AMERICAN NATIONAL BIOGRAPHY

AMERICAN NATIONAL BIOGRAPHY

Published under the auspices of the
AMERICAN COUNCIL OF LEARNED SOCIETIES

General Editors

John A. Garraty

Mark C. Carnes

VOLUME 15

OXFORD UNIVERSITY PRESS

New York 1999 Oxford

OXFORD UNIVERSITY PRESS

Oxford New York
Athens Auckland Bangkok Bogotá
Buenos Aires Calcutta Cape Town Chennai
Dar es Salaam Delhi Florence Hong Kong Istanbul
Karachi Kuala Lumpur Madrid Melbourne Mexico City
Mumbai Nairobi Paris São Paulo Singapore
Taipei Tokyo Toronto Warsaw
and associated companies in
Berlin Ibadan

Published by Oxford University Press, Inc.,
198 Madison Avenue, New York, New York 10016
http://www.oup-usa.org

Funding for this publication was provided in part by
the Andrew W. Mellon Foundation, the Rockefeller Foundation,
and the National Endowment for the Humanities,
a federal agency.

Library of Congress Cataloging-in-Publication Data

American national biography / general editors, John A. Garraty, Mark C. Carnes
p. cm.
"Published under the auspices of the American Council of Learned Societies."
Includes bibliographical references and index.
1. United States—Biography—Dictionaries. I. Garraty, John Arthur,
1920– . II. Carnes, Mark C. (Mark Christopher), 1950– .
III. American Council of Learned Societies.
CT213.A68 1998 98-20826 920.073—dc21 CIP
ISBN 0-19-520635-5 (set)
ISBN 0-19-512794-3 (vol. 15)

Printing (last digit): 9 8 7 6 5 4 3 2 1

Printed in the United States of America
on acid-free paper

CONTINUED

MCCUTCHEON, Floretta Doty (22 July 1888–2 Feb. 1967), bowler, was born in Ottumwa, Iowa. The names of her parents are not known. She moved to Denver, Colorado, in 1901 and Pueblo, Colorado, in 1921. She married Robert McCutcheon, a welfare director for Colorado Fuel and Iron Corporation. They had one daughter, Barbara, before their 1935 divorce (the year of their marriage is not known). By 1935 bowling activities consumed much of her time.

McCutcheon started bowling in 1923 when doctors suggested that she become more physically active. She had nearly suffered a nervous breakdown and her weight had increased to 211 pounds. Her husband organized a bowling league for women employees and persuaded her to join. At the time only 2,000 women were registered bowlers in the United States. McCutcheon rolled an unspectacular 69 in her first game on 23 November 1923 at Pueblo, Colorado. She bowled in two leagues, but illness forced her to give up bowling temporarily after that season. "I didn't like bowling at first," she recalled. "I often wonder why I didn't break my neck running the way I did. I stood as far back as I could and ran to the foul line, swinging the 16-pound ball. My impression of the way to bowl was to throw as hard as possible."

McCutcheon did not bowl again until Jimmy Smith, world champion exhibition kegler, performed an exhibition in 1926 in Pueblo. She adopted Smith's technique, which emphasized rhythm, consistency, timing, and accuracy rather than strength. "I'd been a self-taught bowler because there were not instructors in those days," McCutcheon said. "I tried to alter my style to fit his." She started concentrating on spot bowling, hitting the 1–3 pocket. As her delivery slowed, McCutcheon began demonstrating machine-like accuracy. One writer observed, "You could read the trademark on her ball as it methodically rolled down the lanes. We've seen kids go to their Saturday night baths faster than Floretta's ball went after those pins." The new style quickly paid dividends for McCutcheon. At Pueblo in November 1927, the matronly housewife bowled her first perfect 300-pin game. The following month, she bowled against Jimmy Smith in two special matches at Denver and attained sudden fame by upsetting him, 704 to 697, in the second. McCutcheon astonished the crowd by opening the second match with seven consecutive strikes. Sportswriter Damon Runyon called her scores "unbelievable."

McCutcheon gave professional and exhibition tours from 1928 to 1938; her weight had dropped to 170 pounds. As her fame spread, the Brunswick Company hired her in 1928 for exhibition tours of fifty-one midwestern and western cities. Two years later she formed a partnership with Carl J. Cain, Smith's manager. Cain organized extensive tours where McCutcheon organized schools of bowling instruction and staged exhibitions against local bowlers. The tours financed her daughter's undergraduate education at the University of Colorado. Mrs. McCutcheon's School of Bowling, patterned after contemporary cooking schools, spread the sport's popularity among thousands of women nationally. In the nation's major cities, she offered free instruction during days and exhibitions for women during evenings, frequently sponsored by newspapers and financed by bowling alley owners and operators. Her first bowling school was held in November 1931 at Peoria, Illinois. Two months later over 3,500 women attended her bowling school at Chicago, Illinois. The stocky, quietly charming McCutcheon, with prematurely white hair, impressed other women with her bowling skills because she did not look like an athlete. The *Christian Science Monitor* described her as "looking like she just stepped out of the kitchen after baking a cake." She encouraged women to try the sport and form leagues. The housewife excelled at a traditionally masculine sport associated with working-class culture, and she helped popularize it among working-class women.

Although bowling mostly on unfamiliar alleys, McCutcheon rolled more high scores than any other woman kegler. She averaged 201 for 8,076 games on instructional exhibitions and in unsanctioned match play. According to a press release issued by the Women's International Bowling Congress (WIBC) Hall of Fame on 25 February 1972, "Mrs. Mac" bowled ten perfect 300-pin games, nine 299-pin games, 11 800-pin three-game series, and over 100 700-pin three-game series. One exhibition series saw her average 248 for 12 games. In a much-heralded 1930 tournament at Cleveland, Ohio, McCutcheon finished fourth against 253 male bowlers who had all bowled at least one career official perfect 300-pin game. Her feat drew so many women to bowling alleys that writers nicknamed her "The Pied Piper of Bowling." At Morris, Minnesota, on 20 January 1931, she bowled her highest three-game total of 832 pins. The Women's International Bowling Congress (WIBC) does not count McCutcheon's records because they were made in instructional exhibitions or unsanctioned match play. At the 1932 Los Angeles, California, Summer Olympic games, she performed a bowling exhibition.

McCutcheon settled in New York City in 1938 and began teaching bowling at the Capital Health Center. During the 1938–1939 season, she joined WIBC-sanctioned leagues and averaged 206 pins in league play. Her average remained a WIBC record for sanctioned play until the 1952–1953 season. McCutcheon moved to Chicago, Illinois, in 1944 and taught at the Bowlium. She organized a bowling league there and directed the Windy City Professional Women Bowlers Association for one year. In January 1954 McCutcheon retired to South Pasadena, California, to be near her daughter. At an exhibition in 1959, bowling great Marion Ladewig asked her to start the proceedings. Although age 70, McCutcheon bowled one ball and appropriately made a strike.

McCutcheon wrote bowling instructional booklets and newspaper columns, advocating the four-and-one-half step delivery, rolling the ball, and spot bowling. In 1956 she was inducted into the WIBC Hall of Fame. McCutcheon's other honors include selection to the Colorado Sports Hall of Fame (1973), the Pueblo, Colorado, Sports Association Hall of Fame (1974 or 1975), and the Iowa Sports Hall of Fame (1988). The pioneer in women's sports and bowling superstar died at Pasadena, California.

During three decades, McCutcheon left major legacies as an outstanding bowler, respected organizer, and excellent teacher. She taught an estimated 250,000 women how to bowl and encouraged women to form bowling leagues. McCutcheon held all the bowling records for women without ever participating in a WIBC tournament. Juanita Rich, a women's bowling official, declared, "I don't think anybody will ever set records like Mrs. McCutcheon did. And she bowled under such adverse conditions."

• McCutcheon's files are at the Women's International Bowling Congress Hall of Fame, Greendale, Wisc. For biographical information, see the *Des Moines Sunday Register*, 3 July 1988; Mac Davis, *100 Greatest Sports Heroes* (1954); Phyllis Raybin Emert, "Floretta McCutcheon: Ma Bowl Strikes Again," *Women Sports*, Oct. 1976, pp. 60–62; Phyllis Hollander, *100 Greatest Women in Sports* (1976); and Helen Hull Jacobs, *Famous American Women Athletes* (1964). Further information is in "Lady Bowler," *Literary Digest*, 1 Feb. 1936, pp. 38–39; *Los Angeles Examiner*, 30 Dec. 1927; R. G. Lynch, "Maybe I'm Wrong," *Milwaukee Journal*, 31 May 1942; David L. Porter, *Biographical Dictionary of American Sports: Basketball and Other Indoor Sports* (1989); and George E. Veatch, "Floretta McCutcheon: 1956 Star of Yesteryear," *The Woman Bowler*, June 1956, p. 17. An obituary is in a WIBC Hall of Fame press release, 25 Feb. 1972.

DAVID L. PORTER

MCCUTCHEON, George Barr (26 July 1866–23 Oct. 1928), author, was born in South Raub, near Lafayette, Indiana, the son of John Barr McCutcheon, who after being wounded in the Union army had resumed work shipping cattle and hogs, and Clara Glick, who came from a well-to-do local farm family. John McCutcheon served as commissary manager at Purdue University in Lafayette in 1876–1877 and then as deputy sheriff from 1877 to 1879. In 1879 the McCutcheons moved to Elston, just south of Lafayette, where John resumed work as a livestock shipper. The children were reared in a comfortable home with many advantages, including good books, and they attended local schools with solid curricula. They enjoyed devising their own neighborhood theatricals and delighted in performances by theater and opera companies stopping in Lafayette while on tour.

Well grounded in French and German literature, McCutcheon entered Purdue University in 1882. While there he enjoyed the friendship of George Ade, who later became a well-known writer. McCutcheon worked as a part-time reporter for the *Lafayette Journal* and wrote several plays, none of which were produced. In 1884 McCutcheon flunked out of Purdue at the end of his sophomore year. He continued with the *Journal* and was hired full time in 1889. In 1893 he became the city editor of the *Lafayette Daily Courier*, a position he held until 1902. During these years he wrote in his spare time but published very little, and his ambition to become a famous author was frustrated—until he succeeded with *Graustark: The Story of a Love behind a Throne* (1901).

Graustark capitalized on the American mania for swashbuckling romances set in imaginary kingdoms. The vogue had begun with *The Prisoner of Zenda* (1894) by Anthony Hope, *The Princess Aline* (1895) by Richard Harding Davis, Hope's Zenda sequel *Rupert of Hentzau* (1898), and other such novels. McCutcheon, who had seen melodramas aplenty at the Lafayette Opera House, caught the fever and finished a draft of *Graustark* in 1899. After trying unsuccessfully to get it published, he followed Ade's advice and sold the manuscript to the Chicago publisher Herbert S. Stone for $500. The work became the number one bestseller of 1901. McCutcheon became famous overnight, and Stone made hundreds of thousands of dollars, part of which he voluntarily paid to McCutcheon. Graustark is a mythical Balkan kingdom, in which Princess Yetive is in much danger until a high-minded American named Grenfall Lorry rescues, woos, and wins her. McCutcheon's most frequently quoted passage appears in *Graustark*, when readers are assured that "every born American may become ruler of the greatest nation in the world—the United States. His home is his kingdom, his wife, his mother, his sisters are his queens and princesses; his fellow citizens are his admiring subjects if he is wise and good." The Graustarkian formula represented the jingoistic reversal of the fin de siècle vogue of American millionaires buying their daughters titled but penniless European husbands.

McCutcheon followed his success with five *Graustark* sequels: *Castle Craneycrow* (1902), *Beverly of Graustark* (1904, the heroine being a South Carolinian Calhoun living near Lorry and Yetive), *Truxton King, a Story of Graustark* (1909), *The Prince of Graustark* (1914, the hero being Yetive's son by Lorry), and *The Inn of the Hawk and the Raven* (1927). (Playwright David Belasco unsuccessfully dramatized *Beverly* in 1905.) Meanwhile, McCutcheon, financially secure, had moved to Chicago in 1902. He hit the bestseller lists with more ephemeral fiction but also continually experimented. Between 1901 and 1914 eight of his novels were on the bestseller lists, each quickly selling in excess of 750,000 copies. In 1902 he published his frothy novel *Brewster's Millions*, which, republished in 1903 and marketed by Stone, ultimately sold more than five million copies. In it, Monty Brewster inherits a million dollars from his grandfather, whose rich enemy promises him seven million dollars if he can honestly divest himself of the grandfather's legacy in one year. McCutcheon's more serious writing is represented by *The Sherrods* (1903), widely regarded as his best novel. It is a psychological study of bigamy: an Indiana farmer marries his childhood sweetheart, goes to Chicago to become a painter, and marries his high-society benefactress, who does not know he is already married. Ultimately unmasked, he commits suicide, which leads to the two wives' friendship but more frustration for the would-be lover of the first wife.

Lionized in Chicago and increasingly rich, in 1904 McCutcheon married a lawyer-politician's daughter, the twice-wed but still youngish widow Marie Proudfoot Van Antwerp Fay. McCutcheon adopted Marie's son from a previous marriage, and the couple had one child of their own who died moments after being born. Marie was thereafter unable to have more children.

The McCutcheons moved to New York City in 1910. By then, McCutcheon finished writing *Brood House*, his finest play (although it was never produced), which satirizes his brother John's big-game hunting in Africa with Theodore Roosevelt and offers a profound psychological study of tangled family relationships that is worthy of comparison to plays by Henrik Ibsen and Eugene O'Neill. *Mary Midthorne*, McCutcheon's favorite among his own works, was published in 1911. It is a story of adultery and murder set in the fictional equivalent of Kennebunkport, Maine. McCutcheon expanded a 1904 *Saturday Evening Post* story into *Anderson Crow, Detective* (1920), based loosely on his father's work as a sheriff in Elston.

McCutcheon, ever a workaholic, continued to make money with well-plotted, stylish fiction. But underlying his glittering melodrama is witty criticism of business tycoons and social snobs, prison management, hypocritical clergymen, and the high cost of funerals. He addresses family problems such as alcoholism, child abuse, and mercy killing. McCutcheon was a member of exclusive New York clubs, sold several plots to the movie industry, answered his fan mail courteously, and collected first editions and fine paintings. To the end of his life he remained shyly bitter because serious literary critics had failed to discern his literary ability. McCutcheon died in New York City.

• Most of McCutcheon's manuscripts and letters are in the Berg Collection at the New York Public Library, at the Newberry Library in Chicago, and in the libraries of Indiana University, Purdue University, and Yale University. A. L. Lazarus and Victor H. Jones, *Beyond Graustark: George Barr McCutcheon Playwright Discovered* (1981), is the only book-length treatment of McCutcheon. In stressing his dramas, they do not slight his fiction. *Drawn from Memory* (1950), the autobiography of McCutcheon's brother John T. McCutcheon, touches on the novelist. McCutcheon is also treated in Frank Luther Mott, *Golden Multitudes: The Story of Best Sellers in the United States* (1947), and in Alice Payne Hackett and James Henry Burke, *80 Years of Best Sellers: 1895–1975* (1977). Grant C. Knight, "The 'Pastry' Period in Literature," *Saturday Review of Literature* 27 (16 Dec. 1944): 5–7, 22–23, brilliantly explains the popularity of Graustarkian "tinsel and cardboard." Knight followed with *The Strenuous Age in American Literature* (1954), in which he contrasts McCutcheon's works with those of more vigorous young realists. Erik Löfroth, *A World Made Safe: Values in American Best Sellers, 1895–1920* (1983), emphasizes the conservatism of that era's popular authors, including McCutcheon. An obituary is on the front page of the *New York Times*, 24 Oct. 1928.

ROBERT L. GALE

MCCUTCHEON, Keith Barr (10 Aug. 1915–13 July 1971), U.S. Marine Corps officer, was born in East Liverpool, Ohio, the son of Merle D. McCutcheon, a physician, and Louise Alberta Sturtevant. McCutcheon graduated from East Liverpool High School in 1933 and earned a B.S. in management science in 1937 at the Carnegie Institute of Technology. A member of the Army Reserve Officers' Training Corps, McCutcheon was accepted for flight training. However, with no guarantee of an active duty assignment because of limited funding during the depression, he decided to resign his army reserve commission for a regular appointment as a second lieutenant in the Marine Corps, effective 13 August 1937.

After sea duty on the aircraft carrier USS *Yorktown*, McCutcheon entered flight training at Pensacola, Florida, in 1939. On 3 July 1940 he received his long-desired wings. McCutcheon served for a year with Marine Observation Squadron One and then was selected to attend the prestigious postgraduate engineering school at the U.S. Naval Academy. After finishing first in his class in May 1943, he entered the Massachusetts Institute of Technology, where he received his M.S. in July 1944.

In September 1944 McCutcheon went overseas as operations officer of Marine Air Group Twenty-four at Bougainville in the Solomon Islands. The following month, MAG-24 was given the mission to provide close air support for army troops during the planned invasion of Luzon in the Philippine Islands. Discovering that no standard doctrine for close air support had yet evolved, McCutcheon assembled and studied all existing procedures. He then drew up a course of forty lectures, based on the principle that all close air support should be employed at the discretion of the ground commander.

McCutcheon supervised the training of personnel for air liaison parties, a concept that had first appeared during the New Georgia campaign of June–July 1943. These ALPs, consisting of an officer and an enlisted radioman, would work directly with ground units to control air strikes. McCutcheon's system won high praise from army units on Luzon. "Had he accomplished nothing else in the Marine Corps," noted historian William R. Fails, "this achievement alone would have made him a major figure."

In April 1945 McCutcheon demonstrated a personal courage that complemented his keen analytical mind.

Five days before the planned landing on Mindanao in the Philippines, intelligence received word that Japanese defenders recently had moved into new positions. McCutcheon volunteered to fly into a small airfield behind enemy lines that had been seized by guerrillas. He obtained information on the changed disposition of Japanese forces and then acted as a forward air observer and directed pre-invasion air strikes that contributed to the success of landings in the Malabang area of Mindanao. He received a Silver Star for his exploits.

Following the end of the war, McCutcheon instructed at the Marine Corps Schools at Quantico, Virginia, and then served with the Bureau of Aeronautics, where he concentrated on the development of guided missiles and pilotless aircraft. He also acted as senior Marine Corps aide to the White House in 1947. That same year he married Marion P. Thompson of East Liverpool, Ohio. The union produced two children.

In the summer of 1950 McCutcheon took transitional helicopter training. On 17 August 1950 he assumed command of Marine Helicopter Squadron One, the pioneering Marine Corps rotary wing unit that had been formed in December 1947. In December 1951 McCutcheon left for Korea to command the recently deployed Marine Helicopter Transport Squadron 161. Over the next eight months, he explored the combat capabilities of helicopters, developing new tactics and techniques for what would prove an extremely important tactical innovation for the Marine Corps.

McCutcheon remained involved with helicopters during the 1950s. In August 1957 he took command of Marine Air Group Twenty-six, the corps's main rotary-wing unit. He remained with this organization until June 1959 and then attended the National War College. In July 1960 he became assistant director of aviation at Marine Corps headquarters; in September 1961, director.

Promoted to brigadier general, McCutcheon in March 1962 took command of the First Marine Brigade in Hawaii. The following year, he became assistant chief of staff for operations to the commander in chief, Pacific (CINCPAC). In this position he helped to plan the initial deployment of marines to Vietnam. As American forces grew in size, he was especially concerned with developing procedures to delineate the responsibilities for combat air operations among the marines, navy, and air force.

McCutcheon went to Vietnam in July 1965 as commander of the First Marine Aircraft Wing, where he supervised the aerial component of the growing marine commitment to the war in Southeast Asia. In June 1966 he returned to Washington, D.C., as deputy chief of staff for air. The next four years saw McCutcheon locked in a struggle with the office of secretary of defense over the administration's attempt to fight a war without calling up reserve forces or seeking adequate funding from Congress. Pilots, especially helicopter pilots, were in short supply, as were helicopters. During these bureaucratic battles, McCutcheon earned a reputation, in the words of William Fails, as "one of the most effective promoters and defenders of Marine Corps aviation."

In 1970 McCutcheon was assigned to Vietnam as commander of the Third Marine Amphibious Force. His main task was to direct the redeployment of the unit from Southeast Asia. Selected for promotion to four-star rank, McCutcheon returned to the United States in January 1971 for assignment as assistant commandant of the Marine Corps. Illness, however, prevented him from assuming his new duties. Congress passed special legislation that placed him on the retired list in the grade of general, effective 1 July 1971. Twelve days later, he died of cancer at Bethesda Naval Hospital, Maryland.

McCutcheon made important contributions to the doctrine and practice of close air support during World War II. However, he will be remembered in the Marine Corps as "the Father of Helicopters." From Korea to Vietnam, McCutcheon was the central figure in marine rotary-wing development. Known for his quiet determination and keen intellect, he was preparing to move into the highest echelons of the Marine Corps when his career was cut short by illness.

• The Marine Corps Historical Research Center in Washington, D.C., has an extensive biographical file on McCutcheon as well as an oral history that deals mainly with his bureaucratic struggles during the 1960s. William R. Fails, *Marines and Helicopters, 1962–1973* (1978), discusses McCutcheon's career at length. See also McCutcheon's historical account, "Marine Aviation in Vietnam, 1962–1970," *Naval Review* (1971): 122–55. An obituary is in the *Washington Post*, 14 July 1971.

WILLIAM M. LEARY

MCDANIEL, Hattie (10 June 1895–26 Oct. 1952), film actress and singer, was born in Wichita, Kansas, the daughter of Henry McDaniel, a Baptist minister, and Susan Holbert, and grew up in Denver, Colorado. Former slaves, her parents passed singing abilities along to Hattie and her siblings. During her early education, Hattie's teachers allowed her to sing spirituals and other songs for her fellow students. In 1910 Hattie recited "Convict Joe" for the Denver Women's Christian Temperance Union, winning a gold medal and a standing ovation. This success motivated Hattie to join her father and brother Otis—the two had formed a minstrel company—and become a full-time entertainer. She was dubbed by critics and audiences as a "jazz singer."

Around 1920, after Otis had died and her father had retired, McDaniel joined "Professor" George Morrison and his "Melody Hounds," Denver's most highly respected black musical group. She first sang solo on radio in 1925 on Denver's KOA with Morrison's band. The stock market crash of 1929 left her unemployed. She heard of possible work in Milwaukee at Sam Pick's Club Madrid. There was a job for her—as the attendant of the ladies' washroom, earning one dollar an evening plus tips. When business was slow one night, the manager asked McDaniel to sing. She sang "St. Louis Blues" and never again worked as a ladies' room attendant.

In 1931, as the depression deepened, McDaniel joined her sisters Etta and Orlena and her brother Sam in Hollywood, where they had survived by taking bit parts in movies. At her first job—with KNX's "the Optimistic Do-Nut Hour"—she once arrived in a formal evening gown, causing a cast member to exclaim: "Hattie's gone high-hat." From that day on, she was known as "Hi-Hat Hattie." Like her siblings, McDaniel took bit parts in movies, being paid five dollars for each performance. She also did household work for wealthy Los Angeles and Hollywood families. Later, she estimated that she had washed a million dishes on her way to stardom.

In 1934 McDaniel was first credited in the movie *Judge Priest*, starring Will Rogers, who remarked that McDaniel's acting and singing stole the show. His opinion helped gain her other roles in movies like *Alice Adams* (in which she played a "saucy, talk-back-to whitey" maid), *Show Boat* (as "Queenie"), and *The Mad Miss Manton* (in which she threw a pitcher of water in Henry Fonda's face). By the late 1930s she was known primarily as the maid who loyally criticizes the idiosyncrasies of her white employers.

McDaniel read Margaret Mitchell's *Gone with the Wind* (1936) because her friends thought the role of "Mammy" was ready-made for her. During her audition for the movie, David O. Selznick said he could "smell the magnolias." Her role in *Gone with the Wind* (1939) led to Hattie McDaniel's becoming the first black person in history to win an Academy Award—for best supporting actress. The staircase scene, occurring after Bonnie is accidentally killed in a fall from her pony when Mammy tearfully tells Melanie that Rhett will not allow the child to be buried, was considered by many to be the scene that won McDaniel her Oscar. Accepting the award, McDaniel said that she would always hold her Oscar "as a beacon for anything that I may be able to do in the future. I sincerely hope that I shall always be a credit to my race, and to the motion picture industry."

To some extent, McDaniel's role as Mammy limited the rest of her career because Mammy became the image by which she was remembered. Nevertheless, her part as Minerva Clay in *In This Our Life* (1942) was thought by many to herald a new era for treating blacks in movies. Blacks had always played maids, servants, and lazy ne'er-do-wells. *In This Our Life*, however, depicted a young black who had ambitions to be a lawyer and a servant who was not "live-in" and not afraid to talk back to white people.

Unfortunately, *In This Our Life* did not prevent a confrontation between McDaniel and Walter White, the executive secretary of the National Association for the Advancement of Colored People (NAACP). White demanded the creation of a "Hollywood Bureau" to screen scripts so that roles for African Americans were properly cast. McDaniel and colleagues like Clarence Muse stated that the "Hollywood Bureau" would constitute censorship. White wanted to end what seemed to him a complete reliance on "handkerchief head" roles for blacks. Nevertheless, McDaniel played Aunt Tempey in Walt Disney's *Song of the South* (1946), using black dialect, and, as a result, she was disowned by the NAACP. The intent of the NAACP and the House Un-American Activities Committee in the late 1940s ultimately had its effect. Like many fellow black performers, McDaniel was out of work in movies for several months because of racial and political tensions.

McDaniel did, however, star on the radio in "Beulah"—with its famous "Somebody Bawl for Beulah" introduction—from 1947 to 1951. Her contract with the Columbia Broadcasting System created a non-dialect-speaking character who, though a servant, was the mainstay of the Henderson household. "Beulah," according to the Hooper ratings, became the most listened-to program in radio history. McDaniel became so well known in this role that mail addressed simply to "Beulah, Hollywood, California" usually reached her. She played the television "Beulah," after Ethel Waters relinquished the role but filmed only six video versions, becoming too ill in 1951 to carry on with both radio and television. (None of her television "Beulah" performances was ever aired.)

In public McDaniel was the happy, smiling, "sister full of love," as some friends called her. Privately, her life was frequently somber. She was married four times. Her first marriage to George Langford in 1922 ended when her husband was shot. The other three—to Howard Hickman in the late 1930s, to George Crawford in 1941, and to Larry C. Williams in 1949—ended in divorce. Of particular sadness to McDaniel was her "false pregnancy" while she was married to Crawford. It took the physicians nearly eight months to learn that she was not pregnant but was suffering from a variety of ailments, including diabetes and heart problems. In 1952 a boil under McDaniel's left arm turned out to be breast cancer. She sold her belongings and moved to the Motion Picture Country Home and Hospital in Woodland Hills, and there, a few months later, she died.

Hattie McDaniel did not change the system, as other people tried to do, but in her dignified roles as a household servant and in nondialect "Beulah" she set examples that were followed by other African-American performers on the way up. She believed that more could be accomplished through love and well wishes than through rancor and confrontation, and she taught these values to many up-and-coming entertainers, both black and white.

• McDaniel's most important papers are in the Margaret Herrick Library of the Academy of Motion Picture Arts and Sciences, Beverly Hills, Calif. Other archival sources are the Margaret Mitchell Collection, University of Georgia, Athens; the MGM, Fox, Universal, Paramount, and Warner collections, University of Southern California, Los Angeles; the Collection of the National Association for the Advancement of Colored People, Library of Congress; and the David O. Selznick Collection, University of Texas, Austin. A full-length biography is Carlton Jackson, *Hattie: The Life of Hattie McDaniel* (1990). She is mentioned in Donald Bogle,

Toms, Coons, Mulattoes, Mammies and Bucks: An Interpretive History of Blacks in American Films (1973); Edward D. C. Campbell, *The Celluloid South: Hollywood and the Southern Myth* (1981); and Susan Myrick, *White Columns in Hollywood: Reports from the* Gone with the Wind *Sets* (1982). Useful newspaper and magazine articles include Tamara Andreeva, "Hattie Is Hep," *Denver Post*, 11 Apr. 1948; Hedda Hopper, "Hattie Hates Nobody," *Chicago Sunday Tribune*, 14 Dec. 1947; and Harry Levette, "I Knew Hattie McDaniel," *American Negro Press*, 5 Nov. 1952. Obituaries appear in the *New York Times*, 27 Oct. 1952, and the *Los Angeles Examiner*, 2 Nov. 1952.

CARLTON JACKSON

MCDERMOTT, John J., Jr. (10 Aug. 1891–2 Aug. 1971), professional golfer, was born in Philadelphia, Pennsylvania, the son of John J. McDermott, a postal employee. (His mother's name is unknown.) As a youth the quiet, unobtrusive McDermott was devoted to his family, did not drink alcohol or smoke, and rarely missed Sunday Mass. He performed well academically at West Philadelphia High School but dropped out to pursue a golf career. His first job was at the Merchantville Field Club in southern New Jersey, but he soon moved to the Atlantic City Country Club.

McDermott first played in the U.S. Open while still a teenager in 1909, finishing in 49th place. He won the 1910 Philadelphia Open and again entered the U.S. Open, which that year was played on a course at the Philadelphia Cricket Club in Chestnut Hill, Pennsylvania, near his home. McDermott tied for the championship at the end of regulation play with a score of 298. After a one-day rain delay McDermott participated in an 18-hole playoff with the brothers Alex and MacDonald Smith. Experience paid off for Alex Smith, 20 years older than McDermott, when he shot a 71 to 75 for McDermott and 77 for MacDonald Smith.

The following year the U.S. Golf Association scheduled the Open championship at the Chicago Golf Club. A determined and ambitious McDermott was ready for the challenge. During this period the U.S. Open was played in two days over 72 holes. McDermott did not start well, shooting an 81 in the morning round, but he came back with a strong 72 in the afternoon. The next day he shot 75–79 to finish in a three-way tie with Mike Brady and George Simpson. This time McDermott triumphed in the playoff with a score of 80 to 82 for Brady and 85 for Simpson. For the first time since the U.S. Open had begun in 1895, a native-born American had captured the national championship. In addition, the 19-year-old McDermott was the youngest golfer ever to have won the U.S. Open. In the 1912 championship, held at the country club in Buffalo, New York, McDermott captured his second U.S. Open by two strokes over Tom McNamara.

Anxious to prove he was a world class player, McDermott traveled overseas to participate in the British Open in 1912 and 1913. In 1912, playing at Muirfield Golf Club in Scotland, he shot a 96 and failed to qualify for the championship. The next year in Hoylake, England, he finished fifth with a score of 315, 11 strokes behind the winner, James H. Taylor. Nevertheless, no American had recorded a better finish in the British Open up to that time.

An opportunity to face the best English players came again in 1913 when Harry Vardon and Ted Ray came to the United States to play exhibition matches and compete in the U.S. Open. The challengers met their match in the Shawnee Open when McDermott left Vardon and Ray 13 strokes behind. As the U.S. Open began at the country club in Brookline, Massachusetts, McDermott was viewed as the golfer most likely to retain the title for the Americans. However, Francis Ouimet, a 20-year-old amateur, held the Englishmen at bay and won the championship, while McDermott finished in ninth place. McDermott won the Western Open in 1913 and the North-South Open in 1914, his last victories. He finished ninth in the 1914 U.S. Open, marking his final appearance in that event.

The mashie, the equivalent of the five iron, was McDermott's favorite club. He would open a newspaper and place it on the ground about 150 to 160 yards away from the practice tee. Using the mashie, McDermott would hit one shot after another onto the newspaper. By 1911, possessing a cocky self-assurance, McDermott challenged professional golfers in the Philadelphia area to 18-hole matches, with the winner of each match receiving $1,000 from the loser. After he won three straight matches, other possible opponents would not accept the challenge. Money and fame quickly came his way through his endorsements of golf clubs and golf balls. He also played exhibition matches and frequently gave lessons.

By his early twenties McDermott seemingly had achieved a lasting success. However, the pressure of fame and the burden of quick wealth began to undermine his mental stability. His abrupt departure from competition prior to his 24th birthday came partly because McDermott drove himself hard. He practiced constantly by hitting hundreds of golf balls every day. After practicing at dawn, he tended to his golf shop customers and then played as many holes as possible in the afternoon. After dark he often putted balls on a putting green by lamplight or moonlight. In addition, he lost heavily in some stock market investments. Having never married and living with his parents, he kept this news from his family. He made some remarks upon winning the Shawnee Open in 1913 that were interpreted as being insulting to Vardon and Ray. Although the Englishmen were less offended than the press, undoubtedly McDermott took this criticism to heart. These setbacks changed his demeanor, as he began to brood and to suffer bouts of deep depression.

Never a robust man, the 120-pound McDermott broke down in 1914 while being rescued in the wake of a collision of two cruise ships in the English Channel. He suffered from mental illness for the remaining 56 years of his life, living in hospitals, rest homes, and the residence of his sisters. He occasionally hit golf balls, but he never played actively after his breakdown and was eventually forgotten by the golfing public.

In June 1971 McDermott was escorted by his sister to the U.S. Open at the Merion Golf Club near Philadelphia, sixty years after he had won the event. Within two months of his appearance as a spectator at Merion, he died in his sleep at his sister's home in Yeadon, Pennsylvania. The author Charles Price described McDermott as a perfectionist who made no secret of his belief that he could defeat any golfer. For five years, between 1910 and 1914, McDermott may have been the finest golfer in the world.

• Information on McDermott's career and accomplishments can be found in Herbert Warren Wind, *The Story of American Golf* (1956); Charles Price, *The World of Golf* (1962); and Robert Sommers, *The U.S. Open: Golf's Ultimate Challenge* (1987). An obituary is in the *New York Times*, 3 Aug. 1971.

LEWIS H. CROCE

MCDERMOTT, Robert (7 Jan. 1914–4 Oct. 1963), basketball player and coach, was born in Whitestone, Queens, New York. He left Flushing High School after just one year and began his professional basketball career with the Brooklyn Visitations of the Metropolitan Basketball League in 1932. He and his wife, Virginia, had five children.

The 5′11″, 185-pound guard, who owned the era's best two-handed set shot, helped the Visitations win the 1934–1935 American Basketball League Championship, ranking second among scoring leaders. The following season, he led Tunkhannock, Pennsylvania, to the New York–Pennsylvania League crown. His stellar 32-point performance established a single game professional basketball playoff scoring record, besting Johnny Beckman's previous mark by four points. McDermott excelled for the New York Original Celtics during the 1936–1937 seasons and for the Kingston Colonials during the next two seasons, often tallying at least 50 points per game. Nicknamed "Bobby" and "Mr. Basketball," he rapidly developed into the sport's premier performer and best gate attraction. After leading the American Basketball League in scoring with Kingston in 1939–1940, he spent the 1940–1941 campaign with the Troy/Brooklyn Celtics.

From the 1941–1942 through 1945–1946 campaigns, McDermott starred for the Fort Wayne Zollner Pistons and garnered National Basketball League most valuable player honors for five consecutive seasons. He made the all-NBL first team five straight times as the league's best outside shooter. In 1941–1942, his 13.2 point average ranked him second among NBL scorers. Fort Wayne lost the NBL finals to the Oshkosh All-Stars, but McDermott led his team in scoring. The next season he won both the NBL scoring title with 316 points (13.7 point average) and the field goal crown (132 baskets), leading Fort Wayne, with its 17–6 record, to the regular season title. Although McDermott led all playoff scorers, the Sheboygan Redskins defeated the Zollner Pistons in the NBL finals.

With McDermott at guard, Fort Wayne captured a record three consecutive World Pro Tournament championships at Chicago, Illinois, from 1944 to 1946. Fort Wayne reached the pinnacle of its NBL success between 1943 and 1945. In 1943–1944 McDermott again led the Zollner Pistons in scoring and the NBL in field goals (123) and finished second among NBL scorers with a 13.9 point average. Fort Wayne captured another regular season title with an 18–4 mark and won its first NBL playoff crown, taking all three games from the Sheboygan Redskins. McDermott established the tone for the NBL finals with a long two-handed set shot in the waning seconds of the first game for a two-point victory. In the NBL playoffs, he led all scorers with 27 field goals and 67 points (13.4 point average).

The 1944–1945 Zollner Pistons dominated the NBL from the outset, compiling a sparkling 25–5 mark for another NBL regular season crown. McDermott shattered the NBL field goal record with 258 points and joined leading scorer Mel Riebe of the Cleveland Allmen Transfers as the first two NBL players to attain 20-point averages. McDermott again paced Fort Wayne scorers with 20.1 points per game and broke the NBL single game record with 36 points against Cleveland. In the NBL playoffs, the Zollner Pistons rallied from a two game deficit to defeat Sheboygan for a second consecutive NBL crown. For the third straight time, McDermott led playoff scorers in field goals with 45 points. In November 1945 Fort Wayne defeated the College All-Stars in Chicago before a crowd of 23,912, an attendance record at the time. The successful exhibition contest reflected the revival in popularity of pro basketball following World War II.

In 1945–1946 McDermott led Fort Wayne to a 26–8 record and its fourth straight regular season NBL crown, repeating as the second best NBL scorer with 13.5 points per game. The Rochester Royals, however, ended Fort Wayne's two-year reign as NBL playoff champions, taking three of four games. Besides being most valuable player of the 1944 tournament, McDermott was named to the 1944, 1945, and 1946 All-Star first teams.

Fort Wayne named McDermott as player-coach before the 1946–1947 campaign. After compiling a 7–7 mark with Fort Wayne, McDermott was suspended by owner Fred Zollner on 19 December. McDermott, whom Zollner Piston general manager Carl Bennett described as "a hellion off the court," especially when drinking liquor, had beaten up a teammate on the train one night. The fifth place Chicago Gears NBL club purchased him as player-coach. He made the all-NBL first team and gave the American Gears an outside scoring threat to accompany center George Mikan's devastating inside game. McDermott guided Chicago to a 19–8 record and a third place regular season finish. Chicago defeated the Rochester Royals in four games to capture the NBL playoff title, as McDermott topped scorers in percentage of free throws made. As player-coach of the Tri-Cities Blackhawks, he compiled a 20–18 record in 1947–1948 and a 25–20 mark in 1948–1949. His NBL playing career ended in 1949 with the struggling Hammond, Indiana, Calumet Buccaneers. McDermott joined the Wilkes-Barre, Pennsylvania, Barons in 1949, tallying 48 points in an exhibition game against the New York Knickerbockers and averaging 17 points per game until his career was ended by a back injury. Following his pro basketball career, he worked as a security guard at Yonkers Raceway. He was injured in a September 1963 traffic accident there and died at Yonkers, New York, two weeks later.

McDermott, who achieved professional greatness in 17 seasons although he had no college experience, led three different leagues in scoring and became the first player-coach to direct two professional basketball teams to playoff titles. Despite his small size, he ranked first in NBL career scoring with 3,583 points in 287 games (12.5 point average). McDermott finished second only to Leroy Edwards in NBL career playoff scoring, tallying 494 points in 45 games (11.0 point average). Although games were only 40 minutes long and the pace of play was slower than that of present day teams, 20-point games were not unusual for McDermott. The seven-time NBL All-Star led the NBL in scoring once and finished second five seasons. Under his direction, Fort Wayne captured four NBL regular season titles and three NBL playoff crowns. McDermott led the Zollner Pistons in scoring all six seasons there. In 1945 NBL coaches, managers, and players and sports editors selected the set-shot artist the "greatest player of all time." His other honors included making the *Collier's* "All-World Team" in 1950 and being voted the "greatest Fort Wayne player of all time" in 1954. In 1988 he belatedly was named to the Naismith Memorial Basketball Hall of Fame.

• The Naismith Memorial Basketball Hall of Fame, Springfield, Mass., has McDermott's file. For biographical material on McDermott, see Wayne Patterson and Lisa Fisher, *100 Greatest Basketball Players* (1989), and Robert W. Peterson, *Cages to Jump Shots: Pro Basketball's Early Years* (1990). David S. Neft and Richard M. Cohen, eds., *The Sports Encyclopedia: Pro Basketball*, 5th ed. (1992), treats McDermott's NBL career. An obituary is in the *New York Times*, 5 Oct. 1963.

DAVID L. PORTER

MCDERMOTT, Walsh (24 Oct. 1909–17 Oct. 1981), medical researcher and public health advocate, was born in New Haven, Connecticut, the son of a family doctor and Rosella Walsh. McDermott attended local public schools for his primary education, Phillips Academy in Andover, Massachusetts, for high school, and Princeton College, from which he graduated in 1930. He applied to medical school, although his undergraduate record was not remarkable. However, he was the son of a doctor and had earned honors in biology, and he was accepted into Columbia's College of Physicians and Surgeons. At first, he found medical school as unexciting as the rest of his education; some of his friends suspected that he would have preferred to pursue a career as a writer. In a letter he wrote later in life, commenting on proposed curricular changes at Johns Hopkins Medical School, McDermott recalled his own ambivalence in his first year of medical school: "I learned virtually nothing except for the rudiments of gross anatomy which I promptly forgot." That year he finished eighty-fourth in his class of 103.

Between that year and his graduation in 1934, McDermott became more serious about his career. After finishing medical school, he chose to remain in New York, entering a residency at New York Hospital. In the second year of his residency he contracted tuberculosis, and in August 1935 he entered the Trudeau Sanitarium in Saranac, New York. After seven months at Saranac, he returned to medical practice cautiously, accepting a part-time appointment at an outpatient syphilis clinic of New York Hospital. Tuberculosis would shadow McDermott for the next two decades, bringing him as a patient to New York Hospital nine times until he was finally cured.

Although the outpatient clinic was identified predominantly as a treatment center for syphilitic patients, people also sought help for a variety of other diseases there. In the era before penicillin, patients suffering from syphilis received weekly injections of arsenical compounds. This regular treatment plan allowed them to develop sustained relationships with the clinic doctors, including McDermott, that were akin to private patient-doctor relationships. While working there, McDermott met a volunteer, Marian McPhail, whom he married in 1940. They had no children.

The advent of penicillin ended the need for this clinic. In 1942 David Barr, the chief of medicine at Cornell, appointed McDermott head of the hospital's division of infectious diseases. When World War II ended, McDermott was perfectly positioned to conduct research with the new antimicrobial agents that offered physicians a new weapon against infectious diseases. In an essay written after McDermott's death, his colleague and student David E. Rogers wrote that his mentor had told him that living in this time "gave a physician a profound sense of wonder, coupled with pride in science and in medicine that would sustain him or her the rest of a lifetime." McDermott immediately started conducting clinical research with the new drugs. He soon discovered that although penicillin had a detrimental effect on gastric acid and, therefore, on digestion, in certain instances it could be given orally as well as by injection. In these early years McDermott also traveled to Mexico, where he helped local health officials develop therapies for typhoid fever and brucellosis.

In New York McDermott and his associates worked with animals, studying how microbes reacted to the new class of drugs in living tissues. Among the questions they strove to answer was that of why antimicrobial drugs that had a lethal effect on pathogens in vitro could not kill the microbes in a host organism. After about two decades of studying this phenomenon in mice inoculated with human tubercule bacilli, McDermott and his colleagues concluded that the microbes did not find sanctuaries or pockets within the host, as some had speculated; rather, they mutated rapidly, developing resistance to the drugs. His work on what he called the "adaptive plasticity" of streptococcus suggested that two drugs working together might have an effect greater than either one used alone, because the pathogen would have a harder time adapting to two drugs.

In 1948 McDermott was named managing editor of the *American Review of Tuberculosis*; four years later he became editor, a post he held for the next twenty years. Under his direction the journal changed its name to the *American Review of Respiratory Disease*, reflecting the waning of tuberculosis in society. McDermott, however, continued to fight his own long battle against the disease. Although he tried many of the new generation of antituberculosis drugs, he still resorted periodically to bed rest and occasionally directed the infectious disease ward from his bed. In 1950 he developed a bronchopleural fistula and underwent a risky procedure that finally tamed his tuberculosis, allowing him to return to his work with renewed vigor.

In 1952 McDermott became involved with a project to bring isoniazid, a new antituberculosis drug he and his colleagues had developed, to the Navajo Indian population. Because of their poverty and isolation, many Native Americans could not get access to the daily injections of streptomycin that could cure the tuberculosis that ravaged their reservations. McDermott devised the Many Farms Project, in which a van brought doctors and nurses to sick people's homes. He also used the project as an opportunity to study the relative merits of isoniazid and streptomycin. The project continued for only six years, but McDermott's commitment to public health persisted throughout his life. In 1955 he became chair of Cornell's public health department.

That same year McDermott won the Albert Lasker Award with three of his colleagues for their work on isoniazid. McDermott was already trying to solve more challenging public health problems. Although many medicine departments in this period were criticized for ignoring societal problems, Cornell's public health department under McDermott's leadership was known for its practical approach. McDermott argued that he and his colleagues should care for the underserved populations that generated excessive morbidity and mortality statistics; he referred to such treatment as "statistical compassion." He lobbied for this view from a variety of public health positions he held, from the local to the international level. He was the first chair of the Health Research Council of the City of New York (1960–1966) and a participant on the Agency for International Development's research advisory committee.

McDermott's public health work did not keep him from other jobs. A devoted teacher, he shepherded Russell Cecil's *Textbook of Medicine* through four editions as a co-editor. In the late 1960s he was among the physicians lobbying for a National Academy of Medicine, similar to the National Academy of Sciences. He was one of the founders of the Institute of Medicine, born out of this movement. In 1972 he was appointed as special adviser to the newly created Robert Wood Johnson Foundation. Three years later he retired from Cornell after forty-seven years at the New York Medical Center.

An indefatigable worker throughout his life, McDermott was well-liked by all he met, from the Navajos he encountered on the reservation to the New York colleagues he passed on the medical ward. Many of his colleagues sensed that an era had ended when McDermott died at Pawling, New York.

• The most complete biography of Walsh McDermott is Paul B. Beeson's account in National Academy of Sciences, *Biographical Memoirs* 59 (1990): 283–307. It includes a full bibliography of McDermott's publications. See also *America's Doctors, Medical Science, Medical Care* (1986), a Festschrift for McDermott organized by the American Academy of Arts and Sciences, of which he was a fellow. Another student tribute to McDermott is Gladys Hobby, "In Memoriam: Walsh McDermott, M.D., 1909–1981," *American Review of Respiratory Disease* 125 (1982): 141–43.

SHARI RUDAVSKY

MCDILL, James Wilson (4 Mar. 1834–28 Feb. 1894), U.S. senator and interstate commerce commissioner, was born in Butler County, Ohio, the son of John McDill, a Presbyterian clergyman, and Frances Wilson. As an infant James moved with his family to Hanover, Indiana. After elementary training in the common schools of Hanover, he enrolled in the preparatory department of Hanover College and then transferred to Salem Academy in Ohio. He pursued a college education at Miami University in Ohio, where future president Benjamin Harrison was a fellow student. Following McDill's graduation in 1853, he went west to Kossuth, Iowa, teaching school there for a short time. He then returned to Ohio to study law and was admitted to the bar in 1856. The following year McDill opened a law practice in Afton, Iowa. In 1857 he married Narcissa Fullenwider who had been his pupil in the Kossuth school; they had five children.

In 1858 McDill embarked on his political career, winning election as county judge. A year later the voters chose him to serve as county superintendent of schools. Meanwhile, he became a protégé of Iowa's senator James Grimes, who in 1861 appointed McDill as clerk of the Senate Committee of the District of Columbia. The following year McDill was appointed a clerk in the third auditor's office of the Treasury Department, where he handled war claims. In 1865 he opened a law office in Washington, but by 1866 he had returned to the practice of law in Afton.

A loyal Republican, McDill won his party's nomination for judge of the circuit court in 1868. After two years in that position he was appointed district court judge by Iowa's governor. In 1872 McDill decided to leave the bench and won election to the U.S. House of Representatives, where he served for four years. He was a member of the House committees on the Pacific railroad and public lands. In 1876 he refused to run for a third term, seeking instead to achieve some financial security through a lucrative law practice. Two years later, however, he accepted an appointment to the state board of railroad commissioners. He held that post until 1881, when Iowa's governor chose him to fill the unexpired term of U.S. senator Samuel J. Kirkwood, who had resigned to accept the post of secretary of interior in President James Garfield's cabinet.

McDill served in the Senate from 1881 to 1883 and was a member of the committees on territories, public lands, and the District of Columbia. During his short term he dutifully performed the responsibilities of his office but achieved no special distinction or fame. He introduced a bill to appoint an interstate commerce commission, yet not until 1887 did Congress create such a body. McDill was one of a number of lawmakers who during the 1880s pushed for federal regulation of railroads. He did not seek a full six-year term in the Senate but retired voluntarily after completing his two-year stint.

In 1884 McDill again assumed a place on the Iowa state railroad commission. In his capacity as state railroad commissioner, he testified before a U.S. Senate investigating committee and expressed his support for an effective federal rail commission empowered to order reductions in transportation rates. During the Harrison administration, McDill hoped to be appointed federal district court judge but was passed over for that position. In 1892, however, President Harrison selected him to serve as a member of the federal Interstate Commerce Commission. As a commissioner, McDill was troubled by the federal courts' repeated interference with the work of the commission and complained of the willingness of judges to nullify the regulatory body's decrees. Speaking before an assembly of Iowa farmers, McDill in his last public address criticized the courts for undermining the beneficial work of the commissioners. After two years on the commission, he died of typhoid fever at his home in Creston, Iowa.

Though not one of the preeminent political figures of the late nineteenth century, McDill made his mark as a pioneer in the field of railroad regulation. A staunch Republican lawyer with a judicial temperament, McDill was not a fiery prairie populist crusading passionately against transportation monopolies. Instead, he believed that the state and federal governments could cure the transportation ills of the nation through responsible regulation by men of goodwill and moderation, such as himself. He was a modest, moderate man who pursued modest, moderate goals.

• There are no collections of McDill's personal papers. The best biographical essay is S. R. Davis, "James Wilson McDill," *Midland Monthly* 1 (1894): 383–92. For shorter biographical accounts and reminiscences, see Benjamin F. Gue, *History of Iowa* (1903); David C. Mott, "Pioneer Lawmakers Association of Iowa," *Annals of Iowa* 14 (1925): 564–67; and Edward H. Stiles, *Recollections and Sketches of Notable Lawyers and Public Men of Early Iowa* (1916). Obituaries are in *Annals of Iowa* 1 (1894): 423, *Iowa Historical Record* 10 (1894): 95, and the *Chicago Tribune*, the *New York Times*, and the *Washington Post*, 1 Mar. 1894.

JON C. TEAFORD

MCDONALD, Babe (29 July 1878–16 May 1954), track and field athlete, was born Patrick Joseph McDonnell in County Clare, Ireland, the son of poor farming parents whose names are unknown. McDonald emigrated to the United States in 1901, where, at Ellis Island, immigration officers misunderstood his given name and called him "McDonald." He joined the New York City Police Department in 1905 and remained there for forty-one years.

Now standing 6′5″ and weighing 300 pounds, McDonald joined the famous Irish-American Athletic Club, received the nickname "Babe," and immediately gained notoriety in the peculiar sport of throwing heavy weights. He became highly proficient in the 16-pound shot, the discus, the 35-pound and 56-pound weight throws for distance and height, and the "combined" shot put. In the last event, the athlete hurled the shot with his right hand, had it measured, and returned to put the shot lefthanded. The combined total in feet and inches determined the winner. All of these events, ancient Irish festival sports, were added to the program of the revived Olympic Games in 1896. Competing in these events were fellow immigrants from Ireland and members of the New York City Irish-American Club: James Mitchell, John Flanagan, Matthew McGrath, and Martin Sheridan. McDonald and his four Irish-American teammates were huge men, earning them the title "Irish whales," and all won Olympic gold medals. McDonald was elevated to "prince of whales." The five of them dominated the gold, silver, and bronze medal awards at the Olympic Games in Paris (1900), St. Louis (1904), London (1908), Stockholm (1912), and Antwerp (1920).

McDonald won sixteen first-place championships in the United States from 1907 through 1933 (at age fifty-four). At the Olympic Games in Stockholm, McDonald won the gold medal in the shot with a record 50′4″ and a silver medal in the combined event, his throws adding up to 87′2½″ having been just short of teammate Ralph Rose's 90′5½″. McDonald, the giant New York City policeman, went to the 1920 games in Antwerp, where he won the gold in the 56-pound weight with an Olympic record throw of 36′11½″. Several days earlier, the 42-year-old captain of the American Olympic team had carried his country's flag at the opening ceremonies; four years later in Paris, the prince of whales was selected as "honorable member of the team."

From 1905 through 1920 McDonald was a traffic policeman at one of the world's busiest intersections, New York City's Times Square. On his promotion to sergeant, a *New York Times* writer noted, "Never in the record of the swirling traffic of autos did any chauffeur ever venture to ignore McDonald's great bulk. Newsboys pooled their spare pennies to buy him a loving cup" (25 Dec. 1920). He was like a living Statue of

Liberty, as one writer put it. During the summer of 1926 McDonald plunged into the Atlantic Ocean and rescued two youngsters. "It's part of my job," he was quoted as saying. On 1 October 1926 he was promoted to lieutenant, then elevated to captain on 1 April 1936, and retired on 3 April 1946, "one of the premier heroic figures of American field sport," according to the *New York Times* of the following day. The *New York Herald Tribune* of 4 April 1946 called the massive, white-haired McDonald "a living legend." His six national championships in a single year (1914) "was a feat hailed at that time as one of the most remarkable in athletic annals." McDonald died in New York City; he was survived by his wife, the former Mary McMahan (date of marriage unknown), and a son.

• For biographical information on McDonald and the "Irish whales," see Erich Kamper, *Lexikon der 14,000 Olympioniken* (1983), p. 175; Bill Mallon et al., *Quest for Gold* (1984); p. 324; F. A. M. Webster, *Great Moments in Athletics* (1947), pp. 194–95; Dick Schaap, *An Illustrated History of the Olympics* (1963), p. 164; David Wallechinsky, *The Complete Book of the Olympics* (1991), pp. 108, 140; *Report of the American Olympic Committee, 1920* (1921), pp. 226, 304–5; and Alexander M. Weyand, *The Olympic Pageant* (1952), pp. 119, 138, 140, 166–67. See also the *New York Times*, 11 July 1912; 25 Dec. 1920; 26 Aug. 1926; 2 Oct. 1926; 4 Apr. 1946; 17 May 1954; and 18 May 1954. Also see the *Times* (London), 6 July 1912; Edward Lyell Fox, "Our Olympic Flyers," *Outing Magazine* 60 (July 1912): 397; *New York Herald*, 25 Aug. 1912; *New York Tribune*, 22 Aug. 1920; "Was the Recent Olympiad a Failure?" *Literary Digest*, 16 Oct. 1920, p. 78; *New York Herald Tribune*, 4 Apr. 1946; and *New York Herald Tribune*, 17 May 1954.

JOHN A. LUCAS

MCDONALD, David John (22 Nov. 1902–8 Aug. 1979), labor official, was born in Pittsburgh, Pennsylvania, the son of David McDonald, a steelworker and tavern keeper, and Mary Kelly. McDonald grew up in the Hazelwood district of Pittsburgh and graduated from evening high school in 1919. One year prior to graduation, however, he began working for U.S. Steel and in 1919 was hired as a typist in the Pittsburgh office of Wheeling Steel.

In 1923 McDonald was hired through a neighborhood contact as a traveling secretary for Philip Murray, then the vice president of the United Mine Workers of America (UMWA). Based out of the UMWA headquarters in Indianapolis, Indiana, McDonald traveled throughout the union's territory with Murray. He spent much of 1925 in West Virginia, assisting UMWA leader Van Bittner in a bitter strike. He acted as secretary during national negotiating sessions in the 1920s and assisted in the defeat and suppression of union dissidents. In the late 1920s Murray and McDonald moved back to Pittsburgh, where McDonald attended evening drama classes at Carnegie Technical Institute, completing the program in 1932.

Following the passage of the National Industrial Recovery Act (NIRA) in 1933, McDonald assisted Murray in organizing drives in the Pennsylvania coalfields. When the UMWA and the coal operators formed a joint commission on the elimination of geographic wage differentials later that year, McDonald became its secretary. He was also appointed as Murray's assistant on the NIRA Administrative Board. Then, in 1936, when Murray was named chairman of the CIO's (Congress of Industrial Organizations) Steel Workers Organizing Committee, McDonald became the SWOC's secretary-treasurer. In his new post, McDonald worked on the J&L organizing campaign and in the Little Steel Strike, both in 1937. That same year he married Emmy Lou Price. They had one child before divorcing in 1946, with McDonald retaining custody of the child. In 1950 McDonald married his secretary, Rosemary McHugh; they had no children.

Murray became president of the CIO in 1941, and more of the daily responsibility of administering the SWOC fell to McDonald. When Murray suffered a heart attack later that year, McDonald took temporary charge of the union until he recovered. In 1942 the SWOC became the United Steelworkers of America (USWA), and McDonald ran unopposed for the position of secretary-treasurer. During World War II, he traveled to Europe and Latin America on assignment for the Department of Labor and Office of Inter-American Affairs. Following the war he was active in the 1949 steel strike and was an early and enthusiastic advocate of purging leftists from the USWA and the CIO.

By the early 1950s a rift had developed between Murray and McDonald. Murray was critical of McDonald's expensive and flamboyant lifestyle and may have feared that the younger man was plotting to oust him. At the 1952 USWA convention Murray engineered the stripping of most of the power from the secretary-treasurer position. Many observers felt that McDonald would be removed from his post at the next election. Murray, however, died suddenly in late 1952. McDonald moved swiftly to fill the power vacuum, and the union's executive board named him interim president. In the next election, held one year later, McDonald was elected, unopposed, to the post.

Almost immediately McDonald embarked on a nationwide series of plant tours with Ben Fairless, the Chief executive officer of U.S. Steel. The tours were part of McDonald's conciliatory approach to management, reflecting his belief that a new era of cooperation had arrived. As he told the 1953 USWA convention, managers and workers were both corporate employees, and "together, these two groups have a mutual trusteeship to operate the steel company."

In negotiations in 1953 and 1954, the USWA won wage increases and a noncontributory pension. In 1956 McDonald led the union through a strike before winning an excellent contract, which included a substantial wage hike and a plan for supplementary unemployment benefits. When the CIO merged with the American Federation of Labor (AFL) in 1955, McDonald became a vice president and a member of its executive committee.

At the 1956 USWA convention, McDonald pushed through a dues increase, which provoked considerable opposition. Some of his opponents formed the Dues Protest Committee (DPC). The DPC ran Donald Rarick against McDonald in the 1957 USWA presidential election, and the incumbent's backers used a number of tactics to defeat Rarick, including, the evidence suggests, vote fraud. McDonald was declared the victor, but the 35 percent vote drawn by the virtually unknown and inexperienced Rarick showed that there was considerable opposition to McDonald's lifestyle and policies.

In 1959 contract negotiations led to a 116-day strike in the steel industry, leading President Dwight Eisenhower to invoke a Taft-Hartley back-to-work order. The union was able to win gains in wages and benefits in the settlement reached in early 1960 and to turn back a company attempt to gain greater control over shop floor working conditions.

McDonald was an ardent and early supporter of John F. Kennedy. The Kennedy administration intervened in the 1962 steel contract negotiations in an effort to hold down both wage and price increases. McDonald accepted a contract without a wage increase and with benefit changes amounting to between 2 and 3 percent. The companies then raised prices anyway. In the resulting confrontation between President Kennedy and U.S. Steel, McDonald was a strong supporter of the president. Influenced by calls for restraint from the president and the media, McDonald's 1963 Big Steel contract gained little for labor.

By late 1964 opposition to McDonald's leadership of the USWA had increased. Secretary-treasurer I. W. Abel decided to challenge the incumbent president and was backed by more than half of the union's executive board. Issues included the poor 1962 and 1963 contract settlements, McDonald's lavish lifestyle—characterized by the insurgents as "tuxedo unionism"—and the incumbent's lack of attention to the dull details of union administration and functioning.

McDonald threw himself into the campaign and waged a fairly effective defense of his presidency, emphasizing the gains won for steelworkers in the 1950s. The vote, held in early 1965, was very close. McDonald actually carried the U.S. districts of the union, but his substantial losses in the Canadian districts brought him down. The totals, announced in April 1965, were 309,000 for Abel and 299,000 for McDonald.

McDonald retired to his Palm Springs, California, home following the defeat. His autobiography, *Union Man*, was published in 1969. In his retirement he played almost no role in the affairs of the USWA. Still, during his thirteen years as president of the steelworkers, he was one of the most powerful labor leaders in the country. He died in Palm Springs.

• Some of McDonald's papers as USWA president are in the USWA Archives at Pennsylvania State University. McDonald's autobiography, *Union Man* (1969), is the best source on his early life and his career with the UMWA. McDonald and Edward A. Lynch, *Coal and Unionism: A History of the American Coal Miners' Unions* (1939), is a paean to the UMWA leadership, especially John L. Lewis. John Herling, *Right to Challenge: People and Power in the Steelworkers Union* (1972), is a strong assessment of McDonald's role in the USWA. An obituary is in the *New York Times*, 10 Sept. 1979.

MARK D. MCCOLLOCH

MCDONALD, Donald (?–4 Apr. 1788), British officer, was born in Scotland. Nothing is known of his early life. He participated in the battle at Culloden Moor in Scotland. After coming to America, he was in the battles of Lexington and Bunker Hill and was sent in July 1775 to Cross Creek, North Carolina, to organize the recently settled Highlanders as the chief Loyalist participants in the forthcoming vigorous campaign against the Carolina revolutionaries. Earlier, in response to the often and urgent solicitations of the royal governors for assistance in curtailing the rising revolution, Parliament had proposed using loyal Americans to counter the activities of their rebellious fellow citizens. This special cultivation of the Scots and the former Regulators on the upper Cape Fear River was the first attempt to put the plan into action on a colony-wide scale.

When McDonald and his fellow British officer Donald McLeod appeared during late July in the port city of New Bern, North Carolina, they were immediately summoned to appear before the Committee of Safety to explain their presence in the colony. After falsely convincing the authorities that they were there merely to visit family and friends, they were allowed to proceed to the Scot settlement at Cross Creek.

The first meeting between McDonald and the local Highlander leaders took place in the home of Alexander Morrison. Morrison was very influential in the Scottish settlement, not only because he was a veteran of the battle of Culloden, but also because he had persuaded 300 of his neighbors to emigrate with him to America. Before the meeting adjourned, a number of men were chosen for positions of leadership in the force to be recruited. McDonald was commissioned captain general (brigadier general).

While the new officers recruited men for McDonald's command, royal governor Josiah Martin, in an effort to increase the Loyalist support group, required all new arrivals in the colony to swear an oath of allegiance to the king before they could disembark from their ships. His plan was to embody and arm 3,000 men under McDonald and back them with a support body of 20,000 loyal citizens drawn from the 30,000 residents of the colony.

About 500 men responded to the initial call to arms, mostly members of a colonial militia unit serving under Allen McDonald, the husband of Flora McDonald, the heroine of the 1745 uprising, and Alexander McLeod, a brother of Donald McLeod and a veteran of the battle of Culloden, as well as the son-in-law of Allen and Flora McDonald. These men met General McDonald at Cross Hill, near the present site of Carthage in Moore County.

As the recruiting continued, Governor Martin assured the British authorities that a large body of disaffected men in the interior of the colony were eager to take up arms on behalf of the king. At the same time, McDonald and McLeod put their recruiting plan in full force. They revealed a scheme of eight inducements designed to persuade the undecided and timid to quickly align themselves with the Crown. These inducements included promises of free land, remission of arrears in quitrents, and twenty years of tax exemption. On 10 January 1776 the governor issued orders for the erection of the king's standard, and word went out that Sir Henry Clinton, with the British forces in America, was to unite with Sir Peter Parker's fleet, which was transporting seven regiments of Irish Regulars to the port at Wilmington. The success of the mission rested on the ability of McDonald and his force of "the King's friends" to wrest control of the port from the hands of the revolutionaries and thereby provide a safe landing site for the reinforcements. The generous inducements and the promise of the involvement of such a masterly force brought daily increasing numbers to McDonald's camp.

Meanwhile, McDonald began corresponding with Colonel James Moore, a resident of New Hanover County and the commander of the Second North Carolina Regiment. McDonald hoped to convince Moore to restore his loyalty to the king and to place his command under the king's standard. Although McDonald was persuasive, he failed to reconcile Moore. Convinced that his hope of opening the port without bloodshed would never be a reality, McDonald began final preparations to take the port by force. Yet, even as McDonald redoubled his recruiting activities, he gradually revived his hope that by some means a confrontation could be avoided.

While McDonald rallied the Highlanders and former Regulators around the Union Jack, Colonel Moore marched his regiment to the Widow Moore's Creek Bridge. During the following three weeks, Moore carried out a brilliant campaign that included recruiting revolutionaries as well as harassing and alarming the gathering Loyalists. His immediate field of operations was from Fayetteville to Moore's Creek Bridge, some sixty miles up and down the Cape Fear River. By 24 February 1776 nearly 6,000 patriots were on duty at various points throughout the colony attempting to prevent the junction of Clinton, the Highlanders, and Sir Peter Parker's force. Almost daily, conflicting reports of the strength of McDonald's force reached Moore; various reports gave their strength as from 1,500 to 3,000. Actually, McDonald had about 1,400 men under his command and less than half bore firearms. McDonald and Moore, using their forces as pawns, jockeyed for the upper hand. As McDonald shifted, retreated, or thrust forward, attempting to bypass Moore's force, Moore successfully countered every move and at last held McDonald in check at Moore's Creek Bridge, the last point of defense outside of Wilmington. Here, the revolutionaries under Colonel Richard Caswell, a force of unknown strength and experience to McDonald, sat as a cork in a bottle.

Still hoping to reach the port without a major confrontation, McDonald supported action that would continue the maneuvering and parlaying. Unfortunately, McDonald became ill and could not continue as a member of the officers' council. During the debate that followed McDonald's withdrawal the desire of the younger, less-experienced officers prevailed, and an immediate attack was set in motion.

The result was a rout of the Loyalists by the patriot rebel forces; McDonald received news of the disaster while still on his sickbed. One tradition says that McDonald was found lurking in a hole where he had been hidden by a free black. Another says that he received his captors while sitting on a stump, too ill to stand. However, as soon as the aged warrior reached the camp of the senior patriot office, he insisted, with dignity, on a formal surrender. His sword, having been received by Moore, was returned to the old gentleman as a token of the respect in which the patriot officers and their men held McDonald. Then Moore assured McDonald that he would be treated with respect for his rank, position, and reputation. Moore was inclined to give him parole and allow him to return home because he was ill; however, Colonel Caswell objected and had him taken as a prisoner to New Bern. From New Bern, he was conducted by a guard of horse to Halifax, North Carolina, where he was immediately ushered into jail. McDonald was allowed parole within Halifax on 5 April 1776, but he refused to leave the jail because of the attitude of the citizens. Later, he was sent to a prison in Philadelphia. From there, he and General Richard Prescott were exchanged for General John Sullivan and Lord Stirling about 6 September 1776. McDonald made his way to New York, where he was placed on half pay until 1780.

Early in 1781 McDonald, with a few others from the Cross Creek area, joined Charles, Lord Cornwallis, in North Carolina and became a part of the North Carolina Regiment. From the battle of Guilford to the surrender at Yorktown, McDonald and his forces served with distinction under the command of Lord Cornwallis.

The defeat of the Loyalists at Moore's Creek Bridge dealt the death blow to the British hope to use loyal Americans to defeat the American revolutionaries. Edward Channing correctly observed, "At Moore's Creek and at Sullivan's Island the Carolinians turned aside the one combination of circumstances that might have made conquest possible." It has accurately been stated that the battle of Moore's Creek Bridge was the "Lexington and Concord of the South." McDonald's defeat had far-reaching effects, repercussions that no one, Loyalist or patriot, could have imagined. Regardless, shortly after receiving news of the disaster, Governor Martin spoke lightly of the defeat at Moore's Creek Bridge when he said that the little check they had received would not have any extensive consequences. In his opinion, all was recoverable by a body of troops penetrating into the country. Most probably, Clinton, when he reached the Cape Fear River on 12 March 1776, did not share the governor's enthusiasm. After a brief stay, Clinton, Sir Peter Parker, and the British fleet, having found no organized support, withdrew and put into motion the alternate plan. They sailed away, intending to use a combined attack of army and naval forces to capture Charleston, the port capital of South Carolina. There, they were repulsed as well. The failure of the Loyalists at Moore's Creek Bridge played a major role in keeping the British army out of the South for two years. Even more important, the defeat convinced the Loyalists of the dangers in assisting the British. Therefore, as the king's army drove through the Carolinas in 1780 and 1781, the Loyalists ignored the calls of the army for support. The withholding of food, horses, men, and all other supplies forced Cornwallis to abandon the Carolinas and withdraw to Yorktown in Virginia. There, the British army was trapped and defeated. McDonald was in London in 1784 and later died there. It is not known if he ever married or had children.

• McDonald's military career, traced through consultation of his papers in Audit Office 13/79, Audit Office 13/121, Audit Office 13/122, and Treasury Board Papers, T64/23, housed in the Public Record Office, Kew, London, extends from the battle of Culloden Moor to the American Revolution. Supporting primary information is found in Peter Force, *American Archives*, 4th ser., 4–6, and in the Papers of the Continental Congress. Lorenzo Sabine, *Biographical Sketches of Loyalists of the American Revolution with an Historical Essay* (1864), gives the most concise account of McDonald's life. Hugh F. Rankin, "The Moore's Creek Bridge Campaign, 1776," *North Carolina Historical Review* 26 (Jan. 1953): 23–60, presents a more substantial personality, using Sabine's material and supplementing it with data in "North Carolina Revolutionary Army Account, Secretary of State Treasurer's and Comptroller's Papers Journal A (Public Account) 1775–1776"; *North Carolina Colonial Records*, vol. 10; and *North Carolina State Records*, vols. 11, 12, 15, 17, and 22. Early North Carolina historians Samuel A'Court Ashe, *History of North Carolina* (1908), and Eli W. Caruthers, *Interesting Revolutionary Incidents and Sketches of Characters Chiefly of the "Old North State"* (1856), were the first attempts to show the impact that McDonald had on the history of the state. Later, Duane Myer, *The Highland Scots of North Carolina, 1732–1776* (1961), and Robert DeMond, *The Loyalists in North Carolina during the Revolution* (1940; repr. 1964), explored in greater detail McDonald's influence and actions in rallying the Scot Highlanders of North Carolina in early 1776 and illustrated that his influence extended far beyond the limits of North Carolina.

BOBBY G. MOSS

MCDONALD, Henry (31 Aug. 1890–12 June 1976), professional football player, was born in Port-au-Prince, Haiti. Little is known about his early life except that he was brought to the United States when he was five years old after his natural parents agreed to his adoption by an American coconut and banana importer from Canandaigua, New York. "He was my father's boss," McDonald explained, "and he just took a liking to me. My natural parents realized it was a great opportunity for me to go to America. I didn't see my mother again for over fifty-five years." McDonald was raised in Canandaigua and attended Canandaigua Academy. After the family moved to Rochester, New York, McDonald became the first African-American graduate of East High School, where he was a standout player in both baseball and football. In 1911 McDonald began playing professional football for the Oxford, New York, Pros, beginning a career that would extend through 1920. McDonald was the third African American known to have played professional football. He was preceded by Charles W. Follis, who played for the Shelby Athletic Club (1902–1906), and Charles "Doc" Baker, who played for the Akron Indians (1906–1908, 1911).

In his first professional game, McDonald played halfback for the Oxford Pros against the Rochester Jeffersons, who promptly enticed him to play for them. He spent most of his career with the Jeffersons, later a charter member of the National Football League, occasionally playing for western New York all-star teams, and concluding his playing career in 1920 with the All-Buffaloes team. A handsome, long-legged man, McDonald weighed only 145 pounds but possessed ample speed and was nicknamed "Motorcycle." "Most of the guys were bigger than me," he said, "but I was too quick for them to catch. I could run a hundred yards in ten point two seconds. The world record was ten flat in those days." Rochester owner and coach Leo Lyons agreed, stating that "you can't hit or hurt what you can't see. If you blinked your eyes, McDonald was on his way."

During his pro career, McDonald had a difficult time making ends meet playing football. He recalled that in all the years he played, "I never once took home more than fifteen dollars for one day of football." McDonald added that he "had to play two games to get that much." He often played a morning game in Rochester for the Jeffersons, then took a trolley to Canandaigua and played for the town team in the afternoon. In the summer, McDonald supplemented his income by playing pro baseball for a number of different teams in the New York Negro leagues. In all, he played baseball for seven seasons. Despite his meager earnings, McDonald gloried in being a halfback, because running backs were the star players and received the most money. McDonald recalled that the ball "was soft and shaped like a watermelon. We threw a couple of passes every game, but they were usually a last resort. The ball was made to be carried, not thrown all over the field." Clearly, McDonald was one of the fine professional halfbacks of his era, noted for his long breakaway runs.

Like many early African-American football players, McDonald tended to minimize the problems he faced on the field because of his race. In a 1971 interview, he recalled only one serious racial incident. During the 1917 season, Coach Lyons recruited three college players to bolster the Jeffersons lineup for a game in Ohio against the Canton Bulldogs, who were led by Jim Thorpe. The trouble started when Canton's Earle "Greasy" Neale, a southern-born player, knocked McDonald out of bounds. Raising his fists, he shouted at McDonald, "Black is black and white is white where I come from and the two don't mix." An accomplished boxer, McDonald stood ready to defend himself when

Thorpe intervened. According to McDonald, Thorpe "prevented a real donnybrook. He jumped between us and said, 'We're here to play football.' I never had any trouble after that. Thorpe's word was law on the field." Canton defeated the Rochester team that day by a score of 49–0.

After his retirement, McDonald settled down in Geneva, New York. He was married to Paula (maiden name unknown), with whom he had three children. In 1973 he was among the thirty-eight original inductees into the National Black Sports Hall of Fame. McDonald died in Geneva, New York.

• Materials relating to McDonald's career are in the Professional Football Hall of Fame in Canton, Ohio. All quotes in the text are from newspaper clippings in his file there. See also Ocania Chalk, *Pioneers of Black Sport: The Early Days of the Black Professional Athlete in Baseball, Basketball, Boxing and Football* (1975); Joe Horrigan, "Early Black Professionals," in *Professional Football Researchers Association Annual* (1985), pp. 81–89; Jack Orr, *The Black Athlete: His Story in American History* (1969); Robert Smith, *Illustrated History of Pro Football* (1970); Mike Rathet and Don Smith, *Their Deeds and Dogged Faith* (1984); and Arthur R. Ashe, Jr., *A Hard Road to Glory: A History of the African-American Athlete 1619–1918* (1988). An obituary is in the *New York Times*, 15 June 1976.

JOHN M. CARROLL

MCDONALD, Lawrence Patton (1 Apr. 1935–1 Sept. 1983), U.S. congressman, was born in Atlanta, Georgia, the son of Harold Paul McDonald, a physician, and Callie Grace Patton, who later divorced. McDonald graduated in premed from Davidson College in North Carolina in 1953 and received his doctorate in medicine from Emory University in 1957. From 1957 to 1961 he served as a flight surgeon for the U.S. Naval Reserve Medical Corps, rising to the rank of captain. After fulfilling his military service, McDonald completed a general surgery residency at Grady Memorial Hospital in Atlanta and accepted a postgraduate residency in urology at the University of Michigan, Ann Arbor, from 1963 to 1966. He subsequently established a urology clinic in Atlanta with his brother and father. An enthusiastic booster of laetrile as a cure for cancer, McDonald treated many patients with the controversial drug. In 1978 the family of one of his laetrile patients who had died sued him. A federal jury decided McDonald was not responsible for the death but ordered him to reimburse the family $15,000 in medical fees and expenses.

After serving as the chairman and vice chairman of the Georgia State Medical Education Board from 1969 to 1974, McDonald entered national politics as Georgia's Seventh District congressional representative. He won reelection and served until his death. McDonald's unabashed opinions and tireless efforts on behalf of the Right earned him a reputation as the most conservative member of Congress. In addition to his participation on congressional committees, including the Committee on Armed Services, McDonald was a member of the advisory board of the American Conservative Union, the Committee for Survival of a Free Congress, and the John Birch Society. He also served on the national council of the National Movement to Restore Democracy and belonged to Georgia's Right to Life Movement.

McDonald's efforts on behalf of the John Birch Society earned him the most notoriety. A member of the society's national council, McDonald was elected chair, succeeding the founder and only other chair of the conservative organization, Robert H. Welch. McDonald championed the goals of the Birch Society, which regularly contributed to his election campaigns, by inserting many of its tracts into the *Congressional Record*. He was sharply criticized by congressional opponents and thoughtful observers for his efforts on behalf of his friend and fellow Birch Society member Nelson Bunker Hunt, the Texas silver billionaire. In 1979 McDonald spearheaded a successful effort in Congress to block sales of silver from the government's military stockpile. Government sales would have dumped millions of ounces of silver on the market, depressed prices, and threatened Hunt's bullish investment strategy.

McDonald devoted equal amounts of his personal energy and political influence to support the National Rifle Association and frequently warned that enactment of gun control laws would "leave Americans defenseless against Communist invasion." In 1977 it was revealed that he had accumulated 200 guns in his district residence in Marietta. Responding to public inquiry, McDonald argued, "I think it is foolish to discuss in public your guns or where you keep them . . . I am unaware at any time of having done any violation of law. I have given guns as presents and received guns as presents." Two years earlier, he had expressed similar convictions regarding the right to bear arms in an article on gun control published in *American Opinion*.

McDonald's personal conservative convictions were evident throughout his eight-year career as a representative in Congress. In 1971, in a campaign to rally popular opposition to Senate ratification of the Panama Canal treaties, he traveled across the United States, warning that "anyone who supports or votes for these treaties should be permanently retired from public life." McDonald also opposed a plan to place a memorial of the Reverend Martin Luther King, Jr., in the halls of Congress, maintaining that although the slain civil rights leader had professed nonviolence, he in fact had been committed to violence. Similarly, McDonald voted against making King's birthday a holiday, opposed Justice Department enforcement of fair housing laws, advocated the imposition of a ceiling on food-stamp financing, and opposed controls on hospital costs. A board member of the Christian Voice, one of the early New Right organizations, he also adamantly opposed homosexual rights legislation. In 1981 McDonald sponsored a budget amendment forbidding the Legal Services Corporation to file lawsuits on behalf of people or groups advocating homosexuality as an acceptable lifestyle. At a John Birch Society meeting in the early 1980s he allegedly proposed that homosexuals should be assessed a "user's fee" to pay for AIDS research. Like many other conservatives, the congressman ardently supported a strong military, which he viewed as "America's only hope to avert the destruction threatened by the international Communist conspiracy." McDonald consistently favored defense spending bills and, in particular, lobbied for the controversial MX missile and mandatory draft registration.

McDonald's conservatism placed him at odds with his Democratic colleagues. Finally, his refusal to vote with the Democratic caucus for reelection of Representative Thomas P. O'Neill, Jr., as House Speaker in 1981 cost him his committee assignments.

While traveling to Seoul to attend a ceremony celebrating the thirtieth anniversary of the signing of a mutual defense treaty between the United States and South Korea, McDonald and 268 others died when Korean Flight 007 was shot down after flying into Soviet airspace. The congressman was survived by his wife, the former Kathryn Jackson, their two children, and three children from a previous marriage that had ended in divorce.

• McDonald's papers are not publicly available. Information pertaining to his voting records and interest groups is fully documented in the Library of Congress and the Congressional Quarterly's *Politics in America*. McDonald coauthored (with six others) an article, "Correlation of Urinary Output with Serum and Spinal Fluid Mannitol Levels in Normal and Azotemic Patients," *Journal of Urology* 99 (May 1968): 662–69. He also published articles in various opinion journals of right-wing organizations, notably "Lobbies Control the Congress," *Review of the News* 2 (Feb. 1976): 8, and "Gun Control," *American Opinion* 18 (July 1975): 6. Several articles concerning McDonald and the downing of Korean Flight 007 appear in the *New York Times*, 1, 2, 5, and 12 Sept. 1983. An obituary is in the *New York Times*, 1 Sept. 1983.

SHARON D. RUDY

MCDONNELL, James Smith, Jr. (9 Apr. 1899–22 Aug. 1980), aeronautical engineer and airplane manufacturing executive, was born in Denver, Colorado, the son of James Smith McDonnell, a merchant, and Susan Belle Hunter. He grew up in Little Rock, Arkansas, graduating from the public high school in 1917. After a brief stint in the stateside army during the last part of World War I, McDonnell attended Princeton University, where he studied physics. While there, he became interested both in politics, because of Wilsonian foreign policy, and aeronautics, because of an airplane ride with a barnstormer. His father, believing that McDonnell was "too shy and serious" to succeed in politics, suggested he pursue a career in aviation. Following his father's advice, young McDonnell graduated from Princeton with a bachelor of science degree in 1921 and immediately enrolled in the graduate program in aeronautical engineering at the Massachusetts Institute of Technology. While at MIT he enlisted in the army aviation section and received a reserve pilot's wings in 1923. Two years later McDonnell received his M.S. from MIT.

Although the post–World War I aviation industry employed only about 2,800 individuals, even before completing his graduate studies McDonnell found journeyman work in 1924 as an aeronautical engineer at the Huff-Daland Aircraft Company in Ogdensburg, New York. McDonnell stayed at Huff-Daland only a short time before moving on to the Consolidated Aircraft Company in Buffalo, New York. During the next fifteen years McDonnell was a vagabond aeronautical engineer who moved from one aircraft company to another in search of a challenging assignment, respect, and authority. In all, he worked for eight different firms, accumulated a broad base of experience, and worked on several pioneering aircraft, including the forerunner of the famous Ford Trimotor and two all-metal monoplanes. He was never satisfied unless he controlled the direction of the work.

Nothing pointed up his desire for control better than McDonnell's early venture into business on his own in 1928. In April 1927 the Daniel Guggenheim Fund for the Promotion of Aeronautics announced a competition to design a safer training plane. McDonnell and two colleagues, Constantine Zakhartchenko and James Cowling, resigned their jobs, formed their own company—James S. McDonnell, Jr., and Associates—and entered the competition. What they came up with was the Doodlebug, a two-seat monoplane of all-metal construction. It failed to win the Guggenheim competition, forcing the firm into bankruptcy, but McDonnell thought the experience one of his most satisfying. He and his partners had to find work with other firms, and McDonnell had to wait a decade before he would be able to be his own boss again. He married Mary Elizabeth Finney in 1934; they had two children.

World War II proved a great boon to aeronautical firms in general and in particular to McDonnell's dreams of owning his own aircraft business. He was working for the Glenn L. Martin Company in Baltimore in 1938 when he quit his job, and on 6 July 1939 he organized the McDonnell Aircraft Corporation in Maryland. He quickly moved the firm's offices to St. Louis, because he thought the government would look favorably on the location inland from possible enemy attack on either coast, and rented space in a building owned by American Airlines adjacent to Lambert Field. McDonnell zeroed in on the rapidly expanding military market and sent twelve proposals for airplanes to the army and another four to the navy during his first year of operation. The response was less than impressive, but McDonnell did receive his first government contract, a $3,000 contract to study fighter planes for the army. Nothing came of it. At the end of the first year, McDonnell reported to his stockholders, "Our backlog was zero, sales zero, earnings zero!"

By the fall of 1940 military purchases began to transform McDonnell's firm into a viable aircraft company. The firm won some additional study contracts and received orders to develop and manufacture components that were used in aircraft built by other firms. The bulk of McDonnell's wartime work consisted of manufacturing various parts and subassemblies for Douglas and Boeing aircraft at plants throughout the St. Louis area. It also manufactured under license thirty Fairchild-designed AT-21 trainers for the military.

A turning point in McDonnell Aircraft Corporation's history came in January 1943 when it received a navy contract to design a jet fighter that could fly off an aircraft carrier. The contract pushed McDonnell into the major leagues of aviation with firms such as Boeing, Douglas, and Lockheed. Three years of intense work led to the flight of the FD-1 Phantom from a carrier on 21 July 1946. The company produced sixty of these new fighters for the navy and went on to design and build 895 F2H Banshee jet fighters for carrier operations between 1947 and 1953. McDonnell followed this work in the early 1950s with the design and production of the F-101 Voodoo fighter for the U.S. Air Force. By 1954 the net income of McDonnell's company had reached $3 million per year, but it had received production contracts for only four aircraft of its own design and one designed by Fairchild. All of its contracts, furthermore, were with the military. It had made no attempt to move into the commercial aircraft arena, as had other firms, and throughout the rest of the 1950s McDonnell designed and manufactured a succession of increasingly sophisticated fighter planes. His first wife having died in 1949, McDonnell married Priscilla Graham Brush Forney in 1956; she brought three children to the marriage.

Without question the most successful aircraft built by McDonnell was the F-4 Phantom II, begun in 1953 as a navy attack plane. In the process of design it was transformed into an interceptor, and when production began in 1959 the U.S. military quickly realized that it had a superior aircraft. Within months of entering service, the F-4 set twenty-one world records, including a speed of Mach 2.57 (1,606 miles per hour). Because it was such a successful navy plane, and because of Secretary of Defense Robert S. McNamara's emphasis on commonality among the services, in 1963 McNamara directed the air force to buy F-4s as well. During a production run that did not end until 1981, McDonnell produced 5,057 F-4s, 2,640 of which the air force purchased. The rest went to the navy and eleven foreign countries. The airplane saw active service in numerous military organizations around the globe into the 1990s.

While the F-4 program was getting under way, McDonnell also entered the rapidly developing field of missile and spacecraft technology. The firm had developed several air munitions for use on fighters, but it won its greatest fame in this technical arena for its work on the Mercury and Gemini spacecraft used by the National Aeronautics and Space Administration (NASA) for human spaceflight programs in the early 1960s. In 1965 it was also chosen, along with the Douglas Aircraft Co., by the air force to develop the Manned Orbiting Laboratory (MOL), an ill-conceived effort to build a space station for military purposes.

While the F-4 production line was going strong in the mid-1960s, McDonnell purchased a controlling interest in Douglas Aircraft, which had exhausted its resources in a competition with Lockheed and Boeing to develop the first wide-bodied jetliners. In 1967 the two companies formally merged. With McDonnell at the controls, McDonnell Douglas Aircraft Co. emerged as a giant in the industry and remained so throughout the rest of his life. McDonnell's government contracts, coupled with those of Douglas, made it possible to move into new ventures, and plans proceeded for the building of a wide-body commercial plane, the DC-10, which first flew in 1970.

McDonnell also reorganized the merged companies into several divisions during the mid-1970s. The old McDonnell operation in St. Louis concentrated on military combat aircraft, while the Douglas plant in Long Beach, California, handled commercial transport activities. A Tulsa, Oklahoma, branch of Douglas was dedicated to component design and production, while the McDonnell Douglas Astronautics Company in Huntington Beach, California, managed the expanding rocketry and space hardware orders. A subsidiary of McDonnell Douglas in Canada produced DC-9 and DC-10 wings, and another subsidiary financed commercial aircraft sales. Electronics and automation sections rounded out the company. McDonnell was chair of the board at the time of his death in Ladue, Missouri.

James S. McDonnell, Jr., was one of a cadre of aviation pioneers who established the aerospace industry in the United States. He was enormously successful in obtaining and keeping the federal government as a client for his goods and services, and he did not move beyond those relatively comfortable confines until he bought out Douglas in 1967. That allowed his firm to enter the commercial aircraft production scene with the full experience and reputation of Douglas's legendary efforts in that arena backing the move.

• There is no formal collection of McDonnell's papers. Material by and about him can be found at the McDonnell Douglas Aircraft Co., St. Louis, but access is controlled. Additional material about McDonnell can be found in Douglas J. Ingalls, *The McDonnell Douglas Story* (1979); Rene J. Francillon, *McDonnell Douglas Aircraft since 1920* (1979); and John B. Rae, *Climb to Greatness: The American Aircraft Industry, 1920–1960* (1968). An obituary is in the *New York Times*, 23 Aug. 1980.

ROGER D. LAUNIUS

MCDOUGALL, Alexander (1732–9 June 1786), revolutionary leader and banker, was born on the island of Islay, off the western coast of Scotland, the son of Ronald McDougall, a dairyman and milk dealer, and Elizabeth (maiden name unknown). McDougall migrated to New York with his parents at the age of six. They initially planned to settle on the province's northern frontier but remained in New York City instead. McDougall's father prospered there, but the son went to sea. Returning briefly to Islay in 1751, he married Nancy McDougall, a distant relative. They had three children before her death in 1763. In 1767 he married Hannah Bostwick. They had no children.

During the French and Indian War (1756–1763), McDougall moved from merchant seafaring to privateering, commanding two different vessels. When peace returned, he established himself as a small merchant in New York City. Although he was interested enough in public affairs to attend the provincial assembly as a spectator, he did not take an active role in the Stamp Act crisis (1765–1766). This, apparently, was because he had aligned himself politically with the province's landed leadership, centered on the Livingston family. Their goal was to control and moderate popular resistance to Britain rather than to stimulate it. McDougall's name does not appear on the earliest list of New York's organized Sons of Liberty.

McDougall advanced to popular leadership in 1769, when he published his broadside, "To the Betrayed Inhabitants of the City and Colony of New-York," over the pseudonym "A Son of Liberty." Publishing the piece did not mark a break with the Livingstons, who had lost control of the assembly in the election that year. He charged the provincial assembly with sacrificing New Yorkers' rights for partisan advantage. When he was revealed as the author, the assembly imprisoned him. He was imprisoned twice on the assembly's orders, serving a total of 162 days, but he was never convicted of an actual crime. His jailing had echoes of Parliament's notorious imprisonment of its dissident member John Wilkes, and patriots feted McDougall with imagery recalling the Wilkes case. Thereafter, McDougall was very active in the politics of resistance and revolution. He helped organize New Yorkers for direct resistance to the Tea Act at the end of 1773. The city's initial tea ship turned around at Sandy Hook after a committee including McDougall warned its captain of the consequences should he enter the harbor. When a second vessel did try to bring in dutied tea in April 1774, McDougall had a hand in organizing the dumping of its cargo.

About the same time, McDougall became a member of the city's committee of correspondence. From that, he went on to serve on its committees of Fifty-one, Sixty, and One Hundred, which gave leadership to the growing revolutionary movement and, increasingly, drained power away from established institutions. On 6 July 1774 he presided over a major popular meeting that resolved the city's intention to resist the Coercive Acts, which Parliament had passed to punish Boston and Massachusetts for their more famous tea party. In large part the meeting was a ploy to overcome a reluctance to act within the Committee of Fifty-One itself. It led to the breaking up of the Fifty-one as McDougall, along with others of a militant mind, chose to resign rather than accept the committee's decision to repudiate the public meeting.

Between 1774 and 1775 McDougall served in several of New York's provincial congresses. He was also chosen a member of the provincial assembly at its final election in February 1776. The election had been called by the royal governor in a bid to frustrate the revolutionary movement, but after the new house proved to be dominated by McDougall's sort, the governor decided not to convene it.

McDougall had already become the ranking colonel in New York City's revolutionary militia. He advanced to brigadier general in the Continental service in 1776 and to major general the following year. During the summer and autumn of 1776 he took part in George Washington's defensive campaign against the British that began with the battle of Long Island and ended with the battle of White Plains.

Except for periods of illness, McDougall remained on active service throughout the war. He played a major role in fortifying the Hudson Highlands after the British drove the patriots out of New York City. Washington made him commander at West Point after Benedict Arnold's treason. At the war's end, when the army was encamped at Newburgh, New York, McDougall took a prominent role in focusing the discontent of officers about their pay and conditions. As early as 1780 he led an officers' delegation to Congress, and he campaigned on their behalf when he became a representative from New York the following year. A public dispute with his fellow general William Heath in 1782 led to McDougall's being court-martialed on seven separate charges of "conduct unmilitary and unbecoming an officer." He was found guilty on one and subjected to a public reprimand. Restored to duty, he returned to pursuing the country's debt to the officers. Although he was not a direct member of the "Newburgh Conspiracy" of 1783, which raised the possibility of a coup d'état, he played on the fear of such an event when he again represented the officers' case to Congress.

McDougall was elected to the New York State Senate when peace returned at the end of 1783, serving until his death. His son-in-law John Laurance was a close associate of Alexander Hamilton, both in state and national politics and in the founding of the Bank of New York. By the time he died, McDougall himself was moving into Hamilton's circle, and he became the first president of the bank. He thus moved through the revolutionary era "from the bottom up," making the climb from street radical to high-ranking general, national figure, and emergent capitalist. He died in New York City.

• McDougall's own papers are in the New-York Historical Society. He is the subject of two full-length studies, Roger J. Champagne, *Alexander McDougall and the American Revolution in New York* (1975), and Sister Anna Madeleine Shannon, "General Alexander McDougall: Citizen and Soldier, 1732–1786" (Ph.D. diss., Fordham Univ., 1957). He appears in almost all accounts of the Revolution in New York, including Carl Lotus Becker, *The History of Political Parties in the Province of New York, 1760–1776* (1909), Edward Countryman, *A People in Revolution: The American Revolution and Political Society in New York, 1760–1790* (1981), and Gary B. Nash, *The Urban Crucible: Social Change, Political Consciousness, and the Origins of the American Revolution* (1979).

EDWARD COUNTRYMAN

MCDOUGALL, Frances Harriet Whipple Green. *See* Green, Frances Harriet Whipple.

MCDOUGALL, William (22 June 1871–28 Nov. 1938), psychologist, was born in Chadderton, Lancashire, England, the son of Isaac McDougall, a second-generation Scottish industrial entrepreneur, and Rebekah Smalley. William was a precocious child. His talent for languages, mathematics, and science, coupled with his family's motivation to achieve and its wealth from chemical, iron, and wood pulp industries, enabled him to excel in school, first in a local private school for boys and then abroad in the *Realgymnasium* in Weimar, Germany. His father wanted him to study law or to help manage the family businesses, but William, with his mother's support, decided to pursue a career in science.

At the age of fifteen, McDougall entered the nearby University of Manchester and completed two degrees in four years, receiving a B.Sc. in 1889 and a Geology I in 1890, with a focus on biology and evolution. In 1890 he won a scholarship to Cambridge University, where, under the tutelage of W. H. R. Rivers, he began a lifelong interest in bridging biological sciences, such as neurophysiology, and social sciences, such as anthropology. In 1894 he won a scholarship to St. Thomas Hospital in London for medical studies, where he did experiments on muscle contraction in the laboratory of C. S. Sherrington. In 1896 he won the Grainger Testimonial Prize for research in anatomy and physiology and in 1897 began his medical residency.

McDougall's interests soon shifted from medical science to the new field of psychology as a result of three events. The first was his reading William James's *Principles of Psychology* (1890), which described a science of human behavior based on biology and on experimentation. The second was nomination in 1898 as a fellow of St. John's College at Cambridge University. For this honor, McDougall submitted a proposal for a neurophysiological solution to the mind-body problem. The third event was joining the 1898 Cambridge Anthropological Expedition to the Torres Straits near New Guinea. McDougall's study of the sensory abilities of the straits' inhabitants was perhaps the first empirical cross-cultural research in psychology. After further anthropological studies on cultural diffusion in Borneo, McDougall returned to England in 1899, firmly convinced that psychology was the best bridge between biology and anthropology.

That same year, McDougall married Anne Hickmore, with whom he eventually had five children. They moved immediately to Göttingen, Germany, where McDougall spent a year of study with G. E. Müller on psychophysics, memory, and methods of laboratory experimentation. Having gained perhaps the best and broadest quality of education and training in neurophysiology, anthropology, and experimental methods since Wilhelm Wundt, William James, and Sigmund Freud, McDougall was now set to begin his career.

In 1900 McDougall was appointed lecturer in psychology at the University of London, where he devised experiments on color vision and lectured on child psychology. Here, too, McDougall became a colleague of Francis Galton, Karl Pearson, and Charles Spearman and joined their projects in mental measurements and eugenics. In 1904 he boldly accepted an appointment as reader in mental philosophy at Oxford University, where the notion that the human mind might be understood by experimental research met strong resistance. In 1908 he published *Introduction to Social Psychology*, in which he argued that perceptions, emotions, motivations, and behavior are fundamentally biological, based on inborn purposive dispositions, or instincts. This book enjoyed large sales, as did his *Psychology: The Study of Behavior* (1912), which sold over 100,000 copies.

Taking a bold approach to life, McDougall viewed no topic as taboo for empirical study and experimentation, including psychic phenomena and Lamarkian theories that learning could be inherited. At the start of World War I, he dropped numerous research projects to join the French army as a private driving an ambulance. He soon was serving as a major in the British Army Medical Corps treating shell shock. From observation of these cases, he disputed the Freudian theory that all neuroses are sexual in origin. After the war, he began psychoanalysis with Carl Jung in Zurich, but felt that he gained from this experience little insight or benefit.

In 1920 McDougall emigrated to the United States to fill the chair of psychology at Harvard University, then the world's most prestigious academic position in psychology. At Harvard, however, he immediately entered into controversies because of the racist nature of his lectures and writings on eugenics and because he stood forth in public debates opposing, even ridiculing, the stimulus-response theories of the behaviorists. Nevertheless, during this period, he wrote *Outline of Psychology* (1923), in which he emphasized the goal-seeking, future-oriented aspects of human thought and behavior. He also published a textbook on abnormal psychology, as well as several papers on Freudian theory.

In 1927 McDougall accepted a professorship at Duke University, where he supported J. B. Rhine's laboratory studies of extrasensory perception and continued his own Lamarkian experiments on improved learning across successive generations of white rats. McDougall also wrote numerous books of social commentary, including several opposed to militarism and the arms race. He predicted the development of nuclear weapons and foresaw that they would eventually place the whole human race under threat of doom. He died of cancer in Durham, North Carolina. Ever the psychologist, he left copious notes analyzing the experience of his final pain. Posthumous accounts of McDougall's career by former students reveal that he had anticipated and supported many developments in psychology, for example, that brain cells function in neural networks or cell assemblies, that behaviors satisfy purposive drives, and that the interrelations of many variables can be attributed to underlying factors (see Donald Adam, "William McDougall," *Psychological Review* 46 [1939]: 1–8, and Cyril Burt, "The Permanent Contributions of McDougall to Psychology," *British Journal of Educational Psychology* 25 [1955]: 10–22).

• Although after McDougall's death, many of his personal papers were destroyed by mistake, the Duke University Archives holds 1,800 items and twenty-three volumes of letters, manuscripts, research notes, and many photos from his 1899 travels in New Guinea and Borneo. McDougall's autobiographical accounts of his career are in Carl Murchison, ed., *History of Psychology in Autobiography* (1930), and "Experimental Psychology and Psychological Experiment," *Character and Personality* 1 (1933): 195–213. Bibliographies of McDougall's twenty books and more than 150 articles are May Smith, "William McDougall: Bibliography," *Character and Personality* 7 (1938): 184–19, and Anthony Robinson, *William McDougall: A Bibliography Together with a Brief Outline of His Life* (1943). Obituaries are, by John Flugel, in the *British Journal of Psychology* 29 (1939): 321–28, and in the *New York Times*, 29 Nov. 1938.

FLOYD W. RUDMIN

MCDOWELL, Ephraim (11 Nov. 1771–25 June 1830), surgeon and general medical practitioner, was born in Rockbridge County, Virginia, the son of Samuel McDowell, a jurist, and Mary McClung. McDowell was educated informally by his family members (he had eight older siblings) and by tutors after the family moved to Danville in the Kentucky Territory in 1782. In 1790 McDowell returned to Staunton, Virginia, to join the household of Dr. Alexander Humphreys, where he apprenticed for three years. Humphreys, an Edinburgh University graduate, stressed the importance of anatomical experience for his apprentices.

In 1793 McDowell arranged to go to Edinburgh for further study, although the trip placed a financial burden on the family. While he attended the medical lectures at the university, it was the extramural lectures of John Bell that seemed to have exerted the most profound influence on McDowell's subsequent career. Bell was known as a careful surgeon who placed great emphasis on anatomical knowledge. He taught the best surgical judgment of the day and stimulated his students with the hope for new surgical solutions to clinical problems. McDowell did not take an Edinburgh degree, presumably because of the extra expenses, but returned to Danville in 1795 to begin practice.

Because of his familial connections, a serious lack of competition, particularly in difficult surgical cases, and the eclat of foreign training, McDowell was rapidly successful. In 1802 he married Sarah Shelby, the daughter of the governor of the state, further enhancing his social position. They had six children. He performed operations not previously done in the region. Two operations for which he achieved particular recognition were the radical (surgical) cure of hernia and lithotomy (the operation to remove bladder stones). In the days before anesthesia, speed and precision were particularly important in surgery. To this end McDowell reviewed the regional anatomy prior to any major procedure and drilled his assistants repeatedly in the parts each was expected to play in the operation. He always used the lateral perineal incision, common in Edinburgh during his training. By 1828 he had performed the lithotomy thirty-two times without a fatality. One of his patients was a seventeen-year-old James Polk, who later remembered the surgeon fondly for his cure as well as his care and concern. In 1807 McDowell was elected to the Philadelphia Medical Society as a corresponding member.

McDowell is best remembered for pioneering surgery to remove the ovaries as a treatment for cancerous growth. In 1809 he was called sixty miles to consult on the particularly baffling case of Jane Crawford, who was believed to be pregnant beyond term with twins. McDowell diagnosed an ovarian cyst that would, he believed, be fatal unless removed. This was the opinion he had been taught in Edinburgh, where Bell among others had been aware of drainage operations for cysts containing fluid and had suggested the possibility of surgical removal as a treatment of solid tumors. But no one had yet tried it when McDowell offered to operate on Crawford. With his typical care McDowell would only consider doing the operation in Danville, where he could properly train his assistants before the surgery. Crawford would have to travel sixty miles, mostly on horseback, to undergo the procedure. She surprised McDowell by coming, and on Christmas Day 1809 McDowell undertook the operation. Stories abound of a mob gathering outside the house, but there is no contemporary evidence to support them. The operation was a success, and Crawford was out of bed in five days and shortly returned home.

In 1813 and 1817 McDowell encountered similar cases and again operated successfully. After three cases he was convinced to publish an account of what he could remember. Because he kept no notes he had only his ledgers to re-create the Crawford operation. He submitted a manuscript for publication to Philip Syng Physick of Philadelphia, who rejected it; then editor Thomas James arranged its publication in his *Eclectic Repertory*. A manuscript was sent to Bell in Edinburgh, but he was traveling in Italy and did not receive it. His successor in the surgical program at Edinburgh, John Lizars, eventually published it as part of a paper in which Lizars described his own operative experience (*Edinburgh Medical and Surgical Journal*, Oct. 1824). The account was met with skepticism, but McDowell in 1819 reported two more operations, including his first postoperative death. He eventually operated at least twelve times but paid a price for his diligence: he became viewed as too innovative, too prone to operate, and his practice suffered. However, he was frequently called in cases of ovarian disease.

In 1822 McDowell received what renowned surgeon Samuel D. Gross believed as late as 1860 to be the largest surgical fee paid in the United States when a grateful husband, John Overton of Hermitage, Tennessee, trebled his requested $500. In 1825 the University of Maryland awarded McDowell an honorary medical degree for his achievement, but he was also involved in controversy with a variety of people about the Overton surgery, among them his nephew and assistant, Joseph McDowell, who claimed credit for the operation. McDowell, who served on the Board of Trustees of Centre College in Danville from 1819 to 1829, continued his philanthropic support of the college and St. Paul's Church in Danville despite the decline in his practice. He died in Danville and left an estate in excess of $40,000, an indication of his early successes in practice as well as of his thrift.

• No Corpus of McDowell's professional or personal papers is known to exist. His major letters are reprinted in J. N. McCormack, ed., "Some of the Medical Pioneers of Kentucky," published as a supplement to the *Kentucky Medical Journal*, vol. 15 (1917). His two papers on ovariotomy are in the *Eclectic Repertory and Analytical Review*, no. 7 (1817): 242 and no. 9 (1819): 546. The best biographical sketch is Samuel D. Gross, *Lives of Eminent American Physicians and Surgeons of the Nineteenth Century* (1861), pp. 207–30. Two larger biographies are Mary Y. Ridenbaugh (later editions under the name Mary Thompson Valentine), *The Biography of Ephraim McDowell* (1890), and August Schachner, *Ephraim McDowell, "Father of Ovariotomy" and Founder of Abdominal Surgery* (1921). See also Emmet F. Horine, "The Stagesetting for Ephraim McDowell, 1771–1830," *Bulletin of the History of Medicine*, no. 24 (1950): 149–67.

THE EDITORS

MCDOWELL, Fred. *See* McDowell, Mississippi Fred.

MCDOWELL, Irvin (15 Oct. 1818–4 May 1885), soldier, was born in Columbus, Ohio, the son of Abram Irvin McDowell and Eliza Selden Lord. He attended the Collège de Troyes in France and in 1834 received an appointment to the U.S. Military Academy at West Point. He graduated in 1838, twenty-third in a class of forty-eight. McDowell was commissioned a lieutenant of artillery and was an instructor and staff officer at West Point (1841–1845). In the war with Mexico he served on John E. Wool's staff, was brevetted for gallantry at the battle of Buena Vista, and then was appointed to Winfield Scott's headquarters staff. In 1849 he married Helen Burden, with whom he had four children, and settled into a series of staff assignments. In 1858–1859 he was in Europe, studying military systems there.

When the Civil War began, McDowell was a brevet major and again served on General Scott's staff. McDowell was a man of physical energy, wide interests, and strong opinions with no obvious vices and practically no personal charm or ordinary good manners. He had powerful patrons, especially Salmon P. Chase, but no observable qualifications for high command. In late May 1861 he was given the command of the Union forces in the Department of Northeastern Virginia with expectations of an early offensive. While McDowell took steps to organize his "army," the Confederates took up positions along Bull Run, about five miles north of Manassas, Virginia. Their commander was P. G. T. Beauregard, McDowell's classmate and the victor at Fort Sumter. Elements of both armies faced off near Winchester, the Confederates under Joseph E. Johnston and the Federals under Robert Patterson. In order to prevent Johnston from reinforcing Beauregard, Patterson should have attacked or at least pressed his opponent, or he might have marched his forces to support McDowell. He did neither, although Scott's orders clearly directed him to occupy Johnston. McDowell planned to outflank Beauregard and force him out of his fixed positions along Bull Run, a sensible enough plan, assuming energetic leadership, effective staff work, and experienced soldiers in the ranks. Also, Patterson would have to contain Johnston. These happy circumstances did not occur, and McDowell, for all his outward show of confidence, doubted that he could make the plan work, mainly because his soldiers were without experience or proper training.

Patterson postured and procrastinated while Johnston, on 18 July, dispatched some 9,000 soldiers by rail to Manassas. Most of them arrived on 20–21 July, in time to take part in the fighting. McDowell began his advance on 16 July, unaware of Johnston's movements. On 18 July a brief clash occurred at Blackburn's Ford, and the Federals retreated. This apparently heightened McDowell's lack of confidence in his soldiers, and rather than push the main attack forward, he hesitated. Not until late on 20 July did he order the attack for the following day. Unfortunately, his army was not in place for a concerted effort, while the Confederates were in a strong defensive position and poised for a possible counterattack. A secondary threat and holding movement by General Daniel Tyler was not launched in a timely manner, giving Beauregard time to move against McDowell's main effort. McDowell did not concentrate his forces but fed his brigades in seriatim. His exhausted and poorly led soldiers could not sustain the attack nor withstand the Confederate counter thrust. Thanks to effective delaying actions by regular units, the Federal army escaped more or less intact but thoroughly routed. McDowell, with some justice, blamed the politicians for urging a premature battle. Still, with energetic leadership by their generals, especially McDowell, the Union forces should have carried the day.

Command in the East was now given over to George B. McClellan. McDowell commanded a division and then a corps around Washington, while McClellan took the bulk of the army to the Virginia Peninsula to contend with Johnston and Robert E. Lee. McDowell was to screen the capital against attack or join McClellan in a pincers movement against the Confederates. Thanks to Thomas J. "Stonewall" Jackson's maneuvers in the Shenandoah and the Lincoln administration's fear for the capital, McDowell's force was largely irrelevant to the campaign. In late August

McDowell led a corps in John Pope's disastrous campaign called Second Bull Run (Second Manassas). Lee thoroughly outgeneraled Pope, and McDowell shared in Pope's disgrace. McDowell held no other important commands, and in 1864 he was sent to command a territorial department on the West Coast. From 1868 to 1872 he commanded the Department of the East and from 1872 to 1876 the Department of the South. He then returned to San Francisco until his retirement in 1882. He died there after serving as the city park commissioner.

McDowell was clearly out of his depth as an army commander. Perhaps even a corps was too much for him. Staff duty or service as an artillery officer at a relatively junior rank was his proper niche. He was effective enough as a planner, but in the field he could not fight from the map or react to circumstances. He seemed at times to be thoroughly adrift mentally, as if he were but a passive spectator rather than a leader. He transferred his own lack of self-confidence to his soldiers; never did he believe them to be the equals of the opposition. Such was the cast of mind of the commanders of the Army of the Potomac until George G. Meade took command before Gettysburg.

• McDowell's public career is in Warren W. Hassler, Jr., *Commanders of the Army of the Potomac* (1962); William C. Davis, *Battle at Bull Run: A History of the First Major Campaign of the Civil War* (1977); and John J. Hennessy, *Return to Bull Run: The Campaign and Battle of Second Manassas* (1993).

JOHN T. HUBBELL

MCDOWELL, John (11 Feb. 1751–22 Dec. 1820), educator and lawyer, was born in Peters Township, Cumberland, now Franklin County, Pennsylvania, the son of William McDowell and Mary Maxwell, Scotch-Irish farmers. He lived intermittently within a stockade, his log home having twice been burned in Indian raids during the French and Indian wars. Though living on the frontier, McDowell had a good elementary education and attended John King's Latin school for three years until Indians destroyed it in 1763. His former teacher John King was a graduate of the College of Philadelphia and arranged for McDowell to gain entrance to the institution in 1768. Because he lacked funds, McDowell tutored in lieu of tuition and board, and graduated in 1771, giving the English oration "On the Advantages of Studying History." He continued tutoring at the college for eleven years and taught Provost William Smith's class in natural philosophy. He served as a private in the Continental army in 1777, but his frail constitution forced him to resign after a few weeks.

Judge Robert Goldsborough, the uncle of one of McDowell's former students, Charles Goldsborough, persuaded McDowell to read law in his Cambridge, Maryland, law office in 1782. McDowell taught school in Cambridge while reading law, gained admittance to the Dorchester County bar in 1783, and conducted a lucrative law practice with many of the state's important landholders. Through his important Maryland connections, he was appointed professor of mathematics and acting principal at the new St. John's College at Annapolis in August 1789. He began teaching in November of that year and became principal in 1790. The primarily Episcopalian board of visitors and governors of St. John's were anxious to promote the college as a state-aided nondenominational school to mirror Washington College, founded on the state's Eastern Shore at Chestertown in 1782. McDowell's Presbyterianism, his ties to the nonsectarian University of the State of Pennsylvania (later University of Pennsylvania), and his proven teaching ability prepared him well for the position, even though trustees had advertised for a "Gentleman of Great Character from Europe." As a Federalist, he defended the college's receipt of state funds against Republican legislators who demanded that all public monies for education be given to lower schools. Discouraged by the constant uncertainty about funding, he resigned in 1801. Even though the trustees persuaded him to remain, he resigned again in 1806 when the college lost all state funds. He returned that year to the University of Pennsylvania as professor of natural philosophy and became the university's third provost in 1807, the first graduate of the college to be named to that office.

Historian Edward P. Cheyney called these years the "lowest period in the history of the College" (*History of the University of Pennsylvania, 1740–1940* [1940], p. 186). Because of the trustees' constant interference and the increased competition from area colleges, the university maintained a course of study of only two years, and enrollment fell in 1807 to just seventeen undergraduates. Unlike the robust University Medical School, the undergraduate school was in desperate straits. McDowell was a good scholar, writer, and teacher, but he had little power to improve the situation because trustees allowed the provost little more than disciplinary duties. Ill health forced his resignation in 1810. In recognition of his work, he received an LL.D. from the University of Pennsylvania in 1807 and was elected a member of the American Philosophical Society the same year. In 1811 he returned to live with relatives in Franklin County, Pennsylvania, where he again practiced law.

St. John's College offered him the principalship in 1812, which he declined, but he accepted the post in 1815 after the legislature restored $1,000 to support the college. By 1816 he mourned his decision, blaming the difficulties of higher education in Maryland upon the ill effects of democracy as well as the inaction of the college trustees. He left when the board closed the college temporarily in 1817. Although St. John's reopened in 1818, McDowell was now quite ill and spent much of his last two years at Governor Charles Goldsborough's home near Cambridge, Maryland. Late in 1820 he returned to his sister's home near Mercersburg, Pennsylvania, where he died. Never having married, he left an estate of $40,000 to his relatives and most of his library to the University of Pennsylvania.

As a mature scholar, McDowell maintained that the mental discipline of a classical liberal arts education suited his students for leadership in the new nation, which he fervently believed needed wise counsel. A dignified, kind, Christian gentleman, he was held in high esteem by planters, scholars, trustees, former classmates, and students. St. John's College prospered under him in its first decade until the funding became tenuous, and his second departure, after which the college closed temporarily, prompted alumni such as Francis Scott Key to support the college effectively in the future. Although his impact upon the University of Pennsylvania was less significant, the school's problems at the time were perhaps beyond any one person's capabilities to solve. He was as gracious as a Federalist could be in a Republican era.

• On McDowell's early years, see the *Biographical Annals of Franklin County, Pennsylvania* (1905), and Women's Club of Mercersburg, Pennsylvania, *Old Mercersburg* (1912). Although there is no collection of his papers, some of his letters are in the Gratz collection and Tilghman papers at the Historical Society of Pennsylvania; other contemporary sources are in the Maryland Diocesan Archives and St. John's College Archives at the Maryland State Archives. Charlotte Fletcher, "John McDowell, Federalist: President of St. John's College," *Maryland Historical Magazine* 84 (1989): 242–51, is an excellent overview of his impact upon the college and contains an extensive bibliography. See also W. B. Norris, *Annapolis: Its Colonial and Naval Story* (1925), and Tench Tilghman, *The Early History of St. John's in Annapolis* (1984). Sketches about him at the University of Pennsylvania include the *Alumni Register, University of Pennsylvania* (Oct. 1903); *General Alumni Catalog of the University of Pennsylvania* (1917); George Bacon Wood, *The History of the University of Pennsylvania from Its Origin to the Year 1827* (1834); and Horace M. Lippincott, *The University of Pennsylvania, Franklin's College* (1919).

ROBERT J. TAGGART

MCDOWELL, Joseph Nash (1 Apr. 1805–25 Sept. 1868), anatomist and teacher, was born in Lexington, Kentucky, the son of John McDowell and Lucy LeGrand or Lagrand. McDowell began his medical studies at the medical department of Transylvania University in Lexington, the first medical school west of the Allegheny Mountains, and graduated in 1825. Following graduation, his connection with his uncle, Ephraim McDowell, led to his appointment to the chair of anatomy at Transylvania. Ephraim McDowell was a famed Danville, Kentucky, surgeon who was a pioneer in the field of operative gynecology. A year later Joseph McDowell held a similar position, the chair of anatomy at the newly formed Jefferson Medical College in Philadelphia, but he stayed for just one term, returning to Lexington in 1827. Shortly thereafter he married Amanda Virginia Drake, sister of Daniel Drake, one of the eminent American physicians of the nineteenth century. They had three sons who survived childhood.

The details of McDowell's life between 1827 and 1831 are obscure. He probably was in practice in Lexington during this period. In 1831 he went to Cincinnati, where he taught anatomy at the newly established medical department of Miami University in association with his brother-in-law, Daniel Drake. In 1835 he joined Drake in the establishment of the Cincinnati Medical College, where McDowell was professor of anatomy. When the college ceased existence in 1839, he departed Cincinnati for St. Louis, Missouri, in late 1839 or early 1840.

McDowell soon set about organizing a faculty of medicine under the charter of Kemper College. In 1845, however, Kemper was forced to close because of financial insolvency, but McDowell's College continued until 1846, when it became the Medical Department of the University of the State of Missouri. In 1857 a reorganization of the university required all faculty to be full-time; unwilling to give up private practice, the medical faculty members chose to become independent. Until the outbreak of the Civil War, the school operated as the Missouri Medical College. After the war McDowell reestablished the college, and it continued until its merger with its rival, St. Louis Medical College, in 1899. The merged schools formed the basis of the present School of Medicine of Washington University.

McDowell was highly successful during his years in St. Louis (1840–1860). In addition to his involvement in the college he had a large surgical practice. In 1861, when South Carolina seceded from the Union, McDowell took up the southern cause. He embarked by steamboat for Vicksburg with many of his students to join the Confederate armies. In 1862 he eluded the Union blockade and went to Europe, where he was warmly received by the universities in Edinburgh and Paris. He claimed that he was on a secret mission for the Confederacy, which was probably a fantasy on his part.

After the end of the Civil War McDowell returned to St. Louis and reopened his medical college, but, according to an unpublished memoir of his student J. F. Snyder, "He was heart broken, wrecked financially and physically. . . . Casting his lot with the Confederacy had alienated the esteem and confidence of nearly all his former old and best patrons; and he was in no condition to form new associations of value."

McDowell was a superb anatomist and an amusing and entertaining lecturer as well. A pupil of McDowell's recalled that he "made even the dry bones talk." He was also vain and impetuous, however, and in his conflicts with colleagues he often employed invective and ridicule. Shortly after establishing his medical school in St. Louis McDowell delivered a number of vituperative lectures against Jesuitism, because he felt that the Jesuits of St. Louis University had allowed a rival medical school (the St. Louis Medical College) to organize under its charter. Following these lectures McDowell became so fearful of retaliation that be began carrying a sidearm and had a brass chest-protector made. He was an aggressive champion of the Know Nothing Party and made many speeches on its behalf, railing against foreign immigration and Catholicism. Further, he was proslavery. Reaction to his attacks and political causes merely confirmed his sense of persecution by conspiracies.

Despite McDowell's erratic notions, some contemporaries saw him as a man of genius. Henry Clay, who knew McDowell well, once said, "There never was a greater mind than McDowell's and one so totally disabled by eccentricities." As to his eccentricities, McDowell had his medical college building in St. Louis built like a fortress—a huge, octagonal stone building. His nearby home was similarly constructed. During a bout of severe illness, believing himself near death, McDowell called for Charles W. Stevens, his partner in medical practice, and Drake McDowell, his son, to his bedside to obtain their pledge that, in the event of his death, they would take him in an alcohol-filled coffin to Mammoth Cave, Kentucky, and suspend the coffin from the roof of the cave. He felt that such a burial would preserve the remains in a perfect state and protect them from grave robbers. He had attempted a similar burial of one of his children in a cave near Hannibal, Missouri, but was thwarted when vandals broke into it. It is not known if the men agreed to McDowell's request, but he received an ordinary burial.

McDowell died in St. Louis from what the *Daily Missouri Republican* called a "congestive chill."

The major westward expansion of the United States occurred during the first half of the nineteenth century. Important medical institutions modeled after European schools and particularly those in England and Scotland were already in place along the Eastern Seaboard. A similar development in social infrastructure began west of the Appalachian chain as a result of the efforts of a small group of medical pioneers, McDowell prominent among them. Despite his eccentricities and his advocacy of controversial social issues, he was a superb teacher and a visionary medical educator. He was one of the pioneers who brought medical education to the West.

• The largest collection of resource material, published and unpublished, including material related to McDowell's medical schools, is at the Missouri Historical Society in St. Louis; the collection includes biographies, obituaries, newspaper clippings, memoirs, original journal and magazine articles, letters, and other memorabilia. Detailed biographies include Robert E. Schlueter, "Joseph Nash McDowell (1805–1868)," *Washington University Medical Alumni Quarterly*, Oct. 1937, pp. 4–14; and Marjorie E. Fox Grisham, "Joseph Nash McDowell and the Medical Department of Kemper College: 1840–1845," *Bulletin of the Missouri Historical Society*, July 1956, pp. 358–71. Additional biographical information is in Otto Juettner, *Daniel Drake and His Followers: Historical and Biographical Sketches* (1909).

STANLEY L. BLOCK

MCDOWELL, Mary Eliza (30 Nov. 1854–14 Oct. 1936), reformer and administrator, was born in Cincinnati, Ohio, the daughter of Malcolm McDowell, a manufacturer, and Jane Gordon. She grew up in the large house of her maternal grandfather, a steamboat builder, and mixed freely with children of Irish and German immigrants living in an industrial neighborhood in Cincinnati. McDowell attended public school and for a few years a private girls' school; however, because she was needed at home to help with younger brothers, she did not continue her education, which she later regretted. She followed her father into the Methodist church, shared his sympathy for African Americans, and was proud of his military career and that of her uncle, General Irvin McDowell. Malcolm McDowell, a manufacturer of iron and steel, moved his family to Chicago about 1870. Mary McDowell assisted victims of the 1871 fire and was active in a northside Methodist church and later in a church in Evanston, where the McDowells settled in the 1880s.

In the 1880s McDowell found in the Woman's Christian Temperance Union a way to express her religious beliefs and utilize her outgoing personality. She organized young women's leagues in the Midwest and by 1887 was national director of this activity. Already an experienced Sunday school teacher, McDowell was attracted to the kindergarten movement in 1889 and in 1890 completed Elizabeth Harrison's training school in Chicago. She then taught in New York and supervised WCTU kindergartens until the fall of 1891, when she became the head kindergarten teacher at Hull-House in Chicago. McDowell also drew the pupils' mothers into a club and expanded that into the Hull-House Woman's Club. Called back to Evanston in 1893 by a family illness, she volunteered at Northwestern University Settlement and read widely on social and economic problems. In 1894, upon Jane Addams's recommendation, McDowell was asked to take charge of a small program that members of the University of Chicago Christian Union had started in Back of the Yards, an area near the city's stockyards and packinghouses. She accepted immediately.

University of Chicago Settlement opened in a four-room flat. Within five years it housed a half-dozen residents and sponsored a day nursery and kindergarten, activities for youngsters, and a woman's club. While the academic community provided volunteers, board members, and financial support, the University of Chicago did not own or subsidize the settlement. Adept at fundraising, McDowell purchased land on Gross Avenue (later McDowell Avenue), where she built a combination gymnasium and auditorium in 1899 and a three-story settlement building in 1905. There was then space for more residents and more activities, including classes in English and citizenship for the foreign-born living Back of the Yards. During McDowell's thirty-five years as head resident, she saw mostly Irish, German, and Bohemian immigrants change to Poles, Lithuanians, Slovaks, and Mexicans. A staunch defender of the cultural rights of immigrants, she saw their success as evidence of adjustment to American life. McDowell spoke about settlement work to church groups, women's clubs, the National Conference of Charities and Correction, and the National Federation of Settlements. She was president of the latter organization in 1914–1915.

McDowell had closer ties to the labor movement than did most settlement leaders. Already a convert to trade unionism when she moved to Back of the Yards, she supported Michael Donnelly's efforts to organize packinghouse workers and helped to build the women's local. During the protracted 1904 strike, she stood by the union, interpreting its position to reporters and to the packers. McDowell was a delegate to the 1903 American Federation of Labor convention in Boston and became founding member of the National Women's Trade Union League. She started a Chicago branch early in 1904, served as its president until 1907, and drew Agnes Nestor and Mary Anderson (1872–1965) into the organization. While promoting women's trade unions, McDowell also worked for remedial state legislation. In 1905 she, Sophonisba Breckinridge and Edith Abbott conceived the idea of a federal investigation of women's wages and working conditions, and McDowell played a key role in marshalling the necessary public support to prod President Theodore Roosevelt (1858–1919) and Congress to act in 1907. Using evidence from the multivolume study that followed, she lobbied in many states for shorter hours and during World War I upheld enforcement of those regulations in defense industries.

As a shaper of sanitary policy in Chicago, McDowell mobilized support from Back of the Yards, the university community, women's groups, and the male City Club and Citizens' Association. What started in the late 1890s as a plea to city hall to close an offensive garbage dump in Back of the Yards turned into a campaign for municipal incinerators or reduction plants and improved methods of collection. McDowell not only studied urban waste disposal around the United States and in 1911 in Europe, but as chair of the Woman's City Club's City Waste Committee, she coordinated the campaign. Winning municipal suffrage for Chicago women in 1913 provided crucial leverage for her efforts. The mayor appointed a City Waste Commission, of which McDowell was a member, and he followed through on its 1914 recommendations to close the dumps and build incinerators and reduction plants. The following year McDowell was elected president of Woman's City Club.

In 1914 McDowell ran unsuccessfully for a seat on the Cook County Board of Commissioners, but during mayor William E. Dever's 1923–1927 administration, she served as commissioner of the Department of Public Welfare. In this capacity, she reopened the lodging house for homeless men and added an employment and social service office. Her research department studied the elderly poor and published a study of housing conditions for African Americans and Mexicans. McDowell followed up with a conference on the need for low-income housing and persuaded Dever to appoint Chicago's first Housing Commission. Long a member of the NAACP and the Urban League, she helped integrate women's clubs and publicize African-American contributions to the arts. Throughout the 1920s she kept the problems of women in industry before the League of Women Voters.

McDowell died in Chicago. A memorial service at University of Chicago Settlement recalled her warmth, wit, and determination and paid tribute to her work with ethnic groups in Back of the Yards and on behalf of wage-earning women as well as her unique influence on public policy.

• The Mary McDowell/University of Chicago Settlement Papers at the Chicago Historical Society have extensive settlement records but incomplete McDowell materials—some correspondence, drafts of speeches, and an unfinished autobiography. She published more than five dozen articles in a wide variety of journals, and some speeches appeared in conference proceedings. Caroline M. Hill compiled essays by McDowell and her associates in *Mary McDowell and Municipal Housekeeping* (1938), and in 1928 Howard E. Wilson expanded his master's thesis into a biography, *Mary McDowell, Neighbor*. See also Lea D. Taylor, "The Social Settlement and Civic Responsibility—The Life Work of Mary McDowell and Graham Taylor," *Social Service Review* 28 (Mar. 1954): 31–40; Allen F. Davis, *Spearheads for Reform: The Social Settlements and the Progressive Movement, 1890–1914* (1967); and Mina Carson, *Settlement Folk: Social Thought and the American Settlement Movement, 1885–1930* (1990). For McDowell's work with the Women's Trade Union League, see the autobiographies of Agnes Nestor (*Woman's Labor Leader* [1954]) and Mary Anderson (*Woman at Work* [1951; repr. 1973]) and the monograph by Elizabeth Payne, *Reform, Labor, and Feminism* (1988). An obituary is in the *New York Times*, 15 Oct. 1936.

LOUISE CARROLL WADE

MCDOWELL, Mississippi Fred (12 Jan. 1904–3 July 1972), blues singer, songwriter, and guitarist, was born Fred McDowell in Rossville, Tennessee, the son of Jimmy McDowell and Ida Cureay, farmers. Little is known of his early life, primarily because of his own conflicting accounts. His earliest recollections, aside from those of farm life, focused on weekend parties and the guitar playing of his uncle and main inspiration, Gene Shields, who also may have helped raise young Fred after the death of his father. In a 1969 interview, McDowell recalled: "I was a little-bitty boy. My uncle, he played with a beef bone that come out of a steak. He reamed it out, took a file and smoothed it and wore it on this [little] finger here . . . I said if I ever get grown I'm gonna learn to play a guitar. Boy it sound so good to me."

In his teens McDowell attended country dances, where he would sing rather than play guitar. He picked up pointers from local guitar players, but his own instrumental skill came slowly. It was never clear when McDowell became an accomplished guitarist, since he did not own a guitar early in life.

McDowell left Rossville around age twenty-one to work at various jobs in and around Memphis. Working at a dairy in White Station, Tennessee, he finally acquired a guitar, supposedly a gift from a white man from Texas. Through the late 1920s and 1930s he played at dances and jook joints in the Mississippi Delta region.

In 1928 McDowell saw Charley Patton, perhaps the seminal figure in Delta blues, at a jook in Cleveland, Mississippi. Deeply impressed, McDowell added a number of Patton songs to his repertoire. During his

Delta wanderings, he also ran across Booker White, a bottleneck-style guitar player, who supposedly became belligerent after McDowell stole his crowd. By now an accomplished musician, McDowell could compete with other musicians at dances and in country jooks. He later claimed he and Eli Green, a lifelong friend from whom he learned the song "When You Get Home Write Me a Few Lines," often played around Rosedale and Cleveland.

By his own account, McDowell moved to Mississippi for good sometime around 1940, after the death of his mother. Before she died, he supposedly promised her he would give up blues, a promise he claimed he kept for six years. He settled in Como, northern Mississippi hill country, just east of the Delta. In December 1940 he married Annie Mae Collins, with whom he had a son. He worked a small cotton farm and began playing for local dances. He might have remained an obscure local performer except for a 1959 encounter with folklorist Alan Lomax, who learned of McDowell from other local musicians while doing research in the area around Como and nearby Senatobia. Lomax spent a night recording McDowell in the summer of 1959, and those field recordings were later released in two of Lomax's documentary projects, the Southern Folk Heritage Series for Atlantic Records and the Southern Journey series for Prestige International. The recordings brought McDowell little in the way of royalties but elicited interest among other folklorists and documentary record labels.

While continuing to work on his farm and at a local Stuckey's Candy outlet, McDowell recorded for Testament and Arhoolie, and in 1963 he made his festival debut at the University of Chicago Folk Festival, followed the next year by an appearance at the Newport Folk Festival. He was considered one of the purest "folk" discoveries of the folk-revival era, on a par with such rediscovered "bluesmen" as Mississippi John Hurt, Booker White, and Robert Wilkins—each of whom had recorded commercially before World War II. In 1965 he toured California and then Europe with the American Folk Blues Festival. He continued to take what he referred to as "junkets" throughout the 1960s, working the festival and coffeehouse circuits and winning friends with his soft spoken manner and willingness to share his musical ideas. Throughout the 1960s he recorded extensively for both American and European labels, including Capital which produced his 1969 Grammy-nominated album *I Do Not Play No Rock and Roll.* McDowell also appeared in such films as *The Blues Makers* (1968) and *Fred McDowell* (1969).

A late-life switch to electric guitar in 1969 may have annoyed his folk following, but it won him new admirers among blues/rock fans and musicians. He influenced British rocker Keith Richards and even toured briefly with the Rolling Stones, which had reprised his version of the traditional spiritual "You Got to Move." He also played with leading white blues musicians of the 1960s—Michael Bloomfield, Paul Butterfield, and Elvin Bishop—and worked with and enjoyed a close friendship with guitarist and singer Bonnie Raitt, who recorded his "When You Get Home Write Me a Few Lines."

Despite his celebrity friends, McDowell's music changed very little, although his repertoire did expand. He remained a traditional artist who never forgot his country ties, recording for Arhoolie Records with his old partner Eli Green in 1966 and working with another down-home friend, harmonica player Johnny Woods, at the Ann Arbor Blues Festival in 1969. Continuing to perform at festivals into the early 1970s, he returned to Como in 1971, suffering from stomach cancer. He died at Baptist Hospital in Memphis.

Along with Texas guitarist Mance Lipscomb, Mississippi Fred McDowell was widely considered the most important new rural blues discovery of the 1960s. His music seemed to be frozen in some earlier time, largely untouched by progressive changes in blues. His riff-driven instrumental style, in which complex, repeated melodic figures supported a bottleneck treble lead, paralleled the sound of Mississippi's hill-country fife and drum groups, combining the dual African traditions of complex rhythms and vocal tonality. As McDowell described the style, "I'm trying to make the guitar say what I say." Lionized by folk revival audiences and later by blues/rock fans, McDowell was a singular artist, one of the unmistakable voices of the blues tradition, remembered as a gentleman and teacher as well as an artist.

• For additional information see Sheldon Harris, *Blues Who's Who: A Biographical Dictionary of Blues Singers* (1979; repr. 1989); Alan Lomax, *The Land Where the Blues Began* (1993); Bruce Cook, *Listen to the Blues* (1973); Tom Pomposello, "Mississippi Fred McDowell," in *Blues Guitar: The Men Who Made the Music*, ed. Jas Obrecht (1990); and Hoyle Osborne, "I Been Headed up Ever Since: An Interview with Fred McDowell," *Sing Out* 19, no. 2 (Jul.–Aug. 1967): 16–17, 19. For a discography, see Mike Leadbitter et al., *Blues Records 1943–1970: "The Bible of the Blues,"* vol. 2: *L–Z* (1994). For examples of his music, try *Fred McDowell*, Flyright FLYCD14, and *My Home Is in the Delta: Blues and Spirituals by Fred and Annie McDowell*, Testament TCD 5019.

BILL MCCULLOCH
BARRY LEE PEARSON

MCDUFFIE, George (10 Aug. 1790–11 Mar. 1851), U.S. senator, congressman, and governor of South Carolina, was born in Columbia County, Georgia, the son of John McDuffie and Jane (maiden name unknown). His parents were poor Scottish immigrants, and he was put to work early on farms and in stores. While employed as a store clerk in Augusta, Georgia, he caught the eye of store-owner James Calhoun, brother of John C. Calhoun. After the business failed, McDuffie was put up by another Calhoun brother, William Calhoun, so that he could attend Moses Waddell's academy in Willington, South Carolina. An excellent student, he graduated from South Carolina College in 1813. McDuffie subsequently studied law and practiced briefly in Pendleton, South Carolina, before moving to Edgefield and going into partnership with Eldred Simkins, a prominent politician. McDuffie's practice flourished. He was elected to the South Carolina House of Representatives in 1818 and to the U.S. House of Representatives two years later. He served from 1821 to 1834, chairing the Committee on Ways and Means between 1825 and 1834.

Many prominent Carolinians, notably John Calhoun, made the journey in the 1820s from a distinct, albeit qualified, nationalism to the militant assertion of state sovereignty. Congressman McDuffie's transformation proved as spectacular as any. Early in his congressional career, McDuffie spoke slightingly of strict construction of the Constitution, arguing instead that Congress might exercise considerable discretion in fulfilling its mandate to promote the common defense and general welfare. He exhibited little patience with the claim that states were the repository of liberty against the encroachment of the federal power and accordingly could defy federal law. In an 1821 essay that would come back to haunt him, he warned, "The people of particular states are liable to fall occasionally into a dangerous and morbid excitement upon particular subjects, and that under this excitement they will impel their rulers into the adoption of measures in their tendencies destructive to the Union" (quoted in Green, pp. 31–32). On more than one occasion McDuffie's national orientation and loyalty to Calhoun carried him as far as the dueling ground. A series of challenges and several encounters in 1822 with William Cumming, an adherent of William Crawford, Calhoun's Georgia rival, left McDuffie with gunshot wounds that slowly crippled him. His injuries were said to have deepened an existing reserve but also to have made an already accomplished orator an oddly fascinating one. On the platform, one contemporary said, "He hesitates and stammers; he screams and bawls; he thumps and stumps like a mad man in Bedlam" (Freehling, p. 146).

His oratorical performances moved McDuffie into the van of South Carolinians who in the early 1830s confronted the federal government and President Andrew Jackson over states' power to nullify enforcement of federal laws that they deemed unconstitutional (McDuffie also opposed Jackson on another issue that engaged the president's passions, the Bank of the United States). As cotton prices tumbled and upcountry land wore out, Calhounite nationalists reconsidered their embrace of the federal government. Protective tariffs, they insisted, reduced strapped planters' return on crops sold on the international market. The precedents that broad construction of the Constitution might set for federal interference in slaveholding grew more disturbing as the slavery issue increasingly intruded on national politics. McDuffie could speak at first hand about the plight of upcountry cotton cultivators, having developed his own plantation, "Cherry Hill," in Abbeville County during the 1820s (a careful manager, he owned 5,000 acres and 175 slaves by 1845). He married a rich planter's daughter, Mary Rebecca Singleton, in 1829; she had one daughter before her death in 1830.

By 1828 McDuffie was promoting nonimportation of northern goods, because the manufacturers were thought to profit unfairly by the tariff structure. After Congress in 1830 tabled his attempt to lower rates, McDuffie publicized his "forty bale theory," which argued that by levying 40 percent duties on the sorts of items southern crops were exchanged for in Europe, the existing tariff robbed planters of forty of every one hundred bales of cotton they raised, transferring the proceeds to the federal government and protected northern interests. A striking image, if economically dubious, the theory and McDuffie's speechifying were central to nullifiers' campaigns to persuade the state not merely to protest the tariff but to attempt to abrogate it. He played a key role in convincing his fellows that the tariff reductions Congress passed in 1832 were insufficient, and a state convention late that year passed an ordinance voiding the tariff within South Carolina's borders. McDuffie played a prominent role in the convention, pressing it to declare that South Carolina would secede should the federal government attempt to coerce the state. Having by this time decided the union was a "foul monster," McDuffie, more than some other nullifiers, seemed to welcome the prospect of dissolution. Yet nullification found little support elsewhere in the South, and in Congress early the next year McDuffie voted for the compromise worked out by Calhoun and Henry Clay, which provided for the very gradual lowering of tariff rates, and favored the consequent rescinding of the nullification ordinance. Two years later, having retired from Congress, McDuffie was elected governor with bipartisan backing. His election was part of a compromise that resolved the dispute over a state oath that unionists feared could be interpreted to require officials to pledge more or less exclusive allegiance to South Carolina.

If McDuffie gave a bit of ground on the tariff, he remained militant in defense of South Carolina's distinct interests against a national majority. As governor, he threw himself into strengthening the state's militia so that South Carolina might preserve its "liberties" in future conflicts with the general government. As he wrote in 1836, "I regard a separation of the slaveholding states from the Union, as . . . absolutely inevitable and all my efforts for two years past have been devoted to the work of preparing the state for every possible emergency" (Freehling, p. 323).

At the end of his term in 1836, McDuffie returned to practicing law and tending to his plantation. In 1842, however, the legislature elected him to the U.S. Senate to fill a vacancy. He again made war on protective tariffs, but westward expansion meant that the battle for slavery had to be fought on new fronts. McDuffie, who chaired the Committee on Foreign Relations in 1845 and 1846, would not support an aggressive U.S. claim to Oregon, but he strongly supported the annexation of slaveholding Texas. In a dramatic eyeball-to-eyeball confrontation in 1844 with Missouri senator Thomas Hart Benton, McDuffie suggested Benton was a traitor to his section, and Benton that

McDuffie was a traitor to his country; the South Carolinian demanded annexation, insisting that Texas be allowed to operate as a safety valve for the Old South's "superabundant" slave population.

Increasingly feeble, McDuffie resigned from the Senate in 1846. He died five years later at Cherry Hill. He had done much to move South Carolina to a more ardent defense of the rights of a slaveholding minority within the nation. Within ten years of his death, his state was leading others out of the Union in the name of that same cause.

• Collections of McDuffie papers are at Duke University and at the South Caroliniana Library, University of South Carolina, Columbia. His early nationalist essay was published as *National and States Rights Considered by "One of the People"* (1821). The only full-length biography, Edwin Green's *George McDuffie* (1936), contains little analysis or even insight into its subject's complex character or career. For a more colorful portrait of McDuffie and a more incisive discussion of his role in South Carolina politics, see William W. Freehling, *Prelude to Civil War: The Nullification Controversy in South Carolina, 1816–1836* (1966).

PATRICK G. WILLIAMS

MCELHENEY, Jane (c. 1836–4 Mar. 1874), actress and writer, was born in Charleston, South Carolina, the daughter of James McElhenney, a prominent lawyer, and Joanna Wilson. Her last name is also given as McEhenney, McElhenney, McElhenny, McElheny, McElhinney, McEthenery, and McEthenney. She called herself Ada McElhenny. Her pen names were Clare, Ada Clare, and Alastor. Her stage names were Ada Clare and Agnes Stanfield. By 1847 both of her parents had died, and Jane was taken north by her maternal grandfather, a wealthy planter, and his wife. She evidently quarreled with them; so, when about 1854 she inherited a small annuity, she moved to New York City, ambitious to be a writer and an actress. She published three poems in the *Atlas*, a New York weekly, beginning in January 1855. They are "Lines to . . . " (by Clare), "To Thee Alone" (by Ada Clare), and "To Thee!" (by Ada Clare). "Lines to . . . " begins:

Oh sleep my darling, sweetly sleep,
  No sound shall break thy deepest rest;
Oh! let thy dreamings faintly rise
  From the sweet dreamland of my breast;
Oh! sleep, my darling, sleep!

These poems were so popular that other editors sought her work, and she responded with short stories, amorous sketches, and more poetry. With little or no training, she debuted in a benefit performance of *The Hunchback* on 15 August 1855 and was criticized for having a weak voice.

By this time McElheney knew Louis Moreau Gottschalk, the concert pianist, composer, and international matinee idol. He had met her in 1853 when she was vacationing with her grandparents at a resort hotel, perhaps at Saratoga. She fell in love at once with the dashing, irresponsible man, then twenty-four. Two years later, she read in a New York newspaper that he was ill with malaria and wrote him a note of sympathy and expressed the hope that they might renew their acquaintance. In good health again, he called on her the following day, and a tempestuous, indiscreet love affair followed. She starred in a two-play bill in November 1855. The first, *Love and Revenge*, was a farce; the second, *The Wife*, a tragedy. Gottschalk was in attendance, enthralled by her beauty and vivacity. Later the same month she appeared as Ophelia in *Hamlet*, then in 1856 in *The Marble Heart*, *Jane Eyre; or, The Orphan of Lowood*, and Dion Boucicault's *The Phantom*, with Boucicault himself as the Vampire.

Gottschalk, frequently performing outside New York, went on a summer tour to Canada. After his return, he gave piano lessons, fell in love with the married mother of one of his pupils, and abandoned McElheney. She had been touting his concertizing over that of a distinguished older rival, Sigismund Thalberg, in thinly veiled *Atlas* sketches signed "Alastor." But when Gottschalk told her in December 1856 that he was leaving to perform for two years in the West Indies with the child soprano Adelina Patti, accompanied by her father as chaperon, the pregnant McElheney immediately detailed her love affair with Gottschalk in an *Atlas* sketch titled "Whips and Scorns of Time." In February 1857 he left McElheney, who went to Paris, where in May she gave birth to a son, whom she named Aubrey. She pursued a bohemian life, sent articles on the French theater to the *Atlas*, visited Germany and England, and boldly signed "Miss Clare and Son" at hotels and aboard ships. After returning to New York, she appeared in 1859 in a version of *Antony and Cleopatra* combining lines from William Shakespeare and John Dryden.

McElheney began a weekly column for New York's *Saturday Press* in 1859, often mentioning Gottschalk with reverence for his genius. She frequented Pfaff's famous delicatessen and beer parlor on Broadway so regularly that she became known as "Queen of Bohemia." Her sparkling beauty and liberated manners—including short hair and smoking in public—impressed many frequenters of Pfaff's, notably Henry Clapp (her *Press* editor and "King of Bohemia"), William Dean Howells, Adah Isaacs Menken (another emancipated woman), Fitz-James O'Brien, Bayard Taylor, and Walt Whitman. When the *Press* discontinued publication because of the Civil War, McElheney sent her sketches to the *New York Leader* until early 1864, when she went to San Francisco, accompanied by her son, to be a staff writer for the *Golden Era*. She rendezvoused with the dazzling Menken, took her to some well-known spiritualists, visited the Comstock Lode, met and delighted Mark Twain and Dan De Quille there, spent some time in Hawaii, and sent articles about the islands to the *San Francisco Bulletin*. Back in California, she played the lead in *Camille*, rather badly, late in 1864.

After she returned to New York in 1865, McElheney wrote a wretched novel. Called *Only a Woman's*

Heart (1866, by Ada Clare), it tells how Laura Milsland, her peppy, partly autobiographical heroine, wins the love of Victor Doria, an actor-sculptor based on Gottschalk, only to drown with him. Next, calling herself Agnes Stanfield, she appeared in *The Merry Wives of Windsor* in 1866 in New York and then went on an extensive tour through the South. In 1868, in Houston, Texas, she married actor J. Franklin Noyes (also known as Frank P. Noyes and M. J. F. Noyes). After more itinerant acting in several cities, she returned to New York. About 1873 she gave birth to Noyes's son, who may soon have died. In early January 1874, in search of a new acting assignment, she went to the office of a casting agent, whose sick pet terrier jumped into her lap. As she was petting the dog, it suddenly bit her viciously through the cartilage of her nose. The wound was carefully cauterized by a physician, and she soon seemed well again. But a month later she collapsed while appearing in *East Lynne* in Rochester, New York, and was rushed to her home in Manhattan, where she died two days later of hydrophobia.

McElheney wrote erotic verse and sketches that briefly titillated her readers. She also performed on stage with endearing vivacity. But because of her unconventional behavior in generally conservative times, she is mainly remembered as "Ada Clare," the epitome of the 1850s bohemian who died of the bite of a rabid dog. (Biographical researchers are not in agreement as to her son or sons. She is buried in a Presbyterian cemetery in Hammonton, N.J., beside a son. That son may have been Aubrey, who his mother is reported to have said died in 1868 at age eleven. But it is also said that the deceased son was hers by Noyes and that Gottschalk's son survived, was adopted by Noyes, and grew to adulthood.)

• McElheney family papers are in the South Carolina Historical Society, Charleston, and in the South Caroliniana Library of the University of South Carolina, Columbia. Albert Parry, *Garrets and Pretenders: A History of Bohemianism in America* (1933; rev. ed., 1960), and Franklin Walker, *San Francisco's Literary Frontier* (1939), discuss McElheney in the context of bohemian life in New York and California. Vernon Loggins, *Where the Word Ends: The Life of Louis Moreau Gottschalk* (1958), details McElheney's relationship with Gottschalk. Allen Lesser, *Enchanting Rebel: [The Secret of Adah Isaacs Menken]* (1947), discusses McElheney's sensational friendship with Menken. Roger Austen, *Genteel Pagan: The Double Life of Charles Warren Stoddard* (1991), notes the admiration homosexual California poet Stoddard had for McElheney. Details of McElheney's New York City stage appearances are in George C. D. Odell, *Annals of the New York Stage* (15 vols., 1927–1949), and T. Allston Brown, *A History of the American Stage from the First Performance in 1732 to 1901* (3 vols., 1903). Obituaries are in the *New York Times* and the *New York Tribune*, both 6 Mar. 1874, and the *New York Clipper*, 14 Mar. 1874.

ROBERT L. GALE

MCELROY, John (14 May 1782–12 Sept. 1877), Roman Catholic priest, was born in County Fermanagh, Ireland, the son of farmers (names unknown). In 1803 he emigrated to the United States, where he worked as a clerk in Baltimore and Georgetown (Washington, D.C.), before joining the newly restored Society of Jesus in 1806 as a lay brother. Largely self-educated, McElroy so impressed his religious superiors with his rhetorical skills as an instructor at Georgetown College that they changed his status to candidate for the priesthood in 1816 and ordained him the following year ("I was promised time to study," he wrote thirty years later, "but *as yet* it has not arrived"). As the Jesuit officials had realized, McElroy more than compensated for any lack of formal education by a native shrewdness, strength of character, and zeal that over the next sixty years enabled the indefatigable giant (he was well over six feet) to know seemingly no limits in pursuing apostolic missions that took him from Canada to Mexico.

After serving as an assistant pastor at Holy Trinity Church (1818–1822) in Georgetown, McElroy was appointed pastor in 1822 of St. John's Church in Frederick, Maryland. There, as a circuit rider, he made most of western Maryland and northwestern Virginia his parish by preaching and bringing the sacraments to new communities from Cumberland to Harpers Ferry as well as to mobile groups like the Irish laborers who were constructing the railroad and canal along the Potomac river and beyond. In the town of Frederick, McElroy established St. John's Female Benevolent and Frederick Free School under the Sisters of Charity in 1824, and St. John's Literary Institute (later St. John's College) under the Jesuits in 1829; for both schools he eventually secured state funding even though they were Catholic schools.

Providing week-long missions to his parishioners in Frederick by 1827, McElroy was one of the first American priests to engage in this Catholic equivalent of the Protestant revivals that were sweeping much of antebellum America. For the next thirty-five years McElroy regenerated the faith of thousands of Catholics, religious and laity, native and immigrant through the missions or retreats he gave in hundreds of towns and cities from Nova Scotia to Ohio. "From my little experience in . . . retreats," he wrote in 1840, "I am convinced, it is *the most profitable part of our ministry*, . . . by such [work] it is not only a single city or village, that would profit by our labors; but *the whole United States!*" His attempts to persuade Jesuit officials to make evangelical missions a top apostolic priority in the United States proved premature, but by the 1870s Jesuits, Paulists, and other religious orders had made the parish mission that he had helped to develop a major instrument of revitalization and evangelization within the American Catholic church.

In 1846, at the request of President James Polk, who was concerned about American Catholic support for the war with Catholic Mexico, McElroy became one of two priests who were assigned as noncommissioned chaplains with the expeditionary forces. For a year he served the Catholic soldiers (nearly half of General Zachary Taylor's army) in the American base at Matamoras, Mexico.

In 1847 McElroy became pastor of St. Mary's Church in the North End of Boston, where more than 7,000 Irish immigrants were his charge. He immediately undertook to begin schools for their children. A year and a half later the Sisters of Charity began a school for girls. His attempts to found a college, however, were obstructed by nativist opposition among city officials to the acquisition of land, lack of money for building, and a shortage of Jesuits for a faculty. Not until the eve of the Civil War did McElroy complete Boston College, the first Catholic college to attract large numbers of the sons of immigrants, and its contiguous Church of the Immaculate Conception in the South End. By the time the college officially opened in the fall of 1864, McElroy was eighty-two, blind, and feeble, and had returned to Frederick, where, thirteen years later, he died.

A nationally renowned pastor and preacher, McElroy is remembered for building churches that were monuments to his fine aesthetic sense and colleges that were intended to provide an education for the sons of the Catholic poor.

• The correspondence and journals of McElroy are in the Special Collections at Lauinger Library of Georgetown University. Louis Berkeley Kines, S.J., "Lincoln in a Cassock: The Life of Father John McElroy, S.J., from 1782 to 1847" (master's thesis, Georgetown Univ., 1960), covers the years from McElroy's arrival in the United States in 1803 to his return from Mexico. See also Esmeralda Boyle, *Father John McElroy, the Irish Priest* (1878); J. J. Ryan, S.J., "St. John's College, Frederick, Half a Century Ago," *Woodstock Letters* 30 (1901): 231–46; David R. Dunigan, S.J., *A History of Boston College* (1947); and Robert Emmett Curran, S.J., ed., *American Jesuit Spirituality: The Maryland Tradition, 1634–1900* (1988). An obituary is in *Woodstock Letters* 6 (1877): 178–86.

R. EMMETT CURRAN

MCELROY, John (25 Aug. 1846–12 Oct. 1929), journalist and author, was born in Greenup County, Kentucky, the son of Robert McElroy, an ironmaster, and Mary Henderson. The family background was Scotch-Irish. He left home at the age of nine, after his father's death and his mother's remarriage, dropping his middle name, Henderson, which was his mother's maiden name. He worked his way to St. Louis, where he found a job as a printer's devil. Befriended by journeymen printers, he learned how to set the type for popular songs and sold the songs on the streets of St. Louis. Through a program of reading and independent study he remedied the meagerness of his formal education. He was aided in this project by a photographic memory. He could recite most of Shakespeare's plays, read French and German, and translate Greek and Hebrew. When the country was moving toward war, he traveled to Chicago. In 1862 he enlisted in John Alexander McClernand's "Bodyguard." McClernand, a Jacksonian Democrat who was a friend of Abraham Lincoln, was attempting to raise and arm a brigade in central and southern Illinois to support the Union cause. In the spring of 1863 McClernand's Bodyguard became part of Company L of the Sixteenth Illinois Cavalry. McElroy rose to the rank of sergeant major but was referred to as "colonel" by his friends. On 3 January 1864 he was captured by Confederate forces in Jonesville, Virginia. He spent the rest of the war as a prisoner, mostly in Andersonville in southwest Georgia, officially known as Camp Sumter, which was the largest prison camp in the Confederacy. He kept a journal of his experiences while at Andersonville.

Released from prison at the end of the Civil War, McElroy went to Ottawa, Ohio, where he studied pharmacy while working in a drugstore. In 1866 he married Elsie Pomeroy, the daughter of the drugstore's owner. They had two children.

In 1868 McElroy abandoned his career as a pharmacist and returned to Chicago, where he got a job as a reporter on the *Inter-Ocean*. Later he also became an editorial writer for that newspaper. In 1874 David R. Locke invited him to Ohio to be an editor of the *Toledo Blade*. While in Toledo, Locke published *Andersonville: A Story of Rebel Military Prisons, Fifteen Months a Guest of the So-called Southern Confederacy. A Private Soldier's Experience in Richmond, Andersonville, Savannah, Millen, Blackshear, and Florence* (1879), based on the journal he kept during his imprisonment. *Andersonville* ran serially in the *Toledo Blade* and the *National Tribune*, documenting the horror of the infamous prison camp, where nearly 13,000 of 45,000 prisoners died in the span of fourteen months. His book, which sold 600,000 copies, informed his contemporaries about the atrocities of that prison and provided source material for future writers, who have dealt with Andersonville both as historical fact and as a symbol of the physical, emotional, and spiritual privations endured by prisoners of any war.

By 1884 McElroy became editor of the *National Tribune* in Washington, D.C., founded by Colonel George E. Lemon in 1879. Upon the death of Lemon, McElroy became owner and publisher, a position he held until his own death thirty-three years later. During that time he wrote several histories, including *The History of Slavery in the United States* (1896), *Army of the Cumberland* (1906), *Economic Functions of Vice* (1907), *Army of the Tennessee* (1907), *Army of the Potomac* (1908), and *Struggle for Missouri* (1909). He also wrote a series of fictional accounts of army life including the popular *Si Klegg, His Development from a Raw Recruit to a Veteran* (1897) and *Further Haps and Mishaps to Si Klegg and Shorty* (1898).

McElroy became a political figure as the result of his work on behalf of Union veterans of the Civil War. As managing editor of the *National Tribune*, he spoke out in support of veterans' rights. In 1901 he was senior vice commander in chief of the Grand Army of the Republic (GAR), an organization of Union Civil War veterans that numbered as many as 400,000 members. The GAR supported the Republican party and lobbied for veterans' pensions. McElroy was a member of the legislative committee of the GAR for fifteen years and commanded its Kit Carson post and the Department of the Potomac. He belonged to the Association of the Army of Tennessee and to the National Association of Ex-War Prisoners. He was also a member of the board of trade, a 32d-degree Mason, and a charter member of the Washington Press Club.

In 1925, a widower for several years, McElroy married Mrs. Isabel Worrell Ball. She was an associate editor of the *National Tribune* and shared his interest in patriotic organizations and causes. He died in Washington, D.C.

• McElroy's private papers are in the possession of his son, K. P. McElroy, of Washington, D.C. Other sources include the *Report of the Adjunct General of the State of Illinois*, vol. 8 (1867), p. 512. Roy Meredith, ed., *This Was Andersonville* (1957), is an adaptation of *Andersonville: A Story of Rebel Military Prisons* that provides insight on McElroy's character, literary style, and powers of observation; it also contains photographs and an account of the trial of Captain Henri Wirz, who was executed for atrocities against the prisoners of war at Andersonville. Obituaries are in the *Washington Evening Star*, 12 Oct. 1929, and in the *National Tribune*, 17 Oct. 1929.

SUSAN MCMICHAELS

MCELVAIN, Samuel Marion (9 Dec. 1897–11 Apr. 1973), chemist, was born in Du Quoin, Illinois, the son of Solomon Snyder McElvain and Eliza Childers, farmers. He graduated from high school in 1915 and moved with his family to St. Louis, Missouri, where he enrolled in the St. Louis College of Pharmacy. His primary interest soon changed from pharmacology to chemistry, and so the next year he transferred to Washington University in St. Louis to study chemical engineering. However, he continued to work part-time in a drugstore while in school and eventually passed the state board examination to become a registered pharmacist. He received his B.S. in 1920 and enrolled in the University of Illinois to study organic chemistry. After receiving his M.S. in 1921, he became interested in the anesthetic properties of cocaine, which was first used as a local anesthetic by the Viennese surgeon Carl Koller during eye surgery in 1884. In 1923, the same year he received his Ph.D., he succeeded in rearranging the carbon, oxygen, hydrogen, and nitrogen atoms that comprise cocaine into a different molecular structure, thereby synthesizing a cocaine-like isomer.

In 1923 McElvain accepted a position as an instructor of organic chemistry at the University of Wisconsin. His work with the homococaine isomer convinced him that a cocaine derivative that could produce a greater numbing effect than the natural product without also producing such negative side effects as depression, anxiety, and paranoia could be synthesized by removing some of the atoms from the relatively large cocaine molecule. In 1924 he developed several derivatives from piperidine, itself a derivative of piperine, a sharp-tasting constituent of the fruit of the pepper vine whose molecule contains two fewer hydrogen and one fewer oxygen atoms than cocaine. One of these derivatives, cyclomethycaine, was eventually developed and marketed by Eli Lilly, a pharmaceutical concern, as Metycaine, an ointment that soothes the pain of skin rash, poison ivy, and burns.

McElvain was promoted to assistant professor in 1925, the same year that *Practice of Organic Chemistry in the Laboratory*, a textbook that he coauthored with Homer Adkins, was published. In 1926 he married Helen Sophia Roth, with whom he had two children. In 1928 he became an associate professor and published *Elementary Organic Chemistry*, another textbook coauthored with Adkins. In 1929 he began a series of experiments designed to shed light on the condensation reaction, a chain reaction that involves the catalytic combination of pairs of organic molecules and the concomitant elimination of a simple compound such as water or alcohol, by experimenting with the self-condensation of ethyl acetate. In 1931 he showed that sodium alkoxide serves as the catalyst in this reaction but that the reaction is stopped short of completion by the quantity of alcohol produced during the reaction.

In 1933, the year he was promoted to full professor, he became interested in the suggestion that one of the intermediate products created during the self-condensation of ethyl acetate was ketene diethylacetal, a heretofore unknown compound. Although he quickly demonstrated that the intermediate product was actually a mixture of ethanol and ethyl acetate, he was challenged by the prospect of synthesizing ketene diethylacetal. After succeeding in 1936, he continued to synthesize other ketene acetals and in the process discovered that catalyzing the reaction with aluminum alkoxide, a much stronger base than sodium alkoxide, resulted in the completion of the chain reaction despite the presence of large quantities of alcohol.

Between 1937 and 1959 McElvain used ketene diethylacetal, which proved to have prodigious reactive powers because of its propensity to donate electrons during chemical bonding, to synthesize a number of substances by combining it with halogen compounds and acids, unsaturated carbonyl compounds, diazonium salts, quinones, halides, aldehydes, and ketones. The results of these experiments with ethyl acetate and ketene diethylacetal contributed significantly to a better understanding of base-catalyzed reactions and the principles of chemical reactivity, topics he addressed in his third textbook, *Characterizations of Organic Compounds* (1945; rev. ed., 1953).

In addition to his work with ethyl acetate and ketene diethylacetal, in 1930 McElvain returned to synthesizing painkillers by deriving local anesthetics from quinoline and one of its isomers. By 1948 he had done likewise with a number of piperidine derivatives such as picoline, substituted piperidinoalcohols, and the reduction products of acetylpyridine. One of these derivatives, synthesized jointly by McElvain and Thomas P. Carney, his postdoctoral associate and a future vice president of Lilly, was eventually developed and marketed as the local anesthetic Surfacaine. As a result of this research, McElvain eventually became the holder of a dozen patents covering synthetically derived painkilling substances.

In addition to his interest and skill as a researcher, McElvain was devoted to teaching as well and served as dissertation director for seventy-nine graduate students. He was a consultant for the National Defense Research Council during World War II and served as chairman of the Organic Division of the American Chemical Society from 1945 to 1946 and associate editor of the *Journal of the American Chemical Society* from 1946 to 1956. He was elected to membership in the National Academy of Sciences in 1949. The University of Wisconsin honored him by creating the S. M. McElvain Professorship in 1972 and the S. M. McElvain Visiting Scholarship in 1977 and by naming its organic chemistry laboratories in his honor in 1979. He retired in 1961 and died in Madison, Wisconsin.

McElvain played a pioneering role in the modern development of organic chemistry in the United States. He produced a number of synthetic compounds that proved to be of great utility as local anesthetics. His discovery and study of the ketene acetals informed the scientific understanding of base-catalyzed reactions and contributed significantly to the understanding of the relation between a substance's atomic and molecular structure and its propensity to react with other substances, a major factor in the development of synthetic organic chemistry.

• McElvain's papers have not been located. A biography, which includes a bibliography and list of patents, is Gilbert Stork, "Samuel Marion McElvain," National Academy of Sciences, *Biographical Memoirs* 54 (1983): 221–48.

CHARLES W. CAREY, JR.

MCENERY, Samuel Douglas (28 May 1837–28 June 1910), governor of Louisiana and U.S. senator, was born in Monroe, Louisiana, the son of Henry O'Neil McEnery, a planter and federal land registrar, and Caroline H. Douglas. After attending the common schools of Monroe, Samuel furthered his education at Spring Hill College in Mobile, Alabama, the U.S. Naval Academy, and the University of Virginia. In 1859 he graduated from the State and National Law School in Poughkeepsie, New York, and began to practice law in Maryville, Missouri. By 1860, however, he had returned to Louisiana, and with the outbreak of the Civil War he became a lieutenant in the Confederate army. He apparently spent most of the war in command of a training camp in Louisiana.

Following the war, McEnery practiced law in Monroe and battled the ruling regime of Republican carpetbaggers and their African-American allies. In 1872 his elder brother, John McEnery, was the Democratic candidate for governor of Louisiana and claimed victory in his contest against Republican William P. Kellogg. President Ulysses Grant, however, intervened on the side of Kellogg, and with the help of federal troops the Republicans secured the governor's office. Thus the name McEnery was closely linked to the battle for white Democratic rule, a fact that proved invaluable throughout Samuel's political career. The McEnerys had suffered at the hands of the carpetbaggers and their black supporters, earning the lasting devotion of many white voters.

In 1877 white Democratic rule returned to Louisiana, and a generation of Bourbon Democrats would build a political regime on white fears of a return to carpetbagger-black rule. The next year McEnery married Elizabeth Phillips; they had three children. In 1879, exploiting his reputation as a crusader for white supremacy, Samuel McEnery was elected lieutenant governor. In October 1881 Governor Louis A. Wiltz died, elevating McEnery to the chief executive's office. In 1884 he was elected governor in his own right, serving until the expiration of his term in May 1888.

McEnery's administration was tainted by corruption. State treasurer Edward A. Burke was political boss of the state during these years, and by the close of his term he had stolen almost $1.3 million from the state coffers. Allied with Burke and McEnery were John Morris of the Louisiana State Lottery Company and Samuel L. James, the principal lessee of convict labor from the state penitentiary. James put many of the convicts to work constructing river levees, but he also reaped a handsome profit by subletting prisoners to other entrepreneurs. Both Morris and James were known for their willingness to bribe legislators or any other public official who would support the highly lucrative lottery or the venal convict leasing system. McEnery's close ties with the lottery company earned him the derisive nickname "McLottery."

Rebelling against the corrupt lottery forces, the Louisiana Democratic Convention denied McEnery renomination as governor, selecting instead Francis R. T. Nicholls. In retaliation McEnery threatened to ensure a "fair count" in the upcoming gubernatorial election. A fair count meant that the Republican votes of African Americans would be counted, a practice that could spell defeat for the white Democrats. To placate McEnery and guarantee that he would not enforce honest election practices, Nicholls apparently promised the outgoing governor appointment to the state supreme court. In 1888 incoming governor Nicholls accordingly placed McEnery on the high court.

Four years later, however, McEnery again sought the governor's office, this time as the candidate of the prolottery faction of the divided Democratic party. After a heated battle, the antilottery Democrat Murphy J. Foster won the election. In 1896, seeking to restore party unity, Foster convinced the state legislature to elect McEnery to the U.S. Senate. McEnery assumed his seat in the Senate in 1897 and served there for the rest of his life.

McEnery was not a prominent senator, and during his last years ill health and deafness limited his effectiveness. He was known as an independent who readily deviated from the Democratic party line if Louisiana interests seemed threatened. Thus he consistently took a high tariff stance, voting for both the Republican-sponsored Dingley Tariff of 1897 and the GOP's Payne-Aldrich Tariff of 1909. The high tariff measures protected Louisiana sugar planters from foreign competition, and for McEnery planters' profits were more important than party loyalty. When questioned about his deviation from Democratic policy, McEnery answered, "What have the Democrats ever done for sugar?" During his third term in the Senate, McEnery died in New Orleans.

McEnery exemplified the worst of Bourbon Democracy and Louisiana politics. Exploiting racial fears, he was able to hold high public office for more than three decades. Throughout these years he used his political power to enhance the profits of friends and allies. Ever faithful to the pecuniary interests of his supporters, he helped redeem Louisiana from corrupt Republicans and hand it over to corrupt Democrats.

• Before his death, McEnery destroyed all of his correspondence and personal papers. Joseph G. Dawson III, ed., *The Louisiana Governors* (1990), includes a brief biographical sketch of McEnery. Donna Drew, "The Louisiana Election of 1892 Re-examined," *Louisiana Studies* 15 (1976): 161–77, discusses the McEnery-Foster gubernatorial contest. Berthold C. Alwes, "The History of the Louisiana State Lottery Company," *Louisiana Historical Quarterly* 27 (1944): 964–1118, is the standard account of the battle over the lottery in Louisiana. William Ivy Hair, *Bourbonism and Agrarian Protest: Louisiana Politics 1877–1900* (1969), offers the best account of Louisiana politics during the McEnery era. Obituaries are in the *New York Times* and the *Washington Post*, both 29 June 1910.

JON C. TEAFORD

MCENTEE, Jervis (14 July 1828–27 Jan. 1891), landscape painter, was born at Rondout (now Kingston), New York, the son of James S. McEntee, an engineer, and Sarah Jane Goetsheus. James McEntee directed the building of the Delaware and Hudson Canal, which terminated at Rondout. Jervis attended the Clinton Institute in Clinton, New York, but his early interest in art and literature reportedly was stimulated by Henry Pickering, a boarder in the McEntee home who wrote nature poetry and knew the principal artists and authors of the time.

From 1850 to 1851 McEntee studied landscape painting with Frederic E. Church at the Art-Union Building in New York, where McEntee rented a neighboring studio. During this training period he began exhibiting work at the National Academy of Design. By 1852 he had returned to Rondout to work in the flour and feed business but continued to submit landscape paintings to the academy exhibitions. Two years later McEntee married Gertrude Sawyer, the daughter of a prominent clergyman; the couple had no children. McEntee returned full time to landscape painting around 1858 and was among the earliest artists to rent rooms in the new Studio Building on West Tenth Street, which quickly became the quarters of the chief New York landscape painters. It remained the artist's city residence until his death. He and his wife earned a reputation for hosting lively evening socials of artists and acquaintances. Among his neighbors and close friends at the Studio Building were his former teacher Church, the landscape painters Sanford R. Gifford and Worthington Whittredge, and the genre painter Eastman Johnson. In 1860 McEntee was elected an associate of the National Academy on the strength of his painting *Melancholy Days* (unlocated), one of several works inspired by the poetry of William Cullen Bryant. The artist rose to full academician in 1861.

As a member of the New York fraternity of artists called the Hudson River School, McEntee adopted the pattern familiar among them. Abandoning the Studio Building in late spring following the National Academy exhibition, he made sketching tours with his fellow artists—most frequently Gifford and Whittredge—in the Catskill Mountains and environs, using his hometown of Rondout as his summer residence. He normally returned to the city in late autumn to make paintings from the sketches. In 1868 he planned a trip abroad with Gifford. McEntee and his wife crossed the Atlantic on their own, toured England briefly, then moved on via Paris to Rome, where they met Gifford and stayed in the same pension. The two artists frequently sketched together in the city and countryside. However, it was with Church and the portrait painter George Alexander Healy, who were also in Rome at this time, that McEntee collaborated on a remarkable pictorial document of nineteenth-century Americans on the Grand Tour. *The Arch of Titus* (1871; Newark Museum, Newark, N.J.), a vertical painting six feet high, portrays the three painters at the base of the famed monument discussing a drawing that Church is making, while the poet Henry Wadsworth Longfellow and his daughter Edith stroll beneath the arch. McEntee is said to have painted the arch, Church the Colosseum, and Healy the figures. McEntee's later paintings of Italian subjects exhibited the same preference for ancient ruins. The McEntees departed Rome in March 1869, visiting the north Italian cities and Alpine lakes en route to Brussels and Antwerp. They sailed to England and Scotland before returning to New York in July.

Despite his friendships and European exposure, McEntee had little taste for the frontier locales—the tropics, the Far North, the West—often favored by his colleagues. He visited Fort Halleck, Nevada, in the summer of 1881, chiefly to see his sister and brother-in-law in an effort to alleviate the pall cast over him by the loss of his wife, who had died three years earlier. Stylistically, he rarely exhibited the prevalent taste of the major Hudson River School painters for scenic and panoramic views. He shared with Gifford a preference for the autumn (and later, winter) season, yet he expressed it not in the hazy, luminous Indian summer mountain vistas typical of Gifford's work but in intimate, often gray and moody pasture or woodland scenes in the Catskill valleys or the neighborhood of Rondout. Indeed, McEntee's ouevre, with those of painters such as Alexander H. Wyant and Homer Martin, serves to modify the perception of an abrupt change from the Hudson River School style, informed by British landscape aesthetics, to that of the French-inspired paintings of George Inness, whose subjective approach to landscape painting gained increasing favor by the time of the Centennial. Though McEntee rarely indulged in the conspicuous brushwork and misty introspection of Inness and his followers, almost from the first he paralleled Inness's preoccupation with personal feeling as the determinant of a landscape's extent and complexion. In pursuit of self-expression, McEntee not only anticipated the overcast conditions that would characterize the paintings of Wyant, Martin, Robert Swain Gifford, and Inness but, in some late landscapes such as *Winter in the Country* (private collection) of 1890, seems to have introduced Japanese-inspired elements into his paintings that by that date could have been filtered through the work of James A. M. Whistler, Winslow Homer, or even American impressionists such as John H. Twachtman. At the same time, the figures prominent in this and other of his paintings betray the influence of Eastman Johnson and even hark back to seventeenth-century Netherlandish painting.

Unfortunately for McEntee, his divided loyalty to somber artistic expression and to the clubby company of the New York landscape painters of the Civil War period fostered in him a perceived sense of unsuccess. In the face of the brisk, sometimes phenomenal business enjoyed by his colleagues Church, Gifford, Whittredge, and Johnson, McEntee's was moderate, and his finances were a constant source of anxiety to him. Still, the contemporary critical evaluation of him was warm, sometimes profound. He exhibited at most of the major annual exhibitions, as well as at the Universal Exposition in Paris in 1867 and at the Centennial Exposition in Philadelphia in 1876. McEntee's worries were in some measure self-fulfilling. His wistful meadow vistas and wintry prospects expressed what appears to have been an inherent pessimism that was both aggravated and alleviated by his association with the New York landscape painters.

To McEntee's psychic predisposition is undoubtedly owed a contribution that rivals his paintings. From 1872 nearly until his death two decades later, he kept a highly revealing diary, which ultimately accrued to five volumes of manuscript. It not only illuminates his personality but stands as a vivid if fragmentary narrative of the daily life and inexorable decline of the Hudson River School: the interchange among artists and with patrons in the Studio Building, the rhythm of summer fieldwork and winter studio labor, the entertainments the artists frequented, the personal anniversaries they mutually marked, the deaths among them that they together mourned, the challenge to the established landscape painters at the National Academy by young, foreign-trained figure painters, the tensions among the landscape painters themselves, and the incremental slippage in their popularity.

The routines, events, and trends of artist life in New York are observed not merely in McEntee's remarks about others but in his close record of his own day-to-day thoughts and doings. Resenting the condescension he sensed from more conspicuous talents like Church, McEntee nonetheless entertained the idea of painting more "sunny atmospheric effects" (diary, 19 Feb. 1873) that would reflect the typical Hudson River School style of landscape. Bristling at the art dealers' bias for marketing foreign works at the expense of American artists, he yet tried his hand at figure painting, a concession to the subject matter that dominated foreign imports and was increasingly sought by American patrons. Bemoaning the growing neglect of the National Academy exhibitions by its traditional members in favor of showing privately in their studios, at clubs, and with dealers, he still recognized the unoriginality of much of the work shown at the academy and ultimately conceded the need for dealers to promote artists' interests, including his own.

McEntee never fully rebounded from the death of his wife in 1878. He succumbed to Bright's disease at his birthplace in Rondout. At a memorial meeting there of his colleagues and friends, the artist's "transparent truthfulness," "modesty," "mood of self-disparagement," and the limitations of his art were all acknowledged and ordained attributes of a fine character "beyond the reach of false pride or the vain esteem of self." His "thread of melancholy," moreover, was said merely to have been a foil to his "sparkling wit" (*Jervis McEntee, American Landscape Painter*, 1891). In his diary, McEntee exposed both faces when he blurted out to a reluctant client "to wait until I was dead, perhaps my pictures would be worth more" (27 Jan. 1873). However, like the paintings of his fellow Hudson River School painters, McEntee's art dropped into oblivion for more than a half-century. With theirs, his reputation has recovered since the 1960s, and his known pictures have grown in value, if only in proportion to their relative worth in his own time. His located paintings number about 150; some of his most ambitious and touted pictures remain unrecovered. The subdued tenor that distinguished his work has probably continued to restrain its appeal to modern collectors.

• The Jervis McEntee Diary is preserved at the Archives of American Art, National Museum of American Art, Smithsonian Institution and is available on microfilm at the offices of the Archives of American Art in New York, Boston, and Los Angeles; the first two years of the diary are extensively excerpted in "Jervis McEntee's Diary," *Journal of the Archives of American Art* 8 (July–Oct. 1968): 1–29. A current list of his known pictures is maintained in the Bicentennial Inventory of American Paintings Executed before 1914, Smithsonian Institution. The most useful recent discussion of the artist is Hirschl and Adler Galleries, *A Selection of Drawings by Jervis McEntee from the Lockwood DeForest Collection* (1976; essay by Sarah Kay Feldman). Illuminating contemporary sources for the artist are T. B. Aldrich, "Among the Studios, 5," *Our Young Folks* 2 (Oct. 1866): 622–25; Henry T. Tuckerman, *Book of the Artists* (1867), pp. 543–46; [anon.], "American Painters—Jervis McEntee, N.A.," *Art Journal* (N.Y.) 2 (1876): 178–79; G. W. Sheldon, *American Painters* (1879), pp. 51–56; and *Jervis McEntee, American Landscape Painter* (addresses given at a memorial meeting for the artist, 30 Jan. 1891). See also Clara Erskine Clement and Laurence Hutton, *Artists of the Nineteenth Century and Their Works*, vol. 2 (1880); *National Academy of Design Exhibition*

Record, 1826–1860, vol. 2 (1943); and *National Academy of Design Exhibition Record, 1861–1900,* vol. 1 (1973). An obituary is in the *New York Times,* 28 Jan. 1891.

KEVIN J. AVERY

MCFADDEN, Louis Thomas (25 July 1876–1 Oct. 1936), banker and congressman, was born in Troy, Bradford County, Pennsylvania, the son of Theodore L. McFaddin [*sic*] and Julia Babb, farmers. When his mother died in 1887, McFadden went to live with Dr. T. A. Gamble in East Troy, where he attended school and did farm chores to earn his keep. Several months after the death of his father in 1892, McFadden moved to nearby Canton, where he found a job as an office boy and janitor at the First National Bank. By 1899 he had risen to cashier, and in 1916 he became president, serving in the position until 1926, when he resigned to devote himself full time to politics. McFadden was very active in the Pennsylvania Bankers' Association, serving as president for two years and in a variety of other capacities. He was also an active farmer. In 1898 he married Helen Westgate; they had three children. Beginning in 1914 they made their home at Mourland Park, a local landmark.

McFadden's election to Congress in 1914 as a Republican from Pennsylvania's Fourteenth (later Fifteenth) District commenced a political career that extended from the Sixty-fourth through the Seventy-third Congresses (1915–1935). His profession prompted an interest in financial matters. He became an immediate critic of the fiscal policies of Woodrow Wilson's administration and assumed a role as watchdog of the Federal Reserve System. He supported American entrance into World War I but criticized the war financing plan as inflationary. In 1919, after an unpublicized three-year feud with the comptroller of the currency, John Skelton Williams, McFadden introduced legislation to abolish the comptroller's office. Williams responded by attacking McFadden's banking practices. McFadden's bank later won a suit against the comptroller's office, a case that reached the Supreme Court. McFadden supported national prohibition and tariff protection for industry and agriculture, and he unsuccessfully advocated rural credit legislation to aid farmers.

McFadden gained a reputation as an expert on financial policy based upon his long tenure on the House Banking and Currency Committee, which he chaired from 1920 to 1931. His greatest legislative achievement was the enactment in 1927 of the McFadden-Pepper Act after three years of consideration by the Congress. A provision of the act that regulated branch-banking practices generated much controversy and attracted most of the attention, but the law's broader intent was to make membership in the Federal Reserve System more attractive by strengthening the ability of national banks to compete with state banks operating under less restrictive charters. The act gave banks in the Federal Reserve System indeterminate charters and increased their authority to engage in investment activities and extend loans for real estate. It partly achieved its purpose, but the latter provisions, which permitted banks to dabble in real estate, most likely contributed to the speculation preceding the financial collapse of 1929.

McFadden's last years in Congress were marked by controversy. An isolationist, he constantly suspected plots against the nation's interests. He opposed internationalism in any form (whether the League of Nations, the World Court, or the Kellogg-Briand Pact), had little faith in contemporary disarmament efforts, and attacked the Carnegie Foundation on the grounds that it sought to involve the United States in foreign alliances. The onset of the depression moved him to harsh criticism of his party's financial policies. He charged that European leaders, in collusion with New York bankers (specifically the House of Morgan), Treasury officials, and the Federal Reserve Board, had conspired to make the United States pay the cost of World War I and that the resulting "reckless" loans (Dawes Plan, 1924, and Young Plan, 1929) had drained the country's resources and caused the depression. When President Herbert Hoover (1874–1964) declared a moratorium on the collection of debt payments in 1931, McFadden attacked the president so vehemently that his House colleagues condemned him and the Hoover administration stripped him of his patronage privileges. Nevertheless, McFadden was renominated in 1932 on the Prohibitionist, Democratic, and Republican tickets. (His opposition to Hoover was undoubtedly a factor in winning Democratic support.) McFadden won the Republican primary in a spirited contest with Cornelia Bryce Pinchot, wife of Pennsylvania governor Gifford Pinchot, and was reelected by his biggest margin ever.

Returning to Congress, McFadden twice moved Hoover's impeachment by the House (Dec. 1932 and Jan. 1933). The Pennsylvania Republican delegation removed him as secretary and practically expelled him from the party. Undaunted, he also urged the impeachment of several Treasury and Federal Reserve officials, and he accused Jews of plotting to secure the repeal of the gold clause (May 1933). William Dudley Pelley, founder of the fascist Silver Shirt organization, praised McFadden for circulating anti-Semitic remarks under his frank. While their relationship apparently did not extend beyond friendship, the House Committee on Un-American Activities later noted Pelley's association with McFadden.

McFadden became a foe of the New Deal, but his official opposition ended with his defeat for reelection in 1934. Although his party supported him, he was unable to overcome the addition of two heavily Democratic counties to his district. He attempted a comeback in the next election but lost narrowly in the Republican primary. By then his health was failing, and he died during a visit to New York.

Harboring xenophobic prejudices, conceiving of national interest narrowly, and committed to the issues of farmers and small-town bankers, McFadden opposed a wider federal role in national affairs and a broader national role in world affairs.

• H. C. Bradsby, *History of Bradford County, Pennsylvania with Biographical Sketches* (1891), and *The First National Bank of Canton: A One Hundred Year Start on Tomorrow* (n.d.), contain references to McFadden's family background and business career. His feud with Comptroller Williams is reported in the *New York Times*, 16, 17, and 21 Feb. 1919. Charles S. Tippetts, *State Banks and the Federal Reserve System* (1929), and John M. Chapman, *Concentration of Banking: The Changing Structure and Control of Banking* (1934), discuss the McFadden-Pepper Act. See also *Congressional Record*, 69th Cong., 2d sess., 3 Mar. 1927, vol. 68, pt. 5, 5812–18. McFadden's views on foreign debts are in *Congressional Record*, 71st Cong., 2d sess., 9 June 1930, vol. 72, pt. 10, 10348–51, and a summary of his world view is in *Congressional Record*, 72d Cong., 2d sess., 3 Mar. 1933, vol. 76, pt. 5, 5643–47. McFadden's opposition to Hoover's debt moratorium is in *Congressional Record*, 72d Cong., 1st sess., 18 Jan. 1932, vol. 75, pt. 2, 2179–81. For his attempts to impeach Hoover, see *Congressional Record*, 72d Cong., 2d sess., 13 Dec. 1932, vol. 76, pt. 1, 399–402; *Congressional Record*, 72d Cong., 2d sess., 17 Jan. 1933, vol. 76, pt. 2, 1965–69. The *New York Times*, 5 May 1930, reports his attack on Jews. His efforts to impeach other federal officials are in *Congressional Record*, 73d Cong., 1st sess., 23 May 1933, vol. 77, pt. 4, 4055–58. Obituaries are in the Towanda (Pa.) *Daily Review* and the *New York Times*, both 2 Oct. 1936.

ROBERT C. OLSON

MCFARLAND, Ernest William (9 Oct. 1894–8 June 1984), U.S. Senate majority leader, Arizona governor, and Arizona Supreme Court chief justice, was born in Earlsboro, Oklahoma, the son of William McFarland and Keziah Smith, farmers, who had joined the land rush on the Pottawatomie Strip, formerly Indian Territory. The young McFarland led a demanding life as the child of pioneer farmers in this newly opened section of the American frontier. After graduating from Earlsboro High School in 1914, he completed the two-year program at East Central Normal School (later East Central State Teacher's College) in Ada. Following a brief stint as a rural schoolteacher, he undertook pre-law studies at the University of Oklahoma in Norman, receiving a bachelor's degree in 1917.

In December 1917 McFarland enlisted in the U.S. Navy as a second class seaman, serving for the duration of World War I at the Great Lakes Naval School in Illinois. During this period he suffered from a serious and lengthy bronchial illness that nearly proved fatal. Discharged in January 1919, McFarland moved to Phoenix, Arizona, for health reasons.

After working briefly in a bank, McFarland in 1919 entered Stanford University Law School, where he earned a J.D. in 1922, and he received a master's degree from Stanford in political science in 1924. Already accepted to the Arizona bar, he had opened a private practice in Casa Grande in 1921 and had been appointed from 1923 to 1924 the state's assistant attorney general. He then moved to the Pinal County seat of Florence after being elected county attorney in 1924, serving in that position in 1925–1926, 1927–1928, and 1929–1930. In 1931 he became a defense attorney and counsel for the San Carlos Irrigation and Drainage District, and in 1934 he successfully ran for Pinal County superior court judge. Reelected in 1938, he served as county judge until 1941.

McFarland had married Clare Collins in 1925; they had three children. After the death of all three children, and of his wife in 1930, he married in 1939 Edna Eveland Smith and adopted her daughter. They had no children together.

In a stunning political upset, McFarland defeated 28-year incumbent Henry Fountain Ashurst in the 1940 U.S. Senate Democratic party primary and then triumphed over his Republican opponent, commencing a twelve-year congressional career. In 1941 he won national recognition for his defense of motion picture producers during the 1941 Senate Hollywood film probe. This investigation dealt with allegations that the major film producers attempted to sway public opinion toward intervention in World War II.

During the war McFarland's greatest legislative contribution was in the field of veterans' affairs. Known as the "Father of the GI Bill," McFarland wrote the sections in this landmark legislation that dealt with free educational provisions and home and business loans. He also chaired the Communications Subcommittee that toured both the European and Pacific theaters immediately after World War II to formulate a postwar role for the United States in international communications. His work culminated in the Communications Act of 1952, which revised the 1934 act and established new guidelines for Federal Communications Commission relations with private industry.

Reelected to a second term in 1946, McFarland turned his attention to water affairs, particularly to obtaining Colorado River water for Arizona for irrigation and reclamation purposes. Although he directed the Central Arizona Project to Senate passage in 1950 and again in 1951, the bill did not become law until 1968. He also sponsored the only three successful Social Security increases to occur from 1946 to 1952, and his Navajo-Hopi Rehabilitation Act of 1950, which funded roads, hospitals, and schools, served as an example of improved legislation for Indians.

Acknowledged as an expert in communications, veterans' affairs, and irrigation and reclamation, and known to be skillful at negotiation and compromise, McFarland was elected by his colleagues as the U.S. Senate majority leader for the Eighty-second Congress (1951–1953). Senator Lyndon Johnson served as the "whip"—McFarland's assistant—during these controversial years of McCarthyism and the Korean War. Numbering among the first senators to condemn Senator Joe McCarthy's allegations of communist influence in Washington, McFarland also proved instrumental in maintaining the bipartisan foreign policy that conducted the war effort. In 1951 he stood firmly behind President Harry S. Truman's decision to relieve General Douglas MacArthur of command.

McFarland, closely linked to Truman's declining public approval, lost his Senate seat to Republican Barry Goldwater in 1952. An influx of Republican voters to the postwar Southwest and the popularity of presidential candidate Dwight Eisenhower also contributed to Goldwater's narrow victory. After a brief period as chief attorney for Western Union, McFarland reentered the political arena by defeating incumbent Republican Howard Pyle for Arizona governor in 1954. McFarland served two terms from 1955 to 1959, during which time the state restructured its entire legal code; founded a state parks system; increased aid to health, education, and welfare; established fair employment practices for state offices and publicly financed jobs; increased highway construction; and brought new industry to Arizona. In an unprecedented move for a state governor, McFarland personally argued and won before the U.S. Supreme Court a special Colorado River water case against California, paving the way at last for congressional passage of the Central Arizona Project in 1968.

In 1958 McFarland failed to regain the U.S. Senate seat from Goldwater in a hotly contested election that was marked by controversial campaign tactics and charges of alleged links to unpopular labor organizations brought against McFarland. He then turned to his private law practice and Pinal County farming interests and served as president of the Arizona Television Company, which he had founded in 1953.

In 1964 McFarland successfully ran for the Arizona Supreme Court, serving until 1971, including two years as chief justice. He wrote more than 300 opinions, including one made famous in its reversal in the U.S. Supreme Court as *Miranda v. Arizona*, which established the rights of defendants undergoing arrest. During 1968–1969 he also sat on the thirteen-member National Commission on the Causes and Prevention of Violence in America under Presidents Lyndon Johnson and Richard Nixon.

McFarland retired from active political life in 1971, returning to his television and farming interests. In 1975 he was awarded the Copper Mike for outstanding contributions to broadcasting in Arizona, and in 1978 he donated to Arizona McFarland Historical State Park, formerly the old Pinal County Courthouse constructed in 1878. In 1979 he completed his autobiography, *Mac*, and in 1980 the Stanford University Law School honored him as its "Most Distinguished Living Alumnus." He died in Phoenix.

McFarland's career was characterized by humility, compassion, and practical contribution. Throughout his life, he consistently upheld the interests of the underprivileged, brought attention to the needs of veterans, and supported farm and labor concerns. As an expert at negotiation and compromise, he worked effectively with liberals and conservatives of both political parties, and he is among the few to have held his state's highest offices in the executive, legislative, and judicial branches.

• McFarland's papers are in the Ernest W. McFarland Library and Archives, McFarland Historical State Park, Florence, Ariz. His autobiography is *Mac: The Autobiography of Ernest W. McFarland* (1979). Other sources include *The Ernest W. McFarland Papers: The United States Senate Years, 1940–1952*, ed. James E. McMillan (1995), and McMillan's "Ernest W. McFarland, Southwestern Progressive: The U.S. Senate Years, 1940–1952" (Ph.D. diss., Arizona State Univ., 1990). Articles on McFarland, all by McMillan, include "McFarland and the Movies: The 1941 Senate Motion Picture Hearings," *Journal of Arizona History* 29 (Autumn 1988): 277–302; "First Sooner Senator: Ernest W. McFarland's Oklahoma Years, 1894–1919," *Chronicles of Oklahoma* 62 (Summer 1994): 178–99; and "Father of the GI Bill: Ernest W. McFarland and Veterans' Legislation," *Journal of Arizona History* 35 (Winter 1994): 357–76. Obituaries are in the *New York Times*, the *Arizona Republic*, and the *Phoenix Gazette*, all 9 June 1984.

JAMES E. MCMILLAN

MCFARLAND, George (2 Oct. 1928–30 June 1993), child actor, known as Spanky, was born in Dallas, Texas, the son of Robert Emmett McFarland and Winifred Virginia Phillips. As a baby, he modeled for ads, and in 1931 his aunt mailed his photo, as did many parents of "cute kids" in those days, to the Hal Roach Studio, home of the *Our Gang* comedies (later known, on television and home video, as *The Little Rascals*). Roach, who had created and supervised the popular series of comedy short subjects since 1922, was impressed with the moon-faced child and arranged for a screen test with director James Horne. Studio bosses who saw the test were bowled over by the child's ebullient personality; he was, they agreed, a "natural." (The scene of McFarland in the 1932 short *Spanky*, in which he tries to hit a bug with a hammer, was in fact screen-test footage incorporated into the film.) The studio's title writer, H. M. Walker, gave McFarland's character the name "Spanky" after observing the boy's mother warning, "Spankee-spankee, mustn't touch."

Spanky was in fact the first character to be individually featured and promoted in the series, even winning special "star" billing in the main titles of some series entries. Yet his image in the series changed several times during his eleven-year run. At first, he was an adorable infant. Then he was teamed with fellow ragamuffin Scotty Beckett; the two became a deadpan Greek chorus, commenting sardonically on the failings of the older kids in the gang, who tried their best to ignore these pesky little ones. Fans especially remember their contribution to *Honky Donkey* (1934), in which a mule named Algebra would stop chasing its hapless victim only when it heard a bell ringing. Finally, McFarland as Spanky became the unofficial leader of the gang and the instigator of their many schemes and adventures, from venturing into a pirate cave in *Mama's Little Pirate* (1934) to staging a backyard show in *Pay As You Exit* (1936). By the late 1930s, he and the characters of Alfalfa, Darla, Buckwheat, Porky, and Butch were the seemingly permanent stars of the series.

McFarland's feature-film appearances included *Day of Reckoning* (1933); *Miss Fane's Baby Is Stolen* (1934), with overnight child sensation Baby Leroy; *Kentucky Kernels* (1934), with Wheeler and Woolsey (playing a character billed as Spanky) and directed by Hal Roach Studio veteran George Stevens; *O'Shaughnessy's Boy*

(1935), with Wallace Beery and *Our Gang* alumnus Jackie Cooper; *The Trail of the Lonesome Pine* (1936), in which McFarland played a major part as Sylvia Sidney's baby brother; *Varsity Show* (1937), in which McFarland was billed as George McFarland; and *Peck's Bad Boy with the Circus* (1938), also featuring two Hal Roach comedy stalwarts, Edgar Kennedy and Billy Gilbert.

When producer Roach felt that short subjects were no longer profitable enough to sustain the studio, he tried out each of his series stars in a feature film to gauge audience response. Significantly, the first *Our Gang* feature was titled *General Spanky* (1936). It was a Civil War tale and not sufficiently popular to warrant an encore. The children belonged in shorter, funnier films and Roach knew it. So in 1938 he sold *Our Gang* to Metro-Goldwyn-Mayer, his distributor, along with the contracts of McFarland and the other stars. The series continued at MGM through 1944, and McFarland remained on board until 1943—well past the normal limit for an *Our Gang* actor. He was growing up, literally bursting out of his clothes, and no longer the adorable, spontaneous child actor he had once been.

Once he left the series, McFarland found it almost impossible to get other work on screen. Eventually, he stopped trying. He moved back to Texas and joined the air force, later receiving a hardship discharge. He worked at a soft drink plant and a hamburger stand. In 1958 he hosted a kiddie show on television in Tulsa, Oklahoma, running *The Little Rascals* shorts, but this second brush with show business was short-lived. Eventually McFarland became a successful salesman. He joined Philco-Ford in 1966, becoming a sales executive with the company and remaining there until his retirement. He also married Doris Taulman, with whom he had two children.

It was the continual showings of *The Little Rascals* on TV that eventually made McFarland a celebrity again. In the 1970s he was recruited to appear at a nostalgia convention, and he soon found himself in considerable demand. He also toured college campuses across the country, showing some of the *Our Gang* comedies, answering questions from youthful fans, and showing off the costume that he wore in the 1930s—which had been saved by his mother for all those years. Although he had at times been resentful that he had never earned a dime from the re-use of the films on television, he made peace with his alter ego because it brought him latter-day fame and an income. He served as a spokesman for Justin Boots and for Republic Pictures Home Video, which released the *Little Rascals* films in the 1980s.

Only weeks before his death, McFarland appeared as himself in a cameo on the popular television series "Cheers." The cast members were delighted to have him there; he was, to them, as much a celebrity as any contemporary movie star. In fact, Spanky retained enormous name recognition with people of his own generation as well as their children and grandchildren, who continued to discover his films on home video.

McFarland had just launched an official fan club and had begun mailing out individually signed certificates from his home in Fort Worth, Texas, when he died. He was survived by his mother, who had steered his childhood career some sixty years earlier.

• For a detailed account of McFarland's career and the *Our Gang* series, see Leonard Maltin and Richard W. Bann, *The Little Rascals: The Life and Times of Our Gang* (1977; rev. ed., 1992). For a more personal profile by a fellow *Our Gang* alumnus, see Dick Moore, *Twinkle, Twinkle, Little Star (but don't have sex or take the car)* (1984). Obituaries are in the *New York Times*, 1 July 1993, and *People Weekly*, 19 July 1993.

LEONARD MALTIN

MCFARLAND, J. Horace (24 Sept. 1859–2 Oct. 1948), printer, civic reformer, and rosarian, was born John Horace McFarland in McAlisterville, Pennsylvania, the son of George Fisher McFarland, a schoolteacher, and Adeline Dellicher Griesemer. Following the Civil War, the family moved to Harrisburg, where Horace's father bought and operated the Riverside Nurseries, a large property along the Susquehanna River. When he was sixteen, McFarland started setting type for the *Temperance Vindicator*, a newspaper his father published. He also arranged to print seeds lists for the growers who supplied the Riverside Nurseries. Three years later he formed his own printing firm, incorporating it in 1891 using the imprint Mount Pleasant Press. Seeking wider business opportunities, he began printing horticultural catalogs, featuring attractive graphics. In 1884 he married Lydia Sieg Walters. They had two children.

By the early 1890s McFarland was personally photographing flowers, fruits, and vegetables from Connecticut to Florida and west to Texas. These he used to produce woodcuts, but he introduced photographs into his catalogs when photoengraving plates first became available. During 1896 he worked in New York with William Kurtz, the developer of a color photomechanical process, and soon began producing catalogs in vivid color. Among his customers were many of the nation's major growers.

McFarland came to national prominence between 1895 and 1900 through *Outlook* magazine, first as a special assignment photographer, then as a writer. A series of articles in *Outlook* led to his first book, *Getting Acquainted with the Trees* (1904), which went through ten reprints. The New York Public Library named it one of the "best books" of that year. Through his horticultural and printing interests, he established close ties in New York with publishers Macmillan and Company and Doubleday and Doran. From 1904 to 1935 the Mount Pleasant Press printed books and magazines on horticultural subjects for both firms. The most ambitious of these publications was the 1914 edition of Liberty Hyde Bailey's *Standard Cyclopedia of Horticulture*.

In 1904 McFarland was elected president of the American Civic Association, formed that year in St. Louis by a union of the American Park & Outdoor Art Association and the American League for Civic Improvement. For twenty years, as head of the organization, he led hard-fought campaigns to preserve Niagara Falls from the power industry, protect Hetch Hetchy Valley from despoliation by San Francisco, establish the National Park Service, and clean up American cities. He wrote and lectured widely on park development and civic beautification, assisting more than 400 communities in his "Crusade against Ugliness." City Beautiful scholar William Wilson referred to McFarland as the "leading lay spokesman" for the movement.

McFarland worked closely on these and related campaigns with park authority Frederic Law Olmsted, Jr., the Arnold Arboretum's Charles S. Sargeant, Boston landscape gardener Warren Manning, and Cornell University horticulturist Bailey. The five men shared similar ideas about plants, parks, and gardens, with McFarland playing a large part in the application of those ideas to public policy. The Mount Pleasant Press was the primary platform from which he expressed them, and the American Civic Association was the political forum from which he acted on them.

In 1908 McFarland participated in the White House Governor's Conference on Conservation. His was the only speech advocating the preservationist viewpoint. Although McFarland supported conservation, he argued against the utilitarian emphasis fellow Pennsylvanian Gifford Pinchot gave the movement. McFarland believed that preservation of scenic beauty was the "highest form of conservation" and that sustenance for the spirit was a national resource equally as important as material nourishment for the body. He was never able, however, to convince Pinchot that "preservation of forests, water power, minerals and the other items of national prosperity . . . must be associated with the pleasure to the eye and the mind and the regeneration of the spirit of man."

Between 1909 and 1913 McFarland conducted the congressional phases of the Sierra Club's unsuccessful campaign to protect Yosemite's Hetch Hetchy. In 1910, however, he began the drive that led to the establishment of the National Park Service in the Department of the Interior. Overcoming the powerful influence of Pinchot, who was against the plan, McFarland marshaled sufficient support by 1916 to have the necessary legislation enacted. He served the Department of the Interior as an adviser on parks until his death.

Although his formal education was limited to four years of private schooling, McFarland was highly respected as a master printer. He helped develop the curriculum for the Harvard Graduate School of Business's first course in printing and lectured there for several years beginning in 1912.

In 1915 McFarland and rosarian Robert Pyle proposed to the American Rose Society, a small tradesmen's association, that the organization be turned into a widely held group of amateurs and professionals. McFarland's editorship of the *American Rose Annual* from 1916 to 1948—the centerpiece of the original proposal—has been credited as instrumental in fostering the modern popularity of the rose. The Breeze Hill gardens surrounding his Harrisburg home were among the noteworthy rose gardens of the day.

McFarland wrote more than 200 articles on horticultural, park, rosarian, and civic improvement issues for national magazines, including *Outlook*, *Review of Reviews*, *Ladies' Home Journal*, *Better Homes and Gardens*, and *Saturday Evening Post*. In addition, he was the author of *My Growing Garden* (1915), *Modern Roses* (1930), *Roses of the World in Color* (1936), and *Garden Bulbs in Color* (1938). The keys to his success were single-minded perseverance to his goals, personal integrity, and the ability to find the right individual to do a job and to inspire that person to give his or her best effort. From his earliest years he was a staunch supporter of women in the workplace, employing them in responsible positions at the Mount Pleasant Press and in the American Civic Association. McFarland enjoyed the respect even of his opponents and, according to Bailey, "stood for every good thing." Because of a modest nature and a desire to forward his purposes rather than to have his name "spread wide on . . . attractive volumes," McFarland, who was held in high esteem by his contemporaries, has yet to receive appropriate recognition as an important early twentieth-century civic reformer and parks advocate. He died in Harrisburg.

• McFarland's papers, including his manuscript speeches and much of his correspondence on civic improvement issues, Niagara Falls preservation, and national and state park affairs as well as a broad range of his photographs, are housed at the Pennsylvania Historical and Museum Commission, Harrisburg. *Memoirs of a Rose Man* (1949), a posthumous collection of his writings, is a pleasant vignette of his rosarian interests. A complete assessment is Ernest Morrison, *J. Horace McFarland, A Thorn for Beauty* (1995). For McFarland's role in the battle for Hetch Hetchy see Holway R. Jones, *John Muir and the Sierra Club: The Battle for Yosemite* (1965); and for a survey of his contribution to civic beautification see William H. Wilson, *The City Beautiful Movement* (1989).

ERNEST MORRISON

MCFARLAND, Ross Armstrong (18 July 1901–7 Nov. 1976), psychologist, was born in Denver, Colorado, the son of James McFarland, a Presbyterian minister, and Helen Russell. When McFarland was five years old, his father died and the family moved to Parkville, Missouri, where the children could receive their education free of charge at Presbyterian schools. McFarland graduated from Park Academy, attended Park College for two years, and finished his undergraduate studies at the University of Michigan, earning his bachelor of arts in 1923. He received a fellowship from the National Council on Religion and Higher Education to attend Harvard University graduate school. In 1928 he earned a Ph.D. in psychology from Harvard. He spent the academic year 1927–1928 as a research fellow at Trinity College, Cambridge, England, where he first investigated the effects of oxygen deprivation on human behavior. In September 1928 McFarland became an instructor in the department of psychology at Columbia University.

McFarland's research at Columbia University defined the course of his career. There he investigated the psychological and physiological effects normal and abnormal supplies of such substances as oxygen and glucose had on human performance. His studies were sponsored by the U.S. Department of Commerce and contributed to the development and use of pressurized cabins in airplanes. He also conducted psychoneurotic studies and investigated the effects of fatigue on mental functions.

In 1935 McFarland joined the International High Altitude Expedition to Chile, which studied differences between the behavioral characteristics of natives who lived in the high altitudes of the Andes and those of expedition members to determine the effects of altitude. McFarland conducted sensory, motor, mental, and personality tests to measure psychological changes as physiological changes occurred. He also studied the effects of rapid ascents by airplane and compared them with the effects of gradual ascents by rail in the same region of South America. McFarland's interest in aviation dated from this investigation. In 1936 he became a consultant for Pan American Airways, serving as its medical coordinator until 1952. During this time, McFarland investigated pilot fatigue, physiological and psychological characteristics of pilots, and pilot health.

McFarland left Columbia to join Harvard University's Fatigue Laboratory in 1937. There he worked with physiologists studying a wide variety of conditions that affect human performance. He held positions as assistant professor of industrial research and associate professor of industrial hygiene in the School of Public Health. He also taught highway transport safety and started a program in aviation health and safety whose seminars trained more than two hundred scientists who became leaders in aerospace medicine, occupational health, and highway safety. In addition, McFarland was the first director and chair of the Guggenheim Center for Aerospace Health and Safety at Harvard.

McFarland's expertise was sought in many arenas. He routinely assisted with pilot selection and training in the Boston area for the National Research Council and the Civil Aeronautics Authority and worked with the U.S. Navy to analyze high failure rates among student pilots. For this project, he was commissioned a lieutenant commander and was on active duty from July to September 1940 at the Pensacola Naval Base in Florida. McFarland organized a research team from Harvard, and together they completed the program, the Pensacola Study of Naval Aviators, in 1941. He also worked for the U.S. Air Force in the Solomon Island Campaign. As a civilian operations analyst in 1943 and 1944, McFarland studied combat fatigue in both air and ground forces. It was during this project that he began investigating the relationship between the design of equipment and human performance.

McFarland continued to examine the physiological and psychological relationships between human and machine, and in 1946 he published his first book, *Human Factors in Air Transport Design*. It was one of the earliest books on the subject and established McFarland as a leader in human factors engineering in aviation. Other books followed. *Human Factors in Air Transportation* in 1953 helped develop health and safety standards in civil aviation, and in 1966, *The Human Body in Equipment Design*, with Albert Damon and Howard W. Stoudt, provided important biological and biochemical data that was useful in designing equipment for human use. In addition to these books, McFarland published many chapters in other books, several monographs, and more than two hundred articles. He also lectured extensively on human factors, aviation medicine, and related topics.

McFarland was an active member of several professional and scientific organizations, including the Aerospace Medical Association, Airline Medical Directors Association, American Physiological Society, American Psychological Association, and many others. He was a founding member of the Human Factors Society and served as its president from 1969 through 1971. As McFarland's reputation in human factors grew, his consulting career extended beyond Pan American to Greyhound Lines, John Deere, General Motors, the Federal Aviation Administration, and NASA, among others. He received numerous awards and honorary degrees.

In 1950 McFarland married Emily Frelinghuysen Bilkey and became stepfather to her two children. Though he remained a bachelor for most of his life, McFarland enjoyed his later roles of grandfather, stepfather, and husband. He died suddenly at his home in Dublin, New Hampshire.

McFarland's research laid the foundation for the study of human factors in a wide range of disciplines. From aviation to space flight, from ground vehicle design to health and safety in transportation, McFarland's investigations into the effects of substances such as alcohol, tobacco, and carbon monoxide, his studies of dark adaptation, oxygen deprivation, high altitude physiology, stress and fatigue, accident prevention, and circadian rhythms mark the beginnings of aerospace medicine and human factors engineering as twentieth-century specialties.

• McFarland's papers are in the Fordham Health Sciences Library at Wright State University in Dayton, Ohio. In addition to correspondence, photographs, reprints, and drafts of published and unpublished papers and lectures, the collection includes manuscript copies of his two major books. Important biographical sources include "McFarland, Ross Armstrong: American Physiological Psychologist and Aerospace Scientist," *Modern Men of Science* 2 (1968): 358–60; Malcolm Ritchie, "Ross A. McFarland, 1901–1976," in *Division 21 Members Who Made Distinguished Contributions to Engineering Psychology* (1994), pp. 94–107; and Mary Ann Hoffman and Robert A. Ritchie, *Ross A. McFarland Collection in*

Aerospace Medicine and Human Factors Engineering, vol. 2 (1987), pp. ix–xi. McFarland's obituary is in *Human Factors Society Bulletin* 19 (1976): 1–2.

MAGGIE YAX

MCFARLAND, Spanky. *See* McFarland, George.

MCFERRIN, John Berry (15 June 1807–10 May 1887), editor, administrator, and minister of the Methodist Episcopal Church, South, was born in Rutherford County, Tennessee, the son of James McFerrin, a minister of the Methodist Episcopal church, and Jane Campbell Berry. McFerrin's formal education was meager. Although he completed only a few years of elementary education, McFerrin had a good mind, was eager to learn, and eventually acquired an education through independent study.

Raised in a devout Christian family, it is not surprising that McFerrin prepared for the ministry. At age eighteen he was "licensed to preach" and admitted "on trial as a traveling preacher" in the Tennessee Conference of the Methodist Episcopal church. In November 1825 he was appointed the "junior preacher" on the Franklin circuit of the Huntsville (Ala.) district. (In those years Methodist churches in Alabama were part of the Tennessee Conference.) In 1827 he was admitted into "full connection" in the Tennessee Conference and ordained as a deacon. The final step in ordination took place in 1829 when he was ordained as an elder. In 1832 McFerrin married Almyra Avery Probart, with whom he had six children.

In those years ministers in the Methodist Episcopal church were constantly on the move; indeed, church law limited ministers to two years in a church appointment, with one year being the average. McFerrin's experience was rather typical: three years as a circuit rider and six years as minister at station (single) churches. He also completed a two-year assignment as a missionary to the Cherokee Indians from 1827 to 1829. In 1836, at the age of twenty-nine, he was appointed the presiding elder of the Florence (Ala.) district and the following year the presiding elder of the Cumberland district, positions of supervision normally reserved for persons of more mature status. Such appointments were indications of the respect he had earned from the church's leadership. Similar respect from his circuit-riding peers was evidenced by his election to the quadrennial general conference of the Methodist Episcopal church (1836), the top legislative body of that denomination. He was to be so honored thirteen times, a record at the time of his death.

In 1840 the general conference selected McFerrin to be the editor of the *South-Western Christian Advocate*, a denominational newspaper located in Nashville, Tennessee. For the remainder of his ministry McFerrin worked at senior-level administrative positions in the church's bureaucracy.

The 1840s were tension-filled times in the Methodist Episcopal church. Many members increasingly believed slavery was incompatible with Christian commitment; however, many others in the South disagreed. As a result, southern Methodists formed the Methodist Episcopal Church, South (MEC,S), in 1845, and McFerrin became a leader in bringing this body into being. While he considered slavery evil and never bought or sold slaves, he was convinced of the rightness of the southern position on slavery.

In the new church McFerrin continued his editorial responsibilities. In 1846 he and Moses Henkle were authorized by the general conference to establish and be coeditors of the *Nashville Christian Advocate*. Four years later he was designated sole editor of this journal, a position he held until 1858 when he became the book agent for the southern church, the title given to the chief administrator of the church's publishing house in Nashville. In 1854 McFerrin's wife had died, and in 1855 he married Cynthia Tennessee McGavock, with whom he had two children.

When hostilities commenced between the North and the South, northern armies invaded Tennessee, causing McFerrin and his family to flee south from their Nashville home. No longer able to fulfill his editorial responsibilities, he was appointed by the bishops to serve as a missionary to the Army of Tennessee. In this capacity he functioned as a chaplain, though not under the command of the Tennessee army commanders. When the war ended, he returned to Nashville to find his home destroyed and the publishing facilities of the southern church in desolation.

At the general conference of 1866, McFerrin was appointed to head the Board of Domestic Missions for the MEC,S; four years later he became head of all the missionary activities of the church, both domestic and foreign. In 1878 the general conference prevailed upon him to undertake another challenge—to save the publishing house of the church, which was in severe financial condition. Reluctantly he agreed and was once again elected book agent, a position he held until his death.

In his day McFerrin was well known as a speaker and preacher. One of his contemporaries called him "the best platform speaker in the U.S." His responsibilities required that he constantly travel and speak to groups in every part of the country. Wherever he appeared a large audience gathered; they could be assured of a memorable performance. McFerrin's friends and biographer O. P. Fitzgerald tells of an occasion, which he suggests was typical, when McFerrin engaged another Methodist (Myers by name) in debate. "McFerrin poured in upon him the full torrent of his ridicule, his nasal buglings rising higher and higher until the whole Conference was in an uproar of merriment. 'He has tomahawked Myers, scalped him, and is dancing a war-dance over his remains!' exclaimed a preacher, red in the face from excessive laughter."

McFerrin was also known as a writer, primarily through the pages of the various publications he edited. He was quick to editorialize on all sorts of issues, mostly matters agitating the church. The only book he wrote was the *History of Methodism in Tennessee* (3 vols., 1869–1873). He died at his home in Nashville, Tennessee.

McFerrin represented the best in church leadership of his day. He was devout and utterly selfless in his service to the institution he loved, a fighter to protect "Old Methodism," which to him meant traditional ways of thinking and doing. He was also endowed with an unusual ability to convince others of his version of the truth. He was greatly admired far and wide. In a sense he was representative of a passing era. The bishop who spoke at his funeral probably was correct when he said, "We ne'er shall see his like again."

• McFerrin's papers were left in the possession of his biographer and friend, O. P. Fitzgerald, who included lengthy quotations from many of them in his book *John B. McFerrin: A Biography* (1888). The location of the papers today is not known. Also see James P. Pilkington, *The Methodist Publishing House: A History*, vol. 1 (1968).

FRANK GULLEY

MCGARVEY, John William (1 Mar. 1829–6 Oct. 1911), minister and theological educator, was born in Hopkinsville, Kentucky, the son of John McGarvey, a storekeeper, and Sarah Ann Thomson. McGarvey was four years of age when his father died. His mother married Gurden F. Saltonstall, a physician and hemp farmer. The family migrated to Tremont, Illinois, in 1839 and continued raising hemp for rope. McGarvey attended James K. Kellogg's private school in Tremont.

From April 1847 to July 1850 McGarvey attended Alexander Campbell's Bethany College in Virginia (now West Virginia). His teachers, Alexander Campbell, W. K. Pendleton, and Robert Richardson, were the first-generation faculty of the preeminent college of the Stone-Campbell movement. This movement, also known as the Disciples of Christ, was the result of the efforts, during the United States' early national period, of Barton Stone in Kentucky and Thomas and Alexander Campbell in Pennsylvania and Virginia to restore Christianity to New Testament purity and unity in order to evangelize the world.

At Bethany, McGarvey attended church where Campbell often preached, participated in the Campbells' household devotions, and met Alexander's father, Thomas. Under these influences, he sought baptism. Confessing his faith in Jesus Christ, he was immersed by Pendleton in 1848. Munnell, Robert Graham, Charles Loos, and Alexander Procter were among McGarvey's Bethany compatriots who later became Disciples leaders. At graduation he received first honors.

McGarvey had decided to become a preacher but was dissatisfied with his preparation. Declining "apprenticeship" with an evangelist of the movement, he rejoined his family who had moved to Fayette, Missouri. For two years he studied privately, primarily the Bible, and conducted a school for boys. He was ordained to preach in September 1852.

In January 1853 McGarvey became pastor of the Disciples church in Dover, Missouri. In March he married Atwayanna "Ottie" Francis Hix; they had eight children. In Dover, McGarvey preached, was "houseparent" with Ottie of a girls' school, and defended the Disciples "reformation" in debates with Presbyterian, Methodist, and Universalist opponents. He also began some writing for the *American Christian Review*, a journal edited by Benjamin Franklin of Cincinnati, Ohio.

McGarvey opposed Christians' participation in the Civil War, though his pre–Civil War household had included at least two slaves—the gifts of his father-in-law and his wife's aunt. McGarvey's pacifism led in 1862 to his being invited to become the preacher for Main Street Christian Church in Lexington, Kentucky. His predecessor there, Winthrop Hopson, was openly pro-Confederate. McGarvey's more neutral stance mirrored Kentucky's official war posture and offered more hope for unity in the politically divided congregation.

McGarvey's chief contribution, however, was as a theological educator. Bethany College, the Disciples' most influential educational model, failed to offer sufficient training for preachers, despite its ethos and Campbell's Bible lectures, and prior to 1865 the Disciples had no seminary designed for such training. In 1865 the remnants of the Disciples' oldest college (Kentucky University, formerly Bacon College) and of a struggling Transylvania University were merged and rechartered in Lexington as Kentucky University. Led by John Bowman, this new church-related institution even included the state Agricultural and Mechanical School. McGarvey was appointed professor of sacred history (Bible) of the new university's College of the Bible. Focused on ministerial preparation, this college was the Disciples' first theological seminary. During the next forty-six years, McGarvey became the dominant personality of the College of the Bible, serving as president from 1895 until 1911.

Controversy over the character of Kentucky University led the College of the Bible to become a separate institution in 1877 (known, after 1965, as Lexington Theological Seminary). The remaining colleges of Kentucky University separated (in 1878) into the Agricultural and Mechanical College of Kentucky (after 1916, the University of Kentucky) and Transylvania University.

Under McGarvey, the College of the Bible emphasized the Bible's content; its use in preaching; its geography; "lower criticism" of its text—the application of historical methods to identify or reconstruct the most reliable original text; and its "defense." McGarvey and his early, Bethany-trained colleagues taught from a Campbellian perspective that stressed the Bible's divine origin and veracity, its authoritative character for the church, and its setting forth the successive dispensations that culminated in the Christian "scheme of redemption."

The emphases of McGarvey's teaching were echoed in his two dozen books and pamphlets, several articles and chapters in edited works, and a weekly column in the *Christian Standard* that ran from 1893 until 1911. In his books and *Standard* column, McGarvey increasingly refuted and ridiculed "higher" Bible criticism, such as George Foot Moore's *A Critical and Exigetical Commentary on Judges* (1895) and William Rainey Harper's writings in the *New Christian Quarterly* (1893). McGarvey regarded the higher critics' views as destructive of biblical authority and Christian faith. He strove to prevent their gaining a hearing among Disciples.

No single theological educator in the Stone-Campbell movement's history has had an impact equal to McGarvey's. He shaped ministerial training among the Disciples during their period of relative internal unity, rapid growth, and development of a series of formal organizations for mission, benevolence, and education.

In the twentieth century three distinct bodies emerged in the Stone-Campbell movement, each of which reflects some legacy of McGarvey: Churches of Christ, "independent" Christian Churches and Churches of Christ, and the Christian Church (Disciples of Christ). The Churches of Christ, a rigorously New Testament-restorationist and congregationalist fellowship, are known for their opposition to the use of instrumental music in worship (a position that McGarvey shared) and to missionary societies (a position that McGarvey did not share), and for their numerical strength in and cultural association with the southern United States. Their separate identity was recognized by the United States Census in 1906.

"Independent" Christian Churches and Churches of Christ are also restorationist, known especially for their insistence that the "immersion of penitent adult believers" is the only scriptural form of Christian baptism. By the 1920s these "independent" churches and their leaders were clearly in dissent from the institutions and agencies of what were called "cooperative" Disciples. To a significant degree, the "independents" saw themselves as the defenders, especially during the generation after his death, of McGarvey's approach to the Bible and to theological education. In both Churches of Christ and "independent" Christian Church circles, McGarvey's understanding of the Bible and its critics has continued to be highly esteemed and taught.

Among the "cooperative" Disciples, who constituted themselves the Christian Church (Disciples of Christ) in 1968, McGarvey's approach has given way to historical-critical views of the Bible. This shift in interpretive viewpoint came dramatically to The College of the Bible in 1917; McGarvey's intended successor, Hall Laurie Calhoun, and his supporters were unable to stem the growing influence of theological liberals R. H. Crossfield, William Clayton Bower, A. W. Fortune, and E. E. Snoddy. However, the Bible remains foundational in the theological education curricula there and in the Christian Church (Disciples of Christ) generally. McGarvey's passion for a ministerial education conducted in schools created for that purpose lives on in four Disciples theological seminaries and three university-related foundation houses.

• McGarvey's papers, including his handwritten lecture notes, are in Bosworth Memorial Library, Lexington Theological Seminary. Among McGarvey's major works are *A Commentary on Acts of the Apostles with a Revised Version of the Text* (1863), *Lands of the Bible* (1880), *Evidences of Christianity* (1886), and *The Authorship of the Book of Deuteronomy with Its Bearings on the Higher Criticism of the Pentateuch* (1902). The primary biographical source on McGarvey is DeLoris and Dwight E. Stevenson's edition of *The Autobiography of J. W. McGarvey* (1964). Secondary assessments of McGarvey include W. C. Morro, *"Brother McGarvey": The Life of President J. W. McGarvey of the College of the Bible, Lexington, Kentucky* (1940), David H. Bobo, "John William McGarvey: A Biographical and Theological Study" (master of theology thesis, Christian Theological Seminary, 1963), and John C. Trimble, "The Rhetorical Theory and Practice of John W. McGarvey" (Ph.D. diss., Northwestern Univ., 1966). McGarvey's leadership at the College of the Bible is described in Dwight Stevenson, *Lexington Theological Seminary: 1865–1965—The College of the Bible Century* (1965), and in Richard Harrison, "Disciples Theological Formation: From a College of the Bible to a Theological Seminary," in *A Case Study of Mainstream Protestantism: The Disciples' Relation to American Culture, 1880–1989*, ed. D. Newell Williams (1991), pp. 281–98. McGarvey's role as a Bible critic is discussed in Don Haymes, "'To Honor the God of the Bible': J. W. McGarvey and the 'Higher Criticism,'" *Lexington Theological Quarterly* 29: 160–87, and in M. Eugene Boring, "The Disciples and Higher Criticism: The Crucial Third Generation," in *A Case Study of Mainstream Protestantism*, ed. Williams (1991), pp. 29–70. Boring's essay includes a bibliography of McGarvey's writings. An obituary is in the *Louisville Courier Journal*, 8 Oct. 1911.

ANTHONY L. DUNNAVANT

MCGEE, Anita Newcomb (4 Nov. 1864–5 Oct. 1940), physician and founder of the Army Nurse Corps, was born in Washington, D.C., the daughter of Simon Newcomb, an astronomer at the U.S. Naval Observatory, and Mary Caroline Hassler. Anita's early education combined attendance at private schools in Washington, D.C., with lessons from parents, relatives, and tutors. From 1882 to 1885 Anita, her two sisters, and their mother lived in Europe. Anita studied German literature, European history, German, and French at the University of Geneva in Switzerland, and physiography at Cambridge University in England. After returning to America, she began researching her revolutionary war roots and wrote articles for *Appleton's Cyclopaedia of American Biography* (1886 to 1889). From 1886 to 1902 she studied communal societies, communism, and various religions, publishing occasional articles. She presented a paper to the American Association for the Advancement of Science in 1888, was elected to fellowship in 1892, and became sectional secretary in 1897.

In 1888 Anita Newcomb married William John "W J" McGee, a geologist with the U.S. Geological Survey, and accompanied him on a geological survey north from New Orleans on horseback. Their daughter Klotho, the first of three children, was born in 1889. Anita McGee and her husband lived a life of frequent separations, usually due to his professional commitments. Child care was a constant concern for

McGee, who prided herself on being a "new woman" combining domestic life and career. Their daughter was often under the care of a private nurse but sometimes stayed for months at her paternal grandparents' home in Iowa.

In 1888 McGee joined the Women's Anthropological Society of America, a venue for scientific inquiry by women. Several physician members may have inspired McGee to attend medical school. She served as the society's secretary, established a library of works by and about professional women, arranged joint meetings with the men's anthropological society at which women delivered papers, and succeeded in negotiating a merger with the men's society in 1899.

In 1889, McGee entered medical school at Columbian College (now George Washington University). During her senior year the medical faculty decided to bar women from future entry, and McGee petitioned unsuccessfully to reverse the decision. She received her M.D. with honors, joined the Women's Clinic (an internship opportunity in Washington for white women doctors) as an attending physician, and opened her private medical practice in 1892. In an unprecedented occurrence, a male gynecologist invited her to train with him in a hospital setting for a few months in 1893. McGee's practice, situated at home, enjoyed moderate success. A few months after the unexplained death of her infant son in 1895, she closed her practice. In 1896 she joined the Women's Dispensary in Washington and remained part of its attending staff for several years.

McGee became one of the first members of the new Daughters of the American Revolution (DAR), founded in 1890, serving on the board of trustees, on numerous committees, and as vice president general, surgeon general, historian general, and the first librarian general. She established the library as a repository for documents on women's roles in the Revolution, edited the national DAR journal, organized the association's first chapter and member directory, and from 1893 to 1904 attempted to establish a national coeducational graduate school. McGee also became a founding member in 1890 of the Washington Club, an exclusive women's club to rival the men's Cosmos Club, a center of power founded in 1878 by her father and other eminent men.

As events progressed toward war with Spain in 1898, many untrained women deluged the government, offering to serve as nurses. McGee, a friend of George M. Sternberg, Surgeon General of the Army, encouraged him to use only trained graduate nurses. Once war was declared in April, McGee offered DAR assistance to Sternberg to set criteria and select eligible nurses for war service. Sternberg immediately accepted. McGee, director of the newly formed DAR Hospital Corps Committee, was described in May by the Washington press as "young and charming, possessing unusual magnetism, vivacity, and a gift of language." Professional nurses' organizations and the American Red Cross, however, developed hostility toward McGee because they had not been designated to provide nurses to the military. McGee's first contract nurses were appointed and en route to duty stations in May. DAR volunteers examined five thousand applications in three months and placed almost 1,600 women on duty with the army and navy during the war.

In August 1898 Sternberg appointed McGee as acting assistant surgeon general to supervise the hundreds of contract nurses, the first woman to serve in such a high official position. The only woman authorized to wear a U.S. Army officer's uniform, McGee became an honorary member of the Association of Military Surgeons of the United States, wrote a monthly feature for *Trained Nurse and Hospital Review*, and was an associate editor of the *Woman's Medical Journal*. In addition to her administrative responsibilities, she organized DAR relief efforts, visited army camps and hospitals, and distributed DAR supplies.

In his 1899 report to Congress, Sternberg stated, "American women may well feel proud of the record made by those nurses in 1898 to 1899, for every medical officer with whom they served has testified to their intelligence and skill, their earnestness, devotion and self-service." Nurses served in the United States, Puerto Rico, Cuba, Hawaii, Philippines, and on the new hospital ship, USS *Relief*. Twelve nurses died from typhoid fever and one from yellow fever. Sternberg, McGee, and others believed that the nation should not be left without a permanent nursing corps. Professional nurses submitted a bill to Congress that would separate nursing from the medical department, but it failed. McGee wrote the legislation in the Army Reorganization Act of 2 February 1901, which successfully established the "Nurse Corps (female)" as an integral part of the Army Medical Department. Professional nurses, however, succeeded in obtaining a requirement that the corps superintendent be a trained graduate nurse. McGee appointed her successor and resigned at the end of 1900.

In 1898 McGee founded the Society of Spanish-American War Nurses and served as president for six years. In 1905 the society unveiled a memorial to their fallen comrades at Arlington National Cemetery. McGee remained in touch with her nurses, assisting them in filing for individual pensions. She provided expert assistance to the navy in 1903 when it drafted legislation for its nursing corps. The manual she wrote in 1899 for her nurses remained in effect for both the army and the navy until 1947, when the National Defense Act created the U.S. Air Force and a new nursing corps.

During the Russo-Japanese War in 1904, McGee served the Japanese government for six months as superior of nurses. With the rank of a Japanese army officer, she and nine Spanish-American War nurse veterans inspected hospitals and trained nurses in Japan, Manchuria, and Korea. The emperor and empress of Japan awarded McGee the Imperial Order of the Sacred Crown.

McGee lived in California from 1910 to 1911 and lectured on hygiene. Another son had been born in 1902, and, after her husband's death in 1912, McGee devoted herself to her son's education at boarding schools and college. She divided her time among homes in Washington, D.C.; Woods Hole, Massachusetts; and Southern Pines, North Carolina. McGee died in Washington, D.C. She was buried in Arlington National Cemetery with full military honors and laid to rest beside her father. In 1967 the U.S. Army established the annual Dr. Anita Newcomb McGee Award to recognize outstanding nurses.

McGee's greatest legacy was the establishment of the Army Nurse Corps and the professionalization of the military nurse. Because of her vision, American military personnel received superior care in the twentieth century. Her nursing corps served as the model for the Navy and Air Force Nursing Corps and laid the groundwork for women to enter the military in nontraditional fields.

• The most comprehensive information on McGee is found in the Anita Newcomb McGee Papers at the Library of Congress. Other archival sources are located at the National Archives, the American Red Cross Archives, and the U.S. Army Center of Military History Nursing Archives. McGee testified in *Report of the Commission Appointed by the President to Investigate the Conduct of the War Department in the War with Spain*, U.S. Senate Document, Series 3865, XXIII, no. 221, Vol. 7, 56th Cong., 1st sess. (1899–1900): 3168–81. Sternberg's *Report of the Surgeon General to the Secretary of War*, 1898, 1899; and the *Annual Report of the War Department*, vol. 1, pt. 1 (1898): 690, and vol. 1, pt. 2 (1899): 375–77, discuss McGee's contributions. The *Second Report of the National Society of the Daughters of the American Revolution, October 11, 1897–October 11, 1898* includes comments by McGee. McGee's publications include *Standard for Army Nurses* (1899) and *Colonel John Bull* (1919), as well as many articles. The best treatments of McGee are Gloria Moldow, *Women Doctors in Gilded-Age Washington: Race, Gender, and Professionalization* (1987); Philip A. Kalisch and Beatrice J. Kalisch, *The Advance of American Nursing* (1986); Edith A. Aynes, *From Nightingale to Eagle: An Army Nurse's History* (1973); Ellen Condliffe Lagemann, ed., *Nursing History: New Perspectives, New Possibilities* (1983); Mary M. Roberts, *American Nursing: History and Interpretation* (1955); Lavinia L. Dock, *History of American Red Cross Nursing* (1922); and Portia B. Kernodle, *The Red Cross Nurse in Action, 1882–1948* (1949). See also Emma R. McGee, *Life of W. J. McGee, Distinguished Geologist, Ethnologist, Anthropologist, Hydrologist, etc., in Service of United States Government with Extracts from Addresses and Writings* (1915). An obituary is in the *Washington Post*, 6 Oct. 1940.

CONNIE L. REEVES

MCGEE, Frank (12 Sept. 1921–17 Apr. 1974), television news journalist, was born Doctor Frank McGee in Monroe, Louisiana, the son of Robert Albert McGee, a farmer and sawmill owner, and Calla Brown. His parents divorced when he was a child, and his mother married Lannie Crocker, an oil field worker. His family, like many during the depression, had very little money.

McGee attended school in Monroe and then, after his mother's remarriage, in Seminole and Norman, Oklahoma, but never graduated from high school. He joined the U.S. Army as a private in September 1940 and completed a high school equivalency course while in the service. During World War II he attained the rank of technical sergeant but later was demoted to private first class. He later said it took him three years "to get a glimmering of why I was there." Never involved in combat, he was discharged in August 1945. His war years did influence his choice of a career. He recalled his feelings: "Men who fight wars have a right to know why," and he wanted to try to tell them why.

In 1941 McGee married Nialta Sue Beaird. They had a son and a daughter.

Under the GI Bill McGee attended the University of California at Berkeley in 1945–1946, and to support his family he worked a variety of odd jobs, including board marker in a stockbroker's office and assistant to an interior designer. In 1947–1948 he attended the University of Oklahoma. He began working for KGFF, a 250-watt radio station in Shawnee, Oklahoma, as a jack-of-all-trades: announcer, advertising salesman, disc jockey, commercial copywriter, news broadcaster, and music librarian.

In 1950 McGee transferred to WKY, a radio-television station in Oklahoma City. Four years later he took over as news director at WSAF-TV in Montgomery, Alabama, the only local channel that had fifteen minutes of local news and fifteen minutes of weather. Never part of the Montgomery white-power establishment, McGee began reporting on the Ku Klux Klan. Like most reporters of the era, McGee sympathized with the blacks and, perhaps because of his own background, showed compassion for all poor people, regardless of race. He received constant threats on the street and over the phone but was never assaulted. His coverage competed with that of local newspapers, and his local station managers never dictated what he could air. NBC network news, still in its early stages, began to use his reports on a direct feed.

Impressed with his work, network chairman Julian Goodman and other NBC executives put McGee in charge of the NBC news desk in Washington, D.C., in 1957. One of his first assignments was covering the integration of Central High School in Little Rock, Arkansas.

In 1958 McGee became the announcer for "Monitor," a three-hour NBC weekend network radio program that combined news with music and entertainment. The job paid $150 a week. Even with his increasing responsibilities in other news venues, McGee continued to do "Monitor" until his death. Also in 1958 McGee won a Headliners Award for radio and television news broadcasting. In 1959 he won the Robert E. Sherwood Award.

From 1960 to 1964 McGee anchored WNBC's "Sixth Hour News" and in 1964 switched to the "Eleventh Hour News," which he anchored until his death. In 1960 he hosted "World Wide '60," a Saturday evening program of documentaries. The first program was "Castro's Year of Power"; the most controversial was "Germany: Fifteen Years Later" because in it McGee warned of possible dangers in German rearmament. Also in 1960 he received an award from *TV*

Guide. In 1961–1962 he hosted "Here and Now," a Friday evening news magazine.

McGee's strength as a news commentator lay in his calm, flawless delivery despite turbulent events and in his clear presentation. His voice was crisp with a slight hint of a southern drawl. Rather than pontification and easy witticisms, his scripts demonstrated depth and perception. McGee wrote his own scripts because he believed he could more smoothly ad lib his own material than unfamiliar material written by others. Besides writing his own scripts, he also wrote a book of short stories titled *They Don't Make Depressions Like That Any More*.

In addition to his regular assignments, during the 1960s McGee covered inaugural conventions and presidential elections, the assassinations of John F. Kennedy and Robert F. Kennedy, and the space program. He moderated the second debate between presidential candidates Richard Nixon and John F. Kennedy and served as a panelist in another one of the debates. For more than eleven hours he stayed in front of news cameras reporting John Glenn's orbital flight in February 1962. He repeated the same feat by spending twelve straight hours on the news desk after the assassination of President Kennedy.

McGee was also praised for his work on documentaries and instant news specials. He won the Peabody Award twice, once in 1964 for his television documentary "The American Revolution of '63," on the black struggle for equality, and again in 1966 for his coverage of the visit of Pope Paul VI in New York. After a month in Vietnam with two camera teams, he produced "Same Mud, Same Blood," about relations between black and white soldiers in Vietnam, a one-hour documentary that received a Brotherhood Award from the National Conference of Christians and Jews. McGee preferred documentaries to regular news broadcasts because he felt they allowed more time to develop their stories and viewers could more easily see the subject's importance.

McGee's first "instant special" covered the Khrushchev-Eisenhower Paris summit of May 1960. These instant specials interrupted regularly scheduled programs to inform viewers about important news events as they were occurring. They generally lasted between fifteen and thirty-five minutes. In 1961 Gulf Oil agreed to sponsor the specials for a cost of over $3 million. By February 1962 McGee had done six of them, including reports on the Kennedy administration, Africa, Laos, American military preparedness, and the trial of Adolf Eichmann. During his broadcasting career McGee reported for more than 450 news specials.

An example of the constraints under which McGee worked for these specials is his coverage of the seizure of the SS *Santa Maria* by Portuguese rebels in 1961. In a Pittsburgh hotel room preparing a luncheon talk, McGee learned of the seizure at 11:30 A.M. He gave the talk, boarded a private plane that arrived in New York at 5:00 P.M., and finished his script ten minutes before air time. Instant specials, such as those on the 1963 Supreme Court decision on school prayer, gave greater depth than usual news coverage, and NBC News beat CBS Reports to the subject by two days. In 1968 McGee received an Emmy for his special-event satellite coverage of Konrad Adenauer's funeral.

Also in 1968, McGee became the first television journalist to criticize openly the American presence in Vietnam. He said that the United States appeared to be losing the war and that to destroy Vietnam in an effort to "save it" might not be the best policy.

In 1970 McGee became coanchor of the NBC evening news with David Brinkley and John Chancellor and continued in that position until his death. Chancellor later said of McGee, "Frank McGee was one of the men who gave his life to television, and brought to it a significant measure of decency and integrity."

In 1971 McGee replaced Hugh Downs as host of the NBC "Today" show. Despite severe pain and failing health caused by multiple myeloma, a rare type of bone cancer, he remained on the job until six days before his death. He died at Columbia-Presbyterian hospital in Manhattan of pneumonia.

• A video featuring McGee, "Vietnam: The Home Front," broadcast 1 Apr. 1966, is held by the Library of Congress. Articles on McGee can be found in the *New York Times*, 5 Feb. 1961; *Variety*, 20 Sept. 1961 and 4 Apr. 1962; the New York *Herald Tribune*, 8 July 1963; and *Broadcasting*, 22 Apr. 1974. A tribute to him appears in the *Congressional Record*, 24 Apr. 1974, pp. 11765–66. Information on his life can also be found in Eric Barnouw, *The Image Empire* (1970), and David Halberstam, *The Fifties* (1993). His obituary is in the *New York Times*, 18 Apr. 1974.

ANN W. ENGAR

MCGEE, Sam (1 May 1894–21 Aug. 1975), country music guitarist and singer, was born Sam Fleming McGee in rural Williamson County, due south of Nashville, in Middle Tennessee, the son of John F. McGee, a farmer and well-known local fiddler, and Mary Elizabeth Truett. As a boy, Sam listened to tales about the Civil War battle of Franklin, which was fought near his home, as well as several types of music. From his father he learned a repertoire of old fiddle tunes, from his mother, a battery of old American and British ballads and religious songs. The McGee farmhouse was often the scene of dances and musical jam sessions, with one of the McGee uncles joining in. In 1904, when Sam was ten years old, his father bought him a cheap, $10 banjo, and he learned to "second" (accompany) his father at country dances and in fiddling contests. In 1899 his brother Kirk was born; Kirk learned to play the fiddle and became curator of many of the McGee family fiddle tunes.

Meanwhile, when Sam McGee got his first guitar around 1910, he became fascinated with it. He took some formal lessons from a doctor in nearby Franklin, who taught him to play the guitar as a parlor instrument. But, more important, he also began to hang around black section hands who worked on the nearby railroad and became fascinated with the way they played blues guitar—especially with their unorthodox tunings and use of a piece of steel to do slide noting.

The guitar was just emerging as a folk instrument during McGee's youth, and many rural musicians had never even seen one before. McGee became an early exponent of finger picking the guitar and making it a solo instrument; he did this by combining his interest in blues with his parlor training and his fascination with current ragtime and vaudeville songs.

In this post–World War I era, few in the rural South seriously expected to make a living from music, so McGee began to work as a blacksmith in 1922. He married a local woman, Mary Elizabeth Pate, in 1914, and by 1915 their first child was born. Then in 1925 he met and began touring with the foremost Middle Tennessee banjo player of the day, Uncle Dave Macon. The following year he accompanied Macon to the Vocalion recording studios in New York, where he backed him on a number of historic recordings and then made a series on his own. These included original "Buck Dancer's Choice," a dazzling virtuoso guitar piece that he had derived as accompaniment to a buck dancer touring with Macon. He later recorded a number of other early guitar solos, such as "Franklin Blues," "Knoxville Blues," and "Railroad Blues." All of these became test pieces for young guitarists and helped show the musical world that the guitar could be an effective solo instrument.

From 1926 through 1934 McGee, and often his brother Kirk, traveled and recorded with Macon, winning wide fame for their instrumental dexterity and comic songs. (McGee often wore a red "toby" wig for comic relief in the shows.) He served as a member of Macon's larger recording string band, the Fruit Jar Drinkers, as well as his gospel group, the Dixie Sacred Singers, both of whom also recorded for Vocalion. When Macon became a regular member of the WSM radio show the Grand Ole Opry in 1925, McGee soon joined him there as well. In 1931 he ceased touring with Macon, and he and Kirk began working with Fiddlin' Arthur Smith, performing on the Opry as the Dixieliners. They continued there throughout the 1930s—though the records Smith made during this time do not have the McGees on them.

The Dixieliners broke up when Smith left the Opry in 1938, and McGee joined with Kirk to work as a duet act on the Opry. For a time they worked with the comedy act Sarie and Sallie and also toured with bluegrass maven Bill Monroe. By the 1950s the older McGee style of music was being eclipsed by the newer, electrified, honky-tonk style, and there was a move to fire the brothers from the Opry. They naturally protested, and shortly afterward, in 1956, a new, young, urban audience interested in their music as folk music began to pay attention to the McGees.

They made a couple of new LPs for Folkways Records and, with the help of young folksinger Mike Seeger, began to travel to various folk festivals in Newport, Chicago, and California. This reinvigorated their music and even won them new respect from the Opry management, who now began to see them as an important link to the Opry's rich folk past. McGee did a remarkable solo LP for Archoolie and even formed his own record company, MBA, in Franklin. In 1974, as the McGees played the last Opry show at the historic Ryman Auditorium, reporter Garrison Keilor from the *New Yorker* magazine watched them and got the idea for a similar show that he called "Prairie Home Companion."

By now McGee had become a guru of sorts to all kinds of young acoustic guitar players, who often made the pilgrimage out on Peytonsville Road to his spacious Franklin farmhouse. His guitar solos were transcribed and studied by people fascinated with his playing technique. He was the subject of a BBC film documentary, as well as a book. McGee was killed in an accident while mowing in a field. His brother Kirk kept alive the McGee music for a time, before his own death in 1983.

• Very little has been written about McGee, and most information available on him is based on personal interviews conducted by Charles K. Wolfe. See Wolfe, "Sam McGee," in *Tom Ashley, Sam McGee, Bukka White: Tennessee Traditional Singers*, ed. Thomas G. Burton (1981).

CHARLES K. WOLFE

MCGEE, William John (17 Apr. 1853–4 Sept. 1912), geologist and anthropologist, was born near Farley, Dubuque County, Iowa, the son of James McGee, an Irish immigrant and farmer, and Martha Ann Anderson. McGee attended local schools intermittently until about the age of fourteen. An older brother who had attended college provided education in Latin, German, mathematics, and astronomy, and a maternal uncle helped teach McGee surveying, a skill for which there was much local demand. He learned blacksmithing and in the early 1870s manufactured and sold agricultural implements. With a brother and a cousin he obtained a patent in 1874 on an improved adjustable cultivator, which was not a financial success.

McGee and his brothers explored the countryside, and McGee became interested in caves, aboriginal artifacts, burial mounds, and especially the evidence of glaciers that had once left debris in Iowa. He began reading scientific literature, and he wrote to scientists on these subjects. In 1878 he joined the American Association for the Advancement of Science at its meeting in St. Louis. There he met John Wesley Powell, a chiefly self-taught scientist, who apparently encouraged the young man in his researches. Also in 1878 McGee published his first two scientific papers, on glacial drift and on prehistoric burial mounds in Iowa, in the *American Journal of Science*. From 1877 to 1881 he carried out on his own a topographic and geological survey of 12,000 square miles in northeastern Iowa, which was published in 1891 as "The Pleistocene History of Northeastern Iowa." Through Powell's influence, McGee was hired to examine and report on building stones of Iowa for the tenth census of 1880, the first attempt at a comprehensive study of the nation's mineral resources.

Powell, who had been appointed the first director of the Bureau of Ethnology of the Smithsonian Institution in 1879, also became director of the U.S. Geological Survey (USGS) in 1881. The next year he hired McGee as a field assistant of the survey to work in Nevada and California, and in 1883 McGee became a full-time employee of that agency. His first assignment was to produce a geologic map of the United States. From publications by individual states and regions and from unpublished sources—all of which varied in scale and terminology—McGee compiled a generalized hand-colored map, published in the *5th Annual Report* of the USGS in 1885. Although preliminary and with many uncolored portions for unexplored areas, McGee's map was the first such map of the nation. He also encouraged the production of a geologic map of New York State.

In 1884 McGee also summarized for the USGS available knowledge of the practical uses of petroleum, which was then primarily used for illumination and lubrication. In 1885 he was put in charge of a division to study the geology of the Atlantic coastal plain. In this capacity he participated in and directed the surveying and mapping of 300,000 square miles of the southeastern United States. Performed in a region largely uncharted geologically, this work involved problems of stratigraphy and of elevation and depression of the land. His identification of the sequences of glacial advances and retreats in the upper Mississippi valley was also valuable. McGee is considered a pioneer in geomorphology, the study of land forms. He was one of several geologists who recorded observations of the earthquake of 1886 in Charleston, South Carolina. In 1893 he was again in charge of producing a geologic map of the United States.

McGee became a significant member of scientific circles in the nation's capital. Colleagues considered him cordial, generous, and helpful. For reasons not defined, he preferred to be known only by his initials W J, without periods. In 1888 he married Anita Newcomb, the daughter of astronomer Simon Newcomb; she had academic interests herself and became head of the army nurse corps. The couple had two children.

One of the founders of the Geological Society of America, McGee served from 1888 to 1891 as the first editor of its *Bulletin*. A founder of the Columbia Historical Society, he was also president of the American Anthropological Association from 1898 to 1900 and of the Anthropological Society of Washington in 1911, and he was acting president of the American Association for the Advancement of Science in 1897–1898. He was president of the National Geographic Society in 1904–1905 and editor of *National Geographic Magazine* for several years.

In 1893 Powell, who had resigned as director of the U.S. Geological Survey in 1893, offered McGee a position in the Bureau of American Ethnology. As ethnologist in charge of the bureau from 1894 to 1903, McGee published about thirty reports on native peoples of the Americas, including one on the Sioux. Following a trip in 1894–1895 to their remote islands in the Gulf of California, he also wrote a long report on the Seri (1898). He resigned from the bureau in 1903, after Powell's death, and took charge of an anthropological exhibit of peoples of the world for the St. Louis Exposition in 1903–1904. In 1905 he became the first director of the St. Louis Public Museum. Two years later he was appointed to the Inland Waterways Commission by President Theodore Roosevelt and was also appointed to the Bureau of Soils of the U.S. Department of Agriculture. In the latter position he headed a team that investigated the nation's water resources, and he published significant papers on water supplies and soil erosion. Both appointments continued until his death in Washington, D.C.

Through his published reports and participation in scientific organizations, McGee made significant contributions to American geology and to anthropology. A good administrator, he was also a sage member of organizations and national committees, and he was acknowledged as an early advocate of conservation of natural resources.

• McGee's papers from his years at the U.S. Geological Survey are in the National Archives; others are in the Library of Congress and the Smithsonian's National Anthropological Archives. McGee's report on Iowa was in U.S. Geological Survey, *11th Annual Report*, pt. 1 (1891), pp. 199–557. Most of McGee's anthropological papers were in annual reports of the Bureau of American Ethnology. Biographies are Frank Hall Knowlton in the *Bulletin of the Geological Society of America* 24 (1913): 18–29, which has a bibliography of McGee's geological papers; Nelson Horatio Darton in the *Annals of the Association of American Geographers* 3 (1915), pp. 103–110; and Kenneth E. Peters and Robert B. Herrmann, "First-hand Observations of the Charleston Earthquake of August 31, 1886, and Other Earthquake Materials," *South Carolina Geological Survey Bulletin* 41 (1986), p. 1–5. See also William Culp Darrah, *Powell of the Colorado* (1951).

ELIZABETH NOBLE SHOR

MCGHEE, Frederick Lamar (1861–9 Sept. 1912), lawyer and black activist, was born in Aberdeen, Mississippi, the son of Abraham McGhee and Sarah Walker, slaves. Although his father, a blacksmith, was not afforded a formal education, he learned to read and write, later becoming a Baptist preacher. Abraham McGhee also made certain that his children were literate, teaching each of them how to read and write. Such skills served young Frederick well when his parents died in 1873. Having moved with his family to Knoxville, Tennessee, soon after his parents were freed, McGhee remained there, studying at Knoxville College under the tutelage of Presbyterian missionaries. Without completing his undergraduate studies, he soon ventured to Chicago, working as a waiter for a time and then studying law with Edward H. Morris, a prominent local lawyer.

By 1885 McGhee was admitted to the Illinois bar, and in 1886 he married Mattie B. Crane. The couple had one daughter. For the next three years McGhee engaged in private practice in Chicago, still working closely with Morris, who by then had become an Illinois state legislator and one of McGhee's partners. Despite his apparent success in Chicago, McGhee moved his family to St. Paul, Minnesota, in 1889. There he made a name for himself as one of the most highly skilled criminal lawyers of the Old Northwest.

Although McGhee would eventually become known for his efforts to end racial discrimination, his initial success as a litigator was more of a testament to his eloquence and mental acuity than to any personal ambitions he might have had to test the boundaries of racial equality. The first African American admitted to the bar in Minnesota, McGhee quickly attracted a biracial clientele by establishing a reputation as a tough criminal lawyer whose presence could be felt in the courtroom. Despite his success as a trial lawyer, he was no stranger to discrimination. One writer commented, "He knew by bitter experience how his own dark face had served as an excuse for discouraging him and discriminating unfairly against him" (the *Crisis*, Nov. 1912). Consequently, although McGhee had achieved such accolades as being the first black man allowed to argue cases before the Minnesota Supreme Court, he still resented any sort of racial slight, and by the early 1900s he became interested in the national discussion concerning race.

In 1898 McGhee responded to a formal "call" issued by Bishop Alexander Walters of the African Methodist Episcopal church to revive the defunct Afro-American League. That organization was founded in 1890 upon the views of T. Thomas Fortune that agitation and perhaps even revolution were necessary if African Americans were to achieve racial equality. The meeting convened eight years later as the Afro-American Council, and while its precepts remained unchanged, its resolutions quickly acquired a conciliatory nature under the leadership of Booker T. Washington. Although, like Fortune, Washington advocated both solidarity and self-help, he vocalized his disapproval only when he felt it would be effective, believing that agitation alone could not bring about justice. McGhee, like many other northern lawyers, differed from his southern counterparts. He depended on whites as well as blacks for his living, interacted daily with his Caucasian clientele, and established himself firmly in the upper echelon of St. Paul society. Therefore, McGhee was an improbable ally for Washington and his principles of economic chauvinism and industrial education. McGhee wavered on the issue of social equality, stating as late as 1904 that, while he would not abide racial discrimination, he did not believe in absolute social equality.

McGhee acted as head of the council's legal department, served as program chairman for the 1902 St. Paul meeting, and in 1903 was elected financial secretary. He became disillusioned with Washington's tendency to placate whites in order to win marginal battles, and by 1903 he was urging the Afro-American Council to use more aggressive tactics. Although McGhee, a well-known Catholic layman, never completely sided with the Tuskegeean in the national debate, Washington persuaded him in 1904 to approach the Catholic hierarchy in hopes of enlisting the church's explicit opposition to disfranchisement of black voters in Maryland.

McGhee helped initiate the Niagara movement, an attempt by more radical blacks to directly and openly oppose the conservative actions and views of Washington. Writing for the *Voice of the Negro* in September 1905, W. E. B. Du Bois went so far as to give McGhee full credit for creating the more radical entity, stating, "The honor of founding the organization belongs to F. L. McGhee, who first suggested it." McGhee served the new organization loyally, helping it to take legal action against the Pullman Company for discrimination in 1907. Although the Niagara movement ultimately failed, McGhee, Du Bois, and others did finally see the gradual decline of Washington's influence, as the Tuskegeean lost control of the Afro-American Council in 1907. The Niagara movement's decline was evidence that neither militant nor conservative blacks were representative of the race as a whole. According to author August Meier, without the help of a small number of white progressives, the Niagara movement alone would not have been able to oust Washington or his influential allies in light of the fundamental characteristics of race relations in the United States at the turn of the century.

McGhee was a lifelong Democrat during a period when Republicans continued to experience the residual loyalty of many African Americans. While he supported Theodore Roosevelt for president in 1904, within Minnesota he continued to vote the Democratic ticket because he believed the Democrats were better to African Americans in that state. Furthermore, he rejected Republican imperialism, particularly the violent attempts to crush Filipino independence. In 1900 he wrote:

> Of the number of women and children killed in attacks upon villages defended by men armed with bamboo spears, this with the profoundly and oft-repeated assertion, of late so prevalent, that the proud Anglo-Saxon, the Republican party, by divine foreordination, is destined to rule earth's inferior races. . . . Is it to be wondered then that so little value is placed upon the life, liberty, freedom and rights of the American Negro? Is he not also one of the inferior races which Divine Providence has commissioned the Republican party to care for? (Katz, p. 424)

By 1910 the National Association for the Advancement of Colored People, which would become the most powerful force for African Americans in the United States, had organized and held its first meeting, a tangible sign that Washington's influence was by this point negligible. Although the Niagara movement did not actually merge with the new organization, most of its members soon joined forces with the fledgling entity, including McGhee, who helped organize the St. Paul chapter. McGhee died of pleurisy shortly after its formation and was never able to experience the organization's eventual triumphs.

A tireless opponent of discrimination in this country, McGhee, according to an obituary in the *Crisis*, "stood like a wall against the encroachment of color caste in the Northwest and his influence and his purse were ever ready to help." Despite his loyalty to African Americans and their particular circumstances, McGhee's attentions were never completely self-absorbed. Throughout his life and career he remained acutely aware of the oppression of other races, particularly those overseas, remarking that because blacks had experienced oppression firsthand, they "should be the loudest in the protestations against the oppression of others" (Katz, p. 324).

• Several of McGhee's letters are in the Booker T. Washington Papers in the Library of Congress. For a brief sample of McGhee's writing on the topic of imperialism in the Philippines, see "The Same Thing Cropping Out at Home," *Howard's American Magazine*, Oct. 1900. Short biographies are in William B. Hennessey, *Past and Present of St. Paul, Minnesota* (1906) and *Gopher Historian* (1968–1969). For a thorough discussion of African-American thought in the United States during McGhee's life, particularly the views of Washington and W. E. B. Du Bois, see August Meier, *Negro Thought in America 1880–1915* (1963). Earl Spangler, *The Negro in Minnesota* (1961), and William Loren Katz, *The Black West* (1987), also contain information about McGhee's role as an African-American leader in the West. An obituary is in the *Crisis*, Nov. 1912.

DONNA GREAR PARKER

MCGHEE, Howard B. (6 Mar. 1918–17 July 1987), jazz trumpeter, arranger, and composer, known as "Maggie" in the jazz community, was born in Tulsa, Oklahoma. His parents' names are unknown. His father, seeking factory work, moved the family to Detroit when McGhee was an infant, but his mother died soon thereafter, and he was raised by his grandmother in Bristow and Sapulpa, Oklahoma. His father returned from Detroit but died when McGhee was about five years old. After moving with his grandmother to Boley, Oklahoma, McGhee attended a boys' school, where he learned to play a scale on trumpet; then, to his disappointment, he was started on clarinet, so as not to be ahead of the rest of the class. McGhee lost an eye in a childhood accident and thereafter always wore dark glasses. Perhaps the fashion among beboppers of the 1940s for wearing dark shades in dingy nightclubs has in McGhee's experience a practical origin independent of Dizzy Gillespie and Thelonious Monk's sartorial preferences.

McGhee's first job in music was playing trumpet in a carnival band in Muskogee, Oklahoma, at about age thirteen or fourteen. He was still in school but spent the summer traveling with the carnival. He joined a quartet in a restaurant in Oklahoma City, where he developed his endurance as a trumpeter, but when he traveled to California to join Gene Coy's band it was as a tenor saxophonist. He switched permanently to trumpet to play with Art Bronson's jump band in 1935, at age sixteen. Bronson's men ridiculed McGhee for his intense admiration and excessive imitation of Louis Armstrong, and he left after three months.

McGhee continued playing in obscure territory bands from 1936 to 1940, when he returned to Detroit to lead his own group. He joined Lionel Hampton's big band in September 1941 but quit soon thereafter upon discovering that he could make the same wages in Detroit and not have to travel. The following year, though, he joined Andy Kirk's big band in St. Louis. While with Kirk in New York, McGhee participated in jam sessions at Minton's Playhouse and Monroe's Uptown House. He met Gillespie at Minton's in July and thereby became involved in the emerging bop style. McGhee had begun writing arrangements for Kirk, and that same month, July 1942, he was featured on Kirk's recording of "McGhee Special," which McGhee had composed for his own band in 1940. Like many African-American musicians, he disliked traveling in the South and quit in August when Kirk announced his next tour.

Late in August 1942 McGhee became one of four African-American instrumentalists to join the big band of saxophonist Charlie Barnet, for whom he also supplied arrangements. As a freelancer in New York after August 1943, he served as a substitute in Count Basie's big band late in the year. He recorded with Kirk again in December. During his last tenure with Kirk, from February to 28 June 1944, he tutored his fellow section mate Fats Navarro on how to produce high notes on the trumpet. He then went into another racially integrated endeavor, joining saxophonist Georgie Auld's big band on 30 June as the featured trumpet soloist, a regular member of the trumpet section, and an arranger. He substituted in Billy Eckstine's bop big band during this period and also wrote arrangements for Eckstine and Woody Herman.

In December 1944 McGhee joined tenor saxophonist Coleman Hawkins's five-piece group, including bassist Oscar Pettiford, pianist Sir Charles Thompson, and drummer Denzil Best, at the Three Deuces in New York. He traveled with Hawkins to California, where he participated in Jazz at the Philharmonic concerts. According to McGhee, at one of these concerts producer Norman Granz made a recording of "How High the Moon" without telling the band; the successful disc brought McGhee celebrity but little money. Meanwhile, he worked as Hawkins's sideman in Los Angeles from February to mid-April 1945, when he quit in a dispute over money.

McGhee stayed in California for two years, initially co-leading a group with Teddy Edwards from 1945 to early 1946 and then leading on his own. He participated at the chaotic and controversial Dial recording session of 29 July 1946, preceding alto saxophonist Charlie Parker's admittance to Camarillo Hospital. Three of the four resulting titles, including "Be-bop," were originally issued under McGhee's name. He led his own session for Dial on 18 October and then joined a recovered Parker on 26 February 1947 for celebrated versions of "Relaxin' at Camarillo," "Carvin' the Bird," "Cheers," and "Stupendous," the last three titles featuring themes composed by McGhee. In April he was also captured on record as a soloist on "Groovin' High" at producer Gene Norman's Just Jazz concert, a rival to Jazz at the Philharmonic.

Back in New York, McGhee appeared with Jazz at the Philharmonic at Carnegie Hall late in 1947 and toured with this assemblage of all stars. He also toured and recorded with his own groups, his recordings including a session of 3 December 1947 with saxophonist James Moody, vibraphonist Milt Jackson, pianist Hank Jones, bassist Ray Brown, and drummer J. C. Heard as his sidemen. In Chicago he recorded a further session featuring Jackson in February 1948. In May of that year he took his own group, including saxophonist Jimmy Heath and bassist Percy Heath, to the Paris Jazz Festival; they recorded on 14 May under drummer Kenny Clarke's leadership. In New York, with Jackson playing vibraphone and piano, he recorded a marvelous session with Navarro, the two trumpets exchanging closely matched improvised bop phrases on "Boperation" and "Double Talk" (Oct. 1948). McGhee was a member of singer and percussionist Machito's Afro-Cuban group in the spring of 1949. Saxophonist Brew Moore and he are the jazz soloists on "Cubop City," which Machito recorded in April. In 1949 he was selected best trumpeter of the year in the annual *Down Beat* poll.

McGhee's attempt to found a big band in 1950, at exactly the time when many famous leaders were disbanding, was a financial disaster. As a member of Pettiford's group he embarked on a USO tour of the United States, Japan, Korea, the Philippines, Guam, and Okinawa from late 1951 to early 1952. By this time, if not some years earlier, McGhee was addicted to heroin. He occasionally played with Parker in Boston during the early 1950s, and he led a fine recording session with pianist Horace Silver and guitarist Tal Farlow among his sidemen in June 1953, but he was largely inactive from 1952 through 1959. Arrested for possession of narcotics in 1958, he served about six months at the Tombs and on Riker's Island in New York City. After McGhee's release from jail, Woody Herman gave him a job in 1960. He began recording again, including the albums *Together Again!* with Teddy Edwards in May 1961 and *Maggie's Back in Town* with pianist Phineas Newborn, Jr., in June. He worked in Moody's band in Los Angeles in 1961 and late that year briefly joined Duke Ellington. McGhee received critical acclaim for his performances at the Newport Jazz Festival in July 1963.

From the mid-1960s into the 1970s McGhee led a big band in New York, largely for musical satisfaction rather than as a money-making venture. During this period he often worked with singer Joe Carroll. Reverend John Gensel, the "jazz pastor," had helped McGhee secure a police cabaret card so that he could work in New York again after the narcotics conviction. Subsequently, McGhee often donated his musical services to Gensel's church. He may be seen in the documentary film biography of Gensel, *Shepard of the Night Flock* made between 1972 and 1977. As the festival circuit blossomed in the 1970s, McGhee toured widely, including a visit to Europe with a group that included trombonist J. J. Johnson and alto saxophonist Sonny Stitt. In the mid-1980s McGhee continued his activities with Gensel in the Jazz Vespers series at St. Peter's Lutheran Church. He died in New York City. He was survived by his wife Tina, and their four children; her maiden name and the marriage date are unknown.

McGhee was one of the few trumpeters of the mid- to late 1940s who could play bop well, meeting the technical demands that the style's melodies posed for a brass player and inventing creative lines in the process. Gillespie and Navarro set the standard in this regard; McGhee and Kenny Dorham were not far behind. In fact, distinguishing between Navarro's and McGhee's dovetailing and brilliant melodies on the two takes of "Double Talk" (1948) is almost certainly a matter for the jazz expert, not the general listener. Indeed, on liner notes to the first twelve-inch LP reissue of this session, even bop expert Leonard Feather appears to have confused the two, stating that Navarro played the first two 32-bar choruses before initiating a series of trades back and forth (eight bars each; later sixteen, then eight, then each), when it sounds as if Navarro played thirty-two bars and McGhee the next thirty-two before Navarro began the quicker trading. This observation is not a criticism of Feather but rather testifies to how completely McGhee had absorbed the difficult bop melodic style, considerably removed from his upbringing in the tunefulness of the Swing Era.

• An interview by Ira Gitler (16 and 23 Nov. and 1 and 6 Dec. 1982) is among the oral histories at the Institute of Jazz Studies, Newark, N.J. Further extensive interviews conducted by Scott DeVeaux between 1980 and 1985 are summarized in the context of detailed historical and musical interpretation in his "Jazz in Transition: Coleman Hawkins and Howard McGhee" (Ph.D. diss., Univ. of California, Berkeley, 1985). Published surveys and interviews include Johnny Sippel, "Faster Trumpet Work Tabs 'McGhee' Special," *Down Beat* 11 (15 Sept. 1944): 4; Robert George Reisner, ed., *Bird: The Legend of Charlie Parker* (1962; repr. 1975): and Bill Coss, "Back to Stay: Howard McGhee," *Down Beat* 29 (18 Jan. 1962): 20–21. See also George Hoefer, "The Early Career of Howard McGhee," *Down Beat* 30 (15 Aug. 1963): 33–34; Valerie Wilmer, *Jazz People* (1970; repr. 1985); and DeVeaux, "Conversation with Howard McGhee: Jazz in the Forties," *Black Perspective in Music* 15 (Spring 1989): 64–78. Photos are in Frank Driggs and Harris Lewine, *Black Beauty, White Heat: A Pictorial History of Classic Jazz, 1920–1950* (1982). A catalog of recordings is Richard E. Boenzli, *Discography of Howard McGhee* (1961). These recordings are described from conflicting viewpoints by Demètre Ioakimidis, "Maggie's Back," *Jazz Hot*, no. 201 (Sept. 1964): 34–37, and Jim Burns, "Howard McGhee, with Discography by Alun Morgan," *Jazz Journal* 19 (Jan. 1966): 12–14, 39. Discographical additions and corrections are by Morgan in *Jazz Journal* 19 (Nov. 1966): 38; and by Mark Gardner in 20 (May 1967): 24. Gunther Schuller analyzes "McGhee Special" in his *The Swing Era: The Development of Jazz, 1930–1945* (1989). Obituaries are in the *New York Times*, 18 July 1987, and *The Independent*, 23 July 1987.

BARRY KERNFELD

MCGILL, Ralph (5 Feb. 1898–3 Feb. 1969), journalist, was born in Igou's Ferry, Tennessee, the son of Benjamin Franklin McGill (born Benjamin Wallace) and Mary Lou Skillern, farmers. McGill recalled, "I lived in history," in an area near Civil War battlefields and marked by monuments to war heroes. This region had been predominantly nonslaveholding; McGill's grandfathers had taken opposite sides in the Civil War, and McGill's middle name, Emerson, honored a family friend and admirer of the New England sage.

McGill had an early love of books and often walked two miles to the nearest library. He enrolled at Vanderbilt University in Nashville but did not graduate. He became acquainted with some of the "Fugitive" group of agrarian sympathizers at the university, notably Allen Tate and Robert Penn Warren. His work on the campus newspaper led to his career in journalism. He joined the staff of the *Atlanta Constitution* in 1929, primarily as a sportswriter. He became its executive editor in 1938 and its publisher in 1960. McGill married Mary Elizabeth Leonard in 1929; they had three children, only one of whom survived to adulthood.

McGill made his mark by championing progressive political causes in the South, especially civil rights and racial integration. He saw himself in the tradition of Henry Grady, the late nineteenth-century editor of the *Constitution* and major advocate of the "New South" ideal. In language often blunt and pointed, McGill denounced many aspects of the southern tradition. He saw the region under control of local baronies and regressive demagogues who ruled through corruption. He decried the passions that ruled the southern masses and their easy exploitation by political leaders. He continually advocated for economic growth, looking to new business leaders, and for education to foster a progressive challenge to political and economic stagnation. McGill also championed migration into the South as further leverage against the old order. He often displayed contempt for the old southern myths, particularly doctrines of white supremacy.

McGill constantly faulted the appeal to states' rights among southern politicians and newspaper editorialists. He considered the ideal outmoded and ill-serving of the South's real interests. No region, he said, depended more on the federal largesse. He knew that the states' rights standard served essentially as a cover for racism, and he cited Alabama governor George Wallace as a prime example. McGill gained a national reputation in the Little Rock school integration crisis in 1957. While white anti-integrationists cited states' rights, McGill appealed to a larger progressive ideal, the improvement in schooling for the state's white and black children and the opportunity to change the state's shameful record in public education. He discussed the constitutional crisis surrounding southern schools in frequent public addresses, urging realism.

McGill placed little hope in the southern masses as a source of progressive change. He addressed his pleas more to the southern leadership and to moderates in all fields; he met constant frustrations, however, even among the groups on which he most relied, and his editorials became even more denunciatory. As the South in the late 1950s and early 1960s seemed to tolerate church burnings, murders, and the violence of the Ku Klux Klan, McGill was appalled and depressed. He asked, "Where have the 'best people,' the 'good people' been?" Moderates, he said, "gave consent to immoderation," and the "red-necks and violent haters" had their way.

McGill considered himself a moderate man and espoused moderate means. He wrote in strong moral terms, but he also appealed to a republican tradition in which the public forum was the vehicle of rational debate and discussion. This kind of calm deliberation he believed the South sorely needed, but he found that almost always the extreme voices dominated, to the point that every liberal proposal was denounced as communist-inspired and anti-American. McGill often invoked a progressive southern tradition as modeled by Thomas Jefferson, but he also contrasted the courage and integrity of Confederate leaders like Robert E. Lee with the unprincipled and cowardly reactionaries of the present South. McGill also had strong views on other issues. He supported American policy in the Vietnam War and defended Israel in the 1967 war with Egypt.

McGill endured much. Dubbed "southern enemy number one" by the Klan, he often received abusive phone calls and threatening letters. People threw garbage on his lawn and shot holes in his mail box. His personal life saw tragedy as his wife died in 1962. In 1967 McGill married Mary Lynn Morgan, a dentist.

McGill belonged to a tradition of southern liberalism that has always struggled in a conservative region. To some northerners McGill seemed naive and predictable, but he had a profound sense of the complexity of southern history and expected no easy resolution of its problems. Despite the wrath of so many southern whites, he gained influence among southern moderates weary of racial violence and reactionism. Many sought his counsel. McGill loved poetry and could quote pages by memory; his literary skills and passionate moral feelings produced the animated prose of his editorials. In 1959 he received the Pulitzer Prize for outstanding editorial commentary, and in 1964, the Presidential Medal of Freedom. He died in Atlanta.

• A collection of McGill papers is at Emory University in Atlanta, Ga. McGill's most notable writings are collected in *The South and the Southerner* (1959), which is heavily autobiographical. *Southern Encounters: Southerners of Note in Ralph McGill's South*, ed. Calvin M. Logue (1983), contains essays on such figures as Margaret Mitchell, Martin Luther King, Jr., George Wallace, and Lester Maddox. One may find more of McGill's writings in *No Place to Hide: The South and Human Rights*, ed. Logue (2 vols., 1984), in which Logue has a lengthy introductory essay. Still more from Logue on McGill is *Ralph McGill: Editor and Publisher* (2 vols., 1969). *A Church, a School* (1959) is a small anthology of McGill editorials including important ones on school integration and civil rights. Some of McGill's best essays are in *Saturday Review*, including "The Decade of Slow, Painful Progress," 16 May 1964; "The Case for the Southern Progressive," 13 June

1964; and "Race: Results Instead of Reason," 9 Jan. 1965. An informative biographical study is Harold Martin, *Ralph McGill, Reporter* (1973).

J. DAVID HOEVELER, JR.

MCGILLIVRAY, Alexander (1759?–17 Feb. 1793), member of the Koasati tribe and Great Beloved Man (chief counselor) of the Muskogee or Creek confederacy, was born at Little Tallassee plantation outside the Upper Creek town of Otcipofa (near present-day Montgomery, Ala.), the son of Lachlan McGillivray, a Scottish trader, and Sehoy Marchand, sister of Koasati chief Red Shoes. Raised among the matrilineal Koasati, McGillivray developed close ties to his influential Wind clan relations and was deeply imbued with the culture of his mother's people. He also learned the language and British culture of his father, who took him to Charleston and Savannah for a formal education in 1773. There he studied business and history until his studies were cut off by the outbreak of the American Revolution.

In 1777, McGillivray accepted a commission as a colonel in the army, working for the Board of Trade's superintendent for Indian affairs, and returned to Little Tallassee as the British commissary for the Upper Creek towns. His family and clan connections gave him immediate access to the councils of the Muskogee confederacy. McGillivray was an ideal cultural broker from the Muskogee point of view since he was fluent in both English and Koasati and was also trustworthy. As the distributor of British trade goods and patronage, young McGillivray became the leader of the pro-British faction among the Creeks. Although unable to move the confederacy into an open alliance with England, McGillivray organized raiding parties that inflicted heavy damages throughout the Georgia frontier. As a result, he became widely known as a Muskogee war chief even though he rarely participated in battle.

In the Treaty of Paris, England betrayed its Indian allies and "gave" most of the Creek confederacy's territory to the United States. When Georgia tried to grab three million acres of Muskogee land through fraudulent treaties imposed on a handful of Muskogee chieftains who had been seized and threatened with death unless they agreed to the cessions, McGillivray became the leading defender of Muskogee sovereignty. Trying a balance-of-power strategy, he approached Spain, which had just regained Florida. In the Treaty of Pensacola signed on 1 June 1784, McGillivray secured a Spanish alliance for the confederacy, a Spanish-Creek trade monopoly for the British trading firm of Panton, Leslie and Company (which rewarded him with a partnership), and an annual subvention of gunpowder and trade goods for his people—to be distributed by McGillivray.

Using his control over Spanish largess and British trade to reward his friends and punish his enemies, McGillivray mounted a near revolution in the confederacy and came to dominate a strengthened Creek National Council. When his life was threatened by Georgia officials, he organized some of his supporters into a band of armed "constables." The "constables" introduced the use of force into Muskogee politics by destroying the property of chiefs who signed fraudulent treaties.

When Georgia sent settlers to claim the Creek lands, McGillivray gained National Council authorization to dispatch warriors to block their settlement. Their great success in driving off the invading settlers in 1786 and 1787 made McGillivray famous. It also made his Spanish allies fear being drawn into a wider war, however, and they threatened to cut off his supplies unless he made peace with the United States. McGillivray agreed to negotiate but refused to consider any settlement that included Muskogee recognition of the fraudulent Georgia treaties.

In 1789, faced with a reorganized United States able to provide military backing to Georgia, McGillivray determined to reach a satisfactory settlement. Along with other Creek leaders, he went to the U.S. capital and negotiated the Treaty of New York (7 Aug. 1790). Although the Muskogee confederacy conceded two-thirds of the territory claimed by Georgia, McGillivray won the protection of the United States against further attempts by Georgia to seize Muskogee lands and a guarantee of the new borders. He also won for the confederacy the right to deal freely with any American who invaded Creek lands. McGillivray's victory was sweetened by secret clauses that made him a brigadier general in the U.S. Army (with a $1,200 salary) and gave him control over $60,000 worth of duty-free trade goods a year.

Despite the positive aspects of the treaty, its provisions relinquishing two million acres of Lower Creek towns' land mobilized Lower Creek opposition to McGillivray's leadership, which was based in the Upper Creek towns. When McGillivray's rivals in the Upper Creek towns joined the opposition, McGillivray was forced to repudiate the Treaty of New York and renew the alliance with Spain on 6 July 1792. Having suffered from ill health for some time, he died in Pensacola only months later.

Little is known of McGillivray's personal life. He had at least two wives, as was customary for a Muskogee chief. When he died, he left three plantations and about sixty slaves to his three surviving children, contrary to Muskogee custom, whereby his property would have gone to his sisters.

• Letters from McGillivray have been published in D. C. Corbitt, ed., "Papers Relating to the Georgia-Florida Frontier, 1784–1800," *Georgia Historical Quarterly* 21 (Mar. 1937); *American State Papers: Indian Affairs*, vol. 1 (1832); and John Caughey, *McGillivray of the Creeks* (1938), which includes a short scholarly biography. The most important recent works are James H. O'Donnell, "Alexander McGillivray: Training for Leadership, 1777–1783," *Georgia Historical Quarterly* 49 (June 1965): 172–86; J. Leitch Wright, "Creek-American Treaty of 1790: Alexander McGillivray and the Diplomacy of the Old Southwest," *Georgia Historical*

Quarterly 51 (Dec. 1967): 379–400; and Michael D. Green, "Alexander McGillivray," in *American Indian Leaders: Studies in Diversity*, ed. R. David Edmunds (1980).

STANLEY NADEL

MCGILLIVRAY, Lachlan (1719–16 Nov. 1799), Indian trader, was born at Dunmaglass, Invernesshire, Scotland, the son of William McGillivray, a drover, and Janet McIntosh. The McGillivrays were a sept of the larger Clan Chattan, which supported the Jacobite rising of 1715 and was in political disfavor thereafter. When agents of James Oglethorpe visited the Highlands seeking recruits for Georgia, 163 members of Clan Chattan responded. They settled on the banks of Georgia's southern border, the River Altamaha, in January 1736 and called their town Darien. The Scots preferred fighting to farming and gladly followed Oglethorpe to Florida to do battle with the Spaniards. Military discipline was not a strong point, and the Darien Scots were surprised by a night attack on their outpost; most of them were killed or captured. Many of the Scots who survived abandoned Darien and sought their fortune in Carolina. Lachlan found employment with his relative Archibald McGillivray, head of Charlestown's largest trading company.

In 1741 Lachlan served as Indian interpreter on James Bullock's diplomatic mission to the Creeks. Two years later he began to trade among the Upper Creeks along the Coosa River. In 1744 McGillivray was a founding member of Brown, Rae and Company, which dominated the Creek Indian trade from its base in Augusta. By 1750 McGillivray resided on a plantation near Little Tallassee, only nine miles from the French outpost, Fort Toulouse, in present-day Alabama. McGillivray performed important services to the governors of South Carolina and Georgia as an informant on French intrigues among the Indians. McGillivray followed the Creek marriage ritual when he took Sehoy Marchand as his wife. Sehoy, the daughter of a French officer and a woman of the respected Wind Clan, was an important link between McGillivray and the Creek chieftains. Their three children represented a fusion of the Creek and Scottish clans. Their only son, Alexander, who later became the recognized head of the Creek Nation, was sent to Charlestown to be educated.

Among the services McGillivray performed for his king, as well as his company, was supplying the Choctaws when a faction of that nation broke with the French in 1746. Because of his proficiency in Creek languages, McGillivray was the preferred interpreter for South Carolina governor James Glen. When Georgia's first royal governor arrived in 1754 in the person of John Reynolds, McGillivray served as Georgia's principal intermediary with the Creek Nation.

In 1755 McGillivray left the Indian country and took up residence near Augusta. His house was a popular rendezvous for visiting Creeks. His Creek connection proved invaluable when the Cherokees went on the warpath in the winter of 1760. McGillivray led parties of Creeks and Chickasaws against the besieging enemy. He was thanked by the Georgia legislature for his services in protecting Augusta.

After the return of peace in 1762, McGillivray entered a new phase of his career; he moved to Savannah, acquired rice plantations, and went into the import-export business. With two partners from the old trading company, John Rae and George Galphin, he acquired 50,000 acres on the Ogeechee River and recruited settlers from Northern Ireland for the town of Queensborough. Even after his retirement from the backcountry, McGillivray's skills were in demand for all important Indian negotiations. He was instrumental in persuading the reluctant Creek chiefs to come to Augusta for land cessions in 1763 and 1773. He accompanied the surveyors who marked the boundary line between the Creek hunting grounds and British settlements in 1768. In 1770 he was authorized by Governor James Wright to report on Indian policy directly to Lord Hillsborough, secretary of state for America. In his book on American Indians, published in London in 1775, James Adair praised McGillivray and George Galphin for their contributions to king and country and declared that they had greater influence among the Creeks than any others.

As McGillivray's fortunes waxed, he persuaded his cousin William McGillivray, chief of the McGillivrays, to take up residence in Georgia and donated valuable rice lands to get him started as a planter.

When they heard the news of Lexington and Concord in May 1775, Georgians were forced to take a stand for king or congress. On 26 June prominent Georgians gathered in Savannah to deliberate. As a signal honor, they elected Lachlan McGillivray to the chair, and his name was signed to the resolution to oppose Parliament's efforts to raise revenue in America. In November McGillivray was elected to the extralegal provincial assembly and at the same time appointed by Governor James Wright to the Royal Council. McGillivray cast his lot with the royal government and was forced to leave Georgia in 1776. When Georgia was temporarily restored to the Crown in 1779, he returned and resumed his import business, only to leave again in 1782 when Savannah surrendered to General Anthony Wayne.

McGillivray spent his last years at Dunmaglass, the place of his birth, where, before his death there, he was entrusted with the care and education of John Lachlan, future chief of the McGillivrays, and his grandson Aleck, son of Alexander McGillivray, chief of the Creek Nation.

Lachlan McGillivray was important because he was a liaison between two societies, the Creek and the British colonial, and because he represented in his own career the changes that resulted from the transition of the southern frontier from a socioeconomic hunting-trading system to that of the merchant and planter.

• The manuscript copy of McGillivray's 1755 journal is in the New-York Historical Society. Edward J. Cashin, *Lachlan McGillivray, Indian Trader: The Shaping of the Southern Colonial Frontier* (1992), has an extensive bibliography. No other biographies of McGillivray have been published, and the account of his career must be assembled from original records such as Allen Candler et al., eds., *The Colonial Records of the State of Georgia* (32 vols., 1904–1989); vols. 33–39 are in typescript at the Georgia Department of Archives and History, Atlanta. For his early career, see J. H. Easterby, ed., *The Colonial Records of South Carolina: The Journal of the Commons House of Assembly* (9 vols., 1951–1962). Robert McGillivray and George B. Macgillivray, *A History of the Clan Macgillivray* (1973), is invaluable. (George B. Macgillivray was commander of the clan when this entry was written.)

EDWARD J. CASHIN

MCGILLYCUDDY, Valentine Trant O'Connell (14 Feb. 1849–6 June 1939), physician and Indian agent, was born in Racine, Wisconsin, the son of Irish immigrants Daniel McGillycuddy and Johanna Trant, whose means of earning a living are not known. McGillycuddy attended the University of Michigan in 1866–1867 and received an M.D. in 1869 from the Detroit College of Medicine, where after graduation he served as a lecturer and assistant hospital surgeon until ill health from overwork forced his resignation in 1871. To rebuild his strength, McGillycuddy signed on as a recorder, assistant engineer, and surgeon with the U.S. Survey of the Great Lakes (1871–1874), topographer and surgeon of the British-American Boundary Line Survey (1874), and finally as physician and topographer to Columbia School of Mines Professor Walter P. Jenny's Black Hills Scientific Expedition (1875). He was the first Caucasian to ascend Harney Peak, the highest point in the Black Hills, where now he is buried. Upon his return to Detroit, McGillycuddy married Fanny E. Hoyt, of Ionia, Michigan, in 1875; this union was childless.

In 1876, at the request of General George Crook, McGillycuddy served as a surgeon to the U.S. Second Cavalry, then ordered to Wyoming and Montana, and administered to troops injured at the battle of Rosebud Creek, Montana. The next year McGillycuddy became assistant post surgeon at Fort Robinson, Nebraska. There he treated the wife of Crazy Horse for tuberculosis, and became good friends with the great Sioux chief. McGillycuddy was the attending physician when Crazy Horse died on 5 September 1877 from a bayonet wound suffered in an attempt to escape from army custody.

While visiting Washington, D.C., in January 1879, McGillycuddy complained to Secretary of the Interior Carl Schurz about the recent maltreatment of Cheyenne Indians at Fort Robinson. One hundred and fifty Cheyennes had fled the Indian Territory 600 miles south of the outpost in a desperate attempt to return to their original homeland. The survivors were captured near Fort Robinson on 27 October 1878 and locked up in the barracks. An attempt at escape on 9 January 1879 resulted in the deaths of almost all of the captives. McGillycuddy left for Washington that same night, distressed over the plight of the refugees. Impressed with the doctor's knowledge of Native Americans, Schurz nominated him to be the next agent of the Pine Ridge Sioux Reservation, now in South Dakota; the appointment was approved by the U.S. Senate on 29 January 1879.

Although McGillycuddy's years at Pine Ridge (1879–1886) represented the height of his career, his was a turbulent tenure. The policy of the federal government then was to reduce the power of the traditional chiefs and to "civilize" the Sioux, making them into farmers within a few years. To this end McGillycuddy established a fifty-man Indian police force to keep peace on the reservation, considering this preferable to the presence of the army, which might have sparked clashes. He built schools, forced corrupt white traders to leave Pine Ridge, and engaged in a long series of arguments and confrontations with Red Cloud, chief of the Oglala Sioux, whom most Indians on the reservation regarded as their leader and spokesman. Both men were unyielding, and several times McGillycuddy "deposed" Red Cloud from his authority as chief, but to little effect.

Besides Red Cloud, who sent petitions to the federal government to remove McGillycuddy, the doctor was opposed by what he described as "Eastern sentimentalists" who wanted the Sioux to set their own pace in the process of "civilization," and whites who wanted to exploit the Indians after his dismissal. McGillycuddy thwarted his adversaries' attempts to dislodge him, escaped at least one attempted assassination in 1882, and demonstrated easily that charges of fraud, dishonesty, and misappropriation of funds brought against him were without foundation. His discharge from the Pine Ridge Agency was a political act. The Democratic administration of Grover Cleveland ordered McGillycuddy in 1886 to replace his chief clerk with one of that party's political appointees. When McGillycuddy, a lifelong Republican, refused, he was discharged for insubordination and disobedience.

The McGillycuddys moved to Rapid City, Dakota Territory, where the doctor was chosen as the territorial surgeon general in 1886. In 1888 Rapid City elected him as a representative to the Third Constitutional Convention that partitioned South and North Dakota; he signed the new South Dakota constitution the next year. From 1889 to 1898 McGillycuddy served as the assistant adjutant general for South Dakota.

Commissioned as a colonel of the state militia by Governor Arthur Mellette, McGillycuddy returned to Pine Ridge in 1890 to assess the possible threat posed by a new religious movement, the Ghost Dance. Wovoka, a Paiute from Nevada, had preached that Jesus would return to give a new gospel to the Indians; white men would disappear from the earth, and both deceased Indians and the buffalo would come back. More ominous to the authorities was the belief, discouraged by Wovoka himself, that sacred "ghost shirts" would render their Sioux wearers invulnerable to bullets. McGillycuddy counseled inaction to General John R. Brooke, believing that the movement would burn itself out when the promised Messiah failed to appear before spring. Even Red Cloud requested that McGillycuddy be reinstated at Pine Ridge as agent in place of successor D. F. Royer, and the doctor offered to serve as negotiator between the army and the Sioux. McGillycuddy's services, however, were spurned by Brooke, and the massacre at Wounded Knee—on the reservation about twelve miles to the northeast of Pine Ridge—followed on 29 December 1890. Returning to the agency's headquarters, McGillycuddy treated many of the surviving Indians.

McGillycuddy was named foreman of the federal grand jury that met in Deadwood, South Dakota, early in 1891 to handle cases related to Wounded Knee. He used his influence to dismiss indictments of Indians who had been unjustly accused of crimes at Pine Ridge and to press for the arraignment of white settlers who had taken advantage of the recent paranoia to attack innocent Sioux. McGillycuddy was involved in many business ventures including a hydroelectric power company and two banks. The loans extended by the banks to farmers were large enough to bring him down financially when the panic of 1893 wrought havoc. He then accepted the deanship of the South Dakota State School of Mines, from which he resigned in 1897. A few years after the death of his first wife in 1896, McGillycuddy married Julia E. Blanchard, the daughter of George Blanchard, a trader and friend from his Pine Ridge days; the couple had one child.

From 1898 until 1912, McGillycuddy was the supervising medical inspector for the Pacific Coast and Mountain Division of the Mutual Life Insurance Company of New York. From retirement in Berkeley, California, he was called back into service by the U.S. Public Health Service during the "Spanish Flu" pandemic of 1918–1919 as a physician for remote mountain communities in California, Nevada, and Utah. In the spring of 1919 he was sent to the Aleutian Islands of Alaska, a harrowing assignment that included finding entire villages wiped out by influenza and being attacked by starving dogs. From then until his death in San Francisco, McGillycuddy was the house physician at the Hotel Claremont in Berkeley.

McGillycuddy's only original contributions to medical knowledge came while treating patients at the New Idria Mines in San Benito County, California, during the 1918 influenza pandemic. None of the furnace men involved in extracting mercury from the ore had contracted influenza, which the doctor attributed to either increased salivation induced by exposure to the volatilized element or its antiseptic qualities. Because mercury is poisonous, however, the value of this discovery is questionable. He claimed also to have had success treating paralysis agitans (tremor of resting muscles, slowing of voluntary movements, and muscular weakness) caused by the virus with *Cannabis indica* (an Asiatic variety of marijuana).

Sympathetic to the plight of Native Americans but convinced that they would starve if they continued to lead their traditional way of life, McGillycuddy sought to have his charges adapt to the now dominant culture as quickly as possible, at the cost of angering opponents and quarreling with Sioux leaders. Even McGillycuddy's critics, however, are inclined to agree that the Wounded Knee massacre might not have occurred had he still been the Pine Ridge agent in 1890.

• McGillycuddy's papers, reports, and telegrams from Pine Ridge are in the National Archives; his letters to William Garnett about the death of Crazy Horse have been reprinted in Robert A. Clark, ed., *The Killing of Chief Crazy Horse* (1976; repr. 1988). While much has been written on McGillycuddy's tenure at Pine Ridge, he still lacks a modern comprehensive biography. Julia Blanchard McGillycuddy, *Blood on the Moon: Valentine McGillycuddy and the Sioux* (1990), is laudatory, occasionally exaggerated, inaccurate, and lacking in chronology, but is invaluable nevertheless. Jack Schaefer, *Heroes without Glory: Some Goodmen of the Old West* (1965), is little more than a paraphrase of Julia McGillycuddy's work. George E. Hyde, *A Sioux Chronicle* (1956), takes a dimmer view of the agent's activities. More balanced is James C. Olson, *Red Cloud and the Sioux Problem* (1965). Robert M. Utley, *The Indian Frontier of the American West, 1846–1890* (1984; repr. 1987), analyzes Indian agents, including McGillycuddy, in some detail.

TIMOTHY L. BRATTON

MCGINLEY, Phyllis (21 Mar. 1905–22 Feb. 1978), poet and prose writer, was born in Ontario, Oregon, the daughter of Daniel McGinley, a rancher, and Julia Keisel. As an infant she moved with her family to a Colorado ranch. When McGinley was twelve her father died, and the family moved to Ogden, Utah, where she attended Sacred Heart Academy and the local high school. In 1927 she graduated from the University of Utah and taught high school English for one year in Ogden; in 1929 she took a teaching position in New Rochelle, New York, and began publishing poems in magazines. She wrote frequently for the *New Yorker* and *Town and Country*. In 1934 her first collection, *On the Contrary*, appeared.

After her marriage to Charles L. Hayden in 1937, she published the collections *One More Manhattan* (1937), *A Pocketful of Wry* (1940), and *Husbands Are Difficult* (1941). Following the births of her daughters in 1939 and 1941, McGinley also began to write children's books, the first of which was *The Horse Who Lived Upstairs* (1944). Although she considered herself primarily a poet, the more than a dozen books for children led to her writing lyrics for the 1948 Broadway revue *Small Wonder* and continuity for the 1951 film *The Emperor's Nightingale*. During the 1950s she also began writing essays about women's lives and interests for such magazines as *Vogue*, *Mademoiselle*, *Saturday Evening Post*, *Good Housekeeping*, *Ladies' Home Journal*, and *America*, as well as professional essays about writing in the *American Scholar*, *Saturday Review*, and the *New York Times Book Review*. She published two collections of her essays, *The Province of the Heart* (1959) and *Sixpence in Her Shoe* (1964).

The recipient of the 1961 Pulitzer Prize for poetry for her collection *Times Three* (1960), McGinley also won the Edna St. Vincent Millay Memorial Award of the Poetry Society of America in 1955 for *The Love Letters of Phyllis McGinley*, the Catholic Writers Guild Award (1955), the Christopher Medal (1955), the Golden Book Award (1961), and many other accolades, including the Catholic Institute of the Press Award (1961). She was a member of the National Institute of Arts and Letters and served on the board of the *American Scholar*.

McGinley revived American readers' interest in light verse. She was admired for her skill in using a wide range of poetic forms, writing some of the most interesting sonnets and villanelles of her time. She also experimented with syllabic verse. Among her best-known formal poems are "Ballade of Lost Objects," her choice for entry in the collection *Poet's Choice* (1962); the often anthologized "Midcentury Love Letter"; and "Portrait of Girl with Comic Book," "My Six Toothbrushes," and "Apologia." Her poems showed her dedication to catching the details of ordinary life in her work. Her subjects were often taken from her life as wife and mother leading a middle-class life in the New York suburbs. She gave voice—and value—to events and characters that seldom appeared in poetry. In an *American Scholar* essay in 1965, McGinley called "The Doll House" one of her best poems, "her intimation of mortality." It is her thematic concern with the unheralded events of many women's lives that made McGinley an important influence on such younger women writers as Anne Sexton and Sylvia Plath.

McGinley's skillful writing emphasized the comedic, yet her work was often acerbic and caustic, as she both celebrated and criticized American life. One of her hobbies, she said, was "sticking pins into the smugger aspects of the social scene." Hypocrisy and pretense were often her targets, and she showed political courage during the McCarthy era when asked to write the Columbia University Phi Beta Kappa poem. Her contribution, "In Praise of Diversity" (1954), stood out at a time when official statements rarely championed difference as an aspect of social life. McGinley's wry, careful formality enabled her to make comments her listeners may not have understood or may not have wanted to understand. This tension between the apparent lightness of her verse and the acute skill with which she wrote was praised by countless reviewers.

Near the end of her life, McGinley wrote a collection of holiday poems entitled *A Wreath of Christmas Legends* (1967) and published the prose biography narratives of her favorite saints in *Saint-Watching* (1969). Both were well received.

• Phyllis McGinley's papers are housed at the Syracuse University Library; there is no biography. The critical study is Linda Welshimer Wagner, *Phyllis McGinley* (1971). J. B. Lippincott published the pamphlet *The Wide World of Phyllis McGinley* (n.d.). Discussions of her work are included in Everett S. Allen, *Famous American Humorous Poets* (1968), and W. H. Auden's introductions to McGinley's *Times Three* and his *The Dyer's Hand* (1962). See also biographical features "The Lady in Larchmont" and "Moment with Phyllis McGinley," *Newsweek*, 26 Sept. 1960, pp. 120–22; "The Telltale Hearth," *Time*, 18 June 1965, pp. 74–78; and Mary E. O'Brien, "Poet's Garden," *Popular Gardening*, 16 Sept. 1965, pp. 20–23.

McGinley's other books for children are *The Plain Princess* (1945), *All around the Town* (1948), *A Name for Kitty* (1948), *The Most Wonderful Doll in the World* (1950), *Blunderbus* (1951), *The Horse Who Had His Picture in the Paper* (1951), *The Make-Believe Twins* (1953), *The Year without a Santa Claus* (1957), *Merry Christmas, Happy New Year* (1958), *Lucy McLockett* (1959), *Sugar & Spice* (1960), *Mince Pie and Mistletoe* (1961), *Boys Are Awful* (1962), *The B Book* (1962), *A Girl and Her Room* (1963), *How Mrs. Santa Claus Saved Christmas* (1963), *Wonderful Time* (1966), and *Wonders and Surprises* (1968).

LINDA WAGNER-MARTIN

MCGINNITY, Joe (19 Mar. 1871–14 Nov. 1929), baseball player, was born Joseph Jerome McGinnity in Rock Island, Illinois; his parents' names and other details of his early life are unknown. McGinnity established a reputation as a town ball pitcher before beginning his lengthy professional baseball career in 1893 with Montgomery, Alabama, of the Southern League. After two minor league seasons of indifferent success—the second with Kansas City, Missouri, of the Western League—McGinnity opted to pitch semiprofessionally in his native state; this proved more lucrative for him, given the country's economic depression of that time, than professional baseball had been. Besides honing his pitching skills, McGinnity ran a saloon and toiled in his father-in-law's Oklahoma iron foundry during his three-year hiatus from the minor leagues. (He had married in or around 1895; his wife's name is unknown.) He worked in the foundry during subsequent winters as well, thereby earning the nickname "Iron Man." McGinnity's remarkable durability as a pitcher served to reinforce the sobriquet.

Having returned to the professional ranks as a member of the Peoria, Illinois, Western Association minor league team in 1898, the right-handed McGinnity enjoyed his first winning season with a 10–3 record. He broke into the major leagues—where he would never experience a losing season—in spectacular fashion the next year, tying for the National League lead with twenty-eight wins as a Baltimore Orioles hurler. When Baltimore was dropped from the circuit at season's end, McGinnity joined the Brooklyn Superbas (later known as the Dodgers); he won five games in his first six days with the team in 1900 and again finished the season atop the National League with twenty-nine victories. In rapid succession, McGinnity followed the legendary manager John McGraw in quitting the National League for the newly formed American League's Baltimore franchise (1901) and then leaving Baltimore for the National League's New York Giants (1902). McGinnity played out his major league career with the McGraw-managed Giants, winning 151 games while losing only 88 in seven seasons as Christy Mathewson's pitching partner. McGinnity paced the league's pitchers in wins with 31 in 1903, 35 in 1904, and 27 in 1906; in 1905 he won 26 regular season games and one World Series contest, a 1–0 victory over Philadelphia's Hall of Fame left-hander Eddie Plank.

McGinnity's initial 30-win season in 1903 included three doubleheader victories, all complete game wins in the month of August; he enhanced the drama of one of those six victories by stealing home. He hurled both ends of a doubleheader two other times during that season, winning one game and losing the other on each occasion. Although his 1,658 batters faced and 434 innings pitched that year established league records, McGinnity would pitch 436 innings as a minor leaguer with Tacoma, Washington, of the Northwestern circuit ten seasons later. He eclipsed 400 innings five times during his twenty-five years of combined major and minor league pitching, including a record two times in the National League.

McGinnity won an astounding 471 games, including 246 in the major leagues. He led or tied for league leadership ten times in games pitched, including six times in the major leagues; seven times in innings pitched, including four in the majors; seven times in games won, including five in the majors; twice in the majors in winning percentage; and once in the majors in shutouts. Although McGinnity struck out more than 100 batters in each of ten seasons, he usually induced batters to pop up and often required only a handful of pitches to complete an inning. Reputed to throw at hitters, McGinnity averaged one hit batsman for every nineteen men he faced, setting a major league record; he set another dubious major league mark when he hit forty-one batters with pitches in 1900.

The scrappy McGinnity battled with ball park security personnel and at least one umpire, in addition to opposing players. In an important and controversial 1908 game between the Giants and Chicago Cubs at New York's Polo Grounds, in which Giants baserunner Fred Merkle neglected to touch second base as the Giants' winning run was scored, McGinnity grappled with Chicago players for a ball he then threw into the stands in a futile attempt to prevent a game-ending forceout. Shortly thereafter McGinnity successfully sought his release from the Giants, enabling him to become the playing manager of the Newark, New Jersey, team in the minor Eastern League for 1909. He then pitched and managed minor league clubs in Tacoma (1913–1915); Butte, Montana (1916–1917); and Dubuque, Iowa (1922–1923, 1925). As manager and co-owner of the Dubuque team in the Mississippi Valley League, he continued to pitch—and won six of twelve decisions—at age fifty-four.

After coaching (1926) and scouting (1928–1929) for the Brooklyn Dodgers, McGinnity ended his involvement with professional baseball. Additionally, in the late 1920s he served as assistant baseball coach at Williams College in Williamstown, Massachusetts, and performed laboratory work on behalf of physicians in Brooklyn. He died in Brooklyn of stomach cancer. In 1946 McGinnity was selected for enshrinement in the National Baseball Hall of Fame, which did not exist during his lifetime.

"McGinnity, as his record attests, was a strong man," the baseball writer Tom Meany reported in the 1950s. "He stood just under six feet and weighed a trifle over 200 pounds. He had a deceptive, almost sidearm pitching motion, a good curve ball and what is known as a 'sneaky' fast ball. He also was an exceptional runner and batter for a pitcher" (Meany, "The Real Men of Iron," p. 257).

• A clipping file on McGinnity is at the National Baseball Library, Cooperstown, N.Y. Tom Meany, *Baseball's Greatest Pitchers* (1951), offers a useful account in anecdotal style. Another profile of McGinnity that was written by Meany, "The Real Men of Iron," was printed in *The Second Fireside Book of Baseball*, ed. Charles Einstein (1958), pp. 256–59. See also Arnold Hano, "Iron Man McGinnity," *Sport*, Aug. 1967, pp. 54, 85–86; and Lowell Reidenbaugh, *Cooperstown* (1986).

THOMAS D. JOZWIK

MCGIVNEY, Michael J. (12 Aug. 1852–14 Aug. 1890), Catholic priest and founder of the Knights of Columbus, was born Michael Joseph McGivney in Waterbury, Connecticut, the son of Patrick McGivney, a molder in a brass mill, and Mary Lynch. McGivney received his secondary education at the College of St. Hyacinth in Quebec, then attended Our Lady of Angels Seminary in Niagara, New York (1871–1872) and St. Mary's College in Montreal (1872–1873). He then worked briefly in a spoon factory to help support the family. From 1873 to 1877 he studied philosophy and theology at St. Mary's Seminary in Baltimore, Maryland, and was ordained a priest in December 1877 and assigned to St. Mary's Church in New Haven, Connecticut. On 2 October 1881 he chaired in the church basement the first meeting of what officially became the Knights of Columbus on 29 March 1882, the date of the order's incorporation in Connecticut.

The Knights of Columbus originated as a result of the interaction between McGivney and a small group of Irish-American laymen at St. Mary's Church. As chaplain of the St. Joseph's Young Men's Total Assistance Society, McGivney sharpened his awareness of the rising popularity of fraternalism. The lodge was considered a refuge from the harshly competitive and atomistic character of industrial society. The economic depression of the early 1870s entailed the bankruptcy of many commercial insurance companies. Fraternal insurance societies replaced them with a cooperative rather than a competitive system of sick and death benefits. McGivney realized the value of insurance protection from the early death of his own father and from his ministry to those families suffering from the loss of the breadwinner.

In accord with second-generation Irish-American leadership, McGivney extolled the compatibility of Catholicism and American fraternalism. No doubt the priest was motivated by the wish to keep young Catholics from entering the ranks of condemned secret societies and by the need to protect families during sickness and death. He was equally persistent in his aim to establish a Catholic fraternal society imbued with zealous pride in the American Catholic heritage. Indeed, the order's Columbus motif invoked pride in the Catholic origins of the nation. To assert Catholic legitimacy against nativism and anti-Catholicism, the *Santa Ma-*

ria was promoted as a Catholic counter symbol to the Puritan *Mayflower*.

Prior to the decision to establish an independent fraternal society, McGivney visited with the leaders of the Massachusetts Catholic Order of Foresters with the intention of exploring the foundation of a Connecticut branch of that order. Had the New Haven society affiliated with the Foresters, its fraternal character would have been represented by Robin Hood and England rather than by Columbus and American Catholicism.

In his role as founder McGivney successfully sought his bishop's permission to establish the Knights of Columbus. He then wrote a letter to all the pastors in the Diocese of Hartford, which included all of Connecticut in 1882, in which he asked each of them to establish a Knights of Columbus council in his parish. However, it took several letters and personal visits before the Knights of Columbus became a viable society with several councils.

As the first financial secretary, McGivney was entrusted with daily management of the infant order, a position in accord with his role as founder, organizer, and ambassador. The first council, San Salvador, was founded in New Haven in May 1882, but it was not until 23 April 1883 that Silver City Council No. 2 was instituted in Meriden. After the founder had written a long letter to the editor of the *Connecticut Catholic* in August 1883 in which he outlined the benefits of the order, a new council was instituted in Middletown, a second in Meriden, and another in Wallingford during the following six months.

With expansion of the Knights assured, McGivney announced at the Supreme Council meeting of 15 June 1884 that he would not be a candidate for supreme secretary. However, he was elected supreme chaplain, an office that removed him from daily business concerns and was more compatible with his other priestly duties. The following November Bishop Lawrence McMahon of Hartford, who had become chaplain of a Knights of Columbus council there, appointed McGivney pastor of St. Thomas Church in Thomaston, Connecticut.

The priest-founder vigorously promoted the expansion of the order. He personally was involved in the formation of the Atlantic Council in Thomaston and represented the order in negotiating plans for new-council development with the bishop of Providence, Rhode Island.

Never a man of robust health, McGivney was afflicted with pneumonia in January 1890. After traveling south on two occasions, he died in Thomaston.

McGivney was a priest of the people, a kind, approachable person who evoked confidence and trust. He manifested a strong sense of determination in establishing the Knights of Columbus, dedicated to charity, unity, and fraternity, forging a synthesis between Catholicism and American fraternalism. On 18 December 1997 the Archdiocese of Hartford officially began efforts toward his canonization. Fifteen years after McGivney died the order was in every state and territory, the five provinces of Canada, Mexico, and the Philippines and was poised to enter Cuba and Puerto Rico. The financial success of the Knights owed much to its insurance feature, but the fraternal aspect appealed to all Catholics, regardless of ethnicity or national origins, especially in its formative years. At the close of the twentieth century there were 1.5 million Knights.

• The Knights of Columbus Archives in New Haven, Conn., has papers relating to the origins of the order. For further information see Arthur J. Riley, "With Vision, Zeal and Clarity," *Columbia*, Aug. 1952; Jean Paul Gelinas, "Biography of the Founder," in his *The True Knight of Columbus* (1961); Neil Maloney, "Life and Times of Michael J. McGivney," *Sunday Republican Magazine* (Waterbury, Conn.), 4 Jan. 1987; Joseph Gordian Daley, "The Personality of Fr. McGivney, Founder of the Knights of Columbus," *Columbiad*, June 1900; David Q. Liptak, "Reverend Michael J. McGivney, Heroic Founder of the Knights of Columbus," in his *Pioneer Priests of Early Connecticut*, vol. 1 (1992); Christopher J. Kauffman, *Faith and Fraternalism: The History of the Knights of Columbus*, rev. ed. (1992) and *Columbianism and the Knights of Columbus* (1992).

CHRISTOPHER J. KAUFFMAN

MCGLYNN, Edward (27 Sept. 1837–7 Jan. 1900), Roman Catholic priest and social reformer, was born in New York City, the son of Peter McGlynn, a building contractor, and Sarah (maiden name unknown). His parents, Irish immigrants with a passionate commitment to Gaelic language and traditions, raised their family on the Lower East Side of New York City. Their friendship with Bishop John Hughes provided Edward with educational opportunities in New York's Free Academy and the Urban College of the Propaganda Fide in Rome. McGlynn studied for the priesthood in Rome (1850–1859). Faculty and church leaders recognized McGlynn's theological and pastoral skills, appointing him as the first vice rector of the new American College in Rome (1859). At the close of his years in Rome, the Urban College of the Propaganda awarded McGlynn a doctorate in theology.

Following his ordination in 1860, Bishop Hughes requested that McGlynn be placed on missionary status in New York City. The training at the Urban College instilled in McGlynn a missionary fervor that in 1891 he recounted, "I fain, coming out from the Propaganda a missionary apostolic to preach the gospel to every creature, would have converted my country, converted the whole world." It was, however, the influence of Father Thomas Farrell, abolitionist and radical reconstructionist, that shaped McGlynn into a social reformer.

Farrell was the leader of a circle of clergy known in the archdiocese as the Academia. The pastoral and intellectual company included colleagues from his years in Rome, like Reverend Richard Burtsell, and from his ministry in the United States, like Paulists Isaac Hecker and Augustine Hewitt. They began meeting in 1866, and their conversations focused on the liberal ideas of the day: the abolition of slavery, critical questions concerning scriptural inspiration, the temporal authority of the pope, the vernacular Mass, and the decentralization of Church governance. Farrell encouraged in McGlynn a critical consciousness of the dynamic relationship between theology and social justice; he also stressed awareness of the creative sympathies between the spirit of American democracy and Catholic tradition. Urban ministry under the mentoring of Pastors Farrell and Jeremiah Cummings served as the milieu in which McGlynn won recognition as a sogaarth aroon, which is Gaelic for the "precious priest of the people"—an appellation that he earned from lay Catholics like Hyacinth Archibald Ringrose (1890) and fellow priests like Sylvester Malone (1900). The Academia also introduced the young cleric to the thought of Orestes Brownson, who believed that the Catholic church was better suited than the Protestant church to be a friend of the people and to infuse into the American soul the theological virtues needed to realize its providential destiny.

McGlynn served several interim pastorates in St. Bridget's, St. James's, and St. Ann's parishes. In 1862, after a respite, Bishop Hughes assigned the cleric to a floating parish in Central Park. The multicultural parish consisted of Irish-American laborers and African-American squatters. In one of his annual reports to the Mission Office of the Propaganda Fide, McGlynn reflected on how his ministry of the Word and the sacraments among all of the residents in Central Park refined his theological analysis of social questions and deepened his pastoral commitment to service to the poor.

After the Civil War, Dr. Jeremiah Cummings requested that McGlynn serve as his assistant pastor at St. Stephen's Church, one of the city's largest parishes on the Lower East Side. McGlynn succeeded Cummings as pastor, and he flourished in his ministry with poor and working class parishioners from 1866 until 1887. The *New York Tablet* (7 July 1883) described McGlynn: "devoted as a priest, far-seeing, quick to perceive the wants and needs of his flock, he is prompt and decisive in his measures." He also won high praise from social and religious community leaders like Lyman Abbot, William Lloyd Garrison, and Rabbi Stephen S. Wise.

McGlynn's daily encounters with the poor in St. Stephen's parish convinced him that something more than institutional and personal charity was needed to respond to the social questions of post-Reconstruction America. In 1881 McGlynn read Henry George's *Progress and Poverty* (1880), a text he described as the most compelling analysis of involuntary poverty and its remedy. George's proposal, "The Single Tax," reminded McGlynn of the teachings of the church fathers and doctors as well as of the Irish Brehon Laws on land and its social use.

McGlynn believed that the social application of George's Single Tax theory to land policies and practices in America would yield a community chest with which cities like New York could address the dilemmas of public health, housing, education, and sanitation. Even though McGlynn shared George's confidence in reformed America's ability to realize the kingdom of God's fatherhood and human brotherhood, his social analysis of land and labor reveals a distinctive reliance on the theological teachings of church fathers like St. Ambrose and of schoolmen like St. Thomas Aquinas.

The Cross of the New Crusade (1887) was his most well-traveled piece and the definitive statement of his social theology. Ever the pastoral theologian, McGlynn raised in the speech a clarion call for Catholics to realize America's providential, humanitarian destiny. The spirit of Thomas Aquinas's theology manifested itself as soon as McGlynn moved the speech from a pastoral apologetic to a social analysis of land and labor. He sought to mitigate an American capitalist tendency to define land as an exploitable resource for the benefit of private (self) interest with a thomistic assertion that God created land toward the end of productive social use for the attainment of a common good. Like his theological forebearers, Sts. Basil, Jerome, and Augustine, he saw through the guise of private property the monopolist distortion of the divine intention that land was a common holding.

The vibrant urban pastor underwent ecclesiastical censure and excommunication between 1887 and 1892 on the charges that he had disobeyed his superiors and on the suspicion that he had socialist leanings in his political support of Henry George's campaign for the mayoralty of New York City (1886). George ran as an independent labor candidate (United Labor party) against the wealthy Democratic candidate Abram Hewitt (affiliated with Tammany Hall) and a youthful Theodore Roosevelt. McGlynn clashed with Archbishop Michael Augustine Corrigan over the civil and ecclesiastical rights of the clergy as a consequence of his radically democratic commitments. Contrary to episcopal admonition to refrain from political activity during the municipal elections of 1886, McGlynn fully participated in politics. He spoke in support of George's campaign in church and public periodicals like the archdiocesan *Catholic News* (9 Feb. 1887) and George's newspaper the *Standard* (26 Mar. 1887) to advance his war on poverty. Even though McGlynn did break ties with Henry George in 1888 over the most effective political means by which to initiate social reform, Archbishop Corrigan separated the priest from his parish. After McGlynn twice refused to travel to Rome to answer charges against him, he was excommunicated for his disobedience to his archbishop, unheard-of grounds for excommunication. Despite McGlynn's excommunication, he continued to wage a public battle from Brooklyn against poverty through the Anti-Poverty Society (1888).

It was not until 1892 that the persistent lobby of McGlynn's friends moved the Papal Legate Archbishop Francesco Satolli to review the priest's case. Pope Leo XIII took notice of the activity on behalf of McGlynn, and he instructed Satolli to establish a pontifical committee of scholars from the Catholic University of America to deliberate McGlynn's case. The committee decided that McGlynn's writings were well within the parameters of orthodoxy. A historical reconsideration of Edward McGlynn's social theology in light of Pope Leo XIII's encyclical, *Rerum Novarum* (1891), reveals a sympathy on the issues of land and labor substantive enough to prompt McGlynn's reinstatement to the church and priesthood. In 1892 Pope Leo XIII received the priest in Rome and reinstated him to the church and active priesthood. Edward McGlynn closed his life as pastor of St. Mary's parish in Newburgh, New York. During his last few years, he remained a public advocate for social reform with publications in journals like *Donahoe's Magazine* (July 1895). The "precious priest" died in Newburgh.

American historians tend to identify McGlynn as a Catholic manifestation of the social gospel because of his association with Henry George and because of the priest's appeal to the social gospel principles of the fatherhood of God and the brotherhood of Man. McGlynn's understanding of labor, however, highlights best the distinction between the Protestant social gospel and Catholic social theology. One would be hard pressed to find in the social gospel a sacramental estimation of labor like that in *The Cross of the New Crusade*. McGlynn suggested that just as the Eucharist was the sign of Christ's redemptive sacrifice that fulfilled human supernatural needs, so labor was a natural sign of God's ordered cultivation fulfilling our material needs. Of great historical significance is the sogaarth aroon's pastoral praxis. His social activity emerged from a reflection on life on the Lower East Side of New York City in light of the Word and sacraments of God. McGlynn, much like the French labor priests and pastors of the Base Church communities in Central America during the twentieth century, serves as a reminder of the sacramental role of religion in culture infusing into society a moral consciousness of a common good that transcends particular (self) interests.

• The papers of the case of Edward McGlynn are located in the Propaganda Fide Collection in the Archives of the University of Notre Dame (South Bend, Ind.) and in the Archives of the Archdiocese of New York (Yonkers, N.Y.). The oldest and most accurate copy of McGlynn's speech *The Cross of the New Crusade* is located in Henry George's newspaper the *Standard*, 2–3 Apr. 1887. The most thorough assessment is Dominic Scibilia, "Edward McGlynn, Thomas McGrady and Peter C. Yorke: Prophets in American Social Catholicism" (Ph.D. diss., Marquette Univ., 1991). See also Richard L. Burtsell, *The Diary of Richard L. Burtsell, Priest of New York: The Early Years, 1865–1868* (1978); Sylvester Malone, *Edward McGlynn* (1900); Stephen Bell, *Rebel, Priest and Prophet: A Biography of Dr. Edward McGlynn* (1937); and R. Emmett Curran, *Michael Augustine Corrigan* (1978). An obituary is in the *New York Times*, 8 Jan. 1900.

DOMINIC P. SCIBILIA

MCGOVERN, Terry (9 Mar. 1880–22 Feb. 1918), prizefighter, was born Joseph Terrance McGovern in Johnstown, Pennsylvania. His parents' names are unknown. His family moved to Brooklyn, New York, when he was six months old, and he lived there for the remainder of his life. McGovern's father died when Terry was young. To help support the family, Terry took a job with the Litchfield Lumber Company in Williamsburg. When he was fourteen years of age, his mother married a saloonkeeper and ward politician, Joe "Pop" Kenny.

After McGovern held his own in a fistfight against a boy who was 25 pounds heavier, his boss, Charley Mayhood, encouraged McGovern to become a boxer. Mayhood and Harry Fisher, an ex-boxer, managed McGovern in his early career. Terry won all 31 of his amateur bouts, 21 by knockout. In his first professional bout, at Dan Jackson's boxing club in Brooklyn on 3 April 1897, McGovern easily won with a first-round knockout of Jack Shea. McGovern was undefeated in 15 bouts that year. After a 24th-round knockout of George Munroe on 11 June 1898, Munroe's manager, theatrical entrepreneur Sam Harris, was sufficiently impressed by McGovern's abilities that he negotiated with Mayhood and became a comanager of McGovern. In his next bout, however, McGovern incurred his first loss on an 11th-round foul against Tim Callahan in Brooklyn on 23 July 1898. He then gained the American bantamweight title with a 12th-round knockout of Casper Leon in Brooklyn on 30 January 1899.

Continuing his winning ways, McGovern was matched with Englishman Thomas "Pedlar" Palmer for the world bantamweight title in a 20-round bout in Tuckahoe, New York, on 12 September 1899. The 19-year-old McGovern entered the ring having lost only once in 36 bouts; the 22-year-old Palmer was undefeated in 26 bouts. Although the bout started at 3:00 P.M. on a Tuesday afternoon, it still drew more than 10,000 spectators. Surprising the champion and knocking him out in the first round after only 2:32 of fighting, McGovern won a $10,000 purse.

After winning the title, McGovern won nine nontitle bouts by knockout in three rounds or fewer in the next three months—twice winning two bouts in one night. He then met George "Little Chocolate" Dixon for the world featherweight title in a 25-round bout at the Broadway Athletic Club in New York City on 9 January 1900. Dixon, a Canadian, had become in 1890 the first black fighter to win a world title. After taking a beating from McGovern for eight rounds, Dixon was saved from being counted out by his manager, who called a halt to the bout.

After moving up to the featherweight class, McGovern abandoned the bantamweight title without ever having defended it. He successfully defended his featherweight title six times in 1900 and 1901, including two victories over Oscar Gardner. In the first fight against Gardner, McGovern was knocked down and appeared finished. However, referee Charley White took nearly 20 seconds to reach the count of nine, at which time McGovern was revived by his seconds. When McGovern knocked down Gardner in the following round, White compensated for his slowness by counting out Gardner in fewer than 10 seconds, enabling McGovern to retain his championship. This no doubt pleased the watching fans, as the fight took place in New York, McGovern's hometown.

During those years McGovern also won nine nontitle bouts, one of which against the lightweight champion, Frank Erne. On 13 December 1900 McGovern knocked out Joe Gans, the future lightweight champion, in the second round of a bout that was later disclosed as a fixed fight, although neither McGovern nor Harris was aware of the fix. Gans had been approached by gamblers and had agreed to lose but won more than $10,000 by betting on himself to lose. As a result of the controversial bout, boxing was banned in Chicago shortly afterward.

In 1900 McGovern capitalized on his fame by appearing on the Broadway stage in *The Bowery after Dark* and in 1901 in *The Road to Ruin*. Although he was far from being a polished actor, the audiences were satisfied just seeing their hero McGovern beat up the villain on stage and save the damsel in distress. But McGovern grew tired of the stage and decided to resume his boxing career.

In his seventh title defense McGovern was matched with Young Corbett (William H. Rothwell) in a 20-round bout in the Coliseum in Hartford, Connecticut, on 28 November 1901. Corbett was lightly regarded by McGovern as he was a Denver fighter not well known in the East, all of his 41 bouts having taken place west of the Mississippi. The featherweight limit at that time was 122 pounds, but Corbett was unable to get below 126 pounds; however, Harris agreed to let him fight anyway. Prior to the bout Corbett taunted and mocked McGovern, causing him to lose his composure. After an even first round, Corbett knocked McGovern out at 1:44 of the second round. McGovern demanded a rematch that took place at the 20th Century Athletic Club in San Francisco on 31 March 1903. Although only 23 years old at the time, McGovern's skills had eroded and he was knocked out in the 11th round.

In 1905 McGovern suffered a nervous breakdown and was persuaded to enter the Stamford Hill Sanatorium on 16 April. His breakdown was in part attributed to the recent loss of two of his children (although the details of his probable marriage and his family life are not known). McGovern returned to boxing and met Corbett, who was no longer champion, once more in a six-round bout in Philadelphia in 1906. Although the Pennsylvania state boxing law forbade the use of decisions in determining the outcomes of boxing matches, McGovern was judged the winner by the majority of newspaper writers. Later that year President Theodore Roosevelt invited McGovern to the White House. On the way home, McGovern got into a barroom brawl, and the local police placed him on a train to New York City. Becoming violent on the train, he was forcefully removed and taken to Kings County Hospital in Brooklyn for treatment of mental illness.

McGovern fought two more bouts in 1908 before retiring permanently. The 78 matches in which he had fought had taken their toll, and he was in and out of sanatoriums during the next ten years. In 1918 he fainted while refereeing amateur bouts at Camp Upton and shortly thereafter died in Brooklyn from an attack of pneumonia. His funeral at St. John the Evangelist Church in Brooklyn was attended by 2,000 people.

Nat Fleischer, publisher of *The Ring* magazine, selected McGovern as the all-time greatest featherweight boxer. He was inducted into *The Ring* Boxing Hall of Fame in 1955. His career record was 66 victories, 42 by knockout; 6 defeats; and 6 draws.

• McGovern's complete professional ring record is in Herbert G. Goldman, ed., The Ring *1986–87 Record Book and Boxing Encyclopedia* (1987). Nat Fleischer, *Terrible Terry—The Brooklyn Terror—The Life and Battles of Terry McGovern* (1943), is a brief, 64-page biography. Dan Daniel, "Was McGovern-Gans Fight a Fake?," *The Ring*, June 1960, pp. 8–9, 45, provides insights into the circumstances surrounding the fight and concludes that it was a fake. A report of the McGovern-Palmer match is in Stanley Weston, "Greatest Fights of the Century," *Boxing and Wrestling*, Sept. 1955, pp. 31, 58–59. Bert Randolph Sugar, *The 100 Greatest Boxers of All Time* (1984), rates McGovern as the 30th greatest boxer and includes a two-page sketch of his career. All the above sources report McGovern's death date erroneously as 26 Feb. 1918, which was in fact the date of his burial. The *New York Times*, 23 Feb. 1918, has a death notice listing his death on 22 Feb. 1918 and also contains a full obituary. The issue of 26 Feb. 1918 contains a full report of the funeral. The *New York Times* is also an excellent source for detailed coverage of McGovern's major bouts as well as his mental problems.

JOHN GRASSO

MCGOWAN, William (10 Dec. 1927–8 June 1992), telephone company executive, was born in Ashley, Pennsylvania, the son of Andrew McGowan, a railroad engineer and labor union organizer, and Catherine Mary Evans, a schoolteacher. William McGowan worked as a clerk for the Central Railroad of New Jersey while attending the University of Scranton, until he was drafted in 1945. He served as a medic with the U.S. Army, working with the relocation of concentration camp survivors and the Berlin Airlift; he also attended courses at the University of Munich. After his discharge in 1948 he studied chemical engineering at Kings College in Wilkes-Barre, Pennsylvania, graduated in 1950, and went on to Harvard Business School, where he was a Baker scholar.

During his summer vacations from Harvard, McGowan worked on the corporate staff of Shell Oil in New York City, an experience that soured him on large and inefficient corporate bureaucracies. After receiving his M.B.A. in 1954, McGowan worked for Malcolm Kingsberg, a former investment banker who was organizing the Magna Theatre Corporation with Hollywood producer Mike Todd. McGowan's duties first involved negotiating contracts with movie theater owners for the installation of wide-screen projectors. He later assisted Todd with the production of wide-screen movies, including *Oklahoma!* (1956) and *South Pacific* (1958).

McGowan spent the early 1960s on Wall Street as an independent financial consultant specializing in the reorganization and turn-around of failing companies. His most notable success was the Powertron Company, which he took over for $25,000 in 1959 and sold for $3 million in 1962. A multimillionaire by 1966, McGowan took a lengthy sabbatical from business and traveled around the world twice—once in each direction.

When McGowan returned to the business world in 1968, a friend introduced him to John D. "Jack" Goeken, an Illinois entrepreneur who sold mobile radios. Goeken was trying to obtain government approval to construct a series of microwave radio towers between Chicago and St. Louis. The microwave lines would enable truckers to communicate with anyone along the route and also allow direct communications between the two cities without using American Telephone & Telegraph Corporation (AT&T) long-distance facilities. Goeken's 1963 application to the Federal Communications Commission (FCC) was being bitterly opposed by AT&T, and Goeken needed further financing to continue his application.

McGowan realized that if the FCC granted Goeken's application, his firm could eventually compete with AT&T for long-distance telephone service throughout the nation. McGowan bought a half interest in Goeken's company, Microwave Communications, Inc., for $50,000 and became its chair and chief executive officer. He changed the name to MCI Communications Corporation and set about raising funds to finance its application and future construction.

The FCC granted MCI's petition to construct microwave towers and provide "private line" telephone service along the Chicago–St. Louis route in 1969. McGowan spent 1969–1971 raising money from private investors to finance the new network, whose construction began in 1971. He also prepared petitions for additional routes for Chicago–New York and Chicago-Dallas, laying the groundwork for a nationwide network connecting 165 cities. MCI became a publicly traded company on 22 June 1972, with a public offering of $100 million.

In order to implement MCI's long-distance communications plan, its network would have to be connected with the local telephone networks, which were owned by subsidiaries of AT&T. McGowan and his firm engaged in negotiations with AT&T for interconnection rights. AT&T stalled the negotiations for a lengthy time, finally refusing to allow any interconnections except at exorbitant prices. McGowan and MCI filed a lawsuit against AT&T on 2 March 1974, charging that AT&T was violating antitrust laws by refusing to allow access to its local telephone network. During years of extensive discovery, McGowan obtained numerous AT&T documents that revealed a long-standing policy to destroy any long-distance competition. Partly as a result of McGowan's lawsuit, the U.S. Department of Justice also filed its own antitrust lawsuit against AT&T in November 1974.

Meanwhile, McGowan had discovered that the cost of constructing the proposed intercity network of microwave towers was much more expensive than anticipated. In order to increase MCI's revenues, he wanted MCI's offerings to expand beyond the specialized private line services that had been approved by the FCC. This caused a conflict with Goeken, who did not want MCI to compete head-to-head with AT&T by offering general long-distance telephone service. McGowan prevailed, and on 12 July 1974 Goeken resigned from MCI. He later founded several other companies dealing with specialized telecommunications services.

During late 1974 McGowan and MCI vice president Bert Roberts devised a new type of service called MCI Execunet, which received FCC approval in October 1974. Using this service, MCI customers could dial a twelve-digit sequence of numbers into any telephone to call up MCI's computers, which would then connect the caller with any other telephone number, bypassing AT&T's long-distance facilities. The Execunet service was priced at a fraction of the cost of AT&T's long-distance service and became very popular; within one year Execunet was providing the bulk of MCI's revenues.

The FCC, however, apparently had approved the Execunet petitions without realizing it had permitted MCI to implement general long-distance telephone services. When AT&T brought this fact to the FCC's attention, the FCC conducted a hearing in 1976 and ordered MCI to drop the service. MCI appealed the ruling, and the federal courts eventually ruled that MCI (or any other carrier) had the right to offer long-distance service.

MCI's antitrust lawsuit finally came to trial in February 1980, resulting in a favorable verdict and $1.8 billion in damages for McGowan and MCI. AT&T appealed, and a second trial reduced the damages to $113 million. However, the documents that had been uncovered during the MCI lawsuit were very helpful to U.S. prosecutors litigating the federal lawsuit against AT&T. In order to avoid a trial, AT&T negotiated a settlement whereby it agreed to divest its local operating companies and control over the local telephone networks. The Modified Final Judgment (MFJ) embodying the settlement was approved in early 1982, and the local Bell companies separated from AT&T on 1 January 1984.

Under the MFJ, the local telephone companies had to provide "equal access" to their local networks for all long-distance telephone carriers. In the aftermath of divestiture, AT&T wound up with about 75 percent of the long-distance business, MCI with 15 percent, and the rest divided among a host of smaller competitors.

To provide better service McGowan authorized the construction of a nationwide transmission network of high-capacity fiber optic cables. McGowan relied on Michael Millken, a financial trader at Drexel, Burnham & Lambert, to raise the money to finance MCI's new network. Millken was a pioneer in the development of high-risk securities (junk bonds), which financed much of MCI's later growth.

McGowan received an annual salary of $2 million, which he earned by devoting almost every waking moment to the development of MCI. He was a voracious smoker and coffee drinker, worked fourteen-hour days, seven days a week, and rarely took a vacation. In 1984 McGowan married Sue Ling Gin, a Chicago entrepreneur. They had no children.

In 1985 the FCC revised the access charges that local telephone companies charged MCI and other long-distance carriers for permission to connect to the local networks. The changes reduced the cost disparities between MCI and AT&T, resulting in severe financial losses for MCI. Company stock plummeted, and MCI laid off hundreds of employees. McGowan redoubled his efforts and was rewarded with a heart attack in 1986. He underwent a heart transplant the following year.

While recuperating, McGowan transferred control of MCI to Bert Roberts, then president of a subsidiary, MCI Telecommunications Company. After a six-month leave of absence following his heart transplant, McGowan resumed working, albeit at a slightly slower pace. The board of directors, with McGowan's approval, named Roberts as the company's chief executive officer in late 1991. By that time MCI had about a 16 percent share of the $60 billion long-distance market, with annual revenues of more than $8 billion from all its operations. McGowan died in Washington, D.C.

• McGowan's papers at MCI are not available to the public. The Blackwell Corporation and *Washington* magazine produced a video recording about McGowan and MCI, *Taking on the Giant* (1991), as part of their series Films for Humanities & Sciences. McGowan was the subject of many profiles and interviews, including Ken Adelman, "'Make Some Damn Mistakes!'" *Washingtonian*, Oct. 1990; Reed Abelson et al., "The Book Can Wait," *Forbes*, 28 May 1990; Mitch Betts, "Survivor amid Change," *Computerworld*, 26 Sept. 1988; and Leslie Wayne, "Together Apart," *New York Times Magazine*, 27 Mar. 1988. Larry Kahaner, *On the Line: The Men of MCI—Who Took on AT&T, Risked Everything, and Won!* (1986), is a favorable view of MCI based on extensive interviews. See also Peter Temin, *The Fall of the Bell System* (1987), Steve Coll, *The Deal of the Century: The Break-Up of AT&T* (1986), and Alan Stone, *Wrong Number: The Breakup of AT&T* (1989). Obituaries are in the *New York Times* and the *Washington Post*, both 9 June 1992.

STEPHEN G. MARSHALL

MCGRADY, Thomas (16 June 1863–26 Nov. 1907), Catholic socialist priest and lawyer, was born in Lexington, Kentucky, the son of Hugh McGrady, a tenant farmer and day laborer, and Alicia (maiden name unknown). McGrady's parents were refugees from the Irish famine who had emigrated to Kentucky in the late 1840s. In 1907 McGrady acknowledged the seething effect that stories of the famine had had on him: "Coming from a race that had been oppressed for generations in the old world, I have learned to hate injustice and oppression with a deathless hatred." McGrady received his early education in St. Paul's parish school in Lexington. Where he received his seminary education remains in doubt, but more than likely he went to St. Aloysius Seminary near Columbus, Ohio, where Nicholas Aloysius Gallagher (1846–1918) had been rector from 1871 to 1876. In 1887, after his seminary education, he was ordained a priest by Gallagher, who had become a bishop and the administrator of Galveston, Texas, in 1882. From 1887 to 1891 McGrady served parishes in Galveston, Houston, and Dallas. In 1891, because of poor health, he requested a transfer to his native diocese of Covington, Kentucky, where he became pastor of St. Paul's in Lexington (1891), St. Edward's in Cynthiana (1891–1895), and St. Anthony's in Bellevue (1895–1902).

During his pastorate at Bellevue, which was near Cincinnati, McGrady was struck by the devastating effects of industrialism on his parishioners. The experience led him to begin a serious study of political economy. From the mid-1890s he began reading Edward Bellamy's *Looking Backward*, Robert Blatchford's *Merrie England*, Henry George's (1839–1897) *Progress and Poverty*, and, after a trip to Europe in 1898, Karl Marx's *Capital*. Periodically from 1896 to 1902 he lectured on political economy at Martha Moore Avery and David Goldstein's Karl Marx Class in Boston. By 1899 he considered himself a socialist and began to publish his arguments on the compatibility of Christianity and scientific socialism. "I was firmly convinced," he wrote in 1902, "that the collective ownership and administration of capital for the benefit of all people was the only rational solution of the industrial problem." Such a view contrasted with Pope Leo XIII's encyclical on working conditions, Rerum Novarum (1891), but McGrady believed that that encyclical had misunderstood socialism; by criticizing it, the encyclical had unwittingly supported the capitalist profit motive. The encyclical, moreover, offered no realistic solution to industrial problems.

At the turn of the century McGrady and Father Thomas J. Hagerty were lonely representatives of a Catholic Christian socialism. Although numbers of Catholic workers were attracted to socialism in the late nineteenth and early twentieth centuries and joined the Socialist and Socialist Labor parties, few priests or articulate lay leaders found socialism compatible with Catholic teachings. Most Catholic clergy—following the encyclicals of Popes Pius IX, *Qui Pluribus* (1846), and Leo XIII, *Quod Apostolici Muneris* (1878)—considered socialism a revolutionary movement that created hostility and violence between labor and management; they saw it as a social theory grounded in atheistic naturalism, an ideological assault on the natural rights of private property, and a wrongheaded view of society that absorbed the individual in the state and absolutized the state's powers. McGrady disagreed, and he criticized Catholic leaders for misunderstanding socialism and supporting the injustices of capitalism. McGrady insisted that the Catholic criticism of socialism was based primarily on a European socialist ideology that did not exist in the United States. His own form of American Christian socialism aimed, he argued, to democraticize wealth and property by means of a thoroughly democratic state in which distribution of wealth would occur through governmental ownership of capital and the means of production. His own socialism was what he called social democracy, and it would be achieved gradually by means of popularly mandated state legislation and not by the violence of revolutionary immediacy. McGrady argued that his own understanding of social or economic democracy was consistent not only with American constitutional democracy, but also with the biblical view of Creation and the early church fathers' understanding of a Christian commonwealth.

Between 1895 and 1902 McGrady traveled throughout the country as a Catholic socialist priest who became a popular lecturer and propagandist for various Socialist party locals. During these years he also wrote three books and a number of pamphlets and articles. *The Mistakes of Ingersoll* (1898) was a collection of lectures on the relationship between religion and science, criticizing in particular Robert G. Ingersoll's agnosticism and his attacks on revealed religion. *The Two Kingdoms* (1899) argued for the compatibility of Christianity and socialism, grounding its explanation in a millennialist view of history. McGrady saw the late nineteenth-century struggle between the competitive capitalist economic system and the emerging cooperative economic movements as a historical prelude to the millennial reign of Christ and to the fulfillment of the divine promise of a kingdom of love and peace. The conflict between the two systems was a means through which God was working in history to purify church as well as state. *Beyond the Black Ocean* (1901), a historical-utopian socialist novel, depicted the oppression of minorities and the working class in a capitalist society and looked forward to a time when "the competitive system has been supplanted by the co-operative system; the middle men and parasites of society have long ceased to exist, and the dreams of Socialism have been realized."

McGrady was periodically attacked for his socialist views by many Catholic clergy and the Catholic press and for his religious grounding of socialism by some in the Socialist party. In November 1902 McGrady's bishop, Camillus Paul Maes, also criticized him for being a poor parish administrator and an absentee pastor; a supporter of intellectuals like Emile Zola, Ernst Renan, and Charles Darwin whose works had been condemned by church authority; and an unjust critic of papal encyclical teachings on socialism. Maes also asserted that McGrady had violated church discipline by not seeking an episcopal imprimatur before publishing his books. In response, McGrady insisted that his social teachings were consistent with the early church's teachings. Maes refused to engage him further on the social question, insisting instead on compliance with ecclesiastical discipline. McGrady considered the bishop's demands despotic and a violation of his intellectual and moral freedom as a priest. In December 1902 he resigned from his pastorate. He remained in the diocese of Covington for another year and prepared himself to become a lawyer.

In December 1903 McGrady left Kentucky and moved to San Francisco where he practiced law. Not much is known about his legal work or about his practice of Catholicism in San Francisco. A few months before his death he wrote one article each for *Arena* and the *American Labor Union Journal*, which indicated he was still psychologically and emotionally a Catholic but that his reason had led him to depart from what he criticized as Catholic institutional and political authoritarianism and its unjust and exploitative alliance with capitalism, a system that he predicted would surely die and take with it much of Catholicism. After a lifetime of generally poor health, he died of chronic myocarditis. His death certificate listed his occupation as priest, not lawyer, but his final personal relationship with the church remains uncertain even though he received the church's last rites on his deathbed. That he was buried in consecrated ground in a Catholic cemetery in Lexington indicates that he was not excommunicated from the Catholic church as St. Louis's Arthur Preuss, editor of the *Review*, assumed in 1903.

• McGrady's letters and unpublished papers are located primarily in the Archives of the Diocese of Covington, the Archdiocese of San Francisco, and the Diocese of Galveston-Houston. Among his other published works are *Socialism and the Labor Problem* (1900, 1901, 1903), *The Clerical Capitalist: Reply to Father Mackey* (1901), *City of Angels: Review of Bishop Montgomery's Christian Socialism* (1901), *Unaccepted Challenges* (1901), "How I Became a Socialist," *Comrade* 2 (Oct. 1902): 74; "Why the Catholic Church Opposes Socialism by a Leading Socialist," *Arena* (Boston, May 1907): 520–24; "The Catholic Church and Socialism," *Arena* (July 1907): 18–27. No critical biography exists, but a few studies have examined his life and work: "The Christian Socialist Fellowship," *Christian Socialist* (Chicago), 5 May 1907; Toby Terrar, "Catholic Socialism: The Reverend Thomas McGrady," *Dialectical Anthropology* (1983): 209–35; Terrar, "Thomas McGrady, American Catholic Socialist," *Ecumenist* 21 (Nov.–Dec. 1982): 14–16; Robert E. Doherty, "The American Socialist Party and the Roman Catholic Church, 1901–1917" (D.Ed. diss., Teachers College, Columbia Univ., 1959); Dominic Scibilia, "Edward McGlynn, Thomas McGrady, and Peter C. Yorke: Prophets of American Social Catholicism" (Ph.D. diss., Marquette Univ., 1990). See also Eugene Debs, "Thomas McGrady," *Appeal to Reason*, 14 Dec. 1907; Debs, "Rev. Fr. Thomas McGrady: A Glowing Tribute," *Christian Socialist* (Chicago), 1 Jan. 1908.

PATRICK W. CAREY

MCGRANERY, James Patrick (8 July 1895–23 Dec. 1962), congressman, federal judge, and U.S. attorney general, was born in Philadelphia, Pennsylvania, the son of Irish immigrants Patrick McGranery and Bridget Gallagher. McGranery attended Catholic parochial schools in Philadelphia, but he left before completing his secondary education to work as an electrotyper for the Curtis Publishing Co. While there, he became a member of the city's electrotypers union and carried the union card most of his life. In 1917 he joined the U.S. Army and served in the First World War as a balloon observation pilot and later as an adjutant of the 111th Infantry. After being demobilized in 1919, he returned to Philadelphia and school. He received a law degree from Temple University Law

School in 1928 and was subsequently admitted to the Pennsylvania bar. His clientele included police and the firemen's union.

McGranery became active in South Philadelphia Democratic ward politics while still a law student. In 1928 he managed the local campaign for presidential candidate Alfred E. Smith and ran for public office himself. Although he was unsuccessful in his first three campaigns (in races for court clerk in 1928, district attorney in 1931, and congressman in 1934), he ultimately won a seat in the U.S. House of Representatives in 1936. He represented Pennsylvania's Second Congressional District until his resignation in 1943, winning reelection in 1938, 1940, and 1942. He served as a member of the Banking and Currency Committee, the Interstate and Foreign Commerce Committee, and the House Ways and Means Committee. His voting record was solidly New Deal, and he backed President Franklin D. Roosevelt on such issues as lend-lease, the institution of price controls, and the Supreme Court retirement bill. But he broke with the administration on some Irish Catholic issues, particularly over the 1939 arrest of Irish revolutionary Sean Russell for illegal entry into the United States. McGranery caused some controversy when he implied that the arrest could trigger a congressional boycott of a reception for the king and queen of England. In 1939 McGranery married Regina T. Clark, a former special deputy attorney general of Pennsylvania; they had three children.

McGranery's first stint in the Justice Department came in late 1943, when President Roosevelt nominated him to be assistant attorney general. Serving as second in command under Francis Biddle and then Tom C. Clark, he was responsible for supervising all major units in the Justice Department. For the balance of World War II, he handled reviews of decisions by the Board of Appeals under the Selective Service Act and was awarded a Medal of Merit in 1946 for his wartime contributions to the national defense.

In October 1946 President Harry S. Truman nominated McGranery for a federal judgeship in the Eastern District of Pennsylvania; McGranery was confirmed unanimously by the Senate. *Time* magazine noted that Judge McGranery had "the reputation of being a highhanded pro-Government man" (14 Apr. 1952). His most notable case was the 1950 espionage trial of atomic weapons spy Harry Gold, whom he sentenced to the maximum thirty years in prison. McGranery left the federal bench in April 1952 to become Truman's last attorney general.

In 1952 the Justice Department was deeply demoralized, having been heavily criticized for its poor handling of an investigation of a tax scandal in the Bureau of Internal Revenue. McGranery's predecessor, J. Howard McGrath, was a former Democratic national party chairman known for lax oversight of the Justice Department. To restore public confidence, Truman had earlier considered replacing McGrath with a distinguished lawyer but had decided instead to appoint a special prosecutor. Months later, when McGrath fired the special prosecutor without informing the president, Truman fired McGrath and immediately offered the post to McGranery, who was confirmed by the Senate in a 52–18 vote. The new attorney general characterized his job as restoring "the faith of the American people in the integrity of the government . . . and in the Justice Department" (*New York Times*, 4 Apr. 1952).

McGranery reportedly had been considered earlier for a cabinet post in the Truman administration, but his appointment had been opposed by some factions of the Pennsylvania Democratic party, which was badly split at the time. His appointment in 1952 might have been the result of several factors. First, given his sense of being betrayed by others in the administration, Truman may have wanted a loyal and reliable friend in Justice. The president also was sensitive to election-eve charges by congressional Republicans that his administration was soft on communism; McGranery's role in the Harry Gold case therefore was appealing. Third, both men were prolabor, and Truman was facing a showdown with the steel industry. In fact, five days after firing McGrath, Truman seized the nation's steel mills to avert a labor strike brought on by the intransigence of company owners.

McGranery's appointment was not universally lauded. Anticommunist Republican senators attacked his 1945 criticism of how the Federal Bureau of Investigation (FBI) had handled a search of a left-wing magazine office and suggested that he was less than zealous in prosecuting Soviet espionage. Others opposed to the nomination were concerned about his ability, or willingness, to clean out the scandals in the department. The *New Republic*, for example, described him as "a likeable Democratic politician" but without the technical competence or national stature "to direct a professional job of house-cleaning" (14 Apr. 1952). Some blasted McGranery for not reappointing the special prosecutor after announcing that he would rely on the FBI to conduct an internal investigation of the department. These critics charged that McGranery would cover up the wrongdoing.

Despite these charges, McGranery took the house-cleaning task seriously and, as attorney general, "bounced Justice bureaucrats, freely fired crooked U.S. marshals, and started proceedings to deport . . . Mafia mobsters" (*Time*, 4 Jan. 1963). Also during his brief tenure, the Justice Department was engaged in two significant Supreme Court cases. In June 1952 the solicitor general unsuccessfully defended Truman's seizure of the steel mills in *Youngstown Sheet and Tube Company v. Sawyer*. Justice also filed a historic amicus curiae brief when *Brown v. Board of Education* was first argued in December 1952, explaining that racial discrimination was a concern to the executive branch because it undermined American moral authority in foreign affairs.

McGranery served only eight months as attorney general before the 1952 election brought in a Republican administration and a new attorney general. According to his successor, Herbert Brownell, McGranery felt that his time in office was too short to institute significant reforms, but he made several recommendations to Brownell, including providing a list of twenty-five department attorneys who "were incompetent but had important political sponsors" (Brownell, p. 146). While McGranery had been unable to remove them in his short time, Brownell did investigate and dismiss them. McGranery later said of his tenure in office, "I wouldn't do it again for a hundred million dollars, but on the other hand, I wouldn't have missed it for twice that much" (*Newsweek*, 7 Jan. 1963).

After leaving government service, McGranery practiced law in Philadelphia and Washington, D.C. He remained active as a Roman Catholic layman. In 1950 Pope Pius had awarded him the insignia of Knight Commander of the Order of St. Gregory the Great, and the next year had appointed McGranery a private chamberlain of the Cape and Sword. McGranery died in Palm Beach, Florida.

• The James Patrick McGranery Papers are in the Manuscript Division of the Library of Congress. For information on his appointment as attorney general, see Robert J. Donovan, *Tumultuous Years: The Presidency of Harry S. Truman 1949–1953* (1982); Harold F. Gosnell, *Truman's Crises: A Political Biography of Harry S. Truman* (1980); the *New York Times*, 4 Apr. 1952 and 21 May 1952; *Time*, 14 Apr. 1952, pp. 21, 22; and *Newsweek*, 14 Apr. 1952, p. 27. Herbert Brownell's memoirs, *Advising Ike* (1993), provide some insight into the end of McGranery's time as attorney general. Obituaries are in *Time*, 4 Jan. 1963; *Newsweek*, 7 Jan. 1963; and the *New York Times*, 1 Apr. 1963.

NANCY V. BAKER

MCGRATH, J. Howard (28 Nov. 1903–2 Sept. 1966), U.S. senator and attorney general, was born James Howard McGrath in Woonsocket, Rhode Island, the son of James J. McGrath, an Irish immigrant who became a fraternal insurance association executive, and Ida E. May, a bookkeeper. McGrath received a Ph.B. from Providence College in 1926 and an L.L.B. from Boston University in 1929. From 1924 to 1928 he was president of the Rhode Island Young Democrats. In 1929 he married Estelle A. Cadorette; they had one child, a son. In 1930 he was appointed city solicitor by his father-in-law, the mayor of Central Falls, Rhode Island, and from 1930 to 1934 he also chaired the Democratic State Committee. In 1934, thanks to the patronage of Senator Theodore F. Green, whose law firm he had just joined, he was appointed U.S. district attorney for Rhode Island.

Greatly assisted by his political connections, McGrath also became involved in real estate, insurance, manufacturing, and savings and loan enterprises that made him wealthy. Active in charitable activities, he was a member of numerous fraternal and religious organizations.

McGrath was elected governor of Rhode Island in 1940 and reelected in 1942 and 1944. His most important accomplishment as governor was the establishment of a state juvenile court system. At the behest of Senator Green, President Harry Truman appointed him solicitor general of the United States in October 1945, but less than a year later he returned to Rhode Island to run for the U.S. Senate. His victory capped a meteoric rise that owed more to his ability as a political organizer than to personal magnetism.

In 1947 President Truman selected McGrath to succeed Robert E. Hannegan as chairman of the Democratic National Committee (DNC). Retaining his seat in the Senate, McGrath assumed the role of unifying spokesperson for an ideologically and ethnically divided party. In 1949 McGrath reluctantly gave up his Senate seat to become attorney general, replacing Tom C. Clark, a Protestant, whom Truman had appointed to the Supreme Court position formerly held by Frank Murphy (1890–1949), a Catholic, thus requiring the placement of a prominent Catholic politician as attorney general.

McGrath's tenure in the Department of Justice was undistinguished. His most notable accomplishments were support for black plaintiffs in important civil rights cases and the successful antitrust action against the Great Atlantic & Pacific company. The department's indifference toward organized crime and tolerance of graft were highlighted during congressional inquiries chaired by Senator Estes Kefauver in 1950 and 1952.

By early 1952, the corruption issue had become so serious that McGrath was forced to accept an independent investigator, Newbold Morris, whom he soon fired. On 3 April 1952 Truman dismissed McGrath, who then advised his successor, James P. McGranery, "Bring a pair of asbestos trousers with you."

McGrath devoted most of the rest of his life to his legal practice and business interests, coming out of political retirement, ironically, to manage Senator Kefauver's unsuccessful presidential primary and vice presidential campaigns in 1956. McGrath died at his farm near Narragansett, Rhode Island.

Although primarily a political professional, McGrath was a New Deal–Fair Deal liberal who desegregated the DNC and lectured his fellow Catholics on the Jewish experience in the Holocaust. His weakness was that of many political professionals who start at the bottom, see at close range the deal-making and payoffs that constitute the seamy side of American politics, benefit from such themselves, and take them to be (as McGrath privately remarked in 1955) "only the ordinary run of what goes on." In all these respects, he resembled the president whom he served and was a representative figure in the post–World War II Democratic party.

• McGrath's papers are at the Harry S. Truman Library, Independence, Mo. An acidly critical assessment is in Robert S. Allen and William V. Shannon, *The Truman Merry-Go-Round* (1950), pp. 98–110. A brief, unpublished oral interview with him was done for Truman's *Memoirs* and may be found in the Truman papers, *Memoirs* File, Truman Library. An obituary is in the *New York Times*, 3 Sept. 1966.

ALONZO L. HAMBY

MCGRATH, Matthew J. (20 Dec. 1876–29 Jan. 1941), track and field athlete, was born in Nenagh, Tipperary, Ireland, the son of Timothy McGrath, a poor tenant farmer, and Ann (maiden name unknown). As a youth McGrath began participating in track and field, winning races from 100 yards to the half-mile and excelling in the long jump. His main ambition, however, was to perform in the weight-throwing events and surpass the achievements of his hero, John J. Flanagan, who held the world record in the sixteen-pound hammer throw. In 1897 McGrath immigrated to New York City and worked as a blacksmith, bartender, and salesman before joining the police force in 1902.

From that point, McGrath pursued his goal of becoming history's finest weight-thrower. As a member of the recently organized New York Police Athletic League, in 1906 he achieved national recognition in the hammer throw with a toss of 158′8″. The next year he set his first world record in the event, hurling the hammer 173′7″. A month before that achievement, McGrath had recorded a throw of 175′10″, which the Amateur Athletic Union (AAU) did not recognize as a world record because he had used a nonregulation implement. In 1908 he won the AAU National Championship in the event. Other national titles in the hammer throw followed in 1910, 1912, 1918, 1922, 1925, and 1926. Hampered by a knee injury in the 1908 Olympic Games at London, he finished second in the hammer throw to Flanagan, who won his third consecutive gold medal.

Over the next twenty years McGrath ranked among the world's leading weightmen. As part of the Irish-American Athletic Club, he established world records in 1911 of 40′6⅜″ for the 56-pound weight throw and 53′11″ for the 35-pound weight throw. That year the 6′, 210-pound McGrath also hurled the hammer 187′4″ for a world record. In 1912 he won the Olympic gold medal in the hammer throw at Stockholm and established an Olympic record of 179′7″, which stood until 1936. In 1913 he won the AAU championship in the 56-pound weight throw; more championships came in 1916, 1918, and 1922 through 1925.

Beginning in 1913 McGrath and Patrick J. Ryan, a recent Irish immigrant, competed for supremacy in the hammer throw. On 13 August McGrath achieved a distance of 190′10″, but the effort was not recognized as a world record because it came during an exhibition meet. Four days later, Ryan claimed an official world record with a toss of 189′6½″. In 1918 McGrath set a world record of 61′8″ for the 35-pound weight. Although he was held to fifth place in the hammer throw in the 1920 Olympic Games at Antwerp because of a badly twisted knee, a healthy McGrath won the silver medal in the 1924 Olympic Games at Paris. At the age of fifty-two, weighing 248 pounds, he finished fifth in the 1928 U.S. Olympic Trials.

As a police officer, McGrath demonstrated the same physical prowess that earned him success as an athlete. He dove into the frigid waters of the East River to rescue someone from drowning in 1906, and he subdued an armed murder suspect by rapidly hurling a barrage of bricks at him in 1913. On both occasions he received the police department's citation for valor. In another instance, however, in a personal dispute, he lost his temper and inadvertently shot a man. After being acquitted of all assault charges, he was mobbed by admirers as he left the courtroom. He rose steadily through departmental ranks, becoming a sergeant in 1917, lieutenant in 1918, captain in 1927, deputy inspector in 1930, and chief inspector of traffic control in 1936. In that year McGrath and his wife, Loretta (maiden name unknown), adopted an orphaned Chinese child. (The date of their marriage is also unknown.) McGrath was sick for much of 1940. He died in New York City.

McGrath represented an era in American track and field when Irish immigrants dominated the sport, especially the weight-throwing events. From the late 1880s to the late 1930s Irish Americans took national championships, Olympic titles, and held world records in the hammer throw, discus, shot put, and events requiring great strength and exact technique. Because of their size, McGrath and his national colleagues were nicknamed the "Irish Whales." For them and for other Irish-American men, sport served an important social function. Participation in sport, both as a performer and as a spectator, formed a linchpin for the Irish-American community and provided important avenues to opportunities in mainstream society. McGrath's career as a policeman, especially his rise from patrolman to chief inspector, demonstrated the increasing occupational and social mobility of Irish Americans in early twentieth-century America.

• For a full sketch of McGrath, see his obituary in the *New York Times*, 29 Jan. 1941. Other biographical information can be found in Bill Mallon and Ian Buchanan, *Quest for Gold: The Encyclopedia of American Olympians* (1984). Roberto L. Quercetani, *A World History of Track and Field Athletics* (1964), places McGrath in the context of early twentieth-century track and field. His accomplishments are compiled in Frank G. Menke, *The Encyclopedia of Sports*, 4th rev. ed. (1969), and David Wallechinsky, *The Complete Book of the Olympics*, 2d rev. ed. (1988).

ADAM R. HORNBUCKLE

MCGRAW, James Herbert (17 Dec. 1860–21 Feb. 1948), publisher, was born in Panama, Chautauqua County, New York, the son of Patrick McGraw and Catharine (maiden name unknown), farmers. His parents had left Ireland in 1849 in the wake of the Great Famine, coming by way of Canada to western New York. He excelled in studies at the small local school and then for his further education took advantage of the free State Normal School in nearby Fredonia, New York. While there he earned spending money by working as a book agent and magazine salesman. After graduating as valedictorian in 1884, he spent a year as a teacher and principal in Corfu, New York. About this time his own former principal, Horace Swetland, had become intimately involved with the American Railway Publishing Company—whose *Journal of Rail-*

way Appliances McGraw had previously sold—and in 1885 Swetland called his young protégé to join him in New York City. McGraw promptly complied, but after a year spent canvassing Philadelphia for subscriptions, he was informed that the young company was in deep financial trouble and could not afford to pay him. McGraw borrowed $1,000 from a wealthy Chautauqua farmer and gave it to Swetland in exchange for a vice presidency in the company. McGraw thus staked his entire future on the success of industrial journalism.

In 1887 he married Mildred Whittlesly of Corfu; they had four sons and a daughter. McGraw disagreed with his partners at American Railway, particularly over their refusal to fully recognize the coming role of electricity in industry, as shown by their ongoing focus on horse-drawn trolleys in their *Street Railway Journal*. McGraw broke with them in 1888, buying out the *Journal of Railway Appliances*. With his father-in-law, Curtis Whittlesly, providing much of his capital, McGraw bought a number of small technical and industrial journals. Through consolidation he gained virtual control of the market. His *Electrical World* was a prime example: in 1896 he had begun buying electrical magazines, and after acquiring three, he merged them into this single, successful publication in 1899. The year proved a banner one for McGraw who—always keenly aware of trends in technological development—then purchased the old *Street Railway Journal* from one of his former partners, refashioned it according to his vision of the age of electricity, and made it a key part of the burgeoning empire that he incorporated that same year as the McGraw Publishing Company.

McGraw lived in Madison, New Jersey, for most of his career. His life was almost entirely devoted to his business, and he raised his sons to inherit the dynasty he was building. He did briefly take an interest in politics, serving as chair of the Morris County Republican Committee from 1900 to 1908 and as a delegate to the Republican National Convention of 1904. But his attention was always focused on his expanding business, and in the first decade of the new century he began adding technical books to his publications. His great competitor in this arena, as in the magazine field, was John Alexander Hill. Urged on by the managers of their respective book divisions—McGraw's Martin Foss and Hill's Edward Caldwell—the two publishers, for mutual benefit, merged their book interests in 1909 to create the McGraw-Hill Book Company. Their other publications remained separate until after Hill's death in 1916; his heirs expressed no interest in running his five magazines, and in 1917 McGraw bought them to form the McGraw-Hill Publishing Company. The McGraw-Hill Book Company remained a separate subsidiary.

The McGraw-Hill book list contained approximately 250 titles at the outset of World War I, but preparations for war brought the company orders for twenty textbooks for the armed forces in new fields such as aviation and submarine warfare. After the United States entered the war, the Committee on Industrial Preparedness and the Council of National Defense commissioned books on basic manufacturing. McGraw-Hill's second revision of *American Machinists' Handbook and Dictionary of Shop Terms* (1914), for example, was directly applicable to munitions production—and set records for technical book sales. In the booming 1920s the book list expanded further, to include fields such as chemistry, scientific agriculture, mathematics, medicine, and even accounting and business administration. The publishing company's magazines, such as McGraw's *Power* and Hill's old *American Machinist*, also flourished; thirty-five years after his daring break with Swetland, McGraw had won supremacy in the field of American technical publications.

Having met and exceeded his goals as a businessman, McGraw retired as president of the book company in 1925—he was succeeded by Caldwell—and as president of McGraw-Hill Publishing Company in 1928. He remained chair of the board of the latter until 1935, but he left the running of the firm to his successors. After his retirement the chairmanship was taken by his son James H. McGraw, Jr. He spent his last years in San Francisco, where he died. His sons and grandsons continued to play a prominent role in the business empire that he established.

McGraw's greatest legacy might well be in the textbooks that he created for generations of Americans. For all his apparently single-minded devotion to business, his character was perhaps most profoundly shaped by his youth in a country schoolhouse. "Teaching was the true direction of his genius," and "everything he did was a kind of teaching . . . everything he established was a kind of school" (Burlingame, p. 60). He and his company especially contributed to the advancement and dissemination of scientific and technical knowledge in the United States during the crucial years of the early twentieth century. His idealism shows in the credo that he wrote near the end of his presidency. McGraw believed that an industrial journal must "have no other guides for its opinions and policies but truth and the sound interests of the field it serves" ("Ideals of Industrial Journalism," p. 559).

• Columbia University Libraries holds the McGraw-Hill Oral History Collection, transcripts of tape-recorded interviews with persons associated with the growth and development of the company. McGraw's reflections on his profession are available in his article "Ideals of Industrial Journalism," *Electrical World* 50 (20 Sept. 1924): 559, and in his book *Teacher of Business: The Publishing Philosophy of James H. McGraw* (1944). Roger Burlingame, *Endless Frontiers: The Story of McGraw-Hill* (1959), is a thorough study of the company history and contains biographical information on McGraw. An obituary is in the *New York Times*, 22 Feb. 1948.

W. FARRELL O'GORMAN

MCGRAW, John (7 Apr. 1873–25 Feb. 1934), baseball player and manager, was born John Joseph McGraw in Truxton, New York, the son of John McGraw, an Irish immigrant railroad laborer, and Ellen Comerfort. When he was about twelve, following the death of his mother and four of his brothers and sisters in a diphtheria epidemic, McGraw moved in with neighbors and from then on saw little of his father. He did odd jobs around the village, sold snacks on the rail line from Truxton to Elmira, and played baseball as much as he could. By age sixteen, at 5′6½″ and 115–120 pounds, he was the best player on the town team.

McGraw started playing professional baseball in 1890 for Olean in the New York–Pennsylvania League and then for Wellsville in the New York State League. That winter he joined a team that played a series of games in Cuba. In 1891, performing mostly in the infield, McGraw made a creditable record at Cedar Rapids in the Illinois-Iowa League, and in August of that year he joined the Baltimore Orioles of the American Association, then considered a major league. A mediocre batter at that time and an unreliable fielder, he barely stayed on the team roster in 1892 when the American Association disbanded and Baltimore entered a reorganized, twelve-club National League.

Under manager Edward "Ned" Hanlon, the Baltimore Orioles became one of the league's best teams. Lacking great natural ability, the pint-sized McGraw made himself into an outstanding player—the league's foremost third baseman and leadoff man—by grit, guile, and a fiery disposition. McGraw's no-holds-barred style of play typified the Orioles as they won three consecutive National League championships from 1894 through 1896 and barely missed a fourth in 1897.

Despite his relatively limited athletic skills, McGraw ended his playing days with a .334 lifetime batting average and a remarkable .465 career on-base percentage; in the 10 seasons at the heart of his career he averaged more than 40 stolen bases per season. In 1898 and in 1899 he led the National League in both bases on balls and runs scored. Even by the low fielding marks of his time, caused in large part by poor playing surfaces and rudimentary equipment, McGraw's statistics indicate he was an error-prone third baseman. Possibly his rough, crafty style of play (many fans of opposing teams called it "dirty") made up for his erratic arm and glove. Typically, McGraw would block the path of base runners, forcing them to break stride, swerve, and lose steps. He would stomp on opponents' feet when taking throws at the bag. And he often would hook a base runner's belt with his free hand to slow him down when the umpires were looking elsewhere.

In 1899 McGraw became the Orioles' manager and started to build his reputation as a baseball genius, leading a group of nondescript players to a strong fourth-place finish. His team would probably have finished even higher if not for McGraw's absence during the season's last weeks because of the death of his wife of two years, the former Minnie Doyle. When the National League contracted to eight franchises in 1900, dropping Baltimore and three other cities, McGraw ended up playing for St. Louis. Then he joined Ban Johnson in forming the American League and became player-manager of the new Baltimore club. Within a short time, though, repeated clashes with Johnson, mostly having to do with the abuse of umpires by McGraw and his players, prompted McGraw to desert the new league. On 8 July 1902 he signed a four-year contract to manage the New York Giants for an annual salary of $11,000, highest in baseball up to then.

Meanwhile, McGraw married Blanche Sindall of Baltimore. Although the marriage lasted for thirty-two years, they were childless. The McGraws traveled inveterately, lived high, and made little effort to save from his baseball income, which by the late 1920s exceeded $70,000 a year. McGraw simply gave away much of what he earned—to literally thousands of down-and-out former players and others who sought his help—and he also lost as much as $100,000 when the great Florida land boom collapsed in 1926.

Beginning in 1904, when McGraw's Giants won their first pennant under his direction, the "Little Napoleon," as the New York sportswriters crowned him, was a dominating presence in baseball and especially in National League affairs. Managing in the nation's largest city and its media capital, he became one of the best-known figures in the United States; as a result of many offseason trips to Cuba, an around-the-world tour in 1913–1914, and another to Great Britain and France in 1924, he was an international celebrity as well. From 1904 through 1924 his Giants won ten National League titles, and while they beat their American League opponents only three times in the World Series, McGraw—a master tactician, a bullier of umpires without equal, and a martinet with his players—kept his reputation as baseball's premier manager.

Although the Giants came close several times and featured a galaxy of future Hall of Famers, McGraw's post-1924 teams never won another pennant. In June 1932 McGraw, much overweight and in failing health, and unable to get his ballclub into contention, yielded the manager's job to Bill Terry, his star first baseman.

During a managerial career that spanned three decades in New York, McGraw's Giants amassed the most successful won-lost record in major league baseball. When his three seasons in Baltimore are included, he ranks second only to Connie Mack in games managed (4,845 for McGraw) and in games won (2,816). His Giants' teams finished in the league's second division only twice. He was an outspoken manager, noisy, contentious, brilliant, and inspirational. Some historians credit him with being a major stimulus to baseball's growing success before the lively ball era. Eight Hall of Famers played all or substantial parts of their careers with the Giants under McGraw: Roger Breshnahan, Travis Jackson, Fred Lindstrom, Joe McGinty, Rube Marquard, Christy Mathewson, Mel Ott, and Bill Terry; and by 1932 Carl Hubbell was coming into his own.

A year after retiring, McGraw came back to direct the National League team in the first All-Star game. Eight months later he died in New Rochelle, New York. In 1937 he was elected to the National Baseball

Hall of Fame, which formally opened two years later at Cooperstown, New York.

• McGraw's complete record as player and manager can be found in Craig Carter, ed., *Daguerreotypes*, 8th ed. (1990), pp. 202–3, and the National Baseball Library's McGraw Collection is sizable. McGraw's memoirs were published as *My Thirty Years in Baseball* (1923). The principal biographical items are Charles C. Alexander, *John McGraw* (1988); Frank Graham, *McGraw of the Giants* (1944); Mrs. John J. McGraw, *The Real McGraw*, ed. Arthur Mann (1953); and Joseph Durso, *The Days of Mr. McGraw* (1969). See also Frank Graham, *The New York Giants* (1952); Neil Hynd, *The Giants of the Polo Grounds* (1988); and Fred Lieb, *The Baltimore Orioles* (1955).

CHARLES C. ALEXANDER

MCGRAW, Myrtle Byram (1 Aug. 1899–6 Sept. 1988), developmental psychologist, was born near Birmingham, Alabama, the daughter of Riley McGraw, a farmer, and Mary Byram, a seamstress. Having both training and experience in typing and shorthand, McGraw worked as a secretary to the headmistress of a boarding school in Boaz, Alabama, to pay for the cost of her secondary education. As a fifteen-year-old student there she began a correspondence with John Dewey, who was to be a major influence on her life and career.

After her graduation from Ohio Wesleyan University in 1923, McGraw entered graduate school in religious education at Teachers College, Columbia University, made possible by typing a book manuscript for Dewey. A year's sojourn in a mountain village in Puerto Rico convinced her that religious education was not her field, and in 1925 she returned to Columbia to pursue a Ph.D. in psychology under the direction of Helen Thompson Woolley, director of the Child Welfare Institute, Teachers College. A Laura Spelman Rockefeller fellowship helped subsidize the completion of her course work for the Ph.D., and in 1927 she accepted a teaching position in psychology at Florida State College for Women and began her dissertation research comparing the performance of black and white infants on a battery of standardized tests. In the absence of reliable birth-registration records, she located her subjects by driving around looking for diapers on clotheslines. Returning to New York in 1929, McGraw took a clinical intern position at the Institute for Child Guidance, where she administered standardized tests and wrote reports while finishing her dissertation. Her doctorate was awarded in 1931.

On 1 September 1930 McGraw reported for work at the Columbia Presbyterian Medical Center and entered what was to be the most significant period in her life as a scientist. As the associate director of the Normal Child Development Study at Babies Hospital, she conducted research on the relative contributions of nature and nurture to the behavioral development, particularly the motor development, of infants. The culmination of this work was the publication of her famous study of the Woods twins, *Growth: A Study of Johnny and Jimmy* (1935). In a context in which the focus of infant and child research was the establishment of developmental norms through administration of standardized scales and tests, McGraw was less concerned about the age at which various milestones appeared than she was with understanding the process of growth. She drew on a variety of disciplines to further this understanding. Reflecting on the contributions of neuroembryologist George Coghill to her thinking, she said, "It was he and John Dewey and the babies that got me thinking of process, not end result, or achievement" (Bergenn et al., p. 384). The focus of the Normal Child Development Study was on the relationship between neurological development and behavior—structure and function. Because of the death of Frederick Tilney, neurologist and project director, the data analyses of neuronal development were never completed, but McGraw's work was noteworthy for her emphasis on observation and manipulation of behavior and for the novelty of her methods to challenge infant motor development through special intense exercise.

Experimental psychology at the time was dominated by the views of the behaviorist John Watson, who claimed that given a dozen healthy infants he could, by manipulating their environment, make of them anything he chose. On the other side of the nature-nurture debate was Arnold Gesell, the maturationist, who insisted that no amount of training could influence the development of an infant until that infant's nervous system had reached the appropriate stage of growth. McGraw rejected this maturation-learning dichotomy and instead looked for cues in the infants' behavior suggesting environmental challenges that would stimulate optimal motor development. She was the first to demonstrate the swimming reflex in two- and four-month-old babies. As the infants began to creep, she provided steeper and steeper inclines, and to challenge the development of equilibrium and stepping movements, she put little Johnny Woods on roller skates at thirteen months of age. To the surprise of the research team and to the delight of the media, Johnny became a very skillful skater.

Wrongly classified as a maturationist because of her use of the term "critical period," McGraw's concept of development was more dynamic. As she used it, critical period simply referred to the most opportune time, as indicated by the child's behavior, for training in a particular type of activity, like roller skating or toilet training. Her concept of development included periods of regression and loss as a natural part of the growth process. As she characterized it, "My concept was of multisystems developmental processes emerging and advancing at different times and different rates, but finally interacting, integrating, and synthesizing for the creation of new performances or traits" (McGraw, "Professional," p. 170). The Normal Child Development Study ended in early 1940 when, in part due to the approach of war, grant support was not renewed. McGraw remained at Babies Hospital until 1942, sorting through records and completing her second book, *The Neuromuscular Maturation of the Human Infant* (1943).

McGraw characterized the period from the termination of the child development study to the early 1950s as her D-D (domesticity and diversity) decade, during which she did some writing, but for the most part lived quietly with her husband, Rudolph Mallina, whom she married in 1936, and her daughter. She wrote, "The thirties had been a glorious decade when the babies had been my teacher. Now I should use what I learned to take care of my own" (O'Connell and Russo, p. 51). In 1953 Briarcliff College offered her a position in the psychology department and a schedule that would permit her to be at home when her daughter came home from high school. So, in a smoking room converted to a teaching laboratory, McGraw trained undergraduate women to work with infants and young children. Her educational objectives were to teach students to learn from the babies. In an article published after her death she wrote, "Education should prepare individuals to understand and communicate with different age groups, not build up rigid standards based on age distinction or categories. With the decline of the kinship family and the instability of the nuclear family, it becomes society's responsibility to develop new methods or techniques of inculcating in present-day teenagers the art of observing and interpreting behavior development in growing infants, before they bear their own" (McGraw, "Memories," p. 937). McGraw retired in 1972. She died at her home in Hastings-on-Hudson, New York.

Myrtle McGraw was clearly ahead of her time in articulating a concept of development that has been largely confirmed by more recent research showing the interdependence of structure and function in developing nervous systems. At her memorial service, her daughter, Mitzi Wertheim, may have characterized her best, "My mother was born in the 19th century, lived in the 20th century and thought in the 21st century" (quoted in Lipsett, p. 977).

• No personal papers are available. Autobiographical sources include "Professional and Personal Blunders in Child Development Research," *Psychological Record* 35 (1985): 165–70; "Memories, Deliberate Recall, and Speculations," *American Psychologist* 45 (1990): 934–37; and McGraw's entry in *Models of Achievement: Reflections of Eminent Women in Psychology*, ed. Agnes N. O'Connell and Nancy F. Russo (1983). The most complete source is Thomas C. Dalton and Victor W. Bergenn, eds., *Beyond Heredity and Environment: Myrtle McGraw and the Maturation Controversy* (1995). It contains a number of McGraw's published and unpublished works with introductory essays and commentary by contemporary scholars. Another assessment of McGraw's work can be found in Victor W. Bergenn et al., "Myrtle B. McGraw: A Growth Scientist," *Developmental Psychology* 28 (1992): 381–95. Obituaries include one by Lewis P. Lipsett in *American Psychologist* 45 (1990): 977, and the *New York Times*, 13 Sept. 1988.

KATHARINE S. MILAR

MCGREADY, James (1758?–Feb. 1817), Presbyterian preacher, was reared in western Pennsylvania, the son of James McGready and Jean (maiden name unknown), farmers and recent immigrants from Scotland. His family moved to Guilford County, North Carolina, but in 1778 McGready returned to Pennsylvania, where he studied at Joseph Smith's Latin school in Upper Buffalo. After an emotional conversion experience in 1786, McGready moved to Cannonsburg, Pennsylvania, to study under John McMillan in 1787, who was reputedly the first Presbyterian minister to have a regular congregation west of the Allegheny mountains. McMillan instilled in his students his own "New Side" (revivalist) beliefs. On 13 August 1788 the Redstone Presbytery of Pennsylvania licensed McGready to preach; shortly thereafter he decided to move back to North Carolina. En route he stopped at Hampden-Sydney College in Farmville, Virginia, and observed how John Blair Smith's flamboyant rhetorical style incited a revival among the students. By the time he returned to North Carolina, McGready was well versed in the techniques and powers of revivalism. Within a year of his return to North Carolina, he married Nancy Thompson; they had six daughters, two of whom died in infancy.

Initiating his ministerial career in Orange County, McGready's appearance was plain but his approach direct. Because he judged postrevolutionary North Carolina to be vicious, materialistic, and generally profane, McGready became a "son of thunder," whose role was to damn the guilty and terrify the apathetic. In his sermon, "Doom of the Impenitent," for example, he warned that "Hell burns by fuel," and "the unhappy wretches, filth and refuse of the universe, all ranks and classes of ungodly, impenitent sinners—collected into one horrible company, bound up in bundles and piled together for the vengeance of eternal fire" served as that fuel. Through these sermons McGready inspired several students at David Caldwell's "Guilford Academy," including William Hodge, Samuel McAdow, William McGee, John Rankin, and Barton W. Stone, to become Presbyterian revivalist preachers. Not everyone in Piedmont society was so taken with McGready, however. His attacks on materialism in 1796 offended some of the wealthy parishioners at the Stoney Creek congregation, who responded by sending him a death threat written in blood. McGready decided it was time to move to Kentucky.

By January 1797 McGready had assumed the ministerial duties at the Red River, Gasper River, and Muddy River Presbyterian congregations in Logan County, Kentucky. He found the region unchurched but receptive and initiated a sermon series on "regeneration, faith, and repentance." He also asked the congregations to sign a covenant requiring each member to spend several hours each week praying for revival. The churches experienced moderate growth through 1798, but the antirevivalist (Old Side) Presbyterians, led by James Balch, checked any emerging enthusiasm. In the summer of 1799, however, McGready's preaching at sacramental meetings—modeled on the four-day Scottish communion service—provoked a series of awakenings that attracted attention throughout the region. By the next summer hundreds of people traveled up to 100 miles to attend McGready's revivals. Because the visitors overwhelmed local accommodations, they camped out in the fields surrounding the church buildings. Thus emerged the famous camp meeting pattern of the Second Great Awakening. McGready described how a "divine flame" (a biblical allusion to Pentecost) spread through meetings and incited physical and emotional outbursts. In his "Vindication of the Exercises in the Revival of 1800," McGready defended the unusual demonstrations noting "Christ's coming at the present day in the power of the Godhead to visit his church with the outpouring of his Spirit, is marked with circumstances equally unreasonable in the opinion of the proud and worldly minded. They think the noisy tumult and uproar is mad confusion and cannot believe this falling down and shrieking and crying to be the glorious work of the Eternal God." Moreover, he believed "so intimate is the connection between the soul and body that it is nothing strange if a man fulfilled with an uncommon sense of terror and divine wrath should fall to the ground and his bodily strength be overcome." Not only were these camp meetings notable for their emotional and physical exercises but also for their democratic tendencies. Richard McNemar explained how the 1801 Cane Ridge revival tolerated "neither distinction as to age, sex, color, or anything of a temporary nature: old and young, male and female, black and white, had equal privilege to minister the light which they received." Not surprisingly, camp meetings became a staple of the frontier culture in the early nineteenth century.

Despite their popularity, these revivals further divided the Old and New Sides of the Presbyterian Church. McGready angered his more conservative synod by supporting the use of uneducated preachers; more important, they worried that he had abandoned certain key tenets of Calvinism. Thus the synod suspended McGready and several other ministers of the Cumberland Presbytery in 1805. When some of his more Arminian (advocates of free will as opposed to predestination) colleagues officially formed the prorevival Cumberland Presbyterian Church on 4 February 1810, he decided not to participate in the schism and successfully sought reinstatement by the Transylvania Presbytery. For the final seven years of his life he worked to establish churches in southern Indiana. He died at home in Henderson, Kentucky.

As the father of revivalism in the West, McGready provided a vehicle whereby religion could appeal to the masses and expand with the nation. Consequently Protestantism continued to serve as a powerful force in America's early history.

• Sermons comprise the bulk of McGready's writings, and a selection of these were reprinted in James McGready, *The Posthumous Works of the Reverend and Pious James M'Gready, Late Minister of the Gospel in Henderson, Ky*, ed. James Smith (2 vols., 1831–1833). See also Barton W. Stone, *The Biography of Eld. Barton Warren Stone* (1847); Ben M. Barrus et al., *A People Called Cumberland Presbyterians* (1972); John B. Boles, *The Great Revival, 1787–1805* (1972); Catharine C. Cleveland, *The Great Revival in the West, 1797–1805* (1916); Paul K. Conkin, *Cane Ridge: America's Pentecost* (1990); James Opie, "James McGready: Theologian of Frontier Revivalism," *Church History* 34 (1965): 445–56; and Bernard A. Weisberger, *They Gathered at the River: The Story of the Great Revivalists and Their Impact upon Religion in America* (1958).

RICHARD C. GOODE

MCGROARTY, Sister Julia (13 Feb. 1827–12 Nov. 1901), Roman Catholic educator and provincial, was born in Inver near Donegal, Ireland, and baptized Susan, the daughter of Neil McGroarty and Catherine Bonner, farmers. She was the second daughter and third of ten children. In the spring of 1831 the family followed several of Catherine Bonner McGroarty's relatives to Ohio via Quebec. Neil McGroarty farmed briefly in Fayetteville, then turned to railroad and turnpike building, moving the family to Cincinnati. He died there of pneumonia in 1838. Catherine McGroarty raised her children with the assistance of her relatives, particularly physician brother Stephen Bonner; she did not remarry.

Susan McGroarty was an energetic, engaging child with little self-discipline. Still unable to read at age ten, she got by in school with a retentive memory. When she was thirteen Stephen Bonner arranged for her to enter the convent school of the Sisters of Notre Dame de Namur, a Belgian order that had just opened a Cincinnati house, and whose sisters he served as physician. At the convent school McGroarty flourished academically, and even at this young age she voiced an interest in professing in a religious order, at that time the Sisters of Charity, which an aunt had entered.

Her allegiances shifted, however, and after graduation from the academy in 1845 she obtained her mother's permission to enter the Notre Dame convent on 1 January 1846, becoming the order's first American postulant; she donned the habit and received the name Sister Julia on 25 April 1846. Immediately she began to teach in the order's infant school, or kindergarten. After taking her vows on 3 August 1848, Sister Julia was named head of the day school. Her formation as a sister and potential order leader was personally undertaken by Sister Louise Van der Schrieck, the Cincinnati convent's first superior and, after 1849, provincial of the order's eastern houses.

In 1854 Sister Julia was assigned as mistress of boarders at the order's new academy in Roxbury, Massachusetts. In 1860 she became the order's first American superior at the Philadelphia academy, where she spent the next quarter century. Among her achievements was building a new girls' academy, despite neighborhood anti-Catholic sentiment, and establishing schools for blacks and for immigrant girls.

In 1885 an ailing Sister Louise recalled Sister Julia to Cincinnati to prepare Sister Julia as her successor. After Sister Louise's death in December 1886, Sister Julia was duly elected provincial in 1887, taking charge of twenty-six houses and 1,500 sisters, postulants, and novitiates. She began a sweeping reorganization of the order's schools, instituting a unified curriculum, more stringent teaching standards and training, and common examinations. She also vigorously expanded the order's foundations, building a new novitiate for the eastern houses in Waltham, Massachusetts, and at least fourteen other installations, including The Summit chapel and a new convent in Cincinnati. In 1892 the Notre Dame motherhouse recognized her abilities by placing the California province under her authority.

Sister Julia's crowning educational achievement was the founding of Trinity College, the first Catholic women's college opened independently of an existing academy. While refusing applications by women to the Catholic University of America in Washington, D.C., founded in 1889, university administrators sought an order to undertake the higher education of women. Sister Julia later admitted that she had not been a proponent of women's college education but was persuaded of its necessity by Catholic University administrators; by her closest advisers, Sisters Georgianna Flannelly and Mary Borgia; and by the vigorous superior of the order's small Washington, D.C., convent, Sister Mary Euphrasia Taylor. Finally, in the summer of 1897, with the backing of James Gibbons Sister Julia began formal planning.

Conservative clerics opposed the idea, raising the specter of coeducation and invoking fears of Americanism, a controversy over modernism within the American church that had begun to concern Rome. Working through her own contacts, Sister Julia secured papal approval in November. Notre Dame's mother general, Sister Aimee de Jesus, would continue to have misgivings, however, and removed California from Sister Julia's care in 1901.

College planning included tours of major eastern women's colleges, including Wellesley, Vassar, Mt. Holyoke, and Smith, and correspondence with the order's teacher-training colleges in Liverpool, England, and Glasgow, Scotland. Sister Julia raised funds from private donors and from the public, named the first trustees and an auxiliary board of secular women to assist in fundraising, coordinated the college site and building with Sister Mary Euphrasia, and in the summer of 1900 gathered the entire faculty in Waltham for joint instruction by professors from Harvard and the Massachusetts Institute of Technology. When the college opened in November 1900, it was with the highest entrance requirements and without a preparatory department. Sister Julia maintained control over the curriculum and early faculty appointments, as president of the first corporation; and she resided at the college for much of its first year, acting as its de facto president although another sister held that title.

Throughout her tenure as provincial Sister Julia reformed the work of and to a great degree built the American Sisters of Notre Dame de Namur, particularly in the East. Under her the number of professed sisters rose from 850 to more than 1,300, and the number of pupils taught quadrupled. Sister Julia combined firm governance and innovative educational and administrative methods with personal warmth, inspiring great loyalty. Solidly loyal herself to the church and to the order she loved, her estrangement from the Notre Dame motherhouse over Trinity was the greatest source of pain in her life. Nevertheless, founding Trinity College, she oriented Catholic women's higher education toward academic rigor and the meeting of secular as well as religious standards, sparking, in the process, what would become a flood of college foundings by various orders over the next three decades.

The cares of Trinity exacerbated an existing heart condition, and Sister Julia died of apoplexy at the order's Peabody, Massachusetts, convent. She was buried at The Summit in Cincinnati after a requiem mass offered by Archbishop William H. Elder.

• An important collection of letters written by and to Sister Julia is located at the Archives of Trinity College in Washington, D.C. The archives also contain numerous other documents about the founding and early years of the college. Other documents may be available in the provincial house of the Sisters of Notre Dame de Namur in Cincinnati, Ohio. The best interpretive source is Sister Angela Elizabeth Keenan, *Three against the Wind: The Founding of Trinity College, Washington, DC* (1973), which also profiles Trinity cofounder, Sister Mary Euphrasia, and their relationship. An earlier, and still the only full-length biography, is Sister Helen Louise Nugent, *Sister Julia* (1928). Histories of Trinity College that discuss Sister Julia's role include Sister Columba Mullaly, *Trinity College: The First Seventy-Five Years* (1987), and Sister Mary Patrick Butler, *An Historical Sketch of Trinity College* (1926). Sister Julia's work as provincial is profiled in Sister Mary Patrick Butler, *The American Foundations of the Sisters of Notre Dame de Namur* (1928), and Sister Miriam of the Infant Jesus, *The Finger of God: History of the Massachusetts Province of Notre Dame de Namur, 1854–1963* (n.d.; 1964?). There is some information on her dealings with the California province in Mary Dominica McNamara, *Light in the Valley* (1967). An obituary is in the *Cincinnati Enquirer*, 14 Nov. 1901.

CYNTHIA FARR BROWN

MCGUFFEY, William Holmes (23 Sept. 1800–4 May 1873), textbook writer and teacher, was born in Washington County, Pennsylvania, the son of Alexander McGuffey and Anna Holmes, farmers of Scot and Scotch-Irish ancestry. McGuffey was raised on the family's frontier homestead in Trumbull County in the Western Reserve in Ohio. The family's struggles to clear the land and establish a working farm shaped the values that permeated the *McGuffey Readers*, a series of influential instructional books that William McGuffey later wrote. William's formal education was arranged with a series of Presbyterian ministers in church schools along the frontier, and at the age of fourteen he was considered competent to become a teacher. In the fall of 1814, at West Union, Ohio, a village near the family farm, he offered "to tutor all pupils" in a subscription school; forty-eight paying students arrived to begin a fifteen-week term, six days a week, eleven hours a day. Pupils were expected to bring their own books, which usually meant the Bible, the only book a family was likely to possess. In between teaching and continuing to work on the family farm, McGuffey also pursued his own academic studies, first at a local academy and later at Washington College, a Presbyterian institution in Washington, Pennsylvania. In 1826 he earned a bachelor's degree in ancient languages and in philosophy.

Impressed with McGuffey's academic promise, the president of Miami University, a small, progressive institution in Oxford, Ohio, offered the young scholar an appointment to teach Latin, Greek, and Hebrew. Over the next ten years McGuffey became a leading member of the Miami faculty, celebrated for his language instruction and for his course in moral philosophy. His students remembered him as a stern and austere man but a creative teacher skilled at illustrating abstract principles with concrete examples or an apt anecdote. He was a conservative on social issues and doctrinal matters, often taking positions that irked his more progressive colleagues. He advocated, for example, particularly rigid puritanical constraints on student behavior in the college. A conservative even about clothing, he always appeared in clerical black, dark tie, stove pipe hat, and ebony cane.

McGuffey was married in Oxford in 1827 to Harriet Spining (later spelled Spinning), the daughter of a Dayton judge and landowner. They had five children, only two of whom survived to adulthood. After ordination as a Presbyterian minister in 1829, he took an active part in church affairs and became well known in the region for his eloquence as a preacher. McGuffey was active in the movement in the 1830s in Ohio to support free, tax-supported common schools, joining with Calvin Stowe, the first state commissioner of education, his wife Harriet Beecher Stowe, the physician Daniel Drake, and other advocates of public education.

McGuffey's Miami years ended in 1836 with his appointment as president of the newly reorganized Cincinnati College, which its supporters hoped to develop into an institution worthy of Cincinnati's claim to be the cultural center of the Midwest. The financial panic of 1837, however, led to the closing of the college in 1839. McGuffey was then named president of Ohio University in Athens, the oldest collegiate institution in the state. But after only four years McGuffey resigned the presidency because of a series of disputes with local residents and bitter criticism of his inflexible policies on tax collections in support of the college. McGuffey and his young family returned to Cincinnati where he briefly taught languages at Woodward College, the city's classical high school.

In 1845 the University of Virginia offered McGuffey a position as professor of philosophy. Some members of the Virginia faculty criticized McGuffey's advocacy of emancipationism, the gradual elimination of slavery, but others countered that he was by no means an abolitionist radical. McGuffey gratefully accepted the appointment and remained on the faculty until his death. During the years at Charlottesville he taught "mental and moral philosophy," preached throughout the region, and worked to promote the establishment of public education in Virginia. His wife died in 1850, and the following year McGuffey married Laura Howard, the daughter of a Virginia colleague. Two daughters were born to this marriage.

McGuffey's major work, begun during his Miami years, was the compilation of a series of reading textbooks that came to be widely used across the United States in his lifetime and remained popular long after his death. In 1836 the Cincinnati publishing house of Truman & Smith brought out the first McGuffey textbooks: a primer, a speller, and four readers. These books were anthologies of instructional reading materials, graded for increasing difficulty within each volume and from one volume to the next, with ample woodcut illustrations, and questions and exercises for each lesson. The first series was titled the *Eclectic Readers*; the many later editions were named the *McGuffey Eclectic Readers*. McGuffey cooperated with his younger brother Alexander to bring out a *Fifth Reader* in 1844 and in 1857 a *Sixth*. McGuffey's original publication contract capped his royalties at $1,000, but later revisions increased this amount. Through many editions (major revisions in 1857 and again in 1879) and several publishing firms, approximately 122 million copies of the *Readers* were sold by 1920, with the largest volume of sales in the years from 1870 to 1890.

In these anthologies of American and British stories, essays, verse, historical accounts, and speeches, McGuffey's lessons explicitly and implicitly reflected the Protestant ethic of individualism, work, thrift, perseverance, modesty, truthfulness, the sanctity of property, and, above all, a pious morality. The *Readers* sought to build moral character, not intellectual values. They were imbued with Victorian sentimentality and portrayed women as innately virtuous. The *Readers* represented the self-reliant individualism of the frontier as the road to economic success and celebrated American nationalism through accounts of the heroes of the Revolution. They paid little or no notice to subsequent events such as the Mexican War, the blazing of the Oregon Trail, and, later, the Civil War and emancipation. In sum, the lessons of the *Eclectic Readers* reflect McGuffey's small-town, agrarian America of the early and mid-nineteenth century, creating a common tradition for generations of Americans. Ironically, the *Readers* enjoyed their greatest success during the late nineteenth century when American society was becoming more urban, industrial, and ethnically diverse. The influence of McGuffey and his *Readers*, ideas and attitudes in educating the young, was a major aspect in the forming of American character, for good or ill, well into the twentieth century.

• The main collection of McGuffey papers is held at Miami University, Oxford, Ohio, where there is also a McGuffey museum. A collection of memorabilia can also be found at the Henry Ford McGuffey Museum, Dearborn, Mich. Popular biographies are Alice McGuffey Ruggles, *The Story of the Mc-*

Guffeys (1950), and Harvey C. Minnich, *William Holmes McGuffey and His Readers* (1936). A more scholarly work is James Arnold Scully, "A Biography of William Holmes McGuffey" (Ph.D. diss., Univ. of Cincinnati, 1967). Systematic analysis of the substance of the *Readers* can be found in Richard D. Mosier, *Making the American Mind: Social and Moral Ideas in the McGuffey Readers* (1947), and John H. Westerhoff III, *McGuffey and His Readers: Piety, Morality, and Education in Nineteenth-Century America* (1978).

JOHN HARDIN BEST

MCGUGIN, Daniel Earle (29 July 1879–19 Jan. 1936), college football player and coach, was born in Tinley, Iowa, the son of Benjamin Franklin McGugin, a Union army officer, and Melissa Almeda Critchfield. After graduating from Tinley High School, McGugin entered Drake University, where he played football during his junior and senior years. Although slight of build, he played tackle and guard, positions usually reserved for larger men. After graduating from Drake in 1901, McGugin entered law school at the University of Michigan. There he joined the football team, and the coach, Fielding Yost, recognized McGugin's talent for playing the guard position. McGugin, who often blocked opponents who outweighed him by 20 to 30 pounds, proved Yost's remark that "weight doesn't count for everything; I would rather have a light strong man than a heavy weak one." McGugin played on Yost's legendary "point-a-minute" teams, which enjoyed undefeated seasons from 1901 to 1903. In 1901 Michigan scored 550 points and gave up none against its opponents, and in 1902 the Wolverines won the first Rose Bowl game, 49–0, over Stanford University. McGugin, who graduated from the University of Michigan law school in 1904, served as an assistant coach in 1903.

Admitted to the Michigan bar in 1904, McGugin briefly practiced law in Detroit before settling into a career as a college football coach. That same year Vanderbilt University in Nashville, Tennessee, and Case Western Reserve in Cleveland, Ohio, recruited him to coach their football teams. McGugin selected Vanderbilt because he wanted to "see and know the people" of the South. Under his direction, Vanderbilt developed into one of the South's leading college football powers, winning ten Southern Intercollegiate Athletic Association championships from 1904 to 1907, from 1910 to 1912, and from 1921 to 1923. In 1904 Vanderbilt enjoyed an undefeated season and led the nation in scoring. Vanderbilt lost only one game in each of the 1905, 1906, 1911, and 1916 seasons. Potentially undefeated seasons were spoiled by ties in 1910, 1921, and 1922. Vanderbilt lost one and tied one game each in 1907, 1912, and 1917. McGugin's only losing season came in 1915 when the Commodores won two games and lost six. During his 30-year coaching career at Vanderbilt, McGugin won 197 games, lost 55, and tied 19, for a winning percentage of .762. In that time, his teams scored 6,673 points to their opponents' 1,668 points.

In 1905 McGugin married Virginia L. Fite of Nashville, Tennessee; they had one daughter and two sons. Yost, his football mentor at the University of Michigan, served as his best man and eventually became McGugin's brother-in-law, as he later wed Virginia's sister Eunice. In 1909 McGugin became a partner in the Nashville law firm of Anderson, Aust, McGugin, and Evans. Specializing in corporate law, McGugin included among his clients the Tennessee Electrical Power Company, the Tennessee Manufacturers Association, and the Tennessee Road Builders Association. From 1909 to 1913 McGugin also served as a professor in the Vanderbilt University School of Law, teaching courses in engineering and contract law. Although he did not teach after 1913, he was appointed a full professor in the university. In 1918, during World War I, McGugin did not coach football but directed the university's athletic military activities. After presiding as the president of the Football Coaches Association in 1933, he stepped down as Vanderbilt's football coach to become its athletic director and to devote more time to his law practice. One of McGugin's former players, Raymond Morrison, who played quarterback and halfback from 1908 to 1911, replaced his mentor as football coach, after enjoying a successful coaching career at Southern Methodist University. McGugin died suddenly of a heart attack at the home of law partner John R. Aust in Nashville.

• Materials on McGugin are held at the archives and sports information departments of the University of Michigan and Vanderbilt University. Secondary sources on college football coaches that have useful material on McGugin include Tim Cohane, *Great College Football Coaches of the Twenties and Thirties* (1973); Allison Danzig, *Oh, How They Played the Game: The Early Days of Football and the Heroes Who Made It Great* (1971); and Ivan Kaye, *Good Clean Violence: A History of College Football* (1973).

ADAM R. HORNBUCKLE

MCGUIRE, George Alexander (26 Mar. 1866–10 Nov. 1934), bishop and founder of the African Orthodox Church, was born in Sweets, Antigua, British West Indies, the son of Edward Henry McGuire and Mary Elizabeth (maiden name unknown). He graduated from the Antigua branch of Mico College for Teachers in 1886. Baptized in his father's Anglican church, he was educated in the Moravian tradition of his mother, graduating in 1888 from the Moravian seminary at Nisky, St. Thomas, in the Danish West Indies. Thereafter he pastored a Moravian congregation at Frederiksted, St. Croix. He married Ada Roberts in 1892; they had one daughter.

McGuire emigrated to the United States in 1894. The following year he was confirmed in the Protestant Episcopal Church. He studied for the Episcopal ministry under a fellow West Indian, Henry L. Phillips of Philadelphia. McGuire found himself in a church that desired to minister to African Americans but was generally unwilling to accept any blacks as equal to whites. McGuire's talent and Phillips's mentorship allowed him to advance swiftly through the offices open to him. Ordained deacon in 1896 and priest the next year, he pastored a succession of black congregations, including St. Andrew's, Cincinnati (1897–1899); St. Philip's, Richmond (1899–1901); and St. Thomas', Philadelphia (1901–1904).

In 1905 McGuire accepted the appointment of Bishop William Montgomery Brown as archdeacon for colored work in the diocese of Arkansas. This was the highest position open to a black man serving the church within the United States. The denomination's national General Convention, however, was considering two proposals for allowing blacks to serve as domestic bishops: the first would place black bishops in charge of all-black missionary districts independent of local dioceses; and the second would allow dioceses to elect suffragan bishops who would work under the supervision of the diocesan bishop. Soon after McGuire's arrival, Brown proposed a third plan: black Episcopalians should be separated into an independent denomination. In 1906 McGuire seems to have preferred the missionary plan; later, under his own initiative, he attempted to enact Brown's plan.

Racial conflicts in the Arkansas diocese led McGuire to accept an invitation to return to the North in 1909 to pastor St. Bartholomew's, a young congregation of West Indians in Cambridge, Massachusetts. Under McGuire's leadership the church grew dramatically, but again he was frustrated by the racism of the Episcopal Church, evident in the diocese's refusal to grant the congregation voting rights. In 1911 he moved to New York to become field secretary of the American Church Institute for Negroes. Two years later he accepted a call to serve as rector of St. Paul's Church, Falmouth, in his native Antigua.

While in the Islands McGuire encountered the ideas of racial independence and nationalism advocated by Marcus Garvey. These resonated with McGuire's experience of whites' inability to treat blacks as equals within the church. He returned to New York in 1919 to support Garvey's newly formed Universal Negro Improvement Association (UNIA) and African Communities League. McGuire soon established his own congregation, the Church of the Good Shepherd, which affiliated briefly with the Reformed Episcopal Church but soon united with a few other congregations to form the Independent Episcopal Church.

In August 1920 the first International Convention of the Negro Peoples of the World elected McGuire chaplain-general of the UNIA and "titular Archbishop of Ethiopia." McGuire strengthened the work of local UNIA chaplains and, according to the UNIA's *Negro World*, sought to create a church "big enough for all Negroes to enter, retaining their own worship" (2 Apr. 1921). McGuire linked Christianity and racial independence in *The Universal Negro Catechism* (1921) and *The Universal Negro Ritual* (1921), which he composed for the UNIA. The catechism taught that if one "had to think or speak of the color of God" it should be described "as black since we are created in His image and likeness." The infant baptism rite charged the baptized to "fight manfully . . . for the freedom of his race, and the redemption of African unto his life's end."

The formality of the rituals did not appeal to many Protestant supporters of the UNIA, nor did McGuire's ordination of a UNIA leader as a presbyter of the church. Within a year the *Negro World* was at pains to stress, "We favor all churches, but adopt none as a UNIA Church" (16 July 1921). Although Garvey desired to unite blacks into "a great Christian confraternity," he did not want the church and hierarchy that McGuire sought to create. After a brief period of estrangement McGuire resumed a prominent role in the UNIA, presiding over the movement's "canonization" of Jesus as the "Black Man of Sorrows" in 1924.

Unable to establish a church linked to the UNIA, McGuire sought to provide an independent black church for Anglo-Catholics. Elected bishop of the Independent Episcopal Church in September 1921, he insisted that the church be renamed the African Orthodox Church (AOC) to emphasize its racial leadership. He maintained that his new church was "neither schismatic nor heretical," but a legitimate national or racial "branch" of the one Holy Catholic Church.

When trying to form a church linked to the UNIA, McGuire had been willing to forego apostolic succession, but he believed this was essential to authenticate the claims of the AOC. Refused consecration by Episcopal, Catholic, and Russian Orthodox bishops, he finally received it from Joseph René Vilatte of the Old Catholic Church of America. Having an autonomous church headed by a black bishop in apostolic succession was a great source of pride for McGuire and his followers, but the questionable authenticity of Vilatte's consecrations haunted their relations with other churches.

McGuire crafted a liturgy for his church based largely on the Book of Common Prayer and Anglo-Catholic practices, but also incorporating a few elements from Eastern Orthodoxy. The liturgy included prayers for the race and the redemption of Africa, though less pronounced than those in the *Universal Negro Ritual*. McGuire also founded Endich Theological Seminary in 1923 and edited the church's monthly *Negro Churchman* from 1923 to 1931. By the mid-1920s church membership numbered 12,000, with congregations in the northeastern United States, Nova Scotia, and the Caribbean. In 1927 McGuire was raised to the rank of patriarch and expanded the church to South Africa by receiving a few congregations and consecrating their leader, Daniel William Alexander, as bishop. McGuire died in New York City as head of a slowly expanding church.

McGuire broke new ground in extending the autonomy enjoyed by many black Protestants to black Anglo-Catholics. He was among the most important religious leaders in Garvey's movement and a talented member of the corps of West Indian clergy serving the Episcopal Church in the United States. The churches led by Alexander in Africa proved to be an enduring and significant presence on that continent. Yet in the U.S. the AOC became a small, though enduring, community of less than 6,000 people. As a black church leader who boasted of a claim to apostolic succession that few recognized, McGuire remained a marginal figure in both the church and predominately Protestant black America.

• McGuire's published writings include *The Universal Negro Catechism* (1921), *The Universal Negro Ritual* (1921), and articles in *The Negro Churchman*. His most famous sermon, "What Is in Thine Hand," is reprinted, with a biographical sketch, in Randall K. Burkett, *Black Redemption: Churchmen Speak for the Garvey Movement* (1978). The most complete assessment of McGuire's career is in Elias Farajajé-Jones, *In Search of Zion: The Spiritual Significance of Africa in Black Religious Movements* (1990). Harold T. Lewis, *Yet with a Steady Beat: The African American Struggle for Recognition in the Episcopal Church* (1996), discusses his role among West Indian clergy in the United States and the struggle for black bishops in the Episcopal Church. Burkett, *Garveyism as a Religious Movement: The Institutionalization of Black Civil Religion* (1978), discusses his relationship to Marcus Garvey.

DAVID R. BAINS

MCGUIRE, Hunter Holmes (11 Oct. 1835–19 Sept. 1900), surgeon, was born in Winchester, Virginia, the son of Hugh Holmes McGuire, a physician and surgeon, and Ann Eliza Moss. At seventeen he enrolled in the Winchester Medical College. Founded in 1826 as the Medical School of the Valley of Virginia, it was among Virginia's earliest medical colleges. His father was one of its founders and the professor of surgery. The school ceased operations in 1829 but was revived in 1847 as the Winchester Medical College.

McGuire received his M.D. in 1855 and set up practice with his father. In 1856 he was elected to his alma mater's chair of anatomy and for the next two years taught and practiced medicine. In 1858 he sought further medical training in Philadelphia, the medical center of the nation, at the Jefferson Medical College. Soon after his arrival in Philadelphia, McGuire was invited to join Francis E. Luckett, a fellow Virginian and physician at the Philadelphia Almshouse, in conducting a "quiz class." In this age of didactic lectures and paucity of satisfactory textbooks, medical students generally relied on "quiz masters" to keep up with their classes. McGuire and Luckett were popular tutors and built up a large following, especially among students from the South. In December 1859 they instigated and led the return home of nearly 250 of Philadelphia's southern medical students in the wake of John Brown's raid. Some 144 of them, including McGuire and Luckett, enrolled at Richmond's Medical College of Virginia. After receiving a second M.D. in March 1860, McGuire traveled to New Orleans, where he established a successful quiz class for students in the medical department of the University of Louisiana.

At the outbreak of hostilities between the North and South, McGuire hurried home to volunteer his services to his state. At first, he put aside his medical training to enlist as a private. But he was soon persuaded to accept a commission in the Confederate medical service. In May 1861 Surgeon General Samuel P. Moore ordered McGuire to report to Stonewall Jackson as medical director of the Army of the Shenandoah. Initially, Jackson was unimpressed with the lanky, pale doctor. However, McGuire's intense loyalty, skill as a physician, and administrative ability changed Jackson's mind, and the two became fast friends. McGuire, present when Jackson was struck down by his own men at Chancellorsville, amputated Jackson's wounded arm and was at his bedside when he died. (In 1883 he published the authoritative account of this Confederate tragedy.) After Jackson's death, McGuire served as chief surgeon for Generals Richard S. Ewell and Jubal A. Early. Less well known were his attempts to lessen the horrors of war, most notably the precedent-setting release of captive Union medical officers after the battle of Winchester in May 1862, perfecting the Ambulance Corps (also known as the Infirmary Corps), which was responsible for evacuating casualties from the battlefield to the rear area hospitals, and organizing the Reserve Corps Hospitals, an auxiliary to the Confederate hospital system.

McGuire was paroled at Appomattox and returned to Winchester. In July 1865 he was elected professor of surgery at the Medical College of Virginia in Richmond. McGuire supplemented his meager salary with a large private practice, much of it surgical in nature. Since hospitals were rare, especially in the South, he operated on his patients either in their homes or, if they did not live in the city, in boardinghouses. In 1866 he married Mary Stuart, with whom he had nine children. In response to the growing need for hospitals, McGuire in 1878 helped start the Retreat for the Sick and later, in 1883, founded his own 48-bed St. Luke's Home for the Sick in an old four-story hotel. In 1886 a training school for nurses, one of the first in the South, was added.

In 1878 McGuire resigned his professorship at the Medical College of Virginia because of friction among the faculty and the lack of time for the proper preparation of lectures. But he missed teaching and in 1893 was a founder of the College of Physicians and Surgeons (later the University College of Medicine), also located in Richmond. McGuire was appointed professor of surgery, a position he held until his death. Just as it had been in McGuire's youth, the best medical colleges were in the North, and southern students continued to stream to them. Hoping to reverse this tide, the University College of Medicine took the lead in medical reform in the South. The three-year graded curriculum—the first in the South—was its biggest innovation. The new school was an instant success, forcing its older rivals—the Medical College of Virginia and the University of Virginia—to offer longer courses of instruction and to update teaching methods. The institution eventually fell victim to the very reform movement that it had helped pioneer, as mounting financial pressures growing out of the turn-of-the-century national campaign to improve instruction in medicine forced it, in 1913, to merge with the Medical College of Virginia.

McGuire was one of the most respected physicians and surgeons in the late nineteenth-century South. At one time he had the largest general practice in Richmond. His surgical practice, while not as substantial, was equally significant: he was among the earliest American converts to the germ theory of disease that revolutionized the practice of medicine in the postbellum period; he pioneered standardization in the treatment of appendicitis; he was an early advocate of operative intervention in gunshot wounds of the abdomen; he was the first to recommend suprapubic cystostomy for the formation of an artificial urethra in prostatic obstruction; and he was considered the first to ligate the abdominal aorta (which he did in 1868) since it had originally been done in 1817. But it is as a teacher that McGuire is best remembered. His success in the classroom is attributable to his extraordinary skill as a diagnostician, wealth of surgical experience, and profound humaneness. McGuire also wrote dozens of articles, many of which described his surgical techniques. He was a forceful spokesman for medical organizations and belonged to a variety of local, state, and national ones. He was elected president of the Richmond Academy of Medicine (1869); Association of Medical Officers of the Army and Navy of the Confederacy (1875); Virginia Medical Society (1881), which he had helped found in 1870; American Surgical Association (1887); Southern Surgical and Gynecological Association (1889); and American Medical Association (1893).

Toward the end of his life McGuire, whose southernism remained steadfast, became outraged at what he became convinced was an antisouthern bias in textbooks published by northern publishing houses that were used in Virginia schools. He launched a campaign to eliminate the tainted texts from the state's schools. He rallied concerned citizens and Confederate veterans to his cause. A committee was appointed to examine school histories in use, the Virginia School Board was reorganized, and offending books were condemned and replaced with acceptable ones.

McGuire died in Richmond and was buried in Hollywood Cemetery, the final resting place of hundreds of Confederate soldiers from the battles fought around Richmond. Soon after his death, the Hunter McGuire Memorial Association was formed to erect a commemorative monument to McGuire's public and professional services. The response that ensued allowed the commissioning of a larger-than-life seated bronze statue. The Virginia legislature authorized its placement in Capitol Square on a site near the statue of Stonewall Jackson. It was unveiled on 7 January 1904.

• The two principal collections of McGuire's papers are located in the Huntington Library, San Marino, Calif., and the University of Virginia Archives, Charlottesville. Two biographies, John W. Schildt, *Hunter McGuire: Doctor in Gray* (1986), and Maurice F. Shaw, *Stonewall Jackson's Surgeon: Hunter Holmes McGuire, a Biography* (1993), although useful, fall considerably short of the mark. The best account of McGuire's life remains his son's recollections, Stuart McGuire, "Hunter Holmes McGuire, M.D., LL.D," *Annals of Medical History*, n.s., 10 (1938): 1–14, 136–61. An obituary is in the *Richmond Times*, 20 Sept. 1900.

JAMES O. BREEDEN

MCGUIRE, Peter J. (6 July 1852–18 Feb. 1906), labor leader, was born in New York City, the son of John J. McGuire, a porter, and Catherine Hand O'Riley. One of five children of the Irish immigrant couple, McGuire grew up in the tenements of the Lower East Side. When his father enlisted in the Union army in 1863, Peter left school to become the family breadwinner, hawking papers, shining shoes, and cleaning stores.

At the age of seventeen he began an apprenticeship in woodworking at a piano shop. At night he attended lectures at Cooper Union, a center for continuing education and a meeting place for radical and reform-movement activists. McGuire joined a political debating society and marched in the 1872 demonstration for the eight-hour workday. The following year he led a walkout of workers at his piano shop. Laid off in December 1873, McGuire emerged as a spokesman for the rapidly growing New York City organizations of the unemployed. His participation in the dramatic Tompkins Square rally of 13 January 1874 cemented his vocation as an organizer.

For the rest of the decade McGuire worked in finish shops and piano factories in order to finance his political activities. A gifted orator, he traveled widely to speak on behalf of the socialist Workingmen's party. He urged independent political action and the creation of a working-class party. McGuire managed electoral campaigns in Connecticut and received nine thousand votes when he ran for local office in Cincinnati despite having lived there for only six weeks. After mobilizing St. Louis workers during the 1877 railroad strike, McGuire was appointed deputy commissioner for a new Missouri State Bureau of Labor Statistics.

In August 1881 McGuire convened a meeting to found a national organization of carpenters. He was unanimously elected general secretary, the sole full-time position of the new Brotherhood of Carpenters and Joiners of America (renamed United Brotherhood of Carpenters and Joiners of America [UBCJA] seven years later). That year he set up the Brotherhood's national office in Philadelphia and moved his residence to Camden, New Jersey. The union grew slowly, from a membership of 2,042 in 1881 to 5,789 in 1885, but the militancy and dynamism of the 1886 and 1890 strikes for the eight-hour workday catapulted McGuire and the UBCJA into the forefront of the American labor movement. Membership topped 50,000 in 1890 as the union emerged as the single largest organization of any special trade in the world. Under McGuire the Carpenters Union combined the political vision of his reformer's background with the nuts-and-bolts focus of benefits unionism. The average wage for carpenters doubled during his two decades in office. By 1902 carpenters worked eight-hour days in nearly five hundred cities at a time when ten- and twelve-hour days were common in many industries.

As editor of the monthly *Carpenter* magazine, McGuire created one of the most influential labor journals of the day. He insisted that the union not "sink ourselves into a mere benevolent society or insurance company." He argued that unions should be primary schools for political education. Internal organizational debates were freely aired, and he printed articles by a variety of well-known political writers, including Eugene Debs, Henry George, and George McNeill. While he sharply criticized the sectarian character of the organized socialist parties, he continued to advocate labor's role in building a "co-operative commonwealth," a society free of class distinctions. At the 1894 American Federation of Labor convention, McGuire opposed the proposed Political Programme that endorsed governmental ownership of the means of production. His position drew fire from members and sympathizers of the Socialist Labor party. McGuire responded that he was a "socialist . . . of the trades union kind." Second only to Samuel Gompers, McGuire spoke for the American labor movement as a whole in the late 1800s. He was a pivotal force in the American Federation of Labor and the Knights of Labor and is generally considered the "Father of Labor Day." His belief in the importance of organization for all workers led him to devote considerable efforts to unions other than his own.

His success within the Carpenters Union laid the foundation for his downfall. McGuire's charismatic organizing style had drawn large numbers of carpenters into newly powerful local organizations in major cities across the country. Many building employers had reluctantly accepted the reality of unionism in their industry and sought labor peace by trading higher wages and shorter hours for more amicable relations with local unions. The rise of the "business agent," a full-time local union officer, was often accompanied by a shift from an organizing to an administrative framework. In the manner of a political ward boss, many business agents sought to maximize benefits for their members and demonstrated little concern for unorganized or organized workers outside the borders of the Carpenters Union. McGuire enthusiastically supported administrative efficiency and stability at the local level but not at the expense of a broader vision of worker solidarity and class-based politics.

The competing orientations clashed over McGuire's continuing role as head of the UBCJA. For the two years following the union's 1900 national convention, a group of officers schemed to remove McGuire from his post. On 24 July 1901 the General Executive Board charged McGuire with embezzlement and incompetence and suspended him as general secretary. Led by General President William Huber, a New York City business agent, and aided by several powerful employers, the anti-McGuire forces took advantage of the aging leader's alcoholism, liver disease, frail disposition, and primitive bookkeeping to seize the political initiative. In spite of the concerted campaign, the union's membership overwhelmingly rejected the General Executive Board's actions against McGuire in two successive national referenda. The ceaseless battle took its toll, however, and a beaten and haggard McGuire resigned from office at the union's 1902 national convention.

Peter McGuire's demise marked the end of the UBCJA as a beacon of the reform wing of the American labor movement and established the organization's subsequent identity as the leading voice of conservative craft unionism within the American Federation of Labor. The last years of McGuire's life were spent "in misery and poverty," according to UBCJA official and friend Arthur Quinn. "He was neglected and apparently forgotten by men of labor." He died in Camden, New Jersey, leaving his second wife, Christina Wolff, whom he had married in 1884, and four children.

• McGuire's lengthy testimonies before the U.S. Senate in 1883, the Congress on Industrial Conciliation and Arbitration in 1894, and the U.S. Industrial Commission in 1899, are available at the Tamiment Institute Library at New York University. The single best source of McGuire's writings is the *Carpenter*, the monthly magazine he edited from 1881 to 1902. The only full-length biography is David Lyon, "The World of P. J. McGuire" (Ph.D. diss., Univ. of Minnesota, 1972). Briefer accounts can be found in Mark Erlich, "Peter J. McGuire's Trade Unionism: Socialism of a Trades Union Kind," *Labor History* 24 (Spring 1983): 165–97, and "Peter J. McGuire: The Story of a Remarkable Trade Unionist," *Carpenter*, Mar. 1982, as well as a pamphlet written in 1946 by A. Charles Corotis and Charles Phillips, "The Life Story of a Forgotten Giant," available at the Tamiment Institute Library.

For the history of the UBCJA, see Robert Christie's excellent *Empire in Wood* (1956); Walter Galenson, *The United Brotherhood of Carpenters* (1983); and Thomas Brooks, *The Road to Dignity* (1981). General labor histories that discuss McGuire's career at length include John R. Commons et al., *History of Labour in the United States* (1921); Philip Taft, *The A.F. of L. in the Time of Gompers* (1957) and *Organized Labor in American History* (1964); Gerald Grob, *Workers and Utopia* (1961); William Dick, *Labor and Socialism in America: The Gompers Era* (1972); and Stuart Kaufman, *Samuel Gompers and the Origins of the American Federation of Labor* (1973).

MARK ERLICH

MCHENRY, James (16 Nov. 1753–3 May 1816), physician and merchant, was born in Ballymena, County Antrim, Ireland (present-day Northern Ireland), the son of Daniel McHenry, a merchant, and Agnes (maiden name unknown), both Scotch-Irish Presbyterians. James McHenry emigrated to America in 1771 and lived in Philadelphia with Captain William Allison, a sugar baker. In 1772 McHenry attended or was a tutor at the Newark Academy in Delaware, an institution incorporated by "Old Light" Presbyterians that had an English school offering "Merchants Accounts," navigation, and surveying. After the academy, McHenry studied medicine privately in Philadelphia with the prominent physician Benjamin Rush. In the meantime, McHenry's parents and his brother John had settled in America in 1772; the following year McHenry's father and brother established the Baltimore firm of Daniel McHenry and Son.

An ardent revolutionary, McHenry joined the American army as a volunteer assistant surgeon and in January 1776 was working in a Cambridge, Massachusetts, hospital. In August 1776 Congress appointed him a surgeon in the Fifth Pennsylvania Battalion, and in November he was captured with 2,000 other Americans at Fort Washington on Manhattan Island. Paroled in January 1777, he resided in Baltimore, then his home, until exchanged in March 1778. He reported to the "Flying Hospital" at Valley Forge as senior surgeon, but in May 1778 General George Washington appointed him his assistant secretary without military rank. Although McHenry always described himself as a doctor, his medical career had for all practical purposes ended. Entering the inner circle of Washington's aides, McHenry developed lasting friendships with Washington and Colonel Alexander Hamilton. Washington described McHenry as a "Man of Letters," honorable, amiable, and polished; McHenry even wrote poetry. In August 1780 McHenry became the marquis de Lafayette's aide-de-camp, and, after much lobbying, he was commissioned a major in May 1781, the rank dating from October 1780. Through his friendships with Baltimore merchants and Maryland Governor Thomas Sim Lee, McHenry obtained supplies for Lafayette's division and in October was with Lafayette at Yorktown. McHenry left the army in December 1781 and in 1783 was a founding member of the Society of the Cincinnati.

In September 1781 McHenry was elected to a five-year term in the state senate from Maryland's Western Shore. He attended sessions from 1781 to 1784, resigning his seat in January 1786. As a senator, he opposed paper money and supported the federal impost of 1781 and a protective tariff. McHenry was a justice of the peace of Baltimore County, 1782–1784, and a justice of that county's Orphan's Court, 1783–1784. In January 1784 he married Margaret Caldwell, the stepdaughter of Captain Allison; they had four children.

The Maryland legislature elected McHenry to the Confederation Congress in May 1783 to fill a vacant seat and reelected him in November 1783 and December 1784. In Congress until the following December, McHenry advocated the movement of the federal capital to Annapolis, believing that this would economically benefit Baltimore. Even though McHenry wanted Congress to have sole jurisdiction over foreign commerce and interstate trade, in August 1785 he was reluctant to grant this power because he feared that the North would commercially overwhelm the South.

In the fall of 1786 an association of Baltimore mechanics, supporting protective tariffs and freedom of religion, endorsed McHenry for the state senate, but he lost the election. This loss was softened on 26 May 1787 when the legislature appointed him to the Constitutional Convention, meeting in Philadelphia to revise and amend the Articles of Confederation. McHenry attended from 28 to 31 May, missed all of June and July because of his brother's illness, and returned on 6 August, remaining until 17 September, when he reluctantly signed the new Constitution. A moderate nationalist, McHenry spoke little, but he tried unsuccessfully to resolve the striking differences within Maryland's delegation. He opposed a simple majority vote on navigation acts and heavy taxes on commerce and advocated the establishment of uniform imposts, excises, and duties throughout America, if adopted by Congress. McHenry kept a valuable set of notes of the Convention's debates.

In late November 1787 Maryland's convention delegates were requested by the state House of Delegates to give information on the convention. Acquitting himself "beyond the most sanguine hopes of his friends," McHenry stressed the weakness of the Articles of Confederation and the Constitution's advantages to Maryland's commercial and manufacturing interests. In early April 1788 McHenry and another Federalist, both opponents of prior amendments, were elected (amid charges of fraud) to represent the town of Baltimore in the state convention, where later that month they voted to ratify the Constitution. In October 1788 McHenry and another Federalist were elected to represent the town in the state house of delegates, defeating two Antifederalists (including Samuel Chase) who supported amendments, in a bitterly fought election. In October 1789 McHenry was reelected. He voted for bills providing for the gradual manumission of slaves and for admitting Quakers to office by permitting an affirmation rather than the taking of an oath.

President George Washington repeatedly asked McHenry's advice on federal appointments in Maryland; McHenry, an outright Federalist partisan, became a leading dispenser of administration patronage in Maryland. Both Washington and Treasury Secretary Alexander Hamilton thought that McHenry was more valuable in this capacity than in a diplomatic post that McHenry had sought. Between 1789 and 1795 McHenry successfully nominated or recommended thirty men, many of them former soldiers, for federal jobs in Maryland. In the fall of 1791 McHenry, at Hamilton's urging, ran for and was elected to the state senate. Four years later, the legislature chartered a bank in Baltimore that McHenry recommended to that body in an anonymous 45-page pamphlet titled *A Brief Exposition of the Leading Principles of a Bank*.

In January 1796 President Washington offered McHenry the position of secretary of war after three others had rejected it. McHenry accepted; took the oath of office in February; and divested himself of two mercantile partnerships, one at a loss of £3,000 and the other at an annual loss of £1,000. Nevertheless, he remained a wealthy man, having inherited by 1790 the mercantile and landed property of his father and brother. John Adams, Washington's successor, retained McHenry. McHenry's successes as secretary came early. He put into operation a May 1796 act of Congress that changed the organization of the army from a legionary structure to one organized by combat functions, thereby creating the "New Army." He also created comprehensive rules and regulations for army life. In 1797 and 1798 McHenry reorganized the frontier constabulary, promoted the development of arsenals, and made the secretary the department's sole authority on financial matters. His well-crafted reports stressed the need for a strong military establishment.

McHenry's disloyalty to President Adams and the complexities of his job eventually brought him down. He frequently sought and followed the advice of Hamilton, Adams's bitter enemy. In the spring of 1798 Congress began to prepare for war with France, and Adams appointed Washington commander in chief. McHenry's political maneuvering forced Adams to accept Hamilton as second in command to Washington, a humiliation Adams did not forget. On matters relating to the "New Army," Adams was uncooperative, making decisions slowly, if at all. McHenry even aroused the displeasure of Washington and Hamilton, both of whom seriously questioned McHenry's fitness for office. McHenry also earned the hostility of the Republican party by staffing the army only with Federalists and by using some regular troops (a standing army) to suppress Fries's Rebellion (1799). An ineffective administrator, he became hopelessly mired in detail, incapable of delegating authority. His health was also a problem; he had suffered from a "bilious fever" since 1782.

In late 1799 McHenry ran afoul of Adams again as he and Secretary of State Timothy Pickering tried to prevent Adams's peace commission from leaving for France. On his own authority, an angry Adams ordered the peace commissioners to France, thereby opening a rift in the Federalist party. McHenry was appalled that Adams had ignored the heads of departments who also held "a high and responsible station." Finally, in May 1800 Adams confronted McHenry and brutally browbeat him, accusing him of constantly plotting with Hamilton against his administration. Adams demanded and received McHenry's resignation.

McHenry, the quintessential insider with a superb gift for friendship, never held another public office. He retired to "Fayetteville" (named for Lafayette), his country estate near Baltimore, and engaged in Federalist politics as a leader of the Washington Benevolent Society, a charitable organization fronting for the party. McHenry was a Mason from 1806 to 1809, and he compiled and published the *Baltimore Directory, and Citizens Register, for 1807.* A communicant of the First Presbyterian Church of Baltimore, McHenry was elected president of the Bible Society of Baltimore in 1813. A year earlier his legs had become paralyzed, and by 1814 he was a helpless invalid. McHenry died at his home near Baltimore.

• Collections of McHenry's papers are in the Maryland Historical Society, the Library of Congress, and the William L. Clements Library at the University of Michigan, Ann Arbor. His papers as secretary of war were destroyed by fire in November 1800. Of vital importance is Bernard C. Steiner, *The Life and Correspondence of James McHenry* (1907). Also useful are Frederick J. Brown, *A Sketch of the Life of Dr. James McHenry* (1877), and Emily Stone Whiteley, *Washington and His Aides-de-Camp* (1936). Additional published McHenry correspondence can be found in *A Sidelight on History, Being the Letters of James McHenry . . . to Thomas Sim Lee . . . Written During the Yorktown Campaign, 1781*, foreword by Sarah Redwood Lee (1931), and Harold C. Syrett et al., eds., *The Papers of Alexander Hamilton* (27 vols., 1961–1987). McHenry's notes of the debates of the Constitutional Convention are in Max Farrand, ed., *The Records of the Federal Convention of 1787* (4 vols., 1937).

On McHenry as secretary of war, see Richard H. Kohn, *Eagle and Sword: The Federalists and the Creation of the Military Establishment in America, 1783–1802* (1975). On Maryland politics, see Philip A. Crowl, *Maryland during and after the Revolution: A Political and Economic Study* (1943); L. Marx Renzulli, Jr., *Maryland: The Federalist Years* (1972); and Charles G. Steffen, *The Mechanics of Baltimore: Workers and Politics in the Age of Revolution, 1763–1812* (1984). On national and regional politics, see Stephen G. Kurtz, *The Presidency of John Adams: The Collapse of Federalism, 1795–1800* (1957); Norman K. Risjord, *Chesapeake Politics, 1781–1800* (1978); and Stanley Elkins and Eric McKitrick, *The Age of Federalism: The Early American Republic, 1788–1800* (1993).

GASPARE J. SALADINO

MCHENRY, James (20 Dec. 1785–21 July 1845), poet, novelist, and literary critic was born in Larne, County Antrim, Ireland, the son of George McHenry and Mary Smiley. Little can be ascertained about his early life. Like Alexander Pope, in whose neoclassical tradition McHenry was to place himself, he was hunchbacked, the deformity probably being the result of a spinal injury in his boyhood. Early biographical accounts say that he held degrees in both theology and medicine. A poem dated 21 October 1810, "On Leaving Ireland for the University of Glasgow," refers to his pursuit of science as the reason for leaving Ireland, although neither the University of Glasgow nor the Royal Faculty of Physicians and Surgeons has any record of his studying medicine in Glasgow. It is possible that he gained his medical knowledge as an apprentice to a practicing physician, a common practice of the day.

McHenry's interest in literature began early in his life. In 1808 in Belfast he published *The Bard of Erin*, a small volume containing seventeen poems on Irish themes. In one poem, "Black Cave Shore," he reveals that in 1798–1799 he had been under the tutelage of a clergyman who encouraged his poetic ambitions. The young McHenry's interest in Irish themes was shown again when he published in Glasgow *Patrick* (1810), a narrative poem in heroic couplets. Shortly after this publication he began practicing medicine in Larne. A year later he married Jane Robinson, a woman of English stock, and after the marriage the McHenrys settled in Belfast; they had five children. In 1816, determined to try his fortune, McHenry emigrated with his wife and infant son to the United States, living in Baltimore and then Butler County, Pennsylvania, and Pittsburgh, before settling in Philadelphia in 1823, where as a doctor, draper, politician, and man of letters he remained for nineteen years.

In 1819, while suffering personal misfortunes, McHenry wrote *The Pleasures of Friendship*, a didactic poem undoubtedly influenced by Thomas Campbell's *Pleasures of Hope* (1799). Published in 1822, this was McHenry's first major poem written in the United States; it was well received and enjoyed great popularity, reaching a seventh edition in 1836. *Waltham* (1823), a poetic "tale" presumably based on General George Washington's experience at Valley Forge, is one of the first poems on American patriotic themes. The same year McHenry also published two historical romances. *The Wilderness*, subtitled variously *or, The Youthful Days of Washington* and *or, Braddock's Times*, was written under the pseudonym "Solomon Secondsight" and issued in London. Critics praised McHenry for his account of Protestant Ulstermen in revolutionary America and for his embodiment of Washington and other patriots in the popular novel form. *The Spectre of the Forest; or, Annals of the Housatonic* is a romance based on seventeenth-century witchcraft delusion in New England.

In 1823 McHenry founded the *American Monthly Magazine* (not to be confused with N. P. Willis's *American Monthly Magazine*) as a Philadelphia rival of the *North American Review*. Intended to appeal to "those who are desirous of encouraging the literature of the United States," the magazine failed after a full year of publication because of financial reasons, but not before affording McHenry his first opportunity as a literary critic or before publishing a poem by the youthful Henry Wadsworth Longfellow. McHenry's taste in poetry was very conservative: he supported Samuel Johnson's definition that poetry is "metrical composition" and disputed Hugh Blair's assumption that poetry is "the language of passion, or of enlivened imagination," concluding that William Wordsworth and Lord Byron were the "Shadwells" of the day. Politically, however, he was liberal, supporting the Monroe Doctrine and the Greek struggle for independence.

McHenry continued writing fiction, publishing *O'Halloran; or, The Insurgent Chief* (1824), the first American novel set in Northern Ireland, and *The Hearts of Steel* (1825), an Irish historical tale concerned with the evils of absentee landlordism. After a trip to Europe, he launched an unsuccessful career as a playwright. *The Usurper* (1827), a blank verse tragedy set in pre-Christian Ireland, opened at the Chestnut Street Theatre on 16 December 1827. It failed, although it was called by the *Irish Shield* "an admirable tragedy, which in spite of some defects in incident and character, has in it . . . more force of expression, depth of tenderness and originality of conception, than any American production." McHenry's church prevented him from receiving communion until he gave up the writing of drama. He refused and the next year wrote a comedy, *Love and Poetry; or, A Modern Genius* (1828), the moral of which was to "discourage the unfledged poet." In October 1828 he was naturalized as a U.S. citizen.

Meanwhile, McHenry published poems in literary magazines such as the *Album and Ladies' Weekly Gazette*, *The Casket*, and *Working Man's Advocate*, and resumed writing novels, publishing *The Betrothed of Wyoming* (1830), which deals with strife between Tories and colonists; and the semihistorical *Meredith; or, The Mystery of Meschianza* (1831), which is set in Philadelphia and features Quakers as leading characters. In the 1830s he also became the leading poetry reviewer for the *American Quarterly Review*. Led by his neoclassic bias, McHenry in 1832 made unmeasured attacks of William Cullen Bryant and N. P. Willis as imitators of Wordsworth, and in 1834 he asserted that no good poetry had appeared in the previous five years, a lustrum that saw the publication of Edgar Allan Poe's *Poems* (1831) and Bryant's *Poems* (1832), among other literary works. These reviews stirred up so much criticism—drawing fire from Sidney Willard's *American Monthly Review* and Lewis G. Clark and Willis G. Clark's *Knickerbocker*—that McHenry was effectually finished as a critic.

His final creative attempt was a ten-book epic, *Antediluvians; or, The World Destroyed* (1839), a blank verse chronicle of the Flood. *Blackwood's* scathingly reviewed it and the *Knickerbocker* called it a "tuneless literary abortion . . . which has fallen still-born from the English and American press." In 1843 McHenry returned to his native Ireland, where he served in the Londonderry consulate. He died in Larne two years later.

McHenry was a man with a wide range of interests who developed considerable popularity and reputation. He contributed to American drama its first play on an Irish legendary theme, and he was among the first writers to work with American patriotic themes. His best contribution seems to be his shorter lyric poems, which he valued least of his work. As a literary critic, McHenry held to consistent principles; but because he was a classicist living in the Romantic period, he has not enjoyed the lasting respect accorded some of his contemporaries.

• McHenry published much of his lyric poetry in the periodicals of the period; see, for example, the *Album & Ladies' Weekly Gazette*, 25 Apr. 1827; his own *American Monthly Magazine*, Jan.-Dec. 1824; *The Casket*, Jan. 1828, Apr. 1828; *Literary Messenger*, Oct. 1841; *National Pilot*, 13 June 1822; and *Working Man's Advocate*, 28 Aug. 1830. Examples of McHenry's literary criticism can be found in the *American Monthly Magazine*, Jan.-Dec. 1824, and the *American Quarterly Review*, Mar. 1832, June 1834.

The best discussion of McHenry's life is in Robert E. Blanc, *James McHenry (1785–1845): Playwright and Novelist* (1939), which includes an extensive bibliography of his major works. For selected reviews of McHenry's work by his contemporaries, see *American Monthly Review*, May 1832; *Blackwood's*, July 1839; *Irish Shield*, Oct. 1829; *Knickerbocker*, July 1834, June 1841, Apr. 1859; *The Minerva*, 8 Mar. 1823, 4 Oct. 1823; *Philadelphia Monthly Magazine*, Nov. 1828; *Port Folio*, Oct. 1822; *United States Magazine, and Literary and Political Repository*, Jan. 1823; and F. W. Wemyss, *Theatrical Biography; or, Twenty-six Years of the Life of an Actor and Manager* (1847). Later discussions of McHenry's work are in Edward E. Chielens, ed., *American Literary Magazines: The Eighteenth and Nineteenth Centuries*, (1986); F. L. Mott, *A History of American Magazines, 1741–1850* (1930); A. H. Quinn, *A History of the American Drama from the Beginning to the Civil War* (1923). An obituary is in the *Philadelphia Public Ledger*, 12 Aug. 1845.

DAVID BOOCKER

MCILVAINE, Charles Pettit (18 Jan. 1799–13 Mar. 1873), Episcopal bishop and evangelist, was born in Burlington, New Jersey, the son of Maria Reed and Joseph McIlvaine, a prominent attorney. After attending a local academy, McIlvaine studied at the College of New Jersey in Princeton, from which he graduated with high honors in 1816. During those years he developed a deeply personal affirmation of religious principles and decided to become an Episcopal priest. He read theology at home until entering Princeton Theological Seminary in 1817, there being as yet no divinity school of his denomination in the country. Poor health forced him to leave after eighteen months, and he continued private study until 1820, when he received ordination as a deacon. While at home he organized and superintended one of the nation's first Sunday schools. In 1820 McIlvaine accepted an invitation to serve as rector of Christ Church in Georgetown, District of Columbia. His preaching soon attracted public notice, and in 1821 he also served as chaplain to the U.S. Senate for a one-year term. In 1822 he married Emily Coxe, a friend since childhood; they had four children. The following year he was finally ordained a priest. Pursuing pastoral duties for a short time longer, he made an important career decision late in 1824, moving the following January to the U.S. Military Academy.

The post McIlvaine filled at West Point was that of chaplain and professor of geography, history, and ethics. Always a fervent advocate of emotional religious experience, he preached boldly to officers and cadets on campus, awakening deep feelings in many and causing some to worry that his influence might inhibit martial valor. Such fears were borne out in at least one case. During a season of quickened interest that some called a revival, his preaching affected cadet Leonidas Polk enough to cause him soon to resign his commission and enter the Episcopal priesthood. In 1838, when Polk was made missionary bishop in Louisiana, McIlvaine preached the sermon at his consecration. McIlvaine ended his controversial tenure at West Point by accepting in 1827 the rectorship of St. Ann's Church in Brooklyn, New York. Several invitations had tempted him by then, including that of the presidency of the College of William and Mary, but St. Ann's provided a venerable setting for an influential ministry over the next six years. In 1831–1832 McIlvaine also held a lectureship at the University of the City of New York, where he published a series of essays on the evidences and central values of Christianity. His lectures were published in 1832, and the book went through numerous reprints.

In 1831 events began to move McIlvaine's lifework in another direction. He was elected bishop of Ohio, succeeding Philander Chase, who had recently resigned. He was consecrated in office the following year but did not move to the episcopal residence at Gambier until 1833. In addition to acting ex officio as president of Kenyon College, the new bishop traveled extensively in his diocese, enduring primitive conditions that taxed his precarious health. McIlvaine never enjoyed a robust constitution and often toured abroad, especially England, where he established important contacts in Anglican circles. He became known on both sides of the Atlantic as a staunch "low" churchman, advocating evangelical preaching rather than reliance on sacraments or ceremonies. Though strenuous in ruling his diocese, he retained support among the majority of his followers. One famous example of his stern, imperious manner occurred in 1846, when he refused to consecrate a church in Columbus because it featured a stone altar instead of a modest table for use in the communion service. Such conflict was symbolic of McIlvaine's theological perspective that highlighted modern evangelical faith instead of medieval ritualism. His annual addresses to diocesan clergy stressed themes like justification by faith, the importance of promoting evangelical knowledge, and his own conviction that churches needed fresher and greater revivals of religion. He represented those emphases at nationwide General Conventions too, leading low church clerics from 1844 to 1871.

Though outspoken and heavy-handed, McIlvaine was nevertheless able to keep the affection of most people within his jurisdiction. He also maintained a large number of acquaintances in England. In 1861 English sentiment was inflamed when the *Trent*, a British mail packet, was halted on the high seas by a U.S. warship. Federal forces performed this questionable act in order to prevent Confederate diplomats from reaching their European posts. Most British citizens viewed this breach of international law as an insult. President Abraham Lincoln asked McIlvaine to use his good offices to help smooth things over. This mission as ambassador without portfolio succeeded to some extent in retaining British support of the Union. Beyond that, McIlvaine's lasting image is one whose evangelical theology contained a simple message of salvation through faith, where any stress on ecclesiology substituted churches for Christ, priests for the gospel, superstition for the liberty of enlightened religion. He died in Florence, Italy, while journeying yet again in an attempt to restore his health.

• The bulk of McIlvaine's correspondence, his diary, and materials about the diocese are housed in the Kenyon College library in Gambier, Ohio. The bishop's publications include *The Evidences of Christianity* (1832), *Oxford Divinity: Compared with That of the Romish and Anglican Churches* (1841), *Reasons for Refusing to Consecrate a Church Having an Altar Instead of a Communion Table* (1846), *No Priest, No Sacrifice, No Altar but Christ* (1850), and *Righteous by Faith* (1862). The chief source of information about this prelate is William Carus, ed., *Memorials of the Right Reverend Charles Pettit McIlvaine* (1882). Additional information is available in George F. Smythe, *A History of the Diocese of Ohio until the Year 1918* (1931). An obituary is in the *New York Times*, 15 Mar. 1873.

HENRY WARNER BOWDEN

MCINTIRE, Samuel (c. 1757–6 Feb. 1811), carpenter and architect, was born in Salem, Massachusetts, the son of Joseph Mackintire, a carpenter, and Sarah

Ruck. By the age of nine he was working with some regularity as a carpenter, laying flooring, installing gutters, and making household repairs. His father and older brother Joseph, both carpenters, evidently taught him the trade and allowed him to work with them when he was not at school. By age twenty-one he was a mature carpenter working for wages equal to those of his brother, and he had married Elizabeth Field (1778). Soon the third brother, Angier, joined to form a triumvirate that performed many solid commissions for building or renovating the houses of wealthy local merchants. During the Revolution they also worked on board ships in the port of Salem. At some point he changed the spelling of his last name from Mackintire to McIntire.

The large number of original drawings and documents concerning the McIntires in the collection of the Essex Institute allows the reconstruction of a very clear picture of Samuel McIntire's career and an assessment of the value of his contributions. His work, with or without his brothers, falls into three periods identified by major changes in his designs. In the decade of the 1780s his plans for buildings are roughly drawn and contain many irregularities alien to the work of a close follower of Palladio, the Italian classicist who also inspired Thomas Jefferson. McIntire's houses are planned axially with a central door and bisecting corridor, but rooms vary in size and do not maintain the rigid formality of traditional Georgian houses. Exterior elevations correspond in symmetry, fenestration, and the application of classical orders to any number of houses built contemporaneously in the Boston area. His Peirce-Nichols House (1782) is an outstanding example. Plainness is stressed by using the simple Doric order. Interior architectural embellishment, all tastefully carved, is copied from earlier English sources of the midcentury Georgian period.

The second phase of McIntire's work began in the 1790s, when he suddenly became acquainted with the advanced work of Charles Bulfinch in Boston. Bulfinch's drawings, done meticulously with color wash, were a revelation to him. He imitated the new manner (actually copied by Bulfinch from what he had seen in England and in English architectural books) and found that without much extra effort he could do equally fine drawings. Along with his improved presentation drawings came a close study of recent architectural books that had become available in Boston and even in Salem. He bought a copy of William Pain's *The Practical House Carpenter*, which drew on the fashionable Adam style for many of its designs. In this way both Bulfinch and McIntire introduced the delicate, beautifully carved Adam motifs to America, using them for mantelpieces, door architraves, and other moldings. In the northeastern states decorative parts of the so-called Federal style are largely derived from Robert Adam.

In 1795 the richest merchant in Salem, Elias Hasket Derby (1739–1799), gave his wife permission to build a new and very large mansion. Several architects contributed plans, but the commission went to McIntire, even though Bulfinch wanted the job. It is not known why Derby chose McIntire rather than the famous Bostonian, but McIntire could probably do the work more cheaply, and his drawings looked equally good to Mrs. Derby. In any case McIntire and his brothers constructed the mansion. Although it was demolished less than two decades later, owing to financial difficulties, the mansion was famous for its beautiful carved decorations and its fine proportions.

From 1800 to the end of his life, McIntire continued to show proficiency in drawing while remaining somewhat unprofessional in planning interior spaces. In perhaps his best house of this final period, designed for John Gardner (1804), on Essex Street in Salem, the plan attempts to cope with the use of spaces but fails to make comfortable spatial adjustments. The exterior is of brick and has a very fine semicircular entrance portico with remarkable carving of capitals. The architectural decoration on the interior is equal to that of the great Robert Adam.

It is interesting to note that until 1800 McIntire worked, as did other artisans, for daily wages. After 1800 he worked only on a commission basis, thus raising himself to the rank of a professional. He had become recognized for what he was: a man trained as an artisan but with talents far beyond those of his trade. Other noteworthy buildings designed by McIntire include the Joshua Ward House (1784–1787), Salem Courthouse (1785–1786), the Nathan Read House (1793), the Lyman House in Waltham (1793), the Ezekiel Hersey Derby House (1800), South Church (1803–1809), the Jonathan Hodges House (1805), Hamilton Hall (1805–1807), and the Gideon Tucker House (1808–1809). These and many more graced the streets of Salem, making it a source for architects of the late nineteenth century searching for models to inspire a new interest in what they called Colonial architecture.

McIntire derived great pleasure from carving wood, particularly after 1800 when he produced elaborate figure heads and taffrails for ships, chair backs and other small carvings for furniture, at least two portrait busts (John Winthrop, Voltaire), a large profile medallion of George Washington, and numerous American eagles.

If McIntire had been only an outstanding carpenter-architect he would not have had the immense respect he gained in Salem from persons of every class. From all accounts he was a loyal citizen, unprejudiced, better educated than other artisans, and a staunch supporter of his church, where he arranged music for singing and played the cello.

McIntire left a comfortable estate for his wife when he died in Salem. The Reverend William Bentley, whose diary has contributed so much to the understanding of early Federal Salem, eulogized McIntire thus: "This day Salem was deprived of one of the most ingenious men it had in it. He was distinguished for Genius in Architecture, Sculpture, and Musick; Modest and sweet Manners rendered him pleasing; Industry and Integrity respectable; He professed the Religion of Jesus in his entrance on manly life; and proved its excellence by virtuous Principles and unblemished conduct."

• With only a few exceptions, all McIntire's extant drawings and documents are at the Essex Institute, Salem, Mass. The largest amount of biographical material and the best discussion of McIntire's professional life are in Fiske Kimball, *Mr. Samuel McIntire, Carver, the Architect of Salem* (1940; repr. 1966). Genealogy is covered by Robert H. McIntire, *Descendants of Philip McIntire* (1941). A variety of interesting articles are in Benjamin W. Labaree, ed., *Samuel McIntire: A Bicentennial Symposium 1757–1957* (1957). Several articles by Fiske Kimball and by Mabel Swan discuss furniture and other wood-carving by McIntire (see bibliography in Labaree).

PAUL F. NORTON

MCINTOSH, John Baillie (6 June 1829–29 June 1888), soldier, was born at Fort Brooke (present-day Tampa), Florida, the son of James Simmons McIntosh, a colonel in the U.S. Army, and Eliza Matthews. Enlisting in the navy as a midshipman in April 1848, the teenager saw action aboard the USS *Saratoga* during the last months of the war with Mexico, a conflict in which his father lost his life. Having come to view some aspects of naval service as "distasteful," he resigned on 24 May 1850 and settled in New Brunswick, New Jersey. Later that year he married Amelia Stout, with whose father McIntosh formed a business partnership. The marriage produced one child, a daughter who died in 1861.

Despite family ties to the South (his older brother, James, became a Confederate general), when the Civil War broke out in April 1861 John McIntosh cast his lot with the Union. Early in June he obtained a commission in the Second U.S. Dragoons; two months later he transferred to the Fifth Cavalry, in which he served on the Virginia Peninsula. Throughout the Peninsula campaign McIntosh was cited for gallantry and combativeness, but he found little opportunity to distinguish himself in the subsequent campaign in western Maryland that culminated in the battle of Antietam.

On 15 November 1862 McIntosh succeeded William Woods Averell as commander of the Third Pennsylvania Cavalry. His new command quickly became one of the most effective regiments of volunteer horsemen in the Army of the Potomac. From the start McIntosh proved not only an able tactician but also a highly popular officer; one of his men called him "splendid" and "dashing," while another lauded him as "the bravest of the brave."

McIntosh served competently in a limited role at Fredericksburg on 13 December and was conspicuous in action at Kelly's Ford on 17 March 1863, the first battle in which Union horsemen proved a match for the cavaliers of J. E. B. Stuart. He was one of few participants to emerge with his reputation unscathed from Major General George Stoneman's failed spring 1863 expedition toward Richmond. When his former brigade commander, General Averell, lost his command following that raid—an outcome McIntosh ascribed to army politics—McIntosh threatened to resign in protest; only the entreaties of other superiors persuaded him to remain in the field.

His decision to remain enabled McIntosh to play a conspicuous role in one of the war's pivotal operations. Detached duty in Washington, D.C., prevented him from participating in the 9 June battle at Brandy Station, the opening engagement of the Gettysburg campaign and the largest mounted clash in North American history. Two days later the cavalry was reorganized, and McIntosh received command of a six-regiment brigade in Brigadier General David McMurtrie Gregg's Second Division, Cavalry Corps, Army of the Potomac. He led his new command in brilliant fashion on 2–3 July outside Gettysburg, helping Gregg parry a thrust against the Union rear by Stuart's cavalry in conjunction with Major General George E. Pickett's infantry attack on the Federal center atop Cemetery Ridge.

Late in 1863 McIntosh was placed on inactive duty, the result of a fall from his horse. When partially recovered, he supervised a cavalry depot in Washington. He returned to the field at the outset of Ulysses S. Grant's Overland campaign, fighting in the Wilderness, on Major General Philip H. Sheridan's Richmond Raid, at Haw's Shop, and in the early battles and expeditions around Petersburg. On 21 July 1864 he was appointed brigadier general of volunteers, a promotion his commanders considered long overdue.

Sent to the Shenandoah Valley early in August, McIntosh won plaudits for his performance in the early action of 19 September at Third Winchester, where he received a severe wound that cost him a leg. He finished the war as a brevet major general in both the regular and volunteer services. During the postwar reorganization of the army McIntosh gained the lieutenant colonelcy of the Forty-second U.S. Infantry. At that rank he also served as governor of the soldiers' home at Washington, D.C. (1867–1868), and as superintendent of Indian Affairs in California (1869–1870). On 30 July 1870 he was permitted to retire as a brigadier general. He returned to New Brunswick, where he quietly spent the balance of his life.

McIntosh remains one of the lesser-known figures of the Civil War, despite the variety and magnitude of his contributions to the Union cavalry in the eastern theater. His most conspicuous performance came on the third day at Gettysburg, when he built a formidable barrier against Stuart's advance and maintained it through judicious use of mounted and dismounted troopers and horse batteries, shoring up threatened sectors in timely fashion and taking the offensive as opportunities arose. Superiors as diverse as Averell, Gregg, Sheridan, and James Harrison Wilson considered him one of their most reliable subordinates. Still, McIntosh waited a long time for promotion to brigadier general and never rose above brigade command, a failure partially explained by his lack of a West Point diploma and of active political support in Washington.

Though plagued by an excitable temperament that sometimes expressed itself in violent bursts of anger,

McIntosh maintained the respect and confidence of his troopers. Perhaps the most dramatic evidence of his popularity was a petition that numerous members of his brigade sent to the War Department in January 1864, seeking promotion for "a polished gentleman, a strict disciplinarian, and an earnest Soldier."

• A large collection of McIntosh's wartime and postwar correspondence is in the John Hay Library, Brown University. His Civil War campaign reports can be found in *The War of the Rebellion: Official Records of the Union and Confederate Armies* (128 vols., 1880–1901). Glimpses of his wartime service are offered in William Brooke Rawle, comp., *The History of the Third Pennsylvania Cavalry* (1905); James Harrison Wilson, *Under the Old Flag* (2 vols., 1912); and David McMurtrie Gregg, *The Second Cavalry Division of the Army of the Potomac in the Gettysburg Campaign* (1907). More recent operational studies that highlight McIntosh include Stephen Z. Starr, *The Union Cavalry in the Civil War* (3 vols., 1979–1985), and Edward G. Longacre, *The Cavalry at Gettysburg* (1986). For substantial obituaries, see the *New York Herald*, 1 July 1888, and the *Army and Navy Journal*, 7 July 1888.

EDWARD G. LONGACRE

MCINTOSH, Lachlan (5 Mar. 1727–20 Feb. 1806), planter and Continental army officer, was born in Badenoch, Inverness-shire, Scotland, the son of clan chieftain John McIntosh Mohr and Margaret (or Marjorie) Fraser. McIntosh arrived in Georgia in January 1736 as part of a shipload of Highland Scots sent to guard the colony's southern frontier. Led by McIntosh's father, the expedition founded the Altamaha River town of Darien, which was a military center during the War of Jenkins's Ear. In 1748 McIntosh went to Charleston, South Carolina, where he met Henry Laurens, who would remain his close friend and adviser. He soon returned to Georgia and over the next two decades established one of the largest and most profitable rice plantations in the region. In 1756 he married Sarah Threadcraft, and they had eight children.

McIntosh served briefly in the colonial assembly, but he had little interest in politics beyond the local level. While he did not oppose British attempts to regulate trade after the French and Indian War, by 1775 he had thrown his lot with the Whigs and was recognized as their leader in the southern part of the colony. A member of Georgia's provincial congress, he was the compromise selection to head the state's continental battalion in January 1776, acquiring the rank of colonel. McIntosh gathered what troops he could and blocked British efforts to secure supplies in Savannah. He also attempted to protect the state's exposed frontier, but shortages of men and supplies made his task all but impossible. He was able to lead a raid into Florida and disrupt enemy supply sources, but it provided only temporary relief from pressure being applied by the British and their Indian allies.

McIntosh's inability to secure the state was criticized by more radical Whigs, led by Button Gwinnett. Tensions between McIntosh and Gwinnett grew to the extent that in May 1777 their differences were settled in a duel; McIntosh was wounded and Gwinnett killed. Friends in the Continental Congress had McIntosh transferred from the state and out of the reach of his political enemies. He joined George Washington at Valley Forge in December 1777 and was put in command of the North Carolina Brigade. In the spring he inspected military hospitals in the area, and in May 1778 he was sent to Fort Pitt to command the Western Department. Washington hoped McIntosh could balance the demands of Virginia and Pennsylvania groups who wished to dominate the postwar Ohio Valley; though the Georgian was not entirely successful in this regard, he was able to build two western outposts (Fort McIntosh and Fort Laurens) that gave the United States a presence in the region important in peace negotiations with the British.

Learning his family had been taken prisoner when Savannah fell in December 1778, General McIntosh requested a transfer home. Arriving in Augusta in July, he found himself again in the middle of a political dispute between the survivors of Gwinnett's party and his own supporters. In the fall of 1779 he led Georgia and South Carolina Continentals against Savannah in the doomed Franco-American attack. Shortly thereafter he left for Charleston and the Continental army under General Benjamin Lincoln. While there McIntosh learned that he had been suspended from command on the basis of information sent to Congress by the Georgia assembly and Governor George Walton; it was charged that the people had "such a Repugnance" to McIntosh that they would not serve under him. Before he could respond, however, Charleston fell in May 1780, and he was taken prisoner. Released in the summer of 1781, McIntosh set out to regain his post and to avenge the insult to his honor. Finally the Georgia assembly and the Continental Congress cleared him of charges, but he never felt his enemies had been punished sufficiently for the assault on his character. Later McIntosh held a number of appointed offices, including commissioner of Loyalist estates; delegate to the Convention of Beaufort, which negotiated the Georgia–South Carolina boundary; and state representative to treat with the Indians at Galphinton (1785) and Hopewell (1785). He also served as president of the Georgia Society of the Cincinnati. However, his financial losses during the war were considerable, and though he moved his plantation operation from Darien to Skidaway Island, nearer Savannah, he never recovered his prewar prosperity. He died in Savannah.

• The largest collections of McIntosh papers are in the Georgia Historical Society and the University of Georgia Library, Athens. These collections have been edited by Lilla M. Hawes and published as *The Papers of Lachlan McIntosh*, Georgia Historical Society, *Collections*, vol. 12 (1957), and *Lachlan McIntosh Papers in the University of Georgia Libraries* (1968). See also Kenneth Coleman, *The American Revolution in Georgia* (1958); Edward J. Cashin, "George Walton and the Forged Letter," *Georgia Historical Quarterly* 62 (1978): 133–45; and Harvey H. Jackson, *Lachlan McIntosh and the Politics of Revolutionary Georgia* (1979).

HARVEY H. JACKSON

MCINTOSH, Maria Jane (1803–25 Feb. 1878), author, was born in Sunbury, Liberty County, Georgia, the daughter of Major Lachlan McIntosh, a soldier and lawyer, and his fifth wife, Mary Moore Maxwell, the widow of John Butler Maxwell. McIntosh was raised primarily by her mother, her father having died when she was three. She was educated at Sunbury Academy and Baisden's Bluff Academy in nearby McIntosh County. Her mother died in 1823, and McIntosh managed the family's Georgia plantation estate for twelve years before leaving Sunbury to live with her sister, Anne Ward, and later her half brother, Captain James McKay McIntosh, both of whom lived in New York.

When she lost her fortune in the panic of 1837, McIntosh began to write, since she did not want to be dependent on anyone. Her first published work, *Blind Alice*, published under the pen name "Aunt Kitty" in 1841, is an intensely moral children's story. Between 1841 and 1843 McIntosh wrote four more of these tales, which were published at intervals in 1843 and later bound and sold as *Aunt Kitty's Tales* in 1847. These tales were enormously popular and intensely didactic, so much so that several similar moral tales addressing young boys were published in 1843 and 1845.

In addition to writing children's stories, McIntosh wrote eight women's novels, many of which went into seven or eight editions in less than four years and were reprinted in London and translated into French and German. McIntosh became one of the most popular women writers of her time; sales of her books were exceeded only by Susan Warner and Sarah Willis Parton.

In 1846 McIntosh published her first novel under her own name, *Two Lives; or, To Seem and To Be*, which Nina Baym describes as "the first of the new wave of woman's best sellers" (p. 91). As do many of McIntosh's novels, *Two Lives* juxtaposes a pair of contrasting heroines who will ultimately meet the proper ends for their respective dispositions—the "woman who lives for the esteem of others gets nothing, while the one who lives so as to merit her own esteem gets everything" (Baym, p. 93).

McIntosh's nonfiction writing is equally important. In 1850 she wrote *Woman in America: Her Work and Her Reward*, in which she criticizes the women's rights movement, claiming women should put their efforts into the spiritual influence of the youth rather than attempt to eliminate the inequality between the sexes that was "ordained in Paradise." The political inequality, she felt, was also a factor of socialization and inequitable educational opportunities between the sexes. Because women were morally and ethically superior, according to McIntosh, they should reform society. In addition, in 1852 McIntosh wrote a letter to the *New York Observer* in an attempt to refute the antislavery claims Harriet Beecher Stowe had made in *Uncle Tom's Cabin*; these ideas were published in pamphlet form in 1853. While regretting that slavery need exist at all in the South, McIntosh defended the southern women who cared for and Christianized the slaves, which she argued was far more beneficial to the slaves than the criticism of northern slavery foes. She later put this argument into her novel *The Lofty and the Lowly; or, Good in All and None All-Good*, published in 1853.

Due to the success of her novels, McIntosh was able to live financially independent and never married. In 1859 she traveled to Liverpool, England, with the family of her nephew, John Elliott Ward, and she stayed in Geneva, Switzerland, with his wife and children for some time before returning to Manhattan in 1860. There, she taught school and published her final novel, *Two Pictures; or, What We Think of Ourselves and What the World Thinks of Us*, in 1863. In Manhattan she maintained a salon where women could come and share their creative talents. She moved to Morristown, New Jersey, to live with her niece and namesake, Maria McIntosh Cox, where she died after a painful illness.

Despite McIntosh's popular success in the 1840s and 1850s, only one of her novels, *Charms and Counter-Charms* (1848), her most popular, was reprinted in the twentieth century. McIntosh, however, suffered the same fate as many late nineteenth-century women writers whose works were often not published because they were written by and largely for women. Critics and scholars also ignored or denigrated novels such as McIntosh's partly because they were popular. Nina Baym and other late twentieth-century scholars have attempted to redress this wrong. However, because McIntosh's novels were often seen as proslavery, some are reluctant to champion her.

• The Huxford Genealogical Society in Homerville, Ga., contains manuscripts of McIntosh's family, including her father. A letter from Maria Jane McIntosh to Maria Cummins (Oct. 1857) is in the Clifton Waller Barrett Library at the University of Virginia, Charlottesville. Publication dates of many of McIntosh's works are in dispute, but other novels include *Conquest and Self-Conquest; or, Which Makes the Hero?* (1843/1844), *Woman an Enigma; or, Life and Its Revelations* (1843/1844), and *Violet; or, The Cross and the Crown* (1856). *Evenings at Donaldson Manor; or, The Christmas Guest* (variously dated 1849, 1850, 1851, and 1852, depending on the source), which collects her contributions to magazines and combines them with a loose thread, was intended as a book for the holidays. Nina Baym, *Woman's Fiction: A Guide to Novels by and about Women in America, 1820–70* (1993), has a chapter discussing McIntosh's women's novels, which gives a good sense of the content of the novels as well as how they reveal McIntosh's views of women's place in the nineteenth century. Bashar Akili, "Maria Jane McIntosh: A Woman in Her Time: A Biographical and Critical Study" (Ph.D. diss., Loughborough Univ. of Technology, 1990), gives a thorough biographical account, although sometimes it focuses on the time period rather than on McIntosh herself. Akili discusses McIntosh's nonfiction works in more detail than Baym's study. McIntosh is also discussed in Mary Kelley, *Private Woman, Public Stage* (1984), and Elizabeth Moss, *Domestic Novelists in the Old South* (1992).

MICHELLE PAGNI STEWART

MCINTOSH, William (1778?–30 Apr. 1825), military leader and high-ranking chief in the Creek Nation, was born in Coweta, in present-day Russell County,

Alabama, the son of Captain William McIntosh, a recruiter for the British army, and Senoya, a full-blooded Creek. McIntosh was raised as a Creek, enduring the customary rites of passage and advancing to the rank of chief, *Tustunnuggee Hutke* or "White Warrior." Polygamy being accepted, he had three wives: Eliza, Susannah, and Peggy, and twelve children. There is no record that he ever met his Caucasian father.

McIntosh's career was influenced by Benjamin Hawkins, who became the U.S. Indian agent to the Creek Nation in 1796. Hawkins envisioned a system of Creek government controlled by his carefully chosen National Council. Hawkins was drawn to McIntosh for his oratorical brilliance and willingness to adapt to white culture.

In his late twenties McIntosh achieved national recognition as spokesman for a six-chief delegation selected by Hawkins to negotiate a land treaty in 1805 with President Thomas Jefferson. Skillfully arguing that the 2 million acres of Creek land was worth ten cents an acre (instead of the Senate's one-cent price), McIntosh prevailed, but he conceded rights to a federal road through his nation to Louisiana. As McIntosh predicted, the road brought Indian-white violence.

As roadways proliferated during the years 1807–1811, resentment escalated, particularly among the nativistic, recalcitrant Upper Creeks. Localized primarily in Alabama, they were vulnerable to Tecumseh's bellicose rhetoric in the early fall of 1811. Murders of whites by the Upper Creeks led Hawkins to organize the "law menders," a National Council police force, directed by McIntosh. In one portentous incident, McIntosh killed an Upper Creek seated on a chief's throne, claiming sanctuary.

In 1813 enmity between the Upper and Lower Creeks escalated into the Creek War of 1813–1814, an element of the larger War of 1812. In August 700 Upper Creeks attacked Fort Mims, a pine-log stockade and refuge for white settlers near Mobile. More than 250 whites and friendly Indians were killed. An outcry for revenge swept across the frontier, and the Tennessee governor ordered General Andrew Jackson to call out 2,000 men and attack the Upper Creeks. Other states sent militia, and among the Georgians was William McIntosh, leading a company of Creek warriors wearing white deertails around their necks to mark them as friendly Creeks. Major McIntosh and his men distinguished themselves, particularly at the battles of Autossee (29 Nov. 1813) and Horseshoe Bend (27 Mar. 1814).

In the peace treaty he concluded at Fort Jackson in August 1814, Jackson ignored the loyalty of the friendly Lower Creeks. In effect, he took 20 million acres of good land from them to compensate for damages committed by the Upper Creeks. Later in 1814 Jackson campaigned for Indian removal from Alabama and Georgia, and McIntosh vigorously protested in Washington to President James Madison. At this time the Creeks were in a state of terrible poverty. Hawkins described them as "in a manner naked, their hunting done, their resources destroyed by their civil war."

In 1818 General Jackson assembled 1,800 regular army troops to quell the Seminole uprising along the Georgia-Florida border. He added 1,500 Creek volunteers under newly promoted Brigadier General McIntosh. That same year McIntosh was honored at a banquet in Augusta, where a speaker praised his being at home "both in the bosom of the forest, surrounded by a band of wild savages," and "in the drawing room in the civilized walks of life."

During the period from 1817 to 1821 McIntosh became increasingly wealthy as partner to David Bridie Mitchell, who resigned as governor of Georgia to replace Benjamin Hawkins as Indian agent. They established a commissary and encouraged Creek chiefs to take land payments in goods rather than cash. One Creek chieftain, Little Prince, said, "McIntosh and Mitchell used to steal all our money, because they could write." They were also accused of defying the law by smuggling in black slaves. McIntosh was fully cleared, but Mitchell was found guilty and dismissed as Indian agent in 1821.

McIntosh was a key figure in negotiations in 1821 that allowed the desperately poor Creeks to sell more than 4 million acres of Georgia land for five cents an acre. For his cooperation he was given 1,640 acres of land, on which he built a profitable resort hotel. His material success and his status in the white world angered the Upper Creeks, whose hatred for McIntosh lingered from his leading of the law menders.

Pressures on McIntosh from the white politicians increased in 1823 when his first cousin George M. Troup was elected governor of Georgia with a mandate to remove the Indians. The Upper Creek chiefs responded by demanding death for any Creek who signed away more land. In late November 1824 President James Monroe called a meeting to negotiate Indian removal, and there McIntosh was relieved of his tribal office as Speaker, accused of secret deals with the treaty commissioners and profiting from removal.

In January 1825 treaty negotiators told President Monroe that McIntosh was ready to relinquish the land and move his followers west. A meeting was called on 7 February, and five days later McIntosh and five lesser chiefs, representing only a few of the fifty-six Creek towns, signed a treaty giving up all the remaining Creek lands in Georgia.

After a few months of restless quiet, the notorious Chief Menawa and a company of Upper Creek warriors arrived at dusk on 29 April at McIntosh's plantation on the banks of the Chattahoochee River and concealed themselves in the forest. Just before dawn they set fire to the house, and McIntosh, after shooting at his assailants from the second floor, came down to escape the flames and was shot more than fifty times before being scalped and thrown into the river.

McIntosh's actions aroused strongly partisan positions. To the Upper Creeks, he was a traitor; to the white Georgians, a hero and martyr. Thomas L. McKenney, superintendent of Indian trade, said that McIntosh "probably foresaw that his people would have no rest within the limits of Georgia, and perhaps acted with an honest view to their interests."

• McIntosh papers can be found in the Thomas Gilcrease Museum, Tulsa, and in *Creek Indian Letters, Talks, and Treaties, 1705–1829* in the Georgia Archives in Atlanta. Voluminous papers relating to McIntosh's death and the events leading to it are published in *Report on Messages of the President, Select Committee, House Report*, no. 98, 19th sess., vol. 3, *The Georgia Indian Controversy* (1837). James C. Bonner, "William McIntosh," in *Georgians in Profile*, ed. Horace Montgomery (1958); C. L. Grant, ed., *Letters, Journals, and Writings of Benjamin Hawkins* (2 vols., 1980); Michael D. Green, *The Politics of Indian Removal* (1982); and Benjamin W. Griffith, Jr., *McIntosh and Weatherford: Creek Indian Leaders* (1988), are important sources.

BENJAMIN W. GRIFFITH, JR.

MCINTYRE, James Francis (25 June 1886–16 July 1979), Roman Catholic cardinal, was born in New York City, the son of James Francis McIntyre, a policeman, and Mary Pelley. His mother died when McIntyre was ten. He and his father, who had become an invalid several years earlier, went to live with a married cousin, Mary Conley. Despite feeling called to the priesthood, he quit school three years later to support his father as an errand boy for David Pfeifer, a stockbroker and member of the New York Curb Exchange, which conducted its transactions on the sidewalk at the corner of Broad Street and Exchange Place. In 1902 McIntyre became a runner for H. L. Horton and Company, a Wall Street brokerage firm, and over the next twelve years he worked his way up to office manager. Meanwhile he completed his secondary education at night school and took some courses at City College and Columbia University in the hope of someday becoming a priest. For this reason, in 1914 he turned down a junior partnership with Fahnestock and Company after it had acquired Horton. When his father died the next year, McIntyre left the company and began studying for the priesthood at New York's Cathedral College. He graduated in 1916, spent the next five years studying at St. Joseph's Seminary in Yonkers, and was ordained in 1921.

McIntyre spent the next two years as assistant pastor of St. Gabriel's Parish in Manhattan. In 1923 he was appointed assistant chancellor and assistant diocesan secretary of the archdiocese of New York. In these positions he became heavily involved in its financial affairs, particularly the management of its extensive real estate holdings. In 1934 he was made a monsignor and appointed chancellor, in effect the archdiocese's chief financial and legal officer. Owing in large part to his financial acumen, the archdiocese was able to continue all of its administrative and charitable functions throughout the Great Depression by converting its long-term debt to low-interest loans. He was consecrated an auxiliary bishop of the archdiocese in 1940, appointed vicar general in 1945, and elevated to coadjutor archbishop in 1946. In these positions he became the most trusted adviser of Francis Cardinal Spellman, the archbishop of New York who also served as head of the U.S. Chaplains' Corps and informal leader of all U.S. Catholics. Spellman's frequent absences permitted McIntyre, who was a much sterner taskmaster, to exercise tremendous control over the archdiocese's affairs, and he implemented a number of reforms that reduced significantly the autonomy of the pastors. In 1947 he denounced as communistic a state bill to outlaw racial discrimination in the classroom because the bill's preamble declared education to be the duty of the state. In his opinion, this duty fell to the parent.

In 1948 McIntyre became the archbishop of Los Angeles, California, at the time the fastest growing archdiocese in the United States. During his 22-year tenure, the membership of the archdiocese almost tripled. Despite the fact that the archdiocese was financially troubled, McIntyre immediately implemented a major fundraising and building program that resulted in the establishment of twenty-six new parishes and the construction of sixty-four parochial schools and eighteen high schools in the next four years. Over the next eighteen years he oversaw the establishment of an additional eighty-two parishes and another 115 schools, earning for him the sobriquet "the brick-and-mortar bishop." As a result of this building effort California's parochial schools gained tax-exempt status in 1951. McIntyre successfully defended that status in referenda in 1952 and 1958 by demonstrating that the archdiocesan school system saved the taxpayers of southern California more than $20 million a year.

In 1953 McIntyre was elevated to the Sacred College of Cardinals. Although he continued to administer the archdiocese for another seventeen years, he focused his attention increasingly on matters of church doctrine and policy and emerged as a leader of the Roman Catholic church's conservative element. At the time the hierarchy was debating the necessity of renewing and reforming itself in the face of the challenges of the modern world, a process that resulted in the Second Vatican Council in Rome, Italy, in 1962. Over the next three years the council implemented a number of changes in policy and liturgy, most of which McIntyre resisted. He was particularly opposed to saying the mass in the vernacular instead of Latin because he believed that it detracted from the solemnity of the celebration. He complained loud and long against the U.S. Supreme Court decision to ban Bible reading and prayer in public schools, charging that the decision suggested the United States was dangerously close to becoming a Communist country. He drew fire from all quarters during the civil rights movement for refusing to oppose passage of a discriminatory housing bill in California and for censuring priests under his jurisdiction who worked actively for racial equality.

McIntyre retired as archbishop in 1970 but continued to serve as a priest at St. Basil's Parish in Los Angeles for several more years. He died in Los Angeles. Considered one of the most conservative members of the Roman Catholic hierarchy of his day, he played a central role in the development of the educational and religious life of the two largest cities in the United States.

• McIntyre's papers have not been located. A biography is in Francis Beauchesne Thornton, *Our American Princes: The Story of the Seventeen American Cardinals* (1963). A highly unflattering portrayal of McIntyre is in John Cooney, *The American Pope: The Life and Times of Francis Cardinal Spellman* (1984). An obituary is in the *New York Times*, 17 July 1979.

CHARLES W. CAREY, JR.

MCINTYRE, O. O. (18 Feb. 1884–14 Feb. 1938), newspaper columnist, was born Oscar Odd McIntyre in Plattsburg, Missouri, the son of Henry Bell McIntyre, a hotel manager, and Frances "Fannie" Young. After his mother's death, his father sent Odd (pronounced *ud*) to his paternal grandmother in Gallipolis, Ohio, for upbringing. It was here that he met a neighborhood playmate, Maybelle Hope Small, whom he married on his twenty-fourth birthday. They had no children.

McIntyre was not fond of school and eventually dropped out, leaving him with lifelong weaknesses in grammar and spelling, but he was attracted to a local newspaper and its print shop. When the editor used a personal note of his, he later wrote in 1928, McIntyre was thrilled. "Right then and there I decided I would become a newspaperman and Grandma, bless her, encouraged me." Newspaper work, he added, was "the only kind of labor that has ever interested me." He took his first newspaper job in Gallipolis. His father, however, who disliked journalists, sent McIntyre to a business school in Cincinnati. McIntyre mastered touch typing but little else, and his father called him back to Plattsburg to learn the hotel business. McIntyre chafed under this, and his father sent him away.

After a second position with the *East Liverpool* (Ohio) *Morning Tribune*, he took a position in 1906 with the Dayton *Herald* and moved up rapidly to city editor. A year later he was recruited to the Cincinnati *Post* by Ray Long, soon to be a successful magazine editor, who subsequently convinced McIntyre to come to New York City in July 1911. *Hampton's Magazine* failed financially a few months later, but McIntyre felt himself out of his element in this medium. His fear of failure soon pushed his confidence and morale to a low point, but after a dismissal from the New York *Evening Sun* in 1912 he began, with his wife's encouragement, writing his daily "letter" from New York to newspapers. It was accepted first by the Bridgeport (Conn.) *Post* in October 1912. Mrs. McIntyre, as his office manager, handled the mimeograph machine, the mailings, and their financial affairs. McIntyre combined his writing with effective publicity work for clients such as the Majestic Hotel, into which he moved in 1915, and the showman Florenz Ziegfeld. McIntyre saw his column as "an effort to see the highlights and shadows of America's largest and most interesting city and to chronicle them in an intimate fashion" (1928). Through the "quixotic little adventure" of self-syndication he developed the column on his own before joining the McNaught Syndicate in 1922. By the time of his death the column ran in more than 500 newspapers daily and Sundays, earning him approximately $3,000 per month. Also in 1922, with Ray Long now at *Cosmopolitan*, McIntyre began publishing a brief monthly article that ran continuously until his death.

McIntyre was by all accounts a very popular and successful journalist. He pioneered the Broadway column, with chatty notes and observations on the likes and doings of entertainment celebrities as well as his own activities and memories. The style for his "New York Day by Day" column was a sprinkling of points loosely tied together, frequently run under regular headings of "Thingumabobs," "Reflections while Walking," "Purely Personal Piffle," "Look Alikes," and "Personal Nominations." He wrote about New York City during its heyday and the heyday of competing metropolitan newspapers in the decades before television. He in turn wrote about the values and lifestyle in small-town America, from which many an American moving into large urban areas had sprung. He wrote about intimate conversations with Irvin Cobb or Flo Ziegfeld, Will Hogg and Will Rogers, about glamorous dinners and fancy evenings at the theater, or about his beloved dogs, the Halloweens of his childhood, his family members back home (especially Gallipolis, to which he returned only in death), and bicycle riding as a youngster. His critics decried the fictional quality of the geography in his New York City. He mixed up distances between streets or places to make points seem either closer or farther than they actually were; he made ordinary places seem like palaces. He sought to entertain by reporting on the fabric of life in the big city, celebrating most of all, for the folks back home, individuals who had successfully realized their dreams on a grand scale. He was a man, his friend Will Hays eulogized, "who came from the *soil* of America and won a lasting place in the *heart* of America" (1940). But he manifested a cultivated innocence about the sweeping changes of his era. His essential nostalgia lacked the reflective quality of his contemporaries Sherwood Anderson and Sinclair Lewis. While his influence may seem remote and quaint today, in the decades between the two world wars his appeal to the simple pleasures tapped "a shared outlook on life that made him a beloved national figure" (Huddleston, p. 81).

• A microfilm collection of McIntyre materials, filmed in 1991, is available from the Ohio University Libraries. It is incomplete but includes scrapbooks from earlier years, many columns and articles from later years, and his partial, unpublished autobiography (1928). Collections of selected pieces published during McIntyre's lifetime, giving a sense of his own favorites, are *White Light Nights* (1924), *Twenty-five Selected Stories* (1929), *Another "Odd" Book* (1932), and *The Big Town: New York Day by Day* (1935). Charles B. Driscoll's biography, *The Life of O. O. McIntyre* (1938), is the only book-length study but suffers from exaggeration. Max Shiveley's unpublished dissertation, "The Conte of O. O. McIntyre: An Assessment of His Contributions to Personalized Journalism" (Ohio Univ., 1980), examines McIntyre's career comprehensively. He drew on locally held materials, including those subsequently microfilmed, as well as interviews with Maybelle McIntyre. The most recent study is E. L. Huddleston's analytical "O. O. McIntyre: Broadway Populist," *American Studies* 15 (1974): 79–89. An obituary is in the *New York Times*, 15 Feb. 1938.

GEORGE W. BAIN

MCIVER, Charles Duncan (27 Sept. 1860–17 Sept. 1906), progressive educator, was born on a farm near Sanford in Moore County, North Carolina, the son of Matthew Henry McIver, a farmer and country store operator, and Sarah Harrington. Although McIver liked to refer to his humble country origins, his family was by no means poor. At a time when many North Carolinians were uneducated sharecroppers or farm tenants, his father owned 250 acres of land, employed six tenants, and hired private tutors for his children. The staunchly Presbyterian McIver sons typically attended Davidson College, but Charles broke with family tradition by entering the University of North Carolina. His choice of the state university over the private college was prophetic. For most of his adult life, the devoutly religious McIver pleaded for public support of education against the opposition of church leaders who wished to maintain their own control over educational institutions.

Upon receiving his B.A. in 1881, McIver took a job as assistant principal in a private school in Durham. Realizing that private academies could not meet the educational needs of the masses, he supported the town's effort to establish a public school system and cast his first vote in favor of a local school tax. In 1884 he moved to Winston where he became principal of the high school department of the new graded school. Here he met and in 1885 married a fellow teacher, Lula V. Martin; they had four children. Martin helped convert McIver to the cause of women's higher education. The couple's discussions on education led to McIver's first public speech on the higher education of women at the 1885 Teachers' Institute in Winston. McIver argued that universal education could not be achieved without the higher education of women: "Universal education a necessity, woman the universal educator; therefore, the education of woman the foundation of human progress" (*Charles Duncan McIver Memorial Volume*, p. 266). McIver believed that the higher education of women benefited the whole community, not just the individual. The wives and mothers of the future would be the ones who would educate the next generation of North Carolinians: "If it were practicable," he wrote, "an educational qualification for matrimony would be worth more to our citizenship than an educational qualification for suffrage" ("Two Open Fields for Investment in the South," McIver papers, p. 10). Although he did not oppose the education of blacks, McIver concluded that whites had to be educated first. He was convinced that the education of white women was the "quickest method" of elevating the entire southern population.

From 1889 to 1892 McIver and his college friend Edwin A. Alderman served as state conductors of Teachers' Institutes in North Carolina, campaigning for universal education and offering county institutes and special summer schools for teachers. Elected president of the North Carolina Teachers' Assembly in 1890, McIver was chosen chair of the committee that lobbied the legislature for the establishment of a training school for teachers. Thanks to his efforts the bill to establish the North Carolina State Normal and Industrial School for white women passed in 1891, and McIver was chosen as the institution's first president. The School's central location in Greensboro, its county scholarships and low fees, and its utilitarian curriculum made it immensely popular among the young women of the state, and McIver found it hard to accommodate demand. When the institution opened in 1892, he had to find rooms for 176 students, instead of the 125 he had anticipated; by the following autumn, enrollment was up to 391.

McIver's educational efforts did not stop with the establishment of the women's college. In 1892 he was elected president of the North Carolina Teachers' Assembly and encouraged the formation of the Woman's Association for the Betterment of Public Schools. McIver's efforts for school reform caught the attention of Robert C. Ogden, a wealthy New York industrialist. Ogden brought together a number of southern and northern educators and philantrophists who were connected with the Conference for Education in the South to discuss the educational problems of the region; the result was the formation of the Southern Education Board in 1901. The SEB was essentially a propaganda agency aimed at convincing localities to tax themselves to provide free schools for all the children of the community. McIver served as the organization's first secretary and later as its president. In 1905 he was made chair of the SEB Campaign Committee for the promotion of universal education. In recognition of his contributions to public education in North Carolina, the state university awarded him two honorary degrees (1893 and 1904).

McIver shared a concern for the plight of the common man and woman in industrial America with William Jennings Bryan. The two had been friends since Bryan's speech at the normal and industrial school in 1894. McIver supported Bryan's presidential bid and died of a heart attack aboard a campaign train carrying Bryan from Raleigh to Greensboro.

• McIver's papers are located in the University Archives, Jackson Library, the University of North Carolina at Greensboro. In addition to material on the normal and industrial school (which in 1897 became the State Normal and Industrial College and, in 1919, the NC College for Women), the collection contains McIver's correspondence with other educators and the papers of the SEB from 1901 to 1906. The *Charles Duncan McIver Memorial Volume*, which was prepared by a faculty committee in 1907, includes the text of the memorial exercises held at the college in November 1906, eulogies from various daily and monthly periodicals, testimonials from fellow educators, and the speech given by William Jennings Bryan that mourned McIver's death. A 1957 biography, Rose Howell Holder's *McIver of North Carolina*, provides numerous interesting anecdotes about McIver but no documentation of sources. An earlier study by Frances Gibson Satterfield, *Charles Duncan McIver* (1942), is briefer and more scholarly. References to McIver's role in establishing universal education in the South may be found in Dewey W. Grantham, *Southern Progressivism* (1983), and William A. Link, *A Hard Country and a Lonely Place* (1986). Both authors conclude that McIver's educational efforts, like those of other southern progressives, were for whites only.

AMY THOMPSON MCCANDLESS

MCIVER, Helene Emma. *See* Madison, Helene Emma.

MCKAY, Claude (15 Sept. 1890–22 May 1948), poet, novelist, and journalist, was born Festus Claudius McKay in Sunny Ville, Clarendon Parish, Jamaica, the son of Thomas Francis McKay and Hannah Ann Elizabeth Edwards, farmers. The youngest of eleven children, McKay was sent at an early age to live with his oldest brother, a schoolteacher, so that he could be given the best education available. An avid reader, McKay began to write poetry at the age of ten. In 1906 he decided to enter a trade school, but when the school was destroyed by an earthquake he became apprenticed to a carriage and cabinetmaker; a brief period in the constabulary followed. In 1907 McKay came to the attention of Walter Jekyll, an English gentleman residing in Jamaica who became his mentor, encouraging him to write dialect verse. Jekyll later set some of McKay's verse to music. By the time he immigrated to the United States in 1912, McKay had established himself as a poet, publishing two volumes of dialect verse, *Songs of Jamaica* (1912) and *Constab Ballads* (1912).

Having heard favorable reports of the work of Booker T. Washington, McKay enrolled at Tuskegee Institute in Alabama with the intention of studying agronomy; it was here that he first encountered the harsh realities of American racism, which would form the basis for much of his subsequent writing. He soon left Tuskegee for Kansas State College in Manhattan, Kansas. In 1914 a financial gift from Jekyll enabled him to move to New York, where he invested in a restaurant and married his childhood sweetheart, Eulalie Imelda Lewars. Neither venture lasted a year, and Lewars returned to Jamaica to give birth to their daughter. McKay was forced to take a series of menial jobs. He was finally able to publish two poems, "Invocation" and "The Harlem Dancer," under a pseudonym in 1917. McKay's talent as a lyric poet earned him recognition, particularly from Frank Harris, editor of *Pearson's* magazine, and Max Eastman, editor of *The Liberator*, a socialist journal; both became instrumental in McKay's early career.

As a socialist, McKay eventually became an editor at *The Liberator*, in addition to writing various articles for a number of left-wing publications. During the period of racial violence against blacks known as the Red Summer of 1919, McKay wrote one of his best-known poems, the sonnet, "If We Must Die," an anthem of resistance later quoted by Winston Churchill during World War II. "Baptism," "The White House," and "The Lynching," all sonnets, also exemplify some of McKay's finest protest poetry. The generation of poets who formed the core of the Harlem Renaissance, including Langston Hughes and Countee Cullen, identified McKay as a leading inspirational force, even though he did not write modern verse. His innovation lay in the directness with which he spoke of racial issues and his choice of the working class, rather than the middle class, as his focus.

McKay resided in England from 1919 through 1921, then returned to the United States. While in England, he was employed by the British socialist journal, *Workers' Drednought*, and published a book of verse, *Spring in New Hampshire*, which was released in an expanded version in the United States in 1922. The same year, *Harlem Shadows*, perhaps his most significant poetry collection, appeared. McKay then began a twelve-year sojourn through Europe, the Soviet Union, and Africa, a period marked by poverty and illness. While in the Soviet Union he compiled his journalistic essays into a book, *The Negroes in America*, which was not published in the United States until 1979. For a time he was bouyed by the success of his first published novel, *Home to Harlem* (1928), which was critically acclaimed but engendered controversy for its frank portrayal of the underside of Harlem life.

His next novel, *Banjo: A Story without a Plot* (1929), followed the exploits of an expatriate African-American musician in Marseilles, a locale McKay knew well. This novel and McKay's presence in France influenced Léopold Sédar Senghor, Aimé Césaire, and other pioneers of the Negritude literary movement that took hold in French West Africa and the West Indies. *Banjo* did not sell well. Neither did *Gingertown* (1932), a short story collection, or *Banana Bottom* (1933). Often identified as McKay's finest novel, *Banana Bottom* tells the story of Bita Plant, who returns to Jamaica after being educated in England and struggles to form an identity that reconciles the aesthetic values imposed upon her with her appreciation for her native roots.

McKay had moved to Morocco in 1930, but his financial situation forced him to return to the United States in 1934. He gained acceptance to the Federal Writers Project in 1936 and completed his autobiography, *A Long Way from Home*, in 1937. Although no longer sympathetic toward communism, he remained a socialist, publishing essays and articles in *The Nation*, the *New Leader*, and the *New York Amsterdam News*. In 1940 McKay produced a nonfiction work, *Harlem: Negro Metropolis*, which gained little attention but has remained an important historical source. Never able to regain the stature he had achieved during the 1920s, McKay blamed his chronic financial difficulties on his race and his failure to obtain academic credentials and associations.

McKay never returned to the homeland he left in 1912. His became a U.S. citizen in 1940. High blood pressure and heart disease led to a steady physical decline, and in a move that surprised his friends, McKay abandoned his lifelong agnosticism and embraced Catholicism. In 1944 he left New York for Chicago, where he worked for the Catholic Youth Organization. He eventually succumbed to congestive heart failure in Chicago. His second autobiography, *My Green Hills of Jamaica*, was published posthumously in 1979.

Assessments of McKay's lasting influence vary. To McKay's contemporaries, such as James Weldon Johnson, "Claude McKay's poetry was one of the great forces in bringing about what is often called the 'Negro Literary Renaissance.'" While his novels and autobiographies have found an increasing audience in recent years, modern critics appear to concur with Arthur P. Davis that McKay's greatest literary contributions are found among his early sonnets and lyrics. McKay ended *A Long Way from Home* with this assessment of himself: "I have nothing to give but my singing. All my life I have been a troubadour wanderer, nourishing myself mainly on the poetry of existence. And all I offer here is the distilled poetry of my experience."

• The bulk of McKay's papers is located in the James Weldon Johnson Collection at Yale University. Numerous letters are widely scattered; some sources include the Schomburg and H. L. Mencken collections at the New York City Public Library; the William Stanley Brathwaite Papers at Harvard University; the Alain Locke Papers at Howard University; the NAACP Papers in the Library of Congress; the Eastman Papers at the University of Indiana, Bloomington; the Rosenwald Fund Papers at Fisk University; and the Countee Cullen Papers at Dillard University. *Selected Poems of Claude McKay*, an extensive collection, was published in 1953. *American Mercury*, *The Crisis*, *The Liberator*, and *Opportunity* are among the wide range of periodicals in which McKay's poems, articles, book reviews, and short stories appear. Early poems can be found in the Jamaican newspapers *Jamaica Times* and *Kingston Daily Gleaner*. Late poems appear in *Catholic Worker*. Extensive bibliographies can be found in several unpublished dissertations.

Published full-length biographical and critical studies include Wayne F. Cooper, *Claude McKay: Rebel Sojourner in the Harlem Renaissance, a Biography* (1987); Tyrone Tillary, *Claude McKay: A Black Poet's Struggle for Identity* (1992); and James R. Giles, *Claude McKay* (1976). Stephen H. Bronz, *Roots of Negro Racial Consciousness: The 1920s, Three Harlem Renaissance Authors* (1964); Addison Gayle, *Claude McKay: The Black Poet at War* (1972); and Wayne F. Cooper, ed., *The Passion of Claude McKay* (1973), are also useful bibliographic and biographical resources. An obituary appears in the *New York Times*, 24 May 1948.

FREDA SCOTT GILES

MCKAY, David Oman (8 Sept. 1873–18 Jan. 1970), ninth president of the Church of Jesus Christ of Latter-Day Saints, was born in Huntsville, Utah, the son of David McKay and Jennette Evans, farmers. Both parents were the children of Mormon converts who immigrated to Utah from Great Britain; the paternal grandparents of David McKay were among the first Mormon converts in Britain. When his son was eight years old, David McKay, Sr., received a call from the church to minister as a missionary in Scotland, leaving his son, as the eldest male in the household, in nominal charge of the family farm. Educated at the Weber Stake Academy in Ogden, Utah, McKay read widely in English literature in his free time. He became principal of the community school in Huntsville at age twenty but, feeling the need for better preparation for a career in education, enrolled soon after at the University of Utah, from which he graduated in 1897 as class valedictorian.

McKay was sent to Scotland on a two-year missionary journey in August 1897 and was eventually appointed to preside over the Glasgow district of the British mission. While on this mission he received a personal spiritual revelation, which confirmed his faith and assured him of an important role in church leadership. He returned to Utah in 1899 and taught English at the Weber school until 1908, when his rapidly increasing duties in church educational administration forced him to give up teaching. In January 1901 he was sealed in marriage to Emma Ray Riggs in the Salt Lake City Temple. The couple had seven children.

McKay was called to serve as a member of the Quorum of the Twelve Apostles in 1906, making him at age thirty-two a member of the church's governing body. Education remained the focus of his responsibilities. He served as second assistant general superintendent of the church's Sunday school program and in 1919 became the church's first commissioner of education. McKay believed that education ought to aim at improvement of the whole person, at character development; particular subjects are fundamentally only the vehicles for this aim. He summed up his ideas in *Gospel Ideals* (1953):

> True education—the education for which the Church stands—is the application of knowledge to the development of a noble and Godlike character. . . . The principal aim of many of our schools and colleges seems to be to give the students purely intellectual attainments and to give but passing regard to the nobler and more necessary development along moral lines.

In 1920 McKay inaugurated what became his hallmark missionary emphasis by undertaking a thirteen-month, 62,500-mile tour of Mormon mission sites worldwide. In 1922 he served in Europe as head of the European missions; in 1924 he was given charge of missions worldwide. In Europe he began to reverse the church's long-standing recommendation to converts that they emigrate to Utah, promising instead that temples would one day be built in mission lands, so that converts would be able to participate in the sacred temple ordinances in their native countries.

McKay was elevated to membership in the church's supreme executive body, the First Presidency, in 1934, when he was named second counselor in the First Presidency by church president Heber J. Grant. Grant and McKay had earlier clashed over the issue of U.S. membership in the League of Nations, which McKay opposed. McKay was continued in this office when Grant died in 1945. That year McKay's niece, the historian Fawn McKay Brodie, published a biography of Mormon prophet and church founder Joseph Smith titled *No Man Knows My History*, which was highly skeptical of the divine origins of the church.

Brodie was eventually excommunicated, and her relations with her uncle severed, although the extent of McKay's involvement in the "disfellowship" proceedings was not revealed.

Upon the death of President George Albert Smith in 1951, McKay succeeded to the presidency of the church and began an exceptionally vigorous and successful administration marked by unprecedented expansion of the church worldwide. McKay made popular the slogan "every member a missionary," and in his nineteen years as president church membership increased from 1.1 million—largely concentrated in the western United States—to 2.8 million, spread over such diverse mission territory as Latin America, Oceania, and New Zealand. True to his promise, temples were dedicated overseas, beginning in Bern, Switzerland, in 1955; several new American temples were built, including a $4 million edifice in Los Angeles. McKay encouraged church engagement with civil society and social problems, and while remaining largely nonpartisan, he was considered in church circles to be a liberal. He believed, for instance, that the Mormon prohibition of African Americans from the ranks of priesthood was a matter of practice, not dogma. In this way he anticipated the subsequent dropping of the ban by President Spencer W. Kimball in 1978.

McKay died in Salt Lake City. Throughout his presidency Mormons recognized in his charisma and leadership the marks of his authentic prophetic calling. The church acknowledged his importance as an educator by naming the building housing the College of Education at Brigham Young University in his honor.

• Some of McKay's papers are in the Latter Day Saints Historical Department in Salt Lake City. McKay's publications include *Ancient Apostles* (1918), *Gospel Ideals* (1953), *Stepping Stones to an Abundant Life* (1971), *Treasures of Life* (1963), and *True to the Faith* (1966), and numerous articles in the LDS periodical, *Improvement Era*. Biographical sources include Clare Middlemiss, *Cherished Experiences from the Writings of President David O. McKay* (1955), and Llewelyn R. McKay, *Home Memories of David O. McKay*, as well as Francis M. Gibbons, *David O. McKay* (1986), and James B. Allen, "David O. McKay," in *The Presidents of the Church*, ed. Leonard J. Arrington (1986). An obituary is in the *New York Times*, 19 Jan. 1970.

MICHAEL J. LATZER

MCKAY, Donald (4 Sept. 1810–20 Sept. 1880), master shipbuilder, was born in Nova Scotia, Canada, the second of sixteen children of Hugh McKay, a farmer, and Ann McPherson. He moved to New York in 1827 to study the art and science of shipbuilding, and for the next several years he worked for the firm of Isaac Webb. Later he was employed at Brown and Bell, where he learned his trade in the construction of some of the famous packet ships of the day. Noting McKay's special talents, his employer Jacob Bell recommended him to William Currier, a New England shipbuilder, by whom McKay was employed to build ships at Wiscasset, Maine, and at Newburyport, Massachusetts.

Having demonstrated his skills, in 1841 Currier offered McKay a partnership, and his career as an independent shipbuilder was launched. Shortly thereafter McKay dissolved this partnership and formed the firm of McKay and Pickett with his new partner William Pickett at Newburyport where he built three ships. The last of these, the *Joshua Bates*, was built for the prominent Boston merchant Enoch Train, who was so impressed with the architectural qualities of the vessel that he invited McKay to move to Boston and build ships for his new Boston-to-Liverpool packet line. The move proved to be a fortunate one financially as the Irish famine of 1846 resulted in a dramatic increase in demand for passenger ships.

McKay now enjoyed prosperity, producing between 1845 and 1853 forty-nine ships, vessels that were noted for their speed, skillful design, and beauty. At first he concentrated on the sturdy packet ships that were fully rigged, with three masts and a four-to-one length-width ratio. These crafts were used for both freight and passenger service, and by the 1840s they were averaging more than a thousand tons in displacement.

Although McKay was a latecomer to building packet ships compared to contemporaries such as William Webb and Jacob Westervelt, he would soon match them in fame. In 1846 he built the *Washington Irving*, a ship with many innovations, including sleek lines and plush staterooms, that reflected McKay's architectural skill. One of the last of his packets, the *Daniel Webster*, made its appearance in 1850. At the ship's christening, Webster himself gave the oration—his speech interrupted by the shouts of "Man Overboard!"—as one of the workmen lost his footing and fell into the bay.

McKay was to make his greatest mark, however, in another form of shipbuilding. The sudden discovery of gold in California in 1848 and then in Australia in 1851 created a need for a faster sailing ship than the packets. The answer was the clipper ship. In the next five years McKay became the dominant figure in the brief but dramatic clipper ship era. In designing these ships, every other element was subservient to speed. His first big clipper, the *Stag Hound* (1,534 tons), built in 1850, was a reflection of these principles of design. It was at that time the largest merchant ship in the world and its lines were longer and sharper than any other vessel. McKay's most famous ship, the *Flying Cloud*, was built one year later. Despite its size of nearly 1,800 tons, it was the swiftest of all the clipper ships, setting a record of eighty-nine days from New York to San Francisco, a passage matched only twice, including once more itself. Surpassing the *Flying Cloud* in size but not in speed was another clipper, *Sovereign of the Seas* (2,421 tons), one of three that McKay built in 1852. *Sovereign* featured a main mast ninety-three feet high and, when fully rigged, carried over 12,000 yards of canvas sails. In the next three years five additional ships were completed. Four were similar in size to their predecessors. The fifth, the *Great Republic*, was an exception, displacing 4,500 tons, stretching 335 feet in length, and carrying four masts. The ship was said to be the "darling of the builder's heart." Although McKay had a reputation for using labor-saving devices such as a steam-powered sawmill and specially designed derricks, the construction cost of this ship was high, topping $300,000. Unfortunately, shortly after completion it was destroyed in a fire in New York Harbor. Because it was insured for only $200,000, McKay suffered a financial loss from which he never recovered.

The destruction of the *Great Republic*, McKay's favorite ship, presaged the near sudden end of the clipper ship era. Several forces contributed to the conclusion of this phase of the Transportation Revolution, including the overbuilding of clippers (300 in less than ten years), the decline in trade beginning with the depression of 1857, the emergence of steamships controlled largely by the British to dominate the Atlantic sealanes, and the coming of the Civil War.

McKay reacted to these challenges in several ways. With no ships on order during the brief but severe depression, he made an agreement with the British Admiralty to provide five hundred loads of timber for ship building. This led in time to a year's sojourn in Europe (1859–1860), where he observed the building of new ironclad ships. Returning to the United States, he tried to convince the U.S. Navy in March 1861 to begin a modernization program by ordering an ironclad corvette mounted with twelve nine-inch guns. When his proposal was rejected, McKay returned to Europe for two years. Belatedly the Navy Department saw the importance of armored ships powered by steam. McKay responded by converting his shipyard to build iron ships and marine and locomotive engines in 1863. In 1864 the Navy Department placed its first order with McKay to build steam-powered armored ships, and by the end of the Civil War he had built five such ships for them. Before he sold his shipyard in 1869, he had built several steamships and three sailing ships, including the *Glory of the Seas* that remained in service until 1923. His last building efforts, in the 1870s, were two wooden sloops of war for the navy that he constructed in a yard owned by another shipbuilder. Poor health forced his retirement in 1877 and he died three years later at his home in Hamilton, Massachusetts.

McKay had outlived his first wife, Albenia M. Boole, whom he married in 1829. He was survived by his second, Mary Cressy Litchfield (married in 1845), and most of his fifteen children from the two marriages.

• Letters to and from McKay concerning naval matters can be found in the Navy Department Archives (miscellaneous correspondence with the secretary of navy); the Gideon Welles Papers, Library of Congress; and the Admiralty Papers in the Public Record Office, London. Despite his fame, Donald McKay is the subject of only one biography: Richard C. McKay, *Some Famous Sailing Ships and Their Builder, Donald McKay* (1928), which lists the vessels he built. Two succinct accounts of the shipbuilder appear in Richard C. McKay, *South Street: A Maritime History of New York* (1934), and the introduction to John Robinson and George F. Dow, *The Sailing Ships of New England*, ser. 2 (1924). The best technical account is covered in Arthur H. Clark, *The Clipper Ship Era* (1967), which also includes a dramatic physical description of Donald McKay; see also Octavius T. Howe and Frederick C. Matthews, *American Clipper Ships* (2 vols., 1926–1927), Carl C. Cutler, *Greyhounds of the Sea* (1930), and Howard Chapelle, *History of American Sailing Ships* (1935). The economic and technical problems shipbuilders faced is clearly presented in Robert G. Albion, *Square Riggers on Schedule* (1938). The naval side of McKay's work can be found in James P. Baxter. *Introduction to the Iron Warship* (1933), and "Report of the Joint Committee on the Conduct of the War," Sen. Doc. No. 142, 38 Cong., 2 sess., vol. 3, pt. 2. Letters to and from McKay concerning naval matters can be found in the Navy Department Archives (miscellaneous correspondence with the secretary of navy); the Gideon Welles Papers, Library of Congress; and the Admiralty Papers in the Public Record Office, London.

WILLIAM L. CALDERHEAD

MCKAY, Gordon (4 May 1821–19 Oct. 1903), inventor and industrialist, was born in Pittsfield, Massachusetts, the son of Samuel Michael McKay, a manufacturer and politician, and Catherine Gordon Dexter. Possessing a delicate constitution, he received little formal education. Feeling that outdoor work might improve his health, McKay prepared for a career in engineering. At age sixteen he went to work for the Boston & Albany Railroad in the engineering department, and he later held a similar post with the Erie Canal. Having gained valuable practical experience and eager to direct his own firm, McKay returned to Pittsfield in 1845 and opened a machine shop that specialized in maintaining paper and cotton mill machinery. In that year he married Agnes Jenkins. They had no children, and the union ended in divorce several years later.

McKay's firm prospered and eventually employed at least one hundred men. In 1852, however, a new opportunity presented itself, and he became general manager and treasurer of the Lawrence Machine Shop in Lawrence, Massachusetts. While working at Lawrence, McKay learned of an inventor, Lyman Reed Blake, who had on 6 July 1858 received a patent (no. 20,775) for a machine that sewed the upper portions of shoes or "uppers" to the soles. McKay recognized that the new process, heretofore thought impractical, held the potential for enormous profits. He met Blake through the latter's patent attorney and soon reached an agreement to promote and develop the new process. Strapped for cash and in declining health, Blake accepted $70,000 ($8,000 in cash and $62,000 to be paid out of future profits) for his invention and relocated to Staunton, Virginia, where he ran a retail store.

Although McKay's new investment offered great promise, it still operated imperfectly. Stitching the toe and heel areas of shoes proved especially troublesome, and McKay worked for several years to perfect the machine. In his efforts he was ably assisted by expert mechanic R. H. Matthies and after 1861 by Blake, who was forced by the Civil War to abandon his operations in Virginia. On 6 May 1862 McKay received patent number 35,165 for his "process of sewing soles of boots and shoes." The final resolution of the sewing device's defects could hardly have come at a better time. The Civil War was in full force, and all hope that the conflict would be short in duration had vanished. Given the enormous demand for military footware, McKay soon formed the McKay Association to manufacture the newly perfected machine. Lucrative government contracts for footware, totaling 25,000 pairs of shoes, were shortly forthcoming, and McKay fulfilled the contracts at his factories in Farmington and Rayham, New Hampshire. McKay sensed that by leasing the machines rather than selling them to outside manufacturers outright he could increase overall profits while leaving the market open to improved versions of the machines. Hence, the association built and leased shoe-sewing machines for other manufacturers, who operated on a royalty-based fee schedule of 1 to 5 cents per pair. By the end of 1862 McKay was earning royalties from over sixty factories throughout the northern states, and the basis of his fortune was secure.

Not content to rest on his laurels, McKay constantly worked on improvements in the machine. He obtained five additional patents on the machine with Blake in 1864, and in the following year he also patented a machine that produced shoes with turned soles. McKay and Blake made a good team. While McKay managed the association's day-to-day operations, Blake took to the road to introduce the machine to manufacturers and to instruct them in its operation. The device eventually came into near-universal use. By 1876 over 177 million pairs of shoes had been created by the machine, and McKay was receiving over $500,000 annually. The partnership of McKay and Blake proved to be both long-lasting and mutually profitable. In 1874 the two men successfully fought to have Blake's patents extended, and after receiving another large payment from McKay for his efforts, Blake retired from active participation in the McKay Association.

Although he enjoyed a dominant position in the shoe manufacturing industry, McKay faced a challenge from Charles Goodyear, son of the noted rubber entrepreneur. Goodyear had entered the shoe industry in 1861 as the president of the American Shoe-tip Company. Moving up within the ranks of manufacturers by purchasing the patents of outside inventors, much as McKay had, Goodyear excelled in the production of so-called "welt shoes." By 1876 the competing firms were locked in a heated competition for business, and four additional years of acrimony and litigation followed before an agreement was reached in 1880 that gave the rights to Goodyear's welt shoe machinery to McKay. McKay in return surrendered the rights to his turned shoe machinery patents to Goodyear's interests and spent the remaining years of his career developing and manufacturing machinery for the production of heavier-grade shoes. In 1878 McKay married Marian Treat. They had no children and divorced in 1890. Because he was the patentee or joint patentee of over forty inventions, McKay's wealth at his retirement was estimated at more than $40 million.

McKay sold all of his business interests to the Goodyear Company in 1895 and retired from active business affairs. He then divided his time between homes in Cambridge, Massachusetts, and Newport, Rhode Island, and entered into an active role in local philanthropy. He established the McKay Institute, a school for African-American boys, in Kingston, Rhode Island. Aware of his own lack of formal education and eager for recognition among the Boston Brahmins, McKay found an ideal opportunity for philanthropy. He had enjoyed a long friendship with geologist and Harvard faculty member Nathaniel Southgate Shaler, and upon Shaler's elevation to dean of Harvard's long-struggling Lawrence Scientific School in 1891, McKay agreed to endow the school with a $4 million trust fund. Flexible in structure, the fund was to provide for technical training for students from all walks of life. He also desired adequate faculty salaries, functional facilities, and laboratories with the latest equipment. McKay made provisions that no monies would be forwarded until the last annuitant of his estate died, and the fund eventually rose to a value of $24 million. McKay's health began to decline in 1902, and he died in Newport, Rhode Island. Unfortunately, his bequest never benefited the Lawrence Scientific School. Although Shaler had sought the funding in part as a defense against Harvard president Charles W. Eliot's plans to reorganize the college, the money also attracted the attention of the neighboring Massachusetts Institute of Technology (MIT), which feared that additional Harvard funding would place MIT at a competitive disadvantage. After a proposed merger between the schools was overturned in court, the Lawrence Scientific School was discontinued in 1906 and replaced by a Graduate School of Applied Science.

McKay was one of the leading industrial figures in nineteenth-century America. Although he produced little in the way of original inventions, his willingness to utilize and improve upon the work of others revolutionized the American shoe industry, creating enormous wealth for himself and the opportunity for philanthropy.

• McKay's papers are divided between the Harvard University Archives and the Baker Library of the Harvard Business School, both in Cambridge, Mass. The best secondary sources of information are Blanche E. Hazard, *The Organization of the Boot and Shoe Industry in Massachusetts before 1875* (1921), for his industrial career; and Clark A. Elliott and Margaret W. Rossiter, eds., *Science at Harvard University: Historical Perspectives* (1992), and David N. Livingstone, *Nathaniel Southgate Shaler and the Culture of American Science* (1987), on his philanthropic efforts. Obituaries are in the *Springfield Daily Republican* and the *New York Times*, both 20 Oct. 1903.

EDWARD L. LACH, JR.

MCKEAN, Thomas (19 Mar. 1734–24 June 1817), statesman, jurist, and signer of the Declaration of Independence, was born in Chester County, Pennsylvania, the son of William McKean, an innkeeper and farmer, and Letitia Finney. He studied at Francis Alison's New London Academy (1742–1750), then left to study law (1750–1754) with his cousin David Finney of New Castle, Delaware. He joined the Delaware bar in 1754 and expanded his practice into Pennsylvania (1755) and New Jersey (1765). Following his admittance to practice before the Pennsylvania Supreme Court in 1757, he gained admission to the Society of the Middle Temple in London as a specialiter, which permitted him to earn certification in 1758 as a barrister without attending.

McKean's ability and drive brought him numerous appointments, including deputy prothonotary and recorder for the probate of wills for New Castle County (1752), deputy attorney general (1756), trustee of the New Castle Loan Office (1764–1772), justice of the peace (1765), and despite his criticism of English policies, collector of customs for New Castle (1771). A proponent of public education, he acted as a sponsor of the New London Academy, became a trustee of the Newark Academy, and in 1779 served as a trustee of the University of Pennsylvania. McKean was a longtime member of the Society for Promotion of Agriculture, the American Philosophical Society (which he served as a counselor), and the Order of the Cincinnati. To provide relief for needy Irish immigrants he helped found the Hibernian Society (1790) and served as its president.

In October 1762 McKean was elected to the Delaware Assembly, a body in which he had served as clerk (1757–1759). With the exception of a single year, he served in the assembly from 1762 to 1779. With Caesar Rodney he collected, edited, and published the laws of the Three Lower Counties (1763). He also collected and recopied valuable Delaware land records that were deteriorating in scattered depositories, some as far away as New York. He worked tirelessly to render the colony's judiciary more efficient. Twice he was elected Speaker (1772, 1777).

McKean married Mary Borden of Bordentown, New Jersey, in 1763. The couple had six children before her death a decade later. McKean's second marriage, to Sarah Armitage of New Castle County (1774), produced five children. To enlarge his law practice and to enter more actively in the movement toward independence, McKean moved to Philadelphia in 1773. His prominence and skill led to his being named chairman of the Committee of Inspection and Observation (1776), colonel of the City's Fourth Battalion of Associators, and president of the Provincial Conference called to lay the groundwork for a state constitutional convention (18–25 June 1776).

McKean became an important Presbyterian voice in the opposition to English policies after 1763. He represented Delaware in the Stamp Act Congress (1765), where he argued for a strong statement of American rights. As a county judge he urged others to follow his lead in carrying out judicial proceedings on unstamped paper. McKean also helped to orchestrate Delaware's resistance to the Townshend Duties (1767–1769) and served in the First and Second Continental Congresses. In the months before independence he sat on five standing congressional committees, including the important Secret Committee. He served in Congress from 1774 to 1783. There he saved Benjamin Franklin (1706–1790) from removal as American representative to France (1779), signed the Articles of Confederation (1781), and briefly acted as its president (1781).

McKean embraced the radical position early. On 10 June 1776 he and his battalion of associators announced publicly that they favored independence. And it was he who on 14 June placed before the Delaware Assembly an official copy of Congress's 10–15 May resolve and successfully urged its acceptance and the suspension of the proprietary government. In Congress on 1 July 1776 McKean voted for independence; but finding Delaware's vote split between his positive vote and George Read's negative position, he urgently sent for the absent Rodney, who arrived on 2 July to cast Delaware's deciding vote for independence. McKean then participated in the discussion and acceptance of Jefferson's Declaration of Independence on 4 July. (In later years he correctly disputed the growing assumption that delegates had signed the Declaration on 4 July. When McKean himself signed the Declaration remains a matter of debate. It doubtless was sometime in 1777, but it could have been as late as 1781.) McKean chaired a meeting on 5 July to discuss common strategy for the defense of the middle states and means to correlate congressional and state military efforts before accompanying his battalion to Perth Amboy, where it saw limited action.

McKean returned to Delaware in August 1776 and attended the September constitutional convention in New Castle. Though he later exaggerated his role in drafting the Delaware constitution, clearly he was a prime figure in determining its final form. Nevertheless, it was the Pennsylvania constitution that occupied his attention. Viewing that document as seriously flawed, he joined an open meeting on 17 October in Philadelphia to enumerate its failings. He and John Dickinson were the principal speakers denouncing the new constitution at a second meeting on 21 October. Despite his criticism of the 1776 constitution, McKean supported Pennsylvania authorities seeking to suppress the disaffected. He chaired a meeting of the Philadelphia Committee of Safety on 25 November 1776 at which suspected Tories were "convicted" and jailed, and he provided legal advice to the new government. But during much of this period McKean was in Delaware, carrying out legal business, serving the assembly as Speaker, and acting briefly as president of the state (22 Sept.–2 Nov.).

On 28 July 1777, despite his continuing unhappiness with the Pennsylvania constitution, he accepted the chief justiceship, a position he held for twenty-two years. As chief justice, McKean also sat on the High Court of Errors and Appeals after its inception in 1780 and presided over most sessions in its first decade. McKean's acceptance of the chief justiceship prompted charges of hypocrisy and ambition and sustained protests against his pluralism. Still, he proved to be a forceful chief justice who contributed substantially to the transformation of the supreme court into a formidable and independent institution. Though he was often accused of partisanship, as chief justice he pursued a course independent enough to frustrate all state political factions at one time or another.

McKean urged a middle course for his court. He fostered a policy of moderation in treason prosecutions. He upheld the English concepts of libel and contempt, employed the process of outlawry, and generally defined the legal rights of women in customary terms. He was slow to accept the changes in the status of blacks, encouraged by the state's 1780 gradual abolition act. But he championed penal reforms, expanded defendant rights, resisted military encroachment on civil authority, embraced the state's confiscation policies, and a decade before *Marbury v. Madison* (1803) accepted his court's right to strike down as unconstitutional state legislative acts. McKean's judicial notes contributed heavily to Alexander J. Dallas's *Reports of Cases Ruled and Adjudged in the Courts of Pennsylvania* (1790), a work originally dedicated to McKean.

McKean was an ardent supporter of the federal Constitution. He and James Wilson led the successful effort to have it ratified in Pennsylvania (1787). Their speeches in its behalf were published as *Commentaries on the Constitution of the United States* (1793). McKean's aggressive advocacy of the new national government failed to secure him the federal judgeship, which he actively pursued. Subsequently, he played an important role in producing a new and more conservative state constitution in the Pennsylvania constitutional convention (1789–1790). Chosen as chair of that body, he stepped down to promote his conservative positions more aggressively.

Because McKean nursed serious reservations regarding Alexander Hamilton's (1755–1804) funding bill, after 1790 he worked to promote the state's Republican party. His enthusiasm for the French Revolution notwithstanding, he concurred in Washington's Neutrality Proclamation (1793). On the other hand, he denounced the Jay Treaty. McKean joined Dickinson in 1798 in trying to calm those advocating war with France. McKean's reputation, high profile, and sympathy for the French Revolution earned him the Republican gubernatorial nomination in 1799. He defeated Federalist James Ross in the election. As governor he introduced the spoils system, dismissing Federalists and replacing them with Republicans. He urged upon Jefferson a similar program following Jefferson's election as president in 1800. When Jefferson's election was delayed by an electoral tie, McKean threatened to mobilize the Pennsylvania militia to secure his ascendancy to the office. Even so, McKean's first term generally ran smoothly and he was reelected in 1802 by a margin of more than 30,000 votes.

Fissures within the Republican party deepened in McKean's second term. William Duane, publisher of the *Aurora and General Advertiser*, who became disenchanted with McKean's refusal to accept his advice on political appointees, joined the state's more radical Republicans in protesting the governor's patronage pattern and in denouncing McKean's failure to endorse radical legal and judicial reforms. McKean's vetoes of assembly bills designed to alter the state's legal system and the law that supported it drew Federalist support even as they angered Republicans. Radical Republicans first sought to remove McKean by offering him as the Republican vice presidential candidate and then by endorsing Simon Snyder (Northumberland County) to oppose him. But a coalition of moderate Republicans (labeled Quids by their opponents) and Federalists ensured McKean's reelection.

McKean began his third term by removing Republicans who had opposed him and naming Federalists in their stead. This, his persistent opposition to the push for radical legal and judicial reform, and his ardent support of the state's supreme court justices who faced an assembly intent on impeaching them, exacerbated his relations with the Duane-Snyder faction. So did McKean's nepotism; he named more than a dozen relatives to office. Increasingly scurrilous attacks on McKean and his policies elicited a spate of lawsuits by the governor, and he pressured the assembly to tighten libel laws. In 1807 impeachment proceedings were initiated against him, but his passionate defense of his official conduct combined with maneuvering by his friends to postpone the partisan and generally frivolous charges (27 Jan. 1808) enabled McKean to complete his term.

Despite the turbulence and personal acrimony that characterized his gubernatorial years, McKean served the state well. His warm advocacy of education paid dividends, as did his espousal of moderate judicial reforms and internal improvements. He spent his remaining years overseeing his extensive estate and died at his Philadelphia home.

The indefatigable McKean had offices and responsibilities thrust upon him as often as he sought them. He shouldered the burdens of everyday service and sacrifice during the Revolution on a level matched by few Whigs. He became an outstanding, if unpopular, chief justice. For all his personal failings—his vanity and occasional pettiness and his uncontrollable temper and exasperation with those unable to grasp things as quickly as he did and lacking his knowledge of the law—McKean was superior to any of his predecessors in that office. His friend and colleague Hugh Henry Brackenridge fittingly observed that "As a judge [McKean] has never been sufficiently appreciated. . . . His legal learning was profound, and accurate . . . the lucidity of his explications and the perspecuity of his language was perfect. . . . I never saw equalled his . . . manner in delivering a charge to the jury, or on a law argument, to the bar" (*Law Miscellanies* [1814], p. 87).

• The McKean papers, including an incomplete autobiography, are in the Historical Society of Pennsylvania (HSP) in Philadelphia. Some papers also can be found in the Hampton L. Carson Collection and in the Simon Gratz Collection, both at HSP. The William Atlee Papers, Library of Congress, contain important McKean material, as do the George Bryan Papers, HSP. Important published sources of McKean materials include Edmund C. Burnett, ed., *Letters of Members of the Continental Congress* (8 vols., 1921–1936), and its successor, Paul H. Smith, ed., *Letters of Delegates to Congress, 1774–1789* (18 vols., 1976–1991); Worthington C. Ford, ed., *Journals of the Continental Congress, 1774–1789* (34 vols., 1904–1937); the *Pennsylvania Archives*, ser. 4, vol. 4 (Gov. McKean's papers), and ser. 1, vols. 4–11; Alexander J. Dallas, ed., *Reports of Cases Ruled and Adjudged in the Supreme Court of Pennsylvania* (4 vols., 1790–1807); Jasper Yeates, ed., *Reports of Cases Adjudged in the Supreme Court of Pennsylvania* (4 vols., 1790; repr. 1871); and *Pennsylvania Colonial Records* (16 vols., 1851–1853). Among the more important of McKean's writings are *A Calm Appeal to the People of Delaware* (1793), *A Charge Delivered to the Grand Jury by the Honourable Thomas McKean, at a Court of Oyer and Terminer, and General Gaol Delivery . . . on the 21st Day of April, 1778* (1778), *Commentaries on the Constitution of the United States* (1793), with James Wilson, *Laws of New Castle, Kent and Sussex Counties upon Delaware* (2 vols., 1763), *The Acts of the General Assembly of the Commonwealth of Pennsylvania . . . Passed between the 30th Day of September, 1775 and the Revolution* (1782), and *Votes and Proceedings of the House of Representatives of the Governments of the Counties of New-Castle, Kent and Sussex upon Delaware, for the Years 1765, 1766, 1767, 1768, 1769, 1770* (1931), with George Read. Three modern biographies are G. S. Rowe, *Thomas McKean: The Shaping of an American Republicanism* (1978); James Peeling, "The Public Life of Thomas McKean, 1734–1817" (Ph.D. diss., Univ. of Chicago, 1929); and John M. Coleman, *Thomas McKean: Forgotten Leader of the Revolution* (1975), although Coleman's work ends in 1781. Roberdeau Buchanan, *The Life of the Honorable Thomas McKean* (1890), is still useful. Among specialized studies are Coleman, "Thomas McKean and the Origins of an Independent Judiciary," *Pennsylvania History* 34 (1967): 111–30; Peeling, "Governor McKean and the Pennsylvania Jacobins, 1799–1808, *Pennsylvania Magazine of History and Biography* 54 (1930): 320–54; Thomas R. Meehan, "The Pennsylvania Supreme Court in the Laws and the Commonwealth, 1776–1790" (Ph.D. diss., Univ. of Wisconsin, 1960); and Elizabeth K. Henderson, "The Attack on the Judiciary in Pennsylvania, 1800–1810," *Pennsylvania Magazine of History and Biography* 61 (1937): 113–36. McKean's career as chief justice is examined in Rowe, *Embattled Bench: The Pennsylvania Supreme Court and the Forging of a Democratic Society, 1684–1809* (1994). For genealogical particulars, consult P. F. Thompson, "Narrative of Thomas McKean Thompson," *Pennsylvania Magazine of History and Biography* 52 (1928): 59–77, 111–29; Cornelius McKean, *McKean Genealogies* (1902); and Buchanan, *Genealogy of the McKean Family* (1890). An obituary is in Poulson's *American Daily Advertiser*, 26 June 1817.

G. S. ROWE

MCKECHNIE, William Boyd (7 Aug. 1887–29 Oct. 1965), baseball player, coach, and manager, was born in Wilkinsburg, Pennsylvania, the son of Scottish-immigrant parents. After high school, he signed a baseball contract in 1906 with a Pennsylvania-Ohio-Maryland League club in Washington, Pennsylvania. Although McKechnie showed promise defensively, he was a weak hitter. The Pittsburgh Pirates called him up in September 1907, but he spent most of the month on the bench.

The Pirates assigned McKechnie in 1908 to the Ohio-Pennsylvania League, where he batted a surprising .283 in 118 games for Canton, Ohio. He earned a promotion to the Wheeling, West Virginia, club in the Central League, where he played regularly and batted .274. McKechnie made the Pirates in 1910 as a utility infielder. With Honus Wagner at shortstop and Bobby Byrne having his best season at third base, McKechnie played mostly as a backup to Dots Miller at second base. Pirate player-manager Fred Clarke had the switch-hitting McKechnie battle 31-year-old rookie Newt Hunter for the first base job in 1911. McKechnie fielded well but batted .227 in 104 games. He played twenty-four games with Pittsburgh in 1912 before being demoted to St. Paul, Minnesota, in the American Association. The Boston Braves drafted McKechnie, but he played only one game before being released on waivers to the New York Yankees in 1913.

Although McKechnie's talent as a player was average at best, he possessed other important talents. He was a quick and perceptive student of the game, and while he could not execute some skills perfectly himself, he was able to teach them to others. McKechnie was raised in a deeply religious home, and for twenty-six years sang in the Wilkinsburg Methodist Church choir. His family and church instilled in him a strong character and generous heart that he carried to the ballyard. Nicknamed "Deacon Will," he possessed the valuable assets of a gentlemanly disposition, a team-first spirit, and an exceptional knowledge of baseball. While he batted a dismal .134 for the Yankees in 1913, manager Frank Chance employed him as a bench coach because McKechnie knew baseball better than anyone else on the team.

In 1914 the Federal League opened to rival the other two major leagues. Seeing a chance to be an everyday player, McKechnie signed with Indianapolis, Indiana, in the new league. He played 149 games at third base, stole 47 bases, and batted .304. He moved with the franchise to Newark, New Jersey, in 1915 and recorded 54 wins and 45 losses after he became manager in June. With the demise of the Federal League after the 1915 season, McKechnie returned to the National League and played 108 games with the New York Giants and Cincinnati Reds in 1916. Reacquired by the Pirates, he started 126 games at third base in 1918. He quit baseball in 1919 but accepted an invitation to rejoin the Pirates as a utility infielder in 1920. His eleven-year major league playing career included 845 games, 713 hits, 319 runs, 8 home runs, 240 RBIs, 127 stolen bases, and a .251 batting average.

After McKechnie batted .321 in the American Association with Minneapolis, Minnesota, in 1921, the Pirates hired him as a coach. When Pittsburgh slipped below .500 in July 1922, McKechnie became the manager, leading the Pirates to fifty-three victories in their final eighty-nine games and a third-place finish. In 1923 the Pirates again finished third and in 1924 finished just three games behind the pennant-winning Giants. McKechnie's managerial style included a knack for getting the most out of utility players and careful handling of the pitching staff. He often employed a five-man rotation to avoid overworking even his more durable starters. Whether a star hitter or third-string catcher, every player was made to feel his role and contribution was vital to the team. Hurlers Lee Meadows, Ray Kremer, Emil Yde, Johnny Morrison, and Vic Aldridge compiled their best seasons under McKechnie's tutelage. The 1925 campaign belonged to Pittsburgh as McKechnie's Pirates won the National League pennant by 8½ games over the Giants and fought back from a three-games-to-one deficit to defeat the Washington Senators in the World Series.

In 1926 Fred Clarke was rehired by the Pirates as assistant manager to McKechnie. The Pirates finished third, only 4½ games behind the World Champion Cardinals, but the team was torn by strife as some players openly cast allegiance to Clarke over McKechnie, preferring Clarke's energetic and charismatic style to McKechnie's more methodical and predictable approach. Clarke was virtually a baseball icon in Pittsburgh for his sixteen seasons as player-manager and four National League pennants. Although Pirates owner Barney Dreyfuss supported him, McKechnie accepted an offer from St. Louis general manager Branch Rickey to join the Cardinals' coaching staff in 1927. The following year Rickey named McKechnie manager. McKechnie had future Hall of Famers Jim Bottomley, Frankie Frisch, Rabbit Maranville, and Chick Hafey in his everyday lineup. However, he worked his best magic with the pitching, coaxing a 16–9 season from 41-year-old Grover Cleveland Alexander, a career-high twenty-one victories from veteran Bill Sherdel, and another twenty wins from 35-year-old Jesse Haines. The Cardinals outdistanced John McGraw's Giants to win the National League pennant but lost in four straight games to the New York Yankees in the World Series. Enraged Cardinals owner Sam Breadon demoted McKechnie to manage Rochester, New York, in the International League in 1929. When St. Louis stumbled below .500 through July 1929, Breadon restored McKechnie to the Cardinals' helm.

Although Breadon offered him a contract for the 1930 season, McKechnie instead accepted the job as manager of the Boston Braves. The Braves had finished no higher than seventh place over the previous four years. From 1930 to 1937 McKechnie never took the Braves higher than fourth place; given the glaring lack of talent, he was considered a genius for taking them that far. In 1937 McKechnie was named National League Manager of the Year when his Braves finished fifth. His efforts that year with two rookie pitchers, 34-year-old Jim Turner and 30-year-old Lou Fette, resulted in twenty victories from each.

In 1938 McKechnie became manager of the Cincinnati Reds and immediately went to work on the pitching. Veteran Paul Derringer won sixty-six games for the Reds from 1938 to 1940. Converted third baseman Bucky Walters won twenty-seven in 1939 and twenty-two in 1940 while leading the league in earned run average both years, and Junior Thompson followed a 13–5 rookie season in 1939 with sixteen wins in 1940. Also in 1940, McKechnie acquired Jim Turner, who responded with a 14–7 record. McKechnie's efforts paid handsome dividends when Cincinnati won ninety-seven games in 1939 and one hundred games in 1940, easily capturing the National League pennant both years. The 1939 World Series was hauntingly similar to McKechnie's trip to the World Series with the 1928 Cardinals, as the Yankees defeated the Reds in four games. In 1940, however, with masterful pitching from Derringer and Walters, McKechnie's men won Cincinnati's first world championship since 1919, defeating the Detroit Tigers in seven games. On 10 June 1944 McKechnie called on fifteen-year-old Joe Nuxhall, the youngest player in major league history, to pitch in relief against the St. Louis Cardinals. From 1941 to 1946 McKechnie directed the Reds to one second-place and two third-place finishes. When the team struggled to seventh place in 1945 and sixth place in 1946, McKechnie was fired. From 1947 to 1949 he coached for the Cleveland Indians and played an instrumental role in developing Larry Doby, the first black player in the American League. In twenty-five years as a manager he won 1,898 games and lost 1,724. Remembered as a cautious, patient, "by the book" manager, McKechnie was firm with his players but assumed the best in them and tried to create situations in which they could excel.

McKechnie married Berlyn Bien in 1911. They had four children, and their son, William, Jr., served as president of the Pacific Coast League from 1968 to 1973. The McKechnies moved to Florida in 1953 and invested in produce, real estate, and oil. In 1962 McKechnie was elected to the National Baseball Hall of Fame. He died in Bradenton, Florida.

• The National Baseball Library in Cooperstown, N.Y., has a file on William McKechnie. Shorter biographies are found in Martin Appel and Burt Goldblatt, *Baseball's Best: The Hall of Fame Gallery* (1977); Edwin Pope, *Baseball's Greatest Managers* (1960); Lowell Reidenbaugh, *Cooperstown: Where Baseball's Legends Live Forever* (1983); and Michael Shatzkin, ed., *The Ballplayers* (1990). For complete statistical information on McKechnie's playing career and managerial record see Rick Wolff, ed. dir., *The Baseball Encyclopedia* (1990). Bob Broeg's *Redbirds: A Century of Cardinals' Baseball* (1981) covers his years with the St. Louis Cardinals. Lee Allen, *Cooperstown Corner Columns from the Sporting News (1962–1969)* (1990), provides interesting anecdotes from his career. An obituary is in the *New York Times*, 30 Oct. 1965.

FRANK J. OLMSTED

MCKEE, John (c. 1767–11 Aug. 1832), American Indian agent and congressman, was born on Buffalo Creek in Rockbridge County, Virginia, the son of John (or James) McKee and Esther "Nannie" Houston, farmers. He attended Liberty Hall Academy (now Washington and Lee University). In 1792 Governor William Blount of the Southwest Territory appointed McKee as one of the commissioners to run the boundary line provided for by the Cherokee Treaty of Holston. Difficulties prevented completion of the survey, but Blount sent McKee—"a Trader of Chota"—on a mission to pacify the Cherokees in February 1793. By September McKee was conducting five Chickasaw chiefs to Philadelphia to visit the president. The next year he was temporary Cherokee agent, residing at Tellico Blockhouse, gathering information, and trying to keep the tribe friendly. In November 1794 Blount explained to the secretary of war why McKee should continue as agent, "For besides his having a great share of the confidence of the [Cherokee] Nation, he is from his abilities & knowledge of Indians, their habits & dispositions, the most proper man within my acquaintance or knowledge for a Deputy, and if it should be necessary to his continuance that he should be an officer, I can assure you that he is not only qualified by his bodily & mental abilities to perform the duties of a Captain but of a Field or General Officer." On 28 January 1795 McKee was licensed as an attorney in the Court of Pleas and Quarter Sessions; in August Blount commissioned him a militia lieutenant colonel and the clerk of Blount County, Southwest Territory. In 1797 the United States sent McKee to Pensacola to discuss payment of the debts the Choctaws owed to Panton, Leslie, and Company. McKee was U.S. agent to the Choctaws from about May 1799 until March 1802.

On 5 December 1810 McKee reported to the secretary of war on disturbances in West Florida. The previous September Americans in that Spanish colony had seized the fort at Baton Rogue and asked for annexation by the United States. The next month the United States annexed part of West Florida, but Mobile remained under Spanish control. On 26 January 1811 President James Madison dispatched McKee and George Mathews to West Florida to buy or seize what remained of that Spanish colony. The mission failed to obtain Mobile. In 1813 General Andrew Jackson sent McKee into the Choctaw Nation to keep that tribe loyal to the United States and gather information. On 28 September McKee officially became Tennessee's special agent to the Choctaws. He recruited Choctaw warriors, who fought the Creeks for the United States on the Alabama and Black Warrior rivers in late 1813. On 1 May 1814 McKee replaced Silas Dinsmoor as U.S. Choctaw agent. McKee recruited Choctaw and Chickasaw warriors to fight with Jackson against the British. Harry Toulmin believed "that the exertions of Col M'Kee with the Choctaw Indians did more than any thing else to save us from them" during the War of 1812.

Along with John Coffee and John Rhea, McKee negotiated the Choctaw Treaty of 24 October 1816, by which the tribe ceded territory in western Alabama. In April 1818 McKee, William Carroll, and Daniel Burnet were appointed to negotiate with the tribe for a cession in Central Mississippi. The negotiations failed that fall when the Choctaws refused to sell any more land. Jackson replaced Carroll in 1819, but again the Choctaws refused to agree to a treaty. Because McKee was perceived as too friendly to the American Indians, Jackson and Thomas Hinds were the negotiators in 1820, and the Choctaws ceded five million acres of land in the Treaty of Doak's Stand on 18 October 1820. The previous May President James Monroe had nominated McKee to be register of the land office at Tuscaloosa. The Senate postponed action on the nomination, but once renominated on 3 January 1821, McKee was confirmed. He resigned as Choctaw agent.

McKee represented the Middle District (the central portion of the state around Tuscaloosa) in the U.S. House of Representatives from 1 December 1823 until 3 March 1829. On 14 April 1823 Jackson wished McKee "success" in running for Congress. No speech by McKee is extant, but he served on the Committee on Indian Affairs for six years and in December 1824 was consulted by Secretary of War John C. Calhoun on the negotiations with a Choctaw delegation in Washington. McKee provided additional information to the War Department on several other occasions. The citizens of Tuscaloosa honored him on 19 May 1829 with a public dinner and commended him for "his amiable and gentlemanly deportment as a citizen, added to his faithful, able and patriotic services" in Congress for the last six years.

Sometime in or after 1816 McKee built his house, "Hill of Howth," one mile southeast of Boligee, Greene County, Alabama. He reportedly married a Chickasaw half-breed and had a son and daughter. He died at his plantation.

• Collections of McKee's papers are in the Alabama Department of Archives and History, the Library of Congress, and the Southern Historical Collection at the University of North Carolina at Chapel Hill. Scattered letters are in the David Henley Papers, Tennessee State Library and Archives; the James McHenry Papers, Maryland Historical Society; the Samuel Brown Papers, Filson Club, Louisville; Mississippi Governors' Correspondence, RG 27, Mississippi Department of Archives and History; records of the Indian Office and War Department at the National Archives; and various collections of Andrew Jackson Papers throughout the country. Access to this latter material can be gained through *The Papers of John C. Calhoun*, ed. Robert L. Meriwether et al. (1959); *The Papers of Andrew Jackson*, ed. Sam B. Smith et al. (1980) and the guide to the comprehensive microfilm edition; and Clarence E. Carter and John Porter Bloom, eds., *The Territorial Papers of the United States*, vols. 4–6 and 18 (1934–1975). McKee's activities as Choctaw agent are briefly discussed in Arthur H. DeRosier, Jr., *The Removal of the Choctaw Indians* (1970). See also "Colonel John McKee," *Alabama Historical Quarterly* 3 (Spring 1941): 15–22.

CHARLES H. SCHOENLEBER

MCKEEN, Joseph (15 Oct. 1757–15 July 1807), clergyman and college president, was born in Londonderry, New Hampshire, the son of John McKeen and Mary McKeen, occupations unknown. Coming from a locally prominent family, he was tutored by the Reverend Simon Williams before entering Dartmouth College. In 1774 he graduated with first honors and then taught school in Londonderry until 1782, with a short interruption for duty with General John Sullivan during the revolutionary war. Eager to continue his formal education, McKeen in 1782 entered Harvard, where he studied astronomy, mathematics, and natural philosophy with Samuel Williams. He took time from his studies to marry Alice Anderson in 1785; five children were born of the marriage.

Raised in the Presbyterian faith, McKeen felt a call to the ministry and studied theology with his former teacher, Simon Williams. After being licensed to preach by the Londonderry Presbytery, McKeen spent a brief period assisting at the Phillips Academy in Andover, Massachusetts, and also preached on odd occasions in Boston. Later switching to the Congregationalist faith, similar in creed to the Presbyterians, he received a call to the First Congregational Church in Lower Beverly, Massachusetts, where he replaced the Reverend Joseph Willard, the newly appointed president of Harvard. Ordained in May 1785, McKeen remained in this position for the next seventeen years, steering a middle course between the most orthodox and the most liberal theological leanings of his congregation. His conciliatory approach attracted the attention of officials at the newly chartered (1794) Bowdoin College, and after the college agreed to provide not only a salary but also a dwelling place for his family, McKeen was chosen as the college's first president in July 1801.

Following his selection as president, McKeen set out on a tour of existing New England colleges with the only other faculty member, John Abbot. Visiting Harvard, Brown, Yale, and Williams Colleges, McKeen observed firsthand the varied operations of the schools. Although a newcomer to the field of higher education and selected more for his piety than his academic credentials, as were nearly all of his contemporaries, McKeen nevertheless brought solid credentials to his new post; as a member of the American Academy of Arts and Sciences, he had made several contributions to the publications of that organization.

McKeen and Abbot were installed in their respective posts at Bowdoin's first inauguration on 2 September 1802. In his opening address, McKeen set the tone for his administration, stating: "It ought always to be remembered, that literary institutions are founded and endowed for the common good, and not for the private advantage of those who resort to them for education. It is not that they may be able to pass through life in an easy or reputable manner, but that their mental powers may be cultivated and improved for the benefit of society. If it be true no man should live for himself alone, we may safely assert that every man who has been aided by a public institution to acquire an education and to qualify himself for usefulness, is under peculiar obligations to exert his talents for the public good."

McKeen advocated the training of mental facilities in his students in an era when the development of student character was considered paramount, and he set high standards for Bowdoin. The eight students who gained admittance to the first class had to meet the same entrance requirements that Harvard required of its matriculants. In his teaching, McKeen was noted for his ability to relate examples from ordinary life to his lessons, thereby modifying the then-standard educational practice of learning by memorization and rote recitation. Upon the founding of the college, the library consisted of nearly five hundred volumes, impressive given the meager assets of the school. Bowdoin acquired so much scientific apparatus, such as a telescope and an equatorial, that the college boasted it was second only to Harvard in possession of equipment for scientific study.

Although the faculty grew slowly, no addition proved more significant than Parker Cleaveland in 1805. Holding the first chair of mathematics and natural and experimental philosophy at Bowdoin, he made significant contributions to the school's instruction in chemistry and mineralogy and to the Medical School, which began instruction in 1820.

The onset of dropsy took McKeen from his duties for several months before it caused his death in Brunswick, Maine, although he lived long enough to preside over the school's first commencement. His background was similar to that of many of his contemporaries in higher education, but McKeen was nonetheless a pioneer in many areas, particularly in instruction in the natural sciences.

• McKeen's papers are divided; the Bowdoin College Archives in Brunswick, Maine, holds a small collection, and some additional correspondence is in the Isaac Lincoln Papers at the Pejepscot Historical Society, also in Brunswick. The best source of information on his life and career remains Louis C. Hatch, *The History of Bowdoin College* (1927), although a good recent sketch is Kenneth Charles Morton Sills, *Joseph McKeen (1757–1807) and the Beginnings of Bowdoin College, 1802 . . .* (1945). An obituary is in the *Boston Repertory*, 24 July 1807.

EDWARD L. LACH, JR.

MCKELDIN, Theodore Roosevelt (20 Nov. 1900–10 Aug. 1974), politician, was born in Baltimore, Maryland, the son of James Alfred McKeldin, a stonemason and policeman, and Dora Grief. During his long political career, McKeldin often attributed his success to his mother, who taught him to work hard at every task he attempted. The McKeldin family was large, eleven children, and money was scarce in their South Baltimore, working-class home. Theodore McKeldin was forced to discontinue his full-time education at the age of fourteen, following his graduation from grammar school, to help support the family. He worked during the day as an office boy in a bank while he attended night school. During vacations he worked as a gravedigger to earn extra money. After earning the equivalent of a high school diploma, McKeldin continued his studies in night school at the University of Maryland, where he earned a law degree in 1925. The year before he had married Honolulu Claire Manzer; the couple had two children.

McKeldin began his professional career as a campaign worker for William F. Broening, a prominent Baltimore Republican. Broening was elected the city's mayor in 1927, and McKeldin became his executive secretary, a post he held for four years. In 1931

McKeldin established a private law practice in Baltimore but remained active in Republican politics.

McKeldin first sought political office in 1939, when he ran unsuccessfully for mayor of Baltimore. In 1942 he ran, again unsuccessfully, for governor of Maryland. A year later he was elected Baltimore's mayor in an upset victory that he attributed to his persistent door-to-door campaigning and to his improved speaking abilities. In the ensuing decades, McKeldin was renowned for his often florid oratory and was considered the best Republican orator of his day. Becoming the most prominent politician of his party in the state, he earned the nickname "Mr. Republican."

McKeldin's speeches, with their ringing affirmations of a Bryan-like faith in the common person, were not empty bombast, however. During his years in office, he worked hard to improve the daily lives of ordinary citizens, regardless of their race, creed, or color. Beginning with his first term as mayor of Baltimore (1943–1947), he opposed racial segregation throughout his political career. As mayor he appointed the first black school board member and hired blacks for his personal staff and to work in the city solicitor's office.

While still mayor of Baltimore, McKeldin ran a second time for the governorship of Maryland in 1946 but lost the race. When his term as mayor expired a year later, he returned to private law practice and also studied economics at Johns Hopkins University. He ran a third time for governor in the fall of 1950 and campaigned intensively, making hundreds of personal appearances throughout the state. Although Maryland voters were overwhelmingly Democratic, McKeldin won the race by an unprecedented majority. He took office in January 1951 as only the fourth Republican governor in the state's history.

As governor McKeldin continued to advocate civil rights while vetoing what he considered bureaucratic legislation passed by the state legislature, which was controlled by well-entrenched Democrats. A major achievement of his administration was the dedication of the Chesapeake Bay Bridge, linking Maryland's Eastern Shore with the western half of the state, in the summer of 1952. Although the project had been instigated under the preceding governor, McKeldin had seen it through to completion. At the same time, he strongly supported many of the social reforms introduced by Franklin D. Roosevelt's New Deal and Harry S. Truman's Fair Deal, while criticizing alleged corruption in the Truman administration. He was also an early critic of McCarthyism and what he called its "smear technique," "big lie," and "sly innuendo."

Through public appearances at national gatherings, including the Southern Governors Conference and the Lincoln Day Dinner of the National Republican Club, McKeldin emerged as a leader of Republican moderates. In the spring of 1952 he announced his "favorite son" candidacy for the party's presidential nomination, challenging the powerful conservative Republican senator Robert Taft. Not long afterward, McKeldin met with General Dwight D. Eisenhower, by then the front-runner among moderates for the Republican presidential nomination, and after the meeting implied that he would endorse Eisenhower's candidacy.

When the Republican National Convention opened in early July 1952, McKeldin was chosen to nominate Eisenhower. His speech, televised nationally, made him famous overnight throughout the country and gave an additional boost to Eisenhower's candidacy. McKeldin campaigned widely for Eisenhower in the fall election, which Eisenhower won handily.

McKeldin was reelected governor in 1954 and served another four-year term. After leaving office in 1959, he remained active in state party politics, and four years later he was reelected mayor of Baltimore. The city, like much of the nation, was in the midst of the civil rights movement, and McKeldin continued his stalwart defense of racial equality. On several occasions he was credited with defusing tense situations as rioting erupted in various parts of the city.

McKeldin was also an early opponent of U.S. involvement in the Vietnam War, and in the last years of his political career he worked for the abolition of capital punishment. After leaving the mayor's office in 1967, McKeldin remained active in various community and charitable organizations. In addition to his professional duties, McKeldin taught Sunday school for many years at his neighborhood Episcopal church and during the 1940s taught law courses at the University of Baltimore Law School, the Baltimore College of Commerce, and Forest Park Evening School. He was also the author, with John C. Krantz, of *The Art of Eloquence* (1952), an oratorical handbook that includes a selection of McKeldin's speeches. McKeldin died at his home in Baltimore.

• Most of McKeldin's personal papers are in the Maryland Room of the Theodore R. McKeldin Library at the University of Maryland, College Park. McKeldin's gubernatorial papers are deposited at the Maryland State Archives in Annapolis; his mayoral papers are in the Baltimore City Archives. An extensive clipping file on McKeldin is at the Maryland Historical Society, Baltimore. The society's collections also include some of McKeldin's personal correspondence and the McKeldin-Jackson Oral History Project, a series of interviews with public figures, including McKeldin, who played a major role in the civil rights movement in Md. in the mid-twentieth century. Biographical information on McKeldin is in *Current Biography Yearbook 1952* (1952), pp. 377–79. An obituary is in the *New York Times*, 11 Aug. 1974.

ANN T. KEENE

MCKELWAY, Alexander Jeffrey (6 Oct. 1866–16 Apr. 1918), editor and social reformer, was born in Sadsburyville, Pennsylvania, the son of John Ryan McKelway and Catherine Scott Comfort. Less than a year after McKelway's birth his family moved to Virginia, where he spent his entire childhood. In 1886 he earned his B.A. from Hampden-Sydney College, a Southern Presbyterian school in Virginia, and he received his divinity degree from Union Theological

Seminary in Richmond, Virginia, in 1891. That year he was ordained as a Presbyterian minister and married Ruth Smith; they had four children.

After serving Presbyterian congregations in Johnston County and Fayetteville, North Carolina, from 1891 to 1897, the theologically moderate McKelway in 1898 became the editor of the *Presbyterian Standard* in Charlotte, North Carolina. Under his leadership the paper's quality and themes attracted national attention. As editor McKelway worked fervently to have laws passed in southern states forbidding the sale of alcohol, and he joined many southerners in an effort to close down saloons, which he believed promoted crime and disorder and lowered economic productivity.

Charlotte was located in the center of the North Carolina textile industry, a fact that inspired McKelway to also become involved in the crusade for legislation that would prohibit child labor. He wrote editorials and articles attacking the practice, which was widespread in the South—especially in the textile, tobacco, and canning industries. In 1903 he helped persuade the North Carolina legislature to adopt a law forbidding children under age twelve from working at all and limiting the work of older children to sixty-six hours per week. Although a weak law, it established the principle of government regulation of industry in the state.

McKelway's efforts to end child labor brought him into contact with another leading reformer, Edgar Gardner Murphy, an Episcopalian minister in Alabama. Murphy convinced him to serve as the assistant secretary for the southern states of the new National Child Labor Committee, which Murphy had formed with the assistance of Felix Adler of the New York Child Labor Committee and Florence Kelley of the National Consumers' League. In 1905 McKelway left the *Standard* and began working as a full-time lobbyist and publicist for the organization. He toured New England mill towns to examine their child labor regulations, studied the history of child labor in England, and visited every southern state numerous times to meet politicians and to lobby in legislatures for child labor reform. His well-publicized investigations shocked the public and angered mill owners and their political allies. In response to the charge that he was an agent of New England textile manufacturers seeking to destroy southern industry, McKelway demonstrated that these northern manufacturers owned many southern mills and actually opposed child labor laws in the South.

The failure to persuade any southern states to adopt significant child labor laws led the national committee in 1907 to work for federal regulation. McKelway was sent to Washington, D.C., to lobby for a bill introduced in the Senate by Albert Beveridge of Indiana. Because industry had become nationwide, McKelway argued, it was impossible for the states to regulate it effectively. National legislation prohibiting child labor was needed to control corporations and enable states to compete on an equal level. Congress, however, failed to pass the Beveridge Bill, and the national committee decided not to support other federal regulatory measures except the formation of a Children's Bureau, which was finally established in 1912. While helping to secure the adoption of this bureau, McKelway also continued to aid the state committees in their efforts to improve southern child labor laws. Because his passionate rhetoric had made many enemies in the South, McKelway reduced his traveling in the region and devoted more time to managing the national committee in Washington.

McKelway developed many close relationships with congressmen and cabinet officers, but his most significant relationship was with Woodrow Wilson. McKelway helped his friend and fellow Presbyterian win the Democratic presidential nomination in 1912 by sharing with Wilson his knowledge of southern Democrats. During Wilson's first term, McKelway prodded him to support social justice legislation. After lobbying vigorously for a national child labor bill, McKelway helped convince Wilson to sign the 1916 Keating-Owen Bill, the first federal child labor law, which prohibited products manufactured by children under the age of fourteen from being shipped in interstate commerce. He also helped write the Democratic national platform of 1916, influencing in particular its planks on government employment, prison reform, labor, and public health.

McKelway worked hard for Wilson's reelection in 1916, especially in trying to win over Progressives disappointed that the president had not supported enough of their programs during his first term. Also in 1916 he organized the Bureau of Education and Social Service to appeal for support of Wilson among teachers and social workers; he published two pamphlets for distribution among those groups and spoke extensively throughout New York State on Wilson's behalf. After Wilson was narrowly reelected, McKelway continued his work with the National Child Labor Committee, concentrating on efforts to implement the Keating-Owen Bill.

McKelway's interest in social reform was not limited to the child labor problem. While living in North Carolina he had fought for prohibition and antigambling laws, and during the last fifteen years of his life he sought to pass employers' liability and workmen's compensation laws, as well as the initiative, referendum, and recall, which, respectively, gave voters the right to propose new laws, to accept or reject a proposed law at the ballot box, and to remove an elected official from office. He also worked to abolish the convict leasing system, to establish juvenile courts, to improve housing and public education, to provide state aid to poor families, to gain woman suffrage, and to end international militarism.

Like many other Progressives, McKelway had paternalistic and racial prejudices. He believed he knew what was best for the children of the working class and rarely considered the views of their parents, who may have believed their children should work to augment the family income and who may have preferred to pass to their children their own cultural heritage, not that of the social reformers. He insisted that ending child labor and educating children in the public schools would help end the cycle of poverty, allow children to reach their full potential, and ensure greater social stability in the South. McKelway defended the lynching of blacks as an understandable response to the crime of rape and argued that slavery had uplifted blacks by providing them with civilization and Christianity. He saw blacks as especially predisposed to drunkenness and supported their disenfranchisement on the grounds that they were usually the "pawns of the saloon in the political game." Although deploring the violence involved, he justified the Atlanta race riots of 1906 because black men had assaulted white women.

McKelway's progressivism was grounded in his Christian faith. With other proponents of the social gospel he believed that solving social problems was essential to building the kingdom of God on earth, which was "the chief business of the Church." Establishing God's kingdom required treating children, the nation's principal asset, properly. He believed that children who worked too early in their lives suffered a "stunting of the body, . . . dwarfing of the mind, [and] spoiling of the spirit." Because they were "helpless and dependent," they must be granted the right to play and dream, to sleep at night, and to go to school rather than work long hours in factories or mines. Like many other Progressives and adherents of the social gospel, McKelway insisted that child labor was a structural problem, produced by the industrial system and existing beyond the control of any individuals or groups. Believing it could only be solved by public policies, he spent the last fourteen years of his life trying to secure laws to remedy the tragedy of child labor.

McKelway was an effective pastor, an inspiring editor, a persuasive lobbyist, and a provocative publicist. He was frequently criticized for using a "sharp pen," a charge that his friend and colleague Owen Lovejoy admitted was just but which was rooted in McKelway's belief that the "wrongs against defenseless children . . . deserved the most uncompromising condemnation" (Lovejoy, p. 23). Graham Taylor, a professor at a Congregationalist seminary in Chicago, wrote that McKelway was a "genial yet robust, fraternal yet aggressive, gentle yet brave" crusader who "valiantly, eloquently, and effectively" promoted the welfare of children (Lovejoy, pp. 26–7). Worn out by incessant travel, numerous speeches, and constant controversy, McKelway died of a heart attack in Washington, D.C., prompting Wilson to write to his widow that he lamented the loss of McKelway's "friendship and counsel" (Lovejoy, p. 24).

• McKelway's papers are at the Library of Congress in Washington, D.C., and the Presbyterian Church, U.S.A.'s Department of History in Montreat, North Carolina. His articles include "The Devil Over-reaching Himself," *Charlotte Presbyterian Standard*, 2 Feb. 1899; "Up to Slavery," *Charlotte Presbyterian Standard*, 22 Apr. 1903; "Child Labor in Southern Industry," *Annals of the American Academy of Political and Social Science* 35 (Jan.–June 1905): 430–36; "The Child Labor Problem—A Study in Degeneracy," *Annals of the American Academy of Political and Social Science* 27 (Jan.–June 1906): 312–26; "Child Labor in the Southern Cotton Mills," *Annals of the American Academy of Political and Social Science* 27 (Jan.–June 1906): 259–69; "The Awakening of the South against Child Labor," *Annals of the American Academy of Political and Social Science* 29 (Jan. 1907): 9–18; and "Child Labor and Its Attendant Evils," *Sewanee Review* 16 (Apr. 1908): 214–27. The most complete source on McKelway's life and contributions is Betty Jane Brandon, "Alexander Jeffrey McKelway: Statesman of the New Order" (Ph.D. diss., Univ. of North Carolina, 1969). For McKelway's career see Brandon, "A Wilsonian Progressive—Alexander Jeffrey McKelway," *Journal of Presbyterian History* 48 (1970): 2–17, and Herbert J. Doherty, Jr., "Alexander J. McKelway: Preacher to Progressive," *Journal of Southern History* 24 (May 1958): 77–90. William A. Link, *The Paradox of Southern Progressivism, 1880–1930* (1992), discusses McKelway. Obituaries are "Brilliant Toil in Two Fields," *Continent* 49 (2 May 1918): 484, and Owen R. Lovejoy, "Dr. Alexander Jeffrey McKelway, 1866–1918," *Child Labor Bulletin* 7 (May 1918): 21–27.

GARY SCOTT SMITH

MCKENDREE, William (6 July 1757–5 Mar. 1835), bishop in the Methodist Episcopal church, was born in King William County, Virginia, the son of John McKendree and Mary (maiden name unknown). Reared as an Anglican, McKendree joined a Methodist society sometime before 1777. For ten years during and after the revolutionary war (he was present at the surrender of Cornwallis at Yorktown), he moved in and out of Methodist class meetings before experiencing a profound religious conversion in 1787. Although he had no formal education, McKendree's serious turn of mind and spirit was recognized by the leaders of the Methodist Episcopal church, and he was received on trial in the Virginia Conference in 1788. For six years he served as traveling preacher on several Virginia circuits.

In 1792 McKendree sided with James O'Kelly, his presiding elder, on a General Conference resolution allowing dissatisfied preachers to appeal their appointments. The resolution was defeated, and O'Kelly split off to form the Republican Methodist church, which guaranteed the right of appeal. McKendree left with him, but soon he became disenchanted and began traveling with Bishop Francis Asbury, the founder of American Methodism. After carefully examining the *Rules and Discipline* of the church drawn up by John Wesley, its founder, McKendree became convinced that O'Kelly was in error.

Quickly reestablishing his Methodist Episcopal loyalties, McKendree served on preaching circuits in Virginia until 1796, when he was appointed presiding elder. In 1801 he moved to the Kentucky District of the newly formed Western Conference (including Ohio, Kentucky, Tennessee, western Virginia, and part of Illinois). He was later known as the "father of Western Methodism" for his pioneer work, combining extraordinary gifts of lively preaching and solid administration. McKendree domesticated the high enthusiasm of the frontier camp meeting and harnessed its energy for

Methodist churches, circuits, and districts throughout the conference.

In 1808 McKendree preached at the General Conference of the Methodist Episcopal church. Asbury foretold, "That sermon will get you elected bishop." At that same conference McKendree became the third elected bishop, and the first American-born one, in American Methodism. He made his most significant administrative mark by asking the advice of his presiding elders on the appointment of preachers, over Asbury's reservations. This eventually led to the formation of the cabinet system prevalent in United Methodism today. In 1815 Asbury, in failing health, resigned his "stations" to McKendree. In 1820 McKendree, beginning to feel vulnerable because of the effects of old age himself, rather uncharacteristically opposed a move to limit the power of the bishops in assigning preachers to their charges. Soon after this his health broke under the strain of his responsibilities, and although he continued to travel throughout the conference, he exercised fewer episcopal duties.

In 1830 McKendree donated 480 acres of land to Lebanon Seminary in Lebanon, Illinois, and the name of the institution was immediately changed to McKendree College. He never married. He died at the home of his brother, Dr. James McKendree, in Sumner County, Tennessee.

Historians remind us of McKendree's most significant contributions to both church polity and evangelism. The cabinet effectively molded Methodism's appointment system. In addition, McKendree's founding of churches in what was then the West led to an ever-expanding Methodist influence throughout the nineteenth century.

• The most detailed source is Robert Paine, *Life and Times of William McKendree* (1869; repr. 1880). Another extended biographical sketch is in Benjamin S. Fry, *The Lives of Bishops Whatcoat, M'Kendree, and George* (1853).

ROBERT G. TUTTLE, JR.

MCKENNA, Joseph (10 Aug. 1843–21 Nov. 1926), jurist, was born in Philadelphia, Pennsylvania, the son of Irish famine immigrants. His father, John McKenna, and his mother, the former Mary Johnson, ran a small bakeshop to support their large family but gave it up in 1855 and migrated to California. There Joseph was educated in parochial schools, graduating in 1865 from Benicia Collegiate Institute. That same year he was admitted to the California bar. In 1869 he married Amanda F. Bornemann, with whom he had four children.

McKenna rarely engaged in private practice but used his legal expertise as a stepping-stone to a successful career in politics. He won election to two terms as district attorney of Solano County (1866–1870) and one term to the state legislature (1875–1876). Pointing his sights on the national level, he suffered a series of defeats but finally won election to the House of Representatives where he served four terms as a Republican from California's new Third District (1885–1892).

In Congress he displayed the characteristics that identified him as a loyal party man. He introduced private members' bills for Leland Stanford, a railroad magnate, and supported the extension of California railroad land grants. McKenna proved adept at getting pork barrel legislation for the folks at home, including a $400,000 appropriation for improving harbor and port facilities in the San Francisco Bay Area. He fought hard for high protective tariffs and against any form of railroad regulation, joining the minority vote against the creation of the commission proposed with the Interstate Commerce Act of 1887. He ingratiated himself with Stanford by giving strong support to the allocation of $3 million to Stanford's Central Pacific Railroad for military transportation, although the rail line was already in debt to the government for at least $70 million.

In 1892 he resigned his House seat when President Benjamin Harrison named him to the Court of Appeals for the Ninth Circuit, an appointment influenced undoubtedly by Stanford. After winning a smashing electoral victory in 1896, President-elect William McKinley paid off political debts and established western geographical representation by naming McKenna his attorney general two months before taking office in March 1897. And on 16 December of that same year, he elevated McKenna to the U.S. Supreme Court to succeed Justice Stephen J. Field. McKinley had the opportunity to make only one appointment, McKenna's, to the Supreme Court during his four-and-a-half years in office, but this one selection of an old friend and fellow legislator gave him, if not everyone else, particular pleasure.

Opposition to the appointment was both predictable and loud. McKenna's long association with Stanford, railroad, and other West Coast special interests was cited. The nomination was delayed for about five weeks, but after his opponents had their say the Judiciary Committee and the Senate as a whole voted confirmation on 21 January 1898 without a formal roll call. McKenna took his seat on the Supreme Court that same month.

McKenna served almost twenty-seven years on the high court, among the longest tenures of any justice in its history. There were few majority opinions in the more than 633 he wrote while on the bench, and in the early years many of them were verbose, bewilderingly complex, and studded with numerous established precedents. He served during a period when the Court decided some very important cases and a few of his opinions had long-lasting effects. Over time he gained a better grasp of the responsibilities of an associate justice but never developed any recognizably consistent legal philosophy.

His decisions strengthened the effectiveness of the Interstate Commerce Act and expanded the federal police power, robustly supporting congressional efforts to regulate new areas of the nation's economic and social life under the commerce clause. If his position on railroad rate-fixing seems to be in conflict with his earlier opposition to establishing the ICC, it only serves to underline a certain erratic strain in his decisions, frequently resulting in contradictory opinions.

McKenna, for a unanimous Court, gave the opinion in *Hipolite Egg Co. v. U.S.* (1911), which sustained the validity of the Pure Food and Drug Act of 1906. This and such earlier decisions as *Champion v. Ames* (1903) established him as pursuing a more consistent line of decisions, using a broad interpretation of federal commerce. He ruled, in *Hipolite*, that although Congress could not directly prevent the processing of adulterated foods, it could prevent the transportation of such foods in interstate commerce.

In 1913 the Court gave further support to the growing body of federal police power legislation when it upheld the Mann Act prohibiting the interstate transportation of women for immoral ends (the so-called "white slave trade"), whether for commercial purposes or otherwise. McKenna wrote, "if the facility of interstate transportation can be taken away from the demoralization of lotteries, the debasement of obscene literature, the contagion of diseased cattle or persons, the impurity of food and drugs, the like facility can be taken away from the systematic enticement to and the enslavement in prostitution . . . of women, and, more insistently, of [young] girls" (*Hoke v. U.S.* [1913]).

In 1920 McKenna wrote the majority opinion for the Court in *United States v. U.S. Steel Corporation*, in which he declared that the Sherman Act did not prohibit the mere existence of the power to dominate an industry. In a 3 to 5 decision, the Court ruled that in the absence of some overt action to the contrary, it could be assumed that a corporation was acting "reasonably." In other words, the unconcealed monopolistic tendencies of U.S. Steel were "reasonable," thus expanding the "rule of reason." Some of McKenna's later opinions were characterized by practicality, the application of common sense, logic, and a greater clarity of expression. Overall his performance while on the Court was respectable, in spite of the dire predictions that had preceded his confirmation.

McKenna's dissent in *Hammer v. Dagenhart* (1918), in which he was joined by Justices Brandeis, Holmes, and Clarke, included a vigorous criticism of the doctrine of dual federalism. Proponents of this judicial instrument argued that the Tenth Amendment in the Bill of Rights created a dual system of sovereignty in which both the powers of the states and of the federal government were separable, and in their respective spheres inviolable. McKenna upheld extending federal regulatory power to child labor while the majority of his brethren, turning their backs on logic, history, and working children, upheld the power of the states, in spite of earlier decisions in which they had upheld the federal police power. In this and other cases McKenna demonstrated that he was less friendly to state regulation that allegedly inhibited freedom of contract, and accordingly he voted with the majority in such landmark decisions as *Lochner v. New York* (1905) and *Adkins v. Children's Hospital* (1923).

In his later years McKenna's mental processes began to deteriorate, but when he was at his best his decisions were infused with a strong nationalism, moral vigor, and sound reasoning. Failing to recognize or admit the enfeebling effects of advanced age, he remained on the Court beyond his time. His colleagues, realizing by 1922 that he frequently missed the entire point of a case, agreed internally in November 1924 to postpone decisions in those cases in which McKenna's vote would be crucial. With considerable prodding from Chief Justice William Howard Taft, he retired from the bench on 25 January 1925, and nearly two years later he died in Washington. The other justices were honorary pallbearers at his funeral.

• There is no collection of McKenna's papers, although a few items can be found scattered in other collections, such as the papers of President/Chief Justice Taft in the Library of Congress, Manuscript Division. McKenna is profiled in Matthew McDevitt's *Joseph McKenna: Associate Justice of the United States* (1946); there is no other formal biography. A shorter treatment can be found in James F. Watts, Jr., "Joseph McKenna," in *The Justices of the United States Supreme Court, 1789–1969*, ed. Leon Friedman and Fred Israel, vol. 3 (1969), pp. 1719–36. Brief references are in Alpheus T. Mason, *William Howard Taft: Chief Justice* (1964); John E. Semonche, *Charting the Future: The Supreme Court Responds to a Changing Society, 1890–1920* (1978); and Margaret Leech, *In the Days of McKinley* (1959). For a full account of his resignation see the *New York Times*, 6 Jan. 1925. His obituary is in the *New York Times*, 22 Nov. 1926.

MARIAN C. MCKENNA

MCKENNAN, Thomas McKean Thompson (31 Mar. 1794–9 July 1852), lawyer, congressman, and railroad president, was born in Dragon Neck, New Castle County, Delaware, the son of Colonel William McKennan, a revolutionary war officer, and Elizabeth Thompson, a niece of Thomas McKean, a Pennsylvania chief justice and governor. His grandfather, the Reverend William McKennan, who emigrated from Scotland via northern Ireland and Barbados, ministered to the Presbyterians in Wilmington for over fifty years. When Thomas was just a boy, his family left Delaware, migrating to western Virginia and then western Pennsylvania. They settled in the town of Washington in 1803, and Colonel McKennan served in the administration of Pennsylvania's governor McKean until the end of the governor's term in 1808. Colonel McKennan died in 1810 from the effects of wounds suffered in the revolutionary war.

McKennan graduated from Washington College (now Washington and Jefferson College) the same year his father died. He studied law in the office of Parker Campbell of Washington, Pennsylvania, and during 1813–1814 was a tutor in ancient languages at Washington College. He was admitted to the bar in 1814 and began a law practice in Washington that continued until his death. "He soon won a place in the front rank of his profession" (*Appleton's Cyclopaedia of American Biography*, vol. 4, p. 131). In 1815 he married Matilda Lowrie Bowman; they had eight children. Also in 1815, at age twenty-one, McKennan became deputy attorney general for the county, serving until 1817. He became a member of the town council in 1818. He resigned from the town council in 1831, when he entered the U.S. House of Representatives.

Pursuing an interest in the possibilities of railroad transportation, McKennan became, in 1831, an early official of the projected Washington (Pa.) and Pittsburgh Railroad Company. Washington, because of its location, was in need of connections to the main lines of transportation, but because of opposition from the Baltimore & Ohio and Pennsylvania railroads as well as those promoting the "national road," construction was delayed for many years. Meanwhile, McKennan resigned from the town council to enter national politics.

Elected as an Anti-Masonic candidate to the Twenty-second Congress in 1830, McKennan was reelected to the Twenty-third, Twenty-fourth, and Twenty-fifth Congresses, leaving the House of Representatives in 1839. He was a presidential elector in 1840 on the Whig ticket of William Henry Harrison and John Tyler. Returning to Washington in 1842, he filled out an unexpired term in the Twenty-seventh Congress, where he served as chairman of the Committee on Roads and Canals. As a congressman, he supported the traditional Whig policies, favoring national banking, federal expenditures for internal improvements such as railroads, and protective tariffs for the country's growing industries. In the Twenty-seventh Congress, McKennan "distinguished himself for his bold and able advocacy" of the highly protective Tariff Act of 1842 (*New York Times*, 12 July 1842).

McKennan headed Pennsylvania's electoral college in the election of 1848, when Zachary Taylor became the last Whig to be elected president. With the death of Taylor in 1850, Millard Fillmore became president and, recognizing the Whig loyalty of McKennan, appointed him secretary of the interior. McKennan had the distinction of being only the second person appointed as interior secretary, for the new department had been created by Congress in March 1849. He also had the distinction of serving just a couple of weeks. He resigned in disgust, because "vulgar" politicians were pressuring him over the selection of men to serve in his department. Furthermore, the laws were inadequate to enable him to prevent wild speculation and loss of public lands, yet public lands were in the custody of the new Interior Department.

McKennan returned to his interest in railway transportation. He became the first president of the Hempfield Railroad Company, Inc., which was incorporated in 1850 to build a line west from Washington County to the Ohio River. The Hempfield Company completed the first section of its railroad, between Washington, Pennsylvania, and Wheeling, Virginia (now W.Va.), in 1857, five years after McKennan's death. The company was eventually sold to the Baltimore & Ohio Railroad, becoming part of that major transportation system.

Throughout his life, McKennan was devoted to local educational and agricultural institutions and other community concerns. He was appointed a trustee of Washington College in 1818 and in that position faithfully supported the college until his death. When his law office burned in 1822, he helped establish the Hope Fire Company, and he was elected one of the directors of the local water company. McKennan was one of the incorporators of the Monongahela Bridge Company and was its first secretary. The bridge, completed in 1833, provided a much-needed link in the route of western travel across the Monongehela River. He was a founder of the Washington County Society for the Promotion of Agriculture and Domestic Manufacturers. In McKennan's parlor, plans were developed to establish the Washington Female Seminary, an institution that fifty years later still had a "fine reputation" that followed "its graduates into many States, especially of the West and South" (Crumrine, p. 455). Contemporaries considered McKennan a distinguished gentleman and admired him for his accomplishments. He died in Reading, Pennsylvania.

• Boyd Crumrine, ed., *History of Washington County, Pennsylvania, with Biographical Sketches of Many of Its Pioneers and Prominent Men* (1882), is essential for biographical details and information on McKennan's transportation interests, placing them within the context of rapid nineteenth-century railroad development. *Biographical and Historical Catalogue of Washington and Jefferson College; Containing a General Catalogue of the Graduates and Non-Graduates of Jefferson College, of Washington College, and of Washington and Jefferson College, 1802–1902* (1902) gives the facts of his academic achievements and his support for educational institutions. An obituary in the *New York Times*, 12 July 1852, emphasizes the esteem in which he was held.

SYLVIA LARSON

MCKENNEY, Ruth (18 Nov. 1911–25 July 1972), humorist and political novelist, was born in Mishawaka, Indiana, the daughter of John Sidney McKenney, a factory manager, and Marguerite Flynn, a public school teacher and Irish nationalist who influenced Ruth toward radical politics. She died when Ruth was eight. McKenney grew up in Cleveland, Ohio. At the age of fourteen she began working on the *Columbus Dispatch*, first learning the trade of printer and at seventeen switching to reporting. In 1928–1930 she attended but did not graduate from Ohio State University. In 1932 she started writing for the *Akron Beacon-Journal*, soon winning awards for her feature writing. She then moved to New York City, where from 1934 to 1936 she was employed as a feature writer on the *New York Post*. After this, she used her savings and an $80 loan from a friend to launch herself as an independent author.

McKenney's early writings remain her best known. These are short stories about her zany younger sister, Eileen, which appeared in the *New Yorker* beginning in 1936. The wittiest were collected into the bestselling *My Sister Eileen* (1938). In 1940 Eileen moved to Hollywood, where she married novelist Nathanael West, but the newlyweds were killed in a car accident at the end of that year. The play version of *My Sister Eileen* opened only a few days later, in early 1941, and went on to become a smash hit. It was made into a movie in 1942, a Broadway musical called *Wonderful Town* in 1953, and another film, based on the musical, in 1955. McKenney's madcap tales about her family appeared in three subsequent collections: *The McKenneys Carry On* (1940), *The Loud Red Patrick* (1947), which was also made into a Broadway show, and *All about Eileen* (1952). Less successful were two humorous autobiographical books about her later life, *Love Story* (1950) and *Far Far from Home* (1954).

In 1937 McKenney married a prominent Communist journalist, Richard Bransten, who used the pen name Bruce Minton. After Eileen McKenney's death they adopted her son from her first marriage as well as Bransten's son from his first marriage, and the couple had a daughter of their own, named after Eileen. McKenney's political views were as ardently Communist as her husband's; during the late 1930s and early 1940s she had her own weekly column, "Strictly Personal," in the party's *New Masses*.

McKenney considered her humor writing merely a source of income, "to make a living while composing weightier *opera*." The first of her "weightier" works was a nonfiction novel, *Industrial Valley* (1939), based on events in Akron from 1932 to 1936. The documentary form of the work, which uses experimental techniques to dramatize the Goodyear Rubber strike and the beginnings of the Congress of Industrial Organizations (CIO), led *New Republic* critic Malcolm Cowley to declare it "one of our best collective novels." Her second political novel, *Jake Home* (1943), the story of a Communist labor organizer, was less warmly received.

In 1946 the Communist party went into turmoil when party leader Earl Browder was accused of right-wing deviations by Communist leaders from abroad. Bransten and McKenney were publicly expelled for "ultraleftism." At this time they were living in Hollywood, where McKenney and her husband collaborated on movie scripts.

Subsequently McKenney and Bransten took their family to Western Europe to avoid the conservative atmosphere sweeping the United States with the onset of the Cold War. In April 1947 the family moved to Brussels, where they spent two years. Settling in England for a time, they co-authored a successful travel book, *Here's England* (1950); they also spent time in France and a period back in the United States. Bransten committed suicide in 1955, just before McKenney's last major work appeared. *Mirage* (1956) is a historical novel about Napoleon in Egypt. A few years later McKenney returned to the United States, where she was periodically institutionalized for depression. Suffering from a heart ailment and diabetes, she died in New York City.

• No collection of McKenney papers is known to exist, but there are a few letters in the Matthew Josephsen Collection at Yale University Library. Autobiographical material is in *Twentieth Century Authors*, ed. Stanley J. Kunitz and Howard Haycraft (1942). See also "Two Writers Ousted by Communist Party," *New York Times*, 13 Sept. 1946. An obituary is in the *New York Times*, 27 July 1972.

Alan M. Wald

MCKENNEY, Thomas Loraine (21 Mar. 1785–20 Feb. 1859), government official, was born in Chestertown, on Maryland's Eastern Shore, the son of William McKenney, a merchant, and Anne Barber, both staunch Quakers. He attended Washington College in Chestertown and at age twenty-one married Editha Gleaves, by whom he fathered two children, a daughter, Maria, who died in infancy, and a son, William. In 1809 McKenney moved his family to Georgetown in the District of Columbia, where he operated a dry goods store. After serving briefly in the local militia during the War of 1812, he resumed his mercantile activities until President James Madison appointed him superintendent of Indian trade in 1816.

As superintendent, McKenney coordinated a network of government-owned trading houses known as the factory system. Established by Congress in 1795, the factory system, which was designated for Indians, was intended to furnish them with quality goods in a fair exchange for their furs. McKenney came to view the factories as more than tools to win Indian loyalty and friendship. He saw them as a means to introduce the tribes along the American frontier to the benefits of civilized life. He had little opportunity to implement fully this vision, however, as American interest in the fur trade following the War of 1812 led to a public clamor against government involvement in private enterprise. Congress responded by abolishing the factory system in May 1822.

McKenney immediately became editor of the *Washington Republican and Congressional Examiner*, a semiweekly newspaper he founded to support Secretary of War John C. Calhoun's bid for the 1824 presidential nomination. The *Washington Republican* had a short and turbulent history. In addition to promoting Calhoun's interests, the paper defended McKenney's handling of the Office of Indian Trade, which became the object of a congressional investigation because of the huge financial loss it had suffered. McKenney was exonerated of guilt in the matter. In 1824, after withdrawing from the presidential race in return for the vice presidency, Calhoun, who was still secretary of war, rewarded McKenney by giving him charge of the Office of Indian Affairs, a new bureau Calhoun established without legislative sanction in March 1824. McKenney served as superintendent of Indian affairs until the autumn of 1830, when President Andrew Jackson dismissed him from office.

McKenney is credited with helping secure passage of two major pieces of legislation, the Indian Civilization Act of 1819, which provided the first federal funding in support of Indian education, and the Indian Removal Act of 1830, which was designed to relocate all eastern Indian tribes to new homes west of the Mississippi River. A direct result of the Indian Removal Act was the tragic "Trail of Tears" involving the forced transfer of the Cherokee, Creek, Choctaw, Chickasaw, and Seminoles from the southeastern United States to Indian Territory (Okla.) in the 1830s. McKenney later claimed that his plan for Indian removal was intended to benefit the Indians and that Jackson was to blame for the outrages that resulted. It is probably no coincidence that Jackson dismissed McKenney shortly after signing the removal act into law.

A pioneer in the study of North American ethnology, McKenney used federal funds to assemble in his war department office a virtual "archives of the American Indian," a large collection of books, manuscripts, artifacts, and paintings that constituted the first museum in Washington, D.C. The core of the collection was a gallery of some 150 portraits of prominent Indian men and women, most of them painted by Washington artist Charles Bird King during official visits to Washington. The portraits were later published as part of a mammoth lithography project that McKenney conceived of and launched, with the aid of writer James Hall, after his dismissal from the Office of Indian Affairs. Known as the *History of the Indian Tribes of North America*, the publication features the portraits and biographies of 120 Indian men and women from McKenney's collection. The entire archive eventually ended up at the Smithsonian Institution, where the portraits were destroyed by fire in 1865.

Although the Indian history bears his name, McKenney abandoned the monumental project years before the three folio volumes finally limped to completion in 1844. In the meantime, he worked diligently to overthrow the Democrats, but his hopes for restoration to office under a Whig administration proved groundless. He survived largely through the benevolence of friends and as a public speaker on Indian affairs. His last hurrah came in 1846, when he persuaded the New York City firm of Paine and Burgess to publish his memoirs. Volume one, entitled *Memoirs, Official and Personal; with Sketches of Travels among the Northern and Southern Indians; Embracing a War Excursion, and Description of Scenes along the Western Borders*, is primarily a justification of his controversial actions in public office—and more a government document than a memoir. Volume two, which was not part of the first edition of the memoirs, is entitled *On the Origin, History, Character, and the Wrongs and Rights of the Indians, with a Plan for the Preservation and Happiness of the Remnants of That Persecuted Race* and is little more than a compilation of transcripts of his public lectures.

After failing to receive an appointment in the Whig administration of Zachary Taylor, McKenney faded into obscurity, having outlived both his wife and son. He died penniless and friendless in a Brooklyn boardinghouse. Although his passing received little notice, years earlier he had provided his own fitting epitaph: "The Office I was sent from is my monument—its records, its inscriptions, I stand or fall by them." Indeed, the Bureau of Indian Affairs is a monument that has endured to this day.

A self-impressed, pompous individual who liked to be called "Colonel," McKenney had a mixed reputation. Whereas his proponents cheered him as a sincere advocate who sought to improve the condition and welfare of America's native peoples, his opponents dismissed him as an unprincipled self-promoter who used his offices solely for political and personal advantage. The truth lies somewhere in between. Some of his actions, particularly his efforts to ingratiate himself with Andrew Jackson by promoting the Indian removal program, seem indefensible today. On the other hand, he was a voice of moderation and restraint regarding federal Indian policy at a time when such a position was both unpopular and politically unwise, and he made sincere attempts to treat America's native population fairly while also pursuing the expanding national interests.

• McKenney is one of the least known and therefore one of the least documented figures in the history of American Indian affairs. For a full biography see Herman J. Viola, *Thomas L. McKenney, Architect of America's Early Indian Policy: 1816–1830* (1974). A useful general history is Francis Paul Prucha, *The Great Father: The United States Government and the American Indians* (1984).

HERMAN J. VIOLA

MCKENZIE, Red (14 Oct. 1899–7 Feb. 1948), jazz singer and comb player, was born William McKenzie in St. Louis, Missouri. Raised in Washington, D.C., after his parents' deaths, McKenzie returned to St. Louis, where he worked first as a racing horse jockey and then as a bellhop at the Claridge Hotel. It was while on this job during the early 1920s that he began amusing himself and others by humming jazz melodies into a homemade instrument made of a comb wrapped in newspaper. With kazoo player Dick Slevin and banjoist Jack Bland, McKenzie formed a trio that soon came to the attention of bandleader Gene Rodemich, who took them to Chicago for a recording date. Their February 1924 Brunswick coupling of "Arkansaw (*sic*) Blues" and "Blue Blues" was issued under the name of the Mound City Blue Blowers in honor of their hometown, and from then on McKenzie referred to his form of playing as "blue-blowing." Gifted with a natural ear and grasp of jazz phrasing, McKenzie achieved a trumpet-like sonority and played lively, contrapuntal improvisations along with Slevin's less imaginative, more nasally intoned kazoo.

The Mound City Blue Blowers' first record sold surprisingly well, and in March 1924 Rodemich's star saxophonist Frank Trumbauer was featured with them on "San" and "Red Hot." Working as a novelty act in vaudeville houses, in the summer of 1924 the Blue Blowers played a residency at the Beaux Arts in Atlantic City, in August adding guitarist Eddie Lang for tours, recordings, and appearances at New York's Palace Theater and London's Piccadilly Hotel. In the summer of 1925 they were back at the Beaux Arts, where Lang's frequent musical partner, violinist Joe Venuti, often played with them. McKenzie's collaboration with Lang's equally blues-based but harmonically advanced guitar was especially notable on "Deep Second Street Blues" and "Gettin' Told." The same people also recorded eight more titles for Vocalion under the name of McKenzie's Candy Kids, but guitarist Joe Humby took Lang's place for a March 1927 Brunswick coupling of "What Do I Care What Somebody Said?," McKenzie's first recorded vocal, and "Nervous Puppies." The original group probably disbanded in the spring of 1927, and in June a trio comprising the singer, Lang, and Venuti recorded "There'll Be Some Changes Made" and "My Syncopated Melody Man" under the name of Red McKenzie and His Music Box for OKeh. McKenzie is also prominently featured as a vocalist on "My Baby Came Back" and "From Monday On" from a May recording session with Eddie Condon added on banjo.

Although initially successful with the Blue Blowers, McKenzie was also active as a promoter for other jazz musicians and groups. In his capacity as a talent scout, he lined up the OKeh recording sessions for Trumbauer, whose February 1927 through April 1929 output included some of the greatest work of cornetist Bix Beiderbecke. He was also responsible for the equally historic December 1927 McKenzie and Condon's Chicagoans sessions on OKeh, for which Condon assembled cornetist Jimmy McPartland, clarinetist Frank Teschemacher, tenor saxophonist Bud Freeman, pianist Joe Sullivan, bassist Jim Lannigan, and drummer Gene Krupa for a definitive statement of the then new "Chicago style." In April 1928 McKenzie arranged for recording dates on Brunswick and Paramount for a similarly styled group, but on these sessions, released under the names of the Chicago Rhythm Kings and the Jungle Kings, McPartland and Freeman were replaced by cornetist Muggsy Spanier and tenorman Mezz Mezzrow. In May McKenzie made an even more significant contribution to jazz by setting up recording sessions on Vocalion for Jimmie Noone's Apex Club Orchestra, a favorite of both the Teschemacher-Condon clique and Benny Goodman. McKenzie may have also arranged for the little-known September 1929 Columbia session on which he sings "Swanee Shuffle" and "I Gotta Have You" with the Midnight Airedales, a ten-piece dance band including Krupa, trombonist Glenn Miller, and tenorman Fud Livingston.

In May 1928 McKenzie and Condon left for New York, where they tried to find work. With a revised Blue Blowers combination of McKenzie, Bland, Condon, and Josh Billings, who played whisk brooms on a suitcase covered with wrapping paper, they landed a job in 1929 at the Bath Club on West Fifty-third Street. Between August and November 1929, with varying performers, including violinist Bruce Yantis on "Indiana," trombonist and vocalist Jack Teagarden ("Tailspin Blues" and "Never Had a Reason to Believe in You"), clarinetist Pee Wee Russell, and tenor saxophonist Coleman Hawkins ("Hello, Lola" and "One Hour"), McKenzie documented increasingly inspired examples of small band hot jazz at its best. The last two titles are among the most famous in jazz because they feature Russell and Hawkins, but they also demonstrate some of McKenzie's most heated and inventive comb playing on record. He was only slightly less effective on a long-unissued October 1930 recording with Goodman, Freeman, Hawkins, and pianist Fats Waller, but rebounded with striking force on a June 1931 session featuring Hawkins, Spanier, and clarinetist Jimmy Dorsey.

In the fall of 1931 and spring of 1932, with Joe Sullivan on piano and Slim Kurtzmann playing suitcase, the Blue Blowers worked at the Stork Club. Between October 1931 and April 1932 McKenzie also recorded for Columbia as a solo ballad singer, and his rich baritone voice, melodic inventiveness, and relaxed phrasing were showcased on eight ballads, including "Time on My Hands," "Just Friends," "I'm Sorry Dear," and "Can't We Talk It Over?" Not only did these and earlier recordings serve as influences on the younger Bing Crosby, but they also came to the attention of Paul Whiteman, who signed McKenzie to a one-year contract beginning in the spring of 1932. However, the popular bandleader did not fully utilize McKenzie's talents, for he can only be heard on four titles from this period.

Beginning in December 1928, when he recorded "Can't Help Lovin' Dat Man" with Bud Freeman's band in Chicago, McKenzie's other sideman credits include two dates in New York in 1929 with Red Nichols, a 1933 session with Adrian Rollini, and four titles with Benny Goodman for World Broadcasting System in 1934. When McKenzie left Whiteman in the spring of 1933, he reorganized the Blue Blowers for a return engagement at the Stork Club, but with the repeal of Prohibition in November they lost the job. In September 1934 McKenzie fronted the Spirits of Rhythm, a black novelty group, for a four-title date on the newly formed Decca label and in October returned to sing "It's All Forgotten Now" and "What's the Use of Getting Used to You?" in the manner of his 1931 Columbia sessions. In 1935 McKenzie and Condon formed a group with trumpeter Bunny Berigan and pianist Joe Bushkin for a job at the Famous Door on Fifty-second Street, at the same time recording with Mike Riley and Eddie Farley's Onyx Club Boys and a nucleus of Bob Crosby sidemen. In early 1936 the enterprising singer recorded several sessions with Berigan and opened his own club on Fifty-second Street. For this venture, he and Condon used Bushkin, trumpeter Marty Marsala, clarinetist Joe Marsala, bassist Artie Shapiro, and drummer George Wettling, but because of personal irresponsibility and lack of business experience the club soon folded.

McKenzie had apparently married somewhat early. When his wife, Marie, died in 1937, he returned to St. Louis to see to his son's welfare. However, he was back in New York in time to appear with Condon at the December 1937 opening of Nick's in Greenwich Village. Alternating sets with Sharkey Bonano's band from New Orleans, the Condon group included Pee Wee Russell, cornetist Bobby Hackett, trombonist

George Brunies, pianist Dave Bowman, bassist Clyde Newcomb, and drummer Johnny Blowers. In early 1939 McKenzie sang briefly at Kelly's Stable on Fifty-second Street, after which he settled in St. Louis, where he worked for several years in a brewery. On the 20 January 1939 BBC broadcast of a Joe Marsala jazz concert, host Alastair Cooke announced McKenzie's performance on "I Would Do Anything for You" as possibly being his last. McKenzie did retire from professional music, but he returned to New York in early 1944 to participate in Condon's jazz concerts at Town Hall and elsewhere. McKenzie sang on Condon's World Broadcasting System transcription session in March 1944 and was featured on four of his broadcasts between September 1944 and February 1945. In October 1944 McKenzie had a leader date on Commodore and in December recorded for both V-Disc and World, this time under his own name. After appearing on a Fats Waller Memorial broadcast in February 1945, he made his last recording session in 1947 for the small National label. A heavy drinker for more than twenty-five years, McKenzie spent the last six weeks of his life in St. Clair's Hospital in New York, where he died of cirrhosis of the liver.

Although the homespun instrumental makeup of the first Mound City Blue Blowers was quaint at best, McKenzie's affinity for jazz rhythms and blues tonalities came through with surprising clarity even from the first. It may be difficult for some to take his "blue-blowing" seriously, but as an extension of the human voice it is no less valid a means of expression than the growling effects of Pee Wee Russell on clarinet or Bubber Miley on cornet. However, apart from the role he played as a promoter of jazz and talent scout for recording companies, his most memorable contributions were those he made as a singer in the 1930s and 1940s.

• The primary source of information on McKenzie's activities in Chicago and New York is Eddie Condon, *We Called It Music* (1947), while accounts of his early St. Louis period can be found in Philip R. Evans and Larry F. Kiner, *Tram: The Frank Trumbauer Story* (1994). Broader coverage of the Chicago scene is in Charles Edward Smith, "The Austin High School Gang," *Jazzmen*, ed. Frederic Ramsey, Jr., and Smith (1939), and Richard Hadlock, *Jazz Masters of the Twenties* (1965). See also Robert Hilbert, *Pee Wee Russell: The Life of a Jazzman* (1993) and *Pee Wee Speaks: A Discography of Pee Wee Russell* (1992). Complete discographical information is in Brian Rust, *Jazz Records, 1897–1942* (1982), and Walter Bruyninckx, *Traditional Jazz Discography, 1897–1988* (5 vols., 1988).

JACK SOHMER

MCKIM, Charles Follen (24 Aug. 1847–14 Sept. 1909), architect, was born in Isabella Furnace, Chester County, Pennsylvania, the son of James Miller McKim, an abolitionist, and Sarah Allibone Speakman, a Quaker. The radical politics of his parents appear to have had little impact on McKim, who grew up to become the senior member of the prestigious McKim, Mead & White partnership and was known for his promotion of classicism as the basis for American architecture. However, McKim's devotion to the civic nature of architecture and to developing an art suitable for the United States, combined with his tenacious willpower, undoubtedly owed a debt to his upbringing.

McKim spent 1866–1867 at Harvard University. A growing interest in architecture led him to work for a short time in the New York office of Russell Sturgis. From 1867 to 1870 he studied at the École des Beaux-Arts in Paris and traveled in Europe and England; he was one of the first Americans to be trained in Paris. Upon his return to New York City, McKim worked intermittently between 1870 and 1876 for the architect Henry Hobson Richardson. During this time he contributed to a number of important designs, such as that for Trinity Church, Boston (1872–1877). In 1874 he married Annie Bigelow of New York. They had one child. The McKims spent portions of the next several summers at the home of Annie's family in Newport, Rhode Island. While with Richardson, McKim made the acquaintance of his future partners, William Rutherford Mead and Stanford White. He also became a close friend to a number of artists, such as Augustus Saint-Gaudens, Frank Millet, H. Siddons Mowbray, and John La Farge, all of whom he later commissioned to decorate his buildings. McKim joined in partnership with his brother-in-law William Bigelow and Mead in 1877; Bigelow was replaced by Stanford White in September 1879. In that same year McKim and his wife divorced. He married Julia Amory Appleton of Boston in 1885; she died in 1887, and he never remarried.

By the mid-1880s McKim, Mead & White had become one of the leading architectural practices in the United States, a reputation it maintained until the 1920s. The approximately one thousand individual commissions dating from McKim's period with the firm were concentrated in New York and the Northeast. However, they designed significant buildings in many other states, and their influence was nationwide both through their designs and also from the many architects who trained in their office. McKim, the senior and dominant partner in the firm (although the flamboyant Stanford White gained a posthumous notoriety), clearly was the leader. Mead, with his practical nature, served as office manager and tempered the sometimes impractical whims of his partners. In the early years the three partners collaborated closely, and it is difficult to separate individual designs. After 1887, as both the firm and the projects grew in size and complexity, a single partner would take charge, and the individual hand of each becomes easier to distinguish.

The dominant motif in Charles McKim's work was the establishment of a national style—that is, the development of an architectural imagery appropriate for the United States. To some degree he and his firm were engaged in a stylistic battle as they designed in a number of different idioms, such as English Norman for St. Paul's Episcopal Church (1883), or French Chateauesque for Joseph Choate's house (1887), both in Stockbridge, Massachusetts. But by the late 1880s the firm, with McKim in the lead, had settled upon classicism as the basis from which an American architecture could be developed. The result was known as American Renaissance: an attempt to both import and rival Old World culture and artistic standards. McKim's principal contributions were in three areas: the Colonial Revival, a new American classicism, and the promotion of architecture and the allied arts.

By 1879 McKim had gained a reputation for wooden resort houses in Newport and other East Coast watering spots, and this type of commission dominated the firm's early work. McKim had begun in the mid–1870s to investigate and utilize motifs and features from American buildings dating from the early colonists to the Federal period. He was among the first architects to look at the colonial past, and while in Newport he commissioned the first photographic record of early American buildings. Influenced by the contemporary British Queen Anne movement and the search through the English past for national images, McKim began to apply this same method to developing an architectural language for the United States. The shingled exterior forms of such houses as the Quaker Tom Robinson addition (Newport, 1875), the William Dean Howells (Belmont, Mass., 1878), and the Samuel Gray Ward (Lenox, Mass., 1878) were loosely based on vernacular seventeenth-century structures McKim had observed. Not particularly classical in mass or plan, these houses utilized classical details such as pediments, paneling, and moldings. On the interior the houses were asymmetrical and were organized around a large hall. The firm's early shingle-covered work, such as in Newport with the Casino (1881), the Samuel Tilton house (1882), and the Isaac Bell, Jr., house (1882), all continued this theme, which became known as the "modernized colonial."

A change occurred by the mid–1880s as McKim eschewed the informal-vernacular sources and started to examine very closely the more formal and classical American-Georgian style of the eighteenth century. Designs such as the H. A. C. Taylor house (Newport, 1883–1885) recalled large clapboarded sea captains' houses; the William Edgar house (Newport, 1884–1886) looked to southern plantations; and the John F. Andrew house (Boston, 1883–1886) picked up the bowfront idiom Charles Bulfinch had begun about 1790. In plan these buildings were more symmetrically organized, and although they contained modern functions and were constructed of modern materials, their facades self-consciously recalled the American past of the founding fathers. Even in houses that continued to use the shingled exterior, such as the William G. Low (Bristol, R.I., 1887), the same rigorous symmetry and order was evident. McKim continued to utilize the red brick and light-colored trim of the Georgian style in later buildings such as the Harvard Club (New York, 1894), the Harvard Union (1901) and the Harvard School of Architecture (1902) in Cambridge, and the Army War College (Washington, D.C., 1908). The Harvard Club and the Harvard Union used Georgian details, but the School of Architecture and the War College lacked such specific historicism; their massing ornament drew upon several traditions and was really part of a new American classical idiom.

McKim's shift to the more formal Georgian in the 1880s accompanied a growing recognition that Greek and Roman classicism was the basis of Western architecture, including that of the American colonies. All of the various classical styles—Imperial Roman, Italian and French Renaissance, and English and American Georgian—were part of a larger classical lineage. McKim was not the only one to espouse classicism as the source of an American architecture, but he was one of the most persuasive. The Henry G. Villard houses, a group of six dwellings (New York, 1883–1886), drew on the Palazzo Cancelleria in Rome (c. 1500) for its facade, which was arranged on three sides around a courtyard. McKim's most important design announcing the expanded classical legacy was the Boston Public Library (1887–1895, the decoration continued until 1916), based on French and Italian sources. Although indebted to Italian Renaissance palazzos, the Boston Library was much enlarged and stood free, a solitary object not part of the city's fabric. Constructed out of light pink Milford granite, it marked a definite break with the dark colors common to architecture of the post–Civil War years. The plan was conceived of as a procession through elaborately ornamented spaces. Decorated with sculpture by Augustus and Louis Saint-Gaudens, Daniel Chester French, Frederick MacMonnies, and Bela Pratt, murals by Puvis de Chavannes, Edwin Austin Abbey, John Singer Sargent, and others, it was intended by McKim and the board of trustees to be a demonstration of artistic collaboration and "civic art." It set a new standard for American public buildings and influenced American architecture well into the 1930s.

McKim designed the settings and pedestal bases for some of Augustus Saint-Gaudens's most important sculptures, such as the Colonel Robert Gould Shaw Memorial (Boston, 1884–1903). For the World's Columbian Exposition in Chicago in 1893, McKim acted as the conscience of the chief of construction, Daniel Burnham, arguing forcefully for classicism as the unifying motive for the Court of Honor. McKim's Agricultural Building on the Court of Honor was generally considered to be its most admired structure. Classicism in its various stylistic idioms came to rule the firm's work, and McKim was the primary designer of many buildings, including the new Morningside campus for Columbia University (New York, 1892–1901), the University Club (New York, 1899), the Frederick W. Vanderbilt house (Hyde Park, N.Y., 1899), the old (now demolished) Pennsylvania Railroad Station (New York, 1902–1910), and the J. P. Morgan Library (New York, 1907). In contrast to Stanford White's work, which frequently displayed elaborate decoration, high coloration, and specific quotations from the past, McKim's designs tended toward an austere grandeur, free of historicism. The Low Library at

Columbia, though indebted to the idea of centrally planned domed structures, recalls none specifically. The Pennsylvania Station, commissioned by railroad president Alexander Cassatt, drew on the Roman imperial baths of Caracalla for the main waiting room, though McKim greatly enlarged it, and the main facade was articulated by a giant Doric colonnade. As was typical with many of these buildings, it contained murals and sculptures, provided by Jules Guerin and Adolph A. Weinman, respectively. All of these buildings and sculptures were conceived of as emblems of a new American civilization that would have an impact on all who came in contact with it.

In 1901 the U.S. Senate Committee on Washington, D.C., headed by Senator James McMillan of Michigan, appointed McKim, along with Burnham, Saint-Gaudens, and Frederick Law Olmsted, Jr., to study the public grounds of Washington, D.C., and make recommendations. McKim dominated the so-called McMillan Commission report of 1902 and advocated a return to the classical 1791 design of Major Pierre Charles L'Enfant and the extension of the mall to include the Lincoln Memorial. The subsequent development of the monumental core of Washington largely followed McKim's guidelines, and his plan became a model for the "City Beautiful Movement." In 1902 McKim was selected by President Theodore Roosevelt (1858–1919) to remodel the White House.

As a spokesman for architecture and art, McKim proved to be effective, though he loathed public speaking. Inspired by professional and public sentiment surrounding the World's Columbian Exposition, in 1894 McKim founded the American School of Architecture in Rome, which in 1896 became the American Academy in Rome. Modeling his school on the various European academies there, McKim intended that talented young American architects, sculptors, archaeologists, and painters would complete their training in Rome among the great examples of antiquity. McKim successfully raised funds for the school and convinced Congress to give it a national charter in 1905. He was concerned with developing professional standards for architects and assisted in transforming the American Institute of Architects (AIA) from a small, New York–based gentlemen's club into a national organization with political influence. In 1902–1903 he served as president of the AIA, securing the Octagon in Washington, D.C., as its permanent headquarters.

Along with these accomplishments, McKim received many honors, including the King's Medal of the Royal Institute of British Architects in 1903. Impressed by the esteem in which architects were held in England and abroad, McKim conceived of a similar award to be presented by the AIA. He became the second recipient of the AIA Gold Medal in 1909.

By the time of his death in St. James, New York, McKim had helped reestablish classicism in its various idioms as the appropriate image for America. This conceptualization lasted until the 1930s, when it was overturned by the modernist revolution. McKim's architectural prominence came at a time when the wealthy needed to build lavish private homes and grand public libraries and railroad stations still existed. Lacking both a firm cultural identity and artistic security, many Americans looked to Europe to provide the standards for high culture and noble art. The consequence was the adoption of elements of Old World and early American buildings in the various classical idioms, decorated with murals and sculpture. Ultimately McKim moved beyond specific historicism to create a vision of the American city and, ultimately, a new American classicism.

• McKim's correspondence, both personal and business, is in the Library of Congress; the firm's papers, including drawings, are at the New-York Historical Society and Avery Library, Columbia University. The standard biography is Charles Moore, *The Life and Times of Charles Follen McKim* (1929), which concentrates on his later life, after 1900. Also useful as a memoir is Alfred Hoyt Granger, *Charles Follen McKim: A Study of His Life and Work* (1913). Studies of the firm's work are Leland Roth, *McKim, Mead & White, Architects* (1938) and *The Architecture of McKim, Mead & White 1870–1920: A Building List* (1978); Richard Guy Wilson, *McKim, Mead & White, Architects* (1983); and the Brooklyn Museum (Richard Guy Wilson, Dianne Pilgrim and Richard Murray), *The American Renaissance, 1876–1917* (1979). See also *A Monograph of the Work of McKim, Mead & White 1879–1915* (4 vols., 1915–1920; repr. as *The Architecture of McKim, Mead & White*, ed. Richard Guy Wilson [1990]), and Richard Guy Wilson, *The AIA Gold Medal* (1984). Important articles on McKim and the firm's work are Russell Sturgis, "The Works of McKim, Mead & White," Great American Architects Series No. 1 *Architectural Record* (May 1895): 1–111; Henry W. Desmond and Herbert Croly, "The Work of Messrs. McKim, Mead & White," *Architectural Record* 20 (Sept. 1906): 153–246; and Richard Guy Wilson, "The Early Work of Charles F. McKim: Country House Commissions," *Winterthur Portfolio* 14 (Fall 1979): 235–67.

RICHARD GUY WILSON

MCKIM, James Miller (14 Nov. 1810–13 June 1874), antislavery and freedmen's relief official, was born in Carlisle, Pennsylvania, the son of James McKim, a tanner, and Catherine Miller. In 1831, three years after graduating from Dickinson College, McKim was swept up by the evangelical movement known as the Second Great Awakening and began what would be an often interrupted preparation for the ministry. Then, in 1833, a local black barber persuaded him to read William Lloyd Garrison's *Thoughts on African Colonization* (1832), which attacked the prevailing reformist view that America's racial problems could best be resolved by expatriating slaves and free Negroes to Africa. As McKim later recalled, this experience led to his sudden and complete conversion to immediate emancipation, a cause that seemed to him simply an extension of the Lord's work. Thus it was that in December 1833 the abolitionists of Carlisle, all of whom were black except McKim, chose McKim as their delegate to the founding meeting of the American Anti-Slavery Society in Philadelphia. Although he played only a minor role in the convention, as the youngest delegate, he caught the attention of Lucretia Mott, who was so impressed with McKim that she invited him to be her house guest for the duration of the convention and then kept him on for over a week more. Although his acquaintance with Mott introduced him to new and unsettling ideas, for a time McKim continued down the path to a traditional ministerial career. In 1835 he was ordained as a Presbyterian minister and took up a pastorate in Berks County, Pennsylvania.

In August 1836 McKim was recruited as an antislavery agent into Theodore Dwight Weld's "Band of Seventy," and over the next sixteen months he canvassed Pennsylvania on behalf of the cause. Soon his new vocation drew him again into contact with Lucretia Mott and her Hicksite circle. Here, amid this Quaker faction that emphasized the importance of personal belief guided by spiritual revelation, McKim was further introduced to religious opinions that were so liberal they frightened him. To his diary he confided, "I certainly feel as though I had left my old moorings and were drifting into the unknown depths of radicalism. I sometimes feel I shall lose my character and my opportunities of usefulness" (quoted in Cohen, p. 156). By 1838 McKim had traveled so far from his old moorings that he felt compelled to publish *A Letter to the Presbytery of Wilmington,* renouncing his belief in the doctrine of vicarious atonement, which holds that Jesus Christ died for the sins of humanity. This action was tantamount to inviting the Presbytery to oust him from his ministry for heresy, and it did so in October 1838. At that time, McKim was engaged to Sarah Allibone Speakman, the daughter of a prosperous Hicksite, but their marriage could not take place until he had a secure position. With this purpose in mind, Mott arranged for him to become the publishing agent of the Pennsylvania Anti-Slavery Society in 1840. That year he married Speakman; they had three children, one of whom was the noted architect Charles Follen McKim.

From 1840 to 1862, under one title or another, McKim served as the paid general agent of the Pennsylvania Anti-Slavery Society, administering virtually all of the organization's affairs. He managed and sometimes edited its newspaper, the *Pennsylvania Freeman,* published its tracts, hired its lecturers, organized its meetings, and lobbied state legislators in support of its policies. In addition, he aided fugitive slaves and skillfully turned some rescues into propaganda opportunities for the cause. When John Brown (1800–1859) was executed after his failed attempt to incite a slave insurrection at Harpers Ferry in 1859, McKim escorted Brown's wife to Virginia to retrieve Brown's body and played a significant role in efforts to exploit the incident for the antislavery cause.

Throughout most of his antislavery career, McKim was a dutiful follower of Garrison's brand of abolitionism, which embraced pacifism, rejected human government, and condemned the U.S. Constitution as a covenant with slaveholders. Such beliefs did not, however, prevent him from cultivating good relations with Pennsylvania lawmakers or from becoming an admirer of John Brown. Most important, when the Civil War began, his Garrisonian beliefs did not stop him from immediately welcoming it as an "abolition war." Soon McKim sought to convince his fellow abolitionists that "*the pulling down* stage" of their movement was over and that "the *building-up*—the constructive part—remains to be accomplished" (*National Anti-Slavery Standard,* 3 May 1862). He urged them to stop carping against the government and instead to support the northern cause and work to shape the postwar conditions under which the freedmen would live.

Clearly, this was McKim's own agenda. In March 1862 he organized the Philadelphia Port Royal Relief Committee (later the Pennsylvania Freedmen's Relief Association) to aid the newly freed blacks of South Carolina's Sea Islands. As secretary of this group, he toured the Sea Islands in June, and his public report, *The Freedmen of South Carolina* (1862), was crafted to persuade northerners that former slaves were already showing that they were capable of working independently without compulsion and that, if allowed to do so, the freedmen would fight for their liberty. McKim's trip convinced him that a government commission was needed to study freedmen's issues and to recommend the policies the nation should pursue after the war. In December 1862 he proposed the idea to U.S. senator Charles Sumner, U.S. congressman Thaddeus Stevens, U.S. secretary of war Edwin Stanton, and others. Four months later, his plan was implemented with the government's creation of the American Freedmen's Inquiry Commission. Although McKim had hoped to be appointed the secretary of this body and was quite disappointed when he did not get the post, his efforts continued unabated. In 1863, as a member of the Philadelphia Union League, he launched a drive that recruited ten black Pennsylvania regiments in a ten-month period. In 1865 he was instrumental in the campaign that ended Jim Crow practices on the streetcars of Philadelphia. That same year, he played a leading role in founding the *Nation,* an organ to advocate the cause of the freedmen. His sponsorship had a more personal side as well—he sought to create a secure position for Wendell Phillips Garrison, his future son-in-law, who soon became the magazine's literary editor.

During the war, McKim had unsuccessfully advocated a coordination of the efforts of the various northern relief associations for freedmen. Once the war was over the Freedmen's Bureau was established, however, his position gained more support. In the fall of 1865 he brought into being the American Freedmen's Aid Commission (later the American Freedmen's Union Commission), an umbrella organization uniting virtually all of the secular relief groups. In 1865–1866 the commission played a major role in supporting freedmen's education. Soon, however, the American Missionary Association and other evangelical societies began to take over this educational role, squeezing out the secular organizations as they did, and in 1869, on McKim's motion, the commission disbanded, having nevertheless helped prepare the foundation for public education in the South. After the war McKim moved his family to New Jersey. He retired in 1869 but continued his involvement with the *Nation*. He died at his home in Llewellyn Park, New Jersey.

James Miller McKim was neither a gifted speaker nor an especially talented writer, but for twenty years he was the man who got things done for the antislavery cause in Pennsylvania. One antislavery colleague termed him a "prudent rash man," and he has been well described as an administrator who "applied a fundamentally conservative temperament to the prosecution of a radical cause" (Brown, p. 72). Once the Civil War began, McKim played a more independent and influential role in shaping events. He took the lead in urging his abolitionist colleagues to stop attacking the government from the outside and to instead become insiders with a say in shaping Reconstruction. He worked tirelessly to aid the freedmen, and he was the person most responsible for coordinating the postwar assistance efforts of the secular freedmen's aid societies.

• The main repositories of manuscript sources on McKim are the James Miller McKim Collection at Cornell University, the Maloney Collection at the New York Public Library, and the William Lloyd Garrison Collection at the Boston Public Library. William Cohen, "James Miller McKim: Pennsylvania Abolitionist" (Ph.D. diss., New York Univ., 1968), details McKim's life up to the time of the Civil War and gives a complete bibliography of primary and secondary sources. While not focused exclusively on McKim, James McPherson, *The Struggle for Equality* (1964), is the best source of details on McKim's work during the Civil War and Reconstruction. For genealogical information, see William Lloyd Garrison, Jr., *In Memoriam: Sarah A. McKim* (1891). See also Ira V. Brown, "Miller McKim and Pennsylvania Abolitionism," *Pennsylvania History* 30 (Jan. 1863): 56–72; William Still, *The Underground Railroad* (1872); Charles Moore, *The Life and Times of Charles Follen McKim* (1929). An obituary is in the *New York Tribune*, 16 June 1874.

WILLIAM COHEN

MCKINLAY, Whitefield (15 Sept. 1852–14 Dec. 1941), businessman, was born in Charleston, South Carolina, the son of George McKinlay and Mary E. Weston. His father, a free person of color, had purchased a house on Meeting Street in Charleston in 1848; his grandfather, Anthony Weston, was a well-known mulatto millwright and slave owner in antebellum South Carolina. After the Civil War, Whitefield studied at Avery Institute in Charleston, and in 1874 he enrolled at the University of South Carolina, remaining there for three years until blacks were excluded after the Democrats came to power. After teaching school in South Carolina, he matriculated at Iowa College in Grinnell, Iowa, where he remained until 1881. By the age of twenty-nine, McKinlay could boast of a very strong education.

Although the profession of teaching was open to a person of his talents, McKinlay moved to Washington, D.C., and found a job in the Government Printing Office. In 1887 he married Kate Wheeler; the couple would have two children. That same year he entered the real estate and loan business in the nation's capital. His clients included both whites and blacks, but he built up his business by catering principally to well-to-do blacks, either as a broker for the purchase of their homes or as the manager of their real estate investments. Among his elite black customers were lawyer, editor, and civil rights leader Archibald Grimké; physician, medical educator, and hospital administrator Charles Burleigh Purvis; Memphis real estate executive, banker, investor, and philanthropist Robert Reed Church; and District of Columbia lawyer, Harvard graduate, and municipal court judge Robert Herberton Terrell. McKinlay had a keen eye for realty investment and a penchant for detail. He charged modest fees for his work (usually 5 percent), and he usually managed his investors' property profitably. While estimates of his net worth vary, by the early twentieth century he was one of the wealthiest blacks in the United States, probably worth $200,000.

McKinlay's education, wealth, success, location, and dealings with upper-class blacks made him a natural to serve in some political capacity, but he accepted only two political appointments. In 1907 he agreed to serve on a commission on housing for the poor in the District of Columbia, and he accepted an assignment as collector of the Port of Georgetown, District of Columbia (1910–1913), both presidential appointments. McKinlay's most important political role was as a friend, adviser, and confidant of Booker T. Washington, who stayed in McKinlay's home during his visits to the nation's capital. He advised his friend on who his supporters were in the District of Columbia and on the activities of his enemies. McKinlay gained audiences with presidents at Washington's behest and drove Washington to the White House in his buggy for the educator's famous 1901 supper with Theodore Roosevelt and returned for him afterward.

McKinlay made a strong plea two years later for the appointment of William Demos Crum, a politically active and socially prominent physician, as collector for the Port of Charleston. He wrote Roosevelt, "If the southern opponents of the Negro succeed in defeating this appointment it will establish a precedent which will make it almost impossible for you or any other President to appoint, for years to come, a colored man to any office in the southern states." During a bitter and divisive fight, Roosevelt gave Crum an interim appointment until the Senate finally confirmed him as collector in 1905. McKinlay in 1912 was among the first to protest against segregation of federal employees in government offices, a trend that would become more pronounced during Woodrow Wilson's first administration.

During the 1920s and 1930s, while maintaining his activities as a real estate agent and lessor of District properties, McKinlay became, according to historian Carter G. Woodson, "a faithful coworker of the Association for the Study of Negro Life and History." Along with Woodson, he sought to save primary source records concerning blacks, and he turned over to the association all of his own remarkable correspondence with distinguished persons of both races, including members of the cabinet and presidents of the United States. He also made available his large correspondence with Booker T. Washington. He continued his work in realty until he became enfeebled. McKinlay died in Washington, D.C.

• For McKinlay correspondence, see the Archibald Grimké Papers (Howard University), the Whitefield McKinlay Papers in the Carter G. Woodson Collection (Library of Congress), and Louis R. Harlan and Raymond W. Smock, eds., *The Booker T. Washington Papers* (15 vols., 1972–1989); also see Willard B. Gatewood, *Aristocrats of Color: The Black Elite, 1880–1920* (1990). An obituary is in the *Journal of Negro History* 27 (Jan. 1942): 129–30.

LOREN SCHWENINGER

MCKINLEY, Carlyle (22 Nov. 1847–24 Aug. 1904), journalist and poet, was born in Newnan, Coweta County, Georgia, the son of Judge Charles G. McKinley and Frances C. Jackson. His maternal great-grandfather, James Jackson, served two terms as governor of Georgia and was later elected to the U.S. Senate. Early in the Civil War, the fifteen-year-old Carl McKinley enlisted in the Georgia Cadet Battalion, having left (according to McKinley family history) his studies at the University of Georgia. He served under General Joseph E. Johnston in the battles around Atlanta. His bravery led to his being promoted to the rank of sergeant-major during the last day of fighting.

After the war McKinley worked briefly for a cotton brokerage in Atlanta before accepting a position with the U.S. marshal's office in Savannah. He was then said to have returned to the University of Georgia to complete his studies, though on this point it should be noted that the university has no record (among its authoritative sources) of either McKinley's attendance or graduation. In 1871 he enrolled in the Presbyterian Theological Seminary in Columbia, South Carolina, graduating in 1874. Soon after, he married Elizabeth H. Bryce, the daughter of a Columbia planter and lawyer; they had four children.

Despite his theological training, McKinley chose not to become a minister because of a change in his religious views. Instead, he pursued a literary career and, to augment his income, accepted a teaching position at the grammar school established by Colonel Hugh S. Thompson, who later became governor of South Carolina. During this time McKinley published a number of his most important poems, many pseudonymously.

Believing that journalism would help him develop his literary potential, McKinley began his lifelong association with the Charleston, South Carolina, newspaper, the *News and Courier*. In July 1875 he became head of the paper's Columbia bureau, and in 1879, its Washington correspondent. After a brief departure the following year to work for the Richmond and Danville Railroad, McKinley returned to Charleston in 1881 as associate editor of the *News and Courier*, where he worked until late in life, when his deteriorating health forced him to retire. After an illness of nearly a year, McKinley died at his Charleston home.

As a journalist McKinley was responsible for many of the paper's editorial essays (though it is impossible to identify the specific authors of these unsigned works), which progressively promoted textile industries in South Carolina and encouraged diversified farming. He wrote the widely praised, graphic accounts of two Charleston disasters, "The Cyclone of 1885" and "The Earthquake of 1886." He also received considerable recognition for his monograph on race relations, *An Appeal to Pharoah* (1889), which, when it first appeared anonymously, was assumed to be the work of several different figures, including McKinley's colleagues at the *News and Courier* Yates Snowden, J. C. Hemphill, and F. W. Dawson and even the more moderate Henry W. Grady, the prominent southern orator and owner of the *Atlanta Constitution*. McKinley proposed that the way to solve what was then termed "the negro problem" was to ship black Americans to Africa. This idea, the origins of which go back as far as 1733 in the writings of the New England preachers Samuel Hopkins (1721–1803) and Ezra Stiles, saw concrete development in the establishment of Liberia in 1847. McKinley's contribution to this movement, which in his day counted among its proponents the journalist John Temple Graves, was to detail, in some two hundred pages heavily larded with statistics and census figures, what he saw as the practicability of his "radical" plan of the mass deportation. Favorably received, this work went through three editions (two in New York and one in South Carolina) between 1889 and 1907. It also led the African explorer Sir Henry Morton Stanley to write McKinley's New York publisher on 29 March 1890, praising McKinley as "clearly a seer of a rare type nowadays . . . [who] handles his subject wisely."

But Carlyle McKinley's principal literary achievement lay in his poetry, particularly those works that emerged during the difficult Reconstruction period. One such poem, "South Carolina, 1876," reflects the postwar bitterness that many of McKinley's confederates shared and ends, not surprisingly, on an ominously vengeful note. Other works, such as "Crucifer," reflect the poet's years of theological study. This poem, which he dedicated to a troop of Charleston veterans, takes the form of a parable concerning who would be allowed to pass through "heaven's gate" and who would be condemned. In his elegy "At Timrod's Grave," McKinley praised the Charleston poet and "laureate of the Confederacy" Henry Timrod as the "Harp of the South," whose work could "charm our ears" and "soothe our pain."

McKinley's most notable poem may well be "Sapelo," in which he describes the peace and contentment he experienced on the island of that name off the coast of Georgia. There he found "care ebbs out with every tide, / And peace comes in upon the flood." In its evocation of the pastoral delights of his relatives' island home, it stands in quiet contrast to his other writings, which were informed by the harsh consequences of the Civil War.

As a journalist and poet, McKinley gradually moved from merely cherishing the South of his boyhood years to the more progressive attitude articulated by Henry W. Grady in the latter's advocacy of the New South. Yet, while McKinley deplored the inequities of Reconstruction and lamented the South's state of being "underdeveloped," he also consistently maintained, as he wrote in 1889, that "the whole hope of the South depended upon its recovering its former place in the Union." McKinley used his writing throughout his life to try to help his region achieve that goal.

• Manuscripts of a number of McKinley's poems are in the William A. Courtenay Collection, Charleston Library Society. A small collection of his papers is also in the South Carolina Library, University of South Carolina. Of related interest, at Duke University's William R. Perkins Library, are the papers of Francis Warrington Dawson I (1840–1889) and James Calvin Hemphill (1850–1927), who were editors of the *News and Courier* during the period when McKinley was the newspaper's associate editor.

Shortly after McKinley's death, W. A. Courtenay prepared the biographical pamphlet *In Loving Memory of Carlyle McKinley* (1904), which includes tributes from the poet's friends. Courtenay also contributed the sketch of McKinley's life and career to the *Library of Southern Literature*, ed. E. A. Alderman and Joel Chandler Harris, vol. 8 (1907). See also Mildred L. Rutherford, *The South in History and Literature* (1906); George A. Wauchope, *The Writers of South Carolina* (1910); and John William McCullough, "Carlyle McKinley" (master's thesis, Univ. of Georgia, 1941). An obituary is in the Charleston *News and Courier*, 25 Aug. 1904.

FRANCIS J. BOSHA

MCKINLEY, Ida Saxton (8 June 1847–26 May 1907), first lady, was born in Canton, Ohio, the daughter of James A. Saxton, a banker, and Kate Dewalt. Ida was the second of their three children and the eldest of two daughters. She attended local schools and then went to private schools in Delhi, New York, and in Cleveland, Ohio. In 1869 she graduated from the Brook Hall Seminary in Media, Pennsylvania. At the age of twenty-two she made a six-month tour of Europe with her sister, Mary Saxton, a chaperone, and other companions. When Ida returned to Canton, she worked at her father's Stark County Bank during 1870.

Ida Saxton met William McKinley at this time. He was twenty-seven and had just been elected county prosecutor for Stark County. McKinley fell in love with Saxton and soon proposed to her. They were married in Canton on 25 January 1871. Their first child, Kate, was born on Christmas Day 1871. By mid-1872 Ida McKinley was again pregnant.

This second birth was difficult for Ida McKinley. Her mother died as she was preparing to have her child, and the shock produced a physical reaction when Ida went into what proved to be a hard labor. A daughter was born on 1 April 1873 and survived only until 22 August. Mrs. McKinley experienced a severe response to these events, including convulsions, possible phlebitis, and prolonged depression. Seizures and periodic loss of consciousness led to a diagnosis of epilepsy. For the rest of her married life, Ida McKinley was an invalid. The death of her first daughter on 25 June 1876 added to her sense of loss and melancholy.

In 1876 William McKinley was elected to Congress, where he served until 1891. Ida McKinley accompanied him to Washington, D.C., and their routine reflected the demands of her condition. Because she did not like fresh air, they lived in closed rooms. Her husband smoked his cigars away from her presence. He watched for her attacks and seizures. When they came, he put a handkerchief in front of her face until the episode passed; even at public functions, he continued his conversation as if nothing had happened. She wore her hair short to avoid the strain of pins and curls. She aged prematurely. William McKinley spent all of his spare time with her in what one biographer has called "his secondary career of psychiatric nurse" (Leech, p. 19). Bonds of mutual dependency held the McKinley marriage together.

As her husband's political career prospered, Ida McKinley remained a constant backstage presence, and she could be jealous when he was away. They traveled together and went to official functions. When he became governor of Ohio in 1892, her health improved, and she spent more time with friends, though she was still an invalid. Each day the governor waved his handkerchief from his office window in the capital toward the window of his wife's hotel room across the street where she watched. She loved to have children around her, and she was always staunchly devoted to her husband's career.

When William McKinley was nominated for president in 1896, a biography of Ida McKinley was written to reassure the public about her health and fitness to be first lady. The first campaign book about a future first lady, it represented an innovation in how the wives of presidential candidates were depicted to the nation. After her husband won the presidency, Ida became first lady in March 1897. She tried to discharge the social duties of her new position, but illness made her performance erratic. She insisted on attending the inaugural ball but fainted during the event. Ida was often heavily sedated, but she received callers and appeared at official dinners. She spent her days knitting and ultimately donated to charity 3,500 pairs of bedroom slippers. The president relied on Jennie Tuttle Hobart, the wife of Vice President Garret A. Hobart, to handle the ceremonial duties when Ida could not. William McKinley's affection for his wife never faltered. He often told friends that "Ida was the most beautiful girl you ever saw. She is beautiful to me now" (Leech, p. 30).

Ida McKinley had some influence on her husband in matters of appointments and policy. Leonard Wood had become her friend while he was her doctor in the White House, and that connection helped persuade the president to name Wood to head American occupation forces in Cuba in 1899. She also encouraged the president to pursue private efforts to send Protestant missionaries to the Philippine Islands, which the United States had acquired from Spain in 1898–1899.

Ida McKinley's health fluctuated throughout her husband's presidency. After he was reelected, she was well enough to accompany him on a tour of the country during the summer of 1901. One of her fingers became infected during the journey, and when the infection threatened her life, the tour was canceled. After his wife's recovery, the president went to Buffalo, New York, in September 1901. There, on 6 September, an assassin shot him. As he fell, he told an aide: "My wife, be careful . . . how you tell her—Oh be careful!" (Leech, p. 596). The president died eight days later.

During the funeral ceremonies and the month of national mourning that followed, Ida McKinley performed with few signs of physical distress. She returned to Canton, where she lived for almost six years without the symptoms that had characterized her married life. Out of the public spotlight and away from the pressures of her husband's career and presence, she found relief from the emotional and physical tensions of her married life. She fell ill and died in Canton during the spring of 1907. In her last days she said, "He is gone, and life is dark to me now" (*New York Times*, 27 May 1907). Ida McKinley was very much a nineteenth-century presidential wife. She adopted no causes and attracted less attention from the newspapers and the public than her successors in the twentieth century. Her influence in shaping the character and personality of the twenty-fifth president during their life together was her major impact on the history of the United States.

• The William McKinley and George B. Cortelyou Papers, Library of Congress, Washington, D.C., have much information on Ida McKinley's life. The Stark County Historical Society, Canton, Ohio, has some personal documents and family papers relating to Ida McKinley. Henry S. Belden, comp., *The Grand Tour of Ida Saxton McKinley and Sister Mary Saxton Barber, 1869* (1985), is a collection of her letters from a European trip drawn from the Stark County Historical Society holdings. Josiah Hartzell, *Sketch of the Life of Mrs. William McKinley* (1896, 1897), was written for the 1896 presidential campaign. Murat Halstead, "Mrs. McKinley," *Saturday Evening Post*, 6 Sept. 1902, pp. 6–7, is a biographical sketch of her life after she left Washington. Mrs. Garret A. Hobart, *Memories* (1930), discusses how the wife of the vice president helped discharge some of Ida McKinley's ceremonial duties. See also "Comparison of Mrs. McKinley and Mrs. Bryan," *Harper's Bazaar*, 11 Aug. 1900, pp. 954–56. Margaret Leech, *In the Days of McKinley* (1959), treats Ida McKinley's impact on her husband at length. Howard Wayne Morgan, *William McKinley and His America* (1963), analyzes the marriage too. Edward Thornton Heald, *The William McKinley Story* (1964), prints some local documents. The *New York Times*, 27 May 1907, has a useful obituary.

LEWIS L. GOULD

MCKINLEY, John (1 May 1780–19 July 1852), U.S. senator and justice of the U.S. Supreme Court, was born in Culpeper County, Virginia, the son of Andrew McKinley, a physician, and Mary Logan. Sometime after 1790, Dr. McKinley moved his family to Lincoln County, Kentucky, where John grew up. He read law and was admitted to the bar in 1800. He practiced first in Frankfort and thereafter in Louisville. By 1810 he owned two slaves. He married Juliana Bryan and, later, Elizabeth Armistead, twenty years his junior. He had at least two children.

In 1819 McKinley moved to Huntsville, Alabama, and at once became one of the new state's most prominent attorneys. In November he became a candidate before the legislature for a circuit judgeship, with the support of the element in state politics associated with the Huntsville Bank and led by Governor William Wyatt Bibb and Senator John W. Walker, but he was defeated after four ballots. The following August, however, he was elected a state representative from Madison County and was appointed chairman of the judiciary committee. In November 1822 he ran as the candidate of the Huntsville Bank faction for the U.S. Senate vacancy created by Walker's resignation and subsequent death, but in a heated contest he was defeated 39–38 by the violently antibank William Kelly, the candidate of the faction headed by Governor Israel Pickens and Senator William R. King.

Following his defeat by Kelly, McKinley began severing his ties with the Huntsville Bank forces. Andrew Jackson's overwhelming victory in Alabama in the presidential election of 1824 gave McKinley the means to establish more popular credentials, and in the fall of 1826 he announced himself as a candidate for the U.S. Senate as a committed Jackson man. His opponent, Clement Comer Clay, had also been an important ally of the Huntsville Bank group and also now claimed to be a firm Jackson supporter. In fact, at the same time that they were competing for the Senate seat, McKinley and Clay were serving together as the attorneys for the creditors in the second of the "big interest" cases; they persuaded the state supreme court to reject Kelly's efforts to recover the usurious interest charged Alabama's borrowers. But Clay's tentative effort to obtain the support of the legislature's handful of admirers of John Quincy Adams, by saying that he would offer no factious opposition to the Adams administration, lost him more among the Jacksonians than it gained him among the Adams forces. McKinley was elected with a vote of 41 to 38 and took his seat on 21 December 1826.

In the Senate McKinley devoted his efforts to obtaining federal assistance for internal improvements in Alabama and to gaining the reduction of public land prices and preemption rights for squatters. McKinley introduced and guided to passage the bill granting Alabama 400,000 acres to finance the building of a canal around Muscle Shoals. When Andrew Jackson took office and vetoed the Maysville Road bill, McKinley voted to override the veto. He also voted for the act that would remove American Indians from the lower South but was later accused of having delayed its passage.

McKinley startled the Senate in 1828 by arguing that the United States had no general constitutional power to hold public lands outside the territories and was bound to cede control of them to the new states as each state was created. These views were regarded as outlandish at the time, but McKinley persisted in advancing them throughout his congressional career; seventeen years later as a U.S. Supreme Court justice he was able to write a version of them into antebellum constitutional law through his opinion in *Pollard's Lessee v. Hagan*. All of the federal government's municipal powers over the western lands, he held, passed to the new states as soon as they were created; the federal government retained only the power to regulate public land sales.

McKinley's opposition to the Maysville Road veto and his supposedly lukewarm support of Indian removal led enemies in Alabama to question the orthodoxy of his Jacksonianism. When McKinley sought reelection in 1830, Governor Gabriel Moore opposed him on the ground that Alabama needed a senator whose support for Jackson was ardent and unwavering. The two issues on which McKinley was accused of having deserted the faith were both points of particular concern to the legislature's small bloc of nullifiers, and they joined with Moore's friends to defeat McKinley, 49 to 40.

In the meantime, McKinley had moved from Huntsville to Florence, and in 1831 he was elected a state representative from Lauderdale County. He wrote and obtained the adoption of a memorial urging Congress to replace the existing privately controlled Bank of the United States with a largely governmentally owned one. And he voted against the creation of additional banks in Alabama. By this time, McKinley owned six slaves, but he was one of the dozen state house members who opposed legislation, in response to the Nat Turner insurrection in Virginia, that placed severe restrictions on slaves. He voted to extend Alabama's jurisdiction over the Indian territory within the state but voted to exempt the Indians from taxation.

In 1833, after a heated contest, McKinley was elected to the U.S. House of Representatives with a bit more than 52 percent of the vote. He was appointed a member of the Ways and Means Committee, and he strongly supported Jackson's removal of the government's deposits from the Bank of the United States. He resumed his fight for permanent preemption rights for squatters and lower public land prices, and he denied the power of Congress to abolish slavery, even in the District of Columbia.

McKinley did not seek reelection to a second term, but he accepted nomination as a Democratic presidential elector and conducted a vigorous canvass in behalf of Martin Van Buren. At the same time he ran again for the state legislature, with the intention of replacing Gabriel Moore in the U.S. Senate. That Moore had nullifier support in his victory over McKinley in 1830 had led President Jackson to be suspicious of Moore, and Jackson's coldness had driven Moore into the arms of the opposition. When Moore voted against confirming Van Buren as minister to Britain, Alabama's Jacksonians repudiated him, and the sentiment became widespread that McKinley deserved reelection to vindicate his orthodoxy from the treacherous Moore's earlier questioning of it. On 21 November 1836 McKinley was easily elected to the Senate over the Whig nominee.

In the meantime, the Congress had expanded the U.S. Supreme Court from seven justices to nine, and Jackson had offered one of the new seats to former South Carolina senator William Smith, now a resident of Huntsville. When Smith declined because of his advanced age, the newly inaugurated Van Buren turned to McKinley. McKinley had actively sought the appointment, and, resigning as senator, he accepted it at once. He took his seat on the Court on 9 January 1838.

The new justice lost no time in making his presence felt. That spring, on circuit in Mobile, he ruled in *Bank of Augusta v. Earle* that a corporation chartered in one state could not do business in another without its explicit authorization. When the case was appealed to the Supreme Court, McKinley's new colleagues unanimously reversed him, but, undismayed, he filed a trenchant dissent. The states' rights tenor of this opinion would characterize his general approach to constitutional questions throughout his fourteen years as a member of the Court. He joined with the majority in *Groves v. Slaughter* in believing that, despite the fact that the Constitution vested control of interstate commerce in the federal government, a state could bar the importation of slaves for sale. In *Lane v. Vick*, he dissented from his colleagues' holding that the Mississippi Supreme Court's interpretation of a will was not binding on the U.S. Supreme Court. However, in the Passenger Cases, he filed a concurring opinion arguing the nationalist position that the Constitution forbade any interference by the states with immigration after 1808.

Immediately after his appointment to the Court, McKinley moved back to Louisville, Kentucky. The census of 1850 reported the value of his real estate in that year as $85,000. Initially, he had an enormous circuit to cover, requiring him to travel more than 10,000 miles a year. But in 1842 the circuits were rearranged, and thereafter his burden was somewhat reduced. In presiding on circuit, he apparently was something of a martinet. Future Alabama Supreme Court justice Lyman Gibbons commented, "I have never before seen a judge on the bench so decidedly rude and ungentlemanly, disregarding alike the feelings of the members of the bar and the settled rules of law." In the late 1840s McKinley's health began to fail, and he took a diminishing part in the business both of the court and of the circuit. He died in Louisville.

• McKinley's personal papers have not survived. Jimmie Hicks, "Associate Justice John McKinley: A Sketch," *Alabama Review* 18, no. 3 (July 1965): 227–33, cites the few letters that are extant. John M. Martin, "John McKinley: Jacksonian Phase," *Alabama Historical Quarterly* 28, nos. 1 and 2 (Spring-Summer 1966): 7–31, is a thorough account of his congressional career. Frank Otto Gatell, "John McKinley," in *The Justices of the United States Supreme Court, 1789–1969: Their Lives and Major Opinions*, ed. Leon Friedman and Fred L. Israel, vol. 1 (1969), pp. 769–77, comments on his judicial role.

J. MILLS THORNTON III

MCKINLEY, William (29 Jan. 1843–14 Sept. 1901), twenty-fifth president of the United States, was born in Niles, Ohio, the son of William McKinley and Nancy Allison, both of Scotch-Irish ancestry. McKinley's father managed charcoal furnaces and manufactured pig iron in a small way. McKinley went to school in Niles and later in Poland, Ohio. At seventeen he entered Allegheny College in Meadville, Pennsylvania, but a brief illness and financial problems forced him to drop out after a single term.

When the Civil War began, McKinley was the first man in Poland, Ohio, to volunteer. He joined the Twenty-third Ohio Infantry, which was commanded by Rutherford B. Hayes. During the fighting at Antietam in 1862, McKinley displayed bravery in combat when he brought food and coffee to his regiment under heavy enemy fire. He was promoted to second lieutenant and finished the war with the brevet rank of major. During his entire political career, he was known as "Major" McKinley.

After the war, McKinley worked in the law office of Judge Charles E. Glidden of Youngstown, Ohio, and spent some time at the Albany Law School in New York. Admitted to the Ohio bar in 1867, he opened a practice in Canton, Ohio, where he maintained a home until his death.

McKinley soon became active in the Republican party, and in 1869 he was elected prosecuting attorney for Stark County. In 1871 he married Ida Saxton, daughter of a Canton banker. The couple had two daughters, one of whom died in infancy, and the other died at the age of four. Grief and shock over these tragedies, further compounded by epilepsy, transformed Ida McKinley into a chronic invalid. McKinley, a devoted husband, lavished attention and affection on her throughout his life.

In 1876 McKinley was elected to Congress from Ohio's Seventeenth District. He quickly identified himself with the protective tariff and became a spokesman for the economic nationalism that protection represented. Democratic efforts to gerrymander McKinley's district were a constant threat to his political survival. Nonetheless, he consistently won reelection, except for the 1882 race.

Popular among his House colleagues and a gifted public speaker, McKinley soon became a rising star within the party. Named to the House Ways and Means Committee in 1880, he was a prominent participant in the debates about the Mills Bill, a Democratic tariff measure in 1888. He chaired the Committee on Resolutions at the Republican National Conventions of 1884 and 1888. After he lost a race for the Speakership to Thomas B. Reed in 1889, he was named chairman of the Ways and Means Committee, which drafted the McKinley Tariff of 1890. This measure raised customs duties but authorized trade reciprocity, a provision James G. Blaine had sponsored. From then on McKinley became increasingly convinced of the wisdom of reciprocity.

About this time, McKinley formed a friendship with the Ohio industrialist Marcus Alonzo Hanna. Hanna wanted to be a presidential kingmaker, and their partnership helped lead McKinley to the White House. Political opponents and cartoonists painted Hanna as the dominant figure in their relationship, but McKinley, though he respected Hanna and benefitted from his support, was always his own man.

The McKinley Tariff resulted in the sweeping defeat of the Republicans in the 1890 elections. Even McKinley lost his seat, but the following year he ran for governor of Ohio against the incumbent, James E. Campbell, and was elected. In 1892 McKinley enjoyed some support as a presidential candidate against President Benjamin Harrison (1833–1901), but he was the permanent chairman of the Republican National Convention and resisted efforts to have his name placed in nomination. He knew that the Republicans were likely to lose, and he did not wish to make enemies by opposing President Harrison.

A financial setback in 1893 cast a shadow over McKinley's future. He had endorsed the notes of a friend, Robert L. Walker, who went bankrupt in February of that year. McKinley's obligations approached $130,000. Hanna and other wealthy friends took charge of McKinley's property, raised money from other donors, and retired the debts. Rather than hurt him, the incident won him sympathy as another victim of the financial depression that hit the nation in 1893. He easily won reelection as governor in the fall.

During the 1894 congressional elections, McKinley made 371 speeches for party candidates and emerged as the most prominent candidate for the presidential nomination in 1896. His path to the nomination was relatively smooth. Among his serious challengers, Speaker Reed had strength only in the Northeast, and William Boyd Allison of Iowa never developed much of a following. The only problem that McKinley encountered in winning the party's nomination was his position on the gold standard. During the 1870s he expressed some support for policies that encouraged a wider use of silver—voting, for example, for the Bland-Allison Act of 1878. The progold forces within the Republican party wanted a straight-out declaration of support for gold, but McKinley wanted to leave some room for helping silver in order to conciliate Republicans from the West. The resulting plank in the platform came out "unreservedly for sound money" but also spoke of the possibility of an international agreement for bimetallism. McKinley's caution over the gold standard contributed to his reputation within the Republican party for some political indecision. Nevertheless, he won easily on the first ballot and picked Garret A. Hobart of New Jersey as his running mate.

The Republicans expected an easy campaign against the divided and dispirited Democrats. Instead, the Democratic party nominated William Jennings Bryan on a free-silver platform, and a wave of enthusiasm for the youthful Bryan swept the land as he toured the country endlessly during the summer and fall of 1896. Rather than try to match Bryan's campaign style, McKinley conducted a "front-porch" campaign at his home in Canton. Delegations of visiting Republicans came daily to hear the candidate give short, effective speeches warning of the dangers of free silver and the importance of tariff protection. Meanwhile, Hanna and the Republican campaign raised and spent $4 million on hundreds of millions of pamphlets, numerous columns and advertisements in newspapers, and dozens of party speakers. By October the tide had turned. On election day, McKinley received 271 electoral votes to Bryan's 176. His popular majority of 600,000 was the most decisive result since the election of 1872.

The new president was five foot six but dressed in ways that made himself appear taller. He liked cigars but refused to be photographed with one in his hand. McKinley wrote few personal letters and did not convey his intimate thoughts to friends. "He had a way of handling men," Elihu Root said of him, "so that they thought his ideas were their own." He was an ambitious person who had a clear sense of his own historical destiny. Senator Charles Dick of Ohio said that McKinley "had been petted and flattered until he felt that all the fruit on the tree was his."

At the outset of his administration, McKinley's cabinet was not as distinguished as it would later become. The aged John Sherman (1823–1900), who was appointed secretary of state, was not up to the job and had to be replaced when the Spanish-American War broke out in 1898. McKinley offered Hanna a place as postmaster general, but the latter preferred to replace Sherman as senator from Ohio. For the Treasury Department, McKinley named Lyman J. Gage, a Chicago banker. The secretary of war, Russell A. Alger, proved a weak selection. The other members of the cabinet reflected the usual mix of sectional and political considerations.

When McKinley took office on 4 March 1897, the presidency was in eclipse. Relations with the press were in disarray, and the institution was not prepared for the rapidly expanding duties of the office. Though he never expressed any large theories of presidential power, McKinley proved to be a forceful executive. He traveled extensively, promoted his policies, and sought better relations with the press. Newsmen were given space on the second floor of the White House and received daily briefings from the presidential secretaries. McKinley's first, ineffective personal secretary, John Addison Porter, was soon replaced by the more efficient and bureaucratic operative, George B. Cortelyou. By adroit use of the media and management of the president's travels, Cortelyou emerged as a prototype of the presidential chief of staff.

McKinley's experience in Congress served him well. He called Congress into special session soon after his inauguration to deal with the tariff, and a new measure, the Dingley Tariff of 1897 was passed in July. Going beyond the reciprocity provisions of the McKinley Tariff, it authorized reciprocal trade treaties, which the president pursued during his administration. McKinley also opened negotiations with France and Great Britain for an agreement to encourage a wider use of silver in world commerce, but these talks ended in failure in October. From that point onward the administration moved toward the support of gold that culminated in the Gold Standard Act of 1900.

During the first year of the presidency, McKinley also set in motion negotiations with Great Britain over the longstanding issues of the Canadian boundary with Alaska, Newfoundland fisheries, and fur seals. These talks laid the basis for better relations with the British. The question of the annexation of the Hawaiian Islands also arose after the United States negotiated a treaty with that government, which received Senate consideration early in 1898. Opposition from southern Democrats, who disliked the racially diverse Hawaiian population, stalled the pact until the outbreak of the war with Spain.

The most important foreign policy question that McKinley faced was the rebellion against Spanish rule in Cuba that had been going on since 1895. Close economic ties between the United States and Cuba aroused interest in the war. Reports of atrocities by the combatants touched humanitarian feelings, and sensational stories in popular newspapers kept the issue of intervention in Cuba very much in the public mind. Businessmen looked upon a possible conflict with Spain as bad for the economy, but the American people sympathized with the Cubans and wanted Spain to leave the island. All these forces tested President McKinley as soon as he took office. McKinley believed that Spain should not be granted unlimited time in which to suppress the uprising. He also believed that Spanish tactics must be humane and limited. Finally, any settlement must be acceptable to the Cuban rebels. These assumptions put the president on a course toward war with Spain, where no government could tolerate the loss of Cuba.

During 1897 the administration pressed Spain to make concessions. Some apparent adjustments did occur, including an autonomy plan that gave Cubans greater control over domestic affairs but left foreign policy to Madrid. Spain also ended the "reconcentration" camps into which the Spanish army had sent Cuban civilians. Spanish sovereignty, however, remained in place. The situation worsened as 1898 began. The Spanish in Cuba who were opposed to the autonomy program rioted on 12 January 1898, convincing the president that Spain was not going to meet his expectation that the Cubans should obtain true self-rule. With the situation worsening, the battleship *Maine* was sent to Havana as a sign that friendly relations between Washington and Madrid still existed. On 9 February newspapers in the United States printed a letter that Cubans had intercepted from the Spanish minister to the United States, Enrique Dupuy de Lôme. It criticized McKinley and revealed that Spain was not negotiating in good faith. Six days later the *Maine* exploded in Havana harbor, killing 266 of its officers and crew. Sentiment for war mounted.

While he waited for a naval board of inquiry to report on the sinking, McKinley pressed Spain to agree to an armistice or acceptance of American mediation leading to Cuban independence. When Spain rejected these terms in late March, the president prepared to ask Congress for authority to intervene in Cuba to end the war. Prodded by European governments, Spain finally agreed to a suspension of hostilities that did not involve recognition of the rebels, but Madrid balked at Cuban independence. McKinley sent his interventionist message to Capitol Hill on 11 April 1898. Congress gave him the authority he sought on 19 April, Spain broke diplomatic relations on 20 April, and the two nations were at war by 25 April.

During the brief conflict with Spain, McKinley was the central figure. Preparing for a possible war, the U.S. Navy had developed a plan to attack Spain at a vulnerable place, the Philippine Islands, which Madrid could not easily defend. McKinley gave the attack order on 24 April that sent George Dewey's squadron into action at Manila Bay on 1 May. After that victory, McKinley began sending American troops to the Philippines. Although he had not yet decided to annex the islands, his policies preserved American options to take the Philippines if that seemed necessary.

In the fighting in Cuba, McKinley exercised a close supervision over the army of General William R. Shafter. The switchboard at the White House enabled the president to convey orders to the battlefield within twenty minutes. McKinley was a forceful and effective commander in chief who used the war powers of his office to shape events. Largely through his efforts, the United States stood victorious in Cuba and the Philippines by mid-July 1898.

McKinley also shaped the strategy of the United States in the peace talks that followed the end of the fighting in mid-August. Congress had already voted to annex Hawaii by joint resolution in July. The president had replaced Secretary of State Sherman with William R. Day when the war began. McKinley designated Day to lead the delegation to the peace conference in Paris and named John Hay as secretary of state. Aware of German, Japanese, and Russian interest in the Philippines, McKinley was moving toward a decision to acquire all of the Philippines for the United States.

McKinley put three prominent senators on the peace commission to conduct negotiations with Spain in Paris to end the formal state of war. In this way, he ensured later votes for whatever treaty they negotiated. McKinley toured the Middle West in the autumn of 1898 to arouse popular enthusiasm for acquisition of the Philippines. When the peace commissioners asked him in late October what the nation's position was on the islands, he responded that there was "but one plain path of duty—acceptance of the archipelago." He did not consult with the Almighty in making the judgment, as a later dubious anecdote alleged. The Peace of Paris was signed on 10 December 1898, ceding the Philippines, Puerto Rico, and Guam to the United States.

Republican success in the 1898 elections made McKinley's task easier. The president went on a speaking tour of the South in December 1898 to woo Democratic senators. He wielded patronage, orchestrated public appeals, and did some adroit private lobbying to win over wavering senators. These techniques helped bring narrow Senate approval of the treaty on 6 February 1899 by a vote of 57 to 27, one more vote than the necessary two-thirds.

The aftermath of the war brought many other problems for McKinley. By February 1899 fighting had erupted between Filipino nationalists and American soldiers in the islands. The president did not waver in his assertion of United States sovereignty in the Philippines during the difficult war that followed. He governed the islands through the war powers and established civilian commissions to handle the transition to colonial government once the insurrection was defeated.

Criticisms about the conduct of the army during the fighting and the quality of its supplies led McKinley to form the Dodge Commission to evaluate the army's performance. These hearings led to important military reforms in how the army was organized and the relationship between the regular army and the National Guard. In 1899 the president eased Secretary Alger out of the War Department and replaced him with Root. McKinley had acted cautiously on the unpopular Alger because he believed that the secretary was not to blame for all the problems that the army had encountered.

Rejecting calls for immediate Cuban independence by some in the United States, McKinley established a military government under the president's control in Cuba to oversee the transition to ultimate self-rule. The president and his advisers feared that a Cuba without close links to the United States might fall under the dominance of a European power such as Germany. Therefore, McKinley insisted on congressional passage of the Platt Amendment in 1901 to an army appropriation act. The amendment, to which the Cubans also were compelled to agree, restricted their sovereign right to enter into alliances with other powers or to incur foreign debts.

Another major priority of the McKinley administration was a canal across Central America. Secretary Hay negotiated the Hay-Pauncefote Treaty of 1901 that cleared the way for the United States to build what became the Panama Canal during the presidency of Theodore Roosevelt (1858–1919).

An important achievement of the McKinley administration was the Open Door Policy for China that Hay announced in 1899. The diplomatic notes sought to safeguard U.S. trading rights in China and asserted American interest in Asia. McKinley exercised the war powers again in 1900 when he sent troops to help in the relief of Europeans trapped in Peking (Beijing) during the Boxer Rebellion.

By 1900 returning prosperity and the foreign policy record of the administration made McKinley's reelection chances almost certain. The death of Vice President Hobart in November 1899 led to the selection of Theodore Roosevelt as the vice presidential nominee in 1900. While McKinley worried about Roosevelt's impetuous nature, he had no viable alternative candidate and accepted the enthusiasm of the Republicans for Roosevelt. The Democrats renominated Bryan for another race against McKinley. Observing the custom that incumbent presidents not actively seek another term, McKinley allowed Roosevelt to do most of the campaigning. The result was another decisive victory for McKinley; he had 292 electoral votes to 155 for Bryan. Interpreting the result as an affirmation of his leadership, McKinley told friends, "I am now the President of the whole people."

During a second term, McKinley had plans to travel outside the country to break the informal precedent that confined presidents to the United States. He also intended to push for stronger antitrust laws and to secure Senate approval of reciprocal trade treaties. The early months of the second term went well. The army captured the main Filipino leader, Emilio Aguinaldo, in March 1901; and the Supreme Court upheld the administration's power over the territories won from Spain in 1898 in the Insular Cases. That summer McKinley traveled across the country and decided to visit the Pan-American Exposition in Buffalo. His wife's illness delayed the trip until early September.

On 5 September, in a speech at Buffalo, the president argued for acceptance of his reciprocity treaties. Breaking away from the view that the nation could follow only protectionist policies, he said that "the period of exclusiveness is past" and that a new trade policy based on reciprocal concessions was in order. The next day, as he was greeting citizens during a public reception in the Temple of Music, Leon Czolgosz, a self-proclaimed anarchist, shot him twice in the stomach. McKinley lived for eight more days before he died in Buffalo. The nation mourned; McKinley was buried in Canton, and a memorial to him opened there that same year.

When Americans became disillusioned with the Spanish-American War after 1920, McKinley was criticized as a weak and ineffectual executive whose vacillating policy had yielded to popular hysteria and had failed to prevent a needless conflict. That indictment overlooked the real issues that separated Madrid and Washington in 1898 and Spain's unwillingness to yield to American demands.

McKinley was the first modern president. When he exercised the war powers to govern the first overseas territories that the United States had acquired, when he exerted public pressure on Congress to support his policies, and when he used the press and his travels to rally public opinion, he laid a foundation of activism upon which Theodore Roosevelt and Woodrow Wilson built.

• The main group of McKinley's papers are housed at the Library of Congress and are conveniently available on microfilm. The papers of his terms as governor of Ohio are at the Ohio Historical Society at Columbus. There are smaller collections of McKinley documents at the McKinley Museum of History, Science, and Industry in Canton, Ohio, and at the Western Reserve Historical Society in Cleveland. The papers of McKinley's secretary, Cortelyou, at the Library of Congress also contain extensive materials from the president's administration. For McKinley's writings, *Speeches and Addresses of William McKinley* (1893) covers his prepresidential years, while *Speeches and Addresses of William McKinley from March 1, 1897 to May 30, 1900* (1900) deals with his administration. A guide to the historical literature on McKinley is Lewis L. Gould and Craig H. Roell, eds., *William McKinley: A Bibliography* (1988). Charles S. Olcott, *The Life of William McKinley* (2 vols., 1916), was the official biography. It has been superseded by Margaret Leech, *In the Days of McKinley* (1959), and even more fully by H. Wayne Morgan, *William McKinley and His America* (1963). Lewis L. Gould, *The Presidency of William McKinley* (1980), examines his administration and McKinley's impact on the office. John Dobson, *Reticent Expansionism: The Foreign Policy of William McKinley* (1988), is a critical look at McKinley's diplomacy. Joseph A. Fry, "William McKinley and the Coming of the Spanish-American War: A Study of the Besmirching and Redemption of an Historical Image," *Diplomatic History* 3 (Winter 1979): 77–97, examines the most controversial aspect of McKinley's life. For a list of obituaries and tributes to McKinley after his death, see Gould and Roell, *McKinley*, pp. 171–80.

LEWIS L. GOULD

MCKINLY, John (24 Feb. 1721–31 Aug. 1796), physician and first president (governor) of Delaware, was born in northern Ireland. His parents' names are unknown. Nothing is known of his early life, education, or immigration to North America. While in his early twenties he established a medical practice in Wilmington, Delaware. McKinly soon became active in public affairs, serving as a militia officer in 1747–1748 and 1756 and as sheriff of New Castle County from 1757 to 1759. He was annually elected chief burgess of Wilmington between 1759 and 1762 and from 1766 to 1776.

John McKinly married Jane Richardson probably between 1761 and 1766. He was a Presbyterian; she, a Quaker. The McKinlys had no children and lived in Wilmington throughout their marriage.

Each year from 1771 to 1775, McKinly was elected to Delaware's unicameral assembly. As Delawareans debated the issues that led to independence, McKinly, like many of Irish and Presbyterian background, supported the patriot cause. He emerged as one of its leaders, serving on Delaware's committee of correspondence appointed in October 1773; on the New Castle County committee that urged in July 1774 the appointment of delegates to the First Continental Congress; and, in December 1774, as chairman of the Committee of Vigilance that enforced the Continental Association in New Castle County. In September 1775 McKinly was elected president of Delaware's council of safety and chosen brigadier general of the New Castle County militia. Under Delaware's new constitution of 1776 he became a member and Speaker of the House of Assembly in the bicameral general assembly. The legislature did not immediately elect a state president as authorized by the constitution but chose another council of safety in November 1776, again with McKinly as president.

John McKinly became Delaware's first president in February 1777. Although the more radical patriots distrusted him because of his close alignment with George Read, a conservative Whig, McKinly's election accurately reflected the mood of the state. His moderate approach made him acceptable to a political spectrum that ranged from Whig to Loyalist. In his brief tenure as president, the conscientious but cautious McKinly faced an overwhelmingly difficult situation. The militia was small and ineffective; the court system, under a chief justice of shifting loyalties, was practically at a standstill; and Loyalist insurrection was a constant threat. Holding an office with little constitutional authority, McKinly made scant progress toward solving Delaware's problems. The situation deteriorated as the revolutionary war came to northern Delaware late in the summer of 1777. After a brief skirmish at the battle of Cooch's Bridge on 3 September (Delaware's only battle of the war), the British defeated the Americans at the battle of the Brandywine in nearby Pennsylvania on 10 September. The British immediately occupied Wilmington and captured President McKinly at his home three days later.

Hopes for his quick release faded as McKinly was held on two British ships in the Delaware River (the *Roebuck* and the *Solebay*), imprisoned in the Philadelphia State House, and transferred to Long Island when the British evacuated Philadelphia in July 1778. Delaware's leaders worked reluctantly to free McKinly; some of them wrongly suspected him of harboring British sympathies. In August 1778 McKinly was paroled so that he could persuade Congress to release New Jersey governor William Franklin (1731–1813), a Loyalist, to the British in exchange for McKinly's freedom. John McKinly was finally freed in mid-September 1778.

After his release, McKinly resumed his medical practice in Wilmington. He was elected to Congress in 1784 but for unknown reasons did not serve. McKinly helped found the Medical Society of Delaware in 1789, and he served as a trustee of the First Presbyterian Church in Wilmington and of the Academy of Newark in Newark, Delaware. He died in Wilmington.

• Personal papers of McKinly are in the Historical Society of Delaware in Wilmington. Some letters have been published in Mary T. Evans, "Letters of Dr. John McKinly to His Wife while a Prisoner of War, 1777–1778," *Pennsylvania Magazine of History and Biography* 34 (1910): 9–20. McKinly has not been the subject of a full biography. The best sources are G. S. Rowe, "The Travail of John McKinly, First President of Delaware," *Delaware History* 17 (1976–1977): 21–36, and Roger Martin, *A History of Delaware through Its Governors* (1984).

CONSTANCE J. COOPER

MCKINNEY, Roscoe Lewis (8 Feb. 1900–30 Sept. 1978), educator and anatomist, was born in Washington, D.C., the son of Lewis Bradner McKinney, an employee of the U.S. Printing Office, and Blanche Elaine Hunt. McKinney attended Dunbar High School, the all-black grammar school on M Street in Washington. Dunbar's faculty, comprised of highly motivated African-American scholars, inspired generations of black youth to strive for academic excellence. McKinney himself recalled the atmosphere of "hopeful purpose and tremendous encouragement" that pervaded the school.

After graduating in 1917 McKinney enrolled at Bates College in Lewiston, Maine. Unlike many other white colleges at the time, Bates admitted African-American students. Some of McKinney's Dunbar teachers were Bates graduates; Benjamin E. Mays, later president of Morehouse College in Atlanta, was a year ahead of McKinney, and other blacks were to follow. Nevertheless, McKinney found race to be an issue in at least one Bates program. Following his induction into the army reserve training corps, the commanding officer made it clear that he was personally opposed to the participation of African-American students, even though he tolerated it as required by college policy. Other aspects of campus life, both social and academic, proceeded more smoothly. McKinney joined several clubs, including the Young Men's Christian Association, Outing Club, and Forum, and competed on the varsity track team. Ranked near the top of his class, he earned an award for "declamations," was elected to Phi Beta Kappa, and graduated with the bachelor of science degree in 1921.

At Bates, McKinney developed an interest in biology that carried over into his future academic career. One of his professors told him about the work of the eminent African-American zoologist Ernest Everett Just, whom McKinney came to revere as a role model. This same professor encouraged McKinney's budding interest in cellular research, especially the relation of the cell to extracellular products and connective tissues. Yet, as McKinney approached graduation, he did not seriously consider a career in research or academics. He was hoping, rather, to study medicine and establish himself in practice in the Washington, D.C., area. "Who is the fellow," a contributor to his class yearbook wondered, "that we see over in the zoology laboratory six or eight hours a day, noting a few fine points in the embryological development of the chick or preparing slides for [the professor]? We all shall watch with interest and admiration his work at Harvard Medic for the next four years, and we know he will make some Doctor."

For unknown reasons, McKinney never attended medical school. Instead, he accepted an instructorship in zoology at Morehouse College in 1921. Two years later he joined the faculty of the zoology department at Howard University as an instructor under Just. Also in 1923 he began studies toward the doctorate in anatomy. Each summer he attended the University of Chicago, taking courses and working on various projects in tissue culture under Alexander A. Maximow, the eminent Russian histologist. When Maximow died in 1928, McKinney continued his studies at Chicago under William Bloom and worked with him to complete Maximow's histology textbook. This work, *A Textbook of Histology*, went into several editions and became a standard reference source for medical students. McKinney's contribution, acknowledged in Bloom's preface, included preparation of the figures and the manuscript for publication. The text appeared in 1930, the same year that McKinney received his Ph.D. in anatomy. His thesis, a study of fibers in tissue culture, was published in 1929 in a major German scientific journal.

McKinney was among the earliest African Americans to earn a Ph.D. in anatomy. He returned to Howard University in 1930 and joined the anatomy department in the School of Medicine, where he was soon joined by two other African-American anatomists (William Montague Cobb and Moses Wharton Young) as part of a larger campaign to upgrade the institution's medical teaching and research programs. McKinney served as professor and department head (1930–1947) and as vice dean of the school (1944–1946). He maintained an active research program, despite a heavy administrative and teaching load.

In 1952, on the recommendation of the National Advisory Cancer Council, McKinney was awarded a grant by the National Institutes of Health for "An *In Vitro* Study of the Development of Intercellular Fibers in Tissue Culture of Normal and Cancer Cells." Although he did not publish widely, he worked on several projects in tissue culture, microcinematography, radioactive isotopes in cells and tissues, and the origin and development of connective tissue. He and Just collaborated occasionally, for example, on skin-graft experiments with lower amphibious animals such as tadpoles and frogs. Editions of *Gray's Anatomy* included slides of tissue stains made by McKinney. His doctoral thesis was cited in the medical and scientific literature eleven times between 1955 and 1989.

Along with his departmental colleagues Cobb and Young, McKinney played a role in pressuring scientific associations on key civil-rights issues. In 1950, for example, all three (plus two other members of the Howard anatomy department) boycotted the New Orleans meeting of the American Association of Anatomists to protest a decision to house all nonwhite participants at a remote site where they would "feel comfortable." A similar protest was organized a year later by members of the mathematics department at Fisk University, with regard to arrangements for a Nashville meeting of the Mathematical Association of America. While a few professional groups such as the American Anthropological Association, the Association of American Medical Colleges, the American Psychological Association, and the American Association of Physical Anthropologists had established antisegregationist policies by 1950, in particular by refusing to site meetings in southern cities with racially separate facilities and accommodations, several years were to elapse before most followed suit.

McKinney retired from Howard with emeritus rank in 1968 but was quickly reappointed to the active faculty, serving as professor of anatomy in 1968–1969 and 1971–1976. His career also took him overseas. He served for two years as professor of microscopic anatomy at the Royal Iraq Medical College in Baghdad (first as a Fulbright fellow, 1955–1956; then on the invitation of the Iraqi government, 1956–1957); taught, under the auspices of the U.S. State Department, at Osmania Medical College, Hyderabad, India, 1960–1962; and was a consultant in anatomy to the medical faculty, University of Saigon, Vietnam, 1969–1971. The U.S. ambassador to Iraq wrote that McKinney "made a most favorable impression here during his two years' stay . . . not only in academic circles where his professional competence was readily recognized, but also among a wide circle of Iraqis."

McKinney was a member of the American Association for the Advancement of Science, the American Association of Anatomists, and the Tissue Culture Association. He had married Ethel Berena James in 1937, and they had four children. He died in Washington, D.C.

• Although few relevant archival materials survive, a small file on McKinney's 1929 application for a Rockefeller Foundation fellowship contains useful information on his early years (see "The Rockefeller Foundation: Personal History Record and Application for Fellowship" in General Education Board Records, ser. I, subser. 1, box 29, folder 267, Rockefeller Archive Center, Pocantico Hills, N.Y.; also see references to McKinney in box 28, folders 259–261). Other useful references may be found in Bates College publications, especially Gladys Blickmore, "Bates at Howard," *Bates Alumnus*, Jan. 1949, p. 10, and his class yearbook, *The 1921 Mirror*, p. 52. McKinney's doctoral thesis was published as "Studies on Fibers in Tissue Culture: III. The Development of Reticulum into Collagenous Fibers in Cultures of Adult Rabbit Lymph Nodes," *Archiv für experimentelle Zellforschung besonders Gewebezüchtung* 9 (1929): 14–35. A biographical file comprised of newspaper obituaries and a program for his memorial service is preserved at the Moorland-Spingarn Research Center, Howard University. Published biographical summaries include an obituary notice in *Journal of the National Medical Association* 71 (May 1979): 518, and *TCA Report* 12 (Sept.–Dec. 1978): 144, a publication of the Tissue Culture Association.

KENNETH R. MANNING

MCKINNON, Edna Bertha Rankin (21 Oct. 1893–5 Apr. 1978), birth control reformer, was born in Missoula, Montana, the daughter of John Rankin, a builder and rancher, and Olive Pickering, a teacher. Edna Rankin entered Wellesley College in 1912 but left in 1914 to enroll at the University of Wisconsin. Two years later, she left school again to work on the successful congressional campaign of her sister, Jeannette Rankin. In 1916 she received a B.A. from the University of Montana. At the urging of her brother Wellington, she then studied law—even though she hated it—and public speaking. In 1918 she became the first woman born in Montana to receive a law degree and be admitted to the bar.

She practiced law briefly in Helena, Montana, before her marriage in 1919 to John Wallace McKinnon, Jr., a Harvard graduate from Boston who had come to the Bitterroot Valley to manage a fruit-growing venture. It failed, as did other future ventures. They had two children. Financial difficulties forced Edna McKinnon to seek work in New York City in 1929.

The tragic death of their son from an undiagnosed illness in 1930 may have precipitated the end of their marriage soon thereafter.

In the mid-1930s McKinnon found a job in Washington, D.C., where she attended her first lecture on birth control in 1936. Immediately thereafter she became executive director of the National Committee for Federal Legislation on Birth Control, a division of the Margaret Sanger Research Bureau. Her assignment was to work for the overturn of the Comstock Law, which outlawed the dissemination of birth control information and devices as a form of pornography. A few months later, the Circuit Court of Appeals in New York City issued its landmark decision overturning the Comstock Law in *U.S. v. One Package of Japanese Pessaries*.

Through the intervention of birth control researcher Clarence J. Gamble, McKinnon then became a field worker for the Margaret Sanger Research Bureau in 1937 in Montana. Encountering ridicule and hostility as often as she encountered a warm welcome, she worked to spread the birth control message in both rural and urban areas. Thwarted in the state by the hostility of her conservative and politically powerful brother Wellington, McKinnon was reassigned to Tennessee, where her unwavering faith in her work, effectiveness in recruiting both lay and professional supporters, and articulate explanations of the importance of birth control led to the establishment of five clinics. She then moved on to Kentucky and Alabama and by 1946 had brought the birth control message to thirty-two states.

In 1947 McKinnon became executive director of the Planned Parenthood Association of the Chicago area. During the next ten years, with "unforgettable magnetism and unquenchable enthusiasm" (Dykeman, p. 107), she built a sturdy federation that tripled in size and increased its budget sevenfold. In 1952 McKinnon accompanied Margaret Sanger to the founding conference of the International Planned Parenthood Federation (IPPF) in Bombay.

After resigning from her Chicago post in 1957, McKinnon planned to take a leisurely journey around the world with a friend. At the invitation of Clarence Gamble, she agreed to combine investigating and reporting on the activities of the recently established Pathfinder Fund (a family planning organization founded by Gamble) in Singapore, Manila, and other locations with a personal survey of IPPF projects and her vacation travels. Because the friend with whom she had planned to travel had died suddenly, McKinnon set out in 1960 with her daughter.

After receiving a warm welcome in Tokyo, Taipei, Manila, Hong Kong, Saigon, Bangkok, and Kuala Lumpur, McKinnon stayed on in Singapore to work as a volunteer at Constance Goh Koh Kee's clinic. There, when her association with Gamble became known, she became a target for the hostility of the larger, more bureaucratic IPPF toward the less orthodox Pathfinder Fund, which focused on local organizing by field workers. Determined that group rivalries would not impede her work, McKinnon relocated from Singapore to nearby Johore Bahru in January 1961 and became a paid field worker for the Pathfinder Fund.

During the next five years, McKinnon traveled in Southeast Asia, India, Nepal, Turkey, Iran, Saudi Arabia, Kuwait, and sub-Saharan Africa, spreading her message: "Every single child born on this earth should be wanted and cherished. Birth control and peace are the answers we must give to death control by war and pollution" (quoted in Dykeman, p. 276). She organized government, medical, and popular support for birth control and in many places "broke the barrier of silence."

In 1966 McKinnon was called home to Montana by news of Wellington's death. Except for a trip to Indonesia, Nigeria, and Ethiopia in 1968, she retired after thirty years of tireless work. McKinnon spent her last years in Carmel, California, where she died. The clinics, programs, and organizations that she initiated throughout the world are evidence of the truth of her belief that "one person—in any cause or place—can make a difference."

• McKinnon's papers are preserved at the Schlesinger Library, Radcliffe College, which also houses some of McKinnon's letters in the Jeannette Rankin and Sarah Merry Bradley Gamble papers. McKinnon's scattered reports to the Margaret Sanger Research Bureau, the American Birth Control League (after 1939 the Planned Parenthood Federation of America), and the International Planned Parenthood Federation and a more complete record of her activities for the Pathfinder Fund are in the papers of Clarence J. Gamble, Rare Books Department, Countway Library, Harvard Medical School. The only published biography is Wilma Dykeman, *Too Many People, Too Little Love—Edna Rankin McKinnon: Pioneer for Birth Control* (1974).

PATRICIA MILLER KING

MCKINSTRY, Elisha Williams (11 Apr. 1825–1 Nov. 1901), lawyer and jurist, was born in Detroit, Michigan, the son of David Charles McKinstry, a businessman and entrepreneur, and Nancy Whiting Backus. His family, originally from New York, was prominent in Detroit. His father had moved about 1815 to what was then a small Great Lakes port recently evacuated by the British and in time acquired extensive business enterprises including wharves, a warehouse, a ferryboat between Detroit and Canada, a store, stagelines, a theater, and a construction firm. On one occasion McKinstry's family hosted Martin Van Buren during the president's visit to Detroit.

McKinstry was educated in Michigan and Ohio. His family moved from Detroit to Ypsilanti, Michigan, about 1840, where McKinstry was educated by tutors. After studying law in the offices of his uncles Justus McKinstry and Elisha Williams in Hudson, New York, he was admitted to the New York bar in 1847.

After the discovery of gold in California in 1849 McKinstry migrated west, landing first in San Diego and arriving in San Francisco on 4 June 1849. He later recalled, "How ineffaceable . . . the impressions of the first day in San Francisco! . . . The five dollar breakfast of a pair of eggs and a cup of black coffee!" (Johnson, p. 125). In 1850 he opened a law office near Sacramento and was elected an assemblyman from his district to the tumultuous first California legislature, sometimes termed the "Legislature of a Thousand Drinks" (Sacramento *Daily Union*, 13 Sept. 1871). McKinstry took a leading part in the initial legislature among, as he put it, "distractions of . . . practical jokes—mostly of the sham duel order—of quarter races and bullfights, billiard matches and fandangos" (Sacramento *Daily Union*, 13 Sept. 1871). On one occasion he and another member, D. P. Baldwin, were ordered to apologize to the legislature after an altercation and disorderly conduct in the assembly. In 1850 the governor appointed McKinstry adjutant general of California, administrative head of the state militia, but McKinstry never served in the post because no appropriation was made for it by the legislature.

At the close of the legislature in 1851, McKinstry contracted cholera during an epidemic in Sacramento. Recovering, he went to San Jose, Martinez, and eventually to Napa where he resumed practicing law. There McKinstry in 1852 was elected district judge for Napa and the surrounding region. One commentator observed, "He made an excellent judge amid scenes at times turbulent and without facilities for handling lawbreakers. He always treated the bar with great deference and was accorded a very high measure of esteem by the profession." (Johnson, p. 125). Reelected district judge in 1858, he resigned that position to become the Democratic candidate for lieutenant governor in 1863. Losing the election, toward the end of 1863 he moved to Nevada, where in 1864 he unsuccessfully ran for the state supreme court. Earlier in 1863 McKinstry and eighteen-year-old Annie Livingston Hedges had been married by the Episcopal bishop of California in Marysville; they would have four children.

In the frontier town of Aurora, Nevada, McKinstry participated in an 1864 vigilance committee that seized several men suspected of murder. McKinstry withdrew his assistance when the committee itself became excessively lawless, and several of the suspects were lynched.

McKinstry returned to San Francisco in 1865 to practice law and in 1867 was elected county judge on the Democratic ticket. His participation in the Aurora Vigilance Committee was used against him in the election campaign, and charges were made that he could have prevented the lynchings. He ran in the 1869 election as an independent candidate and was elected judge of the Twelfth District Court for San Francisco and San Mateo counties. He again ran as an independent in 1873, defeating Democratic and Republican candidates for election to the California Supreme Court.

The new state constitution of 1879 reorganized the supreme court, and in that year McKinstry won election to the reorganized court for an eleven-year term on the Democratic and Workingmen's ticket. McKinstry declined appointment as chief justice in 1887. In 1888 he resigned from the supreme court to become professor at the Hastings College of Law in San Francisco, eventually succeeding founder Robert P. Hastings as dean of the school. The University of Michigan awarded McKinstry an LL.D. in 1889. In 1890 he resumed law practice while remaining on the Hastings faculty and eventually was joined by his son, James C. McKinstry, with whom he formed the firm Stanley, McKinstry, Bradley & McKinstry. In 1895 he resigned from the Hastings faculty after the school's trustees disapproved of his mixing practice and teaching, causing "expressions of regret on the part of the students, who respected him highly" (Johnson, p. 126). McKinstry established a reputation as a capable member of the San Francisco bar. He converted to Roman Catholicism late in his life. McKinstry died suddenly during a trip to San Jose.

McKinstry was a "good-sized man, about six feet tall, weighing two hundred pounds, with a commanding and engaging presence" (Johnson, p. 126). He described himself as having a "nervous temperament" but was known to have a good sense of humor. "Not without spirit, McKinstry could be calmness itself in the face of great personal danger" (Johnson, p. 127). A colorful example of a frontier lawyer, legislator, and judge, whose career spanned the formative years of California's development, McKinstry participated in the enactment of many of the initial statutes and in the decision of numerous appellate cases, which for decades shaped the course of his state's law.

• Entries about McKinstry appear in Oscar Tully Shuck, *History of the Bench and Bar of California* (1901), and Edward Johnson, *History of the Supreme Court Justices of California 1850–1900*, vol. 1 (1863). An obituary is in the San Francisco *Chronicle*, 2 Nov. 1901.

FRANCIS HELMINSKI

MCKISSICK, Floyd Bixler (3 Mar. 1922–28 Apr. 1991), civil rights lawyer and activist, was born in Asheville, North Carolina, the son of Ernest McKissick, a hotel bellman, and Magnolia Esther Thompson, a seamstress. When Floyd was four years old, an angry bus driver ordered him to the rear of the bus after he had wandered into the white section to join some white children who were watching the driver. That incident revealed to him that black children did not have the same freedom and opportunity in North Carolina as white children did. Black children attended segregated schools with inferior facilities, sat in the back of the bus, and could not sit down and eat at lunch counters. They received harsh treatment from city employees like bus drivers and police officers. They did not have public skating rinks or swimming pools, and they could not use the public library. As a result of his awareness, McKissick decided early in life that he would study law to fight for equal rights for black Americans. In fall 1939 he began a prelaw course at Morehouse College in Atlanta, Georgia, working his way through the year as a dining hall waiter. At Morehouse he became the personal waiter for black political activist, sociologist, and historian W. E. B. Du Bois. Du Bois's belief that blacks must demand absolute equality without compromise, and his opinion that educated black people had an obligation to improve the condition of the race, had an influence on the young college student.

McKissick left Morehouse in February 1942, after the United States entered World War II. In that same year he married his childhood sweetheart, Evelyn Williams; they would have three daughters and one son. McKissick joined the U.S. Army and was eventually assigned to a field artillery unit. He taught in army literacy programs in the United States for two years before he was shipped overseas. Eventually, he served in battle in Europe, where he earned a Purple Heart.

Eager to continue his education, McKissick applied to the segregated University of North Carolina after his discharge from the army in 1945. His application was not even acknowledged. Unwilling to concede defeat, he got a job as a waiter to earn enough money to reenter college. He began his long career as a civil rights activist in 1947 when he joined Bayard Rustin on the Journey of Reconciliation. The journey, a bus trip, was organized by the Congress of Racial Equality (CORE) to test a recent Supreme Court decision requiring the integration of interstate travel. The objectives of CORE, an interracial organization founded in Chicago, Illinois, in 1942, were to draw attention to and take direct action against racial discrimination in public facilities.

In the late 1940s McKissick returned to Morehouse and again applied to the all-white law school at the University of North Carolina. When he was rejected, Thurgood Marshall and the National Association for the Advancement of Colored People (NAACP) filed a suit on his behalf. While he waited for the case to be decided, McKissick attended the all-black law school at North Carolina College. In 1951 he won his suit and became the first African American to earn the LL.B. degree at the University of North Carolina, although all of his course work already had been completed at North Carolina College.

McKissick passed the North Carolina bar exam in 1952 and began a general law practice in Durham, North Carolina. In 1958 he filed his first civil rights case, a suit on behalf of his eldest daughter to integrate a public school in Durham. Active in Durham's black community, he joined the Durham Business and Profession Chain (a black businessmen's organization), became an adviser to the state's NAACP youth groups, and became the director of Durham's CORE chapter.

Because of his role as adviser to the NAACP youth groups in North Carolina, McKissick was contacted by the students who began the sit-in at the Woolworth's lunch counter in Greensboro, North Carolina, in February 1960. That sit-in marked the beginning of a great increase in the demand by blacks for equal rights. McKissick helped the students expand the sit-ins to other towns, and he led workshops on nonviolence for sit-in participants. During the first half of the 1960s McKissick represented many of the demonstrators who were arrested in direct action campaigns against segregated facilities in the South. He often served as a negotiator between the demonstrators and the local authorities, seeking to secure integrated facilities and fair employment policies.

From 1963 to 1966 McKissick served as the national chairman of CORE's board, the group responsible for determining policy at the national level. In 1966 he replaced James Farmer as the director of the national office, assuming responsibility for implementing CORE's policies. After James Meredith, the first black man admitted to the University of Mississippi, was shot, McKissick joined the Reverend Martin Luther King, Jr., and Stokely Carmichael, president of the Student Non-violent Co-ordinating Committee (SNCC), to complete Meredith's March Against Fear in 1966. McKissick supported Carmichael's effort to change the emphasis of the march to voter registration and the achievement of black power. During the period that McKissick led CORE, it became an all-black organization that was more militant in its demands for black political and economic power. As the decade became more violent, McKissick and CORE moved away from nonviolence as a philosophy and advocated self-defense.

In 1968 McKissick resigned as national director of CORE to pursue his dream of building a black community that would ultimately become economically and politically self-sufficient. Soul City, North Carolina, located about fifty miles from Durham, began with a grant from the U.S. Department of Housing and Urban Development. McKissick hoped that black-owned businesses would be attracted to the area once housing and a community infrastructure were in place. However, his plans for Soul City never materialized, partly because federal money for the project ceased. In 1979 the Department of Housing and Urban Development foreclosed on Soul City although McKissick and others continued to live there.

In 1969 McKissick published *Three-Fifths of a Man*, his analysis of the race problem in the United States. McKissick believed the problem was primarily economic and that a redistribution of the nation's wealth was needed to enable black people to share in the nation's prosperity. In the book, McKissick expressed his belief that the Declaration of Independence and the U.S. Constitution already contained all the tools necessary to solve the nation's racial problems; they only had to be enforced. McKissick continued to practice law in Durham until June 1990, when he was appointed by North Carolina governor James G. Martin as a judge in the state's Ninth Judicial District. McKissick died in Soul City.

As the national leader of CORE from 1963 to 1968, McKissick helped determine the direction of the 1960s civil rights movement. As a result of this movement, Congress passed extensive civil rights legislation in

1964 and 1965. These laws instituted profound changes in American society.

• McKissick's papers are located at the Hayti Heritage Center in Durham. Biographical information appears in Elton C. Fax, *Contemporary Black Leaders* (1970), as well as in Barbara Carlisle Bigelow, ed., *Contemporary Black Biography: Profiles from the International Black Community* (1993). Many books on the civil rights era include information on McKissick and CORE; the most comprehensive accounts are August Meier and Elliott Rudwick, *CORE: A Study in the Civil Rights Movement, 1942–1968* (1973), and James Farmer, *Lay Bare the Heart: An Autobiography of the Civil Rights Movement* (1985). Obituaries are in the *New York Times*, the *Los Angeles Times*, and the *Washington Post*, all 30 Apr. 1991.

JENIFER W. GILBERT

MCKNIGHT, William Lester (11 Nov. 1887–4 Mar. 1978), manufacturer, was born near White, Brookings County, South Dakota, the son of Joseph McKnight and Cordelia Smith, farmers. Born in a sod hut, McKnight attended a one-room primary school and graduated from White High School intent on attending a business college rather than farming.

In the fall of 1906 McKnight hired himself out to haul water for a threshing machine to raise the tuition. By the end of the harvesting season he had earned $280, enough to pay the $60 tuition at the Duluth (Minn.) Business University, where he enrolled in January 1907 to study bookkeeping, business-letter writing, and penmanship. After five months the head of the bookkeeping department sent McKnight to an interview for a bookkeeping job that would change his life forever.

McKnight arrived at the offices of the Minnesota Mining and Manufacturing Company (3M), "the scaredest boy that ever lived when I applied for the job." Sure he had failed the interview, McKnight returned to school. He then interviewed with a Michigan company that hired him. Because his mother became ill suddenly, he notified the Michigan company that he could not take the job. Fortuitously, the 3M Company hired the jobless McKnight, and on 13 May 1907 he joined the firm where he would spend the next seven decades.

McKnight thought he was going to work for "the largest manufacturer of sandpaper in the world," but in fact the company was teetering on bankruptcy. Unaware of the company's financial situation, McKnight happily accepted the $11.55-a-week salary and so impressed the management that they promoted him to cost accountant and office manager in Chicago two years later. The company continued its decline, however, until moving to St. Paul in 1910. When the sales manager resigned because he couldn't sell inferior and inconsistent products, management chose the 24-year-old McKnight as his replacement. Although inexperienced in sales, McKnight had new ideas that would revolutionize the company's business. He sent the salesmen into the shops to talk with and demonstrate 3M's products to the workmen rather than soliciting orders from front-office purchasing agents with a product catalog. Like his predecessor, McKnight found 3M's sandpaper inferior to its competitors', but McKnight pushed quality control and communication between the factory and salesmen.

McKnight abhorred crippling special discounts and determined to have 3M create a quality product for which the customer would be willing to pay a decent price. He also suggested that 3M avoid highly competitive markets. "Our eggs were all in one basket at the beginning," McKnight said. "If, by diversifying products we could be competing with different industrial groups, it was unlikely a trade war would hit them all at the same time. At least part of our business would always be profitable" (Comfort, p. 127). After three years McKnight recommended that 3M's president create a position of general manager to coordinate sales and production. In 1914 president Edgar B. Ober appointed McKnight to the new post. One year later he was named a vice president, and in 1916, for $500, he established a 3M research laboratory for testing and quality control.

World War I brought increased use of abrasives and financial success to the company and McKnight. He established the company's guidelines to diversify, maintain quality control, license patents for new products, increase sales by 10 percent yearly, expand production facilities, and maintain high employee morale. Under McKnight's leadership, company employees developed waterproof sandpaper, masking tape, and Scotch brand cellophane tape. In 1929 McKnight became president of the company. McKnight significantly increased the research budget for engineering and product development in 1937. By the time he became chair of the board in 1949, 3M had grown into an industrial giant with more than $114 million in sales and 8,750 employees. That same year he reorganized and decentralized the company to give the diversified divisions more autonomy and also because one chief executive could no longer have hands-on control.

McKnight's work seemed to take precedence over pleasure. While on a business trip to Europe in March 1924, a colleague persuaded him to visit the Louvre in Paris. McKnight "raced through the galleries, not because he disliked sightseeing or art but because, on a business trip, he wanted to tend to business, not waste time in personal pleasures" (Comfort, p. 107). In the 1950s McKnight, a passionate horse-racing fan, developed the Tartan Stables and Breeding Farm, which bred and raced the notable Dr. Fager. It appeared that McKnight lived and breathed 3M; after a conversation with trainer John Nerud about track conditions, he had the 3M laboratories develop the artificial, all-weather Tartan surface for racetracks, playgrounds, and farms. McKnight retired from 3M in 1966 although he remained on the board of directors until 1973 and as director emeritus until his death. Devoting more of his time to racing, McKnight served as chair of Calder Race Course in Miami and co-owned Hialeah Park from 1972 to 1974.

McKnight served on the board of trustees of the Charles T. Miller Hospital and as a director of the

Minnesota Mutual Life Insurance Company, First National Bank of St. Paul, and Anchor Casualty Company, all of St. Paul; Northwest Bell Telephone Company, Omaha; Durex Abrasives Corporation, New York; and the Great Northern Railway and Crane Company.

In 1915 McKnight had married Maude Gage, with whom he had one child, Virginia Edith McKnight Binger, who continued Tartan Farm and the McKnight Foundation, established in 1953 by her parents to fund social-service causes in Minneapolis; they bequeathed most of their estates to the foundation. After his first wife's death in 1973 he married Evelyn M. Franks, with whom he became a backer of successful Broadway shows. McKnight died at home in Miami Beach.

William L. McKnight took a failing sandpaper company from near bankruptcy to a multimillion dollar diversified conglomerate over seventy-one years, insisting on quality control, new product development, and serving customer needs. McKnight left three legacies—3M, Tartan Farm, and the McKnight Foundation.

• Two important biographical studies of McKnight in his role as president and chair of the board of the Minnesota Mining and Manufacturing Company are Virginia Huck, *Brand of the Tartan: The 3M Story* (1955), and Mildred Houghton Comfort, *William L. McKnight, Industrialist* (1962). For a description of the changes McKnight instituted at 3M, see *Business Week*, 24 Sept. 1949, and "3M," in *Everybody's Business: A Field Guide to the 400 Leading Companies in America*, ed. Milton Moskowitz et al. (1990). John N. Ingham and Lynne B. Feldman provide an overall assessment of McKnight's impact on 3M and horse racing in *Contemporary American Business Leaders* (1990). An obituary is in the *New York Times*, 5 Mar. 1978.

SUSAN HAMBURGER

MCLANE, Allen (8 Aug. 1746–22 May 1829), soldier and politician, was born in Philadelphia, Pennsylvania, the son of a Scottish immigrant, Allen McLeane (as he spelled his name in his will), a leather breeches maker, and Jane Irwin. The son always spelled his first name Allen, although it appears as Allan on his tombstone in Asbury Church cemetery in Wilmington. Details of his rearing and education are unknown, except that he traveled to Europe in 1767. Apparently having previously moved to Kent County, Delaware, he was married there in 1770 to Rebecca Wells, daughter of the sheriff; they had fourteen children, of whom eleven died in infancy.

Settled at Duck Creek Cross Roads (later Smyrna), McLane was working at his father's trade when the Revolution began. He joined a volunteer military company of his neighborhood and in September 1775 was commissioned a lieutenant in the militia. In October McLane went to Virginia to join men skirmishing near Norfolk with troops gathered by the governor, Lord Dunmore. After returning to Delaware in 1776, he set off independently to join Washington's army before the battle of Long Island and continued through the following campaign to Princeton, New Jersey, where he was promoted to captain.

That winter McLane returned home to recruit a company of his own and with it he gained fame for intrepid action on the lines around Philadelphia, which the British occupied from September 1777 to June 1778. His company, often augmented by Oneida Indian scouts, kept watch on the British, interrupted trade between the city and its environs, where many residents were loyalists or neutral, and engaged in a series of bold adventures, some of which were popularized in such novels as S. Weir Mitchell's *Hugh Wynne* (1897) and Howard Fast's *Conceived in Liberty* (1939), as well as memoirs of the war like those of James Wilkinson (1816) and Alexander Garden (1852). An account of McLane's thrilling escape from British dragoons became the subject of a painting by James Peale. Although many of his exploits were merely irritants to the British, occasionally his watchfulness was of critical value, as when, in May 1778, he brought timely warning to Lafayette of a threatened British encirclement of his advanced position. McLane's men were the first Americans to enter Philadelphia when the British finally withdrew, following so closely that they captured more than forty laggards. Subsequently, McLane complained of Benedict Arnold's profiteering as military governor of Philadelphia, but his warnings were not heeded.

By the time the British reached New York, McLane's company was attached to Henry Lee's legion and McLane, though commander of Lee's infantry, lost the independence—and the credit—he had enjoyed. His important role in raids on Stony Point, New York, and Paulus Hook (Jersey City), New Jersey, won little attention. McLane envied the younger Lee, whom he blamed for failing to acknowledge his role.

After being sent to Virginia, McLane undertook a critical mission to the West Indies, where he delivered dispatches to Admiral de Grasse in Haiti that led the French commander to bring his fleet and army to join in the siege of Cornwallis at Yorktown. Denied further promotion during the war because of the lack of openings at the higher ranks, McLane was brevetted major at the war's conclusion. In 1794 he was commissioned lieutenant colonel in the militia and was thereafter commonly referred to as Colonel McLane.

Contingencies of the war, such as inflation and the need to use his private funds, had dissipated a decent inheritance, and so McLane set up a mercantile business at Duck Creek when the war ended. Kent County voters elected him three times to one-year terms in the house of assembly (in 1785, 1789, and 1791, when he became speaker), and he also served on the privy council, an executive body, from 1786 to 1789, as well as in the convention of 1787 that ratified the federal constitution on 7 December (before any other state) by unanimous action. He received some votes for the U.S. House of Representatives in 1789.

On establishment of the new government President George Washington named McLane the first marshal of the District of Delaware, a part-time post of little financial benefit. In 1797 McLane was glad to exchange it for appointment as collector of customs, thanks to action by Washington shortly before his term ended. The collectorship, which McLane held under seven presidents, was very valuable, financially and politically. Fees and commissions varied from year to year, but on occasion this post could bring extraordinary awards through a share in the value of a ship and cargo found violating the navigation laws. Although his office was in Wilmington, his home after 1797, he kept his cutter at New Castle, Delaware, in position to seize ships bound for Philadelphia. He showed the same vigilance in enforcing embargoes that he had shown on the lines outside Philadelphia in 1777–1778.

In politics McLane's enemies said his post was worth fifty to a hundred votes—through the sailors, clerks, and other functionaries he hired, as well as the carters and warehouse owners, the printers, bankers, and lawyers he patronized. He played an important role in assuring that Delaware remained Federalist longer than any other state (to 1827). His friendship was valued by Senator (and later Governor) Richard Bassett and Bassett's son-in-law James A. Bayard, major figures in the local Federalist party at the turn of the century.

The connection of McLane with Bassett was through a common religious experience. Both had become Methodists, and both were frequent hosts to Francis Asbury and other Methodist itinerants. When Thomas Jefferson was on the eve of electoral victory in 1801, Bayard refused to join in a Federalist plot to deny him the presidency and in return relied upon Jefferson's assurance that he would not proscribe worthy public servants because of their political preferences. Delaware Democrats were furious when McLane was left in office, but Jefferson's tolerance, and that of Madison and their successors, was founded on McLane's splendid military reputation, his unquestioned vigilance in enforcing the navigation laws, the greed of his enemies who could not agree on one claimant for his position, and the influence of McLane's friends in high places, including his son Louis, who entered the U.S. House of Representatives in 1817.

The old collector lived to attend Andrew Jackson's inauguration. An abolitionist, and one-time president of the Delaware Abolition Society, McLane also became a supporter of the colonization movement. He was active in the Society of the Cincinnati, owned stock in a turnpike company, and acquired many properties in Wilmington. At a time when Methodists were frequently reviled, McLane clung to his connection with the original Methodist church in his borough. Irascible and cantankerous, he was generous to his church and to his children. McLane died in Wilmington, Delaware.

• The bulk of McLane's papers are in the New-York Historical Society. Copies of them are in the Historical Society of Delaware, Wilmington, along with a few original documents. Other papers are in the Historical Society of Pennsylvania, Philadelphia; the New York Public Library; and the Morristown (N.J.) National Historical Park. Published accounts of his life are in John A. Munroe, *Louis McLane, Federalist and Jacksonian* (1973); Christopher L. Ward, *The Delaware Continentals, 1776–1783* (1941); Steven Hill, *The Delaware Cincinnati, 1783–1988* (1988); Fred J. Cook, *What Manner of Men: Forgotten Heroes of the American Revolution* (1959); and Charles E. Green, *Delaware Heritage: The Story of the Diamond State in the Revolution* (1975). Noble E. Cunningham, Jr., *The Jeffersonian Republicans in Power: Party Operations, 1801–1809* (1963), pp. 44–49, describes some of the partisan politics involved in his retaining the collectorship.

JOHN A. MUNROE

MCLANE, Louis (28 May 1784–7 Oct. 1857), politician, diplomat, and business executive, was born in Duck Creek Cross Roads (now Smyrna), Delaware, the son of Allan McLane and Rebecca Wells. The father, originally a leather worker, was a distinguished partisan commander in the Revolution, after which he conducted a mercantile business until President George Washington appointed him first federal marshal and then customs collector, whereupon he moved his family to Wilmington. Fees he received as a very diligent collector provided a handsome income, and various perquisites of his position gave him—and his son—great influence in the state Federalist party.

After brief service as a midshipman, Louis attended the Academy of Newark (Del.) and then read law in the office of James A. Bayard (1767–1815). Admitted to the bar in 1807, McLane practiced law in Wilmington for the next twenty-two years. In 1812 he married Catherine Mary Milligan, a trusted confidant until her death in 1849; they had thirteen children, one of whom died in infancy. He became president of the local branch of the state bank and co-owner of a millsite on the Brandywine River before 1816, when he won the first of six successive at-large elections to the U.S. House of Representatives, all on the Federalist ticket.

Despite his political affiliation, recognition of McLane's ability gained him appointment as chairman of the Ways and Means Committee in December 1822. In this position, which he held until after his election to the Senate in January 1827, he became a close confederate of Secretary of the Treasury William H. Crawford, for whom he cast the vote of Delaware in 1825, when the presidential election was thrown into the House.

Thereafter, angered by the Adams-Clay alliance, McLane moved into the Jackson party and attempted to lead his Federalist colleagues in Delaware on the same path. Thwarted in this effort, though not until after his election to the Senate, he became dependent on his allies in Washington, especially Martin Van Buren, for his further advancement.

President Andrew Jackson rewarded McLane's support in 1829 by appointing him minister to Great Britain. Here he displayed considerable skill in securing an agreement opening the British West Indies to American shipping. His ability impressed the distinguished legation secretary, Washington Irving, who remained a close friend of McLane and his family for many years.

In 1831 McLane returned to Washington as secretary of the treasury, in which role he proposed a comprehensive financial scheme—much as Alexander Hamilton (1755–1804) had done four decades earlier—to expedite Jackson's wish to eliminate the national debt. Frustrated by developments, such as Nicholas Biddle's (1786–1844) insistence on seeking recharter of the national bank before the election of 1832, McLane accepted a transfer to the State Department to succeed Edward Livingston, who wanted to go to Paris as head of the legation delegation. Livingston's delay in setting out kept McLane in the Treasury until May 1833, but the transfer had been arranged well before removal of government deposits from the U.S. Bank, which McLane opposed, became an important issue.

As secretary of state McLane urged forceful action against France for failure to meet treaty obligations in paying indemnities. Overruled in this instance and clearly losing influence, McLane resigned in June 1834. He blamed Van Buren for deserting him on several key issues and never spoke to his erstwhile friend again. Taking care, however, not to break with the Jackson party, he refused John Tyler's (1790–1862) offer to make him secretary of state in August 1841.

To support his large family, McLane accepted the presidency of the Morris Canal and Banking Company, with a salary of $6,000, in 1835. Though he improved the canal and extended it to Jersey City, his principal interest was in the Morris Canal Bank, which, though a New Jersey institution, conducted its major business through an office in New York, where most of its directors resided.

Under McLane the Morris began to pay dividends, and his success led to an offer of the presidency of the Baltimore and Ohio Railroad. He assumed this position in 1837, and despite a major depression in 1839, he succeeded in doubling the length of the B&O by extending it west to Cumberland while reorganizing its administration and increasing its efficiency. His most difficult problem, however, lay in negotiating with neighboring states that controlled access to the road's Ohio River objective.

In 1845 McLane took leave from the railroad to represent the Polk administration in London. Here he helped smooth the way for the cession of Oregon, though Secretary of State James Buchanan insisted that the final steps and all the credit should go to Washington. James K. Polk offered to make McLane secretary of state, thinking Buchanan was about to accept a proffered seat on the Supreme Court, but when McLane, who had accepted, returned to the United States he learned Buchanan had changed his mind.

After a final year as head of the B&O, McLane resigned under fire from enemies he had made when choosing between various routes westward. He spent his last years between Baltimore, where he died, and his much-loved estate, "Bohemia" (formerly the home of his wife's family), on the upper Eastern Shore. He served in the Maryland constitutional convention of 1850–1851 but otherwise spent these years in concerns related to his investments in securities and in real estate as well as in the affairs of his large family. Three of his six sons had distinguished careers: Robert in politics, Louis and Allan in business.

Intelligent, industrious, and congenial when he chose to be, McLane had a prickly, jealous disposition that caused him to break with many old friends. Short in stature and in temper, dyspeptic, especially when under pressure, McLane possessed talents in finance and in diplomacy that were widely respected. Though reared by ardent Methodist parents who were frequent hosts to Francis Asbury, McLane became an Episcopalian. Remaining faithful to his Federalist beginnings—if not to his father's faith—friendly to England, to the armed forces, to the national bank, to a strong central government, and to the encouragement of manufactures, McLane demonstrated the success that a man from a small state and a minority party could achieve in Congress in the declining days of the first party system. But when he cast his fortunes with the Jackson party his great ambition as well as the intrigues swirling about the new order betrayed him and forced him to transfer his endeavors to the business world. His talents proved useful in the transportation revolution, which provided him with needed income though not with the glory and the power that he had craved.

• Louis McLane papers are in the Maryland Historical Society, Baltimore; in the Library of Congress; and in the Historical Society of Delaware, Wilmington. Copies of most of these and of many more are in the Morris Library of the University of Delaware, Newark, where there are also some McLane manuscripts. His birth date is frequently given incorrectly by two years. The only complete biography is John A. Munroe, *Louis McLane, Federalist and Jacksonian* (1973). See also Eugene I. McCormac, "Louis McLane," in *The American Secretaries of State and Their Diplomacy*, vol. 4, ed. Samuel F. Bemis (1928), and Martin Van Buren, "Autobiography," ed. John C. Fitzpatrick, in *Annual Report of the American Historical Association for 1918* 2 (1920).

JOHN A. MUNROE

MCLANE, Robert Milligan (23 June 1815–16 Apr. 1898), congressman and diplomat, was born in Wilmington, Delaware, the son of Louis McLane, an attorney who served as secretary of the treasury and secretary of state in the Jackson administration, and Catherine Mary Milligan. After attending St. Mary's College in Baltimore and Collège Bourbon in Paris, Robert entered the U.S. Military Academy in 1833. He graduated in 1837 and assumed command of Company E, First Artillery Regiment. After participating in the Seminole War in Florida and in what he termed the "mournful" removal of the Cherokees from Georgia, he transferred in 1838 to the Corps of Topographical Engineers. He went to Italy in 1841 on orders to observe dikes and drainage systems. Having studied law in Washington, D.C., while stationed there with the military engineers, he was admitted to the bars in the District of Columbia (1840) and in Maryland (1843). He resigned his commission in 1843 and began the practice of law in Baltimore. He married Georgine Urquhart in 1841, and they had two daughters.

In 1844 McLane began a career in Democratic party politics by campaigning for James K. Polk for president. McLane was elected to the Maryland House of Delegates in 1845 and saw duty briefly in the Mexican War in 1846 as a volunteer officer. He served in the U.S. House of Representatives from 1847 to 1851. In Congress he was an outspoken expansionist and defended Polk's conduct of the Mexican War. In a House speech in 1848 he proposed the creation of a virtual U.S. protectorate over Mexico. As chair of the House Committee on Commerce from 1849 to 1851, he advocated river and harbor improvements and favored a moderate tariff high enough to meet government revenue needs with protection of American industry only as an incidental consideration. He voted for the Compromise of 1850, which admitted California as a free state while leaving the future of slavery in the remaining territory obtained from Mexico subject to what he termed the nonintervention policy; that is, Congress would take no action and leave the issue to the courts to decide.

Choosing not to run for reelection to Congress, McLane ventured to California in 1851. He conducted a lucrative legal practice, serving as counsel for mining companies and representing prominent clients such as Cornelius Vanderbilt (in his successful litigation to obtain transit rights across Nicaragua) and the Western Pacific Railroad (later purchased by the Central Pacific). Returning to Baltimore in 1852, McLane served as chair of the National Executive Committee of the Democratic party during Franklin Pierce's successful campaign for president.

In October 1853 Pierce appointed McLane to be U.S. commissioner to China with the powers of a minister plenipotentiary. His commission also accredited him to the governments of Japan, Korea, Siam, and Cochinchina. Since Commodore Matthew Perry was already engaged in negotiations with Japan, McLane set sail for China. He arrived in Hong Kong in March 1854 with instructions to seek revision of the existing treaty between the United States and China to allow expanded American commercial privileges. Perry provided McLane the use of an imposing steam frigate to impress the Chinese. On this vessel McLane went to Shanghai and proceeded directly—without awaiting official permission—up the Yangtze River to Nanjing, the capital of the Taiping rebels then challenging the ruling Qing dynasty. The U.S. commissioner decided that the Taiping leader was a "vulgar villain" and incapable of ruling China. McLane made a further demonstration of U.S. determination to obtain treaty revision by taking his ship upriver to Wuhu before returning to Shanghai. In Shanghai he arranged with local Chinese authorities and British and French diplomats for a guarantee of equal commercial rights for all Western nations in China. This precursor of the United States' later "Open Door Policy" was short-lived, however, because Britain still dominated trade through its influence over the Chinese customs service.

In October 1854 McLane and the British minister arrived at the mouth of the Peiho River near Tianjin with five warships. They attempted unsuccessfully to communicate their demands for treaty revision directly to the Qing emperor in Beijing. With winter approaching they sailed back to Shanghai, and McLane recommended to Washington that Britain, France, and the United States join in a blockade of China's principal ports until Beijing agreed to negotiate. Secretary of State William Marcy rejected this "aggressive policy." In November 1854 McLane departed China for Europe, and in April 1855 he sent his resignation from Paris, citing poor health.

In 1859 President James Buchanan named McLane minister to Mexico, a country rent by civil war. McLane went in April to Veracruz, where he met with provisional president Benito Juárez. After assuring Juárez that the United States recognized his authority, in December 1859 the minister signed the so-called McLane-Ocampo Treaty, which gave the United States railroad and canal routes in Mexico and the right to intervene militarily in Mexico to protect commerce. Sectional and partisan divisions within the U.S. Senate prevented ratification of this expansionist convention. McLane resigned as minister in December 1860. With the outbreak of the Civil War, he advocated that his home state of Maryland neither secede nor join in military action against the South. Because of the ascendancy of the Republicans to power in Washington, McLane turned his attention from politics to his law practice during the 1860s and 1870s.

Disgusted over what he considered corrupt political dealing that gave Rutherford B. Hayes the presidency over Samuel Tilden, McLane returned to elected politics in 1877 on a reform platform and won a seat in the Maryland Senate. The next year he was elected to Congress and reelected in 1880. He chaired the House Committee on Pacific Railroads (1879–1880) and supported efforts to lower tariffs.

In 1883 McLane was elected governor of Maryland, and during his term, from 1884 to 1885, he obtained wage and hour regulations for women and child workers and created a Bureau of Statistics and Labor Information but failed to achieve legislation for an eight-hour workday for men. In 1885 McLane resigned as governor to accept President Grover Cleveland's nomination to be minister to France. McLane spoke fluent French and had many friends in Paris. U.S.–French relations were cordial during his ministry, as exemplified by the 1886 dedication of the Statue of Liberty, France's gift to the United States. With the return of a Republican administration in 1889, McLane's ministry to France ended. He continued to live in France in retirement and frequently visited the United States. He died in Paris.

Robert McLane's career reflected an entrepreneurial and democratic spirit. In foreign affairs, especially during his service in China and Mexico, he unabashedly championed U.S. commercial expansion and maintained that "friendship and commerce . . . would result more certainly from intimate commercial relations than from the acquisition of territory." He was proud to be a "steady Democrat" and admired Jackson's Veto Message of 1832 on the Bank of the United States. The president's "powerful paper" asserted, according to McLane, "the grand principle that the laws should not . . . make the rich richer, and the potent more powerful." A half-century after Jackson, McLane still viewed himself as battling "the selfish fears of the Capitalists" as he worked as governor of Maryland to improve conditions of the "laboring population of the world."

• The records of McLane's diplomatic missions to China, Mexico, and France are in the General Records of the Department of State, National Archives, Washington, D.C. His dispatches from China were published in *Correspondence of Robert M. McLane*, Sen. Exec. Doc. no. 22, vol. 1, 35th Cong., 2d sess., and some of his dispatches from France are in *Foreign Relations of the United States, 1885–1889*. His congressional speeches are in the *Congressional Globe*, 30th Cong. and 31st Cong., and the *Congressional Record*, 46th Cong. and 47th Cong.

The best biographical source is McLane's *Reminiscences, 1827–1897: Governor Robert M. McLane* (1903, repr. 1972). His political career in Maryland is described in Frank J. White, Jr., *The Governors of Maryland, 1777–1970* (1970). For critical studies of his mission to China see Tyler Dennett, *Americans in Eastern Asia* (1922); John King Fairbank, *Trade and Diplomacy on the China Coast* (1953); and Te-kong Tong, *United States Diplomacy in China, 1844–60* (1964). On his diplomacy in Mexico, see J. Fred Rippy, *The United States and Mexico* (1931), and Jerome J. Niosi, "The McLane Mission to Mexico, 1859–60" (Ph.D. diss., New York Univ., 1953). Obituaries are in the *Baltimore Sun*, 18 and 19 Apr. 1898, and the *New York Herald*, 17 Apr. 1898.

DAVID L. ANDERSON

MCLAUGHLIN, Andrew Cunningham (14 Feb. 1861–24 Sep. 1947), historian, was born in Beardstown, Illinois, the son of David McLaughlin, a store owner and superintendent of schools, and Isabella Campbell. McLaughlin attended public schools in Muskegon, Michigan, and received an A.B. in classics from the University of Michigan in 1882. After teaching Latin for two years at Muskegon High School, he returned to the University of Michigan, earned an LL.B. degree, and passed the bar exam in 1885. He also received an honorary A.M. in 1896 and his LL.D. in 1912 from Michigan.

McLaughlin taught Latin at the University of Michigan for one session before transferring to the history department as an instructor in 1887. A year later he became an assistant professor in history, and in 1891 he achieved the rank of full professor. Although McLaughlin attracted some national attention with the publication of *The Life of Lewis Cass* (1891), a volume in the American Statesmen series, his *The Confederation and the Constitution, 1783–1789* (1905), a volume in the American Nation series, catapulted him into academic stardom. Declining offers from Johns Hopkins, Yale, and Stanford, McLaughlin chose to succeed J. Franklin Jameson in 1906 as professor and chairman of the history department at the University of Chicago, where he remained until his retirement in 1927. He married Lois Thompson Angell, daughter of James Burrill Angell, president of the University of Michigan, in 1890; they had six children. Rowland Hazard, the McLaughlins' second son, was killed in action in France in 1918. Rowland's death understandably predisposed McLaughlin, as a historian, to react strongly against revisionist interpretations of the origins of the First World War. "I lost a boy in that war," he wrote in 1924, and "I don't take any pleasure in having it announced . . . that he lost his life fighting on the wrong side."

McLaughlin's lasting legacy is his writings on the constitutional history of the United States. In addition to *Confederation and the Constitution*, he produced *The Courts, the Constitution, and Parties: Studies in Constitutional History and Politics* (1912), *The Foundations of American Constitutionalism* (1932), and *A Constitutional History of the United States* (1935), for which he received the Pulitzer Prize in 1936. Three themes characterize McLaughlin's histories. First, he argued that American constitutionalism is best understood not as a product of momentary genius but rather as an achievement of conscious effort, struggle, and experience over the course of centuries. In his examination of such fundamental constitutional issues as the basis of the natural rights philosophy and popular sovereignty, the foundations of federalism, the origins of judicial review, the rise of political parties, the nature of consent and contractual agreements, and the obligations of citizenship, McLaughlin invariably embarked on a search for precedents. He insisted in *The Courts, the Constitution, and Parties* that inherited ideas and principles, "molded and fashioned by the needs of passing generations," were decisive in determining the shape of the American constitutional order. The men who gathered in Philadelphia in 1787 possessed "rare judgment, wide knowledge of men, profound insight into human motives, remarkable sanity, and a capacity for generous appreciation of the sentiments of their fellows," McLaughlin observed in *Confederation and the Constitution*, but the claim that they had made the Constitution "is not true; time made the American Constitution." The founding fathers were practical political thinkers who forged a product that was based on Old World ideas but adapted to New World conditions.

Second, when McLaughlin searched for precedents, he turned to seventeenth- and eighteenth-century England's imperial system and devoted most of his attention to detailing the colonial background of the American nation. According to McLaughlin in *A Constitutional History of the United States*, the revolutionaries did not cast aside old-fashioned colonial practices when they declared their independence from England. Instead, they modified and enlarged upon such practices in order to establish the first state constitutions, the Confederation government, and finally the Constitution. McLaughlin made this point most effectively in his discussion of the origins of American federalism, wherein sovereign power is divided among different levels of government. Even here, in what he deemed to be America's signal contribution to political theory and practice, McLaughlin argued that the American solution to the problem of organizing a national state, a recognition of separate sovereign jurisdictions, was one that the colonists had learned through experience; their federal structure was a modification of the inherited imperial arrangement. Before the Revolution, royal officials had ignored at their own peril the historical fact that competent colonial governments had been operating in America for more than a hundred years. As a practical working system, the relationship between the mother country and the colonies was already federal by 1776. After independence, the problem of national organization passed into the hands of American statesmen. The division of power between the central government and the states was an adjustment of the old practical relationship between England and the colonies. "Thus it may be said that colonial history made the Constitution," McLaughlin concluded.

The final characteristic of McLaughlin's several works is a persistent strain of philosophical progressivism. He was intent on telling, as he pointed out in *Confederation and the Constitution*, "the story of political achievement." No history of the United States could be thought satisfactory if it failed to recount the successes of the "wise and the strong" in establishing a Constitution in the face of political confusion, economic dislocation, and challenges emanating from the "vicious, the restless, the ignorant, [and] the foolish." But McLaughlin's purpose was more than simple celebration. He emphasized that the achievements of the revolutionary generation carried with them certain obligations. The principles of individual liberty, limited government, federalism, and the rule of law, in short, the essence of American constitutionalism, could not be long maintained "unless supported by intelligence and by some portion of that earnestness and consecration which established our constitutional principles" in the first place. By elaborating on the successes of "generations long gone by," then, McLaughlin hoped, as he noted in *The Foundations of American Constitutionalism*, not to inspire "any thoughtless loyalty to the doctrines of the Fathers," but to instill in his audience a conviction that "popular government must find its foundation in the appreciation of responsibility." This, to McLaughlin, was the virtue of teaching constitutional principles historically. "When all is said, the hope for successful popular government—and in very fact its justification—is based upon the willingness of people to think" and act for themselves. Appropriately enough for someone trained initially in the classics, McLaughlin's final message was rooted in an understanding of classical republicanism.

From 1898 to 1914 McLaughlin served as an associate editor, and from 1901 to 1905 as managing editor, of the *American Historical Review*. He was also director of historical research at the Carnegie Institution in Washington, D.C., from 1903 to 1905. He died in Chicago.

McLaughlin's work on the nature of federalism in the revolutionary era influenced American historiography in three important ways. First, McLaughlin's contention that the American federal system was inherited from the British empire dovetailed nicely with the arguments of such imperial historians as George Louis Beer and Charles McLean Andrews. Second, because he continued to insist that custom and tradition effectively shaped American institutions, McLaughlin resisted the appeals of Frederick Jackson Turner who argued that the American frontier environment stripped away the trappings of European culture. Third, McLaughlin's assumption that an understanding of intellectual heritage was essential to comprehending the course of American federalism in the 1780s openly challenged Charles Beard's interpretation of the economic motives of the framers of the Constitution.

• McLaughlin's papers, including his professional and personal correspondence, essays, and lecture notes, are in the Michigan Historical Collections at the University of Michigan. The University of Chicago Library also has a significant collection of McLaughlin's speeches, notes, and manuscript lectures. Among McLaughlin's works that have not already been mentioned are *The History of Higher Education in Michigan* (1891); *Civil Government in Michigan* (1892); *A History of the American Nation* (1899), a widely used textbook in the early twentieth century; *America and Britain* (1918), which contains a summary chapter on "The Background of American Federalism"; *Steps in the Development of American Democracy* (1920); and "American History and American Democracy," *American Historical Review* 20 (1915): 255–76, his presidential address to the American Historical Association in 1914. McLaughlin's place in American historiography and in the professionalization of the study of history is expertly summarized in John Higham, Leonard Krieger, and Felix Gilbert, *History: The Development of Historical Studies in the United States* (1965), and Peter Novick, *That Noble Dream: The "Objectivity Question" and the American Historical Profession* (1988). Henry Steele Commager's entry on McLaughlin in the *Dictionary of American Biography* is worth consulting. Obituaries are in the *American Historical Review* 53 (1948): 432–34, and the *New York Times*, 25 Sept. 1947.

MELVIN YAZAWA

MCLAURIN, Anselm Joseph (26 Mar. 1848–22 Dec. 1909), U.S. senator and governor of Mississippi, was born at Brandon, Mississippi, the son of Lauchlin McLaurin and Ellen Caroline Tullus, farmers. In McLaurin's early childhood his family moved to a farm in Smith County, where he worked in the fields and attended the rural schools. At the age of sixteen he enlisted as a private in the Confederate army and served in a cavalry unit during the last year of the Civil War. After returning home he enrolled at Summerville Institute in Noxubee County, but he had to leave at the end of his junior year to help his father on the farm. Having begun the study of law under the guidance of a professor, he continued his studies at home at night. He obtained his law license in July 1868 and then established a successful law practice in Raleigh, Mississippi. In 1870 he married Laura Elvira Rauch; they had ten children, only seven of whom survived infancy.

Entering politics in 1871, McLaurin conducted a successful campaign for district attorney in the southeastern judicial district and served a four-year term. In 1876 he moved to Brandon, where he soon gained fame for his expertise as a criminal lawyer. Three years later he was elected to a two-year term in the lower house of the legislature. Although highly recommended for a seat on the state supreme court, he failed to secure the gubernatorial appointment. In 1888 he served as a Democratic presidential elector. As a delegate to the constitutional convention in 1890, he opposed restrictions on the suffrage and supported an unsuccessful effort to achieve an elective judiciary. Along with two of his brothers, who also served as delegates, he voted against the new constitution but signed it after final approval and adoption.

In the political discontent of the early 1890s, McLaurin rose to prominence among the younger Democrats, who advocated a platform more sympathetic to the needs of the farmers. In February 1894 the legislature elected him to the vacated seat of Senator Edward Cary Walthall, who had resigned because of poor health before completing his term. An advocate of the free coinage of silver and other flexible monetary policies, McLaurin quickly earned the respect of his colleagues and enhanced his political standing at home. He secured legislation to grant a township of public land to the state's university and each of its three colleges, including the Alcorn Agricultural and Mechanical College for black students. In debate on the Wilson Tariff Bill, he supported an amendment for an income tax and opposed the doctrine of protectionism, which, he declared, "takes money out of the pockets of one class of people and gives it to another" (*Congressional Record*, 53d Cong., 2d sess., p. 5764). While serving in the Senate, he became a close personal friend of the Populist senator from Nebraska, William V. Allen.

At the end of the senatorial term in March 1895, McLaurin returned to Mississippi and announced his candidacy for governor. After securing the Democratic nomination by unanimous vote, he defeated a strong Populist opponent in the general election by a 3–1 margin. National party leaders congratulated McLaurin on his impressive victory. An elated Mississippi Democrat, Joseph Bogen of Greenville, declared that McLaurin had "routed the [Populist] adversaries and sent them to a well merited oblivion" (letter to McLaurin, 6 Nov. 1895).

As governor, McLaurin encountered bitter factional opposition because of disputes over patronage and other issues, but he maintained strong legislative support and his popularity with the voters. His administration successfully prosecuted suits against two railroads for failure to pay taxes. He advocated pensions for Confederate veterans and their widows, and he gained the admiration of white women by vetoing a bill that discriminated against female faculty members at the white women's college. He earned the respect of black Mississippians by firmly opposing any reduction in school funds for black children. In a letter to the governor, a black admirer declared, "You are the man of the people and for the people. . . . Your administration has done more to bring good feelings between the races than any of your predecessors" (letter from D. J. Randolph, n.d.). In 1899 McLaurin won the Democratic nomination for U.S. senator, and the following year the legislature elected him to a full senatorial term.

McLaurin reentered the Senate on 2 December 1901 and served until his death. Characterized by a Jackson newspaper as "the strongest man in public life . . . in Mississippi" (*Clarion Ledger*, 10 Mar. 1905), he encountered no opposition in his ensuing bid for another term. His senatorial assignments included membership on the Committees of Interstate Commerce, Immigration, the Mississippi River and Its Tributaries, and Public Expenditures and the Joint Committee on Revision of U.S. Laws. He served on the U.S. Immigration Commission. An advocate of stringent antitrust legislation and an opponent of high protective tariffs, he also denounced the imperialistic policy of the Republican party and called for the application of the principles of the Declaration of Independence to the people of the Philippine Islands. Jewish leaders praised him for introducing a resolution to condemn Russia's treatment of Jews. A Mississippi editor described him as "a Senator intent upon safeguarding the interests and welfare of his people" (*Clarksdale Daily Register*, 18 Feb. 1909).

While on Christmas vacation, Senator McLaurin died suddenly at his home in Brandon. His death had a significant impact on Mississippi politics. It ended the influence of a strong political force in the state and triggered a factional struggle to determine his successor. "In a worldwide sense," the *Jackson Evening News* editorialized, "'Anse' McLaurin was not a great statesman, but he possessed to an eminent degree many of the essential elements of statesmanship" (25 Dec. 1909). McLaurin was a self-made man who did not resort to blatant demagogy to achieve political success and whose strength lay in his direct appeal to the people.

• A large collection of McLaurin's papers is in the Governors Records at the Mississippi Department of Archives and History, which also holds the A. J. McLaurin Family Scrapbook. Biographical information is in Dunbar Rowland, *The Official and Statistical Register of the State of Mississippi* (1917), and Rowland, *Courts, Judges, and Lawyers of Mississippi, 1798–1935* (1935). George Coleman Osborn, *John Sharp Williams: Planter-Statesman of the Deep South* (1943), and William F. Holmes, *The White Chief James Kimble Vardaman* (1970), include details about McLaurin's political activity. A recent assessment of his political career is in Thomas N. Boschert, "A Family Affair: Mississippi Politics, 1882–1932" (Ph.D. diss., Univ. of Mississippi, 1995). See also William N. Ethridge, Jr., and Walter Nesbit Taylor, eds., *Mississippi: A History*, vol. 1 (1940); Rowland, *Mississippi*, vol. 2

(1907); and Clyde J. Faries, "Redneck Rhetoric and the Last of the Redeemers: The 1899 McLaurin-Allen Campaign," *Journal of Mississippi History* 33 (Nov. 1971): 283–98, on his political career. See the *Congressional Record*, 53d Cong., 2d sess., 4 Dec. 1893–28 Aug. 1894; 3d sess., 3 Dec. 1894–3 Mar. 1895; and 57th Cong., 2 Dec. 1901, through 61st Cong., 3 Mar. 1911, on his senatorial career. An obituary is in the *New York Times*, 23 Dec. 1909.

THOMAS N. BOSCHERT

MCLAWS, Lafayette (15 Jan. 1821–24 July 1897), army officer, was born in Augusta, Georgia, the son of James McLaws and Elizabeth Huguenin (occupations unknown). McLaws entered the University of Virginia in 1837 but left the next year when he received an appointment to the United States Military Academy at West Point. He graduated in the class of 1842, which included his future superior officer James Longstreet, and was commissioned a second lieutenant in the Seventh United States Infantry. After brief service on the frontier McLaws saw action in the Mexican War then returned to the West, where he was promoted to captain by 1851 and where he served until 1861.

McLaws resigned his commission shortly after Georgia seceded and was appointed a major in the Confederate States Army in March 1861. When the Tenth Georgia Infantry was organized he became its first colonel on 17 June 1861 and commanded the regiment until promoted to brigadier general on 25 September of that year. He won the notice of his superiors for his performance at Yorktown and Williamsburg the next spring, and was subsequently promoted to major general and given command of a small division on 23 May 1862.

After the Seven Days' campaign in the summer of 1862 McLaws received two additional brigades, creating a four-brigade division of Georgians, South Carolinians, and Mississippians. This new division, in Longstreet's First Corps, compiled a solid, if not outstanding, combat record under McLaws's command from June 1862 to December 1863, and served in almost all of the major campaigns of the Army of Northern Virginia during that period. McLaws and his division remained in the vicinity of Richmond during the second Manassas campaign but rejoined the army in September 1862 for the Maryland campaign, assisting in the capture of Harpers Ferry, then arriving on the battlefield at Antietam in time to provide badly needed reinforcements.

At Fredericksburg, on 13 December 1862, McLaws achieved his greatest success of the war when his division easily repulsed multiple frontal assaults by the Army of the Potomac against its strong defensive position on Marye's Heights. He later reported that the Federals "advanced with fresh columns to the attack at intervals of not more than fifteen minutes, but they were repulsed with zeal and driven back with much loss on every occasion" (*Official Records*, vol. 21, p. 580). Longstreet, for his part, praised McLaws after the battle "for his untiring zeal and ability in preparing his troops and his position for a successful resistance" (*Official Records*, vol. 21, p. 571). McLaws's troops fought well at Salem Church in May 1863, during the Chancellorsville campaign, and in the Peach Orchard on 2 July 1863 at Gettysburg, but his handling of the division was hampered by his apparent lack of aggressiveness and was not as salient as it had been during earlier campaigns. His division accompanied Longstreet to Georgia and Tennessee in the fall of 1863, participating in the Chickamauga and Knoxville campaigns, but soon became the focus of controversy after its attack on Fort Sanders, at Knoxville, was repulsed on 29 November. Longstreet held McLaws responsible for the defeat, relieved him of command, and charged him with neglect of duty. Although a court-martial found McLaws guilty of a minor offense, its findings were disapproved by Confederate authorities, who ordered him restored to duty. This order notwithstanding, McLaws did not return to the Army of Northern Virginia but was soon transferred out of the eastern theater and spent the balance of the war in Georgia, South Carolina, and North Carolina. He participated in the Savannah and Carolinas campaigns, most notably at the battle of Bentonville, and surrendered with Joseph E. Johnston's Army of Tennessee in April 1865.

McLaws, who had married Emily Allison Taylor shortly after his West Point graduation (they had seven children), spent his postwar years in Augusta and Savannah, Georgia, working in the insurance business and in civil service, including several years as postmaster of Savannah before his death there. He was also active in Confederate veterans' organizations, occasionally giving speeches or publishing articles about his division and its campaigns, and corresponding with former comrades and Union veterans about the war.

Lafayette McLaws's place among Civil War generals is not nearly as secure as that of better-known officers who served under Robert E. Lee, but who had less experience than he did commanding a division. McLaws himself refrained from self-promotion—"There are few men, particularly military men, who are prompted less by love of fame and glory than he is," a wartime sketch of him claimed (*Southern Illustrated News*, p. 30)—but the primary reason for his relative obscurity is that he was not considered a particularly inspiring officer by most of his contemporaries and is not a compelling figure to most students of the war. Edward Porter Alexander, Longstreet's chief of artillery, recalled years later "the pains he took in many matters of little detail. It gave him the reputation of being slow, but he made up for it in having his division always in the best possible condition" (Gallagher, p. 136). Douglas Southall Freeman, eminent historian of the Army of Northern Virginia, observed in *Lee's Lieutenants* that McLaws "was not accounted among the ablest of division commanders, but he was respected as a man and a soldier" (Freeman, vol. 3, p. 299). Perhaps the best assessment of McLaws's Confederate career is that written by G. Moxley Sorrel of Longstreet's staff, who called him "not brilliant in the field or quick in movement there or elsewhere" but "he could always be counted on and had secured the entire confidence of his officers and men" (Sorrel, p. 135).

• McLaws's papers, including his Civil War letters to his wife and postwar correspondence concerning his Confederate service, are in the Southern Historical Collection at the University of North Carolina, Chapel Hill. The most significant source for his career is *The War of the Rebellion: A Compilation of the Official Records of the Union and Confederate Armies* (128 vols., 1880–1901), which include his and others' official reports of his campaigns and battles. See also the contemporary biographical sketch in the *Southern Illustrated News*, 4 Apr. 1863; McLaws, "The Confederate Left at Fredericksburg," in *Battles and Leaders of the Civil War*, ed. Robert U. Johnson and Clarence C. Buel (1888), vol. 3, pp. 86–94, "The Battle of Fredericksburg," *Addresses Delivered before the Confederate Veterans Association of Savannah, Ga.* (1895), "Gettysburg," *Southern Historical Society Papers* 7 (1897): 64–90, and "After Chickamauga," *Addresses Delivered before the Confederate Veterans Association of Savannah, Ga.* (1898); the memoirs of James Longstreet, *From Manassas to Appomattox* (1896), Edward Porter Alexander, *Fighting for the Confederacy: The Personal Recollections of General Edward Porter Alexander*, ed. Gary W. Gallagher (1989), and G. Moxley Sorrel, *Recollections of a Confederate Staff Officer* (1905); and Douglas Southall Freeman, *Lee's Lieutenants: A Study in Command* (3 vols., 1942–1944).

J. TRACY POWER

MCLEAN, Archibald (6 Sept. 1849–15 Dec. 1920), minister and missionary administrator for the Disciples of Christ, was born near Summerside, in Prince Edward Island, Canada, the son of Malcolm McLean, a farmer and stonemason, and Alexandra McKay. After his mother died in 1853, shortly after the birth of her last child, his father married a second time and had nine more children. A tradesman himself, Malcolm McLean apprenticed each of his sons to a master in some skilled occupation. At fourteen Archibald entered an apprenticeship in carriage building. After five years as an apprentice with William Tuplin in his shop in Summerside, McLean departed for Boston, Massachusetts, to work for a year as a journeyman. When he returned home, he built one carriage and decided to attend college to study for the ministry.

Under the guidance of his father, a dedicated Scotch Presbyterian, McLean had always taken the Christian faith seriously. He grew up with twice-daily Scripture readings in the home, followed each morning and evening by the singing of psalms or hymns and a prayer. Presbyterians on Prince Edward Island also watched with interest the missionary career of John Geddie, former pastor of the New London Presbyterian Church, just six miles from the McLean family farm. As a youth, McLean heard stories of Geddie's work among cannibals on Aneityum, one of the South Sea Islands. His religious sensibilities already well tuned by experiences in family and church, McLean came under the influence of Donald Crawford, a minister associated with the reform movement begun by Alexander Campbell and known as the Disciples of Christ.

During a protracted revival meeting held in 1867, McLean heard Crawford preach typical Disciples themes: the Bible as the only rule of faith and practice, the hope to restore the vitality of the early church through the union of all Christians under Christ rather than under denominational names, and believer's baptism by immersion. These "Reformers" had no intention of beginning a new denomination but hoped instead to work within existing denominations to unite the church under the banner of Christ alone. McLean found the message compelling and underwent baptism at Crawford's hands in June 1867. Crawford became the young McLean's mentor as he encouraged him to become involved in the work of the Summerside Christian Church and to consider ministry as his own vocation.

In the fall of 1870 McLean made his way to Bethany College, an institution of higher learning founded by Alexander Campbell in 1840 and associated with the Disciples of Christ. The small college, situated in Bethany, West Virginia, offered him a classical course of studies with few distractions and afforded him the opportunity to study with William Kimbrough Pendleton, Charles Louis Loos, and Robert Richardson, some of the better-known leaders among the Disciples. The faculty awarded him the A.B. on 18 June 1874. Three days later he assumed the pastorate of the Mount Healthy Christian Church, located in a little village about ten miles from Cincinnati, Ohio. He served the church well for eleven years, increasing its giving to missionary causes and completing the building of a new church facility.

In 1874, the year of McLean's ordination, a group of men, partially shamed by the successful activity of Disciples women on behalf of missions work, met in the basement of the Richmond Street Christian Church in Cincinnati to discuss foreign missions. Archibald McLean was among them. The official institution among Disciples concerned with foreign missions, the Foreign Christian Missionary Society (FCMS), grew out of this meeting a year later and established its headquarters in Cincinnati. When the first corresponding secretary of the society resigned in 1882, the executive committee chose McLean as his successor. Although he continued in his pastorate for the next three years, McLean's prodigious leadership, even though part time, brought immediate new life to the society and nearly doubled its income of $13,178 within his first year. The society's first eight missionaries were commissioned to India in 1882. The next year Disciples opened a mission in Japan. By 1900, the twenty-fifth year of the FCMS and the year it officially named McLean as its president, the society reported an income of $180,000 to support missionaries in nine countries. By the time of his death the Disciples budget for missions had reached $2.25 million per year, supporting more than 282 missionaries in ten countries.

For more than thirty-eight years McLean dedicated himself to the cause of Christian missions. Even during his brief two-year stint as the president of Bethany

College (1889–1991), he remained responsible for the major administrative decisions for the society. As a single man without any family responsibilities, he could travel extensively and speak tirelessly on behalf of foreign missions. In addition, his propensity to write and publish brought tremendous benefit to the missionary enterprise among Disciples. Author of seven books and numerous published tracts, he also edited the *Missionary Intelligencer*, a quarterly journal he founded in 1888, which became a monthly the next year. In all his written endeavors, he emphasized themes addressing the history, theology, and contemporary witness associated with Protestant missions throughout the world.

Well known among Disciples for his contribution to the theology, structure, and promotion of missionary activities over three crucial decades, Archibald McLean's most significant contribution to Disciples, and Protestants in general, was his ecumenical spirit. During a time when congregational pressures in his own movement pushed in the direction of an isolationist approach to missions, McLean sought and maintained ecumenical relationships with other Protestant groups and leaders involved in missions. He served as a delegate to most of the major ecumenical missionary conferences held during his lifetime. Through his ecumenical contacts and endeavors in mission, McLean modeled for other church leaders the kinds of relationships that led to Disciples' participation as a founding member of the Federal Council of the Churches of Christ in America in 1908.

Active until the very end, McLean supported the consolidation of intradenominational work among Disciples, including that of the FCMS, into the newly formed United Christian Missionary Society in 1919 and served as its first vice president. McLean died in Battle Creek, Michigan, where he had gone for medical treatment. Although his understanding of mission was colored by the perspectives of nineteenth-century American culture, McLean dedicated his life and resources to reaching others with the good news of the Gospel.

• McLean's papers are at the Disciples of Christ Historical Society, Nashville, Tenn. His books are *Missionary Addresses* (1895), *Handbook of Missions* (1897), *A Circuit of the Globe* (1897), *Where the Book Speaks* (1907), *Epoch Makers of Modern Missions* (1912), *The Primacy of the Missionary* (1920), and *The History of the Foreign Christian Missionary Society* (1921); countless articles appeared in the *Missionary Intelligencer*, *Christian-Evangelist*, *Christian Standard*, and other religious periodicals. For his biography see William Robinson Warren, *The Life and Labors of Archibald McLean* (1923). His funeral address by the Reverend George A. Campbell is in *World Call*, Feb. 1921, pp. 5–8. A memorial issue of *World Call*, containing numerous brief articles and tributes to McLean, appeared in Mar. 1921. An obituary is in the (Cincinnati, Ohio) *Commercial Tribune*, 16 Dec. 1920.

MARK G. TOULOUSE

MCLEAN, Franklin Chambers (22 Feb. 1888–10 Sept. 1968), physician, researcher, and educator, was born in Maroa, Illinois, the son of William Thomas McLean, a physician, and Margaret Philbrook Crocker. McLean was also the grandson of a physician, Chambers Argo McLean, and was given his grandfather's name. His father often took young McLean on his remote farmhouse calls and impressed on him the idea of not only becoming a physician but also of attaining the chair of medicine at the University of Chicago.

McLean entered the University of Chicago in 1905 and obtained his B.S. in three years with no grade below an A. In his junior year he worked with Anton J. Carlson, professor of physiology. He received his M.D. in 1910 from Rush Medical College and his M.S. in pharmacology (1912) and his Ph.D. in physiology (1915) from the University of Chicago.

After his internship at Cook County Hospital in 1910–1911, McLean became professor of pharmacology and materia medica at the University of Oregon Medical School at Portland, where he remained until 1914. During the summers he taught pharmacology at the University of Chicago and became interested in clinical chemistry. His method for blood sugar determination was the first such developed in the United States. He also worked out one of the earliest mathematical formulations for urea clearance. He reported those achievements in 1914–1915.

When McLean left Portland he spent nine months in physiologist Otto Loewi's laboratory in Graz, Austria. Returning to the United States in 1914, McLean was hired as a resident by the Rockefeller Institute for Medical Research in New York City. From 1914 to 1916 he worked with Donald Van Slyke on a study of the chemistry of body fluids. He also spent much time in planning for the establishment of the first western medical school in China, sponsored by the China Medical Board of the Rockefeller Foundation. In 1916 McLean went to China as director and professor of medicine at the new Peking Union Medical College. While the college was being constructed, McLean was granted a leave of absence and enlisted in the U.S. Army, joining the Medical Department of the American Expeditionary Force during World War I as a first lieutenant. He worked as a consultant out of the headquarters at Neufchateau, France, and had experience with victims of mustard gas attacks.

Leaving the army in 1919 as a major, McLean returned to China. Despite some problems in bringing Chinese and Western medicine and physicians together McLean achieved his major goal of providing an excellent medical education at Peking. In 1920 he resigned as director to devote himself full time to research. McLean married one of the younger members of the Peking faculty, obstetrician Helen Vincent, in Tientsin in June 1923. He resigned his professorship at Peking that year and returned with his wife to the United States. The McLeans had one son, who was killed in an accident in his early teens.

In 1923 the University of Chicago offered McLean the responsibility for planning and building their new medical school. He became professor of medicine and chairman of that department in 1923. In an innovative move, McLean set aside time for the students to do research. However, the school soon underwent a battle between those who backed a full-time policy (as at Peking, where the faculty were all on salary and did not receive clinical fees) and those who believed that faculty members should be able to carry on private practices. McLean had assumed that Rockefeller's General Education Board would continue its funding at Chicago beyond the original five-year period as they had done at Peking. When this did not occur, he resigned his chair in 1928 and became director of Chicago's University Clinics, outpatient clinics for the medical school.

George Dick, an opponent of the full-time policy, was offered the chairmanship of the department of medicine but set as a condition for acceptance that McLean would be removed from that department. When the university accepted Dick's terms in 1928, Carlson named McLean professor of pathologic physiology, the title he held until his retirement in 1953. This made it possible for McLean to go back to research.

McLean's interests involved analytical and physiological studies of chemicals in body fluids and the use of such methodology in clinical problems and the study of blood as a physicochemical system. He investigated the physiology of bone, especially calcium metabolism, and the roles of calcium in body fluids. He also explored the mode of action of the parathyroid hormone. Much of his work was done with either A. Baird Hastings or Marshall R. Urist.

In 1943 McLean reenlisted in the army as a lieutenant colonel and was assigned to the chemical warfare service. Here he did considerable research and administrative work for the National Defense Research Committee and traveled widely. He completed his assignment in 1945 as a colonel and was awarded the Legion of Merit. Later he served as a consultant for the Atomic Energy Commission, observed the atomic bomb tests at Eniwetok, and became involved with the medical results of atomic explosions.

In 1928 McLean had become a trustee of the Julius Rosenwald Fund (the philantropist Rosenwald was his patient), enabling him to help minority candidates financially to enter and stay in medical schools. He also helped more than 600 such students through the National Medical Fellowships, Inc. After retiring from the University of Chicago in 1953, he remained active with his government duties and work with black medical education. He died in Billings Hospital at the University of Chicago.

Although he did little to promote his own self-interest, McLean is remembered for his pioneering research in biochemistry and physiology, his planning and leadership in medical schools, his painstaking government service, and his effective labors in behalf of medical education for blacks.

• The University of Chicago Special Collections has a considerable amount of McLean's professional and private papers and related materials. Biographical articles include Marshall R. Urist, "Phoenix of Physiology and Medicine: Franklin Chambers McLean," *Perspectives in Biology and Medicine* 19, no. 1 (Autumn 1975): 23–58; Walter L. Palmer, "Franklin Chambers McLean and the Founding of the University of Chicago School of Medicine," *Perspectives in Biology and Medicine* 22, no. 2, pt. 2 (Winter 1979): S2–S32; and A. Baird Hastings, "Franklin Chambers McLean and the State of Calcium in Body Fluids," in *Cellular Mechanisms for Calcium Transfer and Homeostasis*, ed. George Nichols, Jr., and R. H. Wasserman (1971). An obituary is in the *New York Times*, 11 Sept. 1968.

WILLIAM K. BEATTY

MCLEAN, John (3 Mar. 1785–3 Apr. 1861), associate justice of the U.S. Supreme Court, was born in Morris County, New Jersey, the son of Fergus McLean and Sophia Blackford, farmers. He moved with his family to Morgantown, Virginia (now in West Virginia), in 1789, to Kentucky in 1790, and to Ohio in 1796. He worked on his parents' farm until he was sixteen. At that age he received his first formal education in a local school, where he studied classics for two years.

In 1804 McLean was apprenticed to the clerk of the Court of Common Pleas of Hamilton County, Ohio. During that time he studied law under Arthur St. Clair, Jr., one of Ohio's leading lawyers. In 1807 McLean was admitted to the bar, and on March 20 of that year he married Rebecca Edwards of Newport, Kentucky. They had seven children.

Shortly after their marriage, the couple moved to Lebanon, Ohio, where McLean published the *Western Star*, which supported the administration of Thomas Jefferson. He also practiced law in Lebanon for four or five years. He served as examiner of the U.S. Congressional Land Office in Cincinnati (1811–1812). In 1812 the Ohio congressional delegation was increased from one to six, and McLean was elected to one of the new seats. He supported the administration in the War of 1812. He served in Congress until 1816, when the Ohio legislature elected him to the Ohio Supreme Court, where he served from 1816 to 1822.

President James Monroe in 1822 appointed McLean commissioner of the Public Land Office and postmaster general (1823). He was continued in the latter position by President John Quincy Adams and, for a short time, by President Andrew Jackson. He presided over the U.S. Post Office in a time of expansion and gained a reputation as an able administrator.

McLean was appointed an associate justice of the U.S. Supreme Court by President Jackson in 1829. At that time each justice rode a circuit where he held trial court proceedings with a district judge. McLean served as circuit justice for the Seventh Circuit, which comprised Ohio, Kentucky, and Tennessee from 1830 to 1837, and Michigan, Ohio, Indiana, and Illinois from 1837 to 1861. Throughout his tenure McLean's workload as a circuit justice was heavy. In 1838 he traveled 2,500 miles, more than all but two other justices of the Court. In 1856 the number of new filings in his circuit, the number of cases disposed of, and the remaining cases on the docket, exceeded that of six of the other circuits combined. In the 1850s, when Chief Justice Roger Taney was frequently ill, McLean, as the senior justice, often served as the presiding justice of the Supreme Court.

As an associate justice, McLean authored 160 majority opinions and thirty dissents. He was one of the few justices who published his circuit opinions.

McLean's first wife died in 1840, and on 2 March 1843 he married Sarah Bella G. Garrard, who was known for her abolitionist sentiments. They had one son, who died in infancy.

McLean a wrote of number of antislavery opinions, including one as an Ohio Supreme Court justice in *Ohio v. Thomas D. Carneal* (1817), limiting the ability of slaveholders to take slaves into free states. In his concurrence in *Groves v. Slaughter* (1841), he indicated that the federal government acted on slaves as persons, not property; that federal power over the interstate slave trade was exclusive under the commerce clause; and that slavery was derived solely from local law. He dissented in *Prigg v. Pennsylvania* (1842), which held that the federal Fugitive Slave Act preempted Pennsylvania's freedman's acts. He opposed the Mexican War, in part because he felt it would open new territories to slavery. In 1848 he publicly stated that to exist, slavery needed positive law, and that consequently—unless authorized by Congress—slavery could not exist in a territory. But he also enforced the Fugitive Slave Act of 1793 in cases such as *Jones v. Van Zandt* (1847), and he later upheld the constitutionality of the 1850 Fugitive Slave Act in *Miller v. McQuerry* (1853). This brought him the condemnation of many abolitionists.

McLean's most famous opinion was his dissent in *Dred Scott v. Sanford* (1857). According to his biographer, Francis P. Weisenburger, McLean decided to dissent on the merits after the breakdown of the Court's original decision to dispose of the question on jurisdictional grounds. In contrast to the majority opinion that blacks, free or slave, were not U.S. citizens, McLean held that an American-born person held in slavery became a citizen when he or she became free. He also dissented from the majority opinion that the Missouri Compromise of 1820 was unconstitutional. Although he gave courage to those who opposed the majority's decision, even his biographer stated that the dissent of Justice Curtis was "much the abler."

McLean was frequently considered as a presidential candidate. Although he had managed to stay in favor with President Jackson, he was not a true Jacksonian; he was more comfortable with the Whig party and the wing of the Republican party composed of former Whigs. He refused the nomination of the Anti-Masonic Convention in 1831. He was endorsed by the Ohio legislature as a candidate for president in 1836. He unsuccessfully sought the 1848 Whig nomination and was discussed as a possible Free Soil candidate that same year. He received 196 votes in a straw poll at the 1856 Republican convention and twelve votes on the first ballot at the Republican convention in 1860. His presidential ambitions were heightened, in part, by the low opinion he had of almost every other presidential candidate.

McLean was in good health until the last two years of his life, when illness sometimes kept him from the bench in both his circuit and on the Supreme Court. He died in Cincinnati. McLean was considered an able man, but not one who towered above his contemporaries. Weisenburger noted that while McLean spent most of his public life on the bench, he "was a politician before he became a jurist, and he remained a politician to the end."

• Collections of McLean's papers are held by the Library of Congress and the Ohio Historical Society. Some of his early opinions are found in Ervin H. Pollack, ed., *Ohio Unreported Judicial Decisions prior to 1823* (1952). His circuit court opinions are published in the six volumes of *McLean's Reports* and also in *Federal Cases*. His Supreme Court opinions are found in the *United States Reports*. A biography of McLean is Francis P. Weisenburger, *The Life of John McLean* (1937). A more recent sketch of his life by Frank O. Gatell appears in Leon Friedman and Fred Israel, eds., *The Justices of the United States Supreme Court* (1969), p. 535. Dorothy Ganfield Fowler, *The Cabinet Politician* (1943), treats the office of postmaster general and contains positive references to McLean's administration. Don Fehrenbacher, *The Dred Scott Case* (1978), contains the best account of McLean's role in that case. The context of his life during the time Taney was chief justice is found in Carl B. Swisher, *The Taney Period, 1836–64* (1974). Memorials and obituaries are in 66 U.S. (1 Black) 8 (1861); the *New York Times*, 5 Apr. 1861; and the *Cincinnati Daily Gazette*, 6 Apr. 1861.

RICHARD L. AYNES

MCLEAN, Mary Hancock (28 Feb. 1861–17 May 1930), physician and missionary, was born in Washington, Missouri, the daughter of Elijah McLean, a physician, and Mary Stafford. She enjoyed a privileged childhood. Her father wanted her to succeed academically; he hired a private tutor and provided Mary with an ample allowance throughout her life. At age thirteen she enrolled at Lindenwood College in St. Charles, Missouri. In 1878 she transferred to Vassar College, from which she graduated two years later. McLean aspired to be a physician like her father and was accepted at the University of Michigan Medical School, an institution then more receptive than others to female students.

McLean graduated with an M.D. in 1883. She returned to Missouri to practice, and, because of her father's influence, she did not encounter as many obstacles as did other women physicians. General Stevenson, a family friend, secured McLean a position as an assistant physician at the St. Louis Female Hospital in 1884. She was the first woman allowed to hold an official position in the city hospitals and was treated as an equal. At that time, internships were not required for physicians, and McLean had access to a professional opportunity denied most women doctors.

For a year McLean tended mostly to impoverished patients, primarily prostitutes suffering venereal diseases. Like many Victorian female physicians, McLean was a humanitarian who considered medicine a means of social reform. A deeply religious Presbyterian, she was also concerned for her patients' moral condition. Her protégée, Bertha Van Hoosen, recalled that McLean "approached her hospital service seriously and devoted night and day to her patients." She visited the hospital wards and read case histories every evening. "Her record was so exceptionally high and so unusual," Van Hoosen noted, "that few men in the profession did not know of her accomplishments as a skillful operator and an exhaustive diagnostician."

Despite her successful work in the hospital, however, McLean decided to establish a private practice in obstetrics and gynecology in 1885, and she encountered discrimination doing so. She was unable to rent office space because St. Louis landlords feared that property values would fall owing to the stigma of housing a female physician. When she finally signed a contract for an Olive Street residence, McLean had to agree not to post any signs with her name and designation as a doctor. She arranged her office and living space in the same building. Locals dubbed the seedy neighborhood "Scab Row," and McLean expended energy and money trying to convince residents to benefit from her expertise.

McLean's father financed her practice, and she waited for her first patient. She convinced a black servant named Tillie, suffering from a uterine fibroid, to permit her to operate. Lacking access to a hospital operating room, McLean spent $250 to hire nurses and sterilize instruments and dressings. She successfully operated in Tillie's home, launching her surgical career in St. Louis.

Medical professionals admired both McLean's character and her surgical skills. Her practice expanded quickly. Although some patients sought her services because seeing St. Louis's only woman doctor was a fad, others recognized her abilities. McLean's policy of being more interested in a patient's condition than in her professional advancement earned the respect of her clients and peers.

In 1885 McLean became the first female member of the St. Louis Medical Society and its only woman member for fifteen years. Ophthalmologist Simon Pollak sponsored her application. Previously he had nominated Nancy Levell, but the male physicians refused to accept her. Pollak reminisced, "Later I succeeded in slipping in Dr. Mary McLean" who "has become a brilliant practitioner, and has done remarkably well." McLean presented papers to the society and was allowed to operate at all St. Louis hospitals.

McLean was devoutly religious and prayed before each surgery she performed. Some regarded her zeal as excessive. She devoted time to volunteer work and donated part of her inheritance to the Bethesda Hospital to fund care for geriatric patients.

The twentieth century and the Progressive movement brought McLean new medical and reform opportunities. The 1904 World's Fair at St. Louis attracted many rural women to the city. Many of these impoverished women suffered and were exploited because they lacked employment skills. McLean sponsored the Emmaus Home for Girls, providing pleasant housing, health care, and job training. This facility was the forerunner of the St. Louis Young Women's Christian Association (YWCA), which McLean helped found in 1905; she also served on its board of directors.

McLean was especially concerned with young women's health and hygiene, in addition to their social, intellectual, and spiritual development. She gave them physical examinations (alert for rheumatic fever and heart weakness) and counseled them kindly. She also provided blunt information about sex.

In 1908 McLean established a free evening clinic on Washington Avenue. Described as being "run by women, for women," the clinic made medical care accessible to working women. As medicine became professionalized and scientific research and applications became more valued than social service, McLean focused increasingly on her charity work. "Her instinct for protecting girls in unhappy surroundings led her to devote a great deal of her time to improving their modes of living and she sent several through school," a writer for the *Journal of the Missouri State Medical Association* commented.

Male physicians had advised McLean to pursue surgery and arranged professional opportunities for her, but no women physicians had been available to be her mentors. McLean herself aided women physicians to secure professional roles in St. Louis's medical community. She paid their medical school tuition and boarding expenses, took students to clinics, tutored women in anatomy, notified women of open positions, and otherwise inspired and advised them. (Despite all this, she opposed woman suffrage.)

Interested in missionary work, McLean traveled to China and hoped to move there permanently. The harsh climate deterred her from doing so, but she stayed for several months, operating in hospitals and learning about Chinese medical education. McLean supported at least twenty Chinese students through American medical schools; many of them lived in her St. Louis home. She was angered when several of her Asian protégées were rejected for internships by prejudiced hospital administrators.

McLean broke her wrist in 1928, ending her surgical career. She continued her private medical practice until a few months before her death. She received much recognition during her pioneering medical career. She was one of the few women members of the American College of Surgeons and a fellow of the American Medical Association. She died in St. Louis, having never married.

• McLean's papers are in the Western Manuscript collection and YWCA Archives at the University of Missouri, St. Louis. Biographical information appears in Mary K. Dains, ed., *Show Me Missouri Women: Selected Biographies* (1989), and Bertha Van Hoosen, *Petticoat Surgeon* (1947). For her career in the context of her times, see Marion Hunt, "Woman's Place in Medicine: The Career of Dr. Mary Hancock McLean," *Missouri Historical Society Bulletin* 36 (1980): 255–63;

and E. J. Goodwin, *History of Medicine in Missouri* (1905). An obituary is in the *Journal of the Missouri State Medical Association* 27 (1930): 301–2.

ELIZABETH D. SCHAFER

MCLEAN, William Lippard (4 May 1852–30 July 1931), newspaper publisher, was born in Mount Pleasant, Pennsylvania, the son of Robert Caldwell McLean, the head of a furniture plant, and Augusta Dorothea Voigt. McLean got an early start on his journalistic career by delivering the *Pittsburgh Leader* after school. At the age of twenty he moved to Pittsburgh and took a job in that paper's circulation department selling subscriptions outside the city. He worked in a variety of positions at the *Leader* for the next six years.

In 1878 McLean began his long association with Philadelphia, Pennsylvania, when Calvin Wells, a Pittsburgh iron manufacturer, purchased the *Philadelphia Press* and hired McLean as secretary and treasurer of the paper. He soon became its business manager. The *Press* under McLean was a conservative and well-run newspaper with a growing circulation. In 1889 he married Sarah Burd Warden; they had four children.

In 1895 McLean purchased the *Evening Bulletin*, a 48-year-old paper with a small circulation, for $73,000 of mostly borrowed money. At that time, the Philadelphia newspaper market was highly competitive, with thirteen dailies ranging in sales from about 5,000 to nearly 200,000. McLean declared his policy for the paper in a 1 June 1895 editorial: "It will be the purpose of the Evening Bulletin to present to the people of Philadelphia a complete afternoon newspaper that will be abreast of every improvement in modern journalism. . . . It will register the decrees of no leader or faction, . . . always subordinating party to the advancement of good government."

McLean's *Bulletin* was part of the movement away from the partisan press of the nineteenth century to new journalistic standards. The *Bulletin* under McLean, like the *New York Times* under Adolph S. Ochs, became a paper of record that was committed to reporting the news within the new norm of "objectivity." Virtually every event that happened in or around Philadelphia could be found on the pages of the *Bulletin*. McLean avoided large headlines and sensational stories in the *Bulletin*, making it an accurate, inclusive, but often dull paper.

Because of its exhaustive coverage and modern printing facilities that allowed it to deliver the news quickly, McLean's *Bulletin* soon established itself in the Philadelphia market. In the first year of his management, the circulation rose from approximately 6,000 to more than 30,000 (although this was still well behind the leading morning papers such as the *Philadelphia Record* and the *Item*). Within a decade of his purchase, the *Evening Bulletin* had a circulation of more than 200,000 and was the most widely read newspaper in Philadelphia, a distinction it would not lose until just before it folded in 1982. Under McLean the paper adopted its famous slogan: "In Philadelphia, nearly everybody reads *The Bulletin*." At the time of McLean's death the paid circulation was over 500,000 copies daily. McLean, the son of a Presbyterian elder and the grandson of a minister, never allowed the *Bulletin* to have a Sunday edition while he was alive.

Perhaps the best assessment of McLean and his paper was made by a competitor, David Stern, the outspoken owner of the *Philadelphia Record* and the *New York Post*. The morning after McLean's death, Stern wrote in an editorial in the *Record*: "Conservative by inclination and habit, of thoughtful and judicial rather than crusading temperament, Mr. McLean pursued undeviatingly his ideal of a newspaper that should be a force for civic sanity and righteousness and progress, but at the same time should mold public opinion by quiet persuasion rather than by news-emphasis or argumentative vigor."

McLean's other major role in journalism was as a director of the Associated Press (AP) from 1896 to 1924. He, along with fellow director Victor Lawson of Chicago, helped reorganize the wire service in 1900. It was during McLean's involvement that the AP became the dominant wire service in the United States. He was also a director of the American Newspaper Publishers' Association from 1889 to 1905. In 1921 his wife died. McLean died at his home in the Germantown section of Philadelphia.

William L. McLean took a small newspaper and made it into the dominant journal in Philadelphia by creating a paper that accurately covered the news and offended few readers. His paper reflected his personality and that of the city it served; it was polite, inclusive, and conservative.

• There is no significant collection of McLean's papers. There are brief examinations of his and his family's involvement with the *Evening Bulletin* in Kenneth Stewart and John Tebbel, *Makers of Modern Journalism* (1952), and David G. Wittels, "The Paper That Was Tailored to a City," *Saturday Evening Post*, 7 Apr. 1945. The fullest treatment of his life is in the obituary in the *Evening Bulletin*, 30 July 1931. There is also an obituary in the *New York Times*, 31 July 1931.

JOHN H. HEPP IV

MCLEMORE, Jeff: (13 Mar. 1857–4 Mar. 1929), journalist, state legislator, and congressman, was born Atkins Jefferson McLemore near Spring Hill in Maury County, Tennessee, the son of Robert Anderson McLemore and Mary Howard McEwen, farmers. He had an "aversion to teachers" and recalled that he "never saw the inside of a schoolroom after he was fourteen years of age" (*Congressional Directory*, p. 109). In 1878 he moved to Texas, where he worked as a cowboy, then he spent the next four years as a miner and newspaper reporter in Colorado and New Mexico. After a brief trip to Mexico in 1883, he returned to Texas and resumed his career as a journalist.

McLemore was employed on newspapers in San Antonio, edited a weekly newspaper in Kyle from 1883 to 1886, and started the *Gulf News* in Corpus Christi in 1889. In 1892 he was elected to the Texas House of Representatives as a Democrat from Corpus Christi, serving two terms. Moving to Austin in 1895, he was a member of the city's board of aldermen and became secretary of the State Democratic Executive Committee between 1900 and 1904. In 1903 he founded a weekly newspaper that evolved during the decade that followed into the *State Topics and Texas Monthly Review*. McLemore signed his first name "Jeff:" and he wrote editorials that favored the antiprohibitionist, probusiness, conservative wing of the Democratic party.

Developing friendships with Edward M. House and Senator Joseph Weldon Bailey, McLemore was nominated as the Democratic congressman at large from Texas in 1914 "over bitter opposition" (*Congressional Directory*, p. 109) from the prohibitionist elements in the party. He won the general election easily. He introduced resolutions attacking the Anti-Saloon League and was soon identified as one of the most ardent wets in Congress. He also attacked the Wilson administration's policy toward Mexico. When Woodrow Wilson called for preparedness legislation to deal with the effects of the First World War, however, McLemore was one of the few Texas representatives to endorse the president's position. The Texas congressman wanted to use the nation's enhanced military strength to "help the people of Mexico straighten out their affairs" (*San Antonio Express*, 15 Mar. 1929). In that sense, his support for preparedness did not represent any real sympathy with Wilson's European neutrality policies.

Another foreign policy crisis revealed how much McLemore was at odds with President Wilson. When the administration in early 1916 indicated that it would hold Germany responsible if Americans, traveling on armed Allied merchant ships, were casualties as a result of a submarine attack, McLemore feared that the policy might lead the nation into war. He offered resolutions to keep Americans off the vessels of belligerent powers, believing that the American people "do not want this country plunged into war because of the heedless act of some American citizen" (Kretzschmar, p. 16). While others made similar proposals, McLemore became associated with a resolution offered in the Senate by Thomas P. Gore of Oklahoma. The Gore-McLemore Resolution, as it was called, seemed to the White House to pose a significant threat to President Wilson's power over foreign policy. It would have had Congress dictating the terms under which American citizens might exercise their rights as neutrals. McLemore thus became a symbol of legislative opposition to a Democratic president.

The White House succeeded in quelling the revolt against the president during February 1916, and the Gore-McLemore Resolution was tabled. McLemore's standing with the Wilson administration never recovered, and his patronage requests to the president were rebuffed. Nonetheless, the fame he had attained because of his resolution helped him win reelection in 1916. A friend told him that his constituents said, "Jeff is one Congressman from Texas who has managed to put himself before the public and we are for him" (Gould, p. 165). A perennial bachelor, McLemore married May Clark on 26 Dec. 1916; they had one child.

McLemore took another step into political danger in April 1917 when he was the only Texas congressman to vote against the resolution declaring war with Germany. He told his colleagues that he was "not yet ready to vote absolutism to any President, nor will I ever vote to abrogate the Monroe Doctrine by forming any alliance with the warring nations of the Old World" (Gould, p. 223). Friends of the president in Texas charged that McLemore was doing the work of Germany.

When McLemore faced reelection in 1918, he confronted a changed set of circumstances. The Texas legislature had redistricted the state in 1917, and McLemore now had to run in a specific district if he wished to return to Washington. Rather than oppose an entrenched incumbent in Austin's Tenth District, McLemore decided to contest the Seventh District, an antiprohibitionist area with Galveston as its major city. It was not familiar territory to the congressman, who faced two strong opponents, including the eventual winner, Clay Stone Briggs. The other Democratic candidates charged him with being a tool of the liquor interests and an enemy of President Wilson. McLemore was soundly defeated and told a friend angrily that the voters "wanted a rubberstamp to represent them in Congress, and they got it" (Gould, p. 244). Returning to Texas after his term expired in 1919, he established a newspaper in Hebronville in South Texas. He ran for the Senate in 1928 without success. McLemore died in Laredo.

Because his name became associated with the resolution that assailed Wilson's leadership in 1916, McLemore emerged overnight as a symbol of the forces in the United States opposed to intervention in European quarrels. His mail became filled with letters and documents from groups representing the anti-Wilson, anti-interventionist side of the political debate. McLemore's career is important not for what he did but for what he came to symbolize and the support that he attracted.

• The McLemore papers are a rich collection at the Center for American History, University of Texas at Austin, which includes a biographical file on McLemore. The Clay Stone Briggs Papers at the center also are useful. The Woodrow Wilson Papers, Library of Congress, contain the administration's response to McLemore's actions. The congressman's entry in *Congressional Directory* (1916) is written in an autobiographical style. He also published *Indianola and Other Poems* (1904). Copies of *State Topics* are held at the University of Texas at Austin. For his career in Congress see Timothy G. McDonald, "The Gore-McLemore Resolutions: Democratic Revolt against Wilson's Submarine Policy," *Historian* 26 (1963): 50–74; Robert L. Wagner, "The Congressional Career of Jeff: McLemore as Seen in His Letters," *Historian of the University of Texas* 1 (1962): 65–81; Lewis L. Gould, *Progressives and Prohibitionists: Texas Democrats in the Wilson Era* (1973); and Michelle Kretzschmar, "Jeff: McLemore and the McLemore Warning Resolution" (seminar paper, Univ. of Texas, 1988). An obituary is in the San Antonio *Express*, 5 Mar. 1929.

LEWIS L. GOULD

MCLENDON, Gordon Barton (8 June 1921–14 Sept. 1986), broadcasting innovator and businessman, was born in Paris, Texas, the son of Barton McLendon, a motion picture theater owner, and Jeanette Eyster. Exposed at an early age to the entertainment business through his father's chain of motion picture theaters in Texas and Oklahoma, Gordon also spent hours in front of the family radio entranced by the sportscasts of Ted Husing, Graham McNamee, and Bill Stern. A brilliant student and debater at Kemper Military school, McLendon ranked first in his class and received all four of the school's honor awards. He began his career in communications at age fourteen as assistant editor for the Cass County, Texas, newspaper.

McLendon attended Yale University from 1938 to 1942, earning a degree in oriental languages. As a student he began broadcasting baseball and basketball games on WOCD, the university radio station. McLendon served as a language specialist during World War II, spending much of his time in the Pacific Theater. He observed that U.S. servicemen flocked to hear broadcasts of sporting events on the Armed Forces Radio Network. He then conceived the idea of a national sports radio network.

After attending Harvard Law School and working as a part owner of station KNET in Palestine, Texas, in 1946–1947, McLendon became the owner and principal announcer of radio station KLIF in Dallas on 9 November 1947. In a hotel basement studio he created a radio character, "The Old Scotchman," who rebroadcasted football and baseball games from wire reports; McLendon offered his broadcasts to other stations. By 1949 he had formed the Liberty Radio Network with seventy-one associated stations, mostly in the South and West, regions lacking major league teams and where the only broadcasts were of special events such as the World Series. McLendon made live and re-created baseball and football broadcasts and employed talented announcers, including Lindsey Nelson, Jerry Doggett, and Dizzy Dean.

By 1950 his Liberty network included more than 240 stations and offered sixteen hours of daily programming that specialized in sports. With financial backing from Houston oilman Hugh Roy Cullen, the network expanded in large measure because of McLendon's correct assessment of the demand for sports on radio in the fast-growing Sun Belt region. Sporting events provided the staple of Liberty programming, which claimed audiences in the tens of millions for big games. McLendon's articulate, dramatic style earned him the *Sporting News* Broadcaster of the Year Award in 1951. His live coverage of the Giants-Dodgers playoff game on 3 October 1951 reached more than 450 Liberty stations.

McLendon attracted wide acclaim for his re-creations of games from telegraphic reports. This technique, which he perfected with imaginative, prerecorded and live sound effects, initially was employed to save money, but he also utilized re-creations to establish fixed sports times in Liberty's programming schedule. Decades before ABC's Monday Night Football changed American social habits, McLendon showed that skilled scheduling could establish audience loyalty.

Whether re-creations of contemporary contests from wire accounts or of historic sports events, McLendon's broadcasts attracted large audiences who believed they were real. His most famous re-creation was a 1951 production describing an 1886 St. Louis Browns–Brooklyn Bridegrooms baseball game. It featured the archaic rules of counts of six balls and two strikes, interruptions while the umpire retrieved foul balls, and a live postgame telephone interview with 91-year-old Arle Neff, who had actually played in the contest. In contemporary re-creations McLendon improvised during telegraph breakdowns with accounts of imaginary arguments and fights, animals running loose on the field, and descriptions of people in the stands.

McLendon's success did not endear him to the professional baseball owners, who believed that he benefited financially from their games without paying all of them rights fees and that his re-created broadcasts harmed major and minor league attendance. They wanted to cash in on the revenues from radio. In 1952 the owners severely limited the number of games Liberty could broadcast, effectively killing the network. Denouncing the club owners for "brazenry, ruthlessness, and illegality," McLendon abandoned his sports network but continued to innovate in radio, devising new kinds of station promotions, helping create the "Top Forty" format (news, weather, leading popular songs, and sports), and developing the first all-news radio stations. Although seldom carrying live sports events, his stations gave major emphasis to sports news and the latest scores in their programming. During the 1970s he sold his fourteen radio stations for more than $100 million. He also ventured into the production of motion pictures, producing the film "Victory," which featured Pelé, the legendary Brazilian soccer star.

McLendon married in 1947 Anna Gray Noe, the daughter of a former Louisiana governor; they had four children. He sought without success the Republican nomination for governor in Texas in 1962 as a champion of conservatism, but in business he possessed a Midas touch in broadcasting, real estate, and precious metals. In 1985 *Forbes* estimated his fortune in excess of $200 million and listed him among the 400 richest people in the United States. Former broadcast partner and later Dallas mayor, Wes Wise, declared that McLendon was prouder of his accomplishments in radio than of the fortune his business ventures brought him. McLendon died at his Denton County, Texas, home.

• Gordon McLendon's papers, including sound recordings and a 26 Feb. 1981 interview, are in the Southwest Collection, Texas Tech University, Lubbock, Tex. Jim Harper, "Gordon McLendon: Pioneer Baseball Broadcaster," *Baseball History* 1, no. 1 (Mar. 1986): 42–51, focuses on his work in sportscasting, and Ronald Garay, *Gordon McLendon: The*

Maverick of Radio (1992), is a full biography. Francis X. Tolbert, "The Man Behind a Network," *Nation's Business*, Mar. 1952, pp. 56–60, provides a contemporary biographical account; and Lindsey Nelson, *Hello Everybody, I'm Lindsey Nelson* (1986), delivers the perspective of a co-worker. Willie Morris's autobiography, *North toward Home* (1967), provides insight into McLendon's impact on listeners. An obituary in the *Dallas Morning News*, 15 Sept. 1986, also assesses his place in broadcasting.

JIM HARPER

M'CLINTOCK, Mary Ann Wilson (20 Feb. 1800–21 May 1884), and **Thomas M'Clintock** (28 Mar. 1792–19 Mar. 1876), were Quakers, abolitionists, and key organizers of the first Woman's Rights Convention. The location of Mary Ann Wilson's birth is unknown; she was the daughter of John Pyle and Elizabeth (maiden name unknown). Thomas was born in Brandywine Hundred, Delaware, the son of Thomas M'Clintock and Mary Allen. Nothing more is known of their parents or their early education. Thomas and Mary Ann were married at the Burlington, New Jersey, Friends meetinghouse in 1820 and thereafter lived in Philadelphia, where Thomas had been working as a druggist since about 1814. They had five children.

In the 1820s Thomas was an active adherent of the Hicksite party in the religious controversy that split the Society of Friends. As early as 1822 Thomas was in correspondence with Elias Hicks and William Poole about the activities of Hicks's Orthodox opponents in Philadelphia Yearly Meeting. Hicksite leaders relied on Thomas's extensive knowledge of theology and the writings of the early Quakers to counter attacks by their Orthodox opponents. Though Thomas opposed the evangelical views of the Orthodox leadership, he was more concerned with their tendency to value doctrine over behavior. In a letter to Poole on 20 November 1823, Thomas wrote: "I pity indeed all whose eyes are so blinded by traditions and prejudice, as to place more importance in opinions, than in a life of humble conformity to the Divine will." Although his name does not appear on the printed volumes, Thomas helped edit *A Series of Extemporaneous Discourses . . . by Elias Hicks* (1825) and edited most of the eight-volume set of Quaker founder George Fox's *Works* (1831).

Thomas's public involvement in the antislavery cause began in 1827, when he became a founder and the first secretary of the Free Produce Society of Pennsylvania, a largely Quaker organization promoting the use of goods made without slave labor. Later, Thomas and Mary Ann M'Clintock would be closely associated with the Garrisonian wing of the antislavery movement, with Thomas serving as a manager (1843–1848) and a vice president of the American Anti-Slavery Society.

In 1837 the M'Clintocks moved to Waterloo, New York, where Thomas operated a drugstore. Thomas, who had been acknowledged as a Friends minister around 1835, and Mary Ann took an active part in Genesee Yearly Meeting. Both served on committees, and Thomas was clerk of Genesee Yearly Meeting Men's Meeting in 1840, 1841, and 1843; Mary Ann was assistant clerk of the Women's Meeting from 1839 to 1842. Within the Society of Friends, they promoted temperance, American Indian rights, and antislavery. They organized antislavery fairs, wrote and signed antislavery petitions, cared for African-American children in their home (perhaps as part of an underground railway network), endorsed utopian communities, maintained contact with reformers such as Lucretia Mott, William Lloyd Garrison, Amy and Isaac Post, and Frederick Douglass, and sold goods "free from the labor of slaves."

Thomas clearly rooted his antislavery commitment in his religious ideals. In his address to the "Association of Friends for Advocating the Cause of the Slave, and Improving the Condition of the Free People of Color" (1840), he noted that "religion, in our view, has been emphatically embodied, not in speculative theories, but in practical righteousness, in active virtues, in reverence to God, in benevolence to man—the latter being the only sure test of the former." Although his neighbors in Waterloo warned Thomas that his reform activities were unpopular and would hurt his business, he replied that "I must speak the truth, and abide the consequences" (Stebbins, pp. 70–71).

Though the Society of Friends was opposed to slavery, it was divided on the appropriateness of its members participating in "worldly" reform movements. Some of the radical reformers among Friends rejected the authority of the meeting to discipline its members on what were seen as questions of individual conscience. Partly as a result of this controversy, a schism occurred at the annual meeting sessions of Genesee Yearly Meeting at Farmington, New York, in June 1848. The M'Clintocks helped organize a new group, which called itself the Yearly Meeting of Congregational Friends. Two documents, *An Address to Friends of Genesee Yearly Meeting* and the *Basis of Religious Association*, both probably written by Thomas, explained their beliefs. "The object of religious association," noted the *Basis*, "may be defined in brief to be, the promotion of righteousness—of practical goodness—love to God and man—on the part of every member composing the association, and in the world at large." They believed in the equality of all people, including women and men, and that every person "stands in such contiguity to Omnipresent God as to have immediately revealed to him God's will regarding him. THIS IS THE FUNDAMENTAL FACT IN RELIGION" (repr. in Brown and Stuard, eds., *Witness for Change: Quaker Women over Three Centuries* [1989], pp. 113–14).

The Congregational Friends (renamed the Friends of Human Progress in 1854) met annually at the Junius Friends meetinghouse near Waterloo until the 1880s. They corresponded with other Progressive Friends groups, notably the Pennsylvania Yearly Meeting of Progressive Friends that Thomas helped found in 1853. The Waterloo meeting attracted numerous reformers, Quaker and non-Quaker alike, including Elizabeth Cady Stanton, Frederick Douglass, Susan B. Anthony, Aaron M. Powell, and Samuel J. May. As clerk of the yearly meeting, Thomas signed and probably wrote many of the "Testimonies" and "Epistles" that appeared in the printed proceedings of the Congregational Friends from 1849 to 1858.

In July 1848, just two weeks after the schism in Genesee Yearly Meeting, Mary Ann M'Clintock, Lucretia Mott, Martha Coffin Wright, and Elizabeth Cady Stanton met at the house of Richard and Jane Hunt in Waterloo and there drafted a call for a woman's rights convention, to be held on 19–20 July 1848 at Seneca Falls. A few days later Stanton and the M'Clintocks met at the M'Clintock home to prepare a "Declaration of Sentiments." This document used the Declaration of Independence as a model and declared, "We hold these truths to be self-evident, that all men and women are created equal." At the convention itself, Thomas, Mary Ann, and their daughters, Elizabeth and Mary Ann, Jr., all listed their names in support of the Declaration of Sentiments, the largest nuclear family group to do so. Stanton later recalled that Thomas "was among the first to append his name to the declaration of rights issued at Seneca Falls, and he did not withdraw it when the press began to ridicule the proceedings of the Convention" (Stanton, *History*, vol. 1, p. 539). Mary Ann, Jr., was secretary of the convention; Thomas chaired the evening session on the second day; and both Elizabeth and Mary Ann, Jr., gave speeches and acted as ushers at the meeting. The M'Clintocks also helped organize the second Woman's Rights Convention, held in Rochester on 2–3 August 1848.

Following the convention, Elizabeth M'Clintock and Stanton were "intimate friends for several years" (Stanton, *Woman's Journal* 27 [1896]: 373), and together they wrote newspaper articles to refute critiques of women's rights. Elizabeth M'Clintock, a clerk in her father's drugstore, braved ridicule in 1849 in her attempt to find employment in the wholesale silk business in Philadelphia. Mary Ann, Jr., married James Truman, a dentist who was active with the Progressive Friends in Pennsylvania and at Waterloo and in opening the dental profession to women.

In 1856 the M'Clintock family moved to Easton, Pennsylvania, and about 1860 returned to Philadelphia, where Thomas operated a drugstore until 1866. Both Thomas and Mary Ann, Sr., died in Philadelphia.

The historical importance of the M'Clintock family lies primarily in their role in organizing the first Woman's Rights Convention at Seneca Falls. The largest identifiable group among those present at the convention were Congregational Friends, whose most visible leader was Thomas M'Clintock. Of the several Quaker families who attended the convention, the M'Clintocks brought the largest single family of woman's rights supporters. The M'Clintocks were reformers and religious radicals. Before the 1840s their activities had been primarily within the Society of Friends. In the 1840s, and particularly after the schism in Genesee Yearly Meeting in 1848, they came to reject those elements of Quakerism that they saw as sectarian. In the Woman's Rights Convention and the meetings of the Friends of Human Progress, the M'Clintocks were maintaining what they understood to be the traditions of earlier Quakers: a belief of "that of God" in every person, continuing revelation, no hierarchies, and practical Christianity. This was the basis of the rest of their work, and these beliefs influenced other non-Quaker reformers, including Stanton, to maintain a thoroughly egalitarian stance.

• Letters of Thomas M'Clintock are included in the George H. Burr Papers and the Elias Hicks Papers at the Friends Historical Library, Swarthmore College, and the Women's Rights National Historical Park at Seneca Falls, N.Y., has a small collection of M'Clintock family letters c. 1833–1888. For Thomas's role in the Hicksite-Orthodox separation, see H. Larry Ingle, *Quakers in Conflict: The Hicksite Separation* (1986) and "The Hicksite Die Is Cast: A Letter of Thomas McClintock, [*sic*], February 1827," *Quaker History* 75 (1986): 115–22.

Thomas M'Clintock's earliest publication was *Essays on the Observance of a Sabbath* (1822), under the pseudonym "Leland." The controversy over Thomas's editing of George Fox's *Works* (1831) is documented in issues of the *Friend* and the *Friend, or Advocate of Truth*. Thomas's other publications include *Observations on the Articles Published in the Episcopal Recorder* (1837), *Letter . . . to the Association of Friends for Promoting the Abolition of Slavery* (1840), and letters and articles in the *Friend, or Advocate of Truth*, *Liberator*, *National Anti-Slavery Standard*, and *Pennsylvania Freeman*.

Giles B. Stebbins, *Upward Steps of Seventy Years* (1890), pp. 70–71, includes a description of the family. The M'Clintocks' deaths were noted in the *Friends Intelligencer*. The participation of the M'Clintock family in the woman's rights conventions in 1848 is recorded in the printed proceedings and in Elizabeth Cady Stanton et al., *History of Woman Suffrage*, vol. 1 (1888).

CHRISTOPHER DENSMORE
JUDITH WELLMAN

MCLOUGHLIN, John (19 Oct. 1784–3 Sept. 1857), trader, was born in Rivière du Loup, Quebec, Canada, the son of John McLoughlin and Angelique Fraser, farmers. As a child McLoughlin was probably greatly influenced by two uncles, Alexander Fraser, a fur trader with the North West Company, and Simon Fraser, a physician. Following in Simon's footsteps, McLoughlin studied medicine, apprenticing to Dr. James Fisher of Quebec City for four and a half years. In April 1803 McLoughlin was admitted to medical practice by the board of examiners in Montreal.

McLoughlin did not remain in Canada long, however. Instead he entered the fur trade in the service of the North West Company in the summer of 1803. In letters to his family, he indicated the reason for this move was "my own lack of conduct." A man of great temper, McLoughlin, according to family accounts, had fled the country to avoid the wrath of British authorities after a scuffle with a soldier who had crowded or pushed a young woman McLoughlin was escorting into a muddy Quebec street. McLoughlin's first posting with the North West Company was at Fort William, or Kaministiquia, on Lake Superior. There, McLoughlin worked both as a post surgeon and as a fur trader. Although unhappy with his lot in life, McLoughlin did well enough in the service of the North West Company, advancing to the position of wintering partner—spending the winter in fur country—in 1814. McLoughlin was involved in 1816 in the North West Company's violent suppression of Lord Selkirk's Red River Colony, an agricultural colony that blocked the company's cross-country supply lines, and for his part was tried for murder. He was acquitted in October 1818.

Strong rivalry and fierce competition that occasionally erupted into violence marked relations between the North West Company and the Hudson's Bay Company. Beginning in 1820, however, several disgruntled wintering partners, represented by McLoughlin, began to explore the possibility of a merger with the Hudson's Bay Company. The negotiations were undercut by the agents for the North West Company, who negotiated a merger on their own account, without the wintering partners, in March 1821. Although disappointed, McLoughlin, like others in the North West Company, entered the ranks of the Hudson's Bay Company. One of North America's largest and most powerful business concerns, the Hudson's Bay Company had been chartered in 1670 and was granted authority to make and enforce laws, build forts, and maintain military forces to protect trade over a huge territory that included the shores of Hudson Bay, the Arctic, and vast areas of what eventually would become Canada and the United States. The merger with the North West Company now allowed the company to expand to the Pacific Coast.

After the company initially posted McLoughlin as chief factor for the Lac la Pluie district, he was named chief factor of the company's newly established Columbia Department, on the Pacific Coast, in July 1824. It was the first successful permanent British settlement on the west coast of North America. From his headquarters at Fort Vancouver on the north bank of the Columbia River, presently known as Vancouver, Washington, McLoughlin supervised several forts for the next two decades, including a large area that in time ranged from Alaska to Oregon, as well as roving fur-trapping brigades and a fleet of vessels. Each year an annual supply ship arrived from Britain laden with supplies and the "outfits" for trade. Furs from the previous years assembled from throughout the department at Fort Vancouver were bundled and shipped home.

The development of subsidiary agricultural and industrial enterprises by McLoughlin proved a great boon for the company and led to the establishment of a sawmill, a large orchard, and fields that more than adequately met the needs of the Columbia Department. The fort employed a large force of laborers and included a shipyard. Beginning in 1825, vessels were sent north to compete with American ships buying furs from the coastal tribes. Among the vessels built or acquired for the coastal trade was the *Beaver*, which became the first steamship on the pacific coast of North America in 1836. McLoughlin's fleet carried produce grown at Fort Vancouver, salmon netted on the Columbia, and lumber milled at the fort to Alaska for trade with the Russian America Company, as well as to California and the Hawaiian Islands.

The Columbia Department was the scene of competition between the United States and Britain as well as the Hudson's Bay Company and various American traders. While working to monopolize trade with the Indians to the exclusion of American interests, McLoughlin was a generous host to visitors, including U.S. citizens. He actively aided American settlers coming across the Oregon Trail to farm in Oregon's Willamette Valley. It was expected that the Columbia River would be the international boundary. For this reason, Fort Vancouver was located on the north bank. The majority of Americans settling south of the river's banks were thought to be an ideal market for the fort's goods and produce. McLoughlin's extension of credit and sale of supplies brought him the praise of many settlers, leading to his ultimate reputation as the "Father of Oregon," which led to that state's placement of a statue of him in the Capitol Building in Washington, D.C., despite strong antipathy toward the Hudson's Bay Company, which most viewed as a powerful foreign monopoly encroaching on American territory.

McLoughlin's own relationship with the Hudson's Bay Company began to sour in the 1830s over a variety of issues, including a long-standing dispute with George Simpson, the company's North American governor, over the efficiency of fixed outposts versus coasting ships for trade with the Indians. McLoughlin came to favor forts and did what he could to discourage the use of ships over the company's and Simpson's objections and contrary instructions. McLoughlin's generous extension of credit to American settlers also came in for criticism.

McLoughlin's purchase of property at the falls of the Willamette River, which is today's Oregon City, and his construction of a sawmill with company funds but in his own name led to controversy. McLoughlin avowed that the purchase had been for the company, to protect its rights and trade, but in the end he was maneuvered into paying for the property and improvements on his own account and subsequent retirement from the company. Leaving the service of the Hudson's Bay Company in 1846, McLoughlin relocated to Oregon City, where he lived out his days as a private merchant, although he retained his British citizenship. He subdivided lots in Oregon City and began to sell them, but his claim to the property was invalidated by Congress in 1850. McLoughlin remained in possession of his home and land until his death in Oregon City.

McLoughlin took as a common-law wife Marguerite Wadin McKay, a "half breed" widow of Alexander McKay, a fellow North West Company trader, in 1811. McLoughlin's union was one of many "fur trade marriages" between traders and native or part-native women, sanctioned by the various companies, for they improved relations with the native groups. He and his wife had four children in their lifelong union.

McLoughlin was described in 1832 by his superior, George Simpson, as a "bustling active man" who nonetheless "has not the talent of managing the few associates and clerks under his authority." Simpson and others noted his "ungovernable violent temper." In one famous incident, McLoughlin caned the Reverend Herbert Beaver, Fort Vancouver's chaplain, in March 1838, for referring to McLoughlin's wife as a "woman of notoriously loose character" and the doctor's "kept mistress." As George Simpson noted in 1832, McLoughlin was "a man of strict honour and integrity but a great stickler for rights & privileges and sets himself up as a righter of wrongs."

McLoughlin stood 6′4″ with a large mane of snow-white hair and piercing blue eyes and cut a commanding figure with all who knew him. He was known to the Indians of the region as the great white eagle. His legacies include Fort Vancouver, now a reconstructed national historic site in Vancouver, Washington, and a voluminous correspondence, which chronicles much of the initial European and American development of the Pacific Northwest.

• Most of McLoughlin's papers are in the Hudson's Bay Company Archives in the Manitoba Provincial Archives, Winnipeg. A collection of 118 family and personal letters, dating from 1806 to 1849, are in the collection of the McLoughlin Society in Oregon City. Many were edited and published by Jane Lewis Chapin in the *Oregon Historical Quarterly* 36 (1935): 32–37 and 37 (1936): 45–75, 294–300. The majority of his business letters were published in *McLoughlin's Fort Vancouver Letters*, ed. E. E. Rich (3 vols., 1941), and cover the period 1825–1846. Other Hudson's Bay Company letters by McLoughlin in the Oregon Historical Society's collection were edited by Burt Brown Barker as *Letters of John McLoughlin, Written at Fort Vancouver, 1829–1832* (1948). Another McLoughlin letterbook, in the collection of the National Park Service, Fort Vancouver National Historic Site, was edited by William R. Sampson and published as *John McLoughlin's Business Correspondence, 1847–48* (1973). A second group of his papers is *The Financial Papers of Dr. John McLoughlin, Being the Record of his Estate and of his Proprietary Accounts with the North West Company (1811–1821) and the Hudson's Bay Company (1821–1868*), ed. Barker (1949).

The story of McLoughlin's entry into the fur trade is analyzed by Dorothy Morrison and Jean Morrison in "John McLoughlin: Reluctant Fur Trader," *Oregon Historical Quarterly* 81 (1980): 377–89. There are several dated biographies of McLoughlin and many highly romanticized accounts. Among the better treatments are Richard Gill, *The White-Headed Eagle: John McLoughlin, Builder of an Empire* (1934), and Dorothy Morrison, *The Eagle and the Fort: The Story of John McLoughlin* (1979). The best biography is by W. Kaye Lamb and appears as the introductory essay in *McLoughlin's Fort Vancouver Letters*.

JAMES P. DELGADO

MCLOUGHLIN, Maurice Evans (7 Jan. 1890–10 Dec. 1957), tennis player, was born in Carson City, Nevada, the son of George McLoughlin, an employee and later superintendent of machinery in U.S. mints, and Harriet Verrill. He developed an attacking "big game" style of play on San Francisco's asphalt courts that led to his winning the Junior Parks Championship in 1906. McLoughlin captured the Pacific Coast and San Francisco championships in 1907 and the 1909 National Interscholastic Tournament. After graduating from Lowell High School in San Francisco in 1909, he was accepted into the University of California but decided to pursue a tennis career instead.

McLoughlin's cannonball serves, top-spin groundstrokes hit with a heavy western grip, and nonstop net attacks adapted well to tennis on eastern turf courts. He advanced to the All-Comers final in his first attempt in the men's singles championship, but lost to Bill Clothier, who exploited his backhand weakness.

McLoughlin's entry into and success in the elite, upper-class sport of tennis in the early 1900s caused quite a sensation. With the notable exception of a few Californians like May Sutton, easterners had dominated the game, because only they had access to tournaments at private country clubs and the financial resources and time to participate. In 1912 he proved that a person from the middle class could win the national men's singles championship by playing vigorously rather than at a slower pace. He became a crowd favorite as his spectacular style of dash and power popularized tennis by attracting to the sport well-conditioned male players who wanted to hit the ball hard.

Besides repeating as national singles champion in 1913, he teamed with Thomas Bundy to win doubles titles in 1912–1914. In 1911 McCloughlin lost in the singles finals to William Larned, in 1914 to Richard Williams, and in 1915 to William Johnston. He was a runner-up in the doubles finals in 1909, 1915, and 1916. Between 1909 and 1915 he achieved top-ten rankings, while in 1912–1914 he held the number one position.

In his first Davis Cup play in 1909, he captained the team that lost to Australia. He achieved overall records of 9–4 in singles and 3–4 in doubles in eight Davis Cup competitions in 1909, 1911, 1913, and 1914. His most spectacular Davis Cup performance occurred in the inaugural international match played at Forest Hills, New York, in 1914. McLoughlin won a service-dominated 17–15 first set from Australia's Norman Brookes in one of the more dramatic and acclaimed matches ever. Although McLoughlin defeated Brookes and, the next day, Anthony Wilding, the United States failed to recapture the Davis Cup.

McLoughlin advanced to the finals only to lose to Wilding in his only appearance at the All-England Championships at Wimbledon in 1913, yet his style of play and sunny disposition made him a crowd favorite.

Due to the loss of his cannonball serves, whirlwind speed, and punch on his strokes, an attempted comeback in 1919 met with little success, causing him to retire. For McLoughlin, tennis was replaced by real estate and other businesses, including service in the navy in 1917 during World War I and work with the War Production Board, War Assets Administration, and North American Aviation Corporation. In 1918 he married Helen Mears. They settled in Pasadena and had three children. He was named to the Citizens Savings Athletic Foundation in 1913 and enshrined in the International Tennis Hall of Fame in 1957. He died in Hermosa Beach, California.

The first male national tennis champion from the West, McLoughlin earned the nickname "California Comet" because he introduced the big game to tennis. He showed that tennis could be rugged and strenuous and available to all on public courts, thereby helping to take the sport to the masses.

• McLoughlin wrote *Tennis as I Play It*, an instructional book published in 1915. His career is best described in Parke Cummings, *American Tennis—The Story of a Game and Its People* (1957); Allison Danzig and Peter Schwed, eds., *The Fireside Book of Tennis* (1972); Will Grimsley, *Tennis: Its History, People and Events* (1971); Paul Metzler, *Tennis Styles and Stylists* (1969); Robert Minton, *Forest Hills* (1975); and *Fifty Years of Lawn Tennis in the United States* (1931), published by the United States Lawn Tennis Association. An obituary is in the *New York Times*, 17 Dec. 1957.

ANGELA LUMPKIN

MCMAHON, Brien (6 Oct. 1903–28 July 1952), U.S. senator, was born James O'Brien McMahon in Norwalk, Connecticut, the son of William H. McMahon, a prosperous builder, and Eugenie J. O'Brien. Both parents were Irish Catholic immigrants. He graduated from Fordham, a New York Jesuit university, in 1924 and Yale Law School in 1927. In 1933, after six years with a Norwalk law firm, he became a special assistant to Attorney General Homer S. Cummings, a Connecticut Democrat. From 1935 to 1939, as assistant attorney general, he headed the Justice Department's Criminal Division. He prosecuted many important cases, successfully arguing twenty-one of them before the Supreme Court. His most important case involved the Harlan County, Kentucky, Coal Operators Association whom he prosecuted in 1938 for intimidating union organizers, a violation of federal labor law. Although the case ended with a hung jury, the operators soon signed a contract with the United Mine Workers union. Leaving government in 1939, McMahon practiced law in Norwalk and Washington, D.C., for five years. In 1940 he married Rosemary Turner, with whom he had one child.

McMahon became increasingly active in Democratic politics in Connecticut (a state with many Catholic voters where his religion proved an asset), and in 1944 he was elected to the U.S. Senate. A strong supporter of President Franklin D. Roosevelt's internationalist policies, he successfully portrayed his Republican opponent as an isolationist. As senator, McMahon unfailingly backed President Harry S. Truman's Fair Deal reform program, including the Employment Act of 1946, aid to education, public housing, and civil-rights legislation. A supporter of efforts to contain Soviet expansionism, he also voted for the Marshall Plan and the North Atlantic Treaty Organization.

McMahon's most notable service was in molding U.S. atomic energy policy, initially as an opponent of the proposed May-Johnson Bill. This measure, drafted by the War Department and introduced in October 1945, two months after the atomic bombing of Hiroshima and Nagasaki, would have assigned the nation's atomic program to the military under a strict blanket of secrecy. A group of atomic scientists quickly organized a campaign against May-Johnson, calling instead for civilian control of atomic energy. Seizing the moment, McMahon mastered the issues and introduced legislation establishing a Special Committee on Atomic Energy. The bill passed in October, and McMahon, though a newcomer, became chair of the special committee.

Then, in December 1945, McMahon introduced an alternative to the May-Johnson Bill authorizing the establishment of a civilian Atomic Energy Committee. Chairman of the special committee, McMahon used the hearings as a forum for advocates of civilian control. These hearings, wrote the League of Women Voters, offered "the first bright hope" that legislators could "meet the challenge of the atomic age." Sensing the shift of opinion, President Truman endorsed McMahon's Bill. Support for civilian control, however, wavered early in 1946, when British authorities arrested physicist Alan Nunn May as a Soviet spy. McMahon responded by working with the Republican minority leader, Senator Arthur Vandenberg of Michigan, to toughen his original bill. The resulting Atomic Energy Act of 1946, commonly called the McMahon Act, created a civilian Atomic Energy Commission (AEC) to be appointed by the president and confirmed by the Senate. A military liaison committee was also established with power over bomb production and authority to review all AEC decisions and to appeal them directly to the president if it chose. The law, in addition, created a permanent Joint Congressional Committee on Atomic Energy. As a member of this body from the outset, and its chairman in 1946–1947 and again from 1949 to 1952, McMahon shaped atomic-energy policy. He presided over the confirmation hearings of Truman's AEC appointees, including chairman David E. Lilienthal. McMahon initially supported the international control of atomic energy and urged a policy of maximum openness. As late as January 1949, while addressing the Detroit Economics Club, he deplored the military's monopoly on atomic-bomb production and information as a threat to democracy.

The Soviet Union's atomic-bomb test of September 1949, however, jolted McMahon profoundly. He now lobbied President Truman to authorize research on the hydrogen bomb, or "Super," a weapon a thousand times more powerful than the atomic bomb. To Lilienthal he expressed the view that only a preemptive nuclear attack on Russia could prevent World War III. His committee exhorted the AEC to show "boldness [and] initiative" and spend any sum necessary "[to] maintain our [nuclear] preeminence." McMahon's staff assistant William L. Borden, a fervent anticommunist, buttressed the senator's growing militance.

When the AEC's scientific panel, the General Advisory Committee (GAC), chaired by J. Robert Oppenheimer, opposed research on the Super, McMahon was dismayed. The GAC's position, he wrote physicist Edward Teller, "just makes me sick." In a November 1949 memorandum to President Truman, drafted by Borden, McMahon attacked the GAC's "false, horror-inspired logic" and urged an "all-out effort" to build the hydrogen bomb. In this impassioned 5,000-word document, he pointed out the H-bomb's strategic advantages ("a Super might miss its target by ten miles or more and still serve the purpose intended") and found no "moral dividing line" between it and any other weapon. "If we let Russia get the Super first," he proclaimed, "catastrophe becomes all but certain." While still professing to support disarmament as a long-term goal, he ridiculed a call by physicists Enrico Fermi and Isidor Rabi for a renewed diplomatic effort to restrain the nuclear arms race. While many considerations undoubtedly underlay Truman's January 1950 approval of the hydrogen-bomb project, McMahon's role was crucial.

McMahon's hawkishness did not spare him from becoming a target of the anticommunist crusader Senator Joseph R. McCarthy. Despite McCarthy's attacks, however, he won a second Senate term in 1950. Continuing to press for an ever-larger thermonuclear arsenal, McMahon declared in 1951 that the United States needed "thousands and thousands" of nuclear weapons. In a May 1952 memo to Truman, he called for accelerated H-bomb production.

A shrewd and ambitious politician, McMahon clearly had presidential aspirations, possibly intending to seek the Democratic nomination in 1952. But a fatal cancer intervened, and he died that July in Washington.

Within months of his arrival in the Senate, Brien McMahon had won celebrity by focusing on atomic energy at a moment when this issue dominated the national consciousness. Having initially opposed the militarization of the atom in 1945–1946, by 1949 he was beating the drums for a vast nuclear buildup. In this progression, he both mirrored and contributed to the evolution of American public opinion and of Washington's early Cold War atomic policy. One can only speculate about his career had he lived. Eight years after his death, John F. Kennedy achieved what many had anticipated for McMahon: election as the first Roman Catholic president of the United States.

• The Library of Congress holds a small collection of McMahon papers from 1943 to his death. McMahon's role in atomic policymaking is covered in the first two volumes of Richard G. Hewlett et al., *History of the United States Atomic Energy Commission*, vol. 1 (1962) and vol. 2 (1969). See also John Newhouse, *War and Peace in the Nuclear Age* (1989); McGeorge Bundy, *Danger and Survival: Choices about the Bomb in the First Fifty Years* (1988); Alice Kimball Smith, *A Peril and a Hope: The Scientists' Movement in America, 1945–1947* (1965); Herbert York, *The Advisors: Oppenheimer, Teller, and the Superbomb* (1976); Paul Boyer, *By the Bomb's Early Light: American Thought and Culture at the Dawn of the Atomic Age* (1985); and Benjamin P. Deutsch, "Conviction and Ambition: Senator Brien McMahon and the Politics of Atomic Energy" (M.A. thesis, Univ. of Wisconsin-Madison, 1989). The memoirs, biographies, and diaries of many public figures of the day, including Harry S. Truman, Dean Acheson, J. Robert Oppenheimer, and David E. Lilienthal contain material on McMahon. An obituary is in the *New York Times*, 29 July 1952.

PAUL BOYER

MCMAIN, Eleanor Laura (2 Mar. 1868–12 May 1934), social service worker, was born near Baton Rouge, Louisiana, the daughter of Jacob West McMain, a dean of Louisiana State University, and Jane Josephine Walsh. She was born into the circumstances of economic hardship which beset many formerly prosperous Southern families after the Civil War, but her parents subscribed to the best periodicals and provided their daughter with the finest education locally available for girls. She learned to appreciate outdoor activities, through playing with her numerous brothers, and nurtured her younger siblings. A generally cheerful child, she encountered grief at the age of ten, when her six-year-old sister died during a yellow fever epidemic.

Sometimes called "the Jane Addams of New Orleans," McMain had special skill with children. Beginning her career at the age of eighteen as a governess, she later became a kindergarten teacher and coprincipal of a New Orleans Free Kindergarten Association school. She was appointed head resident of Kingsley Settlement House in 1901. (Settlement houses were community resource centers, funded and staffed by generous upper- and middle-class Americans, where poor European immigrants could be helped to assimilate into modern urban society.) In 1902 she established a summer vacation day camp, Onward City, as well as a year-round supervised playground. The three slogans she chose for the summer day-campers were: "Everything to Help and Nothing to Hinder. Each for All and All for Each. I Must Do My Part." She firmly believed that these children of poverty-stricken, problem-filled families could learn positive values, self-esteem, and habits of cooperative citizenship under the guidance of adult workers at the settlement house. The day camp later evolved into a residential camp.

In addition to her work at Kingsley House, McMain was appointed to serve on the board of governors of the State Milne Home for Girls in 1904. She was an active participant in the New Orleans Women's League, becoming its first president in 1905. The league worked for a variety of social reforms, including improved tenement housing, sanitation, educational campaigns to fight tuberculosis and yellow fever, compulsory state public education, protective legislation for working women and children, and woman suffrage.

After spending the year 1912 studying social work at the University of Chicago, McMain was offered the directorship of a Chicago settlement house. She declined this proposal, as she did later requests from Detroit and Cleveland. Stimulated by her year of study, she joined a psychology professor at Newcomb Women's College in New Orleans in teaching a social work course in 1913. The following year she established the Southern School of Social Science and Public Service on the Kingsley House premises for the purpose of training professional social workers. However, funds were tight, and after Tulane University opened a school of social science in 1920, the task of training social workers shifted there. McMain took part in the New Orleans Central Council of Social Agencies since its inception in 1921 and served as its president in 1927. The council was successful in establishing a community chest fund and in coordinating welfare efforts throughout the city.

The settlement house grew under McMain's leadership, constantly adding new classes and programs for the surrounding population. Among the activities were a hot-lunch service for working women, a dispensary (health clinic) for women and children, an infant and preschool day nursery, outreach training in well-baby care for mothers (stressing nutrition and sanitation), music and drama classes, a circulating library and reading room, interest clubs, home visits for elderly and sick neighbors, public health initiatives, and organized competitive sports. When a newspaper article referred to her community as "the New Orleans slums," McMain wrote in their defense, "The Kingsley House people have a splendid record of loyal service, of unselfish devotion to their churches, to Kingsley House, to their schools. They have given their time and money to every good neighborhood endeavor. . . . People with such a record as this cannot be called 'slum people,' nor their children 'slum children'" (Dubroca, p. 116).

Beloved by those with whom she worked, McMain was the recipient of many honors. These included the *Times-Picayune* Loving Cup in 1918, selection as adviser to help establish a settlement house in Paris in 1923, and the naming of a public high school in her honor in 1930. Her warmth, insight, empathy, good humor, courage, determination, and dedication were noted in tributes paid to her.

Kingsley House operations were outgrowing the building when, in 1924, a generous citizen donated money for improved facilities. An old cotton press plant was purchased five blocks from the original site, and a beautiful new settlement opened in 1925. The move inspired McMain to write a brief history of the settlement house from its beginning in 1896.

McMain suffered numerous relapses of the malaria she had first contracted in 1909, and her health became noticeably worse during her sixties. Though forced gradually to curtail her responsibilities as her condition worsened, she kept her title and spent her last days in the care of friends at Kingsley House. An energetic and innovative administrative social worker and reformer, Eleanor McMain was instrumental in launching the field of social work in the southern United States.

• Unpublished papers, scrapbooks, and photographs concerning McMain's tenure are kept in the Kingsley House Records, 1899–1970, Special Collections, Tulane University Library, New Orleans. For a descriptive narrative of Kingsley House activities under McMain's leadership, see Isabelle Dubroca, *Good Neighbor Eleanor McMain of Kingsley House* (1955). An obituary is in the *New Orleans Times-Picayune*, 13 May 1934.

REBECCA MORROW-NYE

MCMANUS, George (23 Jan. 1884–22 Oct. 1954), cartoonist, was born in St. Louis, Missouri, the son of George McManus, a theater manager, and Kathrine Kenrick. Young George was working as an office boy in the art department of the *St. Louis Republic* by the time he was fourteen, and soon he was doing the sort of graphic reportage that newspaper artists did before photographs could be reproduced—drawing hangings and scenes of murders and other disasters. In 1903, acting on a bootblack's tip, McManus bet $100 on a horse running 30-to-1, and when he won, he used the money to go to New York, where he eventually found a job at Joseph Pulitzer's *New York World*. As a staff cartoonist, McManus produced a considerable share of his paper's cartoon artwork. He drew several short-lived comic strips—*Snoozer*, *The Merry Marceline*, *Ready Money Ladies*, *Cheerful Charlie*, *Panhandle Pete*, *Let George Do It*, and *Nibsy the Newsboy in Funny Fairyland*, an imitation of Winsor McCay's *Little Nemo in Slumberland* (sometimes filling most of the Sunday edition with his work)—and then hit his stride in 1904 with *The Newlyweds*. McManus's insights into married life were mostly vicarious; not until December 1910 did he marry concert singer Florence Bergère. *The Newlyweds* attracted the attention of Pulitzer's adversary in the city's celebrated circulation war, William Randolph Hearst, who lured McManus to his *Journal American* in 1912. For Hearst, McManus reincarnated his *Newlyweds* as *Their Only Child*. He also did *Rosie's Beau* before finding his forte with *Bringing Up Father*, a gag strip that pitted the unaffected low-brow desires of Jiggs against Maggie's vaulting social pretensions in an epic comedy of husband-and-wife strife that would outlast its creator.

The strip everyone called "Jiggs" or "Maggie and Jiggs" began under its proper title on 2 January 1913, inspired by a play that McManus had seen in 1895 as a youth in St. Louis. *The Rising Generation* dramatized the trials and tribulations of an Irish laborer who had struck it rich and moved to Fifth Avenue. In the Irishman's uninhibited naturalness (of which his socially ambitious wife and daughter were ashamed) and in his consequent unflagging desire to escape (for however brief a time) from the pretensions of the social world into which his wealth had thrust him was the quintessential Jiggs. Jiggs's dilemma became central to most of the strip's humor and embodied the theme of the immigrant experience in America—the ascent out of the poverty of the Old World into the relative prosperity of the New World.

Jiggs's abiding affection for a game of cards, a drink, the fellowship of his old cronies at Dinty Moore's corner saloon, for corned beef and cabbage (the strip's ubiquitous symbol of a simpler, more natural life), and for eyeing pretty girls cast him forever in opposition to his wife Maggie's tyrannical efforts to reform him, to force him to adopt tastes and habits appropriate to the dignity of their new status and to her parvenu social aspirations. The comedy arose from the extremes to which Jiggs went to escape from Maggie's world to Dinty Moore's: when she locked him in his room, he'd slip out the window and creep along a cornice twenty stories above the ground, then make his way to the skyscraper next door by means of a balancing act along a telephone wire, descending to the street at last on a swinging steel girder. In Jiggs's unrelenting effort to escape and in Maggie's frequent failure to live up to her own pretensions, we find the seemingly inexhaustible elaboration on the theme that people will be themselves—and that they are the better for so being, regardless of social ambitions. It was, as countless immigrants had found, the message of America. In one of the oft-repeated reversals in the strip, Maggie invariably found that Jiggs was already the intimate companion of some social lion whom she wanted him to meet. And Jiggs had done it by being himself. (Jiggs, incidentally, is a wholly made-up name, McManus once reported—neither first nor last, "and I don't know which its owner prefers it to be.")

When they first appeared, Jiggs and Maggie were the same size, and Jiggs had the build of the hod carrier he had formerly been. But during their first decade, McManus shrank his hero for comic contrast with his wife and to enhance the humor of the strip's most frequent refrain at the punchline—the hail of crockery around Jiggs's ears that proclaimed Maggie's discovery of his latest departure from the path of propriety. After that modification, the strip changed very little, its simple formula repeated with infinite variations throughout the remaining years of McManus's 41-year tenure.

McManus had a marvelously inventive graphic imagination, which he displayed in some of the most elegant penmanship in cartooning. His line was fine and delicate, and once his style matured (by the mid-1920s), *Bringing Up Father* was distinguished by the copiously decorative detail in rococo backgrounds and ornate props—the filigree of a city skyline, the graceful curlicues in the design of a stair railing or of the pattern in Maggie's dress—and by the judicious and telling placement of solid blacks. His tricks with silhouette were striking: in one of Jiggs, the solid black was always accented by the stark white of his shirt collar and cuffs. But McManus also simply "drew funny." No one could surpass him in depicting the hilarious aspect of an unlettered Irish laborer attired in his Sunday best, celluloid collar choking him to such an extent that his ears stand straight out from his head. Other noteworthy aspects of the strip include the gently self-mocking humor of nostalgic reminiscences on Sundays ("Remember, Maggie me darlin', when we kids used to call at the Chinese laundry to get your daddy's shirts—I mean, shirt—and how we envied Jerry McGuire when he had the mumps and didn't have to go to school . . . ") and McManus's comic innovation of putting on the walls pictures in which the figures had miniature lives of their own and emerged beyond the picture frames in their antics, sometimes tossing things from one picture to another.

In 1931 McManus moved to Santa Monica, California, for his wife's health; she remained an invalid most of their married life. McManus died in Santa Monica of hepatitis; the strip was continued by others.

A convivial, short, heavyset man who consumed cigars at the rate of three dozen a day, McManus was often assumed to be himself the model for Jiggs. The cartoonist acknowledged similarities: "Jiggs and I enjoy being ourselves. Hedda Hopper wrote once that I draw Jiggs the way I want to be myself. Maybe. Anyway, we both like people. We like restaurants and round tables, with people sitting around them enjoying themselves." McManus might have been summarizing the appeal of his strip. It was about people enjoying themselves by being themselves, a message McManus dinned into his readers for nearly two generations in a vivid demonstration of the power of the single-situation comedy that so often characterized early comic strips.

• The first year of *Bringing Up Father* is reprinted in a volume of that title by Hyperion Press (1977), with a useful introduction by Bill Blackbeard. A sampling of Sunday pages in color can be found in *Jiggs Is Back* (1986), and a representative selection from the entire run of the strip (albeit with an emphasis on the vintage years of the 1930s and 1940s) is contained in *Bringing Up Father*, ed. Herb Galewitz (1973). Biographical information on McManus is in a three-part article he wrote with Henry La Cossit for *Collier's* in 1952, "Jiggs and I," which appeared in the issues for 19 Jan., pp. 9–11, 66–67; 26 Jan., pp. 24–25, 67–69; and 2 Feb., pp. 30–31, 39, 41.

ROBERT C. HARVEY

MCMASTER, James Alphonsus (1 Apr. 1820–29 Dec. 1886), journalist and Catholic polemicist, was born in Duanesburg, New York, the son of Gilbert MacMaster, a strict covenant Presbyterian minister, and Jane Brown. Along with his two brothers, James studied the classics and the Bible at home in preparation for the ministry. He completed two years (1838–1839) at Union College in Schenectady, New York, and he then entered Columbia College in 1839 to study law. In 1840 McMaster began studies for the Episcopal ministry at New York City's General Theological Seminary.

The Anglican Tractarian Movement, which provided public tracts expressing the Catholic leanings of the Oxford (Eng.) Movement's leaders, had reached America's shores and inspired certain seminarians at General Theological to aspire to an "American Oxford Movement." A concerned administration enforced a close supervision of the seminary students for evidence of Romanizing influences. McMaster, increasingly interested in Roman Catholicism, protested the scrutiny and was dismissed in 1844.

Under the tutelage of the Redemptorist Gabriel Rumpler and Bishop John McCloskey, McMaster converted to Catholicism in 1845. Like other American converts to Catholicism in the mid-nineteenth century, he found in the Roman church a concrete expression of the romantic impulse to join the individual and communal, the material and spiritual, in a synthetic unity and an institutional counter to a perceived religious banality of mainline liberal Protestantism.

Joining two other noteworthy American Catholic converts, namely Clarence A. Walworth and Isaac T. Hecker, McMaster traveled to St.-Trond, Belgium, intending to be ordained as a Redemptorist. On the way he stopped in Littlemore, England, to visit with John Henry Newman, a pivotal figure in the Oxford Movement and convert to Roman Catholicism in 1845. Early in his novitiate with the Redemptorists he and his superiors concluded that he was not suited for a priestly vocation. In 1846 he returned to New York City, penniless and with no hope of familial assistance.

To support himself, McMaster began writing for the *New York Tribune* and the *New York Freeman's Journal and Catholic Register*, the New York Catholic diocesan paper. Journalism quickly became his primary vocation. Using money borrowed from George V. Hecker, the brother of his former companion Isaac, in 1848 McMaster purchased Archbishop John Hughes's shares of the *Freeman's Journal* and became the sole owner of the newspaper. For nearly forty years McMaster's newspaper served as a national organ for militant Catholicism as well as a northern voice defending the Democratic party's prosouthern platform. McMaster feared no opponent, from the U.S. president to the local archbishop, and he employed incendiary language as often as he thought necessary.

McMaster married Gertrude Fetterman in 1856, and they had seven children, four of whom survived to adulthood. The three daughters joined religious orders.

McMaster's national notoriety as a political pundit peaked in 1861 with his denunciation of the policies of the newly elected president, Abraham Lincoln. An outspoken proponent of states' rights and a foe of abolition, McMaster decried Lincoln's summons for men to form a Union army. The U.S. postmaster general declared the *Freeman's Journal* seditious and treasonous and prevented any national mailing from 24 August 1861 to 19 April 1862. McMaster was imprisoned from 16 September through 23 October 1861 at Fort Lafayette, located on Hendrick's Reef in New York City's harbor. His release came without a trial.

McMaster depicted himself as the courageous advocate of freedom of the press and continued denouncing Lincoln's policies, including the 1863 Emancipation Proclamation. Expressing obviously racist views, McMaster linked the 1863 compulsory draft laws with the Proclamation, which had immediately preceded the conscription legislation. He articulated the deep resentment generated by racial and class conflict felt particularly by poor Irish immigrants unable to pay the $300 to free themselves from military obligation. McMaster's 1863 editorials fueled an anger that erupted into a four-day riot in New York City.

Catholics, lay and clergy, also became the butt of McMaster's vituperative rhetoric. He found especially distasteful any Catholic whom he judged to be willing to compromise the faith in favor of modernity. He castigated other lay Catholic journalists and apologists who demonstrated any "liberal" tendencies, including Orestes Brownson, Denis Sadlier, and Thomas D'Arcy McGee.

Among the causes McMaster continually championed was the founding of Catholic schools. He therefore lent strong support to New York archbishop John Hughes in his battle with the New York State legislature to gain the same financial aid for Catholic schools as that given to the Protestant-run common schools. On other issues, however, especially concerning the Union army's drafting of Irish immigrants, Hughes distanced himself from McMaster's acrimonious editorials. After the Civil War and Hughes's death, McMaster continued his battle against the "Godless" public schools.

McMaster expressed his Catholic allegiance through an absolute loyalty to the papacy. He articulated an extreme ultramontane position in defense of papal infallibility and strongly protested the end of the papacy's temporal powers that came about with the success of the Italian unification movement. McMaster criticized less enthusiastic American bishops in attendance at the First Vatican Council (1868–1869), and he censured the secular press for accounts that either trivialized the council's proceedings or disseminated misinformation concerning its decisions.

McMaster's unyielding defense of a centralized papal authority did not extend to defending absolute episcopal powers. Using the pseudonym "Jus," McMaster wrote a series of letters defending clergy's rights as found in canon law and reproaching bishops who acted as despots in their diocese, ignoring priests' canonical rights. His criticism placed him at odds with such influential bishops as John Lancaster Spalding and Bernard McQuaid.

McMaster's fearless apologetics for a thoroughly Roman Catholicism in the United States, coupled with his tenacious defense of political views shared by many poor white immigrants, made him a potent journalistic force in the second half of the nineteenth century. He died in Brooklyn, New York.

• McMaster's papers are located in the archives of the University of Notre Dame, South Bend, Ind. A useful biography is M. A. Kwitchen, *James Alphonsus McMaster* (1949); see also Maurice F. Egan, "A Slight Appreciation of James Alphonsus McMaster," U.S. Catholic Historical Society, *Historical Records and Studies* 15 (1921). The Oxford movement that shaped McMaster's early life is discussed in Clarence A. Walworth's *Oxford Movement in America* (1895). An obituary is in the *New York Herald*, 30 Dec. 1886.

SANDRA YOCUM MIZE

MCMICHEN, Clayton (26 Jan. 1900–3 Jan. 1970), country music fiddler, singer, and composer, was born in Allatoona, Georgia, some forty miles northeast of Atlanta. His family was from a Scots-Irish clan who had been in the area since the 1790s and had absorbed many of the Anglo-American folk-music styles in the area, from shape-note religious singing to playing the fretless banjo. McMichen's own father was what he called "one of those sophisticated Irish violin players" who could read music and play anything from breakdowns to light classics, and young McMichen grew up listening to a wide variety of music. As a youth, McMichen was determined to make his living as an automobile mechanic but was soon drawn into trying to make a living by fiddling.

By 1914 Atlanta had become a center of old-time fiddling, with a national contest held annually at the old municipal auditorium; young McMichen found himself involved in these. About the same time he met another young fiddler, Marcus Lowe Stokes, who taught him to play a more modern "long-bow" style of fiddling—a style in which fingering was more important than bow strokes. This new style soon divided the younger Atlanta fiddlers from the older ones, who relied on short strokes, comedy, and trick fiddling. McMichen was determined to take fiddling more seriously and by the late 1910s even organized an association of younger fiddlers to promote long-bow fiddling.

After several years of traveling around the countryside with various itinerant "medicine shows," McMichen settled in Atlanta and in 1922 organized a band called the Home Town Boys to play on the new radio station WSB. This band included the guitarist Riley Puckett as well as violinist Bert Layne and mandolin player Ted Hawkins. They made a handful of records for the OKeh Company in 1925, which led to McMichen's affiliation with Columbia Records the following year. Columbia had made Atlanta its recording center in the South and were holding long sessions there in fall and spring of each year. Noting McMichen's versatility, A & R (artists and repertoire) man Frank Walker began to use him as a studio musician on records and eventually made him a member of a studio band he was forming called the Skillet Lickers. This band began recording in the spring of 1926 and soon was selling more records than any similar group on the early country music scene. Hits like "Bully of the Town," "Pass around the Bottle," and "Watermelon on the Vine" (all 1926) were soon heard on Victrolas across the South. The records featured Puckett's singing and twin fiddle work by McMichen and Gid Tanner. During their five-year recording run, from 1926 to 1931, the Skillet Lickers generated almost 100 sides for Columbia and became the most famous rural string band of the time.

McMichen, however, did not like having to play the rube for these records and felt that Tanner's older mountain fiddling style was incompatible with his. He began to record a series of fiddle solos under his own name, as well as a series of smooth, pop sides under the name McMichen's Melody Men. He also began to write songs and to sing, using the alias "Bob Nichols" on his Columbia sides. One of the biggest hits of the age, in fact, was a sentimental duet he recorded in 1926 with Puckett called "My Carolina Home." He also began working with Jimmie Rodgers, the most popular country act of the time, playing fiddle on his records, touring with him, and writing songs for him, such as "Peach Picking Time in Georgia" (1926).

In 1931 McMichen quit the Skillet Lickers and organized a new, hot, jazz-tinged band called the Georgia Wildcats. He seemed determined to forge a new brand of string-band music, merging the sound of fiddles with the arrangements and solos of swing-era music. "I can't get nothing for my old-time fiddling," he sang on one of his Decca records, "I'm gonna learn to swing." In doing this, he was anticipating the kind of western swing that Bob Wills would later invent, but for a variety of reasons McMichen could not make his work. Throughout the 1930s he worked on various radio stations and made a string of innovative records for Decca (1936–1938), but he had trouble duplicating the success of the Skillet Lickers. He constantly found himself falling back on his old-time fiddling and was named winner of national fiddling contests eighteen times. By the 1940s he was playing over Louisville radio, leading a small Dixieland band with a horn section and well-crafted arrangements.

By the 1950s McMichen was living in semiretirement in Battletown, Kentucky, keeping his hand in by playing at an occasional fiddling contest. During the early 1960s he was rediscovered by students of the folk-music revival and was interviewed and visited by folklorists. He was coaxed into making "comeback" appearances at the University of Illinois and the Newport Folk Festival, but he was disappointed to find that most of the new fans saw him only as a relic of the Skillet Lickers, not of his 1930s innovations. McMichen did, however, receive accolades for the immense influence he had on fiddlers. Along with Grand Ole Opry star Arthur Smith, he dominated the fiddling world of the 1930s. His long-bow style and his repertoire—including such classics as "Down Yonder," "Boil Them Cabbage Down," and "Georgianna Moon"—had an immense impact on southern fiddlers and are still heard in contests today. Still frustrated and somewhat embittered, McMichen died in Battletown.

• McMichen's large scrapbooks and other documents are housed at the Country Music Foundation and Media Center, Nashville, Tenn. For additional information, see Charles Wolfe, "Clayton McMichen: The Reluctant Hillbilly," in *The Devil's Box: Masters of Southern Fiddling* (1996).

CHARLES K. WOLFE

MCMILLAN, Edwin Mattison (18 Sept. 1907–7 Sept. 1991), physicist, was born in Redondo Beach, California, the son of Edwin Harbaugh McMillan, a physician, and Anna Marie Mattison. When he was one year old his family moved to Pasadena, California, where he grew up. In high school he developed a keen appetite for science, which he fed by attending many of the weekly lectures that the California Institute of Technology (Caltech) offered free to the public. In 1924 he matriculated at Caltech, where he studied physics and received his B.S. degree in 1928 and his M.S. degree in 1929. He then enrolled in the graduate physics program at Princeton University, where he studied the ability of an electric field to deflect a molecular beam, a thin stream of subatomic particles directed into a vacuum chamber so that their behavior can be observed more easily.

After receiving his Ph.D. in 1932, McMillan obtained a fellowship from the National Research Council to conduct postdoctoral research at the University of California at Berkeley. In 1934 he was invited to join the staff of the university's newly established Berkeley (now the Lawrence) Radiation Laboratory as a research associate. There he immediately began experimenting with the laboratory's cyclotron, which was invented by Berkeley's Ernest O. Lawrence and M. Stanley Livingston. The device was popularly known as an "atom smasher" because it accelerates subatomic particles to extremely high velocities and then propels them into atomic nuclei in an effort to create an atomic reaction. During the next six years McMillan used the cyclotron to collaborate on the transmutation of aluminum and nitrogen and the creation of radioactive oxygen. He also used it to investigate gamma rays and artificial radioactivity and to observe the effect of bombarding uranium nuclei with neutrons. In 1935 he was appointed an instructor in the Department of Physics and the next year received a promotion to assistant professor.

In the late 1930s McMillan became interested in the work of the Italian physicists Enrico Fermi and Emilio Segrè, who in 1934 bombarded uranium with neutrons in the hope that one or more of the neutrons would fuse to a nucleus and thereby transmute the uranium, which has the highest atomic number of the natural elements, into an artificial element heretofore unknown to science. Whether they succeeded has remained a matter of conjecture, because most if not all of the neutrons were moving too fast to be captured by the uranium nuclei and instead caused nuclear fission, as the German physicists Otto Hahn, Fritz Strassmann, and Lise Meitner demonstrated in 1938 when they attempted to replicate the experiment. In 1940 McMillan and Philip H. Abelson, in an effort to shed further light on the Fermi-Segrè experiment, used the cyclotron to bombard uranium oxide with neutrons and in the process created and identified for the first time an element with an atomic number of 93, one higher than uranium. This element, a silvery metal named neptunium after the planet Neptune, was the first artificial element created. The discovery inspired researchers the world over, who proceeded to create another fifteen transuranium elements between 1940 and 1984. It also led to McMillan's promotion to associate professor in 1941 and earned for him a share of the 1951 Nobel Prize for chemistry.

After the discovery of neptunium, McMillan took a leave of absence to conduct research on the development of airborne microwave radar at the Radiation Laboratory at the Massachusetts Institute of Technology. In 1941 he married Elsie Walford Blumer, with whom he had three children, and became affiliated with the U.S. Navy's Radio and Sound Laboratory in San Diego, California, where he participated in the wartime application of sonar and microwave radar. In 1942 he joined the Manhattan Project and for the next three years he participated in the development of the first atomic bomb at the Los Alamos Science Laboratory.

McMillan returned to Berkeley after World War II and immediately set out to develop a second generation of cyclotrons. This device accelerates subatomic particles by means of an electromagnetic field; however, as a particle's velocity approaches the speed of light, its mass increases and it decelerates, causing it to lag behind the field's oscillating electric impulses and disappear into the cyclotron. In an effort to remove the "speed limit" at which particles in a conventional cyclotron could travel, he synchronized the electromagnetic field so that the oscillating impulses slow down as the mass of the particles increases, thereby permitting the particles to keep pace with the field. This modified cyclotron, known as a synchrocyclotron, led to his promotion to full professor in 1946 and earned for him a share of the Ford Motor Company's Atoms for Peace Award in 1963.

In 1954 McMillan became the associate director of Berkeley's laboratory; four years later he was promoted to director, a position he held until his retirement in 1973. In addition to his teaching and research duties at Berkeley, he served as a member of the General Advisory Committee of the Atomic Energy Commission from 1954 to 1958, the Board of Trustees of Rand Corporation from 1959 to 1969, the Commission on High Energy Physics of the International Union of Pure and Applied Physics from 1960 to 1966, the Science Policy Committee of the Stanford Linear Accelerator Center from 1962 to 1966, the Physics Advisory Committee of the National Accelerator Laboratory from 1967 to 1969, and the Board of Trustees of the Universal Research Association of Washington, D.C., from 1969 to 1974. He was a member of the National Academy of Sciences and served as its chairman from 1968 to 1971. He received the Research Corporation of America's Science Award in 1951 and was a fellow of the American Academy of Arts and Sciences and the American Physical Society. He died in El Cerrito, California.

McMillan made two important contributions to science. His discovery of neptunium led to the discovery of other artificial elements and informed a more nuanced understanding of chemistry and nuclear theory. His development of the synchrocyclotron from the Lawrence-Livingston cyclotron allowed researchers to continue adding to the body of knowledge on the structure and properties of the nucleus and the forces that hold it together.

• McMillan's papers are in the Bancroft Library of the University of California at Berkeley. Biographies are David E. Newton, "Edwin M. McMillan," in *Notable Twentieth-Century Scientists*, ed. Emily McMurray (1995), pp. 1352–53, and "Edwin M. McMillan," in *Nobel Prize Winners*, ed. Tyler Wasson (1987), pp. 683–84. Additional biographical information is in Glenn T. Seaborg, *Man-Made Transuranium Elements* (1963). Obituaries are in the *New York Times*, 9 Sept. 1991, *Newsweek*, 23 Sept. 1991, and *Nature*, 17 Oct. 1991.

CHARLES W. CAREY, JR.

MCMILLAN, James (12 May 1838–10 Aug. 1902), U.S. senator, was born in Hamilton, Ontario, Canada, the son of William McMillan, a railroad official, and Grace MacMeakin. James completed his studies at Hamilton Grammar School and then began his business career as a clerk in a Hamilton hardware store. In 1855, after four years learning the hardware business, he moved to Detroit, where he worked for two years in a wholesale hardware house. Through his father's influence he was named purchasing agent of the Detroit and Milwaukee Railroad. In 1860 he married Mary L. Wetmore; they had six children.

In 1864 McMillan laid the foundation for his future wealth when he joined with three others to found the Michigan Car Company, a manufacturer of railroad cars. This concern spawned such other McMillan enterprises as the Detroit Car Wheel Company, Baugh Steam Forge Company, and Detroit Iron Furnace Company. McMillan was also largely responsible for the construction of the railroads that opened Michigan's Upper Peninsula to commercial development, and he served as president of the Duluth, South Shore, and Atlantic Railroad. Telephone lines, Great Lakes shipping, banks, and street railways were among his other business interests. By the end of the nineteenth century his wealth was estimated at $15 million.

During the late 1870s McMillan became increasingly involved in politics, assuming a place on the Republican State Committee in 1876 and two years later managing the successful congressional campaign of his business partner, John Newberry (1826–1887). In 1886 McMillan became chairman of the Republican State Committee and was forced to confront the factional rivalry among various ambitious party leaders that was undermining GOP strength in Michigan. He responded by reorganizing the party and placing it clearly under his control. Some attacked him as a political boss, and his "machine" was known as the McMillan Alliance. Though he was not a heavy-handed dictator, he did remain in charge of Republican politics in Michigan for the remainder of his life, and he made effective use of patronage to unite the party behind him. During the 1890s reform crusader Hazen S. Pingree challenged McMillan's leadership, serving six years as insurgent mayor of Detroit and then four years as Michigan's governor. McMillan and Pingree remained archfoes within the Republican party until 1900, when McMillan's forces were able to deny their enemy renomination as the state's chief executive.

In 1889 McMillan used his political influence to secure election to the U.S. Senate. Until his death he continued to serve in the Senate, winning reelection twice. In the Senate he earned the respect of his fellow lawmakers and at the time of his death was generally acknowledged to be among the most influential members. He was not a flamboyant figure who persuaded through oratory, but rather he was a genial, modest man who mastered behind-the-scenes negotiation and compromise. McMillan was one of the group of inner-circle Republican senators who met informally and called themselves the School of Philosophy Club. Like most of these GOP leaders, he favored retaining gold as the standard for American currency. As a member of the Senate Naval Affairs Committee he also strongly supported U.S. naval efforts in the Spanish-American War. Moreover, as expected of a senator from Michigan, he secured federal funding to aid Great Lakes shipping.

McMillan's most notable service was as chairman of the Senate's District of Columbia Committee. As such he had a dominant voice in the government of the nation's capital, earning him the informal title of "mayor of Washington." With the approach of the city's centennial in 1900, McMillan led efforts to initiate a program of beautification. This resulted in the creation of the Senate Park Commission, otherwise known as the McMillan Commission, charged with formulating a blueprint for the future development of the District. The commission consisted of architects Daniel Burnham and Charles McKim, landscape architect Frederick Law Olmsted, Jr., and sculptor Augustus Saint-Gaudens. McMillan worked closely with these experts and introduced their plan to the Senate in January 1902. He wholeheartedly supported the commissioners' goal of restoring the original plan for Washington as conceived by Pierre L'Enfant in 1792. McMillan was especially dedicated to removing the railroad tracks from the Mall and creating a new union station northwest of the Capitol. While fighting for acceptance of the "McMillan Plan," the senator died at his summer home in Manchester, Massachusetts.

McMillan was a plutocratic state party boss, the very type despised by the emerging generation of Progressive Era reformers. Yet he was also instrumental in the beautification of Washington, and the McMillan Plan was a model for city beautiful reformers who sought to improve urban life through comprehensive planning. He thus stood at the juncture of the old and the new. He was a remnant of the Gilded Age who ushered in the city planning ideals of the Progressive Era.

• McMillan's papers are in the Burton Historical Collection, Detroit Public Library. For McMillan's role in Michigan politics, see Marie Heyda, "Senator James McMillan and the Flowering of the Spoils System," *Michigan History* 54 (1970): 183–200, and Melvin G. Holli, *Reform in Detroit: Hazen S. Pingree and Urban Politics* (1969). For the work of the McMillan Commission, see Charles Moore, *Daniel H. Burnham: Architect, Planner of Cities* (1921), and John W. Reps, *Monu-*

mental Washington: The Planning and Development of the Capital Center (1967). Obituaries are in the *New York Times* and the *Washington Post*, 11 Aug. 1902.

JON C. TEAFORD

MCMILLIN, Bo (12 Jan. 1895–31 Mar. 1952), college football player and coach, was born Alvin Nugent McMillin in Prairie Hill, Texas, the son of Reuben Thomas McMillin, an employee of a meat-packing firm, and Matilda Riley. His father moved the family to Waco and finally to Fort Worth in 1901. McMillin delayed his high school education because of his father's death in 1911 and his apparent dislike for school. Nicknamed "Bo" by a cousin, he frequently found himself in trouble because of gambling and various boyhood pranks.

His early plans to become a prizefighter were sidetracked by football coach Robert L. "Chief" Meyers of Fort Worth's North Side High School, where McMillin enrolled as a seventeen-year-old freshman in 1912. Meyers persuaded him to pursue sports, in which McMillin excelled. Also competing in baseball, basketball, and track, the 5′9″, 165-pound McMillin became a star quarterback for North Side's football team.

When Meyers accepted a position at his alma mater, Centre College, a tiny Presbyterian men's college in Danville, Kentucky, in 1916, he persuaded McMillin and several other North Side players to follow him to Danville. Because McMillin lacked enough credits to graduate from high school, Meyers arranged for him to spend a year at nearby Somerset High School, where McMillin completed the necessary credits to enroll at Centre in 1917.

McMillin placed little emphasis on his studies at Centre, but immediately he became the star of the football team under coach Charley Moran. Despite an enrollment of only 200 students, Centre lost only one game in 1917 and shocked the football world by defeating Kentucky, 3–0, on the only field goal McMillin ever attempted.

With the outbreak of World War I, McMillin enlisted in the U.S. Naval Reserve in Dallas. Under the federal Student Army Training Corps program, Centre College became a military camp and McMillin was assigned to duty there. The war and an influenza epidemic shortened the 1918 football season. Consequently, players were given an additional year of athletic eligibility.

Centre's "Praying Colonels," so named for their traditional pregame prayer, achieved national prominence in 1919 with an undefeated record, including victories over Indiana and West Virginia. McMillin and two teammates, James "Red" Weaver and James M. "Red" Roberts, were named to Walter Camp's All-America team, and the Helms Athletic Foundation named McMillin as its Player of the Year.

Centre's success attracted the attention of traditional football powers such as Harvard, which scheduled Centre for a game in Cambridge, Massachusetts, in 1920. After playing Harvard even for a half, Centre finally fell, 31–14, in an impressive enough performance to warrant a rematch the following season. The 1921 Harvard-Centre game established McMillin as a football legend. In what the *New York Times* later called the "upset of the century," Centre defeated Harvard, 6–0, on McMillin's 32-yard touchdown run, ending the Crimson's 25-game unbeaten streak. Seen as a symbol of the common man overcoming insurmountable odds, McMillin became the subject of Ralph D. Paine's novel, *First Down Kentucky!* (1921).

McMillin reputedly supported himself early in his college days by wagering on Centre victories and gambling at pool and card games. Because of his importance to the football program and, consequently, to Centre's enrollment, college officials ignored McMillin's indiscretions and allowed him to continue to participate in sports. After the college offered to pay for his tuition and room and board, McMillin's gambling appears to have diminished.

Although McMillin had not graduated from Centre, in 1922 he accepted a head-coaching position at Centenary College in Shreveport, Louisiana; his salary of $8,000 per year was higher than that of the college's president. Also that year he married his high school sweetheart, Marie Myers, with whom he had one child.

In his three years at Centenary, McMillin's teams won 26 games and suffered only 3 losses. While coaching in 1922 and 1923, he also played professional football with the National Football League's Milwaukee Badgers and Cleveland Indians, but only on those weekends when Centenary played a game in the North. Despite McMillin's success, school authorities decided not to renew his contract when a regional accrediting agency objected to his high salary.

After rejecting an offer from Centre, McMillin accepted another high-paying coaching job in 1925 at Geneva College in Beaver Falls, Pennsylvania. His three years at Geneva, another small school, were again successful, as his teams won 22 of 28 games, including a victory over Harvard. By 1928 McMillin was looking for greater challenges and took a coaching post at Kansas State Agricultural College, a much larger school. During his tenure there, McMillin, a widower since 1926, married Kathryn Gillihan in 1930; the couple had four children. While McMillin's Kansas State clubs met with mixed results (his coaching record in six years was 29–21–1), his reputation as an energetic motivator increased.

In 1934 McMillin agreed to coach at Indiana University, where he spent fourteen years. In 1937 he finally received his bachelor's degree from Centre after the college gave him credit for his military service. McMillin achieved his greatest success as a college coach in 1945, when his Hoosiers were undefeated and captured the school's first Western Conference championship. The American Football Coaches Association rewarded McMillin by naming him Coach of the Year. Appreciative Indiana authorities had already given McMillin a lifetime contract, believing his fame and public relations skills benefited the school.

The Detroit Lions of the NFL enticed McMillin into becoming their head coach and general manager in 1948. McMillin's Detroit teams struggled while he built the foundation for championship teams that included future Professional Football Hall of Fame members Bobby Layne and Doak Walker. McMillin never enjoyed the glory of the Lions' championship because difficulties relating to his players led to his dismissal after the 1950 season. He immediately accepted an offer as head coach from the NFL's Philadelphia Eagles but resigned early in the 1951 season because of illness. It was later revealed that McMillin was suffering from stomach cancer. After his resignation, he returned to Bloomington, Indiana, where he died.

McMillan was honored by being named to the Helms Athletic Foundation's Football Hall of Fame and the College Football Hall of Fame as both a player and a coach. The keys to success from his point of view were hard work and self-discipline, themes that he emphasized in his later years as a prominent public speaker. Despite spending most of his career as a coach, McMillin is most remembered as a player, his status in football lore cemented by his stunning touchdown run in Centre's 1921 victory over Harvard.

• For a full-length biography, see Charles W. Akers and John Carter, *Bo McMillin: Man and Legend* (1989). Aspects of McMillin's life and career are featured in John McCallum, *Ivy League Football since 1872* (1977); Allison Danzig, *Oh, How They Played the Game* (1971) and *The History of American Football: Its Great Teams, Players, and Coaches* (1956); W. F. Fox, Jr., and Robert A. Cook, "The Missing Man of the Year," *Saturday Evening Post*, 28 Sept. 1946, pp. 14–15; and Ashton Reid, "Indiana's Bo," *Collier's*, 31 Aug. 1946, pp. 42ff. An obituary is in the *New York Times*, 1 Apr. 1952.

MARC S. MALTBY

MCMINN, Joseph (22 June 1758–17 Nov. 1824), soldier, planter, and governor of Tennessee, was born in Chester County, Pennsylvania, the son of Robert McMinn and Sarah Harlan, farmers. He grew up in Pennsylvania, but as a young man he moved with his wife, Hannah Cooper, whom he had married in 1785, and their only child to Hawkins County, North Carolina (later Tennessee), where at least one other member of his family had settled. He established himself as a planter and soon was commissioned a militia captain in the Southwest Territory, which was created in 1790 to prepare Tennessee for statehood. He was a member of the territorial legislature in 1794 and of the constitutional convention that assembled in Knoxville in 1796 to draft a constitution and a petition to Congress for Tennessee's admission to the Union. McMinn was entrusted by the assembly to deliver the document and petition to national leaders in Philadelphia. Having presented the documents to the secretary of state, he remained in Philadelphia long enough to sit for a portrait by Rembrandt Peale.

After Tennessee's admission to the Union, on 1 June 1796, McMinn was elected to the state senate. He served continuously, except for one term, until 1811 and was chosen as Speaker and lieutenant governor for three sessions, from 1805 to 1811. At that point he determined to retire from public life but soon was persuaded to run for governor. He was elected in 1815 by a large majority over four opponents.

McMinn's greatest claim to recognition lies in his service as governor. His years as Tennessee's chief executive coincided with a period of considerable state growth. The population more than doubled and the number of square miles was increased by 50 percent. The War of 1812 had ended just six months prior to his election, and the mustering out of soldiers sent hordes westward in search of lands. Andrew Jackson's victory at New Orleans in January 1815 focused increased attention on Tennessee and the West and added to the population increase.

The "extinguishment of Indian claims to land lying within the limits of the state," as McMinn expressed it in his inaugural address in 1815, had been a major goal of Tennesseans since President Thomas Jefferson had suggested a decade earlier that Indians residing east of the Mississippi should surrender their lands in exchange for territory in the Louisiana Purchase. At McMinn's insistence, Chickasaws surrendered lands in the south-central part of the state in 1816, 1818, and again in 1819; the "Jackson Purchase" was consummated in 1818 whereby Chickasaw chiefs, for $300,000, vacated the vast "Western District" between the Tennessee and the Mississippi rivers.

Negotiations with the hard-bargaining Cherokee, however, posed a greater problem. In 1816 the federal government appointed McMinn and Jackson as special commissioners to the Cherokee, and they—in the "Jackson-McMinn Treaty"—set aside land on the Arkansas and White rivers for the Cherokee in exchange for lands in Georgia and the Sequatchie Valley of Tennessee. McMinn was able to persuade several thousand members of that tribe to move west, but the majority remained until forcibly removed during Jackson's presidency.

While McMinn's gubernatorial terms began in prosperity, they ended in the widespread depression that followed the panic of 1819. His last term was devoted primarily to futile attempts to restore the economy to a firm footing. Bank failures, depressed cotton prices, and sagging markets had brought the economy to a standstill, and McMinn called legislators into special session to deal with the problems. A "stay law" enacted in 1819 postponed execution of judgments for two years. In the special session of 1820, a "state loan bank" was established to lend funds to hard-pressed debtors at low interest rates. Paper money issued for this purpose was backed by anticipated proceeds from the sale of state lands. This measure, sponsored by Felix Grundy but opposed by Jackson, did little to end the depression, which continued into the next administration. Other matters did not escape McMinn's attention. Internal improvements, public education, and penal reform were issues addressed by the governor.

After McMinn's wife died in 1811, he married Rebecca Kincade of Hawkins County, who died in 1815. While governor, he married Nancy Williams of Davidson County.

Ahead of his time in his advocacy of many reforms, McMinn was well respected by his constituency—at least until the deleterious effects of the panic of 1819 were apparent. McMinn County and the city of McMinnville (the county seat of Warren County) were named for him, as was McMinn Academy, in Hawkins County. He retired after 1821, purchased a farm with twenty slaves, and served briefly as a Cherokee agent. He died at his home near Calhoun.

• All of the general histories of Tennessee discuss McMinn's gubernatorial administrations. Many of his papers and legislative messages are in Robert H. White, *Messages of the Governors*, vol. 2 (1952), pp. 442–732. Some of his correspondence regarding Indian treaties appears in Albert V. Goodpasture, ed., "McMinn Correspondence on the Subject of Indian Treaties in the Years 1815, 1816, and 1817," *American Historical Magazine* 8 (1903), pp. 377–94. See also Cynthia M. Stone, "The Administration of Governor Joseph McMinn of Tennessee, 1815–1821" (M.A. thesis, George Peabody College, 1940). Scholarly articles include William E. Beard, "Joseph McMinn, Tennessee's Fourth Governor," *Tennessee Historical Quarterly* 4 (1945), pp. 154–66; William R. Garrett, "Letters and Papers of Governor Joseph McMinn," *American Historical Magazine* 4 (1899), pp. 319–35 and 5 (1900), pp. 48–65; and Edwin M. Murphey, Jr., "Joseph McMinn, Governor of Tennessee, 1815–1821: The Man and His Times," *Tennessee Historical Magazine*, 2d. ser., 1 (1930–1931), pp. 1–16.

ROBERT E. CORLEW

MCMURRICH, James Playfair (16 Oct. 1859–9 Feb. 1939), biologist, was born in Toronto, Ontario (Canada), the son of John McMurrich and Janet Dickson. The family was prominent socially and politically; McMurrich's father served in both the Legislative Council of Canada and the provincial legislative assembly, and his older brother William was mayor of Toronto. McMurrich studied science as an undergraduate at the University of Toronto, where he was awarded a B.A. in 1879 and an M.A. two years later. In 1882 he interrupted his graduate career to teach biology at Ontario Agricultural College (now the University of Guelph), and in the same year he married Katie Moodie Vickers; they had two children. In 1884 he resumed his graduate studies at Johns Hopkins University, which offered the leading graduate program in biology. Serving as an instructor in mammalian anatomy, McMurrich completed his Ph.D. work under William Keith Brooks and wrote his dissertation, "The Osteology and Myology of *Amiurus catus*," in 1885.

After teaching biology for three years at Haverford College, McMurrich moved in 1889 to the new graduate program at Clark University, where he became docent and assistant professor of animal morphology, his graduate specialty at Johns Hopkins. Severe financial problems at Clark caused McMurrich to move to the University of Cincinnati in 1892 as professor of biology. In 1894 his career took an abrupt shift when he accepted the position of chair and professor of anatomy in the University of Michigan's medical school. This was one of the first academic appointments of a Ph.D. to a medical school faculty and represented efforts to improve medical education by requiring more exposure of medical students to the basic sciences. McMurrich remained at Michigan until 1907, when he returned to the University of Toronto as professor of anatomy. Here, he continued his important contributions to medical education and helped to organize graduate education and research at the university, eventually becoming the first dean of graduate studies in 1922. He retired in 1930.

McMurrich enjoyed an impressive career in biology, a profession to which he contributed in many important ways. He made significant contributions to understanding the embryology, morphology, and phylogeny of invertebrates and vertebrates. His first book, *A Textbook of Invertebrate Morphology* (1894) was the pioneering text for invertebrate zoology in North America and led to the development in 1895 of the first course in the subject at the Marine Biological Laboratory in Woods Hole, Massachusetts. Much of the background for this book stemmed from his graduate student days at Johns Hopkins, where he studied at the university's Chesapeake Zoological Laboratory and developed an early interest in coelenterates, especially *Actinozoa*. His additional interest in vertebrate development and anatomy led him to numerous research projects and two other texts, *The Development of the Human Body* (1902), and several English editions of Johannes Sobotta's *Atlas of Human Anatomy* (1906). Beginning with his doctoral research on the white catfish, *A. catus*, McMurrich became interested in fisheries biology, to which he contributed several research projects on the Pacific Coast salmon and halibut as well as served on the North American Committee on Fisheries Investigation and the Biological Board of Canada; he was chair of the latter from 1926 to 1935. Finally, McMurrich contributed to a new field, the history of science, both through a scholarly monograph, *Leonardo da Vinci, the Anatomist* (1930), and through his service to the History of Science Society. In all, he published over 107 articles and books.

Perhaps the best indication of McMurrich's character and reputation is his service to academic societies and institutions. A natural leader, skilled administrator, and consummate organizer, McMurrich believed strongly in the importance of the social structure of science. An active member of numerous societies, McMurrich was either appointed or elected to be a trustee of the Marine Biological Laboratory (1892–1896), on the advisory board of the Wistar Institute of Anatomy and Biology, secretary of the American Society of Zoologists (1890–1893), vice president of the History of Science Society (1921), and president of the American Society of Naturalists (1907), the American Association of Anatomists (1908), and both the American Association for the Advancement of Science and the Royal Society of Canada (1922); the latter organization bestowed its Flavelle Medal upon McMurrich posthumously in 1939.

In addition to his successful professional life, McMurrich enjoyed a rewarding family and personal life. His home often served as the gathering place for students and colleagues. He died in Toronto.

In addition to McMurrich's numerous contributions to specific scientific problems, he played an important role in demonstrating the practical nature of science in two important ways. First, McMurrich was the first broadly trained biologist to teach anatomy within a medical setting, moving anatomy from a clinical specialty to an important scientific discipline within medical schools. At both the University of Michigan and the University of Toronto, he established the initial department of anatomy, a tradition soon adopted by most medical schools. Second, McMurrich's lifelong interest in the embryology of fish and in marine biology led him to participate in and then to encourage research activity to enhance salmon and halibut fishery in Canada. These efforts were instrumental in framing much of the work of the North American Committee on Fisheries Investigation and the Biological Board of Canada, and they served an important role in illustrating science's role in fisheries enhancement.

• McMurrich's papers (including correspondence, student notebooks, and manuscript material) are in the University Archives at the University of Toronto. His unpublished "History of Anatomy" is located in the university's Thomas Fisher Rare Book Library. Additional material associated with his long career at Toronto is located in the administrative records of the Office of the President. McMurrich's role in the American Association of Anatomists is described in Nicholas A. Michels, "The American Association of Anatomists: A Tribute and Brief History," *Anatomical Record* 122 (1955): 679–714. Biographical sketches include Frank R. Lillie, "James Playfair McMurrich," *American Philosophical Society Year Book* (1939); Charles C. Macklin, "James Playfair McMurrich," *Canadian Medical Association Journal* 40 (1939): 409–10; James C. Watt, "Obituary: James Playfair McMurrich," *Science* 89 (1939): 307–8; and James C. Watt, C. M. Jackson, and E. Horne Craigie, "Professor James Playfair McMurrich, 1859–1939: In Memoriam," *Anatomical Record* 74 (1939, supplement): 2–5.

KEITH R. BENSON

MCNAIR, Frederick Vallette (13 Jan. 1839–28 Nov. 1900), naval officer, was born in Jenkintown, Pennsylvania, the son of John McNair, an educator, and Mary Yerkes. His father was the head of a private school for boys and later became a Democratic congressman from the Fifth District of Pennsylvania, serving in the Thirty-second and Thirty-third Congresses, 1851–1855. The family then moved to a plantation in Virginia. McNair's grandfather, Alexander McNair, had been elected the first governor of Missouri, serving from 1820 to 1824. Nominated by his father, McNair, at age fourteen, was appointed a midshipman at the U.S. Naval Academy in 1853.

After four years at the Naval Academy, graduating in 1857, McNair served aboard the *Minnesota* in the Far East and then on the U.S. Coast Survey schooner *Varina*. Upon the outbreak of the Civil War, he was promoted to lieutenant. Serving aboard the *Iroquois* in the West Indies, he participated in the pursuit of the Confederate steamer *Sumter*.

On the *Iroquois* McNair served under Admiral David Farragut in the Mississippi River campaign at Forts Jackson and St. Philip, at the Chalmette batteries below New Orleans, and at Vicksburg. He was the officer sent ashore to demand the surrender of the Confederate forts at Natchez and Baton Rouge in May 1862. During a brief leave in 1862 he married Clara Warren; they had one child. Later in 1862 McNair served aboard the *Juanita* and the *Seminole* on the East Coast, then in the Mississippi campaign again aboard the *Pensacola*. In April 1864 he was appointed lieutenant commander. As executive officer on the *Juanita*, he was involved in attacks on Fort Fisher in December 1864 and in January 1865. The commander of the *Juanita*, J. J. Almy, praised the 26-year-old McNair as "a most excellent officer, possessing good judgment."

Following the Civil War McNair's naval career alternated between shore and sea duty. His shore assignments took him to the Naval Academy in 1868, 1871–1875, and 1878–1882, first as instructor, then as head of the Department of Seamanship, and finally as commandant of cadets. At sea he served with the Brazil Squadron, as executive officer of the flagship *Brooklyn* (1866–1867), and then aboard the practice ship *Macedonian* (1868). From 1870 to 1871 he was executive officer aboard the flagship *Franklin* of the European Squadron, and from 1875 to 1878 he was on the Asiatic Station.

McNair was promoted to captain in 1883. He served at the Mare Island Navy Yard in California, then commanded the flagship *Omaha* of the Asiatic Station, 1887–1890. He was a member of the court of inquiry investigating the loss of the Arctic exploration ship *Jeannette* in 1882. In 1890–1894 he served as superintendent of the Naval Observatory, then he commanded the Asiatic Squadron, 1895–1898.

Grounded in technical matters and experienced as a commander and an educator, McNair played an important part in the successful buildup of the Asiatic Squadron before the Spanish-American War. Under his persistent drilling and careful instruction in gunnery, the ships and crews of the Asiatic Squadron reached a high state of proficiency, which Commodore George Dewey, who took command of the squadron early in 1898, considered a prime factor in the victory at Manila. Although McNair could not directly lay claim to the glory of that naval victory, his professional career and his quiet dedication to seamanship drill and training and to technical excellence reaped rewards for his service and his nation.

During the Spanish-American War McNair served under Commodore Dewey. He then was ordered to Annapolis to take charge of Admiral Pasquale Cervera and other Spanish naval officers captured off Cuba on 3 July 1898. Promoted to rear admiral that year, he served as commandant of the Naval Academy until

March 1900, when he was appointed the first president of the Government Lighthouse Board. He remained on "waiting orders" status because of his declining health. He died in Washington, D.C.

Like many naval officers of his generation, McNair gained experience in the Civil War, followed by responsibilities in educational and technical duties ashore and increments of shipboard duty and command. A crucial component of the growing professionalism of the U.S. Navy, McNair and his fellow officers contributed both individually and as a class to the excellent showing of the navy during the brief war with Spain in 1898. McNair's rigorous preparation of the Asiatic Squadron proved decisive at the battle of Manila.

• McNair wrote *Manual of Seamanship Drills* (1874), and as superintendent of the Naval Observatory he was the chief author of *Astronomical, Magnetic and Meterological Observations Made during the Year 1890* (1895). See also L. R. Hamersly, *The Records of Living Officers of the U.S. Navy and Marine Corps*, 6th ed. (1898). An obituary is in the *New York Times*, 29 Nov. 1900.

RODNEY P. CARLISLE

MCNAIR, Lesley James (25 May 1883–25 July 1944), commanding general and educator of U.S. Army Ground Forces in World War II, was born in Verndale, Minnesota, the son of James McNair, a lumber merchant and general store owner, and Clara Manz. Lesley "Whitey" McNair graduated from West Point in 1904, eleventh in a class of 124, and received a commission as an artillery officer. The following year he married Clare Huster; they had one child. Until 1909 he served in a series of artillery and ordnance assignments, including tours at Fort Douglas, Utah, the Office of the Chief of Ordnance in Washington, D.C., and the Watertown arsenal in Massachusetts. McNair then served with the Fourth Field Artillery Regiment at Fort Russell, Wyoming, from 1909 to 1914. In 1912, however, he attended the School of Fire at Fort Sill, Oklahoma. His student thesis, "Probabilities and the Theory of Dispersion," helped to significantly improve gun firing methods throughout the U.S. Army. Because of his rising reputation as an artilleryman, McNair spent most of 1913 in France as a foreign military observer. The experience ensured his return to Europe with the American Expeditionary Force (AEF) in June 1917. Within two months General John J. Pershing selected McNair, then a lieutenant colonel, to join the AEF General Staff, where he subsequently became the senior artillery officer in the training division.

McNair performed his duties so well that at age thirty-five he became one of the youngest American brigadier generals in France. He subsequently distilled his wartime experiences into *Artillery Ammunition and Fuses* (1920), which quickly became a standard reference on the tactical employment of U.S. artillery units in war. In addition to writing, McNair spent the interwar years in a series of education and artillery-related assignments. By April 1939 he was commandant of the Command and General Staff School at Fort Leavenworth, Kansas, where he revised the curriculum to specifically focus on war. At the conclusion of his abbreviated tour at Fort Leavenworth, McNair's rendezvous with history occurred. He was about to become the great educator of American ground combat forces in World War II.

Over his forty-year military career, McNair deliberately avoided publicity. He was soft-spoken and unspectacular, yet to General George C. Marshall he was "the brains of the army" in World War II. McNair was an accomplished mathematician and, in one wag's opinion, a "Scots Presbyterian" thinker, that is, he was all irony and intellect. McNair did not, however, see himself as one of the army's best and brightest. In his own mind, he was a "pick and shovel" man who did the army's dirty work, despite his loathing for paperwork. He also had a "do something!" philosophy that led to a training empire second to none and eventually organized, mobilized, and trained more than 3 million U.S. soldiers for ground combat overseas. McNair accomplished this feat in two phases: as the chief of staff of the newly created Army General Headquarters (Aug. 1940–Mar. 1942) and then as commander of the Army Ground Forces (Mar. 1942–June 1944), where he never had less than 1.5 million men, approximately 200 generals, and 71 domestic military installations under his direct control. As the leader of Army Ground Forces, Lieutenant General McNair was one of only three army commanders in the continental United States. The other two were Lieutenant General Henry "Hap" Arnold, who shepherded the Army Air Forces, and Lieutenant General Brehon Somerwell, who led the Army Service Forces.

As an educator, McNair sought to produce "well-trained, hard-hitting fighting teams" for what he believed was a war of national survival. His avowed goal was "to make killers" of combat recruits, and he had no qualms about his appointed role. To McNair, ultimate victory depended on the "painful progress" of the infantry, which imposed its will on the enemy by seizing territory and defeating hostile armies. To prepare the American fighting man properly, McNair traveled more than 200,000 miles on inspection trips and initiated a series of radical reforms that still define U.S. Army combat training today.

McNair's major reforms were threefold. He started by revising the army's Tables of Organization and Equipment. If the army relied on large units in war (divisions, corps, and armies), McNair concluded, it should organize, train, and administer the selfsame units in peace. In particular, McNair and others transformed the ponderous "square" division of the interwar years into the relatively supple "triangular" division of World War II. By containing three rather than four regiments, the new division proved to be more powerful and efficient than its predecessor. Second, McNair insisted on training army combat units in phases. The standardized phases included fundamentals, small unit operations, combined arms, and lastly, corps and army maneuvers. By adopting this gradualist approach, McNair not only promoted efficiency, he also trained combatants to perform a variety of tasks and therefore protected the U.S. Army from overspecialization. Lastly and perhaps most importantly, McNair introduced realistic training into the American military. He used live ammunition (more than 240,000 tons) in combat education; he turned mere obstacle courses into mock battlefields; he organized twenty-seven large-scale maneuvers in the United States, one of which involved 1.5 million people; he used the 180,000-square-mile Desert Training Center in California and Arizona to simulate theater-level warfare; and he demanded "free" maneuvers, in which local commanders had to solve battlefield problems with little or no guidance from superiors. In short, McNair took over the "wobbly" army ground forces in 1940 and eventually trained 100 hardened divisions from their midst.

Unfortunately, McNair did not live to see the Allied victory in Europe. While observing front-line troops in the Normandy area, McNair and over a hundred others mistakenly died at the hands of Eighth Air Force bombers near St.-Lô, France. The bombers dropped their bombs short of their intended targets, and thus made McNair the highest ranking American officer killed in combat up to that time. A grateful nation posthumously promoted McNair, the great educator of its army, to four-star rank in 1945.

• McNair's voluminous official correspondence is available in the army records of the National Archives and Records Service. A modest collection of his personal papers and effects is in the Library of Congress, and a basic record of his military activities is available in the Office of the Chief of Military History, Department of the Army. E. J. Kahn, *McNair: Educator of an Army* (1945), is a sympathetic profile of the general that first appeared in the *New Yorker* magazine. Interested readers should consult two volumes in the U.S. Army's "Green Series" on World War II, Kent R. Greenfield et al., *The Organization of Ground Combat Troops* (1947), and Robert R. Palmer et al., *The Procurement and Training of Ground Combat Troops* (1948).

PETER R. FABER

MCNAIR, Ronald E. *See* Challenger Shuttle Crew.

MCNALLY, Johnny Blood (27 Nov. 1903–28 Nov. 1985), college and professional football player and coach, was born John Victor McNally, Jr., in New Richmond, Wisconsin, the son of John Victor McNally, manager of the New Richmond Roller Mills, and Mary Murphy, a schoolteacher. A precocious child, McNally graduated from high school at age fourteen. In 1919 he entered River Falls State Teachers College (now the University of Wisconsin–River Falls). The following year he enrolled at St. John's College, a two-year college in Collegeville, Minnesota, operated by the Benedictine friars. Although physically too small for athletics in high school, McNally had matured by the time he entered St. John's, where he earned varsity letters in football, basketball, track, and baseball. He also edited the school newspaper and led the debating team. In 1923 he enrolled at the University of Notre Dame to play football for coach Knute Rockne. However, he was expelled from the university for violating curfew and refusing to identify those who accompanied him. He then moved to Minneapolis, where he worked as a stereotyper at the *Minneapolis Tribune*, which his mother's family owned.

In 1924 McNally rechristened himself Johnny Blood. While on his way to try out for the East Twenty-sixth Street Liberties, a Minneapolis semipro football team, he noticed a movie marquee featuring the Rudolph Valentino film *Blood and Sand*. To protect his amateur status, he assumed the name Blood and was added to the Liberties' roster. For young athletes of this era, playing under a false name was common since it enabled them to earn money without jeopardizing their amateur standing. In McNally's case the pseudonym stuck, and he subsequently played professional football under that name.

McNally began his National Football League (NFL) career in 1925 with the Milwaukee Badgers. He played with the Duluth Eskimos in 1926 and 1927, then moved to the Pottstown Maroons in 1928. In 1929 he joined the Green Bay Packers and quickly achieved stardom playing for a superb team. With the exception of the 1934 season, when he played for the Pittsburgh Pirates (the forerunner of the Pittsburgh Steelers), he remained with Green Bay through 1936. During seven seasons at Green Bay he established himself as one of the early NFL's premier football players, scoring 37 touchdowns and 224 points. In 1931 McNally scored an NFL record of 13 touchdowns. He led the Packers to NFL championships in 1929, 1930, 1931, and 1936. He was selected "All-League" in 1928, 1929, and 1930 and was named All-NFL left halfback in 1931, the first year such a team was officially chosen by position.

McNally was the prototype for the professional football halfback. His slashing style, blinding speed, and great elusiveness made him a devastating runner. He was also an outstanding pass catcher, relying on his exceptional leaping ability. Brimming with self-confidence, he was capable of scoring anytime he handled the football. As was common in the early days of professional football, he played defense as well as offense, making his mark at defensive back as a strong tackler.

Despite his success on the playing field, McNally was a burden for Green Bay coach Curly Lambeau. High-spirited and hard-drinking, he continually broke curfews and missed practices. Lambeau reportedly once offered him a contract for $110 a week if he would not drink after Wednesdays but only $100 a week if he did. McNally took the $100 offer. He spent money as rapidly as he could obtain it, and he supposedly never met a rule that he could not or did not break. Legend has it that, broke and desperate for an advance on his salary, he once leaped across an eight-foot courtyard into the window of a sixth-floor hotel room where Lambeau had barricaded himself to escape him.

Leaving Green Bay in 1937, McNally signed with the Pittsburgh Steelers where he was both a player and the head coach. He began with the Steelers by returning the opening game kickoff for a touchdown against the Philadelphia Eagles. After his run, he reputedly turned to his players and said, "That's the way to do it, fellows." However, such scenes were not often repeated. His Pittsburgh teammates were a subpar lot, and, with advancing age, his once magnificent skills deteriorated rapidly. In a short time his glory days on the field were over.

In choosing McNally to coach the Steelers, Pittsburgh owner Art Rooney made a serious mistake. As engaging a personality as McNally was, he had no use for the discipline, training, organization, and planning required of a head coach. Rooney, realizing his mistake, observed, "On most teams, the coach worries about where the players are at night. Our players worried about the coach." After compiling a record of six wins and 19 losses, McNally was dismissed in the midst of the 1939 season.

McNally played minor league football in 1940 and 1941, and he served in World War II as a cryptographer. After a 1945 comeback attempt with the Packers failed, he returned to St. John's College, where he finally obtained his bachelor's degree in 1949. Between 1950 and 1952 he taught economics at St. John's and coached the football team. He also attended the University of Minnesota between 1947 and 1957 but did not receive a degree.

In 1949 McNally married Marguerite F. Streater. Ten years after a 1956 divorce, he married Catherine I. Kopp. He had no children with either wife. In his later years McNally and his second wife owned several employment agencies. In 1972 he led a short-lived campaign to draft U.S. Supreme Court Justice Byron "Whizzer" White, his former teammate from the Pittsburgh Steelers, for the Democratic nomination for president. In 1979 he retired to Palm Springs, California, where he died.

McNally was selected in 1963 as one of seventeen charter members of professional football's Hall of Fame. He combined exceptional football skills with a unique and likable personality to become a much-needed attraction for the fledgling NFL and eventually a football legend.

• The McNally file at the Professional Football Hall of Fame, Canton, Ohio, contains significant biographical information, including an interview taped shortly before his death and an autobiographical scrapbook he assembled. George Sullivan, *Pro Football's All-Time Greats* (1968), pp. 80–84; Myron Cope, *The Game That Was* (1970), pp. 59–70; Arthur Daley, *Pro Football's Hall of Fame* (1963), pp. 78–92; and Dennis J. Harrington, *The Pro Football Hall of Fame* (1991), all provide biographical sketches emphasizing the antics of perhaps the most colorful man to play professional football. Gerald Holland, "Is That You up There, Johnny Blood," *Sports Illustrated*, 2 Sept. 1963, pp. 18–25, consists of several chats with McNally about his exciting if unconventional life during the early days of the NFL. McNally supplies autobiographical recollections in Richard Whittingham, *What a Game They Played* (1984), pp. 29–41. An obituary is in the *New York Times*, 30 Nov. 1985.

FRANK W. THACKERAY

MCNAMEE, Graham (10 July 1888–9 May 1942), pioneer radio announcer and sportscaster, was born in Washington, D.C., the son of John Bernard McNamee, a lawyer, and Anne Liebold. He grew up in St. Paul, Minnesota, and attended public schools there. As a boy he had a good singing voice, and his mother saw to it that he had singing lessons, although he also participated on sports teams, especially baseball and hockey. McNamee's father hoped that the boy would take up his own profession of the law, but after graduating from high school he drifted for a few years. He worked for a while as a clerk on the Rock Island Railroad and as a traveling salesman for the Armor Meat Packing Company.

McNamee's father died in 1912, and his mother, believing in McNamee's talents as a singer, moved her son to Weehawken, New Jersey, and later New York in the hopes that in the right environment her son might make his way as a professional. To a certain extent he did. Within a short time he was performing in both light and grand opera and making a modest yet precarious living as a singer. And he made a solo debut as a concert singer at New York's Aeolian Hall on 22 November 1920.

McNamee's career as a singer never quite blossomed, however, and in the summer of 1923 he was having a hard time making ends meet. He was called to jury duty at the federal courthouse at Foley Square, which held out the promise of providing a few free meals. While wandering along lower Broadway, where he had seldom ventured, he noticed the call letters of the newly established station WEAF, which was the pioneering radio station of AT&T. (WEAF became the anchor station of the first radio network, NBC, when NBC was formed in 1926.) McNamee knew nothing about radio, but he had heard that radio stations sometimes presented vocal programs, so he thought there would be nothing wrong with inquiring about the possibilities. He spoke to the station manager, Samuel L. Ross, who was impressed with his qualifications as a singer but even more interested in McNamee's speaking voice and by the fact that he knew something about baseball. He told McNamee that he was looking for an announcer and offered an audition. On the basis of the audition, Ross hired the young singer on the spot and told him to report for work at 6 P.M. the following day.

This curious twist of fate changed the course of McNamee's life. His career as a singer would rapidly fade, but within a few years his would be the best-known voice in America. In 1923 radio was still in the incubative stage; accordingly McNamee had been hired as a general purpose announcer. He talked, made station breaks, introduced other singers, and even sang himself when there was free air time. He also did all of his own programming.

WEAF was hoping to broadcast the World Series in 1923—luckily it was a "subway" series between the New York Yankees and the New York Giants. McNamee wanted to broadcast the games, but the station was leery of the idea since he had no background in sports news. The station hired Bill McGeehan, sports editor of the *New York Herald Tribune*, to broadcast the games, but McNamee went along to fill in between innings and perhaps add a little color or commentary. McGeehan apparently had few talents as a sportscaster, and after the first few games the station allowed McNamee to do most of the talking and McGeehan faded into the background.

What nobody realized at the time was that McNamee was embarking on a career as the nation's most recognizable radio personality, its first star announcer. For a number of years McNamee would broadcast nearly all major sports for WEAF and later for the NBC network—baseball, football, title boxing matches, and so on. He would broadcast every World Series game until 1934. In January 1927, in the first nationwide hookup for a sports event, he broadcast the Rose Bowl from Pasadena, California.

During the mid-1920s, however, McNamee continued to be an all-purpose announcer. In 1924, for example, he did the first broadcasts of national political conventions of both the Republican and the Democratic parties. In 1927 he announced in his own inimitable manner the arrival of Charles Lindbergh in Paris. His voice was probably known by more Americans than the voice of any radio announcer before or since. He received hundreds of fan letters a week from listeners, more than even the most popular movie stars.

But it is mainly as an early sportscaster that McNamee will be remembered. He has often been called the "Father of Sportscasting." Veteran sportscaster Red Barber called him the greatest sportscaster of all time. The secret of his success is a bit hard to pin down. He had a superb speaking voice, of course, but he possessed a vivid and colorful imagination and a ready wit. He never settled for a drab play-by-play account of a game, but with a glib tongue he filled in all the dead air space with charming chatter and accounts of what was happening off the field as well as on. He could slip effortlessly from the homespun to a kind of rapid-fire delivery. No announcer in history could better evoke the ambience and feel of a game—the crowd, a fight breaking out in the stands, the sky, the clouds, the windup of a pitcher, or the grimaces of a batter. There was no television eye to do the work in those days, so McNamee supplied that eye.

At the height of McNamee's career, *New York World* columnist Heywood Broun remarked that radio, after all, was only a mechanical medium and everything that goes out over it can be as "dull as dishwater" unless infused with personality. This McNamee had. Broun said, "Graham McNamee has been able to take a new medium of expression and through it transmit himself—to give out vividly a sense of movement and of feeling. Of such is the kingdom of art."

McNamee continued to work in radio for the rest of his life. In the 1930s, however, he was eased aside as a sportscaster by younger men with more specialized expertise in this or that sport. Some have suggested that split-second timing required by station breaks and commercial spots cut into McNamee's expansive and florid style of narration and gift for repartee. Nevertheless, in the 1930s McNamee was the announcer on the first radio program regularly broadcast before a live audience, Ed Wynn's "Fire Chief" program. He was also the announcer for Rudy Vallee's hit variety show.

McNamee was a rather nervous and shy person away from the microphone. He was married twice, first to Josephine Garrett in 1921 (they divorced in 1932) and then to Ann Lee Sims. There were no children from either marriage. McNamee died in New York City of a stroke. In his later years he did voice-over announcing for newsreels, which kept his well-remembered voice before a wide public.

In his book on the history of sportscasting, *The Broadcasters* (1970), Red Barber gave McNamee full credit for inventing sportscasting from scratch. There were no sports booths in those days; sportscasters just had to sit in the stands next to the sportswriters on a hard wooden bench and depend on ready wit and ingenuity:

> Graham McNamee . . . the first sports announcer . . . no preparation . . . took a carbon microphone, walked into the stadium, sat down, . . . told the nation what it was waiting to hear and had never heard before . . . told them about ten different sports. I concentrated on two—baseball and football—and I thought I had my hands full. . . . His sign-off was distinctive. "This is Graham McNamee speaking. Good night all." I don't know what's on his tombstone, but those words would read well on it, wouldn't they?

• McNamee wrote his own memoirs at the height of his popularity, *You're on the Air* (1926). A good account of his days at WEAF can be found in William Peck Banning, *Commercial Broadcasting Pioneer: The WEAF Experiment* (1946). There is much helpful background in Gleason L. Archer, *A History of Radio to 1926* (1938). A short account of McNamee's early career is in George H. Douglas, *The Early Days of Radio Broadcasting* (1987). An early profile by Geoffrey T. Hellman appeared in the *New Yorker*, 9 Aug. 1930. For additional biographical information, see obituaries in the *New York Times*, 10 May and 12 May 1942.

GEORGE H. DOUGLAS

MCNARY, Charles Linza (12 June 1874–25 Feb. 1944), U.S. senator, was born on the family farm five miles north of Salem, Oregon, the son of Hugh Linza McNary and Mary Margaret Claggett, farmers. Orphaned at the age of nine, he lived with his older siblings in Salem, and as a young man worked as a farmhand, paperboy, and apprentice in a tree nursery. He never lost his love of trees and the outdoors. His hobby of working with new plant hybrids resulted in his development of the American filbert and the Imperial prune in 1909.

McNary attended public school and in 1896 entered Stanford University. He left after the first year, however, to read law in his older brother John's law office in Salem. After admission to the bar in 1898, he joined his brother's practice. Real estate became his specialty, and he soon had acquired a large clientele, but he also continued to operate the family's old farm. In 1902 he married Jessie Breyman, the daughter of a prominent Salem merchant. They had no children. His wife was killed in a car accident in 1918, and in 1923 McNary married his former secretary Cornelia Woodburn Morton, with whom he adopted a child.

Local politics soon interested McNary. Between 1892 and 1896 he served as Marion County recorder. In 1904 he managed his brother's successful campaign for county district attorney and then assisted his brother as deputy district attorney from 1904 to 1911. Meanwhile, in 1908 he was appointed dean of the law school at Willamette University, a position he held until 1913. As dean, McNary worked vigorously to expand the curriculum and moved the classes from downtown law offices to the university campus to forge closer links between the school and the university.

Early in his career McNary identified himself with the Progressive wing of the Republican party, a position he maintained throughout his political life. He did not, however, let his more liberal stance hinder his support of President William Howard Taft in 1912 and demonstrated his nascent political skills by working effectively with both wings of his party. The next year Oregon's Democratic governor Oswald West appointed McNary associate justice of the Oregon Supreme Court. His western populism surfaced in opinions he wrote in support of workmen's compensation and the eight-hour workday. His happy tenure on the bench was interrupted, however, when in 1914 he lost a close Republican primary election for a full-term associate justice of the Oregon Supreme Court by one vote. He returned to the political fray two years later as Republican state chairperson and manager of Charles Evans Hughes's presidential campaign in Oregon.

In May 1917 McNary began his lengthy career in the U.S. Senate with his appointment to fill the vacancy caused by the sudden death of Harry Lane, one of the half-dozen senators who had opposed American intervention in World War I. In contrast, McNary supported President Woodrow Wilson's wartime measures declaring, "I am not a standpatter. I am a progressive. Neither am I a hidebound partisan" (Neal, p. 34) This brief statement aptly summarized his political philosophy: he was a pragmatic politician willing to compromise where necessary to achieve a workable solution to the nation's problems. His political flexibility would ultimately take him to the leadership of his party in the Senate.

In 1918 McNary was elected for a full term. His minimalist approach to campaigning (he stayed in Washington the entire time) proved effective, and for the rest of his years in office he seldom campaigned in person, leaving that task to his supporters in the state. During the League of Nations fight, McNary joined the "mild" reservationists, yet he forged a close working relationship with Wilson's nemesis, Henry Cabot Lodge. Lodge educated the new senator in the ways of the Senate, appointing him as western member to the Committee on Committees.

McNary's favorite committee, however, was Agriculture and Forestry, and it was from there that he made his first significant legislative contributions. During the 1920s he sponsored a series of bills protecting the nation's forests. His concern for the welfare of farmers spurred him to design legislation that boosted prices for farm products. With the support of Representative Gilbert N. Haugen, the McNary-Haugen bill sought to stabilize farm income by establishing an Agricultural Credit Corporation to set parity prices for a select number of agricultural products and then purchase surplus production for sale either domestically or abroad. The United States government would compensate the corporation with an equalization fee for any losses realized from sales abroad at lower prices. Passed twice by Congress, the McNary-Haugen bill was twice vetoed by President Calvin Coolidge, who believed that it would lead to an unconstitutional involvement of the government in private business affairs and would raise food prices to the benefit of only a few farmers. McNary's hopes for a more generous hearing from Coolidge's successor, Herbert Hoover, were dashed by the onset of the depression and by Hoover's unwillingness to expand governmental support of agriculture.

McNary was most often allied both politically and personally with other western progressives such as George Norris, William E. Borah, and Robert M. La Follette. Despite his sympathy for the progressive agenda, McNary continued to support mainstream Republicans and backed Coolidge in 1924, when La Follette ran for president on a third-party ticket. McNary was often urged to seek leadership of the Senate Republicans, but he preferred to work within the seniority system and defer to his colleagues with more time in office. He nevertheless created a well-deserved reputation as a man of his word who could be counted on to get accomplished the work of the Senate.

Hoover's defeat in 1932 placed McNary in a new position—Senate minority leader, a position for which he was ably suited. During the early years of the New Deal, he and Franklin Roosevelt developed a mutual respect and liking for each other that lasted until McNary's death. McNary performed admirably as the leader of the loyal opposition, while providing much crucial support for elements of Roosevelt's New Deal. Personally sympathetic with much of the initial New Deal legislation, he backed public distribution of power and supported the Tennessee Valley Authority. Roosevelt rewarded McNary by authorizing the construction of the magnificent Bonneville Dam on the Columbia River.

McNary's support had limits, however. When Roosevelt attempted to change the number of Supreme Court justices in 1937, McNary kept his Republican colleagues quiet while conservative Democrats successfully attacked the plan. Afterward he began to openly oppose Roosevelt more often. An ardent protectionist, he expressed his opposition to Roosevelt's reciprocal trade legislation. He also was not pleased with the Gold Reserve Act, which tampered with the value of the dollar. He underestimated the dangerous situation in Europe in the late 1930s and voted against a repeal of the arms embargo in 1939. Although he supported the Selective Service Act of 1940 and lend-lease in 1941, he generally remained opposed to American involvement in overseas affairs up to Pearl Harbor.

In 1940 McNary, as the most prominent Republican in Congress, was chosen to balance the ticket with the eastern and urban Wendell Willkie. Roosevelt, who had once mentioned his interest in having McNary as a possible running mate, chose Iowa's Henry Wallace. During the campaign McNary and Wallace often rode together to speaking engagements and offered praise more than criticism of each other. After the election McNary turned down Roosevelt's offer to join his cabinet. His first love was the cozy confines of the Senate, where he was recognized as the premier parliamentarian and where he believed he was most productive. He labored there until he fell ill with a brain tumor. He died at Fort Lauderdale, Florida.

In a career that spanned the period between the world wars, McNary represented many of the ideals that characterized the western populists and progressives. His concern for the land and for those who worked it fostered his efforts to have the government protect both. His progressive credentials and his willingness to compromise with his colleagues across the aisle made him a popular and highly effective legislator during the two and one-half decades he served in the Senate.

• McNary's papers are located at the Library of Congress. The University of Oregon and the Oregon Historical Society also have smaller collections. The best biography is Steve Neal, *McNary of Oregon: A Political Biography* (1985). Neal provides a condensed version of his biography in "Charles L. McNary: The Quiet Man," in *First among Equals: Outstanding Senate Leaders of the Twentieth Century*, ed. Richard A. Baker and Roger H. Davidson (1991), pp. 98–126.

EDWARD A. GOEDEKEN

MCNEILL, Daniel (5 Apr. 1748–1833), privateer and naval officer, was born in Charlestown, Massachusetts, the son of William McNeill and Catherine Morrison. Little is known about his early life. He married Mary Cuthbertson in February 1770. She apparently died sometime before 1773. He married a second time, to Abigail Harvey of Nottingham, England. He had at least ten children with her, the first being born in July 1773.

Shortly after the outbreak of the Revolution, McNeill went to sea as a privateer, sailing on vessels holding commissions from the Massachusetts Provincial Congress. Altogether during the war McNeill commanded six privateers, *Hancock*, *America*, *Eagle*, *Ulysses*, *Wasp*, and *General Mifflin*. The last named was his most important command of the war. The *General Mifflin* was one of the most successful American privateers to venture into European waters. Under McNeill's command in 1778–1779 it took thirteen prizes. The *General Mifflin* returned to Boston in February 1779. While McNeill continued to share ownership in local privateers he did not go to sea again during the remainder of the war.

From the end of the Revolution until 1798 McNeill probably owned and perhaps commanded merchantmen sailing from Boston. This was a prosperous period for the port of Boston. Trade with the Northwest coast and China was thriving and was increasing along the traditional routes to Europe and the West Indies, and McNeill would have had considerable opportunity to invest in overseas ventures. With the outbreak of the Quasi-War with France in 1798 McNeill offered his services to the new navy. On 17 July 1798 he was commissioned a captain and assigned command of the *Portsmouth*, a small 24-gun ship built at Portsmouth, New Hampshire, by James Hackett.

The *Portsmouth* sailed on 26 January 1799 to join Commodore John Barry's squadron in the West Indies and was assigned to cruise off the French colony of Surinam. Its mission was to protect American vessels in that area from French warships and privateers. McNeill returned to Boston in May 1799. The secretary of the navy ordered him to refit quickly and return to the coast of Surinam. The *Portsmouth* was back on the coast in July, joined there by the revenue cutter *Scammel*. On his second deployment to Surinam McNeill was able to blockade the French privateer *Hussar*. When the port was captured by the British in August 1799 McNeill gave the *Hussar* over to the Royal Navy. McNeill returned to New York in January 1800.

On 8 April 1800 McNeill received orders to proceed to France under a flag of truce in order to bring home the American ministers who had been in Paris negotiating peace. The *Portsmouth* arrived at Le Havre on 20 May. On 30 September the convention ending the Quasi-War was signed in Paris, and shortly thereafter the *Portsmouth* welcomed aboard the American diplomats and returned to the United States, arriving in early December. With the war at an end, on 1 April McNeill was ordered to remove the *Portsmouth*'s guns and bring the ship to Baltimore to be sold. McNeill himself was furloughed on 19 May and told to await orders.

On 2 July 1801 McNeill was ordered to command the frigate *Boston*, then at Boston. He was told to bring the *Boston* down to New York and prepare it to deliver the new American minister to France. On 1 October he received special orders that after delivering the minister he was to take the *Boston* and join the American squadron in the Mediterranean. Uncertain as to the situation in the Mediterranean, the secretary told McNeill that if peace should have been secured with the Barbary Powers by the time of his arrival, he was to return to the United States. If war still prevailed, he was to remain and assist in suppressing the enemy.

On 25 December the *Boston* arrived at Gibraltar. Learning that Commodore Richard Dale was at Toulon, McNeill proceeded to that port and arrived on 5 January. Since peace had not been secured Dale ordered the *Boston* to Tripoli. The frigate departed Toulon on 19 January but not without some controversy. To avoid being put under quarantine, McNeill did not report to the local authorities that his ship had recently visited other ports. In other words, he filed a false report. Perhaps because he feared being discovered, McNeill took the *Boston* back to sea so quickly that he left several of his crew ashore, including his third and fourth lieutenants, the lieutenant of marines, purser, purser's steward, wardroom steward, and two boys. Indeed, the departure was so sudden that three French officers who were aboard found themselves unexpectedly underway. Dale took serious objection to McNeill's actions and made an unfavorable report to the secretary, in which he questioned McNeill's integrity.

While cruising off Tripoli McNeill captured several small Tripolitan vessels. On 13 July McNeill was ordered to return to the United States with the *Boston*. One month later the secretary altered those orders. The *Boston* was to remain in the Mediterranean and McNeill was to make his way home by the best means available. While the secretary's orders did not specifically mention McNeill's conduct at Toulon, it is clear from other correspondence that the captain was being called home in disgrace. After arriving back in the United States McNeill was left to wonder about his future. No charges were ever brought against him for his conduct at Toulon, but on 27 October 1802 he was dismissed from the service under the provisions of the Peace Establishment Act of 1801.

McNeill returned to Boston and slid into obscurity. Although James Fenimore Cooper, in his *History of the Navy*, refers to McNeill's service in the War of 1812, there is no evidence to support the claim. The vital records of Massachusetts as well as local obituaries reveal nothing about McNeill. Having been dismissed from the service he seems to have faded into obscurity.

• Documents regarding his naval career are in the Naval Historical Center "Z Files." Genealogical information for McNeill may be found in T. B. Wyman, *Genealogies and Estates of Charlestown* (2 vols., 1879). For his naval career see Gardner W. Allen, *Massachusetts Privateers of the Revolution*, Massachusetts Historical Society, *Collections*, vol. 77 (1926); Allen, *Our Naval War with France* (1909); Dudley Knox, ed., *Naval Documents Related to the United States Wars with the Barbary Powers* (6 vols., 1939–1944); Knox, ed., *Naval Documents Related to the Quasi War between the United States and France* (6 vols., 1935–1938).

WILLIAM M. FOWLER

MCNEILL, George Edwin (4 Aug. 1837–19 May 1906), labor leader, was born in Amesbury, Massachusetts, the son of John McNeill (occupation unknown) and Abigail Todd Hickey. He attended local schools until he was fifteen, then got a job in the Amesbury woolen mills, followed by stints as a shoemaker and a salesman.

McNeill moved to Boston in 1856, and three years later he married Adeline J. Trefethen; it is not known if they had children. His life found its professional focus in 1863, when he served for a year as secretary of the Grand Eight-Hour League, a group formed to support labor theorist Ira Steward's call for the eight-hour day. McNeill promoted Steward's ideas while he edited labor papers in New York City and in Fall River and Paterson, New Jersey. He also served as president of the Workingmen's Institute (1867–1869) and the Boston Eight-Hour League (1869–1874), two groups that brought together skilled workmen, legislators, and civic leaders in support of Steward's proposals. So effective was McNeill as a speaker, author, and organizer that the *New York Times* later called him the "father of the eight-hour movement." McNeill helped win passage of a number of federal and state eight-hour laws, but when it became evident that the new laws were not being enforced, he played an important role in encouraging the nation's unions to promote the eight-hour day through economic action. McNeill's influence helped shape the labor agenda for the 1880s.

In 1869 McNeill, abolitionist and reformer Wendell Phillips, and a number of allies organized the New England Labor Reform League to support the goals of the newly formed National Labor Union. Although the Massachusetts legislature refused the group's request for a corporate charter, it sought to keep labor's favor by establishing the nation's first Bureau of Labor Statistics. McNeill became the bureau's first deputy director. The following year McNeill and Phillips helped organize the Massachusetts Labor Reform party, on whose ticket Phillips ran for governor. In 1873 McNeill was dismissed from the Labor Statistics bureau for associating himself too visibly with the labor movement.

McNeill's relations with the movement were often strained. Many trade unionists of the day combined their support for the eight-hour day with advocacy for other causes, including cooperatives and currency reform. McNeill and Steward, however, condemned these activities as frivolous distractions. All energies, they believed, must remain focused on the evils of wage labor and the unfair labor contract. Thus, when Phillips became active in the greenback movement, Steward and McNeill broke with the Labor Reform League and revived their Eight-Hour League. This split significantly weakened labor's position as an independent political force in Massachusetts.

In 1878 McNeill and some of his eight-hour allies cooperated with Marxists from the International Workingmens Association to found the International Labor Union (ILU). The ILU focused exclusively on economic goals—shorter hours and higher pay—yet McNeill, who served as its first president, articulated its social vision when he explained that it intended to organize unskilled workers of every nationality, creed, and color into one "grand labor brotherhood." The union made significant progress in organizing textile workers—many of them female—but a series of lost strikes proved demoralizing, and the organization disbanded within a few years.

With the demise of the ILU, McNeill turned his energies to the Knights of Labor, which in 1874 had adopted almost verbatim a declaration of principles that McNeill had drafted for another labor congress. McNeill joined the Knights in 1883 and became treasurer of District 30 (Massachusetts) the following year. Meanwhile, he supported himself by working as treasurer and general manager of the Massachusetts Mutual Accident Insurance Company, which he organized in 1883. He also worked as a labor arbitrator, helping to settle Boston's bitter horsecar strike in 1885.

In May 1886 a nationwide series of strikes for the eight-hour day ended in bloody confrontations and harsh government reprisals. The Knights' leader opposed the strikes, but thousands of members participated, and in the wave of public reaction against radicals and labor activists of all kinds, the Knights came under sharp attack. In this climate, the "pure and simple unionism" espoused by the new American Federation of Labor (AFL) struck many workers as more practical than the Knights' vision of broader social reform. McNeill was appointed to draft a plan for peace between the two organizations, but it foundered almost immediately. McNeill's single-minded focus on economic issues had always been an uneasy match with the Knights' more sweeping agenda, and in July 1886 he left the Knights for the AFL. Within the next several months he also began editing a Boston paper (the *Labor Leader*) and ran for mayor of Boston on the United Labor party ticket.

George McNeill attended every AFL convention for the next twelve years, wrote and spoke frequently on the organization's behalf, and in 1897 represented the AFL at the British Trade Union Congress. During the terrible depression of 1893 he toured more than a dozen cities as AFL spokesman, rallying the unemployed and demanding government relief for them. Two years later, he generated much discussion—but little response from the AFL—when he called for an all-out drive among unorganized workers, whatever their skill, race, creed, color, or sex. He also served on several Massachusetts state commissions, was vice president of the American Anti-Imperialist League in 1898, and in 1900 sat on the advisory council of the National Civic Federation. At the same time he produced a number of books on labor topics, most notably *The Labor Movement: The Problem of Today* (1887), for which he served as editor and principal author; it is considered the first comprehensive history of the American labor movement. He died in Somerville, Massachusetts.

In 1887 McNeill wrote, "The laborer's commodity perishes every day beyond possibility of recovery. He must sell today's labor today or never. . . . An empty stomach can make no contracts." The only solution, he believed, was for workers to build a truly mass movement whose political and economic strength would equal that of their employers. McNeill was a man of his time, and his commitment to labor solidarity had its limits; he was outspoken, for instance, on the impossibility of making common cause with Chinese workers. Nevertheless, nearly half a century would pass before the mainstream labor movement initiated anything as broadly inclusive as the organizing efforts he proposed.

• McNeill left no personal papers. In addition to the book mentioned above, he published *Eight Hour Primer* (1889); *The Philosophy of the Labor Movement* (1893); *A Study of Accidents and Accident Insurance* (1900); *Unfrequented Paths: Songs of Nature, Labor, and Men* (1903); "Trade Union Ideals," a paper for the American Economic Association (1903); and two novels (dates unknown): *The Slave of Fortune* and *The Story of a Silver Dollar*. For information about his career, see John R. Commons et al., *History of Labour in the United States*, vol. 2 (1918), and *Documentary History of American Industrial Society*, vol. 10 (1910); David Montgomery, *Beyond Equality: Labor and the Radical Republicans* (1967); Norman J. Ware, *The Labor Movement in the United States, 1860–1895* (1929); and Philip S. Foner, *History of the Labor Movement in the United States*, vol. 1 (1947) and vol. 2 (1955).

SANDRA OPDYCKE

MCNEILL, Hector (10 Oct. 1728–25 Dec. 1785), naval officer, was born in County Antrim, Ireland, the son of Malcolm McNeill and Mary Stuart. When Hector McNeill was eight years old the family emigrated to Boston, where their Scotch-Irish antecedents became the subject of derision. McNeill later wrote that "dureing the whole time of my Boy-hood in the town of Boston my life was one continual State of warfare" (Smith, p. 9). McNeill first went to sea in a Boston merchant vessel at the age of sixteen and became captain of his own ship only five years later. In 1750 he married Mary Wilson; they were to have four children, three of whom survived infancy.

In 1755 the vessel under McNeill's command, the schooner *Lawrence*, was taken into British government service to transport a detachment of New England militia in a campaign against the French. Later that year the *Lawrence* was captured by Indians (probably Iroquois), and McNeill was taken prisoner and marched to Quebec. He described his captors as "a Cruel Bloody Bigoted Cowardly race of Vermine" (Smith, p. 10). He apparently escaped or bargained for his release and, according to his own account, he then commanded several other ships in British service. At the end of the French and Indian War he was enjoying a profitable career as a shipowner and master in the New England coastal trade. In 1769 his wife died; the following year he married Mary Watt, with whom he had one child.

Just how McNeill came to be connected with the cause of the American Revolution is unclear. In 1775 he and his family were living in Quebec. When the American army, under Benedict Arnold, laid siege to the city, the British governor, Sir Guy Carleton, ordered its citizens to either take up arms in its defense or leave the vicinity. McNeill was among those who departed. During the next several months he apparently was engaged in a business relationship with Arnold, taking some responsibility for transporting the Continental Army's supplies along the St. Lawrence River.

When the American troops retreated from Quebec, McNeill set out for Philadelphia, arriving there in early June 1776. It seems that McNeill either made a dramatic impression on the Continental Congress or already had some influential connections within it. The Massachusetts delegates may well have been aware of his talents. Barely a week after his arrival the marine committee of the Congress appointed him to the command of the Continental frigate *Boston*, then fitting out at Newburyport, Massachusetts.

The command of a new warship in a new navy taxed McNeill's professional capacity and overtaxed his patience. It took him almost a year to find the guns, supplies, and men the *Boston* needed, as sailors and shipbuilders gave preference to privateers and merchantmen. He complained to the marine committee that "I have Suffer'd so much in fitting out the Ship I now have the Honour to Command, that I do not think I would undertake such a Task again for any Sum whatever unless I was better Supported" (Clark and Morgan, eds., vol. 8, p. 1008). Another frigate, the *Hancock*, was fitting out at the same time under the command of John Manley. When the Congress published a list establishing the relative seniority of captains in the Continental navy, Manley's name appeared second and McNeill's third. The two officers came to detest each other.

The *Hancock* and the *Boston* finally got to sea on 21 May 1777, with orders to seek out and destroy British warships off the coasts of New England and Canada. Captains Manley and McNeill spent most of the cruise verbally sniping at each other, McNeill claiming that Manley had no idea of how to command a naval squadron. On 8 June they encountered a British frigate, the *Fox*, which they captured after a gun duel that lasted an hour and a half. The *Hancock* seems to have born the brunt of the fighting, but McNeill claimed that a crucially timed broadside from the *Boston* had made the British captain strike his colors.

For the next month the *Hancock*, *Boston*, and *Fox*, the latter now commanded by one of Manley's lieutenants, prowled around the Grand Banks. McNeill complained that the area was too dangerous now that the enemy knew the American squadron was at sea; he was proven right. On 7 July the British frigate *Flora* and the 44-gun ship *Rainbow* came into sight. The ensuing action turned into a rout, with neither American captain showing any enthusiasm for supporting the other. The *Flora* retook the *Fox* and the *Rainbow* sailed over the horizon in pursuit of the *Hancock*, which was captured after a chase of thirty-nine hours. The *Boston* escaped.

McNeill, convinced that the entire British fleet would be looking for him, took his ship into the Sheepscot River on the coast of Maine to hide for more than a month. By the time he took her back to Boston in late August, complaints about his conduct were circulating not only among his officers but in the Continental Congress. James Warren wrote to John Adams of McNeill's "overbearing haughtiness and unlimited conceit" (Smith, p. 9); McNeill grumbled that he had only been doing his duty in saving his ship from capture by a superior enemy, and that the loss of the *Hancock* and *Fox* had been the result of Manley's "blunders and misconduct" (Clark and Morgan, eds., vol. 9, p. 804). When Manley was released in a prisoner exchange in the summer of 1778, the Congress ordered a court-martial of both captains. Manley was acquitted but McNeill was dismissed from the navy.

With the end of his naval career McNeill almost disappears from the records. Later in the war he apparently commanded at least two privateers, the brigantine *Pallas* and the ship *Adventure*. With the coming of peace he returned to the merchant service. He was lost at sea on Christmas night 1785.

McNeill seems to have been representative of the characters who were attracted to the officer ranks of the American Continental navy: an adventurous and ambitious man whose understanding of the relationships between seamanship, patriotism, and military discipline was decidedly hazy. His few surviving writings indicate that he was a fine seaman who let his impatience with his superiors interfere with his professional performance.

• Most of the extant papers relevant to McNeill's career are being published in the multivolume *Naval Documents of the American Revolution* series, ed. William Bell Clark and William James Morgan (1964–). The lengthiest biography, Gardner W. Allen, "Captain Hector McNeill, Continental Navy," *Proceedings of the Massachusetts Historical Society* 55 (1921): 46–152, is dated. The best modern account of McNeill's career in the Continental navy is contained in Philip Chadwick Foster Smith's narrative of the battle in which the frigate *Hancock* was lost, *Fired by Manley Zeal: A Naval Fiasco of the American Revolution* (1977). See also William M. Fowler, Jr., *Rebels Under Sail: The American Navy during the Revolution* (1976); William James Morgan, *Captains to the Northward: The New England Captains in the Continental Navy* (1959); and Gardner W. Allen, *A Naval History of the American Revolution* (2 vols., 1913).

JOHN A. TILLEY

MCNEILL, John Hanson (12 June 1815–10 Nov. 1864), soldier and farmer, was born in Hardy County, Virginia (now W.Va.), the son of Strother McNeill and Amy Pugh, farmers. McNeill's childhood and youth were made difficult by the death of his father when McNeill was only four years old. The dire circumstances of his family forced him to abandon school after only a few years and assist his mother in farming while he was still a child. In 1837 he married Jemima Harness Cunningham; they had four sons and one daughter.

From 1837 until the outbreak of the Civil War, McNeill and his family migrated to a succession of farms in search of larger plots of land and more cattle. From 1837 to 1838 he had a small farm in Hardy County, near his childhood home. In 1838 he moved his family to a new farm near Paris, Kentucky, but in 1844 they returned to Hardy County because of his wife's poor health. In 1848, with his wife now recovered, McNeill moved the family to Boone County, Missouri, and in 1855 the McNeills moved again, this time to a 300-acre farm he had purchased in Daviess County in northwestern Missouri. Until the Civil War McNeill was a stockbreeder of some renown, well known in Virginia and Missouri for his herd of Shorthorn cattle, which won many awards in county fairs and agricultural exhibitions. His last farm in Missouri was particularly prosperous. In addition to his land and cattle, he also owned a family of slaves and was a minister in the Methodist Episcopal church.

The secession crisis of 1861 forced McNeill out of farming and into soldiering. Although some sources contend that McNeill opposed secession, he was one of the first men in Missouri to raise a local militia unit in opposition to the federal government. Even before Confederate governor Claiborne Jackson's military proclamation of June 1861, McNeill raised his own cavalry company from Daviess County, led by himself and officered by his sons William, George, and Jesse. On 14 June 1861 they mustered into Confederate service as B Company, First Regiment Cavalry, Missouri State Guards.

From 1861 to 1862 McNeill and his cavalry accompanied Confederate general Sterling Price in the increasingly bitter campaign to win Missouri for the Confederacy. In August 1861 McNeill fought in the battle of Wilson's Creek and pursued Union stragglers after their defeat. In September 1861 he fought at the battle of Lexington, where he was badly wounded and his son George was killed. After Lexington, McNeill recuperated at a friend's home in Boone County, where he was captured by a Union patrol. He was imprisoned first at Columbia, Missouri, and then at St. Louis. On 15 June 1862 he escaped and returned briefly to Daviess County to see his family.

With the failure of Price's conventional campaign to win Missouri, McNeill turned his attention to unconventional means to win Confederate independence. Along with his son Jesse, he made his way across the country back to their ancestral home in Hardy County, Virginia, in July 1862 with the outline of a plan to wage guerrilla war against the Union. Under the terms of the Confederate Congress's Partisan Ranger Act of 28 April 1862, McNeill and a number of other officers were authorized to raise independent commands to raid Union army supply trains and pocket the proceeds. From August 1862 until March 1863 McNeill and his band, recruited from Hardy County, operated under the overall command of Colonel John Imboden, engaging in a series of minor raids that infuriated local Union commanders and eventually provoked stern countermeasures.

In March 1863 McNeill dissolved his formal relationship with Imboden and raised an independent command, known as McNeill's Partisan Rangers. As captain of his own company, he continued to cooperate with Imboden, joining him for larger raids on Morgantown and Gettysburg, but he usually preferred striking out on his own. Altogether his command never numbered more than one hundred men at any given time, but his constant raiding forced Union commanders to tie up large numbers of men attempting to hunt him down and fortifying every minor outpost in northern Virginia and western Maryland. His repeated raids on the critical Baltimore and Ohio Railroad, which ran along the Potomac River, caused numerous crises in troop and supply movements between the eastern and western theaters for Union military planners.

Despite his success as a guerrilla leader, McNeill had his detractors within the Confederate camp. Some Confederate generals were convinced that partisan groups were a magnet for Confederate deserters, drawn by the lure of easy discipline and fast profits from war booty. Others were concerned that partisan activity behind Union lines provoked Federal retaliation that harmed the local population more than the raids hurt the invading Yankee army. In February 1864, with the urging of General Robert E. Lee, the Confederate Congress repealed the Partisan Ranger Act and ordered all partisan commands absorbed into the regular army. Under the terms of the repeal, the Confederate secretary of war, James Seddon, could exempt particular units. He chose only two: McNeill's Rangers and Mosby's Rangers.

In 1864 McNeill took part in the campaign to prevent the invasion of the Shenandoah Valley by Major General Franz Sigel and his replacement, Major General Phil Sheridan. On 3 October 1864 McNeill was mortally wounded while leading a raid on a Union camp near Mount Jackson, Virginia. He died in Harrisonburg, Virginia. After McNeill's death, his son Jesse continued to lead McNeill's Rangers. In February 1865 Jesse McNeill led a daring raid on Cumberland, Maryland, to capture two Union generals, George Crook and B. F. Kelley. This raid was apparently in retaliation for Kelley's arrest and imprisonment of Jemima McNeill, John's wife and Jesse's mother. Jesse McNeill surrendered to Brigadier General Rutherford B. Hayes, a future president of the United States, on 8 May 1865.

Historians debate the effect that guerrilla warfare of the type McNeill waged had on the outcome of the Civil War. Virgil Carrington Jones maintains that Confederate partisans so harassed Union armies in 1864 that they extended the war for eight or nine months. Other historians disagree, noting Ulysses S. Grant's difficulty in coordinating a wide campaign, Lee's skill in parrying Grant's Richmond campaign, and the Confederate hope that Abraham Lincoln would be turned out in the November 1864 presidential election. What is beyond dispute, however, is that the partisan warfare waged by McNeill and others helped make the Civil War more costly and more bitter for both sides. Sheridan reacted to partisan warfare in the Shenandoah Valley by embarking on a scorched earth policy, which not only left the partisans little to subsist on but also caused widespread poverty and deprivation among the populace. The ill will and destruction of this devastation was felt throughout the region for decades after the war ended.

• McNeill's life is covered in W. D. Vandiver, "Two Forgotten Heroes," *Missouri Historical Review* 21 (Apr. 1927): 404–19. Vandiver, as a child, met McNeill and apparently had access to McNeill family papers (current location unknown). The most complete study of McNeill's Rangers, which also includes a detailed roster of the unit and an account of McNeill's antebellum life, is Roger U. Delauter, Jr., *McNeill's Rangers* (1986). McNeill's final days are the subject of J. W. Duffy, *McNeill's Last Charge* (1912). McNeill's role in the overall scheme of Confederate partisan warfare in Virginia is covered in Virgil Carrington Jones, *Gray Ghosts and Rebel Raiders* (1956). See also Stephen Z. Starr, *The Union Cavalry in the Civil War*, vol. 2, *The War in the East from Gettysburg to Appomattox* (1981).

JAMES K. HOGUE

MCNEMAR, Quinn (20 Feb. 1900–3 July 1986), psychologist, was born in Greenland, West Virginia, the son of farmers. He described his rural hometown as a "hillbilly, hollow folk area." The teachers in the one-room school that he attended were often inadequate, but the school permitted the bright McNemar to seek out the books that were available for all grades and to work at his own level. He liked arithmetic and worked his way through the eight-grade text by the end of his fifth year, and the next year he taught arithmetic to the eighth graders because the teacher was unable to do so.

McNemar continued at the school until he was eighteen, having absorbed all that was available there. In 1918 he easily passed the state teachers' examination. His family wanted him to work as a conscientious objector rather than serve in the army and encouraged him to return to school to postpone his being drafted. He attended the University of West Virginia at Keyser, completing his first year at age twenty-two and serving as the class president. From there he went to Juniata College in Huntingdon, Pennsylvania, graduating in 1925 with a secondary teaching certificate. After two years of teaching mathematics and science in a high school in Charles Town, West Virginia, he was admitted to Stanford for graduate study in psychology.

McNemar was introduced to statistics during his first year at Stanford through three one-quarter courses under Truman Lee Kelley, whose book *Statistical Method* (1924) was the standard advanced text for students of psychology and education. After receiving his Ph.D. in 1932, McNemar became a member of the Stanford faculty, rising through the ranks to full professor and remaining until he reached professor emeritus status.

McNemar continued to build his firsthand knowledge of the developments in the new areas of factor analysis and the analysis of variance. In 1929 he attended the International Congress of Psychology at Yale and heard a paper by Charles Spearman, the British founder of factor analysis. The following year he met Olga Williamson, a senior at Stanford whom he married in 1931; they had no children. In 1933 he received a postdoctoral fellowship from the Social Science Research Council and spent the summer at the University of Chicago, where he heard alternative positions on factor analysis presented by four of its distinguished leaders: Spearman, Karl Holzinger, L. L. Thurstone, and Harold Hotelling. McNemar then went to Columbia University for the remainder of the year, studying the analysis of variance, which had been introduced by R. A. Fisher in England. He was aided by study with Hotelling, who had traveled to Oxford to learn directly from Fisher. Hence McNemar was prepared to continue as Kelley's successor when he returned to Stanford.

During World War II McNemar had further opportunities to widen the scope of application of statistical procedures and sampling techniques by working with Samuel Stouffer and others in the initial stages of what became the research leading to the *American Soldier* volumes, studies of the morale of the men in the armed forces. From 1941 to 1943, and again briefly in 1944, he was on the staff of the Social Science Research Council in New York City, serving as the head of the fellowship programs and grants-in-aid. This also gave his wife the chance to pursue her graduate study in psychology at Columbia.

In 1947 McNemar became a professor of statistics in Stanford's newly established Department of Mathematical Statistics while continuing in his professorships in psychology and education. The first edition of his influential book *Psychological Statistics* appeared in 1949, followed by revisions in 1955, 1962, and 1969. Through this book his influence reached a very wide audience of many generations of students and psychologists.

McNemar held many elective offices, including the presidencies of the Psychometric Society (1951), the Division of Evaluation and Measurement of the American Psychological Association (APA) (1952), the Western Psychological Association (1959), and the APA (1963–1964). He had worked closely with Lewis Terman and Maud Merrill in the revision of the Stanford-Binet test, and in 1962 he published the background book on the methodology used in the revision of the earlier scale. He and Terman had published a new scale called the Terman-McNemar Test of Mental Ability in 1941.

McNemar's presidential address before the APA, "Lost Our Intelligence? Why," was widely cited and reprinted in at least fifteen books of readings and in a French translation. When he published his autobiography in volume 7 of *A History of Psychology in Autobiography* (ed. Gardner Lindzey [1980]), he justified his role as a critic, citing the use of his critical skills in editing papers submitted to journals such as the *Journal of Applied Psychology* and the *Annual Review of Psychology*.

McNemar was greatly admired as a teacher and a consultant to graduate students and was always willing to assist them in the design of their investigations and the analysis and presentation of their data. His interest in students, undergraduates as well as graduate students, was personal as well as professional. Having no children of their own, he and his wife entertained many students in their home, helped them financially when needed, and continued to correspond with them later in their careers.

McNemar retired from Stanford in 1965 and spent the next five years as a professor of psychology and education at the University of Texas in Austin. He then returned to Palo Alto, where he died. At his death, psychology lost an able teacher and a distinguished researcher with a host of friends among his professional colleagues and students.

• An obituary is in *American Psychologist* 43 (Mar. 1988): 196–97.

ERNEST R. HILGARD

MCNEMAR, Richard (20 Nov. 1770–15 Sept. 1839), revivalist minister turned Shaker missionary and author, was born in Tuscarora, Pennsylvania. His parents were farmers. His mother's maiden name was Knox. From the age of fifteen, he worked as an itinerant schoolteacher throughout South Central Pennsylvania, laboring on his family's farm between jobs. He moved to Kentucky in 1791 to study languages with Malcolm Worley at Caldwell's Station and theology with the Reverend Robert Finley at Cane Ridge. In April 1793 he married Jane Luckie; they had seven children. The next spring, McNemar, his wife, and their first child moved to Paint Creek, where he taught for a time before moving back to Cane Ridge to preach. He became minister of the Presbyterian church in Cabin Creek in September 1796 and was ordained in August 1798.

Despite achieving popularity, McNemar faced accusations of heresy in 1801 when his preaching to thousands at camp meetings helped to fuel the fires of the "Great Revival." The accusation against him was that he was an Arminian, that is, he denied Calvinistic predestination. With his "New Light" colleagues, McNemar held that "the will of God [is] manifest to each individual who honestly [seeks] after it, by an inward light" (quoted in Phillips, p. 29). "Old Light" Presbyterians increasingly opposed such denials of the Westminster Confession as well as the disorder of revival "enthusiasm." McNemar nevertheless continued in his course and became minister of the church in Turtle Creek, near Lebanon, Ohio. In the fall of 1803, growing tensions with the synod over his unorthodoxy led McNemar and four supporters to secede and form their own Springfield Presbytery. Within a year, however, as these New Lights became more radical, they dissolved their presbytery and refused all labels but that of "Christians." McNemar wrote the presbytery's "Last Will and Testament," calling for Christian unity rooted solely in the Bible.

McNemar grew more radical yet. Inspired by the Great Revival's success, he came to believe in the imminence of Christ's second coming. His millennial fervor prepared him to accept the message of the Shakers, the United Society of Believers in Christ's Second Appearing, who upheld that Christ had in fact already returned in the form of Mother Ann Lee. In 1805 three Shaker missionaries from the central ministry in New Lebanon, New York, traveled west to plant Shakerism in the revival's fertile ground. They sought particularly to convert influential souls like McNemar, and his conversion on 24 April 1805, two days before a camp meeting at Turtle Creek, signaled a victory for their faith. McNemar led his Turtle Creek congregation virtually intact through the New Light schism and into Shakerism. His family converted soon after him, as did his brother, his sister, and her husband, the Reverend John Dunlavy. Despite the fact that the Shaker commitment demanded accepting celibacy, renouncing marital relations, and transferring all property to the community, McNemar was successful in converting scores of people in Ohio during 1805.

McNemar's own land became the site for Union Village, where the Shakers built their first western meetinghouse. Between 1806 and 1825, he took orders from David Darrow, who had come from New Lebanon to lead the western Shakers. McNemar helped to establish and maintain most of the seven Shaker villages founded in Kentucky, Indiana, and Ohio. For instance, in 1808 he made a long winter missionary trip to Busro, Indiana, where the Shakers soon founded West Union village; when the village faltered in the mid-1820s, he supervised the relocation of its residents. In 1806 and 1807 McNemar also participated in a failed mission to a group of Native Americans camped at Greenville, Ohio. After Darrow's death in June 1825, McNemar took assignments from his successors and served as an elder for "families" within Union Village. Without formal legal training but with considerable success, he also represented Shaker interests in lawsuits brought by apostates seeking to reclaim their property and between 1827 and 1831 managed Shaker legal business at Pleasant Hill and South Union.

McNemar was one of the first to realize the importance of the press for the Shaker cause. In *The Kentucky Revival* (1807), one of the earliest Shaker books, he chronicled the revival and defended the Shakers against the criticisms of opponents such as Barton Stone, a former New Light colleague. Throughout the 1820s and 1830s, McNemar continued to write pro-Shaker tracts including *A Concise Answer to the General Inquiry, Who, or What Are the Shakers* (1823), which was republished a dozen times. He also wrote and published many hymns, compiled a grammar for Shaker use, and printed a compilation of Shaker constitutions. From 1832 to 1835 he served as head of the Watervliet, Ohio, village, where he founded the *Western Review* (1834–1837), the first Shaker serial, in which he memorialized the activities of the western faithful. Not only did he do his own typesetting, printing, and binding, but he also had a zeal for more typical Shaker crafts and produced well over a thousand chairs in his lifetime.

Despite McNemar's contributions to western Shakerism, he was expelled from Union Village during the last year of his life. In 1836, not wanting to be hindered in his many established duties, McNemar refused the opportunity to lead Union Village. Freegift Wells, who assumed the office instead, grew jealous of McNemar's status and antagonized him until he found an excuse to eject him from the community in 1839. During a period of spiritualistic revival known as "Mother Ann's work," a young village woman, Margaret O'Brien, received a message from the spirit of Mother Ann Lee rebuking McNemar. This message was followed in early June by another vision: an order to exile McNemar. Although another visionary vindicated him after he made a long journey to the central ministry at New Lebanon, McNemar died soon after his return to Union Village. As the western Shakers eventually learned, McNemar's powerful preaching, cultivated mind, and effective use of the press were assets that they could ill afford to lose.

• The Library of Congress Shaker collection includes many of McNemar's extant letters, journals, and diaries. His important published writings, in addition to those cited above, are *A Selection of Hymns and Poems for the Use of Believers* (1833), which includes some of McNemar's many original hymns and poems, and *The Constitution of the United Society of Believers (Called Shakers)*, which includes Shaker village covenants and a defense of Shaker government "Addressed to the Political World." For a complete bibliography of his published writings (some of which he published under pseudonyms, including his church name, Eleazor Wright) see Mary L. Richmond, *Shaker Literature: A Bibliography* (2 vols., 1977). There are two highly sympathetic biographies of McNemar, neither of them comprehensive: John Paterson MacLean, *Sketch of the Life and Labors of Richard McNemar* (1905), and Hazel Spencer Phillips, *Richard the Shaker* (1972). MacLean's biography includes extensive quotations from McNemar's diaries. For discussions of McNemar within the broader contexts of Presbyterianism and the Great Revival, see Ernest Trice Thompson, *Presbyterians in the South*, vol. 1 (1963), and John B. Boles, *The Great Revival, 1787–1805: The Origins of the Southern Evangelical Mind* (1972). Boles includes a discussion of McNemar's theology. The most comprehensive history of Shakers in America is Stephen J. Stein, *The Shaker Experience in America: A History of the United Society of Believers* (1992), which also provides a good starting place for bibliography.

DAVID J. GRAHAM-VOELKER

MCNICHOLAS, John Timothy (15 Dec. 1877–22 Apr. 1950), archbishop and educational leader, was born in Treenkeel, County Mayo, Ireland, the son of Patrick McNicholas, a steel mill laborer, and Mary Mullany. The family immigrated to the United States in 1881 and settled in Chester, Pennsylvania, a port of entry on the Delaware River about fourteen miles from Philadelphia. At the age of seventeen, John entered the Dominican order at St. Rose Priory in Kentucky and was ordained to the priesthood on 10 October 1901 at St. Joseph Priory in Somerset, Ohio. He then spent three years in Rome, earning a doctorate in theology and gaining many influential friends both in the upper echelons of the Dominican order and in the Roman Curia.

After his return to the United States in 1904, McNicholas served successively as the master of novices in Somerset, Ohio, as a professor of theology and canon law at the Catholic University of America in Washington, D.C., and as the national director of the Holy Name Society in New York City. This last position gave him great prominence since the Holy Name Society was a forceful organization that promoted not only reverence for the name of Jesus but also monthly communion Sundays and annual rallies and parades throughout the country. The frequent reception of communion and the public demonstration of church membership encouraged by the Holy Name Society gave Catholic men a deeper sense of loyalty to their church.

In 1917 he returned to Rome as an assistant to the master general of the Dominican order and as a professor at the Angelicum University. The following year he was appointed bishop of Duluth, Minnesota, and in 1925 he was appointed archbishop of Cincinnati, where he remained for twenty-five years.

In Cincinnati McNicholas was a dynamo of energy, establishing about fifty mission chapels, organizing Holy Name Societies, advocating lay retreats, championing the rights of labor, supporting the foundation of the Home Missioners of America, and promoting the newly established Legion of Decency, a Catholic film review board that provided influential motion-picture ratings and critical evaluations. He put much emphasis on education, building interparochial high schools, establishing a teachers college to improve the quality of instruction in the archdiocesan schools, and sending over 120 priests to graduate schools for further study, many of them to the Angelicum University in Rome to earn doctorates in theology. In 1928 he received a charter from the state of Ohio for the Athenaeum of Ohio, an umbrella organization that gathered several colleges together into one structure: Mount St. Mary's Theological Seminary, St. Gregory's College Seminary, the Archdiocesan Teachers College, and Our Lady of Cincinnati College. In 1935 he founded the Institutum Divi Thomae Graduate School of Science. His ambition was to shape these institutions into an influential Catholic intellectual and cultural center in Southwest Ohio. Only the theological seminary remains today. He was a vigorous crusader for state aid to parochial schools. Although the Ohio state legislature did not, in the end, provide any tax monies for parochial schools, McNicholas succeeded in publicizing the contribution Catholic schools made to the state.

Archbishop McNicholas was a confidant of Pope Pius XI and was the principal author of that pope's encyclical on Christian education. In 1939 Pius XI drew up documents appointing McNicholas to be the archbishop of New York but died before the documents were formally issued. His successor, Pope Pius XII, appointed Francis J. Spellman to that post instead.

McNicholas's intense drive also influenced the national councils and organizations of the Catholic church. He was a member of the Board of Trustees of the Catholic University of America from 1934 until his death, the chairman of the Education Department of the National Catholic Welfare Conference from 1930 to 1935 and from 1942 to 1945, the president of the National Catholic Educational Association from 1946 to 1950, and the chairman of the Administrative Board of the National Catholic Welfare Conference from 1945 to 1950. Archbishop McNicholas died at his residence in the Cincinnati suburb of College Hill.

McNicholas was a typical "builder bishop" of an expansionist era in American Catholic history, an effective orator, an outspoken scrapper who minced no words in advocating his cherished projects, a formidable adversary, and an ambitious and astute politician who, according to the many obituaries published after his death, left a deep impression on all who dealt with him.

• McNicholas's papers are primarily in the Archives of the Archdiocese of Cincinnati and in the Dominican Archives at Providence College in Providence, R.I. Many of his lectures and sermons are collected in Maurice E. Reardon, *Mosaic of a Bishop* (1957). See also Steven M. Avella, "John Timothy McNicholas in the Age of Practical Thomism," in *Records of the American Catholic Historical Society of Philadelphia* (1986).

M. EDMUND HUSSEY

MCNICKLE, D'Arcy (18 Jan. 1904–15 Oct. 1977), author, government official, and anthropologist, was born William D'Arcy McNickle at St. Ignatius, Montana, on the Flathead Indian reservation, the youngest child of William McNickle and Philomene Parenteau, farmers. D'Arcy McNickle's maternal grandparents, Isidore Parenteau and Judith Plante, were members of the Canadian Metis community, which traced its heritage to French, Chippewa, and Cree ancestors. They had fled from Saskatchewan to Montana following their participation in the Metis rebellion in 1885. McNickle's father, the son of Irish immigrants, had come from Pittsburgh to Montana to work on the Northern Pacific Railroad.

McNickle spent his early years on his father's ranch in the Mission Valley near St. Ignatius. In 1905 he was enrolled as a member of the Confederated Salish and Kootenai Tribes. When he reached school age he entered the mission school at St. Ignatius, boarding there during the school year. In 1913 McNickle's parents were divorced, and he was sent to the Salem Indian Training School in Chemawa, Oregon. In 1916 he returned to the Flathead reservation to live with his mother and her new husband, Gus Dahlberg, then lived with them successively in Langley, Washington, and Missoula, Montana. McNickle graduated from Missoula High School in 1921 and enrolled at the University of Montana that fall. The young student began writing as an undergraduate and published several short pieces in the college literary magazine.

In 1925, midway during his senior year at the university, McNickle decided to withdraw from school, sell the land he had been allotted on the Flathead reservation, and complete his undergraduate education in Europe. Before he left Montana, his poem "Old Isidore," written as a memorial to his recently deceased grandfather, won a statewide literary competition and confirmed the young man's determination to be a writer. McNickle sailed for England in September 1925 and made his way to Oxford. Unfortunately, he learned that it would take two additional years of residence to earn an Oxford degree. Discouraged and short of funds, the would-be student moved on to France in early 1926 and spent the next five months exploring the expatriate world of Paris and its environs. He returned to the United States in May 1926 and settled in New York City.

With the exception of a brief stint as an automobile salesman in Philadelphia, McNickle spent the next decade working in various editorial capacities with New York publishers. In September 1935 the Federal Writers Project, based in Washington, D.C., hired him to work on its new series of state guides. Early the following year he was transferred to the Bureau of Indian Affairs (BIA), where he joined the staff of Commissioner John Collier. A former social worker, Collier was the architect of an "Indian New Deal," which attempted to reverse the government's traditional hostility to tribally based communities and initiate a variety of community development projects. As one of the few Native Americans in a senior policymaking position, McNickle played a major role in facilitating communication between local Indian people and the BIA leadership. Like Collier, he also saw the value of applying the insights and expertise of anthropology to the bureau's work. His duties took him to reservation communities across the United States and provided him with a unique vantage point on an exciting period of reform. In 1944, as an outgrowth of his work under Collier, McNickle joined several other Indian leaders to found the National Congress of American Indians (NCAI), the most effective pan-Indian organization of the modern era.

Collier left the government after World War II, but McNickle continued to advocate the former commissioner's agenda, despite rising pressure from Republicans and western representatives to dismantle his reforms. McNickle grew increasingly disenchanted with the authoritarian policies developed under Presidents Harry S. Truman and Dwight D. Eisenhower, and by 1952 he decided to leave his position as director of tribal relations to devote himself to Indian affairs without the restraints of a government position. During the 1950s and early 1960s, McNickle directed American Indian Development, a nonprofit organization devoted to community development; played an active role in the NCAI's campaign to oppose the growing popularity of termination among non-Indian policy makers, and conducted a model project at Crownpoint, New Mexico, on the Navajo reservation. In 1956 McNickle also began to conduct summer leadership training workshops for young Indians, and in 1961 he was one of the principal organizers of the American Indian Chicago Conference, an unprecedented gathering of Native American leaders.

In 1966 McNickle accepted the position of professor and chair of the anthropology department at the University of Saskatchewan's new Regina campus. He held that position until 1971 when he retired and moved to Albuquerque, New Mexico. One year later, McNickle became founding director of the Newberry Library's Center for the History of the American Indian (later renamed the D'Arcy McNickle Center) in Chicago. He remained in that position until 1976 when he became chair of the center's advisory council. In his last years McNickle was a much sought-after speaker, mentor to young Indians engaged in academic life, and consultant to foundations and government agencies. One of his last projects was an extensive review of federal Indian policy prepared for the American Indian Policy Review Commission and published in 1976.

Writing was McNickle's first love, but he pursued his career as a writer outside his daily employment. He rarely had the luxury to devote himself full time to his craft. He wrote his first novel, *The Surrounded*, while living in New York. Based loosely on his own autobiography, and set in the Mission Valley, it was published in 1936 to critical acclaim but weak sales. *They Came Here First: The Epic of the American Indian* (1949), a general history of Indian people, appeared in 1949, while McNickle was still a BIA employee. After leaving the Indian Office he published three other works of nonfiction, *Indians and Other Americans: Two Ways of Life Meet* (with Harold E. Fey, 1959), *The Indian Tribes of the United States: Ethnic and Cultural Survival* (1962), and *Indian Man: A Biography of Oliver La Farge* (1971). McNickle wrote two more novels following his resignation from the government, *Runner in the Sun: A Story of Indian Maize* (1954) and *Wind from an Enemy Sky* (1978). The first, set in the Southwest centuries before the time of Columbus, traced the ways in which an Indian village dealt with internal tension and technological innovation; the second, set on a fictional reservation that resembled the Mission Valley, focused on the cultural distances that separate Indians and non-Indians in contemporary society. McNickle published shorter pieces on Indian-white relations and government policy in a variety of popular magazines, including the *Nation* and *Christian Century*.

McNickle was married to Joran Birkeland from 1926 to 1938, Roma Kauffmann from 1938 to 1967, and Viola Pfrommer from 1969 until her death in 1977. Each of the first two marriages produced one child. He died at his home in Albuquerque.

D'Arcy McNickle's personal journey ran parallel to the course of Indian affairs during the twentieth century. Like many others, he evolved from a youth who felt caught between a native heritage and his society's indifference to a scholar and activist who believed that Native Americans could embrace their Indianness without sacrificing membership in the larger society. His writings and his achievements smoothed the path for Native Americans who came after him, and his ability to bridge the distance between Indian values and the national culture is an enduring legacy.

• McNickle's papers are in the Newberry Library, Chicago. Much of the official correspondence from his years at the Bureau of Indian Affairs is contained in the records of that agency in the National Archives. Others of his letters are part of the Sol Tax Papers at the University of Chicago. McNickle is the subject of a full-length biography, Dorothy Parker, *Singing an Indian Song: A Biography of D'Arcy McNickle* (1992); his literary work is treated extensively in John Lloyd Purdy, *Word Ways: The Novels of D'Arcy McNickle* (1990). Both books contain excellent bibliographies of works by and about their subject.

FREDERICK E. HOXIE

MCNUTT, Paul Vories (19 July 1891–24 Mar. 1955), politician and diplomat, was born in Franklin, Indiana, the son of John Crittenden McNutt, a lawyer and librarian of the Indiana Supreme Court, and Ruth Neely. After a childhood in Martinsville, Indiana, where his father practiced law, McNutt studied at Indiana University. He was an active campus politician who became editor of the school newspaper and president of the student union. He graduated with an A.B. in 1913 and then went on to Harvard Law School, from which he received an LL.B. in 1916. He entered the army during World War I and became a major in the artillery. His duties kept him in the United States. He married Kathleen Timolat in 1918; the couple had one daughter.

The ambitious and handsome McNutt was drawn to political life, and he soon attracted attention as a rising young Democrat. He became a faculty member of the Indiana University law school in 1917 and resumed teaching there after World War I. In 1925 he was named dean. He also identified himself with the American Legion and used that organization to gain national recognition. He was chosen commander of the Indiana Department of the legion in 1927 and from that base ran successfully for national commander of the legion a year later. The power of the veterans in Indiana helped make McNutt a statewide politician. As the depression of the 1930s hit Indiana, McNutt was often mentioned as a possible candidate to win the governorship for the resurgent Democrats.

McNutt announced his candidacy for governor in February 1932, controlled the state nominating convention, and won an easy victory over his Republican opponent in the fall. The newcomer to national politics did make one costly error. At the Democratic National Convention, McNutt led an uninstructed delegation from Indiana that came late to supporting Franklin D. Roosevelt. There is some evidence that McNutt cherished hopes that he might be a compromise candidate at a deadlocked convention. Failure to come out for Roosevelt early poisoned McNutt's relations with the president. Roosevelt's campaign manager called McNutt "that platinum-blond so and so" (Pringle, p. 315).

During his single term as governor, McNutt achieved an impressive record. He believed that "government may be a great instrument of human progress" (Madison, p. 296). McNutt reorganized the state government, pushed through an income tax, and sponsored welfare laws and state pensions. He paid off the state debt and left office with a $17 million surplus in the Indiana treasury. These accomplishments gave him national prominence and presidential hopes for 1940. On the other hand, McNutt had serious liabilities. Under his regime state employees were required to donate 2 percent of their salaries to the Hoosier Democratic Club. To many outside the state the "Two Percent Club" represented Indiana's political corruption. McNutt had established a system of regulating the beer distributors in the state that also seemed unsavory. When McNutt deployed state troops in labor disputes, Norman Thomas said that he was a "Hoosier Hitler" (Blake, p. 162).

Barred by the Indiana constitution from running for a second term, McNutt sought the 1940 Democratic presidential nomination. Roosevelt named him high commissioner to the Philippines in February 1937. While in that post, McNutt questioned whether the islands should be granted rapid independence. He resigned from his diplomatic post in July 1939 and became the director of the new Federal Security Agency, which oversaw federal welfare programs. As McNutt gained attention for his presidential bid, rivals within the Roosevelt administration attacked him. The Treasury Department probed his finances, and the inconclusive end to the inquiry left a cloud over McNutt's chances.

By the spring of 1940 the worsening war situation and the opinion among Democrats for Roosevelt to seek a third term led McNutt to end his presidential candidacy. He was a strong choice among the Democrats at the national convention for vice president, but Roosevelt went with Henry A. Wallace instead. The president told friends that he was "afraid that during the campaign something might break in connection with matters" in Indiana that involved McNutt (*The Secret Diaries of Harold Ickes*, vol. 3, p. 286). McNutt withdrew his name from contention even though the delegates cheered him for twenty minutes.

During the war McNutt remained as the director of the Federal Security Agency and chaired the War Manpower Commission. He was not a notable success in these assignments. The president did not give him much authority, and McNutt himself was an indifferent administrator. After the war, President Harry S. Truman sent McNutt back to the Philippines as high commissioner. In that role he worked for an efficient transition to independence. Once the Philippines were independent, McNutt served as ambassador until May 1947. He ended his political career and practiced law in New York and Washington, D.C., for the next eight years. His corporate clients included the Motion Picture Producers Association and businesses in the Philippines. McNutt died in New York City.

McNutt was an important force in Democratic politics in Indiana and the nation during the New Deal era. His critics called him the "platinum-haired knight from the banks of the Wabash" (Pringle, p. 311), but there was more to his career than just good looks. His moderate views and solid record in state and national posts made him attractive to many middle-of-the road Democrats. His ambition for the presidency was the guiding principle of his political career. When that goal was out of his reach after 1940, he gradually faded from national prominence.

• McNutt's personal papers are in the Lilly Library at Indiana University. The Archives Division, Indiana State Library, Indianapolis, houses the records of his governorship. For his service in the federal government, relevant documents are at the Franklin D. Roosevelt Library, the Harry S. Truman Library, and the National Archives. McNutt wrote frequently on public issues. Some representative examples include "Social Security Bogeyman," *Virginia Quarterly Review* 15 (Spring 1940): 230–40; and "Democracy on Trial in the Orient," *Vital Speeches* 13 (1 Apr. 1946): 362–66. The only full-length biography is I. George Blake, *Paul V. McNutt: Portrait of a Hoosier Statesman* (1966). Among contemporary appraisals of McNutt, Henry F. Pringle, "McNutt Is Willing," *Forum* 103 (June 1940): 311–16, is perceptive. Alva Johnston, "I Intend to Be President," *Saturday Evening Post*, 16 Mar. 1940, pp. 20–21, 67–68, 70, is very critical. Interesting information on McNutt is in the anonymously edited *The Secret Diaries of Harold Ickes*, vols. 2 and 3 (1954); and Bernard F. Donahoe, *Private Plans and Public Dangers* (1965), traces his ill-fated quest for the presidency in 1940. A modern assessment of McNutt appears in James H. Madison, *The Indiana Way* (1986). Iwan Morgan, "Factional Conflict in Indiana Politics during the Later New Deal Years, 1936–1940," *Indiana Magazine of History* 79 (Mar. 1983): 29–60, has more detail about McNutt's political base. Unpublished treatments include Robert R. Neff, "The Early Career and Governorship of Paul V. McNutt" (Ph.D. diss., Indiana Univ., 1964), and John E. Morin, "Paul V. McNutt: A Political Portrait" (Ph.D. diss., Michigan State Univ., 1976). An obituary is in the *New York Times*, 25 Mar. 1955.

LEWIS L. GOULD

MCPARTLAND, Jimmy (15 Mar. 1907–13 Mar. 1991), jazz cornetist, was born James Dougald McPartland in Chicago, Illinois, the son of a former boxer who also played violin and owned a music store. The names of his parents are not known. Between the time that his parents divorced in 1912 or 1913 and their reconciliation seven years later, Jimmy, his older brother Dick, and their sister Ethel lived in an orphanage. Before the divorce, Dick and Jimmy had been given violin lessons by their father, each starting at the age of five. In 1919 or 1920 the reunited family moved to the suburban community of Austin and the boys were enrolled in Austin High School, where in 1922, with Frank Teschemacher, Bud Freeman, and Jim Lanigan, they first discovered the jazz records of the Friars Society Orchestra, a Chicago-based band later known as the New Orleans Rhythm Kings. Though they too had begun on violin, Teschemacher had already started playing alto saxophone, and Lanigan, the eldest, was a pianist. Acting on their example, the McPartlands and Freeman decided to learn instruments more appropriate to jazz. Jimmy chose the cornet, Dick the banjo, and Freeman, the only one without prior musical training, the C melody saxophone. When joined by pianist Dave North and drummer Dave Tough, Lanigan switched to bass, and in 1923 they formed the Blue Friars, named in honor of their initial inspiration.

By 1923 the Blue Friars had become enthralled by King Oliver's Creole Jazz Band and McPartland, who never completed high school, was playing his first professional jobs with Murph Podolsky and other local bandleaders. The Blue Friars also played jobs with the precocious fourteen-year-old clarinetist Benny Goodman, who frequently sat in. In early 1924 McPartland heard Bix Beiderbecke for the first time and quickly began to model his style on that of the slightly older cornetist. In the fall, when Beiderbecke left the Wolverine Orchestra to join Jean Goldkette, McPartland was chosen as his replacement, a position he held on and off through late 1927. In December 1924, after the band dispersed following an aborted job in Miami, McPartland and Dick Voynow, the Wolverines' pianist and manager, reorganized the group using the cornetist's Austin High friends. In 1925 Voynow left and McPartland took on the role of leader. Now booked by Chicago promoter Husk O'Hare, the band was billed as Husk O'Hare's Wolverines for engagements at the Riverview Park in Des Moines, Iowa, and the White City Ballroom in Chicago.

In 1926, along with Freeman and Lanigan, McPartland worked with Art Kassel in Detroit and then at the Friars' Inn in Chicago with Bill Paley before returning to Kassel in 1927. After taking Beiderbecke's place, McPartland had recorded two titles with the Wolverines in December 1924; in October 1927, with a markedly different personnel, he recorded four more numbers with the newly named Original Wolverines. His most important records, however, were made in December 1927 under the name of McKenzie and Condon's Chicagoans. These two records introduced the undiluted, exciting sounds of the Austin High Gang on record and defined for all time the new "Chicago Style" as well. With the clipped, rhythmically incisive, Bixian lead of McPartland, the fiery, almost savage fervor of Teschemacher's clarinet, Freeman's explosive tenor sax, and the heated, propulsive support of pianist Joe Sullivan, banjoist Eddie Condon, bassist Jim Lanigan, and drummer Gene Krupa, a new dimension was brought to the concept of swing in jazz.

At the time he recorded these 1927 sessions, McPartland was a member of Ben Pollack's orchestra, which he joined at the Black Hawk in Chicago in September. After that job the orchestra played at several other venues before opening in September 1928 for a long residency at the Florentine Grill in Manhattan's Park Central Hotel. Pollack had been using Goodman as his featured hot clarinetist and Glenn Miller as his trombonist and arranger since 1925, but shortly after hiring McPartland and Freeman he also brought in trombonist Jack Teagarden, whose unique abilities were recommended to him by several of his sidemen, including McPartland. The Pollack group recorded profusely between 1927 and 1929, not only under its own name but also under a bewildering number of colorful pseudonyms. In addition, McPartland was featured on two small band dates in January and June 1928 under Goodman's leadership. Shortly after its opening at the Park Central, in late December the orchestra also started playing for the Broadway musical *Hello, Daddy*. Combined with recording activities, the orchestra was literally working night and day. McPartland left Pollack in 1929, after being fired for appearing onstage late and dirty from playing handball with Goodman, who subsequently was fired for standing up for McPartland. After a time with Arnold Johnson's orchestra, McPartland worked on Broadway in the pit bands of *Sons o' Guns* and, from 1930 to 1931, *Sweet and Low*. Apart from playing two improvised solos on a 1930 Jan Garber record, McPartland was now effectively out of jazz.

McPartland married singer Dorothy Williams in 1929, and the two worked in Billy Rose's *Crazy Quilt* in 1931; but some time after McPartland went on tour with the show, she divorced him. They had no children. After traveling with both Russ Columbo and Smith Ballew, McPartland returned to New York City in 1933. There was no work for him in jazz, so he took whatever commercial jobs he could get before joining his guitarist brother's Embassy Four at the Palmer House in Chicago, where he remained from 1934 through 1936. McPartland's only opportunity to play jazz during this period was at the jam sessions the lawyer and musician Edwin "Squirrel" Ashcraft held at his home in Evanston, Illinois. Acting on Ashcraft's suggestion, in April 1936 McPartland put together a group to record four titles that were then issued in a limited edition by the Hot Record Society; the personnel of Jimmy McPartland's Squirrels consisted entirely of Chicago-based jazzmen. Though obscure at the time of their release, the numbers they recorded were later widely renowned when they were bought by Decca and reissued several years later as part of its Gems of Jazz series. On the basis of this recognition, in October 1939, while working at Chicago's Brass Rail, McPartland was asked to record another session for Decca's *Chicago Jazz* album. For this date he used his regular rhythm section and added clarinetist Bud Jacobson, alto saxophonist Boyce Brown, his brother Dick, and bassist Lanigan, now the husband of the McPartlands' sister Ethel.

McPartland remained in Chicago through 1940, leading bands from 1937 on at the Three Deuces and the Panther Room of the Hotel Sherman. In early 1941 he returned to New York to play at Nick's Tavern in Greenwich Village with Eddie Condon, and he joined Teagarden's orchestra in January 1942. Later that year he enlisted in the army, volunteering for combat duty. He participated in the D-Day invasion of Normandy and proceeded through Europe to Belgium, where he requested transfer to a musical unit. In 1944, while leading a jazz group for the USO, he met British jazz pianist Marian Page. They married in Aachen, Germany, in February 1945 and in March 1946 settled in Chicago, where they formed a quartet and worked at the Brass Rail and the Zebra Lounge in Green Bay, Wisconsin. With rare exception they continued to work in the Midwest until the early 1950s, when they moved to New York City. Marian had already formed her own trio, and Jimmy went on to lead jazz bands at Nick's, Child's Paramount, and the Metropole.

From 1952 through 1975 Jimmy McPartland recorded and toured extensively. Along with Condon, Teagarden, Freeman, Sullivan, Krupa, and clarinetist Pee Wee Russell he appeared on a November 1961 CBS telecast, "Chicago and All That Jazz." In 1965 he and Marian reunited for a job at the London House in Chicago and also appeared at the *Down Beat* Jazz Festival; from late 1965 to 1971 he worked frequently in New York at Jimmy Ryan's as well as continuing to play at Condon's club. During the 1970s he played at concerts in Durban, South Africa, and appeared at jazz festivals from Newport to Nice to New York. He toured Britain in 1981, played at the closing of Condon's in 1985, and performed in a re-creation of the Wolverines at the 1986 JVC Jazz Festival. In spite of increasing problems with Alzheimer's disease, he continued to play until shortly before his death at home in Port Washington, New York. Although they had agreed to divorce in the 1970s, the McPartlands remained close friends and musical collaborators through the ensuing years and remarried two weeks before his death, which preceded that of his lifelong friend Bud Freeman by only two days.

• Although not a biography per se, Chip Deffaa, "Jimmy McPartland: The Austin High Gang," in his *Voices of the Jazz Age* (1992), is a comprehensive interview-based profile that incorporates as much first-person oral narrative as it does solid historical research. Not limited to the period suggested in the subtitle, about which much had already been written since the 1930s, it also covers the subject's life both before and after the 1920s. Valuable early sources are Charles Edward Smith, "The Austin High School Gang," in *Jazzmen*, ed. Frederic Ramsey, Jr., and Smith (1939); Eddie Condon, *We Called It Music* (1947); and Nat Shapiro and Nat Hentoff, eds., *Hear Me Talkin' to Ya* (1955). More contemporary accounts of McPartland's contributions are Richard M. Sudhalter and Philip R. Evans, *Bix: Man & Legend* (1974); James Lincoln Collier, *Benny Goodman and the Swing Era* (1989); Robert Hilbert, *Pee Wee Russell: The Life of a Jazzman* (1993); and Ross Firestone, *Swing, Swing, Swing: The Life & Times of Benny Goodman* (1994). An especially insightful essay is Marty Grosz, notes to the Time-Life Giants of Jazz album set *Frank Teschemacher* (1982). Complete discographical information is in Brian Rust, *Jazz Records, 1897–1942* (1982), and Walter Bruyninckx, *Traditional Jazz Discography, 1897–1988* (6 vols., 1985–1989) and *Swing Discography, 1920–1988* (12 vols., 1985–1989). An abbreviated biography is in John Chilton, *Who's Who of Jazz* (1985).

JACK SOHMER

MCPHERSON, Aimee Semple (9 Oct. 1890–27 Sept. 1944), evangelist and founder of the Church of the Foursquare Gospel, was born near Ingersoll, Ontario, Canada, the daughter of James Morgan Kennedy, a Methodist farmer and road engineer, and Mildred "Minnie" Pearce, a Salvation Army volunteer. Minnie believed that her own call to preach the gospel had been frustrated by her marriage and therefore promised God that she would dedicate to his service a daughter if he would only give her one. Believing Aimee to be an answer to this prayer, Minnie dedicated Aimee as an infant during a Salvation Army jubilee and nurtured her to fulfill this calling.

Aimee was a precocious child and stubbornly resisted attempts to govern her actions and thoughts. After a somewhat rowdy career at the elementary level of public school, she entered high school at the Ingersoll Collegiate Institute. During her time there she was educated in Darwinism and consequently began to question the truth of her Christian upbringing. Curiosity led her to a Pentecostal Holy Ghost revival meeting where she heard Irish evangelist Robert James Semple, and her crisis of faith became a faith crisis in which she not only fell in love with God but with Robert Semple also. Aimee converted to Pentecostalism, and Semple became her mentor.

In 1908, at age seventeen, Aimee married Robert Semple. After several short-term ministries in North America, the couple moved to China in 1910 to serve as missionaries. On 17 August 1910 Robert died from malaria and other complications. One month later, Semple gave birth to their daughter Roberta Star Semple. Returning to the United States, she continued to engage in Pentecostal ministries and assisted her mother with Salvation Army work. Early in 1912 Semple wed Harold "Mack" Stewart McPherson, an accountant. They had one son, Rolf McPherson, who would later assume leadership of the Church of the Foursquare Gospel. Unhappy in her domestic state, McPherson left her husband in 1915. Asked to speak at a religious meeting in Mount Forest, Ontario, she had an epiphany and turned to the life of a Pentecostal evangelist. Harold joined her in 1916, and for several years they wandered up and down the eastern seaboard, wherever the Spirit led, conducting evangelistic meetings. By 1918 Harold grew weary of their travels and they again parted company; they divorced in 1921.

In 1919 McPherson, also known as Sister Aimee, or even more affectionately as Sister, was joined by her mother, who began to manage her speaking schedule and administrative matters. They traversed the country in McPherson's "Gospel Car," which had "Jesus Is Coming Soon—Get Ready" painted along one side and "Where Will You Spend Eternity" on the other. In the beginning McPherson would use a megaphone, gospel tracts, and a good deal of showmanship to gather a crowd and then encourage them to attend the evangelistic services. Later such tactics became unnecessary as her fame spread and she filled tents, arenas, auditoriums, coliseums, and parks with tens of thousands of listeners. In January 1921 30,000 people attended a single service in San Diego. The press filled columns with stories of her ability to give sight to the blind, hearing to the deaf, and vitality to the infirm. Some of the attendees came seeking God, some were seeking healing, and others were there to be entertained.

From an early age McPherson had entertained at church events, and at one time she had desired to become an actress. Now her sermons were full of drama. They were apocalyptic but without the fire-and-brimstone themes common in the fundamentalist sermons of the early twentieth century. Instead, her sermons were optimistic and emphasized the love of God; she gave glowing accounts of the blessedness of heaven. Her services were alive with music, storytelling, healing, speaking in tongues, narration of visions, and theatrical presentations of biblical stories. McPherson had an intuitive understanding of group dynamics. She could unify a mass audience and move it toward her goal.

Financial receipts from her many campaigns were used to build the Angelus Temple, which opened on 1 January 1923 in Los Angeles, California. This 5,300-seat auditorium contained two balconies and a stage sufficient to hold McPherson's 200-voice choir and theatrical presentations and was crowned with a dome and rotating, lighted cross that was visible from a distance of fifty miles. She had the words "Dedicated unto the Cause of Interdenominational and World-wide Evangelism" engraved upon the cornerstone. The Temple became the home of the Church of the Foursquare Gospel, which was incorporated in 1927. The Church of the Foursquare Gospel was named in response to divine inspiration in which McPherson claimed to be given the interpretation of the vision recorded in Ezekiel 1:10, which describes four living creatures with four faces and four wings. She indicated that the four faces of these creatures represented Christ's fourfold role as Savior, healer, baptizer in the Holy Spirit, and coming king. At this time she did not intend to start a new denomination. She could not have imagined that the Church of the Foursquare Gospel would eventually evolve into an independent Pentecostal denomination that in 1997 would claim more than 2 million members in over 21,000 churches around the world. From the Temple, McPherson preached twenty-one times a week, ministered to the homeless and hungry, started a radio station, made available a telephone counseling ministry, initiated an around-the-clock prayer vigil, founded the Lighthouse for International Foursquare Evangelism (LIFE) Bible College, and personally attended to the spiritual needs of her parishioners and those who traveled from around the world to meet her.

In 1926 McPherson was at the center of a highly publicized disappearance/kidnapping. She disappeared while swimming in the Pacific Ocean off the southern California coast and five weeks later walked out of the desert into Agua Prieta, a Mexican town neighboring Douglas, Arizona, with a story about having been kidnapped. The district attorney claimed that she had spent that time with a married man, Kenneth G. Ormiston, who had previously been employed at the Angelus Temple and with whom she had worked closely. Legal charges were brought against her for obstruction of justice and subornation of perjury. Although the charges against her were eventually dropped, McPherson had been found guilty in the court of public opinion. To vindicate herself she went on a national tour in which she presented her life story, including the kidnapping incident, in dramatic narration. During this three-month odyssey she engaged in behavior believed to be worldly by many of her followers. Upon her return, she quarreled bitterly with her mother about the alleged improprieties. The discord was such that it became impossible for them to continue to work together. McPherson forced her mother out of her position as business manager for the Echo Park Evangelistic Association, which held official ownership of the Church of the Foursquare Gospel.

In subsequent years McPherson was involved in a series of bad business deals and financial difficulties. She was named as defendant in numerous lawsuits and went through a series of broken relationships, including a third marriage to David Hutton in 1931, which was childless and ended with a divorce in 1935. It was McPherson's desire that her daughter, Roberta, follow in her footsteps and inherit the leadership of the Church of the Foursquare Gospel. These plans were abandoned when a schism developed between them after a disagreement regarding Temple management. The situation was exacerbated when they were forced to take opposing sides in a legal battle. Roberta's later attempts to contact her mother were unsuccessful, and they remained permanently estranged. Likewise, McPherson's relationship with her mother, which had suffered after the 1926 disappearance, was never properly restored.

McPherson's admirers included the rich, the powerful, and the colorful. Among them were members of the Ku Klux Klan; a large contingent of gypsies; politicians, such as the governor of Colorado; speakeasy owner Tex Guinan; attorney William Jennings Bryan; and actors, such as Charlie Chaplin. However, as a rule, her followers tended to be ordinary working-class people. During the early decades of the twentieth century many individuals were leaving mainline denominations because of liberalism, and McPherson provided the kind of leadership and religious enthusiasm for which they were looking. She did not offer a new religion, but the old-time religion made new.

McPherson is remembered as a flamboyant performer. She was usually clad in her trademark white dress and blue cape. Her stage shows included camels and macaws, orchestras, bands, and dramatized sermons with texts, such as "Little Red Riding Hood" and *Dr. Jekyll and Mr. Hyde*. These were the tools she utilized to advance the cause of evangelism. Throughout her ministry she employed many novel approaches, but emphasis was always placed upon the spiritual need for personal salvation. In a sermon titled "This Is My Task," which McPherson preached in the Angelus Temple on 12 March 1939, she proclaimed, "What is my task? To get the gospel around the world in the shortest possible time to every man and boy and girl." Toward this end she founded a new denomination that had evangelism as a major tenet, established a Bible college to train evangelists and missionaries, published the periodical *Bridal Call* and several spin-offs, and started the nation's first religious radio station.

Before her death she successfully passed control of the International Church of the Foursquare Gospel to her son, Rolf McPherson. She died in an Oakland, California, hotel after taking an overdose of sleeping pills. Her death was ruled accidental by medical officials.

• McPherson's papers are maintained in the archives of the International Church of the Foursquare Gospel. McPherson published two autobiographies during her life, *This Is That* (1919) and *In the Service of the King: The Story of My Life* (1927). *The Story of My Life* (1951) is a compilation of autobiographical materials taken from her books, sermons, and articles that was edited by Raymond W. Becker, with a foreword by Rolf McPherson. These autobiographical works are highly romanticized and must be balanced against other publications. Two of the better full-length biographies include Daniel Mark Epstein, *Sister Aimee: The Life of Aimee Semple McPherson* (1993), and Edith L. Blumhofer, *Aimee Semple McPherson: Everybody's Sister* (1993). Both of these works recognize the legitimate accomplishments of McPherson while maintaining a critical distance. Shortly after the alleged kidnapping of McPherson, Nancy Barr Mavity published *Sister Aimee* (1931), which deals primarily with the disappearance and subsequent events. Under the pseudonym "Lately Thomas," Robert V. P. Steele published a similar work, *The Vanishing Evangelist* (1959), and followed it with *Storming Heaven: The Lives and Turmoils of Minnie Kennedy and Aimee Semple McPherson* (1970), which focuses on the broken relationships that followed on the heels of McPherson's disappearance. Those seeking to know more about the beliefs of the Church of the Foursquare Gospel and its founder may wish to consult *The Four-Square Gospel* (1969), which contains fourteen of McPherson's sermons intertwined with explanatory chapters by the book's compiler, Raymond L. Cox.

KEVIN E. STILLEY

MCPHERSON, Edward (31 July 1830–14 Dec. 1895), congressman and author, was born in Gettysburg, Pennsylvania, the son of John Bayard McPherson and Katherine Lenhart. He attended public schools in Gettysburg and graduated from Pennsylvania College (now Gettysburg College) in 1848. For a brief period after graduating from college McPherson studied law under Thaddeus Stevens, the U.S. representative who would earn fame by his firm stance in favor of emancipation and equal rights. McPherson eventually decided not to pursue a career in law, but Stevens remained his most influential mentor. Instead of the law, journalism became McPherson's chosen profession. In 1851 he became editor of the *Harrisburg (Pa.) American*, and in that same year he established an affiliation with the *Independent Whig* of Lancaster, Pennsylvania. Beginning in 1855 he also contributed to the *Pittsburgh Daily Times*.

McPherson switched partisan affiliations from the Whigs to the Republicans in the mid-1850s. In 1858 he published a series of articles advocating the sale of state public improvements, a position he had advocated since 1851. These articles brought him some prominence, and he was elected as a Republican representative in 1858 and again in 1860. In 1860 he was a member of the Republican National Committee. As a congressman during the first year of the Civil War, he was fairly innocuous and tended to vote with the more moderate Republicans. For example, he voted against the first "confiscation" act of 1861, which seized as enemy property all slaves used by the Confederacy for military purposes, in effect freeing those slaves. In 1862 he was appointed to replace Francis P. Blair, Jr., of Missouri as a member of the House Committee on Military Affairs. He was defeated for reelection in 1862, losing by a narrow margin to the Democratic candidate, Alexander H. Coffroth. McPherson's district had been considered safe for the Republicans, but in the last days of the election voters lost much of their faith in the Republicans' ability to prosecute the war successfully. McPherson blamed his defeat on Robert E. Lee's invasion of Maryland and Pennsylvania in mid-1862, J. E. B. Stuart's raid on southern Pennsylvania days before the election, and the enforcement of the draft in McPherson's district by federal authorities. In 1862 he married Annie Dods Crawford; they had five children.

Upon leaving the House of Representatives, McPherson was appointed deputy commissioner of internal revenue. He left the position after only six months to become clerk of the House of Representatives, a post he held from 1863 to 1875. As a practiced parliamentarian and an amateur historian, McPherson had an impressive knowledge of governmental procedure and precedent, and he made a first-rate clerk. Usually he was as placid as he had been as a congressman, with one significant exception. In December 1865, when the Thirty-ninth Congress assembled, he was instrumental in barring from their seats those southern representatives newly elected by reconstructed governments. The Republican caucus had determined that these members should not be seated, and McPherson, coached by Stevens, complied. As he called the roll, amidst jeers and protests, he simply omitted the names of the southerners, and he told the excluded members who tried to speak that they had no right to do so because they had not been called and therefore were not legally seated. Likewise, northern Democrats who tried to interrupt the process were informed by McPherson that, by congressional rules, they could not speak until the roll call was completed. In this way, McPherson deftly executed the plan of the Republican majority to deny representation to the former Confederate states.

During his years as clerk, McPherson prepared a number of useful historical and reference works. These include *The Political History of the United States during the Great Rebellion* (1864; 2d ed., 1865; 3d ed., 1876), *The Political History of the United States of*

America during the Period of Reconstruction (1871; 2d ed., 1875), *A Political Manual* (published annually from 1866 to 1869), and *A Handbook of Politics* (published biennially from 1868 to 1894).

Throughout the 1870s and 1880s McPherson was active in Republican party politics at the state and national levels. In 1875 he wrote the Pennsylvania Republican platform, which called for tariff protection, specie resumption, and civil rights for African Americans and which opposed a third term for President Ulysses S. Grant. In 1876, at the Republican National Convention in Cincinnati, he was a leading agent for James G. Blaine, who hoped to secure the presidential nomination. The Blaine faction won an initial victory by obtaining the election of McPherson as permanent chair of the convention, but on the final day of balloting, Blaine's opponents coalesced around Rutherford B. Hayes, who ultimately received the nomination. Many of Blaine's adherents blamed McPherson for the lost nomination, for McPherson had allowed some of the Pennsylvania delegates to vote against Blaine. However, in allowing delegates to vote individually rather than by the "unit rule," under which all state delegates had to cast the same ballot, McPherson was in fact acting under Blaine's orders. McPherson, no longer the clerk of the House of Representatives when Hayes was elected, was appointed by the new president as chief of the Bureau of Engraving and Printing, but he held the post for only a year. In 1880 he was the secretary of the Republican Congressional Committee. From 1881 to 1883 and again from 1889 to 1891 he resumed his position as clerk of the House of Representatives. He served longer in this position than any clerk before him.

During the 1870s and 1880s McPherson continued to be active in journalism. He was a contributor to and frequent editor of the *Philadelphia Press* from 1877 to 1880, and he was the owner and editor of the *Gettysburg Star and Sentinel* from 1880 to 1895. While acting as editor for various newspapers, he edited the *New York Tribune Almanac and Political Register* from 1877 to 1895, and during part of this period he also edited the *Almanack de Gotha*. In those years that McPherson did not hold office in Washington, D.C., he resided in Gettysburg. He spent many of his later years collecting and organizing Stevens's papers, which were ultimately deposited in the Library of Congress. Like Stevens, McPherson was committed to racial equality and a centralized Union, even though his belief in the protection of personal property made him at first reluctant to support the confiscation policy of the Union during the Civil War. He died in Gettysburg after mistakenly taking poison.

• McPherson's papers are in the Library of Congress. Many of his original letters and manuscripts are in the Thaddeus Stevens Papers, also in the Library of Congress. Fawn M. Brodie, *Thaddeus Stevens: Scourge of the South* (1959), and Erwin Bradley, *Simon Cameron, Lincoln's Secretary of War: A Political Biography* (1966), both contain useful information. James G. Blaine, *Twenty Years of Congress* (2 vols., 1884–1886), records many of McPherson's activities in Congress. Particularly relevant to McPherson's activities during the early years of Reconstruction are George Fort Milton, *The Age of Hate: Andrew Johnson and the Radicals* (1930), and Eric L. McKitrick, *Andrew Johnson and Reconstruction* (1960). For McPherson in the 1870s, his busiest period in politics, see Frank B. Evans, *Pennsylvania Politics, 1872–1877: A Study in Political Leadership* (1966). An obituary is in the *New York Times*, 15 Dec. 1895.

MICHAEL VORENBERG

MCPHERSON, James B. (14 Nov. 1828–22 July 1864), soldier and Union general, was born James Birdseye McPherson in Green Creek Township, Sandusky County, Ohio, the son of William McPherson, a farmer and blacksmith, and Cynthia Russell. He attended local schools until the age of thirteen, when he went to work as a general store clerk. At the age of eighteen he returned to school for two years at Norwalk (Ohio) Academy. In 1849 he was appointed to the U.S. Military Academy. Despite an active social life at West Point, he compiled a superb record and graduated at the top of his class in 1853. His roommate was John Bell Hood, whom McPherson would later face on the battlefields of northern Georgia.

McPherson received a coveted assignment to the Corps of Engineers and remained at West Point for a year as assistant instructor of engineering. From 1854 to 1857 he worked on the harbor fortifications in New York City. In 1857 McPherson was transferred to San Francisco, where he supervised the fortification of Alcatraz Island and was promoted to first lieutenant on 13 December 1858. When the Civil War began in April 1861, McPherson was ordered to Boston to supervise harbor fortifications there, being promoted to captain on 6 August 1861.

Desiring an active assignment in the field, McPherson wrote to his former superior officer in California, Major General Henry W. Halleck, who had just taken command of the Department of Missouri. Halleck brought McPherson to St. Louis as aide and assistant engineer with rank of lieutenant colonel (12 Nov. 1861), rising to colonel (1 May 1862). On 1 February 1862 McPherson joined Brigadier General Ulysses S. Grant's campaign against Forts Henry and Donelson as chief engineer. This appointment launched McPherson's rapid rise to field command. Extraordinarily able and industrious, courageous in the face of enemy fire, with an imposing presence but gregarious personality, he won Grant's confidence and friendship by the invaluable services he performed at Fort Donelson, at Shiloh, and in the campaign against the Confederate stronghold at Corinth, Mississippi.

At Grant's recommendation, McPherson was promoted to brigadier general on 19 August 1862 and served as superintendent of railroads in Grant's department, embracing western Tennessee and northern Mississippi. He finally got his chance to command troops in the field after the battle of Corinth, 3–4 October 1862, when Grant ordered him to collect a brigade from the railroad defense units and pursue the retreating Confederates. McPherson moved with dispatch, winning promotion to major general of volunteers on 8 October and command of a division in the XIII Corps. After the repulse of his initial probes against Vicksburg in November-December 1862, Grant reorganized the army and gave McPherson the newly created XVII Corps on 18 January 1863.

As a corps commander, McPherson played a prominent role in Grant's operations against Vicksburg, culminating with its capture on 4 July 1862. In this campaign McPherson's corps was principally responsible for Union victories at Raymond, Mississippi (12 May), the capture of Jackson (14 May), and the decisive battle of Champion's Hill (16 May), which forced the Confederates back into the Vicksburg defenses. After unsuccessful Union assaults on 19 and 22 May, in which the XVII Corps was conspicuous and suffered heavy casualties, Grant settled down for a siege that forced the surrender of this "Gibraltar of the Confederacy" six weeks later. As a reward for his contribution to this victory, McPherson, on Grant's recommendation, was appointed a brigadier general in the regular army (1 Aug. 1863).

For the next six months McPherson remained at Vicksburg in charge of Union occupation forces in the region. When Grant became general in chief of the Union armies in March 1864, William T. Sherman succeeded him as commander of all troops between the Mississippi River and the Appalachian Mountains, and McPherson succeeded Sherman as commander of the Army of the Tennessee on 26 March. McPherson had just started on a furlough to marry Emily Hoffman, whom he had met in 1859 when he was stationed at San Francisco. His furlough cut short, and his wedding postponed, McPherson took command of his army as part of Sherman's campaign against Atlanta. Sherman promised him the furlough after they captured the city.

The campaign began 7 May with a movement establishing a pattern that would be repeated several times over the next eleven weeks. Fixing the Confederate army commanded by Joseph E. Johnston in place at Dalton, Georgia, by feinting a frontal attack, Sherman sent McPherson's troops on a wide swing to the right through Snake Creek Gap to cut the railroad in Johnston's rear at Resaca. Finding Resaca defended by strong fortifications, McPherson overestimated the force holding them (there were only two brigades) and pulled back without attacking. When Sherman joined him three days later, after Johnston's whole army had occupied Resaca, he greeted the chagrined McPherson, "Well, Mac, you have missed the opportunity of a lifetime" (Castel, p. 150).

Sherman retained his confidence in McPherson, however, and used his Army of the Tennessee as the mobile flanking force that compelled Johnston repeatedly to retreat southward to protect his railroad supply line. By 17 July Johnston had fallen back to Atlanta, and Jefferson Davis replaced him with McPherson's West Point roommate Hood, who launched a series of counterattacks that resulted in heavy Confederate casualties. The most grievous casualty, however, occurred on the Union side. During the battle of Atlanta, on 22 July, McPherson rode to the front to realign his troops and close a dangerous gap between two divisions. He encountered Confederate skirmishers who shouted "Halt!" and shot him from his saddle when he tried to spur his horse to the cover of nearby trees. McPherson died almost instantly.

That evening a grieving Sherman told an aide, "I expected something to happen to Grant and me; either the Rebels or the newspapers would kill us both, and I looked to McPherson as the man to follow us and finish the war" (Lloyd Lewis, *Sherman: Fighting Prophet* [1932], p. 387). When Grant learned the news of McPherson's death, he said, "The country has lost one of its best soldiers, and I have lost my best friend" (Whaley, p. 164). It was a fitting epitaph.

• No collection of McPherson's papers exists. The only biography is the unscholarly and anecdotal Elizabeth J. Whaley, *Forgotten Hero: General James B. McPherson* (1955). A great deal of information about McPherson is in *Memoirs of General William T. Sherman* (2 vols., 1875) and *Personal Memoirs of U. S. Grant* (2 vols., 1885–1886). In addition, for McPherson's career under Grant's command in Tenn. and Miss. during 1862–1863, see Bruce Catton, *Grant Moves South* (1960); and for his role in the Atlanta campaign, see Albert Castel, *Decision in the West: The Atlanta Campaign of 1864* (1992). For an obituary, consult *Army and Navy Journal*, 30 July 1864.

JAMES M. MCPHERSON

MCQUAID, Bernard John (15 Dec. 1823–18 Jan. 1909), Catholic bishop and educator, was born in New York City, the son of Mary Maguire and Bernard McQuaid, a laborer. Orphaned at the age of ten, McQuaid found refuge with the Sisters of Charity and under their influence decided to enter the priesthood. After attending local schools he studied at Chambly College near Montreal and finished his training at St. Joseph's, the diocesan seminary in Fordham, New York. Precarious health made him less gregarious than other students, but after ordination in 1848 he proved to be a dynamic ecclesiastical administrator. Beginning with his first pastorate, St. Vincent's Church in Madison, New Jersey, he preached energetically and organized Catholic schools in the surrounding counties.

Transferred in 1853 to St. Patrick's Cathedral in Newark, McQuaid increased his efforts in evangelicalism, charity, and education. He was instrumental in establishing a motherhouse for the Sisters of Charity in 1859, thus enabling them to supervise orphanages and parochial education, especially at a thriving cathedral academy with more than 600 pupils. He also played a central role in founding Seton Hall College and Seminary in 1856, serving in 1857 and 1859–1868 as its president. While he is deservedly known as a missionary leader of urban congregations and as a controversial conservative, his interest in Catholic education is the most significant characteristic of a distinguished clerical career.

Beginning in 1866, McQuaid served as vicar general, administering the diocese of Newark. That experience led to his appointment in 1868 as first bishop of Rochester, New York. Some priests there recoiled at his stern discipline and insistence on ready obedience, but the vigorous prelate soon quelled the discontented and stamped the new diocese with his own image. For more than four decades the ardent bishop pursued his objectives with tenacious purpose. He organized the Sisters of St. Joseph as a diocesan community to aid such activities as parish schools and teacher training programs. McQuaid erected as many as sixty parishes within his jurisdiction in addition to building orphanages, recreational facilities, old age homes, and a Young Men's Catholic Institute. As an advocate of Christian education, the bishop often refused absolution to parents who sent their children to "godless schools" in the public realm when Catholic schools were available. In 1870 he began St. Andrew's, a preparatory seminary, and by 1893 St. Bernard's Seminary crowned all his efforts to provide a self-sufficient complex of mutually supporting Catholic educational institutions.

In addition to embodying brisk, authoritarian tactics in dealing with people, McQuaid also sided with conservative forces on issues that divided late nineteenth-century American Catholicism. Like many other prelates he opposed proclamation of papal infallibility at the Second Vatican Council because he feared a Protestant backlash at home. He left Rome before the final vote was taken, but when *Pastor Aeternus* was issued in August 1870 he read it from his pulpit and affirmed belief in the doctrine.

He allied with Michael A. Corrigan, archbishop of New York, in opposing what he considered debilitating liberal tendencies, especially views on Americanism as espoused by James Gibbons of Baltimore and John Ireland of St. Paul. Those two churchmen erred, in McQuaid's opinion, by trying to align distinctive Catholic loyalties and lifestyles too closely with broader American patterns in education, literature, and politics. In his view, Catholics in the United States were better advised to eschew public education through wholehearted support of parochial training and to conduct their lives—beliefs and behavior—with strict attention to the teachings and moral standards decreed by the authorities in Rome.

As a conservative adhering strictly to the letter of canon law, McQuaid condemned secret societies because Rome said to do so. This obedience led him to oppose serious workmen's unions such as the Knights of Labor and harmless fraternal societies such as the Ancient Order of Hibernians. McQuaid and Ireland patched up their differences and reached a semblance of reconciliation by 1905. But pleas for leniency and moderation did not lessen McQuaid's rigid attitude regarding matters that he thought central to conservative progress in his church. In his very last days Catholic dignitaries from around the world attended his last triumph, the dedication of the Hall of Theology at St. Bernard's. While speaking from a wheelchair to welcome the visitors, he collapsed and died shortly thereafter in Rochester.

Though some remember him only as an outspoken controversialist during various struggles over Americanism, McQuaid's own priorities lay in areas of more constructive and lasting significance. He spent the better part of his life expanding his church's congregations through energetic preaching, educating thousands of Catholics in a self-sufficient system that provided guidance from kindergartens through seminaries and graduate schools, and constantly fulfilling the role of pastor: exhorting people of his diocese to persevere in the godly life that he considered essential to happiness in both this world and the next.

• Official papers and correspondence conducted during McQuaid's episcopate are housed in St. Bernard's Seminary and College Library. Books about him include Frederick J. Zwierlein, *The Life and Letters of Bishop McQuaid* (3 vols., 1925–1927) and *Letters of Archbishop Corrigan to Bishop McQuaid and Allied Documents* (1946). See also Norlene M. Kunkel, *Bishop Bernard J. McQuaid and Catholic Education* (1988). An obituary is in the *New York Times*, 19 Jan. 1909.

HENRY WARNER BOWDEN

MCQUEEN, Peter (?–1822?), Creek war leader, whose tribal name was Talmuchees Hadjo, was born possibly at the Upper Creek town of Tallassee on the Tallapoosa River, Alabama, the son of James McQueen, a Scottish trader, and a Tallassee Creek woman. Peter McQueen became the head warrior of Tallassee, accumulated considerable wealth through trade (he claimed to have owned thirty black slaves in 1813), and was well connected. His wife, Betsy Durant, belonged to the prestigious Wind clan and was a niece of the famous Alexander McGillivray, and his three daughters married the son of Big Warrior, the foremost Creek leader before the war of 1813.

In 1813 the Creeks were deeply divided. Among the Upper Creeks of the Alabama, Coosa, and Tallapoosa a strong anti-Americanism fed upon fears for Indian land, resentment at the activities of filibusters in Florida and at the efforts of the United States to blaze roads through the Creek country, and a rejection of the "civilization" policy promoted by the American agent Benjamin Hawkins. The Shawnee prophet Tenskwatawa and Creek religious leaders such as Josiah Francis reported divine sanction for the repudiation of white influences, while the pan-Indian message of Tecumseh and the outbreak of the War of 1812 encouraged the militant Creeks, known as "red-sticks," to believe that other Indians, the Spanish, and the British would assist them against the United States. McQueen emerged as a leader of the red-sticks.

In July 1813 open warfare between the red-stick and pro-American Creeks broke out, and McQueen led a party of some 300 warriors to Pensacola, seeking arms and ammunition for the civil war and the possible outbreak of a wider conflict with the United States. Securing over 1,000 pounds of powder, as well as other supplies, from the Spanish governor and several merchants, McQueen returned to Alabama, where he was intercepted by a force of Mississippi Territory militia under James Caller. In a skirmish at Burnt Corn Creek

(27 July 1813), McQueen defeated the militia but lost some of his ammunition and suffered casualties. This episode diverted the red-sticks from their plan of attacking the Lower Creeks; they decided instead to avenge themselves on the mixed-bloods and whites who had participated in the attack. Another irritant was the destruction of McQueen's town of Tallassee in August by Creeks sent by Hawkins. Although McQueen and the head civil chief of Tallassee, Hopoithle Micco, evacuated their people before the attack, they were soon calling upon the Upper Creek warriors to assemble for a blow against the whites. On 30 August 1813 McQueen and others fell upon Fort Mims on the Alabama, killing or capturing most of the 400 or so whites, mestizos, Indians, and blacks inside. The "massacre" shocked the South, and Mississippi Territory, Alabama, and Georgia raised armies to invade the Creek country. In truth, many whites were happy to wage a ruthless war to appropriate Creek land.

McQueen was one of the most important leaders of the Indians confronting the Georgian army under John Floyd and the Tennesseans of Andrew Jackson. He helped defend Autosse from Floyd's force on 29 November and then turned to organize resistance to Jackson's army as it marched from Fort Strother to the Tallapoosa. McQueen, Francis, and other Creeks twice struck at Jackson between 22 and 24 January 1814 and, despite being low on ammunition, drove his army back to the Coosa. McQueen was also probably with the force that stopped Floyd's second advance at Caleebe Creek on 27 January, turning it back to the Chattahoochee with 169 casualties. Ultimately the Creeks could not prevail against the superior numbers and resources of the Americans and their Indian allies, and after Jackson's victory at Horseshoe Bend in March many surrendered. The most resolute, under McQueen and Francis, fled to the protection of the Spanish at Pensacola. In August Jackson imposed a treaty at Fort Jackson, stripping red-stick and friendly Creeks alike of about half their land.

The arrival of the British at Apalachicola Bay in Florida in May 1814 encouraged McQueen to believe that the Americans could still be overthrown, and he cooperated with the British invasion of the South later that year. When it misfired and the British withdrew in 1815, both Francis and McQueen attempted unsuccessfully to persuade them to intercede with the United States, claiming that the treaty of Fort Jackson was invalidated by the subsequent peace of Ghent ending the War of 1812. Britain's failure to respond effectively destroyed McQueen's cause, but he remained in Florida, stiffening Seminole animosity to the United States. His warriors participated in the Seminole attack on Lieutenant R. W. Scott's detachment on the Apalachicola River in November 1817.

The Spanish protection of McQueen's rebels encouraged Andrew Jackson to invade Florida in 1818, wage the so-called First Seminole War, and precipitate the eventual extinction of Spanish Florida. Although McQueen's party was dispersed by Jackson's forces in April 1818, and Francis was shortly captured and executed, McQueen himself remained at large. He is reported to have died "on a little barren island on the Atlantic side of Cape Florida" (one of the Florida keys?) soon after, but other evidence suggests that he had a village on Tampa Bay as late as 1821. Whichever, he was remembered as one of the most significant, capable, and determined leaders of the Creek revolt, and he was certainly the most elusive. His legacy continued to trouble the United States for many years. His grandnephew Osceola, who had followed him from Alabama to Florida, was one of the leading movers of the Second Seminole War of 1835.

• Peter McQueen was illiterate, but two appeals written for him, one to Admiral Alexander Cochrane in December 1814 and the other to minister Charles Bagot in November 1816, are in the Public Record Office, Kew, England, filed in Adm. 1/505 and CO 23/66. Thomas S. Woodward, *Woodward's Reminiscences of the Creek, or Muscogee Indians* (1859) is useful but should be treated cautiously. Other essential primary sources are to be found in *American State Papers, Indian Affairs*, vol. 1 (1832–1834); John S. Bassett, ed., *The Correspondence of Andrew Jackson*, vols. 1–3 (7 vols., 1926–1935); and Elizabeth Howard West, ed., "A Prelude to the Creek War of 1813–14," *Florida Historical Quarterly* 18 (1940): 247–66. A comprehensive history of the Creek struggle is still needed, but McQueen figures in H. S. Halbert and T. H. Ball, *The Creek War of 1813 and 1814* (1895); Frank L. Owsley, Jr., *Struggle for the Gulf Borderlands* (1981); John Sugden, "The Southern Indians in the War of 1812: The Closing Phase," *Florida Historical Quarterly* 60 (1982): 273–312; J. Leitch Wright, Jr., *Creeks and Seminoles* (1986); and Benjamin W. Griffith, Jr., *McIntosh and Weatherford* (1988).

JOHN SUGDEN

MCQUEEN, Steve (24 Mar. 1930–7 Nov. 1980), actor, was born Terrence Steven McQueen in Beech Grove, Indiana, the son of William "Red" McQueen, a stunt pilot, and Jullian Crawford. His father deserted the family when Steve was six months old. His carefree, alcoholic mother frequently left him for long periods in the care of relatives in her home town of Slater, Missouri. At fourteen he ran off to join the circus but soon hitchhiked to Los Angeles to again live with his mother. When he became an incorrigible gang leader, his mother obtained a court order remanding him to the Boys' Republic at Chino. There he learned discipline and completed the ninth grade, his last formal education. "The Boys' Republic saved my life," he later said.

After leaving in April 1946 he spent a year in itinerant labors, as a seaman on an oil tanker, a waiter in a brothel, and a lumberjack in Canada. Twelve months later he enlisted in the marines, training as a tank driver and mechanic. He discovered what became a lifelong love of engines and speed. By his own account, he was busted from private first class to private seven times, once spending forty-one days in the brig for a two-week unauthorized absence. He also saved the lives of five corpsmen while on an Arctic exercise and left with an honorable discharge in April 1950.

He drifted to Greenwich Village, where odd jobs ranging from making artificial flowers to repairing televisions paid rent on a $19-a-month cold-water flat. When things were especially hard, he later admitted, he rolled drunks. He had ambitions no loftier than to become a $3.50-an-hour tile layer, but friends persuaded McQueen to try acting. His first role was a walk-on at a Yiddish theater on Second Avenue, where he entered, said "Nothing will help!" and left.

In the fall of 1951 he used the GI Bill to begin a two-year study under Sanford Meisner at the Neighborhood Playhouse, supplementing his income by competing in motorcycle races on Long Island. During this New York period he often shadowed James Dean, tailing the rising actor through the streets to study his mannerisms. Meisner later said McQueen was "both tough and childlike—as if he'd been through the wars of life but had managed to preserve a certain basic innocence." After one year McQueen was in summer stock, appearing first in *Peg o' My Heart* with Margaret O'Brien. He later joined a national road company tour of *Time Out for Ginger* (1952) starring Melvyn Douglas. The veteran actor soon tired of McQueen's rebellious offstage behavior and forced him to resign from the cast. The fallout from this incident kept him off the stage for three years.

He continued to study, receiving a scholarship in 1952 to train with Uta Hagen and Herbert Berghof at their drama school. In 1956 he was one of five accepted from 2,000 applicants for Lee Strasberg's Actor's Studio. That same year he played his only Broadway role, replacing Ben Gazzara as the lead in *A Hatful of Rain*. McQueen was unequal to the part, however, and was replaced in three months. During this period he was seen infrequently in television dramas and in 1956 was in his first movie, a brief bit in *Somebody Up There Likes Me*. That same year he wed Broadway actress and dancer Neile Adams. The marriage produced a boy and a girl, McQueen's only children, before they divorced in 1971.

In 1958 McQueen was paid $3,000 to play the teenage lead in the science fiction cheapie *The Blob*. This was the beginning of the actor's 22-year screen career of twenty-eight movies. That same year he was hired to play western bounty hunter Josh Randall on television's "Wanted Dead or Alive." During the three-year series McQueen was referred to as the "thinking man's cowboy." In reviewing the popular show, the *Saturday Evening Post* described the actor as "believable and sympathetic without resorting to either spurious sentiment or showy heroics."

In 1960 McQueen appeared as Vin in *The Magnificent Seven*, the western film based on Akira Kurosawa's *The Seven Samurai*. Increasingly confident, McQueen held his own with lead Yul Brynner and gained the attention of critics.

Three years later McQueen appeared in a role that established him as a major star. As Captain Virgil Hilts, he defined a cocky, spirited Air Force pilot, impervious to solitary confinement and intent on escape from a German stalag. *The Great Escape*, based on one of the most adventurous stories from World War II, dealt with the clever tunnel breakout of seventy-nine officers from a prison camp, three of whom made it to safety. A one-minute motorcycle chase sequence with McQueen in flight remains one of the most exhilarating moments in cinema.

In 1961 McQueen founded Solar Productions. Initially a tax shelter, in time it produced more than a dozen of his films. Five movies followed in which McQueen honed his identity as the outsider against the system, the volatile, thick-skinned loner hiding sensitivity beneath a cool exterior. Slashing unnecessary dialogue from his scripts, without pretension he relied on subtle gestures and pantomime to convey complex emotion. He became the exemplar of Ernest Hemingway's heroic ideal, displaying "grace under pressure." Actor Edward G. Robinson, who played opposite McQueen in *The Cincinnati Kid* (1965), said, "He comes out of the tradition of Gable, Bogey, Cagney, and even me. He's a stunner" (St. Charnez, p. 105).

In 1965 McQueen traveled to Moscow as the first American to receive Russia's best foreign actor award at the International Film Festival. The next year McQueen starred as ship's engineer Jake Holman in *The Sand Pebbles*. Filmed in Taiwan, the plot concerned doomed American naval folly on the Yangtze River in 1926. McQueen brought maturity and determination to the role, for which he received his only Oscar nomination.

In 1968 McQueen starred in the first U.S. film set on location to use an entire Hollywood crew and received $1 million for his efforts, making him the highest-paid film star at the time. *Bullitt*, shot in San Francisco, brought audiences an authentic, high-speed, nine-minute car chase that set the standard for the genre.

To many, McQueen best exemplified 1960s cool. The actor, despite his inveterate offscreen womanizing and profligate drug use, fulfilled the era's need for a hero. Many of his films have since become minor classics. Critic Ethan Mordden wrote that he gave his fans "a sense that one is seeing one's beliefs affirmed." McQueen kept himself in superb physical shape throughout most of his career and frequently performed his own onscreen stunts. A winning motorcycle and sportscar racer, he competed both in the United States and abroad.

McQueen was the personal choice of Henri Charriere to star in *Papillon* (1973), the film of the Frenchman's autobiography. Portraying Charriere's life and escapes from the notorious French penal colony on Devil's Island, McQueen received an unheard-of $2 million for the role. That same year the actor married actress Ali MacGraw, a union that lasted four years.

From 1974 to 1977 McQueen became a Trancas Beach recluse. He was bearded and overweight, and friends failed to recognize him. In 1978 he returned to film the Ibsen classic *An Enemy of the People*, featuring a notable cast. Despite its ambitions, producers found it impossible to promote. It was never released to the general public. In 1980 two McQueen films were released, *Tom Horn* and *The Hunter*, his last movie. Both were indifferently received. In January of that year he married model Barbara Minty. One month earlier he had been diagnosed with mesothelioma, an inoperable cancer.

In desperation McQueen sought unorthodox treatment at a Mexican clinic and died in Juarez following surgery. A flier in the last years of his life, his ashes were scattered over the Pacific Ocean by airmen friends. Following his death, *Films in Review* noted that "McQueen left behind, on film, more of himself than most people . . . are allowed to leave. It's a worthy legacy."

• Clippings on McQueen can be found in the New York Public Library for the Performing Arts, Lincoln Center. See also Ephraim Katz, *The Film Encyclopedia* (1979); Grady Ragsdale, *Steve McQueen: The Final Chapter* (1983); Casey St. Charnez, *The Films of Steve McQueen* (1984); Penina Spiegel, *McQueen: The Untold Story of a Bad Boy in Hollywood* (1986); Neile McQueen Toffel, *My Husband, My Friend* (1986); and Marshall Terrill, *Steve McQueen: Portrait of an American Rebel* (1993). An obituary is in the *New York Times*, 8 Nov. 1980.

DON STEWART

MCQUILLEN, John Hugh (12 Feb. 1826–3 Mar. 1879), dentist, editor, and educator, was born in Philadelphia, Pennsylvania, the son of Hugh McQuillen and Martha Scattergood, occupations unknown. He attended the Friends' School and worked as a youth as a clerk in an importing firm. In 1847 he began the study of medicine and became particularly interested in dentistry. He studied with Elisha Townsend, a noted Philadelphia dentist, and in 1849 went into dental practice. He continued his medical studies and in 1852 received the M.D. from Jefferson Medical College. That same year he married Amelia Donnel Schellenger. They had five children, one of whom died in infancy. From 1852 to 1861 he was associated with Daniel Neall, another well-known Philadelphia dentist, and then returned to private practice.

McQuillen became "a marked power" in dentistry and "without a doubt the best known dentist of his day in America." A skillful practitioner, his contributions to scientific and operative dentistry were many. He wrote prolifically and addressed many professional bodies on a great many subjects but especially in the area of dental histology and on professional and educational aspects of dentistry. Foremost among his lectures and addresses to appear in print are *Anatomy and Physiology of Expression* (1864) and *Human Teeth in Their Relations to Mastication, Speech and Appearance* (1864). One of the first in America to demonstrate the importance of the microscopical knowledge of human teeth, he contributed also to the field of orthodontics and was also acknowledged as having provided "the most comprehensive description of occlusion." Some of his articles were copied and translated in European journals.

McQuillen's career as a dental educator began in 1857 with his appointment as professor of operative dentistry and dental physiology (sometimes stated as dental pathology) in the Pennsylvania College of Dental Surgery. In 1858 he became professor of general anatomy and physiology, but in 1862, displeased with a faculty appointment, he resigned. In 1863 he and colleagues founded the Philadelphia Dental College, where he became professor of anatomy, physiology, and hygiene. He served as dean of the college from its start until his death. The college prospered under McQuillen; by 1876 it had graduated 385 students.

In 1852 McQuillen had published his first of a number of articles in the *Dental News Letter*. When that journal ceased publication in 1859, it was succeeded by the monthly *Dental Cosmos*, under the editorship of James D. White, George J. Ziegler, and McQuillen. The journal gained the reputation of being "one of the brightest in the journalistic constellation" with a circulation larger than "any other dental journal in the world."

As a prolific contributor and as editor in chief from 1865 to 1872 McQuillen used *Dental Cosmos* as a forum for his constant campaign for the improvement of dentistry both as a science and as a profession. An organizer as well as a teacher and writer, he was a prime mover in the establishment of the American Dental Association. McQuillen's proposal, "Basis of a National Dental Association," which appeared in the *Dental News Letter* of April 1859 under the pseudonym "Junius," was to lead to the organizational meeting of the American Dental Association in Niagara Falls in August 1859, which he attended. He had made certain to involve the Pennsylvania Association of Dental Surgeons in the movement. McQuillen and J. Foster Flagg were authorized by the state association to correspond with colleges and societies on the subject and to publicize the movement in the dental press. His belief prevailed that the national association should be representative of the organized profession, that is, of local and state societies and of faculties of dental schools. There were those who preferred a society of individual dentists and argued that the proposed arrangement was undemocratic and exclusive. McQuillen thought a representative system "eminently democratic" and that the proposed organization was "only exclusive so far as the willfully ignorant are concerned." McQuillen was chair of the committee on the constitution, and that document echoed the ideas he had presented in his "Junius" paper. Both the founding of the association and the character of its constitution reflected not only the ideas of McQuillen but also the intelligent and forceful leadership with which he overcame considerable opposition. He was president of the association in 1864 and played a prominent role in its activities until his death.

McQuillen's interest in dental organization preceded, and continued after, the founding of the American Dental Association. He had become a member of the Pennsylvania Association of Dental Surgeons in 1849—the year he started in practice—and served as its president in 1874–1875. In 1875 he was a member of the committee of the state association that framed a bill regulating the practice of dentistry in the state. In 1863 he was active in establishing the Odontographic Society of Philadelphia, was its first corresponding secretary and its president from 1868 to 1870. In 1866 he was one of the organizers of the Association of Colleges of Dentistry and its first corresponding secretary. He belonged also to the Odontological Society of Great Britain. His scientific interests brought him in 1865 into the Academy of Natural Sciences of Philadelphia, where in 1868 he was active in the founding of the biological and microscopical section. He belonged also to the Union League of Philadelphia and to the Reform Club. During the Civil War he volunteered his services as surgeon in the military hospitals of Philadelphia.

McQuillen played an important role in the scientific development of dentistry and sought to elevate it above the empirical basis on which it was founded. He advocated "a thorough and collegiate education" and believed that laws should be passed that made such an education "not a matter of choice but of compulsion." The American Dental Association, he believed, should not dictate to the profession, but its recommendations should carry a moral force that would be overwhelming and irresistible. The attainment of excellence in the scientific and professional standards of the profession was a consuming passion with him. His colleagues believed that his sacrifice of energy, money, and time in the pursuit of his goals not only did not leave his family "handsomely provided for" but also hastened his early demise. He died suddenly in Philadelphia.

• The best account of McQuillen's career is in Barton L. Thorpe, *Biographies of Pioneer American Dentists and Their Successors*, vol. 3 of Charles R. E. Koch, ed., *History of Dental Surgery* (1910), pp. 297–303. McQuillen's American Dental Association activity is detailed in Robert W. McCluggage, *A History of the American Dental Association* (1959), pp. 123ff. A list of McQuillen's writings is in Arthur D. Black, ed., *Index to the Periodical Dental Literature in the English Language, 1839–1875* (1923), pp. 496–98.

DAVID L. COWEN

MCRAE, Carmen (8 Apr. 1920–10 Nov. 1994), jazz and popular singer, was born in New York City, the daughter of Osmond (or Oscar) McRae, the manager of a health club, and Evadne (maiden name unknown), both immigrants from the West Indies. During her lifetime McRae's birth year was widely reported to be 1922, but according to obituaries she was actually born in 1920.

McRae took classical piano lessons for five years but practiced pop tunes whenever her parents were not around. She attended Julia Richman High School in Manhattan. At age seventeen she won an amateur contest as a singer at the Apollo Theater in Harlem. Pianist and songwriter Irene Kitchings, then the wife of jazz pianist Teddy Wilson, helped McRae begin her career. McRae idolized Billie Holiday, who in 1939 recorded McRae's song "Dream of Life." McRae in turn imitated Holiday closely in performances at the start of her career, during which time, at her parents' insistence, she also took secretarial courses and did clerical work.

After spending two years as a government employee in Washington, D.C., McRae returned to New York City in 1943. She resumed singing at night while continuing her clerical work. In 1944 she married jazz drummer Kenny Clarke; they had no children. During that year she sang briefly as a substitute in the big bands of Benny Carter, Earl Hines, and Count Basie. As Carmen Clarke she joined Mercer Ellington's big band in 1946 and in that same year completed her first recording. Ellington's group disbanded after an engagement in Chicago in 1948. McRae separated from Clarke and took a seventeen-week job as a self-accompanied singer and pianist in a Chicago club. She performed in Chicago for three and a half years, during which time the influence of Holiday gave way to that of Sarah Vaughan, and McRae's own style began to emerge.

McRae returned to New York to record with jazz accordionist Mat Mathews and then took a job at Minton's Playhouse in Harlem, initially as the intermission pianist and then as a member of clarinetist Tony Scott's group. By 1953 she was working as a singer and only occasionally playing piano. She recorded her first album in 1954 and the following year finally gained widespread recognition for her album *By Special Request* which included versions of "Suppertime," "Yardbird Suite," and "You Took Advantage of Me." A career of extensive touring began with stands at the Black Hawk in Los Angeles, the Rainbow Grill in New York, and the Colonial in Toronto. In 1956 she divorced Clarke and married bassist Ike Isaacs; they had no children. For two years he led her accompanying trio. The couple separated in 1958 and later divorced.

Among McRae's albums were *After Glow* (1957), *Something to Swing About* (1959), and *Lover Man* (1961), the last a collection of tunes associated with Holiday but executed in McRae's own style and with the accompaniment of the forcefully energetic tenor saxophonist Eddie "Lockjaw" Davis, in contrast to Holiday's association with Lester Young's understated tenor sax. In 1962 she recorded a version of pianist Dave Brubeck's instrumental hit "Take Five," with lyrics added by Brubeck's wife, Iola, and that June she performed with Brubeck at a *New York Daily News* Jazz Concert in Madison Square Garden.

McRae traveled internationally over the next two decades and continued to make fine albums, including *The Great American Songbook* (1971), *Live at Bubba's* (1981), and, most notably, *Carmen Sings Monk* (1988). This last collection grew out of concerts at the Great American Music Hall in San Francisco, where she performed a number of pianist Thelonious Monk's instrumental compositions set to lyrics (and retitled, for reasons of copyright).

McRae suffered from asthma, which led to respiratory failure after a show at the Blue Note nightclub in New York in May 1991; she was bedridden thereafter. She suffered a stroke in October 1994 and died the following month at her home in Beverly Hills, California.

McRae was a strong, forthrightly honest, and sometimes intimidating woman whose outlook was encapsulated by the subtitle of writer James T. Jones's article: "Cut the Crap." She had an actress's commanding stage presence and sensitivity to the enunciation and meaning of lyrics and a jazz instrumentalist's talent for phrasing. Her cutting, mocking vocal timbre was inimitable, conveying a sound that was, as writer Jack Batten described it, "lazy, sexy, kind of autumnal and a little bittersweet." Perhaps owing to these qualities and a corresponding absence of sentimentality, McRae never achieved the same kind of widespread fame as Sarah Vaughan or Ella Fitzgerald. Her voice simply was not suited to sweet ballads, and indeed it was near the end of her career when she discovered that Monk's angular melodies were the perfect musical match for her singing. These performances are arguably her finest work.

• For interviews of McRae and surveys of her career see "Carmen McRae Looks Back on Her First Big Year," *Down Beat*, 12 Jan. 1955, p. 17; Sammy Mitchell, "The Magic of Carmen McRae," *Down Beat*, 12 Dec. 1968, pp. 18, 41; Barbara Gardner, "On the Threshold: Singer's Singer Carmen McRae," *Down Beat*, 13 Sept. 1962, pp. 19–21; Jack Batten, "Jazz: McRae Nears Peak of Singing Talent," *Toronto Globe and Mail*, 26 Oct. 1971; Les Tomkins, "Carmen McRae: Good New Songs Are Hard to Come By," *Crescendo International* 22 (Apr.–May 1984): 6–7; Bruce Crowther, "I Have to Sing for Myself," *Jazz Journal International* 41 (July 1988): 10; and James T. Jones IV, "Carmen McRae: Cut the Crap," *Down Beat*, June 1991, pp. 24–25. See also Ralph J. Gleason, *Celebrating the Duke, and Louis, Bessie, Billie, Bird, Carmen, Miles, Dizzy, and Other Heroes* (1975), pp. 118–24; Arthur Taylor, *Notes and Tones: Musician-to-Musician Interviews* (1977; repr. 1982); Leslie Gourse, *Louis' Children: American Jazz Singers* (1984); and Gary Giddins, *Rhythm-a-ning: Jazz Tradition and Innovation in the '80s* (1985). Mike Hennessey's *Klook: The Story of Kenny Clarke* (1990) has some information on McRae. A catalog of recordings appeared anonymously, "Carmen McRae," *Swing Journal* 35 (Feb. 1981): 192–97. Obituaries are in the *New York Times* and the *Pittsburgh Post-Gazette*, both 12 Nov. 1994.

BARRY KERNFELD

MCRAE, Edna (15 June 1901–7 June 1990), dancer and teacher, was born in Chicago, Illinois, the daughter of William M. McRae and Marie Watts. McRae's "fancy dancing," as she called it, began beside her sister, Elna McRae, in churches and converted movie houses in musical comedies "in which the entire neighborhood participated." Her understanding of production elements—the importance of costumes, makeup, and lighting—were thus well developed by the time she reached Carl Schurz High School, where she received her earliest formal training in physical education dance classes with Mabel M. Wright. That teacher directed her to Madeline Burtner Hazlitt, who had studied with European-trained teachers. In 1919 McRae graduated from the Chicago Normal School of Physical Education.

From about age thirteen, McRae's ballet technique was directed by a series of European teachers who came to Chicago, notably Andreas Pavley and Serge Oukrainsky, Vecheslav Swoboda, and Adolf Bolm. From 1915 McRae performed in Chicago theaters such as Orchestra Hall; the Masonic Temple, with Pavley; and the Blackstone Theatre, with students from Mary Landry's studio in the Stevens Building.

Adolph Bolm founded a Chicago school in 1923, at which time McRae was both student and part-time teacher at the Pavley-Oukrainsky school. A "fluke," as she told it, brought her to study with Bolm. McRae always believed it "a very fortunate happening" because of Bolm's great musicality, the manner in which he presented his classes, and his choreography. She became a teacher in his school and later in 1923 a member of Adolf Bolm's Company (called variously Ballet Intime), which performed in Chicago and toured much in the Midwest and in the East. McRae was at first part of the ensemble but by 1924 danced solos and was partnered by Bolm. The group also included dancers Harriet Lundgren, Ruth Page, Berenice Holmes, Jorg Fasting, Caird Leslie, and Mark Turbyfill. Bolm became for her a "living link with the great personages of the ballet world, not only dancers but musicians, teachers, choreographers and painters." Through Bolm she met Anna Ludmilla, Anna Pavlova, and Tamara Karsavina, who danced with Ballet Intime at Chicago's Eighth Street Theatre. Nicholas Roerich, designer for Sergey Diaghilev's famous 1909 production of act 3 of Aleksandr Borodin's *Prince Igor*, was also a visitor.

These experiences gave impetus to McRae's further schooling with other notable Russian émigré teachers. Backstage at the Auditorium Theater, a chance view of Pavlova's company in practice also convinced McRae that her technique was incomplete. She and Elna saved their money and went to Europe, where they found classes with other transplanted Russian teachers. She traveled yearly to Europe before World War II and studied with Nicholas Legat (1929, 1932, 1934), Laurent Novikoff, Harcourt and Claudie Algeranoff (1932), and Lydia Kyasht (1934) in London, and in Paris with Mathilde Kschessinskaya, Olga Preobrajenskaya, Vera Trefilova, and Lubov Egorova. McRae also studied in New York City with Michel Fokine and Chester Hale.

In the 1925 season McRae again danced solos with Adolph Bolm's Ballet Intime. From 1925, when she founded her own school in Chicago, McRae also choreographed for her own group as well as a number of other local troupes. The McRae Ballet performed at the Aragon Ballroom for the New Year's Eve party there in 1929. For the Children's Theatre at the Chicago Century of Progress Exposition, 1933, she did a one-act ballet, *The Sleeping Princess*, to Tchaikovsky's score. Other projects were under the auspices of the Chicago Park District Opera Groups, the Chicago

Concert and Opera Guild, the Society of Polish Artists, Sidney J. Page Productions, and the initial season of the Chicago Lyric Opera Company. In the 1920s she also taught at Francis Parker School, Chicago Teachers College, and Perry-Mansfield Camp in Colorado.

After McRae closed her studio in 1964 in order to "give time to special projects," she carried out several other responsibilities with far-reaching consequences to American dance. Until illness brought "an abrupt end" to her work, McRae supervised for a decade (1964–1974) the original Joffrey Apprentice Program in New York City and was briefly on the faculty there of the Juilliard School (1969) and Jacob's Pillow in Massachusetts (1973). *Dance Magazine* (Mar. 1966) noted that she was guest teaching that year and was studying tap with John Bubbles. From 1966 to 1970 she directed the scholarship programs sponsored by Pacific Lutheran University, Tacoma, Washington, held in conjunction with Joffrey Ballet's residency on that campus. In 1971 the University of California, Berkeley, sponsored a similar Joffrey program, which McRae also directed. A near-fatal heart attack in April 1974 prevented her from any further teaching.

Ruth Page summarized McRae's teaching methods in *Class* and wrote also that students "adored her discipline." Strictness, graduated progress, and thoroughness were hallmarks of McRae's class. Her straightforward approach to technique began with basics; that is, each lesson led to a clear grasp of the movement concept and an individual body's command of it. She brought to those meticulous classes experience of some of the century's best teachers and rich performing and choreographing opportunities. Often, through the years, Ruth Page, Walter Camryn, and Bentley Stone took class with her. Dancers on tour in Chicago never failed to visit the studio for her "rigors." Dance historian Selma Jean Cohen is another of McRae's former Chicago students. In 1986 a measure of the Chicago dance community's esteem was evident in two honors given her: Richard Ellis and Christine DuBoulay, directors of Ellis-DuBoulay School of Ballet, established an annual Edna McRae award; in the same year, Chicago Dance Coalition awarded to her the Ruth Page Award for Lifetime Service. Earlier the Cliff Dwellers, an old, prestigious arts group of Chicago, awarded McRae the Merit for Distinguished Service to the Arts. McRae never married. She died in a retirement home in Evanston, Illinois.

• Principal sources on McRae are the McRae papers, the Walter Camryn Papers, and the Ann Barzel Papers in the Newberry Library, Chicago, and the McRae programs and papers in the Dance Collection of the New York Public Library. This material has been augmented by the author's unpublished discussions with McRae and Walter Camryn (1980–1984). See also Walter Terry, "Midwest Ballet: The New and the Old," *Saturday Review*, 11 May 1968, and Ruth Page, *Class: Notes on Dance Classes around the World, 1915–1980* (1984). Obituaries are in the *Chicago Tribune*, 11 June 1990, and the *New York Times*, 13 June 1990.

ELIZABETH WEIGAND

MCRAE, John Jones (10 Jan. 1815–31 May 1868), governor of Mississippi and Confederate congressman, was born in Sneedsboro (now McFarlan), North Carolina, the son of John M. McRae, a merchant, and Elizabeth Mary Hempstead. The third son in a large family descended from Scotch Highlanders, McRae was raised on the frontier of southern Mississippi, where his father had moved the family to pursue mercantile opportunities in the cotton trade. After attending a local academy, McRae was sent north to Miami University in Ohio, from which he graduated in 1834. Returning to Mississippi to read law in Pearlington, in 1835 he joined the bar and married Mary A. McGuire, a widow. The total number of their children is unknown, but one son died in childhood.

Aided by the political connections he had made while establishing his law practice and editing the Paulding *Eastern Clarion*, McRae was elected to the Mississippi legislature in 1848 from Clarke County. He was a states' rights Democrat who followed the leadership of John A. Quitman and Jefferson Davis in opposing the Compromise of 1850 on the grounds that it failed to safeguard the rights of the South within the Union. After his reelection in 1850, McRae served as Speaker of the House and was then appointed to fill the U.S. Senate post vacated when Davis resigned to run for governor. In 1853 McRae was elected to the first of two terms as the governor of Mississippi.

As governor from 1854 to 1858, McRae pushed for a strong developmental role for state government. At his urging some $2 million of state funds were invested in railroads during his administration. Along with his brother Colin McRae, who took over and expanded their deceased father's mercantile business, McRae was a stockholder in both the Mobile and Ohio and the Mobile and New Orleans railroad companies. The brothers also speculated in vast tracts of timberland, which stood to gain in value as the railroad projects were completed. In addition to railroads, McRae's expansive view of state government encompassed the building of levees along the Mississippi River, increased public aid to education, and funding for the Deaf and Dumb Institute, which opened under state control in 1854.

At the expiration of his gubernatorial service, McRae was elected to the U.S. House of Representatives in 1858. A slaveholder, he took an extreme stand in favor of southern rights and aggressively called for the expansion of the United States into Mexico and Central America to gain more territory for slave labor. As part of his program for protecting and expanding slavery, he favored the reopening of the African slave trade, which had been closed by Congress since 1808.

McRae had long warned that the South would never accept a Republican president, and he had no doubts about the legality of secession. He once summarized his states' rights philosophy, "Co-equal rights in the Union, and the rights of the States severally to judge for themselves of infractions of the Constitution, as well as of the mode and measure of redress, is the great distinguishing feature of our republican form of government" (Inaugural address, governor, 10 Jan. 1854). He reacted to the election of Abraham Lincoln with a call for immediate secession and resigned from Congress in January 1861 with the rest of the Mississippi delegation.

McRae was among the most loyal of Davis's supporters during the Civil War. Elected to the first regular Confederate Congress in the fall of 1861, he backed the administration's war measures while serving on the Ways and Means and Special committees. He broke with the administration only over the issues of free trade, which he favored, and of exemptions from military conscription. In place of the unwieldy system of multiple exemptions imposed by Congress, McRae wanted to entrust the secretary of war with full authority for exempting and detailing draftees. He introduced a bill in February 1863 that so empowered the secretary of war, but it was never reported out of committee. As a result of growing disenchantment with the war by the voters in southern Mississippi, McRae lost his bid for reelection in the fall of 1863. He spent the rest of the war assisting Colin, who was a special financial agent for the Confederacy in Europe.

McRae retired from politics after the war and returned to his law practice in an effort to rebuild his personal wealth. Like many other noted Mississippi secessionists, he advised cooperation with the congressional plan of Reconstruction in 1867, which mandated black suffrage. He did so not only to embarrass conservative Whigs, who had staked their political fortunes on the success of President Andrew Johnson's more lenient program of Reconstruction, but also in an effort to secure white control over the newly enfranchised black voters. In the spring of 1868 McRae, who was quite ill at the time, traveled to Belize in British Honduras to visit Colin, an unpardoned Confederate who chose not to return to the United States at the end of the war. McRae died in Belize of the unspecified illness and was buried there.

• Most of the surviving private correspondence of McRae is grouped with that of Colin McRae in the McRae letters at the Alabama State Department of Archives and History in Montgomery. Useful for his public career is the Governors' Correspondence (1853–1858, E, 21–32) in the Mississippi State Department of Archives and History in Jackson. McRae has yet to be the subject of a biography. The best short treatment of his life is Dunbar Rowland, *History of Mississippi*, vol. 1 (1925). Additional material can be found in Charles S. Davis, *Colin J. McRae: Confederate Financial Agent* (1961). An obituary is in the *New York Times*, 12 June 1868.

WILLIAM L. BARNEY

MCREYNOLDS, James Clark (3 Feb. 1862–24 Aug. 1946), associate justice of the U.S. Supreme Court and attorney general of the United States, was born in Elkton, Kentucky, the son of John Oliver McReynolds, a doctor, and Ellen Reeves. He graduated first in his class from Vanderbilt University (Nashville, Tenn.) in 1882. After spending an additional year there as a fellow and assistant in natural history and geology, he entered the University of Virginia School of Law. Earning his law degree in little more than a year, he returned to Nashville in 1884 and opened a law office.

McReynolds remained in Nashville for the next two decades. Although he became known as a successful businessman long before he was recognized as a successful lawyer, his practice grew steadily; eventually he was asked to join the law faculty at Vanderbilt to teach commercial law, insurance, and corporations. Involving himself actively in the affairs of the rapidly growing city, he had by the turn of the century become a leading figure in its legal, political, and social circles.

In 1903 President Theodore Roosevelt's attorney general asked a friend if he knew a $30,000 lawyer who would work for the Justice Department for $5,000. The friend said he did, but warned, "He's a Democrat." Attorney General Philander Knox replied, "I'm hiring a lawyer, not a politician." What Knox got was McReynolds, who became the chief prosecutor of the American Tobacco Trust. After winning the case, McReynolds resigned in a huff in 1911 because he considered the dissolution order to which the government agreed too lenient.

Less than two years later, President-elect Woodrow Wilson plucked McReynolds from his New York law office to become attorney general of the United States. Trusts were then a major issue in American politics, and McReynolds fit Wilson's requirements perfectly: he was a Democrat who had specialized knowledge of corporate law but no connections to the corporations themselves. Though he served as attorney general for only eighteen months, McReynolds filed and successfully settled antitrust suits against American Telephone and Telegraph and several railroad companies. In these cases he pursued a strategy of filing suits and then negotiating out-of-court settlements. The strategy was unprecedented and was hailed as "the most important accomplishment of the executive branch since the Wilson Administration came to power" (*Literary Digest* 48 [24 June 1914]: 142).

Despite his success as a trust-buster, McReynolds irritated many Democrats because he refused to discharge Republican U.S. attorneys wholesale, and he also declined to recommend Democratic "hacks" for the federal bench. His curt dismissal of suggestions from cabinet colleagues exasperated them, and many were relieved when Wilson nominated McReynolds to succeed U.S. Supreme Court justice Horace Lurton in August 1914.

Though an ailing Senator George Norris railed against the nomination, the Senate confirmed McReynolds 44–6. Though most Court observers initially expected the little-known McReynolds to inject a liberal perspective into the Court's deliberations, he became by the 1930s its most conservative member. During the first fifteen years of his service on the Court, McReynolds attracted little public notice. In those years he differed little with the majority of his colleagues. He was at most somewhat more hostile to government action, less willing to permit government regulation of property, and quicker to condemn government interference with individual freedoms. During this period he wrote two opinions that continue to influence constitutional law. *Meyer v. Nebraska* (1923) and *Pierce v. Society of Sisters* (1925) have for decades been frequently cited for their ringing definitions of liberty, which in *Meyer* he declared embraced:

> the right of the individual to contract, to engage in any of the common occupations of life, to acquire useful knowledge, to marry, establish a home and bring up children, to worship God according to the dictates of his own conscience, and generally to enjoy those privileges long recognized at common law as essential to the orderly pursuit of happiness by free men.

Although McReynolds flirted with the idea of retiring from the Court in the late 1920s, he stayed on the bench; once the scope of President Franklin D. Roosevelt's New Deal became clear, he vowed to remain until the president, whom he considered crazy, was thrown out. He dissented from every major decision that sustained New Deal legislation, beginning with the Gold Clause cases in 1935. In an electrifying oral dissent from the bench McReynolds, who had run for Congress as a "Gold Democrat" in 1896, condemned Roosevelt's repudiation of the gold standard as "Nero at his worst" and declared, "Shame and humiliation are upon us. Moral and financial chaos may confidently be expected." He alone dissented from the Court's endorsement of the government's right to construct and operate the Tennessee Valley Authority, declaring that his brethren had permitted Congress to transform a government of limited powers into one of unlimited powers.

In the wake of Roosevelt's court-packing scheme, McReynolds orchestrated the conservatives' last stand against the New Deal in the cases challenging the constitutionality of the National Labor Relations Act (NLRA). Dissenting once again, he lamented the vast powers given the government, predicting that "the authority of the State over its domestic concerns would exist only by sufferance of the federal government." The NLRA decisions reaffirmed his belief, expressed privately to a friend earlier, that "the Constitution is gone."

Judged by some academics to be one of the worst justices who ever sat on the U.S. Supreme Court, McReynolds is thought to have embodied all the ugly qualities imputed to the four conservative justices who opposed Roosevelt's New Deal. The basic charge is that he deliberately perverted the Constitution in his unwavering defense of wealth and privilege. Critics consider it unconscionable that he would willingly have thrown around the rich a constitutional mantle of protection while the poor suffered universal distress. McReynolds has thus come to symbolize intransigent, mean-spirited opposition to democratic progress.

The common judgment is doubtless also reinforced by the equally common belief that McReynolds was a rude, intolerant misanthrope. When he reluctantly retired from the high court in 1941, his colleagues expressed no regret, and none attended his funeral five years later. By then the stories of McReynolds's churlish behavior toward his colleagues and counsel were legion. On hearing that Judge Benjamin Cardozo had been nominated for a seat on the Court, he remarked, "Apparently all one need be [to be appointed] is a Jew and the son of a criminal." Earlier he had declined to accompany his colleagues on a ceremonial visit to Philadelphia, advising Chief Justice William H. Taft that he (McReynolds) "was not always to be seen whenever a Hebrew [presumably Louis Brandeis] was abroad." He often ridiculed counsel and once instructed a lawyer not to answer a question from Justice Felix Frankfurter. No other justice has ever been so consistently portrayed as wanting in good manners. While a critic of Supreme Court justices might not be able to hate the scholarly George Sutherland, the gracious Willis Van Devanter, or the innocuous Pierce Butler, he could hate the aloof, sarcastic McReynolds, and the New Dealers hated McReynolds passionately.

This judgment is an exceedingly harsh one, for McReynolds took very seriously his oath to defend and protect the Constitution, though to be sure it was the Constitution as he understood it or, as McReynolds put it, "the Constitution as written and not as whittled away by tenuous reasoning." McReynolds's constitutional views were those of Thomas Jefferson, as they had been transmitted to him by a father born in the heyday of Jacksonian democracy. Although the Jeffersonian view to which McReynolds adhered rested on a sound exposition of legal principles rooted in precedents reaching back to the beginning of the American republic, his voice echoed from an increasingly distant past, and it seemed outdated to twentieth-century Americans. Yet he did see himself as a judicial Nero, content to fiddle constitutional text while the country burned. He neither consciously sought to make the world safe for capitalism nor for the capitalist. He sought only to make it safe for the individual citizen to exercise his inalienable rights.

Believing that he had failed in that task, McReynolds retired after Roosevelt's election to a third term. He was by then a lonely and isolated figure on the increasingly liberal Court. "I tried to protect my country," he grumbled, "but any country that elects Roosevelt three times deserves no protection." McReynolds, who never married, died in Washington, D.C. He is buried alongside his mother and father in the family plot in Elkton. The inscription he selected for his tombstone captures his disaffection from the modern world: "With Jesus Christ, Which Is Far Better."

• A full-length biography of McReynolds is James E. Bond, *I Dissent: The Legacy of James Clark McReynolds* (1992). Two unpublished doctoral dissertations on the justice's life are D. Blaisdell, "The Constitutional Law of Mr. Justice McReynolds" (Univ. of Wisconsin, 1954), and S. Early, "James Clark McReynolds and the Judicial Process" (Univ. of Virginia, 1954). A brief biographical sketch, based on these dissertations, is David Bruner, "James Clark McReynolds," in *The Justice of the United States Supreme Court 1789–1969*, ed. Leon Friedman and Fred Israel (1969).

JAMES E. BOND

MCSHANE, Edward James (10 May 1904–1 June 1989), mathematician, was born in New Orleans, Louisiana, the son of Augustus McShane, a physician, and Harriet Kenner Butler, a former schoolteacher. McShane grew up in New Orleans and attended Tulane University. He graduated from Tulane in 1925, receiving both a B.E. in engineering and a B.S. in physics. He turned down an offer of a position in industry to continue studies in mathematics at Tulane, where he received an M.S. in 1927. In the summer of 1927 he entered the doctoral program in mathematics at the University of Chicago. His doctoral studies were temporarily interrupted in 1928–1929, when he served as an assistant professor at the University of Wichita. He received a Ph.D. from Chicago in 1930, with a dissertation on existence theorems for isoperimetric problems in the calculus of variations, written under the direction of L. M. Graves and G. A. Bliss. McShane was a National Research Council Fellow for 1930–1932, studying at Princeton, Ohio State, Harvard, and Chicago. In 1931 he married Virginia Haun; they had three children.

There were few jobs for young mathematicians in the United States in 1932, at the depth of the Great Depression. Facing these prospects McShane took advantage of the offer of an assistantship at Göttingen University in Germany, where he worked with Richard Courant, director of the mathematics institute. During this time he translated into English Courant's two-volume *Differential and Integral Calculus*. Upon returning to the United States in 1933 he joined the faculty of Princeton University as an instructor and was promoted to assistant professor in 1934. In the fall of 1935 he became a professor of mathematics at the University of Virginia, a position he held until his retirement in 1974, when he became emeritus professor. At times during his long career at Virginia, McShane took leaves of absence to go elsewhere as a visiting professor, spending a year each at the Institute for Advanced Study in Princeton, the University of Utrecht in the Netherlands, and Rockefeller University, and a semester at the University of Kyoto in Japan.

McShane's early research centered on the calculus of variations for multiple integral problems. In the late 1930s and early 1940s he developed methods to provide existence theorems and necessary conditions for a large class of single integral problems in the calculus of variations. Exemplary of his rising status in the field, McShane was invited in 1938 to give a semicentennial address at the fiftieth anniversary meeting of the American Mathematical Society. In 1943 he was the AMS Colloquium Lecturer. He had also begun to work in other, allied areas. In 1939 he published a paper on Lagrange multipliers that later had a profound effect on the theory of optimal control, being used in 1959 by Lev Semënovich Pontrayagin, professor of mathematics and mechanics at the University of Moscow, in the proof of his eponymous "Maximal Principle."

The entry of the United States into World War II led McShane to work in the war effort as a civilian. From 1942 to 1945 he was in charge of a mathematics group at the Ballistics Research Laboratory at Aberdeen Proving Grounds. With two of his Aberdeen colleagues, J. L. Kelley and F. V. Reno, he wrote *Exterior Ballistics* (1953), for some time the definitive work in the field.

After the war years, integration theory in its various aspects became McShane's main area of interest. McShane had long been attracted to physical science and engineering applications of mathematics. In a natural way this tied in with his interest in the theory of integration. His search for a correct mathematical setting to treat the "infinities" and divergent integrals of quantum field theory led him to write *Order Preserving Maps and Integration Processes* (1953).

In recognition of McShane's outstanding work in pure and applied mathematics he was elected in 1948 to the National Academy of Sciences. In 1950–1951 he served as vice president of the AMS, and in 1953–1954 he was president of the Mathematical Association of America. He served the AMS in several other leadership capacities in the 1950s, culminating in being chosen its president for 1958–1959. In 1953 he was awarded the Chauvenet Prize by the MAA for his expository article "Partial Orderings and Moore-Smith Limits" (*American Mathematical Monthly* 59 [1952]: 1–11). In the 1950s and 1960s McShane was active in the movement to revitalize undergraduate mathematics in the United States, and in 1964 he received the MAA Annual Award for Distinguished Service to Mathematics. From 1956 to 1968 he served as a member of the National Science Board.

During the 1960s and 1970s McShane became interested in developing a stochastic differential and integral calculus, involving random variables or random coefficients and arising in a natural way from problems in the physical world that have a random or probabilistic nature. At that time a stochastic calculus existed, as the result of researchers as Kiyoshi Itô, one of the first and most important in the field, but it did not adequately handle certain types of stochastic differential equations that arise in engineering. McShane introduced a new stochastic calculus to remedy the situation. His 1974 monograph *Stochastic Calculus and Stochastic Models* became the definitive work on this subject.

McShane's abiding interest in integration theory and his keen desire to make this theory both more useful to scientists and engineers and more readily understandable to students came together in his work on a new theory of integration, which had both the power of the Lebesgue integral and the intuitive appeal of the Riemann integral. McShane became an enthusiastic promoter of this new integration process; his work in this area culminated in his last published book, *Unified Integration* (1983).

A man of many talents and varied interests, McShane had a knack for languages and loved music. In his student days he had learned Italian in order to read opera libretti. That language later proved useful when as a doctoral student he needed to read Italian mathematician Leonida Tonelli's new book on calculus of variations. McShane was an accomplished amateur cellist. Late in life he became interested in Chinese calligraphy and painting. He died in Charlottesville, Virginia.

McShane's enduring importance in mathematics derives from the two main avenues of his research: optimization and integration. An assessment of the former was given in 1989, when the Society of Industrial and Applied Mathematics (SIAM) dedicated the September issue of its *Journal on Control and Optimization* to McShane. McShane's work on integration theory and its applications is considered by experts in the field to be important and probably of lasting value. The McShane integral has about the same range and power as the Lebesgue integral, while being more tractable and intuitively appealing, like the Riemann integral.

• Among McShane's major published works are "Recent Developments in the Calculus of Variations," *American Mathematical Society Semi-centennial Publications*, vol. 2 (1938), pp. 69–97; *Integration* (1944); *Real Analysis*, with T. A. Botts (1959); "A Riemann-Type Integral That Includes Lebesgue-Stieltjes, Bochner, and Stochastic Integrals," American Mathematical Society, *Memoir 88* (1969); and "The Calculus of Variation from the Beginning through Optimal Control Theory," in *Optimal Control and Differential Equations*, ed. A. B. Schwarzkopf et al. (1978), pp. 3–49. A list of McShane's published works is given in L. D. Berkovitz and Wendell Fleming, "A Tribute to E. J. McShane," *SIAM Journal on Control and Optimization* 27 (1989): 909–15. See also Wendell Fleming and Victor Klee, "Edward James McShane, 1904–1989," American Mathematical Society, *Notices* 36 (1989): 828–30. An obituary is in the *New York Times*, 6 June 1989.

HENRY E. HEATHERLY

MCTAMMANY, John (26 June 1845–26 Mar. 1915), inventor, was born in Kelvin Row, near Glasgow, Scotland, the son of John McTammany and Agnes McLean. In 1862 the family emigrated and settled in Uniontown, Ohio, midway between Canton and Akron. As a youth, McTammany wanted to become a concert pianist. However, although he played for churches and public functions throughout his adult life, poverty and injury limited him to the status of an amateur musician. He received little formal education and worked at various factories. While employed at a Uniontown company engaged in the manufacture and repair of agricultural implements, he became interested in designing improvements for the reaper and other farming machinery. The Civil War diverted him: in 1863 he enlisted in the 115th Ohio Volunteer Infantry. He was wounded in battle near Chattanooga and recuperated in a military hospital in Nashville, Tennessee. During his convalescence McTammany visited a local pawnshop and volunteered to repair musical instruments and a music box. Repairing the music box inspired him to begin designs for a mechanical piano based on a similar principle and different from earlier devices that were attached to a keyboard rather than constructed as an integral part of a piano (or organ). Many years passed, however, before he was able to construct a working model. Returning to Ohio, McTammany sold pianos and other musical instruments, taught music, and labored in a variety of jobs. At night he continued work on a pneumatic "player" using a roll of paper tape and a depression mechanism to produce the tones.

The first public exhibition of the player took place in June 1876 in St. Louis, Missouri. McTammany constructed several working models and attracted the attention of the president of the Estey Organ Company. He created a new prototype powered by a pedal; a perforated paper roll, mounted within an Estey organ cabinet, activated the values or keys pneumatically. This automatic organ was first exhibited at the music store of Story & Camp in St. Louis. McTammany's creation and subsequent demonstrations of competing organ and piano players at the Philadelphia Centennial Exposition stirred public interest, but the musical establishment ridiculed the invention, and piano manufacturers initially resisted the development of the player mechanism.

Following a move to Boston, Massachusetts, in 1876, McTammany manufactured and sold player organs (called organettes) and other automatic musical instruments there and in Cambridgeport. In 1880 he moved his operation to Worcester to reduce costs but his business acumen did not match his inventive spirit. He was unsuccessful at marketing his invention and was reduced to poverty. McTammany had filed a caveat (an extension of time to file a complete patent application) with the U.S. Patent Office in 1876, but he did not have the money to follow up with patent applications. As the popularity of the player grew, other inventors patented and manufactured devices similar to the McTammany player. McTammany began a lengthy process of litigation and was eventually recognized in federal court as the original inventor of the player piano. He was awarded patents for the player in 1881. His manufacturing business, however, was eventually lost when his competitors acquired stock in his musical instrument company and ousted him.

McTammany redirected his efforts toward new inventions based on pneumatics and the perforated paper roll. He developed the first mechanical voting machine for popular elections (patented in 1892). The progressive movement was seeking to reduce the control of political machines over the election process, and a principal element of electoral reform was the Australian or secret ballot. The Australian system of voting demanded both uniformity in the production of ballots and anonymity in the voter's marking of the ballot. The voting machine provided a means for efficient elections. Opening the cover of the machine advanced a perforated roll on which the voter marked choices for parties, candidates, or ballot questions. Closing the cover caused a pneumatic registering device to add the voter's choices to the total recorded votes. McTammany's voting machine removed the necessity for printing and distributing ballots. Voting machines soon became an important weapon in progressive attempts to combat election fraud. The Massachusetts legislature authorized use of the McTammany device in 1893, and the first popular election using it was held in North Brookfield, Massachusetts, in 1896. The machines, produced in Portland, Maine, were used in many subsequent elections, but McTammany was again overcome by his competition; similar voting machines were devised, patented, and used in elections.

McTammany's other inventions included many automatic musical instruments (such as a mechanical banjo), a tabulating machine for census and other data records, and an automatic typewriter. He was also active in the prohibition movement. He continued to make improvements to his inventions throughout his later years, even though he had little money to fund his projects. He became disillusioned with the U.S. patent system and the legal system. McTammany died at a soldier's home in Stamford, Connecticut. The city staged a public funeral for him, and a grand player piano performed the music.

McTammany's inventions were examples of technological devices that helped to democratize the nation. Music was valued during the Victorian era, but few Americans had access to concerts or professional musicians. The player piano granted the public access to artistic proficiency: professional artists recorded performances for it, and composers wrote music specifically for it. The player piano and other music-reproducing instruments dominated the market through the end of World War I. The player initially surpassed the phonograph in terms of playing time and fidelity, but improvements to the phonograph eventually led to the demise of the player. McTammany's litigation over patent rights led to reforms in the issuance of patents. His balloting devices led to fraud-free mechanized voting in urban America. Although these devices were rendered obsolete by newer ones, McTammany's inventions gave the public some advantages that previously had been available only to the elite.

• Other than his numerous patent applications, few of McTammany's papers survive. His books *The History of the Player* (1913) and *The Technical History of the Player* (1915) describe the invention of the player piano and related business enterprises. The former contains more biographical information, while the latter provides a detailed account of the evolution and the patent history of player mechanisms. William Gemmert's introduction to *Technical History* places McTammany's contribution in the context of events of the time.

JAMES W. ENDERSBY

MCTELL, Blind Willie (5 May 1898?–19 Aug. 1959), blues artist, was born Willie Samuel McTell near Thomson, Georgia, the son of Minnie Watkins and Eddie McTell. Probably blind from birth, he was one of two children. His birth date remains obscure; some sources report 5 May 1901, but in a 1940 recorded interview, folklorist John Lomax announced him to be forty-two years old. Both of his parents played guitar, as did an uncle. McTell told Lomax that he took up music when he was "quite a child," learning mainly from his mother after the family had moved to Statesboro, Georgia, the place he later referred to as his real home. Allegedly he ran away from home as a teenager to work in various traveling shows, although what he did in the shows remains unclear (he told Lomax he quit the guitar for eight years, then returned to playing). According to McTell, he attended several schools for the blind: the state school in Macon from 1922 to 1925, then a school in New York City, and finally a school in Michigan, where he learned to read braille.

He then returned to Georgia and resumed the life of an itinerant musician. Ranging as far afield as Miami and Nashville, he often teamed up with other street musicians, chief among them the legendary Blind Willie Johnson, a religious singer and bottleneck slide guitar virtuoso from Texas. According to McTell, he and Johnson were great pals, traveling together "from Maine to the Mobile Bay." Johnson's music clearly influenced McTell's style and repertoire.

On 18 October 1927 McTell began a productive recording career. His initial session for RCA Victor in Atlanta resulted in four sides. They were artistic successes and did well enough commercially to earn McTell a return session a year later at which he recorded his best-known composition, "Statesboro Blues." On all the Victor sides he was identified as Blind Willie McTell. Over the next five years he recorded for Columbia as "Blind Sammie," for OKeh as "Georgia Bill," and for Victor again as "Hot Shot Willie." In 1933 he did four Vocalion sessions with fellow Atlanta street musicians Buddy Moss and Curley Weaver.

Throughout his recording career, McTell continued to ply his trade on the streets of Atlanta, playing house parties or other informal street corner venues. As pianist Piano Red recalled, McTell, Moss, and Weaver "walked the streets with their guitars on their backs. And during the day they would have them daytime parties, house to house, where they had that white lightning . . . and they made a little money doing that. They'd try this side of town this morning, the other side the next morning. They go in a different territory every day. Just start walking. People call them with their guitars, say, 'How about playing us a number?' About twenty or thirty minutes, they'd have a house full or a porch full."

In 1934 McTell married Ruthy Kate Williams. The following year the couple recorded blues and religious pieces for Decca, accompanied by Curley Weaver. Continuing as a street singer, McTell ranged as far as Tennessee, Alabama, and North Carolina; he toured Georgia and Kentucky with a medicine show and was involved in one unproductive Vocalion session. In October 1940 McTell had a chance encounter in Atlanta with Lomax, who arranged a documentary recording session for the Library of Congress. The session, conducted on 5 November 1940 in Lomax's hotel room, showed the breadth of McTell's repertoire and included spoken interview material. Lomax, who paid McTell a dollar and cab fare for the session, wrote in his field notes how easily McTell got around the city, finding his way by memory. He also reported that

McTell followed tourists to resorts in Florida and the Georgia Sea Islands, going wherever the money went.

Traveling as far as New York City, McTell continued as a street performer, gradually leaning further and further toward religious music. After a nine-year break in recording—indicative of the public's loss of appetite for old-style music—McTell returned to the studio in 1949 and 1950 to record blues and religious songs for two labels, Atlantic and Regal. In both cases, the recordings had more documentary value than popular appeal.

By this time McTell had curtailed his traveling, staying closer to home in Atlanta or Macon. He played religious music with a second guitarist, Little Willie, and played on several religious radio programs. His final 1956 recording session, an informal affair in the back of an Atlanta record store run by Ed Rhodes, was captured on tape and stored away.

According to his wife, McTell devoted himself exclusively to religious songs soon after the 1956 session and became active as a preacher. At this time his health was declining, and he suffered several strokes. In 1959 he entered Milledgeville State Hospital, where he died of a cerebral hemorrhage. He was buried near Jones Grove Church in Thomson.

While McTell left an extensive recorded legacy spanning some four decades, he was never a bestselling blues artist. He spent most of his life traveling the country, playing to diverse audiences, surviving on tips and handouts. He was, however, a fine musician with a remarkably extensive and eclectic repertoire that included ballads, ragtime, pop, novelty tunes, and even pseudocountry tunes, as well as some of the finest religious music ever recorded. An articulate, well-educated man with a clear, well-enunciated vocal delivery, a master of the twelve-string guitar, and the major exemplar of the East Coast/Atlanta sound, McTell was perhaps more appreciated after his death. His "Statesboro Blues" became a blues revival standard after its re-release in 1959 and went on to become a rock classic in the repertoires of artists ranging from Taj Mahal to the Allman Brothers. The tape of his 1956 session in Rhodes's record store was retrieved from storage and issued as part of the Prestige Bluesville series in 1961. McTell was elected to the Blues Foundation Hall of Fame in 1981.

• For discographical information, see Robert M. W. Dixon and John Godrich, *Blues and Gospel Records, 1902–1943* (1982); Mike Leadbitter and Neil Slaven, *Blues Records, 1943–1966* (1968); Paul Oliver, ed., *The Blackwell Guide to Blues Records* (1989); and David Evans, "Blind Willie McTell," notes to *Atlanta Blues, 1933*, JEMF-10C (1979). For more biographical details, see Samuel Charters, *The Blues Makers* (1991); Bruce Bastin, *Red River Blues: The Blues Tradition in the Southeast* (1986); and Sheldon Harris, *Blues Who's Who: A Biographical Dictionary of Blues Singers* (1979; repr. 1989). For a sampler of McTell's repertoire, try *Statesboro Blues: The Essential Recordings of Blind Willie McTell*, Indigo IGOCD2015, and *The Definitive Blind Willie McTell*, Columbia Legacy C21C 53234; for the Library of Congress session, *Blind Willie McTell: 1940*, Melodeon MLP 7323.

BARRY PEARSON
BILL MCCULLOCH

MCTYEIRE, Holland Nimmons (28 July 1824–15 Feb. 1889), bishop of the Methodist Episcopal Church, South, was born near Barnwell, South Carolina, the son of John McTyeire and Elizabeth Amanda Nimmons, farmers. He spent his early years on the family plantation outside Barnwell. While clearly not belonging to the rich planter class, his parents were well-established farmers. In 1838 they took up permanent residence in Uchee, Alabama, near Columbus, Georgia.

Education was important to the McTyeires. At age twelve Holland enrolled in Cokesbury Conference Institute, a Methodist school in Abbeville, South Carolina. Although he remained there for only a year, his experience at the school gave direction to his life. He then studied for almost two years at Collinsworth Institute in Talbotton, Georgia, but it was Randolph-Macon College in Virginia, where he enrolled in August 1841, that shaped him for his future work. There he profited from teachers who instilled in him a love for learning.

Although he was raised in a Methodist family that took its religious commitments seriously, not until his student days at Cokesbury Institute did McTyeire profess "conversion." In time he offered himself for ministry in the Methodist Episcopal church, reaching that decision, after great struggle, as he graduated from Randolph-Macon in 1844. Shortly thereafter he was licensed to preach in the Methodist Episcopal church. Simultaneously, powerful forces were at work (principally over the abolition of slavery), which in 1845 would split the Methodist Episcopal church into northern and southern branches. The northern branch retained the original name of the church; the southern branch took the name Methodist Episcopal Church, South. In November 1845 McTyeire was appointed to the church in Williamsburg, Virginia. Consequently, he would spend his life as a minister in the Methodist Episcopal Church, South. McTyeire was admitted into "full connection" in that church in 1848 and ordained an elder in 1849.

In this period it was rare for Methodist ministers to remain more than a few months in a pastoral appointment. Bishops moved ministers frequently to meet the needs of the fast-growing church. Within six years McTyeire served churches in Virginia, Alabama, Mississippi, and Louisiana. While serving the Methodist congregation in Mobile, Alabama, he married Amelia Townsend in 1847; they had eight children.

McTyeire's talent as a writer earned widespread recognition. In 1851, along with his pastoral duties in New Orleans, he and a colleague inaugurated the *New Orleans Christian Advocate,* a paper designed to keep Methodists in the Southwest abreast of denominational news. It also provided him a forum for comment on a variety of topics agitating the church. When the Methodist Episcopal Church, South needed an editor for its denominationwide periodical, the Nashville *Christian Advocate,* McTyeire was a natural choice. In the summer of 1858 he assumed his new duties.

The General Conference of 1866 elected McTyeire as a bishop. His leadership qualities were so well recognized that his election was virtually inevitable. Like other Methodist bishops, he spent his years traveling across the church, which extended from coast to coast and from Texas and Florida in the south to West Virginia and Utah in the north.

While McTyeire's labor as an episcopal leader should not be minimized, his lasting mark was the founding in 1873 of Vanderbilt University. Others in southern Methodism supported the effort to found a university, but McTyeire pushed for a "great University" in the South comparable to Yale and Harvard in the North. The financial depression of the South following the Civil War did not augur well for the success of such a venture, and if left to their own resources, southern Methodists would have had to abandon the idea. McTyeire rescued the dream by securing a gift of almost $1 million from the railroad and shipping tycoon Cornelius Vanderbilt (1794–1877). Distant family ties brought Vanderbilt and McTyeire together, creating the basis for Vanderbilt's generous gift. In making his gift Vanderbilt insisted that McTyeire be made president of the board of trust for life with veto powers over board actions and that the university be located in or near Nashville. Further, McTyeire personally was given authority to select the site of the university and alone was entrusted with the expenditure of the Vanderbilt money. From the time Vanderbilt committed his financial support (1873) until McTyeire's death, the university was under the direct control of the bishop. During those early years no individual was more responsible for setting its direction.

McTyeire also found time to write books. His first effort was a small monograph, *Duties of Christian Masters to the Servants* (1851; repr. 1859), in which he confronted the volatile issue of slavery, calling for the Christian treatment of slaves within the framework of existing laws. Clearly he was no abolitionist. In 1869 he published *A Catechism of Bible History* and *A Catechism on Church Government.* In the following year he published *A Manual of the Discipline of the Methodist Episcopal Church, South,* which became the authoritative statement on government in the southern church and required reading for those seeking ordination. His magnum opus was *A History of Methodism* (1884). Methodism in the United States had been organized into a church in 1784, and McTyeire was commissioned to publish a history of the movement by the church committee established to design the centenary celebration. McTyeire's history of Methodism received instant acclaim in the North and the South and became one of the bestsellers among religious books. Written from a southern point of view, as McTyeire stated, the study deals with Methodism primarily before the North-South division in 1845 and was noncontroversial. McTyeire's southern sympathies clearly manifested themselves in his discussion of the split in the church. Even here, however, northern Methodists would have to conclude that, on the whole, his analysis was fair.

McTyeire died on the Vanderbilt campus where he lived. McTyeire was a strong personality with a vision of what might be. Though not a charismatic personality, he was able to win others to his point of view. He was the principal force by which post–Civil War southern Methodism was restructured for the new day. Vanderbilt University, to his mind, was clearly part of his grand vision.

• McTyeire's papers are housed in the Special Collections section of the Vanderbilt University Library. The only full-length biography of McTyeire is *Bishop Holland Nimmons McTyeire* (1955) by John J. Tigert IV, grandson of the bishop.

FRANK GULLEY

MCVICKAR, William Neilson (19 Oct. 1843–28 June 1910), clergyman and Episcopal bishop, was born in New York City, the son of John Augustus McVickar, a homeopathic doctor, and Charlotte Neilson. He studied at Columbia College, from which he graduated in 1865. He entered Philadelphia Divinity School in 1865 but transferred after two years to the General Theological Seminary. He received both a bachelor's degree in divinity from General and a master's degree from Columbia in 1868. McVickar was ordained a deacon in the Episcopal church in 1867, and the following year he was ordained a priest. He served briefly as an assistant minister at St. George's Church in New York, but once he became a priest he assumed the rectorship of the Church of the Holy Trinity, recently established uptown in Harlem. Although Holy Trinity had only a few members and no building when McVickar arrived, he helped build the church into a substantial institution during his tenure at the parish.

In 1875 McVickar left New York and accepted the rectorship of the Church of the Holy Trinity in Philadelphia, which was one of the most prominent parishes in the diocese of Pennsylvania. During his twenty-two years in Philadelphia, he distinguished himself both in the work of his diocese and in the national affairs of the Episcopal church. He was also elected a deputy to the five General Conventions that met between 1883 and 1895. In October 1897 the Rhode Island diocesan convention chose him to succeed Thomas March Clark, then the bishop of the diocese. he was consecrated bishop coadjutor (assistant bishop) in 1898 and held that position until Clark's death in 1903. McVickar was installed as the bishop of Rhode Island in September 1903.

Besides supervising church matters, McVickar was extensively involved in social service activities in Rhode Island. He embraced a "Social Gospel" that considered the Christian's duty was not the abandonment of the world but its salvation through moral reform. As a consequence of this belief, he assailed what he considered to be the sins, both private and public, of the citizens of his state. He labored especially hard on behalf of the temperance movement. He was president of the Rhode Island Anti-Saloon League for six years, from 1904 to 1910, and he served as president of the New England Watch and Ward Society, which was affiliated with the Anti-Saloon League. McVickar was also a member of the committee on marriage and divorce of the Federation of Churches of Rhode Island. In that capacity he supported legislation, eventually adopted by the Rhode Island legislature, that reformed the state's marriage laws. The chief aim of the legislation was the prevention of "hasty marriages."

During McVickar's comparatively brief episcopate (1903–1910), the communicant strength of his diocese increased by approximately 12 percent, and several new parishes were founded. He was known as a "broad churchman" who was open to new ideas in science, theology, and biblical studies. In this regard, he was typical of many clergy who guided Protestant urban churches during the critical period of transition in the late nineteenth century. McVickar was successful in maintaining the institutional structures of the Episcopal church at the same time that American society was undergoing profound changes, as non-Protestant immigrants from southern and eastern Europe flooded into cities in the Northeast and Midwest. Meanwhile, church members were confronted with a number of intellectual challenges, as the theory of evolution and the reinterpretation of the Bible imperiled traditional Christian beliefs. McVickar sought a middle ground between these various threats to the stability of his denomination. His social concerns balanced a genuine desire to relieve human suffering with a need to uphold Protestant hegemony in his state. His broad church theological stance, moreover, enabled Episcopalians to accept new scientific findings without entirely abandoning the old, pre-Darwinian faith.

McVickar never married but was close friends with the great Episcopal preacher and fellow bachelor Phillips Brooks of Boston. He continued to serve as bishop and remained active in church and community affairs until his death. McVickar fell ill while on vacation at his summer home in Beverly Farms, Massachusetts, where he died.

• Biographical material on McVickar is quite sparse. Some manuscript papers are in the Episcopal Diocese of Rhode Island Archives at the Special Collections Department, University of Rhode Island Library. Dudley Tyng, *Rhode Island Episcopalians, 1635–1953* (1954), provides useful information about his episcopate. A full description of McVickar's career is in his obituary notice in the *Providence Daily Journal*, 29 June 1910.

GARDINER H. SHATTUCK, JR.

MCWILLIAMS, Carey (13 Dec. 1905–27 June 1980), activist attorney, writer, and editor, was born in Steamboat Springs, Colorado, the son of Jerry McWilliams, a cattle rancher, and Harriet Casley. He entered the University of Southern California in 1922 and pursued a liberal arts curriculum but apparently was permitted to enroll in the university's law school without receiving a B.A. To say that McWilliams was educated in southern California means not merely that he received a J.D. from USC in 1927 but rather, and more importantly, that he learned about the particular injustices that characterized the region in which he lived and committed himself to seeking radical change in those aspects of society.

Admitted to the California bar upon his graduation from law school, McWilliams practiced for eleven years in the Los Angeles firm of Black, Hamond and McWilliams. Researching his earliest books added valuable context to what he had learned from his immediate experience. First, his biography of Ambrose Bierce, published in 1929, immersed him in the life and writings of California's premier iconoclast, a writer for whom the pen was a strategic weapon against entrenched power and received inanities. His next book, *The New Regionalism in American Literature* (1930), allowed him to explore a new way of thinking about social and cultural issues that was also reflected in his next critical volume, *Louis Adamic and Shadow-America* (1935). McWilliams states in his autobiography that he had the same sort of interest in the culture of the western United States as the southern agrarian writers espoused for their region. The choice of Bierce and Adamic as subjects of his monographs suggests, however, that he did not follow the agrarians in their identification of regionalism and conservatism but that he was drawn, rather, to the unconventional and radical aspects of the West.

During the 1930s McWilliams became deeply concerned with racism, particularly prejudice against Mexican immigrants and their descendants and against Japanese Americans. Both of these preoccupations were extremely unusual for a California "Anglo" of McWilliams's generation, particularly one who was not directly affiliated with the labor union movement or the Communist party. In 1938 McWilliams was appointed chief inspector of the California State Division of Immigration and Housing. While there, he began writing about the problems of the Mexicans in southern California, focusing on the lives of migrant agricultural laborers. In all, he published four books about Mexicans and other Latin American immigrant groups. Two of these—*Factories in the Fields: The Story of Migratory Farm Labor in California* (1939) and *Ill Fares the Land: Migrants and Migratory Labor in the United States* (1942)—focus specifically on the farmworkers, whereas his later books, *North from Mexico: The Spanish-Speaking People of the United States* (1948) and *The Mexicans in America: A Student's Guide to Localized History* (1968), are more general treatments of issues concerning the Mexican population north of the border.

McWilliams placed the study of ethnic minorities and the relations between groups at the center of his conception of local history. This approach is reflected in other studies of his home state, *Southern California Country: An Island on the Land* (1946) and *California: The Great Exception* (1949), as well as in his edited collection, *The California Revolution* (1968). McWilliams's work was an early and unusual example of regional studies meant to challenge the local status quo rather than reinforce the self-congratulation of local elites.

It was as a Californian who worked in state government that McWilliams spoke out against discrimination toward Japanese Americans. *Prejudice: Japanese Americans, Symbol of Racial Intolerance* was published in 1944, when most of the West Coast population of Japanese immigrants and their American-born offspring were confined to concentration camps. The wartime "relocation" of Japanese residents and citizens was a federal policy formulated and implemented by government officials who were presumed to have special insight into the threat this population represented to national security. McWilliams, once again, was one of a handful of Anglos and an even smaller number of California state functionaries to protest the arbitrary and racist nature of the internment. In January 1943, before the publication of *Prejudice*, but after McWilliams had already been publicly challenging the relocation policy for more than a year, California's newly elected governor, Earl Warren, announced that his first official act in office would be McWilliams's removal from his state position. From this point on, McWilliams worked full-time as a writer and editor.

McWilliams became West Coast contributing editor of *The Nation* in 1945, remaining in that position until 1951. Issues of racism remained prominent in two books he published during this time, *A Mask for Privilege: Anti-Semitism in America* (1948), and a more general survey of racial issues, *Brothers under the Skin* (1943). At the same time, he devoted many of his articles and editorials to opposing American Cold War policies, particularly the repression of domestic dissent. In late 1950 he was asked to edit a special issue of *The Nation* focusing on the assault on civil liberties. He agreed to spend a month in New York working on the project and stayed for more than twenty-five years, serving the magazine as associate editor in 1951–1952, editorial director from 1952 to 1955, and editor from 1955 until his retirement in 1975.

Through *The Nation*, as well as the bold anti-McCarthy book he published in 1950, *Witch-Hunt: Revival of Heresy*, McWilliams championed civil liberties and constitutional rights in a period when many American journalists acquiesced or even enlisted in the anti-Communist crusade. Subsequently, under McWilliams's editorship, *The Nation* successfully effected a transition from the defensive mood of the 1950s to the activist militancy of the civil rights movement and the struggle against American intervention in Vietnam and elsewhere in the world. Years after his death, McWilliams's exemplary role as an engaged journalist was still being cited frequently in the pages of *The Nation*.

After he retired from the magazine, McWilliams wrote an autobiography, *The Education of Carey McWilliams* (1979). This memoir focused on his public career rather than on his personal life. It has little to say, for example, about McWilliams's two marriages (to Dorothy Hedrick from 1930 to 1941 and to novelist Iris Dornfeld, whom he married less than a week after his divorce) or his relationship with his children (he had a son by each wife). Many reviewers, missing his conscious emulation of Henry Adams's *Education*, criticized this impersonal approach. It does make McWilliams appear more detached and ideological than the man that everyone who knew him remembers. However, the autobiography was controversial chiefly because it revived McWilliams's old political battles, reopening all the wounds of the 1950s, so that evaluation of the narrative divided along predictable ideological lines. The controversy over his account of his life's work was McWilliams's last battle; he died the following year in New York City.

• McWilliams's papers are divided between the Bancroft Library at the University of California at Berkeley and the library of Harvard University, which houses *The Nation* archive. Some material is still in the possession of his widow. A study of his early political education is G. Critser, "The Making of a Cultural Rebel, Carey McWilliams, 1924–30," *Pacific Historical Review* 55 (May 1986): 226–55. An obituary is in *The Nation*, 12 July 1980.

LILLIAN S. ROBINSON

MEACHUM, John Berry (1790?–1854), craftsman, minister, and businessman, was born a slave in Virginia. The names of his father, a Baptist preacher, and his mother are unknown. A skilled carpenter and cooper, he was allowed to save some of his earnings, and eventually he bought his freedom. Moving to Louisville, Kentucky, he married a slave, Mary, and then purchased her out of bondage; they would have an unknown number of children. About 1815 he moved with his wife to St. Louis, reportedly with only $3 in his pocket. There Meachum used the carpentry skills he had learned under slavery to find a job as a cooper. He established his own cooper's shop a few years later and began buying St. Louis real estate.

During the 1830s, in order to help fellow African Americans become free, Meachum started buying slaves, training them in barrel-making, and letting them earn money to pay him back for their liberty. By 1846 he had emancipated "twenty colored friends that I bought." Except for one, who was an alcoholic, they were all successful, as Meachum boasts in *An Address to All the Colored Citizens of the United States* (1846). In fact, one former slave not only acquired his own freedom, but he purchased his wife, built a home for his family, and became a highly proficient blacksmith.

Meachum's *Address* does not include all the facts, however. In 1834 Julia Logan petitioned the Circuit Court of St. Louis claiming that she was entitled to her freedom but that she was being "held as a Slave by Berry Meachum a man of color in St. Louis and [was] bound and imprisoned in his (Meachum's[)] house." Logan feared she would soon be sold "to some distant place." In 1836 the case went to the Missouri Supreme Court, which ruled against Meachum.

By 1850 Meachum owned two brick homes in St. Louis and an Illinois farm. According to the census that year, his $8,000 in real estate holdings made him the third richest free African American in Missouri. Yet Meachum conducted himself modestly, even with this sizable wealth. An 1854 inventory of Meachum's estate listed a few basic chairs, a carpet worth $7, and about forty books valued at $8. The 1850 census showed twelve people living at his home, including his wife, Mary, their two grandchildren, various other adults and children, and two African-American coopers who appeared to be working to reimburse Meachum for buying their liberty.

Meachum also organized and maintained two schools for African-American youth, one even after a state law had been passed prohibiting the teaching of black children. When the Englishman he hired to teach at the school was arrested, Meachum got him out of jail and later reopened the school secretly on one of the steamboats he built and owned.

As the son of a Baptist preacher, Meachum followed his father's lead. He joined the St. Louis Mission Church about 1816 and became its pastor about 1828, when it became an independent black church, called the First African Baptist Church. By the late 1830s his congregation included two hundred slaves and twenty free blacks. Meachum's style as a preacher was so energetic and enthusiastic that in 1846 a small group led by John R. Anderson, a former slave described as "quiet" with "reserved power," left the church. Even the name of Meachum's steamboat—"Temperance"—reflected his concerns as a minister and as a leader in his community.

Meachum died in St. Louis. Despite the Logan case, he left a legacy of remarkable industry and economic success as well as of intellectual and spiritual guidance for blacks emerging from bondage.

• The most useful biographical sources about Meachum include Mechal Sobel, *Trabelin' On: The Slave Journey to an Afro-Baptist Faith* (1979; repr. 1988), and Donnie Bellamy, "Free Blacks in Antebellum Missouri, 1820–1860," *Missouri Historical Review* 67 (Jan. 1973): 198–225. For more on the Logan case, see Missouri Supreme Court Cases, St. Louis District, *Meachum v. Logan*, 1836, Missouri State Archives, Jefferson City.

LOREN SCHWENINGER

MEAD, Elizabeth Storrs Billings (21 May 1832–25 Mar. 1917), educator and college president, was born in Conway, Massachusetts, the daughter of Sally Williston Storrs, the daughter of a well-known clerical family, and Colonel Charles Eugene Billings, a farmer, an early settler of Hartford, and a representative to the Massachusetts General Court. Elizabeth attended the Ipswich (Mass.) Female Seminary, taught high school for one year in Northampton, Massachusetts, headed a girls' school in Andover with her sister for six years, and then married the Reverend Hiram Mead in 1858. Reverend Mead, a graduate of Middlebury College and Andover Seminary, was then the pastor of the Congregational church in South Hadley, Massachusetts. The couple remained in South Hadley for ten years, spent a brief time in Nashua, New Hampshire, and in 1869 moved to Ohio, where Reverend Mead was a professor at Oberlin College until he died in 1881. Throughout her marriage, Elizabeth was active in a variety of activities, including the Oberlin Women's Board of Managers. She taught occasionally while raising her two children; her son George Herbert Mead later became a professor of philosophy at the University of Chicago.

After her husband's death, Mead became an instructor at Oberlin College and then associate principal of Abbott Academy in Andover, Massachusetts. Her major contribution to education began in April 1890 when she was chosen to be the president of Mount Holyoke College, where she remained for ten years. Mead's selection marked a major watershed for Mount Holyoke. Founded in 1837 as a women's seminary with strong evangelical underpinnings, Mount Holyoke found itself in a period of transition and crisis at the end of the nineteenth century. The founding of neighboring women's colleges and the transformation of the modern university challenged the traditional ideas of women's education. A new secular ideology demanded that education for women no longer be tied to doing the Lord's work but rather emphasized women's engagement with ideas and social contribution. The percentage of female students enrolling in women's colleges was diminishing, and the faculty was seriously divided about the proper course for Mount Holyoke. In response to these concerns, the Holyoke faculty in 1888 had successfully pushed for a new collegiate charter, which would allow the seminary to offer the bachelor's degree and change its name.

Elizabeth Mead's selection followed a tragic incident in which the new president-elect, Mary A. Brigham, had been killed in a train accident before assuming office. Mead was the first president who was not an alumna, although she was well known to people at Mount Holyoke because of her long residence in South Hadley and her late husband's earlier service as a member of the board of trustees. The trustees wanted an outsider but one who would have the sympathy of the senior faculty. Mead was known to be worldly, of distinguished appearance, and associated with a fashionable girls' academy. It is unclear whether the trustees understood the magnitude of the changes that Mead would initiate in her tenure as president. Influenced by the popular contemporary English writer Matthew Arnold, Mead was a strong believer in the "perfectibility of man." She espoused ideas about education for women as part of liberal culture and maintained that an educated mind was quite separate from the utilitarian view of education for women. She was quite cautious about taking a stand on woman suffrage or the use of education to upset the established social order in any way.

When Mead assumed the presidency, she found a community disappointed over the death of Brigham and mired in low morale. There was strong competition from the more recently founded women's colleges, and a large portion of the senior faculty who had led the struggle for a college charter was about to retire. The first year of her tenure was difficult, but Mead began to formulate the agenda that would dominate the decade of her presidency. She pushed the trustees to support scholarly development of the faculty and succeeded in encouraging a number of faculty members to earn advanced degrees. She argued for improved salaries and a reduction of nonteaching obligations so that she would be able to hire more qualified faculty rather than young recent graduates.

By 1893 the college had a full collegiate charter, and the seminary curriculum was phased out. Mead followed the lead of other women's colleges in developing a more department-based curriculum, and she adopted a moderate stance on the controversy of the decade—whether to establish a firm core curriculum or to allow a large choice of electives. Progress was severely interrupted by a fire that destroyed the major academic and residential center of the college. Mead persuaded the trustees and all but six students that the college could continue to operate. The fire provided an opportunity to raise money for a new cottage-style residential system and several other new buildings.

By the time of her retirement in 1899 Elizabeth Mead could take satisfaction in a number of accomplishments. An expanded college curriculum was in place, the campus was larger and included new buildings, the endowment had begun to grow, and extracurricular activities reflected the new acceptability of theater and intramural sports as legitimate student endeavors. Perhaps her most important legacy to her successor, Mary Woolley, was the increased power of the presidency. By the end of the 1890s the president attended board of trustee meetings, recommended appointments, and enjoyed expanded administrative authority in the operation of the college. Mead resigned in 1899 but stayed in office until Mary Woolley took over in January 1901. She returned to Oberlin after her retirement and died at her daughter's home in Coconut Grove, Florida.

• Mead's papers are in the archives of Mount Holyoke College. The most complete account of her work is in Charlotte King Shea, "Mount Holyoke College 1875–1910: The Passing of the Old Order" (Ph.D. diss., Cornell Univ., 1983). An additional unpublished account is in Anne Edmonds, "A Memory Book: Mount Holyoke College" (1988).

PENINA MIGDAL GLAZER

MEAD, Elwood (16 Jan. 1858–26 Jan. 1936), U.S. Commissioner of Reclamation, was born near Patriot, Indiana, the son of David B. Mead, a farmer, and Lucinda Davis. Mead spent his early years studying in a one-room schoolhouse, doing chores on his father's farm, and enjoying "long summer days playing in the groves of ash, oak, wild cherry, hickory, poplar, and walnut trees along the slopes of the Ohio River." In this idyllic, mid-nineteenth-century setting he came to value the benefits of rural community life even as he broadened his horizons in his grandfather's library, reputed to be the largest personal one in southern Indiana.

Mead's earliest dream of a military career was abandoned after a few weeks at West Point in 1877, when a bout of malaria forced him to return home. The following fall he enrolled at four-year-old Purdue University, from which he graduated in 1882 with a diploma bearing mention of special work in agriculture and science. That same year he married Florence S. Davis; they had three children. Following his service in the U.S. Army Engineer Corps from August to December 1882, as an assistant engineer surveying the Wabash River, Mead earned a civil engineering degree the following year from Iowa Agricultural College (later Iowa State University). When Mead's mentor at Purdue, Charles Lee Ingersoll, became the president of Colorado State Agricultural College (now Colorado State University) in Fort Collins in fall 1882, he invited Mead to teach mathematics and science at the college. There Mead first became acquainted with irrigated agriculture and found his life's work: "the study of all the physical, human and legal problems of turning on water with a shovel" (Letter to Grace Raymond Hebard, 27 Mar. 1930; Hebard Collection, Univ. of Wyoming).

About the time Mead arrived in Fort Collins, Colorado was beginning to address the problems of distributing a limited supply of water with a growing demand for the precious commodity. Beginning in 1879, a series of laws, including the establishment of the office of state engineer, were enacted to oversee the allocation of water claims. E. S. Nettleton was the first person to hold that position, and Mead began to assist him in his spare time and during the summers and to incorporate this practical experience into his courses. In 1886 he was named professor of irrigation engineering, the first such position in the United States. He quickly mastered the features and flaws of the Colorado system and gained a reputation as an authority on irrigation and water rights.

Mead's growing status as an expert on water issues attracted the attention of officials in neighboring Wyoming. In 1888 officials there consulted him when they created the office of territorial engineer and then named him to the position. His renown was further enhanced two years later when Wyoming became a state. Mead wrote the section of the constitution dealing with water and then put together the code and administrative structure to implement it. The result came to be known as the Wyoming System, the prototype for water distribution throughout the American West as well as in a number of countries around the world.

The 1890s saw a growing movement in the West for a greater role by the federal government in reclamation—that is, the cultivating of desert lands by irrigation. Mead, however, favored a more limited, states-oriented program. When it became clear that some form of federal activity was forthcoming, Mead's supporters got him appointed to head the Office of Irrigation Investigations in the U.S. Department of Agriculture in 1899. They hoped this would lead to his eventual appointment to direct whatever federal program was created.

The Reclamation Act of 1902 did not reflect Mead's views, however, and, when the new Reclamation Service was housed in the Interior Department, he saw his influence in the nation's capital waning. He began splitting his time between his Washington duties and teaching part-time at the University of California at Berkeley. An offer of a professorship there unfortunately coincided with the San Francisco earthquake, which temporarily dried up funds for such a position. In the midst of these frustrations, Mead was involved in a streetcar accident that resulted in the amputation of his right arm. One of the nurses who cared for Mead during his recuperation was Mary Lewis. His first wife having died in 1897, Mead married her in September 1907; they had three children. Shortly thereafter, officials from the Australian state of Victoria approached Mead with an offer to head their State Rivers and Water Supply Commission. In the fall of 1907 he agreed to try the job for six months; in the end he stayed nearly eight years.

Mead characterized his years in Australia as the "most fruitful experience" of his professional life. That evaluation was based on three major accomplishments stemming from his primary task of developing the rivers of Victoria, a complex of streams that encompassed a significant part of the Murray River system, the continent's only significant watershed. Formulating a comprehensive plan not only entailed engineering considerations but also involved settling long-standing disputes with New South Wales and South Australia, Victoria's sibling states, over water rights and allocations, and, ultimately, colonizing the area with settlers.

A compact dividing the Murray River system waters among the three states was the most elusive of Mead's achievements. A formal agreement was not signed until 12 April 1915, only three days before Mead tendered his resignation to return to the United States. While those negotiations dragged on, construction of the facilities necessary to develop the Murray and its tributaries proceeded apace, creating an impressive network of dams and canals for the storage and distribution of water. Victoria's leaders had to show that the enormous cost of all of this activity benefited the general population, and this led to the work Mead found most rewarding—the actual settlement of the land with resident farmers.

Attracting colonists to an agricultural frontier had had a long and unsuccessful history in the "Land Down Under," as Australia is often called. Three major efforts to promote rural communities (known as closer settlements in the jargon of Australians) were made in the nineteenth century; all failed for a variety of reasons. Mead now proposed tying community planning to irrigation. This combination would, he hoped, justify its huge expense by creating opportunities for large numbers of settlers, lessen the continent's chronic dependence on imported foodstuffs, and replicate the bucolic days of his youth.

In 1909 the Victorian government accepted Mead's proposals and named him to the State Lands Purchase and Settlement Board. From that position, he directed the purchase of reclaimed land and its division into three categories: two-acre plots for subsistence laborers to learn irrigation farming, five- to ten-acre allotments for orchard and market gardening, and twenty- to 200-acre tracts for regular farms. Generous repayment schedules, expert advisors, and cooperatives for buying and selling rounded out the main features of these model communities.

A heady sense of accomplishment characterized the first years of this program. In 1910 Mead led a delegation of Victorian officials and a reporter from the Melbourne newspaper *The Argus* to Europe and North America; an aura of success surrounded the enterprise. By 1914, however, discontent had begun to spread as the realities of hard work, poor prices, heavy debts and a severe drought set in. The flaws in the system and a growing cry that they had been deceived by Mead and the government were just beginning to manifest themselves when Mead sailed back to the United States in May 1915. Meanwhile, he saw his program as a great success, blithely choosing to ignore the complaints of a few "pettifogging critics," as he characterized them in a letter to his son Tom. Mead returned to his native country determined to bring the blessings of aid and direction in land settlement to the United States.

In 1915 Benjamin Ide Wheeler, president of the University of California at Berkeley, appointed Mead professor of rural institutions. Concerned about the declining condition of California farm life, Wheeler hoped Mead could revitalize it. In 1917, at Mead's behest, the California legislature created a Land Settlement Board, and the governor appointed Mead to head it. Under Mead's direction, the board established two model rural communities. Patterned on the Australian example, these demonstration projects were designed to show land developers how to run their properties and to serve as inspirations for revitalizing rural life. A 6,239-acre colony near Durham in the Sacramento Valley was opened in 1918; two years later an 8,400-acre track of land near Delhi in the San Joaquin Valley began accepting settlers. Like their Australian counterparts, both settlements began with high hopes and great fanfare, and like their "down under" cousins, they soon collapsed, victims of the 1920s agricultural depression, poorly chosen land, and resentment at the promises and heavy-handed paternalism of the Land Settlement Board and Mead's policies. Settlers believed that they had been deceived and then abandoned by those who had lured them into this experiment, and, as with the Australian experience, Mead had moved on before the full extent of the failure became apparent.

In 1923 Mead took a sabbatical from his teaching duties and went on an around-the-world consulting tour. The trip took him to Hawaii, where he advised the government on land programs for native Hawaiians, then to Australia—this time to New South Wales—for four months, and finally to Palestine, where he assessed the progress of agriculture for the World Zionist Organization. In the Middle East he was particularly attracted to the *kibbutzim* movement, the closest his settlement schemes ever came to achieving success.

While in Australia, Mead received a letter from Secretary of the Interior Hubert Work asking him to serve on another panel reviewing federal reclamation. Mead had been on the 1915 Central Board of Cost Review that had examined problems at that time. The result was a modification of some charges and a few other adjustments that stilled complaints temporarily. High wartime prices followed for several years, but by 1923 U.S. irrigation had reached a critical state. The six-man board, the so-called Fact Finders Committee, submitted a list of sixty-five recommendations that bore the imprint of Mead on every important point, including a call for aid and direction in land settlement, a refrain that recurred in virtually any report Mead had had a part in since 1915. In March 1924, even before the board had finished its work, President Calvin Coolidge named Mead to be commissioner of reclamation. Mead immediately set to implementing the suggestions of the Fact Finders.

The gist of these proposals concerned construction charges that water users were expected to repay. The water users believed that these fees were much higher than income from the land could ever finance, and that they were being expected to absorb the cost of government errors. The Fact Finders investigations bore out these allegations and, under Mead, more than $27 million of charges were written off by Congress. The new commissioner believed that the water users would be much more cooperative and responsible for charges that they felt were legitimate. Mead also began the process of decentralizing the Reclamation Bureau to return day-to-day control of operations over to farmer cooperatives, again believing that "hands-on" management bred good management. By 1929 revenues on the projects and the levels of repayments were both up significantly, and it appeared that federal reclamation was headed at last toward its original goals. But then the Great Depression hit the country, and reclamation, like everything else, went into a tailspin. For the rest of his tenure, Commissioner Mead struggled with repayment issues. Still, the reforms he initiated in his first five years set the bureau on the road to a stability it had never known before he took office.

Besides the day-to-day management of his bureau, Mead's energies were directed increasingly toward one of the outstanding engineering feats of the twentieth century, the building of Hoover Dam, the centerpiece of a massive, multipurpose program for the lower basin of the Colorado River. Construction of this huge dam, begun in 1931, was the capstone of Mead's remarkable life in reclamation. Under his overall direction, the 727-foot arch-shaped structure was finished a full two years ahead of schedule. Unfortunately Mead was unable to attend the dedication in September 1935; he lay ill in a Los Angeles hospital. He recovered and returned to work, only to die soon thereafter in Washington, D.C., so he never saw the dam completed later that year. In recognition of his long service to reclamation, Secretary of the Interior Harold Ickes named the lake then forming behind Hoover Dam in his honor.

For over a half century, Mead was a major figure in the development of the American West. Every significant change in reclamation, from the simple ditch diversions of individual farmers to the behemoth Hoover Dam, was affected by his ideas and deeds. The guiding principle throughout his life was the romantic Jeffersonian vision of the hearty yeoman farmer. He wanted to help men own farms. His aims were noble, but the results were slim. That his goals were not achieved as he envisioned them, however, should not diminish the contributions he made to reclamation.

• Mead's personal papers have almost all been lost. The American Heritage Center at the University of Wyoming in Laramie and at the Wyoming State Archives in Cheyenne contain material dealing with Mead's work in that state. The Bancroft Library and the University of California Archives, both at Berkeley, have a wealth of material relating to his years as a professor there and his work on the Land Settlement Board. The National Archives in Washington, D.C., have his official papers from the various governmental posts he held. Mead's two books, *Irrigation Institutions* (1903) and *Helping Men Own Farms* (1920), are basic to understanding his ideas. The only full-length treatment of Mead is James R. Kluger, *Turning on Water with a Shovel* (1992). To put Mead's early career in perspective, see Donald J. Pisani, *To Reclaim a Divided West* (1992). An obituary is "Dr. Elwood Mead, Commissioner of Reclamation, Dies," *Reclamation Era* 26 (1936): 33–35.

JAMES R. KLUGER

MEAD, George Herbert (27 Feb. 1863–26 Apr. 1931), philosopher and social theorist, was born in South Hadley, Massachusetts, the son of Hiram Mead, a minister and professor of homiletics, and Elizabeth Storrs Billings, professor and president of Mt. Holyoke College. Mead and his elder sister Alice were reared in a home steeped in the traditions of Congregationalism. Although new intellectual and social currents began to stir at Congregationalist Oberlin College during Mead's student years (1879–1883), later in life he could still remark that "it took him twenty years to unlearn what he had been taught the first twenty" (Miller, p. xii). He received an A.B. from Oberlin in 1883 and after a short stint as a grade school teacher spent the next few years alternating between the posts of surveyor with the Wisconsin Central Rail Road Company and private tutor. Correspondence with his close friend and future brother-in-law, Henry Castle, of the influential and wealthy Castle family of Hawaii, led to his enrollment in 1887 at Harvard College, where the focus of his studies was philosophy and psychology. While at Harvard Mead tutored William James's children and lived in his home for a period of time. He received an A.B. from Harvard in 1888, having studied with Josiah Royce, George H. Palmer, and Francis Bowen. Shortly thereafter he left for Europe, where he joined Henry and his sister, Helen Kingsbury Castle, in Leipzig, Germany. During his stay in Europe he studied at the Universities of Leipzig and Berlin, and in 1891 he married Helen; they had one child. Before he could complete his Ph.D. in Berlin he was offered an instructorship in philosophy and psychology at the University of Michigan.

At Michigan Mead came under the influence of the social psychologist Charles H. Cooley and met John Dewey, who became a lifelong friend and ally. Mead taught philosophy at Michigan from 1891 to 1894. In 1894 Dewey agreed to chair the philosophy department at the new University of Chicago, and he helped secure an assistant professorship for Mead. Dewey, Mead, and a number of distinguished colleagues at the university came to be known as the Chicago School of pragmatism. By 1907 Mead had been promoted to full professor, a position he would hold until his death. In the year or so before Mead's death, the new president of the University of Chicago, Robert Maynard Hutchins, sought to change the character of the philosophy department, in part by appointing Mortimer J. Adler to the faculty. Mead decided to leave Chicago for an appointment at Columbia University that was to begin in the fall of 1931 but died in April of that year.

Mead was a dedicated social reformer who worked with many of the leading progressives in Chicago, and he counted Jane Addams among his close friends. He was active in a number of civic associations and supported numerous causes during his years in Chicago. Mead marched with suffragists, supported strikers, served as treasurer of University of Chicago Settlement Board, chair of the City Club Committee on Public Education, and as vice president of the Immigrants' Protective League. Perhaps his numerous commitments help to explain why, with the exception of a coedited volume on vocationalism, Mead never published a book. He was, however, the author of numerous scholarly and civic-minded articles. After his death unpublished manuscripts and students' notes were transformed into the five books that currently bear Mead's name: *The Philosophy of the Present* (1932), *Mind, Self, and Society: From the Standpoint of a Social Behaviorist* (1934), *Movements of Thought in the Nineteenth Century* (1936), *The Philosophy of the Act* (1938), and *The Individual and the Social Self* (1982). Shortly before his death Mead delivered the Carus Lectures. They were published, along with supplementary essays, as *The Philosophy of the Present* (1932).

Mead was a gifted conversationalist whose breadth of knowledge, fine sense of humor, and love of poetry all contributed to his skill. That he was gifted in verbal exchanges is rather fitting, for Mead thought that the development of the mind and the self could be explicated by careful study of animal and human communication. As a naturalist who drew on Wilhelm Wundt's work on the gesture, Mead argued that while animals use gestures, only human beings use what he called significant symbols. If a dog growls at another dog, the second dog may respond to the gesture of the first by running away or growling back. Meaning can be defined in terms of the second dog's response to the gesture of the first. But the dogs are not aware of the meaning of their gestures. On the other hand, human beings become aware of the meanings of their vocal gestures as they use them, learning to modify future responses in light of the anticipated responses of other individuals. This conversation of gestures is repeated on a more complex level with the development of roles. Roles, which Mead believed are complex constellations of behavioral responses, make sense only in relationship to other roles. The child, for example, cannot play at being a doctor without also being able to take the role of a patient. Mead's account of the development of the self turns on his analysis of communicative interaction and focuses on the process of "taking the role of the other." Mead's ideas on language, roles, and the development of the self are perhaps his most widely cited theoretical contributions. His thought in this area has influenced numerous social psychologists and sociologists and has helped give rise to the school of symbolic interaction in sociology.

Mead was, however, first and foremost a philosopher, and he lectured on a wide range of subjects: ethics, politics, metaphysics, epistemology, and the history of philosophy. Early in his career Mead was heavily influenced by the Darwinian revolution in the biological sciences, and he remained committed to explaining human development in naturalistic terms. Mead argued that nature must be understood as a realm of emergence in which novel properties, behaviors, capacities, and creatures find their way into existence. But he also claimed that human beings live, for the most part, in a world of habitual behaviors and expectations, or what he called the world that is there. When novel events, conflicts, and problems arise, they move us to reflect on our circumstances and adjust our behaviors. The capacity to reflect, to think self-consciously about a situation, entails seeing a situation from different perspectives. This ability, which human beings have developed to an extraordinary level, is tied to role-taking and linguistic skills. Science, for Mead, is but a methodical refinement of our capacity for reflective problem-solving thought.

Both Dewey and Alfred North Whitehead spoke of Mead as "a seminal mind of the very first order," and he has had a lasting impact in the field of sociology. Although generally considered a major figure in the history of pragmatism, Mead has not achieved the renown of William James, Charles Sanders Peirce, and John Dewey among philosophers. The 1980s saw newfound interest in Mead's ideas, however, and he has played an important role in the work of the social philosopher Jürgen Habermas.

• Mead's papers are in the archives at the University of Chicago Library. Many of his most important articles are reprinted in Andrew J. Reck, ed., *Selected Writings: George Herbert Mead* (1964). David L. Miller, *George Herbert Mead:*

Self, Language, and the World (1973), has an extended biographical sketch and a bibliography. The most extensive bibliography is Richard Lowy, "George Herbert Mead: A Bibliography of the Secondary Literature with Relevant Symbolic Interactionist References," *Studies in Symbolic Interaction* 7 (1986): 459–521. Dmitri Shalin, "G. H. Mead, Socialism, and the Progressive Agenda," *American Journal of Sociology* 93 (1988): 913–51, addresses Mead's activities as a social reformer. Hans Joas, *G. H. Mead: A Contemporary Re-examination of His Thought* (1985), is an account of Mead's intellectual development and includes a bibliography. A bibliography of literature from the 1980s is in Mitchell Aboulafia, ed., *Philosophy, Social Theory, and the Thought of George Herbert Mead* (1991).

MITCHELL ABOULAFIA

MEAD, Larkin Goldsmith (3 Jan. 1835–15 Oct. 1910), sculptor, was born in Chesterfield, New Hampshire, the son of Larkin Goldsmith Mead, Sr., a lawyer, and Mary Jane Noyes. Young Larkin grew up in a cultured, talented family environment in Brattleboro, Vermont. His sister Elinor married the novelist William Dean Howells and his brother William Rutherford Mead became a partner in the famous architectural firm of McKim, Mead & White. Larkin began the study of sculpture in the Brooklyn studio of Henry Kirke Brown from 1853 to 1855, when Brown, with the assistance of John Quincy Adams Ward, was creating his bronze equestrian statue of George Washington (Union Square, New York). Returning to Brattleboro to establish his studio, Mead first attracted attention with a sculpture of a heroic *Recording Angel*, modeled in snow at a crossroads on New Year's Eve in 1856. This greatly impressed the local folk, and a newspaper account of it somehow reached Nicholas Longworth of Cincinnati, a generous benefactor of artists, who wrote Mead to give him a commission. James Russell Lowell—who many years later, in 1874, visited Mead in his Florentine studio—derived the inspiration for his poem, "A Good Word for Winter," from the account given of Mead's snow angel. In 1857 the young sculptor created his first permanent monumental work, the colossal figure of Vermont, or Ceres, for the dome of the state capitol in Montpelier.

After a brief visit to Washington, D.C., in 1858, Mead returned to Brattleboro to execute a full-length marble figure of Ethan Allen (1861) for the Vermont state capitol; a second version of this statue, in revolutionary war uniform but in a pose based on Michelangelo's *David*, was later sent to Statuary Hall in the U.S. Capitol. With the outbreak of the Civil War, Mead became an illustrator for *Harper's Weekly*, and, like Winslow Homer, made sketches of army camp life. When his sister Elinor left for Europe in 1862, Mead accompanied her, giving her away in marriage to Howells in Paris before he departed for Florence and the newlyweds for Venice, where Howells assumed the post of American consul.

In Florence, Mead was befriended by fellow American expatriate sculptors Hiram Powers, Thomas Ball, and Joel T. Hart. Hart shared his studio with Mead and arranged for him to obtain an apartment in the Casa Grazzini. Occasionally Mead went to Venice to serve as acting consul during his brother-in-law's absence. There he met and, in 1866, married an Italian woman of noble family, Marietta di Benvenuti. They had no children.

Back in his Florentine studio he modeled a small female figure, based on an antique torso, which he called *Echo*. When the Washington art collector William Wilson Corcoran visited the studio he immediately commissioned the piece to be put into marble, and it is now in the Corcoran Gallery of Art in Washington, D.C. Other marble works that date from this period include a country girl, *La Contadinella*, and a Civil War theme, *The Returned Soldier*, or *The Battle Story*. When Mead returned to the United States in March 1866 he brought with him the design for a great memorial to Abraham Lincoln for Springfield, Illinois. A figure of the Great Emancipator stood at the base of a towering obelisk while four groups—representing infantry, navy, artillery, and cavalry—were placed at the four corners. The monument, one of the first Civil War memorials to be designed, was dedicated on 15 October 1874, but the last of the auxiliary groups was not set in place until 1883. The figures were dignified and realistic but undramatic, and sober in the sense that they never romanticized a war that had been so painful. All the figural parts were modeled in Mead's Florentine studio under a $200,000 contract from the state of Illinois. The Meads returned to America only when business or family matters necessitated, living happily in the city on the Arno, where a steady stream of visitors, American and European, called at what had become one of the most famous sculptor's studios in Italy. Even the pedimental group *The Triumph of Ceres*, destined for McKim, Mead & White's Agricultural Building at Chicago's World's Columbian Exposition of 1893, was modeled in the studio in Florence. Mead was especially close to his brother William Rutherford, who had lived with Mead in Florence in 1871 before becoming an architect.

For many years Mead held the position of professor of sculpture at the Academy in Florence, his early biographers noting that he held the same appointment in the same school where Michelangelo had taught. His only major piece from the later 1890s is a reclining male figure, translated into marble, representing the Father of the Waters—a personification of the Mississippi River—which eventually found a home at the Court House in Minneapolis. Mead's career was essentially over by 1900, when his brand of marble neoclassicism had been eclipsed by the livelier style and richly textured bronze surfaces emanating from Parisian studios. Mead was an urbane, gentle person of cultivated tastes and broad intellectual interests. He died in Florence.

• A few letters written between Mead and Hiram Powers as well as photographs of many of Mead's works in Florence are in the Hiram Powers Papers at the Archives of American Art, Smithsonian Institution. Mead's activities are mentioned frequently in the correspondence of his sister and his brother-in-law; see *If Not Literature, Letters of Elinor Mead Howells* ed. Ginette de B. Merrill and George Arms (1988), and *William Dean Howells, Selected Letters* ed. George Arms et al. (1979–). A notice of Mead's early career appeared in Henry T. Tuckerman, *Book of the Artists* (1867), pp. 597–98, and his life and work are summarized in Lorado Taft, *History of American Sculpture* (1903), pp. 236–44, and Wayne Craven, *Sculpture in America* (1968; rev. ed., 1984), pp. 321–25. His obituary is in the *New York Times*, 16 Oct. 1910, and in *American Art News*, 22 Oct. 1910.

WAYNE CRAVEN

MEAD, Lucia True Ames (5 May 1856–1 Nov. 1936), pacifist and suffragist, was born in Boscawen, New Hampshire, the daughter of Nathan Plummer Ames, a businessman and farmer, and Elvira Coffin. (She was initially given the middle name Jane but apparently changed it herself to True.) After her mother died when Lucia was five, the family moved to Chicago. Nine years later she returned east to live with an older brother in Boston; she was educated privately and then attended public high school in Salem, Massachusetts. Her intellectual development was encouraged by her maternal uncle, Charles Carlton Coffin, a well-known author and war correspondent.

After finishing high school Lucia moved to Boston, where she studied with a prominent music teacher, Benjamin J. Lang. She then began teaching music, as well as lecturing to women's clubs on New England poetry. Soon, however, her lectures began to reflect her own growing conviction that educated women of her class should do what they could to address the nation's social problems. These ideas were reflected in her novel *Memoirs of a Millionaire* (1889), in which a young schoolteacher contributes millions of dollars to a variety of reform projects.

In 1898 Lucia married Edwin Doak Mead, editor of the *New England Magazine*, who himself had built a distinguished record crusading for such issues as women's rights and world peace. They had no children. After her marriage Mead participated in a wide range of reform organizations, including the Women's Municipal League, the Women's Educational and Industrial Union, the Consumer's League, the Boston Equal Suffrage Association, the National Association for the Advancement of Colored People, and the American Civil Liberties Union. She also served as president of the Massachusetts Woman Suffrage Association from 1903 to 1909.

Despite her other interests, peace became Mead's most consuming concern. When the conference on world peace took place at The Hague in 1899, she helped organize local discussions of the proceedings, and by the following year she had declared herself a pacifist. She took an active role in the American Peace Society and chaired Peace Committees in both the National Council of Women and the National American Woman Suffrage Association. Along with her husband, Mead traveled to many European peace conferences, and she began writing numerous articles and pamphlets promoting disarmament and international organization. In 1903 she called for a system of international police that would enforce laws made by a world legislature and would bring miscreants to justice instead of killing them, as armies did. "We need not wait until sins and quarrels have been banished from the earth," she wrote, "before we find a rational way of treating them." Three years later her *Patriotism and the New Internationalism* decried the chauvinistic nationalism that had accompanied the rise of imperialism. Instead, she said, "cooperation must be emphasized as the only key to normal human progress." In "Peace and Arbitration" (1914), written only months before World War I broke out, she called the task of replacing war with law "the most pressing reform before civilization to-day and the most hopeful of near accomplishment." She concluded, "World Organization is to be the achievement of the Twentieth Century."

Like many peace enthusiasts, the Meads were appalled by the outbreak of World War I, which occurred while they were on vacation in Switzerland in August 1914. Both pinned their hopes on keeping the United States out of the fighting. Edwin Mead had been employed since 1901 as an editor at the World Peace Foundation. As America intensified its emotional and financial commitment to the Allies, he drew increasing criticism for his outspoken opposition to military preparations and war loans; finally in 1915, he had a breakdown and resigned his position. Lucia Mead devoted part of her time thereafter to caring for her "dear invalid," but she also continued to play her own important role in the peace movement.

Soon after the war began, Mead conceived the idea of having women organize simultaneous peace demonstrations in many cities. The proposal caught the interest of suffragist leader Carrie Chapman Catt, but Catt felt that sponsorship by Mead, whom she described as a "very unpopular woman," would harm the cause. "I confess," said Catt, "that while I cannot name a single sensible reason for my feelings, I always want to run when I see her coming." When the organizing convention of the Women's Peace Party (WPP) was held in January 1915, Mead was selected as one of the party officers, but Jane Addams took the chair.

The next two years saw repeated clashes between the Massachusetts and New York branches of the WPP. Mead and her fellow New Englanders focused principally on encouraging American officials to stay neutral, while the New Yorkers wanted to press for more radical social changes that they believed would prevent future wars. Speaking for the New Englanders, Mead urged the national organization to soft-pedal its commitment to woman suffrage, to make its patriotism "more explicit," to provide more vocal support for the goals being articulated by President Woodrow Wilson, to avoid rhetoric that would offend potential supporters, and to make clear that "there can be no peace until the military domination of Prussia is destroyed." Dismissed by the New York members as "reactionaries," the Massachusetts branch broke with the WPP in 1918 and continued its work under another name.

Despite these strains, Mead remained a committed and active member of the national peace movement. Once the war ended, she warmly welcomed the establishment of the League of Nations and threw herself into the losing fight to persuade the United States to join. She continued to campaign for League membership during the years that followed, and to call for disarmament and international understanding. She held office in many peace organizations, including the National Council for the Prevention of War, the American Peace Society, and the American Committee of the League for Permanent Peace. She died in Boston after being injured while boarding a subway train.

Mead devoted herself to working for peace during a thirty-year period that began shortly before the most devastating war the world had yet known and ended as a second and far more terrible war loomed on the horizon. Yet she remained dedicated, energetic, and hopeful throughout her life, convinced that people everywhere would ultimately turn against war as a "needless peril" and accept world organization as "the primary duty of every voter in the world."

• The papers of Lucia Mead and her husband are in the Peace Collection, Swarthmore College. Besides the works cited in the text, Mead's published books and articles include *To Whom Much Is Given* (1898); *Great Thoughts for Little Thinkers* (1902); "International Police," *Outlook*, 74 (18 July 1903): 705–6; *Milton's England* (1902); *Primer of the Peace Movement* (1904); *Swords and Ploughshares* (1912); "Peace and Arbitration," in *The Woman Citizen's Library*, vol. 11, ed. Shailer Mathews (1914), pp. 2715–35; *Law or War* (1928); and many articles and speeches in the *Advocate of Peace*. Correspondence with her appears in the papers of Lucia G. Wentworth, Henry Wadsworth Longfellow Dana, Emily Balch Greene, George William Nasmyth, the Women's Peace Party, the Massachusetts Peace Society, and the American Peace Society—all in the Swarthmore Peace Collection. Other letters are in the papers of Judith Lyams Douglas, Louisiana State University, and Jabez Thoms Sunderland, Michigan Historical Collections, University of Michigan. Her work is discussed in Harriet Hyman Alonso, *Peace as a Women's Issue: A History of the United States Movement for World Peace and Women's Rights* (1993), and C. Roland Marchand, *The American Peace Movement and Social Reform, 1898–1918* (1972).

SANDRA OPDYCKE

MEAD, Margaret (16 Dec. 1901–15 Nov. 1978), anthropologist, was born in Philadelphia, Pennsylvania, the daughter of Edward Sherwood Mead, a University of Pennsylvania economist, and Emily Fogg, a sociologist and social reformer. Mead's unconventional education provided her with the tools and social attitudes that governed her later career. Before high school, her paternal grandmother, Martha Ramsey Mead, a schoolteacher well versed in progressive educational theory of the day, and her mother, a social scientist, directed her education at home. Young Margaret's education included collecting data for observation and recording; anything from the structure of leaves to the language patterns and personality differences of her younger siblings could be noted as data. Before Margaret Mead reached her teens, she accompanied her mother on field trips to Hammonton, New Jersey, where Emily Mead was engaged in sociological research among Italian immigrants. The mother—a feminist, suffragist, leader in the cooperative household movement, and staunch opponent of nativist and racist attitudes—made it a point to expose her child to other ethnic groups and to instill in her awareness of and respect for human equality and differences. Margaret Mead's M.A. thesis in psychology, in which she argued that linguistic and cultural differences explained lower intelligence-test scores of Italian immigrant children, grew from these early training experiences with her mother.

Edward Mead, a specialist in banking and business, assumed a less active role in his daughter's education, but his discussions of his work instilled in Margaret an understanding of the social scientist's use of case studies as a basis for generalization. The adults in the Mead household were agnostics, but at the age of eleven, the strong-willed Margaret joined the Episcopal church. She remained a devout member of this church for life, finding no conflict between her scientific attitudes and her faith. Although she never directly stated the point, her religious faith seems to have supported her optimism and belief in human potential. In 1923 she married Luther S. Cressman, an Episcopal priest who later became an archaeologist. She and Cressman were divorced in 1928, having had no children.

Mead's early scientific training helps explain why she became one of the outstanding women scientists of her time. "Most of the experiences which young people meet for the first time in college," she once wrote, "I had had by the time I was five. They were part of my whole self" (*History of Psychology*, vol. 4, p. 301). Mead's career can be roughly divided into two periods—before World War II, when she earned her graduate degrees and conducted more than twenty field trips in the South Pacific, and after the war, when she became more and more the public scientist.

Mead earned her B.A. in psychology from Barnard College in 1923; she earned both her M.A. in psychology (1925) and her Ph.D. in anthropology from Columbia University (1929). Her choice of anthropology as a career made sense for a woman of her talents. She had an interest in literature and wrote poetry but realized that she did not have the "superlative" talent needed for a successful career in the arts. "Science," she noted modestly, in retrospect, "is an activity in which there is room for many degrees of giftedness" (*Blackberry Winter*, p. 111). Then there was the sheer excitement of participating in a relatively new academic discipline that had only just begun to explore the meaning of "culture"—the central object of its study—and to establish its unique research method—fieldwork among fast-disappearing primitive cultures of the world. Franz Boas, the dean of American cultural anthropology and a formidable intellect, was willing to train women fieldworkers, including Ruth Benedict, who was to become Mead's lifelong confidante and intellectual collaborator. Women anthropologists were a necessity if the lives of primitive women and children in small primitive communities were to be studied, a fact that Mead quickly realized and turned to her advantage.

Boasian anthropology attacked the concept that there was a racial hierarchy based on innate capacities. Instead Boasians argued that culture, or learned behavior, explained differences among human groups. Such a hypothesis is almost a taken-for-granted truth today, but in the 1920s the idea of culture was as revolutionary as Sigmund Freud's concept of the unconscious mind. By the time Mead came under Boas's tutelage, he was directing his students toward a new analysis of the cultural patterning of the individual's relationship to his or her society. Mead and Benedict, however, are credited as leaders in establishing the culture-and-personality school. Unlike psychologists and Freudians, who were interested in the unfolding of determined biological processes in the individual or in internal cognitive, affective, and conative processes, the culture-and-personality theorists were interested in the cultural patterning of personality. Mead's special contribution was to illuminate the process of how the young are taught to conform to cultural norms. Early in her career she also challenged the ideas of important thinkers such as Freud, Jean Piaget, Lucien Lévy-Bruhl, and other social scientists who described the primitive mind as a childlike version of civilized man's. Mead's early fieldwork in New Guinea in 1928–1929 supported with data culled from psychological tests and children's drawings enabled her to question this position. She pointed out that whatever these famous scientists said about primitive cultures was based on speculation, not anthropological fieldwork such as she had conducted in the South Pacific.

Mead's earliest bestseller, *Coming of Age in Samoa: A Psychological Study of Primitive Youth for Western Civilization* (1928), a study of adolescence, catapulted her to fame. Her novelistic writing style and the book's subject matter made it accessible both to lay audiences and to professionals interested in problems of adolescence. *Coming of Age in Samoa* popularized the idea of culture. In it, Mead pointed out that if it were possible to find one society where adolescence did not throw teenagers into a state of crisis, then something other than biology, namely, cultural patterning of behavior, contributes to the course of human development. *Growing Up in New Guinea* (1930), Mead's next popular book, focused on the early period of child development. She discovered anthropology's public-education potential from the popularity of these two early books and began to develop her role as the self-appointed educator of Americans concerning the anthropological approach to culture. This public role became increasingly dominant in her later years.

In 1926, on her return from Samoa, Mead became a curator of ethnology at the American Museum of Natural History, a position she maintained throughout her life. She understood herself to be working as an individual researcher using the museum as her base. To achieve her goal as a leading figure in academic anthropology, she had to address the work of ethnographers working in Great Britain. British anthropologists, who looked to natural science as a model for anthropology, rejected vague ideas of "pattern" and favored notions of social systems and the study of comparative social systems such as kinship. During Mead's second childless marriage (1928–1935)—to Reo Fortune, who had studied in Britain under W. H. R. Rivers and A. R. Radcliffe-Brown—she wrote the technical study *Kinship in the Admiralty Islands* (1934), which proved her conversant with the British social anthropologists. This book also represented her practice of publishing a scholarly monograph alongside a popular work, in this case *Growing Up in New Guinea*.

Sex and Temperament in Three Primitive Societies (1935), based on Mead's comparative fieldwork (1931–1933) among New Guinea's Arapesh, Mundugumor, and Tchambuli people, was grounded in Benedict's notions of cultural patterning of behavior and, less directly, in Mead's and Benedict's reading of Carl Jung's ideas on psychological types. Each culture, Benedict claimed, chose a standard personality from among a wide variety of possible human temperaments. In *Sex and Temperament* Mead argued that each culture also chose different kinds of personality traits to assign to males and females. Within a few miles of each other, Mead found one New Guinea group where everyone—male and female—behaved in what North Americans would call a "feminine," maternal way, another where men and women behaved in a "masculine," aggressive way, and, finally, a tribe where men behaved like "women" and women behaved like "men." Thus, in the Boasian tradition, Mead's study of sex roles, like her study of adolescence, called into question simple biological determinism of human behavior. Because her field research confirmed that the variations in sex roles were possible, Mead concluded that masculinity and femininity were cultural constructions, not biological givens. Moreover, she understood temperamental differences, whether they resided in males or females, to be as significant as biological sex. In the book Mead made a plea for respect and encouragement of human differences as a means to develop a fully enriched society and fully realized individuals. Published in the mid-1930s, after Hitler's rise to power, the book can be seen as Mead's public statement against totalitarianism and the racism that accompanied it.

Sex and Temperament, Mead later pointed out, was her most misunderstood book. Although she meant to explore differences between males and females (she consistently understood that innate differences exist between humans and between males and females), she ended up emphasizing temperament and arguing for the importance of cultural stylization of sex roles. Her feeling was that in the context of the 1930s scientists could defer their study of the controversial issue of innate biological determinants of human behavior and concentrate instead on the exploration of culture. Later, when she published *Male and Female: A Study of the Sexes in a Changing World* (1949), Mead felt it acceptable to explore the biological determinants of sex-role behavior. This resulted in criticism from American feminists such as Betty Friedan, who in *The Feminine Mystique* (1963) attacked Mead and most of social science for lending support to the "motherhood trap" of postwar America. A half-century after her publications concerning gender, many would argue that Mead, along with the psychoanalyst Karen Horney, who was herself influenced by Mead in her cultural critique of Freud's biological notions of feminine development, was the originator of the social constructivist position on gender. That is, Mead used her evidence of cultural variations in gender roles to argue that sex roles were not universal, "natural" outcomes of biological development but variable cultural creations.

Mead's next major field trip to Bali and New Guinea (1936–1939) was a joint endeavor with her third husband, the British anthropologist Gregory Bateson, to whom she was married between 1936 and 1950. They had one child, Mary Catherine Bateson Kassarjian, who became an anthropologist and writer. Work done with Bateson, the son of one of England's most distinguished families of natural scientists, enhanced Mead's methodological sophistication and scientific rigor. Their objective was to relate childhood and infancy to broad cultural patterns. Mead used her field observations of Balinese ritual, dance, visual art, trance, and child rearing to round out her work on culture and personality. Bateson studied more abstract problems of social interaction and learning, a continuation of his work on circular feedback systems and the epistemological issues in fieldwork observation, which he described in *Naven: A Survey . . . of the Culture of a New Guinea Tribe . . .* (1936).

Each had a profound influence on the other's work. Bateson's consciousness of the observational process, Mead's desire to make her work more scientific in response to critics who found it "impressionistic," and her openness to the possibilities of technological innovations in fieldwork made them pioneers in visual anthropology. They set out to create a visual record that would allow others to examine and verify their findings. They produced thousands of feet of still and moving images taken in Bali and New Guinea. Along with this visual evidence, they produced detailed annotations to describe the action and the fieldworkers' responses to it. Although others had used cameras in the field, nothing so inclusive and systematic had ever before been attempted. One outcome was their jointly authored book *Balinese Character, a Photographic Analysis* (1942). Mead and Bateson later produced several films on Bali and New Guinea that emphasized themes such as child rearing and character formation. Professional anthropologists, filmmakers, and the lay public still acknowledge Mead's influence on ethnographic filmmaking at the annual American Museum of Natural History Margaret Mead Film Festival, which draws contributors from all over the world.

World War II strongly affected Mead's notion of how the discipline of anthropology and she herself should relate to government and to social policy. The war brought a temporary halt to her Pacific fieldwork and stimulated her development as an applied anthropologist, first in government service, then as a private commentator on domestic and international affairs. During the early war years, Mead made several attempts to convince government officials of the significance of anthropology for the war effort. After Pearl Harbor, she worked for the Committee on Food Habits (1942–1945), an arm of the National Research Council, advising on the anthropology of nutrition, rationing, and other home-front morale issues. She took this opportunity to inject anthropology into government programs. True to the anthropological notion of looking at an entire culture in order to understand its parts, she understood food habits as only one aspect of the American national character, a subject she documented fully in *And Keep Your Powder Dry* (1942). She wrote this book, a wartime morale booster, hoping that awareness of their national character would prepare Americans for war.

Restricted from Pacific fieldwork under wartime conditions, Mead developed "culture at a distance" studies together with anthropologists Benedict, Geoffrey Gorer, and others. Later, the culture at a distance studies were taken up by Mead and others, including her longtime collaborator Rhoda Metraux, at the Columbia University Institute for Contemporary Cultures, which Mead directed between 1948 and 1952. Because these studies relied on interviews, films, and expatriate informants, not on direct field observation, they were frequently criticized by anthropologists. On the other hand, Benedict's bestselling *Chrysanthemum and the Sword* (1946), which introduced Americans to the culture of the defeated Japanese, seemed to underscore the practical educational value of this work.

Mead entered the war era with her characteristic missionary zeal for anthropology as a tool for social change. In the war's aftermath her awareness of government's misuse of scientific information, exemplified by the atomic bomb and covert practices, led Mead to create a public role for herself as one of a handful of American science celebrities who used radio, television, and other news media as platforms. Without any formal institutional support or financial backing, she became a self-appointed scientific expert on everything from the nuclear family to nuclear war. She gained the attention of national and international leaders in politics, urban planning, demography, nutrition, child development, race relations, education, psychiatry, economic development, communications, and the environment.

All of Mead's war and postwar work was based on principles of Boasian anthropology, culture, and personality field research and her belief that anthropology, properly applied, could improve the human condition. The variety of organizations with which she worked testifies to her energy. She was president of several scientific organizations, including the World Federation of Mental Health (1956–1957), the American Anthropological Association (1960), the World

Society of Ekistics (1969–1971), the Scientist's Institute for Public Information (1972), and the American Association for the Advancement of Science (1975). She received more than forty awards for science and citizenship, including the Kalinga Prize for the popularization of science and, posthumously, the Presidential Medal of Freedom. Twenty-eight honorary degrees in the humanities, science, and law were conferred on her.

Academic appointments came to Mead late in life, well after she had achieved a distinguished publication record. She became an adjunct lecturer at Columbia University beginning in 1954, was a visiting professor at the University of Cincinnati's Department of Psychiatry in the late 1950s, and served as Sloan Professor at the Menninger Foundation (1959). She also was chair of the Department of Social Sciences and professor of anthropology at Fordham University (1968–1970).

Believing that the atomic bomb and the rate of change that was occurring in the postwar world had marked a turning point in human history, Mead returned to Papua New Guinea in 1953 to the village she had studied in 1928–1929. Her *New Lives for Old: Cultural Transformation—Manus* (1956) documented the impact of rapid change on a Stone Age people who had adapted readily to it and who, she believed, could be a model for the rest of the world.

Mead popularized the term "generation gap." She used the term to refer to generational differences in historical experience between individuals who were born before and after World War II. In her book *Culture and Commitment: A Study of the Generation Gap* (1970), she proposed that the young, accustomed to living in a world of change, were better equipped to understand a changing world than their parents. This and other opinions, including her opposition to the Vietnam War, endeared her to the younger generation.

Upon her death in New York City, several obituaries warmly referred to her as "grandmother to the world," an image she cultivated in her later years with her familiar ample figure and costume of round spectacles, unfashionably cut hair, flaring cape, and four-foot walking stick. When asked what she would like to have as an epitaph, she replied: "She lived long enough to do some good."

Mead was known primarily for her studies of culture and personality, child socialization, gender, generational difference, cultural change, and "applied anthropology," the practice of bringing anthropological insights to practical issues such as nutrition, psychiatry, law, family life, adolescent conflict, population control, and even space travel. Her publishing activity was extraordinary, consisting of more than thirty-five books, hundreds of articles, films, records, and tapes; her work was and is cited both within and outside of anthropology. Psychiatrists, psychologists, population experts, religious groups, and international agencies along with journalists, magazine publishers, and the radio and television media sought her advice and knowledge. She energetically participated in public dissemination of anthropological ideas because she believed scientific knowledge could assist an enlightened citizenry to achieve the highest development of human potential. This enthusiasm distinguished her from other anthropologists who concentrated on purely academic issues. Some academic anthropologists disdain Mead's willingness to engage the general public in discussions of anthropological concepts, while others consider her early field research in Samoa and New Guinea to be oversimplified. Despite these criticisms, Mead remains America's best-known anthropologist.

Her scientific achievements and her active participation in public life also earned Mead the unusual distinction of being one of the best-known women of the twentieth century. An unusual educational and family background, her own determined and energetic personality, the state of anthropology when she entered the discipline, and the events of the twentieth century, most notably World War II and the social changes following it, explain her unique achievements.

• Margaret Mead's papers are at the Library of Congress. A bibliography of her work is Joan Gordon, ed., *Margaret Mead: The Complete Bibliography* (1976). Works by Mead not mentioned in the text include *Cooperation and Competition among Primitive Peoples* (1937); with Rhoda Metraux, *The Study of Culture at a Distance* (1953); *Continuities in Cultural Evolution* (1964); with T. Dobzhansky et al., *Science and the Concept of Race* (1968); with James Baldwin, *A Rap on Race* (1971); her autobiography, *Blackberry Winter: My Earlier Years* (1972); *Twentieth Century Faith* (1973); *Letters from the Field, 1925–1975* (1977); two works on Ruth Benedict, *An Anthropologist at Work: Writings of Ruth Benedict* (1959) and *Ruth Benedict* (1974). Two useful autobiographical accounts are "Retrospects and Prospects" in her *Anthropology and Human Behavior* (1962), pp. 115–49, "Margaret Mead," in her *History of Psychology in Autobiography*, vol. 4 (1974), pp. 295–325. See also her daughter Mary Catherine Bateson's memoir, *With a Daughter's Eye: A Memoir of Margaret Mead and Gregory Bateson* (1984), and E. Rice, *Margaret Mead: A Portrait* (1979). Virginia Yans-McLaughlin, "Science, Democracy, and Ethics: Mobilizing Culture and Personality for World War II," *History of Anthropology* 4 (1987): 184–217, details Mead's work as an applied anthropologist during the war years. Jane Howard, *Margaret Mead: A Life* (1984), is a journalistic account of Mead's life. For an obituary, see the *New York Times*, 16 Nov. 1978.

VIRGINIA YANS-MCLAUGHLIN

MEAD, William Rutherford (20 Aug. 1846–20 June 1928), architect, was born in Brattleboro, Vermont, the son of Larkin Goldsmith Mead, a lawyer, and Mary Jane Noyes. His sister, Elinor, was a painter and his brother, Larkin Goldsmith, a sculptor. From 1861 to 1863 Mead attended Norwich University in Northfield, Vermont, completing an A.B. degree at Amherst College in 1867. In 1868, after a year in a New York City engineering office, Mead became a paid apprentice to the architect Russell Sturgis. In 1871 he traveled to Florence, Italy, studying informally at the Academia di Belle Arti for one year before touring Europe for six months.

On returning to New York City in 1872, Mead met Charles Follen McKim. For five years each developed an independent practice and helped the other, sharing office space and expenses at 57 Broadway. With William B. Bigelow they established McKim, Mead & Bigelow in 1878, but that partnership was dissolved in 1879. Mead and McKim added Stanford White to their practice that year, officially forming McKim, Mead & White in 1880. Mead married Olga Kilyeni in Budapest, Hungary, in 1884; they had no children.

McKim, Mead & White was a partnership of equals with distinct yet complementary strengths. In 1886 Stanford White characterized their respective contributions to the practice thus: "No member of our firm is ever individually responsible for any design which goes out from it" ("Correction," *Art Age* 3 [Jan. 1886]: 100). While McKim and White were the firm's principal designers, Mead was responsible for commissions such as the Rhode Island State Capitol. White's son Lawrence Grant later noted that Mead "often conceived the scheme which was the basis for the whole design . . . and gave timely criticism which had vital bearing upon the finished work" (quoted in Moore, p. 56).

Mead managed the office, was responsible for hiring and mentoring staff, and was in charge of engineering design and construction supervision. Mead himself joked that his primary function was to "prevent [his] partners from making damned fools of themselves" (quoted in Moore, p. 56). A cartoon by Augustus Saint-Gaudens showed Mead struggling with the strings of two kites flying in opposite directions, one labeled "McKim" the other "White."

In his manuscript memoirs, Mead dated the firm's classical bent from a "celebrated" 1877 New England expedition to document Colonial architecture. He credited his own inclination toward classical architecture to visiting the Doric state capitol building in Montpelier, Vermont, as a young man with his brother Larkin. It was Joseph M. Wells, however, who brought the language of the Italian Renaissance to the office in 1879. With the design of the Villard Houses on Madison Avenue the simultaneous simplicity and grandeur of Renaissance proportion, ceremonial order, attention to materials, and precision in detailing became the hallmarks of the firm. The Renaissance style as adapted to the American experience in the nineteenth and twentieth centuries, in combination with the partners' interest in antiquity, made McKim, Mead & White among the most celebrated and prolific architects of the American Renaissance.

The firm of McKim, Mead & White completed numerous important commissions of exceptional quality; it had a profound influence on American architecture. The publication of a four-volume monograph of their work beginning in 1915 brought the ideas of McKim, Mead, and White to a wide audience. By 1900 the firm boasted the largest architectural office in the world. For nearly half a century McKim, Mead & White employed, mentored, and trained hundreds of young architects who carried the classical principles and the perfectionist spirit of their early office experience into private practices around the country.

Because its projects were both public and urban, the firm had a pronounced impact on the shape and character of major American cities. Although many have been demolished, a representative sample of McKim, Mead & White's buildings in New York City alone includes the Pennsylvania railroad station (1910); the Morgan Library (1907); the master plan, libraries, and other structures of Columbia (1892–1918) and New York (1892–1903) Universities; the University (1900) and Metropolitan (1894) Clubs; Madison Square Garden (1891); the Brooklyn Institute of Arts and Sciences (1895–1903); the Madison Square Presbyterian Church (1906); the National City Bank (1910); the Knickerbocker Trust Co. (1904); and the Tiffany and Gorham Buildings (1906). The firm also designed the Boston Public Library (1895) and Symphony Hall (1901); the Rhode Island State Capitol (1894); the War College in Washington, D.C. (1908); and additions and renovations to the White House (1902–1903) and to the University of Virginia in Charlottesville (1896–1913). Underscoring its commitment to a uniquely American classical tradition, the firm designed the New York State Commissioner's Building and the Agricultural Building for the World's Columbian Exposition in 1893.

Mead retired in 1919, after the assassination of White in 1906 and the death of McKim in 1908. He had been a fellow of the American Institute of Architects and served as president of the New York chapter from 1907 to 1908. Mead had also been elected to the American Academy of Arts and Letters and the National Academy of Design. From 1899 to 1909 he was president of the Amherst College Alumni Association in New York. And, in 1909, after the death of founder Charles McKim, Mead had replaced his partner as president of the American Academy in Rome. He retained that post for eighteen years.

In 1913 the American Academy of Arts and Letters conferred its first gold medal to any architect upon Mead "for distinguished service in the creation of original work in architecture." In 1922 he was made a knight commander of the Order of the Crown in Italy. Mead died in Paris, France, and is buried next to his brother at the American Cemetery in Florence, Italy.

McKim, Mead & White practiced at the turn of the twentieth century—years that brought about the industrialization of building. Working contemporaneously with Louis Sullivan and Frank Lloyd Wright, the firm has been criticized for adhering to a classicism that some considered inappropriate to an American democracy and for falling short of new Modern definitions of rationalism and truth in architectural design. Yet McKim, Mead & White practiced a nuanced, often innovative, rational architecture that incorporated new materials and construction technologies. These were placed at the service of an "intuitive classicism" that for many served to bring dignity and beauty to American institutions. Without William Rutherford Mead, whom Royal Cortissoz called "the anchor in practicality and judgement, the coolheaded moderator [of] steadfast wisdom," this work would have been impossible.

• Mead's papers are in the New-York Historical Society, McKim, Mead & White Archives, and Amherst College, William R. Mead Collection. Some additional papers can be found at the Columbia University Avery Architectural Library in the McKim, Mead & White Collection. Useful biographical sketches and bibliographical information appear in Charles Moore, *The Life and Times of Charles Follen McKim* (1929), and Leland M. Roth, *The Architecture of McKim, Mead & White, 1870–1920: A Building List* (1978). The work of McKim, Mead & White can be seen in McKim, Mead & White, *The Architecture of McKim, Mead and White in Photographs, Plans and Elevations* (4 vols., 1990), with an introduction by Richard Guy Wilson. That work is analyzed in Leland M. Roth, *McKim, Mead & White, Architects* (1983); Edward R. Ford, *The Details of Modern Architecture*, vol. 1 (1990); Wayne Andrews, *Architecture, Ambition and Americans* (1964); Frederick Koeper, *American Architecture*, vol. 2, *1860–1976* (1984); and Henry-Russell Hitchcock, *The Architecture of H. H. Richardson and His Times* (1966). Articles and notes written about William Rutherford Mead during his lifetime are in *Brickbuilder* 24 (Dec. 1915); *Country Life in America* 39 (Apr. 1921); and M. R. Cabot, *Annals of Brattleboro, 1681–1895* (1922). Obituary notices are in *American Architect and Building News* 134, *American Art Journal* 25, *Architectural Forum* 49, *Architectural Record* 64, *Journal of the American Institute of Architects* 16, *Pencil Points* 9, the *New York Herald Tribune*, and the *New York Times*, all on or about 20 June 1928.

MARILYS R. NEPOMECHIE

MEADE, George (27 Feb. 1741–9 Nov. 1808), merchant and Roman Catholic layman, was born in Philadelphia, Pennsylvania, the son of Robert Meade, a merchant, and Mary Stretch. The father was born in county Limerick, Ireland, lived in Philadelphia from about 1732, and had commercial interests in St. Croix and Barbados. George Meade was privately educated by his maternal uncle, George Stretch, in Barbados and was resident there in 1754 when his father died in St. Croix. By 1761 he entered into a business partnership with his elder brother in Philadelphia. The firm of Garrett and George Meade imported rum, sugar, and slaves, usually small groups of girls and boys, from Barbados and other West Indian ports. Enslaved Africans were employed as skilled and unskilled laborers by local farmers, artisans, merchants, and urban householders. Both Garrett and George Meade signed the Non-Importation Agreement of 1765 in opposition to the Stamp Act. Since the firm was not engaged in trade with Great Britain, nonimportation had little or no impact on their business, while opposition to the stamp tax was politically popular.

In 1768 George Meade married Henrietta Constantia Worsam. Her father was a prominent planter, a member of the Council in Barbados, and an active member of Christ Church (Anglican) in Philadelphia. The difference in religion reputedly caused the marriage to be delayed until after the death of Worsam's father. The Meades had five daughters and five sons. One son, Richard Worsam Meade, was the father of the Civil War general, George Gordon Meade. The children were baptized at St. Joseph's Roman Catholic Church in Philadelphia, but in the 1790s most of the daughters and one of the sons adopted their mother's faith. Four daughters went to England, their mother's birthplace, in that decade, and their mother followed soon after her husband's death.

In 1772 Garrett Meade left the partnership to pursue other interests. George Meade formed a company with Thomas Fitzsimons, the husband of Meade's younger sister Catherine. The company speculated in western Pennsylvania lands and continued to engage in West Indian trade and shipping. As Pennsylvania moved toward independence from Great Britain, Meade was elected to the Committee of Inspection and Observation for the City and Liberties, better known as the Second Committee of 100, on the Mechanic's ticket on 21 February 1776. While he served on at least one subcommittee, he was not prominent in politics. He joined the Third Philadelphia Battalion and the local militia but did not engage in battle. Meade fled with his family to Chester County during the British occupation of the city in September 1777, returning a year later after British troops were evacuated. He invested 2,000 pounds in Pennsylvania Bank stock and later invested in the Bank of North America. Both banks were designed to raise money to provision troops but were founded too late to have any important impact on the war. His firm was one of the largest provision merchants during the war, engaging in trade with European suppliers through the port of Martinique. The firm also speculated in both American bonds and British stocks during the conflict, seeking to profit, as did other Philadelphia mercantile firms, no matter what the war's outcome. Meade's company prospered during the war, then failed during the economic downturn of 1783–1784. The partnership was dissolved, and Meade owed the large sum of 30,000 pounds sterling to his creditors. A London creditor advanced 10,000 pounds, which allowed Meade to recover.

Meade had earlier been a founding member of the Fishing Company of St. David (1763), a social club, and of the Friendly Sons of St. Patrick (1771), a social and charitable organization. His civic activities peaked during the late 1780s and the 1790s. He was a member of the Common Council of Philadelphia (1789–1792); a member of the Hibernian Society for the Relief of Emigrants from Ireland (beginning in 1790); chairman of the Board of Management of the Inspectors of the Prisons (1792); vice president of the First Day or Sunday Schools (1793); manager of the Philadelphia Dispensary; a trustee of St. Mary's Parish; and a contributor to St. Mary's and St. Augustine's Roman Catholic churches. He was a generous contributor to the African Church of Philadelphia in 1791, a nondenominational forerunner of the African Episcopal Church of St. Thomas, although he held slaves until shortly after Pennsylvania provided for gradual emancipation in 1780. His politics were Federalist, and he marched with nine other "gentlemen" near the head of the Grand Federal Procession in Philadelphia in 1788. The political prominence of his brother-in-law, Congressman Fitzsimons, undoubtedly aided Meade in his civic activities early in this period. By 1796 another economic downturn left Meade bankrupt, but he recovered before his retirement in 1806. He died in Philadelphia.

Meade's reputation as an active patriot was the late nineteenth-century creation of his descendant R. W. Meade, who published an 1891 article on Meade, describing him as "A Patriot of the Revolutionary Era." This hagiographic account seems to have fulfilled the family's desire to locate an ancestor worthy of George Gordon Meade, a prominent participant at the battle of Gettysburg, and was typical of the concern with lineage and genealogy of the late nineteenth-century elite. In his own time, George Meade was not especially remarkable, and only scattered references to his civic and business careers exist in contemporary records. The family did not preserve his personal papers, which were lost by 1830. Meade has been included among several founders of elite Philadelphia families who supposedly formed a cohesive, long-lasting national upper class, but little actual evidence supports this claim of inherited greatness. Meade's firm was not the disinterested, patriotic benefactor of the American Revolution described in nineteenth-century accounts but engaged in speculative activities with both British and American investments. His descendants remembered him as "eccentric in his manners, but social, hospitable and benevolent" (Dallas, p. 3), and as "testy" and given to profanity (Meade, p. 217). These qualities may account for his short terms in minor elected and appointed positions. He did support Roman Catholic and Irish causes in Philadelphia at a time when anti-Catholic and anti-Irish prejudices were rampant, and he served in various ecumenical organizations. However, later biographers considered these quiet virtues insufficiently heroic for the grandfather of a famous general.

• Meade's papers do not survive. A receipt book from the Garrett and George Meade partnership is at the Historical Society of Pennsylvania along with a few other items preserved in the papers of other individuals. The fullest accounts of his life are at the Genealogical Society of Pennsylvania in family histories. See A. J. Dallas, *Pedigree of the Meade Family* (c. 1879); and Thomas Stewardson, "Meade Genealogical Notes" (n.d.). Also useful are R. W. Meade, "George Meade: A Patriot of the Revolutionary Era," *Records of the American Catholic Historical Society of Philadelphia* 3 (1891): 193–220, which must be read with care; and John H. Campbell, *History of the Friendly Sons of St. Patrick and of the Hibernian Society for the Relief of Emigrants from Ireland* (1892). Most mentions of Meade are based on these nineteenth-century sources; see Charles Metzger, *Catholics and the American Revolution* (1962); E. Digby Baltzell, *Philadelphia Gentlemen: The Making of a National Upper Class* (1958); and Baltzell, *Puritan Boston and Quaker Philadelphia* (1979). References to Meade based on twentieth-century research are in Thomas M. Doerflinger, *A Vigorous Spirit of Enterprise: Merchants and Economic Development in Revolutionary Philadelphia* (1986); and Richard Alan Ryerson, *The Revolution Is Now Begun: The Radical Committees of Philadelphia, 1765–1776* (1978). Glimpses of Meade's life surface occasionally in the writings of contemporaries; see *The Letters of Benjamin Rush*, ed. L. H. Butterfield (2 vols., 1951); *Extracts from the Diary of Christopher Marshall, 1774–1781*, ed. William Duane (1877; repr. 1969); *The Diary of Elizabeth Drinker*, ed. Elaine Forman Crane et al. (3 vols., 1991); and *Francis Hopkinson's Account of the Grand Federal Procession, Philadelphia, 1788*, ed. Whitfield J. Bell, Jr. (1962). Information on Meade and slavery is in Darold D. Wax, "Negro Imports into Pennsylvania, 1720–1766," *Pennsylvania History* 32 (1965): 254–87; and Billy G. Smith and Richard Wojtowicz, *Blacks Who Stole Themselves: Advertisements for Runaways in the Pennsylvania Gazette, 1728–1790* (1989).

SUSAN E. KLEPP

MEADE, George Gordon (31 Dec. 1815–6 Nov. 1872), soldier and engineer, was born in Cadiz, Spain, the son of Richard Worsam Meade, a merchant and U.S. naval agent, and Margaret Coates Butler. Meade came to the United States at the age of one and a half years with his mother, who established a home in Philadelphia while her husband, caught up in the aftermath of the Napoleonic Wars, languished in a Spanish prison. Released in 1818, Richard Meade eventually moved his family to Washington in an effort to recover a sizable debt owed him by the U.S. government. The claim was disallowed, and as family finances dwindled, George attended a succession of private schools in Philadelphia, Washington, and Baltimore. After the death of Meade's father, Margaret Meade, seeking the least costly expedient, obtained an appointment for George to the U.S. Military Academy. He entered West Point in September 1831 at the age of fifteen.

Cadet Meade did little to distinguish himself during his four years at West Point. He graduated nineteenth out of fifty-six in the class of 1835 and was assigned to the artillery. In order to purchase his officer's wardrobe, he spent his graduation furlough working on a survey party for the Long Island Railroad. Meade's first military assignment was to Florida. He arrived at Tampa Bay in January 1836 in the midst of the First Seminole War. Unaccustomed to the heat and humidity, he suffered from ill health and was rendered useless for active campaigning. After escorting a large band of peaceful Seminoles to the Indian Territory, he was reassigned to arsenal duty in Massachusetts. Completing his mandatory one year of service, he resigned from the army effective 28 October 1836.

Meade's brief experience in railroad surveying stood him well in obtaining a similar position in Pensacola, Florida, but the project succumbed to the financial panic of 1837. Meade found two more surveying jobs on the Sabine and Mississippi rivers as a civilian employee of the Army Topographical Bureau. These projects kept him engaged until February 1839, followed by nearly a year of unemployment, which Meade spent in Philadelphia. During that time he courted Margaretta Sergeant, daughter of Congressman John Sergeant. In August 1840 Meade received an assignment to the boundary survey of Maine, which promised lengthy employment. During a winter leave in 1840 he married Margaretta; the couple had seven children.

In 1842 Congress passed legislation that excluded civilians from service with the military engineers. Meade consequently applied for reinstatement in the army and was appointed second lieutenant of topographical engineers in May 1842. He remained on the Maine boundary project until November 1843. Thereafter he designed and constructed lighthouses in Delaware Bay until September 1845, when he was sent to Corpus Christi, Texas, to begin service as an engineering officer on the staff of Major General Zachary Taylor.

Meade participated in the opening campaign of the Mexican War, seeing action as a courier during the battles of Palo Alto and Resaca de la Palma. In the predawn hours of 21 September 1846 Meade piloted American troops during the assault on Independence Hill. The resulting capture of a strong Mexican fort opened the way into Monterey. For his conduct Meade was awarded a brevet promotion to first lieutenant.

In March 1847 Meade took part in the invasion of Veracruz, conducted by General Winfield Scott. Meade soon found himself "pretty much of a spectator," owing to the abundance of engineering officers already with Scott. Meade was sent to Washington for reassignment and then reassumed his duties on Delaware Bay. Similar assignments in Florida and on the Great Lakes occupied him for the next fourteen years. At the time of his promotion to captain in 1856, Meade was living with his family in Detroit while supervising the Great Lakes geodetic survey.

Soon after the outbreak of the Civil War, Meade accepted a commission as brigadier general of volunteers and was assigned a brigade in the Division of Pennsylvania Reserves. The division wintered over in the defenses of Washington and then took part in the 1862 Peninsula Campaign. At the battle of Glendale, 30 June, Meade was twice wounded. His injuries necessitated six weeks of convalescent leave.

At the second battle of Manassas, 29–30 August 1862, Meade led his brigade in securing the Warrenton Turnpike for the retreat of Major General John Pope's army. Meade's brigade covered the army's withdrawal and was one of the last units to cross Bull Run Creek. In September Meade took command of the Pennsylvania Division, which was now a part of the First Army Corps under Major General Joseph Hooker. Meade skillfully handled the division as it secured the heights above Turner's Gap in the battle of South Mountain on 14 September. He further established his apparent competency for high command in the 17 September battle of Antietam. On the right wing of the Federal army, he pushed his division forward through the North Woods and the Cornfield against heavy opposition. Though painfully bruised by spent grapeshot, he remained in the thick of the fight, rallying his men and calmly examining the field. In late morning, when the injured Hooker retired from the scene, Meade assumed command of the First Corps.

Meade received promotion to major general of volunteers on 29 November 1862. With Hooker again leading the corps, Meade resumed command of the Pennsylvania Reserves. In conferences with staff officers and in letters written home, he expressed concern over the Union's ill-conceived campaigns in the East. He believed that the high command had erred in its place-oriented approach to attempting capture of the Confederate capital. "I have always maintained that Richmond need not and should not be attacked at all," he wrote. "The proper mode to reduce it is to take possession of the great lines of railroad leading to it . . . , and their army will be compelled to evacuate it and meet us on the ground we can select ourselves." More than two years later this strategy, implemented by Ulysses S. Grant, would decide the war.

In the battle of Fredericksburg, on 13 December Meade's division was arrayed for action toward the far left of the Union assault line. "General Meade was possibly the best general in the Army . . . that day and he had some of the best soldiers," opined one Federal soldier. Enemy gunners under Major John Pelham drew first blood, but Meade's guns eventually silenced the rebel cannons. Soon, however, the opposing forces closed with each other in fierce combat. During a day of desperate fighting, which saw much go very badly for the Federals, Meade's division captured three hundred prisoners. Meade himself came under fire, his hat being pierced by two bullets, and he probably saved his own life by smashing the flat of his saber against the shoulder of a battle-crazed Federal soldier. The man had been ordered to move on but instead had pointed his gun at Meade. The blow Meade delivered was a hard one indeed; the sword blade was snapped off at the hilt. Though Meade's division made meaningful progress, it was inadequately supported and eventually had to fall back in some disarray. To his superior, Major General John F. Reynolds, Meade exasperatingly cried, "Did they think my division could whip Lee's whole army?" Meade's good performance did not go unrewarded; he was elevated to Fifth Corps command, effective 23 December 1862. This was later reconfirmed by General Hooker, who became commander of the Army of the Potomac on 26 January 1863.

Hooker's 1863 campaign entailed crossing the Rappahannock River above and below Fredericksburg and drawing out the entrenched Confederate Army of Northern Virginia. On 30 April the Fifth Corps led the crossing and descended on Chancellorsville. Meade prepared to seize the hills beyond, but Hooker stopped the advance and concentrated the army on poorly chosen ground. On 1 May Meade again sent a division forward to capture heights overlooking a strategic ford. The division took the hill, braced for the counterattack, and requested reinforcements. Instead, Hooker ordered the division back. Frustrated, Meade exclaimed to a fellow officer, "My God, if we can't hold the top of the hill, we certainly can't hold the bottom of it!"

On the next day Hooker seemed to be inviting attack and was overheard by a fellow officer to remark that the enemy would have to fight him on his own ground. As the lines were formed up, Meade wisely extended his troops to the river to protect their flank. Hooker ignored Meade's cautious approach and arrayed other troops more precariously, relegating Oliver O. Howard's Eleventh Corps, probably the poorest trained, to the far right. As it turned out, Howard's flank was woefully vulnerable. Meade was left to pick up the pieces when the army right collapsed after being struck hard late in the day by "Stonewall" Jackson's assault. Meade's trained ear told him at once what had happened, and he ordered a line thrown out along the road, seeking to halt and hold the fleeing Federals from Howard's Corps.

On 3 May Meade learned that the enemy to his front had no reserves, and he was anxious that his Fifth Corps should aid in a counterattack, but he did not receive any orders to do so. He went personally to Hooker to plead the case, but Hooker had been badly dazed when a rebel cannonball hit a column of the "Chancellor House" and dislodged fragments that stunned him. Raising up from his cot, Hooker faulted Meade's actions and forbade detachment of any more troops to him, despite Meade's vehement arguments. Meade later wrote his wife: "I tried all I could . . . but I was *overruled* and censured . . . Hooker never did allow himself to be influenced by me or my advice."

After the battle of Chancellorsville, rumors spread that President Abraham Lincoln would relieve Hooker. Yet the professionals had little desire to obtain the appointment, inasmuch as the leader of the Army of the Potomac would be subject to the political whims of Washington. Meade had already decided not to seek the position, as "it is more likely to destroy one's reputation than to add to it." Others, however, including Pennsylvania Governor Andrew G. Curtin and senior corps commander Major General Darius N. Couch, took up Meade's case, both going to Washington to recommend him for the command. Lincoln, though, at this point still wished to retain Hooker. Not until the rebels crossed into Pennsylvania and Hooker admitted that he did not know what he should do did the president make a hurried decision to elevate Meade.

Orders for the command change arrived at army headquarters at 3:00 A.M. on the morning of 28 June 1863. Meade's immediate concerns were the disposition of his scattered troops and ascertaining the location of the enemy forces. Completely unaware of whatever plans Hooker might have had, Meade quickly had to devise some of his own. "I can only say now," Meade replied to the War Department, "that it appears to me I must move toward the Susquehanna, keeping Washington and Baltimore well covered. . . . If the enemy is checked in his attempt to cross . . . or if he turns toward Baltimore [I intend] to give him battle."

Meade's handling of the subsequent battle of Gettysburg, 1–3 July 1863, did, and perhaps always will, invite criticism. The ground was not of his choosing—he had relied upon the judgment of subordinates. His flanks were vulnerable, and it was merely good fortune for the Federals that they were not turned. Nor did Meade follow up on his victory with any aggressive pursuit. Nevertheless he won, and in the process he clearly hurt the enemy force. Meade had proven the power of the defensive. He learned it, he wrote, from several battles in which the enemy "would play their own game of shooting us [from] behind breastworks—a game we played this time to their entire satisfaction." Meade received a promotion to brigadier general in the regular army and the official Thanks of Congress for his Gettysburg victory.

The ascendancy of Grant to general in chief in March 1864 left Meade's status in doubt. In a meeting on 10 March, Meade told Grant that he was willing to serve faithfully wherever placed and that his personal feelings were subservient to the cause. "This incident," Grant wrote in his *Personal Memoirs* (1886), "gave me even a more favorable opinion of Meade than did his great victory at Gettysburg." Though personally disappointed that Grant chose to remain in the field with his army, Meade continued to command the Army of the Potomac with competence and dedication. It was a complex command relationship, one which the distinguished military historian Russell F. Weigley asserts has never been adequately analyzed. The war, after all, was only a little past its halfway point, and much hard fighting ensued during the long months ahead. Meade's personal contributions to the eventual Federal victory were quite keen, and it is plausible (as some scholars have opined) that Meade was unfairly treated later when he was passed over for elevation to the position of commanding general, which went instead to the younger Philip H. Sheridan.

Meade's postwar career consisted of a series of military administrative posts. In the spring of 1866 he foiled the planned invasion of Canada by the American Fenian Society. Beginning in August 1866 he commanded the Military Division of the Atlantic, headquartered in Philadelphia, while also serving as a commissioner of that city's Fairmont Park. From January 1868 to March 1869 Meade was in charge of the Department of the South. He then returned to the Atlantic Division. He died of pneumonia in Philadelphia. Doctors attributed his death to a physique weakened by war wounds.

The bespectacled Meade resembled more the scholar than the soldier, but being at times short-tempered, he lived up to a popular description of him as a "damned old goggle-eyed snapping turtle." He saw to it that each corps in his army had a gallows or shooting post for "Friday executions." He deserted newspaper correspondents, believing much of their reporting to be inaccurate and to him malicious. Frequently he barred them from his army, only to have them retaliate with still more unfavorable coverage. According to his biographer, Freeman Cleaves, Meade's contributions were so distorted and denigrated by the Radical press that Meade supposed "it soon would be proved that either he was not at Gettysburg at all or that his presence there had been a positive detriment." Press criticism combined with the biased memoirs of grandstanding commanders who had various affiliations with the Army of the Potomac effectively relegate Meade to the background. His reputation has not achieved the high level that it deserves.

• The largest single collection of Meade papers is held by the Historical Society of Pennsylvania. Additional letters are in the Library of Congress, the Virginia Historical Society, and the New-York Historical Society. His engineering notes are in the Topographical Bureau Records of the National Archives. More accessible and ordered are his writings in *Life and Letters of George Gordon Meade* (2 vols., 1913), which was published by his grandson George Meade. Two early biographies of the general are Richard M. Bache, *George Gordon Meade* (1897), and Isaac R. Pennypacker, *General Meade* (1901). While each contributes something to the historical records of Meade's life, neither one brings him clearly into focus. A better view, one that at least provides interesting vignettes of Meade's administration, is George R. Agassiz, ed., *Meade's Headquarters, 1863–65: The Letters of Colonel Theodore Lyman* (1922). Lyman was volunteer aide to Meade and much devoted to him. Warren W. Hassler, Jr., provides a helpful primer on Meade's career in *Commanders of the Army of the Potomac* (1962). Freeman Cleaves, *Meade of Gettysburg* (1960), stands as the strongest effort at modern biography. A substantive obituary of Meade can be found in the *New York Times*, 7 Nov. 1872.

HERMAN HATTAWAY
MICHAEL D. SMITH

MEADE, Richard Worsam, III (9 Oct. 1837–4 May 1897), naval officer, was born in New York City, the son of Richard Worsam Meade II (1807–1870), a naval officer, and Clara Forsythe Meigs. After attending the College of the Holy Cross and Mount St. Mary's College, Meade entered the U.S. Naval Academy in 1850. Graduating fifth in his class in 1856, he was promoted to passed midshipman that year. Commissioned lieutenant (1858), he served aboard the *Cumberland* (1857–1859) and the *Dale* (1859), both off Africa patrolling for slavers. Aboard the *Saranac* (1859–1860), he was court-martialed after a personal dispute with a marine lieutenant erupted in violence.

During the Civil War Meade was promoted to lieutenant commander (July 1862) and then received his first command, the ironclad *Louisville*, Mississippi Squadron (Sept. through Nov. 1862). Commanding a naval division off Helena, Arkansas, he engaged in fierce battle and was nearly killed by Confederate fire. He commanded the *United States* in the search for Confederate raider Charles W. Read, boarding and overhauling twenty-seven vessels (June 1863). During the New York City draft riots (July 1863), Meade commanded the naval battalion in lower Manhattan.

Meade next commanded the *Marblehead*, South Atlantic Blockading Squadron (1863–1864), performing picket duty on the Stono River during the siege of Charleston. On Christmas Day 1863 he was wounded while working his vessel under fierce fire from John's Island and was later recommended for promotion "for gallant conduct in the face of the enemy." Afterward he commanded the *Chocura*, West Gulf Blockading Squadron, capturing or destroying seven blockade runners. In June 1865 he married Rebecca Paulding; they had five children.

Meade headed the Naval Academy's Department of Seamanship and Naval Tactics from 1865 to 1868, increasing scientific education, introducing naval construction, and commanding summer practice cruises. Commissioned commander (Sept. 1868), he took the gunboat *Saginaw* (1868–1869) on one of the first American surveys of the Alaskan coast, where he razed four Kake villages to counter resistance to American traders. In 1869 he published a professional text on naval architecture that placed him on the side of technological reform and against the navy's conservative old guard. In August 1870 he commanded, although he did not actually sail, the yacht *America* in the first challenge for the America's Cup.

Meade's most notable cruise was in command of the *Narragansett* (1871–1873), a voyage of 60,000 miles, mainly under sail, throughout the central and southern Pacific. Shaping an undisciplined crew into an efficient unit, he skillfully sailed a worn-out vessel. In Samoa he engineered a temporary peace among warring tribes and promulgated articles of confederation, a commercial treaty, and a naval treaty granting exclusive American use of Pago Pago. Although the Senate rejected the harbor treaty, Meade's actions laid the groundwork for the 1878 treaty giving the United States rights to a coaling station. In addition, Meade pursued illegal labor traders, engaged in military and quasi-diplomatic activity at Abaiang in the Gilbert chain, took formal possession of Christmas Island, and collected hydrographic, political, economic, and coaling information. Admiral David D. Porter praised Meade and the *Narragansett* for performing "more professional work than any other ship that has been afloat for the past two years in the Navy."

From 1873 to 1876 Meade served at the New York Navy Yard as inspector of ordnance, head of the navigation office, and occasional captain of the yard. He wrote articles displaying his vision for reforming a navy in steep decline. As a progressive navalist and precursor to Alfred Thayer Mahan, he advocated a rationalized naval administrative structure and a technologically advanced steel and steam fleet and promoted the importance of sea power in shaping history. He also testified at congressional hearings into navy yard management (1876), speaking bluntly about the system's inefficiency and corruption, and wrote two unsuccessful House Naval Affairs Committee bills to reform the navy. For two years he received no posting, commonly seen as punishment for his outspoken views.

Meade's next sea command was the *Vandalia* (1879–1882), cruising Newfoundland, the Atlantic Coast, and the Caribbean. The *Vandalia* gathered intelligence in the Isthmus of Panama, a region of growing

American concern. In Newfoundland in 1882, by conferring with civilian and military authorities, Meade smoothed Canadian-American relations in the wake of ill feeling over the 1878 Fortune Bay affair. He was promoted to captain in March 1880.

In 1882 Meade wrote the report recommending the Whitehead torpedo, which was to become a mainstay of the new navy's ordnance. After a leave of absence to work for the Missouri Pacific Railroad (1884–1885), he was given special duty commanding the controversial dispatch boat *Dolphin* (1885–1886), one of the nation's first steel warships. He put the *Dolphin* through rigorous sea trials to test its seaworthiness, reporting it structurally acceptable but of inferior design and workmanship.

Meade became president of a special naval Board of Inventory (1886–1887). His report documented the navy's shoddy and inefficient system of purchasing, accounting, and storage and recommended major restructuring to achieve more "business-like" methods. As a result, the secretary of the navy instituted a system of central purchasing and control of supplies, a system that, along with modern ships and new strategic thinking, helped the United States develop into a modern naval power.

As commandant of the Washington Navy Yard (1887–1890), Meade transformed the facility into a premier center for the development and production of naval ordnance. He served as navy representative to the Board of Managers of the World's Columbian Exposition (1890–1893) and was promoted to commodore in 1892. He conceived of a replica battleship as the navy's exhibit and oversaw its design and construction. The "Brick Ship," one of the exposition's most popular exhibits, introduced hundreds of thousands of Americans to the modern navy.

Meade commanded the North Atlantic Squadron aboard the flagship *New York* in 1894–1895, advancing to rear admiral officially in September 1894. During a short and turbulent cruise, he clashed with civilian authorities over squadron movements in the politically volatile Caribbean. While the department dispatched other ships to trouble spots, it kept Meade's flagship in safer ports. The admiral, by then known as a "rattler" in foreign affairs, pushed for an active role in the region, particularly Nicaragua, Cuba, and Venezuela, while the administration of Grover Cleveland pursued a cautious policy. In protest, Meade surrendered command and retired on 20 May 1895. He died two years later in Washington, D.C., of complications from appendicitis.

Meade was a man of strongly held beliefs, shaped by a keen sense of his family heritage. He was a strict disciplinarian on his ships, yet he was admired and respected by his crews. His career was marked by personal and professional disputes, sometimes heated, and his love of the navy was tempered by the glacial pace of promotion throughout the post–Civil War era and his feelings that the government had mistreated his relatives and ancestors. Continuing health problems, financial worries, and religious doubts detracted from his enjoyment of his professional accomplishments.

Meade's contributions to the "new navy" included administrative innovations, reforms in naval education, advocacy of a multifaceted global fleet with modern ships tailored for particular duties, and his belief in an activist foreign policy. He was a progressive navalist whose fame was eclipsed by lesser contemporaries who lived to serve in the Spanish-American War.

• Meade's official papers can be found in the National Archives: Naval Records Collection (RG 45), General Records of the Department of the Navy (RG 80), Records of the Office of the Judge Advocate General (RG 125), Records of the Bureaus of Yards and Docks (RG 71), and General Records of the Department of State (RG 59). The New-York Historical Society holds a sizable collection of Meade material. The most comprehensive introduction to Meade's thinking on naval topics is his influential series "Thoughts on Naval Administration," *Army and Navy Journal*, 23 Oct. 1875–20 May 1876, published under the byline "A Naval Officer." He published numerous other articles on naval topics—often for the *New York Herald*—using that byline or "Reform." Meade published two translations, Jules Étienne de Crisenoy, *Our Naval School and Naval Officers* (1873), which includes an introduction by Meade, and Paul M. Dislère, *The Iron-Clad Ships of the World* (1875); two introductory texts, *Manual of the Boat Exercise at the U.S. Naval Academy* (1868) and *Treatise on Naval Architecture and Ship-Building* (1869); and numerous professional reports, including *Ordnance Instructions*, with Montgomery Sicard (1880), and *Regulations of the Navy-Yard, Washington, D.C.* (1889). He described some of his *Narragansett* experiences in "A Winter Voyage through the Straits of Magellan," *National Geographic*, May 1897, pp. 129–41. Informative obituaries are in the *New York Tribune*, 5 May 1897, the *New York Times*, 5 May 1897, the *Army and Navy Journal*, 8 May 1897, and *National Geographic*, May 1897. *A Tribute of Respect by Lafayette Post No. 140* (1898) honored Meade posthumously and includes several of his speeches on professional subjects.

KENNETH J. BLUME

MEADE, William (11 Nov. 1789–14 Mar. 1862), Episcopal bishop, was born in Frederick County, Virginia, the son of Colonel Richard Kidder Meade, an aide on General George Washington's staff during the Revolution, and Mary Fitzhugh Grymes. He attended a private school, Carter Hall, in Virginia and then entered the junior class at the College of New Jersey in 1806. Meade said later that he "never attributed an ecclesiastical opinion and hardly a religious impression to Princeton" (Goodwin, *History*, vol. 1, p. 438). He graduated in 1808 and was valedictorian of his class.

Meade studied for the ministry of the Episcopal church under the Reverend Walter Dulaney Addison, the evangelical rector of St. John's Parish, Maryland. It was under "Parson Addison" that Meade learned his evangelical doctrine. He wrote: "It was while reading under his direction, that the first clear, satisfactory and delightful view of the necessity and reasonableness of a propitiation for sin by our blessed Lord was presented to my mind" (Johns, p. 39). As an evangelical, he would always stress the atoning death of Jesus Christ. Many of his friends and members of his family thought he was crazy since he desired to be ordained in the Episcopal church. He later wrote that many thought "that there was something unsound in mind or eccentric in character, at any rate a want of good common sense . . . or I could not make such a mistake as to attach myself to the fallen and desperate fortunes of the Old Church" (*Old Churches*, pp. 30–31). A story was widely circulated that a rabid dog had once bitten his father "and there was a vein of eccentricity in some members of the family" ("Autobiography," p. 392). Before his ordination, Meade married Mary Barnwell in 1810. They had three sons before her death in 1817. In 1820 he married Thomasia Nelson; they had no children.

Meade traveled 200 miles to Williamsburg, where Bishop James Madison was resident, for his ordination. He was informally examined by the bishop before breakfast and ordained deacon by Bishop Madison on Sunday, 24 February 1811 in Bruton Parish Church. It was a most inauspicious beginning according to Meade's description. "On arriving at the church, we found it in a wretched condition, with broken windows, and a gloomy comfortless aspect" (*Old Churches*, p. 29). He said the congregation consisted of two women and about fifteen men, nearly all of whom were relatives or acquaintances. He even had to preach his own ordination sermon. Meade was not guilty of exaggeration. By 1811 the Episcopal church, which had existed in Virginia for 204 years, was almost dead. Of the approximately 250 churches and chapels owned by the church in 1776, only about thirty-five were still in use. Clergy had left, vestries had died out, the state had seized most of the glebe lands, and "a deathlike silence pervaded the churches." As bishop, Meade changed all this.

He began his ministry as rector of Christ Church, Alexandria. Meade was ordained priest on 29 January 1818, by Bishop Thomas Claggett of Maryland, since Virginia had no bishop at that time. In 1814 he became the minister for Frederick County, and in 1821 he became the rector of Christ Church, Winchester. Largely through Meade's influence, Richard Channing Moore became the second bishop of Virginia in 1814, and he and Meade led the evangelical revival of the Episcopal church in that diocese. With Bishop Moore and William Holland Wilmer, he helped to found the Protestant Episcopal Theological Seminary in Virginia in Alexandria in 1823. He was an opponent of slavery and was one of the charter members who met in Washington, D.C., in December 1816 to organize the American Society for Colonizing the Free People of Color in the United States.

On 29 May 1829 Meade was elected assistant bishop of Virginia on the first ballot and was consecrated on 19 August 1829. He served as assistant bishop until 12 November 1841, when Bishop Moore died and he became the third bishop of Virginia. He served in that position until his death. He was strongly opposed to secession, but when Virginia left the Union he supported it. He insisted that it was one's duty to defend one's homeland when it was invaded. The first preliminary meeting of the dioceses in the Confederate States met in Montgomery, Alabama, 3–6 July 1861, and the second preliminary meeting was in Columbia, South Carolina, 16–24 October 1861. As senior bishop he presided at the Columbia meeting that drew up the constitution of the Protestant Episcopal church in the Confederate States. On 6 March 1862 Meade was chief consecrator of Richard Hooker Wilmer as bishop of Alabama, the only bishop consecrated by the southern Episcopal church.

Meade was a refounder of the Episcopal church in Virginia, a leader of the Evangelicals, and helped to found the Protestant Episcopal Society for the Promotion of Evangelical Knowledge in 1847, which was "to maintain and set forth the principles and doctrines of the gospel embodied in the Articles, Liturgy and Homilies of the Protestant Episcopal Church." He believed that the scriptures were the sole rule of faith containing all things necessary for salvation and that tradition was not equal with scripture. The scriptures were "the infallible word of God . . . our only rule of faith and great instrument of conversion and sanctification" (*Lectures*, p. 226). The job of the clergyman was to preach the message contained in these scriptures. The evangelical revival in Virginia was centered in the pulpit. Meade taught that preaching was to convict the hearer of sin and to state the truth as it is in Jesus.

One of the principal means of evangelical revival in Virginia sponsored by Meade was the establishment of "clerical associations," which were much like revival meetings. Usually held day and night from Thursday to Sunday, but sometimes for as long as ten days, they differed from a Baptist or Methodist revival primarily by ending with a service of Holy Communion. These associations were a primary evangelistic method to reach the unchurched and to inspire the indifferent.

Meade was a committed Protestant and a leading Episcopal evangelical bishop in the nineteenth century. He died in Alexandria, Virginia.

• Meade's papers are in the Archives of the Bishop Payne Library at the Protestant Episcopal Theological Seminary in Virginia, in Alexandria. His major publications were *Companion to the Font and the Pulpit* (1846), *Old Churches, Ministers, and Families of Virginia* (2 vols., 1857), *Lectures on the Pastoral Office Delivered to the Students of the Theological Seminary at Alexandria, Va.* (1849), *The True Churchman* (1852), *Reasons for Loving the Episcopal Church* (1851), and *The Bible and the Classics* (1861). A very helpful primary source is "Documentary History of the American Church: The Autobiography of William Meade," *Historical Magazine of the Protestant Episcopal Church* 31 (1962): 379–94. The major scholarly study of Meade is David L. Holmes, Jr., "William Meade and the Church of Virginia, 1789–1829" (Ph.D. diss., Princeton Univ., 1971). Other studies are John Johns, *A Memoir of the Life of the Right Rev. William Meade* (1867), and Philip Slaughter, *Memoir of the Life of the Rt. Rev. William Meade* (1881). William A. R. Goodwin, *History of the Theological Seminary in Virginia and Its Historical Background* (2 vols., 1923), and John E. Booty, *Mission and Ministry: A History of the Virginia Theological Seminary* (1995), are both helpful with regard to Meade and the seminary.

DONALD S. ARMENTROUT

MEAGHER, Thomas Francis (23 Aug. 1823–1 July 1867), Irish-American nationalist, lawyer, and soldier, was born in Waterford, Ireland, the son of Thomas Meagher, a merchant and member of the British Parliament, and (first name unknown) Quan. Both of Meagher's parents came from wealthy and prominent Irish families. His mother died while Meagher was an infant. He was subsequently educated at his father's alma mater, Clongowes-Wood, a Jesuit school in Ireland, and then at Stoneyhurst College in England from 1839 to 1843. Upon graduation he seemed destined to follow his father into a career in business, but in 1845 he joined the Young Ireland party and became embroiled in the rising debate over Irish independence from Great Britain. In the fateful year of 1848, when revolution swept over Europe, Meagher made an impassioned public appeal in Ireland for the violent overthrow of British rule. This advocacy earned him the popular title of "Meagher of the Sword," which he carried for the rest of his life. His determination to overthrow British rule by violence also landed him in difficulty with the British authorities. In July 1848 he was arrested, tried, convicted of high treason, and condemned to death. Partly because of the prominence of his family, his sentence was commuted in 1849, and the British banished him for life to the island of Tasmania (then a British possession) off the southern coast of Australia.

In Tasmania Meagher spent the first several years of exile quietly farming in the countryside. In 1851 he married Catharine Bennett, daughter of a British colonial farmer. They had two sons, but only one survived infancy. In 1852 Meagher escaped from Tasmania alone and made his way to New York City, which at that time had a rapidly expanding Irish immigrant community. Meagher's reputation as an eloquent and fiery proponent of Irish nationalism made him an immediate success on the burgeoning speaker circuit in America and an important voice in local politics of the New York City Irish. In addition to lecturing, he studied law, was admitted to the bar in 1855, and practiced until the Civil War. In his best-known case, the April 1859 murder trial of Dan Sickles, he participated as a junior defense counsel in the first successful use of the insanity plea in U.S. legal history. From 1855 to 1859 Meagher was the editor of the *Irish News*, the leading Irish immigrant newspaper in the country, and became a staunch supporter of the Democratic party in local and national politics. Following the death of his wife, who had returned to Ireland alone after briefly reuniting with Meagher in 1852, he married Elizabeth Townsend in 1855. The wedding ceremony was performed by Archbishop John J. Hughes, a friend of Meagher and the most influential American Catholic clergyman of the time. The couple had no children.

The secession crisis of 1861 plunged Meagher into a deep personal crisis. An ardent Democrat, he had supported the party position of noninterference with southern slavery. Like many European immigrants in the North, however, he was equally attached to the idea of an indivisible Union. News of the Confederate attack on Fort Sumter resolved Meagher's personal qualms, and he threw himself into organizing a company of volunteers for the Sixty-ninth New York Volunteer Militia Regiment, composed primarily of Irish immigrants. While serving as an officer with this regiment, he had his horse shot out from under him at the first battle of Manassas on 15 July 1861.

After the battle and the expiration of the term of service for ninety-day volunteers, Meagher returned to New York City in the fall of 1861 and raised the famed Irish Brigade, which eventually included the 63d New York, the 69th New York, the 88th New York, the 28th Massachusetts, and the 116th Pennsylvania regiments. Most of the soldiers in these regiments were either first or second generation Irish immigrants. In February 1862 Meagher, by now a brigadier general of volunteers in the Union army, became the Irish Brigade's commander. He commanded the brigade in the campaigns of the Peninsula, Second Manassas, Antietam, and Fredericksburg in 1862. At Fredericksburg the Irish Brigade suffered heavy casualties in a series of futile assaults against Confederate general James Longstreet's position on Marye's Heights. After Fredericksburg Meagher petitioned the War Department for authority to recruit replacements for the Irish Brigade, but his request was denied. Personally embittered and deeply dissatisfied with the treatment of his unit, he resigned his commission in early 1863 and returned to New York. Nevertheless, he continued to back the Union war effort at a time when Irish-American resentment of conscription and black emancipation was growing. In 1864 Meagher accepted a new appointment as brigadier general and was assigned as a military administrator with the Union army. In January 1865 he was sent to General William T. Sherman's command to assist with the military occupation of Savannah, Georgia. After the Confederate surrender at Appomattox, he was mustered out of military service.

At the end of 1865 Meagher received a patronage appointment as territorial secretary of Montana from President Andrew Johnson, who had been, like Meagher, a "War Democrat." In October 1865 Meagher became acting territorial governor of Montana, substituting for the absent governor, Sidney Edgerton. Montana at that time was inundated by white settlers and would-be gold miners fresh from the war. Meagher had his hands full attempting to mediate disputes in the mining camps and between restive Native American groups and white farmers hungry for cheap land in the West. Rumors have persisted that he was also involved at this time with the Fenian Brotherhood, a secret society of Irish Americans dedicated to invading Canada to strike at the British, but they have never been substantiated and remain doubtful in light of his public career and pronouncements. On the night of 1 July 1867 he apparently fell from the deck of a steamboat on the Missouri River and drowned near Fort Benton, Montana. His body was never recovered, and it was widely suspected at the time that drinking contributed to his death.

Meagher was a symbolic figure in nineteenth-century Irish-American history. Like many antebellum Irish immigrants to the United States, he ardently believed the ultimate goal of Irish nationalism in the United States to be the establishment of an Irish republic free from British domination. For many of these Irish immigrants, the Civil War was a watershed event that shifted the thrust of their political aspirations away from establishing a temporary refuge in the New World and toward the path of permanent assimilation into American society. Meagher's life and career exemplify that transition.

• Meagher's memoirs are in Michael Cavanaugh, ed., *Memoirs of General T. F. Meagher* (1892). Robert G. Athearn, *Thomas Francis Meagher: An Irish Revolutionary in America* (1949), sheds light on both Meagher's role as an Irish revolutionary and his importance in Irish-American politics in antebellum New York. A recent and comprehensive work on the Irish Brigade of the Union army is Paul Jones, *The Irish Brigade* (1969), which underlines Meagher's role and the assimilation that Union military service encouraged among the Irish Americans. See also David Powers Conyngham, *The Irish Brigade and Its Campaigns* (1867). An obituary is in the *New York Times*, 8 July 1867.

JAMES K. HOGUE

MEANS, Gardiner Coit (8 June 1896–15 Feb. 1988), economist and author, was born in Windham, Connecticut, the son of Frederick Howard Means, a Congregational minister, and Helen Chandler Coit. Means grew up in Massachusetts and Maine and entered Harvard at age eighteen. When the United States entered World War I in 1917, he joined the army. Though still requiring another semester to complete a degree in chemistry, Means received his diploma in absentia when the university awarded the bachelor of arts to students of the class of 1918 who had enlisted in the armed forces.

Commissioned as an infantry lieutenant, Means transferred to the Signal Corps and was sent to aeronautics school, where he survived a harrowing plane crash without injury. Military service did not send Means overseas but work for a charity did. Still hoping to go abroad when the war ended and he was discharged, Means joined Near East Relief, an organization formed in response to the murder and dispersion of Armenians in Turkey. Sent to Harput (now Elizaer) to provide vocational training for orphans, Means set up shops in which the youths learned shoemaking, hand-weaving, and carpentry trades. Having become interested in the textile industry, Means returned to the United States in 1920 and enrolled in the Lowell Textile School. Two years later he established the Means Weave Shop, a business producing hand-woven blankets that he continued until 1933.

Conducting business in the diverse markets of Harput and Boston made Means curious about economic structures in general and led him to graduate study at Harvard in 1924. As he worked through the economics department's rigorous yet largely conservative course of study, Means found it difficult to reconcile the classical economic theories of Smith, Ricardo, and Mill with what he had personally observed as an entrepreneur. Though possibly applicable to pre-industrial Britain or the open bargaining and trading he found in the marketplaces of Turkey, Means decided that models based on atomistic competition and flexible prices did not account for the impact of the Industrial Revolution. Influenced by his instructor William Z. Ripley's analyses of corporations, Means gradually came to believe that the rise of the factory system and major increases in the scale of organization and production made much of the prevailing orthodoxy inapplicable.

In 1927 Means received his master's degree, married economic historian Caroline F. Ware, and accepted an invitation from Columbia Law School professor Adolf A. Berle to work with him on an analysis of corporate development trends. Fellow soldiers at army officer's training, the two had been reintroduced through their wives, who were friends and former classmates at Vassar. Means and Berle's partnership proved exceptionally productive as Berle handled the task of researching the changing nature of corporate law while Means analyzed the degree of corporate economic power. Their work, published in 1932 as *The Modern Corporation and Private Property*, argued that the American economy had changed in two highly significant ways. First, a small number of immense corporations had come to tower over all others. By the 1920s, Berle and Means argued, 200 gigantic corporations controlled nearly half the assets and enjoyed more than 40 percent of all corporate income. Second, the dispersion of stocks had led to a fundamental separation of ownership and control. Rather than the commonly accepted model of a large number of small firms across a variety of industries, Berle and Means found massive corporations run by a separate management structure that conducted business free from any restraint placed on them by stockholders or government. With stockholders reduced to passive agents, a multitude of them had lost the ability to control their property. Power over the American economy, Berle and Means also argued, had become concentrated in the hands of an elite few who could not always be counted on to act in the public interest.

Stunningly successful, *The Modern Corporation and Private Property* ran through multiple printings and several foreign translations. Means's dissertation, "The Corporate Revolution," however, did not enjoy the same reception. In January 1933 Means submitted a compilation of his recent statistical studies and a section describing their theoretical significance to Harvard's economics department. His doctoral committee, however, rejected his theoretical arguments and finally approved his work on the basis of its quantitative analyses alone. Means received his Ph.D. later that year.

Though not fully embraced at Harvard, Means's views proved attractive to New Dealers interested in the potential for government intervention in the economy. Convinced that the problems of the Agricultural Adjustment Administration were linked to industrial issues, economist Rexford Tugwell persuaded Secretary of Agriculture Henry Wallace to hire Means as an economic adviser in the summer of 1933. As a member of committees in the National Recovery Administration and the Consumer Advisory Board, Means noted that some prices seemed more flexible and responsive to market forces than others. When overall demand slackened, agricultural prices had also dropped, just as orthodox models of competitive markets held they would. Many industrial prices, however, had fallen very little.

Through a detailed study Means found inflexible prices most frequently present in the industrial, oligopolistic sector of the economy. Building on his earlier work, he argued that, rather than reducing prices in response to falling demand, many large suppliers had instead kept their prices constant and cut their output, actions that deepened unemployment and diminished consumer purchasing power. Holding these "administered prices" as a significant factor in explaining the severity of the depression, Means concluded that laissez-faire approaches were misguided. In a dual economy of both market and administered prices, government had to take an active role to ensure public welfare.

Circulated through the Roosevelt administration, Means's report also gained the attention of Idaho's Republican senator William Borah, a fierce opponent of monopolies. Wrongly suspecting that distribution of Means's report was being tightly restricted, Borah secured passage of a resolution demanding that the administration submit the report to the Senate. Published in 1935 as *Industrial Prices and Their Relative Inflexibility*, the document spurred a growing debate. Opposed to trust-busting, Means believed that many large firms provided necessary efficiency in a complex, highly technical economy. The solution, he suggested, was to establish committees to balance consumer, labor, and corporate interests. Opponents of big business, however, made the most of Means's ideas in promoting antitrust actions.

Over the next several years Means attempted to develop a comprehensive model of the U.S. economy for policy planning. Serving on the National Resources Planning Board (later designated the National Resources Committee) from late 1934 through the middle of 1940, he projected employment and production patterns at various levels of consumer income and published his studies in 1938 as *Patterns of Resource Use*. During 1940 and 1941 he worked for the fiscal division of the Budget Bureau and studied problems of price control and war mobilization. Though his analytical methods were used by the War Production Board, growing differences of interpretation over postwar planning diminished Means's political influence. Many Keynesian economists and government advisers feared that a postwar drop in government spending would drive the economy back to depression conditions and advocated an increase in the wartime money supply to combat that possibility. Means, however, believed that monetary expansion would lead to dramatic inflation when wartime price controls were abolished. Unable to convince his colleagues, he left the bureau at the end of 1941.

After leaving government service, Means dedicated himself to lecturing, writing, and consulting. From 1943 through 1958 he worked for the Committee for Economic Development, a private business-sponsored research organization. Means also attempted to develop a macroeconomic theory that would include both flexible and administered prices, an effort that more traditional academic economists viewed with skepticism. Although conceding that Means had identified general trends in business concentration and separation of ownership from control, many of his critics maintained that such changes did not fundamentally alter industrial behavior. The interests of stockholders and managers, they argued, were not significantly divergent, and, far from clinging to rigid or fixed prices, firms generally responded to market demands as classical economic theory predicted. According to scholars such as University of Chicago economist George Stigler, Means's scattered evidence did not seriously challenge the traditional framework of analysis.

The recessions of the mid-1950s, however, once more gave Means a chance to play a role in public debate. In 1957 Estes Kefauver, chair of the Senate Subcommittee on Antitrust and Monopoly, started an investigation of the steel, auto, and drug industries and called on Means to testify. Demonstrating that recent price increases occurred primarily in highly concentrated industries, Means argued that post–World War II inflation resulted from the strategies large firms used to maximize profits. Contracting output instead of lowering their fixed, administered prices, firms contributed to higher unemployment and lowered levels of real income. Published as *Administrative Inflation and Public Policy* (1959), Means's analysis played a significant role in the Kennedy administration's decision in 1962 to advocate wage and price guidelines in industry.

Late in life Means continued to write, took an interest in conservation efforts, and returned to business as a partner in a sod company. His death in Vienna, Virginia, at age ninety-one left a divided legacy. Means worked outside the academic career structure, and his unorthodox views about the impact of powerful, institutional forces on the functioning of the market were rejected by most university economists of his time. *The Modern Corporation and Private Property*, his New Deal service, and his later congressional testimony, however, made him one of the most well-known social scientists of his era and gave him a major voice in shaping American public policy.

• The papers of Gardiner Means are housed at the Franklin D. Roosevelt Library, Hyde Park, N.Y. The extensive collection includes material from his service during the New Deal through his business interests in the 1970s. Material by Means pertaining to his service in specific government agencies may also be found in the National Archives. Means also wrote *The Holding Company* (1932), with James Bonbright; *The Modern Economy in Action* (1936), with Caroline F.

Ware; *The Structure of the American Economy* (1939); *Jobs and Markets: How to Prevent Inflation and Depression in the Transition* (1946), with several coauthors; *The Corporate Revolution in America* (1962); and *Pricing Power and the Public Interest* (1962). He also published a large number of articles and comments. Frederic S. Lee and Warren J. Samuels, eds., *The Heterodox Economics of Gardiner Means: A Collection* (1992), provides an assessment of Means's life as well as a selection of his writings. Bernard Nossiter, "The World of Gardiner Means," *New Republic*, 7 May 1962, pp. 17–20, and Alfred S. Eichner, "Gardiner C. Means," *Challenge* 22 (1980): 56–59, provide brief accounts of Means's career. Frederic S. Lee, "A New Dealer in Agriculture: G. C. Means and the Writing of *Industrial Prices*," *Review of Social Economy* 46 (1988): 180–202, offers an in-depth assessment of Means's New Deal activities. Warren J. Samuels and Steven G. Medema, *Gardiner C. Means: Institutionalist and Post-Keynesian* (1990), is useful as an interpretation of Means's scholarly ideas and their value. Obituaries are in the *New York Times*, 18 Feb. 1988, and the *Washington Post*, 17 Feb. 1988.

MICHAEL E. LATHAM

MEANS, Gaston Bullock (11 July 1879–12 Dec. 1938), spy, swindler, and detective, was born in Blackwelder's Spring, North Carolina, the son of William Gaston Means, an attorney, and Corallie Bullock. Means grew up in Concord, North Carolina, in a family that had lost most of its considerable wealth during the Civil War. He left the University of North Carolina in 1900, early in his third year, and served for two years as the superintendent of the elementary schools in Stanly County, adjacent to Concord. In 1902 he took a job as a salesman for the Cannon textile mills, living in New York City and traveling widely.

Means married Julie Patterson in 1913; two children would later be born to them. In 1914 he took a job in New York as an investigator with the William J. Burns detective agency. Before U.S. entry into World War I, Means served as a German spy, relaying information about armaments and ship movements. He was agent E-13 and reported directly to the assistant naval attaché at the German embassy in Washington, D.C. Means placed German agents in U.S. shipyards that were building submarines for shipment to England and France so that they could obtain information to demonstrate that the United States was violating neutrality laws. Means also served as a German propagandist, operating an organization he called the American Peace Society and circulating stories about Americans supplying British ships in New York harbor, also a violation of the neutrality statutes.

Means's subsequent career was marked by bizarre and sensational acts of skulduggery as well as by the probable murder of a millionaire heiress. In 1917 Maude King, the widow of a lumber baron, became the first major victim of Means's extraordinary ability to work his way into a person's confidence. Means's wife, before her marriage, had known King. When the acquaintance was renewed, Means began to gain the widow's confidence and to manage her finances. She apparently began to suspect that he had bled some $400,000 of her fortune for his own benefit. In August 1917 Means invited King to Concord, North Carolina, purchased a gun, allegedly for her, and took her on a barbecue outing that was to include rabbit hunting. Means's tale was that King was killed when she removed the loaded weapon from a tree limb where he had placed it and accidentally shot herself. Authorities in New York were convinced that Means had murdered King. They were, however, unable to have the trial transferred. A Concord jury acquitted Means, despite ballistic evidence that it was impossible for King to have shot herself in the back of her head. In part, the jury appears to have been irritated by the presence in the courtroom of "Yankee" prosecutors monitoring the proceedings.

Despite this episode, William Burns appointed Means as an agent in 1921 when Burns was named head of the newly created Bureau of Investigation in the federal Department of Justice. Soon Means was shaking down criminal suspects, promising that for a payoff he would fix their cases. He also solicited bribes to have liquor released from federal warehouses. Often he failed to deliver on these promises, but his victims were in no position to protest formally. Though earning only $7 a day from the government, Means employed three servants in his house and went about in a chauffeur-driven Cadillac.

Means was suspended by the bureau in February 1922 but was employed by the Treasury Department as a customs agent. In March 1924, while under indictment for federal offenses, Means testified before the Senate committee investigating the conduct of the attorney general of the United States. He brought with him two huge accordion cases that allegedly contained diaries of his government work but that actually had recently been concocted with the assistance of several secretaries. When he later was asked to deliver his materials to the committee, he said that he had given three large suitcases and a trunk containing his records to persons who represented themselves as Senate sergeants-at-arms. Nothing was ever found, undoubtedly because it never existed.

In June 1924 the government began the much-delayed prosecution of Means for violations of Prohibition law. His conviction in this trial and a subsequent one for extortion led to a sentence of four years in prison. At the federal penitentiary in Atlanta, rather predictably, Means worked his way into the good graces of the warden and served his term in cozy quarters with privileges accorded only a few inmates.

Once out of prison, with the collaboration of May Dixon Thacker, a writer and the wife of a prominent southern evangelist, Means wrote a bestseller, *The Strange Death of President Harding* (1930), maintaining that the president had been poisoned by his wife so that she could protect his reputation against allegations that when he was an Ohio newspaper publisher Harding had fathered a child with Nan Britton, a young admirer. The book is striking for its inventive genius and puts on display Means's talent for providing explicit details regarding trivial matters, such as clothing and house furnishings, and ostensibly verbatim quotations from people who were no longer alive. Such information, all secondhand, was intended to show the intimate connection Means enjoyed with the inner White House circle, though in truth he had never met Mrs. Harding. After authorities ridiculed the tale and Means could not supply the supporting documents he had claimed to possess, Thacker wrote, "with humiliation," that she had been duped by Means and that the book was a "colossal hoax."

When renowned aviator Charles Lindbergh's baby boy was kidnapped in 1932, Means thrust himself into that case by persuading Evalyn Walsh McLean, an extremely wealthy woman and a friend of the Lindberghs, that for $100,000 he would get the kidnappers to return the child. Subsequently, Means had a friend impersonate a gangster and demand another $4,000 from McLean. McLean traveled with Means to El Paso, Texas, to pick up the baby, but she reneged, fearing for her life, when he insisted that they proceed to Mexico to establish contact with the kidnappers, whom he said had become suspicious and left the United States. For stealing the $100,000, which never was recovered, Means was sentenced to ten years in prison and to an additional five years for extorting the $4,000.

Means's activities are often viewed as amusing episodes, perhaps because his victims, often shamefaced about their own gullibility, sought to downplay his thoroughly despicable behavior. Edwin P. Hoyt's biography of Means is titled *Spectacular Rogue* (1963), while a *New York Times* (15 May 1932) editorial portrayed him as "incurably romantic," noting, "He belongs to the half-world of facts and fancy, never knowing which is which." In her autobiography, McLean indulgently called Means "a fat and deeply dimpled scoundrel." But Means also can be seen as an unconscionable predator, meanly exploiting those whom he was able to ensnare in a web of deceit, and on at least one occasion he was very likely a cold-blooded murderer.

In his tale of Harding's death, Means wrote that he was "entirely aware of the fact that I am regarded as a consummate liar" but then noted defensively that "it is difficult for the lay mind to distinguish between trained dissimulation and lying." Means often would lie even when it might be to his disadvantage to do so. In a later, even more frantic attempt to get attention, he claimed that he himself had kidnapped the Lindbergh baby. Means died at the Medical Center for Federal Prisoners in Springfield, Missouri, where he had been transferred from the federal penitentiary at Leavenworth, Kansas, to undergo a gall bladder operation.

• A full-length biography of Means is Edwin P. Hoyt, *Spectacular Rogue: Gaston B. Means* (1963). Among others, Andrew Sinclair, *The Available Man: The Life behind the Masks of Warren Gamaliel Harding* (1965), pp. 285–87, provides an accurate portrayal of Harding's death from natural causes. The story of Means's involvement in the Lindbergh case is told in Evalyn Walsh McLean and Boyden Sparkes, *Father Struck It Rich* (1936), pp. 296–300, while his association with the Bureau of Investigation (later the FBI) is detailed in J. Edgar Hoover, "The Amazing Mr. Means," *American Magazine*, Dec. 1936. Obituaries are in the *St. Louis Post-Dispatch*, 12 Dec. 1938, and the *Concord (N.C.) Daily Tribune*, 15 Dec. 1938.

GILBERT GEIS

MEANS, James Howard (24 June 1885–3 Sept. 1967), physician and educator, was born in Dorchester, Massachusetts, the son of James H. Means, a manufacturer, and Helen Farnsworth. His successful father retired early to devote himself to aeronautical studies; his interest in science was an early and strong influence on his son. At age fourteen the young Means read Charles Darwin's *The Origin of Species*, an event that awakened an interest in biology that dominated the rest of his life. After graduating from Boston's Noble and Greenough School, he spent a year as a special student under William Sedgwick at the Massachusetts Institute of Technology; he then attended Harvard College, graduating with honors in 1907. L. J. Henderson was among his most influential teachers. Four years later he graduated from Harvard Medical School, where biochemist Otto Folin was an important figure in his growth. From 1911 to 1913 he was a house pupil on the medical service of the Massachusetts General Hospital, under David Edsall. In 1915 he married Marian Jeffries; they had one son. A fellowship took him to the Carnegie Laboratory in Boston to study calorimetry, then to the laboratory of August Krogh in Copenhagen to study blood flow, and on to England to work with physiologist Joseph Barcroft in Cambridge. He returned to Massachusetts General Hospital to initiate the measurement of basal metabolism, the first quantitative approach to the altered physiological processes in patients, which ushered in the modern era of quantitative medicine.

Recognizing that a principal application of measurements of the basal metabolic rate was in patients with thyroid disease, Means assembled a nucleus of interested physicians that evolved in the early 1920s into the Thyroid Clinic, an enterprise in which he was keenly involved well beyond retirement. This clinic was a model for the unit approach to the organization of the medical services of a hospital, whereby a small number of interested physicians are grouped into specialty services for teaching, clinical care, and research. This model was developed by Means in several subspecialties, including general endocrinology, hematology, pulmonary diseases, and cardiology, and was adopted in teaching hospitals worldwide.

After he was appointed to the staff of Massachusetts General, Means's work on metabolism proceeded in meager facilities. With U.S. entry into World War I in 1917, he joined the Army Medical Corps, serving first in Bordeaux with the Sixth U.S. Army Base Hospital, and then on detached duty in England working on problems of hospitalization for American troops; he attained the rank of lieutenant colonel. After discharge in 1919, he returned to Massachusetts General to work with friends and luminaries such as Paul D. White and

Joseph Aub. In 1923 he was chosen to be Jackson Professor of Clinical Medicine at Harvard and chief of the medical services at Massachusetts General, posts he held until his mandatory retirement in 1951.

Shortly after assuming the professorship, Means set about establishing a research ward, the first of its kind and the model for the Clinical Center at the National Institutes of Health. He considered this one of his most useful accomplishments. He and his staff used it regularly for clinical investigations. One of the most productive staff members was endocrinologist Fuller Albright, who made his seminal investigations on patients on what came to be known as Ward 4. Later Means wrote a charming account, *Ward 4* (1958), on the founding of the ward and of the scientific enterprise it nurtured.

An important milestone for Means and his medical service was a joint effort with investigators at MIT that introduced the use of radioactive iodine in clinical medicine. This began when Means and colleagues learned of the existence of radioactive isotopes of iodine and wondered about its possible use as an investigative tool in thyroid physiology. Robley Evans produced a small amount of a short-lived isotope that was initially tried in rabbits and later successfully used as a therapeutic agent in patients with overactive thyroid glands. Means's chief of the Thyroid Clinic, Saul Hertz, carried out these trials under his supervision. Means advocated such a multidisciplinary approach to problem solving and often spoke of the "fecundity of aggregation," a phrase that he borrowed from L. J. Henderson.

Means contributed more than 200 papers to the medical scientific literature and published several books, including *The Thyroid and Its Diseases* (1937), which went through several editions; *Doctors, People and Government* (1953); a history, *The American Association of Physicians* (1961); and a tribute to his father, James Means, *The Problem of Manned Flight* (1964), published by the Smithsonian Institution. One of his most memorable works was a short pamphlet, *The Amenities of Ward Rounds* (1940), long used as a guide to civil behavior for physicians in the presence of their patients.

In mid-career Means became interested in the medical-political scene. His position was that the people were not well-served by the medical establishment, and he was sharply and publicly critical. He advocated group practice and medical insurance, both of which at the time were anathema to the power structure within the American Medical Association. This earned him the abiding dislike of many in the profession, especially those who were influential in preserving the status quo and the fee-for-service pattern of payment. His thinking was ahead of his times, and much of what he advocated became standard practice within a few years.

In 1950 Means's wife died, and the following year he married Carol Lord Butler. After retiring in 1951, Means joined the staff of the medical clinic at MIT, where he thoroughly enjoyed the practice of medicine uninterrupted by administrative duties and where he developed many warm personal relationships, such as with mathematician Norbert Wiener and MIT's president, Jay Stratton.

Means was an expert watercolorist. He spent summer vacations at his home on Isle au Haut, Maine. There he devoted mornings to writing and keeping up with hospital affairs by mail and afternoons to painting. He held several one-man shows.

To some Means seemed austere, but to those who knew him well, he had a high sense of comedy and a facile turn of phrase; he wrote easily. He could be tough in argument over a clinical point, but he maintained a complete sense of intellectual equality. The door to his office was always open to his staff. Ward rounds were an obligation of staff members, and Means took his share each morning for two hours, for four months each year. His rounds, usually attended by visiting physicians from around the world, were lively and patient-oriented, featuring much give-and-take within the group; he always paid every attention to discretion in front of the patient, and he was always interesting.

Means traveled widely in Europe, South America, and the Far East. One of his proudest moments was being recognized at an event marking the completion of his tenure as visiting professor at Guy's Hospital, London, when he was given a plaque designating him as "perpetual student." Many awards came his way, including the Kober Medal of the Association of American Physicians, membership in many medical societies in the United States and abroad, and many visiting professorships and lectureships. Until his final illness he maintained an active interest in medicine, medical science, his friends and family, and the social and political scenes. He represented the best that American medicine had to offer.

• Among Means's most significant publications are "The Thyroid Hormone: The Use of Hormones, Drugs and Radiations in the Management of Thyroid Diseases," *Bulletin of the Johns Hopkins Hospital* 80 (1951): 90–120; "Government in Medicine: How Much?" *Atlantic Monthly*, Mar. 1953; and "Homo Medicus Americanus," *Daedalus* 91 (1963): 701. For a lengthy portrait of Means and an account of his career and accomplishments, see John B. Stanbury, *A Constant Ferment: A History of the Thyroid Clinic and Laboratory of Massachusetts General Hospital, 1913–1990* (1991). See also the tribute by Howard Sprague on the presentation of the Kober Medal, *Transactions of the Association of American Physicians* 77 (1964): 37. An obituary is in the *New York Times*, 6 Sept. 1967.

JOHN B. STANBURY

MEANWELL, Walter Earnest (26 Jan. 1884–2 Dec. 1953), basketball coach, was born in Leeds, England, the son of a shoemaker (his parents' names are unknown). Three years after his birth, the family emigrated to the United States, taking up residence in Rochester, New York. While attending high school, Meanwell developed an interest in athletics. As a member of the Rochester Athletic Club he served as captain of its baseball and basketball teams and won the Canadian lightweight wrestling championship.

Meanwell earned a medical degree from the University of Maryland in Baltimore in 1909 and served his internship there. In 1911, however, he accepted a position as a park athletic director. The decision set the course of his life over the next two decades. At some unknown date he married Helen Grath; they had three children.

As Meanwell instructed young boys in basketball, the restrictive floor space of one facility forced him to adapt their style of play. What had often been a rough, hectic game gave way to short, crisp passes, patterned plays, and greater finesse. Short in stature, and given to violent outbursts, "Doc" Meanwell earned a variety of nicknames, including the "Napoleon of Basketball," as his career progressed. He worked as Baltimore's supervisor of recreation and as director of athletics at Loyola University in Baltimore before assuming duties as basketball coach at the University of Wisconsin in 1912. Players at the college level did not take well to his martinet style, his tongue lashings, or his quick temper, but they relented when his innovative offense produced an undefeated season. His teams lost only one game over the next two seasons. They won twenty-nine straight games, twenty-three in Western Conference (later Big Ten) play, a record at the time.

Continuing his education while he coached, Meanwell received a doctor of public health degree in 1915. He resigned his coaching duties in 1917 to serve as a captain in the army medical corps for a year during World War I.

He came back from the service to coach at the University of Missouri, producing Missouri Valley Conference championship football and basketball teams from 1918 through 1920. In 1921 he returned to coach basketball at Wisconsin, a job that he continued to do until after the 1933–1934 season when he assumed duties as the school's athletic director. During his tenure as head coach, Wisconsin won nine league championships and finished second four times, compiling a 246–99 won-loss record. Meanwell's cumulative intercollegiate coaching record totaled 290 wins and only 101 losses. He trained many players who became successful coaches in their own right by adopting a well-disciplined motion offense combined with the tenacious defense that marked not only his teams, but his personality. The weave patterns, pivots, and screen plays of the "Wisconsin System" forced opponents out of their zone defenses and presaged the modern era of basketball.

Meanwell shared his knowledge as a clinician and author. He wrote a number of books: *Basket Ball for Men* (1922), *The Science of Basket Ball for Men* (1924), and *Training, Conditioning, and the Care of Injuries* (1931), which he coauthored with Knute Rockne. In addition, Meanwell served on several governance bodies, including the U.S. Olympic basketball committee and the National Basketball Rules Committee. He is credited with developing a basketball shoe and a valve that replaced the laces on a basketball.

On his retirement from the University of Wisconsin in 1935, Meanwell started a medical practice in Madison. In 1953 he was honored by the International Basketball Association for his contributions to the sport. It is not certain where he died. In 1959 the Naismith Memorial Basketball Hall of Fame awarded him posthumous membership as an outstanding coach. Meanwell had been a charter member of the National Association of Basketball Coaches and a member of the Helms Athletic Foundation Hall of Fame.

• Helpful biographical sketches of Meanwell are included in Zander Hollander, ed., *The Modern Encyclopedia of Basketball* (1979), and John D. McCallum, *College Basketball U.S.A.* (1978). An obituary appeared in the *Chicago Tribune*, 3 Sept. 1953.

GERALD R. GEMS

MEANY, George (16 Aug. 1894–10 Jan. 1980), labor leader, was born in New York City, the son of Michael J. Meany and Anne Cullen, both of whom were American-born children of Irish families that had migrated to the United States during the early 1850s. In 1899 the Meanys moved across the East River to a comfortable working-class neighborhood in the Bronx, where George (the first name on his birth certificate, William, seems never to have been used) grew up. Mike Meany was a plumber, and against his father's hopes for something better for his son, George Meany chose to follow in his father's footsteps. He left school at fourteen, worked for over a year as a messenger for an advertising agency, and in 1910 was taken on as a plumber's helper. He was inducted into Local 463 as a journeyman plumber in early 1917. By then his father had died, and when his older brother left for the army in April 1917 he became the sole supporter of his large family. In 1919, after a prolonged courtship, he married Eugenie McMahon, a garment worker. They had three daughters and a happy home life, which Meany assiduously shielded from his public career as a rising labor leader.

Initially, Meany was not much interested in union affairs, but his father had been an active local officer, and when George decided to run for the executive board in 1919, being Mike Meany's son won him the seat. Three years later Meany was elected a business agent—a full-time position—and although he was a first-class plumber he never worked at his trade again. Local 463 was an archetypal building craft union, usually open only to relatives of members, functioning as the organizing agency of the local labor market in conjunction with the contracters' association and concerned primarily with protecting the job interests of its members. The business agent had strictly bread-and-butter duties: he protected the local's jurisdiction, maintained union standards at construction sites, and settled disputes.

Meany proved to be an ace business agent, but his horizons quickly expanded. In the early 1920s the

New York construction trades were wracked by corruption: to cope with the situation, the American Federation of Labor (AFL) in 1923 chartered a new building trades council. Meany, a proponent of clean unionism, became the secretary and thus was thrust into the center of building trade politics in the city. In 1932 he became the building trades' delegate to the New York central labor council and, more important, was elected to the executive board of the New York State Federation of Labor.

The Great Depression was forcing the AFL to abandon its historic voluntarism, a shift signaled particularly by its advocacy of unemployment insurance from 1932 onward. Meany played a key role in fashioning an unemployment bill in Albany and sold it to the 1934 state convention with the kind of speech that became his hallmark—plainspoken and incisive. The speech capped his vigorous campaign for the presidency of the state federation. This full-time post enabled Meany to resign his job as plumber's business agent and begin a lifetime vocation as labor politician and federation leader.

His stint as head of the New York movement shaped Meany as a labor leader. He examined and put on firmer intellectual ground his roots in labor's pure-and-simple traditions. He studied Samuel Gompers's speeches, schooled himself in the AFL founder's labor philosophy, and late in life could still quote copiously from the Gompers canon. Meany was staunchly anti-Communist and opposed to any form of independent labor politics. In the battle over industrial unionism that came to a head in 1935, Meany recognized that the AFL leadership was blundering badly, but he opposed the formation of the Committee on Industrial Organization as a dual movement.

On the other hand, Meany became a New Dealer. The 1934 elections had created an exceptional opportunity in New York State: for the first time in over two decades, both houses were in Democratic hands, and the governor was the liberal Democrat Herbert Lehman. In the 1935 session, Meany later said, "we put more legislation on the statute books . . . in favor of labor than . . . in any period before or since by any other state"—including a model unemployment insurance act, reform of workman's compensation, and fourteen other major bills. The mix of roles—Meany the craft unionist (who still opposed the minimum wage for men at this point) and the New Dealer—was perhaps best exemplified by the successful strike he orchestrated in New York City in 1935 against the Works Progress Administration for refusing to pay the standard union rate to craft workers.

Meany was happy in his work and did not expect to go any higher. He knew that being the head of a state federation was a dead-end job in the American labor movement because the state federations lie outside the real power structure dominated by national unions. But Meany had caught the eye of the national chieftains, and with the aged AFL secretary-treasurer Frank Morrison about to retire in 1940, they tapped Meany as his successor. Initially, Meany did not think he had gotten much of a promotion. His constitutional functions were routine, and AFL president William Green (1870–1952) jealously reserved for himself the important work of making labor's case on Capitol Hill and at the White House. But events soon conspired to give Meany a larger stage.

After Pearl Harbor the AFL needed a strong voice in the wartime administration, which Meany provided as senior labor member of the War Labor Board. More important in the long run, Meany became the architect of an activist international role for the AFL. The key was his unrelenting anti-Communism, which was rooted in union voluntarism. For Meany, the litmus test of any political regime was whether it permitted independent trade unionism, so he remained, even during the Grand Alliance of World War II, an inveterate enemy of the Soviet Union. During the war the AFL began to send missions to Europe to aid in the setting up of non-Communist unions, and when the World Federation of Trade Unions was formed in early 1945 the AFL boycotted it because of the participation of Soviet unions. As the Cold War deepened, other western labor movements, as well as the Congress of Industrial Organizations (CIO), came over to the AFL's position and, with the AFL in the van, created the International Confederation of Free Trade Unions in 1949. Meany was an instrumental figure in this battle, supporting the vigorous pursuit of Harry S. Truman's Cold War policies.

Meany led the fight against the Taft-Hartley Act (1947), which the labor movement considered to be anti-union, and after its passage he helped expand the federation's political activities, which had consisted of little more than letters of commendation to prolabor candidates. With the creation of Labor's League for Political Education in December 1947, the federation joined the CIO as a major player in American electoral politics, bringing to bear large financial and organizational resources on behalf of candidates who supported labor's agenda. In 1948 labor contributed significantly to Truman's upset victory. Although the AFL was for practical purposes now allied with the Democratic party, Meany insisted that the federation was not departing from, but only invigorating, labor's traditional nonpartisanship.

If there were any lingering doubts about Meany's fitness for leadership, they were dissipated in a famous exchange between him and John L. Lewis at the 1947 AFL convention. The issue was the non-Communist affidavit required of union officers by Taft-Hartley. Lewis refused to sign and delivered a withering tongue-lashing against the AFL leaders for failing this test of their manhood. In response, Meany coolly enumerated what Lewis's heroics would cost the unions and then, moving to the offensive, blasted Lewis for having brought on the hated affidavit by recruiting Communists as CIO organizers during the 1930s. No one in memory had ever bested the fearsome Lewis in open debate; Meany's performance earned him widespread gratitude and marked his as the strong voice that the AFL sorely needed. When William Green died in 1952, it was a foregone conclusion that Meany would be his successor; at age fifty-eight he assumed the presidential office that, for practical purposes, he was already filling.

Meany's first task as president was to restore unity to the labor movement. He pushed through a no-raiding agreement with the CIO in 1953, opening the way to a solution of the key institutional problem: the rival jurisdictional claims by AFL and CIO unions. Since these could not be untangled, Meany proposed that the status quo simply be accepted, and insofar as overlapping jurisdictions created problems, these would be resolved over time by mutual consent of the interested parties. Meany also navigated through (or around) the factional quarrels roiling both federations and, despite prickly personal relations, worked well enough with the new CIO president Walter Reuther to solve a multitude of vexing issues. Because the AFL was twice the size of the CIO, there was no question that Meany would retain the presidency. In 1955 the merger was consummated, and labor's twenty-year civil war finally ended.

The next decade saw Meany truly in his element. The political machinery of the AFL-CIO grew formidable in these years. Operating through the Committee on Public Education (COPE), the AFL-CIO became the most important single electoral resource available to the Democratic party. Programmatically, Meany was committed to social unionism, which meant labor's adoption of the larger cause of social justice as its own. This meant a commitment to Keynesian policies as the key to sustained economic growth and an ambitious expansion of federal social welfare programs. Not much headway was possible under the Eisenhower administration (although Meany was on amicable terms with the president), but with the election of John F. Kennedy in 1960, labor's prospects brightened. Initially suspicious of Kennedy's successor, Meany found in Lyndon Johnson the presidential leadership he had been waiting for, and he played a central part in pushing through Johnson's Great Society program.

Meany was an early and consistent supporter of the civil rights movement, but he was cautious about confronting racial injustice within the labor movement and was not sensitive to the crusading dimensions of the civil rights struggle. It was Walter Reuther, not Meany, who spoke for labor at the March on Washington in 1963. But in the halls of Congress, Meany was a determined and effective partisan for civil rights. He stressed particularly the need for legislative action against job discrimination, in part because he knew that the labor movement lacked the capacity to root out discriminatory practices within its own ranks. It was his doing, more than anyone else's, that the Civil Rights Act of 1964 contained its far-reaching prohibition against job discrimination.

Meany was, if anything, even more enthusiastic about President Johnson the cold warrior. He fully backed the war in Vietnam, clung to that position when it destroyed Johnson's presidency, and afterward transferred his anti-Communist loyalties to Richard Nixon (while opposing his domestic policies). He felt betrayed when Nixon initiated the movement toward detente with the USSR and China in 1971.

The cultural revolution that swept the country during the Vietnam years deepened the isolation of the AFL-CIO and intensified the divisiveness within its ranks. Deeply conservative in his personal values, Meany was repelled by the sight of long-haired hippies and student radicals; he had little sympathy for the rioters beaten by the Chicago police outside the Democratic convention hall in 1968. When the Democrats nominated George McGovern in 1972, Meany—and hence the official AFL-CIO—withheld support and sat out the election.

In his final years, George Meany seemed to embody the faults of a declining labor movement, or what were perceived as faults by its critics: remoteness from the rank and file, complacency in the face of shrinking power and numbers, an ambiguous stance toward the claims of minorities and women, and rigidity in an age of sweeping cultural and economic change. Yet it was also true that, with his Bronx accent and gruff manner, his absence of pretence and his outspoken, uncompromising views, the Meany that Americans saw on television and that presidents confronted at the White House conveyed something of the enduring strength of organized working people in America. When the Watergate scandals broke, the AFL-CIO was the first major organization to call for Nixon's resignation. In 1974, in a memorable interview, Meany acknowledged that he had been wrong about Vietnam, that he had been lied to and misled, and that the AFL-CIO had learned a hard lesson about the trustworthiness of governments.

When he finally left office in November 1979, Meany was past eighty-five; he died within two months in Washington, D.C. Many thought he had long outlasted his time, but no national voice for labor's cause replaced Meany's in the increasingly hard times the union movement experienced following his death.

• Meany's official papers are deposited at the George Meany Center for Labor Studies, Silver Spring, Md. His formal positions are best studied in the convention proceedings of the New York State Federation of Labor (1932–1939), the AFL (1940–1954), and the AFL-CIO (1955–1979). Joseph C. Goulden, *Meany: The Unchallenged Strong Man of American Labor* (1972), a knowledgeable and sympathetic biography, covers Meany's life in detail up to 1972. Archie Robinson, *George Meany and His Times* (1981), is essentially an oral history drawing on extended interviews with Meany and others. There is an incisive briefer account by Robert H. Zieger, "George Meany: Labor's Organization Man," in *Labor Leaders in America*, ed. Melvyn Dubofsky and Warren Van Tine (1987). The institutional setting for Meany's career as federation leader is fully treated in Philip Taft, *The AFL from the Death of Gompers to the Merger* (1959). For a more recent synthesis, see Robert H. Zieger, *American Workers, American Unions, 1920–1985* (1986).

DAVID BRODY

MEARNS, Edgar Alexander (11 Sept. 1856–1 Nov. 1916), ornithologist, mammalogist, and army surgeon, was born in Highland Falls, New York, the son of Alexander Mearns and Nancy Carswell. He attended Donald Highland Institute in Highland Falls. When still very young, he grew interested in local plants and animals and planned a book on the natural history of the area, which he was unable to complete at the time. Many years later, in 1898, he did publish a fifty-page account of some of his conclusions as "A Study of the Vertebrate Fauna of the Hudson Highlands, with observations on the Mollusca, Crustacea, Lepidoptera, and the Flora of the Region" in the *Bulletin of the American Museum of Natural History*.

Mearns published his first paper on some rare birds found at West Point, New York, in the *Bulletin of the Nuttall Ornithological Club* (Jan. 1878); he soon followed it with other pieces on New York birds in *Forest and Stream*, *Bulletin of the Essex Institute*, and the *Auk*. He entered the College of Physicians and Surgeons in 1878. In 1881 he received his M.D., and he married Ella Wittich, with whom he had a son and a daughter. Following his graduation Mearns spent some time as a temporary curator of ornithology at the American Museum of Natural History in New York City, working on European birds and making arrangements to store his personal collections there.

Mearns was commissioned an assistant surgeon in the U.S. Army Medical Corps in December 1883. First posted to Fort Verde, Arizona, in 1884, he was transferred to Fort Snelling, Minnesota, in 1888. During his three-year stay there, he received a promotion to captain. He busily collected birds and other vertebrates during his off-duty hours at both posts. In 1891 he was able to spend some months between assignments at the American Museum of Natural History, where he worked up his collections and wrote several papers. Assigned as medical officer and naturalist to the Mexican–U.S. International Boundary Commission, with offices at El Paso, Texas, in 1892, he explored the boundary region west to the Pacific. Over a two-year period he collected more than 30,000 plant and animal specimens, together with many notes, and projected an ambitious report on the natural history and geology of the boundary region. A volume on the mammals, together with some biogeographical observations, would later be published as *The Mammals of the Mexican Boundary of the United States* (1907), but Congress declined to underwrite the larger project.

In the summer of 1896 Mearns was assigned to Fort Myer, Virginia, and in 1897 he was briefly stationed at Fort Clark, Texas. He made additions to his bird and mammal collections at Fort Clark and during his next assignment at Fort Adams, Rhode Island (1898–1900). Mearns spent some sick leave in Florida in late 1900 and early 1901, where he received a promotion to major. Before taking up his next assignment at Fort Yellowstone, Wyoming, Mearns spent some time studying specimens of larger tropical cats at the National Museum in Washington, later publishing several papers on the subject.

In 1903–1904, and again in 1905–1907, Mearns served in the Philippines, his tour of duty there being interrupted by a hospital stay in the United States. In 1903 he was instrumental in establishing the Philippine Scientific Association. Despite strenuous duty, including participation in eight expeditions designed to put down Moro tribesmen, Mearns steadily continued with his collections of birds and other vertebrates. He enjoyed cordial relations with Major General Leonard Wood, then the senior American officer in the islands, who encouraged Mearns's scientific work. In 1906 Major Mearns was placed in charge of a biogeographical survey of a portion of the island of Mindanao, and he later undertook a similar study of Mount Halcon, on the island of Mindoro. Mearns did not allow disease, the tropical climate, difficult terrain, or other impediments to interfere with his assiduous specimen collecting. On one occasion, he secured a choice parrot specimen by climbing a fence into a Moro compound and retrieving the bird from a well-armed tribesman.

Mearns's next assignment, at Fort Totten, New York, was interrupted when the Smithsonian suggested that he accompany Theodore Roosevelt, a friend of many years, on the latter's expedition to Africa. Though obliged to retire from the army, which he did in 1909 with the rank of lieutenant colonel, Mearns was immediately reassigned to active duty with the retiring president "by his consent." During this yearlong expedition Mearns was in large part responsible for the collection of more than 3,000 vertebrate specimens, primarily mammals, birds, and reptiles. Soon after his return to Washington in the spring of 1910, Mearns, who had not yet completed drafting his report concerning the birds collected in Africa, was asked to accompany Childs Frick on yet another trip to that continent. Although he was already suffering from the onset of diabetes, Mearns made the trip, collected some 5,200 additional bird specimens from eastern Africa, and again returned to Washington, hoping to complete the formal reports on both expeditions. The ravages of his illness gradually took hold, however, and despite his best efforts (insulin therapy having not yet been developed), he was soon incapacitated. He died in Washington, D.C. His son, a promising young astronomer, had died during Mearns's second trip to Africa.

Mearns published some 125 articles during his career, the majority of them on biological topics, though some concerned medicine and other subjects. More than fifty species of fauna and flora were named in his honor, together with one genus each of tree, fish, and bird, the latter all from the Philippines. A two-volume work, *Birds Collected by the Childs Frick Expedition to Ethiopia and Kenya Colony*, edited by Herbert Friedmann (U.S. National Museum Bulletin 153, 1937) was for the most part based on Mearns's field work and was considered a memorial to him. Mearns contributed some 37,000 vertebrate specimens to the collections of the National Museum (now the National Museum of Natural History), of which 20,000 were birds, 7,000 mammals, and the remainder divided approximately equally between reptiles and fishes. Mearns also contributed more plants to the National Herbarium than had previously been given by an individual collector.

• Mearns's papers are in the collections of the Division of Birds of the United States National Museum, housed in the Smithsonian Institution Archives. Other papers are in the Manuscript Records of the Surgeon General of the Army, Archives II, National Archives and Records Administration, College Park, Md. The principal biographical accounts are by Edgar E. Hume, in his *Ornithologists of the United States Army Medical Corps* (1942); and a memorial by Charles W. Richmond, in the *Auk* 35 (1918): 1–18. See also memorials in *Journal of the American Medical Association* (1916); *The Ibis* (London), 1917; and an obituary in the *(Washington, D.C.) Evening Star*, 3 Nov. 1916.

KEIR B. STERLING

MEASE, James (11 Aug. 1771–14 May 1846), physician, was born in Philadelphia, Pennsylvania, the son of John Mease, a wealthy merchant, and Esther Miller. His childhood was apparently a comfortable one. In 1784 he entered the University of the State of Pennsylvania, where he received his bachelor of arts degree in 1787 and master of arts degree in 1790. Two years later Mease was a member of the first class to graduate from the Medical Department of the University of Pennsylvania, which was created as a result of a merger between the College of Philadelphia and the University of the State of Pennsylvania.

In 1790, two years before he received his medical degree, Mease published a short paper on rabies in the *American Magazine*. Mease expanded this into his medical school thesis as *An Inaugural Dissertation on the Disease Produced by the Bite of a Mad Dog, or Other Rabid Animal* (1792). It was the first American contribution of note on the subject and was republished in London in 1793. Although his thesis was dedicated to his mentor and friend, Benjamin Rush, Mease's work stirred up a minor controversy between the two. Mease asserted that rabies had a debilitating effect on the system and thus proposed a stimulating regimen of strong tonics, opium, and mercurial ointments. Moreover, he strenuously opposed therapeutic measures that depleted the system, such as bleeding. Rush originally agreed with his student but later changed his mind, arguing that rabies resulted from excess stimulation and thus required bleeding and other methods of depletion. Rush's opposition to his friend's views prompted Mease in 1801 to issue his *Observations on the Arguments of Professor Rush in Favor of the Inflammatory Nature of the Disease Produced by the Bite of a Mad Dog*, wherein he reiterated his arguments against his former teacher. As a result of his work on rabies, Mease became the leading American authority on the subject and was consulted by physicians from across the country for advice concerning its treatment.

In 1793 a deadly yellow fever epidemic appeared in Philadelphia. Mease remained in the city to fight the malady and was one of the first to adopt Rush's controversial regimen of bleeding and purging. Despite their disagreements over the subject of rabies, Mease and Rush remained close friends. When Mease was afflicted with yellow fever during the 1793 epidemic, it was Rush who cared for him. In the wake of the epidemic, the Pennsylvania legislature passed measures to protect the port of Philadelphia from future outbreaks. The measures included the establishment of the post of resident physician of the health office of the port of Philadelphia. In 1794 Governor Thomas Mifflin appointed Mease to this post, in which he served faithfully until 1797. Whereas Mease opposed Rush's depleting therapeutics concerning rabies, he ardently supported Rush's bleeding and purging against the epidemic. Like Rush, Mease was also an advocate of the domestic origin of yellow fever. Mease in 1798 joined the short-lived Academy of Medicine, which was founded that year by Rush and his supporters to promulgate these views in opposition to the College of Physicians of Philadelphia.

Born into wealth, Mease did not require a medical practice to make a living. Moreover, in 1800 he married Sarah Butler, daughter of Pierce Butler (1744–1822), a wealthy planter and U.S. senator from South Carolina. They had five children. A man of many interests beyond medicine, Mease was financially secure enough to dabble in several of them. Although he never held an official appointment in a medical school, he did teach private courses. In 1813 he offered one of the first private courses of lectures on the diseases of domestic animals, and, in 1816 and 1817, presented private courses on pharmacy. From 1814 to 1815 Mease served as a hospital surgeon during the War of 1812.

Mease was associated with many of Philadelphia's learned and scientific institutions. In 1802 he was elected to the American Philosophical Society and served that organization as a curator and councilor. An owner of a large vineyard, Mease was one of the managers of the Company for the Improvement of the Vine, founded in 1802. In 1807 he was involved in the founding of the Philadelphia Mineral Water Association, the purpose of which was to manufacture seltzer water to be bottled or dispensed from fountains. This attempt by Mease and his colleagues to create the first soda fountain failed miserably, however. Mease was elected to the Philadelphia Society for Promoting Agriculture in 1805. An active member for many years, he was named the society's secretary in 1813. One of the founders of the Athenaeum of Philadelphia (1814) and the Pennsylvania Horticultural Society (1827), Mease served both of these institutions as a vice president.

Mease's diverse interests were reflected in his many publications. Besides medicine in general and rabies in particular, Mease wrote on veterinary medicine, geology, agriculture, local history, and penology. In 1795 he edited the third edition of *The Surgical Works of the Late John Jones*, which included his biographical sketch of the surgeon. His *Geological Account of the United States* (1807), *A Picture of Philadelphia* (1811), and *Archives of Useful Knowledge* (2 vols., 1811–1812) are among his many publications.

Although Mease was the leading American expert on rabies during his life, did much to promote the study of veterinary medicine and comparative anatomy by physicians, and was a leading figure in the learned and scientific life of Philadelphia, he is largely forgotten today. He died in Philadelphia.

• A small collection of James Mease's correspondence is at the Portsmouth Athenaeum in New Hampshire. The records of the Athenaeum of Philadelphia, the American Philosophical Society, the Pennsylvania Horticultural Society, and the archives of the Philadelphia Society for Promoting Agriculture, which are housed in the Special Collections of the Library of the University of Pennsylvania, document Mease's activities within these organizations. In addition to those mentioned in the text, Mease's important publications include his *Introductory Lecture to a Course of Lectures upon Comparative Anatomy, and the Diseases of Domestic Animals* (1814); *A Treatise on the Causes, Means of Prevention, and Cure of the Sick-Headache* (1819); "An Account of a Contagious Disease Propogated by a Drove of Southern Cattle in Perfect Health," *Memoirs of the Philadelphia Society for Promoting Agriculture* 5 (1826): 280–83; and "On the Hoof Disease from Eating Hay Affected with Ergot," *Memoirs of the Philadelphia Society for Promoting Agriculture* 5 (1826): 196–202. William Snow Miller, "James Mease," *Annals of Medical History* 7 (1925): 16–30, and J. F. Smithcors, "James Mease, M.D., on the Diseases of Domestic Animals," *Bulletin of the History of Medicine* 31 (1957): 122–31, are the only modern works on Mease available. See also James Boyd, *A History of the Pennsylvania Horticultural Society 1827–1927* (1929), and Simon Baatz, *"Venerate the Plough": A History of the Philadelphia Society for Promoting Agriculture 1785–1985* (1985).

THOMAS A. HORROCKS

MECOM, Benjamin (29 Dec. 1732–1776?), printer, was born in Boston, Massachusetts, the son of Edward Mecom, a saddler, and Jane Franklin, sister of Benjamin Franklin (1706–1790). When he was twelve, his parents apprenticed him to New York printer James Parker (1714–1770). Dissatisfied with the position, Mecom complained to his uncle about harsh treatment, but Franklin dismissed the complaints because he knew Parker was a conscientious employer. Mecom himself was hardly the model apprentice. He had a reputation for staying out all night without reason or excuse, and at one time he temporarily deserted his apprenticeship to board a privateer in search of fortune. Franklin attributed Mecom's restlessness to his youth and continued hoping he would prove himself worthy.

When Antigua printer and bookseller Thomas Smith died, Franklin, who owned the Antigua printing press, offered Mecom the business if he would allow him one-third of the profits. Mecom accepted the terms, and on 20 August 1752 he sailed from Philadelphia. While anxious to help his sister's son, Franklin was uneasy about the young man's business prospects: "I fear I have been too forward in cracking the shell, and producing the chick to the air before its time. . . . if Benny can but be prevailed on to behave steadily, he may make his fortune there. And without some share of steadiness and perseverance, he can succeed no where." Mecom began well, reviving the weekly *Antigua Gazette*, which had not been published since Smith's death, and ordering many books from England. Bookseller William Strahan sometimes refused to fill Mecom's large orders, but Mecom still became increasingly indebted to him. Though book sales were disappointing, the *Antigua Gazette* was popular enough to justify two issues per week starting in February 1755. Franklin offered Mecom more favorable terms, but Mecom longed to own the business outright. By the middle of 1756, he had discontinued the *Antigua Gazette*, shipped the printing equipment to Philadelphia, and returned to the mainland. After Mecom came back, Franklin prophesied: "I fear he will not for some Years be cur'd of his Fickleness, and get fix'd to any purpose" (Franklin to Jane Mecom, 28 June 1756).

Mecom next went to Boston, hoping to start a printing business. Before opening his own shop, he helped Zechariah Fowle print an edition of the *New England Primer*. Fowle's apprentice, Isaiah Thomas, would later remember Mecom as a dandy who set type wearing a powdered wig, ruffles, and gloves. Before the end of 1756, Mecom bought his old Antigua printing press from Franklin and had it shipped to Cornhill in Boston, where he set up shop. Shortly after settling there—the exact date is unknown—Mecom married Elizabeth Ross, daughter of the former mayor of Elizabeth Town, New Jersey; the couple would eventually have six children.

Mecom worked diligently for the next few years. His Boston imprints included almanacs, an introductory music handbook, conduct books, sermons, humorous dialogues, psalters, voyages, and the first separate reprinting of Franklin's *Father Abraham's Speech* (1758). Mecom's most ambitious project was the *New-England Magazine*, which he edited under the pseudonym "Urbanus Filter." The first number appeared in August 1758. Directed to both male and female readers, the periodical contained poetry, extracts from recent histories, burlesques of popular literature, devotional pieces, and original essays. The magazine was well conceived, but Mecom lacked the perseverance to see it through, and it faltered after the third issue (Mar. 1759).

Between September 1762 and June 1763, Mecom moved his family to New York City and, with a timely loan from Franklin, established a printing business there. On 11 July 1763 he published a sample issue of the *New-York Pacquet*. The paper died around six issues later—the latest known issue appeared 22 August 1763. Less than a year later, Mecom was bankrupt. To pay creditors, he surrendered the printing press and his stock of books to James Parker, who let Mecom take over his printing house at New Haven, Connecticut, in 1764 and appointed Mecom New Haven postmaster the following year. Mecom started slowly and was unable to revive the *Connecticut Gazette* until 5 July 1765, almost a year after he arrived. He kept the business afloat mainly by ignoring his creditors. Complaining about Mecom's financial irresponsibility, Parker described him as lethargic, indolent, sluggish, and torpid. But Parker pitied Mecom's large family and patiently urged him to pay his bills. The proud Mecom tired of Parker badgering him for his unpaid rent and resigned his commission as New Haven postmaster.

After printers Samuel and Thomas Green established a business at New Haven during late 1767, Mecom began looking for work elsewhere. He stopped the *Connecticut Gazette* after 19 February 1768 and moved his family to Philadelphia, where he found journeyman's work with printer William Goddard. Not surprisingly, Mecom made a poor employee. He came and went as he pleased and frequently quarreled with Goddard. After being dismissed, Mecom worked unsuccessfully for other Philadelphia printers. He reestablished his own printing business briefly and published the triweekly Philadelphia *Penny Post* starting 9 January 1769, but the paper died within a month.

Remaining details concerning Mecom's activities are sketchy. He was still in Philadelphia in 1770, as indicated by his application for a liquor license that year to help support his wife and children. In the early 1770s, he moved his family to Burlington, New Jersey, where he worked for printer Isaac Collins. Calling Mecom "the first person in the country who attempted stereotype printing," Isaiah Thomas wrote that Mecom cast plate for several pages of the New Testament but never finished the job. No additional evidence survives to confirm the story, but the anecdote jibes with Mecom's characteristic lack of perseverance. In 1776 two friends of his wife wrote that Mecom was "often Depriv'd of his Reason" and "likely to become very Troublesome" (John Lawrence and William Smith to Benjamin Franklin, 19 July 1776). A few years later, Jane Mecom wrote her brother about her son's last known whereabouts, placing him at the battle of Trenton (26 Dec.) or the battle of Burlington (11 Dec.), where he "was wandering about till the Hessians took possession of Burlington, when he disappeared and has never been heard of since."

Mecom never really fulfilled his potential as a printer and publisher. His numerous abandoned projects suggest that his ambition outstripped his perseverance. Still, he deserves to be remembered for his editorial efforts, most notably the *New-England Magazine*.

• For Mecom's American imprints, see Charles Evans, *American Bibliography* (1903–1934). Information concerning Mecom within Evans is easily accessible with Roger Pattrell Bristol, *Index of Printers, Publishers, and Booksellers Indicated by Charles Evans in His American Bibliography* (1961). See also Bristol's *Supplement to Charles Evans' American Bibliography* (1970). Mecom's newspapers are discussed in Clarence S. Brigham, *History and Bibliography of American Newspapers 1690–1820* (1947). Other sources include Isaiah Thomas, *The History of Printing in America*, ed. Marcus A. McCorison (1970); Holman S. Hall, "The First New England Magazine," *New England Magazine* n.s. 33 (1906): 520–25; Wilberforce Eames, "The Antigua Press and Benjamin Mecom, 1748–1765," *Proceedings of the American Antiquarian Society* 38 (1928): 303–48; and Carl Van Doren, *Jane Mecom: The Favorite Sister of Benjamin Franklin* (1950). The vicissitudes of Mecom's career can be traced in the *Papers of Benjamin Franklin* (1959–).

KEVIN J. HAYES

MECOM, Jane Franklin (27 Mar. 1712–c. 9 May 1794), the favorite sister of Benjamin Franklin (1706–1790), was born in Boston to Josiah Franklin, tallow chandler, and his second wife, Abiah Folger. The last of the seventeen Franklin children, Jane formed, with Benjamin and Lydia, a trio separated from their older siblings by a gap of several years. Benjamin and Jane outlived all the others; they were alike in many ways: intelligent, vital, indomitable. But whereas Benjamin rose in the world, Jane never had a chance. Married at fifteen to an almost illiterate and sickly saddler, Edward Mecom, she had twelve children, eleven of whom died before her, as did many of her grandchildren. The deaths were recorded with Christian resignation in her *Book of Ages*. She was forever cramped, spiritually and physically, squeezed in for years in her parents' house, then in her own Boston home, where poverty compelled her to take in lodgers.

Jane had a huge source of strength—her faith—and a huge source of joy, her brother Benjamin. He never let her down. He gave her much more than the money, clothes, flour, and wood recorded in their letters. He gave her a feeling of his need for her good opinion. Spread over sixty years, their extensive correspondence is woven with all the threads of the brother-sister relationship: a rough, teasing loyalty; an undercurrent of squabbling; a shared nostalgia for the world of their childhood, scented by the soap and candles their father made. Franklin's letters to Jane are far more interesting, both politically and personally, than those he sent to his wife.

The problem between brother and sister was always the same: faith. Jane never deviated from her parents' religion, rooted in the Puritanism of the previous century. Benjamin wandered far from it into a rational humanism, later to become a broad-minded deism. Never did he abandon his fundamental tenet that good deeds count more than prayer; never did Jane budge from the opposite position. While not reconciling their theological views, the two remained immensely fond of each other, and Benjamin's tone grew more gentle as his sister's life grew more tragic. He even made peace with what he called her "miffy temper," a tendency to take offense where none was meant.

While they always felt close, they did not spend much time together. Jane was only eleven when her restless, rebellious sibling ran away to Philadelphia in 1723. Every one of his subsequent visits home marked another step in his prodigious ascension. In 1724 he was the saucy adolescent showing off how well he was managing his newfound freedom; in 1733, married and a father, he was doing well as a printer and publisher; in 1743 his stay in Boston, just after he had withdrawn from business, allowed him to witness the first electrical experiments, the field on which his own future fame would be based; in 1753 he was there to receive his honorary degree from Harvard. Josiah Franklin's establishment, the Blue Ball, was sold that very year, and the Mecoms settled in Hanover street. Franklin's 1763 visit lasted all summer because of a fall from his horse. He showed off his daughter Sally's musical accomplishments, and as the Reverend Samuel Cooper (1725–1783), John Winthrop (1714–1779), and other Boston luminaries came visiting, Jane could enjoy the "suitable conversation" she was longing for. The last and most dramatic meeting took place in October 1775, when the brother, fresh from meetings with General George Washington in Cambridge, picked up his sister, who had fled Boston and found refuge in Rhode Island. He brought her back to Philadelphia in a carriage: such was Jane's capacity for happiness that the trip enchanted her in spite of the circumstances. She spent the next two years with Franklin's daughter Sally and her husband, Richard Bache, moving here and there as the war warranted before returning to Rhode Island and eventually to Boston, in 1784.

The disintegration of Jane's family was relentless. Three children died in infancy; most of the others, once they reached their midtwenties, were hit with a mysterious languor, went into a slow decline, and died. The two sons on whom the hopes of the family had once rested—Peter and Benjamin Mecom, apprenticed respectively to Jane's brothers John and Benjamin—both went mad after promising starts and had to be boarded out for years. Her husband died in 1765, having suffered much, she said, "by sin and sorrow"—a cryptic allusion, perhaps, to syphilis. All this was accepted humbly as Jane quoted Alexander Pope's "Whatever is, is right." Only once did she cry out in near revolt, at the death of her favorite child, Polly, who succumbed at nineteen in 1767: "Sorrows roll upon me like the waves of the sea. I am hardly allowed time to fetch my breath. I am broken with breach upon breach, and I have now, in the first flow of my grief, been almost ready to say, 'What have I more?' But . . . God is sovereign and I submit" (Van Doren, p. 98). By the time she was in her sixties, Jane had only one daughter left.

Even her modest business ventures were doomed, through no fault of her own. When Franklin was in London, in 1766, Jane started making artificial flowers "for the ladies' heads and bosoms, with pretty good acceptance" and asked for bright-colored bits of linen or cambric, as well as the latest patterns. Just as sales were picking up, they were hit by the colonists' refusal to buy imported goods—a move Franklin could only approve—and her business came to an end. From France, during the revolutionary war, he sent her various goods, *pacotille*, that she could sell. With the advent of peace, he asked her upon occasion to make batches of their family crown soap, of which she had the secret formula, for distribution among the ladies of Paris. After he settled again in Philadelphia in 1785, and they both knew themselves too infirm ever to meet again, Jane could not help dreaming of them under the same roof, engaging "in a litle familiar Domestic Chit Chat like common folks" (Van Doren, p. 240). He bequeathed her the Boston house and a life income of £50. Jane outlived her brother by four years and reminisced to the end about the pleasures he had given her: "they passed like little streams from a beautiful fountain" (Van Doren, p. 342). She died in Boston.

The significance of her life lies in having brought out, more than any other woman, the protective, tender side of Franklin's nature. She gave him the unconditional adoration that, for all his jesting, he probably craved: "I think it is not Profanity to compare you to our Blesed Saviour who Enploued much of his time while hear on Earth in doing Good to the bodys as well as souls of men and I am shure I think the compareson Just ofton when I hear the calumny Invented and thrown out aganst you while you are Improveing all your Powers for the salvation of them very Persons" (Van Doren, p. 149).

• Correspondence can be found in Carl Van Doren, *The Letters of Benjamin Franklin and Jane Mecom* (1950; in some cases, where original correspondence no longer exists, quotations appear in modern English); Van Doren also has produced *Jane Mecom, the Favorite Sister of Benjamin Franklin* (1950). Also see Claude-Anne Lopez and Eugenia W. Herbert, *The Private Franklin: The Man and His Family* (1975).

CLAUDE-ANNE LOPEZ

MEDARY, Samuel (25 Feb. 1801–7 Nov. 1864), editor, politician, and territorial governor of Minnesota and Kansas, was born in Montgomery Square, Montgomery County, Pennsylvania, the son of Jacob Medary, a farmer, and Mercy Bennett, a member of the Society of Friends. He attended an academy in Norristown, where he wrote poetry for a local newspaper and taught intermittently in a nearby Quaker school to pay for his education. After spending five years in Montgomery County, Maryland, and Georgetown, District of Columbia, he settled in Batavia, Ohio, in 1825 and was elected county surveyor, county auditor, and a school trustee. He married Eliza Scott in 1823; they had twelve children.

In 1828 Medary established the *Ohio Sun* in Bethel but soon moved it to Batavia. He was elected to the Ohio house in 1834, serving one term, and then to the state senate, where he served two terms. Moving his residence to Columbus, he purchased the *Western Hemisphere* in 1837 and changed its name to the *Ohio Statesman*. He made the paper the official organ of the Democratic party in Ohio, and his articles were quoted widely in the state's county presses during the 1840s. By then he was recognized as "one of the leading Democratic journalists north of the Ohio River" (Weisenburger, p. 184). His party associates made him the state's supervisor of printing in 1837, a post he held for the next decade despite being investigated for malfeasance of office in 1839 and 1840. He also served as president of the state board of agriculture and helped found several railroads.

An ardent supporter of Andrew Jackson and Martin Van Buren, Medary was a hard money, antibank

Democrat, although patronage desires caused him to vacillate on these questions, as when he endorsed Senator Lewis Cass for president in 1848. In 1844 Medary was a delegate to the Democratic National Convention in Baltimore. When his candidate, Van Buren, faltered, he threw his support to James K. Polk, embracing the Tennessean's expansionist program. He was recommended by the Ohio congressional delegation for postmaster general but had to settle for the postmastership in Columbus, a job he held for about one year. During this time he relinquished control of the *Statesman*, only to resume it in 1846.

A supporter of the Mexican War, Medary was an ardent expansionist, part of the group referred to as "Young America." In 1843 he helped organize and became vice president of the convention at Cincinnati, which advocated annexing all of the Oregon Territory. He is recognized by some as having coined the slogan "fifty-four forty or fight," a phrase also attributed to his factional opponent in Ohio, Senator William Allen (1803–1879).

Because of the patronage difficulty with Polk and concern for the problem created by the slavery question in Ohio politics, Medary backed Cass for president in 1848. He erroneously believed that "popular sovereignty" would satisfy Ohioans' opposition to the extension of slavery into the territories. When it failed to assuage Ohio voters, he repudiated the idea and changed his positions frequently during the next several years, helping a Free Soil–Democratic alliance elect Salmon P. Chase to the U.S. Senate in 1849 and favoring Stephen A. Douglas's Kansas-Nebraska Act in 1854. He accepted the *Dred Scott* decision as a solution to the issue of slavery in the territories in 1857. His positions were determined not by racial views but by political necessity during this time of turmoil in Ohio politics.

Interestingly, Medary's prestige was at an all-time high during this period. He was elected to preside at the Democratic state convention in 1846 and later became the leader of a successful effort to rewrite the Ohio constitution. As a delegate to the constitutional convention in 1850 and 1851, he advocated limitations on the state's indebtedness and reorganization of the judiciary to make the court system more efficient. He opposed special legislation creating charters of incorporation, helped to secure unlimited individual liability of stockholders in corporations, and championed taxation of corporations and banks the same as individuals.

In 1852 Medary was publicly neutral in the presidential race while privately (but unactively) favoring Douglas. When Franklin Pierce was nominated, the *Statesman* gave him enthusiastic backing. Although Medary once again hoped to become postmaster general, he was appointed U.S. minister to Chile in May 1853 but resigned before assuming the post to campaign for the U.S. Senate. He was the only candidate to endorse Douglas's Kansas-Nebraska Act. Defeated for the Senate, he failed to win the gubernatorial nomination in 1855 and once more became editor of the *Statesman*, continuing until 1857.

Medary opposed James Buchanan in the Democratic convention in 1856 but, after "Old Buck's" nomination, worked hard for him. Buchanan appointed Medary governor of the Minnesota Territory on 13 March 1857. As the territory's last governor, he lived in Minnesota for only a few months and showed little interest in its affairs. Despite a partisan struggle between Democrats and Republicans that led to two separate state constitutional conventions, Medary did not intervene, and when the parties met to compromise their different charters, he did nothing to delay statehood. Although he remained governor until Congress approved the new constitution in May 1858, his duties were in fact handled by a subordinate.

Medary returned to Columbus as postmaster but was chosen on 23 November 1858 to be governor of the Kansas Territory. He made a futile attempt to capture John Brown (1800–1859) and initially supported the proslavery Lecompton constitution. When the failure of Lecompton became apparent, he responded to pressure and called for election of delegates to a new constitutional convention. Meeting at Wyandotte in July 1859, the Kansans drafted a constitution modeled on the Ohio document of 1851 that Medary had helped create. As the Democratic nominee for governor of Kansas in 1859, he was defeated by Charles Robinson (1818–1894). In February 1860 Medary vetoed a bill abolishing slavery in the territory, saying that it was political and premature because it enacted one of the provisions of the new state constitution. The legislature overrode him, but the territorial supreme court later upheld his position.

As Kansas neared statehood, Medary resigned in December 1860 and returned to Columbus, where he began publishing the *Crisis*. He criticized the South for secession and the North for coercion. He tried to be neutral in the war as a leader of the "Copperheads" or "peace faction" within the Democratic party. He presided at the party's state convention in 1862 and in the general election helped make possible its first victory in Ohio in nine years.

At the Jackson Day dinner in January 1863, Medary began a sustained and violent assault on President Abraham Lincoln and his administration. He advocated Lincoln's impeachment for arbitrary arrests and criticized the president for his despotic blockade of the southern ports, expenditure of money on the military without congressional approval, and suspension of the writ of habeas corpus. As a bitter and caustic critic of the administration, Medary and his newspaper became notorious among Republicans and Lincoln supporters. Members of the Second Ohio Cavalry, stationed near Columbus, sacked the *Crisis*'s office in 1863.

Medary made a feeble attempt to secure the gubernatorial nomination in 1864, but wracked by illness, he began to retire from public life. Elected as a delegate to the Chicago convention in 1864, he did not attend and did not support George B. McClellan (1826–

1885), the party nominee. By now he was convinced that the Civil War was hopeless and advocated an end to the fighting and withdrawal from the South. He was arrested and indicted for "disloyal utterances" in 1864 but died in Columbus before being tried.

• A small number of Medary papers are located at the Ohio Historical Society in Columbus. A good short biographical sketch is Helen P. Dorn, "Samuel Medary—Journalist and Politician, 1801–1864," *Ohio State Archaeological and Historical Quarterly* 5 (1944): 14–38. Information on his newspaper career is found in Osman Castle Hooper, *History of Ohio Journalism, 1793–1933* (1933); Hooper, *The Crisis and the Man, an Episode in Civil War Journalism* (1929); and Stuart Sprague, "Sam Medary, Fight for the Press," *Civil War Times Illustrated* 22 (1983): 36–41. For Medary's political involvement in Ohio see Francis P. Weisenburger, *The Passing of the Frontier, 1825–1850*, vol. 3 of *The History of the State of Ohio* (1941); Stephen E. Maizlish, *The Triumph of Sectionalism: The Transformation of Ohio Politics, 1844–1856* (1983); Eugene H. Roseboom, *The Civil War Era, 1850–1873*, vol. 4 of *The History of the State of Ohio* (1944); and Frank L. Klement, *The Copperheads in the Middle West* (1960). Medary's experiences as a territorial governor are discussed in Thomas A. McMullin and David Walker, *Biographical Directory of American Territorial Governors* (1984); Homer E. Socolofsky, *Kansas Governors* (1990); William E. Connelley, *Kansas Territorial Governors* (1900); and W. W. Folwell, *A History of Minnesota* (1956). An obituary is in the *New York Times*, 13 Nov. 1864.

ROBERT S. LA FORTE

MEDILL, Joseph (6 Apr. 1823–16 Mar. 1899), editor and principal owner of the *Chicago Tribune* (1855–1899), was born on a small farm near what is now St. John, New Brunswick, Canada, the eldest son of William Medill and Margaret Corbett. His parents were immigrants from Belfast, Ireland, where his father and grandfather were shipbuilders. The family moved to Stark County, Ohio, near Massillon, when Medill was nine. There he attended the Massillon Village Academy and later studied law for about two years in nearby Canton, Ohio. He established a law practice in New Philadelphia, Ohio, soon after being admitted to the bar in November 1846. There he met Katharine Patrick, daughter of the owner of the *Tuscarawas Advocate,* who taught him how to set type. They married in 1852. The couple had three daughters.

On slow days during his law practice, Medill passed time at the offices of local newspapers, becoming interested in politics and journalism. Starting out as a staunch Whig editor, Medill, along with his three younger brothers, purchased the *Coshocton* (Ohio) *Democratic Whig,* in 1849, but soon renamed it the *Republican.* Medill appointed himself editor-in-chief and made his brothers his assistants. He moved to Cleveland in 1851, and in April 1852 established the *Daily Forest City,* a Whig paper. It was renamed the *Cleveland Leader* in 1854 after Medill became a partner with John C. Vaughan, a South Carolina abolitionist and the editor of the *True Democrat.*

When the Whig party failed in the 1852 presidential election, Medill became involved in the formation of a new, antislavery party to replace it. There is evidence that at a secret meeting in the office of the *Cleveland Leader* in March 1854, plans for a new party were adopted, and that Medill was the first to advocate the name Republican.

Medill became managing editor of the *Chicago Tribune* in the spring of 1855 when the newspaper was floundering and its owners hoped to find a buyer. When Dr. Charles H. Ray heard the paper was for sale, he was interested and wrote to Horace Greeley asking for advice. Greeley suggested that he contact Medill. Medill and Ray entered into a partnership to purchase a controlling interest in the *Tribune.* Both men were confirmed abolitionists, converts to the new Republican party, and bitter opponents of Senator Stephen Douglas. Under the terms of the partnership, Ray became editor in chief, and Medill was general manager and managing editor. Ray wrote the editorials, while Medill supervised the daily news and business operations. When Ray left the newspaper in November 1863, Medill became editor-in-chief. During a financial panic in the winter of 1857–1858, the *Tribune* suffered, and rather than see his newspaper fail, Medill merged it with the *Democratic Press.* From July 1858 to November 1860 the paper published as the *Press and Tribune.*

After John Frémont's defeat in the 1856 presidential election, Medill began planning for the 1860 election. In an interview published in the *Saturday Evening Post* in 1899, Medill recalled that the strategy to secure the 1860 Republican presidential nomination for Abraham Lincoln was devised in the *Tribune*'s offices in the summer of 1859. In December 1859, the strategy was put into action when Medill went to Washington, D.C., as the *Tribune*'s correspondent. Once there, Medill promoted Lincoln's candidacy and boosted Chicago as the site of the 1860 Republican National Convention. When the convention opened, Medill ensured that uncommitted delegations were seated close to delegations that supported Lincoln. Medill and his circle promised cabinet posts in exchange for delegate votes, thus obtaining the support of Indiana, Pennsylvania, and Ohio. When Ohio shifted its support to Lincoln on the second ballot, it began a landslide that gave Lincoln the nomination.

During the Civil War, Medill supported Lincoln's policies, although at times he seemed impatient with the president and even scolded him in person when Lincoln visited the *Tribune*'s offices. *Tribune* editorials harangued Lincoln to declare emancipation, confiscate Southern property, and accelerate the war effort. Medill may have supported the abolition of slavery, but his views on African Americans were racist. In a letter to his brother William, written in 1863, Medill said that "In future wars black and yellow men will be freely used to fight. We will not be so careful about spilling the blood of niggers." However, Medill was among the earliest to advocate the arming of slaves. He insisted that no soldier in the field lose his right to vote during the war; because of Medill's urging, several states passed laws to that effect in 1864.

Medill lost control of his beloved *Tribune* in 1865 when Horace White, Alfred Cowles, and William Bross purchased enough shares of Tribune Company stock to form a majority. Dr. Ray succeeded Medill, but was eventually supplanted by White. Medill still held stock and supervised the editorial department, but was otherwise powerless.

Medill ventured into politics and government service for a brief period following his loss of power at the *Tribune*. He served as a delegate to the Illinois constitutional convention in 1869, and was appointed by President Ulysses S. Grant to the first Civil Service Commission in 1871. Also in 1871, he fell twenty votes short of the Republican state party nomination for Congress. Medill and the *Tribune* became an inspirational force in the recovery of Chicago from the disastrous fire of 1871. As a result Medill was elected mayor of Chicago, serving from 1872 to 1874. Although he worked to reduce patronage and bring civil service reform to the city's government, his term was stormy because his policies reflected the probusiness, antilabor, and xenophobic positions of his newspaper. When he announced in July 1873 that he would not seek reelection, he and his family left for a European trip, not returning until his term had expired.

After his return in 1874, Medill purchased $300,000 of *Tribune* stock, aided by a loan from Marshall Field, to acquire full control of the paper. Under Medill's direct daily control, the *Tribune* supported Republican policies nationally, and Chicago business and industry interests locally. The newspaper supported some labor demands, such as an eight-hour workday and "decent pay" for railroad workers. Medill and the *Tribune* attacked monopolists because he feared that the exploitation of labor would cause labor unrest, which he deeply feared.

The *Tribune*'s antilabor views became strident and vituperative as Medill blamed communists, anarchists, and socialists for the violence caused by labor unrest. The invective nature of the *Tribune*'s attacks on labor, especially following the Haymarket bombing, have lead some historians to accept uncritically a misstatement of fact originated by George Seldes in his *Lords of the Press* (1938). Seldes said an item in the 12 July 1877 issue of the *Tribune* was an example of Medill's inhumane policy toward labor. The item, located at the bottom of page eight under the heading "The City/General News," advised Chicago leaders to place arsenic in the food served at city shelters to the unemployed. It was not a *Tribune* editorial, as Seldes said. Editorials were published on page four at that time. The section containing the item was routinely used to print comments by suburban reporters and stringers. While the item never should have been printed, it cannot be taken as either a statement of *Tribune* policy or the personal view of Medill.

He remained actively in charge of the paper until his death, although during the 1890s he gradually transferred control to his sons-in-law, Robert W. Patterson, Jr., and Robert Sanderson McCormick. Medill died while spending the winter at his ranch in San Antonio, Texas. His physician reported that his last words were "What's the news this morning?" His grandsons, Robert R. McCormick and Joseph M. Patterson, shared control of the *Tribune* until Patterson left for New York to found the *Daily News;* granddaughter Eleanor Medill Patterson, called "Cissy," published the *Washington Times-Herald;* great-granddaughter Alicia Patterson Guggenheim founded Long Island's *Newsday,* and another great-granddaughter, Josephine Patterson, was a reporter for the *Chicago Daily News.*

Medill was a bold and colorful editor with a great degree of national influence. In an era of personal journalism, Medill's newspaper voice was loud and strong. Although he could be vehement and cruel in his attacks on persons or parties he believed threatened what he supported, he vigorously promoted the Republican party, defended American business, and boosted Chicago as the greatest city in America.

• Medill's only published works of significance were the news items and editorials he wrote for the *Tribune.* His personal papers are kept in the Tribune Company Archives in Chicago. Major secondary sources are Philip Kinsley, *The Chicago Tribune: Its First Hundred Years* (3 vols., 1943–1948), a richly detailed, but clearly authorized history. John Tebbel, *An American Dynasty* (1947), is useful but repeats Seldes's error. Lloyd Wendt, *Chicago Tribune: The Rise of a Great Newspaper* (1979), is better balanced. Obituaries appeared in the *New York Times, Chicago Tribune,* and *Chicago Times Herald,* 17 Mar. 1899.

JOSEPH P. MCKERNS

MEDINA, Harold Raymond (16 Feb. 1888–14 Mar. 1990), lawyer, teacher, and judge, was born in Brooklyn, New York, the son of Joaquín Adolfo Medina, a Mexican importer who became a U.S. citizen, and Elizabeth Fash, an Episcopalian of Dutch descent. Medina, a product of Brooklyn's aspiring middle classes, graduated from Princeton in 1909 with an A.B., a Phi Beta Kappa key, and highest honors in French. He received an LL.B. from Columbia Law School at the head of his class in 1912. Starting as a poorly paid law clerk, he became a prominent Manhattan attorney between the two World Wars by teaching, scholarship, and private practice. He was a part-time teacher and scholar of New York procedure at Columbia Law School, founder of a popular bar examination course that made him a millionaire, and a leading appellate advocate.

After Medina's bungled pleading appeared to provoke a client's suicide in 1915, the young lawyer lost his nerve for trials and concentrated on appeals for two decades. Learning from other attorneys' mistakes in more than 1,300 appeals, he returned to trial work in the 1930s, becoming a highly respected trial counsel. His forte was complex litigation requiring a mind for both detail and grand strategy from trial through appeal. His important cases included the 1932 mayoralty succession case that paved the way for Fiorello H. LaGuardia's election as mayor of New York City; the Bank of the United States prosecution of 1931–1933, involving the largest bank failure of the Great Depression; and *U.S. v. Cramer* in 1942–1945, a milestone in American law of treason. As assigned counsel in the *Cramer* case, he saved an alleged harborer of Nazi saboteurs from execution and persuaded the Supreme Court to stiffen standards of proving treason under the historic two-witness rule of the Constitution.

Justice William O. Douglas, a student of his at Columbia, described Medina as "bright, able, and a ham actor." Tall, stocky, and darkly handsome, he was a colorful individualist who converted classrooms and courtrooms into live theater. His daunting energy, systematic mind, warmth, humor, and childlike ego formed a powerful public persona that overshadowed his private erudition, religious faith, and passion for literature. People often said he belonged in Hollywood.

In 1947 President Harry S. Truman nominated Medina as a federal judge in the Southern District of New York in response to a unique campaign by bar associations to sponsor a specific nominee for the federal bench. His appointment over the opposition of local party bosses was hailed as a triumph of professionalism over politics. In 1949 he shot into world fame as the dominant figure in one of the great political show trials in American history, *U.S. v. Dennis*, in which eleven top leaders of the Communist Party USA were tried under the Smith Act for conspiring to advocate violent overthrow of the government. After nine tumultuous months in which the defense attempted to provoke a mistrial and accused the court of trying Marxist-Leninist ideas, all eleven were convicted. Medina then summarily punished Eugene Dennis and five other defense counsel for attempting to obstruct justice and impair his health. These controversial decisions, upheld on appeal by divided courts, advanced popular perceptions of the Communist party as a revolutionary conspiracy controlled by Moscow, reconciled Smith Act prosecutions of Stalinists with the First Amendment, and bolstered judicial contempt powers in political trials. Medina, lionized by the news media as "Judge Patience" and demonized by the left, became a symbol of American justice—or injustice—and a folk hero to millions during the Cold War. He was the most famous trial judge of his time.

He was promoted to succeed Learned Hand on the U.S. Court of Appeals for the Second Circuit in 1951, but he continued to preside over a mammoth antitrust trial of seventeen leading investment banking firms until 1953. After two years of hearing the government's evidence in *U.S. v. Morgan*, he dismissed civil conspiracy charges that the syndicate system of underwriting securities was used to monopolize the industry in violation of the Sherman Antitrust Act. His opinion became a classic in the fields of antitrust and investment banking, and the government did not appeal. The *Morgan* decision, rejecting New Deal premises of a "Wall Street conspiracy," legitimated a prime method of raising capital in the industrial economy and postwar boom.

Medina served on the court of appeals until 1958 and then as a senior circuit judge with a reduced workload. He heard his last case in 1980 at age ninety-two, the oldest judge on the federal bench. His appellate opinions fall into three groups. First were innovations in public law, such as advancing arbitration as an alternative to adjudication and allocating costs of notice in class action suits (*Eisen v. Carlisle & Jacquelin*, 1968 and 1973). Second were so-called "stinkers," cases that clarified complex conflicts, including the French Connection drug smuggling case in 1972 and the Vesco fraud case in 1979. He relished stinkers despite his loud complaints about overwork. Third, and perhaps most revealing, were unconventional solutions for outsiders caught in the maw of bureaucracy. For example, in 1967 he gave draft director General Lewis B. Hershey "a good kick in the pants" for threatening to reclassify students protesting the Vietnam War. His dissent against a ruling that Christmas gifts to private club employees were taxable income began: "Yes, Virginia, there is a Santa Claus."

Medina died at age 102 in Westwood, New Jersey, and was buried near his home at Westhampton, Long Island. To him, the most important event in his life was his marrying, in 1911, Ethel Forde Hillyer, an attractive woman from a socially prominent family, who kept him on an even keel. The couple had two sons, both prominent lawyers, and a large family of which he was a devoted patriarch.

Medina made enduring contributions in each phase of his career. His teaching made bar exam courses respectable parts of legal education in an era of rising professional standards. His dogged defense of Anthony Cramer against treason charges during World War II ranks among the great American cases in which a lawyer, braving public hostility to defend an accused, advanced constitutional rights. Above all, his conduct in the grueling Communist conspiracy case was a watershed in American law. Criticism continues that he contributed to the melee, punished defense counsel without a hearing, and repressed political dissent. Still, he set a lasting example against concerted efforts to make political trials untriable, which Judge John J. Sirica later cited for support in the Watergate case. Medina's charge to the jury significantly enlarged freedom of political expression by requiring acquittal for abstract advocacy of violent revolution and allowing conspiracy convictions only for advocacy intended to incite revolutionary acts when circumstances permit. The Supreme Court endorsed this subtle standard to curb McCarthyism in *Yates v. U.S.* (1957). In retrospect, his *Dennis* charge was a major step in the evolution of free speech.

Medina's lifestyle was perhaps his most original artifact. From his teachers, Woodrow Wilson, Christian Gauss, and Harlan F. Stone, he absorbed professional values and the ancient ideal of "integer"—that life is a process of becoming a whole person. He mastered many hobbies to discipline himself and melded work with play. He collected thousands of great books in English, French, Greek, and Latin to improve his mind, writing skills, and public speaking. He crusaded for court reform, press freedom, and the humanities while translating medieval legal documents, speaking Spanish, and translating *Don Quixote* for fun. Seizing opportunities for "new life" at every stage, Medina embodied Gauss's credo that "the art of living is perhaps the most important of all the liberal arts."

• Medina's extensive papers are in the Seeley G. Mudd Manuscript Library, Princeton University. His reminiscences are in the Oral History Collection, Columbia University. He published several law books, including *Cases on New York Pleading and Practice* (1928); two volumes of speeches, *Judge Medina Speaks* (1954) and *The Anatomy of Freedom* (1959); and many articles, introductions, and reviews. A popular biography is Hawthorne Daniel, *Judge Medina: A Biography* (1952). The best criticisms of the *Dennis* case are Michal R. Belknap, *Cold War Political Justice* (1977), and Stanley I. Kutler, *The American Inquisition* (1982), pp. 152–82. The *Morgan* case is treated in Vincent P. Carosso, *Investment Banking in America* (1970), pp. 458–95. For other episodes, see J. Woodford Howard, Jr., "Judge Medina's School Days," *Princeton Alumni Weekly* 88 (15 June 1988): 22–25; "Advocacy in Constitutional Choice: The *Cramer* Treason Case, 1942–1945," *American Bar Foundation Research Journal* 1986 (1986): 375–413; "The Amateurs Win: Harold R. Medina's Appointment as a Federal District Judge," *New York State Bar Journal* 61 (1989): 14–22; and "Judge Harold R. Medina: The 'Freshman Years,'" *Judicature* 69 (1985): 126–38. An obituary is in the *New York Times*, 16 Mar. 1990. The U.S. Court of Appeals for the Second Circuit held special sessions in honor of his one-hundredth birthday, 859 F2d 85–107 (1988), and in his memory, 917 F2d 91–114 (1990).

J. WOODFORD HOWARD, JR.

MEDWICK, Joe (24 Nov. 1911–21 Mar. 1975), baseball player, was born Joseph Michael Medwick in Carteret, New Jersey, the son of John Medwick, a factory worker, and Elizabeth Schultiz. A star athlete at Carteret High School, Medwick turned down an offer to play football at the University of Notre Dame and signed a contract with the St. Louis Cardinals in 1929.

An outfielder and a powerful hitter, he spent two seasons in the minor leagues with Cardinal farm teams at Scottdale, Pennsylvania, and Houston before he reached the major leagues in 1932. That year as a Cardinal rookie he hit .349 in 26 games. Each season over the next decade he batted above .300 (averaging .332 for that period), and in six seasons he had more than 100 RBIs. In 1936 he married Isabelle Heutel of St. Louis, and they had two children.

Medwick's peak performance came in 1937 when he won the National League's Most Valuable Player Award and the Triple Crown with a batting average of .374, 31 home runs, and 154 runs batted in. He led the league in runs batted in in 1936, 1937, and 1938. In four different years he had more than 200 hits, and six times he scored 100 runs or more. He led the National League in hits twice, in doubles three times, in triples once, and in slugging average once with a .641 mark. Over his entire career he hit .324 with 540 doubles, 113 triples, 205 home runs, and 1,383 runs batted in.

Medwick generated much controversy during his seasons with the Cardinals because of his fiery temper and his tendency to fight with his teammates, opposing players, and occasionally even baseball writers. A woman in Houston gave him his nickname "Ducky" while he was a minor leaguer because she thought that he swam like a duck. Later, his fellow Cardinals called him "Ducky-Wucky." He despised that label, preferring the sobriquet "Muscles." His personality was well suited to the Cardinals of the 1930s—the colorful, combative, freewheeling "Gas House Gang" that included Leo Durocher, Frankie Frisch, Pepper Martin, and Dizzy Dean. A loner who was often surly and selfish, he nonetheless contributed greatly both to the legend of the "Gas House Gang" and the Cardinals' National League and World Series championships of 1934 and their second-place finishes in 1935 and 1939. Although known as a "badball hitter" who would swing at pitches far out of the strike zone, he was one of the National League's most feared batters during the 1930s. A fast runner who regularly missed signals and made bonehead decisions on the basepaths, he was a moody and inconsistent outfielder who occasionally made spectacular, game-saving plays.

The most notorious incident involving Medwick occurred in the seventh game of the 1934 World Series against the Tigers in Detroit. As the Cardinals were routing the Tigers, he slid into third baseman Marv Owen with his spikes high. Knocked down, Owen got up and started to punch Medwick, who retaliated. After a brief scuffle the players were separated, but when Medwick returned to his outfield position the fans pelted him with fruit and garbage. The near riot caused a long delay; the game was finally resumed after baseball commissioner Kenesaw Mountain Landis ordered Medwick out of the game.

After several years of contract disputes with the Cardinals, Medwick was traded to the Brooklyn Dodgers in 1940. His productivity during his later years suffered as a result of a beaning he sustained shortly after the trade. Medwick charged that Cardinals pitcher Bob Bowman intentionally hit him on the head with a fastball, and Brooklyn District Attorney William O'Dwyer and Commissioner Landis investigated the incident but took no action against Bowman. Although Medwick recovered, he never again was as fearsome a batter. In 1943 the Dodgers traded him to the New York Giants, where he competed until 1945. Subsequent trades moved him to the Boston Braves in 1945, the Dodgers again in 1946, and then back to the Cardinals in 1947, where he ended his career in 1948. Although his erratic behavior as a player made him a questionable choice for a managerial position, after he retired in 1948 he served terms as a minor league player-manager in Houston (1948), Miami Beach (1949), Raleigh, North Carolina (1951), and Tampa, Florida (1952). He later became an assistant baseball coach at St. Louis University (1961–1965) and a farm system hitting instructor for the Cardinals from 1966 until his death in St. Petersburg, Florida.

Although only a few players surpassed his lifetime statistics, twenty years passed after his retirement before Medwick was elected to the Baseball Hall of Fame in Cooperstown, New York, in 1968. Many suspected that his frequent battles with sportswriters caused the long delay, which he said was "like a twenty year slump." A tough competitor who alienated many during his stormy career, Medwick was one of the most talented and troubled players of his time.

• There is a clipping file on Medwick in the National Baseball Library, Cooperstown, N.Y. No biography of Medwick exists, but the following books contain detailed information and anecdotes about his life: Bill Borst, *Baseball through a Knothole* (1977); Bob Broeg, *The Redbirds* (1981); Robert Gregory, *Diz: Dizzy Dean and Baseball during the Great Depression* (1992); Robert Hood, *The Gashouse Gang* (1976); and Frederick G. Lieb, *The St. Louis Cardinals* (1945). An obituary is in the *New York Times*, 22 Mar. 1975.

GEORGE B. KIRSCH

MEEK, Alexander Beaufort (17 July 1814–1 Nov. 1865), lawyer and writer, was born in Columbia, South Carolina, the son of Samuel Mills Meek, a minister and physician, and Anna McDowell. The family moved to Tuscaloosa, Alabama, in 1819, the year of Alabama statehood, and after first attending the University of Georgia, Meek became a member of the first regular graduating class of the University of Alabama in 1833. He was elected by his fellow seniors to give the Fourth of July oration, the first of many invited orations on patriotic, literary, historical, and educational topics he would deliver throughout his lifetime. After reading law in the office of the state attorney general Meek was admitted to the bar by the Alabama Supreme Court in 1835. In the same year he also became coproprietor and editor of the Tuscaloosa Democratic newspaper *Flag of the Union*, thus entering two fields, journalism and politics, that would offer him various continuing roles. Following service in 1836 as a volunteer officer in the Seminole War, he served a brief appointment as state attorney general before resuming private law practice. In 1839 he became editor of a short-lived literary monthly, the *Southron*, in Tuscaloosa.

Devoting himself again mainly to the law, Meek compiled *A Supplement to Aiken's Digest of the Laws of the State of Alabama* (1841) and the next year was appointed judge of the county court of Tuscaloosa. When he failed subsequently to win election to that office, he pursued federal political office. A supporter of James K. Polk and bearer of the Alabama electoral vote to Washington in 1844, Meek was first given a position in the U.S. Treasury Department in Washington before being named U.S. attorney for southern Alabama and moving to Mobile in 1847. Between this legal service and his appointment as judge of the probate court of Mobile County in 1854, Meek again pursued journalism, this time as an editor of the *Mobile Daily Register*. Although, as in Tuscaloosa, he failed in an election bid to retain his seat as judge, he was elected to the state legislature in 1853, where he played a primary role in establishing the Alabama public school system. When he was again elected to the legislature in 1859, he was chosen Speaker of the House.

By this time Meek boasted a substantial literary reputation—his poems had appeared widely in southern periodicals, and six of his orations had been issued as pamphlets—but not until the mid-1850s did he secure book publication. *The Red Eagle: A Poem of the South* (1855) is about the leader of the Creek Indians in the Alabama wars of 1813; *Songs and Poems of the South* (1857) is a collection of shorter poems; and *Romantic Passages in Southwestern History* (1857) is a selection of orations, sketches, and essays. All three books were well enough received to merit reprintings. Meek abandoned his long-planned project of a history of Alabama when another writer published such a volume. In his literary approach, Meek was a romantic, a well-known advocate for American, southern, and Alabama perspectives in literature. His prevailing poetic themes, expressed conventionally and lyrically, were love of woman, nature, and country of region. One of his most popular pieces was "The Mocking Bird," but "The Fated City," about Pompeii, and "Balaklava," based on an incident of the Crimean War, were among the best and most frequently reprinted of Meek's poems.

Although all his sympathies were literary, Meek once observed, his habits were not. In 1856 he was chosen an elector on the Buchanan ticket and elected president of the Electoral College; in 1860 he was a delegate to the Democratic National Convention, where he reluctantly sided with secessionists. He married Mrs. Emma Donaldson Slatter in 1856; after her death, he married Mrs. Eliza Jane Cannon in 1864. He had no children. Having become one of the young state's cultural, intellectual, and political leaders, Meek left Alabama in 1863 in order to be with his brother's family during his brother's military service. He died of a heart attack in Columbus, Mississippi.

• The largest collections of Meek papers are in the Alabama State Department of Archives and History, Montgomery, and the Perkins Library of Duke University, Durham, N.C. Important biographical treatments of Meek appear in Charles Hunter Ross, "Alexander Beaufort Meek," *Sewanee Review* 4 (Aug. 1896): 411–27; Herman C. Nixon, *Alexander Beaufort Meek: Poet, Orator, Journalist, Historian, Statesman* (1910); and Margaret Gillis Figh, "Alexander Beaufort Meek, Pioneer Man of Letters," *Alabama Historical Quarterly* 2 (Summer 1940): 127–51. See also William R. Smith, Sr., *Reminiscences of a Long Life* (1889); Jay B. Hubbell, *The South in American Literature, 1607–1900* (1954); and Benjamin Buford Williams, *A Literary History of Alabama: The Nineteenth Century* (1979).

BERT HITCHCOCK

MEEK, Fielding Bradford (10 Dec. 1817–21 Dec. 1876), paleontologist, was born in Madison, Indiana, the son of a lawyer, descended from Irish Presbyterians (names unknown) who came to this country around 1768. His father died when Meek was three years old, leaving a small inheritance for his widow and four children. Little is known of his family.

Meek invested his patrimony in two mercantile ventures—one in Madison, another in Owensboro, Kentucky—both of which failed. He had little aptitude for business, and he was distracted by a serious interest in natural history. He made a modest living at odd jobs, particularly as a portrait painter, and he managed to continue the self-directed studies he had begun as a boy. Although Meek never attended college or gained any formal training in geology, by his thirty-first year his knowledge of fossils attracted the attention of Dr. David Dale Owen, who hired him as a geological assistant for the federal survey of Iowa, Wisconsin, and Minnesota during 1848 and 1849.

Returning afterward to Owensboro, Meek worked on his own again until June 1852, when he moved to Albany, New York, to become an assistant to the paleontologist James Hall, whom Meek met through one of Hall's former students. Because of Meek's skills as a draftsman, Hall hired him to draw fossils. During the six years they worked together, Hall was studying and preparing reports on the invertebrate fossils of the Northwestern Boundary Commission, the Mexican Boundary Survey, the state of Iowa, and, of course, the state of New York. This work gave Meek a broad apprenticeship in what became his specialty.

Meek further expanded his knowledge of western fossils by personal fieldwork. During the summer of 1853 Hall sent him and the young naturalist Ferdinand Vandeveer Hayden to collect specimens in the White River Bad Lands of Dakota (then part of Nebraska Territory). The article Meek wrote with Hall on some Cretaceous formations of Nebraska described the geologic structure of rocks in western America for the first time (*Memoirs of the American Academy of Arts and Sciences*, n.s. 5 (1856): 379–411).

Finding Hall to be a stingy and overbearing employer, Meek sought additional employment in Missouri, even while he continued to work with Hall for half of each year. He worked for George Clinton Swallow on the geologic survey of Missouri for two summers, beginning in 1854. As a part of Swallow's *Second Annual Report* (1855), Meek's resource inventory of Moniteau County showed how little coal existed in Missouri. In 1854 he also agreed to publish descriptions of the abundant invertebrates Hayden began bringing back from his own collecting ventures. Their first five jointly written articles appeared during 1856 and were published in the *Proceedings* of the Academy of Natural Sciences of Philadelphia.

Hall took a dim view of Meek's budding partnership with Hayden, partly because it distracted Meek from working on Hall's materials, but also because it threatened Hall's ambition to become the preeminent authority on America's invertebrates. For his part, Meek feared that Hall had gained much of his knowledge of Paleozoic formations in the Rockies from Meek's own unpublished descriptions of Hayden's fossils from that region. In 1858 Meek and Hayden claimed to have found in Kansas and the Dakotas the first Permian and Jurassic fossils in America. Hall claimed he had found earlier evidence of these fossils in other regions. Clashing ambitions and mutual suspicions growing out of this priority dispute led Meek to break with Hall in the spring of 1858.

That autumn Meek and Hayden made further collections together in Kansas, substantiating their claims on the Permian and buttressing their reputation as the foremost authorities on the geology of the West, especially the Upper Missouri Basin. Their further joint publications established the essential structure of this region and offered pioneering insights on the uniqueness of American geology. During the 1860s Meek elaborated this point in articles written for the *American Journal of Science*. His relationship with Hayden was truly collaborative: while Meek wrote most of the fossil descriptions they published, he depended on Hayden's unsurpassed knowledge of the field setting where he gathered countless specimens. Hayden also wrote some of the general notes on geology for their joint articles.

After leaving Albany in 1858, Meek settled in Washington, D.C., where Joseph Henry, secretary of the Smithsonian, provided him a residence in that institution's first building, the "Castle," where Meek lived and worked for the rest of his life. In return, Meek became the Smithsonian's full-time expert on paleontology, at no salary, and he organized many of the collections deposited at the Smithsonian by federal expeditions during the next two decades.

To earn money Meek prepared official reports for the Northwestern Boundary Commission; the army explorations of Capt. John N. Macomb and Capt. James H. Simpson; the states of Nebraska, California, Ohio, and Illinois; and the Clarence King, John Wesley Powell, George Montague Wheeler, and F. V. Hayden surveys. His correspondence and publications show he examined specimens from all over North America and from virtually every geologic period. Many naturalists submitted their fossils for his authoritative appraisals. James Dwight Dana, for example, acknowledged Meek's many contributions to his own influential *Manual of Geology* (1862 and subsequent editions).

Most of Meek's later publications were for the second geological survey of Illinois (1858–1875) under Amos Henry Worthen and Hayden's Survey of the Territories (1869–1879). Meek's most famous work, "A Report on the Invertebrate Cretaceous and Tertiary Fossils of the Upper Missouri Country," was published by Hayden's survey in 1876 (*Final Reports*, vol. 9). This was a supplement to his earlier "Palaeontology of the Upper Missouri" of 1865 (*Smithsonian Contributions to Knowledge*, vol. 14) on Cambrian through Jurassic invertebrates. He was elected to the National Academy of Sciences in 1869.

Meek's sweeping approach to American paleontology was inspired by his inherent thoroughness, but also by his continuing rivalry with James Hall, whose own grasp extended beyond New York into New Jersey,

Ohio, Iowa, Wisconsin, the Lake Superior region, and Canada and included official work for Clarence King's survey. Between them, Meek and Hall examined every significant fossil retrieved from the western strata. The first comprehensive interpretations of western geology relied on the fruits of their assiduous rivalry. Hall published somewhat more than Meek (both were prolific, however), while Meek was the more exacting researcher.

Meek became deaf during his last years, which only reinforced his solitary nature. An abstemious, even austere man, Meek had many admirers but no close friends. He never married. He suffered from poor health all his life, and he died of tuberculosis in Washington, D.C.

• A large collection of Meek's incoming letters, his field journals, newspaper clippings, and other items is in Record Unit 7062 in the Smithsonian Institution, Washington, D.C. His outgoing letters will be found among the papers of many scientists of the day, notably Hall (N.Y. State Library and N.Y. State Archives), Hayden (Record Group 57, National Archives), Worthen (Univ. of Illinois), Dana (Yale Univ.), Spencer Fullerton Baird (Smithsonian Archives), Joseph Leidy (Academy of Natural Sciences of Philadelphia), George Engelmann (Missouri Botanical Gardens), and C. A. White (Univ. of Iowa). The George P. Merrill Collection at the Library of Congress contains some of his letters. Most of what is known of Meek's life and career derives from Charles Abiathar White, whose best sketch, "Memoir of Fielding Bradford Meek, 1817–1876," was published by the National Academy of Sciences in *Biographical Memoirs* 4 (1902): 75–91. See also White, "In Memoriam, Fielding Bradford Meek," *American Journal of Science*, 3d ser., 13 (1877): 169–71, and "Biographical Sketch of Fielding Bradford Meek," *The American Geologist* 18 (1896): 336–50. G. P. Merrill, *The First One Hundred Years of American Geology* (1924), gives unique details about Meek and quotes several of Meek's letters. Merrill's "Contributions to the History of American Geology," in *U.S. National Museum Annual Report for 1904* (1906), pp. 189–734, also is valuable. Merrill's sketch of Meek in the *Dictionary of American Biography* (1933) is useful for its bibliography. Both White and Merrill allowed their personal fondness for Meek to inhibit their critical insight. Meek was a much bolder man than they allowed.

Several recent studies rely on Meek's papers. See Clifford M. Nelson and Fritiof M. Fryxell, "The Ante-Bellum Collaboration of Meek and Hayden in Stratigraphy," in *Two Hundred Years of Geology in America*, ed. Cecil J. Schneer (1979), pp. 187–200; Nelson and Ellis L. Yochelson, "Organizing Federal Paleontology in the United States, 1858–1907," *Journal of the Society for the Bibliography of Natural History* 9 (1980): 607–18; and Yochelson, "Fielding Bradford Meek," *Dictionary of Scientific Biography* 9 (1974): 255–56. Mike Foster treats Meek's rivalry with Hall in "The Permian Controversy of 1858: An Affair of the Heart," *Proceedings of the American Philosophical Society* 133 (Sept. 1989): 370–90. Foster's *Strange Genius: A Life of Ferdinand Vandeveer Hayden* (1995) discusses the relationship between Meek and Hayden.

MIKE F. FOSTER

MEEK, Walter Joseph (15 Aug. 1878–15 Feb. 1963), physiologist, was born in Dillon, Kansas, the son of William E. A. Meek and Mary Hester White, farmers. Orphaned at age thirteen, he was raised by an aunt and uncle who lived nearby. He received his A.B. from the University of Kansas in 1902 and the next year began teaching biology at Penn College in Oskaloosa, Iowa, while doing graduate work at the University of Chicago. In 1906 he married Crescence Eberley; they had three children. In 1908 he resigned his professorship at Penn to become an instructor of physiology at the University of Wisconsin's new preclinical two-year medical course. In 1909 he received his Ph.D. in physiology from the University of Chicago.

Meek was promoted to assistant professor in 1910 and associate professor in 1912. His primary research interest was the physiology of the heart, particularly the origin and propagation of the heartbeat. Much of his early research involved the form and function of the cardiac branch of the vagus nerve, by which neurological signals are transmitted from the brain to the muscles of the heart to slow the rate of heartbeat. He also studied the sinoatrial node, the small mass of tissue in the right atrium that functions as the heart's sparkplug by emitting the electrical impulses that initiate cardiac muscular contraction. In 1917 he joined the U.S. Army as a major and, as a member of a university-based unit of the Chemical Warfare Service, spent the next two years conducting research on the biological effects on humans of mustard gas, lewisite, and phosgene. In 1918 he became a full professor at Wisconsin, a position he held until his retirement.

After the end of World War I Meek resumed his studies of the heartbeat by using X-rays to make images of the heart during the various stages of the cardiac cycle. He also conducted pioneering investigations into the effects of exercise, hemorrhage, an overabundance of blood, and changes in blood pressure in the veins on the size and pumping ability of the heart. He was one of the first medical researchers to investigate the effect of an enlarged heart on an athlete's performance and health. In 1934 he began studying the effects on cardiac regularity of cyclopropane, an anesthetic gas that was introduced the year before and that represented a major improvement over nitrous oxide and ether because it neither irritates the mucous membranes nor depresses respiration. However, he soon discovered that cyclopropane, when administered to dogs in conjunction with epinephrine—a hormone frequently administered during surgery to increase blood pressure and stimulate the heart by constricting the smaller arteries—often causes ventricular fibrillation, a rapid and spasmodic quivering of the fibrous muscles of the heart that prevents the ventricles from pumping blood through the arteries. By 1940 Meek was able to describe how and why this phenomenon occurs. In 1941 he discovered that phenylephrine, an epinephrine-like substance, produces an increase in blood pressure without affecting the beating of the heart and that its administration in place of epinephrine made cyclopropane safe for use in a number of surgical procedures.

In addition to his achievements as a researcher, Meek also made important contributions as an administrator during the early years of the University of Wisconsin School of Medicine and as a leader of the American Physiological Society. He served as the medical school's assistant dean and dean of admissions from 1920 to 1942, acting dean from 1942 to 1945, and associate dean from 1945 to 1948. He served as secretary of the society from 1924 to 1929, president from 1930 to 1932, and chairman of the Board of Publication Trustees from 1933 until shortly before his death. In this latter capacity he played an important role in the establishment of the *Annual Review of Physiology* in 1937. He also made a minor contribution to the history of medicine by writing more than twenty papers, most of which were not published, on major figures and events of a physiological nature. For many years he was a trustee of Madison (Wis.) General Hospital and a member of Wisconsin's Governor's Advisory Committee on Medical Education.

Meek retired from his teaching and administrative duties in 1948 but remained at Wisconsin for a year as a research professor. In 1950 he lectured on the history of physiology at the University of Texas and then moved to Florida, where he served on an organizing committee for the establishment of a medical school at the University of Florida. He received the Wisconsin State Medical Society's Man of the Year Award in 1944, and he was elected to the National Academy of Sciences in 1947. In 1949 he was presented with a Distinguished Service Award from the University of Kansas. He died in Fort Myers Beach, Florida.

Meek was one of the leading physiologists in the United States for almost fifty years, and he contributed to the advance of American biomedical science in several ways. He performed much of the pioneering research in the United States concerning the origins of the heartbeat. His work with cyclopropane and phenylephrine permitted the widespread use of improved methods of anesthesia during surgery. His role as one of the early administrators of the University of Wisconsin's School of Medicine helped to establish that institution as one of the best of its kind in the Midwest.

• A biography of Meek is Chandler McC. Brooks, National Academy of Sciences, *Biographical Memoirs* 54 (1983): 251–68. Meek is mentioned throughout Paul F. Clark, *The University of Wisconsin Medical School: A Chronicle, 1848–1948* (1967).

CHARLES W. CAREY, JR.

MEEKER, Ezra (29 Dec. 1830–3 Dec. 1928), Northwest settler and Oregon Trail memorialist, was born near Huntsville, Butler County, Ohio, the son of Jacob Meeker and Phoebe Baker, farmers. Meeker grew up in a struggling farm family. In search of better land, his parents twice moved their family during Ezra's youth, first to Lockland, Ohio, and then in 1839 to Attica, Indiana. Ezra worked at home and held odd jobs to augment the family's earnings. He had less than a year of formal schooling.

On 13 May 1851 Meeker married Eliza Jane Sumner and moved with her to Eddyville, Iowa, where inexpensive farmland was available. A harsh winter coupled with exciting reports about the Oregon Territory motivated them to head west in April 1852. They started from Council Bluffs, Iowa, in a small party that included their infant son and Meeker's brother Oliver. Thousands of migrants followed the Oregon Trail westward during the summer of 1852, and the Meeker party encountered many on their journey. They were deeply impressed by the hardships that they and others experienced, including adverse weather, rugged terrain, and cholera.

The Meekers reached Oregon in the fall, and after stays in Portland and two other locations along the Columbia River, they moved to southern Puget Sound, in what would become Washington State. Between 1853 and 1862 they homesteaded at several sites in the vicinity of modern-day Tacoma. Meeker farmed, guided travelers through the Cascade Mountains, and became well known in the lightly settled region. In 1857 he was one of two jurors who refused to convict Leschi, a leader of the indigenous Nisquallies, on murder charges related to conflicts between white settlers and native peoples in 1855–1856. He criticized Leschi's execution, which followed a second trial and subsequent conviction. Meeker's belief that local Indians had often been wronged by whites figured prominently in his first book, *Pioneer Reminiscences of Puget Sound: The Tragedy of Leschi* (1905).

In 1862, with their four children (a fifth was born later), the Meekers settled in the Puyallup Valley, also near Tacoma, where in 1877 he platted the town of Puyallup. Other family members had followed Meeker, and in 1865, with his father and brother John, he began to grow hops. Cultivation of hops became a major industry in the territory. Meeker became a hops broker, spent several years in London selling Washington hops in the European market, and prospered until the hop louse began to damage local crops in the mid-1880s. Resulting setbacks for farmers increased economic and social problems around Puget Sound. In 1885 pressure mounted to drive Chinese workers, some of whom harvested hops, from the area. Meeker publicly denounced the popular expulsion movement. His efforts were in vain, but after vigilantes forced Chinese residents from Tacoma, Meeker's testimony contributed to charges filed (though later dropped) against vigilante leaders. Meeker, nevertheless, was sufficiently popular to be elected Puyallup's first mayor in 1890.

The hops industry continued its decline, due to the louse and outside competition. By 1893, primarily because he had forgiven debts owed to him by many farmers, Meeker had lost the fortune he amassed during the industry's heyday. He invested in banking, local real estate, and railroads but never repeated the success he had with hops. He also traveled to the Klondike between 1898 and 1901, to supply prospectors, but made little profit. In his seventies, Meeker decided to retire from business and devote his energies to public service.

Always interested in western history, Meeker had become increasingly concerned that the sacrifices and hard work of early pioneers were fading from public memories. He decided to draw national attention to the forgotten Oregon Trail and thus renew respect for those who had traversed it. In 1906 he began a publicized journey to mark the trail eastward from Puget Sound. Traveling by covered oxcart, he stopped along the route and encouraged others to memorialize the trail. Many people responded by raising funds to build monuments to Oregon Trail pioneers at various sites along the trail.

En route, he wrote *The Ox-Team; or, The Old Oregon Trail, 1852–1896* (1906), which he published upon reaching Lincoln, Nebraska. With proceeds from the book's sale he shipped his oxcart to cities in the Midwest and East, where he gave popular speeches about the role of the Oregon Trail in American history. An angular man with a dramatic full beard and thick, white hair, the photogenic Meeker seemed to embody the image of westering pioneers, and his appearance added to his appeal to urban, modern Americans. Finally, reaching Washington, D.C., in the fall of 1907, he met President Theodore Roosevelt (1858–1919), who added his support to Meeker's cause.

Meeker returned to Puyallup in 1908 as a nationally recognized spokesman for memorializing pioneers of the Oregon Trail. He traced the trail again by ox team in 1910, by automobile in 1915, and by airplane in 1924. In 1926 he formed the Oregon Trail Memorial Association (OTMA) and persuaded Congress to authorize the minting of Oregon Trail memorial coins, sales of which funded monuments to the trail and projects to explain its use. Although the OTMA dissolved by the 1950s, its endeavors (especially Meeker's) inspired the founding in 1983 of the ongoing Oregon–California Trails Association.

Attempting another automobile trip along the trail in 1928, Meeker became ill and returned to Seattle, where he died. By drawing national attention to the Oregon Trail, he ensured that it would be remembered. Sites along the trail have been designated as state and national monuments, and following hearings in which Meeker's work was cited, in 1978 Congress made it a national historic trail.

An extraordinarily energetic man, Meeker held firmly to his beliefs, even when they were unpopular, and seldom ignored an opportunity to extol them in public. These traits served him well in the two decades that he devoted to restoring public awareness of the Oregon Trail and those who traveled it west.

• Meeker's papers are held by the Library of the Washington State Historical Society. A published guide to the collection, *Ezra Meeker—Pioneer*, by Frank Green, includes a brief biographical essay on Meeker. Other materials owned by Meeker are held by the Ezra Meeker Historical Society, which operates Meeker's Puyallup home as a museum. Meeker's books include *The Busy Life of Eighty-Five Years: Ventures and Adventures of Ezra Meeker* (1916, rev. from a 1909 publication), *Seventy Years of Progress in Washington* (1921), and *Kate Mulhall: A Romance of the Oregon Trail* (1926). Biographical studies of Meeker include Bert Webber, *Ezra Meeker: Champion of the Oregon Trail* (1992), and C. B. Galbreath, "Ezra Meeker, Ohio's Illustrious Pioneer," *Ohio Archaeological and Historical Quarterly* 36 (Jan. 1927): 3–47. For discussions of Meeker's contributions to the preservation of the Oregon Trail and its history, see Gladys Shafer, "Eastward Ho! Ezra Meeker Memorializes the Oregon Trail, 1905–1910," *American West* 5, no. 6 (1968): 42–48, and Merrill Mattes, "A Tribute to the Oregon Trail Memorial Association," *Overland Journal* 2 (Winter 1984): 29–34. Accounts of Meeker's involvement in the trial of Leschi and the expulsion of Tacoma's Chinese residents are included in Murray Morgan, *Puget's Sound: A Narrative of Early Tacoma and the Southern Sound* (1979). Obituaries are in the *Seattle Times*, 3 Dec. 1928, and the *Seattle Post-Intelligencer*, 4 Dec. 1928.

BETH KRAIG

MEEM, John Gaw (17 Nov. 1894–4 Aug. 1983), architect and preservationist, was born in Pelotas, Brazil, the son of John Gaw Meem III and Elsa Krishke, Episcopalian missionaries. From 1910 until 1914 Meem attended the Virginia Military Institute, graduating with a degree in civil engineering. He was an infantry captain in Iowa from 1917 until 1919. After World War I Meem worked as a banker in Brazil, but he had to return to the United States to be treated for tuberculosis. He was admitted as a patient at Sunmount Sanatorium near Santa Fe, New Mexico, in the spring of 1920. Although Santa Fe had a population of only 10,000 in 1920, there was a vocal group of people who wanted any growth in the area to occur within the architectural traditions of the native Pueblos and the Spanish settlers. Meem immediately was drawn into this circle in part because the founder and head of the sanatorium, Frank Mera, and several patients (like the painter Carlos Vierra) were advocates for preserving the distinctive character of Santa Fe.

In October 1922 Meem left New Mexico for the architectural offices of Fisher and Fisher in Denver, Colorado, intent on developing his design skills. In the evenings he attended the Atelier Denver, a studio affiliated with the Beaux-Arts School of Design in New York City and run by architect Burnham Hoyt. One of Meem's drawings received an award in a nationwide competition in April 1923. Meem spent fifteen months in Denver learning the rudiments of architectural design, but he overextended himself and had to return to the sanatorium in Santa Fe in January 1924. In February 1924 Meem and a fellow patient, Cassius McCormick, formed an architectural partnership that lasted until 1928, when McCormick returned to Indiana.

From the start of Meem's career the preservation of traditional buildings and the design and construction of new buildings were intertwined. In 1924 Meem agreed to be Hoyt's assistant in Denver in preserving historic mission churches. An informal Committee for the Preservation and Restoration of New Mexican Mission Churches led this effort. (The group incorporated in 1932.) Meem's experience with this group, among others, gave him invaluable hands-on experience with adobe and the informal accretions of vernacular construction, what he called "freehand architecture" ("Address," *Proceedings of the AIA*, p. 136). The lessons he learned from preservation work enabled him to contribute successfully to what is known as the Pueblo revival style (also known as the Santa Fe style).

Meem's first major commission was the expansion he did for La Fonda Hotel on Santa Fe's plaza from 1926 to 1929. Meem's challenge, besides negotiating with the client, was to respect the original 1920 design and avoid competing with the towers of the nearby cathedral. Having proven himself on the hotel, his practice grew; by 1930 he won a nationwide competition, funded by John D. Rockefeller, Jr., to design an ambitious group of buildings for the Laboratory of Anthropology in Santa Fe. In the end, only two structures were built. Meem's most distinctive designs, including the laboratory, date from the 1930s, when rich clients and a small office made individual attention possible. In residential commissions, Meem used antique beams and doors collected from other adobe structures and combined them in a new, carefully sited adobe structure suited to modern needs, as in the Amelia Hollenback house (1932), overlooking Santa Fe.

By 1930 Meem had added Hugo Zehner to his office staff; Zehner became a partner in 1934. In 1933 Meem married one of his employees, the architect Faith Bemis; the couple had one child. Meem became the architect for the University of New Mexico (UNM) in 1933, a position he held until 1958. His firm built seven buildings for UNM, with the Zimmerman Library (1933–1937) being the most notable. The Public Works Administration provided the funds for the UNM buildings during the depression, making possible the employment of talented craftsmen. While Meem's large-scale works often were built using modern materials like concrete, the building profiles and details recalled traditional construction and forms. As supervisor for the Historic American Building Survey (HABS) in the Southwest from 1934 until 1955, Meem had direct knowledge of many buildings that inspired his own designs. Meem's vision was sometimes denigrated, as when Frank Lloyd Wright visited UNM's campus. Meem reported that Wright declared: "This is imitation and all imitation is base!" (quoted in DeVolder, p. 223).

Meem served as an architectural adviser to the Roman Catholic archbishop Rudolph Gerken from 1933 to 1943. He also built a number of churches for Protestant denominations, including two cathedrals for the Episcopalians (1951 in Albuquerque and 1953 in Gallup, N.Mex.). Meem's church designs often were in medieval revival styles. In addition to creating a substantial number of residences and buildings for educational and religious institutions, Meem built his masterpiece (according to Bunting) in 1936, the Colorado Springs Fine Arts Center. The center won the silver medal at the Fifth Pan American Congress of Architecture in 1940 and brought Meem international recognition. The complex program was fulfilled in a carefully proportioned building of nearly white reinforced concrete with aluminum detailing. An *Architectural Forum* article described the center as the "very essence of the new architecture," wherein memories were evoked with traditional forms that served new purposes.

Postwar work by Meem, which employed prefabricated building materials, was categorically different from his highly crafted work in the 1930s. The results were economical and efficient (as in the UNM Gymnasium, 1955), with minimal ornament on forms abstracted from earlier vernacular works. Edward Holien became a partner in 1944, and the firm became known as Meem, Zehner, Holien and Associates. Holien served as the chief designer, while Meem increasingly was involved in public service (he was chairman of the Santa Fe City Planning Commission from 1945 to 1951, for example). He also worked extensively on drafting and then passing Santa Fe's Historic Zoning Ordinance, one of the country's first, adopted in 1957. Meem died in Santa Fe.

While Meem's career as an architect is appropriately filled with buildings, he was a forceful speaker and writer as well, successfully convincing the public of the value of preserving traditional forms and materials in the face of modern changes. Much of the credit for Santa Fe's distinctive architectural appearance is due to Meem's long and persistent work in cooperation with like-minded others. He took his ideas about preservation and applied them in his own designs, popularizing the Pueblo revival style.

• The primary documents on Meem's career are in the John Gaw Meem Architectural Records Collection at the University of New Mexico in Albuquerque, N.Mex. Meem's 1931 address to the American Institute of Architects on the mission churches of New Mexico is a good summary of his preservation ideas and can be found in the *Proceedings of the Sixty-fourth Annual Convention of the American Institute of Architects* 64 (1931): 135–38. His synthesis of past forms and present needs is well expressed in his "Old Forms for New Buildings," *American Architect* (Nov. 1934): 10–21. "The Colorado Springs Fine Arts Center," *Architectural Forum* 65 (July 1936): 11–20, features descriptions and illustrations of Meem's award-winning work. The main source on Meem is the monograph by Bainbridge Bunting, *John Gaw Meem: Southwestern Architect* (1983), which is amply illustrated with photographs by Ansel Adams and Laura Gilpin, two photographers whom Meem hired to document his work, and which provides a bibliography. Also useful, with citations not in Bunting, is Arthur L. DeVolder, "John Gaw Meem, FAIA: An Appreciation," the *New Mexico Historical Review* 54 (July 1979): 207–25. To put Meem's ecclesiastical work in a broader context, consult George Kubler, *The Religious Architecture of New Mexico in the Colonial Period and since the American Occupation* (1940). For comparisons of Meem's work with that by others, see John Barton, "Spanish-Pueblo Revival," *Architectural Association Quarterly* 13 (Jan.–June 1982): 7–14. "John Gaw Meem and the Regional Tradition," *Mass* 1 (Spring 1983), is a special issue devoted to Meem's work in the Southwest. An obituary by Wolfgang Saxon is in the *New York Times*, 7 Aug. 1983.

SHARON IRISH

MEES, Charles Edward Kenneth (26 May 1882–15 Aug. 1960), chemist and director of industrial research, was born in Wellingborough, England, the son of Reverend Charles Edward Mees, a Wesleyan minister, and Ellen Jordan. After illness limited his outdoor activity, he did chemistry in a well-equipped home laboratory. He attended public schools and earned a B.Sc. in 1903 and a D.Sc. in 1906 from University College, London, doing doctoral research on the rate of chemical reactions related to photography. In 1909 he married Alice Crisp, with whom he would have two children.

At the urging of his professor, Nobel laureate in chemistry Sir William Ramsay, Mees sought work in industry, offering to work on photographic processes for the well-established photographic firm Wratten and Wainwright. That company valued his potential so highly that it set up a subsidiary devoted to scientific consulting in photographic problems with Mees as partner and managing director. Mees successfully developed process improvements and new products, such as improved resolution emulsions for use in dry-plate photography, and did research on color photography.

His growing reputation as one of the world's preeminent students of the chemical processes underlying photography gained the attention of George Eastman, whom Mees had met in a visit to the Rochester, New York, factories of the Eastman Kodak Co. in 1909. That company had won great success selling photography to the public under the slogan "you push the button, we do the rest." Now, in 1912, with early patents expiring and trade secrets insecure, Eastman saw the need for a research laboratory to help rebuild Kodak's competitive advantage and offered Mees the job as its director. Mees agreed on condition that Eastman purchase the Wratten and Wainwright firm, which Eastman did. Mees came to Rochester around 1912, with authorization to hire seventeen researchers, beginning with an annual budget of just over $50,000. He opened the laboratory in 1913 and told Eastman that it might take a decade for significant results to occur.

Unlike other pioneers in U.S. industrial research, Mees had no experience in Germany, where chemical companies had been carrying out research for decades. He instead identified as his positive model William Rintoul, who had organized a productive laboratory at Britain's Nobel's Explosive Company, and as his negative one Willis R. Whitney, creator of the General Electric Research Laboratory, whose methods Mees perceived as anarchic and to be avoided.

Mees early secured assent from Eastman for two policies that proved essential to success: the researchers could publish their results in scientific journals (after making sure that no essential proprietary information was disclosed), and people in different departments could share information within the laboratory. Both these policies were unusual in the highly secretive photographic industry.

The key institution of the laboratory was the weekly conference, at which typically fewer than ten people focused on a key research effort. Mees sought to keep those efforts exclusively focused on photography, a tactic he called "convergent" research (that is, research focused on the technologies critical to current products). The opposed concept of "divergent" research (that is, research on technologies extending beyond those critical to current products) would later lead to Nobel Prize–winning science at Bell Labs, GE, Du-Pont, and IBM/Zurich. However, if the field of study was chosen by management, the specific research topics and methods were not. As Mees put it, "The best person to decide what research work shall be done is the man who is doing the research. The next best is the head of the department. After that you leave the field of best persons and meet increasingly worse groups. The first of these is the research director who is probably wrong most of the time. Finally, there is a committee of company vice presidents, which is wrong all of the time" (*The Organization of Industrial Scientific Research*). The quote catches Mees's authoritative, voluble, and aggressive style. Though his impatience and preference for debate over consensus could be trying, his fairness and enthusiasm made him an inspirational leader.

During its first decade, the laboratory staff increased sixfold, published nearly 200 papers, established important new data and information sources for the photographic industry, and spun off a development department in 1919. Despite Mees's rejection of divergent research, he had convinced Eastman to create a Kodak organic chemistry laboratory in 1918, originally to help the U.S. war effort. Organic chemical manufacture went on to become a major Kodak business. The first important commercial product developed at the laboratory, the Cine-Kodak Process for amateur movie-making, went on the market in 1923. A Kodacolor process for color movies followed. Kodak's biggest innovation of the Mees era, Kodachrome color film, did not originate in his laboratory but began with the work in 1920 of two young New York City musicians, Leopold D. Mannes and Leopold Godowsky. Mees did, however, immediately recognize the value of their work, bring them to the laboratory, surround them with a team, and shepherd the process through the long haul to a 1935 commercial introduction of Kodachrome.

Those are just samples of thousands of improvements to photography and dozens of spinoffs into areas ranging from plastics to chemical tracers that came out of Mees's laboratory. His own scientific and management work provided the basis for some 250 papers and ten books. The best known are *The Organization of Industrial Scientific Research* (1920; rev. ed. 1950) and the collection of papers he edited, *The Theory of the Photographic Process* (1942).

Mees became a director and vice president of Eastman Kodak. He turned over the reins of his laboratory to his successor in 1947, retired to Hawaii in 1955, and spent his last years lecturing, writing, and pursuing his hobbies of astronomy, marine biology, and orchid cultivation. He died in Honolulu. Mees is one of the handful of individuals (others include Whitney, Frank Jewett of AT&T, and Charles Stine of Du Pont) who helped demonstrate to big American companies that operating a research laboratory is good business.

• Mees's papers are at the George Eastman House, Rochester, N.Y. His autobiography is *From Dry Plates to Ektachrome Film* (1961). The best short article on Mees is Walter Clark, "When Industrial Research Was Young," *Research Management* 24 (July 1981): 9–16. The best extended account of his significance is in Reese Jenkins, *Images and Enterprise* (1975).

GEORGE WISE

MEGAPOLENSIS, Johannes (1603–Jan. 1670), minister in the Dutch Reformed church, was born in Koedijk, near Alkmaar, in the province of North Holland. His parents, whose identities are not known, disinherited him when, at age twenty-three, he left the Roman Catholic church for the Reformed church.

Megapolensis pursued a career in the Reformed ministry, serving several congregations in the vicinity of Alkmaar between 1634 and 1642. Married to Machtelt Steengen, his uncle's stepdaughter, he and his wife had four children. (The date of their marriage is unknown.) In 1642 Megapolensis accepted a call to serve as minister in Rensselaerswyck, the patroonship of Kiliaen van Rensselaer on the Hudson River, near present-day Albany, New York.

According to his contract with van Rensselaer, Megapolensis agreed to serve for three years at an annual salary of 1,000 guilders and, provided that his work was satisfactory, for an additional three years at 1,200 guilders. (A master carpenter at Rensselaerswyck was paid about 250 guilders per year.) In addition, a house and 60 guilders worth of food were to be supplied him annually. Besides his pastoral duties and a specific charge to edify and instruct the Indians in the area, the minister was to undertake certain administrative and supervisory tasks for the patroon, who was never to visit his 700,000-acre tract of land. Megapolensis and his family sailed from the Netherlands on 14 June 1642, arriving in New Amsterdam on 4 August after a passage of fifty-one days.

In the storehouse of the patroon at Rensselaerswyck, Megapolensis preached his inaugural sermon on 17 August to a crowd of about 100. Virtually every Rensselaerswyck settler attended as did soldiers, artisans, and traders from nearby Fort Orange.

Van Rensselaer insisted that regular church attendance be compulsory at Rensselaerswyck, with fines levied on nonattenders, and tithing was mandatory. These strictures, however, were unpopular with the independent-minded settlers, and the large turnout for Megapolensis's first service was not a harbinger of things to come. It was as difficult for the patroon's agents to collect the tithes as it was for Megapolensis to persuade his rough-and-ready congregants, who were given to drink, brawling, and thieving, to observe either the Sabbath on a regular basis or customary Christian proprieties.

In his efforts to Christianize the Mohawk Indians who inhabited the area, Megapolensis immediately set about learning their language and customs. In spite of the excellent relations he established with them, his attempts to convert them were largely unavailing—one reason being that the Mohawks were unimpressed with Christianity's effects on the behavior and morals of the local white population. Nevertheless, the minister's friendly demeanor toward them and their evident regard and respect for him enabled Megapolensis to forward the negotiations for the release of Father Isaac Jogues and Father Giuseppe Bressani, two Jesuit missionaries held captive by the Mohawks.

Upon the expiration of his second three-year term at Rensselaerswyck, Megapolensis was persuaded by the classis of Amsterdam, which had jurisdiction over the Reformed church in New Netherland, to accept the pulpit of the Reformed church at New Amsterdam, which was about to be vacated, leaving the colony without an ordained Reformed minister. Megapolensis agreed, and he remained in this pulpit for the next twenty-two years until his death.

Megapolensis's new congregation, described by his predecessor in 1648 as "very ignorant in regard to the true religion, and very much given to drink" and in 1649 by Governor Peter Stuyvesant, an elder, as "feeble lukewarm and faint hearted," was as hard-living and ungovernable as the congregation at Rensselaerswyck. By 1657 the long-suffering Megapolensis had decided that education was the best hope for smoothing the rough edges of his flock and warming their hearts for Christ. He persuaded the classis of Amsterdam and the West India Company authorities in New Amsterdam to encourage the formation of more schools in the colony, and by 1664 nine of the eleven chartered towns in New Netherland had set up schools. The schoolmasters were obliged to supplement the efforts of the Dutch Reformed church by teaching the Ten Commandments, the Heidelberg Catechism, the meaning of the sacraments, and important Christian prayers.

Relations between the staunch Dutch Reformed dominie and the directors of the West India Company became strained in the 1650s over the former's insistence that under the terms of a 1628 regulation, no church but the Reformed was legally permitted to hold public worship in New Netherland. The company, on the other hand, thought it expedient to begin to take a more tolerant attitude toward Lutherans, Quakers, and the plethora of other faiths and sects in the colony. As a former Roman Catholic, Megapolensis was particularly opposed to that faith, and he fired off a ten-page letter to Jesuit priest Simon Le Moyne in which he condemned everything from the popes to the church councils to the monks and nuns in all their orders. And on the question of a Jewish presence in New Netherland, both Megapolensis and his colleague Samuel Drisius took a very dim view. "We have here already," Megapolensis wrote to the classis of Amsterdam, "Papists, Mennonites and Lutherans . . . also many Puritans . . . Atheists and various other servants of Baal . . . [and thus] it would create a still greater confusion, if the obstinate and immovable Jews came to settle here." As in the case of the Christian religions he wished to exclude, however, Megapolensis was overruled by the directors of the West India Company on this matter, their views undoubtedly guided by the fact that a number of influential Dutch Jews owned shares in the company.

Megapolensis and his fellow Reformed ministers in New Netherland may appear to have been intolerant of faiths other than their own, but they were concerned to uphold a regulation of 28 March 1624, and a restatement of it in 1638, restricting public worship to the services of the Dutch Reformed church. As increased colonization produced demand for other public services, the West India Company continued to put pressure on the Dutch church to relax its rules, particularly in relation to the Lutherans, and to this pressure Megapolensis eventually proved amenable. He was also charitable toward a group of twenty-three destitute Jews who landed in New Amsterdam in 1654.

Trouble between Megapolensis and the West India Company in the Netherlands erupted in 1664 when Megapolensis urged Governor Stuyvesant to surrender, without a fight, to an English fleet, which had arrived unannounced in the harbor with the intention of taking over the Dutch colony. Megapolensis's wise advice was based on the fact that New Amsterdam, outnumbered by the English ten to one and with poor defenses, was in no position to mount an offense and could not possibly have withstood a siege of the dilapidated fort.

Apparently, he was severely criticized in Holland for his advice, which had been acted on by Governor Stuyvesant. On 27 August 1668 the governor and various New Amsterdam officials testified that Megapolensis had carried out the duties of a "faithful subject of the States-General and the West India Company" as befitted a "pious and godly minister" on such an occasion. He died in New Amsterdam (renamed New York after the English conquest).

Megapolensis's devotion to the Dutch Reformed church in New Netherland over the long and frustrating years of his ministry was a major factor in enabling the church to endure and to flourish in America after the English conquest.

• Primary sources concerning Megapolensis include Edward T. Corwin, ed., *Ecclesiastical Records of the State of New York* (7 vols., 1901–1916), esp. vol. 1; A. J. F. van Laer, ed., *Van Rensselaer Bowier Manuscripts* (1908); J. Franklin Jameson, ed., *Narratives of New Netherland, 1609–1664* (1909); and Isaac Newton Phelps-Stokes, *The Iconography of Manhattan Island, 1498–1909* (1915–1926). Works about him are Albert Eekhof, *De Hervormde Kerk in Noord-Amerika, 1624–1664* (1913), and Gerald F. De Jong, "Dominie Johannes Megapolensis: Minister to New Netherland," *New-York Historical Society Quarterly* 52 (1968): 7–47.

FIRTH HARING FABEND

MEGEE, Vernon Edgar (5 June 1900–14 Jan. 1992), U.S. Marine Corps officer, was born in Tulsa, Oklahoma Territory, the son of George D. Megee, a rancher, and Alice Ford. Megee's mother died when he was five years old, and he was raised by his father on a small ranch in central Oklahoma. Educated in local schools, he entered Oklahoma A & M College (now Oklahoma State University) in 1917. Two years later, on 8 March 1919, he enlisted in the U.S. Marine Corps. Megee sought and obtained a commission as second lieutenant on 4 May 1922. The following year he married Nell Nemeyer; they had one child.

Megee experienced a variety of assignments as an infantry officer during the 1920s, including expeditionary duties in Haiti, Nicaragua, and China; these expeditionary duties ranged from enforcing domestic order to protecting American lives and liberty. While serving as a quartermaster with an aircraft squadron in 1930, he requested flight training. He entered the naval aviation school at Pensacola, Florida, in January 1931, and in February 1932 he was awarded his wings.

Megee flew as a pilot, instructed in aviation tactics, and, in 1939, commanded Marine Fighter Squadron Two. He also attended the Air Corps Tactical Training School at Maxwell Field, Alabama. In October 1940 he was attached to the U.S. Naval Aviation Mission to Peru, where he acted as special adviser to the government's minister of aviation. Although Megee sought reassignment to combat duty following American entry into World War II in December 1941, he remained in Peru until October 1943.

Megee went overseas with the Third Marine Air Wing in May 1944. Five months later, in the wake of an agreement between the Marine Corps and the navy over responsibility for air support during amphibious operations, General Holland M. Smith, senior marine commander in the Pacific, created the Marine Landing Force Air Support Control Units (LFASCU). He selected Megee, by this time promoted to colonel and known as a close air support enthusiast, to command the new organization.

Megee had recognized the limitations of air support doctrine during the early phases of the war in the Pacific. Developed before reliable aircraft radio equipment existed, the doctrine had failed to address the problem of properly controlling close air support. Until 1944, air strikes had been controlled by amphibious force commanders, a system that had come under increasing criticism from marine ground units. Megee became a strong advocate of shifting control of air support from offshore naval commanders to marine detachments with the troops ashore.

The first test of the new concept came during the invasion of Iwo Jima in February 1945. After the initial assault, Megee came ashore and took over as senior air commander, controlling all aircraft operating over the island. Over the next two weeks he was continuously available to infantry commanders for consultation, planning, and control of air strikes. This provided a flexibility that had been previously absent, winning both the system and Megee high marks from the ground forces.

The control techniques that had been first employed on Iwo Jima saw their finest hour during the battle for Okinawa that began in April 1945. Three LFASCUs coordinated air strikes on Okinawa, one with marines of the III Amphibious Corps, another with army troops of the XXIV Corps, and a third attached to the

Tenth Army, which served as Megee's forward headquarters. Thanks to improved communications, better-trained personnel, and more advanced techniques, historian Robert Sherrod has observed, "Close support was employed more efficiently in the 82-day Okinawa battle than in any other Central Pacific operation."

Following his promotion to brigadier general, Megee was assigned in January 1947 as chief of staff, Fleet Marine Force, Atlantic. In August 1949 he took over as assistant director of Marine Corps aviation. Having transferred credits from courses taken at George Washington University, he graduated from Oklahoma A & M in 1950. Two years later Megee commanded the Marine Corps Air Bases at Cherry Point, North Carolina, then in February 1952 he became commander of the air component of Fleet Marine Force, Pacific.

On 8 January 1953 Megee again went to war, taking over the First Marine Air Wing in Korea. He was, he recalled, "very unhappy about the nature of the air war." His predecessor had allowed the U.S. Air Force to assume operational control of marine aircraft, leaving the wing with only administrative and logistical duties. It took Megee three months to regain control over interdiction, armed reconnaissance, and support missions. Close air support remained under central control at the Joint Operations Center in Seoul. Megee believed that the new arrangement substantially increased the efficiency of Marine Air Wing operations.

Megee served in senior positions in both the Pacific and Atlantic following his Korean tour. On 1 January 1956 he was promoted to lieutenant general and appointed assistant commandant/chief of staff of the Marine Corps. He was the first aviator to hold this position. In his final assignment, from December 1957 until his retirement on 1 November 1959, he commanded Fleet Marine Force, Pacific.

Megee, who received a retirement promotion to four-star general, entered the University of Texas at Austin and earned an M.A. degree in history in 1963. His master's thesis was a study of Marine Corps operations in Nicaragua, where he had served as a junior officer. In 1963 he became the first superintendent of the newly opened Marine Military Academy in Harlingen, Texas, a preparatory school with close if unofficial ties to the Marine Corps. Megee stepped down as superintendent in 1973. He died in a retirement home in Albuquerque, New Mexico.

Megee and Keith B. McCutcheon were instrumental in developing marine close air support doctrine and techniques during World War II. The two men worked on parallel courses. Whereas McCutcheon's emphasis on small forward control parties suited tactical situations like Luzon, where ground units were not in close proximity to one another, Megee's more centralized system of command and control was needed to coordinate air strikes when many units were grouped together along a short front, as happened on Okinawa. Known as both ambitious and brilliant, Megee became the leading advocate for marine close air support, a position that can be largely attributed to his ten years of service as an infantry officer.

• The Marine Corps Historical Research Center, Washington, D.C., has a biographical file on Megee along with a lengthy oral history that covers all phases of his life and career. Megee's role in the development of close air support is discussed in Robert Sherrod, *History of Marine Corps Aviation in World War II* (1952), and Allan R. Millett, *"Semper Fidelis": The History of the United States Marine Corps* (1980).

WILLIAM M. LEARY

MEGGERS, William Frederick (13 July 1888–19 Nov. 1966), physicist, was born in Clintonville, Wisconsin, the son of John Meggers and Bertha Bork, German immigrant farmers. In 1907 Meggers entered Ripon College, from which he received a B.A. in physics in 1910. He remained there the following year as assistant to physics professor William H. Barber, the department head. In 1911–1912 Meggers attended the University of Wisconsin, where he studied physics under Max Mason, Charles E. Mendenhall, and Leonard R. Ingersoll. He moved to Pittsburgh in 1912 to become a physics instructor at Carnegie Institute of Technology. There, after reading Niels Bohr's essay "On the Constitution of Atoms and Molecules," Meggers chose to focus his career on spectroscopy, which had become the most powerful tool for probing the electronic structure of elements and the chemical bonds of compounds. Spectroscopic analysis generated the fundamental data base from which came the second great revolutionary idea of twentieth-century physics after relativity: quantum mechanics.

Meggers was able to do significant research in spectroscopy by qualifying through a civil service examination to join the largest comprehensive laboratory in the physical sciences at the time, the National Bureau of Standards (NBS) in Washington, D.C. Appointed to the position of laboratory assistant in June 1914, he remained at the bureau for his entire career. In his early years at the bureau, Meggers was greatly influenced by Keivin Burns, who taught the young physicist the techniques of photographing spectra, measuring wavelengths of spectral lines, and spectrochemical analysis. Through a novel program of graduate studies inaugurated at NBS in 1908 in conjunction with cooperating research universities, Meggers earned a master's degree in 1916 from the University of Wisonsin and a Ph.D. in 1917 from Johns Hopkins while remaining in full employ. He became chief of the spectroscopy section of the NBS division of light and optical instruments in 1919, a position he maintained until 1958. In 1920 he married Edith Marie Raddant; they had one daughter and two sons.

At the bureau, Meggers was a seminal investigator in several fields, including physical optics, astrophysics, photography, and especially spectroscopy, to every aspect of which Meggers would devote himself tirelessly for half a century. His research was crucial to both of the major components of spectroscopy: the various techniques of separating sources of light using refractive elements (prisms) or interference devices (diffraction gratings) into their constituent wavelengths, or spectra, and the interpretation of observed spectra. He developed several new light standard sources, including a novel mercury lamp and a microwave-excited thorium-iodide lamp. The mercury lamp (1948) produced extremely sharp lines at low pressures and temperatures and thus was superior to the old cadmium light source as a standard for measuring length. The thorium-iodide lamp proved to be ten times as accurate as the old iron standard for measuring spectral-line wavelengths.

One of Megger's most significant contributions to the study of spectra was his work with Chauncey G. Peters to determine precisely the value for the index of refraction of air. The theory of atomic and molecular spectra was developed using models that assumed that the atoms and molecules existed in vacuum. Because, however, the wavelengths of atoms and molecules were being measured in air, the index of refraction of air was necessary to convert the measured wavelengths to their theoretical values in vacuum. Meggers and Peters's 1918 paper, "Measurements on the Index of Refraction of Air for Wavelengths from 2218A to 9000A," provided tables with which the most accurate conversion of wavelengths could be calculated, a crucial element of modern spectroscopy.

Meggers improved detection and recording technology by incorporating various dyes in photographic plates to record long wavelengths into the near infrared portion of the spectrum. This infrared research was of particular importance to solar physics and atmospheric absorption studies. Infrared solar energy, which arrives at the earth's surface largely unimpeded by passing through the earth's atmosphere, gives signatures of the sun's composition and energy profile, but until this time there had been no way to analyze these emissions by wavelength. The extension of the measurement of spectra into the near infrared was also significant to astrophysics because the development enabled the study of a greater region of the spectra of stars. Meggers did extensive cooperative work on the near infrared with the astrophysicists Henry Norris Russell at Princeton and Keivin Burns at Allegheny Observatory. He was also a member of the International Astronomical Union's Commission on Wavelengths.

Meggers contributed volumes of spectral data of atoms and ions (charged atoms) calculated to unprecedented accuracy, including the spectra of rare-earth elements as they were discovered. This large amount of accurate data was obtained primarily by his extension of the atomic and ionic spectra into the near infrared and by his improvement of standards of measurement, particularly for the index of refraction of air. He was also one of the first, beginning in 1914, to pursue spectrochemical analysis, which provided a powerful method for determining the constituents of an unknown compound. Because spectrochemical studies required not only accurate wavelengths but also the spectral line intensities, Meggers's *Tables of Spectral Line Intensities* (1961) proved invaluable for spectrochemical analysis.

Among Meggers's many honors were the Frederick Ives Medal (1947) and the C. E. K. Mees Medal (1964) of the Optical Society of America, the gold medal of the Department of Commerce (1949), the medal of the Society of Applied Spectroscopy (1952), and the Eliot Cresson Medal of the Franklin Institute (1953). He was president of the American Optical Society from 1949 to 1951 and a member of the governing board of the American Institute of Physics from 1952 to 1958. He was elected to the National Academy of Sciences in 1954. He continued performing laboratory investigations and publishing virtually until his death in Washington, D.C.

Meggers's many interests outside of the laboratory included collecting large amounts of Indian relics, phonograph records, and electronic devices. The latter collection was so extensive that he set up a "Museum for Science and Civilization" at his home in suburban Maryland. (It was probably available to friends and associates but was not open to the public.) Meggers's stamp and coin collection was left after his death to the American Institute of Physics to fund a program of training for students interested in a scientific education.

Meggers's scientific personality has been described by many of his colleagues as patient and painstaking. At the presentation of the Ives Medal to him in 1947, Meggers was described as having "a broad perspective of the entire field of atomic structure and a keen realization of the needs of science in this field. He is held in highest esteem by the student of fundamental spectroscopy and atomic structure, and by the user of spectroscopic methods for quantitative and qualitative analysis" (*Journal of the Optical Society of America* 38 [1948]: 2).

• The William Frederick Meggers Papers are at the American Institute of Physics, Center for History of Physics, College Park, Md. His 235 articles, handbooks, and tables, which nearly all present technical-spectrographic research, appeared in many of the primary scientific journals, including *Physical Review*, the *Astrophysical Journal*, and *Zeitschrift für Physik*, between 1915 and 1967. His NBS colleague Paul D. Foote's essay on Meggers in National Academy of Sciences, *Biographical Memoirs* 41 (1970): 319–40, includes a complete bibliography.

NELSON R. KELLOGG

MEGRUE, Roi Cooper (12 June 1883–27 Feb. 1927), playwright, was born in New York City, the son of Frank Newton Megrue, a stockbroker, and Stella Cooper. He attended a private school and was a 1903 graduate of Columbia University, where he engaged in college theatricals. In 1903 he went to playbroker Elizabeth Marbury with a proposal for a dramatization of a popular novel. Though she turned down the idea, she hired him as a clerk and play reader for her office. She wrote in her autobiography, "I wanted someone who could receive the clients with a radiant good humor. Megrue's round face seemed to me encouraging, so he fell into the job." In appearance Megrue was "a plump young man with the merry eyes of one of mirthful bent and the alert gaze of a wide-awake intellect" (*Theatre Magazine*, Dec. 1914).

Megrue spent ten years in the Marbury office. He became, in effect, a professional in the profit-making business of mass entertainment that Broadway was at the turn of the century. He learned what elements of a play producers and stars thought necessary to please audiences, thus minimizing the risks of a production. Reading an estimated 2,000 scripts over the years, he also learned what made most scripts hopeless for the stage. "It . . . certainly taught me what to avoid," he told a *New York Tribune* reporter (29 Sept. 1918).

Megrue wrote plays during the evenings after his office work. He began with one-act plays and in 1911 placed one of them with actress Fanny Ward as a vaudeville sketch. His first full-length play to achieve production was the romantic comedy *White Magic* (1912), written in collaboration with David Graham Phillips. Reviews were scathing, and the production closed almost immediately. Megrue said later, with some curtness, "It ran a couple of minutes at the Criterion" (*New York Tribune*, 29 Sept. 1918). Disheartened by his first play's failure, Megrue did not attach his own name to his next work to achieve production. Only after *Under Cover* (1914) achieved success at its Boston tryout did he drop a pseudonym and make himself known as its author.

Under Cover dealt with the exposure of corrupt customs officials who allowed socialites to smuggle in jewelry in return for a private payoff—a topic from the headlines of the day. The play, a melodrama, proved to be one of the Broadway season's major successes; theater historian Gerald Bordman described it as "a thumpingly gripping crook play—one of the best in the whole history of the genre" (*American Theatre . . . 1914–1930*, p. 6). Audiences enjoyed its unexpected touches of humor amid the suspense, with a surprise plot twist at the end.

Not long after, Megrue had a second solid hit on Broadway. *It Pays to Advertise* (1914) was a farce, co-written with Walter Hackett, that told how the idle son of rich parents was tricked by them into becoming a successful businessman. The *New York Times* review said that "not often in the course of a season is it given to the first-nighters to roar [with laughter] so heartily" (9 Sept. 1914). Comparing the new play to *Under Cover*, the reviewer observed that *It Pays to Advertise* "is of greater skill and shrewder workmanship than that engaging melodrama." With two box-office successes on Broadway at the same time, Megrue was now established as a "money" playwright.

Two more successes for Megrue followed in 1915. One was a war play, *Under Fire*, that built a melodrama on headlines about the war in Europe and added the stage spectacle of German troops marching into a fallen city. The other was a broad ethnic comedy, *Abe and Mawruss*, co-written with Montague Glass as a sequel to the enormously successful *Potash and Perlmutter* of the previous season. To Megrue, both were molded by the same processes for the same purpose: the entertainment of the audience, "from the fifty-center in the last row of the family circle to the three-dollar man in the stage box" (*New York Times*, 28 Nov. 1915).

At one point during this period of career success, Megrue's four plays were being performed by seventeen companies, in New York City, on the road, and abroad. Yet as a theater businessman, he never counted on remaining a success. He saw the theater changing. In an article in the *New York Times* he noted that no longer could a well-crafted play "amble along pleasantly enough for its ten or twelve weeks in New York, and then go on the road to clean up. . . . Nowadays, there are so many theatres, so much competition, so many productions, while all the time the theatregoing public has not increased proportionately, that only the very best plays succeed" (29 Nov. 1914). From 1916 to 1918 his next three plays failed.

Megrue persisted. He told an interviewer: "A man writes a play and sticks to it through all the three-ply agonies of revisions, rehearsals and so on, all because he set out to do it and he can't make himself stop. . . . [He wants] to satisfy his sporting instinct to excel. Making the day's record for the club on the golf-course is exactly the right training for making the right sort of attempt at play-writing. It is the hanging-on that counts" (*Green Book*, Nov. 1916). Meanwhile, he coaxed his friend, novelist Jesse Lynch Williams, into writing a comedy, *Why Marry?*, arranged for its production, and directed it himself. The result was one of the hits of 1917.

Megrue's next play, the light comedy *Tea for Three* (1918), adapted from a German original, proved to be the greatest success of his career. Audiences delighted in its witty aphorisms on love, friendship, and marriage. It ran the entire season of 1918-1919 and toured for several seasons afterward. He still knew himself to have no secure place in the theater. He told the *Tribune* interviewer, "A playwright's place . . . is never assured. The 'good will' value of his business is nil." He was correct. Audience tastes were changing after World War I, and his two plays in 1919 and 1920 failed.

Megrue helped found the Dramatists' Guild, served on its first contract committee, and helped win the guild's first arbitration with theater managers. Personally, Megrue enjoyed the fruits of his past financial successes; he also had inherited the entire estate of an aunt in 1918. He enjoyed living, entertaining, and traveling with his mother, and he was her devoted companion for his entire life. In 1925 he wrote a last play for Broadway, *Venice for Two*, adapted from a French original. It failed. After months of increasing illness, he died in New York City. The *New York Times* obituary gave the cause of death as "a complication of diseases, in which uraemic poisoning was a determining factor."

From start to finish of his writing career, Megrue remained a businessman of the theater rather than an artist. An interviewer described him as "an average looking, blue serge New Yorker," with nothing of the playwright about him except "the traditional tobacco-stained fingers," who wrote what would please a crowded theater's audience. "It is not hard to believe him when he assures one that he writes plays for the pleasure and profit of doing them, with no ulterior motive of reforming anything or any one" (*New York Tribune*, 29 Sept. 1918). He takes his place in American theatrical history as a craftsman from the last years of Broadway as a purveyor of mass entertainment, before moving pictures and radio took over completely in that area. In light of his "sporting instinct to excel," one can say that five hits to seven failures gives him a creditable score among players of the risky game of Broadway.

• Materials on the life and career of Megrue are in the Billy Rose Theatre Collection at the New York Public Library for the Performing Arts, Lincoln Center. Articles written by Megrue are in the *New York Times*, 29 Nov. 1914 and 28 Nov. 1915. Interviews with the playwright are in Ada Patterson, "Roi Cooper Megrue: The Boy with Two Plays on Broadway," *Theatre Magazine*, Dec. 1914, pp. 276, 290; "Playwriting as a Sport," *Green Book*, Nov. 1916, pp. 930–31; and the *New York Tribune*, 29 Sept. 1918. A list of his plays, with the exception of *Venice for Two*, is in *Who Was Who in the Theatre, 1912–1976* (1978). Reminiscences of Megrue's early days are in Crosby Gaige, *Footlights and Highlights* (1948), and Elizabeth Marbury, *My Crystal Ball* (1924). Summaries and comment on his plays are in Gerald Bordman, *American Theatre: A Chronicle of Comedy and Drama, 1869–1914* (1994) and *American Theatre: A Chronicle of Comedy and Drama, 1914–1930* (1995). Mergue's aid to Jesse Lynch Williams is described in the *New York Times*, 30 Dec. 1917. Obituaries are in the *New York Times* and the *New York Herald-Tribune*, both 28 Feb. 1927.

WILLIAM STEPHENSON

MEHEGAN, John Francis (6 June 1920?–3 Apr. 1984), jazz educator, writer, and pianist, was born in Hartford, Connecticut, the son of John James Mehegan, a blacksmith, and Margaret Egan. The *New York Times* obituary gives his birth year as 1916, but Mehegan himself gave 1920 in interviews and standard reference sources.

Mehegan studied violin from 1926 to 1933 but hated that instrument and instead acquired keyboard skills by copying the movement of player pianos. After studies at Hartford Federal College during the academic year 1937–1938, he spent the following year at the Julius Hartt School of Music in Hartford. Refused entry as a piano major, he was told that he would never play professionally; instead he studied composition and theory.

In 1940 or 1941 Mehegan married Doris Crowley; they had two children. Moving to New York City in 1941, he performed at the Nut Club in Greenwich Village and the Hangar Bar in New Jersey. He recorded in March 1945 as the leader of a quartet with guitarist Billy Moore, bassist Al Hall, and drummer Jimmy Crawford and in May as a member of reed player Herbie Fields's group. After a year-long apprenticeship as a teaching assistant to jazz pianist Teddy Wilson at the Metropolitan Music School from 1945 to 1946, he headed the Metropolitan's jazz department from 1946 to 1956 (or 1958). He also taught at the Juilliard School of Music from 1947 to 1964.

Mehegan wrote the score for Tennessee Williams's *A Streetcar Named Desire*, and from 3 December 1947 he served as offstage pianist throughout the show's three-year run of 855 performances on Broadway. Then, while continuing his dual career as an educator and a musician, he embarked on a third career as a writer, contributing an instructional series, "How to Play Jazz Piano," to *Metronome* magazine from 1952 to 1954. Bridging these activities, he recorded the album *A History of Jazz Piano: From Barrelhouse to Bop* in a duo with string bassist Charles Mingus late in 1952. He performed at the Hickory House, Birdland, and the Drake Room. In September 1955 he recorded *Reflections*, an album of unaccompanied solos and duos with drummer Kenny Clarke. Around this time he performed at the Composer Club as the leader of a trio with Vinnie Burke playing bass and Eddie Costa alternating between vibraphone and second piano; they recorded in November. In April 1956 he made the solo album *How I Play Jazz Piano*.

Divorced in 1956, Mehegan married Terry Adelstein in 1957; they had no children and divorced in 1961. He served as jazz critic for the *New York Herald Tribune* from 1957 to 1960 and also contributed to *Down Beat*, *Saturday Review*, and *Music Journal*. While remaining at Juilliard, he left the Metropolitan school to become jazz instructor at Columbia University Teachers College from 1958 to 1961 or 1962. During summer vacation in 1959, he embarked on a concert, lecture, and research tour of South Africa that was cut short because he encouraged black musicians. In 1961 he lectured in twenty-five European cities on a tour sponsored by the State Department. He also tried his hand at radio as the jazz critic on WNYC from 1961 to 1962. In 1961 he married Gay Griscom; they had three children and divorced in 1978.

During these years Mehegan initiated his most important work, the four-volume series *Jazz Improvisation, i: Tonal and Rhythmic Principles* (1959), *Jazz Improvisation, ii: Jazz Rhythm and the Improvised Line* (1962), *Jazz Improvisation, iii: Swing and Early Progressive Piano Styles* (1964), and *Jazz Improvisation, iv: Contemporary Piano Styles* (1965); a revised and enlarged edition of all four volumes was published in 1984. Concurrently, Mehegan wrote a number of instructional booklets: *The Jazz Pianist* (3 vols., c. 1960–1961), *Styles for the Jazz Pianist* (3 vols., c. 1962–1963), *Studies in Jazz Harmony* (c. 1962), *Touch and Rhythm Techniques for the Jazz Pianist* (c. 1962), and *Contemporary Styles for the Jazz Pianist* (3 vols., c. 1963–1970; 2d ed., c. 1980). In 1969 he contributed an instructional series to *Clavier* magazine.

Mehegan founded his own jazz studio in New York City in 1963 before leaving Juilliard. He taught at the University of Bridgeport, Connecticut, from 1968 to 1977. This position overlapped with an appointment as lecturer in jazz improvisation at the Yale School of

Music from 1974 to 1983. On Saturday afternoons from 1980 to summer 1983 he performed at the River Cafe in New York. During this period he also held long engagements at the United Nations Hotel in New York, and the Seascope and Dameon's in Westport, Connecticut. On 23 March 1984, after it became known that Mehegan was suffering from a brain tumor, Gerry Mulligan, Dave Brubeck, and other jazz musicians gave a concert in his honor at Symphony Space in New York City. He died in New Canaan, Connecticut. A last booklet, *Improvising Jazz Piano*, was published posthumously in 1985.

A man whose "glass of water" on the piano was actually vodka, Mehegan was, perhaps not by coincidence, strongly and sometimes outrageously opinionated: of Thelonious Monk, he said, "I can only understand his style as some kind of musical disability" (Lydon, p. 25). But his sometimes eccentric outlook was probably also shaped by the frustrations of trying almost singlehandedly to deal with jazz improvisation in a rigorous musicological and theoretical manner at a time when such an approach was routinely disregarded in the academy. In his response to a *Contemporary Authors* questionnaire, Mehegan stated his aims: "I realized that no vocabulary existed to concisely communicate the functions of this art form. . . . My labors in the field of jazz have been directed toward dispelling this lack." The results, a four-volume survey of improvisation and the numerous instructional booklets, have provided countless readers with insights into the nuts and bolts of mainstream jazz piano styles.

• Filed at the Institute of Jazz Studies, Newark, N.J., is a typescript of an unidentified and undated (c. late 1950s) interview of Mehegan. Michael Lydon surveys his career in "John Mehegan: Jazz Piano Author and Teacher," *Keyboard* 9 (Apr. 1983): 22, 24–25. See also Leonard Feather, *The Encyclopedia of Jazz*, rev. ed. (1960); Feather, *The Encyclopedia of Jazz in the Sixties* (1966); Feather and Ira Gitler, *The Encyclopedia of Jazz in the Seventies* (1976); and *International Who's Who in Music*, 8th ed. (1977). Obituaries are in the *New York Times*, 5 Apr. 1984, and the *Chicago Tribune* and *Washington Post*, both 9 Apr. 1984.

BARRY KERNFELD

MEIGS, Charles Delucena (19 Feb. 1792–22 June 1869), physician and teacher, was born in St. George, Bermuda, the son of Josiah Meigs, an editor, educator, and lawyer, and Clara Benjamin. Josiah, although born and raised in Connecticut, was serving as a proctor in the English courts of admiralty in Bermuda when Meigs, the fifth of ten children, was born. The family moved back to Connecticut in 1794, and soon thereafter Meigs's father was elected professor of mathematics and natural philosophy at Yale College. After six years in New Haven, the family moved to Athens, Georgia, when the father was appointed president of the University of Georgia.

During his youth in the sparsely populated town of Athens, Meigs was encouraged by his father to study classical literature and learn French, in which he later became fluent. Meigs continued his study of the classics at the University of Georgia, graduating with an A.B. in 1809. He apprenticed to Dr. Thomas Hanson Marshall Fendall of Augusta the same year. After completing his three-year apprenticeship, Meigs matriculated in the Medical Department of the University of Pennsylvania. He attended lectures at the university in 1812–1813 and 1814–1815, returning to Georgia to practice medicine between these sessions. Meigs received his medical degree in absentia from the University of Pennsylvania in 1817. His thesis was on the prolapse of the uterus.

In the winter of 1814–1815, while at medical school, Meigs met Mary Montgomery, daughter of a prominent Philadelphia merchant. Married in 1815, they had ten children. Although Meigs had established a successful medical practice in Georgia, his wife's distaste for slavery forced them to leave the South. In 1817 Meigs and his wife moved to Philadelphia, where he soon built an extensive private practice. In the beginning, he devoted his spare time to the study of medical literature and belles lettres, carpentry, modeling clay and wax, and drawing and painting. The artistic skills he developed during this period enabled him to prepare his own drawings and models for teaching.

Meigs quickly became one of the leaders of Philadelphia's medical community. He was active in the Philadelphia Medical Society, the Philadelphia County Medical Society, the College of Physicians of Philadelphia, and the Kappa Lambda Society of Hippocrates of Philadelphia. One of the founding members of Kappa Lambda, a secret organization founded in 1822 to elevate the public's view of the medical profession by regulating the ethical conduct of its members, Meigs was an editor of its publication, the *North American Medical and Surgical Journal*. He was also a member of the Academy of Natural Sciences and the American Philosophical Society. During the 1832 cholera epidemic in Philadelphia, Meigs was in charge of one of the several hospitals established to care for victims of the disease.

It was as a teacher and writer in the fields of obstetrics and gynecology that Meigs was most influential. Although attracted to obstetrics early in his career, Meigs temporarily abandoned the specialty after several difficult deliveries, but he soon overcame his crisis of confidence.

Meigs first ventured into teaching obstetrics in 1830, when he offered lectures in one of the many private medical schools in the city. From 1838 to 1849 he headed the Lying-in Department of the Pennsylvania Hospital. In 1841 he was appointed professor of midwifery and diseases of women and children at Jefferson Medical College, where he would teach for twenty years.

Of medium height, thin, and possessing a large head, Meigs was a showman in the lecture hall. And despite his squeaky voice, Meigs held his students' attention while gaining their affection. His very popular lectures were conversational in tone; Meigs would tell anecdotes, quote Scripture, and use passages from classical literature to make his points. Samuel D.

Gross, who served with Meigs on the Jefferson faculty, wrote in his autobiography that in the lecture room, Meigs "was the best actor I have ever seen."

Meigs was a prolific author. He translated from the French Christoph Wilhelm Hufeland's *A Treatise on the Scrofulous Disease* (1829), Alfred A. L. M. Velpeau's *An Elementary Treatise on Midwifery* (1831), and Marc Colombat's *A Treatise on the Diseases and Special Hygiene of Females* (1845). Meigs's own *The Philadelphia Practice of Midwifery* (1838), later republished as *Obstetrics: The Science and the Art* (1849), appeared in a number of editions and was used as a textbook in many medical schools. Meigs's other publications included *Females and Their Diseases* (1848), *Observations on Certain of the Diseases of Young Children* (1850), *A Treatise on the Acute and Chronic Diseases of the Neck of the Uterus* (1854), and *On the Nature, Signs, and Treatment of Childbed Fevers* (1854), which contains color lithographs made from his original drawings.

Meigs's writings and lectures made him one of the most prominent and controversial figures in American obstetrics and gynecology. Like many other leaders of Philadelphia medicine, who were known for their conservatism, Meigs opposed the use of anesthesia in childbirth and carried on public disputes with those who disagreed with him. Moreover, he was criticized by many of his colleagues for his belief, later proved wrong, that puerperal fever was not contagious and that physicians could not possibly be carriers of the disease. Meigs found unacceptable the idea that he or any other physician posed a threat to obstetric patients. Although Meigs could be courteous and gentle to his friends and patients, he tended to be self-righteous and highly sensitive to criticism. During the debate over the contagiousness of puerperal fever, Meigs argued violently, occasionally using foolish and offensive language with his opponents, most notably Oliver Wendell Holmes and Walter Channing.

By the late 1850s Meigs's grueling regimen of practice, teaching, and writing began to wear him down. In 1856, suffering from nervous exhaustion and longing for retirement, Meigs built a country retreat outside of Philadelphia, which he called "Hamanassett" after a small river in Connecticut. Meigs tried to resign from Jefferson Medical College in 1856, but because of the ill health of his successor, he remained on the faculty until 1861. During the last eight years of his life, Meigs, perhaps due to the professional controversies in which he was involved, lost his interest in medicine. Ensconced in his country estate, he devoted most of his time to horticulture and reading. Depressed over the Civil War, Meigs's last years were filled with bitterness and infirmity. He lost a grandson in the Civil War, and his wife died in 1865. Meigs died four years later at his country estate in Delaware County, Pennsylvania.

Famous during his lifetime as an author and teacher in the fields of obstetrics and gynecology, Meigs is primarily remembered not for his contributions to medicine but rather for his stubborn resistance to the use of anesthesia in childbirth and his unwillingness to accept the evidence that puerperal fever was contagious.

• Small collections of Meigs's papers can be found at the College of Physicians of Philadelphia, Pennsylvania Hospital, and in the archives of Thomas Jefferson University. John Bell, "Obituary Notice of Charles D. Meigs, M.D.," *Proceedings of the American Philosophical Society* 13 (1873): 170–79, and J. Forsyth Meigs, *Memoir of Charles D. Meigs* (1876), are the best contemporary accounts of Meigs's professional career and personal life. Herbert Thoms, "Charles Delucena Meigs," *American Journal of Obstetrics and Gynecology* 31 (1936): 1049–56, is the best modern treatment of Meigs's career. See also [Cato], "Sketches of Eminent Living Physicians. No. V. Charles D. Meigs," *Boston Medical and Surgical Journal* 40 (1849): 313–15, 333–34; Samuel D. Gross, *Autobiography of Samuel D. Gross, M.D.* (1887); A. Levinson, "The Three Meigs and Their Contribution to Pediatrics," *Annals of Medical History* 10 (1928): 138–48; J. Wister Meigs, "Puerperal Fever and Nineteenth-Century Contagionism: The Obstetrician's Dilemma," *Transactions & Studies of the College of Physicians of Philadelphia*, 4th ser., 42 (1975): 273–80, and "Charles Delucena Meigs, M.D. (1792–1869), as Seen by His Great-Great-Grandson," *Transactions & Studies of the College of Physicians of Philadelphia*, 4th ser., 43 (1976): 129–35; and W. Robert Penman, "Charles Delucena Meigs, M.D.: An Assessment of His Role in Philadelphia Obstetrics," *Transactions & Studies of the College of Physicians of Philadelphia*, 4th ser., 43 (1976): 121–24.

THOMAS A. HORROCKS

MEIGS, Josiah (21 Aug. 1757–4 Sept. 1822), educator, was born in Middletown, Connecticut, the son of Return Meigs, a hatter, and Elizabeth Hamlin. In a family in which thirteen children were born, Meigs was one of only four who survived past childhood. His youth in Connecticut was spent in an environment of heated political dialogue as colonists railed against British rule and debated alternative forms of government. His two older brothers eventually fought in the American Revolution, and Meigs himself developed early a commitment to popular government.

Meigs attended Yale College in New Haven, Connecticut, obtaining a B.A. in 1778 along with classmates Noah Webster and Joel Barlow. He took a teaching position in Claverack, New York, but returned to Yale after three years to accept an appointment as a tutor of mathematics, natural philosophy, and astronomy. In 1782 he married Clara Benjamin, with whom he had nine children.

As a young man with wide-ranging interests, Meigs also studied law and was admitted to the bar in New Haven in 1783. A year later, when he was elected the first city clerk there, he resigned his tutor position and went into partnership in a printing and publishing establishment. With Daniel Bowen and Eleutheros Dana he published the weekly *New Haven Gazette*, which by 1787 was renamed the *New Haven Gazette and the Connecticut Magazine* with Meigs as sole publisher. However, in 1788, the financially troubled publication ceased.

In 1789 Meigs again initiated a career shift. He resigned as city clerk and moved his family to the Bermuda Islands to open a law practice that advocated American claims against British privateers in the vice admiralty court. One constant in Meigs's early career meandering was his love of science. After he resigned from Yale he continued to lecture there on astronomy and natural philosophy. In Bermuda he studied geometry and logged official meteorological observations for the Royal Society in London.

Another constant feature in Meigs's life was his outspoken political opinion along republican lines of the day, applauding Jeffersonian democracy and scorning vestiges of monarchy or suggestions of government by a land-owning aristocracy. His immovable stance and candor eventually resulted in his arrest for treason in Bermuda. Quickly released, he returned to Connecticut in 1794 and was appointed professor of mathematics and natural philosophy at Yale. When he joined the faculty, he discovered that his former Yale teacher and mentor Abraham Baldwin had moved to Georgia. There Baldwin and Governor Lyman Hall (also a Yale graduate) were working to secure legislative support for a future college.

Meigs's Jeffersonian sentiments were not widely shared in Connecticut, a stronghold of antirepublican leanings. Yale president Timothy Dwight, an ardent federalist, was particularly opposed to Meigs's views. By 1798 Meigs could retain his professorship only by writing a long letter of atonement to the Corporation of Yale College. In it he explained that he was not an enemy of the Constitution, insisted that his republican opinions reached wider circulation than intended, and pleaded that his termination would "be utterly ruinous to me and my family" (11 Sept. 1798). Although he was retained for another uneasy year, he resigned in 1800 when Baldwin invited him to a professorship at a new university in Georgia that as yet had no campus, no buildings, and no students.

By 1800 Baldwin had obtained a legislative charter for the future University of Georgia, had gathered a board of trustees, and had secured a campus site at Athens, then on the edge of Georgia's rugged western frontier. He also had named Meigs as his successor to the presidency of the planned venture. Meigs took over as president in 1801 when Baldwin, by then also serving as a U.S. senator, resigned the school post.

Hastily and single-handedly Meigs began teaching the first small group of students in the fall of 1801, with classes held under the trees and in a small log cabin at the Athens site. He also managed a fundraising campaign for public subscriptions and legislative support, contracted for the construction of more substantial buildings, and traveled throughout the state to recruit students. When few were found ready for higher education, he started a preparatory academy at the college. A year later finances allowed for hiring a second professor and for construction of a large brick main building, the three-story Franklin College. Within five years Meigs's tireless recruitment efforts netted seventy students in the college and forty in the academy.

Meigs convinced the board of trustees to approve an ambitious and innovative curriculum emphasizing the sciences and de-emphasizing the traditional overtones of clerical training found in New England's colonial colleges. Latin and Greek language and literature were required, along with courses in geometry, trigonometry, astronomy, geography, chemistry, composition, public speaking, and bookkeeping. In 1806 the study of French language was added—a first for American higher education. Courses in the U.S. Constitution and moral philosophy comprised the capstone for seniors. In a 20 May 1802 letter to Meigs, Thomas Jefferson applauded the curriculum, noting, "Science is indispensably necessary for the support of a Republican government, and it is to the middle and southern states we must look for support until the clerical chains in which the New England states are bound can be broken or lightened."

Meigs continued his outspoken support of republican sentiments and soon found himself under fire from federalist trustees and local citizens. Sometimes with biting candor, he squared off with trustees about his objections to their actions with regard to the college. The trustees blamed Meigs and his politics for an enrollment decline that began in 1808. Meigs resigned the presidency in 1810, staying on as a professor of mathematics, natural philosophy, and chemistry. Animosities continued, however, and the trustees dismissed him in 1811.

Meigs barely escaped unemployment again when he was appointed in 1812 to a U.S. surveyor general position in Cincinnati, Ohio. In 1814 he moved his family to Washington, D.C., to become commissioner of the U.S. General Land Office. He immediately found the company of others with scientific interests and in 1816 became a founder of the Columbian Institute for the Promotion of Arts and Sciences. The institute was chartered by Congress in 1818, and land set aside for its botanical interests eventually became the U.S. Botanic Garden. Meigs became its president in 1819. Along with his brother Return J. Meigs, who was U.S. postmaster general, Josiah Meigs became involved in the founding of Columbian College (now George Washington University); when the college was granted a charter in 1821 by the U.S. Congress, Meigs was one of fourteen original incorporators. He also served on the college's first board of trustees and briefly held an appointment as professor of natural philosophy until his death in Washington, less than a year after the college opened its doors.

Meigs's most significant contribution was to higher education in Georgia. However, his energies in recruitment and campus building, and especially his innovative curriculum, also demonstrated beyond Georgia the possibilities for extending higher education to students in sparsely populated and rural areas of the American frontier.

• Papers concerning Josiah Meigs's efforts in the founding and early years of the university are at the University of Georgia Library, Athens, with relevant collections including his letters, minutes of the Board of Trustees of the University of Georgia (vol. 1), and minutes of the Senatus Academicus, University of Georgia, 1799–1842. Minutes of early board of trustees meetings are at University Archives, Gelman Library, George Washington University. Books offering insights into Meigs in Georgia include Augustus Longstreet Hull, *A Historical Sketch of the University of Georgia* (1894); E. Merton Coulter, *College Life in the Old South* (1928); and Thomas G. Dyer, *The University of Georgia: A Bicentennial History* (1985). The most comprehensive account of Meigs's life is the biography by his great-grandson William Montgomery Meigs, *Life of Josiah Meigs* (1887). Additional information about Meigs's early life is included in Franklin Bowditch Dexter, ed., *Biographical Sketches of the Graduates of Yale College, with Annals of the College History*, vol. 4: 1778–1792 (1907). Sources for Meigs's years in Washington, D.C., are William B. Bryan, *A History of the National Capital* (1916), and Elmer Louis Kayser, *Bricks without Straw, the Evolution of George Washington University* (1970). An obituary is in the *Washington, D.C., Daily National Intelligencer*, 5 Sept. 1822.

KATHERINE C. REYNOLDS

MEIGS, Montgomery Cunningham (3 May 1816–2 Jan. 1892), army officer, was born in Augusta, Georgia, the son of Charles Meigs, a physician, and Mary Montgomery. Soon after the family relocated to Philadelphia. In 1831 Meigs briefly attended the University of Pennsylvania there. He transferred to the U.S. Military Academy the following year and on 1 July 1836 graduated fifth in his class of forty-nine. As a second lieutenant, Meigs was initially posted with the First Artillery Regiment but subsequently requested and received transfer to the engineers. He engaged in various construction projects over the next sixteen years, commencing with Fort Mifflin near Philadelphia. He also worked on navigational improvements along the Mississippi River with Lieutenant Robert E. Lee. Meigs rose to first lieutenant on 7 July 1838; he then supervised work on Fort Delaware and the Delaware breakwater, Fort Wayne on the Detroit River, and Fort Montgomery on Lake Champlain, New York. A tenacious and energetic leader, he was also appointed to serve with the Board of Engineers for Atlantic Coastal Defenses from 1839 to 1841. In 1841 Meigs married Louisa Rodgers, daughter of Commodore John Rodgers. The couple had four children.

Meigs continued distinguishing himself in various engineering capacities. In 1853 he was summoned to Washington, D.C., to oversee the Washington Aqueduct Project. This eight-year endeavor was destined to bring year-round supplies of fresh water to the capital. It culminated in the construction across the Cabin John Branch of the world's largest masonry arch, a major technological feat. Meigs advanced to captain on 3 March 1853 and enjoyed such celebrity that he was commissioned to build new wings and domes for the Capitol between 1853 and 1859. In September 1860 he ran afoul of Secretary of War James B. Floyd in a dispute over contracts and was reassigned to Fort Jefferson on the Dry Tortuga Islands off the Florida coast. His exile proved short-lived, and in February 1861 Meigs returned to Washington, D.C., to attend the inauguration of President Abraham Lincoln. He resumed construction activities until the advent of the Civil War.

When hostilities commenced in April 1861, Meigs conferred with Lincoln and Secretary of State William Seward about the possibility of secretly relieving Fort Pickens, Florida. He then accompanied an expedition commanded by Lieutenant Colonel Erasmus D. Keyes and Lieutenant David D. Porter, U.S. Navy, for that purpose. The garrison was successfully reinforced, and on 14 May 1861 Meigs was promoted to colonel, Eleventh Infantry. He disdained a field command, however, and requested reassignment. On the following day Meigs succeeded Joseph E. Johnston (who had joined the Confederacy) as quartermaster general of the Union army. Though never trained as a logistician, Meigs made significant contributions to the war effort.

Meigs inherited a small, disorganized department but rapidly transformed it into a smoothly functioning bureau that supplied the needs of nearly one million soldiers. He was also responsible for overhauling transportation regulations for the railroads, wagons, ships, and pack animals under his charge. Continually beset by corruption, kickbacks, and unscrupulous contractors, Meigs nonetheless administered his affairs efficiently and dispensed nearly $1.5 billion by war's end. No armchair warrior, he repeatedly extended his logistical expertise to field operations and in 1864 personally commanded General Ulysses S. Grant's supply bases in Virginia. In July 1864, when Jubal Early's raid threatened the capital, Meigs directed a division of War Department employees in its defense. He also orchestrated a complicated seatrain of supply ships that victualed the army of General William T. Sherman at Savannah in 1864 and Raleigh in 1865. For brilliantly executing the complicated duties of his department, Meigs received promotion to brevet brigadier general on 5 July 1864.

After the war, Meigs remained with the quartermaster department in Washington, where he supervised plans for a new War Department building and the National Museum, a part of the Smithsonian Institution. He also made several trips to Europe to observe military affairs and in 1876 served with a commission charged with conducting military reforms. Meigs retired on 6 February 1882 but secured appointment as architect of the Pension Office buildings. He also found time to serve as regent of the Smithsonian Institution, join the American Philosophical Society, and become an early exponent of the National Academy of Science. Meigs died in Washington and was interred at Arlington National Cemetery.

Meigs was an irascible man who spent forty-six years in the service of his country. He was a talented architect and engineer, but his tenure as quartermaster general was perhaps more significant as it ushered in a new age of modern military bureaucracy. Meigs's appetite for staff work, insistence on departmental honesty, and attention to the minutiae of supplying troops in the field rendered him one of the most effective administrators of U.S. Army history. His unsung efforts certainly facilitated the eventual Union victory. His eldest son, John Rodgers Meigs, was a talented Union officer who was allegedly murdered by Confederate partisans while scouting the Shenandoah Valley on 3 October 1864. His commanding officer, General Philip Sheridan, was so outraged that he burned all houses and farms within five miles of the place of his death.

• Meigs's official correspondence is in RG 92, Office of the Quartermaster General, National Archives. A large collection of personal papers is at the Manuscript Division, Library of Congress, while his civil engineering papers reside at the Smithsonian Institution Library. The only reliable biography is Russell F. Weigley, *Quartermaster General of the Union Army* (1959). Useful details are also found in Erna Risch, *Quartermaster Support for the Army* (1962), and Sherrod E. East, "Montgomery C. Meigs and the Quartermaster Department," *Military Affairs* 25 (1961): 183–96. For information on other phases of his life consult Carolyn Mulford, "A Monumental Tribute to Architecture," *Historic Preservation* 38 (1986): 58–63; East, "The Banishment of Captain Meigs," Columbia Historical Society, *Records* 40 (1940): 97–143; and "General M. C. Meigs on the Conduct of the Civil War," *American Historical Review* 26 (1921): 285–303. An overview of Meigs's administrative contributions is in Allan Nevins, "A Major Result of the Civil War," *Civil War History* 5 (1959): 237–50.

JOHN C. FREDRIKSEN

MEIGS, Return Jonathan (17 Dec. 1740–28 Jan. 1823), revolutionary war officer and federal Indian agent, was born in Middletown, Connecticut, the son of Return Meigs, a hatter and member of the Connecticut General Assembly, and Elizabeth Hamlin. Nothing is known of his early life and education. Meigs married Joanna Winborn in 1764. They had four children, one of whom was Return Jonathan Meigs, Jr. (1764–1824), governor of Ohio, U.S. senator, and U.S. postmaster general. Joanna died in 1773, and in 1774 Meigs married Grace Starr, with whom he had three children, two of whom survived infancy. Until entering the Continental army, Meigs was involved in a mercantile business.

Meigs served in the Connecticut militia as a lieutenant (11 Oct. 1772) and then as a captain (18 Oct. 1774). Appointed major in the Second Connecticut Regiment (1 May 1775), Meigs held the same position when Congress on 14 June 1775 brought the Connecticut regiments into the Continental army. In September 1775 Meigs and his regiment were detached to Benedict Arnold's force for the invasion of Canada. Meigs kept a journal of his experiences during the trek through the Maine wilderness and also of the military operations outside of Quebec. He wrote the journal using powder and water that he mixed in the palm of his hand. At the assault on Quebec, 31 December 1775, Meigs scaled a wall of the city and was captured. Interned at the Seminary in Quebec, he was paroled in May 1776, returned to Connecticut in July, and exchanged by order of Admiral Richard Howe on 10 January 1777.

Meigs reentered the Continental army as a lieutenant colonel (22 Feb. 1777) in Henry Sherburne's Additional Continental Regiment. Meigs won a reputation as a daring and enterprising soldier in his raid at Sag Harbor, near the eastern end of Long Island, 23–24 May 1777. This was in response to an attack on Danbury, Connecticut, 23–28 April 1777, by the Loyalist governor of New York, William Tryon. Meigs's objective was a British foraging party that had come out of New York City. Taking the enemy by complete surprise, he burned twelve vessels, destroyed military stores, killed six of the enemy, and took ninety prisoners without any loss to his 160-man force. Within twenty-four hours, having covered 100 miles by water, Meigs and his men were back at Guilford, Connecticut. Congress rewarded Meigs by presenting him "an elegant sword" and on 10 September 1777 promoting him to colonel of the Sixth Connecticut Regiment (the "Leather-Cap Regiment"), making the rank retroactive to 12 May 1777.

For the next two years Meigs served in the Hudson highlands. He commanded one of the four light infantry regiments in Anthony Wayne's successful assault on Stony Point, 16 July 1779. Upon disbandment of the light infantry, Meigs returned to his Sixth Regiment. In May 1780, while temporarily commander of the brigade to which he belonged, he quelled, with the assistance of Pennsylvania troops, a mutiny of part of the Connecticut Line, winning the gratitude and praise of George Washington. On 1 January 1781, on the reorganization of the Connecticut regiments, Meigs retired from the army.

In late 1787 or early 1788 Meigs was appointed a surveyor for the Ohio Company. He and a party of New England settlers arrived at the mouth of the Muskingum River on the Ohio in April 1788 and there founded the town of Marietta. Meigs drew up a code of regulations, which was put into effect until the organization of a territorial government. He served as one of the territorial judges, a justice of the peace, clerk of the Court of Quarter Sessions, and a member of the Ohio territorial legislature (1799–1801). In 1795 he was a commissary of clothing for the army in the western country under General Wayne.

In politics, Meigs was a Jeffersonian Republican. In 1801 Thomas Jefferson appointed Meigs agent for Indian affairs in the Cherokee Nation and also agent of the War Department in the state of Tennessee. Meigs's first task was to establish a combined Indian and War Department agency at South West Point (now Kingston), Tennessee. Called "The White Path" by the Cherokees, Meigs endeavored honestly and fairly to support the rights of the Indians. He favored Indian land allotments and encouraged Indian amalgamation into white civilization. He made every effort to protect Indians from trespass and violence on the part of white people.

Meigs was the chief negotiator for Indian treaties involving Chickasaws and Creeks as well as the Cherokees. After the Louisiana Purchase, he promoted Indian removal. In 1817 and 1819 some western

Cherokees opted to relocate in the Arkansas Territory. Meigs prevailed on the Lower Creeks and the Cherokees to side with the United States during the "Red Stick" Creek rebellion of 1813–1814.

Affecting areas under his agency, federal and state governments successfully obtained nine Indian land cessions, most of which were located in northern Georgia. Meigs attempted to convince Indians that payment for lands was in many instances preferable to keeping them, and he helped the Cherokees become farmers. Among his duties were distributing annuities, surveying new borders, advising on the establishment of a republican government for the Cherokees, providing medical aid, and arbitrating disputes among the Indians and with the whites. Generally he acted as a liaison between white and Indian governments. He kept a firm hand in expelling intruders from Indian lands. Though a champion of the Indians, Meigs favored termination of government annuities because he believed the program had sapped Indian initiative.

Meigs was highly regarded in his time by both federal officials and the Cherokees for his efficient and diligent service. His advocacy for firmness in justice, especially as to crimes committed by whites against the Indians, however, was often thwarted by federal and state authorities. Meigs's agency headquarters during most of the period was located at the Hiwassee Cherokee Reservation at the border of southwestern North Carolina and southeastern Tennessee. On one occasion, he gave up his comfortable quarters to a visiting chief and slept outdoors in a tent. There he contracted pneumonia, from which he died.

• The Indian Collection of the Manuscript Division of the Library of Congress has Meigs's "Memorandum Book of Occurrences in the Cherokee Country, 1796–1807." Voluminous correspondence and documents pertaining to Meigs as Indian agent are found in the Records of the Cherokee Indian Agency, Tennessee, Bureau of Indian Affairs (including Meigs's journals); and Bureau of Indian Affairs: Letters Received by the Secretary of War Relating to Indian Affairs, 1800–1823, both collections at the National Archives, Washington, D.C. For sketches of Meigs and his family, see Henry B. Meigs, *Record of the Descendants of Vincent Meigs* (1901), which includes an obituary, originally published as a broadside, on pp. 201–4. Meigs's participation in the Canadian invasion is seen in Kenneth Roberts, ed., *March to Quebec: Journals of the Members of Arnold's Expedition*, 5th ed. (1945), with Meigs's "Journal" on pages 173–92; and Justin H. Smith, *Arnold's March from Cambridge to Quebec* (1903). For other events of Meigs's revolutionary war career, see Henry P. Johnston, "Return Jonathan Meigs: Colonel of the Connecticut Line of the Continental Army," *Magazine of American History* 4 (1880): 282–92, which partially reprints the obituary; and Johnston, *The Storming of Stony Point on the Hudson, Midnight, July 15, 1779* (1900). Treatment of the early years in Ohio is in Israel W. Andrews, *Washington County and the Early Settlement of Ohio* (1877). William G. McLoughlin, *Cherokee Renascence in the New Republic* (1986), is a detailed study of Meigs's Indian agency and Cherokee relations. Henry T. Malone, *Cherokees of the Old South: A People in Transition* (1956), also has a discussion of Meigs as Indian agent.

HARRY M. WARD

MEIGS, Return Jonathan (14 Apr. 1801–19 Oct. 1891), lawyer, abolitionist, and state librarian of Tennessee, was born near Winchester, Clark County, Kentucky, the son of John Meigs and Parthenia Clendinen. After the death of his father in 1807, he lived part of the time with his uncle James Lemme in Bourbon County, where he studied the classics under the tutelage of George Wilson. Subsequently he studied law and was admitted to the bar in Frankfort, Kentucky, in 1822.

In January 1823 the youthful lawyer visited his grandfather, Colonel Return Jonathan Meigs, the famous Indian agent at the Hiwassee Garrison in East Tennessee. Shortly after his arrival there, his 83-year-old grandfather, highly respected by the Cherokees, gave up his bed to a visiting Cherokee chief. As a consequence of sleeping on the floor, Colonel Meigs contracted pneumonia and died. Young Meigs immediately assumed responsibility for the disposition of his grandfather's estate and decided to remain in Tennessee. In 1825 he married Sally Keys Love, with whom he would have five sons. They settled in Athens, where he continued to practice law until removing in 1835 to Nashville to enter into a legal partnership with James Rucks.

In 1834 Meigs was persuaded by friends to be a candidate from McMinn County to the state convention to revise Tennessee's constitution. He was defeated in part because of a popular prejudice against lawyers but mainly because of his avowed abolitionism and open campaigning to amend the state constitution to allow for the gradual emancipation of all slaves. Meigs's sympathy for the plight of both slaves and free blacks was manifested repeatedly throughout his career. One of the incorporators of the Tennessee Society for Colonization of Free Negroes, he fought two highly publicized court battles on behalf of slaves, *Elijah v. the State* (1839) and *Jacob v. the State* (1842). The latter case involved the conviction of a slave, Jacob, who killed his abusive master in self-defense; Meigs and fellow lawyer Thomas Washington made a compelling argument that the case was one of justifiable manslaughter, but they lost before the Tennessee Supreme Court.

In 1838 and 1839 Meigs was attorney general of the state and reporter of its supreme court decisions (*Tennessee Reports* 19 [1839]). Appointed U.S. attorney for the Middle Tennessee District in 1841, he subsequently published between 1848 and 1850 a two-volume *Digest of All the Decisions of the Former Superior Courts of Law and Equity, and of the Present Supreme Court of Errors and Appeals in the State of Tennessee*. His foremost effort at codifying Tennessee's laws, however, came in 1858, when he published with William F. Cooper the *Code of Tennessee*, the only such code legally adopted by the legislature until 1931.

Meigs served as a Whig in the state senate from 1847 to 1848. He advocated state financing of internal improvements such as turnpikes and railroads and sponsored a free banking bill, based on New York's banking laws. He also offered bills on court reform, public support of education, and local aid for internal improvements. Like other Whigs, he saw railroads as a key to Tennessee's future prosperity, and as early as 1831 he had supported proposals for the building of a railroad connecting the state with the Atlantic seaboard. Meigs also introduced legislation incorporating colleges for women and providing appeals for slaves convicted before justices of the peace, as well as a bill incorporating the Sons of Temperance of Tennessee.

Meigs's advocacy of a lengthy list of educational, cultural, and humanitarian reforms is impressive by any standard. The first president of the Tennessee Society for the Diffusion of Knowledge, he subsequently served as corresponding secretary of the Tennessee Historical Society and as trustee of both the University of Nashville and the School for the Education of the Blind. A patron of public lectures, music, and the theater, he declined a position on the state's supreme court to accept in 1856 what would become the major focus of his many interests, the position of first state librarian of Tennessee. His enthusiasm and energy in acquiring new books, despite the legislature's continuing parsimony in appropriations, enabled Meigs to obtain many rare and valuable volumes that formed an excellent foundation for future acquisitions.

At the outbreak of the Civil War Meigs was one of the few prominent inhabitants of Middle Tennessee who remained steadfastly loyal to the Union. Fearing danger to himself and his family because of his outspoken Unionism, he removed to New York in 1861. Subsequently he gave legal advice to his good friend, Andrew Johnson, when the latter became military governor of Tennessee. Meigs was said to have declined both a nomination to the U.S. Senate from Tennessee in 1865 and an appointment to the U.S. Supreme Court later offered to him by President Johnson. One of his sons, Captain Josiah Vincent Meigs, appealed directly to President Abraham Lincoln and received permission during the Civil War to raise a detachment of black troops from Tennessee for the Union.

Appointed clerk of the Supreme Court of the District of Columbia in 1863, Meigs remained in this position until his death in Washington, D.C., never returning to Tennessee. As a consequence of the Civil War and Meigs's unswerving abolitionism and loyalty to the Union, Tennessee thus lost one of its most enlightened, public-minded citizens and possibly the state's most profound legal scholar in the nineteenth century.

• In addition to works cited in the text, Meigs wrote "Second Biennial Report upon the Library of the State," Tennessee General Assembly, *Appendix, 1857–1858*: 241–51; and "Third Biennial Report upon the Library of the State," Tennessee General Assembly, *Appendix, 1859–1860*: 149–50. The best recent summary of Meigs's life and career is Ronnie W. Faulkner, "Return Jonathan Meigs: Tennessee's First State Librarian," *Tennessee Historical Quarterly* 42 (Summer 1983): 151–64. Older sources include John W. Green, *Law and Lawyers* (1950); Marcus J. Wright, "Return Jonathan Meigs, 1801–1891," *Magazine of American History* 28 (Aug. 1892): 128; *Washington Evening Star*, 21 Oct. 1891; Henry B. Meigs, *Record of the Descendants of Vincent Meigs Who Came from Dorsetshire, England to America about 1635* (1901); Joshua W. Caldwell, *Sketches of the Bench and Bar of Tennessee* (1898); Randal W. McGavock, *Pen and Sword: The Life and Journals of Randal W. McGavock* (1959); *Knoxville Register*, 22 Jan. 1834; Chase C. Mooney, "The Question of Slavery and the Free Negro in the Tennessee Constitutional Convention of 1834," *Journal of Southern History* 12 (Nov. 1946): 487–509; Charles T. Trabue, "The Voluntary Emancipation of Slaves in Tennessee as Reflected in the State's Legislation and Judicial Decisions," *Tennessee Historical Magazine* 4 (Mar. 1918): 58–60; Samuel Cole Williams, *History of Codification in Tennessee* (1932); Mrs. John Trotwood Moore, "The First Century of Library History in Tennessee, 1813–1913," *East Tennessee Historical Society's Publications* 16 (1944): 6; and two books by Henry S. Foote, *Casket of Reminiscences* (1874) and *Bench and Bar of the South and Southwest* (1876).

DURWOOD DUNN

MEIGS, Return Jonathan, Jr. (17 Nov. 1765–29 Mar. 1824), governor of Ohio, senator, and postmaster general, was born in Middletown, Connecticut, the son of Return Jonathan Meigs (1740–1823) and Joanna Winborn. Meigs graduated with honors from Yale College (now Yale University) in 1785 and became a lawyer in Middletown. There he met Sophia Wright, a student in a local academy. They were married in 1788; among their wedding gifts were two slaves. They had one child.

Shortly after the marriage, the Meigs household traveled on horseback to the new settlement of Marietta in the Northwest Territory. Meigs's father was an active member of the Ohio Company of Associates, which had founded the town in April 1788. Meigs had high expectations about the settlement, hoping that it would become the commercial and cultural center of the Ohio Valley. In the 1790s, Meigs maintained his household through his legal practice, land speculation, and a partnership in a general store that thrived through trade with the army and river travelers as well as local residents.

Politically, he attached himself to Ohio Company superintendent Rufus Putnam, a staunch defender of the Federalist territorial government. Meigs's loyalty and competence, in conjunction with Putnam's influence, won him appointment as Marietta postmaster in 1794 and, more significantly, as a territorial judge in 1798. He also was elected to the 1799 meeting of the territorial legislature. Shortly thereafter, Meigs began to cultivate friendships with opponents of the territorial regime, such as Edward Tiffin and Thomas Worthington of Chillicothe. He soon became the leader of the pro-statehood forces in the Marietta area. This shift of allegiances was not without a price; in 1802 he was defeated in his bid to serve as a delegate to the Ohio constitutional convention.

By now Meigs had acquired a reputation for being willing to trim his ideological sails to suit the prevailing winds. However, his connections with Worthington and Tiffin helped him secure election in 1803 as the first chief justice of the Ohio Supreme Court. Grand title aside, this was a tedious job, since the constitution required the court to meet in each county once a year. Characteristically, Meigs was soon looking elsewhere.

Resigning as chief justice in 1804, he accepted President Thomas Jefferson's appointment as commander of American forces in upper Louisiana. In 1805 Jefferson appointed Meigs presiding judge of the Louisiana Territory court meeting in St. Louis, but Meigs was unpopular and soon grew disenchanted. Pleading ill health, he went home to Marietta in the fall of 1806. The federal government agreed to transfer him to the Michigan Territory, and he took up his judicial responsibilities there in the spring of 1807. That fall Meigs became a candidate for governor of Ohio. He received more votes than his opponent, but the legislature nullified his election in December 1807 on the grounds that he did not meet the constitutional requirement of having been a resident of Ohio for the previous four years. As a consolation, he was elected to the supreme court again.

This time Meigs's former allies, Worthington and Tiffin, used their influence in the legislature against him. They had begun to doubt the sincerity of his devotion to Republican principles. No doubt, Meigs did keep his eye on public opinion, but he was also simply more suspicious of popular government than were Worthington and Tiffin. Meigs was thus an attractive candidate to many Federalists and conservative Republicans; he was particularly popular among voters from New England. As the Worthington-Tiffin forces began to decline, Meigs's fortunes rose. In December 1808 the legislature chose him over Worthington to fill a seat in the U.S. Senate. Two years later, in a bitter campaign centering on the question of the degree to which the judiciary should be independent of the legislature, the procourt Meigs decisively defeated Worthington to become governor of Ohio.

Meigs served two terms. The first was uneventful; the second coincided with the outbreak of the War of 1812. Governor Meigs eagerly prepared for war and dispatched 1,200 militia to serve with General William Hull. The firestorm that greeted the general's subsequent surrender in Michigan Territory also singed Meigs's reputation. Criticism abated, but Meigs, as usual, did not stay around much longer. In March 1814 he resigned in order to become postmaster general of the United States under James Madison (1751–1836). He held this job longer than any other. During his nine-year tenure, the number of post offices grew from 3,000 to 5,200, the number of miles of post roads doubled from 41,000 to 85,000 miles, and he proved to be an effective administrator.

Meigs spent the last year of his life in his federal-style mansion in Marietta, where he died. Many prominent contemporaries believed him more concerned with personal aggrandizement than principle, as revealed in his 1804 response to George Tod's request for advice on whether he should run for Congress. Meigs responded favorably, because he thought that Tod's election would get him "a Territorial Judgeship [at] $1200 per Annum." The jobs he got, however, were never good enough, and he frequently abruptly resigned from one in order to try another. Still, Meigs's career was hardly unusual in Jeffersonian America, and he generally handled his political positions with skill and integrity. Meigs thus played a prominent role in establishing the authority of American governments in the Trans-Appalachian West.

• The largest collection of Meigs papers is in the Ohio Historical Society in Columbus; there are also some letters in the Library of Congress, the Indiana University Library in Bloomington, and the Campus Martius Museum in Marietta, Ohio. No biography exists. Modern assessments of Meigs can be found in Jeffrey P. Brown, "The Ohio Federalists, 1803–1815," *Journal of the Early Republic* 2 (1982): 261–82; Andrew R. L. Cayton, *The Frontier Republic: Ideology and Politics in the Ohio Country, 1780–1825* (1986); Alfred Byron Sears, *Thomas Worthington, Father of Ohio Statehood* (1958); and William T. Utter, *The Frontier State: 1803–1825*, vol. 2 of *The History of the State of Ohio* (1942). There is a brief but carefully researched outline of Meigs's life in Linda Elise Kalette, ed., *The Papers of Thirteen Early Ohio Political Leaders* (1977).

ANDREW CAYTON

MEIKLEJOHN, Alexander (3 Feb. 1872–16 Dec. 1964), educator and civil libertarian, was born in Rochdale, England, the son of James Meiklejohn, a Scottish textile worker, and Elizabeth France. After his family migrated to Pawtucket, Rhode Island, in 1880, Meiklejohn attended local schools and Brown University (1889–1893). He took a Ph.D. in philosophy at Cornell University (1897) and returned to his alma mater as an assistant professor that fall. He married Nannine LaVilla in 1902, and they had four children. Meiklejohn served as dean at Brown (1901–1912), concentrating on matters of student life and discipline, before being selected president of Amherst College in 1912.

During his eleven years at Amherst, Meiklejohn won a national reputation as a motivator of young men, a curriculum innovator, and a critic of the professionalization of college athletics. A collection of his speeches and occasional papers, *The Liberal College* (1920), summarized his views. He inaugurated an interdisciplinary freshman course in social and economic institutions and hired the first college writer-in-residence, poet Robert Frost. He brought controversial speakers to campus, demanding equal time for opponents as well as supporters of U.S. entry into World War I. He rebuilt the faculty around youthful, provocative teachers. Critics complained about faculty disharmony, student rebelliousness and irreligion, and the Meiklejohn household's allegedly excessive spending. When the trustees, led by financier Dwight Morrow, fired Meiklejohn on the morning of commencement in June 1923, twelve students refused their degrees, several faculty resigned on the spot, and the case occupied New York and Boston newspapers for weeks.

After Amherst, Meiklejohn wrote and spoke widely. A volume of his public addresses, some from Amherst, appeared as *Freedom and the College* (1923). On the lecture platform, he held audiences spellbound. Following the death of his wife in 1925, he married Helen Everett, a Ph.D. in economics and the daughter of a former Brown philosophy colleague, in 1926; they would have no children. Earlier that year he joined the faculty of the University of Wisconsin and designed an Experimental College, which ran from 1927 to 1932. There, students lived together in a university dormitory and had no required classes or exams. They spent their first year studying Periclean Athens and their sophomore year exploring contemporary American society through tutorials and papers, prior to completing their undergraduate studies at the university or elsewhere. The experiment attracted wide notice, placing Meiklejohn on the cover of *Time* magazine in 1928, but also mobilized concerted opposition among traditionalist faculty and administrators, sufficiently alarming Wisconsin parents to the extent that enrollments fell at the Experimental College. Meiklejohn's account of his work, *The Experimental College* (1932), is a classic statement on behalf of a core curriculum and a criticism of lecture- and discipline-based higher education. Numerous alumni of the Ex-College went on to distinguished careers in education and public service.

From the early 1930s until his death Meiklejohn made his home in Berkeley, California. While overseeing a pioneering, privately financed venture in adult education, the San Francisco School of Social Studies, he wrote *What Does America Mean?* (1935) and *Education between Two Worlds* (1942), substantial critiques of American society, educational thought, and what he termed "Protestant capitalist civilization." Neither a pragmatist nor a Marxist, Meiklejohn drew from the philosophies of Immanuel Kant and Jean-Jacques Rousseau. Increasingly, he turned his attention to civil liberties, helping found and then leading the northern California chapter of the American Civil Liberties Union and writing significant articles and two books, *Free Speech and Its Relation to Self-Government* (1948) and *Political Freedom: The Constitutional Powers of the People* (1960), which outline an "absolutist" position on the First Amendment's protection of free speech.

Meiklejohn's theory of the First Amendment gave special privilege to free discussion of political issues. He argued that the public's right to hear any point of view is central to its role in democratic decision making and overrides any governmental interest in silencing it, rejecting Oliver Wendell Holmes's "clear and present danger" test. During the 1940s and 1950s Meiklejohn opposed the ACLU's expulsion of an avowed Communist from its board and wrote on behalf of University of California faculty who refused to sign an anti-Communist loyalty oath. Meiklejohn's views ultimately influenced several Supreme Court decisions, most notably the landmark *Times v. Sullivan* (1964), which greatly broadened the freedom to criticize public officials. Meiklejohn deemed the *Sullivan* decision "an occasion for dancing in the streets." When he received the Presidential Medal of Freedom in 1963, four justices were on hand to greet him. Meiklejohn died in Berkeley.

Meiklejohn's lead in higher education has been taken up in varying ways, from the no-elective Great Books curriculum installed at St. John's College, Annapolis, Maryland, in 1937 by his former Amherst student Scott Buchanan, to the interdisciplinary academic majors at Evergreen State College in Washington state, dating from the 1960s. Meiklejohn had greater influence in small, liberal arts college settings than in large public universities. In the realm of civil liberties, by the 1970s Meiklejohn's views were praised by jurists as divergent as William J. Brennan and Robert Bork, but additional issues arose for which his formulations may not have sufficed. Meiklejohn's emphasis on the public's "right to hear" was by no means identical to an individual's "right to speak," the path most liberals took in the decades after his death. Though Meiklejohn denied that the Constitution protected only "political" speech, others wondered if he would have backed artistic or literary speech or other forms of expression as unyieldingly. He remains a major figure in both of his primary areas of action.

• Meiklejohn's papers are in the State Historical Society of Wisconsin in Madison, but there are substantial collections in the Brown University Archives and the Amherst College Archives. An anthology of his writings with a biographical introduction is Cynthia Stokes Brown, ed., *Alexander Meiklejohn: Teacher of Freedom* (1980). The best brief assessment is Joseph Tussman, "Remembering Alexander Meiklejohn," *Liberal Education* 70 (Winter 1984): 323–42. See also Roland L. Guyotte, *Alexander Meiklejohn: An Introduction* (1991). For Meiklejohn's educational reforms, see Robert F. Brennan, "The Making of the Liberal College: Alexander Meiklejohn at Amherst," *History of Education Quarterly* 28 (Winter 1988): 569–97, and John F. Jenkins and E. David Cronon, *The University of Wisconsin: A History*, vol. 3 (1994), an unsympathetic account. On civil liberties, see William J. Brennan, "The Supreme Court and the Meiklejohn Interpretation of the First Amendment," *Harvard Law Review* 79 (Nov. 1965): 1–20; Frederick Schauer, *Free Speech: A Philosophical Enquiry* (1982); and Lee Bollinger, "Free Speech and Intellectual Values," *Yale Law Journal* 92 (Jan. 1983): 438–73. An obituary is in the *New York Times*, 17 Dec. 1964.

ROLAND L. GUYOTTE

MEIN, John (1732–1810), bookseller, printer, and Loyalist publisher, was born in Edinburgh, Scotland, the son of John Mein, a burgess and guildsman of Edinburgh and a slater by trade. His mother's name is unknown. John, Jr., was also enrolled as a burgess and guildsman in December 1760. Little is known about Mein apart from his role in supporting British policy during the revolutionary crisis. He emigrated to Boston in November 1764 and set up the first of his three shops in company with Robert Sandeman, founder of the Sandemanian religious sect to which Mein adhered. By September 1766 he was located in his third shop, on the north side of King Street, in partnership with John Fleeming. He had also established the first circulating library in the town of Boston.

Mein began to write on behalf of British policy in 1767. His first work, "Four Dissertations on the Reciprocal Advantages of a Perpetual Union between Great Britain and Her American Colonies," was advertised in January, but no copy survives. He achieved notoriety that December, however, when he published the first issue of the *Boston Chronicle*, which patriot leader James Otis claimed printed the "most infamous and reproachful invectives, that ever was invented." For instance, the issue of 26 October 1769 referred to John Hancock as "Johnny Dupe, Esq., alias the milch cow—a good-natured young man with long ears—a silly conceited grin on his countenance—a fool's cap on his head—a bandage tied over his eyes—richly dressed and surrounded with a crowd of people, some of whom are stroking his ears, others tickling his nose with straws, while the rest are employed rifling his pockets."

Mein's politics and violent temper soon landed him in trouble. Criticized as a Jacobite in an article published by patriot printer John Gill—that is, a supporter of the Stuart rebels against the British throne—he assaulted Gill in a Boston street in January 1768 when Gill refused to name the author of the remark. Mein was ultimately fined £75.

Even greater trouble arose that summer. The Boston resistance leaders had taken to printing the names of those who would not honor intercolonial nonimportation agreements. Two years earlier, consortiums of colonial merchants, encouraged where they were not compelled by local meetings, had pledged to cease importing goods from Britain until the Townshend Acts of 1767, which taxed glass, paint, tea, and paper, were repealed. Mein responded by examining the Customs House records and, beginning with his 21 August 1769 issue listed fifty-five patriots who had imported secretly in defiance of their own agreement. He also printed copies of the list and distributed it widely in America and Britain. This was the last straw for the patriots. Mein was threatened by several of them, but when he appealed for protection to Lieutenant Governor Thomas Hutchinson, he was told he could only be helped if he named his adversaries. (When he later returned to England, Mein criticized Hutchinson, who had hoped the resistance would burn itself out if left unprovoked.)

On 28 October several patriot leaders headed by William Molineux accosted Mein and his partner Fleeming. Thomas Marshall, lieutenant colonel of Boston's militia, swung a shovel at Mein's head; Fleeming discharged an empty pistol as the two Loyalists ran for protection to the British soldiers then stationed in Boston. Samuel Adams and Molineux swore out a warrant for Mein's arrest on the grounds he had fired on people "lawfully and peaceably assembled together." Mein hid out for a few days before returning to England in fear for his life: "Their plan was to get me into the custody of the officer, and it being dark, to knock [me] on the head; and then their usual saying might have been repeated, that it was done by boys and negroes, or by nobody."

Mein's troubles were not yet over. John Hancock bought up his debts and sued him for books, stationery, and supplies worth nearly £3,000 he had not yet paid for. This kept Mein tied up in British courts for most of 1770 and 1771. Mein emerged briefly from retirement to defend his reputation and attack the American revolutionaries in 1774. "The threats of an old factious agent, who vomits out his venom in the newspapers, are utterly contemptible; he owes his safety not to his innocence, but to the levity of our laws," was Mein's comment on Benjamin Franklin. Indeed, his general line was that the Revolution occurred thanks to "the timidity of the magistrate and the weakness of the government," a criticism he directed at Hutchinson for not ordering Boston's British garrison to protect him.

Mein lived obscurely for the last thirty-five years of his life, or at least no one has investigated his later career. The place of his death is unknown. His extreme loyalism alienated even supporters of the government like Hutchinson in the mid-1760s, when they were trying to restore social harmony rather than put down a rebellion that had yet to occur. But it was Mein, like Samuel Adams of the patriots, who anticipated the ultimate course of events.

• Readers may consult the *Boston Chronicle* in the microfilm edition of American newspapers published by the American Antiquarian Society. Two articles by John E. Alden deal with Mein: "John Mein, Scourge of the Patriots," Colonial Society of Massachusetts, *Publications* 34 (1945): 571–99, and "John Mein, Publisher," Bibliographic Society of America, *Papers* 36 (1942): 199–214. There is much material on Mein in Hiller Zobel, *The Boston Massacre* (1970).

WILLIAM PENCAK

MEINZER, Oscar Edward (28 Nov. 1876–14 June 1948), hydrogeologist, was born near Davis, Illinois, the son of William Meinzer and Mary Julia Meinzer, farmers. (His parents were not related.) Meinzer's grandparents, who had emigrated from Prussia to escape from a culture they had found oppressive, may have directly influenced Meinzer's future religious convictions, independent thought, hatred of war, and industriousness. As a child, Meinzer exhibited an enthusiastic curiosity about his surroundings, especially about the glacial till that rested on his father's fields and the fluctuating groundwater supply that occasionally left the family well dry. Meinzer gained his early education in local schools, supplemented by study at home. In 1896 he enrolled in Beloit Academy in Wisconsin and, a year later, in Beloit College, from which he graduated magna cum laude in 1901. He served as public school principal for two years in Frankfort, South Dakota, and then taught science for two more years at Lenox College in Hopkinton, Iowa, where he met his future wife, Alice Crawford, whom he married in 1906. The couple had two children, one of whom was adopted.

Beginning in 1903, Meinzer spent the summers studying geology at the University of Chicago, and in 1905 he enrolled full time in the university's graduate school. The following summer, he worked as a geologic aide with the U.S. Geological Survey, thus initiating the contact that was to provide much of the institutional base for his future career. Having completed his residence requirements for a doctoral degree in geology (which he received in 1922) at the University of Chicago in 1907, he returned to the USGS as a junior geologist and began his lifelong study of groundwater. During the next few years, Meinzer's assignments took him to Minnesota, Utah, Iowa, Arizona, and New Mexico. In each location, he carefully studied groundwater resources, occasionally, as in Utah, by traveling alone on horseback and carrying only the supplies he could fit in his saddlebags. This field experience impressed upon Meinzer the urgent necessity of acquiring quantitative data about the country's water resources—knowledge that would have immediate application in many commercial, agricultural, and industrial fields. The data enabled hydrologists to identify suitable areas for digging water wells, which in turn allowed the development of irrigation and the growth of population centers. In 1912 Meinzer became acting chief of the Division of Ground Water, and a year later he became chief, a position he held until his retirement in November 1946. In 1914 he stated, "The principal function of the Ground-Water Division is to make a survey of the water that exists below the surface of the ground; to determine, for every point in the United States, the occurrence, quantity, head, and quality of this subsurface or ground water, and the best method of recovering it for human use" (Sayre, p. 198).

As chief, Meinzer continued the quantitative investigations he had begun earlier. He studied groundwater supplies in various western and midwestern states, Cuba, and Hawaii, all the time refining approaches to make possible the collection of more accurate data. Meinzer realized that users in many parts of the country exploited groundwater reservoirs beyond "safe yield" levels, and he thereupon developed procedures to compute the amount of groundwater available for beneficial use, i.e., for irrigation and residential and industrial water supply. His findings were published in 1920 in *Quantitative Methods of Estimating Ground-Water Supplies* and were republished by the USGS in 1932. During World War I, Meinzer was commissioned a captain of engineers at the request of General John Pershing and was preparing to sail for France when the armistice was signed in November 1918. In 1923 Meinzer published two pioneering studies: *Outline of Ground-Water Hydrology, with Definitions*, an attempt to standardize terminology; and his 1922 dissertation, *The Occurrence of Ground Water in the United States, with a Discussion of Principles*, which became a basic handbook on groundwater.

As head of the Division of Ground Water, Meinzer became known as the father of groundwater hydrology in the United States. He systematized the available information on groundwater, much of which had been developed in Europe. He realized that hydrogeology (the geoscience that focuses on groundwater) descended from two branches, fluid mechanics and geology, but that the two sciences had not been well integrated. Especially in the 1930s, when fluid mechanics began to influence water resource developments in a significant way, he brought together engineers and scientists to collect and analyze data. Foreseeing the importance of groundwater to agriculture and, indeed, to the national economy, Meinzer insisted that hydrogeologists not only collect data on size, location, and physical characteristics of aquifers, but also on the quality of the water available for beneficial use. He attempted to measure the rate of depletion of aquifers but concurrently insisted that hydrogeologists not look at aquifers in isolation but as functional components of the larger hydrologic system. Meinzer had a hydrologic laboratory built, analyzed saltwater encroachment in coastal areas, and supervised dozens of geologists and engineers who significantly influenced the progress of hydrology in the United States. He led the fight to have the American Geophysical Union create a section on hydrology, a recognition that finally came in 1931. Meinzer became the section's first chairman, and Robert E. Horton, sometimes called the father of American hydrology, became the vice chairman.

Throughout his tenure as division chief, Meinzer emphasized interdisciplinary, systematic research. He also strove to share new knowledge with the public as quickly as possible rather than retaining it within the halls of bureaucracy. Although he increased his staff from four to nine between 1911 and 1917, World War I and subsequent reductions interrupted the division's continued growth. Meinzer's staff consisted of only ten geologists and engineers in 1929. Increased attention to resource development during the dust bowl crisis and depression of the 1930s, however, resulted in an expansion of the division to more than eighty members by the end of that decade. In 1940 the Divisions of Ground Water and Quality of Water together composed the largest corps of hydrogeologists in the world. By that time, the science of hydrogeology had developed strong theoretical roots, the result in no small part of the labor of Meinzer and his staff. During and after World War II, these roots provided for the rapid development of the science.

During his career Meinzer wrote or collaborated in writing more than 100 articles and reports and critically reviewed hundreds of others. Among his many honors was his election in 1947 to the presidency of the American Geophysical Union, a position he held at the time of his death in Washington, D.C. While Meinzer's important work was early recognized by his peers, the fact that he was shy, spoke deliberately, and shunned self-promotion kept him from becoming well known outside of professional circles. Meinzer's emphases on interdisciplinary research, water quality as well as quantity, and systematic collection and analysis of groundwater data continue to mark his profession to the present day.

• Some of Meinzer's unpublished notebooks are in the USGS Field Records Library, Central Region, in Denver, Colo.

Other official papers may be found in the records of the USGS, RG 57, National Archives and Records Administration. For Meinzer's own treatment of the history of hydrology, see his introduction as editor of *Hydrology* (1942). See also George B. Maxey, "The Meinzer Era of U.S. Hydrogeology, 1910–1940," in *Contemporary Hydrogeology: The George Burke Maxey Memorial Volume*, ed. William Back and D. A. Stephenson (1979), pp. 1–6; O. M. Hackett, "The Father of Modern Ground Water Hydrology," *Ground Water* 2, no. 2 (Apr. 1964): 2–5. Meinzer's role is put into a larger historical setting in National Research Council, Water Science and Technology Board, *Opportunities in the Hydrologic Sciences* (1991); and in David A. Stephenson et al., "Hydrogeology: It Is," *GSA Today* 1, no. 5 (May 1991): 93–100. Obituaries include, by A. Nelson Sayre, "Memorial to Oscar Edward Meinzer," *Geological Society of America Proceedings for 1948* (Apr. 1949): 197–206, which contains a complete bibliography of Meinzer's publications, and "Oscar Edward Meinzer, 1876–1948: A Memorial," *Economic Geology and the Bulletin of the Society of Economic Geologists* 3 (May 1949): 248–50.

MARTIN REUSS

MEISS, Millard (25 Mar. 1940–12 June 1975), art historian, was born in Cincinnati, Ohio, the son of Leon Meiss, a businessman, and Clara Loewenstein. Educated in public schools, he entered Princeton University in 1923, where he studied art history and architecture. In 1926 he won the Wanamaker Prize in English. After receiving a B.A. in 1926, he chose to continue studies in art history. His father did not approve of his son's choice, so Meiss worked for two years as a supervisor of building construction for a New York City architectural firm while he attended evening language classes at Columbia University.

In 1928 Meiss married Margaret Louchheim of New York City, with whom he had two children. He then went to Harvard, where he earned an M.A. in art history in 1931, working with Walter Friedlander. Returning to New York, he studied at New York University's Institute of Fine Arts with Richard Offner, the renowned authority on the Italian Dugento "primitives," as well as with the great humanist Erwin Panofsky, whom he would later join at the Institute for Advanced Study in Princeton, New Jersey. From 1931 until 1933 when he received his Ph.D. from New York University, he served as lecturer in art history there. In 1934 he was appointed to the faculty at Columbia University, becoming a full professor in 1954. He left Columbia in 1955 for a dual appointment at Harvard as professor of fine arts and curator of paintings for the Fogg Museum. In 1958 he became professor of art history at the Institute for Advanced Study, where he remained until 1974.

Meiss was a leading authority on late medieval and Renaissance painting. He contributed to studies in Flemish, French, and Italian painting of the fourteenth and fifteenth centuries, especially of the Tuscan Trecento. Meiss achieved distinction with the publication of his first book, *Painting in Florence and Siena After the Black Death* (1951). This study noted a change in painting in Florence and Sienna during the fourteenth century, discussing the regression to medieval style after the period of the Black Death. According to Meiss, this stylistic change represented a retrenchment from the development of a new realism begun by Giotto. This move—from a new focus on the human dimension (homocentricity) back to the spirituality, otherworldliness, and mysticism of the Middle Ages—Meiss saw as a reaction to the economic and social disasters of the period. *Painting in Florence and Sienna After the Black Death* was followed by *Andrea Mantegna as Illuminator* (1957), *Giotto and Assisi* (1960), *The Painting of the Life of St. Francis in Assisi* (1962), and *Giovanni Bellini's St. Francis in the Frick Collection* (1964). In 1967 the five-volume work *French Painting in the Time of Jean de Berry* was published. Believing that manuscripts were a major but understudied form, Meiss also published *The Illuminated Manuscripts of the Divine Comedy* (1969), *The Visconti Hours* (1972), and *The Rohan Master* (1973).

One of Meiss's most crucial contributions lay in his work as a preservationist. From 1946 to 1951 he was chair of the American Committee for the Restoration of Italian Monuments. From 1961 to 1964 he served as president of the International Committee of Art History (the first American to hold that position) and called for the creation of photographic archives to document endangered artworks. These efforts led, during the 1966 floods in Florence, to his organization and chairing of the Committee to Rescue Italian Art, which undertook restoration of damaged frescoes and buildings. Paradoxically, the catastrophe allowed for the restoration of many monuments that previously had been neglected. Among the critical landmarks saved were the churches and frescoes of Santa Maria Novella and Santa Croce, and the Church of the Ognissanti, the latter containing paradigmatic frescoes by Botticelli and Ghirlandaio. In the process of excavation and restoration of Santa Croce the original thirteenth-century basilica and nearly 300 sinopia cartoons were discovered. Meiss wrote *The Great Age of Fresco: Discoveries, Recoveries and Survivals* (1970), giving a dramatic account of the technical and logistic intricacies of the rescue mission within a well-documented history of fresco painting.

In 1976 Meiss edited and published *The Painter's Choice*, an anthology including his most celebrated essays: "Light as Form and Symbol in Some 15th-Century Paintings"; "*Ovum Struthionis*," a classic iconographic investigation of the ostrich egg in Piero della Francesca's Montefeltro altarpiece; "Sleep in Venice," on the painting of Giorgione; "A Documented Altarpiece by Piero della Francesca," which reconstructed the Borgo San Sepulcro altarpiece and predicted the discovery of a lost part of the work a few years after its original publication; and studies of van Eyck, Masaccio, Raphael, and others.

Meiss admirably balanced the active and contemplative life, receiving many honors for service as well as scholarly accomplishments. As chief editor of the *Art Bulletin* (1940–1942), he was said to have brought "new intellectual life and impeccable editing" to a faltering publication, and he served on its editorial board thereafter until 1975. He was also on the editorial board of the *Magazine of Art* from 1948 to 1952. He was scholar in residence at Harvard's Villa I Tatti for the study of Renaissance art and served as director of that center from 1967 to 1969.

Upon his retirement in 1974, Meiss became professor emeritus at the School of Historical Studies of the Institute for Advanced Study. Noted for the breadth of his approach to the interpretation of art objects, he applied aesthetic, documentary, literary, and technical perspectives to his investigations, giving equal weight to style, iconography, and sociohistorical context. His connoisseurship was always informed by detailed evidence and analysis of texts, technique, and hand. Lauded for his grace, economy, and exacting approach to judgments about artworks and artists, he was praised for a "historical imagination of a kind few other art historians have possessed" (Pope-Hennessey). He was credited with 19 books, 100 articles and reviews, and numerous editorial projects.

He died in Princeton, New Jersey. Upon his death Rensselaer Lee observed that no better metaphor could stand for Meiss than that found in his own writings: "'Mobile and intangible light,' he wrote, 'has always seemed the natural counterpart of the mind.' How well this association of mind with light applies to Millard himself, to his own eager, agile intelligence and to the light-dispensing efficacy of his life as scholar and teacher."

• Meiss's papers are in the Archives of American Art, Smithsonian Institution, Washington, D.C. Additional information is available in the Archives of the Institute for Advanced Study, Princeton, N.J. For further bibliography see the entry on Meiss in *A Community of Scholars: Faculty and Members, 1930–1980* (1980). See Grace Gluck, "Art History Colleagues Honor Millard Meiss," *New York Times*, 15 Apr. 1974; Rensselaer W. Lee, "Millard Meiss: In Memoriam," *Art Journal* 35, no. 3 (Spring 1976): 261–62; and John Pope-Hennessey, "Depiction of Light," *New York Times*, 8 May 1977. See also Irving Lavin and John Plummer, eds., *Studies in Late Medieval and Renaissance Painting in Honor of Millard Meiss* (1977). Obituaries are in the *New York Times*, 14 June 1975, and *Burlington Magazine* 117 (1975): 544.

AMY WINTER

MELCHERS, Gari (11 Aug. 1860–30 Nov. 1932), painter, was born Julius Garibaldi Melchers in Detroit, Michigan, the son of Julius Melchers, a noted sculptor, and Marie Bangetor. He showed artistic ability at a young age and was apprenticed to his father; his first work of art was a charcoal sketch of his father done in 1871. At the age of seventeen Melcher, encouraged by his parents, went to study at the Düsseldorf Royal Art Academy. The academic training he received there, with its emphasis on the realistic depiction of the human body, permanently affected his painting style. He was also strongly influenced by his teacher Eduard von Gebhardt, who painted religious subjects. From 1881 until 1884 Melchers studied at the Académie Julian in Paris under Gustave Boulanger and Jules Joseph Lefebvre. While there Melchers replaced the brown, gray, and tan tones of the Düsseldorf school with the brighter, more vivid palette of the impressionists. It was also in Paris that Melchers became aware of the *juste-milieu* painters such as Jules Bastien-Lepage, who depicted academic subjects with careful draftsmanship combined with an impressionistic palette and technique. This hybrid style characterized much of Melchers's work.

Melchers's first success was the acceptance of his painting *The Letter* (1882, Corcoran Gallery of Art) into the Paris Salon of 1882. *The Letter* depicted two Breton peasant women reading a letter by a window, demonstrating Melchers's knowledge of Jan Vermeer. This peasant subject and an interest in light were important elements in Melchers's art for most of his career.

In 1884 Melchers, like many other American artists of his generation, decided to remain in Europe. He moved to the Egmonds, three small Dutch villages on the North Sea, where his fellow American artist George Hitchcock had established a studio in 1881. Another American artist, Walter MacEwen, also lived there. Even though MacEwen moved to The Hague in 1885, he continued to influence Melchers. Aware of the continuing popularity of the peasant theme in late nineteenth-century European art, all three artists specialized in the depiction of Dutch peasants.

In the late nineteenth century, depictions of peasant life were often combined with religious themes in response to the growing secularization of the period. (The prototype for this genre was Gustave Courbet's *Burial at Ornans* [1849], though the subject had become more sentimentalized by such artists as Jules Breton in the later nineteenth century.) This trend is evident in many of Melchers's major paintings of the 1880s. *The Sermon* (1886, National Museum of American Art), depicting a young Dutch peasant girl nodding off during a church service, received honorable mention in the Paris Salon of 1886, and it was also chosen to be exhibited at the Paris Universal Exposition of 1889.

The Sermon, along with three other peasant paintings, *The Pilots* (1887, Frye Art Museum, Seattle), *Communion* (1888, Cornell University), and *Shepherdess* (1886, Wheaton College), earned Melchers the highest honors in the American section, which he shared with John Singer Sargent. Other major paintings of the 1880s included *The Choirmaster* (c. 1888, private collection) and *In Holland* (1887, Belmont, Gari Melchers Collection). For these paintings, Melchers used Dutch models from the surrounding villages, as well as interiors of actual buildings. The figures were depicted unsentimentally in sharp detail; the vibrant colors of their clothes often contrasted with the neutral colors of the background walls. In the outdoor paintings, such as *In Holland*, a high horizon line was used, with the land completely dominating the figure.

According to Joseph G. Dreiss, Melchers's paintings of the 1880s were the most successful of his career, as they achieved a balanced synthesis based on the artist's study of European styles. Seen in this light, Melchers's later work, though still technically accomplished, can be viewed as eclectic and not as innovative.

By 1890 Melchers had established his reputation in both Europe and the United States. From 1889 until 1909, while continuing to maintain a studio in Holland, he also spent time in Paris and became associated with Pierre Puvis de Chavannes, a major symbolist painter. De Chavannes's influence can be seen in Melchers's major commissions in the 1890s, which were murals for the World's Columbian Exposition in Chicago (1893) and the new Library of Congress in Washington, D.C. (1895). Both commissions were not murals in fresco but oil paintings on large canvases attached to the wall.

The two murals for the Manufacturers and Liberal Arts Building at the Chicago Exposition were *Arts of War* and *Arts of Peace*. They are characterized by the low-saturation colors, dark outlines, shallow space, and relief-like depiction of the figures often found in symbolist art. These murals now hang in the Library of the University of Michigan. De Chavannes's influence is also seen in the murals for the Library of Congress, *War* and *Peace*, which are similar to the Chicago murals but contain more figures.

Mirroring the fin de siècle interest in religious art, Melchers produced several biblical paintings in the 1890s and early 1900s. These included *The Nativity* (c. 1891), which is characterized by the pale palette and decorative elements of de Chavannes, and *Supper at Emmaus* (c. 1900), after Rembrandt. Other paintings were two versions of the Last Supper, *The Last Supper (Lamplight)* (1902–1903, Virginia Museum of Fine Arts) and *The Last Supper (Daylight)* (1904, Belmont, Gari Melchers Collection). Village men were used as models, recalling the *tableau vivant* technique of the Düsseldorf school. These paintings were Melchers's last major works to focus on religious subjects.

In the 1890s Melchers began painting the theme of the mother and child, a subject that reappeared throughout the rest of his career. Christian Brinton wrote in *Modern Artists* (1908) that "it is in pictures such as these . . . that Melchers strikes his truest, most profound note." Many of his contemporaries—Paula Modersohn-Becker, Eugène Carrière, and Max Liebermann—were also painting the same subject at this time. Mary Cassatt was an important influence on Melchers; for example, the compositional elements of Cassatt's *A Kiss for Baby Ann* (1897) are directly related to those in Melchers's *The Caress* (1923, Belmont, Gari Melchers Collection).

Melchers married Corinne Lawton Mackall, an art student, in 1903. They enjoyed a happy marriage, and Melchers's wife often acted as his model. The marriage coincided with Melchers's financial success as an artist, and this period saw a series of decorative, quasi-impressionistic paintings of upper middle-class domestic scenes in the manner of Sargent and William Merritt Chase, such as *At Home (The Winged Victory)* (1905–1910, Belmont, Gari Melchers Collection).

Melchers lived in the United States from 1905 until 1909, becoming a member of the National Academy of Design in 1906 and maintaining a studio in the Beaux-Arts Building at 80 West Fortieth Street in New York City. In 1908 he was commissioned by Charles Freer to paint President Theodore Roosevelt's portrait at the White House.

From 1909 to 1915 Melchers held a teaching position at the Ducal Academy of Fine Arts in Weimar, Germany. His output lessened during this period because of traveling and teaching as well as a decline in his health. Melchers left Germany in 1915; after that date his primary residence was in the United States.

In 1916 Melchers purchased "Belmont," an eighteenth-century estate near Fredericksburg, Virginia, and established a home and studio there. He continued to paint portraits of the rich and famous, including William K. Vanderbilt and Andrew Mellon. From 1923 until his death he headed the Smithsonian Commission to Establish a National Gallery of Art (now known as the National Museum of American Art), and he was instrumental in obtaining the John Gellatly Collection for the museum.

From 1916 until his death Melchers painted landscape and genre subjects related to his Virginia environment. These included *Native of Virginia* (c. 1925), an American version of a European peasant painting, and *The Hunters*, based on his earlier *juste-milieu* style with a high horizon line, monumental figures, and impressionist brushstrokes.

Despite worsening health Melchers undertook mural projects. In 1921 Cass Gilbert, the architect of the Detroit Public Library, commissioned Melchers to create three murals for the library, which depicted the founding of Detroit with historical and allegorical subjects. Because of this success, the state of Missouri also commissioned Melchers to paint four murals for the Missouri State Capitol. All of these works eschewed Melchers's earlier allegiance to de Chavannes, and they are characterized by depth, bright colors, and detail.

During the last decade of his life, Melchers enjoyed one-person shows in museums and galleries. He died at Belmont. Internationally known at the time of his death, Melchers later sunk into obscurity. However, Melchers, along with many of his contemporaries, was re-evaluated in the 1970s. He was included in Michael Quick's Dayton Art Institute exhibition and catalog *American Expatriate Painters of the Late Nineteenth Century* (1976), in which Quick asserted that Melchers should be honored again for the quality of his late nineteenth-century paintings. The Graham Gallery in New York exhibited and sold paintings from the Melchers collection in 1978 both to endow the artist's estate in Fredericksburg and to restore his reputation.

In another evaluation of Melchers's contribution, Dreiss pointed out that his most successful works were his genre scenes, mothers and children, portraits of the elite, and landscapes and cityscapes, while his religious paintings and murals were less successful. Dreiss summarized the contradictions that are especially found in Melchers's later art in this description of *The Zeeland Madonna* (1930): "The artist was not able to fuse into a synthetic unity the diverse and even contradictory stylistic influence that informs the work. Melchers shared this problem with many of his contemporaries who, like him, tried to retain academic qualities of style while incorporating features from avant-garde art of the day."

• Melchers's former estate, Belmont, is now a historic site, museum, and library. It houses the largest archive relating to Melchers as well as the largest collection of his art. More modest collections of his art are at the Art Institute of Chicago, the Detroit Institute of the Arts, and the Corcoran Gallery of Art. The most comprehensive treatment of Melchers is Joseph G. Dreiss, *Gari Melchers: His Works in the Belmont Collection* (1984), which includes an extensive bibliography, biographical chronology, and exhibition history. A smaller bibliography is found in *Gari Melchers (1860–1932): Selections from the Mary Washington College Collection* (1973). Useful exhibition catalogs include Diana Lesko, *Gari Melchers: A Retrospective Exhibition* (1990), for the St. Petersburg (Fla.) Fine Arts Museum, and Janice C. Oresman, *Gari Melchers, 1860–1932: American Painter* (1978), for the Graham Gallery. An obituary is in the *New York Times*, 1 Dec. 1932.

KAY KOENINGER

MELCHIOR, Lauritz Lebrecht Hommel (20 Mar. 1890–18 Mar. 1973), heroic tenor, was born in Copenhagen, Denmark, the son of Jørgen Melchior, a school principal, and Sofie Møller. He was educated at the Melchior School, a private institution founded by his grandfather, then administered by his father. The Melchior family fortunes were reversed in 1910 when the opening of commune schools forced many private institutions to close.

Kristine Jensen, who had become the family housekeeper after the death of Sofie Melchior soon after Melchior's birth, made it possible for Melchior to receive vocal training after he graduated from high school. A writer of successful cookbooks, Jensen spared neither time nor money to further young Melchior's early vocal and dramatic studies in Denmark. To facilitate his acceptance as an apprentice at the Royal Opera School in 1911, she even paid for his early release from a stint of duty with the Royal Danish Life Guards, an institution to which he remained devoted all his life. Melchior was formally engaged by the Royal Danish Opera company in 1914, one year after his successful apprentice debut as Silvio in Leoncavallo's *Pagliacci*, a baritone role. Acting on the strong recommendation of American operatic contralto Sarah Cahier, the Royal Opera supported Melchior for a year while he worked to develop his voice into that of a heldentenor under the direction of Vilhem Herold, a renowned Danish tenor. In 1918 Melchior debuted for the second time at the Royal Opera, in the Wagnerian tenor role of Tannhäuser.

Melchior married Inger Nathansen Holst-Rasmussen, the daughter of matinee idol Ludvig Nathansen, in 1915; they had two children. From 1920 through 1924 the renowned British novelist Hugh Walpole acted as Melchior's mentor, providing financial support for Melchior's family and his studies with Victor Beigel in London and Anna Bahr-Mildenburg in Munich. Siegfried Wagner, the son of Richard Wagner, summoned Melchior to Bayreuth in 1923. After an audition for Wagner and his mother Cosima, Melchior was engaged to sing at the first postwar Bayreuth Festival, which occurred during the summer of 1924; he sang the role of Siegmund in Wagner's *Die Walküre*. He had performed the same role earlier that year in his first international appearance as a heldentenor during the first British postwar season at Covent Garden.

While studying in Munich, Melchior met Maria Hacker, a diminutive, young film stuntwoman. They were married in 1925, following his divorce from his first wife. Melchior and Kleinchen, as she was nicknamed by him, had no children. Shrewd, beautiful, and charming, Kleinchen successfully managed Melchior's career, proving particularly adept at publicity techniques that were ahead of their time. By exploiting, aggrandizing, and even inventing situations that the press would devour, she successfully trod the line between making Melchior too accessible, thereby losing his credibility as a serious artist, and making him too remote, thereby losing his appeal to the mass audience.

Following his prestigious Bayreuth debut, Melchior was in great demand in Germany. Invited to the Metropolitan Opera in 1926, he made his American debut as Tannhäuser on 17 February. After being assigned only two performances with the Metropolitan during the 1927 season, he was advised to return to a European house to master Wagnerian roles before seeking roles in the best opera houses. Consequently, Melchior spent 1928 in German and French houses, singing such heavy tenor roles as John of Leyden (*Le Prophète*), Siegmund, both Siegfrieds (*Siegfried, Götterdämmerung*), Canio (*Pagliacci*), Radamès (*Aida*), Tannhäuser, and Otello.

Melchior made his Barcelona debut in 1929 as Tristan, the premier Wagnerian tenor role. Shortly thereafter he was hired to sing Tristan at the Metropolitan Opera. Melchior subsequently sang, to great acclaim, in all the important houses, including those in London, Paris, Buenos Aires, Chicago, San Francisco, and Boston. Having conquered the heavy roles of Tristan and Seigfried, the most demanding in the repertoire of a Wagnerian heldentenor, Melchior passed into the first rank of international tenors.

Melchior's easy command of the Wagnerian roles, the longest and most demanding operatic tenor roles, rested upon his capacity to withstand great vocal and physical rigors. His voice, with its lusty Nordic timbre, was the ideal heldentenor sound and the ideal heldentenor size. Melchior is the only heroic tenor in history to survive twenty-five years of Wagnerian roles and still continue to sing with unremitting sonority, authority, color, poetic understanding, and with endurance and power in reserve. Some critics argued that the quality of his voice was too penetrating. Vocal experts, however, have countered that Melchior's purposefully narrow vocal production was not only the hallmark of his tonal quality but also the enabling factor behind his vocal longevity. During his twenty-four years at the Metropolitan, for example, Melchior canceled only three of 515 scheduled performances of Wagnerian operas. Even when Melchior retired, he was still in command of his voice, having sung nearly 1,000 Wagner opera performances—183 Siegmunds, 106 Lohengrins, 81 Parsifals, 107 Siegfrieds (*Götterdämmerung*), 128 Siegfrieds (*Siegfried*), 183 Siegmunds (*Die Walküre*), 40 Tannhäusers (Dresden version), 104 Tannhäusers (Paris version), and 223 Tristans.

In the 1930s, at the height of his career, Melchior would have preferred to sing a variety of Italian and German roles, but most opera companies could not spare him from the Wagnerian roles. The situation intensified when World War II deprived the United States of access to heroic tenors from overseas. The Metropolitan, left with Melchior as the only Wagnerian tenor in the company, limited him to Wagnerian roles, all of which he sang without respite three and four times a week until the end of the war. The Metropolitan's refusal to cast him as Otello was a great disappointment to Melchior. He sang Otello only thirty-one times in his career, Turiddu (*Cavalleria Rusticana*) five times, Radamès twenty-five times, Samson (*Samson et Dalila*) two times, Canio twenty-one times, Florestan (*Fidelio*) nine times, and John of Leyden eleven times.

During the 1930s and 1940s, opera stars were regarded in the United States as pretentious, temperamental persons engaged in an esoteric profession that was devoid of meaning to the average American. Following Melchior's appearance on the popular Fred Allen radio show in 1943, during which he showed that opera stars could be talented comedians who were willing to make fun of themselves, he was invited to Hollywood. Too rotund to play the part of a romantic lover, Melchior was successfully cast by MGM as a funny, grandfatherly figure in five movies: *Thrill of a Romance* (1945), *Two Sisters from Boston* (1946), *This Time for Keeps* (1947), *Luxury Liner* (1948), and *The Stars are Singing* (1952). Frequent radio and movie appearances made Melchior the most well-known opera singer in the country.

In 1950 the Metropolitan engaged a new general director, Rudolf Bing, who advocated greater production values and lesser dependence upon star singers, and he manipulated Melchior into resigning. After Melchior's last performance at the Metropolitan on 2 February 1950, he retired from opera but continued to sing actively in concert, radio, and television appearances for another fifteen years. At the age of seventy, Melchior brilliantly sang the first act of *Die Walküre* on Copenhagen radio, still a heroic tenor of phenomenal stamina.

Melchior died in Santa Monica. After his death, his fame increased yearly, fed by the popularity of his recordings and the absence of a successor. It is generally agreed that since the time of Melchior, no heldentenor has been able to equal him.

• The Lauritz Melchior Memorial Collection, housed in the C. E. Dana Library of Dana College in Blair, Nebraska, contains Melchior's personal scrapbooks, correspondence, record collection, personal tape collection, photograph collection, medals, and mementos. Melchior's son, Ib J. Melchior of Los Angeles, California, retains all other personal papers. The family-authorized biography of Melchior is Shirlee Emmons, *Tristanissimo* (1990), published in Danish as *Lauritz Melchior*, trans. Tove Nørlund (1991). See also Lilian E. Foerster, "Lauritz Melchior and his Roles," *Opera News* 10, no. 13 (23 Jan. 1946): 4–9; Conrad L. Osborne, "For the First Time on Records, 'Siegfried' in its Entirety," *High Fidelity*, April 1963, pp. 70–71; Gerald Fitzgerald, "Speaking of Wagner," *Opera News* 34 (28 Mar. 1970): 6–9; John Rockwell, "The Heroes," *Opera News* 38 (23 Mar. 1974): 12–15; Osborne, "Voices from the Festspielhaus," *Opera News* 41 (August 1976): 28–31; M. Owen Lee, "To See Your Soul: Tannhäuser Holds the Mirror Up to Man's Duality," *Opera News* 46 (30 Jan. 1982): 20–22; Barrymore Laurence Scherer, "Decline and Fall? (What Has Happened to the Art of Singing Wagner?")*, Opera News* 48 (3 Mar. 1984): 18–19; Shirlee Emmons, "Lauritz Melchior and the Heldentenor Crisis," *NATS Journal* 46, no. 5 (May–June 1990): 13–16, 33; and Emmons, "Lauritz Melchior, Heldentenor for the Ages," *American Music Teacher* 40, no. 3 (Dec.–Jan. 1990–1991): 14–17, 64–66. Obituaries are in the *New York Times*, 20 Mar. 1973 and 25 Mar. 1973; the *Washington Post*, 20 Mar. 1973; the *Los Angeles Times*, 19 Mar. 1973; the *Dallas Morning News*, 25 Mar. 1973; and the *Boston Herald*, 20 Mar. 1973.

SHIRLEE EMMONS

MELLEN, Prentiss (11 Oct. 1764–31 Dec. 1840), judge, was born in Sterling, Massachusetts, the son of John Mellen, a prosperous Congregational minister, and Rebecca Prentiss, the daughter of a minister. Prentiss Mellen grew up on the family farm and was tutored by his father. He graduated from Harvard in 1784, apprenticed with attorney Shearjashub Bourne in Barnstable, Massachusetts, and was admitted to the bar in 1788. After several years of searching for a place to practice gainfully, he settled in Biddeford, in the District of Maine, where he stayed for fourteen years. In 1795 he married Sarah Hudson of Hartford, Connecticut; the couple had six children, all born in Biddeford.

With a courtroom presence that was "ardent, earnest, rapid, and impulsive," Mellen flourished in Maine. He developed an extensive practice and, according to attorney and legal scholar Simon Greenleaf, was "retained in nearly every important cause." Mellen's business in Portland grew so large that he moved there in 1806.

Mellen served as a presidential elector in 1816 and as a member of the governor's council several times. In 1818 the Massachusetts legislature elected him a U.S. senator, the first person from Maine to hold that office. A Federalist, he at first opposed the separation of Maine, a stronghold of Jeffersonian democracy, from Massachusetts, but under the pressure of popular opinion, and perhaps mollified by the promise that Federalists would share in the new state's office, Mellen joined the cause of separation. However, as an opponent of slavery, he resisted attempts to link statehood for Maine to statehood for Missouri, a battle he lost when Congress passed the Missouri Compromise in 1820.

That same year Mellen left the Senate to become the first chief justice on Maine's three-person Supreme Judicial Court, a move that probably entailed a substantial cut in income. One of the court's first tasks, assigned by the legislature, was to adapt the Massachusetts statutes for use in Maine. As judges, the three conducted trials individually and heard appeals collectively, riding circuit in both capacities.

As a trial judge, Mellen had no patience for procedural delays, long-winded lawyers, or rambling witnesses; he insisted on moving proceedings along. As an appellate judge, he dominated the early court, writing 80 percent of the decisions published in the first two volumes of the *Maine Reports*. According to his biographer Ellyn C. Ballou, Mellen "evidently saw among the first court's functions a duty to educate the new state's bar." Although Maine, as a part of Massachusetts before 1820, had long benefited from the talents of eminent attorneys, such as Mellen, the new, rapidly growing state attracted many young lawyers who could not compete in the more established areas of New England. Mellen used the court as a forum in which to train the new practitioners. He generally wrote lucid, well-organized opinions, often restating the points under discussion for the edification of his professional readers. A great respecter of precedent, he cited numerous authorities both to buttress his conclusions and to instruct the bar.

Mellen played a key role in establishing a jurisprudence of governmental power in Maine. In *Proprietors of Kennebec Purchase v. Laboree* (1823) and *Lewis v. Webb* (1825), he struck down legislative attempts to interfere with vested rights through ex post facto laws, writing in the latter case, "We trust there is more harmony than this between the principles of morality and those of the constitution." When reviewing regulatory statutes, however, Mellen almost always deferred to the legislature. In one notable opinion, Lunt's Case (1830), involving a challenge to the state's authority to regulate the sale of liquor, Mellen held that the reasonableness of a law was a matter for legislative judgment. The court acknowledged the possibility of "exceptions to the generality" of this proposition; but, Mellen wrote, it was "not disposed to consider them as among the probabilities of legislation."

Although he was conservative in the use of judicial power, guided by precedent and given to broad views of state police power, Mellen was not averse to using the court to foster economic development in the new state. In *Spring v. Russell* (1831), for example, a case involving the competing claims of a logger and a canal company to the use of navigable waters, Mellen pointed out that damage sometimes results "from the application of those principles by which the general good is to be consulted and promoted, though in many respects operating unfavorably to the interests of individuals in society."

During his judicial tenure, Mellen also wrote many poems and stories for newspapers and magazines. His best compositions were historical in nature, and he played an active part in establishing the Maine Historical Society.

In 1834, upon reaching the constitutional age limit for judges, Mellen retired from the bench and practiced law in Portland until his death there. He rendered his last public service by heading a commission to revise the state statutes, the final report of which was presented to the legislature shortly after his death.

While generally not regarded as a jurist of the first rank, Mellen was, in the words of Ballou, "a skilled and experienced attorney, aware of the first court's importance to the new state" of Maine. As reviser and codifier of Maine's statutory law, the author of so many of the Maine court's early decisions, and an educator of Maine's young bar, Mellen left a lasting mark on the jurisprudence of the state.

• The Maine Historical Society in Portland houses a small collection of Mellen Family Papers. Mellen published a memoir, "Old Times and Modern Times, with Certain Law Memories," in *Colman's Miscellany* (1839). His judicial opinions are found in vols. 1–11 of the *Maine Reports*. The most thorough analysis of Mellen's life and career is Ellyn C. Ballou, "Prentiss Mellen, Maine's First Chief Justice: A Legal Biography," *Maine Law Review* 28 (1977): 317–418. Shorter accounts by eminent lawyers of his acquaintance are Simon Greenleaf, "Memoir of the Life and Character of the Late Chief Justice Mellen," *Maine Reports* 17 (1841): 467–76, and William Willis, *A History of the Law, the Courts, and the Lawyers of Maine* (1863), pp. 163–73 and passim. For his work on the Maine statutes, see pp. 5–78 of Samuel S. Silsby, "History of Statutory Law in the State of Maine," in *Maine Revised Statutes Annotated*, vol. 1 (1985).

DAVID M. GOLD

MELLON, Andrew William (24 Mar. 1855–26 Aug. 1937), financier, statesman, and art collector, was born in Pittsburgh, Pennsylvania, the son of Thomas Mellon, a lawyer and later a judge, entrepreneur, and banker, and Sarah Jane Negley. Mellon attended public schools in Pittsburgh and Western University of Pennsylvania (now the University of Pittsburgh). While still a student he observed his father's financial dealings with industrialists Andrew Carnegie and Henry Clay Frick and his friendship with Pennsylvania Republican party politicians Simon Cameron and Matthew S. Quay. Young Mellon, a member of the 1872 class, left three months short of graduating, borrowed money from his father at interest, and started a lumber and construction business in Mansfield (now Carnegie), Pennsylvania. Two years later he sold out advantageously in anticipation of a slump in prices and began to work in his father's bank. In 1880 he accompanied Frick on a European tour, developed a love of art, and bought a painting costing $1,000. Two years later his father made him president of the family bank.

Mellon expanded the bank and invested in promising ventures. In 1887 he made his younger brother Richard Beatty Mellon his partner in the T. Mellon and Sons Bank. Two years later he became president of Pittsburgh's Union Trust Company, which he and Frick had established. In 1890 his father made Mellon virtual owner of all Mellon properties on condition that he treat other members of the family fairly. That same year he helped finance Charles M. Hall's electrolytic process for manufacturing aluminum. In 1895 Mellon invested in Edward Goodrich Acheson's Carborundum Company. In the early 1890s he purchased several western Pennsylvania oil properties and industries, which he profitably sold to John D. Rockefeller's Standard Oil Company in 1895. In 1899 he bought $20,000 worth of European paintings.

In 1900 Mellon married Nora Mary McMullen, a member of a wealthy brewery family in Hertfordshire, England. She was twenty-three years his junior. The couple had two children. Mellon helped found the Gulf Oil Corporation in 1901. After nursing Union Steel along, he oversaw its merger, together with Carnegie's huge steel company, into J. Pierpont Morgan's United States Steel Corporation in 1901. In 1902 T. Mellon and Sons became Mellon National Bank, with Andrew Mellon as president. Ultimately, it evolved into an enormous multibank holding company, specializing in bonds, data processing, and managing personal trusts. By 1910 he had become a money-wielding force behind the scenes in the Republican party. Two of his closest allies were Pennsylvania senators Philander C. Knox and Boies Penrose, both of whom he supported with lavish campaign contributions. Mellon's devotion to business and his wife's summer vacations in England caused their divorce in 1912. He created Koppers-Pittsburgh in 1915, seven years after Heinrich Koppers had invented a process to recover valuable waste products from coke ovens and had begun operations to do so. Mellon's investments in construction processes resulted in partnerships with engineers Howard H. McClintic and Charles D. Marshall, whose firm built, among other major projects, the Panama Canal locks, the George Washington Bridge, Manhattan's RCA Building, and mills in Jamshedpur, India. Mellon became a dominant officer of more than sixty corporations, notably Alcan, Alcoa, Overholt Distillery, and the Mellon-Stuart Company (a heavy construction firm).

Mellon favored high tariffs, opposed workmen's compensation bills, and contributed to Charles E. Hughes's Republican presidential campaign against Democrat Woodrow Wilson, who was reelected in 1916. After World War I Mellon helped finance propaganda that killed U.S. participation in the League of Nations. When Warren G. Harding became Republican president in 1921, Senator Knox persuaded him to make Mellon his secretary of the treasury. Mellon accepted, resigned from his numerous corporate offices, estimated his family fortune at $2 billion, and served under Harding, and then Calvin Coolidge and Herbert Hoover, until 1932. During his tenure, he wrestled with problems such as reducing the national debt, lowering corporate and personal income taxes to stimulate business and industry and hence produce prosperity, and settling with several debtor nations. He favored excise taxes and advocated raising stamp taxes, taxes on bank checks and motor vehicles, and postal rates. He opposed giving veterans bonuses, purchasing excess farm produce for distribution abroad, and expanding federal bureaucracy. His policies, as well as specific advice from the Bureau of Internal Revenue commissioner, suspiciously benefited Mellon family investments. (In 1926 his relatives made $300 million on aluminum and Gulf Oil.)

The economic boom of the 1920s made most of Mellon's policies seem wiser than they actually were. In truth, they may have encouraged stock-market speculation and inflation and thus in part may have caused the crash of 1929. Mellon had much to do with the general beautification of Washington, D.C., during his long residence there. For a year, ending with the inauguration of President Franklin D. Roosevelt in 1933, Mellon was ambassador to Great Britain. While he was socially graceful but politically uncreative there, Congress back home was holding abortive hearings into his impeachment for conflict of interest. Home again, he resumed his manifold duties as the head of his Pittsburgh bank.

In the late 1920s Mellon had turned to art collecting in earnest. Working through New York, London, and Berlin agents, he gradually amassed a matchless collection. For example, beginning in 1930 he bought thirty-eight treasures from the Soviet Union's Hermitage in Leningrad (now St. Petersburg) for $8 million. In 1931, however, he refused two Leonardo paintings and one Giorgione, overpriced, he thought, at $3.5 million. Through the mid-1930s he made many other acquisitions, including some statuary. As early as 1927 he evidently planned to donate his collection to the nation. In 1934 the Department of Justice alleged that Mellon had falsified his 1931 income tax, and the agency sought more than $3 million in taxes and penalties. Appeals followed, and his name was cleared. (In 1938, a year after Mellon's death, however, his estate paid a token settlement, on technical grounds, of $668,000.) Of infinitely greater significance was Mellon's formal announcement in 1937 that he would donate to the federal government all of his art treasures: 369 paintings by Botticelli, Corot, Cuyp, Fragonard, Gainsborough, Hals, Holbein the Younger, Memling, Perugino, Raphael, Rembrandt, Reynolds, Romney, Titian, Turner, Van Dyck, Van Eyck, and others, together with 175 American portraits and twenty-five or so statues. In addition, he provided funds to build and maintain the National Gallery of Art in Washington. When accepted, the gift was valued at $65 million. He participated in architectural planning for the gallery before his death in Southampton, New York.

Mellon was a canny financier, outwardly quiet but in reality fiercely forceful. He provided capital for the beneficial development of the oil, metal, and construction industries, often when other bankers were reluctant to take a chance. He was the most powerful figure in three successive presidential cabinets. And he was the generous donor to a grateful nation of a nonpareil collection of art and the museum of which it is the glowing nucleus.

• Considerable Mellon correspondence is in the Calvin Coolidge Papers in the Library of Congress and in the Carter Glass Papers at the University of Virginia. Other papers are in the National Archives. The extended Mellon family is treated in detail in Frank Richard Denton, *The Mellons of Pittsburgh* (1948); Burton Hersh, *The Mellon Family: A Fortune in History* (1978); and David E. Koskoff, *The Mellons: A Chronicle of America's Richest Family* (1978). The *International Directory of Company Histories* (8 vols., 1988) discusses in particular Mellon and Alcan, Alcoa, Koppers, Mellon Bank, and Mellon-Stuart. Mellon's art-assembling wizardry is detailed in John Walker, *Let's Trade the Van Dyck and the Rembrandt for the Giorgione: The Inside Story of the Mellon Art Collection* (1972). Mellon's father's autobiography, *Thomas Mellon and His Times*, ed. Mary Louise Briscoe, 2d ed. (1994), contains well-annotated information about the younger Mellon as well. See also Paul Mellon, with John Baskett, *Reflections in a Silver Spoon: A Memoir* (1992), the autobiography of Mellon's son, which sheds light on the father-son relationship. An obituary, with a portrait, is in the *New York Times*, 27 Aug. 1937.

ROBERT L. GALE

MELLON, Thomas (3 Feb. 1813–3 Feb. 1908), jurist and financier, was born at Camp Hill Cottage near Omagh, County Tyrone, Ireland, to Andrew Mellon and Rebecca Wauchob, farmers. Despite the relative comfort of their 23-acre farm, Andrew Mellon chose to follow his parents and siblings and emigrate to the United States with his wife and five-year-old Thomas. They arrived in Baltimore in early October 1818 and traveled by Conestoga wagon to Westmoreland County, Pennsylvania. Andrew Mellon purchased a farm in Franklin Township, twenty-one miles east of Pittsburgh.

Although western Pennsylvania would experience tremendous growth during Mellon's lifetime, in both population and industry, the arrival of the family coincided with the economic depression of 1819. In order to make their monthly mortgage payments, young Thomas worked a double shift, tending the fields during the day and spinning bags of flax at night. Later in life he would recall these years of hardship as having impressed on him the values of industry and thrift.

As a boy Mellon displayed high intellectual ability. An eager reader, he took works of Shakespeare and Robert Burns with him into the fields. Like many other American children of the nineteenth century, Mellon was taken with Benjamin Franklin's *Autobiography*; he delighted in the idea that one "so poor and friendless" could grow to be a great merchant and professional man.

Mellon was also captivated by the activities of nearby Pittsburgh, with its iron foundries, glass manufactories, and power looms. In 1823 he made his first trip to the city, where he saw the homes of prosperous citizens, including the mansion of Jacob Negley, which had great impact on him.

Such sights turned Mellon against the idea of spending his life on the farm. In 1832 he rejected his father's efforts to purchase a plot of land for him and instead returned to school, this time mastering Latin and Greek under the direction of Jonathan Gill. To complete his education, Mellon attended the Western University of Pennsylvania (later the University of Pittsburgh). After his graduation in 1837 he read law under Charles Shaler, former judge of the Court of Common Pleas of Allegheny County. He passed the bar in December 1838 and worked briefly as managing clerk for Prothonotary Thomas Liggett.

Not long after starting his own practice in June 1839, Mellon gained the reputation of a leading young lawyer. He was particularly well known for bringing cases to quick settlement. He also proved himself a shrewd investor and businessman by purchasing real estate and arranging mortgages. Mellon was quick to capitalize on investment opportunities, such as the chaos following Pittsburgh's Great Fire of 1845. He entered other businesses, purchasing coalfields and ironworks. One of his largest land gains came after his marriage in 1843 to Sarah Jane Negley, the daughter of Jacob Negley. They had eight children, five of whom, all sons, survived to adulthood.

In April 1859, with his business affairs growing almost burdensome, Mellon was convinced by some politically powerful friends to run for the office of assistant law judge of the Court of Common Pleas. With their help, he secured the Republican party nomination and went on to an easy win in the October election. He proved an adept and active judge, rendering quick decisions in plain language.

Mellon took little part or even interest in the Civil War, which erupted one year into his term. He deplored the waste and damage of war and feared an expanded government. Still, he appreciated the business opportunities presented by the war's conclusion. Feeling shackled by his judicial appointment, he chose not to seek re-election in 1869 and turned to take advantage of the prosperous economy. This time he would bring his sons into business; after carefully tutoring them in everything from business etiquette to penmanship, he lent them money to start their own nurseries, lumberyards, and other enterprises.

In January 1870, only one month after leaving the court, Mellon opened what would become his most lasting business, the private banking house of T. Mellon and Sons. At the bank, Mellon arranged mortgages, took deposits, and made loans to local entrepreneurs. In 1871 the young Henry Clay Frick borrowed $10,000 from Mellon to purchase coalfields and build coke ovens. Through the years the bank would intersect with other Mellon family interests. When workers needed housing, the Mellons sold them the property, constructed the dwellings, arranged for the mortgages, and heated the homes. Mellon also had controlling interest in a transportation system, the Pittsburgh, Oakland, and East Liberty Passenger Railway.

After weathering the depression of the 1870s, Mellon retreated from business. In January 1881 he turned complete control of the bank over to his son Andrew and took a tour of his native Ireland. Back in

Pittsburgh, Mellon sat down to write his autobiography, *Thomas Mellon and His Times* (1885). The book offered sober advice to his children and warned them of what he perceived as the dangers of the times—socialism, taxation, and trade unions. Mellon seemed to be calling for a retreat to rural democracy at a time when other Pittsburgh entrepreneurs, including his children and clients, were constructing the great industrial plants that would dominate the city's landscape.

Although Mellon continued to purchase real estate throughout the 1880s, he was leaving more and more business to his children. On his seventy-seventh birthday he transferred nearly all of his property to the care of his son Andrew. In *Judge Mellon's Sons*, Thomas's grandson W. L. Mellon estimated the amount of wealth turned over to be just under $2.5 million—an extraordinary sum for the time.

Restless and looking to make a fresh start in business, Thomas Mellon set out for Kansas City by himself in 1890. There he attempted to build incline railways for uphill transport, similar to those in Pittsburgh, but he was unable to gain a permit from the city council. While in Kansas City, Mellon also pursued his growing interest in spiritualism, attending séances with the hope of contacting his dead son Selwyn.

Returning from Kansas City in 1895, Mellon spent the last thirteen years of his life at his house at 401 Negley Avenue. He became a fixture on his front porch, rocking back and forth. His eyesight had degenerated, and he paid his children and grandchildren to read to him. In 1885, feeling the press of age, Thomas Mellon had written that a long life was like an ear of corn with the grains shriveled at both ends—the years at either end being of little account. He died in Pittsburgh twenty-three years later on his ninety-fifth birthday.

Mellon's greatest accomplishment lay in the business education of his sons. They would run not only the Mellon National Bank, but also Alcoa, Gulf Oil, Carborundum, the Koppers chemical company, and other corporations. Another major achievement was his autobiography, which was commercially published for the first time in 1994 and was quite popular, with its emphasis on family, integrity, and self-sufficiency echoing political themes of the period.

• Mellon's autobiography, *Thomas Mellon and His Times* (1885, repr. 1994), is the best review of his life, although, like Benjamin Franklin's autobiography (on which it was modeled), it presents a somewhat false image. For a less approving view, see Harvey O'Connor's book about Mellon's son Andrew, *Mellon's Millions: The Biography of a Fortune* (1933). Also helpful are histories of the family, including David Koskoff, *The Mellons: The Chronicle of America's Richest Family* (1978), and Burton Hersh, *The Mellon Family: A Fortune in History* (1978). Also useful are his grandson W. L. Mellon's *Judge Mellon's Sons* (1948) and his son James Ross Mellon's *Letters, 1862–1895* (1928), both privately printed. On his antagonism to labor unions, see Paul Krause, *The Battle for Homestead, 1880–1892* (1992). No personal papers are currently available, but further insight into Mellon's life can be gained by reading contemporary issues of the *Pittsburgh Legal Journal* and *Pittsburgh Banker*.

WALTER FRIEDMAN

MELLON, William Larimer (1 June 1868–8 Oct. 1949), oil industry executive, was born in East Liberty, Pennsylvania, the son of James Ross Mellon, a building materials dealer, and Rachel Hughey Larimer. Born into a closely-knit family, Mellon benefited from the prominence of both sides of his family; his paternal grandfather, Thomas Mellon, was the founder of what later became Mellon Bank & Trust. After receiving his early education at local public and private schools, he attended the Pennsylvania Military Academy in Chester and finished his formal education at Shortledge Academy in Media, Pennsylvania. Too restless to entertain ideas of college, he then went to work at his father's lumberyard, only to quickly tire of the dull routine and low salary. After making a profit of $500 on a modest house that he had built on speculation, Mellon, eager to match the success enjoyed by his uncles (who were then running the family bank), decided to enter business for himself.

Inspired by a nearby oil find in 1889, Mellon soon entered the nascent industry as a dealer in oil leases for his uncles Andrew Mellon (who would go on to become secretary of the treasury) and Richard Mellon. With the continued financial backing of his uncles, he soon began drilling his own wells throughout southwestern Pennsylvania. At first almost compelled to sell his production to industry giant Standard Oil, he soon discovered a new purchaser in the French firm of Fenaille & Despeaux. After quickly adding additional customers (one Spanish firm and Paul Pays & Company—another French firm), he leased a small refinery and also began construction of a limited set of pipelines. Initially dependent on the railroads to carry his production, he soon faced an increase in shipping rates. Eager to escape his dependence on the railroads, Mellon commenced construction of a lengthy pipeline. Running from Gregg Station (just outside Pittsburgh) to Marcus Hook, Pennsylvania (on the Delaware River), the line provided Mellon with direct access to the site of his newly-built refinery at the riverfront. Although the firm grew quickly, the onset of the panic of 1893 as well as depressed prices due to an oversupply of crude gave Mellon and his uncles pause, and in 1895 the firm willingly (like so many other independent oil companies before it) sold the holdings of both Crescent Oil and Crescent Pipeline to John Rockefeller's Standard Oil.

Following his departure from the oil business, Mellon continued to explore investment opportunities for his family's bank. He married May Hill Taylor in Palatka, Florida, in March 1896; they had four children. In the latter part of the 1890s Mellon turned his attention to the development of electric streetcar lines in Pittsburgh. Provided with some technical innovations by local entrepreneur George Westinghouse, Mellon and his uncles soon developed a successful line of fifty-five miles. Competition within the industry was fierce, however, and Mellon eventually leased his interests to a competitor (the Philadelphia Company) for 900 years and turned his attention elsewhere.

Mellon, however, soon became involved in the oil business again, and he was to spend the remainder of his career in the field. With his uncles having heavily invested in the Spindletop oil development in Texas, concern arose in 1902 when oil production in the field dropped alarmingly. Having been lured back into the oil business by Colonel James M. Guffey, the Mellons were eager to protect their interest in the J. M. Guffey Petroleum Company and the Gulf Refining Company, which had been created in November 1901 to initiate refining operations in the area. Mellon made an inspection tour of the field and concluded that although Guffey excelled at finding oil, his business management skills were inadequate to the task of managing the operation. After his appointment as vice president of both Guffey Petroleum and Gulf Refining, Mellon faced a myriad of problems, including poorly executed leasing arrangements that resulted in litigation, haphazardly planned lease purchase, and a refinery that was ill suited to handle Texas oil, which had a high sulfur content.

Mellon met the challenges of Spindletop head-on. He hired competent subordinates to run refining (George Taber), pipeline (George Craig), and production (John H. Fisher) operations and broke a disadvantageous long-term sales agreement arranged by Guffey with the Shell Transport and Trading Company (later Shell Oil) that would have bankrupted Guffey and Gulf had it been allowed to stand. Faced, as were all producers, with a never-ending need for new supplies of crude, he was quick to take advantage of oil discoveries in the Indian Territory near Tulsa (the Glenn Pool in modern-day Okla.) and formed a subsidiary, the Gypsy Oil Company, to develop the area. The new find occurred at a critical time; Texas oil production was in a temporary decline, and the Glenn Pool oil offered the additional bonus of containing both low sulfur content and high gasoline content, which made it increasingly desirable as a fuel source. With the two firms' reorganization as the Gulf Oil Corporation on 13 February 1907, the Mellons completed their investment-salvaging efforts by buying out all of Guffey's stake in the operation. The new firm immediately constructed a 450-mile-long pipeline from Glenn Pool to the Gulf of Mexico and quickly expanded operations into West Texas, northern Louisiana, and eastern Kansas as well. The firm also plunged into the area of scientific research and development, eventually employing hundreds of scientists who helped to transform the art of oil production into a science.

As the president of Gulf Oil from 1909 until 1930 (when he became chairman of the board), Mellon oversaw the operations of a firm that eventually became the world's fourth-largest oil producer. The firm was immediately successful, boasting net profits of $1 million in its first year. Gulf Oil served as an industry pioneer in several areas; it was the first to undertake successful overwater drilling operations (on Ferry Lake on the Texas-Louisiana border in 1910–1911). Retail trade was another company priority, as Gulf initiated the first drive-in service station in the United States in 1913. With a growing number of automobiles on the nation's highways, Gulf continued to expand its retail outlets and by the early 1930s boasted 2,300 service stations. The firm built additional refineries (at Philadelphia; Bayonne, N.J.; and Fort Worth, Tex.) and expanded operations at its Port Arthur, Texas, facility until it stood as the world's largest in 1923. Gulf also expanded its search for oil overseas, initiating exploration efforts in places as diverse as Venezuela and Kuwait. Although the firm suffered as a result of the Great Depression, eventually turning away from direct operation of service stations in favor of leasing arrangements, the ultimate survival of the company was due in no small way to Mellon's foresight and leadership. He retired as board chairman in 1948.

Long active in the Republican party, Mellon at one point served as state party chair of Pennsylvania. An avid sportsman who enjoyed hunting and fishing, he spent parts of the years 1928–1941 cruising the world in his yacht *Vagabondia*. In keeping with the tradition of Pennsylvania industrialists, he also turned to philanthropy in his later years. He established the William L. and May T. Mellon Foundation in 1939, which granted $6 million to the Carnegie Institute of Technology (later Carnegie-Mellon University) in order to create the Mellon Institute, a graduate school of industrial administration. Mellon died at his home in Pittsburgh.

Shrewd, flexible, and quick to take advantage of opportunities when they arose, Mellon parlayed all of the resources at his command (including his own family's considerable financial backing) to create his own niche among the great industrialists of the late nineteenth and early twentieth centuries. Although Gulf Oil was purchased by Chevron in 1984, his role in the firm's growth and development remains his greatest legacy.

• Mellon's work with the Gulf Oil Corporation is reflected in company records. The best source of information on his life and career remains his autobiography, *Judge Mellon's Sons* (1948), written with Boyden Sparkes. Also useful are Frank R. Denton, *The Mellons of Pittsburgh* (1948) and *Since Spindletop: A Human Story of Gulf's First Half-Century* (1951). An obituary is in the *New York Times*, 9 Oct. 1949.

EDWARD L. LACH, JR.

MELMOTH, Charlotte (1749–28 Sept. 1823), actress, was born in Surrey, England, the daughter of farmers whose names are unknown. Her day of birth and details of her childhood are also unknown. In 1772 she eloped from the boarding school she was attending with the recently ordained Samuel Jackson Pratt. "Melmoth" is the stage name that she and her common-law husband used from their first appearance at the Smock Alley Theatre in Dublin in 1773, giving rise to the speculation that Melmoth may have been Charlotte's family name.

After a brief venture in theater management, the couple headed to London, where Melmoth made her debut at Covent Garden as Calista in *The Fair Penitent* on 24 February 1774 and remained through the 1774–1775 season, playing roles that attest to the tragic grandeur that would mark her career: queens in *Richard III*, *King Henry II*, *The Earl of Essex*, and *Hamlet*; Roxana in *Alexander the Great*; and Hermione in *The Winter's Tale*. During the first half of 1776, the Melmoths played at the Theatre Royal in Edinburgh, returning to London for Melmoth's debut at Drury Lane as Lady Macbeth in the fall of 1776. Though she "met with some applause," Melmoth was considered "very wild in the part," and after a final performance at Drury Lane as Roxana in 1777, the Melmoths left London to tour England, Wales, and Ireland, separating in 1781.

By 1793 Melmoth appeared in New York, offering a series of recitations in the City Assembly Rooms at Corre's Hotel that she repeated several times during the month of April. Her program included Antony's soliloquy over the body of Caesar, a scene from *Macbeth*, Satan's soliloquy to the sun and Eve's dream from *Paradise Lost*, and Collins's *Ode to the Passions*. According to *Loudon's Register* (10 Apr. 1793) she "evinced judgement of taste, and the most refined sensibility." In the fall of 1793 she became a member of the Old American Company at the John Street Theatre, under the management of Henry and Hallam. Her debut with the company was as Euphrasia in *The Grecian Daughter* on 20 November 1793. Though "now past her prime" and "not a little too large," William Dunlap asserts that her merit "carried her through with great applause" (vol. 1, p. 203). Within the first months of her engagement with the Old American Company, Melmoth played first line roles in over nineteen plays.

During the next seven seasons, Melmoth became the undisputed grande dame of matronly tragedy. Charles Durang refers to her as "an actress of intellect, which has been greatly cultivated by thorough reading and exemplified by estimable worth" (chap. 30). Some of her most often repeated roles were Calista in *The Fair Penitent*, Lady Macbeth, Matilda in *The Fatal Deception*, Lady Randolph in *Douglas*, Belvidera in *Venice Preserv'd*, Matilda in *The Carmelite*, Arpasia in *Tamerlane*, Lady Ann in *The Deserter's Daughter*, Queen Elizabeth in *The Earl of Essex*, Euphrasia in *The Grecian Daughter*, Mrs. Beverly in *The Gamester*, and the Queen in *Hamlet*. Melmoth also achieved some success in lighter fare, playing Lady Elinor Irwin in *Every One Has His Fault*, Widow Racket in *The Belle's Strategem*, and Mrs. Alford in *The Children of the Wood*, for which she wrote her own entrance song.

On occasion, Melmoth's increasing corpulence caused inadvertent humor amongst members of the audience and the critics. John Bernard relates an instance when Melmoth cried out the line "Tyrant, strike here!—Here you will find blood enough!" in *The Grecian Daughter* and produced peals of laughter from the audience as she indicated her own sizable chest. Durang laments that "she had been handsome, but unfortunately for her professional career, her figure became so extremely *obese* that no art in fitting tragedy robes could lessen her . . . bulk" (chap. 30). In addition, the 4 February 1794 review in the *Minerva* questions the appropriateness of some of the roles essayed by the now middle-aged Melmoth: "The part of Roxalena, the *little, lively, turned-up nosed*, girl, would have delighted under the management of Mrs. Hodgkinson. What Demon, then, could have put it in the head of Mrs. Melmoth to attempt it?"

Nevertheless, by January 1798 Melmoth's salary was $20 per week, according to Dunlap, and she was one of the leading players of the company. Though she rarely appeared in the comic afterpiece, she frequently gave recitations at the conclusion of an evening, *Shelah's Voyage to America* becoming one of the audience favorites. By 1800, however, her leading position in several plays was supplanted by younger actresses and Melmoth was featured in fewer and fewer new productions. In the summer of 1801, Mrs. Merry of Philadelphia was brought in for the first star booking on record in the New York theater and temporarily displaced Melmoth from her accustomed roles. After this turn of events and an argument with theater manager William Dunlap over her benefit night, Melmoth headed her footsteps toward Philadelphia and accepted a place with Wignell's Chestnut Street Theatre for the 1802–1803 season while, according to Durang, entering into "an agricultural speculation on Long Island." She also authored a comic musical piece in 1803, *The Generous Farmers*, from which she frequently performed the song "Drimindoo."

For the season of 1803–1804, Melmoth resumed playing at the Park Street Theatre and remained there until Dunlap's bankruptcy in 1805 forced its closing. Melmoth returned to the Chestnut Street Theatre, reprising some of her former roles (Lady Randolph, Lady Macbeth, Lady St. Valori, and Emilia) and sharing the stage with Mrs. Wignell (formerly Mrs. Merry) in *The Disressed Mother*, *Mary Queen of Scots*, *The Earl of Essex*, and *Pizarro* during the 1805–1807 seasons. Melmoth retired from the stage with her benefit performance as Fiamemetta in *The Tale of Mystery* at the Olympic Theatre in New York on 12 August 1812. In the last years of her life, Melmoth ran a school for elocution and kept the small dairy farm that she had purchased on Long Island. She died on Long Island, New York.

Throughout her career Melmoth established standards of behavior, both on and off the stage, that, according to Durang, "were examples to the younger members of the profession" (chap. 36). Despite her ever increasing age and weight, she excelled as a tragic villainess, and the power of her performances quelled even the harshest critics. *Rambler's Magazine* (Dec. 1809) commented that she was "remarkable for (a superabundance of tears) but she possessed a skill in the management, that enabled her to resist the popular disapprobation." Dunlap commended her as "the best tragic actress the inhabitants of New York . . . had ever seen" (vol. 1, p. 203). She brought a dignity, power, and control to her serious roles and raised the level of tragic acting in the newly formed professional theater of the United States.

• William Warren's records as manager of the company, in the Library of Congress, mention Melmoth. There is a biographical entry in Philip H. Highfill et al., *A Biographical Dictionary of Actors, Actresses, Musicians, Dancers, Managers & Other Stage Personnel in London, 1660–1800*, vol. 10 (1973–1994). *Index to the London Stage, 1660–1800*, pt. 4, ed. G. W. Stone, Jr., and pt. 5, ed. Charles Beecher Hogan (1979), give dates of her Covent Garden and Drury Lane appearances. Her career in New York is chiefly obtained through William Dunlap's *History of the American Theatre, Three Volumes in One* (1963); George C. D. Odell's *Annals of the New York Stage*, vols. 1–3 (1927); George O. Seilhamer's *History of the American Theatre* (1891); and Joseph N. Ireland's *Records of the New York Stage*, vol. 1 (1966). Periodic and newspaper sources include the *American Minerva*, *New York Magazine*, the *New Daily Advertiser*, the *Commercial Advertiser*, the *Evening Post*, and the *Rambler*. Her career in Philadelphia can be traced through Charles Durang's unpublished files, *The Philadelphia Stage. From the Year 1749 to the Year 1855* (of the *Philadelphia Sunday Dispatch*, beginning 7 May 1854), of which the complete files can be found pasted in bound volumes at the University of Pennsylvania, the Historical Society of Philadelphia, and Harvard University; Thomas Clark Pollock's *The American Theatre in the Eighteenth Century* (1933); and Reese Davis James's books, *Cradle of Culture, 1800–1810; the Philadelphia Stage* (1957) and *Old Drury of Philadelphia: A History of the Philadelphia Stage* (1932). Periodic sources regarding Philadelphia include *Port Folio*, the *Aurora*, and the *United States Gazette*. Melmoth is mentioned in the following diaries and account books as well: William Wood, *Personal Recollections of the Stage* (1855); James Fennell, *An Apology for the Life of James Fennell* (1814; repr. 1969); and John Bernard, *Retrospections of America, 1797–1811* (1887). See Susan Porter, *With an Air Debonair* (1991), for Melmoth's musical authorship.

SUSAN F. CLARK

MELTZER, Samuel James (22 Mar. 1851–7 Nov. 1920), physician and physiologist, was born in Ponevyezh, Russia, the son of Simon Meltzer, a teacher, and Taube Kowars. The family were Orthodox Jews, and Meltzer received his early education in a rabbinical seminary. He decided against a religious vocation, however, and entered the University of Berlin in 1876 to study philosophy and medicine, obtaining his medical degree in 1882.

Meltzer's M.D. dissertation, under the direction of the physiologist Hugo Kronecker, dealt with the swallowing reflex. He first outlined his theory of inhibition in this work, noting that the reflex stimulation of one of a pair of antagonistic muscles (e.g., inspiratory muscles) was accompanied by reflex inhibition of the other (e.g., expiratory muscles). He postulated that this reciprocal arrangement must exist for other antagonistic muscles in the body to facilitate efficient motor action; this concept influenced much of his later work.

Upon his graduation from medical school, Meltzer decided to emigrate to the United States because he recognized that anti-Semitism would hamper his career in Germany and in his native Russia. He worked as a ship's surgeon for several crossings in order to earn the fare. Settling in New York in 1883, he entered into private medical practice to support himself and his family. Meltzer had married Olga Levitt in 1870, and the couple had two children.

In order to continue his research, Meltzer made arrangements to have access to the laboratories of colleagues, including William Welch, then at Bellevue Hospital, who was impressed enough by the young physician to share space and equipment with him. For about twenty years Meltzer's research was conducted largely with his own funds and in whatever time he could spare from his medical practice. When the Rockefeller Institute for Medical Research was established in 1904, Meltzer was appointed head of the Department of Physiology and Pharmacology, a position he held until his retirement in 1919.

Meltzer developed the idea of combined action of opposing processes, first expressed in his M.D. thesis, into a general theory. He believed that every excitation or stimulation of a tissue was accompanied by a corresponding inhibitory response, and that physiological phenomena were a compromise between these two fundamental, antagonistic processes, excitation and inhibition.

Although Meltzer's dualistic conception of life processes was never widely accepted, it was an important stimulus to his own experimental work. For example, his animal studies on the pharmacological action of magnesium salts (1905–1909) showed that these compounds produced unconsciousness and muscle relaxation, states readily reversed by the injection of calcium chloride. This research added magnesium to the list of elements known to play a significant part in the activity of the cell. Meltzer believed that magnesium was the element especially concerned with inhibition.

Meltzer also carried out a series of important studies on artificial respiration in collaboration with his son-in-law, John Auer. In 1909 they developed the technique of intratracheal insufflation, whereby the lungs are kept inflated by blowing a stream of air through a tube inserted into the trachea. Including an anesthetic vapor in the air stream made possible anesthetization combined with artificial respiration, making the technique useful in thoracic surgery.

Other scientific contributions of Meltzer include his theory that bronchial asthma is a phenomenon of anaphylaxis, and his introduction of the engineering term "factors of safety" to describe the reserve powers of organisms. He also collaborated with his daughter Clara in important studies on the effects of adrenaline on the blood vessels and on the muscles of the iris.

Meltzer played an important role in the founding and early development of several scientific or medical societies. He was the founder and first president of the Society for Experimental Biology and Medicine (1903), which was familiarly known for years as the "Meltzer Verein." He was also a founding member of the American Society for Pharmacology and Experimental Therapeutics (1908). The breadth of his interests and knowledge is reflected in the fact that he was elected president of half a dozen national medical societies in diverse fields, from the American Physiological Society (1911–1913) to the American Association for Thoracic Surgery (1918). Meltzer's contributions to science were recognized by his election to the National Academy of Sciences in 1912.

Meltzer's strong belief in the international character of science led him to establish an international medical brotherhood, the Fraternitas Medicorum, early in the World War I years. Thousands of Americans joined, but the organization ceased functioning when the United States entered the war.

Familiar with both clinical medicine and biomedical research, Meltzer was also able to serve as a liaison between practitioners and scientific investigators at a time when the rapid rise of biomedical science was creating some tension between the two groups. His colleague W. H. Howell stated in an obituary, "No one in our generation, I venture to say, was more useful in this country in bringing about a helpful and sympathetic understanding between the laboratory worker and the physician" (1921: 105). Meltzer's most important contribution in this area was his instrumental role in the founding of the American Society for Clinical Investigation (1908), which provided a setting where young academic physicians could link laboratory research to clinical problems.

Although troubled by illness in his later years, Meltzer continued to pursue his research until he died while at work in his study in New York. His more than 240 publications enhanced knowledge of important physiological processes and resulted in several practical applications in medicine. He helped to nurture several young societies struggling to carve out professional identities for scientific disciplines such as physiology and pharmacology. At a time of increasing specialization in medicine, Meltzer managed to retain a broad overview of the medical field and to forge a link between practice and research.

• The Rockefeller University Archives holds a small amount of manuscript material related to Meltzer. The only book-length biography is Adolph Meltzer, *Breath of Life: The Life and Works of Dr. Samuel James Meltzer* (1993), which includes a bibliography of Meltzer's publications. The most useful biographical article is W. H. Howell, "Samuel James Meltzer, 1851–1920," *Memoirs of the National Academy of Sciences* 21, no. 9 (1926): 15–23, which also includes a bibliography. See also the obituary by Howell in *Science*, n.s. 53 (1921): 99–106, and A. McGehee Harvey, "Samuel J. Meltzer: Pioneer Catalyst in the Evolution of Clinical Science in America," *Perspectives in Biology and Medicine* 21 (1978): 431–40. A special supplement to vol. 18 (1921) of *Proceedings of the Society for Experimental Biology and Medicine*, a memorial issue for Meltzer, contains several biographical sketches by colleagues.

JOHN PARASCANDOLA

MELVILLE, George Wallace (10 Jan. 1841–18 Mar. 1912), naval engineer, was born in New York City, the son of Alexander Melville, a chemist, and Sarah Wallace. He graduated from Brooklyn Collegiate and Polytechnic Institute and joined the U.S. Navy as a third assistant engineer in July 1861. He saw much hazardous duty during the Civil War, some of it through his own choosing. He volunteered to go aboard the Confederate ship *Florida* as a spy, and he made the critical suggestion to ram and capture that ship as it lay in a neutral harbor (1864). He served with Admiral David D. Porter's fleet at the capture of Fort Fisher, and after the war, he served on the fleet that observed the French evacuation from Mexico. Melville married Henrietta (maiden name and year of marriage unknown); they had three children.

Melville also volunteered to go to the Arctic as chief engineer aboard the *Tigress* in its mission to find the men of the *Polaris*. During this successful mission, he became enamored of Arctic exploration and developed a firm friendship with Lieutenant George Washington De Long. In 1879 Melville volunteered to go with De Long on a voyage of exploration by way of the Bering Strait. As chief engineer aboard the *Jeannette*, he was largely responsible for keeping the craft afloat during nearly two years of drifting in the Arctic ice pack. He contributed notably to the voyage by landing on and claiming Henrietta Island for the United States of America (2 June 1881). De Long afterward wrote that Melville's actions in this regard were "brave and meritorious."

The ship's company made a desperate attempt to reach the Lena Delta in Siberia. The *Jeannette* sank on 11 June, and on 12 June Melville led one of the boats in the attempt to escape. His boat was separated from De Long's, and Melville and his crew landed on the delta's east coast, where they found help in the form of Tungusnatives in two days. Following a rest period (which would later become controversial), Melville made an extensive search for De Long and his men. Failing to find his commander, Melville returned to his camp, wintered there, and then began to search again in the spring. He found the bodies of De Long and his companions on 23 March 1882 and buried them in a cairn overlooking the Lena River. He returned to the United States by way of Irkutsk and St. Petersburg, where he had a brief interview with Czar Alexander III.

Melville returned to a hero's welcome in New York City. However, he almost immediately quarreled with his wife, who was put in an asylum. After two months the doctors determined that she had regained her mental health and released her. Melville's behavior in this regard was viewed with some suspicion by the press. He also found he had to answer charges from relatives of the dead members of the *Jeannette* expedition that he had not searched quickly enough for De Long during the fall of 1881. He responded to the charges in ringing terms at the congressional inquiry, they were dropped, and he then hastened off as chief engineer aboard the *Thetis*, which went in search of the members of the Greely expedition, who were lost north of Greenland. The desire within the navy to prevent a possible scandal in the *Jeannette* affair made it difficult for observers to ascertain for certain whether Melville's three-day delay was completely necessary.

In 1887 Melville was appointed as chief of the Bureau of Steam Engineering of the navy, advanced over forty-four officers who had seniority. Congress also gave Melville a warm endorsement and raised his rank to captain in belated recognition of his search for De Long. As chief of the bureau (1887–1903), Melville was both inventive and farsighted. He superintended the designs of the machinery of more than 120 ships and introduced the water-tube boiler and the triple-screw system. He was responsible for the building of the USS *San Francisco*, *Columbia*, and *Minneapolis*, which were for a time the fastest warships afloat. He served as president of the American Society of Mechanical Engineers in 1899. Melville believed that the USS *Maine*, the destruction of which provided a pretext for the Spanish-American War in 1898, was lost to an internal explosion, not a Spanish mine. His analysis of the *Maine* explosion was published in the North American Review in 1911.

Melville retired from the navy in 1903. As a revered expert on Arctic exploration, he weighed in on the side of Robert E. Peary in the controversy between Peary and Frederick Cook as to who had actually reached the North Pole. Melville divorced his wife (year unknown) and then married Estella Smith Polis in 1907. Melville died in Philadelphia. He left half of his $300,000 estate to establish a home for aged and deserving poor people, but a Pennsylvania statute regarding codicils prevented this from being carried out.

As a sailor, engineer, and naval administrator, Melville was often excellent, at times beyond reproach. He possessed a great self-assurance and inspired confidence in his subordinates. His innovations as head of the Bureau of Steam Engineering made the U.S. Navy competitive with the great European navies. His stellar career was marred by two occurrences, the delay of the search for De Long and the institutionalization of his wife, each of which cast a possible shadow on his character. However, as an explorer, a writer, a naval leader, and a celebrity, Melville loomed large in the age of romantic and inspiring Victorian heroes at the turn of the twentieth century.

• Although no central collection of Melville's papers exists, some of his manuscripts are at the Library of Congress and the Franklin D. Roosevelt Memorial Library, Hyde Park, N.Y. His exploits in the Arctic are chronicled in his own *In the Lena Delta* (1884) and in Emma De Long, ed., *The Voyage of the "Jeannette," the Ship and Ice Journals of George W. De Long* (1884). Melville's life and career are well documented in articles and journals, but there is no comprehensive biography of him. His naval career is described in William L. Cathcart, "George Wallace Melville," *Cassier's Magazine*, Apr. 1897. The *New York Times* reported on his heroic return to the United States, 14 Sept. 1882, and the *Philadelphia Ledger* covered his placement of his wife in an asylum, 18 and 19 Sept. 1882. The most up-to-date and thorough study of the *Jeannette* expedition and Melville's attempts to rescue De Long is Leonard F. Guttridge, *Icebound: The "Jeannette" Expedition's Quest for the North Pole* (1986). The primary documents that Guttridge's work is based on are *Proceedings of a Court of Inquiry into the Loss of the Exploring Steamer "Jeannette"*, 47th Cong., 2d sess., H. Exec. Doc. 108, and *Proceedings of an Investigation into the "Jeannette" by the Naval Affairs Subcommittee*, 47th Cong., 1st sess., H. Misc. Doc. 66.

SAMUEL WILLARD CROMPTON

MELVILLE, Herman (1 Aug. 1819–28 Sept. 1891), novelist and poet, was born in New York City, the son of Allan Melvill (as the name was spelled), an importer of Parisian dry goods, and Maria Gansevoort. The Melvill family was connected to Scottish nobility; Maria was the daughter of General Peter Gansevoort, a hero of the American Revolution, and related to the Van Rensselaers and other Dutch families long dominant in upstate New York. Between 1815 and January 1830 eight children were born to the Melvills, all of whom lived to adulthood. At six Herman entered the New York Male High School; at nine he was enrolled in the Grammar School of Columbia College. After persistently borrowing from his father and his mother-in-law, Allan Melvill in 1827 was duped into a financial scheme that wiped out the rest of his wife's and his own prospective inheritances. In October 1830, eluding creditors, Melvill fled to Albany, where Maria's brother Peter got him work as a clerk; the trauma precipitated the death of old Mrs. Gansevoort.

From the end of 1831, when he was withdrawn from the Albany Academy, Herman's education was catch-as-catch-can. The sudden death of his father in January 1832 was followed that year by the death of his grandfather, the aged Thomas Melvill, a hero of the Boston Tea Party, and early in 1833 by the death of his Grandmother Melvill. The Melvilles (as they began spelling the name) were left in poverty. At twelve Herman was hired as a bank clerk for $150 a year; two years later his mother put him to work in his older brother Gansevoort's cap and fur store. Some years Herman was allowed to spend a week with his uncle Thomas at the Melvill farm south of Pittsfield, Massachusetts. The farm was Herman's "first love," a cousin later declared, and when he managed it in 1837, after his uncle went west to Illinois, he saw in the Berkshires an American paradise. Poorly educated himself, he taught that fall in a rural school nearby, but early in January 1838 he was back in Albany.

In May 1838 Maria Melville moved with six of her children to Lansingburgh, across the Hudson River, to live more cheaply. Herman took a course in surveying and engineering at the Lansingburgh Academy, but he was unable to find maintenance work on the Erie Canal. In May 1839 a Lansingburgh newspaper published his first known fiction, "Fragments from a Writing Desk." That summer he signed on a merchant ship bound for Liverpool (the basis for his *Redburn*), and that fall he taught at Greenbush, across the Hudson from Albany. The school proved unable to pay his salary, and late the next spring he taught briefly in Brunswick, near Troy. In June 1840 he traveled to Illinois hoping in vain that his uncle Thomas could find him work. After job-hunting in Manhattan, Herman and his brother Gansevoort went to the Massachusetts whaling ports. At Fairhaven Herman signed on the whaleship *Acushnet*, which set sail on 3 January 1841.

Passage around Cape Horn led the *Acushnet* to the Pacific Equatorial whaling grounds by summer 1841. In July 1842 the *Acushnet* arrived at Nukuheva, in the Marquesas Islands, where Melville and a shipmate, Richard Tobias "Toby" Greene, deserted and took refuge with the Typees, reputedly cannibals. Because Melville had become lame, Greene left for help; he did not return, and Melville remained with the Typees another two weeks before they let him sign on an Australian whaler, the ineptly captained *Lucy Ann*. In late September some of the crew, including Melville, refused duty in Tahiti and were imprisoned by the British consul. With a companion Melville escaped to a neighboring island, where the two worked on a farm. In November Melville signed on a Nantucket whaler, the *Charles and Henry*, from which he was discharged in April 1843 on Maui in the Hawaiian Islands. There most likely he first heard details of a tragic occurrence on the U.S. Brig *Somers* the previous December, the hanging for mutiny of three men; the second in command on the *Somers*, Melville learned, was his older first cousin, Lieutenant Guert Gansevoort, thenceforth a powerful figure in his imagination. Soon he sailed to Honolulu, where he set pins in a bowling alley and then, expecting to stay indefinitely, became a clerk in a store. In August, homesick, he impulsively signed on the U.S. Navy frigate *United States* as an ordinary seaman. The ship cruised in the Pacific and along the western coast of South and Central America. On the *United States*, as earlier, Melville practiced his yarns about his adventures among the natives in the Typee valley, playing on their reputation as sexually liberal cannibals; he also learned to tell about the mutiny at Tahiti so that his story was as comical as the much-discussed *Somers* mutiny was tragic.

When the *United States* arrived at the Navy Yard in Boston in October 1844, Melville was not immediately discharged. From newspapers he learned that his brother Gansevoort, now a famous orator, was just returning from a western speaking tour on behalf of the Democratic candidate for president, James K. Polk. Melville learned that his older sister Helen and Elizabeth Shaw, born in 1822, the daughter of his father's friend Lemuel Shaw (since 1830 the chief justice of the Massachusetts Supreme Court), had become intimate friends during his absence. Judge Shaw proved so hospitable and encouraging that Herman dedicated *Typee* to him a year and a half later. After seeing the family in Lansingburgh, Herman witnessed the election in New York with his celebrated orator brother and their younger brother, Allan. There he began his own quest for fame by writing out the story of his "captivity" among the Typees.

In the spring of 1845 the Harper Brothers refused the manuscript, thinking it a hoax. Melville returned to Lansingburgh, and his brother Gansevoort, rewarded with the secretaryship of the American legation in London, took the manuscript with him. The English publisher John Murray suspected that the author must have been a practiced fiction writer, but, reassured by Gansevoort, he paid £100 for the exotic narrative. In the absence of an international copyright law Murray was gambling that by being the first publisher of the book he would secure a de facto copyright. Washington Irving was shown proofs of *Typee* by Gansevoort and passed them along to G. P. Putnam, then in London, who bought it for American publication by Wiley & Putnam. The book appeared in London in February as *Narrative of a Four Months' Residence among the Natives of a Valley of the Marquesas Islands; or, a Peep at Polynesian Life*. In New York in March it was published as *Typee: A Peep at Polynesian Life. During a Four Months' Residence in a Valley of the Marquesas*, without some sexual passages hastily censored by John Wiley. Although as Murray had feared, some critics suspected that the narrative was invented by a man who had not been to the Pacific, in Great Britain and the United States the book became a sensation. Melville's fresh handling of Polynesian life contrasted sharply with previous accounts provided by naval officers intent on recording information of economic and military importance and by missionaries intent on furthering efforts to Christianize the natives.

In April 1846 the Presbyterian New York *Evangelist* attacked *Typee* for its portrayal of American Protestant missionaries in the Pacific, thereby initiating a systematic attempt to silence Melville. A Presbyterian himself, John Wiley required Melville to expurgate the book thoroughly for a "Revised Edition." The intermediary, Evert A. Duyckinck, the editor of two series of books for Wiley & Putnam, became a friend of Melville's. Meanwhile, Gansevoort Melville died suddenly in London, leaving Herman launched as an author and the head of the family. The fortuitous reappearance of Toby Greene, Melville's fellow deserter from the *Acushnet*, brought fresh notoriety to *Typee*, some editors apologizing for their previous skepticism, others certain the "resurrection" of Toby was itself a hoax. The ensuing controversy became a publicity bonanza. Late that summer, in Lansingburgh, on the strength of Murray's promise to pay for the story of Greene's escape, Melville proposed to the visiting Elizabeth Shaw and was accepted.

In December 1846 Melville sold his new manuscript to Murray and to the Harpers, now eager to publish him. *Omoo* continued Melville's adventures (dressed out with fictional episodes) from the time he left the Typee valley until he signed on his third whaler. Melville had mastered a personal and, it turned out, reckless way of putting biblically suffused prose to the service of comical rogue adventure. Warned by how little he actually received for the highly publicized *Typee*, Melville hoped for a steady job in a custom house and made a fruitless office-seeking trip to Washington early in 1847. *Omoo* was published in March in London and in April in New York to favorable reviews.

With *Typee* and *Omoo* Melville seized the imagination of readers of English throughout the world. He was a modern Robinson Crusoe, who even skeptical

Britons finally decided was a genuine adventurer. Making the two volumes even more alluring was the element of sexuality, both overt, as in the eyewitness account of the way women swam out to welcome ships to the Marquesas, and more covert. The New York *Tribune* of 26 June 1847 denounced *Typee* and *Omoo* as "unmistakably defective, if not positively diseased in moral tone," and the July *American Whig* proclaimed Melville to be a man glorying in his licentiousness. Melville had become the first American literary sex symbol, associated in readers' minds with his presumed sexual experiences in the South Seas, and Fayaway, the beautiful maiden in *Typee*, had become—as she remained throughout the nineteenth century—the best-known of all Melville's characters. Melville's first two books, the basis of his reputation, remained in print throughout his lifetime, distributed worldwide as part of John Murray's Home and Colonial Library.

In May 1847, at Lansingburgh, Melville began his third South Sea book, *Mardi*, and in June the success of *Omoo* was such that Judge Shaw thought Herman could support a family. The wedding took place in August at the Shaw home, where the groom's admirers could not intrude. After the honeymoon in Canada, Melville, with money from Shaw, bought an indenture of lease on a house on Fourth Avenue in New York City and settled there with his bride, his mother, his four sisters, and his lawyer brother Allan and Allan's own bride, Sophia. Resuming work on *Mardi*, Melville altered it from an adventure story to a romantic and satirical allegory and still later added chapters of political allegory commenting on the 1848 European revolutions and on American politics. The book at last completed, Melville took his wife home to Boston, where in February 1849 their first child, Malcolm, was born. John Murray rejected *Mardi*, but Richard Bentley accepted the baffling book and published it in London in March to mixed reviews and slow sales, a fate the Harpers' edition, published in April, also suffered. In June the expurgated Wiley & Putnam edition of *Typee* was reissued under the Harper imprint, to general approbation.

By May 1849 it was clear that *Mardi* would be less popular than the straightforward *Typee* and *Omoo*. A fit subject came to hand when Melville's youngest brother, Tom, shipped out of Manhattan for China. Tom was nineteen, and going aboard Tom's ship triggered memories. Thinking he could perform easy penance for his self-indulgent *Mardi*, Melville in two months wrote the realistic *Redburn*, based on his voyage to Liverpool. That feat accomplished, in August and September Melville wrote yet another, even longer, sea narrative, *White-Jacket*, based on his naval service. A ruling in London having denied British copyright to any American book, even if published there first, in October Melville sailed for England, determined to sell *White-Jacket* in person, against the odds. With a large enough advance, he could then make a grand tour of Europe and the Levant to gather materials for adventurous books set in new exotic locations. *Redburn*, generously accepted by Bentley, was in bookstores when Melville arrived in London; the Harpers published it in New York in November. Failure to get an advance for *White-Jacket* forced Melville to content himself with a brief visit to Paris and the Rhine country. When Bentley at last paid for *White-Jacket* in advance, Melville sailed for home. During the prolonged voyage, he had time to plan a work yet more ambitious than *Mardi*, a book that would invest an American whaling story with the grandeur of Shakespearean tragedy.

Home in early February 1850, Melville shut himself up and worked so hard that by 1 May he could say in a letter to Richard Henry Dana, Jr., the author of *Two Years before the Mast*, that his whaling book was half done. In July, determined not to enslave himself again all summer, he gave himself and his family a vacation at the Melvill house south of Pittsfield, now run by his cousin Robert as a summer boardinghouse for an elite clientele. On an outing to Monument Mountain in August, Melville and the reclusive Nathaniel Hawthorne met for the first time. The older man was so struck by Melville that he invited him to stay at his cottage outside Lenox. Similarly impressed, Melville dashed off for Duyckinck's *Literary World* an essay on the only Hawthorne book at hand, *Mosses from an Old Manse* (1846). Writing in the splendor of the Berkshires, and daring to compare Hawthorne to Shakespeare, Melville acknowledged to himself the greatness of his own half-finished American (and Shakespearean) tragedy. The anonymously published "Hawthorne and His Mosses" marked a turning point in Hawthorne's reputation, and once its author was identified, it enhanced the warmth Hawthorne and his wife already felt for Melville.

Soon afterward, with more money from his father-in-law, Melville impulsively bought a farm adjacent to the Melvill property, owing the previous owner not just the mortgage but a large part of the down-payment. Melville moved to the farm in October with his wife and son as well as his mother and three of his sisters. "Arrowhead" was an old farmhouse, in disrepair, but it satisfied two reckless desires of Melville's: to finish his great tragic drama in a room with a view of Mt. Greylock, the grandest peak in the Berkshires, and to finish it near the only American writer he could consider his equal.

Once settled in, Melville had little time to see Hawthorne and was bedeviled by money worries. Late in March 1851 he sold the long-empty Fourth Avenue house, for less than he expected; then the Harpers refused him a further advance. On 1 May he made a fateful decision, borrowing $2,050 for six years at 9 percent interest from T.D. Stewart, a Lansingburgh friend. Some of that money—an enormous sum—paid off the down-payment on Arrowhead; some paid for improvements on the farmhouse and barn; and some of it went for plating his new book so that Melville could sell it to the highest bidder. Dollars, he wrote Hawthorne, damned him. In July, under extreme pressure, he completed what he was calling "The Whale."

Melville sold the book to the Harpers, after all, giving it at the last minute a more memorable title: *Moby-Dick*. In October 1851 (the month the Melvilles' second son, Stanwix, was born) Bentley published it in London as *The Whale*, in three volumes, handsome but flawed, since the half-page "Epilogue" had been lost in moving Melville's prefatory "Etymology" and "Extracts" to the back of the third volume. Despite the apparent death of the narrator, Ishmael, with the ship, *The Whale* received much acclaim. The London *Morning Advertiser* of 24 October could not think of works "more honourable to American literature" than Melville's three volumes. In November, during a private dinner in the dining room of the Curtis Hotel in Lenox, Melville presented an inscribed copy of *Moby-Dick* to the surprised dedicatee, Nathaniel Hawthorne, then preparing to leave the Berkshires. Hawthorne praised the book and offered to review it, but Melville declined, already deeply involved with his next book, a novel that he thought of as more profound than *Moby-Dick*. That work, *Pierre*, was a psychological novel based on what Melville had been learning about his own mind. Two years earlier, Melville had naively planned *Redburn* as a fast and easy excursion into his childhood and away again. To use his later words in *Pierre*, he had "dropped his angle" into the well of childhood and gone fishing in his own memory, where who knew what monstrous creatures might be brought up. The intense psychological unfolding that began in the aftermath of writing the autobiographical parts of *Redburn* had precipitated *Moby-Dick* and *Pierre*.

In the first two weeks after its American publication in November, the Harpers sold 1,535 copies of *Moby-Dick*, but in the next two months or so only 471 more; sales after that dwindled rapidly. The highest British praise for *The Whale* might have prepared deferential American reviewers to laud *Moby-Dick*, but in the United States the two widely distributed English reviews happened to be those in the *Spectator* and the *Athenaeum* (both dated 25 Oct. 1851). These were hostile toward Melville on good grounds—because nothing in *The Whale* explained that the narrator survived. It was Melville's bad luck that neither magazine specified precisely what was wrong with the ending, so no American reader had any reason to retort triumphantly that Ishmael assuredly *did* survive in *Moby-Dick*, rescued by the *Rachel*. What praise *Moby-Dick* received in the United States did not last long. Melville's "flings" at religion (comments quietly censored out of the English edition) aroused indignation, and many reviewers were cruel, imperceptive, and contemptuous. When Evert Duyckinck reviewed the book in his influential, tone-setting *Literary World*, he devoted the first week's installment to the coincidence of the book's appearing just as news arrived that the whaleship *Ann Alexander* had been sunk by a whale off Chile. In the second, Duyckinck complained about Melville's irreverence toward religion, the "piratical running down of creeds and opinions." The religious press would have leapt on Melville anyway, but Duyckinck lent intellectual and literary respectability to ferocious reviews such as the one in the New York *Independent* on 20 November 1851, which proclaimed that the "Judgment day" would hold Melville liable "for not turning his talents to better account." Even writers for the secular press lamented Melville's decline from the graphic *Typee* and *Omoo*, still viewed as the best, even if tainted, fruits of his undeniable genius.

In Pittsfield at the end of 1851 Melville finished his latest manuscript and carried it to New York. For *Pierre* the Harpers in early January 1852 offered a punitive contract, twenty cents on the dollar (after costs) instead of the usual fifty cents—an arrangement that doomed Melville's career. Frantic, Melville did everything wrong. Accepting the Harpers' terms, he took up the completed manuscript and crudely inserted into it a lengthy satire on the American literary scene and a distorted history of his own immature ambition to write a great mature book, mingling memories of *Mardi*, *Moby-Dick*, and the short original version of *Pierre* itself. By refusing to let Bentley publish *Pierre* on half profits, without an advance, he destroyed the continuity of his reception in England: London reviewers, some of whom thought him one of the finest new writers in the English language, had no follow-up to *The Whale*. In May 1852 Melville defaulted on the semi-annual interest he owed on his loan from T. D. Stewart. Published in July, the Harper *Pierre* provoked a firestorm of outrage, for it dealt perturbingly with falsity in family relationships in which incest was openly hinted at. The Harpers distanced themselves by spreading the rumor that Melville had become "a little crazy." Everything Melville wrote after *Pierre* was aftermath. Nothing he did could overcome the damage to his reputation. In each successive November and May for four more years, he defaulted on the payments due Stewart; twice he defaulted on a mortgage payment as well.

From August until December 1852 Melville brooded over a true story about a long-suffering Falmouth woman and repeatedly urged Hawthorne to write it. In early 1853 he wrote the story himself, probably transferring the locale to Nantucket, which he had visited with Judge Shaw. The week his first daughter, Elizabeth, was born, in late May, Melville completed "The Isle of the Cross," but in June when Melville offered it to the Harpers he was somehow "prevented" from publishing it. Melville's failure to publish his eighth book was compounded by the failure of the family's efforts to secure him a post in a foreign consulate. Resilient still, Melville started a new career as a writer of magazine short stories. "Bartleby, the Scrivener" appeared in the November and December 1853 *Putnam's*, and "Cock-A-Doodle-Doo!" in the December *Harper's*. Until early 1856 he published stories in both *Harper's* and *Putnam's*, all anonymously, according to custom. Melville received an advance from the Harpers for a new book on tortoise hunting in the Galapagos Islands; abandoning the project, he used some of the material in "The Encantadas," serialized in *Putnam's* of March-May 1854. There he also serialized the novel *Israel Potter* from July 1854 through March 1855 (the month the Melvilles' fourth and last child, Frances, was born), after which Putnam published it as a book. He collected his *Putnam's* stories as *The Piazza Tales*, published in May 1856 by Dix & Edwards, introduced by a new essay, "The Piazza." Already he was at work on *The Confidence-Man*, a satirical allegory on American optimism, which he completed that summer.

From his stories Melville earned little money, but he worked, season after season, denying as best he could the inevitable financial disaster awaiting him when Stewart's note became due on 1 May 1856. Guilty, ashamed, terrified at his inability to meet his responsibilities, the once athletic sailor developed rheumatism in 1855 and then was stricken with sciatica. By early 1856 Stewart was threatening to seize Arrowhead in repayment for his loan, and Melville had to confess his irresponsibility. As Judge Shaw rescued him from financial disaster, Melville put up half the farm for sale. Concerned for Melville's health and even his sanity, Shaw paid for a prolonged recuperative tour. Leaving Allan to handle the publication of *The Confidence-Man*, Melville sailed for Scotland, from which he went to Liverpool (where Hawthorne was the American consul), then by ship to the Mediterranean. After a stopover in Egypt at year's end, he left Alexandria for Jaffa in January 1857 for three weeks in the Holy Land. After visiting Greece, Sicily, and Naples, he toured Italy for an intense self-education in history and aesthetics. Meanwhile, *The Confidence-Man* was published in London (Hawthorne having made the sale) and in New York, both on April Fool's Day (the date the action of the book begins), but neither edition earned Melville a penny. He toured through northern Italy, Switzerland, Germany, and the Netherlands before returning to England and sailing for home in late May. His uncle Peter, in particular, hoped he would write up his experiences in the Holy Land, but the disillusioned Melville had concluded not to write any more at present. His fiction writing over, it seemed as if Melville would be remembered for only two good books, *Typee* and *Omoo*.

Irresolute in many ways, now, in July 1857 Melville agreed to purchase a house in Brooklyn but changed his mind; in the fall he tried to sell Arrowhead but found no buyer. From late November through February he lectured on "Statues in Rome" as far away as Montreal, Clarksville (Tenn.), and Cincinnati. From December 1858 through March 1859, he lectured on a topic intended to be more popular, "The South Seas," this time going as far south as Baltimore and west to Chicago and Milwaukee. Some reviewers were enthusiastic, but on most nights, especially in the Midwest, audiences complained that the man whom Dana had once called incomparable in dramatic storytelling was inaudible and stiff. For his last lecture, "Travel," he could book only three halls between November 1859 and February 1860.

Around 1858 Melville began writing poetry, a secret shared only with his wife. In 1860, when he decided to sail around the world on the *Meteor*, a clipper ship captained by his brother Thomas, he left his brother Allan instructions for publishing a volume of short poems, expecting that when he reached San Francisco he would find "*Poems* by Herman Melville" waiting for him, published in New York and shipped by the Panama route. Sailing up the Pacific, Melville read long poems, preparing to commence an epic poem of his own once the *Meteor* began its voyage across the Pacific to Calcutta. *Poems* was not waiting for him in San Francisco, only news that two publishers had refused to publish the book. Melville went home via Panama, deeply disappointed, and put aside his epic ambitions. Some of the short poems may survive, in altered forms, in manuscript or in the two small volumes he printed privately shortly before his death, or, less likely, they may survive as songs interspersed in *Clarel* (1876).

In 1861, proposed by his family for a consulship, Melville went to Washington, but returned home when word came that his father-in-law was dying. Soon Elizabeth Melville received a portion of her inheritance, freeing the Melvilles to rent a place in New York City early in 1862. There the author of *Moby-Dick* humbly set himself to study what British literary historians, critics, and poets said about how literary greatness could be achieved, taking notes for a personal aesthetic credo. Recovering from a bout of rheumatism, he returned to Pittsfield, where he again put the farm up for sale. In November 1862, moving to a rented house in Pittsfield, he was badly injured when he was thrown from a wagon in a freak accident. Until this time a daring driver, he became excessively cautious.

Selling Arrowhead to Allan for use as a summer home, Melville left for New York City with his family in October 1863, his wife having bought Allan's former house on East 26th Street, near Park Avenue. The family spent the Civil War quietly, living on money Elizabeth Melville had inherited. In 1862 Melville's cousin Guert Gansevoort, now alcoholic, haunted by the Somers hangings, wrecked the ship in his command, the sloop of war *Adirondack*. In April 1864 Melville visited his cousin Henry Gansevoort, who was in the Army of the Potomac, and rode on a scouting party. Realizing that none of his family was playing a genuinely heroic role in the war, Melville saw that as the poet of the war he might emulate the Revolutionary-era achievements of his two grandfathers. Sometime before the fall of Richmond (Apr. 1865), he began recording the conflict in poems published by Harpers in August 1866 as *Battle-Pieces and Aspects of the War*. Reviewers jeered at the book as evidence that the author of the fondly remembered *Typee* and *Omoo* had little or no poetic talent.

In December 1866 Melville at last received a political appointment as an inspector of customs in New York at four dollars a day. The job did not relieve his shame at having been unable to provide for his family and his grief over the loss of his career. In the spring of 1867 Elizabeth Melville was miserable, convinced that her husband was insane. Her minister suggested that she take refuge with her two half-brothers in Boston. The brothers rejected the idea as illegal and imprudent, and she remained with her husband. Tensions in the household went unresolved, and in September the Melvilles' first child, Malcolm, eighteen and a half, died in his bed from a self-inflicted gunshot wound—an accident, the family vehemently insisted. After the glare of new notoriety, the Melvilles became more private than ever.

In the next years, newspapers and magazines seldom mentioned Melville, and then usually as a Berkshire writer or, increasingly, as the friend of the greatest American writer, Hawthorne. Late in 1869, memories of Hawthorne, who had died in 1864, crystallized Melville's inchoate scheme to make literary use of his visit to the Holy Land. Through the characters of Vine and Rolfe (the former based on Hawthorne, the latter an idealized self-portrait), Melville could come to terms with his private memories of his fellow writer and their disparate fates even while portraying Holy Land travelers (American, English, Continental, and Near Eastern) in thoughtful conversations on such topics as the leveling of American values, the unresolved social and political issues of the French Revolution, and the difficulty of retaining faith in Christianity in the new secular world.

In 1872 Melville's brother Allan and his mother died. For months Melville and his family took refuge in Staten Island with his brother Tom, now the prosperous governor of Sailors' Snug Harbor, a home for retired and disabled seamen. Acquaintance with some of the pensioners encouraged Melville to draw on his own sea memories in his late poems and prose. That November, Elizabeth Melville lost income-producing property in the great Boston fire, and the next year Melville's job at the Custom House was threatened. His wife gave up her church pew, unable to pay the rent. At the end of 1875 Melville's salary was temporarily cut to $3.60 a day.

By mid-1875 Melville had finished his epic poem, and with a legacy from his uncle Peter he published it in June 1876. *Clarel: A Poem and Pilgrimage in the Holy Land*, like *Battle-Pieces*, was a failure. The New York *Independent* of 6 July called it "destitute of interest or metrical skill," and the Springfield (Mass.) *Republican* of 18 July pronounced that "Herman Melville's literary reputation will remain, what it has fairly become, a thing of the past." On 8 September, however, the *Republican* took note of praise in the London *Academy*, observing that "Herman Melville's poem, 'Clarel,' receives kindlier countenance in England than it has in his own land"—an early signal of Melville's revival in England. In 1879 the disappointed poet stoically agreed to authorize the publisher (Putnam's) to pulp the remaining bound and unbound volumes of *Clarel* to get them out of the way. After that bitter acknowledgment of the failure of his epic, Melville pursued his work on less ambitious, interrelated poems, "A Symposium of Old Masters at Delmonico's" and "A Morning in Naples," preceded by prose sketches introducing their fictional narrators. These pieces, usually referred to as the "Burgundy Club Sketches," grew out of discussions Melville had participated in since the 1840s, when he first met American artists and became friends with the art historian Henry T. Tuckerman.

In the late 1870s and early 1880s Melville kept his job in the Custom House, taking only a week or two of vacation in August, sometimes to the family house in Gansevoort, sometimes to mountain retreats where his wife sought refuge from her allergies. The second Melville daughter, Frances, married in 1880. Thereafter, the Melvilles lived alone with their severely arthritic daughter Bessie. Melville resigned from the Custom House in December 1885. Early the next year his son Stanwix died in San Francisco. (Among other losses, Melville's sister Augusta died in 1876; his brother Tom in 1884; his younger sister Fanny in 1885; his older sister Helen in 1888.)

Around 1885 Melville wrote a ballad, "Billy in the Darbies," about a mutinous sailor awaiting execution. In his retirement, Melville worked on the "Burgundy Club" material, and at intervals on a prose headnote to the ballad. By 1888, when Melville made a fair copy of *Billy Budd*, the headnote had overwhelmed the short poem. In September 1888 Melville printed *John Marr and Other Sailors with Some Sea-Pieces* in an edition of twenty-five copies. Around 1890 he dropped the prose sketches from the "Burgundy Club" manuscripts, retitling the poems "At the Hostelry" and "Naples in the Time of Bomba." In April 1891 he again thought he had finished *Billy Budd* (and would have published it, for English admirers had made it clear he would have an audience). He continued to work on the manuscript, and in June he printed his *Timoleon and Other Ventures in Minor Verse*, again in an edition of twenty-five copies. On 28 September 1891, with *Billy Budd* not quite completed, Melville died.

Four days after his death, the *New York Times* commented: "There has died and been buried in this city, during the current week, at an advanced age, a man who is so little known, even by name, to the generation now in the vigor of life that only one newspaper contained an obituary account of him, and this was but of three or four lines. Yet forty years ago the appearance of a new book by Herman Melville was esteemed a literary event, not only throughout his own country, but so far as the English-speaking race extended" (2 Oct. 1891). In England, Melville's reputation had been revived, mainly among younger literary people, many of whom championed his works quietly through the next quarter century. The first to praise *Moby-Dick* aggressively was a professor at Dalhousie University in Canada, Archibald MacMechan, who had corresponded with Melville in the author's last years.

The year 1919, the centennial of Melville's birth, precipitated a public revival of his reputation both in England and in the United States, and on new terms—the prose praised as Shakespearean, and the God-defying Captain Ahab's pursuit of Moby Dick seen as an archetypal confrontation with the inscrutable powers of the universe. In the early 1920s an English publisher issued the first collected edition, ending with a volume containing *Billy Budd*, as hastily transcribed by Raymond Weaver, a lecturer at Columbia University, who in 1921 had published the first full-length biography of Melville. Through the 1920s American literary critics slowly came to terms with *Moby-Dick* and with the other books already famous in England, *The Piazza Tales* and especially *Pierre*. American academics began paying attention to Melville in the 1930s, but until after World War II there was in his own country nothing like the general British awareness of his achievement. Then, *Moby-Dick* began to be taught in new American literature classes designed to accommodate veterans attending college on the G.I. Bill. Only in the 1950s did *Moby-Dick* achieve classic status in popular culture.

Since that time, no well-educated American could fail to know about Melville's epic novel. It and other major works (especially *Benito Cereno* and *Billy Budd*) were adapted to other artistic forms, such as movies, radio dramas, plays, operas, and audiotapes. Critics belatedly proclaimed *Clarel* a great poem, and Melville's other poems were granted increasing space in anthologies of nineteenth-century American poetry. Yet Melville remains in the American consciousness primarily as the author of *Moby-Dick*, a novel not equaled in scope by any previous piece of American literature and never matched in its portentous portrayal of human struggle with the forces of the universe.

• The Houghton Library at Harvard holds the largest collection of Melville's papers, but significant holdings are in other libraries, notably the New York Public Library and the Berkshire Athenaeum. The important Lemuel Shaw Papers are at the Massachusetts Historical Society. The standard edition of Melville's works is *The Writings of Herman Melville*, ed. Harrison Hayford, Hershel Parker, and G. Thomas Tanselle (15 vols., 1968–), referred to as the Northwestern-Newberry Edition.

The most important work of Melville scholarship has been Jay Leyda's *The Melville Log* (1951; 2d ed., with a supplement, 1969), which Leyda and H. Parker have undertaken to significantly expand. The most reliable narrative biography is H. Parker, *Herman Melville: 1819–1851* (1996) and *Herman Melville: 1851–1891*. Accounts of different portions of Melville's later life include Stanton Garner, *The Civil War World of Herman Melville* (1993), the editorial sections of the Northwestern-Newberry *Clarel*, and H. Parker's *Reading "Billy Budd"* (1990). Less careful but treating all of Melville's life is Laurie Robertson-Lorant, *Melville: A Biography* (1996).

The most valuable specialized studies are Wilson L. Heflin, "Herman Melville's Whaling Years" (Ph.D. diss., Vanderbilt, 1952); the editorial sections in the Hendricks House edition of *Omoo*, ed. H. Hayford and Walter Blair (1969); Merrell R. Davis, *Melville's "Mardi": A Chartless Voyage* (1952); William H. Gilman, *Melville's Early Life and "Redburn"* (1951); and the University of Chicago Press edition of *Billy Budd, Sailor*, ed. H. Hayford and Merton M. Sealts, Jr. (1962). For information on sources used by Melville, see M. M. Sealts, Jr., *Melville's Reading* (1988), and Mary K. Bercaw, *Melville's Sources* (1987). For criticism during Melville's lifetime, see Kevin Hayes and H. Parker, comps., *Checklist of Melville Reviews* (1991), and Brian Higgins and H. Parker, eds., *Herman Melville: The Contemporary Reviews* (1995). Useful details are to be found in Kathleen E. Kier's careful *A Melville Encyclopedia: The Novels* (2 vols., 1990) and Robert L. Gale's usually reliable *A Herman Melville Encyclopedia* (1995). The best bibliographies of Melville criticism are by B. Higgins: *Herman Melville: An Annotated Bibliography, 1846–1930* (1979) and *Herman Melville: A Reference Guide, 1931–1960* (1987).

HERSHEL PARKER

MEMMINGER, Christopher Gustavus (9 Jan. 1803–7 Mar. 1888), secretary of the treasury in the Confederacy, was born in Nayhingen, Württemberg, Germany, the son of Christopher Godfrey Memminger, an army officer, and Eberhardina Kohler. A naturalized American citizen, Memminger was brought as an infant by his mother and her parents to Charleston, South Carolina, after the death of his father. Only four when his mother died, he was placed in the Charleston Orphan House. Thomas Bennett, a future governor of the state, took him in at the age of eleven and subsequently sent him to South Carolina College. After graduating second in his class in 1819, Memminger returned to Charleston, studied law, and opened a practice in 1824. He married Mary Wilkinson in 1832; they had eight children.

Memminger was a Union Democrat for most of the antebellum period. In the nullification crisis of 1830–1832, he wrote a satirical pamphlet, *The Book of Nullification* (1832), lampooning the nullifiers and went so far as to propose the use of military force against them. He was elected to the lower house of the South Carolina legislature in 1836 and, with the exception of 1852–1853, served continuously up to the outbreak of the Civil War. He specialized in banking and monetary issues and gained a reputation as a fiscal conservative and sound money manager through his long service as chairman of the Ways and Means Committee. When South Carolina threatened to secede over the Compromise of 1850, Memminger again assumed a conservative stance. He agreed that secession was a constitutional right of the individual states but held out for a cooperative movement that would ensure the unity and economic stability of the South.

As late as January 1860, Memminger was still opposed to separate state secession. In that month he was sent by the governor as a special commissioner to Virginia. He addressed the Virginia legislature and urged the state to join South Carolina in its call for a southern convention "to concert measures for united action" in the wake of John Brown's raid. When he sensed that his mission had failed, Memminger concluded that "we farther South will be compelled to act and drag after us these divided states." He actively promoted South Carolina's secession in December 1860 and was selected to the provisional Confederate Congress that met in Montgomery, Alabama, in February 1861. He served on the Commercial Affairs Committee and chaired the special committee appointed to draft a provisional constitution for the Confederate government.

Upon the recommendation of the South Carolina delegation, President Jefferson Davis appointed Memminger to his cabinet as secretary of the treasury. Although regarded as a sound money manager, Memminger was selected for the cabinet more for his representation of South Carolina than for his financial expertise. In fact he had little experience with the intricacies of a complex economy or the problems of supervising an extensive fiscal program. Indeed, his doctrinaire, laissez-faire economic beliefs robbed him of the flexibility and boldness needed for successful planning and administration of Confederate finances. He had proven himself a skilled parliamentarian in the South Carolina legislature, but he was too stiff and caught up in details to be an effective politician in his dealings with the Confederate Congress. Convinced (as were many others) that the war would be of short duration, he failed to move quickly enough to implement measures for raising a large revenue. All of these factors worked against his effectiveness as secretary of the treasury.

Memminger was well aware of the folly of relying on treasury notes or paper money for the bulk of Confederate finances, but he soon found himself trapped in an inflationary spiral fueled by the necessity to issue ever more treasury notes to pay for the mushrooming requisitions made on the government. His initial program called for a small bond issue, a minimal amount of notes to provide for a uniform paper currency, and minor taxes. The first bond issue did raise $15 million in specie, but subsequent issues raised little hard currency. Memminger then relied on produce loans, by which bonds were sold for agricultural produce, most notably cotton. However, in the absence of any government program to exchange the cotton so acquired for specie from Europe, Memminger was forced to print more paper money to meet the government's needs. As early as February 1862, treasury notes constituted 76 percent of the government's income. Congress finally passed a comprehensive tax package in April 1863, but it was too late to undo the fiscal damage. In an effort to reduce the currency in circulation, Memminger called for its compulsory exchange into long-term bonds. Congress belatedly responded with a refunding act in February 1864, but its net effect was to destroy what little confidence remained in Confederate currency.

Memminger was under heavy criticism throughout most of his term as secretary of the treasury, and he finally resigned on 15 June 1864. By then he was widely viewed as a failure. Perhaps no one could have overcome the obstacles he faced in bringing order and stability to Confederate finances. Military reverses, the Union blockade, and the persistence of the Confederate Congress in relying on unsecured paper and bonds as a means of financing the war all undermined much of what Memminger attempted to accomplish. Still, his limited financial background, fear of government intervention, and lack of economic vision were handicaps that he never overcame. These same handicaps also plagued the Confederate Congress and the Davis administration as a whole.

Upon his resignation, Memminger retired to his country home in Flat Rock, North Carolina. He spent the rest of the war there and did not return to Charleston until 1867, when he received a presidential pardon. After resuming his law practice, he was instrumental in founding the Etiwan Phosphate Company in 1868, a manufacturing and chemical concern that launched the phosphate industry in the Charleston area. With the exception of a term in the South Carolina legislature in 1877 after the Democrats had overthrown Reconstruction, he was not politically active after the war. His chief public service came in the fields of transportation and education. He served briefly as president of the Spartanburg and Asheville Railroad, sat on the board of South Carolina College, and continued his prewar work on behalf of the public school system of Charleston. In 1878, upon the death of his first wife, he married her sister, Sarah A. Wilkinson. He died in Charleston and was buried at Flat Rock.

• Most of Memminger's personal papers were destroyed in the burning of Columbia in 1865. Small collections of his private papers can be found at the Duke University Library and in the Southern Historical Collection at the University of North Carolina at Chapel Hill. Much of his public correspondence as Confederate secretary of the treasury is available in the Archives of the Confederate Treasury Department, 1861–1865, National Archives, Washington, D.C. Henry D. Capers, *The Life and Times of C. G. Memminger* (1893), is the standard, but badly outdated, biography. Richard Cecil Todd, *Confederate Finance* (1954), and Douglas B. Ball, *Financial Failure and Confederate Defeat* (1991), provide the best accounts of Memminger's role in the Confederacy. Of the two, Ball is far more critical. An obituary is in the Charlestown *Courier*, 8 Mar. 1888.

WILLIAM L. BARNEY

MEMPHIS MINNIE (3 June 1897–6 Aug. 1973), blues singer and guitarist, was born Elizabeth Douglas in the West Bank extension of New Orleans, Louisiana, known as Algiers, the daughter of Abe Douglas and Gertrude Wells, sharecroppers. In 1904 her family moved, eventually settling in Walls, Mississippi, just outside Memphis, Tennessee. Nicknamed "Kid," she showed an early aversion to farm work and an aptitude for music, talking her father into giving her a guitar for Christmas when she was around eight. By age thirteen she had learned to play both banjo and guitar and was frequently running away to Memphis. There she played for handouts and heard older musicians, including Frank Stokes and Dan Sane, early practitioners of the guitar-duet style favored by the city's street performers. While still in her teens, Douglas joined the Ringling Brothers' Circus in Clarksdale, Mississippi, traveling with the show for several years during World War I. After returning to northern Mississippi, she struck up a partnership with noted Delta blues guitarist Willie Brown and a third guitar player, Willie

Moore, performing for white as well as black audiences at local stores, country dances, and on an excursion boat.

Later, Douglas met guitarist and blues singer Joe McCoy, a member of the musical McCoy family from Jackson, Mississippi. The two formed a guitar duo, performing both in Mississippi and in Memphis, where a scout for Columbia Records heard them playing in a barber shop on Beale Street in 1929. That summer they went to New York and in June recorded six issued sides, including a sizable hit, "Bumble Bee." Columbia listed McCoy as "Kansas Joe" and Douglas as "Memphis Minnie," giving her the name she would use for the rest of her life.

In 1930 Joe and Minnie, now living in a common-law marriage, recorded twice in Memphis. A February session for Vocalion resulted in nine issued sides, including a pair of double-sided songs, "Can I Do It for You?" and "What Fault You Find in Me." A May session for Victor produced four sides credited to "McCoy and Johnson" and two sides with the Memphis Jug Band. (Legend has it that Minnie also was the "Miss Minnie" who sang with Mississippi-born guitarist Bukka White on two religious recordings cut in Memphis in 1930.) In June the couple moved permanently to Chicago, where they logged seven more sessions for Vocalion that summer and fall.

There were nine more sessions for Vocalion in 1931, but only one session in 1932, as the Depression began to take its toll on the music industry. The 1932 session in New York included three sides by an all-star band: Minnie and Joe on guitars, Georgia Tom Dorsey on piano, and Tampa Red on slide guitar. Minnie continued to record, both solo and as a duo with Joe, until December 1934, when she and Joe called it quits. By that time "Kansas Joe and Memphis Minnie" had become "Memphis Minnie and Kansas Joe," and there were rumors—never fully confirmed—that McCoy had grown jealous of his wife's popularity. The break-up, however, had no effect on her popularity, and in 1935 Minnie had seven sessions with three different labels. Besides her own professional name, she recorded as "Gospel Minnie" and "Texas Tessie." She recorded with pianists Jimmy Gordon and Black Bob and guitarists Casey Bill Weldon and Bumble Bee Slim, among others. A popular club performer both in Chicago and on the road, Minnie began to tour with Fiddlin' Joe Martin in the second half of the 1930s and later with guitar virtuoso Big Bill Broonzy, all the while continuing a prolific record output.

On tour in Memphis in the late 1930s, Minnie met Ernest Lawlars, a guitarist and blues singer from Hughes, Arkansas, who was known professionally as Little Son Joe. Minnie and Little Son recorded together in February 1939 and remained in a common-law marriage for the next twenty-two years. Through the 1940s they recorded as a duo and in small-band formats for Vocalion. Later, after Vocalion was absorbed by Columbia, the couple also recorded under that label. In 1940 and 1941 they waxed several classics, including Minnie's biggest hit, "Me and My Chauffeur Blues," and Little Son's "Black Rat Swing."

Minnie remained popular through the 1940s. She was a major club draw in Chicago, particularly at the Club de Lisa and the 708 Club. In the mid-1940s she operated a blues club in Indianapolis in partnership with pianist St. Louis Jimmy Oden and later lived for several years in Detroit. Also in the late 1940s she and Little Son formed a trio with pianist/vocalist Roosevelt Sykes, playing Chicago clubs and touring the South.

Minnie's reign as a big-time recording star ended along with the 1940s. She tried recording with three small independent labels in Chicago in 1949, 1952, and 1953, but the records did not sell well, despite the fact that she remained a solid club attraction.

Although some sources claim Minnie moved back to Memphis for good in the mid-1950s, biographers Paul and Beth Garon place her in Chicago through 1958, when she performed at a memorial concert for her old partner, Big Bill Broonzy. That year, in declining health, she and Little Son relocated to Memphis. They continued to perform, working with a five-piece band for a time, doing radio broadcasts in Memphis and Helena, Arkansas, where they played with harmonica wizard Sonny Boy Williamson No. 2. The couple also returned to the recording studio for one fruitless session and continued working "little gigs over in Arkansas," according to blues musician David Honeyboy Edwards. With Minnie's career now in decline, she and Little Son lapsed into poverty. After he died in 1961, Minnie suffered a stroke and was in and out of nursing homes for the rest of her life. Two periodicals, *Living Blues* and *Blues Unlimited*, solicited contributions for her welfare, but little was raised. Minnie died in Memphis, at the home of her sister Daisy Johnson.

As a woman in the violent, male-dominated world of blues musicians, Memphis Minnie was more than a survivor; she was a tough, aggressive, hard-drinking, tobacco-chewing brawler who cursed, gambled, and fought with fists, knives or whatever was available. Guitarist Homesick James recalled her as "tougher than a man."

Minnie was equally powerful as a performer—one of the principal blues artists of her time. Immensely popular with the African-American blues audience, she recorded more than 180 issued sides over four decades for major blues labels. As an instrumentalist she was an artist who, as Big Bill Broonzy wrote in his autobiography, could "make a guitar speak words . . . make a guitar cry, moan, talk and whistle the blues." She was an innovator, too, performing on electric guitar possibly as early as 1942. Whether Minnie played in solo, duo, trio, or larger-ensemble formats, her music was of consistent high quality, encompassing folk, pop, spirituals, comic-dialogue duets, rocking dance tunes, deep blues, and rhythm and blues. Her life and work, spanning the era of early down-home Delta blues to the electric Chicago ensemble sound of the 1950s, had special resonance for aspiring female musicians in later generations.

• For more biographical information on Memphis Minnie, see Paul Garon and Beth Garon, *Woman with Guitar: Memphis Minnie's Blues* (1992); Sheldon Harris, *Blues Who's Who: A Biographical Dictionary of Blues Singers* (1979); and Mike Leadbitter, "My Girlish Days," *Blues Unlimited*, no. 78 (Dec. 1970): 8–9. For a discussion of her music, see Del Rey, "Guitar Queen," *Acoustic Guitar*, no. 53 (Sept. 1995): 52–61. For discographical information, see Robert M. W. Dixon and John Godrich, *Blues and Gospel Records: 1902–1943* (1982); Leadbitter and Neil Slaven, *Blues Records 1943–1970*, vol. 2 (1994); and Paul Oliver, ed., *The Blackwell Guide to Blues Records* (1989). To hear her music, try *Bumble Bee: The Essential Recordings of Memphis Minnie* (Indigo IGOCD 2005) and *Memphis Minnie: Hoodoo Lady (1933–1937)* (Columbia Legacy CK 46775). An obituary is in *Living Blues*, no. 14 (Autumn 1973): 5.

BARRY LEE PEARSON
BILL MCCULLOCH

MEMPHIS SLIM (3 Sept. 1915–24 Feb. 1988), blues singer and pianist, was born John Len Chatman in Memphis, Tennessee, the son of Peter Chatman, a roadhouse proprietor and musician who played piano and guitar, and Ella Kennedy, who died when her son was only two. Raised by his father, the younger Chatman learned piano by age seven, became a competent blues player at thirteen, and began playing on Beale Street in Memphis while still in his teens. He attended Lester High School, playing bass in the school band, but his main teachers were the itinerant boogie and blues pianists who came to Memphis, particularly Roosevelt Sykes, whose style Chatman clearly emulated early in his career. Sometime around 1931 Chatman succeeded Sykes as house pianist at the Midway Cafe in South Memphis, earning "a dollar and a half a night and two pints of whiskey." As Chatman later recalled, the clubs in Memphis, particularly the clubs run by gangsters, operated with little regard for Prohibition and gambling laws, but they did provide steady employment for blues piano players.

According to another Memphis piano player, Booker T. Laury, a crackdown in 1935 forced many musicians, including Chatman, to look for work across the state line in West Memphis, Arkansas. Chatman already had tested his skills as a musician and gambler in Arkansas, working jooks and levee camps and, by his own account, teaming up briefly with blues guitarist Robert Johnson in Marianna and Marked Tree.

In the late 1930s Chatman joined the migration of southern blues musicians to Chicago, and by 1939 he was firmly established among the city's fraternity of blues players. Blues producer Lester Melrose, who brokered Chicago blues talent through the 1940s, set up Chatman's initial recording date with the OKeh label. Accompanied by a "washboard band," he recorded six songs on 6 August 1940 using his father's name, Peter Chatman. Several months later he was back in the studio, recording seven sides, including his first hit, "Beer Drinking Woman," for RCA Victor's Bluebird label. These were the first sides released as Memphis Slim, the professional name Chatman retained for the next forty-eight years.

In Chicago, Memphis Slim came under the patronage of guitarist and recording star Big Bill Broonzy. After the 1942 death of Broonzy's pianist, Joshua Altheimer, he joined Broonzy's group, which held court at Ruby Lee Gatewood's tavern on the South Side. With Broonzy's encouragement, Memphis Slim began to develop a style more in tune with changing African-American musical tastes, and eventually he put together his own band, the House Rockers. After World War II he returned to the studio with the House Rockers, recording for two small, independent labels: Hy-Tone in 1946 and Miracle in 1947. The band included two saxophones, bass, and drums and later a third saxophone and a guitar. The bassist on the 1947 session was Willie Dixon, a songwriter, vocalist, and blues hustler who stayed with the band for three years, producing hits such as "Rocking the Joint" in a postwar, jump-blues format.

In 1947 Memphis Slim, Broonzy, and another former bandmate from Ruby's tavern, harmonica player John Lee "Sonny Boy" Williamson, participated in folk-song collector Alan Lomax's "Music at Midnight" concert series in New York. The trio also went into the studio with Lomax and recorded what Lomax later titled "Blues in the Mississippi Night," an informal mix of conversation, music, and stories about the living conditions they faced as black men in the South. During the session, Slim talked about working the levee camps in Arkansas, mixing blues with a discussion of the conditions in which blues developed. Although Slim included similar ruminations in performances years later, he and his fellow artists were afraid their off-the-cuff comments would be too controversial in 1947, so they were given pseudonyms—Slim's being "Leroy."

From 1949 until well into the late 1950s, Memphis Slim continued as a major rhythm and blues figure, touring with the House Rockers and jumping from label to label—King, Peacock, Chess, Mercury, Money, Premium, and United.

In 1959 Memphis Slim branched out into the more lucrative "folk blues" market, playing primarily to white audiences. He played the Newport Folk Festival to a standing ovation, did a show at Carnegie Hall in New York with Muddy Waters, began to work upscale nightclubs—the Gate of Horn in Chicago, for one—and hit the coffeehouse circuit. He continued to record rhythm and blues with his band for the independent VeeJay label in Chicago while also cutting albums for Folkways in New York, working solo or as a duo with longtime sidekick Willie Dixon. He even recorded with folk icon Pete Seeger.

In 1960 and 1961, on tours with Dixon, Memphis Slim got his first exposure to the European market. By 1962 he had married Christine Freys, the daughter of a French club owner (he was previously married in the United States to Doris Owens), and had settled permanently in Paris, taking a job as house pianist at a Left Bank jazz club, Les Trois Mailletz. He quickly became a celebrity in France, appearing frequently on television, touring the Continent, and returning occasionally to the United States. He developed a one-man show, the Story of the Blues, which wove together his music and his early recollections; he also worked as an actor and musician in three films. According to Memphis Slim, he moved to France because he could make a better living as a musician there. Indeed he clearly enjoyed the trappings of success, with an elegant wardrobe, a Paris apartment, and a Rolls Royce automobile.

Although he was slowed by heart problems in the 1980s, Memphis Slim returned to the United States in 1983 to perform with B. B. King and Bobby Blue Bland at a Smithsonian Institution program celebrating the Memphis blues tradition. He died in Paris, survived by his wife and six children. A funeral, attended by dignitaries and music celebrities, was held in Memphis, where flags flew at half staff, and he was buried in Galilee Memorial Gardens next to his father.

Memphis Slim wrote 300 songs and recorded almost 500 during his career. His own compositions included his theme song "Every Day I Have the Blues," a hit for Count Basie vocalist Joe Williams in 1955 and, later, B. B. King; it remained a standard among later blues artists.

He worked with a veritable blues who's who: Big Bill Broonzy, Buster Brown, Lowell Fulson, Buddy Guy, Robert Johnson, Little Walter, Muddy Waters, Junior Wells, and both Sonny Boy Williamsons, No. 1 and No. 2. He figured prominently in major blues transitions, first when he merged Beale Street and Arkansas barrelhouse blues with the prewar ensemble sound in Chicago, and later when he helped reshape the prewar sound into the jump-blues and rhythm-and-blues styles that emerged in the 1950s. Later still, he shifted from R-and-B star to become a thoughtful interpreter of the blues for the folk-revival audience. And finally, Memphis Slim became the most successful expatriate blues ambassador ever, bringing his musical stylings to appreciative audiences throughout Europe. Late in his career, he was honored in the U.S. Senate as an "ambassador-at-large of good will" and was named commander of arts and letters by the French government. In 1989 he was inducted into the Blues Foundation Hall of Fame in Memphis.

• For more biographical information on Memphis Slim, see Sheldon Harris, *Blues Who's Who: A Biographical Dictionary of Blues Singers* (1989); Samuel Charters, *The Legacy of the Blues: Art and Lives of Twelve Great Bluesmen* (1977); and Bruce Cook, *Listen to the Blues* (1973). For a discography, see Robert M. W. Dixon and John Godrich, *Blues and Gospel Records: 1902–1943* (1982), and Mike Leadbitter et al., *Blues Records 1943–1970: "The Bible of the Blues,"* vol. 2, *L–Z* (1994). For a sample of his music, try *Memphis Slim: You Got to Help Me Some* (Blues Encore CD 52013 AAD). For an obituary, see Peter Lee, "Memphis Slim," *Living Blues*, no. 80 (May–June 1988): 31–32.

BILL MCCULLOCH
BARRY LEE PEARSON

MENARD, Henry William (10 Dec. 1920–9 Feb. 1986), marine geologist, was born in Fresno, California, and was the adopted son of Henry William Menard, a display manager for a department store, and Blanche Laverne Hodges. Known as Bill, Menard was reared in Los Angeles and received the B.S. degree in 1942 from the California Institute of Technology (Caltech) in Pasadena, California. During World War II he served for three years as a naval reserve officer in the South Pacific, specializing in photo interpretation and air intelligence. He was wounded in action on the aircraft carrier *Hancock* and later decorated with the Bronze Star and a Navy Commendation ribbon with six combat stars. After the war Menard returned to Pasadena to earn a master's degree from Caltech, where he also met his wife, Gifford Merrill, originally of New York. They married in 1946 and then moved to Cambridge, Massachusetts. Menard received the Ph.D. from Harvard University in 1949, completing his dissertation on flume studies of sediment transport.

Menard returned to California as a research scientist in marine geology at the Navy Electronics Laboratory (NEL) in San Diego under the supervision of Robert S. Dietz. In 1955 he joined the faculty of the Scripps Institution of Oceanography in La Jolla, California; he was promoted to full professor in 1961, and except for a few years in government service, he remained at Scripps until his death. He and his wife raised three children in La Jolla, and Menard supervised at least six graduate students who went on to establish distinguished careers. He was particularly notable for his mentoring of female students at a time when ocean scientists were almost exclusively male.

Menard was one of the great explorers of the twentieth century. He participated in approximately thirty deep-sea research expeditions; in the early 1950s he discovered the large fracture zones of the northeastern Pacific. These would a decade later be explained as the fault scars that mark the direction of seafloor spreading in the North Pacific. For this discovery he was elected in 1968 to the National Academy of Sciences at a relatively young age. In 1990 he discovered the Mid-Pacific Mountains, a large chain of submarine volcanoes extending from the Hawaiian Islands to Wake Island. A large fracture zone in the South Pacific and a major deep-sea volcano bear his name.

When Menard began his research in marine geology, it was a new field, made possible by the development of the echo sounder during World War II for measuring the depth of the oceans and encouraged by the U.S. Navy's interest in the deep sea for the purpose of antisubmarine warfare. Great discoveries were waiting to be made, and a host of new problems needed to be solved. In this climate Menard thrived. His contributions extended across a wide spectrum of topics within marine geology, including subsidence of the seafloor, the hydraulics of sediment transport and deposition, dating the seafloor using magnetic anomalies, and studies of the great submarine faults, midocean ridges, abyssal hills, volcanic islands, and seamounts.

In the mid-1960s Menard's research came to the forefront of the field during the early days of the plate tectonics revolution. Aided by a fleet of research ships operated by Scripps and the hard work of his graduate students, he put his encyclopedic knowledge of the Pacific Basin to work in unraveling its plate-tectonic history. At a time when most marine geologists were focusing on the horizontal motions of the earth's surface caused by the drift of tectonic plates, Menard was one of the few who realized that they could learn much about the dynamic interactions of the plates with the convecting mantle by studying the vertical motion of the plates. He worked out the depth distributions in the Pacific 100 million years in the past by using the flat tops of volcanoes to measure their subsequent subsidence, on the reasonable assumption that the beveled summits had been eroded at sea level when the volcanoes were islands. His findings led to much progress in understanding the thermal and mechanical properties of the tectonic plates. In all Menard wrote 115 scientific publications; those written in the 1980s just before his death were as vibrant and timely as those of the mid-1960s.

Menard is almost as well known for his studies on the sociology of science. His books—including *Anatomy of an Expedition* (1969), *Science: Growth and Change* (1971), *The Ocean of Truth* (1986), and *Islands* (1986)—allow the nonspecialist to gain insight into science as discovery, with many examples drawn from his own participation in the greatest revolution in the history of earth science. The stories are told with Menard's trademark wit, charm, and style.

U.S. presidents asked Menard to serve the country twice: first in 1965 and 1966 as a technical advisor in the Office of Science and Technology Policy, and from 1978 to 1981 as the tenth director of the U.S. Geological Survey. Despite the glamor of life in Washington, D.C., Menard was eager to return to his home in La Jolla to the research life he loved best. In 1985, when the American Geophysical Union presented him with the Bowie Medal, its highest honor, for outstanding contributions to fundamental geophysics and unselfish cooperation in research, Menard said, "I cannot call it work because it constantly fills me with joy and wonder, and there is nothing I would rather do." He died in La Jolla.

• An extensive collection of Menard's papers, correspondence, and drafts of books and papers is archived at the Scripps Library, Scripps Institution of Oceanography, La Jolla, Calif. The collection also includes photographs and an oral history interview by Harold Burstyn, conducted in 1981. Other books by Menard not mentioned in the text are *Marine Geology of the Pacific* (1964) and *Geology, Resources, and Society* (1974). Among the most noteworthy of his published articles are "Hawaiian Swell, Deep, and Arch, and Subsidence of the Hawaiian Islands," with R. S. Dietz, in *Journal of Geology* 61 (1953): 99–113; "Archipelagic Aprons," *American Association of Petroleum Geologists Bulletin* 40 (1956): 2195–210; "The East Pacific Rise," *Science* 132 (1960): 1737–46; "Fracture Zones," with T. E. Chase, in *The Sea*, vol. 4, pt. 1, ed. A. E. Maxwell (1971), pp. 421–43; "Fragmentation of the Farallon Plate by Pivoting Subduction," *Journal of Geology* 86 (1978): 99–110; "Lithospheric Flexure and Uplifted Atolls," with M. McNutt, in *Journal of Geophysical Research* 83 (1978): 1206–12; and "Insular Erosion, Isostasy and Subsidence," *Science* 220 (1983): 913–18. An obituary is in the *New York Times*, 11 Feb. 1986 (it contains an error, giving his age as seventy-five rather than sixty-five).

MARCIA K. MCNUTT

MENARD, Pierre (7 Oct. 1766–13 June 1844), frontier trader, merchant, and politician, was born at St. Antoine, Quebec, Canada, the son of Jean Baptiste Menard, a French-born merchant, and Marie Françoise Cirée, a Canadian. He had a common school education. Following in the footsteps of his father, who had supported the American side in the American Revolution and served in the American army, Menard, at age twenty-one, moved from Quebec to find opportunities on the American frontier as a trader or merchant. Rather than following those among the French Canadians who, in response to the Treaty of Paris, tried to continue trading under British control and protection in the western Great Lakes and the Mississippi River valley, Menard moved to Vincennes, Indiana, around 1787 and actively sided with the Americans in their relations with the British and Indians. Menard was employed by Colonel François Vigo and associated with Toussaint Du Bois. Within a few years Menard achieved considerable success and had also acquired extensive experience with the Native Americans, French métis, French, and Americans in the Ohio and Mississippi river valleys. In 1789 he accompanied Colonel Vigo to consult with General George Washington on frontier affairs at Carlisle, Pennsylvania. But still interested primarily in trade and noting the speed at which settlement moved across Ohio and Indiana, in 1791 Menard decided to establish a mercantile agency at Kaskaskia, Illinois, the oldest among the French towns and former capital of French Illinois and still, in spite of the growing competition of St. Louis and the loss of trading connections with French Canada, a vigorous center of trade and local production in the Mississippi River valley. Like other French merchants of Illinois, Menard, because of his French background and knowledge of the Indians of Illinois and the upper Mississippi River valley, prevailed over American and British competitors and prospered. But unlike other French merchants in Illinois, such as Charles Gratiot and Gabriel Cerée, as well as his associate from Quebec Peter De Lorimer, who had come to Kaskaskia with him in 1790, Menard chose to continue to operate out of Kaskaskia rather than move to St. Louis. Therefore, although Menard established numerous connections with the French community of St. Louis, he remained outside its inner circle. After the death in 1804 of his first wife, Thérèse Godin, whom he had married in 1792 and with whom he had six children, Menard sought to alter his social position by marrying in 1806 Angélique Saucier, sister-in-law of Jean Pierre Chouteau, one of the organizing partners of the St. Louis Missouri Fur Company. Menard had four children with his second wife.

This connection drew him into an investment in the company and his decision, in 1809, to accompany Chouteau, Manuel Lisa (a famous Spanish Indian trader from St. Louis), and Governor Meriwether Lewis on the expedition up the Missouri River to return the Mandan chief Shahaka (also known as Big White) and his followers, who had been brought to St. Louis by Lewis and Clark in 1806, to their home village. Another goal of the expedition was to develop trading relations with a number of other Indian tribes on the upper Missouri River. Toward this goal, the expedition constructed Fort Mandan above the village of the Gros Ventre Indians, secured their position at Fort Raymond at the confluence of the Big Horn and Missouri rivers, and, after wintering there, advanced to the Three Forks of the Missouri, with the intention of establishing a fort. They were, however, repulsed by the Blackfeet Indians and returned to St. Louis. Though Menard never went on another expedition, he continued to invest in the efforts of Chouteau to establish more intensive fur-trading connections with the Indians who lived in the upper Missouri River valley. The knowledge and experience Menard acquired from this connection combined with his own continued trading on the upper Mississippi to make Menard one of the most knowledgeable men in the region about the Indians, the French, the French métis, and the relations and trade among these people.

Menard's prominent position in the local and regional economy quickly drew him into local, territorial, state, and even federal politics and government. When Kaskaskia was part of Indiana Territory from 1787 to 1809, Menard served as major of Randolph County's militia (1795–1805) and was promoted to lieutenant colonel commanding the militia in 1806, judge of the county court of common pleas (1801–1811), associate judge of the supreme court of the territory (1802–1809), and delegate to the territorial legislature of Indiana Territory (1803–1809). After the creation of the territory of Illinois, he resigned his judgeship and was elected to the first Illinois Senate, which was called the Council. He served as its presiding officer through 1818. When Illinois became a state in 1818, Menard was the choice for lieutenant governor, to which he was appointed in 1819 and served through 1822—after the state legislature had reduced the residency required for citizenship from thirty to two years, allowing Menard, who had not yet been naturalized, to become a U.S. citizen. In 1828 Menard, having served as a subagent of Indian affairs, was appointed to a commission to establish a treaty with the Winnebago at Prairie du Chien (in present-day Wisconsin) in the wake of the so-called Winnebago War of 1827 across the Lead Region of northwestern Illinois and southwestern Wisconsin. In 1829 he served on a similar commission to negotiate treaties with other Indian tribes in the Northwest. Among the French- and French-Canadian–born merchants of his generation who migrated to the Ohio and Mississippi river valleys in pursuit of trading opportunities, Menard was one of the very few who managed to gain the full respect and esteem of most Americans with whom he came in contact and be appointed to territorial and state government offices. As a trader and "gentleman," he lived a genteel life in an impressive French-style mansion on the bluffs above the town of Kaskaskia and the Kaskaskia River, reassuring American settlers that gentility could prevail amid frontier conditions. He died there high above the rising floodwaters, which crested two weeks later at their highest level between 1785 and 1993 and washed away much of the town of Kaskaskia.

• The Pierre Menard Papers are in the Chicago Historical Society and the Illinois State Historical Library, Springfield. Records of his trip to the upper Missouri River in 1809–1810 are in the Chouteau collection and the Kaskaskia Papers in the Missouri Historical Society. Richard E. Oglesby, "Pierre Menard, Reluctant Mountain Man," *Bulletin of the Missouri Historical Society* 24, no. 1 (Oct. 1967): 3–19, provides the best modern account of Menard. See also William E. Foley and C. David Rice, *The First Chouteaus: River Barons of Early St. Louis* (1983), and Clarence W. Alford, ed., *The Governors' Letter Books*, vol. 4, *Collections of the Illinois State Historical Library* (1904), pp. 10–11. Edward G. Mason, "Pierre Menard, the First Lieutenant-Governor of Illinois," in *Early Illinois*, vol. 1 of the Fergus Historical Series (1890), pp. 17–43, and Sarah Bond Hanley, *Pierre Menard, Pioneer* (n.d.), are also useful.

TIMOTHY R. MAHONEY

MENCKEN, H. L. (12 Sept. 1880–29 Jan. 1956), author, editor, and journalist, was born Henry Louis Mencken in Baltimore, Maryland, the son of August Mencken, a cigar manufacturer, and Anna Abhau. Having emigrated from Germany during the mid-nineteenth century, the Menckens and Abhaus had quickly adapted to life in the United States, and they provided a home more Victorian than German-American for their four children. Henry Mencken, the eldest, did attend a private German school for his earliest education, but he completed his formal education at Baltimore Polytechnic, a high school primarily responsible for producing engineers and technicians.

From the beginning, Mencken was more interested in reading and writing than in applied science, and in his teens he began to write poetry and short stories. He had wanted to become a newspaper reporter after his graduation from Polytechnic, but as a dutiful son he accepted instead a position in his father's now flourishing cigar factory. The two years he spent at Aug. Mencken & Bro. were the most miserable of his young life, and he found release from the work only at the sudden death of his father when he was eighteen.

Within two weeks of his father's death Mencken had applied for a position on the Baltimore *Herald*, and within three months he was a cub reporter. Thus began a meteoric rise to police and city hall reporter, city editor, managing editor, and, at age twenty-five, editor of the *Herald*. In 1906 he took a position as Sunday editor of the Baltimore *Sun*, and soon he gained local fame as a columnist and editorial writer.

Meanwhile, Mencken contributed poetry and stories to national magazines and at age twenty-two published a volume of poetry, *Ventures into Verse* (1903). That volume was inconsequential, but two other works published within the next five years were to gain recognition and praise. *George Bernard Shaw: His Plays* (1905) and *The Philosophy of Friedrich Nietzsche* (1908) launched Mencken as literary and social critic and intellectual historian.

In 1908 Mencken also became literary editor of the *Smart Set*, a New York monthly he would serve for the next fifteen years, six as book reviewer and nine as co-editor, along with drama critic George Jean Nathan. Mencken first gained a national audience as *Smart Set* editor, and with his magazine columns and his "Free Lance" column in the Baltimore *Evening Sun* he found his style and his voice—irreverent, hyperbolic, outrageous. His chief targets were those he was to pursue over the next decade—puritanism, Anglo-Saxons (both in England and in the United States), the English cultural tradition, the American Genteel Tradition in literature, and particularly the American hinterlands, notably the South.

In the early years of World War I Mencken vigorously promoted the German cause, but when the United States entered the war he was silenced by his newspaper and by magazines for which he had written. He used the time to write on other subjects. In *A Book of Prefaces* (1917) he attacked the literary status quo in the United States, blasted professors and puritans and poetasters, and championed such writers as Theodore Dreiser who were challenging traditional Anglo-American literary assumptions. He also produced *In Defense of Women* (1918), a witty discussion of relations between the sexes, and the first edition of *The American Language* (1919), a work that drew on his growing interest in the differences between British and American English.

After the war was over, Mencken was ready to burst forth with an indictment of American life unprecedented in his—or any other writer's—career. His six-volume collection of essays, aptly titled *Prejudices* (1919–1927), scrutinized and often ridiculed American values, politics, religion, education, literature—in short, nearly every aspect of American life. His satires of politicians, professors, preachers, businessmen, and the average "boobus Americanus" gained him enemies in abundance, and he welcomed and enjoyed the battle that ensued. His prose was scintillating, as in his classic indictment of the American South, "The Sahara of the Bozart":

> Nearly the whole of Europe could be lost in that stupendous region of fat farms, shoddy cities and paralyzed cerebrums . . . And yet, for all its size and all its wealth and all the "progress" it babbles of, it is almost as sterile, artistically, intellectually, culturally, as the Sahara Desert. (*Prejudices*, vol. 2 [1920], p. 136)

It was not only the South that Mencken decried; he also derided New England (the ancestral home of Puritanism) and the Midwest and California (the land of quacks, he believed). He satirized Rotarians and Elks and Methodists and Christian Scientists, and he ridiculed presidents. He detested Woodrow Wilson for his moralism, but Mencken was equally critical of (if less passionate about) Warren G. Harding, Calvin Coolidge, and Herbert Hoover. Mencken's influence was enormous in the 1920s. "The most powerful personal influence on this whole generation of educated people," Walter Lippmann pronounced Mencken in 1926, and any number of other commentators agreed.

Mencken was not only writer but also celebrity. When he traveled to Dayton, Tennessee, in July 1925 for the Scopes evolution trial, he was as much participant as reporter. His dispatches to the Baltimore *Evening Sun*, reprinted in dozens of other newspapers, portrayed Tennesseans as "gaping primates of the Cumberland slopes," and there was talk among the Fundamentalists of running him out of town. In fact, he left under his own steam, only to learn of the death of anti-evolutionist William Jennings Bryan a week later and to write, in an obituary essay on Bryan, one of the most savage indictments any American journalist had ever issued. Bryan, he charged, was a "walking malignancy . . . a vulgar and common man . . . ignorant, bigoted, self-seeking, blatant and dishonest . . . deluded by a childish theology, full of an almost pathological hatred of all learning, all human dignity, all beauty, all fine and noble things. He was a peasant come home to the dung-pile" (Baltimore *Evening Sun*, 27 July 1925).

Mencken's primary forum after 1923 was the *American Mercury*, a magazine that he and Nathan founded and that he edited until 1933. It was through the *Mercury* that he reached tens of thousands of apostles and exerted his greatest influence. In the *Mercury* as well as in the earlier *Smart Set*, he published a number of writers whom he had discovered or encouraged—including Sinclair Lewis, F. Scott Fitzgerald, Sherwood Anderson, James Branch Cabell, and Theodore Dreiser—and was largely successful in establishing their brands of literary realism or naturalism and, in the process, putting romance and sentimentalism to rout.

By the late 1920s Mencken had largely tired of literary pursuits and had tired as well of his role as polemicist and public spectacle. He undertook a series of scholarly inquiries that were published as *Notes on Democracy* (1926), *Treatise on the Gods* (1930), and *Treatise on Right and Wrong* (1934). Having been influenced by Nietzsche, he was avowedly antidemocratic (he called himself a monarchist) and uncompromisingly agnostic, but such positions did not prevent him from being fascinated both by democracy and religion. His "serious" inquiries, however, did not fare so well critically as the satires and the polemical works of the 1920s.

By the early 1930s Mencken had fallen out of public favor, although the period from 1930 to 1935 was personally one of the most pleasant of his life. In 1930, just before his fiftieth birthday, he had married Sara Haardt, a writer from Montgomery, Alabama (one of those well-born southerners he preferred, despite his condemnation of the South), but what proved to be a happy marriage ended with Sara's death, at age thirty-seven, in May 1935. After her death Mencken found refuge in work, turning grimly and resolutely to another edition of *The American Language*, a work that occupied him in some manner for most of his adult life. With the publication of the massive fourth edition in 1936, he found that he was again in critical favor.

That favor increased with the publication of a trilogy of autobiographical works, *Happy Days* (1940), *Newspaper Days* (1941), and *Heathen Days* (1943), in which Mencken wrote about earlier, more pleasant years. Virtually an urban *Tom Sawyer* written seventy years after Mark Twain's classic, *Happy Days* recounted his boyhood in Baltimore, a nearly ideal time as he depicted it. *Newspaper Days* and *Heathen Days* were works in the same vein, and Mencken's reputation, so low in the early 1930s that one critic referred to him as "the late Mencken," rose with each volume.

At the same time that he was remembering more carefree earlier days, Mencken was also keeping a darker record, one not intended for publication in his own lifetime, perhaps not intended for publication at all but which nonetheless saw print more than thirty years after his death as *The Diary of H. L. Mencken* (1989). He had begun the diary in 1930, had largely ceased writing in it after Sara's death in 1935, but had returned to it with a vengeance in the early 1940s. Again, in the early forties, he was silenced by war: again, he could not write on international affairs, so strong was his opposition to the pro-British stance of the *Sun* papers. In his diary he entered his displeasure with American life, with numerous friends and writers, with Franklin D. Roosevelt (whom he also excoriated in print), and much else. Roosevelt, he wrote, was not only a betrayer of his class but also a fraud, a political snake-oil salesman. The country in general, he felt, was being taken over by bureaucrats and labor leaders. Internationally, although he abhorred Great Britain, he was forced to admit that the Germany he had loved was no more. At home, in Baltimore, friends were ill and dying, his own health was declining, his neighborhood was deteriorating, and the city he had loved was gone forever.

The diary was only one of Mencken's wartime occupations. He also labored over a personal newspaper history, "Thirty-Five Years of Newspaper Work," which he intended to be published long after his death, and "My Life as Author and Editor," a chronicle of his days as *Smart Set* editor and friend of Dreiser, Lewis, Fitzgerald, and other writers. His "Life as Author and Editor" was not to be published until 1993; "Thirty-Five Years," not until 1995.

After the Second World War Mencken continued to work on *The American Language*. In 1945 he produced a supplement to the 1936 edition and in 1948 another supplement. With the two additional volumes—which, together with the earlier editions, totaled some 3,800 pages—Mencken had solidified his position as the nation's most prominent popular philologist. Earlier he had been interested primarily in the ways in which British and American English had diverged. In the later volumes he maintained that they were drawing closer again, with "American" this time gaining the upper hand. His own preference for American over British English had always been clear: in his opinion, it was more descriptive, more vivid, more colorful.

In late 1948 Mencken's literary career came to a cruel end. The victim of several small strokes over the past decade, in November he suffered a massive stroke that robbed him of his ability to read and write. Although he would regain a measure of his physical health, he would never again regain those functions. A *Mencken Chrestomathy*, a work he had prepared just before the stroke, was published in 1949; it would be the last of his books published in his lifetime. Another book, *Minority Report*—an earlier manuscript found by his secretary in late 1955—appeared just after his death in Baltimore.

Minority Report was the first of a series of works that constitute the posthumous career of H. L. Mencken. Because such works as *My Life as Author and Editor* and *Thirty-five Years of Newspaper Work* were ordered, by Mencken's will, to be kept under lock and key until thirty-five years after his death, and because his diary was tied up for nearly as long, they did not appear in print until the late 1980s and early 1990s. When they did appear, they stirred up a curious kind of Mencken renaissance. "It will be nice being denounced again," Mencken had said shortly before the publication of *Minority Report*—and just three days before his death—and such was the case in the final decade of the century. The publication of the diary brought renewed charges of racism and anti-Semitism, and defenders were as vocal as critics. For a man with no conventional religious faith and no belief in the afterlife, such controversy was indeed a form of immortality.

Mencken's reputation, thus, is still in flux. From the beginning he was a difficult writer to categorize; in an American context he was nearly *sui generis*. His antecedents, if any, appeared to be European—Voltaire, Swift, Shaw, Nietzsche. The earlier American writer he most resembled was Mark Twain, and like Twain his reputation has been revised somewhat, has become darker, with the publication of his posthumous works.

But the Mencken works that will endure are not the *Diary* and *My Life as Author and Editor*, despite their interest. The enduring works will be the volumes of *Prejudices* of the 1920s, the editions of *The American Language* (particularly that of 1936), and the autobiographical *Days* books. If Mencken in his later years was a somewhat subdued soul, ill of health and possessed of a darker vision, the essential Mencken was the writer and editor of the 1920s—a man who damned America with all the relish and gusto (and even underlying affection) with which Walt Whitman had praised it, a man of whom Walter Lippmann once said, "He calls you a swine, and an imbecile, and . . . increases your will to live" (*Saturday Review*, 11 Dec. 1926, p. 414).

• The vast majority of Mencken's letters, papers, and memorabilia is in the Enoch Pratt Free Library of Baltimore and the New York Public Library. On Mencken's life, see William Manchester, *Disturber of the Peace: The Life of H. L.*

Mencken (1950); Carl Bode, *Mencken* (1969); and Fred Hobson, *Mencken: A Life* (1994); as well as *The Diary of H. L. Mencken*, ed. Charles A. Fecher (1989); *My Life as Author and Editor*, ed. Jonathan Yardley (1993); and *Thirty-five Years of Newspaper Work*, ed. Fred Hobson et al. (1995). For discussions of Mencken's work, see William Nolte, *H. L. Mencken: Literary Critic* (1966); Douglas C. Stenerson, *H. L. Mencken: Iconoclast from Baltimore* (1971); Fred Hobson, *Serpent in Eden: H. L. Mencken and the South* (1974); Charles A. Fecher, *Mencken: A Study of His Thought* (1978); Edward A. Martin, *H. L. Mencken and the Debunkers* (1984); Charles Scruggs, *The Sage in Harlem: H. L. Mencken and the Black Writers of the 1920s* (1984); and Vincent Fitzpatrick, *H. L. Mencken* (1989).

FRED HOBSON

MENDEL, Lafayette Benedict (5 Feb. 1872–9 Dec. 1935), physiological chemist, was born in Delhi, New York, the son of German immigrants Benedict Mendel, a merchant, and Pauline Ullman. Mendel showed unusual ability as a scholar from an early age. After studying at a local school in Delhi and at the Delaware Academy, he took the entrance examination for Yale University in Latin, Greek, and math at the age of fourteen and entered the university the following year. In 1891 he received a B.A. for studies in classics, economics, and the humanities. At nineteen he was the youngest member of his graduating class and a member of Phi Beta Kappa.

Despite limited scientific training, Mendel entered Yale's Sheffield Scientific School in the fall of 1891 to study physiological chemistry with Russell Chittenden. Mendel's early research interests centered on nutrition. Chittenden's laboratory was the leading American exemplar of the German model of nutritional research, in which chemists and physiologists worked in close collaboration to identify chemical structures of nutrients and to determine their role in the body's physiology. By virtue of his location there, Mendel was well positioned to make important contributions as the scientific focus of nutrition research shifted from studies of the body's energy requirements to examination of how the body used specific chemical compounds to build tissue, regulate metabolism, and promote growth. Receiving a Ph.D. in 1893, he was appointed assistant to Chittenden and, in 1894, instructor in the department. Mendel took a leave of absence in 1895–1896 to study experimental physiology with R. Heidenhain in Breslau and the biochemistry of amino acids with E. Baumann in Freiburg. Returning to Yale, he was named assistant professor in 1897 and professor in 1903. That year he also became a member of the governing body of the Sheffield Scientific School. Mendel's most important research contributions were in the study of growth and in identification of the role of vitamins and individual amino acids in nutrition.

In 1905 Mendel began a long and fruitful collaboration with chemist Thomas B. Osborne of the Connecticut Agricultural Experiment Station in New Haven. Much of their work was funded by the Carnegie Institute of Washington, D.C. Osborne studied the chemical structure of proteins and provided individual compounds that Mendel fed to animals in carefully controlled experiments. In 1906 Mendel began studies of growth, in which he modified experimental diets given to immature albino rats and monitored their effects on growth to adult size. Mendel found that the rat proved a useful subject animal, since its omnivorous diet resembled that of humans, as did its growth pattern to adulthood (although in a much shorter time span). Moreover, the animal's small size facilitated study of large numbers of individuals and kept feeding costs comparatively low.

In 1909 Mendel and Osborne launched a series of experiments on proteins. They established that rats could live on a diet of milk alone, growing normally and producing a next generation that similarly throve on milk. However, early attempts to develop an artificial diet, in which all components were known and to which individual components could be added or subtracted, were frustrated as rats failed to thrive. In 1911 Mendel and Osborne tried a diet consisting of "protein-free milk," sugar, and starch, to which they added specific isolated proteins or fats. They discovered that when the fat component consisted of lard, the rats failed to grow normally. However, when butter fat was substituted, normal growth patterns resumed. Mendel and Osborne hypothesized that the butter fat must contain minute amounts of some essential nutrient, which was later identified and named "vitamin A." Working along parallel lines, E. V. McCollum of the University of Wisconsin submitted similar findings for publication just ahead of Mendel and Osborne, and the term "vitamin," introduced in 1912 by Casimir Funk, became the accepted name for these trace compounds necessary for health. Mendel and Osborne continued their vitamin studies, especially on the fat-soluble vitamin A and the water-soluble vitamin B (later found to consist of several distinct compounds), in addition to probing the importance of the proteins.

Recognition that a wide variety of proteins occurred in foods of plant and animal origins raised the question of whether all proteins were equally valuable in nutrition. Through painstaking experimentation, in which Osborne synthesized individual proteins made up of characteristic sequences of amino acids and Mendel fed these in controlled diets to rats and other animals, the two elucidated the differing protein requirements of various species. For example, in 1912 they showed that, while rats could live on a diet in which the only protein component was gliadin, they would not grow in the absence of glycin and lysin. Mendel and Osborne established that any given species could synthesize certain forms of protein but was dependent on receiving the correct mix of amino acids in the diet to obtain required proteins its body could not synthesize.

Mendel was a prolific researcher who published more than 330 papers and several books, including *Feeding Experiments with Isolated Food Substances* (2 pts., 1911) and *Changes in the Food Supply and Their Relation to Nutrition* (1916). He delivered the Hitchcock Lectures at the University of California in 1923;

these were published as *Nutrition: The Chemistry of Life* (1923), a slim volume in which Mendel places his and Osborne's work on vitamins and proteins in the context of earlier and other contemporary nutritional research.

Mendel was elected to the National Academy of Sciences in 1913. He married Alice R. Friend in 1917; the couple had no children. In 1921 Mendel was appointed Sterling Professor of Physiological Chemistry at Yale, and in 1922 he succeeded Chittenden, who retired that year, as department chair. Throughout his tenure at Yale, Mendel helped sustain the department's stature as a leading producer of physiological chemists. Mendel excelled as a teacher of researchers. Rather than delivering standard lectures or walking students through experiments to which they already knew the outcome, he gave them just enough background to enable them to learn through the experimental process itself. He insisted that they stay abreast of the latest developments through a weekly seminar in which students presented and critiqued current articles from American and European (especially German) journals.

Through their discoveries of the crucial role of vitamins in maintaining growth and health and of the specific amino acid requirements in protein nutrition, Mendel and Osborne made fundamental contributions to the understanding of animal and human nutritional requirements. Mendel died in New Haven.

• Mendel's papers are in the Yale Medical School Archives. His collaborative work with Thomas B. Osborne was reported in more than 100 coauthored articles, including "The Relation of Growth to the Chemical Constituents of the Diet," *Journal of Biological Chemistry* 15 (1913): 311–26; "Growth and Maintenance on Purely Artificial Diets," *Proceedings of the Society for Experimental Biology and Medicine* 9 (1912): 72; "The Role of Gliadin in Nutrition," *Journal of Biological Chemistry* 13 (1912): 473–510; "Some Problems of Growth," *American Journal of Physiology* 33 (1914): 28; "Amino-Acids in Nutrition and Growth," *Journal of Biological Chemistry* 17 (1914): 325–49; and "The Influence of Cod Liver Oil and Some Other Fats on Growth," *Journal of Biological Chemistry* 17 (1914): 401–8. Mendel and P. H. Mitchell produced "Chemical Studies on Growth," *American Journal of Physiology* 20 (1907–1908): 81–116. Mendel described his and Osborne's work in "Nutrition and Growth," *Harvey Lectures* (1914–1915), pp. 101–31. Russell Chittenden outlived his star student and wrote the memoir "Lafayette Benedict Mendel, 1872–1935" in the National Academy of Sciences, *Biographical Memoirs* 18 (1938): 123–55. William C. Rose, "Recollections of Personalities Involved in the Early History of American Biochemistry," *Journal of Chemical Education* 46 (1969): 759–63, describes Yale's Department of Physiological Chemistry under Chittenden's and Mendel's leadership and recalls Mendel's inspiring teaching methods. An obituary is in *Science*, 17 Jan. 1936.

CAROLINE JEAN ACKER

MENDELSOHN, Erich (21 Mar. 1887–15 Sept. 1953), architect, was born in Allenstein, East Prussia (now Olsztyn, Poland), the son of David Mendelsohn, a businessman, and Emma Esther Jaroslawski, a milliner. One of six children, Erich (also spelled Eric) began his college studies in political economics at the University of Munich in 1907 but quickly changed to an art and architectural emphasis at the technical universities of Berlin-Charlottenburg (1908–1910) and Munich (1910–1912). At the latter he studied under Theodor Fischer, mentor to many of Germany's best architects of the 1920s.

After graduation, Mendelsohn established his own architectural practice in Munich, where he became acquainted with the expressively modern art of the "Blue Rider" group and painters such as Franz Marc and Wassily Kandinsky. The bulk of his commissions at this time were for theatrical sets and costumes as well as shop windows. Shortly after his marriage in 1915 to cellist Louise Maas, who also was Jewish, he joined the Engineering Corps in order to serve in World War I. Trained in Berlin-Spandau, he served on the Russian front in 1917 and on the western front in 1918. During the war years he began to produce the loose sketches of dramatic, curvilinear buildings that would characterize his own form of expressionist architecture in the postwar period. Some of these early wartime fantasy sketches were dedicated in 1916 to his newborn daughter, Marie Louise Esther. At war's end he established his own practice in Berlin (1918–1919).

In 1919 Mendelsohn met his first major client, Gustav Hermann from Luckenwalde, for whom he designed a garden pavilion as well as a hat factory in 1920 (demolished). In 1919 Mendelsohn had his first gallery exhibition; it featured the fantastic, expressionist sketches from the war years and slightly later. Even more important, his friend Erwin Finley-Freundlich, one of Albert Einstein's associates, proposed that Mendelsohn be given the job of designing an observatory. The brick tower surfaced in concentric forms of curvilinear concrete and stucco (1921–1924), built on Telegrafenberg Hill in Potsdam, is still in use as an astronomic research facility. It made Mendelsohn an overnight success, as did his expressively curved remodeling of the Rudolf Mosse publishing house (1921–1923) located on Jerusalemer Strasse in the center of Berlin (later rebuilt to its original appearance). Even the loss of his left eye in an operation to remove a cancerous tumor could not hinder his growing career. More work came in from Hermann's hat factory and other textile works and, most important, from department stores, starting with the Weichmann Silk Workshop and Store (1922–1923) in Gleiwitz (now Gliwice, Poland). Perhaps it was his mother's experience as a milliner and his father's career in business, combined with his own early experiences with stage and storefront design, that helped Mendelsohn garner the hat factory work and, then, major department store commissions throughout the 1920s. Some of his most famous examples of the latter are the Schocken Stores in Stuttgart (1926–1928, demolished) and Chemnitz (1928–1929, altered), the Petersdorf Store in Breslau (now Wroclaw in Poland; 1927–1928, only slightly altered), and the Columbus House in Berlin (1931–1932, demolished), an office building that began its design life as a Galleries Lafayette store. Constructing these buildings constituted the bread and butter of the office, but he also designed movie theaters, housing projects, trade union buildings, and Jewish educational and religious structures. In the 1920s and early 1930s he furthered his career both by traveling to England, France, the United States, Palestine, Holland, and the USSR and by publishing books that were the tangible results of his impressions about architecture and urbanism on those trips: *Amerika: Bilderbuch eines Architekten* (Berlin, 1926) and *Russland, Europa, Amerika. Ein architektonischer Querschnitt* (Berlin, 1929).

Mendelsohn was arguably the most successful German architect until Hilter's takeover in 1933, when because of his Jewishness, he was forced to emigrate. He was fortunate to have the means and connections that enabled him to leave Germany quickly. He first went to England, where he formed a partnership with Serge Chermayoff. They designed a variety of structures, mostly simple private houses with the exception of the spectacular De La Warr Pavilion (1934–1935) in Bexhill-on-Sea, an entertainment building that had the bold curves of some of Mendelsohn's larger Berlin buildings. He commuted between London and Haifa/Jerusalem during the 1930s and designed modernist buildings in both England and Palestine. The structures he planned and executed in Palestine were much larger than those in what he may have felt was a more-restricted environment in England; good examples include the Hebrew University and Hadassah Medical Center on Mount Scopus in Jerusalem (1936–1938, partly completed) and the government hospital in Haifa (1937–1938). These and his other buildings in Palestine, such as the house he built for leading Zionist and, later, first president of Israel, Chaim Weizmann (1936–1937), are a bit more conventionalized by masonry construction, a common characteristic of institutional buildings everywhere but especially so in the hot climate of the Middle East. These structures are particularly conventional compared to the more expressive curvilinear glass walls of his flamboyant department stores in Central Europe. Although Mendelsohn obtained English citizenship in 1938–1939 and became a Fellow of the Royal Institute of British Architects in 1939 (Anglicizing his name to "Eric"), he spent much of the early years of World War II in Palestine, not London, exempt from service in the British army because of his age.

With war raging in Europe and even nearby North Africa, Mendelsohn closed his Jerusalem office in early 1941 and left Palestine for the United States, where he visited a variety of prominent architects, including Albert Kahn in Detroit, Frank Lloyd Wright in Spring Green, Wisconsin, and Sam Marx and German émigrés Ludwig Hilberseimer and Ludwig Mies van der Rohe in Chicago. Afterward he went to New York, where he worked in the office of Ely Jacques Kahn and prepared a traveling exhibition of his work that first showed at the New York Museum of Modern Art and then at the Arts Club of Chicago and later at the San Francisco Museum of Modern Art. During the Second World War he gave lectures at various institutions, particularly at the University of California at Berkeley, and with the assistance of a Guggenheim Fellowship began to prepare a book to be called "A Contemporary Philosophy of Architecture" but only finished part of it. According to some accounts, Mendelsohn was depressed during these years, especially after U.S. entry into World War II, and possibly about his own fate. After all, here was Germany's most-successful architect of the 1920s living far from Germany or his beloved Palestine, reduced to secondary status, without commissions or even a secure economic base—especially in comparison to Walter Gropius, Hilberseimer, and Mies—that would allow him to teach until a peacetime economy catalyzed new construction. Perhaps the stories about the treatment of Jews in German concentration camps and then rumored extermination camps exacerbated an already glum outlook, especially if he feared that the Allies might lose the struggle. These factors could easily help to explain why he, along with other displaced designers such as Konrad Wachsmann and Antonin Raymond, served as a consultant to the U.S. Army in the construction and furnishing of typical German masonry buildings in what was coined "German Village" on an army proving ground in Utah—buildings and interiors that in 1943 the army used to test the effectiveness of incendiary bombs to be dropped on enemy cities. These and an adjacent group of typical Japanese houses designed by Antonin Raymond and built for the same purpose were constructed in conjunction with the Standard Oil Company. This virtually unknown aspect of Mendelsohn's career represents a tangible effort on his part to serve his new homeland.

Mendelsohn became an American citizen in 1946, and with the end of the war, his Francisco practice began to pick up, receiving commissions for private homes as well as synagogues and community centers from Cleveland and St. Louis to Grand Rapids, Michigan, and St. Paul, Minnesota. Probably his largest commission was for Maimonides Hospital on Sutter Street in San Francisco (1946–1950, altered soon after construction). Whereas the smaller Jewish community centers retained some of the bold expressive shapes of his German buildings, the curvilinear forms on the hospital's facade were limited to small nodes that broke the rectangularity of the linear balconies; it was a much more restrained building than his other work, especially his designs from the 1920s and 1930s. Before his death in San Francisco, he reportedly said, "If I had the chance, I would begin again, letting my earliest sketches guide me . . . for a final, newly creative period." Although he was not given that opportunity, his work stands, in the United States, Israel, and Germany, as a precedent for individualized expression within modern architecture, thereby paving the way for like expression in the next generation—from the Air Force Academy Chapel in Colorado Springs (1964) by Walter Netsch of Skidmore, Owings & Merrill to Eero Saarinen's Washington (D.C.) Dulles International Airport (1958–1962) and the TWA Terminal at New York's John F. Kennedy International Airport (1956–1962).

• Some fifteen hundred drawings by Mendelsohn are in the Kunstbibliothek in Berlin, the major repository of his work. Some were published in Sigrid Achenbach, *Erich Mendelsohn, 1887–1953. Ideen Bauten Projekte* (Berlin, 1987), a very informative source. Mendelsohn's letters were published as *Eric Mendelsohn: Letters of an Architect*, ed. Oskar Beye with an introduction by Nikolaus Pevsner (1967). Records on Mendelsohn's traveling exhibition are in the archives on the Arts Club of Chicago at the Newberry Library. Information on his wartime consultancy can be found in a historic properties report prepared by Building Technology, Inc. and the Historic American Buildings Survey/Historic American Engineering Record (July 1984) along with an original report by the Standard Oil Development Co. (1943). These documents are available through the U.S. Army Corps of Engineers. Additional information on and illustrations of the typical Japanese buildings constructed near Mendelsohn's German village can be found in *Antonin Raymond: An Autobiography* (1973), pp. 188–89. Also see Bruno Zevi, *Erich Mendelsohn* (1985).

JOHN ZUKOWSKY

MENDENHALL, Charles Elwood (1 Aug. 1872–18 Aug. 1935), physicist, was born in Columbus, Ohio, the son of Thomas Corwin Mendenhall, a professor of physics at Ohio State University, and Susan Allan Marple. Mendenhall's father served as president of the Rose Polytechnic Institute (now Rose-Hulman Institute of Technology) in Terre Haute, Indiana, superintendent of the U.S. Coast and Geodetic Survey, and then president of the Worcester Polytechnic Institute. When Mendenhall was six years of age, his father took him to Japan for three years during his tenure as a visiting professor at the Imperial University at Tokyo. This left young Mendenhall with a lasting interest in Japanese art and culture.

Mendenhall was educated in public schools in Columbus, Ohio, and Washington, D.C. He graduated with an A.B. from the Rose Polytechnic Institute in 1894. During the summer of 1894 he assisted on a transcontinental survey of the acceleration of gravity conducted by the U.S. Coast and Geodetic Survey. He then served as an instructor of physics at the University of Pennsylvania for one year. In 1895 Mendenhall began graduate studies at the Johns Hopkins University, completing his Ph.D. in 1898. He was an instructor at Williams College in Williamstown, Massachusetts, from 1898 to 1901. Mendenhall became an assistant professor at the University of Wisconsin in Madison in 1901; he was promoted to associate professor in 1903 and to professor in 1905. He married Dorothy M. Reed in 1906; they had two children. Dorothy Reed Mendenhall had received her M.D. from Johns Hopkins in 1900 and was the first woman granted a fellowship from the school in 1901–1902. She had a distinguished research career and maintained a pediatric practice.

From 1917 to 1919 Mendenhall was a major in the U.S. Army Signal Corps, working with the National Research Council on organizing scientific work for the war effort. He ended this service in 1919 as scientific attaché to the U.S. embassy in London. Mendenhall chaired the Division of Physical Sciences of the National Research Council in 1919–1920. In 1926 he was appointed chair of the Department of Physics at Wisconsin, retaining that position until his death. He was elected to the National Academy of Sciences in 1918 and was the chair of its Section of Physics from 1924 to 1927. He was also elected to the American Philosophical Society and the American Academy of Arts and Sciences. His other positions within professional organizations included president of the American Physical Society (1923–1925), with terms as a councillor for and as the associate editor of the *Physical Review*; vice president of the American Optical Society in 1921, and later a member of the editorial board of the *Journal of the Optical Society*; and vice president of the American Association for the Advancement of Science in 1929.

Mendenhall's broad research interests included gravity measurement, galvanometer design, and melting-point determination. Thermal radiation was a common area of study, for which he originated the "V wedge black body." This instrument is essentially an electrically heated thin strip of metal bent to a V-shaped cross section. Its principal use is in the efficient comparison of the radiation from an investigated metal to black-body radiation, the radiation given off by a perfect emitter of any substance at any temperature. Mendenhall often investigated photoelectric effects in his later years. He published twenty-four papers in the *Astrophysical Journal*, *Physical Review*, *Proceedings of the National Academy of Sciences*, and other technical journals. He coauthored two textbooks: *Physics for Students of Science and Engineering* (1912), in which Mendenhall wrote the chapter on heat in the third and subsequent editions, and *College Physics* (1935), with A. S. Eve and D. A. Keys. He avoided coauthorship with his students if he had not actually performed some of the laboratory work; this practice substantially shortened his publication list. He supervised thirty-five doctoral candidates during his career and spent many hours advising students in the Department of Physics. Mendenhall died in Madison, Wisconsin.

• F. G. Benedict, "Charles Elwood Mendenhall," *Proceedings of the American Philosophical Society* 76 (1936): 391–94, is a brief memorial. A comprehensive review of Mendenhall's life is by J. H. Van Vleck in National Academy of Sciences, *Biographical Memoirs* 18 (1937): 1–22. An obituary is in *Science* 82 (1935): 317–18.

RALPH L. LANGENHEIM, JR.

MENDENHALL, Dorothy Reed (22 Sept. 1874–31 July 1964), physician and public health educator, was born in Columbus, Ohio, the daughter of Grace Kimball and William Pratt Reed, a wealthy shoe manufacturer. Although Mendenhall's father died when she was six, the family was left comfortably well-off, and

Mendenhall received an upper-class education at home, including instruction by a governess and frequent European travel.

In 1891 Mendenhall entered Smith College. She intended to study journalism, but in her sophomore year she developed a new interest in biology. She claimed never to have heard of a woman physician until she was grown, but an afternoon spent with a Harvard classmate of her brother's (the future dean of the University of Wisconsin Medical School, Charles R. Bardeen), in which she heard about the "remarkable school of medicine being started in Baltimore," turned her thoughts toward Johns Hopkins and the possibility of a medical career. Her move in this new direction was also spurred by the realization that, because her mother had mismanaged the family's inheritance, there was little money left. In spite of the hostility of her family to the idea of a career in medicine (her aunts were "aghast," and a cousin refused to entertain her after she received the M.D.), Mendenhall began an encouraging correspondence with Dr. William Welch, dean of Johns Hopkins Medical School, and upon graduation from Smith College in 1895, she spent a preparatory year learning chemistry and physics at the Massachusetts Institute of Technology.

In 1896 Mendenhall joined an outstanding cohort of women, a group that included the research scientist Florence Sabin and Margaret Long, the daughter of the former governor of Massachusetts, who attended Johns Hopkins Medical School in the 1890s. Women were admitted to Hopkins because of a determined group of feminists who were willing to relieve financially pressed founders of their money worries for the price of women's equality. As a result, Mendenhall and her peers were exposed to the best teachers and medical education available in the United States at the time. Yet they were never allowed to forget that they were women. For Mendenhall, being a medical student meant the chance to assist in the operating room and bacteriological laboratories of the Brooklyn Navy Yard Hospital in 1898, to win a highly competitive internship at Johns Hopkins under Dr. William Osler in 1900, and to earn a pathology fellowship with Dr. William Welch in 1901. But it also meant enduring constant harassment and barriers to advancement because she was a woman. Mendenhall, unlike her friend Florence Sabin, also had to cope with the gnawing emotional pulls of private life. As a result, although Mendenhall displayed talent and interest in bacteriology and undertook research on Hodgkin's disease that resulted in her discovery of the Reed (also known as the Reed-Sternberg) cell crucial to its diagnosis, she did not pursue pathology as a lifetime career. Personal obligations and the professional obstacles to female success, which she felt acutely at Hopkins, proved too powerful. Indeed, the central challenge of her life was an ongoing struggle to balance an extraordinarily promising professional career with the demands of wifehood and motherhood. In 1903 she left Hopkins to accept a coveted internship in pediatrics with Dr. Emmet Holt at Babies Hospital in New York. Four years and one unhappy love affair later, she married Charles Elwood Mendenhall, a childhood friend. Shortly thereafter she moved to Madison, Wisconsin, where her husband was professor of physics at the University of Wisconsin.

After her superior education at Hopkins, Mendenhall found Madison a professional wasteland; indeed, her firstborn died at birth in 1907 because of poor obstetrical care. Three more children followed, in 1908, 1910, and 1912, prompting her to withdraw temporarily from professional activity, not yet clear about how to manage work and family life.

The death of her sister in 1903 had left Mendenhall with the financial responsibility for the education of her nieces and nephews. This burden and the cooperation of her husband prompted Mendenhall to gradually shape what would become her life's work: public health medicine and education. She began with a part-time commitment: lecturing, preparing correspondence courses, gathering epidemiological data on infant mortality, and producing bulletins on nutrition for the Department of Home Economics at the university, the Wisconsin State Board of Health, and the U.S. Department of Agriculture. In 1917 she joined her husband in Washington, D.C., where he was involved in war work. There she met Julia Lathrop, the director of the Children's Bureau, who immediately offered her a job. Though she returned to Wisconsin after the war, Mendenhall continued to work for the bureau, becoming one of its premier medical troubleshooters. Like many other women physicians in the bureau's employ, she did field work, participated in a nationwide campaign to weigh and measure all children under six, and wrote several bureau publications, including six chapters of the important *Child Care and Child Welfare: Outlines for Study* (1921). In 1926 she surveyed infant and maternal mortality rates in Denmark, comparing them with rates in the United States. Her findings resulted in another groundbreaking bureau study, *Midwifery in Denmark* (1929), which argued that the higher American rates were due to the unwarranted medicalization of childbirth. Mendenhall continued work for the Children's Bureau and local Wisconsin health organizations until her retirement in 1936.

Although Mendenhall provides a striking example of a woman who pioneered in managing the dual burdens of a demanding career and an equally demanding family life, she paid a price for her efforts in the disdain of male medical colleagues, many of whom felt that her work in public health indicated that she had not been serious enough about medicine. Whenever she saw William Welch at meetings in Washington, D.C., he worried out loud that she was not "keeping up" with her reading. In the 1940s Mendenhall learned from Dr. Alice Hamilton that faculty members opposed to the admission of women to Harvard Medical School cited her as an example of "an able woman who had married and failed to use her expensive medical education." But Mendenhall knew better. She left among her unpublished papers a remarkably frank 1,000-page memoir that affords unusual insight into the private struggles and public trials of many women physicians of her generation. She died in her home in Chester, Connecticut, where she had retired after the death of her husband in 1935.

• By far the best sources for Mendenhall's life are her papers, which include the autobiography, letters, and a wide range of other interesting material, located in the Sophia Smith Collection at Smith College. Another manuscript source is the Children's Bureau records at the National Archives, which contain Mendenhall correspondence. She published two papers on Hodgkin's disease: "On the Pathological Changes in Hodgkin's Disease with Especial Reference to Its Relation to Tuberculosis," Johns Hopkins Hospital *Reports* 10 (1902): 133–96, and "A Case of Acute Lymphatic Leukaemia without Enlargement of the Lymph Glands," *American Journal of Medical Sciences* 124 (Oct. 1902): 653–69. In addition to the U.S. Children's Bureau publications mentioned above, see also *Milk: The Indispensable Food for Children* (1918) and *What Builds Babies* (1925). Edmund Wilson, who was Mendenhall's mother's cousin, wrote of Mendenhall in his book *Upstate* (1971). Also worthwhile are Gena Corea, "Dorothy Reed Mendenhall: 'Childhood Is Not a Disease,'" *Ms.*, Apr. 1974, pp. 98–104; Jean Bergman, "Dorothy Reed Mendenhall," *Famous Wisconsin Women* 6 (1976): 48–53; Regina Morantz-Sanchez, *Sympathy and Science: Women Physicians in American Medicine* (1985); and Penina Migdal Glazer and Miriam Slater, *Unequal Colleagues: The Entrance of Women into the Professions, 1890–1940* (1987). Obituaries are in the Madison, Wis., *Capital Times*, 31 July 1964, and the *Wisconsin State Journal*, 1 Aug. 1964.

REGINA MORANTZ-SANCHEZ

MENDENHALL, Thomas Corwin (4 Oct. 1841–22 Mar. 1924), physicist, was born in Hanoverton, Ohio, the son of Stephen Mendenhall, a carriage maker and farmer, and Mary Thomas. In 1852 he moved with his family to Marlboro, Ohio, where six years later he became assistant principal of the local primary school. In 1861 he enrolled at the Southwest Normal School in Lebanon, Ohio, and received an Instructor Normalis degree that same year. He spent the next twelve years teaching mathematics and science at a succession of high schools in his home state, acquiring a reputation for excellence as an educator and public speaker. In 1870 he married Susan Allen Marple; they had one child. In 1873 he became the professor of physics and mechanics at the newly established Ohio Agricultural and Mechanical College, later renamed Ohio State University.

In 1878 Mendenhall accepted an invitation to teach physics at the Imperial University in Tokyo, Japan, where he established a physics laboratory, a weather observatory, and a society for the study of earthquakes. While in Japan he conducted a number of experiments, the most important of which utilized a reversible compound pendulum like the one devised in 1818 by the British physicist Henry Kater to determine the absolute force of gravity at sea level near Tokyo Bay as well as atop Mount Fuji. He then computed the relative force of gravity between these two points to arrive at what was at the time the most accurate estimate of the mean density of the earth.

In 1881 Mendenhall returned to the United States to teach physics at Ohio State and to establish and serve as the first director of the state-run Ohio Meteorological Bureau. In 1884 he resigned both positions to join the U.S. Signal Corps as a professor of electrical science and chief of its Instrument Division. After setting up a physics laboratory, establishing several stations for observing and collecting data pertaining to earthquakes, and making numerous observations of atmospheric electricity, in 1886 he left the Signal Corps to accept the presidency of Rose Polytechnic Institute (now the Rose-Hulman Institute of Technology) in Terre Haute, Indiana. While at Rose he authored *A Century of Electricity* (1887), a history of the development of electrical science from the discovery by the Italian physician and physicist Luigi Galvani of the electrical nature of nerve impulses to the postulation by the British physicist James Clerk Maxwell of the classical theory of electromagnetism.

In 1889 Mendenhall was appointed superintendent of the U.S. Coast and Geodetic Survey. At that time scientists were discovering that gravity, which they already knew varied depending on latitude and elevation, also varied depending on the Earth's internal density distribution and that gravitational data could be used to estimate the depth and density of underlying geologic formations. However, before the survey could begin taking the necessary gravitational readings needed to compile such data for the United States, both a master plan and a portable and accurate instrument for measuring absolute gravity in the country's most inaccessible terrain had to be developed. To this end, Mendenhall devised a short, rigid pendulum that was easier to use and more accurate under field conditions than earlier instruments. He then implemented the strategy necessary for compiling a gravitational map of the United States.

As head of the survey, Mendenhall also supervised the work of the U.S. Weights and Measures Department. In addition to these duties, he served as a member of the U.S. Lighthouse Board in 1889, the first Bering Sea Commission in 1891, and the U.S. and Great Britain Boundary Line Survey Commission to delineate the boundary between Alaska and Canada in 1892. As a delegate to the International Electrical Congress in 1893, he wrote the draft for the internationally recognized definitions of the ohm, ampere, and volt—the three basic units of electricity.

In 1894 Mendenhall resigned from all of his government posts to become president of Worcester (Mass.) Polytechnic Institute. Two years later he also assumed the duties of the chairman of the Massachusetts Highway Commission. When his health declined in 1901, he moved to Italy to recuperate and from there traveled throughout Europe and Asia for the next eleven years. In 1912 he returned to the United States and settled in Ravenna, Ohio. From 1919 until his death in Ravenna he served on the Board of Trustees of Ohio State.

Mendenhall was active in the affairs of the American Association for the Advancement of Science as general secretary and section vice president; he served as its president in 1889. At the Paris Exposition in 1900 he was awarded a gold medal for his work in seismography, cartography, and terrestrial gravity. He also received the American Geographical Society's Cullum Geographical Medal in 1901, Japan's Order of the Sacred Treasures 2nd Class and the National Educational Society of Japan's Gold Medal in 1911, and the Franklin Institute's Franklin Medal in 1918. He was elected to membership in the National Academy of Sciences in 1887 and became the first honorary member of the Society for the Promotion of Engineering Education in 1911.

Mendenhall contributed to the advance of American science in several ways. As an educator and administrator, he contributed significantly to the development of engineering curricula. As a bureaucrat, he oversaw the implementation and completion of several important government scientific projects. As a researcher, he contributed to the growing body of knowledge in the fields of geophysics and electrical science.

• Mendenhall's papers are located in the Collections of the Center for the History and Philosophy of Physics at the American Institute of Physics in College Park, Md. A biography, which includes a bibliography, is Henry Crew, "Thomas Corwin Mendenhall," National Academy of Sciences, *Biographical Memoirs* 16 (1934): 331–51. An obituary is in *Science*, 11 July 1924.

CHARLES W. CAREY, JR.

MENDENHALL, Walter Curran (20 Feb. 1871–2 June 1957), geologist and federal administrator, was born in Marlboro, Stark County, Ohio, the son of William King Mendenhall, a farmer, and Emma Pierce Garrigues, a schoolteacher; both parents were Quakers. Mendenhall lived with his maternal uncle's family while attending high school in Portland, Oregon. Returning to Ohio, Mendenhall taught at a local school and then entered Ohio Normal (now Ohio Northern) University in Ada. While an undergraduate, he spent his summer months as a teamster-laborer (1892) and a geologic assistant (1894) with a U.S. Geological Survey (USGS) field party led by geologist Marius R. Campbell, a family friend and neighbor. After completing a B.Sc. degree in 1895, Mendenhall rejoined Campbell's team to continue areal mapping and detailed studies of Appalachian coal fields. From 1895 to 1898 Mendenhall, promoted to assistant geologist in 1896, aided Campbell and his other geologists in mapping parts of Kentucky, Tennessee, and West Virginia for the folio *Geologic Atlas of the United States*. Encouraged by Campbell, Mendenhall also took leaves of absence to continue his education at Harvard (1896–1897) and Heidelberg (1899–1900) Universities, but he did not complete an additional degree.

The USGS's Geologic Branch reassigned Mendenhall to reconnaissance mapping in the West between 1898 and 1902. Mendenhall and USGS geologist Frank C. Schrader accompanied related army explorations in 1898 for easier routes through Alaska's Copper, Sustina, and Tanana basins to the new gold fields on the Yukon River; with USGS mapping teams in 1902, they combined and expanded the earlier work in more detailed studies of the geology and mineral resources of the Copper River–Wrangell Mountains country. In 1899 Mendenhall helped USGS geologist George O. Smith to analyze igneous rocks and to map two reconnaissance-scale quadrangles in Washington's Cascade Range. Returning to Alaska for the field seasons of 1900 and 1901, Mendenhall (newly promoted to geologist) joined USGS topographers in explorations and mapping of parts of the Seward Peninsula east of Nome and areas north of the Yukon between Fort Hamlin and Kotzebue Sound.

In 1903 Mendenhall and several of his USGS colleagues were transferred from the Geologic Branch to the newly reorganized Hydrologic Branch. Working from district headquarters in Los Angeles, he improved and completed instrument-based analyses and statistical studies of the below-surface water increasingly being drawn from the coastal plains and basins of southern California. Mendenhall then extended his hydrologic investigations to the San Joaquin Valley, to watering places elsewhere in the Southwest, and to Hawaii. In 1909 the USGS and the National Conservation Commission published Mendenhall's overview of underground waters, in which he recommended measures for the conservation of these resources and emphasized their increasing contamination. By that time Smith had become the USGS director, and Mendenhall had been recalled to Washington, D.C., to lead the Ground Water Division of the renamed Water Resources Branch and to serve on Arthur Veatch's Land Classification Board (LCB). The LCB expanded to examine and classify for their highest value for farming, grazing, lumbering, mining, or water power, before their disposition, the public lands increasingly withdrawn from entry during the administrations of Presidents Theodore Roosevelt, William Taft, and Woodrow Wilson.

In January 1911 Smith made Mendenhall the second chief of the LCB, which continued to operate with funds and staff assessed from the agency's three program branches. Smith elevated the LCB to branch status in 1912, but he did not obtain from Congress direct line-item appropriations for the LCB's "classification of lands" until 1917. The passage of federal mineral-leasing and water-power acts in 1920 significantly increased Mendenhall's responsibilities, funds, and staff. Just before leaving the USGS in 1922, to serve one year on President Warren Harding's Coal Commission, Smith renamed the unit the Land Classification Branch and appointed Mendenhall to lead the Geologic Branch as the USGS chief geologist.

As chief geologist, Mendenhall strove to continue the branch's balanced program of applied and basic work to serve society. In the USGS *Fiftieth Annual Report* ([1929], pp. 11–12), Mendenhall emphasized the nation's "need for geologic research" as "an integral part of human progress." "To apply science to human needs," Mendenhall added, "there must be science to apply," a phrase in use within the USGS since the 1890s. Expanding basic studies, in order to gain a better understanding of "general relations and natural laws," would improve the organization's ability to "solve the growing volume of practical problems, which are constantly increasing in complexity." To this end, Mendenhall and Smith sought a new line-item appropriation of $100,000 for "fundamental research in geologic science," which Congress approved, but only for two years. Despite the federal retrenchment and personnel losses to academia and industry that followed World War I, and the onset of the Great Depression, Mendenhall increased the Geologic Branch's total funds from $572,000 to $659,000 and its full-time staff from 134 to 155 persons, while maintaining high standards in appointments and operations. Mendenhall also encouraged increased cooperative mapping and studies with the states. That work led in part to a new geologic map of the United States completed in time for the Sixteenth International Geological Congress held in 1933, for which Mendenhall served as general secretary. He continued to emphasize regional stratigraphic studies (mostly in the West) as frameworks for detailed investigations of energy and metallic minerals, oversaw examinations of sites for dams and reservoirs, and secured direct funding for surveys of volcano hazards in Hawaii.

When President Herbert Hoover, a USGS veteran, appointed Smith chairman of the Federal Power Commission in December 1930, Hoover made Mendenhall the USGS's acting director and nominated him as director a year later. After the Senate confirmed his appointment, Mendenhall took his oath of office on 24 December 1931. In the next dozen years, he acted as his own "chief geologist" and extended his earlier policies to the agency's other program branches to meet two major external challenges—the Great Depression and World War II. The total funds deployed by the USGS increased to $4,927,000, and its staff increased to 1,065 persons during 1931 and 1932, but congressional retrenchment thereafter quickly reduced the agency's direct appropriations and eliminated its line-item for fundamental research in geoscience. Beginning in fall 1933, however, the Public Works Administration (managed by Interior Secretary Harold Ickes), the Tennessee Valley Authority (TVA), and other New Deal agencies transferred to the USGS sums more than three times the bureau's direct appropriations. These funds helped to save the USGS from having to decimate its programs and staff. In the next two years, the agency revived or initiated innovative projects in mapping and water-resource studies that combined applied and basic work in science and technology. Continuing USGS interests in petroleum geology, Mendenhall joined several presidential and secretarial committees created between 1934 and 1940 to ensure adequate fuel supplies for the nation. In those years, Mendenhall also chaired the executive committee of the U.S. Board on Geographic Names.

After 1938, as the USGS's direct appropriations rose above 1932 levels and transfer monies continued to increase, Mendenhall diverted some of the USGS's activities to war preparedness; from 1942 he directed all of its work toward helping the Allies to win the global conflict. USGS teams expanded their searches for domestic and foreign sources of strategic and critical commodities and employed geophysical methods to locate metallic minerals and ground water. They also prepared strategic and tactical intelligence on terrain and engineering locales abroad. Photogrammetric skills gained by the USGS while working with the TVA were improved and extended to map planimetrically and topographically strategic areas worldwide and to compile aeronautical charts and relief maps. USGS hydrologists found sources of water for military and industrial sites at home and for use in the combat theaters overseas. As a measure of the effectiveness of the USGS's contributions to the war effort, President Franklin Roosevelt twice granted Mendenhall one-year extensions beyond the mandatory retirement age of seventy. When Mendenhall departed on 27 February 1943, the USGS had a total of $11,127,000 available for operations by its 2,300 full-time personnel.

During his USGS career, the quiet, unemotional, and imperturbable Mendenhall demonstrated that he preferred discussion over argument and fostering public relations instead of public speaking. As an active member of the USGS Association of Aspiring Assistants, and its equally informal successor the Pick and Hammer Club, his sense of humor served well the yearly in-house satirical reviews. Mendenhall was equally involved in and honored by local and national scientific and social organizations, including the Chevy Chase, Cosmos, Faculty (Cambridge, Mass.), and Harvard (New York City) clubs; the American Association for the Advancement of Science (vice president, Section E, 1922); the Geological Society of America (president, 1936); the Geological Society of Washington (president, 1917); the Mining and Metallurgical Society; and the Seismological Society of America. The American Association of Petroleum Geologists and the American Institute of Mining Engineers made him an honorary member of their organizations. Mendenhall also served on the visiting committees at Harvard and at the Massachusetts Institute of Technology. The National Academy of Sciences elected Mendenhall to membership in 1932, and he received the Society of Economic Geologists' Penrose Medal in 1944. Mendenhall Peak, in the Directors Range part of Antarctica's Thiel Mountains, also honors his half-century of contributions to science in the public service.

Mendenhall married Alice May Boutell, the daughter of a Detroit business executive, in New York City in 1915; they had two daughters. He died at his home in Chevy Chase, Maryland.

• Mendenhall's public documents are in RG 57 (Geological Survey) at the National Archives and Records Administration, College Park, Md., except for his field notebooks

(1898–1910) at the USGS Field Records Library in Denver, Colo. *U.S. Geological Survey Bulletins* 746 (1923): 337, 737–38; 823 (1931): 417; 937 (1944): 637–38; and 1049 (1957): 620 list Mendenhall's principal publications through 1946. These citations also are available on CD-ROM as part of the American Geological Institute's "GeoRef" online bibliographical database. An appreciation by Monroe G. Cheney is in the *Bulletin of the American Association of Petroleum Geologists* 19 (1935): 922–24. Morris M. Leighton, *Journal of the Association of American State Geologists* 14 (1943): 3–5, marked Mendenhall's retirement as USGS director. Memorials published by Mendenhall's colleagues within and outside the USGS include D. Foster Hewett, *Science* 126 (1957): 603–4; Leighton, *Bulletin of the American Association of Petroleum Geologists* 42 (1958): 682–90; and Thomas B. Nolan, National Academy of Sciences, *Biographical Memoirs* 46 (1975): 310–28, which includes a bibliography. Mary C. Rabbitt, *Minerals, Lands, and Geology for the Common Defence and General Welfare*, vol. 2: *1879–1904* (1980) and vol. 3: *1904–1939* (1986), place most of Mendenhall's service in the context of federally sponsored geology. A brief assessment of the remainder of Mendenhall's directorate is in Rabbitt, "The United States Geological Survey: 1879–1989," *USGS Circular* 1050 (1989): 34–35.

CLIFFORD M. NELSON

MENDES, Henry Pereira (13 Apr. 1852–20 Oct. 1937), rabbi and communal leader, was born in Birmingham, England, the son of Rev. Abraham Pereira Mendes, a religious leader, and Eliza de Sola. He attended University College of the University of London from 1870 to 1872 and received private instruction in Jewish studies. A descendant of a long line of religious leaders on both his paternal and maternal sides, he decided early in life to minister to the religious needs of his people. Also interested in medicine, he received an M.D. from New York University in 1884.

From 1875 to 1877 Mendes served as minister to the Sephardic congregation of Manchester, England. He was then invited to become the religious leader of Congregation Shearith Israel, the Spanish and Portuguese Synagogue in New York City, which was founded in 1654. He was associated with Shearith Israel as minister and minister emeritus from 1877 until his death. Mendes married Rosalie Rebecca Piza of St. Thomas, one of the Virgin Islands, in 1890; they had two sons.

Mendes was an eloquent exponent of the Sephardic tradition in Judaism. For him, the Sephardic outlook represented an ideal blending of commitment to tradition and receptivity to general culture. A staunch Orthodox Jew, Mendes was also a man of broad education and experience. Often involved in interfaith activities, he also worked with all Jews—whether Orthodox or not—and won the respect of the various segments of the community. Mendes believed that only through faithfulness to tradition could Jews be true to themselves. He was an outspoken critic of the teachings of Reform Judaism, believing that its deviations from traditional Judaism were destructive of the fiber of Judaism. Reform Judaism had attracted many followers, especially among the more affluent and assimilated members of the Jewish community. Mendes argued that Orthodoxy, if represented by cultured and worldly spokesmen, could offset the inroads made by Reform. To achieve this end, he and his colleague Rabbi Sabato Morais of Philadelphia helped to found the Jewish Theological Seminary in 1887. Mendes served as its president from 1897 to 1902. The purpose of the seminary was to train cultured, English-speaking Orthodox rabbis to serve the Jewish communities of the United States. (When the seminary later identified itself with Conservative Judaism, Mendes separated himself from it.) In 1898 he was among the founders of the Union of Orthodox Jewish Congregations of America and served as its president for its first fifteen years. He felt that a union of Orthodox congregations could provide the needed communal framework for the advancement of Orthodoxy in the United States.

While committed to traditionalism, Mendes was not parochial. He was a founder of the New York Board of Jewish Ministers (later known as the New York Board of Rabbis), of which he also served as president. The New York Board included Orthodox, Conservative, and Reform rabbis and fostered a spirit of cooperation and tolerance. Mendes was also active in many humanitarian endeavors. He founded a society called "The Horeb Home and School for Jewish Deaf-Mutes," which in 1908 became the "Institution for the Improved Instruction of Deaf-Mutes." This school developed into the Lexington School for the Deaf. Mendes was also a founder of Montefiore Hospital in New York. In 1896 he served as vice president for the Guild for Crippled Children, acting as chairman of the committee that organized the "Crippled Children's East-side Free School," which opened in 1901. He worked with the sisterhood of his congregation to establish and operate settlement houses for new immigrants on the Lower East Side. At the same time, he lobbied for a number of causes: in Washington, for more liberal immigration laws; in Albany, for the rights of Sabbath-keeping storekeepers not to be restricted by proposed Sunday laws; at City Hall in New York City, for public schools to be kept free of sectarianism. He helped organize the first Young Women's Hebrew Association. He was also a Mason and became the first Jewish person to serve as a Grand Chaplain of the Grand Lodge of the State of New York (1895–1897). In 1892 Mendes was shot by a demented indigent man to whom he had been giving financial assistance. Mendes survived the gun wound, and the criminal was imprisoned. When the prisoner died some years later, Mendes saw to it that his would-be assassin was given a proper religious funeral.

Mendes was a leading spokesman for Zionism, serving as a vice president of the Federation of American Zionists. He was an exponent of what he called "Bible Zionism" or "spiritual Zionism," contending that the return of Jews to the land of Israel should be accompanied by a religious revival. He was also a prolific author in various genres. Contributing essays regularly to the newspaper the *American Hebrew*, he also wrote children's stories, religious textbooks, sermons, prayers, poetry, and dramatic pieces. Among his books are

Jewish History Ethically Presented (1895); *The Jewish Religion Ethically Presented* (1895); *Jewish Life Ethically Presented* (1917); and *The Way of Life* (1934). In addition to his multiple roles and activities, Mendes was a tireless pastor, maintaining close relationships with the members of his Congregation Shearith Israel. He died in Mt. Vernon, New York.

• Some of Mendes' papers are found in the Archives of Congregation Shearith Israel in New York City. Biographical information is in David De Sola Pool, *H. Pereira Mendes, A Biography* (1938), and in Pool's *An Old Faith in the New World* (1955). An obituary is in the *New York Times*, 21 Oct. 1937. A doctoral dissertation on the life of Mendes was written by Eugene Markovitz, "Henry Pereira Mendes: Builder of Traditional Judaism in America" (Ph.D. diss., Yeshiva Univ. 1961).

MARC D. ANGEL

MENDEZ, José (1888–6 Nov. 1928), baseball player, was born José de la Caridad Mendez into humble circumstances in Cárdenas, Cuba. His parents are unknown. Mendez developed his physique by chopping sugar cane as a boy. At age twenty he startled the baseball world by almost pitching a no-hitter against the touring Cincinnati Reds. A scratch single in the ninth spoiled the bid. Two weeks later, playing with one of Cuba's two leading professional teams, Mendez pitched sixteen more shutout innings against the Reds.

Cuban fans hailed him as "el Diamante Negro" (the black diamond), and newspapers in the United States began calling him "the black Mathewson," after New York Giants star Christy Mathewson. Old-timers said Mendez's fastball "looked like a pea," and his curve "looked like it was falling off a pool table." After his showing against the Reds, Mendez sailed to Key West, Florida, with a Cuban squad and pitched what may have been the first integrated baseball game in the U.S. South—a no-hitter against a local club.

In the winter of 1908–1909 in the Cuban professional league, Mendez won 15 games and lost 6. Barnstorming in the United States with a Cuban professional team the following summer, he was credited with 44 wins and 2 losses, presumably against semipro opponents. That autumn he was back in Havana as the two top Cuban teams, the Havana Reds and the Almendares Blues, won eight of the twelve games against the American League champion Detroit Tigers. Ty Cobb did not play in the series, but the following winter the Tigers brought Cobb along. He had one hit and struck out once facing Mendez, who lost the game, 6–3. Over the winter Mendez's record with Almendares was 11–2.

When New York Giants' manager John McGraw's National League champions arrived in Havana in 1911, the American players spent their World Series money nightclubbing and lost their first two games. "I didn't come down here to let a lot of coffee-colored Cubans show me up," McGraw thundered, and the next day Mathewson beat Mendez, 4–0. However, the following week Mendez and another Cuban pitcher, Eustaquio Pedroso, combined to defeat Mathewson, 7–4. Mendez's totals against major leaguers came to eight victories, including one against Philadelphia Athletics' Hall of Famer pitcher Eddie Plank, and eight defeats.

McGraw was much impressed by the dark-skinned Cuban pitcher, declaring that "José Mendez is better than any pitcher except Mordecai Brown and Christy Mathewson—and sometimes I think he's better than Matty." McGraw said he would have paid $50,000 for Mendez, "if only he were white." Although McGraw, in his wife's words, "bemoaned the failure of baseball, himself included, to cast aside custom or unwritten law . . . and sign a player on ability alone, regardless of race or color," he would not violate existing racial taboos and "thus settled for players who were undeniably Cuban." The first light-skinned Cubans soon appeared on U.S. major league teams, but Mendez was left to a career of barnstorming.

From 1912 until 1915 Mendez's Cuban league win-loss record was 9–5, 1–4, 10–0, and 2–0. He spent summers traveling by bus through the U.S. prairie states with the All Nations team out of Kansas City that included American blacks, Cubans, Asians, and even one female. They barnstormed through small midwestern towns, offering a baseball game in the afternoon and a dance band at night. Mendez played pitcher, shortstop, and cornet. One of his best games took place in Chicago in 1912, when he dueled the great black pitcher Rube Foster to a 12-inning 2–2 tie.

In 1916 Mendez was warmly received on arriving in San Juan, Puerto Rico. He entertained guests with his guitar each evening while coaching baseball by day. He is given much credit for spreading the popularity of baseball to Puerto Rico and from there to other Caribbean nations.

In 1920, when Rube Foster formed the first successful black league in the United States, the Negro National League, Mendez joined the Kansas City Monarchs, owned by former All Nations owner J. L. Wilkinson. Mendez was the manager, the team's shortstop, and on occasion a pitcher. He played nine games at shortstop in 1920, batting .061, but he hit .284 the following season. No records have been found for 1922, but in the Monarchs' pennant-winning season of 1923, Mendez's pitching record was 8–1. Monarch's pitcher Chet Brewer recalled Mendez as "a good teacher, a man of very high character, and a very neat dresser. Just an all-round class guy."

As the manager, Mendez led the Monarchs to two more pennants in 1924 and 1925. The 1924 team faced the Philadelphia Hilldales in the first modern black world series. The series went ten games, including one tie, and Mendez put himself in to pitch the final game. "Gray, gaunt, and grim," as one newspaper described him, he pitched eight shutout innings, and went into the ninth tied 0–0 before the Monarchs won.

No records for Mendez's next few years have been located. He died in Havana, probably in 1927, from tuberculosis. His family asked for government financial help to pay for the funeral.

A striking commentary on how white Americans' prejudice hobbled Mendez's career was provided in 1923, when another great Cuban pitcher, the light-skinned Dolf Luque, returned home in triumph after leading the National League with 27 victories for the Cincinnati Reds. Luque was given a parade, a new car, and more. Spotting Mendez on the sidelines, Luque went over and embraced him. "You should have gotten this car," he said. "You're a better pitcher than I am. This parade should have been for you."

• Further information on Mendez can be found in John B. Holway's *Blackball Stars* (1988), based on U.S. and Cuban newspaper accounts and on interviews with former players. Also see John Miller, *The Ballplayers* (1990), p. 730.

JOHN B. HOLWAY

MÉNDEZ, Rafael (1 Mar. 1906–15 Sept. 1981), trumpeter, was born Rafael Guttiérez Méndez Arceo in the Mexican town of Jiquilpan, Michoacan, the son of Maxìmino Méndez Guttiérez, a musician, and Irene Arceo Galvez. His earliest musical training came from his father, who remained a strong influence throughout his career. As a five-year-old boy, Méndez took up the cornet, becoming a part of his father's family band. His formal education went only through the third grade. In 1916 he came to the attention of the revolutionary general Pancho Villa, and at Villa's command, young Méndez traveled with the army for several months, serving as the general's personal cornetist. After returning home, he was briefly apprenticed to the local shoemaker but soon turned again to music, playing in his father's band and performing with circus bands throughout central Mexico. While he was in his teens Méndez made the change from cornet to trumpet.

In 1926 Méndez emigrated to the United States, settling first in Gary, Indiana, but soon moving to Flint, Michigan, where he won a spot in a company band sponsored by the Buick Corporation. In 1927 he moved to Detroit, where he hoped to make a living as a musician. After some initial financial difficulties—he had to pawn his trumpet and for a time earned a meager living playing the guitar in speakeasies—Méndez was asked to join the orchestra of the Capitol Theater. This proved to be his entrée into full-time employment as a musician, and within a few years he was Detroit's preeminent freelance trumpet player. Financially secure, Méndez was able to send money to his family in Mexico, and in 1930 he married Ann Amor Rodriguez Fernandez in Detroit.

Méndez suffered a severe injury to his upper lip in 1932, and the healing process was to have long-term consequences for his musicianship, forcing him to develop new approaches to playing and strengthening his virtuoso technique. He later credited his recovery to guidance from his father and was able to apply this experience to his own teaching. By 1934 Méndez was achieving popular acclaim in the Midwest as a soloist. He moved to New York City in 1935 and for the next few years played lead trumpet in the orchestra of Rudy Vallee.

Méndez moved to California in 1937 and spent the next several years working in Hollywood, eventually playing in the MGM studio orchestra and in the popular band of Xavier Cugat. During this period Méndez began his career as a composer and arranger, creating many works for himself as a soloist, including adaptations for trumpet of famous virtuoso violin solos. In 1940 he became a citizen of the United States. Méndez's fame as soloist continued to spread, bolstered by several immensely popular concerts at the Hollywood Bowl and by concert appearances and radio programs throughout the country. He appeared as a featured soloist in films, including *Flying Down to Rio* (1933) and *Hondo* (1953) and played on soundtracks for MGM and Disney in the 1940s.

Méndez's contract with MGM was terminated in 1949, providing impetus for him to launch a solo career. He already had a lucrative recording contract with Decca and eventually released twelve LP recordings for that label. Perhaps the most successful of these Decca recordings is *The Trumpet Extraordinary*, which includes his famous rendition of Rimsky-Korsakov's *Flight of the Bumblebee* and several of Méndez's own compositions. (Before signing with Decca, Méndez had recorded as both trumpeter and conductor for the Azteca and PanAmerican labels.) Méndez began to tour the United States as a soloist, appearing with several major symphony orchestras and playing at universities, high schools, and concert halls throughout the country. Many of these appearances included brass clinics, giving younger players the chance to work with Méndez. One eulogy commented, "With the younger, less experienced players, he was always warm, understanding, teaching, and encouraging. . . . no money could buy what this man gave to them" (Ileane McElwee, "Memoriam for Rafael Méndez," *School Musician* 53 [May 1982]: 25). He was also in demand as a featured performer in television variety shows throughout the 1950s and early 1960s. Many of his engagements during the 1950s featured his only children, his twin sons Ralph and Robert, both of whom were trumpeters—Méndez's "Tre Méndez Polka" (c. 1952) was composed expressly for their appearances together. In 1956, when he was at the height of his powers as a performer, he was featured in the series Concerts on Film, a widely distributed set of films featuring the greatest classical performers of the day. Although Méndez was plagued by asthma and other health problems during his late career, he continued to perform professionally until 1975. He died in Encino, California.

Méndez was one of the twentieth century's most influential brass players. Early in the century the trumpet rarely was considered a solo instrument, but it became one through the virtuoso performances of Méndez and other trumpeters of his generation and through Méndez's active advocacy for his instrument. His phenomenal technical abilities were widely praised by fellow musicians. In the 1940s conductor

Edwin Franko Goldman said, "Méndez is the greatest trumpet player in the world, and his virtuosity is the equal of great violinists such as Jascha Heifetz or Fritz Kreisler" (Michel Laplace, "Masters of the Twentieth Century: Rafael Méndez," *Brass Bulletin* 75 [1991]: 48). He created a large repertoire of works designed to showcase his style and technique. Méndez also exerted a profound influence on an entire younger generation of brass players through his many concert performances and countless brass clinics and master classes. Méndez is commemorated by the Rafael Méndez Brass Institute and by the annual Rafael Méndez Prize for young brass players, awarded by the International Trumpet Guild.

• Original recordings, together with papers and memorabilia are held by the Rafael Méndez Library at Arizona State University in Tempe. On Méndez's approach to teaching, see his *Prelude to Brass Playing* (1961). The most comprehensive biography is Jane W. Hickman and Delon Lyren, *Magnificent Méndez* (1994). Méndez's 78 rpm and LP recordings have been rereleased on compact disc by Summit Records.

J. MICHAEL ALLSEN

MENÉNDEZ DE AVILÉS, Pedro (15 Feb. 1519–17 Sept. 1574), captain general of the armada of the Indies and adelantado of Florida, was born in northern Spain, in the Asturian seaport of Avilés, the son of Juan Alfonso Sánchez and María Alonso de Arango. A descendant of minor hidalgos, he was connected by blood and marriage to several noble families, but as one of the youngest of twenty children, he could count on little else. Raised by relatives after his father died and his mother remarried, Pedro married a distant cousin, María de Solís, with whom he would have four children; invested his patrimony in a small, rapid sailing vessel; and became an unlicensed privateer.

Between 1543 and 1545 Menéndez served in the fleet of Álvaro Bazán, a noted corsair fighter. In 1548, having obtained his own letter of marque, he armed a galleon and began taking prizes in the Bay of Biscay. Two years later a second letter of marque licensed him to pursue corsairs in the Indies. There he fell into corsair hands, and while arranging ransom for himself and his ship, learned of French plans to raid the Indies. He gave warning in New Spain, Havana, and Santo Domingo, then went to Spain to present a strategic defense plan to the Council of the Indies. Impressed, the council made him a captain general of the armada of the Indies in 1552. While waiting for a commission, he commanded one of the 150 ships sent to escort Prince Philip to England to wed Mary Tudor. Menéndez conducted his first fleet to and from the Indies in 1555–1556, improving his fortunes with some smuggling, as captains general were wont to do. He then served two years in the armada of Flanders, convoying men, money, and matériel to Spain's armies and allies in the Franco-Hispanic wars. Once he traveled in disguise across France by post. After the peace of Cateau-Cambrésis in 1559, he brought Philip II back to Spain from Flanders.

Although France and Spain were nominally at peace, overseas the corsair war continued, swollen by legions of unemployed, doctrinally combative veterans. Returning to his transatlantic convoy duties, Menéndez continued his covert transactions, accumulating the capital to acquire a small fleet, which he leased to the Crown. In 1563 the House of Trade, in Seville, brought suit against Pedro Menéndez and his brother Bartolomé. While he languished in an Andalucian jail waiting for his case to come to trial, his debts mounted, his vessels ran aground, and his only son disappeared in a storm in the latitude of Bermuda. After twenty months the king intervened, directing the House of Trade to expedite the suit and find in Menéndez's favor. He was needed to defend the royal interests in Florida—Spain's name for eastern North America. Every Spaniard who had tried to plant a settlement on its coasts had failed, from Juan Ponce de León to Tristán de Luna y Arellano. The Spanish feared that the French Huguenot Jean de Ribault, however, might succeed in making permanent the colony of Huguenots he had established in 1562 at a garrisoned fort on Port Royal Sound in present South Carolina.

By 15 March 1565 Menéndez had a contract appointing him adelantado, or frontier governor, of Florida and charging him, within three years and without cost to the Crown, to explore, conquer, and colonize the land and begin its conversion. When, ten days after the signing, Philip II learned of a new French settlement on the St. Johns River—Fort Caroline, under René de Laudonnière—he added 300 royal soldiers and 15,000 ducats, making the Florida enterprise a joint venture. When spies reported that Ribault was on his way to reinforce the fort, the need for haste became critical. The king's champion had readied two fleets, one to sail under his command from Cadiz and the other from shipyards in the north, to rendezvous in the Canaries. Without waiting for his second fleet, Menéndez headed for Puerto Rico, then, with a force of more than 1,000, through the Bahamas and up the Gulf Stream to the mouth of the St. Johns.

Ribault had gotten there first; his unloaded ships, too large to cross the bar, lay at anchor outside the channel. Menéndez gave his challenge, shouting that he had come to burn and hang any "Lutheran French" he found in his king's lands and waters. The French cut their cables and escaped. Menéndez fell back to the nearest harbor to lighten his flagship, the great galleon *San Pelayo*, for action. He had his men fortify the Timucuan Indian village of Seloy; then, on 8 September 1565, he stepped ashore and formally established the municipality of St. Augustine.

A hurricane was approaching, and the *San Pelayo*, still heavy with supplies, had to be sent to safer waters. Menéndez knew that Ribault's ships and most of his forces would be out searching for the flagship. In a bold move, Menéndez divided his forces and marched forty miles through the storm to surprise and capture Fort Caroline, sparing only the noncombatants. He renamed the fort San Mateo. While writing up his report, he learned from Indians that Ribault's galleons had been wrecked far to the south. Grimly, Menéndez prepared to rid the land of Spain's enemies. As two groups of survivors, Ribault included, walked up the beach, soldiers met them at an impassable inlet, took them prisoner, and put them to the sword at a place still known as Matanzas. Menéndez saved a third group found near Cape Canaveral and made them galley oarsmen, trusting that rations for them would soon be arriving from Cuba. His prisoners told him that their expedition was part of another design to seize the Caribbean.

Menéndez acted swiftly. As reinforcements arrived—his own fleet from Cadiz and another fleet in 1566 from the Crown—he established five garrisons in the Antilles and nine on the North American mainland at harbors from Tampa Bay around to Port Royal. Each fort in Indian territory represented a diplomatic coup. To secure an alliance with the Calusas, a powerful nonagricultural chiefdom in southwestern Florida, he married the sister (and former wife) of the chief and took her to Havana, where, like most transplanted natives, she died. His "legitimate" wife remained in Spain.

Florida had yet to be explored, converted, and populated. From Santa Elena, at Port Royal, Menéndez sent two expeditions under Captain Juan Pardo into the interior, intending to open a road to Mexico, with a connector to the gulf. The Jesuits who had come to be missionaries established a school in Havana for the sons of Florida chiefs and sent a mission to Axacán on the Chesapeake Bay, where Menéndez hoped to discover a waterway through the continent. None of these endeavors was successful. To populate his three municipalities—St. Augustine, San Mateo, and Santa Elena—he brought farm couples from Spain and gave them building lots, fields, seeds, and livestock. As governor of the colony, he established commemorative feast days and promulgated the first European ordinances of government in North America.

In 1568 Menéndez returned to Spain to negotiate an extension of his contract and present a new plan for the naval defense of the Indies. Philip II loaded him with honors: a court portrait by Titian, membership in the Order of Santiago, carrying the coveted *don*, the revenues of the seigneurship of Santa Cruz de la Zarza, the right to entail his estate, and a patent for an instrument to measure longitude. He had already been made governor of Cuba, in a move to relieve his supply problems. Menéndez's new strategy called for using shallow-draft galleys and frigates to patrol the coasts of the Greater Antilles and intercept corsairs in the "narrow waters" of the northeastern Caribbean. The king gave him command of the Española Squadron and the title of captain general of the West.

Florida, meanwhile, misgoverned by lieutenants and assailed by corsairs, famine, fire, flood, disease, mutiny, and desertion, came close to extinction. Indians drove the Spaniards from one place after another until only St. Augustine and Santa Elena remained. Unable to make any progress, the Jesuits left. After himself experiencing shipwreck in Indian territory, Menéndez returned to Spain and requested authority to wage war on the "treacherous" nations of Florida and sell them as slaves. The king offered instead to support a permanent force of 300 soldiers and missionaries, this time Franciscans—another step toward transforming the original proprietorship into a Crown colony.

Heartened by the royal vote of confidence, Menéndez made plans to move his wife and household to Santa Elena, which would be the port for his intended marquisate in the interior. His family was on his mind. Of his four legitimate children, María was a professed nun, Juan had drowned, Ana had been murdered, and if Catalina's marriage to Hernando de Miranda continued childless, the direct line would end. In that case he chose to have the entail and title pass to a nephew, bypassing a fifth child, his illegitimate daughter María, wife of don Diego de Velasco.

But the king was not ready to let his servant retire to an American marquisate. With one hand he extended Menéndez's government around the gulf to meet the borders of New Spain; with the other he beckoned him back to Spain to prepare a great armada for use in northern Europe. The adelantado did as commanded, leaving his son-in-law Velasco in his place. He never saw Florida again, for he died in the shipyards of Santander of a stomach disorder, probably one of the "contagions" to which the ports were prone. He had served the king as a captain general of the royal armadas for thirty-two years.

The title of adelantado of Florida continues to this day in the patrimony of the counts of Revillagigedo. The colony that Pedro Menéndez de Avilés founded survived for more than 250 years, to be transferred by sale to the United States in 1821.

• A superb essay on the primary sources relating to Pedro Menéndez is Lyle N. McAlister's introduction to a facsimile edition (1964) of one source, which originally appeared as Jeannette Thurber Connor, ed. and trans., *Pedro Menéndez de Avilés. Memorial by Gonzalo Solís de Merás* (1923). Eugene Lyon, *The Enterprise of Florida: Pedro Menéndez de Avilés and the Spanish Conquest of 1565–1568* (1976), focuses on the first three years of Menéndez's governorship. Paul E. Hoffman, *The Spanish Crown and the Defense of the Caribbean, 1535–1585: Precedent, Patrimonialism, and Royal Parsimony* (1980) and *A New Andalucia and a Way to the Orient: The American Southeast during the Sixteenth Century* (1990), and David J. Weber, *The Spanish Frontier in North America* (1992), situate the colony and its founder in the larger story of Spain in America.

AMY TURNER BUSHNELL

MENETREY, Joseph (28 Nov. 1812–27 Apr. 1891), Jesuit missionary to Native Americans, was born in Siviriez in the canton of Fribourg, Switzerland, where he probably attended the local university. Nothing is known about his parents. After entering the Turin Province of the Society of Jesus in Italy in 1836, he spent ten years completing the regular Jesuit course of studies. Upon his ordination as a priest in 1846, he volunteered for the order's Rocky Mountain Mission in North America, which had been founded five years earlier by the Belgian Jesuit Pierre-Jean De Smet. Sailing from Europe with twenty-one other religious recruited by Archbishop François Norbert Blanchet of Oregon, Menetrey arrived at Jesuit headquarters on the Willamette River near the Oregon coast in August 1847. He served there in various capacities until perhaps as late as 1850 when he was posted into the interior to minister to the Coeur d'Alene tribe at Sacred Heart Mission in present-day Idaho. From there it is likely that he also visited other tribes in the region.

In 1854 Menetrey began work among the Kalispels, and together with Father Adrien Hoecken he established St. Ignatius Mission in Montana's Bitterroot Valley after an earlier site for the outpost proved inadequate. After serving for a while as superior, he was charged with the extensive temporal operations at the mission. St. Ignatius, which claimed nearly 2,000 native converts four years later, was designated the best of the order's missions in the Pacific Northwest by Jan Roothaan, Jesuit superior general. In 1855, when Governor Isaac I. Stevens of Washington Territory summoned the tribes of the interior to the Walla Walla Council to negotiate treaty boundaries, Menetrey was one of several Jesuits invited to attend as an observer. Stevens's secretary recorded that the priest "speaks English fluently and is an agreeable gentleman" (Burns, p. 80). During the hostilities that erupted between natives and settlers as a result of the treaties, Menetrey worked to maintain peace between the races. He also participated in peace negotiations between the government and the Kalispels in late 1855. In 1857 the priest made the first of his pastoral visits to the Flathead tribe, located in the valley below St. Ignatius Mission. Pleased by the reception he received, he urged superiors to reopen the mission to the tribe, which had been closed in 1850, but nine more years passed before that goal was realized.

During most of his long career Menetrey experienced frequent changes of assignment resulting from the large turnover in personnel that typified the administration of the Jesuits' rapidly expanding Rocky Mountain Mission. Thus, 1858 found him back among the Coeur d'Alenes at Sacred Heart Mission, from which he also made periodic pastoral visits to the Kutenais. At the government's invitation he joined Joseph Joset, superior of the mission, in attending the treaty council that ended hostilities between the Coeur d'Alenes and the United States in 1858. The following year he returned to St. Ignatius Mission as superior. His administration was made difficult by the cost of building a new church, by frequent horse stealing between the Kalispels and their Blackfeet neighbors, and by problems stemming from increased white expansion into the area. In 1862 he assisted in reopening St. Peter's Mission among the Blackfeet.

In 1863 Menetrey was assigned to St. Paul's Mission, located at Kettle Falls on the Columbia River near Fort Colville. Closed since 1859, the mission was ordered reopened by Rocky Mountain Mission superior Joseph Giorda. En route from Sacred Heart Mission to his new assignment, Menetrey assisted in founding St. Joseph's Church for métis and white Catholics in Frenchtown, Montana, and in the vast Hell Gate Valley. After arriving at St. Paul's, probably in 1864, Menetrey took up residence at the nearby Immaculate Conception Church, which had been recently established for soldiers assigned to Fort Colville. Although he was summoned to headquarters on the Willamette to manage mission finances in 1867, he spent the fall of that year and part of the next supervising the temporary closure of St. Peter's Mission, Montana. He returned to the Kettle Falls mission in 1868.

During the 1870s the growth of settlements in the Pacific Northwest led the Jesuits to shift more and more of their personnel from native to white ministries. Menetrey's later career reflected that change. During 1874 through 1877 he was occupied by parish work in Helena, Montana, and in numerous neighboring communities. In 1876 he built St. Joseph's Church at Canton, a farming settlement in Montana. In 1877 Menetrey was stationed at St. Mary's Mission, Montana. Three years later he was posted again to St. Ignatius Mission. From 1884 to 1889 he served as assistant pastor at St. Francis Xavier Church in Missoula, which he had built in 1881. From there he continued to supply Frenchtown and other frontier settlements. Faced with failing health, Menetrey retired in 1889 to St. Ignatius Mission where he died. After his funeral, which was attended by a large number of Indians, he was buried under the church he had once helped build.

Unlike many of his Jesuit missionary contemporaries, Menetrey left behind no dictionaries or grammars of the Native-American languages that he mastered in the course of his long career. Nor has his memory been perpetuated by the creation of written memoirs or records of his missionary activities. Instead, his reputation rests on his contribution to the overall Jesuit enterprise in the Pacific Northwest through his work as an early missionary among Native-American tribes, his role in maintaining peace between whites and Native Americans during periods of conflict, and his founding of numerous parish churches in the region.

• A few letters from Menetrey are in the Oregon Province Archives of the Society of Jesus, Gonzaga University, Spokane, Wash.; and in the "Montium Saxosorum" Collection (Rocky Mountain Mission Collection) of the Archivum Romanum Societatis Iesu, Rome, Italy. Extracts of two of his missionary letters were published in *Annales de la Propagation de la Foi* 30 (1858): 406–9, and *Lettres des Scholastiques de Laval* (1869): 21. Brief chronologies of his life are found in William N. Bischoff, *The Jesuits in Old Oregon, 1840–1940* (1945), and L. B. Palladino, *Indian and White in the Northwest* (1894). See also Robert Ignatius Burns, *The Jesuits and the Indian Wars of the Northwest* (1966); Hiram Martin Chittenden and Alfred Talbot Richardson, eds., *Life, Letters, and Travels of Father Pierre-Jean De Smet, S.J., 1801–1873*, 4 vols. (1905); Gilbert J. Garraghan, *The Jesuits of the Middle United States*, 3 vols. (1938); William L. Davis, *A History of St. Ignatius Mission, an Outpost of Catholic Culture on the Montana Frontier* (1954); and Wilfred P. Schoenberg, *Paths to the Northwest; a Jesuit History of the Oregon Province* (1982). An obituary is in "Nécrologie," *Collectión de Precis Historiques* 20 (1891): 583–84.

GERALD MCKEVITT

MENEWA (fl. 1811–1836), second-ranking chief of the Oakfuskee towns, lying on either side of the Tallapoosa River in Alabama, was a mixed-blood Upper Creek of unknown parentage. Though of relatively insignificant rank, Menewa led a colorful life that impinged on southern frontier history at several crucial junctures. As a young man he was known as Hothlepoya (Crazy War Hunter) for his daring horse-stealing forays across the Cumberland River into Tennessee. As he matured, he became wealthy selling horses, cattle, and furs to the Spanish at Pensacola. When Tecumseh came south in 1811, promoting a general confederacy of Indians to oppose the Americans, Menewa's affluence and heroic reputation made him an advantageous ally. Secondary sources indicate that Tecumseh visited Menewa, who was at first reluctant to join forces with the Upper Creeks in their forays against the encroaching whites.

The murder of a settler in the Oakfuskee neighborhood in 1812 was blamed on Menewa's band of warriors, and U.S. Creek Indian agent Benjamin Hawkins dispatched William McIntosh to lead a company of Lower Creeks as "law menders" to impose punishment. They burned one of the Oakfuskee villages, exacerbating the long-standing rivalry between McIntosh and Menewa, who believed a rumor that McIntosh had instigated the murder to expose him to the vengeance of the Georgians.

The Upper Creeks, who came to be known as the Red Sticks, began committing acts of civil war against the Lower Creeks as well as the settlers. In August 1813 the Red Sticks escalated the war by attacking Fort Mims near Mobile in the bloodiest Indian attack in U.S. history. There were an estimated 275 to 300 whites, friendly Indians, and mixed-bloods in the fort, and no more than 40 escaped. Andrew Jackson led an army of militia and regular soldiers, aided by McIntosh and a company of Lower Creeks, on a search-and-destroy mission against the Red Sticks. Although he seems to have been reluctantly drawn into the Creek Indian War, Menewa soon attained a premier position in the Red Stick military leadership.

Menewa was a hero in the final battle of the war on 27 March 1814 at Horseshoe Bend, where the Red Sticks were trapped on a peninsula nearly encircled by a bend in the Tallapoosa River in Alabama. Menewa and the Oakfuskee warriors were misled by their principal chief, a prophet who relied on an incantation and the juggling of herb-filled gourds to repel the enemy bullets. The prophet predicted that General Jackson would attack from across the river at the rear. When the general's cannon began a frontal attack on the log breastworks, Menewa angrily killed the prophet, leaped over the breastworks with a mighty war whoop, and led his warriors to inevitable defeat. Nine hundred warriors followed him into battle; only seventy survived.

According to a frequently told story that may be apocryphal, the severely wounded Menewa regained consciousness to find himself lying in a welter of corpses. When night fell, he was revived enough to crawl to the river and find a canoe. He floated downriver to Elkahatchee, where the women and children had been hidden in a swampy area, and was joined by other survivors, most of whom were wounded. Menewa refused to surrender, returning, stripped of his wealth, to his devastated village, where he became a leader of the Creek faction that opposed further cession of land to the whites.

In the meantime, William McIntosh continued to build a following of Lower Creeks who were willing to sell their lands in Georgia and relocate in the West. He and five lesser chiefs signed a treaty at Indian Springs on 7 February 1825, relinquishing all the remaining Creek land in Georgia. Menewa was appointed to lead a company of Upper Creeks to execute McIntosh, and at dawn on 30 April the deed was accomplished. Because of the controversy surrounding the Indian Springs treaty, it was declared void, but on 24 January 1826 virtually the same treaty was concluded in Washington, D.C., with fourteen signatories, among them Menewa. Menewa, now reconciled to the inevitable, advocated selling most of the land, with the proviso that certain parcels be deeded to individuals choosing to remain. He won the retention of a part of the Oakfuskee lands but lost his own farm in the process. During a negotiating visit to Washington, Charles Bird King painted his portrait for the gallery of the War Department.

Menewa led a company of Upper Creeks against the Seminoles in 1836 and for this service was given the assurance that he could remain in Alabama after the general removal of the Creeks to the West. That same year, however, he was ordered to be included in the forced removal, and he died in Oklahoma at an unknown date.

• Accounts of Menewa's activities are found in *Report on Messages of the President*, Select Committee, House Report No. 98, 2d sess., vol. 3, *The Georgia Indian Controversy* (1837); H. S. Halbert and T. H. Ball, *The Creek War of 1813 and 1814* (1895); Thomas L. McKenney and James Hall, *The Indian Tribes of North America* (3 vols., 1836, 1838, 1844); Frederick W. Hodges, ed., *Handbook of American Indians North of Mexico* (1959); and Theron A. Nunez, Jr., "Creek Nativism and the Creek War of 1813–1814," *Ethnohistory* 5 (1958): 69–72, 131–75, 292–301.

BENJAMIN W. GRIFFITH, JR.

MENJOU, Adolphe (18 Feb. 1890–29 Oct. 1963), film actor, was born Adolphe Jean Menjou in Pittsburgh, Pennsylvania, the son of Jean Adolphe Menjou, a restaurateur, and Nora Joyce. The family moved to Cleveland, Ohio, when Menjou was seven. After completing the primary grades at St. Joseph's Seminary, he attended Rockwell Public School and East High School. When his father learned that he was cutting classes to appear as a stage extra at the Euclid Avenue Opera House, Menjou was sent to Culver Military Academy in Indiana and then to Stiles University Preparatory School in Ithaca, New York. He went on to Cornell University, where he studied engineering before transferring to a liberal arts program. He left Cornell after his junior year to work in his father's restaurant.

The notion of an acting career appealed to Menjou more than the food business, and in 1912 he moved to New York City to seek acting jobs. There he found work in vaudeville and theater as well as earning an extra's wages in early silent films, *The Man behind the Door* (1914) being the first. In 1916–1917 he appeared in about ten more features, most prominently *The Blue Envelope Mystery* (1916).

With the entry of the United States into World War I in 1917, Menjou joined a Cornell University ambulance unit. He served in Europe for a year, seeing combat and rising to a captaincy. After his discharge in 1919, he did a stint as production manager for the A. J. Van Buren motion picture company and married Katherine Tinsley. He and Tinsley were childless and divorced seven years later.

In 1920 Menjou traveled to Hollywood in hopes of returning to screen acting. Bigger and better parts than before the war soon came his way. He played Rudolph Valentino's friend in *The Sheik* and Louis XIII in Douglas Fairbanks's *Three Musketeers* (both 1921). In 1923 he found a villain's part in Charles Chaplin's *Woman of Paris* that ushered him to silent film stardom. In that movie Menjou established the persona of the nattily dressed roué, his signature role for the next thirty-five years.

During the 1920s Menjou was featured in some four dozen pictures. By now he had mastered the characterization of "the other man," a decadent, polished Old World seducer of younger women. He was earning $7,500 a week playing such parts. Actress Louise Brooks forthrightly assessed Menjou's dependable professionalism: "He never felt anything. . . . You never felt anything working with him, yet you see him on the screen—and he was a great actor."

Menjou married Kathryn Carver in 1927; they had no children and were divorced in 1933.

Although Menjou's marvelous voice allowed him to make an easy transition to sound films, his starring roles changed to leading character parts in the 1930s, including three of his finest characterizations. The first was in *Morocco* (1930), directed by Josef von Sternberg, in which Menjou played the world-weary victim of archetypal sex goddess Marlene Dietrich. Next came his role in *The Front Page* (1931), that of the crafty newspaper managing editor, which earned him his only Academy Award nomination. The third was in the best film version of an Ernest Hemingway work, *A Farewell to Arms* (1932), directed by Frank Borzage: Menjou was brilliant as the hedonistic officer friend of the hero (Gary Cooper), who tries out of jealousy to undermine Cooper's love affair with heroine Helen Hayes.

In 1934 Menjou married actress Verree Teasdale. They adopted one child.

Through the rest of the 1930s Menjou scored with other performances, often as a wealthy theater or movie producer, as in *Morning Glory* (1933), *A Star Is Born* (1937), and *Stage Door* (1937). He also made his mark playing against his usual casting in *Little Miss Marker* (1934), as a race-track tout, with six-year-old Shirley Temple; as the widowed, jobless, musician father of fifteen-year-old Deanna Durbin in her springboard film, *One Hundred Men and a Girl* (1937); and as a shady prizefight manager in *Golden Boy* (1939), which introduced 21-year-old William Holden.

In the 1940s Menjou was highly effective in *Roxie Hart* (1942), *The Hucksters* (1947), and especially *State of the Union* (1948), in which he rated critical superlatives for his role as a crooked politician.

The start of the Cold War aroused the House Committee on Un-American Activities (HUAC) in 1947 to look into possible communist influence in Hollywood movies. Menjou, a founder of the Motion Picture Alliance for the Preservation of American Ideals and ten years later a charter member of the John Birch Society, was a fierce detractor of the liberal New Deal; he became one of the House committee's most outspoken champions. At HUAC's Washington, D.C., hearings into the film industry in October 1947, Menjou was the first of fourteen "friendly witnesses," who also numbered studio head Walt Disney, actors Gary Cooper, Robert Taylor, and Ronald Reagan, and screenwriter Ayn Rand.

Unfortunately for Menjou, historians and analysts of the Hollywood blacklist have emphasized his more extreme and careless statements before HUAC, such as "I'd move to the state of Texas if they [communists] came over here, because I think the Texans would kill them on sight" or Hollywood was "one of the main centers of communist activity in America" or "I am a witch-hunter if the witches are Communists. I am a Red baiter . . . I would like to see them all back in Russia." He further testified that for years he had compiled political dossiers on scores of Hollywood figures whom he suspected of being communists, or—as he declared under oath—who acted "an awful lot like" communists.

Menjou made fifteen more films over the rest of his career. His performances in several were memorable, especially *The Tall Target* (1951); *The Sniper* (1952), in which for the first time he shaved off his patented waxed mustache; *Man on a Tightrope* (1953), ironically as an officer of the Soviet secret police; and, most notably, as a textbook French army commander in the Stanley Kubrick–directed antiwar classic, *Paths of Glory* (1957). Menjou's last role, again opposite a popular child star, Hayley Mills, was in the Walt Disney studio's *Pollyanna* (1960).

Menjou was never a great or versatile actor. But his always dependable and sometimes outstanding performances in more than 140 American motion pictures make him an unforgettable presence in film history.

He died in Beverly Hills, California, reputedly one of the wealthiest individuals in Hollywood.

• Menjou's autobiography, *It Took Nine Tailors* (1948), is a familiar, gossipy account of his role in the earlier years of American films, more self-serving than reliable history. Virtually all standard movie reference works briefly cover his career. David Quinlan, *Quinlan's Illustrated Registry of Film Stars* (1991), offers the most complete filmography, while David Thomson, *A Biographical Dictionary of Film*, 3d ed. (1994), is the most insightful into his craft. Menjou's overall career can be traced through different issues of *Film Review*. The best account of events surrounding Menjou's testimony in the HUAC hearings is Larry Ceplair and Steven Englund, *The Inquisition in Hollywood: Politics in the Film Community, 1930–1960* (1980). Some of Menjou's HUAC appearance can be seen in the documentary *Hollywood on Trial* (1976). An obituary is in the *New York Times*, 30 Oct. 1963.

ROBERT MIRANDON

MENKEN, Adah Isaacs (15 June 1835–10 Aug. 1868), actress, was born Ada McCord in Memphis, Tennessee, the daughter of Richard McCord and Catherine (maiden name unknown). Her father died when she was a small child, and her mother married Josiah (or James) Campbell.

Several fundamental facts of Menken's life are in dispute, and as a consequence biographers differ. She herself is small help, having claimed several names and identified several people as parents. She said she was born Marie Rachel Adelaide de Vere Spencer, daughter of an Englishman, Richard Irving Spencer. She also claimed to have been born in Madrid, Spain, Dolores de Ricardo Los Fiertes (or Fuertes). She used biographies as publicity releases, and the first test of data seemed to be viability in image building. Biographers have an extensive palate of choices as they define her birth identity, and they inevitably are guided by their own personalities and agendas. Name confusion is emblematic of contradictions in her character. The Magnificent Menken, as she also was called, deliberately assumed positions calculated to provoke her public to respond. She juxtaposed arresting and contradictory poses, and through the images she thus created, she controlled her audience.

The first twenty years of Menken's life are legend and conjecture. She was said to have been captured by Indians, to have delighted Havana audiences when she was barely a teenager, to have married the Cuban poet-patriot Jean Clemente Zenea, and to have been a sought-after courtesan in Havana. None of these things could have been, but there is a splendid harmony among such fictions of her young life and the facts of her adult years. Her family apparently had moved to New Orleans at some point. Those first New Orleans years must have been hard ones for Catherine and her children in the years after Campbell died, and the sisters Annie and Ada may have danced for their living as they did later. But the real stories from those days probably were more grim than sublime. It is the fictions, instead, that seem true to the Menken we think we know.

The first sure trace of Menken is in Galveston County, Texas, where she was giving readings and writing for the *Liberty Gazette*. There she met and on 4 May 1856 married a pit conductor, Alexander Isaac Menken, and moved with him back to New Orleans, where she began acting major roles without apprenticeship or training. There were stories about other marriages: to a man in Lexington, Kentucky, and to W. H. Kneass of Galveston, but it was Menken's name she used, and it was after being married to Menken that she claimed to be culturally Jewish. At the beginning of her career, she attempted roles in the so-called regular drama, such as *The Lady of Lyons*, by Bulwer Lytton. However, even in her early years, she had more success in the minor forms, especially *The French Spy* (a Mme Céleste vehicle) and *Black-Eyed Susan*. Her professional debut was in March 1857, in Shreveport, Louisiana, with J. C. Charles's company.

In June 1858 they moved from New Orleans to Cincinnati, where Alexander's family were merchants. During this period, if not earlier, she began to spell her first name in the "Hebrew" way, with an *h*. However, the role of Judaism in her life is problematic. Some biographers (notably, Bernard Falk and Allen Lesser) have claimed she was born Jewish. Whatever the truth of that, she conscientiously played the part of a Jewish convert during this phase of her life.

Throughout her life Menken seemed to be most herself when she was an outsider. In fact, as a Jewish wife having a life in the theater she was doubly nonconformist. She championed Jewish civil rights causes and wrote for the *Cincinnati Israelite*. But her acting in breeches and protean roles, the costumes she wore, and her exuberant lifestyle shocked her husband and his family in Cincinnati. He told her to give up theater, but instead she went to New York City. He secured a rabbinical diploma of divorce in July 1859.

Menken's New York debut (1 Mar. 1859) in two burlettas was badly received by the critics. They especially complained about her tight men's costumes and suggestive manner, but behind their censure was a prejudice against minor forms and the growing democratization of theater. She was sacked after only three performances.

While in New York Menken met and fell in love with the boxer John C. Heenan. They were married 3 September 1859, unfortunately before a legal divorce from Menken had been obtained. A scandal ensued after Heenan left to fight Tom Sayers in England. Mrs. Heenan, as Menken briefly billed herself, put up a bold front, but a succession of blows—being pregnant, losing the baby in infancy, her mother's death, being repudiated by both Menken and Heenan (she filed for divorce from Heenan in August 1861)—put her into a depression that plainly shows in the poems that she wrote during this period. She began to withdraw from life.

When she did emerge in the middle of 1861 in a theater in Albany, with most of her clothes off, on the back of a runaway horse, she was not the same Adah Menken. John B. Smith, manager of the Green Street

Theatre, decided to revive Henry M. Miller's adaptation of Byron's heroic epic *Mazeppa* with Menken in the title role. The play concerns a hero who fights against the Poles for his people's freedom. Captured and tied to a horse, he is driven onto the Russian steppes. Publicity emphasized the danger, her vulnerability, and the possibility that she might be naked (actually, she wore a flesh-colored body stocking and a brief tunic). Menken was both a tremendous success and the occasion of moral outrage wherever she played. She tried several ways to expand her repertoire during the rest of her career, but she never got away from that horse.

During this time Menken met the satirist Robert Henry Newell who, though no bohemian himself, introduced her to Walt Whitman and the others who met at Charley Pfaff's beer cellar. She and Newell were married in September 1862, but they were too dissimilar, and the marriage never worked.

Beginning in August 1863, Menken played San Francisco and other communities in Nevada and California to great acclaim. In San Francisco she was paid half the gross receipts for each Friday and matinee and a third for the other nights. She gave good value for the money, performing with vigor. She entered the social life of the city, being most comfortable around Bret Harte, Artemus Ward, and the other bohemians. She generated publicity wherever she went. She left the city in April 1864 at the height of her powers and much, much richer. When she and Newell left the West Coast they went separate ways. They were divorced in August 1865.

The Menken, as her admirers called her, went to London, where she had arranged to play *Mazeppa* at Astley's Amphitheatre (3 Oct. 1864), managed by the circus impresario E. T. Smith. Publicity had been carefully programmed to show Menken to the city and, without arousing the censor, to take full advantage of her reputation, looks, and costume. *Punch* was scandalized, but most other papers did not let Victorian prohibitions detract from "The Mazeppa's" consummate showmanship. She brought fashionable audiences across Westminster Bridge to this horse opera venue on the unfashionable side of the Thames. While she was there she became friendly with several artists and writers, notably Charles Dickens, Dante Gabriel Rossetti, A. C. Swinburne, and the French actor Charles Fechter. Her escort on most occasions was an American southerner, James Paul Barkley. A romantic attachment developed, and although Menken had earlier forsworn marriage, the discovery that she was pregnant led her to marry Barkley on 19 August 1866 in New York. Three days after the wedding she sailed to France, to wait for the baby and her forthcoming debut in Paris. She never saw Barkley again. Her baby, baptized Louis Dudevant Victor Emmanuel Barkley with George Sand as his godmother, lived only a few months.

Menken's reception in Paris was a triumph. She would never again be so important to so many people. On 29 December 1866, about a month after her baby was born, she opened at the Théâtre de la Gaîté in *Les Pirates de la Savane*, playing a leading role that had no lines. Parisians went wild for her, and all over town there were Menken photos for sale, Menken cravats, Menken shaving mugs, and Menken pantalets. Parisians called her "*dada* Menken" (*dada* means hobby horse in French).

Menken also was trying to publish a collection of her own writing, and with encouragement from Rossetti and others, she collected the poems that she had written during the previous fifteen years. Called *Infelicia*, it came out 18 October 1868, too late for Menken to see it. It went through eight editions in England and the United States and stayed in print more than forty years.

After Paris Menken played in Vienna and London, but she did not command the enthusiasm that she earlier had. Finally in London she sold her jewelry to finance her own production of *Mazeppa* at Sadler's Wells. She closed in two weeks and—tired and broke—made her will. She returned to Paris to begin rehearsals, but she was too sick to work; she died within a month from unknown causes. Originally buried in Père Lachaise Cemetery, Paris, she was reinterred eight months later in the Jewish section of Montparnasse Cemetery.

Any assessment of her importance has to take into account the tremendous appeal she had as a performer and acknowledge that she had qualities that made her a superstar in a modern sense. There were other female Mazeppas but none who matched her appeal. Other actresses wore tights but not so fascinatingly, nor were they so elegantly notorious as she. With many other theater artists she contributed to the evolution of the modern musical. It was, however, no one thing she did or had that made her memorable. She won her fame through her energy and her ability to juxtapose strength and vulnerability. It was the inexorable enthusiasm with which she seized freedom whenever it was offered.

• An important collection of unpublished material related to Menken, including photographs, is in the Harvard Theatrical Collection. Her album is in the Brown University Library. A good biography is Wolf Mankowitz, *Mazeppa: The Lives, Loves, and Legends of Adah Isaacs Menken* (1982), which was drawn in part from material in the closed collection of the British Library in documenting A. C. Swinburne's relationship to Menken. Mankowitz's book also discusses the many inaccuracies in Noel Gerson's (pen name Paul Lewis) book about Menken, *Queen of the Plaza* (1964); Mankowitz eventually extracted an admission from Gerson that he had fabricated much of his narrative and invented sources to document it. Allen F. Lesser, *Enchanting Rebel, the Secret of Adah Isaacs Menken* (1947). Menken's own account of 1862 is included as an appendix in Lesser's book. It is not factually reliable, but it is illuminating all the same. Mankowitz's book also has an appendix that includes representative Menken poems, including "Aspiration," which Dante Gabriel Rossetti considered her best. The best genealogical work is by John Cofran, "The Identity of Adah Isaacs Menken: A Theatrical Mystery Solved," *Theatre Survey* (May 1990). Cofran used previously unexamined public records and followed up several clues overlooked by others, and in his closely reasoned, objective analysis of the theories, he neatly distinguishes between reasonable inference and wishful thinking. Bernard Falk, *Naked Lady*, was first published in 1934 and revised in its 1952 edition.

CLAIR O. HAUGEN

MENNIN, Peter (17 May 1923–17 June 1983), composer and educational administrator, was born Peter Mennini in Erie, Pennsylvania, the son of Attilio Mennini, a restaurant owner, and Amelia Bennaci. The elder Mennini was an avid record collector, and music was a central feature of the family environment. (Peter's older brother Louis Mennini also became a professional composer. Peter later changed his name to avoid confusion between the two.) Peter began formal musical study at age five and started to compose at the age of seven. He entered the Oberlin College Conservatory in 1940 but left to join the U.S. Army Air Force in 1942. By this time he had already completed his First Symphony, a large work nearly an hour in duration. On completion of his military service in 1943, Mennin entered the Eastman School of Music, where his major teachers were Howard Hanson and Bernard Rogers. There he earned his B.M. and M.M. in 1945, and his Ph.D. in 1947. While at Eastman he completed two more symphonies, already revealing his predilection for large forms that was to characterize his mature output. Mennin's work immediately began to attract widespread attention. His Symphony no. 2 won Columbia University's Bearns Prize in 1945, and his Symphony no. 3 was performed by the New York Philharmonic before he left Eastman. The Philharmonic recorded the symphony soon thereafter, placing Mennin, still in his mid-twenties, at the forefront of American composers.

In 1947 Mennin married Georganne Bairnson, a young violinist whom he had met at Eastman; they had two children. At this time the Juilliard School in New York was undergoing a major restructuring at the hands of William Schuman, who invited Mennin to join the distinguished composition faculty he was in the process of establishing. Mennin remained at Juilliard until 1958, when he was offered the opportunity to head the Peabody Conservatory in Baltimore. In 1962 he returned to Juilliard as its president, overseeing the school's move to the newly opened Lincoln Center for the Performing Arts. He held this post for the rest of his life. As president, Mennin advocated rigorous training based on the fundamental skills of practical musicianship, and he upheld traditional standards of excellence during a period when educational orthodoxy was under severe attack. At the same time, he inaugurated the Juilliard Theatre Center, the American Opera Center, and a program for the training of conductors, all of which brought international attention to the school and drew talented students from all over the world.

Despite Mennin's important role as an educational administrator, composition remained the driving force in his life. Throughout his career he produced major works that were performed and recorded by many of the world's leading orchestras and soloists. He received awards, honors, and commissions from the most prominent musical institutions and served on the boards of a wide range of arts organizations. Nonetheless, Mennin's administrative identity, and a distaste for promoting his own music, caused his public persona as an administrator to overshadow his contributions as a composer. Furthermore, from about 1950 to 1975 American composition was deeply divided between those who adhered to traditional musical forms and values and those who repudiated them in favor of more novel modes of expression. As a composer of sonatas and symphonies who also served as president of two of the nation's leading traditional music conservatories, Mennin clearly belonged in the former camp. While his positions earned him considerable prestige within institutional circles, it somewhat tarnished his reputation as a creative figure. Consequently, during his later years Mennin's music received little serious attention.

Although Mennin's music conformed to traditional techniques and forms in the most general sense, his evolution as a composer was marked by an independence from prevailing trends and models and by a consistent adherence to his own aesthetic ideals. Mennin was, indeed, a traditionalist in many ways: he never abandoned the principle of tonality, and he remained loyal to the classical forms of symphony, sonata, and concerto, basing his works on centuries-old contrapuntal techniques. But he allied himself with no trends or schools of thought and acknowledged no compositional influences beyond the choral masters of the Renaissance. Furthermore, he made no attempt to embrace the variety of expression sought by most traditionalists. As he stated in an interview,

> Individuality is an inevitable precondition for music of lasting value. Individuality does not mean novelty for its own sake, since novelty, once familiar, becomes a cliché. It does mean a strong musical thrust, unconcerned with convention, or with conformity either to the past or to the fads of the moment. It is concerned with the drive of the composer's musical ideas; it is having one's own voice, one's own face. . . . I don't think any real composer ever aligns himself with a group. . . . A composer has to travel alone. (Quoted in a memorial brochure published by the Juilliard School shortly after Mennin's death)

Mennin's relatively small body of some thirty compositions centers around nine symphonies, a large dramatic work entitled *Cantata di Virtute* (1969) based on Robert Browning's poem "The Pied Piper of Hamelin," and several concertos. His output reveals a preference for large, abstract forms. His style is consistently serious—even grim—in tone and lofty in intent, with no trace of either frivolity or sentimentality. Mennin's music is characterized by nervous contrapuntal activity, intense rhythmic drive, and a propensity for cataclysmic explosions, all of which became more pronounced in his later works. Despite the uncompromising character of his music, its fundamentally expressive orientation and its consistently meticulous craftsmanship have rendered it accessible to audiences. During the years since Mennin's death in New York City, there has been a renewal of interest in the American symphonic school, and Mennin's work is regarded by many to represent this group at its most distinguished.

• Mennin's papers are on file at the Juilliard School. His music is published by Carl Fischer, Inc., New York City. An informative two-part interview with the composer, conducted by David Owens, is in the *Christian Science Monitor*, 29 and 30 July 1981. See also the obituary in the *New York Times*, 18 June 1983.

WALTER G. SIMMONS

MENNINGER, Charles Frederick (11 July 1862–28 Nov. 1953), physician and cofounder of the Menninger Clinic, was born in Tell City, Indiana, near Cincinnati, the son of August Valentine Menninger and Katarina Schmidberger, both German immigrants. August became the prosperous owner of a Tell City saw mill and pushed his children toward practical business and professional pursuits in the locality. But Charles had strong intellectual interests and graduated in 1882 in high standing from Central Normal College in nearby Danville, Indiana. To his parents' distress, he accepted a teaching position at Campbell College in distant Holton, Kansas, where he taught German and several courses in the sciences.

In 1885 Menninger married one of his students, the strong-minded Flora Knisely. At her urging, he left the Lutheran faith under which he had been reared, and both became devout lifelong members of the Presbyterian church. The marriage was always tense. Flora dominated and imposed her concern for financial survival and constant self-improvement over the more easy-going and tolerant Charles, who always acquiesced and often suppressed his anger. Karl Menninger, their first son, was born in 1893 and bound closely with Flora to form the family's ruling alliance. Charles was closest to his amiable, youngest son, William Menninger. Edwin, the middle son, felt estranged from either alliance and moved far away shortly after high school.

At Flora's urging, Menninger left his teaching post in 1887 for the Hahnemann Medical School in Chicago. He received a degree in homeopathic medicine after two years of study and moved to Topeka, Kansas, to establish a practice. He recognized that allopathic medicine also had much to offer and, after twenty years of eclectic homeopathic practice, took an M.D. at the University of Kansas Medical School in 1908. He became one of Topeka's most respected internists. Deeply interested in the pre-insulin treatment of diabetes, Menninger studied briefly with research pioneer Elliott Joslin of Boston. He was also modestly interested in psychiatric disabilities and wrote a paper on the insanity of Hamlet.

As he watched Joslin engage in group research, Menninger acquired a sense of the advantages of group medical practice. A 1908 visit to the Mayo Clinic in Rochester, Minnesota, further demonstrated the benefits if the group consisted of family members. Consequently, he encouraged his sons to join him in a group medical practice. Karl, who had studied psychiatry at the Boston Psychopathic Hospital, insisted that the family practice focus on the treatment of mental abnormalities and consider treatment possibilities through a psychoanalytic approach that was commanding more and more of his interest. Menninger agreed and essentially put Karl in charge when they established a group practice in 1919. Seven years later, his other physician son, William, was persuaded to join the family practice. By then it had become the Menninger Clinic for psychiatric disorders.

As Karl and William assumed control of the clinic in the mid-1920s and early 1930s and made it into a unique and internationally respected psychiatric treatment center, Charles became the house physician. He examined and attended to the physical problems of the patients. He also took special interest in Southard School, the clinic's agency to treat emotionally distressed children, and served briefly as its director. He had a kind and playful manner, and the children loved his presence. From the 1930s until his death, clinic patients and staff referred to him lovingly as "Old Dr. C.F." He was not regarded as a clinic founder so much as a kind, grandfatherly figure.

By the early 1940s, Menninger was largely retired, but he continued to visit the Menninger Clinic regularly and tried to ease the increasing tensions between Karl and William. He took special interest in enhancing the beauty of the trees, lawns, and gardens that surrounded the clinic. When Flora died in 1945, he continued to live with a longtime household border, Pearl May Boam, whom he married in 1948. His relationship with Pearl was considerably more relaxed and fun-filled than his marriage to the austere and anxious Flora, and it made for a happier retirement. He died in Topeka.

• Many of Menninger's letters and unpublished essays are in the Menninger Clinic archives in Topeka. His files in the Menninger family collections there are especially valuable. Walker Winslow lacked these documents when he wrote *The Menninger Story: A Biography of Dr. Charles Frederick Menninger and the Story of the Clinic He Founded* (1956), which nevertheless treats Menninger's family life and enjoys the advantage of lengthy interviews with Charles. See also Flora Menninger's autobiography, *Days of My Life* (1939), and Lawrence J. Friedman, *Menninger: The Family and the Clinic* (1990). An obituary is in the *Topeka State Journal*, 1 Dec. 1953.

LAWRENCE J. FRIEDMAN
JAMES CARNEY

MENNINGER, Karl Augustus (22 July 1893–19 July 1990), psychiatrist and author, was born in Topeka, Kansas, the son of Charles Frederick Menninger, a physician, and Flora Vesta Knisely, a Bible studies teacher. Karl Menninger's upbringing affected both his personal and professional lives. Karl was the Menningers' eldest son. A general practitioner, Charles was the stabilizing force in the Menninger home. Eager to maintain calm, he helped neutralize the anxiousness and mood swings often felt by his wife, who came from economically depressed conditions. Her concern over finances in her adult life remained extreme, although Charles provided a comfortable living. Flora was also anxious about Karl and fretted as she cared for him. His mother's mood swings promoted in Karl an insecurity that drove him to maintain control of his surroundings—often with little apparent regard for others' feelings. While Karl exhibited his mother's emotional fluctuations, his younger brother, William Claire Menninger, resembled their father, who was easy-going and conciliatory. These family dynamics would shape the history of the Menninger Foundation.

Karl Menninger attended Washburn College in Topeka briefly but graduated from the University of Wisconsin. He considered a career in the ministry, a suggestion that was frowned upon by his mother because the profession lacked financial rewards. He finally settled on a career in medicine and attended Harvard Medical School. Rather than focus on physical illnesses as his father did, however, Karl was drawn to psychiatry. During his residency at the Boston Psychopathic Hospital, Menninger studied under Elmer E. Southard. Southard's interest in nosology (identifying and describing psychiatric ailments) was pervasive in early twentieth-century psychiatry, though it held little interest for the cure-oriented Menninger. After completing his M.D. in 1919, he returned to Topeka and formed a medical partnership with his father. This professional arrangement conformed to Menninger family dynamics. Karl, the headstrong son, had already decided to focus the practice on psychiatry. His father, though he had no formal training in psychiatry, acquiesced to his son's decision and essentially made Karl the senior partner in what was to become the Menninger Clinic.

Menninger's reputation in professional psychiatric circles grew rapidly. As an early proponent of the "new psychiatry," he moved beyond the teachings of Southard by attempting to discern more than the specific description of his patients' maladies. Menninger wished to determine the causes of psychiatric symptoms and, if possible, to effect a cure. His belief that psychiatric ailments could be understood and treated placed him in the forefront of a profession that was still largely focused on the custodial care of the mentally ill. By the mid-1920s the Menninger Clinic's reputation had grown far beyond Topeka, and Menninger had become a recognized leader in the emerging "new psychiatry" movement.

Menninger's reputation also increased through his publications. Having taught a course on mental hygiene at Washburn College, he recognized the need for a general textbook on psychological ailments and treatments that was consistent with the tenets of the "new psychiatry" movement. His first book, *The Human Mind* (1930), served as an introduction to psychiatry for students. Written in a popular and accessible style, it also became a Literary Guild selection and a bestseller. Menninger's optimism about the treatment of mental illness appealed to a public that associated psychiatry with the "warehouse-style" care of "crazy" people. He argued that there were no permanently "crazy" people, any more than there were perpetually "sane" people. He sought to demonstrate that psychiatric symptoms were explicable and that treatments were available. In *Man against Himself* (1938), Menninger focused on suicide, noting that suicides occurred for reasons that could be understood and treated. In this, his second book, Menninger broadened the concept of "suicide" beyond its popular meaning. Troubled individuals, he wrote, could commit a "focal suicide," which may be concentrated on a specific part of the body. "Accidents" that produced bodily destruction may not be accidents at all but, rather, limited suicides, whereby subjects destroyed parts of themselves as a substitute for their whole body. An important distinction between Menninger's first two books is the latter's use of psychoanalytic understanding as its conceptual core. Utilizing Sigmund Freud's dual instinct theory, Menninger showed how people fluctuate on a continuum between the extremes of Eros (the life instinct) and Thanatos (the death instinct). (This continuum would form the basis of his book *The Vital Balance* [1963].) In *The Human Mind* Menninger had very briefly described psychoanalytic treatment. By the time *Man against Himself* was written, however, Freudian theory had become central to Menninger's conception of psychological illness and treatment.

At the Boston Psychopathic Hospital, Menninger had been introduced to psychoanalysis through a lecture by Eugene Louisville Emerson, an early American psychoanalytic pioneer. His interest in analysis grew when he met Smith Ely Jelliffe, a New York psychiatrist with an interest in psychosomatic illnesses. In addition to discussing Freud's writings and ideas with Menninger, Jelliffe also analyzed the young Topekan for a few sessions. Analysis soon became the cornerstone of Menninger's psychiatric thinking and practice.

After the publication of *The Human Mind*, Menninger began a training analysis under the Hungarian Franz Alexander. One of Freud's more able pupils, Alexander had recently founded the Chicago Institute for Psychoanalysis. Personally, Menninger hoped that this analysis would enable him to extricate himself from the emotional control that his mother continued to exert over him. He also hoped that the analysis could save his relationship with his wife, the former Grace Gaines, whom he had married in 1916; they had three children. But this first analysis was less than successful. Encouraged by Alexander, Menninger dealt with his marital problems by engaging in affairs and made little headway in becoming independent of his mother's emotional controls.

This unsatisfying analysis under Alexander did not quell Menninger's devotion to psychoanalysis. He visited Vienna with Alexander in 1932 and met Freud, who was ill with cancer and displayed little interest in him. Menninger was especially irritated that Freud seemed unaware of *Man against Himself*, with its support for Freud's dual instinct theory (which had acquired few adherents within American psychoanalytic circles). Decades later, Menninger learned that Alexander had told Freud, in a private moment, that the Kansan was vain and narcissistic and that Freud should limit his praise of the younger man.

His experiences with Alexander and Freud notwithstanding, Menninger sought to make analysis the primary treatment method at the Menninger Clinic. During the 1930s, with few American physicians trained as analysts, he hired European analysts fleeing fascist repression. Menninger surrounded himself with analysts trained by Freud or by Freud's students, making his clinic one of the few psychoanalytically oriented hospitals between the East and West coasts, where a considerable number of émigré analysts practiced. Menninger's reputation as an author and his psychoanalytic émigrés combined to make the clinic a force in the national mental health arena at a time when psychoanalytic treatment was coming to be perceived as the most advanced and sophisticated available.

Aware of the deficiencies of his first analysis, Menninger turned to an analyst who had gained a reputation for reworking failed first analyses. He chose Ruth Mack Brunswick, an American who had spent years in Vienna learning from Freud. After a year and a half in New York City with Brunswick, he returned to Topeka to announce his divorce from Grace. He then married his secretary, Jeanetta Lyle, in 1941, with whom he had been intimate since the mid-1930s; they adopted one child. During the second analysis he also decided to transform the clinic into a nonprofit foundation, which opened the door to tax-deductible donations while enabling him to maintain family control.

While Menninger struggled to manage his tumultuous personal life during the 1930s and 1940s, family-related issues had an impact on the clinic. The attempts by Karl and Will (who had joined the clinic in 1925) to run the clinic as a team were strained. Replaying their roles from childhood (and emulating their parents), Karl's erratic mood swings and bursts of energy required the stabilizing influence of Will. The two often found it convenient to be apart from each other as contact was often exceedingly tense. During this decade, the brothers took on roles that they would maintain for much of their adult lives. Karl became "the innovator," the theorist, author, and creator of new ideas for psychiatric treatment. Will was "the implementor" and manager who worked to put his older brother's ideas into action. This conflict-ridden relationship did not abate after the war.

One of Menninger's most significant "innovations" was in the field of psychiatric education. Influenced in part by Will's experiences with psychiatric casualties during the Second World War, he recognized the postwar need for trained psychiatrists. With funding from the Veterans' Administration, the Menninger Clinic renovated a run-down V.A. hospital in Topeka to give physicians a crash course in psychiatric theory and treatment. Although the Menningers had trained only thirty-six psychiatric residents since 1931, Karl agreed to take on 100 residents in the first Menninger School of Psychiatry class of 1946. By 1949 the MSP also trained psychiatric nurses and social workers.

The accomplishments of the Menninger School of Psychiatry were significant. The quantitative impact of the Menningers on American psychiatry went well beyond the size of their staff. By 1951 the Menningers could boast that they had trained 15 percent of the psychiatrists who practiced in the United States. However, the sudden growth of the Menninger organization also produced a number of problems. The rapid expansion of the 1940s and early 1950s had transformed the foundation from a small, family-centered practice into an impersonal institution that required a concomitant increase in fundraising. During the late 1940s and throughout the 1950s, Will became a full-time traveling fundraiser, while Karl remained in Topeka as chief of staff, trying to oversee the vast and still growing Menninger Clinic. The uncoordinated growth of the clinic, coupled with Karl's attempts to control all facets of the organization, led to disastrous results. With Will away and unable to modify his brother's actions in the interest of prudence, talented staff members began to leave Topeka. As he flitted from department to department, Karl increasingly alienated those department heads whom he tried to control. The situation worsened during the 1950s and early 1960s. In April 1965 the heads of four departments informed Will that they wished to report directly to him instead of to Karl. They explained that the clinic had grown too large to be led by one person and that Karl's inconsistent and meddling attempts to coordinate all the clinic's activities were damaging to staff morale. Will agreed that such a centralized approach was no longer appropriate. A more decentralized structure in which the department heads made their own decisions was needed. Karl was, in effect, removed as chief of staff. His reaction was a mixture of rage and resignation. When he first realized that a "revolt" had begun, Karl attacked. He blamed Will for the events, noting that Will had turned against him and sided with the department heads. Mindful of the clinic's psychoanalytic orientation, Karl reminded the "conspirators" of the fate of the brothers who slew their father in Freud's *Totem and Taboo*; that those who helped bring down the leader would meet a similar end. Karl was sometimes described as "psychotic" as he unsuccessfully attempted to regain his power.

Shortly after the "revolt" of April 1965, Will was diagnosed with lung cancer and died nine months later. Before his death, the clinic began a search for a new president. As it became clear that Will's eldest son, Roy, was the likely successor, Karl maintained that his own son, Robert, should be chosen. Robert's mixed reputation as a therapist and administrator made his appointment unlikely. When Roy Menninger was chosen by the trustees whom his father had appointed, Karl publicly welcomed him and retired to the largely ceremonial position of chairman of the board of trustees.

During the 1970s and 1980s Menninger's significance to the clinic continued to decline. Although he received the Medal of Freedom from President Jimmy Carter in 1981 and met with dignitaries who visited the clinic, his power within the organization that he had helped found had evaporated. His health also deteriorated. An operation for a brain tumor in 1976 was followed by a series of strokes and bouts with pneumonia. He finally succumbed to inoperable stomach cancer and died in Topeka.

Although Menninger counted among his achievements the founding of the Menninger Clinic and a term as president of the American Psychoanalytic Association, he may be remembered most for his belief in hope. The importance of hope was central to *The Human Mind* and each book thereafter. In *Man against Himself* Menninger emphasized that suicidal individuals were not incurable. In *The Vital Balance* Menninger elaborated his conception of a mental health continuum. Noting that no individual remained static on this continuum, Menninger wrote that no matter how psychologically maladapted a person may be, the potential for mental health remained extant. Indeed, hope also motivated Menninger's last large-scale endeavor, the Villages, a series of foster homes in the midwestern United States for abused children. No longer in the vanguard of the mental health profession, the Menninger Clinic's significance has diminished since the 1960s. Through his work with the Villages, however, Karl's insistence on the need for hope never dwindled.

• Menninger's correspondence and manuscripts are located at the Menninger Foundation archives in Topeka, Kans. Edited versions of a small portion of Menninger's correspondence can be found in *The Selected Correspondence of Karl A. Menninger, 1919–1945* (1988). Important volumes by Menninger not mentioned in the text include *Love against Hate* (1942), *A Manual for Psychiatric Case Study* (1952; 2d ed., 1962), *Theory of Psychoanalytic Technique* (1958; 2d ed., 1973), *A Psychiatrist's World: The Selected Papers of Karl Menninger, M.D.* (1959), and *The Crime of Punishment* (1968). Walker Winslow, *The Menninger Story: A Biography of Dr. Charles Frederick Menninger and the Story of the Clinic He Founded* (1956), is helpful in understanding both the clinic's and the Menninger family's histories. Unlike Winslow, Lawrence J. Friedman was granted unrestricted access to the Menninger archives for his *Menninger: The Family and the Clinic* (1990). Menninger's early years are also chronicled in his mother's *Days of My Life: Memories of a Kansas Mother and Teacher* (1940).

LAWRENCE J. FRIEDMAN
J. E. CARNEY

MENNINGER, William Claire (15 Oct. 1899–6 Sept. 1966), psychiatrist, was born in Topeka, Kansas, the son of Charles Frederick Menninger, a physician, and Flora Vesta Knisely. He felt closest to his father and resembled him in personality. Both were amiable, interested in a diversity of hobbies, and acquiescent to the anxious demands of Flora and the oldest son, Karl. In 1918 William briefly interrupted his education at Washburn College in Topeka to enlist in the army. But he saw no military action and graduated from Washburn the following year.

Menninger next pursued graduate work in medicine. He completed a master's degree at Columbia in 1922, an M.D. from Cornell Medical School in 1924, and an internship at Bellevue Hospital in New York in 1925. Although Charles and his brother Karl Menninger were transforming Charles's general medical practice in Topeka during the early 1920s into a psychiatric clinic, William chose internal medicine and cardiology over neuropsychiatry as his medical specialty. In 1925 he married Catharine Wright; they had three children. The couple hoped to become Protestant missionaries in China. But his parents and Karl pressured William to join the emerging Menninger Clinic, and he did so at the beginning of 1926.

Because he had joined a psychiatric specialty firm with no formal training in mental health, Menninger took a four-month residency at St. Elizabeth's Hospital, which was directed by the eminent psychiatrist-psychoanalyst William Alanson White. Nonetheless, Menninger conducted much of this residency independent of White, researching and publishing on juvenile paresis, an inherited form of syphilis that is detectable in teenage populations. (The research culminated in his classic 1936 volume, *Juvenile Paresis*.) When he resumed his duties at the Menninger Clinic, he evidenced greatest interest in diabetes and other maladies with clear "physical-psychical relationships." Unlike Karl and even Charles Menninger, William remained skeptical of the use of Freud's "science of the psyche" in a treatment center that was beginning to emphasize psychoanalytic interpretation. In 1930 William was named director of the major Menninger Clinic institution—the inpatient sanitarium-hospital. This freed up Karl to write, travel, and conduct psychoanalytic training, and allowed Charles (already quite old) to spend fewer hours as a staff physician. When he assumed the directorship, William was acquiring a medical reputation as an expert in paretic neurosyphilis, cerebrospinal fluid, epilepsy, thyroid gland dysfunctions, and chronic appendicitis. In the late 1920s, he had also been investigating a scientifically reputable drug treatment for mental illness, which failed dismally.

Deeply disturbed by this failure in organic psychiatry, Menninger began a lifelong emphasis on environmental and intrapsychic dimensions of mental disturbance. Above all, he concerned himself with the curative powers of a managed social milieu for treatment and, specifically, the benefits of planned interpersonal relationships between patients and staff. Aided by a training analysis under the Hungarian Freudian, Franz Alexander, William structured a "scientific" social regime for treatment during the 1930s around Freud's dual drive theory. His program accented the forces of the life wish and reduced death wish factors that were moving the patient toward self-mutilation and suicide. Instead of allowing patients to harm themselves, for example, the staff encouraged them to sublimate aggressive drives by taking up less destructive activities (splitting logs, for instance). William developed an intricate program for his staff and carefully directed them in their conduct and attitudes toward each individual patient, so that they might enhance patients' fervor for life and diminish their self-destructive propensities. This psychoanalytically informed milieu therapy program became the most distinctive and renowned part of Menninger Clinic treatment during the 1930s and early 1940s. Because it focused on planned staff interactions with patients, it enhanced the role of "auxiliary" personnel—nurses, activities therapists, and attendants—who worked with patients far more than the physicians. The effectiveness of the program is difficult to measure; the preponderance of patients were classified at discharge under the ambiguous category of "slight improvement." Nonetheless, staff morale was high and national leaders of the psychiatric profession regarded the Menninger hospital as a well-run facility.

When William was called to army duties in 1942, Karl took over day-to-day management of the Menninger hospital and largely perpetuated William's treatment program. William rose rapidly and became the most influential American psychiatrist in World War II. By 1943 he was neuropsychiatric consultant for the Fourth Service Command. A year later he was promoted to lieutenant colonel and chief psychiatrist for the entire army. With considerable authority, he set to work reducing psychiatric disorders among the American troops. Menninger pressed for comprehensive neuropsychiatric examinations so that Selective Service boards and army personnel could screen out emotionally disturbed inductees. When soldiers developed "combat fatigue" and other psychiatric maladies, he sought to have them treated immediately at aid stations near the front lines instead of at distant hospitals from which they rarely returned to combat duties and were often discharged. Arguably, these psychiatric first aid stations were forerunners of postwar community mental health clinics. Toward the end of the war, Menninger compiled a comprehensive text of psychiatric disorders and reactions as a guide for army psychiatrists in diagnosing and treating patients. This became an important source for the American Psychiatric Association's first *Diagnostic and Statistical Manual of Mental Disorders*.

After the war William returned to the Menninger Clinic, where he helped Karl to develop the Menninger School of Psychiatry. It trained hundreds of psychiatric residents, clinical psychologists, social workers, and attendants not only on the Menninger grounds, but in a nearby Veterans Administration hospital and the Topeka State Hospital. By the early 1950s the MSP was training roughly 15 percent of all American psychiatrists and large numbers in all of the other mental health professions. Many MSP graduates became national leaders of their professions.

Nonetheless, William found it increasingly difficult to work on the same campus with Karl. Their relationship, always troubled, became so conflict-ridden by the late 1940s that William found himself more comfortable away from Karl. The organization had grown so large and complex, with a diversity of costly needs, that it required a full-time professional fundraiser. William assumed that function, and it kept him on the road much of the time. In 1946 William had become a founding member of the Group for the Advancement of Psychiatry—a collectivity of World War II psychiatric veterans pushing for a more activist, socially obligated psychiatric profession. The following year he was GAP's successful candidate for presidency of the American Psychiatric Association, and did much to transform the APA into an organization atune to social and community applications of psychiatric knowledge. GAP and APA duties, coupled with fundraising plus leadership in the American Psychoanalytic Association, for which he served as president from 1947 to 1949, kept William away from Topeka for all but the summer months.

During the 1950s and the first half of the 1960s Menninger became a psychiatric elder statesman. He often sat in corporate boardrooms advising on psychiatric dimensions of employee management and seeking donations for the Menninger Clinic. He spoke before legislatures in almost every state, pleading for enlarged public appropriations to expand state programs for psychiatric training and treatment. He advised governors, congressmen, and even presidents on the appropriate social and psychological programs for emotional maladies. In addition, he publicized the message of activist, socially oriented, and supposedly effective professional psychiatry in popular books like *You and Psychiatry* (1948) and *Making and Keeping Friends* (1952). As he left clinical duties behind and repeated a basic stock of speeches and observations year after year through the 1950s and into the 1960s, Menninger lost some of his earlier acuity. He favored increased appropriations for state mental hospitals as well as new community clinics, but failed to see the early warning signs that state and federal lawmakers were willing to trade off the hospitals for the clinics. This "deinstitutionalization" policy drastically reduced the number of chronic and deeply disturbed patients in state hospitals, while new community clinics (preoccupied with a less disturbed middle-class clientele) did not care for most of the former hospital patients. As a result, large numbers of the severely mentally ill became street people or entered unregulated nursing homes. To the end of his life, Menninger failed to see this increasingly precarious turn in national mental health policy.

In April 1965 a small group of senior Menninger Clinic department heads pleaded privately with William to exercise his powers as president of the organization. They urged him to fire Karl, the chief of staff, for becoming dictatorial and promoting a demoralized and diffuse facility that was losing its preeminence in American psychiatry. Since childhood, William had suppressed a deep anger at the erratic and controlling ways of his older brother. Tired after years of travel and fundraising on the road, and anxious to return full time to Topeka and the Menninger Clinic, William struck back at Karl directly for the first time in his life. He sided with the department heads and subsumed under his presidential title Karl's chief of staff position and duties. Karl exploited the psychoanalytic implications of this event by drawing upon the Oedipal myth. William and his colleagues had "assassinated" him, the father of the clinic, Karl charged. It was like the killing of the primal father—a self-destructive revolt by the sons, who would struggle among themselves to determine who would succeed him. In the end, they would bring disaster among themselves.

Although Karl's response to his firing did not regain his place in the Menninger Clinic, William and the department heads (firm believers in the Freudian implications of patricide), became deeply disturbed. Several became alcoholic or so incapacitated in their work that they had to be fired. William developed a massive and malignant lung tumor shortly after this "palace revolt." As his death drew nearer, he worked successfully to keep Karl out of power in the Menninger Clinic and to install his oldest son, Roy, as his presidential successor. He died in Topeka.

• Menninger's letters and unpublished manuscripts are partially housed in the Menninger Clinic archives and partially in the residence of his wife, Catharine, who survived him. Regrettably, he lacks a biographer. Bernard H. Hall's *A Psychiatrist for a Troubled World: The Selected Papers of William C. Menninger, M.D.* (2 vols., 1967), reproduces most of his major essays and provides a helpful introduction and annotations. Lawrence J. Friedman, *Menninger: The Family and the Clinic* (1990), places William in the context of his family and his medical workplace. Gerald N. Grob, *From Asylum to Community: Mental Health Policy in Modern America* (1991), thoroughly explains the national mental health policy shifts and the state of the American psychiatric profession during the 1941 to 1970 period when Menninger was perhaps America's most influential psychiatrist.

LAWRENCE J. FRIEDMAN
JAMES CARNEY

MENOHER, Charles Thomas (20 Mar. 1862–11 Aug. 1930), army officer, was born in Johnstown, Pennsylvania, the son of Samuel Menoher, a carpenter, and Sarah Jane Young. His father served as a soldier in the 206th Pennsylvania Volunteers during the Civil War. After attending local schools and teaching school himself, Menoher received an appointment to the U.S. Military Academy at West Point in 1882. "Strong and well developed physically" (Rhodes, p. 234), he became, during his senior year, the cadet first lieutenant of Company A, commanded by Cadet Captain John J. Pershing. Menoher graduated sixteenth in a class with seventy-seven members and selected the artillery as his branch. He was commissioned a second lieutenant in the First Artillery on 1 July 1886. In 1889 he married Nannie Wilhelmina Pearson. They had four sons, three of whom survived to maturity and became army officers.

American artillery regiments of the period were organized for administrative expedience instead of for tactical considerations and consisted of a mixture of Coast Artillery companies and Field Artillery batteries. While the Coast Artillery was gradually modernizing, the Field Artillery was obsolescent if not obsolete by European standards. It was still equipped with guns that recoiled out of position with each shot, used black powder propellant that engulfed the gun position with smoke, and relied on direct (line of sight) fire. Menoher served successively in the First, Third, and Sixth Artillery Regiments and was a student at the Artillery School (1894), which enabled him, like other junior officers, to master both specialties. His professional expertise and reputation for imperturbability led to his appointment as regimental adjutant of the Sixth Artillery in March 1898. This position led directly to successive postings during the Spanish-American War and the Philippine insurrection as aide to Brigadier General E. B. Williston and as a staff officer of first Williston and then Brigadier General James Franklin Bell, which gave him insight into command and policy at higher levels.

These two wars led to modest reforms of American artillery, among them the creation of mountain artillery, small howitzers capable of being disassembled and packed on the backs of mules. Promoted to captain in February 1901, Menoher commanded the Twenty-eighth Battery, Field Artillery (Mountain) from its organization in October 1901 through May 1903. He was then selected as part of the initial increment of officers to serve on the new War Department General Staff (Aug. 1903 until Oct. 1907). He was a member of the board of officers that in 1905 adopted indirect fire as the preferred method of delivering artillery fire and was one of two army planners who worked out in 1907 the War Department's emergency plan for war with Japan. It envisioned concentrating the entire Philippine garrison for a last-ditch defense of Subic Bay on Luzon until the U.S. battle fleet arrived. From October to December 1907 he was provost marshal of the Army of Cuban Occupation.

Upon the separation of the coast and field artillery into two branches, he selected the Field Artillery and in December 1907 assumed command of a battalion of the First Field Artillery. He spent most of the next decade with troops. On 1 July 1916 he was promoted to colonel of Field Artillery, and the War Department assigned him to command the Fifth Field Artillery. During the mobilization on the Mexican border, he commanded a Provisional Field Artillery Brigade from September to November 1916.

Promoted to temporary brigadier general following U.S. entry into World War I, Menoher went to France in August 1917. His classmate, General Pershing, assigned him to command the American Expeditionary Forces' Field Artillery School at Saumur, France (Sept.–Dec. 1917). The school's purpose was to assimilate the best of the field artillery tactics, techniques, and procedures in use by the British and French armies on the western front so as to instruct the half-trained field artillerymen arriving from the United States. Menoher had only laid the foundation for the school when Pershing assigned him to relieve Major General Charles T. Mann as commander of the Forty-second "Rainbow" Division. Menoher, now a major general, oversaw the training of the division and successfully commanded it in combat. The division helped defeat the last German drive in Champagne in July 1918 and then participated in the successful Allied counterattack against the Marne salient. There the Forty-second, advancing against a line of detached machine gun posts in the face of complete German domination of the air, suffered its heaviest casualties of the war. It took part in the St. Mihiel offensive (Sept. 1918) and some of the heaviest fighting in the Meuse-Argonne (Oct.–Nov. 1918). During the fighting, he earned a reputation not only as a skilled tactician but also as a leader of particularly broad vision, a man able to obtain the best out of difficult, often headstrong subordinates, including Brigadier General Douglas MacArthur, Colonel William J. "Wild Bill" Donovan, and Colonel Henry J. Reilly. In recognition of Menoher's talents, Pershing promoted him to command the VI Corps on 10 November 1918, one day before the conflict ended.

Menoher did not remain long in France. Secretary of War Newton D. Baker selected him to head the reorganized Air Service, one of the major disappointments of wartime mobilization. Menoher took up his duties on 2 January 1919. He oversaw its demobilization and secured its legislative charter as a separate branch of the army. His attempts to secure adequate funding for research and development of all combat aircraft floundered on congressional desire to retrench in peacetime. While he attempted loyally to carry out this mandate, he came increasingly in conflict with his assistant, Brigadier General William Mitchell, who by courting popular support sought increased funding for the Air Service at the expense of the navy and independence for aviation from the ground army. Mitchell generated considerable public support for his position when the First Provision Brigade under his command sank the captured German battleship *Ostfriesland* in tests off the Virginia capes in July 1921. As a result, the Joint Army-Navy Board called for the rapid development of aviation, both shore-based and in the fleet. Mitchell submitted his own report advocating a radical reorganization, and then someone in his office leaked it to the press. Regarding this as an attempt to undermine administration policy, Menoher attempted to fire Mitchell, but with Mitchell's popularity at its height Secretary of War John W. Weeks instead accepted Menoher's resignation as chief of the Air Service on 4 October 1921. Menoher served with troops for five more years before retiring for age. His first wife died in 1919, and in 1923 he married Elizabeth Painter; they had no children. He died in Washington, D.C.

Menoher was important in three areas. He was a key figure in the modernization of the U.S. Field Artillery. His work with mountain artillery was directly linked to the development of airborne artillery in World War II and was more circumspectly related to the development of air transportable artillery since that conflict. As a division commander in World War I, he trained and then led one of the most successful divisions in the American Expeditionary Forces. Finally, in his dispute with Mitchell, Menoher displayed the combined arms mentality that has dominated U.S. Army thinking during the twentieth century, while Mitchell exhibited a tendency to exalt military aviation as decisive and virtually self-sufficient. Their conflict proved emblematic of the kinds of tensions that have existed between ground and air officers ever since.

• Menoher apparently wrote only infrequently, and his letters are not very revealing of his personality. The U.S. Military Academy Library at West Point has a small collection of his papers. Only a few of his letters survive in the papers of Pershing, Mitchell, and Baker at the Library of Congress. The correspondence files of the Office of the Chief of Air Service, 1917–1926, are, thus, essential for any detailed study of Menoher. His annual reports as chief of Air Service are available in published form in the *Air Service Newsletter*, an incomplete collection of which is available at the Air Force History Office at Bolling Air Force Base, Washington, D.C. Menoher's often elusive personality is best captured in memoirs by Charles D. Rhodes, "Charles Thomas Menoher," in *Association of Graduates of the United States Military Academy . . . June 10, 1931* (1931), pp. 234–38; and Francis P. Duffy, *Father Duffy's Story* (1919). For background on the three areas in which Menoher played an important role, see Boyd Dastrup, *King of Battle: A Branch History of the U.S. Army's Field Artillery* (1992); Edward M. Coffman, *The War to End All Wars: The American Military Experience in World War I* (1968); D. Clayton James, *The Years of MacArthur, 1880–1941* (1970); Paul F. Braim, *The Test of Battle: The American Expeditionary Forces in the Meuse-Argonne Campaign* (1987); Robert F. Futrell, *Ideas, Concepts, Doctrine: Basic Thinking in the United States Air Force, 1907–1984*, 2d ed. (2 vols., 1989); and Alfred F. Hurley, *Billy Mitchell: Crusader for Air Power* (1975). An obituary is in the *New York Times*, 12 Aug. 1930.

EDGAR F. RAINES, JR.

MENTSCHIKOFF, Soia (2 Apr. 1915–18 June 1984), lawyer, co-drafter of the Uniform Commercial Code, law professor, and dean, was born in Moscow, Russia, the daughter of Roman Sergei Mentschikoff and Eugenia Ossipov. Fleeing the 1917 Russian revolution, Mentschikoff's father, an American citizen, took his family to New York City, where he worked as a typewriter salesman and her mother took in fine sewing. Mentschikoff attended the New York public schools and Hunter College, receiving her A.B. in 1934. She then enrolled in Columbia Law School in a class that was 7 percent women. She worked in the registrar's office and as a research assistant to her contracts professor, Karl Llewellyn, a leading Legal Realist philosopher and a renowned teacher and scholar. She received her law degree in 1937.

In 1937 Mentschikoff took a position at Scandrett, Tuttle and Chalaire, a small New York firm. She was the only woman lawyer at the firm and had accepted the position on the understanding that she would be permitted to do litigation—an area virtually closed to women at that time. In 1941, when some Wall Street firms hired their first women lawyers to replace the young men who went off to World War II, Mentschikoff became an associate at Spence, Windels, Walser, Hotchkiss and Angell, a large corporate law firm with seventeen male partners and ten to fifteen associates. There she honed her arbitration and litigation skills in labor and commercial law.

In the fall of 1943 Mentschikoff took a four-month leave from the firm to act as the assistant reporter for the Uniform Sales Act. Llewellyn, whom she described as her "mentor and best friend," was the chief reporter for this act. It was part of his ambitious project to create a uniform commercial code to modernize and standardize state laws governing sales and financing of personal property, as well as modes of payment and title documents. Mentschikoff recalled that at age twenty-seven she brought the skills of an "innocent, a non-expert" to the eminent "old men" on the drafting committee. "If I could understand it," she said, "anyone could; if I could set it up in a pattern, it would be intelligible to nonexperts. Knowledge of the law can be a great hindrance when your approach is what can we do that is sensible rather than how do we change the existing law" ("Reflections of a Drafter," pp. 535, 542). Her lifetime intellectual focus was always on the craft of the law—determining how it can help the parties in a transaction achieve their objective—rather than on the theory of the law.

After returning to the law firm, Mentschikoff remained closely associated with this law reform endeavor, which, greatly expanded in 1944, became the Uniform Commercial Code (UCC) project. In 1945, when most of the newly hired women lawyers were sent home to make room for men returning from the war, Mentschikoff became the first woman partner in the firm, then called Spence, Hotchkiss, Parker and Duryee; in fact, she was the first woman partner in any Wall Street firm. Although she practiced law for only the first decade of her career, all of her life Mentschikoff described herself as a lawyer rather than a law professor or dean.

Mentschikoff served as the associate chief reporter on the UCC project and, with Llewellyn, retained overall editorial responsibility and control, working intensively with the drafting committees for each article. She also facilitated proposals sent from other drafters to Llewellyn, who was often difficult and unreceptive to criticism. Mentschikoff played a key role in the campaign for passage of the UCC, working with lawyers, legislators, and business people in each state. By 1967 the UCC was adopted by every state except Louisiana and has become the most successful codification in American law. The UCC probably would not have succeeded without the complementary talents of Mentschikoff and Llewellyn. Their partnership "in life as in law" was formalized by their marriage on 31 October 1946. (Thereafter, Mentschikoff used the name Soia Mentschikoff Llewellyn in nonprofessional situations.)

In the course of her work on the code, Mentschikoff gained a reputation that impressed many leading academics, judges, and lawyers. The dean of Harvard Law School, Erwin Griswold, invited Mentschikoff to come to Harvard as a visiting professor in the fall of 1947. She taught commercial law and commercial arbitration, and although she had never taught before she was a great success. Many of her students credit her with teaching them how one apt phrase or word could clarify an issue or protect a client or a nation from catastrophe. She also demonstrated that a sense of timing and balance is crucial to a successful negotiation. They recalled her confidence in them and her advice and support in their professional and personal lives.

During the 1948–1949 academic year Griswold offered Mentschikoff a position on the permanent faculty when women students were not admitted and there had never been a woman of professorial rank. However, he did not extend the same offer to Llewellyn, who had joined her as a visiting professor in her second year in Cambridge. Mentschikoff refused the offer; Griswold believed that for the rest of her life she was angry at him for his failure to make a similar offer to Llewellyn.

Mentschikoff and Llewellyn returned to New York, where he tried unsuccessfully to get Mentschikoff a teaching position at Columbia University Law School. In 1951 Dean Edward Levi of the University of Chicago Law School invited Mentschikoff and Llewellyn to join the faculty, Mentschikoff as a professorial lecturer and Llewellyn as a tenured professor, in conformity with the university's antinepotism rules. Mentschikoff did not care about tenure; "if you're first rate, you'll make it" was her view. In her years at Chicago, Mentschikoff, the first woman on the faculty, was treated in all discernible ways as a tenured faculty member. She was a major force in the faculty and a close friend and trusted adviser to Levi. Her superb negotiating skills, mixed with her powerful charm, served the Law School well in some delicate situations. Her power to persuade any and all recalcitrants was legendary.

Mentschikoff taught commercial law and elements of law, as well as courses on law in the undergraduate school. Her students at Chicago spoke less of her magic in the classroom and more of her skills as a great teacher in discussions outside the classroom and through example. She gave both men and women students counsel, advice, and support in their personal lives as well as in their search for and choice of careers. Many of these relationships continued long after graduation. She simultaneously counseled wives of male law students that their primary job while their husbands were in law school and afterward was to support their husbands' careers in every way. (Mentschikoff did not seem to recognize the potential contradiction for her women students.)

At Chicago Mentschikoff began an ambitious study of commercial arbitration as one of the empirical studies at the Law School funded by the Ford Foundation. She was interested in the social and psychological context of this alternative method for resolving commercial disputes, as well as the implications for conventional legal processes. In an unusual step for that time, she brought a social psychologist in to work on these aspects of the project. Mentschikoff published two articles based on this study, but the projected final volume never appeared. Some of the participants speculated that she had learned what she sought and simply lost interest.

In the mid-1950s, the two young daughters of Mentschikoff's brother came to live with Mentschikoff and Llewellyn, who became, de facto, their parents. In 1962 Llewellyn died very suddenly. Mentschikoff was devastated by his death. In the following years she immersed herself in a number of public organizations. She served as a member of the U.S. delegation to the Hague Conference, the Commission on the Rights, Liberties and Responsibilities of American Indians, the panel of arbitrators of the International Center for the Settlement of Investment Disputes, and the executive committee of the Council for the Study of Mankind; she was also a fellow of the American Academy of Arts and Sciences. Her name was mentioned seriously in 1967 and again in 1975 in connection with a possible Supreme Court nomination.

In 1967 Mentschikoff began a seven-year tradition of teaching the winter quarter as a distinguished visiting professor at the University of Miami Law School. Her mother, who had lived with Mentschikoff virtually all of her life, was finding the Chicago winters hard, so Mentschikoff moved her to Miami. The informality of the Law School and long solitary walks on the beach perfectly suited Mentschikoff's temperament.

In 1972 Mentschikoff was the first woman named as a trustee of the RAND Corporation; in 1974 she became the first woman president of the Association of American Law Schools and one of the first woman deans of a major law school. Mentschikoff accepted the deanship at Miami only after gaining unique independence from the university for the Law School. In her eight-year tenure as dean, she brought in a group of outstanding, dedicated young faculty, instituted a tutorial program, made important additions to the curriculum, closely oversaw the construction of a new law school, and attracted outstanding students. She gained national recognition for Miami as a first-rate law school. The faculty characterized her alternately as "Czarina" and "Earth Mother," reflecting two important aspects of her personality that made this accomplishment possible.

Mentschikoff retired in 1982. In the good periods of her very last days of suffering with cancer, she worked on and finished dictating an expert affidavit for an international commercial arbitration on the significance of "good faith" in the UCC. Mentschikoff died in Coral Gables, Florida.

• Mentschikoff's papers are at the University of Miami. Her scholarly writings include "Unification of International Private Law," *Report of the American Bar Association Special Committee*, with Nicholas DeB. Katzenbach (1961); *Ius Privatum Gentium. Festschrift für Max Rheinstein*, ed. with Ernst von Cammerer and Konrad Sweigert (1969); "The Significance of Arbitration—A Preliminary Inquiry," *Law and Contemporary Problems* 17 (1952): 471, 698; "Letters of Credit: The Need for Uniform Legislation," *University of Chicago Law Review* 23 (1956): 571; "Commercial Arbitration," *Columbia Law Review* 61 (1961): 761, 846; "Highlights of the Uniform Commercial Code," *Modern Law Review* 27 (1964): 167; "Peaceful Repossession under the Uniform Commercial Code: A Constitutional and Economic Analysis," *William and Mary Law Review* 14 (1973): 767; "Llewellyn the Civilian," *Tulane Law Review* 56 (1982): 1125; and "Law: The Last of the Universal Disciplines," *University of Cincinnati Law Review* 54 (1986): 695, with Irwin Stotzky. Her casebooks were *Commercial Transactions: Cases and Materials* (1970) and *The Theory and Craft of American Law: Elements*, with Stotzky (1981). For her recollections of the drafting of the UCC, see "Reflections of a Drafter," in "Origins and Evolution: Drafters Reflect upon the Uniform Commercial Code," *Ohio State Law Journal* 43 (1982): 535, 537. See the *Miami News*, 28 Jan. 1982, for her contributions to the University of Miami Law School. An obituary is in the *New York Times*, 19 June 1984.

ZIPPORAH WISEMAN

MENZEL, Donald Howard (11 Apr. 1901–14 Dec. 1976), astrophysicist, was born in Florence, Colorado, the son of Charles Menzel, railway employee and businessman, and Ina Zint. Raised in the mining town of Leadville, Colorado, Menzel was encouraged to study science by his surroundings, his parents, and the writings of Jonathan Swift and Jules Verne. From about the age of six, he collected minerals, both for sale to passing tourists and for himself. His father taught him Morse code, and he soon built his own wireless transmitter and receiver, beginning a lifelong interest in amateur radio. With his mother's encouragement, Menzel also took up chemistry, establishing a laboratory in the barn and, eventually, setting up an office for analyzing ores at cut-rate prices.

In 1917 Menzel entered the University of Denver, where he continued to study chemistry and took composition courses with a view to becoming a writer. Events in his college years redirected his attention toward astronomy. In 1918 he witnessed a total solar eclipse, the first of sixteen he would see during his career. The next summer an accident in a chemical plant where Menzel was working damaged his lungs, forcing him out of the laboratory. Denver University astronomer Herbert A. Howe allowed him to use the school's telescopes. At the same time, one of his English professors urged Menzel to write to astronomer R. S. Dugan at Princeton. At Dugan's suggestion, Menzel joined the American Association of Variable Star Observers and began observing Mira-type variables. He received his bachelor's degree in 1920, and, the following year, wrote a master's thesis on eclipsing variable stars. The next fall he went on to Princeton to study astronomy with Dugan and his colleagues. Menzel wrote his dissertation on the physical interpretation of the spectra of low temperature stars. Using data from the Harvard College Observatory, he was able to complete this work in 1924. He then went briefly to the University of Iowa as an instructor and to Ohio State University as an assistant professor. In 1926 he married Florence Elizabeth Kreager; they had two children.

In the fall of 1926 Menzel joined the staff of the Lick Observatory on Mt. Hamilton in California. There he analyzed W. W. Campbell's collection of photographs of the chromospheric spectrum, taken at eclipse. Applying atomic theory, he not only found that the atomic weight of atoms in the chromosphere was unexpectedly low, but that the chromosphere was considerably hotter than expected. While he was at Lick, Menzel also began studies of planetary nebulae that would continue over several years. In 1932 Menzel accepted an appointment to the astronomy faculty of Harvard University, where he continued his studies of the spectrum of the solar chromosphere at eclipse. He also was intrigued by the coronagraph designed by French engineer and astronomer Bernard Lyot. This instrument made it possible to observe the solar corona regularly instead of just during eclipses. Using funds from the U.S. Department of Agriculture, Menzel arranged to have a coronagraph built and installed in 1940 at a new High Altitude Observatory (HAO) near Climax, Colorado. By the late 1930s, coronal activity had been linked with terrestrial magnetic storms and hence with radio fadeouts. During World War II, predicting radio transmission was of considerable military importance. Menzel arranged to have coronagraph observations that were made by Harvard astronomy graduate student Walter Orr Roberts at the HAO sent to Washington, D.C., and combined with data from other sources.

During the war years Menzel developed ties to several U.S. government patrons. Long interested in cryptography, he taught a course in the subject at Radcliffe and arranged for similar courses at other women's colleges. He also attempted to design an antiaircraft gunsight to be used against planes that attacked from the direction of the sun. In 1942 Menzel was commissioned as a lieutenant commander with the U.S. Navy, with special responsibilities for radio and radar communications. He moved to Washington, setting astronomy aside for a time. After the war Menzel returned to Cambridge and chaired Harvard's Department of Astronomy until 1949. He arranged for funding for the Climax observatory from both the University of Colorado and the National Bureau of Standards. Menzel also persuaded the U.S. Air Force that coronagraphic studies would aid its program of solar rocket research. A second coronagraph was built by Harvard in 1949 for the air force and installed at Sacramento Peak in New Mexico, near the White Sands Proving Ground. Menzel used observations from new coronagraphs at Climax and at "Sac Peak" to study the structure and motions of solar prominences, the cause of low temperatures in sunspots, and the origin of solar flares.

Menzel's success in funding, building, and using new instruments impressed the administration of Harvard University. In 1952, when Harlow Shapley retired as director of the Harvard College Observatory, Menzel was named acting director. Two years later he became director, a post he held until 1966. Menzel believed that the observatory needed new direction, and his administration was described by some as "the new regime." The observatory underwent a thorough housecleaning, and several new buildings were built. Harvard's Boyden Station, its observatory in South Africa, came to be jointly operated by an international coalition of six observatories. As a director of the Association of Universities for Research in Astronomy from 1957 to 1966, Menzel worked to make better radio telescopes available to Harvard astronomers. The largest change in the astronomy program at Harvard during his administration came in 1956 when the Smithsonian Astrophysical Observatory (SAO) moved from Washington, D.C., to the Harvard College Observatory grounds. Frederick L. Whipple, long a member of the Harvard astronomy faculty, became director of the SAO. This move sealed the transformation of astronomy at Harvard into an activity largely funded by the U.S. government. Menzel himself spent five years as a research scientist at the SAO after his retirement in 1971.

Menzel was elected to the American Academy of Arts and Sciences (1934), the American Philosophical Society (1940), and the National Academy of Sciences (1948). He served as president of the American Astronomical Society from 1954 to 1956 and was active in the International Astronomical Union. In addition to astronomical work, he was active writing popular science and science fiction, inventing, and playing bridge, chess, and musical instruments. He died in Cambridge, Massachusetts.

• Menzel's unpublished correspondence is in the collection of the Harvard University Archives and scattered through the papers of contemporary astronomers. His published books include *A Study of the Solar Chromosphere* (1931), *Our Sun* (1949), *Flying Saucers* (1953), *Mathematical Physics* (1953), and *Writing a Scientific Paper* (1961). An obituary is in *Sky and Telescope* 53 (Apr. 1977): 244–51.

PEGGY ALDRICH KIDWELL

MERCER, Charles Fenton (16 June 1778–4 May 1858), U.S. congressman and colonizationist, was born in Fredericksburg, Virginia, the son of James Mercer, a jurist and planter, and Eleanor Dick. Fenton was raised at "Marlborough," his grandfather's extensive plantation on the Rappahannock River. Slaves performed all work on the estate, which reinforced the child's perception that he held a privileged position in society. Although Mercer later came to loathe slavery in the abstract, a small number of slaves worked his farm and acted as servants throughout his long life.

Mercer's mother died when he was not yet two years old. At age fifteen, following his father's death, he moved to the home of his cousin James Mercer Garnett, where he received a private education. Two years later, he enrolled in the College of New Jersey (Princeton) in the junior class. There he fell under the influence of William Godwin's *Political Justice*, from which he learned that government could be a powerful instrument for promoting social change. In 1797, following his graduation at the top of his class, he remained at Princeton, to work toward a graduate degree in jurisprudence. When the Quasi War with France interrupted his studies in 1798, Mercer approached family friend and Federalist patriarch George Washington in search of a commission. Twice offered an officer's rank in the army, Mercer unexpectedly declined when he discovered that his service in the unpopular conflict would "interfere" with his political "advancement" in the Jeffersonian bastion of Virginia.

In 1804, following a brief tour of Britain and France, Mercer settled in the piedmont county of Loudoun, Virginia. "Solitary and friendless" by nature, the gloomy and egotistical attorney never married. Yet Mercer dreamed of a life in public politics, and in 1810 a retirement in his Federalist district allowed him to win a seat in the Virginia House of Delegates. There the young conservative began to piece together an interlocking economic program that foreshadowed the Whig party's American System, which he would later champion in Washington. An atypical Virginian who saw industrial capitalism as the best hope for his state's financial future, Mercer introduced legislation to reorganize and increase the number of state banks. His 1816 bill creating a Board of Public Works helped to centralize Virginia's haphazard system of roads and canals and transform the state, so he hoped, into "a unit in action."

Mercer supported an equally ambitious bill to fund a system of free primary and secondary education that passed the House but died in the Senate at the hands of Republicans, who instead appropriated the money to finance the University of Virginia. Mercer's reforms earned him the support of progressive elements around the state, as did his liberal-sounding rhetoric and his willingness to serve as a brigadier general in the militia during the War of 1812 (a conflict he had ardently opposed). This public affability, designed to make his minority Federalist party more palatable to the growing electorate, masked his private view that the white working class was "ignorant from birth and habit." His confidential writings demonstrated that he hoped to use the power of the state to discipline and control the working classes while perpetuating the prerogatives of the new business elite.

Mercer's view of humanity as a "corrupt mass" in need of control is best illustrated by the act that produced his greatest fame. In early 1816 an offhand comment led him to examine the unpublished records of the Virginia colonization debates of 1800–1804. Believing that racism (and not inherent ability) permanently relegated free blacks to the working class and thus made them a dangerous, discontented group in an industrializing society, Mercer approached his old Princeton schoolmate Elias B. Caldwell about establishing a West African homeland for free blacks. Together with Caldwell's brother-in-law, Robert Finley, the two men formed the American Colonization Society in Washington the following December. At the same time, Mercer pushed through the Virginia Assembly a resolution endorsing colonization. Until the society was reorganized in 1833, Mercer was nationally recognized as "the father of the Colonization Society." Although he regarded forced labor as a "blot" on American society, Mercer, like most antislavery Virginians, assuaged his embattled conscience by insisting that he could do little about slavery. If he hoped that colonization would allow for gradual emancipation in his home state, he failed to say so in either his public or private writings.

Elected to the House of Representatives in 1817, Mercer abandoned the dying Federalist party and became a Monroe Republican. There he labored with other National Conservatives, most notably Henry Clay and John Quincy Adams, to advance his economic and social agenda. His 1819 Slave Trade Act, ostensibly designed to close loopholes in the 1807 act outlawing the international trade, also appropriated money for the purchase of Liberia. Although most free African Americans resolutely claimed the right of American citizenship, some free blacks, weary of American racism, applied directly to Mercer for passage to Africa. The following year Mercer returned to the topic with a bill that branded the slave trade piracy and thus a capital crime. His later efforts to codify Anglo-American suppression of the trade perished, however, when the Adams-authored treaty became an issue in the presidential election of 1824.

During the Adams administration, Mercer, then chairman of the House committee on roads and canals, introduced legislation to connect the Chesapeake and Ohio Valley by canal. With Adams's endorsement, Mercer became president of the C&O Canal Company, a semipublic corporation. Despite the conflict of interest, the congressman remained company president until 1833, when the board of directors, futilely seeking President Andrew Jackson's support, replaced Mercer with Jackson's Tennessee friend, John Eaton.

Dismayed by both the loss of his company and the American Colonization Society's attempts to appeal to the northern antislavery movement by ridding itself of its southern leadership, Mercer became (according to critics within his own party) "a mere eater and drinker of the good things at Washington." Despite the leading role he played in reforming Virginia's constitution at the 1829–1830 state convention, the younger members of his party wished to replace him with a more active Whig prior to the election of 1840. Although he successfully beat back the challenge, Mercer, humiliated, resigned from Congress at the end of 1839. Accepting the position of cashier at the Union Bank in Tallahassee, Florida, Mercer traveled to Britain on business.

There he met a group of English investors interested in buying land in the Republic of Texas. An 1844 meeting with President Sam Houston resulted in the creation of the Mercer Colony. The venture collapsed, however, in 1848 when a federal court voided his contract at the behest of a group of Texas farmers. Following an unsuccessful attempt to obtain a diplomatic post from President-elect Zachary Taylor, Mercer wandered aimlessly about Europe, finally settling in 1855 in Paris.

Ill with cancer, Mercer returned in 1857 to Virginia, where he was nursed by relatives. After several painful operations, he died in Alexandria one month prior to his eightieth birthday.

• The core collection of Mercer family papers is in the Virginia Historical Society, although the New Jersey Historical Society has a small number of Charles Fenton Mercer's letters. Malcolm Watkins, *A Cultural History of Marlborough, Virginia* (1968), discusses life on the Mercer plantation. Material relating to his Princeton years can be found in the New-York Historical Society and in Arthur Lowndes, ed., *Correspondence of John Henry Hobart* (1912). For Mercer's opinions on the politics of the late 1790s, see his 1849 autobiographical sketch at the Virginia State Library and his anonymous 1845 treatise, *An Exposition of the Weakness and Inefficiency of the Government of the United States of North America*. Mercer's activities on the state level are discussed in his *Report on Banks* (1816) and *Discourse on Popular Education* (1826). For information about the removal of free blacks, which concerned him for most of his life, see his *Address to the American Colonization Society* (1854) and *Colonization of Free People of Colour* (1827) as well as his enormous collection of documents, *Slave Trade* (1830). Mercer's support for internal improvements is chronicled in his *Chesapeake and Ohio Canal* (1834).

Douglas R. Egerton, *Charles Fenton Mercer and the Trial of National Conservatism* (1989), is the only full-length biography. James H. Broussard, *The Southern Federalists, 1800–1816* (1978), puts Mercer's early career in context, as does David H. Fischer, *The Revolution of American Conservatism* (1965). Betty Fladeland, *Men and Brothers: Anglo-American Antislavery Cooperation* (1972), is useful on Mercer as a colonizationist.

DOUGLAS R. EGERTON

MERCER, Henry Chapman (24 Jun. 1856–9 Mar. 1930), archaeologist, collector, and tilemaker, was born in Doylestown, Pennsylvania, the son of William Robert Mercer, a naval officer, and Mary Rebecca Chapman. His father retired from the navy to become a gentleman farmer and gardener. His mother's sister, Elizabeth, came into a sizable fortune when her husband, Timothy Bigelow Lawrence of Boston, serving as a diplomat in Italy, died in 1869. Cultured and widely traveled, and with no children of her own, she returned to Doylestown and became a major influence in the lives of Mercer's family, underwriting the costs of his education and travels. Mercer graduated from Harvard University in 1879 and studied at the University of Pennsylvania Law School. Although admitted to the Philadelphia County Bar in 1881, he never practiced law. Mercer never married or had children.

Mercer's adult life consisted of a sequence of major projects all interconnected by his love of history and all undertaken with an almost religious fervor. In the 1880s he traveled extensively in Europe and Egypt, making long journeys by raft and houseboat down the Danube, Rhone, and Loire rivers. During these travels he took photographs, kept journals, and collected cultural artifacts.

Until the late 1890s he lived the life of a gentleman scholar, focusing his interest on the material culture of the New World and the existence of original man in the Delaware Valley. His first archaeological monograph, *The Lenape Stone, or the Indian and the Mammoth* (1885), a study of a prehistoric artifact found in a local farmer's field, crystalized his thinking about the historical significance of material culture and established him as an important ethnologist.

In 1891 he was invited to join the curatorial staff of the University of Pennsylvania Museum's newly formed Department of Archaeology and Paleontology, where he served until 1897. For the next six years, he explored sites in the Delaware Valley looking without success for evidence of prehistoric toolmaking that would prove the existence of what he termed "original" man in the United States. In 1893 the Spanish government awarded him a bronze medal for his exhibit of American Indian specimens at the Exposición Histórico-Americana at Madrid. In 1893 he was elected a member of the Academy of Natural Sciences of Philadelphia, and in 1895 he was elected to the American Philosophical Society. His fieldwork led to a steady flow of scholarly papers and he was an associate editor of *American Naturalist* from 1893 to 1897. He dug in archaeological sites in Maine, Indiana, Ohio, Virginia, and Tennessee. In 1895 he led the Corwith Expedition to the Yucatán, publishing his findings in *Hill Caves of the Yucatan* in 1896. In that year he left the museum, disgruntled with the politics that were involved. He moved his work to his studio, "Indian House," in Doylestown, and published *Researches Upon the Antiquity of Man in the Delaware Valley and the Eastern United States* in 1897.

Now unaffiliated with any institution, he turned his attention to the affairs of the Bucks County Historical Society, which he helped found in 1880. When, by chance, he attended a penny-lot sale of junk, looking for used fireplace tongs, he was seized with the idea that the cast-off implements of pioneer settlers were in fact archaeological specimens of preindustrial American life that lent themselves to the intellectual and methodological processes that he had used with prehistoric objects. These "Tools of the Nation Maker," as he later described them, satisfied his need to link antiquity to modern man. He continued collecting, cataloging, and exhibiting these implements, as well as writing about them, until his death.

While searching for potter's tools in 1897 he discovered a nearly extinct redware craft tradition. In attempting to resuscitate a local Pennsylvania-German pottery as a living history adjunct to the historical society, he began to work in clay himself, soon settling on decorative tile forms. In 1898, after preliminary experiments, he established the Moravian Pottery and Tile Works in Doylestown, named to honor early settlers of Bucks County. He developed and patented a handwork system of manufacturing relief-decorated tiles. These pictorial tiles for pavings and fireplaces were an immediate success with his architect friends in Philadelphia and Boston, where the new aesthetic of the Arts and Crafts Movement demanded handcrafted products. They influenced the work of other important American tilemakers, including William Grueby, Mary Chase Perry, Ernest Batchelder, and Herman Carl Mueller. His handcrafted tile operation became a successful business, supplying tiles for installations throughout the United States. He adapted many of his early designs from medieval English tiles that he had seen at the British Museum. In 1902 he devised and patented a process for making tile mosaics—akin to the design of stained glass windows—for a large decorative pavement he was commissioned to create for the new Pennsylvania Commonwealth Capitol building in Harrisburg. He drew heavily on his collection of tools for the imagery of nearly 400 mosaics depicting the life and lore of Pennsylvania. In 1904 his tiles won a grand prize at the St. Louis World's Fair. In 1906 he developed his "brocade" style of tiles in which pictorial elements cut in silhouette and modeled in deep relief formed pictures in a background of concrete. This style grew out of his increasing interest in concrete as a primary building material.

Mercer described himself as a rediscoverer of the past. He expressed his discoveries in his tiles. He viewed storytelling—his term for any literary program underlying a work of art—as his essential task. He meant his tiles to be beautiful but never at the cost of surrendering their meanings. As he moved beyond simple relief tiles in standard geometric forms to his mosaic style and then on to sculptural brocades he gained the ability to treat increasingly complex subjects. Through his major theme, the discovery of the New World, he created a new American iconography in tiles. Retiring by nature and disinclined to associate with other makers of decorative objects, he nonetheless became through his tiles a major figure in the Arts and Crafts Movement.

In 1907 Mercer began an architectural career at age fifty-one with the design and construction of the first of his three state-of-the-art exposed, reinforced-concrete buildings. This was his residence, Fonthill, a structure inspired by his "literary and artistic dreams, and memories of travel" (quoted in *Memorial Services*, p. 39). In 1911 and 1912 he designed and oversaw the construction of a new tile works, modeled after California missions. In 1916 he completed and presented to the Bucks County Historical Society a fireproof museum of his own unconventional design to house his now vast tool collection, which remains preeminent in its field. He pioneered the method of visible storage, in which he arranged artifacts in open display, making the entire collection accessible for study.

The Society of Arts and Crafts in Boston, of which he was a master craftsman, awarded him its bronze medal for excellence in 1913. In 1916 he received an honorary Doctor of Science degree from Franklin and Marshall College. In 1921 the American Institute of Architects awarded him its gold medal for distinguished achievements in ceramic art. He continued his active life as a scholar, collector, and writer all the while creating new designs for his thriving tile works. After his last European trip in 1904 he became more reclusive and was periodically beset with illness. He died in Doylestown. The Arts and Crafts Guild of Philadelphia awarded him its first Master Craftsman Medal a month after his death.

His tile works continued to operate under the supervision of his assistant since 1897, Frank Swain, who with his wife Laura resided at Fonthill for many years, preserving Mercer's legacy. The Bucks County Department of Parks and Recreation acquired it in 1967 to operate as a living history museum.

Mercer played a key role in the revitalization of the decorative ceramic tile as an element of architecture, was a major promoter of the Arts and Crafts Movement's handcraft ideology, and innovated the use of exposed reinforced concrete in building construction. In addition, he created a major museum of American preindustrial implements and wrote seminal books on the material culture of Colonial America that remain standard references in the field.

• Mercer's papers are in the Spruance Library of the Bucks County Historical Society in Doylestown, Pennsylvania. Mercer published ten books, including *The Bible in Iron* (1914), *The Origin of Log Houses in the United States* (1926), and *Ancient Carpenter's Tools* (1929), and over 170 articles, reviews, papers, reports, monographs, and other publications. His buildings, Fonthill, the Moravian Pottery and Tile Works, and the Mercer Museum, all located in Doylestown, are primary sources for the study of his architecture and his tiles. All are listed on the National Register of Historic Places and open to the public year-round. The first comprehensive study of his life and work is Cleota Reed, *Henry Chapman Mercer and the Moravian Pottery and Tile Works* (1987), based on a study of primary sources. It contains a bibliography of Mercer's publications. Obituaries and remembrances are collected in Bucks County Historical Society, *Memorial Services* (1930).

CLEOTA REED

MERCER, Jesse (16 Dec. 1769–6 Sept. 1841), Baptist minister, was born in Halifax County, North Carolina, the son of Silas Mercer, a Baptist minister, and Dorcas Greene. Before the revolutionary war, Silas Mercer moved his family to a farm in Wilkes County, Georgia. Jesse Mercer received little formal education in these years.

Mercer married Sabrina Chivers in 1788. Both children of this marriage died young. Mercer began farming 100 acres given to him by his father while also studying diligently and preaching. After two years of this regimen, Mercer was ordained and became pastor of Sardis Baptist Church in Wilkes County, Georgia.

Continuing as pastor of this church, Mercer sold the farm and studied classical languages and theology for two years under John Springer, a Presbyterian minister. The next year he studied at the classical academy established by his father. Upon his father's death in 1796, Mercer accepted the calls of the three churches his father had pastored. For the next thirty years, Mercer pastored four Georgia churches simultaneously, preaching in each church once a month.

Mercer quickly gained a reputation as an intelligent and moving preacher. By 1800 his services were in high demand for weddings and funerals, for which he often was recompensed liberally. When Georgia governor William Rabun died in office in 1819, the state legislature called on Mercer to deliver a memorial sermon before both houses.

Mercer's standing as a respected leader provided opportunities for political influence. In 1798 Mercer was one of three delegates elected from Wilkes County to the convention for amending the Georgia constitution. At the convention he authored the new constitution's article on religious freedom. Mercer regretted, however, having once run for state senate, having become convinced that only the greatest crises should induce ministers to serve in political office. Because of this conviction Mercer refused to listen to the suggestions of his friends that he run for governor, and on another occasion he refused to accept his nomination to the Georgia electoral college. Mercer held that the important duties of ministers should keep them clear of everyday politics, but he believed that ministers had a special duty to speak out regarding constitutional issues.

Mercer applied most of his energies to leadership of the Baptist denomination. He organized the first Powelton Conference, which met at Mercer's church in Powelton, Georgia, in 1801. This conference and its successors effectively promoted itinerant preaching and mission activity among the Creek Indians. In 1815 Mercer organized, and was elected president of, the Powelton Baptist Society for Foreign Missions. Mercer also led Georgia Baptists in the movement to support the missionary initiatives of Luther Rice and of the General Missionary Convention of the Baptist Denomination in the United States, which was largely inspired by Rice's efforts. Mercer attended several of these "triennial conventions," which met for the purpose of Baptist cooperative effort in missions, and from 1830 until his death was president of the convention's Baptist Board of Foreign Missions.

In addition to missions, the need for education drew Mercer's attention. Believing that knowledge was "indispensable to ministers," Mercer served as an advocate, contributor, and trustee of Columbian College (now George Washington University). Mercer's efforts on behalf of theological education were rewarded in 1831 when the Georgia Baptist Convention resolved to establish a "Classical and Theological School." Named in honor of Mercer's labors on behalf of Baptist education, Mercer Institute (now Mercer University) opened in 1833 in Penfield, Georgia.

The authority with which Baptists invested Mercer derived from his steady commitment to both piety and orthodoxy. He expressed this commitment with pathos and intelligence. Mercer's devotion to God and to his ministerial calling won him the esteem of his colleagues and the love of his parishioners. When praying or preaching, it was not unusual for Mercer to weep and to melt his congregations to tears. He often engaged in itinerant preaching tours and encouraged his fellow ministers to do the same. His churches experienced periodic revivals, when unusually large numbers of people were converted. Mercer also gave liberal amounts of money to Christian causes such as education, missions, temperance, and Bible distribution. Although he was accustomed to taking brandy every day on the advice of physicians, he embraced abstinence and advocated temperance once he became convinced that his alcohol consumption had been construed as an encouragement to drunkenness. He even established a temperance newspaper that he underwrote for six years.

Mercer buttressed his piety by an intelligent advocacy of orthodoxy, teaching the Calvinism of English Baptists John Gill and Andrew Fuller. Against the Arminianism of the Methodists and of some Baptists, Mercer advanced the Calvinist view "that the atonement is special, both in its provisions and applications." But he found it necessary to defend his activist Calvinism from "primitive" Baptists whose hyper-Calvinism precluded participation in missionary, educational, and temperance endeavors. Although some primitive Baptists in Georgia seceded from the "missionary" Baptists, Mercer's efforts held the large majority together for the cooperative support of missions and education. In recognition of Mercer's leadership, his colleagues elected him moderator of the Georgia Baptist Association for twenty-two years (1816, 1818–1838) and moderator of the Georgia Baptist Convention for nineteen years (1822–1840).

Mercer acquired an important weapon in his arsenal for the promotion of orthodoxy in 1833, when he purchased the *Christian Index* (still published), a weekly newspaper that had served the interest of Baptist missions since 1822. Mercer served as editor until 1840 and underwrote the paper's losses. In its columns he advanced the causes of missions, education, personal piety, and orthodox theology. Mercer's colleagues apparently valued most his teaching on the nature of church purity and power. Mercer frequently championed the necessity of strict moral discipline in the churches, but he believed that discipline belonged to individual churches alone and not to associations of churches. Hence, Mercer's admirers called him "the able expounder of gospel discipline" and termed the *Christian Index* "the scourge of ecclesiastical tyranny."

In 1827 Mercer married Nancy Mills Simons, Sabrina Mercer having died the previous year. Nancy was the widow of a wealthy merchant and horse breeder, Abraham Simons, who was Jewish. Nancy Mercer died on 21 May 1841 after a long illness. Jesse Mercer died only four months later while visiting James Carter, a Baptist pastor, in Butts County, Georgia.

Mercer left large bequests to Mercer University and Baptist missions, but his greatest legacy was to the Baptist denomination, especially in Georgia, where, more than any other pastor, he solidified Baptist commitment to Calvinist orthodoxy, congregational discipline, local church autonomy, missions, and education.

• Mercer's papers, consisting of a number of letters and an account book, are at Mercer University. Other letters and papers are in the Butler Family Papers and Keith Read Papers, University of Georgia at Athens, and the Luther Rice Papers, George Washington University. Mercer's important works are *The Cluster of Spiritual Songs, Divine Hymns, and Sacred Poems* (multiple editions, 1810–1835), *A History of the Georgia Baptist Association* (1838), *Ten Letters . . . of the Atonement* (1830), and numerous circular letters published in the minutes of the Georgia Baptist Association and of the Georgia Baptist Convention. C. Ray Brewster, *The Cluster of Jesse Mercer* (1983), is a fine edition of Mercer's hymnal and contains a bibliography of Mercer's works and a chronology of his life. Charles D. Mallary, *Memoirs of Elder Jesse Mercer* (1844), is the most important source on Mercer. Samuel Boykin, *History of the Baptist Denomination in Georgia* (1881), also is important. See also, Robert Gardner, Charles Walker et al., *A History of the Georgia Baptist Association, 1784–1984* (1988).

GREGORY A. WILLS

MERCER, John (6 Feb. 1705–14 Oct. 1768), lawyer and writer, was born in Dublin, Ireland, the son of John Mercer, a merchant, and Grace Fenton. He is said to have briefly attended Trinity College. He emigrated to Virginia in 1720 and by 1724 captained a sloop, acting as a merchant until he married Catherine Mason in 1725. The couple settled at Marlborough on the Potomac, and Mercer began practicing law. He gradually built a grand house and large estate at Marlborough.

Mercer compiled *A Compleat Collection of the Laws of Maryland* (1727), for which William Parks paid him £11 10s. He was probably influenced directly or indirectly by the attitudes and writings of Thomas Bordley, the leader of Maryland's bar and assembly, who had repeatedly defended the rights of Americans and expressed contempt for the English authorities who would abridge them. Mercer early demonstrated a similar concern for equality and citizens' rights. In 1727 the Virginia House of Burgesses passed an act exempting from taxes all persons employed in iron works and requiring the public to build roads to the mines. To some, the act seemed to favor Governor Alexander Spotswood and his cronies. Mercer objected, and in 1730 wrote a proposition against the act that was read before the Stafford County Court. The House of Burgesses said on 28 May 1730 that the proposition contained "false and scandalous Reflections upon the Legislature and the Justices of the General Court and other Courts of this Colony." The sergeant at arms was ordered to seize Mercer. He appeared at the assembly on 8 June 1730, was fined, and, after his apology, released. His objection, however, was successful. The act was subsequently amended, and the requirement to build roads at the public expense to the iron works removed. To those persons living in the counties (including Stafford) who would have had to build the roads, Mercer had heroically opposed arbitrary authority.

Mercer's violent temper often landed him in trouble. The Prince William County Court justices complained in 1734 that he was sometimes presumptuous and dictatorial to them. On 13 June the Virginia Council agreed that his behavior was disreputable and suspended him from practicing law in court for six months. During his enforced idleness, he compiled *An Exact Abridgement of the Laws of Virginia* (1737). On 23 April 1735 he petitioned for a new license. It was granted, although excepting "the County Court of Prince William." On 27 November 1738 the council voted to allow him to practice in Prince William County, but within the year its justices again complained of him, and on 28 October 1739 the council found that "Mercer has behaved himself very insolently to the Justices of the County Court of Prince William and excited the People to condemn them and their Authority." Consequently he was "forever disabled" to practice before the Prince William Court. That same year, he brought out *A Continuation of the Abridgement* (1739).

On 16 April 1741 he was readmitted to practice before the General Court in Williamsburg. On 12 November 1748 the council appointed him chief justice of Stafford County. Three Stafford colleagues complained against him on 16 April 1753, but the council merely reprimanded him on 14 June for his "Intemperance opprobrious Language on the Bench and indecent Treatment of the other Justices," retaining him as chief justice. The council turned him out of the commission of 3 May 1757 for acting as an attorney before the Stafford County Court. On 11 November 1758, however, he was reinstated as chief justice of Stafford County, perhaps in part because he had compiled another useful, up-to-date legal treatise, *An Exact Abridgement of the Laws of Virginia* which appeared in Glasgow (1759). He remained chief justice until his death.

Mercer and his contemporaries knew that the American West would be the site of future settlements and that future fortunes would be made there. A group of Virginians and the Maryland frontiersman Thomas Cresap organized the Ohio Company in 1747, petitioned the Crown for a grant for 500,000 acres on the Ohio River, and sent out Christopher Gist to explore the Ohio. The group decided to hire Mercer as their lawyer on 3 December 1750. On 23 May 1751 he drew up the original charter of the Ohio Company, at Stafford Court House. He was then admitted as a partner after "advancing his twentieth part of the whole Expence"; he acted as secretary of the company. The members subsequently established one trading post at the head of the Potomac, the site of Cumberland, Maryland, and a second on the Monongahela River, at the site of the present Brownsville, Pennsylvania. Early in 1754 the company began to build Fort Prince George at the forks of the Ohio. With the beginning of the French and Indian War, the company's activities on the frontier halted. Mercer drew up "The Case of the Ohio Company" in 1759 and 1760 and revised it in 1761 for the Board of Trade. The company's plans to renew its activities on the frontier failed because of the Proclamation of 1763, which forbade settlement beyond the heads of the rivers that flowed into the Atlantic. Subsequently Mercer's son George Mercer visited London several times as the Ohio Company's agent, but failed to gain the grant.

Mercer's major literary contribution occurred in the mid-1750s when he wrote a series of satires in prose and verse, using various mock-illiterate personae, against Governor Robert Dinwiddie. The satires anticipate the techniques of James Russell Lowell, George Washington Harris, and Mark Twain, while using a number of local, American types (the southern moonshiner), products (corn whiskey), and Americanisms ("crap" for "crop"). Mercer's primary reason for satirizing Dinwiddie was because of the tax he imposed on land titles (the Pistole Fee), but he also criticized his supposedly cowardly leadership in the French and Indian War, his favoring of fellow Scotchmen, and his control of the press. Thus Mercer has Dinwiddie, speaking in his Scotch accent, say, "I hae the press, under my thumb, / to spak my pleasure, or be dumb, / so that nathing can be printed, / Until it hath by me been minted" (Davis, p. 25). The collection of mock-illiterate letters and poems was called "The Dinwiddianae" or (in public and in print) "The Little Book." Evidently copies of the manuscript had circulated widely before 1757, when Mercer's fine poem in the 13 October *Maryland Gazette* was attributed to "the author of *The Little Book*."

Mercer's most important political writing occurred in 1765. Edmund Randolph wrote that Mercer "was the first in Virginia who distinctly elucidated upon paper, the principles which justified the opposition to the Stamp Act. He showed them in manuscript to his friends." Mercer had arrived in Williamsburg on 8 April, and news of the Stamp Act's certain passage and the text of the act reached Williamsburg about that time. He immediately prepared an alphabetical table of the taxes "as the most effectual method of demonstrating the exorbitance of the duty" and wrote a preface to the table denouncing the oppressive nature of the act, the "unconstitutional Manner of imposing it," and the basic illegality of taxation without representation. He claimed that the Stamp Act directly violated chapter forty of the Magna Carta, which guaranteed that recourse to law should be cheaply available to all Englishmen. He and his clerk were besieged for copies. Governor Francis Fauquier forbade printer Joseph Royle to publish any remarks or observations on the Stamp Act. Finally, the table alone appeared in the *Virginia Gazette* of 26 April, but Mercer's manuscript preface, circulated widely in Virginia, was summarized in the *New York Gazette*, 23 May, and printed in full in the *New York Gazette*, 4 July, and in the *Maryland Gazette*, 18 July 1765. Mercer's remarks on the Stamp Act and his alphabetical table of the exorbitant taxes must have been known by all the burgesses present in Williamsburg in April and May. His preface prepared the way for the first official American opposition against the Stamp Act, the Virginia Resolves, which Patrick Henry presented in the House of Burgesses on 30 May 1765.

On 5 October 1765 Mercer and the other magistrates of Stafford County wrote Governor Fauquier that they would not serve after 11 November because "that unconstitutional Act of Parliament" would involve them in perjury. Mercer wrote the refusal, which echoed his preface to the alphabetical table of the stamp act. Mercer's son Colonel George Mercer made the mistake of accepting the post of stamp distributor for Virginia. Richard Henry Lee burned him in effigy, an act that initiated a feud between the Mercer and Lee families. John Mercer entered the quarrel with a long letter in the *Virginia Gazette* of 26 September 1766. It is the best and most entertaining of the many epistles in the feud.

In his last years, the indefatigable, ever optimistic, and entrepreneurial Mercer established a brewery and projected a glass factory, but his efforts failed, and when he died at Marlborough, he was heavily in debt. He left behind the greatest law library of colonial Virginia and, after William Byrd's, the greatest personal library.

Mercer's first wife died in 1750, and later that year he married Ann Roy, daughter of Dr. Mongo Roy of Port Royal. With his first wife, he had five children who lived to maturity, including George Mercer, John Fenton Mercer, and James Mercer. With his second wife, he again had five children who lived to maturity, including John Francis Mercer. Mercer also was the guardian of his nephew George Mason, who was brought up in Mercer's home and acquired his education primarily in Mercer's library. The actions, beliefs, and writings of Mercer undoubtedly influenced young Mason, author of the Virginia Declaration of Rights (1776).

• A transcription of Mercer's Bible, with genealogical notes, is at the Maryland Hall of Records. Mercer's Land Book is at the Virginia State Library. Mercer's Ledgers, B (1725–1732, with his journal in the back) and G (1744–1750), are at the Bucks County History Society, Doylestown, Penn. His correspondence with Daniel Parke Custis, Martha Dandridge Custis, and George Washington is in the Custis papers, Virginia Historical Society. Mercer's papers relating to the Ohio Company are at the University of Pittsburgh, and in Lois Mulkearn, ed., *George Mercer Papers Relating to the Ohio Company of Virginia* (1954). A manuscript of "The Dinwiddianae" is extant at the Huntington Library; it is also in Richard Beale Davis, ed., *The Colonial Virginia Satirist*, n.s. 57, pt. 1 of *Transactions of the American Philosophical Society* (1967).

Mercer's difficulties with his fellow lawyers are documented in the *Executive Journals of the Council of Colonial Virginia*, vols. 4 (1930), 5 (1945), and 6 (1966). His law books are studied by Herbert A. Johnson, *Imported Eighteenth-Century Law Treatises in American Libraries 1700–1799* (1978), and by William Hamilton Bryson, *Census of Law Books in Colonial Virginia* (1978). The fullest biography of Mercer, together with a detailed archaeological investigation of the site of Marlborough, is C. Malcolm Watkins, *The Cultural History of Marlborough, Virginia* (1968). Mercer's writings on the Stamp Act are identified and discussed in J. A. Leo Lemay, "John Mercer and the Stamp Act in Virginia, 1764–1765," *Virginia Magazine of History and Biography* 91 (1983): 3–38, where additional references may be found.

J. A. LEO LEMAY

MERCER, John Francis (17 May 1759–30 Aug. 1821), planter and officeholder, was born at "Marlborough Point," Stafford County, Virginia, the son of John Mercer, a lawyer and wealthy landowner, and Ann Roy. John Francis Mercer graduated from the College of William and Mary in 1775. In February 1776 he enlisted in the Third Virginia Regiment. Despite his youth—he was not yet seventeen—his family's social status enabled him to secure a commission as a first lieutenant. In a little more than a year Mercer achieved the rank of captain. He was wounded in September 1777 at Brandywine. In June 1778 he was commissioned a major and became an aide-de-camp to General Charles Lee. Lee's retreat and insubordination to the commander in chief at Monmouth later that month and his subsequent court-martial ended his career, and Mercer resigned as well from the regular army in July 1779. Resuming his military career in 1780 as a lieutenant colonel in the Virginia militia, he served briefly under General Lafayette and commanded a corps of militia grenadiers at the battle of Yorktown.

Mercer read law in 1779 with Thomas Jefferson, who was then governor of Virginia, and at the College of William and Mary, 1782–1783. He began practicing law in Fredericksburg, Virginia, in 1781. His political career began in 1782, when at age twenty-three he was elected as one of Virginia's delegates to Congress under the Articles of Confederation. He remained until 1785, serving on numerous congressional committees involved with defense and military matters. Outraged that American commissioners Benjamin Franklin, John Adams, and John Jay had signed a peace treaty with the British without consulting the French, in violation of specific instructions from Congress, Mercer became an outspoken critic of the treaty.

In 1785 Mercer moved to Maryland to marry Sophia Sprigg. Her father was Richard Sprigg, a wealthy planter at "Strawberry Hill" in Anne Arundel County. Sophia inherited land and slaves from her grandparents and father, including the 1,478-acre "West River Farm." Mercer brought some slaves of his own from Virginia and began planting tobacco at West River Farm. The Mercers had at least two sons and a daughter.

Mercer's first political office in Maryland came in 1787 with his appointment as one of the state's five delegates to the Philadelphia convention that wrote the U.S. Constitution. Mercer's appointment was due more to the prominence of his and his wife's families than to his own demonstrated political abilities. He was willing to serve, a critical factor for the Maryland Assembly, which had previously appointed several better-known men who had declined to represent the state in Philadelphia.

Mercer did not attend the Philadelphia convention until 6 August 1787, nearly two and one-half months after it started, and then he stayed less than two weeks, probably because of a lack of money for his expenses. Despite his brief attendance in Philadelphia, he spoke often and made clear his opposition to the proposed Constitution then taking shape. Mercer allied with Luther Martin, one of the other Maryland delegates in the convention. Both men objected to the strong central government and sharply curtailed role for the states supported by most of the convention's delegates. Mercer opposed popular elections for members of the House of Representatives, believing the large size of congressional districts would make it impossible for the electorate to judge the quality of candidates. He also predicted that urban residents would vote as a block, effectively disfranchising many rural farmers. The premise underlying all of Mercer's objections was the danger of a powerful government distant from the people. He believed that the quality of government and individual liberty were both best assured when government was close to the governed.

Once the proposed Constitution was referred to the states for ratification, Mercer became an outspoken anti-Federalist. However, most Marylanders supported the proposed Constitution, and when elections were held in early April 1788 for delegates to the state's ratification convention, only three counties returned anti-Federalist slates. One of those counties was Anne Arundel, where Mercer joined three others in a last-minute campaign that defeated the heavily favored Federalist slate. Appealing directly to the electorate in the four days before the election, they posted handbills around the county condemning the proposed Constitution for its lack of a bill of rights.

Only twelve of the seventy-six delegates elected to Maryland's ratification convention opposed the Constitution. Being so outnumbered, the anti-Federalists could not hope to win an outright rejection of the new form of government. Instead, under the leadership of former governor William Paca, the anti-Federalists planned to introduce proposed amendments—a bill of rights—for the consideration of the delegates. The Federalist majority, however, successfully barred Paca from even introducing his proposed amendments.

Mercer spoke at length in the ratification convention concerning his objections to the proposed Constitution. He said that the long, hot summer had taken a toll on the delegates in Philadelphia, and in their haste to adjourn, they had made "capital alterations" to the proposed Constitution in the last few days of the convention without considering the full implications of them. As a result, Mercer argued, the Constitution sent to the states was "not the result of Mature deliberations." He denounced the broad taxing power given Congress and the provision that federal treaties would be binding on the states, and he criticized the Constitution's grant to Congress of unlimited authority to create inferior federal courts. Mercer warned of the danger inherent in giving Congress the right to call out the state militias without state approval, a powerful argument, since most free, adult, white males in the states were legally members of the militia. Mercer predicted that a national government would be torn apart by sectional differences. "The Eastern [states] threaten the southern states, about their *negroes*," he proclaimed, "& will always hold up that article to carry other points."

After several days of futile debate, the anti-Federalists struck a deal with the Federalist majority in the convention. Paca agreed to vote for the proposed Constitution in exchange for a special committee that would examine his proposed bill of rights. Mercer was named to the committee. Despite the Federalists' 9 to 4 superiority, by the morning of 28 April the committee had agreed unanimously or by large majorities to support twelve amendments to the Constitution. All of the anti-Federalists except Mercer were willing to satisfy themselves with this and give up the fight for other proposed amendments. Mercer insisted that the Federalists support even more of the anti-Federalist agenda. Finally, he agreed to support the compromise if the Federalists would approve one more amendment—a guarantee that the state militia would not be subject to martial law in peacetime. The Federalists agreed. Despite his promise, however, Mercer then pressed other amendments, and the fragile accord between the opposing members of the amendments committee consequently broke down. The Federalist leaders of the ratification convention called for a vote on the proposed Constitution, and it passed by a large majority. The amendments approved by the special committee were not even considered. Mercer's intransigence may have been due to principle or to his lack of familiarity with Maryland politics and its leaders. Whatever the cause, his refusal to compromise was a blow to Maryland's anti-Federalists. Once the state's ratification convention adjourned, they had lost their best forum for arguing that the proposed Constitution needed a bill of rights. The argument for a bill of rights that Mercer and his fellow anti-Federalists waged in Maryland's ratification convention nevertheless proved a boon to opponents of the Constitution elsewhere, especially in Virginia. That state's ratification convention in June adopted a proposed bill of rights to accompany its ratification of the Constitution. Later states to ratify also endorsed the idea. As a result, the first federal Congress in 1789 approved twelve proposed constitutional amendments. The states ratified ten of these, which became known as the Bill of Rights.

Mercer's distrust of a powerful and distant central government and his insistence on the importance of individual liberty was popular with his Anne Arundel County neighbors. They elected him as their delegate to the Maryland General Assembly in 1788 and again in 1791–1792. In 1792 Mercer was appointed to fill a seat in Congress and was elected to the Third Congress and served until he resigned in April 1794. In Congress, he opposed the George Washington administration's efforts to create a strong federal government and was especially critical of Treasury Secretary Alexander Hamilton's fiscal policies. When William Branch Giles of Virginia introduced nine resolutions censuring Hamilton's conduct in negotiating loans in Europe, Mercer was one of a handful of representatives who spoke in favor of them. Hamilton was exonerated, but Mercer's role in the effort to restrain or remove the Treasury secretary publicly aligned him with Thomas Jefferson and other opponents of a strong central government, who soon formed their own opposition political party.

In 1800 the voters of Anne Arundel County again elected Mercer to the house of delegates, and in 1801 the general assembly elected him to the first of two consecutive one-year terms as governor of Maryland. Maryland's constitution provided for a weak executive, but Mercer did what he could to influence public policy and to make the state more democratic. He initiated the practice of sending formal messages to the legislature to outline his views, supported the successful effort to remove the high property qualifications for state senators and members of the house of delegates, and in 1802 Mercer and his fellow Republicans celebrated the general assembly's approval of a bill that removed property qualifications as a condition of suffrage. For the first time since 1670, all free white males over the age of twenty-one could vote in Maryland.

After leaving the governor's office, Mercer served three more terms in the house of delegates, 1803–1806, then ended his office-holding career. He remained active in democratic politics in the state until 1812, when he announced his support for the Federalists, because they opposed going to war with Great Britain.

Suffering from poor health, Mercer traveled to Philadelphia in 1821 to seek medical attention. He died while visiting the city.

Mercer was a secondary figure among the Marylanders who led the opposition to the U.S. Constitution and the strong national government it proposed. William Paca, Samuel Chase, and Luther Martin were all better known and more politically experienced, but only Mercer remained true to the principles of states' rights and small government, and it was he who made democracy a reality in Maryland politics.

• Few of Mercer's personal papers have survived, and they are scattered. Records relating to his public career and landholdings are at the Maryland State Archives in Annapolis. Notes taken during Mercer's presentation to Maryland's ratification convention in Apr. 1788 and a contemporary memorandum outlining his role in the unsuccessful effort to work out a compromise between Federalists and anti-Federalists on the amendments committee are in MdHR 1592, Maryland State Archives. A copy of the handbill Mercer signed and distributed in his successful campaign for election as an anti-Federalist delegate to the ratification convention is in MdHR 1796-A-152, Maryland State Archives. The biography of

Mercer in Frank F. White, Jr., ed., *The Governors of Maryland* (1970), contains many errors. His family history and public career are outlined in Edward C. Papenfuse et al., eds., *A Biographical Dictionary of the Maryland Legislature, 1635–1789*, vol. 2 (1985). Some additional information is in J. Reaney Kelly, "Cedar Park, Its People and Its History," *Maryland Historical Magazine* 58 (1963): 30–53; and James Mercer Garnett, "John Francis Mercer," *Maryland Historical Magazine* 2 (1907): 191–213. For Mercer's opposition to the proposed U.S. Constitution in the state ratification convention, see Gregory A. Stiverson, "Maryland's Antifederalists and the Perfection of the U.S. Constitution," *Maryland Historical Magazine* 83 (1988): 18–35.

GREGORY A. STIVERSON

MERCER, Johnny (18 Nov. 1909–25 June 1976), popular composer, lyricist, and singer, was born John Herndon Mercer in Savannah, Georgia, the son of George Mercer, an attorney, and Lillian Ciucevich. Throughout his childhood Mercer was fascinated with the popular songs of the day as well as by Gilbert and Sullivan operettas and the blues and spirituals of southern blacks. From 1922 to 1927 he attended Virginia's Woodbury Forest Preparatory School, where he wrote light verse and songs. Shortly after graduation he pursued a career as an actor and singer in New York. There he married Ginger Meehan, a dancer, in 1931 and soon had two children. While his acting career languished, success as a songwriter came in 1933 when he collaborated with Hoagy Carmichael on "Lazybones," a song whose authentic regional flavor provided a refreshing change from the confected sentimentalisms that had long been staples of popular song. In 1933 Mercer also found success as a singer, joining Paul Whiteman's band; he continued to perform as a vocalist through the 1930s, frequently being heard on radio with the Benny Goodman and Bob Crosby bands.

Moving to Hollywood in 1935, Mercer became one of the most prolific songwriters during the next two decades of film musicals. Working with many composers, he wrote songs that became independently popular and have remained so. With Richard Whiting he wrote the lyrics to "Too Marvelous for Words" (1937) and "Hooray for Hollywood" (1938) and in 1938, with Harry Warren, "You Must Have Been a Beautiful Baby" and "Jeepers Creepers," the latter Mercer's first song to be nominated for an Academy Award. In 1942, with Victor Schertzinger, he wrote "Tangerine" and, with Jerome Kern, "I'm Old Fashioned" and "Dearly Beloved," which also was nominated for an Oscar. Mercer found his greatest success in collaboration with Harold Arlen, whose blues-oriented melodies brought out Mercer's distinctively earthy elegance. Together they wrote such classics as "Blues in the Night" (1941), "That Old Black Magic" (1942), "My Shining Hour" (1943), and "Ac-cent-tchu-ate the Positive" (1944)—all Academy Award nominees—as well as the quintessential torch song, "One for My Baby (and One More for the Road)" (1943). In 1946 Mercer, after eight nominations, finally won his first Oscar with "On the Atchison, Topeka, and the Santa Fe," with composer Harry Warren, for the movie *The Harvey Girls*.

In addition to writing songs for more than eighty films, Mercer wrote lyrics for independent songs that were popularized by big bands of the swing era. Mercer's facility with the vernacular, his feeling for jazz, and his skill as a singer enabled him to fit words dexterously to such intricate and sinuous melodies as Ziggy Elman's "And the Angels Sing" (1939), Rube Bloom's "Day In—Day Out" (1939) and "Fools Rush In" (1940), and Carmichael's "Skylark" (1942). In 1945 Mercer set words to David Raksin's haunting theme music for the film *Laura*, producing a standard that was popularized by Woody Herman's orchestra and several other big bands.

Throughout the late 1930s and early 1940s Mercer continued his career as a singer by making numerous recordings, including several duets with Bing Crosby, as well as by performing on network radio shows, including his own "Johnny Mercer's Music Shop." Together with songwriter and producer Buddy DeSylva and Glenn Wallichs, owner of a Hollywood music store, Mercer founded Capitol Records in 1942. The company attracted such young jazz stars as Stan Kenton and Freddy Slack and singers Nat "King" Cole and Jo Stafford. Mercer helped his new company succeed by recording his own songs, such as "G.I. Jive" (1944) and "Dream" (1945), for both of which he also composed the music.

Mercer's only major setbacks as a songwriter came when he wrote songs for the Broadway musical theater. *St. Louis Woman* (1946), *Texas Li'l Darlin'* (1949), *Top Banana* (1951), *Saratoga* (1959), and *Foxy* (1964) were all box-office failures; only *L'il Abner* (1956), with music by Gene dePaul, had a truly successful run on Broadway. Mercer, a great writer of individual songs, had the misfortune to write during an era when Broadway musicals demanded not just good songs, but ones that were integrally related to the plot and characters of the book. Hollywood soon followed suit, but instead of continuing to create their own musicals the studios merely began making film versions of successful Broadway musicals, a development that meant fewer opportunities for songwriters such as Mercer. He continued to write individual songs for films, however, including "In the Cool, Cool, Cool of the Evening" for *Here Comes the Groom* (1951, with Carmichael), which earned Mercer his second Oscar. The last major full-scale original Hollywood musicals for which he wrote lyrics were *Seven Brides for Seven Brothers* (1953) and *Daddy Long Legs* (1955).

Even as the era of original film musicals passed, Mercer continued to contribute to movies, writing songs that became independently popular. Two of these, "Moon River" (1961) for *Breakfast at Tiffany's* and the title song for *Days of Wine and Roses* (1962), both with music by Henry Mancini, won the Academy Award. Mercer also created lyrics in English for such foreign songs as "Autumn Leaves" in 1950, "When the World Was Young" in 1951, and "Glow-Worm" in 1952, and he added lyrics to the jazz instrumentals

"Early Autumn" in 1952, "Midnight Sun" in 1954, and "Satin Doll" in 1958. Even in the face of massive changes in popular music style Mercer continued to be successful with such lyrics as "I Wanna Be Around" (1959) and "Summer Wind" (1965).

He died in Los Angeles, leaving behind a group of song lyrics that not only were enormously popular in their own time, but, in many cases, have endured as some of the great standards of American popular song. Mercer's extraordinary range and versatility, developed through working with a highly diverse range of composers, earned him the distinction of being one of the few lyricists whose fame equaled that of the best popular composers of the century.

• Mercer's papers are located at Georgia State University. While no biography has been written, *Our Huckleberry Friend: The Life, Times and Lyrics of Johnny Mercer*, ed. Bob Bach and Ginger Mercer (1982), contains biographical anecdotes. Max Wilk, *They're Playing Our Song* (1973), and Gene Lee, *Singers and the Song* (1987), offer personal profiles. David Ewen, *American Songwriters* (1987), gives a brief biographical sketch, and Philip Furia, *The Poets of Tin Pan Alley* (1990), devotes a chapter to analyzing Mercer's development as a lyricist. An obituary is in the *New York Times*, 26 June 1976.

PHILIP FURIA

MERCER, Mabel (3 Feb. 1900–20 Apr. 1984), cabaret/concert singer and song stylist, was born Mabel Alice Wadham at Burton-upon-Trent, Staffordshire, England, the daughter of Benjamin Mercer, an African-American tumbler or acrobat, and Emily Mame Wadham, an English-Welsh music-hall entertainer. Her parents were unmarried, and Mabel was reared by maternal grandparents in north Wales in a family of singers, dancers, and painters. At age seven she was placed in a Catholic convent school in Manchester. Her mother, before going on a world tour, took Mabel onto the stage of an empty music hall. Climbing to the balcony, she yelled, "All right, sing! And I want to understand every word!" Mabel experienced the first of lifelong stage fright, but her mother heard every word (Balliett, p. 60).

At the convent school, Mabel was ridiculed as a golliwog and told for the first time she was black (she had her mother's blue eyes, with golden skin and frizzy black hair). To make matters worse she was a "gammy," who crossed herself with her left hand. The white children told her no man would ever marry her because of her kinky hair. Mabel found comfort by becoming the traditional "seven-year-old Catholic for life" who never missed a day at Mass. She left school at age fourteen, and when she learned her father's name, she took Mercer as her surname and began a long but unsuccessful search for him.

Auditioning as a music-hall singer and dancer, she was always fired as soon as the manager noticed her hair. Mercer was rescued by an aunt who, with her husband and sons, had a traveling vaudeville troupe in the Midlands. To accommodate her hair they became "The Five Romanys," a gypsy song and dance group.

During World War I the "orphan" joined a Cockney girl named Kay to sing and dance wherever they could find engagements. They went to France, Belgium, and the Netherlands. As one of "The Chocolate Kiddies," she concealed her frizz beneath an enormous blond beehive wig. Meeting her first black entertainers from America, the girl who had thought herself the only colored person on the planet was transported. In the revue called Coloured Society, she performed minstrel acts mixed with Italian opera, ballads, and spirituals. Mercer starred as the soprano in "Lucia" and was inspired to take concert singing lessons. When the flu pandemic of 1918 swept Europe, the teenager replaced the ill orchestra director, wearing white tie and tails and a monocle.

Mercer sang in both the London and Paris choruses of Lew Leslie's "Blackbirds of 1926," but recognition as a soloist began at clubs in Paris where American jazz was the rage. Soft-voiced and shy, she sang with a small megaphone in a pure soprano as she moved from table to table, enchanting the international set at the famous Bricktop's cafe with her humor and charm. Royalty, diplomats, millionaires, and intellectuals of the Lost Generation were devoted to her; Marlene Dietrich arranged the recording of an early Mercer song, "You'd Better Go Now." Mercer performed the sassy compositions of Cole Porter and met jazz pioneers Duke Ellington and Louis Armstrong and singer Paul Robeson. She became a lifelong friend of the playboy (future) duke of Windsor and of England's King George VI. Songs were composed especially for her. Mercer could belt out "Black Minnie Sings the Blues" and "Mandy," or reduce grown men to tears with ballads by Kern, Hammerstein, and Rodgers and Hart. Her style, enunciation, and phrasing introduced a new style of singing popular songs. The unjudgmental depths of her understanding won her a devoted following, especially among homosexuals.

World War II forced Mercer to flee to New York in 1938. Her mother, now residing in upstate New York and fearing reprisals from white neighbors, pretended to be her daughter's aunt. To Mercer's keen disappointment they seldom met. Mercer lived in Harlem and opened at Le Ruban Bleu at 4 East 56th street. When a tonsillectomy changed her voice to a husky mezzo soprano, she rose to fame. During an unprecedented seven years at Tony's, a small New York night club, the "*doyenne* of American popular singing" introduced a vast range of ballads, poetry, and show tunes, while seated with great dignity in a highbacked chair.

"What a lesson to watch that entrance," said Bobby Short, one of her many disciples. "A monarch adored by and adoring all her subjects. . . . She developed enormous style such as I had never heard. It was a wonderfully warm, entertaining, informing presence. I often saw Sinatra and Billie Holiday and Lena Horne and even Edith Piaff in her audience."

"Her gift with a song is enough to make other vocalists seek a different occupation," said Frank Sinatra. To Leonard Bernstein she was "the eternal guardian of elegance in popular music" (Livingstone, p. 60). Metropolitan opera star Eileen Farrell considered Mercer the best teacher she ever had, despite the fact that the cabaret singer never taught a lesson in her life. Margaret Whiting remembered, "One night Peggy Lee, Duke Ellington, Frank Sinatra, and I were there at the same time and we all agreed that we sat at her feet. . . . When she would start to talk about lyrics, she would say, 'Just mean them.' I think Mabel had the most respect of anyone in entertainment. She was very special and beloved."

Mercer engaged in a "paper marriage" in 1940 to the young African-American singer Kelsey Pharr II, who predeceased her in 1960. She became a U.S. citizen in 1952.

Mercer sang the French street song "Tu reviendras," opening the opera "The Consul," by Gian-Carlo Menotti, which won the New York Drama Critics Award for 1950 and a Pulitzer Prize. However, like most of the great stars of the golden age of cabaret (the 1940s and 1950s), with the closing of night clubs during the next three decades, she found herself with fewer and fewer singing engagements. She bought a farm near Chatham, New York, and moved there in the late 1950s, living happily with her dogs and cats, but returning to New York City for occasional appearances. As she grew older, she suffered financial hardship. Among her close friends were the prolific composer Alec Wilder and her manager and lover, Harry Beard.

Despite her failing voice, Mercer was rediscovered and made more famous in her seventies by the young agent Donald F. Smith. After Beard's death in 1981, Smith revived "Mabel Mercer Madness." She sang to sell-out audiences at the Playboy Clubs in London and Chicago, as well as touring in Los Angeles and San Francisco. Her seventy-fifth birthday was celebrated at an enormous party at the St. Regis Hotel in New York, where a plaque marked the Mabel Mercer Room. Atlantic Records reissued many of her recordings as "A Tribute to Mabel Mercer on the Occasion of Her 75th Birthday." She appeared twice in concert with her friend and "disciple," Metropolitan opera star Eileen Farrell, in the Kool Jazz Festival and at Alice Tully Hall, both in New York City. She was the first distinguished recipient of *Stereo Review*'s Mabel Mercer Award; President Ronald Reagan honored her with the Presidential Medal of Freedom in 1983.

Mercer died in Pittsfield, Massachusetts, and was buried beside Harry Beard. Her fame continued to grow posthumously. The Mabel Mercer Foundation, Inc., a nonprofit corporation organized by Smith and others, launched annual, weeklong Cabaret Conventions at Town Hall, New York City, in 1986. These soon burgeoned into other cabaret events, spreading to San Francisco and elsewhere. Mercer's posthumous influence led to cabaret contagion in the 1990s and created new venues for gifted vocalists and for the classic American popular song.

• Most of Mercer's surviving family records, photos, and letters are at the Schomburg Center for Research in Black Culture, New York Public Library. Important interviews with Mercer appear in the following: Whitney Balliett, "Profiles: A Queenly Aura," *New Yorker*, 18 Nov. 1972, p. 60; Balliett, "Our Footloose Correspondents in the Country," *New Yorker*, 6 Sept. 1982, pp. 40–49, reprinted as a chapter in Balliett, *American Singers* (1988); William Livingstone, "The Singer's Singer," *Stereo Review*, Feb. 1975, p. 60; and Roland Wild, "She Never Looked Back," *Park East*, Mar. 1953, p. 19. Remembrances of Mercer at Bricktop's in Paris are recounted in James Haskins, *Mabel Mercer: A Life* (1987), which also contains a discography, and in Bobby Short, *Bobby Short, the Life and Times of a Saloon Singer* (1995).

MARGARET CHENEY

MERCER, Margaret (1 July 1791–17 Sept. 1846), antislavery reformer and educator, was born in Annapolis, Maryland, the daughter of John Francis, a politician, and Sophie Sprigg. Margaret, a quiet, frail child, spent most of her childhood in Annapolis, where her father held a variety of public offices, including service as governor for one term. Her family also spent time at their ancestral country home, "Cedar Park." Intelligent and scholarly, Margaret completed a postsecondary education under the supervision of her father, a man known for his liberal views. Following in his footsteps, Margaret devoted herself to her church and donated time and money to local Sunday schools, which provided elementary education as well as religious instruction to the poor.

Although she worked for a number of social causes, the one Mercer is probably best known for is her work in the antislavery movement. Arguably the best-known female southern reformer of her era, she had deep-seated convictions about slavery and was an active member of the American Colonization Society (ACS) from almost the beginning of its inception in 1817. This society was an organization of southern origins that aimed to encourage manumission of American slaves and to remove free blacks to Liberia. Mercer not only encouraged her peers to free their slaves, but she set an admirable example by emancipating the slaves she had inherited upon her father's death. She then used her own personal funds to provide passage for her former slaves who were willing to go to Liberia in the late 1820s. Mercer sold her remaining property to purchase the freedom of other slaves and to help relocate them, choosing a life of principled poverty over a life of affluence. After her funds were exhausted, she continued to work to raise funds for the society, and this money was then used to aid educational efforts in Liberia, as well as to emancipate and relocate former slaves.

Although Mercer continued to be an advocate of the antislavery movement throughout her life, she began to focus on a different area, teaching. She taught school for twenty-five years after she freed her slaves, and critics are divided as to whether she taught out of financial necessity or because she felt spiritually led to teach. Both factors may very well have influenced her vocation. It is certainly true that her financial situation after she freed her slaves and sold her property was tenuous, and that for a woman of her background teaching was one of the few respected means of making a living. It is also true that she had already demonstrated through her previous work with the Sunday schools a spiritual fervor and a desire to educate the poor intellectually as well as spiritually, a zeal that led Mercer to found the Cedar Park Institute, originally located on the grounds of her family estate. As the years passed, the school changed locations a few times, moving to Franklin, Maryland, for a short time before being permanently established in Belmont, Virginia. There, on a run-down farm, she began a new boarding school for girls, which gained renown for its strong moral and religious training, along with its emphasis on academic excellence. Mercer, deeply committed to Christianity and to the welfare of her students, wrote religious verse and authored three treatises addressing moral and spiritual development—"Popular Lectures on Ethics; or, Moral Obligation" in 1837, "Studies for Bible Classes" (1841), and "Ethics: A Series of Lectures to Young Ladies"—all written for her students and used as part of the school's curriculum. Over time the institute developed into a kind of community, centered around the school and a church that was built with funds raised from the townspeople. The residents of the Belmont area came to the school leaders for advice and resolution of their problems, familial, social, and economic, and the area children attended the institute's free classes in primary subjects and in agriculture.

Mercer battled tuberculosis for most of her life; she died from that disease at her home in Belmont, where a memorial to her still stands in the old churchyard.

Critics have questioned the success of her various reforming efforts, noting that her efforts with the ACS seem to have been in vain. For example, a black doctor she trained in America died after three years in Liberia. Other former slaves wrote to her of their struggles: "There is no meat . . . the monkeys are wild . . . the leopards howl . . . the savages caught us, but praise the Lord they set us free" (Whitton, p. 162). Liberia proved to be a difficult environment for house servants used to the amenities of Maryland and Virginia. However, while Liberian resettlement was not the solution it was purported to be, the work that Mercer did in rallying antislavery sentiment remains noteworthy, as is her role as a woman reformer in the nineteenth-century South.

Her career as an educator and an author seems to have had a more lasting impact. Both her religious verse and her educational treatises were recognized as valuable both during her lifetime and after her death. The memory of her work among the students and residents of the Belmont area also endures, and the memorial in Belmont is an acknowledgement of her impact on nineteenth-century southern education.

• Biographical and autobiographical information on Mercer can be found in Caspar Morris, *Memoir of Miss Margaret Mercer* (1848); Lucian Lamar Knight, *The Biographical Dictionary of Southern Authors* (1978); Mary Ormsbee Whitton, *These Were the Women, USA 1776–1860* (1954); and Austin Allibone, *A Critical Dictionary of English Literature* (1899). See also *Mrs. Hales Woman's Record* (1853). Obituaries are in the *Maryland Colonization Journal* (Nov. 1846), and in the Washington, D.C., *Daily National Intelligencer*, 22 Sept. 1946.

AMRITA MYERS

MERCIER, Alfred (3 June 1816–12 May 1894), writer and physician, was born Charles Alfred Mercier in McDonoughville, Louisiana, the son of Jean-Baptiste Mercier, a plantation owner, and Marie-Héloïse Leduc. In accordance with the practice common among upper-class French families in Louisiana of educating their Creole sons in Paris, Mercier's parents sent him to the Collège Louis le Grand in 1830. Inspired by his reading there of classical and romantic works—especially those by Sir Walter Scott, Bernardin de Saint-Pierre, Chateaubriand, and Lamartine—Mercier put off his previous intention of studying law in favor of pursuing literary ambitions. In 1838 he went back to Louisiana and then visited Boston to improve his English, but when his brother-in-law Pierre Soulé encouraged him to join the Louisiana bar, Mercier refused and returned to Paris to continue his attempts at writing. He succeeded in 1842 with the warmly received publication of two romantic narrative poems, *La Rose de Smyrne* and *L'Ermite du Niagara*, and a collection of shorter poems, many about Louisiana, called *Erato*. In the 1840s he traveled through Europe gathering much material that would serve him later in his novels, such as *Le Fou de Palerme* (1873). Upon his return to France he wrote a play, *Hénoch Jédésias*, the manuscript of which was destroyed by pillagers during the Revolution of 1848. While in Paris he faced a serious illness but was nursed back to health by Virginie Vezian, whom he married in 1849; they had three children.

Finding his revenues from writing inadequate, Mercier decided to follow in his brother Armand's footsteps and pursue a career in medicine. He received his degree in 1855 upon the completion of his dissertation on the relationship between typhoid fever and consumption. Mercier practiced as a family physician in New Orleans and helped to found the Société Médicale there in 1858. In 1859 he crossed to France again in order to deliver a paper on the treatment of yellow fever in New Orleans, receive an award for his medical scholarship, and temporarily practice medicine in Normandy. From that vantage point he followed the developments of the American Civil War and came to fear for the cultural integrity of the South as the threat of a northern victory increased. In 1863, although Mercier was opposed to slavery, his belief in southern independence led him to appeal for French assistance on behalf of the South in a pamphlet, *Du Panlatinisme: Necéssité d'une alliance entre la France et la Confédération du Sud*.

In the wake of the Confederacy's military downfall, Mercier became intent on preserving his bailiwick of southern culture: the French way of life in Louisiana. Directly after the Civil War he returned to New Orleans to minister not only to the physical but also to the cultural well being of its citizens. Toward these ends, he conceived of an organization devoted to perpetuating the French language in Louisiana; encouraging local scientific, literary, and artistic achievement; and forming an association of mutual assistance. On 12 January 1876 he founded just such an organization in the Athénée Louisianais. With Mercier's guidance, the Athénée attended to immediate political needs, such as lobbying against the 1878 Reconstruction order that eliminated French from elementary education. Furthermore, the organization sought to establish a more permanent legacy by creating the periodical *Comptes Rendues de L'Athénée Louisianais* for the publication of local writing in French. With regard to the latter, Mercier once commented, "Il y a beaucoup de bon dans les *Comptes Rendues*; tout n'est pas de première qualité; néanmoins, ceux qui nous suivront et désireront connaitre l'état de la langue française en Louisiane à notre époque, y trouveront des renseignements utiles." ("There are many fine works in the *Comptes Rendues*, although not all of its publications are of the first order; nevertheless, those who succeed us and want to know the state of the French language during our period will find useful information there.")

At the same time that Mercier served as a physician in New Orleans, he contributed prolifically to the *Comptes Rendues*. As in his youth, he continued to compose much poetry, such as "Esprit Charmant" and "Tawanta." In addition to verse, Mercier generated philological treatises such as the highly acclaimed "Etude sur la langue Créole en Louisiane" (July 1880), literary criticism such as "Dante Alighieri et la *Divine Comédie*" (Jan. 1886), scientific articles such as "Sommeil, rêves, somnambulisme" (Mar. 1889), and travel narratives such as "Excursion dans les Pyrénées" (July 1889). Among his several novels, *L'Habitation Saint Ybars* (1881) is notable for its depiction of antebellum Louisiana plantation life, its portrayal of both positive and negative relationships between masters and slaves, and its rendering of dialogue in Creole patois.

For his many services, the French government recognized Mercier by inducting him into the Legion of Honor in 1885, and upon his death in New Orleans the members of the Athénée Louisianais declared him their secretary in perpetuity. Despite his considerable literary output and public activity, Mercier's works and life have received relatively little sustained critical attention. Even as he was writing, however, Mercier knew that he and his culture existed on marginal terms. Neither fully French nor completely American, the Creole culture of Louisiana faded in its political, social, and cultural influence in a process that began with the Louisiana Purchase of 1803 and intensified after the Civil War. In a long philosophical poem entitled *Réditus et Ascalaphos*, Mercier wrote, "La vie est un naufrage; et l'étude est le port / Où l'homme qui se sauve attend la douce mort." ("Life is a shipwreck, and study is the port where the man who saves himself awaits sweet death.") Through the process of constructing a literary sanctuary wherein French Louisiana was central rather than marginal, Alfred Mercier advanced and inspired a unique culture and created one of its most voluminous and diverse legacies.

• Mercier's other books are *Biographie de Pierre Soulé* (1848), *La fille du prêtre* (1877), *Emile des Ormiers* (1886), *Lidia* (1887), *Fortunia* (1888), and *Johnelle* (1891). Edward Laroque Tinker, *Les écrits de langue française en Louisiane au XIXe siècle* (1932), pp. 359–64, provides a bibliography of Mercier's publications. Rena Marie LaCroix, "Dr. Alfred Mercier: The Man and His Works" (master's thesis, Louisiana State Univ., 1929), and Ruby Van Allen Caulfield, *The French Literature of Louisiana* (1929), discuss Mercier's major works. Personal writing and letters can be found in Gloria Nobles Robertson, "The Diaries of Dr. Alfred Mercier" (master's thesis, Louisiana State Univ., 1947). For a contemporary reflection on Mercier, see Alcée Fortier, "Hommage à la mémoire de Dr. Alfred Mercier," *Comptes Rendues du Athénée Louisianais*, 18 May 1894.

FLOYD D. CHEUNG

MERCK, George Wilhelm (29 Mar. 1894–9 Nov. 1957), pharmaceutical manufacturer, was born in New York City, the son of George Merck, a pharmaceutical manufacturer, and Friedrike Schenck. His early education took place at the Newark and Morristown academies, both in New Jersey. He then attended Harvard University, graduating with an A.B. in 1915. After graduation, he went to work at his father's pharmaceutical firm, Merck & Co. By working in a wide variety of capacities, Merck learned the business thoroughly. In 1917 he married Josephine Carey Wall; they had two children.

Merck became president of Merck & Co. in 1925 while his father, who had resigned the presidency for reasons of health, continued as chairman of the board. In 1926, the year after Merck and his first wife divorced, he married Serena Stevens; they had three children. In 1927 Merck & Co. merged with Powers-Weightman-Rosengarten Company, a pharmaceutical company based in Philadelphia, to become Merck & Co., Inc. Merck became president of the consolidated company, which had assets of $9 million, slightly more than half of which had come from Powers-Weightman-Rosengarten.

The Great Depression did not slow the growth of Merck & Co., largely because of an extensive expansion program that began with the building of an independent nonprofit laboratory, the Merck Institute for Therapeutic Research, in Rahway, New Jersey. Built at a cost of $200,000, it was opened by Merck's father in April 1933. In the following year the firm opened a new plant designed for organic preparations, in 1935 a new administrative building, and in 1936 the renovated power plant. In 1939 the company created Experimental Plantations, Inc., a wholly owned subsidiary whose purpose was to grow tropical plants of possible medical use in Guatemala and Costa Rica.

Under Merck's leadership, the firm produced a significant number of important new pharmaceuticals during the 1930s. Mecholyl, a vasodilator, was discovered in 1933, and in the following year a new inhalation anesthetic, vinethene, was patented. Merck & Co.

also produced anti-syphilis medications and quinine, the drug used to treat malaria. A new process for the synthesis of ephedrine, the stimulant found in the Chinese medicinal plant ma huong, was developed in the Merck laboratories.

The company was a leader in the synthesis and production of vitamins. Vitamin B_1 (thiamin) was first produced synthetically in 1936, followed two years later by the creation of vitamin E. B_6 was synthesized in Merck laboratories and produced in 1939, followed by pantothenic acid, a member of the B vitamin family, in 1940 and biotin in 1942. Merck & Co. made many other vitamins commercially available for the first time, including vitamin C, niacin, vitamin B_2 (riboflavin), calcium panthothenate, vitamin K, and menadione.

The firm led the way in the development of penicillin. Research into the drug began in 1940, and by 1942 the first case of bacteremia was successfully treated with it in the United States. In 1943 Merck & Co. began exporting the drug to England for the use of the U.S. Army Medical Corps. A plant devoted to penicillin production was opened in Merck's Canadian subsidiary, and by 1944 the firm was supplying large quantities to the American armed forces. In the spring of 1945 production of the drug for civilian populations began. Merck & Co. also was primarily responsible for the development of streptomycin, an antibiotic active against both gram-positive and gram-negative bacteria, including species like streptococci that are resistant to other antibiotics. It was especially important in the treatment of tuberculosis. The drug was first produced in 1944, and commercial shipments began two years later.

Merck also served the U.S. government as an adviser on medical supplies and biological warfare, work that would eventually win him the Medal of Merit. He was a member of the advisory committee to the Army and Navy Munitions Board from 1939 to 1951, chairing the committee from 1949 to 1951. He served on the National Research Council's committee on drugs and medical supplies from 1942 to 1945. His involvement with biological warfare research included directing the biological warfare work of the war research service (1942–1944), consulting with the secretary of state on issues of biological warfare, and chairing the U.S. biological warfare committee (1944–1945).

Merck was elected chairman of the board of Merck & Co. in 1949, continuing in this role when Merck & Co. merged with Sharpe & Dohme in 1953. He served on the board of the National Science Foundation from 1951 to 1957, as well as on the boards of numerous other scientific, research, and charitable organizations. He died in West Orange, New Jersey.

Under Merck's leadership, Merck & Co. became one of the foremost American pharmaceutical manufacturers. Besides producing more than 1,500 products, the company was known for the publications it issued, especially *The Merck Index*, an encyclopedia of drugs and chemicals with medicinal or scientific uses; *The Merck Manual of Therapeutics and Materia Medica*, a medical reference work; and the *Merck Report*, a quarterly devoted to pharmaceutical topics. Merck's dedication to furthering scientific research meant that he often funded projects that did not offer immediate remuneration. Especially interested in fostering close ties between industrial and academic research, he established fellowships, scholarships, and grants at universities and research institutions across the United States, including a $100,000 fund in conjunction with the National Academy of Sciences for young researchers in chemical and biological research.

• For further information on Merck's ideas of research and the relationship between industrial and academic research, see his article "An Essential Partnership—The Chemical Industry and Medicine," *Industrial and Engineering Chemistry*, July 1935. Some discussion of the place of Merck & Co. in the chemical and pharmaceutical industry is given in William Haynes, *American Chemical Industry* (6 vols., 1945–1954; see esp. vol. 6), and in Tom Mahoney, *The Merchants of Life* (1959). See articles in *Time*, 18 Aug. 1952; and "The Merck Tradition," *Medical Times*, Oct. 1958. Obituaries are in the *New York Times*, 10 Nov. 1957, and *Chemical and Engineering News*, 25 Nov. 1957.

ELIZABETH ZOE VICARY

MEREDITH, Edna C. Elliott (25 Apr. 1879–1 Jan. 1961), publisher, was born in Des Moines, Iowa, the daughter of Samuel Mathew Elliott and Adeline Mary Jones. She grew up in Des Moines, and after briefly attending Iowa State College (now Iowa State University) she married Edwin Thomas Meredith in 1896. The couple became the owners and publishers of *Farmer's Tribune*, a Populist newspaper, which they had received as a wedding gift from Edwin's grandfather. Edwin-Meredith had worked for the paper for two years already, and understanding its tenuous financial situation, he changed its emphasis from politics to agriculture. The success of this effort inspired him to create a new monthly magazine, *Successful Farming*, which became a major agricultural journal and established him as a spokesman on the concerns of farmers. As a result of his publishing success and his knowledge of agricultural issues, Edwin entered politics. He served as a member of the Advisory Committee on Excess Profits for the Treasury Department, as a representative to the National Industrial Conference of 1919, and as the secretary of agriculture under President Woodrow Wilson. By 1928 Edwin was a serious candidate for U.S. president; however, he had begun to suffer from heart troubles, and he died that year.

During Edwin Meredith's political career, the popular Merediths had become well known for social entertaining, and Edna Meredith received special recognition as a consummate hostess. "Mrs. Meredith's table" was used by many in Washington society to describe exemplary grace and elegance in formal entertaining. Edna had supported Edwin's political forays, distinguishing herself as an encouraging, gracious, and supportive wife. During this time Edna Meredith also displayed her own public spiritedness by taking a noted interest in the needs of the ill and wounded servicemen at Walter Reed Hospital. On Edwin's death most of his estate, including a significant share of the publishing company, went to Edna, with the remainder going to their two children.

Her husband's death did not inhibit Edna Meredith from continuing her political activity. Instead of supporting Al Smith, the Democratic presidential candidate in 1928, she publicly endorsed fellow Iowan Herbert Hoover, the Republican nominee. She did not approve of Smith's anti-Prohibition views, his farm policies, and his ties to the Tammany Hall political machine in New York City.

Meredith continued her public political apostasy in 1932 when she again supported Hoover, this time against Democrat Franklin D. Roosevelt. She also opposed Roosevelt's reelection in 1936 and 1940. She did not approve of the New Deal or of Roosevelt's receiving an unprecedented third term as president. In 1936 she led in founding the National Coalition of Women Supporting Alfred M. Landon for President. In 1940 she declared her support for Republican presidential candidate Wendell Willkie. Despite her actions, though, she still considered herself a Democrat.

In addition to gaining notice for her conspicuous political actions, Meredith assumed the presidency of Meredith Publishing Company, where she earlier had been the business manager, and the company increasingly experienced success. In 1922 her husband had started a new magazine, *Fruit, Garden, and Home*, changing its name two years later to *Better Homes and Gardens*. By 1929, when Meredith became corporate vice president, secretary of the company, and a member of the board of directors and turned the presidency over to her son-in-law, Fred Bohen, Meredith Publishing Company was a prosperous major publishing firm with *Better Homes and Gardens* its premier publication. Meredith's influence coupled with the leadership of Bohen and her son, E. T. Meredith, Jr., who became vice president, treasurer, and general manager in 1935, facilitated the production not only of the two popular magazines (*Successful Farming* continued to thrive as well) but also of the celebrated *Better Homes and Gardens Cook Book*, published first in 1930. The company also profitably marketed many other "family service" books. Meredith and those handling the company's operations remained loyal to Edwin Meredith's concept of "service journalism," publications dedicated to information exchange on practical topics. The Meredith family offered Meredith Publishing Company common stock for public purchase in 1946, and in 1956 Meredith gave up her company titles. By then Meredith Publishing Company was producing 70 million copies of magazines and books each year.

Meredith also became known for her philanthropy, particularly in Des Moines, where, for example, she purchased iron lungs for two local hospitals and provided funds for a journalism building at Drake University. She also received recognition for her support of 4-H clubs in Iowa. Most of all, though, she became noted during World War II for helping military personnel. She spearheaded the establishment of a service club at Camp Dodge in Des Moines and opened up her own home and the Meredith Publishing Company's recreation area to the wounded and the newly inducted.

Edna Meredith died in Des Moines. For thirty-two years she had been the supportive and admired wife of an important publisher and politician. During the rest of her long life she functioned in her own right as a philanthropist, outspoken independent political voice, and prominent stockholder in a major communications firm, which by the time of her death owned radio and television stations as well as several publishing operations.

• Information on Edna Meredith can be found in a scrapbook for 1920 and scattered letters in the Edwin T. Meredith Papers located in Special Collections at the main library of the University of Iowa, Iowa City. Newspaper articles about Meredith are in the clipping files at the State Historical Society of Iowa, Des Moines. Magazine articles focusing on her during her husband's political career are Frederick L. Collins, "Mrs. ???? in the White House," *Woman's Home Companion*, June 1928, and Frances Parkinson Keyes, "The Ladies in the Chase," *Delineator*, Mar. 1928. On the Meredith Publishing Company, see "Meredith's Blossoming Empire," *Iowan* 10 (Summer 1962); Michael Walker, "A Better Home for Meredith," *Iowan* 30 (Winter 1981); Peter Ainsworth, "The Meredith Publications," *Palimpsest* 11 (June 1930); and Carol Reuss, "Edwin T. Meredith: Founder of *Better Homes and Gardens*," *Annals of Iowa* 42 (Spring 1975). Obituaries are in the *Des Moines Register*, the *Des Moines Tribune*, and the *New York Times*, all 2 Jan. 1961, and *Publishers Weekly*, 30 Jan. 1961.

THOMAS BURNELL COLBERT

MEREDITH, Samuel (1741–10 Feb. 1817), treasurer of the United States, was born in Philadelphia, Pennsylvania, the son of Reese Meredith, a merchant, and Martha Carpenter. He attended Dr. Allison's Academy in Philadelphia and then joined his father's business. As a Philadelphia merchant concerned with the American colonies' conflicts with Britain, Meredith signed the nonimportation resolutions adopted in Philadelphia on 7 November 1765. He then served as a deputy to the Provincial Convention held in Philadelphia in January 1775. In 1772 Meredith married Margaret Cadwalader of Philadelphia, daughter of Dr. Thomas Cadwalader. The Merediths had seven children.

Meredith's revolutionary service was extensive. He served first as a major and then as lieutenant colonel of the Third Battalion of Associators, known as the Silk Stocking Company. He fought in the battles of Trenton and Princeton, and in April 1777 he was promoted to brigadier general of the Pennsylvania militia for his services in the battles of Brandywine and Germantown. Meredith resigned from the army on 9 January 1778, and resumed his business as a merchant.

His political career began with three terms in the Pennsylvania colonial assembly (1778–1779, 1781–1783). Meredith's position in the Philadelphia business community subsequently led to his election as one of twelve initial directors of the Bank of North America. He served on the board from 1 November

1781 until 12 January 1784. In 1786 Meredith resumed his political career with his election to the Confederation Congress for 1787 and 1788.

Meredith is best remembered for his appointment as the first treasurer of the United States under the Constitution. Meredith actively sought opportunities as a professional public servant. Like many others in 1789, he solicited President George Washington for a government post in which he might "be of service to the Public, and at the same time benefit myself." He explained that his personal business affairs had suffered from "too great [a] confidence in Continental money," and he needed a salary to support his family. Washington appointed Meredith surveyor of the Port of Philadelphia in August 1789. But Meredith resigned this position before assuming his duties in order to accept the post of treasurer. Michael Hillegas had been treasurer since 1776, and he fully expected that the president would remember his services in the new administration. But Meredith received Hillegas's post. Meredith's successful appointment may have had much to do with his connections with influential Philadelphia businessmen like madeira merchant Henry Hill (1736–1798), who remarked to the president that Meredith's appointment was "a distinguishing instance of your powerful friendship."

Meredith began his duties on 11 September 1789. He carried out the responsibilities of his office even under hardship. A yellow fever epidemic in the summer of 1793 closed down the federal government, then based in Philadelphia. Many government employees fled the city to escape contagion, but Meredith remained. Both he and his wife subsequently contracted the illness, but they were successfully treated by the noted physician Benjamin Rush. Though several treasury clerks later petitioned Congress to cover their expenditures for the time they remained at the Treasury office during the epidemic, Meredith declined to ask for such compensation.

Meredith retired from office on 31 October 1801, citing his declining health and the unsettled state of his business affairs. In 1802 he moved from Philadelphia to his estate, "Belmont," in Mount Pleasant, Wayne County, Pennsylvania. It was here that he spent the remaining years of his life and where he died.

• Many of Meredith's letters concerning both his business interests and his various political positions are in the Dreer collection and the Cadwalader collection at the Historical Society of Pennsylvania. There is no comprehensive biography of Meredith, but several brief biographical sketches exist: S. M. M. Graham, *A Short History of the Three Merediths*, Historical Society of Pennsylvania (1896); Wharton Dickinson, "Brigadier-General Samuel Meredith," *Magazine of American History* (Sept. 1879); F. W. Leach, "Old Philadelphia Families," *Philadelphia North American*, 4 Feb. 1912; and Samuel Whaley, *History of the Township of Mount Pleasant, Wayne County, Pa.* (1856). Meredith's involvement with the founding of the Bank of North America is described in that institution's history: Lawrence Lewis, Jr., *A History of the Bank of North America* (1882). Meredith's career in the Pennsylvania legislature is in Craig W. Horle and Marianne S. Wokeck, eds., *Lawmaking and Legislators in Pennsylvania: A Biographical Dictionary*, vol. 1 (1991). Details of Meredith's official appointment as treasurer are in various letters to the president in *The Papers of George Washington: Presidential Series*, ed. Dorothy Twohig, vols. 1 and 3 (1987–1989). An obituary is in *Poulson's American Daily Advertiser*, 22 Feb. 1817.

SUSAN BRANSON

MERGENTHALER, Ottmar (11 May 1854–28 Oct. 1899), inventor of the Linotype hot-type composing machine, was born in Hachtel, Württemberg, in what is now Germany, the son of Johann Georg Mergenthaler, a schoolteacher, and Rosina Ackermann. As a boy growing up in Ensingen, he earned the nickname "Pfiffikusmärle" (Cleverhead) because of his mechanical ability to start up the long-silent village clock. At age fourteen, after objecting to becoming a teacher in the family tradition, he was apprenticed for four years as a watch- and clock-maker to his stepmother's brother in Bietigheim. Because many soldiers were then returning from the Franco-Prussian War in 1872, Mergenthaler thought work prospects might be better in the United States. After landing in Baltimore, Maryland, he went directly to Washington, D.C., to work for August Hahl, son of his apprenticeship master, in a shop that designed and constructed clocks, bells, weather devices, and patent models.

In 1874 Hahl and Mergenthaler moved to Baltimore, where business prospects seemed better. Mergenthaler, as shop foreman, in 1876 was first introduced to the problems of type composition when inventor Charles T. Moore brought in a typing machine designed to print characters in lithographic ink onto paper strips. The character impressions were to be mounted on a backing sheet and the words transferred to a lithographic stone for printing. Mergenthaler improved the reliability of the typing machine after Hahl had secured financial support from Moore's principal backer, James O. Clephane. A Washington, D.C., court reporter, Clephane had tested early models of Christopher Sholes's typewriters and had envisioned in Moore's invention a machine that would enable the speedy production of court reports and pamphlets. Continuing difficulties in transferring the lithographic images, however, led to abandonment of this process.

In about 1878 Clephane proposed using a stereotypic process in which the typing machine would impress characters into papier-mâché strips. Mergenthaler now devised his rotary impression machine for which he received his first patent. The difficulties in successfully making metal castings from the strips, though, ended progress in this process. Mergenthaler, meanwhile, became Hahl's partner, and in 1881 he married Emma Lachenmayer, with whom he would have five children.

Clephane, however, continued to experiment with possible composing processes. He supported Mergenthaler's plans to open his own shop in 1883 and backed the inventor's efforts to develop a new machine Mergenthaler had first suggested in 1879. Mergenthaler's first band machine used long, tapered metal bands with raised characters that made impressions of character lines in papier-mâché strips. Again, there were difficulties in making satisfactory castings. In 1884 he developed the second band machine; this device used bands of indented characters that were positioned in the machine so that actual lines of type could be cast from molten lead. This was Mergenthaler's first primitive Linotype. Confident of future success, Mergenthaler's backers, principally Clephane, formed the National Typographic Company with a capitalization of $1 million and named Mergenthaler as manager of its Baltimore factory. The company became the Mergenthaler Printing Company in 1885. Although the second band machine attracted wide attention, Mergenthaler nevertheless realized it would not produce type matching the quality of handset type and meeting the demands of a then-skeptical trade. He proposed another machine, one using matrices (molds) of single characters, and his backers reluctantly approved this new direction.

The principle of single matrices that circulate in the machine has been used in all subsequent Linotypes. Mergenthaler's first commercial machine, the 1886 Blower, was named for the air blast used to propel the matrices. It was installed that summer at the *New York Tribune* to set newspaper type and a 500-page book, *The Tribune Book of Open-Air Sports*. Whitelaw Reid, *Tribune* publisher, headed a publishers' syndicate that envisioned the machine's money-making potential and provided additional capital through the Mergenthaler Printing Company.

The stage was set in early 1888, though, for a confrontation between Reid and Mergenthaler. Reid, who is usually credited with naming the machine, and other syndicate members using the new devices complained that the machines were unreliable and unprofitable. Reid wanted a machine produced quickly; Mergenthaler wanted a perfect one. Because of this unresolved difference, Mergenthaler, then thirty-four, resigned under pressure as factory manager.

Reid moved the factory that year to Brooklyn, New York, but disputes between Reid's New York stockholders and the Washington faction of Clephane and Lemon G. Hine led to Reid's ouster and Hine's selection as president. Mergenthaler, meanwhile, reestablished his own machine shop in Baltimore, developing an improved model built in both shops.

The year 1891 marked the formation of the Mergenthaler Linotype Company, the return of control to the New York directors, the selection of Philip T. Dodge as the company's president, and Mergenthaler's perfection of the newer Model 1 Linotype. This machine overcame the objections of newspaper publishers. In 1895 the company reported that 2,608 machines were installed at 385 locations in almost every state or territory. Publishers at last found that the Linotype produced type much more quickly and at less cost than hand composition in addition to providing a "new dress [type] daily." The Linotype thus became the revolutionary advance over the hand process initiated by Johann Gutenberg in the 1450s.

The early 1890s was a period when newspaper, book, and magazine printers tried out the new composing machines entering the market. Various contests and demonstrations were held, with the Linotype usually producing the best records. Organized labor initially had qualms about a machine that they feared would put its printers out of work, but by 1900 their objections had largely subsided as union printers had taken control of the machines and the demand for printed material had increased.

Both before and after Mergenthaler's death, the Mergenthaler company defended its patents against interference and infringement by competing machines. It also bought out a competitor in 1895 to obtain patent rights for the crucial double-wedge spaceband used in justifying the lines of type. The Linotype thus "held the field" until after the inventor's principal patents expired and the competing Intertype was introduced in 1913.

Linotypes were extensively improved over the years as installation proceeded in a majority of the nation's printing plants. The hot-type systems using them began their decline after World War II. Intense labor problems and the adoption of offset printing and cold-type photocomposition methods (and later computers) coincided with publishers' desires for lower costs. The Mergenthaler company ended U.S. production in 1971 after building nearly 90,000 Linotypes. Probably a few thousand were still in use in the United States in the early 1990s.

Mergenthaler built Linotypes for Brooklyn at least until 1894, and his Baltimore shop made parts and other nonprinting devices. By then tuberculosis, the illness that caused his death, forced him to relinquish active management, although he continued to patent improvements to the Linotype. (He was awarded more than sixty patents.) He sought a cure by living in Arizona and New Mexico, where he prepared an autobiography. After a prairie fire destroyed it and his home, he returned to Baltimore to write the briefer version (*Biography*) printed a year before his death there. This autobiography chronicles in part his bitterness toward the Mergenthaler company leaders for forcing his resignation and for reducing the amount of his royalty.

During his lifetime, Mergenthaler received the Elliott Cresson Medal from Philadelphia's Franklin Institute and the John Scott Medal from the City of Philadelphia. In honor of his centenary, the former schoolhouse where he had been born in Hachtel was dedicated as the Mergenthaler Museum, and Berlin issued a 10-pfennig stamp illustrating Mergenthaler and a Linotype. Mergenthaler was posthumously inducted in 1982 into the National Inventors Hall of Fame in Washington, D.C. The display module there describes the Linotype as "one of the most significant technological advances of the 19th Century. . . . It made possible the mass dissemination of information and ideas throughout the world."

• Some of Mergenthaler's papers are in the National Museum of American History, Graphic Arts Division. Others, of the 1885–1889 period, are among the correspondence in the Whitelaw Reid Collection in the Library of Congress, Manuscript Division.

Mergenthaler's autobiography, *Biography of Ottmar Mergenthaler and History of the Linotype* (1898), has been reprinted with additional research by Carl Schlesinger (1989). Three biographies published by the Mergenthaler companies are Thomas Dreier, *The Power of Print—and Men* (1936); Fritz Schröder, *Ottmar Mergenthaler* (1941); and Willi Mengel, *Ottmar Mergenthaler and the Printing Revolution* (1954). Others are I. E. Levine, *Miracle Man of Printing: Ottmar Mergenthaler* (juvenile) (1963), and Frank Romano, *Machine Writing and Typesetting* (1986). See also George Iles, *Leading American Inventors* (1912), pp. 393–432.

Among the articles that appeared at the time of the Linotype's introduction are "A Machine to Supersede Typesetting," *Scientific American*, 9 Mar. 1889, pp. 149–50, and (same title), 9 Aug. 1890, p. 85; "The Linotype," *New York Tribune*, 19 May 1889; and "The Linotype and the Man Who Made It," *The Journalist*, 18 July 1891. Other articles are Edward Mott Woolley, "Forty Years for Forty Millions," *System*, Sept. 1908, pp. 212–23, and Henry Lewis Bullen, "Origins of the Linotype Machine," *Inland Printer*, Feb. 1924, pp. 769–71, and Mar. 1924, pp. 936–38. Two doctoral dissertations supply extensive bibliographies, George Everett, "The Linotype and U.S. Daily Newspaper Journalism in the 1890s" (Univ. of Iowa, 1972), and George Corban Goble, "The Obituary of a Machine: The Rise and Fall of Ottmar Mergenthaler's Linotype at U.S. Newspapers" (Indiana Univ., 1984). An obituary is in the Baltimore *Sun*, 30 Oct. 1899.

CORBAN GOBLE

MERGLER, Marie Josepha (18 May 1851–17 May 1901), physician and surgeon, was born in Mainstockheim, Bavaria, the daughter of Francis R. Mergler, a physician, and Henrietta von Ritterhausen. Her father moved the family to Palatine, Illinois, when Marie was two years old. Mergler received most of her early education from her father. She also assisted him with his medical work. But his example and practical training did not immediately propel her into a medical career. Perhaps because the obstacles against women entering medicine were considerable, she prepared instead for a teaching career. She attended the Cook County Normal School in Illinois and the State Normal School at Oswego, New York. After graduating in 1872, she taught and served as assistant principal at a high school in the Chicago suburb of Englewood.

Frustrated by the lack of opportunity for advancement in the teaching profession, Mergler entered the Woman's Medical College of Chicago in 1877. She excelled in her studies, becoming valedictorian of her class. Following graduation in 1879, she was one of the first women permitted to compete with men for an internship at the Cook County Insane Asylum. Although her performance entitled her to the position, the hospital board refused to appoint a woman. Mergler then spent a year of postgraduate study in Zurich, Switzerland.

Mergler returned to Chicago in 1881 and began practicing medicine. She restricted her practice to obstetrics and gynecology and became the surgical assistant to William H. Byford, an influential Chicago gynecologist. In 1882 she was named professor of materia medica and adjunct professor of gynecology at the Woman's Medical College of Chicago and in 1890 succeeded Byford as chair and professor of gynecology. From 1885 to 1899 Mergler served as secretary of the college faculty and in 1899 was elected dean.

In 1882 Mergler became the second woman to obtain a staff position at Cook County Hospital. She was appointed attending surgeon at the Woman's Hospital of Chicago in 1886, and gynecologist at Wesley Hospital in 1890. In 1895 she was elected head physician and surgeon of the Chicago Hospital for Women and Children, which, in honor of its deceased founder, had been renamed the Mary Thompson Hospital.

Mergler devoted her life to the practice of surgery and to the education of women in medicine. She received high praise for her diagnostic abilities and surgical skills and garnered respect as a leading abdominal and gynecological surgeon. She wrote articles for state and local medical publications, published *A Guide to the Study of Gynecology* (1892), and coauthored a chapter in *An American Textbook of Obstetrics* (1895). Her influence over students and colleagues was substantial. She encouraged and inspired them and, by her example, proved that women could become successful physicians and surgeons. Mergler never married, but she maintained a warm and comfortable home where she enjoyed music, literature, and the companionship of colleagues and students. After two years of failing health, Mergler died of pernicious anemia in Los Angeles, California.

• For an article written by Mergler, see "History of Competitive Examinations," in *Woman's Medical School, Northwestern University: The Institution and Its Founders* (1896), pp. 84–92. The most comprehensive biography of Mergler is William K. Beatty, "Marie J. Mergler: Surgeon and Friend," Institute of Medicine of Chicago, *Proceedings* 36 (1983): 101–4, 136. See also F. M. Sperry, comp., *A Group of Distinguished Physicians and Surgeons of Chicago* (1904), pp. 110–13, and Council of the Chicago Medical Society, "Maria Josepha Mergler," *History of Medicine and Surgery and Physicians and Surgeons of Chicago* (1922). Three tributes to Mergler by her contemporaries appeared in the *Woman's Medical Journal* 11 (Aug. 1901), I. A. Danforth, "Marie Josepha Mergler, M.D.," pp. 291–93; Eliza H. Root, "Dr. Marie J. Mergler as Woman and Physician," pp. 293–97; and "Marie J. Mergler, M.D.," pp. 301–2.

EVE FINE

MERI, La. *See* La Meri.

MERICA, Paul Dyer (17 Mar. 1889–20 Oct. 1957), metallurgist, was born in Warsaw, Indiana, the son of Charles Oliver Merica, a lecturer, and Alice White. Merica attended public schools in Warsaw and then went to DePauw University in Greencastle, Indiana, for three years, where he concentrated on chemistry. In 1907 he enrolled in the University of Wisconsin in

Madison and received his A.B. the following year, majoring in physics under professor Charles Elwood Mendenhall.

From 1908 to 1909 Merica was an instructor in physics at the University of Wisconsin. He then spent two years at Chekiang Provincial College in Hangchow, China, as a professor of chemistry and "western subjects." Having studied both chemistry and physics, he chose to attend the University of Berlin, Germany, to study with metallurgist William Minot Guertler, whose expertise was the analysis of alloys. Merica received his Ph.D. from that university in 1914, with a dissertation on the mechanical and magnetic properties of metals under elastic and plastic deformation.

After returning to the United States in 1914, Merica was briefly a special investigator on caustic embrittlement of steel at the University of Illinois. That same year he became a research physicist at the National Bureau of Standards, where he was associated with physicist George Kimball Burgess, the chief of the division of metallurgy. During the next five years Merica advanced to associate physicist, physicist, and metallurgist. He married Florence Young in 1917; they had no children.

Interest in metallurgical problems increased during the years of the First World War. Before 1914 Alfred Wilm in Germany had created duralumin, an alloy of aluminum containing small amounts of copper, magnesium, manganese, iron, and silicon. Because of its lightness and strength, it was especially suitable for airplane construction. The strength and hardness of the alloy increased while cooling during the few days after its creation, a phenomenon that puzzled Wilm and other metallurgists. At the National Bureau of Standards, Merica, working with R. G. Waltenberg and Howard Scott, concluded that the hardening resulted from precipitation of a compound. According to his co-workers, Merica was primarily responsible for working out the concept. His conclusion was that precipitation occurs in a second phase as very small submicroscopic particles. One metal dissolves in another at high temperatures but not at lower temperatures. Thus, the copper in duralumin dissolved in the aluminum, but as it cooled a new compound of copper and aluminum was created.

This work was published after the war by Merica and his fellow researchers as "Heat Treatment of Duralumin," in the *Bulletin of American Institute of Mining and Metallurgical Engineers* (1919). The analysis of the concept of precipitation hardening opened a new frontier in physical metallurgy that made possible the creation of many new alloys of nearly all the common metals by heat-treatment procedures.

While at the National Bureau of Standards, Merica published approximately twenty-five papers, chiefly on metal alloys, corrosion, and stress in metals. One of these, published by the National Bureau of Standards in 1921, was *Nickel and Its Alloys* (rev. ed., 1924), a highly reliable summary in this subject.

In 1919 Merica was employed as a physical metallurgist by the International Nickel Company at its Orford refinery in Bayonne, New Jersey, and there he became the director of research circa 1922. In 1931 he moved to the New York office and became a technical assistant to the president of the parent company, The International Nickel Company of Canada, Limited, and the next year he became an assistant to its president. He continued working in the parent company as a director in 1934, the vice president in charge of research in 1936, the executive vice president in 1949, and the president from 1952 to 1954, when he retired at his own request. Simultaneously, he held equivalent positions in the U.S. subsidiary. After his retirement he continued as a consultant on the company's projects, policies, researches, and technical activities.

At International Nickel, with "characteristic vigor and determination," Merica joined the company effort to increase the use of nickel, which had been used primarily in armaments until the end of the First World War. He continued his researches on alloys and improved the processes of melting nickel. He determined that a small increase in the amount of nickel, with lowered amounts of silicon and carbon, "substantially increased" the hardness and strength of gray cast iron and made it more machinable. He was "personally and deeply concerned" in developing the nickel-copper alloy trademarked as "Monel K-500" in 1926. He created a nickel-copper cast iron that was durable, tough, and resistant to heat and corrosion. That alloy, trademarked "Ni-Resist" in 1932, became widely used in automobile parts. Another of his cast-iron alloys with an intermediate amount of nickel, called "Ni-Hard," was highly resistant to abrasion. Merica obtained twenty-one U.S. patents, most with coauthors, for his metallurgical concepts.

The contributions by Merica and his colleagues increased the demand for nickel. Its use grew from 1921 to 1929 but was reduced during the depression years until about 1935, when the company's business reached a new peak. From its mines in the Sudbury district of Ontario, Canada, the company continued after his death to produce about one-half of the world's supply of nickel.

As a high official in the company, Merica encouraged the development of new processes for extracting metals from their ores. Such metallurgical techniques were introduced at the company's mines in Sudbury, which resulted in recovery of such other metals as copper, platinum, palladium, rhodium, ruthenium, iridium, gold, silver, cobalt, selenium, and tellurium. Sulfur was also recovered in liquid form. Merica also participated in the appraisal and development of mines in northern Manitoba, Canada.

He was acknowledged as a leader with a "contagious interest in research," who combined "great scientific ability with a keen commercial sense." He published more than fifty technical papers. Merica was a member of many scientific societies and was honored with medals from several societies and with membership in the National Academy of Sciences (1942). He died in Tarrytown, New York.

• Merica's significant paper, "Heat Treatment of Duralumin," was published as *National Bureau of Standards Scientific Paper* 347 (1919). He wrote a chapter on nickel in *Modern Uses of Nonferrous Metals*, ed. C. H. Mathewson (1935; rev. ed., 1953). The primary biography of Merica is Zay Jeffries, National Academy of Sciences, *Biographical Memoirs* 33 (1959): 225–40, which features a bibliography and a list of patents. An obituary is in the *New York Times*, 22 Oct. 1957.

ELIZABETH NOBLE SHOR

MERITT, Benjamin Dean (31 Mar. 1899–7 July 1989), ancient historian and epigraphist, was born in Durham, North Carolina, the son of Arthur Herbert Meritt, professor of Greek and Latin at Trinity College (now Duke University), and Cornelia Dean. After receiving his A.B. from Hamilton College in 1920, Meritt attended the American School of Classical Studies at Athens (1920–1922). He received his M.A. (1923) and Ph.D. (1924) from Princeton University. From 1923 to 1926 he taught Greek at the University of Vermont, Brown, and Princeton, before returning to Athens as assistant director of the American School (1926–1928). In Greece Meritt traveled extensively, excavated at Corinth and Nemea, reconstructed—with A. B. West—the inscribed tribute-quota lists of the Athenian Empire, and published his first book on the Athenian calendar.

From 1928 to 1933 he was associate professor, then professor of classics at the University of Michigan. In 1933 he accepted the White Professorship of Classics at the Johns Hopkins University, which he held until 1935, when he became professor of Greek epigraphy at the Institute for Advanced Study, Princeton. Retiring from this post in 1969, he later went to the University of Texas at Austin as a visiting scholar (1972–1989).

Meritt was active in the academic program of the American School in Athens as visiting professor (1932–1933) and annual professor (1936, 1954–1955, 1969–1970). He was a lecturer (1935) and then George Eastman Professor at Oxford University (1945–1946). He delivered the Sather Lectures in Classical Literature at the University of California, Berkeley (1959).

For his service to Hellenic scholarship the Greek state decorated Meritt as Commander: Order of the Phoenix and the Royal Order of George I. He was elected president of the American Philological Association in 1953 and shared its Award of Merit in 1954. He was also affiliated with numerous learned societies in both the United States and Europe.

Meritt's reputation as America's leading authority on ancient Greek inscriptions rests on an impressive array of publications (fourteen books and about two hundred articles) spanning roughly sixty-five years. He published for the first time thousands of inscriptions discovered in the Agora excavations of the American School between 1933 and 1968. They encompass all categories of inscribed documents, including laws, decrees, treaties, financial records, inventories, leases, catalogues of magistrates, dedications to the gods, honorary statue bases, and gravestones. Many shed new light on important aspects of ancient Athens—its history, economy, political institutions, and religion, for example. Meritt's prompt and authoritative publication of this huge body of invaluable primary data represents a permanent contribution to scholarship.

Meritt will probably be best remembered for his pioneering work on the finances of Athens in the fifth century B.C., culminating in the monumental four-volume *Athenian Tribute Lists* (1939–1953), coauthored with H. T. Wade-Gery and M. F. McGregor. This detailed publication of all the documentary evidence for the administration of the Athenian Empire also contains many novel interpretations that have continued to spark productive debate. Among these are Meritt's views on the impact of imperial revenues on Pericles' building program on the Acropolis, the interaction of the inscriptions and Thucydides' account of the growth of the Athenian Empire, and the date of the imposition of Athenian coinage, weights, and measures on the confederate states. The work has stood up fairly well to the test of later discoveries. The same cannot be said for many of Meritt's numerous publications on chronology and the calendars of Athens. Tenacious defense of his intricate theories led him into a long and bitter controversy with other scholars over such topics as secretary cycles in the list of Athenian archons, the count of days in the Athenian month, the sequence of ordinary and intercalated years, and Aristotle's views on the civic calendar. Many of his calendric reconstructions have won assent only within a small circle of disciples.

At the Institute for Advanced Study in Princeton, Meritt created a marvelous center for the study of Attic epigraphy, consisting of an excellent library, large collections of paper impressions (squeezes) and photographs, and a massive card file of Athenian citizens, which he generously shared with others. Many scholars from the United States and abroad enjoyed his warm hospitality and were stimulated by his exacting and imaginative scholarship.

In 1923 Meritt married Mary Elizabeth Kirkland; they had two sons. After her death, he married Lucy Taxis Shoe, a classical archaeologist and editor of publications of the American School (1950–1972), in 1964. He died in Austin, Texas.

• Meritt's unpublished monthly reports as assistant director of the American School to Edward Capps, chairman of the Managing Committee, vividly document his intensive scholarly and administrative activities in 1926–1928; they are housed in the archives of the school in Athens. He is the author of *The Athenian Calendar in the Fifth Century* (1928); *Supplementum Epigraphicum Graecum*, vol. 5 (1931), with A. B. West; *Corinth*, vol. 8, i., *Greek Inscriptions, 1896–1927* (1931); *Athenian Financial Documents of the Fifth Century* (1932); *The Athenian Assessment of 425 B.C.* (1934), with A. B. West; *Documents on Athenian Tribute* (1937); *Epigraphica Attica* (1940); *The Athenian Year* (1961); and *The Athenian Agora*, vol. 15, *The Athenian Councillors* (1974), with J. S. Traill. A list of his other publications to 1974 appears in D. W. Bradeen and M. F. McGregor, eds., *Phoros: Tribute to Benjamin Dean Meritt* (1974), a collection of essays contributed by twenty-six colleagues to commemorate Meritt's seventy-fifth birthday. Obituaries are in *American Journal of Archaeology* 94 (1990): 483–84, and *Proceedings of the American Philosophical Society* 135 (1991): 111–15.

RONALD S. STROUD

MERKEL, Una (10 Dec. 1903–2 Jan. 1986), actress, was born in Covington, Kentucky, the daughter of Arno Merkel, a salesman, and Bessie Phares. Merkel's father traveled throughout the American South as a salesman, especially of calendars, and his family usually accompanied him. As a result, Merkel's formal education was delayed until age nine, and she reported that she experienced poor health during her early years. Later, after the family moved to the Northeast, she attended the Girl's Annex in Philadelphia and Alviene's, a dancing school in New York City.

While studying drama in New York in 1920, Merkel became a stand-in for Lillian Gish because of her resemblance to that actress, and she appeared in such films as *Way Down East* (1920) and *The White Rose* (1923), directed by D. W. Griffith. She received her first feature film credit in *The Fifth Horseman* in 1924, playing the feminine lead.

Merkel made her stage debut in 1922, playing a cigarette girl in *Montmarte* at the Belmont Theatre in New York. She appeared in small roles in other productions in New York, including *Two by Two* (1925) and *Pigs* (1926), and in 1927 she was cast with Helen Hayes in *Coquette*, which ran for twenty-two months at the Maxine Elliot Theatre.

In 1930 Merkel moved to Hollywood and began a long film career with Griffith's *Abraham Lincoln*, as Ann Rutledge; Walter Huston played the title role. Most of her subsequent parts were considered "character" roles, and for the first part of her career she was a contract player for Metro-Goldwin-Mayer. Notable films in which she appeared early in her film career include *The Maltese Falcon* (1931), *42nd Street* (1933), and *Destry Rides Again* (1939).

Merkel, a blue-eyed blond who spoke with a noticeable southern accent, made as many as six movies a year during the 1930s and 1940s, usually appearing in supporting roles with such established stars as W. C. Fields, Jean Harlow, Harold Lloyd, and Marlene Dietrich, with whom she shared a memorable, hair-pulling fight scene in *Destry Rides Again*. Later film appearances include *The Kettles in the Ozarks* (1956), *The Fuzzy Pink Nightgown* (1957), *The Mating Game* (1959), *Summer and Smoke* (1961), for which she received an Academy Award nomination, and *The Parent Trap* (1961).

During the 1950s Merkel returned to Broadway, and in 1956 she appeared in *The Ponder Heart*, a dramatization of a story by Eudora Welty, and won the Antoinette Perry Award for "best supporting actress" of the year.

Merkel married Ronald Burla, an aviation executive, in 1932; childless, they divorced in 1947. She spent her retirement in Los Angeles, where she died.

• Merkel left no papers, and no biography is available to date. She is mentioned in Arthur McClure and Alfred Twomey, *The Versatiles* (1969), and in Kyle Crichton, "Something to Fight About," *Collier's Magazine*, 2 Apr. 1938, pp. 17, 58. See also John Walker, *Halliwell's Filmgoers and Video Viewer Companion*, 10th ed. (1993), and Larry Laughlan, *Encyclopedia of American Film Comedy* (1987). An obituary is in the *New York Times*, 5 Jan. 1986.

ARCHIE P. MCDONALD

MERMAN, Ethel (16 Jan. 1909–15 Feb. 1984), actress and singer, was born Ethel Agnes Zimmerman in Astoria, Queens, New York, the daughter of Edward Zimmerman, a bookkeeper, and Agnes Gardner. (Her year of birth is sometimes given as 1908, and some sources spell her family name Zimmermann.) After graduating from William Cullen Bryant High School in Long Island City, she worked as a steno-bookkeeper-secretary in Manhattan while singing at social affairs in the evenings. In 1929 theatrical agent Lou Irwin secured for her a film contract with Warner Bros. in New York, but the only engagement that the studio gave her was a small part in a short film. She subsequently joined the team of Lou Clayton, Eddie Jackson, and Jimmy Durante that was performing at Les Ambassadeurs Club. At that point she shortened her name from Zimmerman to Merman.

Merman's big break came when Broadway producer Vinton Freedley heard her perform at the Brooklyn Paramount Theater. Freedley then brought composer George Gershwin to hear her. Impressed with her voice, Gershwin gave her a part in *Girl Crazy* (1930), a musical starring Ginger Rogers. Merman awed Broadway with her powerful rendition of "I Got Rhythm," in which she held a high C-note for sixteen bars. After *Girl Crazy* Merman joined the cast of the *George White's Scandals of 1931*, in which she sang "Life Is Just a Bowl of Cherries."

In 1932, in the musical *Take a Chance*, Merman brought down the house with her performance of "Eadie Was a Lady." In 1934 she sang in the film *We're Not Dressing*, which starred Bing Crosby, Carole Lombard, George Burns, and Gracie Allen. Merman next appeared in *Kid Millions* (1934) with Eddie Cantor, Ann Sothern, and George Murphy. A role in *The Big Broadcast of 1936* followed. Between the two movies she appeared on Broadway in the Cole Porter musical *Anything Goes* (1934), singing "I Get a Kick out of You," "Blow, Gabriel, Blow," and "You're the Top." The show ran for 420 performances. In 1936 she reenacted the starring role in the film version opposite Bing Crosby. Twenty years later Merman recreated the same part for a 1954 installment of the "Colgate Comedy Hour" on NBC-TV. In 1934 radio station WABC began broadcasting "The Ethel Merman Show."

In 1936 Merman appeared with Durante in another Porter musical, *Red, Hot and Blue*, in which she sang "It's De-lovely," "Ridin' High," and "Down in the Depths on the Ninetieth Floor." It ran through 183 performances. In 1938 she signed with 20th Century–

Fox and was immediately cast with Don Ameche and Sonja Henie in *Happy Landing*. That same year she appeared in the box-office blockbuster *Alexander's Ragtime Band*, costarring Tyrone Power, Alice Faye, and Ameche; she sang an Irving Berlin medley in the film. She then appeared with the Ritz Brothers in the movie *Straight Place and Show* (1938).

In February 1939 Merman appeared in *Stars in Your Eyes*, which included the musical number "This Is It" and closed after 127 performances. In December 1939 she was featured with Bert Lahr in the Porter musical *Du Barry Was a Lady*, which ran for 408 performances and featured Betty Grable in her Broadway debut. Lucille Ball was cast in Merman's stage role in the 1943 film adaptation of the play. In 1940 Merman appeared in her fourth Porter production, *Panama Hattie*, which ran for 501 performances and established Merman as a Broadway star. Her musical numbers included "I've Still Got My Health," "Let's Be Buddies," "I'm Throwing a Ball Tonight," and "Make It Another Old-Fashioned, Please." That same year she married William Smith, a Hollywood actors' agent. They were divorced the following year and had no children. In 1942 she married Robert D. Levitt; the couple had two children before divorcing in 1952. In 1943 she made a guest appearance in the film *Stage Door Canteen*.

Merman's fifth Porter musical was *Something for the Boys* (1943). Her songs included "Hey, Good Lookin'," "He's a Right Guy," and "The Leader of a Big Time Band." The show enjoyed tremendous success in wartime New York and ran for 422 performances. During World War II Merman entertained frequently at USO (United Service Organizations) and military bases, efforts for which she was presented with a special citation.

By 1946 Merman was ready for a change from her customary musical roles. Berlin provided it with his western musical *Annie Get Your Gun*, which opened on 16 May and ran for 1,147 performances. The comedy, starring Merman as sharpshooter Annie Oakley, featured a memorable score that included "There's No Business Like Show Business" and "Anything You Can Do." Mary Martin took Merman's role in the road company, while Betty Hutton played Annie in the film version (1950).

In 1949 Merman made her television debut as a guest host for "Thru the Crystal Ball." The next year she had another hit, Berlin's *Call Me Madam*, directed by George Abbott and produced by Leland Hayward. The show ran for 644 performances. Merman received a Tony Award for her leading role, which was based on Washington hostess Perle Mesta, who had been appointed ambassador to Luxembourg by President Harry S. Truman. In 1953 Merman starred in the motion picture version, which was produced by 20th Century–Fox and costarred George Sanders, Donald O'Connor, and Vera Allen. The next year the same studio cast her in the vaudeville-style film *There's No Business Like Show Business* (1954), which was made in the new widescreen CinemaScope technique. Merman sang a medley of Berlin's songs in the movie. In 1953 she had married Robert Six, the owner of Continental Airlines. They were divorced in 1960.

In 1956 Merman was cast in the musical-comedy *Happy Hunting*, written by Howard Lindsay and Russel Crouse and based on the wedding of actress Grace Kelly and Prince Rainier of Monaco. It costarred Fernando Lamas and ran for 412 performances. During this time Merman also played a straight dramatic role for the U.S. Steel Hour segment "Honest in the Rain." It aired on CBS television on 9 May 1956.

In 1959 Merman starred in *Gypsy*, which was based on Gypsy Rose Lee's autobiography. Merman played the stripper's stagestruck mother. Written and composed by Jule Styne and Stephen Sondheim, the show ran for 702 performances on Broadway and included the songs "Some People," "Small World," "Together," and "Everything's Coming Up Roses." The role was one of Merman's favorites; she was disappointed when Rosalind Russell was cast in the film version (1962). In 1963, after more than thirty years in show business, Merman went on her first tour, taking *Gypsy* on the road.

In 1963 director Stanley Kramer cast Merman in his all-star zany comedy *It's a Mad, Mad, Mad, Mad World*. That same year she drew crowds with her rare nightclub appearance at the Persian Room in New York's Plaza Hotel. In March 1966 she was named Woman of the Year by the Harvard University drama club, the Hasty Pudding Theatricals.

In June 1964 Merman married Academy Award–winning actor Ernest Borgnine. They separated after only thirty-eight days and were divorced the next year. After costarring with James Garner in the film *The Art of Love* (1965), Merman recreated her role as Annie for a Broadway revival of *Annie Get Your Gun* (1966). Berlin added the song "Old Fashioned Wedding" for her to sing in the new production. The play was televised on NBC on 19 March 1967. That same year Merman's daughter died of an overdose of barbiturates. There were rumors of suicide and drug addiction at the time, but Merman vehemently denied them. Merman was subsequently appointed coguardian of her daughter's two children.

In March 1970 Merman took over the title role in the long-running Broadway hit *Hello Dolly!* Producer David Merrick added to the score two songs for her, "World Take Me Back" and "Love, Look in My Window." She stayed with the show until its final curtain, after 2,844 performances. In 1972 she received a special Tony Award in recognition for her lifetime contribution to the musical theater. On 15 May 1977 the Museum of the City of New York sponsored a concert of songs from the musical theater titled *Together on Broadway*. It starred Mary Martin and Merman with Cyril Ritchard as the narrator.

In August 1977 Merman, backed by the entire Los Angeles Philharmonic Orchestra, performed in front of more than 17,000 fans at the Hollywood Bowl in a one-woman tribute concert to Irving Berlin on the occasion of his ninetieth birthday. Included in the program were songs by Berlin, Jack Whiting, Porter, Sondheim, and Styne. In 1979 Merman, with Carol Burnett, Rock Hudson, and Richard Chamberlain, taped songs from four American musical comedies for public television.

During the 1960s and 1970s Merman appeared in many television productions, including "Batman" (1967), "That Girl" (1967, 1968), the Mormon Youth Symphony concert saluting George Gershwin (1972), "Ed Sullivan's Broadway" (1973), "The Ted Knight Musical Comedy Variety Special" (1976), and "The Love Boat" (1979, 1980, 1981, and its two-hour special in 1982). She also made cameo appearances in the movies *Won Ton Ton, the Dog Who Saved Hollywood* (1976) and *Airplane!* (1980). She became a frequent guest on talk shows and in 1979, falling in with the spirit of the decade, made the *Ethel Merman Disco Album*.

Merman died in her Surrey Hotel apartment in New York City, where she had lived since 1979. The evening she died all Broadway theaters dimmed their lights for thirty seconds at curtain time.

• The collection of the theater and music department of the Museum of the City of New York contains sheet music, printed and manuscript music, programs, catalogs, memorabilia, and pictures of Ethel Merman. Merman wrote two autobiographies, *Who Could Ask for Anything More* (1955) and *Merman* (1978). The earlier book was serialized under the title "That's the Kind of Dame I Am" in the *Saturday Evening Post*, Feb. and Mar. 1955. A biography is Bob Thomas, *I Got Rhythm: The Ethel Merman Story* (1985). Also see George Bryan, *Ethel Merman: A Bio-Bibliography* (1992). James Robert Parish and Michael R. Pitts, *Hollywood Songsters* (1991), devotes a chapter to Merman. An obituary is in the *New York Times*, 16 Feb. 1984.

SHOSHANA KLEBANOFF

MERRIAM, Charles (31 Nov. 1806–9 July 1887), publisher, was born in West Brookfield, Massachusetts, the son of Daniel Merriam, a newspaper publisher and editor, and Thirza Clapp. The Merriam family was heavily involved in the printing and publishing business in West Brookfield. Besides the newspaper, the *Political Repository; or, Farmer's Journal*, Daniel Merriam and his brother Ebenezer published, among others, William Perry's *Royal Standard English Dictionary*. Charles's father apprenticed him at the age of fourteen to a printer in Hartford, Connecticut, continuing his practice of apprenticing his sons to master printers in Hartford and Boston. The apprenticeship was cut short in 1823 because of his father's death, and Charles returned to West Brookfield to work in the family business and continue his apprenticeship under his elder brother George and his uncle Ebenezer.

After completing his apprenticeship, Charles Merriam left West Brookfield and worked as a teacher for a few months before moving to Philadelphia. Then he settled in Boston, working as a journeyman and foreman with the printing shop of T. R. Marvin. Early in 1831 he was invited to Springfield, Massachusetts, to establish a local paper. Together with George, he scouted the territory, and they decided against a newspaper, establishing a printing shop and bookstore instead. The brothers officially named their fledgling business G & C Merriam, and Co. in 1832. A third brother, Homer, joined the company in 1855.

Craftsman-trained, the brothers were soon able to produce quality books at an economical cost. Charles, the major influence in the bookstore, also brought to the firm an excellent grasp of the art of selling, and the brothers learned to promote their works heavily. By the end of the 1830s they had a well-established business in schoolbooks, Bibles, and law books. Charles married Sophia Eleanor Warriner in 1835; they had five children.

Around this time the firm of D & J Ames offered the Merriams their rights to the octavo abridgement of Noah Webster's *American Dictionary of the English Language*. Sorely tempted and perhaps remembering their father's involvement with Perry's dictionary, they lacked the capital to make the purchase. In 1841 Webster published a new edition of his dictionary as *An American Dictionary of the English Language, 2nd Edition, Corrected and Enlarged*. The lexicographer was by then in his eighties and had entered into considerable debt to publish the dictionary, which was in two volumes and priced too high to sell well. Webster was not an astute publisher, and a number of unbound copies of the publication were still in his possession when he died in 1843.

J. S. & C. Adams purchased the dictionary at the time of Webster's death but soon discovered it had taken on too much. The Merriams stepped in at this point and purchased the unbound sheets and the rights to the 1841 edition. Charles saw the potential of the dictionary as an important resource tool for Americans. That it also complemented other works they were publishing, such as the law books of Joseph Chitty, appealed to the businessman in him and added to the dictionary's lure.

The first decision regarding the dictionary was to make it salable. This was accomplished with an expanded, revised edition in one volume that sold at a considerably lower price. The first Merriam-Webster dictionary was published in 1847 to great success and high acclaim, prompting what was then called the "Battle of the Dictionaries" between the Merriam-Webster and James Worcester's *Universal and Critical Dictionary* (1846). This so-called battle showed the advertising genius of the Merriams, especially when their slogan "Get the Best!" was picked up by reviewers and newspapers. In 1864 a new edition of the Merriam-Webster dictionary was published, though Charles Merriam was strongly opposed to such an extravagance at a time of national crisis. This edition permanently established the Merriam-Webster dictionary as the primary dictionary of American English.

Merriam's wife died in 1858. Two years later he married Rachel White Capen Gray, and they had one daughter. During this time the company became highly successful with the publication of the dictionary, earning the Webster estate alone more than $250,000 and making the brothers wealthy. They were able to opt out of the bookselling business and concentrate on publishing only. The company formally acknowledged its debt to the dictionary in 1981, when it was renamed Merriam-Webster, Incorporated. After retiring in 1876, Merriam became a great philanthropist, endowing a library in West Brookfield and funding another in Springfield, Massachusetts. He died in Springfield.

While a lot of credit has been given to George Merriam for continuing Webster's monumental work, mainly because of his insistence on publishing the 1864 edition at the height of the Civil War, Charles Merriam's contribution should not be underestimated. Described as the most scholarly of the four brothers and noted as a diplomat, Charles also was the quintessential businessman. He actively supervised the publication of the dictionary, often acting as a proofreader. Without him, Merriam-Webster as an international brand name would not have existed.

• Little has been written on the life of Charles Merriam. His name and those of his brothers have become synonymous with the dictionary that they so skillfully saved from oblivion. Thus, the most extensive biography of Charles Merriam and his brothers can be found in the celebration of the dictionary's first century, Robert Keith Leavitt, *Noah's Ark, New England Yankees and the Endless Quest* (1947). Charles's death did not warrant an obituary in the *New York Times*, although the reading of his will earned a description in the 19 Aug. 1887 edition.

JOHN J. DOHERTY

MERRIAM, Charles E. (15 Nov. 1874–8 Jan. 1953), political scientist, was born in Hopkinton, Iowa, the son of Charles Edward Merriam, a merchant and postmaster, and Margaret Campbell Kirkwood, a schoolteacher. Charles Edward Merriam, Jr., was raised in a home and community devoted to Presbyterianism and Republican politics. Charles Merriam, Sr., desired a career in law and politics for his son, but after preparing for law school at Lenox College in Hopkinton and the State University of Iowa (B.A., 1895), "Ed" decided to pursue his interest in the emerging field of political science. Enrolling at Columbia University in 1897, he studied under John W. Burgess and William A. Dunning and soon became active in Columbia president Seth Low's mayoral campaign.

Practical experience and scholarly theory were thus intertwined in Merriam's developing understanding of politics. After a year of study in Germany under Otto von Gierke and Hugo Preuss, Merriam returned to Columbia in 1900 to complete his dissertation, published that year as *A History of the Theory of Sovereignty since Rousseau*. Also in 1900 he was hired as an instructor at the University of Chicago. As the first "political scientist" employed by that institution, Merriam strongly identified himself with the new discipline. In 1903 he became one of the founding members of the American Political Science Association. Merriam also quickly established roots in Chicago. In 1901 he married Elizabeth Hilda Doyle, with whom he had four children. He became involved in local reform politics and was elected to the city council in 1909. With Harold L. Ickes as his campaign manager, Merriam waged an aggressive yet unsuccessful run for mayor in 1911. More defeats followed: he lost his city council seat in 1917 and finished a distant third in the 1919 Republican mayoral primary.

Despite these political defeats, Merriam became an increasingly prominent figure in national progressive politics. Professional advances also compensated for political setbacks. As he ascended the ladder of academic promotion, becoming a full professor in 1911, his work gradually minimized the theoretical and abstract approaches of Burgess, Dunning, and the Germans and took on a more empirical orientation, as in his *Primary Elections* (1908). Merriam's developing empiricism, joined with his political experiences and his work for the Committee on Public Information during the Great War, spurred an interest in the statistical and psychological study of political behavior. After the war, Merriam began to articulate this new agenda for the profession of political science, one that culminated in his *New Aspects of Politics*, published during the year of his presidency of the American Political Science Association (1925). *New Aspects*, possibly Merriam's most influential book, emphasized the need for scientific, cooperative, and impartial inquiry in politics. Although the decline of progressivism had taught that American "jungle politics" and "laboratory science" were "incompatible," Merriam retained the characteristically postprogressive hope that "the laboratory will master the jungle of human nature and turn its vast, teeming futility to the higher uses of mankind."

Despite his influential demands for more scientific and behaviorist political analysis, Merriam produced few such studies himself. Rather, Merriam was most concerned with creating the conditions that would make such research possible, not only in political science, but in what he believed to be the larger cooperative venture of social science. He thus turned his energies toward the organization and financing of social research and of building bridges between the social sciences and government policy making. Merriam played an instrumental role in the formation of the Social Sciences Research Council (SSRC) in 1923 and served as its first president from 1924 to 1927. Displaying an unparalleled gift for persuading philanthropists of the value of social science, he forged a significant alliance between the SSRC and the Rockefeller Foundation. These sources of financial and organizational support allowed Merriam to hire promising students such as Harold Gosnell and Harold Lasswell and build his department into the "Chicago School" of political science, a school renowned for such methodologically innovative studies as Merriam and Gosnell's *Non-Voting* (1924).

The alliance between the Rockefeller Foundation and the SSRC also provided the financial support and personnel for President Herbert Hoover's Research Committee on Social Trends, formed in 1929 with

Merriam as its vice chairman and Wesley Clair Mitchell of Columbia University as its chair. The committee's report, *Recent Social Trends in the United States* (1933), stood as one of the most extensive and comprehensive works of cooperative social science research ever produced. Though the report came too late to salvage Hoover's presidency, it did much to establish the relevance of social science to the New Deal initiatives that would follow and pushed Merriam further into the arena of government policy making. Merriam's old ally Ickes, now President Franklin D. Roosevelt's secretary of the interior, brought Merriam into the New Deal in 1933 as a member of the National Resources Planning Board (NRPB). Opposed, obstructed, and eventually abolished in 1943 by a Congress fearful of "socialist" planning agencies, the NRPB never fulfilled its aims. Under the leadership of Merriam, it acted primarily as a conduit between academic research and public policy. As a member of the President's Committee on Administrative Management (1936–1937), Merriam also played a crucial role in the reorganization of the presidency into its more powerful, modern configuration.

In the 1930s and 1940s Merriam's work in the New Deal was paralleled by a renewed concern with the elaboration of a "systematic politics" in response to a "storm of attack upon democracy converging from the Right and from the Left." In part, this concern evolved from an earlier interest in civic education and an international SSRC project that he had organized and summarized in his *The Making of Citizens: A Comparative Study of Methods of Civic Training* (1931) as well as in his *Civic Education in the United States* (1934). Democracy, Merriam contended in *The New Democracy and the New Despotism* (1939), arose from a commitment to the "essential dignity of man" and was the only form of government worthy of human nature. Moreover, democracy rested on the assumption that the "gains of commonwealths are essentially mass gains and should be diffused" through social-scientific planning and policy.

By the time of his retirement from Chicago in 1940, Merriam was recognized as the doyen of American political science and as one of the founders of the discipline in its modern form. His belief in the necessity of conscious and purposive control for the realization of democratic ideals was expressed in his scholarly work, and it left its impress on the organization of modern American social science and government. Merriam died in Rockville, Maryland.

• Merriam's papers, collected in the Regenstein Library of the University of Chicago, are extensive and of use to historians of Chicago politics, social science, and government administration. Merriam's *Chicago: A More Intimate View of Urban Politics* (1929) contains interesting autobiographical elements. Leonard D. White, ed., *The Future of Government in the United States: Essays in Honor of Charles E. Merriam* (1942), contains both a nearly complete bibliography of Merriam's work (Merriam's only important post-1942 publication was *Systematic Politics* [1945]) and an autobiographical fragment, "The Education of Charles E. Merriam." Barry D. Karl, *Charles E. Merriam and the Study of Politics* (1974), is a comprehensive and definitive account of Merriam's life and career. Other historical interpretations and critiques of Merriam's political science can be found in Bernard Crick, *The American Science of Politics, Its Origins and Conditions* (1959); Albert Somit and Joseph Tanenhaus, *American Political Science* (1964); Raymond Seidelman with Edward J. Harpham, *Disenchanted Realists: Political Science and the American Crisis, 1884–1984* (1985); and Dorothy Ross, *The Origins of American Social Science* (1991). An obituary is in the *Chicago Daily Tribune*, 9 Jan. 1953.

MARK G. SCHMELLER

MERRIAM, Clinton Hart (5 Dec. 1855–19 Mar. 1942), zoologist and government official, was born in New York City, the son of Clinton Levi Merriam, a businessman, banker, and two-term Republican U.S. congressman, and Caroline Hart. A younger sister, Florence, became a notable ornithologist. Merriam spent his early years at "Homewood," the family farm in the Adirondack Mountains region. His father encouraged Merriam's keen interest in natural history, principally in insects and birds, and later, when his son was at Yale University, built a three-story frame museum building on the family property to house the younger man's burgeoning natural history collections.

While paying a visit to his father's congressional office in 1871, Merriam met Spencer F. Baird, then assistant secretary of the Smithsonian Institution, who encouraged the young naturalist to acquire training in taxidermy. He did so informally. In the summer of 1872, Merriam, then only sixteen, was invited by Baird to serve as naturalist to the second division of the Hayden Survey, which visited northwestern Wyoming. Merriam spent a productive summer in the Yellowstone, and his "Report on the Mammals and Birds of the Expedition" appeared in Ferdinand Vandeveer Hayden's *Sixth Annual Report of the United States Geological Survey . . . Being a Report of Progress of the Explorations for the Year 1872* (1873). Although Hayden wanted Merriam to return the next summer, Baird argued that the lad would never be anything more than a competent collector unless he continued his formal schooling. After spending a year at Williston Seminary in Massachusetts, Merriam entered Yale's Sheffield Scientific School, where he studied biology and anatomy for three years and left without graduating. His first major work, *A Review of the Birds of Connecticut* (1877), covered nearly 300 species and won critical acceptance from professionals in the field.

Merriam entered the College of Physicians and Surgeons in New York in the fall of 1877 and completed the three-year course in two years, receiving an M.D. He then embarked on a highly successful medical career in the Locust Grove, New York, area, specializing in the diseases of women, while he maintained his active interest in natural history. His two-volume *The Mammals of the Adirondack Region, Northeastern New York*, published between 1882 and 1884 and based on his extensive field work, remains one of his most highly regarded works. After 1881 he focused his research principally on mammals.

By 1883, Merriam had become restless with his medical practice and decided to undertake full-time scientific work. Baird arranged for Merriam the temporary post of surgeon on the sailing steamer *Proteus*, which visited the sealing grounds off Newfoundland and Labrador during March and April 1883. Concentrating his energies on natural history, Merriam became a charter member of the newly formed American Ornithologists' Union in the fall of 1883 and chair of the AOU Committee on the Migration of Birds the same year. This group of volunteers was soon overwhelmed with information about bird migration. They appealed to Congress for a modest subvention to complete analysis of the data on grounds that the nation's farmers would benefit from information concerning the distribution of birds and their role in the control of noxious small mammals and insects. With the aid of Senator Warner Miller of New York, a cousin and old family friend, $5,000 was appropriated to create an Office of Economic Ornithology, which would be attached to the Bureau of Entomology in the Department of Agriculture. In the spring of 1885, Merriam took his only trip to Europe, for the purpose of studying mammal and bird specimens in private collections and museums in Germany, the Netherlands, and England. When he returned that summer, he accepted the post of economic ornithologist in the Bureau of Entomology. Within a year, he had added economic mammalogy to his responsibilities and had been named chief of his own independent Division of Economic Ornithology and Mammalogy. He married Virginia Elizabeth Gosnell, his secretary, in 1886. The couple had two daughters.

In 1890 Merriam's agency was renamed the Division of Biological Survey, and in 1906 it became the Bureau of Biological Survey, the name it retained until its reorganization in 1940. Merriam was originally expected to examine the economic effects of birds and mammals on American agriculture, but he spent the first two decades of his tenure essentially pushing his own research agenda. This effort entailed comprehensive studies of the taxonomy and geographic distribution of the nation's vertebrate fauna, principally birds and mammals. This was done in the context of his life zone theory, which posited that temperature extremes were the principal desiderata in determining the geographic distribution of organisms. He utilized new types of traps, which had been invented for the capture of smaller mammals, and developed more systematic methods of field work, enabling him and his field men to identify and describe hundreds of new species. Some Biological Survey naturalists, young men of modest educational attainments whom Merriam trained on the job, became noted mammalogists and ornithologists in their own right; they included Vernon Bailey, Theodore Sherman Palmer, Wilfred Osgood, and Gerrit Smith Miller, Jr.

The Biological Survey's many publications, notably those in the North American Fauna series (1889 on), some written by Merriam, were valuable additions to the literature on mammals and biogeography. His own contributions included *Results of a Biological Survey of the San Francisco Mountain Region and Desert of the Little Colorado Region, Arizona* (1890), *Life Zones and Crop Zones of the United States* (1898), and taxonomic revisions of North American pocket mice, pocket gophers, shrews, and weasels. For more than half a century, Merriam spent half of each year in Washington, D.C., and the other half in the field, mainly in the West.

From 1891 to 1911 Merriam advised several government departments concerning the problem of fur seals being hunted to near extinction in the waters of the Bering Sea. His membership on the Fur Seal Advisory Board continued until the United States, Great Britain, Japan, and Russia signed an international agreement in 1911 providing effective protection for the fur seals of that region.

In 1899 the railroad magnate Edward H. Harriman organized an elaborate scientific expedition to Alaska, and Merriam was asked to select most of the participants, coordinate their work, and edit their published results, which appeared in thirteen volumes between 1901 and 1914 as *Reports of the Harriman Alaska Expedition*.

After 1905 Merriam had to deal with an array of new professional and bureaucratic challenges. The late nineteenth-century vogue of establishing new species on the basis of very narrowly drawn physical distinctions ("splitting") was giving way to an opposite tendency among zoologists, known as "lumping." With his training in mammalian anatomy, Merriam could not accept this change. His last major taxonomic revision, *Review of the Grizzly and Big Brown Bears of North America* (1918), demonstrated his excessive tendency to "splitting" and was highly controversial. Developments in genetics provided new means of reaching more accurate conclusions about the nature of mammal populations and speciation. Merriam's life zone theory gave way to more sophisticated biogeographic models. Congress, increasingly reluctant to support Merriam's research agenda, compelled his agency to focus more effort on practical advice to farmers and ranchers. Staff time was also increasingly given to the enforcement of game laws and conservation legislation, beginning with the Lacey Act of 1900 (which he had helped promote, not knowing his own agency would be responsible for enacting its conservation measures) and including territorial game laws in Alaska. Merriam, who had little patience with these changes of emphasis and abhorred the congressional budget process, failed to persuade Congress of the need to raise appropriations for his agency, which had risen from $5,000 to only $62,000 by the end of his quarter-century tenure in 1910.

In 1910 E. H. Harriman's widow, Mary Harriman, responding to the urgings of colleagues who wanted Merriam freed of bureaucratic responsibilities so that he could complete several long-term projects on mammals, set up a trust fund for him. Under this arrangement, Merriam received an annual salary of $5,000 and an annual research subvention of $7,000 for the remainder of his productive career. He resigned from the Biological Survey and, until 1939, focused much of his attention on North American bears, but his syntheses dealing with these mammals and with North American mammals in general were never completed. Although he had no training in the field, Merriam spent much time in his later years on studies of the vocabularies of disappearing California Indian tribes, which remained unpublished at his death.

Merriam was a founder and first president of the Linnaean Society of New York (1878); a founding member, fellow, and president (1900–1903) of the American Ornithologists' Union; a founder and first president (1919–1921) of the American Society of Mammalogists; and president (1924–1925) of the American Society of Naturalists. He was also a founder and longtime trustee of the National Geographic Society and was elected to the National Academy of Sciences in 1902. He lived with his older daughter in Berkeley, California, following the death of his wife in 1937, and he died there five years later.

Trained as a physician and anatomist, Merriam came of age before the development of modern graduate programs in zoology. He pioneered new methods of field investigation in mammalogy but distrusted conclusions reached by better-trained laboratory scientists. His biogeographic theories were outmoded by the mid-1930s. Nevertheless, many of his methods and conclusions continue to influence modern mammalogy. He named twenty-four genera and about 660 species and subspecies of mammals new to science. A complex and controversial administrator, he was a transitional figure between traditional naturalists and modern zoologists.

• Many of Merriam's papers and complete sets of his home and field journals (1873–1938) are in the Manuscripts Division of the Library of Congress, which also contains useful materials in the papers of Theodore Roosevelt and of two Biological Survey associates, Albert Kenrick Fisher and Theodore Sherman Palmer. Several file cabinets of Merriam's manuscripts and clippings are held at the Museum of Vertebrate Zoology, University of California, Berkeley. The Bancroft Library at Berkeley has some 15,000 of Merriam's photographs, slides, and other illustrations. The papers of Merriam's brother-in-law Vernon Bailey, at the University of Wyoming Library in Laramie, contain many Merriam letters. Smaller collections of letters are in the Departments of Ornithology and Mammalogy, American Museum of Natural History, New York; the Museum of Vertebrate Zoology, Harvard University; and the Smithsonian Institution Archives, Washington, D.C. The only biography is K. B. Sterling, *Last of the Naturalists: The Career of C. Hart Merriam* (rev. ed., 1977). See also Donald Hoffmeister and K. B. Sterling, "Origin," in *Seventy-Five Years of Mammalogy (1919–1994)*, ed. E. C. Birney and J. R. Choate (1994), and K. B. Sterling, "Builders of the Biological Survey, 1885–1930," *Journal of Forest History* (Oct. 1989). A biographical appreciation by Wilfred H. Osgood, with a bibliography of Merriam's works by Hilda W. Grinnell, is in the National Academy of Sciences, *Biographical Memoirs* 24 (1947): 1–26. Jenks Cameron, *The Bureau of Biological Survey: Its History, Activities and Organization* (1929), is an excellent institutional history with a valuable bibliography. Useful critiques of Merriam's life zone theory are by S. Charles Kendeigh and Victor E. Shelford in *Wilson Bulletin* (Sept. 1932) and by Rexford F. Daubenmire in *Quarterly Review of Biology* (Sept. 1938). Alfred Kroeber, "C. Hart Merriam as Anthropologist," in C. Hart Merriam, *Studies of California Indians* (1955), pp. vii–xiv, is a sensitive appreciation of Merriam's work in this field. William H. Goetzmann and Kay Sloan, *Looking Far North: The Harriman Expedition to Alaska, 1899* (1982), is the best account of that undertaking. Obituaries are in the *New York Times*, *New York Herald Tribune*, *New York Sun*, and *Baltimore Sun*, 21 Mar. 1942; the *New York Herald Tribune* also published an editorial appreciation of Merriam's career. See also obituaries by T. S. Palmer in *Auk* (Apr. 1954), A. K. Fisher in the *Journal of the Washington Academy of Sciences* (15 Oct. 1942), and Charles L. Camp in *California Historical Society Quarterly* (Sept. 1942).

KEIR B. STERLING

MERRIAM, Henry Clay (13 Nov. 1837–18 Nov. 1912), soldier, was born in Houlton, Maine, the son of Lewis Merriam and May Ann Foss. He was initially educated at Houlton Academy, then he entered Colby College in Waterville, Maine, to study law. His law studies were interrupted in 1862, when he joined the Twentieth Maine Volunteer Infantry Regiment as a captain to participate in the Civil War. Owing to his distinguished military service in the war, Colby College subsequently granted him a bachelor of arts in 1864 and a master of arts in 1867.

Merriam demonstrated great bravery during the early campaigns of the Civil War, and he was given command of black troops. In 1862 he fought at the battles of Antietam, Shepherdstown, and Fredericksburg. In 1863 he was transferred to the Eightieth Colored Infantry and sent southward. On 27 May 1863 he participated in the Union attack on Port Hudson, Louisiana, where he was cited for gallantry in action and earned a promotion to lieutenant colonel. On 9 April 1865, at the battle of Fort Blakely, he achieved lasting fame. Leading the assault on this Confederate bastion, a vital part of the outer defenses of Mobile, Alabama, his courage was so pronounced that he was awarded the Congressional Medal of Honor. His gallantry contributed to the capture of 6,000 Confederates, and he was brevetted a colonel in the regular and volunteer army.

After the Civil War Merriam left the army to resume his law studies, but he soon returned to the army and began an eventful career in the American West. In October 1865 he was again a civilian, pursuing his studies. In 1866 he married Lucy J. Getchell; the couple had one daughter. Later that year he decided to return to uniform and was commissioned a major in the regular army. He was sent to Texas to command Fort McIntosh along the Mexican border. Tragedy struck on 24 April 1870, when Lucy Merriam and the couple's infant daughter drowned in a cloudburst at Staked Plains, Texas. In 1874 Merriam married Una Macpherson-Macneil; they had three sons and two daughters.

In early April 1876 Merriam became involved in a serious border incident, when in reprisal for the maltreatment of U.S. citizens, he fired on Mexican army units. He was promoted to lieutenant colonel on 10 June. In August 1876 he led American troops across the border and rescued an American commercial agent being held by Mexican revolutionaries.

Transferred to the North and West, Merriam participated in active operations against American Indians for the next fourteen years. His initial campaign in these operations was against the Nez Percé tribe in 1877. His performance of duty won commendations from Generals Oliver O. Howard and Nelson A. Miles and the thanks of civil authorities in Idaho and Washington. On 10 July 1885 Merriam was promoted to colonel in command of the Seventh Infantry Regiment. Five years later he was involved in the final disarming of the Sioux in the 1890–1891 campaign, and during this period he had the delicate task of taking rifles and pistols away from 300 of Sitting Bull's veteran warriors. On 30 June 1897 he was promoted to brigadier general in the regular army.

Merriam did not see active operations during the Spanish American War, being charged with mobilization duties and keeping the peace at home. He was elevated to major general of volunteers and was instrumental in preparing troops for deployment to the Philippines. During the next year, as the commander of the Department of Colorado, he was ordered to dispatch troops to quell labor unrest at the Coeur d'Alene lead mines, coming to the assistance of overwhelmed Idaho civil officials. Using tact and good judgment, he declared martial law and acted quickly and firmly to restore order and civil control. An investigation of the incident later concluded that Merriam's management of the dangerous incident was judicious and appropriate.

Merriam retired from the army after almost forty years of active duty. In recognition of his long and faithful service to the United States, Congress advanced him to the rank of major general. He died in Portland, Maine.

Among his many accomplishments, Merriam invented a soldier's pack. This innovation was of such merit that the French Academy of Inventors awarded him a gold medal. However, his chief contribution was to consistently lead with bravery and sound judgment in storming Confederate defenses, commanding black troops, dealing with explosive border disputes, or quelling emotion-packed labor riots for almost four decades.

• Merriam's ancestry is in C. H. Pope, *Merriam Genealogy* (1906). His career is traced in the *Official Army Register* (1903). His Civil War service is in *The War of the Rebellion: A Compilation of the Official Records of the Union and Confederate Armies* (128 vols., 1880–1901). The events of the 1899 Idaho riots are detailed in Samuel H. Hayes, Attorney General, *Report to the Governor of Idaho on the Insurrection in Shoshone County, Idaho*. Obituaries are in the *New York Times* and the *New York Herald*, both 19 Nov. 1912, and the *Army and Navy Journal*, 23 Nov. 1912.

ROD PASCHALL

MERRIAM, John Campbell (20 Oct. 1869–30 Oct. 1945), paleontologist and science administrator, was born in Hopkinton, Iowa, the son of Charles Edward Merriam and Margaret Campbell Kirkwood. Merriam's father, following four years of service in the Union army, became a merchant, a leader in local church and civic affairs, and a trustee of the local college. His mother encouraged the boy's interest in natural history.

After being educated at home and in public schools, Merriam received a B.S. at age sixteen from Lenox College in Hopkinton, Iowa, in 1887. The family then moved to Berkeley, California. Merriam attended the University of California at Berkeley, where he was an assistant in mineralogy and studied geology with Joseph Le Conte and botany with Edward Lee Greene. At Le Conte's urging, Merriam attended the University of Munich, Germany, where he studied with paleontologist Karl Alfred Von Zittel. He received a Ph.D. there in 1893 in vertebrate paleontology, with a dissertation on fossil reptiles.

In 1894 Merriam became an instructor in geology at the University of California, Berkeley. He married Ada Gertrude Little in 1896; they had three children. He advanced to assistant professor in 1899, associate professor in 1905, and professor in 1912, teaching courses in the departments of zoology and geology, until a separate department of paleontology was established in 1909, with Merriam as chairman. He then increased the number of courses offered in paleontology and developed an undergraduate course that was widely attended. Some support for this department and its collections was provided by philanthropist Annie M. Alexander, who had taken courses from Merriam.

At the University of California Merriam began researches in both vertebrate and invertebrate paleontology and published papers on a fossil beaver, Tertiary mollusks from Vancouver Island, and on fossil echinoids (sea urchins and sand dollars) from California. He pointed out the significance of the evolutionary changes of the echinoids during the Tertiary epoch in defining the age of geologic deposits and their correlation. He also identified collections of invertebrate fossils for other geologists.

Merriam focused more on vertebrate paleontology from 1899 and 1900, when he led field trips with students and colleagues to the John Day Basin in southwestern Oregon to collect large numbers of fossil mammals. This area had been sampled by earlier vertebrate paleontologists, but Merriam was the first to work out the stratigraphic sequence. He published "A Contribution to the Geology of the John Day Basin" in 1901 (*University of California Publications, Bulletin of Department of Geology* 2, no. 9: 269–314), and he described fossils from the area in several later papers.

The existence of the tar pits of Rancho La Brea in southern California had been known for some years, and in 1906 Merriam began collecting Pleistocene fossils there. "With characteristic energy and thoroughness," wrote biographer Ralph W. Chaney, "he supervised the removal of what has become the largest and most complete collection of vertebrate fossils ever made from one locality" (p. 384). Merriam included his students in the fieldwork, and he cooperated with paleontologists from other California institutions. He described the locale in "The Fauna of Rancho La Brea: Part I, Occurrence" (*University of California Memoirs* 1, no. 2 [1911]: 197–213), and he published many other papers on its fossil mammals, some coauthored with his former student Chester Stock. The area has continued to yield Pleistocene fossils and some early human remains.

Merriam collected fossils in various areas of California and other western states. Most of his studies were on mammals, but he continued his first interest in reptiles with several papers and a monograph, "Triassic Ichthyosauria, with Special Reference to the American Forms" (*University of California Memoirs* 1, no. 1 [1908], pp. 1–196). Always interested in archeology, he also studied and published on human remains found in some western caves.

In 1917 Merriam, with Henry Fairfield Osborn and Madison Grant, founded the first organization to set aside coastal redwoods in public reserves, the Save-the-Redwoods League. From 1917 to 1920 he was chairman of the Research Committee of the California State Council of Defense. He was elected into the National Academy of Sciences in 1918 and was chairman of the National Research Council in 1919. The next year he became dean of the faculties of the University of California but served only one year.

In 1920 Merriam became president of the Carnegie Institution of Washington in Washington, D.C., where he became noted for cooperating with other research organizations. He increased the number of the institution's research associates who were located elsewhere, and he encouraged them to publish their scientific researches and to give popular lectures. He appointed committees to recommend interdisciplinary programs. One of these compiled information about the surface of the moon. Another committee recommended a program of research on earthquake hazards of the Pacific coast. As a result, between 1922 and 1931, a network of stations with newly developed seismographs was established in California, surveying monuments were installed by the U.S. Coast and Geodetic Survey, geological mapping of faults in California was conducted, and the California Institute of Technology established the Seismological Laboratory in Pasadena. Merriam encouraged studies of archeology in southern Mexico and Guatemala and later in the United States and in Asia, and he organized an international symposium on early man in 1937. At some time in his later years he founded a private research organization, John Day Associates, to continue scientific studies in that basin.

During his tenure at the Carnegie Institution of Washington, Merriam published many articles on the role of science, education, conservation, national parks, and ancient human history. He also wrote *The Living Past* (1930), a collection of previously published articles on human history and values. When he retired in 1938, he was honored with the book *Cooperation in Research* (1938), written by members and research associates of the institution about scientific advances in programs that he had encouraged. He returned to California and continued writing on the significance of science. His final book, *The Garment of God* (1943), expresses his philosophy that understanding nature enriches human experience.

Merriam's wife died in 1940, and the next year he married Margaret Louise Webb. They had no children. He died in Oakland, California.

• Merriam's archival papers are in the Manuscript Division, Library of Congress, and in the Archives of the Bancroft Library, University of California, Berkeley. All of his publications are collected in *Published Papers and Addresses of John Campbell Merriam* (1938). Significant publications not cited above include "The Thalattosauria: A Group of Marine Reptiles from the Triassic of California," *Memoirs of California Academy of Sciences* 5, no. 1 (1905): 1–52; "Tertiary Vertebrate Faunas of the North Coalinga Region of California," *Transactions of American Philosophical Society* 22, pt. 3 (1915): 191–234; and *The Felidae of Rancho La Brea*, with Chester Stock (1932). Among his articles for the layman is the three-part "The Beginnings of Human History Read from the Geological Record: The Emergence of Man," *Scientific Monthly* 9, no. 3 (1919): 193–209; 10, no. 4 (1920): 321–42; and 10, no. 5 (1920): 425–37.

The volume *Cooperation in Research* (1938) includes summaries of many of Merriam's accomplishments, including Chester Stock, "John Campbell Merriam as Scientist and Philosopher," pp. 765–78; Stock also wrote memorials in the *Proceedings Volume of Geological Society of America, Annual Report for 1946* (1947), pp. 183–198, and in *National Academy of Sciences, Biographical Memoirs* 26 (1951): 206–32, with bibliography. A memorial by Ralph W. Chaney is in *American Philosophical Society Yearbook 1945* (1946), pp. 381–87.

ELIZABETH NOBLE SHOR

MERRIAM, William Rush (26 July 1849–18 Feb. 1931), banker, Minnesota governor, and director of the 1900 census, was born at Wadham's Mills, Essex County, New York, the son of John Lafayette Merriam, a merchant and iron ore dealer, and Mahala Kimpton De Lano. His mother died in 1857, and his father married Helen M. Wilder. In 1861 he moved with his family to St. Paul, Minnesota, joining his stepuncle, Amherst H. Wilder, who had moved from New York two years earlier. Merriam's father, who was often associated in business with Wilder, soon achieved prominence and wealth through investments in stagecoaches, railroads, and banks.

From 1864 to 1871 Merriam was educated at the prep school and college in Racine, Wisconsin. After graduating from Racine College as class valedictorian, he began his banking career. In 1871 he clerked briefly in the First National Bank of St. Paul, which was owned principally by his father and stepuncle. Later in the year he was named cashier of the Merchants' National Bank, which had just been organized by his father and other investors. He became the institution's vice president in 1880 and four years later succeeded his father as president. In 1872 he married Laura E.

Hancock, daughter of Colonel John Hancock (1824–1893). The couple had five children.

Following in his father's footsteps, Merriam was elected to the Minnesota House of Representatives in 1883. Early in his first term he made his mark in Republican party politics as a leader of the younger Republican faction by blocking the third-term bid of William Windom, Minnesota's old-guard, senior U.S. senator. In 1886, during his second legislative term, Merriam was chosen Speaker of the house, a position his father had held in 1870–1871.

In 1888 Merriam challenged Governor Andrew R. McGill for the Republican gubernatorial nomination and won the support of the nominating convention despite his party's tradition of renominating incumbents. Merriam and his supporters played on the fear that McGill, a narrow victor in 1886 and the champion of controversial high liquor license fees, could not win the general election and thus would jeopardize Benjamin Harrison's (1833–1901) prospects of carrying Minnesota in the presidential race.

Merriam's strength was his popularity in rural Minnesota. As Speaker he was sympathetic to Farmers' Alliance aims such as state railroad controls and creation of a grain inspection system, and in 1886–1887 and 1887–1888 he served as vice president and president of the Minnesota State Agricultural Society. Consequently, many Republicans regarded him as their party's best answer to the demands of the increasingly strident Farmers' Alliance. Following the bitterly contested convention, Merriam was easily elected governor, but his tactics offended many former Windom and McGill supporters. His popularity declined during his first term, because he and the Republican-controlled legislature failed to support Farmers' Alliance goals. The disappointed alliance nominated its own gubernatorial candidate in 1890. Despite considerable rural opposition, the lingering hostility of some members of his own party, and appealing alliance and Democratic candidates, Merriam was narrowly reelected. During his second administration the legislature enacted a statewide Australian ballot and refunded the state's debt.

Having attracted considerable attention as the nation's second youngest governor, Merriam was regarded as a prospect for the U.S. Senate to replace Cushman K. Davis, Minnesota's senior senator. In a move that ruined Merriam's political future, he and his supporters unsuccessfully tried to block Davis's reelection by the legislature to open the way for Merriam's bid. Merriam was an influential delegate to the Republican National Convention in 1896. As a strong gold standard advocate, he served on the Platform Committee and was instrumental in helping William McKinley carry Minnesota. Despite his key role in McKinley's victory, Merriam was never named to the major diplomatic post he anticipated, because the resentful Davis would not support him.

Finally, three years after the campaign, McKinley named Merriam to direct the Twelfth Census. Because of the recent sharp growth of the nation, this was an enormous task. Merriam hired prominent statisticians to conduct the technical aspects of census taking and through his administrative and organizational skills supervised the rapid completion of the project and the dissemination of its results. S. N. D. North, Merriam's successor, praised the outcome as the best of the nation's first twelve censuses. During his directorship Merriam publicized the census extensively by contributing articles to leading magazines, such as the *North American Review* and the *Atlantic Monthly*. Perhaps his greatest contribution was in convincing Congress to establish a permanent census bureau.

Merriam resigned in 1903 to devote himself to various businesses in Washington, D.C. While he was governor and census director, the Merriams were known for their lavish entertainment of prominent people. He served as president of the Shenandoah Coal and Iron Company and the Liberty Furnace Company, both based in Virginia, and as president of the Tabulating Machine Company of Washington, D.C. In retirement he and his family maintained their Washington residence but spent their winters at their Fort Sewall, Florida, home where he died.

• Archival records of Merriam's governorship are in the Minnesota Historical Society, St. Paul. Extensive biographical sketches of Merriam are in James H. Baker, *Lives of the Governors of Minnesota*, vol. 13 (1908), and "State Builders of the West: William Rush Merriam, Eleventh Governor of Minnesota," *Western Magazine*, 1 Sept. 1919, pp. 133–35. For the Merriam-McGill competition in 1888, see H. P. Hall, *Observations* (1904). Merriam's role in the Minnesota State Agricultural Society is described in Darwin S. Hall and R. I. Holcombe, *History of the Minnesota State Agricultural Society* (1910). Events of Merriam's gubernatorial administration are covered in William Watts Folwell, *A History of Minnesota* (4 vols., 1921–1930). For the history of the Merriam family, see Charles Henry Pope, *Merriam Genealogy in England and America* (1906). Obituaries are in the *St. Paul Pioneer Press*, the *Minneapolis Tribune*, and the *New York Times*, 19 Feb. 1931.

WILLIAM E. LASS

MERRICK, Edwin Thomas (9 July 1809–12 Jan. 1897), lawyer and jurist, was born in Wilbraham, Massachusetts, the son of Thomas Merrick and Anna Brewer. His father died when Merrick was very young, and he was raised by an uncle, Samuel Brewer of Springfield, Massachusetts, where he received his early education. In 1828 Merrick entered the Wesleyan Academy in Wilbraham, from which he graduated in 1832. While attending the academy, Merrick began to read law in the office of William Knight. After his graduation, Merrick studied law in the office of his uncle, Alonzo Brewer, in New Lisbon, Ohio. Admitted to the Ohio bar in 1833, Merrick began practice in Carrollton. The following year he assumed his uncle's practice in New Lisbon, forming a partnership with William E. Russell. After Russell's retirement, Merrick moved to Louisiana in 1838, opening an office in Clinton in partnership with James H. Muse.

Making special study of Louisiana's unique civil law, a system unlike the common law found in other states, Merrick mastered it and was admitted to the Louisiana bar in 1839. His practice in Clinton flourished, and Merrick's statewide distinction was such that in 1845 he was elected judge of the Seventh Judicial District of Louisiana, which covered the parishes of East and West Feliciana. In 1855 he successfully ran on the Whig ticket for the office of chief justice of the Louisiana Supreme Court for an eight-year term. Called "a born judge" in an obituary published in *Reports of the American Bar Association* (20 [1897]), Merrick reportedly had a "straight-forward mind, a legal mind, fortified by incessant study, well conducted" and was "thoroughly equipped for the arduous and responsible duties of the magistrate" (p. 535). Lawyers later commented that "references and citations, from the fruit of unremitting research, crowded and would perhaps sometimes incumber [*sic*] his opinions." Merrick was called "exact and formal," enforcing "every one of the rules" of the supreme court; he "repressed at once anything which bordered on improper line of remark, or on light conduct, on the part of counsel" (*Louisiana Report*, p. viii).

The northern-born Merrick opposed Louisiana's secession from the Union, but when secession occurred he remained loyal to his adopted state. He moved the supreme court to the western part of Louisiana after the capture of New Orleans by Union forces in 1862. Reelected chief justice in 1863, Merrick was removed from office at the close of the Civil War by the Reconstruction government and was disbarred when he refused to take a loyalty oath. After achieving a pardon for his participation in the secessionist government, Merrick recovered his home in New Orleans and his plantation in West Feliciana, which had been confiscated during the war. He was reinstated as an attorney and resumed a distinguished law practice that included the argument of successful appeals to the U.S. Supreme Court.

Merrick was married in 1840 to Caroline E. Thomas of Jackson, Louisiana; they had four children. Caroline Merrick eventually became a noted suffragist. Merrick toward the end of his life became law partners with one of his sons, Edwin Thomas Merrick, Jr. A Methodist, Merrick was an administrator of Centenary College in Jackson, Louisiana. He also wrote several legal works, including *The Laws of Louisiana and Their Sources* (1871), a treatise about Louisiana's peculiar mixture of civil and common law, which one source reported was so remarkable it caused "worldwide comment" (*Louisiana*, p. 146).

Merrick continued practicing law to his final days, appearing before the state supreme court a week before his death. He died at his home in New Orleans, at age eighty-seven, the oldest member of Louisiana's bar. His death brought gushing praise, the New Orleans Law Association describing him as "singularly pure" and "domestic, temperate, simple in all his habits, modest, patient, punctual and exceedingly studious . . . a good husband and a loving parent" (*Louisiana Reports*, p. viii). One lawyer found him "extraordinarily industrious; devoted to his books, and particularly of the driest and most abstruse works" (*Louisiana Reports*, p. ix).

Merrick experienced a most unusual life, stretching geographically from Yankee New England to the frontier Midwest to antebellum Louisiana and professionally from the English-based common law to the French-based civil law. He appeared to master all settings in which he found himself, through diligent hard work if not through brilliance. "Pure as a puritan, but not of their thinking" (*Louisiana Reports*, p. x), Merrick, through his term as chief justice, his writings, and his long career at the bar, left his mark as much as any lawyer of his day on the jurisprudence of Louisiana.

• A collection of Merrick papers is in the Historic New Orleans Collection. Entries on Merrick are in vol. 2 of Alcée Fortier, *Louisiana* (1914), and in the *New Orleans Times-Democrat*, 13 Jan. 1897. An extended memorial by the Louisiana Supreme Court is in *Louisiana Reports* 49 (1897). See also Caroline Merrick's autobiography, *Old Times in Dixieland* (1901).

FRANCIS HELMINSKI

MERRICK, John (7 Sept. 1859–6 Aug. 1919), insurance company founder and entrepreneur, was born a slave in Sampson County, North Carolina. Merrick never knew his father, but his mother, Martha, was a strong presence in his life. Little is known of Merrick's early years, except that, to help support his mother and brother, he began working in a brickyard in Chapel Hill when he was twelve. In 1877 he moved with his family to Raleigh, where he worked as a helper on the crew that constructed the original buildings on the campus of Shaw University. Merrick could have remained in the construction trade—he advanced to brick mason, a highly skilled and relatively well paid occupation—but he had far greater aspirations. Merrick's first goal was to open his own barber shop, one of the few business opportunities open to black southerners at that time. So he soon quit being a brick mason and took a menial job as a bootblack in a barber shop, in the process learning the barbering trade. After becoming a barber in Raleigh, Merrick began to attract as his customers several of the area's most prestigious men, among them tobacco magnates Washington Duke and Julian S. Carr, who convinced him and another barber in the shop, John Wright, to move to the nearby tobacco town of Durham and open a decent barber shop there.

Durham was a quintessential "New South" city. Created in the wake of burgeoning industrialization in the region, Durham was a frontier of sorts, undeveloped and open, one of the few places in the South where African Americans had a chance of achieving success on their own terms. Merrick and Wright opened a shop in Durham in 1880 and ran it together until 1892, when Wright sold out to Merrick. Soon after arriving, Merrick began to branch out, purchasing in 1881 the first of many lots in Hayti, the developing African-American section of town, where he himself lived. Merrick constructed small rental houses on these lots, eventually becoming one of Hayti's largest landholders. In the late 1890s he expanded his barbering business—at one time owning as many as nine shops—and also developed a broadly advertised cure for dandruff.

Merrick's most significant involvement during his early years in Durham was his purchase, along with several others, of the Royal Knights of King David, a black Fraternal order, in 1883. An important feature of the Royal Knights, as with other fraternal orders of the era, was the provision of insurance plans to its members. Merrick came to realize, however, that the meager death benefits offered by the Royal Knights were not enough to provide adequate coverage for African Americans. As a result, in conjunction with several other prominent blacks in Durham and Raleigh, Merrick founded the North Carolina Mutual and Provident Insurance Company in Durham in 1898. The firm began operations in April 1899 but almost failed after six months, primarily from lack of adequate attention by the founders. At that point Merrick and Aaron McDuffie Moore, Durham's first black physician, bought out the other investors and reorganized the firm as the North Carolina Mutual Insurance Company. They also hired Charles Clinton Spaulding, a relative of Moore's, to take over full-time management of the concern. Although Merrick was not the firm's operating manager, he was the primary figurehead during its first two decades. Initially, North Carolina Mutual only underwrote industrial insurance, but the firm soon expanded into industrial straight life and, later, into other policies. Income, which was just $840 in the company's first year, had surged to about $1.7 million by 1919, the year of Merrick's death.

North Carolina Mutual was only one of Merrick's many business enterprises in Durham. He was vice president of the Mechanics and Farmers Bank, organized in 1907. A vitally important element in the development of local capitalist ventures by African Americans, Mechanics and Farmers Bank helped Durham become what sociologist E. Franklin Frazier called the "capital of the black middle class." By the early 1920s, when the bank had more than $600,000 in deposits and assets of $800,000, it had become a crucial source of capital for blacks who wanted to purchase homes and start small businesses. In 1910, when Booker T. Washington visited Durham, he described it as the most progressive city in the South and praised Merrick for his incomparable leadership in the black business community.

Merrick's real estate purchases led him to join with Moore and Spaulding in organizing the Merrick-Moore-Spaulding Land Company to own and manage properties owned by Merrick and by North Carolina Mutual. In 1906 North Carolina Mutual established its own newspaper, the *Durham Negro Observer*. Its more successful successor, the *North Carolina Mutual*, was for decades the city's only African-American newspaper. In 1908 Merrick and several others started Bull City Drug Company to operate drugstores in Hayti. One of Merrick's most important, though short-lived, ventures was the Durham Textile Mill, established in 1914 to manufacture socks. The mill was historically significant because it attempted to show, contrary to white southern myth, that African Americans could profitably be employed as textile workers.

At Merrick's death, from cancer, he was survived by his wife, Martha Hunter, and four of their five children. His son Edward later served for many years as treasurer of North Carolina Mutual, which eventually became the largest black business enterprise in America (until after World War II) and which still operates in virtually every state. It was John Merrick's organizational ability, his contacts with the white community, and his status in the broader African-American community that did much to make the venture the success it became. His influence with wealthy whites was well known. It was Merrick who persuaded the Duke family to provide funds for the establishment of private Lincoln Hospital in 1901. Indeed, Merrick's greatest talent was perhaps his ability to push for greater economic and social opportunities for blacks while adapting those efforts to the realities of the time. In seeking white investment for various black business concerns, he never put the independence of those ventures in jeopardy.

• There is no collection of Merrick's private papers, and just one of his letters is in the Duke University Archives, along with a scattering of his letters to Booker T. Washington in the Booker T. Washington Papers in the Library of Congress. Material on North Carolina Mutual is in that company's archives in Durham, but it is not open to researchers. Some material on the early operation of the firm is in the Southern Oral History Program in the Southern Historical Collection at the University of North Carolina at Chapel Hill. A full-scale biography of Merrick is Robert McCants Andrews, *John Merrick: A Biographical Sketch* (1920). By far the best account of North Carolina Mutual is by Walter B. Weare, *Black Business in the New South: A Social History of the North Carolina Mutual Insurance Company* (1973), but see also an insider account, William J. Kennedy, *The North Carolina Mutual Story* (1970). Some additional information can be found in Jesse E. Gloster, "North Carolina Mutual Insurance Company: Its Historical Development and Current Operations" (Ph.D. diss., Univ. of Pittsburgh, 1955). For insight into the importance of Durham for blacks during the first few decades of the twentieth century, see Booker T. Washington, "Durham, North Carolina: A City of Negro Enterprise," *Independent*, 30 Mar. 1911; W. E. B. Du Bois, "The Upbuilding of Black Durham," *World's Work*, Jan. 1912; Clement Richardson, "What Are Negroes Doing in Durham?" *Southern Workman*, July 1913; and E. Franklin Frazier, "Durham, Capital of the Black Middle Class," in *The New Negro: An Interpretation*, ed. Alain Locke (1925).

JOHN N. INGHAM

MERRICK, Myra King (15 Aug. 1825–10 Nov. 1899), physician and educator, was born in Hinckley, Leicestershire, England, the daughter of Richard King, a brickmaker, and Elizabeth (maiden name unknown). In 1826 the family emigrated to the United States and settled in Taunton, Massachusetts. At the age of eight, Myra began working in Taunton's textile mills, helping to support a family that now numbered five children. In 1841 the family moved to Cleveland, Ohio, where she secured employment as a nurse to several physicians in the area and developed an interest in medicine as a profession. After her marriage to builder and machinist Charles H. Merrick in 1848, the couple moved to Connecticut, where she began the study of medicine under New Haven physicians Eli Ives, professor of theory and practice of medicine at Yale University, and his obstetrician son, Levi Ives.

Completing her apprenticeship, Merrick sought additional medical education in New York City. There she attended medical lectures at Hyatt's Academy and studied privately with Mary Gove Nichols, one of the pioneers of the hydropathic movement in the United States. Merrick's search for clinical experience led her to the Nichols's Hydropathic Institute in Brooklyn, where, according to her daughter-in-law, Eliza J. Merrick, she was "sent all over the city to give packs" or applications of cold water to the body with the intent of relieving discomfort and disease (letter to Mason-Hohl, 30 Oct. 1945).

In 1851 Merrick secured admission to one of the few medical institutions that admitted women at that time, the Central Medical College in Syracuse, New York, an eclectic institution that promoted botanical substitutes for drugs used by regular physicians. Graduating in 1852 at the top of her class, she and Charles returned to Ohio, where she set about building a medical practice and a family at the same time. The couple's two sons were born in 1854 and 1858. When Charles left to join the Union army during the Civil War, Merrick moved to rural North Eaton, Ohio, where she attempted to sustain the family with income from her medical practice and by managing her husband's financially precarious sawmill and lumber business. Overburdened with debt, Merrick returned to Cleveland in 1863 to reestablish her urban medical practice.

At some point, Merrick developed an interest in homeopathy, a medical system based on infinitesimal doses of drugs prescribed according to the "Law of Similars," or "let likes be treated by likes." One of the first women members of the American Institute of Homeopathy, Merrick was a staunch advocate of women in the medical profession, allying with women students in Cleveland when they were unexpectedly barred from that city's homeopathic medical college. When the faculty of the Cleveland Homeopathic Medical College reversed its position on the admission of women and suddenly excluded them from matriculation beginning in the fall of 1867, Merrick, along with Augusta Cleora Seaman, M.D., founded the Cleveland Homeopathic Hospital College for Women. Merrick became professor of obstetrics and diseases of women, and Seaman, president of the board of trustees. Merrick took over as president upon Seaman's death in 1869.

Besides establishing a degree-granting program for women intending to become physicians, the new college offered an innovative program of lectures designed to increase the knowledge of women who sought to enhance their ability to care for family members in times of illness and disease. Opening its door in 1868, the college enrolled approximately forty women during its three years of operation while the all-male homeopathic college suffered a drop in tuition revenue. In the spring of 1871 the Cleveland Homeopathic College reversed its position and again welcomed women to its courses, promising a curriculum of joint education of the sexes. Despite support by some women to maintain a separate educational institution, the board of trustees voted to merge with the men's college. Merrick was appointed special lecturer in obstetrics at the newly named Cleveland Homoeopathic Hospital College. Learning that she would not be permitted to teach male students, however, she resigned on 16 October 1871 but continued as preceptor to several women students throughout the 1870s.

The social and professional associations Merrick developed during her tenure with the women's college offered her an opportunity for a more prosperous private medical practice. She became friends with oil magnate John D. Rockefeller, who favored homeopathic medicine, and numbered among her patients the wives of Standard Oil Company executives; her name is listed as attending physician on the birth records of many prominent Cleveland residents. Her relatively lucrative medical practice enabled her to contribute $10,000 toward a new building at the homeopathic Huron Road Hospital, where she was a member of the staff.

With the help of former students and friends, Merrick organized the Cleveland Medical and Surgical Dispensary Society and devoted herself to the cause of providing health care to Cleveland's most disadvantaged and vulnerable women and children. In May 1878 that organization opened the city's first free dispensary, the "Open Door," serving mothers and children of a social class very familiar to Merrick from her childhood labor in Taunton's mills. In addition to working one morning each week in the clinic, she served as the dispensary's president for a period of twenty years. Merrick was an effective fundraiser, providing for the institution's continued growth and usefulness to the city's poor throughout her life. Before her death, Merrick and others connected with the dispensary incorporated the Women's and Children's Free Medical and Surgical Dispensary, formalizing its provisions to care for poor women and their children while providing clinical opportunities for women physicians.

Merrick died in Cleveland. Divorced from Charles Merrick in 1881, she was survived by her son Richard and her daughter-in-law Eliza J. Merrick, M.D., a graduate of the Homeopathic Hospital College of Cleveland who carried on the private medical practice of her mother-in-law.

• Information on Merrick's life between the years 1861 and 1865 can be found in a collection of letters written to her by

Charles Merrick during the Civil War (Charles H. Merrick Papers, Western Reserve Historical Society, Cleveland, Ohio). Other sources on her life include a letter to Dr. Elizabeth Mason-Hohl from Eliza J. Merrick, 30 Oct. 1945, Miami, Fla. (vertical files, Archives and Special Collections on Women in Medicine, Allegheny Univ. of the Health Sciences); Marion N. Gibbons, "A Woman Carries the Caduceus—Myra K. Merrick," in *Pioneer Medicine in the Western Reserve*, ed. Howard Dittrick (1932); Kent Brown, ed., *Medicine in Cleveland and Cuyahoga County, 1810–1976* (1977); and Charlotte Newman, "Cleveland's First Woman Physician," *Gamut*, no. 26 (Spring 1989), pp. 17–29. An obituary is in the *New York Times*, 11 Nov. 1899.

ANNE TAYLOR KIRSCHMANN

MERRICK, Samuel Vaughan (4 May 1801–18 Aug. 1870), manufacturer and railroad pioneer, was born in Hallowell, Maine, the eldest son of John Merrick, a Unitarian minister and author, and Rebecca Vaughan. His father, who came from England in 1798, provided Merrick with a rich cultural environment in which to develop. He attended Hallowell schools and in 1816 left Maine to work for his bachelor uncle, John Vaughan, in Philadelphia. His four-year apprenticeship in Vaughan's wine importing business was quite successful and revealed that Merrick had much to offer to the mercantile world.

Between 1820 and 1836 Merrick exhibited an interest in mechanics and engaged in an important engineering project to improve Philadelphia. In 1820, after Vaughan purchased an insolvent fire-engine plant in Philadelphia, Merrick decided against a career in the wine business and that same year formed a partnership with John Agnew to operate the plant. During this period, in 1823, he married Sarah Thomas; they had six children. The firm of Merrick and Agnew became quite profitable, for Merrick quickly acquired a basic knowledge of the principles of mechanics and capably marketed in Philadelphia and in other eastern cities two products: powerful and well-designed fire engines and machine gearing. Another significant technical matter also occupied Merrick's attention during the early 1830s; in 1833 he proposed using gas to light Philadelphia streets and that year was elected to the city council to implement his proposal. In 1834 city authorities named him chairman of a committee to explore this topic and that year sent him to Europe to learn about methods of gas manufacturing. When he returned, Merrick presented an extensive account of his findings to the city council, who appointed him chief engineer for the construction of the city's gas plant. On 8 February 1836 he completed the plant, which distributed gas throughout Philadelphia. The next year Merrick resigned from the city council to devote attention to his thriving manufacturing business.

Between 1836 and 1860 Merrick became the leading manufacturer of heavy machinery in Philadelphia. With John H. Towne as junior partner, in 1836 he set up the Southwark Foundry, in which they made boilers, steam engines of all kinds, and a wide assortment of mill machinery. Even after Towne retired in 1849, Merrick continued to expand the product line. He brought his son, J. Vaughan Merrick, into the company, and in 1852 they changed the name of the firm to Merrick and Sons. By the time of Merrick's retirement in 1860, his firm became Philadelphia's leading manufacturer of brass and iron castings, bone black furnaces, and steam hammers. The company also constructed sugar mill machinery and built iron lighthouses along the Florida coast. Merrick became known for constructing a marine engine for the steam frigate *Mississippi* and for building the first engine with a screw propeller for a ship of any kind, for the *Princeton*. Merrick's firm also received recognition for building the *New Ironsides*, a pioneer armor-clad vessel.

As Boston, New York, and Baltimore competed with each other between 1845 and 1860 for control of western markets, Merrick attempted to develop Philadelphia into a railroad hub. After the Pennsylvania Railroad was set up on 13 April 1846, Merrick, who had been an active member of the Philadelphia Board of Trade, was elected as the railroad's first president on 31 March 1847. He brought the company executive expertise and the ability to raise capital. Merrick succeeded in securing $3.5 million for the railroad and established its first line between Philadelphia and Harrisburg. He resigned from the presidency on 1 September 1849 to spend more time on his business; however, he continued to provide leadership to the railroad, serving as one of its directors until 2 February 1852. He also rendered support to the Sunbury and Erie Railroad, a small and financially troubled line, which, once completed, would link Philadelphia with Lake Erie. Merrick in 1856 reluctantly agreed to serve as its president and, as a result of poor health, resigned from the position the next year; thereafter, he continued to back this railroad, providing personal funds to enable it to complete its construction to Lake Erie. He also served as a director of the small Catawissa Railroad, for it would help to foster the commercial development of Philadelphia.

Merrick contributed to Philadelphia in other ways. With Professor William H. Keating of the University of Pennsylvania and with the banker Frederick Fraley, in February of 1824 he established the Franklin Institute to promote the study of the mechanical arts and the physical sciences. Between 1828 and 1831 he chaired the institute's publications committee and greatly improved the quality of its journal by publishing only substantive articles about mechanics and science. From 1842 to 1854 he served as president of the institute and recruited to its ranks prominent members from Philadelphia's business and cultural circles. Merrick was affiliated with another significant learned society; in 1833 he was elected to membership in Franklin's American Philosophical Society. He also held other important positions in Philadelphia. He served on the Sanitary Commission and was a founder of the Western Savings Fund. He belonged to the city's Grace Episcopal Church and was one of its wardens. He was known for his benevolence. In addition to contributing to schools in the South after the Civil

War, he made large donations to the Episcopal Hospital in Philadelphia. He died in Philadelphia.

Merrick was an enterprising and a civic-minded individual; he helped to establish an industrial base in Philadelphia during the first half of the nineteenth century. He also provided leadership in the attempt to transform the city into a major railroad center. However, his creation of and involvement in the Franklin Institute was his most noteworthy achievement and reflected his belief that the advancement of Philadelphia and other cities depended on practical inventions in technology and in science.

• Some letters and papers of Merrick are in the Franklin Institute and in the American Philosophical Society. The career of Merrick is described by D. R. Goodwin, "Samuel Vaughan Merrick, Esq.," *Proceedings of the American Philosophical Society* 11 (1871): 584–97, and by Charles Penrose, *Samuel Vaughan Merrick (1801–1870): Merchant, Engineer, Industrialist, and First President of the Pennsylvania Railroad* (1946). However, the most comprehensive biographical account is Thomas Coulson, "Some Prominent Members of the Franklin Institute: 1. Samuel Vaughan Merrick, 1801–1870," *Journal of the Franklin Institute* 258 (Nov. 1954): 335–46. E. T. Freedley, *Philadelphia and Its Manufacturers in 1857* (1858); Ellis Paxson Oberholtzer, *Philadelphia: A History of the City and Its People*, vol. 2 (n.d.); J. T. Scharf and Thompson Westcott, *History of Philadelphia*, vols. 1 and 3 (1884); E. Digby Baltzell, *Puritan Boston and Quaker Philadelphia: Two Protestant Ethics and the Spirit of Class Authority and Leadership* (1979); and Russell F. Weigley, ed., *Philadelphia: A 300-Year History* (1982), mention the contributions of Merrick to manufacturing in nineteenth-century Philadelphia. For his involvement in the Franklin Institute, consult Ellwood Hendrick, *Modern Views of Physical Science: Being a Record of the Proceedings of the Centenary Meeting of the Franklin Institute at Philadelphia, September 17, 18, and 19, 1924* (1925), and Bruce Sinclair, *Philadelphia's Philosopher Mechanics: A History of the Franklin Institute, 1824–1865* (1974). An obituary is in the *Philadelphia Public Ledger*, 19 Aug. 1870.

WILLIAM WEISBERGER

MERRILL, Charles Edward (19 Oct. 1885–6 Oct. 1956), investor and founder of Merill Lynch securities brokerage house, was born in Green Cove Springs, Florida, the son of Charles Morton Merrill, a physician and drugstore proprietor, and Octavia Wilson. The youngest of three children, Merrill sold newspapers as a young man, and in his early teens he attended a college preparatory school associated with Stetson University in De Land, Florida, before attending Worcester Academy in Massachusetts under an athletic scholarship. He continued his education at Amherst College in Massachusetts from 1904 to 1906 while he sold clothing, waited on tables, and participated in sports. However, he left Amherst without graduating and worked at the West Palm Beach (Fla.) *Tropical Sun* as reporter, editor, and occasional typesetter, calling it "the best training I ever had."

Merrill enrolled at the University of Michigan Law School, but he did not find law attractive and he spent the summer of 1907 playing baseball for a minor league team in Mississippi. By that time, at age twenty-two, Merrill went to New York City, where he worked in the city office of Patchogue Plymouth Mills, a textile firm that operated its main factory in Patchogue. In New York he met Edmund Lynch at a Young Men's Christian Association facility, and the two became close friends and associates.

In September 1909 Merrill took a job with a Wall Street firm, George H. Burr & Company, where he performed financial services. When the owner, George Burr, wanted to move into corporate bond sales, he hired Merrill, who in turn hired Lynch. Merrill wanted to use direct mail solicitations for bond sales, but with a change from traditional newspaper ads of the day: Merrill insisted on accuracy and solid information in the circulars. *Leslie's Illustrated Weekly* carried an article by Merrill, titled "Mr. Average Investor," in November 1911, in which he stressed obtaining information about the investor before recommending a security. He also appreciated the potential of a broad market for securities. The major firms had relied on relatively small groups of investors for their business and had adopted a somewhat elitist attitude toward securities investment. Merrill sought to change all that. "The customer," he observed, "may not always be right but he *has* rights."

Merrill continued to focus on those two themes throughout the remainder of his career: Broaden the market to average citizens by providing accurate investment information. Under Merrill, the bond department at George H. Burr quickly turned a profit, and the firm ventured into underwriting equities. Burr sponsored an offering of $2 million in preferred stock plus 10,000 shares of common stock for the Kresge chain stores. Merrill thus formed an important alliance with chain stores, then a novel approach to retailing.

But the compensation at Burr did not satisfy Merrill, and he moved to Eastman, Dillon & Company in 1913 but resigned to establish his own securities firm, Charles E. Merrill & Company in January 1914. Lynch joined him, and the two made a formidable team. The firm underwrote securities for two chain stores—McCrory Stores and Kresge (whose account Merrill brought with him)—in 1915, and these partners soon made the emerging chain store business their primary area of specialization. World War I interrupted Merrill's career, however, and he volunteered for service in 1917, serving as a flight instructor for the army's air force.

When the war ended, Merrill Lynch prepared itself for the securities boom of the 1920s. Merrill sensed that Americans had developed the habit of investing in securities through their purchase of war bonds, and that he could convince them to invest in securities markets. To do so he had to reshape public opinion about Wall Street bankers as either elitist stuffed shirts or unprincipled speculators. The firm accomplished that, in part, by keeping its focus on the customer of moderate means. For example, Merrill Lynch opened its uptown New York office every weekday from 7:00 A.M. to 9:00 P.M. for the convenience of customers, breaking Wall Street tradition. Merrill also hired Annie Grimes, Wall Street's first bond saleswoman, and never hesitated to advertise.

Increasingly, Merrill Lynch emphasized the chain store sector, with half of its underwritings going to retailers such as J. C. Penney, Kresge, and McCrory. Although the firm invested in early films, Merrill Lynch recognized that it did not have the capital to support a national theater chain, and sold out to Cecil B. DeMille and Joseph P. Kennedy. With the cash from that sale, the partners acquired Safeway Stores, a southern California food chain, in 1926. In 1929 he formed another food chain under the name Mac Marr Stores, starting with nearly forty retail outlets. Merrill transferred the sales concepts that fueled his mass marketing of securities into the mass marketing of goods at a high volume in the retail sector. He then transferred those same practices back to securities.

Merrill anticipated the stock market crash of 1929, urging investors to sell with discretion as early as March 1928. Lynch was more optimistic about the market's future, but Merrill persuaded Lynch to reduce the firm's own exposure. The most important result for the firm of Merrill's prescience, however, came after the crash, when the customers who had saved millions of dollars owed their fortunes to his advice. Nevertheless, Merrill Lynch could not capitalize fully on its reputation due to the low regard the public in general had of securities firms after 1929.

Merrill Lynch focused more sharply than ever on food chain stores, and Merrill himself was Safeway's largest stockholder. He aided Safeway management in fighting back a punitive tax in California designed to restrain the large stores' penetration of the "mom and pop" grocery market.

Edmund Lynch died in 1938, and Merrill reorganized the company over the next several years to include E. A. Pierce and Company in 1940. That brought Merrill back to active management in the securities business, and he found upon his return that the image of the investment and securities brokerage industry had sunk to new lows. Merrill took the challenge personally and made it the top priority of his company to change attitudes. He devoted substantial resources to advertising, and within the first year after reorganization the company opened 12,000 new accounts. Throughout the 1940s and 1950s Merrill Lynch expanded its network, opening its 100th office. The success of Merrill's marketing concept was seen in a 1947 poll of fifty outstanding business leaders: Merrill was the only one on the list with a securities background.

Merrill died in Southhampton, New York. His success in the financial world came at a personal price. He married Elizabeth Church in 1912, and they divorced in 1925; he married Helen Ingram in 1925, and they divorced in 1938; and he married Kinta Des Mares in 1939, and they divorced in 1952. Merrill had two children by his first wife and a son by his second wife. But Merrill had a strong philanthropic side, donating substantial sums to educational institutions, charities, Amherst College, Stetson University, and Harvard Medical School. At the time of his death, he had an estate valued at $25 million, most of which went to establish the Merrill Trust for educational, medical, and religious purposes.

• Information on Merrill is in Edwin J. Perkins, "Charles E. Merrill," in *The Encyclopedia of American Business History and Biography: Banking and Finance, 1913–1989*, ed. Larry Schweikart (1990). See also Donald T. Regan, *The Merrill Lynch Story* (1981), and Henry R. Hecht, ed., *A Legacy of Leadership: Merrill Lynch, 1885–1985* (1985). An obituary is in the *New York Times*, 7 Oct. 1956.

LARRY SCHWEIKART

MERRILL, Elmer Drew (15 Oct. 1876–25 Feb. 1956), botanist, was born in East Auburn, Maine, the son of Daniel Cummings Merrill and Mary Adelaide Noyes, shoe factory workers and farmers. He had originally planned to enter his parents' occupations; however, when his mother died in 1893 she bequeathed to him a small sum of money for the express purpose of funding his college education. After switching from engineering to general science, Merrill received his B.S. from the University of Maine in 1898 and then stayed on for an additional year as an assistant in natural science. In 1899 he took a position with the U.S. Department of Agriculture in Washington, D.C., as an assistant agrostologist (a botanist specializing in the study of grasses) and spent the next three years classifying North American grasses while familiarizing himself with herbarium methods and practices as well as the methodology of botanical nomenclature and taxonomy. From 1900 to 1901 Merrill also studied medicine at George Washington University but abandoned whatever plans he may have had to become a physician when he accepted an assignment in the Philippine Islands.

From 1902 to 1912 Merrill worked in Manila as a botanist for the Insular Bureaus of Agriculture, Forestry, Government Laboratories, and Science. In 1904 he received his M.S. from Maine, and in 1907 he married Mary Augusta Sperry; they had four children. In 1912 he was promoted to head of the Bureau of Science's botany department and was made an associate professor of botany at the University of the Philippines. In 1916 he was promoted to full professor, a position he resigned three years later to become the director of the Bureau of Science. In these capacities he established a botanical library and a herbarium with more than 275,000 specimens from the Philippines and Malaya at the university, served as editor of the *Philippine Journal of Science*, and classified for the first time thousands of plants indigenous to the Philippines. The results of this latter endeavor were published in *Enumeration of Philippine Flowering Plants*, a four-volume series published between 1922 and 1926 that identified more than 8,000 species. He also published enumerations of the flora of southeastern China, Guam, Indochina, French Polynesia, and the Dutch East Indies.

In 1923 Merrill returned to the United States to become the dean of the College of Agriculture of the University of California at Berkeley. Later that year he was also made the director of the university's agricultural experimental station. As dean he overhauled the curriculum so that the college's students received a university education instead of vocational training, and he stimulated faculty research by implementing a number of long-range investigations into fundamental aspects of agricultural science. He also added more than 100,000 specimens to the university's herbarium, founded and edited from 1925 to 1929 the agricultural journal *Hilgardia*, and served as the first director of the California Botanical Garden in Los Angeles.

In 1930 Merrill became a professor of botany at Columbia University and the director of the New York Botanical Garden. He added more than 300,000 specimens to the garden's herbarium and supervised the rehabilitation of its buildings and grounds while also serving from 1931 to 1935 as founder and editor of the botanical journal *Brittonia*. In 1935 he became affiliated with Harvard University as Arnold Professor of Botany, director of the Arnold Arboretum, and administrator of the university's botanical collections, which included the Harvard Forest in Massachusetts, a tropical substation in Cuba, and various herbariums, museums, research facilities, and libraries. From 1943 to 1945 he assisted the American effort during World War II by lecturing on tropical medicine at the U.S. Army Medical School in Washington, D.C., and by writing *Emergency Food Plants* (1943), a manual for troops stationed in the Pacific theater that identified the region's poisonous and edible plants.

Merrill retired from his administrative duties at Harvard in 1946 and from teaching in 1948. That same year he played a major role in introducing to the American West a "living fossil," the dawn redwood tree, a relative of the sequoia that was thought to be extinct until its discovery in China in 1941. In 1951 he undertook the study of the Malaysian collection in the British Museum of Natural History and in 1954 published "The Botany of Cook's Voyages" (*Chronica Botanica* 14), a debunking of many theories regarding the origin and spread of European plants throughout Oceania. He died in Forest Hills, Massachusetts.

Merrill was a corresponding member of botanical societies in Argentina, Austria, China, Cuba, France, Germany, Great Britain, Honduras, India, Japan, Malaya, the Netherlands, Sweden, Switzerland, Tahiti, and the United States. He was elected to membership in the National Academy of Sciences in 1923. In 1930 he was the vice president and chairman of the section of nomenclature at the International Botanical Congress (IBC) in Cambridge, England, and he was the president of the section of nomenclature at the IBC in Amsterdam, the Netherlands, in 1936 and in Stockholm, Sweden, in 1950. He served as acting president of the American Association for the Advancement of Science in 1931 and as president of the American Botanical Society in 1934, the International Union of Biological Sciences in 1935, the Herb Society of America in 1936, the New England Botanical Club from 1937 to 1939, and the American Society of Plant Taxonomists in 1946. In 1939 he became the first American to receive the Linnaean Society of London's Linnaean Gold Medal. He also received the French Ministry of Agriculture's Gold Medal in 1939, its Grand Medal of Geoffrey St. Hilaire in 1950, and the Massachusetts Horticultural Society's George Robert White Medal of Honor in 1947. He was made a commander in the Netherlands Order of Orange-Nassau in 1948. Seven plant genera and 220 species were named in his honor.

In his day Merrill was one of the most highly regarded botanical taxonomists in the world. He procured more than 1 million specimens for the botanical collections under his administration and published more than 500 botanical treatises. His pioneering contributions to the classification of Oriental and Oceanic flora coupled with his activities as an administrator, author, builder of botanical collections, editor, organizer, and researcher earned for him an international reputation as "the American Linnaeus."

• Merrill's papers are in the archives of the New York Botanical Garden. A biography and bibliography is by William J. Robbins in National Academy of Sciences, *Biographical Memoirs* 32 (1958): 273–333. Other biographies are Richard Evans Schultes, "Elmer Drew Merrill: An Appreciation," *Taxon* 6 (1957): 89–101, and Ivan M. Johnson, *A Correspondence between a Professor at Harvard and the University* (1957). Obituaries are in the *New York Times*, 26 Feb. 1956, *Nature*, 14 Apr. 1956, and *Science*, 11 May 1956.

CHARLES W. CAREY, JR.

MERRILL, Frank Dow (4 Dec. 1903–11 Dec. 1955), army officer, was born in Hopkinton, Massachusetts, the son of Charles William Merrill, a carriage trimmer, and Katheryn Donovan. Merrill, who wore glasses to correct astigmatism, hoped to attend the U.S. Military Academy after graduating from high school in Amesbury, Massachusetts, but was rejected because of his vision. He then enlisted in the army as a private but kept on applying to the Military Academy. He was finally accepted on his sixth attempt and graduated from West Point in 1929. Merrill then served with the Third Cavalry at Fort Ethan Allen, Vermont, and with the Second Armored Car Squadron at Fort Eustis, Virginia. In 1930 he married Lucy Kelsall Wright. The couple had two children.

Merrill returned to the classroom in 1931 to study special weapons at the Ordnance School of the Watertown Arsenal in Watertown, Massachusetts, and to enroll in the military engineering program at the Massachusetts Institute of Technology. He received the B.S. from MIT in 1932. Between 1932 and 1934 Merrill served as regimental motor officer with the Thirteenth Cavalry at Fort Riley, Kansas, except for a four-month period when he was detached for duty with the Civilian Conservation Corps at Brownbranch, Missouri. After completing Cavalry School at Fort Riley (1934–1935), Merrill remained on the post as an instructor. Promoted to first lieutenant in 1934 and to captain in 1939, Merrill began a new phase of his career in July

1938 when he was sent to Tokyo for three years to study the Japanese language and to serve as assistant military attaché. Merrill cultivated friendships with several Japanese officers and became familiar with Japanese military thought and doctrine. In 1941 Merrill was transferred to General Douglas MacArthur's command in the Philippines as an intelligence officer. When war began in December, he was in Rangoon, Burma, on a special assignment and received orders to stay there as a liaison officer with the British army.

In March 1942 Merrill, now a major, was attached to the staff of Lieutenant General Joseph Stilwell as operations officer. Stilwell, who headed the newly established China-Burma-India (CBI) theater, had many responsibilities, among them helping to organize the delivery of military supplies to China. While the English regarded Burma as an outpost on the periphery of empire, American leaders saw the region as the key link between India and China, which had been at war with Japan since 1937. Continued control of northern Burma would allow military supplies to be delivered to China by land. Once the Japanese attacked Burma in January 1942, British forces defending the south and both British and Chinese in the north experienced defeat after defeat. Allied efforts collapsed in April, and the exhausted defenders attempted to escape to India. Stilwell, who had gone to Burma in March in an unsuccessful effort to galvanize Chinese resistance, personally led a group of about 100 men and women (many of them medical personnel) on the well-known walkout to India. The group's trucks had to be abandoned, so jeeps and pack animals were primarily reserved for carrying supplies. En route Merrill collapsed from heat exhaustion and a flareup of a heart condition and had to be taken by litter part of the way. He recovered and, when the group safely reached India, continued to serve as Stilwell's operations officer. Merrill received promotions (all temporary) to lieutenant colonel in 1942, to colonel in January 1943, and to brigadier general in November 1943. Since the United States did not commit a significant number of ground combat troops to the CBI theater, Stilwell's hopes for regaining control of northern Burma and reopening land communications with China depended on his ability to utilize Chinese personnel sent to India for training by American instructors. Larger forces were trained under American supervision in China itself.

In 1943 Stilwell received authorization to retake northern Burma. The Chinese would provide much of the personnel for the daunting operation, but Stilwell was able at last to secure some American ground troops, the 5307th Composite Unit (code-named Galahad), which he placed under Merrill's command. The outfit, like the British Chindits after whom it was modeled, was in concept supposed to be an elite unit able to function behind enemy lines. In practice many of its 3,000 men were already worn down from prior service in the Pacific or were misfits from the Pacific and Caribbean. Merrill was able to give the unit three months of training, and most reports indicate that the 5307th—Merrill's Marauders, reporters soon named it—did shape up.

Stilwell told Merrill what he wanted the Marauders to accomplish, and Merrill planned the details of the campaign. It opened in February 1944, about three months after the overall effort to retake Burma had begun. The Marauders, or Galahad, as the outfit was also known, went behind enemy lines to disrupt Japanese communications and seize important but lightly garrisoned objectives. With Merrill leading them in the field, the Marauders operated in a difficult terrain and a tropical climate that exacted their toll on the men. Merrill suffered a heart attack late in March and was evacuated, but Stilwell's orders kept Galahad in the field, its personnel marching some 500 miles and fighting Japanese forces on some two dozen occasions.

Key to the entire operation was the transportation hub of Myitkyina and its airfield. Merrill had planned for the Marauders to approach the city on the ground, quickly seize the airfield so that supplies and reinforcements could be flown in, and then fly out while the fresh personnel continued the task of ousting the Japanese from northern Burma. Merrill did not accompany the Marauders on their difficult trek in but did arrive by plane soon after the Myitkyina airfield was seized to take control of both American and Chinese personnel. However, he suffered another heart attack and had to be flown to a hospital in a rear area. Fighting at Myitkyina continued. British Empire troops also participated. Contrary to plans, the Marauders, already worn by a ten-day battle at Nhpum Ga, were not relieved, for Japanese resistance proved even more tenacious than anticipated. When Myitkyina was at last secured after a siege of more than ten weeks, the 5307th was so decimated by wounds, illness from malaria and other diseases, and combat fatigue that it was considered unfit for further battle. Its remnants were reorganized under a different name and placed under another officer's command.

Merrill, who had returned to Myitkyina in June, was hospitalized with malaria in July and did not again see combat. He was promoted to major general in September and, once he recuperated, was named deputy commander under Lieutenant General Daniel Sultan of the Burma-India theater, which had been separated from the now defunct CBI. Merrill ended the war on Okinawa, serving as chief of staff for the Tenth Army, then commanded by Stilwell. In January 1946 Merrill became chief of staff of the Sixth Army, headquartered in San Francisco. Stilwell, who was in command of the Sixth Army at this time, died in October 1946. Merrill subsequently became chief of staff to the Military Advisory Group in the Philippines. He had still another heart attack in 1947 and retired from the army in 1948. Merrill settled in Concord, New Hampshire, where his family had resided during the war, and in 1949 was named the state's commissioner of public works and highways. He supervised planning of the New Hampshire Turnpike and also developed plans for the roads that eventually became New Hampshire's segment of the Interstate Highway System. In December 1955

Merrill was elected president of the American Association of Highway Officials at the group's annual meeting in New Orleans. Merrill died of a heart attack in Fernandina Beach, Florida, while driving home from the convention with his wife.

Merrill was a fine staff officer for most of the Second World War. He was already in the Far East when war began and was kept there to become an indispensable member of Stilwell's staff, representing Stilwell as needed at various planning sessions in Chungking (Chongqing), China; Delhi, India; Quebec, Canada; and other places. Exhibiting confidence in him, Stilwell named Merrill to his first and only combat command during the war. In actuality Merrill commanded only a regiment, normally a colonel's billet, but, since he was already a brigadier general, the 5307th was designated a composite unit. The press soon made the outfit famous as Merrill's Marauders, for the idea of a group of men trained to operate behind enemy lines for weeks at a time, dependent for survival on aerial resupply and their resourcefulness, caught the public's imagination. Merrill's continuing heart problems kept him out of actual combat for much of the Marauders's ordeal, but he did organize the training of the 5307th so that when it did take the field in 1944 it did everything it was trained to do, and more.

• Information about Merrill can be gleaned from records in the Army Center of Military History, Washington, D.C. Merrill authored "Technique of Fire of the Light Machine Gun," *Cavalry Journal* (Jan.–Feb. 1937). Of the numerous books about the war in Burma, among the best are Charlton Ogburn, Jr., *The Marauders* (1959): Barbara W. Tuchman, *Stilwell and the American Experience in China, 1911–1945* (1971): and Charles F. Romanus and Riley Sunderland, *The China-Burma-India Theater* (3 vols., 1953–1959). Also valuable is Charles N. Hunter, *Galahad* (1963). Hunter was the regiment's original commanding officer and no fan of Merrill's. The film *Objective Burma* (1945), starring Errol Flynn, gives an idea of the public's fanciful image of how a fictional unit, obviously meant to resemble the Marauders, functioned. Obituaries are in the *New York Times*, 13 Dec. 1955, and *Time*, 26 Dec. 1955.

LLOYD J. GRAYBAR

MERRILL, George Perkins (31 May 1854–15 Aug. 1929), geologist, was born in Auburn, Maine, the son of Lucius Merrill, a carpenter and cabinetmaker, and Elizabeth Jones. He attended the town schools in Auburn and the Lewiston Falls Academy before entering the Maine State College of Agriculture and Mechanic Arts in Orono (now the University of Maine). Working his way through his college years, he received his B.S. in chemistry in 1879 and an M.S. in 1883. He worked on food chemistry as an assistant chemist at Wesleyan University (1879–1880), and during this time he met Dr. G. Brown Goode, who was then in charge of the U.S. National Museum in Washington, D.C.

Merrill then moved to Washington as an assistant in the fisheries census at the Smithsonian Institution (1880–1881). There he met Dr. George W. Hawes, the curator of geology at the National Museum, who aroused his interest in geology. In 1881 he became an assistant in the geology department of the National Museum, and upon Hawes's death in 1882, Merrill became acting curator of geology. He married Sarah P. Farrington in 1883; they had one son and three daughters. He became a curator in 1889 and head curator of the Department of Geology in 1897, a position he held until his death. Concurrently he was a lecturer at the Maryland Agricultural College (1890–1891) and part-time professor of geology and mineralogy at the Columbian (now George Washington) University from 1893 to 1916. In 1894 his wife Sarah died, and in 1900 he married Katherine L. Yancey; they had one daughter. In 1903 in a poll conducted by *American Men of Science* of the leaders of science in America, Merrill was ranked thirty-ninth (out of eighty-one) in geology.

Much of Merrill's work was derived from his activities at the U.S. National Museum and can be divided into four areas. First was his work at the museum, which he tirelessly pursued with the goal of making the geological holdings one of the world's best and most extensive collections. In his first annual report (1883) he indicated an inventory of less than fifteen thousand items, while his final report (1929) reported more than two million items. Likewise, under his guidance the staff grew from one to fifteen workers. During his tenure there, he had ten major expositions, and these were accompanied by the issuance of handbooks and catalogs that furnished a guide to the collection. Merrill personally prepared seven of these, and the two-volume fossil guide (1905, 1907) ran to more than a thousand pages.

Second, he did pioneering work in the study of building stones, the process of weathering, and the occurrence of nonmetallic minerals. Each of these led to books that saw several editions. The first of these was *Stones for Building and Decoration* (1891), which was primarily concerned with stones employed in the United States. This was his most popular book, and it got him involved as a consultant for the types of stone to be employed in government buildings, e.g., the Lincoln Memorial. *A Treatise on Rocks, Rock Weathering, and Soils* (1897) was the first book-length study of its kind and won him international acclaim. Among agricultural experts he became known as the outstanding authority of his time on soils.

Third, Merrill was a pioneer investigator in the application of petrology to the study of meteorites, and he was the foremost American authority on meteorites. He was fascinated by the phenomenon and constitution of meteorites, and in 1917 a mineral that he discovered in them was called merrillite in his honor. One of his most important functions was in connection with the Great Meteor Crater in Coconino County, Arizona. In 1891 the leading geologist (then the chief geologist of the U.S. Geological Survey), Grove K. Gilbert, had dismissed the possibility that the crater was caused by a meteor. Merrill visited it in 1907 and, citing new evidence unavailable to Gilbert, correctly identified it as a meteor crater (1908). He wrote several reports on it, and while the issue of influence remains controversial, there is no doubt that Merrill's stature as a representative of the Smithsonian Institution was a factor in the preservation of the site for future study.

Finally, Merrill was an early leader in the task of compiling a history of North American physical geology. He wrote two large reports—*Contributions to the History of American Geology* (1906) and *Contributions to a History of American State Geological and Natural History Surveys* (1920)—and a book, *The First Hundred Years of American Geology* (1924). All of these were highly regarded by his contemporaries, who hailed them as both scholarly and useful contributions.

Merrill was president of the Washington Academy of Science (1906–1907) and vice president of the Geological Society of America in 1920. He was elected a member of the National Academy of Sciences in 1922, and during the same year he was awarded their J. Lawrence Smith gold medal for his research on meteorites. He was the recipient of honorary doctorates from the University of Maine (1889) and George Washington University (1917).

In a centenary address on the birth of James D. Dana, Merrill expressed his ideas on the qualities that a geologist should possess. First, a geologist must be a good observer. Second, a geologist must be sufficiently well versed in the basic sciences to permit the derivation of legitimate conclusions from observations. Third, a geologist must be knowledgeable about what other investigators have done and be able to make use of their work and conclusions. Fourth, a geologist must have staying power. Finally, to be truly great, a geologist must possess a creative imagination and be a master of both inductive and deductive reasoning. Unquestionably, Merrill himself satisfied the first four of these criteria, and perhaps his only failing in the last one was in his conservatism. He preferred to keep close to the facts, and rather than draw conclusions, he tended to let time and the accumulation of data decide the final result. As he said, in his daily work he tried "to be always afloat in regard to opinions in geology." However, not withstanding such caution, Merrill was one of the most influential and respected American geologists of his time. He died in Auburn, Maine.

• Merrill's personal papers are in the archives of the Smithsonian Institution. Merrill's tribute to Dana is "Dana, the Geologist," *Bulletin of the Geological Society of America* 24 (1913): 64–68. Extensive retrospectives on Merrill's work, with portraits and complete lists of his publications, are Waldemar Lindgren, National Academy of Sciences, *Biographical Memoirs* 17 (1935): 31–53; and Charles Schuchert, *Bulletin of the Geological Society of America* 42 (1931): 95–122. Another detailed notice by Schuchert is *Annual Report of the Board of Regents of the Smithsonian Institution for 1930* (1931), pp. 616–34. Additional personal information is in Samuel Merrill's two-volume mimeograph, "A Merrill Memorial 1917–1928," in the Library of Congress; and James H. Benn, "Testimonial Dinner to Dr. Merrill," *Science* 70 (2 Aug. 1929): 122–23, prepared on the occasion of Merrill's seventy-fifth birthday. An obituary is in the *New York Times*, 15 Aug. 1929.

JOSEPH D. ZUND

MERRILL, John Ogden (10 Aug. 1896–10 June 1975), architect, was born in St. Paul, Minnesota, the son of Henry Alexander Merrill, a wholesaler of crockery, lamps, and glassware, and Mabel Elizabeth Baldwin. Merrill studied at the University of Wisconsin for two years before serving as a captain in the Coast Artillery of the U.S. Army from 1917 to 1919. He married Ross MacKenzie in June 1918; they had three children before the marriage ended in divorce. Following the war, he attended the Massachusetts Institute of Technology, where he received a bachelor of science degree in architecture and engineering in 1921.

Merrill began his architectural career with the firm of Granger & Bollenbacher in Chicago, Illinois. A fellow of the American Institute of Architects, he served as president of the Chicago chapter from 1931 to 1933. From 1934 through 1939 he served with the Federal Housing Administration (FHA) as the chief architect for the midwestern states. During this period, the fledgling FHA expanded its services in order to stimulate building during the lean years of the depression. In addition to crucial financial measures, the FHA sought to stabilize home values by improving housing standards and conditions. Merrill's Chicago office was at the forefront of this movement. To create housing on existing narrow lots, FHA architects in Chicago designed a new type of row house that was considered more attractive and economical than previous styles.

In 1939 Merrill accepted a limited partnership with the three-year-old firm of Skidmore and Owings, which then became Skidmore, Owings and Merrill (SOM), with offices in New York and Chicago. According to architects already in the firm, such as Gordon Bunshaft and Larry Perkins, Merrill was hired in order to obtain government commissions for public housing. Original partner Louis Skidmore felt that bringing a civil engineer into the firm, and adding his name to the title, would also help attract large, multidisciplinary projects. The strategy paid off. In the 1940s SOM received the monumental commission to design and build the community of Oak Ridge, Tennessee, a covert town for scientists engaged in the Manhattan Project. To meet the diverse demands of town planning, land surveying, utilities, and the design of housing and community facilities, Merrill opened an on-site office and oversaw the expansion of a relatively small staff to nearly 500 by 1946. Oak Ridge established a bond between the government and both SOM and Merrill, which led to several more large-scale, government commissions.

Following World War II Merrill was chosen by the Atomic Energy Commission to direct the redesign of Oak Ridge as a permanent, self-sustaining community. At this same time, in conjunction with the military's postwar plans, he oversaw the creation of permanent military facilities in Okinawa, Japan, and

Morocco. For a civilian populace in 1946, he guided SOM's design and construction of the Fort Hamilton Veterans Hospital in Brooklyn, New York. Part of a $770 million government campaign to build veterans' facilities, this hospital was lauded by *Architectural Record* in June 1947 as a "tour de force in contemporary directness toward achieving smooth functioning, design simplicity and structural economy" (p. 114).

In the late 1940s Merrill directed the revision of Chicago's building code, published between 1947 and 1949. The Housing Act of 1949 required the revision as a qualification for federal urban redevelopment funds. Along with other cities, such as Pittsburgh, Cleveland, Denver, and Kansas City, Chicago was forced to examine building regulations that had long become restrictive and costly. Merrill and his committee recommended the adoption of performance codes that permitted the use of new materials and construction methods as long as they withstood tests of wear, health, and safety. This was more flexible than the specification code then in place, which restricted construction to certain materials and building techniques. Concerned for the redevelopment of Chicago's blighted areas, Merrill stated in *Engineering News-Record* (3 July 1947), "Existing building codes have definitely discouraged urban redevelopment. The unprecedented volume of construction required for such redevelopment requires the unhampered ingenuity and skill of the building industry" (p. 9).

From 1954 to 1958 Merrill oversaw the planning of the $152.5 million Air Force Academy in Colorado Springs, Colorado. Nestled on a mesa against the foothills of the Rocky Mountains, the vast facility expresses, according to Henry Russell Hitchcock, the regimentation of military life. Merrill retired from SOM in 1958 and lived until his death in Colorado Springs with his wife Viola Berg, whom he had married in April 1946.

Throughout his career in the public and private sectors, he strove to advance construction and design standards through practice and legislation. His efforts came at a crucial point in history when the building boom following World War II necessitated major reforms in the construction industry. Furthermore, his pioneering work with colleagues at SOM, specifically his organization of a multidisciplinary work force for large government projects, set the standard for the large-scale corporate practice of architecture.

• Merrill wrote "Planning a Town for Atom Workers," *Engineering News Record*, 21 July 1949, pp. 48–49, which presents the plan for one of his major commissions. Discussions of Merrill's work with Skidmore, Owings and Merrill can be found in Nathaniel Owings, *The Spaces In Between: An Architect's Journey* (1978). Observations on his joining Skidmore, Owings and Merrill are included in the Art Institute of Chicago, *The Oral History of Laurence Bradford Perkins* (1986) and *The Oral History of Gordon Bunshaft* (1990). An obituary is in the *New York Times*, 13 June 1975.

LISA A. TORRANCE

MERRILL, Paul Willard (15 Aug. 1887–19 July 1961), astrophysicist, was born in Minneapolis, Minnesota, the son of Charles Wilbur Merrill, a Congregational minister, and Kate Amelia Kreis. Merrill's family moved a number of times during his youth but by 1900 had settled in Saratoga, California. Merrill attended Stanford University and obtained an A.B. in mathematics in 1908. He did some surveying work in Iowa during the summer of 1907, and this experience helped him obtain a position with the U.S. Geological Survey as a field assistant in California in July 1908. By December of that year, however, he began pursuing an earlier interest in astronomy by taking a position as an assistant on Mount Hamilton at the Lick Observatory of the University of California at Berkeley. He eventually enrolled in the university's graduate school in July 1910 and received a Ph.D. in astronomy in 1913. During these years he was a fellow at the Lick Observatory, a leading center of stellar spectroscopy, where he obtained a great deal of experience in this field. Also in 1913 Merrill married Ruth Leslie Currier. They had one child, an adopted son.

In October 1913 Merrill became an instructor of astronomy at the University of Michigan. There he worked at the university's Detroit Observatory but was dissatisfied with the poor spectroscopic facilities and salary as well as with his assigned tasks that were unrelated to astronomy. In 1916 he received a year's leave of absence to take up spectroscopic work at the National Bureau of Standards in Washington, D.C. At the bureau, Merrill conducted research in interference methods and physical investigations relating to astronomy. Specializing in infrared research, he studied the use of the application of dyes to extend the sensitivity of photographic emulsions well into the infrared region of spectra. With the entry of the United States into World War I, Merrill's research drew interest from the military because of the ability of infrared aerial photography to peer through atmospheric haze. In this research, he was one of the early pioneers of aerial photography and performed a number of experiments from aircraft at Langley Field, Virginia.

Merrill preferred research at the bureau much more than his work at Michigan, and in 1917 he was given a one-year extension of his leave of absence. As he became engaged in military research at the bureau, Merrill came to the attention of the Mount Wilson (Calif.) Observatory director George Ellery Hale, whose involvement with the National Research Council had brought him to Washington, D.C. Hale offered Merrill a job as an astronomer at Mount Wilson. Merrill accepted Hale's offer and joined the staff at the end of the war when his services were no longer needed at the bureau. Merrill was well suited to the position of astronomer at Mount Wilson, where his experience with spectroscopy and photography enabled him to make the best use of its excellent research facilities.

Merrill arrived at Mount Wilson at the end of January 1919 and worked in the observatory's Stellar Spectroscopy Division. Hale's research agenda for Mount Wilson was to achieve an understanding of the problem of stellar evolution. Within this broad framework, the astronomers were given a great deal of latitude in what they chose to study. Merrill's overriding interest throughout his career at Mount Wilson was the study of abnormal stars. Merrill believed that an abnormal star's unusual behavior was an exaggeration of what was considered normal behavior, and he hoped that understanding these unusual processes might lead to greater insight into stellar phenomena in general.

In particular, Merrill focused on long-period variable stars (red stars that undergo luminosity variations over irregular periods on the order of three months to two years). Merrill studied the spectra of many of these variable stars, gathered data on their physical properties, and correlated this data so as to understand the stars' complex behavior. This approach would also be useful in dealing with a problem of great concern to all stellar astrophysicists at this time: what are the abundances of the chemical elements in the universe? Merrill's research led to the establishment in 1923 of a new class of red stars called S-type stars, whose spectra were rich with the signature bands of zirconium oxide molecules. Much later in his career (1952), Merrill's study of S-type stellar spectra resulted in his finding evidence of the element technetium in their atmospheres. Technetium does not occur naturally on Earth, and no stable isotopes are known. Its presence in stars implied that nuclear processes were occurring that produced new technetium atoms (which have a short half-life compared to the age of a star).

Merrill was also a key figure in the study of a class of stars known as emission-line B stars, or Be stars. Normal B-type stars are white stars with temperatures around 20,000K and prominent dark spectral lines of hydrogen and helium. The Be stars, however, also exhibit bright spectral lines of hydrogen superposed on the dark lines (the bright lines are produced by a region of gas surrounding the star). Merrill discovered a large number of these stars and from 1933 to 1949, together with Cora Burwell, produced a series of catalogs of over one thousand Be stars.

Another area in which Merrill made a significant contribution was in the study of symbiotic stars. In 1933 he began investigating in detail stars whose spectra exhibited bright lines of ionized helium and dark bands of titanium oxide, normally only found in very hot and very cool stars, respectively. He showed that the spectra were of a distinct type of stars, which he called symbiotic stars, indicating the apparent coexistence of two very different types of stars (eventually, symbiotic stars were shown to be binary stars). Merrill also contributed greatly to the research on interstellar absorption and in the use of infrared photography in astrophysical work. Greatly concerned about many aspects of scientific writing, he served as editor of the Mount Wilson Observatory publications for twelve years as well as on a number of editorial boards of scientific journals.

Merrill, a staunch Republican, was always interested in politics and was elected a city director of Pasadena, California, in 1927–1931. His political career ended there, however, and he concentrated solely after that on his astrophysical research. His scientific nature was evident in his bout with arthritis. Not content with existing medical treatments, Merrill hunted down potential new treatments or cures, which he examined carefully and scientifically, often in consultation with eminent physicians. Although he never found a cure and continued to suffer at times from extreme pain, he did not let the condition interfere with his work.

Merrill officially retired in 1952 but continued to maintain an office and work regular hours as a research associate of the Carnegie Institution of Washington at the Mount Wilson Observatory until his death in Los Angeles. He was a skilled and painstaking observational astronomer, and many consider him one of the leading figures in the study of abnormal stars. Merrill's data provided a large part of the foundation on which theoretical astronomers have developed their models of stellar behavior.

• Merrill's papers are in the Collection of the Observatories of the Carnegie Institution of Washington in the Huntington Library, San Marino, Calif. A good source of biographical information, including a complete bibliography, is Olin C. Wilson, "Paul Willard Merrill, 1887–1961," National Academy of Sciences, *Biographical Memoirs* 37 (1964). Otto Struve, "Paul Willard Merrill (1887–1961)," *Year Book of the American Philosophical Society* (1962), provides a slightly different perspective on Merrill's life. Merrill's research is discussed within the overall context of stellar spectroscopy in J. B. Hearnshaw, *The Analysis of Starlight* (1986).

RONALD S. BRASHEAR

MERRILL, Stephen Mason (16 Sept. 1825–12 Nov. 1905), Methodist bishop and author, was born near Mount Pleasant, Ohio, the son of Joshua Merrill, a farmer and shoemaker, and Rhoda Crosson. The fifth child of eleven, Merrill moved with his family to Clermont County in southeast Ohio as a youth. While growing up, he learned the trade of shoemaking from his father but was not interested in continuing the trade, having decided to become a preacher. By the time he was seventeen, he had moved to Greenfield, Ohio, and there joined the local Methodist Society. By 1845 he had been licensed to preach and was teaching school. The next year he was admitted to the Ohio Conference and received a circuit of twenty-two stops in the Georgetown area. After spending three years on the circuit, he married Anna Bellmire in 1848; they had one child.

A year after his marriage Merrill was ordained a deacon in the Methodist Episcopal Church, North, which had been formed in 1844 when the Methodist Episcopal church split along geographical lines because of the issue of slavery. The split resulted in declining membership and a sense of drift in the leadership of the northern church. It was during this time of crisis that Merrill shone brightly. Once he was appointed to the pastorate, he rose from pastor to district captain to presiding elder (ordained in 1851). In the late 1850s he was transferred to the Kentucky Conference, returning to the Ohio Conference in 1863.

Merrill attended his first General Conference in Chicago in 1868, the same year he received a doctor of divinity degree from Ohio Wesleyan University. During the conference, he argued clearly and soundly to defeat a motion for admitting laymen to the Methodist legislature without an amendment to the constitution. His demeanor and argument so impressed the members of the General Conference that they selected him to succeed John M. Reid as editor of the Methodist newspaper, *Western Christian Advocate*, a post he would hold until 1872. He brought more politics to the editorial of the *Advocate* than some of his predecessors. He advocated the disfranchisement of former Confederates and openly disapproved of the candidacy of Ulysses S. Grant for president.

Merrill was elected a bishop in 1872 (a title he held until his retirement from active service in 1904) and moved to St. Paul, Minnesota. During this time he wrote *Christian Baptism* (1876), followed by *The New Testament Idea of Hell* (1878), *The Second Coming of Christ* (1879), and *Aspects of Christian Experience* (1882).

In 1880 Merrill moved to Chicago, Illinois, where he became more involved in the administrative offices and the governing body of the Methodist Episcopal church. His knowledge and recall of Methodist law was indisputable, and his works on the subject, *A Digest of Methodist Law* (1885) and *The Doctrines and Disciplines of the Methodist Episcopal Church* (1888), are his most significant contributions to Methodism. It has been said that his knowledge was second only to that of Joshua Soule, another prolific leader in early American Methodism. The episcopal address that he presented to the General Conference in 1888 has become the basis of standard laws of the powers and limitations of the governing body of Methodism.

At the age of seventy-nine, Merrill retired. His work helped to unify the American Methodist church through his fair and just treatment of his fellow administrators, and his writings contributed a great deal to the knowledge of Methodist law. He died in Keyport, New Jersey.

• Among Merrill's writings not cited in the text are *An Oral Discussion of Justification* (1858), *Sanctification* (1901), *Atonement* (1901), and *Recollections of a Superannuate*, ed. Merrill (1857). In 1899 he published a work of family history titled *Joshua Merrill and Family: A Family Record*. An autobiographical essay is in the *Journal of the Twenty-fourth Delegated General Conference* (1904). See also Richard J. Cooke, "Bishop Stephen Mason Merrill," *Methodist Review* 89 (May 1907), and Samuel Merrill, "A Merrill Memorial," in *Methodism: Ohio Area, 1812–1962*, ed. John Marinus Veersteeg (1962). An obituary is in the *New York Daily Tribune*, 14 Nov. 1905.

DAVID B. MALONE

MERRIMON, Augustus Summerfield (15 Sept. 1830–14 Nov. 1892), U.S. senator and jurist, was born in Transylvania County, North Carolina, the son of Branch H. Merrimon, a Methodist minister, and Mary Paxton. Meager family finances limited his formal education. At age nineteen he attended the Asheville Male Academy for eight months, and he used six additional months as an assistant teacher there for further study. Self-educated well beyond his formal schooling, the young Merrimon read *Towne's Analysis* while plowing and often referred to it "as if it was his Alma Mater." He considered books his friends and wrote that "[n]othing is calculated to make a more ready man than reading." Law study in the office of Asheville attorney John W. Woodfin commenced a process that Merrimon presciently foresaw would "be ended only with [his] life." He read extensively in *Blackstone's Commentaries*, the staple of nineteenth-century legal education.

In 1853 Merrimon began to practice law in Asheville. He traveled a large circuit and complained of bad lodging, unpleasant rides, and "half freezing almost all the time." The sloth and unprofessional conduct of other lawyers also caused him discomfort. He viewed some lawyers as "censurable with intolerable sloth" and others as "highly dishonorable" for bewildering juries. "It is not part of the duty of a lawyer," he wrote, "to assist a scoundrel at law." Merrimon took a simultaneous interest in politics. In 1852 Zebulon B. Vance, his "brother student in Law, and . . . one whom [he] esteem[ed] much," defeated him for Buncombe County solicitor (now district attorney). Merrimon later served as county solicitor, however, and in the 1860–1861 North Carolina House of Commons. In 1852 he married Margaret Baird; they had eight children.

The Civil War curtailed Merrimon's legislative service but boosted his political career. He defended slavery as "of divine appointment" and deprecated *Uncle Tom's Cabin* as "only prov[ing] that Slavery . . . is abused." Abolition, he wrote, "would be very dangerous to the government and institutions of our country." Still, his prewar sentiments were those of a strong Union Whig, who foresaw the futility of secession. "If unfortunately the Union should be dissolved," he said, however, "I shall be for the South alone, and as true to its interests as I now feel . . . to the interests of the . . . Union." When secession came, he supported his state and region. After first joining a local company, he received an appointment as commissary, with the rank of captain, in the Confederate army. He served until he was appointed solicitor of the Buncombe circuit in 1861, a responsibility he discharged until the end of the war. The position was difficult and dangerous. It required prosecuting Confederate and Union deserters as well as numerous offenses against the public peace. Following the war Merrimon became a superior court judge. In 1867 he resigned rather than execute military orders that required state judges to disregard state statutes and "proceed in the execution of their office according to the direction prescribed." He wrote Major-General D. E. Sickles that, although he did not "wish to hinder or delay the reconstruction of the government," his "convictions of duty" would not allow him to violate his oath of office by "recogniz[ing] or obey[ing] any Military order" in contravention of the laws of the State.

In 1868 Merrimon was defeated for associate justice of the supreme court. In 1872 he lost the governorship to Republican Tod R. Caldwell by less than 2,000 votes. The Merrimon forces considered contesting the election by charging the Republicans with interference by federal officers, with bringing large numbers of Negroes into the state to vote, and with false registration of voters. The Republicans refused "to be Ku Kluxed out of their victory," however, and the charges were dropped. The Conservative-Democrats had promised Merrimon a seat in the U.S. Senate if he lost the governorship. With the aid of Republican votes (designed to disorganize the Democrats), he was elected to the Senate and served there from 1873 to 1879. He was a member of the committees on the post office, post roads, privileges and elections, claims, rules, and the District of Columbia. He served on a select committee to investigate problems in the presidential election in South Carolina. He once was described as "the ablest lawyer on the floor of Congress."

As a senator, Merrimon represented the then traditional views of white southern Democrats. Civil rights legislation, he conjectured, would cause the state legislature to choose no schools over racially mixed schools. Passage, he thought, would result "in the degeneracy and eventual extinction of the two races." While Merrimon "ardently desire[d] the progress . . . of all races," he viewed federal civil rights legislation as "destructive of such ends." Without federal legislation, he saw the "colored man" as "slowly and surely improving" and "cheerful and hopeful."

Defeated by Vance in the 1879 Senate election after a campaign based on personal animosity rather than issues, Merrimon returned to law practice in Raleigh. He was an associate justice of the N.C. Supreme Court from 1883 to 1889 and chief justice from 1889 until his death. One of Merrimon's more notable opinions was a solitary dissent (*Barksdale v. Commissioners*, 1885) in which he disagreed with the majority's holding that the North Carolina constitution limited the amount of taxation that counties could levy to support the public schools. The court later held with his views in *Collie v. Commissioners* (1907), noting the "acknowledged power and force of reason" of Merrimon's dissent.

As a delegate to the prohibition convention in 1880, Merrimon stated that nine-tenths of the cases in his law practice "had been brought about by liquor." He "often . . . raise[d] his voice for the temperance cause" (*Biographical History of North Carolina*, vol. 8 [1907], p. 340).

Shortly before his death Merrimon joined the Methodist church. He died in Raleigh.

• The Augustus S. Merrimon Papers are located in the Southern Historical Collection, the University of North Carolina at Chapel Hill. Biographical accounts include Maud L. Merrimon, *A Memoir, Augustus Summerfield Merrimon* (1894); A. R. Newsome, ed., "The A. S. Merrimon Journal," *North Carolina Historical Review* 8 (1931); and Armistead Jones, "Address at the Presentation of the Portrait of Judge Merrimon to the North Carolina Supreme Court, 27 Mar. 1894," *North Carolina Reports* 114 (1894). Articles relevant to Merrimon's career include Douglass C. Dailey, "The Elections of 1872 in North Carolina," *North Carolina Historical Review* 40 (1963), Fannie Memory Farmer, "Legal Practice and Ethics in North Carolina," *North Carolina Historical Review* 30 (1953); and Daniel J. Whitener, "North Carolina Prohibition Election of 1881 and Its Aftermath," *North Carolina Historical Review* 11 (1934). Obituaries include "In Memoriam," *North Carolina Reports* 111 (1892); and R. H. Hayes, "August S. Merrimon," *Guilford Collegian* 5, no. 3 (1892): 94–96.

WILLIS P. WHICHARD

MERRITT, Anna Massey Lea (13 Sept. 1844–7 Apr. 1930), painter, printmaker, and writer, was born in Philadelphia, Pennsylvania, the daughter of Joseph Lea, Jr., a textile manufacturer, and Susanna Massey. Her Quaker-turned-Unitarian parents sent her to progressive schools, including abolitionists Theodore and Angelina Grimké Weld's Eagleswood School in New Jersey from 1858 to 1860 and the Agassiz School in Cambridge, Massachusetts, in 1861. She was also instructed by private tutors in classics, languages, mathematics, and music. Anna Lea learned to paint from instruction books and studied anatomy at the Women's Medical College in Philadelphia.

In 1865 the family moved to Europe. Anna Lea studied with Stefano Ussi in Florence, Italy, and with Heinrich Hoffman in Dresden, Germany. She worked with the artists privately because women were excluded from the academies. Her studies interrupted by the turmoil at the beginning of the Franco-Prussian War in 1870, Anna Lea settled in London when the rest of her family returned to Philadelphia. In 1872 she began to study with her neighbor, art critic and restorer Henry Merritt. He and fellow artists William Holman Hunt, Sir Edward Burne-Jones, Dante Gabriel Rossetti, and George Frederic Watts encouraged her to adopt elements of the Pre-Raphaelite style, which suited her realistic portrait and narrative subjects. Although she continued to live in England, she returned to the United States more than sixty times, usually for several months at a time, painting portraits in Philadelphia, New York, Boston, and Ottawa. Her style was largely realism with Pre-Raphaelite elements of "finish" and sculpture quality.

Henry Merritt and Anna Lea were married in 1877; he died three months later. With technical help from their friends Charles West Cope and Elizabeth Ruth Edwards, Merritt learned to etch so that she could illustrate a book of her husband's art criticism and fiction that she arranged to have published. Her etchings in the book *Henry Merritt: Art Criticism and Romance, with Recollections and Twenty-three Etchings by Anna Lea Merritt* (1879) are narrative scenes illustrating his stories. For its frontispiece she etched a portrait of Merritt, which has become one of her best-known pieces.

Merritt etched many frontispieces for books and made etchings after her own and other artists' paintings. Individual etchings were published in the United States by Christian Klackner and Wunderlich and Co.

and in England by Eyre & Spottiswood. In 1886 Klackner published two Pre-Raphaelite allegorical subjects after Merritt's paintings *Eve (Eve Repentant)*, her diploma etching for the London Society of Painter-Etchers; and *St. Cecilia (St. Cecilia Asleep)*. Sylvester Koehler included her etching *Sir Gilbert Scott*, after an oil painting by George Richmond, in the *American Art Review* in 1879. He commented in his essay that accompanied the etching, "This plate may justly claim rank among the best of modern etched portraits." Koehler also published Merritt's work in *American Etchings; A Collection of Twenty Original Etchings* (1886). In addition, one of her etchings was published in *American Artists and Their Works* (c. 1889–1891), and three portrait etchings were included in *The Etcher* (1879, 1880, and 1883), which was produced in England.

Merritt retired to Hurstbourne-Tarrant, a village on the Hampshire Downs, in 1891. Inspired by the beautiful countryside, she turned to landscape painting in a realistic style with strong effects of atmosphere and light and also developed her career as a writer. She produced an article on mural painting, books about rural village life and her carefully designed English-style garden, and articles on gardening, which she illustrated with her paintings. Merritt died in Hurstbourne-Tarrant.

Merritt exhibited her paintings and etchings regularly throughout her life. Her works were shown at London's Royal Academy, the Royal Society of British Artists, the Pennsylvania Academy of the Fine Arts, the Brooklyn Art Association, the Philadelphia Society of Artists, the National Academy of Design in New York, the Museum of Fine Arts in Boston, the Boston Art Club, the National Arts Club in Washington, D.C., and the Paris Salon. She was a member of and exhibited with the Plastic Club, an association of women artists. She also participated in the 1887 exhibition *Women Etchers of America* at the Museum of Fine Arts in Boston, the first museum show to exhibit women's work separately. An enlarged version of the exhibition was held the next year at New York's Union League Club.

At the 1876 U.S. Centennial Exposition in Philadelphia, Merritt won two awards. She also exhibited in both the American and British painting sections of the 1893 Columbian Exposition in Chicago and won two medals. For the vestibule of the exposition's Woman's Building she was commissioned to paint three mural panels representing women's work, *Needlework*, *Benevolence*, and *Education*. Other expositions in which she exhibited include the 1881 Massachusetts Charitable Mechanic Association, the 1888 Ohio Valley Centennial in Cincinnati, the 1889 Exposition Universelle in Paris, the 1895 Cotton States Exposition in Atlanta, the 1901 Pan-American Exposition in Buffalo, the 1904 Louisiana Purchase Exposition in St. Louis, and the 1915 Panama-Pacific Exposition in San Francisco. Merritt exhibited etchings with the New York Etching Club, the Salmagundi Club in New York, the Boston Art Club, the Philadelphia Society of Etchers, the Berlin Society of Etchers, and the Royal Society of Painter-Etchers in London, of which she was an associate member.

Merritt's contributions to the dialogue on women artists are often cited. Most quoted is her article "A Letter to Artists: Especially Women Artists," published in *Lippincott's Monthly Magazine* in March 1900. In it she lamented that women artists did not have the benefit and support of someone to serve as homemaker and free the artist to primarily make art. Although she participated in many separate exhibitions of women's work, Merritt wrote some of the earliest criticism of the practice. In "A Letter to Artists" she declared that "separate exhibitions of women's work were in opposition to the views of the artists concerned, who knew that it would lower their standard and risk the place they already occupied. What we so strongly desire is a place in the large field: the kind ladies who wish to distinguish us as women would unthinkingly work us harm."

Further commenting on the separation of women's and men's spheres, Merritt wrote in her 1926 memoirs that during the late 1860s, when she was studying in Europe, she "longed to be a man, freed from the tiresome conventions of young ladyhood." Yet at the same time she denied the existence of discrimination against women, as expressed in the *Lippincott* article: "There has never been any great obstacle for women to overcome, . . . and modern conditions affect men and women equally." Her statement reveals the deeply internalized sexism that has been so much a part of women's experience.

• The New York Public Library and the Museum of Fine Arts in Boston have the largest collections of Merritt's etchings. Most of her paintings are unlocated, but a few are known to be in private and public collections, including the Tate Gallery and the Guildhall, London; the Pennsylvania Academy of the Fine Arts and the Historical Society of Pennsylvania, Philadelphia; and the Hudson River Museum, Yonkers, N.Y. Merritt's 1926 memoirs are published in Galina Gorokhoff, ed., *Love Locked Out: The Memoirs of Anna Lea Merritt with a Checklist of Her Works* (1981). Her letters are in the Anna M. Lea Merritt Papers, Manuscript Division, New York Public Library, and in the Sylvester Rosa Koehler Papers, Archives of American Art, Smithsonian Institution, Washington, D.C. Merritt wrote about art and artists in "A Talk about Painting," *St. Nicholas*, Dec. 1884, pp. 85–92; and "A Letter to Artists: Especially Women Artists," *Lippincott's Monthly Magazine*, Mar. 1900, pp. 463–69. See also Austin Chester, "The Art of Anna Lea Merritt," *Windsor Magazine*, Nov. 1913, pp. 605–20; Phyllis Peet, "The Emergence of American Women Printmakers in the Late Nineteenth Century" (Ph.D. diss., Univ. of California, Los Angeles, 1987); and Peet, *American Women of the Etching Revival* (1988). Obituaries are in the *Philadelphia Public Ledger*, 7 Apr. 1930; the *New York Times*, 9 Apr. 1930; and the *Philadelphia Evening Bulletin*, 1 May 1930.

PHYLLIS PEET

MERRITT, Ernest George (28 Apr. 1865–5 June 1948), physicist, was born in Indianapolis, Indiana, the son of George Merritt and Paulina Tate McClung. A gifted child, he began publishing an illustrated newspaper at age seven and built a home observatory and transit house when he was fourteen. He graduated from the Indianapolis Classical School, where he won first prizes in foreign languages and mathematics. Merritt attended Purdue University in 1881–1882, before entering Cornell University, where he received an M.E. in 1886. He then studied under the popular Cornell physics professor William A. Anthony. In 1887 Merritt accompanied his family to California, where he built a darkroom, learned to play the guitar, and carefully recorded observations of nature.

During this period Anthony left Cornell, and upon Merritt's return there Merritt received a fellowship and spent the next year working under Edward L. Nichols, Anthony's replacement, who had worked with inventor Thomas Edison. At Cornell, Merritt extended and published his earlier researches on the energy of light in incandescent lamps (*American Journal of Science* 37 [1889]: 167–78) and was named an instructor in 1889, advancing to assistant professor in 1892. In 1893 Merritt participated in founding the *Physical Review*, which he coedited for the next twenty years.

To help a faculty member interested in phonetics, Merritt designed an improved method for photographing the manometric flame, a device for making sound vibrations visible. Five years later Merritt worked with Nichols to further improve the method, which unfortunately remained incapable of recording the complexities of human speech (*Physical Review* 1 [1893–1894]: 166–76, and 7 [1898]: 93–101).

Between 1893 and 1895 Merritt studied at the University of Berlin, where he attended Max Planck's courses on heat theory and the foundations of physics. Absorption and dispersion of light and their relations to double refraction were of considerable theoretical interest in Germany. Properties of infrared rays were also under scrutiny. Advised by August Kundt, Henri du Bois, and Heinrich Rubens, Merritt examined the absorption of several doubly refracting minerals in the infrared. He found that infrared rays behaved like visible light in the crystals. (*Annalen der Physik und Chemie* 55 [1895]: 49–64; *Physical Review* 2 [1894–1895]: 424–41).

Returning to Cornell, Merritt published papers on electrical topics and on cathode rays. Contemporaneously with J. J. Thomson, he found that photoelectric rays behaved similarly to cathode rays (*Physical Review* 11 [1900]: 230–50, with O. M. Stewart). Some of Merritt's early researches were inspired or influenced by his lecture demonstrations. He married Bertha Sutermeister, with whom he would have five children, in 1901 and was named a full professor in 1903. In 1895 Merritt and Nichols had developed a course on spectroscopy. Methods taught in the course later became useful for their joint research on luminescence. These researches would be seen as Merritt's most significant contribution to physics, bringing him international status as a leader in the field.

Fluorescence and phosphorescence had intrigued researchers for both theoretical and practical reasons, yet the complexities and limitations of "cold light" were daunting. Perhaps not fully aware of the problems, Merritt and Nichols fearlessly attacked the controverted question of Stokes's law of fluorescence, an empirical relation between the wavelengths of fluorescent light and the light that produced it. Though chided by Heinrich Konen, a leading German spectroscopist, for their "relatively crude" methods, Merritt and Nichols produced results that were widely cited (*Physical Review* 18 [1904]: 403–18). Over the next thirteen years Nichols and Merritt used the spectrophotometer to determine fluorescence spectra of organic dyes and uranium compounds and to probe the luminescence of zinc sulfate. They analyzed decay rate, effects of temperature and excitation mode, and spectral energy distribution, as well as relations of luminescence to exciting wavelength, absorption, and electrical conduction. Significant support was provided by the Carnegie Institution.

Nichols and Merritt coauthored more than two dozen articles and monographs published primarily in the *Physical Review* between 1904 and 1917. Their intensive collaboration faded, however, during the First World War, when Merritt worked on submarine detection at the U.S. Naval Experimental Station in New London, Connecticut. Later his administrative responsibilities as chair of the physics department (1919–1935), afforded him less time for research. Merritt's friendship with Nichols nevertheless continued throughout his life.

Radio attracted many researchers during the early twentieth century. In 1911 Merritt had used the silicon detector to study radio waves and had given a theoretical explanation of contact rectification. After the war he investigated contact rectifiers and radio transmission, on which he published in 1925, 1928, and 1931. Merritt also published on his spectrophotometric studies of iridescent bodies in 1925. Several papers on fluorescence (published 1925, 1926, and 1930) rounded out his career.

Though firmly rooted in the experimental physics tradition, Merritt retained a lifelong interest in theory. He supported an electrical theory of luminescence (*Physical Review* 27 [1908]: 367–99). Underlying his research was a conviction that luminescence would provide important clues to atomic structure. Merritt taught theoretical physics, having received a firm foundation from Planck. After the war he applied quantum theory to studies of luminescence (*Physical Review* 28 [1926]: 684–94).

Merritt was a cofounder in 1899 of the American Physical Society and oversaw much of the organization's administration during its first forty-nine years, first as its secretary (1899–1912), then as president (1912–1914). He also served as councilor and editor of its *Bulletin*. Merritt was a fellow of the American Academy of Arts and Sciences and the American Association for the Advancement of Science (secretary of Section B, 1895; vice president, 1900), and a member of the National Academy of Sciences, the Optical Society of America, and the American Academy of Sciences, among other organizations.

Reflective, systematic, courteous, and modest, Merritt was liked and respected by the Cornell faculty, who chose him as their representative to the university's board of trustees from 1931 to 1933. Merritt was an early champion of faculty research, maintaining (in spite of his inability to attain this goal himself) that half of a university professor's time should be devoted to research. In 1909 he was named dean of the graduate school. Merritt resigned this position in 1914 in order to return to teaching. He taught a series of demonstration lectures on recent developments in physics to enthusiastic students for twenty years. Merritt was known for his ability to lead his students through the discovery process and to create striking demonstrations with crude apparatus. During his career, more than 400 physicists either taught or received advanced degrees at Cornell. Kind and fair-minded, he was supportive of women students. On his retirement in 1935, more than 100 physicists gathered in his honor. Merritt retained the title of professor emeritus until his death in Ithaca, New York.

• Merritt's papers, in Cornell University's Department of Manuscripts and University Archives, include correspondence, administrative records and documents, records of his war research, laboratory notebooks, lecture notes, a diary, publications, biographical material, and photographs. Much of Merritt's work on luminescence is contained in *Studies in Luminescence*, with E. L. Nichols (1912); *Fluorescence of the Uranyl Salts*, with Nichols, H. L. Howes et al. (1919); and *Selected Topics in the Field of Luminescence*, with Nichols and C. D. Child (1923). A survey article is "The Optics of Radio-Transmission," *Journal of the Optical Society of America* 21 (1931): 90–100. Merritt contributed numerous book reviews to the *Physical Review* and wrote an article on the history of the American Physical Society (*Review of Scientific Instruments* 5 [Apr. 1934]: 143–48. A short biographical sketch is in *American Journal of Physics* 33 (Feb. 1965): 87–88. An article on the occasion of Merritt's retirement appeared in *Science* 81 (31 May 1935): 530. Obituaries are in the *New York Times*, 6 June 1948; *Physics Today* 1, no. 4 (Aug. 1948): 30; and *School and Society* 67 (1948): 442.

MARJORIE C. MALLEY

MERRITT, Wesley (16 June 1834–3 Dec. 1910), army officer, was born at New York City, New York, the son of John Willis Merritt, a lawyer, and Julia Anne de Forest. Several years after Wesley's birth a failing law practice forced the family to move to Illinois, where John Merritt was eventually elected to the state legislature. After a brief legal apprenticeship, in 1855 Wesley enrolled at the U.S. Military Academy. Graduating twenty-second in a class of forty-one, he was appointed brevet second lieutenant, Second Dragoons, in 1860. He joined his regiment in Utah and received his regular commission the following year.

After the Civil War broke out, Merritt served as aide to cavalryman Philip St. George Cooke. Promoted to captain, he served in the peninsular campaign. He joined George Stoneman's cavalry raid on Richmond in spring 1863, and he was subsequently commissioned a brigadier general of volunteers for his actions in the skirmish at Beverly Ford. He commanded the reserve cavalry brigade, First Division, Cavalry Corps, Army of the Potomac, at the battle of Gettysburg, winning a brevet regular promotion to major. Succeeding to division command, Merritt distinguished himself in numerous skirmishes in central Virginia in 1863 and 1864. For his actions at the battle of Yellow Tavern (11 May 1864), he secured a brevet lieutenant colonelcy; service at the battle of Haw's Shop (28 May 1864) led to a brevet colonel's appointment.

Merritt's aggressive leadership won the notice of General Philip Sheridan, and he was transferred to the latter's Army of the Shenandoah and given command of a cavalry division. He was appointed major general of volunteers for his service at the battles of Winchester (19 Sept. 1864) and Fishers Hill (22 Sept. 1864). Commanding the Cavalry Corps of the Army of the Shenandoah and subsequently the Army of the Potomac, he won a brevet brigadier generalship for his leadership at the battle of Five Forks (1 Apr. 1865). Merritt was at Appomattox Court House for the surrender of the Confederate Army of Northern Virginia eight days later. He then participated in the final movement of the war against Joseph E. Johnston's Confederate army in North Carolina. After the war he became a brevet major general (regular army) and major general of volunteers.

Merritt was transferred to the Military Division of the Southwest and in July 1865 given command of the cavalry in the Department of Texas. He spent a brief tenure in the Department of the Gulf, and on 1 February 1866 he was mustered out of volunteer service. After a visit to Europe he was appointed lieutenant colonel of the Ninth Cavalry Regiment in July 1866. He assumed effective regimental command the following year, setting up headquarters at Fort Davis, Texas. Membership on the army's tactics board at St. Louis and a leave of absence interrupted his Texas duty in 1870 and 1871. He married Caroline Warren in 1871. He later served at Forts Stockton, Clark, and Concho.

Merritt sought transfer from his regiment, whose enlisted personnel were all black. From his patron, Sheridan, in 1875 he secured temporary appointment as inspector of cavalry for the sprawling Division of the Missouri, thus relieving him from regular duty in Texas. The following summer, Merritt was promoted to colonel and immediately assumed command of the Fifth Cavalry Regiment, then near the Powder River campaigning against the Sioux and the Northern Cheyennes. Inexperienced in fighting Indians, on 17 July Merritt engaged a party of Cheyennes at War Bonnet Creek. Though the skirmish convinced many of the tribe to remain at their Red Cloud Agency, the action forced Merritt to be late in joining the main army column, drawing the wrath of its commander, General George Crook. Merritt then participated in Crook's September pursuit of the Indians, which culminated in the indecisive battle of Slim Buttes.

Merritt was next assigned to Fort D. A. Russell (renamed Fort Francis E. Warren in 1930) in Wyoming. He commanded U.S. troops at Omaha during the July 1877 railway strike and joined in the famous pursuit of Chief Joseph later that year. With the outbreak of violence on the Ute Reservation at Milk Creek, Colorado, in September 1879, Merritt marched south, but negotiations ended the conflict before his command saw any combat. After two and a half years at Fort Laramie, Wyoming, Merritt assumed the superintendency of the U.S. Military Academy in September 1882, which he held for five years. Promoted to brigadier general in the regular army, he commanded the Departments of the Missouri, the Dakota, and the East from 1887 to 1898 and was appointed major general in April 1895.

The war against Spain again brought Merritt into the national limelight. George Dewey's naval victory at Manila Bay prompted President William McKinley to send ground forces to the Philippines, with Merritt second in rank to commanding general Nelson A. Miles. By the end of May his command, which eventually became the Eighth Army Corps, had increased to 20,000 troops. Though he had hoped to lead troops in the Caribbean, which he presumed would prove a more glamorous command, Merritt whipped his regulars and volunteers into condition as they poured into San Francisco, taking great pains to load his transports so that the troops would be properly equipped upon their arrival. Lead elements of the Eighth Corps landed in the Philippines on 30 June; Merritt and staff, along with steamers bulging with reinforcements, followed on 25 July.

Merritt inherited a difficult situation. Although Dewey's fleet controlled the bay, monsoon weather had rendered the countryside a quagmire. Governor-General Firmin Jaudenes, the Spanish commander in Manila, had a 13,000-man garrison; between the Americans and the Spanish were over 10,000 Filipino insurgents led by Emilio Aguinaldo. Following the policy of the McKinley administration, Merritt avoided direct contacts with the rebels while he and Dewey pressed the Spanish to capitulate. Jaudenes, well aware that the big guns of the American ships far outranged his own artillery, agreed provided his garrison be allowed to surrender with a modicum of honor. Informally, he proposed to give up after a brief battle on condition that the insurgents not be allowed to enter the city. Wary of the arrangement, Merritt had to pass his troops through the Filipino lines without completely breaking the uneasy peace between the U.S. Army and Aguinaldo. On 13 August, after a token naval bombardment, lead elements of the Eighth Corps occupied outlying Spanish strongpoints and moved into Manila. The Americans suffered fewer than 150 casualties. Merritt accepted the formal Spanish surrender the next day.

Washington and Madrid had agreed to a formal cessation of hostilities on 12 August (13 Aug. Manila time), but slow cable transmissions delayed the news from reaching the Philippines for three days. Merritt set up a military government even as Aguinaldo's angry followers, having been barred from entering Manila, lingered outside the city. Two weeks later, McKinley called Merritt to Paris to advise the American peace commission, which would negotiate final terms with Spain and determine the fate of the Philippines. Like Dewey, whose views he also reported, Merritt tried to remain noncommittal about U.S. annexation of the archipelago, leading some to suggest that he shared the political aspirations of his naval counterpart. Merritt traveled to London to marry his second wife, Laura Williams, then returned to the United States on 19 December 1898. He completed his military career in command of the Department of the East, retiring in June 1900.

Merritt's military service against the Confederates has won high praise. He seemed less comfortable, however, combating the more unconventional methods of the Indians. During the war against Spain, he prepared his command well for the rigors of a long ocean voyage followed by almost immediate service in a difficult environment, especially when compared to William R. Shafter, who led the assault on Cuba. He showed some diplomatic skill in helping to secure the relatively bloodless capture of Manila, although the failure to include the Filipino rebels in the process posed serious consequences for subsequent American occupation forces. After retirement he testified in favor of the organizational changes espoused by Secretary of War Elihu Root. He died at Natural Bridge, Virginia, and was buried at West Point.

• Don E. Alberts, *Brandy Station to Manila Bay: A Biography of General Wesley Merritt* (1980), offers a full-length account of Merritt's life. Shorter treatises may be found in Lewis Randolph Hamersly, *Records of Living Officers of the United States Army* (1884); George W. Cullum, *Biographical Register of Officers and Graduates of the U.S. Military Academy at West Point* (1901); and Francis B. Heitman, *Historical Register and Dictionary of the United States Army* (1903). Merritt's relationship with Sheridan is examined by Paul Andrew Hutton, *Phil Sheridan and His Army* (1985); his role in the war against Spain is seen in David F. Trask, *The War with Spain in 1898* (1981).

ROBERT WOOSTER

MERRY, Anne Brunton (30 May 1769–28 June 1808), actress and manager, was born in London, England, the daughter of John Brunton, a tea dealer turned actor and manager, and his wife, whose maiden name was Friend. When Anne Brunton was only fifteen her debut on the stages of Bristol and Bath, where her father performed, created such a sensation that Thomas Harris, the manager of Covent Garden Theatre, offered her a three-year contract beginning the following season. She was an immediate success. For the next seven years she remained a leading actress in sentimental comedy and tragedy at Covent Garden and in the provinces during the summer months. Although she performed for the season following her marriage in 1791 to a minor poet, wit, and playwright, Robert Merry, she left the stage in 1792 when her husband's republican sympathies for the French Revolution took them to Paris. They returned to England a year later, settling near Norwich. But his financial problems and her inability to return to the stage because of her husband's politics created such a desperate situation that the couple accepted Thomas Wignell's offer for Anne Merry to join his two-year-old Chestnut Street Theatre company in Philadelphia.

Within a few weeks of her American debut on 5 December 1796 as William Shakespeare's Juliet, Merry quickly established her superiority as an actress "without rival." She remained attached to the Philadelphia theater throughout her American career. She also carried new standards of excellence to Baltimore and Annapolis, Maryland, two cities in the Chestnut Street company's regular circuit. The difficulties of drawing summer audiences forced the company to seek support in other towns such as Georgetown, District of Columbia, Alexandria, Virginia, and Washington, D.C., where she was the key attraction.

Merry also captivated New York audiences. After the sudden death of her husband in December 1798, William Dunlap, manager of the Park Theatre in New York, offered her a permanent position with his company. Although Merry declined Dunlap's offer, he succeeded in persuading her to appear as a featured attraction to revitalize his flagging box office in the summer of 1801. Highly paid guest appearances were an uncommon practice at the time, but Merry's six performances established her as both a decided advantage to the box office and a "prodigious favorite in New York." Her subsequent starring appearances in New York in 1802, 1805, and 1807, and in Boston in 1807, continued to command unprecedented compensation, demonstrating to actors as well as managers the advantage and vast potential of importing actors of great reputation to perform with local companies. Her five visiting engagements launched the star system that soon became widespread and ultimately weakened and did away with resident repertory companies.

In early 1803 Anne married Wignell, who died seven weeks later and with whom she had her only child. She now assumed the responsibilities of comanaging the theater as well as acting but after two years turned over her share of the management to a fellow actor, William Warren, whom she married in 1806. She died in childbirth two years later in Alexandria, Virginia.

Described by her contemporaries as having "agreeable features" and not very tall, she was noted for the "magic sweetness" of her voice, graceful movement, and a face whose every feature "bespeaks the emotions of her soul." Her "mobile face," "vivacious countenance," "expressive eyes," and "tenderness of look" became the distinguishing features of her performances. She reflected the tendency toward more naturalistic acting with "her expressive manner of filling up pauses and listening to the conversation of others." Although versatile, Merry identified most with tragic characters of a loving, passionate, but gentle nature, in contrast to forceful, queenly types such as Lady Macbeth. Juliet, Desdemona, and Ophelia were her most successful Shakespearean roles. She was also well suited to the tender heroines of sentimental comedy and melodrama whose loving, patient natures helped them endure and triumph over hardship and deprivation. From the outset of her career her personal life reflected the virtuous, brave heroines she often portrayed.

Merry was one of the first successful professional women in America. Dunlap described her as the "most perfect actress America has seen." As the country's foremost actress, Merry developed new standards consistently higher than those of any other performer. Because of her "spotless and unsullified fame," she was invited into some of the most prominent homes in Philadelphia and traveled in a social sphere usually closed to actors. Her unblemished personal reputation contributed to the new respectability of the acting profession in America.

• For details of Merry's career, see the Channing Pollock Theatre Collection, Howard University, Washington, D.C., which also holds the unpublished journals of William Warren (1796–1831). A biographical treatment is Gresdna A. Doty, *The Career of Mrs. Anne Brunton Merry in the American Theatre* (1971). Information on Merry and late eighteenth-century theater can be found in Joseph Haslewood, *The Secret History of the Green-Room*, vol. 2 (1795); *The Thespian Dictionary* (1802); Thomas Gilliland, *The Dramatic Mirror*, vol. 2 (1808); John Bernard, *Retrospections of the Stage, 1756–1787*, vol. 2 (1832); William Dunlap, *History of the American Theatre* (1833); John Genest, *Some Account of the English Stage*, vols. 6 and 7 (1832); [anon.], "Biographical Sketch of Mrs. Warren," *Mirror of Taste and Dramatic Censor* 1 (Feb. 1810): 121–22; William B. Wood, *Personal Recollections of the Stage* (1855); and James Fennell, *An Apology for the Life of James Fennell* (1814). Also helpful is Charles Durang, "The Philadelphia Stage," published serially in the *Philadelphia Dispatch* (1854–1860). An obituary is in *Gentleman's Magazine*, Aug. 1808.

GRESDNA A. DOTY

MERRY, William Lawrence (27 Dec. 1842–11 Dec. 1911), sea captain, merchant, and diplomat, was born in New York City, the son of Thomas Henry Merry, a merchant and sea captain, and Candida Isbina Xavier, apparently Brazilian. Merry attended the Collegiate Institute in New York City during the 1850s. He became a junior officer on the *George Law* at sixteen and temporarily commanded the clipper ship *Tornado* before commanding the New York clipper *White Falcon* in the Pacific when he was only twenty years old.

In 1863 Merry became the agent for the United States Mail Steamship Company in Panama. From 1864 until 1867 he captained the *America* between San Francisco and Nicaragua. Merry married Blanche Hill of Scarsdale, New York, in 1866; they had seven children. In 1867 he became the general agent in charge of Nicaraguan transit for the Central American Transit Company and the North American Steamship Company, but the Nicaraguan route, always used primarily for passenger movement, ceased operations after 1869. About 1871 he returned to Panama to represent the Pacific Mail Steamship Company.

Merry's impact on the debate among proponents of Nicaragua, Tehuantepec, and Panama for the canal site rested on his various experiences during a fifty-year period. He held elevated positions in the shipping industry, had merchant enterprise and chamber of commerce ties to Pacific Coast trade, and held important diplomatic and consular offices for both Nicaragua and the United States. During these years, he studied on site the potential Panamanian and Nicaraguan canal routes. He was convinced that the Nicaraguan route was vastly superior because it demanded less time and was judged to be cheaper. In the 1860s and 1870s, the typical ship size made a suitable route easier to build and placed lower requirements on the harbors at both ends of the passage. It was rumored that he held land interests along the potential San Juan River canal route which, if true, may have influenced his determination to have Nicaragua chosen as the transit route.

In 1874 he resigned from the Pacific Mail Steamship Company and moved to San Francisco, where he formed Merry, Faull, and Company, a wholesale provision merchant firm that operated until liquidated in 1892. He also served as president of the North American Navigation Company, a Pacific Coast ship line, for several years. He presided over the San Francisco Chamber of Commerce for seven years.

Merry lobbied for and publicized his support of the Nicaraguan canal in several pamphlets, *The Nicaragua Canal* (1890), *The Nicaragua Canal: Its Political Aspects* (1892), *The Nicaragua Canal: The Gateway between the Oceans* (1895), *The Nicaragua Canal and the Railroads* (1897), and in various articles. Samples of his articles are in *The Californian* (July 1880), the *Overland Monthly* (Apr. 1888, May 1894, and Nov. 1897), and *California Bankers' Magazine* (Oct. 1890). His speech before the Trans-Mississippi Commercial Convention in St. Louis, Missouri, on 28 November 1894 also was printed. His works, which supported a Nicaraguan canal and San Francisco trade, were widely read and often cited in the late nineteenth century. Despite the appreciable efforts of Merry, Admiral Daniel Ammen, and Ulysses S. Grant, all outspoken supporters of a Nicaraguan canal, the Panama route was chosen because it was technically superior and considerably cheaper. By the early twentieth century, steam engines and metal ships required a canal able to handle larger and deeper draft vessels.

In 1890 the Nicaraguan government appointed Merry its consul general for the Pacific Coast area of the United States. He left this service when President William McKinley named him minister to Costa Rica, Nicaragua, and El Salvador on 17 July 1897. He served for fourteen years in Central America although El Salvador was made a separate legation on 31 December 1907 and Nicaragua on 24 August 1908. State Department officials valued his experience. He spoke a fairly fluent, if abominable, Spanish, but most of his predecessors and successors in the legation spoke no Spanish at all. The State Department respected his views on isthmian transit and trade and shipping ties with Central America, until some began to hold his age against him.

From 1903 until 1909 Merry played an active role in a disagreement between Salvadoran presidents Fernando Figueroa and Manuel Enrique Araujo and U.S. consul John Jenkins who was allied with the Moisant family (emigrants from San Francisco to El Salvador) and Salvadoran dissident leader Prudencio Alfaro. Merry criticized the conduct of Jenkins and his allies but tacitly supported them when he refused to sustain Salvadoran positions in opposition to U.S. officials. The Jenkins group wanted the Salvadoran government to adopt policies more favorable to trade with California. Merry was engaged in the persistent effort of the U.S. government (from 1904 until 1910) to compel Nicaraguan President José Santos Zelaya to resign. Initially Merry spoke well of Zelaya, a strong, determined figure whose administration significantly improved Nicaraguan society. But Zelaya resisted U.S. domination, so the State Department wanted him removed. Under constant bombardment of correspondence from his superiors critical of Zelaya, Merry finally concurred in the condemnation. Zelaya's fall led to the rise of U.S. puppet regimes in Nicaragua, which lasted for the next seventy years. Illness forced Merry to leave Costa Rica on 4 March 1911, and he went to the Battle Creek Sanitorium in Michigan, where he died.

• There are no Merry papers, but a typescript biography of Merry is at the Bancroft Library, University of California, Berkeley, which also has the best collection of his printed materials. The U.S. State Department's microfilmed records contain his official correspondence from Costa Rica, Nicaragua, and El Salvador (microfilm M219, reels 82 and 94) and for Costa Rica (M669, 670, and 671). In addition, Record Group 84 (Post Records) contains several bound volumes of Merry's official correspondence for the years 1906–1911.

No book or article-length biography of Merry has been published. Some aspects of his diplomatic career in Central America are touched on in Thomas Schoonover, *The United States in Central America, 1860–1911: Episodes of Social Imperialism and Imperial Rivalry in the World System* (1991), and Karl Bermann, *Under the Big Stick: Nicaragua and the United States since 1848* (1986). Obituaries are in the *New York Times* and the *San Francisco Examiner*, 16 Dec. 1911.

THOMAS SCHOONOVER

MERTON, Thomas (31 Jan. 1915–10 Dec. 1968), Trappist monk and writer, was born in Prades, France, the son of Owen Merton, a New Zealand–born painter, and Ruth Jenkins, an American. In 1916 the family returned to the United States. Following Merton's mother's death of cancer in 1921, his father took him to Bermuda for a year and, after a return to New York, left for France where he enrolled Merton in the Lycée Ingres at Montauban in 1925. In 1928 Merton's father moved to England to exhibit his paintings. Merton himself left Montauban to enter Oakham School. In 1931 Merton's father died of a brain tumor while still resident in England. In 1933, thanks to a scholarship, Merton entered Clare College, Cambridge, where he remained until 1934.

For reasons that are not absolutely clear (but most likely the pregnancy of a young woman was involved) Merton's guardian removed him from Cambridge and sent him back to the United States. Merton entered Columbia University as an English major in 1935. After finishing his B.A. in February 1938, he began work on an M.A. thesis on William Blake, written under his friend and mentor Mark Van Doren. During this year, influenced in part by his studies in medieval philosophy, he showed an intense interest in Catholicism. After having a course of instructions at Corpus Christi Church near the Columbia campus, he was received into the Catholic church in November 1938.

Between 1939 and 1941 Merton finished his M.A. and began thinking about the Ph.D. with a prospective dissertation on Gerard Manley Hopkins. He also made a journey to Cuba, worked one summer in a settlement house in Harlem, and taught as an instructor at St. Bonaventure's College (now St. Bonaventure University) in Olean, New York. In the midst of this he also thought about a vocation to the priesthood. After an abortive attempt to enter the Franciscans (was the illegitimate child a cause of his rejection?), he decided to enter the monastery of the Cistercians of the Strict Observance (known familiarly as the Trappists) near Bardstown, Kentucky, having made a Holy Week retreat there in the spring of 1941.

Merton entered the monastery in December 1941 as a postulant. He made his final vows in 1947 and was ordained to the priesthood in 1949. Encouraged, against his own inclinations, to write, Merton published under his secular name (he was known as Father Louis in the monastery) *Thirty Poems* (1944). In 1947, prompted by his abbot and his college friend Robert Giroux, he wrote the story of his conversion. Published under the title *The Seven Storey Mountain* (1948), it began with slow sales but, largely through word of mouth, became a bestseller. It sold 600,000 copies in hardcover. Translated into fourteen languages, *The Seven Storey Mountain* is widely regarded as a classic of spiritual autobiography.

After this success, Merton published prolifically on a wide range of subjects. He continued with his autobiographical reflections in the form of spiritual diaries and journals, only some of which were published in his lifetime, including *The Sign of Jonas* (1953) and *Conjectures of a Guilty Bystander* (1965); among the posthumously published volumes are *The Asian Journal of Thomas Merton* (1973) and *A Vow of Conversation: Journals 1964–1965* (1988).

Merton's writings from the 1940s into the late 1950s focused on his convictions about the need for prayer, penance, an ascetic approach to life, and the value of contemplative silence. These sentiments touched a deep nerve in American Catholicism, whose beau ideal had been the gregarious priest exemplified by Bing Crosby in the film *Going My Way* (1944) or the popular preacher Archbishop Fulton J. Sheen. Merton not only found millions of lay readers, but many men, inspired by his example, came to the monastery to try their vocation.

In the late 1950s Merton refocused his energies outward from the monk's interior life to the needs of the world. He wrote on issues of peace and racial harmony. His interest deepened in the religions of the East, especially Zen Buddhism. He wrote widely on literature. He also carried on a wide-ranging correspondence with religious leaders, literary figures, activists, and old friends like the poet Robert Lax and the abstract expressionist painter Ad Reinhardt (both of them Columbia classmates).

Merton's enormous literary activities in the 1960s did not deter him from seeking permission to leave the monastic community at the Abbey of Gethsemani to live as a hermit in a small cottage on the grounds. Despite this solitary life, he received a stream of visitors ranging from the folk-singer activist Joan Baez to the eminent philosopher Jacques Maritain and activists like Daniel Berrigan. His writing took on more of an experimental cast (reflected in the journal *Monk's Pond*, which he edited), while his interest in Eastern mysticism continued.

In 1968, after persistent negotiations with his superiors, Merton was allowed to take a trip to the Orient. It was to be the first trip over a significant length of time that he had made since he entered Gethsemani. After stops in California, he met religious figures and monastics in India, which culminated in a visit to the exiled Tibetan leader, the Dalai Lama. Merton went to Thailand for a meeting of contemplative monks. Outside Bangkok, he gave his presentation to the assembled contemplatives. When they went to call him for an afternoon session, he was found dead, apparently of a heart attack triggered by electrical shock from a defective fan. The date was 10 December, twenty-seven years to the day from his entrance into the monastery. He is buried close to the abbey church with his fellow monks. Like them, his grave is marked with a simple cross and his name in religion: Fr. Louis Merton.

Merton's influence continues long after his death. The posthumous publication of *The Collected Poems* (1977), *The Literary Essays* (1981), a Thomas Merton letters series, and several volumes of private journals have fueled an intense interest in this polymath monk by scholars and students as well as serious Christians and other religious seekers. He remains one of the most influential American Catholic writers of the twentieth century.

• The most extensive collection of Merton's papers and writings is at the Thomas Merton Study Center at Bellarmine College in Louisville, Ky. St. Bonaventure University, Syracuse University, and Columbia University also have important holdings. Marquita Breit and Robert Daggy, *Thomas Merton: A Comprehensive Bibliography* (1986), is standard. The authorized biography is Michael Mott, *The Seven Mountains of Thomas Merton* (1984), although other biographies and memoirs by friends are of interest. Studies of Merton appear in *The Thomas Merton Annual*, which began in 1988, while *The Thomas Merton Seasonal* (published at Bellarmine

College) provides shorter articles, reviews, and a running bibliography of Merton articles and translations. *Cistercian Studies*, a scholarly journal, prints hitherto unpublished Merton articles on occasion. The International Thomas Merton Society meets for the presentation of scholarly papers and discussion every other year; many of the better papers appear either in the society's *Annual* or the *Seasonal*. A front-page obituary of Merton is in the *New York Times*, 11 Dec. 1968.

LAWRENCE CUNNINGHAM

MERVINE, William (14 Mar. 1791–15 Sept. 1868), naval officer, was born in Philadelphia, Pennsylvania, the son of John Mervine, whose occupation is unknown, and Zibia Wright. No information is available on Mervine's early education. Appointed midshipman in 1809, his first assignment was the Philadelphia Navy Yard. Aboard the *Adams* when war with England was declared in 1812, Mervine was assigned to the Black Rock flotilla on Lake Erie. He was wounded during the naval engagement at Black Rock. Reassigned to the *Hamilton*, Mervine—already an acting lieutenant—was officially promoted to that grade on 4 February 1815. Also in 1815 he married Amanda Maria Crane. No record of any children exists.

Routine sea duty and time in grade brought Mervine promotion to master commandant in June 1834 and to captain on 8 September 1841. In 1845 he was assigned command of the *Cyane* and, soon afterward, the *Savannah*. Stationed off the California coast in 1846, Mervine—following orders from Commodore John D. Sloat—landed at Monterey with a detachment of sailors and marines and took possession of the town in the name of the United States. Shortly thereafter, when war with Mexico became "official," Mervine became military commander of Monterey. His single military encounter with the Mexicans while commanding an expedition of some 300 sailors and marines (Oct. 1846) proved less than distinguished. Mervine's force was headed for Los Angeles but never got there. Encountering a body of armed Mexicans, Mervine, according to Marine captain Archibald H. Gillespie, began acting like an "insane man." Uncoordinated patrols, lacking proper guidance, began shooting at one another in the dark. Finally, Mervine ordered a retreat just as Gillespie's marines were on the verge of capturing an enemy gun. Thoroughly disgusted, Gillespie summarized the affair as "one of the most disgraceful defeats our arms have ever sustained" (Ames, pp. 335, 341). Commodore Robert F. Stockton, who had replaced Sloat as supreme naval commander in California, concurred that the engagement was "a very bad defeat" (Marti, p. 90). Lieutenant Tunis A. M. Craven, also serving in California, characterized Mervine as "much puffed with conceit & self-importance . . . an officer who has never enjoyed any degree of favor among officers who have sailed with him" (Kemble, ed., p. 216).

Despite his lackluster naval career, as Mervine advanced in seniority, so did his responsibilities. From 1855 to 1857 he commanded the Pacific Squadron and was employed on the coast of Central America in 1857 to curtail the activities of American filibusterer William Walker 1824–1860 in Nicaragua.

On 6 May 1861 Mervin's seniority brought him appointment as flag officer of the newly created Gulf Blockading Squadron. The blockade was intended to prevent the South from receiving arms and other goods from abroad and from exporting cotton, thereby contributing to its defeat. Mervine's orders were "to establish and enforce a blockage . . . of all the ports south of Key West to the Rio Grande." With only seventeen vessels to effect this blockade, the task was nearly impossible. Soon after leaving Boston, Mervine's flagship, the USS *Mississippi*, was compelled to return to port because of a breakdown of the ship's condensers, believed by Mervine to have been caused by sabotage. Finally, in June 1861 the *Mississippi* was on station off Fort Pickens, Florida, and the blockade was initiated. By the end of July thirteen warships were dispersed off nine Gulf ports, and four others were guarding passes to the Mississippi River. Nevertheless Navy secretary Gideon Welles was displeased at what he perceived as Mervine's "apparent inactivity and indifference." Welles was especially irritated by two serious setbacks he blamed on Mervine's supposed lack of action: the escape of the Confederate raider *Sumter* from New Orleans and the Confederate fortifying of Ship Island without interference. In fairness to Mervine, it is unlikely that any commander could have satisfied Welles at this point in the war, when so few Federal ships were available. Exasperated, judging Mervine as an "utter failure," Welles abruptly relieved him of his command. (Mervine's replacement was Captain William W. McKean, whose own tenure was cut short because of ill health.) Indignant at his dismissal, Mervine demanded a court of inquiry, which Welles refused, claiming to be acting in "the public interest."

Although officially retired, Mervine was promoted to commodore, 16 July 1862, and assigned administrative duty at Washington, D.C., and later at Philadelphia. At war's end he was at New York, serving as president of the retiring board. On 25 July 1866 Mervine was promoted to rear admiral on the retired list. He died at his home at Utica, New York.

A telling characterization of Mervine was made by Secretary Welles in 1862. While recognizing Mervine's patriotism and "correct deportment and habits," Welles saw that officer utterly lacking in executive and administrative ability. "In ordinary times," Welles observed, he "would float along the stream with others, but such periods as [the current national crisis] bring out the stronger points of an officer, if he has them."

• No Mervine papers have survived. RG 45, Naval Records Collection, National Archives, contains information; and Mervine's official correspondence as flag officer of the Gulf Blockading Squadron is in *The Official Records of the Union and Confederate Navies in the War of the Rebellion*, ser. 1, vol. 16 (30 vols., 1894–1922). Welles's feelings toward Mervine are revealed in Howard K. Beale, ed., *The Diary of Gideon Welles*, vol. 1 (1960). See also H. H. Bancroft, *History of Cali-*

fornia, vol. 5 (1890); John H. Kemble, ed., "Naval Conquest in the Pacific: The Journal of Lieutenant Tunis Augustus Macdonough Craven, U.S.N.," *California Historical Society Quarterly* 20, no. 3 (1941): 216; Werner H. Marti, *Messenger of Destiny: The California Adventures . . . of Archibald H. Gillespie . . .* 1960; and George W. Ames, Jr., "Gillespie and the Conquest of California," *California Historical Society Quarterly* 17, no. 4, pt. 1 (1938): 335, 341. An obituary is in the *Utica Daily Observer*, 16 Sept. 1868.

NORMAN C. DELANEY

MERWIN, James Burtis (22 May 1829–3 Apr. 1917), temperance reformer, was born in Cairo, New York, the son of Joseph R. Merwin and Emily Parker (occupations unknown). Much of his personal life and much of his career is obscure. Merwin claimed to have been educated at Brookfield Academy in Connecticut in preparation for college, which he did not attend; he also said that he had learned the jewelry trade but did not take it up. In 1850 he married Margaret Andrews of New Britain; after her death (date unknown) he married (date unknown) Mary G. Shipman, also of New Britain. It remains unknown whether Merwin fathered any children. By the early 1850s he was a public speaker and journalist advocating temperance and prohibition in Connecticut and other states. He was a member of the Connecticut Temperance Society and editor of a Hartford temperance paper, *The Fountain.*

Merwin first began to play a role in national public life during the Civil War. In July 1861 the governor of Connecticut and temperance advocates persuaded President Abraham Lincoln to name Merwin as temperance lecturer to the army. Merwin's activities included handing out temperance tracts and delivering anti-liquor talks to the troops. According to the testimonials of various generals, Merwin's 1861 and 1862 temperance addresses to assemblies of troops were well received. In June 1862 he was appointed as a hospital chaplain with the rank of major. What survives of his diary from the war years (May–Sept. 1864) depressingly chronicles his caring for wounded soldiers in hospitals and transport ships, writing letters of condolence to the families of the dead, and seeking to arrange better care of the wounded with various authorities and organizations.

After the war, Merwin continued his reform activities. In August 1865 he was one of the leaders at the Saratoga convention, which formed the National Temperance Society and Publication House. Organized along the lines of a tract society, the National Temperance Society was the chief propagandizing arm of the prohibition movement until the 1880s. The society went into eclipse, however, when new temperance organizations, especially the Woman's Christian Temperance Union (WCTU), founded in 1874, and the Prohibition party, established in 1869, pushed beyond the society's means of moral suasion. Merwin's role in temperance advocacy weakened along with that of the National Temperance Society. His declining influence in temperance circles may also have resulted from his moving to St. Louis and focusing his reform energies on education. In 1867 he founded the *American Journal of Education* (not to be confused with Henry Barnard's well-known publication of the same name). With the support of William T. Harris, superintendent of public schools in St. Louis and later U.S. Commissioner of Education, Merwin edited the periodical until 1891, advocating liberal education as a means of bettering the lives of individuals and producing better citizens for the nation. He also continued his public speaking on various topics, including education, literature, and reform.

In a 1904 speech at Lincoln's tomb, and then in a subsequent article in the *New Voice* (a Prohibition party paper), Merwin asserted, for the first time, that Lincoln had been a prohibitionist. With this claim, Merwin suddenly recaptured the attention of those in the prohibition movement as well as the public eye. Indeed, avowing that Lincoln had been a prohibitionist became the fixation of his final years.

To prove his point, Merwin repeatedly told of three incidents involving the president, which he claimed to have witnessed. The first was that Lincoln wrote and campaigned for passage of the 1855 Maine-style prohibition law in Illinois. Merwin, who had traveled west to become corresponding secretary of the Maine Law Alliance of the State of Illinois, claimed to have developed a friendship with Lincoln, who he claimed joined him on the stump at least six times. In recounting this tale, Merwin said that on the stump Lincoln used almost the same language to attack liquor as he later used against slavery and that he also coined the aphorism, "The saloon and the liquor traffic have defenders but no defense." Merwin's second assertion was that Lincoln had opposed the liquor tax levied by the federal government in 1862 to finance the war. Merwin claimed that the president had believed it was immoral for the government to profit from or sanction the liquor trade and that he had signed the bill grudgingly and had planned to repeal the tax soon after war's end. Merwin's third claim was that he had dined with Lincoln at the White House on the day of the president's assassination. During the meal, according to Merwin, Lincoln prophesied that with the ending of slavery the next great moral crusade would be the suppression of liquor.

Prohibitionists embraced Merwin's view of Lincoln, making all three tales staples of their propaganda, but there is no evidence to support his assertions. Merwin's silence on the issue for forty years seems too convenient; his tales emerged only after the principals had died and could not confirm or deny his assertions. Also, Merwin lacked documentation to prove his contentions, and no one offered independent confirmation of any of the tales. Merwin held fast to his beliefs, however, until his death in Brooklyn, New York. Indeed, his death notice in the *New York Times* (5 Apr. 1917) reads in full, "He took the stump in Illinois with Abraham Lincoln in 1855 for temperance." Thus Merwin's chief contribution to American history was his effort to perpetuate the myth that Abraham Lincoln was a prohibitionist.

• Indispensable to understanding Merwin are two manuscript collections: the James B. Merwin Papers, Manuscript Division, Library of Congress, which includes leaflets and a typescript copy of his diary covering 10 May to 5 Sept. 1864 as well as other documents; and the Temperance and Prohibition Papers, Howard Hyde Russell Series (microfilm ed. by the Ohio Historical Society), folders 41a-e, which includes interviews and correspondence with Merwin, reprints, and clippings. Useful in delineating and assessing Merwin's assertions about Lincoln are Ervin Chapman, *Latest Light on Abraham Lincoln and War-Time Memories* (1917); Duncan C. Milner, *Lincoln and Liquor* (1920); and William H. Townsend, *Lincoln and Liquor* (1934).

RICHARD F. HAMM

MERZ, Charles (23 Feb. 1893–31 Aug. 1977), editor and author, was born in Sandusky, Ohio, the son of Charles Hope Merz, a physician, and Sakie Emeline Prout. Merz edited the Sandusky High School newspaper and in the summer worked on the city's local dailies. In 1911 he entered Yale University, where he concentrated in English, history, and economics. He became editor of the *Record*, Yale's humor magazine, and was elected to Phi Beta Kappa. In 1915 he graduated with an A.B. and took a position at *Harper's Weekly* in New York City, becoming managing editor that same year. In 1916 he left *Harper's* to become the Washington, D.C., correspondent for Herbert Croly's *New Republic*. He soon developed a close friendship with Walter Lippmann, who, along with Croly and Walter Weyl, had founded the liberal-progressive journal of opinion in 1914. When the United States entered World War I, Merz received a commission as first lieutenant in the American Expeditionary Force, working in military intelligence. Sent to France in 1918, he became an assistant to the American delegation to the peace negotiations.

Merz returned to the *New Republic* in 1919 and began working with Lippmann on an analysis of the *New York Times*'s coverage of the Russian Revolution during the period between 1917 and 1920. The results of their study were published as "A Test of the News" in the 4 August 1920 issue of the *New Republic*. Significantly, Lippmann and Merz demonstrated that the *Times*'s performance failed to live up to its standards of objective reporting. They presented substantial evidence demonstrating that the paper often made reference to events that did not occur, reported on atrocities that were never committed, and claimed on several occasions that the Bolshevik regime was about to fall. The problem, according to Lippmann and Merz, was that the *Times* overly relied on anonymous sources, made excessive use of partisan correspondents, and allowed editorial opinion to color the news. In sum, they charged that *Times* coverage had presented readers with a biased and propagandistic account of the Bolsheviks' rise to power.

Merz remained at the *New Republic* until 1921, when he followed Lippmann to the *New York World*. He served as staff correspondent in Europe and Asia until 1923 and joined Lippmann to produce the editorial page in 1924. Before Merz became associate editor, he frequently contributed to *Collier's Weekly* and *Century*. Merz's first book, *Centerville, U.S.A.*, was published in 1924. Drawing mainly from his experiences as a youth in Sandusky, he portrayed everyday life in small-town America. In June of that year he married Evelyn Scott. They had no children. Four years later *The Great American Band-Wagon: A Study in Exaggerations* was published. A satire of 1920s American popular thought and culture, Merz's second book appraised the appeal of radio, jazz, boxing, sensationalist murder trials, beauty contests, golf, motion pictures, and other standardized forms of entertainment. Mark Van Doren noted in the *Nation* (22 Feb. 1928) that Merz had insightfully observed that mass culture not only provided an escape from the tensions of modern society but also represented a nostalgic yearning for the simpler days of frontier life.

In 1931, when the *World* ceased publication, Merz joined the editorial board of the *New York Times*. That year he completed *The Dry Decade*, a study of the successes and failures of Prohibition. At the *Times* he quickly developed a close friendship with Arthur Hays Sulzberger, the paper's publisher and president. In 1938, when editor in chief John H. Finley retired, Merz was named as his replacement.

When Merz assumed responsibility for the editorial page on 18 November 1938, debate over U.S. foreign policy in Europe had reached a fever pitch. Merz, a political liberal and ardent anti-Fascist, took a hard line against Hitler and pressed for an end to American isolationism. "In any ultimate test of strength between democracy and dictatorship," Merz wrote in a 15 June 1938 editorial, "the good will and the moral support—and in the long run more than likely the physical power of the United States—will be found on the side of those nations defending a way of life and the only way of life which Americans believe to be worth living." When the United States entered World War II, Merz's editorials supporting the draft were accorded great influence in breaking down political resistance to conscription.

In 1941 Merz edited *Days of Decision*, a volume of *Times* war editorials, and in a January 1942 article in the *Annals of the American Academy of Political and Social Science*, he took stock of changes in editorial journalism since World War I. The trends he pointed out were a response to the shortcomings of American journalism identified in the 1920s and 1930s by liberal observers of the press such as his mentor Lippmann. As Merz observed, contemporary editorial writing placed more and more emphasis on interpretation and analysis, made a concerted effort to separate fact from opinion, and had come to rely authoritative and expert sources to give the social, economic, and political issues of the day depth and perspective. After the war, Merz's internationalist leanings ensured that the *Times* played a central role in the campaign in support of the United Nations. In the early 1950s his editorials vigorously denounced Joseph R. McCarthy's virulent anticommunism and called for the Wisconsin senator's censure.

In 1961 Merz became *Times* editor emeritus. Upon retirement, he and his wife lived part of the year in New York City and the other in a small cottage on Cape Cod near Falmouth, Massachusetts. Merz died in New York City.

For nearly twenty-five years, Merz presided over the editorial pages of one of the world's most influential newspapers and was recognized by contemporaries as an important figure in the development of modern editorial journalism.

• Merz collaborated with Walter Lippmann to produce *The United States in World Affairs in 1932* (1933). For information on Merz's early career, see "Editor of the Times," *Newsweek*, 28 Nov. 1938, p. 28; "Merz for Finley," *Time*, 28 Nov. 1938; and David W. Levy, *Herbert Croly of the "New Republic": The Life and Thought of an American Progressive* (1970). On the significance of "A Test of the News," the best account remains Ronald Steel, *Walter Lippmann and the American Century* (1980). See also John Luskin, *Lippmann, Liberty, and the Press* (1972), and Michael Schudson, *Discovering the News: A Social History of American Newspapers* (1978). On his career at the *New York Times*, see Meyer Berger, *The Story of the "New York Times"; The First One Hundred Years, 1851–1951* (1951), Gay Talese, *The Kingdom and the Power* (1969), Harrison Salisbury, *Without Fear or Favor: The "New York Times" and Its Times* (1980), and Ward Morehouse, "Editor Charles Merz Sparks *New York Times* Staff," *Editor and Publisher*, 15 Apr. 1944, pp. 12, 59. An obituary is in the *New York Times*, 1 Sept. 1977.

ANDREW FELDMAN

MESERVE, Nathaniel (c. 1705–28 June 1758), shipbuilder and provincial military leader, was born in Newington, New Hampshire, the son of Clement Meserve, a joiner, and Elizabeth Jones. In 1725 he married Jane Libby; they had two children. Meserve soon afterward moved to Portsmouth, where he prospered as a shipbuilder and, in 1740 built one of the town's more elegant houses adjoining his shipyard.

In 1745 he was lieutenant colonel of the New Hampshire regiment in the successful New England expedition against the French fortress of Louisbourg during King George's War. There his skills and experience enabled him to provide an ingenious solution to the crucial problem of transporting cannon and mortars to a strategic hilltop across a two-mile marsh that supported neither wheels nor oxen. Meserve supervised the construction of timber sledges, which were each dragged by two hundred men over a period of fourteen successive nights to do the job. Meserve's shipyard had also furnished several of the transports that carried troops to Louisbourg. Besides giving the expedition an immense tactical advantage by the placement of artillery, Meserve made more conventional contributions to the siege in the form of bridges, breastworks, and barracks. Thus he was recognized at home as an important element in the New England victory, though the New Hampshire troops grumbled when their extraordinary efforts in placing the cannon, planned and supervised by Meserve, did not get the specific acknowledgment they thought they deserved in official reports to London.

Shortly after his return from Louisbourg, in 1746 Meserve joined with eleven other leading citizens of the province in purchasing from John Tufton Mason the original Mason family claim to much of the territory in New Hampshire. This was a somewhat controversial move in that the private purchase of the claim took place quietly during a protracted discussion in the New Hampshire Assembly of acquisition of the Mason title by the province itself. Governor Benning Wentworth was especially annoyed, since the deal was carried off without his knowledge even though the purchasers included several of his closest relatives. However, the "Masonian proprietors," as the purchasers were called, were careful to respect the interests both of the province government and of those who already lived on some of the lands in question. Harmony among the Portsmouth elite, of which Meserve as a Masonian proprietor and high-ranking war hero was now an unquestioned member, was quickly restored, and the Portsmouth elite's power and prestige in New Hampshire was more firmly established than ever.

In 1749 Meserve gained the most notable ship contract of his career, partly in recognition of his contributions at Louisbourg. The British admiralty commissioned him to build the 44-gun warship *America*, the first of its class to come from an American shipyard. The Royal Navy career of this vessel and even its rating—a ship named *America* is described as everything from a frigate to a ship-of-the-line, bearing anywhere from forty to sixty guns—are obscured by conflicting records. It may have been part of the fleet to which the Dutch garrison at Capetown surrendered in 1795 and finally retired and converted to a masting hulk in 1799. Other sources say it was so badly built it was never sent to sea after its maiden voyage to England in 1750.

In the same eventful decade of Meserve's achievement at Louisbourg and his rise to wealth and local prominence, he was married a second time, in 1747 to Mary Odiorne Jackson, his first wife Jane having died some time previously. Meserve and his second wife had nine children.

Soon after the outbreak of the French and Indian War, Meserve again went to war, this time as colonel in command of the New Hampshire regiment that took part in expeditions against Crown Point in 1756 and 1757. He won particular praise even from the imperious John Campbell, earl of Loudon, the British commander in chief, who overcame his general contempt for provincial soldiers and their officers sufficiently to commend Meserve for his diligence and skill in building fortifications and commanding the defense of Fort Edward in the summer of 1756. In 1757 he headed a detachment of carpenters from the regiment who went with Loudon's army to Halifax to build barracks and storehouses.

In 1758 the brief military future that remained to Meserve was determined by his reputation as builder and engineer. At the express desire of the new Pitt administration, which replaced Loudon in the American command with General James Abercromby, Meserve relinquished command of his New Hampshire regiment altogether in order to accompany Major General Jeffrey Amherst to Louisbourg at the head of another company of carpenters. Amherst succeeded in the conquest, but not before 92 of Meserve's 108 men succumbed to smallpox while at Louisbourg. Meserve and his son Nathaniel were among the casualties.

Nathaniel and Jane Meserve's other son, George Meserve, commanded a company in the 1745 Louisbourg expedition but is more lastingly remembered as the unfortunate appointee as stamp agent for Portsmouth in 1765 who was forced to resign under popular pressure and considerable ill-will during the crisis over the Stamp Act.

Meserve's early death at Louisbourg interrupted a promising career of leadership in the public and business life of his province. He remains significant primarily for his contributions as a military engineer to British successes in the colonial wars of the eighteenth century.

• Meserve's military role in King George's War and the French and Indian War is covered in Jeremy Belknap, *The History of New-Hampshire*, vol. 1 (1831), and in *Report of the Adjutant-General of the State of New-Hampshire*, vol. 2 (1866). A discussion of Meserve as shipbuilder, with particular attention to HMS *America*, may be found in William G. Saltonstall, *Ports of Piscataqua* (1941). The Portsmouth (N.H.) Atheneaum has a model of the *America* on display and also holds a large file of miscellaneous materials detailing the somewhat conflicting histories of that vessel. For genealogical and other biographical information, see Sybil Noyes et al., *Genealogical Dictionary of Maine and New Hampshire* (1972), and Charles W. Brewster, *Rambles About Portsmouth*, 1st ser. (1873; repr. 1971).

CHARLES E. CLARK

MESSER, Asa (31 May 1769–11 Oct. 1836), educator, was born in Methuen, Massachusetts, the son of Asa Messer and Abiah Whittier, farmers. Young Asa was a farmboy and then a grocery clerk in nearby Haverhill until in his mid-teens he began to prepare for college under Haverhill Baptist minister Hezekiah Smith, who sent him on to Rhode Island College in Providence. Matriculating as a sophomore in 1788, Messer graduated in 1790. Probably because of Smith's influence, Messer flirted with the ministry, acquiring his license to preach from the First Baptist Church in Providence in 1792 and his ordination in 1801, yet he never sought a pastorate and made only sporadic pulpit appearances during his career. His greater calling was to his college.

Messer began a 36-year career on the faculty of Rhode Island College in 1791 when he accepted a tutorship. He then served as professor of learned languages from 1796 to 1799 and as professor of natural philosophy from 1799 to 1802. Upon the resignation of his predecessor, Jonathan Maxcy, the trustees selected Messer as president pro tempore in September 1802 and made the appointment permanent in 1804. Messer married Deborah Angell in 1797, and the couple had four children, one of whom died in infancy.

Under Messer's conservative leadership, the college made slow, steady progress. It acquired a patron in Nicholas Brown (1769–1841), a Providence merchant, whose name the institution adopted in 1804. The college increased its number of students and courses and augmented its library while retaining the curriculum of the late eighteenth century. In 1811 it established a medical school that at first was understaffed and ill equipped but which grew in stature as the years went by.

To the students Messer was friendly and good humored but also a stern, if fair, disciplinarian. He was more comfortable teaching mathematics and natural philosophy wherein he could use his flair for the material and his practical, inventive nature than he was teaching moral philosophy (the usual lot of the college president) wherein he was handicapped by a lack of eloquence. Still, like most of his fellow presidents, he attempted to inculcate in his students his moral, political, and philosophical views, which, in Messer's case, initially took the form of a zealous Federalism that linked religious orthodoxy and proper governmental administration. In a 1799 discourse to the graduating seniors, he condemned deism and urged them to support the established civil government, warning that criticism of it would pave the way for the terrors of the French Revolution to cross the Atlantic and infect the United States. Messer's 1810 and 1811 commencement addresses reiterated his attacks on infidelity, but the latter address deviated from the standard Federalist rhetoric of the day by admonishing students "never to allow any other nation the right of abusing or controlling, or directing your own," a veiled reference to the United States's dispute with Great Britain, which would lead to the War of 1812.

Until about 1820 Messer was well regarded by all associated with Brown. During the early 1820s, however, Brown students, who like their fellow students elsewhere had always chafed at strict discipline, escalated their protests to mean-spirited pranks. By 1824 their behavior was riotous. At the same time, Messer came under attack from the trustees, whose criticism undoubtedly weakened the president's authority over the students. The underlying problem was Messer's increasingly apparent deviation from religious orthodoxy. In fact, his religious beliefs underwent change throughout his adult life. He moved from an adherence to evangelical Christianity to Arianism as early as 1805 but revealed nothing of this in his college sermons. By the teens, he was offering prayers at a Unitarian church in Providence, and in 1820 he accepted an honorary degree from Unitarian-dominated Harvard. Messer denied that his religious position was Unitarian, arguing that Christ was the Son of God but not God Himself. More important, he asserted that his religious beliefs were no one else's concern, protesting in 1818, for example, that "I abhor a bigot, and I should be unwilling to live among men unwilling that I should think for myself."

Messer's position reflected those parts of Brown's charter that proscribed religious tests and provided for religious toleration, but the majority of Rhode Island's Baptists had condemned Arianism for years and could not abide the spectacle of the denomination's first college being led by someone they considered a heretic. Having irreconcilably alienated both his students and his governors, Messer resigned amid disorder and criticism in 1826. The departure of the educationally conservative, religiously unorthodox Messer led to the appointment of the religiously orthodox, educationally reform-minded Francis Wayland (1796–1865), who became one of the most famous college presidents of the nineteenth century.

Messer lived quite comfortably after leaving Brown. Freed of the college's constraints, he joined a Freewill (Arminian) Baptist church. His practicality extending to the management of money, he had acquired farm property and an interest in a cotton mill while still at Brown, and these ventures provided him an adequate income. Continuing to live in Providence, he mounted something of a political career. He had refused a seat on the Rhode Island Supreme Court in 1818 but served as a Providence alderman for some years during the 1820s and 1830s and waged an unsuccessful campaign for the governorship of Rhode Island in 1830 on the "National Republican and Landholders Prox" ticket. He refused renomination for governor in 1836 and died shortly thereafter in Providence.

Messer was a man of solid academic and administrative talents. He gave Brown University competent, conservative leadership for more than twenty years, but his public departure from Baptist orthodoxy could not be tolerated in one who presided over the denomination's premier educational institution during an era of religious enthusiasm.

• Messer papers (sermons and essays) are in the Brown University Archives and some correspondence appears in the Horace Mann Papers, 1829–1856, in the Brown University Library. Some of his published addresses are reprinted in Romeo Elton, *The Literary Remains of the Rev. Jonathan Maxcy* (1844); all can be found on microfiche in the American Antiquarian Society's Early American Imprints series. There is no modern biography of Messer. An older sketch, reflecting its author's religious concerns, appears in William B. Sprague, ed., *Annals of the American Pulpit*, vol. 6 (1865; repr. 1969). Useful histories of Brown University that cover Messer's tenure there are Walter C. Bronson, *The History of Brown University, 1764–1914* (1914), and Reuben A. Guild, *Early History of Brown University, Including the Life, Times, and Correspondence of President Manning, 1756–1791* (1897). The reflections of an admiring pupil may be found in An Alumnus, *Brown University under the Presidency of Asa Messer, S.T.D., LL.D.* (1867). Baptist attitudes toward unorthodox beliefs such as Messer's find treatment in William G. McLoughlin, *New England Dissent, 1630–1833*, vol. 2 (1971).

DAVID W. ROBSON

MESSERSMITH, George Strausser (3 Oct. 1883–29 Jan. 1960), educator and diplomat, was born in Fleetwood, Pennsylvania, the son of Charles Messersmith, an entrepreneur, and Sarah Strausser. George Messersmith was raised in Berks County, Pennsylvania, and was educated at home by his mother until he was eleven years old. He then went to public schools, graduated from high school, and continued on with a two-year course of study at the normal school in Kutztown in 1900. There he received sufficient training to allow him to teach school. According to the Department of State *Biographical Register*, he attended Delaware College, but there is no record of any coursework. He probably stopped with the degree in 1900 but, unwilling to admit his lack of education, claimed to have had a college background. He taught and later served as a principal in Delaware schools, but after more than a decade in this field, he took three major steps in 1914: first, he decided to leave his position; second, he decided to join the consular service; and third, he married Marion Mustard, a union that never produced any children.

Messersmith's first assignment was in Fort Erie, Canada, where he focused on improving bilateral commercial relations. After two years at that station, he was transferred to Curaçao, where he concentrated on building better trade relations and preventing German espionage activities from damaging U.S. efforts in World War I. After the fighting ended in 1919, Messersmith moved to Antwerp and five years later was promoted to consul general. Once again he emphasized increased trade, and, to reach this goal, he advanced the cause of American-Belgium cooperation. In 1928 he was assigned to Buenos Aires, Argentina, the first capital to which he was stationed, and during this posting he also inspected several American consulates in Latin America.

In the darkest days of the Great Depression, in 1930, Messersmith returned to Europe, where he served as consul general in Berlin and was one of the first American diplomatic observers to report on Adolf Hitler's ascension to power in 1933 and the growth of German militarism and anti-Semitism. Messersmith offered no solutions to the growing threat of the Third Reich's expansionist tendencies, nor did the Western European nations, who passively watched German rearmament. After four years in Germany, he was promoted to American minister in Austria, where he continued to report on the increased tensions in Central Europe and the events leading up to the Anschluss, the absorption of Austria into the Third Reich. During this period of Messersmith's crescendoing voice against nazism, many Jews erroneously labeled him the most philo-Semitic member of the foreign service, but that distorted his position. Messersmith clearly held that Germany's Jewish population was mistreated, but this did not translate into a welcome for the persecuted minority into the United States. Those who met the legal requirements to come to American shores were accepted, but he never favored relaxing or altering immigration restrictions.

While Messersmith was earning a reputation as an anti-Nazi, the State Department was undergoing a major reorganization in 1937. His part in this change was the assumption of the role as assistant secretary of state in charge of budgetary affairs, enforcement of immigration regulations, and foreign commercial interaction. While stationed in the capital, Messersmith also supported the president's unsuccessful efforts to check Hitler's aggression. The assistant secretary also supported Secretary of State Cordell Hull in his efforts to increase American foreign trade through the reciprocal trade agreements program.

By early 1940 Messersmith completed his tour as assistant secretary and became ambassador to Cuba. Willard Beaulac, his closest assistant, captured his chief's character, emphasizing that his "greatest merit was that he was always successful. . . . Serious and grim, Messersmith had no hobby but his work and no recreation except mystery stories and an occasional game of Chinese checkers. . . . [He] hammered away at every problem until it was solved. He never gave up. He never relaxed. He complained continually about the delicate state of his health while doing the work of three men without apparent fatigue." He reported in minute detail, and Beaulac labeled him "the No. 1 letter writer in the service." Messersmith often wrote the president and the secretary of state letters that were fifteen typewritten pages, single-spaced, with several more pages of postscripts (Beaulac, *Career Ambassador* [1951], pp. 147–50).

While in Havana, Messersmith worked to improve bilateral economic relations and prevent the Nazis from having any meaningful fifth-column impact on the island. As always, he warned against the menace of the Third Reich as its troops swept across Europe and that effect on the Americas. The day that France signed the armistice with Germany, Messersmith concluded: "The news from Europe this morning is so devastating that I think we must now seriously face practically complete collapse and we simply cannot permit the British and French fleets to fall into the hands of the Germans. If we do that we will put our defense program two years back and will open the way to almost immediate developments among the other American Republics where our second line of defense now lies, with the first one gone or also gone" (Gellman, *Good Neighbor Diplomacy*, pp. 133–34).

Just after the United States entered World War II, Messersmith became ambassador to Mexico and remained there until 1946. He again sought to emphasize trade, and under the administration's drive for hemispheric solidarity, he worked to modernize Mexican railroads, enhance petroleum production, and assist with the passage of a bilateral water rights treaty. Toward the end of this assignment, he helped plan and execute the agenda for the Chapultepec conference, the meeting that started multilateral discussions on the future of postwar hemispheric cooperation and the seating of Argentina at the upcoming United Nations gathering.

Messersmith's last hemispheric assignment was in Buenos Aires as the successor to Ambassador Spruille Braden, who had become deeply involved with trying to remove Juan Perón from power by preaching democracy and publishing a book that recounted the contacts between Argentina's military rulers and the Axis. Instead of losing power, however, Perón used Braden's efforts to rally nationalistic sentiment against the United States and emerged as president; Braden was recalled to the United States as the assistant secretary of state in charge of Latin American affairs. Messersmith was sent to Argentina to repair the breach in bilateral relations, but this proved impossible with Braden's opposition to the ambassador's efforts. The acrimony that erupted between the two diplomats forced both of their resignations by the summer of 1947. After his separation from the foreign service, Messersmith quickly accepted the presidency of Mexican Power and Light Company. He retired from that post in 1954 in declining health. He died in Houston, Texas.

Messersmith has been almost exclusively remembered for his early stance against the Nazis, but his significance reached much further. He rose in the consular service until his Berlin assignment. He then became minister to Austria, which reinforced his claim as a champion against the venality of the Third Reich. Although mistaken for his philo-Semitic feelings, he certainly did not reflect the anti-Semitism of many of his colleagues. As assistant secretary of state, he did not eliminate visa requirements, but he did apply the rules fairly, which radically altered the anti-Semitic practices of his predecessors. He never forgot the rise of the Nazis and the holocaust they had unleashed. From many perspectives, Messersmith considered the advent of the Cold War and the growth of Soviet totalitarianism as a similar menace. Using this reasoning, he recommended that the United States engage in a preventive war against Stalin at the end of the 1940s to stop Soviet expansionism, although he was ignored as he had been in the 1930s. When he returned to the field as ambassador to Cuba, Mexico, and Argentina, he reiterated several themes: improved trade, closer bilateral cooperation, and inter-American solidarity. Messersmith opposed Latin American authoritarianism throughout his diplomatic career. He decried communism, fascism, and nazism as nearly identical evils that threatened the growth of stability in the Western Hemisphere. The United States, he believed, needed to counteract these influences by committing to strong inter-American ties. As Jesse Stiller has concluded, throughout his life Messersmith championed justice and empathy, which were then and are now enduring principles of American foreign policy (Stiller, p. 271).

• The George Messersmith Papers are housed in the University of Delaware, Department of Special Collections, Newark, Del. These manuscripts include a great deal of his official correspondence as well as his memoirs. His diplomatic correspondence is primarily in the U.S. Department of State, Central Decimal File, RG 59, National Archives, Washington, D.C. The definitive biography of Messersmith is Jesse H. Stiller, *George S. Messersmith: Diplomat of Democracy* (1987). See also Irwin F. Gellman, *Good Neighbor Diplomacy: United States Policies in Latin America, 1933–1945*

(1979), and see Gellman, *Roosevelt and Batista: Good Neighbor Diplomacy in Cuba, 1933–1945* (1973), for Messersmith's tour of duty in Cuba.

IRWIN F. GELLMAN

MESSMER, Sebastian Gebhard (29 Aug. 1847–4 Aug. 1930), fourth Roman Catholic bishop of Milwaukee, was born in Goldach, Switzerland, the son of Sebastian Messmer, a farmer, innkeeper, and local politician, and Rosa Baumgartner. He attended the village school and spent three years at the *Realschule* in Rorschach. From 1861 to 1866 he studied at St. George College near St. Gall and from there undertook philosophical and theological studies for five years at the University of Innsbruck, Austria. He was ordained to the priesthood on 23 July 1971 by Bishop Athanasius Edward Zuber in Innsbruck. In October 1871 he accepted the invitation of Bishop James Roosevelt Bayley of Newark to teach theology and canon law at Seton Hall College in South Orange, New Jersey. He spent eighteen years at Seton Hall while serving as a pastoral assistant to St. Mary's Orphanage in Newark.

He played an important role at the Third Plenary Council of Baltimore in 1884, drafting the decrees, acting as one of the council secretaries, and preparing a report of its deliberations for publication in 1886. As a reward, Pope Leo XIII conferred on him an honorary doctorate in divinity. Although he was opposed to the foundation of the Catholic University of America in Washington, D.C.—he shared the sentiments of many German-speaking bishops that the university was dominated by Americanists and detracted from local institutions of higher learning, more directly under their control—Messmer was selected in 1889 to teach canon law at the newly opened institution and spent a year of preparation at the Apollinaris College in Rome, where he earned a doctorate in canon law. He served at the Catholic University until 1891, when he was appointed Bishop of Green Bay, Wisconsin. He was consecrated 27 March 1892 in Newark by Bishop Otto Zardetti. Despite his later absorption with administrative duties, Messmer retained his love for scholarship. He published articles in *Catholic Encyclopedia* and in such journals as *Salesianum*, *American Catholic Historical Review*, *American Ecclesiastical Review*, and *Pastoral Blatt*. He wrote *Praxis Synodalis* (1883), a pamphlet that laid out the deliberations of the Provincial Council of New York that met in 1882; he translated *Canonical Procedures in Disciplinary and Criminal Cases of Clerics* (1887) from the German by Franz Droste and edited *Spirago's Method of Christian Doctrine* (1901), William Devivier's *Christian Apologetics* (1903), and the *Works of the Rt. Rev. John England*, which filled seven volumes (1908). Messmer also wrote *Outlines of Bible Knowledge* in 1910 and 1927, basing it on Andrew Bruell's *Bibelkunde*.

He served ten years as the leader of the Green Bay diocese, building schools and social welfare institutions. As a result of his long years in academe, Messmer had very carefully worked out positions on the issues of his day. For example, he was an outspoken defender of the rights of German ethnics in the Catholic church, arguing for the retention of distinctive German parishes and schools and the maintenance of the German language in work and worship as a means of preserving the faith of German immigrants. Messmer was also critical of certain aspects of American reform movements. He spoke out against Prohibition and woman suffrage and was particularly adamant against socialism. His disagreements with American Socialists attracted a good deal of attention after he became archbishop of Milwaukee in 1903 and had to contend with the rising socialist political influence in the city. An important forum for his ideas was the American Federation of Catholic Societies, which Messmer and Trenton, New Jersey, bishop James A. McFaul had sponsored in 1901 to coordinate the activities of lay Catholic organizations. The organization flourished briefly and collapsed in 1919.

In Milwaukee Messmer effected a major centralization of archdiocesan offices, creating the post of superintendent of schools and drawing power to himself and his chancery staff, especially his chancellor and vicar general, Bernard Traudt. Messmer's pro-Germanism was in evidence throughout his years in Milwaukee, though it was somewhat muted during World War I. He reversed his earlier support of ethnic diversity, however, in the wake of serious clashes between himself and militant Polish Catholics led by Father Wenceslaus Kruszka and his brother, layman Michael Kruszka, who wanted greater Polish representation in the hierarchy. Messmer did secure the appointment of the Polish priest Edward Kozlowski as auxiliary bishop in 1914, but after Kozlowski died a year later, the Poles insisted that another Polish auxiliary bishop be appointed and that there be more Polish representation in the upper echelons of the archdiocesan administration. Messmer resisted, and the simmering tensions erupted into open confrontation when Messmer taxed Polish parishes and clergy to fund an over-built Polish church that was unable to meet its debts. Polish leaders considered this unfair and protested the move. The situation nearly resulted in a major schism, but eventually tempers cooled and the controversy died down with time.

Messmer's earlier sponsorship of the American Federation of Catholic Societies led to his backing similar organizations, such as the National Catholic Welfare Conference and the Catholic Hospital Association of the United States and Canada. He also encouraged progress in higher education by substantially improving the quality of the staff and buildings at St. Francis Seminary, encouraging the efforts of the Jesuits at Marquette University, and welcoming into the diocese Mount Mary College, a women's school operated by the School Sisters of Notre Dame. He also established a Catholic chaplaincy at the University of Wisconsin in 1904.

Messmer's health declined steadily during the 1920s, and he spent increasingly longer amounts of time away from his duties. When the aging archbishop traveled to Switzerland in 1930, apostolic delegate Pietro Fumasoni-Biondi gently suggested that Messmer accept a coadjutor. He died in Switzerland later that year and was buried in his native Goldach.

Messmer's career can truly be characterized as transitional. Beginning as a firm proponent of accentuated ethnic rights, Messmer dramatically shifted his position in the early twentieth century and sought to homogenize the American Catholic population. This he felt would give the church more authority and influence in dealing with pressing social and economic problems in the United States. A broadly educated man with a number of publications, Messmer could not be characterized a true scholar. Many of his published works were translations or compilations of the writings of other authors. Nonetheless, he was a strong advocate of a principled and rational debate in confronting challenges to the church from contemporary society.

• The archives of Seton Hall University, South Orange, N.J., the Archdiocese of Milwaukee, and the Diocese of Green Bay, Wis., contain material related to Messmer's career. See also Benjamin Blied, *Three Archbishops of Milwaukee* (1955); Alfred J. Ede, *The Lay Crusade for a Christian American: A Study of the American Federation of Catholic Societies* (1988); and Anthony Kuzniewski, *Faith and Fatherland: The Polish Church War in Milwaukee* (1980). An obituary and related article are in the *New York Times*, 5 and 8 Aug. 1930.

STEVEN M. AVELLA

MESTA, Perle (12 Oct. 1889 or 1891–16 Mar. 1975), political activist, businesswoman, diplomat, and hostess, was born Pearl Skirvin in Sturgis, Michigan, the daughter of William Balser Skirvin, a salesman, and Harriet Reid. The actual year of her birth was one of her best-kept secrets. Early in the twentieth century her father left Michigan for the oil fields of South Texas, where he made a fortune in the famed Spindletop field. The feisty "Billy" Skirvin moved to Oklahoma City, where he founded the American Oil and Refinery Company and built the luxurious fourteen-floor Skirvin Hotel. Pearl was educated in private schools in Galveston and studied voice and piano at the Sherwood School of Music in Chicago. In 1917 she married 54-year-old George Mesta, founder and president of the Mesta Machine Company located in Pittsburgh. During her years living in the nation's steel capital she changed her name to the distinctive "Perle."

Mesta accompanied her husband to Europe on twenty business/pleasure trips before his death in 1925, at which time she inherited nearly $1 million. They had no children, and she never married again. Upon her husband's death she was appointed to the Mesta Machine Company's board of directors, a responsibility she took seriously, immersing herself in all aspects of the steel production and manufacturing business. When her father died in 1944, she inherited an estimated additional $.5 million. Mesta managed her dual inheritances skillfully, investing successfully in stocks, oil, and real estate. She purchased a mansion along "millionaires' row" in Newport, Rhode Island, in 1929 and a luxurious residence, "Les Ormes," in Washington, D.C., in 1941.

During the late 1930s Mesta became actively involved in politics on behalf of women's rights. She joined the National Woman's party and in the 1930s and early 1940s doggedly lobbied for the Equal Rights Amendment. She worked on behalf of Alf Landon's presidential campaign in Oklahoma in 1936 but left the Republican party in 1941 in protest against the shabby treatment she perceived Wendell Willkie received from party regulars.

Mesta had always enjoyed entertaining, but after moving to Washington, D.C., she made it an integral part of her life. Her first major event was a reception in honor of Vice President Harry S. Truman. Her relaxed style of entertainment placed a premium on having her guests enjoy themselves and was appreciated by the unpretentious Trumans. She became the "unofficial hostess" of the Truman administration, a title Bess Truman encouraged because of her strong personal dislike for formal entertaining. In 1948 Mesta played an important role in raising funds for Truman's underfinanced reelection campaign, and she served as cochair of his 1949 inaugural committee.

During the early years of Truman's presidency, Mesta established herself as the capital's premier hostess, presiding over dinner parties large and small, enormous buffets, crowded receptions, and intimate cocktail parties. She took pride in bringing leading political figures of both parties together with prominent members of the judiciary, the press, the Foreign Service corps, and the entertainment world. Her parties were recognized for their convivial informality. President Truman frequently played the piano, and President Dwight D. Eisenhower once sang a memorable solo of "Drink to Me Only with Thine Eyes."

Invitations to Mesta's events were highly prized during the Truman and Eisenhower years. She stocked her bar with ample quantities of the best wines and liquors, although as a Christian Scientist she drank only Coca Cola. Always dressed stylishly and adorned with expensive jewelry, she presided over her zestful events with sparkle and élan, her hearty voice and booming laugh often floating above a crowded room of dignitaries.

Although Mesta was widely known as the "Hostess with the Mostes'," not everyone in the cutthroat world of Washington society was enamored with her lofty reputation. Alice Roosevelt Longworth complained, "She's amiable, of course, but commonplace." The haughty Lady Astor proved even less charitable, "She gives enormous parties that nobody who's anybody ought to go to." But these were minority views expressed most likely out of pique and jealousy of Mesta's ability to attract prominent individuals to her highly publicized events.

In 1949 Truman nominated Mesta as minister to the Grand Duchy of Luxembourg, making her only the third woman to become the head of an American embassy. This surprising appointment prompted many a humorous comment, but Mesta took her job seriously and performed her duties admirably. Her business experience enabled her to engage in serious dialogue with the political and business leaders of this tiny country, which was nonetheless the world's seventh largest producer of steel. Mesta assisted in establishing libraries, toured factories and mines, founded a scholarship program to enable Luxembourg students to study at American universities, and, of course, entertained an estimated 25,000 guests, including many American servicemen and servicewomen. After a much publicized three-month tour of the Soviet Union as a private citizen, she returned to Washington in late 1953. Although she now lacked the political clout she had enjoyed during a Democratic administration, her parties remained a highlight of the Washington social scene throughout the Eisenhower years. In 1950 Irving Berlin's *Call Me Madam*, a rollicking musical comedy based on Mesta's years as hostess and diplomat, became a Broadway hit. Its gentle satire met with her approval as well as adding to her fame. In 1953 a popular film version appeared. Both the stage and motion picture versions starred Ethel Merman.

In 1960 Mesta once again shifted political allegiances, supporting Richard Nixon for the presidency. This meant that she was definitely out of favor during the John Kennedy years, but she made a comeback of sorts during the Lyndon Johnson administration, hosting many large events as well as small dinner parties for the president and his wife when they wished to dine with individuals outside of a formal White House setting. By this time, however, her style had fallen out of favor in a city where the clouds of Vietnam put a damper on social gaiety. Advancing years slowed her once frenetic pace, and in 1972 she suffered a broken hip, which forced her to use a walker and a cane. With declining health, she entered a managed care facility in Oklahoma City, where she had moved to be near her brother. Mesta died in Oklahoma City.

• Mesta wrote an autobiography, *Perle: My Story* (1960). Her role on the margins of the Truman administration is discussed briefly in David McCullough, *Truman* (1992), and more thoroughly by Alonzo Hamby in *Man of the People* (1995), but the best sources on her life are the large number of newspaper and news magazine articles that were written about her diplomatic and social adventures. See Martha Gellhorn, "Party Girl in Paradise," *Saturday Evening Post*, 7 Jan. 1950; Flora Lewis, "Madam Minister to Luxembourg," *New York Times Magazine*, 25 Dec. 1949; Horace Sutton, "Lady Minister," *Saturday Review of Literature*, 11 Aug. 1951; "What's a Woman to Do?" *Life*, 18 May 1953; and "Mesta Machine," *Newsweek*, 25 Apr. 1960. An obituary is in the *New York Times*, 17 Mar. 1975.

RICHARD O. DAVIES

MEŠTROVIĆ, Ivan (15 Aug. 1883–16 Jan. 1962), sculptor and architect, was born in Vrpolje, Croatia, the son of Mate Meštrović, a poor migrant farmworker and stonemason, and Marte Kurabasa. Shortly after his birth the family returned to its home in Otavice, a Croatian village in the Dalmatian Alps. Meštrović never attended school, and he spent his early years as a shepherd and farmer. Immersed in the peasant folk traditions of his native area, he achieved a local reputation for carving religious figurines. At the age of fourteen Meštrović was taken to Split and apprenticed to a master mason. These experiences were the foundation for his later career as an accomplished carver who worked directly with his media. He attracted the attention of a Viennese mine owner who financed his move to Vienna in 1899. There Meštrović studied with Otto Koenig, a retired professor of sculpture, to pass the entrance examination at the Vienna Academy of the Fine Arts, where he studied from 1900 until 1904.

Beginning in 1903 Meštrović became a regular exhibitor at the Vienna Secession. Proceeds from the sale of some sculptures to a wealthy patron enabled him to visit Italy, where he saw the work of Michelangelo. The following year he married Ruža Klein, the daughter of a Croatian sculptor. In 1905 Meštrović moved to Paris, where he befriended Auguste Rodin, who pronounced him "the greatest phenomenon among the sculptors." From then until 1914 Meštrović worked on the Kossovo Temple, a large-scale national shrine with a complex sculptural program devoted to the theme of Yugoslav nationalism. Although it was never built, individual pieces exhibited at the 1909 Vienna Secession brought him great critical acclaim and recognition as an artist of international repute.

Forced to flee Yugoslavia at the outbreak of World War I because of his vocal opposition to the policies of the Austro-Hungarian Empire, Meštrović found refuge in Rome, London, Geneva, and Cannes. His interest in religious subjects steadily increased as his career progressed. He was active in the Yugoslav Committee on National Liberation, and exhibitions of his work inevitably assumed a political significance because they drew public attention to the plight of his native country. He moved to Zagreb in 1919, remaining there for the most part until 1942. Opposed to a predominantly Serbian regime that did little to further the interests of Croatia, he refused a number of positions in the Yugoslavian government and served as director of the Zagreb Academy of Fine Arts. In addition to receiving commissions for large public sculptural monuments such as *Gregory, Bishop of Nin* (1926, Split), he designed churches and memorial chapels, most notable among them the Račić Memorial Church (1922, Cavtat). After his first marriage ended, in 1923 he married Olga Kesterčanek, with whom he had four children.

Meštrović spent 1924 and 1925 in the United States, where he exhibited in several major cities and was commissioned to execute the *Indian with Bow* and *Indian with Spear* for Grant Park, Chicago. In 1933 a major traveling exhibition of his work was seen throughout Europe. In 1941, during the Italian occupation of Yugoslavia, he was imprisoned by the secret police until his release was negotiated by the Vatican. This harrowing experience had a decisive influence on Meštrović's creativity and engendered an outpouring of intensely spiritual religious imagery. Early in 1942 he went to Rome and commenced work on his 12′ by

5½′ Carrara marble *Pieta* (Sacred Heart Church, Univ. of Notre Dame), a work that he regarded as most expressive of his religious convictions. When Rome also became dangerous he was forced to wait out the war in Switzerland.

After the war Meštrović refused to return to a Yugoslavia governed by Josip Broz Tito's dictatorship, and in 1947 he emigrated to the United States, where he taught at Syracuse University. His exhibition at the Metropolitan Museum of Art that year was the first time that institution granted a one-man show to a living artist. In 1952 he was elected an honorary member of the Art Academy of Vienna. In 1953, the year that his 24-foot bronze *Man and Freedom* was installed at the Mayo Clinic in Rochester, Minnesota, he was awarded the American Academy of Arts and Letters Award of Merit. In 1954 he became an American citizen. The following year Meštrović accepted an appointment as professor of sculpture at the University of Notre Dame in South Bend, Indiana, where he found the atmosphere conducive to his interest in creating religious art. The sculptor lived there for the rest of his life. In 1959 he visited Yugoslavia for the last time. Despite suffering a severe stroke that affected his sight the following year, Meštrović continued working until his death in South Bend.

Meštrović's place within the history of twentieth-century European sculpture is difficult to assess; his biographers often assume a hagiographic tone, while most art historians have unjustly ignored him. His major sculptures, whose subjects are drawn almost exclusively from either Yugoslavian history and folklore or Roman Catholicism, display an austere, monolithic quality that relates them to the art of the ancient Near East, Egypt, and archaic Greece. Meštrović was a prolific artist who worked in the neoclassical, art nouveau, and expressionistic styles. Believing that his work should be intelligible to the masses, he never ventured into non-objective art. His insistence that art communicate specific concerns and his failure to espouse avant-garde tendencies have adversely affected his reputation for posterity. He was a figure sculptor who closely adhered to the tradition of Michelangelo and Rodin, the two dominant influences on his work. Meštrović's aesthetic goal is best described in his own words:

> What I sought to create was a synthesis of the popular national ideals and their development, to express by stone and architecture the depth of the memory of our greatest moments and the most characteristic phases of our history—forming at the same time an apex for hopes in the future, amidst nature and under the free sky.

• Meštrović wrote two studies on Michelangelo, *Michelangelo* (1926) and *Michelangelo's Dialogues with His Friends* (1957–1958). The definitive study of the artist's career is Laurence Schmeckebier, *Ivan Meštrović: Sculptor and Patriot* (1959). See also Milan Curcin, ed., *Ivan Meštrović: A Monograph* (1919), which includes a number of essays by critics; Ernest H. R. Collings, *Ivan Meštrović* (1933), which contains an introduction by the artist; and Harry H. Hilberry and Estelle S. Hilberry, *The Sculpture of Ivan Meštrović* (1948). The most important exhibition catalogs devoted to Meštrović's work are Christian Brinton, *The Meštrović Exhibition* (1924), Andre Dezarrios and R. Warnier, *Ivan Meštrović* (1933), *Katalog Galerije Ivana Meštrovića U Splitu* (1957), and Anthony J. Lauck et al., *Ivan Meštrović: The Notre Dame Years* (1974). Dean A. Porter and James Flanigan, *Ivan Meštrović, 1883–1962: A Centennial Exhibition* (1983), concentrates on his drawings.

ROBERT WILSON TORCHIA

METACOM. *See* Philip.

METALIOUS, Grace (8 Sept. 1924–25 Feb. 1964), writer, was born Grace DeRepentigny in Manchester, New Hampshire, the daughter of Albert DeRepentigny, a printer, and Laurette Royer. Her parents, working-class, French-Canadian Catholics, divorced when she was twelve. Subsequently she and her younger sister were raised by their maternal grandmother and their fairly independent but socially ambitious mother. Through most of Grace's childhood she was considered "a little princess" by her grandmother and mother, who impressed on her a strict sense of class and ethnic hierarchy that often bordered on snobbery.

Although she was an average student, Metalious began writing at an early age, partially as a means to escape her troubled depression-era family life. She was a voracious reader, wrote her first novel in the seventh grade, and continued writing plays with friends through high school. She graduated from Manchester's public Central High School in January 1942, worked as a typist for one year, and then married high school boyfriend George Metalious in 1943, much to the dismay of both the bride's and the groom's families. George worked odd jobs until he enlisted in the army in the summer of 1943. Grace gave birth to their first child in October 1943 and spent the remainder of the war years working at an air force base. After George returned from the war in early 1945, the young couple found their finances and their marriage continually strained. Another child was born in February 1947, and in 1948 George enrolled at the University of New Hampshire in hopes of becoming a teacher. In July 1950 Grace gave birth to the couple's third child after a long and difficult labor during which she almost died. When her doctors informed her that another pregnancy would probably prove fatal, she was significantly disturbed by the news, considering herself a failure as a woman and a wife.

Grace again turned to writing as a means to channel her creative energy, occupy her time, and escape from what she saw as the lackluster reality of her life. By 1952 George had graduated and was working as a social studies teacher in rural Belmont, New Hampshire, and Grace found small-town family life largely unsatisfying. As a result, she began working on the novel that would eventually make her famous: *The Tree and the Blossom*, later titled simply *Peyton Place*.

The year 1955 was critical for the Metaliouses. George accepted a job as school principal at nearby

Gilmanton Corners School, and Grace finished what she now called her "fourth baby." *The Tree and the Blossom* was meant to be an exposé of small-town hypocrisy and corruption drawn from Grace's own experience and observations. For months rumors had been flying about Belmont and Gilmanton that she had written and was attempting to publish a scandalous book about real townspeople, and George was threatened with the loss of his job by angry school board members. He prevailed, and finally, after a number of failed attempts to secure a publisher, in August 1955 the book was accepted by Messner Inc., a small New York publishing firm. This news, coupled with a $1,500 advance, thrilled both Grace and George, who were still living in reduced financial circumstances. However, Grace soon encountered difficulties with the way in which editor Leona Nevler was handling her book. Nevler was released, and Grace began working directly with Kitty Messner, head of the Messner publishing firm. This partnership proved more successful, both personally and professionally, and *Peyton Place* was finally published in September 1956.

The novel was an immediate success, appearing on the bestseller list within a month of publication, where it would remain for more than a year. Readers were attracted by the lurid "real-life" aspects of the book as well as its racy love scenes. The publicity surrounding the novel was likewise remarkable. After it was discovered that George Metalious finally had been fired from his job as school principal, Gilmanton was besieged by media searching for the "real" Peyton Place. Grace Metalious herself became instantly famous, and *Peyton Place* became a popular subject for discussion. Although it was criticized by many for its stylistic shortcomings and was banned in parts of the country for its subject matter, it ultimately sold over eight million copies. Later the novel was adapted into a successful film and a television series.

After the astounding success of *Peyton Place*, Grace Metalious assumed that "life was going to be all beer and skittles and nothing unpleasant was ever going to happen to me again." Unfortunately, her personal life grew more complicated. Her marriage to George Metalious disintegrated, and she began an affair with T. J. Martin, a disc jockey. In 1958 Grace and George divorced, and T. J. and Grace were married. After two years of lavish living and partying, they divorced in 1960. Grace reunited with George, and they announced their remarriage in October 1960, although no records have been found to verify this. In any case, their second union ended in 1963.

During this time, Grace Metalious continued to turn out bestselling novels based on a theme similar to that of *Peyton Place*. *Return to Peyton Place* appeared in 1959, followed by *The Tight White Collar* (1960) and *No Adam in Eden* (1963). Although none of her novels received critical praise, Metalious enjoyed continued financial success and fame. She died in Boston of advanced cirrhosis.

The enormous popularity of *Peyton Place* and its successors allows us insight into the tastes of readers of popular literature in the mid- and late 1950s. Metalious's explicit love scenes and the sexual nature of her novels separated her work from the typically more conservative popular literature of the era, and her work opened the doorway to a whole new generation of similar writers who were encouraged by her success. Although Metalious never won critical recognition for her work, she was highly successful at reaching and appealing to a mass audience. The publicity techniques pioneered by the writer/editor team of Metalious and Messner continue to serve as models for reaching a wide audience. Reviews may have been consistently poor, but Metalious and Messner were able to positively manipulate them by stressing their emphasis on the racier aspects of the work. In addition, by publicizing the real-life scandal behind a novel such as *Peyton Place*, Metalious and Messner also showed skill in generating enormous media and popular interest. These techniques assisted Metalious in her career and still play an important role in the publishing industry today.

• "All About Me and *Peyton Place*," a series of autobiographical articles written by Grace Metalious, was published in the *American Weekly* (Sunday supplement), 18, 25 May, 1, 8 June 1958. An important biography is Emily Toth, *Inside Peyton Place* (1981), which also contains a complete bibliography and criticism of Metalious's work. See also George Metalious and June O'Shea, *The Girl from "Peyton Place"* (1965). An obituary is in the *New York Times*, 26 Feb. 1964.

KIMBERLY MARKOWSKI

METCALF, Willard Leroy (1 July 1858–9 Mar. 1925), painter, was born in Lowell, Massachusetts, the son of Greenleaf Willard, a violinist with the Boston Orchestra, and Margaret Jan Gallop. In 1863 the Metcalfs moved to a farm in Maine and in 1871 they bought a home in Cambridgeport, Massachusetts, where Metcalf attended public school. His parents believed in ghostly phenomena and actively participated in occult activities. When a medium at a seance convinced them a supernatural spirit had revealed that their son was to become a famous painter, they encouraged his artistic efforts.

Metcalf apprenticed as a wood engraver at age sixteen and attended the Massachusetts Normal Art School in Boston. In 1875 he apprenticed with landscape painter George Loring Brown in South Boston and studied with Munich-trained Ignaz Gaugengig at the Lowell Institute two nights a week. Brown taught Metcalf to draw truthfully from nature and to execute accurate pictures of judges, Roman figures, and wreathed heads. The next year Metcalf enrolled at the school of the Museum of Fine Arts in Boston, where he studied the Dutch tradition of painting with Otto Grundmann and was the first scholarship recipient of the Museum School in 1878. Soon he became known for his *plein air* paintings.

Struggling to earn enough money to eat and buy painting supplies, Metcalf drew scenes of people for *Harper's* in 1882. That same year, *Century* magazine commissioned him to travel with Frank W. Cushing of the Smithsonian Institution and Boston newsman Sylvester Baxter to draw and paint illustrations of Zuni Indians in Arizona and New Mexico. Uncomfortable in the Southwest heat, Metcalf returned to Boston in 1884. That year the Chase Gallery exhibited seventy-five of his paintings.

When some of his works sold, Metcalf decided to leave for Europe. He sketched for two months in England and in October joined fellow Boston artists Edmund C. Tarbell and Frank W. Benson in Paris to study figural drawing with Jules-Joseph Boulanger and Gustave-Rodolphe Lefebvre at the Académie Julian. During 1885–1886, Metcalf painted in Pont Aven in Brittany, Grez-sur-Laing, Dieppe, and in Giverny with Claude Monet.

In the fall of 1887 Metcalf painted in Tunis, Algeria, and Morocco, where he finished a canvas titled *Arab Market* for which he won an honorable mention at the Paris Salon in 1888. Returning to the United States that year, he shared a studio with impressionist painter Robert Reid on West Tenth Street in New York City and opened a summer studio with fellow artist William H. Howe in Old Lyme, Connecticut. It was there that he painted *May Night* (1906), a view of Miss Florence Griswold's home. He also taught at the Art Students League in New York (1898–1908) and did illustrations for *Scribner's*.

In 1889 Metcalf had a one-man show at Boston's St. Botolph Club at which he exhibited his paintings of daily life in North Africa. To his surprise, conservative Bostonians liked his work. From 1893 to 1903 he taught painting classes at Cooper Institute in New York.

In 1898 Metcalf joined an independent group of painters known in art circles as "The Ten," who seceded from the more staid Society of American Painters. The Ten consisted mainly of impressionist artists, including Childe Hassam, William Merritt Chase, and John Henry Twachtman, who decided to exhibit together and stand against the stale academic traditions and rigid juries of the National Academy of Design (Metcalf was elected into the NAD, but he refused) and the Society of American Painters. The Ten gained instant recognition for their French-influenced paintings.

By 1899 Metcalf had become a heavy drinker, but he nonetheless continued painting and often traveled to Gloucester, Massachusetts, to paint with Twachtman and Charles Allen Winter. In 1901 he married his model Marguerite Beaufort Haile, an aspiring actress from New Orleans, but when she ran away that same year with his student Robert Nisbet, the marriage ended in divorce. Metcalf's drinking increased.

When his colleague Twachtman died in 1902, Metcalf became despondent. In 1903 he moved with his parents to Clark's Cove, Maine, and stopped drinking long enough to paint New England landscapes. He soon lightened his palette, loosened his brush work, and focused on how light filters through nature and settles on, behind, around and in objects and the atmosphere. Metcalf later referred to this period of his career as the beginning of his "new-birth," or "Renaissance." In 1904 Metcalf returned to New York City and exhibited twenty-one impressionistic landscapes at Fishel, Adler, and Swartz Gallery.

Becoming intensely fascinated with the mysteries found in nature, Metcalf, beginning in 1905, attended seances hoping to resolve questions he had about how best to see nature and its atmospheric changes. From 1909 to 1925 he painted snowscapes, a genre that served for him as the primary vehicle to explore mood and tonal nuances. In the winter of 1909 he painted in Cornish, New Hampshire. He felt at one in the solace and silence of nature. Charles DeKay wrote in the *New York Times* (22 Mar. 1909) that Metcalf "had never shown a finer canvas" than his snowscape of Cornish titled *The White Veil #1. Icebound*, another work of this period, was included in 1909 in a one-man exhibition at the Montross Gallery in New York; the *New York Herald* (4 Jan. 1909) wrote that it revealed "the poetry of winter."

In 1911 Metcalf married Henriette Alice McCrea; they had two children. She, however, soon learned that Metcalf was a loner who preferred to drink, paint, or fish rather than spend time with her. They divorced in 1921.

Metcalf continued to paint in delicate, muted color tonalities. The *New York Herald* (21 Mar. 1920) noted that in the study of winter Metcalf had "achieved his special metier." Two months before he died in New York City, the *Washington Post* wrote: "No one has ever painted lovelier snow pictures than he. . . . Metcalf shows us the winsome side of winter . . . the caressing touch of the golden sunlight, the soft mantle of snow resting ever so lightly on the shoulders of the world." Metcalf remains one of America's finest impressionist painters.

• For consideration of Metcalf by his contemporaries, see "Mr. Metcalf's New Landscapes," *New York Tribune*, 21 Mar. 1920; John H. Raftery, "Paintings by Metcalf," *New York Telegram*, 31 Mar. 1920; Milch Galleries, N.Y., *Exhibition of Paintings by Willard L. Metcalf* (1920); Bernard Teevan, "A Painter's Renaissance," *International Studio*, 82, no. 341 (Oct. 1925); Catharine Beach Ely, "Willard L. Metcalf," *Art in America* 13 (1925); and Royal Cortissoz, "Willard L. Metcalf," *American Academy of Arts and Letters* 60 (1927). For his place in American art, see Patricia Jobe Pierce, *The Ten* (1976); Spanierman Gallery, N.Y., *Ten American Painters* (1991); *Willard Leroy Metcalf, An American Impressionist* (1996); Elizabeth DeVeer, "Willard Metcalf in Cornish, New Hampshire," *Antiques*, Nov. 1984, pp. 1208–15; and Elizabeth DeVeer and Richard J. Boyle, *Sunlight and Shadow: The Life and Art of Willard L. Metcalf* (1987). An obituary is in *International Studio* 82 (Oct. 1925).

PATRICIA JOBE PIERCE

METCALF, William (3 Sept. 1838–5 Dec. 1909), steel manufacturer, was born in Pittsburgh, Pennsylvania, the son of Orlando Metcalf, a prominent attorney, and Mary Mehitabel Knap. Metcalf attended the city's public schools before entering Rensselaer Polytechnic Institute, one of the country's first engineering schools. After graduating in 1858, he returned to Pittsburgh and was hired by the Fort Pitt Foundry, a leading ironworks noted for heavy casting and forgings, as assistant engineer and draftsman. Within a year Metcalf became general superintendent of the works and supervised the production of heavy armaments for the Union army after 1861. By the end of the Civil War the foundry had produced more than 3,000 artillery pieces, ranging in size from eight-inch to twenty-inch cannons for the army, nine-, eleven-, and fifteen-inch guns for the navy, and eight -, ten-, and thirteen-inch mortars. Thirty of the largest mortars were used by Ulysses S. Grant at the siege of Vicksburg, while the forty-ton, twenty-inch naval guns were the heaviest cast up to that time. Metcalf later recorded that "not one gun of Fort Pitt make was ever reported as failing in service" (Raymond, p. 866). Given the limited understanding of iron metallurgy at the time, this was an impressive record.

In 1865 Metcalf's uncle leased the Fort Pitt Foundry; Metcalf remained on as general superintendent. But in late 1867 he joined Miller, Barr & Parkin, which had been organized in 1865 to produce cast crucible steel using the Huntsman process developed in England in the 1740s. Huntsman placed high-quality wrought iron mixed with charcoal in a closed graphite pot or crucible and heated it until it melted. When poured or cast, this steel was homogeneous, unlike steel produced by other methods. Even after the cast crucible process was developed, steel was a rare and expensive metal used primarily for razors, edge tools, knives, and for other specialty purposes. Only the Bessemer process, introduced in the late 1850s and perfected over the next twenty years, allowed quantity steel production. American firms struggled until the mid-1850s to break an English monopoly on crucible steel, with the first successes coming in Pittsburgh. Miller, Barr & Parkin followed on the heels of several firms that pioneered in making crucible steel. Metcalf became a partner in 1869, and the firm was renamed Miller, Metcalf & Parkin. The partnership's Crescent Works soon achieved a reputation for quality steel, an important consideration since the British competition was severe despite tariff protection for American producers. Output grew steadily, with annual capacity reaching 4,000 tons in 1876 and more than 15,000 tons a decade later. Crescent steel was used in reapers, needles, railroad car springs, saws, springs, drills, corsets, scissors, and in many other implements. In 1889 the partnership was ended with the incorporation of the Crescent Steel Company.

Metcalf played an important role in the firm's growth, winning a reputation as a steel manufacturing expert who provided a crucial advantage to the company. For example, Metcalf and another crucible steel producer attempted to build an experimental facility to produce wrought iron in 1877. Even in failure, this effort demonstrated an approach that combined hands-on experience with study of a growing technical literature. His deep knowledge of steel was apparent in a little book he wrote in 1896, *Steel: A Manual for Steel Users*. In its preface Metcalf explained that he hoped to answer questions "involving an intimate acquaintance with the properties of steel, which is only gained by contact with both manufacturers and users. In this little manual the effort is made to fill this gap and to give all steel-users a systematic, condensed statement of facts that could not be obtained otherwise, except by travelling through miles of literature." His expertise was affirmed by frequent appearances as an expert witness in patent cases.

In late 1895 Metcalf sold his interest in the Crescent Steel Company, but in 1897 he reentered the steel industry by founding the Braeburn Steel Company, which opened in 1898 in Pittsburgh. The firm was a model producer of cast crucible steel, although both Bessemer and the new open hearth production methods were beginning to cut into specialty markets previously held by crucible steel. Open hearth steel soon approached, although it never surpassed, the quality of cast crucible steel. Metcalf remained the president and principal stockholder of Braeburn Steel until his death.

Metcalf's considerable technical ability naturally connected him to the emerging community of professional engineers in this country. Here, too, he was a leader, founding and serving as first president of the Engineers Society of Western Pennsylvania in 1880; he read the first paper before the organization. He was a member, vice president, and in 1881 president of the American Institute of Mining Engineers and a member and in 1893 president of the American Society of Civil Engineers. He was also a vice president of the American Society of Mechanical Engineers (1882–1884), a member of the British Institution of Civil Engineers, and a fellow of the American Association for the Advancement of Science. He read papers before most of these associations on the subject of steel making and treating. His technical reputation, along with the sense of trust that he generated, led to his appointment to a commission assigned to appraise the value of the Monongahela Navigation Company before it was purchased by the federal government in the 1890s. The proposed price was accepted by all parties. Like many leading business figures of the time, Metcalf was actively involved in charitable activities. He was a founder of the Homeopathic Hospital in Pittsburgh and remained its president until his death. In 1864 Metcalf had married Christiana Fries, with whom he had six children. He died in Pittsburgh.

William Metcalf combined technical expertise with business acumen to build a career in the steel industry. The crucible steel industry in Pittsburgh—and its leaders—have been overshadowed by the Bessemer steelworks dominated by Andrew Carnegie. With his technical ability, Metcalf was not completely typical of the businessmen and merchants who built Pittsburgh into the steel city, although his combination of business and technical skills was hardly unique. Also somewhat atypical was Metcalf's formal engineering education, for few steel men began in the classroom at this time. That background, however, explained Metcalf's leading role in the emerging professional organizations for engineering during the last third of the century.

• Biographical sketches of Metcalf are in several engineering journals, including *Transactions of the American Society of Mechanical Engineers* 32 (1911): 1491–92; R. W. Raymond, "Biographical Notice of William Metcalf," *Transactions of the American Institute of Mining Engineers* 41 (1911): 865–68; and *Transactions of the American Society of Civil Engineers* 74 (1911): 490–91. Spotty information on the cast crucible steel industry can be found in [anon.], *Pittsburgh and Allegheny in the Centennial Year* (1876); [anon.], *Cities of Pittsburgh and Allegheny: Leading Merchants and Manufacturers* (1886); and George H. Thurston, *Pittsburgh's Progress, Industries, and Resources* (1886). A detailed view of the industry is in Geoffrey Tweedale, *Sheffield Steel and America: A Century of Commercial and Technological Interdependence, 1830–1930* (1987). John Ingham, *Making Iron and Steel: Independent Mills in Pittsburgh, 1820–1920* (1991), discusses the social background of Pittsburgh's crucible steelmakers. Obituaries are in the *Pittsburgh Dispatch*, 6 Dec. 1909, and the *Pittsburgh Post*, 7 Dec. 1909.

BRUCE E. SEELY

METCALFE, Ralph Harold (30 May 1910–10 Oct. 1978), track and field athlete and U.S. congressman, was born in Atlanta, Georgia, the son of Clarence Metcalfe, a stockyard worker, and Marie Attaway, a seamstress. He moved to Chicago, Illinois, in 1917, grew up in a slum area on the South Side, and attended Tilden Technical High School. Metcalfe won the 1929 interscholastic track-and-field sprint championship and, as a member of the Chase Athletic Club, captured the 1930 Amateur Athletic Union (AAU) junior 100-yard title in 9.7 seconds.

A 5′11″, 180-pound speedster, Metcalfe attended Marquette University, breezing through the 1932 track-and-field season undefeated in both the 100-meter and 200-meter dashes and taking both events at the NCAA and AAU championships. That same year Metcalfe dethroned Eddie Tolan as the dominant American sprinter. On 11 June he tied Tolan's world mark in the 100-yard dash and shattered the world record in the 220-yard dash. At the Olympic trials Metcalfe bested Tolan in both the 100-meter and 200-meter dashes.

During the 1932 Los Angeles, California, Summer Olympic Games, however, Tolan edged Metcalfe in the 100-meter dash in 10.3 seconds in one of the closest races in Olympic history. Tolan's time broke both Olympic and world records. Although favored to take the gold medal, Metcalfe false-started and did not respond quickly to the second shot of the starter's pistol. Tolan led the race until Metcalfe pulled even at 80 meters. Several hours later, seven judges viewed a film of the race and determined that Tolan crossed the finish line two inches ahead of silver medalist Metcalfe. Metcalfe won the bronze medal in the 200 meters, trailing Tolan's record-breaking 21.2 seconds by three-tenths of a second. Metcalfe may have been deprived of a gold medal because his lane was inadvertently two meters longer than it should have been. He did not protest the results, however, because other African Americans had garnered the gold and silver medals.

Following Tolan's departure, Metcalfe dominated the sprints from 1933 to 1936. Noted for his strong finishes, Metcalfe tied the world 100-meter record three times officially and the world 200-meter mark once. His victories included the 100-yard and 220-yard dashes at the 1933 and 1934 NCAA championships, the 100-meter dash at the 1933 and 1934 AAU championships, and the 200-meter dash at the 1933, 1934, 1935, and 1936 AAU championships. In 1936 he repeatedly defeated Jesse Owens in 100-yard dash competition until one week before the U.S. Olympic trials. Metcalfe may have been a better sprinter than Owens, capturing two more NCAA crowns and five more AAU titles.

The politically charged 1936 Berlin, Germany, Summer Olympic Games showcased Adolf Hitler's Nazi dictatorship and Aryan supremacy beliefs. Hitler boasted publicly that his athletes would prevail and scorned what Nazi newspapers termed "America's black auxiliaries." America's black athletes, however, quickly demolished Hitler's supremacist propaganda. Owens earned a gold medal with a 10.3-second time in the 100-meter dash, edging Metcalfe by one second. The 400-meter relay team, consisting of Owens, Metcalfe, Foy Draper, and Frank Wykoff, romped to a gold medal by 15 yards. The quartet covered the 400-meter distance in 39.8 seconds, setting a world record that endured for twenty years. This historic race marked Metcalfe's final track-and-field competition.

Metcalfe earned the Ph.B. from Marquette University in 1936 and an M.A. in physical education from the University of Southern California in 1939. From 1936 to 1942 he taught physical education and political science and coached track and field at all-black Xavier University in New Orleans. Metcalfe served in the U.S. Army as a first lieutenant from 1943 to 1945, receiving the Legion of Merit for directing the physical training of troops.

After moving to Chicago in 1945, Metcalfe operated an insurance agency. He directed the Department of Civil Rights for the Chicago Commission on Human Relations from 1945 to 1949 and headed the Illinois State Athletic Commission from 1949 to 1952. Metcalfe married Madalynne Fay Young in 1947; they had one child.

Metcalfe joined the Chicago Democratic party organization as an assistant precinct captain in 1949 and controlled patronage as Third Ward committeeman from 1953 to 1972. He served on the Chicago City Council from 1955 to 1971, becoming president pro tempore in 1969. Metcalfe, a close ally of Mayor Richard Daley from 1955 to 1972, advanced rapidly because of his loyalty to the political machine and his popularity as a former sports hero. He chaired the powerful Building and Zoning Committee.

In 1970 William Dawson, political boss of the South Side ghetto in the overwhelmingly black First Congressional District, retired from the U.S. House of

Representatives after serving fourteen terms. Metcalfe was elected to Dawson's seat in 1970 after defeating Alderman A. A. "Sammy" Rayner in a spirited Democratic party primary. He was reelected to the House in 1972, 1974, and 1976 and won the 1978 Democratic primary, but he died a few weeks before the general election.

Metcalfe fought discrimination in transportation and consumer affairs while serving on the House Committee on Interstate and Foreign Commerce and its subcommittees on Transportation and Commerce and Consumer Protection and Commerce. He insisted that the administration of federal programs remain equitable for all Americans. Metcalfe wrote comprehensive antidiscrimination provisions in the Railroad Revitalization and Regulatory Reform Act, added two antiredlining amendments to the no-fault auto accident insurance legislation, and helped defeat the Waxman amendment, which would have prohibited special programs for minorities in medical schools.

Housing and employment issues particularly interested Metcalfe. He insisted that homeowners be compensated for deficient appraisals and helped secure a $22 million Housing and Urban Development grant for the huge Robert Taylor Housing Project in his congressional district. Metcalfe protested discrimination in the treatment of minority prisoners and deplored widespread unemployment among black people, urging adoption of the Humphrey-Hawkins bill of 1978.

Metcalfe also belonged to the House Committee on Merchant Marine and Fisheries and chaired its subcommittee on the Panama Canal. Besides wholeheartedly supporting the Panama Canal treaties in 1977, he diligently sought to protect human rights, improve housing conditions, and expand educational and job opportunities of Panamanians.

Metcalfe served as secretary of the Democratic Study Group, as vice chairman of its task force on crime and drug abuse, and as a member of the Democratic Steering and Policy Committee. He authored the Amateur Sports Bill of 1978, which provided federal funds to sponsor American Olympic athletes.

In 1971 Metcalfe joined the black caucus, comprising all thirteen African-American members of the House of Representatives. The group, which monitored federal enforcement of civil rights laws, consisted of Democrats representing poor, urban, predominantly black congressional districts. He and Louis Stokes of Ohio co-chaired the Health Brain Trust.

Low-income and middle-class constituents provided the core of Metcalfe's support within his congressional district. The poor were attracted by his control of patronage jobs, while the middle class liked his law-and-order stance against South Side ghetto youth gangs. Metcalfe represented his constituents in a methodical, reserved style, mastering political detail and working deliberately.

Black militants, meanwhile, opposed Metcalfe until 1972, when he broke with Mayor Daley and spoke out against alleged police brutality toward black Chicagoans. The Afro-American Patrolmen's League charged that the Chicago Police Department had abused South Side ghetto residents verbally and physically. Metcalfe arranged extensive negotiations with police superintendent James Conlisk on ways of increasing confidence among blacks in the police department and enlisting black community support for work against street crime. Mayor Daley, however, abruptly terminated the talks and made only minor changes.

Metcalfe also opposed Mayor Daley's attempt to renominate Edward Hanrahan as state's attorney for Cook County in 1972 and declared that it would be impossible for him to deliver the Third Ward. According to Metcalfe, Hanrahan had supervised a 1969 raid fatal to two Black Panther party officials and had tried to frame the raid's survivors for attempted murder. Hanrahan won reelection despite being indicted for obstruction of justice.

Metcalfe continued to criticize the Chicago police, exploiting the law-enforcement issue among South Side blacks. Daley, fearing that Metcalfe might use Chicago's African Americans, one-third of the city's population, as a base to capture the entire party organization, unsuccessfully ran formidable opponents against Metcalfe in subsequent Democratic congressional primaries. Metcalfe retaliated by supporting an unsuccessful liberal challenger to Daley in the 1975 Democratic mayoral primary.

In 1973 Metcalfe arranged a panel of concerned Chicago citizens to help protect South Side residents from alleged mistreatment by police. The same year he sponsored congressional legislation to make municipal corporations legally and financially responsible for damages assessed against an individual police officer. Metcalfe's measure encouraged cities to improve selection, training, and supervision of police officers. He also served as a director of the National Council to Control Handguns.

Metcalfe participated in several civil rights and athletic organizations. His civil rights activities included work with the National Association for the Advancement of Colored People, the Urban League, the Joint Negro Appeal, the Mahalia Jackson Scholarship Fund, and the Dr. Martin Luther King Urban Progress Center. He co-chaired the organizing committee for the 1959 Pan American Games at Chicago, was elected to the U.S. Olympic Committee in 1969, and served on the President's Commission on Olympic Sports from 1975 to 1977. His Ralph H. Metcalfe Foundation promoted athletic, health, and educational programs for ghetto youth and support for needy Chicago families.

Metcalfe held enormous athletic and political significance for African Americans. He, along with Eddie Tolan, began a long period of dominance by African-American sprinters in track and field. Metcalfe was elected to the Helms Athletic Foundation Hall of Fame, Black Athletes Hall of Fame, U.S. Track and Field Hall of Fame, National Track and Field Hall of Fame, and Wisconsin Hall of Fame. His political independence of the Daley machine paved the way for the rise of Harold Washington as the first black mayor of Chicago. Metcalfe died at his Chicago apartment.

• The Ralph H. Metcalfe Papers are in the possession of Ralph H. Metcalfe, Jr., Chicago, Ill. Clippings and press releases on Metcalfe are at Memorial Library, Marquette University, Milwaukee, Wisc. Michael Cornfield, *Ralph H. Metcalfe: Democratic Representative from Illinois* (1972), provides brief biographical information. For Metcalfe's athletic accomplishments, see Arthur Ashe, Jr., *A Hard Road to Glory* (1993); William J. Baker, *Jesse Owens: An American Life* (1986); Reid M. Hanley, ed., *Who's Who in Track and Field* (1973); Bill Mallon and Ian Buchanan, *Quest for Gold: The Encyclopedia of American Olympians* (1984); Richard D. Mandell, *The Nazi Olympics* (1971); and David L. Porter, ed., *Biographical Dictionary of American Sports: Outdoor Sports* (1988). Ralph Whitehead, Jr., "Black Politics in Cook County: The Metcalfe Rebellion," *The Nation*, 10 July 1972, pp. 14–17, details Metcalfe's problems with Mayor Daley. Obituaries are in the *Chicago Tribune* and the *Chicago Sun-Times*, both 11 Oct. 1978.

DAVID L. PORTER

METCALFE, Samuel Lytler (21 Sept. 1798–17 July 1856), scientist and physician, was born near Winchester, Virginia, the son of Joseph Metcalfe and Rebecca Sittler, farmers. When Metcalfe was a toddler, the family moved to Shelby County, Kentucky, and in 1802 settled on land near Lynch's Station. Metcalfe received his early education in this frontier community. In 1819, contrary to his father's wish that he take over the family farm, he entered the medical school of Transylvania University at Lexington, Kentucky. In 1823, after writing a thesis titled "The Malignant Fever of Louisville," he received an M.D.

Metcalfe published two books before and during his years in medical school. *The Kentucky Harmonist* is a 130-page compilation of hymns along with a lengthy essay by Metcalfe in which he evaluates the moral content of music as well as its origins and character. A second edition was published in 1820. Metcalfe's earnings from the two editions helped finance publication of *A Collection of Some of the Most Interesting Narratives of the Indian Warfare in the West* (1821), in which he recounts the major battles between Native Americans and European settlers that had taken place in Kentucky.

Between 1823 and 1830 Metcalfe pursued a career as a physician. After a stay in New Albany, Indiana, he moved to Mississippi, residing for several years at Natchez. During his stay in Mississippi, Metcalfe was married (wife's name unknown), but the marriage ended with her death four years later. Toward the end of this period, Metcalfe embarked on a walking tour of east Tennessee and North Carolina and wrote several articles on the chemistry, geology, zoology, and botany of the areas he had visited. To pursue his growing interest in the sciences, Metcalfe in 1831 traveled to England to study chemistry and geology. He sought to have full access to scientific books and periodicals available overseas. He later returned to the United States and settled in New York City, where he published *A New Theory of Terrestrial Magnetism* (1833). In 1834–1835 Metcalfe contributed several scientific articles (signed merely "M") to the *Knickerbocker Magazine*.

Like many of his contemporaries, Metcalfe was interested in the nature of heat and had come to believe that "caloric" as a self-active principle could be the key concept to unlocking the secrets of nature. Metcalfe made a second trip to England in 1835 to pursue the practical implications of this view. Intent on focusing on his scientific work, Metcalfe declined an invitation to become a candidate for the Gregorian chair at Edinburgh University and instead worked in London (perhaps at the Library of the British Museum) to develop, prove, and elaborate on this cherished theory. In 1837 he completed the first version of *Caloric: Its Mechanical, Chemical, and Vital Agencies in the Phenomena of Nature*, books 1–3, but did not publish it yet. Metcalfe expanded his research to apply his theory to physiology and pathology, and in 1843 he completed an enlarged, two-volume version of the work, which was published by William Pickering in London.

Metcalfe's book came out at the critical time when the concept of caloric was being gradually discarded and the law of conservation of energy was about to appear (although he did not know it). Instead of calling for the "correlation of forces" (what today is called "conservation of energy"), Metcalfe relied wholly on caloric to explain every phenomenon. His theory can be regarded as an alternative (though incorrect) version of the law of energy that sought to synthesize a wide variety of natural phenomena. Like Julius Robert von Mayer, James Prescott Joule, and others of his contemporaries who simultaneously and independently discovered the law of energy, Metcalfe was initially concerned with the phenomena involved in heat and sought to explain all natural phenomena in terms of a single, indestructible agent. Metcalfe's caloric, however, differed widely from what was to become known as "energy." His was "a material agent" and "a self-active principle, capable of moving itself, and of generating motion in all other bodies. . . . Caloric repels its own particles, and attracts those of ponderable matter, with forces that vary inversely as the square of the distance."

Metcalfe returned to the United States in June 1845. In 1846 he married Ellen Blondel, whom he had met in London. They had one child. Also in 1846 a publisher in Philadelphia agreed to print the revised edition of his *Caloric*, which was published posthumously in 1859. (The new theories described in the appendix were added by the editor of the revised edition.) Metcalfe died at Cape May, New Jersey.

• Biographical sources on Metcalfe are scarce. See the preface to *Caloric* (1843), pp. xv–xvi, and "Dr. Metcalfe's Life," in *Caloric*, vol. 1 (1859), pp. xv–xviii. See also Masao Watanabe, "The Caloric Theory of S. L. Metcalfe," *British Journal for the History of Science* 17, pt. 2, no. 56 (1984): 210–13, on his caloric theory.

MASAO WATANABE

METCALFE, Thomas (20 Mar. 1780–18 Aug. 1855), congressman, governor of Kentucky, and U.S. senator, was born in Fauquier County, Virginia, the son of John Metcalfe, a farmer and revolutionary war veteran, and Sarah Dent Chinn. His family, of modest circumstances, migrated to Fayette County, Kentucky, around 1784; they later moved to Nicholas County in north central Kentucky. Thomas received a perfunctory education at common schools, and in 1796 he was apprenticed to an older brother, who was a stonemason. Before Thomas served his indenture, however, the death of his father in 1799 forced him to return home to support his mother and four siblings. For the next twelve years Metcalfe worked as a stonemason, earning his nickname, "Old Stonehammer." In 1806 he married Nancy Mason, with whom he had four children. Ambitious and self-disciplined, Metcalfe studied in his leisure time and acquired a substantial education despite very little formal schooling. A self-proclaimed "plain man . . . inheriting no part of this World's wealth, an orphan yet in his minority," Metcalfe found that his humble origins served him well in his political life, especially as the democratizing currents in American society gained momentum in the early nineteenth century (*General Metcalfe's Circular Address to the People of Kentucky*, broadside in McCalla Papers, West Virginia University).

Like other ambitious westerners, Metcalfe parlayed military distinction into a career in politics. In 1803, with the threat of a Spanish closure of the port of New Orleans, Metcalfe raised a company of volunteers and awaited orders to sail down the Mississippi River. Although confrontation was averted, the episode demonstrated the growing esteem with which Metcalfe was held in his community. When tensions arose with Spain once again in 1809, Metcalfe made his first formal public speech in which he displayed a remarkable talent for oratory. During the War of 1812 he organized and led a company of volunteers that saw action at the battle of Fort Meigs in Ohio.

Eloquent, hospitable, and fond of socializing, Metcalfe was well regarded among his neighbors, and in 1812 he was elected to the first of four consecutive terms as state representative from Nicholas County. Metcalfe then served five terms as a U.S. congressman from 1819 to 1828, during which time he aligned himself with fellow Kentuckian Henry Clay and his "American System." Metcalfe consistently supported protective tariffs and federally funded internal improvements, although he parted company with Clay on the issues of public land sales and the expansion of the nation's banking system. A slaveholder himself, Metcalfe also looked after the interests of his section, steadfastly asserting that slavery should be allowed to expand into Missouri and the rest of the lands acquired in the Louisiana Purchase.

Residing in Washington, Metcalfe was able to avoid direct involvement in Kentucky's "Relief War," an eight-year, impassioned political struggle over the propriety of enacting debt-relief legislation in the wake of the panic of 1819. In December 1827, with the remnants of the state factions aligning themselves with the emerging national parties, the National Republican (Whig) state convention nominated Metcalfe for the governorship of Kentucky. The Jacksonians countered with William T. Barry, a former leader of the pro-relief faction. Metcalfe's campaign stressed his "plain and unostentatious manner," assuring his prospective constituents that "he remains the unassuming and condescending stone-mason and farmer" (*A Sketch of the Life*, p. 26). Although Metcalfe won by a narrow margin, the victory not only demonstrated the efficacy of the "common man" appeal to the state's anti-Jacksonians, but it also inaugurated an era of Whig domination of Kentucky politics that would last a generation.

As Kentucky's tenth governor, Metcalfe was faced with the challenge of uniting a state that had been riven by intense political dispute for almost a decade. As a means of achieving unity, Metcalfe seized upon internal improvements, for "nothing tends more certainly to assimilate the diverse tastes and sentiments of the citizens, and to harmonize the discordant elements of the body politic" (*Journal of the Senate of the Commonwealth of Kentucky* [1828], p. 19). Moreover, as Metcalfe recognized, transportation projects would more closely connect Kentucky with the market economy; he had few reservations about the benefits of such projects: "Whatever facilitates and cheapens the process of exchanging one commodity for another, increases the capacity to produce; enriches the nation; adds to her offensive, or defensive strength; [and] diffuses happiness, comfort and joy amongst her own citizens" (*Journal of the Senate of the Commonwealth of Kentucky* [1831], p. 11). Like many of his political compatriots, Metcalfe saw internal improvements as a means of achieving the goals of social order and centrally planned commercial growth. He therefore continually prodded the legislature to expend ever more amounts of money for turnpikes, roads, and canals, all the while promising that "every dollar of revenue judiciously applied to the improvement of the country will soon be returned . . . manyfold" (*Journal* [1831], p. 11). By the end of his administration, Kentucky had firmly committed itself to state-sponsored internal improvements. Metcalfe also advocated reform of the state's schools, prisons, tax code, and court system, but a lethal combination of legislative apathy and Metcalfe's own obsession with transportation projects ensured that little change was effected.

After leaving the governor's chair in 1832, Metcalfe stayed active in politics. From 1834 to 1838 he served as a state senator, and from 1840 to 1848 he was chairman of the Kentucky Board of Internal Improvements. In 1839 Metcalfe delivered the speech nominating William Henry Harrison at the national Whig convention in Harrisburg, Pennsylvania. Upon Harrison's victory, Metcalfe was offered the position of secretary of war but turned it down for reasons of health. Metcalfe served briefly as a U.S. senator in 1848 and 1849, replacing John J. Crittenden while he ran for governor of Kentucky. At the age of sixty-nine Metcalfe retired from public life and returned to his Nicholas County farm, "Forest Retreat," where he died of cholera.

• A few of Metcalfe's papers are at the University of Kentucky, Lexington, while a more substantial collection is found at the Kentucky Historical Society. A detailed account of Metcalfe's early life is *A Sketch of the Life of General Thomas Metcalfe* (1828), a campaign biography written during his run for the Kentucky governorship. A few details of Metcalfe's 1828 campaign may be gleaned from Leonard Curry's "Election Year—Kentucky, 1828," *Register of the Kentucky Historical Society* 55 (1957): 196–212. For an overview of Kentucky society and politics during Metcalfe's early career, see Stephen Aron, *How the West Was Lost: The Transformation of Kentucky from Daniel Boone to Henry Clay* (1996). For an incisive study of the cultural values that informed the Whig party leadership, see Daniel Walker Howe, *The Political Culture of the American Whigs* (1979).

MATTHEW G. SCHOENBACHLER

METTAUER, John Peter (10 Apr. 1787?–22 Nov. 1875), physician, was born in Prince Edward County, Virginia, the son of Francis Joseph Mettauer, a French surgeon who served with Rochambeau's troops at Yorktown. His mother may have been Jemima Crump Gaulding, a widow who married the elder Mettauer on 5 May 1791 and gave birth to a son, Francis Joseph Mettauer, later the same year. Mettauer's father subsequently learned that his second son was fathered by his brother and petitioned the Virginia General Assembly for a divorce in 1804.

In spite of this scandalous and unsettling home life, John Peter was an assiduous student. He attended a local grammar school in Prince Edward County that was connected with Hampden-Sydney College. In 1805 he enrolled in the college where he was a founding member of the Philanthropic Literary Society. After just two years at Hampden-Sydney, Mettauer left to study medicine in Philadelphia. He matriculated at the University of Pennsylvania in 1806, where he attended the last lecture of the distinguished professor of anatomy and midwifery William Shippen. Mettauer was also a student of Benjamin Rush and came to embrace the latter's bloodletting practices and aggressive dosing with drugs to treat inflammatory disorders. Following his graduation in 1809, Mettauer worked for a year at the Philadelphia Dispensary before returning home to join his father in practice.

When his father died in 1812, Mettauer moved to Norfolk, Virginia, where he hoped to gain some surgical experience treating members of the military mobilized in the area for the war with Great Britain. His brother apparently followed him and the two established a practice in the city by 1815. In the same year Mettauer married Mary Woodward; the couple had two children before Mary died in December 1823. A devastated Mettauer returned to Prince Edward County after her death.

Mettauer reestablished his practice and began contributing to medical literature. He married Margaret Elizabeth Carter of Prince Edward County in 1825, and the couple had one daughter and three sons. With a new mother for his children, Mettauer was able to focus on his medical practice. Unlike most of his contemporaries, Mettauer did not make rounds on horseback. Instead he was driven to his patients' homes in a carriage so that he could use the time "to continue my studious habits and, if possible, not fall behind the daily improvements of my profession" (Kelly, p. 1912). In 1827 he performed the first operation in the United States for the repair of cleft palate with instruments of his own design. Following this work, Mettauer began experimenting with the use of metallic sutures, an idea that may have originated with his professor of surgery, Phillip Syng Physick. He first published in 1833 on the use of metallic sutures for the repair of laceration of the membrane between the rectum and vagina. He published actively for a twenty-five year period beginning in 1833, initially in the *American Journal of the Medical Sciences* and the *Boston Medical and Surgical Journal* and subsequently in local Virginia medical journals. The majority of his articles described his work in the area of genito-urinary surgery, but he also wrote on epilepsy, fevers, and diseases of women.

In 1835 Washington Medical College of Baltimore, Maryland, elected Mettauer to the chair of surgery and surgical anatomy. While preparing for his lectures, Mettauer began work on a surgical treatise that analyzed much of the surgical literature and procedures of the first half of the nineteenth century. The manuscript was never published. Mettauer, longing for his rural home in Virginia, left Washington Medical College after just two terms. He did reside in Baltimore long enough to marry Louise Mansfield of Connecticut in 1836 (his second wife had died sometime after 1828). The couple had one daughter following their return to Prince Edward County.

Mettauer served as preceptor for a number of aspiring Virginia physicians. He decided to formalize this instruction following his tenure at Washington Medical College. In 1837 he organized the Prince Edward Medical Institute, where he taught the entire medical curriculum. Within ten years, Mettauer felt the need to affiliate his school with a college. He convinced the board of Randolph-Macon College in Boydton, Virginia, to accept his proposal for affiliation. Teaching with his two oldest sons, Mettauer designed a ten-month course of study that regularly attracted about thirty students from 1848 until the Civil War closed the program.

In August 1838 Mettauer operated to relieve a case of vesico-vaginal fistula (an abnormal passage between the bladder and the vagina) that he reported to the medical press two years later. Using metal sutures and a urinary catheter, he designed a method to cure this complication of childbirth five years before J. Marion Sims, who is generally credited with this surgical advancement, began his work. For the next ten years Mettauer continued to perfect what he considered the definitive cure. Some of his surgical success resulted from his insistence on extreme cleanliness in the era before wide-spread antisepsis and his pre- and postoperative care of patients. According to Mettauer's unpublished "Treatise on Surgery," a surgeon "should manage the case himself, because he is in a degree the author of it, and because too, his reputation as a surgeon depends on the result" (p. 20).

After his third wife's death and sometime in the late 1840s, in the middle of the most active phase of his career, Mettauer married for the last time. He and his fourth wife, Mary Elizabeth Dyson of neighboring Nottoway County, had two daughters and a son. The size of his family did not limit his ability to maintain a large surgical practice. Mettauer performed more cataract operations and lithotomies, a procedure for removing bladder stones, than almost all his contemporaries. His reputation as a surgeon attracted patients from all over the Commonwealth and he is known to have traveled as far as Georgia to perform an operation.

Mettauer was an eccentric who was known for his trademark high hat, used to shield his baldness. He was, nevertheless, held in high esteem by his neighbors and colleagues. As the editors of the *Virginia Medical Monthly* noted: "He won for himself at home and abroad an enviable reputation" (Dec. 1875, p. 692). Mettauer made significant contributions to the field of medicine through his design of surgical instruments and development of innovated surgical procedures. His universal fame was probably limited by his decision to remain in his rural hometown. He continued his active medical practice until his death at his home in Worsham, Virginia. Mettauer was buried in the church cemetery at Hampden-Sydney College.

• The two largest collections of manuscript materials are the Mettauer Collection, Historical Library, College of Physicians of Philadelphia; and the Mettauer correspondence and ledgers, Eggleston Library, Hampden-Sydney College. Mettauer's most significant works include "On Staphylorophy," *American Journal of the Medical Sciences* 21 (1837): 309–32; "Practical Observations on Those Malformations of the Male Urethra and Penis, Termed Hypospadias and Epispadias, with an Anomalous Case," *American Journal of the Medical Sciences* 4 (1842): 43–57; "On Vesico-Vaginal Fistula," *American Journal of the Medical Sciences* 14 (1847): 117–21; "A Case of Un-United Parturient Laceration of the Recto-Vaginal Septum, Successfully Treated with Metallic Ligatures," *American Journal of the Medical Sciences* 13 (1833): 113–15; and "Prophylaxis of Childbed Fever," *Virginia Medical Monthly* 2 (Apr. 1875): 1–11. The best biographical sketches are George Ben Johnston, "A Sketch of Dr. John Peter Mettauer of Virginia," *Transactions of the American Surgical Association* 23 (1905): 1–18; W. L. Harris, "John Peter Mettauer, A.M., M.D., LL.D.,—A Country Surgeon," *Virginia Medical Monthly* 53 (Nov. 1926): 485–90; Charles E. Horton et al., "John Peter Mettauer—America's First Plastic Surgeon," *Plastic and Reconstructive Surgery* 27 (Mar. 1961): 268–78; John R. Kight, "In Rural Virginia, World-Class Medicine: John Peter Mettauer, 1787–1878," *Virginia Medical Monthly* (Feb. 1989): 66–70; and Howard A. Kelly, *Cyclopedia of American Medical Biography* (1912). Obituaries are in the *Virginia Medical Monthly* 2 (Dec. 1875): 692 and the *Richmond Dispatch*, 23 Nov. 1875.

JODI L. KOSTE

METZ, Christian (30 Dec. 1794–27 July 1867), a spiritual leader of the Community of True Inspiration (Amana Society), was born in Neuwied, Prussia, the son of Wilhelm Metz, a tanner, and Johannette Catharina Cassell, both of whom were active in the Inspirationist movement. At age seven his family moved to the Inspirationist center at the Ronneburg castle in Hesse, north of Frankfort am Main. As a youth, he was apprenticed as a carpenter.

The Community of True Inspiration was a radical Pietist sect formed in 1714 in Wittgenstein, Germany. An important characteristic of the Inspirationists was the belief that certain leaders were "inspired" to speak with divine authority equal to that of the Bible. Following a period of decline, a spiritual awakening began in 1817 when young Metz was twenty-three years old. Under the influence of Michael Krausert of Strassburg, Metz and Barbara Heinemann of Leitersweiler, Alsace, were recognized as "New Prophets," or "Instruments" (*Werkzeuge*), with the gift of divine inspiration. Krausert, however, was soon forced to leave the group, and Heinemann lost her gift for several years following her marriage in 1823. Leadership thus fell primarily on Metz, who remained until his death the undisputed spiritual and temporal head of the movement. He never married.

Like other radical Pietists, the Inspirationists opposed military service and taking oaths and avoided sending their children to orthodox Lutheran schools. Political pressures in the 1820s prompted the faithful to migrate to a few centers in Hesse, whose government was more tolerant of religious dissenters. The sect grew slowly and Metz leased large estates so that the members could live in close proximity as a church community. Eventually, however, high rents and the desire for religious freedom prompted Metz to seek the future of the Inspirationists in the New World. In 1842 he sailed to New York and purchased a 5,000-acre tract of Seneca reservation land a few miles from Buffalo in Erie County. Here more than 800 colonists built the thriving community of Ebenezer between 1843 and 1845. This settlement grew to six villages, including two in Canada. The gift of prophecy was restored to Barbara Heinemann in 1849, and together she and Metz prepared the Inspirationists for a further move west. In addition to their leadership, a council of elders helped administer the affairs of the colonies. Ebenezer's growing numbers and prosperity required additional land, and the two *Werkzeuge* also wanted more seclusion from their worldly neighbors.

In 1854 Metz again led the faithful to a tract of 3,000 acres (later expanded to approximately 26,000 acres) on rolling farmland along the Iowa River in Iowa County, Iowa. Through divine inspiration he christened their new home Amana, after a word in the Song of Solomon. The Ebenezer holdings were sold off systematically to good advantage, and the exodus to Iowa was completed by 1865. The colony was incorporated under Iowa law as the Amana Society in 1859. Seven villages were eventually established, all named with variations on the word Amana (with one exception,

Homestead). Each village had its own meetinghouse, school, and communal buildings. The Amana constitution and bylaws operated with only minor changes until 1932 when a reorganization resulted in the introduction of capitalism and the separation of church and business affairs. Under Metz's direction the various Amana industries flourished, including communal farms, grain and textile mills, furniture shops, and a bakery.

His writings include a history of the community from 1817 to 1845, *Historische Beschreibungen der Wahren Inspirations-Gemeinschaft* (1845). His prophecies may be found in *Jahrbücher der Wahren Inspirations-Gemeinden* (1842–1871). These prophecies, as well as published accounts by others, suggest that Metz was a man of profound piety and personal magnetism, with keen insight into human nature. Under divine inspiration he presided at the Lord's Supper, started new businesses, approved new members, settled disputes, named church elders, and sought to keep the society separate from worldly influences. By all accounts he was a talented administrator and organizer who deeply felt the responsibilities of being God's divine *Werkzeug*. At the time of his death in high Amana, the society had grown to more than 1,200 colonists. It was among the largest and most successful communal experiments in nineteenth-century America. Metz died in Amana and is buried in a simple grave with an unadorned marker in the community cemetery at main Amana.

• Many of Metz's papers are in the Amana Society's archive at Amana, Iowa. An important source for Metz and the society that contains excerpts from key sources in Bertha M. H. Shambaugh, *Amana That Was and Amana That Is* (1932). The early years of the Inspirationists are treated in Walter Grossman, "The European Origins of the True Inspired of Amana," *Communal Societies* 4 (Fall 1984): 133–49; the New York settlement is considered in Frank James Lankes, *The Ebenezer Community of True Inspiration* (1963). Helpful essays include "Amana the Church and Christian Metz the Prophet," *Midland* (Aug. 1915); Jonathan G. Andelson, "Postcharismatic Authority in the Amana Society: The Legacy of Christian Metz," in *When Prophets Die*, ed. Timothy Miller (1991); and Andelson, "The Community of True Inspiration from Germany to the Amana Colonies," in *America's Communal Utopias*, ed. Donald Pitzer (1997). See also Andelson's *Communalism and Change in the Amana Society, 1855–1932* (1974). The most complete study of Metz is Francis Adam Duval, "Christian Metz, German American Religious Leader and Pioneer" (Ph.D. diss., State Univ. of Iowa, 1948). The most thorough study of Amana in the nineteenth century is Gottlieb Scheuner, *Inspirations-Historie*, vol. 1, *1714–1728*, vol. 2, *1729–1819*, vol. 3, *1817–1850*, trans. Janet W. Zuber (1978; orig. pub. 1884–1891). For a more recent interpretation, see Diane Barthel, *Amana: From Pietist Sect to American Community* (1984). Two earlier works that survey Metz's leadership are William F. Noe, *Brief History of the Amana Society, 1714–1900* (1904), and William Rufus Perkins and Barthinis L. Wick, *History of the Amana Society or True Inspiration* (1891).

DAVID B. ELLER

MEUSEL, Bob (19 July 1896–28 Nov. 1977), baseball player, was born Robert William Meusel in San Jose, California, the son of Charles F. Meusel, a teamster, and Mary Smith. Meusel began his baseball career with Vernon, California (Pacific Coast League), after graduation from Los Angeles High School in 1915. He played three seasons, the second shortened by service in the U.S. Navy, before being purchased by the New York Yankees in 1920. The Yankees, a team in transition, also had acquired the dynamic Babe Ruth, who became Meusel's good friend on and off the field. At 6′3″ and 190 pounds, "Long Bob" was basically a left fielder, but with the retirement of veteran Frank "Home Run" Baker, he also played half a season at third base. Throughout Meusel's decade with the Yankees, his arm was considered the best in the American League and possibly in the majors. From his customary left field spot, the "sun field" in Yankee Stadium, he threw with speed on the ball and accuracy to any base. Since his throws tended to skip erratically when they reached the catcher in the traditional one-bounce throw from the outfield, he always threw home on the fly. Casey Stengel, who played against him in several World Series, said: "He had lightning on the ball." Meusel led the league in outfield assists in 1922 with 24 and shared the lead in 1921 with 28. Even Ty Cobb usually remained at third base, rather than test Meusel's arm on sacrifice flies to left field.

In 1921 Meusel married Edith Cowan. The couple had one daughter.

Meusel, a consistent extra-base hitter, excelled as a worthy member of the Yankees' fearsome "Murderers' Row." He batted above .300 in seven of his first eight seasons with the club and reached a high of .337 in 1927, the year he made his top salary of $13,000. He hit .309 for his career, which ended in 1930 with the Cincinnati Reds. Thirty-seven percent of his 1,693 hits were for extra bases, and he is one of only a handful of players to hit for "the cycle" (single, double, triple, and home run in one game) three times. Batting fifth behind Lou Gehrig, Long Bob knocked in 1,067 runs, or .76 per game played, which placed him thirteenth on the all-time list as late as the mid-1990s. The first year that his batting average fell below .300 was 1925, when the Yankees suffered a disastrous slump to seventh place. Although hitting only .290, Meusel led the American League in home runs with 33 and RBIs with 138.

Meusel performed poorly in World Series competition, batting .225 and striking out 24 times. Three of his six World Series pitted him against his elder brother, Emil Frederick "Irish" Meusel (9 June 1893–1 Mar. 1963), an outfielder for the New York Giants.

Unlike lively Irish, handsome Bob was taciturn and withdrawn. Nevertheless, as Ruth's close friend, he was also an occasional roisterer. In 1921 he and Ruth suffered the full weight of Commissioner Kenesaw Mountain Landis's disapproval by ignoring the ban on postseason barnstorming for World Series players. The commissioner withheld their World Series shares—$3,362 each—and suspended them for the first six weeks of the 1922 season. (The money was returned, but the suspension stuck.)

Depending on his mood, Meusel could be "Languid Bob." He occasionally did not run out a grounder or was less than eager in pursuit of a fly ball. Pleas, threats, or criticism left him unmoved. He spoke in monosyllables, or less. An effort to lighten up toward the end of his career prompted one sportswriter to say, "Poor Bob. He's finally learned to say 'Hello' when it's time to say 'Good-bye.'"

Meusel played two years of minor league baseball after spending the 1930 season with Cincinnati, and he worked for fifteen years as a security guard at a U.S. Navy installation in southern California. He died in Downey, California.

• Meusel's role with the 1927 Yankees is outlined in John Mosedale, *The Greatest of All: The 1927 New York Yankees* (1975). Robert W. Creamer, *Babe* (1974), relates some stories about Meusel and Ruth. Also see the entry on Meusel by A. D. Suehsdorf in David L. Porter, ed., *Biographical Dictionary of American Sports: Baseball* (1987). An obituary is in the *New York Times*, 30 Nov. 1977.

A. D. SUEHSDORF

MEXIA, Ynes Enriquetta Julietta (24 May 1870–12 July 1938), botanical collector, was born in Washington, D.C., the daughter of Enrique Antonio Mexia, a representative of the Mexican government, and Sarah R. Wilmer. Her mother left her husband in 1873 and moved with her children to a ranch owned by the Mexia family in Limestone County, Texas. Ynes Mexia probably attended local schools, and for short periods she was at Quaker schools in Philadelphia, Pennsylvania, and Ontario, Canada. From 1886 to 1887 she attended Saint Joseph's Academy in Emmitsburg, Maryland. She then moved to Mexico City to a property owned by her father. In 1897 she married Herman Lane (or de Laue), a merchant in Mexico City; they had no children, and he died in 1904. When her father died in 1898, a long lawsuit over his will finally left Ynes Mexia as an inheritor. She had established a business of raising poultry and other animals on her property in Mexico City. In 1907 or 1908 Mexia married Agustin A. de Reygados, one of her employees; they had no children. In 1909 she went to San Francisco for medical advice, probably for a nervous breakdown. Reygados almost bankrupted her business, so she sold it, divorced him, and stayed in San Francisco. There she resumed her maiden name and did social work. She became a U.S. citizen in 1924.

In 1920 Mexia began participating in trips of the local Sierra Club and took courses at the University of California, Berkeley, as a special student in natural sciences, without obtaining a degree. In 1922 she accompanied University of California paleontologist Eustace L. Furlong to Mexico, where she collected plants. A summer course in 1925 at Hopkins Marine Station in Pacific Grove, California, taught by LeRoy Abrams, drew her interest even more to botany. That fall she went to western Mexico with botanist Roxanna Stinchfield Ferris of Stanford University. Mexia collected about 500 species of plants (3,500 specimens) before she was injured in a fall from a cliff and returned home. Familiar with the language and customs of Mexico, she decided to collect botanical specimens in unexplored areas there to sell to museums. She arranged with an assistant in the herbarium of the University of California, Nina Floy Bracelin, to care for her specimens, arrange sales of them, and find specialists to identify and name new plants she discovered.

With some financial support from the University of California, and advice on caring for specimens from botanist Alice Eastwood of the California Academy of Sciences in San Francisco, Mexia returned to Mexico in 1926. For seven months she traveled alone, staying with local families in remote locations and finding local guides. She collected in the states of Nayarit, Sinaloa, and Jalisco, along the coast and by pack train to the crest of the Sierra Madre.

Political unrest deterred her from returning to Mexico. In the summer of 1928 she collected more than 6,000 plants in Alaska, at various altitudes in the area of Mount McKinley, traveling at times with pack horses or pack dogs.

William Albert Setchell, professor of botany at the University of California, urged Mexia to collect in South America, which she did from October 1929 to March 1932. For a year and a half she was in the highlands of Brazil at Vicosa in the state of Minas Gerais, where P. H. Rolfs was in charge of the State College of Agriculture. In addition to obtaining specimens for herself, she collected for his herbarium.

After returning to the coast, Mexia decided to try crossing South America at its greatest breadth; no one was known to have crossed it there from east to west. By motorship, river steamer, and dugout canoe she traveled to the highest point of a tributary of the Amazon. For three months in the rainy season she camped near friendly natives with a guide and two helpers. "The 'boys' hunted toucans, monkeys, and parrots—I can assure you, they are not bad eating," she wrote ("Three Thousand Miles up the Amazon," *Sierra Club Bulletin* 18 [1933]: 95). Unable to travel farther west, she returned downriver by balsa raft to ship her specimens. Then she crossed South America from east to west by hydroplane up the Amazon, airplane to the lower Andes, and the Transandean Railroad through a high pass down to Lima, Peru. In 1933 she made a short collecting trip to Nevada, Utah, and Arizona. She accompanied the noted botanists Alice Eastwood and John Thomas Howell.

Mexia traveled again in South America from 1934 to 1936, first visiting a remote mountain area in Ecuador to find a little-known wax palm, then joining an expedition with University of California botanist T. Harper Goodspeed in Peru; she continued south to the Straits of Magellan. Finally, in 1937 she returned to Mexico and collected specimens in Guerrero and Oaxaca. There in the spring of 1938 she became ill and returned to San Francisco. She died in Berkeley.

Goodspeed described Mexia as "the true explorer type and happiest when independent and far from civilization" (*Plant Hunters in the Andes* [1961], p. 12). She is said to have had an uncertain temperament, impulsive and sensitive to criticism. Not a systematic botanist, she was greatly pleased when her name was given to a new identification; these included a composite genus, *Mexianthus*, and about fifty species. Her ability to prepare specimens in the field was remarkable, especially under moist tropical conditions. She saved all significant parts of plants for identification, kept detailed fieldnotes, and took excellent photographs. Bracelin estimated that Mexia collected 145,000 specimens; these were mostly flowering plants, mosses, and ferns but included some insects, birds, and other animals.

• Mexia's correspondence and notebooks are at the Bancroft Library, University of California, Berkeley; correspondence with Alice Eastwood is at the California Academy of Sciences, San Francisco. Specimens she collected are at many museums. In addition to the article cited, Mexia wrote "Botanical Trails in Old Mexico—The Lure of the Unknown," *Madroño* 1 (1929): 227–38, and "Camping on the Equator," *Sierra Club Bulletin* 22 (Feb. 1937): 85–91. Biographies include Mrs. H. P. [Nina Floy] Bracelin, "Ynes Mexia," *Madroño* 4 (1938): 273–75, with a list of expeditions and total of collections; Patricia Joan Siegal and Kay Thomas Finley, "Ynes Enriquetta Julietta Mexia," *Women in the Scientific Search* (1985), pp. 101–5, which lists other sources; Marcia Myers Bonta, "Ynes Mexia," *Women in the Field: America's Pioneering Women Naturalists* (1991), pp. 103–14; and Rebecca Lowe Warren, "Ynes Mexia," in *Notable Women in the Life Sciences*, ed. Benjamin F. Shearer and Barbara S. Shearer (1996).

ELIZABETH NOBLE SHOR

MEYER, Adolf (13 Sept. 1866–17 Mar. 1950), psychiatrist, was born in Niederweningen, Switzerland, near Zürich, the son of Rudolf Meyer, a minister, and Anna Walder. Meyer completed his medical studies at the University of Zürich in 1892, where he studied under August Forel, who worked on hypnotism and advocated complete abstinence from alcohol. That same year Meyer emigrated to the United States.

Meyer's first position in the U.S. was as pathologist for the Illinois Eastern Hospital for the Insane at Kankakee (1893–1895). Meyer intended to conduct neurological research by performing autopsies on deceased patients in an attempt to correlate brain lesions with diagnostic categories. He soon realized that such correlations could be valuable only when extensive, accurate, and uniform observations had been made of the behavior, symptoms, and course of the illnesses of the patients when they were still alive. At the time, such observations were made only informally and recorded haphazardly if at all. To change this situation, Meyer educated the staff in the principles of neurology and psychiatry, observation, history taking, and record keeping. As a consequence, Meyer himself became more interested in observing individual mental patients rather than in post-mortem brain studies, which did not yield particularly interesting results. Meyer's contacts with Chicago's Hull House (in particular Julia Lathrop) and John Dewey at the University of Chicago, whose psychological functionalism Meyer found inspiring, reinforced this change of interest.

Subsequently, Meyer was appointed pathologist at the Massachusetts State Lunatic Hospital at Worcester (1895–1901). In this capacity Meyer implemented the ideas he had developed at Kankakee. He emphasized the necessity of integrating patient care and scientific research—no longer merely neurological in character but based on the observation of patients and on their life histories as they were collected through their own accounts and those of their friends and relatives. These ideals required improved methods of record keeping and extensive training for the staff. By integrating research and treatment, Meyer hoped to raise the level of care for mental patients. While at Worcester, Meyer lectured to psychology students at Clark University, who regularly came to the wards for observation. He also maintained contact with neurologists and psychologists in Boston, among them William James and James Jackson Putnam, who were particularly interested in psychotherapy.

In 1902 Meyer married Mary Potter Brooks, a psychiatric social worker; the couple had one daughter. That same year he was appointed director of the Pathological Institute of the New York State Hospitals for the Insane (1902–1909). He transformed the institute from a center for neurological research into a center for coordinating research and training in New York State mental hospitals. The institute offered training, consultation, and continuing education in trends in psychiatric research to all physicians in the state's employ. Meyer introduced standardized methods of record keeping for all New York State mental hospitals, which made it possible to draw up statewide statistics and to conduct research in psychiatric epidemiology. During his tenure at the New York Pathological Institute, Meyer opened an outpatient clinic to assist former mental patients' transition back to the community and to counsel individuals before commitment to a mental hospital was warranted. Meyer promoted outpatient clinics as the centers of preventative work in psychiatry. In 1904 Meyer was appointed professor of clinical medicine at Cornell University Medical College. He renewed his acquaintance with John Dewey after the latter moved to Columbia University Teachers College and maintained close social contacts with the historian James Harvey Robinson.

During his tenure at the New York State Pathological Institute, Meyer articulated his dynamic psychiatry or psychobiology as a framework and method for studying the life histories of individual patients. Meyer's approach was holistic, pluralistic, and pragmatic; it was inspired by the pragmatism of Charles S. Peirce and William James and the functionalism of John Dewey. Meyer replaced the then-pervasive neurological approach of correlating psychiatric diagnoses with brain lesions with an emphasis on the study of the individual's life history from an evolutionary perspective. According to Meyer, mental problems or maladjustment occurred when an individual lacked the skills for meeting the particular challenges that were facing him or her. Central in Meyer's work is his conceptualization of schizophrenia (or dementia praecox, as it was called at the time). He explained schizophrenia as a progressive disorganization of an individual's habits; as a mental disorder rather than a mental illness, essentially behavioral in nature. According to Meyer, individuals suffering from dementia praecox had shied away from the challenges of life by daydreaming, rationalization, and inaction, thereby becoming increasingly unable to deal with reality.

In Meyer's approach, centered around the concept of maladjustment, the differences between normal functioning, neuroses, and psychoses were only a matter of degree; they all appeared as more or less serious forms of maladjustment. Meyer developed a psychiatry that considered a wide range of human problems, including life problems, asocial behavior, and mental illness, within its domain. Socially disruptive behavior, such as criminality, homelessness, prostitution, alcoholism, and the like, could easily be subsumed under the concept of maladjustment, thereby providing a seemingly medical label for social ills. Psychiatrists used this conception of maladjustment to enlarge the domain of life problems that warranted their professional intervention.

Meyer strongly doubted the usefulness of the extensive nosological and diagnostic systems then common among European psychiatrists. According to him, a diagnostic label in itself did not improve the condition of patients nor was such a label very informative. Meyer was opposed to those who exclusively emphasized psychological factors, most notably psychoanalysts. In his perspective, mental, physiological, neurological, and behavioral factors were all relevant; consequently, they all had to be taken into account. In his psychobiology Meyer attempted to integrate all these factors.

His subscription to the ideal of prevention made Meyer participate in the organization of the National Committee for Mental Hygiene, which was founded in 1909 by ex-mental patient Clifford W. Beers. This committee aimed to develop initiatives aimed at preventing mental disorders though public health education and the establishment of outpatient clinics. Meyer's psychobiology provided the theoretical framework for the mental hygiene movement, which proceeded to increase the domain of psychiatry beyond the mental hospital by including outpatient work, child guidance clinics, industrial psychiatry, and public health education.

In 1909 Meyer was appointed the first professor in psychiatry at the Johns Hopkins Medical School and director of the Henry Phipps Psychiatric Clinic; he held both positions until his retirement in 1941. The Henry Phipps Psychiatric Clinic integrated research, treatment, and teaching. The career of a great number of leading American psychiatrists began in the Phipps Clinic under Meyer's tutelage.

Meyer's psychobiology emphasized the significance of environmental factors and life events in the development of mental disorders. From the beginning of his career, Meyer emphasized the importance of integrating the mental hospital with the surrounding community. At Johns Hopkins, he partially realized this ideal. The Phipps Clinic had an outpatient clinic where patients were seen after their discharge and where an investigation of their home and work environment could be made. In addition, the clinic treated conditions that were not severe enough to warrant institutionalization. Meyer stimulated the development of psychiatric social work for these new tasks. Ideally, Meyer proposed, the country would be divided into mental health districts organized around mental institutions. The psychiatrists working there would acquire intimate knowledge of the conditions in their district. They would coordinate activities promoting mental health in the community which would thereby become more effective. Psychiatrists and social workers would make mental health insights available to the population, which would aid in the prevention of mental disorders. The Phipps Clinic succeeded in developing relations with a few neighborhoods in Baltimore where school surveys were undertaken and special classes for mentally retarded pupils were organized. In addition, a Child Guidance Clinic was opened.

Throughout his life Meyer attempted to improve the status of psychiatry within the medical curriculum. He was instrumental in establishing standards for training and certification in the field. When he was appointed to Johns Hopkins, very few medical schools offered courses in psychiatry. To change that situation, Meyer was convinced that more psychiatrists needed to be educated who could then be appointed to medical school faculties. In addition, uniform standards for psychiatrists had to be formulated. In his presidential address to the American Psychiatric Association in 1927, Meyer mentioned these issues. In 1931 the National Committee for Mental Hygiene established a Division of Psychiatric Education in order to survey the quality of psychiatric education in American medical schools and to recommend improvements. Meyer and his student, Franklin G. Ebaugh, played a central role in these surveys and the subsequent conferences on psychiatric education. In 1934 the American Board of Psychiatry and Neurology was founded to certify members in both professions; Meyer chaired the organizational meeting.

Meyer's influence on American psychiatry has been profound. Nevertheless, his influence on the field of psychiatry was mostly through his teaching at Johns Hopkins University. His writings are infrequently consulted because they are notoriously obscure and poorly organized. His psychobiology was overshadowed by the enormous popularity of psychoanalysis after World War II. Meyer died in Baltimore, Maryland.

• The Johns Hopkins University Medical School holds a collection of Meyer's papers; the G. Stanley Hall Papers at the Clark University Archives include some material related to Meyer. See *The Collected Papers of Adolf Meyer*, ed. Eunice

E. Winters (1950–1952), for a published edition of his papers. Published works by Meyer that are worth noting include "The Dynamic Interpretation of Dementia Parecox," *American Journal of Psychology* 21 (1910): 2–3 and 139–57; and *The Commonsense Psychiatry of Dr. Adolf Meyer*, ed. Alfred Lief (1948), for which Lief also wrote a biographical article. See also Ruth Leys, "Types of One: Adolf Meyer's Life Chart and the Representation of Individuality," *Representations* 34 (1991): 1–28; and Eunice E. Winters, "Adolf Meyer's Two and a Half Years at Kankakee: May 1, 1893–Nov. 1, 1895," *Bulletin for the History of Medicine* 40 (1966): 441–58. An obituary is in the *New York Times*, 18 Mar. 1950.

HANS POLS

MEYER, Albert Gregory (9 Mar. 1903–9 Apr. 1965), Roman Catholic prelate, was born in Milwaukee, Wisconsin, the son of Peter Meyer, a grocer and factory worker, and Mathilda Thelen. After attending parochial schools, he entered St. Francis Seminary in 1917 and began his preparation for the priesthood. In 1921 he went to Rome to study at the North American College and subsequently at the Urbanian College of the Sacred Congregation de Propaganda Fide, where he completed a doctorate in theology (S.T.D.) and was ordained to the priesthood in 1926. He remained in Rome to study at the Pontifical Biblical Institute, where he completed his licentiate (S.S.L.) in 1930.

The same year Meyer, a rather serious and painfully shy young man, returned to Milwaukee and was assigned a parish in Waukesha, Wisconsin. The following year he joined the faculty of St. Francis Seminary as a professor of dogma, biblical geography, and religion. In 1937 he became rector of St. Francis and administered the affairs of the seminary until 1946, when he was selected to head the diocese of Superior, Wisconsin. He was formally installed as the sixth bishop of Superior in May of that year. His was a rural diocese that comprised the sixteen northernmost counties of Wisconsin. Meyer used his episcopate to build up the diocesan clergy and foster closer ties among the widely scattered parishes and mission stations. He inaugurated some limited building projects and established a Catholic newspaper and a diocesan council of Catholic women.

In September 1953 Meyer was installed as the seventh archbishop of Milwaukee. His five-year administration witnessed a burst of growth for the archdiocese reflected in a rapid expansion of its parochial and educational institutions, including thirty-five new grade schools, four new high schools, and new facilities for all the major institutions of higher education. Twenty-five new parishes were created, mostly in newly developed suburbs. Meyer also served a term as president (largely an honorary position) of the National Catholic Educational Association and issued a major pastoral letter in 1956 entitled "Modesty and Decency."

In 1958 Meyer replaced Cardinal Samuel Stritch as the tenth bishop and the fifth archbishop of Chicago. The archdiocese of Chicago had the largest concentration of Catholics in the United States (about two million) as well as a host of urban and racial tensions that demanded the attention of ecclesiastical and civil officials. The first days of Meyer's reign were marred by a tragic fire at Our Lady of the Angels parish grammar school on the north side of the city that killed over ninety children and three teachers. Subsequent investigations stimulated major changes in construction codes for school buildings and the upgrading of fire safety procedures and equipment in schools nationwide. Meyer supported such changes and, as in Milwaukee, oversaw an extensive building program concentrating in new suburban parishes.

Though not identified up to this point as especially progressive in his religious or social thinking, Meyer—unlike his less forceful predecessor—moved actively to put the Catholic church in Chicago firmly behind efforts to bring about racial integration. He was inspired, it seems, more by obedience to existing church teachings against discrimination than by the burgeoning civil rights movement. In a firmly worded instruction to his priests in 1961, Meyer forbade racial discrimination in Catholic schools and vigorously confronted pastors and school administrators who attempted to circumvent his order. He pressured suburban pastors to welcome African-American families to their parishes and called for open housing throughout the city and the nation. In 1963 Meyer served as a host to, and delivered a major address at, the National Conference on Religion and Race. Dr. Martin Luther King, Jr., also participated. This interest in civil rights brought Meyer into an uneasy alliance with Saul Alinsky and his Industrial Areas Foundation in establishing community organizations. An archdiocesan subsidy helped set up the Woodlawn Organization, an all-black group on Chicago's South Side that effectively fought the expansion plans of the University of Chicago.

Meyer's efforts in Chicago, however, were soon overshadowed by his role in the Second Vatican Council (Vatican II). His appointment to the Sacred College of Cardinals in 1960 assured him a prominent place in the planning and administration of the council. He soon allied himself with the progressive forces of northern and western European bishops and eventually came to be considered the leading American bishop at Vatican II. With help from his theological advisers, Barnabas Mary Ahern and Francis McCool, Meyer delivered well-thought-out speeches in ecclesiastical Latin and made major contributions to documents relating to sacred Scripture and the constitution of the church. The nature of tradition was an important point of controversy among various Council Fathers. Meyer accepted the basic principles of the historical-critical method of scriptural interpretation and with that a more dynamic view of the meaning of tradition, viewing it as an evolving reality rather than a fixed set of truths unchanged through history.

Meyer was also a forceful voice for ecumenical amity and in 1964 issued a pastoral letter to his archdiocese encouraging interdenominational cooperation. Because of his belief in the ecumenical movement, Meyer, like many other American bishops, wanted Vatican II to issue a strong statement in defense of religious liberty. When the council president in late 1964 announced a delay in a critical preliminary vote on such a document—prepared by Jesuit John Courtney and others and submitted the year before—Meyer joined in a minor revolt on the floor of the council, which yielded a petition to Pope Paul VI requesting a reversal of the decision. The pope upheld the delay, but Meyer and others redoubled their efforts and reworked the document. The Declaration on Religious Liberty, passed in the council's final session, stands as one of the most distinctly American contributions to Vatican II.

Unfortunately, Meyer did not live to witness the declaration's passage. In February 1965 he was diagnosed with a malignant brain tumor. He died shortly thereafter in Chicago.

• An extensive collection of Meyer's personal papers is in the archives of the archdiocese of Chicago. Smaller collections of official papers are in the archives of the archdiocese of Milwaukee and the diocese of Superior, Wis. The details of Meyer's life are in Steven M. Avella, *This Confident Church: Catholic Leadership and Life in Chicago, 1940–1965* (1992). See also Avella, "The Era of Confidence: Albert G. Meyer and the Transitional Church," *U.S. Catholic Historian* 7 (Winter 1988): 91–111; and Vincent A. Yzermans, ed., *American Participation in the Second Vatican Council* (1967). An obituary is in the *New York Times*, 10 Apr. 1965.

STEVEN M. AVELLA

MEYER, André Benoit Mathieu (3 Sept. 1898–10 Sept. 1979), investment banker, was born in Paris, France, the son of Jules Meyer, a small-business man, and Lucie Cerf. In 1914 he left public school and began his financial career as a messenger for a small Paris bank, Baur and Sons. The next year he moved onto the trading floor as a Paris Bourse broker. In 1922 he married Bella Lehman, with whom he had two children.

Meyer's enterprise and skill as a trader brought an invitation in 1925 from David David-Weill to join an elite Paris bank, Lazard Frères et Compagnie. Meyer became a partner in 1928. Meyer's first notable achievement in investment banking was the proposal to develop SOVAC, the credit arm of financially troubled Citroën, into the first French consumer-finance company. When Citroën itself foundered during the depression, Meyer negotiated the purchase of a controlling interest by the French tiremaker Michelin. The French awarded Meyer the Legion of Honor for financial services to his country, and he served on the French delegation in the Young Plan negotiations on German reparations.

In 1940 Meyer and his family were forced into exile just ahead of the German occupation. Meyer settled in New York City and was naturalized in 1948. Within three years, Meyer had taken charge of the rather lackluster Lazard Frères and Company, New York; by 1944 he was a senior partner. During the next thirty-six years he would transform Lazard into what his biographer, Cary Reich, called "the most venturesome investment bank in America" (p. 19). As one partner noted, Meyer built up the firm singlehandedly, while the other partners were miles behind him. Lazard did not try to compete with the big-money investment houses but prospered as an elite or private bank that provided financial advice for a fee to a select few. In the postwar period Meyer steered the firm into venture capital and concentrated on developing deals in which the partnership could take a stake. The fortunes made for himself and the partners gained Lazard a reputation as a "millionaire factory." Estimates of his own personal fortune ranged from $200 million to $800 million.

Meyer launched in 1950 the first of his big money-making ventures in Texas ranch land, realizing a profit of $10 to $15 million. In the merger-mad 1960s he engineered notable mergers and acquisitions, including Loew's Theaters' takeover of the Lorillard Corporation; RCA's of Hertz and Random House; Atlantic Richfield's of Sinclair Oil; Kinney National Service's of Warner Brothers–Seven Arts; McDonnell Company's of Douglas Aircraft; and R. J. Reynolds's of McLean Industries. The bank's relationship with International Telephone and Telegraph was especially successful; Lazard assisted ITT's relentless drive to acquire diversified holdings such as O. M. Scott & Sons Company and Avis Rent-a-Car System and its controversial takeover of the Hartford Fire Insurance Company. Lazard bought Avis in 1962 for roughly $7 million, returned the company to profitability, and resold it three years later to ITT for stock worth more than $20 million.

Meyer liked to call his work "financial engineering" and relished complex, even Byzantine, financial problems. David Sarnoff, chair of the RCA Corporation and an old friend, observed that at the heart of Meyer's success was his lightning-quick, almost intuitive analytical powers that enabled him to grasp the subtleties and implications of even the most complicated transactions while others were still thinking things over.

Some critics accused Meyer of ruthlessness and of helping to foster the conglomerate movement in the United States. The ITT acquisition of Hartford Fire brought nothing but trouble from the beginning because the deal embroiled Lazard in U.S. government antitrust investigations that were to haunt the firm and Meyer for years. Meyer had always striven to be a banker whose "highmindedness and probity were beyond question" (Reich, p. 332), and the Securities and Exchange Commission (SEC) suit seemed to him a plot to tarnish his image in his late years. Although never prosecuted, Meyer testified before the SEC in the 1970s as the commission filed suit against ITT and Lazard, accusing them of violating the Securities Act of 1933. Both Lazard and ITT negotiated a settlement with the commission.

Meyer's friendships with the rich and powerful, including Jean Monnet, chief architect of the European Economic Community, French prime minister Georges Pompidou, Fiat boss Giovanni Agnelli, and President Lyndon Johnson, were as indispensable to his business as was his ability to put together complicated deals. A trustee of Joseph Kennedy's estate, Meyer was a valued financial adviser and confidant of the Kennedys throughout the 1960s. He occasionally was seen escorting Jacqueline Kennedy in the years before her remarriage, thereby giving credence to the Wall Street saying that Meyer loved three things in life: beautiful women, great art, and complex deals. Asked about that once, Meyer shrugged his expensively tailored shoulders and answered, "The first two are really one, and the third is not always the case." Meyer became the "financial guru" of the postwar power elite because of his investment genius, contacts, and influence.

Meyer sat on many corporate boards, including Allied Chemical, Fiat, Montecatini, and RCA, as well as Lazard in Paris, London, and New York. He was a ferociously hard and self-disciplined worker, never took vacations, and had a telephone beside him constantly. He expected his partners and employees to be accessible on weekends. Friends and enemies alike said Meyer ran the firm with an extraordinary tight authoritarian rein and insisted on knowing even the most minute details of his partners' dealings. Said one partner, "No other partner has any say whatsoever if André doesn't want to do something." Often irrational and arbitrary, Meyer would have violent fallings out, but the incident would be entirely forgotten after passionate reconciliation. His associates sometimes referred to him as "Zeus," the most powerful of the gods. He forever maintained a touch of hauteur and mystique, and always a sense of elegant style and showmanship.

Meyer's generous philanthropies included financing the construction at the Metropolitan Museum of Art of the André Meyer Gallery for nineteenth-century European art. His Manhattan apartment at the Carlyle Hotel contained an extensive art collection, with works by Cézanne, Dégas, Pissaro, Picasso, and Manet. In poor health since 1977, Meyer died in Lausanne, Switzerland, near his second home in Crans-sur-Sierre.

Vast wealth and power came to André Meyer. He was among the most brilliant financiers of the twentieth century, and under his leadership Lazard essentially invented modern aggressive deal making and dominated the field as the most important investment house in mergers and acquisitions during the 1950s and 1960s.

• André Meyer refused to write his memoirs and rarely gave interviews. He believed that secrecy was an essential element of investment banking and deliberately did not commit to writing his ideas and reflections. He wrote very few letters or memos, preferring to deal face to face with people. The only biography is Cary Reich, *Financier: The Biography of André Meyer* (1983), which is based extensively on interviews. Michael C. Jensen, *The Financiers* (1976), has a chapter on Meyer and Lazard Frères. Several articles about Meyer and Lazard are in *Institutional Investor*, *Fortune*, *Business Week*, and *Financial World*; see especially Reich, "Legacy of André Meyer," *Institutional Investor*, 13 Apr. 1979, pp. 30–35, and Thomas Wise, "In Trinity There Is Strength," *Fortune*, Aug. 1968, pp. 100–103. An obituary is in the *New York Times*, 11 Sept. 1979; also see the *New York Times* Biographical Service article by Eric Pace, Sept. 1979.

CAROL M. MARTEL

MEYER, Annie Nathan (19 Feb. 1867–23 Sept. 1951), volunteer activist, was born in New York City, the daughter of Anne Augusta Florance and Robert Weeks Nathan, a businessman. Descended from a distinguished Sephardic Jewish family, Meyer was always conscious of her background. A member of a large extended family, among her cousins was Benjamin Cardozo, a distinguished jurist who eventually served on the U.S. Supreme Court, and Emma Lazarus, a well-known poet.

Although the Nathan family was affluent, Annie's father lost his fortune in the stock market crash of 1875, and they moved to Green Bay, Wisconsin, to avoid social shame. While Annie's older sister Maud attended public high school in Green Bay, Annie went to elementary school and exhibited a keen interest in learning. Some years later when the family returned to New York, Annie wished to continue her education, but in the 1880s studious women could enroll only in Columbia University's Collegiate Course for Women, a course of study that allowed women to take examinations and earn a certificate of completion, though they were not permitted to take classes with Columbia's male students. Neither was separate instruction available for the women. Meyer found this situation appalling and vowed to work for a women's college attached to Columbia.

After participating in the collegiate course from 1885 to 1886, she left the following year to marry a prominent New York doctor, Alfred Meyer, thirteen years her senior; they had one child. Annie Meyer campaigned vigorously for the creation of a woman's college, and in 1889 she witnessed the formation of Barnard College, the separate women's college attached to Columbia. Meyer became a trustee of Barnard, a position she held all of her life. In 1940, at a Barnard function, Mayor Fiorello La Guardia called her "New York's first high-pressure group," public acknowledgement of her prominent role as fundraiser and advocate of Barnard.

Though she supported higher education for women, Meyer did not support many of the leading women's causes of the period. In contrast to her sister Maud Nathan, who was a prominent suffragist and leader of the National Consumer's League, Meyer spoke publicly against suffrage. She argued that educated women could control their husbands' ballots; thus, obtaining an education was the chief priority. Meyer's attitudes on the subject of women's rights and opportunities, however, appear to be paradoxical. While she criticized both woman suffrage and women in business, she believed women had to become independent. In 1888, for example, she began collecting material from eighteen women contributors for a book, *Woman's Work in America*, published in 1891. In her introduction, she stated, "This book is nothing else than a history of woman's slow, but sure, training to stand balanced upon her own feet. She has looked upon the thousands of falling sisters, and has very reasonably reached the conclusion that the only way to make sure of standing is to make use of her own feet."

Although she never considered herself a professional writer, Meyer went on to write plays, novels, and short stories that featured women often in difficult circumstances. In a short story called "Vorbei," published in 1893, for example, she depicted a woman of twenty-five, ostensibly "over the hill," who decided to marry a decent man rather than the romantic love of her life who had years earlier avoided offering her a marriage proposal. When she reencounters her first love and tells him of her earlier feelings, he professes love for her and proposes marriage, only to be turned down when she realizes that youthful love has been replaced with a mature love for another man.

Meyer wrote two plays criticizing the role of women in business, *The Dominant Sex* (1911) and *The Advertising of Kate* (1921). While her sister was speaking at street corner rallies for woman suffrage, Meyer countered that most women were uneducated and therefore incapable of making wise political choices. One apocryphal story that circulated at the time describes a rare meeting between the sisters. Annie asked Maud, "How would you like your cook to vote?" Maud replied, "He does!"

The sisters differed in their views toward their Jewish heritage as well. Nathan was active in Jewish social welfare organizations as well as secular ones; Meyer confined her public activities to lectures on education and art and to her writings. Though an early critic of Hitler, Meyer believed that Zionism raised the specter of dual loyalties for Jewish Americans, whom she believed should be assimilated into the American mainstream. Meyer was sympathetic to and interested in the rights of African Americans. She sponsored the admission of anthropologist-writer Zora Neale Hurston into Barnard in 1925.

In 1951 Meyer published her memoirs, *It's Been Fun*, which portrayed her growing-up years in less than idyllic terms. She chronicled her father's unfaithfulness and her mother's addiction to morphine. By contrast, Nathan's 1933 autobiography, *Once upon a Time and Today*, was a much sunnier version of their childhood, a portrait that avoided all unpleasant references. As the youngest of four children, Meyer had lost her mother when she was only twelve and apparently had felt the effects of the unstable household during her vulnerable years.

Meyer's contributions to Barnard College and education for women are undeniable. Though her fiction and plays have not stood the test of time, they reflect a prominent woman's contrary and traditional view in a time—and a family—that took the opposite position. Meyer never believed that Barnard College gave her proper recognition for her role in its founding, but she remained optimistic that someday her singular accomplishment would be noted. Barnard diplomatically maintained that she was among the group that founded the college but not the sole founder. Meyer died in New York City.

• Annie Nathan Meyer's papers are at the American Jewish Archives and the Barnard College Archives, both in New York City. General information on her family and personal anecdotes are in Stephen Birmingham, *The Grandees: America's Sephardic Elite* (1971). Her writings also include *Barnard Beginnings* (1935). Recent scholarship on Meyer includes an excerpt from the introduction to *Woman's Work in America* in Jacob Marcus, *The American Jewish Woman: A Documentary History* (1981), and Lynn D. Gordon, "Annie Nathan Meyer and Barnard College: Mission and Identity in Women's Higher Education, 1889–1950", *History of Education Quarterly* 26 (Winter 1986): 503–22. An informative interview-essay of both Meyer and her husband is Robert Taylor Lewis, "Profiles: The Doctor, the Lady, and Columbia University," *New Yorker*, 23 Oct. 1943, pp. 27–32, and 30 Oct. 1943, pp. 28–32, 34, 36.

JUNE SOCHEN

MEYER, Eugene Isaac (31 Oct. 1875–17 July 1959), investment banker, government official, and newspaper publisher, was born in Los Angeles, California, the son of Marc Eugene Meyer, a retail merchant, and Harriet Newmark. After growing up in San Francisco, Meyer attended the University of California for one year in 1892. He was a mediocre student who spent much of his time drinking and gambling. After his freshman year, his family moved to New York City and he transferred to Yale. By working much harder academically at Yale, Meyer earned excellent grades and was elected to Phi Beta Kappa. After skipping his junior year, he graduated with an A.B. with honors in 1895, ranking nineteenth in a class of 250. Meyer then spent two years in Europe learning French and German and gaining work experience in banking and international finance. On returning to the United States, Meyer was employed by the international banking firm of Lazard Frères, where his father was a partner. However, because his duties there were menial compared with the work he had been doing in Europe, Meyer left the firm in 1901, much against his father's wishes, to open his own investment firm.

Meyer's life plan, conceived when he was a young man, was to accumulate enough money to leave the business world at fifty, devote ten years to public service, and then to retire from public life at sixty. Starting with $600 that his father had given him as a reward for not smoking, Meyer began speculating in the stock market. His first real success was on the eve of the 1900 presidential election when, betting on a victory for McKinley that would inflate stock prices, Meyer purchased options to buy almost $5,000 of railroad stocks. Four months after the election, he sold the shares he had bought with those options for $50,000 and with the money bought a seat on the New York Stock Exchange. With this seat, Meyer made his fortune during panics by acquiring undervalued stocks and reselling them later at their true value. Meyer married Agnes Elizabeth Ernst in 1910; they had five children. At the age of forty, Meyer's fortune was estimated to be between $40 and $60 million.

When the United States entered World War I in 1917, Meyer closed his investment firm and took a government job in Washington, D.C., for the nominal yearly salary of one dollar. He advised the army on shoe purchases and advised the Committee on Raw Materials (later the War Industries Board) on purchases of nonferrous metals. In 1918 President Woodrow Wilson named Meyer head of the War Finance Corporation (WFC). He continued working with the WFC after the war, extending its range of involvements to include farmers caught in the postwar depression. The success of this work prompted Calvin Coolidge to appoint Meyer head of the Federal Farm Loan Board in 1927.

Named governor of the Federal Reserve Board by Herbert Hoover in 1930, Meyer set about trying to institute reforms of the banking system. However, these attempts were quickly disrupted by the Great Depression. Meyer promoted the idea of the Reconstruction Finance Corporation, which attempted to save failing banks by making loans easier for them to obtain, and became its first head when the program was begun in 1931. Because Meyer did not support Franklin Roosevelt's New Deal, he resigned his government positions in 1933.

For $825,000 Meyer bought the troubled *Washington Post* at a public auction in June 1933. He often worried about the wisdom of this purchase, since he had no experience in the world of journalism and the *Post* had been running at a large deficit for several years. He was, however, optimistic; although the paper was heavily in debt, its printing presses in bad condition, and its management in chaos, the *Post* did have a valuable Associated Press franchise and a prestigious name. He reorganized the staff, instituting much tighter hierarchical control and replacing many news editors and managers, and, with the help of experts in journalism, began extensive analysis of the appeal (or lack thereof) of each page of the *Post* and competing newspapers. Under Meyer's leadership the *Post* weathered early losses and then grew into a major national newspaper.

Meyer's ideas of public service were reflected in the paper's editorials promoting international cooperation and stable democratic government. The editorials often criticized Franklin Roosevelt, especially his 1934 devaluation of the dollar and his unsuccessful 1937 attempt to pack the Supreme Court by increasing the number of justices.

Meyer was the source for one of the *Post*'s most brilliant scoops. From hints dropped by his friend Lord Lothian, Meyer managed to guess the impending scandal that would shake the foundation of the British monarchy. On 17 October 1936 the *Post* was the first major newspaper to break the story that King Edward VIII of Great Britain intended to marry the divorcée Mrs. Wallis Simpson, a marriage that would require him to abdicate the throne.

In June 1946, at the request of President Harry S. Truman, Meyer took on the leadership of the newly formed World Bank, turning the leadership of the *Post* over to his son-in-law, Philip S. Graham. Meyer's presidency was short-lived; he stayed only long enough to organize the bank and put it on a firm structural footing. Returning to the *Post*, he resumed the chairmanship of the board but left the office of publisher to Graham. The newspaper soon acquired several television stations and the rival paper, the *Washington Times-Herald*. Meyer died in Washington, D.C.

Although Meyer's unpaid government service during and after World War I was both extensive and influential, his lasting historical importance rests on his transformation of the *Washington Post* from a poorly written, financially ailing paper into an influential, profitable, and widely read publication. Although at the time of his purchase many suspected Meyer's motivations behind acquiring the paper to be political, he insisted on fair, nonpartisan editorials that established the paper as a trustworthy independent voice in the U.S. political arena.

• Meyer's papers are in the Library of Congress, Manuscripts Division, along with Sidney Hyman's unfinished manuscript, "Life of Eugene Meyer." See also Agnes E. Meyer, *Out of These Roots* (1953), and Merlo J. Pusey, *Eugene Meyer* (1974). An obituary is in the *Washington Post*, 18 July 1959.

ELIZABETH ZOE VICARY

MEYER, George von Lengerke (24 June 1858–9 Mar. 1918), diplomat and secretary of the navy, was born in Boston, Massachusetts, the son of George Augustus Meyer, an East India merchant, and Grace Parker. He was raised in a patrician society that was becoming disaffected from national affairs because of the unfamiliar political alignments created by industrialization, immigration, and the problems of urbanization. Young Meyer, however, did not withdraw from politics. After graduating from Harvard in 1879, he became a merchant and married Marion Alice Appleton in 1885; they had three children. Meyer joined a movement of bluebloods who wished to reassert patrician influence. As an established State Street merchant residing on Beacon Hill, he launched a political career that took him to Boston's Common Council in 1889, to the Board of Aldermen in 1891, and to the Massachusetts House of Representatives in 1892. In 1894 he was elected Speaker and served three relatively undistinguished terms. Upon leaving office in 1896 he returned to his State Street business and became an effective fundraiser for Republican presidential candidates in Massachusetts.

In 1900 William McKinley, whom Meyer initially had opposed for the presidency in 1896, reluctantly appointed him ambassador to Italy. Meyer mingled comfortably with the European aristocracy, who still held power there. While in Rome he developed such a close relationship with Kaiser Wilhelm II of Germany that Theodore Roosevelt (1858–1919), who succeeded to the presidency upon McKinley's assassination in

1901, sometimes used Meyer to deliver and receive messages instead of Charlemagne Tower, the official ambassador to Germany. In 1905 Roosevelt, whom Meyer had actively supported for the presidency in 1904, made him ambassador to Russia. Arriving in April, Meyer played an important role in the delicate negotiations leading to the Treaty of Portsmouth, which ended the Russo-Japanese War. He was especially effective in personal diplomacy with Tsar Nicholas II.

In 1907 Meyer returned to the United States to become Roosevelt's postmaster general, a position from which he led unsuccessful fights for postal savings and extension of parcel post. In 1909 President William Howard Taft appointed him secretary of the navy and largely left Meyer alone to run the navy by himself. After spending nine months learning his job, Meyer instituted a reorganization scheme that profoundly affected the Navy Department. He reversed the trend toward staff control by creating a system of "aids" through which line officers would report directly to him, allowing line officers to assume control of all facets of the fighting fleet. He also increased retention of recruits for second and third enlistments by implementing a more humane system of discipline and augmented the efficiency of the fleet. Although the navy's budget was cut by $14 million during his four-year tenure, the number of vessels in commission during that same period increased 25 percent.

Retiring when Woodrow Wilson became president in March 1913, Meyer was the chief Republican critic of the Wilson administration's naval policies. In 1916 he joined the effort to bring Roosevelt back into the Republican party in hopes of reelecting him president. Meyer died at his home in Boston.

• Meyer's personal diaries are in the Manuscripts Reading Room Collections at the Library of Congress; his personal and much of his professional correspondence is at the Massachusetts Historical Society. Some of his diary entries and letters can be found in M. A. DeWolfe Howe, ed., *George von Lengerke Meyer: His Life and Public Services* (1920). See also Paolo E. Coletta, "George von Lengerke Meyer, 6 March 1909–4 March 1913," in *American Secretaries of the Navy*, vol. 1: *1775–1913*, ed. Coletta (1980), and Wayne A. Wiegand, *Patrician in the Progressive Era: A Biography of George von Lengerke Meyer* (1988).

WAYNE A. WIEGAND

MEYER, Henry Coddington (14 Apr. 1844–27 Mar. 1935), manufacturer, editor, and public health reformer, was born in Hamburg, Germany, the son of American citizens Meyer Henry Meyer, a merchant, and Anne Maria Price. He attended private schools in Montclair, New Jersey, and Tarrytown and Yonkers, New York. Meyer's parents refused to allow the seventeen-year-old Henry to enlist at the start of the Civil War, but in the summer of 1862 Meyer, then age eighteen, joined the Second New York Cavalry (the Harris Light) as a private. In 1863, at Brandy Station, he received a saber wound but returned to duty. In February 1864 he joined the Twenty-fourth New York Cavalry as a second lieutenant. He fought through Pope's Campaign and in the battles at the Wilderness, Fredericksburg, Gettysburg, Spottsylvania, North Anna River, Cold Harbor, and Petersburg, Virginia. At Petersburg, on 17 June 1864, following an assault on Confederate forces, Meyer, by then a captain, received his second wound. He had returned to the battlefield to assist a fellow officer who had been wounded, but Meyer, suffering from malaria, was unable to carry the officer to safety. After turning the officer over and clearing his mouth to let him breathe, Meyer headed back to find help, only to be shot in the back. After spending eleven months in the hospital recovering from his wounds, Meyer received a brevet Major commission and was discharged for his disability. For his "distinguished gallantry in action," which saved his fellow officer's life, Meyer was awarded the Congressional Medal of Honor in 1899.

Before the Civil War Meyer had worked under his uncle, T. B. Coddington, at the New York Shot and Lead Company, making shot and lead pipe. After recovering from his war wounds, Meyer returned to the company, where his uncle had by then become president. In 1868 he married Charlotte English Seaman; they had two children. That same year Meyer formed the Henry C. Meyer Company, to manufacture plumbing fixtures. In about 1880 Meyer, having become occupied with other matters, brought Samuel F. Sniffen on board as a partner and renamed his company the Meyer-Sniffen Company. Meyer retired from the manufacturing business in 1883, though he continued as a stockholder and director.

In 1877 Meyer and several family members suffered from an outbreak of diphtheria. Finding that the outbreak had been the result of a buildup of sewer gases in his house, Meyer designed a venting system to solve the problem. Disappointed by the lack of information available on plumbing and public health, in December of that year Meyer founded the *Plumber and Sanitary Engineer*. He intended this monthly magazine "to make every plumber a sanitary engineer" by discussing "the fullest and latest information on all matters pertaining to the Plumbing, Gas and Steam Fitting Trade." Meyer hired journalist Charles F. Wingate as editor and called on the likes of Dr. John Shaw Billings, Colonel George E. Waring, and American Society of Civil Engineers president J. J. R. Croes to contribute to and advise on the magazine's contents. When Wingate retired in 1881, Meyer took over as editor until his own retirement in 1901. The magazine underwent a series of name changes over the years and was known as *The Engineering Record, Building Record, and the Sanitary Engineer* in 1902, when Meyer sold the magazine to James H. McGraw, founder of the McGraw-Hill Publishing Company. In 1917 the magazine, by then a weekly named *Engineering Record*, merged with *Engineering News* to form *Engineering News-Record* (*ENR*). *ENR* and its predecessors became among the most widely distributed engineering magazines in the United States.

Meyer had founded his magazine largely out of his interest in improving plumbing and housing conditions, but he was not content with merely circulating information. Throughout his years as owner and editor, he used the magazine to push for reform in legislation dealing with housing, plumbing, and a variety of safety issues in engineering. In 1879 Meyer sponsored a contest for architects, asking them to design an improved tenement house. These overcrowded, dark, and unventilated urban dwellings, with little or no plumbing and electricity, had become notorious public health threats. The magazine received over 200 submissions, and the local newspapers reported on the contest. The lobbying that followed this publicity soon led New York state to pass the 1879 Tenement Act, which restricted the area taken up by a building to 65 percent of a standard 25 by 100-foot lot, as opposed to the 90 percent previously allowed. Meyer's next reform effort focused on the poor state of plumbing in much of New York City. The 1881 New York City plumbing laws required all buildings in the city to conform to the standards Meyer had laid out in his publication and for the first time gave the health authorities control over the plumbing and drainage of buildings in the city. Meyer then lobbied in favor of replacing the stoves then commonly used to heat railroad cars. The stoves had caused a number of deadly fires in the wooden railway cars, and Meyer advocated developing a steam heating system to replace them. His efforts to demonstrate the feasibility of heating railway cars by steam led to New York becoming the first state in the country to legislate against the use of car stoves. Though Meyer was not trained as an engineer, in 1885 the members of the American Society of Civil Engineers elected him a fellow of their society (their highest membership status) in recognition of his contributions to the field of sanitary engineering.

Meyer's first wife died in 1915, and in 1921 he married her cousin, Mrs. Gertrude Seaman Merrill, in Montclair, New Jersey. He died in Montclair after a brief illness.

• Meyer's *Plumber and Sanitary Engineer*, which he founded in 1877, went through nine name changes, to become *ENR* in 1987. The intervening names are *The Plumber and Sanitary Engineer*; *Sanitary Engineer*; *Sanitary Engineer and Construction Record*; *Engineering and Building Record and the Sanitary Engineer*; *Engineering Record, Building Record and the Sanitary Engineer*; *The Engineering Record, Building Record and the Sanitary Engineer*; *Engineering Record*; and *Engineering News-Record*. Meyer also wrote three books, one in each of the main areas of his career: *Water Waste Prevention* in 1884 or 1885, on the importance of conservation of resources; *Civil War Experiences: Under Bayard, Gregg, Kilpatrick, Custer, Raulston, and Newberry, 1862, 1863, 1864* (1911), on his military service; and *The Story of the Sanitary Engineer* (1928). One of the most thorough and useful secondary sources on Meyer's life and career is Henry Coddington Meyer, Jr., "Henry Coddington Meyer, F. Am. Soc. C. E.," *Transactions of the American Society of Civil Engineers* 101 (1936): 1719–21. See also, E. J. Mehren, "Development of the *Engineering Record*," *Engineering News-Record* 78 (5 Apr. 1917): 2–5. A newspaper obituary is in the *New York Times*, 28 Mar. 1935.

SARAH K. A. PFATTEICHER

MEYER, Karl Friedrich (19 May 1884–27 Apr. 1974), pathologist, was born in Basel, Switzerland, the son of Theodor Meyer, a merchant, and Sophie Lichtenhahn. He attended universities in Basel, Zurich, Munich, and Bern, studying zoology, comparative anatomy, and veterinary medicine. At the recommendation of Paul Langerhans, Meyer began his thesis work on paratuberculosis infection in cattle under the direction of Wilhelm Kolle, a former pupil and assistant to microbiologist Robert Koch. When Meyer received his doctorate in 1909 in veterinary medicine from the University of Zurich, he followed Kolle's advice about pursuing an academic career. Although Kolle could not find him a paid position in any of the Swiss universities, he was able to arrange an appointment for Meyer as a pathologist at a newly created institute for the study of animal infections in South Africa. A dispute with the institute's director, Swiss veterinarian Arnold Theiler, prompted Meyer's return to Switzerland in 1910. There he learned of a vacancy for an assistant professor of pathology at the University of Pennsylvania School of Veterinary Medicine.

In Philadelphia Meyer rose quickly through the ranks. He was promoted to full professor in 1911 and was also named director of the laboratory and experimental farm of the Pennsylvania Livestock Sanitary Board (with an increase in annual salary from $1,800 to $4,000). Meyer's abrasive personal style, especially his outspoken criticism of colleagues and students, led his mentor, physiologist Richard M. Pearce, to advise Meyer to pursue career opportunities in the West. In 1913, after much deliberation, Meyer accepted an appointment as associate professor of bacteriology and protozoology at the University of California, Berkeley. Before taking up his new post, he married Mary Elizabeth Lindsay; they had one daughter.

In 1915 physiologist George Hoyt Whipple invited Meyer to join the research staff of the newly established George Williams Hooper Foundation for Medical Research in San Francisco, an institution focusing on research involving tropical and exotic diseases. When Whipple accepted the deanship of the University of Rochester School of Medicine, he recommended that Meyer succeed him as director of the Hooper Foundation. After serving as acting director for three years, Meyer was named director, a position he retained from 1924 to 1954.

Meyer's research at the Hooper Foundation reflected his interests in both human and animal diseases and his concern about the transmission of animal diseases to human beings. Throughout his career he worked closely with public health authorities. At the request of the California State Board of Health, he conducted field surveys in 1915 of the incidence of malaria in the San Francisco Bay area. Together with his colleagues at the institute, from 1915 to 1920 and again in 1927 he made an extensive series of studies of a group of organisms (*Brucellae*) responsible for outbreaks of contagious abortion in cattle and for Malta fever in humans. Following reports of widespread disease among horses in California's San Joaquin Valley, Meyer worked from 1930 to 1933 to isolate the viral cause of western equine encephalitis. The use of methods introduced by Meyer in research on equine encephalitis led to the discovery of similar viruses, the causative agents of several forms of human encephalitis. In the 1930s, while researching an outbreak of psittacosis, a viral infection of birds, Meyer fell ill for several months with the disease. Before the advent of antibiotics, psittacosis was responsible for a number of deaths, including those of several laboratory workers. Meyer and his longtime coworker Bernice Eddy were able to trace the disease outbreak to sales of infected parakeets and parrots; they demonstrated that the disease, subsequently renamed ornithosis, occurred in many avian species. Meyer investigated several outbreaks of pneumonic plague in California and demonstrated a reservoir of plague bacillus infection in the state's wild squirrel and chipmunk populations. During World War II he served as a consultant to the U.S. armed forces, helping to mass-produce a vaccine to protect U.S. troops from pneumonic plague.

In 1919 Meyer began a career-long association with the California canning industry, a major economic force in the state. Repeated, in some cases fatal, outbreaks of botulism traced to olives canned in California threatened the state's packers. Approached by an industry association, Meyer outlined a research program to establish a scientific basis for the safety of canned olives and other processed foods. Although criticized for accepting industry money to fund botulism-related research, Meyer and his colleagues conducted comprehensive studies of the botulism organism and of methods to ensure that the manufacturing process adequately protected consumers from spoiled foods. In addition, Meyer pressed for legislation to require canners to process foods safely and conducted on-site inspections of canneries to see that regulations were enforced. His extensive work on the botulism problem enabled public health authorities in 1940 to report that since 1925 no outbreak of botulism had been caused by foods commercially processed in the United States.

In 1954 Meyer formally retired as director of the Hooper Foundation, but he remained active as an emeritus professor of experimental pathology for twenty years. After the death of his wife in 1958, he married Marion Lewis in 1960. He died in San Francisco.

Meyer's work on infectious disease earned him both professional honors and popular acclaim. In popular journals, he was celebrated as one of the courageous medical researchers risking disease and death in the name of science. Paul de Kruif, a chronicler of medical science, called him "a champion among microbe hunters." Meyer, who had earned a doctorate in philosophy from the University of Zurich in 1924 during a sabbatical leave, was the recipient of numerous honorary degrees for his work in infectious disease. His professional honors and awards included the Sedgwick Award from the American Public Health Association (1946), the Lasker Award from the Albert and Mary Lasker Foundation (1951), the Walter Reed Medal from the American Society for Tropical Medicine and Hygiene (1956), and the Jessie Stevenson Kovalenko Medal from the National Academy of Sciences (1961).

• The Bancroft Library at the University of California houses a collection of Meyer's papers, including an oral history memoir, "Medical Research and Public Health" (1976), and the transcript of a 1961–1962 taped interview with Meyer. Meyer's correspondence, including laboratory notebooks, can be found in the papers of the George Williams Hooper Foundation at the library of the University of California, San Francisco. The best source for Meyer's life, including a list of his publications, is a memoir by fellow virologist Albert D. Sabin, "Karl Friedrich Meyer," National Academy of Sciences, *Biographical Memoirs* 52 (1980): 269–331. Other useful accounts include Meyer's "Acceptance of the Walter Reed Medal," *American Journal of Tropical Medicine and Hygiene* 6 (1957): 341–46; James H. Steele, "Karl Friedrich Meyer," *Journal of Infectious Diseases* 129, supp. (1974): S1–S10; and Dan C. Cavanaugh, "K. F. Meyer's Work on Plague," *Journal of Infectious Diseases* 129, supp. (1974): S10–S12. A 1973 film interview with Meyer is available in the series Leaders in American Medicine, sponsored by the National Medical Audiovisual Center of the National Library of Medicine. An obituary is in the *New York Times*, 29 Apr. 1974.

SUSAN E. LEDERER

MEYER, Lucy Jane Rider (9 Sept. 1849–16 Mar. 1922), educator and Methodist deaconess, was born in New Haven, Vermont, the daughter of Richard Dunning Rider and his second wife, Jane Child, farmers. After a happy childhood in a loving and supportive family, she obtained her secondary education by alternately teaching and attending school. At the age of sixteen she held a teaching position in a high school in Brandon, Vermont. She spent another year with a French family in Canada and one teaching in a Quaker school for freedmen in Greensboro, North Carolina. Entering Oberlin College in September 1870 at age twenty-one, she was granted junior standing in recognition of her experience and knowledge. She graduated with an A.B. degree in 1872. While at Oberlin she met and became engaged to a young man who had dedicated himself to service as a medical missionary. In support of him and his vocation, after graduation she entered the Woman's Medical School of Philadelphia to become a doctor. During the winter of her second year, however, her fiancé died, and she left school, returning home to recover from the shock and to be with aging parents who needed her care.

There she directed her energy and talent to the Sunday school and soon became known in a wider circle through contributions to Methodist periodicals, especially the weekly lessons used by Sunday school teachers. In 1876 she became principal and taught natural science at the Troy Conference Academy in Poultney, Vermont. While there she copyrighted twenty "Whisper Songs" for children and published a book, *Real Fairy Folks: Explorations in the World of Atoms* (1887). She studied chemistry for a year at Boston School of Technology and then accepted an appointment as professor of chemistry at McKendree College in Lebanon,

Illinois, in 1879. Continuing her active interest in the Sunday school and Bible study, in 1880 she was chosen a delegate to the World's Sunday School Convention in London. Upon her return she resigned her position at McKendree College to become field secretary of the Illinois State Sunday School Association.

It was during this period of her life that she began to dream of establishing a school to train women for Christian service in home and foreign missions. A winter spent teaching Bible in Dwight L. Moody's Northfield Academy (1884-1885) put her in touch with the great evangelist and his work, but he declined to support her since he was committed to the work of Emma Dryer. In May 1885 she married Josiah Shelley Meyer, who was to become her partner in founding the Chicago Training School for City, Home and Foreign Missions. Theologically conservative, Josiah Meyer was working as secretary for the Chicago Young Men's Christian Association when they married. They had one child.

The Chicago Training School was formally opened on 20 October 1885 with four students. "Built from nickels," it grew steadily until it reached its peak enrollment of 256 in 1910. From its opening until their retirement in 1917, the Meyers had to assume responsibility for the support of the school. In time, deaconess homes for women in full-time Christian service were established in five cities, and Wesley Hospital and the Lake Bluff Orphanage were also created and operated by deaconesses. Lucy Rider Meyer also began publication of the *Message* as the organ of the Chicago Training School in 1886. It later became the *Deaconess Advocate* and was continued until 1914. Meyer completed the requirements for her M.D. degree from the Woman's Medical College of Northwestern University in 1887.

During the summer of 1887 several of the Chicago Training School's students remained in the city to complete the missionary work their curriculum required by doing social work among the city's poor. They received no salary but were allowed to live without cost in the school. That fall the first deaconess home was opened with Isabella Thoburn, a former missionary to India and the sister of Bishop James M. Thoburn, as housemother. The distinctive costume worn by Methodist deaconesses—a long black dress with white cuffs and collar and a black bonnet—was designed by Meyer. Official recognition of the office of deaconess, strongly advocated by Bishop Thoburn and others, was given by the General Conference of the Methodist church in May 1888. The Methodist Deaconess Association was organized by the Meyers in 1908. Because women were not allowed to serve as clergy, the deaconess movement provided recognition and status for those engaged in full-time Christian service within the church. They taught and worked with children, women's groups, in hospitals, and in settlement houses in inner city slums.

Other movements for women were being organized and supported by various groups, including a group of deaconesses led by Jane M. Bancroft under the Woman's Home Missionary Society. She and Meyer were to vie with one another for leadership in the deaconess movement for twenty-five years. Throughout this conflict, the Meyers remained committed to the idea that their work should have no corporate relation to any existing body but should be directly under the supervision of the church. Despite the fact that the General Conference of 1912 affirmed the right of the deaconess work under Meyer's direction to remain separate, the struggle for control continued. Partial resolution was achieved when the Board of Hospitals, Homes and Deaconess Work was formed in 1924. A single board charged solely with the oversight of deaconess work was not created until the Methodist church was formed by the union of the Methodist Episcopal church, the Methodist Episcopal Church South, and the Methodist Protestant church in 1939. Meyer was a delegate to three General Conferences of the Methodist Episcopal church, beginning in 1904. She died in Chicago.

The deaconess movement was a victory in the long struggle to give women recognition and status in the church. The vision and determination of persons like Lucy Rider Meyer and Jane Marie Bancroft were key to its existence. They provided educational opportunities and were role models for the women who worked in the slums, hospitals, and settlement homes as deaconesses.

• Meyer's own account of the deaconess movement is in Lucy Rider Meyer, *Deaconesses, Biblical, Early Church, European, American with the Story of How the Work Began in the Chicago Training School* (1892). Her work on the Sunday school movement is in Meyer and Nellie M. Carman, *Children's Meetings and How to Conduct Them* (1886). Isabelle Horton, *High Adventure: Life of Lucy Rider Meyer* (1928; repr. 1987), is Meyer's biography. Mary Agnes Theresa Dougherty, "The Methodist Deaconess: 1885–1919: A Study in Religious Feminism" (Ph.D. diss., Garrett Evangelical Seminary, 1979), is a scholarly version of the deaconess movement.

JAMES E. KIRBY

MEYER, Max Friedrich (15 June 1873–14 Mar. 1967), psychologist, was born in Danzig (now Gdansk), Poland, the son of Hermann Meyer, a goldsmith, and Sophie Luschnath. Meyer succeeded brilliantly at the local Gymnasium and was awarded free tuition when his family's declining fortunes threatened to terminate his education. As a child he developed a passion for music that later stimulated his interest in the psychology of hearing. At the age of sixteen he was deeply influenced by the work of Lazarus Geiger, an obscure philologist who held that all thinking was unverbalized speech—a notion that was later revived by American behaviorists.

In the spring of 1892 Meyer entered the University of Berlin. Lacking the means to support his education, he earned his board and tuition as a tutor. A seminar with Hermann Ebbinghaus convinced him to pursue studies in psychology. In 1894 Carl Stumpf replaced Ebbinghaus, who departed for Breslau. Stumpf's interest in music and psycho-acoustics attracted Meyer, who served as Stumpf's laboratory assistant until 1898. Meyer completed his doctoral work in 1896 under Stumpf, with the additional supervision of physicist Max Planck, who believed that a mathematical model of reality was possible. Meyer was also influenced by the positivism of Ernst Mach, who held that reality was perceived only through the sensations experienced by the immediate observer.

A falling out with Stumpf led to Meyer's dismissal from the laboratory at Berlin and his move to the University of London in the fall of 1898. Welcomed there by James Sully, Meyer stayed until the following spring. Through correspondence, Hugo Münsterberg, a native of Danzig who had been called to Harvard by psychologist William James, and Columbia psychologist James McKeen Cattell assured Meyer that he would be able to find a position in the United States. Arriving in April 1899 with only his meager savings, Meyer accepted an offer from G. Stanley Hall of an unpaid fellowship at Clark University. There he managed to develop the first version of his theory of music, which he presented at an 1899 meeting of the American Psychological Association in New Haven. His paper, however, received little notice, and owing in part to his unfamiliarity with American academic culture, he failed to make an impression on the inner circle of professional psychologists.

In 1900 Meyer became a professor of experimental psychology at the University of Missouri and, with the help of only occasional assistants, assumed sole responsibility for instruction in psychology. He nevertheless established a laboratory, constructing much of the apparatus himself. In 1904 he married Stella Sexton, one of his students; they had five children. Over the next thirty years, Meyer continued his studies of music and auditory function and authored several textbooks, which include *The Fundamental Laws of Human Behavior* (1911) and *The Psychology of the Other-One* (1922). These books, especially the former, established Meyer as an early proponent of behaviorism in America; some scholars see Meyer's first textbook as embodying the essentials of behaviorist psychology two years before the acclaimed founder of behaviorism, John B. Watson, published his views.

Meyer's behavioristic views, however, were never as radical as Watson's. Although he rejected the use of the introspective method in experimental psychology, Meyer never denied the existence of consciousness or the concept of mind, as did Watson. Moreover, Meyer's psychology, with its mathematical models of reality, had more in common with nineteenth-century German physics—especially that of Max Planck—than with American behaviorism, which had its roots in animal and comparative psychology. Even so, Meyer was part of a cohort of psychologists who provided a context for the acceptance, propagation, and ascendance of behaviorism in the United States in the years immediately preceding and following World War I. His only doctoral student, Albert Paul Weiss, went on to become one of behaviorism's most ardent supporters and helped develop a major program in applied psychology at Ohio State University.

Meyer's career at the University of Missouri came to an abrupt end in 1929 when a questionnaire that one of Meyer's undergraduates had developed for a class assignment came to the attention of a Missouri state legislator. The survey, which contained questions that related to undergraduate sexual mores, caused a political furor, and Meyer was suspended without pay. After a year at the University of Chile, in Santiago, Meyer returned and would have been reinstated had he not made his low opinion of the university's board of governors known in a public speech. Tried for insubordination, he was placed on permanent leave without pay. Meyer spent the next two years as a research professor at the Central Institute for the Deaf in St. Louis.

Despite his solid achievement, Meyer remained on the periphery of American psychology, in part, because of personal characteristics. Trained in the disputations style of the Prussian professoriate, he had difficulty accommodating himself to at least the appearance of collegiality that characterized American academics. The relative isolation of the University of Missouri also prevented him from establishing networks within the influential centers of the profession in the Northeast. Meyer's professional strains were not without their personal cost. In 1936 he and his wife of thirty-two years divorced.

From 1932 to 1940, Meyer was a visiting professor at the University of Miami. In 1950 he published *How We Hear: How Tones Make Music*, and well into his nineties he continued to publish articles on audition, learning, and emotion. Though isolated by temperament and circumstance from the mainstream of American psychology, Meyer made significant contributions to the historical development of thoughts on human behavior and the theory of hearing. He died in Miami.

• Meyer's unpublished autobiography and other bibliographical materials are in the Archives of the History of American Psychology at the University of Akron. Documents and articles from Meyer's Missouri years, including correspondence and transcripts relating to his dismissal, are in the University of Missouri Library's Special Collections and Western Historical Manuscript Collection, the University of Missouri Archives, and the State Historical Society of Missouri. The most thorough accounts of Meyer's career are Erwin A. Esper, "Max Meyer: The Making of a Scientific Isolate," *Journal of the History of the Behavioral Sciences* 2 (1966): 341–56, and "Max Meyer in America," *Journal of the History of the Behavioral Sciences* 3 (1967): 107–31. John M. O'Donnell, *The Origins of Behaviorism* (1985), contains a useful appraisal and provides a context for evaluating Meyer's work.

KERRY W. BUCKLEY

MEYERHOF, Otto Fritz (12 Apr. 1884–6 Oct. 1951), biochemist, was born in Hanover, Germany, the son of Felix Meyerhof, a Jewish merchant, and Bettina May. Early in Meyerhof's life his family moved to Berlin; there Meyerhof completed his secondary education at the Wilhelms Gymnasium. When he was sixteen Meyerhof contracted severe kidney disease, and during the months required for recovery he read extensively, particularly Goethe. Once ambulatory, Meyerhof traveled to Egypt with his cousin Max Meyerhof and spent four months recovering his strength and visiting the temples along the Nile. This time spent among the Egyptian antiquities stimulated an interest in archaeology that lasted throughout Meyerhof's life. With his health restored, Meyerhof continued his original plans to study medicine and, in accordance with existing German custom, he attended universities in Freiburg, Berlin, Strassburg, and Heidelberg. Meyerhof received his M.D. from Heidelberg in 1909. His interest at that time was in psychology and psychiatry, and his thesis, *Beitrage zur psychologischen Theorie der Geistesstorungen* (Contributions to a psychological theory of mental disturbances), was published in 1910. This was, however, not an indication of his future career. At about this time he also published a thesis on Goethe's methods for scientific studies. Meyerhof was attracted to Goethe's interest in a deeper meaning of nature. For three years after graduation, Meyerhof served as Ludwig Khrel's assistant in the medical clinic at Heidelberg, where he met Otto Warburg, who shifted his interest from psychiatry and psychology to experimental biological research, especially the oxidation of carbohydrates and the activation of oxygen in energy metabolism. Shortly thereafter, Meyerhof spent some time at the Zoological Station in Naples, Italy, working with Warburg. In 1912 Meyerhof joined the physiology staff at the University of Kiel, and one year later he was appointed lecturer in physiology. In 1914 he married Hedwig Schallenberg; they had three children. At Kiel, Meyerhof became interested in understanding carbohydrate metabolism, and in 1913 he gave his pioneering lecture describing for the first time the application of thermodynamics to cell (carbohydrate) metabolism. When Meyerhof began this metabolic work, it was known that carbohydrates were stored in the liver and muscle as glycogen and that glycogen and glucose are degraded through two pathways: an anaerobic pathway requiring no oxygen and an aerobic pathway requiring oxygen. The end product of the anaerobic route is lactic acid (lactate) in animals (alcohol in yeast), and carbon dioxide and water are the products of aerobic metabolism. Meyerhof studied carbohydrate breakdown in these processes by comparing oxygen consumption of cells, cellular heat production, and the mechanical work performed by the (muscle) cells. Meyerhof's research led him to conclude that the enzyme systems of animal and yeast cells are essentially the same, a finding that supported the biochemical unity of life.

During World War I Meyerhof served as a medical officer on the western front. After the Armistice he returned to the University of Kiel and continued his work on carbohydrate metabolism. He measured oxygen consumption and lactic acid production in the presence and absence of oxygen. These measurements indicated that in the absence of oxygen (anaerobic glycolysis) lactic acid is produced, but in the presence of oxygen only one-fifth of the lactic acid is oxidized to carbon dioxide and water. Meyerhof interpreted the finding to indicate that the energy generated in the cell by the oxidation process is used to resynthesize glycogen from the lactic acid.

Meyerhof was passed over for the chairmanship of physiology at Kiel. In 1923, however, he shared with A. V. Hill the Nobel Prize in physiology or medicine for his discovery of the fixed relationship between oxygen consumption and the metabolism of lactate by muscle. After the award of the Nobel Prize, Meyerhof was appointed professor at the Kaiser Wilhelm Institute in Berlin. There he continued his work on the metabolism of carbohydrate. While carrying out these studies, he trained or influenced a number of prominent biochemists, including future Nobel Laureates Hans Krebs, Fritz Lipmann, and Severo Ochoa.

In earlier studies Meyerhof had concluded that lactic acid furnished the energy for muscle contraction. After Karl Lohmann discovered adenosine triphosphate, Meyerhof realized that this high-energy phosphate—and not lactate—supplied the energy for muscle contraction.

In 1929 Meyerhof was named director of the Department of Physiology at the Kaiser Wilhelm Institute for Medical Research in Heidelberg. There he continued his work on the anaerobic breakdown of sugars, and by 1932 Meyerhof and his colleagues had isolated and studied the numerous enzymes involved in the degradation of glucose to lactic acid. The anaerobic pathway of carbohydrate degradation is now known as the Embden-Meyerhof pathway.

Disturbed by the Nazi takeover of Germany, Meyerhof and his wife left Germany for Switzerland in 1938. They then moved to Paris. In 1940, when the Germans invaded Paris, Meyerhof and his wife narrowly escaped capture by fleeing across the Pyrenees mountains into Spain. Finally Meyerhof reached the United States, where through the Rockefeller Foundation and the work of A. N. Richards, he was awarded a position as research professor of physiological chemistry at the Medical School of the University of Pennsylvania in Philadelphia. He continued to work on carbohydrate metabolism, spending his winters at the University of Pennsylvania and his summers at Woods Hole in Massachusetts. In 1944 Meyerhof was stricken with a severe heart attack, which incapacitated him for ten months. He became a U.S. citizen in 1946 and a member of the National Academy of Sciences in 1949.

Throughout his life Meyerhof was interested in archaeology, philosophy, art, and poetry. A great concern of his was the effect of science on society. He died at the King's Court Apartments in West Philadelphia.

• Complete summaries of Meyerhof's life are in the memoir by David Nachmanson et al. in National Academy of Sciences, *Biographical Memoirs* 34 (1960): 152–82, in Tyler Wassen, ed., *Nobel Prize Winners* (1987), and in *Biographical Encyclopedia of Scientists*, ed. John Daintith et al., vol. 2

(1981). A good summary of some of Meyerhof's work is in Hans Adolf Krebs, *Otto Warburg, Cell Physiologist, Biochemist, and Eccentric* (1981). References to numerous obituaries written throughout the world and a list of most of Meyerhof's significant publications are included in J. C. Poggendorph, *Biographische Literaresches Handeworterbuch der Exacten Naturwissenschaften* (1959).

DAVID Y. COOPER

MÉZIÈRES, Athanaze de (26 Mar. 1719–2 Nov. 1779), soldier and colonial administrator, was born Athanaze Christofe Fortunat Mauguet de Mézières in Paris, France, the son of Christophe Claude Mauguet, sieur de Mézières, an eccentric mathematician and reputable lawyer, and Marie Antoinette Clugny. After Athanaze's father died in 1734, Madame de Mézières married the marquis de la Haye de Riou, a man of great means who had amassed his fortune partially from his business activities as a slave trader from Saint-Malo and partially from his social contacts at the court of Louis XV, king of France. Conscious of his privileged position in French society, Athanaze de Mézières grew up in the comfort of wealth. At the Collège de Beauvais, where he pursued his advanced education, he was exposed to the whole fabric of the French legal system and excelled in Latin poetry and rhetoric. Trained as a lawyer, Mézières emerged from his upbringing as a brilliant and discerning intellectual whose development was to be irremediably shaped by the Spirit of the American frontier.

Inextricably tied to his family background, Mézières's future could only be enhanced by a military career. On 28 November 1738 he left for Louisiana as a cadet in the army of the king of France. He arrived at New Orleans on board *La Somme* on 23 May 1739. Mézières was twenty years old. He was immediately drafted in a military campaign against the English-allied Chickashaw, whom he fought over a period of eight months under the command of Lieutenant Vieuchatel. He quickly learned as many as six Indian dialects in which he became very proficient during the course of his life on the American frontier.

Over the forty years that he spent in Louisiana, crossing over to Texas, Mézières had many opportunities to leave the colony and settle back in France. But he preferred the difficult challenges of the American frontier to the elegant circles of French society, and in 1740 he established himself at the trading post of Natchitoches on the Texas-Louisiana border. In 1746 Mézières married the very young Marie Petronilla Feliciano de Saint-Denys, daughter of the charismatic Louis Juchereau de Saint-Denys, founder and commandant of Natchitoches. They had one child. When Marie Petronilla died in 1748, Mézières returned to France, where he stayed for a year. In 1749 Mézières came back to Louisiana aboard *La Charmante Esther*. Promoted to the rank of *lieutenant-reforme* with half pay, Mézières lived at Natchitoches with his second wife, Dame Pelagie Fazende, the daughter of a well-to-do New Orleans family. They had seven children.

In 1754 he was promoted to the rank of *capitaine-reforme*. In a military report dated 1758, French military authorities referred to Mézières as "a man of great wisdom, capable of undertaking the most delicate missions mostly when the Spaniards are involved. He speaks Spanish fluently." In 1759, as a retired officer from the French infantry, Mézières was cashing a pension of some 720 livres a year. By 1769 he had become a rich and successful planter settled at Natchitoches, where he owned substantial property, livestock, and slaves.

In 1773 Mézières returned to France to attend the royal wedding of his sister Madame de Montesson to the duc d'Orléans. He was promoted to the rank of lieutenant colonel and was knighted in the Royal and Military Order of Saint-Louis, an honor bestowed only to French Catholic officers who had distinguished themselves in the service of their country.

France had long yielded any political authority on Louisiana to the kingdom of Spain, however, and Mézières had since then responded to the needs of Spain on the American frontier. In 1769 the Spanish Crown appointed him to the position of lieutenant governor of Natchitoches with administrative command over a very large region that included the Red River Valley, northern Texas, Arkansas, and Oklahoma. He took official possession of the Natchitoches commandancy in early January 1770. His appointment was crucial to the Spaniards who had for years experienced endless difficulties with Indian tribes along their northern American frontier, which stretched from Mexico to Louisiana. It was in 1769 that Spanish Indian policy in northern Mexico was redesigned to fit the new frontier demands. Mézières was specifically instructed by the Spanish Crown to establish peace with the Indian tribes of northern Texas formerly controlled by French traders and to win their allegiance over to Spain. Trade in furs, skins, oils, and tobacco as well as a variety of other crops made Natchitoches the strategic port of entry to the whole of the Southern Great Plains. With access to the Plain tribes, namely the Comanche, the Lipan, the Wichita, and other surrounding tribes, Natchitoches was very active in trading with Indians. It was therefore paramount to Spanish interests that peace with the Indians be established and maintained. It was also crucial that the administration of justice on the American frontier be handled firmly and fairly according to the general laws of the country. Using his diplomatic skills and linguistic abilities, Mézières successfully managed relations with American Indian tribes, and trade flourished. He summoned Indian chiefs to Natchitoches, made treaties with them in the name of Spain, issued trading licenses, supervised the supply and price of commodities, cut off trade with hostile tribes, and expelled outlaws living among the Indians. From 1770 thru 1778 he made numerous expeditions through northern Texas and to San Antonio. The wealth of information that he provided in his letters and reports to the Spanish administration of the period remains an invaluable source of historical documentation on the Spanish Borderlands of the New World.

Within the broader context of frontier justice, beyond his efforts to manage Indian policy for the benefit of Spanish interests in the American Southwest, Mézières proved his ability to transcend the fears and insecurities that crippled the colonial slaveholding society of his time in which it was affirmed by political theorists that black slaves had no natural right to liberty and justice. In his capacity of both judge and post commandant, Mézières was routinely called on to legislate on situations that involved interaction between masters and slaves, whites and blacks. During a famous trial at Natchitoches in 1770, he extended equal protection under the law to a black slave suspected of assaulting his white supervisor. Because he firmly believed in the universal natural right to equal justice, he saw no difficulty in applying in his court the concept of due process of law to all regardless of status or color. The concept of due process, however, had yet to be articulated in 1770, let alone applied to black slaves on American soil. In the history of the American Southwest, Mézières was a pioneer who believed in moral progress that to a great extent was the symbol of the New World. In 1779 the Spanish administration appointed Mézières governor of Texas. On his way to assume his new political responsibilities, he died in San Antonio.

• Athanaze de Mézières's reports and letters referring to his activities in Louisiana and Texas were published in 1914 by Herbert Eugene Bolton in a two-volume edition titled *Athanase de Mézières and the Louisiana-Texas Frontier, 1768–1780.* The most complete biographical assessment of Mézières is in Jacqueline R. Crosby, "Frontier Justice on the Texas-Louisiana Border in the Year 1770" (Ph.D. diss., Univ. of Texas at Arlington, 1988). This work contains an extensive bibliography with collection and individual manuscript sources as well as printed sources.

JACQUELINE R. CROSBY

MEZZROW, Mezz (9 Nov. 1899–5 Aug. 1972), clarinet and sax player and promoter, was born Milton Miserow (or Misirow) in Chicago, the son of middle-class Jewish parents whose names are not available. Although reared in a well-to-do family on the north side of Chicago, Mezzrow says in his autobiography that he first learned to play the saxophone while serving a jail term in 1917. The story may be more colorful than true, yet it is not inconsistent with the authenticated events one finds in the life of this fascinating jazz figure. Whatever may have been the timing and site of his earliest musical studies, he achieved professional notoriety primarily through his organizational energies and from frequent ventilations of an ever-ready opinion. Eddie Condon was perhaps both accurate and charitable in his autobiography *We Called It Music* (1947) when he referred to Mezzrow's professional image as that of "a hanger-on."

During the early 1920s Mezzrow jobbed in small bands around his hometown, his grand musical inspiration coming, he claimed, while listening to some of the contemporary jazz giants on Chicago's south side. In his own words, it was "the night I really began to live." Thereafter, on occasion, he played dates with members of the famed Austin High School Gang, which included cornetist Jimmy McPartland and clarinetist Frank Teschemacher, and he made recordings as early as 1927 with both the Chicago Rhythm Kings and the Jungle Kings. He fronted his own small group at the Martinique Inn, at Indiana Harbor (just southeast of Chicago), during the summer of 1924. For a short period in 1928 he organized and fronted for a larger "hot band," this one taking wing under the incomparable name (even for the period) of the Purple Grackle Orchestra.

Before making his first trip to Paris in 1929, Mezzrow moved to New York City, performing frequently as a substitute sideman with the Ben Pollack Band and playing occasional dates with Condon. While in Paris he led a quartet at L'Ermitage Muscovite, returning to New York City that same year to tour with Red Nichols. But Mezzrow's playing usually took a backseat to his managerial drive. Throughout his career he revealed a distinct flair for organizing people into playing dates and recording sessions, usually with musicians whose talents and eventual fame eclipsed his.

In addition to earnings gained from producing record dates for Brunswick and Victor-Bluebird between 1933 and 1938, it was widely reputed that his principal source of income came from marijuana sales to colleagues. For this highly profitable—if illegal—sideline, he was convicted and incarcerated in the prison on Riker's Island from 1940 until 1942. His drug-dealing was immortalized in song (yet apparently never committed to paper or wax) by singer Alberta Hunter. The beginning of her lyric went something like "The Mezz dreamed 'bout a reefer, five foot long; / A mighty mezzrole, but not too strong."

Mezzrow interacted professionally with most of the legendary jazz artists of his time as co-performer and/or as contractor. His career through the 1940s was stunningly filled with performance dates and recording sessions incorporating such talents as Teschemacher, Muggsy Spanier, McPartland, Russell, Joe Sullivan, Art Hodes, Jess Stacy, Bud Freeman, Lionel Hampton, Dave Tough, Gene Krupa, Jack Teagarden, Fats Waller, and Sidney Bechet. In 1945 Mezzrow organized his own record label, called "King Jazz," but that enterprise dissolved in February 1948 when he organized a new band and launched a European tour that would terminate at the jazz festival in Nice, France. (It is not known whether this venture was the cause or effect of the King Jazz label's demise.) He subsequently began spending more time in France, recording and touring with small combos whose personnel he hired from the United States. Like many of his black colleagues, in 1950 he became an expatriate, settling in Paris, which would become his home base until his death. In 1951 he was playing with Claude Luter at 'Au Vieux Columbier in Paris, then toured an all-star band that included Zutty Singleton through western Europe. Other tours covering the same territory (always touted as "All-Star," usually a mere euphemism for "imported from the U.S.") kept him busy and solvent from 1952 until 1955. He continued making successful guest appearances throughout western Europe into the 1960s, although his actual performing was reduced drastically toward the end of that decade.

Mezzrow devoted more and more of his time to his tireless (and often selfless) promotion of jazz as the native American art form, with special attention given to his two all-time musical heroes, Bechet and Louis Armstrong. He championed New Orleans–style jazz throughout his life, helping in the process to preserve the memory of some of the pioneers who otherwise might have been lost to posterity. He often cited the Original Dixieland Band's recording of "Livery Stable Blues" as an epochal memento of his own musical life, as well as a singularly sufficient justification for his stylistic convictions. He died at the American Hospital in Paris.

Few chroniclers of his era, with the notable exception of Mezzrow's fellow promoter and friend, critic Hughes Panassié, reported positively about his musicianship or his playing. Exceedingly, Panassié pronounced Mezzrow the greatest white jazz clarinetist of the time, "perhaps even the greatest musician of the white race." (And Panassié was not unfamiliar with Pee Wee Russell, Benny Goodman, and Artie Shaw, or from another era, J. S. Bach.) In recordings one hears Mezzrow's crudely shrill tone executing patterns that, although appropriate, lack fluency and evident conviction. The larger line and the fresh new melodic slant seem to have eluded him.

Mezzrow felt a sincere and deep affinity for blacks and for the black culture of urban America, remaining especially critical of the unjust plight suffered by those whose creative genius was not adequately recognized and appreciated. He frequently characterized himself as a "voluntary Negro," and he was continually pushing to dissolve racial barriers wherever he found them. During 1937 he led a racially mixed band called "The Disciples of Swing," playing such hard-core jazz havens in Harlem as the Uproar House and the revered Savoy Ballroom. The autobiography he wrote with Bernard Wolfe in 1946, *Really the Blues*, echoes the lifelong obsession he felt, as he put it, to "turn myself black." That volume is the most direct conduit to his ideas and the major events of his colorful life.

Recordings of Mezzrow's playing are hard to find. Reissues in historical series such as the Smithsonian tend to pick players of higher star status, and the sessions Mezzrow produced with those star talents have been passed over in favor of more choice material from other sessions. Some of the 78 rpm Victor-Bluebird and Brunswick pressings from the 1930s can be found in antique stores of large cities and in the collections of some libraries, such as the Brand Library in Glendale, California. As a leader as well as performer he is represented on Riverside 9348 of 1960, and he plays on the Bessie Smith session for Columbia Records (14095D) recorded in 1925.

• More than passing mention of Mezzrow is made in Eddie Condon's autobiography mentioned above, and his name invariably turns up as a supporting player in historical accounts of jazz in New York and Europe between 1920 and 1960, in John Chilton's *Who's Who of Jazz* (1970), Ralph Gleason's *Celebrating the Duke* (1975), and Gunther Schuller's *The Swing Era* (1989). An obituary is in *Down Beat*, 12 Oct. 1972.

WILLIAM THOMSON

MIANTONOMO (c. 1610?–Sept. 1643), joint chief of the Narragansett tribe of the western shore of Narragansett Bay. His name is also rendered as Miatunnomoh or Miantonomy; the stress is on the penultimate syllable. He was joint chief with his uncle Canonicus and soon became the tribe's spokesman. Roger Williams called him Canonicus's "marshal and executioner."

He first appears on record on 3 August 1632, when he visited Boston with his wife and some retainers. Since the founding of Massachusetts in 1630, it had become the great power of the region that Miantonomo was eager to conciliate. As he represented the largest tribe of the region, some 30,000 strong, Boston's Puritans were also eager for his friendship. On this first visit they made much of him.

Such harmony was immediately strained by Puritan intentions to dominate and conquer. By 1636 Puritan policies had so angered the Pequots, western neighbors of the Narragansetts, that they approached the latter with a proposal to forget former disputes and attack the English. The alliance was not concluded, however. Indeed, historian Neal Salisbury thinks that the Narragansetts listened to the Pequots only "to dissuade them from fighting the English" (p. 213).

Further difficulties occurred in 1636, when Massachusetts's influential trader Captain John Oldham was killed at Block Island, then tributary to the Narragansetts. Miantonomo was summoned to Boston for explanations. Clearing himself and Canonicus of blame, he was nevertheless required to cede Block Island and to agree to a treaty of alliance. The treaty is among key documents that later vanished. It seems to have specified Narragansett alliance against the Pequots in a campaign for which they would be rewarded with Pequot captives and hunting rights in Pequot territory.

In the same year Roger Williams fled the Puritans to found the town of Providence Plantations at the head of Narragansett Bay. Canonicus and Miantonomo gave him leave to settle and in 1638 conveyed the land by the first written deed in Rhode Island history. The chiefs seem to have reasoned that they needed political advice, and they welcomed more dissident Englishmen after Williams. When another heresy hunt drove magistrate William Coddington and followers from Massachusetts, Miantonomo and Canonicus deeded the island of Aquidneck (Rhode Island) on 24 March 1637. (Newport stands there now.) The price was forty fathoms of white wampum, and the right of the chiefs to make the sale is attested by their agreement to give twenty hoes and ten coats to compensate the evicted Indian residents.

Besides Massachusetts, the Narragansetts had to cope also with the colonists of Connecticut, who patronized Chief Uncas's Mohegans, enemies of the Narragansetts. This complicated the 1637 conquest of the Pequots undertaken by both Connecticut and Massachusetts. Narragansett warriors fulfilled their treaty with Massachusetts by joining the campaign against the Pequots and were horrified by the massacres perpetrated by the English. Narragansett appeals "that it would be pleasing to all natives, that women and children be spared" (*Collections of the Rhode Island Historical Society* 3: 138) and "that such Pequots as fall to them be not enslaved . . . but . . . be used kindly, have houses, and goods, and fields given them" (*Publications of the Narragansett Club* 6: 34) were brushed aside. Overriding Miantonomo's treaty with Massachusetts, Connecticut's men made their own assignment of Pequot captives, meting eighty to Miantonomo and an unstated but apparently greater number to their own ally Chief Uncas. Furthermore, in 1638 Connecticut imposed a "treaty" under which Miantonomo could not war against Uncas without appealing to "the English Inhabiting the Jurisdiction of the River of Connecticut . . . and *they* are to decide" (emphasis added; *Collections of the Rhode Island Historical Society* 3: 177–78). Annual wampum tribute to Connecticut also was imposed, and the Narragansetts were ordered to keep out of former territory of the Pequots. This treaty overrode the earlier 1636 agreement in which Miantonomo was not permitted to war against Uncas without the permission of Massachusetts.

Miantonomo thus found himself caught between the two colonies' contradictory demands. He had no reason to trust anything but threats from either colony. Plymouth had cut off the Narragansetts' Wampanoag tributaries, Massachusetts had stripped them of Block Island and its Indians, and Connecticut had taken the fruits of their campaigning against the Pequots. As Roger Williams reported in May 1637, "The Nanihiggonsicks are at present doubtfull of Realitie in all our promises" (*Winthrop Papers*, vol. 1, p. 411).

In 1642 tensions came to a head, provoked by the arrival on Narragansett Bay of a new group of dissidents, the followers of Samuel Gorton, known by the Indians as "Gortonoges." Miantonomo deeded to them "Shawomet Neck" (12 Jan. 1642), on which they established their town of Warwick. Four Rhode Islanders opposed to the Gortonoges put themselves under Massachusetts's protection. John Winthrop, Sr., confided that "the place was like to be of use to us," denied the right of Miantonomo to sell it, and declared that it rightfully belonged to subchiefs Pumham and Saconoco, who also accepted Massachusetts's protection. Miantonomo was warned off and accepted the coup.

Miantonomo could no longer tolerate Uncas's Mohegans killing his men hunting in former Pequot territory. He appealed to Boston for leave to war against Uncas and was told he might do as he wished. Notably, Boston ignored the treaty imposed by Connecticut in 1638, in the same way that Connecticut had ignored Massachusetts's treaty of 1636. Because of rumors that Miantonomo plotted a general uprising of all the tribes except Uncas's, he was summoned to Boston in 1643 to answer these charges. Although he managed to clear himself with the magistrates, he was charged with having gone to Long Island to recruit support and was reported to have made a speech there that, whether accurate or not, reflects the dilemmas of New England's Indians. As reported by Long Island chief Waiandance, Miantonomo urged the Indians to "be one as the English are, or we shall soon all be destroyed" and lamented the colonists' destruction of the land and its bounties.

With Massachusetts's sanction, but necessarily violating Connecticut's treaty, Miantonomo marched against Uncas but lost the battle and was taken captive. His men raised a large ransom for him to be delivered to "the English," and Uncas took him to the commissioners of the New England Confederation meeting at Hartford. They decided he must die; but, without legal grounds to execute him themselves, they ordered Uncas to kill him in Uncas's jurisdiction rather than in theirs, carefully appointing an agent to see it done. Although some historians contend that the commissioners merely permitted Uncas to act, the general opinion is that Miantonomo was the victim of judicial murder.

• Puritan sources were written by men who were Miantonomo's enemies and ruthless war propagandists bent on conquest. Thus Massachusetts's treaties with Pequots and Narragansetts have vanished, and Connecticut's treaty is found only in the *Collections of the Rhode Island Historical Society*. Other sources include the *Publications of the Narragansett Club* and *Rhode Island Colonial Records*. A convenient compilation is in *The Correspondence of Roger Williams, 1629–1682* (1988), ed. Glenn W. La Fantasie. Some data must be sought in John Winthrop, Sr., *The History of New England From 1630 to 1649* (1690), ed. James Savage, 2d ed. (2 vols., 1853), and in *The Winthrop Papers*, ed. Allyn B. Forbes (5 vols., 1929–1947), but must be used warily because of the anti-Indian tendentiousness of these writings. Samuel G. Drake, *The Biography and History of the Indians of North America*, 11th ed. (1856), is the best nineteenth-century account. Francis Jennings, *The Invasion of America* (1975), is the most comprehensive modern account, but Neal Salisbury, *Manitou and Providence* (1982), is more equable and fully reliable. Vol. 15, *Northeast*, of the Smithsonian Institution's *Handbook of North American Indians* (1978) has much anthropological material and Wilcomb E. Washburn's excellent article on New England's Indian wars.

FRANCIS JENNINGS

MICHAEL, Arthur (7 Aug. 1853–8 Feb. 1942), organic chemist, was born in Buffalo, New York, the son of John Michael, a real estate investor, and Clara Pinner. Michael attended public and private schools in Buffalo and also received private instruction in chemistry. He planned to enter Harvard, but an illness prevented this, and he never received a college education. In his youth he developed interests in chemistry and mountain climbing, and the family's affluence enabled him to become expert in both through private instruction, a home laboratory, and vacations in mountainous regions of Europe and North America. He made the first ascent by anyone of two peaks in the Canadian Rockies. In 1871 the family went to Europe for an extended stay. From 1872 to 1879 Michael did research with Europe's best chemists: Robert Wilhelm Bunsen at the University of Heidelberg, August Wilhelm von Hofmann at the University of Berlin, Charles Adolphe Wurtz in Paris, and Dmitri Ivanovich Mendeleev in St. Petersburg. In 1881 Tufts College appointed him professor of chemistry. The school was not a center of research, and Michael used his own money to buy apparatus, books, and journals and to pay salaries for assistants. He won international fame at Tufts as a chemist equal to the best in Europe.

Helen Cecilia de Silver Abbott, an affluent Philadelphian, came to work with Michael in 1887. She had already gained a reputation in plant chemistry for her studies on the chemical constituents of plants in relation to morphology and evolution and also had careers as a talented pianist and writer. They married in 1889 and went on an eighteen-month world tour. The marriage produced no children.

In 1891 Michael accepted a professorship at newly established Clark University, but he found that the task of building a department of chemistry restricted his freedom and resigned after several months. The Michaels established a private laboratory on the Isle of Wight where they did their research until 1894, when they returned to Tufts. Helen Michael died in 1904.

Michael left Tufts in 1907, continuing his research in a home laboratory in Newton Center, Massachusetts. In 1912 Harvard appointed him professor of organic chemistry with no teaching duties and no obligation to set foot on campus. He supervised Harvard doctoral students in his laboratory until his retirement in 1936.

Michael was the most productive and original American organic chemist between 1880 and 1920. His research career began with studies in organic synthesis. In 1879 he synthesized the glycosides helicin and salicin. The latter, a fever-reducing agent in willow bark, was the first naturally occurring glycoside to be synthesized, and his method became a standard route to this class of carbohydrates. Another important synthetic method was his 1883 preparation of pyrimidines, the organic bases present in the nucleic acids found in all organisms. His best-known synthesis, the Michael reaction, came in 1887. It was the first general method for converting an organic compound having a carbon-carbon double bond into a saturated bond of a higher carbon series. A 1959 review of the reaction cited 1,045 references to its use, a testimony to its being one of the most commonly employed and versatile synthetic procedures in organic chemistry. A variety of complex molecules can be synthesized by this method, and there is a long list of biologically active natural products that have been produced by its use, including cholesterol, reserpine, and many alkaloids.

Michael's work in synthesis, however, was not his primary concern. He sought the basic principles of his science, and for over three decades he introduced original concepts and formulated a theoretical system. A lasting contribution was his interpretation in 1899 of substitution reactions as involving a preliminary addition reaction to form a "polymolecule," an unstable intermediate that then split into the final products. This notion became an integral part of organic chemistry as chemists found compelling evidence for such intermediate and mobile combinations in many types of reactions.

By the 1880s structural theory had achieved spectacular success. The theory, however, was only a pictorial and mechanical one. To give it a foundation in physical chemistry, Michael introduced the thermodynamic concepts of free energy and entropy into organic chemistry. He converted the second law of thermodynamics (the entropy of the universe tends toward a maximum) into a chemical principle (every chemical process tends toward the maximum neutralization of free energy) and interpreted organic reactions in terms of changes in free energy and entropy. His system, which he applied in detail to many types of reactions, did not gain wide acceptance. In his time, no way had been determined to measure the preferred thermodynamic course of a reaction, and there was no adequate understanding of the nature of chemical bonds and how such bonds formed. Thus, his theory was not too relevant to contemporary chemists, and he was almost alone in applying his way of reasoning.

Michael was most influential as a vigorous critic of current thinking, especially concerning the stereochemical system of the European chemists Jacob van't Hoff and Johannes Wislicenus. During the 1870s and 1880s they developed a theory of the three-dimensional arrangement of atoms in molecules. Applying this to molecules with a double bond, they proposed the existence of cis-trans isomers, isomers with different spatial arrangements about the double bond, and also assumed that all additions to the double bond were cis additions. Michael, in a long series of papers from 1888 to 1908, revealed the inadequacy of the scheme and between 1910 and 1920 reached the conclusion that all the spatial configurations assigned by the assumption of cis addition had to be reconsidered, since both cis and trans addition may occur depending on the reactants and conditions. His studies laid the basis for doubt about theories of spatial arrangements of molecules and for the need of fresh investigations.

After 1930 Michael was not very active in research. He immersed himself in his hobbies, maintaining the beautiful gardens on his estate and his art collections. He was an expert on oriental art; his home contained centuries-old paintings on screens and scrolls, jade carvings, lacquered chests, bronzes, and porcelains from China and Japan. He bequeathed this collection to the Albright-Knox Art Gallery in Buffalo. He also had a major collection of early American silverware that went to the Smithsonian Institution.

Michael was a little-known person. He was reluctant to attend meetings, present papers, or popularize his views, and he refused an award from the American Chemical Society because he did not want the publicity that went with it. He did accept election to the National Academy of Sciences in 1889. He died in Orlando, Florida. Although childless, he was concerned with the welfare of children, and after disposal of his collections and large scientific library he bequeathed the residue of his estate to Buffalo institutions for the care of blind, crippled, and needy children.

Michael was a liberating influence on American organic chemists when they were still under apprenticeship to European masters. He had tried to link physical and organic chemistry in his theorizing, but until the development of electronic theories of chemical bonding, the two fields remained separate. With the appearance of physical organic chemistry in the 1930s, thermodynamics and chemical bonding came together to produce a deeper understanding of organic reactions. American chemists were leaders in the new field, and they referred to Michael as the "grandfather" of physical organic chemistry, the man who foreshadowed the rise of this new field.

• Michael wrote no books. There are no archival collections and no extensive biographical studies. A bibliography of his nearly 300 publications is included in Louis F. Fieser, *National Academy of Sciences, Biographical Memoirs* 46 (1975): 331–66. Fieser et al., *Harvard University Gazette*, 22 May 1943, pp. 246–48, contribute a memorial essay. A brief but valuable portrait by a chemist who personally knew Michael is W. T. Read, *Industrial and Engineering Chemistry* 22 (Oct. 1930): 1137–38. Helen Abbott Michael, *Studies in Plant and Organic Chemistry and Literary Papers* (1907), contains reprints of her publications and a biography based on her diaries, which provides information on Michael. For analyses and evaluations of Michael, see D. Stanley Tarbell and Ann Tracy Tarbell, *Essays on the History of Organic Chemistry in the United States* (1986), pp. 45–54, and Albert B. Costa, "Arthur Michael: The Meeting of Thermodynamics and Organic Chemistry," *Journal of Chemical Education* 48 (Apr. 1971): 243–46. An obituary is in the *New York Times*, 12 Feb. 1942.

ALBERT B. COSTA

MICHAELIS, Leonor (16 Jan. 1875–8 Oct. 1949), medical scientist, was born in Berlin, Germany, the son of Moriz Michaelis, a small-business owner, and Hulda Rosenbaum. He received a humanistic education in a Berlin Gymnasium before entering the University of Berlin in 1893 to study medical science. He received his M.D. degree in 1896. He had a talent for seizing upon important concepts and developments in the medical sciences and translating them into clear and forceful prose. This talent became evident soon after he completed his education. His first book, a treatise on embryology for medical students, underwent nine German editions and translations into several languages after its appearance in 1898.

Also in 1898 Michaelis became an assistant to Paul Ehrlich at the Institute for Serum Research in Steglitz, a Berlin suburb. Given the task of studying the staining of cells with new synthetic dyes, he discovered in 1898–1899 the specific staining of cellular mitochondria by Janus green. His second book was a 1902 treatise on the chemistry of histological dyestuffs.

In 1900 Michaelis became a physician at a Berlin hospital. In the time free from clinical duties he established a laboratory in the hospital and in 1904 published a study on the tumors of the urinary bladder, which led to a position at the Institute for Cancer Research in Berlin. One year later he married Hedwig Philipsthal. They had two children.

In 1905 the University of Berlin appointed Michaelis to a professorship but with no salary, research funds, or laboratory. Because of the widespread anti-Semitism in German universities, he believed that an academic career was hopeless and instead joined the staff of another Berlin hospital. The next seventeen years were his most prolific in research. Working in a hospital laboratory, he completed a remarkable series of papers in biochemistry and biophysics and became a pioneer and leading figure in the application of physical chemistry to biomedical problems. He made major contributions to the kinetics of enzyme-catalyzed reactions, laid the foundation for the understanding of enzyme-substrate interaction, and pioneered the exploration of protein behavior in living systems. By 1920 he was perhaps the most influential medical scientist in Germany. Yet he never obtained an important academic or research position.

In 1922 Michaelis decided to leave his homeland. He accepted a professorship in biochemistry at the medical school in Nagoya, Japan, where he initiated the research that would bring him to the United States, on the surface membrane of cells as a semipermeable membrane. His studies accounted for the physical behavior of the large and small molecules present within cells. Jacques Loeb at the Rockefeller Institute for Medical Research in New York was so impressed that he invited Michaelis to the United States. In 1926 Michaelis became a lecturer at Johns Hopkins and in 1929 a member of the Rockefeller Institute and director of a new laboratory for the application of physical chemistry to biology and medicine. He also became a member of the Woods Hole Marine Biological Laboratory in 1928 and lectured there for ten years.

Michaelis's American career included several major achievements, foremost being his discovery of free radicals in biological oxidations. During the 1930s he proposed that biological systems oxidize with the transfer of two electrons in two one-electron steps. The notion of entities having unpaired electrons was so daring that his contemporaries reacted in disbelief, and the leading American journals of chemistry and biochemistry rejected his paper. He sought more convincing evidence and in 1938 found the paramagnetism associated with free radicals in several biological oxidations. Since then the role of free radicals in biological oxidation has been widely studied with free radicals shown to have important consequences for health and disease.

A relatively minor project in 1933 had as an unintended consequence the creation of a new American business enterprise. Michaelis investigated how a fungus parasite could digest hard proteins such as keratin, the protein of hair. He found that keratin needed its disulfide bonds to retain its crystalline structure. By chemically reducing these bonds with thioglycolic acid, keratin became a noncrystalline, soluble protein. The American cosmetic industry used his findings to create the cold permanent wave process. Michaelis had no patent and gained no recognition or financial reward for what became a major commercial success.

Michaelis continued to work at the Rockefeller Institute after his retirement in 1940, discovering a free radical form of vitamin E and also how the body stores iron in the form of a protein-iron complex that releases iron when needed for the creation of new red blood cells. He was elected to the National Academy of Sciences in 1943.

Michaelis was cosmopolitan and knowledgeable about science, art, and world affairs. His interests included mountain climbing, photography, and, above all, music. He was a composer and an accomplished pianist, capable of improvising in the style of many composers and delighting audiences by requesting a melody and then creating a complete sonata at the piano in perfect classical form. He died in New York City.

Michaelis was a remarkable scientist who made important contributions as an embryologist, histologist, bacteriologist, oncologist, biophysicist, biochemist, and colloid chemist. His influence stemmed both from his efforts to apply physical chemistry to biology and how this approach revealed the mechanisms underlying biological phenomena and from the educational quality of his many books.

• Michaelis papers are in the Rockefeller University Archives, Rockefeller Archive Center, Tarrytown, N.Y. Some of his books are in English translation: *The Dynamics of Surfaces* (1915), *The Effect of Ions in Colloidal Systems* (1925), *Practical Physical and Colloidal Chemistry for Students of Medicine and Biology* (1925), *Hydrogen-Ion Concentration, Its Significance in the Biological Sciences and Methods for Its Determination* (1926), *Permeability and Electric Phenomena in Membranes* (1927), and *Oxidation-Reduction Potentials and Their Physiological Significance* (1930). He wrote a semipopular review of his discovery of free radicals in "Fundamentals of Oxidation and Respiration," *American Scientist* 34 (1946): 573–96. The Michaelis entry in the *Biological Memoirs of the National Academy of Sciences* 31 (1958): 282–321 is an autobiography with an addendum by his co-workers, Duncan MacInnes and Sam Granick, and a bibliography of his nearly 500 publications. E. S. Barron, another co-worker, edited *Modern Trends in Physiology and Biochemistry* (1952), which consists of Woods Hole lectures dedicated to Michaelis, including a biographical essay by Barron. His career at the Rockefeller Institute is traced by George Corner, *A History of the Rockefeller Institute* (1964). Obituary notices are in the *New York Times*, 10 Oct. 1949, and *Nature*, 25 Feb. 1950, pp. 299–300.

ALBERT B. COSTA

MICHAELIUS, Jonas (1584–?), first ordained clergyman in New Netherland, was born in Grootebroek, in the province of North Holland, the Netherlands, the son of Jan Michielssz, a minister of the Reformed Dutch church. His mother's name is unknown. After the death of the father in 1595, the Michaelius family moved to nearby Hoorn, where Jonas attended the Latin school and distinguished himself sufficiently to win a scholarship at age fourteen to the University of Leiden. For six years, at the theological college, he studied theology, philosophy, languages, mathematics, rhetoric, dialectics, dogmatics, and homiletics, leaving the university in 1604 and subsequently accepting appointment as minister of a Reformed church in Brabant.

For twenty years, from 1605 to 1625, Michaelius served various Reformed churches in the province of North Holland. He married in about 1612 and had three children. His wife's name is unknown. In 1624 Michaelius asked to serve a church in San Salvador in Brazil, which the Dutch had recently captured from the Portuguese. En route it became known that the Portuguese had successfully retaken Brazil, and the fleet turned instead to Fort Nassau, in the Dutch colony of Guinea on the coast of West Africa. Here Michaelius ministered for about two years.

At age forty-three Michaelius accepted a call to New Netherland, arriving on 7 April 1628 after an arduous passage, with his pregnant wife, then age fifty, and their two daughters. The couple's son had remained in the Netherlands for his schooling. Soon after their arrival, Michaelius's wife died, leaving him bereft but stoic—and hopeful that "neither through this nor through any other trial I shall lose the courage I need so much in this ministry, in order that my work, or rather His, may be successful."

Michaelius found both success and trials in the wild frontier town of New Amsterdam. His primary objects in New Netherland were to further the "glory of God in the building up of his kingdom and the salvation of many souls," and his first achievement was to gather the settlers into an organized church. In August 1628 he reported to a colleague in Amsterdam that, at the first administration of the Lord's Supper in the little trading community, fully fifty communicants, both French-speaking Walloons and Dutch, participated. Though the settlers were, for the most part, "rather rough and unrestrained," Michaelius found them responsive to the church's teachings and filled with love and respect toward himself. He ministered to the congregation with the assistance of two elders and occasionally a deacon.

By 1630, however, the church, which had at first grown in "numbers and piety," was threatened by a "nefarious enterprise of wicked men"—the civil authorities who governed New Netherland for the West

India Company, which owned it. Director General Peter Minuit, Michaelius reported to authorities at home, was a slippery and dishonest man, "most unworthy of his office." Immoral and cruel, according to the minister, Minuit ruled an iniquitous council comprised of the "most pestilent kind of people"—cheating, wicked, and self-interested. When Michaelius took it upon himself to admonish Minuit, who was also an elder in the consistory, Minuit responded by turning Michaelius's congregation against him and plotting "indefatigably to disperse all the fruit of . . . [his] ministry and . . . labours."

Part of the problem between Michaelius and the civil authorities was that Michaelius had interpreted his mission in the New World as including the conversion of the Native Americans—a people he regarded as "entirely savage and wild, strangers to all decency," uncivil, stupid, ungodly, devil-worshiping, and thoroughly wicked. His plans for converting them involved separating children from their parents and placing the children under the instruction of an "experienced and godly schoolmaster" until such time as they could speak, read, and write Dutch and understand the fundamentals of Christianity. Michaelius's hope was that the children would ultimately be returned to their own nation to spread the knowledge of Christianity. Indian parents, however, were "very loth" to be separated from their children in this fashion. Minuit and his council also opposed Michaelius's plan, for they feared antagonizing the company's partners in the lucrative fur trade.

Thwarted by Minuit in the two directions in which he had advanced—the establishment of a harmonious congregation in New Amsterdam and his missionary crusade among the native peoples—Michaelius became increasingly bitter. To impress on the directors of the West India Company in the Netherlands the gravity of his charges against Minuit and his council, Michaelius, in addition to writing to them, secured permission in 1632 to return to Amsterdam and appear before them in person. But the directors seem not to have appreciated either his concerns for their interests or his well-taken criticisms of their own policies, which were to favor the fur trade to the neglect of the agricultural development of the rich wilderness they controlled. Though the Classis of Amsterdam recommended him for another tour of duty in the New World in 1637 and again in 1638, Michaelius was rejected by the governing board of the West India Company for the post, probably because he had stirred up trouble with Director General Minuit. He subsequently served a Dutch Reformed church in Yarmouth, England, returning to the Netherlands in 1641 to a Reformed pulpit in Zeeland. No further mention is made of him in any historical records located to date.

• Primary materials relating to Michaelius may be found in *Ecclesiastical Records of the State of New York*, vol. 1 (7 vols., 1901–1915). His biographer is Albert Eekhof, whose work *Jonas Michaelius: Founder of the Church in New Netherland* (1926), includes Michaelius's three surviving letters, which provide important information about life in New Netherland. Other useful sources of information about his life and times are Eekhof, *De Hervormde Kerk in Noord-Amerika, 1624–1664* (2 vols., 1913); J. Franklin Jameson, ed., *Narratives of New Netherland, 1609–1664* (1909); and I. N. Phelps Stokes, *The Iconography of Manhattan Island, 1498–1909* (6 vols., 1915–1928).

FIRTH HARING FABEND

MICHAUX, André (7 Mar. 1746–Nov. 1802), botanist, was born at Satory, the royal estate adjacent to Versailles, France, where his father, also named André Michaux, was employed as overseer. His mother's name is unknown. His early formal education consisted of four years at a boarding school after which he was instructed by his father in the practical aspects of horticulture and botany. Both parents were dead by the time Michaux was twenty, and he and his younger brother jointly managed the Satory estate. He married Cécile Claye, daughter of a prosperous farmer, in 1769, but she died shortly after the birth of their only child, François-André Michaux.

A sympathetic and influential friend, Louis-Guillaume Lemonnier, physician to the king and professor at the Jardin du Roi in Paris, became aware of Michaux's unusual talent for the naturalization of exotic plants (the cultivation of plants so that they will maintain themselves and reproduce in areas in which they are not native) and encouraged Michaux in the study of botany. He introduced Michaux to Bernard de Jussieu, who found a position for him at the Trianon gardens. In 1779 Michaux moved to Paris and lived near the Jardin du Roi (Jardin des Plantes after the Revolution), where he met André Thouin, the chief gardener, also a skilled naturalizer of plants. In 1780 he went on a botanical tour in the Auvergne with Jean-Baptiste de Lamarck and Thouin.

Two years later Michaux received a commission to undertake a trip to Persia. He made a dangerous trek through Turkey and Mesopotamia (then part of the Ottoman Empire) and traveled into the comparative safety of the northern provinces of Persia as far as the Caspian Sea. He continually sent back seeds and specimens to Lemonnier and on his return in 1785 brought back rich plant and natural history collections.

The French government, concerned about the dwindling supply of good timber for the navy, appointed Michaux in 1785 to visit North America in search of suitable trees that could be cultivated in France. Traveling with his young son and Pierre-Paul Saunier, a gardener from the Jardin du Roi, Michaux arrived at New York on 13 November 1785. He had been expressly instructed to set up a nursery from which seeds and seedlings could be shipped to France, and, by special permission, he acquired land for the purpose in 1786 near Hackensack, New Jersey. On a visit to Philadelphia, he met William Bartram and William Hamilton and saw their gardens. He went south in the following year with his son and established a second nursery at Charleston, South Carolina, which was to be as much of a home as he ever had in

North America. He and his son explored the southern Appalachians and early in 1788 set out on a three-month trip through Spanish Florida. At the end of the year he again explored the area of Oconee County, South Carolina, and Georgia.

In mid-January 1789 Michaux went to the Bahamas, returning to Charleston with a collection of more than 1,500 trees and seeds from about sixty species. After that he and his son visited the mountains of Carolina on their way to Philadelphia. The fall of the Bastille on 14 July and the ensuing revolution portended difficulties for Michaux in obtaining funds from France to support his work, but he continued to make journeys on his own resources. He sent his son back to France for further education at the end of the year or at the beginning of the new year.

In April 1790 Michaux visited Cumberland Island, the largest of the Sea Islands, off the coast of southeast Georgia. In the following year the Comte d'Angiviller, his chief supporter, fled France. In the last week of May 1792 Michaux set out from Philadelphia to Canada almost as far as Hudson Bay, the longest and most arduous of his expeditions, arriving back in Philadelphia on 8 December. There he conferred with Thomas Jefferson about a possible expedition to the West by way of the Missouri River, and funds were raised by the American Philosophical Society for it. Before Michaux could leave, Edmond-Charles Genet, the new minister plenipotentiary from France, arrived in Charleston and preempted Michaux's trip to the West by proposing that he undertake a different trip. Genet sent him to Kentucky and Tennessee with the object of encouraging American settlers there to join General George Rogers Clark in an attempt to subvert the Spanish holdings in Louisiana. President George Washington opposed this project and requested the recall of the controversial ambassador. The proposed trip up the Missouri River was canceled.

Michaux made further trips to the Carolina mountains in 1794 and in the following year to the Mississippi River, returning in April 1796 for the last time to Charleston. Since he had exhausted his own finances and had not received any money from the French government for some time, he decided to abandon further exploration and return to France.

On the way back Michaux's ship was wrecked off the Dutch coast. He himself nearly lost his life, but almost all his collections were washed up on the shore and survived. He was discouraged to find that the greater number of the 60,000 trees and seeds that he had shipped to France over many years had been given to aristocratic friends of the king and queen and that only a small proportion had found their way into the royal park at Rambouillet. He was received with honor nevertheless by the revolutionary government, but he saw no possibility of its funding his return to collect in America again. On 18 October 1800 he sailed with Nicolas Baudin's expedition to Australia. He left ship at Mauritius on 15 March 1801 and proceeded to Madagascar to conduct further botanical explorations. Not long after he arrived there, he succumbed to fever in November 1802.

Michaux's manuscripts on the oaks and on the flora of North America were seen through the press by his son, possibly with the help of Claude Richard. They were published in Paris as *Histoire des chênes de l'Amérique* in 1801 and *Flora Boreali-Americana* in 1803, both illustrated by Pierre-Joseph Redouté. *Flora Boreali-Americana* was the first major work to attempt to cover the whole area of the new republic as then constituted, and both works are landmarks in the botany of North America. Michaux described nearly a thousand different species of North American plants and introduced a large number of American trees into France. Among the trees Michaux introduced to the United States are the crape myrtle, the chinaberry, the silk tree, and the ginkgo or maidenhair tree. His name is commemorated in *Michauxia campanuloides*, a Mediterranean plant, and in *Quercus michauxii*, an American oak.

Michaux's journal reflects that he was warm and sociable, a person who had the "grace," in the words of Henry and Elizabeth Savage, to move "from weeks in the forest in the company of Indian guides to the elegant society of a president, a governor, or an ambassador, at ease wherever his mission led him."

• The American Philosophical Society in Philadelphia has André Michaux's manuscript botanical journal in North America, 1787–1796, in nine volumes, and microfilms of documents from the Bibliothèque Nationale, the Archives Nationales, and the Jardin des Plantes, Paris. Selections from the journal, edited by C. S. Sargent, are in the *Proceedings of the American Philosophical Society*, vol. 26 (1889). The only full-length biography is *André and François André Michaux* by Henry Savage, Jr., and Elizabeth J. Savage (1986). The most detailed bibliography is in the Morton Arboretum's *André and François-André Michaux* (1981). An interesting uncompleted manuscript at the Bibliothèque Centrale of the Muséum National d'Histoire Naturelle in Paris, written by Léon Rey, "Deux botanistes français aux Etats-Unis: Les missions de Michaux père et fils (1785–1806)" (c. 1950), provides a history of the introduction of American trees into France by father and son.

IAN MACPHAIL

MICHAUX, François-André (16 Aug. 1770–23 Oct. 1855), plant explorer and silviculturist, was born at the royal estate at Satory, next to Versailles, France, the son of André Michaux, then overseer of the estate, and Cécile Claye, daughter of a local farmer. His mother died shortly after his birth. Little is known of his early education, but he appears to have been brought up by an aunt. In 1785 he accompanied his father to North America on a royal commission to explore the forests for trees that could be grown in France. Though the elder Michaux sometimes took his son on his journeys, he generally left him to look after the nursery that he had established near Charleston, South Carolina, in 1786.

Michaux returned to France for further education in 1790. He matriculated in medicine and after graduation, most probably from the old Medical School (now known as René Descartes University), spent time studying botany at the Jardin des Plantes. His father returned to Paris in 1796 but left again on the Baudin voyage to Australia in 1800. Michaux began to seek an opportunity to continue his father's work in North America. With the support of Jean Chaptal, minister of the interior, he sailed for America and arrived at Charleston, South Carolina, on 9 October 1801. He had been instructed to close down the nursery at Charleston for economic reasons, and he sent back to France those seedlings he thought worthy of cultivation. A New Jersey nursery established by his father had also been slated for closure, but a compromise was worked out so that Pierre-Paul Saunier, who had accompanied Michaux and his father to America, could continue to operate it on his own.

In the spring of 1802 Michaux toured the forests of New Jersey with David Hosack and also visited Hosack's newly established Elgin Botanic Garden in New York. From there he made an extended visit to Philadelphia, where he met William Bartram and saw William Hamilton's fine collection of trees at Woodlands. He then made a journey through Pennsylvania, Kentucky, and Tennessee before returning to Carolina, and he met on the way many of his father's old acquaintances. From this trip he produced *Voyage à l'ouest des monts Alléghanys*, which was published in Paris in French in 1804 and published in London the year after in three different English versions. He returned to France at the end of 1803 to organize the shipments of plants and seeds that he had sent back and to make a series of reports on his work. Clearly by then he had formed the idea of producing a major work on the trees of North America.

In the meantime he devoted himself to a detailed report on American trees, *Mémoire sur la naturalization des arbres forestiers de l'Amérique septentrionale*, published originally in the *Mémoires de la Société du Département de la Seine* (1805) and published separately in the same year. The report caused considerable interest. The French government accepted his recommendation to send someone to America to continue the shipment of trees and seeds and appointed Michaux to the task, as he no doubt had hoped. He was in Paris until late January 1806 and then sailed for Charleston on 5 February. Three days out of Bordeaux his ship was seized by an English man-of-war, and he was taken prisoner. When his captors realized that he was a botanist, they treated him with respect and put him ashore at Bermuda. There he was permitted to make a survey of the natural history of the islands before being freed to continue his journey. He arrived in America in the middle of June 1806.

In the late summer he made a trip through western New York, Pennsylvania, and northeastern Ohio. In the spring of the following year he visited Maine and all the Atlantic states and later in the year made an expedition to Lake Champlain. The records of his travels during 1808 are scanty, but in September of that year he visited South Carolina and Georgia and set out again to traverse the states on the west side of the Alleghenies. He then announced his imminent return to Paris to work on his proposed book. Before he left he arranged to carry out commissions for his friends in North America including dealings with booksellers in Paris.

Returning to Paris in November 1808, he began work on *Histoire des arbres forestiers de l'Amérique septentrionale*. The first edition appeared in Paris in three volumes between 1810 and 1813. As early as 1811 there was talk of an American edition to be published by Samuel Bradford, the Philadelphia publisher, but when his business failed Michaux had the English edition published in Paris in 1817–1819 under the title *The North American Sylva, or a Description of the Forest Trees, of the United States, Canada and Nova Scotia*. In 1820 Michaux moved to the country at Vauréal, not far from Paris. He was having difficulties with his sight and decided to cut back his business ventures with American correspondents.

In 1828 Michaux accepted the position of administrator of the Harcourt estate in Normandy and, about that time, he married his housekeeper, Marguerite Guierdet, a cousin, thirty-one years his junior. They had no children. On 9 January 1830 Michaux wrote to John Vaughan, secretary of the American Philosophical Society, his most faithful American correspondent, that he was disturbed to learn that Scottish philanthropist William Maclure was about to publish an American edition of the *Sylva*. Maclure had purchased the copper plates of the *Sylva* (from paintings by Pierre-Joseph Redouté and Pancrace Bessa) from Michaux in 1824 with the intention of producing an American edition but had apparently not consulted the author on his plans. When Maclure joined Robert Owen's utopian community at New Harmony, Indiana, in 1826 he took the plates with him and there set about organizing the printing of the work. There were many delays, and the new edition was not published until 1841–1842, by which time Maclure was dead. This is the rarest of all editions of the *Sylva*, and it is unlikely that Michaux ever saw it or even learned of it, as most of the copies were destroyed in a fire. In 1832 Michaux informed Vaughan that he was planning a legacy to the American Philosophical Society, a gift that was intended to contribute to the promotion of agriculture and silviculture in North America. Among the results of the gift were a series of influential forestry conservation lectures by Joseph T. Rothrock, professor of botany at the University of Pennsylvania, given in Philadelphia over a period of fifteen years beginning in 1877; the establishment of a grove of oak species at the Morris Arboretum at Chestnut Hill, Pennsylvania, in 1953; and the purchase of books on agriculture and forestry for the society's library.

Michaux spent the years 1833–1848 in extensive planting of the estate at Harcourt, which contains the first established public arboretum in France (1851); it is still functioning today. Vaughan died in 1841, and Michaux's ties with the United States began to dwindle so that he probably was not aware of the three volumes of the supplement to the *Sylva* by Thomas Nuttall, published in Philadelphia between 1842 and 1849, or of the later Philadelphia editions of the combined work. Michaux died at Vauréal, reportedly after a day spent directing the planting of American trees. Elias Durand, who met him and wrote a biographical notice of him, describes him as modest, simple, and unaffected, with the manners of a country gentleman.

Michaux ably continued the work that his father had begun, displaying the same botanical skills. His contributions to the study of the trees of North America were considerable, and his *Sylva* remained the major work on the subject until the end of the century, when Charles Sprague Sargent's *Silva of North America* began to be published. Through his legacy to the American Philosophical Society and his own writings, he played a significant role in the establishment of American forestry and forest conservation.

• Michaux's papers are in the American Philosophical Society, Philadelphia; the Academy of Natural Sciences of Philadelphia; and in the Archives Nationales and the Muséum National d'Histoire Naturelle, Paris. The only full-length biography is *André and François André Michaux* by Henry Savage, Jr., and Elizabeth Savage (1986). The most detailed bibliography is *André and François-André Michaux* by Ian MacPhail (1981). An interesting uncompleted manuscript by Léon Rey is at the Bibliothèque Centrale of the Muséum National d'Histoire Naturelle, Paris. It is entitled "Deux botanistes français aux États-Unis: Les missions de Michaux père et fils (1785–1806)" and provides a history of their introduction of American trees into France.

IAN MACPHAIL

MICHAUX, Lewis H. (4 Aug. 1885–25 Aug. 1976), bookseller and black nationalist, was born in Newport News, Virginia, the son of Henry Michaux and Blanche Pollard. Some uncertainty about his birthdate exists because his death certificate from the New York Vital Records Department lists it as 23 August 1884. Before coming to New York, Michaux worked variously as a pea-picker, window-washer, and deacon in the Philadelphia church of his brother, Solomon Lightfoot Michaux. According to Edith Glover, his secretary while a deacon, Michaux started selling books in Philadelphia with an inventory of five. When he founded his bookstore in 1932 in Harlem, he still had only a few books with him, including *Up from Slavery*, plus a bust of Booker T. Washington. Michaux initially sold books from a wagon, then moved to a store on seventh Avenue (later renamed Adam Clayton Powell Jr. Boulevard).

Sleeping in the back of his new shop, Michaux quickly realized the necessity for a bookstore in Harlem. "You couldn't find 15 to 20 books by black people," he said (*New York Times* obituary). When the bookstore first opened, his daily receipts were often less than a dollar; when Michaux retired they totaled up to $1,500 per day and the National Memorial African Bookstore had become a Harlem landmark.

Michaux called his bookstore, which was to become the largest in Harlem, the "House of Common Sense and the Home of Proper Propaganda" and installed a sign over it reading, "Knowledge is power; you need it every hour. Read a book."

Michaux's bookstore attracted customers and visitors from all over the world, including fellow black nationalist Malcolm X, Kwame Nkrumah (later the first president of Ghana), W. E. B. Du Bois, Langston Hughes, Joe Louis, Eartha Kitt, and Louis Armstrong. The store became a landmark for black scholars and for anyone who was interested in literature by or about African Americans, Africans, Caribbeans, and South Americans. Michaux almost single-handedly operated his bookstore for forty-four years and increased his inventory to 200,000 volumes, making it the largest in the nation devoted entirely to subjects concerning blacks and Africa. Professor John H. Clark of Hunter College called the bookstore an "intellectual haven." Michaux influenced and advised many people of all ages, white and black. He encouraged average customers to begin home libraries and invited those who could not afford to buy books to sit down and read them without charge. "The ambition of our people was to make ends meet," he once said in response to the difficulty in getting Harlemites to read (*New York Times*, 31 Aug. 1976). This aspect of African-American life, it was recalled at his eulogy, led Michaux to observe, "The way to hide something from the black man is to put it in a book."

In 1968 Michaux's store was moved from Adam Clayton Powell Jr. Boulevard to West 125th Street to accommodate the State Harlem Office Building, despite strong protests by Michaux and the community. In 1974 the store was closed after additional conflict with state authorities over its location.

Active in the black nationalism movement in Harlem from the 1930s to the 1960s, Michaux served as leader of the African Nationalists in America, backed Marcus Garvey's back-to-Africa movement, picketed in Harlem to promote black business, and protested the United Nations' actions in Zaire (then the Republic of the Congo) in 1960–1964. He also sat on the advisory board of the *Liberator* (established in 1961), a magazine that published the early work of many now-famous black authors and critics, such as LeRoi Jones, James Baldwin, Langston Hughes, Ishmael Reed, Ossie Sykes, and Clebert Ford. Michaux deplored the term "Negro." He felt that it was a derogatory term used for slaves and that it denied African Americans their heritage. He preferred to use "black man." In addition, despite his brother's career as an evangelist and his own upbringing, Michaux shunned the church, claiming it robbed him of his individuality and saying, "No white God answers no black prayers. The only lord I know is the landlord, and I don't have to pray for him, he comes every month for the rent" (*New York Times* obituary).

Michaux was married to Bettie Kennedy and had one son. The first of three annual Lewis H. Michaux Book Fairs was held in May 1976, just three months before his death in the Bronx, New York. In 1978 Ishmael Reed and Toni Morrison were the first recipients of the Lewis H. Michaux Awards, sponsored by the Studio Museum in Harlem.

Practical, outspoken, and self-reliant, Michaux was known as the world's greatest seller of books. He actively worked to understand himself as well as other blacks worldwide.

• The Schomburg Center for Research in Black Culture of the New York Public Library holds an extensive collection of taped interviews, photographs, and published articles from sources such as the *New York Amsterdam News*, *Jet*, the *New York Times*, the *New York Daily News*, and the *New York Daily Challenge*. Obituaries are in the *New York Times*, 27 Aug. 1976, and *Publishers Weekly*, 6 Sept. 1976, p. 18.

BARBARA KRALEY YOUEL

MICHAUX, Lightfoot Solomon (7 Nov. 1884–20 Oct. 1968), radio evangelist, was born in Newport News, Virginia, the son of John Michaux, a fish peddler and grocer, and May Blanche. Lightfoot, whose ancestry was African, Indian, and French-Jewish, spent his formative years in Newport News among Jewish and white gentile merchants on Jefferson Avenue, the main commercial street where the Michauxs lived in quarters above the family's store. He attended the Twenty-second Street School, quitting after the fourth grade to become a seafood peddler. Impressed with the town's commercial atmosphere, he aspired to be a successful businessman. While engaged in one business venture, he met Mary Eliza Pauline, a mulatto orphan. They married in 1906; the couple had no children of their own but helped raise Michaux's two young sisters.

During World War I, Michaux obtained government contracts to furnish food to defense establishments. With the profits from his enterprises he moved his business to Hopewell, Virginia, in 1917. Finding no churches in that wartime boom town, he and his wife joined with a Filipino evangelist to found a church there. Michaux's wife subsequently convinced him to accept the call to preach, and in 1918 he was licensed and ordained in the Church of Christ (Holiness) U.S.A. He returned to Newport News in 1919, went into business with his father, and launched a tent revival. The first 150 of Michaux's converts formed a congregation within the Church of Christ denomination. In 1921 the Michaux congregation seceded from the Church of Christ to establish an independent church, calling it the Church of God. This church, along with its other related operations, was incorporated under an umbrella grouping known as the Gospel Spreading Tabernacle Association. In 1922 Michaux and several of his members were arrested for singing on the streets of Newport News during early morning hours while inviting townsfolk to join the church. When Michaux was fined, he unsuccessfully appealed to the Virginia Supreme Court, contending that his actions were based on a directive from God. In 1924 he began to establish branch churches in cities along the East Coast as he followed members who had migrated north to find jobs during the postwar recession.

Michaux began his radio ministry in 1929 at station WJSV in Washington, D.C., and became famous as a radio evangelist. The broadcast moved to the Columbia Broadcasting System (CBS) in 1932, the eve of radio's golden era. As a result of the radio program's syncopated signature song, "Happy Am I," Michaux became known from coast to coast and overseas as the "'Happy Am I' Preacher." His aphorisms and fundamentalist-like sermons of hope and good neighborliness caught the attention of millions. His wife, an exhorter and the premiere broadcast soloist, was a regular on the radio program. Michaux's radio program was so popular that American and foreign dignitaries flocked to his live, theatrically staged radio broadcasts. The British Broadcasting Corporation contracted with him for two broadcasts in the British Empire, in 1936 and 1938. Booking agents and moviemakers offered him contracts. In 1942 he collaborated with Jack Goldberg to make one commercial film, *We've Come a Long, Long Way*.

During the Great Depression, Michaux used his radio pulpit to offer free housing and employment services to the black and white indigent, and he invited the hungry to sell copies of the church's *Happy News* paper in exchange for meals in the Happy News Cafe. After President Herbert Hoover evicted the Bonus Army (15,000 unemployed World War I veterans and their families who converged on the capital in 1932 to demand immediate payment of bonuses that were not due until 1945) for which Michaux had been holding worship services, Michaux used his radio pulpit to campaign for Franklin Delano Roosevelt in 1932, 1936, and 1940. For this reason, observers credit Michaux with influencing the first African Americans to leave the Republican party and enter the Democratic fold in 1932. Political observers were baffled therefore when, in 1952, Michaux campaigned as vigorously for Republican candidate Dwight Eisenhower as he had for Roosevelt and Harry Truman.

Crowds attended Michaux's annual baptisms, which he moved from the Potomac River bank in 1938 and held in Griffith Stadium until 1961. These patriotically festooned stadium services were full of pageantry, fireworks, and enthralling precision drills and choral singing from the 156-voice Cross Choir. Vocal renditions were supported by the syncopated instrumentation of the church band, while hundreds were baptized annually in a canvas-covered tank at center field. About Michaux and his baptismal services, Bill Sunday quipped that "any man who had to hire a national baseball park, seating 35,000 to hold . . . meetings is the man to preach the gospel."

One reporter observed that Michaux should "not be passed off as just another gospel spreader . . . but should be regarded as a shrewd businessman." He had made lucrative deals in real estate, such as the 1934 purchase of 1,800 acres of land along the beachfront in Jamestown, Virginia, where he intended to develop a National Memorial to the Progress of the Colored Race of America. His plans for selling investment shares fell through when lawsuits that alleged mismanagement of monies were filed against him. Around 1940 he purchased the old Benning Race Track in Washington and received $3.5 million from the Reconstruction Finance Corporation to construct Mayfair Mansions, a 594-unit housing development, which was completed in 1946. Despite allegations on Capitol Hill in the 1950s of favoritism from federal lending agencies, in 1964 he acquired $6 million in FHA loans to build Paradise Manor, a 617-apartment complex adjacent to Mayfair Mansions. These successes were due in part to his friendship with prominent Washingtonians, some of whom were honorary members of the "Radio Church."

While Michaux initially espoused race consciousness and proclaimed the brotherhood of all races, he became increasingly conservative in his later years. In the 1960s he criticized the civil rights and black nationalist movements and alleged that the activities of Elijah Muhammad and Martin Luther King, Jr., were contributing to racial polarization.

Because of his successful radio ministry in the nation's capital, Michaux had moved the church's headquarters there in 1929 and had renamed and reincorporated it several times. During the forty-nine years of his career he established seven churches and several branches and attracted a membership that numbered in the thousands. He amassed and bequeathed to the church an estate, consisting of temples, apartment dwellings, cafes, tracts of land, and private residences in several cities, that was estimated to be in excess of $20 million in 1968. When Michaux died in Washington, D.C., his radio program was estimated to be the longest continuous broadcast in radio annals.

Continuing to operate under the name Church of God, the institution founded by Michaux had 3,000 members and eleven churches by the mid-1990s. Michaux's most significant contribution was in religious broadcasting, where he pioneered in the use of electronic and print media for worldwide evangelism.

• Michaux's written correspondence to the presidents of the United States and papers related to his interests in real estate are located in the Franklin D. Roosevelt, Harry Truman, and Dwight D. Eisenhower papers and in Department of Interior Correspondence in the National Archives. Two sets of sound recordings from Michaux's radio ministry are listed in the holdings of the Library of Congress. The bulk of film, audio tapes, *Happy News* papers, church records, and other sources for research are located in the Church of God's headquarters in Washington, D.C. For a collection of Michaux's aphorisms see Pauline Lark, ed., *Sparks from the Anvil of Elder Michaux* (1950). The most comprehensive account to date of Michaux's life is Lillian Ashcraft-Eason (Webb), *About My Father's Business: The Life of Elder Michaux* (1981). Obituaries are in the *Washington Post* and the *New York Times*, 21 Oct. 1968.

LILLIAN ASHCRAFT-EASON

MICHEAUX, Oscar (2 Jan. 1884–25 Mar. 1951), novelist and motion picture producer, was born near Cairo, Illinois, the son of Calvin Swan Micheaux and Belle Willingham, farmers. This information derives in part from Oscar Micheaux's death certificate and in part from his semiautobiographical work of fiction, *The Conquest*. Little is documented on Micheaux's early years; therefore, *The Conquest*, which appears to be more fact than fiction, provides a basis for reconstructing this period of his life. Micheaux's early years, according to this work, were spent in Metropolis, Illinois, where he attended an all-black school and where he helped out on the family farm—work for which he felt ill suited. At age seventeen, Micheaux left home seeking employment. He held a variety of jobs (coal miner, laborer, steel mill worker, bootblack, and Pullman porter), none of which resulted in economic success.

However, according to *The Conquest*, Micheaux's employment as a Pullman porter did prove to be advantageous, enabling him to travel throughout the Midwest and to acquire the capital needed to become a landowner. U.S. Department of Interior documents reveal that in 1904 Micheaux purchased the first of two 160-acre tracts of land in Gregory County, South Dakota, becoming one of the few African-American homesteaders on the Rosebud Indian Reservation. Valuing the acquisition of his landholdings, Micheaux, who became a government crop expert for Rosebud County, submitted an article to the *Chicago Defender* (28 Oct. 1911) titled "Colored Americans Too Slow to Take Advantage of Great Land Opportunities Given Free by the Government," in which he encouraged other blacks to migrate to the Midwest and purchase land.

Micheaux's journalistic interests, according to *The Conquest*, were shared by a white Scottish woman to whom he was attracted and with whom he considered marriage. Uncomfortable with the concept of mixed-race marriage, Micheaux instead married, in 1910, an African-American woman, Orlean E. McCracken, daughter of N. J. McCracken, an elder affiliated with the AME (African Methodist Episcopal) denomination of Chicago.

This marriage is believed to have dissolved in 1911. According to the *Defender*, Micheaux filed a $10,000 lawsuit against his father-in-law with the Circuit Court of Cook County, Illinois, for interfering with the marriage, for taking his wife from South Dakota to Chicago, and for making a claim against his homestead. Micheaux's deteriorating marriage may have provided the impetus for him to launch his writing career.

In 1913 Micheaux published the first of seven novels, *The Conquest: The Story of a Negro Pioneer*, dedicating it to Booker T. Washington. Although a work of fiction, this novel focuses on Micheaux's early years growing up on the family farm in Illinois, his experience as a Pullman porter, his life as a homesteader in the Midwest, and his deteriorating marriage. Advertised in the *Chicago Defender* (16 Aug. 1913), *The Conquest* was described as the "great narrative of the year." According to this source, the novel was favorably reviewed by a variety of publications such as the *Sioux City Tribune* and apparently was well received by white readers in the Midwest. Micheaux's *The Forged*

Note: A Romance of the Darker Races was published in 1915, and his *The Homesteader* in 1917. Both novels bore striking resemblance to Micheaux's own life. Micheaux continually utilized events from his own experience to develop the characters in these works. For example, in *The Forged Note*, the protagonist is a novelist who, like Micheaux, attempts to promote and distribute his works; in *The Homesteader*, Micheaux provides an expanded version of his earlier work *The Conquest*, whose protagonist is a homesteader living in the Midwest. As to the success of these works, Micheaux reported that as many as 2,500 whites in South Dakota and Nebraska had purchased *The Forged Note*.

Micheaux's entrepreneurial drive kept surfacing in new ventures. One of these was book publishing. Although exact dates and transactions are scant, there is evidence that many of Micheaux's literary works were published by his own book publishing company, the Western Book Supply Company of Sioux City, Iowa.

In 1918 Micheaux, eager to have his novel *The Homesteader* transferred to the motion picture screen, proposed that the Lincoln Motion Picture Company of Omaha, Nebraska, operated by George and Noble Johnson, produce the picture. When this idea failed to materialize, Micheaux entered still another business venture; he decided to produce the picture himself. With the production of his first film, *The Homesteader*, Micheaux established his own filmmaking company in 1918. Combining two ventures, he established the Micheaux Book and Film Company, which later became the Micheaux Film Corporation. This company had offices in Sioux City, Iowa; Chicago, Illinois; and New York City.

Between 1918 and 1948 Micheaux produced nearly fifty films in two periods of filmmaking (1918–1929 and 1930–1948). Micheaux often shot his films on location, as he did in Roanoke, Virginia, and in West Virginia while shooting *The House behind the Cedars* (1923); in studios in New York for *The Gunsaulus Mystery* (1921); in Atlanta, Georgia, for *Body and Soul*; and in studios in Fort Lee, New Jersey, for *The Exile* (1931). Micheaux even began shooting in Florida for films unnamed, but his filmmaking in this state was halted because of the hostility he experienced from both blacks and whites in this area. Films produced in these two periods reflect Micheaux's ingenuity in popularizing his motion pictures by placing in the foreground and capitalizing on the controversial issues of the day, such as passing, intraracial prejudice, lynching, incestuous relationships, hypocritical ministers, and the intimidation tactics of antiblack groups such as the Ku Klux Klan.

In the first period, from 1918 to 1929, he produced many films of high quality and received favorable reviews from the African-American press. Some of his most popular films were among his most controversial, such as *The Homesteader*. According to Micheaux, this film, nearly three hours in length, took more than six years to write and nine months to adapt to the screen. In *The Homesteader*, Evelyn Preer, a prominent black actress who appeared in several of Micheaux's films, is involved in a domestic tragedy. The film provoked controversy both because it portrayed a disputatious interracial relationship and because it portrayed a character of striking resemblance to Micheaux's despised father-in-law. The latter portrayal resulted in the film experiencing difficulty in receiving censor approval because it portrayed a hypocritical minister whose actions were "based upon the supposed hypocritical actions of a prominent colored preacher of this city [Chicago]" (*Chicago Defender*, 1 Mar. 1919).

Equally controversial was Micheaux's second motion picture, *Within Our Gates*, alternately titled *Circumstantial Evidence*, produced in 1919. This film was a murder mystery in which a black sharecropper accused of killing a white plantation owner is lynched. In addition to the fact that the film re-created a lynching, Micheaux was attempting to release the film in Chicago following the city's worst race riot in its history, in July 1919, referred to as the "Red Summer." Micheaux seemed always to provoke controversy. *Within Our Gates*, not surprisingly, had difficulty receiving censor approval.

Symbol of the Unconquered, alternately titled *The Wilderness Trail*, was produced in 1920. This daringly confrontational motion picture focused on the intimidation of African Americans by such groups as the Ku Klux Klan. A review of this film stated,

> It tells the struggles of a young man to retain possession of a piece of valuable oil land against tremendous odds, which includes everything from intimidation at the hands of his neighbors to a narrow escape from death for him at the hands of the Ku Klux Klan. A love story of beautiful texture lends added interest and some red-blooded scrapping and hard-hard riding furnishes the picture with the amount of exciting action required to make the blood tingle through your veins at high speed. (*Chicago Defender*, 8 Jan. 1921)

The House behind the Cedars (1923), based on Charles Waddell Chesnutt's similarly titled book, focused on an interracial relationship between a white millionaire and a woman later discovered to have been of African-American descent. Micheaux promoted this motion picture by linking it to a real-life case involving a white millionaire, Kip Rhinelander, who attempted to annul his marriage to Alice Jones Rhinelander upon discovering that she was an African American. One advertisement for *The House behind the Cedars* stated, "The story of an aristocratic young white millionaire's passionate love (played by Andrew S. Bishop) for a beautiful mulatto being passed off as white—and the discovery! An amazing parallel to the famous Rhinelander case" (*Afro-American* [Baltimore], 28 Mar. 1925).

Micheaux was again accused of using his father-in-law, whom he viewed as the classic example of a hypocritical minister, to re-create the clergyman in *Body and Soul*, produced in 1924. This film featured actor and singer Paul Robeson in his first motion picture appearance as a "jack-leg" preacher. An advertisement for this film stated that it was the "story of a good but helpless girl in the toils of a hypocritical beast who ruins her very *Body and Soul* for his greed and lust" (*Afro-American* [Baltimore], 25 Sept. 1926). The African-American community publicly condemned Micheaux for this portrayal.

On 20 March 1926 Micheaux married Alice Burton Russell of Montclair, New Jersey. Russell, ten years younger than Micheaux, was a concert soloist at the time of their marriage but later became an actress, appearing in several of Micheaux's films and later working for his company. Although born in Maxton, North Carolina, Alice Russell, daughter of Robert Russell and Mary J. Malloy, later moved to New Jersey with her family. The Russell-Micheaux marriage did not produce children. The union apparently remained compatible on a personal and professional level for some twenty-five years. In 1928 Micheaux's company filed for bankruptcy, forcing him to reorganize. A combination of factors was involved, not least among them his inability to obtain financial backing, his sometimes questionable business practices, and the limited number of theaters catering to black audiences to exhibit his films (even though his films were often shown to white audiences at midnight showings). Thus ended his first period of filmmaking.

In his second period of filmmaking, Micheaux produced fewer films, fewer good-quality films, and an increase in rereleases or remakes of earlier films. Micheaux received fewer favorable reviews in the African-American press. As he continued to popularize his films, further provoking controversy, he seemed to be inviting adverse criticism. Color divisions among African Americans, where Micheaux used "light-complexioned" actors for positive characters and "dark-complexioned" actors for negative characters, surfaced in his *A Daughter of the Congo* and became the subject for attack. One film critic charged,

> The first offense of this new film is its persistent vaunting of intraracial color fetishism. . . . All the noble characters are high yellows; all the ignoble ones are black. . . . As a matter of fact, the picture is thoroughly bad from every point of analysis, from the continuity which is unintelligible, to the caption writing which is a crime. (*New York Amsterdam News*, 16 Apr. 1930)

In 1937 Micheaux's *God's Stepchildren*, advertised as one of the greatest films since *Imitation of Life* (1934) and which focused on a black woman whose attempt to pass as white ultimately led to her suicide, was boycotted when it was shown in New York and Boston. Protesters were disturbed by a particular scene in the film that "showed an actor, playing the part of a white man, knocking down a young girl and spitting upon her because she had 'colored blood in her veins'" (*Afro-American* [Baltimore], 28 May 1938). During this period Micheaux even patterned a few of his films after the gangster genre films produced by the major motion picture studios in an attempt to heighten his appeal during a time of declining popularity. Limited financial resources and an inability to attract a new generation of moviegoers by addressing new and current issues rather than those he had introduced in his first period of filmmaking in part explain his declining popularity.

Micheaux did not resume writing novels until 1941, when he wrote *The Wind from Nowhere*, which was followed by the publication of *The Case of Mrs. Wingate* (1944), *The Story of Dorothy Stanfield, Based on a Great Insurance Swindle* (1946), and *The Masquerade* (1947). These works, published by his own company, achieved some degree of success. According to the *New York Amsterdam News*, *The Wind from Nowhere*, *The Case of Mrs. Wingate*, and *The Story of Dorothy Stanfield* became bestsellers with a circulation of over 25,000. Among Micheaux's bestsellers, his most successful novel was *The Case of Mrs. Wingate*, which had a circulation of over 55,000. *The Masquerade* was the least successful of Micheaux's novels. Four years after his last novel, *The Masquerade*, was published and three years after his last film, *The Betrayal*, was produced, Micheaux died. He had been hospitalized in Charlotte, North Carolina.

• Biographical information on Oscar Micheaux is in John Wakeman, ed., *World Film Directors,* vol. 1, *1890–1945* (1987); *New York Amsterdam News*, 7 Apr. 1951 (obituary); Marriage License, Cook County, Ill.; Certificate of Death, North Carolina Department of Vital Statistics; Marriage Certificate, Essex County, N.J., Bureau of Vital Statistics; and Land Documents, U.S. Department of Interior. Compilations and reviews of Micheaux's films cover a wide range of sources. They include Henry T. Sampson, *Blacks in Black and White: A Source Book on Black Films* (1977); Bernard L. Peterson, Jr., "The Films of Oscar Micheaux: America's First Fabulous Black Filmmaker," *Crisis* 86 (Apr. 1979): 136–41; Bernard L. Peterson, Jr., "A Filmography of Oscar Micheaux: America's Legendary Black Filmmaker," in *Celluloid Power*, ed. David Platt (1992); Donald Bogle, *Toms, Coons, Mulattoes, Mammies, and Bucks* (1989); Thomas Cripps, *Slow Fade to Black: The Negro in American Film, 1900–1942* (1977); *Chicago Defender*; *Afro-American* (Baltimore); *Pittsburgh Courier*; *New York Amsterdam News*; *The Freeman* (Indianapolis); *New York Age*; and other African-American newspapers. Literary works have been analyzed and evaluated by Chester J. Fontenot, Jr., "Oscar Micheaux, Black Novelist and Film Maker," in *Vision and Refuge: Essays on the Literature of the Great Plains*, ed. Virginia Faulkner and Frederick C. Luebke (1982); Janis Herbert, "Oscar Micheaux: A Black Pioneer," *South Dakota Review* 11 (1973–1974): 62–69; Joseph A. Young, *Black Novelist as White Racist* (1989); and "Micheaux Writes New Novel but Doubts Viewpoint of the Whites," *Chicago Defender*, 6 Sept. 1941. Films housed at the Library of Congress include *Within Our Gates* (1919), *Birthright* (1924, trailer), *Darktown Revue* (1931), *The Exile* (1931), *Ten Minutes to Live* (1932), *Veiled Aristocrats* (1932, fragments, trailer), *The Girl from Chicago* (1932), *The Temptation* (1936, trailer), *The Underworld* (1937), *Swing* (1938), *Lying Lips* (1939), *Murder in Harlem* (1939, alternately titled *Lem Hawkins' Confession* [1935]), and *The Notorious Elinor Lee* (1940, incomplete).

CHARLENE B. REGESTER

MICHEL, Virgil (24 June 1890–26 Nov. 1938), monk, was born George Francis Michel in St. Paul, Minnesota, the son of Fred Michel and Mary Griebler. His father owned a large general store and speculated in real estate and insurance. At the age of thirteen Michel was sent to St. John's Preparatory School at Collegeville, Minnesota. He stayed there to complete college at St. John's University; he then entered the Benedictine community, taking the name Virgil, in 1909. He made profession of monastic vows in 1913 and was ordained to the priesthood in 1918.

After ordination he was sent to Catholic University, where he completed a doctoral dissertation on Orestes Brownson in 1918. After finishing his dissertation, he returned to St. John's to teach English and philosophy and to serve in various administrative positions. Early in 1924 he was sent to Rome to study scholastic metaphysics but found himself more interested in moral philosophy, social ethics, and economic theory. There he met Lambert Beauduin, the Belgian Benedictine monk who had launched the pastoral-liturgical movement, learning from him the doctrine of the church as Mystical Body of Christ, which was to provide the theological underpinnings of the liturgical movement, also known as the liturgical renewal. This movement, which Michel would champion in the United States, aimed at increasing an understanding of the liturgy and encouraging greater participation in the Mass and other sacraments by all Catholics. After a semester in Rome, he moved to Louvain to study moral philosophy but took the opportunity to study further with Beauduin and to familiarize himself with monastic life, liturgical renewal, and social developments in Germany, France, and the Low Countries. From his studies, his contacts, and his observation of European society, he formed a synthesis between his theology of the church as an organic communion of all the baptized and his social views on the organic nature of human society, between the movement for liturgical renewal in the church and the need for a new social order.

Returning to St. John's in 1925, he plunged into the work of awakening Catholics to the social doctrine of the church as represented by the papal encyclicals, *Rerum novarum* of Pope Leo XIII (1891) and *Quadragesimo anno* of Pope Pius XI (1931), as well as to furthering the liturgical movement in the United States. Michel's contribution consisted less in the originality of his thought than in the connection he saw between liturgical life and the social order, especially in view of the Great Depression, a connection that became the hallmark of the American liturgical movement but that had little echo in Europe.

To spread these ideas, which were shared by a small but growing network of collaborators, Michel with the approval (if not at the instigation) of his abbot, Alcuin Deutsch, established the Liturgical Press at Collegeville in 1926 to publish his translations of European authors such as Beauduin and Guardini and in the same year launched a periodical under the name of *Orate Fratres* (published under the name of *Worship* beginning in 1951). At the same time, he was teaching in the college and serving in a number of administrative positions for a school that was striving for academic recognition. His convictions about the holistic character of the Christian life led to his interest in catechetics and to the Christ-Life series of religious education textbooks, which he wrote in conjunction with the Dominican Sisters of Grand Rapids. All this was rooted in his ongoing interest in philosophy, which yielded two books and twenty-five articles, written mainly from the personalist perspective.

In 1930 his health gave way, and he was forced to abandon his projects for a quieter life as a pastor to the Chippewa Indians on various reservations in northern Minnesota. Characteristically, he developed a number of ideas for improving the situation of Native Americans but was recalled to the abbey before these could be brought to fruition. In 1936 he was back at St. John's to head up the school's drive for accreditation, while taking over the leadership once again of the Liturgical Press and the periodical *Orates Fratres* as well as traveling about the country promoting social reconstruction and liturgical renewal. He died of a streptococcal infection in Collegeville.

• Michel's personal papers are preserved at St. John's Abbey in Collegeville. A full list of his publications is provided by Paul Marx in his biography, *Virgil Michel and the Liturgical Movement* (1957). A selection of Michel's essays was published as *The Social Question. Essays on Capitalism and Christianity by Fr. Virgil Michel, OSB* (1987).

MARK SEARLE

MICHELSON, Albert Abraham (19 Dec. 1852–9 May 1931), physicist, was born in Strelno, Prussia (later Strzelno, Poland), the son of Samuel Michelson, a merchant, and Rozalia Przylubska. His parents immigrated to the United States when Albert was age two and, after a brief stay in New York City, settled in Murphy's Camp (now Murphys) in Calaveras County, California, near Yosemite. There his father found prosperity supplying miners during the gold rush. After graduating from high school in San Francisco, Albert was admitted to the U.S. Naval Academy in Annapolis, Maryland, only after a personal interview with President Ulysses S. Grant. It appears that politics, specifically a need to reach Jewish voters, played a decisive role in his admission. He graduated from the academy in 1873, placing first among the twenty-nine graduates in optics but only twenty-fifth in seamanship, causing the academy superintendent to observe that if Michelson were to devote more attention to his naval gunnery and less to his "scientific things" he could be of service to his country.

After two years of active duty in the navy, Michelson was commissioned an ensign, and he returned to the academy as an instructor in physics and chemistry. In 1877 he married Margaret Heminway, the niece of his commander, William T. Sampson; the couple had three children. His commander, recognizing Michelson's skills in optics, suggested that he set up as an instructional aid an experiment to measure the speed of light. In the process of assembling the apparatus, it became apparent to Michelson that he could make a better measurement if he used high quality mirrors and lenses and a longer baseline. This would cost more money than the academy had budgeted for his project, and his father-in-law, a successful Wall Street businessman, provided an additional $2,000—a large sum at the time. With his improved setup, Michelson was able to measure the speed of light with much higher accuracy than had previously been achieved; indeed, no more accurate measurement was made for a generation, and then it was made by Michelson himself. This accomplishment hit the national press and made Michelson famous while he was still in his twenties. Nonetheless, the United States was still very much a scientific backwater, and Michelson took a leave from his academy position to spend two years studying optics at the major scientific centers of the time, the universities in Paris, Berlin, and Heidelberg. He resigned his navy commission in 1881.

In Europe, Michelson became familiar with contemporary thinking on the nature of light. It had been established since about 1800 that light was some kind of wave, but it was not clear what sort of wave it might be; most waves propagate through a medium, and there was no obvious medium to support light waves. For this reason, scientists postulated the existence of an invisible "luminiferous ether" to serve as a medium for light. This ether was believed to permeate all space, even out to the distant stars, since the light from them could only reach us through the ether. Yet the earth must be able to pass freely through this ether, or it would be slowed down in its orbit around the sun. In the 1860s the brilliant work of Scottish physicist James Clerk Maxwell had unified electricity and magnetism, previously thought to be distinct phenomena. His theory predicted the existence of electromagnetic waves, which were promptly discovered by German Heinrich Rudolf Hertz. The speed of these waves, also predicted by Maxwell's theory, turned out to be the speed of light, and it was therefore natural to assume that light was simply rapidly varying electromagnetic waves propagating through the ether. The calculated speed of light was presumably the speed relative to the ether, just as the speed of sound is relative to the air, the medium through which sound waves travel. The speed of light should therefore change as the earth moved through the ether in its orbit around the sun. Michelson resolved to prove the existence of the mysterious ether by detecting these changes in the speed of light.

Michelson already had in mind the ideal instrument for his proposed experiments. While in Europe, he had begun work on what would occupy much of his scientific career: the interferometer, one type of which bears his name. In a Michelson interferometer, a single beam of light is split into two parts, which follow different paths to a detector. Since light is a wave, the two parts of the beam interfere with each other. If the two paths are the same length, and light travels at the same speed in each path, the beams will reach the detector at the same time and produce an interference pattern. However, if light travels at different speeds in each path, the beams will reach the detector at different times, changing the interference pattern. Michelson arranged his interferometer so that the two paths were perpendicular to each other. Then the motion of the earth through the ether should affect the speed of light; one path would be "upwind" with respect to the ether and the other "crosswind," and the speed of light in each path would correspondingly differ. His initial experiments in Berlin failed to detect any such differences, but he continued them on his return to the United States. In 1883 he became a professor of physics at the Case School of Applied Sciences (later Case Western Reserve University) in Cleveland, Ohio. There he worked with Edward Williams Morley, a professor of chemistry at the adjoining Western Reserve University, on improvements to his interferometer. By 1887 it was capable of detecting changes in speed of only one or two miles per second (less than the speed of the earth in its orbit). Yet Michelson and Morley saw no changes at all.

This famous "Michelson-Morley" experiment may be the most important null result in the history of science. Subsequent improvements demonstrated that there was also no change in the speed of light due to the earth's rotation on its axis. Nor could a later experiment on a high mountain detect any changes, making untenable the hypothesis that the earth was "dragging along" the ether near its surface. This is a complete paradox in classical Newtonian physics, in which it is incomprehensible that the speed of light plus another speed should add up to the speed of light. The only reasonable conclusion was that the concept of an ether pervading all space was wrong. The problem was not resolved until 1905, when Albert Einstein published his special theory of relativity, which recast the definition of space and time and allowed science to dispose of the ether. There is a double irony here: Einstein's solution was so radical that Michelson himself was very reluctant to accept it, and it appears that the results of the Michelson-Morley experiment—originating from what were from a German perspective provincial American scientists—were not even known to Einstein at the time he did his work, although they are now viewed as primary evidence for the theory of special relativity.

In 1888, in one of the first of many honors he was to receive throughout his career, Michelson was elected to membership in the prestigious National Academy of Sciences, an organization he later served as president from 1923 to 1927. Michelson left Case in 1889 to become a professor of physics at Clark University in Worcester, Massachusetts, motivated at least in part by the fact that at Clark, unlike at Case, he would have graduate students to help him with his research. Three years later he joined the new University of Chicago, then being organized by John D. Rockefeller, as a professor and the first head of the physics department. He remained at the university for thirty-seven years, until his retirement in 1929.

At Clark, Michelson continued his work with interferometry, realizing that this permitted accurate measurements of the wavelength of light that could form the basis for a new length standard—one to replace the old definition of the meter as the distance between two marks on a particular metal bar in Paris, which was both imprecise and insecure. He campaigned energetically for an optical standard, which promised great practical advantages to the growing need of American industry for precise measurement techniques. Indeed, it was for his spectroscopic and metrological work (not the more famous but more controversial Michelson-Morley experiment) that in 1907 Michelson became the first American Nobel laureate in physics. However, it was not until 1960 that the meter was officially redefined in terms of the wavelength of light produced by a specific optical transition in the cadmium atom. Subsequently, the speed of light that Michelson spent so much of his life measuring became a defined quantity, and it and the second came to specify the meter.

Michelson developed an interferometric technique to measure the diameter of astronomical objects, essentially using the main lens or mirror of a telescope as an optical bench. The initial experiments, conducted in 1891, used a telescope at the Lick Observatory in California with a 36-inch lens, which he covered with a screen with pairs of holes at various separations to simulate different baselines. He was able to obtain estimates of the diameter of the Galilean moons of Jupiter that are close to the correct values, but to measure the diameter of stars required a much longer baseline.

By 1919, working with Francis G. Pease, Michelson had designed an interferometer that was installed atop the 100-inch telescope at Mount Wilson, California, (then the largest telescope in the world). This consisted of a twenty-foot bar, the length chosen to avoid hitting the interior of the telescope dome. An observer would move mirrors on the bar and watch for interference fringes that indicated the size of the object being studied. This turned out to be both difficult and time-consuming, a particular problem since the telescope was in great demand. It was possible to measure the diameter of only seven relatively nearby stars, all red giants much larger than the sun. Measurement of other stars would require baselines much larger than twenty feet. Nevertheless, the Michelson-Pease experiments were the first to accurately measure the diameter of stars. They played an important role in later studies, and the first result, the diameter of the star Betelgeuse 150 light-years away, caused a sensation in 1920. It was one of the scientific events of the century, the first time an object outside the solar system had been shown to have a definite size. A few years later, in 1923, Michelson returned to the problem of the accurate determination of the speed of light, using a twenty-mile baseline between two mountains in California that he measured to an accuracy of less than one inch. To eliminate the effects of air, later experiments were conducted in a long evacuated tube through which light was bounced back and forth a total distance of ten miles. With this equipment, the speed of light was measured to within a thousandth percent of the value accepted today.

Late in his life, Michelson, motivated by the work of Dayton Clarence Miller, his successor at Case, once again revisited his most famous work, the measurement of changes in the velocity of light due to the motion of the earth. Miller, encouraged by a 1921 visit by Einstein to Case, conducted experiments away from the earth's surface on Mount Wilson that were designed to check the Michelson-Morley null result of thirty years before. His experiments, announced in 1925, attracted great public interest because they appeared to show a measurable effect, implying that the absolute motion of the earth had been determined. This inspired an exhaustive and systematic series of experiments by many scientists, including Pease and Michelson, who were by then over seventy-five years old. They once again obtained a null result, confirming the predictions of relativity, whose two founding fathers—Einstein the eager theorist and Michelson the reluctant experimentalist—met for the first and only time at the California Institute of Technology in 1931.

Most of Michelson's time and energy was dedicated to science, leaving little for other activities, and the strain of overwork may have contributed to a breakdown in 1885. His devotion to his work contributed to his marital difficulties, which culminated in divorce in 1897. He overcame these setbacks; in 1899 he married Edna Stanton, with whom he had three children, and in later years he was devoted to his family and children and even found time to pursue a love of violin playing. Michelson, the first prominent American physicist of his day, called by some the "Apostle of Light," whose optical instruments are still valuable analytic tools in industry and science throughout the world, died in Pasadena, California.

• The Library of the University of Chicago maintains a collection of Michelson's papers and photographs, and a variety of his equipment may be viewed in the Michelson Museum at the U.S. Naval Weapons Center in China Lake, Calif. His own books provide an interesting historical perspective. These include *Light Waves and Their Uses* (1902; repr. 1961) and *Studies in Optics* (1927; repr. 1962); the latter is particularly revealing about his continued ambivalence about the abandonment of the ether hypothesis even at that late date. Informative biographies include John Henry Wilson, *Albert A. Michelson: America's First Nobel Prize Physicist* (1958); Bernard Jaffe, *Michelson and the Speed of Light* (1960; repr. 1979), which includes a description of his research; and Dorothy Michelson Livingston (his youngest daughter), *The Master of Light: A Biography of Albert A. Michelson* (1973), which includes many personal anecdotes. Valuable descriptions of Michelson's work and his many scientific contributions can be found in Stanley Goldberg and Roger H. Stuewer, eds., *The Michelson Era in American Science, 1870–1930* (1988), the proceedings of a symposium on Michelson held at Case Western Reserve University. Loyd S. Swenson, Jr., *The Ethereal Aether: A History of the Michelson-Morley-Miller Aether-drift Experiments, 1880–1930* (1972), is an insightful survey of these experiments and their impact on science, and it includes reprints of a few original papers. William Fickinger and Kenneth L. Kowalski, eds., *Modern Physics in America: A Michelson-Morley Centennial* (1988), the proceedings of an American Institute of Physics conference, focuses on the effect of this experiment on science.

MARTEN DEN BOER

MICHELSON, Charles (18 Apr. 1869?–8 Jan. 1948), journalist and political publicist, was born in Virginia City, Nevada, the son of Samuel Michelson, a storekeeper, and Rosalie Przlubska, both emigrants from Prussia. His brother, older by seventeen years, was Albert Abraham Michelson, a Nobel Prize–winning physicist. Charles Michelson did not take to the studious ways of the rest of the family, left school as an adolescent, found odd jobs, and became "a frontier tramp," a time he recalled as "the most perfect period of my life" (*The Ghost Talks*, p. 73). Summoned back to high school by his parents, he managed to graduate and worked for a time as a bookkeeper and reporter at the *Virginia City Chronicle*.

About 1887 he went to San Francisco, where a brother-in-law, Arthur McEwen, gave him a job on the *Evening Post*. He moved over to the *San Francisco Examiner* about the time that young William Randolph Hearst took over the paper from his father. Michelson remained eight years, honing the techniques of Hearst's sensational journalism. He quit when he was passed over for a promotion. He moved to the *San Francisco Call* and became one of the city's star reporters. He wed Lillian Sterrett of Brooklyn in 1896, and they had one child.

Hearst lured him back, probably in late 1895, by sending him to cover the Cuban insurgency for his newly acquired *New York Journal*. In February 1896, Spanish officials in Havana arrested Michelson and held him overnight in Morro Castle (or perhaps longer; he wrote an account claiming ten days' imprisonment) before sending him back to Florida. The Hearst press, which was supporting the Cuban revolt, transformed the incident into "a major example of Spanish cruelty" (Brown, pp. 30–31). He was assigned for a time to Hearst's "navy"—the vessels that Hearst had hired to report on hostilities in Cuban waters. However, when war was declared in 1898 Michelson covered no combat; he came no closer to the Spanish-American War than concocting an "eyewitness" story of the battle of Manila Bay from his newspaper office in New York.

Michelson settled into a typically uneven career in the Hearst organization, moving from New York to San Francisco to Chicago and back to New York. He served as a city editor, a managing editor, and an editorial writer. After his salary was reduced in the interests of "efficiency," he supplemented his slender income by writing movie scenarios for the pioneering Essanay Company and earned as much as $20,000 on a single film. When World War I started in 1914, Hearst promised him a war correspondent's job but kept him at home. His last job with Hearst was writing editorials for Hearst's New York papers; he disliked Hearst's pro-German positions and left to be a Washington correspondent for the *Chicago Herald*. But Hearst soon bought the *Herald*, and Michelson was discharged.

In 1917 Michelson found a new journalistic base at the Pulitzer family's *New York World*, which named him its chief Washington correspondent. He specialized in politics but covered a variety of national stories, among them the Scopes "monkey" trial in Tennessee and the sudden death of President Warren G. Harding. The *World* gave him a column, "The Political Undertow," one of the first of the insider type, and he provided Democrat-oriented comment throughout the 1920s.

In June 1929 Michelson was named the first director of publicity for the Democratic National committee (DNC). The Democrats had suffered a decade of disastrous electoral defeats culminating in the victory of Herbert Hoover over Alfred E. Smith in the presidential election of 1928. John J. Raskob, the DNC chairman, set up a new party headquarters and brought Michelson in to create anti-Hoover publicity. He started at the then substantial annual salary of $20,800 and later won a raise to $25,000 a year.

The productivity, timing, and fluency that had served Michelson as a journalist now found a new purpose. He turned out almost daily statements to be planted in newspapers or voiced by prominent Democrats in or out of Congress. Because so many politicians used his words, he was sometimes called "Hundred-Tongued Charley." With the deepening of the Great Depression, the Michelson publicity machine concentrated on blaming the incumbent for hard times, and Republicans accused him of smearing the president. Michelson wrote that he had merely concentrated "on various acts and omissions of [Hoover's] administration" (*The Ghost Talks*, p. 41). When the governor of New York, Franklin D. Roosevelt, was nominated for president in 1932, Michelson abandoned Raskob to work for the candidate. Michelson shunned any credit for Roosevelt's landslide victory: "We performed no miracles. The table was spread and there was nothing to do but eat the meal" (*Current Biography*, 1940).

Named an aide in the New Deal's Treasury Department, Michelson wrote an early draft of the first of Roosevelt's famous fireside chats, delivered in the depths of the banking crisis of 1933, and served as American press officer during the critical World Economic Conference in London. Later he was appointed director of public relations for the sprawling, short-lived National Recovery Administration, headed by General Hugh S. Johnson, who called Michelson "the wise Ulysses who kept my erring feet on the path" (Johnson, *The Blue Eagle from Egg to Earth* [1935], p. 310). In 1934 Michelson returned to the Democratic National Committee and never held another government appointment. But he was active in the 1936 campaign, writing speeches and distributing a column to newspapers called "Dispelling the Fog," in the style of his old *World* column.

After Roosevelt's landslide reelection, Michelson stayed on at the national committee, although he was subjected to increasing criticism both from the opposition and from New Dealers, who suspected him of being sympathetic to Roosevelt's conservative opponents in the party. In fact, he turned down a lucrative job offer from the conservatives to work for the anti-Roosevelt Liberty League. He remained on the job until

November 1942 and helped out in the 1944 campaign, Roosevelt's last. He died at his home in Washington of congestive heart disease.

As a journalist, Michelson gained respectability by abandoning the Hearst press, only to return to its techniques as a political ghost writer and propagandist. As a result, he won a reputation for being skilled at a disreputable trade. At his death, his political work was criticized for blurring representative government by putting fabricated words into politicians' mouths. An editorial in the *Washington Post* at his death deplored his partisanship: "To the extent that he resorted to smearing, public issues were subordinated to scintillating phrases and animosities" (11 Jan. 1948). From this perspective, Michelson's work can be seen as the forerunner of the aggressive, negative campaigning employed by both parties in subsequent years.

• Michelson's own account of his life is a loosely written chronicle, *The Ghost Talks* (1944). His adventures as a war correspondent are described in Charles H. Brown, *The Correspondents' War* (1967). His pre–New Deal publicity work is discussed in Thomas Barclay, "The Publicity Bureau of the Democratic National Committee," *American Political Science Review* 25 (Feb. 1931): 68–72; and 27 (Feb. 1933): 63–65. Contemporary appraisals include Frank R. Kent, "Charley Michelson," *Scribner's*, Sept. 1930, pp. 290–96; and Alva Johnston, "Hundred-Tongued Charley, the Great Silent Orator," *Saturday Evening Post*, 30 May 1936, pp. 5–7, 32, 37. Memoirs by Roosevelt's colleagues give him scattered attention. See Raymond Moley, *After Seven Years* (1939) and *27 Masters of Politics* (1949); James A. Farley, *Jim Farley's Story* (1948); and *The Secret Diary of Harold Ickes*, vol. 1 (1953). Obituaries are in the *Washington Post* and the *New York Times*, both 9 Jan. 1948.

JAMES BOYLAN

MICKLEY, Joseph Jacob (24 Mar. 1799–15 Feb. 1878), numismatist, was born in Catasauqua, Northall Township, Northampton County, Pennsylvania, the son of John Jacob Mickley and Eva Catherine Schrieber, farmers. At seventeen Mickley moved to Philadelphia, where he finished an apprenticeship in making pianos and in 1822 began a musical-instrument-making business. He developed a fine reputation for repair and restoration of stringed instruments. In 1831 the Franklin Institute awarded him a prize for his skill in manufacturing pianos. Mickley was married twice, first to Cordelia Hopfeldt and then to Diana Blummer, and had six children (dates and number of children for each marriage are unknown).

Mickley, who has been called the father of American numismatics, amassed one of the earliest important coin collections in America. His numismatic interest was piqued in 1816 or earlier when he attempted to find a very rare 1799 cent, from his birth year. In locating the sought-after cent, he had enlisted the help of his friends and at first settled for an uncirculated 1798 cent but finally obtained the coveted 1799 cent (which brought $40 when his collection was sold). Mickley soon had a host of extremely rare pieces. His two most expensive acquisitions were a Lord Baltimore penny and a Somers Islands shilling, both considered unique at the time.

Mickley, who in 1859 published *Dates of United States Coins and Their Degrees of Rarity*, a four-page pamphlet, was a founding member and the first president of the Numismatic and Antiquarian Society of Philadelphia, serving from 1858 until 1867, and several of its early meetings were held at his home. He was also a "well known" member of the Franklin Institute and the Pennsylvania Historical Society and an honorary member of the Boston Numismatic Society and the New York Numismatic and Archeological Society.

Mickley was proud of his coin collection and showed it freely to friends and strangers, even though he often lost a coin or two when showing it. Besides earlier thefts, twenty half dollars disappeared in 1848 and three scarce half eagles in 1854. In 1867 approximately half of Mickley's collection was taken from his third-floor front room. Taking that traumatic event as "a warning to desist from collecting any more," Mickley shifted his interest to books about coins rather than the pieces themselves. Although it was never determined how much was stolen, Mickley, who had been offered $30,000 for his entire collection, received in 1867 over $10,000 for what was left of his collection.

In addition to his legitimate collecting, Mickley was involved in illegal activities. The Philadelphia Mint customarily sold its worn dies in random batches to scrap-metal dealers. Mickley acquired at least one group of these dies and produced a one-cent forgery from them (in sufficient numbers to make it "by far the most common of many U.S. coins privately issued"). Using an engraving tool, he changed 1803 into 1804 on the obverse die of a cent, because 1804 cents were rare and in great demand. The reverse die of the forgery (which has been designated S-261) was from an 1818 to 1820 cent (reverse O). Either to repair damage or to obscure the fact that it was not the correct reverse for the date, the reverse side of the forgery was "heavily ground down." There is general agreement that these forgeries were struck between 1858 and 1860, but speculation that they were struck at the Philadelphia Mint is not supported by facts. Mickley apparently was involved in a "restrike" scheme involving 1823 cents. Apparently he obtained an 1823 Newcomb 2 obverse die and matched it with a reverse from the period and produced a few coins (one source claims forty-nine) before the obverse die broke, creating a nearly full-diameter crack. Mickley either gave or sold these coins to Dr. M. W. Dickeson, who later sold them to John W. Haseltine, an auctioneer. Mickley also altered to 1804 an obverse 1807 half eagle die (although both years were scarce) and mated it with an 1804 reverse. Examples of these coins were struck between 1858 and 1859 in silver and copper with and without reeded edges. Shortly before his death, Mickley struck other specimens in tin and white metal. He was also definitely identified with making 1811 half-cent forgeries from an 1811 obverse and an 1802 reverse. After Mickley's death, the U.S. government confiscated and destroyed twenty of his dies.

Mickley had other interests besides coins. He had important collections of autographs and books, which were sold at auction the year of his death. His autograph collection included all the signers of the Declaration of Independence and all the presidents through Grant. Mickley also interested himself in historical research and traveled extensively. In 1875 he published *A Brief Account of Murders by the Indians, and the Cause Thereof, in Northampton County, Penn'a., October 8th, 1763*, which had been written a decade earlier as a family memoir for a centennial reunion. "Some Account of William Usselinx and Peter Minuit: Two Individuals Who Were Instrumental in Establishing the First Permanent Colony in Delaware," a paper he had presented before the Historical Society of Delaware in 1874, was published in 1881. Mickley, who was fluent in French, German, and Swedish and familiar with Italian, Spanish, and Russian, visited every mint in Europe. He was empowered as an agent for the Philadelphia Mint to collect coins and medals for its Mint Cabinet. After traveling throughout Europe, including Lapland and Russia, he visited Asia and Africa.

Mickley died in Philadelphia. A year after his death a medal was executed in his honor at the Royal Swedish Mint of Stockholm by its chief medalist, Lea Ahlborn, who was also Mickley's friend. Engraved from a photograph taken shortly before Mickley's death, the medal was executed in silver and later in bronze. Its reverse side celebrates the Numismatic and Antiquarian Society of Philadelphia, and besides containing the portrait of Mickley, its obverse side documents his term as president of that society and the years of his birth and death.

Mickley's significance is that he brought a cosmopolitan intellectualism to coin collecting, which advanced it in America beyond mere accumulation of interesting oddities to a focused study of coins with a full knowledge of their historical and intellectual significance. Mickley gave a tremendous boost to coin collecting in America, despite his unethical sideline in forged rarities. Knowledgeable collectors were not fooled by his forgeries, because they invariably contained obvious "errors," and ironically they bolstered informed collecting by making an awareness of numismatic lore more necessary. Of course, this fortunate outcome in no way excuses Mickley's illegal behavior.

• Mickley's history is relatively well preserved, although much has been lost. Apparently Mickley was an enthusiastic journal writer, but only one year (1852) of his journals has survived. It, along with collateral material from his research in Sweden on the founding of Delaware and on early Pennsylvania immigrants, is in the collections of the Pennsylvania Historical Society in Philadelphia. An extensive research by Minnie Mickley, *The Genealogy of the Mickley Family of America* (1893), pp. 96–121, provides a wealth of personal information on his family as well as a reprint of J. Bunting, "Joseph J. Mickley: A Biographical Sketch," originally published in *Lippincott's Magazine*, July 1885. A sympathetic account of Mickley's life was given in his main obituary, written by his close friend William E. DuBois, in *American Journal of Numismatics* 12 (Apr. 1878): 103–5; repr. in *Pennywise* 8 (15 July 1974): 180–83. Further information can be found in William H. Ruddiman, "Memorial Notice of Joseph J. Mickley," *Pennsylvania Magazine of History and Biography* 2, no. 4 (1878): 457–58. For information on Mickley's involvement with the Numismatic and Antiquarian Society of Philadelphia, see *Proceedings of the Numismatic & Antiquarian Society of Philadelphia*, vol. 26 (1910–1912); minutes and organizational information from the group's founding, 28 Dec. 1857, were published in the proceedings volume for 1913. Information on the medal struck in Mickley's honor for the Philadelphia Numismatic Society is presented in Raymond Williamson and Warren A. Lapp, "The Second Mickley Medal," *Pennywise* 8 (15 July 1974): 184–85.

Mickley's career as a maker of forgeries is well documented in a series of four columns by Tom DeLorey, "What Would You Call It," in *Numismatic Scrapbook* 41 (May 1975): 50–52, (June 1975): 46–48, (July 1975): 58–60, and (Dec. 1975): 90–92. Material on the 1811 half cent is illustrated in detail in Q. David Bowers, *United States Copper Coins* (1984), pp. 31–32, and in *Walter Breen's Encyclopedia of United States Half Cents 1793–1857* (1983), pp. 315–17.

ERIC P. NEWMAN

MIDDLETON, Arthur (1681–7 Sept. 1737), planter, politician, and acting governor of South Carolina, was born in Carolina in 1681, the son of Edward Middleton and Sarah Fowell. In 1678 and 1679, respectively, his father and uncle had emigrated from England to South Carolina, where they accumulated large landholdings and founded a political dynasty that survived until after the American Civil War. Edward Middleton and his wife acquired a land grant of 1,500 acres near Charles Town, in the Goose Creek region of the province, and established "The Oaks," the family's first plantation. Arthur Middleton augmented the family's landholdings throughout his life but made The Oaks his home.

Middleton received his primary education in Charles Town. In 1697 his half-brother Henry Middleton visited the family and took 16-year-old Arthur back to England with him to complete his education. The character of his English education is not known. He did not attend the universities and, instead, was probably apprenticed to a London counting house. Indeed, Arthur's education may have been similar to his future brother-in-law, Thomas Amory, who left Charles Town in 1694 and was apprenticed to "Mr. Osell," a London merchant. Arthur had two uncles, William Middleton and John Harewood, both of whom were London merchants and may have managed his education. Arthur returned to Carolina in late 1703 or early 1704 to claim his patrimony. On 29 October 1706 he married Sarah Amory, daughter of Jonathan Amory, a leader of the South Carolina Assembly. They were the parents of eight children, five of whom died in infancy. One son, Henry, founded the Ashley River plantation called "Middleton Place," and Henry's son Arthur was a member of the Continental Congress and signer of the Declaration of Independence. Sara Amory Middleton died in late 1721. Middleton then married Sarah Wilkinson Morton, widow of Joseph Morton, in 1723.

Middleton began his political career in 1706 when he was elected to represent Berkeley and Craven counties in the South Carolina Commons House of Assembly. He served five terms in the Commons House (1706–1707, 1708–1709, 1716–1717, 1717–1720, and 1720–1721) and was a member (1711–1716) of the Proprietors' Council, the upper house of the Carolina General Assembly. In both the Commons House and Council Middleton opposed the proprietors' government and was a leader in a movement to place South Carolina under direct royal control. Local opposition to the proprietors boiled down to one thing, Carolinians' wish to govern the province to serve their own ends, not those of absentees across the water. In this situation the proprietors were at a considerable disadvantage. They could not govern the province directly from London, so they had to rely on Carolinians of questionable loyalty. Hence, Arthur Middleton frequently held office despite his well-known disagreement with proprietary policies. In the winter of 1719 Middleton was president of the revolutionary convention that ousted proprietary governor Robert Johnson (c. 1676–1735) and proclaimed James Moore, Jr., acting governor of the colony "in the King's name." When he arrived in May 1721, Sir Francis Nicholson, first royal governor of South Carolina, named Middleton to his Council. Middleton was president of the Council from 1721 to 1737 and, when Nicholson left the colony in May 1725, was acting governor until 1730.

During Middleton's long term as president of the Council, and particularly during his years as acting governor, South Carolina was beset by economic and political disorder. The unanimity between the colony's planters and Charles Town merchants that had accomplished the revolution of 1719 broke down in the 1720s. Bitter wrangles in the general assembly and occasional street riots resulted from disputes over the colony's currency policy. Planters wanted to print and use local paper currency to alleviate their indebtedness and speed up commodity exchanges. Merchants, on the other hand, sought to restrict the issuance of paper money and demanded hard currency for debt payments and for international trade. Paper money, especially colonial currency, was rarely backed by gold or silver. It was subject to constant inflation as hard-pressed colonial governments printed more and more unsecured paper money. Colonial debtors were eager to pay their overseas debts in inflated paper money while creditors fought to collect their debts in hard currency—gold and silver—that had a more stable monetary value. On the positive side, paper currency was easily transported and met local, colonial monetary needs. Although a planter himself, Middleton opposed the planter party in the general assembly. He summoned and dissolved five assemblies within two years because he could not cooperate with them. Of these assemblies one lasted two weeks, and another lasted but a single day. In December 1730 Robert Johnson succeeded in obtaining royal appointment as governor of South Carolina. Ousted by rebels against the proprietors in 1719, Johnson was welcomed back to Carolina by loyal subjects of King George II. When Johnson arrived in Charles Town, Middleton reclaimed his Council seat and held it until his death.

In addition to his colonywide offices Middleton held a variety of commissions and local offices. He was commissioner of the Church of England (1706), vestryman of St. James Goose Creek Parish (1707–1708), Charles Town free school commissioner (1710, 1712), and commissioner to construct a state house (1712) and to establish a provincial library (1712). After the outbreak of the Yamasee War in 1715 Middleton traveled to Virginia to negotiate the dispatch of Virginia volunteers to assist the South Carolinians' war effort. He was also a militia captain (1717), tax assessor (1715–1716), and Revenue Act commissioner (1719). In his later years Middleton was free school commissioner at Dorchester (1734), justice of the peace (1734), and justice of the quorum (1737).

After returning to the Council in 1730 Middleton continued to acquire land through grants and purchase. He amassed large tracts on the Savannah River and in Colleton and Granville counties southwest of Charles Town. In addition he owned town lots in Charles Town and Dorchester on the Ashley River. He utilized his plantations according to an efficient system. The Oaks produced the cash crop rice while other plantations yielded provisions and timber. His death in late summer suggested that he may have succumbed to malaria or another "country fever" of the region. According to family oral tradition he was buried behind the chancel at St. James Goose Creek Church.

Middleton was the archetype of a low-country South Carolina planter during the colonial era. Throughout his life he labored to expand his landholdings and to increase his and his family's wealth and prestige. Contemporary descriptions of his plantation homes reveal that he was a man of cultivated taste in the approved English manner. He entered politics at the age of twenty-five and was in public office for the remainder of his life. Although he was a successful leader during the Proprietary era and of the revolution of 1719 that ended the proprietors' rule, he was less successful in later years. His term as acting governor (1725–1730) was marked by so much domestic turmoil and partisan politics that the colonial historian M. Eugene Sirmans called it a period of near-anarchy.

• Arthur Middleton letters and documents are in the Amory Family Papers, Library of Congress, and in the microfilm edition of *The Saumarez Papers: Materials Relating to South Carolina Drawing from the Middleton Family in the Ipswich and East Suffolk Record Office*, with an introduction by William P. Sergeant (1974). A biographical sketch of Middleton can be found in the *Biographical Directory of the South Carolina House of Representatives*, vol. 2, ed. Walter B. Edgar and N. Louise Bailey (1977). Langdon Cheves published a genealogy, "Middletons of South Carolina," in *South Carolina Historical Magazine* 1 (July 1900): 228–62. The most comprehensive study of Middleton, his forebears, and descendants is George Winston Lane, "The Middletons of Eighteenth Century South Carolina: A Colonial Dynasty, 1678–1787" (Ph.D. diss., Emory Univ., 1990). M. Eugene Sirmans, *Colonial South Carolina, a Political History, 1663–1763* (1966), describes Middleton's political career. See also Mills B. Lane, "Middleton Place," in *Architecture of the Old South: South Carolina* (1984). An equestrian drawing of Arthur Middleton by surveyor John Herbert embellishes a 1716 plat of The Oaks in the collections of the Charleston Museum, Charleston, S.C.

ALEXANDER MOORE

MIDDLETON, Drew (14 Oct. 1913–10 Jan. 1990), journalist and author, was born in New York City, the son of Elmer Thomas Middleton, a businessman, and Jean Drew. His mother died in the influenza epidemic of 1918, and he was raised primarily by his grandmother, theatrical producer Isabel Drew, in New York City and South Orange, New Jersey. Middleton attended high school in South Orange before entering Syracuse University, where he was sports editor of the college newspaper, the *Daily Orange*, and campus correspondent for the *Syracuse Herald*. After graduating in 1935 with a B.S., he was the sports editor of the *Poughkeepsie (N.Y.) Eagle News* (1936) and a reporter for the *Poughkeepsie Evening Star* (1936–1937). In 1937 he was hired for the Associated Press sports department by Alan J. Gould, the sports editor. Middleton went to Europe in 1939 to cover sports, but after World War II began, he became the youngest reporter with the British Expeditionary Force in France and Belgium (1939–1940). Middleton says in his memoirs (*Where Has Last July Gone? Memoirs* [1973], p. 14), "Because of the shortage of experienced men I skipped much of the dreary apprenticeship."

After covering the war from Britain (1940–1941) and Iceland (1941–1942), Middleton accompanied the Dieppe Raid on the French coast. His dispatch on the raid won the International News Service medal and the admiration of Raymond Daniell, head of the *New York Times* London bureau, who hired Middleton in September 1942. Middleton was sent to North Africa, where *Time* (12 Apr. 1943) called his work "the best U.S. reporting." Returning to London in 1943, he shared an apartment with journalists Gladwin Hill and Clifton Daniel. He met Estelle "Stevie" Mansel-Edwards, a British woman who worked in the British Foreign Press office. She lost her job in 1943 for marrying a reporter; they had one child. Middleton especially admired leaders who tried to protect the troops they led. On President Harry S. Truman's decision to use the atomic bomb to end World War II, Middleton writes in *Retreat from Victory* ([1973], p. 63), "Remembering the apprehensions of that summer about the estimated butcher's bill for a landing on Japan's home islands, who can doubt that, had they been consulted, Americans would have said almost unanimously, 'Go ahead, anything to get it over.'"

Middleton covered the Nuremberg Trials (1945–1946) and was later bureau chief in Moscow (1946–1947). He was bureau chief in Germany from 1947 to 1953. After his 1947 articles charging that the denazification program did not go far enough, American officials in Germany complained about Middleton to Arthur Hays Sulzberger, publisher of the *New York Times* (1935–1961). Sulzberger supported his reporter, which, Middleton says in his *Memoirs* (p. 172), "explains why reporters trusted that sensible gentleman."

As bureau chief in London (1953–1963), Middleton was happiest. He had been awarded the Order of the British Empire, military division (1947), later commander (1986), and had also received the U.S. Medal of Freedom (1948). Colleagues admired his conversation as well as his writing, and his memoirs are "for absent friends." He was the chief correspondent for the *Times* in Paris (1963–1965) and at the United Nations (1965–1968) before becoming European affairs correspondent (1968–1970).

Middleton was the *Times* military correspondent from 1970 to 1984 (after which he continued to write a twice-weekly column and articles). Middleton had no military background, yet his columns and books were highly regarded by the professional military, who invited him to lecture at the Command and General Staff College at Fort Leavenworth, Kansas, and other military posts. American military historian Russell F. Weigley said in the *New York Times Book Review* (29 May 1983, p. 13) of Middleton's *Crossroads of Modern Warfare*, "Middleton gives us a modern version of [Sir Edward] Creasy's 'Fifteen Decisive Battles,' but there is a thoughtfulness here beyond anything to be found in Creasy's book." Arthur Ochs Sulzberger, publisher of the *New York Times* (1963–1992) and a U.S. marine, recalled Middleton's "enormous admiration for the military."

Unlike many journalists, Middleton supported the war in Vietnam. He attributed the U.S. defeat there to a lack of will, especially in Washington, where, according to his *Retreat from Victory* (p. 141), "The country was in a war, but the government didn't know what kind of a war nor how to fight it." Middleton was willing to express unpopular views, remarking, in his *Memoirs* (p. 74), "Disparagement of West Point . . . is fashionable nowadays. . . . What I found . . . in West Pointers is a high level of professional accomplishment and cold courage untainted by self-advertisement."

Despite changing vogues in academia and journalism—especially in the 1960s and 1970s—Middleton still believed that the United States had a responsibility to defend freedom and should maintain the Truman Doctrine of resistance to the Soviet Union. Middleton's point of view did not arise from partisanship. "In retrospect," he remarks in his *Memoirs* (p. 2), "I count myself fortunate that I came to Europe without deep political commitments. . . . I had never demonstrated for or against anything; nor have I to this day." His long career, during which he wrote fourteen books, may be partly a result of his seeing romance in his work, for which he never lost his enthusiasm. At the Garrick Club in London, where Middleton had been the only American honorary member, Arthur Ochs Sulzberger said, "In the history of the *New York*

Times, there are certain correspondents whose names come to mind when you search for the best. Drew Middleton is at the top of that list—brave, accurate, thoughtful." Middleton died in New York City.

• There are no Middleton papers. His library is at the American Heritage Center at the University of Wyoming in Laramie. Middleton is the author of *Our Share of Night: A Personal Narrative of the War Years* (1946), *The Struggle for Germany* (1949), *The Defense of Western Europe* (1952), *These Are the British* (1957), *The Sky Suspended* (1960), *The Supreme Choice* (1963), *The Atlantic Community* (1965), *Can America Win the Next War?* (1975), *Submarine* (1976), *The Duel of the Giants: China and Russia in Asia* (1978), *Invasion of the United States* (1985), and, with Gene Brown, *Southeast Asia* (1985). Middleton's articles in the *New York Times Magazine* include "Rallying the Marines," 4 Dec. 1983; "Barring Reporters from the Battlefield," 5 Feb. 1984; and "The World Has Never Been Quite the Same," 3 Sept. 1989. See also "Jimmy James's Boys," *Time*, 12 Apr. 1943, and "Middleton Matures," *Newsweek*, 17 May 1943. Arthur Ochs Sulzberger's reflections on Middleton were given at the Garrick Club, London, on 21 Mar. 1990. Obituaries are in the *New York Times*, 12 Jan. 1990; *The Times* (London), 13 Jan. 1990; and the *Century Yearbook 1990* (1991), by Clifton Daniel.

RALPH KIRSHNER

MIDDLETON, Henry (1717–13 June 1784), planter and second president of the First Continental Congress, was born at "The Oaks," his father's plantation near Charlestown, South Carolina, the son of Arthur Middleton (1681–1737) and Sarah Amory. Like the sons of many southern planters of the time, he was educated in England. In 1737 he inherited a large amount of property in South Carolina, Barbados, and England. Through land speculation and marriage, he expanded his holdings to over twenty plantations totaling 50,000 acres and about 800 slaves. "Middleton Place" became his in 1741 when he married Mary Williams. Laying out beautifully proportioned gardens and grounds, he made it his residence and the home of their twelve children. His wife died in 1761; the following year he married Maria Henrietta Bull, daughter of William Bull (1710–1791), lieutenant governor of the colony.

Middleton became active in public life upon his return from England when he was appointed a justice of the peace. First elected to the Commons House of Assembly from St. George, Dorchester County, in 1742, he served as its Speaker in 1747 and from 1754 to 1755. In 1755 he became a member of the Royal Council. As such, he fervently supported the Crown and in 1769 opposed the assembly's gift of £1,500 sterling to the Society of Gentlemen Supporters of the Bill of Rights, associated with the British radical John Wilkes. In September 1770, however, Middleton resigned his seat on the council and joined other South Carolinians in opposing royal policies. This action placed him in conflict with his father-in-law. In July 1774 a mass meeting in Charlestown chose Middleton and four others to represent the colony in the First Continental Congress. In Congress he said little, but behind the scenes he urged moderation in the hope that British commissioners would arrive to seek peace on reasonable terms. On 22 October he succeeded Peyton Randolph as president of the Congress and as such signed the "Declaration of Rights" prepared by the Congress for presentation to the king.

South Carolina returned Middleton to the Second Continental Congress in 1775, where on 24 May he declined the nomination as its president. Instead he continued to advocate moderation and delayed independence from behind the scenes. He returned to South Carolina in late 1775 and married his third wife, Lady Mary Mackenzie, the following year. (His second wife had died in 1772.) Middleton refused reappointment to Congress in February 1776 because, he claimed, he was physically unable to perform the duties of the position. His more radical son, Arthur Middleton (1742–1787), succeeded him in Congress. Henry Middleton later served as president of the South Carolina Provincial Congress, on the state's council of safety, and on the committee that in February 1776 framed a temporary state constitution. Pursuant to that document Middleton served on the legislative council and under the state's new 1778 constitution became a member of the senate in January 1779.

When Charlestown fell to the British in 1780, Middleton acknowledged defeat and accepted their protection. Despite this action, he suffered neither confiscation nor amercement of his property after the war, perhaps owing to his earlier service or his willingness to invest a significant portion of his wealth in the war efforts. Following the fall of Charlestown, Middleton's health began to decline; he died in Charlestown.

• Few letters from Middleton survive today. His correspondence on behalf of the South Carolina delegation or the Continental Congress is found in the Papers of the Continental Congress in the Library of Congress. See also *South Carolina Historical and Genealogical Magazine* (July 1900): 228–62, (Apr. 1919): 75–122, and (July 1926): 107–55; Alicia Hopton Middleton, *Life in Carolina and New England* (1929); Edward McCrady, *The History of South Carolina under the Royal Government*, 2d ed. (1901) and *The History of South Carolina in the Revolution*, 2d ed. (1902); William Smith, *The History of South Carolina as a Royal Province* (1903); Walter B. Edgar and N. Louise Bailey, eds., *Biographical Directory of the South Carolina House of Representatives*, vol. 2 (1977); and Paul A. Horne, Jr., "Forgotten Leaders: South Carolina's Delegation to the Continental Congress, 1774–1789" (Ph.D. diss., Univ. of South Carolina, 1988).

PAUL A. HORNE, JR.

MIDDLETON, Henry (28 Sept. 1770–14 June 1846), planter, politician, and diplomat, was born in London, England, the son of Arthur Middleton, signer of the Declaration of Independence, member of the Continental Congress, and governor of South Carolina, and Mary Izard. He was educated in classical studies by private tutors at Middleton Place, the family plantation near Charleston, and in England. While residing in Great Britain, on 13 November 1794 he married Mary Helen Hering, the daughter of Juliness Hering of Heybridge Hall, captain of his Majesty's Thirty-

Fourth Regiment. The couple had twelve children, eight of whom survived infancy. Upon Middleton's permanent return to the United States in 1800, he inherited Middleton Place, where he planted the first camellias in the United States, and the family estate at Newport, Rhode Island.

A Democratic-Republican because of his opposition to the Jay Treaty and affinity toward Thomas Jefferson as a southern agrarian slaveowner, Middleton represented the parishes of St. Philip and St. Michael in the South Carolina House of Representatives (1802–1810) and Senate (1810). During his tenure as governor (1810–1812), a free system of public education was instituted and the Bank of South Carolina was incorporated. While governor and after the expiration of his term, he supported the war policies of fellow South Carolinians John C. Calhoun, Langdon Cheves, and William Lowndes. He was elected to the U.S. House of Representatives in 1814 and reelected in 1816. While in Congress he embraced the trinity of postwar economic nationalism—protective tariffs, chartering a second national bank, and federally funded internal improvements.

From 6 April 1820 to 3 August 1830 Middleton served as American minister to Russia, the longest tenure of any American minister or ambassador appointed to the Court of St. Petersburg. On the recommendation of John C. Calhoun, the Monroe administration selected Middleton for the post to influence Tsar Alexander I's arbitration of an Anglo-American dispute regarding slaves liberated by British forces during and after the War of 1812, in violation of the Treaty of Ghent. Middleton's memoir on the subject contributed to an award of $1.2 million to American slaveowners as compensation for their lost property. In addition, Middleton's protest against the Russian government's claim of exclusive commercial and territorial rights north of 51° extending 100 miles into the Pacific Ocean (the ukase of 1821) and his defense of the noncolonization principle of the Monroe Doctrine resulted in the negotiation of the Russo-American Treaty of 1824. The agreement protected American rights to trade and fish along the Pacific Northwest Coast for ten years and asserted an American territorial claim to the area as far north as 54°40′. Consciously cultivating a Russo-American entente by exploiting Russian fears of an Anglo-American rapprochement, Middleton succeeded in dissuading Tsars Alexander I and Nicholas I from supporting Spain's effort to recapture its Latin American empire. He also settled the *Pearl*, *Commerce*, and *Hector* claims and obtained assistance from the Russian government in negotiating a commercial treaty with Turkey in 1830 that allowed American merchant ships to freely enter the Black Sea.

Middleton's unwavering support of Russia's anti-British policies in Greece, Persia (later Iran), and Turkey led to his recall as the Jackson administration attempted to settle longstanding Anglo-American differences regarding British West Indies trade. Criticism of the minister's aristocratic manner and a personal feud with secretary of the legation Beaufort Watts also contributed to the termination of his mission. Despite his failure to conclude a commercial treaty with Russia—the Russian government refused to accept America's definition of neutral rights associated with the principle of "freedom of the seas"—Middleton was one of the few American representatives who actually enjoyed a successful residence in St. Petersburg.

Before retiring from public service, Middleton helped organize the Union party, low-country planter opposition against Calhounite nullifiers. Sympathetic to southern opposition toward the "Tariff of Abominations," Middleton submitted a memorial to Congress in 1831 proposing a restoration of import tax rates of 1816 to settle the growing controversy between national supremacy and states rights. In November 1832 the nullifiers gained control of the two-thirds of the state legislature that was required to call a state convention; they then adopted the Nullification Ordinance despite Middleton's opposition. At a Union party convention the following month, Middleton served as vice president and petitioned the legislature of Tennessee to send delegates to a meeting of southern states that would consider measures other than nullification to resist enforcement of the 1828 and 1832 tariffs. Following the settlement of the controversy, he returned to private life at Middleton Place. He died in Charleston.

• Middleton's papers are in the South Carolina Historical Society, Middleton Place Plantation, the Caroliniana Library at the University of South Carolina, and the Southern Historical Collection at the University of North Carolina. On his diplomatic correspondence, see Diplomatic Despatches, Russia, RG 59, National Archives, and *The Papers of Henry Clay*, vols. 4–7, ed. James F. Hopkins (1959–1991). On his political career, consult Emily Reynolds and Joan Reynolds Faunt, comps., *Biographical Directory of the Senate of the State of South Carolina, 1776–1964* (1964); Robert Sobel and John Raimo, eds., *Biographical Directory of the Governors of the United States* (1978); and Kathryn Allamong Jacob and Bruce A. Ragsdale, eds., *Biographical Directory of the U.S. Congress, 1774–1989* (1989). See also William W. Freehling, *Prelude to Civil War* (1966), and William A. Schaper, *Sectionalism and Representation in South Carolina* (1968), on his involvement in the Nullification Crisis. For Middleton's service as American minister in Russia, see the following by Harold Edward Berquist, Jr.: "Russian-American Relations, 1820–1830: The Diplomacy of Henry Middleton, American Minister at St. Petersburg" (Ph.D. diss., Boston Univ., 1970); "Russo-American Economic Relations in the 1820s: Henry Middleton as a Protector of American Economic Interests in Russia and Turkey," *East European Quarterly* 11 (1977): 27–41; "Henry Middleton and the Arbitrament of the Anglo-American Slave Controversy by Tsar Alexander I," *South Carolina Historical Magazine* 82 (1981): 20–31; and "Henry Middleton as Political Reporter: The United States, the Near East, and Eastern Europe, 1821–1829," *The Historian* 45 (1983): 355–71.

DEAN FAFOUTIS

MIDDLETON, Peter (?–9 Jan. 1781), physician, left no information about the date and place of his birth in Scotland. What is known, however, is that he studied medicine under Dr. Thomas Simson at the University of St. Andrews, where according to the university's records Middleton applied on 27 February 1752 for examination for the degree of Doctor of Medicine. He went to New York City, probably in the same year, and entered into the practice of medicine with Dr. John Bard. Middleton became a prominent physician in New York, performing with Bard one of the first recorded dissections of a human body for the purpose of anatomical instruction in America. As suggested by his medical ledgers, preserved at Queens College, Middleton developed an extensive and lucrative practice, treating such eminent New York families as the DeLanceys, the Livingstons, the Schuylers, the Franks, the Hayses, and the Myerses. During the French and Indian War he was surgeon-general of provincial armies and rendered medical services during the Crown Point expedition.

In the 1760s and early 1770s, Middleton played an active part in fostering medical education in New York. On 14 August 1767, he and five other New York physicians presented to the governors of King's College (now Columbia University) a proposal "to institute a Medical School within this College for instructing Pupils in the most useful and necessary Branches of Medicine." The governors assented to this proposal. The medical school of King's College, the first institution of its kind in the city, was opened on 2 November 1767, with "a very elegant and learned Discourse" by Middleton, who reviewed the development of medicine from antiquity. (The event was reported by the *New-York Mercury* on 9 November 1767; the discourse was published as a pamphlet in New York in 1769.) Middleton was named professor of theory in 1767; he took on the teaching of materia medica in 1770. In 1771 he participated in proposing the establishment of a hospital in New York and became one of its incorporators that same year. He was appointed an attending physician in 1774, but the building burned down in 1775. (After being rebuilt, it was requisitioned by the British army in New York; the hospital was not opened for the reception of patients until 1791.) Aside from the *Discourse* given at the opening of the medical school, Middleton's only publication appears to have been a short paper of observations on the croup in a letter to Dr. Richard Bayley, published in Bayley's *Cases of the Angina Trachealis* (1781).

Middleton was active in the civic and cultural activities in New York before the American Revolution. He was a trustee of the New York Society for Promoting Useful Knowledge, a learned society that sponsored lectures given by the city's leading gentlemen-scholars. He was one of the founders of the St. Andrew's Society of New York and served as its president from 1767 to 1770. He was elected one of the governors of King's College in 1773. And he occupied an important position in Freemasonry, serving as deputy grand master of the "Modern" Grand Lodge of New York between 1771 and 1774.

Middleton married Susannah Nicholls Burges, the widow of a New York merchant, in 1766; she died in 1771. They had one daughter. In 1776 Middleton refused to support the cause of the patriots. Spurred by "prudential motives," he left New York for Bermuda in April of that year. After the British occupied the city, he returned to New York, conducted a limited medical practice between 1777 and 1780, and died there in early 1781.

The career of Middleton is intimately associated with significant aspects of eighteenth-century America. American medicine is indebted to him, for he was one of the first eminent contributors to surgery in colonial America. More important, Middleton, by our standards, was a visible and civic-minded person. He played a major role in promoting medical education and institutions in eighteenth-century New York.

• Middleton's life is briefly described in James J. Walsh, *A History of Medicine in New York*, vol. 1 (1919), pp. 46–49. Middleton's behavior as a physician and as a civic leader is examined in W. B. McDaniel, "The Beginnings of American Medical Historiography," *Bulletin of the History of Medicine* 26 (1952): 46–50; in Leo Hershkowitz, "Powdered Tin and Rose Petals: Myer Myers, Goldsmith and Peter Middleton, Physician," *American Jewish History* 70 (June 1981): 462–67; and very briefly in Thomas Bender, *New York Intellect* (1987). Ossian Lang refers to Middleton's role as a New York Masonic leader in the *History of Freemasonry in the State of New York* (1922). Middleton's will can be found in the New-York Historical Society, *Collections for the Year 1901* (1902). Some manuscripts and medical ledgers of Middleton are in the Historical Documents Collections of Queens College of the City University of New York and provide valuable insights into his medical practice.

WILLIAM WEISBERGER

MIDDLETON, William Shainline (7 Jan. 1890–9 Sept. 1975), medical educator and administrator, was born in Norristown, Pennsylvania, the son of Daniel Shephard Middleton, a grocer and wholesale confectioner, and Ann Sophia Shainline. He received an M.D. from the University of Pennsylvania in 1911. While at Pennsylvania, he developed an interest in the history of his profession through contact with John G. Clark, professor of gynecology, and David Riesman, professor of clinical medicine and later professor of the history of medicine.

Following graduation, Middleton did a one-year internship at Philadelphia General (Old Blockley) Hospital. Still uncertain about where and what his medical career should be, he took a position in 1912 at Babies Hospital (a division of Philadelphia's Children's Hospital). That same year Dr. Joseph Spragg Evans, head of the University of Wisconsin's newly established Student Health Service, traveled to Philadelphia in search of an assistant. On the recommendation of Dr. Charles Fife of Babies Hospital, Middleton received the appointment.

William Snow Miller, professor of anatomy at the Wisconsin Medical School, had begun the famous Wisconsin Medical History Seminars in 1909. After his arrival, Middleton became the seminar's most highly regarded and productive member. He eventually wrote nearly forty articles on medical history, many of them on distinguished early Philadelphia physicians. These did much to call attention to the prominence of that city in early American medical history. Middleton was a charter member of the American Association for the History of Medicine and was elected its president in 1934.

In May 1917 Middleton joined the U.S. Army Medical Officers' Reserve Corps. He served in France, first with the British expeditionary forces and then with the American. For a time in 1918 he was stationed at the Central Medical Laboratory unit in Dijon, France, where he met and worked with the famous Harvard physiologist Walter B. Cannon.

Upon his return to the Wisconsin Medical School in March 1919, Middleton was put in charge of the new student infirmary. In September 1921 he married Maude H. Webster, whom he had met while she was a nurse at Madison General Hospital; they had no children.

Shortly after World War I, the medical school at the University of Wisconsin became a four-year institution with its own teaching hospital. Taking full advantage of these improvements, Middleton achieved a national reputation as a teacher, diagnostician, and clinical investigator. In 1933 he attained the rank of full professor of medicine. That same year he was elected president of the Central Society of Clinical Research. Middleton also served as consultant to the Veterans Bureau (later the Veterans Administration) and the U.S. Public Health Service.

In 1935 Middleton became the second dean of the University of Wisconsin Medical School while continuing an active role as professor of medicine, spending his mornings conducting teaching rounds and overseeing hospital consultations and his afternoons attending to administrative duties. His reputation as an exceptional diagnostician and clinical teacher brought him visiting professorships at the Universities of Michigan (1940), Oregon (1941), and Illinois (1941).

After the United States entered World War II, Middleton was encouraged to remain as dean, but he insisted on serving once more in the military. In July 1942 he was made chief consultant in medicine in the Office of the Chief Surgeon, European Theater of Operations. While serving in that capacity he obtained the services of Howard W. Florey of Oxford University to supervise the introduction and use of the new wonder drug penicillin. For his outstanding work in the European Theater, Middleton received the Legion of Merit with Oak Leaf Cluster and Distinguished Service Medal from his own government and the Croix de Guerre with Palm from France, while Britain made him an honorary officer, Order of the British Empire, and fellow of the Royal College of Surgeons of London.

By the fall of 1945 Middleton had resumed his role as dean and professor of medicine at Wisconsin. His services to the military did not cease, however. From 1956 to 1960 he served as expert and consultant to the Department of the Army. In the winter of 1948 he served briefly in active duty as adviser to the Pentagon on improving certain administrative aspects of the Army Medical Department. The following year he was chosen chairman of the Armed Forces Medical Advisory Committee. He also served on the Defense Department's Civilian Health and Medical Advisory Council.

In 1950 Middleton was elected president of the American College of Physicians. At that time the American hospital system was rapidly expanding, and he lobbied vigorously for a greater role for doctors in the survey, inspection, and certification of hospitals. In 1962 the ACP awarded him the Alfred Stengel Memorial Award. In 1951 Middleton served as visiting professor of medicine at the University of Pennsylvania Medical School.

Middleton's postwar period as dean at Wisconsin began auspiciously enough, with the endowment of new chairs in biophysics and the history of medicine, areas proposed by him. Middleton then became increasingly concerned that the nation's medical schools were giving too much emphasis to research and service at the expense of training "thoughtful physicians and co-professionals." He also opposed the use of federal and pharmaceutical monies for research. Middleton's positions on these and other matters led to strained relations between him and the university administration as well as some of the medical faculty. In 1955 he resigned as dean.

Immediately appointed chief medical director of the Veterans Administration, Middleton held the post for two terms. During this time he strongly supported a policy of linking VA hospitals to nearby medical schools and providing a greater role for research at these institutions. He also worked ceaselessly to assure quality care, visiting hospitals regularly and often conducting teaching rounds.

Following his two terms as medical director, Middleton, now seventy-three, served a year as visiting professor of medicine at the University of Oklahoma and accepted the chairmanship of the new National Drug Research Board. Between 1964 and 1970 he acted as consultant in research and education to the VA hospital in Madison, Wisconsin. As a tribute to his accomplishments, the medical library at the University of Wisconsin and the VA hospital in Madison were named after him.

In 1968 Middleton's first wife died, and in 1973 he married Ruth Addams, a longtime friend and former assistant chief of nursing for the Veterans Administration in Washington. They had no children. Middleton died in Madison, Wisconsin.

As teacher, scientist, administrator, and historian of his profession, Middleton played a prominent role in the rise of American medicine to world leadership.

• The two main repositories for Middleton's papers are the National Library of Medicine, Bethesda, Md., and the University of Wisconsin Archives in Madison. Important oral interviews with Middleton were done by Steven Lowe, University Archives Oral History Project, William S. Middleton

Papers, University of Wisconsin Archives; and by Peter D. Olch, Microfilm Reel 76–4, National Library of Medicine. Most of Middleton's essays are collected in *Medical History Essays* (1965) and *Values in Modern Medicine* (1972). His medical writings are listed in "Collected Papers," *Wisconsin Medical Journal* 63 (1964): 548–53. His historical writings are listed in "Medico-Historical Publications of William S. Middleton," *Bulletin of the History of Medicine* 50 (1976): 131–32. The most complete biography of Middleton is Irvin M. Becker, "William Shainline Middleton, 1890–1975" (master's thesis, Univ. of Wisconsin–Milwaukee, 1989), which was reproduced as a supplement to the *Wisconsin Medical Alumni Quarterly* 30, no. 4 (1990). Two other important sources are Paul F. Clark, *The University of Wisconsin Medical School: A Chronicle, 1848–1948* (1967), and John B. Coates, Jr., ed., *Medical Department, United States Army, Internal Medicine in World War II*, vol. 1: *Activities of Medical Consultants* (1961).

PHILIP CASH

MIDGLEY, Thomas, Jr. (18 May 1889–2 Nov. 1944), industrial chemist, was born in Beaver Falls, Pennsylvania, the son of Thomas Midgley, an inventor and manufacturer, and Hattie Emerson. He grew up in Columbus, Ohio, where his father managed a bicycle factory and subsequently started his own automotive tire company. Midgley attended public schools, then transferred to the Betts Academy in Connecticut to complete his secondary education. Intending to follow in his father's footsteps as an inventor, Midgley enrolled in the mechanical engineering program at Cornell University. There he took such a wide range of courses that his future boss and collaborator Charles Kettering often pointed to Midgley's undergraduate experience as a model of the kind of broad, fundamental education that was essential for a successful career in industrial research.

Midgley graduated from Cornell in 1911 and took a job as a designer with the inventions department of the National Cash Register Company in Dayton, Ohio. That year he married Carrie May Reynolds; they had two children. After a stint with his father's tire company, he joined Kettering's Dayton Engineering Laboratories Company, or Delco, in 1916. Because of Midgley's grasp of fundamentals, Kettering put him to work studying "knock," a perplexing malfunction of contemporary gasoline engines that seriously limited performance and efficiency.

Starting with what he knew best, mechanical design, Midgley devised an improved engine indicator, which revealed, contrary to expectation, that knock was more a failing of the fuel than of the engine. He concluded that the basic problem was poor vaporization and tried a red dye, iodine, in the hope of increasing fuel volatility. Iodine did suppress knock effectively, though other dyes did not. Demonstrating a knack for isolating the significant result in an experimental failure, Midgley deduced that iodine worked not because of its color, but because it somehow acted as a catalyst, and so he began testing compounds with related chemical structures. Midgley later dubbed this phase of the research a scientific "fox hunt," though a colleague more accurately recalled it as "a succession of failures with just enough successes to keep us going." Even the "successes" had their drawbacks. Tellerium, for instance, worked well, but the exhaust smelled so bad that the researchers took to calling their test car "The Goat."

General Motors acquired Delco in 1919 and put Kettering in charge of its new research laboratory. Midgley became head of the laboratory's fuel section. Because he anticipated a post–World War I fuel shortage, Kettering gave top priority to Midgley's antiknock research. Midgley tested thousands of potential antiknock additives until he noticed that all the best ones had been derived from a group of elements in one corner of a specially arranged periodic table. He then began concentrating on compounds that were made from those elements. In December 1921 he hit upon tetraethyl lead (TEL), an obscure organic lead compound that suppressed knock completely, even in concentrations as low as one part to 1,300 parts of gasoline. To exploit leaded gasoline commercially, General Motors turned to the chemical engineering expertise of Standard Oil of New Jersey. Together they formed the jointly owned Ethyl Gasoline Corporation in 1924. Kettering became president, and Midgley vice president and general manager. As a corporate executive, Midgley immediately faced some serious technical and safety problems with leaded gasoline. Early road tests revealed that TEL fouled spark plugs and exhaust valves, which forced Midgley back to the laboratory to look for a chemical corrective for this unexpected side effect. He discovered one in ethyl bromide. To ensure an adequate supply to treat the nation's four-billion-gallon-a-year gasoline habit, he worked with Dow Chemical to develop a process for extracting bromine directly from the sea and subsequently became a director of the Ethyl-Dow Chemical Company.

More challenging still was the potential public health threat posed by TEL. Early in the TEL research, Midgley had been forced to take an extended vacation to throw off the toxic effects of organic lead exposure. Two of his General Motors workers had even died from lead poisoning at the Dayton laboratories. Then in October 1924, just after leaded gasoline had gone into full-scale production, four workers were killed and dozens were hospitalized after an accident at Standard Oil's TEL plant in New Jersey. The incident made national headlines and led to local restrictions on the sale and use of leaded gasoline as well as an investigation by the U.S. surgeon general. Midgley and other Ethyl representatives argued that unproven environmental risks should not be allowed to keep leaded gasoline off the market. They offered evidence from their own studies of mechanics and garage workers, which suggested that TEL, once diluted in gasoline, was no more hazardous than most chemicals. The surgeon general's study reached similar conclusions and recommended only stricter manufacturing controls. By 1926 leaded gasoline was back on sale nationwide, with Du Pont taking over TEL production.

Though Midgley recognized and acted upon the short-term health threat of TEL, he and his colleagues did little to monitor the possible dangers from long-term, low-concentration exposure. The full public health risks of leaded gasoline became apparent only in the 1960s, when more sophisticated measuring instruments disclosed just how much lead had actually accumulated over the years and how seriously it was affecting those exposed to it. Strict federal automotive emissions standards in the late 1970s effectively forced leaded gasoline off the market in the United States.

When General Motors moved its research laboratories to Detroit in 1924, Midgley stayed behind in Dayton as a consultant and Ethyl executive. He and his family subsequently moved to Worthington, Ohio. From 1926 to 1930 General Motors supported Midgley's independent studies of synthetic rubber in an attempt to head off steep price increases in natural rubber. Midgley always regarded the rubber research as his most purely scientific contribution, although as he once explained, "Perhaps I consider the work on synthetic rubber more scientific because nothing commercial ever came of it."

Midgley's next consulting job turned out to be more profitable both financially and scientifically. Looking to revitalize General Motors' slumping Frigidaire division, Kettering asked Midgley to study chemical refrigerants with the goal of finding something safer than the highly toxic and flammable refrigerants then in common use. Midgley again put his special periodic table to work and narrowed his search to a handful of compounds. From them, he and collaborator Albert Henne identified and synthesized dichlorodifluoromethane, the first in the family of Freon refrigerants. Midgley introduced it in April 1930 at the annual meeting of the American Chemical Society, where in a theatrical gesture he breathed in a bit of Freon and then slowly exhaled it to extinguish a candle flame, so demonstrating both its nontoxicity and nonflammability.

Once again, General Motors capitalized on its discovery by going into partnership with an established chemical company, this time Du Pont. In August 1930 the two corporations formed the Kinetic Chemical Company to manufacture and market Freon. Midgley became vice president. Despite the relatively high cost, Freon proved so superior to the competition that by the end of the 1930s it had become the standard refrigerant for domestic use. Freon's unique properties also made it an ideal aerosol propellant. Once released into the atmosphere, however, Freon reacted with the earth's ozone layer in unexpected ways, as scientists would begin to discover in the 1970s. So, ironically, a compound that Midgley had developed specifically for its safety features turned out to be an even greater environmental threat than TEL.

Struck down with polio in 1940, Midgley kept as active as possible at his home in Worthington and even rigged up a system of ropes and pulleys to help him to move about his bed more easily. He became increasingly despondent, however, began to drink heavily, and finally took his own life by strangling himself in his own device.

Midgley's achievements earned him four major awards in American chemistry, the Nichols (1922), Perkin (1937), Priestley (1941), and Gibbs (1942) medals; two honorary degrees; election to the National Academy of Sciences (1942); and the presidency of the American Chemical Society (1944). He also held more than one hundred patents and generally disproved his own contention that scientists should move into management by age forty before they ran out of fresh ideas. He believed that the proper measure of a scientific accomplishment was as much its contribution to human welfare as its contribution to human knowledge, and he took well-deserved pride in the great industries that his ideas had built. Perhaps the title of one of his last articles, "Problem + Research + Capital = Progress" (*Journal of Industrial and Engineering Chemistry*) 31 [1939]: 504–6), best summarized Midgley's philosophy. He could not, of course, have anticipated the environmental consequences of some of his work, but he would have accepted them as an inevitable cost of trying to make the world a better place. Like his good friend Kettering, he often insisted that "the price of progress is trouble, and I don't think the price is too high."

• Some of Midgley's correspondence and other papers can be found in the General Motors Institute Alumni Collection of Industrial History in Flint, Mich. The collection includes oral histories with some of his associates and a manuscript history of ethyl gasoline. Midgley provides a good overview of his own career in "From the Periodic Table to Production," *Journal of Industrial and Engineering Chemistry* 29 (1937): 241–44. Two appreciations by close associates are Charles F. Kettering, "Biographical Memoir of Thomas Midgley, Jr., 1889–1944," *National Academy of Sciences, Biographical Memoirs* 24 (1947): 361–80, and Thomas A. Boyd, "Thomas Midgley, Jr.," *Journal of the American Chemical Society* 75 (1953): 2791–95. Both include comprehensive bibliographies. Seth Cagin and Philip Dray, *Between Earth and Sky: How CFCs Changed Our World and Endangered the Ozone Layer* (1993), includes a detailed account of Midgley's work on TEL and CFCs and provides new evidence on the details of his death. See also, Thomas P. Hughes, "Inventors: The Problems They Choose, the Ideas They Have, and the Inventions They Make," in *Technological Innovation: A Critical Review of Current Knowledge*, ed. Patrick Kelly and Melvin Kranzberg (1978), pp. 166–82. Stuart W. Leslie, *Boss Kettering: Wizard of General Motors* (1983); Thomas A. Boyd, *Professional Amateur* (1957); and Joseph C. Robert, *Ethyl: A History of the Corporation and the People Who Made It* (1983), all include chapters on the development of tetraethyl lead. David A. Hounshell and John Kenly Smith, Jr., *Science and Corporate Strategy: Du Pont R & D, 1902–1980* (1988), has a good chapter on the development of tetraethyl lead and Freon from the Du Pont perspective.

STUART W. LESLIE

MIELZINER, Jo (19 Mar. 1901–15 Mar. 1976), stage designer, was born in Paris, France, the son of Leo Mielziner, a portrait painter, and Ella MacKenna Friend, a fashion and arts journalist and the first female member of the Foreign Press Association. (The last name is pronounced mellzeener.) In 1909 the family moved to the United States, where Mielziner was enrolled in the Ethical Culture School in New York City. He also studied for one year at the National Academy of Design and the Art Students League. In 1915 he was awarded a scholarship to study at the Pennsylvania Academy of the Fine Arts. Except for a brief stint in the U.S. Marine Corps during World War I, he remained at the academy until 1919. That year the academy awarded him a Cresson traveling fellowship, which allowed him to tour Europe, then the center of innovation in theatrical and stage design. His travels brought him into contact with designers Oscar Strand in Vienna, famous for having invented a rotating stage, and Gordon Craig in Italy. Mielziner was awarded a second Cresson in 1922.

After Mielziner returned to the United States, he began working as an actor, stage manager, and assistant designer for Jessie Bonstelle's theatrical company in Detroit. He soon moved to New York City, where he apprenticed himself to Joseph Urban, Robert Edmund Jones, and Lee Simonson. After joining the Theatre Guild, Mielziner worked briefly as a stage manager and an actor, performing minor roles in *Saint Joan* and *The Failures* (both 1923). His first major design project was the set for Ferenc Molnár's *The Guardsman* (1924). By the end of 1924 Mielziner's career as a designer had taken off, and he had more commissions than he could complete. By the following season he was designing the backdrops for eight plays, an enormous number by the standards of the day. By 1927–1928 he was of a stature to be the set designer for Eugene O'Neill's *Strange Interlude*, which won the Pulitzer Prize for drama in 1928. One of Mielziner's most noted designs was for the initial production of Maxwell Anderson's *Winterset* (1935), a tragedy of ghettoes and gangsters based on the Sacco-Vanzetti case. He convinced the initially skeptical director to allow him to create a backdrop that was moody, softly lit, and hazily suggestive, instead of the harshly lit, realistic, urban scene Anderson had initially envisioned.

In 1938 Mielziner married Jean MacIntyre, an actress; they adopted three children. In 1942 he was a founding member of the Camouflage Society of Professional Stage Designers, who worked with the military to learn how they might professionally help the war effort. Shortly afterward Mielziner volunteered for two years of service with the U.S. Army Air Corps, in which he reached the rank of major. During this time he wrote a technical manual on camouflage. Mielziner's first stage design upon his discharge was for Tennessee Williams's *The Glass Menagerie* (1945), which earned him a New York Critics' Circle award. At the end of the war, at the request of the State Department, he designed the lighting and interior appearance of the first United Nations session in San Francisco.

Mielziner won his first Tony Award in 1949; it was given for the body of his work created in the 1948–1949 season, which included ten different set designs. The set for Arthur Miller's *Death of a Salesman* (1949), described in the *New York Times* (16 Mar. 1976) as "mordantly moody," was especially lauded. By extending the stage into the seating area, Mielziner created an effect that drew the audience into Miller's poignant drama. Mielziner's credits following World War II also include *A Streetcar Named Desire* (1947) by Tennessee Williams; *Carousel* (1945), *South Pacific* (1949), and *The King and I* (1951) by Richard Rogers and Oscar Hammerstein, Jr.; and *Guys and Dolls* (1950) by Frank Loesser.

Mielziner continued to work in stage design during the 1950s. For his color art direction in the film *Picnic*, he was awarded an Academy Award in 1955. During the 1960s Mielziner accepted several commissions to design entire theaters, including the Vivian Beaumont at Lincoln Center in New York City and the Mark Taper Forum in the Los Angeles Music Center. He also created a portable stage for the White House's East Room in 1964 and a setting for the display of Michelangelo's *Pietà* in the New York World's Fair of 1966. Mielziner's later years were occupied with the writing of *Designing for the Theatre* (1963) and *The Shapers of Our Theatre* (1970). One of his last completed projects was the scenery for Mozart's *Don Giovanni* at the Metropolitan Opera, which opened after his death. Mielziner's designs for the set of a musical adaptation of the French film *The Baker's Wife* were left uncompleted. He died in New York City while writing a work on the importance of collaboration in the theater.

Mielziner's work was part of a new movement in set design that valued atmosphere, illusion, and color over detail and realism. His designs favored minimalism over clutter, symbolism over naturalism. Scenery, he thought, should never occupy more than thirty seconds of an audience's conscious attention. As one of America's most important set designers from the late 1920s into the 1970s, Mielziner created the backdrops for more than 300 dramas, comedies, operas, and ballets.

• Mielziner's papers are at the New York Public Library for the Performing Arts, Lincoln Center; some scrapbooks are in the Special Collections Division of Boston University. For further information on Mielziner, see John Mason Brown, "Youngsters in Stage Designing," *Boston Transcript*, 6 June 1925; *Literary Digest*, 18 July 1925; *New York Times*, 28 Mar. 1942; and *Variety*, 18 Oct. 1944. An obituary is in the *New York Times*, 16 Mar. 1976.

ELIZABETH ZOE VICARY

MIES VAN DER ROHE, Ludwig (27 Mar. 1886–17 Aug. 1969), architect, was born Ludwig Mies in Aachen, Germany, the son of Michael Mies, a stonemason, and Amalie Rohe. His professional name was created by inserting the artificial "van der" between the surnames of his father and mother. Mies received no formal schooling in architecture. Coming from a long line of sober, middle-class Rhenish craftsmen, he attended trade school in Aachen until the age of fifteen and then worked briefly as a bricklayer's apprentice and later as a draftsman in a stucco factory. A natural gift for drawing attracted the attention of several professionals, who encouraged him to consider a career in architecture. In 1905 Mies left his native city for Berlin, where a job as a studio assistant to the municipal architecture office of suburban Rixdorf (known today as Neukölln) awaited him.

Following a tour of duty with designer-architect Bruno Paul, Mies completed his first independent commission in Neubabelsberg, an affluent Berlin suburb. It was a country residence for the distinguished Nietzschean scholar Alois Riehl, who was sufficiently impressed by Mies to finance the 21-year-old's study tour of Italy that carried him to Vicenza, Florence, and Rome.

In 1908 Mies joined the office of Peter Behrens, an architect whose prominence, especially in progressive circles, may be inferred from the fact that two later luminaries of the twentieth-century avant-garde, Le Corbusier (then Charles Jeanneret) and Walter Gropius, worked in the Behrens office, alongside Mies, for a short time in 1910. Behrens's practice was divided between bold, stylistically direct factory structures and more formal residences, the latter markedly indebted in style to the nineteenth-century German romantic classicist Karl Friedrich Schinkel. Mies's own well-documented admiration for Schinkel owed much to time spent in the company of Behrens. Indeed, the project Mies designed for Mr. and Mrs. A. G. Kröller, a villa near The Hague meant to accommodate the owners' huge modern art collection, drew heavily on the example of Schinkel as well as on a design conceived earlier for the Kröllers by Behrens himself. Both the Mies and Behrens projects were rejected by the Kröllers in favor of yet another—likewise never realized—by Hendrik Berlage. By that time, in 1913, Mies had married Ada Bruhn; they had three daughters.

Mies saw the work of Frank Lloyd Wright for the first time in 1911 at an exhibition in Berlin. His later claim that Wright's work affected him deeply is borne out by many of his mature designs, but he stayed true to a neoclassical, Schinkelesque manner until the early 1920s. Then, with army service in World War I behind him, he reestablished himself in Berlin and in 1921 separated from his wife. He met and befriended several avant-garde figures in the German capital, chiefly Hans Richter, El Lissitzky, and Theo van Doesburg, and made a sudden, radical stylistic shift, embracing the abstract forms associated with modernism. Between 1921 and 1924 Mies designed five spectacular projects that catapulted him to the forefront of the modernist movement in Germany. Two of the five works were high-rise buildings, vaguely expressionist in profile but notable more for their reductivist form and audacious treatment of reflective glass skins. A third project was a concrete office building that featured an early and inventive use of ribbon windows, while the remaining two were villas remarkable for their centrifugal reach into surrounding space and, in the later of the two, for a highly original development of the Wrightian open plan.

During the period in which Mies produced these works—none of them ever completed—the German economy languished at a postwar ebb, and Mies kept his practice alive by building residences in traditional styles for mostly conservative clients. By the mid-1920s the nation's financial condition had improved, and Mies was free to work in an increasingly popular modernist idiom, his professional reputation growing correspondingly. The German Werkbund, a professional organization renowned for various endeavors in behalf of the vanguard, directed Mies to supervise the creation of a housing colony near Stuttgart that was intended to demonstrate the attractiveness of the *Neues Bauen* (the New Building). The Weissenhofsiedlung, as it was called, opened in 1927, with a brace of buildings by Le Corbusier, Gropius, J. J. P. Oud, and Mies himself, among others. Not the least notable feature of the event, which sympathetic critics hailed as the triumph of modern architecture, was the unified appearance of the structures: their mostly white facades, flat roofs, asymmetrical plans, and membranous volumes, all studiously devoid of historical ornament.

The strikingly similar appearance of the new buildings in Stuttgart and elsewhere in Europe prompted a pair of American architectural historians, Henry-Russell Hitchcock and Philip Johnson, to claim in a highly influential book of 1932 that an "International Style" (the book's title) had developed in the course of the 1920s. The name eventually became a worldwide commonplace of architectural parlance, exemplified in large part by Mies's work of the late 1920s and early 1930s, especially the two most celebrated works of his European career: the German Pavilion of the Barcelona International Exposition of 1929 (rebuilt 1983–1986) and the Tugendhat House in Brno (1928–1930). Both buildings, notable for Mies's use of a variety of patrician marbles and glass, featured the open plan, with major walls defining rather than enclosing space. They are also remembered as settings for which Mies designed several pieces of furniture, most memorably the "Barcelona Chair" and the "Tugendhat Table," that have come to be recognized as masterpieces of modernist furniture.

Mies also left his stamp on architectural education in Germany during the Weimar period. He was the director of the famous Bauhaus in Dessau from 1930 to 1932, when representatives of an increasingly aggressive local political right wing, long hostile to the Bauhaus's modernist inclinations, forced a shutdown of the state-financed school. Mies reopened it as a private academy in Berlin, where it lasted about a year before pressure from the Nazis, newly in command of the national government, induced the faculty themselves to close the institution's doors.

Mies remained in Germany during the early phase of National Socialism. To all appearances as indifferent to politics as he was devoted to his art, he tried for several years to approach his own architectural practice in a manner and with an attitude he hoped might find acceptance by the Nazi authorities, who, briefly in 1933 and 1934, argued among themselves over the potential worthiness of certain aspects of modernism in the arts. He failed at these attempts at compromise. His 1933 design for a new Reichsbank aimed at a monumentality uncommon in his earlier work, but the project was rejected by a government-appointed jury. Thereafter, laboring mainly on designs of houses surrounded by walled courts—all unbuilt—and living until 1937 mostly on royalties gained from his furniture designs, he accepted a commission from Mr. and Mrs. Stanley Resor of New York City to build a country house for them in Wyoming. Traveling the full 5,000 miles to the site, he stopped en route in Chicago, where he agreed to assume the headship of the School of Architecture at Armour Institute of Technology (later Illinois Institute of Technology). He took up his academic duties as well as residence in Chicago in 1938.

The Resor House never materialized, but its loss was more than compensated by Mies's first large-scale American commission, the reconstitution of the entire Armour campus, an undertaking delayed by World War II but largely realized in the decade thereafter. By 1956 he had completed the premier component of the ensemble, S. R. Crown Hall, the School of Architecture building, a vast unitary space whose roof was hung from four plate girders. Crown Hall was a prime example of the single-story column-free pavilion, one of two genres that most interested him in his American years. The other was the high-rise building, which Mies conceived, in his typical bow to reductive geometry, as a great rectangular prism clad in a steel and glass curtain wall, a slab form that broke with the setback volumetrics characteristic of pre–World War II American skyscrapers. The 860–880 Lake Shore Drive apartment buildings in Chicago (1948–1951) are early examples of this type, while the Seagram Building in New York (1954–1958) is commonly regarded as his masterpiece in the idiom.

Mies's American work was shaped to a significant extent by his ready access to steel. Given his lifelong tendency to stress the importance of technology in the building art, he saw steel as the primary modern constructive material and structure itself as the element closest to the nature of a rational, objective architecture. In view further of his yearning to reduce his work to its sparest essentials ("beinahe nichts"—almost nothing, as he put it), space took on an importance reciprocal to structure. A resultant dialogue between bare material structure and unimpeded, immaterial space was enunciated in later projects both large and small. His 1954 design of a convention hall consisted of a unitary, column-free space more than 700 square feet, roofed over by a three-dimensional truss resting on the slenderest of posts, while the Farnsworth House of 1946–1951 was a bandbox—a single room walled totally in glass and supported by a roof slab and a floor slab held in place by eight wide-flange columns, four to each side.

Mies taught at Illinois Institute of Technology (IIT) until 1958; however, in a sense his significance as an educator was more dramatically evident in the virtually iconic influence he had on international architecture in the 1950s and the early 1960s. Following his retirement from IIT in 1958, Mies confined himself to his practice, which he maintained until his death in Chicago. Mies's position among the several most important architects of the twentieth century was a matter of global consensus by the time he had established a career in the United States, little more than a decade following his emigration in 1938. He is customarily said to have shared in many of the expressive habits of the modernist movement, which in seeking to free architecture of dependence on traditional historical styles tended to emphasize the building as a self-referential object more or less independent not only of past time but of present space—that is, of existent physical context. That viewpoint has been challenged at the end of the century by the architectural postmodernists, who have come to regard history as a stimulus rather than a hindrance to creativity, and context more as a determinant of design than an irrelevance. Despite this significant shift in collective attitude, the qualities with which Mies endowed his work—a rigorously logical reduction of structure and space to their formal essences, a superb use of materials, and an uncommon sense of rightness in proportion—have been enough to keep his reputation secure in the minds of many contemporary critics and historians.

• The Library of Congress has most of Mies's personal papers. The Mies van der Rohe Archive at the Museum of Modern Art contains his professional papers, including thousands of drawings. The most complete biography is Franz Schulze, *Mies van der Rohe: A Critical Biography* (1985). The most complete record of his work is *The Mies van der Rohe Archive: The Museum of Modern Art*, vols. 1–4, ed. Arthur Drexler (1986), vols. 5–6, ed. Schulze (1990), and vols. 7–20, ed. Schulze (1991). Other major books include Jean-Louis Cohen, *Mies van der Rohe* (1996), a brief but informative summary of Mies's life and career; Ludwig Glaeser, *Ludwig Mies van der Rohe: Furniture and Furniture Drawings from the Design Collection of the Mies van der Rohe Archive* (1997), the best discussion of Mies's furniture designs; Henry-Russell Hitchcock and Philip Johnson, *The International Style* (1932, 1966), which fixes Mies's place in European modernist architecture of the 1920s; Johnson, *Mies van der Rohe* (1947, 1978), the earliest monograph on Mies, still highly instructive; Fritz Neumeyer, *The Artless Word: Mies van der Rohe on the Building Art* (1991), an insightful study of Mies's architectural philosophy; and Schulze, ed., *Mies van der Rohe: Critical Essays* (1989), four authoritative articles of recent scholarship.

FRANZ SCHULZE

MIFFLIN, Lloyd (15 Sept. 1846–16 July 1921), poet and painter, was born in Columbia, Pennsylvania, the son of John Houston Mifflin, a moderately well-to-do landowner, portrait painter, and poet, and Elizabeth Ann Bethel Heise. Mifflin's mother died when he was a child, after which his father gave up his career to care for the five children. Mifflin attended elementary schools in Columbia and the Washington Classical Institute there. He was also tutored by his father and by Howard W. Gilbert, who had studied in Heidelberg, Germany. When he began to show an interest in sketching at age fourteen, his father warned him of the problems most artists encounter. Soon recognizing that the boy was serious, however, he proceeded to train him in the basics of draftsmanship and the harmonious use of colors and also encouraged him in landscape drawing.

Mifflin studied briefly under Isaac Williams of Philadelphia and then under Thomas Moran there in 1869 and 1870. Moran, who later distinguished himself as a painter of Yellowstone and other western scenes, became his lifelong friend. In 1869 Mifflin exhibited an early painting titled *An Autumn Evening* at the Pennsylvania Academy of the Fine Arts in Philadelphia. During this period he sculpted a bust of his father, tried to make a bust of himself, then concentrated on painting. He copied a big painting by J. M. W. Turner and worked too strenuously for his delicate health. He especially loved the Susquehanna Valley, made many sketches of scenes along the Susquehanna River, and in August and September 1871 toured and sketched along the entire river from Cooperstown, New York, to the Chesapeake Bay.

Determined to study art in Europe, Mifflin sailed from Boston in January 1872 to Liverpool. From there he visited galleries, cathedrals, and cemeteries in England, France, and the Netherlands, relishing, as he moved about, the freedom of moderate bohemian living, which was new to him. By June he was in Düsseldorf, studying under German painter Herman Herzog for a period of a few months. He sailed up the Rhine, traveled through the Alps, and sketched many challenging scenes. He crossed into Italy, where he gloried in its colorful scenery and art masterpieces, especially in Venice and Rome. Among the great artists, he revered Rembrandt most of all and also admired Paul Gustave Doré, Titian, Tintoretto, and Paolo Veronese. A philosophical change came over him, probably in Venice in June 1873. He began to feel that the beauties of nature were not art subjects as ends in themselves but should together act as a bridge to a harmonious, spiritual ideal—to be somehow captured on canvas and in poetry.

In September 1873 Mifflin returned to Columbia. Inspired by his beloved Susquehanna River anew, he painted several charming views, including *Looking toward Turkey Hill* and *View from Grubb's Hill above St. Charles Furnace*. The following summer he took a leisurely walking trip down the Brandywine River and made 145 sketches for a book of drawings he never assembled. Shortly after falling in love with a local girl named Barbara Peart, he confided to his cousin George Mifflin that he was going to ask her to marry him—only to be permanently downcast when George said that she had already accepted his own proposal. He hints at his sorrow and recovery in a few of the poems making up his first collection. It is titled *Ventures in Verse* and was privately printed in 1876, under the pen name Victor Leon and not for sale. Among his unpublished poems is one with these lines about unconsummated love: "Lovers who would love for aye / Must forever love apart." In many other poems, some published and others found only after his death in a file marked "confidential," he made an obsessive topic out of the notion that there is something unique about such love.

Remaining single all his life, Mifflin became a country squire, managed his "Norwood" estate, and wrote and published poetry in earnest—all bookish and conventional. His literary inspirations included the works of Heinrich Heine, John Keats, Thomas Moore, and Alfred, Lord Tennyson. He also admired Henry Wadsworth Longfellow and William Wordsworth, mainly for their sonnets. He found Robert Browning unmelodic and unfathomable. Never forward-looking, never experimental, Mifflin found it relaxing to read works on Greek mythology, and he responded to the poetry of Bacchylides, Bion, Moschus, and Theocritus. He continued to paint for a while, until at one point he decided that fumes from the paints on his palette were worsening his delicate health. He suffered the first of several heart attacks in 1892 but continued writing, mostly sonnets.

Mifflin published *The Hills* (1896), which contains sixteen poems and was illustrated by Thomas Moran. Following it rapidly was *At the Gates of Song: Sonnets* (1897); its 150 poems were so popular that additional printings were issued later in 1897 and in 1901. Mifflin once boasted that he wrote fifteen sonnets in a single day and that only lack of time kept him from writing five more. His manuscripts reveal a curious method of dating his work—not simply the day, month, and year, but even the hour. He steadily produced book after book of verse from 1898 through 1916. *The Slopes of Helicon, and Other Poems* (1898) contains eighty-five sonnets and lyrics. The nicely titled *Echoes of Greek Idyls* (1899) rewrites eighty-five Greek poems as sonnets. *The Fields of Dawn and Later Sonnets* (1900) contains 104 sonnets, some in pastoral form. *Castalian Days* (1903) offers fifty sonnets. *Lyrics* (1904), privately printed, on one side of the page only and in fifteen copies, contains only four poems. The title poem of *The Fleeing Nymph, and Other Verse* (1905), a miscellany, is a long blank verse narrative. Also in 1905 appeared *Collected Sonnets of Lloyd Mifflin*, which was favorably reviewed in the United States and England and was reissued in 1907. Many of its 350 sonnets had appeared earlier. *My Lady of Dream* (1906) is an old-fashioned paean to Mifflin's one responsive love—the muse of poetry. *Toward the Uplands: Later Poems* (1908) includes new sonnets and a poem called "The Thrush" in praise of Mifflin's avowedly favorite bird. *Flower and Thorn: Later Poems* (1909) offers fifty sonnets.

A final volume, aptly titled *As Twilight Falls* and including some verses originally published in periodicals, appeared in 1916, not long after Mifflin had suffered a paralytic stroke the previous November. Thereafter, he endured two more strokes, was attacked by epilepsy, and was bedridden, but he remained serene and uncomplaining, though often in pain. He died at his home in Columbia. His best poems are sonnets, of which he published more than 500 and left additional dozens never published. His poetry reveals his respect for romantic love; his worship of beauty in its natural, idealized, and imagined forms; the pleasures he discovered in isolation; and his faith in life after death. He also poetized, often resignedly, on the subject of his own literary inadequacies. And well he might, for readers of later generations have demanded more energetic, less lofty, more pragmatic forms of utterance.

• Mifflin's papers are in the Library of Congress, Washington, D.C.; the New-York Historical Society, New York City; the Pennsylvania Historical and Museum Commission, Harrisburg; the Lancaster County Historical Society, Lancaster, Pa.; and the libraries of Columbia University, New York, and Franklin and Marshall College, Lancaster. His life and accomplishments are discussed in E. Hershey Sneath, *America's Greatest Sonneteer* (1928), which includes thirty-seven of Mifflin's sonnets, and in Paul A. W. Wallace, *Lloyd Mifflin: Painter and Poet of the Susquehanna* (1965). An obituary is in the *New York Times*, 17 July 1921.

ROBERT L. GALE

MIFFLIN, Thomas (10 Jan. 1744–20 Jan. 1800), merchant, soldier, and politician, was born in Philadelphia, the son of John Mifflin and Elizabeth Bagnell, Quakers. His father, a wealthy merchant, held numerous significant political posts including that of provincial councilor. Thomas graduated from the College of Philadelphia in 1760 and then spent four years learning the merchant trade with William Coleman. After visiting England and France during 1764 and 1765, Mifflin formed a mercantile partnership with his brother George and in March 1767 married Sarah Morris, a cousin. The couple quickly took a prominent place in Philadelphia's elite social circle. Contemporaries described Mifflin as an affable gentleman and fine sportsman. Elected to membership in the American Philosophical Society in 1768, he actively participated in that organization thereafter.

Mifflin, who was universally described as a persuasive public speaker, joined in resisting British imperial policy. He sat on nonimportation committees in 1769 and 1770 and on four important Philadelphia extralegal committees established between 1773 and 1775. Elected to the Pennsylvania assembly in 1772, he served until October 1775. Mifflin joined forces with moderate Whigs who championed colonial rights but not democratic reforms at home. Mifflin did so believing, as he had phrased it when just fifteen years of age, that "Power wherever lodged will never be stable unless it has large Property for its Foundation." He attended both sessions of the Continental Congress, during which he worked principally on the details for possible economic warfare against Britain.

When war commenced in April 1775, Mifflin became major of a voluntary company; in June he left Congress to become George Washington's aide-de-camp. For such activities, the Quaker Meeting disowned him in July. Mifflin rose to the rank of major general in the Continental army, saw some combat, routinely requested more, and displayed bravery on the battlefield. He also used his oratorical skills to convince troops to stiffen their resolve or to extend their service periods. But controversy marked his military career. Appointed the army's first quartermaster general in August 1775, he resigned in October 1777 pleading ill health. Congress accepted his resignation but asked that he continue serving as quartermaster and also appointed him to the Board of War; he apparently simply stopped functioning as quartermaster in December. In August 1778 he resigned from the military, in large measure because Congress had impugned his conduct as quartermaster. Despite Mifflin's call for a public hearing, none was held on the matter. Although Mifflin had run the quartermaster department under great difficulties and with apparent honesty, he quit his post at a critical juncture and seemed more interested in protecting his reputation than in furthering the war effort.

Mifflin was also closely linked with the "Conway Cabal," a group of army officers that supposedly conspired in the winter of 1777–1778 to have Congress replace Washington with General Horatio Gates. While admitting that he believed some officers had too much influence with Washington, Mifflin adamantly denied being involved in any action against Washington. The evidence suggests that there was, in fact, no organized plot to replace Washington. Nevertheless, many believed it existed, and, to some extent, the charge of cabaling forever haunted Mifflin.

Mifflin invested in privateering ventures during the war and remained interested in promoting manufacturing, but he appears to have retired from most active business pursuits by 1783. In fact, from the time he left the military in 1778, Mifflin became a career public official. He held some important positions at the federal level. In 1780 Congress appointed him one of three commissioners to make recommendations for reorganizing the military staff departments. He served in Congress from 1782 to 1784 and was elected its president in 1783. As president, he persistently and successfully cajoled enough state legislatures into sending representatives so that the Treaty of Paris (Jan. 1784) could be ratified. Mifflin attended the Constitutional Convention of 1787, signed the Constitution, and supported its adoption. However, he is recorded as speaking only once at the convention and then merely to second a motion on a procedural matter.

Mifflin's political career was rooted in Pennsylvania. As an assemblyman in 1778 and 1780 he opposed the radically democratic Pennsylvania Constitution of 1776 that had substituted a supreme executive council for the office of governor and put virtually all political power in the hands of a unicameral legislature. In 1779 he helped create Pennsylvania's Republican Society, which worked to overthrow the 1776 constitution. After returning from Congress, Mifflin became speaker of the Pennsylvania assembly (1785–1788) and then president of the Supreme Executive Council (1788–1790). He presided at Pennsylvania's 1790 constitutional convention, which created a new frame of government that restored a governor with limited veto power and created a bicameral legislature. Mifflin clearly was not captivated by political theory. Although he had ample opportunity to participate in the Pennsylvania convention debates, he was as inactive as he had been at the 1787 federal convention: he rarely spoke and then only on procedural questions.

Despite Mifflin's political popularity and long association with the Republicans, leaders of that group passed over Mifflin and nominated Arthur St. Clair for governor of Pennsylvania. Given his performance at the two constitutional conventions, perhaps they considered Mifflin a political lightweight. But Mifflin, who actually liked the rough and tumble of the political fray, had become accustomed to the status and trappings that accompanied high political office. He had friends nominate him for governor and ran as a supposed champion of democracy. After a short, nasty campaign that left some leading Republicans livid and convinced that Mifflin had come to support the friends of the 1776 Pennsylvania Constitution, Mifflin won by a margin of almost ten to one. Because Sarah Mifflin died the summer before the 1790 election, Mifflin's daughter Emily served as acting first lady.

With good reason, people called Mifflin the state's most popular politician. An advocate for internal improvements, reform of the justice system, and reducing the state's debt, he was reelected governor in 1793 by a three-to-one margin and ran virtually unopposed in 1796. Then and later, many accounted for this extraordinary popularity as governor by emphasizing that Mifflin knew how to flow with the political currents and was personally honest, friendly, and extraordinarily generous. It must be added that, at a time when national political parties were forming and political ideologues routinely slandered one another, Mifflin strove for a measure of balance. Although over time increasingly identified with the Democratic Republicans, Mifflin, who had tremendous patronage power, probably appointed more Federalists than Democratic Republicans to state posts. More important, he championed states' rights but never to the point of undermining the national government.

Mifflin's response to the Erie Triangle problem shows his balanced approach. Having first obtained title from Native Americans, Pennsylvania acquired the Erie Triangle area, now the northern section of Erie County, from the United States in 1792. When Pennsylvania's legislature authorized settlement of a township at Presque Isle in 1793, Native Americans threatened violence. Mifflin proposed sending Pennsylvania troops, but President Washington requested that the settlement plan be delayed. Mifflin eventually acquiesced, but only after asserting that Pennsylvania's rights be protected and only after the state legislature had been maneuvered into ordering a delay in executing the settlement plan. Mifflin accordingly emerged as a champion of western and Pennsylvania rights who nevertheless recognized and acceded to the superior claims of the national government. The same kind of process occurred in the Whisky Rebellion of 1794. When western Pennsylvanians rioted against federal excise taxes, Mifflin pleased them and defended states' rights by saying that no military action should be taken until all the state's judicial remedies had been exhausted. But when President Washington officially declared that a rebellion existed, Mifflin proclaimed that Pennsylvania must follow the federal government's directives. Moreover, Mifflin industriously raised troops and took to the field himself to help put down the lawlessness. Those efforts earned him sincere praise from Washington.

The same generally balanced and politically effective approach marked Mifflin's responses to international diplomacy. Mifflin, whose chief assistant Alexander J. Dallas was a principal founder of the anti-Federalist, pro-France Philadelphia Democratic Society, praised the French Revolution and its firebrand ambassador Citizen Genet. But when Genet violated American law by fitting up a warship for France, Mifflin promptly warned the national government and attempted to thwart Genet's plan. Mifflin judiciously kept a low profile when partisan warfare erupted over Jay's Treaty. Then, when the 1798 XYZ affair raised the specter of war with France, Mifflin aggressively supported military preparedness and proclaimed that, in the face of detestable French insults and abuses of power, Americans must extinguish their former admiration for the French Revolution.

As the 1790s progressed, Mifflin increasingly experienced bouts of illness that were exacerbated by heavy drinking. By the late 1790s Alexander Dallas was performing many of Mifflin's official duties. Limited by the Constitution to three terms, Mifflin's governorship ended in late 1799. In part to help the Democratic Republicans, Mifflin stood for office and was elected to the Pennsylvania House. By then his finances, more and more dependent on loans from friends such as Charles Biddle, were as muddled as his health was precarious. While attending sessions of the House held at Lancaster, he died and was buried there at public expense.

• Although only a limited number of Mifflin's personal papers have survived, manuscript materials exist in many archives. The most important holdings are located in the Historical Society of Pennsylvania (Philadelphia), the Library of Congress, the New-York Historical Society (New York City), the New York Public Library, the Pennsylvania State Archives (Harrisburg), the National Archives, and the Clements Library in Ann Arbor, Mich. Useful guides to the Mifflin holdings of these and other archives are contained in the volumes by Kenneth Rossman cited below.

Mifflin figures prominently in Harry M. Tinkcom, *The Republicans and Federalists in Pennsylvania 1790–1801* (1950). William Rawle's "Sketch of the Life of Thomas Mifflin," in *Memoirs of the Historical Society of Pennsylvania*, vol. 2. (1830), pp. 105–26, is rather evenhanded but thin. The essential details of Mifflin's financial history through the 1780s are covered in Forrest McDonald, *We the People* (1958). The only published scholarly biography is Kenneth R. Rossman, *Thomas Mifflin and the Politics of the American Revolution* (1952). Rossman's "Thomas Mifflin, the Revolutionary Patriot from Pennsylvania" (Ph.D. diss., Univ. of Iowa, 1940) remains important because it is much more fully documented than the published biography.

JOHN K. ALEXANDER

MIGNOT, Louis Rémy (3? Feb. 1831–22 Sept. 1870), landscape painter, was born in Charleston, South Carolina, the son of Rémy Mignot, a confectioner of French birth; the identity of his mother is undetermined. The details of Mignot's childhood are difficult to sort out; tradition has it that he was raised by his grandfather. On 15 August 1848 Rémy Mignot died, and seventeen-year-old Louis apparently left Charleston around that time, registering for drawing classes at The Hague, Netherlands, in January 1849. He remained there for about the next five years, taking instruction from Andreas Schelfhout, an important landscapist and popular teacher. While at The Hague, Mignot became friends with compatriot painter Eastman Johnson. Although previous biographies have stated that Mignot was of Huguenot descent, recently discovered census records at The Hague indicate that he registered himself as a Roman Catholic.

By 1855 Mignot had returned to the United States and settled in New York City. He traveled to upstate New York, finding subjects in Cooperstown and the Adirondacks; he visited Virginia and Maryland; and he sketched along the Susquehanna River. From studies made on these trips he worked up finished compositions, which he exhibited at the National Academy of Design, the Pennsylvania Academy of the Fine Arts, the Boston Athenaeum, the Maryland Historical Society, and elsewhere.

An important turning point in Mignot's career came in the summer of 1857, on a four-month trip to Ecuador, where he discovered the scenery that provided the subject of some of his finest works. His companion on that trip was Frederic Edwin Church, one of the leading New York painters, who had already made one trip to Colombia and Ecuador in 1853. Mignot and Church sailed from New York on 5 May, and by the twenty-seventh they had arrived at the Ecuadorian port of Guayaquil. Throughout June and July they visited the Andean peaks made famous by German naturalist Alexander von Humboldt, including Chimborazo, Cotopaxi, and Sangay. Mignot was also inspired by the tropical coast.

After his return to New York in September, Mignot's reputation grew. Soon after its opening in December 1857 he moved into the Tenth Street Studio Building (at 15 Tenth Street), where most of the city's leading artists worked. In June 1858 he was invited on the artists' excursion sponsored by the Baltimore and Ohio Railroad. He was elected to many prestigious organizations, including New York's Century Association (in 1858) and the National Academy of Design (1858 ANA; 1859 NA), where he exhibited regularly. In 1859 he completed, in collaboration with Thomas Rossiter, *Washington and Lafayette at Mount Vernon, 1784* (Metropolitan Museum of Art), engraved the same year by T. O. Barlow. He began to produce increasingly original South American scenes, complemented by those of North America. In 1860 Mignot married Zairah "Saidee" C. Harris, the daughter of Lucinda Hawley and Chapin Aaron Harris of Baltimore. The couple had one child.

The outbreak of the Civil War made it increasingly difficult for the southern Mignot to remain in New York. On 2 June 1862 a collection of about forty-seven of his works was auctioned off by Leeds at Snedicor's Gallery, 768 Broadway (which was reported to have netted more than $5,000). On 26 July 1862 he sailed to Liverpool and later settled in London. Henry T. Tuckerman and Tom Taylor—critics who knew him personally—mentioned his intention to visit India and paint the Himalayas, a trip never realized.

In London Mignot immediately began to submit paintings to important exhibitions. His debut work at the Royal Academy in 1863 was extensively praised in the *Athenaeum*: "We have not often seen a landscape so brilliantly or artistically painted as Mr. Mignot's *Lagoon of the Guayaquil*." He exhibited there in 1865–1867, 1870, and (posthumously) in 1871, at the British Institution from 1863 until its closing exhibit in 1867, and at other locations. Throughout this period he made something of a specialty of his tropical subjects; these he alternated with local British scenes, including landmarks such as Warwick and Kenilworth castles, Tintern Abbey, and a much-appreciated view of Hastings at the Royal Academy in 1870. He also began to seek literary inspiration in Tennyson, Keats, Coleridge, and Byron. Once more he demonstrated his range and versatility as he sought to adapt himself to the prevailing artistic climate. His work was purchased by English connoisseurs, including Tom Taylor, playwright and editor of *Punch*; watercolorist G. P. Boyce; and Henry Willett, founder of the Art Museum, Brighton. But in London he never achieved the popular appreciation with the general public he had enjoyed in the United States. Consequently during these years he suffered financial hardship, borrowing money and moving from one residence to another. This may explain why in 1868 he sent a collection of his works back to New York City to be auctioned at Leeds & Miner.

Mignot visited Switzerland in 1868 and 1869. These trips resulted in several important canvases, including the much-praised *Lake of Lucerne, with the Rigi* (unlocated), which comprise an important grouping of his mature British career.

Mignot's *Sources of the Susquehanna* (then in the Derby collection) appeared in 1867 at the International Exposition, Paris. Apparently he made several prolonged stays in the French capital beginning about this time, although details remain sketchy. In December 1867 he painted local subjects such as *Bal du Nuit, Paris* (private collection) and *Tours de Jeans Sans Peur, Quartier St. Denis, Paris* (unlocated). In 1870 he exhibited two works at the Paris Salon with an address on the Avenue des Champs-Élysées.

Mignot was apparently caught in Paris during the outbreak of the Franco-Prussian War and had to flee, leaving pictures and other belongings behind. He and his family sought refuge in Brighton, where he died of smallpox. Having remained in Britain, the artist's widow put together a memorial exhibition of the Mignot collection in 1876, which included 119 works.

From early June to mid-September it was shown at 25, Old Bond Street, London, and subsequently at the Pavilion, Brighton.

Mignot's background as a southerner and a romantic offers a key to understanding his art. His canvases are suffused with a poetic sensibility; they are more concerned with interior responses to the picturesque beauty and mystery of a region than with the external details of its botany or geology. Although he left Charleston while still in his teens, his regional affiliation helped define his artistic sensibility; critics interpreted his works in terms of his "southern effects" and, long after he had attained national and international prominence, continued to identify him as the artist from South Carolina.

Mignot left a body of work broad in scope and impressive in quality; in particular he possessed a rare skill as a colorist. He painted the grand landscape monuments, including Niagara Falls, Mount Chimborazo, and Lake Lucerne. But he was most at home in more modest corners of nature, where the play of light and atmosphere became the subject of his work. Among Mignot's significant North American works are his *Sources of the Susquehanna* (1857, National Academy of Design) and *Niagara* (c. 1866–1870, Brooklyn Museum). Important South American pictures are housed in the North Carolina Museum of Art, the Detroit Institute of Art, and the Greenville County Museum of Art, South Carolina. Such works confirm the opinion offered by S. G. W. Benjamin that Mignot was "one of the most remarkable artists of our country."

• Limited Mignot family records are in the South Carolina Department of Archives and History, Columbia. A definitive monograph and catalogue raisonné by Katherine E. Manthorne, with John W. Coffey, was published in conjunction with the 1996 exhibition *The Landscapes of Louis Rémy Mignot: A Southern Painter Abroad* at the N.C. Museum of Art, Raleigh. The following essays by Manthorne assess his tropical works particularly: chap. 6 in her *Tropical Renaissance: North American Artists Exploring Latin America, 1839–1879* (1989) and "On the Road: Louis Rémy Mignot's *Landscape in Ecuador*," *North Carolina Museum of Art Bulletin* 16 (1993): 13–30. Henry T. Tuckerman offers an acquaintance's overview of his work in *Book of the Artists* (1867), pp. 563–64, as does Tom Taylor in *Catalogue of Mignot Pictures with Sketch of the Artist's Life by Tom Taylor, Esq. and Opinions of the Press* (1876). Sales records can be found in *Catalogue: Special Sale of Fine Oil Paintings Including the Collection of Well-Known American Artist, Mr. L. R. Mignot, Now in London, Comprising Some of His Latest and Best Works* (1868). One of the more complete obituaries is in "Fine Arts," *Illustrated London News*, 8 Oct. 1870, p. 386.

KATHERINE E. MANTHORNE

MILES, James Warley (24 Nov. 1818–14 Sept. 1875), Episcopal clergyman, was born in Orangeburg District, South Carolina, the son of James Sanders Miles, a planter, and Sarah Bond Warley. He was educated at Waddel's academy at Willington in 1834–1835 and late in 1835 entered the South Carolina College in Columbia, but he was expelled from the latter school in 1837 for engaging to fight a duel with another student and so did not graduate. After briefly reading law, he gained admission to the General Theological Seminary in New York City, graduating in 1841. He returned to South Carolina and for nearly two years served various missionary charges there, primarily at St. David's Church, Cheraw. Parish work did not satisfy him, and in 1843, after securing the promise of his diocese to provide the means for his support, his bishop agreed to permit him to fulfill a longstanding desire and join the Near Eastern mission of the Reverend Horatio Southgate in Constantinople. Ordained to the priesthood before he sailed, Miles remained with the mission from early 1844 until the summer of 1847 when he was compelled by illness and the prospect of a lack of funds to return to South Carolina.

Miles began publishing articles on philological and philosophical subjects in the *Southern Quarterly Review* in 1848, while rector of St. John's Church, Colleton, on John's Island, and he continued to be an important contributor to the review into the early 1850s. He also assembled a series of sermons that he delivered while serving as acting assistant minister at St. Michael's Church, Charleston, and published them under the title *Philosophic Theology; or, Ultimate Grounds of All Religious Belief Based on Reason* (1849). In 1850, partly on the strength of this book, he was elected professor in the newly established chair of the history of intellectual philosophy and Greek literature at the College of Charleston. He lectured and wrote prolifically in the next four years, developing a system of thought that was eclectic and unoriginal but, cast in the terms of romantic idealism, provided a coherent and reassuring articulation of views widely shared by the slaveholding interests of the South.

As his epistemological foundation, Miles adopted the Coleridgian distinction between Reason and Understanding, asserting that his personal consciousness of God as Perfect Being was a conception of Reason and hence necessarily true though not empirically verifiable. The Understanding provided confirmation for the intuition, however, in the analogical argument that the existence of finite beings possessing essential natures that defined them bespoke an Absolute Being similarly possessed of a self-defining nature and that it was the nature of Being to manifest itself, through time, in the discrete forms of the phenomenal world. Ideal Being was gradually becoming itself in physical reality through an evolutionary process occurring inevitably throughout nature, except in the case of man, for whom free will provided moral choices. Miles taught that moral distinctions were rooted immutably in the nature of things and so were never relative but always absolute. Reason apprehended them, and its conviction declared the moral life to involve strenuous, voluntary effort to develop human nature. Individual men and women met this moral obligation as members of such larger social organic forms as nations and races, expressing the constitution or "genius" of each in their collective activity. Although national differences were important, they were relatively slight in comparison with the radical differences that Miles perceived among races, both in the degree of their voluntary striving and in the variations of human nature they exhibited, and he came close to declaring his assent to polygenesis, the view that the races were in fact distinct species created separately in widely different places of the earth and over an immense span of time. The theory conflicted with the Old Testament account of a single creation and the common exegetical doctrine that it had occurred no more than 5,000 or 6,000 years in the past, but on the basis of textual criticism Miles rejected the literal veracity of Scripture, and his own studies in philology convinced him that the human family was at least 10,000 years old. Responding to fears that his views threatened the authority of revealed religion, Miles declared that as a matter of Understanding they did not affect Christianity, whose truth Reason affirmed. Even had there been a single creation, however, Miles beheld differences between whites and blacks that were great enough to insist upon an original diversity of human races that had fixed their characters forever, directing their development and binding them by an "ethnological law" in an immutable relation of black subordination and white control. Slavery in the South reflected this natural relation; its abolition, Miles claimed, would sacrifice black freedmen to white "tyranny," a temporary condition in which unnatural power, not natural law, prevailed until the law of nature exacted "a necessary retribution" and restored proper order.

In the spring of 1853 Miles, complaining of overwork and poor health, showed signs of extreme depression, and in the following year he resigned from the college, sold his impressive private library (to anonymous friends who later magnanimously returned it to him), and sailed for Europe. His movements there are uncertain, but he spent time in Germany and gave a formal Fourth of July address at the residence of the American minister in Berlin in 1855. Turning down a more lucrative position at the University of Virginia, he returned to Charleston in 1856 to become the librarian of the college and there sank into relative inactivity, contented to be among the library's books pursuing without interruption his favorite studies of literature and languages. (It was said at his death that he had a reading knowledge of over thirty ancient and modern languages.) Still, he remained in close touch with the inner circle of literati who congregated at Russell's bookstore and produced *Russell's Magazine*; his writings appeared in several issues of the journal.

In the secession crisis Miles declared publicly in favor of the cause of southern independence, which he hailed as a providential mission to work out a "great thought of God." He remained in Charleston until 1863 and then spent the last two years of the war with relatives in the upcountry village of Anderson. Certain of victory as late as February 1865, he was bitterly disappointed in defeat but consoled in the reflection that it was only a momentary retrograde movement in a great historical cycle whose end remained the expression of the divine "Idea of Humanity."

Early in 1866 Miles returned to the College of Charleston as professor of ancient languages, a position he held until 1871 when, pleading failing health, he resigned. In 1872 he traveled to Boston, Massachusetts, in response to a request to accept a church there, but finding the social climate uncongenial to his "southern temperament," he returned to Charleston. He spent the last years of his life there, giving private language classes, delivering public lectures on history, Greek drama, and Shakespeare, and substituting in various churches. For a few months in 1874 he served as rector of Grace Church, Camden. He died in Charleston.

Miles never married. In physical appearance he was "spare and fragile" with "keen, vivid" eyes, occasioning the impression that he was at once "ethereal, yet passionate . . . a man of air and fire. . . . " Withdrawn, diffident, and given to self-pity, he was largely isolated from the orthodox majority around him because of his unshakable conviction that personal, intuitive apprehensions of God and absolute moral verities were prior to and independent of Scripture. Yet he was in constant demand as a public speaker for he was intimately identified with the dominant interests in his section of the country, and if his theological liberalism had at best a limited influence, the idealism of which he was an early and consistent exponent had profound and enduring influence in the South as a bulwark of conservatism well into the twentieth century.

• The largest collection of letters is in the James Warley Miles Papers, Duke University, but see also the James Warley Miles Papers in the South Carolina Historical Society, Charleston, and the James Warley Miles Papers in the College of Charleston Library. Ralph E. Luker, "God, Man and the World of James Warley Miles, Charleston's Transcendentalist," *Historical Magazine of the Protestant Episcopal Church* 39 (June 1970): 101–36 and his *A Southern Tradition in Theology and Social Criticism, 1830–1930: The Religious Liberalism of James Warley Miles, William Porcher DuBose and Edgar Gardner Murphy* (1984), present the most complete accounts of Miles's life and thought together with a full bibliography. A brief but valuable review of Miles's thought is in E. Brooks Holifield, *The Gentlemen Theologians: American Theology in Southern Culture, 1795–1860* (1978). William Henry Longton, "The Carolina Ideal World: Natural Science and Social Thought in Ante Bellum South Carolina," *Civil War History* 20 (June 1974): 118–34, describes the local context of Miles's thought. For an older but still useful short sketch, see George W. Williams, *The Reverend James Warley Miles* (1954).

WILLIAM HENRY LONGTON

MILES, Lizzie (31 Mar. 1895–17 Mar. 1963), blues singer, was born Elizabeth Mary Landreaux Miles in New Orleans, Louisiana, the daughter of J. C. Miles. His occupation is unknown. Her mother (named Landreaux, presumably) was a singer. Her stepbrothers were trumpeter Herb Morand, who at some point during the 1920s played in New York in a band accompanying Miles, and drummer Maurice Morand. Miles first sang in church at age five. She also sang in school before dropping out to perform at parties and dances, while continuing to sing at services. From 1909 to 1911 she sang with cornetist King Oliver, trombonist Kid Ory, trumpeter Bunk Johnson, and violinist A. J. Piron at numerous venues in New Orleans. Around this time Miles married; no other details are known. Her second marriage was to August Pajaud; again details are unknown.

Miles toured southern theaters as a member of the Benbow Stock Company. She rode elephants and other animals while traveling with the Jones Brothers and Wilson Circus, which billed her as "Queen Elleezzee," and the Cole Brothers Circus. She then toured with the Alabama Minstrels and the Rabbit Foot Minstrels. She sang with pianist Manuel Manetta in New Orleans in 1917, and around this time she began working as a song-plugger for composer and publisher Clarence Williams. The sequence of these activities is unclear, as are reports of a serious illness, perhaps a heart attack, in 1918 or 1919, when she was with pianist George Thomas's band at the Pythian Temple Roof Garden in New Orleans. Evidently she had to stop singing for some time.

In 1921 Miles was in Chicago, where she continued to promote Williams's songs. She sang with Oliver at the Dreamland Ballroom, as well as in bands led by Freddie Keppard, Carroll Dickerson, Wilbur Sweatman, Charlie Elgar, and Glover Compton. Late that year she moved to New York City, where in February 1922 she made her first recordings, "Muscle Shoals Blues" and "She Walked Right Up and Took My Man Away." While in New York she recorded regularly into 1923, she sang with Piron's orchestra at the Cotton Club that same year, and in 1924 she sang with Sam Wooding's orchestra at the Nest Club. She performed in Paris at the nightclub Chez Mitchell, where she was billed as "La rose noire," and she toured Europe into 1925, at which time she returned to New Orleans to perform with the New Orleans Creole Jazz Band.

While singing in New York clubs from 1926 to 1931, Miles resumed recording. Her work included a session accompanied by Oliver's trio in 1928, "I Hate a Man Like You" and "Don't Tell Me Nothin' 'bout My Man" with pianist Jelly Roll Morton late in 1929, and "My Man O'War" and "Electrician Blues" with pianist Harry Brooks early in 1930. Early in the 1930s she appeared in two little-known films, *The Stardust Ring* and *Tick Tack Toe*, but from 1931 she was mainly inactive, initially because of a serious lung illness and then owing to her determination to stick to a religious resolution that if she recovered—she did—she would cease touring in stage shows.

In 1935 Miles resumed regular nightclub work, performing with drummer Paul Barbarin at the Strollers Club in New York. She sang with Fats Waller in New York in 1938 and then began working in Chicago, where the following year she recorded "Stranger Blues" and "Twenty Grand Blues." Miles performed in Chicago until 1942 and then left music for the remainder of the decade.

Ending her retirement in 1950, Miles performed with clarinetist George Lewis's band at the Hangover Club in San Francisco from 1953 to 1954; at the Blue Note Club in Chicago in 1954; with trumpeter Bob Scobey's band in the San Francisco Bay Area, the Los Angeles area, and Las Vegas from 1955 to 1957; with clarinetist Joe Darensbourg's band in San Francisco in 1958; and at the Monterey Jazz Festivals of 1958 and 1959. She also worked regularly in New Orleans, including residencies at the Parisian Room and with drummer Freddie Kohlman's band at the Mardi Gras Lounge (both perhaps before the engagement in San Francisco, although the chronology is unclear), and in 1958 with Barbarin on a riverboat.

During the final segment of her career Miles recorded two titles at a session with trumpeter Sharkey Bonano in 1952; several tracks on the album *George Lewis Live at the Hangover Club* (1953–1954); and her own albums *Moans and Blues*, *Hot Songs My Mother Taught Me* (both c. 1954), *Torchy Lullabies My Mother Sang Me* (c. 1955), and *Music from Bourbon Street*, with Scobey's band (1956). She also appeared on Paul Gregory's network television show and in 1957 sang on a Voice of America broadcast.

Miles retired to New Orleans in 1959 and became active with the Sisters of Holy Family Chapel and Jesuit Church. She died in New Orleans.

Miles sang in English, in Louisiana Creole patois (known as "gombo French"), and in a Creole that is closer to Parisian French. Like other classic female blues and vaudeville singers, she often performed sexy lyrics replete with double entendres of the sort popularized during the latter half of the 1920s. Miles occasionally pushed what was, in her lifetime, the boundary of propriety, passing from the risqué into obscenity, although in the context of some late twentieth-century rap and rock her lyrics may no longer seem shocking.

A characteristically cynical Darensbourg remembered Miles thus: "She was a typical New Orleans broad, just as evil as hell. What's that song? *Go to church all day Sunday and barrel-house all day Monday*. That was Lizzie. She was supposed to be a great church broad, went to church almost every day, yet she had a young-assed pimp on the side, taking all her money" (p. 151). Interviewer Berta Wood painted a much brighter portrait, recalling Miles's "zest and seemingly boundless energy." She was "a virtuoso conversationalist. . . . She skims, dips, wheels about, breaks up with laughter and darts off again with such rapidity that it would take an ambidextrous shorthand writer to come out about even with her. . . . Her incredible mental agility and powerful spirit are the natural manifestations of a woman who does her own thinking."

• A taped interview of Miles from 1 Jan. 1951 is in the archives of Tulane University. For more on Miles and her musical milieu, see Berta Wood, "Lizzie Miles from New Orleans," *Jazz Journal*, June 1957, pp. 1–2; Samuel Barclay

Charters IV, *Jazz: New Orleans, 1885–1957: An Index to the Negro Musicians of New Orleans* (1958); Laurraine Goreau, "An Evening with Lizzie Miles," *Jazz Journal*, Jan. 1964, pp. 8–10; Derrick Stewart-Baxter, *Ma Rainey and the Classic Blues Singers* (1970); Linda Dahl, *Stormy Weather: The Music and Lives of a Century of Jazzwomen* (1984); and Joe Darensbourg, *Telling It Like It Is*, ed. Peter Vacher (1987; American edition as *Jazz Odyssey: The Autobiography of Joe Darensbourg*).

BARRY KERNFELD

MILES, Manly (20 July 1826–15 Feb. 1898), physician, biologist, and professor of agriculture, was born in Homer, New York, the son of Manly Miles and Mary Cushman, farmers. When he was eleven, his family moved to a farm in eastern Michigan, near Flint. Trained in farm labor and deeply interested in science, especially chemistry and biology, in which he was ambitiously self-educated, he earned an M.D. from Chicago's Rush Medical College in 1850. He married Mary E. Dodge in 1851. After practicing medicine in Flint for nine years, he became zoologist for Michigan's new state geological survey. As its physician and zoologist he gathered collections of mollusca, birds, reptiles, and other animals, some of which he shared with scholars, including Louis Agassiz and Spencer Baird.

In 1860, when Miles's catalogs of Michigan fauna were published in the geological survey's report, he became professor of zoology at the Michigan Agricultural College (later Michigan State University). He taught courses on physiology and geology and by 1863 developed what Madison Kuhn, a historian of the university, believes was the first American course on economic entomology. One of very few agricultural college teachers who then combined much understanding of science with practical knowledge of farming, Miles became acting superintendent of the college farm in 1864 and farm superintendent and professor of animal physiology a year later. In 1869 he let other faculty members teach his various natural science courses and focused his own attention on agriculture. He introduced a course on breeding farm animals, the subject of his 1879 textbook *Stock-Breeding*, and campaigned to have the college's barns and land used for experiments. He also devised a course on practical agriculture that offered a unique combination of scientific lectures with field instruction. On at least one occasion an admiring visitor found him teaching field drainage, the subject of his 1892 book *Land Draining: A Handbook for Farmers on the Principles and Practice of Farm Draining*, while at work in a ditch, laying tile. Professor and students tested a haymower, experimented with hog foods, built barns and a windmill, and in 1871 left Sunday afternoon worship to build backfires that saved the campus woods from a forest fire.

In the early 1870s Miles lectured at farmers' institutes in several Illinois communities and gave lectures in Urbana, where he was hailed as this country's first genuine professor of agriculture and "as an agricultural scientist comparable to . . . Lawes and Gilbert in England and Baron Von Liebig in Germany." Invited in the early 1870s to join the Illinois Industrial University (later the University of Illinois), Miles stayed at East Lansing until he was convinced that Michigan's governor and others wanted someone different from himself, more a practical farmer and less a scientific physician, to teach agriculture there. A biographical essay, "Sketch of Manly Miles," published and republished soon after his death, suggests that Miles was "loved by his students" but "not appreciated by the politicians, or by all of the Board of Agriculture," which ruled the agricultural college, "or even by the public at large." Those constituencies wanted the college farm to be profitable, which was not Miles's goal.

Miles enjoyed a leave of absence, partly spent on a tour of English experimental farms, and in 1875 moved to the Illinois Industrial University, with a salary a third higher than that of any other member of its faculty. There he ambitiously redesigned the campus barns' interior arrangements, rearranged the horticultural grounds, installed a windmill, and campaigned for other improvements in physical arrangements and in the agricultural curriculum. But his drive for change was soon halted by the school's financial weakness and the opposing ideas of regent John Milton Gregory, who as Michigan's superintendent of public instruction had been responsible for bringing Miles to East Lansing. Unwilling to accept Miles's costly ambitions for agriculture at the university, Gregory gave the trustees the choice of accepting his own resignation or driving Miles away. Miles left Illinois in 1876, after only six months of service and conflict.

Three years later Miles became director of experiments at Houghton Farm in New York, seven miles west of the U.S. Military Academy. Lawton Valentine, who bought the farm in 1876, wanted it to be a lovely rural home near his work in New York and an important agricultural research center. Miles designed fields, supervised drainage, visited European research stations, and planned crop experiments. His *Description of Houghton Farm. Experiments with Indian Corn, 1880–1881* (1882) explained his seed selection, work schedule, fertilization, and results. In 1883 he started brief service as professor of agriculture at Massachusetts Agricultural College. Three years later he was back in Michigan, operating a private office and laboratory over a Lansing pharmacy. Most of his publications, including *Silos, Ensilage and Silage* (1889) and *Land Draining* (1892), were written in that last part of his career. A wide-ranging scientist particularly devoted to agriculture, Miles's memorial plaque in Michigan State University's Agriculture Building honors him as this country's "first Professor of Agriculture" who linked "the rapid developments of science with progressive agriculture." Miles died in Lansing.

• Some of Miles's papers are in the Michigan State University Archives. Walter B. Barrow, secretary of the Michigan Academy of Science, wrote an appraisal of Miles's career in science for the *Bulletin of the Michigan Ornithological Club* 2 (Apr. 1898): 13–14. A longer "Sketch of Manly Miles" appeared in

Appleton's Popular Science 54 (Apr. 1899): 834–41 and was reprinted in *Second Report of the Michigan Academy of Science* (1901) and revised in William J. Beal, *History of the Michigan Agricultural College* (1915), pp. 403–6. Madison Kuhn, *Michigan State, The First Hundred Years* (1955), Richard Gordon Moores, *Fields of Rich Toil: The Development of the University of Illinois College of Agriculture* (1970), and Winton U. Solberg, *The University of Illinois 1867–1894: An Intellectual and Cultural History* (1968), discuss Miles's academic career.

DONALD B. MARTI

MILES, Nelson Appleton (8 Aug. 1839–15 May 1925), soldier, was born in Westminster, Massachusetts, the son of Daniel Miles, Jr., a farmer and businessman, and Mary Curtis. With options limited in the rural township of Westminster, Nelson Miles moved to Boston while still a teenager and worked in a store. Following the first battle of Bull Run (Manassas), he borrowed enough money to organize and outfit a company of volunteers. The men elected their benefactor captain, but Governor John A. Andrew offered Miles only a first lieutenancy.

Though boasting but a smattering of military training, acquired through a personal tutor, Miles overcame the disappointment stemming from the governor's slight and distinguished himself as an exceptionally able field officer. Suffering a minor foot wound at the battle of Fair Oaks during the 1862 Peninsula campaign, Miles subsequently took a lieutenant colonelcy in the Sixty-first New York Infantry Regiment. Promoted in September to full colonel for his leadership at Antietam, he took a bullet in the throat during the army's failed advance at Fredericksburg that December. Miles was wounded even more severely during the battle of Chancellorsville (May 1863), for which he would in 1892 be awarded a Medal of Honor for personal bravery. Following a brief convalescence, he was appointed brigadier general of volunteers and brevet major general in May 1864 for his leadership in the fighting at Spotsylvania and Reams' Station, respectively. Slightly wounded at Petersburg, Miles again distinguished himself at Sutherland's Station and Sayler's Creek in the final weeks of the war.

Following the collapse of the Confederacy, Miles, who was recognized as one of the most aggressive and effective officers in the Army of the Potomac, was assigned command of the Military District of Fort Monroe, Virginia. Concerned that his famous prisoner, the recently captured Jefferson Davis, might escape, Miles ordered him placed in leg irons. Although improved facilities soon allowed the removal of the shackles, Miles's action was roundly criticized in many circles. Happy to be rid of the thankless task, in September 1866 Miles accepted the colonelcy of the Fortieth Infantry Regiment, comprised of white officers and black enlisted men, in the greatly reduced postbellum army. He took up Reconstruction duties with the Freedmen's Bureau in North Carolina the following year, and in 1868 he married Mary Hoyt Sherman, daughter of a district court judge and niece of Senator John Sherman and General William T. Sherman.

In mid-March 1869 Miles secured a transfer to the all-white Fifth Infantry Regiment, then stationed in Kansas. His first major western campaign came five years later during the Red River War. Leading a column south from Kansas into the Indian Territory and the Texas panhandle, Miles doggedly pursued Comanches, Kiowas, and southern Cheyennes deemed hostile by the federal government well into the winter. Shifted to Montana in the wake of the battle of the Little Bighorn, Miles's command won a sharp skirmish in October 1876 at Cedar Creek against a large Indian coalition, which included Sitting Bull. Defying the northern Montana winter, Miles drove many of the tribes into Canada. In January 1877 Miles won another victory, this time against Crazy Horse and an assortment of Oglala Sioux and northern Cheyennes, at the battle of Wolf Mountains. As increasing numbers of Plains Indians turned themselves in to the federal government, Miles shattered resistance among Lame Deer's defiant Minneconjou Sioux in May at the battle of Muddy Creek.

Now recognized as one of the army's most effective Indian fighters, Miles further enhanced his image during the 1877 campaigns against the Nez Percé. From the Tongue River Cantonment, through a series of forced marches, his command cut off the attempted flight of many Nez Percé to Canada. An attack on the Nez Percé encampment at Bear Paw Mountain failed, but a subsequent siege of the Indian camp forced the surrender of Chief Joseph and some four hundred followers. One year later Miles routed a small party of Bannock Indians near Clarke's Fork (now Clark Fork) Pass in the eastern Yellowstone Mountains.

In 1880 Miles received his first regular general's star and—after presiding over the controversial court-martial hearing of U.S. Military Academy cadet Johnson C. Whittaker, a black cadet whom officials accused of having staged an incident in which he was found beaten and bound in his own room, and serving on the Ponca Commission—assumed command of the military Department of the Columbia. He was transferred to head the Department of the Missouri in 1885 and replaced his rival, George Crook, in the Department of Arizona the following year. From Arizona, Miles mounted an elaborate campaign against Geronimo and his Chiricahua Apache followers. Initially depending heavily on regular army personnel, Miles's troopers chased their foes across southern Arizona and into northern Mexico without much success. He then changed his tactics, employing smaller teams of Indian auxiliaries led by officers of proven abilities in frontier conditions. After five months of exhausting pursuits, Geronimo gave himself up to Miles in September 1886 amid complaints in some quarters that Miles had made unauthorized promises to his foe.

Although widely acknowledged to be among the nation's premier soldiers, Miles had throughout his career frequently clashed with military superiors, civilian authorities, and fellow officers. Intensely ambitious, his unseemly lobbying engendered the jealousy of many rivals for the infrequent promotions available in the postbellum army. As his rivals within the army reached mandatory retirement, Miles gained successively more important posts: the Division of the Pacific in 1888 and a major generalship and command of the sprawling Division of the Missouri, which encompassed most of the Plains region, in 1890. From the latter he directed army operations during the Ghost Dance campaign, during which the bungled attempts to disarm Big Foot and many Minneconjou Sioux by a subordinate, Colonel James W. Forsyth, led to a disastrous slaughter of some one hundred and fifty Indian men, women, and children at Wounded Knee. During the 1894 Pullman strike Miles, a confirmed nativist, asked permission to allow his troops to fire on protesters, who he believed threatened American institutions. Later that year Miles secured a transfer to command the Department of the East. With the retirement of John M. Schofield in 1895, President Grover Cleveland appointed Miles commanding general.

Miles's greatest challenge in his new post came with the outbreak of war with Spain in 1898. With a standing force of only 25,000 men and virtually bereft of strategic planning, the regulars in blue were overwhelmed by the onslaught of volunteers and the political pressure to act quickly against Spain. Dissatisfied with Miles's suggestions that the United States adopt a defensive posture until healthier fall weather allowed an invasion of Puerto Rico, President William McKinley directed the war from his executive office. Only after the Cuban expeditionary force was well established was Miles allowed to strike Puerto Rico. Benefiting from lessons learned in the near-disastrous Cuban invasion, Miles's Puerto Rico operations proved a model of efficiency and order, overrunning disorganized Spanish troops in a lightning campaign in late July and early August and paving the way for U.S. annexation of the island.

Following the war's conclusion, Miles accused the War Department of having issued the troops chemically "embalmed beef." Although an investigating committee found no evidence to substantiate these charges, Miles still enjoyed enough political support to secure an appointment to lieutenant general in 1900. However, his continuing reluctance to acknowledge the need for substantive military reforms in the wake of the recent near debacle against Spain left him increasingly isolated. Miles eventually broke with both the reform-minded Elihu Root, appointed secretary of war in 1899, and President Theodore Roosevelt, who as a veteran of the Cuban expedition knew firsthand the army's logistical and organizational problems. Through much of the latter half of the nineteenth century controversies between the commanding general and the secretary of war had disrupted relations between the nation's leading military officials. Root and Roosevelt resolved to break the impasse by creating a general staff, designed to institutionalize and rationalize planning, and abolishing the office of commanding general. The president ordered that Miles "be reprimanded severely" and threatened to force him to retire immediately. But Miles still retained the support of many in Congress, which in a compromise measure adopted the general staff bill and abolished the office of commanding general effective on Miles reaching his mandatory retirement in 1903.

Determined to secure revenge against his Republican enemies, Miles mounted an unsuccessful campaign for the Democratic party's 1904 presidential nomination. Although his wife died that year, leaving him with two children, Miles maintained a vigorous schedule through his waning years, participating in a motion picture project with his old friend William "Buffalo Bill" Cody in 1913 and proposing that he be dispatched at the head of an American expeditionary force to Russia during the First World War. He died in Washington, D.C.

In compiling an impressive record against his Confederate, Kiowa, Comanche, Cheyenne, Sioux, Nez Percé, Bannock, Apache, and Spanish opponents, Miles became one of his nation's greatest fighting soldiers. Yet his immense personal ambition rivaled his enormous martial talents. Like many of his peers, he believed the nation had not adequately rewarded him for his military services. Further disappointed by the failure to secure immediate promotion for his victories against Indian opponents, Miles was sometimes too eager to share his dissatisfaction with the press and the general public. His enormous ego was perhaps reflected in the fact that he published two book-length autobiographies as well as a volume describing his 1897 military tour of Europe. Further, Miles's refusal to cooperate with Root's plans for reform marked him a hero of the old frontier army rather than a visionary leader who might help pull the army into the twentieth century. "The future historian," the editors of the *Nation* (13 Aug. 1903) accurately concluded upon his retirement, "will find few if any searching reforms due to Gen. Miles's advocacy," but "if the historian then turn[s] to this officer's purely military services he will find much to praise."

• Miles's papers are in the Library of Congress and the U.S. Army Military History Institute (Carlisle Barracks, Pa.). His books include *Personal Recollections and Observations of General Nelson A. Miles* (1896; repr. in 2 vols., 1992), *Military Europe: A Narrative of Personal Observation and Personal Experience* (1898), and *Serving the Republic: Memoirs of the Civil and Military Life of Nelson A. Miles, Lieutenant-General, United States Army* (1911). Brian C. Pohanka, *Nelson A. Miles: A Documentary Biography of His Military Career, 1861–1903* (1985), contains published versions of many of his official reports. For a complete biography, see Robert Wooster, *Nelson A. Miles and the Twilight of the Frontier Army* (1993).

ROBERT WOOSTER

MILES, Richard Pius (17 May 1791–21 Feb. 1860), Catholic bishop, was born on a farm in southern Maryland, the son of Nicholas Miles and Ann Blackloc, farmers. A few years after his birth his parents migrated, along with many of their mostly Catholic neighbors, from the thin soil of their part of Maryland to the richer virgin land of central Kentucky, settling in Nelson County. The Miles were not indigent. Nicholas Miles bought land and had sufficient resources to set himself and his family up in good style. He became a leading citizen of the region.

This migration to Kentucky made that area one of only two Catholic rural enclaves in the South, the other being southern Louisiana. Most other Catholic immigrants flocked into cities. Prosperous rural areas, on the Maryland pattern, were rare and, along with the mostly French-born clergy, gave an unusual tone to the region. The French-born clergy had immigrated to the United States to escape the persecution of the French Revolution. They had been posted to Kentucky and other western missionary places woefully short of priests. Their superior education did not exactly qualify them for missionary activity, but they founded schools where possible. This was a great boon to students like Richard Miles, who, at the age of fifteen, chose to join the French-American Dominicans and was schooled by them at the convent of St. Rose, not far from his home. The center of Kentucky Catholicism was Bardstown, seat of the first Catholic bishop of the West, whose enormous diocese covered practically all the trans-Appalachian West from the Great Lakes to the Gulf.

The geographical territory of the diocese was plainly too much for one bishop. The diocese of Nashville, created in 1837, was an early spin-off. Miles was chosen as Nashville's first bishop. Since his ordination, probably in 1816—the exact date is nowhere clear—he had lived the life of a missionary, traveling by horseback to minister to his widely scattered flock, doing the work of the convent by teaching and serving as master of its music, along with carrying out housekeeping chores. Gradually he became prominent in Dominican affairs, founding a second priory in Somerset, Ohio, as well as helping to found a sisters' Dominican convent in Springfield, Kentucky. In 1833 he was elected prior of St. Rose's. After a term there he became prior of St. Joseph's in Ohio, then provincial superior of the entire province of St. Joseph. Neither he nor his brother Dominicans were happy to see him named bishop of Nashville. They knew what hardships lay ahead for him. Their farewell gift was a saddle horse.

Consecrated bishop at Bardstown in September 1838, Miles rode his new steed to Nashville as soon as he could set his Dominican affairs in order. He took possession of his see on 14 October 1838. He was leader to the approximately 300 Catholics in the state; there was not a single priest to help him. His first job was to recruit additional priests, which he finally accomplished after many setbacks. But his recruitment of priests, some veterans of the missions, some would-be seminarians, some vagabonds, some men of accomplishment who responded to his call out of sheer charity, was a continuing challenge. Like so many bishops in the South and West, his preeminent desire all his Tennessee life, and doubtless his prayer as well, was for a devout native clergy. He knew the best way to develop them was through education, and he tirelessly set up schools for the purpose, including even early attempts at the instruction of blacks. One by one the schools failed, usually through the lack of competent teachers rather than students. But Miles kept at it.

What Miles brought to Tennessee was a good education formed in him by his religious community. Miles was a cultivated gentleman. As soon as possible, in 1844, he began St. Mary's Cathedral. "It will be the prettiest thing in Nashville," he wrote on 6 February 1840 to his friend Martin A. Spalding, the future bishop of Louisville. One of his first priorities in its furnishings was a good organ, echoing his love of music and his days as organist at St. Rose's. The church's architecture is so good it was usually attributed to William Strickland, the designer of the Tennessee capitol further up the hill from the cathedral. It stands there to this day, continuing to give Nashville Catholicism a tone of elegance. As bishop, Miles was of necessity unusually peripatetic. He traveled throughout the state, bringing his Dominicans to stabilize Memphis Catholicism and attracting communities of religious women to found educational institutions. Above all he ministered to the various enclaves of Irish Catholics brought to Tennessee to work on the railroads. These communities became the nuclei of Catholicism everywhere in the state. Miles himself took happily to "the cars" as soon as they were opened. But he did not foresee how important the Irish would become in the future. In the 1840s and 1850s Miles helped to found Catholic schools, hospitals, orphanages, and churches in all the principal cities and some smaller places throughout the state. He was a shrewd and adroit participant in community affairs, accurately anticipating the Know Nothing riots of the 1840s but carefully refraining from overt politics and maintaining amicable relations with his non-Catholic neighbors. Unlike other sections of the country, which witnessed violent confrontations between Protestants and Catholics in these decades, Tennessee suffered no anti-Catholic riots. How much of this was owing to Miles's dignity and style is of course impossible to say.

All through his life Miles had the character of a devout and stalwart Dominican priest. He was probably happiest in the Dominican institutions he lived in until he came to Nashville at the age of forty-seven. His arrival there was marked by a near-fatal illness in the fall of 1839, from which he never completely recovered. He was often plagued by colds and bronchitis, and he died as a result of one such attack in Nashville. At sixty-nine he had been a bishop for twenty-two years and was the oldest member of the American Catholic hierarchy.

• The most nearly complete collection of the letters of Bishop Miles is in the manuscript collection of the Hesburgh Library, University of Notre Dame, Notre Dame, Ind. The standard biography is Victor F. O'Daniel, *The Father of the Church in Tennessee* (1926). A shorter journalist account is in Thomas Stritch, *The Catholic Church in Tennessee* (1987).

THOMAS STRITCH

MILES, William Porcher (4 July 1822–11 May 1899), U.S. and Confederate congressman, was born in Walterboro, Colleton District, South Carolina, the son of James Saunders Miles, a planter, and Sarah Bond Warley. Neither academics nor politics interested Porcher (pronounced Poor-shay) Miles as a young man, though he graduated from the College of Charleston in 1842 with honors. For a year after college Miles read law, but he abandoned that profession when the College of Charleston appointed him professor of mathematics in 1843. He stayed at the school for twelve years and in time cultivated such friends as Robert Barnwell Rhett, William Gilmore Simms, Laurence M. Keitt, and James Henry Hammond. His first opinions on the course of the South, however, fell between the radical and the cautious; indeed, the different views and jockeying for position among his South Carolina friends was always a source of tension for him. On his twenty-seventh birthday, Miles made his public debut with an "earnest and zealous" speech that was radical in tone and partisan in the way it drew upon the legacy of the American Revolution but in which he maintained that a united South was the "best means of preserving the union of the States."

Miles's political career owed its beginnings to an epidemic of yellow fever that struck Norfolk, Virginia, in 1855. That summer, while vacationing near the town, he volunteered as a nurse. Reports of his compassion reached home, where local elites were fighting the Know Nothing party. He ran for mayor of Charleston as a candidate of the Southern Rights party and won by 423 votes. Among the many reforms Miles introduced during his two-year tenure, he reorganized the city's police force, developed a system of sewers and tidal drainage, and consolidated the city's debt.

Miles was elected to Congress in 1856 and was reelected in 1858. By then he had lost whatever feeling he had for the Union. Although his polished manners sometimes disguised his radicalism, his role in the movement toward secession was pivotal. He understood, as many radicals did not, that civil war would mean full-scale bloodletting. He became one of the secession movement's most abstract thinkers and passionate orators as well as one of its most important engineers. Miles urged like-minded but tempestuous radicals to tread lightly with Virginia, lest that Border State slip away from a southern Confederacy, and he in turn was urged to agitate the slavery issue lest the whole idea of a Confederacy slip away. He was one of twenty-nine congressmen who signed the so-called Southern Manifesto, a document issued on 14 December 1860 that convinced many moderates in Washington that compromise was hopeless.

Miles served as a member of South Carolina's secession convention and then accepted an appointment to the Provisional Congress of the Confederacy. He was elected twice to the Confederate House of Representatives, running unopposed for each term. As chairman of the Committee on Military Affairs, he earned a reputation for being one of Jefferson Davis's staunchest allies. The Richmond newspapers called him the president's "mouthpiece" and "Wamba the Witless," a reference to the jester in Sir Walter Scott's *The Legend of Montrose and Ivanhoe* (1819) that Miles considered "most discourteous and offensive." Yet his support of the administration had more to do with a zealous pursuit of the war effort than it did with Davis personally. His own views and his circle of friends, which now included General P. G. T. Beauregard, made it impossible for him to give unfettered allegiance to the president. Miles instigated the first controversy of the war by reading on the Confederate House floor a letter written by Beauregard after the battle of Manassas in which he intimated that Davis did not support a quick and decisive follow-up to the Confederate victory at Bull Run. Later, when disillusioned friends such as Rhett and Hammond began furious attacks on Davis, Miles told Mary Boykin Chestnut that such attacks were necessary and healthy. He understood the importance of loyal opposition and nationalism to the southern war effort, even if nationalism benefited from opposition and criticism at his expense.

Miles's chairmanship made him one of the most powerful politicians in Richmond. His influence, as the newspapers suggested, was mainly in developing political support for the administration's war policies. He was among the first politicians to urge ending exemptions to the draft. He also supported military detail, a system by which the War Department gained control of all southern labor, white and black. He could not, however, bring himself to support the use of African-American soldiers. To him such a step meant sacrificing the political principles and the social system that the Confederacy was fighting to protect. On 14 January 1865 he wrote to Beauregard: "I cannot bring my mind to the conviction that arming the slaves will add to our military strength and the prospective and inevitable evils resulting from the measure make me shrink back from the step as only to be taken when on the very brink of the precipice of ruin" (Southern Historical Collection).

At the height of the war, in 1863, Miles married Betty Beirne, the daughter of wealthy Virginia planter Oliver H. Beirne; from then on Oliver Beirne was the chief financial support for Miles, his wife, and their six children. Miles's financial condition was so poor in 1879 that Beirne asked the family to move in with him. The offer embarrassed Miles and may have contributed to his move to South Carolina College, where he served as president from 1880 to 1882. Finally in 1882, when Miles left Columbia, South Carolina, to manage Beirne's sugar plantations in Ascension Parish, Louisiana, he began to enjoy some level of financial comfort. But he never again entered politics after the war. He died near Burnside, Louisiana.

• Almost 3,000 items of Miles's correspondence and thirty-one diaries are in the Southern Historical Collection at the University of North Carolina at Chapel Hill. A vast majority of the correspondence consists of letters written to Miles, and the diaries all date from the postwar period, but the collection has rightly been called a seminal source for the study of southern politics before the war. A smaller cache of Miles papers is at the South Caroliniana Library at the University of South Carolina; a reflection on the Confederacy that Miles wrote in 1882 is of special interest. A few of his letters are in other collections at the Southern Historical Collection and in the Pettigrew Family Papers at the North Carolina Department of Archives and History in Raleigh. Many of his speeches, including his 1849 debut (*Oration Delivered before the Fourth of July Association*) and *An Address Delivered before the Alumni Society of the College of Charleston, on Commencement Day, March 30th, 1852* (1852), were printed as pamphlets or in newspapers and government journals. Miles's wartime writings are in *The War of the Rebellion: A Compilation of the Official Records of the Union and Confederate Armies* (128 vols., 1880–1901). Two helpful portraits are Eric H. Walther, *The Fire-eaters* (1992), and Ruth McCaskill Daniel, "William Porcher Miles: Champion of Southern Interests" (M.A. thesis, University of North Carolina at Chapel Hill, 1943). On the formation and operation of the Confederate government, consult Emory M. Thomas, *The Confederate Nation* (1979), and William C. Davis, *"A Government of Our Own"* (1994). For Miles's relationships with other South Carolina secessionists, see Jon L. Wakelyn, *The Politics of a Literary Man: William Gilmore Simms* (1973), and Steven A. Channing, *Crisis of Fear: Secession in South Carolina* (1970). Miles also appears frequently and his engagement and wedding are described at some length in the diary of Mary Boykin Chestnut, *Mary Chestnut's Civil War*, ed. C. Vann Woodward (1981).

PAUL CHRISTOPHER ANDERSON

MILESTONE, Lewis (30 Sept. 1895–25 Sept. 1980), film director, screenwriter, editor, and producer, was born Lewis Milstein in Chisnau, near Odessa, Russia, the son of Emanuel Milstein, a clothing manufacturer. His mother's name is unknown. In 1900 the family moved to Kishinev, Russia, where Milestone attended Jewish schools. His family was disturbed when he showed an avid interest in acting, so after he completed high school he was sent to study engineering at a college in Saxony. When his father sent him money to travel home for the holidays in 1913, Milestone instead used the funds to immigrate to the United States with two school friends. They arrived in Hoboken, New Jersey, with a mere six dollars among them. Milestone was assisted financially by an aunt for a brief time but ended up working at odd jobs (factory sweeper for a raincoat manufacturer, salesman, photographer's assistant) until he became an American citizen. With the country's entry into World War I, he joined the Army Signal Corps to work stateside as an assistant director of training films.

After the end of the war, Milestone became an assistant film cutter in Hollywood. He worked as an assistant to director Henry King beginning in 1920 for the film *Dice of Destiny*. He signed on with the Ince Studios to work as general assistant on *The Foolish Age* (1921). At Ince, he began a four-year apprenticeship under director William A. Seiter. Milestone later remembered that Seiter was more interested in playing golf than in directing and let Milestone take over much of the directing of his films during this time. Over the intervening few years he moved up officially to assistant director and screenwriter before being allowed to direct his first feature, *Bobbed Hair* (1925), a troubled farce that had had as many as twenty writers working on it before Milestone was assigned. He resolved many of the script's problems, and the craftsmanship he had learned over the previous few years helped him complete a satisfactory picture. *Bobbed Hair* was well received, and Milestone gained a reputation as an excellent film doctor, able to spot deficiencies in films and correct them through editing. Milestone worked on numerous pictures in this era, either as a screenwriter or director. For *The New Klondike* (1926), which was set in Florida, Milestone took the entire cast and crew there to film on location, a notion that was virtually unheard of at the time.

Producer Howard Hughes signed Milestone as a director, and in 1927–1928 he won the Academy Award for best comedy director at the first Oscar ceremonies for *Two Arabian Knights* (1927), a light-hearted comedy about two doughboys who escape from a German prison and end up in a variety of misadventures. Milestone's other early directorial efforts included varied successes with a sophisticated comedy, *The Garden of Eden* (1928); a gritty gangster picture, *The Racket* (1928); a melodrama (and his last silent feature), *Betrayal* (1929); another gangster film and Milestone's first "all-talkie," *New York Nights* (1929); and the classic aerial thriller, *Hell's Angels* (1929), which he codirected with Hughes, although he was uncredited.

All of these projects added cachet to his reputation, but it was Milestone's sensitive and insightful direction of Erich Maria Remarque's *All Quiet on the Western Front* in 1930 that elevated his reputation to eminence. Remarque's powerful indictment of war and its destructiveness was recognized at once as one of the first great films of the sound era, winning plaudits for actors Lew Ayres and Louis Wolheim, and especially for Milestone as director. *All Quiet* included a number of memorable images of the horrors of war and features some striking battle scenes, which Milestone shot with no more than 150 extras and a minimum of film stock because of his proficiency as a film editor. *All Quiet on the Western Front*, an often sentimental and uneven picture, was unlike anything that had been seen before, and the movie won the Academy Award for best picture; Milestone received the Oscar for best director.

Demonstrating remarkable versatility, Milestone followed *All Quiet on the Western Front* with three vastly different projects: *The Front Page* (1931), a screen adaptation of the rambunctious stage comedy-drama that was nominated for Oscars for best picture and best director (and was also Milestone's last film for Hughes); *Rain* (1932), starring Walter Huston and Joan Crawford (playing Sadie Thompson against Milestone's wishes) in a stagey film version of Somerset Maugham's steamy novel; and *Hallelujah, I'm a Bum* (1933), an experimental Richard Rodgers and Lorenz Hart musical in which all of the dialogue was set to music that starred Al Jolson. *Hallelujah, I'm a Bum* was a significant failure at the box office, both stalling Jolson's screen career and harming Milestone's reputation, although film historian Charles Shibuk later called it "one of the most underrated films ever made, and one of Milestone's best." Despite its failure, a poll taken by *Film Daily* of 300 movie critics at the time placed Milestone at the top of the ten best directors list.

Although few of Milestone's subsequent films equaled the impressive quality of his earliest classics, his output, which included *The General Died at Dawn* (1936), *Of Mice and Men* (1939), and *A Walk in the Sun* (1945), was similarly diverse, highly proficient, and always interesting. *A Walk in the Sun*, particularly, was a compassionate and sensitively directed war film that harked back to the best qualities of *All Quiet on the Western Front*.

Milestone's later films spanned all of the genres available within the Hollywood studio system, from musicals to dramas to historical epics. The finest of these included *Paris in Spring* (1935), *Anything Goes* (1936), *The Night of Nights* (1939), *Lucky Partners* (1940), *Edge of Darkness* (1943), *The North Star* (1943), *The Strange Love of Martha Ivers* (1946), *Arch of Triumph* (1948), *The Red Pony* (1949), *The Halls of Montezuma* (1951), *Les Miserables* (1952), and *Mutiny on the Bounty* (1962).

In 1946 Milestone testified as an unfriendly witness before the House Committee for Un-American Activities, but his appearance there did not significantly damage his career. Suspicions about him had apparently been raised in regard to a documentary he had made with Joris Ivens during World War II called *Our Russian Front* (1942), which praised the valor of the Soviet army in the face of a fierce onslaught by the Nazis.

After Milestone's disastrous remake of *Mutiny on the Bounty* in 1962, which starred a troublesome Marlon Brando, the director was not credited with any subsequent features. The expensive and difficult production received some critical plaudits but failed to attract audiences. Milestone did direct numerous television episodes in the last decade of his career in which his high level of professional craftsmanship was evident but hardly used to maximum advantage.

During the last few years of his life, Milestone suffered from a series of debilitating strokes that finally confined him to a wheelchair. He had married actress Kendall Lee Glaezner in 1935, after meeting her on the set of *Rain*, and they were still together at the time of her death in 1978. The marriage was childless but reportedly one of the happiest in Hollywood. Milestone's health declined further after the death of his wife, and he died in Los Angeles.

Although his career as a leading film director went into some eclipse in the last decades of his working career, Milestone lived long enough to see his reputation as one of the forerunning directors of the early sound era confirmed by critics, scholars, and film festivals celebrating his work. Movie historian Stephen L. Hanson has written of Milestone's reputation: "Films as diverse as *A Walk in the Sun* and *The Strange Loves of Martha Ivers* indicate that his later films contain moments of high achievement comparable to his two great early efforts, and that there is also a great correlation between his technical innovations and his sensitively-handled theme of men in groups than many scholars give him credit for."

• For additional information on Milestone, see "The Big Screens," *Sight & Sound* (Spring 1955): 209; Kingsley Canham, *The Hollywood Professionals: Lewis Milestone* (1973); Clive Denton et al., *The Hollywood Professionals: Henry King, Lewis Milestone, Sam Wood* (1974); D. Diehl, "Directors Go to Their Movies," *Action*, July–Aug. 1972, p. 2; William Everson, "Thoughts on a Great Adaptation," in *The Modern American Novel and the Movies*, ed. Gerald Peary and Roger Shatzkin (1979); H. Feinstein, "Interview," *Film Culture* (Fall 1964): 25; Otis Ferguson, "Lewis Milestone 'Action!'" *Film Comment*, Mar.–Apr. 1974; "First Aid for a Sick Giant," *New Republic*, 31 Jan. 1949, p. 15; Ezra Goodman, "Directed by Lewis Milestone," *Theatre Arts*, Feb. 1943, p. 111; R. T. Jameson, "Style vs. 'Style,'" *Film Comment*, Mar.–Apr. 1980; Richard Koszarski, "The Reign of the Director," *Hollywood Directors: 1914–1940* (1976), and "First Aid for a Sick Giant," *Hollywood Directors: 1941–1976* (1977); Amy Lawrence, "*Rain*: Theorizing the Transitional Film," *Quarterly Review of Film and Video* 11 no. 4 (1990): 21–33; "Lewis Milestone," *Films & Filming*, Dec. 1962, p. 7; and J. McCarten, "Current Cinema," *New Yorker*, 13 June 1959, p. 117. See also Joseph R. Millichap, *Lewis Milestone* (1981); G. J. Mitchell, "Making *All Quiet on the Western Front*," *American Cinematographer*, Sept. 1985; "Personality of the Month," *Films & Filming*, July 1959, p. 5; Karel Reisz, "Milestone and War," *Sequence*, 1950; Q. Reynolds, "That's How Pictures Are Born," *Colliers*, 6 Jan. 1940, p. 14; Andrew Sarris, "Fallen Idols," *Film Culture* (Spring 1963): 30; Charles Shibuk, *An Index to the Films of Lewis Milestone* (1990); "Should Directors Produce?" *Action*, July–Aug. 1968, p. 10; Gaetano Strazzulla, *All'ovest niente di Nuovo un film di Lewis Milestone* (1990); Jon Tuska et al., *Close-Up: The Contract Director* (1976); "The Work of Lewis Milestone," *Newsweek*, 21 Jan. 1946, p. 98; C. Young, "The Old Dependables," *Film Quarterly* (Fall 1959): 2. An obituary is in the *New York Times*, 27 Sept. 1980.

JAMES FISHER

MILEY, Bubber (3 Apr. 1903–20 May 1932), jazz trumpeter and composer, was born James Wesley Miley in Aiken, South Carolina, the son of Valentine Miley, an amateur guitarist. Nothing is known of his mother, but his three sisters sang professionally as the South Carolina Trio. In 1909 the family moved to the San Juan Hill section of Manhattan, where at age fourteen Miley began studying trombone and cornet in school. In 1918 he enlisted in the navy and, after eighteen months of duty, started playing locally with the Carolina Five and in Harlem with pianist Willie Gant. In late 1921 Miley replaced Johnny Dunn, then New York's leading trumpeter, in vaudevillian blues singer Mamie Smith's Jazz Hounds and did much traveling and some recording with her popular act. At this time, Miley was playing in the stiff, ragtime-based style common to early New York jazzmen. While on tour with Smith in mid-1922 he heard cornetist King Oliver's Creole Jazz Band at the Lincoln Gardens in Chicago.

Deeply impressed with both the rhythmic drive of authentic New Orleans jazz and Oliver's use of blues inflections and the "wa-wa" plunger mute, Miley quickly began to incorporate these elements into his own playing.

In December 1922 he left the Jazz Hounds and played at O'Connor's in Harlem and Reisenweber's in Manhattan before going on tour with *The Sunny South* revue. Following his childhood friend trombonist Charlie Irvis, in September 1923 Miley joined Elmer Snowden's Washingtonians at the Hollywood Club in Times Square, but the following February Snowden was ousted from the band and its leadership was turned over to the group's pianist, Duke Ellington. In the spring of 1924 Ellington added New Orleans clarinetist and soprano saxist Sidney Bechet to the band. However, because of his temperamental nature, frequent lateness, and ongoing friction with Miley and Irvis, Bechet was fired in the late summer, albeit having wielded a powerful stylistic influence on both Miley and Ellington during his brief stay. In addition to the Hollywood Club—remodeled and reopened as the Club Kentucky, or more popularly, the Kentucky Club—the Washingtonians also played in Harlem and at various venues in New England.

Between 1923 and 1928 Miley also freelanced as an accompanist on many blues record dates, as well as recording with the Kansas City Five, the Texas Blues Destroyers, and Clarence Williams. Although few of the singers or other musicians involved in the earlier New York sessions were experienced in southern blues expression, Miley demonstrates that by 1924 he had already succeeded in adapting Oliver's blues inflections, plunger mute facility, and rhythmic swing to the staccato attack and double-timed triplets that were his legacy from Dunn. He had also contributed an element of his own to this synthesis, the pronounced guttural rasp known as "growling," a timbral effect that quickly distinguished him from his colleagues. Miley first recorded with the Washingtonians in November 1924 and again in June 1926, but the results are, with the exception of a fairly competent solo on "Animal Crackers," largely unimpressive, primarily because of Ellington's own misguided band style, one still rooted in the rigid, unswinging, bouncy syncopations of white dance bands. The leader, however, did continue to assimilate the lessons learned from Bechet's earlier example, as well as recognizing Miley as his most promising jazz soloist and a valuable source of melodic ideas and orchestral color.

From November 1926 on, the band's musical identity started to develop at a fairly rapid pace, largely because of Miley but also because of some important changes and additions in personnel. Trombonist Joe "Tricky Sam" Nanton, a ready student of Miley's plunger-muted growling, had replaced Irvis in late June, while the addition of alto and baritone saxist Harry Carney and bassist Wellman Braud in mid-1927 and clarinetist Barney Bigard and altoist Johnny Hodges in 1928 provided the final touches to Ellington's first stylistically integrated orchestra. Especially important was the presence of the New Orleanians Bigard and Braud, for their grounding in blues and swinging rhythm set off the necessary sparks missing from the previous lineups, while Hodges, already a confirmed disciple of Bechet, lent a grandeur and majesty to the band sound. Through the combination of these unique soloists, Miley's guiding hand, and the fortuitous circumstance of the band's employment, which necessitated a steady flow of "primitivistic" music, was the Ellington "jungle style" born. Growling brass, wailing clarinets, ominously moaning saxophones, dissonant blues sonorities, and "savage" tom-tom rhythms were the basic ingredients of the style, but, rather than being mere formulaic effects, they provided a colorful foundation for the melodic ideas of both Miley and the other soloists. As a major voice in shaping this revolutionary orchestral timbre, Miley was responsible, either in part or in whole, for the composition of "East St. Louis Toodle-Oo," "Black and Tan Fantasy," "Creole Love Call," "The Blues I Love to Sing," "Blue Bubbles," "Goin' to Town," "Doin' the Voom Voom," and perhaps several more as well. Miley's horn is prominent throughout most of Ellington's recordings through January 1929 and can also be heard in stylistically definitive solos on "Immigration Blues," "New Orleans Low-Down," "Song of the Cotton Field," "Red Hot Band," "Take It Easy," "Jubilee Stomp," "Got Everything But You," "Yellow Dog Blues," and "The Mooche."

The Ellington band played at the Kentucky Club and other venues for more than four years before entering the Cotton Club in December 1927, where they continued to present a Harlem Renaissance view of African mystique for their wealthy, all-white clientele. Like many of the sidemen, Miley was a heavy drinker, but even in this carefree, hedonistic company he stood out for his lack of professional responsibility. Like Bechet before him, he often showed up late for work, and on two occasions in 1927 he failed to appear at all for scheduled record dates. Worst of all, he was frequently absent when important club owners and bookers came to hear the band, a behavior that so tried the patience of Ellington and his manager, Irving Mills, that in January 1929 Miley was fired. His replacement was Cootie Williams, a highly flexible Armstrong disciple who would soon learn the now-essential growl technique directly from Nanton.

Miley freelanced for a while in New York and in May 1929 went to Paris with Noble Sissle, in whose orchestra he narrowly escaped another encounter with the bellicose Bechet by virtue of the latter's incarceration some months before. After two weeks with Sissle, Miley returned to New York, where he worked with Zutty Singleton's band at the Lafayette Theater and with Allie Ross at Connie's Inn. In January 1930 society bandleader Leo Reisman hired Miley as a featured "hot" soloist for both records and theater performances, but for the latter he was required to play behind a screen or in the guise of a special act so as not to outrage the public with the sight of a racially mixed orchestra. In 1931, though, he was asked to play onstage while accompanying dancer Roger Pryor Dodge in Billy Rose's *Sweet and Low*.

The records that Miley made in 1930 do not always present him in the most ideal settings, but his solos on King Oliver's "St. James Infirmary" and Jelly Roll Morton's "Little Lawrence" and "Pontchatrain" from January and March 1930, respectively, are undoubtedly among his best. Apart from his work with Ellington, perhaps the most interesting session of his career was with Bix Beiderbecke, Joe Venuti, and Bud Freeman on a Hoagy Carmichael date in May. He also appeared on several sides with Reisman between January 1930 and June 1931, of which "What Is This Thing Called Love?" "Puttin' On the Ritz," "Happy Feet," and "Take It from Me" warrant attention. However, the six titles from his own Mileage Makers dates between May and September yield only "I Lost My Gal from Memphis," "Without You, Emaline," and "Chinnin' and Chattin' with May" as being performances worth hearing. With Irving Mills's backing, in late 1931 Miley formed his own band for a *Harlem Scandals* revue at the Lincoln Theater in Philadelphia and the Lafayette Theater in Harlem. But he became ill during the Philadelphia run and was feeling even worse on returning home. In January 1932 he was diagnosed with tuberculosis and, weighing only seventy-six pounds, was admitted to Bellevue Hospital and then transferred to Welfare Island in New York City, where he died.

Although he possessed neither the soaring passion, creativity, swing, and emotional depth of Louis Armstrong nor the lyrical beauty, harmonic adventurousness, and stylistic self-reliance of Bix Beiderbecke, Miley nevertheless emerges as one of the three most influential trumpeters of the 1920s. As the first to develop and master a style almost wholly based on plunger-muted growl effects, his impact, both direct and indirect, can be heard in the playing of such other trumpet stylists as Sidney De Paris, Rex Stewart, Bobby Stark, Ed Allen, Henry Goodwin, Cootie Williams, Ray Nance, Hot Lips Page, and Max Kaminsky, as well as all of the trombonists who based their plunger growl techniques on what Tricky Sam Nanton had learned from him.

• Much about Miley's life and music can be learned from the many books written on Duke Ellington. For history as well as critical appraisal, see Mark Tucker, ed., *The Duke Ellington Reader* (1993), an anthology containing several dozen references to Miley's style, contributions, and personality, while a more concentrated discussion of Miley and the Ellington band is Tucker, *Ellington: The Early Years* (1991). The most probing discussion of his style and contributions to the Ellington band is Gunther Schuller, *Early Jazz* (1989), while musicological analyses of several compositions and their relation to Miley's influence are in Ken Rattenbury, *Duke Ellington: Jazz Composer* (1990). Background information on Harlem jazz in the 1920s is in Samuel B. Charters and Leonard Kunstadt, *Jazz: A History of the New York Scene* (1962), but Duke Ellington, *Music Is My Mistress* (1973), while informative, should not be relied on for chronology. Valuable reminiscences by Miley's colleagues are in Stanley Dance, *The World Of Duke Ellington* (1970), an interview-based collection that is the source of many quotations found in later material. Equally important in this respect are the relevant passages in Nat Shapiro and Nat Hentoff, *Hear Me Talkin' to Ya* (1955). The history of Miley and the Washingtonians is also in John Edward Hasse, *Beyond Category: The Life and Genius of Duke Ellington* (1993), and James Lincoln Collier, *Duke Ellington* (1987). Complete discographical information is in Brian Rust, *Jazz Records, 1897–1942* (1982).

JACK SOHMER

MILEY, John (25 Dec. 1813–13 Dec. 1895), clergyman and theologian in the Methodist Episcopal church, was born on a farm near Hamilton, Butler County, Ohio. Nothing is known about his parents. He was a graduate of Augusta College, a Methodist school in Augusta, Kentucky, where he received an A.B. in 1834 and an A.M. in 1837. During his college life he was particularly influenced by three professors, Joseph Tomlinson, Joseph Trimble, and Henry Bascom. Miley entered the ministry of the Methodist Episcopal church through its Ohio Conference in 1838. Between 1838 and 1852 he served appointments in Ohio at Batavia, Cincinnati, Hamilton, Chillicothe, Columbus, Zanesville, and Wesley Female College. In 1852 he transferred to the New York East Conference and from 1852 until 1866 served as a pastor in Brooklyn, New York; Danbury, Connecticut; New York City; Bridgeport, Connecticut; and New Rochelle, New York. In 1866 he transferred to the New York Conference and from 1866 to 1873 served pastorates in Newburgh, Sing Sing, and Peekskill, New York. He was widely known as an excellent preacher and theologian. In 1840 he married Olive Chichester Patterson; they had four children.

In 1873 Miley was appointed professor of systematic theology at Drew Theological Seminary, Madison, New Jersey, where he became one of American Methodism's most distinguished theological personalities. He held this teaching position until the time of his death.

Miley was an acknowledged leader in the Methodist Episcopal church. He was elected a delegate to its quadrennial General Conferences in 1864, 1872, 1876, 1888, and 1892 and took an active role in the proceedings of this important legislative body. He also served as a member of the Centennial Conference of 1884 and in 1886 was a fraternal delegate to the General Conference of the Methodist Episcopal Church, South.

During the years of his professorship at Drew, Miley was especially interested in developing a Methodist theology for his time. He set forth his views in several published articles and in two important works, *The Atonement in Christ* (1879) and *Systematic Theology* (2 vols., 1892, 1894), which were widely studied by persons preparing for the Methodist ministry. These volumes exhibit Miley's commitment to what he considered the main principles of Methodist Arminian theology. He was committed to formulating a theology that was both scientifically certain and logically systematic. "He displays a comprehensiveness and consistency unsurpassed by any other Methodist theologian of the century, paralleled only by [William Burt] Pope in England, and approached only by [Thomas Osmond] Summers and [Miner] Raymond in America" (Chiles, p. 102).

Miley's theology also reflects the problems and issues of late nineteenth-century American Protestant thought. For example, he differed from those theologians who chose either revelation or nature as sources for Christian theology. Both were necessary, and Miley believed that there was a basic compatibility between natural and revealed religion. They complemented each other and offered greater access to the truth. Miley was suspicious of any of his contemporaries who did not allow sufficient place for the role of reason in the formulation of their interpretations of the Christian faith. He held that reason demonstrated the legitimacy of belief in God, and it was absolutely necessary for interpreting the Bible and systematizing theology. Miley made the human intellect a greater factor in creating a theology than had John Wesley, the founder of Methodism, and the principal Methodist theologians who preceded him.

Although Miley considered all human beings in a state of moral ruin in which they were dependent on the grace of God for their salvation, he rejected the notion of original guilt and inherent human depravity based on Adam's sin in favor of free personal agency. By claiming that humans inherit from Adam a nature that provokes them to sin but cannot be considered truly guilty until they freely choose to transgress the laws of God, Miley assumed that he had avoided modern objections to the traditional doctrine of original sin and had preserved the Arminian doctrine of free will. Regrettably, he wrote, everyone chooses to sin. Therefore, all must freely rely on divine grace, which moves the sinner to repentance, forgives the transgression, and encourages a holy life. Miley's death in Madison, New Jersey, came one day after he had delivered his final seminary lecture.

• In addition to the theological treatises mentioned in the text and articles published in a number of periodicals, Miley's most important work is *Treatise on Class Meetings* (1851). Principal sources of information about Miley's life and thought are Robert E. Chiles, *Theological Transition in American Methodism, 1790–1935* (1965), and James Richard Joy, *Teachers of Drew, 1867–1942* (1942).

CHARLES YRIGOYEN, JR.

MILGRAM, Stanley (15 Aug. 1933–20 Dec. 1984), social psychologist, was born in the Bronx, New York, the son of Samuel Milgram, a baker, and Adele Israel. Both parents were Jewish immigrants from Eastern Europe. After growing up in a neighborhood "abuzz with people" of all backgrounds, Milgram attended Queens College from 1950 to 1954, majoring in political science. He became vice president of both the International Relations Club and the Debating Club and graduated Phi Beta Kappa.

Although already accepted to the School of International Affairs at Columbia University with the aim of entering the foreign service, Milgram changed his career plans during the last semester of his senior year when he heard about and was intrigued by Harvard's Department of Social Relations, an innovative attempt at interdisciplinary cooperation whose diverse faculty contained such social science luminaries as Gordon Allport, Talcott Parsons, Jerome Bruner, Erik Erikson, and Roger Brown. The department combined social psychology, clinical psychology, social anthropology, and sociology, and the resulting smorgasbord of ideas about human social behavior provided very satisfying intellectual fare for Milgram and, as he later recalled, "stimulated in [him] a broad ranging interest in the social sciences." Milgram entered the program in 1954 and received his Ph.D. in social psychology in 1960.

It was also at Harvard that Milgram met the man who became his most important intellectual and scientific influence: Solomon E. Asch. Asch had brought a rational approach, grounded in Gestalt psychology, to social psychology. In 1955–1956 he came to Harvard as a visiting lecturer, and Milgram became his teaching and research assistant. Milgram also worked with Asch at the Institute for Advanced Study in Princeton in 1959–1960.

Asch had become famous for inventing an elegantly simple but powerful experimental paradigm to study conformity. In Asch's experiment, a subject is asked to view a vertical line and to indicate which of three other lines it matched in length, after several other persons have, in turn, announced their judgments. What the subject did not know was that the others were accomplices of the experimenter who were instructed to give identical incorrect matches on critical trials. Asch found that subjects conformed to the bogus majority about one-third of the time.

Asch's paradigm inspired Milgram's doctoral dissertation research—a comparison of conformity levels in Norway and France using auditory rather than visual stimuli. He spent one year (1957–1958) in Norway and the next year in France collecting the data. He found that Norwegians conformed more than French participants, and a report of his findings resulted in his first scientific publication, "Nationality and Conformity" (*Scientific American* [December 1961]: 45–51). It was a groundbreaking study; as Milgram put it, it was "the first attempt to study national characteristics by the direct, experimental assessment of behavior of two national groups."

In the fall of 1960 Milgram went to Yale as an assistant professor in the Department of Psychology. From the summer of 1961 to the end of May 1962, he carried out a series of twenty-four experiments on obedience to authority involving hundreds of subjects, funded by a grant from the National Science Foundation. This set of experiments came to be regarded as one of the most important and controversial pieces of social science research in the twentieth-century. Readers of his first report, "Behavioral Study of Obedience" (*Journal of Abnormal and Social Psychology* 67 [1963]: 371–78), were stunned by his startling discovery: that an average, presumably normal group of men would readily inflict what they believed to be very painful and possibly harmful electric shocks on an innocent victim. Specifically, as part of an experiment supposedly dealing with the effects of punishment on learning, subjects were required by an experimenter to shock a learner every time he made an error on a verbal-learning task, and to increase the intensity of the shock in fifteen-volt increments from 15 to 450 volts on each subsequent error. The results were that 65 percent of the subjects continued to obey the experimenter to the end, simply because he commanded them to.

These experiments generated a great deal of public interest (for example, the *New York Times*, 26 Oct. 1963, reported them under the headline "65% in Test Blindly Obey Order to Inflict Pain") and a whirlwind of controversy, with praise by some and vilification by others. For example, while some clergymen drew moral lessons from the experiments in their sermons, a Benedictine monk from Washington, D.C., wrote a letter to Milgram stating that his "immediate reaction to reading your report on obedience was one of sheer revulsion. Mostly revulsion for the extremely callous, deceitful way in which the experiment was conducted." As suggested by this letter, much of the controversy surrounding the obedience studies had to do with the ethics of subjecting participants to a very stressful experience without their prior knowledge or consent, deceiving them into believing that they may have harmed an innocent human being. In actuality, the victim did not receive shocks; he was only an actor pretending that he did. The participants were enlightened about this after the experimental session was over. But during the experimental hour itself, prior to the debriefing, subjects typically experienced a genuine, emotionally wrenching conflict between the promptings of their conscience and the insistent demands of the scientific authority.

In December 1961 Milgram married Alexandra "Sasha" Menkin; they had two children. Milgram returned to Harvard in 1963 as an assistant professor of social psychology in the Department of Social Relations. There he continued research using the "lost-letter technique" he had devised at Yale as a way of measuring community attitudes. Its innovation was in the fact that it used actions (deciding to mail or not mail a "lost" letter) rather than words as indicators of attitudes. He used this technique at Harvard to predict the outcome of the 1964 presidential elections. He also turned his attention to something new—the "small-world problem," which Milgram described as follows: "Given any two people in the world, person X and person Z, how many intermediate acquaintance links are needed before X and Z are connected." To answer that question he devised the "small-world method," in which a number of people are given packets to send to a stranger in a distant city using only intermediaries that they know on a first-name basis. The main finding was that, among the completed connections, it took a surprisingly small number of intermediaries (about five) to reach the target.

Harvard did not offer Milgram tenure so in 1967 he accepted an offer from the Graduate Center of the City University of New York (CUNY) to head its social psychology program as a full professor: he thus skipped the associate professor level. At CUNY the psychology of city life became the primary focus of his research interests, resulting in the publication of a seminal article titled "The Experience of Living in Cities" (*Science* 167 [1970]: 1461–68), which provided a needed impetus for the newly emerging field of urban psychology. A spin-off of Milgram's interest in city life was his research on the subjective maps (the geography of a place as perceived by residents) of people in New York and Paris.

Soon after Milgram's arrival at CUNY, the CBS network sent out requests for grant proposals to study the relationship between television violence and viewer aggression. Milgram responded with an application and was awarded a very large grant that enabled him to conduct a series of field experiments that remain unique. He was the first and only researcher who was able to get a major TV network to create segments of an ongoing popular prime-time program tailored to meet the needs of an experiment. Specifically, Milgram worked with the writers of the dramatic series "Medical Center" to create a segment with three different endings, two depicting an antisocial act and the third a prosocial one. Across a series of field experiments—some of which involved potentially millions of viewers—subjects saw one of the three versions or a totally different segment (a control program) from the same series; they were then provided with an opportunity to carry out the act depicted in the antisocial versions of the episode. Despite the inventiveness of the study, those who watched the antisocial versions of the program were no more likely to act in an antisocial manner than those who had watched the prosocial or control program.

Observing the production of the "Medical Center" episode whetted Milgram's appetite for making his own films. As a result, from 1972 to 1976, together with documentary film director Harry From, who was a student in the doctoral program in social psychology at CUNY, Milgram made five educational films on various topics in social psychology. One of them, *The City and the Self*, won the silver medal of the International Film and Television Festival of New York. These films continue to be shown in college classes throughout the country.

The last innovative research program that Milgram developed before his death concerned what he called "Cyranoids." Cyranoids are persons who converse with another person with words transmitted to them by yet another person through an inconspicuous earphone. Milgram found that the human tendency to perceive others as possessing a coherent personality exerted a powerful influence on the interviewers of the cyranoids. For example, no one suspected that an eleven-year-old cyranoid's words were not his own even when the "sender" was a fifty-year-old professor of psychology.

In 1980 Milgram was appointed distinguished professor of psychology at CUNY. Later that same year he suffered a massive heart attack, the first of a series occurring over a five-year period. The fifth one, on the afternoon of 20 December 1984, proved to be fatal. Milgram died at the age of 51 in New York City.

Milgram's personality was complex. Depending on the situation or the person he could be profound or playful, friendly or brusque. His students found him to be a marvelous teacher who had a talent for extracting the essence from complicated material and conveying it in an absorbing manner. Yet many also remembered his classes as an emotional roller coaster ride in which exhilaration brought on by flashes of insight would alternate with the terror of waiting to be picked on by Milgram. But his harshness would fade as students progressed through the graduate program; some saw it in retrospect as a kind of rite of passage. And once Milgram became a student's mentor, he or she had a lifelong advocate.

Milgram's research on obedience has had a profound effect on contemporary thinking about the human propensity for evil. As Irwin Katz, his colleague at CUNY, said about these studies at his funeral, "They remain one of the most singular, most penetrating, and most disturbing inquiries into human conduct that modern psychology has produced in this century." Because of its broad relevance, the obedience research has continued to receive attention from journalists, political and social commentators, and a surprising diversity of disciplines outside of psychology. The societal reverberations of the ethical controversy surrounding this work are still felt in the form of a greater sensitivity to the welfare of the human research subject. More concretely, they are among a handful of studies that led the federal government in the 1970s to formalize review procedures for the protection of human subjects (for example, mandating and formulating guidelines for institutional review boards). The variety of Milgram's research endeavors are among the most inventive and interesting in social psychology, energized by a playful curiosity that led him to study even less weighty but intriguing questions such as: "Would New York City subway riders give up their seats if asked to?" Milgram left a legacy of lucid, jargon-free writings that make his works accessible to a wide readership.

• Milgram's papers are located at the Yale University Library. His most complete work on the obedience studies is *Obedience to Authority: An Experimental View* (1974). A full description of the research involving television viewers' behavior is in Stanley Milgram and R. Lance Shotland, *Television and Antisocial Behavior: Field Experiments* (1973). Most of Milgram's other published writings, with additional narrative material, are reprinted in his *Individual in a Social World: Essays and Experiments* (1977); the second edition of that book came out posthumously in 1992 and was edited by his former students John Sabini and Maury Silver. A detailed biography of Milgram is in a chapter by Thomas Blass, "Stanley Milgram: A Life of Inventiveness and Controversy," in *Portraits of Pioneers of Psychology*, vol. 2, ed. Gregory A. Kimble et al. (1996). Arthur Miller, *The Obedience Experiments: A Case Study of Controversy in Social Science* (1986), is an important work. A complete review of the literature on the obedience paradigm is Blass, "Understanding Behavior in the Milgram Obedience Experiment: The Role of Personality, Situations, and Their Interactions," *Journal of Personality and Social Psychology* 60 (1991): 398–413. The relevance of the obedience experiments to the Holocaust is explored in Blass, "Psychological Perspectives on the Perpetrators of the Holocaust: The Role of Situational Pressures, Personal Dispositions, and Their Interactions," *Holocaust and Genocide Studies* 7 (1993): 30–50. A review and analysis of the whole corpus of Milgram's work is in a chapter by Blass, "The Social Psychology of Stanley Milgram," in *Advances in Experimental Social Psychology*, vol. 25, ed. Mark P. Zanna (1992), which also contains the most complete bibliography of Milgram's published writings. An obituary is in the *New York Times*, 22 Dec. 1984.

THOMAS BLASS

MILK, Harvey (22 May 1930–27 Nov. 1978), politician and gay rights activist, was born Harvey Bernard Milk in Woodmere, Long Island, New York, the son of William Milk and Minerva Karns. His father operated a department store in Woodmere that was founded in 1882 by his grandfather, Morris Milk (originally Milch), a Lithuanian immigrant. Before she married his father, Milk's mother was an early feminist activist who joined the Yoemanettes, a group agitating for the inclusion of women in the U.S. Navy during World War I.

Milk graduated from Bayshore High School in 1947 and from the New York State College for Teachers at Albany, where he majored in math and minored in history in 1951. In college Milk was a sportswriter for the *State College News*, serving as sports editor during his senior year. He was also active in Kappa Beta, a Jewish fraternity. Following graduation, Milk joined the U.S. Navy in September 1951. He attended Officer Candidate School (OCS) in Newport, Rhode Island, and was commissioned a lieutenant (j.g.). Milk was based in San Diego, California, where he served until his discharge in August 1955.

After leaving the navy Milk taught high school math and history in Woodmere from 1955 to 1957. In 1957 he moved to Dallas, Texas, where he worked in a department store. The following year he took a position as an actuary at the Great American Insurance Company in New York City. In 1963 he began working as a statistical analyst and supervisor of the information center at Bache & Company in New York City. Milk remained with Bache & Company for several years, building a reputation as an astute financial analyst. After leaving Bache he held a series of positions with various companies in the finance field in both New York and San Francisco.

As with many gay men and lesbians of his generation, the Stonewall Riot marked Milk's emergence as a political and social activist. In the early morning hours of 28 June 1969 New York City police engaged gay men and lesbians in a fierce and protracted clash outside the Stonewall Bar, a popular gay gathering spot in

Greenwich Village. Claiming that the Stonewall was operating in violation of the bar's liquor license, the police conducted a raid. Although that was the immediate spark, the riot was actually a response to long-simmering hostility within the gay community over regular and repeated police harassment and officially sanctioned "gay bashing."

In 1972 Milk moved permanently to San Francisco, which since the end of World War II had become a relatively safe haven for openly gay men and women and the center of gay culture in the United States. Milk opened a camera store on Castro Street, in the center of the gay community, and quickly moved to the forefront of gay political activism. Outspoken, brash, impulsive, passionate, and charismatic, he challenged San Francisco's traditional gay political leadership and its strategy of crafting alliances with the city's liberal establishment in exchange for modest, incremental advances in political recognition and power. Milk's confrontational style brought him into conflict with Jim Foster and the other gay power brokers of the Alice B. Toklas Memorial Democratic Club. In 1973, a San Francisco resident for little more than a year, he declared his candidacy for the San Francisco Board of Supervisors, the powerful legislative body for the combined city and county of San Francisco. Although he was opposed by Foster and the gay power structure, Milk commanded the support of many in the angry and impatient younger gay community. His candidacy received an important boost when José Sarria, a prominent San Francisco gay activist since the 1940s, endorsed him. Although he lost that race, Milk garnered more than 17,000 votes and finished tenth in a 32-candidate field for five at-large seats.

Milk emerged from the 1973 campaign as a new force in San Francisco politics, an urban populist whose platform, while founded on gay rights, also embraced those who sought an uncompromising political voice against the real estate developers, tourist industry, and downtown corporate interests that controlled the city's governance. Milk provided a model of involvement in community and political affairs that encouraged others in the gay community to follow. In 1974 he revitalized the Castro Village Association as a vehicle for gay merchants to exercise economic power. After a second race for supervisor in 1976, which he barely lost, finishing seventh behind six incumbents, Milk was firmly established as the leading political spokesman for the city's gay community, and the election of his friend and ally George Moscone as mayor gave him access to the center of power.

In 1976 Mayor Moscone appointed Milk to the city's board of permit appeals, making him the first openly gay city commissioner in the United States. Less than five weeks after taking office, however, Milk alienated Moscone by filing candidacy papers for the state assembly. His candidacy in the Sixteenth Assembly District disrupted a carefully crafted agreement among the city's top Democratic politicians—Moscone, John Foran, and Leo McCarthy—to divide the political spoils in the wake of Moscone's mayoral victory. Milk lost the race to the Moscone-Foran-McCarthy choice, Art Agnos, a young aide to Assembly Speaker Leo McCarthy. Politically savvy, Milk then sought passage of an amendment to the city-county charter that would replace at-large elections for the board of supervisors, which served to diffuse the gay vote, with district elections, which would result in a concentration of voting power. In 1977, following the achievement of that structural change, Milk was elected to the board of supervisors from District 5, the Castro area. Receiving more than 30 percent of the vote in a sixteen-candidate field, Milk far out-polled his nearest rival.

From his first day as a San Francisco supervisor, Milk pursued an ambitious agenda of political, economic, and social reform that included protection of gay rights, reform of the city's property tax structure to entice light industry back to the deserted factories and warehouses of the inner city, an innovative proposal for citywide day care centers for working mothers run by senior citizens, the enactment of a commuter tax on the 300,000 corporate commuters who worked in the city and used its services but lived—and paid taxes—in the suburbs, the enactment of an anti-speculation tax to combat escalating housing costs that were driving moderate and low-income San Franciscans from the city, the conversion of soon-to-be abandoned military facilities within the city to low-cost housing for senior citizens, and the preservation of the integrity and character of the city's varied neighborhoods. Though his success with these reforms was mixed, given his short tenure in office, many of the programs he promoted were established after his death.

Milk emerged as an ardent proponent of strong, safe, cohesive neighborhoods as essential to high-quality urban life. He paid special attention to his own district, relentlessly pressuring the Moscone administration to improve traffic control, make street repairs, expand library services, and augment street cleaning and police patrols.

As the nation's first and only openly gay elected official, Milk also spoke out on state and national issues affecting gays, including pending antigay legislation in Florida, Minnesota, Kansas, Oregon, and California, among other states. His promising career abruptly ended within a year of his election to the board. Milk and Mayor Moscone were assassinated in their city hall offices by Dan White, a former supervisor and political opponent.

• The most complete and accurate source of information is the biography by Randy Shilts, *The Mayor of Castro Street: The Life and Times of Harvey Milk* (1982). Milk's significance to, and role in, gay political liberation is discussed in Karen A. Foss, "Harvey Milk: You Have to Give Them Hope," *Journal of the West* (Apr. 1988): 75–81. Foss's "The Logic of Folly in the Political Campaigns of Harvey Milk," in *Queer Words, Queer Images: Communication and the Construction of Homosexuality*, ed. R. Jeffrey Ringer (1994), provides useful insight into Milk's campaign rhetoric and style. Two works concentrate on Milk's murder and include valuable biographical information and political analysis: Mike Weiss, *Double Play: The San Francisco City Hall Killings* (1984), and Emily Mann, *Execution of Justice* (1986). The Academy Award–winning documentary *The Times of Harvey Milk* (1986) is a compelling portrait of Milk's life and career through television news footage and interviews. An obituary is in the *New York Times*, 28 Nov. 1978. His murder and White's subsequent trial and reaction to it received extensive press coverage, especially in San Francisco.

FREDERICK J. SIMONELLI

MILLAND, Ray (3 Jan. 1907–10 Mar. 1986), motion picture actor, was born Reginald Truscott-Jones in Neath, Glamorganshire, Wales, the son of Alfred Jones, a construction engineer, and Elizabeth Truscott. After his parents' divorce, Milland (his professional name) had no single home but lived at various times with his mother, his father, and other relatives. He spent his happiest years with his Aunt Luisa (one of his father's half sisters) on her horse-breeding farm in Wales.

When he reached his teens Milland, who had grown into a slender six-footer, worked at various jobs during summers: as a farmhand, a laborer in a steel mill, and a cabin boy on a ship owned by an uncle. Although his frequent moves had caused his schooling to be erratic, Milland was bright and well read and entered the University of Wales in Cardiff to study architecture. He left school after a year to live with an uncle and to work in the office of a steel mill. Still dissatisfied, in 1926 he enlisted in the Household Cavalry. Milland passed the unit's demanding tests in fencing, boxing, shooting, and riding, after which he took months of additional training in horsemanship. His three-year stint in the Household Cavalry was spent in London, where the regiment served as guards to the royal family and was popular with tourists for its elegant (but uncomfortable) attire and pageantry. Milland won celebrity as the British army's champion in both pistol and rifle marksmanship. He never took regimental life seriously, however, and viewed duty in London as an opportunity to party. He left the military as soon as he legally could and at the suggestion of an acquaintance, the American actress Estelle Brody, got a small role in a Wardour Films production, *The Plaything*. He then changed his name to Ray Milland. He enjoyed acting, liked the pay, and secured an agent. He received bit roles in two other 1929 movies, *The Informer* and *The Flying Scotsman*. The last was released before either of the other two films.

Milland performed in one other film in London in 1929, got a role as the juvenile lead in the touring company of the drama *The Woman in Room 13*, and then went to Hollywood at the invitation of a producer at Metro-Goldwyn-Mayer (MGM) whom he had met in London. MGM paid his expenses and signed him to a short-term contract, casting him in small parts in several 1930 productions. The following year Milland was loaned out to Warner Bros. and Fox, both of which, like MGM, gave him bit parts, usually as a playboy. Milland concluded that he had no future at MGM and returned to London. But before doing so, in 1932 he married Malvina Muriel Weber. They had two children, one of whom was adopted.

After his marriage Milland went to England to appear in *Orders Is Orders* and *This Is the Life*, both released in 1933. Back in Hollywood later that year, he made his first significant impression, playing an English lord in the Paramount film *Bolero* (1934), starring Carole Lombard and George Raft. Lombard suggested that Milland be cast (again as an aristocrat) in her next film, the comedy-musical *We're Not Dressing*, which featured Lombard, Bing Crosby, George Burns, and Gracie Allen. Milland was billed eighth, but Paramount nevertheless signed him to a seven-year contract at $300 a week, twice what he had earned at MGM.

For a few years thereafter Milland starred in low-budget films and played supporting roles in first-run films. He was one of several young actors at Paramount who had the status of "hopefuls." His fan mail increased noticeably after he played Dorothy Lamour's love interest in *Jungle Princess* (1936), the film in which Lamour introduced the sarong to American popular culture. In 1937 Milland's performance in the comedy *Easy Living* earned him still more attention. In the early 1940s he attained stardom, showing a deft touch in the popular comedies *The Doctor Takes a Wife* (1940) and *The Major and the Minor* (1942) and also handling himself well in dramatic roles in *Arise My Love* (1940), *I Wanted Wings* (1941), and *Reap the Wild Wind* (1942), in which he co-starred with John Wayne.

Milland was eligible for service in the British army during World War II but was not called to duty. He tried to enlist in the U.S. Army Air Force but was rejected for service because of a chronic problem with his left hand. He continued to make films but also spent considerable time entertaining servicemen at the Hollywood Canteen and at United Service Organizations (USO) camp shows. During a 1944 tour Milland appeared at several U.S. bases in the Solomon Islands and other South Pacific sites. In one of his early appearances he was heckled by a GI who wanted to know why Milland was not in the military himself. Milland responded, "What, with a war going on? Think I'm crazy?" His retort silenced the heckler. Word of the incident spread rapidly throughout camps where Milland was scheduled to appear and did much to establish rapport between the star and his audiences. Fluent in Spanish, he also spoke regularly on government-sponsored broadcasts to Latin America.

Distributors rated Milland as Paramount's most marketable star, and critics gave him many favorable reviews, especially for his performances in the espionage drama *Ministry of Fear* (1944) and in *The Lost Weekend* (1945). In the latter, marred only by an unexpectedly upbeat ending, Milland played Don Birnam, a troubled writer battling an addiction to alcohol and an inability to write the successful novel he also craved. The action takes place over a five-day period, with interior shots filmed at Paramount but with street scenes filmed on location on New York City's then-seedy Third Avenue. For his role Milland spent weeks reading about alcoholism, interviewing physicians, and observing the behavior of compulsive drinkers in bars. Milland's characterization earned him the Oscar for best actor in 1945.

Milland remained a star for another decade, showing his skills as a performer with his first appearances in westerns and especially in two mysteries, *The Big Clock* (1948) and the Alfred Hitchcock production *Dial M for Murder* (1954), co-starring the young Grace Kelly. Nearing fifty at a time during which the major studios were retrenching, Milland soon began experiencing difficulty in getting suitable parts. Consequently he turned to television. In 1954–1955 he played an absent-minded professor in the CBS series "Meet Mr. McNutley," which was renewed for a second season under the new title "The Ray Milland Show." Milland also accepted numerous guest roles and returned to series television in 1959–1960, when he portrayed a wealthy lawyer-sleuth in "Markham." In 1955 Milland fulfilled a long-held ambition when he directed *A Man Alone*, a western filmed by Republic Pictures. The following year he starred in and directed the suspense drama *Lisbon*, one of his last major screen roles.

Over the next two decades Milland continued to be active in several areas. He appeared primarily in low-budget horror films, some of which, such as *The Man with the X-Ray Eyes* (1963), are regarded as minor classics of the genre, and he had an important supporting part as the father of the male lead in the popular tearjerker *Love Story* (1970). In 1965 he returned to the stage for the first time since his struggling days in England when he played Professor Henry Higgins in a road production of *My Fair Lady*. He next appeared in *Hostile Witness*, which ran on Broadway for several months in 1966. Milland also had success as a writer, completing numerous short stories and articles under a variety of pseudonyms. Several of his selections were published in national magazines. He also completed his memoir, *Wide-Eyed in Babylon* (1974). Milland died at the Torrance Memorial Medical Center in Torrance, California.

A man who had never expressed interest in an acting career, Milland initially got parts in films in both London and Hollywood because of his good looks and suave style. He had no formal training in drama but developed insight into the demands of acting by watching numerous films and by asking questions of skilled performers. At the end of the 1930s Milland emerged from a group of other young actors under contract to Paramount to become one of the studio's top box office attractions, able to handle comedy with aplomb and also showing depth as a performer in *Lost Weekend* and in a variety of other roles.

• The best sources are Milland's memoirs, which are strongest on his youth and his first fifteen years in Hollywood, and "Ray Milland," in James Robert Parish and Don E. Stanke, *The Debonairs* (1975). It contains a filmography but is at odds with Milland's memoirs about several facts pertaining to his childhood. An obituary is in the *New York Times*, 11 Mar. 1986.

LLOYD J. GRAYBAR

MILLAY, Edna St. Vincent (22 Feb. 1892–19 Oct. 1950), poet, was born in the small town of Rockland, Maine, the daughter of Henry Tollman Millay, a schoolteacher, and Cora Buzzelle. In 1900 Cora Millay divorced her husband for financial irresponsibility and soon thereafter moved to Camden, Maine, with Edna and her sisters. The hardworking mother supported them by nursing—often overnight—and encouraged her daughters to love reading and music and to be independent. Millay attended public high school, where she wrote for and served as editor in chief of the school magazine (1905–1909). She also published several juvenile pieces in the *St. Nicholas Magazine* (1906–1910). Her first great poem, "Renascence," was published in an anthology called *The Lyric Year* in 1912. When a Young Women's Christian Association education officer heard Millay read this poem, she helped obtain a scholarship for the talented girl to attend Vassar College.

Millay took preparatory courses for one semester at Barnard College and then entered Vassar in 1913. While there she wrote poetry and plays (published in the Vassar *Miscellany*), acted, starred in her own play, *The Princess Marries the Page*, and studied literature and languages. Although she frequently rebelled against rules designed to protect female students, Millay graduated with an A.B. in 1917. That year Millay published *Renascence and Other Poems*. She moved to New York City, where she acted with the Provincetown Players, lived impecuniously in Greenwich Village, and indulged in love affairs with several men, including the novelist Floyd Dell and, briefly, the married poet Arthur Davison Ficke. She earned a little money by publishing short stories (under the pseudonym Nancy Boyd) and poems in *Ainslee's* magazine (1918–1921). In 1919 she wrote and directed a one-act, antiwar verse play with a fairy-tale motif titled *Aria da Capo*, for the Provincetown Players. During this period she also met the critic Edmund Wilson, at that time the managing editor of *Vanity Fair*, which had published some of her work (1920). Millay won a $100 prize from *Poetry: A Magazine of Verse* for "The Bean-Stalk" in 1920. She also published her second book of verse, *A Few Figs from Thistles* (1920; rev. eds., 1921 and 1922), and *Aria da Capo* (1920), which sold well.

With an agreement to write for *Vanity Fair*, the hardworking Millay enjoyed a varied sojourn in Europe from 1920 to 1923. In 1921 she published two more plays and a solid collection of poetry, *Second April*. Meanwhile, she had other love affairs, including a reported relationship with a French violinist that led to an abortion. She encouraged but soon decided not to marry the poet Witter Bynner. After obtaining a $500 advance from Horace Liveright for a novel titled "Hardigut" that was never completed, she sent for her mother, and the two toured France and England; they then returned to New York. In 1923 Millay was honored as the first woman to be awarded the Pulitzer Prize for poetry. In that same year she published *The Harp-Weaver and Other Poems*, and after a brief courtship she married the 43-year-old widower Eugen Jan Boissevain; they had no children. He was a burly American importer of Dutch-Irish extraction who was sensitively intelligent, profeminist, and considerate. Millay went on arduous reading tours and sailed around the world with her husband in 1924. The couple bought and occupied "Steepletop," their permanent home on 700 acres of farmland near Austerlitz, New York, during 1925. Shortly thereafter Millay created the stirring libretto for *The King's Henchman*, Deems Taylor's splendid opera, which premiered at the Metropolitan Opera of New York in 1927 starring the American baritone Lawrence Tibbett. The libretto was published and went through four quick editions, reportedly earning Millay $100 a day for a while.

Later in 1927 Millay became involved in the Sacco-Vanzetti case. Nicola Sacco and Bartolomeo Vanzetti, Italian-born anarchists and labor agitators, had been convicted in 1921 of the 1920 murder of two payroll guards in South Braintree, Massachusetts. The verdict was challenged by those who felt that the two were being persecuted for their history as social activists and anarchists. Although questions about their innocence remained, they were executed on 23 August 1927. Millay and many other intellectuals had joined in a sensational protest, in which she personally appealed to Governor Alvan T. Fuller and was arrested and jailed for joining the "death watch." In response, Millay wrote and published "Justice Denied in Massachusetts" (*New York Times*, 22 Aug. 1927). Her involvement in the protest was evidence of her long-standing sympathy for the socialistic aspects of communism. Despite or perhaps partly because of this notoriety, many honors came to Millay, including her election to the National Institute of Arts and Letters (1929) and the American Academy of Arts and Letters (1940). During approximately this same period, however, three deaths severely depressed her. Her close friend, the poet Eleanor Wylie, died in 1928, her mother died in 1931, and her estranged father died in 1935.

Given her psychological makeup, Millay had found the ideal husband in Boissevain. He attended to all the household chores, traveled widely with his "Vincent"—often to Florida, the Riviera, and Spain—and cooperated with her intellectual and linguistic interests. He catered to her whims and even condoned her having an occasional lover. One, George Dillon, who was fourteen years her junior and whom she met in 1928 while giving a reading at the University of Chicago, inspired *Fatal Interview* (1931), a 52-sonnet sequence. In one sonnet she snarls: "Love me no more, now let the god depart, / If love be grown so bitter to your tongue!" Nonetheless, Dillon and Millay collaborated later on translations from Charles Baudelaire's *Les Fleurs du Mal* (1936). Still later, in a sonnet in *Huntsman, What Quarry?* (1939), she says, "As God's my judge, I do cry holy, holy, / Upon the name of love however brief." Beginning in 1933, Millay and her husband enjoyed summer retreats on tiny Ragged Island, having bought the 85-acre spot in Casco Bay, Maine. Her other pre–World War II works include *The Buck in the Snow* (1928), *Wine from These Grapes* (1934), and *Conversation at Midnight* (1937); the original, unique manuscript of this dialogue of seven men was burned in a Sanibel Island hotel fire a year earlier.

In *Huntsman, What Quarry?* Millay had included stirring poems against the brutalities of Fascist Spain, Nazi Germany, and imperialistic Japan. Other events, such as Italy's attacks on Ethiopia and the German-Russian nonaggression treaty, caused the once-pacifist poet to call for preparedness and then to dash off pro-British and pro-French propaganda verse. Most of her poetry of World War II, much of which she collected in *Make Bright the Arrows: 1940 Notebook* (1940), has proved vapid, but a memorable exception is *The Murder of Lidice* (1942). This long, dramatic verse narrative is based on the depraved German army butchery of an entire Czech village.

In 1944 Millay suffered a nervous breakdown and was unable to write for two years. During this time and later, her husband catered to her so selflessly that he depleted his own reserves of strength and died in 1949 of lung cancer followed by surgery and a stroke. Millay, who with her husband had drunk to excess since the 1930s, evidently grew more dependent on alcohol during her brief, inconsolable widowhood. She died sitting at the foot of her staircase, alone, at Steepletop.

Millay is the poetic voice of eternal youth, feminine revolt and liberation, and potent sensitivity and suggestiveness. Her best and most representative themes are bittersweet love, sorrow, the inevitability of change, resignation, death, and ever-abiding nature. One of her very best poems is her early, mystical "Renascence," about spiritual interment and resurrection through the cycles of nature. It smoothly combines naiveté and profundity and modern and archaic diction. In "Afternoon on a Hill" (published in *Renascence* [1917]) the delicate persona says, "I will touch a hundred flowers / And not pick one." She occasionally takes a snide tone in *A Few Figs from Thistles* (1920); for example, she begins one sonnet with these lines: "I shall forget you presently, my dear, / So make the most of this, your little day." But the collection also includes "Recuerdo," which memorably describes the dawn that a happy couple sees from a ferryboat: "The sky went wan, and the wind came cold, / And the sun rose dripping, a bucketful of gold."

Second April (1921) contains tender elegies to a Vassar friend who died of influenza in 1918. "The Ballad of the Harp-Weaver," the technically brilliant title poem of Millay's 1923 collection, dramatizes a mother's love: a woman too poor to provide necessities for her little son weaves clothes for him by magically playing her harp. In the same book "The Spring and the Fall" bitterly contrasts a lover's vernal attention and his autumnal gibes and concludes that "'Tis not love's going hurts my days, / But that it went in little ways."

The Buck in the Snow (1928) proved unpopular, perhaps because it features much experimental verse; for example, "The Pigeons" contains one line of twenty-five syllables. Her imagery grows startling, as when in "On First Having Heard the Skylark" the bird's cry is "like a crystal dart."

The bitter philosophical poems in *Wine from These Grapes* (1934) are well represented by "Apostrophe to Man," in which, seeming to anticipate World War II, Millay exhorts everyone to "expunge yourself, die out, / *Homo* called *sapiens*." The mounted huntsman in the terse title poem of *Huntsman, What Quarry?* is tempted to enjoy "a one-night's bride" but decides instead to go kill the fox. Notable from the posthumous *Mine the Harvest* (1954) are Millay's delight that "thought unbraids itself" ("Ragged Island"), her conceited disgust with time-consuming visitors—"What chores these churls do put upon the great" ("Cave Canem"), and Christ's warning to His followers, "No shelter will be found / Save in my shadow" ("Jesus to His Disciples").

Millay will always be remembered for her flippant quatrain, which she titled "First Fig" (1920):

> My candle burns at both ends;
> It will not last the night;
> But ah, my foes, and oh, my friends—
> It gives a lovely light!

She should also be remembered, however, for her "Second Fig" (1920): "Safe upon the solid rock the ugly houses stand: / Come see my shining palace built upon the sand!" Her "shining" poetry should never fall out of fashion. Its lyricism, praise of beauty, freedom, and individualism, and technical virtuosity are timeless.

• Most of Millay's papers are at the New York Public Library, Yale University, and the Library of Congress. See also *Letters of Edna St. Vincent Millay*, ed. Allan Ross Macdougall (1952). Primary and secondary bibliographies are Karl Yost, *A Bibliography of the Works of Edna St. Vincent Millay* (1937); John J. Patton, "A Comprehensive Bibliography of Criticism of Edna St. Vincent Millay," *Serif* 5 (Sept. 1968): 10–32; and Judith Nierman, *Edna St. Vincent Millay: A Reference Guide* (1977). Biographical studies include Jean Gould, *The Poet and Her Book: A Biography of Edna St. Vincent Millay* (1969); Joan Dash, *A Life of One's Own: Three Gifted Women and the Men They Married* (1973); and Anne Chaney, *Millay in Greenwich Village* (1975). The best critical study is Norman A. Brittin, *Edna St. Vincent Millay* (1967; rev. ed., 1982). Discerning evaluations of Millay's early poetry are in Alfred Kreymborg, *Our Singing Strength: An Outline of American Poetry (1620–1930)* (1929), while generally derogatory comments are in Hyatt H. Waggoner, *American Poets from the Puritans to the Present* (1968; rev. ed., 1984). *Edna St. Vincent Millay: Selected Poems*, ed. Colin Falck (1991), provides a provocative introduction. David Felix, *Protest: Sacco-Vanzetti and the Intellectuals* (1965), chronicles the crime, trial, reviews, and executions and concludes that both men were probably guilty. Katherine Anne Porter, *The Never-Ending Wrong* (1977), describes the actions of the protestors, including Millay and Porter herself, during the Sacco-Vanzetti tragedy. An obituary is in the *New York Times*, 20 Oct. 1950.

ROBERT L. GALE

MILLEDGE, John (1757–9 Feb. 1818), governor of Georgia, was born in Savannah, the son of John Milledge, a planter who was one of the original English colonial settlers, and Ann Skidaway Smith. He was studying law under the tutelage of James Hume, the colony's attorney general, when the American Revolution erupted in Georgia. On the night of 11 May 1775 he joined a group of young rebels who broke into the powder magazine at Savannah and stole 600 pounds of gunpowder. In December he compounded this treasonous deed by placing the colony's royal governor under house arrest. In 1778 he served as an aide to Governor John Houstoun in an abortive campaign against the British in East Florida and as a militia captain in the defense of Savannah. Following that city's fall in late 1779, he fled to South Carolina to join the Continental army forming there and fell in with a group of patriots who almost hanged him in the mistaken notion that he was a British spy. The following year he took part in the unsuccessful French-Continental attempt to relieve Savannah, and in 1781, as a colonel in the Georgia militia, he helped to recapture Augusta. Afterward he fought with General Anthony Wayne until the war ended, whereupon he returned to Savannah, completed his legal studies under Hume, and opened a law practice. In 1786 he married Martha Galphin, with whom he had one child who died in infancy. After the baby's death, the couple officially adopted Martha's nephew and served as surrogate parents to a number of orphans.

Milledge's political career began in 1779, when he was elected to the patriot general assembly. In 1780, despite his legal inexperience, he became the state's attorney general. He served in the general assembly's lower house from 1789 to 1792 and in the state senate from 1794 to 1795. While in the general assembly, he spoke out forcefully against the Yazoo Land Acts, whereby the Georgia legislature sold most of present-day Alabama and Mississippi to four land companies for a pittance, because he believed that western lands should be sold in small plots to individual farmers rather than in huge tracts to speculators.

Milledge served three times in the U.S. House of Representatives (1792–1794, 1795–1798, and 1801–1802), where he generally supported the Democratic Republicans against the Federalists and worked to involve the federal government more fully in the defense of Georgia's frontiers against the Creeks, Cherokees, and Spanish. During his last term in the House, he served as one of Georgia's commissioners in the cession of its western land claims. Partly because of his skill as a negotiator, Georgia was able to obtain a large cash settlement as well as a federal promise to purchase all American Indian lands within the state's borders and turn them over to Georgia.

In 1802 Milledge was elected governor, a position he held for four years. During his term, the state negotiated land cessions with the Creeks and Cherokees, organized three new counties on these lands, built a road from Tennessee to Augusta, implemented a land lottery, reorganized the militia, and built a new capital on the cession, named Milledgeville in his honor. In 1806 he was elected to the U.S. Senate, where he was a loyal and enthusiastic supporter of the policies of President Thomas Jefferson. He served briefly as president pro tempore of the Senate in 1809 but resigned later that year because of his wife's illness. In 1812, the year after Martha died, he married Ann Lamar, with whom he had three children, two of whom died in childhood.

From 1809 until his death, Milledge lived a life of leisure as a gentleman farmer on his plantation in Augusta, having made his fortune not from practicing law or from politics but by his skill as a planter. In 1777 he bought fifty prime indigo-producing acres on Skidaway Island near Savannah; twelve years later, his holdings on the island comprised a large plantation. Shortly after the end of the American Revolution, he bought 200 acres that had been confiscated from Loyalists, and eventually he acquired 5,000 acres on the outskirts of Augusta. After suffering a severe financial setback in 1798 when his cotton crop failed, Milledge devoted much of his energy to finding a hardier cotton seed for his Augusta plantation as well as experimenting with sea-island cotton on his Skidaway holdings. He also experimented with sheep raising in an effort to improve the quality of domestic wool and discovered a way to extract oil from the benne seed for use as a suitable replacement for olive oil.

Milledge's wealth allowed him to play a prominent role in the creation of the University of Georgia. In 1785 he helped write a charter for the state's university system, which was to include elementary schools and academies. However, the resultant land grant was deemed unsuitable for the location of a university, and in 1801 an alternate site was selected. Unfortunately, the state had no money with which to acquire this 600-acre tract, so Milledge purchased it for $4,000 and donated it to the university. He continued to support the university with generous gifts of money and equipment until his death in Augusta.

Milledge was one of the most prominent figures in the early history of the state of Georgia. After playing an active role in the military campaign whereby it won its independence from Great Britain, he contributed to its well being by serving prominently in its early governmental affairs, by securing peacefully large tracts of frontier land within its borders, and by serving as the first patron of its state university.

• Milledge's papers are in the John Milledge Collections of the Duke University Library, the Georgia Department of Archives and History, the Georgia Historical Society, the Library of Congress, and the University of Georgia Library. A number of his letters written after 1785 appear in *Correspondence of John Milledge, Governor of Georgia, 1802–1806*, ed. Harriet Milledge Salley (1949). The best overall treatment of his life is Barbara Buckley Brown, "John Milledge: Patriot, Politician, Philanthropist, 1757–1818" (M.A. thesis, Georgia State Univ., 1980). An excellent brief biography appears in James F. Cook, *The Governors of Georgia, 1754–1995* (1995).

CHARLES W. CAREY, JR.

MILLEDOLER, Philip (22 Sept. 1775–22 Sept. 1852), Dutch Reformed minister and president of Rutgers College, was born in Rhinebeck, New York, the son of John Muhlithaler and Anna Mitchell. Milledoler experienced religious conversion at fourteen, received some classical training in Boston, and graduated from Columbia College in 1793, delivering a commencement oration on natural philosophy. However, the ministry was his calling.

In late 1793 or 1794 Milledoler joined New York City's Nassau Street German Reformed Church and began theological study under its pastor, John D. Gros, who also was the moral philosophy professor at Columbia. He proceeded quickly to licensure and took over the church following Gros's death in 1795, commencing a spiritual and pastoral odyssey. Milledoler kept his pulpit in the German Reformed church, but due to what church historian William Sprague called "peculiar circumstances," Milledoler became a Dutch Reformed minister in May 1800. Still uneasy, he assumed the pulpit of Philadelphia's Pine Street Presbyterian Church in October 1800. (The Dutch Reformed and Presbyterians differed in polity but were theologically quite similar.) Ill health sent him back to New York and the Rutgers Street Presbyterian Church in 1805, where he served as pastor until June 1813, when he took up the pastorate of the city's Collegiate Dutch Reformed Church, where he stayed until 1825.

Through all of this, Milledoler was a successful minister, gaining converts wherever he preached through an evangelical style featuring fervid, captivating prayer. He was also a religious activist, serving as moderator of the Presbyterian General Assembly in 1808, as teacher of didactic and polemic theology for the Presbyterians in 1811 (the year before their seminary opened in Princeton, New Jersey), as founder of the American Bible Society in 1816, as founder and president of the American Society for Evangelizing the Jews, and as corresponding secretary of the United Foreign Mission Society. He was doctrinally conservative and actively opposed the Hopkinsian idea that people were guilty only of the actual sins they committed and did not share in guilt for Adam's sin, a controversy among New York Presbyterians that may have induced his alliance with the Dutch Reformed.

Milledoler's conservative beliefs also affected his career in higher education. After a dozen successful years at the Collegiate Dutch Reformed Church, in 1825 Milledoler accepted two new positions that thrust him into a contest for control of the Dutch Reformed church in the United States. He answered the synod's call to become professor of didactic and polemic theology at the Theological Seminary of the Reformed Church in America in New Brunswick and simultaneously accepted the trustees' offer of the presidency of Queen's College, also in New Brunswick. Milledoler's selection supposedly marked a truce between the two groups, which had been contending for oversight of the denomination, and it allowed the college to revive undergraduate education, which it had lacked for some years. Yet the Covenant of 1825, the agreement enabling Milledoler to serve both institutions, placed effective control of the college with the synod and would eventually lead to Milledoler's undoing.

From his assumption of the presidency until about 1832, Queen's College prospered. In 1825 it gained the name Rutgers College in anticipation of the philanthropy of a Milledoler parishioner and friend, Henry Rutgers. Rutgers did give the college $5,000 in 1826, but more than that never materialized. It increased enrollment to approximately eighty-five, with about twenty-five graduates per year, enlarged the faculty, added chemistry as a branch of instruction, improved its scientific apparatus, and flirted unsuccessfully with establishing both law and medical schools. But by the early 1830s the college's enrollment and improvements had peaked, and criticism of Milledoler and the institution precluded any growth thereafter.

The problem lay in Milledoler's conservatism and his sensitivity to criticism. Rutgers after 1825 still offered an eighteenth-century curriculum that emphasized the classics, mathematics, and the several branches of philosophy. Milledoler taught the seniors Christian ethics, moral philosophy, and political economy. He allowed little adaptation to changing curricular concerns. His students condemned his pedagogy, which stressed rote memorization of eighteenth-century texts. In religion, too, Milledoler sought to preserve the old ways in the face of attacks by liberals who wanted to modernize church doctrine, cooperate more with other denominations, change the management of the church's mission societies, and alter the instruction in Sunday schools. This dispute hurt Rutgers because Milledoler thought that some of his colleagues were among his doctrinal enemies, and internal factionalism resulted.

An absence of progressive thought underlay the criticism of Milledoler, but the specific charge, stemming from the continuing antagonism between synod and trustees, obscured the problem. Under the Covenant of 1825, several professors served both the college and the seminary. Critics alleged that college duties took up too much time of these men, and therefore, the seminary—the darling of the synod—suffered. Rutgers' trustees had to spend so much time defending the college from this criticism and others (such as the high cost of boarding, too few students were sent from the college on to the seminary, and college finances were improperly managed) that they lost their ability to govern campus affairs and to raise funds. In 1839 a crisis developed when the theological professors withdrew from college instruction. Milledoler resigned over the incident but stayed on for a year because Rutgers could not afford to pay a successor. Milledoler's departure in 1840 was part of a negotiated settlement through which the trustees obtained some independence from the synod; but the issue of control was not resolved, and Rutgers would be plagued by factionalism during the ensuing years.

Returning to New York City, Milledoler held no more permanent posts but preached over the years as a guest in many pulpits throughout the city. His first marriage, to Susan Benson of Harlem, lasted from 1796 until her death in 1815; they had six children. In 1817 Milledoler married Margaret Steele of Philadelphia, with whom he had four more children. Milledoler died at the Staten Island home of one of his daughters; his wife died the following day.

Milledoler's attributes, including an extraordinary evangelical fervor, a devotion to the principles of the late eighteenth-century Dutch Reformed church, and a winning personality, made him more effective as a minister than as a college professor and president. His capacity to inspire revival within his congregations and religious reform activities among his peers contrasted sharply with his inability to mediate between church factions and between himself and discontented students and colleagues while at Rutgers. Even though he was largely responsible for Rutgers' resurrection, he was miscast as a college president, and both he and the college suffered for it.

• The Philip Milledoler Papers are in the New-York Historical Society. A biographical sketch of Milledoler is in William B. Sprague, ed., *Annals of the American Pulpit*, vol. 9 (1869; repr. 1969), which also lists his major published sermons and addresses. The standard histories of Rutgers, W. H. S. Demarest, *A History of Rutgers College, 1766–1924* (1924), and Richard P. McCormick, *Rutgers University: A Bicentennial History* (1966), discuss Milledoler's presidency. George M. Marsden, *The Evangelical Mind and the New School Presbyterian Experience* (1970), surveys the Hopkinsian controversy in the Presbyterian church. An obituary is in the *New York Times*, 23 Sept. 1852.

DAVID W. ROBSON

MILLER, Alden Holmes (4 Feb. 1906–9 Oct. 1965), biologist, was born in Los Angeles, California, the son of Loye Holmes Miller, an ornithologist, and Anne Holmes. Through his father he was introduced early to the outdoors and natural history, as well as to music by both parents. Miller attended the University of California at Los Angeles, where his father was professor of biology, and received his A.B. in 1927. The next year he married Virginia Dove, a fellow student at UCLA; they had three children. After considering a career in music, he instead chose biology and entered the University of California at Berkeley for graduate studies. There, for many years, his mentor was Joseph Grinnell, a widely recognized leader in the distribution and ecology of birds and mammals. Miller received his M.A. (1928) and Ph.D. (1930) and was promptly appointed an associate in the department of zoology at the University of California. He advanced to professor in 1945.

Miller was associated with the Museum of Vertebrate Zoology at the university from his student days. When its first director, Grinnell, died, Miller became director of that facility in 1940. He served in this post until his death. He enlarged the museum's programs into herpetology, with the appointment of Robert C. Stebbins, and into the biology of game animals, with the appointment of conservationist A. Starker Leopold.

Miller's Ph.D. dissertation on American shrikes was considered by his biographer Ernst Mayr as outstanding in its precision. Mayr notes that it includes "detailed statistics of differences in measurable characters of sexes, age groups, and geographic races. . . . and had a lasting impact on American ornithology." Miller followed Grinnell's approach of field studies to determine the precise distribution of each species, its geographic limits, and its variation as affected by the geography. He made many trips within California, and he traveled far afield, to Mexico, Panama, Colombia, El Salvador, Peru, the Galapagos Islands, Jamaica, Australia, and New Guinea. For the museum he collected more than 12,000 specimens.

In his 259 publications, Miller's primary theme was evolution. He dealt with the classification of birds, their distribution, the physiology of their reproduction, and their general ecology. He also carried out significant studies of fossil birds, which included analyses of past environments.

At a time that students of evolution were endeavoring to define its mechanisms, Miller proposed that species and subspecies should be considered variable populations only. In "Speciation in the Avian Genus Junco," *University of California Publications in Zoology* (44 [1941]: 173–434), he showed that geographic races of this bird are incipient species, in contrast to the viewpoint of Richard B. Goldschmidt that geography is not a factor in the formation of species. Miller found hybridization among members of subspecies that had been separated by geography and later came into contact again. He followed this by rearing hybrid juncoes in his laboratory.

As had been the custom of the museum under Grinnell's direction, Miller participated in regional studies, and he coauthored significant monographs, including *The Vertebrate Animals of the Providence Mountains Area of California* (1948, with D. H. Johnson and M. D. Bryant) and *The Lives of Desert Animals in Joshua Tree National Monument* (1964, with R. C. Stebbins).

As a member of the committee that prepared the fifth edition of the *Check-List of North American Birds*, Miller was responsible for the information on birds of western North America. He also contributed to the *Distributional Check-List of the Birds of Mexico* and *Check-List of Birds of the World*.

Miller became interested in the factors that determine the breeding season in birds and concluded that day length is not a significant contributor but that the entire hormonal system, governed by the pituitary gland, regulates the bird's breeding cycle. He found that the response to stimuli differs from one species to another. His first studies were of birds in temperate localities, and then he turned to investigating birds near the equator, where variation of day length is at a minimum. In 1949–1950 he carried out a major study of the annual cycles of the Andean sparrow in Colombia, accompanied by his wife, who was often his field assistant. In this species he found that each individual bird normally has two complete breeding cycles each year, of about six months in duration.

Miller was noted as a conscientious committee member, for the university and for scientific organizations. He was president of the American Ornithologists' Union (1953–1955), and president of the International Commission on Zoological Nomenclature (1964–1965). He became editor of the journal of the Cooper Ornithological Society, *Condor*, in 1939, following Grinnell, and continued until his death. In that journal he sponsored a policy of including manuscripts on ecology, physiology, and behavior, beyond its prior emphasis on systematics. Miller received the Brewster Medal of the American Ornithological Union in 1943, and he was elected to the National Academy of Sciences in 1957.

In all, thirty-one students earned their Ph.D. under Miller's direction. It was his custom to be available when a student sought him, but not to supervise the work closely. The students admired his capabilities and endurance in the field, his complete integrity, and his intense work habits. Miller died after suffering a coronary occlusion at Clear Lake, California.

• Miller's papers are at the Museum of Vertebrate Zoology and Bancroft Library, University of California, Berkeley. His studies of the Andean sparrow were summarized in "Reproductive Periods in Birds near the Equator," *Caldasia* 8 (1958): 295–300, and were published posthumously with his wife, Virginia D. Miller, as coauthor in "The Behavioral Ecology and Breeding Biology of the Andean Sparrow, *Zonotrichia Capensis,*" *Caldasia* 10 (1966): 83–154. Biographies are by John Davis, *Auk* 84 (1967): 192–202, and by Ernst Mayr, National Academy of Sciences, *Biographical Memoirs* 43 (1973): 176–214, which also includes a bibliography.

ELIZABETH NOBLE SHOR

MILLER, Alfred Jacob (2 Jan. 1810–26 June 1874), painter, was born in Baltimore, Maryland, the son of George Washington Miller, an innkeeper, sugar refiner, and grocer, and Harriet Jacob. Miller was educated by tutors and attended a private academy in Baltimore. Details of his early artistic training are sketchy. He appears to have been self-taught but may have studied briefly with Thomas Sully. He had access to Rembrandt Peale's Baltimore Museum and Gallery and may also have seen works by John Vanderlyn when they toured the area. In 1833 Miller traveled to Europe for formal training, possibly with the financial support of Baltimore collector Robert Gilmor, Jr. He began his studies in Paris, where he was admitted as an auditor into life class at the École des Beaux-Arts. In the Louvre, Miller copied paintings by Rembrandt, Veronese, and Delacroix. He then went on to Rome, where he and other young artists frequented the Café Greco. There he met influential sculptors Albert Bertel Thorwaldsen and Horatio Greenough and the head of the French Academy, Horace Vernet. He studied the Titians, Coreggios, and Caravaggios at the Borghese Gallery and visited the Vatican, where he copied Raphael's *Stanze*. In December 1834 he returned to Baltimore, where he briefly established a painting studio, offering portraits, original works, and European copies. In December 1836 Miller moved to New Orleans, possibly in search of a steadier clientele for his work.

Sometime in 1836–1837 Miller received his most important commission. Captain William Drummond Stewart, a Scottish nobleman who would inherit the title of seventh baronet of Murthly Castle in 1838, had been making annual hunting excursions to the Rocky Mountains since 1832, and he invited Miller to accompany him on his next journey to record scenes of his adventures. Miller departed from St. Louis with Stewart's party in May 1837. Their destination was the fur trade rendezvous, a meeting held each year between eastern traders, Indians, and Rocky Mountain trappers. The 1837 rendezvous took place at Horse Creek, a tributary of the Green River, near the present-day border of Colorado and Wyoming. The party went from St. Louis to Westport and then traveled northwest along the Kansas River to the Platte, passing such landmarks as Scott's Bluff and Chimney Rock on their way to Fort Laramie. From Fort Laramie they continued west through the South Pass and north to the rendezvous. After the rendezvous, Stewart and his band headed into the Wind River Mountains to the source of the Green River. There they spent their time hunting before returning to St. Louis in the fall of 1837.

Miller returned to New Orleans shortly thereafter and began work on eighty-seven wash and watercolor drawings and several oil paintings for Stewart that were based on sketches he made in the field. In 1838 Miller moved back to Baltimore, and by July he was exhibiting some of the oil paintings in Baltimore to favorable reviews. By May 1839 Miller had finished eighteen oils, which were exhibited at the Apollo Gallery in New York City before being shipped to Scotland. The show was well attended and garnered good reviews from critics. In 1840 Miller traveled to Murthly Castle, where he continued to work on other monumental oils that Stewart commissioned. In 1841 he completed one of his most famous western scenes, *The Trapper's Bride*, showing a marriage between a white trapper and an Indian woman, and traveled to London to work on a religious commission for a chapel at Murthly.

In the spring of 1842 Miller returned to Baltimore and purchased a 165-acre farm outside the city. His account book indicates that he was well occupied for the next three decades painting portraits and completing a variety of commissions for copies of his western scenes. This activity culminated in a series of 200 watercolor sketches with accompanying notes for Baltimore patron William Walters in 1858–1860 and eighty western watercolors for Alexander Brown in 1872. He also taught painting, and two of his pupils, Frank Blackwell Mayer and A. J. H. Way, became prominent artists in the Baltimore area. Miller was able to support himself through sales of his work and through substantial investments in business and real estate. He never married. He died in Baltimore, leaving a comfortable estate to his sister, Harriet Miller.

Miller is best known for his western subjects, which include sketches produced in the field along with finished oil-on-canvas and watercolor paintings made for Stewart. Although Miller's early works are undated, it is likely he completed as many as 150 sketches in the field. Most of these are executed in watercolor or wash over pencil with gouache on a variety of papers and are small in size. In the years following his return from Scotland, Miller continued to produce versions of these initial sketches in oil and watercolor. More than half of Miller's paintings show Shoshone, Sioux, and Nez Percé engaged in a variety of activities: caring for children, preparing meat, sewing, chasing horses, or hunting. Miller also painted scenes of the caravan en route and of trappers at the rendezvous, along with mountain landscapes. Many of the earlier works show Stewart hunting or visiting Shoshone camps. In later watercolor copies, Miller replaced Stewart's figure with others.

Miller was the first Anglo-American painter to travel as far west as the Rocky Mountains, and the only one to paint a comprehensive view of the Rocky Mountain fur trade. In the past Miller's sketches have been used as sources of ethnographic or historic information about the fur trade and its participants (see, for example, John C. Ewers, "Deadlier Than the Male," *American Heritage* 16, no. 4 [1965]), yet arguably they contribute most as indexes of nineteenth-century attitudes toward the peoples they portray. Miller is also important as an example of an American Romantic painter and as a member of a younger generation who studied in France and Italy rather than England. In addition to his western work Miller painted illustrations of scenes from Sir Walter Scott and Washington Irving and numerous portraits of leading Baltimore citizens.

• Major collections of Miller's watercolors include the Gilcrease Institute of American History and Art, Tulsa, Okla.; the Joslyn Museum of American Art, Omaha, Neb.; the Buffalo Bill Historical Center, Cody, Wyo.; the Amon Carter Museum, Fort Worth, Tex.; the Public Archives, Ottawa, Ontario, Canada; and the Walters Art Gallery, Baltimore. Miller's hand-written memoirs are in a private collection; an account book of his paintings is housed at the Walters Art Gallery. Excerpts from the account book are reprinted in Marvin Ross, "A List of Portraits and Paintings from Alfred Jacob Miller's *Account Book*," *Maryland Historical Magazine* 48, no. 1 (Mar. 1953), and Marvin Ross, *The West of Alfred Jacob Miller* (1968), which also includes a discussion of the watercolor sketches made for Stewart, and reproduces the watercolor commission completed for William T. Walters alongside Miller's accompanying notes. Miller's handwritten notes for the Walters commission are at the Walters Art Gallery, and rough drafts of those notes are housed at the Gilcrease and available in the Archives of American Art. Transcripts of his correspondence are available in the Mae Reed Porter Papers, the American Heritage Center, Laramie, Wyo, and the Maryland Historical Society; selected reprints can be found in Robert Combs Warner, *The Fort Laramie of Alfred Jacob Miller* (1979). The Public Archives of Canada's *Braves and Buffalo: Plains Indian Life in 1837* (1973) illustrates the watercolor commission completed for Brown. Ron

Tyler, ed., *Alfred Jacob Miller: Artist on the Oregon Trail* (1982), provides an overview of Miller's career and a catalog of his oeuvre. Bernard DeVoto's *Across the Wide Missouri* (1947) includes chapters on Miller and Stewart's travels, and Mae Reed Porter and Odessa Davenport's *Scotsman in Buckskin* (1963) provides a biography of Stewart and a history of the commission.

LISA STRONG

MILLER, Alice Duer (28 July 1874–22 Aug. 1942), poet, novelist, and dramatist, was born Alice Maude Duer at Staten Island, New York, the daughter of James Gore King Duer, a banker, and Elizabeth Wilson Meads. Miller grew up on the family estate at Weehawken, New Jersey. When her father's private bank failed during the Baring Bank crisis, Miller, soon after her debut, decided to go to college to study mathematics and astronomy, supporting herself by tutoring and by writing stories and poems for *Harper's* and *Scribner's*. She completed her B.A. at Barnard College, the women's college of Columbia University, in 1899. Always dedicated to Barnard College, she wrote the history of its first fifty years in 1939. In October 1899 she married Henry Wise Miller; they had one child.

The Millers spent the first years of their marriage in Costa Rica. While her husband looked for possible sites for rubber plantations, Miller supplemented their meager income by writing for magazines. Returning to New York in 1903, she taught composition at a girls' school and tutored mathematics at Barnard College as well as writing. By 1907 her husband's financial situation had improved and she was able to write full time.

Miller's short stories and serialized novels were published in *Woman's Home Companion*, *Collier's*, *Saturday Evening Post*, *New Republic*, and other magazines and then published as books. *The Modern Obstacle* and *Calderon's Prisoner* appeared in 1903, *Less Than Kin* in 1909, with a string of novels to follow. Her short stories and novellas were published in several collections, including *Are Parents People?* (1924), *Taxi* (1931), and *Summer Holiday* (1941).

For many years a neighbor of Alexander Woollcott, Miller was a charter member of his literary colony on Neshobe Island, Lake Bomoseen, Vermont. She used her literary background to good advantage, sometimes taking old stories and making them new, as in "Instruments of Darkness," a tale of a modern Macbeth, which appeared first in *Saturday Evening Post* (10–24 Nov. 1923) and then as the title story of a collection published in 1926. Setting her story in modern times, the castle on Long Island Sound near New York, and using the stock market as her battlefield, Miller followed Shakespeare's plot quite closely, evoking the mood and emotions of the original story through her vivid descriptions, the vocabulary employed, and her choice of names. Alice Lawton of the *Boston Transcript* described the story as "an unusually clever and original piece of fiction. Its characterization is vivid and convincing."

Because of her deft creation of characters and her simple, dramatic plots, Miller's stories and novels were soon being transferred to the stage and movie screen. She wrote or helped to write many of the stage plays and screenplays. *Come Out of the Kitchen* (1916) brought Miller her first real success. This novel became a Broadway play; two films, *Come Out of the Kitchen* (1919) and *Honey* (1930); and a musical comedy, *The Magnolia Lady* (1924). *The Charm School* (1919) underwent even more adaptations, a play with the same title; a musical, *June Days* (1925); and five films: *The Charm School* (1921), *Someone to Love* (1926), *Sweetie* (1929), *Collegiate* (1936), and *College Swing* (1938). *Gowns for Roberta* (1933) became the Jerome Kern musical *Roberta* (1933) and film versions *Roberta* (1935) and *Lovely to Look At* (1952).

Miller traveled extensively, lived in Scotland, London, and the French Riviera, and spent time in Hollywood where she worked on scripts for movies. She even tried acting, playing the spoiled daughter of a millionaire in the Ben Hecht-Charles MacArthur film *Soak the Rich* (1936).

Active in the woman suffrage movement, Miller wrote for *The Masses*, a radical political and literary magazine edited by Max Eastman, who also founded the first men's league for woman suffrage. A member of Heterodoxy, a club for unorthodox women of widely varied views, women devoted to the idea of equality, Miller wrote and lectured in support of woman suffrage. Through her column "Are Women People?" in the *New York Times* (1914–1917) she reached a wide audience. A collection of those columns was published as *Are Women People? A Book of Rhymes for Suffrage Times* (1915). In the introduction to the book, Miller wrote:

> Father, what is a legislature?
> A representative body elected by the people of the state.
> Are women people?
> No, my son, criminals, lunatics and women are not people.
> Do legislators legislate for nothing?
> Oh, no, they are paid a salary.
> By whom?
> By the people.
> Are women people?
> Of course, my son, just as much as men are.

The reviewer for *Bookman* (Oct. 1915) wrote: "Mrs. Miller has a specially keen faculty, the endowment of the logical mind, for seeing the weak point in an argument, singling it out and developing it to its ridiculous conclusion." Zita Dresner called Miller "one of the wittiest exponents of women's equality." More of her columns were collected in *Women Are People!* (1917).

Although the major part of Miller's work was in prose, her first published writing was poetry in a book called simply *Poems* (1896) that she wrote with her sister Caroline Duer. *Forsaking All Others* (1933) also was written in verse. But it was her poem *The White Cliffs* (1940) that brought Miller the most fame. Spanning the time between the two world wars, the narrative tells a story of love and sacrifice, patriotism and praise for England. One reviewer, commending the book-length poem, predicted that it would be popular, and it was; within four years 700,000 copies had been sold. An abridged version appeared in *Life* (31 Mar. 1941), accompanied by the announcement that *The White Cliffs* had been number two on the bestseller list for nonfiction for two months and that it was a "rare event in publishing" for a book of poetry to be a bestseller. Miller read the poem in many places in the United States and Canada. Stage actress Lynne Fontanne read it on the radio and recorded it, and it was made into the 1944 film *The White Cliffs of Dover*. Miller died in New York City shortly after finishing *Cinderella*, her retelling of the story in verse; it was published in 1943.

• A collection of Miller's letters written to Alexander Woollcott in the 1930s is in the Houghton Library, Harvard University. Henry Wise Miller, *All Our Lives: Alice Duer Miller* (1945), gives biographical information and titles and dates of much of her work. For an early evaluation of her work see G. M. Overton, *Women Who Make Our Novels* (1918). See also Francis Hackett, *On Judging Books* (1947; repr. 1971), and Max Eastman, *Enjoyment of Living* (1948). For a discussion of Miller's prosuffrage work, see Zita Dresner, "Heterodite Humor: Alice Duer Miller and Florence Guy Seabury," *Journal of American Culture* 10 (Fall 1987): 33–38. Obituaries are in *Newsweek* and *Time*, both 31 Aug. 1942, and *Publishers Weekly*, 5 Sept. 1942.

BLANCHE COX CLEGG

MILLER, Bertha Everett Mahony (13 Mar. 1882–14 May 1969), editor and magazine founder, was born in Rockport on Cape Ann, Massachusetts, the daughter of Daniel Mahony, a passenger agent and telegraph operator for the Boston and Maine Railroad Station, and Mary Lane Everett, a music teacher. Despite his Catholic heritage, Daniel Mahony was not religious and sent Bertha to the Congregationalist church because he felt it had the best influence. Bertha's mother, an accomplished pianist, instructed fifty music students at the time of her marriage in 1881 and continued teaching while raising her children. During Bertha's childhood music could be heard night and day, accompanied by her mother's folk and fairy tales and her father's suspenseful stories of youthful adventures. Throughout her life these family gatherings and an enjoyment of the outdoors would be inspirational to her desire to create and promote children's literature.

When Bertha turned eleven her mother died. Wishing to emulate her mother's care of the family, she took over the household. The emotional strain became too much for her, and in her junior year she dropped out of school for a brief period. She reentered school in time to graduate with her class and managed to receive excellent grades. Following her graduation in 1901, she entered the training class of the public schools of the city of Gloucester to become a pupil-teacher, although she never taught. Instead she became a student at Simmons College for Women in Boston, where she had wanted to enroll in the School of Library Science but did not have the funds. Ultimately, she had to complete her education at the college's School of Secretarial Studies as a special one-year graduate student.

After her graduation Mahony accepted a position as an assistant in the New Library bookshop. Although sometimes left in charge of the shop, her employer was prejudiced against the young woman's Irish-Catholic ancestry. Treated as an inferior, Mahony felt the tension and gratefully accepted a position as assistant secretary of the Women's Educational and Industrial Union (WEIU), a nonprofit, social service agency concerned with the working woman. Her working experience at the WEIU gave her the financial management and organizational skills she needed, introducing her to economics, sociology, and education. As her creativity blossomed, her assignments increased to handling publicity and advertising and preparing informational leaflets.

Mahony's childhood interest in storytelling led her to start the Children's Players. In her search for material for theatrical productions, she discovered a whole range of new children's literature. The executive committee that helped her with the reading of children's books in search of material for the plays also found there were marvelous books available but nothing worth dramatizing. Despite some initial successes, the theater project was short-lived because committee members felt that books were of greater benefit and that occasional attendance at the theater provided for children's dramatic education. Although the Children's Players ended, Mahony's endeavor gave birth to her enthusiasm for children's literature. She then realized her professional vision by becoming the proprietor of a bookshop. In 1915, aided by other women, she and the WEIU created a special department to establish the Bookshop for Boys and Girls.

Mahony quickly sought advice from women librarians. Setting up strict guidelines for book titles, she determined to provide the bookshop with children's literature that had both excellent writing and the best illustrations. In order to publicize her new business, she put together a commercial list of children's books, the first ever to be published. Her 110-page publication, *Books for Boys and Girls—A Suggestive Purchase List*, contained a listing of 1,200 children's books. Criticized by the WEIU for the expense it incurred, the list was nevertheless an innovative step, and a few years later she began the book caravan, a traveling truck that had an interior of shelves holding 1,200 books.

The bookshop expanded in 1919 when Elinor Whitney joined the venture. Their friendship and partnership continued for fifty years, and they coauthored a number of books. In 1924 they also collaborated on another enterprise to publicize the bookshop, founding the *Horn Book Magazine*, the first magazine designed exclusively to "blow the horn" in an effort to introduce children's literature. In addition to writing columns and editorials, Mahony served as editor and was responsible for bringing in numerous literary and artistic contributions.

Mahony married William Davis Miller in 1932. Miller was the president of W. F. Whitney Company, a firm that reproduced colonial furniture. Four years later Elinor Whitney married William Field, and the partnership of two women extended to two entire families as the Millers and Fields began a publishing company. Horn Book, Incorporated ended Bertha Miller's connections to the WEIU, but the new company was instrumental in the discovery and promotion of children's writers and artists. In 1955 Miller received the Constance Lindsay Skinner Award from the Women's National Book Association. She was also honored by the American Library Association in 1959, and in 1967 she received the Regina Medal from the Catholic Library Association. Miller died in Ashburnham, Massachusetts, but her "sense of wonder" and her "lifelong exploration in words" left their imprint on the children whose eyes she helped open to the marvels of literature.

• Bertha Mahony Miller's published and unpublished writings, as well as a bound set of *Horn Book Magazine*, are located in the offices of the *Horn Book Magazine*, Boston, Mass. With Elinor Whitney Field, Miller coauthored *Realms of Gold in Children's Books* (1929), *Contemporary Illustrators of Children's Books* (1930), *Five Years of Children's Books* (1936), *Newbery Medal Books: 1922–1955* (1955), and *Caldecott Medal Books: 1938–1957* (1957). Miller also coedited and helped to compile *Illustrators of Children's Books, 1744–1945* (1947), *Illustrators of Children's Books, 1946–1956* (1958), and *Writing and Criticism: A Book for Margery Bianco* (1951). For biographical information see Eulalie Steinmetz Ross, *The Spirited Life: Bertha Mahony Miller and Children's Books* (1973), which also includes a bibliography of Miller's writings. *Horn Book Magazine* (Oct. 1969) was dedicated to Miller. For a critical assessment of the magazine, see Joan B. P. Olson, "An Interpretive History of the *Horn Book Magazine*, 1924–1973" (Ph.D. diss., Stanford Univ., 1976). For an accurate representation of the bookshop see Annie Carroll Moore, "The Bookshop for Boys and Girls," *ALA Bulletin*, July 1917, and Alice Jordan, "The Bookshop That Is Bertha Mahony Miller," *Atlantic Bookshelf*, June 1939. There is a short tribute in *The Times* (London), 15 Nov. 1969. Obituaries are in the *Boston Globe*, 15 May 1969, and *Simmons Review*, Summer–Fall 1969.

MARILYN ELIZABETH PERRY

MILLER, Charles Henry (20 Mar. 1842–21 Jan. 1922), doctor of medicine, artist, and writer, was born in New York City, the son of Jacob H. Miller, an architect, and Jayne M. Taylor. He attended Mount Washington Collegiate Institute to prepare for a career in law or medicine, although early on he had displayed an interest in painting and drawing. In 1860 Miller exhibited his first painting at the National Academy of Design, and the following year he sent two more paintings for exhibition. His father, unhappy with his son's interest in art, urged him to enroll in the New York Homeopathic Medical Institute. Miller acquiesced to his father's wishes and completed his medical studies in 1863, receiving his degree from William Cullen Bryant, then president of the medical college. Miller's only job in the medical field was a position as a surgeon aboard the emigrant ship *Harvest Queen*. He sailed for Europe in 1864, and when he was given leave from his medical responsibilities, he spent time visiting museums in London, Antwerp, and Paris. Seeing the art of Europe rekindled Miller's interest in pursuing a career as an artist, and upon his return to the United States he decided to give up medicine to paint full time.

Miller resumed exhibiting paintings at the National Academy of Design in 1865. In 1867 he returned to Europe to complete his artistic training, settling in Munich. He enrolled in the Bavarian Royal Academy, choosing to study with the landscape artist Adolf Heinrich Lier. Lier's painting style was influenced by the Barbizon School and John Constable; thus Miller's paintings are closer stylistically to the French and English landscape tradition than to the Munich school.

After three years in Munich, Miller returned to New York City, established a studio, and once again began exhibiting at the National Academy. He was elected an associate member of the National Academy of Design in 1873, and in 1875 he was honored as one of the youngest artists to become an academician after exhibiting two of his most well-known paintings, *Washing Sheep on Long Island* (1874), which was acquired by the National Academy of Design for its own collection, and *High Bridge from Harlem Lane, 1873* (private collection). The latter, awarded the place of honor in the National Academy's 1875 exhibition, also won a gold medal at the Philadelphia Centennial in 1876.

In 1877 Miller was appointed a member of the hanging committee for the National Academy's annual exhibition and broke with academy tradition by giving the best exhibition space to young, unestablished artists. This action caused quite a controversy among the academicians, who retaliated by instituting a rule that guaranteed older, established artists the best hanging spaces. Because of this new rule the younger artists formed their own organization, the Society of American Artists. Miller is first listed as a member of the Society of American Artists in 1879; he exhibited with them from 1878 to 1883 but resigned in 1884, at which time he re-established his association with the National Academy of Design.

Among the Society of American Artists, he met William Merritt Chase, Walter Shirlaw, Augustus Saint-Gaudens, Frederick Stuart Church, and Robert Swain Gifford. With this new circle of friends, Miller formed the Art Club in 1879 and served as the club president. The Art Club existed for five years, during which time Miller played a key role in the organization of exhibitions. He also raised funds to send a selection of works to the International Exhibition held in Munich in 1883, the first time a group of American artists submitted work to an international exhibition held abroad.

Throughout his career Miller wrote in support of American artists. In 1885 he published *The Philosophy of Art in America: A Dissertation upon Vital Topics of the Day; Perhaps of All Time* under the pseudonym Carl De Muldor, which was the family name of his father's Dutch ancestors. The progressive ideas Miller promoted in this work included many improvements to documentation and indexing of late nineteenth-century art. He hoped the U.S. government would play a strong role in encouraging American talent by forming a U.S. Department of Fine and Industrial Arts and a National Gallery of Painting, Statuary, and Art Treasures; and he called for the preservation of works by American artists including Washington Allston, Gilbert Stuart, Charles Willson Peale, Benjamin West, John Vanderlyn, Chester Harding, Thomas Cole, Samuel F. B. Morse, and William Sidney Mount.

Miller is best known today for his views of Long Island, with its mill-ponds, oak trees, and seashores. He received his greatest acclaim as an artist from the late 1870s through the mid-1880s, winning gold medals for paintings of Long Island scenery at the 1878 Massachusetts Charitable Mechanic Association Exhibition held in Boston and at the World's Industrial and Cotton Centennial Exposition held in New Orleans in 1884–1885.

For the rest of his life Miller continued to extol American art and Long Island's historic sights in local newspapers and periodicals. He spent most of his time on his estate in Queens, "Queenlawn," although he did maintain a studio in New York City. He married Elizabeth Dorothea Herdfelder Mosback in 1900. In 1910 he formed an organization called the Queens Borough Allied Arts and Crafts Society, which was concerned with promoting the arts of Long Island. Serving as the society's president until his death, Miller devoted himself to appeals for support of the group's plan to establish a gallery in Queens, a goal realized only many years later with the creation of the Queens Museum in Flushing.

Highly acclaimed in his own day, Miller's paintings have since been relegated to near obscurity. He achieved success early in his career, but later in his life, as he devoted more and more time to the Queens Borough Allied Arts and Crafts Society, the quality and output of his own art declined. Most of the works produced late in his life tended toward mystically allegorical landscapes, although his forte remained the peaceful, idyllic landscapes of Long Island. He died in Queens, New York.

• Miller's own published articles and books (excluding his published poetry) include "Awakening Appreciation of American Art," *Long Island Review* (May 1920): 6–8; "The Noblest Motive Is the Public Good," *Long Island Life* (Jan. 1919): 4; "Old Long Island Mills: 1st Article," *Long Island Life* (Nov. 1917): 5; "A Home for American Art," *New York Times*, 30 Dec. 1917; and Carl De Muldor [Charles Henry Miller], *The Philosophy of Art in America: A Dissertation upon Vital Topics of the Day; Perhaps of All Time* (1885). Twentieth-century sources on Charles Henry Miller include Ronald G. Pisano, *Charles Henry Miller: The Artistic Discoverer of the Little Continent of Long Island* (1979); Rhode Island School of Design, *American Paintings from the Museum's Collection, c. 1800–1930* (1977), p. 62; Lois Marie Fink and Joshua C. Taylor, *Academy: The Academic Tradition in American Art* (1975), pp.77–78; G. W. Sheldon, *American Painters* (1879; repr. 1972), pp. 44–45; Nassau County Historical Museum, *Charles H. Miller, an Artist's Record of Long Island Circa 1880* (Winter 1968); Memorial Hall, Hofstra College, *Charles H. Miller: Exhibition of Paintings* (5–16 Mar. 1951); and the artist's former home, *A Collection of Paintings by Charles Henry Miller* (25–30 Apr. 1950). Nineteenth-century references on Miller include Lillie H. French, "The Artistic Discoverer of Long Island," *Monthly Illustrator* 12 (1894): 54–56; S. G. W. Benjamin, "An American Landscape Painter," *Magazine of Art* 7 (1884): 94–98; and "American Painters—Charles Henry Miller," *Art Journal* (1876): 54–55. An obituary is in the *New York Times*, 22 Jan. 1922.

ANNE R. NORCROSS

MILLER, Cincinnatus Hiner. *See* Miller, Joaquin.

MILLER, David Hunter (2 Jan. 1875–21 July 1961), lawyer, State Department official, and historian, was born in New York City, the son of Walter Thomas Miller, a stockbroker and a member of the New York cotton exchange, and Christiana Wylie. He was educated in private and public schools in New York. Soon after the United States declared war with Spain, Miller enlisted in the Ninth New York Volunteers, serving in the army from May to November 1898. After his military service he began working in his father's brokerage. In 1900 he married Sarah Whipple Simmons; they had no children. In 1904 he decided to prepare himself for a legal career and entered the New York Law School, where he earned an LL.B. in 1910 and an LL.M. the next year. Admitted to the New York bar, he began the general practice of law.

In 1915 a fortuitous decision altered the direction of Miller's career and his life. He and a friend, Gordon Auchincloss, formed the legal partnership of Miller & Auchincloss, which soon prospered. Auchincloss was a son-in-law of Colonel Edward M. House, President Woodrow Wilson's confidant and adviser on foreign affairs. Through Auchincloss, Miller's intellectual qualities and legal skills were brought to the attention of Colonel House and the White House. Two months after the United States entered World War I in April 1917, Miller was appointed to the legal staff of the Department of State even though, as he later testified before the Senate Foreign Relations Committee, he had no prior experience in international law. But Miller learned quickly under the careful tutelage of James Brown Scott. That fall, when President Wilson delegated to Colonel House the task of organizing the American preparations for the eventual peace settlement, known by the code name "the Inquiry," House selected Miller to serve as the Inquiry's treasurer and chief of the division of international law. As the war wound down and defeated Germany communicated its intention to surrender, Wilson deputized House to represent him at the Supreme War Council's sessions in Paris, where the armistice terms would be decided. Miller accompanied House as legal aide. Once the peace conference assembled in Paris, Miller was appointed chief of the legal section of the American Commission to Negotiate Peace, headed by President Wilson. Miller's work brought him into daily contact with efforts to create the League of Nations Covenant.

He attended all sessions of the international commission that framed the covenant and participated in drafting the final version. His efforts in Paris extended beyond the work on the league covenant, for Miller also advised on terms for the settlement of the Adriatic question, provisions governing the treatment of minorities in the new Polish state, and the Sino-Japanese controversy in the Far East. Soon after Miller returned to the United States, he was one of the few members of the American delegation called in 1919 to testify before the Senate Foreign Relations Committee concerning his involvement in the peace negotiations, especially the work on the league covenant.

Although America's participation in the peace negotiations ended in December 1919, Miller's personal commitment to the cause of international peace and to the work of the peace conference occupied him for another decade. He served as legal adviser to the German government in litigation regarding the status and boundaries of Silesia. In 1924–1925 he was a leading advocate of the Geneva Protocol, which attempted to define aggressor states, and he was active in organizing American plans for disarmament. He worked as publicist within the Democratic party, believing that it offered the best political means in the United States for realizing the Wilsonian dream of permanent peace. In this latter connection, Miller led the unsuccessful campaign to nominate William G. McAdoo for president at the Democratic National Convention in 1924.

At least among historians, Miller is remembered for his diary of the peace conference that he privately published in 1924 along with a massive collection of documents as *My Diary at the Conference of Paris, With Documents*, twenty-one volumes in all. Miller donated copies of the limited edition to selected research libraries in the United States and Europe. His *Drafting of the Covenant* (2 vols., 1928) has remained the standard interpretation of how the league covenant evolved at the peace conference and also includes a volume of documents. Until the State Department published the thirteen-volume supplement on the peace conference in the 1940s, Miller's editions provided the chief sources for research concerning the conference. Miller's documentary collections have continued to be consulted by scholars interested in the establishment of peace after the Great War.

In 1929 Miller returned to the State Department. He embarked on the assignment of editing all the international treaties and agreements of the United States, but his collection was like no other edition of American treaties. Miller's series includes extensive annotations, a model of scholarship that became the principal reference tool used by students and diplomats seeking to understand America's international relations. Unfortunately, the series was halted for lack of funding just as Miller reached the year 1863.

The 1920s and the 1930s were periods of great creativity for Miller. Even after he and his wife moved their residence temporarily to Victoria, British Columbia, during the 1940s, he continued to write articles and books, mainly legal treatises and diplomatic history. Beginning in 1932, Miller dropped his first given name from his later publications and official records, preferring to be known as Hunter Miller. He died in Washington, D.C.

• Miller's papers are at the Manuscripts Division, Library of Congress. His State Department collection is Hunter Miller, ed., *Treaties and Other International Acts of the United States of America, 1776–1863* (8 vols., 1931–1948). See also L. E. Gelfand, *The Inquiry: American Preparations for Peace, 1917–1919* (1963); and U.S. Congress, Senate, *Hearings before the Committee on Foreign Relations, United States Senate, on the Treaty of Peace with Germany Signed at Versailles on June 28, 1919, and Submitted to the Senate on July 19, 1919, by the President of the United States*, 66th Cong., 1st sess., 1919, S. Doc. 106. An obituary is in the *New York Times*, 24 July 1961.

LAWRENCE E. GELFAND

MILLER, David Louis (6 May 1903–8 Jan. 1986), philosopher, was born on a farm near Lyndon, Kansas, the son of Otto William Miller and Lucy Augusta Plettner, both German immigrants. He attended the College of Emporia from 1923 to 1927, graduating with majors in physics and mathematics. An accomplished football player, Miller was named all-conference guard in his senior year. He did graduate work in philosophy at the University of Chicago from 1927 to 1932 and in 1932 was awarded a Ph.D. In 1929 he married Mary Evelyn Harsh, and they had one child.

In 1934 Miller took a position as instructor in the Department of Philosophy at the University of Texas, where (with the exception of appointments as visiting professor at the University of Hamburg [1960], Kansas State University [1967], and the University of Miami [1970]) he served continuously until his retirement in 1978. Promoted to full professor in 1945 Miller served as department chairman from 1940 to 1944 and again from 1949 to 1959. During his second tenure as chairman the philosophy faculty more than doubled, and a graduate program was established. Miller is widely credited with building the foundation on which, by 1970, the department had become the largest in the country.

The most profound intellectual influence on Miller was American pragmatist and social psychologist George Herbert Mead. As a student and assistant of Mead's at the University of Chicago, Miller had planned to do his dissertation on the concept of "emergent evolutionism" with Mead's supervision. After Mead's unexpected death in 1931, Miller completed his dissertation ("Emergent Evolution and the Scientific Method") under Charles W. Morris. A leading editor of Mead's writings and expositor of his thought, Miller developed a social philosophy strongly influenced by Mead's ideas, as well as those of such twentieth-century process philosophers—thinkers who believed that evolutionary change is the key to reality—as Alfred North Whitehead.

Miller's writings on Mead include editorial, expository, and critical works. Among them are several books, a large number of journal and encyclopedia articles, and many invited lectures, including several in Japan and Switzerland. At the time of his death Mead had published only a few reviews and articles in professional journals, leaving behind a mass of unpublished manuscripts, including class notes taken by his students. Miller helped to prepare many of these materials for publication. The first collection of Mead's papers, which Miller coedited with Charles W. Morris, John M. Brewster, and Albert M. Dunham, was *The Philosophy of the Act* (1938). The second collection, which Miller alone edited, was titled *The Individual and the Social Self* (1982). In 1973 Miller published a comprehensive account of Mead's philosophy, *George Herbert Mead: Self, Language, and the World*, which has proven to be a central secondary work in the field and a model for future scholarship. At the time of his death Miller was preparing a third collection of Mead's writings for publication. Well before the end of his career, he achieved the distinction of being the foremost authority on Mead's philosophy.

Miller's own philosophy is a naturalistic process metaphysics that unites pragmatism (chiefly Mead's) with emergent evolutionism (essentially that of Alfred North Whitehead). Whitehead, though he does not deny pragmatism's emphasis on practical problem solving, emphasizes creativity and purpose in nature and human history. Mead includes many of Whitehead's insights in his own writings, but he often states them tentatively or implicitly. By contrast, Miller assertively develops many Whiteheadian ideas concerning creativity, perception, and internal relationships. Nature, for Miller, is the fundamental reality, though it is neither fully mechanical nor predetermined.

Miller's dependence on Mead is especially clear in his treatment of the emergence of the self. Mead holds that the self and consciousness arise through a process of social interaction. That is, selves emerge when, through language gestures ("significant symbols"), one person is able to consider the possible responses that his or her actions will elicit in another. Through significant symbols human beings are able to play social roles and to participate in their societies. On the basis of this theory mind is neither presupposed prior to experience nor imputed to the individual independently of the social process. Mind arises in nature, in society.

Though he agrees with Mead's explanation of the genesis of the self, Miller draws significantly stronger conclusions concerning its character. Like many pragmatists, including Mead's friend the philosopher and educator John Dewey, Mead not only insists that the social sciences can fully understand the self; he is convinced that they can, by themselves, solve basic social problems. Miller denies both claims. The social sciences cannot account for human creativity, especially in the sphere of values; and in spite of the usefulness of the knowledge they provide, these sciences can not by themselves provide the solutions to our social problems.

If the solutions to social problems are never merely technical in nature, it is precisely because such solutions leave open so many questions of value. In real world situations, Miller insists, the basic problem is "the ethical one of selecting and agreeing on the goals selected, and not the lack of means for the accomplishment of these goals." The ethical awareness involved in considering these goals and attempting to put them into effect is, he argues, in a manner reminiscent of Immanuel Kant, grounded in human freedom. This freedom is found in the individual. While Mead sometimes writes as if the individual is wholly a product of society, Miller asserts that society can be changed by creative acts springing from the individual.

Because human selves are capable of acts that express creative freedom, it does not follow that they can not be studied or that they evade understanding. The self has a definite, intelligible structure that Miller, following Mead, analyzes into three parts: behavior, the "I," and the "me." Behavior, outward and observable, consists in the effort to achieve goals. The "me" is the self's social component; it is a system of attitudes acquired through interaction with others. Most, though not all, behavior is a function of the "me." The "I," by contrast, is the self's personal component. It is at the same time thinker, willer, judge, and creator. Miller stresses this third aspect of the self, developing the concept and enlarging the function of the "I" in ways that Mead omits or only adumbrates.

To those who would object that such analysis of the self is incompatible with the achievements of modern science in predicting events, including behavior, Miller makes an interesting and original response. Since prediction presents us with future events that we may choose to avoid, as science advances, events become less instead of more predictable. Paradoxically, as science advances men become more, not less free. Karl Popper made this same point independently.

Some existentialists, notably Jean Paul Sartre, attempt an analysis of the "I" in many respects similar to Miller's. But for Sartre, the "I" finds itself alienated in a universe (a vast "in itself") entirely strange to man. For Miller, man and nature are not alien presences. Rather, human freedom exists in the context of a cosmic metaphysics of emergent evolution. Human creativity, an emergent—a new feature in the world that cannot be predicted or reduced to its antecedents—flowers throughout human history in new scientific, technological, social, and ethical concepts, just as, prior to the emergence of man, biological evolution gave rise to new species and subspecies that could not have been predicted. The most that can be said is that once a new state of affairs emerges, one is able to determine the causal factors to explain it.

It is often held that the final test of a philosophy lies in its political implications. If a philosophy cannot lead to a workable, morally defensible politics, it is not, according to this view, an acceptable system of thought. The political implications of Miller's philosophy are certainly clear. A democratic society, he insists, is one in which individuals can best flourish, and, in turn, best contribute. Such societies presuppose pluralism, mutual respect, and a climate of openness. Miller's philosophy, essentially social and ethical in its implications, is a defense of these qualities.

The three fundamental parts of the self discussed above, understood as three basic commitments of social life, function in Miller's thought to reinforce democratic ideals. Behavior, he argues, is best understood through "work," that is, achievement. According to Miller, in a democratic society work should not be understood as a means to money, though many treat it as such. Rather, human accomplishments should be regarded as proof of personal value, whether in the arts, scientific research, business, or elsewhere.

Though the "I" is the source of personal autonomy, its freedom does not consist of isolated independence. No person loses selfhood, individuality, or creativity by cooperating with others. The "I" can function as a source of choice, flexibility, and reformulation only through its participation in a society of selves. Mutual participation is, in turn, possible only through a complex of internalized, shared values. Democratic societies best utilize the threefold commitment to work (behavior), enterprise (the "I") and mutual participation (the "me"). Against those who argue that society should overrule the individual and those who insist that the individual should dictate to society, Miller argues that the three aspects of democratic life strengthen and enrich each other, reconciling the social and the individual.

Miller's carefully crafted prose and painstaking arguments are not intended to dazzle or to impress. An expert carpenter and cabinetmaker in private life, his writing exhibits a craftsmanlike determination to construct stable and enduring structure. He is remembered as an eminent twentieth-century interpreter of Mead who extended the ethical and social content of the latter's thought. Miller, who remained an active and productive scholar until the end, died in Austin, Texas.

• Miller's personal library and papers are in the library at Baylor University. For assessments of his life and writings, see Michael P. Jones et al., eds., *The Individual and Society: Essays Presented to David L. Miller on His Seventy-fifth Birthday* (1978).

PETE A. Y. GUNTER

MILLER, Dayton Clarence (13 Mar. 1866–23 Feb. 1941), physicist, was born near Strongsville, Ohio, the son of Charles Webster Dewey Miller, a street railway executive, and Vienna Pomeroy. Dayton showed both mechanical and musical talents from early childhood. He took a keen interest in playing and tinkering with the workings of pianos, organs, wind-instruments, especially flutes, and many intricate devices like clocks, telescopes, and business machines.

As a student at Baldwin College in Berea, Ohio, Miller sought a liberal education in the arts and sciences, receiving a bachelor's degree in 1886. After working as a banker for a year, he taught mathematics at Baldwin, received a master's degree there in 1889, and enrolled at Princeton University for graduate studies in astronomy. He first encountered an optical interferometer when assigned the task of measuring wavelengths of incandescent sodium. His successes in experimental physics led him toward astrophysics, in which he obtained a Ph.D. in 1890 with an analytical dissertation on behaviors of comets.

Miller visited Cleveland, Ohio, in 1890 in order to seek advice on a set of faulty prisms. In conversation with Edward W. Morley, a physical chemist at Western Reserve College, he learned of the recent departure of Albert A. Michelson from the neighboring Case School of Applied Science. Morley arranged for Miller to take a temporary job at the Case School, teaching introductory courses in mathematics, physics, and astronomy. Morley greatly influenced Miller during almost fifteen years of active cooperation. Morley was hard at work on his primary goals of refining more precisely the elemental compositions of atmospheric air and of distilled water. Miller helped develop better instruments, such as Morley's eudiometer and differential manometer. He also learned to operate a precision Ruprecht balance on loan from the Smithsonian Institution. While Morley determined the atomic weights and densities of hydrogen and oxygen in molecular combinations, Miller began comparing the velocity of light in two half-beams running along perpendicular paths. Teaching wave theory for both acoustics and optics, Miller learned as much as possible from Morley about the optical apparatuses that Michelson and Morley had developed to measure "ether-drag" and "ether-drift," as well as the length of the standard meter-bar in Paris. Most especially, Miller was challenged by and responded immediately to all the scientific news out of Europe about the new phenomena of wireless waves, radio, radioactivity, and X radiation. Having married Edith C. Easton in 1893 (they had no children), he photographed his wife's hand by X rays immediately after reading Wilhelm Konrad Roentgen's account of his discovery. Miller also used X rays to show the fractures of broken bones and the shapes of impacted teeth, perhaps the first use of X rays for density.

In 1897 Morley and Miller published their first joint paper, "On the Coefficient of Expansion of Certain Gases." They collaborated on three other sets of experiments before the turn of the century while simultaneously pursuing individual projects. Miller was becoming deeply immersed in wave theory and in precision instruments to analyze longitudinal waves for sound and transverse waves for light and electromagnetic radiation. Miller's new textbook, *Laboratory Physics* (1903), became a classic manual for three decades. He continued to seek more accurate ways to demonstrate how musical qualities were related to the physical characteristics of tones. In 1908 he announced his invention of the "phonodeik," a type of mechanical oscilloscope, making available a new tool of high precision for harmonic analyses and syntheses. This device recorded sound patterns photographically and was utilized during World War I for locating long-range enemy artillery.

In 1915 Miller published his Lowell Lectures at Harvard, *The Science of Musical Sounds*. There he demonstrated his virtuosity as a flutist. His lifelong hobby with keyboards and player-pianos enlivened his extensive lecturing, and he was widely consulted after the war as an expert on architectural acoustics designing auditoria.

Morley and Miller had attended together the Paris Exposition of 1900, where they heard British physicist William Thomson Kelvin address the International Congress of Physics about "two clouds" that shadowed the dynamical theory of heat and light. Since one of these "clouds" was that of the classic Michelson-Morley ether-drift experiments of 1887, they were urged to repeat with more powerful apparatus those tests of relative motion of the Earth against the background of a presumed luminiferous ether. This they did with progressively more refined interferometers from 1902 through Morley's retirement in 1906. The results, however, continued to be disappointing. In 1905 Albert Einstein suggested that the ether was superfluous. Most experimentalists however were not persuaded.

The results of the Michelson-Morley experiments of 1884–1889 and the Morley-Miller repetitions of 1900–1907 became widely discussed after the theory of special relativity was published, even after the solar eclipse expeditions of 1919 gave apparent confirmation of Einstein's general theory. Michelson, Morley, and Miller were all skeptical of the theoretical wars and partisan use of their results to justify relativity. Encouraged by George Ellery Hale and funded by Eckstein Case, a Cleveland industrialist, Miller alone returned his attention to ether-drift tests with improved apparatus at higher elevations. Between 1921 and 1926 Miller took more than 250,000 readings, most of them at Mount Wilson Observatory, almost 6,000 feet above Pasadena, California. By 1925 he had convinced himself and many others that he had at last found positive results for "ether-drift" showing the absolute motion of the whole solar system. As retiring president of the American Physical Society, he was honored with a $1,000 prize that year by the American Association for the Advancement of Science.

Einstein visited Miller in Cleveland and was quoted as summing up the interview by saying in German, "God may be subtle, but He is not malicious." Although all three experimentalists were reluctant to accept Einstein's theory of relativity, Miller carried on this analyses of data and studies of the properties of the astrophysical motions of the solar system, until his own death by heart attack in Cleveland. With the advent of computers in the 1950s, some of his students, led by Robert S. Shankland, Miller's successor, reanalyzed all Miller's ether-drift data and concluded that very small temperature variations, especially at high altitudes, were the primary causes for the shifts of interference fringes that Miller had observed.

In the last decade of his life Miller wrote four more books: *The Flute* (1935); *Sound Waves: Their Shape and Spread* (1937); *Anecdotal History of the Science of Sound* (1935); and *Sparks, Lightening and Cosmic Rays: An Anecdotal History of Electricity* (1939). In all, he published more than ninety-eight scientific papers and six books. His collection of almost 1,000 flutes was bequeathed to the Music Division of the Library of Congress.

• Miller's personal papers and research notebooks are at Case Western Reserve University. Miller's "The Ether Drift Experiment and the Determination of the Absolute Motion of the Earth," in *Reviews of Modern Physics* 5 (July 1933): 203–42, is a comprehensive résumé of all Miller's repetitions of the Michelson-Morley experiment. Biographical accounts with bibliographies are Harvey Fletcher, "Dayton Clarence Miller," in National Academy of Sciences, *Biographical Memoirs* 23 (1945): 61–74; and Robert S. Shankland, "Dayton Clarence Miller: Physics across Fifty Years," in *American Journal of Physics* 9 (Oct. 1941): 273–83. See also William J. Maynard, "Dayton C. Miller: His Life, Work and Contributions as a Scientist and Organologist" (master's thesis, Palmer Graduate Lib. School, Long Island Univ., 1971). Miller's ether-drift data is assessed in Shankland et al., "New Analysis of the Interferometer Observations of Dayton C. Miller," *Reviews of Modern Physics* 27 (Apr. 1955): 167–78; and his research is set in context in Loyd S. Swenson, Jr., *The Ethereal Aether: A History of the Michelson-Morley-Miller Aether-Drift Experiments, 1880–1930* (1972). Oral history interviews, contained on tapes and transcripts, were conducted by Loyd Swenson, Jr., with R. S. Shankland for the AIP Bohr Library Archives (Aug. 1974). Obituaries are by H. W. Mountcastle in *Science*, 21 Mar. 1941, pp. 270–72; G. Walter Stewart in *Journal of the Acoustical Society of America* 12 (Apr. 1941): 477–80; W. F. G. Swann in American Philosophical Society, *Year Book* (1941); and J. J. Naussau in *Case Alumnus*, May–June 1936.

LOYD S. SWENSON, JR.

MILLER, Dickinson Sergeant (7 Oct. 1868–13 Nov. 1963), teacher of philosophy and writer, was born in Philadelphia, Pennsylvania, the son of Elihu Spencer Miller, a professor of law, and Anna Emlen Hare. He graduated in 1885 from Episcopal High School in Philadelphia. Having a delicate constitution, he spent his hours after school in the library where, he said in conversation, he "got ideas" that "did not grow in school."

At the University of Pennsylvania, where Miller received the A.B. in 1889, he learned from George Fullerton, his "best" teacher, a method of philosophical analysis that he used the rest of his life. Fullerton insisted that the "somewhat startling analyses" of John Locke, George Berkeley, and David Hume should be seen not as destructive or skeptical of causality and knowledge but as explanatory, providing new insight into what we assume to exist all along.

In 1889 Miller entered Clark University to study under psychologist G. Stanley Hall but withdrew the next year to enroll in Harvard University, where he was most influenced by William James and became his lifelong friend. He also studied under Josiah Royce, George Santayana, and George Herbert Palmer. From Harvard he received the A.B. and A.M. in 1892 and, encouraged by James, went abroad to study at the Universities of Berlin and Halle under psychologist Hermann Ebbinghaus, idealist philosopher Friedrich

Paulsen, and neo-Kantian philosopher Max Dessoir. A year later he received the Ph.D. from Halle with a dissertation, "Das Wesen der Erkenntnis und des Irrthums" (slightly revised and published as "The Meaning of Truth and Error" [1893]). It was directed, Miller told a fellow student, not to the *Geschichte*, the history, of the problem, a common German propensity, but to its *Lösung*, its solution. At the outset of his dissertation Miller echoed what he had learned from Fullerton: he saw the analysis of terms rather than the discovery of the existence or nonexistence of certain supposed facts as the most important business of philosophy. Seeking to understand how ideas can know objects external to them, Miller rejected the "metaphysical hypothesis," in which some self-transcendent mental states can report something not of themselves. Instead, he held that ideas are appearances or images before the mind; "belief" is their spontaneous self-maintenance apart from any effort of will. So truth is not a thought's agreement with a transcendent object but with an object in consciousness embodying "belief" in which thought, after development, terminates. James acknowledged in his article "The Function of Cognition" that this view of truth led him to see that any "experienceable workings" would serve as intermediaries between idea and object quite as well as their inclusion in an all-embracing, universal consciousness, an Absolute Mind, as Royce held. James called this debt to Miller "the *fons et origo* of all *my* pragmatism." A few years later Charles A. Strong of Columbia University applauded "the James-Miller theory," saying that it was an original, naturalistic view of knowledge whose "subjective side" had been ably developed by Miller.

Returning from Halle, Miller became an associate in philosophy at Bryn Mawr College in 1894. There he became an admiring friend of Woodrow Wilson but suffered a crisis in health that left him with "crippling neurasthenia," partially paralyzing him for the rest of his days. Because of this, a serious courtship broke off, and he became a permanent bachelor. In 1899 he became an instructor at Harvard. There he became increasingly critical of James's thought, particularly the "will to believe," which asserted that belief involves inclination, motive, or will. Miller, in contrast, maintained that belief is entirely distinct from will; "voluntary belief" is a contradiction in terms that undermines claims to objective knowledge. We do not accept the foundations of knowledge because we have a certain will to do so. Rather, we find them in our minds "without our forth-putting" as "the shape the images take of their own accord."

Miller also questioned the view of truth that James later developed as pragmatism: that truth might follow from linkage of meaning with practical results. "Belief," Miller noted, "enters into a composition of causes with desire, since two sets of desires, with the same belief, may produce different courses of conduct." Thus Miller objected to James's views of both truth and belief. Miller thought that his criticism of James strained their friendship, but James, in a letter to Miller on 18 January, 1900 (deleted from publication at Miller's request), assured Miller that he was an "ideal responder" who genuinely met his views while others "glance side-ways off the surface."

After an acerbic, quarreling correspondence with his chairman over library book orders, his inordinate eccentricity, and, according to some of his colleagues, his "lunacy" and "paranoia," and with failure of promotion, Miller left Harvard in 1904 to teach at Columbia, where he became professor until 1919, with John Dewey, C. A. Strong, and Wendell Bush among his colleagues. There he turned to criticism of James's "radical empiricism" and "realism" with an article entitled "Naive Realism: What Is It?" (in *Essays Philosophical and Psychological* [1908], in honor of William James). That criticism was elaborated in his article "A Debt to James," published in the volume *In Commemoration of William James* (1942).

In his "radical empiricism" James held that in "knowledge by acquaintance" our percept "in its wholeness" is part of the physical world, and the object "in its wholeness" is part of the stream of consciousness. The object-matter of the mind and the object-matter constituting nature are a single fact, "pure experience," without transcendent reference from consciousness to object. At the same time James affirmed "natural realism," the continuous existence of the physical world independently of any knower.

Miller objected, noting that James's view of consciousness in *Principles of Psychology* as the "field of experience" did not allow its identification with physical objects since consciousness has only one aspect, but physical objects have many. James's "natural realism" would imply a contradiction: that one and the same pencil, for example, may be perceived by two different knowers and thus constitute two different fields. Also the percept "in its wholeness" cannot be a new object confronting us because the percept in large part is subjective interpretation. It was unfortunate, in Miller's view, that James saw "radical empiricism" as a theory of the universe, a view of the nature of physical objects in relation to mind, when empiricism had always meant a way of justifying propositional knowledge. Philosophy, Miller held, is not served by such swapping of definitions.

Though Miller partly agreed with "natural realism" as healthy for philosophy, it would have to be interpreted differently. Perception should be seen as possession of certain aspects of the object as well as preparedness for others through the associative function of elements in consciousness and "motor processes half awakened." On this basis Miller subsequently criticized efforts of E. A. Singer and Gilbert Ryle to identify mind with objective behavior.

In 1908 Miller was ordained deacon in the Episcopal church, and in 1911 he became professor of Christian apologetics at General Theological Seminary in addition to his Columbia professorship. In subsequent years until his retirement from teaching in 1926 he wrote many articles on theological matters but increasingly attended to ethics and social philosophy. He also published noteworthy studies of Santayana, Henri Bergson, Matthew Arnold, James as teacher, and problems of education; several of these were for the *New Republic*, whose social outlook—liberal reform—he shared.

In 1923 a commission of Episcopal bishops condemned interpreting words in the creed in any but a literal sense. Miller found this contrary to precedent, inimical to the growth of interpretation, and justification for his resignation from General Theological Seminary. For years he had held that reference in the creed to virgin birth and Jesus as son of God was an important "historic and poetic symbol" for ideal human values, not the "bad science" in metaphysics and theology purporting to purvey cosmic matters of fact. He had been, he said in conversation, a naturalist in his world view since childhood, not a supernaturalist.

After resignation from the seminary in 1924, Miller taught philosophy for two years at Smith College and then began his "European retirement," mainly in Vienna and Florence. He met with the Vienna Circle of logical positivists—Moritz Schlick, Rudolf Carnap, Otto Neurath, Herbert Feigl, and others—and reportedly showed great acuity in individual discussion. Miller also associated with Ludwig Wittgenstein, whom he found working as a carpenter on a house Wittgenstein had designed for his sister. To Wittgenstein's assertion that pleasure or pain were intrinsically neither good nor bad Miller responded with an article entitled "The Pleasure-Quality and the Pain-Quality Analysable, Not Ultimate" (*Mind* 38 [1929]: 215–18), arguing that pleasure and goodness as benefit or welfare are conjoined as "the beneficial becomes the attractive and the attractive *is* the pleasant." He occasionally joined Santayana from Rome and Feigl from Vienna for philosophical discussion in C. A. Strong's villa near Florence. Though Miller had once considered sharing an apartment with Santayana, he twice broke off assisting him in Rome because he could not tolerate his illiberalism. In this period Miller wrote "Hume without Scepticism" and "Free Will as Involving Determination and Inconceivable without It" (*Mind* 39 [1930]: 273–301, 409–25; *Mind* 43 [1934]: 1–27) under the name of R. E. Hobart because some readers might otherwise regard him, he said, as "too old." In addition, an eminent British scholar had dismissed his article on Hume as unworthy of publication, a judgment with which the editor of *Mind* disagreed. The article on free will has been reprinted or cited several times as acute analysis, ably extending Mill's view on the subject.

In 1934 Miller returned to Boston to spend his remaining years in his "American retirement." A year later he was ordained to the priesthood, did considerable preaching, but devoted most of his time, so far as ill-health allowed, to philosophical articles, chapters of projected books, and university addresses. He wrote on Ralph Barton Perry's monumental biography of James, on James's thought for commemorations in 1942, on "Hume's Deathblow to Deductivism," and on the current plight of philosophy. From 1937 to 1944 he was assisted by graduate students from Boston University who sometimes manned his little sloop on the Charles River much as Max Eastman at Columbia had paddled Miller's canoe on the Hudson. Then Miller's usual formality gave way to geniality as he talked about philosophical issues and philosophers he had known. In 1941 he began a book, never published, utilizing his essays on free will, Hume, and James, as well as new pieces on the method of analysis and universals. It would be called "Inquiry, Analytical or Skeptical" or, rather inappropriately, "Some Settled Questions in Philosophy." As early as 1905 James had urged him to take his manuscript "thunder" out of the cupboard and publish it. Miller later lamented that he had had no career in philosophy because he had never published a book. Around 1960 he said he had "substantially completed" books on "Inquiry, Analytical or Skeptical" and intelligence in ethics as well as "thick manuscripts" on James and Santayana. None of these was found among his papers after he died in Boston.

In important respects Miller resembled his description of Fullerton—"limited in health and nervous force" yet "strong in command of himself" and with an engaging smile; always bringing abstractions back to concrete daily experience; like Socrates, always seeking the soundness of each step of an argument. With students he was kindly and patient though at the theological seminary, said one former student, he was not well understood because he spoke a different language, the language of current philosophy rather than theology. He had a wry and sly sense of humor as when he said that no one can make a mark in philosophy without an "-ism" and has really arrived when he has an "-istic -ism."

There were gaps in Miller's accomplishment, many the result of his chronic ill health. He was never consistently clear as to whether his method of analysis aimed to give insight into the nature of things or to clarify meanings to dissolve problems, whether its subject matter was complex existences or conceptions expressed in words and statements. His view of "belief" as entirely distinct from "our forth-putting," a main theme, failed to account for the element of adoption or abandonment in it. But he accomplished much in redirecting philosophy on the functioning of ideas laid out in "the James-Miller theory" of knowledge, in criticisms of James, in practicing conceptual analysis long before its current prominence, and in articles on Hume, free will, and knowledge—articles often recognized as "outstanding," even "remarkable."

• Miller's surviving letters and papers are in Harvard's Houghton Library. Most of his doctoral dissertation, translated as "The Meaning of Truth and Error," *Philosophical Review* 2 (1893): 408–25, was refined in later articles and hence is not included in his *Philosophical Analysis and Human Welfare*, ed. Loyd D. Easton (1975), which contains twenty-one articles—four previously unpublished, two as revised by Miller—an extensive bibliography of his writings and the few articles about him, and an introduction by Easton, with biographical details and the interrelated content of his writings. *The Letters of William James*, ed. Henry James (2 vols., 1920), tells much about James's relation to Miller.

LOYD D. EASTON

MILLER, Donald C. *See* Four Horsemen of Notre Dame.

MILLER, Dorie (12 Oct. 1919–24 Nov. 1943), African-American war hero, was born Doris Miller in Waco, Texas, the son of Conery Miller and Henrietta (maiden name unknown), sharecroppers. Miller attended Waco's segregated Moore High School and became the school's 200-pound star fullback. As the third of four sons in a family engaged in subsistence farming, however, he was forced to drop out of school to find work. In September 1939 he joined the navy as a mess attendant.

The navy was then rigidly segregated. Except for a small group of black sailors in the general service, survivors of the mostly integrated pre–World War I fleet, blacks were restricted to the steward's branch, where they wore distinctive uniforms and insignia. Even chief stewards could not exercise authority over men with lower ratings in the general service. Stewards manned the officers' mess, maintained the officers' billets aboard ship, and, in some instances, took care of the quarters of high officials ashore. Despite the fact that their enlistment contracts restricted their training and duties, stewards, like everyone aboard ship, were assigned battle stations, including positions at the guns and on the bridge. Miller received the standard eight-week training course given mess attendants at the Naval Receiving Station, Norfolk, Virginia, and, after a brief stint on an ammunition ship was assigned to the battleship *West Virginia*.

In the early hours of 7 December 1941, the *West Virginia* was at its berth in Pearl Harbor, Hawaii, and Miller was going about his daily chore of collecting officers' laundry when the call to battle stations sounded. Miller arrived at his station in the antiaircraft battery magazine amidships to find it aflame, a victim of the initial Japanese torpedo attack. Hurrying topside, he followed his supervisory officer to the bridge where, despite enemy strafing and in the face of a serious fire, the powerful young sailor carried the ship's mortally wounded captain to a safer place.

The officer then loaded the two 50-mm bridge guns and ordered the untrained Miller to man one of them. Asked later about his subsequent actions, Miller said, "It wasn't hard. I just pulled the trigger and she worked fine. I'd watched others use those guns. I guess I fired her for about fifteen minutes. I think I got one of those Jap planes. They were diving pretty close to us." In fact Miller continued firing at the enemy planes until ordered to abandon the burning bridge.

In the confused aftermath of Pearl Harbor, Miller's feat, although noted in naval dispatches, went unheralded. Rumors continued to circulate, however, and on 14 March 1942 the Pittsburgh *Courier*, a widely read black newspaper, broke the story, demanding official public recognition of Miller's heroism. Secretary of the Navy Frank Knox, an ardent defender of the navy's racial exclusion policy, reacted belatedly by writing Miller a letter of commendation, but this only fueled the growing demand for public honors. Edgar Brown, representing the National Negro Council, urged congressmen to pass a bill introduced by Senator James M. Mead of New York and others to award Miller the Medal of Honor, and Wendell Willkie, the Republican leader, called on President Franklin D. Roosevelt to intervene.

Knox argued that his letter of commendation and Miller's anticipated promotion to mess attendant, first class, provided sufficient recognition, but the president, no doubt reacting to widespread charges of racism in the navy, overruled Knox. In an extraordinary move, Roosevelt personally ordered Miller awarded the Navy Cross. On 27 May 1942, the commander of the Pacific fleet, Admiral Chester W. Nimitz, bestowed the navy's second-highest award on Miller with due ceremony.

Despite Knox's intransigence, the position of blacks in the navy had changed considerably by mid-1942. Forced to open its general service to African Americans and now dependent exclusively on the Selective Service with its 10 percent black quota for manpower, the navy witnessed a dramatic increase in the number of black sailors in all jobs and ratings. The Bureau of Naval Personnel faced the daunting task of training and assigning thousands of minority members while maintaining their morale in a segregated environment. Civil rights spokesmen deftly connected recognition of Miller's heroism to the growing aspirations of the new black sailors and the black public at large, and the bureau readily endorsed the *Courier*'s suggestion that Miller come home to speak to the young black draftees.

Miller, the high school dropout, proved surprisingly effective at his public affairs assignments, speaking before large audiences throughout the United States. In due course, however, he was promoted to petty officer rank (cook, third class) in the general service and was reassigned to sea. He returned to the fleet in time to participate in the battle for Tarawa, but on 24 November 1943 he was among the 644 men lost when the escort carrier *Liscome Bay* sank during the battle for Makin.

Almost thirty years after Miller's death a more racially enlightened navy, desiring to honor the exploits of its minority heroes, named the Service School Command barracks at Great Lakes Naval Station, Illinois, in Miller's honor, and in June 1973 his mother christened the USS *Miller*, a Knox-class destroyer escort. But again such honors were not without controversy because they followed closely another effort to use the memory of Miller's experience to advance the general civil rights agenda. The navy opposed an effort, this time led by Senator Edward M. Kennedy, among others, to award Miller the Medal of Honor posthumously. The chief of naval operations, Admiral Elmo M. Zumwalt, himself an ardent champion of minority rights in the navy, rejected the demand on the grounds that, in the absence of new evidence, the Navy Cross had been the appropriate award and that naming a ship and barracks in Miller's honor constituted sufficient recognition. In the late 1980s Representative Joe DioGuardi of New York, chagrined that no black serviceman was awarded the Medal of Honor in either world war, again nominated Miller for the nation's highest decoration as representative of all the black heroes of World War II, but to no avail.

Ironically, this son of humble sharecroppers, who during his short life knew nothing but segregation and discrimination, was transformed by an extraordinary act of personal heroism into an enduring symbol of the struggle of African Americans for equal treatment and opportunity.

• Details about Dorie Miller's training and assignments, copies of pertinent official commendations, and a clipping file detailing his exploits and subsequent efforts to award him the Medal of Honor are in the Operational Archives Branch, U.S. Naval Historical Center. Miller's experiences at Pearl Harbor are summarized in Jack D. Foner, *Blacks and the Military in American History* (1974); Gordon W. Prange, in collaboration with Donald M. Goldstein and Katherine V. Dillon, *At Dawn We Slept: The Untold Story of Pearl Harbor* (1978); and Bernard C. Nalty, *Strength for the Fight: A History of Black Americans in the Military* (1986). For an extended discussion of racial policy in the World War II navy, see Morris J. MacGregor, *Integration of the Armed Forces* (1981).

MORRIS J. MACGREGOR

MILLER, Edward (9 May 1760–17 Mar. 1812), physician and teacher, was born in Dover, Delaware, the son of John Miller, a clergyman, and Margaret Millington. Miller was born to devout Presbyterian parents. His father, an eminent classical scholar, was pastor of a Presbyterian church in Dover for more than forty years. Until he reached the age of fourteen, Miller was taught by his father at home, where he learned Latin and Greek and was introduced to classical literature. In 1774 Miller enrolled in a Presbyterian seminary school in Newark, Delaware, under the direction of Francis Alison and Alexander M'Dowell. During his four years at this institution, Miller became an accomplished classical scholar.

Miller began studying medicine in Dover in 1778 as an apprentice to Dr. Charles Ridgely. After spending two years with his preceptor, Miller joined the army in the revolutionary war as a surgeon's mate in a military hospital at Basking Ridge, New Jersey, from 1780 to 1781. He then traveled for a year as a surgeon on an armed ship bound for France. While in France, Miller learned the language and acquainted himself with French medicine. When his military career ended in 1783 with the Treaty of Paris, Miller established a private practice in Frederica, Delaware, in 1784 and, at the same time, began attending medical lectures at the University of Pennsylvania. With little prospect for success in Frederica, Miller moved to Somerset County on the eastern shore of Maryland, where he practiced from 1784 to 1786. Although his practice in Maryland was lucrative, Miller's desire to be near his family and his former preceptor led to his move back to Dover. Meanwhile, he had received his bachelor of medicine degree from the University of Pennsylvania in 1785. Four years later Miller graduated from the university with an M.D. after successfully defending his thesis on the enlargement of the spleen as evidence of chronic malaria, a disorder he encountered frequently in his private practice as a result of remittent and intermittent fevers in the Dover area.

Miller practiced in Dover until 1796 when in response to a request from his brother, Samuel Miller, a theologian on the faculty at Princeton, he moved to New York City. Soon after his arrival Miller became a member of the Friendly Club, a literary society that included many leaders of New York's legal, medical, and religious professions. In 1797 he joined Elihu Hubbard Smith and Samuel Latham Mitchell in founding the *Medical Repository*, this country's first private medical journal. He served as one of the journal's editors through its first fourteen volumes. Miller was an active member of the American Mineralogical Society, which was established in New York in 1798 to promote the development of the mineral resources of the United States.

In 1798, when a yellow fever epidemic broke out in New York City, Miller was among those physicians who stayed in the city to fight the dreaded malady. A devoted friend of Benjamin Rush since his medical school days at the University of Pennsylvania, Miller agreed with his former professor who espoused bleeding and purgatives as treatments for yellow fever, although he showed more caution in his use of the latter. The New York legislature in 1803 enacted a measure to prevent the introduction of pestilential diseases into New York City, which included the creation of the office of resident physician for the port of New York. In 1803 Miller was appointed to this post and served the city in this capacity—except for one year—until his death. When yellow fever returned to New York City in 1805, Miller, as resident physician, prepared a report on the epidemic for the governor. In his report, published in New York in 1806, Miller argued that the disease had a domestic origin, and he concluded that it was caused by a pernicious vapor in the atmosphere. Furthermore, Miller believed that yellow fever was noncontagious. Accordingly, he recommended improvement in sanitation rather than quarantine measures.

Miller was elected a corresponding member of the American Philosophical Society in 1805. Two years later the College of Physicians and Surgeons was founded, and Miller was appointed professor of theory and practice of medicine by the regents of the school. Concerned about the state of American medical education, Miller advocated expanding the curricula of medical schools to include pathology and—almost unheard of at the time—medical history. In 1809 Miller joined the staff of the New York Hospital and subsequently introduced clinical lectures there.

Modest and unassuming, Miller added little to the literature of medicine. Besides his editing duties with the *Medical Repository* and his report on the 1805 yellow fever epidemic in New York City, Miller wrote nothing more than a few articles. He did, however, write most of the chapter on medicine in Samuel Miller's *A Brief Retrospect of the Eighteenth Century* (1801), which was a historical survey of the previous century. Committed firmly to popular government, Miller supported the Democratic-Republican party of Thomas Jefferson and James Madison. A bachelor, Miller died in New York of an acute respiratory infection. His modern views on medical education and his only acknowledged contribution to medical science—the recognition of an enlarged spleen as the best evidence of chronic malaria—are largely forgotten today.

• No sizable collection of Edward Miller's personal papers has been located. The archives of the New York Hospital–Cornell Medical Center and the College of Physicians and Surgeons in New York City contain material that document Miller's activities at these institutions. David Hosack, "Account of the Life and Character of Edward Miller, M.D.," *American Medical and Philosophical Register* 3 (1813): 1–8, and Samuel Miller, *The Medical Works of Edward Miller, M.D., Collected and Accompanied with a Biographical Sketch of the Author* (1814), are the best contemporary accounts of Miller's life and career. The latter work also contains Miller's medical publications. Francis P. Chinard, "Edward Miller—American Physician (1760–1812)," *Journal of the Medical Society of New Jersey* 78 (1981): 296–99, is a useful modern treatment of Miller. See also an unsigned book review of *The Medical Works of Edward Miller* in the *North American Medical and Surgical Journal* 5 (1828): 127–48.

THOMAS A. HORROCKS

MILLER, Elizabeth Smith (20 Sept. 1822–22 May 1911), feminist and designer of the Bloomer costume, was born in Hampton, New York, the daughter of reformer and philanthropist Gerrit Smith and Ann Carroll Fitzhugh. Miller's grandfather, Peter Smith, a partner of John Jacob Astor (1763–1848) in the early nineteenth-century fur trade and a speculator in real estate, amassed a considerable fortune, freeing his son to pursue his interests in the temperance, antislavery, and women's rights movements and ensuring that his granddaughter would become (as her cousin, the feminist Elizabeth Cady Stanton, later put it) "the heiress to a vast estate."

Soon after her birth, Elizabeth and her parents returned to the Smith family home in Peterboro, New York, where she was raised. Except for a brief period during the depression of 1837, when the family temporarily abandoned their "mansion house" for a nearby cottage and she and her mother labored as clerks in Gerrit Smith's land office, she enjoyed a life of prosperity. Relatively unencumbered by parental discipline—a consequence of her father's views on child rearing—the young Elizabeth was strong-willed and exuberant; she delighted in playing practical jokes on relatives and friends with her cousin, Elizabeth Cady Stanton, a frequent guest at Peterboro. As the daughter of a prominent reformer, Miller was reared in an atmosphere that was unusual by the standards of her day. Reformers of various stripes flocked to the Smith home, where they vigorously debated such issues as women's rights, temperance, and, especially, slavery. This socially conscious milieu seems to have had a profound effect on Miller herself; at age twelve she wrote to her father that she was planning to organize a children's "Abolition meeting." Miller was educated, first at home, by tutors and governesses (many years later she would express the belief that girls should be educated at home); she subsequently attended a "manual training school" in Clinton, New York, and the Friends' School in Philadelphia where, as her obituary in the *Woman's Journal* explained, "she learned the simplicity of dress that she practiced through life."

In October 1843 she married banker Charles Dudley Miller, insisting, contrary to her father's wishes, on a fashionable wedding. The couple lived at various locations in upstate New York, first at Charles Miller's home in Cazenovia, then at Peterboro, finally settling at Geneva in 1869. In 1851, after having given birth to three children (a fourth was born in 1856), Miller designed what would later be called the Bloomer costume. Finding long skirts less than suitable for gardening and other household chores, she devised an outfit that, as she later recalled, consisted of "Turkish trousers to the ankle, with a skirt some four inches below the knee." Thus attired, she went to Seneca Falls and visited Stanton, with whom she had long discussed "the toils of crippling fashion" and the inconvenience and unhealthiness of trailing skirts. Impressed by the comfort and freedom of movement that the costume afforded, Stanton and other leading feminists, including Susan B. Anthony and Lucy Stone, adopted it themselves. Stanton's neighbor, Amelia Bloomer, popularized Miller's creation in the pages of her newspaper, *The Lily*; hence the garment became associated in the public mind with Bloomer's name.

Subjected to constant ridicule, most proponents of the Bloomer costume soon abandoned it, but Miller, buttressed by the support of her father and husband, persisted, even wearing the ensemble to official dinners and receptions in Washington during her father's congressional term in the winter of 1852–1853. But at the end of seven years, she decided that the dress "was a perpetual violation of my love of the beautiful" (although one suspects that she also had tired of attracting notoriety) and returned to conventional attire. Nevertheless she continued to eschew corsets, "heavy, trailing skirt[s]," "choking collar[s]," and high heels.

Perhaps of greater significance to her contemporaries was Miller's immensely popular *In the Kitchen*, first published in 1875. Described by its author as "a book of most minute directions in all things pertaining to housekeeping," it contained instructions for everything from "directions for killing chickens" to "disinfecting rooms." Miller's interest in homemaking suggests that she perceived few conflicts between feminism and domestic life; Stanton herself, who suggested the title for Miller's book, believed that "cooking is a high art."

Although she never equaled the activism of her cousin, Miller remained a staunch supporter of women's rights throughout her life, hosting an annual "Piazza Party" for local suffragists, occasionally attending conventions of the National American Woman Suffrage Association, and lending generous financial support to national and local suffrage organizations. She also promoted female education, contributing substantial sums to William Smith College, located in her hometown of Geneva. Possibly in recognition of her own brief experience with financial adversity, she marketed homemade marmalades and jellies in order to provide an example for needy women who otherwise might be deterred from making a living by the generally held perception that it was not ladylike for women to earn money. Miller died at her home in Geneva.

Her achievements overshadowed by those of her more famous cousin, Miller is perhaps best described as an ardent advocate of the feminist cause rather than an active crusader for women's rights. Although her wealth and family connections render her less than representative of the movement as a whole, her life provides insights into the attitudes of rank-and-file feminists whose support proved crucial to the ultimate success of woman suffrage.

• Miller's letters are in the Gerrit Smith Collection at the New York Public Library and in the Syracuse University Library. In "Reflections on Woman's Dress, and the Record of a Personal Experience," *The Arena*, Sept. 1892, pp. 491–95, Miller recounted her reasons for designing and later abandoning the Bloomer costume. See also Dexter C. Bloomer, *Life and Writings of Amelia Bloomer* (1895). Elizabeth Cady Stanton, *Eighty Years and More: Reminiscences 1816–1897* (1898), describes Miller's girlhood; for other biographical information see Ralph Volney Harlow, *Gerrit Smith: Philanthropist and Reformer* (1939). Theodore Stanton and Harriot Stanton Blatch, eds., *Elizabeth Cady Stanton as Revealed in Her Letters, Diary and Reminiscences*, vol. 2 (1922), contains numerous letters written to her cousin. Elizabeth Cady Stanton et al., eds., *The History of Woman Suffrage* (6 vols., 1881–1922), is a good source of information about Miller's role as a supporter of woman suffrage. Lois Banner, *American Beauty* (1983), includes a discussion of nineteenth-century dress reform and the significance of the Bloomer costume. An obituary is in the *Woman's Journal*, 17 June 1911.

WENDY GAMBER

MILLER, Emily Clark Huntington (22 Oct. 1833–2 Nov. 1913), author, Methodist temperance worker, and educator, was born in Brooklyn, Connecticut, the daughter of Thomas Huntington, a physician and Baptist minister, and his second wife, Paulina Clark. Receiving her early education at local schools, she graduated from Oberlin College in 1857 and stayed on briefly to teach in the college. While at Oberlin she met John Edwin Miller, a graduate of the Oberlin Theological Institute and a teacher, whom she married in 1860; they had four children.

During the early years of her marriage, Miller moved between the various towns in Illinois and Ohio where her husband held teaching positions. In 1868 the couple settled in Evanston, Illinois. John Miller gave up teaching to join Alfred L. Sewell as co-publisher of the *Little Corporal*, a children's magazine. Emily H. Miller, a frequent contributor to the magazine, served as its sole editor from 1871 until 1875, when the publication was absorbed by another children's magazine, *St. Nicholas*. Throughout her life, Miller continued to write for various magazines, including the *Atlantic Monthly*, the *Century, Cosmopolitan, McClure's* and *Scribner's*. In addition she published several books, mainly novels, as well as didactic stories for children and poetry. Miller's writing generally dealt with conventional themes, treated in a moralistic manner. Some of her bestselling titles included *The Parish of Fair Heaven* (1876), *Kathie's Experience* (1886), and *The King's Messengers* (1891). Although not of lasting literary significance, her works were popular in her day and brought her a wide reputation as an author and poet.

Miller was also known for her activities on behalf of foreign missions, Sunday schools, women's education, and temperance. In each case, her involvement grew out of her membership in the Methodist church. She participated in the denomination's Woman's Foreign Missionary Society from the early 1870s, holding various offices in Chicago and serving as president of the Minnesota branch from 1883 until 1889. Together with her husband she was an active sponsor of Methodist Sunday school programs and wrote a number of stories over the years to be used in the classroom. After moving to Evanston in 1868 she joined an organization of Methodist women, known as the Women's Educational Association, whose aim—in the words of Frances Willard—was "to found a woman's college, in which women should constitute the board of trustees, a woman should be president and confer diplomas, and women should be, for the first time, recognized and proved peers of men in administrative power" (*Glimpses of Fifty Years* [1889], p. 199). In 1870 this group established the Evanston College for Ladies, with Willard as president and Miller as corresponding secretary of the all-female board of trustees. Despite the founders' desire to be independent, financial difficulties that arose from the great Chicago fire of 1871 forced the trustees in 1873 to cede control of the institution to Northwestern, the Methodist university also located in Evanston. The principle of female authority was not abandoned entirely, however; in transferring the institution, provision was made for five women to act in perpetuity as trustees of the university. Miller was one of those originally elected to serve, and she remained on Northwestern's board for the next twelve years.

In the early 1870s Miller's work on behalf of Sunday schools led to her involvement in the nascent Chautauqua movement and to her role in the organization of the Woman's Christian Temperance Union (WCTU). In the summer of 1874 she attended a Sunday school conference at Lake Chautauqua, in upstate New York, and thereafter participated regularly in the growing movement, lecturing frequently, contributing to the *Chautauquan*, and serving for four years as president of the Chautauqua Woman's Club. At the 1874 conference Miller and other women temperance advocates issued the "Call" that resulted in the organization of the WCTU. As corresponding secretary of the organizing committee, Miller took a leading role in helping to create a national body. Thereafter her involvement in the WCTU was more limited, although she continued to write and occasionally lecture on behalf of the cause.

The Millers moved in 1878 to St. Paul, Minnesota, where John Miller worked for a harvester company until his death in 1882. Emily H. Miller returned to Evanston in 1889 and in 1891 became principal of the Woman's College and assistant professor of English literature at Northwestern. She served in the former capacity until her retirement in 1898 but continued to teach for two more years. Miller's tenure as head of the Woman's College was successful, and in 1897, in recognition of the scope of her responsibilities and her competency in carrying them out, the title of her office was changed to "dean of women." From her early involvement with coeducation at Northwestern, she believed in the ability of women students to profit from higher education and resisted attempts to treat them differently in the classroom. "I always deprecate setting the achievements of women by themselves for valuation," she wrote in a letter, "as if they were not to be judged as work, but as women's work" (excerpted in Wilde, p. 99).

The remaining years of Miller's life were spent in St. Paul and at her summer residence in Englewood, New Jersey. She died at the home of her brother in Northfield, Minnesota.

Miller's life is perhaps best summarized in the words of her friend and colleague Frances Willard: "All objections to an exceptional career for women (and especially for women who have husbands, children, and homes), find conspicuous refutation in the fragile yet indomitable, modest yet independent, loving and beloved, yet brave and business-like little woman whom I have here the honor to introduce" (*Woman and Temperance*, p. 159). Though not as famous as some of her peers, Miller epitomized the educated, reform-minded woman of the second half of the nineteenth century. While committed to her family, her literary skills and her activities on behalf of the Methodist church drew her into the world outside her home, where she sought to make a difference in the lives of others.

• A small collection of Miller's papers can be found at the Minnesota Historical Society in St. Paul and in the university archives at Northwestern. Her published works, which amount to some twenty volumes, also include *The Royal Road to Fortune* (1869); a series of stories published by the Kirkwood Library (1877); *Thorn Apples* (1887); *For the Beloved* (1892), a book of poems; *Home Talks about the World* (1894); and *From Avalon* (1896). She is the subject of entries in Frances Willard and Mary Livermore, eds., *A Woman of the Century* (1893), and Frances Willard, *Woman and Temperance* (1883). See also Ruth Bordin, *Woman and Temperance* (1990), pp. 35–36, 54; Arthur Wilde, ed., *A History of Northwestern University*, vol. 2 (1905); and the *Northwestern*, 25 Sept. 1891 and 21 May 1896. An obituary is in the *New York Times*, 5 Nov. 1913.

SARAH VIRGINIA BARNES

MILLER, Emma Guffey (6 July 1874–23 Feb. 1970), Democratic party activist and feminist, was born Mary Emma Guffey in Guffey Station, Pennsylvania, the daughter of John Guffey, a developer of coal, oil, and gas land, and Barbaretta Hough. Her early education was in the Greensburg, Pennsylvania, public schools and at the Alinda Academy in Pittsburgh, where the family lived after 1891. In 1899 she graduated from Bryn Mawr College, whose president, M. Carey Thomas, awakened in her a feminist concern for women's status in public life. Thomas likely influenced Miller to major in history and political science, although the Guffey family's long involvement in Democratic party politics probably evoked an even earlier commitment to public service. After teaching in Pittsburgh and Allegheny, Pennsylvania, for three years, Miller met Carroll Miller, an engineer, on a trip to Japan. They married in 1902 and lived in Osaka for five years because of Carroll Miller's assignment there. They had four sons. For a time, Miller also taught in Japan.

After returning to Pennsylvania in 1907, Emma Miller entered volunteer work for one organization after another in the fields of education, welfare, and politics. She became an ardent suffragist in 1910, was effective in the campaign in Rhode Island while living in Providence, and subsequently promoted the League of Women Voters (LWV) during 1920–1925 while living at the Millers' permanent home near Slippery Rock, Pennsylvania. Before she turned almost exclusively to women's advancement in politics, she was active in the National Consumers' League and the parent-teachers' organization.

Convinced that the LWV's nonpartisan stance was ineffectual in advancing women in politics, Miller enthusiastically devoted her energies to the Democratic party. She attended every national convention from 1924 to 1968, was a member of the platform committee from 1944 to 1964, and served as Pennsylvania national committeewoman from 1932 until her death. At the 1924 convention she became the first woman to receive a courtesy nomination for president. Seconding the nomination of Alfred E. Smith in 1924 and 1928, Miller, an Episcopalian, drew considerable attention in 1924 for her staunch endorsement of the Catholic candidate and for her indictment of the Ku Klux Klan. She concurred with Smith on the repeal of the Prohibition Amendment, which she declared was "a colossal mistake." Because of her forthright stand and service on the advisory board of the Women's Organization for National Prohibition Reform (1929–1933), she joked, "Everybody in Slippery Rock thought I was a drunk" (*Washington Post*, 25 Feb. 1970).

Similarly, Miller was devoted to Franklin D. Roosevelt, whose nomination she seconded in 1932 and

1936. Her influence with the president and her patronage expanded through the offices of her brother, Joseph F. Guffey, an unswerving New Dealer and senator from Pennsylvania from 1935 to 1947, who lived with the Millers at their Washington home. Emma Miller never received a presidential appointment, but Roosevelt in 1933 named Carroll Miller to the Interstate Commerce Commission (ICC), which he later chaired. Under Harry S. Truman, Carroll Miller remained on the ICC until his death in 1949. During these years, Emma Miller maintained two homes, one in Washington and the other at her legal residence in Slippery Rock.

Emma Miller was relentless in her pursuit of Democratic jobs for women under the New Deal, from clerical posts to the most prestigious offices under administrative appointment. She had major encounters with Mary W. "Molly" Dewson, the director of the Women's Division of the Democratic party. During Roosevelt's second term, Miller challenged Dewson's behind-the-scenes operations by advocating more open confrontations with men who dominated party affairs. Miller never succeeded in supplanting Dewson as head of the Women's Division. Dewson and her allies thwarted the attempt of Miller and other members of the National Woman's party (NWP) to have the Equal Rights Amendment (ERA) placed before an Inter-American Peace conference held in Buenos Aires in 1936. At one point Dewson referred to Miller as "Her Nuisance" in correspondence with Eleanor Roosevelt, who sided with Dewson. Miller's insistence that only loyal women Democrats hold offices in New Deal agencies led to a protracted struggle in Pennsylvania and brought her into conflict with Ellen S. Woodward, head of successive work programs for women. Miller's quarrels with Dewson and Woodward, among others, diminished her standing with Eleanor Roosevelt and created a serious breach over passage of the ERA. When Miller attempted to maneuver Eleanor Roosevelt to endorse the ERA in 1944, the first lady responded with a cursory rebuke. Two years later, as head of the United Nations Human Rights Commission, Roosevelt again withstood Miller's request for her support of the ERA.

Miller spent half her life in advocacy of the ERA. "We should have an Equal Rights Amendment because justice should not be based on sex," she wrote in 1944. Active with the NWP for passage of the ERA, Miller served as chairman from 1960 to 1965 and was life president from 1965 until her death. She lobbied President Truman for his acceptance of the ERA, but he declined to make public his support. Miller was disappointed that Democratic candidate Adlai Stevenson was not forthcoming on the amendment in 1956. She was no more successful with John F. Kennedy, and he declined to name her to his President's Commission on the Status of Women. After the 1964 convention she wrote candidate Lyndon B. Johnson of her dismay that the amendment was omitted from the platform. She carried on despite disabilities caused by a partial loss of hearing and crippling arthritis and spoke one last time at the convention in 1968.

In other endeavors, Miller served on the Pennsylvania State Council of Education and the State Welfare Commission. She was chair of the Pennsylvania advisory board of the National Youth Administration (1935–1943). She was a longtime trustee of Slippery Rock State Teachers College (1933–1968) and was chairman of the trustees during 1933–1937. In 1940 she was a member of the Governor's Defense Commission for Pennsylvania and over the years served by appointment on a number of committees commemorating events in her state's history.

Miller died in Grove City, Pennsylvania. She did not live to see the ERA proposed by Congress in 1972, but its supporters credited her long and vibrant espousal of the amendment before Democratic conventions as highly significant in its eventual acceptance. Miller's stamina, intelligence, and indomitable spirit, tempered by her sparkling wit, made her one of the most popular and important figures in the women's rights movement over a period of six decades.

• Miller's papers, including extensive correspondence, are at the Arthur and Elizabeth Schlesinger Library, Radcliffe College. Some material is in the Schlesinger Library Vertical Files and in the Slippery Rock State University archives. Her correspondence is also in the papers of Eleanor Roosevelt and Mary W. Dewson in the Franklin D. Roosevelt Library, the papers of the National Woman's party, the early records of the League of Women Voters, and in the Harry S. Truman Library. Two representative statements by Miller are "Equal Rights: A Debate," *New York Times Magazine*, 7 May 1944, and a lengthy speech printed in the *Congressional Record*, 26 Feb. 1945. An able assessment of her influence is in Leila J. Rupp and Verta Taylor, *Survival in the Doldrums: The American Women's Rights Movement, 1945 to the 1960s* (1987). Numerous references are in Susan Ware, *Beyond Suffrage: Women in the New Deal* (1981). Obituaries are in the *New York Times* and the *Washington Post*, both 25 Feb. 1970. A eulogy appears in the *Congressional Record*, 91st Cong., 2d sess., p. 4718.

MARTHA H. SWAIN

MILLER, Fishbait (20 July 1909–12 Sept. 1989), doorkeeper of the U.S. House of Representatives, was born William Moseley Miller in Pascagoula, Mississippi, the son of Albert Magnus Miller, a sea captain, and Nettie Maddox. Perhaps because his father abandoned the family, Miller actively developed people-pleasing skills at a very young age. During these years he acquired the name of Fishbait due to his small size; he retained it all his life, although at times he weighed as much as 275 pounds.

Working as a soda jerk in Pascagoula, Miller was befriended by the local district attorney, William M. Colmer, who helped him attend Harrison-Stone Junior College (1929–1932). When Colmer was elected to Congress, he brought Miller to Washington, D.C., as a mail carrier at the Capitol, which is a patronage position. Colmer would ultimately rise to chair of the Committee on Rules, and in a system such as the

House bureaucracy, the more powerful the patron, the more the patronage employee can advance.

Miller briefly attended George Washington University (1933) while he worked at his mail carrier's job (1933–1939). In 1937 he married Mabel Breeland; they had one child. He then advanced up through the House bureaucracy, serving as messenger to the doorkeeper (1939–1943), then as assistant to the sergeant at arms (1943–1947), then as Democratic doorkeeper (1947–1948). The doorkeeper is chosen by the majority party in the House. Miller had support from a majority of Democratic members, and when the Democrats gained control of the House in the 1948 elections, Miller was elected doorkeeper (1949–1953). With a Republican majority in the House, he became Democratic doorkeeper (1953–1954). As minority doorkeeper, of course, Miller lost his supervisory authority over the House bureaucracy. As he described his job during those years, it was "to be so helpful and efficient that if ever the Democrats came back in power I would stand a chance of becoming Majority Doorkeeper." He was elected doorkeeper in 1955 when the Democrats returned to power and remained doorkeeper until he was defeated in balloting for the position within the Democratic Caucus in 1974.

Miller's long patronage career was not simply due to Colmer's influence. His colorful and folksy style and his willingness to serve members of Congress brought him friendships with other congressional leaders, such as Sam Rayburn and John W. McCormack. Miller made himself useful to politicians. He possessed an uncanny ability to remember names and was often used by congressmen at receptions and other public events to identify people for them. He went to great lengths to please members of the House. One of them was quoted in the press as saying that Miller "turned obsequiousness into an art form." It was known that Miller was willing to perform almost any task for members, including baby-sitting their children.

Miller's personal style was seen as entertaining by some. Harry S. Truman, for example, thought it funny that Miller greeted then Princess Elizabeth of Great Britain with, "Howdy Ma'am." Later, however, women were known to be offended by Miller's practice of trying to kiss all females in his presence, his habit of referring to women as "honey," and his repeated promises to single women that he would help them find rich husbands.

With the entrance in 1974 of a new group of Democrats in the aftermath of Watergate, Miller's candidacy for doorkeeper was defeated. It was the first time he had been opposed for the position since 1949. Miller was shocked and embittered by his defeat, describing it as a "mighty hard bump." He blamed the defeat on Congressmen James V. Stanton and Morris Udall. Stanton, Miller claimed, thought he was too old and was hostile in spite of Miller's efforts to be of assistance. Miller asserted that Udall had been his friend but showed his lack of faithfulness to friends when he claimed that he could not have Miller's name associated with his since it would hurt his presidential prospects. Actually, there were other reasons for Miller's defeat. He was increasingly viewed as an anachronism whose folksy ways were an embarrassment to sophisticated, reform-minded members.

Miller never had influence over the policy process, but he was seen as a valuable and colorful functionary. His loud, thickly accented announcement of the president's entry into the House chambers for the State of the Union address became a Capitol tradition. He was the subject of considerable publicity and enjoyed the media attention. As doorkeeper, Miller supervised a substantial bureaucracy that was based on congressional patronage. That bureaucracy consisted of a $3.5 million budget and over 350 employees, including assistant doorkeepers who guard the House chamber, messengers, pages, cloakroom attendants, barbers, rest room attendants, telephone operators, and document room and publication service employees.

As an administrator, Miller wrote that he "was engaged full-time in making all the congressmen feel like kings, and some—the leadership—more kingly than others." While dedicated to providing support services to members of Congress, he could switch from being overly polite to dictatorial when he felt he was enforcing House traditions. He insisted, for example, in a widely publicized confrontation, that Congresswoman Bella Abzug remove her hat before she entered the House chamber. In his retirement, he wrote a book with Frances Spatz Leighton, *Fishbait: The Memoirs of the Congressional Doorkeeper* (1977), which largely detailed the drinking, spending, and sexual activities of a substantial number of congressmen. Miller died in Greensboro, North Carolina.

Miller's advancement in the House bureaucracy was due to the dominance of southern Democrats in the House. It was a time when the leadership and committee chairs were so powerful that they were known as "barons." In that era, personal bonds between politicians were important, and loyalty to one's friends was treasured. Objectives were accomplished through personal contacts and mutual favors that had been traded with other senior politicians over many years. To maintain his position during this era, Miller had to please the "barons" and perform personal favors for them. They, in exchange, would support him as doorkeeper. Miller's problem, however, was that his career went beyond that era. By 1974 the remaining "barons" were threatened by post-Watergate reformers. Fewer rural southern Democrats were in control, and the values were different. Miller was shocked because he thought Congressman Udall was his friend, and Udall refused to support him for the doorkeeper's job. Miller could not understand a new-era politician like Udall, who did not cultivate long-standing friendships and would not reciprocate favors or show personal loyalty. Ultimately, Miller lost his position because the era of the "barons" in the House was at an end, and he could not adapt to changed customs and power relationships.

• Although much of Miller's book is a treatment of congressional improprieties, a significant amount of biographical material is interspersed throughout. Obituaries are in the *New York Times* and the *Washington Post*, 15 Sept. 1989.

ANTHONY CHAMPAGNE

MILLER, Freddie (3 Apr. 1911–8 May 1962), featherweight boxer, was born Friedrich Mueller in Cincinnati, Ohio, the son of German immigrants Wilhelm Mueller, a baker, and Elisabeth Ponnenmacher. He became a professional boxer at the age of sixteen and fought under the anglicized version of his name. By 1929 he had 60 bouts to his credit and was fighting in main events. Managed by Danny Davis and fighting mostly in Cincinnati and nearby cities, he then won a series of victories over featherweight contenders, including Tommy Paul, Roger Bernard, Eddie Shea, Cecil Payne, and Johnny Farr; Miller lost only to Farr and boxed a draw with former bantamweight champion Bushy Graham.

On 23 July 1931 Miller met champion Christopher "Battling" Battalino for the world featherweight title in Cincinnati. Staggered by Battalino's first punch, Miller was knocked down in the eighth and tenth rounds, and he suffered a decisive beating. However, he so favorably impressed Pete Reilly, Battalino's manager, that Reilly afterward acquired Miller's contract and became his manager. Knowing that Battalino had grown too heavy to make the featherweight limit of 126 pounds without being weakened, Reilly arranged a championship rematch between Miller and Battalino in order to keep the title in "the family." Because Battalino was unable to make the weight, the two men instead fought a non-title bout on 27 January 1932 in Cincinnati. During the third round Battalino went down without adequate cause, apparently in an attempt to get Miller recognized as his successor. However, the referee ruled the fight a "no contest," the National Boxing Association stripped Battalino of the featherweight title, and the title then became vacant. Miller's involvement in these shenanigans, perhaps inadvertent, marked the only occasion in his boxing career in which he was associated with dishonest dealings.

On 13 January 1933 Miller defeated Tommy Paul in Chicago to win recognition from the National Boxing Association as featherweight champion. He defended his title successfully in February against Baby Arizmendi and in March against Speedy Dado, both fights occurring in Los Angeles. On 1 January 1934 he made a third successful defense against Jackie Sharkey in Cincinnati. Very active in non-title fights during this period, he defeated future featherweight champions Petey Sarron and Chalky Wright, among others. However, European boxing agencies did not recognize Miller as world featherweight champion until 20 September 1934, when he decisively defeated Nel Tarleton in 15 rounds in Liverpool, England.

The 5′5″, left-handed Miller was clever and extraordinarily nimble afoot. Possessing a wide array of punches, he landed them often and with pinpoint accuracy. To confuse his opponents he would often shift from a left-handed to a right-handed stance and then back again. He usually won on points but was a sufficiently punishing hitter to score several important knockouts, including a one-round knockout of José Girones in defense of his title in Barcelona, Spain, on 17 February 1935. Clever enough to avoid heavy punishment in most of his fights, he was able to withstand heavy blows when hit and was not knocked out until his last fight.

After defeating Tarleton, Miller remained in Europe and fought there with great success, one of his victims being the world bantamweight champion, Panama Al Brown. On 12 June 1935 he successfully defended his title against Tarleton. Soon afterward he returned to the United States, where he made three successful defenses against Vernon Cormier in Boston, Johnny Pena in Seattle, and Petey Sarron in Coral Gables, Florida. Finally, in a rematch with Sarron in Washington, D.C., on 11 May 1936, Miller lost his title in a very close fight.

Later in 1936 Miller fought four times in South Africa, winning all of his matches. He returned to the United States for several fights, then went again to South Africa and lost another close featherweight title fight to Sarron on 4 September 1937 in Johannesburg. In 1938 he boxed in Great Britain and Europe, winning all but one of his fights there. In 1939 he boxed in Venezuela, where he won twice, and he lost twice to Simon Chavez. By this time Miller was losing more frequently, and he retired after a career that involved travel to ten countries and included 246 fights, of which only 27 were defeats.

Miller was dapper and rather handsome, although his facial appearance was somewhat marred by the effects of his long career. He had married Louise Somhorst in 1931, and they had one daughter. Having looked on boxing as a business, he had saved his earnings and lived comfortably in Cincinnati with his family after leaving the ring. He was a good dancer and golfer, and after his retirement he sometimes trained boxers and coached softball. He also engaged in a variety of occupations, including selling insurance, working in an aircraft plant during World War II, and during his last eight years serving as a field engineer for the Hamilton County government. He died in Cincinnati after a heart attack.

Miller was one of the first left-handed fighters to hold a world title, thereby overcoming an ancient prejudice against left-handers in boxing. Fighting in a weight division that was unprestigious in the United States, he traveled abroad and successfully met foreign challengers on their home grounds. He was perhaps the best fighter in the three lighter weight divisions during the 1930s.

• Miller's complete record appears in Herbert G. Goldman, ed., *The Ring Record Book and Boxing Encyclopedia*, 1986–1987 ed. (1987). A useful article about his early career, "World Featherweight Bout: How Freddie Miller Became the Outstanding Challenger," is in the British publication

Boxing, 12 Sept. 1934, p. 20. His activity in South Africa is described in Chris Greyvenstein, *The Fighters* (1981). His major fights were covered in various issues of the *Ring* magazine, and the series of reports from southern Ohio in that magazine, by J. Jimmie Amann, contain many comments on his activities after he retired from the ring. Obituaries appear in the *New York Times*, the *Cincinnati Enquirer*, and the *Cincinnati Post & Times-Star*, all 9 May 1962.

LUCKETT V. DAVIS

MILLER, Frieda Segelke (16 Apr. 1890–21 July 1973), labor official and feminist, was born in La Crosse, Wisconsin, the daughter of James Gordon Miller, a lawyer, and Erna Segelke. Her mother died when Miller was five, at which time she was sent to live with her maternal grandparents. When she was thirteen her grandfather was lost in a boating accident and her father died soon thereafter. She was subsequently raised by her grandmother and an aunt.

In 1911 Miller graduated with a B.A. from Milwaukee-Downer College. She spent the next four years doing graduate research work in economics, political science, law, and sociology as a fellow at the University of Chicago. In 1916 she began working as a research assistant at Bryn Mawr College in Pennsylvania, where she taught social economics. By 1918 she had become the secretary of the Philadelphia Women's Trade Union League (WTUL), a position she held until 1923. While in that post, Miller participated in the creation of the Trade Union College, serving as its secretary and teaching several classes in economics. She was also involved in the founding of the Worker's Education Bureau of America.

Miller explained in *Current Biography* (Feb. 1945) that her entrance into the realm of labor activities came through the "intellectual back door": "I began as a highbrow," she stated, but "if you're interested in labor problems, you find more interesting material if you go out into the world where those problems exist rather than pondering them behind the protection of a charming campus." In the spring of 1923 Miller left the "charming campus" behind and traveled to Vienna, Austria, as a delegate to the International Conference of Working Women. She was accompanied by Pauline Newman, her lifelong companion who was also an organizer for the WTUL. Miller stayed an entire year in Europe, studying labor conditions in Austria, England, and Germany. She returned to the United States in 1924, bringing with her a baby she had adopted while in Germany. She settled with Newman in New York City, working for the next two years for the Joint Board of Sanitary Control as an inspector in the women's garment industry. In 1926 she became a researcher for the New York City Committee of State Charities Aid and then served as a research investigator for the Welfare Council from 1927 to 1929.

Miller's entire career was devoted to the improvement of labor conditions and standards, especially for women. As director of the Division of Women in Industry of the New York State Department of Labor from 1929 to 1938, she spearheaded the development of the state's first minimum wage law for women during the early 1930s. Miller continued in this capacity until 1938, at which time New York governor Herbert H. Lehman appointed her the state's second female labor commissioner, succeeding Frances Perkins, who had gone to Washington, D.C., to become the U.S. secretary of labor. As labor commissioner, Miller transformed the state employment agency into a reliable mechanism for matching the right worker with the right job. She did so in part by creating a series of special services for various individualized occupational groups, such as domestics, seamstresses, nurses, and office workers.

Miller's efforts in New York soon gained her recognition on a much wider stage. By 1940 she had become an internationally known expert in the field of labor law administration. In that year she was named president of the International Association of Government Labor Officials. She resigned from her post as labor commissioner in December 1942 as a result of a dispute with incoming governor Thomas E. Dewey involving the administration of worker's compensation. She became special assistant on labor to U.S. ambassador John G. Winant in London in 1943. Upon her return to the United States in the spring of 1944, Miller played a significant role in a conference of the International Labor Organization (ILO), a world organization working for the improvement of labor conditions for which she served as an adviser from 1936 to 1952. At that 1944 meeting she endorsed the controversial principle of equal opportunity and equal pay for male and female workers.

In August 1944 Miller went to Washington, D.C., to serve as director of the Women's Bureau of the U.S. Department of Labor, replacing the original director, Mary Anderson. In 1945 Miller created the Labor Advisory Committee, which invited trade union women to come to the bureau for the first time. During her tenure she communicated with women's leaders from all over the world as part of the agency's Exchange of Persons Program, sharing with them studies on the status of women in the United States and comparing the plight of women in other nations.

Although Miller was an unabashed advocate of women's rights, she quietly led a fight in opposition to a proposed equal-rights amendment while at the Women's Bureau. She explained that such an amendment, while sounding like a good idea, would actually "take away from women hard-earned industrial gains which have led to a better standard of living." She believed that "no amendment can give women consideration at the hands of the employers who hold the jobs in this country. It is a matter of prejudice and I have fought that prejudice."

Miller resigned as director of the Women's Bureau in 1953 but remained active in the ILO, traveling to South America and the Far East in 1955–1956 to study the changing economic status of female laborers. In the 1960s she served as a representative at the United Nations for the International Union for Child Welfare.

Throughout her career, Miller persisted in seeking improvements not only in the economic conditions of labor but the social conditions as well. She was able to champion the cause of women in the workplace without ever failing to comprehend matters from the perspective of management. Secretary of Labor Perkins praised Miller as a practical administrator who understood the problems facing both employers and employees. Miller died in New York City.

• Miller's papers, including her private letters, diaries, public papers, and published articles, are at the Schlesinger Library, Radcliffe College. The records of the Women's Bureau, which include Miller's reports and publications, are in the National Archives in Washington, D.C. For biographical profiles see *Independent Woman*, July 1943, p. 201, and Sept. 1944, p. 296; Josephine Nelson, "Frieda Miller, the Only Woman Industrial Commissioner in the U.S., Voices Hope," *Christian Science Monitor*, 22 Nov. 1940; and the *New York Times*, 30 July 1938 and 28 Aug. 1938. Obituaries are in the *New York Times*, 22 July 1973 and *Time*, 6 Aug. 1973.

FRANCESCO L. NEPA

MILLER, George (16 Feb. 1774–5 Apr. 1816), preacher, was born in Pottstown, Pennsylvania, the son of Jacob Miller, a miller and millwright, and Elizabeth (maiden name unknown). His parents were German Lutherans. Soon after George's birth, the family moved to Alsace Township, Berks County. Jacob Miller died when George was eleven. Within months, the boy suffered a serious illness, probably rheumatic fever, that confined him for nearly two years. Though his education was limited, he received a Bible while a teenager and read it through in eighteen months, which especially pleased his mother. In his sixteenth year he attended catechetical instructions at Trinity Lutheran Church in Reading, Pennsylvania, where he was confirmed in 1789, though he lacked a sense of salvation at the time. For a time he desired a "change of heart," but his growing disinclination toward any vital experience of religion soon suppressed any continued awakenings of his conscience.

At age nineteen Miller went to live with his brother John Miller and soon became a master millwright. In 1798 he purchased land and built a gristmill in Brunswick Township, Schuylkill County. Two years later he married Magdalena Brobst.

Miller began again to read the Bible and to discourse with some people who were persecuted for their "experiential" religion. Through the preaching of Jacob Albright, Methodist exhorter, he came to realize that true religion required more than virtuous conduct and that religious conversion entailed a renewal of heart. Although resolute and penitent for some three years, Miller felt no assurance of acceptance by God.

In 1800 Albright began to organize his German converts into small groups, or classes, that would become known for a while as "Albright's People." On 3 June 1802, shortly after Albright preached in the Miller home, Miller felt an assurance of salvation by faith while at work in his mill. As he said later in his autobiography, "A stream of his love flowed into my soul, and I was certain that God was surely my friend and I his accepted child." Many evangelical groups in Albright's circle subsequently adopted Miller's phrasing, "God is my friend," to show a conscious link to divine favor.

Though at first he was too timid to claim his experience in public, Miller vowed to serve God entirely. His brother Solomon Miller and Solomon's wife (Magdalena's sister) soon were converted under the preaching of Albright and John Walter. Albright appointed George Miller as a class leader, although Miller's own wife did not fully accept his new religious stance. Neither did the many people who began persecuting Miller. Neighbors tried to ruin his mill, customers left their bills unpaid, and creditors pressed for payment. His father-in-law also actively opposed Miller's new profession of faith and its consequences.

In 1803 Miller attended and served as secretary of a small council that decided to ordain Albright as an elder, a move suggesting that Albright's People were becoming a distinct denomination. After selling his land and setting up a new mill in Albany, Miller resolved "to forsake all for Jesus and the Gospel." He rented his house and in April 1805 became an itinerant preacher under Albright and Walter in Lancaster, Dauphin, and Berks counties. He began revivals in several places, including Jonestown and the Northumberland circuit, and set up new class meetings in many homes, such as that of Michael Becker in Mühlbach.

For four years Miller was a circuit-riding preacher through nineteen counties in eastern Pennsylvania. In May 1806 Albright named him as one of three itinerant preachers in full connection with Albright and Walter. In November 1807 the first regular "annual conference" was held at Becker's home. Albright was elected a bishop, and Miller was elected an elder (the first after Albright) of the 200-member group that now called itself the "Newly Formed Methodist Conference," indicative of Albright's Methodist background and inclinations. Albright was asked to put together a book of discipline for the organization, but he died in May 1808 before completing the task.

Later in 1808 some friends asked Miller to assume work on the discipline. On Christmas, after a portentous dream, Miller awakened with chest pains, became more ill as the day progressed, and finally decided to go home. He never fully regained his health, and he never again traveled extensively in the connection but "located" instead on his farm. Under these circumstances, he completed the book of discipline, *Glaubenslehre und allgemeine Regeln christlicher Kirchen-Zucht und Ordnung der sogenannten Albrechts-Leute*, which the conference published in 1809. He based this work largely on material translated by Ignatius Roemer from *The Doctrines and Discipline of the Methodist Episcopal Church* (1792; rev. ed., 1808). Miller's book included rules of organization, articles of religion, and selections from the writings of John Wesley and John Fletcher.

Miller chaired several successive annual conferences of the leaders of Albright's People from 1809 (meeting in his home) to 1813. Three years after election as an elder, he was ordained at the 1810 session. That conference also adopted a set of procedures and rules, which Miller had compiled to facilitate the business of the conference. The 1812 conference asked Miller to draw up an episcopal plan of government for the group, which numbered nearly a thousand members. During that period he also wrote and published the first biography of Albright and a devotional book, *Thätiges Christenthum* (1814), which was published in English as *Practical Christianity* in 1871.

Miller spent the last four years of his life on a new farm in Dry Valley, Union County. He preached locally as much as possible but suffered prolonged bouts of illness, which kept him from the annual conference in 1815. In July of that year he began writing his autobiography, which he finished in four months. Early in 1816 he was confined to bed, where he remained for the last three months of his life, with chest pains then thought to be consumption but now thought to be heart disease resulting from his childhood rheumatic fever. He died in New Berlin, Pennsylvania.

In the year of Miller's death, Albright's people called a general conference, at which they renamed their new denomination the Evangelical Association. Miller must be counted as one of the pillars of the group. In 1946 it became a part of the Evangelical United Brethren church, which merged in 1968 with the Methodist church to form the United Methodist church. With only a meager education, Miller was the first author in the original Evangelical fellowship. His writing has been described as "severely plain" but "truly practical." He was a powerful preacher, who, it was said, could "shine and thunder," and his preaching emphasized sanctification (the possibility of the believer being sanctified, or made holy, by the work of the Holy Spirit). He was one of the denomination's primary organizers, its most effective evangelist after Albright, and having lived what he preached, one of its best-remembered saints.

• Miller's autobiography, first published in *Leben, erfahrung und amtsfuhrung zweyer evangelischer prediger, Jacob Albrecht und George Miller* (1834), was translated in Reuben Yeakel, ed., *Jacob Albright and his Co-Laborers* (1883). Miller's brief biography of Albright, *Kurze Beschriebung der workenden Gnade Gottes bey dem erleuchteten evangelischen Prediger Jacob Albrecht* (1811), was translated by George E. Epp, *Jacob Albright, the First Biography of the Founder of the Evangelical Association* (1959). Major attention is given to Miller in Yeakel, *History of the Evangelical Association*, vol. 1 (1894), and J. Bruce Behney and Paul H. Eller, *The History of the Evangelical United Brethren Church* (1979).

RICHARD P. HEITZENRATER

MILLER, George Abram (31 July 1863–10 Feb. 1951), mathematician, was born on a farm near Lynville, Pennsylvania, the son of Nathan Miller and Mary Sittler. Miller began teaching in the public schools at the age of seventeen to earn money for college. He spent the year 1882–1883 at Franklin and Marshall Academy, a subdivision of the College at Lancaster. He then attended Muhlenburg College in Allentown, Pennsylvania, where he received a bachelor of arts degree with honorable mention in 1887 and a master of arts degree in 1890. During the year 1887–1888 Miller served as principal of schools in Greeley, Kansas, and from 1888 to 1893 was professor of mathematics at Eureka College in Eureka, Illinois.

In 1890, when many American institutions taught little beyond calculus, Miller offered advanced mathematics courses and the doctoral degree at Eureka. He gave instruction, for example, in higher algebra, probability, determinants, and number theory. Unsatisfied with the available textbooks, Miller wrote his own, which appeared in 1892 under the title *Determinants*. He received his Ph.D. from Cumberland University in Lebanon, Tennessee, in 1892; at that time, courses could be taken by correspondence and examinations substituted for a thesis. Miller spent the years from 1893 to 1895 as an instructor in mathematics at the University of Michigan. While there, he lived in the home of Frank Nelson Cole, a professor of mathematics and prominent figure in the development of group theory. This experience set the course of Miller's research for the rest of his career.

Like many promising mathematicians of the time, Miller traveled to Europe for further study. During his mathematical sojourn from 1895 to 1897, he attended lectures by the world's two leading group theorists, Sophus Lie in Leipzig and Camille Jordan in Paris.

On returning to the United States, Miller served as assistant professor at Cornell University from 1897 to 1901 and assistant and associate professor at Stanford University from 1901 to 1906. He then began his 41-year affiliation with the University of Illinois in Urbana-Champaign. From 1906 to 1931 he passed through the ranks of associate professor and professor, after which he continued his research and writing as professor emeritus until 1947, when his inability to hold a pen curtailed his scholarly pursuits. He married Cassandra Boggs in 1909; they had no children.

Miller studied substitution groups, an important area of research at the turn of the twentieth century, and began publishing his work in 1894. His early papers concerned the determination of certain types of finite groups. These works corrected and completed the work begun in 1872 by Camille Jordan and extended by Arthur Cayley and Frank Nelson Cole. In 1894 Miller also enumerated the groups of degree ten. This result earned him the prize offered by the Cracow (Poland) Academy of Sciences, the first prize in pure mathematics given to an American by a foreign academy. Miller continued to investigate finite groups throughout his long career.

In addition to his interest in group theory, Miller also pursued the history of mathematics, which he taught at Eureka, Cornell, Stanford, and the University of Illinois. He studied this aspect of mathematics longer than he studied groups. His *Historical Introduction to Mathematical Literature* (1916) grew out of his lectures at Illinois and his belief that students of mathematics needed both a comprehensive and a detailed view of the subject. As a result of his involvement in group theory, Miller's best historical works were about this field. His historical writings outside the theory of groups often depended on secondary sources and reflected an attitude overly concerned with pointing out error in published accounts. As the culmination of his work in the history of finite group theory, Miller wrote three comprehensive articles on the time periods covered in the first three volumes of his *Collected Works*.

Miller was elected to the New York (later American) Mathematical Society in 1891, the American Academy of Arts and Sciences in 1919, and the National Academy of Sciences in 1921. He helped organize the San Francisco Section of the American Mathematical Society in 1902 and the Mathematical Association of America in 1915. He was also a member of the London Mathematical Society and the Deutsche Mathematiker-Vereinigung, a corresponding member of the Real Sociedad Matematica Española, and an honorary life member of the Indian Mathematical Society.

The University of Illinois began to publish Miller's collected works in 1934 in recognition of his contributions both to mathematics and to the university. By the time the last volume appeared in 1959, the five volumes contained more than 800 articles, with about 400 devoted to finite group theory. Miller also left a financial legacy. "Everything I have," he once commented to his lawyer, "I received from the university, and I want to repay my obligation." Having carefully invested his retirement pay, he left the University of Illinois nearly a million dollars on his death. He had never mentioned these intentions to his friends and colleagues, and astounded those who knew him well when his bequest was made public after his death in Urbana, Illinois.

Perhaps his contemporaries offered the best assessment of his career. In 1903, nine years after he began his mathematical research, ten leading American mathematicians rated Miller tenth in their ranking of the top eighty American men and women mathematicians for James McKeen Cattell's *American Men of Science*. His steady contributions to the theory of finite groups prompted distinguished Harvard mathematician George David Birkhoff to describe Miller in 1938 as "perhaps the outstanding authority on special finite groups" (Birkhoff, p. 290).

• Miller's papers are at the University of Illinois, Urbana-Champaign. His writings are gathered in *The Collected Works of George Abram Miller*, ed. H. R. Brahana et al. (5 vols., 1935–1959). In addition to the books already mentioned, Miller wrote *Theory and Application of Finite Groups* (1916), with H. F. Blichfeldt and L. E. Dickson. He also authored "Substitution and Abstract Groups" and "The Algebraic Equation" in *Monographs on Topics of Modern Mathematics Relevant to the Elementary Field*, ed. J. W. A. Young (1911). On his life and work, see Raymond C. Archibald's biographical sketch in *Scripta Mathematica* (1935): 353–54; G. Waldo Dunnington, "G. A. Miller as Mathematician and Man: Some Salient Facts," *National Mathematical Magazine*, May 1938, and H. R. Brahana, "George Abram Miller, 1863–1951," *Bulletin of the American Mathematical Society* 57 (1951): 377–82. Brahana, "George Abram Miller," National Academy of Sciences, *Biographical Memoirs* 30 (1957): 257–312, contains a portrait of Miller as an older man and a complete bibliography. For a view of Miller's work set within the broader mathematical context, consult E. T. Bell, "Fifty Years of Algebra in America, 1888–1938," and G. D. Birkhoff, "Fifty Years of American Mathematics," in *Semicentennial Addresses of the American Mathematical Society 1888–1938*, ed. Raymond C. Archibald (1938), pp. 1–34 and 270–315, respectively. Miller's million-dollar bequest prompted "Old Prof," *Newsweek*, 5 Mar. 1951; B. Fay, "Miller's Million," *Collier's*, 21 July 1951; and "Papa Pays Off," *Time*, 7 Dec. 1953.

DELLA DUMBAUGH FENSTER

MILLER, George Augustus, Jr. (24 Sept. 1894–15 Mar. 1983), armorer, was born in St. Augustine, Florida, the son of George Augustus Miller, Sr., a railroad executive, and Minnie Leonora Wilson. In 1911 he received a diploma scientific from Tennessee Military Institute. He studied chemistry at Georgia Institute of Technology from 1911 to 1914 and was awarded a B.Sc. in metallurgy from the Alabama Polytechnic Institute (API) in 1916. That same year he married Lillian Odell Alvis of Auburn; they had no children. After graduation Miller worked for Riverside Metals in Irvington, New York, manufacturing munitions for the Russian imperial government. In late 1916 he moved to Remington Arms–Union Metallic Cartridge Company in Bridgeport, Connecticut, and from there in 1917 to the Frankford Arsenal in Philadelphia, Pennsylvania. In these positions Miller honed his chemistry and metallurgy skills in armaments manufacturing, bullet design, and industrial photography, and by 1919 he had developed an advanced system to photograph bullets in flight.

Miller left Frankford in 1922 to establish a private agricultural laboratory in Florida, but the Great Depression sent him back to the arsenal in 1934. When gathering war clouds in Europe and Asia threatened America's supplies of tungsten, Miller joined the search for an alternative superhard metal for bullet cores; by 1940, in concert with the commercial steel industry, he had developed manganese molybdenum steel to replace tungsten chromium type WD-74100. Tungsten was produced in electric furnaces, but manganese molybdenum steel could be produced in open-hearth furnaces, the predominant furnaces in the United States. The substitute steel not only cost half as much as tungsten but was easier to grind; bullet cores consequently cost half as much to make. The steel was adopted for small caliber bullets and artillery projectiles by the United States and, through lend-lease, by the British and Russians.

Miller used his metallurgical research as the basis for a thesis that he submitted to API (now Auburn University), "The Physical Properties of a Series of Heat-Treated Silico Manganese Molybdenum Steels as Influenced by Slight Differences in Carbon Content," and in 1936 was awarded a chemical engineering degree for his work.

World War II's aerial warfare increased the need for tracers to reveal the path of fire; armor-piercing rounds to break engine blocks and sever important metal parts (whereas conventional bullets might well pass through an airplane without putting it out of service); and incendiary bullets to set the target (especially fuel tanks) afire. Miller worked on red trace for .30 and .50 caliber bullets, led the development of an inexpensive, easy-to-manufacture armor-piercing bullet core, and designed an effective incendiary.

During 1941–1942, Remington Arms and Frankford Arsenal competed for the government contract to develop and manufacture a .50 caliber incendiary. Frankford's round, designed by Miller, equaled the Remington incendiary in effectiveness but was easier and cheaper to manufacture because the Remington round required special powders and machines while the Miller bullet used stock charges and machinery. Miller's bullet consequently became the standard for Allied gunners in World War II. The bullet got good reviews. General Henry H. "Hap" Arnold wrote to Frankford Arsenal in August 1942, "Extremely favorable results with the caliber .50 incendiary ammunition you make are reported by army flyers," and a year later he wrote, "The outstanding small arms development for use against airplanes was the incendiary caliber .50 cartridge." In 1945 Miller received the Legion of Merit for his work with manganese molybdenum steel and the incendiary bullet. A patent for the .50 caliber incendiary bullet in the name of Miller, its design engineer, was issued on 5 December 1950.

Miller entered the army as a lieutenant colonel in July 1942 and was promoted to colonel in June 1945. During the war he commanded the Small Arms Ammunition Department at Frankford Arsenal and helped private manufacturers make the transition from automobiles and other products to bullets. At war's end he turned his talents to directing the construction and equipping of arsenals for U.S. allies around the world. Frankford became a training ground for the military men who took American industrial munitions technology to Iran, Japan, Korea, Spain, Syria, Taiwan, Thailand, Turkey, and Vietnam.

Before World War II most large-caliber cartridge cases had been made of brass, but shortages of copper had forced the Allies to develop the technology for manufacturing steel cartridge cases. After the war, the technology was shared among NATO allies. In 1951 Miller chaired the NATO Steel Cartridge Case Committee that prepared standards for steel cartridge case manufacturing in NATO countries.

Miller retired to Florida in the summer of 1961, sixteen years before the Frankford Arsenal itself was decommissioned. He died in Weirsdale, Florida. An accomplished armorer and design engineer, Miller deserves recognition for his contributions to arming the Allied forces in World War II.

• Miller's papers and his professional thesis are in the Ralph Brown Draughon Library, Auburn University. His papers include carbon copies of his correspondence for fifty years, manuals and reports that he prepared to guide his management of facilities at Frankford, detailed logs of his many trips abroad, and some 5,000 35 mm slides, from work assignments and personal tours at home and abroad. The photographic collection comprises an estimated 25,000 personal and professional photographs. Also on deposit are artifacts such as the impressive display of bullet manufacture awarded to Miller by the Chinese arsenal in Taiwan. A short biography of Miller is David O. Whitten, "An American Armorer: George Augustus Miller, Jr., 1894–1983," *Essays in Economic and Business History* 9 (1991): 1–11.

DAVID O. WHITTEN

MILLER, Gerrit Smith, Jr. (6 Dec. 1869–24 Feb. 1956), mammalogist, was born in Peterboro, New York, the son of Gerrit Smith Miller, cattle breeder, and Susan Dixwell. The elder Miller, the grandson of noted abolitionist Gerrit Smith, is credited with inventing the American game of football and organizing the first American team, the Oneida Club, in Boston in 1862. Miller's maternal aunt Fanny Dixwell was the wife of Oliver Wendell Holmes, Jr., associate justice of the U.S. Supreme Court, with whom young Miller would later develop a close friendship. Educated in private schools and by tutors, Miller did not enter Harvard until 1890, when he was twenty-one. A competent musician, he also had an interest in art, but he sought academic training in zoology.

Graduating with a B.A. in 1894, Miller immediately went to work for the U.S. Biological Survey in Washington, D.C. During the next four years he completed several important taxonomic studies in the Survey's *North American Fauna* series, including "The Long-Tailed Shrews of the Eastern United States" (No. 10 [1895]); "The Genera and Subgenera of Voles and Lemmings" (No. 12 [1896]); and "Revision of the North American Bats of the Family Vespertilionidae" (No. 13 [1897]).

Becoming somewhat restive under the supervision of survey chief C. Hart Merriam, Miller resigned his post in 1898 and began an association with the U.S. National Museum of the Smithsonian Institution (now the National Museum of Natural History) that would last more than four decades. He served as assistant curator of mammals from 1898 to 1909, and as curator of mammals from 1909 to his retirement in 1940. For part of this period, he also served as acting head curator of the museum. He remained with the Smithsonian Institution as an associate in biology from 1940 until his death.

Miller's contributions to mammalogy were many and varied, although he also spent some time during his career working on amphibians, reptiles, birds, and plants. He published occasional papers on plant subjects until 1912. His "Brief Directions for Preparing Study Specimens of Small Mammals," one of the earliest guides for neophyte collectors, first published privately in 1894 and then by the National Museum in 1899, underwent six revisions, the last in 1932. During his earlier years Miller devoted considerable attention to mammalian systematics and distribution. His *Preliminary List of New York Mammals* (1899), included a discussion of the state's zoogeography and its effects on the distribution of the state's mammals, together with some mention of fossil species. His *Key to the Land Mammals of Northeastern North America* (1900) provided wider coverage, still in the context of zoogeographic zonation. In his *Systematic Results of the Study of North American Land Mammals to the Close of the Year 1900*, with James A. G. Rehn (1901), Miller chiefly summarized events of the nineteenth century, and pointed out that the number of known species had risen from 363 to 1,450 in the fifteen years since 1885. This was attributed to better methods of specimen collection and to the fact that the National Museum and other repositories had rapidly been amassing more substantial numbers of specimens for taxonomic analysis. Miller returned to his interest in bats with the publication of his *The Families and Genera of Bats* (1907), a work that, supplemented by later research, remained standard for many years.

Miller's *Catalog of the Land Mammals of Western Europe* (1912), now considered a classic work, was probably his most outstanding contribution to mammalogy. It was based on his examination of some 12,000 specimens found in the collections of the British Museum (Natural History) in London, the U.S. National Museum, and Miller's own collections. Miller began giving his full attention to this project in 1905, and his independent means enabled him to take leave from his post in Washington for much of the period from 1908 to 1911, most of it spent making comparative studies in European museums. Miller's influence on European mammalogy was greater than this one publication would suggest; while abroad he also introduced American methods of mammal study, including collection of substantial series of specimens of each species for purposes of comparison, systematic trapping, and study skin preparation. His own collections of North American and European mammals were later purchased by the British Museum (Natural History).

In 1912 Miller produced the first of three checklists of mammals represented in the collections of the U.S. National Museum. This *List of North American Land Mammals in the United States National Museum* was revised in 1923 and again in 1954, the latter with the assistance of Remington Kellogg. Beginning in the 1920s Miller took a number of collecting trips to Haiti, the Dominican Republic, Puerto Rico, Jamaica, Panama, and several other West Indian islands, studying the small mammals of the Caribbean region. One objective of this effort, which entailed careful investigation of pre-Columbian kitchen middens on the island of Hispaniola, was to demonstrate that *Solenodon*, a foot-long shrew-like mammal, had been used as food by Carib chiefs who retreated to caves there following the Spanish conquest. Miller was at home in several languages, and in 1921 he translated Herlauf Winge's *A Review of the Interrelationships of the Cetacea* from the Danish original. In later years Miller's interest in mammals became increasingly varied, and he published papers on peccaries, wolves, dolphins, bears, and primates, among others. The 400 titles in Miller's bibliography also included papers on paleontological, anthropological, and musical subjects.

Miller was a shy and reserved person who was rarely seen by the public and who once had to be escorted from a hall when he attempted without success to deliver a scientific paper. He was a fellow of the American Association for the Advancement of Sciences, the American Philosophical Society, and the Academy of Natural Sciences of Philadelphia. A charter member (1919) of the American Society of Mammalogists and a member of its first council (later board of directors), he was elected an honorary member in 1941. Miller had married in 1897 Elizabeth Eleanor Page, a widow with three children. She died in 1920. In 1921 Miller married Anne Chapin Gates. He had no children from either marriage. Largely inactive during the last ten years of his life, he died in Washington, D.C.

• Some of Miller's personal papers and manuscripts are in the archives of the Smithsonian Institution. A biographical sketch by H. H. Shamel et al., "Gerrit Smith Miller, Jr." *Journal of Mammalogy* (Aug. 1954), includes Miller's complete bibliography. See also Elmer C. Birney and Jerry R. Choate, eds., *Seventy-Five Years of Mammalogy (1919–1994)* (1994); and Keir B. Sterling et al., eds., *Biographical Dictionary of American and Canadian Naturalists and Environmentalists* (1997). An obituary is in the *New York Times*, 26 Feb. 1956.

KEIR B. STERLING

MILLER, Gilbert Heron (3 July 1884–2 Jan. 1969), theatrical producer and director, was born in New York City, the son of Henry Miller, a leading actor-manager, and Helene Stoepel, an actress who used the stage name Bijou Heron (she was the daughter of Matilda Heron, acclaimed for her translation and portrayal of *Camille*). Miller was educated privately in New York City until the age of twelve; then his mother took him to Europe, where he was educated at schools in Paris, Dresden, and Spain. A cosmopolitan from childhood, he was fluent in French, German, Spanish, and Italian and able to communicate in Hungarian. Returning home to New York, he worked briefly at several jobs, then joined the U.S. Marine Corps and spent two years (1904–1906) in Haiti. Next, following in his father's footsteps, he tried acting in a London production, *Julie Bon-Bon* (1906), and some other small parts in the United States, without success.

Though relations were never easy between Miller and his temperamental star father, Henry Miller made him company manager for a touring production of his hit play *The Great Divide* in 1907. Miller became manager for all his father's productions from 1910 through 1915. During this time he married Jessie Glendenning at a date unspecified in biographical sources. They had one child before the marriage ended in divorce. An early sign of his eye for talent came in 1912, when he hired young actress Ruth Chatterton for a key role in *The Rainbow*, though his father had wanted another, better-known actress. Chatterton proved very successful in the role. In 1916, anxious to be on his own, he asked producer Al Woods to put him in charge of his *Daddy Long-Legs* production in London. Woods did so, despite the violent objections of his New York coproducer, Henry Miller. Gilbert Miller had the satisfaction of seeing the play succeed in London.

Except for service in Paris as a lieutenant in U.S. Army intelligence during World War I, Miller remained in London and produced a number of plays there from 1916 through 1922. One of his London productions, a musical version of *Monsieur Beaucaire*, moved to Broadway in 1919. He developed friendships and business relations with important British theater figures, including actor-manager Sir Charles Hawtrey. At unspecified dates during this period, he married and divorced Margaret Allen.

Miller returned to New York City in 1921 as producing director of Charles Frohman Inc., whose founder had perished on the *Lusitania* in 1915. Miller followed the example of Frohman in being a true internationalist, producing plays, importing productions, and controlling theaters both on Broadway and in the West End. However, whereas Frohman had feared and resisted moving pictures as a threat to the stage, Frohman's successor at the production company had sold it to a motion picture corporation, Paramount–Famous Players–Lasky. Therefore, Miller found himself the head of an organization that invested quietly in plays that might become valuable film properties, both for the profits and prestige of the Broadway run, and for the sake of being able to obtain movie rights to a hit for less than top dollar.

Miller worked for Charles Frohman Inc. through the 1920s as a producer for the stage and became one of the most eminent theater figures on both sides of the Atlantic as his successes mounted. He introduced numerous British actors and playwrights to New York, and New York successes to London. He also brought in plays from the theaters of France, Germany, Austria, and Hungary. At times he made successes of foreign plays no one else believed had a chance to succeed. During the 1927–1928 season he had four successes of foreign origin running simultaneously on Broadway: *The Play's the Thing* was Hungarian, *The Captive* and *Her Cardboard Lover* were French, and *The Constant Wife* was British. After selling out for eighteen weeks, *The Captive* was closed briefly by the police for its delicate suggestion of a lesbian love affair, and Miller and the play's leading actors were arrested. The control Paramount–Famous Players–Lasky exerted over Charles Frohman Inc. was revealed by its refusal to let the play reopen.

Miller married for the third time, in 1927, to Kathryn "Kitty" Bache, daughter of financier Jules Bache; they had no children. He continued to have more successful productions than failures, even while other producers were going bankrupt in depression years. His hallmarks were "elegant characters, stylish sets and cultured dialog" (*Variety*, 15 Jan. 1969). Miller's opening nights were known as social events calling for white-tie and chinchilla-wrap attire. His preference for European playwrights was evident: of some ninety New York productions by Miller, only twenty were the work of American playwrights. Miller's association with Charles Frohman Inc. ended in 1932; thereafter, productions were in his own name. He directed one movie for the Columbia movie studio, *The Lady Is Willing* (1934), made in England with British actors. Otherwise he avoided Hollywood in future years, except to sell movie rights to his stage successes. By this period, he had established a pattern of living six months of every year in England and the other six in the United States. He continued to produce plays in both London and New York.

Socially, he was American theater royalty, as his wife Kitty was American financial royalty, and the couple lived a life of aristocratic high society in both countries. The Millers owned seven residences. Among Miller's nontheatrical interests were being a raconteur, a gourmet, a marksman, an owner of a racing stable, a yachtsman, and a licensed air pilot. For some years he also profited by dealings in foreign currency. He was part-owner of restaurants and a small airline, in addition to owning three theaters in New York and London. Miller was known for lightning changes of mood that could send him in an instant from geniality to violent rages, even with those closest to him.

In theatrical circles much was forgiven Miller because of the quality and taste of his productions. He was producer for a number of the most distinguished plays of the 1930s, such as *The Animal Kingdom* (1932), *The Petrified Forest* (1935), a classic revival of *The Country Wife* (1936) with Ruth Gordon, and *Oscar Wilde* (1938). The greatest success of his career was *Victoria Regina* (1935), starring Helen Hayes. It ran four years in New York City and on tour. Hayes played in six of Miller's productions, Katharine Cornell in five, and British actor Leslie Howard in four. Also in the 1930s, Miller helped found the American National Theatre and Academy, though ANTA flourished only after World War II.

Miller's career as a producer faltered during World War II, when the theaters of Europe languished under wartime difficulties, and Miller served for a time as civilian aviation technician aboard the USS *Shangri-La*. After the war came a decade of further memorable productions with their sources abroad, including *Ring Round the Moon* (1950), *Gigi* (1951), the Olivier-Leigh double bill of *Caesar and Cleopatra* and *Antony and Cleopatra* (1951), and *Witness for the Prosecution* (1954). One success of American origin was *The Caine Mutiny Court-Martial* (1956). Miller's last success was with *The Caretaker* (1961). Thereafter, his increasing age and 1960s changes in public taste, plus rising theatrical costs, brought him to decline. His last production, when he was eighty years old, was *Diamond Orchid* (1965); it failed after five performances. He was given the Tony award for lifetime achievement in the theater that year. He was also the recipient of the French Legion of Honor. He died in New York City.

Miller's significance in American theatrical history is the record of his distinguished productions, both in the United States and Britain, for more than fifty years. He brought the public to share his taste for literate, cosmopolitan, elegantly stylish theater. He backed his own tastes with his own money, often in the face of conventional wisdom, and was responsible for many of the theater's finest moments during his decades of production.

• Materials on Miller's life and career are in the Billy Rose Theatre Collection at the New York Public Library for the Performing Arts, Lincoln Center. For further biographical information and anecdotes, see Margaret Case Harriman, "Mr. Miller and Mr. Hyde," *New Yorker*, 29 May and 5 June 1943; Ward Morehouse, "Portrait of a Producer," *Theatre Arts*, July 1956; and Morton Gottlieb, "Gilbert Miller: Fantasy of a Producer," *New York World-Journal-Tribune*, 11 Dec. 1966. For discussion of Charles Frohman Inc. and its stage/screen interconnections, see Robert McLaughlin, *Broadway and Hollywood* (1974). Obituaries are in the *New York Times*, 3 Jan. 1969, and *Variety*, 15 Jan. 1969.

WILLIAM STEPHENSON

MILLER, Glenn (1 Mar. 1904–15? Dec. 1944), musician and band leader, was born Alton Glenn Miller in Clarinda, Iowa, the son of Lewis Elmer Miller, a building contractor, and Mattie Lou Cavender. Miller attended high school in Fort Morgan, Colorado, where he first studied the trombone and played with the Boyd Senter Orchestra in 1921. He spent two years at the University of Colorado but did not earn a degree.

In 1924 Miller joined Max Fisher's band and also played with Ben Pollack's dance orchestra, an ensemble that included clarinetist Benny Goodman. He followed Pollack from the West Coast to New York in 1928 and established himself as a freelance player, performing with and arranging music for such artists as Red Nichols, Smith Ballew, and the Dorsey Brothers. During this period he studied theory and composition with Joseph Schillinger and played at the Paramount Theater in Paul Ash's dance orchestra. He married Helen Burger in 1928, and they adopted two children. In 1930 he played in the pit orchestra for George Gershwin's *Strike Up the Band* and *Girl Crazy*.

Miller helped organize a swing band with the Dorsey Brothers in 1934, and wrote arrangements for this group. In 1934 Miller helped put together an orchestra for British conductor Ray Noble, which gained a following through its radio performances. The success of this orchestra encouraged Miller to start a band of his own in 1937, but this group failed to capture much public attention and disbanded after only ten months. He organized a second Glenn Miller Orchestra in March 1938. This group fared better with its recordings and as the featured band at the Glen Island Casino in New Rochelle, New York, during the summer of 1939. This was the Miller band that achieved nationwide popularity with its weekly radio broadcasts for Chesterfield cigarettes, its RCA Victor recordings, and its appearances in the films *Sun Valley Serenade* (1941) and *Orchestra Wives* (1942). Known as a perfectionist, Miller created a smooth, immediately recognizable sound with disciplined section performances and well-honed arrangements by himself and, most prominently, Bill Finegan and Jerry Gray. The Miller orchestra's arrangements often featured a clarinet lead above the saxophone section, muted trombone choirs, and shifting ensemble textures. The band recorded many hits, including "In the Mood," "Tuxedo Junction," "A String of Pearls," "Little Brown Jug," "Moonlight Serenade" (the band's theme), and "Chatanooga Choo Choo." During a three-year period at the height of their popularity, Miller and his musicians put out forty recordings that over a stretch of weeks or months had sales among the *Billboard* magazine Top Ten—an unprecedented distinction. Miller disbanded the orchestra after its performance on 27 September 1942 so that he and his players could contribute to the war effort.

Miller volunteered for the Army Air Corps in October 1942. He was commissioned a captain and assigned the job of forming a band to entertain troops in the European theater of operations. Using classically trained musicians as well as jazz players, he put together an ensemble of high quality that traveled to England in June 1944. After performing there for six months, with regular radio broadcasts over the U.S. Armed Forces Network, the group was ordered to travel to Paris. On 15 December, Miller began the flight to France to make final arrangements. His plane presumably went down over the English Channel in bad weather, as it disappeared with no trace.

For many years after World War II various Glenn Miller orchestras, led by Tex Beneke, Ray McKinley, Buddy DeFranco, and others, achieved success, largely because their arrangements closely echoed the Miller originals. Miller's most important contribution to popular music was as a band leader rather than as a performer. He brought together talented musicians and arrangers and forged a unique sound that captivated the imaginations of generations of listeners and dancers. The commercially successful 1953 film *The Glenn Miller Story* also strengthened the legacy of Miller's swing band style, a style that has remained perennially popular since his death.

• For a discussion of Miller's life and works, see George T. Simon, *The Big Bands* (1967, rev. 4th ed., 1981); Stephen F. Bedwell, *A Glenn Miller Discography* (1955, rev. 1956); John Flower, *Moonlight Serenade: A Bio-discography of the Glenn Miller Civilian Band* (1972); Simon, *Glenn Miller and His Orchestra* (1976); Geoffrey Butcher, *Next to a Letter from Home: Major Glenn Miller's Wartime Band* (1986); and Edward F. Polic, *The Glenn Miller Army Air Force Band* (1989). See also *Metronome* (Mar. 1936); *Who Was Who in America, vol. II* (1950); *Current Biography* (1942); and Irving Kolodin in *Saturday Review*, 28 Nov. 1953.

BARBARA L. TISCHLER

MILLER, Harriet Mann (25 June 1831–25 Dec. 1918), author and naturalist known by the pseudonym Olive Thorne Miller, was born in Auburn, New York, the daughter of Seth Hunt Mann, a banker, and Mary Field Holbrook. During her youth she lived in Ohio, Wisconsin, Illinois, and Missouri and was educated in private schools.

As a child Miller delighted in writing and reading, calling books her greatest pleasure. In school she and six friends formed a secret society for writing stories, and as a young adult she published a few pieces in newspapers. In 1854 she married Watts Todd Miller; they had four children. They lived first in Chicago and later moved to Brooklyn. When Miller married she devoted herself completely to her household and children. Later she said, "Many years I denied myself the joy of my life—the use of my pen, and it was not until my children were well out of the nursery that I grew wise enough to return to it." During those years she told stories to her children, becoming skillful in the use of language, sharing with them her interest in learning and her appreciation of nature. It was natural, then, that her first published works were what she called "sugar-coated pills of knowledge" for children.

In 1870 the first of these "pills," a piece on china-making, was published on the children's page of a religious weekly. Many more short articles, stories, and nature sketches followed, published in *St. Nicholas*, the *Youth's Companion*, the *Independent*, *Harper's*, *Scribner's*, the *Chicago Tribune*, and other magazines and newspapers. At first Miller used the pen name Olive Thorne, later changing to Olive Thorne Miller, the name by which she was most widely known.

Miller collected a number of nature sketches to be published under the title *Little Folks in Feathers and Fur; and Others in Neither* (1875). In the preface Miller wrote,

> This book makes no pretensions to be a scientific work. Indeed it is scrupulously otherwise. Long words are carefully left out, nothing is said of scientific classification and very little of scientific names. . . . Far be it from me to intrude upon the field of the scientific naturalist. I merely take his discoveries and translate them into the vulgar tongue.

Nimpo's Troubles (1879) is a collection of Miller's stories for children. Some other stories appear in *Our Little Newsboy and Other Stories* (1879), *Tales from Storyland* (1890), and *Meadow Blossoms* (1908), with stories by Louisa May Alcott and Mara Louise Pratt-Chadwick.

But it was Miller's interest in nature, especially birds, that led to her greatest successes. A Chicago friend, a bird enthusiast, visited Miller in Brooklyn in 1880. The day the two women spent in Prospect Park watching birds changed the direction of Miller's interest and of her writing. Her earlier nature sketches were derived from research; now she wrote from close observation and focused on birds. In *Bird-Ways* (1885), her first adult book, Miller wrote both of birds observed outdoors and in her "birdroom," where she kept birds through the winter, birds "liberated," as she said, from bird stores. More bird books followed, among them *In Nesting Time* (1888), *Little Brothers of the Air* (1892), *Upon the Tree Tops* (1899), *True Bird Stories from My Notebooks* (1903), and *With the Birds in Maine* (1904).

A member of the American Ornithological Union and other nature societies, Miller lectured as well as wrote about birds, becoming known for her strong opinions and her insightful observations. She was part of the humanitarian movement of the late nineteenth century and its efforts to curb the wanton slaughtering of birds. In "These Are Your Brothers," the final chapter of *Bird-Ways*, Miller is grieved that men "can be so carried away by the excitement of the hunt as to lose sight of the terror and pain of the victims. . . . even more strange that a gentle woman can endure the beautiful plumage of a delicate winged creature, whose sweet life of song and joy was rudely cut short by brutal men."

Miller recounted studies of birds made during short visits to Colorado, Utah, and other western places in *A Bird-lover in the West* (1894). Ahead of her time in her concern for the environment and for wilderness preservation, Miller bemoaned the taking of wildflowers in Colorado, where she saw tourists filling their arms and carriages with flowers. "A few more years of plunder," she wrote, "and Colorado will be left bare and lose half her charm." In Utah she observed the damage being done by the "wandering cows that regale themselves upon nearly every flower-plant that shows its head" and that "pull down a tall sapling to despoil it of its foliage."

In American Fields and Forest (1909) featured Miller as one of six eminent nature writers, along with Henry David Thoreau, John Burroughs, and John Muir. Miller is one of twenty-one naturists included in Tracy's *American Naturists* (1930). Tracy spoke of Miller's "quiet unassuming study of common birds," said she might be called a "worker in miniatures—portraits of birds," because her observations were of individual birds, not of the species as a whole.

A strong supporter of women's clubs, Miller wrote of their importance in broadening and elevating women in *The Woman's Club* (1891). "It took a long time to rouse woman out of her lethargy," she said, "but once her eyes are open, she walks down her path as resistless as fate."

From 1870 to 1915 Miller published more than seven hundred articles and twenty-four books, eleven of them on birds. Through her writing and lecturing, Miller shared with countless adults and children her respect for and love of birds. Florence Merriam Bailey said that Miller was one of those who "have enabled us to see nature in its entirety." Miller died in Los Angeles, California, where she had spent the last years of her life in a cottage named "El Nido" ("the nest"), on the edge of a bird-filled arroyo.

• A collection of Miller's papers is in the Library of Congress. Much biographical information is found in Miller's own writings, especially *What Happened to Barbara?* for an account of early childhood experiences and in books from her field notes. Florence Merriam Bailey, "In Memorium: Olive

Thorne Miller," *Auk* (Apr. 1919): 163–69, and Henry C. Tracy, "Olive Thorne Miller: An Artistic Biographer of Birds," in *American Naturists* (1930), both give full biographical information. See also Laura C. Holloway, "Olive Thorne Miller," *The Woman's Story: As Told by Twenty American Women with Portraits, and Sketches of the Authors* (1889), for an early biographical sketch. An obituary is in the *Los Angeles Times*, 26 Dec. 1918.

BLANCHE COX CLEGG

MILLER, Henry (12 Mar. 1702–31 Mar. 1782), colonial printer, was born Johann Heinrich Möller at Rhoden, Waldeck, near Kassel, Germany, the son of Heinrich Möller, a journeyman mason of Altstätten, Switzerland, and Anna Maria Faust. When he was twelve, the family returned to Altstätten (near Zürich). Miller learned the printer's trade at Basel, spent a brief apprenticeship in Brussels and Paris, and then spent some time in London. In 1741 he took ship to New York and a week later arrived in Pennsylvania, where he began printing under Benjamin Franklin's patronage. Converting to the Moravian Brethren from Lutheranism, Miller returned to England in 1742 under orders from the Moravians to set up a printshop at The Hague. By 1744 he was in Marienburg, West Prussia, and returned again to England. Sometime during these years he met Johanna Dorothea Blanner of Switzerland, whom he married in 1744. In 1751 he returned to America, this time founding with Samuel Holland a bilingual paper, *Die Lancastersche Zeitung*, and working for the printer William Bradford. He returned to Europe three years later and published a German-language paper for Hanoverian and Hessian troops during the French and Indian War.

Miller sailed for America again in 1760. He translated what became the only German-language legal handbook published in America before the Revolution, David Henderson's *Des Landsmanns Advocat*. On 18 January 1762 he began publishing a newspaper, which changed titles several times but was known best as *Der Wöchentliche Philadelphische Staatsbote*. It appeared with only brief interruptions until 1777 and ceased publication with his retirement. This four-page paper was available to subscribers for six shillings a year; occasional special broadsides or extra editions were printed on particularly important public occasions. Miller's paper became the only successful challenger to the near-monopoly on the German-language press which had been enjoyed by Christopher Sower, Sr., and his son, Christopher, Jr. Miller turned his back on the Moravians in the same year, publishing a broadside that celebrated his liberation from what he noted had been "the garden of errors." Wholly secular in outlook and purpose, the *Staatsbote* undertook to educate German-speakers about European and North American political matters and concerns. Miller began publishing an almanac in 1763, which he explicitly called the "newest, improved and dependable American Calendar," eschewing a "German" identifying tag in the title. Unlike the Sowers, both father and son, who targeted the German-speaking farmers and religious free-church dissenters, Miller seems to have taken for granted a degree of political sophistication and anglicization among a smaller readership, and he was determined to serve this more elite group. He may have had a circulation among about 1,000 persons, who found his perspective more persuasive than the pacifist and domestic-religious press of the Sowers.

Miller's rise to fame as a publisher of politically controversial subjects began as he allied himself with Benjamin Franklin and the political faction that sought a royal charter for Pennsylvania in 1764. He followed his translation of Henderson's lawbook with the publication of Thomas Godfrey's English-language *Juvenile Poems* in 1765, further signaling his commitment to an anglicized, cosmopolitan audience. The defeat of the Franklin party's plans, however, did little to undercut Miller's success as a printer, for within the year the Stamp Act crisis erupted. In his paper Miller explicated British political terms and concepts, continuing in the *Staatsbote* the task he had first set himself in translating Henderson's book of legal terms and procedures. Miller allied himself immediately with the protests against the act and suspended publication from 31 October to 18 November. Confident that the British ministry had learned to respect the rights of "Americans," a term he had used to identify his own readership since 1764, Miller became disillusioned by the passage of the Townshend Duties in 1767.

Within a year of the passage of the duties, Miller began reaching into his own Swiss past for images of resistance. He published a pamphlet on William Tell and the Swiss fight for independence in 1768 and supported nonimportation. When the crisis with Britain escalated sharply in 1775, Miller again identified himself with Swiss liberties. He published the essay "The Law of Liberty" by his fellow Swiss American Johann Joachim Zübly, followed in 1776 by another heroic Swiss poem connected with the 1388 battle of Näfels commemorating the defeat of the Austrians, and a front-page advertisement for the German translation of Thomas Paine's *Common Sense*. Miller carefully avoided an explicit call for independence during the critical winter months of 1776, but the accumulating logic of his essays and what he chose to advertise to his readership could not have been mistaken.

The *Staatsbote*, being the only paper to appear in Philadelphia on a Friday, managed on 5 July 1776 to scoop the news of the impending appearance of the Declaration of Independence. The German translation of the text followed the next week. Miller's political allegiances were too well known for him to escape the consequences when the British occupied Philadelphia; he was forced to suspend publication of his paper from 17 September to 5 August 1778. Miller ended his career in May 1779, retiring to Bethlehem, Pennsylvania, having made his peace with the Moravians six years earlier. He died and was buried in Bethlehem.

In many respects Miller must be credited with raising the political consciousness of German-speakers in North America during the 1760s and 1770s. His clever use of his own Swiss past, coupled with the cosmopolitan, urbane perspective he had developed on his many journeys in Europe and to the New World, prepared him precisely for this role. Perhaps sooner than almost any other recent immigrant German-speaker, he grasped the significance of mastering legal and political concepts as the key to full participation in the possibilities offered by the New World. Yet Miller was also critical of anti-Indian sentiments among some Pennsylvanians and approved of controls that restrained westward movement of his fellow Europeans. In such controversial public matters Miller immersed himself for most of the half-century he spent as a printer. Yet, in the end, he retreated from the world of political contention to die among the Moravians who had attracted him early in his career in the New World.

• There are no known Miller papers. The best secondary sources include Isaiah Thomas, *The History of Printing in America*, 2d ed., vol. 1 (1874), p. 253; Karl John Richard Arndt and Reimer C. Eck, eds., *The First Century of German Language Printing in the United States of America: A Bibliography Based on the Studies of Oswald Seidensticker and Wilbur H. Oda*, vol. 1 (1989); Willi Paul Adams, "The Colonial German-Language Press and the American Revolution," in *The Press and the American Revolution*, ed. Bernard Bailyn and John B. Hench (1980), pp. 151–228; and A. G. Roeber, "Henry Miller's *Staatsbote*: A Revolutionary Journalist's Use of the Swiss Past," *Yearbook of German-American Studies* 25 (1990): 57–76, and *Palatines, Liberty, and Property: German Lutherans in Colonial British America* (1993), pp. 175–205, 300–303.

A. G. ROEBER

MILLER, Henry (1 Feb. 1859–9 Apr. 1926), actor, manager, and director, was born John Henry Miller in London, England, the son of John Miller, a railroad contractor, and Sophia Newton. In 1873 the family relocated to Toronto, Canada, where Miller spent his adolescent years. Infected from an early age with the theatrical virus, the young Henry studied elocution in Toronto with the American actor Charles W. Couldock, playing whatever small parts the local theaters offered him.

In 1876, at the age of seventeen, he was lured to Baltimore by the promise of a role—which failed to materialize. The disappointed young man decided to remain in the United States, embarking on the usual young-actor period of struggle and starvation on the streets of New York's theater district. Within ten years, however, his beautiful, melodious voice and carefully understated acting made him a favorite leading man of established stars such as Adelaide Neilson, Clara Morris, Fanny Janauschek, and Helena Modjeska. He played an assortment of Shakespearean roles early in his career, including Hamlet; but at this time the classic drama was waning in popularity. After several seasons with Daniel Frohman's Lyceum Theater stock company, in the 1890s he became firmly established as a star with Charles Frohman's Empire Theatre stock company. Here he appeared in popular but undistinguished London imports such as *Liberty Hall*, *The Councillor's Wife*, *Sowing the Wind*, and *Gudgeons*. Miller served a portion of his theatrical apprenticeship under Dion Boucicault; the Irish-born playwright-actor provided his disciple with an excellent model of the *régisseur*, someone who controlled every aspect of theatrical production.

Already an established star, Miller became infuriated when he was forced to wait two hours in Frohman's steamy reception room in midsummer 1905. Storming out of Frohman's offices, he walked down the street and signed a contract with the upstart Shubert organization. Leasing the Princess Theatre, he produced and directed William Vaughn Moody's *The Great Divide*, a poetic drama of love, loss, and redemption set in the rugged American West, casting himself and Margaret Anglin in the main roles. This play struck a resounding chord in America's consciousness. With its emphasis on the conflict between stultifying East Coast puritanism and freedom-loving frontier joie de vivre, the critical and financial success of this play established Miller's reputation as a director and producer as well as a leading man.

Miller's one brush with the new naturalistic playwriting and acting occurred at this time. In 1906, at the request of the Shuberts, he agreed to share the Princess Theatre, where he was presenting nightly performances of *The Great Divide*, with Alla Nazimova, who was appearing in matinees of *The Doll's House* and *Hedda Gabler*. Miller was nominally billed as the director of these Ibsen plays, but he evidenced little interest in the new drama, and the Russian actress took total charge of her English-speaking debut. Then, as throughout his career, Miller showed a preference for the conventional literary drama of the period and for the writings of poet-dramatists such as Moody, Percy MacKaye, and Charles Rann Kennedy.

Miller was a man of firm if conservative principles. Feeling indebted to the author of *The Great Divide*, who was then dying of a brain tumor, he produced Moody's *The Faith Healer* knowing it was destined for failure. And when playing Jack in a San Francisco production of *The Importance of Being Earnest* at the height of Oscar Wilde's homosexual notoriety, he refused to conceal authorship of the play, explaining that "no one had the right to expect a man who was abnormal in his genius to be normal in other respects" (Morse, p. 184).

The remarkable impact of *The Great Divide* was followed by seven intermittently fat years at the Princess, during which, as Miller's press agent recalled, "He won two fortunes, dropped most of his winnings into new theatrical ventures, and fought his way back to a third period of affluence" (Morse, p. 145). In 1909 the actor-manager took his company to London. His performance in *The Great Divide* was well received: the *Times* (London) critic wrote that the "rough diamond of a hero is played with quiet strength and sincerity by Mr. Henry Miller." The play, however, did not fare as well: "Altogether you feel that there has been much superfluous casuistry and mental gymnastics over what is, or would be elsewhere than in America, a very simple business" (16 Sept. 1909). The *Times* had similar reactions to *The Servant in the House*, Miller's other London offering, admiring the acting but not the play: "Well, the whole thing was very fervent; but it is possible to be at once fervent and tiresome, fervent and silly" (26 Oct. 1909). Miller never brought another production to London.

The zenith of his career was reached on 1 April 1918, when Henry Miller's Theatre, on West Forty-third Street, opened its doors with a performance of *The Fountain of Youth*. George M. Cohan remembered that "money was not spared to make it a thing of beauty and a worthy temple of Thespis. When the finishing touches were being put on it he [Miller] fairly lived in the building. He stormed and raced when things were not right, and cried to high heaven to give him patience. He knew what he wanted, and in the end he got results." The newly constructed building was described as "notable for elegance and decorative beauty and pays tribute to the popular tradition of the older drama in having a gallery, elsewhere discarded since the rise of moving pictures" (*New York Times*, 12 Apr. 1926). An opening night review observed that "every detail of the new house is studied with intelligent regard to comfort of the body and repose of the eye. The single scene which suffices for *The Fountain of Youth* is perhaps the most solid and satisfactory drawing room ever presented on our local stage" (*New York Times*, 2 Apr. 1918).

Miller settled down to a comfortable if peripatetic existence as a "man of the theater": leading man, director, producer, theater manager, and occasionally collaborating playwright. The *New York Times*, in an editorial-page encomium appearing at the time of Miller's death, added the then-unusual title of "dramaturge," pointing out that *The Great Divide* originally had a tragic ending, with the hero killed by the woman he adored. Under Miller's guidance, however, the author was induced to create a more palatable love-conquers-all conclusion.

At his own theater Miller presented and acted in successes such as *Her Husband's Wife*, *The Rainbow*, *Daddy Long Legs*, *The Famous Mrs. Fair*, and *The Changelings*. Ruth Chatterton was one of his important acting discoveries, and she remained for many years under his management.

Miller developed a reputation as a perfectionist. Augustus E. Thomas, the author of seven plays produced by Miller, wrote that "when the curtain rose for the first time upon a play of his direction one could be sure that, fail or succeed, that play would be shown to the public as only a master of the theatre could exhibit it. . . . I once saw him rehearse and dismiss seven leading women one after the other, all of them competent enough, because he could not get the right tone from them" (*New York Times*, 18 Apr. 1926).

In his quest for theatrical perfection Miller was often abrupt and irascible. His rehearsal rages became legendary, although he usually later regretted these outbursts. "My life," he confided to his biographer, "is one continual apology."

In 1883 (or 1884) Miller had married Helene Stopel (or Stoepel), whose stage name was Bijou Heron. (Her mother was the actress Matilda Heron.) The couple appeared together in several productions before she began a career as a homemaker and mother. The union produced four children, one of whom died in infancy. The firstborn, Gilbert, became a well-known theatrical producer in the United States and England. The Miller's marriage may have been somewhat strained; Helene Miller, abroad at the time of her husband's death, was left only a $3,000 annuity by the terms of his will, two of his children receiving the remainder of the estate (the third was serving a drug-related sentence in a California prison). Miller's death in New York City came as he was preparing to open still another production of *A Stranger in the House*, one of his most popular plays.

The *New York Times*, in an editorial, summed up his career:

> He was a product of the then vanishing Shakespearean tradition. . . . To the last, he retained the sound method of that tradition, together with a deliberation and an emphasis not always in keeping with the more realistic modern acting. He retained also its idealism, his productions being uniformly true to the elder good taste. . . . It was as a producer that he achieved his highest, though less recognized, claim to distinction. (12 Apr. 1926)

• The Theatre Collection of the New York Public Library for the Performing Arts has photographs, scrapbooks, and other archival materials relating to Miller. Frank P. Morse, *Backstage with Henry Miller* (1938), is the only book that deals extensively with Miller. Morse worked as Miller's press agent, and he assembled data for the memoirs that the actor-manager intended to write "as soon as he found time." Morse's account, while overadmiring, provides an enlightening look at theater from behind the footlights. Details are probably more accurate here than in other sources; the birth date of 1859 differs from that of 1860 given in standard references, as does the given names of "John Henry" rather than "Henry John." Unfortunately, Miller's personal life is almost totally ignored, leaving an incomplete picture of the subject. Augustus E. Thomas wrote an admiring farewell in "Henry Miller," *New York Times*, 18 Apr. 1926. See also the *New York Times*, 2, 7 Apr. 1918; 10 (obituary), 12, 14, and 21 Apr. 1926.

CLIFFORD ASHBY

MILLER, Henry (26 Dec. 1891–7 June 1980), author, was born Henry Valentine Miller in New York City, the son of Heinrich Miller, a tailor, and Louise Marie Neiting. Both of Miller's grandfathers had emigrated from Germany in the middle of the nineteenth century, and his first language was German. Born in the Yorkville area of Manhattan, Miller moved with his family to the Williamsburg section of Brooklyn before he was a year old, and his early life in Brooklyn provided him with scenes and recollections that pervade much of his mature writing.

Very early he displayed an adventurous spirit. As a child and young man he wanted to be a riverboat pilot, a clown, an actor, a six-day bicycle rider—anything but a tailor like his father. He enrolled in the City College of New York in 1909 but dropped out during his freshman year. He decided he would be an author and early promised himself that "some day I will write an enormous, alternate book in which everything will be recorded: . . . all, all of life." But he wrote nothing at that time and was finally forced into his father's tailor shop, where there was scarcely enough business for one. Sitting in the tailor shop, he read Friedrich Nietzsche, Jack London, Knut Hamsun, Herbert Spencer, Rabindranath Tagore, and Henri-Louis Bergson, dreaming of being a writer and resenting the work he did. He traveled to California in 1913 and worked there; later, in 1917, he lived briefly in Washington, D.C., but he always returned to New York, convinced that he was a failure, yet still full of dreams.

Early in his life, and continuing to the time of his death, relations with women troubled him; he was hungry for love and obsessed with sex, but as a youth he regarded sex as "naughty" and was awkward about it, even as he developed an intense idealism about romantic love. Before he was twenty he became attached to a woman old enough to be his mother and remained with her for five years. In 1917, partly to avoid the draft, he married Beatrice Wickens. His alliance with Beatrice was unhappy from the start, and after two years, during which a child was born, this marriage failed. The couple divorced in 1924.

Two events occurred in the early 1920s that importantly influenced his later career as a writer. First, in 1920 he became employment manager for the Western Union Telegraph Company. For the next three years he was in constant contact with thousands of job applicants and got an intimate view of the underside of American life. This experience undermined his smug view of his own superiority and made him identify instead with the down-and-out losers and riffraff who were forgotten in American society. This change in his experience and attitude was fundamental and permanent.

The second great event of this period occurred late in the summer of 1923, when he met June Edith Smith, the woman who was to become his second wife. The couple married in 1924. (They had no children.) His intense obsession with her eventually provided him with the core of the literary materials for several of his most important books. *Tropic of Cancer*, *Tropic of Capricorn*, and the trilogy of novels titled "The Rosy Crucifixion" were all inspired by his troubled and ecstatic relations with June. She came to represent all that he desired, along with all he feared in women. She fascinated and troubled him in equal measure.

From 1923 to 1930 Miller made several failed attempts to write seriously. He managed to publish a few minor pieces, but all of his book-length projects were failures, beginning with a novel, "Clipped Wings," in which he attempted to write about the people he encountered at Western Union; continuing through an autobiographical novel, *Moloch* (1992); and ending in *Crazy Cock* (1991), a novel about his tormented relations with June. He worked at dozens of jobs and traveled to Florida and Asheville, North Carolina, in hopes of making fortunes in the real estate business. There, he and June practiced many scams, but all came to nothing.

In February 1930, with June's aid, he sailed alone for Paris, dreaming that he could become a writer there. With little money, however, he was forced into a variety of odd jobs and schemes merely to survive. He observed flatly, "I have no money, no resources, no hopes." Long delayed in realizing his literary aspirations and often frustrated, lonely, and sometimes close to complete despair, Miller reached a psychological "bottom" in 1931, which prepared him to write a new kind of book, as different from the conventional, popular novel as it was from the experimental novels of the 1920s.

This book, which he titled *Tropic of Cancer* (1934), was, as he famously described it, "a gob of spit in the face of Art, a kick in the pants to God, Man, Destiny, Time, Love, Beauty." He denied that the book was a novel at all, and he allied himself with the tradition of Walt Whitman in American letters by claiming that the book was wholly an expression of himself: the story was his story and his "hero" was himself. He called it an "auto-romance." Into the book went all of his experiences on the margin in Paris. Bawdy, offensive, rebellious, and reveling in the life of the lowest depths, *Tropic of Cancer* was also full of good humor, wonder, and spiritual passion. Miller had tried so long to succeed that he now seemed almost determined to offend; ironically, this effort won him the acceptance that had so long eluded him. His book was immediately praised extravagantly by the most influential modernist critics of his time. T. S. Eliot wrote that "*Tropic of Cancer* seems to me a . . . magnificent piece of work." Ezra Pound added that it was one of only a few modern books that could be set beside James Joyce's *Ulysses*, and he pointed to its "ethical discrimination." Inevitably the book attracted not only well-established critics but also young writers who declared themselves disciples of Miller's. Lawrence Durrell, then in his early twenties, wrote a fan letter to Miller stating that *Tropic of Cancer* was "the only man-size piece of work which this century can really boast of." Even George Bernard Shaw, though troubled by the excess of sexuality in the book, acknowledged, "This fellow can write." *Tropic of Cancer* continued to attract favorable comment for a long time. Edmund Wilson praised Miller's "sure hand at color and rhythm" in 1938, and in 1940 George Orwell extolled his book as a revelation of "the disintegration of our society and the increasing helplessness of all decent people." Later, in the 1970s, Norman Mailer championed his work.

Even as *Tropic of Cancer* was receiving its first favorable commentary in the mid-1930s, the sexually explicit and offensive character of the book resulted in its being banned from sale in the United States and Great Britain and, indeed, from regular commercial distribution anywhere. Thus Miller became the most famous banned author in American history. He became as famous for the censorship of his books as he was for writing them. So for a long time, while his reputation grew, income from his books remained abysmally low.

The likelihood that sales of the book would be limited was recognized before publication, and Miller had to pay the printing expenses of Obelisk Press. This money was actually provided by a young writer, Anaïs Nin, with whom Henry had fallen in love. The love triangle between Henry, Anaïs, and June became an important concern for Henry and an important literary subject for Nin. At the time that he met Nin, she had published only one book, a study of D. H. Lawrence; but she showed Miller her unpublished diaries, and he declared them a major work of "autobiographical romance" and continued to speak and write about her achievement in them until they were finally published to critical acclaim in the 1960s. She was one of a score of writers and artists whose work Miller generously promoted. She, in turn, signed the preface (which Miller actually wrote) to *Tropic of Cancer*, lending it her authority as a critic.

Henry Miller was forty-two years old when *Tropic of Cancer* was published. His creative talent had long been pent up. Once it was released in this book, however, it flowed freely, and he never again experienced writer's block. Novels, auto-romances, books of travel, personal reminiscences, letters, literary criticism, commentaries on art and artists, meditations, and reflections on every possible subject poured from his typewriter. Many pieces first appeared as pamphlets and were later collected into volumes so that it is not possible to give a precise account of how many works Miller actually did publish. The bibliography of primary works in Ronald Gottesman's *Critical Essays on Henry Miller* (1992) lists sixty-five separate books.

Tropic of Capricorn (1939) is Miller's best-known work published in the years following *Tropic of Cancer*. Obviously conceived as a companion book of self-exposure and self-celebration to the earlier work, and written in the same spirit, *Tropic of Capricorn* deals with the period 1920–1930 in Miller's life, before he left New York for Paris. He writes of his experiences at the "Cosmodemonic Telegraph Company" and of his tormented life with June, of his voracious reading, and of his frustrated attempts to become a writer. But far from treating any of these with bitterness, the book is remarkable for the fullness of its humor, its surrealistic exuberance, and its mythical dimensions. In it Miller proclaims that sexual ecstasy, together with awareness of the chaos of modern civilization, can liberate the individual. At the end of the book he frees himself to become the first American dada-surrealist writer; he takes a new name—"Gottlieb Lebenrecht Muller," the God-loving, right-living man—and is born anew through the powers of imagination that derive from natural sensuality.

During the decade that Miller spent in Paris, he wrote several other books. *Black Spring* (1936) is a vivid sequence of sketches, personal recollections, and dreams. *Hamlet*, in two volumes (1939, 1941) consists of a series of remarkable letters exchanged with Michael Fraenkel. A book that was Miller's personal favorite, and which many critics have regarded as his best work, *The Colossus of Maroussi* (1940), was inspired by the period he spent in Greece during 1939–1940. Lawrence Durrell had spoken to him about Greece as an archetypal "heraldic world"; there Miller expected to find deep satisfaction of his spiritual needs, and he did. *The Colossus of Maroussi* is a book wholly without sex, a celebration of the grace and wisdom of the Greek spirit. He told one of the leading Greek intellectuals whom he met there, "I do not consider myself a writer. . . . I am a man telling the story of his life, a process which appears more and more inexhaustible as I go on." The story of his life in Greece is radiant with the peace of inner illumination.

When Miller returned to the United States in 1940, fleeing from the war in Europe, he was as broke as when he had left. Despite his reputation in Europe, few people in America had read his books, and in America at this time he made almost as much money from his watercolors as he did from his writing. At loose ends, he spent nearly a year traveling around his native land. He had hoped to discover in America what he found in Greece; but he was thoroughly disappointed, and he wrote his most bitter book about this American excursion, *The Air-Conditioned Nightmare* (1945). He was bitter, too, about the failure of his hope to make his romantic relation with Anaïs Nin intimate and permanent. June had divorced him in 1933.

A new phase in his life began in mid-1944, when he moved to Big Sur, on the remote rugged coast of northern California. He felt refreshed. "I get an idea a day up here," he told a friend. He put those ideas on paper and began the most productive period of his life. The most important project that he completed during his years at Big Sur was the massive "Rosy Crucifixion" trilogy, consisting of *Sexus* (1949), *Plexus* (1953), and *Nexus* (1960). In these volumes he returned to his years in New York, especially to the time of his liaison with June, but now he wrote in a style much more naturalistic than that of *Tropic of Capricorn*. Norman Mailer later pronounced this 1,600-page work "one of the great picaresque novels of the English language."

In 1961 Barney Rosset, editor of Grove Press, published *Tropic of Cancer* in the United States; it was the most famous banned book in the world. This publication initiated a long series of legal trials concerning the book's protection under the first amendment, as well as personal attacks on Miller. The trials were landmarks in American intellectual history, breaking down the last remnants of censorship of expression and thereby profoundly influencing the changing mores of American life. Miller was one of those rare artists who lived to see the changes in society brought about by his works. As Isaac Bashevis Singer wrote, Miller "kept on fighting for what he considered just [and thus] . . . became a literary leader of the highest magnitude." Litigation against *Tropic of Cancer* lasted for two years and eventually drove Miller out of Big Sur, where he was pestered both by intruders who hated him and by the beatnik generation who idolized him. The price that he paid for "success," when it at last arrived, was worry, sleepless nights, and unwanted notoriety. In 1963 he moved to Pacific Palisades, in southern California, where he remained until his death there.

Miller had married Janina Martha Lepska in 1944. They had a daughter and a son but divorced in 1952. That same year Miller married Eve McClure; they had no children and divorced in 1961. In 1967 he married Hiroko Tokuda, a Japanese jazz singer. After two years, however, this marriage also failed, although the couple did not divorce. They had no children. Miller spent the last decade of his life painting and writing with scarcely diminished fecundity. To the end he remained in advance of his time. In the late 1970s he pronounced himself "amazed and disgusted" by the shallowness of "liberated" sexual mores in America. "Neither man nor woman has yet found the way to freedom," he insisted.

Miller remains an important writer because he focused on fundamental human concerns: the impulse to love, the capacity for wonder, the importance of the inner life, the divinity of each individual, and the obligation of humanity to experience a widening and deepening of consciousness. Of these, love—love in all its forms—is his most basic subject. "There can be no broadening of one's vision without a corresponding leap of love," he insisted. As Erica Jong observed, he was "a wisdom writer like Hesse or Krishnamurti." In one of his later works, *Insomnia* (1971), he declared, "The one thing we can never get enough of is love. And the one thing we never give enough of is love." For Miller, love makes man and woman human. He was both a radical experimentalist and, at the same time, a very traditional writer.

• Miller's papers are widely scattered among American libraries; the most important collections are in special collections at the University of California, Los Angeles; the University of Texas, Austin; and Southern Illinois University, Carbondale. The best biography is Jay Martin, *Always Merry and Bright: The Life of Henry Miller* (1978; rev. ed., 1980). But two more recent biographies should be consulted: Mary Dearborn, *The Happiest Man Alive* (1991), and Robert Ferguson, *Henry Miller: A Life* (1991). Two good personal memoirs well convey the impact of Miller's personality: Alfred Perlès, *My Friend, Henry Miller* (1956), and Erica Jong, *The Devil at Large* (1993). Two excellent bibliographies of Miller are Lawrence J. Shefreen and Roger Jackson, *Henry Miller: A Bibliography of Primary Sources* (1993), and Lawrence J. Shefreen, *Henry Miller: A Bibliography of Secondary Sources* (1979). The most interesting critical studies are collected in Ronald Gottesman, *Critical Essays on Henry Miller* (1992), which also contains an excellent introduction by Gottesman. An obituary by Martin is in the *Los Angeles Times*, 8 June 1980, and is revised and reprinted in Martin, *A Corresponding Leap of Love: Henry Miller Living and Dying* (1996).

JAY MARTIN

MILLER, James (25 Apr. 1776–7 July 1851), army officer, territorial governor, and customs official, was born at Petersborough, New Hampshire, the son of James Miller and Catharine Gregg. He entered the Andover Academy in 1794, obtained a common education, and briefly attended Williams College in Massachusetts. Miller returned to New Hampshire, studied law under James Wilson, and gained acceptance to the bar in 1803. He was the first practicing attorney in nearby Greenfield and there developed an interest in military affairs. Miller commanded a local artillery company, but upon the recommendation of General Benjamin Pierce, he was commissioned a major in the Fourth U.S. Infantry on 8 July 1808. He performed garrison duty at Fort Independence, Boston, for several years, and rose to lieutenant colonel on 30 November 1810. In this capacity Miller accompanied Indiana territorial governor William Henry Harrison during his western campaign of 1811. He missed the battle of Tippecanoe owing to illness but did valuable work at Fort Harrison forwarding supplies. That winter Miller convalesced at the home of Governor Harrison.

When the War of 1812 commenced, Miller's regiment was at Dayton, Ohio, as part of General William Hull's Northwestern army. This force entered western Upper Canada on 14 July 1812, but a few weeks later the vacillating Hull crossed back to Detroit. The general, wishing to restore his lines of communication, dispatched Miller southward toward the River Raisin with 600 men. On 8 August the Americans encountered a mixed force of British and Indians at Maguaga, Michigan Territory. Miller fought off their ambush, charged bayonets, and drove his assailants off in confusion. This skirmish constituted the first land victory by American forces in the War of 1812 and gained Miller promotion to brevet colonel. Unfortunately, Hull surrendered Detroit a week later, and Miller became a prisoner. He was subsequently exchanged at Montreal for Lord Dacres, captain of HMS *Guerierre*, and appointed to the Sixth U.S. Infantry.

Miller took post at the Niagara frontier as part of General John P. Boyd's brigade. He fought at the 27 May 1813 capture of Fort George and was complimented in Boyd's official dispatches. That winter Miller accompanied the ill-fated Montreal expedition of General James Wilkinson and endured harsh winter conditions at the inadequate cantonment at French Mills, New York. There, on 9 March 1814, the rank of colonel, Twenty-First U.S. Infantry, was conferred.

In the spring Miller transferred to Buffalo, New York, as part of a brigade commanded by General Eleazar W. Ripley. The Americans then embarked on the celebrated 1814 Niagara campaign during which the veteran British army was defeated on several occasions. At the desperate 25 July battle of Lundy's Lane, Major General Jacob Brown asked Miller if he could storm a British battery at night. He laconically replied, "I'll try, Sir!" Stealthily approaching the enemy position, he captured it in the best-executed infantry attack of the war. Two months later Miller fought conspicuously at the 17 September sortie from Fort Erie where he stormed another battery. For his Niagara services Miller received brevet promotion to brigadier general, a gold coin from Congress, and a sword from New

York State. He was the only regimental-grade officer of this war so honored.

Miller was retained in the peacetime establishment as colonel, Fifth U.S. Infantry, and stationed along the northwestern frontier. On 3 March President Monroe tendered him the appointment of governor of the Arkansas Territory and he resigned his commission on 1 June 1819. Miller arrived in Arkansas on 26 December and directed relocation of the capital to its present site of Little Rock. He also worked vigorously with the legislature to formulate law codes, raise revenues, and conclude favorable treaties with the Indians. Finding the climate disagreeable to his health, Miller spent increasing amounts of time away from the territory while Secretary Robert Crittenden governed in his place. Miller resigned his post in 1823 and was succeeded by another War of 1812 veteran, George Izard.

In the fall of 1814 Miller ran for Congress and was elected from his native district of Petersborough. When poor health precluded taking his seat, he opted to serve as collector of Salem, Massachusetts, where he remained twenty-four years. There Miller became favorably associated with coworker Nathaniel Hawthorne, who dedicated the introductory chapter of his *Scarlet Letter* to the old soldier. Miller functioned effectively as collector until 1849, when he was paralyzed by a stroke. He retired to his farm at Temple, New Hampshire, where he died of a second stroke.

Despite a lengthy bureaucratic career, Miller is best remembered as the finest regimental officer of the War of 1812. Tactically astute and a strict disciplinarian, he was uniformly successful at Maguaga, Fort George, and especially Lundy's Lane, where his desperate charge saved the army. Miller's exclamation of "I'll try, Sir!" also passed into the national lexicon and is preserved as the motto of the Third U.S. Infantry, a lineal descendant of his old Twenty-first. Miller was married twice, first to Martha Ferguson, who died in 1805, and then to Ruth Flint in 1808.

• The principal caches of Miller letters are at the U.S. Military Academy Library, West Point, and the Lilly Library, Indiana University, Bloomington. Lesser collections reside at the Burton Historical Collection, Detroit Public Library; the Clements Library, University of Michigan; the Historical Society of Pennsylvania; and the Massachusetts Historical Society, Boston. His portrait and sword are preserved at the Essex Historical Institute, Salem. Printed matter is in John G. Biel, "The Savage Preface to the War of 1812," *Society of Indiana Pioneers Yearbook* (1956): 5–11. Panegyrical sketches include Chandler E. Potter, *Military History of New Hampshire* (2 vols., 1856), and R. Thomas, *The Glory of America* (1843). A more objective treatment is Robert J. Holden, "General James Miller, Collector of the Port of Salem," *Essex Historical Institute Collections* 104 (1968): 283–302. Details on Miller's political career are in Clarence E. Carter, ed., *Territorial Papers of the United States: Arkansas*, vols. 19 and 20 (1950); Lonnie J. White, "James Miller: Arkansas's First Territorial Governor," *Arkansas Historical Quarterly* 19 (1960): 12–30; and Carl Ledbetter, "General James Miller: Hawthorne's Hero in Arkansas," *Arkansas Historical Quarterly* 47 (1988): 99–115.

JOHN C. FREDRIKSEN

MILLER, Joaquin (10 Mar. 1839–17 Feb. 1913), writer, was born Cincinnatus Hiner Miller near Liberty, Indiana, the son of Hulings Miller, a laborer and schoolteacher, and Margaret DeWitt. Movement marked Miller's earliest days, as his usually unsuccessful father moved from job to job and from home to home. What stability there was in the family was furnished by his proud mother. Hulings Miller, sometime farmer and merchant, after desultory sojourns in Indiana's Miami Reserve and a number of small towns, in 1852 finally committed his six-member family to the grand progress, the determined trek to what his son would later hyperbolically dub the "ultimate West." Early nurtured by legends of the Pacific slope, Miller in retrospect considered these months on the Oregon Trail a notable adventure, satisfying and symbolic in "an age of active and mighty enterprises" (*Overland in a Covered Wagon: An Autobiography*, ed. Sidney G. Firman [1930]). The gold fever of 1849 having somewhat abated, Miller was freed to associate the West not just with riches, but also with intellectual, emotional, and spiritual fulfillment. From the Midwest, he could hold the idea of the Far West in anticipation, in imagination, and make myth of that golden never-achieved land of the future.

Shortly after the family settled in Oregon, Miller left for the mines of northern California and the frequent companionship of Joseph "Mountain Joe" DeBloney, adventurer, onetime scout of John C. Frémont, and teller of tales drawn upon by Miller in his early books. Miller had embarked on a colorful career in the West, often fancifully embellished in the retelling, all the details of which are not definitively substantiated. For a time he worked as a miner. He attended Oregon's Columbia College for perhaps three months in 1857–1858. He also briefly taught school. Intermittently, he lived among the Native Americans whose rights he was later to champion, claiming a truelove and a daughter, although on other occasions he found himself involved in skirmishes against Native Americans. By the late 1850s he had adopted the name "Joaquin," after the Mexican desperado Joaquín Murieta, whose cause Miller had taken up in print. (However, fellow western author Ina Coolbrith reported having suggested that he use Joaquin as a pen name over a decade later.) Certainly he seemed to deserve the sobriquet after stealing a horse, escaping from jail, wounding a constable, and achieving a reputation for horsemanship on a pony-express route that extended all the way from Oro Fino, Idaho, to the Oregon coast. Selling to Wells Fargo his half-interest in this last business, Miller in 1862 invested in, and wrote editorials for, the Eugene City, Oregon, *Democratic Register* (ever siding with the underdog, he identified himself as a southern partisan), which survived for twenty-nine weekly issues.

Later in 1862 Joaquin Miller met and, four days later, married Theresa Dyer in Port Oxford, Oregon. He had known of her through her published poetry, written under the pseudonym "Minnie Myrtle," and had corresponded with her. They later had two children.

Back in Eugene City, Miller founded the *Review*, a short-lived literary paper for which he served as editor and nearly sole contributor. San Francisco, however, seemed the West's flourishing cultural center, with such journals as the *Golden Era* and writers as eminent as Bret Harte, Mark Twain, and Charles Warren Stoddard. But the couple's foray to San Francisco failed to bring them fame. Although both published stories and poems, clearly they could not make a literary living. Now, Miller made use of his minimal training in jurisprudence (under George Williams (1820–1910), later attorney general in the Grant administration) to become a lawyer and, from 1866 until 1869, judge of Grant County, Oregon. Mutual accusations of financial irresponsibility, if not infidelity, brought the Millers' marriage to an end in 1869. A decade later Miller wed well-to-do eastern hotel heiress Abigail Leland, a marriage that resulted in a separation after a few years.

A crucial turning point in Miller's career occurred in 1870, as he gave himself more completely to literary uses of his western experience and sought fame—and a publisher—in London. Among the British literati he not only became popular, but he made a sensation (although this sensation waned over the years as he and his literary materials gradually lost the appeal of the exotic and novel). In this unlikely setting, Joaquin Miller, unorthodox and striking in sombrero, cape, and boots, became the "Poet of the Sierras," the "Byron of Oregon," the "Buffalo Bill of Poesy." Miller played to foreign stereotypes of the authentic and wild westerner so well that he became for years a public figure as well as successful writer, all the more popular for his audience's lack of detailed knowledge about the actual West. His widely read poetry and prose of the 1870s present a West colored by the idyllic and the exaggerated, his romantic effusions often expressed in an inflated yet conventional style. Witness the infelicitous forced rhymes of "The Tale of the Tall Alcade," in which the town of Renalda lies "Where mountains repose in their blueness, / Where the sun first lands in his newness, / And marshals his beams and his lances, / Ere down to the vale he advances," and so forth. Yet for many, Miller and compatriots like Harte created the appealing images of the West. The brief *Pacific Poems* (1871) was soon expanded and revised as *Songs of the Sierras* (1871) and was immediately praised by general reader and critic alike. Miller mined his characteristic subjects and themes for a long time but never again achieved the success of such early books as *Songs of the Sierras* and the prose autobiography *Life amongst the Modocs* (1873). Danger, romance, and adventure on a landscape of mountain, desert, and prairie abound in "Arizonian" and "Kit Carson's Ride." The first peoples of the West are memorialized in poems such as "The Last Taschastas," in which the ancient lands are violated by "the savage white-man's ploughshare." *Modocs* describes tribal ways and attempts to found a Native-American republic in northern California, and it tells the tale of Miller's wooing and tragically losing Paquita, whose daughter becomes the symbol of the pathos of the "vanishing American," "the last of the children of Shasta."

Miller continued to write verse and personal reminiscence as well as drama and fiction for over three decades. No more polished, precise, or profound than his early works, his writings after 1873 showed little improvement and, in many cases, necessarily lacked thematic novelty. Notable novels include *First Fam'lies of the Sierras* (1876), an improbable tale of the California mining camps very much akin to Harte's "The Luck of Roaring Camp." Rewritten as *The Danites in the Sierras* (1881), the dramatic (and equally melodramatic) version of the book was popular on American and British stages. (The "Danites" of the title are the Mormons, maligned here as in many popular westerns of the time.) *Forty-Nine—An Idyl Drama of the Sierras* (1882), also predictable and sentimental, exhibits an early nostalgia for an imagined "Old West." Miller turned away from the West in novels like *The One Fair Woman* (1876), whose unabashed American abroad, young Mollie Wopsus, is more memorable than the idealized female of the title, based on Lily Langtry. In *Songs of Italy* (1878) and other volumes, Miller wrote poetry set in Europe. With *The Building of the City Beautiful* (1893) Miller joined in the vogue for the utopian romance. His later writings often exhibit a vague and placeless philosophical speculativeness.

After his return from his London triumph and European travel, Miller resided in New York and in his picturesque Washington, D.C., cabin. During the late 1890s he accompanied the gold seekers to Alaska, Klondike, and the Yukon, from where he sent vivid accounts of the exhausting enterprise to American newspapers. (Frank Norris modeled a character in his 1901 novel *The Octopus: A Story of California* on the Miller of this period and thereby addressed Miller's fame and impact on western literature, acknowledging his influence while at the same time castigating Miller's sentimentalizing and his romanticizing the West.) From 1887 until his death Miller otherwise lived in a home in the hills above Oakland, California, where he received guests, wrote, gazed at setting suns, and built monuments to three men whom he honored but who, in fact, embodied his own various roles as explorer, poet, and prophet: Frémont, Robert Browning, and Moses. He died in Oakland.

Miller conceived, created, and enacted a memorable and influential image of the western hero. As writer, he is perhaps at his best in suggestive passages that create a myth of the West as the land of the future and the sunset of death, at once the beginning and the end, opportunity yet unfulfilled longing. Christopher Columbus's voyage was to the West—all of America in the fifteenth century—in Miller's most enduring poem, long a classroom favorite, "Columbus" (in *Songs of the Soul* [1896]). Although he "gained a world," Columbus's inspiriting motto remains "On! Sail on!" Yet Miller's mystic monolith, Mount Shasta, stands forth grandly even in the rampart of the High Sierra "as lone as God, and white as a winter moon"

(*Life amongst the Modocs*). "Our pilgrimage," he wrote, "is simply that of thousands and thousands who peopled the ultimate west" (*Overland in a Covered Wagon*).

• Many of Miller's letters are in the Huntington Library, San Marino, Calif. Other materials are deposited in the Bancroft Library of the University of California, Berkeley. Among many other titles by Miller are *The Destruction of Gotham* (1886), a city novel, *Songs of the Mexican Seas* (1887), local color verse, and *Memorie and Rime* (1884), an autobiography. Miller's collected poetry was published in San Francisco in 1909–1910. Modern introductions to his life and works are O. W. Frost, *Joaquin Miller* (1967), and Benjamin S. Lawson, *Joaquin Miller* (1980). The most thorough, if dated, treatment of Miller's books is Martin S. Peterson, *Joaquin Miller, Literary Frontiersman* (1937). Balancing Peterson's generally favorable view of Miller's writings is the biography by M. Marion Marberry, *Splendid Poseur: Joaquin Miller—American Poet* (1953).

BENJAMIN S. LAWSON

MILLER, John (25 Nov. 1781–18 Mar. 1846), soldier and governor of Missouri, was born near Martinsburg, Virginia (now West Virginia), the son of a farmer. Virtually nothing else is known of his parents, including their social and economic status, and his youth is also undocumented. His formal education was limited to an unknown period in the state common schools, but his career suggests thorough literacy, implying additional schooling at home and thus an above-average socioeconomic background. At the age of twenty-two Miller moved to Steubenville, Ohio, where he published and edited the *Steubenville Gazette* and the *Western Herald*. These activities gained him enough political influence that he was appointed as a general in the Ohio militia shortly before the outbreak of the War of 1812. This commission was quickly followed by an appointment as a lieutenant colonel in the Seventeenth Infantry Regiment of the U.S. Army and a promotion to colonel of the Nineteenth U.S. Infantry three weeks after the war began—an indication that his public reputation was thought valuable for recruiting. Miller distinguished himself in the defense of Fort Meigs on the Maumee River in northwestern Ohio, where he commanded the successful wing of the American sortie against the British batteries on 5 May 1813. William Henry Harrison singled out Miller for commendation, providing renown essential to his postwar political career.

In August 1814 Miller was temporarily made the theater commander in the Northwest. British pressure in other theaters made it impossible to organize a western offensive that fall, and the remainder of Miller's wartime career was uneventful. His services (and his consequent political stature in the West) were rewarded when he was retained without demotion during the massive army reduction of 1815, taking command of the Third U.S. Infantry as one of only ten regimental commanders in the army. In July 1815 Miller commanded the U.S. troops overseeing the treaty council with the Indians at Portages des Sioux near the confluence of the Missouri and Mississippi rivers, a show of force that effectively brought hostilities in that region to a halt, permitting Anglo-American immigration on an ever greater scale. Three years later Miller resigned from the army to take up private business and to further his political future. In 1821 he received a federal appointment as the registrar of the public land office in Franklin, Missouri, in the heart of the booming Boone's Lick region at the center of the state. This prominent position brought him to the attention of the powerful "Central Clique" faction (known among their supporters as the "Boone's Lick Democracy") in state politics, and in December 1825 he was the victor against three opponents in a special election held to replace the deceased governor, Frederick Bates.

Historians once viewed Miller's election as nonpartisan in character, but more recent chroniclers have recognized the active support he received from Thomas Hart Benton against the proto-Adamsite faction led by U.S. Senator David Barton, Benton's principal antagonist within Missouri. During the campaign Miller identified his candidacy with adherence to traditional Jeffersonian principles and hostility to aristocracy, the rhetoric of the evolving Jacksonian party. Always a fiscal conservative, Miller spoke out against legislation for debtor relief, declaring that the state loan office was unconstitutional; he later sought to withdraw the state's paper money from circulation. He sought a more liberal public land policy, including the opening of mineral resources on federal land to private lease; encouraged the production of hemp through a bounty; and advocated more extensive public education (including a state university and library) to be funded by the sale of public lands. The legislature was not responsive enough to satisfy him, so Miller shifted the focus of his expansive interests to the federal level, seeking lower public land prices, tariffs to protect state products, the extension of the National Road through Missouri, and federal aid to protect the Santa Fe Trail.

Miller's role in the development of the Jacksonian party in Missouri remains unclear. Although he made some appointments on a nonpartisan basis, he also applied his patronage powers to aid Benton and the Central Clique, and his efforts were rewarded when he was reelected without opposition in 1828. Two years later he came before the legislature as Benton's preference to succeed Barton as senator, but the Jacksonians split their votes among several candidates and were surprised by the election of an advocate of the American System of federally directed internal improvements, who had posed as a Jacksonian. Indeed, it was not until the election of 1836 that the Jacksonians were able to clearly distinguish themselves from the National Republicans within the state. Miller was constitutionally forbidden from running for another term as governor in 1832, so he retired to private life as a planter near St. Louis. His most significant public policy stance during the remainder of his life was support for western internal improvements, particularly railroads and a canal to link the Illinois River with Lake Michigan. In 1836 Miller was elected to the House of Representatives, but his three terms there were undistinguished, and in 1842 he retired again. Two years later he was the choice of Missouri's Hard Money Democrats (largely members of the Central Clique) to replace the deceased Lewis F. Linn as senator, but Governor Thomas Reynolds appointed David R. Atchison in order to garner support from the state's peripheries. Miller died two years later at his plantation in Florissant. He never married and does not appear to have had children.

The significance of Miller's career lies more in what he represented than in his actions themselves, for there is little to indicate that he was an active leader in the Boone's Lick Democracy. As a soldier, editor, politician, and planter, Miller followed the diverse yet closely interwoven career path characteristic of public men on the frontier of Anglo-American expansion, and his public policy concerns reflected the needs of that frontier—including the demand for internal improvements, more liberal terms for the sale of public lands, and defense against Indians and British influence. Miller may have been personally disposed toward nonpartisanship, but his career was thoroughly intertwined with the development of the Jacksonian party in Missouri, whose policy stances and ideology he generally shared. In doing so, and in his career itself, Miller reflected the suitability of that party's ideas for an expanding frontier suspicious of, yet dependent on, centralized power.

• Very few of Miller's papers have survived; they are located in the Western Historical Manuscripts Collection in Columbia, Mo. His public pronouncements as governor are collected in Buel Leopard and Floyd C. Shoemaker, eds., *The Messages and Proclamations of the Governors of the State of Missouri*, vol. 1 (1922). Background on the political scene in Miller's Missouri can be found in Leota Newhard, "The Beginning of the Whig Party in Missouri, 1824–1840," *Missouri Historical Review* 25 (1931): 254–80; Hattie M. Anderson, "The Jackson Men in Missouri in 1828," *Missouri Historical Review* 34 (1940): 301–34; Robert E. Shalhope, "Thomas Hart Benton and Missouri State Politics: A Re-Examination," *Bulletin of the Missouri Historical Society* 25 (1969): 171–91; Shalhope, "Jacksonian Politics in Missouri: A Comment on the McCormick Thesis," *Civil War History* 15 (1969): 210–25; John Vollmer Mering, *The Whig Party in Missouri* (1967); and Rudolph E. Forderhase, "Jacksonianism in Missouri: From Predilection to Party, 1820–1836" (Ph.D. diss., Univ. of Missouri at Columbia, 1968). Dorothy J. Caldwell, "The Big Neck Affair: Tragedy and Farce on the Missouri Frontier," *Missouri Historical Review* 64 (1970): 391–412, discusses Miller's rather indecisive involvement in an inconclusive scare brought on by white intrusions into Indian territory. See Perry McCandless, *A History of Missouri*, vol. 2: *1820 to 1860* (1972), for the most thorough treatment of the state's history during this era, including several direct references to Miller. Sympathetic obituaries are in the *Jefferson City Enquirer*, 25 Mar. 1846, and the *Boonville Weekly Observer*, 24 and 31 Mar. 1846.

SAMUEL J. WATSON

MILLER, Kelly (18 July 1863–29 Dec. 1939), educator and essayist, was born in Winnsboro, South Carolina, the son of Kelly Miller, a free black who served in the Confederate army, and Elizabeth Roberts, a slave. The sixth of ten children, Miller received his early education in one of the local primary schools established during Reconstruction and later attended the Fairfield Institute in Winnsboro from 1878 to 1880. Awarded a scholarship to Howard University, he completed the Preparatory Department's three-year curriculum in Latin, Greek, and mathematics in two years (1880–1882), then attended the College Department at Howard from 1882 to 1886.

After his graduation from Howard, Miller studied advanced mathematics (1886–1887) with Captain Edgar Frisby, an English mathematician at the U.S. Naval Observatory. Frisby's chief at the observatory, Simon Newcomb, who was also a professor of mathematics at Johns Hopkins University, recommended Miller for admission. The first black student admitted to Johns Hopkins, Miller studied mathematics, physics, and astronomy there from 1887 to 1889 but did not graduate because he ran out of funds. After teaching mathematics briefly at the M Street High School in Washington, D.C. (1889–1890), he was appointed to the faculty of Howard University in 1890. Five years later Miller added sociology to Howard's curriculum because he thought that the new discipline was important for developing objective analyses of the racial system in the United States. From 1895 to 1907 Miller was professor of mathematics and sociology, but he taught sociology exclusively after that, serving from 1915 to 1925 as head of the new sociology department. In 1894 Miller had married Annie May Butler, a teacher at the Baltimore Normal School, with whom he had five children.

Noted for his brilliant mind, Miller rapidly became a major figure in the life of Howard University. In 1907 he was appointed dean of the College of Arts and Sciences. During his twelve-year deanship the college grew dramatically, as the old classical curriculum was modernized and new courses in the natural sciences and the social sciences were added. Miller's recruiting tours through the South and Middle Atlantic states were so successful that the enrollment increased from 75 undergraduates in 1907 to 243 undergraduates in 1911.

Although Miller was a leader at Howard for most of his tenure there, his national importance derived from his intellectual leadership during the conflict between the "accommodationism" of Booker T. Washington and the "radicalism" of the nascent civil rights movement led by W. E. B. Du Bois. Critical of Washington's famous Cotton States Exposition Address (1895) in 1896, Miller later praised Washington's emphasis on self-help and initiative. He remained an opponent of the exaggerated claims made on behalf of industrial education and became one of the most effective advocates of higher education for black Americans when it was attacked as "inappropriate" for a people whose social role was increasingly limited by statute and custom to agriculture, some skilled trades, unskilled labor, and domestic service.

In the *Educational Review*, *Dial*, *Education*, the *Journal of Social Science*, and other leading journals, Miller argued that blacks required wise leadership in the difficult political and social circumstances following the defeat of Reconstruction, and only higher education could provide such leaders. Moreover, the race required physicians, lawyers, clergymen, teachers, and other professionals whose existence was dependent on higher education. Excluded from most white colleges, black Americans would have to secure higher education in their own institutions, Miller argued, and some of them, like Howard, Fisk, and Atlanta Universities, would emphasize liberal education and the professions rather than the trades and manual arts (industrial education) stressed at Hampton and Tuskegee Institutes. In the debate between the advocates of collegiate and industrial education, Miller maintained that the whole matter was one of "ratio and proportion" not "fundamental controversy." Recognized as one of the most influential black educators in the nation because of his extensive writing and his leadership at Howard, Miller was sought out by both camps in the controversy but was trusted by neither because of his refusal to dogmatically support either of the rival systems.

Miller's reputation as a "philosopher of the race question" was based on his brilliant articles, published anonymously at first, on "radicals" and "conservatives" in the *Boston Transcript* (18, 19 Sept. 1903). With some alterations, these articles later became the lead essay in his book *Race Adjustment* (1908). Miller's essays insisted on the right of black Americans to protest against the injustices that had multiplied with the rise of the white supremacy movement in the South, as the Du Bois "radicals" did, but he also advocated racial solidarity, thrift, and institution-building as emphasized by the followers of Washington. Characteristically, Miller had two reputations as a public policy analyst, first as a compromiser between black radicals and conservatives, and second as a race spokesman during the prolonged crisis of disfranchisement and the denial of civil rights by white supremacists and their elected representatives in Congress. *The Disgrace of Democracy: An Open Letter to President Woodrow Wilson*, a pamphlet published in August 1917, was Miller's most popular effort. Responding to recent race riots in Memphis and East St. Louis, Miller argued that a "democracy of race or class is no democracy at all." Writing to Wilson, he said, "It is but hollow mockery of the Negro when he is beaten and bruised in all parts of the nation and flees to the national government for asylum, to be denied relief on the basis of doubtful jurisdiction. The black man asks for protection and is given a theory of government." More than 250,000 copies of the pamphlet were sold, and the military authorities banned it on army posts.

Although Miller was best known as a controversialist, he also made important but frequently overlooked contributions to the discipline of sociology. His earliest contribution was his analysis of Frederick L. Hoffman's *Race Traits and Tendencies of the American Negro*, published by the American Economic Association in 1896. Hoffman attempted to demonstrate that the social disorganization of black Americans (weak community institutions and family structure) was caused by an alleged genetic inferiority and that their correspondingly high mortality rate would result in their disappearance as an element of the American population. Miller's refutation of Hoffman's claims, *A Review of Hoffman's Race Traits and Tendencies of the American Negro*, published by the American Negro Academy in 1897, was based on a technical analysis of census data.

Perhaps Miller's most lasting contribution to scholarship was his pioneering advocacy of the systematic study of black people. In 1901 he proposed to the Howard board of trustees that the university financially support the publications of the American Negro Academy, whose goals were to promote literature, science, art, higher education, and scholarly works by blacks, and to defend them against "vicious assaults." Although the board declined, it permitted the academy to meet on the campus. Convinced that Howard should use its prestige and location in Washington to become a national center for black studies, Miller planned a "Negro-Americana Museum and Library." In 1914 he persuaded Jesse E. Moorland, a Howard alumnus and Young Men's Christian Association official, to donate to Howard his large private library on blacks in Africa and in the United States as the foundation for the proposed center. This became the Moorland Foundation (reorganized in 1973 as the Moorland–Spingarn Research Center), a research library, archives, and museum that has been vital to the emergence of sound scholarship in this field.

The years after World War I were difficult ones for Miller. J. Stanley Durkee, the last of Howard's white presidents, was appointed in 1918 and set out to curtail the baronial power of the deans by building a new central administration. Miller, a conspicuously powerful dean, was demoted in 1919 to dean of a new junior college, which was later abolished in 1925. A leader in the movement to have a black president of Howard, Miller was a perennial favorite of the alumni but was never selected. Although his influence at Howard declined significantly by the late 1920s through his retirement in 1934, Miller's stature as a commentator on race relations and politics remained high. He had become alarmed by the vast social changes stimulated by World War I and was seen as increasingly conservative. He opposed the widespread abandonment of farming by black Americans and warned that the mass migration to cities would be socially and culturally destructive. At a time when many younger blacks regarded labor unions as progressive forces, Miller was skeptical of them, citing their history of persistent racial discrimination. He remained an old-fashioned American patriot despite the nation's many disappointing failures to extend democracy to black Americans. As a weekly columnist in the black press, Miller's views were published in more than one hundred newspapers. By 1923 it was estimated that his columns reached half a million readers. Miller died at his home on the campus of Howard University.

• A limited collection of Miller's papers, including an incomplete autobiography and a scrapbook, is at the Moorland–Spingarn Research Center at Howard University. His other writings include *As to the Leopard's Spots: An Open Letter to Thomas Dixon*, a pamphlet published in 1905, and *Appeal to Reason on the Race Problem: An Open Letter to John Temple Graves* (1906), a searching commentary on the Atlanta race riot. Among Miller's sociological articles are "The Ultimate Race Problem," *Atlantic Monthly*, Apr. 1909, pp. 2–8; "Eugenics of the Negro Race," *Scientific Monthly*, July 1917, pp. 57–59; and "Enumeration Errors in Negro Population," *Scientific Monthly*, Feb. 1922, pp. 168–77. Useful biographical accounts are D. O. W. Holmes, "Kelly Miller," *Phylon* (Second Quarter 1945): 121–25, and August Meier, "The Racial and Educational Philosophy of Kelly Miller, 1895–1915," *Journal of Negro Education* (July 1960): 121–27. An obituary is Carter G. Woodson, "Kelly Miller," *Journal of Negro History* (Jan. 1940): 137–38.

MICHAEL R. WINSTON

MILLER, Kenneth Hayes (11 Mar. 1876–1 Jan. 1952), artist and teacher, was born in Oneida, New York, the son of George Miller and Annie Elizabeth Kelly, both active members of the Oneida Perfectionist Community, a utopian religious society that practiced open marriage and genetic selection. Miller's father was an author and salesman; his mother worked in the community's printing shop. Miller's family moved to Manhattan during his teens, when his father became sales manager of the community's New York City office.

In New York City Miller attended the Horace Mann School, although there is no record of his having graduated. Miller began his formal art training at the Chase School of Art (later the New York School) in about 1890, studying under its founder, William Merritt Chase. In 1892 he continued his art studies at the Art Students League under J. Carroll Beckwith, Kenyon Cox, H. Siddons Mowbray, F. Luis Mora, and Frank Vincent duMond. In 1900 Miller traveled to Europe to see and examine firsthand the works of the Old Masters.

After working briefly as an illustrator, Miller began his long and successful teaching career alongside Robert Henri at the New York School, where he remained from 1899 until it closed in 1911. That same year, Miller accepted a position teaching life classes at the Art Students League, and he taught there for the rest of his life. At his death, Stewart Klonis, former director of the Art Students League, asserted that Miller had been "the only teacher working in America who, in the tradition of the Renaissance, produced a school of painters" (cover, *Art Students League News*, 1 Mar. 1952). Miller made a lasting impression on his students, many of whom became significant American artists, including Yasuo Kuniyoshi, Reginald Marsh, Edward Hopper, Isabel Bishop, George Bellows, Marsden Hartley, Peggy Bacon, and Rockwell Kent. Bishop later recalled that Miller had an "aura" about him that spread to his students, particularly when he discussed his firm belief that "the pursuit of the Art of Painting is of an *absolute* importance" (Reich, p. 27).

Miller's early depictions of nudes in landscape settings were romantic in nature and much indebted to the older American artist Albert Pinkham Ryder, who became a mentor and friend. Miller's portrait of Ryder (1913) is part of the Phillips Collection in Washington, D.C. By 1920 Miller had fallen under the spell of the French painter Auguste Renoir's impressionistic paintings. Renoir's late paintings of nudes were perhaps Miller's only acquiescence to modernism. Both of these influences were to translate into a lifelong interest in large, robust figures.

In 1923 Miller established a studio in New York City at 30 East Fourteenth Street, near Fifth Avenue. Shortly thereafter former students Marsh and Bishop moved to studios in the neighborhood; along with the Soyer twins, Raphael and Moses, among others, they established what later became known as the "Fourteenth Street School." Miller's painting technique and choice of subject (physically imposing women) strongly influenced this informal group of artists. In his works Miller depicts either saleswomen assisting female customers or content patrons strolling downtown New York streets, elegantly dressed in the latest fashions and sporting their newly acquired accessories, talking among themselves, or stopping to examine window displays. These paintings include *Department Store* (1930), *The Fitting Room* (1931), *The Box Party* (1936), and *Sidewalk Merchants* (1940). There was no attempt at satire or social commentary in Miller's work; rather, the artist appreciated and sought to depict realistically this aspect of contemporary life. At the same time, he sought to relate his Manhattan women to those of the Old Masters. Indeed, his emphasis on line and solid forms (aspects central to both his teaching and his paintings) recalls the weight and solidity of the figures of Giotto and Peter Paul Rubens. His frequent borrowing from the compositions as well as painting techniques of the European masters, particularly in the mixing of oil glazes and opaque tempera, further emphasized his indebtedness to that epoch.

Miller, who constantly sought new and enduring friendships, developed long-term relationships with many of his former students, including Kent, Marsh, and Bishop. For thirty years his studio was a regular meeting place for his students and friends. According to art historian Alan Burroughs, the atmosphere was that of an "informal salon." The tall, lean, and earnest Miller was also a voracious reader, and among his most notable acquaintances was the American novelist Theodore Dreiser. Miller practiced a stringent work ethic. As Bishop recalled, "he was always working . . . a visit at any time of the day or of the year would unfailingly find him engrossed in the making of a picture" (Reich, p. 27). Miller never used models, and he worked in a slow, methodical manner on each canvas. He reportedly stated, "In painting I am an inch worm. . . . No, a half-inch worm" (cover, *Art Students League News*, 1 Mar. 1952).

Miller was married twice. His first marriage, in 1898, was to Irma Ferry, a resident of Oneida, although not associated with the Perfectionist Community; they divorced in 1910. The following year he married Helen Pendleton, a suffragette and former student. Together they had a daughter, Louise, his only child.

Miller exhibited four paintings in the momentous Armory Show of 1913 and was one of the first painters to be included in the permanent collection of the Museum of Modern Art, founded in 1929. He was elected to the National Academy of Design in 1944 and to the National Institute of Arts and Letters in 1947 and was a member of the American Society of Painters, Sculptors and Gravers. Owing to his interest in etching, he joined three organizations that solely promoted printmaking activities: the American Print Makers, the Philadelphia Society of Etchers, and the Society of American Etchers. He died in New York City.

Miller enjoyed his greatest influence on American art between the two world wars, when his work with solid figures and tight compositions had a particularly strong impact on many of the urban realists. His popularity declined after his death, when continuing interest in his work focused primarily on his etchings. These prints, however, reflect the figurative concerns found in his other works. Today his work is important primarily for its evocation of a long-faded artistic fashion and the urban culture relating to the first half of the twentieth century in America.

• Documents, correspondence, and transcribed interviews with former students of Miller, such as Peggy Bacon, Isabel Bishop, Lloyd Goodrich, Reginald Marsh, Rockwell Kent, and others, are in the Archives of American Art, Washington D.C.; see also Sheldon Reich, *Isabel Bishop* (1974), and Lloyd Goodrich, *Reginald Marsh* (1972). The National Academy of Design owns a portrait of Miller painted by Reginald Marsh in 1943. For a detailed account of Miller's life, see Lincoln Rothschild, *To Keep Art Alive: The Effort of Kenneth Hayes Miller, American Painter (1876)–1952)* (1974); see also Alan Burroughs, *Kenneth Hayes Miller* (1931), and Lloyd Goodrich, *Kenneth Hayes Miller* (1930). For an assessment of Miller see Hilton Kramer, "The Unhappy Fate of Kenneth Hayes Miller," *New York Times*, 11 Mar. 1979. For feminist scholarship on Miller see Ellen Wiley Todd, *The "New Woman" Revised: Painting and Gender Politics on Fourteenth Street* (1993). An obituary is in the *New York Times*, 3 Jan. 1952. The 1 Mar. 1952 issue of the *Art Students League News* is a special memorial issue devoted to Miller.

EFRAM L. BURK

MILLER, Marilyn (1 Sept. 1898–7 Apr. 1936), dancer and actress, was born Mary Ellen Reynolds in Evansville, Indiana, the daughter of Edwin D. Reynolds, a lineman for the Cumberland Telephone Company, and Ada Thompson, who had theatrical aspirations. The Reynolds' marriage broke up when Edwin was reassigned to another locale, and Marilyn's mother rejected transferring the family. Marilyn was brought up by her mother and a stepfather, Oscar Caro Miller, who had sung, danced, and performed acrobatics in vaudeville and Gilbert and Sullivan operettas.

Marilyn gradually rearranged her name, adopting her stepfather's last name and her mother's middle name, Lynn, and adding it to her given name, finally shortening it to Marilyn Miller on producer Florenz Ziegfeld's advice. Her career began in 1903 when she joined her mother, her stepfather, and her two sisters in an act billed as "The Five Columbians." Presenting a mix of dancing, singing, and light patter, they were popular on the vaudeville circuit in the Midwest. Marilyn made her appearance as a surprise guest artist, "Mademoiselle Sugarplum," and she danced and played the drums. Bookings became difficult in the larger cities, however, because she was underage, so the family left the country, touring in Canada, the West Indies, and England.

While performing in a London club in 1914, Miller attracted the attention of Broadway producer Lee Shubert, who brought her to the Winter Garden in New York, where she made an appearance in his annual revue, *The Passing Show of 1914*. Although her role was minor, her graceful, versatile dancing, complemented by her petite, doll-like beauty, was instantly acclaimed. Miller was fifteen years old at the time. She remained with Shubert for the next three years, her dancing reputation escalating in *The Passing Show of 1915*, *The Show of Wonders* (1916), and *The Passing Show of 1917*.

However, it was the eminent producer Florenz Ziegfeld who catapulted Miller into stardom by inserting her into his annual summer *Follies* of 1918 at the New Amsterdam in 1918. Ziegfeld recognized Miller's potential and expanded her repertoire by furnishing singing and acting lessons. By combining classical ballet with contemporary dance, along with singing and acting, Miller propelled herself into the first rank of the performers on Broadway.

Her first full performance was in Ziegfeld's *Sally* in 1920, the decade's most popular musical show, which ran for more than two years and toured in Boston and Chicago. Miller's hit number was a Jerome Kern song, "Look for the Silver Lining." But personal and financial difficulties led to a split between Ziegfeld and Miller, and Miller was offered a contractual arrangement with Charles Dillingham, a prestigious rival producer. Dillingham recommended that she play the lead in *Peter Pan*. Although Miller had qualms because the role of *Pan* had been made famous by the inimitable Maude Adams, she accepted, and the play opened in 1924. It was to be her only foray in a dramatic production. The critics were ambivalent, comparing her unfavorably with Adams while praising her dancing and gracefulness. The influential writer Alexander Woollcott wrote that "She may be said to have danced the part."

Miller returned to her forte the following year in *Sunny*, Dillingham's next production written by Otto Harbach, Oscar Hammerstein, and Jerome Kern. The show ran for fifteen months and played in New York, Boston, and Philadelphia. Her numbers, "Who?" and "D'Ye Love Me?," became bestselling sheet music, and as a result Miller's salary soared to $3,000, making her the highest-paid musical comedy performer at that time on Broadway.

Reconciling with Ziegfeld in 1928, Miller performed in the successful show *Rosalie*, a half-operetta, half-musical comedy written by George and Ira Gershwin, Sigmund Romberg, and P. G. Wodehouse. It was immediately followed by *Smiles*, which also featured Fred and Adele Astaire but had a short run. In between productions Miller went to Hollywood and starred in the film version of her first hit, *Sally*. Then in 1930 she made a couple of other films, the screen version of *Sunny* and *Her Majesty, Love*, the latter with W. C. Fields.

Miller's last production was *As Thousands Cheer*, a popular satirical revue by Moss Hart and Irving Berlin that was suddenly terminated by contractual difficulties in 1934. She left the stage for a while, hoping to return in another production, but her health began to deteriorate. She died the following year at the age of thirty-seven from complications arising from recurring sinus infections and questionable medical treatment.

The fulfillment that Miller experienced in her theatrical career was not matched in her personal life. Her first marriage had ended in tragedy in less than a year when her husband, Frank Canter, was killed in a car crash. She divorced a second husband, Jack Pickford, who was addicted to drugs and alcohol, in 1927. Her last spouse was Chester O'Brien, a young actor who made only sporadic attempts to secure work on the stage; they were still married at her death, but she left him out of her will.

Musical comedy in the decade of the 1930s was markedly different from the type that had produced Marilyn Miller. The economic depression and competition from film musicals with their lavishly designed costumes and sets and expressively vigorous choreography led to a new style of performer. Miller's delicate and ingénue presentation gave way to a more assertive, sophisticated style.

During her heyday, however, Miller was the reigning star, and her legacy to musical comedy was substantial. Because of her infusion of dancing modes that ranged from classical ballet to clog to contemporary, her elegant and captivating numbers enlarged the musical form. Her statue on the I. Miller building at the corner of Forty-sixth Street and Seventh Avenue in New York City—designed by A. Stirling Calder, father of Alexander Calder—attests to her continuing presence on Broadway.

• Primary materials relating to Miller's life and career are in the Harvard Theatre Collection, Harvard University, and the Billy Rose Theatre Collection at the New York Public Library for the Performing Arts, Lincoln Center. Her place in the pantheon of musical comedy is succinctly but astutely summed up in Gerald Bordman, *American Musical Comedy: From Adonis to Dreamgirls* (1982), but see also his *American Musical Revue: From the Passing Show to Sugar Babies* (1985). An excellent article assessing her career is by Noreen Barnes in Alice M. Robinson et al., eds., *Notable Women in the American Theatre: A Biographical Dictionary* (1989). Important pieces of information can be gleaned from Marjorie Farnsworth, *Ziegfeld Follies* (1956), Abel Green and Joe Laurie, Jr., *Show Biz—From Vaude to Video* (1951), Ethel Mordden, *Better Foot Forward: The History of American Musical Theatre* (1976), Cecil Smith, *Musical Comedy in America*, 2d ed. (1981), and Patricia Ziegfeld, *The Ziegfelds' Girl* (1964). Magazine articles of the period provide insight into her popularity: *Cosmopolitan*, Nov. 1914, *American Magazine*, May 1921, and *Motion Picture Magazine*, Oct. 1923, Oct. 1929, and Sept. 1931. A spritely written biography is by Warren G. Harris, *The Other Marilyn* (1985), but it lacks documentation. Obituaries are in the *New York Daily News* and the *New York Times*, 8 Apr. 1936.

JOSEPH BOSKIN

MILLER, Merle (17 May 1919–10 June 1986), novelist and biographer, was born in Montour, Iowa, the son of Monte Merle Miller and Dora Winders, farmers. He graduated from high school in nearby Marshalltown, Iowa, and then attended the University of Iowa from 1935 to 1938 and 1939 to 1940; he spent the intervening year on scholarship at the London School of Economics. Miller excelled in college, winning numerous writing and speech awards as well as editing the undergraduate daily paper, but his personal dislike of required ROTC classes led him to depart without graduating.

Miller was not, however, a pacifist in principle, as he soon showed in his support of the war effort. After beginning a civilian career in journalism—he was a Washington correspondent for the *Philadelphia Record* from 1940 to 1941—he joined the Army Air Corps in 1942. He spent the next three years as an editor of *Yank* magazine, serving first in the Pacific theater and then in Europe; he won the Bronze Star with oak-leaf cluster for his contributions. Discharged in September 1945, he moved to New York City and became an associate editor at *Time* (1945) and then an assistant editor at *Harper's* (1947–1949). During these years he began writing novels as well, and in 1949 he became a full-time freelance writer. His most notable works of fiction include *That Winter* (1948), a novel about veterans readjusting to postwar life, which received strong contemporary reviews, *The Sure Thing* (1949), and *A Day in Late September* (1963).

Active on the board of directors of the American Civil Liberties Union in the early 1950s, Miller wrote a nonfiction work condemning blacklisting, *The Judges and the Judged* (1952). He also contributed to numerous magazines and wrote screenplays and television plays. Disappointed by his failed attempt to write a pilot episode acceptable to television networks obsessed with sheer profit, Miller—with collaborator Evan Rhodes—countered by writing the satirical nonfiction work *Only You, Dick Daring! or, How to Write One Television Script and Make $50,000,000* (1964).

At the end of the 1960s Miller had made a living as a writer, but he had as yet left no lasting mark in literary or intellectual circles. That changed radically on 17 January 1971, when the *New York Times Magazine* ran an article bearing his name and the title "What It Means to Be a Homosexual." Miller, as he detailed in the piece, had been a homosexual since youth. (In what he called a vain attempt at a "cure," he had married Elinor Green in 1948, but after four years—and no children—they were divorced.) But despite his outspokenness in other areas, he had not to that point publicly admitted his sexual orientation. After being outraged by the aversion to homosexuality shown by an allegedly liberal writer in an article in *Harper's*, however, Miller—despite having "no taste for self-revelation"—felt compelled to record his painful personal experiences of rejection by American society. He wrote of therapists who only sought to cure his "sickness" and of friends who would not trust him alone with their children. His piece provoked strong reactions, both positive and negative, which he chronicled in *On Being Different: What It Means to Be a Homosexual* (1971). This brief book incorporated the original article with a similarly personal afterword detailing its origin and aftermath and has been called nothing less than a "gay Declaration of Independence."

Having done his part in starting a small revolution, Miller returned to broader literary endeavors. Despite his earlier negative experiences with the medium, television ultimately—though indirectly—led him to his greatest popular success. In the early 1960s Miller had been chosen as the researcher and writer for a planned television series on Harry S. Truman and had begun conducting multiple interviews with the former president; when the series was scrapped, Miller salvaged the remains and eventually published the successful *Plain Speaking: An Oral Biography of Harry S. Truman* (1974). Here—interspersing interviews with Truman's colleagues and acquaintances with those of Truman himself and providing only minimal commentary—Miller succeeded in showing the Missourian as a "four-dimensional" man who might well have been "the last human being to occupy the White House" (p. 15).

Miller's success with this form—and his accompanying interest in the occupants of the Oval Office—shaped the rest of his career. Having explored the life of the national leader who oversaw the completion of America's greatest military victory, he next turned to one who had led the nation during its greatest defeat: Lyndon B. Johnson. Miller had opposed the Vietnam War and, like many others, blamed Johnson for dragging the United States deeper into it, but the act of writing *Lyndon: An Oral Biography* (1980) changed his mind at least partially. Using the same format—he conducted 180 interviews and consulted almost 400 oral histories—he presented a portrait of Johnson as "one of the most complex, fascinating, difficult, colorful personages in American history" (p. xiv). Once again Miller juxtaposed bare-bones factual information with recorded testimony from the late president and his colleagues, producing a "mosaic" effect that some critics claimed lacked strong narrative control. Nonetheless, his book received general critical acclaim and became a bestseller.

Returning to the war in which he himself had served, Miller chose another occupant of the White House for his next subject: Dwight D. Eisenhower. This work was slightly different, as he noted in his introduction; it was not an oral biography about a president but rather a biography about a soldier. Two days after completing the manuscript at his Brewster, New York, home—where he had lived since the early 1950s—Miller was hospitalized in Danbury, Connecticut, and diagnosed with an abdominal infection and peritonitis. He died there. *Ike the Soldier: As They Knew Him* was published posthumously in 1987.

Miller has often been called an "oral historian," though he occasionally questioned this categorization and—in what may have been an attempt at self-disparagement—called himself a "reporter." Nonetheless, in his introduction to *Lyndon* he cites his admiration of and debt to pioneer oral historians such as Studs Terkel and T. Harry Williams, biographer of Louisiana governor Huey Long. The popularity of his works bespeaks his contributions to the field. And his outspokenness in *On Being Different* made him an unforgettable figure in the gay rights movement. One of his final statements there might be taken as its credo: "No minority in this country or anywhere else has gained its rights by remaining silent, and no revolution has ever been made by the wary. Or the self-pitying" (p. 64).

• Boston University Library holds Miller's correspondence, typescripts of his works with holograph corrections, preliminary notes, galleys, and publicity materials. Biographical sources include an interview in Roy Newquist, *Conversations* (1967). Also see the *New York Review of Books*, 4 Nov. 1971, and the *New York Times*, 15 Aug. 1980. An obituary is in the *New York Times*, 11 June 1986.

W. FARRELL O'GORMAN

MILLER, Nathan Lewis (10 Oct 1868–26 Jun. 1953), lawyer and politician, was born in Solon, Cortland County, New York, the son of Samuel Miller and Almera Russell, farmers. After graduating from normal school in 1887, he taught school for three years, then clerked in a local law office, and in 1893 was admitted to the New York bar. In 1896 he married Elizabeth Davern, a preceptress at the Marathon Academy; they had seven children. Miller practiced law in Cortland and was elected school commissioner, a position that he held until his appointment in 1900 as corporation counsel. In 1897 he became chairman of the Cortland County Republican Committee.

Miller's activities in Republican politics earned him the respect of New York GOP chairman Benjamin B. Odell, and in 1901 Odell, now governor, appointed him state comptroller to fill a position left vacant by resignation. The next year he won the office in his own right but resigned in 1903 to become a justice of the New York Supreme Court. One year later Odell named him an associate justice of the appellate division, and in 1912 Governor John A. Dix promoted him to the prestigious Court of Appeals, the state's highest tribunal. Here Miller sat in judgment, along with his colleagues and the state senate, as a court of impeachment against Governor William Sulzer in the fall of 1913. He voted with the majority for Sulzer's conviction on two counts (violation of the Corrupt Practices Act and perjury) and for the governor's removal from office. Miller's record as a judge was progressive: he subscribed to the doctrine that the law changes with changing conditions. He wrote decisions that affirmed the constitutionality of a state law prohibiting the employment of minors in hazardous occupations, the Workmen's Compensation Act of 1913, and New York's recently adopted public health law. In less than three years as an appeals court judge, Miller penned eighty-one opinions, most of which were written for the majority. In 1915 he resigned from the Court of Appeals for financial reasons and removed his large family to Syracuse, where he resumed private practice. He became general counsel for the Solvay Process Company and helped form the Allied Chemical and Dye Corporation, a leading American firm in the world's chemical industry.

In 1920 Miller attended the Republican National Convention in Chicago, where he joined in the nomination of Herbert C. Hoover for the presidency. Later that year leaders of the New York GOP persuaded him to run for governor against the popular incumbent, Alfred S. Smith. He defeated Smith by the narrow margin of approximately 74,000 votes, while the Harding-Coolidge national ticket won the state by a plurality that exceeded one million. During Miller's two-year term as governor, he scuttled the sweeping recommendations of his predecessor's Reconstruction Commission and instead instituted piecemeal administrative reform. For a "constitutional" executive budget, he substituted a board of estimate and control, created by statute. He consolidated the offices of state engineer, highway commissioner, tax commissioner, and industrial commissioner. His program of efficiency and economy also included the establishment of the office of budget director and the department of purchase and supply, the elimination of approximately 2,000 civil service jobs, and a reduction in expenditures that by 1923 left a surplus in the state treasury that he estimated at $40 million. Miller's reorganization of the Public Service Commissions and the Industrial Commission generated criticism for undermining the regulatory authority of these bodies. His pay-as-you-go approach allowed him to undertake only a modest hospital construction program, but he did oversee the introduction of new methods of psychiatric care and occupational therapy in the state hospitals.

Miller's record in other areas of governance placed him somewhere between Smith's progressivism and the laissez-faire conservatism of that era. He supported several measures for the protection of women and children, but he refused federal aid for maternity care under the Sheppard-Towner Act (1921) for fear of growing federal power. He favored hydroelectric development but established a water power commission to lease out to private utilities choice sites in the state. At the same time, Miller supported the establishment in New York City of a Transit Commission to straighten out tangled subway problems, and he strongly encouraged the formation of the Port of New York Authority, for which he received the backing of former governor Smith. He signed into law the notorious Lusk bills, which licensed schools and mandated a loyalty oath for teachers, and he reluctantly approved the Mullan-Gage bill, which provided for state enforcement of the prohibition amendment and the Volstead Act.

Miller was defeated for reelection in 1922 by the ever popular Al Smith. He rejected feelers for higher office, including an appointment to the U.S. Supreme Court, and instead returned to private law practice, this time in New York City. He became general counsel for the United States Steel Corporation and represented this company, as well as several other large corporations, before the federal courts. In 1952 he was a member of a team that argued the "steel seizure" case in which the Supreme Court denied the president the authority to take over a private industry. No longer ambitious for public office, Miller remained an outspoken Republican partisan in his later years. He was a founding member in 1934 of the anti–New Deal American Liberty League, and he continued his attacks on Democratic presidents through the Truman era, criticizing what he regarded as a dangerous expansion of federal power, profligate spending, and foreign policy blunders that resulted in the Cold War.

Miller was active in his profession until shortly before his death in New York City. He was widely known as a "lawyer's lawyer" for his vast legal knowledge, thorough preparation, and great eloquence in the courtroom. In 1952 the New York State Bar Association awarded him its first gold medal for distinguished service in the law. As a politician he is remembered as a skillful debater, an expert on finance, and an ardent champion of conservative values.

• There is a small collection of Miller manuscripts in the George Arents Research Library at Syracuse University. Included among the papers are several typescript biographical sketches, a genealogical chart, and a privately published autobiography, *Recollections* (1953). Obituaries are in the *New York Times* and the *New York Herald-Tribune*, 27 June 1953.

ROBERT F. WESSER

MILLER, Olive Beaupré (11 Sept. 1883–25 Mar. 1968), author, editor, and publisher of books for children, was born in Aurora, Illinois, the daughter of William Beaupré, a banker, and Julia Brady. Miller liked to describe herself as "born with pencil in hand." Before she learned to write, she recorded her first stories in picture form. By the age of seven, she was filling homemade notebooks with stories. Following a comfortable and carefree childhood, she went to Smith College, where she studied French and German, sharpened her writing skills, and contributed to college publications. After her graduation in 1904, she returned home and for several years taught English at the local high school. On 2 October 1907 she married Harry Edward Miller, a successful, self-made salesman, first of textbooks, then of commodities.

In 1908 Miller faced a major change in her life. Because of her husband's job transfer, the young couple moved to Streator, Illinois. Separated from family and friends for the first time, once again she turned to writing, cramming her notebooks with ideas for a great American novel. In 1912 her husband was transferred to Chicago, and their daughter was born. Miller soon found that writing interfered with her determination to be a good mother to her long-awaited baby. The writing was set aside, but she always found time to read to her daughter.

Selecting stories for reading eventually helped Miller realize her vocation. In her view, the available children's literature left much to be desired. "Grimm seemed much too grim," she said. Moreover, she thought most stories and poems for children did little to help develop character. She began to write verses for her daughter. Generally these drew on familiar situations and surroundings to celebrate the joy of life. Her husband found her poems engaging and submitted them to a publisher. Much to her surprise, they were accepted. *Sunny Rhymes for Happy Children* was published in 1917, followed by *Come Play with Me* in 1918. Meanwhile, she began collecting more stories and verses to read to her daughter and filled her notebooks with stories for children that would teach as well as entertain. Other mothers expressed interest in what she was doing and asked her help in selecting reading for their children.

Miller's husband, observing this response to his wife's project, envisioned favorable prospects in publishing books for children. Together, they decided to produce a set of carefully edited and graded books of stories for children that would be sold door-to-door on a subscription basis. Printed on the highest-quality paper and attractively illustrated, the books were designed to be read over and over again. The Millers published the first volume of *My Book House* in 1920. It was an immediate success. Miller's husband resigned his job to devote his considerable energy and sales talent to the development of their new company, The Book House for Children.

Olive Miller worked hard selecting, editing, and, if necessary, writing material for the other five volumes of *My Book House*, published in 1920 and 1921. She used three criteria in selecting stories: (1) Does the story have literary merit? (2) Will it interest the child? (3) Will it develop character? Acceptable stories were then graded according to vocabulary, complexity of plot, and the age of the child. Like many educators and child-development professionals of her time, she believed that education has a function in character development, that children pass through developmental stages, and that parents who follow proper procedures can foster character development and enhance their child's readiness to learn. A *Parents' Guide Book* accompanying each volume explained these ideas and showed parents how using *My Book House* could support and enrich their child's educational experiences.

In the 1920s and 1930s Miller and her husband took many trips throughout the world to gather material for their books. From 1921 until her retirement in 1965, Miller's work schedule included preparation of *My Book House* for additional printings or for revised editions. An expanded twelve-volume set was published in 1934 and contained almost 800 selections from about 180 authors in various parts of the world. Another new edition, which also was the thirty-third printing of *My Book House*, came out in 1950. In all these editions, Miller sought to give the child "an association with the greatest authors in English literature" (introd. to vol. 7, 1950 ed.). One can find, for example, selections from such English writers as Shakespeare, Milton, Keats, Tennyson, and Shelley; works by Emerson, Longfellow, Alcott, and Pyle are typical of the American writers in the collection. An article in the education section of *Newsweek* (16 Oct. 1950) reported that the 1950 edition also included "220 pages of new material from such authors as Kenneth Grahame, A. A. Milne, and Pearl Buck."

For the most part, Miller seemed unaffected by the depression of the 1930s. The business continued to prosper and the Millers lived well. Encouraged by letters and words of praise from her readers and their parents, Miller became more and more immersed in her world of writing and editing stories for children. Meanwhile, her marriage foundered, and the Millers were granted a divorce in May 1935. Miller bought out her husband's interest in the company. In addition to being editor, she became vice president of the board of directors. The directors hoped this position would keep her from demanding a more managerial role in the company, but she wanted to be chair, a position she attained in 1939. She remained chair until her retirement. In the 1960s poor health prompted her to move to Tucson, Arizona, where she lived with her daughter until her death. In Tucson, her thoughts turned once again to writing the great American novel. Now, however, she often was too weak to hold a pen and so had to dictate her ideas to her nurse.

Olive Beaupré Miller is remembered primarily as editor of *My Book House*. Through these books, she played a major role in the imaginative experiences and reading pleasure of several generations of twentieth-century American children.

• The Olive Beaupré Miller Papers are in the Sophia Smith Collection, Smith College. They include published and unpublished manuscripts, drawings, correspondence, research materials, reviews, promotional material for her books, and published and unpublished articles about her. See also her *Engines and Brass Bands* (1933), based on her childhood memories of life in a small midwestern town. Miller's involvement in introducing sex education to the public schools of Winnetka, Illinois, led her to edit, with George L. Bird, *How Life Begins* (1935). Miller's other works include *Heroes, Outlaws, and Funny Fellows of American Popular Tales* (1939) and *Heroes of the Bible* (1940).

JANE L. ANDREWS

MILLER, Olive Thorne. *See* Miller, Harriet Mann.

MILLER, Perry (25 Feb. 1905–9 Dec. 1963), intellectual historian and scholar of American literature, was born Perry Gilbert Eddy Miller in Chicago, Illinois, the son of Dr. Eben Perry Sturgis Miller, a physician, and Gertrude Eddy. Miller attended the Tilton School and the Austin School, and matriculated at the University of Chicago in 1922. The following year he dropped out, headed west, where he lived for a time in a Colorado mountain shack, then reversed direction to try New York City, where he picked up acting jobs in several small repertory companies. His theatrical career peaked with a walk-on role in the original production of *Desire under the Elms*.

Finding work as a merchant sailor, he traveled by sea to Mexico, Europe, and eventually to Africa, where, he later recalled, he went in search of the adventure that "had been offered . . . [to] older contemporaries . . . by the First World War." What he experienced there, "while supervising, in that barbaric tropic, the unloading of drums of case oil flowing out of the inexhaustible wilderness of America," was a sudden flood of intellectual and spiritual purpose. "It was given to me," he wrote in the 1950s (explicitly comparing himself to Edward Gibbon amid the ruins of Rome), " . . . to have thrust upon me the mission of expounding what I took to be the innermost propulsion of the United States."

With characteristic ferocity, Miller now embarked upon the task of training himself for his mission. He returned in 1926 to the University of Chicago, earned his Ph.B. there in 1928, and went on to graduate study under Percy Holmes Boynton. In 1930 Miller married Elizabeth Williams; the couple had no children. With his wife Miller went to Cambridge, Massachusetts, in order to research his thesis on the ecclesiastical polity of early New England. He had always thought of himself as a transplanted New Englander, for his mother, related to Mary Baker Eddy, had been born there, and his father also came from New England stock. At Chicago he had been discouraged by several professors from venturing into what they described as the arid, overworked field of early New England history, but he was determined now to begin at the beginning of the American experience because he "could see no [other] way of coping with the problem" of understanding "the republic's appalling power."

The move to Cambridge turned out to be a permanent one. The critic and scholar Ann Douglas, who as an undergraduate attended Miller's lectures in the last year of his teaching, has speculated that he was driven by the conviction that "the Puritans' real heirs went west to Ohio and beyond with the Transcendentalists in the late 1840s and 1850s, [from] where, a century later, Perry Miller would reincarnate their spirit and storm their old Northeastern citadel now occupied by sons they would have disowned." Catching the notice of the senior Harvard scholars Samuel Eliot Morison and Kenneth Murdock, who had already begun to challenge prevailing views of early New England as an intellectual and literary wasteland, Miller produced a dissertation (still under Boynton's sponsorship) that eventually became his first book, *Orthodoxy in Massachusetts* (1933). In this work he introduced the still-controversial notion that the Puritan founders of Massachusetts Bay had developed, *before* their emigration, a casuistical justification for leaving England that he called "non-separating congregationalism."

Although in appearance and scope a monograph in ecclesiastical history, *Orthodoxy* was actually the first hint of what would become Miller's exceptional power as an intellectual historian. He wrote of ideas not as if they were disembodied concepts that existed in an ideal universe uncontaminated by petty human strife, but as expressions of the full range of human experience—from the disinterested quest for truth to base forms of self-promotion. He also wrote with an acute sense of how thin was the divide between conviction and self-deception, and how often belligerence and self-doubt ran together. He brought, in other words, an entirely new kind of psychological drama to American intellectual history, a field previously dominated by a form of hagiography and, in the vibrant volumes of Vernon Louis Parrington (with whom Miller sometimes caustically disagreed, but whom he angrily defended when students had the nerve to disparage him), by a form of political advocacy.

After *Orthodoxy*, Miller embarked on work of an entirely different scale. The capstone of his labors of the 1930s, *The New England Mind: The Seventeenth Century* (1939), was an anatomy of the whole range of Puritan belief. Its magnificent opening chapter, entitled "The Augustinian Strain of Piety," is an overture that presents in compressed form many of the themes of his future work and remains in some respects Miller's most fluent and sensitive summation of the spiritual hunger that he felt lay at the heart of the early American experience. The book itself is a demanding account of the chief Puritan beliefs as they were inherited from the Reformation (particularly Calvinist) tradition. Read alone it seems to suspend time by surgically detaching a body of doctrine from the social and material circumstances in which it functioned. In fact it constitutes a prelude to a projected sequel, *The New England Mind: From Colony to Province* (1953), whose completion was delayed by Miller's service in World War II, and which narrates the slow disintegration over the course of the seventeenth century of the intellectual coherence that is the subject of the first volume.

In the decades since their appearance, these works have been subject to cogent criticism. Miller overstated the degree to which the Puritan concept of "covenant" was a departure from Calvinist doctrine; he overlooked certain important differences among Puritan thinkers, whom he used as more or less interchangeable sources; and he committed himself to a theory of "declension" that is a form of nostalgia (in the tradition of Henry Adams [1838–1918] and other historians who expressed themselves best through the rhetorical mode of lamentation) for a past moment of intellectual integrity that can never be retrieved. Miller has also been criticized for making overblown claims for the comprehensiveness of his reading and, perhaps most seriously, for bequeathing (because of the sheer power of his exposition) a notion of New England as a place of incessant and rarefied theological dispute—an account from which the ordinary person is excluded.

Most of these criticisms, however, have proved to be glancing blows against what has become an enduring monument of American historiography. Subsequent scholarship has revealed a high degree of harmony between the doctrines of the "elite" and the beliefs of the "people," and although some of Miller's emphases have been appropriately corrected, his work remains by far the best representation of early American consciousness ever conceived or composed. It has also taken its place as a work of literature in its own right, expressing the dark mood of the 1930s and finding in the Puritans an impressive awareness of the monstrous human capacity for delusion that was being examined at the same time by neo-orthodox theologians like Paul Tillich and Reinhold Niebuhr. Miller never counted himself a believer in any conventional sense, but his fundamental sympathy for the doctrine of original sin (and his skepticism toward the Enlightenment rationalism that began to eat away at it in the later seventeenth century) gave his writing an unscholarly urgency.

After these heroic works on early New England, Miller continued to march forward through American history, producing a formidable body of scholarship (and many pedagogically useful anthologies) along the way. *Jonathan Edwards* (1949) remains one of the most potent intellectual biographies of any American thinker. The book, driven by the postwar sense of impending catastrophe, discovers in Edwards a world-class philosophical mind on a par with George Berkeley and confronts the perennial issue of how certain historically recurrent attitudes and ideas accommodate themselves to what nowadays would be called "epistemic" shifts. There followed, as well, a sourcebook of writings by the Transcendentalists, interpretive anthologies of the work of Henry David Thoreau and Margaret Fuller, a study (*The Raven and the Whale* [1956]) of the feverish atmosphere of literary nationalism in the 1840s and 1850s, a collection of American intellectual prose from the Civil War to World War I, an anthology that traced the American legal tradition, and many remarkable essays that were eventually collected in *Errand into the Wilderness* (1956) and posthumously in *Nature's Nation* (1967) and *The Responsibility of Mind in the Age of Machines* (1979). In 1957 the first volume (*The Freedom of the Will*, ed. Paul Ramsey) of *The Works of Jonathan Edwards* was published by Yale University Press—an ongoing project of which Miller was general editor. At the time of his death, Miller was at work on a book that was subsequently published as *The Life of the Mind in America from the Revolution to the Civil War* (1965), and that won a posthumous Pulitzer Prize. Although truncated, this work reveals Miller's growing interest (the better word for all his work is obsession) in how the intellectual system of the law was becoming, in the early republic, both the complement and successor to the theological structure of Puritanism.

Miller's other great contribution to his lifelong aim of fostering awareness of the complexity of the American past was as a teacher. He had joined the Harvard faculty as instructor (in the new undergraduate program, History and Literature) in 1931 and was promoted to associate professor in 1939 and to professor in 1946. He was named the first Powell M. Cabot Professor of American Literature in 1960. Never the nurturing type like his colleague F. O. Matthiessen, but blustering, impatient, larger-than-life, he is recalled by David Levin, one of his many students who went on to distinguished academic careers, as a "priceless teacher" with an unparalleled gift for "dramatizing intellectual history so that young students who had virtually no knowledge of theology" would come to share his passion for understanding the mind of the past. Levin recalls his initial appointment with Miller in his Leverett House office, where the great man received him in a room furnished with a Nazi battle flag emblazoned with an immense swastika, and a pair of captured gleaming German combat boots. Then, without delay, there came, Levin recalls, "the simplest question he ever asked me": "'I got the flag and the boots when I liberated Strasbourg with Leclerc,'" said the professor to his new tutee, and then "laughing away the bravado in his reduction of Leclerc's role," he asked, "'Where were you?'" After the Hemingway-esque strut there usually followed a smile of self-mockery.

Miller's power as a teacher was, as Levin puts it, "exemplary rather than sympathetically imaginative." He allowed his students to glimpse him in his personal struggle with the exigencies of serious thinking. He was, in Ann Douglas's words, engaged "without counting the cost, in the romance of the mind, the hubris of striving for perfect intellectual command." For many who witnessed this struggle, it was the privilege of a lifetime.

Perry Miller died of heart disease complicated by alcoholism in Cambridge, Massachusetts, a few weeks after the assassination of President John F. Kennedy, by which his depression had been deepened and had taken the final turn toward despair. He had been seeking psychiatric help to cope with his bouts of depression and drinking and had turned over his undergraduate lecture course, the legendary English 7, to his protégé, Alan Heimert, while continuing to struggle on his own through his graduate course on American Romanticism. His projected lifework of coming fully to terms with the "innermost propulsion of the United States" was far from finished, but he left a body of work unrivaled by any contemporary and by few predecessors. As Heimert wrote in a memorial essay, Miller's "efforts to impart . . . coherence to . . . the materials of American intellectual history . . . [constituted a] quest for a sublime that both stretches the mind to the utmost and arouses the power and passion of the soul."

• The main repository of Miller's papers is the Harvard University Archive, where some personal letters, lecture notes, and professional correspondence are preserved. Smaller holdings are in the Jonathan Edwards Papers at Yale and the papers of Paul Ramsey (Miller's colleague on the Edwards edition) at Duke University. Among the more substantial assessments of Miller's life and work are three essays in a special commemorative issue of the *Harvard Review* 2, no. 2 (1964): Alan Heimert, "Perry Miller: An Appreciation"; Reinhold Niebuhr, "Perry Miller and Our Embarrassment"; and Edmund S. Morgan, "Perry Miller and the Historians." See also Ann Douglas, "The Mind of Perry Miller," *New Republic*, 3 Feb. 1982, pp. 26–30, and David Levin, "Perry Miller at Harvard," *Southern Review* 19, no. 4 (1983): 802–16. Other student recollections include Robert Coles, "The Bible and the Puritans," in *In Praise of What Persists*, ed. Stephen Berg (1983), pp. 45–55; Robert Middlekauff, "Perry Miller," in *Pastmasters: Some Essays on American Historians*, ed. Marcus Cunliffe and Robin W. Winks (1969), pp. 167–90; and Kenneth Lynn, "Perry Miller," *American Scholar* 52, no. 2 (1983): 221–27. Other valuable essays are David Hollinger, "Perry Miller and Philosophical History," *History and Theory* 7 (1968): 189–202, and David D. Hall's introduction to the 1970 reprint of *Orthodoxy in Massachusetts*. The most comprehensive bibliography of Miller's writings is Kenneth Kinnamon, "A Bibliography of Perry Miller," *Bulletin of Bibliography* 26 (1969): 45–51. It is not an exaggeration to say that the entire range of scholarship published since the 1950s on early American intellectual life, especially on New England, constitutes an extended commentary on Miller's work.

ANDREW DELBANCO

MILLER, Roger (2 Jan. 1936–25 Oct. 1992), musician, was born Roger Dean Miller in Fort Worth, Texas, the son of Jean Miller and Landine Burdine, farmers. Miller was thirteen months old when his father died, and rather than commit her children to an orphanage, his mother sent her three sons to live with her late husband's brothers. From the age of three, Roger Miller was raised by Elmer D. Miller and Armelia Miller in Erick, Oklahoma.

Miller's first contact with music came from Sheb Wooley, who later scored pop hits such as "The Purple People Eater" and acted in the film *High Noon* and the television series "Rawhide." Miller later cited Hank Williams and Will Rogers as his major influences. He admired William's songwriting skills, and he admired Rogers's individuality. "Rogers was completely himself," Miller later said. "He was interested in politics and he had a great vein of humor."

Miller's first public appearance, probably in 1952, came when he played the fiddle on a show hosted by Fort Worth radio personality Bill Mack, who was appearing in Delhi, Oklahoma. After quitting school in the eighth grade, Miller went first to Oklahoma City, then Amarillo. He hung out at radio station KGNC in Amarillo, where western swing bandleader Bob Wills had a regular show in 1953 and 1954, and he went regularly to a fiddle repair shop that was run by Texas fiddler Eck Robertson.

Miller served in the army in Korea, and it was there that he met servicemen interested in country music who taught him to play the guitar. Miller's playing quickly progressed to the point that he was transferred to Special Services in Fort McPherson, Georgia, where he led a country band. His sergeant, Horace J. "Happy" Burns, was the brother of Jethro Burns, half of the country comedy duo Homer and Jethro, and Burns offered to help Miller get an audition with RCA Records.

The 1955 RCA audition was unsuccessful, and, as Miller himself later wryly observed, "it took seven years for me to become an overnight sensation." He worked as a bellhop at the Andrew Jackson Hotel in Nashville, and during a disc jockey convention he met country star George Jones, who introduced him to H. W. "Pappy" Daily and Don Pierce, co-owners of Starday Records, which then had a distribution and manufacturing agreement with the larger Mercury Records. Daily and Pierce took one of Miller's songs, "Happy Child," and placed it with one of their artists, Jimmy Dean. They also sent Miller to Houston with Jones to record some songs. Miller's first record, "Poor Little John"–"My Pillow," was released on Mercury-Starday in October 1957. Miller also did "sound-alike" recordings for Starday in which he imitated current hit artists on records designed to be sold through dime stores.

Probably in 1958, Miller got his first professional job playing in a band backing Grand Ole Opry comedienne Minnie Pearl. At the same time, he started writing songs and placing them with Tree Music. He formed a particularly close working relationship with Buddy Killen, then a songplugger for Tree Music—later the president of the company.

In late 1957 or early 1958 Miller left Nashville to work as a fireman in Amarillo to support his wife and three young children, but he continued to attend all the country music shows that came to Amarillo. After being dismissed by the fire department for sleeping through a fire alarm, he joined country singer Ray Price's Cherokee Cowboys, replacing Van Howard as a harmony singer and fiddle player. Price recorded one of Miller's songs, "Invitation to the Blues," in 1958. It became his first charted hit as a songwriter. Other hits quickly followed: Ernest Tubb recorded "Half a Mind" in June 1958, Faron Young recorded "That's the Way I Feel" in August, and the following month Jim Reeves recorded "Billy Bayou." Within a space of several months, Miller became the most in-demand songwriter in country music. Reeve's recording of "Billy Bayou" replaced Price's rendition of Miller's "Invitation to the Blues" in the number one position on *Billboard*'s country charts.

Miller wrote several more hits, including "Old Man and the River" for Donny Young, "Home" for Reeves, and "Last Night at a Party" for Faron Young, before he finally got another chance to record his own songs. By then he had left Price's band and was a drummer and front man in Faron Young's. However, he recorded for Decca in 1959 without success. Only after he signed with RCA Records in August 1960 did he finally hit the charts as a performer. His first recording for RCA, "You Don't Want My Love," made in August, exemplified the style that he carved out for himself. The lyrics bordered on nonsensical, some lines were scatted, and he introduced quotations from other songs (in this instance, he quoted from "Nobody Knows the Trouble I've Seen").

"You Don't Want My Love" was a minor hit but did substantially better when Andy Williams rerecorded it for the pop market. Miller's second RCA single, "When Two Worlds Collide" (written in collaboration with country songwriter-performer Bill Anderson), did even better, peaking at number six on *Billboard*'s country charts. In 1960 and 1961 Miller continued to write songs for other artists. Claude Gray did well with Miller's "My Ears Should Burn (When Fools Are Talked About)." George Hamilton IV's first top ten country hit, "Before This Day Ends," had Miller's "Loneliness All Around Me" on the B side, and both Jan Howard and Jaye P. Morgan recorded Miller's "A World I Can't Live In." Miller insisted that Patsy Cline had intended to record his song "Lock, Stock and Teardrops" had she lived, and it was later recorded in the Cline style by k. d. lang in 1988.

Miller continued to record for RCA with diminishing success until November 1963. By then he had established a reputation for eccentricity. His telling of humorous anecdotes earned him guest appearances on several television shows, including "The Jimmy Dean Show," "The Steve Allen Show," "The Tonight Show," and a regular slot on "The Merv Griffin Show." Miller decided to try to parlay his success on television into an acting career, and in February 1964 he recorded an album of novelty songs (first called *Roger and Out*, subsequently *Dang Me*) for the Smash imprint of Mercury Records, intending to use the session fees and advances to go to Hollywood for acting classes. Miller moved his family to California, but he soon gave up his acting aspirations to promote his records. His Smash recordings, including "Dang Me" and "Chug-a-Lug" (1964) were unlike any other recordings in country music at that time. They featured sparse instrumentation, fronted by Miller's own acoustic guitar, and had a predominantly loose, jazz feel. Miller gave free rein to his inventive wordplay, free-associating and lapsing often into zaniness.

Miller's most successful recording, "King of the Road" (1964), was inspired by a sign he had seen outside O'Hare Airport in Chicago that read "Trailers for Sale or Rent." Miller worked on the song over the next few weeks. He said he had to "induce labor to get it completed" and purchased a statuette of a hobo, staring at it until the words fell into place. In May 1965 Miller's recording of "King of the Road" was certified gold for one million sales. He received Grammy awards for Best Country Song, Best Country and Western Recording (Single), Best Contemporary Vocal Performance—Male, and Best Contemporary Rock 'n' Roll Single. Miller's second Smash Records LP, *The Return of Roger Miller*, received a Grammy for Best Country and Western Album. Miller later invested in a chain of motels called King of the Road. It was successful for a while but ultimately failed, he insisted, because of bad management.

In 1965 and 1966 Miller scored a consistent string of hits with "Engine, Engine #9," "One a Dyin' and a Buryin'," "Kansas City Star," "Husbands and Wives," "You Can't Rollerskate in a Buffalo Herd," "My Uncle Used to Love Me but She Died," and "Walkin' in the Sunshine." Miller had a television series, "The Roger Miller Show," on NBC-TV from September to December 1966. He was profiled in all the major magazines and appeared on many television shows as well as a Ford-sponsored twenty-city tour in 1967. "My face," Miller said later with typical humor, "was on everybody's lips." Reflecting on his sudden success, Miller said, "Suddenly I was Elvis, and I didn't have very good role models: Hank Williams and Elvis and those people, who were pretty wild people, and so I got into some pretty wild times."

Miller's first marriage ended in divorce, and in 1965 he married Leah Kendrick in Las Vegas. They had two children. Miller and Kendrick divorced in 1974, and four years later he married Mary Arnold, who had been a member of Kenny Rogers's First Edition. They had two children.

In common with many other performers who achieve overwhelming success after years of struggle, Miller was ill equipped to cope with the new pressures, especially as his success was tied so closely to his ability to write his own material. Miller's career went into a fairly precipitous downturn in the late 1960s. It was indicative of his decline and of his dry spell as a writer that his last major hit, "Little Green Apples," was not written by him but by Bobby Russell. He left Mercury Records in 1972 and signed with Columbia Records the following year. This was followed by affiliations with Windsong, Twentieth Century–Fox, Elektra, and MCA Records. In 1973 he sang in and narrated Walt Disney's animated version of *Robin Hood*. Miller's last top twenty country hit, "Old Friends" (1982), also featured Ray Price and Willie Nelson.

Miller's contract with MCA came in the wake of his last major success with the Tony Award–winning Broadway show *Big River*. Miller had been approached by producer Rock Landisman in 1983 with the idea of creating a musical that explored the parallels between Mark Twain and Roger Miller. He began writing in October 1983 and completed the assignment in mid-1985. An early version of the musical with seven or eight songs appeared at the American Repertoire Theater in Boston for a six-week run. Then it opened in La Jolla, California, with twelve or thirteen songs. Finally, with eighteen songs, the show opened on Broadway in April 1985. It ran for two and a half years. Miller briefly played the role of Pap. A road company took the show out in February 1986.

Miller's songs are still among the staples of the country music industry. Jerry Lee Lewis revived "When Two Worlds Collide" in 1980, David Frizzell and Shelly West had a top twenty hit in 1981 with "Husbands and Wives," Ricky Van Shelton had a number one country hit with "Don't We All Have the Right" in 1988, and Highway 101 revived a song that Miller and Justin Tubb wrote for Johnnie Wright, "Talkin' Cryin' Barely Beatin' Broken Heart." Miller was elected into the Nashville Songwriters Hall of Fame in 1973, and his last collaboration was with Dwight Yoakam on "It Only Hurts When I Cry" (1990), which used many of the same lyrical devices that had always been his trademarks.

In 1992 Miller was diagnosed as having throat cancer. He died in Los Angeles. Although his career was rooted in country music songwriting orthodoxy, he was perhaps the most iconoclastic performer in country music, and his work crossed the boundaries between popular and country music. His lyrics and the manner in which he phrased them on recordings were unprecedented in country music, and his success as a songwriter who sang his own songs laid the groundwork for singer-songwriters such as Kris Kristofferson.

• The best source of information on Miller is the essay by Otto Kitsinger that appeared in the booklet accompanying the compact disc *King of the Road* (1990), which is based on original interview material. Details of *Big River* can be found in Paul Grein, "Miller Rides 'River' to Deal with MCA," *Billboard*, 23 Nov. 1985. Miller's career is also synopsized in Rich Kienzle, "Roger Miller," *Country Music*, July–Aug. 1993. Obituaries are in the *New York Times*, 27 Oct. 1992, and *Variety*, 2 Nov. 1992.

COLIN ESCOTT

MILLER, Samuel (31 Oct. 1769–7 Jan. 1850), minister and professor, was born near Dover, Delaware, the son of John Miller, a Presbyterian minister, and Margaret Millington. Miller received his early education from his family. From 1788 to 1789 he studied at the University of Pennsylvania and then returned home to read theology with his father. After the death of the elder Miller in 1791, Samuel continued his theological studies with Charles Nisbet, the first president of Dickinson College. Miller later confirmed his intellectual indebtedness to Nisbet in *Memoir of the Rev. Charles Nisbet, D.D.* (1840).

Miller was ordained in 1793 and, in conjunction with John McKnight and John Rodgers, served three Presbyterian churches (Brick, Rutgers Street, and Wall Street) in New York City. At Miller's instigation, these bodies became separate congregations in 1809, at which time he assumed the pastorate of the Wall Street (later First) Church. He was elected moderator of the General Assembly, his denomination's governing body, in 1806. The following year he was named a trustee of the College of New Jersey (later Princeton University) and in 1813 was designated official historian of the Presbyterian church. His marriage in 1801 to Sarah Sergeant, daughter of the Pennsylvania attorney general Jonathan D. Sergeant, further contributed to his prominence. The couple had ten children.

In New York, Miller established himself as a man of letters. He was a member of the Friendly Society, a group of young intellectuals who gathered to read the works of various writers of the Enlightenment. Included in the society were the novelist Charles Brockden Brown, the jurist James Kent, and the Columbia University scientist Samuel Latham Mitchill. In 1803 Miller produced his best-known work, *A Brief Retrospect of the Eighteenth Century*, the first significant intellectual history written by an American. Although the book was largely derivative, it surveyed with remarkable breadth developments in the sciences, agriculture, medicine, philosophy, art, literature, and education. Despite his criticisms of the *philosophes*, Miller affirmed their talents and achievements. *A Brief Retrospect* rejoiced in the scientific progress as well as the diffusion of knowledge brought by the eighteenth century and predicted greater triumphs in the nineteenth, but the book also warned against confusing progress with human perfectibility or scientific advance with moral improvement.

Unlike many orthodox clergy of the era, Miller supported Thomas Jefferson's Democratic-Republican party. He greeted the French Revolution with enthusiasm. Sometime after 1810 he concluded that Jefferson held unreligious views. Miller declared that he wished "unsaid and unwritten everything I ever said or wrote in his [Jefferson's] favor."

As early as 1805, Miller recommended that the Presbyterian church create a theological seminary. He believed such an action was necessary to remedy the shortage of ministers and to equip his co-religionists for effective competition with other denominations. He also argued that a single seminary for Presbyterian ministers would promote unity within the church. When the General Assembly decided in 1810 to proceed in this direction, it appointed Miller to a committee assigned to draft a plan; two years later the assembly established a theological school in Princeton, New Jersey. In 1813 Miller became the second professor at Princeton Seminary; he taught ecclesiastical history and church government.

A number of Miller's publications addressed the nature of ecclesiastical offices. In *Letters Concerning the Constitution and Order of the Christian Ministry* (1807), Miller rejected the episcopal office on the grounds that it was unscriptural, encouraged corrupt prelates to usurp power, and was out of accord with the democratic spirit of the times. He averred that Presbyterian polity, emphasizing the parity of the clergy, better suited that ethos.

Although he never repudiated these sentiments, Miller subsequently struck a more conservative note. *Letters on Clerical Manners and Habits* (1827) described the ideal minister as one whose gentility, learning, and devotion to sound doctrine promoted stability in both church and society. Disagreements within his own denomination increased Miller's fear of disorder. In the late 1820s and early 1830s Presbyterians were polarizing into Old and New School factions. The New School was more open to extra-ecclesiastical voluntary societies, doctrinal innovation, and congregational theories of church government. Decidedly Old School in outlook, Miller moved to combat New School errors. In *Letters to Presbyterians*, which was first published as a series of articles in 1831, he warned that duly-constituted church courts must not surrender their power to supervise doctrine and practice. Miller's signal effort to promote correct order in the church was his *Essay on the Warrant, Nature, and Duties of the Office of Ruling Elder in the Presbyterian Church* (1832). Under the Presbyterian system, elected ruling elders, along with ministers, governed congregations. Wishing to exalt the office, Miller insisted that ruling elders held a position virtually equal to ministers, that they should hold their posts for life, and that they should function as assistants to the pastor. In this fashion, Presbyterianism would achieve a balanced republicanism, for ruling elders would check the ambitions of the clergy but also serve as a bulwark against the chaos of popular rule by the congregation. Miller's *Essay* strongly influenced Scottish Presbyterianism as well as the American church.

Despite his sympathies for the Old School, Miller and most of his seminary colleagues sought to educate the church to their views rather than to divide it. They were aloof from the more ardent partisans of the cause, but when the Old School secured a majority in the 1837 General Assembly and expelled its opponents from the denomination, Miller supported that action.

Although his most-noted publications during the Princeton years dealt with church government, Miller retained the breadth of interests and urbanity that had characterized his *Brief Retrospect*. Among other topics, he wrote on slavery, the Masonic movement, and temperance. Due to failing health, he resigned his position in 1849 and was named professor emeritus at full salary by the General Assembly. He died in Princeton.

• The Miller papers are in the Firestone Library at Princeton University. Samuel Miller (the subject's son), *The Life of Samuel Miller* (1969), remains the fullest biographical treatment. See also Gilbert Chinard, "A Landmark in American Intellectual History: Samuel Miller's *A Brief Retrospect of the Eighteenth Century*," *Princeton University Library Chronicle* 14, no. 2 (1953): 53–71; Bruce M. Stephens, "Watchmen on the Walls of Zion: Samuel Miller and the Christian Ministry," *Journal of Presbyterian History* 56, no. 4 (1978): 296–309; Belden C. Lane, "Presbyterian Republicanism: Miller and the Eldership as an Answer to Lay-Clerical Tensions," *Journal of Presbyterian History* 56, no. 4 (1978): 311–24; and Anita Schorsch, "Samuel Miller, Renaissance Man: His Legacy of 'True Taste,'" *American Presbyterians, Journal of Presbyterian History* 66, no. 2 (1988): 71–88. Useful information may also be gleaned from Lefferts A. Loetscher, *Facing the Enlightenment and Pietism: Archibald Alexander and the Founding of Princeton Theological Seminary* (1983), and Henry F. May, *The Enlightenment in America* (1976).

JAMES H. MOORHEAD

MILLER, Samuel Freeman (5 Apr. 1816–13 Oct. 1890), associate justice of the U.S. Supreme Court, was born in Richmond, Kentucky, the son of Frederick Miller and Patsy Freeman, farmers. He received the doctor of medicine degree from Transylvania University in 1838 and practiced medicine in Barbourville, Kentucky, for twelve years. Circa 1839 he married Lucy Ballinger, with whom he had three children; she died, and in 1857 Miller married Elizabeth Winter Reeves, with whom he had two children. Meanwhile his professional ambitions shifted from medicine to law, and in 1847, after training himself in this field, he was admitted to the bar. The controversy over slavery led Miller, a Whig emancipationist, to move to Iowa in 1850. He became a successful lawyer, specializing in land title, commercial, and transportation cases. In 1854 he joined in organizing the Republican party in Iowa. Although he did not hold an elected office, he became a prominent Republican and a strong supporter of Abraham Lincoln. Politically well connected, Miller sought appointment to the U.S. Supreme Court, and in 1862 President Lincoln appointed him to the high bench.

Practical and nondoctrinaire in his approach to the law, Miller was a statesmanlike judge whose leading opinions tended to be grounded in prudential judgments and fundamental constitutional principles. Concerning the nature of the Union, the central constitutional problem of his time, he was a states' rights nationalist who sought to balance affirmation of federal sovereignty and recognition of local autonomy. Outstanding expressions of his support for national sovereignty appeared in his dissenting opinion in *Ex parte Garland* (1867), where he voted to uphold a federal loyalty test oath applied to members of the federal bar in peacetime. In *Hepburn v. Griswold* (1870), the first of the legal tender cases, he wrote a dissenting opinion advancing a powerful argument for the constitutionality of congressionally authorized paper money as legal tender. He gave the opinion of the Court in *Wabash v. Illinois* (1886), striking down a state regulation of interstate commerce and practically necessitating the Interstate Commerce Act of 1887. Miller also spoke for the Court in *Crandall v. Nevada* (1867), invalidating a state tax on persons leaving the state as a violation of national citizenship rights.

In several notable cases Miller took the side of state authority. He dissented in *Gelpcke v. Dubuque* (1864), objecting to the Supreme Court's overruling of a state court's interpretation of the state constitution. One of the most significant affirmations of state power in American constitutional history was Miller's opinion in the *Slaughterhouse Cases* (1873). Upholding a state legislative grant of monopolistic privilege against a claim that it violated the due process clause of the Fourteenth Amendment, he said that to invalidate the act would make the Supreme Court "a perpetual censor upon all legislation of the States, on the civil rights of their own citizens." While recognizing the substantial alteration in the federal system that resulted from the Civil War, he gave the privileges and immunities clause of the Fourteenth Amendment a moderate interpretation that augmented federal authority without subjecting the states to the dominance of the national legislature or judiciary.

During Reconstruction Miller joined the majority of the Court in resolving civil rights questions in a way that sustained national authority to protect fundamental rights while acknowledging the states' primary responsibility to regulate relations among citizens at the local level, including the issue of private discrimination because of race. He wrote a nationalist opinion in *Ex parte Yarbrough* (1884), upholding federal authority to protect the right of U.S. citizens to vote in elections for national officers. Miller demonstrated concern for individual liberty in *Kilbourn v. Thompson* (1881), where his opinion for a unanimous Court struck down a resolution of the House of Representatives punishing a witness for contempt in a matter over which Congress had no jurisdiction to inquire.

As problems of economic regulation emerged in the 1870s, Miller generally approved state police power measures limiting the freedom of action of corporate persons. Yet he was not hostile to private property rights and, on occasion, as in *Loan Association v. Topeka* (1874), invoked natural rights reasoning that contributed to the development of substantive due process under the Fourteenth Amendment as a guarantee of economic liberty. By comparison with the dominant style of constitutional interpretation that prevailed in the late nineteenth century and early twentieth century, however, Miller was an exemplar of judicial restraint who believed the political branches should decide public policy issues. He served on the Supreme Court until his death, which occurred at his home in Washington, D.C.

• Miller's jurisprudential views are presented in his *Lectures on the Constitution of the United States* (1891). A listing of his Supreme Court opinions is found in Charles Gregory, *Samuel Freeman Miller* (1907). The only full-scale study of Miller's legal career and contribution to constitutional law is Charles Fairman, *Mr. Justice Miller and the Supreme Court, 1862–1890* (1939), which may also be consulted for information about miscellaneous manuscripts pertaining to the subject. Perceptive recent analyses of Miller are Robert C. Palmer, "The Parameters of Constitutional Reconstruction: *Slaughter-House, Cruikshank,* and the Fourteenth Amendment," *University of Illinois Law Review* (1984): 739–70; Charles W. McCurdy, "Samuel F. Miller," in *Encyclopedia of the American Constitution,* ed. Leonard Levy et al., vol. 3 (1986), pp. 1256–58; William Gillette, "Samuel Miller," in *The Justices of the Supreme Court, 1789–1978: Their Lives and Major Opinions,* ed. Leon Friedman and Fred L. Israel, vol. 2 (1969), pp. 1011–24. David P. Currie, *The Constitution in the Supreme Court: The First Hundred Years, 1789–1888* (1985), presents concise accounts of Miller's most significant opinions.

HERMAN BELZ

MILLER, Stephen Decatur (8 May 1787–8 Mar. 1838), congressman, governor of South Carolina, and U.S. senator, was born in the Waxhaw settlement of the Lancaster district, South Carolina, the son of William Miller and Margaret White, farmers. Though William Miller died during Stephen's childhood, leaving only a modest farm and a few slaves, private tutors prepared the youngster for entrance to South Carolina College in Columbia, from which he graduated in 1808. Thereafter, he studied law under John S. Richardson of Sumterville and joined the bar in 1811. A few years later, he married Elizabeth Dick, of the Sumter district; the couple had three children who died before reaching adulthood. After her death in 1819 Miller married Mary Boykin of the Kershaw district, with whom he had four children.

At age twenty-nine Miller won a seat in the U.S. House of Representatives, filling a vacancy caused by the resignation of William Mayrant. Miller's first stint in Washington offered few signs of the strict constructionism that would later characterize his politics. In one of his few House speeches, Miller defended the authority of the president to use the army to build and repair roads; it was unnecessary, he thought, to limit that power to wartime. He developed a stricter interpretation of the Constitution after the panic of 1819, a crisis that he and fellow upland cotton planters blamed on protective tariffs that they believed were unconstitutional. After serving a full term in the House, 1817–1819, Miller decided to resume his South Carolina law practice.

In a time of economic distress, Miller's service in the state senate, from 1822 to 1828, reveals the origins of his fervid states' rights ideology. Their legitimacy rooted in popular election, the legislators wielded extensive powers, electing the governor as well as the state's U.S. senators and presidential electors. The political influence of the wealthy low country remained strong, despite South Carolina's adoption of universal white male suffrage in 1810. Representing not the established elite of the coast, but the emerging planters of the backcountry Sumter district, Miller identified at first with the colorful U.S. senator William Smith, who rejected the economic nationalism propounded in the early 1820s by another noted South Carolinian, John C. Calhoun. Under Smith's influence, Miller emerged as a proponent of the "compact theory," which denied the supremacy of the federal government over the states, and he spearheaded the legislature's 1825 declaration—the "Miller Resolutions"—that protective tariffs, federal appropriations for roads and canals, and any congressional encouragement of the American Colonization Society were unconstitutional.

Miller parted company with the Smith faction in 1828 over the question of a state's right to nullify federal tariff law. Like Calhoun, who renounced his earlier protariff position in favor of South Carolina's prevailing sectionalism, Miller struggled with the problem of reconciling unionism with the conviction that southern states must defend their vital interest, whether it be cotton-growing, or slavery, or both. With political passions nearing fever pitch in December 1828, state legislators chose Miller, the "backcountry candidate," for the governorship. Just nine days later, they adopted resolutions condemning the "Tariff of Abominations" and released Calhoun's anonymously written *South Carolina Exposition and Protest.* The new governor tried to shape the crisis that brewed over tariff policy and federalism. An engaging speaker, Miller used his oratorical skills to swing public sentiment in favor of nullification doctrine. In their sovereign capacity, he insisted, South Carolinians might elect conventions to nullify protective tariffs or, if pushed to the extreme, resist federal coercion by force of arms. Also in his governor's messages, Miller advanced preliminary arguments for slavery as a positive good and proposed state bankruptcy legislation to discourage debt-ridden planters from flocking westward.

At the close of his two-year governor's term, Miller was persuaded by Calhoun's lieutenants in South Carolina to challenge his one-time mentor, William Smith, for the U.S. Senate seat opposite that of Robert Y. Hayne, another Calhounite. The key issue in the 1830 campaign was the one that divided Miller and Smith in 1828: state defiance of federal law. Once elected, Miller declared himself for the "old radical party"—another term for "old republican or state rights party." He opposed recharter of the Second Bank of the United States and condemned the Supreme Court's 1819 ruling in *McCulloch v. Maryland*, declaring in June 1832 that states have as much right to tax branches of the national bank lying within their borders as the federal government had to tax state banks. He voted against Henry Clay's Land Bill of 1832 and, to invite western support against the tariff, favored George M. Bibb's Senate resolution to reduce public land prices.

The Nullification Crisis of 1832–1833 was the event that defined Miller's importance as a public figure. While serving in the Senate, he participated in the South Carolina nullification conventions and voted for the Ordinance of 1832, which condemned the tariffs of 1828 and 1832 as unconstitutional, unjust, and unequal in their application. Like Calhoun and others who sought preservation of the union with southern institutions still protected, Miller held with a moderate element of the nullification movement, in contrast to budding southern nationalists like Thomas Cooper. He saw the crisis as resistance to an alien and hostile use of federal power, not as open revolution: "There is scarcely any law in which I would not acquiesce, when enforced by neighbors and friends—by those having similar rights and feelings. This is our last refuge—the sanctuary which is not to be violated without State authority interposing to punish the sacrilege." Miller also scorned the Force Bill, which empowered a resolute President Andrew Jackson to use the army to enforce federal law in South Carolina. In passing it, Congress was "putting at the disposal of the Executive the whole physical force of the United States—not for the purpose of putting down unlawful acts of the people, but for the purpose of putting down the rightful act of a sovereign and independent member of the confederacy." Like most southerners, however, Miller was anxious to resolve the crisis short of civil war and welcomed the tariff compromise of March 1833.

With his health failing under the stress of political battle, Miller resigned from the Senate in 1833 and retired to the rich soil of Mississippi, where he had purchased a cotton plantation in 1830. There, in the town of Raymond, he died.

• Significant deposits of Stephen D. Miller papers are in the Miller-Chesnut-Manning collection at the South Carolina Historical Society and in the Perkins Library at Duke University. The South Caroliniana Library at the University of South Carolina also contains valuable material. For his career in the Fourteenth, Fifteenth, and Twenty-second Congresses, see Joseph Gales and William W. Seaton, comps., *Annals of Congress, 1789–1824* (42 vols., 1834–1856) and *Register of Debates in Congress, 1825–1837* (29 vols., 1825–1837). Indispensable studies of South Carolina politics during Miller's era include William W. Freehling, *Prelude to Civil War: The Nullification Controversy in South Carolina, 1816–1836* (1965), and Lacy K. Ford, Jr., *Origins of Southern Radicalism: The South Carolina Upcountry, 1800–1860* (1988). Of more general importance on the tariff crisis of 1832–1833, see Richard E. Ellis, *The Union at Risk: Jacksonian Democracy, States' Rights and the Nullification Crisis* (1987).

JOHN R. VAN ATTA

MILLER, Thomas Ezekiel (17 June 1849–8 Apr. 1938), political leader and educator, was born in Ferrebeeville, South Carolina, the son of Richard Miller and Mary Ferrebee, occupations unknown. Miller's race was a source of periodic concern and speculation. Although he always considered himself to be black, Miller's very fair complexion led to allegations during his political career that he was white, the abandoned child of an unmarried white couple.

Miller moved to Charleston with his parents in the early 1850s, where he attended schools for free black children. His mother died when he was nine. As a youngster he distributed the Charleston *Mercury* to local hotels, and during the Civil War he worked aboard South Carolina Railroad trains delivering newspapers between Charleston and Savannah. When the Confederate government seized the Railroads, Miller found himself in the service and in the uniform of the Confederacy. Union forces captured him as they advanced into South Carolina in January 1865 and confined him for two weeks in a Union stockade.

Following the war Miller accompanied Union troops to Long Island, New York, and then pursued his education at Hudson School, north of New York City. After graduation from Pennsylvania's Lincoln University in 1872, he returned to South Carolina and enrolled at South Carolina College (now the University of South Carolina), where he took at least one law course. He read law with both state solicitor P. L. Wiggins and state supreme court chief justice Franklin J. Moses, Sr., and was admitted to the South Carolina bar in 1875, moving to the city of Beaufort to set up practice. Miller had married Anna M. Hume, probably in 1874; they had nine children, seven of whom survived him.

Miller spent most of the next two decades active in politics and the Republican party. He was elected to the Beaufort County School Commission in 1872, and he represented Beaufort in the state House of Representatives from 1874 to 1880. Elected to the state Senate in 1880, Miller resigned two years later. He lost a bid for a seat in the U.S. House of Representatives in 1886, but in 1888 he challenged William Elliott's election to the U.S. House, and following a protracted House investigation Miller was seated. He represented South Carolina's Seventh District from September 1890 to March 1891. In reaction to white Southern Democratic attacks on the Lodge Federal Elections bill (also known as the "Force Bill"), a proposal created to protect the voting rights of Southern black men, Miller passionately defended the progress made by blacks since emancipation. He also condemned white landowners for exploiting black farmers, charging that they negotiated unfair contracts and paid blacks in often worthless scrip. Miller defeated Elliott again in the 1890 congressional election but lost the subsequent challenge in the South Carolina Supreme Court when the justices ruled that though Miller's ballots were printed on the required white paper, it was "white paper of a distinctly yellow tinge." The 1892 congressional election went to black candidate George W. Murray when Miller's too-light coloring became an issue in the campaign. Miller returned to the South Carolina house in 1894 to serve until 1896. When not in public office, Miller returned to his position as an attorney on the payroll of Beaufort merchant D. H. Wall, an association he maintained for fifty years until Wall's death in 1935.

Miller was one of six black men elected to the 1895 state constitutional convention called expressly for the purpose of disfranchising black voters. Tenaciously and eloquently he defended black voting rights, rejecting claims that black political leaders had proven more corrupt and dishonest than white politicians. He challenged the convention's presiding officer, U.S. Senator Benjamin R. Tillman, to recognize the contributions and sacrifices made by black Americans to the nation:

> Mr. President, this country and its institutions are as much the common birthright and heritage of the American negro as it is the possession of you and yours. We have fought in every Indian war, in every foreign war, in every domestic struggle by the side of the white soldiers from Boston commons and Lake Erie to the Mississippi Valley and the banks of the Rio Grande.

He tried to reassure whites by insisting that black people neither sought political control nor opposed segregation: "The negroes do not want to dominate. They do not want and would not have social equality, but they do want to cast a ballot for the men who make their laws and administer the laws. Is there anything new in this plaintive appeal to the nation[?]" He concluded by "pleading for justice to a people whose rights are about to be taken away with one fell swoop." Most of the 154 white delegates were unmoved. Urged on by Tillman, they fabricated an array of disfranchisement measures—the principal one of which required potential voters to demonstrate an understanding of the state constitution—allowing election officials to exclude black voters at will. Miller and the other five black delegates refused to sign the new constitution.

Miller was more successful in demanding the establishment of a black college. Beginning in 1872 most of the state's federal land-grant funds were appropriated to State A&M College, an institution operated by Claflin University in Orangeburg. Claflin, a Methodist school for freedmen that opened in 1869, was run by northern white teachers and administrators. Miller and other black leaders wanted the land-grant monies allocated to an autonomous black institution. Miller convinced Tillman and his lieutenants to support legislation creating the Colored Normal, Industrial, Agricultural and Mechanical College of South Carolina (currently South Carolina State University) by severing the State A&M College's ties with Claflin. By law, the awkwardly named new institution could admit and employ only blacks. Miller later exclaimed, "Thank God the College is in the hands of Negroes."

Four days after the legislation creating the college passed, Miller resigned his house seat, and a few weeks later Governor John Gary Evans and the all-white board of trustees selected Miller as the institution's first president. The new college became a training school modeled after Hampton Institute and Booker T. Washington's Tuskegee Institute. Opened in 1896, it did not grant four-year bachelor's degrees until 1925. In an 1897 speech Miller explained the purpose of the new institution: "The work of our college is along the industrial line. We are making educated and worthy school teachers, educated and reliable mechanics, educated, reliable and frugal farmers."

In 1910 Miller publicly opposed the election as governor of Coleman Blease, a demagogue devoted to white supremacy. Following Blease's victory, the new governor demanded and received Miller's resignation as president of the college. Miller moved to Charleston, where he retired but remained active in community affairs. He enthusiastically supported U.S. entry in World War I and offered to help recruit 30,000 black men. When an all-white state committee on civic preparedness decided to appoint a black subcommittee to aid the war effort, Miller agreed to serve on it. He was a prominent figure in the successful effort in 1919 to replace white teachers with black teachers in Charleston's black public schools. In 1923 Miller moved to Philadelphia but returned in 1934 to Charleston, where he died.

Deeply devoted to American ideals, Thomas E. Miller fervently believed black people should enjoy every right and privilege accorded whites. He defiantly opposed efforts to disfranchise black men. He endorsed hard work, frugality, and industrial training as means to success. While he accepted segregation, he sought to turn it to the advantage of black people through establishing a black college and by insisting that black teachers have the opportunity to teach in black schools. The inscription on his tombstone reads: "Not having loved the white man less, but having felt the Negro needed me more."

• Some information on Miller is located in the Carter G. Woodson Papers in the Library of Congress. For his speech on the Lodge Federal Elections bill, see the *Congressional Record* 22 (1891): 2691–96. His brief recollections are contained in George P. Rawick, ed., *The American Slave: A Composite Autobiography*, supp., ser. 2, vol. 1 (1979), pp. 392–96. No full-length biography of Miller has been written. See also *The Suffrage: Speeches by Negroes in the Constitutional Convention* (c. 1896); George B. Tindall, *South Carolina Negroes 1877–1900* (1952); I. A. Newby, *Black Carolinians: A History of Blacks in South Carolina from 1895 to 1968* (1973); Thomas Holt, *Black over White: Negro Political Leadership in South Carolina during Reconstruction* (1977); and Edmund L. Drago, *Initiative, Paternalism, and Race Relations: Charleston's Avery Normal Institute* (1990). Obituaries are in the (Charleston) *News & Observer*, 9 Apr. 1938, and the *Journal of Negro History*, July 1938.

WILLIAM C. HINE

MILLER, William (15 Feb. 1782–20 Dec. 1849), lay Baptist preacher and father of the Adventist movement, was born in Pittsfield, Massachusetts, the son of William Miller, farmer and revolutionary war soldier, and Paulina Phelps. The family soon moved to upstate New York opposite Rutland, Vermont, where young Miller grew up steeped in the unsophisticated Bible-centered culture of his Baptist minister grandfather and uncle. As a youth he evinced a great desire for learning. In 1803 he married Lucy Smith, with whom he would have ten children, and soon afterward settled across the New York border on a farm near Poultney, Vermont, later entering public life as a constable and then sheriff. After friends introduced him to the writings of Voltaire, Thomas Paine, David Hume, and other Deists Miller grew convinced that the Bible and belief in God were mere superstitions. Joining the Vermont militia in 1810, he was soon transferred to the regular army. As captain of a company, he saw action at the battle of Plattsburgh during the War of 1812.

The wartime scenes of death, together with the death of his father in 1812, apparently led Miller to experience a renewed religious conviction. Upon returning to farming, he began to study the Bible intensively, developing fourteen rules of interpretation, including "figures always have a figurative meaning, and are used much in prophecy . . . such as mountains, meaning governments, Dan. 2: 35, 44; beasts, meaning kingdoms, Dan. 7: 8, 17; . . . day, meaning year, &c. Ezk. 4: 6" (Bliss, p. 71). Miller's rules echo a long, orthodox tradition of interpretation of the Bible's language code and would be unremarkable except for the relentless literalism with which he treated the prophecies. In the Book of Daniel and elsewhere, he found evidence that proved that the second Advent (Second Coming of Christ) would occur "about" 1843, ushering in Christ's reign of a thousand years (the Millennium).

Miller continued to study the Bible for more than a decade, keeping his views mostly to himself until 1831, when he was persuaded to give a series of lectures in hamlets near his home in western Vermont. Following publication of the lectures in a local Baptist newspaper in 1832, and as a pamphlet the next year under the title, *Evidences from Scripture and History of the Second Coming of Christ about the Year A.D. 1843, and of His Personal Reign of 1000 Years* (1833), demand for Miller's appearances grew. Licensed to preach by his congregation in 1833, he took up the mission to warn the world in earnest. By 1836 he had broadened his lecture circuit to include churches and camp meetings in the Hudson and Mohawk River valleys.

Miller might have remained a minor local phenomenon had he not attracted several promoters who began distributing his lectures in book form and arranging his public appearances. Chief among these men was Joshua V. Himes, minister of Boston' Chardon Street Christian Chapel and an ally of various reform movements. Himes arranged for the reprinting of Miller's book as well as for the publication of sermons and lectures delivered by Miller's followers; founded Adventist newspapers; published an Adventist hymnal as well as elaborate illustrated charts based on Miller's calculations; oversaw the opening of tabernacles and reading rooms in various cities; organized a series of "general" conferences to control the movement and codify its principles; and orchestrated speaking tours and rallies. In 1842 Himes acquired a "Great Tent" fifty-five feet high capable of seating 3,000. This novelty, together with the growing number of Miller's publications in circulation and the inevitable suspense as the predicted date of the Second Advent neared, helped to transform Millerism into a mass crusade reaching hundreds of thousands, perhaps millions. Because adherents generally remained within their own churches, exact figures will never be known.

At the opening of 1843 the ever cautions Miller, under pressure by many followers to be more specific about the Second Advent, finally announced that it was to occur within the twelve months beginning 21 March 1843. This additional specificity fanned the growing excitement, drawing even more Millerite preachers and messengers into the field. For the first time, the West and, to a lesser extent, the South became targets of proselytizing. Ill health briefly kept the 61-year-old Miller on the sidelines in 1843, but by the end of the year, as excitement built toward the 21 March 1844 deadline, he was again lecturing almost continuously. By then increasing hostility of many mainstream churches, which barred Millerite meetings and even expelled vocal Millerite congregation members and clergy, had led some Millerite leaders to call openly upon followers to separate themselves from their churches or "come out of Babylon." Miller, who had opposed separation, tolerated but never really accepted the "come-outer" movement.

When 21 March 1844 passed without the longed-for Second Advent, the Millerite movement endured much ridicule and lost some followers. Nevertheless, the movement was able to overcome the setback because Miller had claimed all along that his calculations might be off by weeks or months. Freely admitting that he had been in error, he continued to exhort his followers to wait patiently for the Advent. During the summer of 1844 adherents seized hope from a biblical passage that seemed to explain the delay as a "tarrying time." Then late in the summer the conviction spread that the correct date for Christ's Second Coming was actually 22 October and for a few months this "seventh month" interpretation redoubled the excitement of the previous spring.

The "great disappointment," as the failed Advent of October 1844 came to be known, left the Millerite movement confused and fragmented. Stories circulated that many of Miller's followers had sold their property, failed to harvest their crops, or been driven insane. Miller and his adherents among his Low Hampton Baptist congregation were expelled from the congregation. Soon, the hostility of the press and the churches, together with a strategic reinterpretation of the key biblical passages, was providing Millerites with a rationale for a formal Adventist denomination. Conflicting interpretations within the remaining body of followers, however, slowed the organizing process. One radical group held that the 22 October date of the previous year had actually witnessed the fulfillment of the parable of Matthew 25: "The bridegroom [Christ] came; and they that were ready went in with him to the marriage: and the door was shut." Some of these "shut-door" Millerites, believing that the Millennium had already begun in heaven rather than on earth, demonstrated their good fortune in having been converted in time by entertaining visions, shaving their heads, crawling through the streets, and the shocking practices of "spiritual wifery," "holy kissing," and "promiscuous" (mixed-sex) footwashing (Knight, pp. 251–52). Most Millerite leaders condemned these extremists, maintaining that the Second Advent was still imminent. Miller himself vacillated before finally siding with Himes and others in the "open door" groups.

Long before his death in Low Hampton, the movement Miller had inspired had passed largely from his hands. While he continued in his role of adviser and spokesman, Himes and other moderate leaders worked out the central tenets and congregational organization for the majority faction of the Adventist movement. Modern scholars have pointed to many factors, including clever promotion and anxieties provoked by increasing urbanization and industrialization, to explain the success of these efforts as well as that of the original campaign. Both Adventist and non-Adventist scholars now agree that deeply rooted millennial strands of American thought and rhetoric inherited from the Puritans and the Revolution played a significant role in the growth of Millerism. When Miller began his end-of-the-world campaign, millennial and apocalyptic rhetoric could be found woven into the hymns and sermons of mainstream Christian sects and was the stock in trade of evangelical Protestant revivalism of the 1820s and 1830s as well as of radical new sects like the Mormons and the Shakers. The Shakers had prefigured Millerism in their acceptance of their founder, Mother Ann Lee, as the female Christ. Understood in the context of these related phenomena, Miller no longer wears the tag "fanatic" and his message is no longer automatically labeled a "delusion."

Miller's contributions to American religion are numerous. His message hewed closely enough to orthodox Christianity to make his unsettling prediction at least marginally acceptable to established churches, at least while the critical day remained at some distance, and the tincture of rationalism provided by his calculations made his predictions palatable to many middle-class Americans. To his missionary enterprise he brought an unusual energy (by 1843 he had delivered several thousand lectures) and an extraordinary zeal. Although the movement that he began had nearly collapsed after the failed Advents of 1844, it was to have a lasting impact on the American religious scene. By the end of the Civil War, the fragmented Millerite movement had produced at least six denominations or proto-denominations with varying tenets and agendas. Several of these groups later passed out of existence, but others survived. One splinter group, the Seventh-Day Adventists, who continue to believe in the imminent return of Christ but who believe the actual date of the second Advent to be unknowable, had succeeded in attracting a following of 800,000 in America and another eight million worldwide by the late twentieth century.

• Aurora University, in Aurora, Ill., has a large collection of the papers and publications of Miller and his followers; Seventh-Day Adventist and Millerite materials can also be found at Andrews University, Berrien Springs, Mich. Edwin S. Gaustad, ed., *The Rise of Adventism: Religion and Society in Mid-Nineteenth-Century America* (1974), contains an extensive bibliography of primary materials. Sylvester Bliss, *Memoirs of William Miller, Generally Known as a Lecturer on the Prophecies, and the Second Coming of Christ* (1853), is still useful particularly for its generous quotations from Miller's memoirs and works. In addition to Gustad, standard modern treatments of Miller and Millerism are Ruth Alden Doan, *The Miller Heresy, Millennialism, and American Culture* (1987); George R. Knight, *Millennial Fever and the End of the World: A Study of Millerite Adventism* (1993); Ronald L. Numbers and Jonathan M. Butler, eds., *The Disappointed: Millerism and Millennialism in the Nineteenth Century* (1987); and David L. Rowe, *Thunder and Trumpets: Millerites and Dissenting Religion in Upstate New York, 1800–1850* (1985).

GARY L. COLLISON

MILLER, William Edward (22 Mar. 1914–24 June 1983), U.S. congressman and Republican vice presidential nominee, was born in Lockport, New York, the son of Edward J. Miller, a janitor, and Elizabeth Hinch, who ran a millinery shop. He attended the University of Notre Dame from 1931 to 1935. Upon graduating with a B.A. in economics, he entered Union University Law School in Albany, New York, receiving an LL.B. in 1938. After his admission to the New York State bar that same year, Miller was appointed U.S. commissioner for the western district of New York. Soon thereafter, In a case involving a "routine" auto accident, he met Stephanie Wagner. They were married in 1943, a year after he had joined the army. The couple had four children.

As an army officer Miller first served in Military Intelligence and then was assigned to the War Criminals Branch in Washington. Upon leaving the army as a first lieutenant in 1946, he was appointed assistant district attorney and then district attorney in Niagara County. In 1948 he was officially elected district attorney.

Two years later Miller was elected to the U.S. House of Representatives as a Republican. Coming from New York's "poor and unsophisticated" Niagara County area, he was assigned to the House Expenditures and Government Operations Committee and then to the Judiciary Committee.

In Congress Miller introduced little legislation and had below average attendance. He was "a staunch advocate of private power," which led to the only controversy of his congressional career. Although supporting the Civil Rights Bill of 1956 in committee, Miller switched his position during the final vote, citing constitutional considerations as his reason. When revisions were made, Miller supported similar legislation in 1957, 1960, and 1964. Some believed Miller had made a deal with southern congressmen, in which the southerners, in return for Miller's vote against the Civil Rights Bill, would block legislation giving the federal government control of electrical power generated by the Niagara River. However, earlier in 1956 a landslide caused one of the main private power plants to collapse into the river. Since power was needed immediately, Miller was forced to abandon support for privatization. Since these events occurred before he switched votes on the Civil Rights Bill, the possibility of a "deal" seems unlikely.

In 1960 Miller became chairman of the Republican Congressional Campaign Committee. Focusing on defeatable opponents, he secured victory for twenty-two Republican House candidates that year. In 1961 Miller was appointed chairman of the Republican National Committee. As chairman he downsized the committee's bureaucracy, improved the party's southern strength, and orchestrated Republican comebacks in major cities. He also revolutionized Republican fundraising through direct solicitation of $10 donations, replenishing the party's assets. Miller's hard work earned him the second spot on the Republican national ticket in 1964. Many have asked the question, "Why Bill Miller?" The obscure Miller was a persuasive orator and a master of organization. His quick wit and proficiency for debate made him the suitable man for clarifying careless statements made by the Republican presidential nominee, Barry Goldwater. Miller, it seems, was not picked to hurt Democrats but to punish liberal Republicans. His staunch conservatism offered no balance to a divided party.

During the campaign, Miller spent much of his time denouncing the Great Society and attacking the Democratic vice presidential candidate, Hubert Humphrey. One of his most important tasks involved convincing people that Goldwater would not take the country to war. He also focused on the need to end agricultural subsidies and to reform Social Security. Although some commentators questioned Miller's passion for the campaign, evidence shows he did everything the Goldwater people asked of him without complaint. A week before the election, Miller was upbeat, saying, "The Republicans are on the threshold of victory." Nevertheless, suffering a landslide electoral defeat did not seem to come as a surprise to Miller, who played golf and took a nap on election day.

After the 1964 election, Miller never ran for elective office again. In 1966 he offered assistance to Nelson Rockefeller's reelection campaign for governor of New York. Although he appeared to accept Miller's offer, Rockefeller later said, "There had been a misunderstanding of his original remarks." Evidently, Baseball Hall of Famer Jackie Robinson threatened to withdraw his support for Rockefeller if Miller took an active part in the campaign. Miller quietly campaigned for Rockefeller anyway. Miller's postpolitical life was reclusive; he lived in Lockport, where he practiced law. He died in Buffalo, New York.

Miller will always be the unfamed Republican vice presidential candidate of 1964. Although his obscurity was by choice, Miller enjoyed the debate and energy that came with national politics. Though his trenchant speech earned him many enemies, Miller was respected. His contributions as a party leader were significant and progressive. His role in the 1964 election exhibited professionalism, loyalty, and commitment to the Republican party.

• Miller's papers are in the Division of Rare Books and Manuscript Collections, Cornell University Library. For information on Miller's life and career before the election of 1964, see the *Saturday Evening Post*, 29 Sept. 1962, pp. 33–38. For information on Miller and the campaign of 1964, see Theodore H. White, *The Making of the President 1964* (1965). To put Miller in historical context, see Mary C. Brennan, *Turning Right in the Sixties: The Conservative Capture of the GOP* (1995). See also Barbara Carter, "Who Was Bill Miller?" *The Reporter*, 5 Nov. 1964, pp. 21–24; Ben H. Bagdikian, "They Want to Be Second," *New York Times Magazine*, 11 Oct. 1964, pp. 31–32; and Roger Kahn, "Bill Miller: The G.O.P.'s Tough, Shrewd Pro," *Saturday Evening Post*, 8 Aug. 1964, pp. 81–83. An obituary is in the *New York Times*, 25 June 1983.

RICHARD S. WHITE

MILLER, William Henry Harrison (6 Sept. 1840–25 May 1917), attorney general of the United States, was born in Augusta, New York, the son of Curtis Miller and Lucy Duncan, farmers. After attending an academy in Whitestown, New York, William entered Hamilton College, graduating from that institution in 1861. He then headed west to Maumee, Ohio, where he enlisted in the Eighty-fourth Ohio Volunteer Infantry for a three-month term, serving as a lieutenant. After this short service in the Civil War, Miller moved to Toledo and began to study law under the future chief justice of the United States, Morrison R. Waite. In 1863 Miller married Gertrude Bunce; they were the parents of seven children.

A need for money forced Miller to abandon his apprenticeship with Waite to accept the position of superintendent of schools in Peru, Indiana. There he continued the study of law in his spare time. In 1866 Miller left Peru for Fort Wayne, Indiana, where he practiced law for the next eight years. While arguing cases before the federal courts in Indianapolis, Miller became acquainted with Benjamin Harrison (1833–1901), and in 1874 he was invited to join Harrison's law firm. For the next fifteen years, Miller practiced law in Indianapolis and became one of Harrison's closest friends and confidants. Though not himself a candidate for public office, Miller worked loyally on behalf of Harrison's interests at the Republican National Convention of 1884 and served as his closest adviser in the presidential election of 1888.

Following Harrison's victory in 1888, the new president-elect selected his law partner and close friend as attorney general. Some politicians complained about the appointment, claiming that more worthy Republicans deserved the cabinet position as a reward for their services, but Harrison wanted to make sure that there was one cabinet member in whom he could confide and whom he could trust without question. The *New York Times* said of the appointment, "The President has . . . provided himself with at least one advisor on whose sincerity of purpose and unselfishness of motive he feels that he can place absolute reliance" (5 Mar. 1889). Moreover, Miller was expected to check the influence of Secretary of State James G. Blaine and ensure the president's dominance within the administration. The *Indianapolis News* reported of Miller, "He is combative and outspoken, and will permit no encroachments upon the rights or authority of the President" (18 Feb. 1889).

During his four years as attorney general, Miller fulfilled his role as best friend and stalwart supporter. No one in the Harrison administration was closer personally to the president. Effectively administering the business of the Justice Department, he handled significant litigation involving the McKinley Tariff Law, the Interstate Commerce Act, the Anti-Lottery Act, and the international dispute over seal hunting in the Bering Sea. He was neither vigorous nor effective in enforcing the newly enacted Sherman Antitrust Law, and his lack of success in this regard earned him some criticism.

Miller's most notable achievement was his victory in *In re Neagle* (1890). On hearing rumors that California's former chief justice David Terry was threatening violence against U.S. Supreme Court justice Stephen Field, Miller ordered that a bodyguard be assigned to protect Field. In August 1889 in Lathrop, California, Terry confronted Field and struck him twice. Believing that Terry was about to pull a knife on Field, the bodyguard, Deputy Marshal David Neagle, drew his revolver and killed Terry. The state of California sought to try Neagle for murder, but Miller intervened on his behalf. Taking the case to the U.S. Supreme Court, Miller argued that it was within the prerogatives of the executive branch to protect the judiciary. Consequently, Neagle's deputation as a federal officer was valid, and he could not be prosecuted by the state. The Supreme Court upheld Miller's argument, ruling in favor of Neagle.

Harrison's defeat for reelection in 1892 marked an end to Miller's career in government. He returned to Indianapolis and resumed the private practice of law. Miller died in that city.

Miller played a significant role in the nation's government and politics for only a few years before fading into obscurity. He was Harrison's closest friend, and because of this he rose temporarily to national prominence. Like Harrison, Miller was an honest Presbyterian, competent but unexciting, decent but uninspiring. Like Harrison, he caused few problems but solved even fewer.

• Some of Miller's papers are in the Indiana State Library. Short biographical sketches are in *Pictorial and Biographical Memoirs of Indianapolis and Marion County, Indiana* (1893); Jacob Piatt Dunn, *Greater Indianapolis: The History, the Industries, the Institutions, and the People of a City of Homes* (1910); and Dunn, *Indiana and Indianans: A History of Aboriginal and Territorial Indiana and the Century of Statehood* (1919). A more thorough account is found in Sister Maria Margaret Quinn, CSJ, "William Henry Harrison Miller" (Ph.D. diss., Catholic Univ. of America, 1965). Obituaries are in the *Indianapolis News* and the *Indianapolis Star*, both 26 May 1917.

JON C. TEAFORD

MILLER, William Snow (29 Mar. 1858–26 Dec. 1939), anatomist and medical historian, was born in Sterling, Massachusetts, the son of William Miller, a Congregational minister, and Harriet Emily Snow. He was schooled at home in the classics and later attended Williston Academy in Easthampton, Massachusetts. The family's financial problems prevented him from attending college. Instead, in 1877 he began a preceptorship with a physician, C. H. Hubbard of Essex, Connecticut, primarily studying anatomy by dissecting animals. His high score on a competitive test secured his medical school tuition, and he entered Yale Medical School, where he received his medical degree in 1879. He married Carrie M. Bradley of Clinton, Connecticut, in 1881. She died in 1901, and in 1912 he married Alice L. Burdick of Madison, Wisconsin. He had no children from either marriage.

Miller's own medical problems steered his early career. He worked for a while as a laboratory instructor at Yale under Benjamin Silliman, but after almost dying from an infection acquired during a postmortem examination, he went into private practice. He had a general medical practice for several years, first in Clinton and later in Southbury, Connecticut; however, that career path too was cut short by his own infirmities. Miller's developing deafness prompted him to leave private practice and devote his career to research. In 1887 he entered the College of Physicians and Surgeons in New York City, where he worked in pathology with Francis Delafield. There he was first attracted to the study of the lung, the field in which he would later earn distinction.

As he came to realize how little was known about disease processes, especially tuberculosis, which he saw often in patients, Miller chose to further his study of histology through a fellowship at Clark University in Worcester, Massachusetts. He entered Clark in 1889 and that same year became pathologist for City and Memorial hospitals in Worcester. He was a scholar in anatomy at Clark (1889–1890) and then a fellow in anatomy (1890–1892). He was influenced there by the innovative anatomist Franklin Paine Mall.

The dissolution of Clark's scientific faculty led Miller to join the faculty of the University of Wisconsin in 1892 as an instructor in vertebrate anatomy; he also taught histology and embryology. The University of Wisconsin had no medical school at the time, but, together with Charles R. Bardeen, Miller helped to establish a medical school there and rose through its ranks, becoming a full professor in 1916. He was known as a meticulous laboratory instructor and gifted teacher who took a strong interest in students; he maintained a devoted following of former students around the country.

Except for a one-year leave of absence, which he spent at the University of Leipzig in Germany (1895–1896), and two years at Johns Hopkins (1906–1907 and 1918–1919), the University of Wisconsin remained Miller's academic home for the rest of his career. He retired in 1924, serving as professor emeritus until his death. He continued to come into the laboratory after his retirement and achieved some of his greatest professional renown in that period.

Miller's work focused on the anatomy of the lung and on medical history and biography. He had exceptional skill in the microscopic study of the lung. He is credited with systematizing the lung's physiology, and he made critical contributions to the understanding of lung anatomy. His accomplishments included the discovery of the lung's atria and the discovery that the lobule is the significant unit of the lung's architecture. In 1934 he won the Trudeau Medal, an award given annually by the National Tuberculosis Association "to that individual who has made the most meritorious contribution on the cause, prevention or treatment of tuberculosis."

Miller won worldwide acclaim with the publication in 1937 of his book, *The Lung*, which summarized his research. It was an immediate classic; the first printing of 1,500 copies sold out in two weeks. *Time* magazine hailed it as the "most thoroughgoing study of the human lung in the history of medicine." He also authored 127 articles in medical and scientific journals on histology, lung anatomy, and tuberculosis.

Miller's interest in anatomy extended to historical works in the field. He had one of the finest private collections of classical works on anatomy and, to a lesser extent, other historical medical texts. His own scholarly interest and writing in the history of medicine focused on early anatomists, especially William Beaumont, and on Wisconsin medical history.

In 1909 Miller conceived of seminars on the history of medicine and invited some students to join him at the University Club for an informal discussion of pioneering people and achievements in anatomy. Those seminars developed into regular meetings, moving to his home library on alternate Wednesdays from November to May. Most participants were medical or graduate students. The seminars continued after his retirement, then attended primarily by his older medical school colleagues. Others continued the seminars after his death in Madison. Miller has been called the U.S. pioneer in the seminar method of graduate instruction in medical history. His model was instituted at other medical schools across the country, often by his former students.

Miller received many prestigious honors. He was a fellow of the American Association for the Advancement of Science and of the American Medical Association; he served as vice president of the American Association of Anatomists and the American Association of History of Medicine. Phi Beta Pi medical fraternity established the William Snow Miller Lecture in Medical History at the University of Wisconsin; and with his landmark studies of the lung, Miller established his own place in the history of medicine.

• The University of Wisconsin library purchased Miller's private library, a centerpiece of its historical collection, and also holds bound volumes of papers presented at his seminars. *The University of Wisconsin Medical School: A Chronicle, 1848–1948* (1967) describes Miller's role at the university and his personal style; *The William Snow Miller Festschrift, Assembled on the Occasion of his 70th Birthday* (1928) includes a chapter about him by F. H. Garrison, "Professor Miller as a Pioneer in Postgraduate (Seminar) Training in the History of Medicine," as well as a bibliography of his writings. Obituaries are in the *New York Times*, 12 Dec. 1939; *Science*, 2 Feb. 1940; the *Wisconsin State Journal*, 27 Dec. 1939; and the *Wisconsin Medical Journal*, Feb. 1940. His writings also include *William Beaumont and His Book: Elisha North and His Copy of Beaumont's Book* (1929).

RENIE SCHAPIRO

MILLER, Willoughby Dayton (1 Aug. 1853–27 July 1907), dental scientist, was born in Alexandria, Licking County, Ohio, the son of John Hinkle Miller and Nancy L. Somerville, farmers. He attended the University of Michigan, majoring in science, and received his A.B. degree in 1875. He went to Edinburgh, Scotland (1875–1876) for further study in chemistry and applied mathematics, with the goal of becoming a mining engineer. A lack of funds caused him to interrupt his studies, and he subsisted by teaching adults in night school. In 1876 he went to Berlin for advanced study in physics. There he met Frank P. Abbott, a dentist, who was the unofficial leader of the American colony. Abbott was greatly impressed with young Miller and urged him to study dentistry, because he felt the profession needed men with scientific training, especially in physics and chemistry.

After a short stint in Abbott's office, Miller returned to the United States and enrolled in the Pennsylvania

College of Dental Surgery, transferring in 1878 to the newly organized Dental Department of the University of Pennsylvania, where he received the D.D.S. degree in the school's first graduating class in 1879. Miller then returned to Germany and began dental practice as an associate of Abbott. In October 1879 he married Abbott's daughter, Caroline; they had three children.

In 1884 Miller received an appointment as professor of operative dentistry in the Dental Institute of the University of Berlin, the first American ever appointed to a professorial position in a German university. The appointment of a non-German to such a position created consternation in the German academic community.

In addition to his academic career, Miller continued his studies in medicine at the University of Berlin; in 1887 he was granted the M.D. degree, after receiving a remarkably high grade in an exhaustive examination. In addition, he carried out extensive research on various topics in dentistry and during the period 1880 to 1906 published more than 160 research papers. His work had a profound impact on biologists as well as on the dental and medical professions. His research on the causes of dental caries was published as a series of reports in both German and English journals throughout the 1880s, with the principal vehicle for the English-language articles being the *Independent Practitioner*. During this period Miller had come under the influence of the great microbiologist Robert Koch, and as a result Miller's researches led him into bacteriology. This culminated in the publication of his greatest work, *Die Mikroorganismen der Mundhöhle* (1889), issued in English as *The Microorganisms of the Human Mouth* (1890). The book revolutionized thinking about dental decay and its prevention. Miller promulgated the theory that dental caries is a two-step process: first there is the dissolution of the enamel as a result of acid produced by bacterial action on food residues; second is the penetration, through the break in the enamel, into the underlying dentin, by microorganisms that attack the organic matrix of the tooth. He summed up his theory of the causation of dental decay by stating that acids, pathogenic bacteria, putrefactive bacteria, or all together are not the sole cause of decay of the human teeth. He did state unequivocally, however, that "there is not a single case of caries in which microorganisms do not play a very important part."

The impact of Miller's work was immediate and worldwide. Measures were advanced to prevent decay, and new emphasis was placed on scouring teeth to free them of adherent food. In addition, additives to counteract acid production were combined in dentifrices, and this started the toothpaste industry on its path of tremendous growth in the United States. Nevertheless, because little was known of the role that plaque plays in both caries and periodontal disease, it became clear that tooth-brushing alone failed to stop the ravages of decay.

Miller's reputation was firmly established and he was considered the outstanding dental scientist of his day, with numerous honors bestowed on him. In 1894 he was named Professor Extraordinarius in the medical faculty of the University of Berlin. The University of Pennsylvania in 1902 conferred its highest honor, a Doctor of Science degree. In October 1906 the German Emperor gave him the title *Geheim Medizinalrat* (privy medical councilor). During his career Miller was elected to honorary membership in more than forty dental societies. For six years he served as president of the Central Association of German Dentists; he was also president of the American Dental Society of Europe and of the Association of Dental Faculties of Germany. One of the highest forms of recognition came with his election in 1904 to a five-year term as president of the Fédération Dentaire Internationale.

Miller visited the United States almost every summer. He had purchased a farm not far from his family home in Alexandria, Ohio. In 1906 the University of Michigan named him the first dean of its new School of Dentistry, effective the following year, and Miller returned to his farm for a short vacation before taking up his new duties; he developed appendicitis, and in spite of an operation, he succumbed to peritonitis in a Newark, Ohio, hospital.

Miller's death came as a shock to the worldwide dental community, and funds were raised for the creation of a bronze statue of him. This was placed in front of the library of the Ohio State University and dedicated on 8 December 1915; it was later moved to the grounds of the university's College of Dentistry.

• The Dentistry Library of the University of Michigan has a collection of Miller's letters and some personal papers. Miller early on attacked the theory that decay was a result of an electrolytic process in "Chemical versus the Electrical Theory of Caries," *Dental Cosmos* 23 (1881): 91–98. His *Lehrbuch der Conservirenden Zahnheilkunde* (Textbook of conservative dentistry, 1896) was published in Leipzig. One of the best of the many obituaries of Miller is Edmund Cameron Kirk, *Dental Cosmos* 49 (1907): 1009–12. An obituary is in the *Detroit Free Press*, 30 July 1907.

MALVIN E. RING

MILLET, Francis Davis (3 Nov. 1846–15 Apr. 1912), artist and writer, was born in Mattapoisett, Massachusetts, the son of Asa Millet, a physician, and Huldah A. Byram. He served as a drummer boy in the Union army in 1864. During this time he also acted as an assistant surgeon in the Army of the Potomac, helping on one occasion to amputate a wounded soldier's arm. Millet graduated from Harvard in 1869 and was granted a master's degree in modern languages and literature three years later. Meanwhile, he worked on the *Boston Advertiser* and the *Boston Courier* and learned lithography under D. C. Fabronius. In 1870 he successfully exhibited "Beware," his third lithograph after only three months of lessons. By saving his money, Millet was able to go to Antwerp, where he studied painting at the Royal Academy with Jan van Lerius and Nicholas DeKeyser from 1871 through 1873. He won two academy prizes, one for excellence in his antique class, the other for excellence in painting. He was also publicly commended by King Leopold II of Belgium.

Because of publicity surrounding his awards, in 1873 Millet was appointed secretary to Charles Francis Adams, the head of the Massachusetts commission attending the Vienna Exposition. Adams became his close and admiring friend from that time on. At the close of the meetings, Millet traveled through the Near East, Greece, Turkey, and Hungary. He painted on Capri during that summer and studied painting in Rome during the winter of 1873–1874. He enjoyed leisurely travel through northern Italy—especially delighting in Venice—Switzerland, and Germany before returning to the United States in 1876 to be a newspaper correspondent for the *Advertiser* at the Philadelphia Centennial Exposition. He also worked as one of John La Farge's assistant muralists in decorating the Trinity Church in Boston in 1877.

In 1877 Millet was hired as a special correspondent by the *New York Herald* to cover the Russo-Turkish War. From vantage points with the hospitable Russian army, he worked closely with the brilliant and daring American correspondent Januarius Aloysius MacGahan, the British correspondent Archibald Forbes, and Michael Skobelev, a dashing Russian general who became Millet's closest military friend. Millet also wrote and sketched for the *London Daily News*, replacing Forbes in this capacity, and was employed as a special artist by the *London Graphic* toward the end of the war. Observing, sketching, and vividly describing combat action, he at one time told Russian officers about the location of a ford, enabling them to mount a successful surprise attack on a Turkish flank. For this act he was awarded the Cross of St. Stanislaus and the Cross of St. Anne by the Russian government. Millet advanced alongside General Joseph Gourko to Adrianople, where he was awarded the Iron Cross of Rumania. Following the Turkish surrender of Plevna, Bulgaria, in December, Millet rode into the ruined city, observed the horrific carnage there, and reported his observations graphically. At war's end in December 1877, he and MacGahan telegraphed the last major war dispatch from Constantinople to the *Daily News*. Millet also covered postwar and peace negotiations by the former combatants. He received three other official decorations for bravery under fire. His reports make up part of *The War Correspondence of the "Daily News," 1877–78* (1878).

Soon after the war ended, Millet proceeded to Sicily and Spain and then went on to Paris, where he was active as a member of the Fine Arts jury at the Paris Exposition. He also exhibited his paintings in the Paris Salon and at the Royal Academy in London. He returned to Boston and married Elizabeth Greely Merrill in 1879; the couple had three children. Millet established a studio in nearby East Bridgewater and tried portrait painting, but he soon moved to New York City. In 1881 he accepted an assignment from *Harper's Magazine* to prepare art work in the Baltic Sea region, a job that took him to Denmark, Sweden, and northern Germany. He then enjoyed a sketching tour in England. In 1883 he began painting and showing Greek and Roman costume subjects, on which he later both lectured and published.

In 1884 Millet purchased a summer home at Broadway, in Worcestershire, Great Britain, and helped establish an art studio there, sharing it with Edwin Austin Abbey, Edwin Howland Blashfield, John Singer Sargent, other American colleagues, and the British artist Alfred Parsons. Millet frequently left this studio to winter in New York. In 1885 he toured widely in the American West. In 1887 he published his English translation of a French translation of Leo Tolstoy's *Sebastopol*; Millet's version contained an introduction by William Dean Howells. In 1888 he traveled in the United States and also in Mexico. In 1891 he took a 1,700-mile trip, partly by canoe, down the Danube River on assignment with *Harper's*. His companions were Parsons and the author Poultney Bigelow. Millet wrote five of the seven installments of the serial "From the Black Forest to the Black Sea" and provided sixty-six beautifully detailed illustrations of peasants, sailors, soldiers, and farm and water scenes. Bigelow wrote two other installments, and Parsons also provided many illustrations. From this work Millet created his first book, *The Danube from the Black Forest to the Black Sea* (1892). His second book, *The Capillary Crime and Other Stories* (1892), was a collection of seven short stories, some ghostly in nature. "The Capillary Crime," for example, concerns the death of an artist caused by a gun firing through force of capillary attraction.

At the Columbian Exposition in Chicago Millet was director of decorations at the White City in 1892–1893, working closely with architect and city planner Daniel H. Burnham. Millet was also director of exposition functions in 1893. Burnham and Millet then coauthored *World's Columbian Exposition: The Book of the Builders, Being a Chronicle of the Origin and Plan of the World's Fair . . .* (1894). Millet lived in England from 1894 to 1896, with time off to visit Algiers, Tripoli, and Tunis. In 1898, during the Spanish-American War, he served in Manila as a special correspondent for *Harper's Weekly*, the *London Times*, and the *New York Sun*. He gathered his correspondence into his third and last book, *The Expedition to the Philippines*, in 1899. After a trip through the Far East, including stops in Japan, China, Java, the Straits, Burma, and India, he went on to France. He represented the United States at the Paris Exposition of 1900, supervised the decoration of the American pavilion there, was a member of the Fine Arts Jury, and was appointed Chevalier of the Legion of Honor of France.

Returning to the United States, Millet devoted a good deal of his creative energy to painting large historical murals and similar decorations. In the course of several years, he provided colorful and harmonious art work for the capitol buildings of Minnesota and Wisconsin, the Baltimore Custom House, the Court House in Newark, and the Cleveland Trust Company Building. His murals were usually ambitious but somewhat placid. The capitol in St. Paul, Minnesota, has *The Treaty of the Traverse des Sioux*, Millet's most ambitious single scene, depicting more than sixty figures. The Baltimore Custom House is decorated with twenty-eight panels and five lunettes. For the Cleveland bank, he and his assistants created twelve long panels depicting the pioneering movement that opened the Great West.

Millet's mural work was interrupted in 1908, when President Theodore Roosevelt's Secretary of State Elihu Root named him American commissioner general, with the temporary rank of minister plenipotentiary and envoy extraordinary, to help represent the United States at the Tokyo Exposition. Millet traveled there by way of Europe and the Siberian railway. In Tokyo he and his party had an audience with Emperor Mutsu Hito and Empress Haru. After being accorded the First-Class Order of the Sacred Treasure, he went by way of the Yangtse River and the Hankow-Peking railroad to Shanghai and Peking, studied Chinese methods of preserving art monuments, and finally returned home via Port Arthur, the Yellow Sea, and Tokyo again.

Long a member of special commissions, Millet helped create the American Federation of Arts and the National Commission of Fine Arts in 1910. He reluctantly accepted the directorship of the American Academy in Rome a year later. After serving in Rome for a short time early in 1912, he and his old friend Archibald Butt, President Howard Taft's military aide, booked passage on the *Titanic* in 1912 to return to the United States. They were two of the 1,513 people lost at sea when that ship sank.

Millet's war dispatches are still enormously valuable. His illustrations are regularly competent, but his abiding worth is best seen in his numerous oil canvases, which display sound draftsmanship and fine graphic placement of elements. They also demonstrate skillful use of harmonious, gentle colors suffused by mellow lighting. In their picturesqueness and rendering of costume details, furniture, bric-a-brac, and food, cutlery, and napery, they often resemble Dutch interior scenes. One such painting, *At the Inn* (1884, Union League Club, New York City), is representative. It shows a neatly dressed gentleman, seated at table, about to be served by a courteous young woman. Light comes through large latticed windows, and details of clothing, food, furniture, and room decorations are meticulously rendered. The canvas is exquisite but may be said to resemble an exact copy of a posed photograph. Often displaying much technical skill but little feeling, these highly adept paintings generally seem more illustrative than painterly. Millet's best works are part of many permanent collections both in the United States and abroad.

• Many of Millet's letters are at the American Academy of Arts and Letters, New York, and in the Butler Library of Columbia University and the Houghton Library of Harvard University. The American Federation of Arts, *Francis Davis Millet Memorial Meeting* (1912), lists most of his paintings and literary works. *Art and Progress* 3 (July 1912): 643–54, contains four memorial essays on Millet. Henry James, *Picture and Text* (1893), includes essays on Millet and his Broadway colleagues. Francis Hopkinson Smith, *American Illustrators* (1894), mentions Millet but only slightingly. Leila Mechlin, "A Decorator of Public Buildings," *World's Work* 19 (Dec. 1909): 12378–86, praises Millet's Cleveland Trust Company Building murals and has biographical details. See also Eugen Neuhaus, *The History & Ideals of American Art* (1931). Michael Quick, *American Expatriate Painters of the Late Nineteenth Century* (1976), pp. 114–16, 153–54, covers Millet well and contains an extensive secondary bibliography. Millet's work as a war correspondent is detailed in F. Lauriston Bullard, *Famous War Correspondents* (1914), and in Dale L. Walker, *Januarius MacGahan: The Life and Campaigns of an American War Correspondent* (1988). Millet's work at the Columbian Exposition is touched on in Charles Moore, *Daniel H. Burnham: Architect, Planner of Cities* (2 vols., 1921). An obituary, with portrait, is in the *New York Times*, 16 Apr. 1912.

ROBERT L. GALE

MILLETT, Fred Benjamin (19 Feb. 1890–1 Jan. 1976), educator and literary critic, was born in Brockton, Massachusetts, the son of Daniel Edwin Millett, a skilled shoe factory worker, and Mary Avalina Churchill Porter. A Phi Beta Kappa graduate of Amherst College (A.B., 1912), he taught at Queen's University, Kingston, Ontario (lecturer in English, 1912–1916), the University of Chicago (fellow in English, 1916–1918), and—after service as a U.S. Army private from May to December 1918—at the Carnegie Institute of Technology (assistant professor, 1919–1926; associate professor, 1927). In 1927 he returned as an assistant professor to the University of Chicago, where he received his Ph.D. in 1931 and was promoted to associate professor in 1933. In 1937 he joined the faculty of Wesleyan University in Middletown, Connecticut, as a visiting professor of English on a two-year appointment that became permanent.

Named a university in its 1831 charter, Wesleyan was in fact a traditional liberal arts college with an enrollment of about 800 men. In this favorable environment Millett experimented with courses in the humanities, including a basic offering staffed by professors from various departments who discussed with students the same great works of literature, philosophy, history, and the fine arts as subjects of common concern rather than of personal professional interest. In *Rebirth of Liberal Education* (1945), a report on his visits to several campuses in 1942–1943 as a consultant in the humanities division of the Rockefeller Foundation, he praised the work of committed students and teachers in maintaining promising programs at a time when the humanities were being curtailed in favor of studies deemed more relevant to the national wartime effort. Millett believed that "liberal education . . . may be reborn wherever the humanities . . . are restored to the primary position in the college curriculum," a position merited because "the humanities transcend the other disciplines because of their concern, not with material or physical or social values but with intellectual, esthetic, moral, and spiritual values." This belief was evident in all of his classes and in his work as head of the Honors College (acting director, 1943–1946; director, 1946–1958). For him, true scholarship in liberal education, at whatever level in college or graduate school, involved seeing connections. He called for "training students, not to become specialists in English, philosophy, music, or the fine arts, but to become oriented in all the aspects of a particular culture and skilled in interpreting the relationship between those aspects."

Rebirth of Liberal Education was favorably reviewed in *College English* (May 1945) and the *Weekly Book Review* (25 Mar. 1945) and elsewhere. Writing in the *New Republic* (2 Apr. 1945), Granville Hicks remarked that "Millett's forthright attack on the Ph.D. system, if one considers by whom and under what auspices it was made, is an event in academic history," but found that the book offered little beyond "the patching up of courses and curricula . . . [that] must go on and . . . can be done relatively well rather than relatively badly." Millett regarded his own work at Wesleyan not as patching up but as renovation. His classroom success with the kind of close textual analysis advocated by I. A. Richards in *Principles of Literary Criticism* (1925) and *Practical Criticism* (1929) led to his three companion volumes *Reading Drama*, *Reading Fiction*, and *Reading Poetry* (1950). In a note "To the Teacher" in all three, he stated that "the most meaningful approach to literature [is] the aesthetic, the study of a work of art as a work of art, and not as a footnote to biography, social or literary history, or ethics." Emphasis on the aesthetic element was a matter not just of pedagogical convenience but of personal conviction. In "What I Live By," written for the student newspaper in 1953, Millett declared that he regarded the artist as "the noblest manifestation of man's potentialities, the most God-like of creatures." With no illusions about his own creative powers, he had devoted himself to "reading, teaching, and writing about the literary works produced by artists, in the hope, first, of gleaning from them something of their insight, wisdom, compassion, and joy, and, second, of making students as conscious as possible of these values as expressed in literature."

Fred Millett was a lively presence in the classroom; his well-crafted lectures, leavened with wit, made him a popular teacher and a favorite speaker at alumni gatherings. In his published work he drew on a fund of knowledge acquired through a lifetime of critical reading and study; it underpinned his extensive reviews in *American Literature* from 1933 to 1965, his *Contemporary American Authors: A Critical Survey and 219 Bio-bibliographies* (1940), and other works, especially his successive revisions (in 1943, 1956, and 1964) of the durable *History of English Literature* by William Vaughn Moody and Robert Morss Lovett, originally published in 1902. He was active in many areas: he served on editorial boards (*American Literature* [1948–1952]; *College English* [1948–1950]) and held office in several organizations, among them the College English Association (president, New England section, 1956). His devoted service to the academic profession was recognized by his election as president of the American Association of University Professors (1952–1954). His presidential address, "The Vigilantes," delivered at the fortieth annual meeting in Buffalo, New York, in April 1954, drew national attention as a vigorous attack on censorship in all its forms. Millett charged that "the general atmosphere of hysteria and fear of communism that is being systematically engendered in America and . . . nowhere else in the world" was the cause of "the intensified impulse to censorship" of literature and the arts. Communism had been converted into "the national bogey-man," and to combat communism by censorship was to work in a way "fundamentally opposed to the philosophy of democracy" (*AAUP Bulletin*, Spring 1954).

For his many achievements Fred Millett was gratefully recognized. He was named Olin Professor of English at Wesleyan in 1952 and was invited to teach as distinguished professor of English at the State University of New York, Albany, in 1961–1962. A lifelong bachelor who cherished family ties, he lived in retirement in Whitman, Massachusetts, near close relatives whose families had lived in the area for generations. There, in the home built by his grandfather Benjamin Churchill in 1854, he continued to write. One product of this period, *Professor: Problems and Rewards in College Teaching* (1960), was addressed to young people contemplating an academic career. It was well received, but at least one reviewer had reservations about it as a career guide. Paul Lauter in a *Nation* review (4 Nov. 1961) said that although the book was "stimulating and healthy," Millett was mistaken in assuming that a teacher shortage would continue, or that the old familiar route to success and security would survive the great changes looming in the college world. While the point was a valid one (as the academic upheavals of the next two decades were to prove), the book is of permanent interest in a way not intended: it is a perfect description of the way the academic world had worked for at least sixty years, by one who had known it intimately.

Fred Millett died in Brockton.

• Pertinent materials are in the archives of Amherst College and Wesleyan University. Those at Amherst are a general biographical file, folders of news clippings and photographs, a bibliography, three typed essays, and a folder of pamphlets published by the Washington Street Press (Millett's own private imprint). The Wesleyan archives hold many items for the permanent record contributed by Millett during his lifetime and large quantities of papers received after his death; the papers were as yet unprocessed in 1994 and so unavailable for use. Many of the pamphlets contain intimate family information and recollections; two are *My Father* (1943) and "*Over Home*" (1945). Exemplary pamphlets on academic life include *Edith Rickert, a Memoir* (1944) and *Introduction to a Small Liberal Arts College* (1967). Many of Millett's publications, whether produced by himself or in collaboration, were textbooks, such as *The Art of the Drama*, with G. E. Bentley (1935); anthologies, such as *The Play's the Thing* (1936) and *The College Survey of English Literature*, with others (1942); or authoritative reference books that, though initiated by predecessors, became substantially Millett's own through his successive, thoroughly updated, revised editions, which reflected evolving critical evaluation. These last include *Contemporary British Literature*, 3d rev. ed. (1935), and, notably, *Contemporary American Authors* (1940) and *A History of English Literature*, 8th ed. (1964), both mentioned above. Among his last publications were an essay on Thomas Love Peacock, in Charles A. Hoyt, ed., *Minor British Novelists* (1967), and one on James Branch Cabell, in Hoyt, ed., *Minor American Novelists* (1970). Obituaries are in the *New York Times* and the *Middletown (Conn.) Press*, 2 Jan. 1976.

VINCENT FREIMARCK

MILLIGAN, Lambdin P. (24 Mar. 1812–21 Dec. 1899), lawyer and defendant in a notable U.S. Supreme Court case, was born in Belmont County, Ohio, the son of Moses Milligan and Mary Purdy, farmers. (It is not known what his middle initial stood for.) He attended only one term of a subscription school but read widely in his father's library. He left home during his late teens and worked as a farm hand and schoolteacher for several years before choosing law over medicine as a career. In 1835 he passed his oral bar exam, scoring highest in a class of nine, which included Edwin M. Stanton. On the same day he married Sarah L. Ridgeway; they had two children.

After ten years as a lawyer in Belmont County, Milligan acquired a farm one mile west of Huntington, Indiana. Bothered by ill health (epilepsy and spinal meningitis), he gave up farm work to devote himself full-time to law and became "one of the foremost members of his profession in northern Indiana" (*History of Huntington County* [1914], p. 289). Credited with a "remarkable memory" and characterized as "a man of sterling character and inflexible honesty," he prospered and became a leader in local Democratic circles as a states' rights Jeffersonian with a contempt for New England and its "isms": abolitionism, prohibitionism, Know Nothingism, and protectionism (high tariff policy).

First and foremost a strict constitutionalist, Milligan opposed the Civil War from its beginning, calling his governor's military proclamations "silly twaddle" and the war "unjust, unnecessary, infamous." In August 1861 he led the antiwar faction at the Democratic county convention, chairing the committee that drafted resolutions excoriating the Lincoln administration and "the overthrow of constitutional liberty in America." At the Democratic state convention of January 1862, moderates sidetracked the views of Milligan's antiwar faction. He received another setback when moderates selected James F. McDowell instead of him as the party's congressional candidate in the Eleventh Congressional District.

When Alexander J. Douglas, a state senator from Columbia City, was arrested in May 1863 for antiwar utterances, Milligan served as his counsel before the military commission convened in Cincinnati. Milligan argued that a military court had no right to try a civilian, but the commission brushed aside his Sixth Amendment arguments.

Promoted by friends for their party's gubernatorial nomination at the Democratic state convention of 12 July 1864, Milligan lost to Joseph E. McDonald by a 1,097 to 160 vote. An antiwar speech that he gave on 13 August at Fort Wayne angered Republicans, especially Indiana's governor. Later in the month Milligan was a delegate to the Democratic National Convention in Chicago, at which he reluctantly accepted General George B. McClellan (1826–1885) as the party's presidential nominee.

On 5 October 1864, at the urging of Indiana's governor, General Alvin P. Hovey arrested Milligan and others. They were charged with "disloyal practices" and "conspiring against the government of the United States," supposedly via a secret society, the Sons of Liberty. As far as Milligan was concerned the so-called "conspiracy" was mostly a fantasy devised by Republicans for political gain. Tried by a military commission that convened in Indianapolis in October 1864, he and his counsel argued that the military court had no jurisdiction over civilians. The commission, nevertheless, found four prisoners "guilty as charged" and sentenced three (including Milligan) to be "hanged by the neck."

Milligan's lawyer sought a writ of habeas corpus in a U.S. circuit court, and, meanwhile, the execution of the three was postponed. The case was certified to the U.S. Supreme Court. Federal "agents" offered the four prisoners their freedom if they begged the president for a pardon and if Milligan dropped his suit. Contemptuously, Milligan retorted "that the President should ask *his* [Milligan's] pardon for violation of law by approving a false finding of an illegal body." Early in 1866 the U.S. Supreme Court rendered its decision in *Ex Parte Milligan*. The Court overturned Milligan's conviction, ruling that it was unconstitutional for a military commission to try a civilian where the civilian courts were open and functioning. This decision has been called "one of the bulwarks of American civil liberty" (James G. Randall, *Civil War and Reconstruction* [1937], p. 398).

Freed after eighteen months of imprisonment, Milligan returned to Huntington to receive "one of the greatest ovations ever given to any man in the State" (*History of Huntington County* [1887], p. 515). Seeking revenge, he sued James R. Slack, the Huntington attorney who publicly had urged the arrest of Milligan, and twenty-three others for $500,000 in damages for trespass and false imprisonment, claiming that statements made during the Indianapolis-based trial were false and defamatory. The case went through several name changes and evolved into *Milligan v. Hovey*. The jury decided for Milligan, but a law limited damages in these cases to five dollars.

Milligan's law practice flourished in the postwar era. His wife died in 1870, and three years later he married Maria L. Cavander, a widow. At the age of eighty-five Milligan retired from the bar. His once "rugged physique" gave way to ill health and age, and he died in Huntington, three months after the death of his second wife.

• There is no biography of Milligan and only one known letter written by him. Darwin Kelley, *Milligan's Fight against Lincoln* (1973), is sketchy. Frank L. Klement, "The Indianapolis Treason Trials and *Ex Parte Milligan*," in *American Political Trials*, ed. Michal R. Belknap (1981), pp. 101–28, covers two major events of his life. Obituaries are in the *Huntington Herald*, 22 Dec. 1899, and *Huntington News Democrat*, 26 Dec. 1899.

FRANK L. KLEMENT

MILLIGAN, Robert Wiley (8 Apr. 1843–14 Oct. 1909), naval engineer and officer, was born in Philadelphia, Pennsylvania, the son of James Milligan and Mary Thornton. After attending Philadelphia primary and secondary schools, he entered the U.S. Navy during the Civil War as a third assistant engineer. He served aboard the *Mackinaw*, participating in the battles at Fort Fisher and at Wilmington and the campaign in the James River leading to the fall of Petersburg and Richmond. In 1870 he married Sarah Ann Du Bois; they had two children.

After the Civil War, Milligan's professional career was shaped by the deep social division in the navy. The line officer class was selected and nominated from prominent families across the nation for admission to the U.S. Naval Academy at Annapolis and did not at first admit the equal rank or importance of men like Milligan, shop-trained engineers who had not attended college or the Naval Academy. However, with the growth of the steam-driven steel navy in the late 1870s, the importance of engineers and engineering training gained gradual recognition. Milligan's career reflected this changing perception, and his exploits contributed to the eventual revolution in the status of the naval engineer. His postwar service as an engineer aboard ships was interrupted by two periods as an instructor in engineering at the Naval Academy in 1879–1882 and in 1885–1889, just as the new ships of the steel navy were being introduced to the fleet. From 1893 to 1896 he served on the Board of Inspection and Survey, which insured performance on contracts for engines, fuels, and auxiliary equipment.

In January 1897 Milligan was appointed to the *Oregon* as chief engineer. His service aboard this ship brought him personal recognition and helped change the perception of engineers' crucial role in modern warfare. At the opening of the Spanish-American War in 1898, the *Oregon* was based in San Francisco Bay. Prior to construction of the Panama Canal, the voyage to Cuba around Cape Horn normally required three months or more, including stops for shore leave, coaling, repairs, and maintenance. The *Oregon* left San Francisco on 19 March 1898 and arrived in Florida sixty-eight days later, averaging over eleven knots on the 14,000-mile trip. The cruise experienced no mechanical accidents or delays caused by machinery problems and spent only fourteen days in ports for bringing on fuel, water, and supplies. The press and the public followed the progress of the ship, focusing attention on the chief engineer, who operated the engines and supervised round-the-clock overhauls during the port stays. Milligan personally contributed a small solution to the problem of the two-ocean navy by bringing his ship around a continent in time to be of service in the short war.

Years later, at the Panama Pacific Exposition in November 1915, Admiral C. F. Pond, quoted in the San Francisco *Army and Navy News*, said that the success of the *Oregon* was owed to Milligan "more than to any other one man." During the war in Cuba, the *Oregon* participated in the blockade of Santiago and the battle that ensued as Spanish ships fled the harbor under hot pursuit from the U.S. Navy. During these engagements, Milligan used only fresh water in the boilers and kept all four of the ship's boilers in operation at the same time. Furthermore, he had locked away a quantity of high-quality coal, which he brought out only during the *Oregon's* chase of the Spanish ship *Cristobal Colon*. Colleagues were startled to see the *Oregon* shoot ahead of the other U.S. naval ships at an average of 12.9 knots. Milligan and his engine crew, working in the sweatshop conditions of the engine rooms during the tropical heat of July in Cuban waters, were hailed as heroes.

Milligan's performance during the long cruise from San Francisco and in the battle of Santiago was rewarded with both personal promotion and recognition of the crucial role of the engineer in the age of steam. He was advanced five numbers in the list of naval officers eligible for promotion and was made fleet engineer. In 1902, with the amalgamation of the line officer and engineer ranks, he was promoted to captain. He served at the Norfolk Navy Yard until 1905, retiring with the rank of rear admiral. He resided in Annapolis after his retirement and died in that city.

• There is no known collection of Milligan's papers. Sources on Milligan include L. R. Hamersly, *The Records of Living Officers of the U.S. Navy and Marine Corps* (1902), and C. A. E. King, "Recent Performances of the USS *Oregon*," *Journal of the American Society of Naval Engineers* 9 (Aug. 1898) Obituaries are in the *Baltimore Sun*, 15 Oct. 1909, and the *Army and Navy Journal*, 16 Oct. 1909.

RODNEY P. CARLISLE

MILLIKAN, Clark Blanchard (23 Aug. 1903–2 Jan. 1966), aeronautical engineer, was born in Chicago, Illinois, the son of Robert Andrews Millikan, a physicist, and Greta Irvin Blanchard. Millikan's father was a distinguished physicist (Nobel Prize, 1923), and one of the founders of the California Institute of Technology. Millikan attended the preparatory high school of the University of Chicago and upon his graduation in 1919 studied for one year at the University of California at Berkeley and Throop College of Technology (later California Institute of Technology) in Pasadena. In 1920 he entered Yale, where he majored in mathematics and physics and received his A.B. in 1924. He then began graduate work at Caltech, where he was awarded his Ph.D. in physics with a dissertation, "Some Problems in the Steady Motion of Viscous, Incompressible Fluids, with Particular Reference to a Variational Principle," under the direction of Harry Bateman. He joined the Caltech faculty as a research fellow in aeronautics (1928–1929) and then served as assistant professor (1929–1934), associate professor (1934–1940), and finally as professor of aeronautics (1940–1966). He was acting director of the Guggenheim Aeronautical Laboratory at the California Institute of Technology (GALCIT) from 1944 to 1949 and then director from 1949 to 1966. During World War II he was a lieutenant commander in the U.S. Navy (Reserve) and extremely active in advising and consulting on aeronautics and ballistics for the air force, army, and navy. In a ceremony at Caltech on 22 March 1949, both Millikan and his father were awarded the Presidential Medal of Merit for their wartime service in the development of rocket and jet propulsion. The British government also honored Clark Millikan with the King's Medal for Service in the Cause of Freedom. He was a fellow of the American Physical Society and the Royal Aeronautical Society and an honorary fellow of the Institute of Aeronautical Sciences, of which he was president in 1937. Millikan was elected a member of the National Academy of Sciences in 1964, and in the same year he was a founding member of the National Academy of Engineering.

The career of Millikan was remarkable in its scope; it included outstanding contributions in the worlds of academia (administration, research, and teaching), government service, and industry. His student years prepared him well for research work and developed his passion for all things related to aeronautics. His dissertation showed the impossibility of a variational approach to viscous fluid flow, and he immediately followed it with a basic paper on aircraft performance (1929). Likewise, his paper on boundary layer theory and skin friction for figures of revolution (1932) and his use of dimensional analysis in the study of turbulent flow in channels and tubes (1938) were noteworthy and are frequently cited. He also wrote several papers with Theodor von Kármán (1934–1935). However, his interests lay not in theory, but in the practical design of aircraft and wind tunnels. In 1928–1929 he and his colleagues Arthur L. Klein and Albert A. Merrill designed and flew a revolutionary new type of biplane that had a built-in stability and could be flown "hands off." Millikan and Klein also built the first wind tunnel at Caltech before the formal establishment of GALCIT.

Millikan was an excellent teacher whose lectures were meticulously prepared and up to date, and he gave his listeners the benefit of his personal experience, both in theory and practical applications. His textbook *Aerodynamics of the Aeroplane* (1940) offers a glimpse of his style and taste. He strove to be on the cutting edge of developing technology and in 1945, in cooperation with Frank J. Malina, he offered the first course on jet propulsion at an academic institution. Furthermore, both as a teacher and as an administrator, he made a special effort to get to know and advise students. Much of the success of GALCIT during the von Kármán years was due to Millikan's skill and talent as an administrator. His government work included service on the Air Force Scientific Advisory Board as member-at-large (1952); chair of the ad hoc Committee of Project Atlas (1952); chair of the Aerospace Vehicles Panel (1953–1957), member of its executive committee (1953–1966), and senior statesman (1959–1966); and member of the Department of Defense Strategic Missile Evaluation Committee (1953–1966). The latter played a crucial role in the decision to develop and deploy intercontinental ballistic missiles, and upon the death of J. von Neumann in 1957, Millikan succeeded him as the committee chair. In industry, he was the director of the Southern California Cooperative Wind Tunnel (1945–1960), which was funded by Convair, Douglas, Lockheed, McDonnell, and North American and operated by Caltech. Millikan was also involved in the establishment of Caltech's Jet Propulsion Laboratory, the Aerojet-General Corporation, and the National Engineering Science Company of Pasadena.

Millikan was a gregarious, outgoing man who had a genuine affection for people. This, coupled with his many interests (which he pursued with seemingly boundless energy), and his gentle, soft-spoken wisdom, enabled him to serve the needs of his profession, Caltech, and the American aeronautical engineering community with unique effectiveness. He is remembered as a pioneer in aeronautics, an adviser at the highest levels of government; a distinguished engineer, scientist, and teacher; and a good companion and friend. His contributions to the growth of Caltech as a major center of aeronautics, and indeed to American aviation at large, live on in the memory of his students, his colleagues, and his many friends.

In 1928 Millikan married Mrs. Helen Staats Battle of Pasadena; they had three children. They were divorced in 1958, and in 1959 he married Mrs. Edith Nussbaum Parry, also of Pasadena. In his later years he suffered from high blood pressure and heart disease, but it was not in his makeup to allow these to interfere with his duties or admit that he was tired, sick, or needed a rest. Finally, his health broke, and he died at the Huntington Hospital in Pasadena.

• Millikan's papers are held by the Institute Archives at the California Institute of Technology. Millikan's early views on open questions in aeronautics appear in his expository paper, "The Physicist Gets Air Minded," in *Physics in Industry* (1937), an American Institute of Physics monograph. Also see Judith R. Goodstein, *Millikan's School: A History of the California Institute of Technology* (1991); and three booklets produced by Caltech: *The Guggenheim Aeronautical Laboratory of the California Institute of Technology: The First Twenty-five Years* (1954); Edmund Beard, *Developing the ICBM: A Study in Bureaucratic Politics* (1976); and Fred E. C. Culick, ed., *Guggenheim Aeronautical Laboratory at the California Institute of Technology: The First Fifty Years* (1983). Obituary notices appear in National Academy of Sciences, *Biographical Memoirs* 40 (1969): 210–25, the Caltech publication *Engineering and Science*, Jan. 1966, pp. 211–25, and the *New York Times*, 3 Jan. 1966.

JOSEPH D. ZUND

MILLIKAN, Robert Andrews (22 Mar. 1868–19 Dec. 1953), physicist, was born in Morrison, Illinois, the son of Silas Franklin Millikan, a Congregational minister, and Mary Jane Andrews, a college and preparatory school teacher. Millikan spent most of his childhood in Maquoketa, Iowa, raised on tales of his New England pioneer ancestors and liberal Christian lessons of ethical and social betterment. These lessons instilled in Millikan a strong sense of continuity and progress, to which he was expected to make his own contribution. Although he achieved high grades in mathematics and science at Maquoketa's new academy, he later recalled being unstimulated by the lecture demonstrations of a poorly educated science teacher.

Millikan's initial appreciation of physics came as a teacher of preparatory students while he was enrolled at Oberlin College, which he entered in 1887 and with which two generations of his family had been associated. Upon discovering that an integration of problem solving and laboratory experiments excited both him and his students, he began to consider a career in physics rather than in medicine. Millikan's two physics professors, Charles Churchill and Elisha Gray (an early inventor of telegraph and telephone devices), turned Millikan's attention toward electricity. Both in and out of the classroom, Oberlin reinforced the Christian values and goals Millikan's parents had inculcated. He was introduced to the belief that science and Christianity were complementary ideological paths that could enable a Christian to fulfill his God-given duty to better himself and society. This faith in the moral and material progress of humanity animated his fervent idealism throughout his life and work.

Upon earning a master's degree in physics from Oberlin in 1893, Millikan went to Columbia University on scholarship to pursue graduate studies. There Professor Ogden Rood suggested doctoral research on the emission of polarized light, which led to a summer of research in 1894 under the esteemed optical researcher Albert A. Michelson at the new University of Chicago. Millikan's doctoral research, which involved careful observations with a polarimeter of his own design to resolve an important theoretical issue—whether the polarization of incandescent light obeyed the Cauchy-Fresnel laws of reflection and refraction—presaged his later research style at the University of Chicago.

At Columbia Millikan studied the new mathematical physics of electromagnetism with Michael Pupin, who also gave Millikan a loan that further encouraged him to travel to Europe for a year of postgraduate study in the hope of becoming a first-class experimental physicist. He attended the lectures of Europe's premiere physics researchers and witnessed an early demonstration of Röntgen's new X-rays. Under the close guidance of Walter Nernst at the University of Göttingen, Millikan learned how instruction and investigation could be fruitfully interwoven.

In 1896 Millikan reneged on a better paying job offer from Oberlin to take an inferior position as an assistant at the young but more promising and research-oriented University of Chicago. He soon discovered, however, that his primary responsibilities at Chicago would be pedagogical. Millikan revised the undergraduate physics curriculum around new laboratory experiments and demonstrations, with related practical problem solving in the classroom. These courses, which led to the publication of three popular textbooks that Millikan wrote or co-wrote, served as the basic format for introductory college physics at Chicago for over two decades. Millikan also became involved in debates over the coordination between high school and college physics. With Henry Gale, he wrote an extremely popular series of textbooks for secondary school students, *A First Course in Physics*, which sold more than a million copies in four revisions into the 1930s. He disseminated his pedagogical ideas to secondary school physics teachers in a summer course, "The Pedagogy of Physics," in the University of Chicago's School of Education from 1904 to 1913. On the basis of these educational achievements, he rose steadily up the academic ladder at Chicago to the tenured rank of associate professor in 1906. Royalties from his successful textbook sales even enabled Millikan to build a new house for his wife, Greta Blanchard, whom he had married in 1902, and their three sons.

Although Millikan knew well that highest praise and honors were reserved for those who excelled in research, not teaching, his early research efforts had fallen far short of his ambition for recognition as an experimentalist. Rather than turn away from pedagogy, however, he developed a successful strategy of integrating undergraduate and graduate classroom and laboratory studies and coordinating his own research with that of his graduate students. Millikan offered graduate courses in the most recent developments of X-rays, radioactivity, and quantum and electron physics; in 1910 he taught one of the first university courses in the United States on quantum theory. These courses became research seminars for doctoral candidates on topics of the new physics he wanted to investigate. Students interested in the latest developments in physics were drawn in growing numbers to Millikan's classroom. There his informal question and answer style of teaching and his enthusiasm appealed to fledgling experimentalists. Michelson was glad to turn over the responsibility for supervising the research of doctoral candidates and the internal administration of the physics department to Millikan, who in turn benefited by gathering a growing team of well-trained assistants and, later, collaborators, who would help him resolve a number of his research problems.

By 1916, with the assistance of a succession of eight graduate students, Millikan had achieved the experimental verification of Albert Einstein's photoelectric equation and a more precise determination of Max Planck's constant. Millikan's students made significant contributions to the progress of his photoelectric studies and used their findings for their own doctoral research. They also corroborated Millikan's work, helping him to defend himself against attacks from physicists with conflicting data, such as Carl Ramsauer.

Between 1912 and 1924, Millikan struggled with his assessment of the many theories of the photoelectric effect. He even proposed a modified version of Planck's atomic resonance mechanism. Millikan's classroom discussions reveal how he misunderstood Einstein's light quantum hypothesis. When compared with other quantum theories, Millikan admitted, Einstein's theory, however radical and erroneous, did explain the data most completely. Like most of his fellow physicists, Millikan rejected Einstein's quantum theory of radiation because it could not be reconciled with the well-established facts of defraction and interference. Progress in science, Millikan argued, was primarily by the accretion of experimentally established facts rather than revolutionary conceptual change. He recognized, however, that some quantum theory of radiation that could be reconciled with the electromagnetic theory of light had to come.

Millikan's cooperative and integrative approach to teaching and research also had a positive impact on his second major research program: his famous "oil-drop experiment," which precisely measured the elementary electrical charge and established conclusively the unity of electrical charge. Working closely again with graduate students, particularly Louis Begeman and Harvey Fletcher, between 1907 and 1912, Millikan discovered a new experimental method (based on C. T. R. Wilson's cloud chamber) that convincingly demonstrated electric charge was always an integer multiple of some fixed unit and accurately determined the value of that fundamental constant: the electron charge. This achievement was hailed in the popular press and by his colleagues. Niels Bohr relied on Millikan's 1909 value in his pivotal 1913 paper on the quantum theory of electron orbits in the hydrogen atom. The Nobel Prize Committee for Physics later cited Millikan's findings in support of their decision to award Bohr the prize in 1922. For the next half century, the Millikan oil-drop method became one of the standard experiments in the American college physics laboratory repertoire.

Important achievements such as these often lure detractors. From 1909 to 1916 Millikan became embroiled in a long and acrimonious dispute with Felix Ehrenhaft, who had used similar apparatus but found conflicting evidence for an elementary unit of electricity. Millikan marshaled Fletcher and at least nine other graduate students to conduct research in response to Ehrenhaft's criticisms. This dispute delayed Millikan's selection as a Nobel laureate and may have even driven Millikan to omit a few conflicting results from his later measurements.

Millikan's successful measurements of the photoelectric effect and the electron charge earned him the much-desired esteem of his peers, resulting in his promotion in 1910 to full professor, awards, and election to high offices in prestigious professional societies. In 1923 he received the highest international recognition with awards of the Hughes Medal of the Royal Society of London and the Nobel Prize in physics. Millikan had become the United States' most honored scientist. His enhanced status soon propelled him into the loftier professional circle of national science policy makers. He was elected to the National Academy of Sciences in 1915. When the NAS created the National Research Council (NRC) in 1916 to mobilize cooperative research efforts for national security, Millikan was named a vice chairman on its executive committee and director of research.

As soon as the United States joined the war in Europe, Millikan took a leave of absence from his academic duties in Chicago and went to Washington, D.C., to become chairman of a new General Antisubmarine Committee of the NRC. He now redirected his energy and enthusiasm to a demonstration that academic science could contribute to national defense. Members of Millikan's submarine detection team, particularly physics professor Max Mason, created new sensitive listening devices credited with helping defeat the German U-boats in the North Atlantic. Millikan accepted an army commission as major (later promoted to lieutenant colonel) in the Army Reserve and served as chief of the Signal Corps Science and Research Division for the rest of the war. Millikan left military service more self-confident in his administrative and persuasive abilities, and a respected member of a new network of influential leaders in government and business.

In 1919 Millikan and fellow directors of the the NRC persuaded the Rockefeller Foundation to fund a postdoctoral fellowship program for promising young physicists and chemists, which they could use at a few prominent research universities in the United States or Europe. This program, administered by Millikan and colleagues at the NRC, played a vital role in bringing American physical science to international prominence by the 1930s.

Millikan's ideas about national science policy remained at the forefront of the debates on the role of business and government in science education and research for the next two decades. He had an unreserved faith in the progress of science and society. If science could be sufficiently financed by private enterprise, it would lead inevitably to both material and moral prosperity in a democracy. To advance science he advocated a selective and diversified approach: the best scientific research was the product of a few prominent scientists and their students at the finest, best-funded facilities throughout the nation, rather than centralized at a single institution. This would keep academic scientific research free of interference from politicians and the federal government, which he distrusted, because he believed in a "pioneer mix of self-reliance and local solidarity" to meet the nation's social, economic, and scientific needs (Kargon, p. 162). On the other hand, he endorsed controlling scientific research funding through the centralized administrations of the NAS and the NRC. After the next world war, he actively opposed the new, closer government-science alliance created by the National Science Foundation.

Millikan returned to his academic duties at the University of Chicago in 1919 wanting to take advantage of his new influential circle of friendships with prominent men in business, foundations, and academia. The most significant and long-lived relationship in this potent network was with the highly respected astrophysicist George E. Hale. In 1917 Hale had convinced Millikan to join the faculty of the Throop College of Technology in Pasadena, California, for a quarter session annually. Throop had been a manual training school that Hale was reconfiguring into an engineering school. He hoped to create at Throop an elite scientific research center that could be associated with his nearby Mount Wilson Observatory.

Hale first recruited Arthur Noyes, the celebrated chemist, and then set his sights on Millikan. Hale saw in Millikan just the eminent researcher, talented teacher, capable organizer, and dynamic spokesman needed to realize the grand plans he had for Throop. After the war, Hale continued to court Millikan, who at first was reluctant to leave the reputable University of Chicago for such a risky venture in the West. But Millikan's many successes and growing reputation had fired his ambitions. He tried to persuade Chicago's president Harry Judson to fund his own grand plans for a major research institute, but he failed. Finally, in 1921, with a multimillion dollar bequest to Throop from a local lumber tycoon and the donation of a million-volt laboratory from California Edison, Millikan accepted Hale's challenging offer to become the chairman of the Executive Committee and director of the Norman Bridge Physics Laboratory at the new California Institute of Technology.

Millikan arrived at Caltech with the ambition of creating a world-class research center in pure science; he planned to recruit the most talented scientists and students and organize them into cooperative research projects at the finest facilities. Bringing with him several of his promising graduate students and recruiting some accomplished Chicago graduates, Millikan demonstrated an eye for talent. The quality of a candidate could even overrule his anti-Semitism. His connections with the NRC enabled him to attract bright NRC fellows, such as Carl D. Anderson. Most stimulating, perhaps, was his visiting scholars program, which attracted many famous physicists, such as Max Born, Paul Dirac, Peter Debye, Einstein, Werner Heisenberg, and Erwin Schrödinger, to Caltech as visiting faculty over the next two decades. Capitalizing on a distinguished faculty and students, excellent laboratory facilities, and well-financed research projects, Millikan was able to lure brillant young scientists, such as J. Robert Oppenheimer in 1929, and eminent experienced researchers, such as Theodore von Kármán in 1926.

Within ten years, under Millikan's close supervision, the Caltech physics department became one of the most productive research institutions in the world. Millikan extended this effective enterprise to other disciplines, such as biology, by recruiting the world-renowned Thomas H. Morgan. He persuaded industrialist and philanthropist Harry Guggenheim to finance an aeronautical research center, headed by von Kármán. This laboratory established close ties with the nascent aircraft industry and helped southern California become a world center of aircraft manufacture. With achievements such as this, Millikan believed that he had accomplished his dream of demonstrating that science could stimulate the nation's growth and prosperity.

These many administrative accomplishments did not diminish Millikan's own research into new phenomena. At Chicago, Millikan had demonstrated that an ultraviolet spark could be maintained in a high vacuum with a sufficiently large potential difference. In his early years at Caltech, Millikan and a graduate student, Ira S. Bowen, used improved gratings, from Hale's observatory, to study the spectra of these "hot sparks." With their refined vacuum spectrograph, Bowen and Millikan were able to measure for the first time the extreme ultraviolet spectra of atoms stripped of their valence electrons. Their work demonstrated the unity of optical and X-ray spectra and laid the experimental foundations for the concept of electron spin.

Millikan had a remarkable ability to recognize what significant new phenomena should be investigated, by means of student research teams, and the entrepreneurial skills to persuade wealthy patrons and foundations to finance complex and long-term projects. These talents proved most fruitful at Caltech with his studies of cosmic radiation. Millikan proposed in 1919 a novel experimental technique (using self-recording instruments in unmanned balloons such as he had known in his wartime service) to determine whether the source of highly penetrating radiation in the upper atmosphere was either terrestrial or celestial. Funding from the Carnegie Institution in 1922 enabled Millikan to employ this scheme, with Bowen, and to make nearby mountain-top measurements with other students. Millikan's findings were inconclusive, but they aroused the interest of the scientific community. To settle the question of the genesis of this radiation, Millikan devised a new, elegant experimental arrangement, with graduate student G. Harvey Cameron, to compare the ionization in two deep southern California mountain lakes at different altitudes. This study decisively demonstrated that there was an extraterrestrial source of this radiation, which Millikan named "cosmic rays."

Millikan proposed in 1928 that these cosmic rays were not charged particles, but photons produced by fusion or electron capture. He described them colorfully in *Science and the New Civilization* (1930) as the "birth cries" of nascent atomic elements. Millikan had speculated years before about some atomic synthesis that could counterbalance the heat death of the second law of thermodynamics and the dissipation of radioactive decay. Millikan fervently believed he now had found just such a regenerative phenomenon. He melded this hypothesis with his theistic belief in an omnipresent God. This synthesis met with popular acclaim but usually with derision from his colleagues. Millikan grudgingly abandoned this viewpoint in the mid-1930s, when his own data revealed energies of these cosmic rays were too great to be produced by atomic synthesis.

One important reason Millikan believed that cosmic rays were photons was the lack of effect of the earth's magnetic field on their motion, based on experiments he had conducted in the Pacific and in South America. But a growing number of scientists had found evidence of such a "latitude effect" (different intensities of cosmic rays coming from the East versus the West). Arthur H. Compton, the United States' third Nobel prize winner in physics and head of the physics department at Chicago, mounted a worldwide survey in 1932 that dramatically demonstrated existence of the latitude effect. Compton and Millikan stridently disputed their methods, data, and interpretations in print and public debates. Millikan had graduate student H. Victor Neher repeat their measurements from Los Angeles to Peru. Neher initially found no evidence for the effect as a result of faulty apparatus at a critical location but did confirm the latitude effect in 1933. Millikan nevertheless clung for many years to his conviction, contrary to scientific consensus, that the primary radiation was photons, which produced charged particles when colliding with atmospheric nuclei. Only a few years before his death, Millikan finally admitted that the primary cosmic rays must be charged particles (protons) and not photons.

Millikan's cosmic rays research program had one triumphant consequence. He directed a graduate student, Carl D. Anderson, to find a way to measure directly cosmic ray energies. Anderson combined the same Wilson cloud chamber method used by Millikan with a large magnetic field. By abandoning his mentor's cosmic ray hypothesis, Anderson was able to discover the positron (positively charged electron), a discovery that some regard as the birth of modern elementary particle physics.

Millikan's notoriety during his years at Caltech extended far beyond academic campuses. He helped promote the Science Service news agency, wrote articles for magazines like the *Atlantic Monthly* and books such as *Science and Life* (1924) that popularized the latest achievements in science and technology, and heralded their benefits for the average American. By the mid-1920s, Millikan had become not only the United States' most respected scientist, but its best-known spokesman for science. His face appeared in 1927 on the cover of *Time*, which described him as a "man [who] knows how to make scientific complexities charming as well as awesome."

In the face of growing attacks on modern science by fundamental religious groups, Millikan earnestly spoke out and wrote articles and books, such as *Evolution in Science and Religion* (1927), on the harmony between science and religion. In 1923 he organized a group of prominent businessmen, academics, and religious leaders to sign a joint statement on the complementary role science and religion play in the progress of humanity. During the Great Depression, Millikan spoke out ardently against communism and Franklin D. Roosevelt's New Deal policies, in the belief that they would deter the ability of free enterprise and science to respond to the United States' hard times.

After twenty-four years as chief executive officer at Caltech, Millikan finally had to be maneuvered into retirement because he was neither capable of participating nor actively involved in Caltech's administration. He remained for eight more years in Pasadena, where he died just three months after his wife's demise.

Despite his personal deficits—racism, pride, and a jealous unwillingness to recognize the contributions of others—Millikan left an exceptional four-fold legacy for the next generation of American scientists and citizens. As an educator, his textbooks and laboratory demonstrations set the standard for how to introduce physics principles to thousands of high school and college students for over three decades. As an investigator, Millikan's research teams developed innovative and often-imitated experimental schemes to study electrical properties of new subatomic phenomena. As an administrator, he transformed Hale's dream into a reality: Caltech became one of the finest research institutions for science and engineering in the world. Lastly, as a national science policy maker and spokesman, Millikan's views of the proper relation of science to government, business, religion, and society were widely accepted for over two decades.

• Millikan's family documents and memorabilia, autobiographical and scientific writings, and personal and professional correspondence primarily from after 1921 are located in the Robert A. Millikan Collection and other collections at the Archives of the California Institute of Technology. Materials on his twenty-five years at the University of Chicago are located in various files in the Department of Special Collections of the Regenstein Library of the University of Chicago. Papers describing his familial connections with Oberlin and his college education are found in the Oberlin College Archives. Millikan's own *Autobiography of Robert A. Millikan* (1950) is informative but leaves out or distorts many important episodes of his life. The most extensive bibliography of Millikan's scientific writings is in Lee A. Du Bridge and Paul Epstein, "Robert Andrews Millikan," National Academy of Sciences, *Biographical Memoirs* 33 (1959): 241–82. A list of Millikan's textbooks and laboratory manuals is compiled in Alfred Romer, "Robert A. Millikan, Physics Teacher," *Physics Teacher* 31 (1978): 78–85. Notable and differing biographical accounts are Daniel J. Kevles's essay in *Scientific American* 240 (1979): 141–51, and Robert H. Kargon, *The Rise of Robert Millikan: Portrait of a Life in American Science* (1982). More recent analyses of Millikan's scientific research and teaching are John L. Michel, "The Chicago Connection." in *The Michelson Era in American Science, 1870–1930*, ed. Stanley Goldberg and Roger H. Stuewer (1988); Allan Franklin, *The Neglect of Experiment* (1986); and Peter Galison, *How Experiments End* (1987). Millikan's entrepreneurship and research at Caltech are discussed in Robert W. Seidel, "Physics Research in California: The Rise of a Leading Sector in American Physics" (Ph.D. diss., Univ. of California, Berkeley, 1978); the history of his administration is covered in Judith R. Goodstein, *Millikan's School: A History of the California Institute of Technology* (1991).

JOHN L. MICHEL

MILLIKIN, Eugene Donald (12 Feb. 1891–26 July 1958), U.S. senator, was born in Hamilton, Ohio, the son of Samuel Hunter Millikin, a dentist, and Mary Shelly. In 1913, after graduating from the law school of the University of Colorado in Boulder, Millikin began his legal career in Salt Lake City, Utah. His political life began two years later, when he served as executive secretary to Colorado governor George Carlson. After military service in France as a lieutenant colonel during World War I, Millikin resumed his legal practice in Denver, Colorado, establishing a successful partnership with Karl Schuyler. Schuyler, a prosperous oilman with a keen interest in politics, won a U.S. Senate seat in 1932 and hired Millikin as his secretary. Schuyler's political career was cut short by a fatal automobile accident the following year. Millikin returned to Colorado, where he resumed his corporate law practice and served as president of the Kinney-Coastal Oil Company. In 1935 he married Schuyler's widow, Delia Alsena Shepard Schuyler. The couple had no children.

In 1941 Millikin, a Republican, was appointed to fill a Senate vacancy caused by the death of Democrat Alva Adams. He was elected in his own right in 1944 and reelected in 1950. Adhering firmly to the Capitol Hill norm that emphasized seniority, he waited a year and a half before delivering his first Senate speech, a terse 108-word oration in defense of civil liberties. Even after becoming one of the Senate's most influential and respected members, Millikin chose to avoid the limelight and worked behind the scenes to achieve his most important goals. His favorite technique for eluding publicity was his penchant for profanity. Knowing that strict rules governed what could and could not be printed, he peppered his press conferences with bawdy descriptions of Capitol Hill's political scene.

Millikin's Senate leverage increased when the Republican party won control of both houses of Congress in the 1946 midterm elections. He was respected for his expertise on issues of trade and taxation, and his colleagues elected him chairman of the Senate Finance Committee. While distinguishing himself as a committed internationalist and providing important support for Senate ratification of the United Nations Charter and the North Atlantic Treaty and approval of the Marshall Plan, Millikin objected to most of the Harry Truman administration's social legislation, including the Full Employment Act of 1946, public housing, and federal aid to education. From his position as chairman of the Finance Committee (1947–1948), however, Millikin pursued a more constructive course. Though he usually worked to cut Democratic programs, he cooperated with senior Republican Robert A. Taft of Ohio to oppose the more aggressive cuts favored by their more conservative colleagues. Millikin never shrank from his belief that protecting the prosperous advanced the national interest. The man earning $500,000 a year, he once argued, "has the big estate . . . to maintain. . . . He has three Cadillacs. . . . They must be garaged, oiled, greased, and driven."

In 1952 Millikin supported Taft for the Republican nomination. When the more moderate Dwight Eisenhower prevailed, however, Millikin was a crucial mediator as the Republican party succeeded in rallying its forces for the general election. When the Republicans won control of the Senate during the 1952 congressional elections, he again became chairman of the Finance Committee, where he exercised enormous influence on public policy. In January 1954 *Business Week* described him as "probably the most influential Republican in the Senate." Millikin's unwavering commitment to Eisenhower's legislative program of accepting the parameters of the New Deal while opposing its extension marked the remainder of his Senate career.

In contrast to his obstreperous counterpart Daniel Reed (R.-N.Y.), who as chairman or ranking Republican on the House Ways and Means Committee sometimes abandoned the administration, Millikin won Eisenhower's respect and admiration for his devotion to the White House. Though he generally favored lower taxes and smaller federal programs, Millikin's pursuit of a balanced budget far outweighed any other policy priority. In 1953 he maneuvered through the Finance Committee a controversial six-month extension of the excess profits tax. Later that year he provided crucial opposition to a conservative Republican amendment to increase the business tax credit from $25,000 to $100,000. He spoke for the administration when he objected to any Senate amendments to the House bill, likening the passage of a revised bill through the House to "passing a kidney stone."

Millikin's Democratic adversaries nonetheless described the Coloradan as an accomplished defender of the wealthy elite. In 1954 he battled for a provision that would exempt from taxation a portion of income derived from stock dividends. In the same year he rallied Republican forces to defeat a Democratic proposal to raise the personal tax exemption from $600 to $700. Paul Douglas (D.-Ill.) scorned Millikin's legislation as an "economic, social and moral monstrosity." But Millikin had won the respect of other prominent Democrats. Senator Hubert Humphrey (D.-Minn.) characterized his political adversary as "one of the smartest men they've got . . . the most noble kind of conservative."

More important to his Colorado constituents was Millikin's ability to win federal contracts. In this regard he cooperated with his senatorial colleague, Ed C. Johnson (D.-Colo.). Though the two legislators hailed from opposing parties, Millikin and Johnson established a "joint projects" office upon the outbreak of the Korean War in June 1950. They shared the costs of the office, which was run as a sort of clearinghouse for all requests addressed to the Colorado senators. The two veteran legislators instructed its administrator, Ed

Keating, to give primary credit to whichever senator needed it the most at the time. The Air Force Academy in Colorado Springs stands as the greatest example of their common endeavors.

Suffering from a case of acute arthritis, Millikin chose not to seek reelection in 1956. Confined to a wheelchair by this time and unable to speak from the Senate floor, he continued his practice of drafting important pieces of legislation until his retirement. Known for his expertise on matters of finance and admired for his abilities as a storyteller, Millikin, along with Taft and Arthur H. Vandenberg (R.-Mich.), was one of the three most influential Senate Republicans in the years immediately after World War II. He ended his career as a devoted Eisenhower Republican, and his greatest political contribution may have been his ability to moderate the extremes of his party in the postwar era. He died in Denver.

• The Millikin papers are held by the University of Colorado Libraries in Boulder. The Senate Historical Office in Washington, D.C., houses important biographical information on Millikin. The published accounts of several Washington insiders speak to his impressive intellect and political importance; see especially Richard Langham Riedel, *Halls of the Mighty: My 47 Years in the Senate* (1969), and George E. Reedy, *The U.S. Senate: Paralysis or a Search for Consensus?* (1986). For a more contemporary account, see Douglass Cater, "'Mr. Conservative'—Eugene Millikin of Colorado," *The Reporter*, 17 Mar. 1953, pp. 26–31. Obituaries are in the *New York Times*, the *Washington Post*, and the *Denver Post*, 27 July 1958.

BYRON C. HULSEY

MILLINDER, Lucky (8 Aug. 1900–28 Sept. 1966), bandleader and composer, was born Lucius Venable Millinder in Anniston, Alabama. The identity and circumstances of his parents are unknown. He was raised in Chicago, Illinois, where he attended Wendell Phillips High School.

As Lucius Venable he began to work as a master of ceremonies and danced in nightclubs, including one run by Al Capone's brother Ralph in Cicero, Illinois. He became a bandleader in 1931, touring the RKO theater circuit. Early in 1932 he took over the little-known Doc Crawford band. Later that year he moved to New York.

Millinder appeared in the film short *Scandals of 1933*. In 1933 promoter Irving Mills began grooming Millinder to take over the Mills Blue Rhythm Band by making him the "front man" for the Congo Knights, a ten-piece band. They worked locally and then played on the French Riviera from July to October 1933, at which time the group was billed as Lucky Millinder and His Orchestra. He disbanded it upon returning to New York.

Late that year or early in 1934 Millinder took over the Mills Blue Rhythm Band. Its members included trumpeter Henry "Red" Allen, trombonist J. C. Higginbotham, clarinetist Buster Bailey, and a rhythm section of Edgar Hayes (pianist and arranger), Lawrence Lucie (guitar), Elmer James (bass), and O'Neill Spencer (drums). In 1935 they recorded "Spitfire" and the band's best-known piece, "Ride, Red, Ride," composed by Millinder and Mills and featuring Allen, whose showy trumpeting is encouraged by Millinder's speech-song. Alto saxophonist Tab Smith joined in the fall of 1935. One year later pianist Billy Kyle joined; bassist John Kirby is also believed to have become a bandmember at this time, though discographies list Hayes Alvis as the group's bassist.

From 1936 onward the group's recordings were sometimes issued under the name Lucky Millinder with the Mills Blue Rhythm Band, and from 1937 the group performed as Lucky Millinder and His Orchestra. Among his sidemen from this period were trumpeters Harry "Sweets" Edison and Charlie Shavers, trombonist Wilbur De Paris, Tab Smith, guitarist Danny Barker, and Bitty Kyle. "Jammin' for the Jackpot," recorded in 1937, was notable for a couple of melodic snippets that would soon form the core of Count Basie's masterpiece "Jumpin' at the Woodside," but otherwise this piece was the work of a well-accomplished but not especially memorable big band of the Swing Era. They disbanded in 1938.

In late May 1938 Millinder took over Bill Doggett's big band, with Doggett remaining as pianist. They toured until January 1939, when Millinder went bankrupt. He appeared in the film *Paradise in Harlem* (1939), featuring singer and actress Mamie Smith, and the film short *Readin', 'Ritin' and Rhythm*, including performances by trumpeter Frankie Newton and tenor saxophonist Don Byas.

In September 1940 Millinder formed a long-lived and significant big band that initially worked regularly at the Savoy Ballroom in Harlem. Early on, the band featured singer and guitarist Sister Rosetta Tharpe. Having already recorded blues and gospel pieces on her own, she made several sensational recordings of blues and secularized gospel themes (gospel music with secular lyrics substituted for the original religious texts) for Millinder, including "Trouble in Mind," "Rock, Daniel," "Shout, Sister, Shout" (composed by Doggett and Millinder), and "Rock Me" (all from 1941). That same year she appeared with the band in three "soundies" (film shorts for juke boxes): "The Lonesome Road," "Shout, Sister, Shout," and "Four or Five Times." As a response to the orchestra's "Big Fat Mama" and soundie "I Want a Big Fat Mama" (also from 1941), Tharpe recorded Millinder's song "I Want a Tall, Skinny Papa" in February 1942, at which time she had a change of heart and abandoned the group to devote herself exclusively to religious music.

Millinder's recordings of "Apollo Jump," from September 1941, and "Savoy," from February 1942 (the latter not to be confused with "Stompin' at the Savoy," popularized by Benny Goodman) are bouncy instrumental performances anticipating his later involvement in rhythm-and-blues. He claimed credit as composer on both titles (the latter again with Doggett), as well as on "Mason Flyer" (with Tab Smith) and "Little John Special," this last recording featuring trumpeter Dizzy Gillespie, who joined in 1942. During this period trumpeter Freddie Webster played alongside Gillespie. The rhythm section comprised Doggett, who was replaced by pianist Clyde Hart at some point that same year; guitarist Trevor Bacon, who in July 1942 sang on another incipient rhythm-and-blues hit, "When the Lights Go On Again"; bassist George Duvivier; and drummer Panama Francis. Tenor saxophonist David A. Young told writer Dempsey J. Travis that while touring as accompanists to the Ink Spots, Millinder's sixteen-piece band also included Thelonious Monk on piano. Nevertheless, around this time, in April 1942, Millinder's orchestra was outplayed by Jay McShann's big band, featuring alto saxophonist Charlie Parker, in a battle of the bands at the Savoy.

Further soundies include two from around 1942 featuring Mamie Smith, "Harlem Serenade" and "Because I Love You," and "Hello Bill," from around 1943. In October 1943 the group recorded "Shipyard Social Function." In May 1944 singer Wynonie Harris was featured on "Hurry, Hurry!" and an irreverant account of a drunken preacher, "Who Threw the Whiskey in the Well?" These two recordings moved Millinder more firmly into the rhythm-and-blues camp, but apart from tenor saxophonist Bull Moose Jackson, featured from 1945 to 1947, Millinder's most distinguised sidemen during this period were mainly associated with jazz: saxophonists Lucky Thompson, Eddie "Lockjaw" Davis, Frank Wess, and Paul Quinichette, pianists Ellis Larkins and Sir Charles Thompson, bassist Al McKibbon, and drummer Panama Francis.

Around 1946 the band made another soundie, "I Want a Man," followed by "Let It Roll," recorded in 1947. The next year Millinder was featured in the film *Boarding House Blues* and on NBC radio's "Swingtime at the Savoy," an African-American variety show. In June 1952 the big band accompanied Harris on "Night Train" in a raucous vocal rendition of tenor saxophonist Jimmy Forrest's instrumental rhythm-and-blues hit. At this point Millinder disbanded.

Millinder became a disc jockey, hosting the "Harlem Amateur Hour," a late-night show broadcast from the Apollo Theater on station WJZ. He also worked as a liquor salesman, a publicist, and a fortune teller, while reconstituting a big band for specific occasions. Millinder died in New York City. He was survived by his wife, Vivian Brewington, and their two children.

Millinder was an acrobatic showman and an exceptional big band conductor. As Francis recalled for writer Stanley Dance, "He couldn't read a note. But if you gave him a bunch of guys who could read, in one week's time he'd have them sounding like a band that had been organized for a year. He could remember everything in an arrangement after it was run down once. He was a genius in that way." Gillespie added, "He was the greatest conductor I'd ever seen. He had the biggest ears of anybody. He didn't know anything about music, and all he could do was rely on his memory—but his memory was astounding. He knew arrangements. He knew what everybody was playing all the time—the whole band—and if you missed something, he'd look at you."

• Useful sources include "Lucky Millinder and the Mills Blue Rhythm Band," *Record Research*, no. 88 (June 1968): 9; Stanley Dance, *The World of Swing* (1974; repr. 1979); Albert McCarthy, *Big Band Jazz* (1974); Arnold Shaw, *Honkers and Shouters: The Golden Years of Rhythm and Blues* (1978); Dizzy Gillespie with Al Fraser, *To Be, or Not . . . to Bop: Memoirs* (1979); Alain Gerber's liner notes to the LP *Lucky Millinder's Orchestra with Sister Rosetta Tharpe: Lucky Days 1941–1945* (1980); and Dempsey J. Travis, *An Autobiography of Black Jazz* (1983). See also Danny Barker, *A Life in Jazz*, ed. Alyn Shipton (1986); Gunther Schuller, *The Swing Era: The Development of Jazz, 1930–1945* (1989); and Paul Oliver, ed., *The Blackwell Guide to Blues Records* (1989; rev. as *The Blackwell Guide to Recorded Blues* [1991]). Recordings are cataloged in *Discography of Lucky Millinder* (1962). Obituaries are in the *New York Times*, 30 Sept. 1966, and *Down Beat*, 3 Nov. 1966.

BARRY KERNFELD

MILLNER, Wayne Vernal (13 Jan. 1913–19 Nov. 1976), college and professional football player and coach, was born in Roxbury, Massachusetts, the son of Charles E. Millner, who worked for a machine belt manufacturing company (his mother's name is unknown). An outstanding athlete at Salem, Massachusetts, High School, he was named to the 1928 All-Boston, All–North Shore, All-State, and All–New England football teams. He also played guard on the school's basketball team. Millner worked during the next two years before enrolling at Malvern Preparatory School in Philadelphia with the intention of later entering Villanova University. In the fall of 1932, however, he chose instead to enroll at the University of Notre Dame. He was named starting end on Notre Dame's team in the second game of his sophomore season. That 1933 team suffered a 3–5–1 record, but Millner established his reputation as a big-game player. In the last game of the season against undefeated Army, he recovered a blocked punt for a touchdown to lead Notre Dame to a 13–12 upset.

Millner was named to a number of All-American teams in 1934 when the Fighting Irish won six of nine games under first-year coach Elmer Layden, who had been one of Notre Dame's famous Four Horsemen of the 1920s. The highlight of Millner's college career occurred in the 1935 game against Ohio State. The Buckeyes were leading 13–12 in the waning minutes of the fourth quarter. However, Notre Dame put together a dramatic, last-minute, 51-yard drive, capped by a touchdown pass from tailback Bill Shakespeare to Millner, that gave them an 18–13 victory and ruined Ohio State's undefeated season. Millner was named a consensus All-American at end following that season. He graduated from Notre Dame in 1936 with a bachelor's degree in commerce. In 1934 Millner married Ann Marie Perry (he was one of only a few Notre Dame students given permission to marry at the time). They had two daughters but were divorced in 1948.

The Boston (later Washington) Redskins drafted Millner in the seventh round of the 1936 National Football League draft. He quickly established himself as a tough and versatile end. He played strong defense and was a tenacious blocker despite being only six feet tall and 190 pounds. In 1936, Millner's rookie season, he led Boston in pass receiving with eighteen catches, helping the Redskins to the Eastern Division championship. A conflict between Redskins owner George Preston Marshall and the Boston press and fans over an unannounced increase in ticket prices immediately before a late season game prompted Marshall to move the 1936 NFL championship game with the Green Bay Packers (which the Packers won 21–6) from Boston to New York. The following season Marshall moved the franchise to Washington. The Redskins again won the Eastern Division championship, behind rookie quarterback Sammy Baugh. Millner had his biggest game as a professional in the 1937 championship game against the Chicago Bears. With the Redskins trailing 14–7, he caught a 55-yard touchdown pass from Baugh to tie the score. Later he caught a 78-yard touchdown pass to tie the score again at 21–21. The Redskins subsequently won the game 28–21.

Millner played for the Redskins through the 1941 season. He then served three and one-half years in the navy during World War II as a gunnery officer. Following his discharge from the navy, Millner rejoined the Redskins for the 1945 season as a player-coach. He contributed to another Eastern Division championship team by catching thirteen passes and scoring two touchdowns.

Millner retired before the beginning of the 1946 season to serve as a full-time assistant coach. He had 124 career receptions for 1,578 yards and 12 touchdowns. During his years with the Redskins, they won four Eastern Division championships and one NFL title.

Always a student of the game and respected by his fellow players for his serious hard-nosed play, Millner remained associated with professional football for the rest of his life. From 1946 through 1948 he was an assistant coach with the Redskins. In 1949 he worked as an assistant coach with the Chicago Rockets of the professional All-American Football Conference, and the following season he served as an assistant with the Baltimore Colts. In 1950 Millner started the season as an assistant with the Philadelphia Eagles but was promoted to head coach midway through the season when Bo McMillin resigned because of stomach cancer. Millner himself resigned before the 1952 season when he developed cardiac problems.

He then returned to the Washington area, where he worked for several businesses. He was also a part-time scout for the Redskins until 1974, when he served one season as an assistant coach with the Florida Blazers of the short-lived World Football League. He returned to work part-time with the Redskins until his death.

Millner was inducted into the Professional Football Hall of Fame in 1968. He died in Arlington, Virginia, survived by his second wife, Sara (full name unknown), whom he had married shortly after his 1948 divorce. Wayne Millner was a quintessential two-way player in the era before specialization became part of professional football. He was noted for valuing friendship and for his dedication to football.

• Little of significance has been published about Millner. Small clipping files on his life are held at the Professional Football Hall of Fame in Canton, Ohio, the Notre Dame Sports Information Office, and the Notre Dame University Archives. Also see Beau Riffenburgh, ed., *The Official NFL Encyclopedia* (1986), and David Neft et al., *Pro Football: The Early Years* (1978). Obituaries are in the 20 Nov. 1976 issues of the *New York Times, Washington Post,* and *Washington Star.*

C. ROBERT BARNETT

MILLS, Benjamin (12 Jan. 1779–6 Dec. 1831), lawyer and jurist, was born in Worcester County, Maryland, the son of Edward Mills and Phoebe Byram. While Benjamin was still an infant, his family moved to Washington, Pennsylvania, where he spent his childhood. After completing his elementary education, he was apprenticed to a local doctor. Despite his interest in medicine, Mills chose to postpone a career as a practitioner in order to serve for several years as principal of Washington Academy (now Washington and Jefferson College). As a young man, he married Mary Reade; they had two children.

Mills's interest in teaching, much like his interest in medicine, was tenuous at best, and after moving with his father to Bourbon County, Kentucky, he began to study law. By 1805 he had been admitted to the bar and was practicing in Paris, Kentucky. Within a year he was elected as a Jeffersonian Republican to the Kentucky General Assembly, where he developed a reputation for integrity and steadfastness if not for imagination and brilliance. Between 1806 and 1816 he was reelected for six nonconsecutive terms. In the latter part of his tenure in the state house of representatives, he also served on the Committee on Courts of Justice, a position that prepared him for his later contentious service on the bench.

Mills ran unsuccessfully for the U.S. Senate in 1816 and lost by one vote. A year later he won an appointment as judge of the Montgomery County Circuit Court, and in 1818 he petitioned successfully for a transfer to the Fayette County tribunal in Lexington, home of the state's most prestigious lawyers and cultural organizations. In 1820, because of his solid track record on the bench and impeccable political credentials, Mills was appointed an associate justice on the three-man Court of Appeals, the state's highest appellate court, with Chief Justice John Boyle and Associate Justice William Owsley.

After mid-1818 Kentucky, along with other western and southern states, had experienced severe monetary and commercial contractions, in part because of unwise expansions of credit and currency in the post-1815 economic boom. By 1819–1820 a cataclysmic depression settled over the landscape. Proponents of debtor relief swept to power in annual legislative elections, and by 1821–1822 the so-called Relief party dominated the assembly and, with the election of Governor John Adair, the statehouse. Between 1819 and 1822 the Relief party adopted a sweeping legislative program designed to ameliorate economic hardship by postponing debt settlement. The legislature propped up state banking with a state-funded bank, the Bank of the Commonwealth, and encouraged what Relief partisans called "the best relief," especially an intensified internal improvement program, to make Kentucky less susceptible to complete economic devastation in the future.

In 1820–1821 the judges of the Court of Appeals took firm positions against the Relief party's most innovative relief measures, notably but not only the so-called "debtor bank" and long-term stay or replevin laws. Together these measures allowed debtors, including wealthy speculators, to offer either worthless commonwealth paper in debt settlement or, if creditors rejected the paper, a state-backed bond promising payment in good money some years hence.

Mills and his colleagues soon became political pariahs. When they unanimously declared the Relief party's replevin statute a violation of the federal Constitution's contract clause in the October 1823 cases of *Blair v. Williams* and *Lapsley v. Brashear*, Relief partisans took action. The public did not welcome the court's decision. A majority of Kentuckians believed that the state had every right to render a particular law of the United States null and void if such a law were not in Kentucky's best interest. The Relief party was outraged by the court's decision and attempted to remove Mills and his colleagues by means of a gubernatorial declaration. When removal attempts failed, in 1824 the majority in the state legislature repealed the act that had originally established the court, thus dissolving Kentucky's highest constitutional court, and established a new court with an ordinary statute.

Mills and his fellow jurists, however, refused to step down, standing by their original decision and maintaining that the legislature had no authority to disband the court. For several terms, two appellate courts held sessions in Frankfort, Kentucky. In public prints, Mills came to be synonymous with the most stringent Anti-Relief positions; indeed, he seemed to take great delight in Relief party hostility. But, gradually, both Relief partisans and rhetorical violence lost electoral favor, in part because of the return of economic prosperity but also because tampering with the judiciary made the electorate skittish. In 1825–1826 the Relief (or New Court) party was routed, and a measure removing "unconstitutional obstructions" (the New Court) within the judiciary was adopted. The Court of Appeals returned to work with the universally respected George Robertson as chief justice.

Mills's shrillness, high visibility, and seeming insensitivity to public hardship came back to haunt him. In December 1828 he resigned from the Court of Appeals. The new governor promptly reappointed him, but the state senate refused confirmation. He spent the last few years of his life practicing law in Frankfort, Kentucky, where he died of apoplexy.

Perhaps unfairly, Mills's professional reputation was both made and broken during Kentucky's "court crisis." A magnanimous man well known for lavish charitable gifts, he is primarily remembered for his defense of the old Court of Appeals. According to one account, "a great majority of the bar of Kentucky recognized them as the true court, and brought their causes by appeal before their tribunal. A great majority of the circuit judges, also, obeyed their mandates as implicitly as if no organizing act had passed" (Perrin et al., p. 316). Also known for his forcible (although not silver-tongued) oratory, Mills was a brittle political and legal thinker rarely given to stretching rules of law to meet altered circumstance. His scruples, which one nineteenth-century biographer termed "inflexible integrity," came to be indistinguishable from partisanship and so destroyed him.

• Information about Mills's life and career is sparse. James Kleber, ed., *Kentucky Encyclopedia* (1992), does not include a biography, but its essays on the Relief and Anti-Relief parties and the old court–new court struggle are useful. The brief sketch in W. H. Perrin et al., *Kentucky: A History of the State*, 8th ed. (1888), is favorable to Anti-Relief. For additional information see the terse sketch in the classic *Biographical Encyclopedia of Kentucky of the Dead and Living Men of the Nineteenth Century* (1878); Elizabeth Kinkead, *History of Kentucky* (1896), which also favors Anti-Relief; A. M. Stickles, *The Critical Court Struggle in Kentucky, 1819–1829* (1929), a dated but still useful account; Lewis Collins and Richard Collins, *History of Kentucky* (1874); and Sandra VanBurkleo, "'The Paws of Banks' . . . ," *Journal of the Early Republic* 9 (1989), for early Court of Appeals activity and relief programs. Obituaries are in the (Lexington) *Kentucky Gazette* and the *Louisville Focus*, 8 Dec. 1831.

DONNA GREAR PARKER
SANDRA F. VANBURKLEO

MILLS, Benjamin Fay (4 June 1857–1 May 1916), evangelist and independent religious leader, was born in Rahway, New Jersey, the son of Thornton A. Mills, a Presbyterian minister, and Anna Cook. His mother had seen missionary service in India, and his father had served as moderator of his denomination's General Assembly. After early training at Phillips Andover Academy, Mills attended Hamilton College briefly, then worked as a real estate agent in San Francisco. He returned to college, however, and obtained a degree at Lake Forest University in 1879. That same year he married Mary Russell; they had six children. The independent-minded Mills visited several seminaries and found none that met his expectations for ministerial preparation, so he pursued a personally-designed program of theological study, showing early in life that he would not readily conform to convention.

Mills began his pastoral career in 1878 with a Congregationalist church in Cannon Falls, Minnesota, where he received ordination. He apparently did missionary work in the Black Hills of South Dakota for a while and then accepted a pastorate in Greenwich, New York. From 1884 to 1886 he served a Congregationalist church in Rutland, Vermont, but the confinements of small parishes grew increasingly irksome to him. Mills became interested in evangelistic efforts sponsored by the Young Men's Christian Association, and in 1886 he began concentrating exclusively on such meetings. For the next ten years he devoted himself to itinerant, interdenominational evangelism, visiting every major city in the country during that time. Newspaper accounts stated that millions of people heard him preach a simple, vigorous gospel of personal salvation. Reported thousands converted to some form of Protestant Christian belief as a result of his activities.

What form that belief took became problematic, for the preacher if not for the converted. Mills was increasingly influenced by the writings of George D. Herron, an early Social Gospel thinker. Convinced that applying Christian principles to social problems was more important than saving individual souls, in the early 1890s Mills shifted from concern with personal salvation to a more socially-oriented gospel. He stressed such themes as poor relief, better housing, and improved conditions for workers as aspects of transforming society according to Christian standards. By 1897, however, he felt constricted by this version of religious emphasis as well. Accordingly, after two more years of preaching in Boston, he moved in 1899 to Oakland, California, where he assumed the pulpit of the First Unitarian Church. In 1904 he moved on to Los Angeles to found and preside over an autonomous religious institution known simply as the Fellowship. There, and later in Chicago (1911–1916) at a similar Fellowship, Mills based his ministry on broad concepts such as the organic salvation of society, the brotherhood of all people, and righteousness defined as civic cooperation.

Mills once said that the fundamental problem of his independent religious organization was, "What is the living thing to do?" He was interested in deeds, not creeds—in universal principles that enhanced human welfare, not dogmas that suppressed the search for knowledge. He sought to put the religion of Jesus into practice, not to speculate theologically. Mills advocated the Sermon on the Mount as a practical guide for living, and he considered unselfishness the best philosophical basis for proper behavior. His sermons, self-consciously offered as harbingers of "Twentieth Century Religion," ranged across such topics as learning to love, the riddle of the universe, the gospel of going on, the divinity of man, the pathos of poverty, the woman of today, the psychic powers of man, and ideologies like Unitarianism and Theosophy.

By 1915 Mills, without completely forsaking Protestant liberalism and social reform, once again embraced a more orthodox creed. He had at first accepted uncritically the popular evangelicalism of his youth, then embraced social reform, and mellowed to view religion as practical self-help and community service; finally, he returned to combine his early orientation toward revivalism with a mainstream denominational setting. He sought ordination as a Presbyterian minister, and with this new status he also assumed evangelical pursuits. It was on one such venture that he died, in Grand Rapids, Michigan.

• Mill wrote *Victory through Surrender* (1892), *God's World and Other Sermons* (1894), *Twentieth Century Religion* (1898), and *The Divine Adventure* (1905). Biographical information about him is in his obituary in the *New York Times*, 2 May 1916.

HENRY WARNER BOWDEN

MILLS, Clark (13 Dec. 1810–12 Jan. 1883), sculptor in plaster, stone, and bronze, was born in New York State, probably in Syracuse. The names of his parents are unknown. He was orphaned at the age of five and lived with an uncle until he was twelve or thirteen, leaving the uncle for alleged abuse. He held various jobs between 1823 and 1830, including running a plaster and cement factory in upstate New York. In 1829 he drifted to New Orleans. In 1830 or 1831 he arrived in Charleston, South Carolina, and began to work as a house plasterer. He was apparently a success and had more than one employee in this business.

In 1835 Mills became interested in sculpture, probably as a result of his encounter with a phrenologist, and sought instruction from an Italian sculptor working in Charleston in molding a plaster bust. Mills developed his own technique for taking a life mask in plaster that was far quicker than existing methods. In 1837 he married Eliza S. Ballantine; they had four sons. Mills also had a foster daughter. The first record of his exhibiting a bust from life is in December 1844, when his bust of Dr. B. B. Simmons was exhibited in Charleston's Exchange Reading Room and pronounced "an elegant specimen of art." From modeling in plaster Mills proceeded to carving in stone. He presented his earliest effort, a bust of John C. Calhoun in white freestone quarried near Columbia, to the city of Charleston and received from the city council a gold medal as a testimony of their appreciation. So gifted was Mills that three gentlemen of Charleston contributed a total of $1,000 to send him to Italy to study. However, he was persuaded by William C. Preston that before his departure he should first see the sculpture in Washington, D.C. Preston offered to pay Mills's expenses there and back, and he commissioned busts of his friends Daniel Webster and John Jordan Crittendon, then residing in Washington. Mills accepted Preston's offer, a choice that resulted in his never going to Europe. On his way to Washington, Mills stopped in Richmond to view Jean-Antoine Houdon's statue of George Washington.

At the time of Mills's visit to the nation's capital, the Jackson Monument Committee was meeting to commission an equestrian statute of Andrew Jackson for the city of Washington. In May 1847 Mills presented a proposed design to the committee and secured a commission to make a life-size model. He returned to Charleston to prepare the model. He chose to portray Jackson reviewing his troops on the morning of 8 January 1815, the day the battle of New Orleans was fought. In eight months Mills finished his model. He left Charleston for Washington on 7 March 1848, presented his model, and was awarded a contract. He erected a studio and brick furnace to cast the statue on the grounds of the Treasury Building, adjacent to Lafayette Square, where the statue was to be erected. His material, bronze cannon captured from the British in the War of 1812, was furnished by the government. Mills studied books on casting. Not only did he have to teach himself the technique of casting in bronze, but he chose a pose that had never before been successfully executed. His design called for Jackson sitting astride his horse while the horse reared on its hind legs, so that those legs were supporting the weight of the entire group. On 7 January 1853 Mills's statue was erected, and the following day, the anniversary of the battle of New Orleans, the statue was dedicated. Democratic senator Stephen A. Douglas of Illinois, the orator for the event, opened his remarks with a tribute to the genius of the young, self-taught American sculptor. Identical statues were commissioned for the cities of New Orleans, Louisiana (completed in 1855), and Nashville, Tennessee (completed in 1880). Prior to fulfilling the commission for New Orleans, Mills settled permanently in Washington. He purchased a farm on the Baltimore-Washington Turnpike, three miles north of Washington, where a permanent studio and foundry were constructed.

Mills was commissioned by Congress to produce a colossal equestrian statue of Washington at the battle of Princeton. For the face, he copied Houdon's life mask of Washington. The Washington statue was dedicated on 22 February 1860. In June of that year he commenced work on casting the statue of *Liberty* that crowns the dome of the U.S. Capitol after the design of the late Thomas Crawford. Designed by Crawford in Rome in 1856, the plaster model had been shipped to the United States in 1858. In 1863 *Liberty* was completed.

The remainder of Mills's career was spent primarily in making portrait busts. Two of his sons became artists, one of whom assisted him in the bust business. He worked in a naturalistic style, sculpting from what he saw before him and refusing to romanticize or idealize in the manner of the prevailing neoclassical style. A total of 128 known works are attributable to Mills. He died in Washington.

• The Historic New Orleans Collection, New Orleans, La., is an excellent source for material on Mills in the nineteenth-century New Orleans press. The most recent and most comprehensive source on the life and career of Mills is Rosemary Hopkins, "Clark Mills: The First Native American Sculptor," (M.A. thesis, Univ. of Maryland, 1966). The earliest biography of Mills is in Hannah Lee, *Familiar Sketches of Sculpture and Sculptors* (1854). Another is "Mr. Clark Mills, the Sculptor," *Round Table*, 4 May 1864, p. 340, which is reprinted in Henry Theodore Tuckerman, *Book of the Artists: American Artist Life* (1867). For more information on Mills's experience with phrenology, see Charles Colbert, "Clark Mills and the Phrenologist," *Art Bulletin* 70 (1988): 134–37, which cites *American Phrenological Journal* 17 (1853): 77–78. A list of Mills's work undertaken before he lived in Washington is in Anna Wells Rutledge, "Cogdell and Mills," *Antiques* 41 (Mar. 1942): 192–93, 207–8. With each piece on her list, Rutledge cites the Charleston newspapers that mention it, providing a valuable bibliography.

CYNTHIA SEIBELS

MILLS, C. Wright (28 Aug. 1916–20 March 1962), sociologist, was born in Waco, Texas, the son of Charles Grover Mills, an insurance agent, and Frances Ursula Wright, a housekeeper. (His first name was Charles.) His upbringing was distinctly urban, his boyhood having been spent in Sherman, Fort Worth, and Dallas, where he attended Catholic parochial schools and public high schools.

After an unproductive year as an engineering student at Texas A&M, Mills enrolled at the University of Texas, where he received a B.A. in 1938, an M.A. in philosophy and sociology in 1939. From Texas he went to the University of Wisconsin, where, working under Howard Becker and Hans Gerth, he received the Ph.D. for a dissertation on pragmatism and the rise of professionalism in America that he submitted in 1942. He taught sociology at the University of Maryland from 1942 to 1946 and also conducted research for a variety of government agencies, such as the Smaller War Plants Corporation. He then moved to Columbia University in New York, where he taught sociology for the rest of his life. Much of his time was spent at the Bureau of Applied Social Research, where he worked closely with Paul Lazarsfield, its director. During his years at Columbia he had several visiting professorships, including stints at the London School of Economics (where he worked with Ruth and David Glass); the National University of Mexico (where he was invited by Pablo Gonzales Casanova); and Brandeis University in its new history of American ideas program. Mills was highly regarded as a teacher, especially at the undergraduate level. Many of his students later expanded their work for Mills into books and journal articles.

Mills's work can best be seen in tripartite terms, roughly corresponding to three periods of his life. His earlier work at Texas and Wisconsin was dominated by themes in the sociology of knowledge, such as those explored in essays on philosophical sociology, ranging from Chinese thought to German *Wissensoziologie*. Also during this period he wrote *Sociology and Pragmatism* (1939–1941, not published until 1964). In this period he displayed a deep interest in the relationship of power to culture on a vertical axis, and of professionalism to advanced industrial society on a horizontal axis. Mills put to good use his interdisciplinary training; some scholars in the history of sociology believe his contribution was a unique effort to bring the abstractions of the European tradition in the sociology of knowledge into a concrete American setting.

The years Mills spent at Columbia and the Bureau constitute the second period of his life. Between 1948 and 1956 he produced the three books on social and political stratification upon which most of his posthumous reputation rests. The first, *The New Men of*

Power (1948), was a study of labor leaders and their political attitudes. It reflected the currents of the 1940s by integrating narrative and data characteristic of such scholars as Samuel Stouffer, Robert K. Merton, and Robert S. Lynd, as well as Paul Lazarsfield. *White Collar: The American Middle Classes* (1951), Mills's classic study of varieties of professional labor, continued his concern with work and society but introduced a concern with alienation, culture, and anxiety. This latter focus derived in part from his work with Hans Gerth, which produced the co-written *Character and Social Structure: The Psychology of Social Institutions* (1953), and from his growing interest in problems of contemporary American capitalism. Mills portrayed the concerns of a postwar generation caught up in the business of service rather than production. His third contribution to stratification added a political dimension derived from the European tradition of Vilfredo Pareto, Gaetano Mosca, and Robert Michels; here the theme of power displaced an earlier interest in the Weberian view of authority displayed in *From Max Weber* (1946). In this work, *The Power Elite* (1956), Mills also exhibited a tendency toward didacticism and tendentiousness, which characterized his final period. The work greatly influenced the social and political theorizing of the Eisenhower years, emphasizing as it did the relationship of military, industrial, and executive power. Even the president took note of this when, in his farewell address, he expressed concern about the "military-industrial complex" that was emerging in the 1950s.

In the last period of his brief life, Mills was increasingly concerned with the threat of nuclear warfare, as is demonstrated in *The Causes of World War Three* (1958). He then embarked on a polemical tract in support of the Castro revolution in Cuba, which was published as *Listen Yankee! The Revolution in Cuba* (1960). This work had a galvanizing effect on Mills's reputation: it was widely read, and it produced strong critical responses from colleagues. Mills became a pariah to the extent that his field, or many of his sociological colleagues, no longer saw him as a bona fide sociologist. His final work, a collection titled *The Marxists* (1962), appeared within days of his untimely death. In it, Mills sought to link the Marxist tradition with the open society—offering hope for the socialist critics of Stalinism and showing the thread of pragmatic concerns that characterized such Marxist leaders as Marshal Tito of Yugoslavia. This work also closed out a period of intense political concerns first put forth in *The Sociological Imagination* (1959), in which Mills sought to mix history and biography in order to create a sociology more global in perspective and more personally important than the established orthodoxies of the time.

Mills was married four times: twice to Dorothy Helen "Freya" Smith, from 1937 to 1940 and then from 1941 to 1947; to Ruth Harper, from 1947 to 1959; and to Gloria "Yaroslava" Surmach, from 1959 until his death. He had a daughter by each of his first two wives and a son by the third. He was diagnosed as having heart problems in 1942, but apparently did little about it. His fourth and fatal heart attack came at his home in West Nyack, a suburb of New York City.

Mills left a variety of unfinished tasks and incomplete manuscripts, including "Contacting the Enemy," which was to have been a study of the Soviet power elite similar in tone and substance to his analysis of the American power elite. Mills had begun to think about problems of underdeveloped regions, and he contemplated a multivolume work on international social stratification. He had also contracted to do volumes complementing *The Marxists* on the anarchists, Trotskyists, and other "deviant" socialist and libertarian types.

• Selected correspondence and manuscripts are in the Barker Texas History Center, located at the University of Texas Libraries in Austin, and also in the private collection of Irving Louis Horowitz at Princeton, New Jersey. Essays by Mills on philosophical sociology appear in two collections edited by Horowitz: *Power, Politics and People* (1962) and *On Social Men and Political Movements* (1965). A full-scale intellectual biography can be found in Horowitz, *C. Wright Mills: An American Utopian* (1983). See also Giandomenico Amendola, *Metodo Sociologico e Ideologica: Charles Wright Mills* (1971); John Eldridge, *C. Wright Mills* (1983); Howard Press, *C. Wright Mills* (1978); Joseph A. Scimecca, *The Sociological Theory of C. Wright Mills* (1977); and Martin J. Wibier, *C. Wright Mills als Socioloog en Wetenschapstheoreticus* (1976). A memorial volume in tribute to Mills contains additional information on his life and career: *The New Sociology*, ed. Irving Louis Horowitz (1964), to which Ralph Miliband, Rose K. Goldsen, Anatol Rapaport, Erich Fromm, and Andrew Hacker, among others, contributed.

IRVING LOUIS HOROWITZ

MILLS, Darius Ogden (5 Sept. 1825–3 Jan. 1910), banker and mining and railroad entrepreneur, was born in North Salem, Westchester County, New York, the son of James Mills, a town supervisor of North Salem (1835), and Hannah Ogden. From a prominent family, Mills was educated at the North Salem Academy and then at the Mount Pleasant Academy at Ossining, New York. His father's death in 1841 deprived Mills of a college education. Instead he became a clerk in a mercantile establishment in New York City. In 1847, at the invitation of a cousin, he became cashier of the Merchants' Bank of Erie County in Buffalo, New York.

Discovery of gold in California enticed Mills's older brothers, James and Edgar, to embark for California on a vessel sailing around Cape Horn, with intentions of becoming merchants. Mills hesitated, but late in 1848 he set out via the Isthmus of Panama to join them. He arrived in San Francisco on 8 June 1849 and proceeded to establish himself as a trader in gold dust and a general merchant in Stockton. He shortly shifted his base to Sacramento, where in 1850 he established the Bank of D. O. Mills & Company, which he first operated with a cousin, E. J. Townsend, but later alone. He reorganized the bank in 1858 in partnership with his brother Edgar and his cashier, Henry Miller.

The bank prospered, and by the time of the Civil War, Mills was already a rich man.

In 1864 in San Francisco, jointly with William C. Ralston and others, Mills established the Bank of California, which became one of the dominant banks of the state and, indeed, one of the most important in the nation. He remained president until July 1873, when he turned the office over to Ralston. The panic of 1873 brought about the collapse of some grossly overextended financial arrangements of Ralston and caused the bank to suspend payments in 1875. Mills and other directors forced Ralston to resign. Ralston drowned on the day of his resignation, an apparent suicide, and Mills returned to the presidency. Mills subscribed $1 million of his own funds to a total of some $7 million that he raised to allow the bank to reopen. He was able to resign again in 1876 and prepared to move to New York City.

Mills had, meanwhile, become involved in gold mining in the Comstock Lode at Virginia City, Nevada. The Bank of California through its local agent, William Sharon, gained control of seven mills for ore processing, which it consolidated in June 1867 into the Union Mill & Mining Company. By 1869 what was locally called the "Bank Ring" controlled seventeen mills and processed most of the Comstock ore. The group came into direct control of at least eight mines. Because operation in the area had been handicapped by dependence on mule-drawn wagons, Mills and his associates broke ground in 1869 for a railroad, the Virginia & Truckee, to connect Virginia City with the Central Pacific at Reno. Between the mines, the milling company, and the railroad, the group was able to capture much of the economic rents that the Comstock Lode produced, and Mills gained the reputation of a Midas. He expanded his interests to the Eureka mining area and was among the incorporators of the Eureka & Palisade Railroad in 1873, although he turned over its presidency to Edgar Mills.

Once relocated to New York City, Mills diversified his activities. He built large office buildings in both San Francisco and New York. He became a director of the New York Central, Erie, and Southern Pacific railroads, several steamship companies, and various industrial firms. He became interested in the development of hydropower at Niagara Falls and became president of both the Niagara Falls Power Company and the Niagara Junction Railway. He undertook what seems to have been his favorite philanthropy, a series of three "Mills Hotels" in New York City in which workingmen could rent rooms at 25 cents to 40 cents per day and take meals for 5 cents to 15 cents apiece. By the time of his death the three hotels had a total of 4,029 rooms and, characteristically, made money. Mills served as trustee of the Metropolitan Museum of Art, the American Museum of Natural History, and the American Geographical Society; he contributed extensively to the Metropolitan Museum and the New York Botanical Garden and gave $100,000 to Bellevue Hospital for construction of a school for nurses.

Although Mills retired from active business activities in California in March 1878, he never lost interest in the San Francisco Bay area, which he correctly felt had great growth potential. He maintained an estate at Millbrae on the San Francisco peninsula, which served both as his winter home and as a dairy farm that Mills intended to use to improve the area's milk supply. He was a regent of the University of California, served as its treasurer, and endowed a Mills Professorship of Moral and Intellectual Philosophy. He was a trustee and a financial contributor to the Lick Observatory and a financial supporter of the Protestant Orphan Asylum and St. Luke's Hospital in San Francisco.

Mills traveled extensively in Europe during his long retirement, collecting both books and works of art. He had a mild, unassuming manner, and reportedly moved with ease among the British upper classes. He had married Jane Templeton Cunningham of New York City in 1854; she died in 1888. The couple had two children. Their son Ogden assumed responsibility for the estate, which was variously estimated between $60 million and $100 million at the time of Darius Mills's death at the Millbrae estate. Their daughter Elizabeth had married Whitelaw Reid, who at the time of her father's death was American ambassador to Great Britain. Edward VII sent his personal condolences to the Mills family.

• For additional information on Mills, see Gilbert H. Kneiss, *Bonanza Railroads* (1941); David F. Myrick, *Railroads of Nevada and Eastern California* (2 vols., 1962–1963); and John Steele Gordon, "Opportunities," *American Heritage*, Nov. 1989, pp. 20, 22. Obituaries are in the *San Francisco Chronicle* and the *New York Tribune*, both 4 Jan. 1910.

GEORGE W. HILTON

MILLS, Elijah Hunt (1 Dec. 1776–5 May 1829), lawyer, educator, and politician, was born in Chesterfield, Massachusetts, the son of the Reverend Benjamin Mills and Mary Hunt. The youngest of five children, Mills was orphaned before he was ten. He moved to Northampton, Massachusetts, and was adopted by his maternal uncle Elijah Hunt. Mills was schooled by private tutors before attending Williams College, from which he graduated in 1797. Returning to Northampton, he read the law, was admitted to the bar in 1803, and served as the town clerk from 1804 to 1814. Mills married twice: the first time in 1802 to Sarah Hunt, who died soon after their wedding, and the second time in 1804 to Harriette Blake, with whom he had seven children.

Mills appears to have entered state politics in response to the Embargo Act of 1807 and the effects of that embargo on the people of western Massachusetts before the War of 1812. Serving in the Massachusetts House of Representatives (1811–1814), Mills authored the "Address of the House of Representatives to the People of Massachusetts" (26 June 1812), which fulminated against the declaration of war on Great Britain. Mills urged his constituents to "Organize a *peace party* throughout your country and let all other party distinctions vanish." Influenced by both his mother's family and his college education, Mills came to represent the interests of the commercial classes of Massachusetts, even though he was originally from the agricultural hilltown of Chesterfield. As the War of 1812 imperiled those commercial interests, Mills expressed his views in his most notable speech, "An Oration Pronounced at Northampton . . . on the Thirty Seventh Anniversary of American Independence" (4 July 1813).

Mills began the oration by praising George Washington and the state of neutrality that Washington had announced in 1793 at the start of the war between Great Britain and revolutionary France. Mills went on to attack Thomas Jefferson and James Madison, claiming that both presidents were unduly sympathetic to France. Mills was especially furious that the United States appeared to be in league with Napoleon, "this modern Attilla, 'this Scourge of God.'" Mills denounced the Louisiana Purchase as a waste of $15 million and claimed that the politicians of the southern and western states had hoodwinked the nation into fighting the War of 1812, which, he asserted, would ruin New England's commerce. After taking time to celebrate the successes of the small American navy, Mills enjoined his fellow New Englanders to defend their commerce and their constitutional liberties from encroachment by the southern and western states. Following in the style of Josiah Quincy's speech (14 Jan. 1811) against the statehood of Louisiana, Mills called for New Englanders to act, "PEACEABLY IF YOU CAN, FORCIBLY IF YOU MUST." Mills's speech was one of the dramatic moments in New England political history during the War of 1812, a time leading to the Hartford Convention, where New Englanders would gather to discuss possible secession from the Union.

Mills was elected to the U.S. House of Representatives and served in the Fourteenth and Fifteenth Congresses (1815–1819). He then returned to state politics. He served again in the Massachusetts House of Representatives and was elected the speaker of that body on 31 May 1820. Mills held the office for only two weeks; he was elected to the U.S. Senate to fill the unexpired term of Prentiss Mellen, who had resigned as a consequence of the creation of the separate state of Maine.

Mills's years in the U.S. Senate (1820–1827) were not memorable. He appears to have become milder in tone and was not a vigorous legislator, although he supported a national system for bankruptcy and voted against the tariff of 1824. In 1823 Mills joined with Judge Samuel Howe to create a law school—one of the first in the United States—on Round Hill Road in Northampton, the same road on which George Bancroft was simultaneously developing a preparatory school based on a European model. Mills and Howe charged an all-inclusive fee of $100 per year; the instruction was delivered through lectures, recitations, moot court, and discussions. The school drew ten to fifteen students a year; Franklin Pierce, the future president, studied there, but did not graduate. In 1827 Mills experienced poor health and questions were raised about his seat in the Senate. Daniel Webster wrote to a friend that, "If Mr. Mills lives, he is second to no man in the Senate among our friends" (Curtis, p. 292). When Mills withdrew his name from the contest, Webster himself was elected to serve in Mills's place. Mills retired to Northampton, where he died.

Mills was a figure in Massachusetts politics for fifteen years. His "Address" and "Oration" are reminders of the resistance within New England to the War of 1812. Although he came from the western Massachusetts area that had spawned Shays's Rebellion in 1786, Mills was no populist—his profound dislike for the French Revolution and Napoleon made that clear. Mills favored a strong central government as long as that government allowed New Englanders to pursue their commercial livelihood without restraint. Mills's career symbolized the rift between the northern, southern, and western states in the Union. Had he lived and remained in Congress, he would have had to respond to the Nullification Crisis (1832–1833), whose leaders made many of the same arguments for nullification as Mills did in his "Oration."

• Few sources exist for a study of Mills's life and career. His "Oration" and a description of the Northampton law school can be found at the Forbes Library, Northampton, Mass., and the Massachusetts Historical Society has some of his letters. Mills's "Address" is in *Niles' Weekly Register* (29 Aug. 1812), and the high points of his political career are reported in Northampton's *Daily Hampshire Gazette*, with his obituary on 12 May 1829. Basic genealogical data can be found in Ruth Baker, *History and Genealogy of the Families of Chesterfield* (1962). There are several short profiles on Mills in reference works, the most accurate is found in Cornelius Dalton et al., *Leading the Way: A History of the Massachusetts General Court, 1629–1980* (1984). Mills's relations with Daniel Webster are chronicled in George Ticknor Curtis, *Life of Daniel Webster*, vol. 1 (1870).

SAMUEL WILLARD CROMPTON

MILLS, Enos Abijah (22 Apr. 1870–22 Sept. 1922), nature writer, was born near Pleasanton, Linn County, Kansas, the son of Enos Abijah Mills, Sr., and Ann Lamb, farmers. Suffering from a digestive illness, young Mills went west in 1884 to Estes Park, Colorado, where a cousin, the Reverend Elkanah Lamb, had established the Longs Peak House guest lodgings. Mills soon built a cabin nearby and in 1885 made his first ascent of Longs Peak—he eventually climbed the 14,255-foot summit some forty times by himself and 257 times as a guide.

Restored to health, in 1887 Mills went to the mining town of Butte, Montana, where he worked intermittently until 1902. Largely self-taught, he furthered his education with books from the Butte library and spent many summers traveling from Alaska and the western United States to Europe. In 1889 on a San Francisco beach Mills met a "small gray bearded little man" (quoted in Pickering, *The Rocky Mountain Wonder-*

land, p. xv) who turned out to be the famed naturalist John Muir, the inspiration for Mills's lifework of conservation activism, lecturing, and writing. Within a few years Mills had given his first public address (on forestry) and begun his literary career with contributions about the Estes Park area to a Denver newspaper.

In 1902 Mills bought the Longs Peak House from Lamb's son, transforming it into the more extensive Longs Peak Inn. Rebuilt after a 1906 fire, the inn with its rustic main building and surrounding cabins reflected the interests and eccentricities of its proprietor—no firearms, no pets, no alcohol, no dancing, and no tips. Instead, the exuberant host treated visitors to wilderness excursions and evening nature talks. "He has a unique personality," one guest wrote in 1912, "he is a law unto himself, wears a hat only when he pleases and under no circumstances will he don evening dress" (quoted in Pickering, *Wild Life on the Rockies*, p. xix).

Running the Longs Peak Inn was only one of Mills's many activities. From December 1902 through the winter of 1905–1906 he served as the official Colorado State Snow Observer, a position that required him to "ramble the wintry heights in sunshine and storm" (*Wild Life*, p. 4), measuring snow depth to predict the spring and summer runoff. After completing this assignment he accepted the invitation of President Theodore Roosevelt to become a government lecturer on forestry in January 1907, continuing in that role until May 1909. Concurrently, Mills began contributing essays to national magazines such as the *Saturday Evening Post, Atlantic, Colliers, Country Life*, and *Youth's Companion.* His first article, "A Western Artist," appeared in *Outdoor Life* in 1902, while his first book, the privately published *Story of Estes Park and a Guide Book*, came out in 1905.

Four years later, *Wild Life on the Rockies*, a collection of Mills's nature stories, was published. Dedicated to Muir, the volume included two pieces subsequently published as books, *The Story of a Thousand-Year Pine* (1914) and *The Story of Scotch* (1916). Additional collections appeared in 1911 (*The Spell of the Rockies*), 1913 (*In Beaver World*), and 1915 (*The Rocky Mountain Wonderland*). Reviewers lauded Mills as a storyteller who could construct an interesting and readable narrative, although some criticized him as a "nature faker" who gave animals the capacity to think and anthropomorphized his subjects as, for example, "Dr. Woodpecker, Tree-Surgeon."

As Mills was gaining a reputation as nature writer and innkeeper, he also led the fight to preserve the area around Longs Peak as a national park. "It is a marvelous grouping of gentleness and grandeur," he wrote in *The Spell of the Rockies* (p. 337), "an eloquent, wordless hymn, that is sung in silent, poetic pictures; a sublime garden miles in extent and all arranged with infinite care." Aided by a large and diverse coalition that included the Sierra Club, the Daughters of the American Revolution, and the Colorado Mountain Club, Mills lectured and lobbied from 1909 to 1915, when Congress passed the legislation establishing Rocky Mountain National Park. Within a few years, however, he was mired in controversy with the National Park Service when it gave one firm the exclusive right to operate transportation in the park. Along with other entrepreneurs, Mills had previously transported guests around the park, and he contended that the government had illegally granted a monopoly to one company. Whatever the merits of his position, the independent Mills was often at odds with authority; his colleague James Grafton Rogers, a Denver lawyer and first president of the Colorado Mountain Club, wrote in 1914 that Mills had "a genious [*sic*] for making enemies" (quoted in Abbott, 1979, p. 59).

Nonetheless, the "Father of Rocky Mountain National Park," as Mills was often called, continued to write, producing another six books between 1917 and 1922. At the age of forty-eight he married Esther Burnell in 1918; they had one child. Just three years later Mills died at his Longs Peak Inn home, probably from blood poisoning caused by an abscessed tooth. Four additional book collections were published posthumously; the last, *Bird Memories of the Rockies*, appeared in 1931.

In the following years, however, Mills's books failed to attract new readers; his work was seen as old-fashioned and dated. Although one reviewer wrote in 1915 that "Mills is to the Rockies as Muir to the Sierras" (quoted in Pickering, *Rocky Mountain Wonderland*, p. xxxvii), Mills was not in fact equal to the Californian in terms of intellectual competence or vision. Yet the publication in 1979 of *Enos Mills* by Peter Wild provided a fresh and appreciative look at the long-neglected writer. Calling Mills "a popularizer rather than an original thinker" (p. 33), Wild points out that his works were full of enthusiasm, humor, and astute observations, even as they tended to be repetitive and disorganized. In 1988, *Wild Life* was reissued with a detailed introduction by James H. Pickering. Subsequently three additional volumes were reprinted with introductions also by Pickering, who noted that Mills's "books and articles remain interesting and important documents in the history of early twentieth-century American conservation" (*Wild Life*, p. xxxvi). Thus Mills, renowned in his own time as author and activist, speaks to succeeding generations who share his love of nature and his concern for the preservation of the environment.

• A collection of Mills's papers is held at the Western History Department, Denver Public Library. The best modern biographical information can be found in James H. Pickering's introductions to the reprint editions of *Wild Life on the Rockies* (1988), *The Spell of the Rockies* (1989), *In Beaver World* (1990), and *The Rocky Mountain Wonderland* (1991). See also Pickering's introduction to the 1988 reprint edition of *A Mountain Boyhood* (1926) by Enos Mills's brother Joe Mills. Mills's widow, Esther Burnell Mills, coauthored an earlier biography, *Enos Mills of the Rockies*, with Hildegarde Hawthorne (1935). Peter Wild, *Enos Mills* (1979), includes a selected bibliography of material about Mills. For another assessment, see Carl Abbott, "The Literary Career of Enos

Mills," *Montana*, Apr. 1981, pp. 2–15. Mills's role in the creation of Rocky Mountain National Park is traced in C. W. Buchholtz, *Rocky Mountain National Park: A History* (1983); see also Carl Abbott, "The Active Force: Enos A. Mills and the National Park Movement," *Colorado Magazine*, Winter/Spring 1979, pp. 56–73. Obituaries are in the *Denver Post*, 21 Sept. 1922, and the *New York Times*, 22 Sept. 1922.

MAXINE BENSON

MILLS, Florence (25 Jan. 1895–1 Nov. 1927), entertainer, was born Florence Winfree in Washington, D.C., the daughter of John Winfree, a carpenter, and Nellie Simons, who did laundry. Educated locally, by age five Mills was winning contests in cakewalking and buck dancing. Her first professional engagement came as Baby Florence Mills in the second company (1902) of the Williams-Walker *Sons of Ham*, singing a song she had learned from its originator, Aida Overton Walker, entitled "Miss Hannah From Savannah," the tale of a high-class African American who had come north.

Mills served a lengthy apprenticeship before becoming an "overnight" sensation in *The Plantation Revue* in 1922. After several years in vaudeville with the Bonita Company as a "pick"[aninny], she and her sisters, Olivia and Maude, became the vaudeville Mills Sisters. When this act broke up, Mills joined others until 1914, when she began to sing in Chicago nightclubs. Jazzman Mezz Mezzrow recalled her "grace and . . . dignified, relaxed attitude. Florence, petite and demure, just stood at ease and sang like a humming bird" (Mezzrow, p. 22).

At the Panama Club Mills formed the singing Panama Trio with Ada Smith (later known as "Bricktop," a favorite of American expatriates in Paris) and Cora Green; the trio toured the Pantages vaudeville circuit, where in 1916 Mills joined the Tennessee Ten. After four seasons with the group as the female singer/dancer in a trio with U. S. (Slow Kid) Thompson and Fredi Johnson, Mills married Thompson. The year of their marriage is not firmly established, and they had no children. (She may have had an earlier marriage, in 1912, to James Randolph.)

Mills and Thompson were recruited into *Shuffle Along*, the 1921 black musical comedy by Noble Sissle and Eubie Blake that began a decade-long Broadway vogue for shows featuring African-American performers. *Shuffle Along* lured predominantly white audiences farther "uptown" than before to the Sixty-third Street Theater and ran for a year and a half before enjoying a two-year road tour.

Shuffle Along coincided with a general post–world War I upsurge in theatrical, musical, and literary achievement by African Americans. Because many of its luminaries lived in the northernmost part of Manhattan, "Harlem Renaissance" served as a blanket term for this "advancement" away from racial stereotyping through the use of what W. E. B. Du Bois had called special gifts. Even the militant poet Claude McKay, who characterized Harlem as "the glorified servant quarters of a vast estate" expressed the hope that *Shuffle Along* might help black performers break through the "screen of sneering bigotry" to express their authentic "warmth, color and laughter."

Replacing *Shuffle Along*'s original female star, Gertrude Saunders, Mills soon stopped the show singing "I'm Craving for That Kind of Love" with her particular blend of ethereality and sensuality. Shortly her picture appeared on the sheet music of the show's hit, "I'm Just Wild about Harry." White entrepreneur Lew Leslie hired Mills to star in his 1922 black revue at the Plantation Club at Fiftieth and Broadway. Adding a few acts, he then moved the entire show into the Forty-eighth Street Theatre.

Sometimes dressed in feathers and sometimes in male evening clothes, Mills created a sensation, particularly by her spontaneous dancing. She said, "I just go crazy when the music starts, and I like to give the audience all it craves. I make up the dances to the songs beforehand, but then something happens like one of the orchestra talking to me and I answer back and watch the audience." Musical historian Allen Woll quoted an uncredited critic: "In that season not to have seen and heard Florence Mills was to be quite out of the know on Broadway" (Woll, p. 96).

Leslie took the Plantation Revue to London in 1923 as the second (and most effective) half of an Anglo-American revue, *From Dover Street to Dixie*; Mills sang "I'm a Little Blackbird Looking for a Blue Bird," a poignant piece that wrung audiences dry. Impresario Charles B. Cochran wrote of the tension on its opening night, partly due to the recent failure of another black American revue. Upon Mills's appearance, he told his companion, "She owns the house—no audience in the world can resist that. . . . [She] controlled the emotions of the audience as only a true artist can . . . there was a heart-throb in her bird-like voice . . . her thin, lithe arms and legs were animated with a dancing delirium. It was all natural art" (Cochran, pp. 97–98).

After further European touring with *Dixie*, Leslie brought an enhanced version, built around Mills, to the Shuberts' Broadhurst Theatre in the heart of Times Square as *Dixie to Broadway*, and Mills was also added to the *Greenwich Village Follies of 1923*. James Weldon Johnson wrote that *Dixie to Broadway* "broke away entirely from the established tradition of Negro musical comedies" in starring one woman. Writing in the *New York World* (23 Nov. 1924), Lester Walton said that "The long cherished dream . . . to see a colored musical comedy successfully playing in the very heart of Broadway" had become a reality. *Dixie to Broadway*, like other African-American shows of the era, however, was produced by whites, who made most of the money. Still, Mills was quoted as saying that attitudes toward "colored people" were gradually changing; she saw a great future for "high browns."

After *Dixie to Broadway*, Mills settled in Harlem amidst leaders of the "Renaissance" such as Johnson, poets Langston Hughes and Countee Cullen, authors Zora Neale Hurston and Jean Toomer, National Association for the Advancement of Colored People secretary William White, and actor Charles Gilpin. In 1925

Mills turned down an offer to star in a revue at the Folies Bergère in Paris; after Ethel Waters also declined, Josephine Baker took the job and became famous. Artist Miguel Covarrubias caricatured Mills, and in 1926 the classical composer William Grant Still wrote a jazz piece for her. Likewise, the choreographer Buddy Bradley wrote that prima ballerina Alicia Markova reminded him of Mills. Theater historian Loften Mitchell wrote that in the Harlem of the 1920s her name "was on the lips of everyone in the community. People sat in parlors, on stoops, or stood in hallways, trying to find words that might describe her" (Mitchell, p. 78).

Leslie's next show *Blackbirds*, named for Mills's trademark song, was built around Mills. After six weeks early in 1926 at the Alhambra Theater in Harlem, it opened in Paris, where it ran for six months, moved to London, and continued until August 1927. With slick bobbed hair and soft eyes, she was, Cochran wrote, the only performer he had ever seen who could count on an ovation upon entry and before doing a number. The prince of Wales confessed to seeing *Blackbirds* twenty-two times. In London there were Florence Mills dolls, and the most fashionable shade for clothing was the "Florence Mills shade." The black British jazz musician Spike Hughes, however, questioned her authenticity: whites who thought she epitomized "Negroes" also thought the for-whites-only shows at the Cotton Club in Harlem were authentic. Comparing her unfavorably with Bessie Smith, who sang mainly for black audiences, Hughes said he could not tell from her singing whether she was black or white, British or American.

Mills returned to New York in late September 1927, and huge crowds turned out in Harlem to greet her. The 14 October 1927 edition of the *Inter State Tatler* called on her "to give the people the one great gift within her power . . . a national, or if you please, a race drama. . . . Miss Mills can do more than anyone else to satisfy the latent, unexpressed hunger for race drama."

Mills was twice operated on for appendicitis in late October 1927 and died in New York City of peritonitis and paralytic ileus resulting from the appendicitis. Tributes came from London, where composer Constant Lambert wrote an "Elegiac Blues" for her, and Paris, where, according to the *New York Times* correspondent, she was lauded as greatest of all. More than 75,000 mourners viewed her body before her funeral, which was attended by 5,000 people in a church meant for 2,000, while thousands waited outside. Jazz composer Andy Razaf contributed a poem beginning "All the World is Lonely / For a Little Blackbird" and ending "Sadness rules the hour / Left us only in tears." A chorus of 500 sang to the accompaniment of a 200-piece orchestra. An estimated 150,000 watched the funeral procession. Johnson wrote, "An airplane . . . released a flock of blackbirds. . . . They fluttered overhead a few seconds and then flew away" (p. 201).

• Contemporary material concerning Florence Mills can be found in the Arthur A. Schomburg Center for Research in Black Culture of the New York Public Library and in the Billy Rose Theatre Collection of the New York Public Library for the Performing Arts, Lincoln Center. Reviews of her performances can be found there and in the archives of the Theatre Museum, London. Valuable contemporary sources include Gilbert Seldes, *Seven Lively Arts* (1924); Charles B. Cochran, *Secrets of a Showman* (1929); and James Weldon Johnson, *Black Manhattan* (1930). Also useful are Claude McKay, *Harlem: Negro Metropolis* (1940); Mezz Mezzrow, *Really the Blues* (1946); Nat Shapiro and Nat Hentoff, *Hear Me Talkin' to Ya* (1955); John Henrik Clarke, ed., *Harlem USA* (1964); Loften Mitchell, *Black Drama* (1967); Allon Schoener, ed., *Harlem on My Mind* (1968); Michael Anglo, *Spotlight on the Twenties* (1976); Henry T. Sampson, *Black in Blackface: A Source Book on Early Black Musical Shows* (1980); Bruce Kellner, ed., *The Harlem Renaissance: A Historical Dictionary for the Era* (1984); Richard Long, *The Black Tradition in American Dance* (1989); and Allen Woll, *Black Musical Theatre from Coontown to Dreamgirls* (1989). An obituary appears in the *New York Times*, 2 Nov. 1927.

JAMES ROSS MOORE

MILLS, Harry (19 Aug. 1913–28 June 1982), and **Herbert Mills** (2 Apr. 1912–12 Apr. 1989), singers, were born in Piqua, Ohio, the sons of John Hutchinson Mills, a barber, and Eathel Harrington. Harry and Herbert Mills, with younger brother Donald, had a 57-year career in which they made 2,246 records and helped to found modern-day black harmony singing. With an older brother, John, Jr., the boys began singing in the choir of the Cyrene African Methodist Episcopal Church in Piqua. They also sang Sundays at the Park Avenue Baptist Church in the same city. After their lessons at the Spring Street grammar school, they would gather in front of their father's barber shop on Public Square and begin singing to draw a crowd. Sometimes they sang at the corner of Greene and Main or at the Hardin Road monument, and passersby threw coins at their feet. To improve business John, Jr., began accompanying the four-part harmony with a ukelele and then a guitar. The boys practiced imitating orchestras they heard on the radio. Summer nights they could hear the Roof Garden Orchestra at the local Knights of Columbus hall and would practice every note. John, as the bass, became the tuba. Harry, at baritone, "played" first trumpet. Herbert did the second trumpet and Donald, the trombone. At house parties, lawn fetes, music halls, and supper clubs each brother would double as a saxophone or clarinet when needed.

The brothers' big break came in 1925. After playing May's Opera House in Piqua between silent film features, they accompanied the Harold Greenameyer Band to Cincinnati for an audition with radio station WLW. The band was not hired, but the Mills Brothers were. The station kept them so busy they moved to Cincinnati and took a tutor. For Sohio Motor Oil they were billed as the Steamboat Four. For Tasty Yeast they became the Tasty Yeast Jesters. At other times they were Four Boys and a Guitar, and on Sundays they were billed as the Mills Brothers.

In 1929 friends at WLW arranged an audition for the Mills Brothers at CBS radio in New York City. After broadcasting executive William S. Paley heard the performance in his office on a speaker phone, he put them on CBS radio that same night. When the Mills Brothers signed a three-year contract the next day, they became the first African Americans to have a network show on radio. The exposure gave them a national following and a recording contract. "Tiger Rag," which the Mills Brothers had first recorded in Indianapolis while imitating the Roof Garden Orchestra, was rerecorded for Brunswick Records and became a number-one seller. Other hits quickly followed: their theme song "Goodbye Blues," "You're Nobody's Sweetheart Now," "Ole Rockin' Chair," "Lazy River," "How'm I Doin'," "Paradise," "Oh, I Heard," and "Sweet Lucy Brown."

The brothers' popularity brought sponsorship from the largest advertisers in early radio: Standard Oil, Procter & Gamble, Crisco, and Crosley Radio. They began appearing in films. Their first, *The Big Broadcast* (1932), was an all-star radio revue that included Bing Crosby, Cab Calloway, and the Boswell Sisters. They shared the bill at New York's Paramount Theatre with Crosby, Kate Smith, and George Burns and Gracie Allen. By 1934 the Mills Brothers were in Hollywood, starring with Crosby for Woodbury Soap and recording their classics "Lazy Bones," "Sweet Sue," "Lulu's Back in Town," "Bye-Bye Blackbird," "We're in the Money," "Sleepy Head," and "Shoe Shine Boy." Film appearances included *Twenty Million Sweethearts* (1934) and *Broadway Gondolier* (1935), both for Warner Bros.

The Mills Brothers were the first African Americans to give a command performance for British royalty, playing the Paladium before King George V and Queen Mary. While performing at the Regal Theatre, John, Jr., became ill with pneumonia. He never recovered and died in 1936. The group had lost its leader and considered breaking up. Then their father, John, Sr., joined his sons in the quartet, imitating the tuba and singing bass as his son had.

The group's greatest success was still ahead of them. "Lazy River" was rerecorded and quickly surpassed 1931 sales. It was followed by "Someday You'll Want Me to Want You," "Swing Is the Thing," "'Long about Mid-night," "Organ Grinders Swing," and "The Song Is Ended." They honored their idol, Duke Ellington, with a swinging version of his "Caravan" and then produced a series of classic recordings: "South of the Border," which they performed in a tour of South America, along with "Ain't Misbehavin'," "It Don't Mean a Thing, If It Ain't Got That Swing," "Jeepers Creepers," "Three Little Fishes," "If You Can't Sing It, You'll Have to Swing It," and "Basin Street Blues." But this served only as prelude for a string of successes rarely matched in recording history. In 1943 Donald Mills chose "Paper Doll" as the B-side of "I'll Be Around." Recorded in fifteen minutes, it sold 6 million copies and became the group's biggest hit.

In their 24-year association with Decca, the Mills Brothers continued their enduring barbershop harmonies with a flurry of top-ten hits that included "You Always Hurt the One You Love," "Till Then," "Across the Alley from the Alamo," and "Someday." Film appearances included *Reveille with Beverly* (1939), which helped launch Frank Sinatra, and *Chatterbox* (1943). The rise of rock and roll did little to diminish the brothers' success. "Glow Worm," their first recording with an orchestra, rose to number two on the pop charts in 1952. Soon "Opus One," an updated version of the Tommy Dorsey hit, was keeping it company, along with "You're Nobody 'til Somebody Loves You," "Yellow Bird," "Standing on the Corner," and "If I Had My Way."

In 1954 John, Sr., then seventy-two, reluctantly stopped touring with the group. As a trio in the 1960s the Mills Brothers recorded for Dot Records and were frequent guests on "The Jack Benny Show," "The Perry Como Show," "The Tonight Show," and "Hollywood Palace." They played theaters and clubs, touring forty weeks a year. They were financially independent but sang, according to Harry, "because we love singing and love an audience." Harry and his wife, Ruth (they had no children), and Donald were neighbors in Los Angeles. Herbert lived with his wife, Dorothy, in Las Vegas; they had one child. "Cab Driver," recorded in 1968, was their last great hit. Harry explained five decades of success by saying, "Maybe people want to hear plain, simple songs and easy harmony." By this time Harry, a diabetic, was losing his sight. After the death of Harry's wife in 1974, Donald's son, John, became Harry's valet and helped his uncle onstage.

The brothers celebrated their fiftieth anniversary in show business in 1975 with a nostalgic tribute hosted by Bing Crosby at the Dorothy Chandler Pavilion in Los Angeles. A 1981 historical tribute to harmony groups in New York's Savoy Theatre opened with the Temptations doing a medley of Mills Brothers hits. The evening underscored the significance of the Mills Brothers in the development of the doo-wop style of rock and roll. The death of Harry Mills in West Los Angeles, California, ended a musical partnership that had been as long and as successful as any group in the country's history. Herbert Mills died in Las Vegas, Nevada. Even into the 1990s Donald and his son, John, continued performing under the name the Mills Brothers. They were in Piqua, Ohio, on 3 June 1990, when the town unveiled a monument to their favorite sons on the public square where they had first sung. The plaque reads, "The Mills Brothers . . . America's greatest singing group . . . and musical ambassadors to the world."

• A vertical file on the Mills Brothers is in the History Department of the Flesh Public Library in Pisqua, Ohio. Biographical articles include Doris Black, "Yesterday's Hitmakers: The Mills Brothers," *Sepia*, Feb. 1976, p. 80; Louie Robinson, "The Eternal Mills Brothers," *Ebony*, Sept. 1979, pp. 60–63, 66–68; Vic Bellerby, "Swing Is the Thing: The Mills Brothers," Decca Records, MOR 535, Mono (1982); *Black Perspective in Music* 10 (1982): 229; and Edward Mapp,

Directory of Blacks in the Performing Arts (1990). The relationship of the Mills Brothers to the evolution of African-American and popular music in America is described in David Ewen, *All the Years of American Popular Music* (1977); *New York Times*, 17 July 1981; Gunther Schuller, *The Swing Era: The Development of Jazz, 1930–1945* (1989); William Barlow and Cheryl Finley, *From Swing to Soul: An Illustrated History of African-American Popular Music from 1930 to 1960* (1994); and Thomas J. Hennessey, *From Jazz to Swing: African-American Jazz Musicians and Their Music, 1890–1935* (1994).

BRUCE J. EVENSEN

MILLS, Irving (16 Jan. 1894–21 Apr. 1985), singer, music publisher, and manager, was born in New York City, the son of working-class Russian Jewish immigrants whose names are unknown. He was educated in New York City public schools but did not attend college. He married Bessie (maiden name unknown) at the age of seventeen; they had five children.

Mills began his career around 1911 as a vaudeville singer, a sheet music song demonstrator in dime stores, and a song plugger for Broadway producer Lew Leslie, visiting bandleaders to persuade them to buy Leslie's songs. He also worked as a songwriter, talent scout, and producer for budget-price record labels. In July 1919 Mills and his brother Jack borrowed $4,500 to establish Mills Music. Jack, also a song plugger and manager, tended to finances while Mills made deals around New York. He bought songs from unemployed songwriters and recorded uncopyrighted numbers at inexpensive record studios, pioneering the use of records to sell new songs. The brothers' second publication, "Mr. Gallagher and Mr. Shean," sold two million copies, and by 1924 their company was a major force in song publishing.

As the blues and jazz became popular, Mills investigated the black music scene. He hired the brother of composer-pianist Noble Sissle and the daughter of blues composer W. C. Handy as assistants and bought blues songs from Harlem musicians. He signed black bandleaders James P. Johnson, Will Vodery, and Lovie Austin to promote songs written by black songwriters in his employ. Around 1923 Mills met Duke Ellington, a recent arrival from Washington, D.C. On 8 June 1925 Mills hired Ellington as a pianist to accompany him on a recording. Mills recognized Ellington's talent as a bandleader and composer, and in 1926 the two men began a formal arrangement, each holding a 45 percent interest in a new corporation. The publisher prodded the pianist to write songs—always Mills's main interest—and then claimed cowriting credit (a deceptive but common publisher's practice). Mills often appended lyrics to Ellington's melodies, transforming the instrumental "Concerto for Cootie" into the popular song "Do Nothing 'til You Hear from Me" and providing words for "Solitude" and "Sophisticated Lady." He partially influenced Ellington's musical composition as well, by ordering him to write many songs in standard genres (which were decidedly second-rate Ellington creations).

Ellington was generally satisfied with Mills's management, however. It brought him publicity, lucrative tours, prestigious nightclub jobs, and artistic control of his band. Mills expanded the band's recording schedule, and in 1927, through connections with gangland nightclub operators, he secured a booking at Harlem's Cotton Club. Jimmy McHugh, a Mills Music staff writer, wrote music for the club's famed "jungle" floor shows, which delighted the elite, all-white audiences. Mills also arranged Broadway appearances, and in 1933 the ensemble made its first European tour. Mills's management allowed Ellington to concentrate on composing and rehearsing, allowing him to create the most extraordinary early jazz band music.

Mills continued to sing, although he avoided public performances and generally sang only on recordings made to promote his songs. In the 1920s he formed the Hotsy-Totsy Gang, which recorded and popularized dozens of Mills Music songs for more than a decade. Young white musicians such as Ben Pollack, Benny Goodman, and Hoagy Carmichael gained early experience in these sessions. Jack Mills diligently expanded the company's song holdings, buying bankrupt or faltering publishers. Mills expanded his stable of black bands, creating one for Ellington trumpeter Bubber Miley, another for singer Cab Calloway (who replaced Ellington at the Cotton Club in 1931 and became Mills's highest-earning musician), and many others.

The Great Depression threatened, however, and Mills weathered the hard times by associating himself with major record companies. During 1933 he worked for RCA Victor, building its roster of black performers and handling much of Victor's publicity (foreshadowing the work of artists-and-repertory specialists in later decades). Mills then worked for American Record (AR), the parent company of many labels. By 1935 AR was paying him $60,000 annually, guaranteeing the release of 120 recordings featuring Mills songs, and giving him full marketing rights to broadcasters. In 1937 Mills created the Variety and Master record labels. The latter pioneered the issuing of small jazz "combo" recordings, many of them made by Ellington band members. Mills's attempt to distribute recordings in Great Britain, however, was thwarted by the EMI monopoly.

Mills was a unique figure in the 1930s. At a time when music industries battled each other for royalties and product control, Mills pioneered a creative and profitable synergy among them. He later boasted that Mills Music owned "the world's largest collection of copyrighted tunes" and that he turned down a purchase offer of $750,000 from 20th Century–Fox. The music business remained turbulent, though. By 1939 Mills's record labels had failed, and Duke Ellington, now an established star, wanted a manager who could focus on his needs. Black critics had also condemned Mills's obvious profiteering from Ellington's work; the Reverend Adam Clayton Powell, Jr., called Ellington "a musical sharecropper" picking "Massa Mills' cotton." The subsequent disassociation of Ellington and Mills was amicable, however.

During World War II, as the music business confronted more upheavals, Mills maintained his eclectic enterprises. He continued to manage Cab Calloway and helped to produce and write music for the 1943 all-black film *Stormy Weather*, in which Calloway and other musicians appeared. By 1950 Mills Music owned more than 25,000 copyrights and subsidiaries in Canada, Europe, and Latin America, and entertainment corporations remained eager to purchase it. In 1957 the United Artists studio offered $4 million but was rebuffed. Ignoring the rock-and-roll market, the company specialized in publishing school choral and band arrangements of items in its vast catalog. Mills Music was finally sold in 1965 to a New York conglomerate for about $4.5 million, of which Mills received $1.755 million. The company was soon merged with Belwin, and in the 1970s Belwin Mills became the largest music publisher and song copyright holder in the nation. Mills remained active, purchasing jazz promoter Norman Granz's catalog, but by 1973 he entered permanent retirement. Mills died in Palm Springs, California.

Mills's creative entrepreneurship in a time when music became a major American industry, as well as his promotion of Duke Ellington and many other black musicians in a prejudiced environment, mark him as a colorful pioneer in the history of the American music business.

• Biographies may be found in Barry Kernfeld, ed., *The New Grove Dictionary of Jazz* (1988); and *The Faber Companion to Popular Music* (1987). Mills's business career is covered in Russell Sanjek, *American Popular Music and Its Business: The First Four Hundred Years*, vol. 3, *1900–1984* (1988). An obituary is in the *New York Times*, 23 Apr. 1985.

BURTON W. PERETTI

MILLS, Ogden Livingston (23 Aug. 1884–11 Oct. 1937), lawyer, legislator, and secretary of the treasury, was born in Newport, Rhode Island, the son of Ogden Mills, a business entrepreneur, and Ruth T. Livingston. His father's family had made a fortune in California following the gold rush of 1849. Mills attended the Browning School in New York City and in 1901 was admitted to Harvard University, where he received his A.B. in 1905. He remained at Harvard to study law and was awarded the LL.B. in 1907. Admitted to the New York bar in 1908, he joined the important firm of Stetson, Jennings and Russell in New York City.

Almost immediately following his graduation from Harvard, Mills entered Republican politics, becoming party treasurer of the New York County Republican Committee in 1910 and a national committeeman two years later. In 1911 he married Margaret Stuyvesant Rutherford. They had no children, and the marriage ended in divorce in 1919. In 1912 he was defeated in a campaign for the U.S. House of Representatives, but in 1914 he was elected to the New York State Senate, where he became an advocate of social, political, and financial reforms, including workmen's compensation, certain widows' pensions, and both court efficiency and enlightened prison reform. He became particularly adept in the field of taxation, serving as chairman of a joint legislative committee to investigate the New York tax system. In 1917 he left the senate to enlist in the army. In 1920 he was elected to the U.S. House of Representatives from the Seventeenth Congressional District of New York City and served until 1927. In the same year his strong party and legislative leadership led to his nomination for governor. His opponent was Governor Alfred E. Smith, and during the campaign Mills chose to divert attention away from important ideological issues by blaming the state for "bad milk" in New York City. Smith was easily reelected. In 1924 Mills had married Dorothy Randolph Fell. They had no children.

In 1927 President Calvin Coolidge appointed Mills undersecretary of the treasury, to serve under the older and aloof head of the department, Andrew Mellon. When Herbert Hoover became president in 1929 and kept intact the top Treasury Department leadership, he relied far more on Mills than he did on Mellon for fiscal and monetary advice. After 1929 Mills also became the leader of a group of undersecretaries known as the "New Patriots," who took an active role in departmental improvement and policy making.

Mills's role as ad hoc adviser to President Hoover became a formal one in 1932, when he was appointed secretary of the treasury following Mellon's departure to serve as ambassador to Great Britain. As departmental head, Mills's first important action was to work with conservative Democrats in the Congress to attempt passage of a 2.5 percent manufactures sales tax, which would be less onerous to the business community. Eventually Mills and Hoover had to forgo the sales tax and support a revenue act that increased corporate, estate, and certain excise taxes. On other issues, Mills took conservative positions in urging Hoover to resist federal relief legislation but showed flexibility on fiscal and monetary matters. He advised the president to reduce the gold backing of the dollar, as was done in the Glass-Steagall Act of 1932; to support the Reconstruction Finance Corporation Act, making available $2 billion of funding to ease credit pressures on the banking, insurance, and railroad industries; and to establish a moratorium on the collection of European debts owed to the United States. Being a politically sensitive New Yorker, Mills also opposed the Prohibition amendment and was influential in persuading Hoover to take a quasi-repeal position on it in the Republican convention of 1932.

Ironically, perhaps, the high point of Mills's political contribution was his staying on in the first days of the New Deal to offer the new secretary of the treasury, William H. Wooden, a plan that effected the closing and reopening of the nation's banks. It became the essence of the Banking Act of 1933, the occasion for the first of Franklin Roosevelt's fireside chats. In so doing Mills annoyed Hoover, who complained about the outgoing secretary concerting with the New Deal. Mills exasperatedly replied: "This job had to be done and unless . . . I stayed here it would not have been done. We have a country you know." He would soon be returned to Hoover's good graces. In the mid-1930s the principal defenders of the Hoover presidency, particularly books by Ray Lyman Wilbur and Arthur Mastick Hyde, *The Hoover Policies*, and by William Starr Myers and Walter H. Newton, *The Hoover Administration: A Documented Narrative*, would rely heavily on Mills's correspondence and public statements.

Mills's strong state and national political roles over a period of twenty years earned him a claim to his party's presidential nomination in 1936. That nomination, however, went to the more progressive Alfred M. Landon. Mills died in New York City of a coronary thrombosis.

• Mills's papers are in the Library of Congress. Writings by Mills that defend the ideology of the Hoover presidency include *What of Tomorrow* (1935), *Liberalism Fights On* (1936), and *The Seventeen Million* (1937). For additional information on Mills's career, see Martin L. Fausold, *The Presidency of Herbert C. Hoover* (1985); Susan Kennedy, *The Banking Crisis of 1933* (1973); and Harris Gaylord Warren, *Herbert Hoover and the Great Depression* (1959). Obituaries are in the *New York Times*, 12 Oct. 1937, and *Political Science Quarterly*, Dec. 1937.

MARTIN L. FAUSOLD

MILLS, Robert (12 Aug. 1781–3 Mar. 1855), architect, engineer, and writer, was born in Charles Town (Charleston), South Carolina, the son of William Mills, a tailor, and Ann Taylor. Raised a Presbyterian, he was educated privately in Charleston, possibly in part by his brother Thomas. Mills studied architecture with James Hoban (1800–1802), Thomas Jefferson (1802–1803), and, most important, Benjamin Henry Latrobe (1803–1808), for whom he worked as an assistant in Philadelphia. Impressed by Mills's diligence, Latrobe introduced him to Enlightenment thought and taught him to conceive architectonically, to appreciate the abstract dimension of stylistic expression, and to apply such progressive technical methods as the use of fire-resistant, lightweight brick and cement vaulting.

The course of Mills's stylistic maturation is recorded in a series of ecclesiastical schemes, in which he increasingly adapted the heavier, more decorative Gibbs-Palladian forms to rational classical values. The series commenced with an unexecuted design for a temple-fronted church on Johns Island, South Carolina (c. 1803), continued with the Circular Congregational Church in Charleston (1804–1806) and the plainer, neo-Greek auditorium of Dr. William Staughton's Baptist church in Philadelphia (1808–1811), and culminated in the innovative octagonal Monumental Church in Richmond, Virginia (1812–1814).

While living in Philadelphia between 1808 and 1814, Mills established his professional independence. Following the rejection of his proposal for the South Carolina penitentiary (1806–1807), which was inspired by the reforms to the planning and organization of prisons propounded by John Howard, Mills reworked the design on a reduced scale for the county jail in Mount Holly, New Jersey (1808). He undertook a broad range of commissions, including row housing for naval captain John Meany (1809), additions to Independence Hall to house state offices and the Peale Museum (1809–1812), the capacious Washington Hall (1813), and numerous houses in both Philadelphia and Richmond. Mills married Eliza Barnwell Smith in 1808; they had six children. Mills also served as secretary in 1811–1812 of the short-lived Columbian Society of Artists, which sought to promote American artists; drafted an unpublished architectural handbook; and invested in real estate. Despite his increasing prominence, some significant commissions eluded him, including the Pennsylvania Capitol in Harrisburg (1810), the Richmond City Hall and Courthouse (1812), and a house for Philadelphia lawyer Benjamin Chew, whose dismissive view of the nascent architectural profession Mills courageously challenged by seeking proper recompense for the possible design of his house.

In 1814 Mills won a commission to design the Washington Monument in Baltimore, where he lived from 1814 to 1820. Mills initially envisioned an ornamented Greek Doric column, boldly elevated on a Roman triumphal arch, but budgetary constraints forced him to restrict his design to a simple plinth supporting a column capped by a statue (1814–1829; iron railing installed 1842). Thereafter he gravitated toward a more Jeffersonian classicism, epitomized by the Pantheon-influenced First Baptist Church in Baltimore (1816–1818) and the temple-fronted First Baptist Church in Charleston (1818–1822). A collapse of the Baltimore economy had precipitated the bankruptcy of Mills's Waterloo Row housing development (1816–1818) and the abortion of a progressively planned city workhouse scheme (1818), but patronage in South Carolina alleviated his financial difficulties.

Mills's work in South Carolina between 1820 and 1829 is characterized by functionalism tempered by an adept use of more monumental features, especially the raised portico with side steps so favored in southern Palladian architecture. His style is at its most refined in the Ainsley Hall House in Columbia (1823–1825). From 1820 to 1823 Mills was employed by the state of South Carolina, first as an acting commissioner of the Board of Public Works and then, from 1822, as superintendent of public buildings. As a state employee he designed five standard courthouses, in which he placed the courtroom over vaulted government offices, and designed two types of district jails, intended to be secure yet to provide more humane conditions for prisoners. He best combined utility and dignity in his designs for the insane asylum in Columbia and the Fireproof Building in Charleston (1822–1827), both efficient in arrangement and elegant in their Greco-Roman Palladianism. Mills evaluated canal and road construction, and he published proposals for further internal improvements in the *Atlas of the State of South Carolina* (1825) and in *Statistics of South Carolina* (1826). Mills moved from Columbia to Abbeville,

South Carolina, in 1828, partly to supervise the erection of a courthouse to his designs and partly to reduce household expenditures. There he addressed steam locomotion and railroad development; his idea for an elevated iron-rimmed wooden track was adopted for the pioneering Charleston to Hamburg, South Carolina, line (1828–1829; later replaced because of rot).

Mills's endeavors from 1827 to secure appointment with the U.S. Army Engineers in Washington, D.C., failed. However, in 1830, again aided by southern patronage, he was engaged to reconfigure the acoustically defective Congress (executed 1833). He thereby acquired additional government work. Mills's designs for the masonry-vaulted Appraisers' Stores in Baltimore (1835–1839) and for five New England customhouses (1834–1835; four adhering to a similar plan) exhibit a liberal use of classical motifs. Greek influences are evident in the Treasury (1836–1842) and the Patent Office (1836–1842), both commissions awarded him by Andrew Jackson; Mills's design for the latter is a revision of a design by Ithiel Town, Alexander Jackson Davis, and William P. Elliott, Jr. As unofficial "Architect of the Public Buildings," Mills effected reforms in building practice, as evidenced in the General Post Office (1839–1842), for which he melded classical and Italianate elements. Other projects include his innovative design for the Rational Gothic Washington Gaol (1839–1841) and two standard U.S. Marine hospital designs (published in 1837); Mills had earlier designed the Marine Hospital in Charleston (1832–1833) and would later implement one of his standard designs in Key West, Florida (1844–1845). Mills's reputation was marred by political animosity that caused his dismissal from federal employ in 1842. He was reemployed in 1849 to supervise the designs for the Patent Office east wing. Between 1842 and 1845 Mills submitted entries to the War and Navy departments, for whom he planned a conjoined building, but they were rejected, owing in part to his antipathy for revivalism and metal construction. He was successful, however, in being commissioned to design the Winder Building, leased for the War Department (1847), the National and Smithsonian institutions (1841 and 1846), and the Capitol extension (1850–1853).

Concurrent with his other activities, Mills continued promoting railroad and civic projects. In 1845 he was commissioned to design the national Washington Monument. Construction of the sublime obelisk was begun in 1848 but was temporarily halted in 1854. Completed between 1880 and 1884, the final edifice did not include the encircling American Doric Pantheon base that Mills had originally envisioned. His last major commission was his design of a large multifacility block gracefully attached to Jefferson's rotunda at the University of Virginia in Charlottesville (1851–1852). Both this project and the Washington Monument underscore Mills's tenacity of purpose, breadth of practice, and practical and aesthetic sense.

Mills died in Washington, D.C., close to the major public edifices he designed that established the monumental symbolism of the nation. Among the first professionally trained American architects, he forged a consciously national architectural idiom that integrated current international revivalist styles with traditional Georgian conventions. He also raised the technical level of American design and the level of official patronage and contributed significantly to the implementation of progressive concepts of institutional architecture.

• A sizable body of Mills's personal and professional papers and designs remains, concentrated chiefly in Washington, D.C., at the U.S. National Archives, Library of Congress, Office of the Architect of the Capitol, and Archive of American Art in the Smithsonian Institution. Other repositories include the South Carolina Library at the University of South Carolina and the South Carolina Department of Archives and History, Columbia; the South Carolina Historical Society and the City Archives, Charleston; and the Southeastern Architectural Archive of the Howard-Tilton Memorial Library at Tulane University. Further documents are preserved at the Historical Society of Pennsylvania and the Athenaeum, Philadelphia; Huntington Library, San Marino, Calif.; City Archives, Historical Society of Maryland, and Peale Museum, Baltimore; the libraries of the University of North Carolina and the University of Virginia; Massachusetts Historical Society; and, particularly valuable regarding Mills's private life, in the Richard X. Evans Collection at Georgetown University. The majority of these documents have been gathered on microfilm under the editorship of Pamela Scott as *Papers of Robert Mills* (1990).

The chief studies of Mills are John M. Bryan, ed., *Robert Mills, Architect* (1989), the catalog of an exhibition concentrating on his architectural practice, with critical essays; and R. Windsor Liscombe, *Altogether American, Robert Mills, Architect and Engineer, 1781–1855* (1994), which examines Mills's design and thought in the context of his private life and the contemporary United States and which includes a full bibliography. Aspects of his career in South Carolina are related in greater depth in Gene Waddell, *Mills's Atlas of the State of South Carolina* (1980); Waddell and Liscombe, *Robert Mills's Courthouses and Jails* (1981); and Liscombe, *The Church Architecture of Robert Mills* (1985).

R. WINDSOR LISCOMBE

MILLS, Roger Quarles (30 Mar. 1832–2 Sept. 1911), U.S. congressman and senator from Texas, was born in Todd County, Kentucky, the son of Charles Henley Mills and Tabitha Buckner Daniel, slaveholding farmers. Roger completed his education at Dickey and Horner Academy in Kentucky and in 1850 went to live with a sister in Palestine, Texas. He served as a clerk for the Texas legislature and became an attorney in 1851. In 1852 Mills opened a practice in Corsicana, Texas, where he became a road overseer and supporter of prohibition. In 1856 he was named an alternate delegate to the national convention of the American party. On 7 January 1858 he married Caroline R. Jones, a member of a planter family; they were to have five children. The American party having disappeared in Texas, he was elected as a states' rights Democrat in 1859 to the eighth Texas legislature where he also defended frontier concerns. In 1860 Mills supported John C. Breckinridge for president, and he favored secession in 1861.

Mills fought with the Confederates at Wilson's Creek, Missouri, in 1861, then helped raise the Tenth Texas Infantry. He was promoted to colonel in 1862. Captured with the Arkansas Post garrison in January 1863, he was soon exchanged to the Army of Tennessee. Mills temporarily commanded a brigade at the battle of Chickamauga and was wounded at Chattanooga in the fall of 1863. In 1864 at New Hope Church he again led his regiment, but a wound at the battle of Atlanta ended his military service.

After the war Mills farmed, joined the Methodist Episcopal Church, South, and practiced law. In 1872 he won election to the U.S. House of Representatives, beginning a 26-year career in Congress. During the 1870s he voiced southern views on Reconstruction and urged frontier protection and federal aid for Texas railroads and harbors. He supported the increase of currency circulation as a solution to debtors' problems. Beginning in 1879 he focused on tariff reduction as a way to increase trade and aid consumers. After a change of views, Mills publicly opposed, as an invasion of individual rights, the prohibition amendment to the Texas constitution, which met defeat in 1887. As chairman of the House Ways and Means Committee he carefully gathered information and forcefully presented his Mills Bill to lower tariff rates, which became an issue in the presidential race of 1888. He spoke often in eastern and midwestern states during the campaign, but the Democrats' candidate, Grover Cleveland, lost the election. Mills expressed his views on tariffs and other issues in the *North American Review* and *Forum* from 1889 to 1891. Silver coinage displaced the tariff as the dominant issue, contributing to Mills's defeat in a bid for Speaker of the House in 1891. Nevertheless, Texas Democrats in the state legislature elected him to the U.S. Senate in 1892. In 1894 Senator Mills supported passage of the Wilson bill, which lowered tariff rates. He opposed the annexation of Hawaii but supported Cuban rebels in the mid-1890s. Because Mills did not strongly advocate free silver coinage, he lost some of his popularity and withdrew from a reelection race in 1898.

With the discovery of oil on his land, Mills retired comfortably. He died in Corsicana, Texas.

• Collections of Mills's papers are at the Dallas Historical Society and at the Barker Texas History Center at the University of Texas at Austin. There are unpublished theses about Mills by Durell Carothers at Rice University, by Myrtle Roberts at the University of Texas at Austin, and by Russell L. Purifoy, Jr., at the University of North Texas. See also Alwyn Barr, "The Making of a Secessionist: The Antebellum Career of Roger Q. Mills," *Southwestern Historical Quarterly* 79 (Oct. 1975): 129–44; and H. Wayne Morgan, *From Hayes to McKinley: National Party Politics, 1877–1896* (1969). An obituary is in the *Dallas Morning News*, 3 Sept. 1911.

ALWYN BARR

MILLS, Samuel John (21 Apr. 1783–16 June 1818), initiator of American foreign mission societies and philanthropic agencies, was born in Torringford, Connecticut, the son of Samuel John Mills, a Congregational minister, and Ester Robbins. Influenced by his mother's piety and a religious revival in 1798, Mills experienced conversion in 1801. He then sold his inherited farm and entered Morris Academy in Litchfield, Connecticut. In April 1806 he entered the freshman class at Williams College, where in 1808 he organized a society called the Brethren, which collected and republished missionary materials. Mills graduated with an A.B. in 1809 and attended Yale briefly but failed there to recruit candidates for missions. In 1810 he enrolled in Andover Theological Seminary in Massachusetts, where the following year he organized the Society of Inquiry on the Subject of Missions that did work similar to that of the Brethren at Williams. In 1812 he received his B.D. and was licensed to preach by the General Association of Massachusetts. He was ordained on 21 June 1815 at the Presbyterian church in Newburyport, Massachusetts.

At Yale, Mills had befriended Henry Obookiah, a native Hawaiian. This relationship prompted Mills to raise funds in 1816 for the founding of a Foreign Mission School in Cornwall, Connecticut, to prepare persons to minister to the North American Indians and to the inhabitants of the Pacific Islands and the Asiatic countries. The school was one of the first in the United States designed to train workers for foreign missions.

The Connecticut and Massachusetts Home Missionary Societies commissioned Mills and John L. Schermerhorn to conduct a tour of the southern section of the United States in 1812–1813. The Society for Propagating the Gospel among the Indians and others in North America and the Philadelphia Bible Society were joint sponsors. The team was to locate, identify, and number the Indian tribes west of the Alleghany Mountains and assist in the creation of local Bible societies; they recounted their efforts in *Communications Relative to the Progress of Bible Societies* (1813) and *A Correct View of That Part of the United States Which Lies West of the Allegany Mountains, with Regard to Religion and Morals* (1814). A second tour (1814–1815) was sponsored by the Massachusetts Missionary Society, with Daniel Smith as Mills's associate. Their *Report of a Missionary Tour through That Part of the United States Which Lies West of the Allegany Mountains* (1815) is a record of their journey. All three reports stressed that there was a need for "the united support and energies of all denominations of Christians" to do the work of missions.

In 1816 at the General Assembly of the Presbyterian church in Philadelphia, Pennsylvania, Mills urged the formation of what became in 1817 the United Foreign Missionary Society, whereby Presbyterian, Dutch Reformed, and Associated Reformed churches cooperated in preaching the gospel to peoples in North and South America. Having participated in the creation of local and state Bible societies, Mills was a principal promoter of the formation of the American Bible Society in 1816 to coordinate this work. That year he helped organize the African School in Parsippany, New Jersey, to prepare young African Americans as preachers and teachers for service in the United States,

West Indies, and Africa. He also cooperated with the Female Missionary Society for the Poor of New York and Vicinity. In 1817 Mills and Ebenezer Burgess were commissioned by the American Colonization Society to visit Africa to select a site to purchase for an American colony of free blacks. The place chosen became Liberia in 1821. On the return voyage, Mills died of what was labeled "incipient consumption" and was buried at sea.

Mills's missionary vision encompassed the world. Evangelical in appeal, it included academic training as a prerequisite for missions. Although he was not an eloquent preacher or scholar, Mills was tireless in his efforts to promote an ecumenical missionary movement in the United States.

• For information on Mills, see Calvin Durfee, *Williams Biographical Annals* (1871), John H. Hewitt, *Williams College and Foreign Missions* (1914), Samuel Orcutt, *History of Torrington, Connecticut* (1878), and Gardiner Spring, *Memoirs of the Rev. Samuel J. Mills* (1820). Thomas C. Richards, *Samuel J. Mills: Missionary Pathfinder, Pioneer and Promoter* (1906), and Elizabeth G. Stryker, *Missionary Annals: A Story of One Short Life* (1888), are also helpful.

FREDERICK V. MILLS, SR.

MILLS, Susan Lincoln Tolman (18 Nov. 1825–12 Dec. 1912), educator and college president, was born in Enosburg, Vermont, the daughter of John Tolman, a tanner, and Elizabeth Nichols. She graduated from Mount Holyoke Seminary (now College) in 1845 and taught there until 1848. Introduced to Cyrus Mills, a Presbyterian minister, by Mount Holyoke's founder and principal, Mary Lyon, Susan Tolman accepted his proposal on their third meeting and married him a year later, in September 1848. Soon they traveled as missionaries to Ceylon, arriving at Batticotta in March 1849. Cyrus Mills headed the Batticotta Seminary for boys while Susan Mills taught girls from local schools. Soon after her arrival, Mills became ill with amoebic dysentery followed by internal ulcerations. Her continuing ill health forced their return to the United States in 1854.

Cyrus Mills served as a guest preacher at various churches while Susan partially recovered her health. In 1860 her husband was appointed president of Oahu College (later Punahou School), a school for missionaries' children in Honolulu. At Oahu Susan Mills managed household affairs and taught physical geography, physiology, chemistry, botany, natural theology, Milton, drawing, and calisthenics.

Tired of merely operating academic institutions, the couple left the school in early 1864, and in October 1865 they bought the Young Ladies' Seminary of Benicia, California, a school enrolling approximately ninety girls. In 1870 they sold the Benicia Academy and, the next year, moved to land they had purchased southeast of Oakland and supervised the building of an impressive hall, the first structure of the new Mills Seminary. In partnership with her husband for the next thirteen years, Susan Mills served in many capacities at the seminary. She was the equivalent of dean of students and dean of faculty, taught classes, and supervised the affairs of the academy's household, including room assignments, maintenance, food service, staffing, and financial responsibilities. After her husband's death in 1884, she continued as principal, manager, comptroller, and member of the board of trustees. In 1890 the board of trustees appointed her president of the school.

Between the death of her husband and her resignation from the presidency in 1909, Mills was primarily responsible for the growth of the institution. Chartered as a college by the state of California in 1885, the seminary graduated its first baccalaureate class in 1889. It was the first women's college on the West Coast. In 1900 Mills reluctantly recommended to the board of trustees that the institution drop its pre-college school so that its curriculum could be directed solely to the demands of a baccalaureate program. Mills College discontinued its seminary in 1901, the same year in which Mills received an honorary doctorate from her alma mater, Mount Holyoke College.

Through a series of gifts and leases, the Millses had transferred governance of the school to its board of trustees. Susan Mills signed over the balance of the estate to the board in 1901, thus ensuring the perpetuity of the institution. During her presidency, five major buildings were added to the campus, including three designed by architect Julia Morgan. Mills vigorously recruited new faculty who raised the level of academic achievement at the college during her tenure. After she retired from the presidency in 1909, she continued to teach a class in ethics for two years. She died at Mills College.

• Letters, notebooks, and newsletters from Mills are in the Susan Tolman Mills Papers in the Mills College library and in the Mount Holyoke College library. A biography with thorough references is E. O. James, *The Story of Cyrus and Susan Mills* (1953). Biographical material is included in Rosalind Keep, *Fourscore Years: A History of Mills College* (1931). Anecdotal material has been compiled in Clara Wittenmyer, ed., *The Susan Lincoln Mills Memory Book* (1915).

MARGARET MISKELLY THOMAS

MILLS, Wilbur Daigh (24 May 1909–2 May 1992), congressman, was born in Kensett, Arkansas, the son of Ardra Pickens Mills, the owner of a general store, and Abbie Lois Daigh. The family was prosperous by local standards, and an acquaintance remembered that the Millses owned "what there was to own" in Kensett (Associated Press, 25 Apr. 1971). Wilbur Mills graduated from Hendrix College in Conway, Arkansas, in 1930. He attended Harvard Law School for the next three years but returned home before earning an LL.B. Though he was admitted to the Arkansas bar in 1933, he worked briefly in a Kensett bank his father had purchased. In 1934 he married Clarine "Polly" Billingsley; the couple had two daughters.

Mills entered politics in 1934, when he was elected county and probate judge for White County. He was reelected in 1936. Two years later his largely rural north Arkansas district sent the young Democrat to

Congress. Because he had apprenticed in both the law and banking, Mills was assigned to the House Banking and Currency Committee in 1939 and, in 1943, to the Ways and Means Committee. Rarely facing even primary opposition, Mills became one of those inevitably reelected white southerners who accrued seniority and, therefore, power in Congress at the expense of other parties to the Democratic coalition, particularly African Americans and organized labor. Though not particularly outspoken in the cause of segregation, he in 1956 signed the Southern Manifesto, the declaration of southern members of Congress to seek to reverse the Supreme Court decision in *Brown v. Board of Education* (1954), and consistently opposed civil rights initiatives, including the landmark legislation of 1964–1965. He firmly supported the Taft-Hartley Act and voted for harsh anti-Communist laws through the 1940s and 1950s.

By 1957 Mills had worked his way up to the chairmanship of Ways and Means, the committee that exercised jurisdiction over tax and tariff legislation as well as over the Social Security system and had also come to control congressional committee assignments. The complex bills that Ways and Means reported could not be amended on the floor of the House but only approved or rejected on a take-it-or-leave-it basis. Choosing not to disperse its work among subcommittees, Mills became an unusually powerful head of an unusually powerful committee, a situation President John Kennedy acknowledged ruefully: "Wilbur Mills knows that he was chairman of Ways and Means before I got here and that he'll still be chairman after I've gone—and he knows I know it. I don't have any hold on him" (Theodore Sorensen, *Kennedy* [1965], p. 426). Yet as formidable a figure as he became on Capitol Hill, Mills was apparently not heavy-handed in the committee room. Seeking to build consensus, he would on occasion yield his own sometimes hazy positions, allow members to have their say, and accommodate their need to look after special friends and backers just as he kept an eye out for Arkansas banking and industrial interests. On his own tax forms. Mills took the standard deduction so no one could say that he had profited by arcana in the bills he had authored, but in terms of campaign contributions, he did well by the industries he cultivated. Not surprisingly, Mills was also a master at the pork barrel, and his district received a disproportionate share of federal money.

As Democratic administrations in the 1960s proposed that the federal government do more and spend more, Mills publicly identified himself with the cause of fiscal conservatism. He extracted promises of spending limits or actual budget cuts in return for both embracing the lower taxes Kennedy proposed and tolerating the higher ones to which Lyndon Johnson eventually resigned himself. Yet Mills proved more than simply a tight-fisted naysayer, as illustrated in his tortuous but ultimately creative role in the development of the Medicare and Medicaid programs. For several years he had ensured that proposals to finance hospital care for the elderly through the Social Security system gathered dust, indicating that he was worried about Medicare's potential to impoverish the larger program of old-age pensions. But in the wake of Johnson's landslide election in 1964 and with sentiment for Medicare growing within Congress and the committee, Mills went to work. He combined elements from competing plans offered by Democrats, Republicans, and the American Medical Association to create a bill that, in fact, broadened benefits beyond what had been originally proposed. In addition to hospital care for the elderly funded through the Social Security payroll tax, the Mills legislation provided for coverage of doctors' bills in a voluntary program financed by low-cost premiums and subsidized health care for poor people not covered by Social Security. The Medicare system that was ultimately established followed the Mills outline closely. Though he continued to emphasize the desirability of balancing the budget and lessening the tax burden on the middle class, Mills also oversaw hikes in Social Security benefits.

Republican Richard Nixon won the presidency in 1968, but with Democrats still in control of Congress, Mills remained one of the most influential members. Journalist Hugh Sidey wryly noted in 1971, "If the White House were to rate the independent powers of this world with which it must deal according to their formidability, Arkansas Congressman Wilbur Mills probably would rank just below Germany and above France" (*Life*, 19 Feb. 1971, p. 4). He was willing to make common cause with the administration in opposition to busing and in support of the Vietnam War, the supersonic transport (SST), and a reform of the welfare system that would put more recipients to work. Evidently worried about loosening Congress's grip on the public purse strings, however, Mills became a prime obstacle to Nixon's plans for revenue sharing, which would have turned over part of the money raised by federal taxation to states and localities for their own use. Relations between the White House and the chairman deteriorated to the point that Mills even flirted with the prospect of challenging Nixon for the presidency in 1972, but the effort stalled in that year's Democratic primaries.

Two years later, at the end of a twelve-month period that had seen both Nixon and Vice President Spiro Agnew toppled, Mills fell too. But it was not abuse of his considerable power that undid him but rather alcohol, painkillers, and an Argentine stripper named Fanne Foxe (nee Annabel Battistella). Late one October night in 1974, U.S. Park Police in Washington discovered Mills in the midst of what appeared to be either a drunken romp or a drunken quarrel. He won reelection in November, but after appearing later that month on stage with Foxe at a Boston burlesque house, he consented to be hospitalized for alcoholism and stepped down from the chairmanship of Ways and Means. He served out his term but did not run again. His immediate successors did not exercise the same undivided authority he had enjoyed. Ways and Means established subcommittees and was divested of its power over committee assignments.

In 1977 Mills began work as an attorney, lobbyist, and tax consultant in Washington and New York. He retired and returned to Arkansas in the early 1980s. Mills collapsed at his home in Kensett and was pronounced dead at a hospital in nearby Searcy.

• Mills's papers are at Hendrix College in Conway, Ark. A hefty clippings file is in the Special Collections Division, University of Arkansas Libraries, Fayetteville. For Mills's leadership of the Ways and Means Committee, see John F. Manley, *The Politics of Finance: The House Committee on Ways and Means* (1971), and Julian E. Zelizer, "Taxing America: Wilbur Mills and the Culture of Fiscal Policy, 1949–1969" (Ph.D. diss., Johns Hopkins Univ., 1996). Ralph Nader's Congress Project issued a useful pamphlet, Stephen Merrill, *Wilbur D. Mills, Democratic Representative from Arkansas* (1972). Obituaries are in the *Arkansas Democrat Gazette* and the *New York Times*, 3 May 1992.

PATRICK G. WILLIAMS

MILLS BROTHERS. *See* Mills, Harry, and Herbert Mills.

MILMORE, Martin (14 Sept. 1844–21 July 1883), sculptor, was born in Sligo, County Sligo, Ireland, the son of a schoolmaster. His parents' names are unknown. Shortly after his father's death in 1851, Martin, along with his mother and three young brothers, immigrated to Boston, Massachusetts. He was enrolled at the Boston Latin School and studied art at the Lowell Institute for seven years. He learned wood carving from his older brother, Joseph, who was an accomplished stonecutter.

During these early years Milmore decided to become a sculptor, and when Thomas Ball opened his studio in Boston in 1858, Milmore applied for training. As it turned out Ball did not accept students, but he provided Milmore with materials and room to work in return for Milmore's assistance around the studio. Milmore gained valuable experience over the next four years while Ball worked on an equestrian portrait of George Washington, one of the first monumental bronze equestrians made in the United States. Under Ball's direction Milmore produced a self-portrait, a bust-length marble relief of Edith Rotch (Museum of Fine Arts, Boston, 1862), several statuettes, and an idealized bust-length marble relief of the mythological son of Aurora, Phosphor (MFA, Boston, 1862–1863), which was purchased by Turner Sargent, a Boston lawyer who became Milmore's benefactor.

When Ball returned to Italy, Milmore opened his own studio in Boston. There he modeled from life small busts of Henry Wadsworth Longfellow (New Hampshire Historical Society, 1863) and Charles Sumner (now lost, 1863). In 1864 Milmore received a commission for granite figures of Ceres, Flora, and Pomona for Horticulture Hall in Boston. The Ceres was twelve feet tall and the other two figures were eight feet tall. Milmore's brothers helped carve the figures, which he had modeled in plaster, a technique he had learned from Ball.

In 1867 Milmore designed a soldiers' monument for Forest Hills Cemetery in Roxbury, Massachusetts. The sculpture features a Union volunteer in a long coat, leaning on his rifle and surveying the graves of his loyal comrades. The heroic-scale bronze figure, cast at the Ames foundry in Chicopee, Massachusetts, is a simple and dignified, humble private soldier, fitting for a memorial to a war in which the common soldier was widely recognized as the real hero. The work's success reinforced Milmore's reputation, and he received orders for monuments from Fitchburg, Massachusetts; Keene and Claremont, New Hampshire; and Erie, Pennsylvania. Moreover, the Roxbury statue became an important prototype for the "parade rest" or "sentinel" figures that proliferated on Civil War monuments erected in small towns, North and South, from the 1870s until about 1920. Milmore's Civil War memorial (1872) for Mount Auburn Cemetery in Cambridge was not so influential. He modeled and his brother Joseph carved in granite a colossal American sphinx that symbolizes through the strength of a lion and the benign grace of a woman, the preservation of the Union and the defeat of slavery. The iconography is unique among American Civil War memorials.

In 1874 Milmore was commissioned to make a soldiers' and sailors' monument for the Boston Common. His design consisted of a tall granite pillar topped by a bronze statue of Liberty and surrounded by two tiers of four allegorical figures each, plus pictorial reliefs showing Boston's role in the Civil War. Milmore executed the design in Rome, where he lived from 1870 until 1876. The monument was dedicated in 1877 and became an influential prototype for Civil War memorials in other metropolitan areas. In 1903 Lorado Taft praised the work in his *History of American Sculpture* for its "simple, quiet dignity . . . the proportions of base and column and figures" and the "simple and chaste, yet decorative" lines of the figures. He considered the realistic soldier and sailor the best statues of their type in the United States. Regarding Milmore's total oeuvre, Taft acknowledged his craftsmanship and sense of monumentality. Adeline Adams considered his monuments among the best of their time, but Wayne Craven detected a "competent naturalism that is somewhat limited in expressive power."

Despite Milmore's rather bland realism, his services were in great demand. His bronze statue of John Glover stands in Boston, and one of General Sylvanus Thayer, the father of the U.S. Military Academy, is at West Point. He also completed portraits of George Ticknor (1868), Wendell Phillips (c. 1870), Cardinal John McCloskey, Ralph Waldo Emerson (c. 1870), Daniel Webster, Ulysses S. Grant, and Abraham Lincoln, as well as several ideal sculptures.

Daniel Chester French remembered Milmore, who never married, as "a picturesque figure . . . somewhat of the Edwin Booth type, with long dark hair and large dark eyes. He affected the artistic . . . wearing a broad-brimmed soft black hat, and a cloak. His appearance was striking and he knew it." Milmore died, probably of tuberculosis, in Boston. He was laid to rest in Forest Hills Cemetery near his first Civil War monument. His grave is marked with a memorial by French in which a majestic angel of death stays the hand of a handsome young sculptor who is carving a sphinx in relief.

• There is no known collection of Milmore's papers. Wayne Craven, *Sculpture in America*, rev. ed. (1984), provides the fullest account of Milmore's life and work. Greenthal, Kozol, and Ramierez, *American Figurative Sculpture in the Museum of Fine Arts, Boston* (1986), clarifies several details and illustrates two marble reliefs. Lorado Taft, *History of American Sculpture*, rev. ed. (1930), elucidates Milmore's achievements. The quote from Daniel Chester French appears in the entry on Milmore by Adeline Adams in the *Dictionary of American Biography*. Obituaries are in the *American Architect and Building News*, 18 Aug. 1883, and the *Boston Evening Transcript*, 23 July 1883.

MICHAEL W. PANHORST

MILNER, Lucille Bernheimer (1888?–14 Aug. 1975), civil libertarian, social worker, and cofounder and long-time secretary of the American Civil Liberties Union, was born in St. Louis, Missouri, the daughter of Marcus Bernheimer, a wealthy Jewish wholesale grocer, and Ella Hayman. When she was five, Lucille's father suffered losses in the depression of 1893 from which he never recovered; two years later her mother died of cancer. Lucille attended local public schools until she was diagnosed at sixteen with tuberculosis. She spent a year in the Rocky Mountains in Colorado, after which she was pronounced cured and returned home to care for her ailing and financially distressed father.

When her father died several years later, Lucille lived first with her eldest sister and then moved to the outskirts of Mobile, Alabama, to live with cousins. She married her first cousin Reece Bernheimer in 1912; he died less than a year later of kidney disease. A widow at twenty-five, Lucille returned to St. Louis, where she lapsed into a deep depression; she reported in her autobiography that she wanted to end her life and drank only orange and lemon juice for a month in an effort to acquire "pernicious anemia." Her health actually improved on this regimen, however, and on the advice of a family friend, she entered the New York School of Philanthropy in 1914 to train as a social worker.

While in New York, she studied socialism at the Rand School in the evenings. She supported socialist causes for the rest of her life, although she never joined the Socialist party. After graduating from social work school in 1916, she returned to St. Louis, where she met civil libertarian Roger Baldwin. She worked with Baldwin in the St. Louis Civic League, lobbying on behalf of child labor laws. When war was declared, she turned to antiwar activities in New York in Baldwin's newly organized National Civil Liberties Bureau. After the war, she turned her attention primarily to pro-suffrage and labor organizing. For a time, she worked in a factory in New York City to learn firsthand what it was like to participate in labor organizing. She became secretary of the American Civil Liberties Union (ACLU) when it was formed in 1920. Later that year she married Joseph Milner, a real estate broker and philosopher, with whom she had twin girls two years later.

For the next twenty-five years Milner was deeply involved in all ACLU activities, including the famous Scopes "monkey" trial, the Sacco and Vanzetti defense, and the defense of Communists threatened with deportation. Milner handled all correspondence for the union and clipped newspaper stories on potential cases, including Tennessee's ban on the teaching of evolution, and sent them to the board of directors for possible action. During the 1930s, she was also a delegate to the Congress of the League against Anti-Semitism, the Conférence Mondiale des Femmes in Paris, and the World Peace Congress in Brussels, and she was an investigator for the American Committee against Fascist Oppression in Germany.

Milner's long-standing relations with the ACLU began to sour in the late 1930s. As the anti-Communist polemics of the Red Scare grew more intense, the board of directors of the union first forced the resignation of Dr. Harry Ward by adopting a qualification for membership, known as the 1940 resolution, that excluded anyone who supported "any form of totalitarian government." The board later voted to oust Elizabeth Gurley Flynn for her open membership in the Communist party. As secretary, Milner had no vote on the board, but she was present at all the meetings at which the fate of Ward and Flynn were discussed. In her autobiography, published more than a decade later, she called her failure to protest the purge of Communists in the ACLU a source of continual regret. Moreover, the purge was undertaken with what Milner called the "collaboration" of her old friend Roger Baldwin. She speculated that the divisions within the ACLU surfaced only because the Roosevelt administration was so protective of civil liberties, and thus liberals had leisure to contemplate their differences, instead of battling governments to protect the rights of dissidents. There is evidence, however, that the ACLU was a potential target of the Dies Committee, a congressional body hunting for Communists.

Milner's final split with the ACLU did not come until 1945, after she and others on the Left unsuccessfully attempted to keep the organization from intervening on behalf of American fascist groups, which had been indicted for seditious conspiracy. As she wrote in her autobiography, her investigations for the ACLU's Committee on War Cases convinced her that hundreds of these groups had in fact been employed by Adolf Hitler and had plotted "to destroy American national unity." She resigned in protest, saying that the "Civil Liberties Union had lost its old meaning for me."

Upon her "retirement," as she called it, Milner spent ten years writing her autobiographical account of her political education and her activities on behalf of the ACLU. After the publication in 1954 of her book, which received little notice, Milner faded from public view. She died in New York City.

• The primary source on her life is Milner's own political autobiography, *The Education of an American Liberal* (1954). She also defended the rights of free speech, labor unions, and conscientious objectors in "Freedom of Speech in Wartime," *New Republic*, 25 Nov. 1940, pp. 713–15; "Labor in a National Emergency," *New Republic*, 7 Apr. 1941, pp. 57–59; and, with Groff Conklin, "Conscience in Wartime," *Harper's*, Oct. 1939, pp. 503–9. Her role in the ACLU is discussed in Samuel Walker, *In Defense of American Liberties: A History of the ACLU* (1990), and is mentioned in many of the works cited in Walker's bibliography. An obituary appears in the *New York Times*, 18 Aug. 1975.

SARAH BARRINGER GORDON

MILROY, Robert Huston (11 June 1816–29 Mar. 1890), soldier and lawyer, was born in Washington County, Indiana, the son of Samuel Milroy, a soldier and farmer, and Martha Huston. Samuel Milroy was a major general in the Indiana militia, seeing active service in the War of 1812 and minor campaigns against American Indians in Kentucky and Indiana. From an early age Robert Milroy wanted very much to pursue his father's career. He attended Norwich University in Northfield, Vermont, from 1840 to 1843 and graduated with a bachelor of arts and a master of military science. His failure to secure an appointment to the U.S. Military Academy at West Point (and thereby an appointment in the regular army) almost certainly initiated a pattern of resentment toward professional soldiers that characterized much of his later life.

Returning to Indiana after graduation, he farmed until the outbreak of the Mexican War in 1846. Milroy enthusiastically raised a company of volunteers from Carroll County, Indiana, that was sent to New Orleans after being mustered into federal service on 20 June 1846. Despite his martial ardor, his unit did no fighting, and he was mustered out along with his unit at New Orleans on 16 June 1847.

Milroy then returned to Indiana and civilian life. In 1849 he married Mary Jane Armitage; they had seven children. After studying law at Indiana University, he received a bachelor of laws degree in 1850 and was admitted to the bar. In the next few years his law practice flourished, allowing Milroy to become a prominent man in Indiana legal and political circles. In 1850 he was elected a delegate to the state's second constitutional convention. In 1851 he was appointed as a circuit court judge for the Eighth District, but he resigned that position in 1854 to take up a law practice in Rensselaer, Indiana. In 1856, primarily because of his staunch abolitionist convictions, he joined the infant Republican party and supported John C. Frémont for president.

With the election of Abraham Lincoln in 1860 and the outbreak of the war in the following year, Milroy again served as an important organizer for Indiana volunteers. He raised a company of ninety-day volunteers from Rensselaer in April 1861 and was elected captain of the company and later colonel of its parent regiment, the Ninth Indiana Volunteer Infantry. After the company's term of service expired, he reenlisted for three years. On 3 September 1861 he was appointed brigadier general of volunteers, and in March 1863 he was promoted to major general, to rank from November 1862.

From June to September 1861 Milroy was assigned to the command of George B. McClellan, who was operating in the mountainous western region of Virginia (now W.Va.). Under McClellan, Milroy waged a relentless counterinsurgency campaign against Confederate guerrillas operating throughout the region. While Milroy was successful in suppressing these guerrillas, his tenacity and at times heavy-handed dealings with Confederate sympathizers among the civilian population made his name odious among many Virginians. The Confederate government in Richmond reacted by putting a bounty on his head.

Milroy's promotion to major general was given in a recognition of his success in western Virginia against the Confederate guerrillas. Upon his promotion to major general, he was made commander of the Second Division of the VIII Army Corps. In the spring of 1863 his command was headquartered at Winchester, Virginia, a strategic location near the intersection of the Shenandoah and Potomac river valleys. From 13 June to 15 June 1863 his division came under fierce and repeated attack by Richard Ewell's corps of Robert E. Lee's Army of Northern Virginia, intent on the invasion of Pennsylvania. Milroy resisted as best he could, but all of his positions were overrun, and the remnants of his forces retreated in the direction of Harpers Ferry. Major General Henry W. Halleck, in Washington, D.C., blamed Milroy for the critical loss of Winchester and the advance of the Confederates into Pennsylvania. Milroy insisted that he had deterred the advance of the Confederate army for several critical days, allowing the bulk of George G. Meade's army to catch Lee at Gettysburg. In August 1863 a military court of inquiry exonerated Milroy's conduct at Winchester, but he was not offered a significant command for the remainder of the war. Milroy attributed this slight to Halleck and the "West Point clique" that he felt was ascendant within the Union army.

After the war ended Milroy held a number of prominent positions in business and government. In 1868 he became a trustee of the Wabash and Erie Canal. From 1872 until 1885 he held a succession of federal patronage positions under Republican administrations within the Bureau of Indian Affairs in the state of Washington. He died in Olympia, Washington.

Milroy was known to his soldiers as the "Gray Eagle" for his tall, gaunt frame and flowing hair. His impressive outward appearance, though, concealed a man consumed by slights both real and imagined. His most important contribution to the war effort was his stern campaign to keep western Virginia in the Union, which contributed to the creation of the state of West Virginia in 1863. The loss at Winchester, however, sent his military career into permanent decline, a fate he unfortunately shared with many other regular and volunteer generals in the Civil War. To his last days he remained resentful that his talents as a soldier were not realized to the extent he had always hoped.

• Milroy is mentioned in *The War of the Rebellion: A Compilation of the Official Records of the Union and Confederate Armies* (128 vols., 1880–1901); see esp. 1st ser., 30; 3d ser., 2 and 3; and 4th ser., 2. An article-length account of his military career and life in Indiana is Cary C. Collins, "Gray Eagle: Major General Robert Huston Milroy and the Civil War," *Indiana Magazine of History* 90 (Mar. 1994): 48–72. An account of the battle at Winchester covering Milroy's defensive preparations is in Richard Wheeler, *Witness to Gettysburg*, chap. 4 (1987). The Confederate side of the battle of Winchester, emphasizing Milroy's unpopularity with the Confederate population, is covered by Douglas Southall Freeman, *Lee's Lieutenants*, vol. 3, *Gettysburg to Appomattox*, chap. 2 (1944).

JAMES K. HOGUE

MILSTEIN, Nathan Mironovich (31 Dec. 1903–21 Dec. 1992), concert violinist, was born in Odessa, Russia, the son of Miron Milstein, a fabric importer and merchant, and Maria Bluestein. Born into an assimilated Russian Jewish family, Milstein was educated by a governess and tutors rather than at the Gymnasium. His mother encouraged him to learn the violin at an early age, and he later recalled the two pianos in his home and reminisced that "our house was filled with music." As a child he also learned to play the cello (well enough to teach his brother and, years later, accompany David Oistrakh) and viola (well enough, years later, to accompany Sergey Rachmaninoff). His sister Sara studied piano and accompanied him during some of his first recitals. He also showed an early interest in art, and, though he received no formal training, painting remained a serious hobby for the rest of his life.

Milstein studied violin first with Pyotr Stolyarsky in Odessa, where fellow students included Josef Roisman and David Oistrakh. At age eleven he performed Aleksandr Glazunov's violin concerto at a concert in Odessa in honor of the composer's anniversary. He liked to tell the story of how Glazunov encouraged him to perform his own innovative interpretation. In 1916 Milstein and his mother moved to St. Petersburg where he studied with the celebrated professor Leopold Auer at the St. Petersburg Conservatory. Auer's students included Jascha Heifetz, Mischa Elman, and Efrem Zimbalist. From the start Auer prepared Milstein for a career as a soloist.

In the wake of the February Revolution in 1917, Milstein and his mother returned to Odessa where he began to perform as a soloist throughout Ukraine. In the winter of 1921 he met and began playing regularly with Vladimir Horowitz. Anatoly Lunacharsky, the commissar of education, promoted their careers, dubbing them "Children of the Soviet Revolution." They moved to Moscow and played throughout the Soviet Union to enthusiastic audiences, especially in St. Petersburg. In 1923 they presented the Russian premiers of Karol Szymanowski's and Sergey Prokofiev's first violin concerti.

Milstein and Horowitz were officially encouraged to travel to the West for purposes of cultural propaganda. Milstein left for Berlin on Christmas Day 1925. There he joined Horowitz; the two soon moved to Paris, where they formed part of a vital émigré community. Disenchanted with developments in Russia, they eventually decided not to return, and Milstein remained critical of Soviet communism for the rest of his life. He never returned to perform.

Milstein's first concerts in Germany had little effect, perhaps in part because of an inadequate instrument. But with successful recitals in Spain and South America, he began a series of international tours that continued for over half a century. His Viennese debut (featuring works of Glazunov and Pyotr Ilich Tchaikovsky) was attended by Alban Berg and Arnold Schoenberg. He played with all the major orchestras. Skeptical of the competence of many conductors, he occasionally performed (and recorded) without a conductor. Avoiding overperforming, he also avoided taking a "sabbatical" from his concert tours; consequently, he enjoyed one of the longest and most successful careers of any concert violinist.

In 1926 Milstein sought to continue his formal study with Eugène Ysaÿe, but he remarked that he "learned almost nothing" from that master. Joachim W. Hartnack concludes in *Grosse Geiger unserer Zeit* (1968) that Milstein's artistic conception and his technique were largely self-formed. His playing was distinguished by a lightly balanced bow grip, an exceptionally warm, radiant tone, and restrained vibrato.

Milstein made his United States debut in 1929 under Leopold Stokowski and the Philadelphia Orchestra and appeared that same year with the New York Philharmonic. In 1929 he moved to New York, and in 1942 became a U.S. citizen. After the war he moved to London and spent most of his time in England and Switzerland. After a first marriage, to Rita (maiden name unknown), ended, in 1945 he wed his second wife Thérèse Kauffman, and they had a daughter, Maria Bernadette. He named his 1716 Stradivarius, which he acquired in 1945, the "Maria Thérèse" in their honor.

In addition to a distinguished career as a performer, Milstein offered master classes in Zurich and at Juilliard. He composed pieces that have been widely performed, including "Paganiniana," an arrangement of themes by Niccolò Paganini, cadenzas for the Beethoven and Brahms concerti, and transcriptions of pieces by Prokofiev, Tchaikovsky, Modest Petrovich Mussorgsky, Frédéric-François Chopin, and Franz Liszt.

Milstein's special passions included the music of Johann Sebastian Bach, the Romantics, and works of Glazunov, Rachmaninoff, and other Russians. He helped popularize Bach's violin repertoire, twice recording Bach's unaccompanied sonatas and partitas. A friend of Rachmaninoff since 1931, Milstein paid moving tribute to him in his autobiography at a time when most serious musicians no longer esteemed Rachmaninoff's music. An enthusiastic follower of futurist theater in Russia, he admired some avant-garde music, especially Berg's violin concerto, though he was critical of much twentieth-century music. Milstein's early tastes ran to bravura performers, and in Russia he had bought every record available by Fritz

Kreisler, whose technique he thought exceptional. But in later years he insisted on the need for restraint, particularly in interpreting baroque and classical works.

Popular with audiences and among the highest-paid classical soloists of his time, Milstein stood out in an age of extraordinary virtuosi. His interpretations were also widely praised by critics. Harold C. Schonberg wrote that he may have been "the most nearly perfect violinist of his time." Bernard Gavoty hailed him as "one of the four or five best violinists of his time." Milstein's masterly technique appealed to the younger generation of violinists. Pinchas Zukerman praised him as a violinist of "perfect technique and profound feeling."

Milstein received many honors, including the Légion d'honneur, the Ehrenkreuz, and the Academy of St. Cecilia. His recording of Bach's unaccompanied sonatas and partitas won a Grammy Award in 1975. He was honored with the Kennedy Center Award for lifetime achievement in 1987. Milstein gave his last public recital in Stockholm in 1986. A broken arm subsequently forced his complete retirement. He died at home in London.

• Some of Milstein's letters are included in the Henry Edward Voegili Collection, Chicago Historical Society Library. Important biographical details are in his charming memoirs, written with Solomon Volkov, *From Russia to the West: The Musical Memoirs and Reminiscences of Nathan Milstein*, trans. Antonina W. Bouis (1990). Milstein was the frequent subject of critical reviews and articles. Monographs include Bernard Gavoty, *Nathan Milstein* (1956), and David Ewen, *Men and Women Who Make Music* (1939; repr. 1945). Milstein shunned media attention, but his performance of the Kreutzer Sonata during his last recital was widely televised, and much of that concert, together with documentary interviews, is available on video as *Nathan Milstein: Master of Invention: Some Memories of a Quiet Magician* (1992). An obituary by Harold C. Schonberg appears in the *New York Times*, 22 Dec. 1992.

MICHAEL H. HOFFHEIMER

MILTON, John (20 Apr. 1807–1 Apr. 1865), Confederate governor of Florida, was born in Louisville, Georgia, the son of Elizabeth Jane Robinson and Homer Virgil Milton, a moderately successful planter. He was educated at the local academy, read law in the office of Roger Gamble, and set up practice in his hometown. In 1826 he married Susan Amanda Cobb, with whom he had three children.

After two years in Louisville, Milton moved to Columbus, where he gained his first experience in politics, running unsuccessfully for Congress as a Nullifier in 1833. He is reported to have killed a man in a duel, which perhaps hastened his relocation to Mobile, Alabama, soon after the election. From 1835 to 1837 he served as a captain of Alabama volunteers in the Seminole War and subsequently lived in Marion, Alabama. His first wife died in 1840. That same year, he married Caroline Howze; they had nine children. In the early 1840s they lived in New Orleans, then in 1845 or 1846 they settled in Jackson County, Florida, outside of Marianna, where Milton built his "Sylvania" plantation. The estate grew from 2,480 acres to 7,326 by 1859, and by the outbreak of the Civil War Milton owned fifty-two slaves.

Milton returned to politics, serving as a Democratic presidential elector in 1848 and the next year winning a seat in the state senate. An active legislator, he chaired the Militia Committee but did not seek a second term. In the mid-1850s he was nominated to run for both chief justice and associate justice of the recently formed state supreme court but received neither. He remained an influential member of the Democratic party, however, and in the spring of 1860 was chairman of the state delegation at the Charleston convention. Milton worked to keep the party together, but when the split occurred, he declared that it came about because of fundamental differences between North and South.

Although not favored by incumbent Madison S. Perry, Milton gained the Democratic nomination for governor on the twenty-third ballot in 1860. That November he defeated the Constitutional Union candidate, Edward Hopkins, 6,937 votes to 5,215. Because of a peculiarity of Florida law, however, he did not take office until October 1861, leaving him technically without an official position during the secession crisis.

Animosity between Milton and Perry grew during the formative days of the Confederacy. The governor-elect felt that his predecessor was appointing unqualified men to important positions and wasting precious funds on unwise purchases. Soon after taking office, Milton wrote Jefferson Davis that Perry was "a man of strong prejudices, without very extraordinary intellectual abilities." Undoing Perry's handiwork was not an easy task. When Milton replaced many of Perry's appointees, he angered Perry's friends in the legislature, who responded by reassembling the state convention in January 1862. Milton, they charged, had concealed $21,000 of the state treasury, which he admitted, explaining that he did not want it known that this was all that was left in the treasury. Nevertheless, the convention created an executive council, composed of the lieutenant governor and three convention members, that was to share power equally with the governor.

The challenge to Milton's authority failed, however, as most of the council's resolutions actually expanded the governor's powers. The council also countermanded a convention order that a group of state troops be disbanded. The radicals rapidly lost influence, the council stopped meeting in May, and Milton was left to run the state as he saw fit. Milton could not do much without money, however, and Florida had very little. Income from taxes was minimal, and the $500,000 of state bonds authorized in February 1861 did not sell. In 1864 Milton asked the legislature to double the tax rate, but the necessarily drastic measure did not pass.

Milton was a strong believer in states' rights and protested Confederate intrusions on state sovereignty, particularly in matters that he felt threatened Florida's defense. In general, however, he was one of the most cooperative Confederate governors. The only part of the controversial conscription laws that he questioned was the "most unfortunate blunder" of not allowing for the exemption of overseers, especially since Florida law required that at least one white male live on any plantation where there were slaves. Unlike several other governors, he embraced the concept of conscription, proclaiming in August 1862, "I know no good reason why [militia officers] should not volunteer to aid in filling up the gallant regiments whose ranks have been attenuated upon the battle-field." He explained that "to maintain the Confederate Government in the existing war in support of constitutional liberty, in support of the right of free men to govern themselves for the protection of life, freedom, and property, is a sacred duty which brave and honorable men should cordially and proudly perform." When Georgia governor Joseph E. Brown asked him to join in a protest against the Confederate administration, Milton pointed out, "If each of the States should undertake to supply the wants of their citizens respectively, whether in military service or at home, the result would be alike disastrous to the Confederate States and the several States." In fact, Milton thought so highly of Davis that he named a son after him.

As the Confederacy crumbled in early 1865, Milton became physically ill from stress, and while recuperating at his plantation outside of Marianna he committed suicide. Considering the extreme difficulties that faced him while in office, he was an effective administrator and leader for his state.

• Collections of Milton's papers are at the Florida Historical Society in Tampa and the Supreme Court Library in Tallahassee. Some of his wartime correspondence is in *The War of the Rebellion: A Compilation of the Official Records of the Union and Confederate Armies* (1880–1901), especially in the fourth series, and *The Papers of Jefferson Davis*, ed. Haskell M. Monroe, Jr., et al. (1971–). Milton is the subject of William L. Gammon, "Governor John Milton of Florida . . ." (master's thesis, Univ. of Florida, 1948); and Daisy Parker, "John Milton, Governor of Florida, 1861–1865" (master's thesis, Univ. of Virginia, 1940). See also Parker, "Governor John Milton," *Tallahassee Historical Society Annual* 3 (1937): 14–21, and "John Milton, Governor of Florida: A Loyal Confederate," *Florida Historical Quarterly* 20 (Apr. 1942): 346–61. The best summary of his gubernatorial career is W. Buck Yearns's article in Yearns, ed., *The Confederate Governors* (1985). Milton is prominent in William Watson Davis, *Civil War and Reconstruction in Florida* (1913); John E. Johns, *Florida during the Civil War* (1963); and William H. Nulty, *Confederate Florida* (1990).

KENNETH H. WILLIAMS

MILTON, Tommy (1893–10 July 1962), race car driver and engineer, was born Thomas W. Milton in St. Paul, Minnesota, the son of a prosperous dairy farmer. At six feet tall and 175 pounds, Milton was a talented athlete, focusing on hockey, but an indifferent student. After only three semesters in high school in St. Paul, Milton left to pursue a newly found fascination with racing. Despite having full sight in only one eye, he soon became a champion motorcycle racer and helped to design the steel-soled boot that created the modern style of cycle racing. Increasingly intrigued by auto racing, Milton ran in his first sanctioned contest at the Minnesota Fairgrounds in 1914. He mixed his early racing career with appearances in auto daredevil shows until the famed driver Eddie Rickenbacker helped him to hone his racing skills.

During the early 1920s Milton became renowned as a driver-mechanic who relied as much on engineering talent and driving skills as a leaden foot. As a result, although he was only in his early thirties, Milton became known as the "Old Fox." In 1921 he forever solidified his reputation as a thinking person's speed demon during the Indianapolis 500. As Milton's Frontenac began to falter toward the end of the race, he doubted that he could overtake and beat back a challenge from Roscoe Sarles's smooth-running Dusenberg. Hoping to deceive Sarles instead, Milton pushed his engine to the limit and managed to pass the front-running Sarles. He grinned widely and patted his car with a gesture that Sarles interpreted to mean that Milton's car was running and could easily outrun its competition. Sarles thus decided to settle for a sure second place rather than risk a duel with Milton. Even when Milton was forced to slow down, Sarles cut his own speed, incorrectly believing that Milton was simply coasting home. Milton's maneuver not only gained him the victory at Indianapolis but also the points that ultimately marked his margin of victory over Sarles in the 1921 American Automobile Association (AAA) championship; thus Milton, who had captured the same championship in 1920, became the first driver to win consecutive driving titles.

Milton could also race "flat out," breaking Ralph De Palma's world land-speed record in 1920 by driving a Dusenberg more than 156 miles per hour on the sands at Daytona Beach, Florida. On 25 April 1920 he set the world record for the five-mile run, a mark that held up for nearly a decade. Two days later he set world land-speed records at distances of one-half and two miles. In a three-day period Milton established six speed records.

For the 1922 season Milton designed and developed his own racing engine for a Miller-built chassis; he dubbed the car the "Durant Special" in honor of his financial backer, the wealthy race car enthusiast Cliff Durant. (Milton's engine became the basis for the famed Offenhauser and Meyer-Drake engines that dominated Indianapolis-style racing for decades.) Running on the new board race tracks in California, the Durant Special proved virtually unbeatable. But in midseason Milton ran afoul of an AAA rule that required full disclosure of all sponsorship arrangements when Durant's father, who owned a car-manufacturing business in Chicago, ran advertisements that touted Milton's engine as a "Durant 4." Although Milton himself had no knowledge of this spurious claim, the AAA penalized Milton by refusing to allow him to drive his own car in any sanctioned race. As a result, he was forced to enter the 1922 Indianapolis 500 in a vehicle so hastily constructed that its gas tank fell off early in the race. Although the inexperienced Cliff Durant could do no better than eleventh place driving the Durant Special, Milton himself always insisted that he could have easily piloted it to victory in 1922.

In 1923, driving a single-seat "HCS Special" (built by Stutz) at a dirt track in Syracuse, New York, Milton set a world record for a one-mile track by turning the distance in 42.28 seconds, or 85.14 miles per hour. That same year he recorded his second victory in the Indianapolis 500, a feat that made him the first two-time winner of the Memorial Day classic. After qualifying his HCS Special at a record-breaking speed, Milton—with relief-driving from Howdy Wilcox—won without resort to the kind of psychological ploy he had used two years earlier.

Although Milton felt that he should have been Indianapolis's first three-time winner, his 1923 win brought vindication; it also marked the apogee of his racing career. Despite capturing Indianapolis and setting his dirt track speed record, Milton failed to win that year's driving championship. In the 1924 Indianapolis 500, after having qualified third, he encountered valve problems and became the second driver to leave the race that year. Milton rebounded to finish in fifth place in 1925 and in eighth in 1927, his last year of racing at Indianapolis.

After many years of working for Packard and heading his own successful engineering company in Detroit, Milton returned to Indianapolis in 1949 as the chief steward of the race. During the 1950 race his decision to halt the contest after 138 laps, during an apparently brief rainshower, sparked immediate complaints from drivers who had hoped to overtake the leader (and winner), Johnny Parsons. But Milton's reputation as the "Old Fox" was quickly confirmed when the speedway was engulfed in a sudden deluge that could have produced a series of catastrophic accidents. Milton remained a beloved figure at the Indianapolis Motor Speedway, greatly respected for his command of racing lore; he returned every year until illness forced him to miss the 1962 running of the 500. Despondent over his failing health, Milton committed suicide at his palatial home in Mount Clemons, Michigan.

• Milton's career is nicely covered in Peter De Paolo, *Wall Smacker* (1935). See also Lyle Kenyon Engel, *The Indianapolis "500": The World's Most Exciting Auto Race*, rev. ed. (1972); and John Bentley, *Great American Automobiles* (1957). The story of Milton's travail with his "Durant Special" is recounted in Jack C. Fox, "What's in a Name," *The Indianapolis 500 Year Book* (1975), pp. 148–49. A very informative obituary-homage to Milton is in the *Detroit News*, 11 July 1962.

NORMAN L. ROSENBERG

MINER, Alonzo Ames (17 Aug. 1814–14 June 1895), Universalist minister, was born in Lempster, New Hampshire, the son of Benajah Ames Miner and Amanda Carey, farmers. He was self-educated although he did study from time to time at several New Hampshire and Vermont town schools. By the time he was sixteen he had acquired sufficient knowledge to become a teacher and for several years taught at Hanover, New Hampshire, and Cavendish, Vermont, before becoming head from 1835 to 1839 of the Unity (N.H.) Scientific and Military Academy. In 1836 he married his childhood friend, Maria S. Perley, who then became the academy's preceptress; they did not have children.

Miner's parents were intensely devout Universalists and reared their children in what Universalists liked to call "the larger faith." It was natural for him, therefore, while teaching also to preach at the Universalist congregations adjacent to Unity. He soon realized that ministry was his true vocation, and in 1838, while continuing to teach, he accepted the pulpit of the Universalist society at Chester, Vermont. The next year he gave up his teaching career, was ordained by the New Hampshire Universalist Convention, and faithfully promoted the larger faith until his death.

After brief pastorates at Methuen, Massachusetts (1839–1842), and at the Second Universalist Church, Lowell, Massachusetts (1842–1848), he succeeded Hosea Ballou, the denomination's most prominent theologian and minister in the early part of the nineteenth century, as pastor of the Second Universalist Society in the town of Boston. He occupied this pulpit for the next forty-three years. Its first building was on School Street, but in 1872 the society, responding to commercial developments and to the resulting shift of Protestant families from the north and west ends to the south end of the city, relocated to Columbus Avenue, where they erected a large stone Victorian Gothic structure.

Although Miner was a more conservative theologian than most of his denominational colleagues, he nonetheless was highly regarded by them. An example of their esteem was his selection as preacher of the centennial sermon to be delivered at the great gathering of the Universalist General Convention at Gloucester, Massachusetts, in 1870, during which the movement celebrated its first one hundred years in America. In his sermon Miner, after dismissing the discoveries of modern science, surveyed in great detail the concept of the salvation of all souls from the first Christian century down to the nineteenth century. For him the love of God for all persons, as revealed by God's Son, the Christ, and taught by John Murray, Hosea Ballou, and the other founding fathers, remained the firm foundation of the Universalist church. As a result, eloquent as the sermon was, it was in many ways the "last hurrah" for this interpretation of Christian Universalism, for the next generation of church leaders would accept the ideas behind the findings of science and use them to build a different framework for the Universalist faith.

In 1852 the Universalists founded their first institution of higher learning, Tufts College, in Medford, Massachusetts. After the death of its founding president, Hosea Ballou 2nd in 1861, the trustees, faced with growing financial problems, the outbreak of the Civil War, and the refusal of several Universalist leaders to accept the job of president, finally approached

Miner. He accepted on the condition that he be allowed to continue as pastor of the Second Society. His chief accomplishment as president (1862–1875) was in the area of fundraising. During his tenure the school's endowment increased by more than $700,000, and the first three endowed teaching chairs were created. After he had established a strong financial base for the college, Miner moved to broaden its student base by initiating an engineering department and a divinity school. It was largely through Miner's efforts that Tufts did not close its doors in the 1860s.

Miner was not a significant author; neither was he extremely active in the reform movements of his time. He was, however, a vigorous opponent of alcohol and twice ran for governor on the Prohibition ticket. As president of the Massachusetts Temperance Alliance for ten years he enjoyed debating against those who favored the "liquor interests." Ever committed to education, Miner also served for twenty-four years on the Massachusetts State Board of Education. Both Tufts and Harvard awarded him honorary degrees for his contributions to higher education.

He died in Boston. At his memorial service Edward Everett Hale spoke for the larger Boston community:

> He was not one of those speculative theorists who had to sit back in a closet because the hands were rough from hard work, or the language was ungrammatical, or the dress of the people with whom he was to meet in the cause of duty was unfashionable. He was democratic through and through. . . . He believed in the people, and he threw himself upon the people in the discharge of any duty. I have no wonder that the people recognized the courage of such a leader and were ready to follow where he went before.

Miner's great legacy to the future, however, remains the work he accomplished at Tufts.

• The bulk of Miner's papers is at Wessell Library, Tufts University, which also has the archives of the university for the period when he was its president. His marriage and funeral records (1838–1895) and the records of the Second Universalist Church in Lowell and those of the Second Universalist Society in Boston are at the Library of the Harvard Divinity School, Cambridge, Mass. An example of his lecture style is *The Old Forts Taken* (1878). The standard biography is George H. Emerson, *Life of Alonzo Ames Miner* (1896). For a modern assessment see Russell E. Miller, *Light on the Hill: A History of Tufts College 1852–1952* (1966); also see his *The Larger Hope: The First Century of the Universalist Church in America 1770–1870* (1978). George Huntston Williams, *American Universalism: A Bicentennial Historical Essay* (1971), is the best source for an understanding of Miner's theology.

ALAN SEABURG

MINER, Dorothy Eugenia (4 Nov. 1904–15 May 1973), curator of manuscripts, librarian, and art historian, was born in New York City, the daughter of Roy Waldo Miner, a marine biologist, and Anna Elizabeth Carroll. In 1906 Miner's father became a curator at the American Museum of Natural History in New York.

Miner graduated from Barnard College in 1926, majoring in English and classics, and then studied medieval literature at Bedford College, University of London, as the first Barnard International Fellow. In February 1928 she began her graduate studies in art history at Columbia University as a Carnegie Fellow. Graduate instruction in the history of art, and in particular in medieval illuminated manuscripts, was just beginning at this time. Under the direction of Meyer Schapiro, Miner began a doctoral dissertation on an illustrated Carolingian Apocalypse manuscript of about A.D. 800 in Trier. Her research took her to Europe again in 1929 to 1930 to study manuscripts in European libraries. On her return she studied for another year at Columbia on a President's Fellowship, and from 1931 she taught art history at Barnard. She never completed her dissertation; her entry into the museum world soon directed her energies elsewhere.

In 1933 Miner was hired by the Pierpont Morgan Library to assist with the catalog of the country's first exhibition devoted to illuminated manuscripts. The director of the Morgan Library, Belle da Costa Greene, became her mentor and no doubt recommended her for the position of keeper of manuscripts at a new museum in Baltimore, the Walters Art Gallery, housing some 23,000 works of art bequeathed to that city by Henry Walters in 1931, was scheduled to open in November 1934. For the next thirty-nine years, it was the center of Miner's life.

When she arrived in Baltimore in September 1934, Miner was one of five young art historians faced with preparing the Walters collection to open just two months later. The exhausting work was tempered by excitement at the daily discovery of unknown works of art. During this process, which continued through the 1930s, Miner regularly sought the advice of specialists and thus forged lasting ties with other medieval scholars.

Researching and caring for the Walters Art Gallery's varied and undocumented collections broadened Miner's knowledge and honed her professional skills. In addition to being keeper of manuscripts, she took charge of the collections of Islamic art and acquired expertise in that field; she served as librarian for both the rare book collection and the reference library; and she edited the Walters publications. Like many professional women of her time, she never married and was therefore able to devote most of her extraordinary energy to serving the gallery. Despite her active support of many outside organizations and institutions, her dedication to the Walters was total and uncompromising: in later life, she chided a younger colleague for having held positions in several museums, which she considered flighty.

Miner's scholarly writing grew largely out of her interest in solving problems posed by the books and manuscripts in her care and by their history. "A manuscript, like a person, is often more interesting if it has faced the world instead of leading a life of seclusion," she once wrote in a short article titled "Manuscript Sleuthing" (*Bulletin of the Walters Art Gallery*, Nov.

1950). Her daily contact with the manuscripts in her charge heightened her innate sensitivity to their physical structure and design. At a time when many art historians studied manuscript illumination out of context, she focused on the interrelationship between page, text, image, decoration, and binding as quintessential to the nature of a manuscript, anticipating the discipline of codicology, which came into its own only after her death. Equally in advance of her time was her interest in the ways medieval books were made and used in their social context. A study published in collaboration with Grace Frank in 1937, *Proverbes en rimes: Text and Illustrations of the Fifteenth Century from a French Manuscript in the Walters Art Gallery*, analyzes a book made for merchant-class readers, exploring the relationship between text and image, a subject that did not become popular for another forty years or more. It also broaches another unstudied topic on which she was to become an authority, that of how illustrations and ornament were copied and transmitted in the Middle Ages. Her efforts to expand the Walters collection led to detective work and to an art-historical analysis of her acquisitions, culminating in a two-part article, "Since De Ricci: Western Illuminated Manuscripts Acquired since 1934" (*Journal of the Walters Art Gallery* [1966–1967, 1968–1969]).

Miner's most enduring writings were the exhibition catalogs she produced for the Walters. Preparing exhibitions gave Miner particular pleasure, and she did so on a small scale from the 1930s on. It was not, however, until after World War II that resources permitted her to mount major exhibitions. These were installed at the Baltimore Museum of Art for want of sufficient space at the Walters. Four pioneering exhibitions constituted landmarks: *Illuminated Books of the Middle Ages and Renaissance* in 1949 and *The History of Bookbinding, 525–1950 A.D.* in 1957, both entirely organized and cataloged by Miner; in 1952, *The World Encompassed: An Exhibition of the History of Maps*, organized jointly with the Peabody Institute Library and the John Work Garrett Library of the Johns Hopkins University; and in 1965, *2,000 Years of Calligraphy*, a three-part exhibition at the Baltimore Museum of Art, the Peabody Institute Library, and the Walters Art Gallery. All were unprecedented surveys of American holdings in particular areas. Miner was also the major instigator of *Early Christian and Byzantine Art* (1947) and *The International Style: The Arts in Europe around 1400* (1962). She put many of her talents to use in preparing both the exhibitions and the catalogs: her ability to elicit the collaboration of collectors and of colleagues in other institutions; her meticulous research skills; her talent for bringing objects to life in descriptions of the greatest technical precision; her ability to synthesize a subject in a manner instructive to both the layman and the specialist; and her pleasing sense of design.

Miner's critically acclaimed exhibition catalogs, which remain important reference works, are among the publications that she edited anonymously, insisting that the credit should go to the Walters Art Gallery. In the same way, she tirelessly edited exhibition catalogs outside her own field as well as several major catalogs of the Walters collections. She was the initiator of the *Journal of the Walters Art Gallery* and was its editor from 1938 until 1969. The *Journal* was the first scholarly periodical produced by an American museum and became the model for many others. Miner's tact and hard work obtained articles of the highest standard from carefully chosen contributors. Similar but still more exacting effort went into her greatest editorial endeavor, *Studies in Art and Literature for Belle da Costa Greene* (1954), a monumental tribute comprising articles by fifty-one authors, including the foremost authorities in their fields.

Those who knew Miner were struck by the warmth of her personality, the enthusiasm with which she discussed the works in her care, and the generosity with which she shared her learning and love of books with scholars, students, and the general public. To stimulate children's interest in the Middle Ages, she designed the first museum coloring book. Her gift for communicating excitement as well as knowledge inspired her students at the Johns Hopkins University, where she served as a visiting lecturer, as well as the specialist and lay audiences of her many lectures. Her festschrift, *Gatherings in Honor of Dorothy E. Miner*, testifies to the admiration, gratitude, and friendship of a distinguished roster of medievalists and other scholars. Learning and teaching were central to Miner's work. As scholar and educator, she made a lasting impression on academic art historians and museum professionals.

• Miner's professional correspondence and papers are preserved at the Walters Art Gallery, Baltimore, Md. A complete bibliography of her published writings is to be found in *Gatherings in Honor of Dorothy E. Miner*, ed. Ursula E. McCracken et al. (1974), pp. xiii–xviii. The most extensive published account of Miner's life is Claire Richter Sherman, "Dorothy Eugenia Miner (1904–1973): The Varied Career of a Medievalist: Scholar and Keeper of Manuscripts, Librarian and Editor at the Walters Art Gallery," in *Women as Interpreters of the Visual Arts, 1820–1979*, ed. Claire Richter Sherman with Adele M. Holcomb (1981), pp. 377–409. This includes a selective bibliography. Obituaries are in the *Baltimore Sun*, 16 May 1973, and the *New York Times*, 17 May 1973.

ELIZABETH BURIN

MINER, Sarah Luella (30 Oct. 1861–2 Dec. 1935), missionary educator in China, was born in Oberlin, Ohio, the daughter of Daniel Irenaeus Miner, a missionary and teacher, and Lydia Jane Cooley. One of seven children and the only survivor among the eldest four, Luella received the special and solitary attention of her father in the family's posts on the Kansas plains and at Tougaloo University in Mississippi. She graduated from the normal department at Tougaloo, the only white student in her class.

From Tougaloo she went to Oberlin, where she graduated in 1884 with a reputation for skill as a debater in the sex-segregated debating societies. (She was elected to Phi Beta Kappa when the Oberlin chapter was established in 1905.) Although she felt she lacked a clear call, a strong tradition on both sides of her family made missionary service a "natural development," as her sister observed. She taught in Lexington, Kentucky, and at Fisk University with the American Missionary Association from 1884 to 1887 in preparation for the foreign field.

Miner arrived at the American Board of Commissioners for Foreign Missions (ABCFM) station in Paotingfu, Chihli (Baoding, Hebei), China, in 1887. Initially restricted from free movement outside the mission compound and overcome by loneliness, she threw herself into the study of Chinese, developing close relationships with her language tutors and completing in five months a course of study expected to take eighteen months. Miner's linguistic expertise, which included training in *wenli*, the literary language, distinguished her from other missionaries of both sexes.

In 1888 Miner was transferred to teach at North China College for men at Tungchow (Tongxian). The college was perpetually understaffed, and Miner taught theology and geology (for which she wrote a standard Chinese text) and, by 1890, biology, political economy, and international law. Despite her own reserve, Miner found that her fluency in Chinese and her foreign status earned her free passage across China's strict gender barriers. She did not receive the same respect at mission meetings, however, where Miner, like other women, was neither allowed to vote nor expected to speak.

Imprisoned by antiforeign Boxers in 1900, Miner published "Prisoner in Peking" in the November issue of the *Outlook* and returned to the United States something of a celebrity. She remained until 1903, partially supporting herself through translations and her writing for mainstream journals. During those years Miner published two books, *China's Book of Martyrs* (1903) and *Two Heroes of Cathay* (1903), both of which celebrated the sufferings and heroism of Chinese Christians. Miner also went on speaking tours, noting that her writing gave her "access to pulpits which otherwise might be closed to a woman."

In 1903 Miner returned to Peking as principal of Bridgman Academy for girls. In 1905 she organized China's first women's college, North China Union Women's College (NCUWC). Miner responded to the challenges of modern China with political and curricular progressivism and moral conservatism, lamenting that university students had "learned far more of 'liberty' . . . than they have of self-control." Sometimes uncomfortable with her role "as female seminary ogre," she gained entrance to Peking reform circles, which had emerged in elite society following the Boxer defeat, where she provided lecture series and support for Manchu women newly emerging in public. She responded with excitement to the 1911 revolution and with her Chinese friends helped form the Committee for the Protection of Women and Children.

Miner headed both Bridgman (until 1913) and NCUWC (until 1920) regularly laboring with inadequate funding and staff and sometimes teaching overflow classes to give her new faculty time to study Chinese. She took a year off from her duties in 1914–1915 in order to restore her energies and to assist in the reorganization of a training school for Chinese "Bible women," lay workers who proselytized among women and children. Thereafter she negotiated the merger of NCUWC with the Methodist Board's Peking University and the American Board's North China College to constitute the new Yenching University, which would become one of China's preeminent universities in the interwar years. Following the merger, in 1920 Miner assumed the title of dean of the women's college, which she held until 1922, resigning from that position under pressure from some faculty and the president of Yenching, John Leighton Stuart. Some accounts suggest that Miner's efforts to preserve the autonomy of the women's college had drawn her into conflict with Stuart, a situation that continued to plague her associate of several years, Alice Seymour Browne Frame. After this painful separation from the institution that she had built, Miner went to Cheeloo (Shantung Christian) University in Tsinan (Jinan), where she served as professor of religious education and sometime dean of women until her death.

Miner's institutional contribution lay in women's education, but her writings, in the mission press and in regular long journal-letters circulated at home, especially championed Chinese political and cultural autonomy. When she unsuccessfully backed a former student to become principal of Bridgman Academy in the 1910s, she was among the first missionaries to support the replacement of foreign with indigenous leadership. At the conclusion of World War I, when the Versailles signatories acquiesced to Japan's claims in Shantung (Shandong), Miner joined in the nationalist outcries of the May 4 Movement. She was especially proud of her participation in the interdenominational and Chinese-dominated National Christian Council in the 1920s and made a marked contribution to the politics of missions in 1927 when, as a Chinese delegate to the International Missionary Council at Jerusalem, she sponsored and spoke for a motion renouncing foreign military protection. China's "awakening," as she saw it, was the great drama and joy of her life.

• The vast ABCFM Papers at Houghton Library, Harvard University, Cambridge, Mass., include materials on Miner in several different subcollections. Miner's personal papers, including her formal writings, excerpted letters to her family, her journal-letters designed for circulation, and tributes by others, are archived in the Personal Papers section. See the Women's Board section for Miner's correspondence to the Woman's Board of Missions of the Interior from her North China postings. Oberlin College in Oberlin, Ohio, has a file on Miner and information about her parents in the Alumni and Development Records in the College Archives. Miner wrote frequently for the *Missionary Herald*. The most complete biography is unpublished, Robert E. Chandler, "Woman—Pioneer—Saint," and is located in the Biographical Collection of the ABCFM papers. For particularly valuable additional accounts of her life, see Mary H. Porter, *Luella*

Miner: A Sketch, a pamphlet of the Woman's Board of Missions of the Interior (1916). See also Dwight W. Edwards, *Yenching University* (1959); Jane Hunter, *The Gospel of Gentility: American Women Missionaries in Turn-of-the-Century China* (1984); Harold S. Matthews, *Seventy-Five Years of the North China Mission* (1942); and Philip West, *Yenching University and Sino-Western Relations, 1916–1952* (1976). Obituaries are in the *Missionary Herald*, Feb. 1936, and the *New York Times*, 4 Dec. 1935.

JANE H. HUNTER

MINER, Worthington (13 Nov. 1900–11 Dec. 1982), theater director and television producer, was born Worthington Coswell Miner in Buffalo, New York, the son of Worthington C. Miner, a lawyer, and Margaret Willard, a dressmaker. After interrupting his studies at Yale University to join the U.S. Army and serve in France and Germany during World War I, Miner graduated with Phi Beta Kappa honors from Yale in 1922 and went to England to study at Cambridge University's Magdalene College. "Had it not been for my two years at Magdalene College," Miner reminisced in an interview with Franklin Schaffner, "my career in theatre would never have been. I might have become a teacher, I might have imported woolens and worsteds from Verviers, I might have built mousetraps, but I would never have known the feel or the smell of a Broadway stage." After some work as a prompter and stage manager at a dramatic club in England, Miner decided to try his luck in New York, where he returned in late 1924.

Between 1924 and 1929 he worked regularly as an actor, a stage manager, and an assistant to prominent Broadway producers such as Guthrie McClintic and Jed Harris. Then between 1929 and 1939 he directed a string of thirty plays, including Robert E. Sherwood's *Reunion in Vienna*, starring Alfred Lunt and Lynn Fontanne (1931); Maxwell Anderson's *Both Your Houses* (1933); and Irwin Shaw's *Bury the Dead* (1938). During the summers of 1933 and 1934 Miner also worked as a film director and writer at RKO Radio Pictures. In 1938 he was elected to the executive board of the Theatre Guild.

For all of these accomplishments, however, Miner had still yet to enter the profession for which he is most remembered. In 1939 he became director of program development at the Columbia Broadcasting System's new television network, and by 1942 he was managing the entire television department, producing and directing all fifteen hours of CBS's weekly schedule of news, sports, music, variety, and quiz programs. Miner developed and produced many series during his tenure at CBS, four of which set standards for the emerging genres of the infant medium. "Toast of the Town" (later retitled "The Ed Sullivan Show"), which debuted in 1948, became the longest running variety show in television history, juxtaposing standard vaudeville acts with both popular and classical musical performances. The following year saw the start of the TV version of radio's "The Goldbergs," one of television's earliest situation comedies, and "Mr. I. Magination," an enduring model for future children's shows.

Worthington Miner is best remembered, however, as the producer and principal force behind "Studio One," a live dramatic anthology series that ran from 1948 through 1958. An anchor series in what became known as the "golden age of television," Miner's leadership was unique because he concentrated on the visual qualities of a medium that was at the time almost entirely dependent on writers. "With Studio One," Miner reported in his oral memoirs, "with all my productions, in fact, the accent was to be on direction." Future luminaries such as Schaffner, George Roy Hill, and Sidney Lumet received early training as directors of "Studio One." Miner also hired a stable of highly qualified writers. Rod Serling, Gore Vidal, and Reginald Rose, all celebrated authors of the golden age, contributed to the show. Rose wrote one of the era's most memorable episodes, "Twelve Angry Men," for a 1954 installment of "Studio One."

Miner in 1952 left CBS for NBC, where he is most remembered for developing "Medic," a breakthrough program treating medical issues in graphic detail, and "Frontier." After leaving NBC in 1959, he continued to bring the New York theater to television screens with "Play of the Week," a syndicated anthology that aired until 1961. The show staged the best of modern dramas with well-known actors, who accepted modest salaries in return for the chance to appear in quality productions.

During the 1960s and 1970s Miner devoted most of his energies to the American Academy of Dramatic Arts in Manhattan. He had served as a trustee of the academy since 1948 and eventually became its chair. His wife, actress Frances Fuller, with whom he had three children, became president and director of the academy in 1954 and continued as director until 1974.

Because Miner began working in television before the conventions and aesthetics of the medium were established, and because he was both a network executive, deciding what type of programming to develop, and a producer, making the programs he developed, he played a truly pivotal role in shaping the first two decades of American TV. CBS chair William S. Paley called Miner the network's "earliest pioneer." Bringing experience from a long career in the theater to the new medium, Miner was influential in making the golden age of television so rich in theatrical productions and adaptations. Miner died in New York City.

• Videotapes of "Studio One" and other productions by Miner can be screened at the Museum of Television & Radio in New York City. Franklin J. Schaffner, a director who worked for Miner, served as moderator of Miner's oral memoirs, which were published in *Worthington Miner: A Directors Guild of America Oral History* (1985). Max Wilk, *The Golden Age of Television* (1976), contains a useful chapter on Miner's TV work. An obituary is in the *New York Times*, 13 Dec. 1982.

ROBERT J. THOMPSON

MING, John Joseph (20 Sept. 1838–17 June 1910), Jesuit sociologist, was born in Giswyl, Unterwalden, Switzerland. Knowledge about his parents and other early biographical data is unavailable. He graduated from the classical course at Benedictine College of Engelberg and on 7 September 1856 entered the Society of Jesus to begin his theological studies. Just over twelve years later, on 13 September 1868, he was ordained and assigned as a preacher at Kreuzberg. In 1870, after completing a demanding tertianship, a final year of ascetic training and study, Ming became a professor of theology on the faculty at the Jesuit seminary in Gorizia, Austria.

In 1872 the German government's decision to expel the Jesuit order resulted in Ming's reassignment, along with a large number of fellow German-speaking scholars, to the Buffalo Mission at Canisius College in New York. After an initial period of parish work in Milwaukee, Ming began a career of collegiate teaching and writing that would stretch over the next thirty-six years. While lecturing widely on philosophical, theological, and sociological questions, he fulfilled faculty assignments at Springhill College, Alabama (1874–1878), Canisius College (1879–1881, 1886–1888), St. Louis University (1883–1884), and Campion College at Prairie du Chien, Wisconsin (1882–1883, 1888–1889, 1891–1892, and 1899–1906). These rotating faculty positions, along with extensive contacts at other institutions, reflected a commitment that he shared with other Jesuits at the time to advancing a collective educational effort in the United States.

Starting in the late 1870s, after he had mastered the English language, Ming published essays and book reviews with increasing frequency in Catholic periodicals. These efforts came as the result of a sustained inquiry into the widening philosophical, and specifically sociological, debate over the meaning of late nineteenth-century social change and economic progress. He took sharp exception to evolutionists and socialists, particularly those advocating Marxian dialectics. Drawn into the broader discourse then under way and primarily driven by the need to reaffirm a Christian theological perspective, Ming nevertheless demonstrated a detailed knowledge of the Darwinian hypothesis and Marxist analysis.

In a remarkable series of seventeen articles that Ming published in *American Catholic Quarterly Review* between 1879 and 1898, he confronted directly the new scientific theories of the period. In such pieces as "Modern and Ancient Philosophy Compared" (1879), "Science and Speculative Philosophy" (1887), "The Idea of Evolution" (1893), and "Biologic Sociology" (1898), Ming argued forcefully that neither evolutionary nor Marxian models provided a meaningful alternative to Christianity as a socially redemptive set of beliefs.

Over the course of three decades of scholarly activity, Ming's writings also appeared in the *American Ecclesiastical Review*, *Catholic Encyclopedia*, *Messenger of the Sacred Heart*, and *America*. As his research on the question of modern sociological questions expanded, he authored three monographs that incorporated his views: *The Data of Modern Ethics Examined* (1894), *Morality of Modern Socialism* (1909), and *The Characteristics and the Religion of Modern Socialism* (1908). In *The Characteristics and the Religion of Modern Socialism*, Ming acknowledged that fundamental economic and social divisions existed in modern society, and that these divisions constituted a maladjustment in the distribution of wealth. He argued, however, that Marxian socialism would not resolve the deeper moral and spiritual crisis. "This new religion," he wrote, "lacks the light of eternal truths, unchangeable principles, and the direction of a higher law. Being based merely on evolutionary materialistic science, changing with time and circumstances, it is unable to generate firm convictions, or to afford fixed rules of conduct or to restrain disorderly propensities." Ming urged readers to reject the tenets of Marxian socialism as a flawed response to the social and economic crisis of the early twentieth century.

In 1907 Ming retired from teaching and took up residence in the Saint Stanislaus' Jesuit Home in Parma, Ohio. He continued to write, however, and at the time of his death in Parma was preparing a critical study on the American labor movement. Reviewing Ming's accomplishments in *America* shortly after Ming's death, historian Joseph C. Husslein, S.J., praised the scholar's clarity of expression and attention to detail, concluding that "he has given to the Catholic writer . . . a model of the most modern laboratory criticism as applied to questions of our day." Conservative in both his theological and social views, Ming provided his students and colleagues with an informed and balanced Catholic critique of social and economic questions throughout his years as a teacher and scholar.

• No known collection of Ming's personal papers and writings exists. In addition to the articles and books already mentioned, he published *The Temporal Sovereignty of the Holy See* (1894), a brochure that attracted considerable attention among Catholic theologians at the time. An insightful assessment of Ming appears in Joseph C. Husslein, S.J., "Rev. John J. Ming, S.J., Philosopher and Author," *America* 3 (2 June 1910): 307–8. *Woodstock Letters* 40 (Oct. 1911): 91–92, and *The Catholic Encyclopedia and Its Makers* (1917), p. 116, also provide brief accounts of Ming's life and work.

RONALD M. JOHNSON

MINGUS, Charles (22 Apr. 1922–5 Jan. 1979), jazz musician, was born in Nogales, Arizona, the son of Charles Mingus, a postal worker and army sergeant, and Harriett Sophia Philips. The family moved to the Watts section of Los Angeles shortly after Mingus's birth to seek medical care for his mother, who died soon thereafter. Mingus first studied trombone and then cello. At the age of sixteen he switched to the bass, studying with the well-known jazz player Red Callender, and he also began to study the piano.

Mingus's father was a Methodist, but his stepmother, Mamie, brought the young Mingus to the Holiness church where he heard gospel music and experienced the interaction between audience and preacher—the call and response—that influenced much of his own music. As he matured musically, he played with Barney Bigard and toured with Louis Armstrong (1942–1943). He also studied for five years with the former New York Philharmonic bassist Herman Rheinschagen, who provided him with the basis for the astonishing technique he developed. He continued to play and record in the late 1940s, but financial and family pressures (he married Canilla Jeanne Gross in 1944 and was by then the father of two sons) forced him to seek temporary employment at the post office in 1946 and again in 1950.

Mingus's first major break came in 1950 when he joined the Red Norvo Trio. He traveled with the group to Chicago, San Francisco, and New York, but he was barred from appearing on a television show with Norvo and guitarist Tal Farlow because he was not a member of Local 802, the musicians' union; disillusioned, he quit the group. After brief gigs with Miles Davis and pianist Billy Taylor, he found it necessary to again work at the post office (this time in New York City) during the winter of 1952; he then played briefly with both Charlie Parker and his most important musical influence, Duke Ellington. During the early fifties he also worked with Stan Getz, Miles Davis, and Art Tatum. Along with Max Roach, he founded Debut Records in 1952, hoping to bypass the white-controlled and exploitative record business. During this period he helped organize the famous concert at Massey Hall in Toronto in May 1953, reuniting Parker, trumpeter Dizzy Gillespie, and drummer Roach, with Mingus on bass and Bud Powell on piano.

In 1953 Mingus cofounded the Jazz Composers Workshop with saxophonist-composer Teo Macero and others, and in 1955 he established the shifting ensemble known as the Charles Mingus Jazz Workshop. This group lasted for several years. The drummer Dannie Richmond was with him from 1956 on, and such prominent musicians as Jimmy Knepper, Booker Ervin, John Handy, Eric Dolphy, and Ted Curson were members at various times. Mingus honed his unique compositional approach with the Workshop, expanding on methods pioneered by Ellington and Jelly Roll Morton. He brought sketches to the rehearsals, used the piano to illustrate what he wanted the musicians to do, and often gave them chords to explore for as long as they chose, with the rest of the group joining in spontaneously. He also discussed the emotional effects he was looking for, expecting the soloists to develop their improvisations to support the desired effect. All of this gave the players both enormous opportunity for creative expression and a burdensome responsibility to live up to Mingus's expectations. Mingus often sought to evoke very specific emotions in his compositions. "Fables of Faubus," for instance, was a satirical portrayal of the Arkansas governor whose defense of racial segregation led to the Little Rock school integration crisis in 1957, and the poignant "Goodbye Pork Pie Hat" expressed Mingus's grief at Lester Young's death.

Mingus's musical breakthrough came in 1956, with the album *Pithecanthropus Erectus*. In the title composition Mingus sought to portray the pride of the first modern man at standing erect, his attempts to impose his will on the world, and his subsequent destruction by his own greed and ambition. The piece makes strong emotional impact, heightened by cries and shouts (to suggest primordial sounds) and by the excitement of spontaneous group improvisation. Mingus followed this stunning album with another in 1957, *The Clown* (not released until 1962), which included the innovative "Haitian Fight Song." Seeking to depict the black struggle for freedom, Mingus opened this piece with a superb bass solo steadily mounting in intensity, a touchstone of technical skill and emotional expressiveness; the rest of the group then joined in with headlong patterns of riffs, call-and-response figures, and Mingus's own shouts and cries, culminating in a searing trombone solo by Knepper. Mingus followed this effort with a third pathbreaking album, *Tijuana Moods* (1957), highlighted by the sensuous "Ysabel's Table Dance," and with the albums *East Coasting* and *Scenes in the City* (both 1957). Around the same time he composed and recorded music to accompany several Langston Hughes poems and wrote the score for John Cassavetes's film, *Shadows* (1960).

Even amid this astonishing burst of creativity, Mingus continued to face financial pressures. He had married Celia Nielson in 1951, and the two had a son late in 1957. His wife left him the following April, and the split apparently pushed Mingus to the emotional edge. He admitted himself to Bellevue Hospital, but he did not receive the help he sought. Bureaucratic obstacles prevented his release until friends intervened.

Mingus regained his artistic momentum and recorded three outstanding albums in 1959. By now he had expanded his group to include seven to nine pieces, and instead of treating this larger ensemble as a miniature big band (the common approach) and orchestrating his compositions, he continued to use the Workshop technique of dictating lines for each player while allowing the overall structure to emerge spontaneously. An excellent example is "Wednesday Night Prayer Meeting," from the album *Blues and Roots*. After completing this project, he signed with Columbia Records and recorded *Mingus Ah Um*, which included the masterpieces "Better Get It In Your Soul" and "Goodbye Pork Pie Hat."

Early in 1960 Mingus began a ten-month stay at the Showplace on West 4th Street with Eric Dolphy, Ted Curson, Dannie Richmond, occasional pianists, and a variety of drop-ins, including the tap dancer-percussionist Baby Laurence. This was perhaps his most consistently innovative group. That summer, he and Max Roach led a protest against the growing commercialization of the Newport Jazz Festival. He and Roach organized a counterfestival at Cliff Walk Manor, handling advertising and promotion themselves. The two men also established the short-lived Jazz Artists Guild, another attempt to bypass the recording establishment. Over the next several years Mingus recorded several triumphant albums, including *Money Jungle* (1962), a trio album with Duke Ellington and Max Roach; a solo effort, *Mingus Plays the Piano* (1963); and the classic *The Black Saint and the Sinner Lady* (1963), a powerful work that he conceived of as a single, extended composition. He toured Europe and established his third independent record label. He married again (to Judy Starkey) in 1960 and had two more children. But he abruptly withdrew from public performance in 1966, again stricken by psychological problems. Evicted from his apartment, he moved to the Lower East Side, where, amid poverty and crime, he found renewed hope and friendship in the area's multiethnic community. He began a relationship with Susan Graham Ungaro (whom he married in 1975) and seemed happier than he had been in years.

Mingus reemerged with a new quintet/sextet in 1969. In 1971 Alfred A. Knopf published *Beneath the Underdog*, the autobiography Mingus had been working on for years, and he was awarded a Guggenheim Fellowship that same year. He recorded one of his most successful albums, *Let My Children Hear Music*, and enjoyed a highly successful European tour in 1972. He recorded several outstanding albums with both his quintet and larger groups over the next several years. At the peak of his powers, he was diagnosed in 1977 as suffering from amyotrophic lateral sclerosis (Lou Gehrig's disease). He continued to compose and direct recordings from his wheelchair until January 1978. He sought experimental treatment in Mexico later that year and died of a heart attack in Cuernavaca.

Mingus was one of the most imposing and creative figures in the history of jazz. As a bassist, he helped free his instrument from the constraints of rhythmic accompaniment and enhanced its melodic function. As a composer, he incorporated a spectrum of jazz's various styles in his work, his influences including black church music, the blues, Ellington, Parker, and twentieth-century classical compositions. *The Black Saint and the Sinner Lady* contains everything from nineteenth-century piano music to flamenco guitar. His frequent use of varied tempos and meters was widely influential, and his employment of dynamics and instrumental textures greatly expanded the possibilities of small-group jazz. In its focus on collective improvisation, his work was also an important precursor of the free jazz of the 1960s. His fascination with extended forms is revealed in his posthumously published work, *Epitaph*, which consists of nineteen interconnected segments. Finally, his compositions have a rhythmic force and energy almost unparalleled in modern music; there is no mistaking "Mingus music."

At the same time, Mingus's high artistic standards and volatile personality made him often difficult to work with; his constantly shifting personnel resulted at least in part from musicians rebelling against his dictatorial demands and frequent criticisms, which he leveled at them even during live performances. Yet Mingus also possessed a rare degree of self-awareness. He spoke of being both a frightened animal "that attacks for fear of being attacked . . . " and "an over-loving gentle person" who trusted everyone (Hentoff, p. 161). He found solace and fulfillment in his music. "Most people are forced to do things they don't want to most of the time," he once noted, "and so they get to the point where they feel they no longer have any choice about anything important, including who they are. We create our own slavery. But I'm going to keep on getting through and finding out the kind of man I am through my music. That's the one place I can be free" (Hentoff, p. 158).

• An outstanding study of Mingus is Brian Priestley, *Mingus: A Critical Biography* (1982), which offers a thorough overview of his life and a perceptive analysis of his music and career. Mingus worked on his autobiography, *Beneath the Underdog*, for much of his adult life, and it remains an invaluable source. It also mixes fact and fiction indiscriminately, though, and it should be used in conjunction with Priestley. Several brief introductions to Mingus and his music are excellent: Nat Hentoff, *Jazz Is* (1976), pp. 150–65; Whitney Balliett, *Goodbyes and Other Messages: A Journal of Jazz, 1981–1990* (1990), pp. 149–56; 247–51; Gary Giddins, *Riding on a Blue Note: Jazz and American Pop* (1981), pp. 170–78; Martin Williams, *The Jazz Tradition* (1993), pp. 219–24; James Lincoln Collier, *The Making of Jazz: A Comprehensive History* (1978), pp. 442–49; Lewis Porter and Michael Ullman, with Edward Hazell, *Jazz: From Its Origins to the Present* (1993), pp. 271–77; and David H. Rosenthal, *Hard Bop: Jazz and Black Music, 1955–1965* (1992), pp. 136–41. Also see the two informal but revealing memoirs in Janet Coleman and Al Young, *Mingus/Mingus: Two Memoirs* (1989). Tom Reichman's classic film *Mingus*, shot in the middle 1960s and focusing on Mingus's 1966 eviction from his apartment, is well worth viewing. An obituary is in the *New York Times*, 9 Jan. 1979.

RONALD P. DUFOUR

MINNELLI, Vincente (28 Feb. 1910–25 July 1986), film and stage director, was born in Chicago, Illinois, the son of actors Vincent Charles Minnelli and Mina Gennell. He acted as a child, most particularly in the Minnelli Brothers' Dramatic Tent Show between 1913 and 1918. Educated at the Art Institute of Chicago during the mid-1920s, Minnelli worked for a time as a billboard painter and a window dresser for the Marshall Field department store in Chicago.

Minnelli returned to the theater in the early 1930s, first as a stage manager and costume designer for the Balaban and Katz theater chain in Chicago and then as a scene and costume designer for the Paramount Theatre in New York between 1931 and 1933. He also designed some visual elements for producer Earl Carroll's *Vanities* (1931) and the musical comedy *DuBarry* (1932). In 1934 Minnelli became the art director for New York's Radio City Music Hall, and for nearly two years he designed scenic elements and lighting for all of the productions, directing some as well. Following his Radio City stint, Minnelli designed and directed several Broadway musicals and revues, including *At Home Abroad* (1935), *The Show Is On* (1936), *Hooray for What?* (1937), and *Very Warm for May* (1939). He also contributed designs for the Ziegfeld *Follies* of

1936. His designs were celebrated for their elegance and tastefulness as well as for his striking and adventurous use of color. Minnelli went to Hollywood for a time in 1936 under contract to Paramount Pictures, but he was given little to do and after a few months bought out his contract in order to return to the New York theater. In 1940 he was signed by the Metro-Goldwyn-Mayer producer Arthur Freed to stage musical sequences in the movies *Babes on Broadway* (1941) and *Panama Hattie* (1942) before he was assigned to direct *Cabin in the Sky* (1943), an all-black musical feature starring Ethel Waters, Eddie "Rochester" Anderson, Dooley Wilson, and Lena Horne. *Cabin in the Sky* was not only an all-too-rare opportunity for African-American performers to appear in a major studio product, but a significant social harbinger of changes to come, both on the screen and in American society. However, a favorite sequence of Minnelli's, featuring Horne singing in a bubble-bath, was considered by censors to be too daring a portrayal of a black woman. The scene was deleted, much to Minnelli's chagrin.

After directing a Red Skelton comedy, *I Dood It* (1943), Minnelli was given the plum assignment of directing MGM's outstanding musical actress, Judy Garland, in *Meet Me in St. Louis* (1944). Minnelli's sensitive direction of Garland and his eye for color and period detail made this nostalgic turn-of-the-century musical a screen classic. In 1945 he married Garland, and they had one child, Liza Minnelli, born in 1946. Minnelli directed Garland's next film, the nonmusical feature *The Clock*, in 1945, as well as the critically applauded but financially unsuccessful Fred Astaire musical *Yolanda and the Thief*. He codirected the revue film *Ziegfeld Follies* (1946) and directed *Undercurrent* (1946), a brooding mystery starring Katharine Hepburn and Robert Mitchum, as well as the Garland sequences in *Till the Clouds Roll By* (1947). One of Minnelli's outstanding films of the era was his highly stylized satiric musical *The Pirate*, starring Garland and Gene Kelly (1948). Although this movie failed to find an appreciative audience at the time, its witty direction, Cole Porter score, and superb performances by the stars made it a cult favorite with film buffs. At about this time, Garland's struggles with addiction to pills began to seriously undermine her ability to perform consistently under the stressful rigors of studio life. By the time Garland was fired by MGM in 1950, the Minnelli marriage was unraveling. Minnelli and Garland divorced in 1951, and he subsequently married Georgette Magnani in 1954, with whom he had another daughter, Christiana Maria, born in 1955. Minnelli and Magnani divorced in 1958, and he subsequently married twice more, to Denise Gigante in 1961, a union that ended in divorce in 1971, and to Lee M. Anderson in 1982, a marriage that lasted until his death. Despite his personal woes, Minnelli continued to direct successfully and demonstrated his versatility with the drama *Madame Bovary* (1949) and the light comedy *Father of the Bride* (1950), starring Spencer Tracy. In 1951 *An American in Paris* won an Academy Award as the best picture of the year under Minnelli's direction. This musical profited from Minnelli's visual artistry, particularly in a lengthy stylized ballet featuring Gene Kelly at the end of the picture. The same year Minnelli directed *Father's Little Dividend*, again starring Spencer Tracy, in a popular sequel to highly successful *Father of the Bride*. Next, he directed a few elaborate episodes in two films, *Lovely to Look At* (1952) and *The Story of Three Loves* (1953), before yet another display of remarkable versatility with the hard-hitting melodrama *The Bad and the Beautiful* (1952) and another classic musical, *The Band Wagon* (1953), starring Fred Astaire, that many critics rate as the finest of all MGM musicals. Over the next few years, Minnelli continued to move freely among the screen genres by directing the Lucille Ball–Desi Arnaz comedy *The Long, Long, Trailer* (1954), the musicals *Brigadoon* (1954) and *Kismet* (1955), the gritty drama *The Cobweb* (1955), the acclaimed Vincent van Gogh biographical film *Lust for Life* (1956), the Broadway drama *Tea and Sympathy* (1956), and the brittle, sophisticated comedy *Designing Woman* (1957). In 1957 Minnelli replaced Ronald Neame as the director of *The Seventh Sin*, but he refused to accept screen credit for his contributions. The musical with which Minnelli's name is most often associated, *Gigi*, was filmed in 1958 and is frequently referred to as the last outstanding musical of the Hollywood studio system. Capitalizing on Minnelli's visual gifts, elegant taste, and mastery of the musical genre, *Gigi* became one of the most honored films in movie history. It won numerous Academy Awards, including a Best Director statuette for Minnelli.

Minnelli's later films were often polished and critically applauded, but he seemed to function less successfully during the declining days of the lavish Hollywood studio system. These later films include *The Reluctant Debutante* (1958), *Some Came Running* (1959), *Home from the Hill* (1960), *Bells Are Ringing* (1960), *The Four Horsemen of the Apocalypse* (1962), *Two Weeks in Another Town* (1962), *The Courtship of Eddie's Father* (1963), *Goodbye, Charlie* (1964), *The Sandpiper* (1965), *On a Clear Day You Can See Forever* (1970), and *A Matter of Time* (1976), this last starring his daughter in their only joint screen effort. His sole return to the theater for the Broadway musical *Mata Hari* (1967) was a failure, closing after a mere two weeks. Minnelli died in Beverly Hills, California.

• Minnelli's memoirs, with Hector Arce, are published as *I Remember It Well* (1974). Other works on Minnelli are Stephen Harvey, *Directed by Vincente Minnelli* (1989); James Naremore, *The Films of Vincente Minnelli* (1993); Patrick Brion et al., *Vincente Minnelli* (1985); Roberto Campari, *Vincente Minnelli* (1975); Catherine De la Roche, *Vincente Minnelli* (1959); and Joseph Andrew Casper, *Vincente Minnelli and the Film Musical* (1977). An obituary is in the *New York Times*, 12 Aug. 1986.

JAMES FISHER

MINOKA-HILL, Lillie Rosa (30 Aug. 1876–18 Mar. 1952), physician, was born on the St. Regis reservation in New York State, the daughter of Joshua G. Allen, a

Quaker physician from Philadelphia, and a Mohawk Indian woman whose name is unknown. Her mother died following childbirth. Her father renamed her Rosa because of her dark complexion and sent her to live with maternal relatives on the reservation. At five years of age she was enrolled at the Grahame Institute in Philadelphia, a Quaker boarding school for girls. She graduated from the high school at Grahame in 1895.

Following graduation Rosa Minoka went to live in a convent in Quebec. At the convent she studied French and rejected her Quaker upbringing to become a convert to Catholicism. In 1896 she was admitted to the Woman's Medical College of Pennsylvania and became the second American Indian to study there. She graduated in 1899, serving her internship at the Woman's Hospital in Philadelphia and working in a dispensary known as the Woman's Clinic connected with the Woman's Medical College. After her internship she set up a successful practice with a fellow woman graduate.

In 1905 she married Charles Abram Hill, an Oneida Indian and a graduate of the Carlisle Institute, an Indian school. Hill was eager to return to his home in Wisconsin where he expected his wife to farm alongside him. Rosa Minoka-Hill accepted these conditions and gave up her medical practice. They moved to her husband's farm in Oneida where the couple raised six children.

Minoka-Hill's life changed dramatically in Oneida. Living on an Indian reservation far from modern conveniences was difficult. Urban life had given her no training for farming, and she had to learn how to plant and tend to crops, cook on a wood stove, and pump water. Although she knew some of the tribal customs of her mother's Mohawk family, Minoka-Hill had to learn the different traditions of the Oneida. As she learned more about the Oneida's use of various roots, weeds, and barks, Indians on the reservation began to seek her out for treatment of their ailments.

Minoka-Hill's services were sorely needed. The community's medical, emergency, and surgical needs were met by a single government hospital, nicknamed "The House of Death," and a sole licensed doctor who treated 1,500 Indians. By combining ancient Indian herbal remedies with her medical training, Minoka-Hill was eventually accepted by the local doctor, the medicine men and women, and her husband as she became the area's informal physician.

When Charles Hill suddenly died of appendicitis in 1916, Minoka-Hill and her family faced hardship. Although friends urged her to return to Philadelphia, she was determined to stay in Oneida where she knew she was desperately needed. Because she was not licensed in the state she was unable to collect fees for her medical services. Support for her family came from whatever she earned from the farm and from a small trust fund her father had left her. Area doctors and friends often supplied her with needed medicines.

During World War I the only physician departed from Oneida. In 1917 Minoka-Hill took over his responsibilities and opened a "kitchen-clinic" and traveling practice, taking care of the medical emergencies in non-Indian as well as Oneida communities. Forging ahead to meet the necessary tasks, Minoka-Hill saw patients in her home from early morning until late night, rode miles in her buggy, and saw to the large numbers of Indians suffering from tuberculosis and malnutrition. Many times she traveled eleven miles to the nearest town of Green Bay to get medication for a single person.

When the 1929 stock market crash wiped out her trust fund, Minoka-Hill had to rely only on the generosity of her patients. Some were able to pay her a few dollars or supply her with food. Without a license she could not obtain medicines, get insurance and welfare reimbursements, or admit those needing surgery or emergency treatment to a hospital but had to send them to a licensed physician. Physicians in Green Bay persuaded her to take the examination for her license and loaned her the application fee. In 1934 after four months of study she passed the two-day examination receiving her license some thirty-five years after her medical school graduation.

Even after she received her license Minoka-Hill fixed her fees according to what patients were able to pay. The government aided in the patient overload by sending out a public health nurse three days a week and a doctor once a week, and by contributing food supplies that lessened problems of widespread malnutrition. While tending to their medical ailments, Minoka-Hill instructed the Oneida on preventive measures by stressing better nutrition and sanitation. In 1946 a heart attack curtailed much of her normal routine as a physician, but she continued to see patients in her kitchen.

In 1947 the Indian Council Fire in Chicago named her the outstanding American Indian of the year. The Oneida honored her in 1947 by adopting Minoka-Hill and naming her You-da-gent or "she who serves." In 1948 friends, neighbors, and patients memorialized her with a monument inscribed with "physician, good samaritan, and friend to all religions in this community, erected to her memory by the Indians and white people. 'I was sick and you visited me.'" The State Medical Society of Wisconsin honored her with a lifetime membership and in 1949 sent her to the American Medical Association national convention. She was also given an honorary membership in the Outagamie County Medical Society. In the same year the agriculture department of the University of Wisconsin cited her for her outstanding service to rural people. She continued her practice into the 1950s and died in Fond du Lac, Wisconsin.

In a time when women physicians were rare and Native American physicians rarer, Lillie Rosa Minoka-Hill combined her medical skill and knowledge with American Indian cures. Blending both methods she created an atmosphere of trust that earned her the respect and love of the Oneida Indian community, which she served with ceaseless dedication and a disregard for material rewards or accolades.

• Clipping files for Minoka-Hill are in the Archives Division at the State Historical Society of Wisconsin, Madison, and at the Alumnae Office of the Medical College of Pennsylvania, Philadelphia. Biographical sources include Robert E. Ritzenthaler, "The Oneida Indians of Wisconsin," *Bulletin of the Public Museum of the City of Milwaukee* 19 (Nov. 1950): 3–52; "An Indian Physician Remembers," *Crusader of the Wisconsin Anti-Tuberculosis Association*, May 1951, pp. 8–9; Marion E. Gridley, *American Indian Women* (1974); Victoria Brown, *Uncommon Lives of Common Women: The Missing Half of Wisconsin History* (1975); Rima D. Apple, "In Recognition of Lillie Rosa Minoka-Hill (1876–1952)," *Women and Health* 4 (Winter 1979): 329–31; and David Hurst Thomas et al., *The Native Americans: An Illustrated History* (1993). Obituaries appear in the *New York Times* and the *Chicago Tribune*, 19 Mar. 1952, and in the *Wisconsin Medical Journal* 51 (Apr. 1952): 427–28.

MARILYN ELIZABETH PERRY

MINOR, Benjamin Blake (21 Oct. 1818–1 Aug. 1905), editor, educator, and lawyer, was born in Tappahannock, Essex County, Virginia, the son of Dr. Hubbard Taylor Minor, a physician, and Jane Blake. Both parents were from prominent Virginia planting families. In 1835 Minor enrolled at the University of Virginia, an institution he much preferred to Bristol College, a small mechanical school near Philadelphia where he had earlier studied. For the next three school terms Minor pursued his studies there, eventually receiving several diplomas in various schools. In 1836 Charles Bonnycastle, one of Minor's professors, offered him a principalship at a Baton Rouge academy. Although Minor did not accept the offer, he was persuaded to lodge with Professor Bonnycastle and tutor his children.

Subsequently, Minor entered the College of William and Mary, where he studied moral philosophy and political economy under the guidance of the college's president, Thomas R. Dew, completing his law degree under Judge N. Beverly Tucker in 1839. Considered too young to practice law, however, Minor decided to work a year in the Fredericksburg circuit court clerk's office, during which time he visited sessions of the legislature in Richmond. In October 1840 Minor began practicing law in Petersburg, but the following spring he moved his practice to Richmond. In 1842 Minor married Virginia Maury Otey, the eldest child of James Hervey Otey, an Episcopal bishop of Tennessee. The couple had eleven children, six of whom predeceased them.

During this time Minor was proposed by Professor Dew as a candidate for the chair of moral philosophy and political economy at the University of Virginia; however, the position was given to a more experienced scholar. Disillusioned with practicing law and becoming increasingly interested in literary matters, in July 1843 Minor purchased the *Southern Literary Messenger*. Lacking editorial experience, he nevertheless guided the literary magazine with enthusiasm, hope, and determination. Another trademark of Minor's editorship was explicitness of purpose, which was evident in his efforts to make the publication a showcase for southern writers and views. Although primarily concerned with southern interests such as slavery, states' rights, and the annexation of Texas, the publication also took on a national flair, publishing pieces on the U.S. military, ancient and American history, international copyright issues, insanity, cooking, and other topics. During this period, articles by various writers and southern figures, including Edgar Allan Poe, John Esten Cooke, General Braxton Bragg, Philip P. Cooke, Dr. Samuel Henry Dickson, and Henry Charles Lea, filled the pages of the *Messenger*. Because it featured fiction, poetry, nonfiction, commentary, and reviews, the *New York Tribune* said that the magazine's span of concern was "almost as broad as the whole field of human interest."

In 1845 Minor acquired the *Southern and Western Monthly Magazine and Review* from William Gilmore Simms, merging it with the *Messenger*. In addition to his journalistic endeavors, Minor also remained publically active, serving as a delegate to and a vice president of the Memphis Commercial Convention (also known as the Southern and Western Convention). A large number of delegates from the southern states, as well as men from Illinois, Indiana, and the Iowa Territory, attended the meeting. The convention's main purpose was the improvement and expansion of river and rail transportation in the South.

In 1847 Minor sold his magazine to John Reuben Thompson, and the October issue of that year was the last to bear Minor's name as editor. One month earlier Minor had accepted an unsolicited position as principal of Virginia Female Institute (renamed Stuart Hall in 1907) in Staunton, although he held this position for only one year, voluntarily resigning due to "promises made and broken" by the school's trustees. According to the institute, however, legend has it that after two weeks at school, Minor wrote the bishop stating, "I pray to be delivered from adolescents and their detestable enormities."

In late 1848 Minor returned to the law. Opening an office in Richmond, he practiced there for the next twelve years. Using his position in the community, he attempted to encourage moral behavior and lawful conduct by establishing the Home School for Young Ladies, and although he refused to take a faculty position, Minor actively directed its growth. While an attorney, Minor also aided in drafting a request to the Virginia legislature that led to the erection of the Washington Monument. In addition to his law practice and his educational pursuits, he served as a commissioned lieutenant colonel of the Nineteenth Regiment of the Virginia militia, as a diocesan delegate and warden of St. James Church, and as a founder of the Richmond Male Orphan Asylum. An avid joiner, while living in Richmond Minor became corresponding secretary of the Virginia Bible Society, and participated in the Virginia Historical Society. He was also a corresponding member of the New-York Historical Society, a founder of the Richmond Library Company, and the director of the Richmond Athenaeum.

In July 1860 Minor closed his Richmond practice in order to accept a post as president of the State University of Missouri. At the university, Minor also served as professor of mental and moral science and political economy. During the Civil War the campus was occupied by Federal troops; however, at the urging of faculty, it remained open until March 1862, when it was closed by curators appointed by the newly designated provisional government. Forced to resign, Minor stayed with his family near Columbia, opening a small boy's school in what had previously been the Columbia Female Academy, where he delivered lectures on astronomy. As a Confederate sympathizer, Minor encouraged two of his sons to enlist in the conflict, one in the army, the other in both the army and the navy. A conservative states' rights Whig, Minor had favored John Bell and Edward Everett for president and vice president in 1860. Earlier, he had also served as secretary of the Virginia African Colonization Society, which advocated sending freed African Americans to parts of West Africa.

In September 1865 Minor opened Minor's Female Seminary in St. Louis, a proprietary school, which he ran for the next four years. Although supported by local residents, he ultimately suspended the seminary in 1869, assigning his interests to a competing academy.

Minor's next position was that of general agent for Missouri Mutual Life Insurance Company. While occasionally selling insurance, after 1870 Minor spent most of his time on a seven- or eight-state lecture circuit gaining prominence with his series titled, "Evenings with the Stars and the Bible."

Returning to Richmond in 1889, Minor spent much of his time reading and writing for the local newspapers. He also became active in the Virginia Society of the Sons of the American Revolution, serving as the society's secretary. He died in Richmond.

Minor's editorial definiteness aided in introducing the works of many gifted southern writers to the American public. While under Minor's direction the *Messenger* also became a focal point for sociopolitical discussion. Minor showed the same enthusiasm and explicitness of purpose in his aid of the southern cause and his undaunted efforts in helping the youth of the period. He also helped to improve southern transportation and supported the construction of the Washington Monument. His persistent dedication and guiding role were evident in many nineteenth-century American historical, religious, and patriotic organizations.

• A few of Minor's letters are in the Garland Carr Broadhead Papers and the President's Office Papers in the Western Historical Manuscript Collection, University of Missouri at Columbia. Minor's own works include *An Appeal to the Legislature of Virginia in Behalf of the Colonial History of Virginia* (1844); *An Appeal to the Whole Country, for an Union of Parties, on the Basis of the Principles of Washington, Jefferson, Madison and Monroe . . .* (1850); and *The Southern Literary Messenger, 1834–1864* (1905). For a text edited by Minor, see George Wythe, *Decisions of Cases in Virginia by the High Court of Chancery* (1852). A biography of Minor is in *Encyclopedia of Virginia Biography*, vol. 3, ed. Lyon Gardiner Tyler (1915). For a useful history of the Minor family see John Barbie Minor, *The Minor Family of Virginia* (1923). Frank Luther Mott, *A History of American Magazines, 1741–1850* (1930), also provides insight into Minor's activities and contributions as editor of the *Messenger*. Some of Minor's accomplishments and social activities while living in Richmond are covered in James Lawrence Blair Buck, *The Development of Public Schools in Virginia, 1607–1952* (1952), and W. Asbury Christian, *Richmond: Her Past and Present* (1912). Obituaries are in the *Evening Journal* and the *Richmond News Leader*, both 1 Aug. 1905, and the *Richmond Times Dispatch*, 2 Aug. 1905.

C. E. LINDGREN

MINOR, Raleigh Colston (24 Jan. 1869–14 June 1923), law professor, was born in Charlottesville, Virginia, the son of John Barbee Minor, a law professor, and Anne Jacquelin Fisher Colston. In 1897 he married Natalie Embra Venable, who, like Minor, was a member of a well-known Virginia family and the child of a professor at the University of Virginia; the couple would have two children. Minor maintained strong connections with the University of Virginia throughout his life. He entered the university at the age of fourteen, receiving his B.A. in 1887, his M.A. in 1888, and his LL.B. in 1890.

After practicing law in Richmond, Virginia, from 1890 to 1893, Minor returned to Charlottesville, where he spent the remainder of his career as a law professor at the University of Virginia. He was appointed an instructor in 1893, an assistant professor in 1894, an adjunct professor in 1895, and a full professor in 1899. Minor served as acting dean of the law school in 1907–1908, and in 1910 he was named James Monroe Professor of Law. He also commuted to Georgetown University between 1904 and 1921 to lecture on conflict of laws, and he taught at the University of California in the summer of 1915.

Minor was known as a hard-working, analytical teacher and scholar. Dean William Minor Lile noted Minor's "wonderfully terse and accurate presentation of principles in the class-room," and his students valued his "calm gentleness" and "steadfast earnestness." His subjects were real property, conflict of laws, international law, and constitutional law. In 1901 Minor wrote *Conflict of Laws*, a doctrinal treatise that was used as a standard reference. It emphasized the use of territorial principles to select the law governing cases in which persons or aspects of a transaction were located in more than one jurisdiction. Minor's two-volume *The Law of Real Property*, published in 1908, was a well-received revision and expansion of the second volume of his father's *Institutes of Common and Statute Laws*, which focused on the law of Virginia. His *The Law of Real Property* was followed in 1910 by a single-volume text of the same title, coauthored with Professor John Wurts of Yale, which deemphasized the local focus of the earlier book.

Minor's most creative work related to international and constitutional law. In 1918 he published *A Republic of Nations*, in which he proposed a constitution for a federal union of nations and analyzed in depth both the nature and specific clauses of the proposed constitution. Writing while World War I was still in progress and persuaded that "the vague and tardy influence of public opinion" provided an ineffective limitation on the tendency of nation-states to have recourse to war, Minor proposed a significantly more detailed structure of international governance than was contained in the League of Nations charter. Under his scheme, nation-states would surrender to a federal international government certain "political," "war-breeding" powers, notably powers relating to the regulation of international trade, the acquisition of territory, and the oppression of citizens of other nation-states. Robert Tunstall suggested that Minor's "constructive idealism" stemmed from his belief in the "sanctity of contracts," even among governments. According to Tunstall, this belief led Minor, in *A Republic of Nations*, to attribute "too strong a power for erring humanity."

Minor's proposal for a federal union of nation-states was consistent with his view of constitutional law. He believed that the U.S. Constitution embodied an arrangement in which sovereign states had ceded only limited functions to the central government. The states of the United States kept control over localized issues and surrendered specific political and military powers to the federal government, leaving a situation in which any dispute arising between two states "must always be within the limit of legal and justiciable questions." Minor consistently stressed that various levels of government—state, national, and international—should be organized to carry out effectively powers assigned to them under federal constitutional arrangements.

Minor's treatises in the areas of real property and conflicts have been supplanted by more recent works, and prevailing conceptions of the law in these areas have been modified in many respects. Although Minor's work on international institutions is no longer invoked, ideas similar to his about the need for such institutions remain popular. Debates over the need for and the structure of various international judicial and administrative bodies continue to occupy diplomats and international lawyers. Minor died in Charlottesville following a long illness. (No specific information about the nature of his illness is available.)

• Minor's papers are in several different collections at the University of Virginia. In addition to the books noted above, he wrote *The Law of Tax Titles in Virginia* (1898), *Notes on the Science of Government and the Relations of the States to the United States* (1913), and numerous articles. Biographical information and assessments of Minor's work appear in W. Hamilton Bryson, *Legal Education in Virginia* (1982); Paul B. Barringer, *University of Virginia*, vol. 2 (1904); American Historical Society, *History of Virginia*, vol. 4 (1924); John B. Minor, *The Minor Family of Virginia* (1923); Robert B. Tunstall, "Raleigh Colston Minor," *Proceedings of the Thirty-fourth Annual Meeting of the Virginia State Bar Association* (1923); and Edward James Woodhouse, "Raleigh Colston Minor, Scholar, Teacher, Jurist, Leader of American International Thinking," *Virginia Law Review* 12 (1926): 295–318. Four recollections of Minor's life and work written by William Minor Lile, Charles A. Graves, Murray M. McGuire, and Robert B. Tunstall are in *Virginia Law Review* 10 (1923): 89–105. An obituary is in the *Richmond Times Dispatch*, 16 June 1923.

JOHN E. NOYES

MINOR, Robert (15 July 1884–26 Nov. 1952), cartoonist and Communist party leader, was born in San Antonio, Texas, the son of Robert Minor and Routez Houston. Although both parents had distinguished forebears (his mother was related to Texas hero Sam Houston), Minor grew up in poverty. His father, an unsuccessful lawyer, did not achieve financial stability until his election as a district judge in 1910.

After four years of formal schooling, Minor began working at fourteen. He was a sign maker, clerk, farmhand, and railroad worker before his self-taught artistic skills enabled him to become the cartoonist for the *San Antonio Gazette* in 1904. He soon moved to St. Louis and was hired by the *Post-Dispatch*. By 1911 he was chief editorial cartoonist and reputedly the highest-paid cartoonist in the United States. He was one of the first newspaper cartoonists to abandon the brush and crayon for modern engraving processes.

Minor joined the Carpenter's Union in 1903; in St. Louis he became a Socialist under the influence of a doctor treating him for his growing deafness. He joined the Socialist party in 1907 and gravitated toward its syndicalist faction led by William "Big Bill" Haywood, who was expelled from the party in 1912 for advocating violence. A year's leave to study art in Paris (1912–1913) encouraged Minor's identification with anarcho-syndicalism.

Returning to the United States in 1913, he became cartoonist for the Pulitzer-owned *New York Evening World*. When World War I began, his antiwar position coincided with the newspaper's, but when the paper switched to support the Allies, Minor refused to tone down his position and was fired in 1915. His cartoons began to appear in anarchist journals like *Mother Earth* and socialist papers like the *Call*.

In the next several years, Minor served as a war correspondent for the *Call* and the Newspaper Enterprise Association in Europe and in Mexico, where he covered American forces in pursuit of Pancho Villa. He was the chief organizer of the defense committee for Tom Mooney, the labor leader charged with responsibility for bombing a Preparedness Day parade in San Francisco. Mooney was convicted, but a worldwide campaign finally got his sentence reduced from death to life imprisonment.

In mid-1918 Minor sailed to Russia to observe the revolutionary upheaval. After nine months, he returned to Paris where he was arrested by the French police and jailed by the U.S. Army, which charged him with undermining troop morale by distributing Bolshevik propaganda. Sentenced to be shot, Minor was saved by the intervention of Lincoln Steffens, an old acquaintance from the Mooney campaign. Still strongly influenced by anarcho-syndicalism, Minor criticized Soviet communism and Lenin for authoritarian practices and centralizing power.

In 1920 Minor made a sudden about-face, writing an article "I Change My Mind a Little," in which he endorsed bolshevism, the dictatorship of the proletariat, and Lenin—commitments he held for the rest of his life. He joined the Workers party (as the Communists were then known) that same year and went to work for the *Liberator*, a party magazine. He quickly was elevated to the leadership of the movement; he served on the first Central Executive Committee of the Workers party and attended the Third Communist International Congress as a party delegate in 1921. By the mid-1920s he had given up his artistic career to become a full-time Communist party functionary.

In 1915 Minor had married Pearl Bazaric, from whom he was divorced in 1919. For two years (1920–1922) he was married to the radical journalist and writer Mary Heaton Vorse.

Although he was at first a member of the wing that wanted to maintain a Communist party underground, Minor (he used the pseudonym Ballister for a while) quickly learned the virtue of attaching himself to the dominant Moscow-favored faction. As a member of the Ruthenberg-Lovestone grouping, he was in charge of Negro work in the party, and in 1928 he became editor of the *Daily Worker*. The following year Jay Lovestone, on being called to Moscow to battle for his political life, appointed Minor acting general secretary with orders to seize Communist party property should things go badly in the USSR. His trust was misplaced; Minor betrayed Lovestone and, as a reward, was named to the four-member secretariat that ran the CPUSA until Earl Browder became party leader.

Minor served Browder as diligently as he had served Lovestone. During the 1930s he led party demonstrations (he was arrested and jailed for six months for one 1930 unemployed demonstration), ran for mayor and governor of New York on the Communist ticket, traveled to Spain as a war correspondent during the Civil War, and undertook a variety of tasks for the party. During one of them he was briefly kidnapped by vigilantes in Gallup, New Mexico, while investigating labor violence. When Browder, whom Minor had praised in 1936 as "a new John Brown (1800–1859) of Pottawatamie," was imprisoned in 1940, he named Minor as acting general secretary of the CPUSA. He did little while serving in the post, which he held until 1942 when Browder was released from prison. In 1945, however, when Browder was deposed as party leader after being criticized on orders from Moscow, Minor denounced him, insisting that personal friendship could not stand in the way of political differences.

Despite his political shift, Minor's long and close association with the deposed Communist party leader adversely affected his career. He was appointed southern editor of the *Daily Worker*, a relatively minor position. After suffering a heart attack in 1947, he withdrew from active participation in party affairs. He retired to his home in Croton-on-Hudson with his wife, Lydia Gibson, an artist whom he had married in 1923. He died in Ossining, New York.

• The Robert Minor Papers are housed at Butler Library, Columbia University. The only biography of Minor is a frequently inaccurate and unreliable Communist-line work by Joseph North, *Robert Minor, Artist and Crusader* (1956). See also Theodore Draper, *The Roots of American Communism* (1957) and *American Communism and Soviet Russia* (1960), and Harvey Klehr, *The Heyday of American Communism: The Depression Decade* (1984). An obituary is in the *New York Times*, 28 Nov. 1952.

HARVEY KLEHR

MINOR, Virginia Louise (27 Mar. 1824–14 Aug. 1894), suffragist and reformer, was born in Goochland County or Caroline County, Virginia, the daughter of Warner Minor, a landowner, and Maria Timberlake. When she was two years old the family moved to Charlottesville, where her father took a supervisory position in the dormitories of the University of Virginia. She spent a short time in a local female academy but otherwise was educated at home. In 1843 Minor married an attorney and distant cousin, Francis Minor; they had one child. She went to live with him in Mississippi, and a year later the couple moved to St. Louis.

During the Civil War, Minor and her husband took a firm stand for the Union, despite the fact that both were Virginians. As a founding member of the St. Louis Ladies Union Aid Society, which soon became an important affiliate of the Western Sanitary Commission, Minor helped to organize public meetings, raise funds, and nurse wounded soldiers. She also provided local army hospitals and camps with daily supplies of milk and fruit from her estate. The work was exhausting but engrossing, and like many wartime volunteers Minor missed the intense activity when it ended. Her life became emptier still in 1866 when her only child died at fourteen in a shooting accident.

Minor soon began focusing her energies on the struggle for women's rights. In a political atmosphere dominated by the postwar debate over the rights of emancipated slaves, she became convinced that women as well as freedmen should have the right to vote. With the enthusiastic support of her husband, she became the first woman in Missouri to speak out on the subject. In 1867 she circulated a petition to the state legislature asking that a constitutional amendment that was under consideration for black male suffrage be expanded to include women. Although she obtained several hundred signatures, her request was soundly defeated. A few months later she helped organize the Woman Suffrage Association of Missouri—the first organization in the world dedicated solely to that aim. Minor served as the association's president for the next five years.

In 1869 the Missouri association organized a national suffrage convention in St. Louis. Minor electrified the participants with a speech asserting that women already had the right to vote since the Fourteenth Amendment (ratified the year before) had guaranteed "equal protection of the laws" to all American citizens. Suffrage, she maintained, was a privilege of citizenship. Striking a note that sometimes characterized suffragism during these years, Minor deplored the fact that a "free, moral intelligent woman, highly cultivated," who paid taxes just as a man did, should be placed below black males and naturalized foreigners and reduced to "a level with the savage"—American Indians, who also could not vote. She called on women to demand their rights in state legislatures, and if they were rejected to take their case to the Supreme Court. Her position was outlined in a set of resolutions written by her husband, which was adopted by the convention.

Minor made her speech just as the national suffrage movement was splitting into two rival organizations, the American Woman Suffrage Association (AWSA) and the National Woman Suffrage Association (NWSA). She steered a resolution through the Missouri association permitting members to join either group, but in 1871, when the association voted to align itself solely with the AWSA, Minor—who sided with the more militant NWSA—resigned her presidency.

By this time the NWSA had endorsed Minor's view that women already had the constitutional right to vote. This strategy, which came to be called the "New Departure," gained even more attention when the charismatic Victoria Woodhull made it the centerpiece of her testimony on woman suffrage to the House Judiciary Committee. To test the new idea, NWSA president Susan B. Anthony organized seventy women around the country, including Minor, to vote in the presidential election of 1872. When Minor tried to register, she was rejected by the county registrar, Reese Happersett, on the grounds that the state constitution permitted only males to vote.

None of the other suffragists succeeded either, but Minor and her husband added their own chapter to history by suing the registrar. Defeated in the lower courts, they appealed to the U.S. Supreme Court, where Minor's husband argued the case (*Minor v. Happersett*) in 1874. Once again they were defeated. Speaking for the unanimous court, Chief Justice Morrison R. Waite declared that each state had the power to grant or deny women the right to vote, since "the Constitution of the United States does not confer the right of suffrage upon anyone." This decision demolished the strategy that Minor had been advocating since 1869.

Minor continued to be active in suffrage activities until the end of her life. She maintained her membership in the NWSA and became the president of the local chapter when it was established in 1879. Although she and her allies made no headway on the vote during her lifetime, they helped reform a number of Missouri laws relating to women's property and personal rights. In 1890, when the two rival suffrage organizations reunited to form the National American Woman Suffrage Association (NAWSA), Minor was elected president of the Missouri branch. She served only two years before ill health forced her retirement. She won her last office when she was elected an honorary vice president of the Interstate Woman Suffrage Convention in Kansas City, Missouri, in 1892. She died two years later in St. Louis.

Minor stands out from other suffragists because of the constitutional case that bears her name and because of her husband's active participation in her work. But in other respects her experience is evidence of how much the suffrage movement benefited from (and how much it gave to) upper middle-class women like Minor in communities all across the country. Putting aside the more genteel volunteer activities expected of them, these women dedicated themselves to a cause that many people of their day thought misguided or even unnatural. And although few of them would live to see the ballot won, the suffragists of Minor's generation often found through the movement itself the opportunity for the active citizenship that they hoped the right to vote would give to all women.

• Minor's life is discussed in Monia Cook Morris, "The History of Woman Suffrage in Missouri, 1867–1901," *Missouri Historical Review* 25, no. 1 (Oct. 1930): 67–82; Marjorie Spruill Wheeler, ed., *One Woman, One Vote: Rediscovering the Woman Suffrage Movement* (1995); Alma Lutz, *Susan B. Anthony: Rebel, Crusader, Humanist* (1960); Elizabeth Cady Stanton et al., eds., *History of Woman Suffrage*, vols. 2 and 3 (1886), and Susan B. Anthony and Ida Houston Harper, eds., *History of Woman Suffrage*, vol. 4 (1902).

SANDRA OPDYCKE

MINOT, Charles Sedgwick (23 Dec. 1852–19 Nov. 1914), biologist, was born on a suburban estate in West Roxbury, Massachusetts, the son of William Minot, a wealthy Boston lawyer, and Katherine Maria Sedgwick. Minot's boyhood interest in collecting insects took definite form at fifteen, when he joined the Boston Society of Natural History. He immediately began publishing short papers in entomology and enrolled at the Massachusetts Institute of Technology the same year. Upon graduation in 1872 he began advanced work in natural history, working for a year with Louis Agassiz and Henry Pickering Bowditch at Harvard and then studying physiology and zoology for three years at the universities of Leipzig, Paris, and Würzburg. He returned to Harvard to complete the requirements for the doctor of science degree in 1878.

Minot was significant as an upper-class Boston leader of the late nineteenth-century movement to establish laboratory-based biomedical science in America. Up to the mid-1880s he cultivated a broad interest in pure science, publishing on vertebrate physiology, comparative embryology, anatomy and taxonomy of insects, and the general contours of a "theory of life" based on vital force. He publicized German approaches to zoology and argued that American medical schools should support autonomous professorships of biology. He was also an active member of the American Society for Psychical Research, an organization created to foster open-minded but rigorous inquiries into spiritualist phenomena.

Although his degree was in science rather than medicine, Minot was able to obtain a lectureship with a nominal salary at the Harvard Medical School (where his uncle Francis Minot was professor of medicine) in 1880. Over the next decade he gradually accommodated his science to the long-term interests of academic medicine. He invented the automatic rotary microtome, a tool for cutting specimens into a series of thin sections ready for microscopic analysis. He developed a laboratory course in histology and embryology for medical students, work that culminated in *A Laboratory Text-book of Embryology* (1903). He also prepared a large amount of reference material designed to make current work in medical science accessible to advanced students; the most notable example was his 800-page treatise, *Human Embryology* (1892). As professor of embryology at Harvard beginning in 1892, he was an influential member of the American Association of Anatomists, the American Society of Naturalists, and the American Association for the Advancement of Science.

During his mature years Minot focused his research on cell division and growth in vertebrates. His more general writings sought to address large questions and at the same time transform metaphysical anxieties into routine research. For example, in his 1907 Lowell Lectures, published as *The Problem of Age, Growth, and Death* (1908), he argued that aging was a cell phenomenon that was essentially complete before the individual left the womb. Although he rejected spiritualism, he continued to maintain—most notably in *Modern Problems of Biology* (1913)—that "consciousness" was a nonphysical cause of biological effects.

Minot married Lucy Fosdick in 1889. They had no children. With his carefully groomed Prince Edward beard and orderly work habits, Minot blended Brahmin gentility and modern scientific professionalism. His chief recreation was breeding new varieties of peonies. He died at his home in Milton, Massachusetts.

• A modest collection of Minot's correspondence is preserved at the Harvard Medical Library; the Charles W. Eliot Papers in the Harvard University Archives contain some administrative exchanges. The best sources on Minot are two biographical sketches: Frederic T. Lewis, "Charles Sedgwick Minot," *Anatomical Record* 10 (1916): 132–64, and Edward S. Morse, "Charles Sedgwick Minot, 1852–1914," *National Academy of Sciences, Biographical Memoirs* 9 (1920): 263–85; both include portraits as well as bibliographies of Minot's books (mentioned above) and his more than 180 scientific papers and lectures.

PHILIP J. PAULY

MINOT, George Richards (2 Dec. 1885–25 Feb. 1950), physician and pathologist, was born in Boston, Massachusetts, the son of James Jackson Minot, a physician, and Elizabeth Frances Whitney. His parents, believing Minot frail during his childhood, took him to Florida or California to spend winters. There Minot developed a lifelong interest in natural history; while still in his teens he published two papers, "The Chrysalis of Malitaea Gabbi" (1902) and "The Tussock Moth Peril" (1903). In 1904 Minot entered Harvard, after finishing his secondary education at a Boston private school. He received his B.A. in 1908; in 1912 he received his M.D. from the Harvard Medical School.

While a medical student, Minot became interested in hematology during work in the outpatient clinic with Homer Wright, who had developed the staining procedure for the microscopic examination of blood. While he was an intern at the Massachusetts General Hospital, Minot pursued this interest by studying anemic patients. To learn more about the physiology and pathology of the blood, he spent the years 1913 to 1915 in the laboratory of William Henry Howell at the Johns Hopkins Medical School. Because of Howell's interest in the mechanism of blood clotting, Minot was assigned the problem of studying the blood's antithrombin content. Minot's work on this problem became important for Howell's later work that resulted in the isolation of the anticoagulant heparin.

Minot married Marian Linzee Weld on 29 June 1915; they had two daughters and a son. That year he returned to Harvard and joined the medical staff of the Massachusetts General Hospital (MGH) as an assistant in medicine. Scientific investigation of patients' diseases was encouraged at MGH, so Minot, with Roger Lee, a professor of clinical medicine, investigated the role of blood platelets and found they were involved in blood clotting. At this time Minot also became interested in various types of anemia, especially pernicious anemia (resulting from impaired absorption of vitamin B_{12}). His first work on this problem was a study of patients suffering what was then called "blood thinning," a condition characterized by dangerously low red blood cell counts. Physicians had speculated that these low counts resulted from an unknown substance that destroyed the red blood cells. Most of these cases were unresponsive to treatment, and therapies such as arsenic or splenectomy brought only temporary remission. In most cases, pernicious anemia was fatal. While at Johns Hopkins, Minot had made a significant observation that during remission, there was a large increase in reticulocytes (new red blood cells), and he concluded that an increased reticulocyte count was a sign of clinical improvement. This observation proved useful in his future work.

During World War I, Minot investigated workers exposed to toxic chemicals. In 1923 he became physician in chief at the Collis P. Huntington Memorial Hospital in Boston, having begun work at the hospital in 1917. At this clinical cancer research center, he initiated a study of leukemia and continued his studies of pernicious anemia.

Minot developed diabetes in 1921, just a year before the isolation of a clinically usable insulin preparation by James B. Collip. Minot was treated by the accepted therapeutic routine, a semistarvation diet. Elliot Joslin, the famous Boston diabetes specialist, obtained batches of the first insulin produced in 1922, and with a regimen of strict dietary control and insulin, Minot was able to continue his productive life.

Minot became associated with William P. Murphy in a private practice in 1921. In 1923 he was appointed chief of the medical service at Huntington Hospital and a staff member at Peter Bent Brigham Hospital. These appointments placed Minot in a position to study pernicious anemia more intensely. His earlier interest in the influence of diet on disease led him to investigate the diets of patients with pernicious anemia. He found that the diets of anemia patients were unbalanced and lacking in vitamins, and that their symptoms resembled those seen in sprue, pellagra, and other dietary deficiency diseases.

George Hoyt Whipple, an acquaintance Minot had made while at the Johns Hopkins Medical School, had recently carried out a series of experiments in which he produced anemia in dogs by bleeding them; he had then studied which foods were most effective in restoring their red blood cell count. His experiments showed that although any meat and certain vegetables caused the red blood cells to return to normal levels, the best food for overcoming the anemia was liver. Minot fed liver to some of his private patients and found their red blood cell counts improved. Based on this success, Minot and Murphy began feeding liver to hospital patients with pernicious anemia. At the meeting of the American Association of Physicians in 1926, they reported that this had resulted in obvious clinical improvement, usually within two weeks. Minot used his previous observation that an increase in reticulocytes was an index of improvement.

Edwin Cohn at Harvard aided this work by preparing liver concentrates that were fifty to one hundred times more potent than liver. The rise in blood reticulocytes served as an index for standardization of the liver concentrates. Minot played an important role in working out the standardization procedures while serving on the Pernicious Anemia Committee at Harvard and on the Anti-Anemia Preparation Advisory Board of the U.S. Pharmacopoeia. In 1928 Minot was appointed professor of medicine at Harvard University, as well as director of the Thorndik Memorial Laboratory at Boston City Hospital. In these positions he continued his studies of anemia and became an internationally known consultant on blood diseases. For their discovery of the treatment of pernicious anemia, Minot, Murphy, and Whipple received the 1934 Nobel Prize for Physiology and Medicine.

In 1940 Minot developed vascular and neurological diseases brought on by his diabetes. A stroke in 1947 left him partially paralyzed, and at this time he gave up his active appointments at Harvard. He died in Brookline, Massachusetts.

• A detailed biography is W. B. Castle, "George Richards Minot, December 2, 1885–February 25, 1950," National Academy of Sciences, *Biographical Memoirs* 45 (1974): 337–83. Frances Rackemann, *The Inquisitive Physician: The Life and Times of George R. Minot* (1956), is a full-length biography. Minot's contributions are summarized in Paul DeKruif, *Men Against Death* (1932), and W. B. Castle, "The Contributions of George R. Minot to Experimental Medicine," *New England Journal of Medicine* 247 (1952): 585–92. A summary of the early treatment of pernicious anemia by diet is Minot's "The Treatment of Pernicious Anemia," *Harvey Society Publications* (New York) 23, no. 151 (1929): 154–77.

DAVID Y. COOPER

MINTO, Walter (6 Dec. 1753–21 Oct. 1796), mathematician, was born in a village near the Cowdenknows in the Merse district of Scotland. His family originated from Spain and once held elevated rank; however, his parents at the time of Minto's birth possessed meager resources. He somehow acquired enough education by the age of fifteen to enter the University of Edinburgh, where after completing his preparatory requirements he studied theology and literature. He became acquainted with the philosopher David Hume, who in retirement had become the patriarch of intellectual activity in Edinburgh. He also was a student of the noted professors Adam Ferguson, William Robertson, and Hugh Blair at the university. During this time Minto was a frequent contributor to literary periodicals, particularly *The Gentleman and Lady's Magazine of Edinburgh*, writing articles and essays on poetry, humor, and the arts.

Minto had a strong desire to visit Italy, and this was made possible when Hume recommended him to George Johnstone as a traveling tutor for his sons who were to study on the Continent. Minto and his charges left in May 1776. They ultimately settled in Pisa, where they had lodgings in the home of Joseph Slop von Cadenberg, then assistant to the professor of astronomy at the University of Pisa (becoming his successor in 1780). During this time Minto developed an interest in mathematics and astronomy. The Pisan sojourn was cut short by an illness of one of the Johnstone boys, as well as by a disagreement with their father. Minto returned to Edinburgh in early 1779 and began to teach mathematics there, probably in a temporary capacity with the university.

In March 1781, when William Herschel announced his finding of what was later identified as the planet Uranus, Slop sent Minto his observational data on the new planet. This led Minto to write a booklet, *Researches into Some Parts of the Theory of Planets in Which Is Solved the Problem, to Determine the Circular Orbit of a Planet by Two Observations; Exemplified in the New Planet* (1783). He was engaged in correspondence with members of the professional scientific community, notably the astronomer royal, Nevil Maskelyne, and most likely this booklet enhanced his popularity in Edinburgh. David Stewart Erskine, the eleventh earl of Buchan, invited him to contribute the technical part of his book, *An Account of the Life, Writings, and Inventions of John Napier of Merchiston* (1787). Napier had invented logarithms, and he was selected as the first person to be treated in the earl's elaborate plans for a *Biographica Scotia*. This project further increased Minto's stature and led to his being awarded an LL.D. by the University of Aberdeen; more important, it gained him a lifelong patron in the earl of Buchan.

In 1786 Minto chose to immigrate to the United States. Whether he did so out of liberal political principles (as evidenced in his early writings), a sympathy with the cause of American independence, or a lack of prospects for a permanent position in Scotland, is not known. Probably all three were factors in his decision. Almost immediately upon his arrival in America, Minto was appointed the principal of Erasmus Hall in Flatbush, Long Island, New York. Subsequently, with the support of the earl of Buchan, he was elected professor of mathematics and natural philosophy at the College of New Jersey (later Princeton University). He held this position from 1787 until his death. There he wrote the essay, *An Inaugural Oration, on the Progress and Importance of the Mathematical Sciences* (1788), which was his only other substantial publication. Noteworthy for its eloquence, his argument refuted the charge that the study of mathematics made men skeptical of everything that was not susceptible of a mathematical demonstration. On the contrary, Minto maintained that mathematics was the very handmaiden of religion, and that a student who lacked religious reverence did so because God had not bestowed him with sufficient understanding. The essay concluded with a prayer to the Supreme Being to let prosper the interests of science and literature in the United States, and to guide them to be ever subservient to the promotion of liberty, happiness, and virtue. By all accounts Minto was an enthusiastic and engaging teacher as well as a great asset in attempting to expand and rebuild the college following the revolutionary war. He is credited with the liberalization of the college curriculum to offer mathematics and the physical sciences in place of the traditional requirements of Greek and Latin. While at Princeton Minto married Mary Skelton; they had no children. He died, apparently quite unexpectedly, in Princeton.

Minto was at best an amateur in mathematics whose knowledge did not extend beyond rudimentary algebra, trigonometry, and analytic geometry. While this was not uncommon, or really unsuitable for his elementary teaching at Princeton, it was woefully inadequate for doing research in theoretical astronomy. Hence *Researches into Some Parts of the Theory of Planets*, with Minto's assumption of a "circular" orbit, did not impress professional astronomers. All the known planets had elliptical, or noncircular, orbits and there was no a priori reason to entertain such an assumption for the new planet. Moreover, although this may not have been known by Minto, the ongoing contemporary work of the French savants Joseph Louis Lagrange and Pierre Simon de Laplace (1766–1784) had established a level of accuracy that was wholly inconsistent with Minto's naive assumption. This is perhaps echoed by Minto's remarks to the earl of Buchan, in his few surviving letters, that the astronomers in London were very odd in that they neither acknowledged nor published the papers he sent them. Thus Minto's significance rests in being a historic personage rather than an astronomical or mathematical figure of distinction.

• The manuscript division of the Princeton University Library has a collection of Minto's correspondence, as well as his partial translation of the books of Charles Bossut, *Cours de mathématiques à l'usage des écoles militaires* (1782), which presumably was the basis of his Princeton lectures. There are few available reference sources on Minto, and none are completely reliable. These include the articles, "Walter Minto, LL.D.," *Princeton Magazine* 1 (Mar. 1850); and Luther Pfahler Eisenhart, "Walter Minto and the Earl of Buchan," *Proceedings of the American Philosophical Society* 94 (June 1950).

JOSEPH D. ZUND

MINTON, Sherman (20 Oct. 1890–9 Apr. 1965), U.S. Senator, associate justice of the U.S. Supreme Court, son of John Evan Minton, a farmer, and Emma Lyvers, was born on a farm near Georgetown, Indiana. After graduating from New Albany High School, he attended Indiana University, graduating at the head of his class in the law college in 1915. A scholarship enabled him to earn an L.L.M. degree at Yale Law School in 1916. Minton's law practice in New Albany, Indiana, was interrupted by service overseas as an infantry captain in World War I. Following his military discharge, he returned to his law practice in New Albany and became very active in the Democratic party. He married Gertrude Gurtz in 1917; they had three children.

In 1933 Indiana governor Paul McNutt, who had been a university classmate, inaugurated a "little New Deal" and named Minton to the state Public Service Commission. The following year he was elected to the U.S. Senate, where he was assigned a seat next to newly elected Harry S. Truman. His legal knowledge and activist manner made a quick impression in the Senate. As Democratic whip and assistant majority leader, he vigorously attacked the conservative decisions of the Supreme Court and supported President Franklin D. Roosevelt's "Court-packing" plan. He also proposed that a vote of seven justices be required to hold a federal statute unconstitutional. However, when the first Court vacancy occurred, Roosevelt's appointment went to another senator, Hugo L. Black. Subsequently, Roosevelt named Stanley Reed, Felix Frankfurter, William O. Douglas, and Frank Murphy to the bench, and the "Roosevelt Court" began its historic constitutional revolution.

In 1940 Minton was defeated for reelection to the Senate when the Republican presidential candidate, Wendell L. Willkie, carried the majority in Indiana. Moreover, he had advocated American intervention in Nazi-threatened Europe, and Indiana was an isolationist state. Roosevelt promptly rewarded Minton for his Senate service by appointing him first as a presidential assistant and liaison to military agencies, then, in May 1941, to the Court of Appeals for the Seventh Circuit (covering Indiana, Illinois, and Wisconsin). On the appeals court, he tended to favor labor, but he also upheld the anticommunist affidavits required for labor leaders under the Taft-Hartley Act.

The accession of Harry Truman to the presidency in 1945 was of major consequence for Minton. In addition to his Senate years with Truman, as presidential assistant to Roosevelt Minton had sponsored Truman's proposal for a Senate committee to investigate defense activities. The subsequent work of the "Truman committee" had made the senator widely and favorably known. So when Justice Wiley B. Rutledge died in 1949, Truman appointed Minton to that seat. Some conservative senators, opposing the nomination because of his support for the New Deal and "Court packing," made an effort to call him before the Senate Judiciary Committee to investigate his qualifications. Minton declined an appearance, citing Felix Frankfurter's recent refusal to appear before the committee at the time of his nomination.

Minton was Truman's fourth appointee to the Court, following Chief Justice Fred Vinson and Associate Justices Tom C. Clark and Harold Burton. Five Roosevelt appointees of varying views remained on the Court as he joined it: Hugo L. Black, Stanley Reed, Felix Frankfurter, William O. Douglas, and Robert H. Jackson. The heyday of New Deal liberalism was over, and Minton, contrary to expectations, proved to be a part of a reaction against the use of judicial power. He joined with Vinson, Clark, Burton, and Reed to constitute a majority undisposed to stress First Amendment rights or insist on strict criminal procedures. In a major anticommunist case, *Dennis et al. v. United States* (1951), he voted with the majority to convict the leaders of the American Communist party for conspiring to overthrow the government in violation of the Smith Act. He would even have upheld a state anticommunist law in *Pennsylvania v. Nelson* (1956) that the Court majority struck down as conflicting with the federal Smith Act. But Minton's amiability, warmth, and frankness enabled "Shay," as he was called, to get along well with the entire spectrum of the Court.

Minton consistently supported legislative power to deny government employment and other privileges to alleged subversives. He voted to uphold the procedures of President Truman's federal loyalty program in *Joint Antifascist Refugee Committee v. McGrath* (1951). He wrote the opinion in *Adler v. Board of Education of the City of New York* (1952), upholding a New York State law authorizing the firing of public school teachers on grounds of disloyalty and accepting membership in certain organizations as evidence of disloyalty. Justice Douglas, dissenting, thought that "the guilt of the teacher should turn on overt acts," not membership.

Minton almost never voted against the government in claims by defendants in criminal cases. For example, he wrote the opinion in *United States v. Rabinowitz* (1950), overruling a recent holding that search warrants had to be secured when practicable in searches incident to arrest. He was equally averse to interfering with administration of criminal justice in the states. He wrote, in *Lutwak v. United States* (1953), "A defendant is entitled to a fair trial but not a perfect one."

Minton consistently supported the government's power over economic matters. When the Court majority declared unconstitutional President Truman's seizure of the steel mills during the Korean War in *Youngstown Sheet & Tube Co. v. Sawyer* (1952), Minton joined in Vinson's dissenting opinion supporting the president's action.

Only in confronting racial discrimination did the Vinson Court, with Minton's full support, begin to show liberal concern. Restrictive property covenants operating to exclude minorities from home ownership were declared contrary to public policy and judicially unenforceable in *Shelley v. Kraemer* (1948). Five years later he added, in *Barrows v. Jackson* (1953), that state courts could not force a property owner to pay damages to neighbors for failure to observe a covenant's restrictions.

Cases involving racial discrimination in education also began to appear on the Vinson Court docket. *Sweatt v. Painter* (1950) held unanimously that the exclusion of a black student from the University of Texas Law School was unconstitutional. However, the Court avoided the major issue of racial discrimination in the public schools; with the sudden death of Chief Justice Vinson on 8 September 1953 that dilemma became the responsibility of the new chief justice, Earl Warren.

Justifiably, Minton regarded his vote in *Brown v. Board of Education* (1954) as his most important action on the Court. Chief Justice Warren's strategy called for a simple, strong, and unanimous opinion declaring racial discrimination in the public schools unconstitutional. At the Court's initial conference on this issue, 12 December 1953, Minton forcefully supported this strategy. The concept of a "separate" equality, he said, had been read into the Constitution by the Supreme Court in *Plessy v. Ferguson* (1896) and should now be read right out of it. The world of 1953, he continued, was very different from that of the 1890s, and no justification remained for racial barriers except an avowed belief in black inferiority. As for the enforcement of the judicial decision, he preferred to leave that to the federal district courts to settle in keeping with local conditions, a procedure very close to that actually provided for in the *Brown* decision.

In other areas, however, Minton opposed the judicial liberalism of the Warren Court majority. Poor health forced him to retire from the bench in 1956 at the early age of sixty-five. He died in New Albany, Indiana.

• Richard Kirkendall summarizes Minton's judicial career in Leon Friedman and Fred L. Israel, eds., *The Justices of the United States Supreme Court 1789–1969* (1969). Harry L. Wallace, one of Minton's law clerks, favorably appraises his career in "Mr. Justice Minton: Hoosier Justice on the Supreme Court," *Indiana Law Journal* 34 (1959–1960): 145–205, 383–424. C. Herman Pritchett presents Minton in the context of the Vinson Court in *Civil Liberties and the Vinson Court* (1954). A small collection of Minton papers in the Harry S. Truman Library deals with Minton's work on the Supreme Court.

C. Herman Pritchett

MINUIT, Peter (1589?–1638), director general of New Netherland and governor of New Sweden, was born in Wesel, duchy of Cleves, the son of Jean Minuit and Sarah Breil. His parents were Walloons, French-speaking members of the Reformed church, but they lived in an area with a large Dutch-speaking population. Peter undoubtedly knew both languages. He spelled his name Minuit, French for "midnight," rather than the Dutch spelling Minnewit. His surviving letters, however, are in Dutch. In 1613 he married Gerdruudt Raets in Wesel. Her father was burgomaster of Kleve. Minuit moved to Utrecht and was living there in 1615 while learning diamond cutting. He apparently later returned to Wesel, where he served as a ruling elder of the Walloon church. In May 1624 the city records noted that Minuit was about to undertake a long voyage. His wife returned to Kleve in 1625.

Minuit's experiences in America began when he sailed to the Dutch West India Company's new colony of New Netherland in January 1625. He accompanied the provisional director Willem Verhulst, whose instructions mentioned Minuit as a "volunteer" charged with investigating the "condition of the land" and bartering with the Indians. Verhulst's second set of instructions named Minuit to the director's council. Later in 1625, for unknown reasons, Minuit returned to Holland, but he was on his way back to New Netherland in January 1626. Upon his arrival on 4 May the council appointed him director general. It had removed Verhulst from office for bad behavior, and the colony was in turmoil. Legend states that Minuit then purchased Manhattan Island from the natives for beads worth $24. The documentary evidence is incomplete, and the story of Minuit's role has accumulated many myths since 1626. Surviving letters indicate that he ordered Jan Lampo, his *schout* (a Dutch administrative officer), to organize a meeting with local Delaware Indian leaders to discuss the Dutch interest in buying Manhattan. Circumstantial evidence suggests that the purchase was completed in mid-May so that the Dutch could complete Fort Amsterdam and plant crops on the southern tip of the island. In all probability, Minuit was director of the colony when Manhattan was purchased and played a leading role, but by no means did he act alone. Minuit's letters to the company have not survived. The purchase is only mentioned in a letter of Peter Jansz Schagen, who reported in November that "they have purchased the Island of Manhattes from the Indians for the value of 60 guilders." The legend of twenty-four dollars' worth of beads used in the purchase is a fabrication. There is no evidence that beads were included in what must have been a wide variety of trade goods, and the $24 equivalent is an estimate that became outdated and woefully inaccurate long ago. Delaware Indian versions of the purchase do not indicate that the natives felt cheated by the Dutch. In fact, the sachems who sold Manhattan may have been the ones who took advantage of their trading partners' naiveté, for they probably had no authority to sell the land.

Minuit's reorganization of New Netherland is more important than his role in the purchase of Manhattan. In 1624 the company had scattered the first colonists, Walloon families, at posts on the North (now Hudson) and South (now Delaware) rivers, with only a small fort on Noten (now Governor's) Island. Minuit ordered the consolidation of settlement at Manhattan, which thereby became the political and economic center of the colony, leaving vacant Fort Nassau near present Gloucester, New Jersey, and reducing Fort Orange (now Albany) to a trading post staffed by company officers and soldiers. Minuit spent much of July soothing relations with the Mohawks around Fort Orange. He appointed a successor to the commissary killed in a skirmish with the Mohawks. He sent the trader Pieter Barentsen to renew the Dutch friendship with the Mohawks. Minuit also established relations with Plymouth Colony in 1627. Indians carried letters in Dutch and French from the director to Governor William Bradford. Minuit reminded the English of the long-standing affinities between Holland and England, in particular their recent alliance against the Spanish, and hoped that trade between the two colonies could begin. He presented "our good will and servise unto you, in all frendly-kindes and neighbourhood." Bradford replied amicably, and the relationship remained competitive but cordial for many years.

In 1628 the Reverend Jonas Michaëlius arrived in New Netherland as its first minister. He chose Minuit and Minuit's brother-in-law Jan Huyghens, the company storekeeper, to serve as elders of the Reformed church. Michaëlius described them as "persons of very good character." Meanwhile, the director increased the colony's exports of furs and timber and experimented with tobacco cultivation. Minuit encouraged the company to increase trade even more by ending the company monopoly and opening settlement to patroons who would develop the colony at their own expense. As an advocate of this view he became embroiled in a bitter dispute that split the colony's leadership. Michaëlius among others turned on Minuit in 1630, calling him "a slippery fellow who, under the painted mask of honesty, was a compound of all iniquity and wickedness."

In 1631 the company recalled Minuit and his nemesis Johan van Remunde, the colony's secretary. The directors examined Minuit for several months, then dismissed him. In his six years as director, the Dutch exported beaver and otter pelts worth 400,000 guilders, but the colony remained unprofitable. Minuit sold his farm and livestock in 1632 to the new director Wouter van Twiller and the patroon Kiliaen van Rensselaer. At about this time he is thought to have produced a map of New Netherland known as the Buchellius Chart. Kleve granted him citizenship in May 1635.

That his parting with the company was not altogether amicable is indicated in the threats of another company official who in 1662 declared that he would follow Minuit, who "had not been well treated by the Company" and "had brought the Swedes here." Minuit's actions in 1636–1638 support the spirit of this later account. In 1636 Swedish chancellor Axel Oxenstierna sought the advice of Dutchmen to help his nation enter the race for international trade. Samuel Blommaert, who knew Minuit from their involvement in the West India Company, drew him into the scheme to create a Swedish colony in North America. In June 1636 Minuit wrote a letter to Oxenstierna that outlined his vision for New Sweden, a colony to be planted across the Delaware River from the east bank claimed by the Dutch. In early 1637 Minuit embarked for Sweden to brief the council of state. He fell ill and was not able to leave Stockholm until August. At Gothenburg he supervised the loading of two ships for the expedition. The New Sweden Company, financed equally by Swedish and Dutch investors (including Minuit), ordered him to sail to the Minquas Kill in present-day Wilmington, Delaware, and there to avoid the Dutch, purchase land from the Indians, and establish a trading post. Undoubtedly Minuit's experience as the director of New Netherland shaped in large measure these plans for New Sweden.

After an unplanned stop in Holland for repairs, the expedition sailed late in December 1637, carrying cargo and Arent van Curler for van Rensselaer's patroonship in New Netherland. In March Minuit chose "the Rocks" two miles up the Minquas Kill as the site for Fort Christina. In the months that followed he met with local sachems and purchased the land along the kill, attempted unsuccessfully to trade for tobacco in Virginia, and sparked the first conflict with the Dutch by sailing beyond nearby Fort Nassau (by then reoccupied) to trade with Indians. With a garrison of twenty-four in place, including his grandnephew, Minuit sailed in June to the Caribbean in search of Spanish prizes. He stopped in St. Christopher, where he and his captain visited a ship in the harbor from Rotterdam. While they were on board, sometime around 5 August 1638, a hurricane blew the ship out to sea. Minuit was never seen again. Nevertheless, his enthusiasm for American colonies and his leadership of the first Swedish expedition had convinced the Swedes that they could tap a profitable trade in furs and tobacco.

Unfortunately, Minuit has been mythologized in American history as the man who swindled Manhattan Island from the Indians for a handful of trifles. His real significance lies in a wider range of actions from 1626 to 1638 when he set New Netherland on firm footing and helped launch New Sweden. Both colonies challenged the English and Spanish grip on North America. In this commercial and political drama, Minuit had risen to a leading role that was cut short by his unfortunate death at the peak of his career.

• Few of Minuit's papers have survived. Letters from his involvement in New Sweden are in the Riksarkivet, Stockholm. Documents that illustrate his directorship of New Netherland have been published in A. J. F. van Laer, ed. and trans., *Documents Relating to New Netherland, 1624–1664, in the Henry E. Huntington Library* (1924); J. Franklin Jameson, ed., *Narratives of New Netherland, 1609–1664* (1909); William T. Davis, ed., *Bradford's History of Plymouth Plantation* (1908); and A. J. F. van Laer, ed. and trans., *Van Rensselaer Bowier Manuscripts* (1908). Minuit's role in the purchase of Manhattan is debated in George Olin Zabriskie and Alice P. Kenney, "The Founding of New Amsterdam: Fact and Fiction; Part V.—The Purchase of Manhattan," *De Halve Maen* 51 (Jan. 1977): 11–12, 15–16; Charles Gehring, "Peter Minuit's Purchase of Manhattan Island—New Evidence," *De Halve Maen* 55 (Spring 1980): 6–7, 17; and Peter Francis, Jr., "The Beads That Did *Not* Buy Manhattan Island," *New York History* 67 (1986): 5–22. Friedrich Gorissen, "Peter Minuit und die Stadt Kleve," *Kalendar für das Klever Land* (1982): 112–18, discusses his years in Kleve. Minuit's involvement in New Sweden is covered in Amandus Johnson, *The Swedish Settlements on the Delaware* (2 vols., 1911). C. A. Weslager, *A Man and His Ship: Peter Minuit and the Kalmar Nyckel* (1989), while not only a biography, is a thorough treatment of his life that also includes the first translation of Minuit's plan for New Sweden.

James Homer Williams

MIRANDA, Carmen (9 Feb. 1909–5 Aug. 1955), star of stage, screen, and recordings, was born Maria do Carmo Miranda da Cunha in Marco de Canaveses, a small town in Portugal, the daughter of Jose Maria Pinto da Cunha, a barber, and Maria Emilia Miranda. Her father immigrated to Brazil in 1909, and the family followed when Miranda was three. "Carmen," as she was always called, grew up in Rio's Lapa waterfront district, a haven for sailors and prostitutes. At a convent school Miranda became interested in singing. She later told interviewers, "From a very early age, I knew I felt the need to be in show business." When Olinda, the eldest daughter, died in 1923, Miranda quit school to work as a window decorator and as a salesclerk in a hat shop. She learned broken English from watching American movies, especially westerns. She modeled hats and began making them for society clients.

Miranda began singing in carnival samba parades when she was sixteen and developed an act in which she imitated Argentina and Brazil's popular vocalists. High society considered her common and vulgar, and her sister Aurora said Miranda traveled with a "fast" artistic crowd and had a "shocking mouth." In 1928 she was discovered by composer-guitarist Josué de Barroso. She became a successful radio singer and in 1930 was signed by RCA. Her demonstration record, "Tai," was her first release and became an instant hit. Miranda soon became one of the largest-selling female artists in Brazil. Tourists clamored to see her stage show, "a rebellious act to assert myself apart from prevailing fashion," in which she dressed in colorful *bahianas*, ruffled and billowy costumes derived from those common in Brazil's eastern state of Bahia. At the age of twenty-four Miranda appeared with her sister Aurora in *A Voz Do Carnaval* (1933), the first of Miranda's six Brazilian *chanchadas* (comic musicals). As early as 1934, stars Ramon Novarro and Tyrone Power saw her act and promoted her to Hollywood producers as a "vibrant bundle of fireworks." But it was New York that beckoned first.

At the urging of Norwegian Olympic ice skater and Hollywood star Sonja Henie, Broadway impresario Lee Shubert signed Miranda after seeing her performance at the Cassino da Urca. In 1939 she became an overnight sensation in the revue *Streets of Paris*, costarring with film and vaudeville comic Bobby Clark and with comedy duo Abbott and Costello. Influential columnist Walter Winchell dubbed Miranda the "Brazilian Bombshell." Darryl Zanuck of 20th Century–Fox signed her. Miranda's Hollywood debut was *Down Argentine Way* (1940), which starred Betty Grable as a rich American in love with a horsebreeder, played by Don Ameche. Brilliantly decked out as, in one writer's description, "a bird of paradise," Miranda stole the film, singing Al Dubin and Jimmy McHugh's "South American Way."

In *That Night in Rio* (1941), a story of mistaken identities costarring Alice Faye and Ameche, Miranda introduced Harry Warren and Mack Gordon's "I, Yi, Yi, Yi, Yi" and "Chic Chica Boom Chic," both of which became bestselling records. During a scene for *Week-end in Havana* (1941), after a quick change for a dance number with Cesar Romero, Miranda was photographed sans undergarment during a dashing spin. The incident was quickly laughed off on the set, but a photo in *Confidential* magazine created quite a scandal. On completion of the film Miranda in 1941 returned to New York to record for Decca Records. She created pandemonium on Broadway in November 1941, when she starred opposite Olsen and Johnson in the critically and commercially successful *Sons o' Fun*. A year later she resumed her film career.

In her fourteen films Miranda—sexy, naughty, and fantastically and hilariously overdressed—literally burst from the screen. Only 5′3″, she wore seven-inch "elevator" wedges. She claimed to wear them "so that when I dance with big men, I can see over their shoulder. I don't want them flirting with other girls." In spite of her quick delivery of broken English, she established a love affair with the camera, and when she danced (and how she managed to dance in those platform shoes remains a mystery) it seemed she was flirting with the men in the audience. Her ebullient routines were marked by constant movement of hands and arms adorned with pounds of bracelets. Her Technicolor outfits were always topped with an exotic turban or a gigantic headdress stacked with bananas, other tropical fruits, flowers, and tiny umbrellas.

Writer John Kobal observed that Miranda "chewed the English language around until it came out sounding like an ancient Inca dialect." Nonetheless she imbued the pervasive wartime escapism with an unflagging pace and became one of the country's highest-paid entertainers. She became the first mainstream camp icon since Mae West in the 1930s. Her exaggerated mannerisms, costumes, and headdresses became a staple of female impersonators. Women adopted her hairstyles, and turbans became the rage, especially among female wartime defense factory workers. President Franklin D. Roosevelt, pushing his Good Neighbor policy, named Miranda Latin America's Ambassador of Good Will.

In *The Gang's All Here* (1943), directed by Busby Berkeley, Miranda sang Leo Robin and Harry Warren's "The Lady in the Tutti-Frutti Hat" in a typical Berkeley extravaganza. Surrounded by sixty scantily clad "native" girls, a banana-bedecked Miranda entered on a cart pulled by gold-painted oxen. Her headdress was further exaggerated by a surrealistic backdrop of bananas that soared to the heavens. Miranda then made four films in quick succession: *Springtime in the Rockies* (1942), *Four Jills in a Jeep*, in which she was sent to cheer the troops, *Something for the Boys*, and *Greenwich Village*, in which she added tropical spice to Manhattan (all 1944).

In 1943 Miranda underwent cosmetic surgery on her nose, which turned out disastrously. Throughout her career she experienced bouts of depression, culminating in a nervous breakdown. And though she never drank, she suffered a series of liver ailments. She took a leave of absence to recover her health. On her return nearly a year later, her crown of bananas began to wear thin, and Miranda became captive to formula routines in lackluster musicals. She was even briefly rejected by the Brazilian public, who found her sketches insulting. After she appeared in two more Fox films (*Doll Face*; *If I'm Lucky*, both 1946), Zanuck decided not to renew her contract. Miranda and her agent David Sebastain decided to rethink her career. She made the independent *Copacabana* (1947), in which she was paired with Groucho Marx, but the film was not a great success.

In March 1947, after a long trail of lovers and fiancés and after declaring "I need a man to sustain me," Miranda married Sebastain (they had no children). MGM signed her in 1948 for *A Date with Judy*, in which she costarred with Jane Powell, Elizabeth Taylor, and Wallace Beery. Beery was her dance partner, and Miranda appeared without her usual headdresses and *bahianas* but rather in plain yet flattering clothes. Though *A Date with Judy* was one of the top-grossing films of the year, it proved not very profitable for Miranda's career. That spring she journeyed to Britain for a ten-week sold-out engagement at London's Palladium.

In the summer of 1950 Miranda appeared with Mickey Rooney, Jack Dempsey, Rudy Vallee, and George Burns on the Hadacol Caravan, a tour sponsored by the cough elixir and TV game show sponsor that traveled 4,000 miles through the South on a special train. Also in 1950 Miranda appeared in the film *Nancy Goes to Rio*. Sebastain booked Miranda for top-dollar engagements at Las Vegas's El Rancho Hotel and Casino (1950) and Desert Inn (1951). She made guest appearances with Milton Berle on his NBC TV show "Texaco Star Theatre." In 1953 Miranda undertook a European tour to great acclaim.

After what proved to be her last film, *Scared Stiff* (1953), Miranda was diagnosed with a heart ailment. In 1954, seriously ill, she returned to Brazil. On a trip to Havana in July 1955 Miranda contracted a mild case of pneumonia. She returned to Hollywood at the end of the month to rest. However, incapable of refusing any offer that might further her career, she performed a demanding routine during a taping of the "Jimmy Durante Show," against her doctor's orders. While dancing with Eddie Jackson she suddenly became short of breath but refused medical attention. Her husband discovered her body the next morning; she had suffered a fatal heart attack. More than 4,000 people attended her funeral in Hollywood. Her body was then returned to Brazil, where a day of national mourning was declared. On the Rio de Janeiro oceanfront there is a small but impressive museum containing some of Miranda's costumes, jewels, and career memorabilia. Thanks to film revivals and videos of her movies and countless parodies in films and TV commercials, Miranda and her unique style are well remembered.

• Martha Gil-Montero, *Brazilian Bombshell* (1989), is a biography available in English. Abel Cardoso, Jr., *Carmen Miranda: A Cantora do Brasil* (1978), is in Portuguese. Anecdotes and scenes from her memorable production numbers appear in several Hollywood print anthologies, including John Kobal, *Gotta Sing Gotta Dance: A Pictorial History of Film Musicals* (1970), and Tony Thomas and Jim Terry with Busby Berkeley, *The Busby Berkeley Book* (1973). In 1994 Miranda was the subject of the documentary film *Carmen Miranda, Bananas Is My Business*, directed by Helena Solberg and written by Solberg and David Meyer. An obituary is in the *New York Times*, 9 Aug. 1955.

ELLIS NASSOUR

MIRÓ, Esteban Rodríguez (1744–4 June 1795), Spanish army officer and governor of Louisiana and West Florida, was born in Reus, Catalonia, Spain, to Francisco Miró and Mariana de Miró y Sabater, a middle-class family with ties to the lower nobility. He entered the Zamora Regiment in 1760 as a cadet during the Seven Years' War and served in the Spanish invasion of Portugal in 1762. About 1765 he went to Mexico in the Corona Regiment, serving as an adjutant and rising in rank to lieutenant. He returned to Spain by the early 1770s. He participated in General Alejandro O'Reilly's ill-fated expedition against Algiers in 1775 designed to punish the North Africans for raids on the Spanish coast. He completed a course of study at the Avila Military School in 1777, after which O'Reilly selected him to be the sergeant major (second in command) of the Fixed Louisiana Infantry Battalion, with the rank of brevet lieutenant colonel. He arrived in Louisiana in June 1778.

When Spain entered the American revolutionary war in 1779, Miró accompanied Governor Bernardo de Gálvez as his aide in the expedition that seized British garrisons at Manchac and Baton Rouge in West Florida. In 1780 he traveled to Havana to obtain troops for Gálvez's attack on Mobile, and he served as the governor's aide-de-camp in the 1781 conquest of Pensacola. For his services he gained promotions, becoming colonel in 1781 and commandant of the Fixed Louisiana Infantry Regiment in 1782.

Gálvez appointed Miró acting governor of Louisiana and West Florida on 20 January 1782 and proprietary governor in August 1785. In 1788 Miró also became intendant. In June 1782 he personally led troops to reinforce Natchez against threats from the British Loyalist James Colbert.

Miró encountered problems after the war because Great Britain had negotiated two different boundary settlements with Spain and the United States. Britain recognized the Spanish conquest of West Florida in the war. At the same time, it ceded to the Americans West Florida to the thirty-first parallel and the right to navigate the Mississippi River even where Spain owned both banks of the river. Because he had few soldiers and limited funds, Miró worked to attract the southern Indians to Spanish allegiance and to form a buffer zone against the United States. He used the British trading firms of Mather & Strother and Panton, Leslie & Company to provide the southern Indians with arms to halt American encroachment on Indian and Spanish lands. After the Spanish court ordered Miró to stop, he ceased arming the Indians in the late 1780s, which temporarily turned them against Spain. In June 1784, the Spanish government also closed the Mississippi River to the Americans, which they had used during the war, and that brought rumors of invasion nearly every summer from the angry western Americans.

In 1785 the state of Georgia claimed, under the 1783 Anglo-American peace treaty, "Bourbon County" on the banks of the Mississippi in Spanish-held West Florida. Georgia commissioned four justices of the peace for Bourbon County, who assumed greater authority. They called themselves commissioners and attempted to take possession. Miró refused to acknowledge their claim and rushed troops to defend Natchez, the principal settlement on the Mississippi in West Florida. While the American government disavowed the actions of Georgia, threats to Spanish control of West Florida continued.

As western American settlements increased in population, Miró needed immigrants to help defend Louisiana and West Florida. He believed that the Anglo-American population of the Natchez district inherited after the war was loyal to Spain, and he hoped to encourage additional American settlers. When James Wilkinson arrived in New Orleans in 1787 with a proposal to detach the American West and form an alliance with Spain in order to gain trading advantages, Miró endorsed the plan and added a second proposal for American colonists to settle in West Florida. The Spanish government was already sending English-speaking Irish priests living in Spain to convert the Protestant Anglo-Americans of West Florida; Miró now asked for more Irish priests for the expected Protestant immigrants. In December 1788 the court accepted his immigration proposal and sought to woo the Natchez planters by buying their tobacco. Western Americans were also permitted to export their goods via Louisiana, subject to a 15 percent tariff. Plans to detach the American West and to countercolonize lower Louisiana, however, had largely failed by 1791. Because the threat of war continued, Miró began construction of fortifications at Nogales (Vicksburg) and near the Mississippi's mouth (Plaquemines) to protect Louisiana.

As governor, Miró was an able, imaginative, and popular administrator. He worked to reconcile different social groups in the colony. He encouraged agriculture and industry by securing royal purchases of tobacco and permitting greater commerce overseas. Additional growth would have been possible had royal funds been available. In 1788 when a fire destroyed much of New Orleans, he initiated its reconstruction and trade with American cities on the Atlantic coast.

In 1779 Miró married Marie Céleste Elenore de Macarty, daughter of the prominent New Orleans merchant Bartolome de Macarty. Their only child, Matilde Ana Francisca, died in infancy.

Miró surrendered the governorship on 30 December 1791 and returned to Spain, where he served the Ministry of War. He became a field marshal and returned to active duty in 1793 in Spain's war against the French Republic (1793–1795). He died on the Franco-Spanish front from natural causes.

• In addition to Caroline Maude Burson, *The Stewardship of Don Esteban Miró, 1782–1792* (1940), see Gilbert C. Din's studies: "The Immigration Policy of Governor Esteban Miró in Spanish Louisiana," *Southwestern Historical Quarterly* 73 (1969): 155–75; "War Clouds on the Mississippi: Spain's 1785 Crisis in West Florida," *Florida Historical Quarterly* 60 (1981): 51–76; and *Francisco Bouligny: A Bourbon Soldier in Spanish Louisiana* (1993). There is much information on Miró in the Spanish archives and in New Orleans: Archivo General de Indias (Seville); Archivo Histórico Nacional (Madrid); Archivo General de Simancas (near Valladolid); Louisiana Historical Center (New Orleans); New Orleans Notarial Archives; and Tulane University Special Collections.

GILBERT C. DIN

MIRSKY, Alfred Ezra (17 Oct. 1900–19 June 1974), biochemist and cellular biologist, was born in New York City, the son of Michael David Mirsky, a manufacturer of nurses uniforms, and Frieda Ittelson. After his 1918 graduation from the Ethical Culture School in New York, Mirsky enrolled at Harvard College. He received a bachelor of arts degree in 1922 and began graduate study at Columbia University's College of Physicians and Surgeons. In 1924 a fellowship to study biochemistry at Cambridge University in England resulted in his doctoral dissertation, "The Hemoglobin Molecule," and a Ph.D. from Cambridge in 1926. In the same year he married Reba Paeff, a Radcliffe College graduate and a harpsichordist who performed with early music groups. She was also an award-winning author of children's books. The couple had two children.

In 1927 Mirsky joined the Rockefeller Institute for Medical Research in New York City. He spent his entire career there as an assistant (1927); an associate (1929); an associate member (1940); a member (1948); and, when the Institute became a graduate university, a professor (1954). From 1965 until his retirement in 1972 he was librarian of Rockefeller University. His wife died in 1966, and the following year he married Sonia Wohl, a Rockefeller associate librarian.

Mirsky first worked for Rockefeller as an assistant to the physiologist Alfred Cohn, an expert on the use of the new electrocardiograph machine to study heart function. However, by 1929 Cohn was no longer active in research, leaving Mirsky free to pursue his own interests. A friendship at Cambridge with another American student, Mortimer Anson, led to a collaboration when Anson joined the Institute. They believed in the molecularity of proteins, contrary to the prevailing view that proteins were undefinable colloidal aggregates with no specific molecular structure. Mirsky and Anson developed methods to investigate protein properties and, in 1931, discovered the reversibility of protein denaturation. Although denaturation by heat or acid involved a drastic change in properties, they proved that the natural and denatured forms of a protein were in equilibrium, and they argued that the process was explainable in terms of molecular structure. They proposed that the amino acid peptide chains were coiled in the natural state, denaturation being an unfolding of the coils and renaturation a return to the original condition.

Mirsky spent his 1935–1936 sabbatical year with Linus Pauling at the California Institute of Technology. Pauling was a pioneer in the use of X-ray diffraction to determine molecular structure and a leader in developing the ideas of Gilbert N. Lewis on chemical bonds formed by electron pair sharing. Mirsky and Pauling found that two types of such bonds existed in a protein: covalent bonds in the peptide chains and weaker hydrogen bonds within the molecule. Small changes in heat or acidity would not disrupt the covalent bonds but would destroy the hydrogen bonds, with serious effects on the properties of a protein. In 1936 Mirsky and Pauling proposed that the amino acid peptide chains were not arranged in a stringlike fashion but folded back on themselves, with the folds maintained by the weak intramolecular hydrogen bonds between the side groups of amino acids. These bonds gave to the chains a specific geometrical configuration. Denaturation consisted of the loss of a well-defined configuration for a more random one caused by the destruction of the hydrogen bonds by heat or acid. Their model agreed with the chemical data on denaturation and with data from X-ray diffraction studies of proteins. This general theory of protein structure provided the first clear view of proteins having a precisely arranged three-dimensional structure and represented the appearance of a new approach to molecular structure, one in which informed guesswork and model-building were prominent.

On his return to the institute Mirsky demonstrated that muscle contraction was a denaturation involving changes in the muscle protein myosin. In 1938 his line of investigation took a new direction. He isolated a protein complex from what other scientists claimed came from the cytoplasm of the cell. However, he found it to be a fibrous material from the cell nucleus. This material contained large amounts of deoxyribonucleic acid (DNA), and he wondered about the significance of DNA and its associated protein. With this in mind he established a partnership with Arthur Pollister, a cytologist at Columbia University. During the 1940s Mirsky and Pollister developed methods to extract DNA from cell nuclei and demonstrated that the DNA came from the chromosomes in the nucleus. In 1942, using salmon sperm obtained from city fish markets, they isolated a viscous, colorless solution of nuclear material that contained a mass of delicate threads. The threads were easily lifted out of the solution by inserting a rod and twisting it; the threads matted tightly to the rod. The threads were chromatin, almost pure chromosomes, the first time extracted intact from the nucleus. Chromatin consisted of more than 90 percent DNA combined with histone, a protein rich in basic amino acids, with the remainder being nonhistone protein. They achieved similar results with a variety of animal, plant, and bacterial cells. DNA with its combined histone was the universal constituent of chromosomes.

The Mirsky-Pollister methods proved useful to Oswald Avery, Colin Macleod, and Maclyn McCarty at the institute. They showed in 1944 that the DNA of one strain of pneumococcus, when extracted and inserted into another strain, produced a genetic transformation. This suggested that DNA must be the material that transmits hereditary traits.

In 1946 Hans Ris joined Mirsky's research group. Five years later Mirsky and Ris established the constancy of DNA in cells. They isolated large amounts of chromosomal material from about sixty different species and discovered how to determine quantitatively the amount of DNA in a nucleus. This DNA count revealed that DNA was present in the same amount in all body cells of a given species, with the germ cells having one-half that amount. Mirsky concluded from his work and that of Avery, Macleod, and McCarty that DNA must be closely associated with the hereditary factors of the chromosomes, most likely as part of the stuff of which hereditary material is made. He was not willing to state that DNA is the genetic material, because he believed that the chromosomal proteins might also be involved.

In 1948 Mirsky became a full member of the institute and director of a new laboratory with an enlarged staff. During the 1950s his contributions became part of the worldwide explosion in DNA research, especially after the 1953 appearance of the Francis Crick and James Watson double helix model with its strands of nucleotides held together by Mirsky-Pauling hydrogen bonds. Mirsky enthusiastically accepted the double helix model and focused his research on the roles of DNA and nuclear proteins in the biosynthetic processes of the cell. In the 1950s, with Vincent Allfrey and Marie Daly, he proved that protein synthesis in cells depends on ribonucleic acid (RNA). Protein synthesis took place in the cytoplasm, and they found that the tissues associated with synthesis were rich in RNA. RNA assembled and incorporated amino acids into the peptides of the proteins in cells in specific sequences determined by the RNA nucleotides. These findings became part of a larger picture developed by many scientists in which DNA in the nucleus transcribes its coded information into RNA, with RNA serving as the messenger that conveys the information for assembling the amino acids into the proteins unique to each cell.

Mirsky also contributed important findings on the chromosomal histone and nonhistone proteins, demonstrating that they were the regulators of gene action. DNA contains histone proteins, and in 1968 Mirsky and Allfrey announced that histones inhibit gene action by binding tightly to DNA, making segments of DNA nucleotides unavailable for RNA synthesis. In contrast, the nonhistone proteins serve to pry the histones loose from their binding sites on DNA. Naked areas of DNA thus become available for RNA synthesis and gene action. Much of Mirsky's work on the chromosomal proteins was unfinished at the time of his death, with proposed mechanisms remaining speculative.

Mirsky was also an important educator, editor, and critic of genetic determinism. He helped shape the graduate program at Rockefeller University, successfully arguing for an expansion of the research and educational endeavors to include more fields. He was the chairman of the committee on educational policy and an adviser to the first two university presidents. The editor of the *Journal of General Physiology* from 1951 to 1961, he was responsible for shaping the journal into a more modern form. With Jean Brachet he created and served as coeditor of the six-volume reference work *The Cell* (1959–1964), an essential treatise for those wanting to master the new molecular biology and its picture of the cell based on an understanding of cellular events at the molecular level. Mirsky also engaged in the heredity-environment debate. In critical book reviews, addresses, and essays in the 1950s and 1960s, he attacked the arguments of genetic determinists who asserted that heredity was all-important in shaping human traits and who saw backwardness and crime in some classes and races as largely genetic in causation.

Mirsky felt scientists had a responsibility to present their discoveries to the public in ways that were both accurate and understandable. To this end he founded in 1959 the Rockefeller University Christmas Lecture Series for high school students, which eventually was named for him. A consultant to *Scientific American* magazine, he wrote significant, widely read articles between 1953 and 1968 on the new knowledge of nucleic acids, heredity, and cellular processes. These were superb accounts for the nonscientist, several of which made the reading lists of high school and college courses across the nation.

Mirsky pursued interests outside science. In the 1930s he traveled to China and became a collector of Chinese ceramics. He was an expert on Asian and ancient art and on archeology. His fine collection of art and historical objects became the Alfred E. Mirsky Collection of the Rockefeller University.

Mirsky died in his New York City home. His research from the beginning involved a molecular view of the substances found in living tissue, and his findings were central to the establishment of molecular biology. He discovered methods to isolate the genetic material of cells, helped unravel the chemistry of cellular processes, and made discoveries that merged into an international stream of advances and understanding of cellular events at the molecular level.

• Mirsky's papers are in the Rockefeller University Archives and include correspondence, autobiographical and historical material, notebooks, and photographs. A list of his publications is available from the Archives. Carolyn Kopp presents salient features of the collection in "The Alfred E. Mirsky Papers at the Rockefeller University Archives," *The Mendel Newsletter*, Nov. 1983, pp. 1–5. Mirsky wrote several reviews in biochemistry and molecular biology: "Chromosomes and Nucloproteins," *Advances in Enzymology* 3 (1943): 1–34; "The Chemistry of the Cell Nucleus," *Advances in Enzymology* 16 (1955): 411–500; and "The Nucleus and the Synthesis of Proteins," in *The Chemical Basis of Heredity*, ed. William D. McElroy and Bentley Glass (1957). Three widely read articles by Mirsky in *Scientific American* are "The Chemistry of Heredity," 188 (Feb. 1953): 47–57; "How Cells Make Molecules," 205 (Sept. 1961): 74–82, with Vincent Allfrey; and "The Discovery of DNA," 218 (June 1968): 78–88. For his life and career, see George W. Corner, *The History of the Rockefeller Institute* (1964), and Bruce S. McEwen, "Alfred Ezra Mirsky," in *American Philosophical Society Yearbook 1976*, pp. 100–103. For analyses of his accomplishments and their significance, see Joseph S. Fruton, *Molecules and Life* (1972); Ruth Moore, *The Coil of Life* (1961); and Garland E. Allen, *Life Science in the Twentieth Century* (1975). For his collaboration with Pauling, see Linus Pauling, "Fifty Years of Progress in Structural Chemistry and Molecular Biology," *Daedalus* 99 (Fall 1970): 988–1014. An obituary is in the *New York Times*, 21 June 1974.

ALBERT B. COSTA

MISES, Richard Edler von. *See* Von Mises, Richard Marten Edler.

MITCHEL, John (3 Nov. 1815–20 Mar. 1875), Irish nationalist and journalist, was born near Dungiven, County Derry (Londonderry), Ireland, the son of John Mitchel, a Presbyterian (and later Unitarian) clergyman, and Mary Haslett. In 1819 Mitchel's family moved to Derry City and then in 1823 to Dromalane near Newry, County Down, where he spent the rest of his childhood. From 1830 to 1834 Mitchel was enrolled in Trinity College, Dublin. In late 1835 or early 1836 he began studying law in the office of a Newry solicitor. In February 1837, during his legal apprenticeship, he married Jane (Jenny) Verner of Newry. The couple had six children. In 1840 Mitchel completed his legal training and moved to nearby Banbridge, where he practiced law.

Unlike most Irish Protestants, Mitchel identified with the mainly Catholic-supported Irish nationalist cause. In 1843 he joined the Repeal Association, the organization established by Daniel O'Connell to dissolve the union between Great Britain and Ireland through peaceful means. During this time Mitchel was associated with the Young Irelanders, a group of cultural nationalists who supported repeal. In the fall of 1845, Mitchel joined the staff of their popular newspaper, the *Nation* and moved to Dublin.

In July 1846 the Young Irelanders, including Mitchel, broke with the Repeal Association after it adopted an O'Connell-supported resolution declaring that violence must never be used on behalf of the Irish nationalist cause. In January 1847 they established another repeal organization, the Irish Confederation. During 1847, as thousands of Irish continued to die in the Great Famine while Britain prospered, Mitchel's views became more radical. Before the end of the year he was advocating the abolition of the landlord system and was urging a civil disobedience campaign by an armed people, which he hoped would escalate into a rebellion when the people were prepared.

Mitchel's more radical views led to a friendly split between him and the majority of Young Irelanders. In December 1847 he resigned from the *Nation* and in February 1848 he left his leadership position in the Irish Confederation and launched the *United Irishmen* as "an Organ of Revolution." Because of his *United Irishmen* articles, in May 1848 he was tried and convicted of treason-felony in a celebrated trial and sentenced to fourteen years transportation.

In June 1848 Mitchel was sent to Bermuda to serve his sentence, but was eventually transferred to Tasmania. Arriving there in April 1850, he was allowed to live freely, subject to certain restrictions, and in June 1851 his family joined him. In mid-1853 he escaped from Tasmania and, after a brief stay in California, he arrived in New York in late November 1853, where he was hailed as an Irish hero.

Mitchel instantly became a leader among the New York Irish. In January 1854 he began publishing the *Citizen*, which stirred up anti-English sentiment, most notably with the serialization of *Jail Journal.* Written during his years as a prisoner and published in book form toward the end of 1854, it is still considered one of the most eloquent indictments of British rule in Ireland. In 1854 Mitchel encouraged the formation of a revolutionary society that hoped to assist an Irish rebellion, while Britain was occupied in the Crimean War against Russia. Mitchel in fact met with the Russian minister to the United States to explore the possibilities of Russian aid. Stepping recklessly into local political strife, the *Citizen* gave unabashed support for slavery and attacked Archbishop John Hughes, the spiritual leader of many of the newspaper's readers.

Toward the end of 1854 Mitchel sold his interest in the *Citizen*. Wishing to "fly from the turmoil of New York," and preferring the slaveholding and agrarian South to the North, he moved with his family in the spring of 1855 to a farm about thirty miles from Knoxville, Tennessee. In the fall of 1856, they moved into Knoxville. During his years in Tennessee, Mitchel went on speaking tours to several American cities. In October 1857 he began publishing with a partner the

Southern Citizen to promote white southern interests including "the value and virtue of slavery." The newspaper also carried a series of articles on events in Ireland during the 1840s, which was later published as *The Last Conquest of Ireland (Perhaps)* (1861). In this work Mitchel condemned the British famine policy, declaring that a million and a half Irish "were carefully, prudently, and peacefully *slain* by the English Government."

In December 1858 Mitchel moved to Washington, D.C., where he continued to publish the *Southern Citizen*, until it folded in the summer of 1859. He then went to Paris, believing he might be useful to the Irish cause, should increased Anglo-French tensions lead to war. Nothing happened, and in early 1860 Mitchel returned to America, though that summer he returned to Paris with his family, where he remained until September 1862, working as a foreign correspondent. After leaving Paris, Mitchel took up residence in Richmond, Virginia, where, devoted to the Confederacy, he worked as editor of the *Enquirer* and then as a writer for the *Examiner*. These were difficult years for him as one of his daughters died and two of his three sons were killed fighting for the South.

After the Civil War ended, Mitchel became editor of the New York *Daily News*, but in June 1865 federal authorities arrested him for writing articles critical of the government. He was imprisoned at Fortress Monroe until the end of October. In November he went to Paris as the financial agent of the Fenians, an Irish revolutionary group. Convinced it was not a sound organization, Mitchel resigned as its agent in June 1866 and returned to America in October. For the next year he lived in Richmond, writing a history of Ireland. In October 1867 Mitchel moved to New York and founded the *Irish Citizen*, a newspaper critical of both the fractionalized Fenians and the moderate Home Rule movement. Mitchel, in failing health, continued to live in the New York area after the *Citizen* folded in July 1872. In 1874 he visited Ireland. He returned to Ireland again in February 1875 after being elected to Parliament in a County Tipperary by-election. The government declared his election invalid because he was a felon. In March Mitchel ran again and won, but died in his childhood home near Newry days after the election. He was buried in Newry.

Mitchel was revered as an Irish patriot by the Irish at home and abroad during his lifetime and long after his death. He was admired for the bold stand he took against the British in 1848, for the imprisonment he endured, and for the long years thereafter he spent defending the Irish cause. Mitchel's form of Irish nationalism, however, has been criticized for lacking a broader commitment to human rights, as witnessed, most notably, by his support for slavery.

• Some of Mitchel's papers are among the Fenian Brotherhood Papers at the Catholic University of America; others are among the Mitchel and Purroy Family Papers at Columbia University. The New York Public Library has some letters of Mitchel's wife. Besides those already mentioned, Mitchel's books include *The Life and Times of Aodh O'Neill* (1846), *An Apology for the British Government in Ireland* (1860), *The History of Ireland from the Treaty of Limerick to the Present Time* (1868), and *The Crusade of the Period: And Last Conquest of Ireland (Perhaps)* (1873). Several of Mitchel's books have more than one edition. William Dillon, *Life of John Mitchel* (2 vols., 1888), gives a thorough account of Mitchel's life and contains a wealth of primary source materials. P. S. O'Hegarty, *John Mitchel, an Appreciation* (1917), and Seamus MacCall, *Irish Mitchel: A Biography* (1938), concentrate mainly on Mitchel's years in Ireland. See also P. A. Sillard, *Life of Mitchel* (1889). Charles Gavan Duffy, *Four Years of Irish History, 1845–1849* (1883), discusses Mitchel's activities in Ireland in the 1840s. Emile Montégut, *John Mitchel: A Study of Irish Nationalism* (1915), provides a short but interesting view of Mitchel by a Frenchman. Rebecca O'Conner, *Jenny Mitchel: Young Irelander: A Biography* (1985), contains a good deal of information on Mitchel.

MICHAEL F. FUNCHION

MITCHEL, John Purroy (19 July 1879–6 July 1918), reformer and mayor of New York City, was born at Fordham (now Bronx), New York, the son of James Mitchel, a New York City fire marshal, and Mary Purroy, a schoolteacher until her marriage. After graduating from Columbia College (1899) and New York Law School (with honors in 1902), Mitchel practiced law as a private attorney. In 1909 he married Alice Olivia Child; they had no children.

Mitchel's career took a fateful turn in December 1906, when William B. Ellison, a family friend and New York City corporation counsel, hired the young lawyer to investigate charges of incompetence, waste, and inefficiency in the office of John F. Ahearn, borough president of Manhattan. First as assistant corporation counsel and then as a member of the Commissioners of Accounts, the municipal office empowered to audit and investigate city departments, Mitchel's thorough and professional probes into the operations of several city departments and offices resulted in the dismissal of numerous city officials, including the borough presidents of Manhattan and the Bronx. Mitchel established close working relations with Henry Bruere and other staff members of the Bureau of Municipal Research, who aided him in his investigations and, according to Edwin R. Lewinson, Mitchel's biographer, helped Mitchel transform a relatively insignificant Commissioners of Accounts office into "a valuable arm of municipal administration."

In 1909 Mitchel was elected president of the board of aldermen on an anti-Tammany Republican fusion ticket, which saw its entire slate of candidates except for mayor and Queens borough president elected, all promising New Yorkers a more efficient government run on business principles. The Mitchel-led board of aldermen and the board of estimate, of which he was a member by virtue of his office, again with the help of the Bureau of Municipal Research, enacted numerous administrative and fiscal reforms. Alone among the board of estimate members, Mitchel voted against granting the Interborough Rapid Transit and the Brooklyn Rapid Transit companies permission to extend their existing subway and elevated lines, calling the dual contracts "a bad business bargain for the city." Instead he unsuccessfully fought for a municipally owned rapid transit system. Serving as acting mayor for six weeks in 1910 while Mayor William J. Gaynor recuperated from a bullet wound inflicted by a would-be assassin, Mitchel called for police neutrality during a garment industry strike and initiated an antivice crusade. Before Mitchel's term as president of the board of aldermen expired, President Woodrow Wilson appointed him collector of the Port of New York, a position he held for five months.

As the mayoral election of 1913 approached, New York's reform forces, elated by their success in the election of 1909, organized a Citizens Municipal Committee of 107 to select another anti-Tammany fusion ticket committed to giving New York "a non-partisan, efficient and progressive government." Because of a split among the reform forces, it took the Citizens Committee nine ballots to nominate Mitchel for mayor. Mitchel's candidacy was formally endorsed by the Republican and Progressive parties, William Randolph Hearst's Independence League, and several anti-Tammany Democratic organizations. Theodore Roosevelt (1858–1919) reportedly thought candidate Mitchel "an engaging character, of the required forcefulness and the necessary progressive tendencies." Even President Wilson gave Mitchel his blessing.

Mitchel made Tammany Hall the chief issue of the campaign, telling New Yorkers he was leading a struggle "between the forces of decency, honesty and public service, and the forces of public plunder." He also promised voters a business government, one that would modernize the administrative and financial machinery, methods and processes of city government and, as he told one audience, "secure a dollar's worth of result for every dollar spent." Mitchel won an overwhelming victory, defeating Democratic candidate Edward E. McCall by 121,000 votes, thus becoming the youngest mayor of New York City to that date. Moreover, fusion candidates won all the citywide posts and control of the board of estimate and board of aldermen. Mitchel's election as mayor culminated progressive efforts to gain power to restructure and modernize New York City's government.

The "Boy Mayor," as Mitchel became known, appointed experts and professionals as heads of departments, including the first woman commissioner, and enlisted the help of outside civic and reform groups, especially the Bureau of Municipal Research. His administration created new agencies, such as the Markets Department and the Board of Child Welfare, even while it consolidated, reorganized, and generally increased the efficiency of numerous existing city departments, offices, and bureaus; reformed the city's budgeting, accounting, and purchasing systems; enacted the nation's first comprehensive zoning ordinance; replaced the outmoded elected county coroner system with appointed medical examiners; expanded the city's regulatory activities; ran the police department more honestly and efficiently; and maintained impartiality during garment and transportation workers strikes in 1916. Less popular were the mayor's fiscal policies of funding non-income-producing city improvements such as new buildings on a "pay-as-you-go" basis out of annual tax revenues and limiting appropriations for welfare and the city's schools. Mitchel also was heavily criticized for introducing into the school system the Gary Plan, which combined vocational with academic courses, for cutting the size of the board of education and attempting to gain control over teachers' salaries, and for failing to secure the removal of the New York Central tracks from Manhattan's West Side. After the outbreak of World War I Mitchel's uncompromising advocacy of military preparedness and universal military training alienated many New Yorkers, as did his failure to deal effectively with high food costs and unemployment.

Mitchel's indifference to politics, his social climbing (or hobnobbing with the city's social elite), his excessive concern with economy and efficiency, and his militant patriotism cost him a great deal of support in his reelection bid in 1917. He ran on yet another fusion ticket, only this time minus several independent Democratic groups and the Republicans, whose registered voters preferred another candidate in the city's first direct primary; Mitchel, in a four-man race, came in a poor second to Tammany winner Judge John F. Hylan, who received 297,282 votes to Mitchel's 147,975. After leaving the mayor's office, Mitchel secured a commission in the air force. Tragically, he died when, seat belt unfastened, he fell out of his airplane while engaged in advanced military flight training at Gerstner Field, Lake Charles, Louisiana. He was buried in New York City.

• Mitchel's personal papers are at the Library of Congress; his mayoralty papers are at the Municipal Archives and Records Center, New York City. The only biography is Edwin R. Lewinson, *John Purroy Mitchel: The Boy Mayor of New York* (1965). Other modern assessments of Mitchel's political career are Augustus Cerillo, Jr., *Reform in New York City: A Study of Urban Progressivism* (1991), and Richard S. Skolnik, "The Crystallization of Reform in New York City, 1890–1917" (Ph.D. diss., Yale Univ., 1964). Bibliographies in the above works provide further sources on Mitchel's career. The memorial piece "Mitchel Inherited Fighting Qualities," *New York Times*, 7 July 1918, provides a summary of his life and career.

AUGUSTUS CERILLO, JR.

MITCHEL, Ormsby Macknight (28 July 1809–30 Oct. 1862), astronomer and advocate of science, was born in Morganfield, Kentucky, the son of John Mitchel and Elizabeth McAllister, farmers. His father died less than two years after Ormsby's birth, necessitating the sale of the family farm and forcing the widow and boy to shuttle between the homes of his grown siblings in Ohio. Despite that hardship, Ormsby Mitchel gained a reputation as a prodigy, which he parlayed into an appointment to the U.S. Military Academy at West Point in 1825. At the time he attended, West Point offered the finest training in science and engineering in the United States. Following graduation in 1829, Mitchel taught mathematics at the academy for two years. He married Louisa Clark Trask in 1831; she had a son by a previous marriage, and they had at least six children together.

Mitchel served out the remainder of his commission at Fort Marion in St. Augustine, Florida. In 1832 he returned to Cincinnati, where he studied law and opened a practice with Edward D. Mansfield, also a West Point alumnus. When the Cincinnati College reopened in 1836, Mitchel returned to academia, teaching mathematics, civil engineering, mechanics, and machinery. He also cultivated his oratorical skills through a number of social organizations, the most significant of which was the Semicolon Club, an informal group of New Englanders devoted to literary pursuits. Six years later he presented a series of public lectures on astronomy that catalyzed the formation of the Cincinnati Astronomical Society (CAS) and led to the development of the Cincinnati Observatory.

In 1842 the board of directors of the CAS appointed Mitchel astronomer, and a year later they approved funding for him to make a trip to Europe to procure instruments. Originally, Mitchel presented an admittedly vague plan to mount a powerful telescope in a public place, with which people could observe the wonders of the heavens that he described during his lectures. As he and the CAS pursued the effort, however, they decided to expand the enterprise. From 1841, when Mitchel first broached the idea, to 1845, when he officially opened the building, the plan grew to include a hilltop site, an observatory building, a large equatorial telescope with mounting, and ancillary instruments. Mitchel championed the effort in every way imaginable, raising funds, planning and constructing the building, acquiring the instruments, and even organizing a gala grand opening.

In 1845 a fire leveled Cincinnati College, destroying Mitchel's primary source of income. Because he had agreed to direct the observatory without pay for ten years, he decided to turn adversity to advantage, and he undertook an expanded series of lectures based on those he had delivered in Cincinnati. His circuit ran from Boston to New Orleans, from November through March, when observing conditions in Cincinnati were marginal. His audiences soon began overfilling the theaters, spilling into hallways and aisles, and establishing his reputation as one of the most erudite and inspirational speakers of the antebellum period. His lectures introduced astronomical concepts to the public and connected those ideas to a growing body of natural theology that represented scientists' efforts to reconcile scientific thought to the biblical account of creation.

Although he possessed a functioning observatory by 1846, research required a social infrastructure as well. Mitchel linked himself to George Airy's group at the Royal Observatory in Greenwich, England. Airy advised that Mitchel utilize the superb refractor for the resolution of double stars, for which it was well suited. Mitchel did so; the result was an updating of a double-star handbook, Elijah Burritt's *Geography of the Heavens*. In a broader sense, the partnership was valuable because it gave focus and direction to Mitchel's program. Their correspondence continued into the 1860s.

Mitchel was also involved with other American research endeavors. Alexander Dallas Bache, the superintendent of the U.S. Coast Survey in Washington, D.C., developed a network of astronomers to help fix points of reference for use in the survey. Mitchel joined Bache's effort, a collaboration that led to the development of Mitchel's "automatic clock register," which he regarded as his most significant technical achievement. Situated about 450 miles west of Washington, Mitchel's observatory occupied the westernmost position then available, and Cincinnati's importance as a commodities trading center led to the rapid introduction of telegraph lines. His position on the banks of the Ohio put him in a perfect place for telegraphic experiments that Bache had undertaken to enhance the speed and accuracy of the survey, because differences in longitude yield differences in time. Working with Bache's assistant, Sears Cook Walker, Mitchel automated the time signal of a pendulum clock in 1848, such that its beats could be sent across telegraph wires to any station connected to the line. The mechanism was elegant in its simplicity—Mitchel attached one end of a spider's silk to the pendulum and the other end to a tiny tilt hammer that, at the bottom of the pendulum's swing, dipped into a cup of mercury. He later added a mechanism by which one could record the time of astronomical phenomena. This mechanism rotated a paper disk onto which a pencil imprinted dots to mark seconds, while a second pencil marked the precise moment of an astronomical event. This invention vastly improved both the accuracy and number of observations an astronomer could make in a night of observing. It became known as the "American method" of observing and was adopted first by Airy, then globally.

Off and on, Mitchel served as an engineer for local railroad companies, an activity that interrupted his astronomical research. Between his lectures and his success as an agent of railroads, he moved into the ranks of the wealthy in the early 1850s, but his successes in business activities exacted a toll through diminishing involvement with his scientific peers. He later found himself at odds with Bache during the debates over the role of the standing committee of the AAAS in 1852 and again over the directorship of the Dudley Observatory in Albany, New York, in 1858. Mitchel's wife suffered a series of strokes that left her an invalid from 1857 to her death in 1861, and he refused to leave her side for long. His fortune also suffered reversals during the latter half of the 1850s.

West Point's founding fathers designed the academy to produce leaders who could take command of militia units in a time of war but fade into civilian life and put to use their engineering skills in times of peace. When the Civil War broke out, Mitchel requested of President Lincoln a commission as general, which he received in August 1861. He proved an adept general, driving his army from Cincinnati down through Kentucky, into Tennessee, and ultimately into Huntsville, Alabama, before conflicts with his superiors led them to reassign him. He took charge of the Department of the South in Beaufort, South Carolina, in September 1862. While leading an expedition up the Pocotaligo River, he contracted yellow fever and died in Beaufort.

Mitchel's career lasted barely two decades. His scientific contributions may seem relatively slight, but one must consider the difficulties he overcame. First, in order to validate his credentials as an astronomer he had to transform his observatory into a research institution, which eventually cost him community support despite the innovation and resiliency of the CAS. Second, the same qualities that made him a brilliant lecturer—his quick mind and powerful ego—led to conflicts with his peers that were difficult to reconcile, given the fluidity of antebellum scientific organizations. His mercurial relationships made it hard to undertake long-term research projects. His peers did, however, recognize his contributions—his election to the Royal Astronomical Society in 1850 proceeded from a solid contribution to astronomy. To view his life as reaching an apex in astronomy misses the mark: his first love was the stage, and applause motivated him more than income. His contemporaries honored him because they recognized that, despite his failings, he accomplished more than anyone had dreamed possible.

• Mitchel's papers are held by the Cincinnati Historical Society. His publications include *Planetary and Stellar Worlds* (1848), *Popular Astronomy* (1860), and *Astronomy of the Bible* (1863). His *Sidereal Messenger*, an informal astronomical journal, ran for two years, ending in 1848. Good secondary sources include Robert V. Bruce, *The Launching of Modern American Science 1846–1876* (1987); Stephen Goldfarb, "Science and Democracy: A History of the Cincinnati Observatory, 1842–1872," *Ohio History* 78 (1969): 172–78; Mary Ann James, *Elites in Conflict: The Antebellum Clash over the Dudley Observatory* (1987); Sally G. Kohlstedt, *The Formation of the American Scientific Community: The American Association for the Advancement of Science, 1848–1860* (1976); Russell McCormmach, "Ormsby Macknight Mitchel's *Sidereal Messenger*, 1846–1848," *Proceedings of the American Philosophical Society* 10 (1966): 35–37; Howard S. Miller, *Dollars for Research* (1970); Frederick Augustus Mitchel, *Ormsby Macknight Mitchel, Astronomer and General* (1886); Philip S. Shoemaker, "Stellar Impact: Ormsby Macknight Mitchel and Astronomy in Antebellum America" (Ph.D. diss., Univ. of Wisconsin, 1991); and Hugh Richard Slotten, *Patronage, Practice, and the Culture of American Science* (1994).

PHILIP S. SHOEMAKER

MITCHELL, Arthur Wergs (22 Dec. 1883–9 May 1968), U.S. congressman, was born in Chambers County, Alabama, the son of Taylor Mitchell and Alma (maiden name unknown), farmers and former slaves. At the age of fourteen, Arthur ran away from home, traveled sixty-six miles to Booker T. Washington's Tuskegee Institute, and paid his way through college as a farmhand and office boy for Washington. He came to revere Washington as a father, and the Tuskegean's philosophy of free enterprise and political moderation would profoundly shape Mitchell's future career. Mitchell then earned a teacher's certification from Snow Hill Normal and Industrial Institution in Alabama and taught in rural schools until 1908, when he founded Armstrong Agricultural College in West Butler, Alabama. In 1904 Mitchell married Eula King; they had one child before she died in 1909. In 1911 he married Annie Harris; they had no children.

Following service in the army during World War One, Mitchell, like many black Alabamians, migrated north, yet unlike many of his fellow migrants, he prospered. He began a successful real estate business in Washington, D.C., and studied law at Harvard and Columbia. He was admitted to the bar in 1927.

Increasingly, Mitchell's interests turned to politics. In 1928 he campaigned for Republican candidates, including Chicago's Oscar De Priest, the first black elected to Congress since 1898. Settling in Chicago, Mitchell hoped to carve out his own political career but found his ambitions thwarted by De Priest's GOP machine. The depression opened up new possibilities for ambitious politicians, however, and Mitchell bolted to the Democrats in 1932, winning party backing to contest Illinois's First Congressional District, De Priest's seat, two years later. In a tight race, two-thirds of the black voters cast their ballots for the more race-conscious De Priest, but Mitchell won massive support in white wards loyal to the New Deal and defeated the Republican by 3,000 votes. Although Mitchell owed his margin of victory to whites, his triumph integrated the Democratic congressional caucus and gave legitimacy to his party's effort to woo African Americans. For the next fifty-eight years all blacks elected to the House would be Democrats.

Mitchell's freshman term was shaped by a conflict of loyalties to his party and to his race. Believing that good relations with southern Democrats might soften their racial prejudices, he constantly reminded colleagues of his love for his native Alabama, a strategy that won plaudits from moderate southerners but left conservatives unmoved. When Mitchell, the first African American to speak from the floor at a Democratic convention, rose to second Franklin D. Roosevelt's renomination in 1936, Senator "Cotton" Ed Smith of South Carolina stomped out of the hall, protesting it "humiliated the South" (Weiss, p. 186).

To black critics like Walter White of the National Association for the Advancement of Colored People (NAACP), Mitchell put party before the interests of 12 million African Americans. White particularly resented Mitchell's ties to Hatton Sumners of Texas, chairman of the House Judiciary Committee and chief foe of the 1937 Gavagan antilynching bill. Sumners believed that the NAACP would not "have the nerve to oppose" Congress's sole black member and persuaded Mitchell to introduce a rival, much weaker bill (Zangrando, p. 141). When the House refused to consider his proposal, Mitchell duly backed the Gavagan measure, but the episode further strained his relationship with civil rights activists.

Mitchell's record in Congress was modest but more consequential than his critics charged. He exposed racial discrimination in the Civil Service, nominated black cadets to West Point and Annapolis, and while many others remained silent condemned anti-Semitism in Germany. Above all, he pledged unswerving loyalty to Roosevelt's New Deal. When northern Republicans attacked Jim Crowism in New Deal agencies, Mitchell retorted that blacks should have no quarrel with policies that provided relief, jobs, and housing for Americans of all races. Increasing numbers of blacks voted for Mitchell and his party after 1936, appearing to vindicate his emphasis on class issues.

Mitchell made a more lasting contribution to civil rights in the courts. Traveling from Chicago to Hot Springs, Arkansas, in April 1937, the congressman purchased a ticket guaranteeing first-class Pullman service. When the train crossed the Arkansas border, however, a conductor ordered him to a second-class coach reserved for blacks. That Mitchell was a member of Congress, the conductor remarked, "didn't make a damn bit of difference . . . , that as long as [Mitchell] was a nigger [he] couldn't ride in that car" (Barnes, p. 1). Fearing a violent confrontation, Mitchell duly moved but later filed suit with the Interstate Commerce Commission (ICC) against the Chicago, Rock Island and Pacific Railway. When the ICC and a federal district court dismissed his claim, he took the case to the Supreme Court and won a unanimous ruling. The railroad, Chief Justice Charles Evans Hughes concluded, had violated Mitchell's "fundamental right of equality of treatment" (*Mitchell v. United States*, 1941). Although *Mitchell* prompted southern rail lines to integrate first-class carriages, second-class rail travel remained segregated until 1956. The case was nonetheless significant in setting a precedent for postwar challenges to Jim Crow transit. The solicitor general's brief supporting Mitchell also foreshadowed growing support for civil rights in the executive branch.

In his final two terms in Congress, Mitchell pledged blacks' loyalty to the United States against enemies at home and abroad. Blacks, he claimed, would be the last Americans to succumb to communism and among the first to give their lives in a war against fascism. Yet if blacks were good enough to die for their country, he reminded Congress after Pearl Harbor, they should also be given the "opportunity to live for [their] country without any type of racial discrimination" (*Congressional Record*, 8 Dec. 1941, p. 9526).

Mitchell retired from Congress in 1942 and settled in Petersburg, Virginia. His second wife died in 1947, and Mitchell married Clara Smith one year later. They had no children. By the 1960s he devoted his energies to farming. He kept his own counsel on the new generation of civil rights leaders but noted that the moderate, interracial Southern Regional Council offered the best hope for change in the South.

Born in the year that the civil rights cases symbolized the end of the first Reconstruction, Mitchell died in Petersburg just as the assassination of Martin Luther King, Jr., signaled the end of the second. In breaking the color line among congressional Democrats and in challenging segregated transportation, Mitchell played a singular role in bridging the two eras.

• Mitchell's personal and congressional papers are in the Chicago Historical Society. Copies have been deposited at Virginia State University at Petersburg. For Mitchell's staunch loyalty to Roosevelt, the Democratic party, and the New Deal, see his speech, "The New Deal and the Negro," *Congressional Record*, 18 Mar. 1940, pp. 3019–27. Mitchell outlines his case against the Rock Island railroad in "My Fight before the Interstate Commerce Commission," *Congressional Record*, app., 18 Sept. 1941, pp. 4294–97. For Mitchell's opposition to communism, see his "The Communist Party and the Negro in the United States," *Congressional Record*, app., 14 May 1941, pp. 2944–45; for his comments on Pearl Harbor see the *Congressional Record*, 8 Dec. 1941, p. 9526. A biography of Mitchell is Perry Duis, "Arthur Mitchell: New Deal Negro in Congress" (master's thesis, Univ. of Chicago, 1966). For a list of articles on Mitchell, see Mary Mace Spradling, *In Black and in White: A Guide to Magazine Articles, Newspaper Articles, and Books Concerning Black Individuals and Groups* (1980). Nancy Weiss, *Farewell to the Party of Lincoln* (1983), places Mitchell in the context of black partisan realignment in the 1930s, while Robert Zangrando, *The NAACP Crusade against Lynching, 1909–1950* (1980), notes Mitchell's tensions with Walter White on antilynching legislation. The Supreme Court's ruling is given in *Mitchell v. United States*, 313 U.S. 80 (1941), and Catherine A. Barnes, *Journey from Jim Crow* (1983), places *Mitchell* in the broader context of the desegregation of southern transit. See "Ex-Solon Still Active 20 Years after Retirement," *Ebony*, Aug. 1963, pp. 40–46, for Mitchell's postcongressional activities. An obituary is in the *New York Times*, 10 May 1968.

STEVEN J. NIVEN

MITCHELL, Billy. *See* Mitchell, William Lendrum.

MITCHELL, Blue (13 Mar. 1930–21 May 1979), jazz musician, was born Richard Allen Mitchell in Miami, Florida. Information about his parents is not available. He began his musical career studying the trumpet in high school; he excelled early, touring by the age of twenty-one. Mitchell's early career was with R & B groups. From 1951 to 1955 he performed with bands led by Paul Williams (1951–1952), Earl Bostic (1952–1955), and Chuck Willis. His trumpet style—characterized by blues elements, occasional punctuated high notes, and a soulful sound—was enhanced by his knowledge of jazz, especially chord changes. It was his knowledge and familiarity with bebop concepts that led Cannonball Adderley, a fellow Floridian, to arrange a recording date for Mitchell with Riverside in 1959 in New York City. Two albums, *Big Six* (Riverside 273) and *Blue Soul* (Riverside 309), were produced with Mitchell as leader.

Mitchell became an exponent of a new trumpet aesthetic. Whereas the bebop and hard-bop eras produced trumpeters emphasizing technique, endurance, high notes, and a strong adherence to the contrafact, trumpeters like Mitchell, Miles Davis, and Lonnie Hillyer adopted a less technical and more subtle approach. Mitchell was not as technically proficient as either Clifford Brown or Dizzy Gillespie, and rather than projecting loudly he would use a quieter dynamic to stress emotion and feeling in his music, thereby crafting his own musical identity. Examples of his style can be heard on his recordings with jazz pianist Horace Silver on compositions like "Finger Poppin'," "Cookin' at the Continental," "Come on Home," and "Mellow D" from the *Finger Poppin'* album (1959, Blue Note 4008); "Me and My Baby," "Nica's Dream," and "Horace-Scope" from the *Horace-Scope* album (1960, Blue Note 4042); and his work on *Doin' the Thing* (1961, Blue Note 84076). Mitchell had been hired by Silver in 1958 and remained with the group until 1963; the quintet featured Junior Cook (tenor), Gene Taylor (bass), and Ray Brook (drums).

After Silver disbanded the quintet, Mitchell formed his group with Cook and Taylor. At the piano was Chick Corea, and Al Foster was on drums; they were later replaced by Harold Mabern (piano), and Billy Higgins (drums). Although Mitchell played an electric repertoire with Silver, both his group and Silver's became known as "funky style" bands that retained a conventional tunefulness in contrast to the dissonant, "outside" sounds prevailing in free jazz. Their style was permeated with blues and gospel elements featuring inside solos, a complementary, often repetitious rhythmic feel, repetitious melodies, and a trumpet-tenor front line harmonized in fourths.

After limited success as a bandleader, Mitchell resumed his career as a sideman. Between 1967 and 1978 he performed with a diverse group of musicians. He toured with R & B singer Ray Charles (1967–1971) and with blues singer and guitarist John Mayall (1971–1973), recording *Jazz Blues Fusion* in 1971 (Poly 5027). From 1974 until his death, he worked with Louis Bellson, Tony Bennett, the Bill Berry Big Band, Harold Land, and Lena Horne and Bill Holman. During this time he also recorded several jazz fusion albums (1975–1977), and with Land he made *Mapanzi* (1977, Con 44).

Mitchell was diagnosed with cancer in October 1978 and was thereafter unable to perform. He died in Los Angeles and was honored with memorial services in Los Angeles, New York, and Miami. He and his wife, Thelma (maiden name unknown), evidently did not have children. Mitchell left a legacy of having developed his own sound and aesthetic, fitting any jazz or jazz-related situation.

• Articles that contain an overview of Mitchell's musical life, his career highlights, and his approach to trumpet playing are Mark Gardner, "Blue Mitchell on Blue Note," *Jazz Festival* 23, no. 2 (1979): 2; Barry Kernfeld, "Blue Mitchell," in *The New Grove Dictionary of Jazz* (1988); and H. Nolan, "Blue Mitchell: Able to Leap All Genres with a Single Blast," *Down Beat*, 20 May 1976, pp. 19–20, 44. An obituary is in *Down Beat*, 12 July 1979, p. 12.

EDDIE S. MEADOWS

MITCHELL, Clarence Maurice, Jr. (8 Mar. 1911–18 Mar. 1984), civil rights lobbyist, was born in Baltimore, Maryland, the son of Clarence Maurice Mitchell, a waiter, and Elsie Davis. He attended St. Katherine's Episcopal Church and later became a member of the Sharp Street Memorial Methodist Church. From Douglass High School in Baltimore, he entered Lincoln University in Pennsylvania in 1928 and was graduated in 1932 with a B.A. In 1938 Mitchell married Juanita Elizabeth Jackson, daughter of Keiffer Bowen Jackson and Lillie May Jackson of Baltimore; they had four children. President of the Baltimore branch of the National Association for the Advancement of Colored People (NAACP) and Maryland State Conference of NAACP Branches, Lillie Jackson spearheaded the freedom movement in the state and became a celebrated historical figure.

From 1933 to 1936 Mitchell was a reporter for the Baltimore *Afro American*. He left for a year of graduate study at the Atlanta School of Social Work as a National Urban League fellow. After completing the program in 1937, he served for six months as director of the Maryland office of the Division of Negro Affairs of the National Youth Administration, developing training and jobs program for blacks. In November 1937 he became executive secretary of the Urban League office in St. Paul, Minnesota, where his primary concerns were breaking down racial barriers in housing and fighting employment discrimination. He was especially effective in attacking closed-shop agreements in union contracts that barred blacks from jobs.

In 1941 Mitchell assumed a new job as field employment assistant under Robert C. Weaver, who headed the Negro Employment and Training Branch in the labor division of the Office of Production Management in Washington. Soon afterward he was named assistant director of the department. In January 1943 Mitchell was appointed associate director of the division of field operations for the Fair Employment Practice Committee (FEPC) and in 1945 director of field operations. In 1946, after Congress had discontinued the agency, Walter White, executive secretary of the NAACP, hired him as labor secretary in the organization's Washington bureau to carry on the FEPC's work. Four years later Mitchell became director of the bureau.

One of Mitchell's early accomplishments was helping to secure passage in Congress of an amendment to the Railway Labor Act through his vigorous lobbying efforts. This act prohibited both unions and railroads from dismissing workers who refused to join Jim Crow unions and locals. He prepared another provision, which Congressman Adam Clayton Powell, Jr., of Harlem successfully introduced in 1955 as an amendment to the National Reserve Training Act. The amendment blocked adoption of a proposal to give the Department of Defense authority to transfer draftees to segregated units in the national guard. Mitchell also authored a provision to bar discrimination in federally funded education programs that became known as the "Powell Amendment" because the Harlem congressman introduced it in the House in the 1950s repeatedly without success. Nevertheless, Mitchell helped to persuade President Dwight D. Eisenhower to implement through executive action a policy barring discrimination in the spending of federal funds. His other early accomplishments included lobbying the Eisenhower administration to bar segregation at military facilities and, ultimately, to complete the desegregation of all branches of the armed services in 1954. Crucial aspects of Mitchell's strategy included persuading Eisenhower to publicly commit himself to ending such discrimination and exposing administration officials who contravened the president's expressed views that such practices were wrong and harmful to the services.

Mitchell was the principal force in the struggle for the passage of the 1957 Civil Rights Act. His strategy included winning the support of Attorney General Herbert Brownell for a broad civil rights bill and organizing bipartisan coalitions in the House and Senate that included powerful conservatives like two California Republicans, Congressman Thomas Kuchel and Senator William F. Knowland. Of the act, Mitchell said:

> In due time, this legislation will make the Congress itself a more realistic reflection of the American scene because it will guarantee that future southern delegations in the nation's highest legislative body will include qualified colored men and women. After the stern restraint of a Federal injunction has been applied, those who use force, economic pressure and deception to keep voting lists lily white will realize that the ballot is for all without regard to race.

Even though the 1957 act was primarily an inadequate voting rights law, it created the Civil Rights Division of the Justice Department and the U.S. Civil Rights Commission, both of which became important instruments in the struggles to pass and enforce subsequent laws. In an effort to strengthen the 1957 act, Mitchell lobbied for passage of the 1960 Civil Rights Act, although it was a weak amendment of the 1957 law. Persevering, he spearheaded the struggle for passage of the omnibus 1964 Civil Rights Act. Acknowledging his vision, Roy Wilkins, executive director of the NAACP, said, "Clarence Mitchell was the man in charge of this operation. He perfected and directed flawlessly a wonderful group of representatives of church, labor and all facets of the community to make this possible." As with the previous acts, this coalition of groups worked with the NAACP through the Leadership Conference on Civil Rights, which Mitchell served as legislative chairman. The following year, Mitchell utilized the same strategy to win passage of the 1965 Voting Rights Act.

Of all the civil rights leaders and activists at a White House meeting on 18 March 1966, Mitchell was the only one who supported President Lyndon B. Johnson's decision to seek a fair housing law in Congress. Johnson did not want to deal with the problem piecemeal. The other leaders, however, suspicious of Johnson's intentions and fearing that Congress would not pass the law, wanted the president to issue an executive order barring discrimination in housing. Mitchell was opposed, and he convinced them that a law was permanent whereas an executive order lasted only as long as a presidential administration. His vision and determination paid off when on 10 April Congress passed the 1968 Fair Housing Act. The next day President Johnson signed the measure into law. This success finally won him the recognition from the civil rights community he deserved as one of the most skillful and effective lobbyists in the nation's history. Among other things, the *Washington Post* (28 Apr. 1968) noted that the *Congressional Quarterly* (26 Apr. 1968, pp. 931–34) had documented extensively his role in passing the law.

The next phase of Mitchell's work involved getting enforcement of the laws for which he fought so hard and seeking adoption of strengthening provisions. Those efforts included lobbying for passage of extensions of the 1965 Voting Rights Act in 1970 and 1975.

The central thrust of Mitchell's life's work, as he himself said, was

> . . . to make the Constitution a meaningful document for all people. I began this job by, first, trying to make the executive branch of government work properly. We needed not only just laws but also right national policies. Second, we had to get Congress to enact laws for the protection of our rights. Third, we had to make sure that the laws were enforced. Without enforcement, it would not have been worth getting the laws in the first place.

He said he felt "privileged to live in a time when we have gotten all three branches of our national government to work for civil rights."

Among his awards were the NAACP's Spingarn Medal, which he received in 1969, and the Medal of Freedom, which President Jimmy Carter presented to him in 1980. Mitchell died at his home in Baltimore.

• The personal papers of Clarence Mitchell, Jr., are in the Manuscript Division of the Library of Congress. Oral histories of both Mitchell and his wife Juanita Mitchell are at the Maryland Historical Society. Other materials are in the Civil Rights Documentation Project of the Ralph J. Bunche Oral History Collection located in the Manuscript Department of the Moorland–Spingarn Research Center at Howard University. For additional information on the struggle for passage of the civil rights laws, see the NAACP Washington Bureau papers and general legal files also at the Library of Congress as well as presidential papers from Harry S. Truman to Jimmy Carter. Denton L. Watson's biography of Mitchell, *Lion in the Lobby* (1990), chronicles his civil rights activities and documents this phase of the NAACP's political struggles in Washington. Senate tributes are in the *Congressional Record*, 6 Feb. 1979 and 22 Mar. 1984. Obituaries are in the *New York Times* and the *Baltimore Sun*, both 20 Mar. 1984.

DENTON L. WATSON

MITCHELL, David Brydie (22 Oct. 1766–22 Apr. 1837), governor of Georgia and U.S. Indian agent, was born near Muthill, Perthshire, Scotland, the son of John Mitchell; his mother's name is unknown. He originally came to the United States in 1783 to claim a Georgia estate left to him under the terms of an uncle's will. On 19 January 1792 he married Jane Mills, with whom he had four known children. Mitchell read law in the Savannah office of William Stephens, at which time he also served as a clerk for the committee to revise the state criminal code. This experience led to his election as state attorney general in 1795 as a Democratic-Republican. In 1796 Mitchell was elected to the first of two consecutive terms as a representative in the Georgia General Assembly, where he became known for his opposition to the fraudulent Yazoo land sales. From 1798 to 1801 he served as the eastern district judge in the state superior court, after which he was elected mayor of Savannah. His popularity and legal skills led to his appointment as U.S. attorney general for Georgia in the following year, a post he held until his selection as major general of the state militia in 1804.

In 1809 the Georgia General Assembly selected Mitchell as governor over former governor Jared Irwin, and in 1811 the assembly reelected him over Irwin. As a Jeffersonian Republican, he supported various internal improvements that would be funded from local, not national, sources. During Mitchell's tenure as governor, the state commissioned its first permanent highway board and founded the Agricultural Society of Georgia. To pay for these and other infrastructure improvements, Mitchell supported the legislature's charter of the Bank of Augusta, the state's oldest banking institution, from which the state drew dividend shares. Although he had earlier killed a Federalist political opponent in a duel, he signed the state's first law outlawing dueling. The War of 1812 and Indian relations dominated his second term as governor. Mitchell had foreseen the conflict with Great Britain and wisely convinced the general assembly to devote $30,000 for state defenses. His prior military experience proved to be invaluable shortly after the declaration of war, when Georgia's militia, following Mitchell's orders, captured seventeen British ships in the St. Mary's River. Mitchell declined to run for reelection in 1813; he preferred instead to lead forces in the field during an incursion into Florida after the 1813 Fort Mims massacre, in which hostile Creek Indians murdered several hundred settlers in the Mississippi Territory.

Following the war, Mitchell returned to the office of governor in 1815 after defeating the incumbent, Peter Early. His Jeffersonian idealism continued into his third term with his support for the founding of the Savannah Library Society. Following the previous financial success of the Bank of Augusta, Mitchell advocated the incorporation of the Bank of the State of Georgia in order to provide the University of Georgia with its first regular appropriated income, approximately $8,000. Indian relations during this term grew increasingly strained, but Mitchell proved to be a strong, effective, and respected negotiator. His reputation led President James Monroe to appoint him federal Indian agent to the Creek Indians. Mitchell accepted the post and resigned as governor on 4 November 1817.

Mitchell was a progressive as well as a popular governor of the state of Georgia during his three terms. His political career benefited the residents of Georgia through his support of internal improvements and his military leadership. His turbulent tenure as Indian agent, however, virtually ended his aspirations for higher office.

Events soon tested his skill as a mediator. By 1817 tensions had increased after rumors circulated that the federal government planned to designate a large amount of the state's most desirable acreage as permanent Indian territory. Mitchell successfully negotiated a treaty in 1818 whereby the Creek Nation surrendered 1.5 million acres. Despite this success, his term as Indian agent swirled with controversy after Governor John Clark accused him of involvement with slave smuggling along the Florida border. These charges may have been politically motivated. Previously, Mitchell had refused to allow Clark to command troops sent to invade Indian lands during the Creek War of 1813, commenting, "in the field, brains and money are both indispensable to a commanding general and of the former it is thought Clark is miserably lacking" (*Exposition*, p. 162). Mitchell had also hindered Andrew Jackson's dubious operations in Florida in 1818 when he discouraged Creek participation in the invasion of Spanish-held territory. Jackson and Clark's testimony, along with claims of other misdealings, led to Mitchell's dismissal on 4 March 1821.

Mitchell retired to his home near Milledgeville and spent the next several years attempting to refute the charges against him. His popularity among the local residents resulted in his return to politics in 1828, when he was elected judge of the Inferior Court of Baldwin County, a seat he held until his death. In 1836 Mitchell was elected to the Georgia Senate on the ticket of the newly-formed State Rights party, but he fell ill and died at his home shortly after taking his seat.

• Mitchell's papers are in the Georgia Department of Archives and History in Atlanta. Additional letters are in the Library of Congress and the Telamon Cuyler Collection held at the University of Georgia, Athens. C. M. Drestler edited two published collections of Mitchell's letters, "Correspondence of David Brydie Mitchell," *Georgia Historical Quarterly* 21 (1937): 382–92, and "Additional Correspondence of David Brydie Mitchell," *Georgia Historical Quarterly* 28 (1944): 93–104. Thomas Henry Rentz, "The Public Life of David B. Mitchell" (M.A. thesis, Univ. of Georgia, 1955), is also a useful resource. The controversy surrounding Mitchell's career as Indian agent has been documented in various works. Daniel F. Littlefield, Jr., *Africans and Creeks: From the Colonial Period to the Civil War* (1979), and Michael D. Green, *The Politics of Indian Removal: Creek Government and Society in Crisis* (1982), develop the case against Mitchell. On the opposing side, Benjamin W. Griffin, Jr., *McIntosh and Weatherford, Creek Indian Leaders* (1988), and James F. Doster, *The Creek Indians and Their Florida Lands, 1740–1823* (1974), claim Mitchell was the victim of political deception. Mitchell attempted his own defense in *An Exposition of the Case of the Africans, Taken to the Creek Agency by Captain William Bowen on or about the 1st December 1817* (1822). An obituary is in the (Savannah) *Daily Georgian*, 28 Apr. 1837.

JAMES W. STENNETT

MITCHELL, David Dawson (31 July 1806–31 May 1861), fur trader and government American Indian agent, was born in Louisa County, Virginia. Nothing is known about his parents. Mitchell's youth remains wrapped in mystery. He arrived in St. Louis as a young man and quickly became involved in the Rocky Mountain fur trade. Employed by the American Fur Company as early as 1828, he was assigned first to the Ioway country and then to the Upper Missouri River, where he displayed considerable skill in dealing with the Blackfoot and Assiniboine Indians. During the period between 1828 and 1838 he headed several trading outfits and built Fort McKenzie in Montana in spite of American Indian objections to the construction at the mouth of the Marias River. Noted for a cool head in stressful situations, Mitchell managed to keep tensions from reaching a boiling point, especially over the issue of which native groups might be favored in trade. Bernard De Voto referred to him as a man of extreme courage and extraordinary skill who rose to prominence on "proved merit."

Mitchell attained national recognition by hosting the artist Carl Bodmer and Maximilian, Prince of Wied, on an expedition up the Missouri in 1833. Maximilian spent most of the trip recording the efforts of the American Fur Company to conduct business among potentially hostile American Indians. The German prince took to Mitchell, admiring how he used diplomacy to negotiate with Indian leaders, tempting them with presents or a bit of liquor without offending them as customers. Meanwhile, Bodmer produced exquisite paintings of Indian life and scenes from the fur trade. Under Mitchell's tutelage, Maximilian's trip turned into one of the most important ethnohistorical expeditions of the early nineteenth century. Bodmer's paintings, in particular, are priceless.

Mitchell eventually became a partner in the Upper Missouri Outfit (1835), commanding a number of rugged and remote outposts—Fort McKenzie, Montana; Fort Clark, North Dakota; and finally Fort Union, North Dakota. In 1840 he married Martha Eliza Berry, daughter of a prominent Kentuckian, Major James Berry. The couple had six children. His acknowledged skill in handling American Indian affairs attracted the government's attention, and in 1841 he accepted the office of superintendent of Indian affairs at St. Louis, a post that supervised Indian relations on the Upper Missouri River. Although his former partners probably expected him to cooperate with trading establishments, Mitchell launched an effort to abolish the illegal importation of alcohol into the American Indian country. Indian and white officials had long complained that the whiskey trade led to violence and starvation, thus defeating the government's program to preserve peace. Mitchell agreed, and his success in enforcing the liquor laws irritated trading interests. In October 1843 Missouri senator Thomas H. Benton pressured President John Tyler into replacing Mitchell.

With the outbreak of war with Mexico in 1846, Mitchell joined the Second Regiment of Missouri Volunteers. A lieutenant colonel attached to the command of Colonel Sterling Price, he arrived in Santa Fe shortly after its occupation by American forces. He then led a detachment south into Mexico, where his skill and leadership earned him accolades at the battle of Sacramento. He headed one group of American troops occupying Chihuahua City on 1 March 1847. Mitchell reportedly led a select force searching the city for contraband. His activities immediately following the war are not documented, but he soon returned to St. Louis.

On 30 March 1849, following the election of Zachary Taylor and the return of the Whig party to political power, Mitchell was reappointed to the office of American Indian superintendent at St. Louis. During the next four years he proved himself to be an able government employee, operating independently of the trading companies and playing a significant role in mapping the direction of national Indian affairs. For some time Mitchell had advocated a treaty with the powerful Plains tribes in order to purchase a right of way for American emigrants headed to California and Oregon. He well understood that the tide of emigration would continue, and the only way to assure peace was to compensate the tribes for their losses. He, therefore, suggested that all Plains tribes be brought together for a major council to clear the routes of travel, force the American Indians to stop fighting each other, and provide them with some sort of formal boundaries.

In September 1851 Mitchell led a government negotiating team into council near Fort Laramie with the Teton Sioux, Cheyenne, Arapaho, and others. Distributing over $100,000 in presents to the approximately 10,000 natives on hand, Mitchell concluded the most significant treaty of the era. The 1851 Fort Laramie document brought the Central Plains tribes into official relations with the government, assigned tribal boundaries, and secured an agreement to permit white emigrants to cross the Plains along the Oregon Trail unmolested. In essence, the American Indians agreed to live in peace and accommodate American expansion. The treaty failed to assure permanent peace, however, and also marked a philosophical turning point in American Indian policy; placing Indians on restricted reservations became standard procedure after this event.

Mitchell left his post with the American Indian service in 1853. By 1855 he was involved with the Missouri and California Overland Mail and Transportation Company, serving as its president for several years. His involvement in transportation led him to furnish hundreds of mules to the army during its expedition to Utah in 1858. He died in St. Louis.

• Most of Mitchell's official correspondence while employed in the American Indian service is in the National Archives. Other materials are scattered. Ray H. Mattison, "David Dawson Mitchell," in *The Mountain Men and the Fur Trade of the Far West*, vol. 2, ed. LeRoy H. Hafen (1965), is the only concise biography. For references to his activities as a trader, see Bernard De Voto, *Across the Wide Missouri* (1947), and John Sunder, *The Fur Trade of the Upper Missouri, 1840–1865* (1965). His role as American Indian superintendent is discussed in Robert A. Trennert, *Alternative to Extinction* (1975).

ROBERT A. TRENNERT

MITCHELL, Edward Page (24 Mar. 1852–22 Jan. 1927), editor and writer, was born in Bath, Maine, the son of Edward H. Mitchell, a businessman, and Frances Page. Receiving a strong foundation in Congregationalist religious principles from his family, Mitchell was brought up under a strict moral and behavioral code. His family also introduced him to a variety of good literature, leading to his lifelong appreciation for belles lettres. In 1860 the family moved to New York City and then lived in 1866–1867 in North Carolina, where Mitchell's father tried his hand at farming. In 1871 Mitchell enrolled at Bowdoin College; initially interested in medicine, his literary talent led him to pursue a degree in humanities.

While undertaking his studies, Mitchell worked part-time for the *Boston Daily Advertiser*, and shortly before graduation from Bowdoin in 1874, he accepted a position with the *Lewiston Journal* in Maine, where he remained for almost two years. He married Annie Sewall Welch in 1874; they had four children. Part of his duties at the *Journal* was to read the major city papers, and as a result he became increasingly interested in the *New York Sun*, then edited by Charles A. Dana. He was fascinated by the crisp writing style and was particularly intrigued by the editorials, which covered a wide range of topics succinctly and perceptively. Mitchell began submitting short pieces of fiction and satire to Dana, who printed several of them, paying Mitchell well. In 1875, at Dana's encouragement, Mitchell moved from Maine to New York City and joined the staff of the *Sun* at a handsome weekly salary of $50.

At the time that Mitchell joined the *Sun*, the paper had already established a reputation as an innovative publication and was famous for its feature articles and its fiction. Working under the tutelage of Dana, Mitchell developed his talents as both writer and editor. He became acquainted with important figures from the world of politics, literature, and journalism, notably Goldwyn Smith, John Bigelow, Walt Whitman, William Dean Howells, and Joseph Pulitzer, who worked with him briefly on the staff. Working for the paper provided Mitchell the opportunity to travel throughout the American continent and to Europe, broadening his appreciation for the political and social differences that shaped the United States and its relationships with other nations. This knowledge served as inspiration for more than two decades of editorials in which he criticized politicians on both the right and the left, expressing values that the majority of Americans held in common: belief in individual freedoms tempered by a need to fulfill social and political responsibility; commitment to hard work in the hope of receiving the rewards such labor should bring; strong attachment to the family and the community; and a love of country but a willingness to criticize political mismanagement and corruption.

During the 1870s and 1880s, the *Sun* printed several of Mitchell's short stories that displayed a bent toward what is now called science fiction; time travel, invisible people created by experimentation, and tree-sized plants with intelligence were but a few of the subjects he introduced to avid readers. Although many of his stories were published anonymously, Mitchell achieved sufficient fame that two were published under his name in Charles Scribner's Sons' ten-volume *Stories by American Authors* (1884–1885). He earned the friendship and respect of fellow science fiction writers Frank Stockton, Edward Bellamy, and Brander Matthews, all of whom admired the imaginative qualities of his fiction.

By the turn of the century, Mitchell had become Dana's principal deputy at the *Sun*. He continued the policy of promoting vivid writing and unusual feature stories that made the paper one of the most popular dailies in the United States. He frequently was responsible for the editorial page, and his contributions to political debate helped shape U.S. opinion on topics such as the construction of the Panama Canal and the U.S. decision not to join the League of Nations. Though not overtly political himself, Mitchell had monitored the pulse of the nation for decades. As a consequence, the same man who encouraged editorial writer Frank Church to take seriously a young girl's query about the reality of Santa Claus was willing to put himself on the firing line against the pet project of a popular president because he believed that much might be lost if the United States became too involved in matters beyond its shores.

Although he received frequent offers to move to other papers at a considerably higher salary, Mitchell remained with the *Sun* for his entire career. Upon the death of Charles Dana in 1897, Mitchell gave his strong support to Dana's son Paul, who succeeded his father. In 1903, the same year that William Mackay Laffan bought the *Sun*, Mitchell was rewarded for his loyalty by being named its editor. Laffan eventually turned over daily control of the publication to Mitchell, who in 1909 was named president of the Sun Printing and Publishing Corporation. He handled this extra administrative burden for two years, after which he returned to full-time editorial duties. Mitchell's wife died in 1909, and in 1912 he married Ada Burroughs; they had one child.

Mitchell retired in 1922 and was celebrated by more than 600 journalists and prominent citizens of New York City at a gala held in his honor. He then moved from his suburban home in Glen Ridge, New Jersey, to a farm near Kenyon, Rhode Island. He died in New

London, Connecticut, where he had been hospitalized after an apparent heart attack.

• No collection of Mitchell's papers has survived. The best biographical summary of his life and career is Sam Moskowitz's introduction to *The Crystal Man: Landmark Science Fiction* (1973), an anthology of Mitchell's creative work. Additional information can be found in Frank M. O'Brien, *The Story of the Sun* (1928), and in Mitchell's autobiography, *Memoirs of an Editor: Fifty Years of American Journalism* (1924). A lengthy obituary is in the *Literary Digest*, 12 Feb. 1927.

LAURENCE W. MAZZENO

MITCHELL, Elisha (19 Aug. 1793–27 June 1857), geologist and mineralogist, was born in Washington, Connecticut, the son of Abner Mitchell and Phoebe Eliot, farmers. In 1813 he graduated from Yale University, where he studied under Benjamin Silliman, the noted professor of chemistry and natural history. After teaching briefly at Union Hall Academy in Jamaica, Long Island, and serving as principal of Union Academy in New London, Connecticut, he returned to Yale in 1816 as a tutor.

In 1817 Mitchell received an appointment as professor of mathematics and natural philosophy at the University of North Carolina, having been recommended by U.S. Senate chaplain Sereno Dwight (son of Yale president Timothy Dwight [1752–1817]) to William Gaston, a North Carolina congressman and member of the university's board of trustees. Before assuming this position, Mitchell spent nearly a year studying theology at Andover Theological Seminary and continuing to work with Silliman.

Mitchell served the University of North Carolina from 1818 until his death. In 1825 he assumed the professorship of chemistry, geology, and mineralogy when Denison Olmsted, a Yale classmate, left that position to return to Yale. Mitchell also served the university as bursar, collecting tuition and overseeing the grounds and buildings, at first informally, then officially assuming the post in 1837. Following his ordination by Orange Presbytery in 1821, Mitchell frequently presided over university chapel services and occasionally filled local pulpits as well. In 1835, as faculty president, he served briefly as the chief executive officer of the university when President Joseph Caldwell died.

Despite his New England heritage, Mitchell adapted readily to life in the South. Several of his Yale classmates had been from the South, so he was not unfamiliar with the region. Mitchell returned to New Haven shortly after beginning his career in Chapel Hill to marry Maria Sybil North, whom he had met during his tenure at Union Academy; thereafter he made only infrequent trips to Connecticut for family reasons. The Mitchells enjoyed a comfortable home near the campus for their growing family (four of their seven children survived infancy). They also purchased a small family of slaves.

Although his university administrative and teaching duties and his sometime service as a pastor provided for a full schedule, Mitchell found time to write. He published a number of articles, primarily accounts of his geological observations, in the *American Journal of Science*, edited by Silliman. The issues of the day also attracted his attention. He conducted a lengthy dispute in the Raleigh newspaper with Episcopal bishop John Stark Ravenscroft, whose relatively liberal views on religious interpretations upset the Calvinist Mitchell. Mitchell also grounded his defense of slavery on a literal interpretation of the Bible, claiming in an 1848 pamphlet that although the Bible does not refer to slavery as a sin it makes many references to the dangers of riches. Mitchell concluded that abolitionists who had not abandoned their wealth were hypocrites.

Primarily, however, Mitchell was a scientist and an educator. Most university vacations would find him traversing the state to study its geology. During the 1820s he continued the geological survey of North Carolina begun in 1824 by Olmsted. When the state appropriation for this project ceased in 1828, Mitchell, intrigued by the insistence of John Caldwell Calhoun that the Appalachian Mountains contained peaks higher than any others east of the Mississippi River, focused his attention on the western portion of the state.

Mitchell is most widely remembered for his measurement of the Black Mountain, near Asheville, and for his subsequent controversy with Thomas Clingman over which man had actually found the highest peak in the region. Mitchell first measured the Black Mountain in 1835; in 1838 he reconfirmed his assertion that it was higher than Mount Washington, in the White Mountains of New Hampshire. In 1844, with improved equipment, Mitchell measured the height of the mountain at 6,672 feet. In 1855 Clingman claimed that Mitchell had not been on the highest peak, insisting that he (Clingman) had climbed and measured one at 6,941 feet. Given the time lag since his 1844 measurement, Mitchell returned to the region in June 1857 to settle the controversy. Leaving the rest of his party, Mitchell set out to visit the man who had served as his guide in 1835; on a steep descent Mitchell slipped and fell down a waterfall to his death. He was buried in Asheville, but the following year his remains were reinterred on top of Mount Mitchell. In 1881–1882 the U.S. Geological Survey confirmed Mitchell's measurement of this peak, which is the highest east of the Rocky Mountains, and officially named the peak Mount Mitchell.

Mitchell was well known within the state of North Carolina and maintained some contacts with scientists in other areas of the country. However, he was not a major participant in the nascent move toward professionalization. His sparse papers contain remnants of correspondence with Benjamin Silliman, and he was elected as corresponding member to both the Boston Society of Natural History and the Academy of Natural Sciences of Philadelphia. He joined the American Association for the Advancement of Science in 1848, when the organization was founded, but was not an active member and allowed his membership to lapse in 1854.

Kemp Plummer Battle, a student of Mitchell's in the 1840s who became president of the University of North Carolina in 1876, remembered Mitchell as a man whose "eager curiosity urged him to more or less partial dipping into many subjects" and concluded that this lack of focus had cost Mitchell the opportunity to be numbered among the outstanding scientists of his era. Mitchell's journal does indeed reflect a widely read man, as does the number of different courses that he taught and the contents of his library at the time of his death. Mitchell did not join the small vanguard of professionalism as it existed before the American Civil War, but his geological work, his service to the University of North Carolina, and his concern for his students serve as a true measure of his significance.

• Mitchell's papers are in the Southern Historical Collection, University of North Carolina at Chapel Hill. Although he has not received major scholarly attention, he has been the subject of three biographical sketches in the *Journal of the Elisha Mitchell Scientific Society*: Charles Phillips, "A Sketch of Elisha Mitchell," 1 (1884): 9–18; Kemp Plummer Battle, "Elisha Mitchell, D.D.," 30 (1915): 157–64; Archibald Henderson, "Elisha Mitchell: Scientist and Man," 73 (1957): 204–12. Also see Thomas Lawrence Jones, "Elisha Mitchell: The Man and His Mountain" (honors thesis, Univ. of North Carolina, 1973), and Hope Summerell Chamberlain's 1945 memoir of her grandfather, "Life Story of Elisha Mitchell, D.D., 1793–1857," also housed in the North Carolina Collection.

NANCY MIDGETTE

MITCHELL, George (8 Mar. 1899–27 May 1972), jazz trumpeter and cornetist, was born in Louisville, Kentucky. Nothing is known of his father. His widowed mother worked as a maid. When Mitchell was about twelve years old he became interested in music via a boyhood friend, Leonard Fields, who had a cornet (or, by another account, an alto horn). He began taking lessons from Fields's father, a member of the Louisville Musical Club Brass Band, the leading African-American ensemble in the city. A year later Mitchell's mother bought him a trumpet. By 1912 or 1913 he was a member of the congregational marching brass band of St. Augustine Church, and soon thereafter he joined the Louisville Music Club Brass Band, playing concert band music and ragtime. He learned to improvise while working with this ensemble and with dance and theater orchestras drawn from within the club's ranks and led by Wilbur Winstead and trombonist John Emory. At some point he acquired the nickname "Little Mitch" because of his hunched back and small frame.

Mitchell toured the South for a year with the Rabbit Foot Minstrel Show (1917–1918). Back home, he rejoined Winstead and Emory; a photo from July 1919 shows Mitchell on stage at the Hawaiian Gardens in Louisville as a member of Emory's eight-piece dance band. Late that year a job in Chicago with John Wickcliffe's band fell through, and instead Mitchell joined the pit band for Irving Miller's *Brown Skin Models* revue at the Grand Theater. He also worked at the Club Alvadere for eight months while taking every opportunity to hear the great New Orleans musicians resident in Chicago, especially cornetist King Oliver.

Mitchell worked with pianist Tony Jackson and drummer Tubby Hall in a band at the Deluxe Cafe from late 1920 into 1921. With Hall he toured Canadian theaters in Clarence Miller's band from 1921 into 1922, when they were stranded in Hamilton, Ontario. He performed in Detroit, briefly returned to Louisville, and then joined Doc Holley's band at the Castle Ice Garden in Milwaukee.

Early in 1923 he settled in Chicago, where he first joined Wickliffe's band. In late summer he joined violinist Carroll Dickerson's band at the Sunset Cafe, and early in 1924 they were at the Mahjong Club. In late summer 1924 he was with Doc Cook's orchestra at Harmon's Dreamland Ballroom, and concurrently he worked with clarinetist Jimmie Noone, replacing Freddie Keppard, at the Paradise Gardens. At this time Mitchell switched permanently from trumpet to a hybrid trumpet-cornet, which offers something of the more compact tubing shape and darker sound that distinguishes a cornet from a trumpet. He left Cooke in 1925 and became a member of pianist Lil Armstrong's band at the Dreamland Café to spring 1926. Her husband Louis often sat in, replacing Mitchell. He also worked during 1926 with Vernon Roulette's band, and until at least 1927 he continued doubling after hours at Paradise Gardens, where earnings from tips exceeded his nightly wages elsewhere. He became a member of Dave Peyton's orchestra in spring 1927, and he doubled with saxophonist Verona Biggs's band until he once again replaced Keppard in Cook's orchestra, then at the White City Ballroom. He stayed with Cook for two years.

In these same years, Mitchell became a distinguished recording artist. On 10 March 1926 he entered the studio with pianist Luis Russell's band, soloing and leading the ensemble on "Sweet Mumtaz" and "29th and Dearborn," and accompanying blues singer Ada Brown on "Tia Juana Man." For contractual reasons Mitchell rather than Louis Armstrong recorded with Lil Armstrong in the New Orleans Wanderers and New Orleans Bootblacks sessions of July 1926, including "Papa Dip" and "Perdido Street Blues."

Between September 1926 and June 1927 he was the trumpeter-cornetist in pianist and composer Jelly Roll Morton's Red Hot Peppers, playing on some of the most significant jazz recordings ever made. He can be heard on titles familiar to any fan of early jazz, including "Black Bottom Stomp," "Smoke-House Blues," "The Chant," "Sidewalk Blues," "Dead Man Blues," "Grandpa's Spells," "Original Jelly-Roll Blues," "Doctor Jazz," "Wild Man Blues," "Beale Street Blues," and "The Pearls." Following in a tradition established by cornetists Oliver and Armstrong, Mitchell was paired with trumpeter Natty Dominique in October 1927 for recordings by clarinetist Johnny Dodds's Black Bottom Stompers, including "Come on and Stomp, Stomp, Stomp" and "Joe Turner Blues."

His last recording of any consequence was "Let's Sow a Wild Oat," made at a session with Noone in December 1928. He may also be the unidentified brassman on a session from February 1929 directed by Oliver.

Mitchell joined Earl Hines's big band at the Grand Terrace from summer or autumn 1929 to spring 1930. He was fired for alleged incompetence, rehired in summer 1930, and then fired again the following spring, for reasons unknown, though it seems not a wild guess to suggest that his ragtime-based style had become too old-fashioned for Hines. He worked for the little-known banjoist Jack Ellis that summer. Thereafter he had difficulty securing work in music, and he became a clerk in a financial firm in Chicago. After performing with the little-known Freddie Williams Gold Coast Orchestra in 1934, a Works Progress Administration concert orchestra around 1935, and Charles Elgar's Federal Concert Orchestra in 1936, he abandoned music. He retired from his clerkship in the early 1960s and died a decade later in Chicago.

Mitchell was not a dominating, showy trumpeter-cornetist. Often utilizing mutes for discreet timbral effects, he led ensembles and played polite, precise, lyrical melodies in a manner that conveyed a lilting sense of swing and a rhythmic punch, despite its delicacy. He was a player perfectly suited to Morton's conception of a New Orleans jazz in which composed themes within intricate instrumental structures carried more weight than improvisation and personal glory.

• The archives of Tulane University hold a copy and written summary of an interview of Mitchell taped on 1 July 1959. For a discography, see Walter C. Allen, "Trumpet Giants, 1: George Mitchell" and "George Mitchell Discography," *Hot Notes* 1 (Jan. 1947): 2–5; additions and corrections to the discography are in *Hot Notes* 2 (May–June 1947): 17. The few useful sources on his career are "Little Mitch," *Jazz Journal* 12 (Sept. 1959): 32; Gilbert M. Erskine, "Little Mitch," *Down Beat*, 7 Nov. 1963, pp. 22–23, 38; Peter Bright, "Little Mitch: An Appreciation of George Mitchell," *Jazz Journal* 20 (Mar. 1969): 12–13; John Randolph, "Lucien Brown," *Storyville*, no. 47 (June–July 1973): 180–83; Rolf von Arx, "George Mitchell Revisited," *Storyville*, no. 52 (Apr.–May 1974): 136–42; and John Chilton, *Who's Who of Jazz: Storyville to Swing Street*, 4th ed. (1985). Gunther Schuller discusses Mitchell's contributions to Morton's historic recordings in *Early Jazz: Its Roots and Musical Development* (1968). An obituary is in *Down Beat*, 21 Dec. 1972, p. 12.

BARRY KERNFELD

MITCHELL, George Edward (3 Mar. 1781–28 June 1832), soldier and politician, was born in Elkton, Maryland, the son of Abraham Mitchell, a physician, and Mary Thompson. He studied medicine under his father, took classes at the University of Pennsylvania, and on 5 June 1805 received a permit to practice. Soon afterward Mitchell developed an interest in politics, and in 1808 he was elected to the Maryland House of Delegates as a Democratic Republican. The following year he gained appointment as a member of the state executive council, and from 1809 to 1812 he served as president of this body. Mitchell had previously been tendered a captain's commission in the light dragoons, but he declined military service until war with Great Britain proved imminent. Accordingly, on 1 May 1812 he resigned from office to accept the rank of major in the newly formed Third U.S. Artillery Regiment.

Mitchell spent the first months of the War of 1812 at Albany and Plattsburgh, New York, where Colonel Alexander Macomb transformed the Third Artillery into one of the army's crack outfits. Mitchell so successfully implemented his duties that on 3 March 1813 the rank of lieutenant colonel was conferred. In this capacity he accompanied the amphibious expedition of General Zebulon M. Pike against York (Toronto), Canada, in April 1813. The town was carried but when Pike fell mortally wounded from a magazine explosion, Mitchell tended to him until he died. Mitchell next fought at the 27 May 1813 battle of Fort George and subsequently assumed command of Fort Niagara, across the river, for many months. In the spring of 1814 he formed the rear guard of the Left Division as it marched from French Mills to Sackets Harbor, New York. En route, Mitchell was commanded by General Jacob J. Brown to take charge of the strategic entrepôt at Fort Ontario, Oswego, New York.

The ensuing defense of Oswego became one of the most celebrated actions of the war. Prior to Mitchell's arrival, the navy had been stockpiling heavy guns and naval stores intended for shipment to Sackets Harbor and the U.S. fleet there. Owing to military negligence, however, Oswego and its valuable stores remained ungarrisoned and vulnerable to attack. Accordingly, Mitchell force-marched 300 artillerists from Batavia, covering fifty miles a day for three days, and arrived there on 30 April 1814. He spent several days shoring up the defenses of Fort Ontario, which had lapsed into decay, and shipped the heavy cannon upriver to Oswego Falls. Mitchell's alacrity proved necessary, for on 5 May a British squadron of seven ships under Commodore Sir James Lucas Yeo appeared and attempted to land. Boisterous weather postponed the attack until the next day, but Yeo successfully landed 700 soldiers and marines. Mitchell's gunners resisted tenaciously and at one point advanced on the beach to meet the enemy. After two hours numbers prevailed, and the Americans abandoned Oswego with the loss of sixty men. British casualties totaled ninety, including Yeo's second-in-command, Captain James Mulcaster, and no pursuit was mounted. Mitchell's determined stand spared the valuable naval ordnance from capture. For his exploits he received promotion to brevet colonel as of 5 May 1814 and was appointed garrison commander of the strategic base at Sackets Harbor until war's end. The Maryland state legislature also passed complimentary resolutions on his behalf and presented him with a sword.

Mitchell was retained in the postwar establishment and succeeded General Winfield Scott as commander of the Fourth Military District, headquartered at Baltimore. In 1816 he married Mary Hooper; they had seven children. Mitchell administered his charge competently, but a reawakened interest in politics prompted him to resign his commission on 1 June 1821. He won election as a Democrat to the U.S. House of Representatives in 1822 and again in 1824. During this time he drafted the resolution of Congress that invited the marquis de Lafayette to return to America, and he personally greeted Lafayette upon his arrival in the capital. The two former soldiers struck up a relationship that lasted until Mitchell's death. Declining to run in 1826, Mitchell successfully returned to Congress in 1828, and the following year he was defeated in a bid for the governorship. He was reelected the following year, but in October 1831 he was struck by paralysis and partially disabled. Mitchell died while in office in Washington, D.C.

Mitchell was a talented physician and politician but is best remembered as one of the outstanding regimental leaders of the War of 1812. An ardent Jeffersonian, he owed his rank to political patronage but nonetheless proved himself adept as a drillmaster, administrator, and tactician. His actions at Oswego were justly celebrated, spared the United States an embarrassing and costly setback, and was proof of the growing proficiency of American arms.

• Mitchell's military correspondence is in RG 94, Records of the Adjutant General, National Archives. Some personal correspondence also exists in the Roger Jones Papers, Manuscript Division, Library of Congress, and the Cecil County Historical Society, Elkton, Md. Detailed, if laudatory, biographical sketches are in George Johnston, *History of Cecil County, Maryland* (1881); and George W. Archer, "George Edward Mitchell, Physician and Soldier," *Military Surgeon* 88 (June 1941): 670–73. His wartime activities are clearly delineated in Anthony M. Slosek, *Oswego and the War of 1812* (1989); John C. Fredriksen, ed., "The War of 1812 in Northern New York: Observations of Captain Rufus McIntire," *New York History* 68 (July 1987): 297–324; and Bob Malcomson, "War on Lake Ontario: A Costly Victory at Oswego, 1814," *Beaver* 75 (Apr./May 1995): 4–14. An informative obituary is in the *Daily National Intelligencer*, 30 June 1832.

JOHN C. FREDRIKSEN

MITCHELL, Harry Leland (14 June 1906–1 Aug. 1989), union organizer and activist, was born in Halls, Tennessee, the son of James Young Mitchell, a tenant farmer, and Maude Ella Stanfield. The great-grandson of eighteenth-century Irish immigrants, Mitchell began working on a farm at the age of eight. He first experienced aversion to racism at the age of eleven when he witnessed the lynching of a young black man by a group of whites. Struggling to understand his environment, he turned to books. After graduating from high school, Mitchell worked at a number of jobs, including bootlegging during Prohibition and sharecropping.

Mitchell married schoolteacher Lyndell Carmack in 1926; they raised three children before their divorce in 1948. In 1951 he married Dorothy Dowe, office manager of the Southern Tenant Farmers' Union who was later elected secretary-treasurer, the second woman in the labor movement to hold such a post.

Attracted to the theories of Norman Thomas, Mitchell became a socialist. During Thomas's campaign in the 1932 presidential election, Mitchell and his socialist friend Clay East established a "Red Square" around Mitchell's dry-cleaning store and East's gas station in Tyronza, Arkansas.

Mitchell and East organized black and white sharecroppers in the Southern Tenant Farmers' Union in 1934. Mitchell and his union believed that "nothing will win the battle quicker than by having members of all races, creeds and colors united in one strong union." Mitchell's talents at organizing laborers and East's position as constable of the township insured the success of the union. In his work for the STFU, Mitchell began a lifelong mission to lobby the rich and powerful on behalf of the nation's have-nots. He championed the cause of farm laborers before every president from Franklin Roosevelt to Ronald Reagan. Mitchell's contributions to labor organization border on the legendary. Walter Reuther of the United Auto Workers proclaimed that Mitchell was "already a legend in the South when I was just a punk in an auto plant in Detroit."

According to a 1984 National Public Radio broadcast, many historians believe that the Southern Tenant Farmers' Union "helped poor southern families more than anything since the Homestead Act" of 1862. The union protested sharecropper evictions, lobbied for federal legislation to improve agricultural conditions in the South, and organized strikes to raise wages. The most successful project of the union was the formation of the Delta Cooperative Farm in 1936 at Rochdale, Mississippi, by tenant farmers who had been evicted from plantations in Arkansas for joining the STFU. The Farm Security Administration, created in 1937 to address mounting national concern over the plight of the southern tenant farmer, was modeled on the project.

STFU membership grew to 35,000 members. In addition, the union published a Memphis newspaper, the *Sharecroppers' Voice*, and enjoyed public-relations triumphs in the national press and politics, such as New York mayor Fiorello La Guardia's declaration of a Sharecroppers Week. The STFU, along with the Communist Alabama-based Sharecroppers Union, helped forge the most important links between rural, radical southern blacks and whites since populism and fostered cooperation that would lead to the future civil rights movement.

Mitchell does not fit the profile of the typical southern reformer, most of whom were steeped in the Social Gospel movement. An agnostic, he approached the problems of rural Americans from an economic perspective. Evelyn Smith Munro, an STFU office secretary, described the young organizer: "Mitchell . . . was the Man with the Hoe, Billy the Kid, and Abraham Lincoln, with a little of Jesse James thrown in. His drawl was authentic if his simplicity was not. . . . Mitchell's imagination always kept him one idea ahead of the rest of the union leadership. . . . His work, his recreation and his consuming interest was the Union and the Socialist Party."

Several formidable obstacles blocked Mitchell's hopes for a sustained, mass movement of sharecroppers. Although Eleanor Roosevelt often expressed sympathy with Mitchell's cause, Franklin Roosevelt avoided any major federal commitment to southern social change in his efforts to appease southern planters. Furthermore, the growing mechanization of southern agriculture and the low prices of commodities drastically diminished the bargaining power of sharecroppers.

Union politics also hindered the sharecroppers. In 1937 the Congress of Industrial Organizations invited the STFU to join its international union for agricultural and cannery workers. Some locals refused to join; others joined and then withdrew when in 1938 the Communist party attempted to take over the STFU. A year later, officially withdrawing from the CIO, the STFU was very much weakened. After World War II and the passage of the Taft-Hartley Act of 1947, which placed limitations on union activities, the STFU leadership felt the union needed to join a larger labor organization to insure its own survival. Mitchell maneuvered the STFU, renamed the National Farm Labor Union, into the American Federation of Labor, and for twelve years he and his wife lobbied in Washington, D.C., on behalf of farm workers. In 1959, after the AFL and CIO merged, Mitchell was frequently embroiled in controversy, as his efforts on behalf of his agricultural union were often opposed by AFL-CIO president George Meany.

Mitchell continued to use his organizing talents on behalf of the National Agricultural Workers Union, which in 1955 merged with the Amalgamated Meat Cutters and Butcher Workmen of North America, one of the largest unions in the AFL-CIO. His heart was still in organizing field laborers, however, and he worked desperately for unionization and decent housing for workers on sugarcane plantations. Mitchell also successfully organized fish plant workers in 1964 and pioneered the movement supporting California farm workers' unionization.

During the 1970s and 1980s, Mitchell devoted his energies to encouraging interest in the history of the STFU. He delivered lectures on campuses and at scholarly meetings, promoted the sale of microfilm editions of the STFU papers to libraries, wrote an autobiographical account of his work with the union, and encouraged the media to treat the subject.

Mitchell was one of a group of idealistic reformers in the 1930s and 1940s who worked in the South for economic and racial justice, appropriately labeled "southern radicals and prophets" by Anthony Dunbar in his study *Against the Grain* (1981). In 1948, in honor of his work in race relations, Mitchell was named vice president of the National Association for the Advancement of Colored People. He continued this struggle for justice until his death in Montgomery, Alabama. After his death, the Southern Historical Association established the H. L. Mitchell Award for distinguished books on the history of the southern working class.

• The bulk of Mitchell's papers are in the Southern Historical Collection, University of North Carolina, Chapel Hill, which also houses the STFU papers. Earlier papers of the STFU are at the New York Public Library. Most of Mitchell's extensive interview and history tapes are at the Tamiment Institute, Bobst Library, New York University. His papers dealing with organizing activities in Louisiana are still in the possession of the estate attorney, Micki Beth Stiller. H. L. Mitchell, *Mean Things Happening in This Land* (1979) and *Roll the Union On: A Pictorial History of the Southern Tenant Farmers' Union* (1987), are invaluable autobiographical accounts. A careful scholarly study of the STFU is Donald H. Grubbs, *Cry from the Cotton: The Southern Tenant Farmers' Union and the New Deal* (1971). Anthony P. Dunbar, *Against the Grain: Southern Radicals and Prophets, 1929–1959* (1981), treats Mitchell in the context of other white southern reformers and radicals. Jack Temple Kirby, *Rural Worlds Lost: The American South, 1920–1960* (1987), is the best account of the general significance of Mitchell and the STFU in the American South.

ORVILLE VERNON BURTON

MITCHELL, Hinckley Gilbert Thomas (22 Feb. 1846–19 May 1920), biblical scholar and theologian, was born in Lee, New York, the son of James Mitchell and Sarah Gilbert Thomas. During his childhood, Mitchell's family moved several times, finally settling in Remain, New York. He was educated at Talley Seminary in Fulton, New York, and at Wesleyan University in Middletown, Connecticut, where he received his B.A. (1873), and was ranked as the top student of his class, and M.A. (1876, with honors). During this time, he also studied theology at Boston University, graduating with an S.T.D. in 1876. Encouraged by Dean Latimer, he developed an interest in biblical criticism and exegesis and went to the University of Leipzig in Germany, where he studied under Franz Julius Delitzsch, earning a Ph.D. in 1879.

Upon his return to the United States, Mitchell became a member of the Central New York Conference of the Methodist Episcopal church, which appointed him pastor at Fayette, New York. Within a year, he was invited to teach Latin and Hebrew at Wesleyan University, where he remained from 1880 to 1883. In June 1880 he married Alice Stanford. In 1883 he joined the faculty of Boston University as a professor of Hebrew and Old Testament; later he also taught Semitic languages and literatures, including Assyrian. Strife occurred between Mitchell and the Board of Bishops of the Methodist Episcopal church owing to Mitchell's denial of the historicity of the early chapters of Genesis. Consequently, he left Boston University in 1906 and apparently spent the following four years intensively studying biblical criticism, possibly on his own. In 1910 he became a professor of Hebrew and exegesis at Tufts University, where he remained for the rest of his academic career.

Mitchell contributed regularly to academic journals and edited the *Journal of Biblical Literature* for six years. Between 1901 and 1902, he served as the director of the American School for Oriental Study and Research in Palestine; he wrote his reminiscences of this experience in *Tales Told in Palestine* (1904, with J. E. Hanauer).

Mitchell's first academic work was *Hebrew Lessons* (1884), a textbook of biblical Hebrew for college and seminary students. The book included biblical texts and a sizable glossary, and although more recent textbooks have superseded it the grammar he composed is still remarkably lucid.

It was, however, the question of the Mosaic authorship of the Pentateuch that became Mitchell's major preoccupation, starting with his publication of *The World before Abraham* (1901). Both Jewish and Christian theologians had for centuries assumed the Mosaic authorship. Mitchell based his arguments on the documentary hypothesis, a theory that claims "that the Pentateuch is a mass of fragments, whose authorship it is useless to discuss, thrown into its present form at a comparatively late date by a careless or incompetent compiler" (*The World before Abraham*, p. 23). This theory was developed by early pioneers of modern biblical criticism such as Hugo Grotius (Huigh de Groot), Thomas Hobbes, Baruch Spinoza, Richard Simon, and Jean Astruc. Mitchell embraced the idea that the Pentateuch was a compilation from various sources, edited by a number of authors and editors, not written by Moses. Accepting the theory that the four main sources, J (Judean or Jahwist), E (Eloist), D (Deuteronomist), and P (Priestly), were composed in different periods Mitchell argued that the Old Testament was not completed until between 458 and 444 B.C.E. Mitchell's exposition identified Moses as the initial lawgiver and the "actual founder of the Hebrew Church," but he contended that the Mosaic laws merely began a long, complex process stretching over centuries, from Moses in the thirteenth century B.C.E. to Ezra in the sixth century B.C.E. Mitchell undertook to divide the first eleven chapters of Genesis among the four main sources, thus illustrating the strengths and weaknesses of the documentary hypothesis. In exposing the different sources of these chapters, he claimed to have revealed an inner plan that was likely designed by the P (Priestly) author, who was, according to Mitchell, the most eloquent writer of the Old Testament.

In his last published work, *Ethics of the Old Testament* (1912), Mitchell investigated what he deemed to be the exclusivity of Judaism, which resulted from embracing the Priestly legislation. Arguing for an evolutionary development of ethics in the Old Testament, Mitchell followed the accepted scholarly view of the chronological order of the biblical books and discovered increasingly refined views of the relationship between Yahweh and the Hebrews, the status of women, and social ethics, including attitudes toward slaves and foreigners. The Hebrews started, he argued, as an ethically undeveloped nation, but over the generations, especially during the Prophetic period, they finally recognized the high ethical character of Yahweh. Again, Mitchell described the Bible not as a "homogeneous" text but as the work of several authors with different viewpoints in different periods; a composite work, it was revised and enlarged up until its final canonization.

Mitchell died in Boston, Massachusetts. He is remembered as an American pioneer in the theory and practice of modern biblical criticism and as a scholar who preferred personal integrity to the conventions of the church.

• For Mitchell's other works on biblical exegesis see *Isaiah, a Study of Chapters I–XII* (1897), *Genesis* (1909), and *A Critical and Exegetical Commentary on Haggai, Zechariah, Malachi and Jonah* (1912). His autobiography is titled *For the Benefit of My Creditors* (1922). An obituary is in the *Boston Evening Transcript*, 20 May 1920.

DINA RIPSMAN EYLON

MITCHELL, Joan (21 Feb. 1926–30 Oct. 1992), painter, was born in Chicago, Illinois, the daughter of James Herbert Mitchell, a physician, and Marion Strobel, a poet. Her mother's position as co-editor of *Poetry* magazine made Mitchell's childhood home a stopover for leading modernists such as Ezra Pound, Edna St. Vincent Millay, and T. S. Eliot; Thornton Wilder read bedtime poems to Mitchell and her older sister Sally. Mitchell's father, an amateur artist, introduced her to Chicago's Art Institute, where she first became fascinated with the work of Vincent van Gogh. Mitchell herself began painting as a child; she later claimed to have sold her first landscape while in the eighth grade. While at the progressive Francis W. Parker School, she definitively decided to become a painter.

Mitchell attended Smith College for two years (1942–1944), then transferred to the Art Institute of Chicago, where she received a B.F.A. in 1947. She went to Mexico to paint social-realist landscapes during summer vacations in 1945 and 1946 and met Mexican muralist José Clemente Orozco. In 1948 she won an Edward L. Ryerson traveling fellowship from the Art Institute. Wanting to go to France but wary of conditions in postwar Europe, Mitchell delayed her departure. Rather than remain in Chicago, however, she spent the interim year in New York, where abstract expressionism was at its height. She studied with Hans Hofmann and got her first look at the art of Arshile Gorky and Jackson Pollock.

Mitchell did not immediately embrace expressionism but rather experimented with various styles as she moved away from figurative painting during her yearlong residence in Paris. She also traveled in Europe with her childhood friend, writer and filmmaker Barney Rosset. Mitchell and Rosset married after their return to Greenwich Village in 1949; they had no children. Deeply impressed by the painting *Figure*, Mitchell sought out its creator, Willem de Kooning. She gradually developed strong friendships with de Kooning and another influential young artist, Franz Kline. Through these contacts she gained a place among the so-called second generation of abstract expressionists, thriving in the competitive, hothouse circle that included Pollock, de Kooning, Helen Frankenthaler, and Lee Krasner. She set up her studio at St. Marks Place, frequented the Cedar Tavern and other hotspots of the downtown art scene, and participated in the Ninth St. Show organized by the exclusive Artists' Club. Her first professional exhibition was at the St. Paul Gallery in St. Paul, Minnesota, in 1956. At the same time she continued the formal study of art, earning her M.F.A. from New York University in 1950. Her first one-person show opened in New York in January 1952 and was very well received, marking Mitchell as one of few contemporary women painters to find critical approbation. Reluctant to identify herself as a "woman artist" or as part of any feminine tradition in art, Mitchell kept pace with her male peers by adopting their combative manners, their hard-living ethos, and above all their outsider status. By 1957 the Artists of the New York School: Second Generation exhibition, organized at the Jewish Museum in New York by Meyer Schapiro, recognized her importance within what had become an international art movement.

Mitchell and Rosset had separated in 1951 and divorced in 1952. Mitchell returned to Paris with increasing regularity; she said New York was too "big, successful, and public" for her artistic needs. In France in 1955 she met Canadian painter Jean-Paul Riopelle, who would be her companion for the next twelve years; they had no children. Though she scoffed at the label "expatriate," Mitchell increasingly identified herself with her life in France and moved to that country permanently in 1959. She lived in Vetheuil, a town near Paris where Claude Monet had lived and painted roughly a century earlier. Through the 1960s Mitchell's calligraphic early paintings grew denser and more painterly. She worked on large-scale subjects, inspired by landscape, such as *Blue Tree* (1964). "Music, poems, landscape, and dogs make me want to paint," she explained (Tucker, p. 7). Mitchell rejected drawing from nature and tried to keep "variable" sunlight out of her studio. As a committed (if experimental) expressionist, her painting remained predominantly about "feeling." She wanted to depict a remembered landscape, a felt landscape, an imagined landscape. Thus, her paintings of trees, fields, and water defied the rules of composition and repudiated all formalism except for figure-ground relationships. "The freedom in my work is quite controlled. I don't close my eyes and hope for the best," she told historian Irving Sandler ("Is Today's Artist with or against the Past? Part 2," *ArtNews* 57 [Sept. 1958]: 41). She also became known as a colorist for the first time in her career. Her "black paintings," ironically containing no black pigment, were created in 1964, a year after her father's death; critic Holland Cotter has called them "an extended gesture of mourning." The dark tonality of the 1964 paintings were repeated in *Chicago* (1966–1967), painted while her mother was dying. Her various stylistic changes in this period would have been extremely difficult to develop within New York's minimalist and pop art scenes. Though her *Skyes* (1960–1961) was featured on the cover of *ArtNews*, Mitchell for the most part remained out of fashion in the United States. She continued to reference French masters Cezanne, Matisse, and van Gogh, while American trends dictated a repudiation of the past.

In July 1967 a family inheritance enabled Mitchell to buy the two-acre estate in Vetheuil, where she lived for the rest of her life. She extended a kind of gruff hospitality toward the friends and fellow artists who came to learn from her—while she kept her house open to all visitors, she locked her studio. Like her paintings, Mitchell was daring, energetic, "and always in a state of dissatisfaction" (Somers, p. 77). Van Gogh's work directly inspired her series of *Sunflower* paintings in 1969. Spurred by the brilliance of triptychs such as *Bonjour Julie* (1971) and *Wet Orange* (1972), American art museums began to rediscover Mitchell in earnest. In 1972 she had her first one-artist exhibition at an American museum (Everson Museum of Art, Syracuse, N.Y.), followed by another at the Whitney Museum of American Art in New York in 1974. In this same period she came closer than ever to "all-over painting," giving her canvases a newly luscious, tactile quality. The style is evident in her work through the early 1980s, for example in *Cypress* (1980). Many consider her work in the last decade of her life to be her most powerful and lyrical. Critic Klaus Kertess described paintings such as the renowned *La Grande Vallee* group (1983–1984) as "storms of paint" with "contemplative power." Pained by the end of her relationship with Riopelle, and even more deeply by the deaths of her friend and psychoanalyst Edrita Fried in 1981 and her sister Sally Perry in 1982, Mitchell returned to themes of death and abandonment in her art, declaring that "painting is what allows me to survive."

By the late 1980s Mitchell's artistic reputation became formally acknowledged and widely celebrated. Cornell University organized a retrospective exhibition of her work in 1988, and the same year Robert Mapplethorpe commemorated her with a photographic portrait. In 1989 she received France's Grand prix national de peinture. She continued to work despite declining health and died in Paris.

Joan Mitchell occupies a central place within an international art movement. She worked as an abstract expressionist until the end of her life, and her artistic success convinced younger artists that abstract expressionism, oil as a medium, and France as a source of inspiration were indeed still valuable aesthetic resources. Her influence extended to contemporary musicians and poets as well; poet Frank O'Hara mentions Mitchell in several works, and some of her own paintings—such as *To the Harbormaster* (1957)—were inspired by his poems. Mitchell was one of very few painters who devoted themselves to landscape while remaining outside realist or figurative traditions. In her lifetime she participated in more than twenty-five solo exhibitions and fifty group exhibitions; her work continues to be collected by major museums such as the Museum of Modern Art in New York, the Art Institute of Chicago, and the Phillips Collection in Washington, D.C.

• Mitchell is the subject of two monographs, Judith E. Bernstock, *Joan Mitchell* (1988), and Michel Waldberg, *Joan Mitchell* (1992); literally hundreds of articles and reviews; and a documentary film directed by Marion Cajori, *Joan Mitchell: Portrait of an Abstract Painter* (1992). Catalogs of Mitchell's exhibitions include Marcia Tucker, *Joan Mitchell* (1974); Marcelin Pleynet et al., *Joan Mitchell: Choix de peintures, 1970–1982* (1982); and Robert Storr, *Joan Mitchell* (1994). Her work is cited in numerous books about abstract expressionism, such as B. H. Friedman, ed., *School of New York: Some Younger Artists* (1959), and in studies of women artists, such as Nancy Heller, *Women Artists: An Illustrated History* (1987). Ora Lerman illuminates van Gogh's influence on Mitchell's work and identifies her as part of an aesthetic movement that emphasized the subjective instead of the perceptual and the rational in "The Elusive Subject," *Arts Magazine*, Sept. 1990, pp. 42–46. Deborah Solomon interviewed Mitchell in depth near the end of the painter's life in "In Monet's Light," *New York Times Magazine*, 24 Nov. 1991, pp. 6–13. See also Klaus Kertess, "Joan Mitchell: The Last Decade," *Art in America*, Dec. 1992, pp. 94–101. Bill Scott, "In the Eye of the Tiger," *Art in America*, Mar. 1995, pp. 70–78, and Marion Somers, "Creative Exit," *Art Journal* 53 (Spring 1994): 76–78, offer personal reminiscences of Mitchell. The Jeu de Paume in Paris hosted Joan Mitchell: The Last Years, 1983–1992 in the summer of 1994, with a concurrent exhibition of her earlier works at the Musée des Beaux-Arts in Nantes. An obituary is in the *New York Times*, 31 Oct. 1992.

LAURA PRIETO CHESTERTON

MITCHELL, John (1690?–1768), physician and naturalist. His birthplace and parentage are now unknown. The details of Mitchell's early life remain obscure. In all likelihood, he was born in Britain around 1690. He studied medicine at the University of Edinburgh, where he apparently learned the experimental method and became interested in plant taxonomy. A few sources suggest that Mitchell was born in Virginia and went from there to Edinburgh and perhaps Leiden for his formal education. Sources agree that Mitchell had established a medical practice in Virginia at least by 1738, for in that year he sent his former Edinburgh botany professor, Charles Alston, a collection of American plant specimens and seeds. Also in 1739 he submitted a manuscript to the chief American correspondent for the Royal Society of London, Peter Collinson, describing several new genera of Virginia plants.

Thereafter, and possibly earlier, Mitchell participated in the famed "Natural History Circle" of Europeans and colonists engaged in systematically collecting and classifying plants and animals in parts of the world then being settled by northern Europeans. Mitchell served primarily as a minor collector in that enterprise, though he occasionally speculated about the proper method of classifying plants according to their natural relationships. He corresponded with many of the leading naturalists of Europe, including J. J. Dillenius, J. F. Gronovius, Mark Catesby, Peter Kalm, and the great Carolus Linnaeus, who named the American partridgeberry *Mitchella repens* in Mitchell's honor. Despite his persistent complaints about the lack of scientific expertise in the New World, Mitchell's own work benefited from his contact with prominent American naturalists such as John Bartram, John Clayton, and Cadwallader Colden, as well as with the premier colonial experimenter, Benjamin Franklin.

During his residence in America, Mitchell also investigated other aspects of the natural history of the New World. His most significant papers pertained to his study of reproduction by that curious American marsupial, the opossum; his attempt to apply Newtonian color theory to explain the skin pigmentation of Native and African Americans; and his account of three supposed yellow fever epidemics that struck Virginia during his stay there.

Mitchell's writings from Virginia regularly criticized the state of science and medicine in the American colonies, but it was the very weakness of colonial science and medicine that enabled Mitchell to make his greatest contributions. In a land new to European science and medicine, it took only a little training and curiosity for Mitchell to collect unknown plants, make novel observations, and establish a successful medical practice. Indeed, several other English colonists did as much as Mitchell in these areas, or more. After his return to England for health reasons in 1746, Mitchell joined the prestigious Royal Society but conducted little original scientific research.

Mitchell's most significant endeavor following his return to England and a second enduring achievement of his life was making the definitive map of colonial boundaries within eastern North America. Collinson commented when he wrote to Linnaeus in 1755, "Dr. Mitchell has left Botany for some time, and has wholly employed himself in making a map, or chart, of all North America. . . . It is the most perfect of any published, and is universally accepted." His assessment proved accurate, at least from an English point of view. Mitchell devoted most of five years to the project and drew on the latest British government surveys as well as private correspondence with colonists and the accounts of English and French explorers.

Mitchell prepared his map both as a commercial venture and to boost British interests in the New World. He succeeded on both counts. It was widely published throughout Europe during his lifetime and continues to be reprinted as a historical reference. The map first appeared under the auspices of England's Board of Trade and Plantations in 1755, just in time to support British claims to disputed portions of the Ohio Valley at the outset of the French and Indian War. After that war it was used by Parliament to establish the expansive boundary for Britain's new Canadian colonies, which enraged the American colonists. When the United States gained its independence a few years later, Mitchell's map served as a reference for drawing the international boundary, first in the peace negotiations concluding the American Revolution and later in settling a succession of border disputes that arose between the new nation and English Canada. Negotiators, arbitrators, and courts have regularly relied on the map to resolve conflicting claims to the boundaries of various American states and Canadian provinces, including twentieth-century cases involving the extent of Labrador and Upper Michigan. In a 1933 article Library of Congress map expert Lawrence Martin, a former geographer of the Department of State, described it as "the most important map in American history."

Apparently Mitchell did not practice medicine after his return to England. He contributed anonymous material to a series of undistinguished books about American politics and history that sought to capitalize on the popularity of such publications in England. These writings were marked by a pro-British slant and a recurring lament about the unhealthy climate of the eastern seaboard. Accordingly, he proposed that settlement concentrate in the Mississippi River valley, where colonists could readily produce the agricultural products needed for British markets. These writings had little appreciable impact. He died in London.

Although he lived most of his life in Great Britain, Mitchell is chiefly remembered for his scientific collections and observations of native flora and fauna made during his residence in colonial Virginia from about 1735 to 1746. These contributions resulted from Mitchell's willingness and ability to apply the new scientific methods of the European Enlightenment to the study of the plants and animals easily found in the New World. His American plant collections and map survive as Mitchell's best-remembered legacy while details of his personal life largely have been forgotten.

• Some of Mitchell's letters appear in James E. Smith, *A Selection of the Correspondence of Linnaeus and Other Naturalists* (1821), and in other published collections of Natural History Circle correspondence. Herbert Thatcher reprints several Mitchell letters with his article, "Dr. Mitchell, M.D., F.R.S., of Virginia," *Virginia Magazine of History and Biography* 39–41 (1931–1933). Three of Mitchell's scientific papers first appeared in the Royal Society's *Philosophical Transactions* 43 (1744), 45 (1750), and 51 (1761). His later books included *The Contest in America between Great Britain and France* (1757) and *The Present Status of Great Britain and North America* (1767). The Library of Congress houses the most complete collection of original copies of Mitchell's map. The best secondary accounts about Mitchell are Edmund Berkeley and Dorothy Smith Berkeley, *Dr. John Mitchell* (1974); Theodore Hornberger, "Scientific Ideas of John Mitchell," *Huntington Library Quarterly* 10 (1947): 277–96; Lyman Carrier, "Dr. John Mitchell, Naturalist, Cartographer, and Historian," *Annual Report of American Historical Association* 1 (1918): 201–19; and the section on Mitchell in Raymond P. Stearns, *Science in the British Colonies of America* (1970), pp. 539–54. For further discussion of Mitchell's map and its significance, see Lawrence Martin's article in Hunter Miller, ed., *Treaties and Other International Acts*, vol. 3 (1933), pp. 328–51.

EDWARD J. LARSON

MITCHELL, John (4 Feb. 1870–9 Sept. 1919), labor leader, was born in Braidwood, Illinois, a small coal-mining village, the son of Robert Mitchell, a coal miner and farmer, and Martha Halley. Both his parents having died by the time he reached the age of six, Mitchell was raised by a devout Presbyterian stepmother. He left public school before adolescence to work in the local mines. As a teenager, he moved to the western mountain region in 1886, where coal miners earned higher wages. After an unsuccessful time there he returned to Illinois in 1887.

Back in Braidwood, Mitchell devoted himself to improving the material circumstances of fellow coal miners. The rapid rise and decline of the Knights of Labor, the organization to which Mitchell and most union miners belonged between 1885 and 1890, taught him that miners needed their own union, one that would be better organized, more stable, and totally devoted to the interests of coal miners. He thus became a founding member of the United Mine Workers of America (UMWA) in 1890. In 1891 he married Katherine O'Rourke, a miner's daughter, with whom he had six children. Soon after, Mitchell began to read law and investigate social problems. He then rose rapidly in the hierarchy of the UMWA. He first served as secretary treasurer of Illinois District 12 between 1895 and 1897. He then became a member of the Illinois state executive committee (1897) and an international organizer, becoming vice president of the union that same year. A year later, in September 1898, the union's national executive board appointed him acting president, and the following year members elected him president, an office Mitchell held for ten years. His presidency of the UMWA also earned him the position of fourth vice president of the American Federation of Labor (1898–1900) and then that of second vice president (1900–1914).

Between 1899 and 1903 Mitchell built a national reputation as a successful and responsible labor leader, largely through his efforts to organize the anthracite coal miners of northeastern Pennsylvania. During the protracted anthracite strike of 1902, which many observers lauded as a triumph for the union, Mitchell discouraged bituminous coal miners from striking in sympathy with hard-coal miners; he also proved more receptive than the operators to President Theodore Roosevelt's initiatives to settle the strike. Roosevelt reciprocated Mitchell's cooperation, citing the UMWA president as a "good" labor leader and model citizen. So responsible was Mitchell's behavior during the strike and in his negotiations with the president and employers that he accepted a settlement from the presidential arbitration commission that failed to grant strikers either the union shop or solid union recognition—their basic, original demands.

An unprepossessing person whose conservative dress and demeanor mirrored his union policies, Mitchell's reputation rivaled that of Samuel Gompers. His advice on public issues being avidly sought, Mitchell wrote two books, *Organized Labor* (1903) and *The Wage Earner and His Problems* (1913); these encapsulated the essence of his approach to labor-management relations, which was that the two parties should coexist harmoniously to promote their mutual prosperity. In 1905, for example, he told union delegates that "I am not here to denounce them [mineowners]; I am anxious for their friendship for you." Throughout his tenure as president of the UMWA, Mitchell discouraged precipitate strikes by coal miners and strove to suppress militancy among the rank and file. Yet during his tenure the membership of the UMWA increased from 34,000 to about 300,000 members.

Lionized by Roosevelt and prominent business leaders as a responsible labor leader, Mitchell began to associate more closely with men of wealth than he did with coal miners. He served as a vice president of the National Civic Federation (NCF), an organization founded in 1900 by large industrialists and bankers to foster nonconflictual relations between business and labor. He also used his contacts with influential businesspeople to solicit "tips" on personal investments, with the goal of enriching himself and his family. Mitchell's increasing conservatism, close association with business leaders, and personal financial investments estranged him from the UMWA's rank and file. Working miners and many district officials began to suspect that Mitchell sacrificed his members' welfare in order to maintain harmonious relations with employers.

While his wealth increased, Mitchell's health deteriorated, leading him to resign as union president in 1908. Preferring to amass money and maintain good relations with his business allies, he continued to serve simultaneously as the paid director of the NCF's trade-agreement department and as second vice president of the AFL. Finally, in 1911, insurgents in the UMWA demanded that Mitchell choose between his union and the NCF; he resigned from the latter organization. In 1915 he accepted appointment as chairman of the New York State Industrial Commission, a position he held until his death in New York City as a result of pneumonia following an operation for the removal of gallstones. At his death Mitchell received many tributes from business and political leaders, a further indication of how he had built his career as a responsible labor statesman.

• The John Mitchell papers are located at the Catholic University of America, Washington, D.C., and are also available in a microfilm edition. The best biography of Mitchell remains Elsie Gluck, *John Mitchell, Miner* (1929). Two excellent scholarly articles are Joseph M. Gowaskie, "From Conflict to Cooperation: John Mitchell and the Bituminous Coal Operators, 1898–1908," *The Historian* 38 (1976): 669–88, and James O. Morris, "The Acquisitive Spirit of John Mitchell, UMW President (1899–1908)," *Labor History* 20 (1979): 5–43.

MELVYN DUBOFSKY

MITCHELL, John (1913–1988). *See* Mitchell, John Newton.

MITCHELL, John, Jr. (11 July 1863–3 Dec. 1929), newspaper editor and banker, was born near Richmond, Virginia, on the estate of James Lyons, where his parents, John Mitchell and Rebecca (maiden name unknown), were house slaves. After gaining their freedom, the Mitchells were employed by Lyons as servants in his mansion in the city, where their son performed various chores and became a keen observer of the rituals of polite society practiced there. Mitchell's mother exerted the decisive influence on him during his formative years: she instilled in him a fierce sense of racial pride, instructed him in the ways of gentlemanly conduct, and insisted on his regular attendance at the First African Baptist Church, where he was baptized at the age of fourteen. Over the objections of her white employer, Rebecca Mitchell arranged for her son's education, first in a private school and later in public schools. An intensely competitive student with considerable artistic ability, Mitchell regularly won medals for superior performance and graduated at the head of his class at the Richmond Normal and High School in 1881.

Failure to obtain an apprenticeship in architecture prompted Mitchell to seek employment as a teacher. In 1883, after teaching for two years in Fredericksburg, Virginia, he returned to Richmond where he had secured a post in the city's public schools. A conspicuous figure in the social, cultural, and religious life of Richmond's black community, he also served as a correspondent for the *New York Globe*, a leading black newspaper. For several years beginning in 1883 he contributed a weekly column to the *Globe* on events in black Richmond under the pen name "More." A strikingly handsome, courtly man, always fashionably attired, Mitchell never lacked for female companionship. Although he carried on a courtship over several decades with Marietta Chiles, a normal school classmate, he remained a bachelor. An intensely private man, he impressed many as a lonely, solitary figure.

When after a year Mitchell lost his teaching job in Richmond because of political changes in the city, he embarked on a career in journalism as editor of the *Richmond Planet*, a black weekly founded in 1883. Assuming direction of the virtually bankrupt newspaper with the help of friends in December 1884, Mitchell remained its editor for the next forty-five years. In time he modernized the newspaper's equipment, enlivened its pages with his own art work, increased its circulation, and ultimately transformed the Planet Publishing Company into a modestly profitable enterprise. Active in the Colored Press Association by the mid-1880s, he served as its president from 1890 to 1894. Despite a succession of legal battles that challenged his ownership of the *Planet*, Mitchell managed to retain control and to pursue his intensely personal style of journalism.

The Planet was in many respects a model weekly paper, but its principal distinction lay in Mitchell's pithy and fiery editorials. Known as "the fighting editor," Mitchell continually protested all forms of racial discrimination and ridiculed the pretensions and hypocrisies of white prejudice. As the racial climate deteriorated in the late nineteenth century, he advised blacks to arm themselves in self-defense on the grounds that quiet submission to white oppression only increased assaults on their dignity. Described as "courageous almost to a fault," the *Planet*'s editor on one occasion wrote that the South needed "Jim Crow beds" far more than it needed "Jim Crow cars" and advocated legislation to penalize white men who kept black mistresses. Oblivious to threats on his life, Mitchell, on another occasion, armed himself and personally went into the countryside to investigate a lynching.

In addition to gaining recognition as a crusading editor who boldly defended the civil rights of African Americans, Mitchell also achieved considerable prominence in Virginia's Republican party. Chosen as a delegate to the party's national convention in 1888 and as an alternate delegate four years later, he served as a member of the Richmond City Council from the predominantly black Jackson Ward between 1888 and 1896. Convinced that the repeated use of fraud and racism by Democrats and the spread of lily-whitism among Republicans precluded any chance of blacks and poor whites uniting politically, Mitchell sought to enlist the support of upper-class, conservative whites. But his efforts were futile, as evidenced by his losing a bid to regain his seat on the city council in 1900 and the disfranchisement of Virginia blacks two years later.

Although Mitchell moderated the militancy of his rhetoric late in the 1890s, he was still capable of wielding a pen "dipped in vitriol." As an opponent of imperialism, for example, he denounced the Spanish-American War as "a war of conquest" that would subject the dark-skinned inhabitants of Cuba and the Philippines to the horrors of racism rampant in the South. After the turn of the century Mitchell moved closer to, but never fully embraced, the accommodationist philosophy of Booker T. Washington. Differences in their styles and tactics were abundantly evident in Mitchell's outspoken condemnation of disfranchisement in 1902, his leadership of a boycott to protest Richmond's segregated street cars two years later, his vocal opposition to the city's successful effort to legalize residential segregation in 1911, and his futile campaign for governor of Virginia on a "lily-black" ticket in 1921.

When disfranchisement effectively ended his political career, Mitchell turned to economic development as a means of assisting blacks in their struggle for first-class citizenship. In 1902 he founded the Mechanics Savings Bank, which grew rapidly—in part because of funds deposited by the Virginia chapter of the Knights of Pythias that he headed. As the founder and president of what was publicized as a showpiece of black enterprise, Mitchell won the support and admiration of much of the white business community and for many years was the only African-American member of the American Bankers Association. When the bank failed in 1922, he was indicted for mismanagement. Although he was not convicted of the charge, depositors blamed him for their misfortune. Unable to regain the respect he had so long enjoyed among African Americans, Mitchell died a poor man seven years after the bank's failure and was buried in Richmond's Evergreen Cemetery.

• The extant files of the *Richmond Planet* (1883–1929) provide essential information on the career of John Mitchell, Jr., while Ann F. Alexander, "Black Protest in the New South: John Mitchell, Jr., 1863–1929, and the Richmond *Planet*" (Ph.D. diss., Duke Univ., 1972), is the most thorough scholarly treatment of his life. Also useful are William J. Simmons, *Men of Mark: Eminent, Progressive and Rising* (1970); I. Garland Penn, *The Afro-American Press and Its Editors* (1891); Henry Lewis Suggs, ed., *The Black Press in the South, 1865–1979* (1983); Willard B. Gatewood, "A Negro Editor on Imperialism: John Mitchell, 1898–1901," *Journalism Quarterly* 49 (Spring 1972): 43–50, 60; and Clay Perry, "John P. Mitchell, Virginia's Journalist of Reform," *Journalism History* 4 (Winter 1977–1978): 142–47, 156.

WILLARD B. GATEWOOD

MITCHELL, John Hipple (22 June 1835–8 Dec. 1905), attorney and U.S. senator, was born John Hipple in Washington County, Pennsylvania, the son of John Hipple and Jemima Mitchell, farmers. The family moved to neighboring Butler County where young John attended a country school. As an adolescent he enrolled in the county's high school, Butler Academy, and later studied at the Witherspoon Institute. While teaching in the public schools to support himself, he studied law and subsequently was admitted to the Pennsylvania bar at the age of twenty-two. At about this time he married Sadie Hoon, had two children with her, and then left his family for California in 1860. He remained in California only for a brief period, because he subsequently showed up in Portland, Oregon, where he arrived on 4 July of the same year.

After his arrival in his newly adopted state, he assumed the name Mitchell and quickly became involved in politics. Within four years he was twice elected to the state senate, serving as the president of that body during his second term. An outspoken proponent of the Union cause during the Civil War, Mitchell gained prominence in the newly emerging Republican party. At the same time he began providing legal counsel to Benjamin Holladay's newly formed Oregon and California Railroad Company, an expertise that eventually brought him fame as a powerful attorney for large railroad companies, including the Northern Pacific. With Holladay's powerful influence with the Oregon legislature (he reputedly bought votes to ensure the election), the state senate elected Mitchell to the U.S. Senate in 1872 and thereby subjected the new senator to more careful political and public scrutiny, including charges of bigamy. Before divorcing his first wife, Mitchell had married Mattie Price, an Oregon woman, in 1862. The number of their children, if any, is unknown. Despite the charges of bigamy, of reputedly assuming a false name, and of being the corporate tool of the controversial Holladay, Mitchell remained a key player in state politics for thirty years.

Physically impressive in appearance and an exceptionally gifted public speaker, Mitchell was touted by some as "the most popular political leader of his generation in Oregon." A consummate promoter of the interests of Oregon and the Pacific Northwest, he was successful in obtaining federal funds for harbor improvements, including the building of a jetty at the mouth of the Columbia River, monies to begin construction of the Cascade Canal and Locks on the same waterway, and funds for federal buildings in his home state. He also joined the popular anti-Asiatic movement on the West Coast in the mid-1880s to oppose further Chinese immigration to the United States. But the public clamor against him continued, much of it led by Harvey W. Scott, the influential editor of the Portland *Oregonian*. The enmity between the two was exacerbated further when Mitchell engineered Scott's removal as the customs collector at the Port of Portland in 1876.

The one constancy of Mitchell's public and private career was his unstinting belief that the interests of business and government were one. He carried that conviction into the courtroom, where he defended the interests of the large corporations that conducted business in the state of Oregon. When "free silver" became the rallying cry for many politicians in both major parties in the American West in the early 1890s, Mitchell supported the gold standard. As a representative of a resource-dependent region, the Oregon Republican also invited controversy when he supported a protective tariff and federal funding for the nation's major railroad systems. With fellow Republican party boss, Joseph Dolph, Mitchell was the stalwart spokesman for conservative business causes.

Finally, the veneer of comfortable, statesmanlike rectitude proved to be Mitchell's undoing. The morality of mixing private gain with the public's business eventually made him anathema to the reform wing of his own party shortly after the turn of the century. Caught in the midst of widespread graft involving massive transfers of public land to the private sector, Mitchell was charged with accepting bribes to facilitate fraudulent claims before the General Land Office. Hence, in the midst of his fourth elected term to the U.S. Senate, he was convicted in a federal court in Portland, Oregon, of betraying the public trust. Mitchell died in Washington, D.C., before he was formally sentenced.

• Primary materials on the life of Mitchell are sparse. The best repository is the Oregon Historical Society, although materials are scattered through numerous collections. The indexes of the *Oregon Historical Quarterly* (1940, 1960, and 1980) include several entries that mention Mitchell. In addition, the Portland *Oregonian*, although largely unsympathetic to Mitchell, includes important materials on his career. For secondary sources, consult Joseph Gaston, *The Centennial History of Oregon* (1877); Horace S. Lyman, *History of Oregon* (1890); Harvey W. Scott, *History of the Oregon Country* (1924); Dorothy O. Johansen, *Empire of the Columbia* (1968); Gordon B. Dodds, *Oregon: A History* (1977); and Carlos A. Schwantes, *The Pacific Northwest: An Interpretive History* (1989).

WILLIAM G. ROBBINS

MITCHELL, John Kearsley (12 or 17 May 1793–4 Apr. 1858), physician, was born in Shepherdstown, Virginia (now West Virginia), the son of Alexander Mitchell, a physician, and Elizabeth Kearsley. Orphaned at the age of eight, Mitchell was put in the charge of his maternal grandmother and, after her death, was sent to his father's family in Ayr, Scotland, arriving there when he was about thirteen. He was educated at Ayr Academy, where he excelled scholastically, and at the University of Edinburgh. He returned to the United States in 1814 almost penniless, freed the two or three slaves he had inherited and whose rental had paid his expenses at Edinburgh, and with the financial support of the Kearsleys, began the study of medicine in 1815 or 1816. Taken in first as a student by Dr. Samuel Powel Griffitts, he later enrolled at the University of Pennsylvania, from which he received his medical degree in 1819.

Impaired health led Mitchell to accept a post as ship surgeon. In 1817–1818 he made his first voyage to China and made at least two more trips to the Far East after receiving his medical degree. Writing poetry, compiling a dictionary of quotations, and composing verses to Sarah Matilda Henry (who became his wife in 1822 and with whom he had nine children, eight of whom lived to adulthood) kept him occupied on these voyages. Edgar Allan Poe, when assistant editor of *Graham's Magazine*, in which several of Mitchell's poems later appeared, wrote that "Dr. Mitchell has published several pretty songs which have been set to music and become popular . . . also . . . a volume of poems of which the longest was remarkable for an old-fashioned polish and vigor of versification." Mitchell's volume of poetry was called *Indecision: A Tale of the Far West and Other Poems* (1839), and Poe's euphemistic appraisal probably reflected his regard for Mitchell, who had apparently shown him some kindness.

Mitchell established his medical practice in Philadelphia in 1822 and soon began to lecture in the institutes of medicine at the Philadelphia Medical Institute. Subsequently appointed professor of chemistry, he retained a connection with the institute until 1841. In 1833 he was appointed professor of chemistry at the Franklin Institute and devoted his major efforts during this period to chemistry. His work on the "Liquefaction and Solidification of Carbonic Acid," published in the *Franklin Institute Journal* in 1838, was probably the first demonstration of the procedure in the United States. He experimented with the use of the solid to produce blisters or sloughs in medical practice, and he had visions of the expansion of the gas from the frozen state creating a force akin to steam. His studies of osmotic pressure and of gases—studies then in their infancy in Europe—"On the Penetrativeness of Fluids" and "On the Penetration of Gases" appeared in the *American Journal of the Medical Sciences* in 1830 and 1833. In 1831 he edited and annotated an American edition of Michael Faraday's *Chemical Manipulation*. When he accepted the post of professor of the theory and practice of medicine at the Jefferson

Medical College in 1841, he gave up the teaching of chemistry, according to his son, neurologist Silas Weir Mitchell, "with a pang . . . [and] burned a drawerful of memoranda for future research."

Mitchell had not forsaken medicine. As visiting physician to the Pennsylvania and city hospitals, he ministered during the smallpox epidemic of 1825 and the cholera epidemic of 1832, work that earned him commendations from the city authorities. Once he had joined the Jefferson faculty, on which he remained active until his death, he devoted his energy to teaching and writing in medicine. A profusion of articles and orations flowed from his mind and pen. Many were hortatory, for example, "The Value of a Great Medical Reputation and Suggestions for Its Attainment" (1834). In 1851 his introductory lecture at Jefferson "On the Progress of Recent Science" was a masterful review of the contributions of Franklin, Herschel, Kepler, Laënnec, and many others.

Mitchell's more scientific and clinical endeavors in medicine began as early as 1824, after which he published articles on varied and unrelated subjects. In 1845 he edited an American edition of R. W. Bampfield's *An Essay on the Curvatures and Diseases of the Spine*, and in the 1830s he published an article on the fungus basis of febrile disease and another on rheumatism. Mitchell never pursued the latter subject, but he was later credited—not correctly—by J. M. Charcot with being the first to describe neuropathic arthritis.

In 1849 Mitchell published *An Essay on the Cryptogamous Origin of Malarious and Epidemic Fevers*, which brought him considerable professional notice. The most original and important of his works, this essay brought together ideas that had first occurred to him in 1829 and that he had presented in six lectures to his students during 1846–1847. In a speculative, theoretical, and well-reasoned discussion, Mitchell rejected the explanations of the etiology of malaria then current and postulated the idea that malaria and other fevers were caused by fungi. The diseases caused by fungi, he posited, were specific and contagious. His thesis was received with skepticism, particularly for its speculative nature and lack of experimental evidence. William Henry Welch, a leader in American medical science, later contended, however, that "this book deserves to rank with the more frequently quoted work of Henle relating to the same line of argument." Mitchell recognized that the demonstration of his theory "must exact, for years, the enlightened and patient toils of many philosophers," but, unlike Jacob Henle, the noted German medical scientist whose *Von den Miasmen und Contagien* had appeared in 1840, Mitchell had no devoted followers to perpetuate his theory.

Although Mitchell's "An Essay on Animal Magnetism" was never published during his lifetime, it was included in a volume called *Five Essays* that S. Weir Mitchell issued in 1859 as a memorial to his father. It was also read before the College of Physicians of Philadelphia in 1842, though only in summary, for, as the son pointed out, his father recognized the cold reaction his presentation would receive from that orthodox body of physicians. The essay rejected the clairvoyance that had enveloped mesmerism but went beyond espousing hypnotism. Citing illustrations from Mitchell's own practice, it suggested that the magnetic influences of the practitioner moving his hands above the affected parts of the patient had salutary effects.

The social graces that Mitchell learned as a young man in Edinburgh never left him. His lecture style was described by Cato, the pseudonymous biographer of contemporary medical notables, as "soft and sweet," conversational, and without pretensions or oratorical flourish. His son was to describe him as a tall man, "strongly built . . . a great shot, skilful in all games and ever a gay and resourceful companion," and as "a model of manly beauty, of perfect courtesy." Interested in literature, Mitchell was long a member of the American Whig Society for the Promotion of Literature, Friendship and Morality, and as a Whig, he actively supported Zachary Taylor's presidential candidacy in 1848. In "A Lecture on Some of the Means of Elevating the Character of the Working Classes," he reported broad-mindedly in 1834 that he "had not been able to perceive any necessary connection between manual labor and degradation," a rather unorthodox view. He served as physician, vice president (1840–1841), and president (1849–1850) of the St. Andrew's Society of Philadelphia. An active Mason, he was grand master of the Grand Lodge of Pennsylvania at his death. Professionally, he was a member of the Philadelphia Medical Society (of which he served as corresponding secretary in 1825), the American Medical Association, the Academy of Natural Sciences of Philadelphia, the American Philosophical Society (to which he was elected in 1827), and the College of Physicians of Philadelphia (of which he was elected a member in 1827 and a fellow in 1834). He died in Philadelphia.

• A collection of Mitchell's papers at the Library of the Philadelphia College of Physicians includes a diary he kept on his sea voyages, correspondence with family members, and other papers. There is considerable information about Mitchell in Anna Robeson Burr's biography of his son, *Weir Mitchell: His Life and Letters* (1929). "Cato" devoted the ninth of his series on "Sketches of Eminent Living Physicians" to Mitchell, *Boston Medical and Surgical Journal* 41 (1849): 38–41. Chapter two of R. D. Walker, *S. Weir Mitchell, M.D.—Neurologist* (1970), is devoted to John Kearsley Mitchell and gives concise summaries of his various publications. Mitchell's work on the fungus origins of disease is analyzed in Raymond N. Doetsch, "Mitchell on the Cause of Fevers," *Bulletin of the History of Medicine* 38 (1964): 241–59; his work on rheumatism is analyzed in Michael Kelly, "John Kearsley Mitchell (1793–1858) and the Neurogenic Theory of Arthritis: A Reappraisal," *Journal of the History of Medicine and Allied Sciences* 20 (1965): 151–56. The most complete obituaries are R. Dunglison, *Proceedings of the American Philosophical Society* 6 (1854–1858): 340–42; *Transactions of the Medical Society of the State of Pennsylvania* 11 (1859): 93–98; and S. H. Dickson, *The Late Professor J. K. Mitchell, M.D. Inaugural Lecture . . . in the Jefferson Medical College* (1858).

DAVID L. COWEN

MITCHELL, John Newton (15 Sept. 1913–9 Nov. 1988), lawyer and U.S. attorney general, was born in Detroit, Michigan, the son of Joseph C. Mitchell and Margaret McMahon. He was raised in Blue Point and Patchogue, Long Island, and Queens, New York. An outstanding student and top athlete, Mitchell attended Jamaica High School and graduated from Fordham Law School in 1938. In the same year he joined the New York City law firm of Caldwell & Raymond, where he specialized in municipal and state bond financing. During World War II Mitchell served as a naval officer, winning a Silver Star. After returning from the war, he resumed his law practice. In 1957 he divorced his first wife and married the outspoken Martha Beall Jennings. He had two children by his first marriage and one by his second.

John Mitchell first met Richard Nixon in 1967, when Nixon became a partner in the New York law firm of Nixon, Mudge, Rose, Guthrie, Alexander & Mitchell. He and Nixon developed as close a relationship as Nixon had during this period. Although he was relatively unschooled in politics, Mitchell served as campaign manager of Nixon's successful 1968 run for the presidency and afterward was appointed attorney general. Upon taking office in 1969 Mitchell declared, "I am first and foremost a law enforcement officer."

As attorney general, Mitchell was responsible for a wide range of legal and political activities in the Nixon administration, including the selection of Supreme Court nominees, the policy of "benign neglect" on civil rights, the anticrime policy, the so-called Southern Strategy, Nixon's reelection, and elements of the political surveillance, espionage, and dirty tricks campaign, many of which predated but later came to be known as Watergate. Almost immediately upon taking office Mitchell authorized a series of actions that the courts later determined to be in violation of the law: illegal wiretaps, dirty tricks, political espionage, misuse of intelligence agencies, and other activities that Mitchell himself later characterized as the "White House horrors."

On 15 February 1972 Mitchell resigned as attorney general to head Nixon's reelection organization, called the Committee to Reelect the President. During this time a variety of crimes and dirty tricks were committed against Nixon's political adversaries; the most notable was a break-in at Democratic Party Headquarters in the Watergate complex in Washington, D.C., on 16 June 1972, after which five men were arrested. Subsequent investigations led to the apprehension of G. Gordon Liddy and E. Howard Hunt (former or current Nixon White House aides) and to the disclosure that the break-in had been funded by campaign contributions to the Committee to Reelect the President. Two weeks later, on 1 July, Mitchell resigned from the committee, citing his desire to spend more time with his family. At the time, most people accepted Mitchell's resignation as being unconnected to the Watergate incident. Having successfully contained this potentially serious scandal, Nixon was reelected that November in a landslide over George McGovern, winning 60.7 percent of the popular vote and achieving an even more overwhelming 520 to 17 electoral college victory.

At least as early as 23 June 1972, White House officials had initiated a campaign to cover up the Watergate break-in and earlier illegal programs, some of which had been authorized by the president. On 22 March 1973, referring to efforts to maintain the silence of the Watergate burglars during the forthcoming Senate inquiry to be headed by North Carolina senator Sam Ervin, Nixon said to Mitchell, "I want you all to stonewall it, let them plead the Fifth Amendment, cover up or anything else, if it'll save it—save the plan." Slowly at first, but with increasing speed, press and congressional revelations began to unravel the Watergate affair. The cover up began to unfurl at the edges, and as damaging evidence got closer and closer to Nixon, the president sought a sacrificial lamb, or, as Nixon himself referred to it, "an hors d'oeuvre strategy," believing that if they gave the prosecutors an hor d'oeuvre, "they won't come back for the main course." He tried to make Mitchell the scapegoat, but Mitchell demurred.

As the cover up continued to unravel throughout 1973, John Mitchell was at the center of the controversy. Mitchell protégé and Nixon aide Jeb Stuart Magruder later commented regarding the cover up, "I don't think there was ever any discussion that there would not be a coverup." As the special prosecutor (appointed in May 1973) got closer and closer to Mitchell, his personal life began to fall apart. In 1974, when John and Martha Mitchell separated, she blamed her husband's refusal to break with Nixon. "He fell into the clutches of the King," she commented.

Mitchell, along with Nixon chief of staff Bob Haldeman and top domestic adviser John Ehrlichman, was indicted for conspiracy, obstruction of justice, and perjury. At his 1974 trial, Mitchell remained loyal to Nixon and tight-lipped concerning his role in the crimes and cover up. He denied most of the charges; those he admitted to he said had been done for sound political reasons: to safeguard the national security or guarantee the reelection of Richard Nixon. On 1 January 1975 Mitchell, along with Haldeman and Ehrlichman, was convicted on all counts and sentenced to from thirty months to eight years in prison. One of the twenty-five Watergate defendants who went to jail, Mitchell became the nation's only attorney general ever to have been imprisoned. Nixon resigned as president in August 1974, and shortly thereafter President Gerald R. Ford granted him a full, free, and absolute pardon.

Mitchell served nineteen months in prison, leaving federal custody in 1979. Disbarred from practicing law, he lived quietly in the Washington, D.C., area, rarely made public appearances, and almost never discussed Watergate. He died in Washington, D.C.

John Mitchell's relationship with Richard Nixon ensured him access to political power and influence. During Nixon's first term, and as the president's trusted adviser, Mitchell was close to the center of power. Believing that the ends (reelecting Nixon) justified the means, he paid a heavy price for the crimes of Watergate, as did the nation whose laws he had sworn to uphold.

• Mitchell left no papers, and a biography has yet to be published. For his role in the Watergate affair, see Carl Bernstein and Bob Woodward, *All the President's Men* (1974); John Dean, *Blind Ambition: The White House Years* (1976); Michael A. Genovese, *The Nixon Presidency: Power and Politics in Turbulent Times* (1990); Dan Rather and Gary Paul Gates, *The Palace Guard* (1974); and Theodore H. White, *Breach of Faith: The Fall of Richard Nixon* (1975). An obituary is in the *New York Times*, 10 Nov. 1988.

MICHAEL A. GENOVESE

MITCHELL, Jonathan (1624–9 July 1668), Protestant clergyman, was born in the parish of Halifax, Yorkshire, England, the son of Matthew Mitchell and Susan Butterfield (occupations unknown). His parents were influenced by the Puritan minister Richard Mather of Lancashire, and immigrated to Massachusetts with the Mathers in the same ship in 1635. After many vicissitudes, the Mitchells settled in Connecticut. Jonathan was prepared for Harvard College, which opened in 1638, by his brother-in-law Abraham Pierson. Mitchell entered Harvard at the mature age of eighteen in 1642, performed brilliantly, and by 1649 was one of the first teaching fellows or tutors.

In partnership with the college, which had been founded to prepare young men for the ministry, and situated next door to the college building, was the Puritan church of Cambridge. The gifted minister from 1636 to 1649 was Thomas Shepard. Mitchell joined his church between September 1648 and March 1649. Shepard died unexpectedly in the summer of 1649 at the age of forty-four, and Mitchell was invited by the church elders to succeed him in 1650. He also married his predecessor's young widow, Margaret Boradel Shepard, in November 1650; they had six children.

All members of the college, including the students, attended the church next door every Sunday and listened to the sermons. The senior members of the college, from the president, Henry Dunster, to the tutors, were expected to undergo rigorous religious self-examination, make a public declaration of their faith, and join the church. This made church membership a vital part of the college's program, and gave the local pastor an especially important role in educating young Puritans. Until his own early death, Mitchell was pastor of the church in Cambridge, and guardian of its members' orthodoxy.

As a spokesman for the second generation of Massachusetts Puritan ministers he played an important role on four different fronts. First, he was preacher and pastor to his congregation. Second, he had a direct role at Harvard College, raising money and counseling the students. Third, he negotiated the compromise that kept the New England churches publicly unified at the time of the "Half-Way" Synod. Fourth, as overseer of the press, he helped to define Puritan orthodoxy at a time when it was breaking up under the relentless pressures of modernity.

Mitchell was a famous preacher, admired as "Matchless Mitchell." The title of a collection of his sermons, *A Discourse of the Glory to Which God Hath Called Believers by Jesus Christ* (1677), shows that he preached a hopeful message. As a pastor Mitchell had the unenviable task of dismissing President Dunster from his congregation, when, after long study of the Bible, Dunster publicly announced that infant baptism was not biblical. Mitchell and a whole battery of divines tried to argue him out of this belief, but to no avail. In 1654 Dunster resigned from the presidency of Harvard because a commission felt that he could no longer be trusted with the education of young people. Dunster never blamed Mitchell, whom he made appraiser of his library.

Mitchell's great public skills were shown in the manner he managed the Synod of 1662, which adopted the Half-Way Covenant. Membership in the Puritan churches was dropping because relatively few laymen could be persuaded to undergo the public examination necessary for full membership. Perhaps fewer than one-third of those who attended the church services were full members. Yet all who attended wanted their children baptized as infants. The Half-Way Covenant was a compromise: only the regenerate, full members were to be admitted to the Lord's Supper, but the children of all those who agreed with the tenets of the church and lived decorous lives were allowed to be baptized. This was an obvious compromise that held the churches together in a period when revivalism was not in fashion. Mitchell published the official results of the Synod of 1662, and *A Defence of the Answer and Arguments of the Synod Met at Boston in the Year 1662* (1664), in which his arguments for its adoption convinced many to support the Half-Way Covenant.

Mitchell made great contributions to Harvard. His *Modell for the Maintaining of Students and Fellows of Choise Abilities at the College in Cambridge*, addressed to the General Court (the Massachusetts legislature) in 1663, pleaded for more money to train learned ministers, masters for the grammar schools, and educated laymen for the magistracy. He asked for endowed fellowships for a linguist, a historian and antiquarian researcher, a "polemical divine," someone knowledgeable in the laws of England, and others to prepare the students to become schoolteachers, teachers of mathematics, and physicians. Mitchell's *Modell*, which stressed training young men in practical matters, became the model of the Dissenting Academies in England. The academies were founded by the spiritual descendants of the Puritan intellectuals when they lost control of the English universities to the Anglican Royalists, who had returned to England with Charles II in 1660. The *Modell* did not have much immediate impact on the teaching at Harvard; the college was never well funded during Mitchell's lifetime and persisted in offering little more than training in the classical languages and Hebrew.

Mitchell served on many college committees of a practical nature, but his great contribution was as a spiritual mentor to undergraduates. His "Letter to His Friend in New England," written while he was still a young tutor at Harvard and first published in 1664, was considered a model of advice for religiously scrupulous young men.

Mitchell, Captain Daniel Gookin, and Thomas Danforth, president of the college, were appointed censors of the press in May 1665. The press had been founded in 1638, the first press in the English colonies, and the first in North America north of Mexico. From the beginning it had a dual role: to publish books and pamphlets that set forth religious and governmental orthodoxy and to print material in the local Algonquian language to convert the Indians to Christianity. During the 1640s and 1650s the Massachusetts Puritans had kept their one press modestly employed in printing small runs of orthodox material. The results of the "Half-Way" Synod, however, had not been accepted with grace by many of the Massachusetts clergy. Many of the senior men dissented, and the governor and elders wanted to ensure that the final report was correctly printed. In this way censorship before publication became the rule with the Cambridge press.

The two types of material printed by the press, government documents and material in the Algonquian language of the Indians, had different sources of funding. The government material was funded in Massachusetts; the Indian material depended on charitable donations from England. Samuel Green had been put in charge of the press in 1649. Running the press was a sideline for Green, and he did not depend on it for a living. He was both too busy with other duties and without the advanced skills necessary to oversee the printing of John Eliot's *Indian Bible* (1661–1663), so the English trustees had sent over Marmaduke Johnson in 1660 with a second press and a supply of special type. Johnson was a skilled workman but a restless man who wanted to run his business in the English manner by reprinting English bestsellers when there was not enough material to keep his press busy. Mitchell as overseer had to mediate between the demands of Puritan orthodoxy and the marketplace. Neither he nor his successors ever solved the problem to their satisfaction.

Mitchell died in Cambridge. He left a reputation as "The Churches Gemme, the Colledge Glory," as John Sherman called him in a poetical epitaph. His influence went well beyond his Cambridge pulpit. He was well known to all Puritan pastors and thinkers in both New and Old England. Many of his actions show him to have been deeply conservative, trying to hold together an outmoded code, but his genuine care for his flock in the largest sense make him one of the most appealing of the Puritan ministers.

• A contemporary biography of Mitchell is in Cotton Mather, *Magnalia Christi Americana*, vol. 2 (1853), pp. 67–113. Mather had use of a Latin diary of Mitchell's that has not survived. John Langdon Sibley, *Biographical Sketches of Graduates of Harvard University*, vol. 1 (1873), pp. 141–57, gives a brief bibliography at the end of his sketch. Samuel Eliot Morison, *Harvard College in the Seventeenth Century* (2 vols., 1935–1936), and *The Founding of Harvard College* (1935), discusses Mitchell's role at Harvard as tutor and as author of the *Modell*. The account of his relationship to the Cambridge press is in George P. Winship, *The Cambridge Press, 1638–1692* (1945). Mitchell's "Relation of Conversion" is in Mary Rhinelander McCarl, ed., "Thomas Shepard's Record of Relations of Religious Experience, 1648–1649," *William and Mary Quarterly*, 3d ser., 48 (1991): 432–66.

MARY RHINELANDER MCCARL

MITCHELL, Julian (Nov. 1852–23 June 1926), dance director, was born probably in New York City, the son of Alfred Mitchell, a stationer, and Sophia Lomax. He made his performing debut as an actor in the 1873 revival of the musical *The Black Crook* at Niblo's Garden, where he worked as a call boy, summoning the players from their dressing rooms when it was time for them to appear on stage. Mitchell continued working as a comic actor, and from 1879 to 1882 he performed in the touring company of his aunt, the actress Maggie Mitchell.

In 1883 Julian Mitchell appeared in *A Bunch of Keys*, the first of playwright Charles Hoyt's series of farce-comedies with music. He became the playwright's assistant director and for the next fourteen years helped stage the comic antics that characterized Hoyt's productions, including *A Trip to Chinatown* (1891), the longest-running Broadway show of its time.

During the 1890s Mitchell became increasingly hearing-impaired and was forced to abandon his performing career. He was able to continue staging productions, however, and was thankful that he had discovered his directorial talents, thereby saving himself from what he believed would have been the drudgery of a career as a stage manager.

In 1897 Mitchell was hired to direct the musical burlesques produced by comedians Joe Weber and Lew Fields. As director of these productions, which included *Poussé Café* (1897), *Hurly Burly* (1898), *Helter Skelter* (1899), *Whirl-I-Gig* (1899), *Fiddle-Dee-Dee* (1900), *Hoity-Toity* (1901), and *Twirly-Whirly* (1902), Mitchell created complex choreography, designed innovative scenic effects, and established his reputation as the disciplinarian of the most beautiful and well-trained line of chorus girls on Broadway.

During this period Mitchell also staged operettas, including composer Victor Herbert's *Idol's Eye* (1897), *The Fortune Teller* (1898), *The Three Dragoons* (1899), and *The Singing Girl* (1899), as well as *An Arabian Girl and Forty Thieves* (1899) and *The Princess Chic* (1900). In 1901 he staged the musical extravaganza *The Girl from Up There* and in 1903 the season's biggest hit, *The Wizard of Oz*, followed by *Babes in Toyland*, a lavish Herbert operetta of which Mitchell was also coproducer. Mitchell garnered critical praise for the spectacular visual effects and ensemble choreography he designed for these productions and soon became the highest-paid director on Broadway.

When Weber and Fields dissolved their partnership, Mitchell staged productions for each of them, individually. For example, in 1904 he was a partner with Fields and Fred Hamlin in the Lew Fields Stock Company, which produced the musical *It Happened in Nordland* under Mitchell's stage direction. For Weber, Mitchell staged *Hip! Hip! Hooray!* (1907) and *The Merry Widow Burlesque* (1908). Mitchell also continued his association with Herbert, producing and staging his 1905 musical play *Wonderland* and creating dances for his 1907 comic opera *The Tattooed Man.* In addition, Mitchell staged shows that Fields produced in partnership with the Shuberts, including the 1906 revue *About Town* and the 1907 musical comedy *The Girl Behind the Counter.*

Limited by budgetary restraints imposed by the Shuberts, Mitchell felt unable to fully create the magnificent dance and stage effects he envisioned. He therefore accepted the invitation to stage the first edition of Florenz Ziegfeld's *Follies* (1907). While Ziegfeld managed the finances, Mitchell was the artist responsible for filling the stage with the sophisticated glamour that came to characterize these dazzling revues. By 1908 he had signed an exclusive contract with Ziegfeld and staged every edition of the *Follies* (except 1914) through 1915. Some in the entertainment industry believed Mitchell discontinued his work on the *Follies* after arguing with Ziegfeld, who he felt was short-changing him on royalties. Near the end of his life, however, Mitchell returned and staged the *Follies* of 1924 and 1925.

Mitchell also created acts for the "advanced vaudeville" circuit of producers Marc Klaw and Abe Erlanger and staged the ensemble numbers for about a dozen of their Broadway musicals from 1909 to 1919. He was sought after by all the leading Broadway producers of his day. George M. Cohan hired him to co-stage many of the musicals he produced, including *The Royal Vagabond* (1919), *Mary* (1920), *The O'Brien Girl* (1921), *Little Nellie Kelly* (1922), and *The Rise of Rosie O'Reilly* (1923). Mitchell also staged comedian Ed Wynn's revues *The Perfect Fool* (1921) and *The Grab Bag* (1924).

In 1924 Mitchell directed the dances for the all-black musical *The Chocolate Dandies*, though jazz dance historians suggest that dancer Charlie Davis devised much of the show's choreography. Mitchell's final Broadway production was the 1925 musical *Sunny*, for which he codirected the dances along with Fred Astaire and others.

A highly respected member of New York's theatrical community, Mitchell joined the Lambs in 1892 and the Players in 1893. He was married in 1889 to Georgia Adele Lake. They were probably divorced by 1894, when Mitchell married acrobatic ballet dancer Bessie Clayton, with whom he had one child. Clayton unsuccessfully sued Mitchell for divorce in 1910, naming, as co-respondent, actress Louise Alexander; the couple remained estranged until their divorce in 1923.

Mitchell's theatrical career spanned the embryonic development of the American musical. His work helped to shape each of the different genres of popular entertainment that contributed to the musical's creation, including the nineteenth-century comedies and extravaganzas in which he performed and the farce-comedies, burlesques, operettas, vaudeville acts, revues, and early musical comedies that he staged.

Though almost completely deaf, Mitchell's abilities to conceive and direct visual elements of musicals made him one of the wealthiest theatrical artists of his time. He was the first to integrate chorus routines into the plot of a show and to give an individuality to each chorine: he directed his chorus girls to act by listening and reacting to the drama on stage. Mitchell served as the inspiration for the character Julian Marsh in the musical *42nd Street* but was largely forgotten after his death. He worked during a time when the director had not yet been acknowledged as the controlling figure in shaping a Broadway musical and before the artistry involved in musical theater dance direction was recognized by the title "choreographer."

Before he died Mitchell was working on the dances for the 1926 *Ziegfeld's American Revue*, but illness prevented him from finishing the project. He died in Long Branch, New Jersey. One of Broadway's most prolific dance directors, Mitchell was a highly organized, strict taskmaster with a soft-spoken, gentle manner. He avoided personal publicity but should be remembered for the wealth of visual delights he provided to thousands of American musical theatergoers.

• Unidentified newspaper clippings titled "Mitchell Rehearses Ardently" and "Problems of Directing a Production: Julian Mitchell, Veteran Stage Manager, Tells How He Builds a Show" are housed in the Shubert Archives in New York City. A few samples of Mitchell's correspondence can also be found at the Shubert Archives as well as in the Townsend Walsh Papers, housed in the manuscripts collection of the New York Public Library. The Billy Rose Theatre Collection at the New York Public Library for the Performing Arts, Lincoln Center, has photographs, clippings, and programs from Mitchell's productions. Mitchell discussed his work and ideas about musical theater staging in newspaper and magazine articles, including "Why the American Chorus Girl Is Queen," *New York Herald*, 26 Jan. 1902; "Is Musical Comedy Worn Out?" *Evening Telegram*, 14 Oct. 1905; "Julian Mitchell Tells of an Art Still in Its Infancy," *New York Sun*, 1907; and John Peter C. Stubbs, "Spending the Other Fellow's Millions," *Green Book*, Aug. 1912, pp. 327–32.

LISA JO SAGOLLA

MITCHELL, Langdon Elwyn (17 Feb. 1862–21 Oct. 1935), playwright, was born in Philadelphia, Pennsylvania, the son of Silas Weir Mitchell, a physician and novelist, and Mary Middleton Elwyn. Mitchell graduated from St. Paul's School, Concord, New Hampshire, after which he studied abroad for three years. He then studied two years at Harvard Law School and one year at Columbia Law School and was admitted to the New York bar in 1886. Initially, however, he practiced law in Philadelphia, in the firm of Cadwalader, Wickersham, and Taft; the Cadwaladers were relatives of his mother. In 1883, at Harvard, he had already published some poetry and drama. In 1885 *Sylvian and Other Poems* was published under the pseudonym John Philip Varley, to avoid comparison with his father, a bestselling author. *Sylvian* was a verse tragedy set in seventeenth-century Cordoba. In 1897, inspired by a sojourn in rural West Virginia, he published *Love in the Backwoods*, composed of two novelettes: *Two Mormons from Muddlety* and *Alfred's Wife*. His first produced play, *Deborah*, opened in London in 1892. That year he married Marion Lea of Philadelphia, whom he had seen perform on the London stage. They had three children. *In the Season* premiered in 1893, also in London. His later plays included *Ruth Underwood, Don Pedro*, and *Step-by-Step*.

His first critical and commercial stage success, however, was *Becky Sharp*, Mitchell's adaptation of William Makepeace Thackeray's *Vanity Fair*. It was written specifically for Minnie Maddern Fiske (Mrs. Harrison Grey), whose performance in the title role helped it run for two seasons in New York (1899–1900). Its immediate popularity inspired an American imitation—closed by an injunction—and two alternate versions in England in 1901. Fiske played this satiric comedy extensively on tour, reviving it in New York a decade later. In 1929 it was revived briefly by the Players, the theater and literary club founded by Edwin Booth, which Mitchell joined just two years after its inception. Long after the premiere, Mitchell told an interviewer that the entire second act of *Becky Sharp* was his own invention, to bridge a gap in Thackeray's tale, but even Thackeray experts had not seemed to notice this in performance. In 1935 it was filmed as the first technicolor movie.

Mitchell's next project was adapting his father's *The Adventures of Francois*, a romantic novel of the French Revolution. He simplified some of the complicated and melodramatic situations in the narrative, but even with Henry E. Dixey, a handsome leading man, in the title role, the play was not a success in 1900, when it opened in Philadelphia. In 1906, however, he had two successes within weeks of each other. The first was *The Kreutzer Sonata*, which opened in New York at the Lyric Theatre in September. He adapted the drama from a Yiddish melodrama by Jacob Gordin for the Polish actress Bertha Kalich, who had previously played it to great effect in that language on the Lower East Side. Now playing in English, Kalich became an overnight star of the Broadway theater.

Mitchell's second vehicle that season was written for Fiske, a long-established star taking a chance on a new play with a provocative theme: *The New York Idea*. It opened in November, an instant popular success, partly because several influential critics—among them Mitchell's friend William Winter—denounced the modern morality demonstrated on stage. Divorce was the satiric mainspring of *The New York Idea*, with characters such as the attractive John and Cynthia Karslake and Judge Philip Phillimore and his former wife Vida, just divorced and preparing to change partners. Interviewed that season by the *New York Times*, Mitchell was modest about his contributions to the developing American drama but also insisted: "Today, we stand on the eve of a dramatic awakening . . . no question that a great advance is imminent." Mitchell confided to American theater historian Arthur Hobson Quinn that he was really writing about the upper stratum of Philadelphia society rather than that of New York—a distinction in morals and manners which ceased to be sharply discernible after World War II, if not before. Although the play is witty and highly civilized and remains the sole American comedy of this period to continue to elicit admiration when read or performed, it was sharply attacked by some reviewers. It is in the tradition of social comedies such as Richard Brinsley Sheridan's *The School for Scandal* and Anna Cora Mowatt's *Fashion*, a nineteenth-century satire on New York society. Clearly, Mitchell had touched a raw nerve. Even the *New York Dramatic Mirror*, published by Fiske's husband, complained that divorce was not a funny subject, though Mitchell had made it seem so.

In 1933 the Snarks—an amateur Manhattan theater group—revived the play, after which Mitchell told a reporter that he had just looked at the 1906 reviews, never having read them before. Considering that the play had been sold out almost every night during its original run, he confessed he was shocked at the notices: " . . . very bad press here in New York, rather amazingly bad." A typical comment: "Mr. Mitchell has no respect for women. His women are coarse. They should never have been seen on any stage. Let Mr. Mitchell learn that the women of the country are chaste and pure, home-loving, husband-loving, calm and peaceful creatures" (Langdon Mitchell file, N.Y. Public Library, n.d.). Nevertheless, it was translated into German as *Jonathan's Tochter* and staged in Berlin by Max Reinhardt in 1916. It was also seen in Hungarian, Danish, and Swedish versions.

Fiske tried out Mitchell's *The New Marriage* in 1911 but not on Broadway. Even in Syracuse, in upstate New York, it did not please audiences or critics. Later, on tour, it did not repeat the success of *The New York Idea*, nor did Mitchell's 1916 Thackeray adaptation, *Major Pendennis*. Even with John Drew in the title role on Broadway, the comedy ran only twelve weeks. When Mitchell died he left a large number of unpublished and unproduced plays. One of his favorites was *A Kentucky Belle*, but Arthur Quinn has suggested that he was too dissatisfied with most of them to attempt production.

Mitchell had an academic side as well. In 1906 he was made a member of the National Institute of Arts and Letters. He lectured on poetry for several years at George Washington University, and, in 1928, he was one of five playwrights invited to lecture on drama at the University of Pennsylvania, which led to his being named Mask & Wig Professor of Playwriting. For health reasons, he gave up both appointments in 1930. During this period, his opinion of society—once so liberal in the theater—became extremely conservative. A decade after his last major disappointment on

Broadway, Mitchell turned his attention to a different kind of social critique in *Understanding America* (1927). As early as 1923, however, he told a Lynchburg, Virginia, audience that a "low moral tone" was sweeping America, in the wake of the hate generated by World War I. Appealing to southern sentiments, he said that Robert E. Lee was the ideal man; Abraham Lincoln and Ulysses S. Grant were not good models for youth. He denounced the loss of individual freedoms and the erosion of states' rights. Shortly before his death, he told an audience in Charleston, South Carolina, of his love for plantation life before the Civil War—though he admitted he'd not experienced it. He modulated into his real agenda: "Fascism is the hope of the nation to escape Communism." It had recently arisen in Germany and Italy, he said, out of necessity.

A man of two cities, Mitchell was a member of the Jury and the Rittenhouse clubs in Philadelphia and of the Century and the Players in Manhattan, where he maintained a residence at 14 Beekman Place. A self-styled "damn yankee," he was a frequent and popular guest in the South. He had a summer home in Santa Fe, New Mexico, where his waxed moustache and lavender shirts and socks were topics of comment. He died in a Philadelphia hospital from an infection contracted on a New Mexico bear hunt. One of his daughters, Susanna Valentine, also became a poet and a playwright, under the name of S. Valentine Mitchell.

• Mitchell's papers are in the University of Pennsylvania Library. Most of his plays were not published, but some manuscript copies are in the Library of Congress for copyright purposes. For interviews, reports of speeches, news items, and programs of his lectures, see the Langdon Mitchell clipping file in the Billy Rose Theatre Collection of the New York Public Library at Lincoln Center. (Also included are materials on his father, S. Weir Mitchell, his wife, Marion Lea, and his daughter, Susanna Valentine.) His best-known plays, *Becky Sharp, The Kreutzer Sonata*, and *The New York Idea*, have all been published in acting editions, and the latter has also been anthologized several times. For a sketch based on personal knowledge, see Arthur Hobson Quinn's essay on Mitchell in the *Dictionary of American Biography*, supp. 1 (1944). Commentary on Mitchell and his plays, notably *The New York Idea*, can be found in Quinn, *History of the American Drama from the Civil War to the Present Day* (1936); Thomas Dickinson, *Playwrights of the New American Theatre* (1925); Alan S. Downer, *Fifty Years of American Drama: 1900–1950* (1951); James Metcalfe, "Langdon Mitchell's *New York Idea*," in *The American Theatre as Seen by Its Critics: 1752–1934*, eds. Montrose J. Moses and John Mason Brown (1934); Brooks Atkinson, *Broadway* (1970); and Garff B. Wilson, *Three Hundred Years of American Drama and Theatre* (1973). Obituaries are in the *New York Times*, the *New York Herald-Tribune*, the *Philadelphia Bulletin*, and the *Philadelphia Inquirer*, 21 and 22 Oct. 1935.

GLENN LONEY

MITCHELL, Lucy Sprague (2 July 1878–15 Oct. 1967), educator, was born in Chicago, Illinois, the daughter of Otho Sprague and Lucia Atwood. Migrating from Vermont to Chicago with his young bride shortly after the Civil War, Otho Sprague and an older brother had opened a dry goods business that soon became the largest wholesale grocery in the world. Members of Chicago's merchant elite, the Sprague brothers helped established many of Chicago's leading cultural institutions; they were among the benefactors of Hull-House, the settlement led by Jane Addams, who served as a personal inspiration to Lucy Sprague during her early adolescence.

In 1893 the family moved to Pasadena, California; Lucy entered the Marlborough School, a girls' private preparatory academy in nearby Los Angeles. In 1896, over her father's strong objection, and with the intervention of former Wellesley College president and family friend Alice Freeman Palmer, she enrolled at Radcliffe College as a special student. Sprague studied with the great Harvard philosophers: Josiah Royce, George Santayana, Hugo Munsterberg, George Herbert Palmer, and William James; at her graduation in 1900, she was the only Radcliffe student to receive honors in philosophy.

After college, Sprague returned home to care for her invalid father; rescued again by Alice Palmer, she traveled abroad with the Palmers until Alice's sudden death in 1901. She lived with George Herbert Palmer briefly, helping with housekeeping, while at the same time working for Radcliffe's dean, Ada Comstock, and taking graduate courses in philosophy at Harvard. When, at the suggestion of Palmer, President Benjamin Wheeler of the University of California offered her a position assisting the university's women students, Sprague accepted; in 1906 she was officially appointed dean of women, the university's first. Sprague was appointed assistant professor of English as well; she and economist Jessica Peixotto were the first women on the faculty.

Rejecting the "bog of discipline and decorum," which her successor, Lucy Stebbins, described as customary for deans of women, Sprague was an activist administrator who attempted to give women a more visible presence on campus. Concerned about the isolation of women students, she held poetry readings for women, helped establish women's clubs and housing facilities, and was a powerful advocate of student self-government. Sprague also initiated courses in sex education and introduced a "curriculum of experience," taking women students to explore social problems in Oakland and San Francisco. With her 1912 "Partheneia: A Masque of Maidenhood," a pageant with 500 women students, Sprague began an annual tradition of women's drama festivals that lasted until the 1930s at Berkeley.

In 1912, at the age of thirty-three, Sprague married economist Wesley Clair Mitchell, five years her senior, with whom she had four children. The couple spent a year in Europe and then moved to New York City, where Wesley Mitchell joined the faculty of Columbia University. After a brief apprenticeship in 1911 with Julia Richman, principal of a Manhattan high school, Lucy Sprague Mitchell decided on a new career devoted to educating young children; exposure to innovative schools during a stay in London during her honeymoon confirmed this goal. Now she took courses at Columbia University with John Dewey on the philosophy of education and Edward Thorndike on educational psychology. Although she never completed a degree, studies with these men, who led the two main wings of the progressive education movement, deepened her knowledge of experimental education and established the main lines of her own interests in the field. Mitchell also taught nursery school and kindergarten classes at Caroline Pratt's Play School in Greenwich Village, volunteered as a visiting teacher for Harriet Merrill Johnson at the Public Education Association, and conducted psychological tests on city school children.

In 1916, after her cousin Elizabeth Sprague Coolidge offered to support an educational project of Mitchell's choosing, she, her husband, and Harriet Johnson established the Bureau of Educational Experiments to teach and develop research concerning progressive education and educational experiments. The bureau was cooperatively governed, although as chair of its Working Council Lucy Mitchell acted as catalyst, spur, and dominant influence of the twelve-member group. In its first years, the bureau sponsored a variety of projects, including educational testing, rural schools, play materials, school nutrition, day nurseries, sex and vocational education, and the Gary School "platoon" idea. In 1919 it launched one of the first laboratory nursery schools in the country. The school, for children aged fifteen months to three years, was joined to Caroline Pratt's Play School (later known as City and Country School) for children aged three to seven, and a special class for eight-year-olds taught by bureau staff. Emphasizing the physical, social, intellectual, and emotional needs of children, the school combined comprehensive research into the quantitative indices of children's growth with child-centered expressive curricula. Harriet Johnson directed the innovative school; as chair of the bureau's Working Council, Mitchell helped coordinate the laboratory program while providing overall direction to bureau projects.

Moving away from the quantitative approach that characterized the bureau's research in the 1920s, in 1931 Mitchell and Johnson joined with colleagues from experimental schools to establish the Cooperative School for Student Teachers. The school's goal—to train teachers to work in experimental schools—was "almost as much a pioneer front in 1930 as the study of children and experimental schools for them had been in 1916," Mitchell later recalled. Its innovative curriculum aimed to help students develop an "experimental, critical and ardent" approach to education that combined a "scientific attitude" with the "attitude of the artist." From Monday through Thursday, students were placed at participating experimental schools (in Manhattan, these included the Bureau Nursery School and the Little Red School House, where Mitchell also taught, beginning in 1929). From Thursday afternoon to Saturday, students took courses at "Bank Street," as the school and its parent body, the Bureau of Educational Experiments, was known after its move to 69 Bank Street. These offerings consisted of Mitchell's core courses on language and the environment, and courses taught by Barbara Biber, Jessie Stanton, Harriet Johnson (until her death in 1934), and others. In addition to such "intake" courses, as Mitchell named them, there were "outgo" courses in painting, dance, music, and dramatics to help student teachers experience the world as openly and directly as did children. Mitchell also provided her characteristic "curriculum of experience," taking students to observe tenements, jails, courts, clinics, political rallies, and labor unions and having them spend one morning a week doing fieldwork for social organizations.

In 1938 Mitchell established the Writers' Laboratory at Bank Street in order to help potential writers of books for children understand the dynamics of children's growth and to aid them in developing language, rhythms, and forms based on children's own speech. Modeled after the principles Mitchell first enunciated in her influential *Here and Now Story Book* (1921), which argued that children's stories should be developed from their immediate, firsthand experiences, the Writers' Laboratory trained many outstanding children's writers, including Margaret Wise Brown, author of *Good Night Moon*, Eve Merriam, Edith Thatcher Hurd, and Mary Phelps.

In 1943 Mitchell brought Bank Street's experimental teaching methods to a public school in Harlem, where she taught teachers and children in an experimental program; when the board of education extended the Bank Street workshop to other public schools, one of her fondest hopes—to train public school teachers in experimental methods—was realized.

Bank Street received its charter as a college of education in 1950. Mitchell stayed on as chair of its board and as acting president until 1956, when she retired to Palo Alto, California, to be near one of her children. Until her death there eleven years later, she served as a consultant to Bank Street and continued her writing. In addition to many books for children, Mitchell was the author of several important works for adults, especially *Young Geographers: How They Explore the World and How They Map the World* (1934; repr. 1963), *Our Children and Our Schools* (1950), and *Two Lives: The Story of Wesley Clair Mitchell and Myself* (1953), a book that the *New York Herald Tribune* reviewer described as offering a "better look at changing human and sex relationships than Simone de Beauvoir gives."

A leader in the twin fields of progressive education and child development, Mitchell helped pioneer a new model of women's professional development in the postsuffrage era. Her personal wealth and the coincidence of family and personal interests (her life was "highly focused," she said, "with everything concentrated on children, each aspect of my work illuminating the others") made a full-time career possible, even with four young children. Bank Street's influential nursery school and its dissemination of innovative research involving children, teachers, and parents helped other working women combine parenthood with full-time work.

Under Mitchell's leadership, Bank Street became an organization distinctive not only for its contributions to early childhood education but also to the development of faculty and student teachers; her support and nurturance shaped the careers of many in her field and gave Bank Street a strong cooperative emphasis. Although Mitchell disliked being called Bank Street's leader, she was its "prime mover," as colleague Barbara Biber put it. Mitchell preferred to think of herself as a teacher, and by all accounts, she was brilliant at it; many who studied with her were transformed by the experience. Drawn to children's education because of her belief that "whole" children were the best guarantors of a progressive and humane society, she adapted the political and social reform goals of Dewey-inspired progressivism to a newer, female-based professionalism rooted in modern currents of behavioral and social science. To make teaching into a respected profession with opportunities for continued growth—to create "whole" teachers as well as whole children—remained her urgent and simultaneous objective.

• Lucy Sprague Mitchell's papers are at Columbia University. Additional works by Mitchell include *My Country 'Tis of Thee: The Use and Abuse of Natural Resources*, with Eleanor Bowman and Mary Phelps (1940), and *Know Your Children in School* (1954). Among Mitchell's best-known works for children are *Another Here and Now Story Book* (1937), *Believe and Make-Believe* (1956), *The Here and Now Primer: Home from the Country* (1924), *The Here and Now Story Book* (1921; rev. ed., 1948), *Horses Now and Long Ago* (1926), *Manhattan Now and Long Ago*, with Clara Lambert (1934), and *North America: The Land They Live in for the Children Who Live There* (1931).

The major source on Mitchell is Joyce Antler's biography, *Lucy Sprague Mitchell: The Making of a Modern Woman* (1987). Also see Bank Street College of Education, *Lucy Sprague Mitchell, 1878–1967* (1967); and Esther Raushenbush, "Three Women: Creators of Change," in *The Higher Education of Women: Essays in Honor of Rosemary Park*, ed. Helen S. Astin and Werner Z. Hirsch (1978). Obituaries appear in the *New York Times*, 17 Oct. 1967, and *Publishers Weekly*, 30 Oct. 1967.

JOYCE ANTLER

MITCHELL, Maggie (14 June 1837–22 Mar. 1918), actress, was born Margaret Julia Mitchell in New York City, the daughter of Charles S. Mitchell, an actor in Scotland before he immigrated to the United States with his wife, Ann Dodson. Margaret Mitchell's early life and career are often reported with many variations because of confusion between herself and two older half sisters, Mary and Emma, who appeared in the theater as child actors before Margaret was a teenager.

Contrary to her mother's wishes, young Margaret became interested in the theater and eventually convinced her mother to let an acquaintance of the family, the elder English actor John Moore, coach her. Moore was connected with the stage direction at William E. Burton's theater in Chambers Street, and he secured for Mitchell the role of Julia in *The Soldier's Daughter* for a benefit performance on 2 June 1851. The fourteen-year-old impressed everyone, and at the beginning of the 1851–1852 season, when Moore joined the Bowery Theatre as prompter, T. S. Hamblin, the manager, engaged Mitchell as a regular member of the company at a salary of $4 a week. She began her professional career playing mostly young men's roles and dancing between acts with Gertrude Dawes. Her portrayals of Rosina Meadows, the Prince of Wales (*Richard III*), and especially Oliver Twist earned her increased recognition and a raise in pay.

After a disagreement between Hamblin and Mitchell's mother, the young starlet started her life as a touring soubrette playing innumerable (and largely forgettable) "protean" roles requiring great versatility in theaters around New York and throughout the eastern United States. In these roles, Mitchell paralleled her younger contemporaries, Charlotte "Lotta" Crabtree and Minnie Madden Fiske.

By the time Mitchell reached Cleveland in 1853, her popularity, based on a fine natural acting style and vivacious stage presence, was soaring, and her affectionate nickname, "Maggie," had become a household word. Indeed, a "Maggie Mitchell craze" became popular among the young men in the towns she played, her fans sporting "Maggie Mitchell" hats, scarves, and other paraphernalia.

Later that year, in Pittsburgh, Mitchell appeared for the first time in a piece written especially for her by James Pilgrim called *Our Maggie*. During this first decade of her career, Mitchell expanded her repertory but remained closely tied to the soubrette and young men lines. Roles from this period include Harry Halcyon in *A Middy Ashore*, Margery in *A Rough Diamond*, Paul in *The Pet of the Petticoats*, and the Countess in *The Wild Irish Girl*.

In about 1854 Mitchell married for the first time (husband's name unknown) and had a son, Julian Mitchell. Her mother quickly put an end to the marriage, but Julian Mitchell had a long career in the theater, acting in his mother's company in the late 1870s and working as a playwright and successful stage director into the twentieth century.

On 29 January 1861, at Ben De Bar's St. Charles Theatre in New Orleans, Mitchell struck gold with the play that would be her trademark for the next thirty years: *Fanchon the Cricket*. Adapted by August Walduer, the orchestra leader at the St. Charles Theatre, from the popular German dramatization by Charlotte Birch-Pfeiffer of George Sand's story "La Petite Fadette," the play's principal role was created specifically with Mitchell's style in mind. The capricious, sprightly character suited Mitchell's own "elf-like . . . piquant and winsome" stage demeanor; it also allowed her the scope to create crowd-pleasing interpolations such as a "weird elfish dance" and "a pretty maypole dance."

The opening of *Fanchon*, however, coincided with the beginning of the Civil War, and Mitchell headed north. After a very successful run of her new star vehicle in Boston, she brought it to New York on 9 June

1862, appearing at Laura Keene's Theatre (New Olympic) to a rave public. Although Mitchell's success would always be identified with her Fanchon character (many others tried to imitate her, but none could match her appeal), it was not her only celebrated role. She also won audience approval with her roles in *The Pearl of Savoy* as well as in various translation/adaptations such as *Little Barefoot*, *Lorle*, and *Mignon*, but her most remembered portrayal after Fanchon was her Jane Eyre. Created by Clifton W. Tayleure, the Mitchell version was not the first dramatization of Charlotte Brontë's novel but nonetheless won accolades for the actress on both sides of the Atlantic. Her admirers were said to include President Abraham Lincoln as well as Ralph Waldo Emerson, who wrote verses after seeing her Fanchon, and Henry Wordsworth Longfellow, who tried to convince her to bring her Jane Eyre to England.

Mitchell married Henry T. Paddock, her manager of many years, in October 1868 after a long courtship. This marriage produced two children, neither of whom took up a theater career. The marriage lasted nearly twenty years, ending in divorce amid a fury of press speculation. In 1889 Mitchell married Charles Abbot, the handsome, athletic leading man in her company.

Her contemporary biographer, Luther L. Holden, described Mitchell as "petite . . . with a wealth of sunny, golden hair, whose nervous energy and sprightliness, no less than an exquisite form and face, gave picturesque presence to the line of child heroines she made peculiarly her own" (p. 309). Despite her "youthful spirits and animation" on stage, Mitchell was a reticent, strict company disciplinarian as well as a very good businesswoman, prudent and hard working; she held onto her star wages and after retiring in 1892 lived very comfortably in New York City and Elberon, New Jersey, until her death in New York City.

Holden concludes his biography with the following accolades:

> Favored by nature with a youthful presence, . . . her portrayals were unique. . . . It was the art which made a pure and ennobling stage creation all the more impressive by reason of the soul behind it. . . . Good actors there are, and always will be; but there can never be one who will exert a purer and better influence upon the American stage than [this] genial and winsome *comédienne*.

• Luther L. Holden's biography is contained in Frederic Makay and Charles Wingate, *Famous American Actors of Today* (1896), pp. 309–20. See also T. Allston Brown, *A History of the New York Stage* (1903); John Bouvé Clapp and Edwin Francis Edgett, *Players of the Present* (1899–1901), pp. 251–56; and Lillian Hall, *Catalogue of Dramatic Portraits in the Theatre Collection of the Harvard College Library* (1931), pp. 207–9. Mitchell's obituary is in the *New York Times* and the *New York Tribune*, both 23 Mar. 1918. (The differing birthdates reported have been corrected to 1837 with reference to New York City birth records contained in the holdings of the Church of the Latter-day Saints' Genealogical Library.)

GLEN NICHOLS

MITCHELL, Margaret (8 Nov. 1900–16 Aug. 1949), novelist, was born Margaret Munnerlyn Mitchell in Atlanta, Georgia, the daughter of Eugene Muse Mitchell, an attorney, and May Belle Stephens. Mitchell attended the public elementary schools in Atlanta and graduated from Washington Seminary, an elite girls' finishing school in her native city, in 1918. Her mother had always stressed education, but Mitchell disliked formal schooling and never performed particularly well academically, and this was a major source of conflict between them. At her mother's insistence, Mitchell enrolled in Smith College in Northampton, Massachusetts, in September 1918, but her mother's death in the influenza epidemic that winter made it unnecessary for her to continue, and in 1919 she returned to Atlanta to take her mother's place in society and in the household of her very proper father, one of the most conservative but best-connected men in the New South city.

In the two years after her return south, Mitchell acted out the role of the twenties flapper, careening from social crisis to personal disaster. Her social career culminated in her marriage to a ne'er-do-well, Berrien K. Upshaw, in September 1922. Three months later, she used the excuse of Upshaw's erratic employment to take a job as a newspaper reporter. Literature had obsessed her from her childhood: she was a compulsive, omnivorous reader, and she had always written—letters, plays, short stories, novels and novellas. Her employment at the *Atlanta Journal*, however, concentrated her literary energies. During her four-year tenure at the paper she wrote more than 200 articles, essays, book reviews, and miscellaneous pieces.

Mitchell's working exacerbated her husband's insecurities and eccentricities. After a tempestuous ten-month marriage, Mitchell demanded that Upshaw leave. He returned at least once, battered her, and then abandoned her permanently. The courts finalized their divorce in the fall of 1924. During this entire period, she had kept up social relations with a former suitor, John Robert Marsh, another journalist and later chief publicist for the Georgia Power and Light Company. He had also been Upshaw's roommate and his best man. Mitchell wed Marsh on 4 July 1925. Neither marriage produced children.

Although this second marriage provided a haven from many of the most obvious conflicts of Mitchell's life as a divorced single woman, it also came with liabilities. On the one hand, she sympathized with her husband's masculine honor and her family's skepticism of her professional employment; on the other, she remained as ambitious, driven, and imaginative as before. Illness helped resolve the dilemma. Ever since her mother's death she had been plagued by physical maladies, which often provided convenient means of resolving difficult social circumstances. After she separated from Upshaw, for example, she determined, over her family's violent objections, that she would work her way around the world. She got as far as Havana. Ready to come home but unwilling to admit her plan's failure, she became ill with what she described variously as flu or pneumonia. The pattern repeated itself over and over in her life. It occurred again nine months after her marriage to Marsh, when she developed a mysterious infection that settled in her ankle. Under pressure from her body and the men in her family, she resigned her newspaper job in May 1926. Six months later, bitterly unhappy, she began writing what would become her epic historical novel, *Gone with the Wind*, as a means of occupying her time and distracting her from her physical suffering.

Mitchell completed the main draft three years later. Very reluctant to submit the manuscript to outside readers, she spent more than five years polishing and revising. In one of the great stories of American publishing, Harold Latham of the Macmillan Company managed to separate the novelist from her manuscript in the spring of 1935. Although the manuscript was an open secret among Atlanta's literati, Latham also had heard of its existence through a coworker at Macmillan, Lois Dwight Cole, one of Mitchell's old friends from Atlanta. Mitchell herself repeatedly denied even the existence of the manuscript, but an offhanded remark by another aspiring novelist, she later recounted, challenged her to surrender the enormous manuscript after all. She caught Latham just before he departed Atlanta on his book-collecting trip. Even a partial reading convinced him immediately that he had a prizewinner, which outside readers confirmed. The novel appeared to overwhelming popular and critical acclaim in the summer of 1936. It immediately broke all sales records, and it won the Pulitzer Prize the next year.

David O. Selznick's 1939 film version, which won ten Academy Award nominations and seven Oscars, including best picture, guaranteed the novel's immortality, and the novel itself remains a popular classic. Twice since its original publication it has reappeared on the *New York Times* bestseller list, in 1986 and again in 1991. It also has been translated into every major language of the world and many more obscure tongues. It has spawned a minor industry in publishing and spin-offs (from Mammy dolls and china to housing developments), and Mitchell's language has become a part of American lingo. In all probability it is the most popular and widely read novel in the world and the most famous novel in the English language.

A classic expression of the genre of the historical novel, *Gone with the Wind* plots the rise and fall of the Confederate States of America from the bombardment of Fort Sumter in April 1861 (with flashbacks to the thirty years that preceded the conflict) to the end of Reconstruction in the early 1870s in Georgia, the setting of the entire narrative. Against this historical background of an ill-fated southern cause, Mitchell plotted a romance of four chief characters whose lives, affections, and relations were as ill-starred as the Confederacy's. One measure of Mitchell's literary skill lay in her ability to meld these two narratives, the fiction lending passion and immediacy to the history, the history contributing drama, authenticity, and verisimilitude to the romance. Her art reached a peak in those chapters on the siege of Atlanta and the birth of Melanie Wilkes's baby and Scarlett O'Hara's return to her plantation in the wake of Sherman's destruction—key chapters also in understanding Mitchell's personal values in the novel insofar as they dwell insistently upon mothers, childbirth, and women's lives.

While Mitchell herself protested that her fiction was pure imagination, the novel drew considerable power from the circumstances of the writer's own life. Culturally, Mitchell was the grandchild of the Civil War generation, and like most of her peers of the "Generation of 1900" in the southern literary renaissance—the likes of William Faulkner, Allen Tate, and Caroline Gordon, for example—she used her fiction to work out conflicts about the heroes who had plunged the region into disaster two generations before. The novel also provided the means of chronicling the history of her own beloved city, Atlanta, where she spent her entire life. More personally, she used her epic as a kind of genealogy to explore anomalies of her own Irish Catholic ancestry in a virulently nativistic and Protestant South.

More critically and still more personally, the novel served as both focus and projection of Mitchell's ideas about women. Indeed, she declared to friends that she had intended to tell women's untold history in her novel. Along the same lines, the novel allowed an artful resolution to the somewhat paradoxical relationship she had with the most important woman in her life, her mother. May Belle Stephens Mitchell was an extraordinary woman in her own right, a leader of the Georgia Suffrage Movement and one of the founders of the Catholic Laymen's Association, a political action group in her native, antipapist state. She had constantly held out the idea of achievement and worldly success to her daughter and son, Mitchell's brother, Stephens, but she also had pressed upon her daughter the importance of proper deportment for genteel southern women. This seemingly conflicting advice caught Mitchell in a particular squeeze, which was exacerbated by the peculiarities of regional society.

Mitchell wrote no other fiction during the thirteen years of her life after publication of *Gone with the Wind*, but she made letter writing an art, producing thousands of epistles in this period. A deep commitment to the Allied war effort also distracted her from other writing. While her own sicknesses increased, she also nursed ailing family members and friends. Finally, legal matters, particularly relative to domestic and foreign copyrights of *Gone with the Wind*, absorbed much of her waking hours. She became almost compulsively litigious.

Her social and political conservatism grew exponentially as well during the war and afterward. While she had welcomed Franklin Delano Roosevelt's election in 1932, she described herself as a "Tory Democrat" and had turned against the New Deal by 1936. Profoundly skeptical of centralized governance and bureaucratic officialdom, she opposed communism, socialism, and any government intervention in social problems. She sided with such ardent anti-Leftists as

Westbrook Pegler and Eugene Lyons. Generous in her personal relations with blacks, she nonetheless rejected the growing agitation for civil rights reforms after the war. Originally she had rejected any political interpretation of *Gone with the Wind*; after the war she explained her novel as the search for individual freedom.

Although she continued aspects of old liberality, as with prisoners at the federal penitentiary in Atlanta, Mitchell grew increasingly isolated, bitter, and reactionary during the war and later. She died in her native city after being struck by a drunk driver.

• For compilations of Mitchell's personal correspondence, see *Margaret Mitchell's "Gone with the Wind": Letters, 1936–1949*, ed. Richard B. Harwell (1976), and *Margaret Mitchell, Dynamo Going to Waste: Letters to Allen Edee, 1919–1921*, ed. Jane Bonner Peacock (1983). For biographical information on Mitchell and analyses of her literary importance, see Darden Asbury Pyron, *Southern Daughter: The Life of Margaret Mitchell* (1991) and *Recasting: "Gone with the Wind" in American Culture* (1983); Finis Farr, *Margaret Mitchell of Atlanta* (1965); and Anne Goodwyn Jones, *Tomorrow Is Another Day: The Woman Writer in the South, 1859–1936* (1981).

DARDEN ASBURY PYRON

MITCHELL, Maria (1 Aug. 1818–28 June 1889), astronomer and teacher, was born on Nantucket Island, Massachusetts, the daughter of William Mitchell, a banker and astronomer, and Lydia Coleman, a former librarian. Mitchell attended a school for young ladies conducted by the Reverend Cyrus Peirce, who later oversaw the first normal school in the United States. She exhibited an early fascination with mathematics and learned to assist her father with astronomical observations from the "widow's walk" on their home and later from the top of the Pacific Bank, where her father worked as a cashier. Theirs was a practical interest, established in part by the need of Nantucket whalers for calculators to correct chronometers but also by the excitement of rapidly improving instrumentation and consequent new astronomical discoveries. Mitchell's capacity for precision and persistence contributed first to her national recognition as an astronomer and subsequently to her commitment to education as a means for women to raise their lifetime aspirations.

Mitchell was Peirce's assistant for a short time, then in 1835 she started her own school on Trader's Lane, where she experimented with different teaching methods, including the Lancastrian tutorial system. Unlike the local free school, she allowed students of color from the Portuguese quarter to attend. In 1836 she accepted a position as librarian at the new public Atheneum. Mitchell found it a congenial place to continue to study texts such as Charles Hutton's *Mathematics* and Henry Bowditch's *Practical Navigator* as well as the works of Lagrange and Laplace in French and of Karl Friedrich Gauss in Latin; she also studied German. In the evenings, assisted by a circle and transit on loan from West Point Academy and a four-inch equatorial telescope and other instruments provided by the U.S. Coast Survey (USCS), she and her father made thousands of observations of the stars that improved the determination of time and latitude. Mitchell, again with the cooperation of her father, surveyed Nantucket Island in order to produce a more accurate map of the coastline.

A well-respected community member, Mitchell nonetheless struggled with the increasingly restrictive demands made on members by the Nantucket Quaker meeting, and in 1843 she left the group to attend, although never to join, the Unitarian church. Throughout her life she retained Quaker friendships and speech. The Atheneum, destroyed by fire with all its manuscripts and books in 1846, was rebuilt and subsequently became the center for local learned societies and for the lyceum lecturers who came to the island to share their literary, scientific, and artistic insights. Many of them went away and recorded their impressions of the people of Nantucket, remarking about the fact that women there were unusually committed to literature and science and sometimes noting as well the frequent absences of seafaring men. Mitchell inevitably met with the speakers, and a few, like Ralph Waldo Emerson, were invited to view the skies from the vantage point of the Mitchell observatory.

On the night of 1 October 1847, while sweeping the skies as usual, Mitchell observed a comet that was previously unrecorded; she and her father watched it for several days and contacted their friend George Bond of the Harvard College Observatory. This first discovery of a telescopic comet won her a gold medal from the king of Denmark and brought her opportunities within the U.S. scientific and educational community. Her trips to visit the Harvard observatory became more frequent, and she made the acquaintance of leading scientists such as Charles H. Davis and Alexander Dallas Bache. In August 1849 Davis offered her a position as a computer for the new *American Ephemeris and Nautical Almanac*; not coincidentally, she was asked to compute the position of the planet Venus. Several weeks later she and her younger brother Henry were invited to join Bache for several summer months with USCS observers at Mount Independence, Maine, where she learned to use the zenith sector and the zenith telescope. Mitchell was the only American woman to gain self-supporting scientific employment and international recognition in the 1850s.

In her midlife years, Mitchell sometimes grew impatient with aspects of her position at the Atheneum, particularly when handling summer visitors. She began to travel more outside of Nantucket and thus became increasingly aware that the status and role of women elsewhere lacked the substance of the island community, where wives and mothers ran much of the economic and social life while men were at sea. In 1857 a wealthy Chicago banker offered her the opportunity to travel as chaperon for his daughter, and for the first time Mitchell saw conditions of slavery in the South that had been much discussed by her Quaker friends. Later, carrying letters of introduction from Edward Everett, the president of Harvard; Joseph Henry, secretary of the Smithsonian Institution; and the bonds of Harvard observatory, she met prominent English scientists and traveled the countryside of England. Most important to her, however, were her visits to the world-renowned observatories at Greenwich and Cambridge. When the financial panic of 1857 forced her young charge to return home, Mitchell stayed on for several months and during a trip to the Continent visited the Vatican observatory guided by Angelo Secchi.

On her return, she was given a five-inch telescope built by Alvan Clark by the "Women of America" (an effort coordinated by Elizabeth Peabody) that allowed her to make more accurate and detailed observations. A few years later, after her mother died, she and her father moved to Lynn, Massachusetts, where she set up a small observatory for research. Shortly afterward, however, a trustee of Vassar College asked to meet with her concerning a position at the new women's college being planned in New York state. Like virtually all women of her generation, Mitchell had never had any higher education. She was, however, intrigued by the aspirations of the founder, Matthew Vassar, and followed the debate among administrators and trustees about the appropriateness of women faculty members. When the official offer came, just before the college opened in 1865, Mitchell quickly accepted the opportunity to contribute to the movement for women's education and to utilize the new twelve-inch telescope made by Henry Fit for the Vassar observatory. She and her father moved into the apartment adjoining the campus observatory. Mitchell chafed against the circumstances that held her salary below that of male colleagues and resisted compulsory chapel attendance, but she remained deeply committed to Vassar College and its pioneering efforts for women's education.

A direct and plainspoken woman, Mitchell nonetheless had a sense of humor that made her much beloved by students, especially those who shared long evenings in the observatory. As on Nantucket, she arranged at Vassar for well-known authors, political commentators, and advocates for women's rights such as Lucy Stone and her husband, Henry Blackwell, to come and discuss their ideas. Although her courses were reputed to be challenging, for those who persisted Mitchell offered sustained support in their studies and careers and reminded them, "we are women studying together." Some, like Mary W. Whitney, followed Mitchell into astronomy. Others, like Ellen Swallow Richards, who organized the field of home economics, became leaders in higher education and in opening new fields of opportunity for women. In 1873 she returned to Europe to visit major observatories. This time, however, her journals were filled with references to women educators and women's education. Back home, Mitchell lectured outside the college and wrote articles on astronomy and the need for more study of science in magazines such as *Scientific American* and *Hours at Home*. Her advocacy and influence are fundamental in understanding the significant numbers of women who were accepted as astronomical computers at the end of the century throughout the United States.

Mitchell was elected vice president at the first meeting of the Social Science Association in 1873. Later that year she helped draft a national notice for a congress of women and subsequently helped organize the Association for the Advancement of Women, precursor of the General Federation of Women's Clubs. The initial organization sought to raise the aspirations of women by organizing local clubs and providing nationally known speakers on a range of then controversial topics such as higher education for women, temperance, women's exercise and health, and women's potential role in science. Over the next decade Mitchell remained active and attended annual meetings held primarily in northeastern and north central states. She formulated a questionnaire to determine more about those women who were active in science. Somewhat reluctantly she allowed herself to be elected president more than once. At her presidential address in 1876 she observed, "In my younger days when I was pained by the half-educated, loose and inaccurate ways which we all had, I used to say, 'How much women need exact science.' But since I have known some workers in science who were not always true to the teachings of nature, who have loved self more than science, I have said, 'How much science needs women.'"

Mitchell could also be high-handed. She refused to give in to a local committee that, for example, wanted to bar speakers who advocated woman suffrage. She had a way with words that allowed her to elaborate her ideas clearly and with meaning that could be understood readily by a large audience; even the newspapers, often critical of strong-minded women, usually expressed approval of her logical arguments on topics such as women's education. Genuine and uncompromising, she was well liked and well remembered by those who felt her influence and benefited from her advice. She had embarked on her Vassar career when she was nearly fifty years old, and declining health led her to resign from Vassar in early 1888, after more than twenty years of service. Having never married, she retired to Lynn, where she could use the small observatory built there for her by her nephew, until her death there. During her lifetime she had also been elected to the American Academy of Arts and Sciences in 1848, was the first woman member of the American Association for the Advancement of Science in 1850, and was invited to join the American Philosophical Society in 1873.

• Mitchell corresponded with various friends and scientific colleagues, and thus letters are to be found among those of scientists and educators. The bulk of her papers not destroyed by fire or by her overconscientious sister are in the Maria Mitchell Association of Nantucket and are available on microfilm; correspondence, lectures, and related materials from her years as a faculty member are in the Vassar College Special Collections.

The two life studies are usually but not inevitably accurate and lack documentation; best is Helen Wright, *Sweeper in the Sky: The Life of Maria Mitchell, First Woman Astronomer in America* (1950), and her sister Phebe Mitchell Kendall's more circumspect and sometimes peevish *Maria Mitchell: Life, Let-*

ters, and Journals (1896). Kendall apparently destroyed some of Mitchell's correspondence, particularly personal and family materials. The best obituary is by her pupil and successor at Vassar, Mary W. Whitney, "Life and Work of Maria Mitchell," *Papers Read before the Association for the Advancement of Women* (1891); also see Sally Gregory Kohlstedt, "Maria Mitchell and the Advancement of Women in Science," *New England Quarterly* 51 (Mar. 1978): 39–63. There are also numerous children's biographies of Mitchell.

SALLY GREGORY KOHLSTEDT

MITCHELL, Martha (2 Sept. 1918–31 May 1976), controversial political wife, was born on Labor Day in Pine Bluff, Arkansas, the daughter of George Virgil Beall, a cotton broker, and Arie Ferguson, a teacher of elocution. She studied drama, under Maude Adams, at Stephens College in Missouri, attended the University of Arkansas, and in 1942 was graduated from the University of Miami with a bachelor of arts degree. After briefly teaching sixth grade in Mobile, Alabama, she joined the war effort, working first in Pine Bluff and later in Washington, D.C., for the army's Chemical Warfare Service (later the Army Chemical Corps). There she met army Captain Clyde Jennings, Jr., whom she married in October 1946. Their only child, Clyde Jay Jennings, was born in 1947. By the time of their divorce, in August 1957, the couple was living in New York City. There, on 30 December 1957, she married Wall Street lawyer John Newton Mitchell. A daughter, Martha Elizabeth Mitchell, Jr., was born in 1961. After John Mitchell managed the successful 1968 presidential campaign of his law partner Richard M. Nixon, he was appointed U.S. attorney general, and the Mitchells moved to Washington, D.C.

Nothing in Martha Mitchell's past had prepared her for the life of a cabinet wife. Open, candid, and uninhibited, she did not fit the mold of the traditional political wife—one who keeps quiet and lets her husband do the talking on all issue-oriented subjects. She continued to make frank and forthright statements, speaking out forcefully against liberals, the press, educators, and students (their dress, sex code, and drug use), and she soon became a folk heroine. Middle America loved her; the Silent Majority embraced her as its own; and, surprisingly, she even struck a cord with students. When asked why students were among her staunchest admirers, especially since she had been their harshest critic, a Sweet Briar student said, "Because she was honest, she let it all hang out" (quoted in *Martha*, p. 110). When one administration official suggested that her flamboyant style and unrestrained remarks were becoming an embarrassment and that she should be silenced, White House Chief of Staff H. R. Haldeman was reported to have countered by saying she was the "best thing we've got going for us to keep the Conservatives pacified" (quoted in *Martha*, p. 100). The president urged her on, as did her husband and other officials, who even offered suggestions as to what she might say and do. They believed that because she was a woman, she would not be subjected to the kind of attacks that would befall the attorney general if he were to make such comments. They also thought that they too would not be held responsible for her remarks. Even the timing of her late-night telephone calls to the media and Senate wives (to lobby for or against certain legislation) was programmed. She later said that her husband had told her, "That's the time when you get their attention."

Martha Mitchell soon became the most talked about, written about, adored or hated, praised or maligned, admired or ridiculed cabinet wife in the history of the United States. She also became the only cabinet wife ever voted, in a women's magazine survey, one of the ten most admired women in the world and, according to a Gallup poll, the only one whose name was recognized by three-quarters of the American people. The American Institute of Public Opinion reported that no woman in public life had achieved so quickly the national awareness of Martha Mitchell. This notoriety surprised no one more than members of the Nixon administration. As former White House speech writer Pat Buchanan has said, "Frankly, it was a mild startlement among us in the White House and elsewhere when she suddenly became a folk hero and . . . on the list of most-admired women in the world. There was general amazement and astonishment that this was happening" (quoted in *Martha*, pp. 109–10). The administration used her for a long time, another aide said, "even in the Campaign . . . until the Watergate scandal broke. Then they wanted no part of this woman who said what she thought and had it come through as the truth" (Clark Mollenoff quoted in *Martha*, p. 101).

Martha Mitchell's unofficial role as spokeswoman for the administration's conservative views ended the weekend of 17 June 1972, when five men were caught breaking into the Watergate offices of the Democratic National Committee. The leader of the group was an employee of Richard Nixon's 1972 presidential campaign committee, which was headed by former attorney general Mitchell. Martha, who regularly eavesdropped on her husband's telephone conversations and riffled through his briefcases after he was asleep at night, became convinced that the president, senior White House officials, and her husband were behind the break-in. She soon became equally convinced that her husband was going to be made into a fall-guy for the administration. She begged him to stop protecting the president and to "tell the truth." He did not heed her pleas and refused to turn state's witness or to plea bargain. As Martha saw it, her husband's only chance of staying out of prison was a presidential pardon. "But," she predicted, "he'll go to jail and [King Richard, as she now called the president], who planned the whole . . . thing, will go scot-free" (*Martha*, p. 239). Believing that only she could save him, she accelerated her telephone calls, but instead of railing against liberals she now talked about administration "dirty tricks" and "White House Horrors" and called for the president's resignation. The administration and even her husband tried to discredit her by secretly putting out stories that she had mental problems. (Two of her doctors would later deny these accusations.)

On 10 September 1972, John Mitchell left his wife without saying goodbye; she never saw him again. His departure, however, did not stem her efforts to help him. To her telephone calls she added newspaper and magazine interviews and appearances on radio and television talk shows—one as far away as London, England. There, she surprised her host David Frost and his BBC audience by claiming that President Nixon had planned the whole Watergate affair and that he had "cut a deal" with Vice President Gerald Ford whereby he would be pardoned after he resigned and Ford became president. A BBC staff member later recalled that because of how she presented her claim, people did not believe her and thought she was "a nutter, when in fact all the rest of them were . . . She probably was the most underestimated person within the whole of the Watergate tale" (quoted in *Martha*, p. 321).

Martha Mitchell continued her campaign to rescue her husband until she was stopped by multiple myeloma, a malignant blood cell disease. She died alone in a New York City hospital with neither her estranged husband nor her estranged daughter by her side. (Her son could not be reached in time to make it to the hospital before she died.) As she had requested, Martha was buried in her beloved Pine Bluff, alongside her mother. Prominent among the many floral displays, including one from President and Mrs. Gerald Ford, was a large green and white spray with white chrysanthemums that spelled out in block letters the message MARTHA WAS RIGHT. Many Americans agreed. As Mark Goodman, writing in *New Times Magazine*, said, "She first sounded the alarm . . . we did not listen to Martha Mitchell and we paid for it." In the *St. Petersburg Times*, Eugene Patterson wrote, "Because she told the truth indiscreetly . . . she was written off as a kook in Washington." He later said, "She married the wrong man, connected with the wrong political crowd, and tried to find her place in the wrong town at the wrong time" (both quotes in *Martha*, p. 384). Martha Mitchell would have agreed. She once said that leaving Pine Bluff and moving North had been her biggest mistake. "I would have been all right if I'd stayed in the South."

• Martha Mitchell's childhood home in Pine Bluff has been turned into a museum listed on the National Register of Historic Places. She is one of the subjects in Madeleine Edmondson and Alden Duer Cohen, *The Women of Watergate* (1975). UPI reporter Helen Thomas dedicated a chapter to her in *Dateline: White House* (1975). A full biography is Winzola McLendon, *Martha: The Life of Martha Mitchell* (1979). Also see Martha Mitchell with Winzola McLendon, "I Went to London to Visit with the Queen," *Ladies' Home Journal* Nov. 1971, pp. 82–84, 88, 190; McLendon, "People I'd Love to Call," *Ladies Home Journal*, July 1971, pp. 68–70, 151; McLendon, "Martha Mitchell's Lonely Dream House," *Ladies' Home Journal*, Mar. 1974, p. 68–71, 113–15; Mitchell with McLendon, "My Life in Washington," *McCall's*, Mar. 1974, pp. 106–7, 147–48; Mitchell with McLendon, "A Visit with Cornella Wallace," *McCall's*, Sept. 1974, pp. 75, 120–22; and Mitchell with McLendon, "How Politics Wrecked My Marriage," *Ladies' Home Journal*, Dec. 1974, pp. 52–54, 56, 148–49. Hundreds of newspapers throughout the United States and abroad ran front-page obituaries and related editorials in the first week of June 1976, among them, the *New York Times*, London *Times*, *Chicago Tribune*, and the *Oregonian*, all 1 June 1976, and the *Washington Post*, 1–3 June 1976.

WINZOLA POOLE MCLENDON

MITCHELL, Robert Byington (4 Apr. 1823–26 Jan. 1882), politician and Civil War general, was born in Mansfield, Richland County, Ohio. The names of his parents are not known. Claims made in several historical studies that Mitchell attended Kenyon College in Ohio or Washington College in Pennsylvania cannot be confirmed by school records; all that is known for certain of this period in his life is that in the early 1840s he moved to Mount Vernon in Knox County, Ohio, and studied law under John K. Miller. In 1844 he was admitted to the bar and returned to Mansfield, where he established a practice.

At the start of the Mexican War in 1846, Mitchell enlisted in the Ohio Volunteers and was commissioned a second lieutenant. Shortly after his promotion to first lieutenant, he was wounded during the climactic battle of Chapultepec. Mustered out of the service in July 1848, he resumed his law practice and became active in Democratic politics. In the early 1850s he relocated to Morrow County and in 1855 was elected mayor of Mount Gilead, the county seat. In 1855 Mitchell married Jennie St. John, daughter of Ohio congressman Henry St. John; they had two children.

A journey to Kansas during 1855 in connection with a legal case convinced Mitchell that the rapidly growing territory offered opportunity for personal advancement despite the increasingly bitter strife between proslavery and antislavery forces that followed its organization under the terms of the Kansas-Nebraska Act of 1854. Undeterred by news accounts of killings in Kansas, Mitchell in October 1856 settled his family at Paris in Linn County near the Missouri border.

Rather than join the territorial Democratic party, which was proslavery, Mitchell aligned himself with the conservative faction of the Free State party, which urged prohibition of slavery in Kansas but opposed nationwide abolition. Mitchell claimed in his speeches that free-state principles "could triumph without resort to violence." In 1857 he ran for a seat in the territorial house and won, despite strong proslavery sentiment in the eastern counties. In early 1858 he was among the signers of a proposed state constitution drafted at Leavenworth, and he was a delegate to the Free State convention held at Topeka. Later in the year he was elected to a second term in the legislature. In February 1859 Governor Samuel Medary appointed Mitchell territorial treasurer, a post he held until February 1861.

During 1859 Mitchell switched allegiance to the Democratic party when the Free State party dissolved itself and most of its followers moved into a newly formed territorial Republican party. Objecting to domination of Republican meetings by abolitionists from the radical wing of Free Staters, Mitchell joined the Democrats despite their minority status and their support for "peaceful coexistence for slavery and freedom." In the first state election, held prior to the admission of Kansas to the Union in January 1861, Mitchell lost as a candidate for associate justice of the state supreme court. As a delegate to the Democratic National Convention at Charleston, South Carolina, in April 1860, Mitchell did not join southern Democrats, who split the party rather than accept Illinois senator Stephen A. Douglas as their presidential nominee. During 1861 Mitchell served as the new state's first adjutant general under Governor Charles Robinson (1818–1894).

In response to Abraham Lincoln's April 1861 call for volunteer troops, Mitchell joined the newly formed Second Kansas Volunteer Infantry and was elected colonel. His unit fought under General Nathaniel Lyon at Wilson's Creek near Springfield, Missouri, on 10 August 1861. While fighting at Lyon's side, Mitchell was wounded, and Lyon himself was shot dead moments later. Cited for bravery, Mitchell was given command of a cavalry regiment following his recovery. On 8 April 1862 he was commissioned brigadier general by Lincoln. At the battle of Perryville in southern Kentucky in October, Mitchell commanded the Ninth Division, Third Army Corps of the Army of the Ohio, which sustained over 500 casualties. Posted to Nashville, he participated in the Union offense in Tennessee during 1863. On 19–20 September he led the Cavalry Corps of the Army of the Cumberland in the battle of Chickamauga near Chattanooga.

Mitchell was respected by fellow officers for decisive leadership in battle but also was known as a stern disciplinarian. During the Tennessee campaign he had 350 of his troops arrested on charges of having threatened mutiny. In making his case to his superiors, Mitchell insisted it might be necessary to shoot some of the men in order to make an example of them to the others. No one was shot, but the incident established Mitchell's reputation as an unyielding officer.

After being wounded in Tennessee, Mitchell was ordered to Washington for court-martial duty in late 1863. Early in 1864 he was assigned to the Nebraska Territory Military District, where he participated in campaigns against the Plains Indians. In early 1865 he was moved to the North Kansas District, and when the military districts of Kansas were combined in June, Mitchell was given command of the Kansas Department.

On 14 December 1865 President Andrew Johnson appointed Mitchell governor of the territory of New Mexico. Mitchell was among the Kansas Democrats supporting the president's anti-Radical program. On 16 July 1866 Mitchell took the oath of office in Santa Fe, where expectations were high that the large but thinly populated territory would soon experience rapid growth. Shortly after his inauguration Mitchell toured new gold and silver mines in the mountains and then went to Washington to promote New Mexico to investors.

Returning in March 1867, Mitchell found that territorial secretary W. F. M. Arny, acting governor in his absence, had made appointments that were confirmed by the territorial council. Arny and Mitchell had known one another as fellow Democrats in Kansas but became implacable enemies in New Mexico, where Arny had built a strong base of political support well before Mitchell's arrival. Despite a congressional resolution declaring valid the actions taken in his absence, Mitchell replaced Arny's appointments and further inflamed the situation by usurping the secretary's prerogative and issuing a certificate of election to his personal choice for Congress.

The legislature unanimously passed a memorial asking Congress to refuse recognition of the Mitchell appointees and to change the organic act that gave the governor absolute veto power. Mitchell vetoed the memorial. In January 1868 the legislature passed a resolution requesting that the president remove Mitchell on grounds of exercising unauthorized power. Johnson, reluctant to lose a political ally as he faced an impeachment effort, did not remove Mitchell from office, but Congress changed the organic act to allow override of a veto with a two-thirds majority vote, in effect rewarding a territorial legislature whose members had shown substantial support for the Radical majority in Congress.

Unable to heal political wounds largely of his own making, Mitchell could not persuade the legislature to raise the revenues needed to reduce a large budget deficit. He also faced newspaper charges that he had attempted to sell "bogus gold mines" to eastern investors on his own behalf. A discouraged Mitchell again went to Washington, this time offering his resignation to President Ulysses S. Grant on 30 March 1869. Although it was accepted, the Confederate veteran appointed as Mitchell's successor failed to be confirmed, and on 24 May Mitchell arrived back in Santa Fe still holding office. Mitchell inadvertently hastened his departure from office by issuing an unauthorized proclamation, declaring that all Navajos and Apaches encountered away from reserve areas were enemies subject to immediate arrest. Congress, the army, and the State Department united in vigorous protest of the governor's assumption of authority vested by law in the Department of the Interior and the military. The president responded quickly, and on 16 August 1869 William A. Pile arrived in Santa Fe to replace Mitchell.

In March 1870 Mitchell returned to Kansas and reentered Democratic politics in the now increasingly Republican state. When a rump faction of Liberal Republicans joined the Democrats in 1872 to nominate a slate of candidates promising opposition to corruption, Mitchell was chosen as a candidate for one of three at-large congressional seats. He lost the election, tallying the second lowest vote total among six candidates. Deciding his prospects were dim in Kansas,

Mitchell relocated to Washington, where he spent the last decade of his life. Upon his death in Washington he was buried with full military honors in the Congressional Cemetery.

Consistency of character unites the political and military periods of Mitchell's career. Often contentious, sometimes intemperate, Mitchell always spoke out on matters he considered important, without regard to the effects such behavior would have on his career. His New Mexico years were marred by a failure to understand that the dictatorial methods appropriate to military life were not suitable to political affairs in civilian society. In the end, Mitchell was unable to fulfill the expectations for a role at the national level engendered in him both by his early political successes and his military leadership during a national crisis, for reasons having less to do with competence than with temperament. His record as a dedicated and effective Civil War general stands as his finest achievement.

• The State Records Center and Archives at Santa Fe, N.Mex., contains the records of Mitchell's territorial administration and includes speeches, legislative bills, resolutions, and documentation of appointments. Public documents that shed light on his political activities in Kansas are located in the Kansas Collection of the University of Kansas Library at Lawrence. Of particular relevance as a source is D. W. Wilder, *The Annals of Kansas, 1541–1885* (1886), which includes records of state constitutional conventions, territorial government organization, appointments made by government officials, territorial legislative actions, and election results. Mitchell has not been the subject of a full biography. For material related solely to Mitchell, see "Sketch of the Career of General Robert B. Mitchell," in *The Kansas Historical Collection*, vol. 16 (1923–1924), pp. 632–37, a reprint of a two-part article that originally appeared in *La Cygne Weekly Journal*, 26 Apr. and 3 May 1895. William Frank Zornow, *Kansas: A History of the Jayhawk State* (1957), provides information essential for understanding the complex political situation between 1854 and 1861. Information concerning Mitchell's tenure as governor as well as his Civil War service is found in Calvin Horn, *New Mexico's Troubled Years: The Story of the Early Governors* (1963); William A. Keleher, *The Fabulous Frontier* (1962; repr. 1982); Robert W. Larson, *New Mexico's Quest for Statehood 1846–1912* (1968); Frank D. Reeve, *History of New Mexico*, vol. 2 (1961); and Ralph Emerson Twitchell, *The Leading Facts of New Mexican History* (3 vols., 1911–1917). An obituary and funeral account are in the *Washington Evening Star*, 28 and 30 Jan. 1882.

CAROLE LARSON

MITCHELL, Samuel Alfred (29 Apr. 1874–22 Feb. 1960), astronomer, was born in Kingston, Ontario, Canada, the son of John Cook Mitchell and Sarah Chown. Mitchell was educated through the Canadian school system and received an M.A. in mathematics from Queen's University in 1894. He then entered the Johns Hopkins University fully intending to study mathematics, with minors in physics and astronomy. There, however, he was so impressed with the work of astronomy professor Charles Poor that he opted to major in astronomy with a first minor in physics and a second in mathematics. Poor had the grating ruling engines of Rowland at his disposal and an aggressive agenda for applying the gratings to astrophysical problems. The talented and ambitious Mitchell, with his penchant for hard work and study, fit in well. It is possible his interest in astronomy had started at Queens University, where, as a student, he was given custody of the observatory with its two telescopes and two clocks.

Mitchell received a Ph.D. in astronomy from the Johns Hopkins University in 1898 with a dissertation on the applications of a concave grating to stellar and solar spectroscopy as well as a detailed analysis for calculating the magnitude of aberrations at various orientations of the grating. The following year he married Milly Gray Dumble. They had one son, Allan Charles Gray Mitchell, who would become chairman of the physics department at Indiana University.

Mitchell was a volunteer research assistant at Yerkes Observatory in 1898–1899. In 1899 he became an instructor at Columbia University and was later named adjunct professor. He held an overlapping appointment as assistant professor of astrophysics at the University of Chicago (Yerkes Observatory) in 1909–1913.

In 1913 Mitchell succeeded Ormand Stone as director of the Leander McCormick Observatory, professor of astronomy, and chairman of the Department of Astronomy at the University of Virginia. He was named professor emeritus and director emeritus upon his retirement in 1945 and continued to publish his research through the late 1950s.

Mitchell's early work on concave gratings led him to apply them to the sun, which produced adequate light to make use of their high dispersive power. Techniques such as aluminizing and blazing of gratings had not yet been developed. This work in turn led to studies of the sun's chromosphere and upper atmosphere during eclipses. He assisted or was in charge of a total of ten expeditions to observe solar eclipses. As a result Mitchell attended more solar eclipses than any person up to his time, and he often noted that he had spent more time in the shadow of the moon than any previous human being. He himself organized eclipse expeditions, which, at that time, required considerable long-term planning. It took more than two months to travel to Sumatra for the eclipse of 1901 and back. Planning for one eclipse expedition often overlapped with planning for the next. He also organized numerous cooperative research efforts with the American Association of Variable Star Observers, the most notable being the observations of long-period variable stars.

His work on the sun was highly regarded, and Charles Abbott, the ranking solar scholar of that time, often cited Mitchell's work. The first person to note that the "flash" spectrum of the sun was the reversal of the Fraunhofer spectrum (the detailed absorption line spectrum of the sun), Mitchell became recognized as the world's authority on the "flash" spectrum. He was able to identify the noble gases neon, argon, krypton, and xenon in the solar atmosphere in 1902, and he published this in 1903 (*Astrophysical Journal* 17: 224).

Mitchell's other major research areas included the measurement of the distances (parallaxes) of stars; studies of variable stars, especially long-period variables; and stellar spectroscopy. He was arguably the first to obtain a spectrum of a star using a concave grating and published as part of his dissertation in 1898. In the field of stellar parallaxes, his first publication (in the *Astronomische Nachrichten* in 1914) was with observations made with the Yerkes Observatory refractor. His first paper in this area at the McCormick Observatory was published in the *Astronomical Journal* in 1916 on Barnard's Star, the star with the highest proper motion.

In 1913–1914 Mitchell set up the University of Virginia parallax program, and during his tenure 2,001 parallaxes were published. Considering that there were only about 100 parallaxes published from all sources before 1914, this is quite an accomplishment. During the midnight hours, which are of little value for a parallax program because the parallactic angle is small, he and his colleagues obtained visual magnitudes (photographically) of all of the reference stars used in the parallax program. During the same period, his colleague Alexander Vyssotsky obtained spectra for all of these stars using a ten-inch astrograph and an objective prism.

A well-regarded scientist, Mitchell was elected to the National Academy of Sciences in 1933. In addition he enjoyed a reputation as a solid administrator and organizer. These abilities placed him in high demand within the various organizations in which he was active. He was president of the American Association of University Professors (1934–1935), vice president of the American Association for the Advancement of Science, vice president of the American Astronomical Society (1925–1927), chairman of the Parallax Commission and the Commission on Solar Eclipses of the International Astronomical Union, chairman of the Astronomy Section of the National Academy of Sciences, and a member of numerous other organizations.

Perhaps Mitchell's best organizational effort was that of putting together an outstanding group of talented astronomers at the University of Virginia. Included in that group were Peter van de Kamp, Alexander Vyssotsky, Emma Williams (later married to Vyssotsky), Carl Wirtanen, Michael Kovolenko, Dirk Reuyl, and Rupert Wildt. Harold Aldan, Mitchell's successor at the University of Virginia, was a student of Mitchell's and an early member of the group prior to going to Africa to be astronomer in charge of the Southern Station of the Yale University Observatory in South Africa. Mitchell and his wife also served as the official hosts of the University of Virginia for almost all formal functions during President John Lloyd Newcomb's tenure (1931–1946). Newcomb, who was a bachelor, felt that receptions at the Director's House atop Mount Jefferson with Mrs. Mitchell as hostess were more fitting of the University of Virginia than those held at his own residence.

Mitchell's classic book, a mixture of popular and serious science, *Eclipses of the Sun* (1923), went through five editions up to 1951. Mitchell also coauthored with Abbott an introductory text, *The Fundamentals of Astronomy* (1927). He died in Bloomington, Indiana, in the home of his son.

• Most of Mitchell's professional papers are in archival journals such as *The Astronomical Journal* and *The Astrophysical Journal*. His dissertation is in the Johns Hopkins Library; the essence of that work appears in *The Astrophysical Journal* 8 (1998): 102, and in the *Monthly Notices of the Royal Astronomical Society* 58 (1997–1998): 291–95. His parallax observations appear in the Leander McCormick Observatory Publications, the last one appearing in vol. 14, pt. 1 (1958). A complete listing of Mitchell's scientific publications is appended to a memorial written by C. G. Abbot in National Academy of Sciences, *Biographical Memoirs* 36 (1962): 254–76. For collateral information and a brief autobiography see *Leander McCormick Observatory of the University of Virginia* (apparently self-published in Charlottesville in 1947); a copy is in the Rare Book Collection of the University of Virginia Library. Obituaries are in the *New York Times*, the *Richmond Times Dispatch*, and the Cavalier Daily, all 23 Feb. 1960. A touching tribute, penned by Ross Valentine, appeared in the *Richmond Times Dispatch*, 29 Mar. 1949.

LAURENCE W. FREDRICK

MITCHELL, Stephen Mix (9 Dec. 1743–30 Sept. 1835), lawyer, was born in Wethersfield, Connecticut, the son of James Mitchell, a Scottish immigrant and merchant, and Rebecca Mix, daughter of the Reverend Stephen Mix of Wethersfield's First (Congregationalist) Church. Mitchell became a devout churchman. A Scottish tutor prepared him for Yale College, which he attended from 1759 to 1763. Mitchell, a Berkley scholar after graduation, was a tutor at the college from 1766 to 1769. In the latter year he married Hannah Grant, who brought £3,000 to the match. This marriage was burlesqued by student John Trumbull, later one of the "Connecticut Wits," in a poem entitled "Epithalamium" (1769). The couple had six sons and four daughters who survived infancy. Mitchell studied law with Jared Ingersoll of New Haven and in 1770 was admitted to the Fairfield County bar. He practiced in Newtown from 1770 to 1772 and then returned to Wethersfield.

In 1774 Mitchell joined the revolutionary movement against Great Britain, serving on the Wethersfield Committees of Correspondence and Surveillance. The well-propertied Mitchell practiced law until the decade's end, when he embarked on a long political career that marked him as one of Connecticut's ruling elite. Mitchell sat in the state house of representatives from 1778 to 1784, serving as its clerk in 1782. He was elected an assistant or councilor to the state council in 1784 and was reelected annually through 1792. He was clerk of the council from 1785 until 1793. Mitchell was a justice of the Hartford County Court from 1779 to 1795 and served as presiding judge from 1789 to 1795.

Elected to the Confederation Congress in 1783, Mitchell did not attend its sessions. He was reelected in 1785, 1786, and 1787 and sat from December 1785 to May 1788. "Well-intentioned," Mitchell spoke little "but with assurance," according to a French diplomat, though he was often awed by the brilliance of his colleagues. With the aid of fellow Connecticut delegate William Samuel Johnson, on whom he depended for counsel, Mitchell employed all his "*Caledonian skill*" (as Johnson termed it) to broker an agreement in 1786 with fellow Scotsman, the intimidating James Wilson of Pennsylvania, that permitted Connecticut to retain a portion of its land claims west of Pennsylvania. Located in northeastern Ohio, the retained land became known as Connecticut's Western Reserve.

A supporter of Congress, Mitchell encouraged the states to pay their congressional requisitions and to adopt the Impost of 1783, or else Congress would become "the most contemptible political Body" that ever met. Mitchell advocated a strong federal militia and defended the Society of the Cincinnati, whose members he called those "deserving Sons of Mars," against its critics. He advocated a strong national government but did not believe that Americans of the revolutionary generation would ever give up enough of their liberties to attain one. Shays's Rebellion terrified Mitchell, who thought other "Revolutions" would follow. In early 1787 he was delighted that the rebellion had failed, but he and Johnson voted against calling a constitutional convention to revise and amend the Articles of Confederation. Mitchell and Johnson distrusted conventions because of Connecticut's unhappy experience with popular conventions earlier in the decade. Conventions, they believed, destroyed constitutions rather than erecting them. Consequently, Mitchell refused in late September 1787 to attend the Congress that transmitted to the states the new federal Constitution just adopted by the constitutional convention.

Mitchell's position changed, however. In November 1787 he moderated the Wethersfield town meeting that elected him and another townsman to the Connecticut ratifying convention, where both men voted to ratify the Constitution in January 1788. Nevertheless, Mitchell's federalism was suspect, and he was defeated for election to the U.S. House of Representatives in 1788 and 1790. Finally elected in 1792, he did not take his place because in 1793 he was appointed to fill the U.S. Senate seat vacated by the death of Roger Sherman.

Mitchell was a U.S. senator from December 1793 until March 1795. Upon arriving in the Senate, the Federalist Mitchell was appointed to the committee to consider a petition requesting that Albert Gallatin, a talented Republican leader, not be seated in the Senate because he had not fulfilled the citizenship requirements for the office. Mitchell voted with the Federalist majority in the committee and the Senate to unseat Gallatin. He supported the Bank of the United States and a conciliatory policy toward Great Britain, which had encroached on American commerce. Mitchell was a Federalist presidential elector for John Adams in 1800.

In October 1795 Mitchell was appointed a justice of the Connecticut Superior Court and held this position until 1814, when he was forced by law to retire, having reached the age of seventy. In 1807 he became chief justice of the court, which was then called the Connecticut Supreme Court of Errors. His judicial opinions were noted for their terseness and scholarship.

In 1818 Mitchell was one of Wethersfield's two Federalist delegates to the Republican-dominated state constitutional convention called to adopt a constitution for Connecticut, which was still operating under its colonial charter. Mitchell was appointed to a committee to frame the convention's rules, and he participated in the convention's debates. In particular, he unsuccessfully opposed the inclusion of a bill of rights because no such document could enumerate all of the people's rights. Only a constitution, an authoritative document, could limit a government's powers. Nevertheless, Mitchell voted with the Republican majority to adopt the new constitution. Wethersfield rejected the constitution three to one. Mitchell died in Wethersfield.

• Mitchell's papers are not extant. Some of his letters, largely from the William Samuel Johnson Papers, are in Edmund C. Burnett, ed., *Letters of Members of the Continental Congress*, vol. 8 (1936). The fullest biography is Royal Robbins, "Sketch of the Life and Character of the Hon. Stephen Mix Mitchell, LL.D.," *Quarterly Christian Spectator* 8 (June 1836): 205–25. Indispensable for Mitchell's extensive officeholding is Charles J. Hoadly et al., eds., *The Public Records of the State of Connecticut* . . . (1894–). For Mitchell and the state constitutional convention of 1818, see Hoadly, ed., *Journal of the Proceedings of the Convention of Delegates* . . . (1873). Mitchell's opinions as chief justice of the Supreme Court of Errors are in Thomas Day, *Reports of Cases, Argued and Determined in the Supreme Court of Errors, of the State of Connecticut* . . . , vols. 3–5 (1811–1813).

GASPARE J. SALADINO

MITCHELL, S. Weir (15 Feb. 1828–4 Jan. 1914), physician and writer, was born Silas Weir Mitchell in Philadelphia, Pennsylvania, the son of John Kearsley Mitchell, a physician and professor of medicine, and Sarah Matilda Henry. He entered the University of Pennsylvania at the age of fifteen and in his second year was ranked first in his class, but withdrew after three years because of the illness of his father. He enrolled in 1848 in Jefferson Medical College, where his father taught, and finished the two-year course at age twenty-one. He continued his studies in Paris, where he spent a year in research with several eminent scientists such as the physiologist Claude Bernard and the microscopist Charles Phillippe Robin. In 1851 he returned to Philadelphia to help with the medical practice of his ailing father and by 1855 was the sole supporter of the family. In 1858 he married Mary Middleton Elwyn, who bore him two sons before her death, from diphtheria, in 1862. When his father died in 1858, Mitchell took over his practice.

Engaged in scientific research from the beginning of his career in medicine, Mitchell published his first scholarly paper, "Observations on the Generation of Uric Acid and Its Crystalline Forms," in the *American*

Journal of Medical Sciences in 1852. The next year he was elected a member of the Academy of Natural Sciences. An ardent researcher, he wrote more than 170 specialized papers, making important contributions to the fields of physiology, neurology, pharmacology, and toxicology. His investigations into the nature of snake venom and its effect on the nervous system, begun in 1855 and published in 1860, and his research on the physiology of the cerebellum, carried out from 1863 to 1869, were especially influential and led to important further work by others. He also studied the effects of drugs such as opium and atropine and did original work on the use of amyl nitrate inhalation as a treatment for epilepsy.

During the Civil War Mitchell served as a contract surgeon and a member of the Sanitary Commission with the Union army, and his experience with wounded soldiers resulted in several valuable studies, including *Gunshot Wounds and Other Injuries of Nerves* and *Reflex Paralysis*, both published in 1864. His scientific writing was praised for its clarity, simplicity, and precision. Mitchell left the army in 1864 and toured England and France for two months before returning to private practice in Philadelphia, where he became a leading specialist in nervous disorders. In 1870 he was appointed to the Philadelphia Orthopedic Hospital and Infirmary for Nervous Diseases and served as a professor of medicine at the Philadelphia Polyclinic. In 1874 he took a second wife, Mary Cadwalader, the daughter of General Thomas Cadwalader. His marriage into one of the most prestigious families of Philadelphia gave him entry to that city's highest social circles and assured him the leisure necessary to conduct his scientific investigations.

Mitchell's greatest contemporary fame as a medical man came from a method he developed in the early 1870s for the treatment of a variety of nervous conditions, emphasizing isolation, bed rest, and a rich but bland diet. Recommended especially for women, the "Weir Mitchell Rest Cure" was recognized throughout the United States and Europe and won the support of Austrian neurologist Sigmund Freud and the prominent French neuropathologist Jean Martin Charcot. Mitchell's *Wear and Tear; or, Hints for the Overworked* (1871) and *Fat and Blood: An Essay on the Treatment of Certain Forms of Neurasthenia and Hysteria* (1877) were bestselling popularizations of his theories, published in many editions and translated into French, German, Italian, and Russian. Although the regimen, when applied to women diagnosed as victims of "hysteria," was condemned by some for the assumption of women's natural dependency and weakness on which it was based and for the authoritarian role it assigned to the physician, it was regarded in its time as an enlightened and humane procedure for its sympathetic treatment of women.

Devoted throughout his life to literature, Mitchell wrote poetry and short stories from the age of fourteen. His first published work, a brief poem titled "To a Polar Star," appeared in the *Nassau Monthly* in 1846, and he became a regular contributor of verse to the *Atlantic Monthly* in 1862. He also produced works for children from 1866 until the year of his death. His early poetry and fiction were published anonymously or under the pseudonym of Edward Kearsley in order to keep his literary and his medical careers separate, but the growing popularity of his writing led him to acknowledge his authorship after the publication of his first book of fiction, the novelette *Hepzibah Guiness*, in 1880.

Mitchell's poetry was skillful and widely respected but was generally regarded by serious critics as lacking originality and depth; Walt Whitman described it, in a conversation with Horace Traubel, as "non vital" and "stiff at the knees." Nevertheless his six volumes of poems, from *The Hill of Stones* (1882) to *The Wager* (1900), earned the praise of such personal friends as James Whitcomb Riley, Oliver Wendell Holmes, John Greenleaf Whittier, and James Russell Lowell, and Mitchell received the honor of a collected edition in 1896 and the publication of his *Complete Poems* in 1914. His most admired poem, "Ode on a Lycian Tomb," was written in memory of the only child of his second marriage, Maria, who succumbed to diphtheria at the age of twenty-two in 1898.

Mitchell earned his popularity for the historical accuracy and psychological insight of his fiction. His first published story, "The Case of George Dedlow," published in the *Atlantic Monthly* in 1866, anticipated Stephen Crane's 1895 novel *The Red Badge of Courage* in its perceptive rendering of a young soldier's first experience of battle. Mitchell's first adult novel, *In War Time*, published serially in the *Atlantic* in 1884, also provided a vivid description of the Civil War and its psychological effects on those it touched. His most popular book was *Hugh Wynne, Free Quaker* (1898), a sprawling historical novel set in Philadelphia during the American Revolution. Like all of Mitchell's fiction, it reflects the scientific discipline of its author's medical training in the precise and accurate detail of its observation. Although it has been criticized for its loose plot, it was a great success and was much honored for the psychological depth of its characterization. Mitchell's fiction was warmly received by the literary establishment of his time and included among its most vocal admirers George Meredith and William Dean Howells. The latter praised the "artistic fineness" and "scientific thoroughness" of Mitchell's style, for which he coined the term "psychologism."

Mitchell always considered himself a physician who wrote novels rather than a novelist who practiced medicine, and when asked what he was writing would usually answer "prescriptions!" The many honors he received were equally divided between his two careers: For his work as a scientist he was made a trustee of the University of Pennsylvania in 1875, awarded an honorary M.D. by the University of Bologna in 1888, elected the first president of the American Congress of American Physicians and Surgeons in 1889, and made a trustee of Carnegie Institution of Washington in 1902. His fiction brought him honorary LL.D.s from Harvard, Princeton, and the Universities of Edinburgh and Toronto. A stately, distinguished-looking figure with a patrician manner and a keen wit, Mitchell was a congenial host to his many friends and admirers and a generous help to the young, though in his old age he was prone to personal vanity and fiercely defensive of his legal rights as an author. A leader in Philadelphia society and the moving spirit of its literary community, he served as the first president of Franklin Inn, a writers' association, and presided over its meetings with convivial charm until his death. His complete works were published in twelve volumes in 1909 and in sixteen volumes in 1912–1913.

Mitchell's scientific research has been largely superseded, and his Rest Cure, attacked by feminists during his lifetime, was to fall into disrepute among later psychologists. His contribution to medicine lies rather in the experimental rigor and acute observation he employed in his investigations and in the new areas of research he pioneered. His studies of toxicology, immunology, and the use of drugs were significant in their time, and the high standards of his laboratory methodology had a great influence on subsequent scientific research.

Mitchell's literary reputation has fared less well. His poetry, labored and conventional to later eyes, has been largely forgotten, and his once popular fiction has been described as derivative and "conforming to the sentimental conventions" of the earlier "genteel tradition" in American literature. But though Mitchell's thirteen novels and numerous short stories have received little critical attention since his death, his flair for dramatic narrative, historical color, and insightful characterization remain fresh and vital.

• Mitchell's diaries, personal papers, and letters are in the libraries of the College of Physicians and the University of Pennsylvania in Philadelphia. Among his most influential medical treatises are *Wear and Tear; or, Hints for the Overworked* (1871), *Rest in the Treatment of Disease* (1875), *Fat and Blood, and How to Make Them* (1878), and *Doctor and Patient* (1878). His other novels include *In War Time* (1885), *The Autobiography of a Quack* (1900), *Constance Trescott* (1905), and *Westways* (1913). The most authoritative biographies are Anna Robeson Burr, *Weir Mitchell, His Life and Letters* (1929), Ernest Earnest, *S. Weir Mitchell, Novelist and Physician* (1950), Richard D. Walter, *Weir Mitchell, M.D., Neurologist: A Biography* (1970), and Joseph Lovering, *S. Weir Mitchell* (1971). See also Arthur Hobson Quinn, "Weir Mitchell, Pioneer and Patrician," in *American Fiction: An Historical and Critical Survey* (1936). An obituary is in the Philadelphia *Public Ledger*, 5 Jan. 1914.

DENNIS WEPMAN

MITCHELL, Thomas (11 July 1892–17 Dec. 1962), playwright and actor, was born Thomas Gregory Mitchell in Elizabeth, New Jersey, the son of James Mitchell, a merchant, mortician, and newspaperman, and Mary Donnelly. Mitchell was one of seven children of Irish immigrants who came to America in 1868. Like both his older brother, John, and his father, Mitchell spent time in the newspaper business. He started out as a cub reporter on the *Elizabeth Journal* and, after graduating from Elizabeth High School, went on to work as a reporter for papers in Newark, Washington, Baltimore, and Pittsburgh.

Mitchell's attraction to the stage, originally just a hobby, became a professional pursuit in 1914. He appeared as Trinculo with the Ben Greet Players in Shakespeare's *The Tempest* in Madison Square Garden. After his debut in New York City, he embarked on a two-year tour of the United States as a member of Charles Coburn's Shakespearean troupe. In June 1916 he married Anne Stuart Brewer; they had one daughter.

Mitchell triumphed early as a playwright. After collaborating on *Glory Hallelujah* with Bert Bloch in 1925, he co-wrote *Little Accident* with Floyd Dell in 1928. *Little Accident* had a successful 38-week run on Broadway in the late 1920s, with Mitchell as star and director, earning him a Roi Cooper Megrue Prize for playwriting. In 1931 he played the role of John "Killer" Mears in *The Last Mile* on Broadway, after the leading man, Lawrence Leslie, suddenly became ill. The next year he teamed up once more with Dell to write *Cloudy with Showers*. For this play, Mitchell did triple duty as playwright, director, and leading man. He spent most of the early 1930s treading the New York stage in plays such as the murder tale *Riddle Me This!* and the comedy *Clear All Wires!* (in which he played an American newspaper correspondent in Moscow). Nevertheless, Hollywood was beckoning.

Mitchell's first work in film was an adaptation of the screenplay of *Little Accident* (1930), which was followed by *All of Me* (1934). The latter project involved his talents as both a collaborator and actor. But when he realized his literary talents were being wasted in Hollywood, he returned to New York City, this time solely as an actor. Then, in 1936, he appeared in three Hollywood movies, and for a decade he was one of the most recognizable faces on film, usually in supporting roles. He was nominated for an Academy Award in 1937 for his role in *Hurricane*.

In 1939—a landmark year for Mitchell—he won the Oscar as best supporting actor for his role as the drunken Doc Boone in *Stagecoach*, also appearing in three films nominated for best film of the year. Mitchell played Gerald O'Hara, Scarlett's father, in the winner, *Gone with the Wind*; a crusty newspaperman who befriends Jimmy Stewart in *Mr. Smith Goes to Washington*; and opposite John Wayne in *Stagecoach*.

The demand for Mitchell as an actor was apparent after he suffered a fractured skull during a rehearsal in 1940. The horses pulling a carriage in which he was riding suddenly bolted. Mitchell managed to save the child actor who was riding with him, but he was thrown into a car when the carriage rammed a fire hydrant. Hollywood offers began to roll in even before he had fully recovered. So much prosperity came to Mitchell in the 1940s that he was juggling roles simultaneously. Films for which Mitchell is well known during this period include *Swiss Family Robinson* (1940), *Our Town* (1940), *Bataan* (1943), and *It's a Wonderful Life* (1946).

Mitchell left Hollywood in 1947, however, to divide his time between the new medium of television and the stage. His television career, like his films before, garnered him critical acclaim. He was nominated for an Emmy Award as best actor in 1951, winning the following year. His return to the stage in the 1950s was likewise a professional triumph. He followed a seventeen-month run as Willy Loman in Arthur Miller's classic *Death of a Salesman*, with an award-winning musical role. Although he neither sang nor danced, he took an Antoinette Perry (Tony) Award in 1953 as best actor in a musical for his portrayal of Dr. Enoch Downer in *Hazel Flagg*. In 1954 he was also nominated for another Emmy as best actor in a single performance for his work in *Good of His Soul*.

The stage, however, remained a love for Mitchell. During his film heyday, it was reported in the *New York Times* (13 Aug. 1944) that "another project very close to Mr. Mitchell's heart is his perennial plan to make a huge phonograph album re-creating [seventeenth-century dramatist] Ben Jonson's 'Mermaid Tavern.'" In the same interview, the actor was also quoted as saying he was working on another play. "If it's produced, I'll probably be back to direct it," Mitchell said. In fact, he did write *I Am I*, but it was never produced, and Mitchell himself called it "lousy."

Mitchell's television work in the late 1950s included starring as an affable community leader in "Mayor of the Town" (1955). Mitchell believed in filmed television over live shows. "A lot has been said about the spontaneity and excitement of a live show," he said in an interview with the *New York Times* (15 May 1955). "But what it amounts to is the substitution of nervous energy for vitality. I've been on more than one live television show where we got by, but we were just lucky." He also appeared in plays broadcast on television, such as *Ah Wilderness!* and *The Skin of Our Teeth*, another television series, "Glencannon" (1958), "The O. Henry Theatre" (1957), and other television specials.

In his private life, Mitchell was an avid collector of art. It was noted in the *New York Times* that in 1940 the actor purchased a Rembrandt painting that had been brought to the United States by a Polish prince fleeing the war in Europe. The painting, a study for the head of Christ in Rembrandt's *The Supper at Emmaus*, was just part of Mitchell's collection, which included works by Cezanne, Modigliani, Picasso, and Renoir. Although most of his later work was for television or stage, Mitchell did appear in nine films from 1948 until 1961, including *High Noon* (1952), *Destry* (1954), and his last film, *Pocketful of Miracles* (1961). Interested in actors' welfare, Mitchell served two terms as a council member of Actors Equity Association, an actors' union, from 1933 to 1938 and from 1953 to 1958. He died in Beverly Hills, California.

• As a playwright, there are a number of examples of Mitchell's voice as storyteller. Mitchell's own article in the *New York Times* (22 June 1930) gives some insight into the challenge of suddenly taking over the part of "Killer" Mears in *The Last Mile*. Like many other entertainers, Mitchell was profiled often in the popular press of the day. For such profiles, see *TV Guide*, 8 June 1957 and 14 Feb. 1959; the latter issue looks at Mitchell's visit to England. Obituaries are in the *New York Times*, 18 Dec. 1962, and *Variety*, 9 Dec. 1962.

MARIANNE FEDUNKIW STEVENS

MITCHELL, Thomas Duché (1791–13 May 1865), physician and educator, was born in Philadelphia, Pennsylvania. While biographers note that his family was of "proved respectability and morality" (Payne, p. 350) and had for three or four generations resided in Philadelphia, we know nothing of his parents. His early formal education was exceptionally rich for the day. He received traditional college preparation at the Carson Academy and the Friends' Academy in Philadelphia. After working for a year in Dr. Adam Seybert's drugstore and chemical laboratory, he began a three- or four-year apprenticeship with Dr. Joseph Parrish. He may have begun course work for his medical degree while serving his apprenticeship. His long publishing career began at the age of eighteen with the appearance of three articles in *Medical Museum* (1809). Under the pseudonym "Duché," he probably was the author of "Application of Chemistry to Some of the Purposes of Life," in the *Philadelphia Aurora* (1811).

In 1812 Mitchell received an M.D. from the medical department of the University of Pennsylvania. His thesis on acidification and combustion was published in the *Memoirs* of the Columbian Chemical Society (1813). He also published three other articles that year in *Medical Repository*. The year of his graduation he accepted an appointment as professor of vegetable and animal physiology at Saint John's Lutheran College in Philadelphia. In 1815 he published three more articles in *Medical Repository*. The following year the governor of Pennsylvania appointed him to the office of Lazaretto Physician of the Port of Philadelphia, basically a protoepidemiological post. By identifying the sources of infectious diseases, he advised on the necessity of quarantine to prevent the importation and spread of disease into the city. Illness forced his resignation in 1816. While convalescing he wrote "Remarks on the Quarantine System of the State of Pennsylvania" and "On the Medical Character," for *Medical Repository* (1818), and *Medical Chemistry; or, A Compendious View of the Various Substances Employed in the Practice of Medicine* (1819).

In 1820 *Medical Repository* published three more of his articles. That year, Ohio University in Athens offered him a professorship in chemistry, but he declined the offer. While in active practice at Frankford, near Philadelphia, from 1822 to 1831, he continued or initiated scientific research and writing. At Frankford he led an effort in 1826 to create the Total Abstinence Temperance Society. A strict Presbyterian, his therapeutics contraindicated the internal administration of alcohol. In recognition of his militant social and professional temperance stand, in 1830 Princeton College awarded him an honorary A.M. Between 1826 and

1830 three more of his articles appeared in the *North American Medical and Surgical Journal.* During the winter of 1830–1831, had he remained in Philadelphia, he could have assumed the chair in materia medica at the Jefferson Medical College upon the resignation of Dr. John Eberle. Instead, he joined Eberle as professor of chemistry and pharmacy on the proposed medical faculty at Miami University in Athens, Ohio. When that institution failed to open, in 1831 he accepted the chair in chemistry at the Medical College of Ohio, which would later merge with Miami. He served as dean of the medical college and coeditor of the *Western Medical Gazette* (1832). In 1832 he published the 700-page *Elements of Chemical Philosophy*, which was influential in the western states. In 1833 the *Western Medical Gazette* published his "Treatise on Pharmacy," in which he argued against the use of ardent spirits. In 1833 he was lecturer on chemistry in the preparatory department during the summer session at the Lane Seminary.

In 1837 he accepted the chair in chemistry at the newly founded Louisville Medical Institute, but a month later he resigned to assume a professorship in chemistry in the medical department of Transylvania University in Lexington. The following year he assumed the chair in materia medica that he would retain until 1849. He was dean of the faculty from 1839 to 1846 and during 1845–1846 also served as professor of obstetrics. From 1847 to 1849 he served part-time as visiting professor of the theory and practice of medicine, obstetrics, and medical jurisprudence at the Philadelphia College of Medicine. In 1849 he resigned from Transylvania to work full-time at Philadelphia. In 1850 he published *Materia Medica and Therapeutics.* An expanded edition of this work was published in 1857. That same year he produced a revision of Eberle's *A Treatise on the Diseases and Physical Education of Children.* In 1852 he resigned at Philadelphia, declined offers to go to schools in Tennessee and Missouri, and joined the new Kentucky School of Medicine in Louisville as professor of theory and practice. Ill health forced his resignation in 1854, and he returned to Philadelphia to convalesce. In 1857 he accepted the chair in materia medica and general therapeutics in the Jefferson Medical School, which he occupied until his death in Philadelphia. He never married.

Mitchell was an atypical early nineteenth-century practitioner in many important ways. During the latter part of his career he practiced little medicine and concentrated on writing. He was a prolific writer on such themes of contemporary concern as medical ethics and therapeutics. Acquiring some of his reform zeal and zest for publishing from his medical school professor Dr. Benjamin Rush, Mitchell dedicated his life to reforming society and the medical profession. This task took him on trips around the expanding nation, on which he gained supporters. A consistently vocal critic of his colleagues' personal and professional uses of alcohol, he created tensions everywhere he went. His harshest critics wrote of him as "being a narrow-minded, bigotted, presumptuous puritanical Presbyterian" (Eberson, p. 353). He was an idealist and crusader who worried that the virtues that had created the nation were vanishing. He often expressed these concerns and fully developed them in *Tripod of the American Revolution, viz. Voluntary Association, Pledge, and Self-denial* (1838).

• There are some Mitchell papers and correspondence in the Rare Books Department of Transylvania University Library. Robert and Johanna Peter, *The History of the Medical Department of Transylvania University* (1905), offer a positive assessment of his person and career. Frederick Eberson, "Crusader Extraordinary: Thomas Duché Mitchell, 1791–1865," *Filson Club Historical Quarterly* 52 (1978): 263–79, offers a more balanced account. V. F. Payne, "Thomas Duché Mitchell," *Filson Club Historical Quarterly* 31 (1957): 349–57, provides valuable insights into Mitchell's role in the 1837 exodus of Transylvania professors to a Louisville school and a comprehensive listing and brief explanation of his publications.

ERIC HOWARD CHRISTIANSON

MITCHELL, Wesley Clair (5 Aug. 1874–29 Oct. 1948), economist, was born in Rushville, Illinois, the son of John Wesley Mitchell, a physician, and Lucy Medora McClellan, both ardent abolitionists. Mitchell's mother's family members were associates of the abolitionist Lovejoy brothers and assisted the Underground Railroad. His father volunteered as a surgeon to the Fourth U.S. Colored Infantry during the Civil War and was seriously wounded, and his injuries hampered his later practice. The family moved about Illinois during Mitchell's childhood, supplementing his father's income with farming and minor commercial ventures.

Mitchell entered the University of Chicago in its first class of 1892 and came under the influence of the philosopher John Dewey and the economist Thorstein Veblen. Mitchell credited Dewey with helping him deconstruct the evangelical Protestantism of his youth by pointing out the inevitable personal, social, and economic biases of all ideologies. Dewey's social perspective on thought influenced all of Mitchell's work, especially his analysis of economic theory. The acerbic Veblen continued what Mitchell called this "vivisection without an anesthetic" during Mitchell's sophomore year, and Mitchell began to follow Veblen's lead and study philosophy, ethnology, and psychology in order to critique the allegedly outmoded assumptions of classical economics. Mitchell, Veblen's best and favorite student, would carry on his mentor's institutional brand of economics and its emphasis on the cultural preconceptions of the "money economy."

A third intellectual influence at Chicago was J. Laurence Laughlin, chairman of the economics department and a dogmatic proponent of laissez-faire, who interested Mitchell in monetary issues. After receiving his undergraduate degree in 1896, Mitchell began graduate study in economics and philosophy at Chicago; he wrote his dissertation on the greenback phenomenon during the Civil War as a case study in how the money economy actually worked. In *A History of the Greenbacks with Special Reference to the Economic*

Consequences of Their Issue: 1862–1865 (1903), Mitchell found the primary influence on prices to be not the amount of paper money in circulation but the changing fortunes of the Union army. More importantly, he pioneered in developing more sophisticated forms of statistical accounting as a means of determining actual relationships among various aspects of the economy. Although Mitchell always decried his own lack of statistical ability, he consistently insisted on the importance of statistics for economic study. As he wrote in a 1909 letter to his future wife, "I want to *prove* things as nearly may be and proof means usually an appeal to facts—facts recorded in the best cases in statistical form."

Mitchell received his doctorate in 1899, worked unhappily for the U.S. Census Bureau for a short time, then returned to Chicago as an instructor in 1900. He was appointed assistant professor of economics at the University of California at Berkeley in 1903 and became a full professor in 1909. In 1912 he married Lucy Sprague, the dean of women at Berkeley and a pioneer progressive educator who later founded Bank Street, a cooperative school for experimental teachers. Sprague inherited a considerable fortune from her Chicago mercantile family, and the couple consequently were able to take numerous academic chances. They had four children and by all accounts a mutually satisfying emotional and intellectual partnership.

During his years at Berkeley, Mitchell became convinced that the future of economics lay in the collection and analysis of records of business enterprise in quantitative form. Moreover, as a child of reformers and the late nineteenth century, he not surprisingly perceived the booms and busts of the capitalist economy to be the most troublesome economic and social problem. If economists had sufficient information on business cycles, he believed, they could begin to determine the interrelationships among the various aspects of the economy and, he hoped, control these fluctuations. In *Business Cycles* (1913) Mitchell discussed the various theories about business cycles and then provided elaborate statistical records on cycles between 1908 and 1911. He freely admitted that he could neither test the existing theories nor provide a new one that explained all of the current information, but he insisted that his work provided the data on which later economists could base such approaches. In *Methods in Social Science* (1929) economic theorist John Maurice Clark called *Business Cycles* the "formative type" for the explosion in quantitative economics.

Immediately after their marriage, the Mitchells moved to New York City, where Mitchell joined the Columbia faculty in 1913, first as a lecturer and then a year later as a full professor. Only in New York did Mitchell feel he would have access to the economic data necessary for the development of a science of business cycles. He soon became acquainted with Edwin Gay, an economic historian and dean of Harvard Business School, who shared Mitchell's passion, and the two, with American Telephone and Telegraph's chief statistician Malcolm Rorty, planned an economics research institute dedicated to gathering scientifically verifiable economic data. Before they could obtain funding, however, World War I intervened and Gay became the director of the Central Bureau of Planning and Statistics of the War Industries Board. In 1918 Gay brought Mitchell to Washington, where he quickly began a collection of statistical information from all government agencies, including the armed services. Policymakers required such information because they were called on to achieve an effective economic and military mobilization yet lacked meaningful figures. By the end of the war Mitchell was head of the Price Division of the War Industries Board and had supervised a massive study of the wholesale prices of more than 1,500 commodities for the years 1917–1918.

Businessmen as well as policymakers found such information invaluable in helping them predict future demands and plan intelligently. They petitioned for the economic sections of the War Industries Board to be incorporated permanently into the Department of Commerce. When President Woodrow Wilson rejected this idea, Mitchell and Gay dusted off their plans for the National Bureau of Economic Research (NBER) and quickly obtained financial support from foundations and private businesses. The NBER was officially launched in 1920.

Mitchell understood the dilemma of contemporary social science research. Researchers needed independent funding for the large-scale, quantitative studies that seemed to be necessary for the development of an empirically based science of society. Yet, potential supporters of such research often tried to influence not only the choice of subject but even the results. Mitchell as research director of the NBER from 1920 to 1945 developed an institutional framework that successfully allowed some influence by funders, avoided political controversies, and permitted significant academic freedom. He established an executive board composed of representatives from business, labor, and consumer interests that had a final veto over all research topics and reports in the planning, methodological, and final stages. Such a procedure weeded out all opinions and recommendations, leaving only factual studies. While such measures ensured continued funding and freedom from specific interest groups, it also led to an elimination of alternative perspectives and an unquestioning acceptance of the ongoing economic system. Nevertheless, the bureau's ability to provide factual information about the economy in a time when such important simple tasks as the determination of the gross national product had been perceived as unrealizable quickly made it indispensable.

Throughout his career Mitchell insisted that scientists had a "moral" duty toward society and should direct their research toward areas where they could do the most good. He believed that economists' statistical work during the war proved the utility of quantitative work. In a letter to his wife, he proclaimed "My world is the world of thought, but the world of thought has a realm of action and I live there."

Mitchell was a founder of the New School for Social Research, and he served on numerous government commissions. In 1921 Secretary of Commerce Herbert Hoover pleaded with Mitchell to become the department's official economic adviser. Although Mitchell turned down this request, he became Hoover's contact with other social scientists, first organizing an investigation into unemployment during postwar depressions and then becoming director of a comprehensive two-volume survey of the American economy by many of the nation's prominent economists. Although this study, *Recent Economic Changes* (1929), provided the type of information needed for economic planning, its failure to predict the Great Depression caused it to be ignored. As president, Hoover continued these fact-finding commissions and appointed Mitchell to direct an ambitious survey of all of American society. The resultant *Recent Social Trends in the United States* (1933) reflected Mitchell and Hoover's shared belief in the primacy of accurate data. It received considerable acclaim for its comprehensiveness, although it was also criticized by many for its purely factual nature and unwillingness to suggest solutions to the problems caused by the Great Depression. During the New Deal, Mitchell continued his government work, most notably as a member of the National Planning Board.

Despite Mitchell's emphasis on quantitative work, he was almost as well known as a historian of economic theory. Early in his career he produced several influential essays along the lines of his teacher Veblen. These essays, as well as several of his later calls for a purely empirical economics, were collected in *The Backward Art of Spending Money and Other Essays* (1937). By this time, however, Mitchell had denied the utility of this type of theoretical work and turned to analyzing others' economic thinking. He argued that one could study economic theory in two very different ways. One could either examine particular theories in depth and try to prove or disprove their validity or take a historicist approach and determine why people came to believe certain things at particular times. Mitchell chose the latter, and his Columbia courses on the history of economic theory became famous with experts such as Robert Heilbroner proclaiming Mitchell's lectures the best survey ever.

As the Great Depression worsened, more and more individuals called on Mitchell, the country's leading expert on business cycles, to turn away from their quantitative description to possible solutions. Although he expressed sympathy for this perspective, he continued to insist that empirical research was ultimately more useful. In a 1940 semiautobiographical essay, "Feeling and Thinking in Scientific Work," Mitchell argued that while "feeling" was helpful in selecting important research topics and providing commitment to research, it could skew the results of research. The scientific method, which Mitchell usually equated with quantification, was the only acceptable approach. Mitchell continued and even intensified his empirical research, finishing *Measuring Business Cycles* with Arthur Burns in 1946 and working on *What Happens during Business Cycles: A Progress Report* (1951) until shortly before his death in New York City.

In 1947 Mitchell was awarded the first Francis Amasa Walker Award, given to the individual who contributed most to the study of economics. His presidencies of the American Statistical Association (1919), the American Economic Association (1925), the Social Science Research Council (1927–1931), the American Association for the Advancement of Science (1938), the Academy of Political Science (1940–1941), and the Econometric Society (1943) as well as his appointment to the leading government commissions and advisory boards of the 1920s and 1930s attest to the wide respect he earned in his lifetime. Many of the leading economists of the twentieth century trained under Mitchell at Columbia and the National Bureau of Economic Research, and the NBER itself served as the prototype for the many social science research institutes and think tanks of the twentieth century. His research on business cycles had a profound impact on economics, pushing it toward the largely quantitative study it became. Indeed, Mitchell's sometimes naive faith in the power of numbers and his almost obsessive need to obtain all the facts helped to create the false hope of a truly predictable science of economics. The collection of the requisite data for a comparison of the relationships between all factors in the business cycle remains as chimerical as it was in 1913.

• The Butler Library at Columbia University possesses an excellent collection of Mitchell's correspondence and publications. A good compilation of personal and analytical essays on Mitchell is the memorial volume, *Wesley Clair Mitchell: The Economic Scientist*, ed. his student and NBER successor Arthur F. Burns (1952). It also contains a complete bibliography of his works. A short but extremely useful autobiographical piece is "The Author's Own Account of His Methodological Interests," *Methods in Social Science, a Case Book*, ed. Stuart A. Rice (1929), pp. 673–80. Guy Alchon, *The Invisible Hand of Planning: Capitalism, Social Science and the State in the 1920s* (1985), analyzes Mitchell's role in the origins and development of the National Bureau of Economic Research. Mark C. Smith, *Social Science in the Crucible: The American Debate over Objectivity and Purpose, 1918–1941* (1994), emphasizes Mitchell's commitment to quantification and its significance for social science methodology. Joseph Dorfman, a student of Mitchell, discusses his teacher's work in several places in his classic *Economic Mind in American Civilization*, most notably in vol. 3 (1950), pp. 455–73, and vol. 4 (1959), pp. 360–77. A work that emphasizes Mitchell's institutional economics is Alan Gruchy, *Modern Economic Thought: The American Contribution* (1947), pp. 247–333. Lucy Sprague Mitchell, *Two Lives: The Story of Wesley Clair Mitchell and Myself* (1953), and Joyce Antler, *Lucy Sprague Mitchell: The Making of a Modern Woman* (1987), give good insights into Mitchell's personal life. Several memorial addresses are included in the Burns volume; obituaries are in the *New York Times*, 30 Oct. 1948, and *Political Science Quarterly* 63 (Dec. 1949): 639–40.

MARK C. SMITH

MITCHELL, William (1798–11 May 1856), actor and manager, was born in Billquay, Durham, England, the son of a merchant ship captain. He enjoyed a comfortable childhood and apprenticed as a clerk in the office of a West Indies merchant at age fifteen. Sometime during the next five years, he became stagestruck and abandoned the world of commerce for the world of the theater. Obtaining his first professional engagement in 1820, he played for two years with a minor provincial troupe in Kent, honing his skills as a broadly comic character actor—a low comedian—and then joined the excellent provincial comedy of DeCamp in Sheffield in 1822. This troupe was one of the best of its kind and included several young actors who later became well known in the United States, among them Thomas Flynn, George Holland, and Thomas S. Hamblin.

By 1831 he was acting in London at the minor theaters (those operating on the periphery of the licensing act of 1737 by presenting short plays and musical dramas that were classified as "irregular" and therefore did not violate the monopoly of Covent Garden and Drury Lane, the only two theaters in London legally entitled to present the regular drama). In 1834 Mitchell was fined fifty pounds for acting at the Strand when that theater was found to be in violation of its limited license. Unable to achieve his goal of becoming principal low comedian at either Drury Lane or Covent Garden, Mitchell decided to immigrate to the United States in 1836.

He began his American career as principal low comedian for his old friend Thomas Flynn at New York's National Theatre in the autumn of 1836. He stayed the season and then spent most of 1837 and 1838 as a traveling star, rapidly establishing himself as an audience favorite in a wide range of broadly comic characters. As an actor, Mitchell was a broad farceur. Stout, physically well coordinated, possessing a flexible and humorous countenance, and a master of vocal mimicry, he was an excellent "funny fat man" and established a number of comic vehicles in which he was, according to his contemporaries, unsurpassed.

During 1838 and 1839 he worked as principal low comedian and stage manager for J. W. Wallack, Sr., at New York's National Theatre until Wallack abandoned theatrical management after his theater was destroyed by fire on 28 September 1839. On 9 December 1839 Mitchell began his management of New York's Olympic Theatre. Recruiting a company initially composed primarily of the remnants of Wallack's troupe, Mitchell rapidly made the previously unsuccessful Olympic the city's most popular theater. The playhouse, located at 444 Broadway halfway between Howard and Grand streets in what was then the center of the city, was less than half the size of the city's two leading theaters, the Park and the Bowery. From almost the outset of his tenure as manager, Mitchell relied exclusively on his stock company rather than hiring expensive touring stars as his competitors had done since the end of the War of 1812. Moreover, Mitchell specialized in short, light comic entertainment, providing his audiences with three to four short pieces nightly, many of which were hilarious topical burlesques that lampooned virtually everything of passing import to his fellow New Yorkers. During eleven seasons Mitchell staged thirty-two topical burlesques that ridiculed subjects ranging from the affectations of the English tragedian William Charles Macready and the phenomenal international popularity of the German ballerina Fanny Ellsler to the rival claims of the "hard" and "soft" money men during the national elections of 1840.

In addition to operating New York's most financially successful theater during the depressed decade of the 1840s without stars, Mitchell made other farsighted and innovative changes in managerial policy that later became normative. Since the days of Shakespeare, English-speaking acting companies had relied on the tradition of lines of business. Members of a company played a narrowly specific range of roles in all plays and complained loudly if they were cast outside of that range. Mitchell abolished this time-honored practice. Actors in his employ were contractually obliged to perform any role he assigned to them. Relying on the efforts of a resident company and abolishing lines of business led George Odell to credit Mitchell with developing "the first distinctive stock company of modern times in New York."

After his inaugural season as the Olympic's manager, Mitchell hired primarily young, inexperienced performers and was instrumental in developing their talents, making him the New York theater's first starmaker a quarter of a century prior to Augustin Daly. Because he did not pay the lavish salaries that traveling stars demanded, he was able to spend more on physical production. New scenery and costumes for most of his productions made his theater unusual, and contemporary press accounts are lavish in their praise of the physical aspects of the theater's productions. It was Mitchell's scene painter, Richard Bengough, who first reproduced well-known locations in the city as part of his scenery. Mitchell's careful attention to his repertory, development of his acting company, and attention to scenic detail suggest that the phrase "produced under the direction of Mr. Mitchell," which appeared at the head of the Olympic's playbills, was no mere boast. He was in many ways America's first modern theater director. Additionally, he was an early force in the development of local-color realism prior to the Civil War with his production of *A Glance at New York in 1848*, with the then stock actor F. S. Chanfrau as the Bowery B'hoy hero "Mose."

Throughout most of the 1840s, Mitchell's was the only theater in New York to consistently show a profit. His health began to fail in 1847, the result of either a heart attack or a mild stroke precipitated by both his gustatory personal habits and his exhausting work schedule. Thus in 1848 William E. Burton was able to lure many of Mitchell's actors to his new managerial venture at the Chambers Street Theatre. Burton's theater, initially using both many of the personnel and types of entertainment the Olympic had made famous, rapidly eclipsed the ailing Mitchell's theater.

Mitchell abandoned his management of the Olympic on 9 March 1850. In spite of having earned a profit of more than $10,000 annually during the entire decade of the 1840s, he was penniless when he died in New York City.

• The New York Public Library for the Performing Arts, Lincoln Center, holds clippings on Mitchell and the Olympic, as well as numerous illustrations and photographs of his roles and productions. The Harvard Theatre Collection contains clippings, contract books between Mitchell and his actors from 1843 to 1845, and a complete file of playbills for the entire history of Mitchell's management of the Olympic. See also David L. Rinear, *The Temple of Momus: Mitchell's Olympic Theatre* (1987), George C. D. Odell, "Some Theatrical Stock Companies of New York," *Theatre Annual*, vol. 9 (1951), pp. 7–26, and Claudia D. Johnson, "Burlesques of Shakespeare: The Democratic Americans' 'Light Artillery,'" *Theatre Survey* 21 (1980): 49–62.

DAVID L. RINEAR

MITCHELL, William (24 Feb. 1801–6 Oct. 1886), lawyer and jurist, was born in New York City, the son of Edward Mitchell, a Universalist minister, and Cornelia Anderson. Mitchell received his preparatory education at the school of a blind teacher, Joseph Nelson. In 1820 he graduated with high honors from Columbia College, especially excelling in mathematics and classics. Mitchell delivered a Latin commencement oration, "De Julii Caesaris vita et nece," and enjoyed the study of Greek and Latin for the remainder of his life.

Mitchell studied law in the office of William Slosson and was admitted in stages to the various New York common law and equity bars between 1823 and 1827. In 1832 he published an edition of Sir William Blackstone's important *Commentaries on the Laws of England*, annotated with American cases and citations for American practitioners. Apparently unwilling to acknowledge his editorship publicly, Mitchell attributed the work merely to "A Member of the New York Bar." Blackstone's eighteenth-century *Commentaries* was for decades a crucial work for the new American legal profession. Annotations such as Mitchell's provided lawyers and judges in the United States an opportunity to build gradually a distinctively American legal foundation rooted in English common law rather than attempting a radically different approach to jurisprudence.

After practicing law in New York, Mitchell began his New York judicial career in 1840, when he was made master in chancery. In 1841 he married Mary Penfold Berrien of New York City. They had at least six children. He was elected justice of the state supreme court (the trial court for New York) for the first judicial district in 1849. In 1854 Mitchell became presiding justice of the supreme court and continued in that position until he retired in 1858, although in 1856 and 1857 he also sat as a member of the New York Court of Appeals, the highest court in the state. Mitchell was so well-regarded by attorneys as a judge that after his retirement from the bench he was often chosen by litigants to referee important cases. He received an honorary LL.D. from his alma mater, Columbia College, in 1863.

Mitchell served two terms as vice president of the New York State Bar Association. At his death at the home of a son in Morristown, New Jersey, Mitchell was said to be the oldest member of the New York bar.

Mitchell's career as a trial and appellate judge in the nation's most populous and commercially important state alone would earn him a certain distinction in American legal history. Add to that his annotation of Blackstone's *Commentaries*, and he must be regarded as a significant participant in the formative decades of New York's modern law.

• Memorials of Mitchell appear in the 1887 *Report* of the Association of the Bar of the City of New York and in the general minutes of the New York Supreme Court for the October general term, 1886. Obituaries are in the *New York Times* and the *New York Evening Post*, both 7 Oct. 1886.

FRANCIS HELMINSKI

MITCHELL, William Lendrum (29 Dec. 1879–19 Feb. 1936), army officer, commonly known as "Billy," was born in Nice, France, the son of John Mitchell, a U.S. senator from Wisconsin, and Harriet Danforth Becker. Three years after his birth, Mitchell and his family returned to their estate at "Meadowmere" near Milwaukee. After a brief period of private tutoring, Billy spent six years in an Episcopalian prep school—Racine College of Wisconsin. Tired of Racine's strict discipline, Mitchell transferred before his final year to Columbian Preparatory school in Washington D.C. In the fall of 1895, he entered the college division of Columbian Prep (now George Washington University).

In 1898 Mitchell served in the infantry as a private during the Spanish-American War and later received a commission in the Signal Corps as a second lieutenant. During his tenure in the Signal Corps, he served in Cuba, the Philippines, and Alaska. While in Alaska from 1901 to 1903, Mitchell and the Signal Corps helped end Alaska's isolation by laying a seventeen-hundred–mile telegraph line. Back stateside in 1903, Mitchell met Caroline Stoddard and married her that December. They had three children. He graduated with distinction from the Army Command and General Staff College in 1909. He divorced his first wife in 1922. The next year he married Elizabeth Trumbull, with whom he had two children.

Mitchell was assigned to the aviation section of the Signal Corps in 1915 and soon became one of the outstanding combat air commanders of World War I. At the battle of Saint-Mihiel in September 1918, he commanded a French-U.S. air armada of some fifteen hundred airplanes, the largest concentration of allied air power during the war. By striking first, he quickly gained air superiority over a German air force of 243 planes. In the Meuse-Argonne campaign the same year, Mitchell deployed as many as two hundred airplanes in bombing formations to strike and soften enemy positions for allied ground attacks. In recognition of his service during the war, he received the Distinguished Service Cross and the Distinguished Service

Medal, in addition to the *Croix de Guerre* and other foreign honors.

After World War I, Mitchell was appointed assistant chief of the Army Air Service. From his experience in World War I, he knew that air power would forever change the face of war. He used his new position to argue for the importance of air power, emphasizing the need for unified control of an independent air force. He also advocated the development of an Alaskan air base, arguing that it would put U.S. planes within easy operating distance of "all the vital centers of the United States and of Eastern Asia, including Japan," which he already saw as a potential enemy. To support his public statements that airplanes had made battleships obsolete, in July 1921 he conducted a test bombing mission that sank the ex-German battleship *Ostfriesland* off Hampton Roads.

The army general staff and the navy strongly opposed Mitchell, and he soon became an outspoken critic of the entire military hierarchy. At the end of his term as assistant chief in April 1925, he was ordered to Fort Sam Houston in San Antonio, Texas, then a remote army post, as punishment for his public demonstrations and remarks and to remove him from public attention. Nevertheless, Mitchell continued his criticism, and after the loss of the navy dirigible *Shenandoah* in a violent storm in September 1925, he accused the War and Navy departments of "incompetency, criminal negligence, and almost treasonable administration of the national defense." As a result, he was court-martialed and found guilty of insubordination. General Douglas MacArthur presided over the trial. Mitchell was demoted to colonel and sentenced to five years' suspension of rank and duty. He resigned from the army in February 1926. He died in New York City.

Mitchell was influenced by General Gulio Douhet, an Italian aviator who, in several books and articles, advocated a separate and independent air force consisting of both military and civilian airplanes. Douhet also advanced the idea of producing a super plane that could carry a huge payload and defend itself against enemy fighters, making fighter escorts unnecessary. The purpose of these bombers would be to saturate designated areas, destroying not only strategic targets, but also the enemy's will to fight.

Mitchell's importance in aviation history lies in his efforts to advance Douhet's theories of military air power in an era when few people saw the true capabilities of concerted attacks from the air and the devastating effects of strategic bombing. He is the best-known and earliest U.S. Army officer to advocate a separate air force and an increase in the military understanding of aviation tactics. To further his pursuit of an independent air force, Mitchell published three books: *Our Air Force* (1921), *Winged Defense* (1925), and *Skyways* (1931).

Unfortunately, Mitchell died before World War II, during which his prophecies concerning strategic bombing, mass airborne operations, the emergence of Alaska and the polar region as strategic military areas, and the eclipse of the battleship by the airplane were fulfilled. In 1946, in recognition of his work toward the establishment of a separate air force, he was posthumously awarded the Congressional Medal of Honor. The importance of strategic bombing and the use of air power in the 1991 war in the Persian Gulf further confirmed his position. He remains the person most quoted at military academies and professional schools on the subjects of strategic bombing and the employment of air power.

• Papers and letters pertaining to Mitchell are in the Air Force Historical Archives at Maxwell Air Force Base in Alabama, the Office of Air Force History in Washington, D.C., and the Archives of the Air and Space Museum at the Smithsonian Institution in Washington, D.C. Alfred Hurley, *Billy Mitchell: Crusader for Air Power* (1964), is an important source. The most complete modern assessment is Anthony Sommer, "Billy Mitchell: Aviation's Prophet," *American History Illustrated* 8 (1974): 32–43. See also Roger Burlingame, *General Billy Mitchell, Champion of Air Defense* (1952); Emile Gauvreau and Lester Cohen, *Billy Mitchell, Founder of our Air Force and Prophet without Honor* (1942); and Isaac Don Levine, *Mitchell, Pioneer of Air Power* (1943). Other sources are Timothy E. Kline, "Where Have all the Mitchells Gone," *Air University Review* 4 (1982): 28–31; Fred S. Roach, "Reality Revisited: Will Rogers' Support of Military Aviation," *Military History of the Southwest* 1 (1990): 43–60; and George Hall, "When Honor Conflicts with Duty," *Air University Review* 6 (1980): 45–60; Robert S. Egan and Richard M. Anderson, "S.M.S. *Ostfriesland*," *Warship International* 2 (1975): 113–54; and Melody Webb, "Billy Mitchell and the Alaska Telegraph," *American History Illustrated* 9 (1986): 22–25. An obituary is in the *New York Times*, 20 Feb. 1936.

DONALD GOLDSTEIN

MITCHILL, Samuel Latham (20 Aug. 1764–7 Sept. 1831), physician, scientist, and legislator, was born in Hempstead, Long Island, New York, the son of Robert Mitchill, a farmer and overseer of highways, and Mary Latham. He learned the fundamentals of medicine from his uncle Dr. Samuel Latham, who also underwrote the cost of his nephew's education. Mitchill served as a medical apprentice for Dr. Samuel Bard in New York City between 1781 and 1783. He then proceeded to more formal study at the University of Edinburgh in Scotland, receiving his M.D. with honors there in 1786.

Following the customary grand tour of Europe, Mitchill returned to New York and received an honorary M.A. from Columbia College in 1788. He began practing medicine that same year, and soon afterwards he began to study law with Robert Yates, then the chief justice of New York State. He was appointed to a state commission that was directed to study the purchase of lands from the Iroquois Indian Nation in 1788. He was elected to the first of three separate one-year terms in the New York State Legislature in 1791, serving in 1792; his other two terms were served in 1798 and 1810. During his second term Mitchill was successful in securing exclusive rights to steamboat experimentation in the waters of the state for Robert Fulton and Robert Livingston.

In 1792 Mitchill began a fifteen-year tenure as professor of natural history, chemistry, and agriculture at Columbia College. There he lectured on botany, zoology, and mineralogy, and he began a lifelong practice of collecting, identifying, and classifying many species of flora and fauna, particularly aquatic organisms. He personally collected specimens in his native state and along the Atlantic coast as far south as Virginia. In 1807 he began teaching at the College of Physicians and Surgeons in New York, first as professor of chemistry (1807–1808), then as professor of natural history (1808–1820), and subsequently as professor of botany and materia medica (1820–1826). With several associates, notably David Hosack, J. W. Francis, W. J. MacNeven, and Valentine Mott, Mitchill then left the College of Physicians and Surgeons and organized the short-lived Rutgers Medical College of New Jersey; he served as its vice president from 1826 to 1830.

While at Columbia, Mitchill taught the then-new antiphlogistic chemistry of Lavoisier. He served as mediator between pro- and anti-Lavoisier groups in the United States and became involved in a controversy with the prophlogistic Joseph Priestley. In 1801 Mitchill published *Explanation of the Synopsis of Chemical Nomenclature and Arrangement*, which was an attempt to defend and organize pro-Lavoisier chemical understandings and to end the controversy. In the process he developed his own fallacious "septon" theory of disease, in which he argued that disease-carrying fluids formed from oxygen and nitrogen compounds might be prevented and eradicated with the use of "anti-septic" alkalis such as lime, soda, and potash. This concept was the basis of Mitchill's promotion of personal hygiene and better sanitation. In concert with Elihu H. Smith and Edward Miller, Mitchill instituted and edited the *Medical Repository* (1797–1820), the nation's first medical journal, in which many of Mitchill's articles on medicine and natural history were published.

In 1796 Mitchill carried out a mineralogical survey of the Hudson River basin under the aegis of the Society for the Promotion of Agricultural Arts and Manufactures of New York. This study provided the basis for his *Sketch of the Mineralogical and Geological History of the State of New York*, published between 1798 and 1801. In 1814 he published his *Discourse Embracing a Concise and Comprehensive Account of the Writings Which Illustrate the Botanical History of North and South America*, an effort to organize all that was then known concerning the plant life of the Western Hemisphere. His "Fishes of New York" (*Transactions of the New York Literary and Philosophical Society* 1 [1815]: 355–92) was recognized by contemporary observers as a major contribution to ichthyology. He maintained correspondence with other contemporary American natural scientists, including John James Audubon, William Cooper, Constantine S. Rafinesque-Schmaltz, and Alexander Wilson.

In his political outlook, Mitchill was a Jeffersonian Republican who strove to reform working conditions of sailors in the U.S. Navy, attempted to strengthen quarantine laws, and sought ways to prevent American shipping from the depredations of Tripolitan Pirates. He also offered the secretary of the navy technical assistance in a variety of areas, including the protection of naval property, the manufacture of gunpowder, and the health of sailors. He served in the House of Representatives from 1801 to 1804 and from 1810 to 1813, and he was a U.S. senator from 1804 to 1809. His political expertise was such that Thomas Jefferson referred to him as the "Congressional Dictionary."

Mitchill was a prolific author of periodical literature on a wide range of subject matter, notably natural history, geology, and chemistry. His 200 biological articles embraced such topics as Galapagos tortoises, the fish of New York, and Spanish chestnuts. These not only appeared in his own *Medical Repository*, but also in the *American Monthly Magazine and Critical Review* and the *American Journal of Science*.

Mitchill also authored books on cultural and political subjects, including *Life, Exploits and Precepts of Tammany, the Famous Indian Chief* (1795), *A Tour through a Part of Virginia in the Summer of 1808* (1809), *Address at the Completion of the Erie Canal*, of which Mitchell was a vigorous champion (1825), and *Discourse on the Character and Services of Thomas Jefferson, More Especially as Promoter of the Natural and Physical Sciences* (1826). Mitchill also edited new or American editions of works written by European and American authors, notably Thomas Bewick's *A General History of Quadrupeds* (1st American ed., 1804), to which he added notes concerning American species; Erasmus Darwin's *Zoonomia, or Laws of Organic Life* (1806); and William Philips's *Elementary Introduction to the Laws of Mineralogy* (1818). His essay, "Observations on the Geology of North America" appeared in the American edition of Georges Cuvier's *Essay on the Theory of the Earth* (1818).

Mitchill was secretary of the American Philosophical Society of Philadelphia (1797), and he was elected president of the Society for the Promotion of Agricultural Arts and Manufactures of New York (1797) and the American Mineralogical Society (1799). In 1814 he was a founder of both the New York Literary and Philosophical Society and the Lyceum of Natural History of New York (later the New York Academy of Sciences). He was for several decades a physician on the staff of the New York Hospital, was appointed surgeon general of the New York State Militia (1818), and was elected president of the New York State Medical Society (1821).

Once described as a "chaos of knowledge," Mitchill was generally more admired for his encyclopedic breadth of understanding than for much originality of thought. An affable person, he was sometimes criticized for being egotistical and pedantic. He was unusually responsive when asked to speak on scientific subjects and placed a priority on making scientific knowledge generally available to the public and in promoting the practical applications of scientific inquiry.

Mitchill had married Catherine Akerly Cock, a wealthy widow, in June 1799. They had no children but adopted two daughters. Mitchill died in Brooklyn, New York.

• Mitchill's papers are in the Osgood papers, Miller papers, and Miscellaneous Manuscripts at the New-York Historical Society. Mitchill's handwritten natural history lectures are in the Morton Pennypacker Long Island Collection, Gardiner Memorial Room, East Hampton (N.Y.) Free Library, and his notes on botany and materia medica lectures are in the Thomas A. Brayton Papers, New York Public Library. Some of Mitchill's letters to his wife while he was in Congress are in the library of the Museum of the City of New York. Letters to Thomas Jefferson are in the Jefferson papers, Manuscript Division, Library of Congress. An incomplete list of Mitchill's scientific papers is in vol. 4 of the *Catalogue of Scientific Papers (1800–1863)*, published by the Royal Society of London in 1879. Mitchill's autobiography is *Some of the Memorable Events and Occurences in the Life of Samuel L. Mitchill of New York from 1786 to 1826* (1826). Biographical studies include Alan David Aberbach, *In Search of an American Identity: Samuel Latham Mitchill* (1988); Courtney Robert Hall, "An American Scientist: Samuel Latham Mitchill" (Ph.D. diss., Columbia Univ., 1933); Hall, "Samuel Latham Mitchill: A Queens County Polymath," *New York History*, Apr. 1933; and Hall, *A Scientist in the Early Republic: Samuel Latham Mitchill* (1934, repr. 1968). See also Félix Pascalis-Ouvière, *Eulogy on the Life and Character of the Hon. Samuel Latham Mitchill* (1831); John Wakefield Francis, *Reminiscences of Samuel Latham Mitchill* (1859), reprinted in S. D. Gross, *Lives of Eminent American American Physicians and Surgeons* (1861); and E. F. Smith, *Samuel Latham Mitchill: A Father of American Chemistry* (1922), reprinted from the *Journal of Industrial and Engineering Chemistry*, June 1922. Other useful sources include H. L. Fairchild, *A History of the New York Academy of Sciences* (1887), and George B. Goode, *The Beginnings of American Science: The Third Century* (1888).

KEIR B. STERLING

MITROPOULOS, Dimitri (1 Mar. 1896–2 Nov. 1960), conductor, pianist, and composer, was born in Athens, Greece, the son of Jean Mitropoulos, a leather merchant, and Angeliki Anagnostopoulos. He was musically precocious and began to play the piano at the age of seven. He studied at the Athens Conservatory of Music, where Ludwig Wassenhoven taught him piano and Armand Marsick taught him composition. After fighting on the Bulgarian front during World War I, Mitropoulos returned to the conservatory and graduated in piano in 1918 and in composition in 1920. During these early years Mitropoulos composed several songs to Greek and French texts, a symphonic poem entitled *La mise au tombeau de Christ* (1916), and the opera *Soeur Béatrice*, based on Maeterlinck's play. The rest of his early musical training took place outside Greece. He received a government grant to study composition with Paul Gilson in Brussels and composition and piano with Ferruccio Busoni in Berlin.

Mitropoulos worked as a rehearsal pianist at the Berlin Staatsoper during the early 1920s. Conductor Erich Kleiber promoted him to assistant conductor, and Mitropoulos learned his craft from working in the opera house and from watching Kleiber, Leo Blech, Wilhelm Furtwängler, Bruno Walter, and Richard Strauss conduct. In 1925 Mitropoulos became conductor of the Athens Concert Society orchestra. Two years later he was appointed conductor of the State Symphony Orchestra of Greece, and in 1930 he was named professor of composition and conductor of the orchestra at the Athens Conservatory. His reputation soon spread. His most important composition, *Concerto Grosso*, was premiered in 1929. He conducted in Berlin and Paris in the early 1930s. In 1934 he toured Italy, France, Belgium, Poland, and Russia. Mitropoulos conducted an annual series of concerts in Monte Carlo from 1934 until 1937. By then he had settled into a conducting career and had virtually abandoned composition.

Mitropoulos made his greatest impact as a conductor in the United States. His American debut occurred on 20 January 1936, when he appeared as guest conductor of the Boston Symphony Orchestra at the invitation of its conductor, Serge Koussevitzky. In 1937 Mitropoulos succeeded Eugene Ormandy as the music director of the Minneapolis Symphony Orchestra; he remained there until 1949. His programs there included classical and early romantic works, but he was most interested in presenting contemporary scores by Arnold Schoenberg, Alban Berg, Ernst Krenek, and radical American composers such as Roger Sessions. He championed Gustav Mahler's music and in 1940 received the American Mahler Medal of Honor for his work in promoting the composer. In 1946 Mitropoulos took up American citizenship. He greatly improved orchestral standards in Minneapolis but resigned from his position because of clashes with management, who wanted more traditional programs.

In 1949–1950, Mitropoulos shared a season with Leopold Stokowski as conductor of the New York Philharmonic Orchestra. In 1951–1952 he was appointed music director of the orchestra. He continued in that position until the 1957–1958 season, when he was listed equally with Leonard Bernstein as principal conductor. Mitropoulos was much admired in New York by the musical vanguard for presenting difficult contemporary music. He was especially renowned for his performances of late romantic and modern works such as those by Richard Strauss, Mahler, Anton Bruckner, and the composers of the Second Viennese School. He toured Europe and Latin America with the Philharmonic in 1955 and 1958, respectively. During the 1950s Mitropoulos was also active in opera, conducting at the Metropolitan Opera, La Scala (Milan), the Maggio Musicale (Florence), and the Salzburg Festival. He died in Milan during a rehearsal of Mahler's Third Symphony with the La Scala orchestra.

Mitropoulos had a remarkable photographic memory and, in his earlier years, was a brilliant pianist. He always conducted without a baton and was prone to shouts and wild hysterical gestures on the podium, as if he were possessed by the music. Dedicated to his art, he felt a burning mission to present highly complex modern scores to the musical public, and he sometimes neglected and became bored with more standard repertoire. He gave the premieres of Paul Hindemith's Symphony in E-flat, Aaron Copland's *Statements for Orchestra*, Krenek's Third Piano Concerto, and Samuel Barber's opera *Vanessa*.

The grandson of a priest and the grandnephew of an archbishop, Mitropoulos was a devout member of the Greek Orthodox church. Early in his career he had considered joining a monastic order. He admired St. Francis of Assisi, lived simply, and was a sincere, kind, and generous man. Discreetly homosexual, he never married and sired no children. He worked for the Red Cross during World War II and used his money to pay for extra rehearsals of modern pieces and to help musicians in financial difficulty. He was the person who first urged Leonard Bernstein to take up conducting, and the two became lifelong friends. Instantly recognizable by his tall figure, bald head, and piercing eyes, Mitropoulos's kindness with musicians and absorption in the complexities of contemporary music got the better of him. During his tenure at the New York Philharmonic, he was heavily criticized for allowing lax discipline among the players, as well as coarseness of tone and poor intonation.

Mitropoulos made many recordings, especially for the Columbia label. He recorded works such as Peter Mennin's Third Symphony, Leon Kirchner's Piano Concerto, Sessions's Second Symphony, Schoenberg's *Verklaerte nacht*, and Vaughan Williams's Fourth Symphony. He also recorded several operas, including Verdi's *Un ballo in maschera*, Mussorgsky's *Boris Godunov*, and Berg's *Wozzeck*. His recordings were always individual and interesting, but only those recorded live truly capture the intensity that characterized his performances. As a memorial after his death, the Dimitri Mitropoulos International Competition for Conductors was established for young conductors up to the age of thirty-three. It is still held annually in New York.

• Manuscript scores of works by Mitropoulos are kept in holograph in the Gennadius Library, Athens; microfilms are available at the New York Public Library for the Performing Arts, Lincoln Center. There are also some manuscripts of Mitropoulos's deposited at the National Theater, Athens. A comprehensive biography is William R. Trotter, *Priest of Music: The Life of Dimitri Mitropoulos* (1995). Some of Mitropoulos's letters and a list of his compositions are in *Dimitri Mitropoulos–Katy Katsoyanis: A Correspondence, 1930–1960* (1973). For interviews with Mitropoulos, see Henry Marx, "A Life for Modern Music," *Music News* 41 (Jan. 1949): 3, 49; and Dimitri Mitropoulos, "The Conductor Speaks," *Opera News* 19, no. 9 (3 Jan. 1955), and "The Making of a Conductor," *Etude*, Jan. 1954. Mitropoulos wrote introductions to Louis Biancolli and Herbert F. Peyser, *Masters of the Orchestra* (1954), and Olin Downes, *Ten Operatic Masterpieces* (1952). His career is appraised in Donald Brook, *International Gallery of Conductors* (1951); Howard Taubman, "Mitropoulos, Unpredictable Maestro," *House & Garden*, Oct. 1952; Roland Gelatt, *Music Makers: Some Outstanding Musical Performers of Our Day* (1953); Hope Stoddard, *Symphony Conductors of the U.S.A.* (1957); David Wooldridge, *Conductor's World* (1970); Maria Christopoulou, *Dimitri Mitropoulos: His Life and Works* (1971); David Ewen, *Musicians Since 1900* (1978); John K. Sherman, *Music and Maestros: The Story of the Minneapolis Symphony Orchestra* (1952); Howard Shanet, *Philharmonic: A History of New York's Orchestra* (1975); Apostolos Kostios, *Dimitri Mitropoulos* (1985); and Ekkehard Pluta, "Der Dirigent Dimitri Mitropoulos: Augenblicke der Wahrheit," *Fono Forum*, May 1990. Mitropoulos's recordings are discussed in John L. Holmes, *Conductors on Record* (1982), and are listed in Stathis Arfanis, *The Complete Discography of Dimitri Mitropoulos* (1990). A tribute to Mitropoulos is in the *New York Times*, 3 Nov. 1960.

KENNETH MORGAN

MITSCHER, Marc Andrew (26 Jan. 1887–3 Feb. 1947), naval officer, was born in Hillsboro, Wisconsin, the son of Oscar August Mitscher, a store manager, and Myrta V. Shear. The family relocated to Oklahoma City, where Mitscher's father served as mayor and Indian agent. Mitscher attended schools in Washington, D.C., and in 1906 he received appointment to the U.S. Naval Academy. His performance was mediocre—he graduated 108th in the 1910 class of 131—but after two years of sea duty be became an ensign, on 7 March 1912. The following year he married Frances Smalley of Tacoma, Washington; they had no children. Mitscher served on a variety of warships, including the battleships *Colorado*, *South Dakota*, and *California*, before advancing to lieutenant (junior grade) in 1915. That year he volunteered for flight training at the Pensacola Naval Air Station and received pilot's wings as aviator No. 33 in June 1916. Over the next forty-one years, Mitscher became indelibly identified with American naval aviation, of which he helped lay the foundation. He spent World War I commanding naval air stations at Montauk Point, Long Island, and Miami, Florida, rising to lieutenant commander in July 1918. The following May Mitscher piloted *NC-1*, one of three giant Curtiss seaplanes attempting the first transatlantic flight. Fog detained him at the Azores, but determined flying nevertheless won him a Navy Cross. By February 1919 he was posted to the aviation section of the Office of the Chief of Naval Operations.

Mitscher functioned in this capacity until September 1919, when he joined the Pacific fleet aboard the aircraft tender *Aroostook*. Between 1919 and 1922 he also commanded at the San Diego Naval Air Station. From May to November 1922 Mitscher directed the Anacostia Naval Air Station near Washington, D.C., before transferring to the Plans Division of the Naval Bureau of Aeronautics. He then led a team of navy pilots participating in the International Air Races at Detroit in 1922 and at St. Louis the following year. In May 1926 Mitscher reported to the experimental carrier *Langley* and further honed his skills in air operations. In 1927 he became executive officer on board the *Saratoga*, the first U.S. warship designed specifically as an aircraft carrier. In October 1930 Mitscher was promoted commander and returned to the Naval Bureau of Aeronautics for three years. He assumed command of the tender *Wright* in 1937, rose to captain in 1938, and until 1939 directed operations of Patrol

Wing One. In 1939 Mitscher returned to the Bureau of Aeronautics as assistant chief and on 20 October 1941 received appointment as captain of the newly commissioned carrier *Hornet.*

Mitscher was active throughout the Pacific war and emerged as a leading exponent and practitioner of naval aviation. In April 1942 the *Hornet* served as the base from which Colonel James H. Doolittle's raiders bombed Tokyo and four other Japanese cities. Two months later Mitscher's air groups fought brilliantly at the decisive battle of Midway and helped sink four Japanese carriers. In July he advanced to rear admiral and, following a brief stint with Patrol Wing Two at Hawaii, assumed control of Allied airpower during the closing phases of the Guadalcanal campaign. By April 1943 Mitscher was leading a mixed force of army, navy, marine, and New Zealand airpower, which covered Allied advances through the Soloman Islands. His force is credited with sinking seventeen Japanese vessels and downing 470 aircraft, including a bomber carrying Admiral Isoroku Yamamoto, commander in chief of the Combined Fleet. In August 1943 a respite was conferred when he took control of air fleet elements along the West Coast.

Mitscher resumed sea duty in January 1944, commanding the Fast carrier Task Force of the Central Pacific. This armada was alternatively known as Task Force 58 or Task Force 38, depending on whether it functioned under Admiral William F. Halsey's Third Fleet or Admiral Raymond A. Spruance's Fifth Fleet. In the spring, Mitscher conducted operations against the Marshall Islands, Truk, and Tinian and Saipan in the Marianas. Promoted to vice admiral, he distinguished himself during the 19–21 June battle of the Philippine Sea, the so-called "Marianas Turkeyshoot," whereby 400 Japanese aircraft were destroyed at a loss of sixteen aircraft.

The most-celebrated event of Mitscher's career occurred on the night on 20 June 1944, when he disregarded submarine threats and turned on all ship lights to enable weary pilots to safely land. Task Force 58 subsequently supported amphibious operations in the Bonin Islands and at Mindanao in the Philippines, and also launched airstrikes against the Ryukyus. Mitscher again distinguished himself during the 23–26 October battle of Leyte Gulf, where some of the last remaining warships of the Imperial Japanese Navy were sunk. From January to May 1945, Task Force 58 bombarded Iwo Jima and Okinawa and also launched the first carrier-based air raids against the Japanese mainland since the 1942 Doolittle raid. Though severely lashed by kamikaze attacks, Mitscher's force scored its last notable victory on 17 April 1945 by sinking the redoubtable superbattleship *Yamato.* In the course of these final operations, the Americans also sustained tremendous damage, and Mitscher was forced to transfer his flag to other vessels no less than three times.

Shortly before hostilities concluded, Mitscher returned to Washington to serve as deputy chief of operations in the Navy Department. He remained there until March 1946, when he achieved the rank of four star admiral. Mitscher was commander of the Eighth Fleet, headquartered at Norfolk, Virginia, until 20 September 1946, when he became commander in chief of the Atlantic Fleet. He held this position until his death at Norfolk by coronary thrombosis. He was interred at Arlington National Cemetery.

Mitscher proved himself a pivotal figure in the annals of U.S. naval history. He became associated with naval aviation in its infancy and guided its tactics and technology for nearly four decades. His labors were instrumental in elevating the aircraft carrier from an experimental novelty to the centerpiece of American naval doctrine. Every facet of naval aviation, from dive-bombing and combat air patrols to deckhandling, fell within his purview. Quiet and unassuming, Mitscher was an offensive-minded commander who always strove to take combat to the enemy, wherever he could be found.

• Mitscher's official correspondence is in the Naval Records Department of the National Archives, Washington, D.C. Large collections of personal papers are at the Manuscript Division, Library of Congress, and the State Historical Society of Wisconsin, Madison. The only reliable biography remains Theodore Taylor, *The Magnificent Mitscher* (1954). Briefer but still informative are Arleigh Burke, "Marc Mitscher, a Naval Aviator," *Proceedings of the United States Naval Institute* 101 (1975): 53–63; Paolo E. Coletta, "Admiral Marc A. Mitscher, U.S.N.: A Silhouette," *American Aviation Historical Society Journal* 38, no. 1 (1993): 66–74. His early exploits are amply covered in Richard K. Smith, *First Across! The U.S. Navy's Transatlantic Flight of 1919* (1973), and George Van Deurs, *Wings for the Fleet* (1966). For detailed discussion of Mitscher's wartime endeavors see Clark G. Reynolds, *The Fast Carriers* (1978), and Joseph Bryan and Philip Reed, *Mission beyond Darkness* (1945).

JOHN C. FREDRIKSEN

MITTY, John Joseph (20 Jan. 1884–15 Oct. 1961), Catholic prelate, was born in Greenwich Village, New York City, the son of John Mitty and Mary Murphy. Mitty's mother died in 1894, as did his father in 1898, leaving Mitty an orphan at the age of fourteen. He attended St. Joseph's Grammar School, De La Salle High School, and Manhattan College, all in New York City, graduating from the latter in 1901. The same year he entered St. Joseph's Seminary in Dunwoodie, New York, to study for the priesthood for the Archdiocese of New York. He was ordained a priest on 22 December 1906 by Cardinal John Farley at Dunwoodie. He then pursued graduate studies at the Catholic University of America, where he received a bachelor of sacred theology in 1907. The following year he studied in Rome, where he received a doctorate in sacred theology from the Lateran Seminary (1908). Mitty also completed additional study in psychology at the University of Munich during the summer of 1908.

In 1909 Mitty returned to New York, where he served for a brief time as assistant pastor at St. Veronica's Church before being appointed to teach dogmatic theology at his alma mater, St. Joseph's Seminary. His eight-year tenure as professor there ended in 1917 with the outbreak of World War I. Mitty left the seminary faculty to serve as a military chaplain to the 49th and 101st regiments of the U.S. Army at Camp Merrit, New Jersey, and in France, where he participated in the famed Meuse-Argonne offensive. Following the war, in 1919, he was appointed pastor of Sacred Heart Church in Highland Falls, New York, where he served until 1922, when he was appointed pastor of St. Luke's Church in the Bronx. On 21 June 1926 Pope Pius XI named Mitty bishop of Salt Lake City, Utah. He was consecrated at St. Patrick's Cathedral in New York by Cardinal Patrick Hayes and was installed in Salt Lake on 7 October. For six years Mitty labored in the Mormon heartland, struggling to place the diocese on firm financial standing, which he did, and stepping up evangelism efforts by revitalizing the diocesan newspaper, the *Intermountain Catholic*, and by sponsoring radio talks. In January 1932 Mitty was appointed coadjutor archbishop of San Francisco with the right of succession. He succeeded Archbishop Edward Hanna upon Hanna's resignation on 2 March 1935 and was invested with the pallium on 4 September 1935. Mitty would continue to serve as archbishop until his death.

Mitty's episcopate began when San Francisco, jolted by a general strike the previous year, along with the rest of the nation, remained mired in the Great Depression. His administration spanned World War II, during which time San Francisco served as a major debarkation point for American servicemen and as the site of the initial meeting of the United Nations, and culminated during the explosive population growth that began during the war, stretching finally into the postwar era, when California was well on its way to becoming the most populous state in the union. Mitty's thirteen-county archdiocese grew from 405,000 Catholics in 1935 to 1,125,000 in 1961. Despite the challenge posed by such numbers, Mitty ushered in what many consider to be the golden age of Catholicism in the San Francisco Bay area. Mitty responded to the rapid growth by creating eighty-five new parishes, by sponsoring 563 major building projects, and by overseeing the massive growth of Catholic schools, religious education programs, and charitable organizations.

Though regarded as a stern, aloof man, Mitty was an able administrator and financial genius whose qualities sharply contrasted with those of his predecessor, Hanna, who was widely regarded for his kind, loving demeanor, but who was a poor administrator. Mitty effectively organized and centralized the administration of the archdiocese, streamlining and energizing the church's bureaucratic agencies. He also revolutionized archdiocesan finances. Mitty was one of the national pioneers in the creation of a central archdiocesan banking system, a system in which parishes that had previously established their own bank accounts were required to deposit all surplus funds with the archdiocesan chancery. Consequently, all parish loans had to be obtained through the archdiocesan bank, thus giving the archbishop a better understanding and some control over the entire financial situation of the archdiocese as a whole. The central banking system is now standard in most dioceses throughout the United States.

Mitty's greatest achievement, however, and the one in which he took the most pride, was the creation of a highly motivated and well-trained diocesan clergy, which Mitty asserted was the equal of any religious order of priests. During Mitty's episcopate, clerical morale reached an all-time high. Priests chosen to head archdiocesan agencies were first sent to pursue postgraduate studies at the Catholic University of America in Washington, D.C., along with various other schools, to assure that they were well trained in their fields. Various agencies of the archdiocese, especially the different branches of Catholic Charities and the Catholic Youth Organization, were the beneficiaries of this policy. Though seemingly authoritarian, Mitty was an able delegator, providing ample support with a minimum of meddling to the leaders he had placed in charge. Mitty also encouraged specialized, innovative apostolates, most significantly the Spanish Mission Band—a group of priests freed from parochial duties in order to minister to the bracero and migrant workers in the fields of California. From this program emerged Cesar Chavez, Dolores Huerta, and the United Farmworkers movement.

Mitty, as a result of his tenure in Salt Lake City, was especially sensitive to ecumenical issues. He fought to make the experience of marriage between Catholics and non-Catholics more dignified and less opprobrious to the non-Catholic party. At the national level, he eventually succeeded in establishing the practice of allowing such marriages to occur within the parish church. Mitty also succeeded in creating a positive, dynamic archdiocese in San Francisco. Beset by a variety of illnesses his last few years, he spent much of his time at St. Patrick's Seminary in Menlo Park, California, where he died.

• Mitty's personal papers are housed in the Archdiocesan Archives of the Archdiocese of San Francisco, Menlo Park, Calif. A biographical article is Walter Tappe, "Our Archbishop," *San Francisco Monitor*, 4 Sept. 1953. Obituaries appear in the *San Francisco News Call Bulletin* and the *San Francisco Examiner*, both 16 Oct. 1961.

JEFFREY M. BURNS

MIX, Edward Townsend (13 May 1831–23 Sept. 1890), architect, was born in New Haven, Connecticut. His father was a ship's navigator who left his trade for farming in 1836, when he purchased a large farm at Andover in western Illinois and moved his family there. In 1845 they moved to New York City. Three years later, it is believed, young Mix began an apprenticeship with Richard Upjohn, a major midcentury American architect who pioneered a historically accurate Gothic Revival style and led in the founding of the American Institute of Architects in 1857.

Mix went to Chicago in 1855 and in the next year located in Milwaukee, where he practiced briefly in partnership with prominent Chicago architect William W. Boyington before establishing his own independent practice in 1857. He associated with Boyington again in 1866 in an unsuccessful attempt to obtain the Kansas Capitol commission and, at various times, with several other architects who appear to have influenced the designs of many of his buildings. From 1874 to 1879 he was Wisconsin state architect in charge of construction of state buildings, and from 1882 to 1889 he practiced in partnership with Walter A. Holbrook, who had been his employee. Mix moved to Minneapolis in 1889, where he died. His wife, Mary Hayes of New Haven, was a relative of President Rutherford Hayes.

During Mix's professional career, Milwaukee's population increased more than two and a half times. Starting as a trade center and Great Lakes port of around 45,000 people, the city prospered through railroad building, increases in hinterland wheat production, and Civil War profiteering to become a major midwestern commercial center of some 120,000 people. Mix's practice grew along with the city, of which he was the leading architect for a number of years. Through his training with Upjohn and his own membership in the American Institute of Architects, he was identified as a professional of the highest level, in contrast to the prevalent self-trained carpenters of the times who called themselves architects and usually functioned as builders. During the third quarter of the century, he was one of only four professional architects in the city. In his last years he was president of the Wisconsin Architectural League.

Mix designed in the many architectural styles of his time. Among his homes for wealthy Milwaukee families, the Matthew Kennan house (1860), the Alexander Mitchell house (early 1870s), and the Judge Jason Downer house (1874) followed the Italian villa, the French Second Empire, and the Victorian Gothic styles, respectively; and "Montauk" (1874) in Clermont, Iowa, followed the Italianate style. The National Soldiers' Home in Wood, Wisconsin, begun in 1868, was one of the first institutions of its type. It followed the Victorian Gothic style. He designed several Milwaukee churches, among them St. James' Episcopal Church (1867–1868); Olivet Congregational Church (1868–1869), which became All Saint's Episcopal Cathedral in 1872; Immanuel Presbyterian Church (1873–1874); and St. Paul's Episcopal Church (1883). The earlier churches followed the Gothic Revival style. The last was in a modified Richardsonian Romanesque style, as was his design of the Milwaukee, Chicago and St. Paul Railroad Depot (1886). This was a common style in the last two decades of the nineteenth century. Two important commissions came through wealthy businessman Alexander Mitchell: the Mitchell Building (1876–1878) and the Chamber of Commerce (later the Mackie) Building (1879–1880) next to it, landmarks of their time that followed, respectively, the Second Empire and Italianate styles. His largest building was his last, the twelve-story Guaranty Loan (Metropolitan) Building in Minneapolis (1888–1890), which featured a full-height, glass-roofed central court.

Mix's significance in midwestern architectural circles lay in his thorough professional competence, ranging from his command of architectural styles to the ability to solve complex problems of construction and engineering. He always practiced as a trained professional according to the standards of the American Institute of Architects, founded in New York in 1857, the same year in which he began independent practice in Milwaukee.

• Biographies of Mix appear in Alexander Carl Guth, "Early Day Architects in Milwaukee," *Wisconsin Magazine of History* 10 (Sept. 1926): 17–28; *Dictionary of Wisconsin Biography* (1960), p. 257; and Richard W. E. Perrin, *Milwaukee Landmarks* (1968), p. 15. The last also provides photographs and information on Mix's buildings, as do Perrin, *The Architecture of Wisconsin* (1947), and Perrin, "Richardsonian Romanesque in Wisconsin" and "Wisconsin's Victorian Houses," *Wisconsin Magazine of History* 45 (Winter 1961–1962): 95–98, and 45 (Summer 1962): 290–95. Additional sources on Mix's buildings are Randy Garber, ed., *Built in Milwaukee* (1983); Henry-Russell Hitchcock and William Seale, *Temples of Democracy* (1976); Wesley I. Shank, *The Iowa Catalog: Historic American Buildings Survey* (1979); Donald D. Torbert, "The Advent of Modern Architecture in Minnesota," *Journal of the Society of Architectural Historians* 13 (Mar. 1954): 18–23; and H. Russell Zimmermann, *Magnificent Milwaukee* (1987).

WESLEY IVAN SHANK

MIX, Tom (6 Jan. 1880–12 Oct. 1940), cowboy and motion picture star, was born Thomas Hezikiah Mix in Mix Run, Pennsylvania, the son of Edwin Elias Mix, a teamster in the lumber industry, and Elizabeth Smith. When Tom was eight, his father moved the family to DuBois, Pennsylvania, where the elder Mix took a job as stableman and chauffeur for the wealthy John E. DuBois family. It was in DuBois that Tom, who quit school after the fourth grade, developed an interest in his father's work, especially the handling of horses. The locals would frequently comment that "Tom learned to ride anything that could walk." This early experience laid the foundations for the trick riding and roping that was to become an integral part of Mix's identity as a western film star.

On 26 April 1898, one day after war was declared against Spain, eighteen-year-old Mix enlisted in the army. He was assigned to Battery M, Fourth Regiment, of the U.S. Artillery, in Delaware. Although he never saw combat, Mix received several promotions and was honorably discharged at the rank of first sergeant on 25 April 1901. Almost immediately, Mix reenlisted and was assigned to Fort Hancock, New Jersey. There, in 1902, Mix married Grace I. Allin, a schoolteacher he had met while visiting friends in Norfolk, Virginia. Their marriage was annulled the following year; they had no children. Grace is frequently cited as the reason Mix failed to return from a furlough in October 1902. He was listed as absent without leave and later as a deserter. Unsure of his status with the army, Mix left the East Coast to pursue his longtime fascination with the West. In 1902 he and his wife moved to Guthrie, Oklahoma, where for the next three years Mix held a variety of jobs, including drum major of the Oklahoma Calvary Band, bartender, law enforcement officer, and ranch hand. In later years movie studios would exploit Mix's experiences in Oklahoma for the purpose of establishing him as a "real" western cowboy.

In 1905 Mix accepted a full-time job with the famous Miller Brothers 101 Real Wild West Ranch near Bliss, Oklahoma. The 101 was both a working ranch and an entertainment center. There was a Wild West show performed on the grounds, and the movie industry frequently used the ranch for location shooting. Mix's outgoing personality landed him the responsibility of greeting and coordinating the activities of the ranch's eastern visitors. However, his riding and roping skills would eventually catch the eye of those from the film industry. Mix seemed completely content with his life at the 101, but Kitty Perrine, his wife, whom he had married in 1905, was not. She divorced him in 1906; they had no children. In 1909 Olive Stokes, whom Mix had met at the 1904 World's Fair, became his third wife. They would have a daughter.

Mix became involved in the film industry in 1909 after W. A. Dickie, an employee of the Chicago-based Selig Polyscope company, visited the 101 Ranch. Dickie initially hired Mix to locate stock and wranglers for Selig's western films. However, before completing his first full month at Selig, Mix had already been given a small part in the film *The Range Riders* (1909), and he later starred in the semidocumentary *Ranch Life in the Great Southwest* (1910). In the film Mix is shown bulldogging steers and performing other ranch-related activities. This tough cowboy image, combined with Selig's promotion of him as a U.S. marshal (not exactly accurate), firmly established Mix's identity as a natural for western films. William Selig was so impressed with Mix's on-screen performance that he advanced him $250 to put together his own film unit. The unit's first assignment was in Florida, where Mix was given supporting roles in a series of jungle pictures with Selig's top female star, Kathlyn Williams, including *Back to the Primitive* (1911) and *Hearts of the Jungle* (1915).

In 1913 Mix moved to Prescott, Arizona, to work at Selig's Diamond S Ranch. Selig wanted to give Mix his own series, but before making the final decision Selig decided to test him in two special productions. First, Mix appeared in a three-reel version of Peter Kyne's *Chip of the Flying U* (1914). This was followed by a five-reel feature, *In the Days of the Thundering Herd* (1914). Selig considered both of Mix's performances successes and soon offered him his own series.

The first film in the Tom Mix series was the single-reeler *The Real Thing in Cowboys* (1914). With little interference from Selig, Mix went about assembling his own production unit consisting of Hoot Gibson, Leo Maloney, and close friend Sid Jordan, among others. By 1915 Mix and his unit were rapidly turning out two-reelers for Selig. However, a dispute over production costs between Mix and the company eventually led Mix to sign with William S. Fox in 1917. He also made changes in his personal life that year by divorcing his third wife. Five years later he married his Fox costar Victoria Forde, with whom he had a daughter in 1922.

While working for the Fox company, Mix perfected his brand of western film. He combined good looks, fancy boots, and a ten-gallon hat with his skills as a trick rider and roper to produce action-packed stories. It was a formula that proved extremely popular with young and old alike. Throughout the 1920s Mix and his horse, Tony, would play to packed theaters around the country.

When the talkies came in the late 1920s, Mix, like many other stars of the silent era, found himself facing an uncertain future. Rather than make any immediate decisions, Mix dropped out of motion pictures for approximately two years. During this period, he toured with the Sells-Floto Circus as its main attraction, performing roping and horseback-riding stunts. After divorcing his fourth wife in 1930, Mix married Mabel Hubbell War, an aerial performer with the circus, in 1932; they had a daughter. He also returned to the big screen that year in such features as the original *Destry Rides Again*, *Rider of Death Valley*, and *My Pal, the King*. These films proved moderately successful for Mix, but he would never again attain the stature he had as a silent-film star. After 370 productions and a career that spanned twenty-four years, Mix retired in 1932. He returned three years later to make his last feature, *The Miracle Rider* (1935). Following his retirement from the film industry, he formed his own touring circus and Wild West show and took part in several international rodeos.

Mix died from injuries suffered in a one-car accident near the city of Florence, Arizona, and was buried in Forest Lawn Memorial Park in Los Angeles. His close friend Gene Autry commented, "Tom Mix contributed a great deal to the betterment of the American cowboy and cowboy sports" (*New York Times*, 13 Oct. 1940). In fact, Mix was one of the few western "cowboys" whose career encompassed motion pictures, Wild West shows, rodeos, and circuses.

• The Tom Mix Museum is located in Dewey, Okla. Mix's personal writings include *Tom Mix, My Life Story* (1925) and "How I Was Roped for the Pictures," *Ladies Home Journal*, Mar. 1927. The most thorough biography is Paul E. Mix, *The Life and Legend of Tom Mix* (1972). Another source of information about Mix is Elinor Hughes, *Famous Stars of Filmdom (Men)* (1932). Obituaries are in the *New York Times* and the *New York Herald Tribune*, both 13 Oct. 1940; *Variety*, 16 Oct. 1940; *Motion Picture Herald*, 19 Oct. 1940; and *Newsweek*, 21 Oct. 1940.

GINGER CLARK

MIZENER, Arthur Moore (3 Sept. 1907–11 Feb. 1988), biographer and educator, was born in Erie, Pennsylvania, the son of Mason Price Mizener and Mabel

Moore. The Mizener family came to America from Germany in the second half of the nineteenth century. Mizener's grandfather had a coal company and at one point was mayor of Erie. Mizener's father ran the company for some years before he had a nervous breakdown. The family was comfortably well off and part of the small-town aristocracy of Erie. Mizener graduated from Princeton University in 1930 and earned his M.A. in 1932 at Harvard University. In 1934 he received his Ph.D. from Princeton and also began teaching at Yale. In July 1935 he married Elizabeth Rosemary Paris, with whom he had two children.

In 1940 Mizener became an assistant professor at Wells College in Aurora, New York, and four years later was promoted to associate professor. In 1945 he went to Carleton College in Northfield, Minnesota, where he was later promoted to full professor and chairman of the English department. In 1951 he became Mellon Foundation Professor of English at Cornell University, where he remained until his retirement in December 1975.

Mizener's first book was a catalog of first editions of Archibald MacLeish prepared for an exhibition of MacLeish's works at Yale University Library in 1938. His second work, *The Far Side of Paradise* (1951), the first full-length study of F. Scott Fitzgerald's life, established his reputation as one of the finest literary biographers of the twentieth century. Mizener had first read Fitzgerald's *This Side of Paradise* as a sixth grader at Hill School in Pottstown, Pennsylvania, and began dreaming about Princeton. As an undergraduate at Princeton, he often frequented a classmate's room because it supposedly had been Fitzgerald's. In his first year of teaching, Mizener read *Tender Is the Night* and said he was "haunted by it." Mizener began writing about Fitzgerald in an article entitled "Scott Fitzgerald, Poet of Borrowed Time" for Willard Thorp's volume of biographies of Princetonians, *The Lives of Eighteen from Princeton*. Soon after Mizener published biographical and critical essays about Fitzgerald for *Sewanee Review, Partisan Review, Furioso*, and the *Kenyon Review*.

In preparation for writing *The Far Side of Paradise*, Mizener examined Fitzgerald's manuscripts, correspondence, scrapbooks, and ledger and interviewed his friends, relatives, and associates. Mizener argued that Fitzgerald was a writer of outstanding power, not just a producer of slick fiction or the Jazz Age laureate whose talent quickly deteriorated in the 1930s. While covering the more harrowing aspects of Fitzgerald's life, Mizener emphasized Fitzgerald's artistry and thoughtfully evaluated his accomplishments and aspirations. He thus treated Fitzgerald as a major writer worthy of close study. On a personal level Fitzgerald in Mizener's view was a divided man: handsome and talented on the one hand but lacking in self-confidence and wary of others on the other. Fitzgerald's attitude toward money exemplified his dualism to Mizener. Fitzgerald often owed money but was surprised by the magnitude of his indebtedness, and he put his talent to work for money so that he could participate in a life of wealth with those whom he did not trust. Mizener claimed that Fitzgerald's best work resulted from the tension between his two sides: Fitzgerald could experience "luxuriant emotion under strict discipline."

In the early part of the biography, Mizener focused on Fitzgerald as a young man rather than as a writer-in-embryo. Covering Fitzgerald's later life, Mizener discussed his novels thoroughly. He did, however, omit some information, including Fitzgerald's dying in his lover Sheilah Graham's home, in order to protect her from scandal. In later works Mizener decided to be more forthcoming about events that he thought he had covered inadequately. *The Far Side of Paradise* received generally favorable reviews, was condensed in *Atlantic Monthly*, and became a bestseller. It remained the standard biography of Fitzgerald for over thirty years. After completing *The Far Side of Paradise*, Mizener edited Fitzgerald's writings, collected critical essays on him, and wrote his own critical analyses of Fitzgerald's work.

Though his greatest accomplishment was as a chronicler of Fitzgerald's life and rescuer of Fitzgerald's artistic reputation, Mizener also enjoyed teaching. He was assistant to the chief reader in English for the College Entrance Examination Board from 1955 to 1960; he was a Fulbright lecturer in American Studies at King's College, University of London, in 1955–1956; and he wrote several texts for college students and teachers. Of his teaching he once said, "I'm an impassioned teacher. I love teaching. . . . [it] is not deadening. I get interested in many things. Teaching drives you if you take it seriously, and it makes you more productive. . . . My self-starter is almost always teaching something."

In the early 1960s Mizener began work on his second major biography, this time of Ford Madox Ford. Ford's literary executor, Janice Biala, gave her collection of Ford's papers to Cornell University so that Mizener could use them easily. The Cornell library also had the Violet Hunt and Stella Bowen papers, which contained important information on Ford, and Mizener also consulted Edward Naumburg's private collection of Ford material. *The Saddest Story: A Biography of Ford Madox Ford* (1971) took six years to complete. Using similar analytic techniques, Mizener posited that Ford, like Fitzgerald, had a dual nature. Ford was both a poet who longed to live the uncomplicated life of an English gentleman and at the same time a critic of human foibles. Mizener recognized that Ford's life was the sad story of a gifted man frustrated by his own defects of character.

The reviews of *The Saddest Story* were favorable, though the book did not become a bestseller. Like *The Far Side of Paradise, The Saddest Story* soon became the standard biography of its subject because of its exhaustive examination of a complex figure. Both of Mizener's biographies led to greater valuing of the literary excellence of the two writers, but *The Far Side of Paradise* and the subsequent work that Mizener did on Fitzgerald remains his most important achievement. Mizener died in Bristol, Rhode Island.

Mizener had an analytical mind and demonstrated meticulous attention to detail. It was important to him to separate the men he wrote about from the legends that surrounded them by attention to demonstrable fact. While fascinated by the psychology of the two writers and their tendencies toward self-destruction, Mizener emphasized the quality of their work independent of the nature of their lives. He had sharp analytical powers, which he tried to pass on to students in widely used college texts such as *Modern Short Stories: The Uses of Imagination* with its accompanying guide, *A Handbook of Analyses, Questions, and a Discussion of Technique for Use with Modern Short Stories: The Uses of the Imagination* (1962, rev. 1966, repr. 1979). Mizener's legacy lies in securing Fitzgerald's reputation as a major American author, in providing models for carefully crafted literary biographies, and in helping generations of students and readers to appreciate close and critical reading of literature.

• Mizener's materials on Fitzgerald are at the Princeton University library. A draft of *The Far Side of Paradise* with comments by Edmund Wilson and the correspondence between Mizener and Wilson on Fitzgerald can be found at the University of Delaware library. Correspondence on and the typescript for *The Saddest Story* are located in the Ford Madox Ford Collection, Cornell University. Other works by Mizener not mentioned above include *F. Scott Fitzgerald: A Biographical and Critical Study* (1958); *The Cornell Joyce Collection, Given to Cornell University by William G. Mennen* (1958); *The Sense of Life in the Modern Novel* (1964); *Twelve Great American Novels* (1967); and *Scott Fitzgerald and His World* (1972). He also edited *Reading for Writing* (1958); *F. Scott Fitzgerald: A Collection of Critical Essays* (1963); *The Fitzgerald Reader* (1963); Anthony Trollope's *The Last Chronicle of Barset* (1964); and *Teaching Shakespeare* (1969). The original review of *The Far Side of Paradise*, with information about its writing, appeared in the *New York Times*, 28 Jan. 1951. Obituaries of Mizener are in the *New York Times*, 15 and 16 Feb. 1988, and *Newsweek*, 29 Feb. 1988.

ANN W. ENGAR

MIZNER, Addison Cairns (12 Dec. 1872–5 Feb. 1933), architect, was born in Benicia, California, the son of Lansing Bond Mizner, an attorney, and Ella Watson. His father, who supported Benjamin Harrison (1833–1901) for the presidency in 1888, was appointed American minister to the five Central American republics and moved the family to Guatemala City the following year. In 1890 Mizner studied for a year at the University of Salamanca in Spain, which deepened his appreciation for Spanish art and architecture and prompted his choice of a career. After apprenticeship with San Francisco architect Willis Polk, Mizner opened a small architectural office in New York City in 1904.

From the first, Mizner was determined to become a society architect with ambitions of designing country houses for the wealthy. Through childhood friends from San Francisco, the young architect received the introductions and made the social contacts necessary to build his New York practice. In 1907 Mizner gained his first major commission, the completion of a partially built townhouse in the city. Over the next ten years the architect's projects included country houses in Connecticut, and Dutchess County and Long Island in New York. For Mizner this was stylistically an eclectic period as he produced Japanese houses and gardens, Norman mansions, and his first Spanish villas. It was also a period of growth in which his tightly contained, almost academic houses gave way to the randomly massed and romantic Spanish buildings for which he became known. By the time Mizner arrived in Palm Beach, Florida, in January 1918, he had established himself in society and built a successful career.

Mizner lived in the home of Paris Singer, who decided to build a hospital for shell-shocked soldiers of World War I. Singer asked Mizner to design a building that could be used for a private club after the war. The building, completed in January 1919, after the war had ended, became the Everglades Club. It opened as one of America's most exclusive clubs, with members drawn from the resort's wealthiest visitors.

Club members now called upon Mizner to design "cottages" for them in the resort. Between 1919 and 1925 the architect completed nearly forty large Palm Beach villas for the leading society figures of the town, including Edward T. Stotesbury, the brothers Charles and Gurnee Munn, Harold S. Vanderbilt, Rodman Wanamaker, Angier Duke, Edward Shearson, Preston P. Satterwhite, Joshua Cosden, John S. Phipps, and George Mesker. These villas, and commercial structures such as the Via Mizner and Via Parigi, the Plaza Building, Mizner Plaza, and the Singer Building, assured Mizner's position as the area's leading architect and established a new style of architecture for South Florida.

Mizner's Palm Beach buildings, with their handmade red-tile roofs, rough textured stucco walls, restrained decorative detail, and rambling plans, introduced a new form of Mediterranean architecture to Florida that drew upon the traditions of Spain, Venice, and northern Africa. He also exploited the Palm Beach climate by the extensive use of windows and doors. Mizner's rooms opened to broad terraces overlooking the ocean or Lake Worth and to private patios and secluded courts. His Palm Beach work made Mediterranean architecture fashionable in the resort. Moreover, it set the style for architecture in Florida for the 1920s.

The Florida land boom, with its attendant stories of gigantic profits made by early investors, led Mizner to announce in April 1925 his Boca Raton project, with plans for an oceanfront hotel. When he and a group of associates acquired 16,000 acres of land with two miles of beachfront, the very size of the undertaking made it one of the largest of the Florida boomtime developments. In less than a year, Mizner's company sold over $30 million in real estate and began construction of a small lakefront inn, two administration buildings, and twenty-nine small houses. Unfortunately, before these structures were completed, the land boom in Florida ended and Mizner's company went bankrupt. Later Clarence Geist, the Philadelphia utilities magnate, purchased Mizner's holdings and, after enlarging the hotel, opened it as the Boca Raton Club.

Although Mizner returned to his Palm Beach architectural office, declining health and changes in fashion reduced his practice. While he continued to design for Palm Beach, his major projects in his last years, such as The Cloister of Sea Island, Georgia, were outside of Florida. Mizner never married. He died in his Via Mizner apartment in Palm Beach after a long illness.

• Office tracings and other Mizner papers and photographs are at the Historical Society of Palm Beach County, as is a copy of the unfinished second volume of his autobiography. The first volume is *The Many Mizners* (1932). *The Florida Architecture of Addison Mizner* (1928; repr. 1992) illustrates most of his Florida building to that date. Christina Orr, *Addison Mizner: Architect of Dreams and Realities (1872–1933)* (1977), is a catalogue for a Norton Gallery show. The story of his life and work can be found in Donald W. Curl, *Mizner's Florida: American Resort Architecture* (1984).

DONALD W. CURL

MOBLEY, Hank (7 July 1930–30 May 1986), jazz musician and composer, was born Henry Mobley in Eastman, Georgia; his parents (names unknown) moved to Elizabeth, New Jersey, in 1932. His parents later separated, and Mobley's father moved to Philadelphia, where he remarried. Hank lived with his mother in New Jersey. An uncle, Danny Mobley, a pianist and bandleader, helped to inspire his musical endeavors and provided him with early instruction in jazz. Mobley learned to play alto saxophone on his own at age sixteen and worked at a bowling alley to earn enough money to buy an instrument. According to noted jazz critic and historian John Litweiler, it was a shop teacher who encouraged Mobley to abandon machinist training and devote himself to music.

Rhythm-and-blues bandleader Paul Gayten selected Mobley in 1949 for his orchestra. In addition to playing alto, tenor, and baritone saxophone, Mobley also wrote for the group. Around this time, he also worked with pianist Walter Davis, Jr., playing tenor saxophone in a house band at a Newark club. Artists such as Billie Holiday, Bud Powell, Miles Davis, and Max Roach performed with the band during Mobley's stint in Newark. It was after Roach's 1951 performance that he hired Mobley as a sideman and brought him to New York, where Mobley achieved immediate success.

Mobley worked with Roach until 1953, during which time he came into contact with musicians such as Charlie Parker, Sonny Rollins, Jackie McLean, Kenny Dorham, and Gerry Mulligan and his first song, "Mobleysation," was recorded by Roach. When Roach's group broke up in 1953, Mobley was not left without playing opportunities. In addition to freelance jobs, he worked with Gayten and, briefly, with Duke Ellington (substituting for Jimmy Hamilton). In the summer of 1953 Mobley worked alongside Clifford Brown in Tadd Dameron's band at the Club Harlem in Atlantic City. It was at this time that Mobley almost became a member of the renowned Brown-Roach Quintet, but Roach, who was in California, was unable to reach Mobley when the historic group was being organized. Later in 1953 Mobley joined Dizzy Gillespie's big band on the recording of two band dates and one sextet date. It was in Gillespie's band that he made the acquaintance of pianist Wynton Kelly and trumpeter Lee Morgan, future sidemen on Mobley's solo sessions for Blue Note.

Mobley began to emerge as one of several recognized successors to Charlie Parker (along with Sonny Rollins, Sonny Stitt, Jimmy Heath, and John Coltrane) on the hard-bop scene. Mobley considered Parker by far the most significant source of inspiration for his style; other musicians who influenced him included Bud Powell, Lester Young, Don Byas, Ben Webster, and Dexter Gordon. A very consistent musician with a preference for the middle register, Mobley reached a maturity of style relatively early in his career. Aspects of his style—and traits that were very much in keeping with that of Parker—included a remarkable mastery of formal structure, a subtle yet complex rhythmic juxtaposition, a highly developed sense of organization within the framework of his solos, and an uncanny knack for presenting original material at unexpected, yet highly effective, moments in his solos, an ability that altered the audience's sense of expectation. Mobley's overall musical expressivity was unparalleled.

Mobley joined hard-bop pianist Horace Silver in late 1953, performing at Minton's Playhouse and recording with the Horace Silver Quintet, which included drummer Art Blakey. Mobley remained with Silver for the next four years, recording several albums with him and forming a new group that included trumpeter Kenny Dorham, Silver, Blakey, and bassist Doug Watkins. Together they decided to establish a cooperative venture called the Jazz Messengers, in which any job that a member got was performed by all of the members of the group, with all proceeds to be divided equally. The first of its kind—later groups included the Modern Jazz Quartet, the Miles Davis Quintet, and the Brown-Roach Quintet—the Jazz Messengers established a structure for performing groups that soon became standard among jazz musicians. Mobley performed with the group until 1957; it was to be his crowning achievement in ensemble work.

During the period 1954–1956, Mobley also recorded a great deal of material for solo albums, much of which he composed. These albums are considered by many to contain the best playing of his career. The labels on which Mobley recorded these solo albums included Prestige, Savoy, and Blue Note, the last of which maintained a long-standing relationship with Mobley. From late 1956 to mid-1958 Mobley recorded ten solo albums and performed on twelve more. By this time, however, he was addicted to heroin, which significantly interfered with his playing; although he remained prolific, the quality of his playing generally was not as strong as it had been previously.

Mobley's career was interrupted in 1959 by a drug conviction and one-year prison term. Following his release in 1960, he returned to Art Blakey's Jazz Messengers, which at that time featured Lee Morgan. Later that year Mobley joined the Miles Davis Quintet, replacing Sonny Stitt. Present on such Davis sessions as *At Carnegie Hall*, *Someday My Prince Will Come*, and *In Person at the Blackhawk*, Mobley recorded with one of the legendary jazz rhythm sections (Wynton Kelly on piano, Paul Chambers on bass, and Philly Joe Jones, Jimmy Cobb, and Art Blakey on drums) as well as one of its greatest artists. Mobley also hired Miles Davis's rhythm section for a series of four solo albums—*Soul Station*, *Roll Call*, *Workout*, and *Another Workout*—also acknowledged to be some of Mobley's best work.

Mobley remained with Davis until 1961. Miles had almost finished his exploration of hard bop by the time Mobley joined the group, and it took little time for Davis to become bored with Mobley's playing. This, combined with the implicit comparisons that were constantly being made between Mobley and his tenor predecessors John Coltrane and Sonny Rollins, had a devastating effect on the sideman. Dejected and discouraged, Mobley returned to drugs and in 1964 was arrested and imprisoned a second time on narcotics charges. Once he was out of prison, Mobley formed another cooperative group with Lee Morgan. In addition, he worked with Kenny Dorham, wrote for Blakey, and freelanced. Mobley recorded eighteen dates for Blue Note from 1965 until 1968, when he was arrested a third time for drugs.

A tour of London in 1967, including a seven-week stay at Ronnie Scott's, was followed by a tour of Europe, which lasted until mid-1970. While in Europe, Mobley performed in Paris—where he wrote a score for a movie set during the French-Algerian War—Munich, and Rome as well as throughout Poland, Hungary, and Yugoslavia. He led a sextet session (*The Flip* [1969; Blue Note]) and played sideman with Archie Shepp for a European label. Among the many musicians with whom Mobley performed are Ben Webster, Kenny Clarke, Ornette Coleman, Johnny Griffin, Steve McCall, Don Byas, and Art Taylor.

Returning to the United States, where jazz was being overshadowed by rock 'n' roll, depressed Mobley, who became addicted to alcohol. Nonetheless, by 1973 he had made twenty-three solo albums, participated as sideman on fifty-six others, and written eighty songs. A brief stay that year in Chicago led to dates with pianist Muhal Richard Abrams, bassist Reggie Willis, drummer Wilbur Campbell, and late-bop trumpeter Frank Gordon. Mobley lived in Philadelphia for the remainder of his life but performed very little after 1975 and was hospitalized periodically in the mid-1970s with tuberculosis. He performed briefly in New York City in 1986 before dying later that year in Philadelphia after a bout with pneumonia.

• John Litweiler's interview, "Hank Mobley: The Integrity of the Artist—The Soul of the Man," *Down Beat* 40, no. 6 (1973): 14–15, 30, is a comprehensive look at Mobley and his music through 1973; Dave Gelly's retrospective in *Jazz Journal International* 39 (Sept. 1986): 23 offers stylistic analysis. See also *Miles: The Autobiography of Miles Davis with Quincy Troupe* (1989) for Mobley's period with Miles Davis and Steve Bloom, "Hank Mobley: Requiem for a Blue Note Heavyweight," *Musician*, Nov. 1986, pp. 19–22, for historical and social context.

DAVID E. SPIES

MODJESKA, Helena (12 Oct. 1840–8 Apr. 1909), actress, was born in Cracow, Poland, the daughter of Jozefa Misel, whose husband, Szymon Benda, a businessman, died ten years before Modjeska was born. Although Modjeska's paternity is not certain, she was called Helena (originally Jadwiga) Opid, after the music teacher Michael Opid, who lived in the Benda home until his death (c. 1847). She was given private lessons in music from the age of four and attended a local convent school until she was fourteen. The Cracow fire of 1850 left the family destitute until they were befriended by Gustav Sinnmayer, a wealthy Austrian who came to live with them. Under his guidance, Helena spent her evenings avidly studying German and dramatic literature. In theatrical circles Sinnmayer used the name Modrzejewski; thus it was as Helena Modrzejewska that she made her theatrical debut in July 1861 at a charity event in the salt-mining town of Bochnia, where Sinnmayer and she had gone to live when it was learned that she was pregnant. They had a son, Rudolph, on 27 January 1861; it is not known whether they ever married. A daughter, Marylka, was born the following year but died at the age of three.

Capitalizing on Modjeska's evident talent, Sinnmayer formed a theater company to tour the provinces under the management of Konstanty Lobojko. Acclaimed for the charm and passion of her acting as well as for a repertoire that reflected Polish nationalist sentiment, Modjeska enjoyed four years on the road in Poland. In 1865 her half brother Felix Benda, a popular actor in Cracow, obtained a place for her with the Cracow theater company, for which—under difficult circumstances—she left Sinnmayer; he died a year or two later.

At the Cracow theater Modjeska was able to extend her dramatic range, taking special pleasure in the chance to perform some Shakespearean roles: Portia, Ophelia, and Hero. In 1866 on a company tour to Poznán, she met Karol Chlapowski, a member of the wealthy Polish aristocracy who had been recently released after twenty-one months in prison for anti-Prussian revolutionary activities. They married on 12 September 1868 despite objections from members of his family, and they defied convention by her continuation of her stage career. On 4 October 1868 she made her Warsaw debut in the difficult role of Adrienne Lecouvreur, the title role in the historical drama by Eugène Scribe; it brought her overnight stardom and the offer of a lifetime contract at the Warsaw Imperial Theatre. She accepted with the proviso that she be allowed to choose six new plays each season to be added to the repertoire.

For eight years Modjeska remained as a leading actress with the Warsaw company and performed 284 different roles, but eventually she longed for greater challenges. When the American actor Maurice Neville visited Warsaw in 1874, he performed Hamlet and Othello in English to her Polish-language Ophelia and Desdemona. So impressed was he by the quality of her acting that he encouraged her to learn English to facilitate touring abroad. The death of her brother Felix in 1875 and her husband's increasing frustrations over political conditions in Poland led to their decision to emigrate. Along with the author Henryk Sienkiewicz and a few other friends, they planned a utopian Polish colony in California. After spending a month in San Francisco, where Modjeska saw performances by Edwin Booth, the group settled on a farm near Anaheim in November 1876.

Modjeska began an intensive study of her great roles in English. By January 1877 she was ready to audition at the California Theatre in San Francisco, where she was granted a one-week engagement, opening with *Adrienne Lecouvreur* on 20 August 1877. Eyewitness accounts testify that she "gripped" audiences "by the heartstrings" (*Fair Rosalind*, p. 94), thus winning an extended run. There she also played Ophelia to the Hamlet of John McCullough, endearing herself to San Francisco's large Polish community by switching into Polish for Ophelia's mad scene. It was McCullough, then managing the California Theatre, who shortened her stage name from Modrzejewska to Modjeska. The American press further dubbed her "Countess," borrowing for her husband the title "Count Bozenta" from another branch of his family.

Modjeska's first American tour began in Virginia City, Nevada, on 23 October 1877. Her repertoire consisted of *Adrienne Lecouvreur*, *Romeo and Juliet*, and *Camille* (*The Lady of the Camellias*). She played Carson City, Reno, Sacramento, San Jose, and various small towns before returning to the California Theatre. Reviews typically praised "her grace of movement, her striking physical expressions of the passions and emotions, and her womanly sensibility" (*San Francisco Call*, 2 Dec. 1877) but expressed reservations about "the mincing of a foreign accent" (*San Francisco Bulletin*, 28 Nov. 1877).

For her New York debut at the Fifth Avenue Theatre on 22 December 1877, Modjeska was rehearsed by Dion Boucicault. On a budget so tight that her husband could not afford to accompany her from the West Coast, she was responsible for providing her own costumes. She opened her run with *Adrienne Lecouvreur*, garnering extravagant praise from the leading critic William Winter, who wrote "that her intonation, gesture, movement and play of countenance were all spontaneous, that even her garments, devised and fashioned in a sumptuous and delicate taste not precedented on a stage in this country, seemed a part of the outgrowth and fragrance of the character, and that all her looks and actions sprung from and crystallized around her condition. The spectator could not know that she was acting; and art, of course, can do no more than to perfect and sustain the illusion which genius creates" (*New York Tribune*, 24 Dec. 1877).

The rapturous critical response to Modjeska's refined and sensitive interpretation of the fallen woman in *Camille* signaled what was to be regarded as one of her greatest roles. Reviewers cited her "subtlety" and "powerful . . . intensity" (*New York Herald*, 15 Jan. 1878). Even the prompter was said to have been so overcome with emotion during her scene with Armand's father in act 3 that he threw down the promptscript, reduced to sobs (Modjeska, *Memories and Impressions*, p. 356). She repeated her triumphs in Philadelphia, Washington, D.C., Baltimore, Boston, and elsewhere, all the while studying hard to improve her English. Following her third successful American season she paid a return visit to Poland, and by giving performances at the Warsaw Theatre from December 1879 to February 1880 she was able to pay the 5000-ruble penalty she had incurred when she broke her contract to leave Poland. Modjeska made her London debut at the Court Theatre on 1 May 1880, triumphing once again. She played two seasons there, then returned to Poland to produce Ibsen's *A Doll's House*, the first of his plays seen in Poland. She also gave the play its first professional American production—retitled *Thora*—at McCauley's Theatre in Louisville, Kentucky, on 7 December 1883; Maurice Barrymore played Torwald. Over the years, Modjeska won her greatest renown as an actress in her favorite roles, the women of Shakespeare: Rosalind, Ophelia, Juliet, Beatrice, Viola, Portia, Queen Katharine. Indeed, when she bought a ranch in El Toro, California, she named it Arden. In the 1889–1890 season she toured with Edwin Booth. When they played in Cincinnati and Booth was asked about Modjeska, he replied: "She is a genius. I learn something from her every day" (*Fair Rosalind*, p. 538).

Modjeska's career was frequently interrupted by ill health, which was exacerbated by the strain of touring, a necessity for a career on the American stage at the time. She longed to return to acting with a resident company in Poland, but the financial burden of supporting her husband and son as well as dependent family members in Poland kept her in the American theater for most of her career. Her husband and son became American citizens on 4 July 1883. His name altered to Ralph Modjeski, her son Rudolph became a civil engineer. Modjeska's nearly three decades on the American stage culminated in a benefit performance arranged for her by the pianist Ignacy Jan Paderewski at New York's Metropolitan Opera House on 2 May 1905. She performed several selections, including scenes as Lady Macbeth opposite James O'Neill. After a final season of touring in 1906–1907, she and her husband moved to a small house on Bay Island in Balboa Bay, East Newport, California, where she died of Bright's disease. Funeral services were held in Los Angeles on 17 July 1909. Her husband later returned her remains to Poland to be buried in Rakowicki Cemetery in Cracow, among her ancestors.

Modjeska had strong facial features, but her stage presence was often described as refined and dainty. According to Charles E. L. Wingate, she gave all her roles "a womanly earnestness, an artistic sincerity, and an aesthetic beauty, that have made them warm, breathing characters of genuine interest and ennobling effect" (*Famous American Actors of To-Day*, ed. Frederic Edward McKay and Charles E. L. Wingate [1896], p. 80). In addition to the accomplishment of an illustrious career as a performer in a language she began to study only in her twenties, Modjeska is remembered for her gracious and womanly refinement and for her emphasis on a classic repertoire, especially Shakespeare, in an era when melodrama dominated the American stage.

• A Modjeska clipping file is in the Billy Rose Theater Collection of the New York Public Library for the Performing Arts. Modjeska's autobiography is *Memories and Impressions of Helena Modjeska* (1910). Many nineteenth-century biographies and journal articles contain spurious details—for example, Jameson Altemus, *Helena Modjeska* (1883). Reliable accounts are Arthur Prudden Coleman and Marion Moore Coleman, *Wanderers Twain: Modjeska and Sienkiewicz: A View from California* (1964), which incorporates material supplied by Modjeska's granddaughter Marylka Modjeska Pattison, and Marion Moore Coleman, *Fair Rosalind: The American Career of Helena Modjeska* (1969). The latter includes a complete listing of Modjeska's known professional performances on the American stage, but omits her two London seasons as well as appearances in Poland and France. A feature article, "Modjeska," by Charles deKay, appeared in *Scribner's Monthly*, Mar. 1879, pp. 665–71, with a follow-up letter of correction from her husband (May 1879). Substantial entries appear in the standard sources. An obituary is in the *New York Times*, 9 Apr. 1909.

FELICIA HARDISON LONDRÉ

MODJESKI, Ralph (27 Jan. 1861–26 Jun. 1940), civil engineer, was born Rudolphe Modrzejewski in Bochnia near Kraków, Austrian Poland, the son of Gustav Sinnmayer Modrzejewski, a theatrical promoter, and Helena Opid, an actress. He attended schools in Kraków until the summer of 1876, when he emigrated to the United States. Modjeski, his mother, his stepfather Karol Bozenta Chaplowski (Modjeski's parents had divorced), and several Polish compatriots ostensibly traveled to Philadelphia to visit the Centennial Exhibition. But, motivated by a desire for independence and escape from the political turmoil in their homeland, they continued westward via the Isthmus of Panama, finally settling in Anaheim, California. There they bought land with the intention of developing a self-sufficient farm.

In the summer of 1877, with the farming venture failing fast, mother and son moved to San Francisco. At that time she was about to make her American stage debut and, in deference to her English-speaking audience, shortened her last name to Modjeska. Her son did likewise, assuming the masculine form Modjeski. Believing that Americans preferred short names, he also Americanized his given name to Ralph. Because he had a facility for languages, he quickly learned English and not only resumed his education, but also worked as his mother's stage manager.

Since early childhood Modjeski had studied the piano and for a time was a fellow student with Ignace Jan Paderewski. There is little doubt that he too could have, with modest effort, become a classical pianist. But he chose instead to become an engineer. Nonetheless, playing the piano remained a part of his daily routine throughout his life.

Having set his goal to become an engineer, Modjeski went to Paris in 1878 to enroll in one of the leading civil engineering schools, the state-run École des Ponts et Chaussées. Although he failed to be admitted, he remained in France for three years to prepare for reexamination. In 1881 he was admitted to the École and four years later graduated at the head of his class with a degree in civil engineering. He then returned to the United States, where on 4 July 1883 he had become a citizen, and embarked on an engineering career in Chicago as an assistant to America's leading bridge designer, George S. Morison.

Modjeski's first work was in connection with the construction of a bridge over the Missouri River at Omaha for the Union Pacific Railroad. During the course of this project his knowledge of the profession was broadened. From 1887 to 1889 he served as a mill and shop inspector. During the following two years he further refined his design and drafting room techniques. While with Morison, his most noteworthy work took place during the construction from 1889 to 1892 of the Mississippi River Bridge at Memphis. He supervised the design and also served as inspector of shop work and assistant engineer of construction.

Leaving Morison's employ in 1893, Modjeski established his own Chicago office as a consulting engineer. He also entered into a partnership with Ernest Nickerson, who had been with the Atcheson, Topeka, & Santa Fe Railroad. They planned to make a specialty of civil engineering in its broadest terms—designing and building railway bridges, viaducts, trestles, and metallic structures. When the partnership agreement expired in October 1894, Modjeski returned to independent practice. In that same year his first major contract placed him in charge of the design, construction, and supervision of a seven-span double-deck railroad and highway bridge across the Mississippi River at Rock Island, Illinois.

Always a supporter of the engineering profession, Modjeski participated in various organizations that promoted the field. In 1899 the Western Society of Engineers made Modjeski chairman of a committee to assemble an exhibit designed to demonstrate American engineering prowess at the world's fair to be held in Paris in 1900. Also in 1899 he served as president of a small group of investors in the less-than-successful Bonanza Cripple Creek Gold Mining Company in Colorado.

From 1898 to 1900 Modjeski was engaged by the Northern Pacific Railway Company to create a series of standard designs for steel railroad bridges. With dramatic increases in the weight of rolling stock throughout the industry, there was an immediate need to replace many of the system's bridges with ones capable of carrying the new heavier loads. These bridges ranged from ten feet to 250 feet in length.

Like most consulting engineers Modjeski found it advantageous to enter into temporary professional partnerships when projects were particularly large or challenging. One of the most significant of these relationships began in 1902 when he joined with Alfred Noble, another leading figure in American bridge engineering. Until 1905 they were retained by the Southern Illinois and Missouri Bridge Company to build a double-track railway bridge over the Mississippi River at Thebes, Illinois. The contract called for them to handle all aspects of the bridge construction, including grading the approaches. With Modjeski as chief engineer, a massive through-truss was, in what was common practice, designed to be pin-connected. Using this method, prefabricated parts were quickly assembled in the field as their joints were linked together by the simple insertion of a pin.

Modjeski's success at Thebes led to contracts for projects in the Midwest and the Northwest, where railroad expansion was most active. From 1905 until 1912 his work included bridges in Bismarck, North Dakota; Portland, Oregon; Peoria, Illinois; and St. Louis, Missouri.

Modjeski established his international reputation in 1908 when he was hired to replace the collapsed cantilever bridge then being erected over the St. Lawrence River at Quebec. To assure that the new structure would be successful, the government of the Dominion of Canada named a three-member board to design the bridge and oversee its construction. Modjeski represented the entire American engineering profession on this board, which also included representatives from Canada and Great Britain. He held this position for the ten years it took to plan and build what became the world's longest cantilever span.

Modjeski was never wedded to a particular type of bridge. His designs ranged from simple steel trusses to cantilevers and movable-type bridges. The Cherry Street Highway Bridge over the Maumee River at Toledo, Ohio, completed in 1915, was his first concrete-arch bridge. In 1929 his steel tied-arch Tacony-Palmyra highway bridge opened to traffic in Philadelphia.

Perhaps the most remarkable work for which Modjeski was responsible was the Philadelphia-Camden suspension bridge across the Delaware River. Begun in 1921 it opened the era of the modern suspension bridge design. It was the first bridge of this type to exceed the span and load capacity of the 1883 Brooklyn Bridge, and as such it was necessary to develop new theories of design and new methods of construction. Modjeski was appointed in 1920 as chairman of the three-member board of engineers that prepared plans and estimates for a bridge that would carry highway, rapid transit, and foot traffic. Completed in 1927, the structure is noted for Modjeski's engineering mastery and its artistic symmetry. It was renamed the Ben Franklin Bridge in 1956.

Work on other record-setting suspension bridges followed. When completed in 1930, the Ambassador Bridge linked Detroit, Michigan, and Windsor, Ontario, Canada. Acting as a consulting engineer, Modjeski reviewed all plans and supervised construction of what was briefly the world's longest suspension bridge. For this project he entered into a partnership with Clement E. Chase, an associate of long standing. Also completed in 1930 was the Mid-Hudson Bridge at Poughkeepsie, New York. To carry out this project Modjeski formed a partnership with Daniel Moran, one of the nation's leading foundation experts. The need for particularly deep foundations on which to build the towers made the choice of someone with Moran's skills essential. This bridge has been cited for the beauty of its gothic-like steel towers.

The Mississippi River had always challenged bridge engineers, and a proposed crossing at New Orleans presented particularly difficult conditions. The low marshy surroundings meant that a bridge high enough to clear river traffic needed extremely long, well-founded approaches. When completed in 1935, the Huey P. Long Bridge accommodated four lanes of highway traffic and two railroad tracks. At the time that it was constructed, the bridge was remarkable for the huge amount of steel in the trusses of its superstructure. Overall the bridge and its approaches measured more than four and one-third miles.

Modjeski's final undertaking was by far his largest and most ambitious project. In 1931 he was appointed chairman of a six-member board of consulting engineers to design the San Francisco–Oakland Bay Bridge. The project was unique in that it provided a highway and rapid-transit crossing over five miles of deep water. The main structure would consist of two separate suspension bridges. The most daring aspect of the design was the use of a common concrete cable anchorage between the two suspended sections. The opposing forces from the massive cables would balance each other in the single modest-size anchorage. Although he had moved to San Francisco to be near the project, failing health had by 1936 forced Modjeski to abandon his role in it. He spent his remaining years in retirement.

Although Modjeski is known primarily for his work on bridges, he was responsible for other structures as well. In 1903 he was called on to plan and build a fireproof warehouse for the federal government at the Rock Island, Illinois, arsenal. He was appointed in 1916 to a three-member commission by the Public Service Corporation of New Jersey to report on the feasibility of a vehicular tunnel under the Hudson at New York City and to prepare preliminary plans and estimates. One of his most unusual projects was the Palace of the Soviets. He entered into an agreement with the government of the Soviet Union in 1934 to prepare a formal design and general plans for a monumental cathedral of sciences and arts proposed to be built in Moscow. Plans called for a space frame structure with a circular colonnaded facade to house an auditorium seating 20,000 people. Designed to be the tallest building in the world, it was to stand some 1,360 feet high, including its 450-foot semidome and

210-foot-tall statue of Lenin. It was not built, however.

Rather than maintaining a permanent staff, Modjeski added assistants, designers, and draftsmen as needed. He was willing to give a good deal of responsibility to young engineers. Perhaps the assistant who would achieve the most fame was Joseph B. Strauss, whom he had hired in 1899. Strauss later designed and built San Francisco's other landmark bridge, the Golden Gate. Modjeski's longest-lasting partnership began in 1924 when he was rejoined by Franklin M. Masters. The firm of Modjeski and Masters included other engineers such as Chase, who became a partner in 1927. Following Chase's death in 1933, Montgomery B. Case, also a co-worker of longstanding, became a principal.

Modjeski wrote numerous professional reports and papers. Although a prolific engineer responsible for as many as fifty major bridges, he was not innovative. His work is noted for its unfailing strength and unencumbered clean lines with an emphasis on purpose. All of his structures embody a clear sense of artistic expression.

Modjeski had married Felicie Benda in 1885 and they had three children. They were divorced on 6 July 1931, and on the next day he married Virginia Mary Giblyn. He died in Los Angeles.

• Modjeski's comments on bridges and other matters can be found in the letterpress books of his office correspondence (1898–1921); these are located in the Division of Engineering and Industry, Smithsonian Institution. Articles in the *Journal of the Franklin Institute* (1913 and 1925) reveal Modjeski's thoughts on large bridge design. Although details of Modjeski's early life are few, some facts may be gleaned from his mother's autobiography, *Memoirs and Impressions of Helena Modjeska* (1910). It lacks candor, however, and is at times embellished. Marion Moore Coleman, *Fair Rosalind: The American Career of Helena Modjeska* (1969), offers facts in a more balanced, albeit brief, discussion. Franklin M. Masters recounts his long-time partner's professional life and accomplishments in a "Memoir of Ralph Modjeski," *Transactions of the American Society of Civil Engineers* (1941). An obituary is in the *New York Times*, 28 June 1940.

WILLIAM E. WORTHINGTON, JR.

MOELLER, Henry (11 Dec. 1849–5 Jan. 1925), third archbishop of Cincinnati, was born in Cincinnati, Ohio, the son of Bernard Drugemöller, a cabinetmaker, and Teresa Witte, both of whom had emigrated from Westphalia, (in what is now Germany) in about 1845. Bernard shortened his surname to Möller, and Henry later began using the more anglicized Moeller. The parents, devout Catholics, were delighted when three of their sons were ordained priests and their daughter entered the Sisters of Charity. Moeller was educated at St. Joseph Parochial School and St. Xavier College in Cincinnati and at the American College in Rome. He was ordained at St. John Lateran in Rome on 10 June 1876.

Two years after his return to Cincinnati, Moeller was appointed secretary to the coadjutor-bishop, William Henry Elder, whom he assisted with the complicated legal and pastoral problems caused by the 1878 financial failure of a private banking enterprise operated by the brother of the previous archbishop, John Baptist Purcell. Depositors sued for the sale of 200 churches and schools in order to recover their money. The courts eventually ruled that these properties could not be sold to pay the creditors; nevertheless, the archdiocese and the venerable Archbishop Purcell were humiliated and distressed by the bankruptcy.

In 1900 Moeller was appointed bishop of Columbus, which also was in such dire financial straits that the dissolution of the diocese was being seriously considered. Within three years Moeller put that diocese on a more solid financial footing, almost erasing its $200,000 debt.

In 1903 Moeller returned to Cincinnati as coadjutor-archbishop to assist the aged and frail Archbishop Elder. After Elder's death the following year, Moeller became the first native archbishop of Cincinnati and the first German-American archbishop of that still largely German city. Although the archdiocese had recovered from its 1878 financial failure, the great growth of the city itself had now slowed, for new railroad centers and the Great Lakes steamships had drawn economic momentum away from the old river cities. Nevertheless, forty-four new parishes were established, a new seminary was built, St. Rita's School for the Deaf was established, and offices of Catholic charities and of superintendent of schools were organized during Moeller's 21-year tenure.

Moeller's most significant innovation may have been in the area of Catholic education. Cincinnati's parishes had already established strong grade schools, but the few Catholic high schools were private schools that charged a tuition only the affluent could afford. In 1921 Ohio passed the so-called Bing Law, which provided that youngsters must remain in school until they graduated from high school or reached the age of eighteen. Moeller was well aware of the lack of free secondary schools in the archdiocese, referring to them as the "missing link" in the Catholic school system. He wished to establish interparochial schools that were "free" in the sense that students would not be charged tuition, because expenses would be shared by all of the parishes in the district that the high school served. Thus a Catholic secondary education would also be available to youngsters from poorer families.

In September 1921 the first interparochial school in the archdiocese opened on Cincinnati's Price Hill and was named Elder High School in honor of Moeller's predecessor. Archbishop John Timothy McNicholas, Moeller's successor in Cincinnati, would build a fine secondary school system on the foundation Moeller had established.

When the United States declared war on Germany during World War I, Archbishop Moeller assisted the process of "Americanizing" the largely German Catholic church of Cincinnati, especially by directing that the parochial school classes be conducted in English.

He died at his residence in the Cincinnati suburb of Norwood.

• Moeller's personal and official papers are located in the Archives of the Archdiocese of Cincinnati. See also John H. Lamott, *History of the Archdiocese of Cincinnati, 1821–1921* (1921).

M. EDMUND HUSSEY

MOELLER, Philip (26 Aug. 1880–26 Apr. 1958), playwright and theater director, was born in New York City, the son of Frederick T. Moeller, a prosperous dealer in yarns, batts, and wicks, and Rachel Kate Phillips. He attended public school in Manhattan, studied at New York University, and by 1905 had earned both his A.B. and M.A. from Columbia University.

As a young bachelor of means Moeller had the leisure to write plays, compose music, and travel extensively in Europe to observe theater practice. In New York City he and his friends organized amateur theatricals that were sponsored by the Ethical Culture Society and the Socialist Press Club.

Moeller's real apprenticeship in the theater, however, began in 1914 when he became deeply involved with the Washington Square Players, a fervent group bent on reforming the crude commercialism that then characterized the American theater. During the three and one-half seasons of the Players' existence, Moeller directed twenty-three plays, including short works of his own published as *Five Somewhat Historical Plays* in 1918. *Helena's Husband*, Moeller's most successful one-act play in this collection, became a staple of amateur performers across the country.

Though devoted to the crusading aims of the Washington Square Players, Moeller was not indifferent to the siren call of the commercial theater. Broadway producer Arthur Hopkins staged his *Madame Sand* in 1917, with the popular Minnie Maddern Fiske in the title role. The prominent actor-manager Henry Miller appeared in Moeller's historical romance *Molière* in 1919. For the most part the critics liked the plays, but they were only moderately successful at the box office. In 1920 Moeller himself directed his next historical comedy, *Sophie*, in which Emily Stevens, a well-known actress, struggled to make herself believable as an eighteenth-century courtesan. On its tryout tour the play shocked some out-of-town critics. In New York it lost money. Mrs. Patrick Campbell, the celebrated British actress, opened his *Madame Sand* in London that same year, a production that both Moeller and the critics found slipshod. It would be the last work from Moeller's pen to be performed professionally.

After the dissolution of the Washington Square Players in 1918, Moeller became a part-owner and member of the board of managers of the Theatre Guild, an organization destined to become one of the most important and influential American theater companies in the period between the two world wars. Though sometimes referred to as the inheritor of the mantle of the Washington Square Players, the Guild was far more successful in developing new audiences for significant plays often neglected by Broadway producers.

From 1919, when Moeller staged its first play, *The Bonds of Interest*, until the reorganization of the Theatre Guild board in 1939, Moeller pursued an extraordinary career as a director, easily ranking among the most distinguished American theater directors of the period. Staging more than sixty-two productions for the Theatre Guild, he was responsible for most of the Guild's successes and, it should be added, not a few of its failures.

In 1934 the press referred to Moeller as Eugene O'Neill's favorite director, for in the years between 1928 and 1932 he staged five out of the six O'Neill dramas produced under Guild auspices: the Pulitzer Prize–winning *Strange Interlude* (1928), *Dynamo* (1929), *Mourning Becomes Electra* (1931), *Ah, Wilderness!* (1933), and *Days Without End* (1934). He directed five revivals of plays by George Bernard Shaw—at the time essential for the financial well-being of the Guild—as well as the world premieres of Shaw's *Back to Methuselah* (1922) and *Saint Joan* (1923) and the American debut of *The Apple Cart* (1928).

Moeller directed for the Theatre Guild original works by a number of emerging American playwrights: Elmer Rice's *The Adding Machine* (1923); Sidney Howard's Pulitzer Prize–winning *They Knew What They Wanted* (1924) and his *Ned McCobb's Daughter* (1926); John Howard Lawson's *Processional* (1925); S. N. Behrman's *The Second Man* (1927), *Meteor* (1929), *Biography* (1932), and *Rain from Heaven* (1934); Maxwell Anderson's *Elizabeth the Queen* (1930) and *The Masque of Kings* (1937); and Philip Barry's *Hotel Universe* (1930). He also directed plays of all varieties from the pens of Jacinto Benevente, A. A. Milne, Luigi Pirandello, Franz Werfel, Sil-Vara, Stefan Zweig, and James Barrie.

Moeller made two motion pictures for RKO-Radio: *The Age of Innocence*, starring Irene Dunne and John Boles, in the summer of 1934, and *Break of Hearts*, with Katherine Hepburn, Charles Boyer, and Jean Hersholt in the spring of 1935. Neither was particularly successful, and Moeller, who chafed under the technical requirements of filmmaking, broke with RKO over the story treatment of a third film he was scheduled to direct the following year.

Moeller rarely theorized about his directing, but when he did he advocated an "inspirational" approach. He wanted, through his own concentration and attention during rehearsal, to become inspired, to become moved by what he saw and heard to fresh insight and energy, developing a creative engagement between himself and his actors. It was a concept suited to the incandescent persona he presented in the rehearsal hall as he reclined on an old steamer chair wreathed in smoke and gestured with a Rooseveltian cigarette holder. But it was also a concept that gave rise to the legend, largely untrue, that Moeller never read a play before rehearsals began.

Motivated by the belief that he was serving the author and not himself or the Guild, Moeller displayed tact and consideration when working with playwrights on scripts he favored. But he eschewed any preplanning on paper. His system worked fairly well with playwrights and actors he knew. It unnerved actors who wanted more certainty in rehearsal and irritated playwrights who thought he was meddling. It failed when he could find nothing inspiring in the frothy comedies he was asked to direct in the late 1930s. During a stormy tryout tour of Behrman's comedy *Wine of Choice* in February 1938, Moeller, frustrated and exhausted, abandoned the cast in Philadelphia.

Moeller's vexation with the *Wine of Choice* experience was but a symptom of the policy disagreements and financial stresses that beset the Guild in the late 1930s. The once-unified managers had become irreconcilably split along the fault lines of temperament. In 1939 Moeller and his friends on the board—Helen Westley, a noted character actress, and Lee Simonson, a prominent scene designer—resigned. Philip Moeller's theater career was over. He would never direct again.

Moeller spent a lengthy retirement in a comfortable apartment overlooking Central Park in the company of his sister Hannah. There were small pleasures: trips to see grandnieces and nephews, days with the piano, evenings with friends playing scrabble and bridge. He and his sister went to the movies often, rarely to the theater. Toward the end of his life he would jocularly complain that the illnesses and pain that beset him were somehow the legacy of the excessive nervous strain of his theater days. He died in New York City almost twenty years after leaving the Theatre Guild.

• Moeller papers and related Theatre Guild material may be found in the Billy Rose Theatre Collection at the New York Public Library for the Performing Arts, Lincoln Center; the Manuscript Division of the New York Public Library; the Theatre Guild Collection at the Beinecke Library at Yale University; and the Hoblitzelle Theatre Arts Library at the University of Texas. Bibliographies may be found in the Ph.D. dissertations of David W. Wiley, "Philip Moeller of the Theatre Guild: An Historical and Critical Study" (Indiana Univ., 1973), and Edmond Lawrence Kiser, "The 'Inspirational' System of Philip Moeller, Theatre Guild Director" (Wayne State Univ., 1981). Dissertations that in part deal with Moeller's career are Mary Hedwig Arbenz, "The Plays of Eugene O'Neill as Presented by the Theatre Guild" (Univ. of Illinois, 1961); Helen Krich Chinoy, "The Impact of the Stage Director on American Plays, Playwrights, and Theatres: 1860–1930" (Columbia Univ., 1963); and Eugene Miller Wank, "The Washington Square Players: Experiment toward Professionalism" (Univ. of Oregon, 1973). Published works that in part focus on Moeller's career are Roy S. Waldau, *Vintage Years of the Theatre Guild, 1928–1939* (1972); and Ronald Harold Wainscott, *Staging O'Neill: The Experimental Years, 1920–1934* (1988).

DAVID WILEY

MOFFAT, David Halliday (22 July 1839–18 Mar. 1911), capitalist and railroad executive, was born in Washingtonville, Orange County, New York, the son of David Halliday Moffat, a farmer and storekeeper, and Katherine Gregg. Moffat went to work at the age of twelve, after only a few years at the local school. He commuted from his home to nearby New York City to work as a messenger for the New York Exchange Bank, where he later became an assistant teller. In 1855 he joined his older brother Samuel in Des Moines, Iowa, where Samuel was a teller in the banking firm A. J. Stevens & Company.

In 1857 Moffat moved farther west to Omaha where he was employed as a cashier at the Bank of Nebraska. He prospered in land speculation in the late 1850s but lost a "paper fortune" when the bottom fell out of the land boom. When the bank closed in 1860 Moffat decided to move to Colorado. He became a partner with C. C. Woolworth, a book dealer and stationer. Woolworth remained in the East as a buyer, while Moffat filled a covered wagon with stationery and books, joined a wagon train, and arrived to set up shop in the booming mining town of Denver in March 1860. His shop was soon selling groceries, eastern newspapers, and wallpaper in addition to books and stationery. Before long the small store also contained a post office and was the agency for the Western Union Telegraph Company. With the business well established, Moffat headed back East. He married his childhood sweetheart, Frances A. Buckhout of Mechanicsville, New York, in 1861. He returned to Denver with his bride. They had one child.

Moffat was a tall, thin youth, weighing no more than a hundred pounds, but his faith and belief in the great future of his adopted town was huge. His Denver store was so prosperous he soon moved to larger quarters. In the mid-1860s Moffat was made the adjutant general of the Colorado Militia. In 1866 he became the cashier of the new First National Bank in Denver. His additional duties kept him busy, and in 1870 he gave up his partnership in the stationery business. Like other leaders in Denver, Moffat believed the future of the area depended on a railroad to the East. When it became clear that the Union Pacific would bypass Denver, he invested in the Denver Pacific, which was completed from Cheyenne to Denver in 1870. Moffat was treasurer, and John Evans was president of the new road.

In the early 1870s both Moffat and Jerome B. Chaffee, the president of the First National Bank, made investments in Colorado mining. Moffat was reported to have invested in more than a hundred mines, some located in Leadville, Creede, Aspen, and Cripple Creek. Moffat invested and traded his mining shares astutely, and soon he was a millionaire. He was territorial treasurer of Colorado from 1874 to 1876. In 1880 Chaffee retired as president of the First National Bank, and Moffat was elected to the presidency, a position he retained until his death. He helped organize the Denver Clearing House in 1885. Until 1902 Moffat was one of the owners of the *Denver Times*, and he was a director and later president of the Denver Water Company, which built the Cheesman Dam, and also a promoter and director of the Central Colorado Power Company.

In his banking and mining affairs Moffat was a shrewd and hard-headed businessman, but he actively sought to serve the best interests of Denver.

In the last thirty years of his life Moffat's greatest interest was in railroads that could serve both Denver and Colorado. Colorado's mines and railroads were closely connected. New railroad lines permitted more mines to open, and the mines provided both rail freight and the money to build more branch lines. Moffat helped finance the short Boulder Valley Railroad. He had a major interest in the Denver, South Park & Pacific, built southwest of Denver, before it was sold to Jay Gould and the Union Pacific in 1880. Moffat also had a minor interest in the Denver and New Orleans, which was being projected by John Evans from Denver south to Texas and the gulf. Moffat's major railroad concern in the 1880s was the Denver & Rio Grande (D&RG) Railway, organized in 1870 by William Jackson Palmer, who built its first line from Denver to Pueblo. By 1881 the narrow-gauge three-foot line was extended into northern New Mexico and had branches reaching Leadville, Gunnison, and Durango in Colorado.

Moffat became a director of the D&RG in 1883 and was president of the line from 1884 to 1886 and from 1887 to 1891. During his years as president he added a third rail to much of the narrow-gauge mileage, permitting the use of standard-gauge trains. He also generally upgraded and improved the entire system. The D&RG directors objected to the costly improvements and also accused Moffat of running the road for the benefit of Denver interests rather than the stockholders. Moffat resigned in August 1891. In the early 1890s Moffat acquired a valuable gold mine at Cripple Creek, on the southwestern slopes of Pikes Peak. He built the forty-mile narrow-gauge Florence & Cripple Creek Railroad, which for a few years carried a profitable freight and passenger traffic. During the 1890s Moffat made investments in the Denver Tramway Company, which built and controlled the extensive Denver streetcar system.

At the turn of the century Moffat was a multimillionaire, a banker who in the depression of the 1890s had saved many other bankers from bankruptcy. He was a power in the local Republican party and a major mining king in the state. He still retained an old dream—to build a railroad directly west from Denver to the coal deposits of western Colorado. In 1902 Moffat organized the Denver Northwestern & Pacific Railway, generally known as the "Moffat Road." The new road would reduce the distance from Denver to Salt Lake City by about 200 miles. Moffat had the support of Denver, but the D&RG was naturally opposed. When he sought money in the East, he was blocked by E. H. Harriman and James J. Hill, who did not want any competition for their own western lines. Depending chiefly on his own money, Moffat built the 211-mile scenic route that crossed the continental divide at 11,600 feet and reached Steamboat Springs in 1908. Steep grades and mountain snows kept the line's traffic very light, and the new line did not prosper. Moffat needed more money to build a two-mile tunnel under the divide. Moffat died while on a trip to New York City to finance the tunnel. After his death the six-mile Moffat Tunnel, at an elevation of 9,100 feet, was opened in the late 1920s. Later, the Moffat Road merged with the D&RG.

• Moffat's career in Colorado is reviewed in Glenn C. Quiet, *They Built the West: An Epic of Rails and Cities* (1965). His years with the Denver & Rio Grande are found in Robert G. Athearn, *Rebel of the Rockies* (1962), and Robert A. Le Massena, *Rio Grande—to the Pacific* (1974). The review of narrow-gauge Colorado lines can be found in George W. Hilton, *American Narrow Gauge Railroads* (1990). Moffat's efforts to build a road west of Denver are described in Edward T. Bollinger and Frederick Bauer, *The Moffat Road* (1962). Obituaries are in the *New York Times* and the *Denver Republican*, both 19 Mar. 1911.

JOHN F. STOVER

MOFFETT, William Adger (31 Oct. 1869–4 Apr. 1933), U.S. Navy rear admiral, was born in Charleston, South Carolina, the son of George Hall Moffett, a partner in one of the city's mercantile firms, and Elizabeth Simonton. The young Moffett graduated from the High School of Charleston and entered the U.S. Naval Academy in 1886. Plagued by health problems, he graduated near the bottom of his class in 1890 and two years later received his commission as ensign. From 1893 to 1895 he toured European waters and the Mediterranean in the cruiser *Chicago*, commanded by Captain Alfred Thayer Mahan. During the Spanish-American War, Moffett served in the armored cruiser *Charleston*, which participated in the capture of Guam and formed part of the American blockading fleet following the battle of Manila Bay. He married Jeannette Beverly Whitton of Kingston, Ontario, in 1902; they had six children.

Having advanced to lieutenant commander in 1905 and commander in 1911, Moffett saw duty as navigation officer in the armored cruiser *Maryland* (1908–1910), as inspector of the Eighteenth Lighthouse District in San Francisco (1910–1912), and as executive officer of the battleship *Arkansas* (1912–1913). He won the Congressional Medal of Honor while in command of the cruiser *Chester* during the American invasion of the Mexican city of Veracruz in 1914. Moffett's service as commandant of the Great Lakes Naval Training Station from 1914 to 1918 gained him administrative experience and exposed him to the potential of aviation. During World War I, he encouraged the formation of aviation instruction programs at the base and, equally important, forged links with members of Chicago's North Shore business elite, who became valuable political allies in the congressional and interservice battles over aviation appropriations. In 1917 he attained the rank of captain.

From December 1918 to December 1920 Moffett commanded the battleship *Mississippi*. On his initiative, the ship was fitted with flying-off platforms, used for the operation of aircraft for gunfire spotting and scouting. The experience with *Mississippi*'s ship plane unit gave Moffett an increased understanding of aircraft operations at sea and brought him into direct contact with officers who were committed to naval aviation. Largely through the influence of pioneer naval aviator Henry C. Mustin, Moffett became director of naval aviation in March 1921 and in July assumed the position of chief of the new Bureau of Aeronautics (BuAer) with the rank of rear admiral. The bureau reflected Moffett's organizational and leadership qualities, becoming a close-knit, informal organization, with emphasis on individual initiative and personal loyalty.

In the summer of 1921, the navy arranged a series of bombing experiments with captured German warships in order to determine their vulnerability to aerial attack. The tests culminated in the sinking of the German dreadnought *Ostfriesland*, convincing Moffett that ships could be sunk by airplanes and that it was imperative to make aviation an integral part of the U.S. fleet. Throughout his first term as chief of BuAer he worked to achieve that end by forcefully advocating the development of the aircraft carrier and a program to equip nearly all battleships and cruisers with catapults and aircraft. Moffett's service as a technical assistant at the Washington Naval Conference in 1921–1922 helped sharpen his focus on the future role of the carrier and fleet aviation.

During this period, Moffett became embroiled in a controversy with General William "Billy" Mitchell and the advocates of a unified air force. In 1925 the navy lost one of its flying boats on a flight from San Francisco to Hawaii and experienced the destruction of the rigid airship *Shenandoah* in a storm over Ohio. Although the aviators on the Hawaii flight were subsequently rescued, fourteen airmen lost their lives in the *Shenandoah* crash. Mitchell used the disasters as evidence of the need for a separate air service and criticized the naval leadership for "criminal negligence" in ordering the Hawaii and *Shenandoah* flights. Incensed, Moffett took the offensive against Mitchell in the popular media, excoriating Mitchell for demagoguery and accusing him of using the tragic and near-tragic events for propaganda purposes and personal political gain. Later in the year, a court-martial trial found Mitchell guilty of insubordination and forced his resignation from the army.

Of all the obstacles Moffett faced, however, personnel was one of the most challenging. In a decade-long battle, he wrested control over aviation personnel training and assignments from the powerful Bureau of Navigation. He also defended flight pay as one of the perquisites enjoyed by flying officers and enlisted men. Moffett brought aircraft and engine procurement under the authority of the Bureau of Aeronautics and worked out a flexible system combining negotiated and competitive contracts for aircraft, engines, and equipment. His greatest accomplishment was legislation enacted in 1926 providing for the acquisition of 1,600 naval aircraft over five years. The measure not only provided the navy with new airplanes, but it helped bring badly needed stability to the nation's aircraft-manufacturing industry.

In 1930 Moffett served as a technical adviser at the London Naval Conference. Following the conference, which had approved continuation of restrictions on aircraft carrier tonnages, Moffett emphasized the need for the navy to acquire as many operational platforms as possible. In accordance with this, he urged the development of the small aircraft carrier and what was known as the flying-deck cruiser, a hybrid warship combining elements of the scout cruiser and aircraft carrier. Neither was a success. The small aircraft carrier, in the form of *Ranger*, proved to be deficient in operating capabilities and more vulnerable to bombing attack than larger ships; the flying-deck cruiser never moved beyond the preliminary design phase.

Moffett was one of the navy's most persistent advocates of the rigid airship, the range and payload capabilities of which made it an attractive complement to cruisers in scouting and reconnaissance operations in the Pacific. He viewed the navy as playing a major part in the development of an airship industry in the United States, convincing Congress to fund the construction of two large fleet airships. *Akron*, the first of these large craft, was completed in 1931, followed two years later by her sister ship, *Macon*. The large airships never realized their full potential in limited operations with the fleet. Ironically, Moffett and seventy-two others died when *Akron* went down in a storm off the New Jersey coast on 4 April 1933.

Moffett recognized that the technological, bureaucratic, and economic realities of the twentieth century demanded that he play an activist political role. A visionary and master of the art of compromise and public relations, he carefully balanced his own ambitions against what he considered the best interests of the nation, the navy, and naval aviation. The result was that on the eve of World War II the United States had the most powerful and efficient naval air arm in the world.

• The William Adger Moffett Papers are in the Nimitz Library of the U.S. Naval Academy. Moffett's service records are in file 662 at the National Personnel Records Center in St. Louis. For Moffett's career as chief of BuAer, the correspondence of the Bureau of Aeronautics, RG 72 in the National Archives, is essential. See also William F. Trimble, *Admiral William A. Moffett: Architect of Naval Aviation* (1994), and the older but still useful biography by Edward Arpee, *From Frigates to Flat-Tops: The Story of the Life and Achievements of Rear Admiral William Adger Moffett, U.S.N., "The Father of Naval Aviation"* (1953). Valuable briefer works on Moffett and his career are Paolo E. Coletta, "The Apotheosis of Political Strategy: The Third Appointment of Rear Admiral William A. Moffett as Chief of the U.S. Bureau of Aeronautics, 1929," *American Aviation Historical Society Journal* 36 (Spring 1991): 24–29; Thomas C. Hone, "Navy Air Leadership: Rear Admiral William A. Moffett as Chief of the Bureau of Aeronautics," in *Air Leadership: Proceedings of a Conference at Bolling Air Force Base, April 13–14, 1984*, ed. Wayne Thompson (1986), pp. 83–117; and Clark G. Reynolds, "William A. Moffett: Steward of the Air Revolution," in

Admirals of the New Steel Navy: Makers of the American Naval Tradition, 1880–1930, ed. James C. Bradford (1990), pp. 374–92. An obituary is in the *New York Times*, 5 Apr. 1933.

WILLIAM F. TRIMBLE

MOHOLY-NAGY, László (20 July 1895–24 Nov. 1946), artist, was born László Weisz in Bácsborsod, a small village in southern Hungary, the son of Lipót Weisz, who was probably a wheat farmer, and Karolina Stern. His father abandoned the family and went to the United States in 1897. After the father's disappearance, László's mother moved him and his younger brother first to nearby Ada and then to the town of Mohol (now in Yugoslavia). By 1905 he was attending a Gymnasium in Szeged (at the time the second largest city in Hungary) and living with his maternal uncle Dr. Gusztav Nagy, a lawyer whose last name he adopted. Although born Jewish, he was raised a Calvinist. He drew and painted from the time he was six or seven, but as an adolescent he expressed his creative tendencies through writing poems and short stories, several of which were published in magazines and newspapers in Szeged. In 1913 he graduated from college preparatory high school and moved to Budapest, where he enrolled in law school at Magyar Királyi Tudományegyetem, the Royal Hungarian University of Sciences.

His studies were interrupted by his enlistment in the artillery division of the Austro-Hungarian army in May 1915. In February 1916 he started frontline service near Galicia, close to the Russian border. On 1 July 1917 he suffered a severe wound to the left hand and began a lengthy rehabilitation at military hospitals at Odessa, Szeged, and Budapest. It was during this convalescence that he first seriously explored the medium of drawing with a series of sketches on the backs of military field postcards. He completed his service and returned to Budapest in September 1918 to continue his legal studies. He also continued to write poetry, albeit without the same intensity of his earlier years, and he made several contributions to the avant-garde periodical *Jelenkor* (Present day), edited by a friend, critic Iván Hevesy.

By late 1918 László had enrolled in classes at the private art school of Róbert Berény, a move representing both the start and end of his formal art training. In 1918 he also began his close association with Hungarian writer Lajos Kassák and the circle of artists known as "the Activists" surrounding Kassák and his avant-garde journal *MA* (Today). Through his involvement with Kassák and the other "Ma" artists, he experienced a transformation in his thinking regarding the role of art and its power to affect social and political change. This stance was reinforced by the progressive cultural revolution experienced in Hungary with the Bolshevik takeover led by Béla Kun in March 1919.

By 1919 he had hyphenated his name to Moholy-Nagy, likely in recognition of his childhood home and to distinguish the common surname Nagy. It was during this time that he began to have modest success as an exhibiting artist, and a number of his early representational works were acquired by the National Museum in Budapest. By the summer of 1919, however, the socialist regime had fallen, and the political climate in Hungary had shifted dramatically to the right. Many of the left-leaning artists, Moholy-Nagy among them, left Budapest in late 1919 for exile in Vienna.

Moholy-Nagy stayed in Vienna for a brief and difficult period characterized by extreme poverty and poor health. He left Vienna for Berlin in early 1920, joining a large contingency of Hungarian émigrés in that city. He was immediately energized by the highly industrial urban landscape of Berlin and the dynamic interaction on an international scale that existed among artists there. In this environment his painting evolved from its representational phase to the nonfigurative, geometric, abstract style known as constructivism.

By the next winter Moholy-Nagy became a prominent member of the international avant-garde, associating with artists such as dadaists Raoul Hausmann and Hans Richter, de stijl leader Theo van Doesburg, and Russian constructivist El Lissitzky. In January 1921 he married Lucia Schultz, who was to collaborate with him on many of his pioneering efforts in the field of photography. They had no children. Along with the dadaist American photographer Man Ray and the German Christian Schad, the Moholy-Nagys established the photogram technique (whereby a cameraless image is created by placing objects on photographic film or paper and exposing the material to light).

Moholy-Nagy continued his close association with the Hungarian Ma group and was named the Berlin correspondent for the periodical *MA*. In 1922 he and Lajos Kassák designed and published the groundbreaking *Buch neuer Künstler* (Book of the new artists), both in German and in Hungarian (Uj muvészek könyve). The book, which used photographic illustrations as the primary tool of analysis of the artwork of masters from Pablo Picasso to Kasimir Malevich, is an anthology of the modernist movement that was influential in spreading the cause of constructivism.

Moholy-Nagy's first exhibition outside of Hungary was in a group showing in 1920 at the Fritz Gurlitt Gallery in Berlin. His later exhibition at Galerie der Sturm in 1922, with fellow Hungarian László Péri, brought him greater acclaim and the attention of Bauhaus director Walter Gropius. By April 1923 Gropius invited Moholy-Nagy to join the faculty of this famous design school in Weimar. At the age of twenty-seven Moholy-Nagy became the youngest master teacher at the institution, where he was appointed to head both the metal workshop and the preliminary course (Vorkurs).

Perhaps his greatest contribution to the Bauhaus was his collaboration with Gropius in the compilation and design of the series of fourteen Bauhaus books (*Bauhausbücher*), in which his own *Malerei, Fotografie, Film* (Painting, photography, film) appears. In 1929 his landmark text, *Von Material zu Arkitektur* (From material to architecture) was published. Based on his pedagogical approach to the Bauhaus preliminary course, the book was later translated into English under the title *The New Vision.*

Moholy-Nagy stayed at the Bauhaus on its relocation to Dessau, but he, along with Gropius, Marcel Breuer, and Herbert Bayer, finally resigned in 1928 because of political pressures and philosophical differences with the direction of the school. He returned to live for the next five years in Berlin and opened a commercial design office, where he received important commissions to create stage designs for the Kroll Opera and the Piscator Theater. His innovative stage work included the sets for *Tales of Hoffman* (1929), *The Merchant of Berlin* (1929), and *Madame Butterfly* (1931). In 1931 he had his first exhibition in the United States, a presentation of his photographs at the Delphic Studios in New York.

During the same period Moholy-Nagy experimented successfully with filmmaking and produced the black-and-white films *Berliner Stilleben* (Berlin still life, 1926), *Marseille Vieux Port* (1929), and *Ein Lichtspiel: Schwarz, Weiss, Grau* (Lightplay: Black, white, gray, 1930), in which the *Light-Space Modulator,* Moholy's famous kinetic sculpture for light display, is featured. He also made *Grosstadt-Ziguener* (Gypsies, 1932), which emphasized motion characterized by jumpcut editing, and his most commercial film, *Lobster (The Life of the Lobster),* commissioned by a London documentary film company in 1935.

By 1929 Moholy-Nagy had separated from Lucia, and they finally divorced. In 1932 he married his second wife, writer and teacher Sibyl Pietzsch; they had two children. Eventually finding conditions as an artist under the Nazi regime untenable, Moholy-Nagy left Germany and emigrated to Amsterdam in 1934, his family following shortly after. He continued his work in photography, focusing his experiments on color processing. In the summer of that year he was given a major exhibition of his paintings at the Stedelijk Museum and was also commissioned to create an exhibition of its methods and materials for the Dutch rayon industry.

In May 1935 Moholy-Nagy once again moved, this time to London. He remained there two years producing films, display, and art design for the menswear store Simpson's of Piccadilly. He also collaborated on three books, *The Street Markets of London* (1936), with Mary Benedetta; *Eton Portrait* (1937), with Bernard Fergusson; and *An Oxford University Chest* (1937), with John Betjeman. While in England he also made the film *The New Architecture of the London Zoo* (1936).

In June 1937 Moholy-Nagy received an invitation to come to the United States from the Chicago Association of Arts and Industries. On the recommendation of Walter Gropius (who was by this time the head of the Department of Architecture at Harvard), he was appointed the director of the New Bauhaus, American School of Design. Backed by Midwest businessman Marshall Field and corporations like Avery, Gypsum, and Kohler, the school opened its doors on 18 October 1937, with the hope that the industrial design methodology of the German Bauhaus would transplant easily to American soil. However, financial conditions forced the closing of the school by December 1938. Undaunted, Moholy-Nagy used his own financial resources and the support of Walter Paepcke of the Container Corporation of America to open the School of Design, later known as the Institute of Design, or the "I.D.," in 1939.

Moholy-Nagy's last years were spent in a flurry of activity typical of his entire career. In 1941 he designed the Parker "51" pen, and in 1943 he developed an art program for the rehabilitation of wounded veterans. He also began writing *Vision in Motion* (published posthumously in 1947), his pedagogical treatise that became a standard text for art and design education worldwide. He painted and drew almost daily, and by 1945 his experimentation in Plexiglas sculpture led him to discover new interpretations of his lifelong preoccupation with light and spatial relationships.

Moholy-Nagy was a twentieth-century visionary whose pioneering efforts in art and design influenced generations after him. His commitment, generosity, and enthusiasm as a teacher were legendary. In July 1945 he was diagnosed with leukemia, but he continued to maintain a heavy workload. A retrospective exhibition (the only one held in his lifetime) was mounted on 12 February 1946 at the Cincinnati Museum of Art. By April Moholy-Nagy finally attained his U.S. citizenship, but he died in Chicago seven months later.

• Materials related to Moholy-Nagy are included in the public collections of the Chicago campus of the University of Illinois; the Archives of American Art, Washington, D.C.; and the Bauhaus Archiv, Berlin. Major bibliographical references include Krisztina Passuth, *Moholy-Nagy* (1985); Sibyl Moholy-Nagy, *Moholy-Nagy, Experiment in Totality* (1969); *Marginal Notes, Documentary Absurdities* (1972); Belena S. Chapp, ed., *László Moholy-Nagy: From Budapest to Berlin, 1914–1923* (1995); and Richard Kostelanetz, *Moholy-Nagy* (1970). There is an obituary in the *New York Times*, 25 Nov. 1946.

BELENA S. CHAPP

MOHR, Hal (2 Aug. 1894–10 May 1974), cinematographer, was born in San Francisco, California, the son of a prominent businessman. Raised in an upper-middle-class family, Mohr demonstrated his interest in motion picture technology from an early age. His childhood toys included a magic lantern slide projector. He was exposed to moving pictures at age eleven, when films depicting the devastation of the 1906 earthquake were screened widely in his hometown. "That was a miracle," he recalled to an American Film Institute seminar in 1973, "I had no idea how it was done. So that became the aim of my life, to find out how that picture was made to move. It's been the aim of my life ever since." In 1909 he began working for the Miles Brothers film company, inspecting movie prints. There he got his hands on a projector and with some inventive tinkering turned it into a camera. He shot news events and sold his short, amateurish films to local theaters, dropping out of high school to pursue filmmaking.

Mohr worked for most of the Bay Area's film producers. In 1913 he made industrial films for Sol Lesser. At the California Motion Picture Company he shot both newsreels and story films. On his own time, he recorded the notorious redlight district in his film *The Last Night of the Barbary Coast* (1913). His documentation of the quarter's infamous nightlife sold hundreds of prints nationwide. Mohr next ventured to build his own film studio in Berkeley. He scripted, directed, and shot most of *The Daughter of the Gods* but lacked the money to complete and distribute it. He was, however, already experimenting with camera movements, dollies, and tracking devices that would later become essential to filmmaking.

In late 1914 Mohr took a job as a film editor at the new Universal Studios in Los Angeles. A strict division of labor had yet to develop in the studio system, so Mohr continued to be a jack-of-all-trades. He worked as a cinematographer and, in 1917, was also hired by producer Hal Roach to direct comedies starring Harold Lloyd. Mohr's career was interrupted by two years of service in France (1917–1918) as a U.S. Army photographer.

After World War I, Mohr returned to San Francisco to work once again for the Miles Brothers. He spent 1920 making low-budget films in Seattle and Portland, returning to Hollywood at year's end, when he began to concentrate on his craft as a camera operator. Mohr hired himself to several "Poverty Row" companies, often doing his own lab work as well as cinematography for cheap films. He soon got more prestigious projects. His technical talent was in demand at most of the major studios by the end of the 1920s. His exceptional work in creating richly textured, soft-focus photography for Mary Pickford (*Sparrows* [1926]) and other stars raised his status among his peers. In 1926 he shot many of the extravagant scenes for Erich von Stroheim's spectacular *The Wedding March*. He indulged Stroheim's love of excess, shooting what he called "a series of artistic orgasms," lush candlelight scenes on the set of a Viennese cathedral. In classic Hollywood fashion, the director served as best man when Mohr wed film actress Clara Pegel on the cathedral set in 1926 (though the marriage soon ended in divorce).

In 1927 Warner Bros. enlisted Mohr's technical expertise for the landmark talkie *The Jazz Singer*. Working with director Alan Crosland (with whom he had served in the army), Mohr helped solve the many problems involved with the conversion from silent to sound pictures. The following year the strong-willed Mohr walked out on a studio because Warner Bros. was endangering extras in filming an elaborate flood scene for *Noah's Ark* (1928). He then returned to Universal, where he shot some of the most innovative films of the period, including the Technicolor spectacle *King of Jazz* (1930) and Paul Fejos's *Broadway* (1929), for which he developed an elaborate camera crane. Mohr used his "Broadway crane" liberally. As Richard Koszarski put it, Mohr became known for trying camera stunts "for the sheer, extravagant fun of succeeding at the impossible."

Mohr shot dozens of features for the major studios. In 1935 he won an Academy Award for his shimmering black-and-white cinematography in Max Reinhardt's *A Midsummer Night's Dream*. He was the only person ever awarded an Oscar on a write-in vote. He had been snubbed in the nominations because, as president of the American Society of Cinematographers, he had gone against the union and ended a bitter 1933 strike of the studios.

Mohr pioneered techniques of deep-focus photography in such films as *Bullets or Ballots* and *Green Pastures* (both 1936), which became an important tool for cinema aesthetics. He also proved equally adept at color cinematography, winning another Oscar for his work on *The Phantom of the Opera* (1943).

During the 1950s Mohr worked increasingly in television, performing the less challenging but better paying camera duties on TV commercials and several popular series, including "I Married Joan," "The Bob Cummings Show," and "Father of the Bride." His final film credits came in the 1960s, with the film noir *Underworld U.S.A.* (1961) and Alfred Hitchcock's *Topaz* (1969). Despite his gradual retirement from creative work, Mohr remained active in the industry. He served as head of the International Photographers union in Los Angeles and as a governor of the Academy of Motion Picture Arts and Sciences until his death in Santa Monica, California. In 1934 he had married the actress and classics scholar Evelyn Venable; they had a son and four daughters.

Although seldom before the public eye, Mohr was recognized by his peers as one of the best directors of photography in the history of Hollywood. From his pioneering days in the motion picture industry until his retirement, he proved adept at technical innovation, gaining a wide knowledge of cameras, film stocks, and lighting effects. Rather than developing a particular photographic style, Mohr adapted his technical virtuosity to meet the artistic needs of whatever picture he worked on. "I think that the photography of a motion picture is most brilliant in its inconspicuousness," he told interviewer Leonard Maltin. "I think that a cameraman should be versatile enough to conform to whatever the story would be."

• Mohr wrote "A Lens Mount for Universal Focus Effects," *American Cinematographer*, Sept. 1936, p. 371, in which he explained how his device "could be of inestimable value in the Cinematographer's efforts to reconcile the dramatic purpose of Cinematography with the mechanical limitations of the camera." The two essential accounts of Mohr's career are *Hal Mohr: An American Film Institute Seminar on His Work* (1977) and a lengthy interview published in Leonard Maltin, *Behind the Camera: The Cinematographer's Art* (1971; repr. as *The Art of the Cinematographer: A Survey and Interviews with Five Masters* [1978]). Richard Koszarski also interviewed Mohr, resulting in two publications in *Film Comment*, "The Men with Movie Cameras," Summer 1972, pp. 217–57, and an account of Mohr's work with directors Paul Fejos and Paul Leni in the late 1920s and early 1930s, "Moving Pictures: Hal

Mohr's Cinematography," Sept.–Oct. 1974, pp. 48–53. See also the special cinematography issue of *Focus on Film*, 13 (1973). An obituary is in the *New York Times*, 12 May 1974.

DAN STREIBLE

MOÏSE, Edward Warren (21 May 1832–8 Dec. 1903), soldier and politician, was born in Charleston, South Carolina, the son of Abraham Moïse, a shopkeeper, and Caroline Agnes Moses. Moïse was a Sephardic Jew. His grandparents moved from France to St. Eustatius and then to Haiti, where they became plantation owners. They fled to Charleston during the slave uprisings in the 1790s. Moïse studied in classical academies in Charleston until the age of fifteen, at which time he had to begin work because of family financial problems. While working in the county registry office, he studied law.

Moïse married Esther Lyon in 1854 and two years later, at the age of twenty-four, moved from Charleston to Columbus, Georgia, where he opened a law office. The couple had either eleven or twelve children.

Before the Civil War Moïse opposed secession and was a Douglas Democrat. Joining the Confederacy when the war broke out, he immediately raised a company of 120 men, 50 of whom he equipped at his own expense, a sum of $10,000, his entire fortune at the time. He served as captain of his company until 1863, when he was promoted to major. Near the end of the war he commanded the Seventh Regiment of Georgia but was never promoted to colonel. During the war his unit served in the Army of Northern Virginia and saw action in many important battles, including Gettysburg and Petersburg. He played an important role in the battle of Bentonville and was later charged with burning a bridge at Smithfield, North Carolina, to cover the retreat of generals Wade Hampton and M. C. Butler, both of whom played important roles in postwar South Carolina.

After the war Moïse moved to Sumter, South Carolina, which became his permanent residence. At that time he owned only a wounded horse, which he sold to support his family. He began to practice law again in the provost court and enjoyed considerable success. He was known as an outstanding orator and a provider of charity for the needy, regardless of their status, religion, or race. His reputation for charity followed him for the rest of his life.

Although Moïse served in the convention of 1865, which rewrote the constitution of South Carolina, he is best known for his support of General Hampton and his Red Shirts in the disputed elections of 1876. With the presidency at stake as well as state offices, Hampton led the Democrats in South Carolina. In an effort to keep Republicans from voting, the red shirts generally terrorized African Americans with their rifle clubs and played on the emotions of the white voters with dramatic speeches. Moïse abandoned his law practice and rode through the state with Hampton. He was noted as "one of the most effective stump speakers in the country. He had fine dramatic instinct and could alternate fire and pathos and humor with the skill of a master and apparently without effort" (Williams, p. 228).

Moïse also ran for the position of state adjutant and inspector general. Like the national elections of that year, the elections in South Carolina remained disputed for five months, with both Republicans and Democrats claiming victory. Eventually the Republicans resigned, and the Democrats took over the state. Hampton became governor and Moïse the adjutant, marking the end of Reconstruction in South Carolina.

Moïse believed in public education and donated his entire first year's salary for that purpose. He was reelected as adjutant and inspector general in 1878 but declined to serve after that. However, he continued to be known as General Moïse. In 1880 he served as a Democratic presidential elector. He then returned to private life and did not play a notable role in politics. He died in Sumter, South Carolina.

Moïse's career stands in contrast to that of Franklin J. Moses, another Jew from Sumter, who served as a "scalawag" governor from 1872 to 1874 and was charged with corruption. In neither case, though, was the man's religion a major concern of South Carolinians.

• An account of Moïse's life, including obituaries from various newspapers, is in *Edwin Warren Moïse: In Memoriam. 1831–1903* (1903). Other sources include Harold Moïse, *The Moïse Family of South Carolina* (1961); Barnett A. Elzas, *The Jews of South Carolina* (1905); and Alfred B. Williams, *Hampton and His Red Shirts: South Carolina's Deliverance in 1876* (1935).

JAMES W. HAGY

MOÏSE, Penina (23 Apr. 1797–13 Sept. 1880), poet, was born in Charleston, South Carolina, the daughter of Abraham Moïse, a merchant, and Sarah (maiden name unknown), French refugees who apparently fled from Santo Domingo after the slave insurrection of 1791. Following her father's death when she was twelve, she was forced to leave school in order to help support her family. To do so, she began working at home in embroidery and lace making. According to family biographer Harold Moïse, even as a young girl Penina Moïse was a "frail, romantic figure fairly bursting with poetic sentiment." She apparently had an unquenchable thirst for knowledge and spent whatever free time she had reading and cultivating her literary talents.

Her first-known published work, a poem entitled "France after the Banishment of Napoleon," appeared on 31 July 1819 in the *Southern Patriot*, a Charleston newspaper. For the next sixty years her poems, as well as occasional short stories and essays, appeared in the *Charleston Courier*, to which she was a regular contributor, and in newspapers and magazines throughout the United States, including the *Home Journal*, *Godey's Lady's Book*, the *Boston Daily Times*, the *Washington Union*, *Heriot's Magazine*, and *The Occident, and American Jewish Advocate*. Themes on which she wrote included the beauty of nature, religious faith, loyalty, self-sacrifice, and the attainment of social justice. She also wrote a number of poems that focused on contemporary political events and leaders. In 1833 she published a collection of her poems in a volume entitled *Fancy's Sketch Book*. It was the first volume of poetry published by an American Jewish woman and may well have been the first volume of poetry published by an American Jew.

Devoted to her family and to the Charleston community, she spent a number of years caring for her paralyzed mother and younger brother, who suffered from severe attacks of asthma, and throughout 1854, despite her failing eyesight, nursed those who were ill or dying from the yellow fever epidemic that had swept through the city. She later served as superintendent of the second Jewish Sunday school in the United States, founded in Charleston in 1838 at Congregation Beth Elohim, the congregation to which she belonged. As superintendent, Moïse wrote a number of hymns, poems, and recitations for the school's use. During and after the Civil War, she ran a small school with her sister and niece in the home she shared with them and continued to teach even after she lost her vision. Yet despite the devotion she received from her students and the acclaim she was accorded as a poet, Moïse's long life was marked by poverty, blindness, and great physical pain caused by neuralgia.

Penina Moïse is best remembered as the primary author of the first American Jewish hymnal entitled *Hymns Written for the Use of Hebrew Congregations*. It was published by Congregation Beth Elohim in 1842. This congregation, established in the eighteenth century as an Orthodox synagogue, became in 1824 the first Jewish congregation in America to ally itself with the nascent Reform movement. Jubilant over the victory of the Reformers, Moïse wrote: "The struggle is over—the victory ours, / And grateful emotion my bosom o'erpowers / As ushered by Harmony's spirit divine, / The return, Gracious Judge of the world! to thy shrine." Sixty of the seventy-four hymns that appeared in the first edition were composed by Moïse. The revised and enlarged edition published in 1856 contained 190 of her hymns.

Moïse's hymns, many of which were originally written as poems, clearly reflect the overarching universalism of classical Reform Judaism. Describing faith as the commending of one's soul to God, she viewed the religious life as one of "high concerns," including concern for all those who suffer alone and thus are in need of comfort. She exhorts the reader in her hymn entitled "Piety" to "Forsake the scene of heartless mirth; / Seek those who weep without a friend, / Bring wine and oil to suff'ring worth." At the same time, many of her poems revealed the great importance that Moïse, like many other nineteenth-century Reform Jews, attached to particularistic allegiance. She retained belief in God's election of the Jewish people and stood opposed to intermarriage. To her, the synagogue stood in opposition to the temptations of the outside world, calling the Jewish people to a life of divine service rewarded by immortality.

Never married, Moïse spent many of her later years living with her niece and sister. She died in Charleston. The *Union Hymnal*, published in 1897 as the standard hymnal to be used by American Reform congregations, included eleven of Moïse's hymns. Still widely used, the *Union Hymnal* is said to contain more of her hymns than those of any other author.

• To date, no full-length study of Penina Moïse's life or works has been undertaken. Many of her poems can be found in *Secular and Religious Works of Penina Moïse, with a Brief Sketch of Her Life*, published by the Charleston Section of the National Council of Jewish Women (1911). The first biographical sketch of Moïse was written by her niece, Mrs. S. A. Dinkins, "Penina Moïse," *The American Jew's Annual* (1885–1886). Other biographical studies include L. C. Harby, "Penina Moïse, Woman and Writer," *The American Jewish Year Book* (1905–1906); Harold Moïse, *The Moïse Family of South Carolina: An Account of the Life and Descendants of Abraham and Sarah Moïse* (1961); and Solomon Breibart, "Penina Moïse, Southern Jewish Poetess," in *Jews of the South*, ed. Samuel Proctor and Louis Schmier with M. Stern (1984).

ELLEN M. UMANSKY

MOISSEIFF, Leon Solomon (10 Nov. 1872–3 Sept. 1943), engineer, was born in Riga, Latvia, the son of Solomon Moisseiff, a merchant, and Anna Bloch. Young Moisseiff attended the Emperor Alexander Gymnasium from 1880 to 1887 and the Baltic Polytechnic Institute in Riga from 1889 to 1891, when his political activities as a student contributed to the family's decision to emigrate to the United States. The family settled in New York City, and Moisseiff began working as a draftsman before enrolling in Columbia University in 1892. While a student at Columbia, he was also employed by one of his professors, William H. Burr, in Burr's practice as a consulting engineer. Moisseiff married Ida Assinofsky in 1894; they had three children. He became a naturalized citizen of the United States in 1896.

After receiving his civil engineering degree in 1895, Moisseiff took his first job with the New York Rapid Transit Railroad Commission. In 1896 he joined the Dutton Pneumatic Lock & Engineering Company to work on proposed improvements to the Erie Canal, and in 1897 he worked for a brief time for the Bronx Department of Street Improvements. With the establishment of Greater New York City, which was legislated in 1896 to occur on 1 January 1898, Moisseiff joined the new city's Department of Bridges. Over the next decade he was to oversee the design and construction of some of the largest bridges in the world, including the Williamsburg, Manhattan, and Queensboro bridges over New York's East River. During his nearly two-decade tenure in this department, Moisseiff rose successively to the positions of chief draftsman, assistant designer, and finally, in 1910, engineer of design and was in a position to make the acquaintance of such important bridge engineers as Gustav Lindenthal, the commissioner of bridges from 1903 to 1905; Othmar Ammann, who worked on the Queensboro

Bridge as an engineer with its builder, the Pennsylvania Steel Company; and Ralph Modjeski, who reviewed the design of the Manhattan Bridge.

It was Moisseiff's work on the Manhattan Bridge, which began about 1900, that established him as the premier theorist of bridge design. Moisseiff recognized the significance of what has come to be called deflection theory, the foundations of which were first published in German in 1888 by the Austrian engineer Josef Melan. Moisseiff showed that this method of calculation, which took into account the flexibility of major bridge components, enabled the development of relatively light bridge designs for which there was considerable savings in the amount of steel employed. This naturally translated to reduced cost. His effective development and application of the deflection theory provided a standard by which subsequent suspension bridges were built.

Like many a successful engineer of the period, Moisseiff went into private practice as a consulting engineer. He opened his office in 1915, but for the next five years he engaged in little bridge design, World War I having generally put bridge building projects on hold. In 1920 Moisseiff was appointed engineer of design for the Delaware River Bridge, for which Modjeski was chief engineer. This bridge, connecting Philadelphia and Camden, New Jersey, and now known as the Benjamin Franklin Bridge, was the longest suspension bridge in the world when completed in 1926. For the next decade, Moisseiff was actively involved with the design of virtually every large suspension bridge built in the United States, including the Ambassador, George Washington, Triborough, Golden Gate, San Francisco–Oakland Bay, Bronx-Whitestone, and Tacoma Narrows bridges. Indeed, he was directly responsible for the dominant features of many of these bridges, having redesigned the basic proportions of the Golden Gate and Tacoma Narrows bridges to achieve a long, slender profile that conformed to his sense of what a bridge should look like.

Moisseiff's interest in bridge aesthetics was implicit in his striving for lighter and lighter designs that were also tours de force in steel. As designer in the mid-1920s of the George Washington Bridge towers, components of a suspension bridge that he saw exerting "a preponderant influence on the aesthetic impression of the observer," Moisseiff wrote explicitly about matters of appearance. When appointed consulting engineer to Joseph Strauss, chief engineer of the Golden Gate Bridge, Moisseiff recommended that Strauss's hybrid cantilever-suspension conceptual design be replaced with a pure suspension bridge with a record main span of 4,200 feet. Completed in 1937, the Golden Gate Bridge, which had the slender proportions that Moisseiff championed, proved to be more flexible in the wind than anticipated. This was a harbinger of how a half-dozen or so contemporary suspension bridge designs, all following the aesthetic dictated by and made possible by Moisseiff's deflection theory and its refinements, were to behave.

Among the most flexible of the suspension bridges designed and built in the late 1930s was the Tacoma Narrows. This bridge, whose preliminary design was produced by the Washington State Highway Department, was redesigned by Moisseiff to be the third longest suspension bridge in the world. When called in as a consultant to the project, he criticized the Highway Department's design on aesthetic grounds and produced a sleek design that employed solid girders rather than a more conventional deck truss and that had a ratio of span to width that was unprecedentedly large. The narrowness of the design, prompted in part by the low traffic volume projected for the bridge location, was the focus of considerable reservation expressed by Theodore L. Condron, advisory engineer for the Reconstruction Finance Corporation, which was being asked to purchase bonds to pay for the bridge. However, Moisseiff's overwhelming reputation, backed by his continued development with his associate Frederick Lienhard of analytical theories for dealing with lateral wind forces on suspension bridges, prevailed, and the bridge was built to Moisseiff's specifications. Upon completion, in July 1940, the bridge displayed unprecedented vertical flexibility, and on 7 November 1940, in a 42-mile wind, a twisting motion developed that within a matter of hours caused the bridge to tear itself apart.

Moisseiff's overlooking completely the aerodynamic consequences of a relatively light and narrow steel deck design was excused by an investigatory committee chaired by Othmar Ammann and including the West Coast bridge designer Glenn B. Woodruff and the aerodynamical engineer Theodore von Kármán. The bridge engineers, who knew from personal experience that Moisseiff had not only designed the Tacoma Narrows Bridge to the state of the art but had in fact more than any of them defined what the state of the art was, convinced von Kármán that the failure could not have been anticipated within the culture of bridge design as it had existed in the 1930s. After the collapse of the Tacoma Narrows Bridge, Moisseiff did little by way of direct design, but according to a memoir composed by Ammann and Lienhard, which made no mention of the tragic failure that capped an otherwise brilliant career, Moisseiff acted as "a consultant to consulting and executive engineers" (p. 1511).

Moisseiff joined the American Society of Civil Engineers in 1895 and remained active in the organization throughout his career, publishing some of his most important papers in its *Transactions*. He received the society's Norman Medal in 1934, for his paper on the towers of the George Washington Bridge, and in 1939 he received the society's James Laurie Prize. The Franklin Institute awarded him its Gold Medal in 1933. He was also associated with the American Society for Testing Materials, the American Railway Engineering Association, and the American Welding Society, as well as being a member of Sigma Xi and Zeta Beta Tau. He died in Belmar, New Jersey.

• By Moisseiff, see "Theory and Formulas for the Analytical Computation of a Three-Span Suspension Bridge with Braced Cable," *Transactions of the American Society of Civil Engineers* 55 (1905): 94–113; "The Towers, Cables and Stiffening Trusses of the Bridge over the Delaware River between Philadelphia and Camden," *Journal of the Franklin Institute* (Oct. 1925): 436–66; "George Washington Bridge: Design of the Towers," *Transactions of the American Society of Civil Engineers* 97 (1933): 164–205; and, with Frederick Lienhard, "Suspension Bridges under the Action of Lateral Forces," *Transactions of the American Society of Civil Engineers* 98 (1933): 1080–95. Obituaries are in the *New York Times*, 4 Sept. 1943, and *Engineering News-Record*, 9 Sept. 1943. A remarkable group of tributes followed two weeks later in the letters column of *Engineering News-Record*, 23 Sept. 1943, pp. 74–75. A memoir by O. H. Ammann and Frederick Lienhard is in the *Transactions of the American Society of Civil Engineers* 111 (1946): 1509–12. An assessment of Moisseiff's role in suspension bridge building can be found in Henry Petroski, *Engineers of Dreams: Great Bridge Builders and the Spanning of America* (1995).

HENRY PETROSKI

MOLE, Miff (11 Mar. 1898–29 Apr. 1961), jazz trombonist, was born Irving Milfred Mole in Roosevelt, Long Island, New York, the son of a house painter and amateur violinist. His parents' names are unknown. At age eleven he began playing violin and piano, and at age fourteen he worked in a local theater accompanying silent movies. In 1911 he started playing alto horn but soon switched to trombone, teaching himself the positions by matching his notes with corresponding pitches on the piano. Between 1914 and 1916 he played with Gus Sharp's band in Brooklyn, during which time he studied trombone with Charlie Randall. After leaving Sharp, he played briefly with Jimmy Durante at the Alamo Club before joining trumpeter Phil Napoleon and pianist Frank Signorelli in their newly formed Original Memphis Five (OM5), a group based on the style of the Original Dixieland Jazz Band.

The OM5 played its first job at Coney Island in the summer of 1917, moved to the Ritz in Brooklyn in the winter, and then embarked on a tour of vaudeville theaters with the dance team of Quinn and Farnum. When internal dissension brought about the end of the tour in Los Angeles, Mole remained in California, where he worked in theater orchestras and with Abe Lyman's band at the Sunset Inn in Santa Monica. In 1919 he returned to New York and rejoined the OM5. The band next played for five months in Montreal before moving to the Rosemont Ballroom in Brooklyn.

In late 1919 Mole started a lengthy working relationship with bandleader and recording contractor Sam Lanin, during which time he also began recording regularly with the OM5. Mole worked for Lanin on and off through 1926, but in May 1924 he formally joined Ray Miller's orchestra in Atlantic City, New Jersey. The Miller band next played briefly in Manhattan. It was at the Hippodrome in early September that Bix Beiderbecke, then in New York with the Wolverines, first heard Mole and saxophonist Frank Trumbauer, a meeting that led to the Sioux City Six recordings of October 1924. In June 1925 Mole left Miller to play in both Don Voorhees's pit orchestra and Ross Gorman's intermission dance band for *Earl Carroll's Vanities*. Also working in the show was Red Nichols, the cornetist with whom Mole was most closely associated between 1925 and 1929. In addition to his evening job with *Vanities*, from January 1926 through May 1927 the trombonist also played late night sets with Roger Wolfe Kahn at the Biltmore Hotel. In September he joined radio station WOR's staff orchestra under the joint leadership of Voorhees and Nichols and that same month participated in the first CBS national network broadcast. In 1929 Mole left CBS to join NBC, where he remained on staff for the next nine years, playing in a wide variety of settings, from the NBC Symphony under Arturo Toscanini to dance and jazz bands. Mole also led a group that backed blues singer Bessie Smith on her early 1930s broadcasts.

In August 1938 Mole played briefly in Charlie Margulis's band before replacing Jack Teagarden in Paul Whiteman's orchestra in December, but he left in 1940 to resume his position with NBC. In late November 1942 he joined Benny Goodman's band for hotel and theater engagements in New York and Chicago and a March 1943 trip to Los Angeles, where the band appeared in the film *The Gang's All Here*. Mole returned to New York with Goodman and played at the Hotel Astor from April through early August, after which he briefly led his own sextet at Toronto's Top Hat Club. In October he began a long residency at Nick's in Greenwich Village, leading a house band composed of Muggsy Spanier, Pee Wee Russell, and Eddie Condon's regular rhythm section. Russell was a constant fixture throughout, but in April 1944 Spanier was temporarily replaced by first Bobby Hackett and then Sterling Bose, and in December 1945 Condon left to open his own club.

In early 1944 Mole made his first recordings as leader since 1937 and in May, September, and October he appeared on Condon's weekly concert/broadcast series. After some time off in early 1945 to undergo hip surgery, he returned to Nick's and remained until the spring of 1947, when once again he had to leave for reasons of health. In late 1947 Mole went to Chicago, where he played with the house band at Jazz Ltd. and, with Spanier and occasionally Russell, at the Bee Hive and the Blue Note, interrupting his stay once in June 1948, when he and Russell worked in Max Kaminsky's band in Boston. After he returned to New York in 1954, Mole underwent further operations on his hip. During his later years, dependent on crutches, he frequently had to support himself by nonmusical means, but he did participate in an all-star "Dixieland at Carnegie Hall" concert in February 1958 and worked once more at Jazz Ltd. in 1959. In June 1960 Mole played his last job with Russell on Long Island. He died in New York City.

Despite the fact that Mole's first inspiration on the trombone was the Original Dixieland Jazz Band's Eddie Edwards, a rudimentary player limited to raggy rhythmic punctuations and circus-like glissandos, from his earliest records with the OM5 he exhibited a technical fluency and imagination far in advance of any of his contemporaries, his superiority evident in both his crisp ensemble playing and his cleverly conceived, expertly articulated breaks and solos. Departing from the conventional "tailgate" style of Edwards and the New Orleans Rhythm Kings' George Brunies, Mole fashioned a trumpetlike approach that emphasized technical facility, tone, range, and rhythmic flexibility. Indeed, until the emergence of the more earthy, blues-based Jimmy Harrison and Jack Teagarden, Mole was the major influence on scores of younger trombonists; his best-known disciples were Tommy Dorsey and Glenn Miller.

Between 1922 and 1927 Mole recorded extensively with the OM5, not only under that band name but also under a number of equally colorful pseudonyms such as Jazzbo's Carolina Serenaders, the Cotton Pickers, Ladd's Black Aces, the New Orleans Black Birds, and others obviously designed to capitalize on the exotic appeal of southern black music. Between 1925 and 1930 Mole also recorded with many larger, jazz-tinged dance bands, including the California Ramblers, Ross Gorman, Roger Wolfe Kahn, Sam Lanin, Bert Lown, Ray Miller, Adrian Schubert, and Don Voorhees. But his most influential work was with Red Nichols's various recording bands—the Five Pennies, the Arkansas Travelers, the Charleston Chasers, the Hottentots, Lanin's Red Heads, the Louisiana Rhythm Kings, Miff Mole's Molers, the Red Heads, Red and Miff's Stompers, the Six Hottentots, the Tennessee Tooters, and the Wabash Dance Orchestra.

The 1930s, when he was on staff at NBC, saw a drastic reduction in his recording activities; his only performances during the decade were on a commercial date of his own in 1937 and two sessions in 1939 with Whiteman. Mole's jazz career resumed in January 1940, though, when he began a fruitful association with Condon. From this point on his style became less cerebral and began to display touches of both Brunies and Teagarden, broadening elements that first became evident on a December 1943 session with Yank Lawson and continued through a March 1945 leader date. Throughout this period he performed at his latter-day best and particularly so on a series of radio transcriptions for World Broadcasting Systems and on the Commodore label with Spanier, Hackett, Russell, and Condon. Of somewhat lesser stature are the records he made in Chicago in 1949 and 1950, a date with Max Kaminsky and Russell in 1954, an OM5 reunion backing Connee Boswell in 1956, and a second session at Jazz Ltd. in 1959.

• The style of jazz that Miff Mole played with Phil Napoleon, Red Nichols, and others during the period of his greatest influence was generally derided by later critics and historians, and therefore virtually nothing is available about him in jazz literature prior to the 1970s. Not even Eddie Condon, one of Mole's most prominent associates in the 1940s, saw fit to mention him in his 1947 autobiography, *We Called It Music*. For a general understanding of Mole's era and milieu, however, see Samuel B. Charters and Leonard Kunstadt, *Jazz: A History of the New York Scene* (1962); Herb Sanford, *Tommy and Jimmy: The Dorsey Years* (1972); Richard M. Sudhalter and Philip R. Evans, *Bix: Man & Legend* (1974); and Robert Hilbert, *Pee Wee Russell: The Life of a Jazzman* (1993). Direct quotations of Mole and others in his circle can be found in Nat Shapiro and Nat Hentoff, eds., *Hear Me Talkin' to Ya* (1955), while the booklet accompanying the 1959 Columbia album set, *Thesaurus of Classic Jazz*, offers informative historical and analytical notes by Richard Du Page and Frank Driggs. Gunther Schuller, *The Swing Era: The Development of Jazz, 1930–1945* (1989), includes a thoughtful discussion of the Nichols-Mole recordings of the 1920s and a good description of Mole's style. Complete discographical information is in Brian Rust, *Jazz Records, 1897–1942* (1982), and Walter Bruyninckx, *Traditional Jazz Discography, 1897–1988* (6 vols., 1988), and *Swing Discography, 1920–1988* (12 vols. 1988). A detailed listing of Condon's 1944–1945 broadcasts and all records that Mole made with Russell is in Hilbert, *Pee Wee Speaks: A Discography of Pee Wee Russell* (1992). A short career chronology of Mole is in John Chilton, *Who's Who of Jazz* (1985). An obituary is in the *New York Times*, 30 Apr. 1961.

JACK SOHMER

MOLEY, Raymond (27 Sept. 1886–18 Feb. 1975), professor of public law and presidential adviser, was born in Berea, Ohio, the son of Felix James Moley, proprietor of a "gent's furnishings" store, and Agnes Fairchild. With the onset of the 1893 depression, the family moved to the nearby hamlet of Olmsted Falls. After graduating from Cleveland's Baldwin-Wallace College (B. Phil., 1906), he became a teacher and superintendent of schools at Olmsted Falls (1906–1910). Stricken by tuberculosis in 1909, Moley sought a cure by moving to New Mexico and Colorado. Upon his return to Ohio in 1912, he pursued an M.A. in political science at Oberlin College (1913) while teaching at West High School in Cleveland. He then earned a Ph.D. at Columbia University (1918) while serving as instructor and then assistant professor at Western Reserve University (1916–1919). Moley married Eva Dall in 1916; they had two sons. In 1946, after divorcing Eva, he married Frances S. Hebard, with whom he had one daughter.

Born to a traditionally Democratic family, Moley admired William Jennings Bryan and the progressive spirit that dominated the city of Cleveland during the reform mayoralty of Tom L. Johnson. Like Johnson, he was profoundly influenced by the works of Henry George (1839–1897). He believed that the author of *Progress and Poverty* had touched on concerns that had later fired progressivism, especially concentrated economic power and the need for regulation of public utilities. Drawn at an early age toward involvement in the political arena, he modeled his preparation on that of Woodrow Wilson, focusing on political science and administrative law.

Moley wrote his doctoral dissertation under the direction of Charles A. Beard. It was the beginning of a lifelong friendship. Sons of the Midwest, they shared the view that eastern creditor interests exploited agrarians, and they opposed U.S. involvement in the two world wars of the twentieth century.

Moley's *The State Movement for Efficiency and Economy*, published by the New York Bureau of Municipal Research in 1918, dealt with growing pressures on state government for administrative efficiency and set the stage for the next step in his career. An address on the necessity for a stronger federal presence in the spheres of social and industrial planning caught the attention of social reformer Belle Sherwin, who proved instrumental in securing Moley's appointment as director of the Cleveland Foundation in 1919. The nation's first community trust, a fact-finding agency and funnel for business-sponsored civic improvement projects, it revived the reform spirit embodied in the mayoralties of Tom Johnson and Newton D. Baker.

Moley attained national prominence through the Cleveland Foundation's sponsorship of a survey of the administration of justice in the lake city. He gave prestige to the project by recruiting the services of Roscoe Pound and Felix Frankfurter of the Harvard Law School. The resulting Cleveland Crime Survey (1922) served as a model for other cities and states for a decade. Moley's developing reputation, and probably also his interest in the political education of women, brought him to the attention of the dean of Barnard College, Virginia Gildersleeve, and in 1923 he was appointed to the faculty of that institution.

Moley directed crime surveys in Missouri and Illinois in the 1920s, resulting in the publication of *Politics and Criminal Prosecution* (1928) and *Our Criminal Courts* (1930). Appointment in 1926 as research director of the New York State Crime Commission resulted in his acquaintance with Louis M. Howe, Franklin D. Roosevelt's political mentor, who was then serving as executive secretary of the National Crime Commission. Moley's first encounter with Roosevelt came in connection with Moley's authorship of an address on the administration of justice delivered during Roosevelt's 1928 gubernatorial campaign in New York. The political scientist's reputation in the field led to his appointment as research director in the investigation of New York City's magistrates' courts and their enforcement of the criminal law, the first of the famous Seabury investigations. There followed service in Judge Samuel Seabury's (1873–1958) investigation of the District Attorney's Office and publication of *Tribunes of the People* (1932), a summary of Moley's research findings.

Moley was convinced that Roosevelt would be the Democratic candidate for the presidency in 1932, and he offered his services to the governor in early January. Their collaboration, soon after, on a statement explaining the removal from office of Sheriff Thomas ("tin box") Farley, a consequence of the third Seabury investigation, demonstrated Moley's talents as a writer. Taciturnity and the ability to organize and simplify technical material also added to the academician's appeal to Roosevelt, who was facing a heavy speaking schedule in the presidential campaign. In March, Judge Samuel I. Rosenman, a Roosevelt intimate, proposed recruiting Moley and other Columbia University academics to serve in an advisory role. The initial Roosevelt-Moley effort, the "Forgotten Man" address of 7 April 1932, caused a sensation by arguing that rural poverty and collapsed commodity prices were the principal causes of the Great Depression.

Moley and Roosevelt recruited two other Columbia University professors, Rexford Guy Tugwell, an expert in agrarian economics, and Adolf A. Berle, Jr., a member of the law faculty who was about to publish a definitive work on corporate structure and finance. Dubbed the "brains trust" initially by Louis M. Howe, and a term popularized by *New York Times* reporter James M. Kieran, the group of academicians was enamored of planning or enlarged federal management of the economy.

In a series of memoranda, especially one dated 19 May 1932, Moley distilled for Roosevelt much of the basic content of the early New Deal program, screening a mass of material and ideas solicited from Berle, Tugwell, and other academic sources. Moley's proposals, reflecting views long held by Roosevelt, included liberalization of the Democratic party as a vehicle for progressivism; the necessity for business-government cooperation; legislation of the social minima, such as unemployment reserves and old-age insurance; massive spending for public works; regulation of securities issuance; the separation of commercial from investment banking; federal oversight of private utilities; restoration of predepression price and wage levels; and federal capital investment in regional power development as a yardstick for the fair pricing of private electric power. A gifted phrasemaker, Moley authored the "Concert of Interests" speech, which pointed to growing interdependence of sectors and sections, and he coined the term "new deal," which Roosevelt used in the Chicago convention address accepting his party's presidential nomination. Also demonstrating a capacity for political compromise with party's elders, Moley drafted statements on the tariff, budget balance, industrial controls, and acreage allotment in the 1932 campaign.

During the 1932–1933 interregnum, Moley's role as adviser included foreign policy matters, particularly when the defeated Herbert Hoover sought to commit Roosevelt to international remedies for the Great Depression. Hoover's agenda included World War I debt reduction and maintenance of the United States on a deflationary gold standard. Moley insisted on Roosevelt's adherence to domestic priorities, believing that recovery required insulation from international economic pressures that would vitiate the New Deal program. This Roosevelt pledged as they jointly drafted his first inaugural address.

As assistant secretary of state from 4 March to early September 1933, Moley served as the president's contact with powerful Democratic party legislators in the fashioning of the Hundred Days program. But conflict with his nominal superior, Secretary of State Cordell Hull, was inevitable. Hull was a free-trader, committed to tariff reciprocity agreements at the World Monetary and Economic Conference, scheduled to meet in London in June 1933. Moley and Roosevelt, convinced that overseas trade constituted a relatively small percentage of gross national product, believed that reduction of trade barriers would jeopardize artificially high domestic prices for the products of farmers and manufacturers induced by agricultural and industrial recovery legislation.

To secure dollar depreciation and reflation of domestic price levels, the president was equally determined to take the United States off the gold standard, which he accomplished in April 1933. He sent Moley as an emissary to affirm these views to treasury and central bank negotiators in London. But when Moley, in fact, agreed on 29 June 1933 to a de facto currency stabilization agreement with British and French representatives, Roosevelt dispatched his "bombshell" message of 2 July 1933 in which he condemned the proposed stabilization of the pound, dollar, and franc as an attempt to restrain his options, including, by inference, possible dollar devaluation. The conference, he protested, was not called to discuss the monetary policy of one nation. The gathering was brought to a standstill, with Moley's standing as Roosevelt's principal economic adviser undermined. Hull, who headed the delegation, was convinced he had been undercut by his subordinate, and on his return to Washington, he insisted on Moley's removal. Roosevelt complied, shifting Moley to the Justice Department. But Moley was already negotiating for the creation of an organ of New Deal opinion, founded as *Today* magazine and subsequently merged with *Newsweek*, and he resigned from the administration.

Though the Roosevelt-Moley relationship lasted until the early stages of the 1936 campaign, it sundered on ideological grounds. From the president's perspective, the magazine editor was increasingly responsive to conservative, anti–New Deal business opinion; from Moley's perspective, the president was becoming the captive of the anticorporate views of Felix Frankfurter's protégés, notably Thomas G. Corcoran, and the Democratic party was becoming overly responsive to the newly empowered labor movement.

In the late 1930s Moley edged toward the Republican party. He established a lifelong friendship with Herbert Hoover and then published *After Seven Years* (1939), an acerbic memoir of his association with Roosevelt. Intended to forestall a third-term bid, it argued that there had been a mid-course shift in the New Deal years from economic coordination to business hostility. Moley endorsed Wendell L. Willkie in 1940. In subsequent years, opposed to the eastern internationalist wing of the GOP, he served as an occasional adviser to Republican party aspirants, including Robert A. Taft, Barry Goldwater, and Richard Nixon. In 1964 he authored *The Republican Opportunity in 1964*, an attack on enlarged federal power, which was followed in 1966 by *The First New Deal*, a detailed analysis of his public service.

In his twilight years, Moley published a biography of the Irish patriot Daniel O'Connell (1974), a lifelong hero, and retired to Phoenix, Arizona, where, just prior to his death, he penned a memoir of his early career, which was published posthumously in 1980.

• Moley's papers, including speech drafts and memoranda submitted to Roosevelt, exchanges between the principals and advisers in the Hoover-Roosevelt interregnum, and a diary of his participation in the World Monetary and Economic Conference of 1933, are located at the Hoover Institution, Stanford, Calif. In addition to the two memoirs of his service with Roosevelt, *After Seven Years* (1939) and *The First New Deal* (1966), he authored a brief autobiography, edited by Frank Freidel, *Realities and Illusions* (1980). A detailed study of the way in which the Roosevelt-Moley collaboration shaped the content of the 1932 campaign is found in Elliot A. Rosen, *Hoover, Roosevelt and the Brains Trust* (1977). An obituary is in the *New York Times*, 19 Feb. 1975.

ELLIOT A. ROSEN

MOLYNEAUX, Tom (c. 1784–4 Aug. 1818), pugilist, first appeared on the London boxing scene in 1809. All that is known of his earlier life is that he was a freed slave, probably from Baltimore. He had come to Great Britain by way of working on the New York docks. No evidence supports the fanciful claims of the journalist Pierce Egan that he was descended from a warlike hero who had been the all-conquering pugilist of America.

Molyneaux appeared at Bill Richmond's "Horse and Dolphin" tavern in St. Martin's Lane. The tavern, next door to the Fives Court where sparring exhibitions took place, was a natural magnet for a big, tough, aspiring fighter. Richmond, himself an African American, was well established in the ring and had a high reputation among wealthy backers. He was so impressed by the newcomer that he set about promoting him with such success that after only two easily won fights—one a pickup match following a bullbait, and another against a hardy old London fighter, Tom Blake—Molyneaux was matched against Tom Cribb, the champion.

Richmond's training added some science to Molyneaux's original wild, rushing methods, while Cribb prepared little for the fight. When it took place, at Cropthorne, near East Grinstead in Sussex, on 18 December 1810, the champion was overweight and out of shape. The fight was the highlight of Molyneaux's career and was eventually to be the subject of some twentieth-century controversy over its fairness. The crowd, apart from Molyneaux's backers, were certainly on Cribb's side and showed it, but the contest's questionable events were not unusual by the undemanding standards of the day—the breaking of the ring by spectators when Molyneaux was gaining the upper hand and the delays by Cribb's seconds when their man needed a longer break to recover. In the end, Cribb did win, possibly after Molyneaux had fallen against one of the ring posts or had banged his head on the ground in a wrestling fall. The few eyewitness accounts vary, but none at the time alleged any unfairness. It was nearly twenty years later, when moral expectations about sport were beginning to be raised, that a reminiscing Pierce Egan, who almost certainly saw the fight, referred to a possible injustice toward

Molyneaux. Molyneaux himself made no such accusations in his letter to Cribb (doubtless the literate Richmond's work) challenging him to a return match.

Cribb at once began preparing for this contest under the strict training regime of Captain Allardyce Barclay, who had just won national fame by covering 1,000 miles in 1,000 hours on foot. By contrast, Molyneaux went on a lucrative provincial tour with Richmond, intermittently exhibiting and sparring; took on a relatively meaningless fight with Rimmer, a rough and ready Lancastrian, in May 1811; and relished his fame and the chance to live the good life as he saw it. The outcome was defeat in the rematch, in September 1811, at Thistleton Gap, near Leicester, where Cribb was the fit man and Molyneaux the jaded fighter.

Molyneaux's career was now all anticlimax. An attempt by Richmond to rehabilitate his man in a match against Jack Carter ended with Carter's dubious surrender after he appeared to be winning throughout the fight. Carter and Molyneaux went on tour together, and Richmond broke with his now unmanageable countryman who was giving full rein to all his passions—for fine clothes, food, drink, and the indiscriminate company of women. There was one more fight in Scotland in 1813, against the young William Fuller who, by a fine irony, was in his turn to move to the United States and do much to promote the cause of boxing in North America. Molyneaux moved on to Ireland, where his damaging life-style took its final toll. He died in the arms of two other African Americans serving in the 77th Regiment in the guardhouse of Galway Barracks, where he was taking refuge. It was a mere seven and a half years after his first famous battle with Tom Cribb.

The impact made by Molyneaux's achievements in his own country was minimal and scarcely noted in the press. However, his importance in the history of prizefighting was considerable. While he was by no means the first black fighter in the British ring, he made the path somewhat easier for the dozen or more black boxers who appeared during the next twenty years. His challenge, too, raised the issue of the nature of the "Championship," and the question, scarcely asked at the time, as to whether it was a solely British preserve. Finally, the sight of a white and a black fighter struggling against each other at the highest levels of sport had a significance that went beyond boxing and sport itself.

• The most contemporary account of Molyneaux's fighting career is in Anon., *Pancratia, or a History of Pugilism*, 2d ed. (1815). Other early histories of the sport rely heavily on press reports, in the case of Pierce Egan, *Boxiana* (5 vols., 1812–1829), usually his own. Press accounts of the first Cribb fight are analyzed in Carl B. Cone, "The Molneaux-Cribb Fight, 1810: Wuz Tom Milineaux Robbed," and in Dennis Brailsford, "Morals and Maulers: The Ethics of Early Pugilism," *Journal of Sport History*, vol. 9, no. 3 (1982), and vol. 12, no. 2 (1985). See also Eliot J. Gorn, *The Manly Art: Bare Knuckle Prize Fighting in America* (1986); John Ford, *Prizefighting: The Age of Regency Boximania* (1971); and Dennis Brailsford, *Bareknuckles: A Social History of Prize-Fighting* (1988).

DENNIS BRAILSFORD

MONCKTON, Robert (24 June 1726–21 May 1782), army officer and colonial administrator, was born in Yorkshire, England, the son of John Monckton, who was later the first Viscount Galway, a landowner, and member of Parliament, and Lady Elizabeth Manners, daughter of the second duke of Rutland. At age fifteen Monckton was commissioned in the Third Foot Guards. He fought against the French in the major battles of Dettingen (1743) and Fontenoy (1745), gaining promotion to captain in 1744, major in 1747, and lieutenant colonel in 1751. Becoming a member of Parliament for the family-controlled seat of Pontefract from 1751 to 1754, he showed his preference for the military life by joining his regiment in Nova Scotia in 1752.

Monckton distinguished himself as a soldier and administrator in Nova Scotia. After ten months commanding Fort Lawrence, facing the French Fort Beauséjour at Chignecto Bay, he joined the colonial council at Halifax. When new German settlers rioted against the garrison at Lunenburg, Monckton volunteered to lead 200 men to restore order. His humane and judicious approach to settler grievances, in contrast to Nova Scotia lieutenant governor Charles Lawrence's wish for retribution, was successful. Monckton spent the winter of 1754–1755 in Boston, helping Massachusetts governor William Shirley with preparations for the only successful British expedition of that year. Monckton led the 2,000 New England volunteers and 270 British regulars who sailed from Boston near the end of May 1755. The mission's careful planning and complete secrecy resulted in an unopposed landing at Fort Lawrence on 2 June. The badly outnumbered defenders of Fort Beauséjour, unable to disrupt Monckton's systematic siege, surrendered two weeks later. Monckton granted them passage to Louisbourg and pardoned the Acadians who apparently had been forced to assist the defenders. The other French fort on the isthmus, Fort Gaspereau, surrendered two days later without a shot being fired. The unexpected speed of these conquests prompted Lieutenant Governor Lawrence to force the Acadians to take an unqualified oath of allegiance, an action they had successfully resisted for decades. They refused, and Monckton followed Lawrence's orders to lure the Acadians into custody, burn their villages, and supervise their transport to other British American colonies. Appointed lieutenant governor of Nova Scotia later that year, Monckton became acting governor twice during the next three years, each time working on preparations for the calling of the colony's first legislature.

Monckton returned to active military duty in late 1758 when he was assigned to destroy Acadian settlements for seventy miles along the St. John's River. Although General Jeffrey Amherst appointed him to command the army in the southern colonies, Monckton was chosen by William Pitt and James Wolfe to be second in command in the 1759 siege of Quebec. Monckton led the four battalions that by 30 June had gained control of Point Levis, a position that soon allowed twenty-nine cannon to protect the British fleet in the river and to bombard the town mercilessly. Although skeptical of the plan, he led the ill-fated 31 July attack on the Beaufort shore. Monckton delayed and moderated the enforcement, on the south shore, of Wolfe's harsh measures against unsympathetic Canadians. Tensions between Monckton and Wolfe were never serious, and the campaign moved quickly to its successful conclusion after Wolfe accepted a plan prepared by Monckton and the other brigadiers. Monckton was in command when British forces landed at Anse au Foulon and received a chest wound while commanding the right wing of Wolfe's army in that day's battle on the Plains of Abraham. Recovering quickly, Monckton commanded the conquered city for a month, showing special concern for protecting civilians from soldiers.

Promoted to colonel of the seventeenth Foot, Monckton served as commander of the British troops in the southern colonies in 1760. By March 1761 he was a major general and governor of the colony of New York. The following winter he commanded 14,000 soldiers in the successful invasion of Martinique, undertaken in conjunction with a fleet under Rear Admiral George Rodney. After another uneventful year as governor of New York, Monckton returned to England in June 1763. He became governor of Berwick-on-Tweed in 1765 and lieutenant general in 1770. In 1773 he declined an offer to become the next commander in chief in North America. The following year he became the member of Parliament for Pontefract once again; although he never spoke in Parliament, Monckton was regarded as a "friend of America." In 1778 he became governor of Portsmouth and member of Parliament for the town, holding both positions until his death in London. Though he never married, Monckton fathered three sons and a daughter.

• The largest collection of Monckton papers is in the National Archives of Canada, MG 18, M, which is very well calendared in *The Northcliffe Collection* (1926); there are also papers in the British Library; the Henry E. Huntington Library, San Marino, Calif.; the Library of Congress; the Northamptonshire Record Office, Northampton, England; the Public Record Office, London; and the University of Nottingham. See also D. H. Monckton, *A Geneological History of the Family of Monckton* (1887), and J. C. Webster, *The Forts of Chignecto; a Study of the Eighteenth Century Conflict between France and Great Britain in Acadia* (1930).

IAN K. STEELE

MONDAVI, Rosa Grassi (28 Mar. 1890–4 July 1976), boardinghouse operator and company president, was born in Sassoferrato, Italy. Her parents, Giovanni Grassi and Lucia (maiden name unknown), were farmers. She had no formal schooling and was trained in the domestic arts of cooking and home maintenance, by which she earned her living.

In 1908 Rosa married Caesare Mondavi, who had emigrated from Italy to the United States to work in the iron ore mines of northern Minnesota in 1906 and had returned to Italy to choose a wife from among his family's acquaintances. They settled in Ely, Minnesota, where Rosa ran a boardinghouse in their home and Caesare worked in the mines.

In the next fourteen years Rosa provided lodging and board for fifteen or more (sometimes as many as twenty-one) lodgers at a time, while also tending to the needs of her growing family. By the age of twenty-six she had given birth to her fourth and last child. Her daughter Helen recalls that in Minnesota her mother was "always busy," her work days lasting from 4:30 A.M. to 11:30 P.M. Her tasks included washing clothes, cleaning rooms, cooking meals, and packing lunches for her boarders.

The role of the boardinghouse operator during this period in reinforcing cultural traditions for single immigrant men has received scant attention in scholarly studies. Women like Rosa Mondavi established rules of conduct and companionship for their lodgers whereby they learned to respect the social graces of family life even though they were distant from their own kin.

By 1911 Rosa's earnings enabled the family to move to Virginia, Minnesota, where Caesare bought a saloon. After the arrival of Prohibition in 1921, he changed his stock to groceries.

In 1922 the Mondavis moved to Lodi, California, then the grape capital of the United States. Caesare started a small grape-shipping business, mainly to areas in the East populated with Italians interested in making wine for home consumption.

After Prohibition ended in 1933, the Mondavis expanded their business to producing bulk wine. At one time all the children worked in the business. At home they followed the traditions of the Italian peasant lifestyle their parents had brought from Italy, including maintaining a close, friendly relationship with the nearby farmers, many of them Italian, who grew the grapes the Mondavis shipped.

Rosa concentrated her energies on creating a home noted for its good food and hospitality. Local friends and business contacts of the Mondavi family considered Rosa's kitchen the social extension of the workplace. Every day she prepared meals ample to feed the grape growers and wine makers involved in the family business.

In 1943 the Mondavis had the opportunity to buy the neglected historic Krug winery in St. Helena, Napa County. Robert, the eldest son, remembers that it was the intercession of his mother, as well as the fact that the setting reminded Caesare of Italy, that convinced his cautious and traditional father to agree to the purchase. Caesare placed Robert and Peter in charge of the operations of Krug full-time, while he and Rosa remained in Lodi. The Mondavis transformed Krug into one of California's major table wine producers.

In Lodi, Caesare continued to supervise his shipping business while participating in the Krug partnership. After he died in 1959, Rosa became president of the company and moved to St. Helena permanently, still maintaining her home in Lodi. Accustomed to caring for others, she invited her widowed brother, Nazzareno Grassi, to leave Italy and live with her.

As company president, Rosa Mondavi did not conform to the Wall Street image of corporate power. Much of her business activity took place in her kitchen, where the company's board members and associates gathered to conduct business during an elaborate lunch or dinner. More the official hostess of the winery, her major role was to create a congenial atmosphere that created a business-social bond among board members. Keeping within the tradition of the Italian immigrant gender roles, Rosa Mondavi offered her advice and business opinions in private, mainly to board member Joseph Alioto, former mayor of San Francisco. She respected the tradition of permitting the men to govern in the public sector of community and family life, while reserving her right to exercise influence in private.

The Krug winery symbolized the Mondavis' pride and strength. Rosa's granddaughter Serena Ventura recalls, "For Rosa, the family and the company are one." Rosa said that Caesare, on his deathbed, had told her never to sell what they had worked so hard to achieve. In 1964 President Lyndon B. Johnson in recognition of the family's achievements invited Rosa and her sons to attend a state dinner. The guests represented a cross section of operators of key businesses founded and developed by Italian immigrants to the United States. Robert and his wife Margaret represented the family at the White House gathering.

After arguing with Peter over the mission and scope of Krug, in 1965 Robert left Krug to start his own winery. The discord between the brothers increased over the years. Rosa's loyalty remained with Krug and Peter, who took full control of its operation. Robert, accusing Peter of "persistent mismanagement" and violation of trust agreements, instituted a lawsuit against Krug in 1976. During the hearings on the case, Rosa died in St. Helena.

Rosa Mondavi's pioneering spirit and enterprise as boardinghouse operator created the foundation that launched the family wine-shipping business. Her central role as business partner and hostess at the Krug winery contributed to the success of that operation.

• Angelo M. Pellegrini, "Rosa Mondavi: Mother to Winegrowers," in *Americans by Choice* (1956), offers an in-depth look at Rosa Mondavi's personality. Serena Ventura, "Meet Signora Rosa Mondavi," *San Francisco Chronicle*, 15 Feb. 1976, documents the major developments of her grandmother's career. J. Vincenza Scarpaci, "La Contadina, The Plaything of the Middle Class Woman Historian," *Journal of Ethnic Studies* 9, no. 2 (Summer 1981), uses Rosa Mondavi's experience to discuss the central role of Italian immigrant women in family economics and cultural preservation. James Conaway, *Napa* (1990), provides a dramatic version of the Mondavi family saga. See also "Judge Orders Krug Winery Sold," *San Francisco Chronicle*, 14 Aug. 1976. An obituary is in the *Los Angeles Times*, 7 July 1976.

VINCENZA SCARPACI

MONDELL, Frank Wheeler (6 Nov. 1860–6 Aug. 1939), congressman, mine operator, and lawyer, was born in St. Louis, Missouri, the son of Ephraim Wheeler Mondell, a laborer, and Nancy Brown. Orphaned at the age of six, Frank lived for a short time with relatives in Iowa. When he was eight, he moved with an itinerant Congregational minister named Upton to Dickinson County, Iowa. Mondell did not graduate from high school and, at the age of eighteen, held various jobs in Chicago for a year, then migrated to Colorado in 1879. For the next eight years, he pursued employment in engineering and construction projects, roaming over a ten-state area. In 1887 the Kilpatrick Brothers and Collins, railroad contractors from Beatrice, Nebraska, hired Mondell to prospect for coal in northeastern Wyoming. His discovery in 1886 of a major bituminous coal deposit at Cambria altered his life. Mondell became the mine manager at Cambria. In 1889 the town of Newcastle, Wyoming, was surveyed, and Mondell became Newcastle's first mayor, 1889–1895. Concurrently with his mayoralty, he served two terms in the Wyoming State Senate, 1890–1894; he was elected president of the senate in 1893 and declined that position in 1894.

Mondell's early immersion into the economic and political life of northern Wyoming molded his approach to western institutions and federalism for the rest of his life. A strong advocate of states' rights, he steadfastly championed, throughout his political career, the transfer of public lands to private ownership. A traditional, loyal Republican, he gained the reputation of being the quintessential "party man" in and out of Washington. However, Mondell seldom hesitated to deviate from that party line when Republican philosophy threatened what he perceived as the best interests of the West.

After a brief flirtation as a Republican gubernatorial candidate, Mondell was elected to Congress in 1894. As a testimony to his personal concerns and those of his constituency, Mondell was assigned membership on the Committees of Mines and Mining and the Irrigation of Arid Lands. Though initially indecisive, he eventually adhered to the Republican platform of bimetallism, a stand that brought about his defeat in the congressional election of 1896. For the next two years, Mondell remained in Washington as assistant commissioner of the General Land Office. Elected again to Congress in 1898, Mondell served consecutively as "congressman from Newcastle" for the next twenty-four years. In 1899 Mondell married Ida Harris; they had five children. When the Republicans secured control of the House in the 1918 elections, Mondell became majority floor leader, a position he held until 1922, when he was defeated for the U.S. Senate by John B. Kendrick.

In Congress, Mondell quickly gained recognition for his espousal of "all things western." He vigorously protested the "locking up" of coal and agricultural lands in the West. Hence, he sponsored the 320-acre Homestead Law passed in 1909. When Mondell retired from Congress in 1922, he looked back proudly on various public domain laws relating to the separation of agricultural entry from minerals. Never an admirer of conservationists, Mondell dissented from the conservation philosophy of Theodore Roosevelt. However, he endorsed the National Reclamation Act of 1902, because it provided for private ownership of agricultural lands and state sovereignty over water allocation. States' rights were inevitably the litmus test for Mondell in all legislation on western resources.

As a fervent proponent of western economic interests and sovereignty, Mondell's "standpat protectionism" was applauded by the Wyoming electorate. Indeed, in 1906 Mondell decisively split with the Republican leadership when a powerful and persistent segment of the party advocated tariff reduction on sugar imported from the Philippine Islands. Mondell, in congressional debate, noted that the Republican party by its tariff stand had nurtured the sugar beet industry but now was threatening to kill that very industry. Though the Underwood Tariff temporarily decreased the rates on sugar, soon the Republican party returned to protectionism, which became the hallmark of Republicanism until the Second World War.

Mondell's stand on military affairs was consistent, conservative, and at times at odds with the West. A lifelong, bitter opponent of compulsory military service, Mondell voted for army appropriations but vehemently opposed a standing army of any significant size. In 1917 he admonished the House that standing armies were a favorite creation of tyrants—therefore compulsory universal military training was a tyrannical weapon. However, Mondell's primary protest against the military centered on his innate fiscal conservatism and fear that the enormous appropriations for the military build-up would create economic disaster. He concluded that European countries had become so heavily armed that they would never fight for fear of bankruptcy.

Aside from military budgets and conscription, Mondell followed the Republican leadership in foreign affairs. He supported the annexation of the Philippines on the basis that it was America's duty to emancipate the islands from a despotic government. He castigated Woodrow Wilson for his "meddlesome interference" in the Victoriano Huerta government of Mexico. In 1914 Mondell backed the president's neutrality stand on Europe, but in 1917 he voted for America's entrance into the First World War. On the Treaty of Versailles, Mondell agreed with the position of his Republican friends in the Senate. He accused Wilson of wanting "to go it alone," ignoring the sentiment of the Senate. Mondell's final war cry before the House was a warning that all World War I debts to the United States must be paid in full; otherwise, he warned, the country was courting economic disaster.

Mondell was a spellbinding orator, a westerner first and foremost, a party man, an agrarian, and a conservative. After his defeat in the senatorial campaign of 1922, he became a director of the War Finance Corporation, having declined Warren G. Harding's offers of the positions of ambassador to Japan or governor of Puerto Rico. In 1924 Mondell passed the Wyoming bar, and he practiced law in Washington, D.C., until his death. He received his law degree in 1926 from George Washington University. He died in Washington, D.C.

• A small, erratically diffuse collection of Mondell's personal papers is in the American Heritage Center, University of Wyoming. The most complete and pertinent source on Mondell's life is his autobiography, "My Story," which was published serially in the *Wyoming State Tribune*, 1 Aug. 1935–4 Feb. 1936. A summary of his legislative career is in Donald H. Werniment, "Frank W. Mondell as a Congressman" (M.A. thesis, Univ. of Wyoming, 1956). Additional biographical data is in T. A. Larson, *History of Wyoming* (1965; 2d ed., 1990), and Virginia Trenholm, ed., *Wyoming Blue Book*, vol. 2 (1974). Useful biographical obituaries are in the *Newcastle Letter Journal*, 10 Aug. 1939, and the *Wyoming State Tribune* and the *New York Times*, 7 Aug. 1939.

GENE M. GRESSLEY

MONEY, Hernando de Soto (26 Aug. 1839–18 Sept. 1912), congressman and senator, was born in Holmes County, Mississippi, the son of Pierson Money, a planter, and Triphena Vardaman. During Money's early childhood, his family moved to Carrollton, where he attended the local schools and also studied under a private tutor. Enrolling in the literary department at the University of Mississippi in 1856, he entered the law school two years later and received his degree in 1860. He practiced law in Carrollton until the outbreak of the Civil War and then enlisted as a private in the Confederate army. Wounded and captured by Union forces in 1863, he spent several months in prison. Although promoted to lieutenant after his release, he retired from military duty in September 1864 because of problems with his eyesight. In November 1863 he married Claudia Jane Boddie; they had six children, five of whom survived infancy.

At the end of the war, Money resumed his law practice in Carrollton and operated a cotton plantation that he had acquired in Leflore County. He also edited a newspaper in Carrollton until 1873 and then moved to Winona to publish and edit another newspaper. He served briefly as mayor of Winona in 1875. A successful Democratic candidate for Congress in 1874, he resigned his mayorship and discontinued his editorial duties to take his congressional seat in December 1875. After five consecutive terms, he decided not to run for reelection but remained in Washington for eight more years practicing law. He then returned to Mississippi and regained his congressional seat in 1892. He represented the state's north-central district for two more terms.

During Money's fourteen years as a congressman, he became the ranking Democrat on the Committee on Post Offices and Post Roads, presiding as chairman four years. Believing that the postal system should serve the public interest, he supported a reduction of postage rates and the establishment of a postal savings depository. He also worked to break up the star route postal ring, a fraudulent scheme by which postal officials awarded mail contracts to low bidders who later charged large sums for fictitious extra services. An influential member of the Committees on Naval Affairs and Foreign Affairs, he advocated a strong navy to protect the country and its commerce, declaring, "No nation can so readily secure peace as by being prepared for war." In January 1897 Congressman Money went to Cuba on a controversial fact-finding mission that received widespread coverage in the press and influenced passage of a bill to provide relief funds for the Cuban people.

In October 1897 Money was appointed to fill the seat of the deceased senator James Z. George, his close friend and political mentor. Money subsequently served two full senatorial terms. Although he had held high rank in the House of Representatives, he achieved greater prominence in the Senate. He served on the important Committees of Finance and Foreign Relations and, despite failing eyesight, performed extensive research on major issues. A member of the Democratic Steering Committee, he was party whip before his election as minority leader in December 1909. Under Money's leadership, the Democrats in the Senate became more united and aggressive in support of their party's goals, which included an income tax, lower tariffs, and other economic and social reforms. A Washington journalist reported that the Mississippi senator was "among the very few" who understood "the art of being severe and parliamentary at the same time."

An authority on international affairs, Senator Money supported the annexation of Hawaii and intervention in Cuba but opposed the acquisition of the Philippine Islands. "The pretense that we are to hold the Philippines for the moral, political, or spiritual benefit of their inhabitants," he asserted, "is fraudulent and hypocritical" ("Conquest and the Constitution," p. 339). In response to U.S. participation in the Moroccan Conference in 1906, Money questioned American involvement in the political affairs of another hemisphere. He also criticized President Theodore Roosevelt's decision to intervene in the affairs of the Dominican Republic, telling the Senate, "I do not believe the American people have conferred any power upon the President of the United States to interfere in settling the debts of other people and maintaining order in other countries."

Along with other southern Democrats, Senator Money stood as a staunch defender of white supremacy. In opposition to a bill to reduce a state's representation for denial of the elective franchise, he argued that he knew of no state that discriminated against race or color and that literacy qualifications did not violate the Fourteenth Amendment. "Suffrage is not a natural right," he declared. "It is a privilege based upon a capacity to do a duty. An ignorant vote . . . is felt everywhere . . . [and] may determine a national contest" ("Shall Illiteracy Rule?" *Independent* 52 [18 June 1900]: 175). He retired from public office in March 1911 after serving in Congress for twenty-eight years, longer than any other Mississippian before him, and never suffering political defeat.

In retirement Money lived on the Mississippi coast and continued to be active in public service. As a member of the National Monetary Commission, he visited Europe to study financial affairs and then reported the commission's findings to Congress. He also served on the Lincoln Memorial Commission. He died at his home in Mississippi City.

In a memorial address in the House of Representatives, 26 February 1913, Congressman B. P. "Pat" Harrison of Mississippi characterized Money as "true at all times to the Democratic theory of government and . . . an intense partisan and party man." With superior knowledge of constitutional law and keen analytical skills, Money made a significant contribution to the national legislative process, and in doing so he helped shape the post–Civil War Democratic party into a stronger, more viable political force.

• In the absence of any known collection of Money's papers, microfilmed newspapers of the period are the best primary sources for his public career. Some of his letters are in the Governor's Records and other manuscript collections in the Mississippi Department of Archives and History. His published speeches are in Special Collections at the University of Mississippi. See the *Congressional Record* (44th Cong.–48th Cong. [1875–1885] and 53d Cong.–62d Cong. [1892–1913]) for other details of his speeches and his political views. Among the periodical articles by Money are "The United States and the Spanish American Colonies: A Reply," *North American Review* 165 (Sept. 1897): 356–63; "Our Duty to Cuba," *Forum* 25 (Mar. 1898): 17–24; "Conquest and the Constitution," *Arena* 23 (Apr. 1900): 337–42; and "The Latest Appointments to the Supreme Court: Chief Justice White," *Independent* 70 (2 Mar. 1911): 455–56. Detailed biographical sketches are in Dunbar Rowland, *Mississippi*, vol. 2 (1907), and Clayton Rand, *Men of Spine in Mississippi* (1940). William F. Holmes, *The White Chief James Kimble Vardaman* (1970), provides brief information on Money's personal and public life. A recent assessment of his political activity is in Thomas N. Boschert, "A Family Affair: Mississippi Politics, 1882–1932" (Ph.D. diss., Univ. of Mississippi, 1995). Obituaries are in the *Memphis Commercial Appeal*, the *New Orleans Times Picayune*, and the *Jackson (Miss.) Clarion Ledger*, all 19 Sept. 1912.

THOMAS N. BOSCHERT

MONINGER, Mary Margaret (23 Sept. 1892–21 Mar. 1950), missionary, was born near Marshalltown, Iowa, the daughter of William Ringland Moninger and Mary Helen "Minnie" Kellogg, farmers. Called Margaret from birth, Moninger graduated Phi Beta Kappa from Grinnell College, her parents' alma mater, in 1913 and received an M.A. from Grinnell in 1922. She did not marry. In 1911 she joined the Student Volunteer Movement for Foreign Missions (SVMFM), which was active on many campuses in the early twentieth century, and also belonged to the Young Women's Christian Association and Christian Endeavor. Following graduation she taught mathematics and Latin for two years at the New Providence, Iowa, high school.

Like many brilliant women of her generation, Moninger decided to become a missionary to see the world and have an adventurous, yet totally respectable, life while escaping the confines of American society, which offered women few career opportunities. She applied to the Presbyterian Board of Foreign Missions in 1913 while at an SVMFM meeting in Kansas City, requesting assignment to China. She was assigned to Nanking in 1914 but declined the appointment, explaining she had given her word to the principal that she would teach another year and would not break her word. In January 1915 she was assigned to Hainan and sailed from San Francisco on 2 August. She reached Hainan via Hawaii, Japan, the Philippines, and Hong Kong. During her years in China she was supported by the Waterloo, Iowa, Presbyterial, her home group.

In Hainan Moninger was the first of the missionaries taught to speak the Kachek (Jiaji) dialect, and her colleagues acknowledged her the best among them at the written language. She compiled a massive, two-volume dictionary of the Hainanese colloquial and English, which she carried home in 1942 but never published. She was likely the only female missionary in China to produce a dictionary of the Chinese language.

She collected botanical specimens in Hainan's rain forests and sent them to E. D. Merrill at the Manila Bureau of Science and to Henry S. Conard at Grinnell. Merrill named a plant for her, and her specimens are today at Harvard and Iowa State universities and the national arboretum of the Philippines.

Moninger taught and served as principal of girls' schools at the mission's three stations, Kachek, Nodoa (Nada), and Kiungchow (Ch'iungshan) and, with her students, participated in the many public meetings that accompanied the arrival of the May Fourth movement in Hainan in the 1920s. She was a lifelong advocate for the education and emancipation of women. She served as mission secretary, treasurer, and agent for many years and was one of six women to serve on the countrywide Presbyterian China Council, which met in Shanghai and set policy for the church's missions. She was a delegate to the general assembly of the Church of Christ in China in Amoy in 1933. She wrote most of the articles in and edited the mission's 1919 publication, *The Isle of Palms: Sketches of Hainan*. Republished in 1980 as part of the Hoover Institution's series on the economy of modern China, it is the only work in the series by a missionary and was, for many years, the only book in English about modern-day Hainan.

The Hainan mission required all its members to take yearly vacations, and Moninger customarily took hers in Hong Kong in the summer, following the end of the school term. She spent 1922–1923 at home on furlough. With her colleagues she fled violence in Hainan for the safety of Haiphong, French Indochina, for six weeks in 1925 (where she edited *Refugee Rampage*, a humorous newsletter), and more unrest sent her home on furlough from 1927 to 1929. During these years she taught at the Washington, Iowa, high school and did graduate work at the State University of Iowa, Iowa City. Her last furlough at home was in 1933–1934.

Moninger edited the mission's *Hainan Newsletter* during most of the years she was in China. In the 1930s she published several anthropological articles in the *Lingnan Science Journal* and the *Journal of the North China Branch of the Royal Asiatic Society* on the lifestyles, textiles, decorative symbolism, and agricultural techniques of the aboriginal Miao people (now identified as Yao) of Hainan; on the lifestyles of the Hainanese; and on the island's flora. She wrote articles for church periodicals and Hong Kong newspapers and for the *Marshalltown* (Iowa) *Times-Republican*. Her testimonial for Ivory soap was published in U.S. women's magazines in 1922, and she used her payment to educate a Hainanese girl for a year.

The Japanese invaded Hainan in 1937 and held Moninger and her colleagues at the Nodoa station under virtual house arrest from May 1939 to March 1940. With her irrepressible sense of humor intact, she issued the *Sing Sing Sentinel*. Finally permitted to leave Nodoa she took a vacation in Hong Kong and on return to Hainan was assigned by the mission to Kiungchow. With a colleague she was placed under house arrest in July 1941 in Kiungchow and was later moved to Hoihow (Haikou), the adjacent port, where she joined three more colleagues. The five missionaries were humanely treated by their captors, whom they entertained at tea on Christmas 1941 (when propaganda pictures published in Japanese newspapers were taken) and in January 1942, on the same day newspapers in the United States were printing front-page stories of their murders by the Japanese. Moninger and her colleagues were repatriated via Taiwan, Shanghai, Lorenco Marques, Africa, and Rio de Janeiro, in the first exchange of noncombatants on the *Conte Verde* and the *Gripsholm* in the summer of 1942. During her years in China she wrote home every Sunday, and in retirement she wrote unpublished accounts of her career, her house arrest, and her repatriation. Returning to Iowa, Moninger taught school at Buffalo Center until a stroke in 1944 forced her retirement. She died in Marshalltown, Iowa.

• Mary Margaret Moninger's papers are located primarily at the Presbyterian Historical Society, Philadelphia, and at the University of Oregon Library, Eugene. Grinnell College, Iowa, has a few of her papers. Her SVMFM application is in the SVMFM collection at the Yale University Divinity School Library, New Haven. The *Hainan NewsLetter* identifies her only as M. M. M., editor, and the microfilm edition identifies her as the Reverend Moninger. Her major articles are "The Hainanese Miao," *Journal of the North China Branch of the Royal Asiatic Society* 52 (1921): 40–50; "The Hainanese Miao and Their Food Supply," *Lingnan Science Journal* 11, no. 4 (1932): 521–26; "Paper Making in Stone Bridge Village, Hainan Island," *Lingnan Science Journal* 12, no. 3 (1933): 441–44; "Picturesque Hainan," *Forward*, 21 Jan. 1922, p. 18, 28 Jan. 1922, p. 26, and 4 Feb. 1922, p. 34; "Salt Making in Kheng-dong District, Island of Hainan," *Lingnan Science Journal* 13, no. 4 (1934): 697–98; "Trees and Typhoons in Hainan," *Lingnan Science Journal* 13, no. 2 (1934):

323–25ff; and "Times of Testing in China," *Women and Missions* 4 (Jan. 1928): 384–85. The only biography of Moninger is Kathleen L. Lodwick, *Educating the Women of Hainan: The Career of Margaret Moninger in China, 1915–1942* (1995).

KATHLEEN L. LODWICK

MONIS, Judah (4 Feb. 1683–25 Apr. 1764), Hebraist and educator, was born to parents of unknown name and origin, although, according to at least one contemporary source, he was born in Italy (probably Venice) and was educated at the Hebrew academies in Leghorn and Amsterdam. Some scholars believe he may have been a member of a Portuguese Marrano family (on the evidence of his name), but his pronunciation of Hebrew—as indicated in the transliterations he used for his students—is "unmistakably that of the Italian Jews of his time" (Moore, p. 288).

Monis was in New York City by 28 February 1716 when, according to a municipal register, "Judah Monis, merchant" was admitted as a freeman of the city. He was also reported to have been a rabbi in New York and in Jamaica, Long Island (or, more likely, the island of Jamaica); some historians think he may instead have been a rebbe, or Jewish teacher. It is known, however, that Monis by this time was in correspondence with some of the New England intellectual community. A letter in Hebrew to Samuel Johnson, later the first president of King's College (now Columbia University), dated 2 March 1716, is preserved in the Johnson archives at Columbia; Monis also wrote to the Harvard Corporation about the Hebrew grammar he had completed. In June 1720 he was in Boston with the manuscript of his book and proposed to the members of the corporation that he be given an appointment as a teacher of Hebrew, then a required but unpopular subject.

On 27 March 1722 Monis was baptized a Christian at a public ceremony in the College Hall. On that occasion the new convert delivered a discourse titled "The Truth," one of three theological essays he had written in defense of Christianity, countering the rabbinical view that the Messiah was still to come with arguments that demonstrate his knowledge of the Talmud, Midrash, and cabalistic writings. (This knowledge perhaps made Monis a more accurate interpreter of the Bible than colleagues who depended on Christian-oriented biblical commentaries.) His three-part work, *Three Discourses: The Truth, the Whole Truth, and Nothing but the Truth*, was published in one volume in Boston later that year; the first essay featured a preface by Increase Mather. Monis's own dedicatory preface to the discourse is an apologia for his conversion. Nevertheless, Monis allegedly continued all his life to observe the Saturday Sabbath. In the opinion of Rabbi George Kohut, a late nineteenth-century scholar, Monis converted solely for practical reasons.

A month after his conversion, Monis received an appointment as the first instructor of Hebrew at Harvard, teaching four classes a week. The next year he was awarded an honorary M.A. from Harvard, becoming the first Jew to receive an academic degree in the North American colonies. In 1723 Monis married Abigail Marrett (or Maret), the Christian daughter of a Cambridge storekeeper. The couple had no children. The Harvard Corporation, satisfied with his first year of teaching, voted to renew Monis's appointment and did so each year thereafter until his retirement in 1760. (Not until after Monis's death was an endowed professorship of Hebrew established at the school; Samuel Sewell, one of Monis's former students, was the first incumbent.)

Monis's students, however, were bored by his teaching style, which was still based on drill and recitation rather than the new lecture method; Sewell, for example, later wrote that Monis's instruction never gave him any sense of the "form or comeliness" of the language (Goldman, p. 239). His students also complained that they had to make their own copies of his Hebrew grammar because the manuscript was not actually printed until 1735. In retaliation for this inconvenience, they subjected their teacher to continual harassment, and by 1755 he was giving only one class per week.

Monis's grammar, titled (in his transliteration) *Dickdook Leshon Gnebreet: A Grammar of the Hebrew Tongue*, together with his translations into Hebrew of the Lord's Prayer and the Apostles' Creed, was published in Cambridge and made use of a complete font of Hebrew type sent from London by a Harvard benefactor. It was the first such font in the colonies, and Monis's work, therefore, ranks as the "earliest specimen of Hebrew scholarship in America" (Kohut, p. 226); the grammar was used at Dartmouth College and other New England institutions as well. About 1735 Monis also wrote "A Dissertation upon the 24th and the Beginning of the 25th Verses of the 49th Chapter of Genesis, with an Historical Narrative of the Present Jewish Creed about the Two Messiahs"; it seems never to have been printed and neither was his dictionary of postbiblical Hebrew. Further evidence of Monis's scholarly interests appears in the record of his borrowings from the Harvard library between 1712 and 1747, showing that he was among the most frequent users of the library and read works on law and modern British history as well as theology.

To augment his meager salary—never higher than that of a tutor—Monis opened a general store in Cambridge. Proficient in Spanish, he in 1735 translated official letters in the language for Jonathan Belcher, the governor of Massachusetts. In 1740 Belcher nominated Monis for justice of the peace in Middlesex County, but nothing came of this. Monis's wife died in 1760, whereupon he resigned his instructorship and lived the rest of his life with his wife's brother-in-law, the Reverend John Martyn, in Northborough, Massachusetts. He became a pillar of Martyn's church and, after his death in Northborough, was eventually buried there. In 1767 Martyn presented Monis's books and manuscripts (many in Hebrew) to the Harvard College Library.

Monis's career has aroused the interest of contemporary Jewish scholars, who debate the significance of his conversion and the degree of his proficiency in Hebrew. Clearly his scholarly attainments must have been considerable, enabling him to convey the principles of Hebrew grammar in English. Despite his difficulties as a teacher, Monis managed to impart a knowledge of the language to two generations of Harvard students, some of whom, in turn, became teachers of Hebrew.

• Material on Monis's life after he came to the American colonies is held at the Harvard University Archives. In addition to Shalom Goldman, ed., *Hebrew and the Bible in America: The First Two Centuries* (1993), recent scholarly assessments of Monis's position as convert and teacher, considered in the context of his time, include Milton M. Klein, "A Jew at Harvard in the Eighteenth Century," *Proceedings of the Massachusetts Historical Society* 97 (1985): 135–45; Jacob Rader Marcus, *The Colonial American Jew*, vol. 2 (1970); and Eisig Silberschlag, "Judah Monis in Light of an Unpublished Manuscript," *Proceedings of the American Academy for Jewish Research* 46–47 (1980): 495–529. George A. Kohut, "Judah Monis, M.A.: The First Instructor in Hebrew at Harvard University," *American Journal of Semitic Languages and Literature* 14 (1898): 217–26, evaluates the sincerity of his conversion and analyzes the pronunciation system used in the grammar. Extensive extracts from Monis's writings and the archival sources are usefully provided in Clifford K. Shipton, *Sibley's Harvard Graduates*, vol. 7 (1945); George Foote Moore's untitled address on Monis, read at a meeting of the Massachusetts Historical Society and published in *Proceedings of the Massachusetts Historical Society* 52 (1919): 285–312; Lee M. Friedman, "Judah Monis: First Instructor in Hebrew at Harvard University," *Proceedings of the American Jewish Historical Society* 22 (1914): 1–24; and Friedman, "Some Further Notes on Judah Monis," *Proceedings of the American Jewish Historical Society* 37 (1947): 121–34.

ELEANOR F. WEDGE

MONK, Maria (27 June 1816–4 Sept. 1849?), purported author of an anti-Catholic text, was born in Dorchester, Canada, the daughter of William Monk, a noncommissioned soldier stationed in Montreal, and Isabella Mills. After William Monk's death, Isabella Monk cleaned houses in the army camp. The children, four sons and Maria, were raised as Protestants. In interviews she gave after the publication of *Awful Disclosures of the Hotel Dieu Nunnery of Montreal* (1836), Monk's mother said that as a child of seven Maria had been injured when she pushed a "slate pencil" into her head. After this event, said her mother, Maria's behavior became more and more erratic and uncontrolled. As a teenager Monk worked as a servant. When Monk became sexually active, her mother placed her in a "Magdalen asylum" for the redemption of prostitutes, which was operated by an order of Catholic nuns in Montreal.

In November 1834 Monk, who was pregnant, was expelled from the asylum and may have attempted suicide by drowning. If the attempt was made, it failed when she was pulled from the river. In any event, in 1835 Monk and William K. Hoyt (or Hoyte), an anti-Catholic agitator who may have been the father of her child and was widely believed to be her lover, left Montreal for New York City. In New York, Hoyt introduced Monk to other anti-Catholic propagandists, including John Jay Slocum, Arthur Tappan, George Bourne, and Theodore Dwight. The group began to promote Monk throughout the city as an "escaped nun" and claimed her pregnancy was the result of sexual abuse by a Catholic priest, the "Abbe Patrick Phelan."

Monk's child (a son, according to the *New York Herald*) was born in July 1835; meanwhile the text that would become *Awful Disclosures* was written and published in an anti-Catholic weekly. What part Monk took in the writing of the book is unclear. At the time, George Bourne claimed to have been merely the scribe who took down Monk's recollections; later, Bourne, J. J. Slocum, and Theodore Dwight all claimed to be or were identified by others as being the principal writers. The story told in *Awful Disclosures* draws on familiar anti-Catholic tropes and myths and includes enough salacious material that the Kinsey Institute collection identifies it as the first pornographic text published in America.

The text was offered to Harper's for publication, but the firm decided that its details of rape, infanticide, and other scandalous activities made it an unsuitable book to bear the Harper's imprint. Instead, a dummy firm (Howe & Bates) was established in the name of two Harper's employees, and *Awful Disclosures* was published in January 1836. Initial sales were brisk, and support for Monk was widespread. Samuel B. Morse's enthusiasm was such that James Fenimore Cooper joked in a letter to a friend that Monk was likely to become Mrs. Morse.

Even while the book and Monk were enjoying their greatest popularity, responses from the Catholic church and from individuals questioned the "facts" in the book and the veracity of the supposed author. By summer, those voices were growing louder, so that by 12 August 1836 the *New York Herald* titled one editorial denouncing the text "Great Conspiracy of Religious and Literary Impostures against Public and Private Morals." The *Herald* kept up a steady stream of ridicule and analysis throughout the month of August, arguing on 18 August, "No doubt now exists but the story of Maria Monk is a gross and atrocious fabrication from first to last." Other mainstream journals joined in analyzing and condemning the text. William L. Stone's investigation of the Hotel Dieu convent, published first in the *New York Commercial Advertiser* in October 1836, was especially damning since it came from a respected voice in the anti-Catholic community. Although the *American Protestant Vindicator* and the Protestant Reform Society supported Monk's claims long past the time that ample evidence disproved them, by 1837 Monk was believed to be an escaped nun only by the most willfully blind anti-Catholic.

In 1837 Monk left New York for Philadelphia, where she spent some time with Dr. W. W. Sleigh, who called her "mentally unfit to be at large." On being found, she claimed to have been kidnapped by

Catholic priests, but this story did not find many believers. Monk, once again pregnant and increasingly erratic in her actions and speech, was no longer useful to the anti-Catholic cause and faded from the scene. The birth of a second child, a subsequent marriage, divorce, and descent into prostitution are less well documented. Most accounts have her dying in custody at Rikers Island in 1849, having been arrested for theft in a house of prostitution.

The young woman who was the real Maria Monk was known to the public for only a few years, when she was between the ages of eighteen and twenty-two. The fictional Maria Monk, the escaped nun who had been abused and horrified in the Hotel Dieu nunnery in Montreal, has had a much longer life. Sales of *Awful Disclosures* in the 1830s were large enough to make it one of the decade's bestselling books. In the 1850s, as another wave of anti-Catholicism provoked a new round of "escaped nun" tales, *Awful Disclosures* was reprinted, again to great sales. The book is still available from anti-Catholic groups, who offer it today as it was offered in the 1830s and 1850s, as "proof" of the perfidy of the church and its ministers.

• Most accounts of Maria Monk's life depend on Ray Allen Billington's accounts in "Maria Monk and Her Influence," *Catholic History Review* 22, no. 3 (Oct. 1936): 283–96, and *The Protestant Crusade* (1938). Richardson Wright's profile in *Forgotten Ladies* (1928) is a well-done popularization. Phillippe Sylvain has used Canadian sources to develop another view in "L'affaire Maria Monk," in *Cahiers des Dix* (1983), and the *Dictionary of Canadian Biography* (1966–). Billington warns against the account in John Gilmary Shea's three-volume *History of the Catholic Church in America* (1890), calling it "not only prejudiced but inaccurate." But whether anyone's account can accurately represent Monk's life is doubtful. Although the events around the publication of *Awful Disclosures* can be teased from the various lawsuits brought by the parties (see, for instance, *Colophon*, pt. 17 [1934]), the actual events of Monk's life are much less clear. Critical discussions of *Awful Disclosures* are in David Reynolds, *Faith in Fiction* (1981); Barbara Welter, "From Maria Monk to Paul Blanshard: A Century of Protestant Anti-Catholicism," in *Uncivil Religion: Interreligious Hostility in America*, ed. Robert N. Bellah and Frederick E. Greenspahn (1987); Jenny Franchot, *Roads to Rome* (1994); and Susan M. Griffin, "Awful Disclosures: Women's Evidence in the Escaped Nun's Tale," *PMLA*, Jan. 1996, pp. 93–107.

JoAnn Castagna

MONK, Thelonious (10 Oct. 1917–17 Feb. 1982), composer and pianist, was born Thelonious Sphere Monk in Rocky Mount, North Carolina, the son of Thelonious Monk and Barbara Batts. Raised in the San Juan Hill area of New York City, Monk became interested in the piano around age six. A largely self-taught musician who only later studied formally, Monk played piano and organ in church while in his teens and toured briefly with an evangelist. By age seventeen he began performing in jazz groups around New York.

From 1941 to 1952 Monk performed and recorded with groups that included Charlie Christian, Coleman Hawkins, Charlie Parker, Kenny Clarke, and Dizzy Gillespie. According to jazz historian James Lincoln Collier, his early work exhibited influences of Earl "Fatha" Hines and Art Tatum.

During this period Monk began to develop his individuality not only in performance and composition but behavior as well. He became the focal point of bebop culture through his wearing of dark glasses, dancing on stage, and adopting a lax attitude toward promptness. Monk was seen as the epitome of the cool, hip, counterculture revolutionary that was in vogue in bebop. He was a cultural hero of the "hipsters," men who dressed in zoot suits and uttered phrases such as "be cool, man."

Monk developed his individual piano style in the early 1940s as well. Unlike the styles of pianists Al Haig, Billy Taylor, Bud Powell, and George Wallington, Monk's style was that of a leader and composer rather than a sideman. His sideman recordings, nonetheless significant, are limited primarily to sessions with Art Blakey, Miles Davis, Coleman Hawkins, Gigi Gryce, and Sonny Rollins.

As an improviser Monk played in a unique style. Sparse and punctuated with silence, his chord voicings often consisted of only two notes (third and seventh). His lines display jagged contours, tone clusters, whole-tone scales, uneven rhythms, and a tendency to play behind the beat. Monk's infatuation with scales other than major and minor was also hinted at as early as *Brilliant Corners* (1956; Riverside 226), which includes melodic segments that evoke both the Lydian mode and the whole-tone scale.

Monk's style is intimately bound with the way he used his fingers and hands. His flat-fingered technique meant that each finger had the capacity to play two adjacent notes. Monk's recording of "Misterioso" provides many examples. He also made use of large intervals in his right hand. Monk was distinguished from other beboppers in that he usually used unpredictable off-beat phrasing, generally on two and four, especially when playing eighth- and sixteenth-note runs. He was not as technically proficient as pianists Haig and Powell and he instead incorporated chord clusters, the whole-tone scale, and unresolved chromatic tones as focal points to create tension. His improvisations often featured jagged contours, and like other beboppers, he used many altered chords (such as flatted fifths and sharp ninths). Monk also used stride piano techniques reminiscent of Hines and Fats Waller. When comping or improvising, his approach was more vertical than linear and more harmonic and rhythmic than technically fluent.

Monk's influence on modern jazz oddly parallels that of Tatum. Where Tatum featured an impeccable technique, full chords on all four beats of a measure, extended chord structures, nondiatonic progressions, and embellished runs to connect phrases, Monk was known for chord clusters, substitutions, and altered harmonies. Monk's style suited bebop, where Tatum's style was that of a solo performer. The influence of both men can be heard in later generations' adoption of their styles.

Monk's compositions "Round about Midnight," "Off Minor," "Misterioso," "Blue Monk," "Bemsha Swing," and "Straight, No Chaser" have become jazz standards. His tune "Rhythm-n-ing," based on "I've Got Rhythm," features a challenging use of accents. Interesting uses of metrical displacements can also be heard in "Bemsha Swing," a 32-bar AABA composition that begins with two notes, then continues the theme on the upbeat of four. He also includes an imitation in canon between the piano and the saxophone (Johnny Griffin) at the interval of one beat. In "Straight, No Chaser," a blues, Monk uses a single rifflike idea that is repeated throughout the composition and is accompanied by shifting accents. It does not break down neatly into the three four-bar phrases of a standard blues. Instead, it is divided into two six-measure sections with the melody beginning with a three-beat pattern, followed by five beats.

A large portion of Monk's compositions are written in 32-bar AABA form ("Epistrophy," "Round about Midnight"). He also wrote several blues in addition to "Blue Monk." Earlier compositions like "Evidence," "Misterioso," and "Criss Cross" feature motivic development, angular melodies, and rhythmic displacements. In later compositions like "Jackie-ing" and "Crepuscule with Nellie" Monk features many dissonant and unresolved intervals. He creates in his compositions an openness that allows the improviser to play outside the stated chord-scale relationships.

In 1944, the year Monk performed with Gillespie's orchestra at the Spotlite Club, "Round about Midnight" was recorded by Cootie Williams. Monk led his own sextet in recordings for Blue Note from 1947 until 1952, and several more of his classics date from this period, including "Straight, No Chaser," "Ruby My Dear," "Criss Cross," and "Evidence." Two of his recordings made in 1950, "Bloomdido" and "My Melancholy Baby," feature Parker. After leaving Blue Note, Monk recorded both as a leader and as a sideman (with Rollins, Davis, and Milt Jackson) for Prestige Records. In 1954 his first solo album, *Thelonious Monk* (Swing 33342), was released.

In 1955 Monk signed with Riverside Records, where he remained under contract until 1961. Ostensibly to counter criticism that he could only play his own compositions, he included on his first two Riverside albums several Duke Ellington compositions and a set of jazz standards. In 1957, after his second solo LP, *Thelonious Himself* (Riverside 235), appeared, he held a long-running engagement at the Five Spot Cafe, resulting in the classic *Thelonious Monk with John Coltrane* (Jazzland 946).

By the late 1950s Monk was widely regarded as a unique and creative composer and improviser. Besides Coltrane, his groups included, at different times, Johnny Griffin, Charlie Rouse, and Roy Haynes. Important dates in Europe and at home led to the blossoming of his career in the early 1960s. He signed a contract with Columbia Records in 1962, and two years later he toured Japan. During the late 1960s he again performed in Europe, with both an octet and a quartet. Around 1970 he disbanded his group and joined the new Giants of Jazz, which also featured Blakey, Gillespie, Al McKibbon, Sonny Stitt, and Kai Winding. He continued to record separately, however, and in November 1971 he made solo and trio recordings for Black Lion Records in London. Soon afterward he went into semiretirement, limiting his performances to three with an orchestra at Carnegie Hall and an appearance with his quartet at the 1975 and 1976 Newport Jazz Festivals. Monk was married to Nellie (maiden name unknown); they had two children. Nellie served as a pillar of strength in his life. As both wife and confidante she helped him cope with bouts of depression and drug addiction at home and on the road. She traveled extensively with his bands, an uncommon role for the wife of a jazz musician. Monk spent his last years in seclusion at his home in Weehawken, New Jersey, and at the home of the Baroness Pannonica de Koenigswarter, a friend and patron. He died in Weehawken.

The significance of Monk's career can be assessed in two different but connected ways. His musical compositions endure because they cover the gamut of jazz concepts and techniques. In "Smoke Gets in Your Eyes," "Crepuscule with Nellie," and "Carolina Moon," he altered the existing material to produce compositions permeated with harmonic clusters and dissonances. Rhythmic surprises can be heard in "Straight, No Chaser," and innovative melodies using aspects of the chromatic and whole-tone scales and the Lydian mode can be heard in "Brilliant Corners." Monk's improvisations are also important because he used an unconventional approach to performing on the piano. Since he lacked the right-hand dexterity of some of his contemporaries, especially Tatum, Powell, and Taylor, he was often accused of playing wrong notes. His style, rooted in the Harlem stride piano style of Luckey Roberts and Waller, featured rhythmic surprises, tone clusters, a descending whole-tone scalar passage, and an ability to craft a logical and coherent improvisation from tunes as diverse as blues such as "Misterioso" and "Blue Monk" and standards such as "Round about Midnight" and "Smoke Gets in Your Eyes." Because his compositions and improvisations are strikingly memorable for their approaches to harmony, melody, and rhythm, and because both have been emulated extensively by other jazz artists, Monk continues to be an influence and inspiration.

• Bob Houston, *Thelonious Monk* (1989), covers Monk's life from his ragtime influences to his significance as a bebop composer and pianist. Houston includes an analysis of Monk's music by Dave Gelly and comments on several Monk arrangements by Brian Priestly. A discussion of Monk's life and music can be found in the following: Ran Blake, "Thelonious Monk," in *The New Grove Dictionary of Jazz* (1988), pp. 121–23; "The Pianists: Tadd Dameron, Bud Powell and Thelonious Monk," in *Jazz: A History* (1993), pp. 316–23; James Lincoln Collier, *The Making of Jazz: A Comprehensive History* (1978), pp. 382–89; J. Langford, "Monk's Horns," *Jazz Journal* 23, no. 11 (1970): 2; J. R. Mitchell, "Thelonious Monk: The Man and His Music,"

Jazz Spotlite News 2, no. 3 (1981): 51; and Ran Blake, "Thelonious Monk: The Music," *Wire*, no. 10 (1984), pp. 28–31 (a scholarly assessment of Monk's music). Discographies of Monk's music can be found in J. G. Jepsen, *A Discography of Thelonious Monk and Bud Powell* (1969), and M. Ruppli, "Discographie de Thelonious Monk," *Jazz Hot*, no. 331 (1976), pp. 21–23. An interview of Monk that details his musical philosophy and comments regarding his life can be found in L. Tomkins, "The Classic Interview: Thelonious Monk," *Crescendo International* 24, no. 6 (1987): 11–16. Also see Nat Hentoff, "The Private World of Thelonious Monk," *Esquire*, Apr. 1960, pp. 133–37; Orrin Keepnews, "Thelonious Monk," *Record Changer*, 7, no. 4 (1948): 5; and Martin Williams, "Thelonious Monk: Modern Jazz in Search of Maturity," in *The Jazz Tradition* (1970), pp. 117–31.

EDDIE S. MEADOWS

MONROE, Charlie (4 July 1903–27 Sept. 1975), country music guitarist, vocalist, and bandleader, was born in Rosine, Kentucky, the son of James Buchanan "Buck" Monroe, a farmer and buck dancer, and Melissa Vandiver, a singer, fiddler, and accordion and harmonica player. Monroe was raised in rural western Kentucky, where his family operated a large, successful farm and sawmill. He was exposed to music from an early age by his mother and her brother Pendleton Vandiver ("Uncle Pen"), one of the best-loved fiddlers of the region. Charlie took up guitar, while his elder brother Birch played fiddle; the youngest brother, William Smith ("Bill") played guitar as well but soon switched to mandolin. After working for a while for their father, in the late 1920s Charlie and Birch relocated to the industrial North, first trying to find work in Detroit, Michigan, apparently unsuccessfully, returning to Kentucky, and then finally settling in Hammond, Indiana, where they held jobs in local oil refineries unloading drums of oil. Bill joined them there, and by the early 1930s the three began performing locally as musicians and dancers, while continuing to work for the oil companies. Charlie was less interested in manual labor than the others and pursued more actively a performing career. The three brothers were eventually discovered by a producer of Chicago's WLS's "National Barn Dance" program, and they toured with a group from the show as dancers. However, in 1934, when the group became a full-time professional outfit, Birch bowed out, returning to work in the refineries.

Now working as a duo, with Charlie singing lead vocals and playing guitar and Bill adding high tenor and playing lightning-speed mandolin runs, the two were hired to perform on radio in 1933 first in Iowa, and then in Omaha, Nebraska, where they met announcer-promoter Byron Parker, who went by the colorful nickname of "The Old Hired Hand." Parker began aggressively promoting their career, leading to radio work through the Carolinas, and by 1936 the brothers had a contract with Bluebird (the budget division of RCA Victor Records). The brothers dressed in natty white suits, ranger-style hats, and boots and played matching Gibson instruments. They recorded many classic songs, including "Nine Pound Hammer Is Too Heavy," an up-tempo retelling of the John Henry story; "Feast Here Tonight"; and "Roll in My Sweet Baby's Arms." The duo recorded about sixty sides through spring 1938 that became highly influential because of Bill's increasingly recognized talent. The more laidback Charlie was willing to take a secondary role, although his rowdy behavior and increasing failure to show up for performances irked his more serious younger sibling; this led to a quarrel between the brothers in mid-1938, and they split up.

Charlie Monroe began gathering a group of musicians for a band, eventually called the Kentucky Pardners, who worked a variety of rural radio stations in Tennessee, Virginia, West Virginia, and Kentucky through the mid-1940s. Some noteworthy musicians played with him, including mandolinists Zeke Morris, Curly Sechler, and Lester Flatt (who later switched to guitar when he joined Bill Monroe's band), and banjo player David Akeman, who performed under the name "Stringbean," adding a rural comedy element to the act; both Akeman and Flatt would eventually go on to work with Bill Monroe, as members of his Blue Grass Boys group.

Charlie Monroe rejoined RCA Victor records in 1946, staying with the label for five years, primarily recording traditional country songs, including "Down in the Willow Garden" and "Rose Lee McFall." His band was much more low-keyed than brother Bill's, and his sweet vocals, sung in a relaxed style, were in keeping with the band's soft-country approach. He recorded sporadically through the mid-1950s for Decca and then, with his style of old-time country music fading in popularity, retired to work a farm on the outskirts of Beaver Dam, Kentucky, in 1957.

Monroe performed only rarely through 1972, when his wife died of cancer. Then living in Cross Plains, Tennessee, he was coaxed out of retirement by bluegrass guitarist-vocalist Jimmy Martin and resumed a recording career, performing on the festival circuit until his death. During these later years, he reconciled with his brother Bill, and the duo appeared together at the Bean Blossom Bluegrass Festival, a Monroe family–organized event.

• Ralph Rinzler discusses the Monroe brothers' career in his chapter on Bill Monroe in *Stars of Country Music*, ed. Bill C. Malone and Judith McCulloh (1975); further information is given by Douglas Green in his excellent liner notes for the out-of-print reissue set, *Feast Here Tonight*, issued on RCA (5510) in the mid-1970s. Also noteworthy is Green's interview with Monroe in "The Charlie Monroe Story," *Muleskinner News* 4, no. 1, 4, no. 2, and 4, no. 3 (Feb./Mar. 1973), and Ivan Tribe, "Charlie Monroe," *Bluegrass Unlimited* 10, no. 4 (Oct. 1975): 12–21. Monroe's radio transcriptions from the 1940s were reissued on County Records in 1974 as *Noonday Jamboree*, also out of print. An obituary is in the *New York Times*, 29 Sept. 1975.

RICHARD CARLIN

MONROE, Elizabeth Kortright (c. 1763–23 Sept. 1830), wife of James Monroe, fifth president of the United States, was the eldest daughter of Lawrence Kortright and Hannah Aspinwall. Her place of birth is not definitely known, but it was probably New York City. Although Lawrence Kortright lost much of his large fortune during the American Revolution, Elizabeth Kortright was reared in the exclusive circle of New York mercantile society. Considered one of the great beauties of the day, she married James Monroe, then a delegate from Virginia in the Confederation Congress, in 1786. They settled first in Fredericksburg, Virginia, where he practiced law. In 1789 they moved to Albemarle County to be closer to Thomas Jefferson, Monroe's close friend and patron. She was welcomed in Virginia by her husband's friends, although they found her habitual formality somewhat forbidding. She never felt completely at ease in the more casual social atmosphere of Virginia.

The marriage was a happy one cemented by a deep bond of affection apparent in their few surviving private letters; as was then the custom, most of her letters were destroyed after her death. Throughout her husband's long public career they were rarely separated for more than a few weeks. Their three children were born in Virginia. Until 1813 they lived in a simple farmhouse on a 2,500-acre plantation, "Ashlawn-Highland," adjoining Jefferson's "Monticello." When public responsibilities required longer stays in the capital, the Monroes began to reside at "Oak Hill," a plantation near Leesburg, Virginia, twenty miles from Washington. Here they erected a substantial residence designed according to Mrs. Monroe's wishes. Although they retained the Albemarle estate until 1826, Mrs. Monroe rarely joined her husband on his visits to manage the farm.

In conformity with the conventions of the day Mrs. Monroe played no role in political affairs. The only occasion on which she momentarily stepped on the public stage was during her husband's tenure as minister to France (1794–1796). At the time of their arrival Madame de Lafayette was imprisoned. When the Directory ignored Monroe's appeal for her release, he arranged for his wife to visit Madame de Lafayette at the prison. After the emotional meeting of the two women, observed by a sympathetic crowd, the Directors ordered Madame de Lafayette's release. Residence in France had a lasting impact on the Monroes' manners, dress, and taste in the decorative arts. While in France they purchased furniture, silver, ornaments, and tapestries. Contemporaries often commented upon the magnificent dining table *plateau* (now in the White House) and the adoption of the French custom of having the dishes passed by servants rather than all placed on the table. In refurnishing the White House during his presidency, Monroe ordered all the furniture, mantelpieces, and ornaments from France.

After her husband's appointment to the State Department in 1811 and his election as president in 1816, Mrs. Monroe was constantly in the public eye but remained an intensely private person. The only surviving accounts stress her beauty, the elegance of her dress, her regal bearing, and the formality of her manners. As First Lady she was unfavorably compared to her gregarious predecessor, Dolley Madison, who had always greeted guests warmly even on formal occasions. Mrs. Monroe's decision not to make or return calls (she would be at home one afternoon a week during congressional sessions) caused much unfavorable comment. She was supported by Louisa Catherine Adams (wife of Secretary of State John Quincy Adams), who agreed that the practice of making or returning calls was an intolerable burden in view of the growing population of Washington. Moreover, Mrs. Monroe was acting in accordance with European social customs. On both public and social occasions the Monroes returned to the formality of the Washington administrations, observing strict rules of precedence. At the biweekly receptions (called drawing rooms) guests were received by the president standing in the oval room. The guests were then presented to Mrs. Monroe, who sat beside him. Since Mrs. Monroe presided only at state dinners, wives were usually not invited to the receptions. Neither the president nor Mrs. Monroe accepted invitations from diplomats or residents of the capital.

Washingtonians saw little of the private family life in the White House. There were frequent visits by relatives and close friends. Eliza, who was devoted to her parents, lived at the White House with her husband. Mrs. Monroe regularly spent several weeks each year visiting her relatives in New York. As her health failed during Monroe's second term, she rarely appeared in public, often remaining at Oak Hill and letting Eliza preside on formal occasions.

After her husband's retirement in 1824, she lived quietly at Oak Hill. When her health permitted, she still made annual visits to her New York relatives. She was much concerned about the welfare of her grandchildren and shared her husband's interest in advancing the career of his nephew, James Monroe, Jr., who had entered West Point to prepare for a military career. She died at Oak Hill and was buried there. Monroe, shattered by his wife's death, moved to New York in 1830 to live with his daughter Maria Hester and her husband, Samuel L. Gouverneur, Mrs. Monroe's nephew, who had been Monroe's private secretary at the White House. He died there. In 1903 Mrs. Monroe was reinterred beside her husband in Hollywood Cemetery, Richmond, Virginia.

• The only autograph letters of Mrs. Monroe are in the library of the College of William and Mary. References to her are in the Monroe papers, Monroe Memorial Law Office and Library, Fredericksburg, Va.; Harry Ammon, *James Monroe: The Quest for National Identity*, new ed. (1990); Mary C. Crawford, *Romantic Days in the Early Republic* (1912); George Morgan, *Life of James Monroe* (1921); Laura C. Holloway, *The Ladies of the White House* (1880); and Mary O. Whitton, *First First Ladies, 1789–1865* (1948).

HARRY AMMON

MONROE, Harriet (23 Dec. 1860–26 Sept. 1936), poet and editor, was born Hattie Monroe in Chicago, Illinois, the daughter of Henry Stanton Monroe, a lawyer, and Martha Mitchell. Her parents, both of Scotch ancestry and moderately wealthy, came to Chicago in the early 1850s. Their differing personalities created tension that colored Harriet's childhood. The family enjoyed material prosperity until bad decisions in rebuilding his law practice after the Chicago fire of 1871 caused serious career reverses for Henry Monroe.

From her father, Monroe learned to love literature and the arts. Her education began in his library, where Harriet, a shy, frail, and nervous child, spent hours reading Shakespeare, Byron, Shelley, Dickens, and Thackeray. After suffering a severe unidentified illness in 1876, she was sent the next year to Visitation Convent in Georgetown, D.C. Although her family was neither Catholic nor religious, it was believed that a milder climate would improve her health. At Visitation, her health improved, she became more independent, and her intellectual and literary aspirations were encouraged by the faculty, especially by Sister Pauline, her instructor in English literature and composition.

After graduating from Visitation in 1879, Monroe returned to the family home in Chicago, where she would remain until her father's death in 1903. During the next ten years she participated in the social and intellectual life of the rapidly growing city. She continued to try her hand at prose and poetry, while declining family funds motivated her to search for work. She began a career in journalism, writing freelance reviews of art, music, and drama for Chicago and New York papers. As her literary experience grew, so did her circle of friends, which included influential writers and journalists such as Margaret Sullivan, Eugene Field, and Robert Louis Stevenson, with whom she carried on a long-distance correspondence. Throughout the 1880s trips to New York with her sister Lucy continued to widen her social and professional circle, and Monroe became a regular attendant at the literary salons of important figures such as Edmund C. Stedman and Richard Watson Gilder. In 1888 her first published poem, "With Shelley's Poems," appeared in *Century Magazine*. That same year, while working as an art critic for the *Chicago Tribune*, she was commissioned by the city fathers to write an ode of dedication for the new Chicago Auditorium. Another commission followed in March 1891 for the Chicago's World's Columbian Exhibition. On 21 October 1892 "The Columbian Ode" was read at the fair's dedication, where it was well received.

From 1895 to 1910 Monroe's life was occupied with travel, continuing her career as a freelance journalist, teaching, and writing. Efforts to become a major literary presence were continually frustrated, and finances continued to be strained, but early in 1911 at age fifty, she began a project that would have a major impact on the literary world of the twentieth century. Partially in response to the difficulty encountered in finding a publisher for her own verse, she conceived the idea of *Poetry*, a magazine devoted exclusively to the publication of poetry and the advancement of promising young poets. At the time, no such periodical existed in the United States, and other popular literary journals were often hesitant to publish poetry. However, Monroe asserted that "poetry cannot sing into a void" and began her project in the hopes of reenergizing the somewhat stagnant state of American poetry. With the help of close friends Hobart Chatfield-Taylor and Henry Fuller, she used her extensive social and professional connections to compile a list of financial contributors that included many of Chicago's wealthiest art patrons. Reading a considerable portion of available published poetry also provided her with a substantial list of possible contributors. Finally, after publication funds for the magazine's first five years were secured, *Poetry: A Magazine of Verse* was born in October 1912. Alice Corbin Henderson was the magazine's first associate editor, while Ezra Pound served as its foreign correspondent. *Poetry* gained immediate national attention in the popular press, and the magazine soon became an important forum for critical discussion and a showplace for promising new poets. Robert Frost, Wallace Stevens, T. S. Eliot, and James Joyce were among the many major literary figures to have their early work published in *Poetry*.

The final twenty-four years of Monroe's life were occupied primarily with *Poetry*; she was the main force that ensured the magazine's success during the tumultuous years of the early twentieth century. She also continued to enjoy travel, and she spent time exploring Europe, Mexico, and China during the 1920s and 1930s. In August 1936 Monroe, then seventy-six, attended a conference of the International Association of Poets, Essayists, and Novelists (PEN) in Buenos Aires, Argentina. She died while visiting Inca ruins and was buried at the foot of Mount Misti in the Andes. She had never married.

In *Poetry*, Monroe created an exciting new forum in which modern poetry could flourish. As a skilled editor, she was instrumental in unearthing and encouraging promising new poets. While today she is often less remembered as a poet, her dedication as an editor and lover of poetry had a strong impact on the literary world of the early twentieth century.

• The main sources on Monroe's life are her personal papers in the Harriet Monroe Library of Modern Poetry, Harper Memorial Library, University of Chicago; her autobiography, *A Poet's Life: Seventy Years in a Changing World* (1938); and her editorials and essays in *Poetry* (1912–1936). A complete list of Monroe's published work includes *Valeria and Other Poems* (1891), *The Passing Show: Five Modern Plays in Verse* (1903), *The Dance of Seasons* (1911), *You and I* (1914), *The Difference and Other Poems* (1924), and two collective volumes, *The New Poetry: An Anthology* (1917), which Monroe edited with Alice Corbin Henderson, and *Chosen Poems* (1935). See also her *John Wellborn Root* (1896), a biography of her friend and brother-in-law, and *Poets and Their Art* (1926), a collection of essays. For more information about her association with *Poetry*, see Bernard Duffey, *The Chicago Renaissance in American Letters* (1954), Daniel Cahill, *Harriet Monroe* (1973), and Ellen Williams, *Harriet Monroe and the Poetry Renaissance: The First Ten Years of Poetry, 1912–1922* (1977). Memorial tributes are in *Poetry* (Nov. and Dec. 1936 and Oct. 1937).

KIMBERLY MARKOWSKI

MONROE, James (28 Apr. 1758–4 July 1831), fifth president of the United States, was born in Westmoreland County, Virginia, the son of Spence Monroe and Elizabeth Jones, owners of a modest 600-acre plantation. He entered William and Mary College in 1774 but left two years later to enlist as a lieutenant in the Third Virginia Regiment, fighting in the battles in New York. After being seriously wounded at Trenton, he was promoted to major. From 1777 to 1778 he held a colonelcy as an aide to General William Alexander (Lord Stirling). Unable to obtain a field command after the battle of Monmouth, he entered the Virginia state line. At that time he began to study law with Governor Thomas Jefferson, who became a lifelong friend, patron, and intellectual influence.

Monroe was elected to the Virginia House of Delegates in 1782 and in the following year was chosen a delegate to the Confederation Congress, sitting until 1786. In Congress he organized the opposition to the Jay-Gardoqui proposals to close the Mississippi to Americans in return for trade concessions in Spain and drafted the form of territorial government incorporated into the Northwest Ordinance. He had long advocated strengthening the central government but opposed ratification of the Constitution because he believed it granted too much power to the Senate and authorized direct taxation.

In 1786 he married Elizabeth Kortright, daughter of a once-wealthy merchant. She was admired for her beauty, but contemporaries found her formal manner forbidding. The bond between Monroe and his wife was indeed close, rarely were they separated for more than a few weeks. After his marriage he began practicing law in Fredericksburg, Virginia, moving to Albemarle County three years later to be near Jefferson's estate, "Monticello." Here his daughters Eliza and Maria Hester were born, as well as a son who died in infancy.

Elected to the U.S. Senate in 1790, Monroe worked with his friend Congressman James Madison (1751–1836) in establishing the Republican party to combat the Federalist-dominated policies of President George Washington. When Washington appointed John Jay (1745–1829) minister to England in 1794, he also named Monroe minister to France to appease Republicans who condemned his neutrality policy as harmful to the cause of revolutionary France. Interpreting his mission as the preservation of Franco-American amity, Monroe often seemed a party spokesman rather than a representative of his government. When Washington recalled him in 1796 Monroe defended his actions in a book harshly critical of administration policies, *Conduct of the Executive . . . during . . . 1794, 5, 6* . . . (1798).

Monroe demonstrated solid administrative ability as governor of Virginia from 1799 to 1802. He was praised for his decisive action in 1800 in checking the threat posed by Gabriel's Rebellion, a slave uprising. In Monroe's opinion such uprisings were inevitable unless slavery were eliminated. In order to encourage manumission, Monroe recommended the removal of free blacks to the West. Jefferson agreed in principle but opposed colonization of land adjacent to the United States, preferring Africa. Without federal support the legislature declined to consider Monroe's plan. The rediscovery in 1816 in the legislative archives of the confidential Monroe-Jefferson correspondence revealing their interest in colonization was an important factor in the formation of the American Colonization Society.

In 1803, when Spain suspended the right of deposit at New Orleans to complete the retrocession of Louisiana to France, Jefferson appointed Monroe special envoy to assist resident minister Robert R. Livingston (1746–1813) in buying a port of deposit on the Mississippi. Monroe arrived just as Napoleon, having abandoned his plan of reestablishing France's American empire, offered to sell all Louisiana to the United States for $15 million. Authorized to obtain only a limited area, the American diplomats ignored their instructions and accepted the offer. In spite of doubts about the constitutionality of such a large territorial acquisition, Jefferson submitted the treaty for ratification. Popular approval of the purchase established Monroe as a national figure.

Except for an unsuccessful trip to Madrid to persuade Spain to acknowledge the Louisiana Purchase, Monroe was minister to Great Britain from 1803 to 1807. Monroe and special envoy William Pinkney concluded a treaty in 1806 reducing British commercial restrictions. Confident that the administration would trust his judgment, Monroe was dismayed when Jefferson rejected the treaty because it lacked a formal ban on impressment.

In 1808 dissident Republicans entered Monroe for president against Madison in the Virginia election. Monroe did not participate in the campaign and received little support. Jefferson, aware that Monroe blamed Madison for the rejection of the 1806 treaty, arranged for a reconciliation in 1810. Jefferson's influence assured Monroe's election as governor of Virginia and established that Monroe had the support of party regulars. In 1811 Madison, faced by internal party divisions and resurgent Federalism, appointed Monroe secretary of state. Monroe's popularity with younger Republican congressmen (the so-called War Hawks), enabled Madison to adopt a firmer policy toward Great Britain and to secure the passage of defense measures culminating in 1812 in a declaration of war.

Monroe's desire for a military command was frustrated by the animosity of Secretary of War John Armstrong (1758–1843), who believed Monroe had deprived Robert Livingston (Armstrong's brother-in-law) of credit for the Louisiana Purchase. Armstrong, who preferred to be with the army in the field, discounted warnings from Monroe and others of the danger of a British descent on the capital. After the invasion of Washington, D.C., Armstrong was forced to resign. He was replaced by Monroe, who continued as acting secretary of state. Monroe brought order into the tangled affairs of the Department of War, but his reorganization was too late to affect the military outcome of the war. As acting secretary of state he drafted the instructions authorizing the commissioners at Ghent to abandon the demand that the treaty include a formal ban on impressment. After the war he returned to the Department of State and began the negotiations that culminated in 1817 in the Rush-Bagot agreement demilitarizing the Great Lakes.

Although Monroe was expected to be the party's nominee in 1816, many Republicans weary of the long tenure of Virginians favored forty-year-old William Harris Crawford, who had succeeded Monroe in the Department of War. Although reputedly reluctant to challenge his senior colleague, Crawford's failure to withdraw formally further aggravated the administration. In the congressional caucus, the party nominating agency, Monroe defeated Crawford by sixty-five to fifty-four votes. The Federalists, weakened by their opposition to the war, mustered only thirty-four electoral votes to the 183 cast for Monroe. This was the last significant appearance of the Federalists on the national scene and marked the end of the first two-party system.

Monroe welcomed the new political development. Like others of his generation, he considered parties a destructive element and let it be known that he intended to be the head of a nation and not merely the chief of a party. To publicize his commitment to the "Era of Good Feelings," a term coined by a Federalist newspaper, he undertook a tour of the nation—the first president to do so since Washington. He began the tour in the summer of 1817, visiting first New England where he was given an enthusiastic reception in this bastion of Federalism. Two years later he toured the South and West.

Monroe's cabinet was the ablest since Washington's first administration: Secretary of State John Quincy Adams, Secretary of the Treasury William H. Crawford, Secretary of War John C. Calhoun, and Attorney General William Wirt. All remained in office during both terms. But with the demise of the two-party system Monroe could not invoke party loyalty to gain congressional support for his policies. Instead, he relied on personal contacts and the congressional followings of his cabinet members. A major purpose of his frequent cabinet meetings was to establish a consensus. This method of leadership proved effective until it was shattered by personal and sectional conflicts during his last years in office.

The last of the revolutionary generation to hold the presidency, Monroe seemed to contemporaries a rather old-fashioned figure. He was usually clad in the black small clothes of an earlier generation, his graying hair worn long and tied in a queue with a black ribbon. Tall and angular, he maintained the formal courtesy of his youth. The dominant features of his plain face were his gray eyes, which radiated warmth and kindness—the traits of character most often noted by his associates. He was admired for the soundness of his judgment, although many (like John Quincy Adams) were irked by his habit of reviewing every aspect of an issue, which made him slow to reach conclusions.

The presidential family that moved into the refurbished White House included Elizabeth Monroe; Eliza and her husband, George Hay, who often acted as an informal political agent for the president; Monroe's youngest brother, Joseph Jones, acting as a private secretary; and Mrs. Monroe's nephew, Samuel L. Gouverneur, who served as a private secretary until he returned to New York in 1820 after marrying Maria Hester, Monroe's youngest daughter. Their wedding, the first in the White House, was attended only by family and close friends.

Monroe returned to the formality of the Washington administration, observing strict precedence on formal occasions. Neither the president nor members of his family accepted invitations from diplomats or residents of the city. During congressional sessions the president continued the biweekly receptions open to all who were properly dressed. He received guests in the oval room, standing while his wife and Eliza sat beside him. Servants passed refreshments. The new formality seemed to many an unhappy contrast to the more casual affairs of his Republican predecessors. Monroe received a steady stream of callers in his White House office. Most expected an invitation to dinner (then at two o'clock): when Congress was in session it was not unusual for twenty to be seated at dinner. Monroe left office heavily in debt since his salary of $25,000 without an allowance was inadequate to pay for staff or entertainment.

In the nation's domestic affairs Monroe followed the program of moderate nationalism outlined in his inaugural address, which was couched in his characteristic ponderous and platitudinous style. He accepted without question the constitutionality of the Bank of the United States. In 1819, however, his recommendation of a protective tariff did not evoke a response in Congress. Until the decline in federal revenue after the panic of 1819 he obtained appropriations for the construction of coastal fortifications he deemed necessary after the experiences of the war.

On one issue he adhered to the states' rights views of Jefferson and Madison: he regarded federal support of internal improvements as unconstitutional. In accordance with current opinions about the limited role of government in the economy, the administration did little to alleviate the distress of the panic of 1819. Public expenses were drastically reduced, and the time limit for payments on public lands was extended. During his last two years in office Monroe's attempt to continue the Indian policy of his predecessors involved him in a bitter dispute with the Georgia congressional delegation over Indian treaty rights.

The harmony of the Era of Good Feelings was shattered by the Missouri crisis of 1819–1820. Monroe let it be known that he would veto any bill that granted statehood to Missouri conditional on the abolition of slavery. Fearful that the issue might destroy the Union, he approved the compromise of 1820 admitting Maine as a free state and Missouri without restriction, although he had doubts about the constitutionality of the ban on slavery north of 36°30′ north latitude as binding on future states.

Monroe's most significant achievements as president were in foreign affairs. The collaboration between Monroe and Adams was unique; it was based on mutual respect and a common view of national goals. Monroe formulated broad policy leaving Adams to handle all day-to-day negotiations. They conferred regularly, and Monroe reviewed all dispatches. Both understood that the end of the European wars provided an opportunity to advance existing policy aims with less reliance on the support of France than had been possible under Jefferson. Monroe was convinced that an independent course of action would win from the European states acknowledgment that the United States was the paramount power in the Americas. His major objectives were the acquisition of Florida and obtaining from Spain a definition of the Louisiana boundaries.

Late in 1817 Monroe put his convictions into practice by sending a military force to occupy Amelia Island in the St. John's River. The island, technically within Spanish jurisdiction, had become a base for pirates and privateers with questionable letters of marque from Latin American revolutionary governments. The following year he authorized General Andrew Jackson to pursue into Florida the Indians raiding the southern frontier. As Monroe anticipated, Spain was forced to negotiate. In the Adams-Onís Treaty of 1819, Spain ceded Florida and defined the Louisiana boundaries as extending from the Sabine River to the Canadian border and westward to the Pacific. Jackson's seizure of the Spanish posts led to a national outcry that he be reprimanded for exceeding his orders. Monroe silenced the clamor by shrewdly informing Congress that, while the general had indeed overstepped his orders, he had acted on the basis of information received during the campaign that made the seizure seem necessary. Jackson, however, never forgave Monroe for not fully endorsing his conduct.

In his annual messages Monroe frequently expressed sympathy for the Latin American independence movement but maintained a policy of neutrality. Although pressured by Congress, he declined to recognize the new states until 1822 when he was certain that they had established stable regimes and Spain had ratified the Adams-Onís Treaty. In 1823 when France was seeking to promote European intervention to restore Spanish authority in Latin America, George Canning, the British foreign minister, proposed that the United States and Britain jointly declare their opposition to intervention. Although Jefferson and Madison urged acceptance, Monroe after numerous cabinet discussions opted for a separate statement of policy. In his annual message of 2 December 1823 he declared that the political systems of the two hemispheres were fundamentally different and that any European interference would be regarded as an unfriendly act. At the suggestion of Adams, who was concerned about Russian activities on the Pacific coast, Monroe included a statement that the United States considered the Americas closed to further colonization. His declaration, later known as the Monroe Doctrine, received little notice at home or abroad and had no effect in checking intervention. When Monroe delivered his message in December 1823 he did not know that British opposition had effectively blocked plans for intervention.

Early in Monroe's first administration the British foreign secretary, Viscount Robert Castlereagh, seemed receptive to rapprochement. Negotiations undertaken by Richard Rush, minister to Great Britain, and Albert Gallatin, minister to France, culminated in 1818 in a convention providing compensation for slaves removed by the British during the War of 1812 and making substantial concessions in the fisheries. The convention also fixed the northwestern boundary with Canada along the forty-ninth parallel from the Lake of the Woods to the Rocky Mountains. The British refusal to abandon impressment made further progress impossible.

Midway during Monroe's second term the British again indicated an interest in reopening negotiations. At Monroe's instructions, Adams in the summer of 1823 drafted dispatches to Rush covering outstanding issues and stressing the question of the West Indian trade closed since the Revolution. Among the dispatches was one proposing a radical change from the established American interpretation of neutral rights on the high seas. Monroe sent a draft treaty committing the United States to joining the British-sponsored international patrol for the suppression of the slave trade if Britain would condemn it as piracy. Since pirates could not claim the protection of any flag, suspected ships could be searched.

This proposal, which accorded with Monroe's personal views, stemmed from the lobbying of the American Colonization Society, founded in 1817. The main interest of the society was the colonization of free blacks, but its members had targeted the slave trade as the best means of arousing public interest and securing administration support. In 1822 the House adopted by a large majority a resolution condemning the slave trade as piracy. Monroe interpreted this as a sufficient indication of a shift in public opinion to justify a concession on an issue obviously important to the British. The treaty was approved by all the secretaries except Adams, who argued that any departure from existing policy would expose the administration to attack for yielding a vital right. The British promptly accepted, but just as Adams predicted, the agreement encountered opposition from Crawford's backers in the Senate, led by Senator Martin Van Buren. Crawford, originally an ardent supporter of the agreement, was seriously ill and declined to intervene. The treaty was ratified with such restrictive amendments that the British refused to reconsider it, thus closing the door on the rapprochement Monroe so much desired.

During his last two years in office, Monroe, following the example of Jefferson and Madison, remained neutral as a bitter contest over presidential succession ensued between the 1924 presidential candidates, all members of the Democratic-Republican party. The supporters of Henry Clay, Crawford, and Jackson considered it essential to isolate their candidates from administration policy. Diplomatic and military appointments were assailed. Even such minor issues as the alleged mismanagement of funds for refurnishing the White House were subjected to harsh attacks. Adams and Crawford remained loyal to the president, however, and did not join the clamor.

In deteriorating health by 1827, Monroe was happy to retire to his estate, "Oak Hill," in Loudoun County where he had moved in 1813 to be closer to Washington, D.C. He avoided all political activity, regularly visiting Charlottesville to see Jefferson and Madison and to attend meetings of the Board of Visitors of the University of Virginia. To ease his burden of debt he sold his Albemarle estate, "Highland" (now called "Ashlawn-Highland"). He applied to Congress for compensation for expenses from past diplomatic missions—his accounts had never been fully settled. Opposition by Jacksonians delayed action until early in 1831 when Congress finally allowed $30,000, a sum still insufficient to pay his debts. His last public service came in 1829 when he presided over the Virginia constitutional convention. Grief-stricken by his wife's death in 1830 and too ill to remain at "Oak Hill," he moved to New York City to live with his youngest daughter and died there. The nation solemnly commemorated his death as the passing of one of the last heroes of the Revolution. Originally buried in New York, he was reinterred in Richmond in 1858.

• Monroe's papers are in the Library of Congress, the New York Public Library, the James Monroe Law Library and Memorial Museum (Fredericksburg, Virginia), and in the National Archives. Many letters are also in the papers of contemporaries, notably Thomas Jefferson, James Madison, and John Quincy Adams. Selected published correspondence is in Stanislaus Murray Hamilton, ed., *Writings* (7 vols., 1898–1903). The most recent biography is Harry Ammon, *James Monroe, The Quest for National Identity* (1971; repr. 1990). Among older biographies the best remains George Morgan, *The Life of James Monroe* (1921). Monroe's foreign policy is definitively presented in Samuel Flagg Bemis, *John Quincy Adams and the Foundations of American Foreign Policy* (1949). A complete chronology and annotated bibliography is in Harry Ammon, ed., *James Monroe, A Bibliography* (1991).

HARRY AMMON

MONROE, Marilyn (1 June 1926–5 Aug. 1962), film actress and sex symbol, was born Norma Jean Mortensen (and was also known as Norma Jean Baker in her youth) in Los Angeles, California, the daughter of Gladys Monroe Baker Mortensen, a film cutter, who was unmarried when she gave birth to Monroe (her father has never been positively identified). Gladys Mortensen was an avid movie fan, but Monroe spent very little time with her often unstable mother. Within two weeks of her birth, Monroe was placed in the first of what would be a succession of foster homes, guardianships, and orphanages. This experience convinced her that she was a "mistake," a person easily abandoned. Given an insecure childhood that included the trauma of sexual molestation and an early marriage (to James Dougherty in 1942; they were divorced in 1946) arranged in part to prevent her return to an orphanage, it is a testament to Monroe's tenacity, personal strength, and resilience that she managed to achieve the heights in her career that she did.

Her marriage to Dougherty compelled Monroe to quit high school, and her lack of formal education furthered her sense of inadequacy. While her husband served in the merchant marine during World War II, Monroe found a job inspecting parachutes at the Radioplane Company (1944–1945). Army photographers who had arrived at the plant to take commercial and military pictures of female war workers discovered her. From this first successful posing arose Monroe's fabled "love affair" with the camera (particularly with still photography). She was sensual and at ease before the camera, and her direct sexuality—mingled with her beauty, her innocence, and her now lightened blonde hair—accounted for her popularity with photographers and filmmakers.

At age twenty Monroe had her first screen test, signed a contract with 20th Century–Fox, and adopted her stage name of Marilyn Monroe (she legally changed her name in 1956). Roles were few, though, and her contract was not renewed. It has been suggested that she became a prostitute in order to support herself and that she at times engaged in sexual affairs with men who could advance her career. Through her judicious selection of "contacts," Monroe landed a new contract with Fox in 1948, but her first noticeable roles did not reach the screen until 1950.

Although typecast as the "dumb blonde," an unfair stereotype that bothered her throughout her career, Monroe transcended the limitations of her image in *The Asphalt Jungle* (1950) and *All About Eve* (1950). Working with two of the most lauded directors of the era, John Huston and Joseph Mankiewicz, she brought humanity and intelligence to her small roles in these films. Even though the studio did not consider her a serious actress, Monroe signed a seven-year contract with 20th Century–Fox in 1951. Her grossly underpaid bondage to Fox became symbolic of the many exploitative qualities of the studio system. Monroe nonetheless continued to overcome the deficiencies of her roles, and three films showcased her dramatic abilities: *Clash by Night* (1952), *Don't Bother to Knock* (1952), and *Niagara* (1953). In *Clash by Night* and *Niagara*, Monroe played darker, more demanding roles. Her Rose Loomis in *Niagara* is a steamy, cheating wife intent on murdering her veteran husband. In *Don't Bother to Knock* she portrays a psychotic babysitter.

Such "dangerous" sexuality in Monroe's acting was, however, all too often domesticated. Her sensuousness, independence, and intelligence were tamed once again in the role of the dumb blonde, a part she nonetheless played with sensitivity in *Gentlemen Prefer Blondes* (1953). The film, perhaps Monroe's most famous, features her as Lorelei Lee, a beautiful but dim golddigger, who sings what became Monroe's trademark song, "Diamonds Are a Girl's Best Friend." Monroe infused life into this femme fatale stencil, mocking the sexual greed of "Diamonds" and offering a commentary on postwar male American expectations in her line "I can be smart when it's important, but most men don't like it."

In the early and mid-1950s Monroe became one of the most publicized and popular actresses in America, her sexuality and vulnerability proving to be a potent and attractive mixture. She actively involved herself in her own image making and publicity, turning events from her private life to her professional advantage. Her relationship with baseball icon Joe DiMaggio created a great stir in the press (they were briefly married in 1954), as did the revelation of Monroe appearing nude in photographs for a 1952 calendar. Monroe had posed for the calendar shots when she was the proverbial starving actress, and she openly admitted this to the press, effectively forestalling criticism and in fact creating more sympathy for herself as a waif-like star. Despite Monroe's popularity and visibility, the studio still forced her to play parts she considered less than rewarding, usually rehashes of the dumb blonde role, including her parts in *There's No Business Like Show Business* (1954) and *The Seven Year Itch* (1955).

In *The Seven Year Itch*, Monroe plays a character significantly named "The Girl," and this film thus embodied much of what defined Monroe as an abstract sex symbol. The object of a married man's fantasies and desires, The Girl represents an honest and delighted sexuality—which she revels in as she stands over a subway grate and the cool air billows her white skirt around her thighs. This vision of Monroe created a lasting impression on the American psyche, but it remained wedded to the type of role she increasingly disdained. (The scene also precipitated the Monroe-DiMaggio divorce; DiMaggio, never accepting of Monroe's status and career, became incensed at her public display and reportedly beat her afterward.)

After filming *The Seven Year Itch*, Monroe broke her contract with 20th Century–Fox and attempted to mature into a more serious actress. She made only five more films, and her life from 1955 to 1962 proved how far removed she was from the stereotype she so often portrayed. Her intellectual aspirations found expression in her dedication to acting lessons, guided by the coaches famous for "the Method," Lee and Paula Strasberg. She sought companionship and, one suspects, a sort of apprenticeship with playwright Arthur Miller (whom she married in 1956 and divorced in 1961). A finely tuned sense of political morality also emerged from Monroe during these years. She stood by Miller throughout his ordeal with the House Un-American Activities Committee, risking her reputation and career to combat the committee's unseemly challenges to First Amendment rights in its pursuit of "communist corruption" in the arts. She likewise spoke out against the terrors of the Atomic Age, supporting the National Committee for a Sane Nuclear Policy and saying to reporters, "My nightmare is the H-bomb. What's yours?"

Monroe lent her prestige to such political causes, but her attention remained riveted on the further development of her career and on her personal life. Monroe offered some of her finest performances in the late 1950s and early 1960s, particularly in *Bus Stop* (1956), *Some Like It Hot* (1959), and *The Misfits* (1961). Increasingly, however, her personal problems interfered with her career. Long perceived as a "difficult" actress (for her tardiness, her terror of live filming, and her reliance on drugs, barbiturates in particular), Monroe's troubles worsened during this era. They were not the peevishness of a movie star, and the solutions she chose were grounded in the culture. She had chronic gynecological problems that often accounted for her absence from the set and that in all likelihood prevented her from having the child she so desperately wanted (she had a number of failed pregnancies during these years). Her fears stemmed from her childhood and from the excessive expectations attached to a sex symbol and superstar. She resorted to psychotherapy and drugs, which did little to relieve her anxieties or alleviate her problems. Monroe was forced to live out these agonies in her own life as well as on film in *The Misfits*, where her failed marriage to Miller was torturously recorded.

For all her difficulties, Monroe at the end of her life demonstrated the same sort of resilience that she had as a child. She wrought wonderful images in her last films through all her trauma, and she had plans for reordering her life and for new film projects when she died of a drug overdose at her home in Brentwood, California. Controversy has surrounded Monroe's death, and the initial finding of suicide has become increasingly suspect in recent years. While some sensational but widely accepted theories focus on Monroe's reputed involvement with John F. Kennedy and Robert Kennedy and the Mafia to suggest murder scenarios, her biographer Donald Spoto rather persuasively exonerates the Kennedys (she had only a brief fling with President Kennedy and had a strictly platonic relationship with Robert Kennedy) and lays the blame on her physicians and helpers. According to this theory, Monroe was accidently killed by a drug overdose (Nembutal ingested by mouth combined with a chloral hydrate enema) administered on the orders of her psychiatrist.

In Monroe's last interview with the press, she pleaded with *Life* magazine writer Richard Meryman, "Please don't make me a joke." The often bizarrely explained circumstances of her death and her image as a sex goddess/dumb blonde have at times prevented Monroe from being perceived as more than a caricature. She was, however, much more, and even in those "dumb" roles she displayed an elegance worthy of respect. Her director in *The Seven Year Itch* and *Some Like It Hot*, Billy Wilder, recognized this quality and called her "an absolute genius as a comic actress." Monroe never lost her desire for life or her sense of humor despite her tribulations, and she treated with humor and insight the depersonalization that came with her status and that often tormented her life and career: "I thought symbols were something you clash."

• The writings on Marilyn Monroe are legion, from press clippings and interviews to formal and not so formal biographies, and only a few of the book-length treatments are listed here. For Monroe's own reflections on her life, see her *My Story* (1974), and W. J. Weatherby, *Conversations with Marilyn* (1976). The most recent and well-balanced portrait is Donald Spoto, *Marilyn Monroe: The Biography* (1993), which challenges the sensational accounts of the Kennedys and Monroe and also includes a complete filmography. Representative of the more sensational (but still well-received) accounts of Monroe's life is Anthony Summers, *Goddess: The Secret Lives of Marilyn Monroe* (1985; 1986). A thoughtful analysis of Monroe's life, films, and changing cultural meaning can be found in Graham McCann, *Marilyn Monroe* (1987). Norman Mailer, *Marilyn* (1973), and Gloria Steinem, *Marilyn* (1986), perhaps illuminate as much about their authors as they do about Monroe. Many people who knew Monroe have written accounts of her, including Norman Rosten, *Marilyn: An Untold Story* (1973); Eunice Murray, *Marilyn: The Last Months* (1975); and James Dougherty, *The Secret Happiness of Marilyn Monroe* (1976). Newspaper coverage of Monroe's death was extensive; see especially the *Los Angeles Times* and the *Los Angeles Herald-Examiner*, 6–20 Aug. 1962.

MARGOT A. HENRIKSEN

MONROE, Paul (7 June 1869–6 Dec. 1947), educator, was born in North Madison, Indiana, the son of William Y. Monroe, a Baptist minister, and Juliet Williams. Monroe's father was active in local politics, serving at various times as sheriff, county treasurer, and representative to the Indiana legislature. Monroe attended Hanover College for one year and graduated from Franklin College in 1890. He began his long career in education in 1890 as a high school principal in Hopewell (1890–1891) and Martinsville (1891–1894), Indiana. In 1891 Monroe married Mary Emma Ellis of Franklin, Indiana; they had three children. In 1894 Monroe enrolled in the University of Chicago to study sociology and political science. He was awarded a fellowship in 1895 and received his Ph.D. in 1897. Upon graduation from Chicago, Monroe became an instructor of history at Teachers College, Columbia University, and was appointed adjunct professor of the history of education in 1899. After studying at the University of Heidelberg in 1901, he returned to become a full professor at Teachers College in 1902. He served as director of the School of Education at Teachers College from 1915 to 1923 and director of its International Institute from 1923 until his retirement in 1938.

Monroe made significant contributions to education in three capacities, as a historian of education, as editor in chief of the *Cyclopedia of Education*, and as director of the International Institute. His early years at Teachers College focused on his work in the history of education. He wrote numerous important works in that field, including *Source Book of the History of Education for the Greek and Roman Period* (1901), *Thomas Platter and the Educational Renaissance of the Sixteenth Century* (1904), *Text-Book in the History of Education* (1905), and *Brief Course in the History of Education* (1907).

As important as his own publications was his work with a generation of Teachers College students, many of whom became well-known scholars in education. Especially in his practicum seminar on the history of education in the United States, Monroe encouraged students to begin the task of building a monographic literature in the field. Among his students who later achieved distinction in education were Henry Suzzallo, Harlan Updegraff, Alexander James Inglis, William Heard Kilpatrick, Edgar W. Knight, Willystine Goodsell, Robert F. Seybolt, Stuart G. Noble, Jesse B. Sears, Forest C. Ensign, and I. L. Kandel.

The historical scholarship of Monroe and his students, immensely influential in the first half of the twentieth century, came under severe criticism in the late 1950s and early 1960s. Critics such as Bernard Bailyn argued that, in their passion to promote the emerging profession of education, these scholars had written an uncritical history that equated the triumph of public schooling with progress itself. In their eagerness to provide a sense of dignity to teachers, they had overestimated the importance of schooling, ignored the social context of education, and isolated themselves from the mainstream of American historical scholarship. If they had performed a lasting service by producing a prodigious number of monographs, their celebratory view of American educational history was largely discredited by several mid- and late twentieth-century revisionists.

Monroe was best known not for his work in educational history, but rather for his editorship of the *Cyclopedia of Education*. This vast, five-volume compendium was published between 1911 and 1913. Containing articles by more than a thousand scholars, the *Cyclopedia* was an impressive effort to summarize what was known about education at a time when knowledge was expanding and education was finding a place as a professional school or department in research universities across the country. Monroe's effort surpassed anything previously done and remained for many years the best encyclopedia of education published in the United States.

In the second half of his career, Monroe focused on international and comparative education. He was the first director of the International Institute at Columbia. This institute was created in part to serve foreign students at Teachers College, but it also encouraged research in comparative education and provided research services to foreign educational systems, often undertaking vast surveys at the request of countries around the world. Monroe himself chaired commissions that conducted studies of school systems in the Philippines (1913 and 1925); Puerto Rico (1926), and Iraq (1933). After travel in China, Japan, Korea, India, and Europe, he published a survey of educational facilities for American children in foreign lands.

On leave from Teachers College from 1932 to 1935, Monroe served as president first of Robert College in Istanbul (1932) and then of Istanbul's American College for Girls (1932–1935). Widely known in educational circles around the world, Monroe received several honorary degrees from international universities. He was a founder of the World Federation of Educational Associations and served as its president from 1931 to 1933 and from 1935 to 1943.

• Other important books by Monroe are *Essays on Comparative Education* (2 vols., 1927–1932) and *China: A Nation in Evolution* (1928). The best sources on Monroe are I. L. Kandel, ed., *Twenty-five Years in American Education: Collected Essays* (1924); Lawrence A. Cremin et al., *A History of Teachers College, Columbia University* (1954); William W. Brickman and Francisco Cordasco, "Paul Monroe's *Cyclopedia of Education*: With Notices of Educational Encyclopedias Past and Present," *History of Education Quarterly* 10 (Fall 1970): 324–37; and Sol Cohen, "The History of American Education, 1900–1976: The Uses of the Past," *Harvard Educational Review* 46 (Aug. 1976): 298–330. See also Bernard Bailyn, *Education in the Forming of American Society: Needs and Opportunities for Study* (1960), and Lawrence A. Cremin, *The Wonderful World of Ellwood Patterson Cubberley: An Essay on the Historiography of American Education* (1965).

B. EDWARD MCCLELLAN

MONROE, Vaughn Wilton (7 Oct. 1911–21 May 1973), bandleader, singer, and businessman, was born in Akron, Ohio, the son of Ira C. Monroe, a supervisor in a rubber tire factory, and Mable Louisa Maahs. Following World War I, the family moved to Monroe's grandmother's farm in Cuyahoga Falls, Ohio, where he grew up and went to school. The family also lived for a time in Kent, Ohio. Monroe's musical career began when he was eleven and was given an old, beat-up trumpet. He soaked it in coal oil for a week to get the valves to work and then proceeded to teach himself to play.

With lessons his playing improved so much that when Monroe finished eighth grade, his father gave him a new trumpet as a graduation present. The family moved again to Cudahy, Wisconsin, where Monroe entered high school. In Cudahy the school band was an even more important activity than the football team. Monroe became one of the star brass players and at age fourteen won the Wisconsin State trumpet championship with his interpretation of "Pearl of the Ocean." At the conclusion of the competition, John Philip Sousa directed the combined high school bands, and Monroe decided he wanted to be a bandleader.

The family's next move was to Jeannette, Pennsylvania, where Monroe completed his last two years of high school and met his future wife, Marian Baughman. One evening he dropped in at the Methodist church, picked up a hymnal, and joined the choir rehearsal. The director told him she needed another bass and to come regularly; this was the beginning of his dream of becoming a concert singer. At Jeannette High School he was elected president of the senior class, had the lead in the class play, and was voted most likely to succeed. During the evenings he played trumpet for Gibby Lockard's Jazz Orchestra.

When Monroe finished high school, in 1929, there was no money for college, and he went to work, wrestling heavy tire molds in the rubber factory where his father worked. Two or three nights a week he played trumpet for Lockard, trying to save enough money to pay for college. In 1930 Monroe entered Carnegie Tech in Pittsburgh as a music major, but he was forced to withdraw in 1932 for financial reasons.

Monroe joined Austin Wylie and His Gold Pheasant Orchestra and after six months switched to Larry Funk and His Band of a Thousand Melodies as a vocalist and trumpet player. He stayed with Funk for about three and a half years. These were tough times. Monroe was paid seven dollars a week or, sometimes, not at all. The band was continuously on the road, and in 1936 it suddenly disbanded, as Monroe recalled, somewhere between Chicago and Pittsburgh. Remembering a previous job offer, Monroe went to Boston to work for Jack Marshard.

Jack and Harry Marshard had a number of orchestras that would play at society functions and college dances. Monroe was promoted, eventually, from trumpet player to bandleader and vocalist of a six-piece Marshard unit. Still wishing to become a concert baritone, Monroe took voice courses at the New England Conservatory of Music. In 1940 he had a lucky break. Monroe's unit was playing in Miami when Marshard and his friend Willard Alexander, a music promoter, decided to look in on the band. When Alexander realized that Monroe could sing, he signed him to a contract, noting, "There hasn't been a top-flight singing band leader since Rudy Vallee" (quoted in Davidson, p. 66).

Finally, with the promise of a steady job and some real money, Monroe was able to marry his high school sweetheart. He and Marian were married in April 1940; they would have two daughters. The Monroes had a one-day honeymoon en route to Boston, where Monroe was to take over the new band. Marshard transferred twelve of his best musicians from his other bands into Monroe's band and hired Ticker Freeman, Dinah Shore's voice coach, to work on Monroe's singing style. Marshard also got the new band on NBC radio four nights a week, broadcasting from Old Seiler's Ten Acres Restaurant in Wayland, Massachusetts. Monroe's theme song, which started every broadcast, was "Racing with the Moon," written by Monroe, Johnny Watson, and Watson's wife. Almost from the beginning, the band's popularity centered on Monroe's vocals.

Alexander booked the band into a succession of big city hotels and procured a Victor recording contract. The band played at Frank Dailey's Meadowbrook in New Jersey in 1941 and then had its first big dates at the Paramount Theater and the Hotel Commodore, both in New York City. In 1941 a *Billboard* poll of colleges and universities named Monroe's the most popular young band, and soon it was playing at hotels and dance halls all over the country. By 1945 the band had a radio show, "The Vaughn Monroe Show," which originated from the Century Room at the Commodore Hotel. In 1946 the CBS variety show "Camel Caravan," which over the years had different stars, took over "The Vaughn Monroe Show," which ran until 1954.

With his increasing popularity, Monroe and his band had a call from Hollywood and made their first film in 1944, *Meet the People* for Metro-Goldwyn-Mayer. In his next film, *Carnegie Hall* (1947), Monroe was no longer leading his own band; instead he led the New York Symphony Orchestra. Subsequent films, such as *Singing Guns* (1950) and *The Toughest Man in Arizona* (1952), portrayed Monroe as a singing cowboy.

It was Monroe's recordings, however, that brought him his greatest success. In 1945 he recorded a hit song, "Rum and Coca-Cola," but it was the filler on the other side of the record that became a top seller. "There, I've Said It Again" sold more than 1.2 million copies, and Monroe's one-night stand price of $1,500 jumped to $3,500. A stream of hits followed, including "Ballerina" (1947), which sold 1.8 million records, and "Ghost Riders in the Sky" (1949), which sold 1 million copies.

Monroe lived in West Newton, Massachusetts, but traveled sometimes 200 nights out of a year during the late 1940s and early 1950s. This extensive commuting was facilitated by the fact that Monroe was a licensed pilot and flew his own plane. But the strain of being away from his family for long stretches of time and increasing commitments to television and other guest appearances forced him to dissolve the band in 1953.

In 1950 Monroe turned to television with a musical variety show; "The Vaughn Monroe Show" ran from October 1950 to September 1955. Monroe served as host and also provided most of the singing, beginning each broadcast with his trademark song, "Racing with the Moon." From December 1956 through April 1957 he hosted another musical variety show: "Air Time '57."

When Monroe starred on "Camel Caravan," he had often handled the commercials himself. Therefore, when RCA was looking for a spokesperson in 1954, Monroe was considered, along with four established emcees. Monroe won the job and was the voice of RCA for fifteen years. His job was to deliver television and radio commercials and do public appearances; his salary was more than $100,000 a year.

Unlike many entertainers, Monroe had good business sense and used his income during his "big" years for prudent investments. He owned a fleet of taxicabs, a Boston office building, a song-publishing firm, and the publishing concern Stories for Young America, which produced children's records, books, and toys. He also had a Hollywood film production unit and a catch-all corporation, Vaughn Monroe Productions. In 1947 he became part-owner, with the Marshard brothers, of a successful restaurant, the Meadows, on Route 9, outside of Boston. When Monroe was not traveling, he would sing a couple of songs for his delighted diners, concluding the evening with "Racing with the Moon."

By the late 1950s Monroe's recording dwindled, but he continued to appear in nightclubs and on occasional television shows. In the 1960s Monroe spent most of his time at his Jensen Beach, Florida, home but continued to travel to club dates and to operate the Meadows. He died in Stuart, Florida.

Although Monroe did not become everyone's idol, he did achieve great popularity with his band and his singing during the 1940s and 1950s. Teenagers swooned over his good looks and screamed for his voice. Adults either loved or hated it.

• A collection of Monroe's correspondence, manuscripts, and pictures is at the Mugar Library, Boston University. See also the clippings file at the Boston University School of Communication. Monroe published several songbooks, including *Vaughn Monroe Sings: His All-Time Favorite Songs* (1939), *Vaughn Monroe's Favorite Songs: Old and New Successes as Played and Recorded by Vaughn Monroe and His Orchestra* (c. 1942), and *Vaughn Monroe's Musical Caravan* (c. 1943). Biographical information is found in Alberta Powell Graham, *Strike up the Band* (1949); Richard Lamparski, *Whatever Became of . . . ?* (1973); and George T. Simon, *The Best of Music Makers* (1979) and *The Big Bands* (1981). See also "Boss Record Man," *Newsweek*, 12 Jan. 1948, p. 74; Bill Davidson, "Voice with Muscles," *Collier's*, 20 Aug. 1949, pp. 30ff; Jack Long, "Pied Piper of West Newton," *American Magazine*, Jan. 1951, pp. 26–27ff; Sam Boal, "The Musical Moods of Vaughn Monroe," *Coronet*, Dec. 1951, pp. 85–89; and "Vaughn Monroe Renews Unique Pact as Voice of RCA," *Advertising Age*, 24 July 1961, p. 40. Obituaries are in the *Boston Globe* and the *New York Times*, both 22 May 1973.

MARCIA B. DINNEEN

MONROE, Will Seymour (22 Mar. 1863–29 Jan. 1939), author and educator, was born in Hunlock, Pennsylvania, the son of Ransom Monroe, a storekeeper, and Emeline Womelsdorf. He attended Huntington Mills (Pa.) Academy. Monroe began his career as first a teacher and then superintendent of schools in Luzerne County and Nanticoke, Pennsylvania, from 1881 to 1888. From 1889 to 1892 he served as the second superintendent of the Pasadena, California, school system and in 1892 began his studies at Stanford University. At Stanford Monroe worked with education professor Earl Barnes, who directed Monroe's compilation of bibliographies of works in the history of education, education in Europe, and related areas. These eventually were expanded to produce a *Bibliography of Education* (1897; repr. 1968), which referenced, often with annotation, 3,200 books and pamphlets. He received an A.B. from Stanford in 1894.

Monroe also continued his study of and correspondence with Henry Barnard, who had been the first commissioner of education in the United States. Monroe published a brief biography, *The Educational Labors of Henry Barnard* (1893), and *A Bibliography of Henry Barnard* (1897). He also began a correspondence with William Torrey Harris, then the fourth commissioner of education in the United States, who served as a reference for Monroe both in the United States and abroad. Monroe continued his studies in 1894–1895 at Leipzig, Jena, and Paris, taking courses in education and in psychology, especially of children.

In 1896 Monroe became professor of psychology, education, and geography at the Westfield (Mass.) Normal School. He introduced the "New Psychology" to the curriculum and began work in child study. The "old psychology" was based on a rationalist philosophy, with a strong emphasis on the proper nature of moral conduct. In contrast, the New Psychology emphasized empirically based research as the method for understanding the mind. By 1893 G. Stanley Hall, a psychologist and the first president of Clark University, had become an influential advocate for what he perceived as an example of the new approach—child study. Hall argued that children could be observed and studied scientifically and to this end recruited educators, especially teachers. Typically, questionnaires were given to teachers, who collected data from their students. Results from a large number of children were tabulated and conclusions drawn. While the scientific validity of such studies was questionable, they served to bring teachers and psychologists into proximity and to emphasize an empirical approach to understanding development; this led, for example, to the development of the first intelligence tests.

Monroe had become interested in child study while working with Barnes, who was the major worker in the field along with Hall. At Westfield, Monroe conducted and published such studies, and for some twenty years he was an assistant editor of Hall's *Pedagogical Seminary*, then one of the three professional psychology journals in the United States. Monroe also encouraged his students—all women—to be involved in such research, and some published their work. Likewise, in 1896 he organized Saturday classes in child study for local teachers. Typically a problem was presented, data were collected during the week and discussed at the next meeting, and the results were published. This work received both popular and professional acclaim, and Monroe published a series of three *Child Study Outlines* (1897, 1898, and 1899). Some of these studies were compiled with others in *Die Entwicklung des sozialen Bewusstseins der Kinder* (1899), later translated into Swedish, Flemish, Bulgarian, Bohemian, and Russian. At Westfield, Monroe also continued his work in education, editing *Comenius' School of Infancy* (1896) and writing *Comenius and the Beginnings of Educational Reform* (1900) and the *History of the Pestalozzian Movement in the United States* (1907, repr. 1969), his last major work in education.

Monroe took a leave for the academic year 1900–1901 to travel and study at Leipzig and Grenoble, and he often traveled to Europe during the summers; he eventually spent over six and a half years there. He drew on these experiences for his teaching not only of psychology and education, but now also geography. He would routinely summarize his researches and experiences in a "travel" book about the region, summarizing the history and the cultural and physical geography of the country. These included books on Turkey (1905), Norway (1908), Sicily (1909), *Bohemia and the Czechs* (1910), and *Bulgaria and Her People* (1914). The latter two were the only comprehensive books about those areas available in English prior to World War I, and Monroe was later honored by the governments of both countries for his portrayals.

In 1909 Monroe took a position as head of the psychology department at the New Jersey State Normal School (Montclair), which he held until his retirement in 1925. While there he completed his last major academic project as one of thirteen associate editors for Paul Monroe's *Cyclopedia of Education* from 1911 to 1913 and in this capacity contributed over 600 articles, primarily in the area of educational biography. When not traveling to Europe, Monroe often lectured in the summer at universities, including the University of Illinois (1903), Columbia University (1904), and the University of Chicago (1908). World War I forced a curtailment of European travel, so he lectured at the University of Vermont in the summers from 1914 to 1920.

Near the end of the war President Woodrow Wilson established a peace inquiry commission to study political, economic, geographic, and ethnographic considerations that were likely to be of importance in the peace conference at the end of the war. Monroe was appointed head of the subcommittee on the Balkans based on his travels in and writing about the area. Monroe began to devote more time to hiking and mountain climbing and founded the New York branch of the Green Mountain Club. During his summers in Vermont during World War I he led a group that blazed a 32-mile stretch of the Long Trail through the Green Mountains. The Monroe Skyline began at the base of Couching Lion (Camels Hump) Mountain in Waterbury, Vermont, where Monroe purchased a farm to which he retired in 1925. He never married. His sister, who had moved in with him in 1917, lived with him until her death in 1934. Following his death the farm was willed to the state, where it remains the starting point for that part of the long trail.

In retirement Monroe contributed occasional professional articles—for example, a piece on Barnard for the *Encyclopedia of the Social Sciences* in 1930. He helped found the Great Pyrenees Dog Club of America, served as its first president, judged at numerous dog shows around the United States, and wrote for the *American Kennel Club Gazette* and *Dog News*. He also returned to a lifelong interest in American poetry. Monroe had written *Poets and Poetry of the Wyoming Valley* (1887) and been especially interested in the work of Walt Whitman. In retirement he began work on a volume on Whitman and his contemporaries. While he never finished the project, he amassed extensive notes and correspondence and published articles on Whitman in *Revue Anglo-Americaine* (1930 and 1931) and the *American Mercury* (1933). He also contributed to a volume on Edward Carpenter.

Monroe was important in part because he amassed large collections of scholarly works. For example, Barnard left his papers to Monroe, who cataloged many of the 14,000 items before passing them along to New York University in 1925. He accumulated a professional library of some 5,500 volumes, which he sold to New York University. He also willed Stanford his Whitman-related papers and approximately 2,500 volumes by and related to Whitman. Personally, Monroe was described as a "gentleman of the old school": courteous, with the ability to put others at ease. He knew people in a wide variety of areas. He was a member of the American Psychological Association, the American Anthropological Association, the Geological Society, and the Author's Clubs of New York and of London, and was a fellow of the American Association for the Advancement of Science. He was a representative at at least six international expositions and educational congresses, receiving gold medals in Paris (1900) and St. Louis (1903).

As a scholar Monroe's contribution was primarily in compiling, summarizing, and popularizing. In psychology he did little original research but instead introduced the New Psychology to thousands of teachers through his teaching at normal schools and his writings in educational journals. In education he was a biographer and a bibliographer, and he reported on educational trends in the United States and abroad; he was not a theoretician. His travel books were of a popular, rather than scholarly, nature. They reached a wide audience and were well received abroad; when Monroe died at Burlington, Vermont, telegrams of mourning were received from seven heads of state, including President Franklin D. Roosevelt.

• The only significant group of Monroe's papers remaining is in the Vermont Historical Society, Montpelier. Some correspondence is included in the Barnard papers, New York University. Academic files for Monroe exist at Stanford University and Westfield State College, Westfield, Mass. An obituary is in the *New York Times*, 30 Jan. 1939.

HORACE MARCHANT

MONRONEY, Mike (2 Mar. 1902–13 Feb. 1980), congressman and U.S. senator, was born Almer Stillwell Monroney in Oklahoma City, Oklahoma, the son of Almer Ellis Monroney, a businessman, and Mary Wood Stillwell. He attended public elementary and secondary schools in Oklahoma City, graduated from Central High School, and received a B.A. from the University of Oklahoma in 1924.

Following graduation, Monroney worked as a reporter and political writer for the *Oklahoma News* from 1924 to 1928, serving also for a time as the state capitol reporter. In 1927 he interviewed Charles A. Lindbergh and afterward became a lifelong fan of aviation, an interest that was later reflected in his committee assignments and bill sponsorships while in Congress, as well as in his post-congressional consulting work. He married Mary Ellen Mellon, also from Oklahoma City, in Chicago in 1932, and the couple had one son. After four years with the *Oklahoma News*, Monroney entered his father's furniture business in Oklahoma City and remained there until 1938. During this ten-year period he served terms as president of the Oklahoma City Rotary Club and president of the Oklahoma City Retailer's Association.

In 1938 Monroney was elected to the House of Representatives along with all the other Democratic candidates from Oklahoma. He served six terms in the House as the representative from Oklahoma's Fifth Congressional District. While there he supported the expansion of U.S. naval capabilities, Lend-Lease, and most other prewar and wartime efforts of Democratic presidents Franklin D. Roosevelt and Harry S. Truman. He also served on the Banking and Currency Committee for twelve years, working for price and wage controls during the war. Monroney supported the establishment of the United Nations and of international agencies designed to aid developing countries; he also favored the use of U.S. foreign aid as a means to help ameliorate the conditions of the postwar world. After the war he worked for higher wages for federal employees; helped to improve mail delivery, particularly promoting the increased use of air mail; and pushed for more efficient government. While in the House, Monroney and fellow Oklahoman Elmer Thomas fought to convince the War Department to locate a major aircraft repair center in Oklahoma City during the war. This action quickly established Monroney as a supporter of both aviation and enhanced job prospects in Oklahoma. He co-chaired the Joint Committee on the Organization of Congress in the 1940s, and along with Senator Robert M. La Follette, Jr., of Wisconsin, he introduced the Legislative Reorganization Act of 1946. For that work Monroney received the first *Collier's* Award for Distinguished Congressional Service that same year.

Monroney remained in the House until 1950, when he decided to seek the seat of Senator Thomas, an incumbent Democrat. In the race against Thomas, Monroney launched an energetic campaign based partly on Thomas's age. He also noted Thomas's vote to cut U.S. Air Force appropriations at the time when tensions in Korea were heightening before the war. Thomas, on the other hand, charged that Monroney had opposed President Truman's loyalty program. Described as a contest of "image and personality—Thomas, the aging champion of farmers, versus Monroney, the young advocate of industry and city," the election resulted in victory for Monroney who defeated the veteran senator by about 27,000 votes. Monroney then went on to an easy victory over the Reverend Bill Alexander of Oklahoma City in the November elections.

As a senator Monroney continued to work for the projects and ideas he had supported while in the House. He favored the oil depletion allowance and introduced bills providing grants to airports of all sizes, thereby garnering the support of many who represented the nation's rural areas. He continued to push for greater use of aviation, sponsoring legislation in both 1956 and 1958 that led to the establishment of the Federal Aviation Administration. Aviation legislation eventually became his primary area of interest in the Senate, and as a result the Regional FAA Center in Oklahoma City was later named the Mike Monroney Aeronautical Center. He also supported foreign aid, federal grants for education, civil rights legislative efforts, and most of the tenets of the War on Poverty. In addition to obtaining millions of dollars for aviation and aeronautics projects in Oklahoma, he supported agricultural price supports, soil conservation programs, rural electrification projects, and resource management initiatives. Consequently, as a political idealist and an internationalist, Monroney often clashed with Senator Joseph McCarthy over foreign aid, loyalty programs, and other issues involving international initiatives.

Monroney's committee assignments in the Senate also reflected his interests. He was co-chair of the Joint Committee on the Organization of Congress from 1965 to 1966, a member of the Interstate and Foreign Commerce Committee and chair of its Aviation Subcommittee, and chair of the Post Office and Civil Service Committee from 1965 to 1969. In his only real effort to obtain a leadership position, he ran unsuccessfully for the post of majority whip in 1965, a position that he lost to Senator Russell Long.

Although Monroney had easily defeated Republicans Douglas McKeever in 1956 and B. Hayden Crawford (who charged that Monroney was "soft on Communism") in 1962, he ultimately lost to former governor Henry Bellmon by a sizable margin in 1968. Bellmon's gubernatorial popularity, the death of Senator Robert Kerr in 1963, and the strong presidential race run in Oklahoma by Richard Nixon all contributed to a weak showing by Democrats statewide in 1968.

Following his defeat Monroney continued to support both commercial and military development of aviation, working as a consultant to several aviation companies until he retired in 1974. He died in Rockville, Maryland. He was eulogized as a political idealist in the tradition of Adlai Stevenson, and in Oklahoma he was remembered as a man who worked diligently for his home state and for the development of aviation.

• Monroney's papers are in the Western Historical Collection in the Bizzell Memorial Library at the University of Oklahoma. Three articles in the *Chronicles of Oklahoma* that provide information on Monroney's political career are Philip A. Grant, "A Tradition of Political Power: Congressional Committee Chairmen from Oklahoma, 1945–1972," 60, no. 4 (Winter 1982–1983): 438–47; James N. Eastman, Jr., "Founding of Tinker Air Force Base," 50, no. 3 (Autumn 1972): 326–46; and Stephen F. Lalli, "The *Oklahoma Rural News*: Roots of an Electric Cooperative Newspaper," 71, no. 4 (Winter 1993–1994): 438–49. A detailed study of Monroney's role in the aviation debates of the 1950s and 1960s may be found in Randall B. Ripley, "Congress Champions Aid to Airports, 1958–59," in *Congress and Urban Problems*, ed. Frederic N. Cleaveland et al. (1969); and Ripley, *Power in the Senate* (1969). Several studies that provide insights into Monroney's work in the Senate, as well as his relationship with other politicians, are LeRoy H. Fischer, *Oklahoma's Governors, 1955–1979: Growth and Reform* (1985); Anne Hodges Morgan, *Robert S. Kerr: The Senate Years* (1977); Henry Bellmon, *The Life and Times of Henry Bellmon* (1992); Arrell M. Gibson, *Oklahoma: A History of Five Centuries* (1965); Stephen Jones, *Oklahoma Politics in State and Nation* (1974); and James R. Scales and Danney Goble, *Oklahoma Politics: A History* (1982). Additional information may be found in H. L. Fitzpatrick, ed., *The Oklahoma Almanac 1961* (1960). Obituaries are in the *New York Times* and the *Washington Post*, both 14 Feb. 1980.

JUSTUS F. PAUL

MONSKY, Henry (4 Feb. 1890–2 May 1947), lawyer and Jewish communal leader, was born in Omaha, Nebraska, the son of Abraham Monsky, a fish dealer, and Betsy Perisnev Greenblatt, both of whom had been born in Poland. Monsky was raised in an Orthodox Jewish home; his father was a cantor and was active in synagogue and Jewish communal activities. After graduating from Central High School in 1907, he entered Creighton College of Law as a night student in 1909. There he demonstrated leadership and oratorical skills and in 1911 was president of the Omaha Hebrew Club, a group that had been founded by his father in 1892. He earned his law degree in 1912 and embarked on a corporate practice. He married Sadie Lesser in 1915; they had three children.

Monsky joined B'nai B'rith, a major Jewish fraternal organization, in 1912 and was lodge president in 1913. A lifelong Zionist, he attended the first American Jewish Congress convention in December 1918 and supported the postwar relief of the American Jewish Relief Committee (1919), the Palestine Restoration Fund (1920), and the Joint Distribution Committee meeting. He longed to unite Jews to work for a common purpose.

Monsky's wide-ranging concern for juvenile issues caused him to become a benefactor in 1917 of Father Flanagan, the founder of Boys Town, an orphanage and home for troubled boys. His role is depicted in the film classic *Boys Town* (1938). His concern for the spiritual vitality of Jewish youth facilitated the transformation of an Omaha Central High School Jewish club in 1922 into the B'nai B'rith–sponsored Aleph Zadik Aleph junior order, a program for young boys. Soon thereafter Monsky encouraged the establishment of the Hillel Foundation on many college campuses. In 1923 he introduced Community Chest united fundraising to the Omaha Chamber of Commerce rather than ignoring urban social problems or tackling them piecemeal through multiple, competing, and fragmented charitable organizations.

Monsky aspired to lead B'nai B'rith. An indefatigable fundraiser, he was elected the organization's international president in May 1938, becoming the first Eastern European to lead the group. He pledged all his energy "no matter what the sacrifice may be." Membership rose dramatically, from 45,000 in January 1936 to 82,860 in October 1939, spurred by continuous crises: Hitler's Nazi party, the Nuremberg laws, Kristallnacht, immigration restrictions, and World War II. By the end of the war B'nai B'rith had 300,000 members.

Monsky's 1938 Rosh Hashanah article "A Jewish Inventory" (*B'nai B'rith Magazine*, Oct. 1938, p. 51) identified five outstanding problems facing Jews: (1) relief for refugees; (2) assistance to rebuild Palestine; (3) unswerving defense of Jewish rights; (4) loyalty to democracy in the face of subversive forces; and (5) building a "richer and more vital Jewish life." That same year Monsky attended a meeting of the "big four" in Pittsburgh, Pennsylvania. Together, B'nai B'rith, the American Jewish Committee, American Jewish Congress, and the Jewish Labor Committee created the General Council for Jewish Rights. Monsky served as vice chairman and repeatedly called for a "united front."

When the British government vacillated in the 1930s on honoring the Balfour Declaration, which declared British sympathy with Zionist aspirations and had been signed in 1917, an Emergency Committee of Zionists—comprising Monsky; Dr. Solomon Goldman and Dr. Stephen S. Wise, both rabbis; and Louis Lipsky, an author and journalist—interviewed Sir Roland Lindsay, British ambassador to the United States, and the following day presented a plea to Secretary of State Cordell Hull requesting that U.S. pressure be brought on the British. Monsky sent Prime Minister Chamberlain a number of telegrams urging him to uphold the declaration.

Monsky condemned communism, fascism, and nazism as equal threats to democracy. He fought anti-Semitism at rallies in Madison Square Garden, by supporting the Anti-Defamation League and lobbying elected officials. To his anti-Semitic enemies, such as the American fascists and nativists, he symbolized the "international Jew," part of an alleged Jewish conspiracy featured in the spurious *Protocols of the Elders of Zion*. Monsky involved B'nai B'rith in Red Cross and civil defense programs. President Franklin D. Roosevelt named Monsky to the National Volunteer Participation Committee in July 1941. B'nai B'rith raised over $135 million in war bond sales.

On 25 May 1941 Chaim Weizmann, president of the World Zionist Organization, met with New York governor Herbert H. Lehman, Monsky, Stephen Wise, and Louis Lipsky and others at New York's St. Regis Hotel. Weizmann and Monsky, realizing the fractiousness and disarray in organized American Jewish life, searched for a compromise agreement to establish Jewish unity to rebuild Palestine. As European Jewry's situation further deteriorated during the Second World War, American Jewry created numerous ad hoc committees and programs. Following the verification between June and November 1942 of Hitler's "final solution" and Jewish leadership's ineffectiveness in persuading Cordell Hull and President Roosevelt to take effective action, Monsky in December 1942 almost single-handedly convened the American Jewish Assembly, initially comprising thirty-two different and contending organizations. Subsequently renamed the American Jewish Conference, it concerned itself with European Jewry and Palestine. Monsky served as a delegate to the United Nations conference in San Francisco in 1945.

After Monsky's first marriage ended in divorce in 1937, he married Daisy Hirsch, the widow of Albert Rothschild and a University of Chicago graduate and social worker who had one child, that same year. In 1947 he suffered a fatal heart attack while addressing the American Jewish Conference on the pressing need for unity.

Monsky played a significant role in the B'nai B'rith, Omaha Jewish communal affairs, Jewish-Catholic relations, combating juvenile delinquency, coordinating private sector social welfare, and creating the internationally oriented American Jewish Conference, which disbanded in 1948. Through statesmanship and dedication to fundamental Jewish spiritual concepts, mediated by his midwestern experience, he attempted to bridge divergences and rivalries in Jewish life.

• *Henry Monsky: The Man and His Work* (1947), by his second wife and B'nai B'rith secretary and longtime friend Maurice Bisgyer, was written and published within months of his death. Albert Vorspan, *Giants of Justice* (1960), contains a thumbnail biography, "Henry Monsky—Gambler in Futures," pp. 117–31. Max F. Baer, *Dealing in Futures: The Story of a Jewish Youth Movement* (1983), provides valuable firsthand information and intellectual analysis. More recent academic literature includes a study by Deborah Dash Moore, *B'nai B'rith and the Challenge of Ethnic Leadership* (1981), and a biographical treatment that carries Monsky's life to the eve of the Second World War, Oliver B. Pollak, "The Education of Henry Monsky—Omaha's American Jewish Hero," in *Crisis and Reaction: The Hero in Jewish History*, ed. Menachem Mor (1995). An obituary is in the *New York Times*, 3 May 1947.

OLIVER B. POLLAK

MONTAGUE, Henry James (20 Jan. 1843–11 Aug. 1878), actor, was born in Staffordshire, England, to parents not named in biographical sources. The family name was Mann, and the father was a clergyman of the Church of England. Henry's education was cut short in adolescence when his father suffered financial reverses. He became a clerk in a London banking house, but after hours he began taking part in amateur theatricals. One of his performances was seen by actor-manager Dion Boucicault, a leading stage figure of the day both in England and the United States. Boucicault gave him a small part in his dramatization of Sir Walter Scott's *Heart of Midlothian* (1863). The twenty-year-old took the stage name of Montague as his professional career began.

Montague was hired by the management of the St. James Theatre, London, to play small parts. After gaining stage experience and learning by observing the skilled actors of the company, he gained considerable notice for his portrayal of a minor role in the comedy hit *Woodcock's Little Game* (1864). He went on from there to larger parts with other managements. A personal success in T. W. Robertson's *For Love* (1867) brought him to the attention of two of the leading stars of the day, Squire Bancroft and Marie Wilton of the

Prince of Wales Theatre. Bancroft and Wilton were exponents of the style of playwriting done by Robertson and others: sometimes called "cup and saucer drama," it was more domestic in theme than the heavily romantic melodramas of earlier days and allowed for comic touches from everyday life. Montague joined their company at the St. James in 1867 and became a public favorite in plays like Robertson's *School* (1867) and *Caste* (1868). William Winter wrote that "he reflected perfectly a popular spirit of his day . . . [one of social] satire . . . piquant drollery [and] half-playful, half-bitter cynicism. . . . His manner was elegant. He possessed repose, sentiment, a kind of wistful aspect, sensibility, a certain sapient drollery, and a telling quality of demure banter" (p. 145). In large part, Montague played himself in these plays, bringing to the stage outstanding personal charm rather than the versatility of a skilled player who could take many different roles. His likable personality made him a favorite in the theatrical world. Many years later, Squire Bancroft recalled: "When in his company he somehow had the gift of impressing the idea upon you that he had thought but of you since your last parting, and when he said 'goodbye,' that you would remain in his memory until you met again" (*Mr. and Mrs. Bancroft*, vol. 2, pp. 145–46).

In 1870 Montague, feeling the pressure of providing financial support for his mother and sister, went into management himself. With two others, he leased the Vaudeville Theatre. He had great success that year in *The Two Roses*, which had a long run and two successful provincial tours. Encouraged, the next year Montague became sole lessee of the Globe Theatre. Two successes there were in *Partners for Life* (1871) and *False Shame* (1872). But by 1874 he was in financial straits and giving dramatic readings for additional income: "It is one thing to be a popular actor and quite another to successfully manage a theatre" (*New York Times*, 13 Aug. 1878).

Boucicault knew from experience that there were rich rewards for English actors on the American stage. In the summer of 1874 Montague accompanied him to New York City. He was soon hired by actor-manager Lester Wallack to appear with the acting company at Wallack's Theatre, frequented by fashionable New Yorkers. He opened that autumn in *Partners for Life* to favorable audience reaction. His next performance, as an impoverished marquis in *The Romance of a Poor Young Man* (1874), made him wildly popular: "He became a theme of conversation . . . young women began to adore him, and the young men to ape his manners, and his likeness was displayed in the shop windows" (*New York Times*, 13 Aug. 1878). That same season he appeared as Captain Molyneux in Boucicault's *The Shaughraun* to further acclaim. A *New York Times* writer noted, "At this time Montague was undoubtedly the most popular actor on the American stage."

Offstage, Montague charmed American theatricals as he had those in London. Convivial, "Harry" to his friends, he suggested the formation of the Lambs Club in New York City in 1875. Actor John McCullough recalled that Montague had "a loving, generous, whole-souled disposition . . . he didn't know what it was to be mean. He loved art, sport, dogs, children, and people, went enraptured over pictures in the clouds when we were yachting, played the child . . . he was simply good" (*New York Telegram*, 13 Aug. 1878). Montague became nearly a member of the Wallack family. Looking back, McCullough thought "he made a mistake in estimating his physical power." Besides his constant round of offstage social gatherings, sports, and club activities, he had to bear "the fearful strain which actors and actresses undergo during a performance."

In the next few years Montague gave capable performances in various time-tested plays in the Wallack's repertoire: *The Road to Ruin*, *The Overland Route*, *London Assurance*, and *The Lady of Lyons*. In the summer of 1876 he returned to London and there appeared in *The Two Roses* at a benefit performance. The 1876–1877 season was spent in touring, under the arduous travel conditions of the day. Back in New York for the 1877–1878 season at Wallack's, he repeated his London success in *False Shame*, played his most demanding role as a loveless husband in *Won at Last* (1877), and after other plays in the company repertoire took the juvenile lead in a first production of one of the era's enduring hits, *Diplomacy* (1878).

Conscious of the need to make money from his success, Montague arranged in the summer of 1878 to take a company on tour in *Diplomacy* and *False Shame*, opening in San Francisco after a transcontinental train trip. He was doubtful about the undertaking because of the state of his health. He had been suffering hemorrhages from his lungs and was forced to take "stimulants" to carry on his performances in *Diplomacy* that spring, his theater dresser later revealed (*New York Telegram*, 13 Aug. 1878). Furthermore, he had a heavy cold as he prepared to leave. Before his departure in July, Montague made a will leaving everything to his mother and sister. He also had an insurance policy in their names.

On 10 August, during a Friday performance of *False Shame* in San Francisco, Montague began to hemorrhage. After an apparent recovery that had him packing to leave for the tour's next stop, he began hemorrhaging again on Sunday and died that evening. Death was caused by loss of blood from weakened lungs "superinduced by pneumonia" (*New York Times*, 13 Aug. 1878). He was widely mourned by the acting profession, was buried in the Wallack family cemetery plot in Brooklyn, and a memorial window in his honor was placed in the "Little Church around the Corner" that he attended.

Though obituaries were frank about his limitations, an actor essentially only able to play himself, he was long remembered for his charm and the romantic tragedy of his short life. He stands in American theatrical history as a very early example of the "personality" star who succeeded by projecting his own charm across the footlights and as a prototype of the matinee idols of decades to come.

• Materials on the life and career of Montague are in the Billy Rose Theatre Collection at the New York Public Library for the Performing Arts, Lincoln Center. Reminiscences are in Marie Bancroft and Squire Bancroft, *Mr. and Mrs. Bancroft: On and Off the Stage*, 3d ed. (2 vols., 1888); George Odell, *Annals of the New York Stage* (15 vols., 1927–1949); and William Winter, *Vagrant Memories* (1915). Portraits are in Odell, vols. 9 and 10, and in Daniel C. Blum, *A Pictorial History of the American Theatre* (1960). Obituaries are in the *New York Times* and the *New York Telegram*, both 13 Aug. 1878.

WILLIAM STEPHENSON

MONTAGUE, William Pepperell (11 Nov. 1873–1 Aug. 1953), philosopher and professor, was born in Chelsea, Massachusetts, the son of William Pepperell Montague, a lawyer, and Helen Maria Cary. Only after he was suspended by Harvard in his sophomore year did he take his education seriously. The Harvard philosopher Josiah Royce took an interest in Montague and encouraged him to pursue an academic career. Montague returned to Harvard with new enthusiasm and completed his B.A. in 1896. That same year he married Helen Weymouth Robinson; they had two sons.

Montague did his graduate work in philosophy at Harvard under Royce, William James, and George Santayana. He credited Royce with providing essential support and grounding in the history of philosophy, even though Montague quickly dissented from Royce's own philosophy. He was more attracted to the mystical elements of James's philosophy and to Santayana's theory of substances. He received his M.A. in 1897 and his Ph.D. in 1898. His first regular academic appointment was at the University of California at Berkeley from 1899 to 1903. He moved to Barnard College in 1903. Beginning in 1907, he served on the Columbia University graduate faculty in philosophy. He was promoted to associate professor in 1910, professor in 1920, and Johnsonian Professor at Columbia in 1941. In 1928 he was appointed as Carnegie visiting professor and taught in Japan, Czechoslovakia, and Italy. Montague also participated in professional activities, chairing three U.S. delegations to international philosophical congresses (1920, 1934, 1937) and serving as president of the American Philosophical Association in 1923. He delivered the Terry Lectures at Yale (1930), the Ingersoll Lectures at Harvard (1932), and the Carus Lectures at the University of Chicago (1933). Montague retired in 1947; he died in New York City.

Montague first came to attention as one of the young realists who launched the twentieth-century attack on philosophical idealism, especially as identified with Royce. Montague, in his article "Professor Royce's Refutation of Realism," defended the independence of objects known from the knowing relation. This was a central belief of the New Realists, with whom Montague published *The New Realism* (1912). He considered their effort "a prolegomenon to philosophy and a declaration of independence that would make it possible to investigate the nature of things on their own merits" (Adams and Montague, p. 145). Disagreements among themselves soon split the New Realists, but Montague always retained features of their program: that the real world existed independent of thought, that the world can be known without violating its independence, that scientific method was the surest method to knowledge of the world, and that the world was pluralistic rather than monistic in substance. His own variant of realism was "subsistent realism." He held that substance included everything that could be studied or analyzed. Drawing on Charles Sanders Peirce, Montague argued that the world is known through propositions and terms, which are themselves substances, and thus can be known directly, though the objects to which they refer remain independent of the knowing mind.

Although problems of knowledge first engaged Montague, he became known primarily for the breadth of his philosophic vision. The mind-body problem—how to maintain their separate existence yet explain their complex interaction—underlay much of Montague's philosophizing. His solution, animistic materialism, held that the soul represented a kind of private, internal energy that could be perceived as a sensation. This energy was only potential until stimulated by some external motion. When stimulated, the potential energy was released and perceived psychically. He often used the analogy of the energy stored in a coiled spring, which can not be perceived until released by some action. In this way, Montague believed he could retain the separate existence of mind and body while bringing them into relation with one another.

Montague's ethical theory developed out of his notions of psychic substance. He defined the good life as "the most abundant life. Happiness was increment of psychic substance—fulfilment of tendencies and capacities" (Adams and Montague, pp. 147–48). His religious notions built on his moral theories. He argued that there was too much goodness in the world for it to be the result of chance or of mechanistic determinism. That argued for "a God, a force or trend upward." The existence of evil, however, argued for a limited God. Though he could give no proof, Montague believed that the existence of goodness and such integration and order as existed in the universe gave him grounds for believing in the high probability of such a deity or universal force.

Montague remains important for his formative role in the twentieth-century revival of realism and for the range of his philosophic vision.

• The best autobiographical source is "Confessions of an Animistic Materialist," in *Contemporary American Philosophy*, vol. 2, ed. George P. Adams and Wm. Pepperell Montague (1930), pp. 135–59. Major writings by Montague include "Professor Royce's Refutation of Realism," *Philosophical Review* 11 (1902): 43–55; "A Realistic Theory of Truth and Error," in *The New Realism*, ed. E. B. Holt et al. (1912): 251–300; *The Ways of Knowing; or, The Methods of Philosophy* (1925); *The Ways of Things: A Philosophy of Knowledge, Nature, and Value* (1940); and his Carus Lectures, *Great Visions of Philosophy: Varieties of Speculative Thought in the West from the Greeks to Bergson* (1950). Montague's role in the realist revolt is discussed in Herbert W. Schneider, *Sources of Contemporary Philosophical Realism in America* (1964).

DANIEL J. WILSON

MONTEUX, Pierre Benjamin (4 Apr. 1875–1 July 1964), conductor, was born in Paris, France, the son of Gustave Elie Monteux, a shoe salesman, and Clémence Brisac, a piano teacher. Monteux's honors included commander of the Légion d'honneur and knight of the Order of Orange-Nassau. His early musical education was at the Paris Conservatory, where he studied violin and composition. In 1896 he shared the conservatory's *premier prix* for violin with the young French violinist Jacques Thibaud, who after the turn of the century became one of the most well known violinists of his generation. During his student years Monteux played a viola with the orchestra at the Opéra-Comique, participating in the premiere of Debussy's *Pelléas et Mélisande* in 1902, and with the Concerts Colonne, one of the main subscription concert series in Paris at the time. He later became chorus master and assistant conductor of the Concerts Colonne. In 1894 he became a member of the Geloso String Quartet and remained with that ensemble until 1911. Between 1908 and 1914 he conducted the Casino Orchestra in Dieppe. In 1911 Monteux was engaged by the Russian impresario Serge Diaghilev to conduct concerts of his Ballets Russes. As a result of his association with the Ballets Russes, Monteux's international reputation as a leading exponent of contemporary music, especially by French composers, was established. Notable premieres conducted by Monteux during this period include Debussy's *Jeux* (1913), Ravel's *Daphnis et Chloé* (1912), and Igor Stravinsky's *Le sacre du printemps* (1913), a premiere infamous for the riotous audience reaction to the unusual music and choreography. During this early period of his life Monteux was married twice: first to a pianist from Bordeaux (name unknown), and then to Germaine Benedictus, with whom he had three children.

Following wartime service in the French Thirty-fifth Territorial Infantry, Monteux came to the United States for the first time, in 1916–1917, on a tour with the Ballets Russes. From 1917 to 1919 he was engaged by the Metropolitan Opera in New York City as conductor of the French repertory. While at the Metropolitan in 1918 he conducted the American premiere of Rimsky-Korsakov's last opera, *The Golden Cockerel* (1909), and the ballet version of Henry F. Gilbert's *The Dance in Place Congo* (1913).

After a brief period as guest conductor, Monteux was engaged as conductor of the Boston Symphony Orchestra in 1919, a position he held until 1924. He came to Boston in the midst of an acrimonious strike by the musicians, and after almost thirty players walked out, he had to rebuild the orchestra nearly from scratch. While in Boston, Monteux worked to acquaint his audience with both new works and music outside the Germanic repertoire that had previously been the standard fare in Boston under a series of German-born conductors. Though he was well liked personally in Boston, the music he performed was not always given the same respect. He laid the groundwork, however, for his successor, Serge Koussevitzky, who was also a devoted proponent of new music. In 1924 he moved to Amsterdam to become the principal guest conductor, under Willem Mengelberg, of the Concertgebouw Orchestra. Monteux married Doris Gerald Hodgkins, of Hancock, Maine, in 1928; they had no children.

In 1929 Monteux founded the Orchestre Symphonique de Paris, which presented concerts, including many premieres, until the onset of World War II in 1938. Like many European musicians, Monteux then found a position in the United States that provided a haven from the upheavals in Europe. In 1936 he was engaged as conductor of the San Francisco Symphony Orchestra, a position he held until 1952. He became a U.S. citizen in 1942. Monteux's tenure in San Francisco propelled the orchestra's rise to international stature, enhanced by forty recordings and a successful national tour in 1947.

Following his retirement from the San Francisco Symphony, Monteux performed widely in the United States and Europe as a guest conductor, often conducting opera. In 1961 he signed a twenty-five-year contract with the London Symphony Orchestra. With this orchestra, he conducted the fiftieth anniversary performance of *Le sacre du printemps* in 1963.

Monteux was involved throughout his career with the education of musicians. He was the first in a generation of French-born musicians, including the pianist E. Robert Schmitz, who built their reputations on profound musicianship, restrained yet vigorous performances, and a commitment to the musical education of both aspiring musicians and audiences. In 1932 he established the École Monteux in Paris to coach young conductors, and he continued this work during his summers in Maine after immigrating to the United States. His students include Neville Marriner and André Previn.

Monteux disliked recording because of the lack of spontaneity inherent in the process. However, Monteux's recordings, while not plentiful, are among the finest ever made of the French repertory. His aesthetic restraint and thorough preparation of his orchestras resulted in sensitive, energetic, and authoritative readings of the scores.

In performance, Monteux was, as Stravinsky once said of him, "the [conductor] least interested in calisthenic exhibitions for the entertainment of the audience and the most concerned to give clear signals for the orchestra." For all of his precision, however, it was the lyricism and grace of Monteux's performances that remain their most memorable characteristic.

• Most of Monteux's personal papers and scores were destroyed during World War II. His career is covered in two books by his wife, Doris G. Monteux: *It's All in the Music* (1965, with discography by Erich Kunzel), and, under the pseudonym Fifi Monteux, *Everyone Is Someone* (1962). Other books with information on Monteux during his years in San Francisco include L. W. Armsby, *We Shall Have Music* (1960) and David Schneider, *The San Francisco Symphony: Music, Maestros and Musicians* (1983, with a foreword by Edo de Waart). Evaluations of Monteux may be found in the following general surveys: David Ewen, *Dictators of the Baton* (1948), Hope Stoddard, *Symphony Conductors of the U.S.A.* (1957), and Harold C. Schonberg, *The Great Conductors* (1968). Monteux's career and recordings are sympathetically surveyed in Samuel Lipman, "A Conductor in History," *Commentary* 77 (Jan. 1984): 50–56, and J. Canarina, "Pierre Monteux: A Conductor for All Repertoire," *Opus*, Apr. 1986, pp. 14–19. The following is a list of CD reissues of recordings by Monteux made during the 1950s and 1960s: Beethoven, Symphony no. 3 (Philips 420 853–2); Berlioz, *Overture: Béatrice and Bénédict* (RCA GD 86805); Chausson, *Poème de l'amour et de la mer* (EMI mono CMS7 63549–2); Debussy, *Images* and *Le Martyr de St. Sébastien* (Philips 420 392–2); Franck, Symphony in D Minor (see Berlioz); d'Indy, *Symphonie sur un chant montagnard français* (see Berlioz); Massenet, *Manon* (see Chausson); Ravel, *Boléro, Ma Mère l'Oye, La Valse* (Philips 420 869–2); Ravel, *Daphnis et Chloé, Pavane pour une infante défunte, Rapsodie espagnole* (Decca 425 956–2); Rimsky-Korsakov, *Scheherazade* (Decca 421 400–2); and Tchaikovsky, *Swan Lake* (Philips 420 872–2). An obituary is in the *New York Times*, 2 July 1964.

RON WIECKI

MONTEZ, Lola (1818–17 Jan. 1861), dancer and actress, was born Marie Dolores Eliza Rosanna Gilbert in Limerick, Ireland, the daughter of Edward Gilbert, a professional soldier, and Mary Oliver. At age four Eliza, as she was known, left with her parents for Calcutta, where her father had been posted. After his death in 1824, her mother remarried, and Eliza was sent by her stepfather, John Craigie, to live in Montrose, Scotland. Rebellious and individualistic even at this early age, Eliza was placed in the care of Sir Jasper Nicholls, a distinguished soldier and friend of her stepfather, with whose daughter Fanny she continued her education in Paris and Bath. In 1837 she eloped with Thomas James, an officer in the Indian army on leave in England; they had no children.

James was posted to Calcutta and then to Karnal during the first Afghan war. However, he deserted Eliza in 1841, and after her return to London a legal separation was granted in December 1842. No longer able to depend on relatives and keen to establish her own independent identity, Eliza decided to train as a dancer. After a brief period in Spain, she returned to London in 1843 and assumed the name Lola Montez, by which she was to be known both privately and professionally for the remainder of her life. Although the name had no legal basis, her claim that her mother's family had Spanish ancestors may have been true.

Montez's first performance at Her Majesty's Theatre in June 1843 was a disaster. Her rawness as a dancer could be compensated for by what critics took to be her Andalusian beauty, but she could not escape talk of her recent separation, and some in the audience knew her well enough to see through her thin Spanish disguise. Nevertheless, her dancing attracted the attention of Edward Fitzball, the prolific writer of melodramas, for whose benefit she performed with great success.

After leaving England in 1843, Montez remained on the Continent until 1848 and acquired a reputation as a flamboyant adventuress. Undoubtedly she was attracted to wealthy and powerful people, who, in turn, found her independence, fluency with languages, and capacity for risk taking attractive. After touring Brussels, Warsaw, and St. Petersburg, she spent most of the period in Paris, becoming part of the glittering literary and social scene of the Second Empire.

Montez's debut at the Court Theatre in Munich in October 1846 attracted the attention of Ludwig I of Bavaria. She stayed on not only to become his favorite but also to exert considerable influence over Bavarian politics. Her radical anticlericalism hastened the collapse of the Catholic government in Bavaria and its replacement by a liberal one. Ludwig created her countess of Landsfeld in 1847, but what was seen as her meddling in politics brought her many enemies, including Otto Metternich, the reactionary Viennese chancellor. When the wave of popular unrest swept Europe in early 1848, she was forced to flee Munich.

After some months in Switzerland, she returned to England, where she married George Trafford Heald in 1849. Heald left her in 1850, and the marriage was subsequently annulled. Once again without a stable financial base, Montez began to tour as a Spanish dancer throughout France and Belgium. In Paris in 1851 she met P. T. Barnum, who suggested that he might manage her on a tour of the United States. The negotiations failed, but Montez decided to try this for herself. She arrived in New York on 5 December 1851.

Audiences were attracted to Montez as a personality rather than as a performing artist. After all, she was a celebrity in her own right who had associated with some of the most famous artistic personalities of the nineteenth century and was keenly aware of her own persona and ready to exploit it on stage. She was also sufficiently aware that her repertoire needed to be extended. When she arrived in New York, therefore, she had accumulated a repertoire of dramatic pieces that she was to retain until the end of her career. These included *School for Scandal*, Charles Selby's burlesque *Antony and Cleopatra*, J. T. Haines's *Maidens Beware*, and Thomas Morton Junior's *The Eton Boy*. However, she opened in New York in a mime part in *Betley the Tyrolean* on 29 December 1851 at the Broadway Theatre with little critical but considerable financial success. The following year in New York she premiered in a play she had commissioned from C. P. T. Ware, *Lola Montez in Bavaria*. Although critics denigrated her performance together with the piece as romantic self-aggrandizement, the play remained the centerpiece of her repertoire.

Montez next moved to California by way of New Orleans and arrived in May 1853 in San Francisco, where she made her debut at the American Theatre. During her journey from New Orleans, she had met Patrick Purdy Hull, the editor of the *San Francisco*

Whig, whom she married in San Francisco in July 1853. Again the relationship was to be a brief one; they separated later the same year.

During her California theatrical career, Montez developed her particular trademark, a dance based on the tarantella called the Spider Dance. The renowned Romantic-era ballerina Fanny Elssler, as part of her strategy to employ folk-dance elements in ballet, had introduced the tarantella, calling it *La Tarantule*. Montez converted it into a display of physical freedom that shocked or delighted her audiences by its suggestion of exuberant eroticism. When all else failed, she would perform this dance to acclaim by firemen in San Francisco and gold miners in Sacramento and Nevada City. After her separation from Hull, she settled in Grass Valley, where she remained until 1855.

In June 1855 Montez left on her last theatrical tour. She gathered a scratch company in San Francisco, intending to travel to Australia, Hong Kong, and possibly India. In fact, she only managed the Australian part, arriving in Sydney in August and opening at the Victoria Theatre. She retained the same repertoire as in the United States, augmented by performances of Thomas Archer's comic drama *Asmodeus, the Little Demon*, and Charles Dance's farce *A Morning Call*. She subsequently played in Melbourne, Adelaide, and the gold rush towns of Ballarat and Bendigo. She returned to Sydney and sailed for California in June 1856.

The tour, marked by strenuous travel, physical fights between Montez and her agents, legal battles, and a disintegrating company, had exhausted her. Although Montez performed in New York during 1857, her days as an actress were over. In 1858 she began the last phase of her career, as a public lecturer. That same year she published her autobiography, ghostwritten by Charles Chauncey Burr, together with her lectures on subjects such as the art of beauty and chivalry. In November 1858 she returned to Ireland for the first time since 1837 and began an extensive tour, lecturing on "America and Its Inhabitants," which took her to Manchester, Bath, and eventually London in April 1859. She subsequently returned to the United States, where her career ended. Although she had known periods of great wealth, her prodigality and lifelong devotion to luxury had depleted her financial resources. Partially paralyzed in December 1860, she died in New York City in penury and was buried in Greenwood Cemetery, Brooklyn.

• Clippings can be found in the Montez scrapbooks in the New York Public Library for the Performing Arts, Lincoln Center. Some original letters are located among the Lola Montez Papers and the T. W. Norris Collection, with additional material in the Isaac Goldberg Papers, at the University of California, Berkeley. Further contemporary accounts can also be found at the Harvard Theatre Collection and among the Thomas Ely Buchanan Letters and Crawford Theatre Collection, Yale University, and the La Trobe Library, Melbourne. See also C. Chauncey Burr, *The Autobiography and Lectures of Lola Montez, Countess of Landsfeld* (1858), which tends to perpetuate her self-constructed legend. Her career, especially during the period 1843–1860, was widely reported in contemporary newspapers and journals, especially *The Times* (London), the *Era*, and the *New York Herald*. An interesting and sympathetic evaluation of the period with Ludwig I can be found in G. H. Francis, "The King of Bavaria, Munich, and Lola Montez," *Fraser's Magazine*, Jan. 1848, pp. 89–104. The most reliable published biography is Ishbel Ross, *The Uncrowned Queen: Life of Lola Montez* (1972), which nonetheless owes much to the earlier biographies of Edmund B. D'Auvergne, *Lola Montez: An Adventuress of the 'Forties* (1909), and Horace Wyndham, *The Magnificent Montez: From Courtesan to Convert* (1935, repr. 1969). A particular emphasis on her California tours can be found in Doris Foley, *The Divine Eccentric: Lola Montez and the Newspapers* (1969), and a useful survey of iconography appears in Diane Day, "Lola Montez and Her American Image," *History of Photography* 5 (1981): 339–53. Obituaries are in the *New York Herald*, 20 Jan. 1861, and the *New York Times*, 21 Jan. 1861.

VICTOR EMELJANOW

MONTEZUMA, Carlos (1866?–31 Jan. 1923), American Indian activist and medical doctor, was born in central Arizona, the son of a Yavapai mother and Yavapai father, both of whom died in his early childhood. At the time of Montezuma's birth, the Yavapais had not yet been confined to reservations. But their world, an area of perhaps 20,000 square miles, was becoming rapidly enclosed and invaded by Anglo-Americans and other Indian communities. The Yavapai territory in which they gathered the foods of the region and hunted also possessed gold, which attracted miners to the area during this decade.

Carlos Montezuma's first name was Wassaja, which in English might be translated as "signaling or beckoning." The Pima Indians captured young Wassaja in 1871 and sold him for $30 to an Italian immigrant photographer visiting Arizona. Carlos Gentile named his charge Carlos, after himself, and Montezuma, to give him an Indian name as well. Although there were no Aztecs in Arizona, nearby Indian sites had been named Montezuma's Castle and Montezuma's Well, and it is probable that Gentile appropriated the name from such sources.

Gentile took Carlos Montezuma to his home in Chicago but proved unable to care for him and gave up his custody of the boy. Montezuma eventually wound up in the home of William Steadman, a Baptist minister in Urbana, Illinois. He advanced quickly in his studies and entered the University of Illinois, where he earned a degree in chemistry in 1884. By 1889 he had completed his M.D. at the Chicago Medical College. At a time when few American Indians had access to much schooling, he had become a physician.

After a brief and not very successful stint in private practice in Chicago, Montezuma decided to gain employment as a physician with the Bureau of Indian Affairs (BIA). He worked in North Dakota, Nevada, and Washington before taking a position at the famous Carlisle Indian Industrial School in Carlisle, Pennsylvania, in 1893. Montezuma had not liked what he had seen of reservation life. He thought the government agents had too much power, particularly in the economic realm. Reservations seemed to resemble prisons. Residents had to seek permission to leave its boundaries and were denied freedom of speech and worship.

Montezuma had corresponded with the founder of Carlisle, Richard Henry Pratt, well before going to Pennsylvania. Pratt believed that one had to "kill the Indian" in order to "save the man," and he ran Carlisle along military lines. Pratt also believed, however, in the potential of Indian students to learn as well as to change. At a time when few white Americans saw any promise in Indians, Pratt at least saw what they might achieve. This perspective and Pratt's strong personality won him many disciples among Indian people; Montezuma was strongly influenced by him at this time.

Leaving Carlisle in 1896, Montezuma returned to Chicago to prove himself in the white man's world. In 1900, however, he accompanied the well-known Carlisle football team on a trip west. The journey took them to Arizona, where Carlisle defeated a thoroughly outmatched Phoenix Indian School, 83-6. In 1901 Montezuma returned to Arizona and met relatives he had not seen since his childhood. Thus began a set of relationships and a process that dramatically altered Montezuma's understanding of contemporary Native American life.

Montezuma's relatives and other Yavapais now lived on a newly established reservation not far from the emerging community of Phoenix. Fort McDowell had been a frontier military post before it had been abandoned by the army. In 1903 the site had become the center of a new reservation. Situated in beautiful desert foothill country, the Yavapai lands were not only scenic but also bisected by the Verde River. Access to water was already precious in southern Arizona, and the Yavapais learned quickly that they would have to fight to protect it. They now had a well-educated, articulate ally in the combative doctor from Chicago.

Although Montezuma remained highly critical of Indian agents and government restrictions on Indians, he began to perceive that reservations were homes and that Indian residents deserved protection so that they would not be cheated out of their property rights. He also started to appreciate that the Yavapais at Fort McDowell as well as Indians on other reservations were quite attached to their communities. Even though Montezuma had been critical of how reservations had been administered, he began to see the need for reservations to continue as native enclaves. Thus he differed from his old mentor, Richard H. Pratt, who remained an unabashed assimilationist.

In addition to renewing his ties at Fort McDowell, Montezuma spent the first years of the twentieth century becoming increasingly active in national Indian concerns. His home in Chicago provided a convenient stopping place for other Indian leaders. Montezuma spoke earnestly with other Native Americans who had had educational opportunities and had taken advantage of them. They agreed that a new organization should be founded to meet the challenges of the new century. This organization, the Society of American Indians (SAI), was founded in 1911. Unlike early associations, such as the Indian Rights Association, this group would be a society for Indian members and would present less assimilationist views. Established during the Progressive era, the society also embraced a view of progress. Through education, hard work, and informed leadership, Indians could look forward to a better future. Yet SAI leaders differed about how to realize such goals. Montezuma would at times be the organization's staunchest advocate and its most severe foe, depending on the positions taken by the society. For example, Montezuma argued strongly for the abolition of the BIA, contending the bureau could not be reformed. In his view, the BIA had become corrupt, and too many of its employees could not shed their views of Indians as incompetent. Given the drastic problems facing Indians in the areas of health care, economic development, and education, a gradual approach could not be tolerated. Many people shared his unhappiness with the bureau but opted for the possibility of reform. Arthur C. Parker, a Seneca anthropologist who was also a leader in the SAI, criticized Montezuma for his position, including his unwillingness to offer a clear alternative to the BIA.

In the final decades of his life Montezuma experienced both national recognition and personal happiness. He had been engaged years before to Gertrude Simmons, or Zitkala-Sa, a talented Lakota musician and writer, who was also active in the SAI. It is not surprising that Montezuma refused her terms for marriage. Zitkala-Sa had wanted them to live on one of the South Dakota reservations so she could be with some of her relatives, and Montezuma had had quite enough of reservation life. In September 1913 he married a non-Indian, Maria Keller, a Rumanian immigrant to Chicago. They had no children.

Carlos Montezuma's final years were marked by a continuous whirl of activity on behalf of Indian wellbeing. Troubled by the unwillingness of the SAI's own journal to take strong stands, he started his own newspaper, *Wassaja*, to speak out on the controversies of the day. First published in April 1916, it had a limited number of paid subscribers yet reached a national audience as its readers shared copies of the publication. In addition to advocating the abolition of the BIA, the newspaper spoke out about Indian land and water rights, including the challenges faced by the Yavapais at Fort McDowell.

Montezuma also advocated citizenship for all Indian peoples. His dreams were realized in the passage of the Indian Citizenship Act of 1924. The act symbolized Montezuma's belief that Indians were not second-class members of American society but were entitled to the same privileges, rights, and responsibilities as all Americans. But Montezuma did not live to see the act become a reality. Ill with tuberculosis, he traveled one final time to the land of his people and chose to die with relatives at Fort McDowell, refusing the attention of white physicians who wanted to treat him.

The memory of Carlos Montezuma lived on at Fort McDowell. In the 1970s and 1980s the Yavapais fought against the building of Orme Dam, which would have flooded most of their lands. They refused offers of considerable compensation, saying they wanted to stay with their homes and that they did not want the place where Carlos Montezuma was buried to be covered with water. Despite strong political pressure for powerful state residents, the people won the battle. Orme Dam was defeated.

• Collections of Montezuma's papers are at the State Historical Society of Wisconsin and at Arizona State University. The State Historical Society of Wisconsin papers are available on microfilm, as is a microfilm collection containing theses and other materials. The latter collection, "The Papers of Carlos Montezuma, M.D.," was produced in 1984 by Scholarly Resources. Peter Iverson, *Carlos Montezuma and the Changing World of American Indians* (1982), is the standard biography. Additional information about the Society of American Indians may be found in Hazel Hertzberg, *The Search for an American Indian Identity: Modern Pan-Indian Movements* (1971).

PETER IVERSON

MONTGOMERY, Benjamin Thornton (1819–12 May 1877), businessman, was born a slave in Loudoun County, Virginia. As the boyhood companion of his owner's son, Montgomery completed in the afternoon the lessons the young white boy learned from his tutor in the morning. In this manner Montgomery gained a basic education. In 1836 he was sold to a trader who transported him to Natchez, Mississippi, where he was purchased by Joseph Davis, elder brother of Jefferson Davis, and settled on Davis Bend below Vicksburg. Davis had determined to apply the reform principles of Robert Owen, who sought order and efficiency in the management of industrial labor, to the management of his plantations. This required a rational relationship between owner and worker that, in Davis's application, meant a relationship between master and slave based on kindness, not cruelty, and on wholesome living conditions, not squalor. Davis sought and gained the confidence of Montgomery in his reform endeavor and gave the young slave access to his library. Montgomery learned to survey the land, construct levees, and design architectural plans for the construction of plantation buildings. He also gained the mechanical skills necessary to operate the plantation's steam-powered cotton gin. As a slave on Davis Bend, Montgomery enjoyed significant privileges and emerged as the leading figure of the slave community.

On Christmas Eve 1840 Montgomery formed a conjugal union with Mary Lewis, the daughter of Virginia slaves who had been among the earliest settlers on Davis Bend. Marriage among slaves had no legal standing, but Montgomery worked successfully to establish a nuclear family. From his earnings, Montgomery paid Davis the equivalent of his wife's earnings to ensure that she would live and labor only in the Montgomery household. Four of their children lived to become adults, but slavery severely limited Montgomery's ability to maintain an independent household. When Davis and his wife Eliza wanted to take the Montgomerys' youngest son, Isaiah, into their house as a servant, the child's parents could only express their anguish. Davis, in his role as Owenite manager, attempted to console the Montgomerys by promising to oversee the boy's education.

With the initial assistance of Davis, Montgomery became a successful merchant, importing manufactured goods from New Orleans and selling them to the slaves on Davis Bend in exchange for chickens and vegetables they raised on their garden plots. Davis subsidized Montgomery's first consignment from New Orleans in 1842, but thereafter Montgomery maintained his own account with his New Orleans suppliers. Montgomery's store also provided the white planters and their families with a convenient means of purchasing goods from distant points of manufacture. The produce that Montgomery acquired in this trade supplied the Mississippi River steamboats with fresh food. Montgomery's combined store and home were located near the Davis Bend steamboat landing, where he became a key figure in Davis's efforts to achieve, within a slave labor system, aspects of the Owenite ideal of harmonizing the moral virtues of agrarian life with the material benefits of industry.

The Civil War and, specifically, General Ulysses S. Grant's campaign against Vicksburg thoroughly disrupted life and labor on Davis Bend. Joseph Davis sought refuge for himself and his family in the interior of the state, but most of his slaves, Montgomery included, did not follow. Freed under the terms of the Emancipation Proclamation on 1 January 1863, Montgomery resettled his family in Cincinnati in June 1863. Both of his sons briefly served with Admiral David D. Porter's Mississippi Squadron before joining their father in Cincinnati. After Vicksburg fell on 4 July 1863, Union forces commanded by Admiral Porter took control of Davis Bend. Almost completely surrounded by the Mississippi River, the bend was easily defended by gunboats. With a detachment of black soldiers guarding the neck of the bend, Porter reported in the fall of 1863 that about six hundred freedmen had returned to the bend and were preparing enthusiastically for the 1864 agricultural season.

In March 1864 President Abraham Lincoln placed freedmen affairs in the Mississippi Valley under the control of the army, whose Bureau of Negro Affairs appointed Colonel Samuel Thomas as superintendent for the bend. Federal authorities confiscated the Davis plantations as "abandoned lands," and Treasury Department agents leased much of the Davis plantation to white speculators. Nevertheless, under Thomas's direction 180 black lessees farmed an average of thirty acres each on the bend during the 1864 season and raised 130 bales of cotton despite an army worm infestation. When leases expired in November 1864, Thomas excluded white planters from the bend, declaring that the land was reserved for "military purposes" and that it would be devoted to the "colonization, residence and support of the Freedmen." In March 1865 Congress created the Freedmen's Bureau (officially the Bureau of Refugees, Freedmen, and Abandoned Lands), and Thomas became bureau commissioner for Mississippi. In the spring of 1865 the Montgomery family returned to Davis Bend. Montgomery became a central figure in a dispute between Thomas and Davis as Davis led his family's efforts to regain control of their antebellum plantations.

Early in October 1865 Davis, now eighty years old, moved to Vicksburg. Since his only remaining assets, the Davis Bend plantations, were a prime target for federal confiscation, Davis eagerly sought a business partnership with Montgomery. On 21 October Davis leased the Davis Bend land to Montgomery for the 1866 agricultural year. Thomas fought this effort to wrest the Davis plantations from bureau control and described Montgomery as a "shrewd and intelligent" agent serving the interests of his former master. In April 1866 President Andrew Johnson replaced Thomas as bureau commissioner. In September the president pardoned Davis, and the Freedmen's Bureau settled its dispute with the Davis family by agreeing to pay Davis the income from the Montgomery lease while maintaining management of the estates until January 1867. Rather than resume direct control of the Davis Bend estates, Davis agreed to sell the land to "Montgomery & Sons" for $300,000 over a period of ten years. With the approbation of the *New York Times* and the suspicion of whites in Vicksburg, the Davis Bend estates began production in 1867 entirely under black direction and control.

In partnership with Davis, Montgomery flourished as a merchant on the bend. Montgomery & Sons extended credit to 80 percent of the freedmen on the bend, accepting cotton in exchange for merchandise. Montgomery had become a prominent figure in Reconstruction era Mississippi. In 1867 he became Mississippi's first black justice of the peace, and by 1872, despite serious financial difficulties, the Montgomerys were the wealthiest black family in the South.

Unfortunately for Montgomery & Sons, the spring of 1867 brought devastating floods that cut a channel across the narrow western neck of the peninsula, turning Davis Bend into the more isolated Davis Island. The 1867 and 1868 seasons put Montgomery & Sons—plantations and store—in debt, and although their fortunes improved somewhat over the next several years, the Montgomerys were never able to pay any of the principal of the debt they owed Davis.

Late in December 1874, while Montgomery was working with a crew to raze an old building, a wall collapsed. Montgomery sustained severe injuries from which he never fully recovered. His death, combined with repeated floods, poor crops, and declining cotton prices, made the economic status of the Montgomery firm increasingly unstable. In 1878 the Mississippi State Supreme Court awarded one of Joseph Davis's plantations to Jefferson Davis. In 1881 foreclosure proceedings forced the Montgomery family to sell all their mortgaged lands to Jefferson Davis and the heirs of Joseph Davis. In 1887 Isaiah Montgomery, already a prominent spokesman for black accommodation to segregation, relocated his family to 700 purchased acres in northern Mississippi, where he founded the new black town of Mound Bayou.

• Approximately two hundred letters from Montgomery and his sons are in the Joseph E. Davis Family Papers in the Mississippi Department of Archives and History, Jackson, Miss. Substantial materials relating to Montgomery and his activities on Davis Bend during the Civil War and Reconstruction, including his disputes with the Freedmen's Bureau, are located in the Records of the Bureau of Refugees, Freedmen, and Abandoned Lands, Mississippi, Assistant Commissioner, Letters Received, RG 105, National Archives, Washington, D.C. On Reconstruction in Miss. see the classic study by Vernon Lane Wharton, *The Negro in Mississippi, 1865–1890* (1947), and Eric Foner, *Reconstruction: America's Unfinished Revolution, 1863–1877* (1988). The history of Montgomery's enterprise is the subject of Janet Sharp Harmine, *The Pursuit of a Dream* (1981). The family's status as the wealthiest black family in the South is recorded in Loren Schweninger, *Black Property Owners in the South, 1790–1915* (1990). The hopes that abolitionists attached to the Davis Bend community and the impact of Federal wartime policies toward southern blacks on that community are treated in Louis S. Girds, *From Contraband to Freedman: Federal Policy toward Southern Blacks, 1861–1865* (1973).

LOUIS S. GERTEIS

MONTGOMERY, Charles Franklin (14 Apr. 1910–21 Feb. 1978), museum curator and art historian, was born in Austin Township, Macon County, Illinois, the son of William Norton Montgomery, a farmer, and Grace Louisa Albert. An aunt, Alberta Montgomery, was an important influence in his developing academic interests and loaned him money to attend Harvard University. He graduated from Harvard in 1932 with a B.A. in art history. For the next eight years he worked as a staff member for the education and promotion departments of the *New York Herald Tribune*. In 1932 Montgomery married Evelyn Reed; they had one child.

In 1937 he purchased the Theophilus Jones homestead (c. 1740) in Wallingford, Connecticut, which he carefully restored to exacting historical standards. He ran an apple business from the farm under the name Cook Hill Orchards (1937–1941) and spent what time he could combing the countryside for antiques and materials to restore his house. In 1939 Montgomery opened an antique shop there called At the Sign of the Tankard and became well known as an expert on American pewter after publishing "Important Early American Pewter" (*Antiques* 36, no. 3 [Sept. 1939]: 118–21). Having been divorced from his first wife, in 1946 he married Florence Elizabeth Mellowes, an expert on early American textiles, with whom he continued a lifelong professional collaboration. They had two children.

By 1949 Montgomery was able to establish himself as a professional consultant for the country's leading collectors of American antiques, especially Henry

Francis du Pont. With the creation of du Pont's Winterthur Museum at Wilmington, Delaware, Montgomery joined the museum staff as executive secretary and associate curator (1951–1954), later becoming director (1954–1961) and then senior research fellow (1962–1970). He was instrumental in creating the Winterthur Program in Early American Culture, which offered graduate training in museum operation, restoration, connoisseurship, and scholarly study of American decorative arts and material culture. Begun in 1952 his master's program in early American culture and the decorative arts, administered through the University of Delaware, was the first of its kind in the country.

Montgomery published numerous studies of objects at Winterthur and a general *Guide* to the collection (1962, rev. 1966, 1970). From 1952 to 1967 he was adjunct professor of American art at the University of Delaware and in 1965 visiting lecturer at the University of Pennsylvania. His numerous brief studies dealt with subjects such as tinware, use of documentary evidence for early furniture, early windows, cabinetmakers, clocks, and textiles. He supervised a project to catalog British prints with American scenes, *Prints Pertaining to America* (1963). He also supervised the reprinting, with introductions, of several eighteenth- and nineteenth-century cabinetmaker's manuals. The culmination of his work at Winterthur was his volume *American Furniture: The Federal Period* (1966), primarily a catalog of pieces from the Winterthur collection, which was one of the largest concentrations of American antiques in the world. This became a standard work on the subject. Montgomery went beyond the traditional method of illustrating and describing choice pieces to consider production and artisans, patterns of furnishing in American home life and art of the period, regional styles and variations, attribution, dating, and connoisseurship.

In 1969 Montgomery was invited to Yale University, first as a visiting lecturer and then as professor of art history and curator of the Mabel Brady Garvan and Related Collections in the Yale Art Gallery. His second major work, *A History of American Pewter* (1973), summed up his forty years of interest in pewter. He was well known as an inspiring and exacting teacher of American art and saw a great expansion of American public interest in the subject. In response to this, he created in 1973 the Friends of American Arts, a national organization of collectors of American painting and decorative arts. Montgomery undertook to reinstall the Mabel Brady Garvan and Related Collections in the Yale Art Gallery under the title American Arts and the American Experience (*The Mabel Brady Garvan Galleries* [1973]). This displayed a comprehensive sample of American furnishings and accessories of all periods. Montgomery was considered the leading expert on American decorative arts, that is, art in all its aspects excluding painting and sculpture. His essay "Some Remarks on the Practice and Science of Connoisseurship" in the *Walpole Society Note Book 1961* (1962) offers a concise statement of his personal approach and standards (pp. 56–69).

To commemorate the American bicentennial, Montgomery supervised preparation of a major exhibition at the Yale Art Gallery drawn from numerous American collections, American Art: 1750–1800: Towards Independence. When it opened in the Victoria and Albert Museum in London (July 1976), it was the first exhibition of early American art abroad (Charles F. Montgomery and Patricia E. Kane, eds., *American Art: 1750–1800: Towards Independence* [1976]) and drew 62,000 visitors in eight weeks.

Montgomery was a tall, strong presence, with great vitality and vigor, fond of debate, and an accomplished lecturer, teacher, and raconteur. His remarkable visual memory, aesthetic sense, and integrity of judgment won him great respect among scholars and museum curators and a unique position in the secretive and intensely competitive group of major American art collectors of the mid-twentieth century. He was a member of numerous professional organizations, including the Northeast Museums Conference, American Antiquarian Society, American Studies Association, the International Council of Museums, the Society for the Preservation of New England Antiquities, the National Trust for Historic Preservation, and the Walpole Society. The Charles Montgomery Professorship in American Decorative Arts at Yale was endowed in his honor.

Montgomery was a significant figure in the creation of a formal academic discipline focused on American decorative arts. His dynamic personality and enthusiasm led to the formation of several important collections, and his teaching abilities inspired many of his students to become curators, connoisseurs, and scholars of American material culture. Montgomery died suddenly in New Haven, Connecticut, while attending a lecture.

• Montgomery's papers and professional correspondence are in the Yale Art Gallery, New Haven, Conn. A bibliography of his publications, a biographical sketch, and appreciations are in Barbara M. Ward and Gerald W. R. Ward, eds., *Charles F. Montgomery and Florence M. Montgomery: A Tribute* (1978); additional information was provided by Florence M. Montgomery (Hamden, Conn.), Norma Montgomery Jones (Maroa, Ill.), and Jules Prown (Yale Univ.). Obituaries are in the *New Haven Register* and the *New York Times*, both 22 Feb. 1978.

BENJAMIN R. FOSTER

MONTGOMERY, Elizabeth Rider (12 July 1902–19 Feb. 1985), writer of books for young people, was born in Huaras, Peru, the daughter of Baptist missionaries Charles Quantrell Rider and Lula Tralle. She came to the United States at the age of a year and a half and grew up in Independence, Missouri, "a combination," in her words, "of a tomboy and a bookworm." She read widely as a child. When she was six her essay, "The Good and Bad Uses of the Apple," won first prize in a contest sponsored by the Woman's Christian

Temperance Union. Despite this and other contest victories, she never intended to become a writer, hoping to be an artist when she grew up.

Elizabeth Rider attended Washington State Normal School (later Western Washington University) between 1924 and 1925 and later spent a year at the University of California, Los Angeles. Finances forced her to give up her dream of studying art. Instead she taught elementary school, first in Aberdeen, Washington, and later in Los Angeles. In 1930 she married Norman A. Montgomery, whom she later divorced; the couple had two children. She continued to teach.

According to Montgomery, she became discouraged by the poor quality of the textbooks available to her students: "While teaching, I decided that the world needed a better primer than any I had yet used and that I would write it." A frequent speaker later in life to libraries, schools, and writers' groups, Montgomery always stressed the length of time and number of rejection letters she endured before having a manuscript accepted by Scott-Foresman and Co., a company specializing in elementary-school textbooks. Once published, however, she remained successful; she eventually stopped teaching and remained on the Scott-Foresman payroll as a staff writer from 1938 to 1963.

One of Montgomery's major responsibilities with the company was work on the Dick-and-Jane primers, which became the most popular reading books in schools in the United States. Although the series had begun in 1930, Montgomery's first text, *We Look and See* (1940), established the long-term "Dick-and-Jane" pattern. It proved popular and was frequently reissued as were *We Work and Play* (1940), *We Come and Go* (1940), *Good Times with Our Friends* (1941) and *Three Friends* (1944). The perky and helpful Dick and Jane, their slightly crazy baby sister Sally, and their pets Puff the kitten and Spot the dog trained several generations of American readers. These characters and their parents projected a world in which gender roles were set, nobody was unhappy for long, and family closeness prevailed.

Montgomery did not limit herself to textbooks or to the everyday suburban situations of Dick, Jane, and Sally, however. Her interest in history led her to research and write about a number of nonfiction figures and situations as well. In 1944 she moved from very young readers to the teenage market with *The Story behind Great Inventions*, which led to a series of financially successful "Story behind . . ." books. In a 1945 piece in the *Author and Journalist*, Montgomery explained the appeal of teenage nonfiction for her:

> You need never run out of material. Everything is grist to your mill. . . . Contrary to popular opinion, I believe (and I've had considerable experience to back this belief) that children *want* to learn. They want to learn *everything*. Only—and this is where the juvenile non-fiction writer comes in—they want the process of learning to be painless. They prefer to assimilate knowledge by a sort of osmosis, rather than having to chew and swallow it.

In addition to the "Story Behind . . ." series, Montgomery wrote biographies of Alexander Graham Bell, Albert Schweitzer, Duke Ellington, and Dag Hammarskjold. She also produced a number of theatrical works for young people, including radio and television plays. Montgomery prided herself on her thorough research methods and believed that her work, particularly her historical work, had the potential to inspire as well as educate children. She took her audience seriously. When outlining her own work methods to aspiring writers, she suggested: "If possible, get two or three children of the right age to read your manuscript. You may not learn a thing, if they are the type that says everything is either 'swell' or 'lousy.' But, again, you may learn a good deal—especially where you bogged down in too much technical information."

In 1963 Montgomery married Arthur Julesberg. She continued publishing into the 1980s, producing more than seventy books in the course of her career. "As long as my books are read," she said, "I'll keep on writing." Although the Dick-and-Jane books, eventually viewed as old-fashioned and unrealistic by teachers and students, went out of educational fashion in the 1970s, Montgomery's nonfiction books are still used in many public and school libraries in the United States.

Montgomery received several national awards, including one from the National League of American Penwomen. She was a lifetime member of the Parents and Teachers Association. Elizabeth Rider Montgomery Julesberg died in Seattle.

• Montgomery's discussion of her nonfiction series appeared in "Nonfiction Books for Boys and Girls," *Author and Journalist* (Oct. 1945): 12–13. She was discussed twice, as a prominent children's book author, in *Contemporary Authors*, vols. 1–4, and New Revision Series, vol. 3, and twice in *Something about the Author*, vols. 3 and 34. *Current Biography* treated her in 1952, reprinting an article from the *Wilson Library Bulletin*, May 1952. She was also listed in Martha E. Ward et al., *Authors of Books for Young People*, 3d ed. (1990). A brief history of the "Dick and Jane" series can be found in Joanne Trestrail, "Dick and Jane's Long Run," *Chicago* 37 (Sept. 1988): 173–74. Obituaries are in *Something about the Author*, vol. 41, and *Contemporary Authors*, vol. 115.

TINKY "DAKOTA" WEISBLAT

MONTGOMERY, Helen Barrett (31 July 1861–19 Oct. 1934), Baptist church leader, civic reformer, and educator, was born in Kingsville, Ohio, the daughter of A. Judson Barrett and Emily Barrows, teachers. Her school years were spent in upstate New York, first in Lowville, then in Rochester. Her father, who she later said was a dominant influence in her life, left his teaching career to attend Rochester Theological Seminary, later assuming the pastorate of the Lake Avenue Baptist Church in Rochester.

She graduated in 1884 from Wellesley College, with concentrations in education and Greek. She taught for one year at the Rochester Free Academy and two years at the Wellesley Preparatory School in Philadelphia. Although she was offered a faculty position at Wellesley and was considered for presidencies of two women's colleges, she returned to Rochester to marry William A. Montgomery in 1887. He was a successful businessman who shared her faith and purpose. She was licensed to preach in the Lake Avenue Baptist Church in 1892 and taught a women's Bible class there for forty-four years, building a life of community and world service that was a model for educated, upper-middle-class women of her time.

In 1893 Helen Montgomery, along with Susan B. Anthony, formed the Women's Educational and Industrial Union, and she became its first president. The Union sought to meet the needs of poor working women and their families by providing a legal aid center, public playgrounds, factory schools, and safe milk stations that eventually became public health centers.

As president of the Union, Montgomery was active in the Good Government movement for civic reform and became one of its candidates for school board. When she joined the Rochester school board in 1899, she was the first woman ever elected to public office in the city. Her ten years on the board brought many innovations: kindergartens, vacation schools, manual and domestic training, modern equipment, school lunches, night schools and mother's clubs. The schools became neighborhood social centers, much needed by the growing immigrant population. Montgomery was recognized as one of the six most influential people in the city in this period of civic reform.

Montgomery was president of the New York State Federation of Women's Clubs (1896–1897) and became well known for her public speaking on educational topics. From 1898 to 1900 Montgomery and Anthony worked to raise $50,000 for the University of Rochester so that the trustees of the university would admit women as regular students. When women gained the right to vote in 1920, Montgomery urged church women to join with other women's organizations "to exert the pressure of intelligent public opinion upon state and national government," especially in areas of concern to women and children.

Montgomery's concern for women and children worldwide became the focus of her later writing and speaking. She wrote a number of books on Christian missions; one, *The King's Highway* (1915), sold more than 160,000 copies. Her book *Western Women in Eastern Lands* (1910) examined the status of women, especially in the Orient, and surveyed the development of women's mission boards and the need for women missionaries, as well as the right of women to control their own mission funds and programs. In this book she wrote, "The Gospel is the most tremendous engine of democracy ever forged. It is destined to break in pieces all castes, privileges, and oppressions. Perhaps the last caste to be destroyed will be that of sex" (p. 206). As president of the Woman's American Baptist Foreign Mission Society (1914–1924), she advocated for meeting the educational and medical needs of women and children.

Montgomery's work was not limited to Baptist missions. In 1910–1911 she was the spark for a national celebration of the jubilee of Protestant women's mission work. She traveled all over the country, speaking at large rallies of Protestant women and helping to raise $1 million, primarily for Christian women's colleges in Asia. She was also president of the National Federation of Women's Boards of Foreign Missions (1917–1918).

In 1921 Montgomery was elected president of the Northern Baptist Convention, becoming the first woman chosen to head a major Protestant denomination. In the face of the divisions caused by the Fundamentalist-Modernist controversy, she spoke out for religious liberty and freedom of conscience, for support of world mission and education, and for political and civic responsibility.

After her presidency Montgomery continued her writing and translated the Greek New Testament into contemporary English (*The Centenary Translation of the New Testament*, 1924), the first translation completed by a woman scholar. An elementary school in Rochester bears her name. She died at the home of her adopted daughter, Edith Simson, in Summit, New Jersey.

Montgomery's life was an example of the growing leadership of women in civic and national organizations in the early twentieth century. Her broad understanding of Christian mission continued to influence her own Baptist denomination as well as other Protestant church bodies well into the later part of the century.

• *Helen Barrett Montgomery: From Campus to World Citizenship* (1940), a memorial volume, contains Montgomery's own account of her early years, and tributes from friends that tell of her later life.

In addition to works cited in the text, she wrote *Christus Redemptor* (1906), *Following the Sunrise* (1913), *The Bible and Mission* (1920), *Prayer and Mission* (1924), *The Story of Jesus as Told by His Four Friends* (1927), *From Jerusalem to Jerusalem* (1929), and *The Preaching Value of Mission* (1931). Montgomery's papers and material about her are in the archives of the American Baptist Historical Society, Rochester, N.Y., and at the Lake Avenue Baptist Church, also in Rochester. Blake McKelvy, *Rochester: The Quest for Quality 1890–1925* (1956), notes her work on civic reform. Louise A. Cattan, *Lamps Are for Lighting* (1972), tells of Montgomery's participation in the foreign mission movement, and Edith Deen, *Great Women of the Christian Faith* (1959), has a chapter on her.

BEVERLY CORBETT DAVISON

MONTGOMERY, Isaiah Thornton (21 May 1847–6 Mar. 1924), African-American planter and founder of Mound Bayou, Mississippi, was born on the "Hurricane" plantation of Joseph Davis at Davis Bend, Mississippi, the son of Benjamin Montgomery, the plantation business manager and later a planter and owner of a mercantile store, and Mary Lewis. As a result of his father's prominent position among the slaves, Montgomery was chosen at the age of nine or ten to serve as Davis's personal secretary and office attendant. Davis, the older brother of Confederate president Jefferson Davis, granted Montgomery full access to all the books, newspapers, and periodicals within his home, enabling Montgomery to continue the education begun first by his father and later continued by another slave. Following the Civil War, in November 1866, Davis sold his two plantations to the Montgomery family. During the next fifteen years, the Montgomerys struggled and ultimately failed to make the plantations profitable, yet they still succeeded in garnering numerous prizes for the quality of their cotton and consistently high ratings from national credit firms. The Montgomery family lost both plantations in 1881. In 1871 Montgomery married Martha Robb; they had twelve children, only four of whom survived to adulthood.

In 1877 Montgomery embarked on his most successful venture, the founding of the all-black town of Mound Bayou in the Yazoo-Mississippi Delta. The Louisville, New Orleans, and Texas Railroad, which actively sought farmers to settle the land alongside the newly laid tracks between New Orleans and Memphis, hired Montgomery as a land agent with the understanding that he would choose an area of land within the delta for exclusive purchase by blacks. Montgomery enlisted the support of family and friends, especially former residents of Davis Bend, in purchasing the plots, and the group quickly cleared and settled the heavily overgrown land. During the early years, Montgomery and his cousin Benjamin Green, the town's generally acknowledged cofounder, established several joint ventures, including the town's first cotton gin, mercantile firm, and post office.

In 1890 Montgomery was the only African-American delegate elected to the Mississippi constitutional convention. The convention delegates drafted a constitution that effectively disfranchised African-American Mississippians. During the proceedings, Montgomery gave a speech supporting disfranchisement. He described his support as "a fearful sacrifice laid upon the burning altar of liberty." In an interview published in the *New York World* (3 Oct. 1890), he explained that the temporary disfranchisement of blacks would hopefully signal "the beginning of the end of the great race question," allowing political division along lines other than race. Montgomery mistakenly believed that as African Americans became better educated, white Mississippians would allow them to vote and integrated parties would be formed based on political beliefs, not race. Not surprisingly, most white leaders, including former president Grover Cleveland, applauded Montgomery's position, while most black leaders initially expressed surprise and then dismay. According to Frederick Douglass: "We may denounce his policy, but must spare the man . . . He has made peace with the lion by allowing himself to be swallowed." In many ways, Montgomery's stance foreshadowed Booker T. Washington's infamous Atlanta Compromise of 1895. Washington and Montgomery maintained a correspondence throughout their lives, and Washington often pointed to Mound Bayou as a model African-American community. Later in his life, Montgomery privately lamented the impact of the disfranchisement proposals, expressing frustration with the racist application of the law. Publicly, he never rescinded his initial stance.

In 1898, following the incorporation of Mound Bayou, Montgomery was elected the town's first mayor. He held that office until 1902, when President Theodore Roosevelt, under guidance from Washington, appointed him as receiver of public monies in Jackson, Mississippi. The honor proved short-lived, however, as Montgomery was forced to resign in 1903 amidst controversy over the alleged placement of $5,000 in government funds in his personal account. While he never held another elective or appointive office, Montgomery maintained an active role in both Mississippi Republican party and local politics throughout the remainder of his life.

Montgomery's political ambitions, however, remained secondary to his efforts on behalf of Mound Bayou. In a letter to the director of the U.S. Land Office in Mississippi upon acceptance of his position as receiver of public monies, Montgomery noted that in the previous fourteen years he had expended his "best energies" to ensure the "advancement materially, morally, and socially" of his community and thus he was "loath to turn aside for political preferment." During his lifetime, Montgomery had a hand in almost every project that concerned Mound Bayou. He played a key role in the founding and improvement of the town's educational institutions, joined with his son-in-law E. P. Booze to establish the Farmer's Cooperative Mercantile Company in 1909, and helped with the development of the Mound Bayou Oil Mill & Manufacturing Company between 1911 and 1913. Montgomery's importance to the town was suggested by Charles Banks, a banker and community leader, who insisted in a letter to Washington's secretary that "no work or statement on Mound Bayou, however brief, should be without [Montgomery's] name." Montgomery died in Mound Bayou.

Montgomery's historical significance derives from his role as an African-American accommodationist and entrepreneur. Through his 1890 address and his activities on behalf of Mound Bayou, he displayed a consistent belief that educational and economic advancement, not political activity, offered the best means for African Americans to improve their plight. He closely monitored his own actions and those of his fellow Mound Bayou citizens to ensure the continual support of the white community. As a result, he earned nearly universal acclaim from white Mississippians, and upon his death, local whites purchased a lavish headstone. In contrast, the reaction among the African-American community was decidedly mixed and increasingly hostile after his death. The African-American Mississippi politician Sidney Redmond declared fifty years after Montgomery's speech that Montgomery would always be remembered as "the Judas of his people." Montgomery's actions, however, highlight the horrific conditions for African Americans in Mississippi at the turn of the century and demonstrate the pragmatic philosophy that was necessary for survival and limited success.

• Montgomery's papers are scattered throughout several collections, including the Benjamin Montgomery Family Papers and the Booker T. Washington Papers at the Library of Congress. The Mississippi Department of Archives and History in Jackson contains a substantial collection of material on Mound Bayou. Janet Sharp Hermann, *The Pursuit of a Dream* (1981), chronicles the consecutive efforts of Joseph Davis, Benjamin Montgomery, and Isaiah Montgomery to create a model African-American community. Hermann, "Isaiah T. Montgomery's Balancing Act," in *Black Leaders of the Nineteenth Century*, ed. Leon Litwack and August Meier (1988), provides a concise analysis of Montgomery's historical significance. See Kenneth Marvin Hamilton, *Black Towns and Profit: Promotion and Development in the Trans-Appalachian West, 1877–1915* (1991), and Norman L. Crockett, *The Black Towns* (1979), on Mound Bayou and its position among other black towns. See Neil R. McMillen, *Dark Journey: Black Mississippians in the Age of Jim Crow* (1989), on Montgomery and other African-American Mississippians of his period. An obituary is in the *Vicksburg Evening Post*, 24 Mar. 1985.

DAVID MARK SILVER

MONTGOMERY, James Alan (13 June 1866–6 Feb. 1949), Semitist and clergyman, was born in Philadelphia, Pennsylvania, the son of Thomas Harrison Montgomery and Anna Morton. In 1887 he graduated with a B.A. degree from the University of Pennsylvania, where in 1904 he also received his Ph.D., having specialized in biblical Hebrew. During the same period he studied theology at the Philadelphia Divinity School from which he was graduated in 1890 and became a deacon of the Protestant Episcopal church. In 1893 he was consecrated as a priest. That same year he married Mary Frank Owen; they had no children. He was a curate at the Church of the Holy Communion in New York City in 1892–1893; at St. Paul's in West Philadelphia from 1893 to 1895; and at St. Peter's in Philadelphia from 1895 to 1899. From 1899 until 1903 he was rector of the Church of the Epiphany in Germantown, also serving as assistant editor of the *Church Standard* from 1897 to 1899.

Early in his career Montgomery had to accept the fact that it was no longer possible to combine scholarly and ecclesiastical careers at a high level and that, to live up to his ideals, he had to choose. He remained an Episcopal priest, but biblical and Semitic research, publication, and teaching became his professional calling. Because Germany was the center of Hebraic and Semitic scholarship, he sought and received a traveling fellowship that enabled him to study at the universities of Berlin and Greifswald from 1890 until 1892.

His first wife died in 1900. In June 1902, he married Edith Thompson, with whom he had three sons. This marriage was close and enduring, lasting nearly half a century; she died first, and he did not long survive her. The couple lived in Germantown, in a big old house with a well-cultivated flower garden. His income was modest, their life-style simple, but gracious. He had a large professional library and kept extensive data on three-by-five-inch index cards, enough information to fill eight books and about 100 articles.

During the academic year Montgomery taught at both the University of Pennsylvania (1909–1939) and Philadelphia Divinity School (1899–1935). His archaeological field experience in the Near East was limited to the year 1914–1915, when he, his wife, and their three young sons lived in Palestine, where he served as the annual director of the American School of Oriental Research in Jerusalem. Although Palestine was then part of the Ottoman Empire, which sided with Germany in World War I, the family survived the dangers, and Montgomery's relationship with the American Schools of Oriental Research in both Jerusalem and Baghdad remained close. He was president of both schools from 1921 to 1934.

Among his many time-consuming commitments were his duties as editor of the *Journal of Biblical Literature* from 1910 to 1914 and the *Journal of the American Oriental Society* from 1916 to 1922 and in 1924. Although he was best known for his contributions to the study of the Hebrew Old Testament, he spent much time on Aramaic dialects, including Syriac and Mandaic. His expertise and teaching covered the large field of ancient Near Eastern studies, except for Mesopotamian cuneiform and Egyptian hieroglyphs, nonalphabetic systems of writing that were too ambiguous phonetically for Montgomery's strict nineteenth-century grammatical standards. His command of the medieval Near East included a detailed knowledge of classical Arabic, which was then regarded as the cornerstone of comparative Semitic linguistics. Montgomery's merits were recognized by his peers. He was elected a fellow of the American Philosophical Society (1925) and was president of the Society of Biblical Literature (1918) and the American Oriental Society (1926–1927).

Montgomery kept abreast of new discoveries into his later years. His contributions to the study of the cuneiform tablets unearthed at Ras Shamra (ancient Ugarit), Syria, in 1929 and yearly thereafter were characterized by keen insights at a time when most writing on the subject was undisciplined and chaotic. He sensed that the language of the Ras Shamra tablets (now called Ugaritic) is closer than any other known language to biblical Hebrew and that their content reflects the mythology of pre-Hebraic Canaan. He pursued his research in the pioneering field of South Arabic epigraphy into his eighties, and he left extensive files on the subject.

Montgomery was never in a hurry to publish, however. His first book, *The Samaritans: The Earliest Jewish Sect*, did not appear until 1907, when he was past forty. His *Aramaic Incantation Texts from Nippur* (1913) remains the foremost study in the field of Mesopotamian bowl magic; no publication since has contained such a breadth of knowledge of the use of magic in the Greco-Roman Near East. In 1927 his commentary on the Book of Daniel appeared in the prestigious *International Critical Commentary* series. Still a leading work on Daniel, the commentary reflects Montgomery's mastery of Aramaic and Hebrew as well as the whole range of apocalyptic literature. It is characteristic of Montgomery that he thereafter refused to teach Daniel. After publishing a book on any topic, he never wanted to deal with that subject again. Also in 1927 he translated from the Syriac, and annotated, *The History of Yaballaha III*, a study of the Nestorian patriarch and his vicar, Bar Sauma, Mongol ambassador to the Frankish courts at the end of the thirteenth century. His grasp of global history enabled Montgomery to not only translate a Syrian text but also to examine the larger study of Mongol-Frankish relations. In 1934 Montgomery's *Arabia and the Bible* opened a new frontier in biblical studies. Until then biblical scholars had recognized only three frontiers: to the south of the Holy Land was Egypt; to the west was the Mediterranean; while the north provided the gateway for many Asiatics, including the Mesopotamians. Montgomery added an eastern frontier, for Arabia had access, by land, to western Palestine only through Transjordan.

The accolades Montgomery received for his work on Daniel led to an unprecedented honor: an invitation to write another *International Critical Commentary*, on I and II Kings. His wide-ranging knowledge of ancient Near Eastern history made him especially suited for the assignment. He was familiar with the histories of the many varied peoples with whom the Hebrews had relations as well as with the extrabiblical sources essential to understanding the two historical books. Montgomery died before the commentary was published, but he left the project in the capable hands of his colleague Henry Snyder Gehman, whose editorship led to its publication in 1951.

James Montgomery was, in the true and old sense of the expression, a scholar and a gentleman. Although he was gaunt and aristocratic in appearance, his pace was so lively that younger men had a hard time keeping up with him. His students noticed, but never said in his presence, that he bore a striking resemblance to the well-preserved mummy of Ramses II.

• For the standard biographical details, see *Who's Who in America*, vol. 24 (1946–1947). The best-documented obituary is by Montgomery's junior colleague E. A. Speiser in the *Bulletin of the American Schools of Oriental Research* 115 (Oct. 1949). For an intimate portrayal by a disciple and friend, see C. H. Gordon, "A Scholar and a Gentleman," *Biblical Archaeologist* 46 (Summer 1983): 187–89; see also Gordon, *The Pennsylvania Tradition of Semitics: A Century of Near Eastern and Biblical Studies at the University of Pennsylvania* (1986).

CYRUS H. GORDON

MONTGOMERY, Little Brother (18 Apr. 1906–6 Sept. 1985), blues and jazz pianist, singer, and bandleader, was born Eurreal Wilford Montgomery in Kentwood, Louisiana, the son of Harper Montgomery and Dicy Burton. His father led mule and horse teams, set railroad times, hauled wood, farmed cucumbers, and had a log pond in which Montgomery himself assisted, riding logs to help chain them for the trip to the mill. Most significantly for Montgomery, his father also ran a barrelhouse—a southern saloon that often had a piano and a dance floor, where alcohol was served from barrels. Montgomery claimed that his father served no hard liquor, just food and soft drinks, and that patrons brought their own alcohol. In any event, there he had an opportunity to listen to many accomplished pianists, including the great "Jelly Roll" Morton and numerous now-forgotten players whom Montgomery recalled fondly. His father played cornet, his mother, organ, and his father's uncle Gonzy Montgomery was a multi-instrumentalist and bandleader who worked with Armand J. Piron in New Orleans.

At age five Montgomery began to teach himself to play piano. From age ten he regularly visited an aunt in New Orleans and was able to hear music there. He attended Tangipahoa Parish Training School but ran away before finishing the seventh grade. During the early 1920s he traveled throughout Louisiana and Mississippi, playing in juke joints and barrelhouses as a soloist and occasionally as a member of jazz bands, including an affiliation with clarinetist George Lewis around 1921.

While in Ferriday, Louisiana, Montgomery and other pianists worked out a tune that came to be known as the "44 Blues." By one account, one of these pianists, Delco Robert Johnson (not to be confused with blues guitarist and singer Robert Johnson), was known as "Big Brother," and Montgomery, owing to his height, thus became "Little Brother" when they played together; but others claim that he received the nickname in infancy, as the sixth of ten children.

Montgomery worked with cornetist Buddy Petit around 1925, and he toured logging camps with blues singer and guitarist Big Joe Williams (c. 1926) and guitarist Danny Barker (c. 1927). In 1928 he left the South to tour with New Orleans bandleader Clarence Desdune's band, dropping out when they reached Omaha, Nebraska, later that year. By 1929 he was in Chicago, where he played house parties. Pianist Bob Alexander, from whom Montgomery took some lessons, and Alexander's wife Aletha Dickerson were talent scouts for Paramount Records. In 1930 they hired Montgomery to accompany singer Irene Scruggs. In addition, he made several solo titles, including "No Special Rider Blues" and his best-known recording, "Vicksburg Blues," an elaboration of "44 Blues" (which had already been recorded by pianist Roosevelt Sykes). Montgomery then toured with Dickerson, accompanying her on the Theater Owners' Booking Association circuit as far as Atlanta.

After recording "Frisco Hi-ball Blues" at the beginning of 1931, Montgomery came to Jackson, Mississippi, to organize an eight- to fourteen-piece southern and midwestern touring band, the Southland Troubadours. As a soloist, he recorded "Something Keeps Aworryin' Me," "Farish Street Jive," "Crescent City Blues," and "Shreveport Blues," in New Orleans in 1936. He continued to lead the Southland Troubadours until the late 1930s. He then turned the group over to his sideman Doc Parmley and resumed working in Mississippi and Texas as soloist or in a duo with a drummer.

Montgomery settled in Chicago in 1942. He worked in a defense plant and resumed playing at house parties. In 1947 he recorded "El Ritmo" and "Long Time Ago," and the following year he toured briefly in trombonist Kid Ory's band and continued to work for various "race" labels. Over the next three decades Montgomery worked extensively in Chicago clubs as a bandleader and as a member of reed player Franz Jackson's Original Jass All-Stars. He toured England in 1960, and, after recording singer Queen Victoria Spivey's album *The Queen and Her Knights* in 1965, he went to Europe in 1966 with the touring American Folk Blues Festival.

In 1967 Montgomery suffered a stroke that affected his left hand, but he kept playing and continued to appear at folk and blues festivals as a singer and pianist. He also led his own jazz band in Chicago clubs. Montgomery was married to Gladys Hawthorne (date unknown) and Janet A. Floberg (1967), and he had a son from one of the marriages; details of his marriages are unknown. Montgomery and his second wife, who often recorded as a duo, formed a record label, FM, in 1969, while continuing to record for many other labels as well. He toured Europe again in 1972 and recorded the unaccompanied album *Deep South Piano* in Copenhagen. He performed at the Berliner Jazztage in 1974 and at the New Orleans Jazz and Heritage Festival in 1976. Another fine solo album, *Tishomingo Blues*, dates from his last visit to England in 1980. He died in Chicago.

Montgomery was equally comfortable with earthy and heady material. Indeed, though he was much in demand as a blues soloist, he preferred to be associated with jazz bands, where the level of technical instrumental playing tended to be higher. "He is quick to tell you that most all the blues players break time, and that most of them couldn't tell one note from another any more than a pig knows when it's Sunday." Nonetheless, it was in this domain, the blues, that Montgomery left his most memorable recordings.

• Taped interviews of Montgomery are held at the University of Chicago and Tulane University, the latter material dating from May 1958 and Aug. 1960. The essential source is Karl Gert zur Heide, *Deep South Piano: The Story of Little Brother Montgomery* (1970). Further interviews and surveys are by Tony Standish, "'Billed out and Bound to Go': The Story of Little Brother Montgomery," *Eureka* 1 (Sept.–Oct. 1960): 18–20; Derrick Stewart-Baxter, "Blues," *Jazz Journal* 20 (Apr. 1967): 14; Terry Kent, "Down There in Vicksburg," *Storyville*, no. 55 (Oct.–Nov. 1974): 4–9; Paige Van Vorst, "Little Brother Montgomery: A Jazzman Sings the Blues," *Mississippi Rag* 1 (Apr. 1974): 10–11; "Little Brother Tells His Story," *Mississippi Rag* 1 (Jan. 1975): 1–2; Art Hodes, "Little Brother," and "Eurreal Montgomery, 'Little Brother,'" in *Selections from the Gutter: Jazz Portraits from "The Jazz Record,"* ed. Hodes and Chadwick Hansen (1977). Recollections of Montgomery are in Barker, *A Life in Jazz*, ed. Alyn Shipton (1986). A catalog of his recordings is by Dietrich von Staden, "A Little Brother Montgomery Discography," *Storyville*, no. 111 (Feb.–Mar. 1984): 94–99; no. 112 (Apr.–May 1984): 147–50; no. 113 (June–July 1984): 169–71; and no. 114 (Aug.–Sept. 1984): 206–11. Obituaries are in the *Chicago Tribune*, 9 Sept. 1985, and *Footnote* 17 (Dec. 1985–Jan. 1986): 23–25.

BARRY KERNFELD

MONTGOMERY, Richard (2 Dec. 1738–31 Dec. 1775), soldier, was born at Swords, County Dublin, Ireland, the son of Thomas Montgomery, a baronet and member of the Irish Parliament, and Mary Franklin (or Franklyn). As befitted a son of landed gentry, he received a liberal education. After attending St. Andrews School, he enrolled in Trinity College, Dublin, in 1754 but remained there for only two years. Following the advice of his father and his brother, Alexander Montgomery, he joined the British army on 21 September 1756 as an ensign in the Seventeenth Regiment and began service in the Seven Years' War. He was sent to Canada in 1757, and a year later he took part in the siege of Louisbourg, where he was promoted to lieutenant. In 1759 he accompanied Sir Jeffery Amherst on his expedition against Forts Ticonderoga and Crown Point. The following year he was appointed regimental adjutant by Colonel William Haviland and served with Haviland during successful summer operations against Montreal. In late 1761 he joined Major General Robert Monckton at Barbados, in the West Indies, where preparations for an attack on the French island of Martinique were going forward. Early the following year, Montgomery participated in the capture of Martinique and on 6 May 1762 was promoted to captain in the Seventeenth Regiment. In the summer of 1762 he was with General George Keppel, earl of Albemarle, during siege operations against Havana, Cuba. He was stationed in New York for two years after the Seven Years' War ended in 1763 and then went home with his regiment.

In the decade after his return to England, Montgomery became more and more disgruntled with Britain's policies toward the American colonies and his own lack of advancement in the peacetime British army. He formed friendships with several liberal members of Parliament who sympathized with the Americans, including Isaac Barré, Edmund Burke, and Charles James Fox, and apparently they contributed to his growing discontent with his situation. In 1771 he eagerly pursued a chance to purchase a major's commission, but the majority went to a political favorite of Prime Minister Frederick, Lord North. Disgusted at his lack of political patronage, Montgomery sold his captain's commission on 6 April 1772 and moved to New York in late 1772 or early 1773. He purchased a farm of sixty-seven acres near Kings Bridge, thirteen miles north of New York City, and established himself as a gentleman farmer, far removed from the vexations of politics and public service. Meanwhile he became reacquainted with Janet Livingston, whom he had met briefly eight years before, and in July 1773 they were married. They had no children. Montgomery and his wife established their home at her residence, near Rhinebeck, New York.

He built a mill and began construction of a house to be called "Grassmere," but work was interrupted by deteriorating relations between Great Britain and the American colonies in the mid-1770s.

At that time, Montgomery joined with his neighbors in protesting British policies toward America. Having established himself in New York as a man of integrity and procolonial views, he was elected on 16 May 1775 to represent Dutchess County in the New York Provincial Congress, even though he had not sought the position. Almost inevitably, because of his years of service in the British army, he was destined for a command in the American Continental army. On 22 June 1775 he was appointed brigadier general by the Continental Congress, ranking second among eight brigadiers approved at that time. Although he did not wish to leave his new wife, he bowed to his fate with sadness and reluctance, his only consolation being that "the will of an oppressed people . . . must be respected." On 26 June 1775 he was ordered by General George Washington to assume duty as second in command in New York under Major General Philip Schuyler. Three days later, he and Schuyler were directed by Congress to invade Canada, and the two officers established their headquarters at Fort Ticonderoga. Appalled at the quality of the troops he was to command, Montgomery declared that the officers were "vulgar for the most part" and the privates the "sweepings" of society. Nevertheless, largely through personal example, he shaped these heterogeneous materials into an effective army. In late August 1775 he and Schuyler moved down Lake Champlain, seized Isle aux Noix, and commenced siege operations against St. Johns and Chambly on the Richelieu River.

After Schuyler removed himself from command in favor of Montgomery on 16 September, Montgomery redoubled his efforts against these positions, finally capturing them on 19 October. On 11 November he seized Montreal and then advanced down the St. Lawrence River to Quebec. There, on 2 December, he joined forces with General Benedict Arnold, who had marched an army through Maine to the same destination, and assumed overall command. For three weeks Montgomery and Arnold besieged the city while working on a plan to capture it. With American troop enlistments about to terminate at the end of the year, they audaciously decided upon a two-pronged assault. At 4:00 A.M. on 31 December they attacked in a blinding snowstorm, with Montgomery leading one column against the lower town and Arnold another against the upper town. As Montgomery stormed toward enemy cannon, shouting "Push on brave boys: Quebec is ours," he was killed instantly by a point-blank storm of grape and canister shot, without ever knowing that Congress had promoted him to major general on 9 December. The attackers, thrown into confusion, retreated, leaving Montgomery's body where it had fallen and in the spring of 1776 withdrew from Canada. Montgomery's frozen corpse was retrieved by the British the following day and buried with full military honors within the walls of Quebec. On 25 January 1776 Congress ordered that a marble memorial be erected to him in the graveyard of St. Paul's Episcopal Church, New York. In 1818 the government of Canada permitted the removal of Montgomery's remains to St. Paul's Church, where they were interred beneath the monument. On a rock at Cape Diamond is carved an inscription marking the spot where the general fell.

• Major collections of Montgomery papers are in the William L. Clements Library, Ann Arbor, Mich.; the New-York Historical Society; and the New York Public Library. Montgomery letters are also in the Philip Schuyler Papers, New York Public Library, and the George Washington Papers, Library of Congress. An important printed source is Peter Force, ed., *American Archives: A Collection of Authentick Records, State Papers, Debates, and Letters and Other Notices of Publick Affairs*, 4th and 5th ser. (9 vols., 1837–1853). Hal T. Shelton, *General Richard Montgomery and the American Revolution* (1994), is the best biography. Others are John Armstrong, *Life of Richard Montgomery*, vol. 1 of *Library of American Biography*, ed. Jared Sparks (1836); George W. Cullum, *Biographical Sketch of Major-General Richard Montgomery of the Continental Army* (1876); Percy K. Fitzhugh, *The Story of General Richard Montgomery* (1906); Charles W. Allen, *Memoir of General Montgomery* (1912); Alden L. Todd, *Richard Montgomery: Rebel of 1775* (1967); and *Major General Richard Montgomery: A Contribution toward a Biography from the Clements Library* (1970). Shorter sketches are George W. Cullum, "Major-General Richard Montgomery," *Magazine of American History* 11 (Apr. 1884): 273–99; Louise L. Hunt, "General Richard Montgomery," *Harper's New Monthly Magazine* 70 (Feb. 1885): 350–59; Vincent F. O'Reilly, "Major-General Richard Montgomery," *American Irish Historical Society Journal* 25 (1926): 179–94; and Thomas P. Robinson, "Some Notes on Major-General Richard Montgomery," *New York History* 37 (Oct. 1956): 388–98. Montgomery's service in Canada is discussed in Justin H. Smith, *Our Struggle for the Fourteenth Colony: Canada and the American Revolution* (2 vols., 1907).

PAUL DAVID NELSON

MONTGOMERY, Robert (21 May 1904–27 Sept. 1981), actor, director, and producer, was born Henry Montgomery, Jr., in Beacon, New York, the son of Mary Weed Bernard and Henry Montgomery, vice president of the New York Rubber Company. Montgomery attended private school until his father's death in 1920, after which he supported the family by laboring in a railroad yard and later on an oil tanker. Montgomery first appeared on stage in New York in September 1924 as a butler in William Faversham's *The Mask and the Face*. Two years later he made his film debut in the silent film *College Days* while continuing to act regularly on Broadway. His performance in *The Possession* (1928) attracted the attention of producer Sam Goldwyn, who invited him to Hollywood. There he signed a contract with Metro-Goldwyn-Mayer, for whom his first picture was *So This Is College* (1929). In the meantime he changed his first name and in 1928 married actress Elizabeth Bryan Allen. Montgomery and Allen later had a son and a daughter, actress Elizabeth Montgomery.

His stage experience had prepared him well for talking pictures, and he quickly became one of Hollywood's most popular leading men, starring opposite actresses such as Norma Shearer (*The Divorcee*, 1930; *Riptide*, 1934), Joan Crawford (*Our Blushing Brides*, 1930; *Letty Lynton*, 1932), Greta Garbo (*Inspiration*, 1931), and Carole Lombard (in director Alfred Hitchcock's comedy *Mr. and Mrs. Smith*, 1941). Not one to be typecast, however, he took on more challenging roles, such as the prison whistle-blower in *The Big House* (1930) and the psychotic killer in *Night Must Fall* (1937), for which he received an Academy Award nomination for best actor. He received his second nomination for the comedy *Here Comes Mr. Jordan* (1941), in which he played a prizefighter accidentally sent to heaven before his time. His film career spanned nearly a quarter century and included more than sixty films, in which his personae ranged from steely detective to dashing playboy to honorable war hero.

Montgomery's role in the film industry was not limited to acting. In 1933 he helped found the Screen Actors' Guild and served as its first president. In his four terms of service (1935–1938, 1946), he negotiated successfully for higher pay and better working conditions for actors. He played a pivotal role in the union's rise to power within the studio system.

In 1940 Montgomery became one of the first in Hollywood to join the war effort. He drove ambulances for the American Field Service in France before becoming a navy commander. He was on the first destroyer to enter Cherbourg harbor during the 1944 invasion of Normandy and received the Bronze Star for his bravery.

After the war director John Ford cast Montgomery opposite John Wayne in the war film *They Were Expendable* (1945). The film became Montgomery's directing debut when Ford became ill during the last days of its production, and Montgomery took over the direction of the final scenes. The film's success led to his first full-fledged directing job, *Lady in the Lake* (1946), based on the Raymond Chandler novel. The film attracted attention not only for Montgomery's performance as detective Philip Marlowe, but for its unique stylistic approach: the entire film was photographed from a "first-person" perspective, through the eyes of the detective. Apart from the beginning and end of the film, Montgomery appeared on screen only when the camera caught his "reflection" in a mirror. Montgomery went on to direct himself in *Ride the Pink Horse* (1947), *Once More, My Darling* (1949), and the British film *Eye Witness* (1950), which was also his final appearance on film. His last film-directing effort was *The Gallant Hours* (1960), a biography of navy admiral William Halsey.

Montgomery's broadcasting career began in 1939 with a leading role in "The Grand Duchess and the Waiter" on CBS's "Lux Radio Theatre." He made ten appearances on the program between 1939 and 1944 before moving on to a one-season stint as commentator on ABC-Radio's "Robert Montgomery Speaking" in 1949. The following year he moved into television, where he became executive producer–director-adviser to NBC. He created and independently produced the acclaimed anthology drama series "Robert Montgomery Presents." The program, which boosted the early careers of actors such as Jack Lemmon and Joanne Woodward and occasionally starred Montgomery himself, ran on NBC for seven years.

In later years, Montgomery expressed frustration with the network system and became an advocate of public television. In 1968 he published a critical assessment of network television programming titled *Open Letter from a Television Viewer* and the following year became a member of the National Citizens Committee for Broadcasting.

Divorced from his first wife in 1950, Montgomery married Elizabeth Grant Harkness that same year. They had no children. He became increasingly involved in Republican politics after the war, and in 1947 he appeared on the industry's behalf before the House Committee on Un-American Activities. Having coached Dwight D. Eisenhower's campaign speeches, in 1953 he became the president's adviser on radio and television appearances; Montgomery was thus the first professional entertainer to occupy an office in the White House and one of the first presidential media consultants.

He returned to the stage in 1955 to direct *The Desperate Hours*, for which he received a Tony Award, and in 1962 directed *Calculated Risk*, starring Joseph Cotten, which lasted an impressive 222 performances. In 1969 he served a one-year term as president of Lincoln Center Repertory Theater. In later years he devoted his time to the lecture circuit and to his farm in Canaan, Connecticut. He died in New York City.

• For more information, see George Frazier, "Nobody Pushes Bob Around," *Collier's*, 4 June 1949, and DeWitt Bodeen, "Robert Montgomery," *Films in Review*, Feb. 1981. Substantial obituaries are in the *New York Times*, 28 Sept. 1981, and *Daily Variety*, 29 Sept. 1981.

JENNIFER M. BARKER

MONTGOMERY, Thomas Harrison, Jr. (5 Mar. 1873–19 Mar. 1912), zoologist, was born in New York City, the son of Thomas Harrison Montgomery, an insurance executive, and Anna Morton. When the boy was nine, the family moved to a country property near West Chester, Pennsylvania. There Montgomery explored the nearby woods and fields, taking a special interest in birds. He collected about 450 bird skins, wrote extensive notes on his observations of bird life, and made detailed drawings of the anatomy and skeletons of birds.

Montgomery attended a private school in West Chester, then completed high school at the Episcopal Academy in Philadelphia, from which he graduated at the age of sixteen. In 1889 he entered the University of Pennsylvania, where he studied for two years and was especially interested in a course on comparative anatomy and paleontology given by vertebrate paleontologist Edward Drinker Cope. Montgomery spent much of his free time at the museums and library of the Academy of Natural Sciences of Philadelphia.

On a trip to Europe with his father in the summer of 1891, Montgomery decided to continue his studies at the University of Berlin. There he concentrated on human anatomy and invertebrate morphology and received a Ph.D. in 1894, with a dissertation in which he described in detail a new genus and species of nermertean worm.

On his return to the United States in 1895, Montgomery became a researcher at the Wistar Institute of Anatomy in Philadelphia, serving for three years. He spent the summer of 1895 at the laboratory of Alexander Agassiz in Newport, Rhode Island, and at the U.S. Fish Commission Station in Woods Hole, Massachusetts. The next summer he was at the marine laboratory of the University of Pennsylvania at Sea Isle City, New Jersey. He spent the summer of 1897 at the Marine Biological Laboratory in Woods Hole, to which he returned for many summers.

In 1897 Montgomery became a lecturer in zoology at the University of Pennsylvania, where he advanced to instructor, then assistant professor in 1900. From 1898 to 1903 he was also professor of biology and director of the museum at the Wagner Free Institute of Science in Philadelphia. He married Priscilla Braislin in 1901; the couple had three sons. In 1903 he became professor of zoology at the University of Texas at Austin. While there he published *The Analysis of Racial Descent in Animals* (1906).

In 1908 Montgomery returned to Philadelphia as professor and chairman of the department of zoology at the University of Pennsylvania. In addition to teaching classes and directing graduate students, he worked with members of the department to plan a new, well-equipped zoological laboratory and to see it constructed. He served as coeditor of the *Journal of Morphology* from 1908 until his death.

In his short career Montgomery published more than eighty papers on various subjects in zoology. These included observations on birds, nemertean (ribbon) worms, parasitic hairworms (Trichostrongylidae), spiders, and insects. He summarized the taxonomy and habits of spiders in "The Significance of the Courtship and the Secondary Sexual Characters of Araneids" (*American Naturalist* 44 [1910]: 151–77). From his own observations on spiders he disagreed with English naturalist Charles Darwin's idea that sexual selection is significant in evolution.

Montgomery's taxonomic work included naming many new species of spiders and some aquatic invertebrates such as nemertean worms, hairworms, and rotifers and was characterized by descriptions of the anatomy and by excellent accounts of the life histories and habits of animals. He devoted a great deal of time to observing each animal in the field, from owls at night to spiders in daytime, and he always preferred to collect his own specimens. His biographer Edwin G. Conklin observed that "the many newly turned stones in the fields about Woods Hole were a sign that Montgomery had been collecting there" (p. 211).

Montgomery's other papers were on cytology—the analysis of the details of cells by microscope—a field that was becoming of great interest to biologists as they tried to determine the mechanism of evolution and the development of organisms. His most outstanding work was in spermatogenesis, the origin of reproductive cells. A significant paper was "A Study of the Chromosomes of the Germ Cells of Metazoa" (*Transactions of American Philosophical Society* 20 [1901]: 154–236). In it, according to Conklin, "a discovery of really epoch-making importance was his observation of the conjugation of separate chromosomes in preparation for the maturation divisions, and his clearly reasoned conclusion that one chromosome of each pair is of paternal and the other of maternal origin" (p. 210). In studying the nucleus of cells in many different animals, Montgomery concluded that the conspicuous nucleolus is actually relatively unimportant, so he turned to studies of the chromosomes as more significant. In the insect order Hemiptera ("true bugs") he made the unexpected discovery that in the genus *Euschistus* certain lobes of the testis are unusually large or unusually small, through differential growth, and that they produce kinds of sperm that differ from the sperm of normal lobes. His last paper, published posthumously for the centennial volume of the Academy of Natural Sciences of Philadelphia (1912), was "Human Spermatogenesis, Spermatocytes and Spermiogenesis: A Study of Inheritance."

Montgomery, who had been generally robust and healthy, died of pneumonia in Philadelphia just after his thirty-ninth birthday. Had he lived longer he might have settled into either field biology with its emphasis on taxonomy or the growing subject of cytology with its emphasis on cell structure. Montgomery contributed significantly in both aspects of biology.

• The primary biography of Montgomery is by Edwin G. Conklin in *Science* 38 (1913): 207–14. An obituary is in *Proceedings of Academy of Natural Sciences of Philadelphia* 64 (1912): 154–55.

ELIZABETH NOBLE SHOR

MONTGOMERY, Wes (6 Mar. 1923–15 June 1968), jazz and popular guitarist and bandleader, was born John Leslie Montgomery in Indianapolis, Indiana. His parents (names unknown) separated. Until about age seven Montgomery lived with his mother and stepfather, who both worked as laborers making sleeve fittings for pipes. He and his brothers then moved to Columbus, Ohio, to live with his father, a truck driver who delivered wholesale fruits and vegetables. Around 1935 his older brother, bassist Monk (William Howard) Montgomery, bought Wes a four-string tenor guitar.

Montgomery attended Champion High School. When he was seventeen, the family moved back to Indianapolis, where he apprenticed as an arc welder. After hearing a record featuring electric guitarist Charlie Christian, Montgomery bought a six-string electric guitar and began practicing incessantly. Self-taught, he never learned to read traditional music notation or even to read jazz chord symbols, and yet his ear, memory, and technique were so extraordinary that he was able to fit into any of the diverse musical situations that would come his way. He had trouble playing with a guitar pick and thus inadvertently developed a beautifully rounded timbre by the ad hoc method of strumming the strings with the soft part of his right thumb. Somehow he managed to do this without restricting the speed and clarity of his playing.

In 1943 Montgomery married Serene (maiden name unknown), a dancer. They had seven children. Around this time he began working with some regularity as a musician, occasionally abandoning his various day jobs when an opportunity to tour arose. He was a laborer at Pope's Milk Company for several years until 15 May 1948, when vibraphonist Lionel Hampton heard him and immediately hired him for two years of touring. Montgomery recorded a few solos with Hampton, and he may be seen performing in the film short *Lionel Hampton and His Orchestra* (1949). But he grew tired of being apart from his family, and he returned home to once again take jobs outside of music.

In Indianapolis clubs Montgomery worked in pianist Eddie Higgins's quartet with bassist Bob Cranshaw and drummer Walter Perkins, and then in trumpeter Roger Jones's quintet, which included bassist Leroy Vinnegar. From 1955 to 1957 he was a member of the cooperative Montgomery-Johnson quintet, based at the Tropics Club; the quintet included Monk Montgomery and their brother, pianist and vibraphonist Charles F. "Buddy" Montgomery.

Montgomery traveled to San Francisco to play briefly with Monk and Buddy's new group, the Mastersounds, at the Jazz Workshop, and he occasionally returned to the West to perform with his brothers. Their recordings include his celebrated solo on "Falling in Love with Love" from the album *Montgomeryland* (1958–1959). During 1959, to support his family, Montgomery worked days as a welder while holding two nightclub jobs, these activities together allowing perhaps an hour for sleep; his biographer Adrian Ingram speculates that this impossibly grueling schedule, together with Montgomery's chain smoking, may have set the stage for his early heart disease.

In September 1959 alto saxophonist Cannonball Adderley heard Montgomery and was so impressed that he persuaded Orrin Keepnews of Riverside Records to offer him a contract. Keepnews brought Montgomery, organist Melvin Rhyne, and drummer Paul Parker to New York City for the guitarist's first album as a leader, *A Dynamic New Sound: The Wes Montgomery Trio* (1959). The trio then toured for four months.

In January 1960 Montgomery recorded perhaps his finest jazz album, *The Incredible Jazz Guitar of Wes Montgomery*. The Mastersounds disbanded and a new Montgomery Brothers quintet formed that included Wes. He continued to make a number of jazz albums on his own, as well as with tenor saxophonist Harold Land, with Adderley, with an all-star group headed by vibraphonist Milt Jackson, and with his brothers. Apart from Montgomery's own playing, these recordings are consistently pleasant but perhaps somewhat cautious and uninspired; this is particularly true of his work with his brothers, who were greatly overmatched by Wes's talent. Montgomery himself seemed unaware of his special talent. Ingram reports that in September 1961, while tenor saxophonist John Coltrane was at San Francisco's Jazz Workshop and the Monterey Jazz Festival with wind player Eric Dolphy, pianist McCoy Tyner, bassist Reggie Workman, and drummer Elvin Jones, Coltrane had Montgomery play with the group. Coltrane was so impressed that he asked the guitarist to join permanently; Montgomery declined, feeling that he was not good enough and instead resumed touring with his brothers.

The Montgomery Brothers disbanded in the spring of 1962 for lack of steady work, and Montgomery rejoined Rhyne's organ trio in Indianapolis. He left home for only a few days in June 1962 to visit Berkeley, California, where he performed and made the album *Full House* in the company of tenor saxophonist Johnny Griffin and the rhythm section from trumpeter Miles Davis's current band—pianist Wynton Kelly, bassist Paul Chambers, and drummer Jimmy Cobb. Late in 1963 Montgomery's trio with Rhyne disbanded.

In 1964–1965 Montgomery performed on a segment of the BBC television series "Jazz 625." Late in 1964 he began recording for the Verve label. Under the guidance of producer Creed Taylor, the guitarist turned from hard-bop groups to studio orchestras from 1965 onward, beginning with the album *Bumpin'* (May 1965). He continued to play hard bop in clubs, as documented on *Smokin' at the Half Note*, recorded live with Kelly, Chambers, and Cobb between late spring and early autumn in 1965. But *Goin' Out of My Head* (Dec. 1965) won a Grammy Award for its title track, and from that point on Taylor's authorized mix of jazz standards and instrumental versions of pop hits moved increasingly toward the latter, as heard on *Tequila* (Mar. 1966); *California Dreaming*, with its hit single "Bumpin' on Sunset" (Sept. 1966); *A Day in the Life* (June 1967), which held the number-one position on the *Billboard* magazine jazz charts for thirty-two weeks; and *Down Here on the Ground* (Dec. 1967–Jan. 1968). At the height of his commercial success Montgomery died of a heart attack in Indianapolis.

Translating into English an interview from the French magazine *Jazz Hot* (Feb. 1979), Ingram quoted Griffin's description of Montgomery: "Wes was a marvellous person. He didn't drink, and was very difficult about what he ate. . . . He was the perfect father. He spoke slowly, . . . never letting out a word he did not want, and all with great humour. . . . no drugs, no drink, only rarely jamming in the clubs, no women."

Given his gentle and responsible outlook, Montgomery in his final years found himself caught between a rock and a hard place, lambasted by jazz critics for selling out and disappointing live non–jazz oriented audiences whenever he focused on improvising rather than delivering literal versions of his greatest hits. In the latter capacity Montgomery's role on record became increasingly restricted to rendering melodies in octaves, though it must never be forgotten that he, like Louis Armstrong, had a rare ability to bring a special vitality to the task, as writer Pete Welding explained in a March 1968 *Down Beat* review of the album *The Best of Wes Montgomery*: "It's a pleasure to hear him just state the melody: his sound and control are lovely, and his sense of time, of note placement is uncanny." By contrast, writer Gary Giddins took a harsh view of these activities. Given Montgomery's struggle to support his family, no one could possibly object to his having finally found commercial success, but Giddins rightly took Taylor to task for defining Montgomery's work in an ever-more limited way, so that the greatest jazz guitarist after Charlie Christian was not afforded any further opportunity to record as a jazz guitarist.

In contexts where his hands were not, in effect, tied to octaves, Montgomery's solos often followed a pattern of increasing fullness: a single-note line continued in parallel octaves and brought to a climax with the melody fully harmonized in block chords. His perfect dexterity in executing the parallel octaves astonished listeners, but for Montgomery what was most impressive was not this subsequently widely imitated technical gimmick, but the fact that it served to support an exquisite sense of melody and tone.

• For further information on Montgomery's family, see his brother Monk Montgomery's oral history, held on tape and in transcript at the Institute of Jazz Studies, Newark, N.J. The single essential source is Andrian Ingram, *Wes Montgomery* (1985; repr. 1993), which includes a full biography of Montgomery, a detailed catalog of recordings, a full list of Montgomery's recorded compositions, references to essential books on Montgomery's guitar method and a summary thereof, and an extensive bibliography, including the material cited from Griffin, Welding, and Giddins.

BARRY KERNFELD

MONTOUR, Madame (1684?–1752?), translator, was born possibly Cathérine Montour in Trois Rivières, Canada. Her parents were probably Louis Couc Montour, who emigrated from Cognac, France, around 1667, and Mitewamegwakwe, an Algonquian Indian. Montour later claimed her father was a governor of Canada, but it is more likely that he was a coureur de bois (trapper). Montour was captured by warriors from the Five Iroquois Nations of Mohawk, Oneida, Onondaga, Cayuga, and Seneca around 1694. Taken to New York, she was probably raised by the Oneidas and in 1711 married an Oneida chief, Carandowana (Big Tree), who later took the honorary name Robert Hunter. The couple had at least four children.

Montour and her family were actively involved in Anglo-French rivalry during the eighteenth century. While the fur trade was the initial issue, the ultimate concern was control of the continent. In the early eighteenth century, the French traded extensively with the Great Lakes Indians. Since the mid–seventeenth century the Five Nations had tried to eliminate the Great Lakes Tribes, who were trading with the French, so they could divert the fur trade to themselves. Although the Five Nations professed neutrality in the Anglo-French conflict, they most often allied with the English. Iroquois control of the Great Lakes trade would benefit both the Iroquois and their neighbors in New York.

The "farr Indians" were persuaded to bring their furs to Albany by Montour's brother. Before his murder by French agents in 1709, Montour supplied English officials in New York with vital information about French military strength in Canada. Acting on this information in 1711, the English and the Five Nations planned a military campaign against Canada. New York governor Robert Hunter (1666–1734) was in Albany in August 1711 to welcome a fighting force of 800 braves from the Five Nations and subordinate tribes. Madame Montour, fluent in several Indian languages and in French, served as one of the interpreters at the many planning conferences that were held between the Iroquois sachems and the English governor.

Governor Hunter realized that remaining on good terms with the Iroquois, the most powerful and strategically placed tribes in North America, was vital to England's imperial design to gain control of that continent. Montour's skill as an interpreter made her services extremely valuable to the governor. Other translators served the governor, but Hunter found that they altered what the Indians said to serve their own best interests. Hunter respected Montour's ability and frequently entertained her at dinner, where she appeared in full Indian regalia. He was convinced that he would "never be able to hear the truth but by her means."

Hunter again used Montour's services in 1712, when war broke out between an Iroquois tribe in the south, the Tuscarora, and English settlers in North Carolina who were expanding westward onto Indian territory. Afraid Iroquois intervention would spark a full-scale Indian war, Hunter was determined to keep the Five Nations from assisting the Tuscarora. To accomplish this, Hunter sent Peter Schuyler, commissioner of Indian affairs, and Montour to the Onondaga territory in central New York. Hunter's agents were successful. The unaided Tuscarora were defeated by the English, and remnants of the tribe moved to New York to become the sixth Iroquois nation.

Montour probably did not accompany her husband, Carandowana, to Pennsylvania in 1714 when he was chosen as leader, or king, of the Shawnee, whose Pennsylvania territory was near the Susquehanna River. In 1719 the French sent Montour's sister, who was married to a Miami warrior, to persuade Montour to abandon the English and return to Canada. Montour refused but Schuyler was concerned enough by the French attempt to investigate Montour's complaint that she had not been paid for her services for a year. Schuyler promised she would be paid the same salary as a male interpreter. To ensure that her salary was paid regularly, Schuyler, as acting governor, put her on the imperial, rather than the assembly, payroll.

In 1727 Montour moved to Pennsylvania. That year and the next she served as an interpreter at conferences held in Philadelphia among the Six Nations and the proprietors and governor of Pennsylvania. During her stay the English women of Philadelphia vied to entertain Montour. Her warrior husband was killed around 1729 in the ongoing Catawba War. After his death Montour continued to live in Pennsylvania at Otstonwaken on the Susquehanna, today the site of Montoursville in Lycoming County. In 1734 she was again in Philadelphia when several Oneida Indians called on the proprietors and governor.

In 1742 Johann Conrad Weiser, Indian agent for the colony of Pennsylvania, visited Madame Montour with Count Nicholas Ludwig von Zinzendorf, bishop of the Moravian church. Moravians, fleeing persecution in their native lands, were usually sympathetic to the plight of the Indians. The count proved the exception. Montour, a Christian, asked Zinzendorf to baptize two of her children, but he refused on the grounds that there were no local clergy to continue Christian education after his departure. Montour was deeply offended by this slight.

In 1744 Montour was present at, but apparently did not take part in, the Treaty of Lancaster, in which the Six Nations ceded to the English vast territory in the Shenandoah and Ohio valleys. Maryland's representative, William Marshe, visited "the celebrated Mrs. Montour" in her "wigwam" and was impressed with her civility and "polite manner." Montour recounted her life story for Marshe and told him of her late husband's exploits against the Catawbas. Her daughters had followed her example by marrying war chiefs.

Shortly after Marshe's visit, Montour moved to an island in the Susquehanna (Shamokin, present-day Sunbury) and in 1745 was visited there again by Weiser and some Moravian missionaries. The village was struck by smallpox shortly after Weiser's visit and by 1748 was deserted. Montour, aged and blind, moved to Logstown near Pittsburgh, where she resided until her death, just before the outbreak of the French and Indian War, which ended French claims in North America.

Madame Montour was typical of the thousands of Indians, both full- and half-blooded, who were caught in the middle of Anglo-French rivalry as each country tried to achieve its imperial goals. Accommodation was forced on her, as it was on all Native Americans who had ongoing relationships with Europeans, but she responded with grace and acumen. As was true of many Indians in the path of white expansion, Montour moved to escape land-hungry whites, warfare, disease, starvation, and economic distress. As was also true of many white or half-white captives of Indians, Montour remained part of Native American society despite numerous opportunities to return to European-American communities. The resulting life was, by all contemporary accounts, full and rewarding.

• Madame Montour left no correspondence. For references to her and members of her family, see John Jay Papers, Miscellaneous Manuscripts, New-York Historical Society; New-York Historical Society, *Collections* vol. 1 (1868), p. 200; William Smith, Jr., *The History of the Province of New York*, ed. Michael Kammen, vol. 1 (1972), p. 305; E. B. O'Callaghan, ed., *Documents Relative to the Colonial History of New York*, vol. 5 (1856–1887), pp. 65, 268, 273; *Minutes of the Provincial Council of Pennsylvania*, vol. 3 (1851–1852), pp. 570–71, 573; William Marshe, "Journal of the Treaty Held with the Six Nations at Lancaster, June 1744," in Massachusetts Historical Society, *Collections*, 1st ser. (1800), pp. 189–91; Peter Wraxall, *An Abridgment of the Indian Affairs*, ed. Charles Howard McIlwain (1915), pp. 64–66, 68. See also William M. Darlington, "The Montours," *Pennsylvania Magazine of History and Biography* 4 (1880): 218–24; Paul A. W. Wallace, *Conrad Weiser, 1696–1760, Friend of Colonist and Mohawk* (1945); Anthony F. C. Wallace, *Death and Rebirth of the Seneca* (1969); Francis Jennings, *The Ambiguous Iroquois Empire* (1984); and Thomas Elliot Norton, *The Fur Trade in Colonial New York, 1686–1776* (1974).

MARY LOU LUSTIG

MONTOYA, Joseph Manuel (24 Sept. 1915–5 June 1978), senator and lawyer, was born in Peña Blanca, New Mexico, the son of Tomás O. Montoya, a county sheriff, and Frances de La, an elementary school teacher. While attending parochial elementary schools, he began at age nine to earn money for college by delivering newspapers. When Montoya was fourteen his father became sheriff of Sandoval County and moved the family to Bernalillo, the county seat. There he worked part-time in a drug store and sold produce from his own vegetable garden. In 1931 Montoya graduated from Bernalillo's Our Lady of Sorrows High School and that same year enrolled at Regis College in Denver. Three years later he transferred to Georgetown University Law School and, while there, worked at the U.S. Department of the Interior. He earned his LL.B. in 1938 and gained admission the next year to the New Mexico bar. While still a law student, Montoya became the youngest person ever elected to New Mexico's House of Representatives, representing Sandoval County and, following reelection, serving as majority leader. In 1940 he married Della Romero, a graduate nurse, and the couple would have three children. That same year Montoya won a state senate seat and, after serving six years, was elected lieutenant governor in 1946, 1948, 1954, and 1956. During this postwar decade, he spent two more years in the state senate, practiced law in Santa Fe, and pursued various business ventures. Montoya bought Western Freight Lines in 1945, securing a lucrative contract to truck and haul materials for the Los Alamos Scientific Laboratory. When New Mexico Congressman Antonio M. Fernández died in 1956, Democratic leaders elected Montoya as a temporary replacement. He won the special election to fill the seat in April 1957. In Washington, D.C., Montoya developed a reputation as a hardworking and moderate Democratic party regular.

New Mexico voters reelected Montoya with large majorities to four straight terms in Congress. A tireless and colorful campaigner known for fiery, though often stilted speeches, his support for farm subsidies and funding to retrain seasonally unemployed agricultural workers contributed to his popularity, as did his vigorous endorsement of poverty programs. He supported the redevelopment of depressed rural and industrial areas, stricter water pollution standards, and federal funding for mass transit systems and education. Fate intervened again to advance his career when U.S. Senator Dennis Chávez died in 1962. With the support of labor and a large Mexican-American electorate, Montoya easily defeated conservative Republican Edwin L. Mechem, Chávez's replacement, and took office immediately in November 1964. As senator, he continued to champion the poor, especially New Mexico's Mexican Americans.

As the only member of the U.S. Senate who spoke Spanish, Montoya logically cosponsored with Texas Democratic Senator Ralph Yarborough the nation's first bilingual education bill in 1967. He frequently served as a U.S. delegate to inter-American conferences, firmly opposing communist penetration of Latin America. A vocal defender of the Alliance for Progress, Montoya in general opposed military aid to foreign nations. Although he voted for the Gulf of Tonkin resolution, he became an early critic of U.S. military action in Vietnam and, beginning in 1967, called for phased disengagement. Later, Montoya advocated immediate withdrawal and denounced spiraling defense spending, causing Vice President Spiro Agnew to label him one of the Senate's "professional pessimists." He was also a harsh critic of the Nixon administration's domestic policies. While supporting the equal rights amendment, gun control, and legal assistance for the poor, he voted for greater police power to fight crime and limits on busing to achieve school desegregation. Always conscious of New Mexico's interests, Montoya worked to expand the power of Native Americans in the Bureau of Indian Affairs and federal job opportunities for Mexican Americans.

In 1970 Montoya won reelection against Republican Anderson Carter, who attempted to portray him as a captive of special interests. Appointed to the bipartisan seven-member Watergate Committee in 1973, Montoya carefully composed questions on index cards, asking them methodically even if they were repetitive or immaterial. Columnist Art Buchwald advised that when Montoya began questioning, it was a good time for television viewers to visit the bathroom. His defenders, however, blamed the image he projected on inadequate staff work and the disadvantage of being the last questioner. Later, Montoya worked effectively to reduce President Richard Nixon's "transitional allowance" and floor-managed a law requiring Nixon to pay his own legal expenses.

The post-Watergate emphasis on government honesty and openness ironically led to allegations of unethical behavior against Montoya himself. Newspaper reports revealed that the Internal Revenue Service had refused to audit his tax returns for twenty years despite a history of late filings presumably because Montoya was chair of the treasury, postal service, and general government subcommittee that reviewed the agency's operations. Another investigation probed charges that he had created seven dummy committees to launder $100,000 in campaign contributions. His reputation suffered further damage when he released information late in 1975 revealing that he was a millionaire with extensive real estate investments. Critics charged that Montoya had exploited his position to lease his property for post offices and other federal buildings.

Montoya categorically denied that he ever used his political influence for personal financial gain. "I'm clean," he insisted, distributing as evidence his income tax records and detailed financial statements listing all his real estate and business holdings. Montoya stated that he neither had asked for nor was aware of special treatment regarding audits of his income tax forms. An internal Revenue Service investigation begun in October 1975 found that auditors had halted an examination of Montoya's returns after misinterpreting a directive at a time when the agency was receiving adverse publicity for alleged harassment of Nixon's political enemies. Montoya's failure in 1970 to report in New Mexico out-of-state campaign contributions violated a state law passed in 1972. No hard evidence ever surfaced to justify legal action to disprove Montoya's claim that he was not guilty of wrongdoing.

Republican newcomer Harrison "Jack" Schmitt, a geologist and former astronaut, ran against Montoya in 1976, promising "honesty for a change." Montoya's slogan, "seniority is the name of the game," only advertised his inability to understand recent political changes. Shortly after Schmitt's overwhelming victory, Montoya's implication in "Koreagate" brought more unwelcome publicity, stemming from a $3,000 campaign contribution he had accepted from unregistered foreign agent Tongsun Park allegedly to oppose economic sanctions against South Korea's repressive regime. This latest indignity, coming less than a year after his return to New Mexico early in 1977, surely accelerated Montoya's declining health. In the spring of 1978 he left his home in Santa Fe to seek medical care in Washington, D.C., where he died of liver and kidney failure.

In assessing Montoya's career, detractors would have reason to characterize him as a traditional pork barrel politician who was the captive of special interests and who exploited public office for personal gain. But Montoya deserves high praise for his contributions to improving social conditions and expanding economic opportunities for average people, especially minorities. Tough, hardworking, and unpretentious, this New Deal liberal sincerely believed that in bringing numerous programs and projects to the poor, rural, and underpopulated state of New Mexico, he was doing his job. Following his death, native New Mexicans retained a deep affection for "Little Joe" and appreciated how the state had benefited from the career of "the barefoot boy from Peña Blanca."

• Montoya's papers are in the library of the University of New Mexico Law School. Few sources focus exclusively on the life of the New Mexico senator; probably the best assessment is Maurilio Vigil and Roy Luján, "Parallels in the Career of Two Hispanic U.S. Senators," *Journal of Ethnic Studies* 13 (Winter 1986): 1–20. See also Maurilio Vigil, *Los Patrones: Profiles of Hispanic Political Leaders in New Mexico History* (1980), and Al Martínez, *Rising Voices: Profiles of Hispano-American Lives* (1974). Specific information on Montoya's personal and political activities appears in Grace Lichtenstein, "New Mexico Race Close for Montoya," *New York Times*, 24 Oct. 1976, p. 28; Anthony Marro, "Indictment of Park Charges 36 Crimes, Bell Seeking Return," *New York Times*, 22 Oct. 1977, pp. 1, 9; "Montoya Denies Hiding Origins of Campaign Funds," *New York Times*, 29 June 1973, p. 28; James M. Naughton, "Senate Watergate Panel," *New York Times*, 30 May 1973, p. 18; and David E. Rosenbaum, "Each Senator on His Own in Questioning Witnesses," *New York Times*, 12 July 1973, p. 24. Obituaries and tributes are in the *New York Times*, 6 June 1978; *Santa Fe New Mexican*, 6 and 9 June 1978; and *Albuquerque Journal*, 6 June 1978.

JAMES I. MATRAY

MONTRÉSOR, James Gabriel (19 Nov. 1702–6 Jan. 1776), British military engineer, was born at Fort William, Scotland, the son of James Gabriel Le Trésor, an army officer, and Nanon de Hauteville. Educated by his father in things military, Montrésor joined the Royal Artillery as a matross in 1727 and saw action at Mahon, Minorca. A year later he was at the siege of Gibraltar, serving as a bombardier and distinguishing himself in that role. He was commissioned a practitioner-engineer at Gibraltar on 2 October 1731 and was appointed ensign in the Fourteenth Regiment on 5 April 1732. On 11 June 1735 he married Mary Haswell, with whom he had several children (the exact number is unknown). Skilled as a military engineer, he advanced steadily in the service over the next few years. He was promoted to lieutenant in the Fourteenth Regiment on 23 July 1737, sub-engineer on 7 February 1739, and engineer extraordinary on 3 July 1742. Ordered to Mahon, Minorca, on 5 October 1743 as engineer in ordinary, he served there for four years then returned to Gibraltar on 2 January 1747 as chief engineer. Working assiduously to fortify Gibraltar, he was promoted to subdirector on 17 December 1752.

Montrésor returned to England in June 1754 and on 9 November was appointed chief engineer in North America, to serve under Major General Edward Braddock. On 24 December he sailed in the company of his eldest son, John Montrésor, for America. In the spring of 1755 he commanded a party clearing a road through the wilderness for Braddock's advance from Alexandria, Virginia, toward Fort Duquesne in western Pennsylvania. He was with Braddock on 9 July 1755, when the British army was ambushed by French and Indians near Fort Duquesne and Braddock was killed. Wounded in the debacle, compelled to abandon his personal belongings and the army's engineer stores, Montrésor fled with the retreating army to Fort Cumberland in western Maryland. On 2 August he reached Philadelphia and was ordered by Major General William Shirley, Braddock's successor, to Albany, New York. For seven months in 1756 he surveyed the Lake Champlain district, drawing a map of the southern end of the lake. Also, he designed and built a model defensive redoubt for use in the American wilderness, which General Shirley ordered to be emulated by the British army. Establishing a rapport with Shirley, Montrésor became the general's adviser and troubleshooter, carrying out a number of engineering projects around Lake Champlain and Lake George and serving on the general's councils of war. He impressed Shirley's successor, John Campbell, Lord Loudoun, much less. Loudoun accused Montrésor of jumping from one task to another without informing Loudoun, and never completing anything. "Business will not go on under his direction," declared the new commander in chief; "Mr. *Montresor*, I dare not trust a Siege to" (Pargellis, pp. 266, 277).

Despite Loudoun's negative comments about him, Montrésor was promoted to major on 14 May 1757. That summer he was stationed at Fort Edward with General Daniel Webb when nearby Fort William Henry was captured by French general Marquis de Montcalm. Later that year and into early 1758 he served at Saratoga. On 4 January 1758 he was promoted to director and lieutenant colonel. He was ordered to Halifax, Nova Scotia, on 3 March 1758, "to provide Materials, Fascines & Gabions &c" for fortifications at that post. In early 1759 he returned to New York and accompanied General Jeffery Amherst, the latest commander in chief, to Philadelphia in April. During the summer of 1759 he served under Amherst in New York, impressing Amherst by accomplishing a number of engineering projects under difficult conditions and with a paucity of materials. He designed fortifications for construction at Oswego and a road with defensive blockhouses along the Mohawk River. More importantly, he rebuilt the field works at the head of Lake George in June, and for the remainder of the year, with Amherst's assistance, he constructed a completely new fortification, later named Fort George, to replace the older, inadequate works. While carrying out these engineering duties, he also was ordered by Amherst in July to take command of all troops and posts between Albany and Lake George, as Amherst conducted operations against Fort Ticonderoga on Lake Champlain.

Montrésor remained on duty at Fort George until the spring of 1760, when his failing health finally compelled him to return to England. For two years he had been suffering from fatigue brought on by overwork. In July 1758, while at Halifax, he was incapacitated for a time and in June 1759 received permission from the Ordnance Board to relinquish his duties whenever the service would allow. Then on 29 September he fell and strained himself "in such a manner that [he] was hardly able to get home," even with "the help of 3 persons." In England on 1 October 1760 he was commissioned chief engineer of an expedition against Belle Isle, off the French coast, but was too unwell to accept the post. His wife, Mary, died in 1761, and for the next year he traveled in an attempt to restore his health. On 3 February 1762 he relinquished his commission as lieutenant colonel in the Fourteenth Regiment. Returning to duty in 1763, he spent two years designing and building powder magazines at Purfleet. On 25 August 1766 he married Henrietta Fielding, who died shortly after. He later married Frances Nicholls. Neither marriage produced any children. He served as chief engineer at Chatham in 1769, and on 25 May 1772, despite his earlier relinquishment of his lieutenant colonelcy, was promoted colonel. He died at New Gardens, Teynham, Kent, having achieved a solid record as a designer and constructor of military works, particularly in the wilderness of North America.

• Some of Montrésor's correspondence and journals, as well as a number of his plans and maps of Gibraltar's fortifications, are in the War Office and Ordnance Board papers in the Public Record Office, Kew, Surrey, England. Other of Montrésor's Gibraltar engineering drawings are in the British Library. The National Archives of Canada possesses Montrésor's maps and plans of the Montreal and southern Lake Champlain regions. Montrésor's service journals for 1757–1759, and a useful sketch of his life, are in Gideon D. Scull, ed., *The Montresor Journals*, New-York Historical Society, *Collections, 1881* (1882). One of his letters, and comments about him by his military colleagues, are in Stanley Pargellis, ed., *Military Affairs in North America, 1748–1765: Selected Documents from the Cumberland Papers in Windsor Castle* (1936). His family history is sketched in Sir Bernard Burke, *A Genealogical and Heraldic History of the Landed Gentry of Great Britain and Ireland* (1898). For his role in the engineers, see Whitworth Porter, *History of the Corps of Royal Engineers* (2 vols., 1889). Some of his military contributions in North America, and general background history, are provided by Lawrence Henry Gipson, *The British Empire Before the American Revolution*, vols. 6 and 7 (1946–1949).

PAUL DAVID NELSON

MONTRÉSOR, John (6 Apr. 1736–26 June 1799), British military engineer, was born in Gibraltar, the son of James Gabriel Montrésor, a military engineer, and Mary Haswell. He was educated in military engineering by his father, and in 1754 he accompanied the elder Montrésor to America when the latter was appointed chief engineer of General Edward Braddock's army during the French and Indian War. Joining the Forty-eighth Regiment as an ensign, Montrésor was commissioned a lieutenant in the same regiment on 4 July 1755, while serving with Braddock on an expedition against Fort Duquesne in western Pennsylvania. He was wounded in a disastrous French ambush of Braddock's army on 9 July and ever afterward carried a "restless ball" in his body, despite numerous "incisions cut to extract it." In 1756 Montrésor was stationed at Fort Edward and twice commanded detachments of troops sent to relieve outposts under enemy attack. Two years later he was with Sir Jeffery Amherst during the capture of Louisbourg. On 19 May 1758 Montrésor was commissioned a practitioner engineer in the corps of engineers, and on 17 March 1759 was promoted to subengineer. In late 1758 he conducted a perilous scouting expedition on snowshoes into the heart of Cape Breton Island, "to drive the Indians and Acadians off the Island." Although an engineering officer, he served under General James Wolfe at Quebec in 1759 as commander of the Forty-eighth Regiment's light infantry, storming two enemy posts under fire. On 26 January 1760, while serving under General James Murray at Quebec, Montrésor was ordered to lead a scout through deep snow to New England to deliver dispatches. Almost starving during the desperate, month-long journey in the dead of winter, he declared that Murray was "a madman" for demanding such duty. In the summer of 1760 he carried dispatches from Amherst in New York to Murray in Canada by a ship that he was forced to take command of to escape capture by French men-of-war. For the remainder of the French and Indian War, Montrésor conducted an engineering survey of the St. Lawrence River.

During Pontiac's Rebellion in 1763, Montrésor served under General Amherst, British commander in chief in North America, in carrying much-needed provisions to Major Henry Gladwin, who was besieged by Indians at Detroit. In 1764 he married Frances Tucker. They lived on Montrésor (Randall's) Island in New York harbor and had ten children. In the summer of 1764 Montrésor constructed a chain of redoubts near Niagara and Fort Erie on the shore of that lake and also led a Canadian regiment on a forced march to Sandusky to conclude a treaty of peace with the western Indians. While on the latter service, he survived many perils, including shipwreck, near starvation, and Indian attack. In 1765 he was at Albany, removing old government buildings and erecting new ones, and later in the year, during the Stamp Act disturbances, he was stationed at Fort George, in New York City. He returned to England for six months' leave in November 1765 and while there successfully sought advancement in his career. He was promoted to engineer extraordinary and captain lieutenant on 20 December 1765, as well as being appointed barrackmaster for the ordnance in North America. He continued to serve in America for the next ten years, working on barracks and fortifications in Boston, New York, Philadelphia, and the Bahamas. In 1769 he surveyed the northern boundary line between New York and New Jersey "by astronomical observations."

When the American Revolution commenced in 1775, Montrésor was put to use by British commanders on a variety of engineering projects. He was at the battles of Lexington and Bunker Hill, making a survey of the position and a plan of the works at the latter site. On 18 December 1775 he was appointed chief engineer in America and on 10 January 1776 was promoted to captain and engineer in ordinary. When the British evacuated Boston in March 1776, he blew up Castle William at the mouth of the harbor to keep it from falling into American hands. He saw action under General William Howe as one of the general's aide-de-camps at the battle of Long Island on 17 August 1776, and in the subsequent fighting on Manhattan and in New Jersey. He was with General Howe at the battle of Woodbridge on 26 June 1777; the battle of the Brandywine, 11 September, directing the position and attack of most of the artillery; the occupation of Philadelphia, 25 September; and the battle of Germantown, 4 October. He constructed the lines of defense around Philadelphia in the fall of 1777 and in the spring of 1778 organized the "Meschianza," an extravagant farewell entertainment given in honor of General Howe by his officers before Howe departed for England. He was with General Sir Henry Clinton during the British army's march across New Jersey to New York in the summer of 1778, and he fought at the battle of Monmouth on 28 June. Later that year, having lost Clinton's confidence, Montrésor departed America with his family for England and on 26 March 1779 resigned his commission. He was called upon by General Howe in May to give testimony before a committee of the House of Commons regarding Howe's conduct of the war in America. Although he had come to doubt Howe's military abilities, he generally testified in favor of the general and blamed Howe's ministerial superiors for bungling the war effort. He settled his family on an estate named "Belmont" near Faversham, Kent, and by 1781 had purchased considerable property nearby as well as a London townhouse in Portland Place. Also, he negotiated with the government for reimbursement of personal expenses incurred during his years of military service. Called before the commissioner of public accounts in 1782 to answer questions about his expenditures, Montrésor convinced them that many of his charges were valid. In October 1785 he left with his family for a year-long visit to France, Germany, and Switzerland. He purchased "Huntingfield," near Faversham, in 1787 and lived there for the next decade. In 1798 he still was arguing with the commissioner of public accounts over thousands of pounds in expenses that were disallowed. The government seized much of his property, and he was thrust into Maidstone prison, where he died.

• Montrésor correspondence with the War Office and Treasury Office is in the Public Record Office; some of his plans and drawings are in the British Library. "The Montrésor Journals," ed. Gideon D. Scull, New-York Historical Society, *Collections, 1881* (1882), contain not only many of Montrésor's service journals but also letters, treasury correspondence, and a useful sketch of his life. See also Scull, "Journal of Captain John Montrésor, July 1, 1777, to July 1, 1778 . . . ," *Pennsylvania Magazine of History and Biography* 5 (1881): 393–417; and Kenneth L. Roberts, ed., *March to Quebec: Journals of the Members of Arnold's Expedition* (1940). For his parliamentary testimony, see *The Detail and Conduct of the American War under Generals Gage, Howe, Burgoyne, and Vice Admiral Howe* . . . (1780). Short biographical sketches are Frank M. Montrésor, "Captain John Montrésor in Canada," *Canadian Historical Review* 5 (1924): 336–40; John Clarence Webster, "Life of John Montrésor," Royal Society of Canada, *Proceedings and Transactions*, 3d ser., 22 (1928): 1–31, issued as an offprint the same year; and Francis L. D. Goodrich, "John Montresor, 1736–1799, Engineer and Cartographer," *Michigan Alumnus Quarterly Review* 64 (1958): 124–29. For Montrésor's engineering work near Niagara in 1764, see Frank H. Severance, "The Achievements of Captain John Montresor on the Niagara and the First Construction of Fort Erie," Buffalo Historical Society, *Publications* 5 (1902): 1–19; and Robert W. Bingham, *The Cradle of the Queen City: A History of Buffalo to the Incorporation of the City* (1931). His part in the Stamp Act disturbances is described in Wilbur C. Abbott, *New York in the American Revolution* (1929). John W. Jackson, *With the British Army in Philadelphia, 1777–1778* (1979), discusses Montrésor's role while serving in that city.

PAUL DAVID NELSON

MONTROLL, Elliott Waters (4 May 1916–3 Dec. 1983), mathematical physicist, was born in Pittsburgh, Pennsylvania, the son of Adolph Baer Montroll and Esther Israel. From an early age he demonstrated an interest in chemistry and in 1933 matriculated at the University of Pittsburgh with the intention of becoming a chemist. After receiving a B.S. in chemistry in 1937, he decided instead to become a mathematician and enrolled in graduate school at the University of Pittsburgh, from which he received a Ph.D. in mathematics in 1939. His dissertation, which combined both disciplines by applying integral equations to the analysis of imperfect gases, served as his entry into the field of statistical mechanics, a branch of physics that employs the mathematical tools of statistics, such as probability theory, to study the motions of bodies of planetary and ordinary size as well as particles of atomic and subatomic size.

Montroll's scientific curiosity and mathematical ability led him to undertake a variety of research projects in a number of settings during the first twelve years of his professional career. As a postdoctoral fellow at Columbia University from 1939 to 1940, he and Joseph E. Mayer developed a mathematical technique for analyzing the behavior of imperfect gases that was eventually adapted and used in a number of applications related to statistical mechanics. As a Sterling Research Fellow at Yale University in 1940–1941, he worked out a solution for one dimension of the three-dimensional Ising model, a special problem related to probability theory that at the time had a direct bearing on the study of ferromagnetism. This solution was eventually adapted and used to solve Markov processes, wherein the future value of a random variable is determined to a certain extent by its present value. As a research fellow at Cornell University in 1941–1942, he studied the thermodynamic properties of crystalline solids, a topic that had important implications for the growing field of solid-state physics because metals in their solid state possess a crystalline structure. This study yielded a method for calculating the frequency spectrum of the Born-von Karman model, which held that crystalline solids are formed from elastic lattices of discrete atoms that vibrate in relation to one another as if they were connected by springs.

In 1942, the year before he married Shirley Abrams, with whom he had ten children, Montroll taught physics as an instructor at Princeton University. In 1943 he became chief mathematician at the Kellex Corporation in New York, where he contributed to the development of the first atomic bomb by using the principles of statistical mechanics to predict the behavior of neutrons in an uncontrolled chain reaction. After teaching for a year at Brooklyn Polytechnic Institute, he returned to the University of Pittsburgh in 1946 as an assistant professor of physics and was promoted to associate professor the next year. In 1948 he joined the U.S. Office of Naval Research (ONR) in Washington, D.C., as head of the physics branch, and in 1950 he became a research fellow at New York's Courant Institute.

In 1951 Montroll joined the University of Maryland's Institute for Fluid Dynamics and Applied Mathematics as a research professor, a position he held until 1960. Between 1952 and 1954 he also served as ONR's director of physical science. While at Maryland he made several important contributions to statistical mechanics. He expanded on his earlier work with lattice dynamics by developing a way to calculate the effect of defects in the lattice on its thermodynamic properties and vibrational frequencies. He later adapted this work to the study of harmonic oscillators, diatomic molecules that vibrate harmonically because their two nuclei are continually moving first toward and then away from one another in much the same way as do atoms in a lattice, and contributed to a better understanding of what causes diatomic molecules to split apart. He also investigated the phenomenon of unimolecular relaxation, the split-second period that occurs between an abrupt physical change in a molecule's equilibrium and its response to that change, and as a result provided insights into the rates and mechanisms of chemical reactions.

In the latter half of the 1950s Montroll adapted and applied his work with lattice dynamics to the study of random walks, sequences of steps of the same length but of variable number taken randomly along either the *x*- or *y*-axis of a flat rectangular grid, in an effort to calculate the probability distribution of the distance of the endpoints of a given number of random walks from the starting point. By studying random walks on a lattice structure, thereby making the problem three-dimensional, and by introducing intervals of random duration between steps, he and several collaborators developed an analytical tool that could be used by physical chemists to predict behavioral parameters during the production of long chains of polymers, as well as by solid-state physicists experimenting with the photoconductivity of amorphous semiconductors.

In 1958 Montroll, as a consultant to General Motors Corporation, contributed to a better understanding of the dynamics of automobile traffic by developing the linear theory of car-following. He demonstrated that the tendency of streams of traffic to destabilize as they lengthened was due to a cumulative increase in driver reaction time, resulting in an increase in the frequency of rear-end collisions toward the end of the stream. He later expanded on this study to show that traffic instability also results in increased acceleration noise. These findings served to elevate the study of traffic dynamics to a higher level of respectability and won for him and his collaborators the Operations Research Society's Lancaster Prize in 1959.

In 1960 Montroll rejuvenated the defunct *Journal of Mathematical Physics* and served as its editor until 1970. Having grown restless at Maryland, where he had been for almost ten years, he decided to venture into industrial research by becoming, in 1960, the vice president in charge of physics research at the IBM Corporation Research Center in Yorktown Heights, New York. In 1963 he was made vice president of the Institute for Defense Analysis in Washington, D.C. Three years later he was appointed Albert Einstein Professor of Physics at the University of Rochester and served as the director of its Institute of Fundamental Studies. In this capacity he broadened the application of the methods of statistical mechanics to study problems related to model building for the biological and behavioral sciences. His efforts in this regard included conducting statistical analyses of a variety of subjects from the equilibrium of copolymeric DNA to price fluctuations in a 75-year run of Sears Roebuck mail-order catalogs. In 1981 he retired from his duties at Rochester and returned to the University of Maryland, where he became affiliated with the Institute for Physical Science and Technology. He was named a distinguished professor the next year, a position he held until his death in Chevy Chase, Maryland.

A member of the American Academy of Arts and Sciences and the National Academy of Sciences, Montroll was one of the foremost practitioners of statistical mechanics in the United States. He contributed greatly to its applicability as a discipline by adapting and modifying for its use many of the esoteric mathematical theories and concepts of combinatorial analysis. His particular genius consisted of his ability to develop elegant and powerful mathematical formulae capable of explaining complex physical and social relationships.

• Montroll's papers are located in the Science Archives of the University of Maryland Library. A biography, which includes a partial bibliography, is George H. Weiss, "Elliott Waters Montroll," National Academy of Sciences, *Biographical Memoirs* 63 (1994): 365–80. An obituary is in the *New York Times*, 8 Dec. 1983.

CHARLES W. CAREY, JR.

MOODY, Deborah, Lady (1586–1659?), English colonist and early proponent of religious liberty, was born Deborah Dunch in London, England, the daughter of Walter Dunch and Debora Pilkington, members of the landed gentry. Her father had read law at Gray's Inn and was a member of Parliament at the time of Moody's birth. Her mother's ancestors included churchmen noted for their radical Puritan leanings. Moody probably grew up at the family estate in Wiltshire, where she would have received an education in reading, writing, and accomplishments customary for girls of her class. In 1606 she married Henry Moody. Shortly thereafter, Henry was knighted by James I, making his wife Dame, or Lady, Deborah Moody. Henry Moody would go on to become sheriff of Wiltshire, a baronet, and a member of Parliament. The couple had two children.

After her husband's death in 1629, Moody moved to London, where she associated with nonconformists and may have first developed her Anabaptist convictions. In 1635 she was charged by the Court of the Star Chamber with defying Charles I's edict that the gentry limit their time in London and reside upon their country estates, a law designed to control dissent in London. Moody's initial response to this summons is unknown. Between 1635 and 1639 she immigrated to Massachusetts Bay colony. She settled in Lynn, about ten miles outside of Boston, purchasing a farmhouse and farm of 500 acres, called "Swampscott," in addition to 400 acres granted her in 1640. She also owned a house in Salem.

Although Moody had joined the Salem church in May 1640, her Anabaptist leanings soon involved her in trouble with the colony's ministers and magistrates. In December 1642 the Quarterly Court of Massachusetts Bay charged her with holding Anabaptist beliefs. Rather than submit to a public trial and probable banishment, she went into voluntary exile. She led a small group of men and women to the Dutch colony of New Amsterdam, hoping that as Holland had served as a refuge for fleeing English dissenters, the Dutch in the New World would extend a similar degree of toleration to her and her followers. After she departed, the Salem church excommunicated her.

Sailing from Boston, Moody arrived in Manhattan in mid-1643. She managed to obtain from the Dutch governor Willem Kieft permission to settle in an area of Long Island, which she would name Gravesend. She moved there with her followers from Massachusetts Bay and with English settlers from New Amsterdam who had joined her band. Before the year was out, however, she was back at Fort Amsterdam, having been driven out by warring Mohicans angry over the loss of their lands. After this setback, Moody considered returning to Massachusetts. But on 30 August 1645 a treaty between Governor Kieft and Indian leaders put an end, at least temporarily, to the intermittent warfare between the settlers and the local tribes.

Now able to return to Gravesend, Moody negotiated with Kieft for a new patent, which was granted on 19 December 1645. The patent permitted Moody and her associates self-government, subject to the jurisdiction of Kieft, as well as "free liberty of conscience." Moody would not be permitted to build her own church or hire her own minister, only to practice her religion peaceably in private. Nevertheless, this clause made the Gravesend patent one of the first documents in the New World to bestow this great a degree of religious freedom.

Relations between the settlers and the Dutch were strained first by Kieft's recall to Holland and replacement by Pieter Stuyvesant, and then by war between the English and the Dutch. The situation became critical when two of Gravesend's elected magistrates signed a remonstrance protesting Stuyvesant's arbitrary rule. To defuse the conflict, on 23 November 1654 Stuyvesant met with Moody and the Gravesend citizenry at her home. She brokered a settlement in which Gravesend agreed to retain and be represented by its three remaining magistrates loyal to Stuyvesant. Moody's actions in preserving the freedom of Gravesend were a testament to her power and prestige in the settlement, even though she herself was ineligible, because of her gender, to ever hold elective office. One year later, in 1655, she managed to make the election of magistrates acceptable to Stuyvesant and the Dutch directors.

Remarkable for her era, Moody was willing to extend to others the religious toleration she sought for herself. In 1657 she protected Quakers fleeing persecution in other colonies and permitted them to meet in her own house. Some historians believe that she herself became a Quaker before the end of her life. Throughout the 1650s her friendship with Stuyvesant, a strict Dutch Calvinist, had forestalled his encroachments upon Gravesend's religious liberty, and Quakers there were safe from persecution during Moody's lifetime. Moody died some time between November 1658 and 11 May 1659 (when documents record her son's disposal of some of her property). Five years after her death the English succeeded in conquering New Amsterdam, and the settlement she founded became part of Brooklyn.

The historian Linda Biemer, comparing Moody and her more famous contemporary Anne Hutchinson, attributed Moody's greater success to her rank and her willingness to keep her religious views private. Even John Winthrop, Hutchinson's great opponent, would refer to Moody as "a wise and anciently religious woman" (Cooper, p. 86), deferring to her rank even after her censure and self-imposed exile. Yet Moody's political savvy and what must have been a tremendous degree of personal courage must also be acknowledged; Gravesend owed first its religious liberty and then its very survival to her diplomacy. If the privilege to which she was born granted her the freedom to act as few seventeenth-century women did, still it was her extraordinary energy and ability that earned her a place in American history.

• The best full-length biographical source for Moody is Victor H. Cooper, *A Dangerous Woman* (1995). The second chapter in Linda Biemer, *Women and Property in Colonial New York* (1983), is a shorter, but equally good and comprehensive reference. Deborah Crawford, *Four Women in a Violent Time* (1970), is also useful, though aimed primarily at adolescents and somewhat novelized. Shorter and more general discussions of Moody's life and importance include Martha B. Flint, *Long Island before the Revolution* (1967); Alexander C. Flick, "Lady Deborah Moody: Grand Dame of Gravesend," *Long Island Historical Quarterly* 1 (1939): 69–75; and James W. Gerard, *Lady Deborah Moody: A Discourse Delivered before the New-York Historical Society* (1880).

ANNE SHEEHAN

MOODY, Dwight Lyman (5 Feb. 1837–22 Dec. 1899), evangelist, was born in Northfield, Massachusetts, the son of Edwin Moody, a bricklayer, and Betsey Holton. Raised in western Massachusetts, he deeply imbibed semirural New England values—a sense of family and place and personal attitudes emphasizing thrift, sobriety, and hard work. Yet as a teenager Moody was also drawn away from Northfield by the magnet of urban America. He went to Boston at the age of seventeen, then in 1856 he moved westward to the booming city of Chicago. His rural to urban migration and movement from New England to the Midwest replicated the experience of thousands of other young people. Moreover in 1875, almost at the height of his fame as an urban revivalist, Moody established his permanent home in Northfield, oscillating thereafter between that community and his revival work in great industrial centers. Both city and small town were embedded in him, as was true for many Americans of the late nineteenth century.

In Boston and Chicago Moody worked first as a boot and shoe salesman, but increasingly his interests turned to religious matters. He joined the Young Men's Christian Association in Boston and intensified that interest after moving west. In 1866 he became the president of the Chicago YMCA, the first salaried director of that organization. He always maintained membership in a local evangelical Protestant church (he was a Congregationalist), but his religious commitments grew along nondenominational lines, both in the Chicago YMCA and in a sabbath school–mission church he established in 1859 among the poor folk of the near North Side. Nondenominational evangelicalism became an essential characteristic of Moody's later work as a revivalist. In 1862 he married Emma C. Revell, with whom he had three children. Emma Moody was a major influence on the revivalist, although in quiet, unobtrusive ways. Moody relied on her judgment often, and over the years she did a great deal to smooth over his brusque personality.

After the Civil War, Moody's horizons expanded rapidly. Aided by his recognition as the president of the Chicago YMCA, he began to preach regularly in evangelical churches and in small, local revivals throughout Illinois. First in 1867 and then again in 1872, Moody visited and preached in England, widening to transatlantic dimensions his network of religious friends and supporters. He was also testing his preaching tactics and his undeniable ability to evoke public conversions of people both within and outside evangelical circles. The great Chicago fire of 1871, which destroyed Moody's Illinois Street Church and the Chicago YMCA's headquarters, and almost simultaneously a powerful conversion experience that provided the young evangelist with a renewed sense of inner well being and personal confidence, led to a major vocational gamble that transformed Moody's life. In 1873 he left Chicago and went to Great Britain to launch a two-year revival "campaign" in the large cities of Scotland and England.

The unqualified success of this extended trip had several important consequences. First, Moody created in England the techniques of mass, urban revivalism that he applied in the United States equally effectively throughout the last quarter of the nineteenth century. Second, the popular acclaim the evangelist received in Great Britain assured acceptance upon his return to America in 1875 as this country's premier popular revivalist. He remained so until his death. The inauguration of Moody's formal, full-time career as a popular revivalist in England also underscored the transatlantic dimensions of nineteenth-century evangelical Protestantism. Religious leaders in England and the United States frequently had moved back and forth; but Moody's debut as a revivalist in Great Britain, not in the United States, was a spectacular reminder of the close relationship between the religious communities of the two countries.

Moody was a layperson. Indeed, he never received any formal theological or biblical training. His personal letters were crudely written, filled with grammatical errors—a reflection of his grammar school education approximating fifth grade. His meager education fit the image of the popular revivalist, a man sprung from the soil of democracy, a religious representative of "the people." He also reflected the decline of revivalism as a serious intellectual and theological force, beginning with the highly educated and intellectually sophisticated Jonathan Edwards (1703–1758), continuing through the lawyer Charles Finney, then on to Moody, and later Billy Sunday, a converted ex-ballplayer. Yet a review of Moody's career makes clear the man's personal integrity and his irenic spirit. Although an evangelical conservative (the term "fundamentalism" had not yet been coined at the time of his death), even late in life he included among his friends theological liberals, like William Rainey Harper, the first president of the University of Chicago, and the Englishman Henry Drummond. Unlike some of his conservative evangelical friends (and sometimes to their distress), he did not lead the growing attack on liberal Protestants but embraced such people personally even when he could not agree with their views about the Bible or theology.

Possessing an aura of integrity seemed an important part of his appeal to the thousands who crowded into his revival meetings. His simple "talks" in a near-conversational tone; his business background and dark business suits combined with his rugged physique; his simple message of a God of love, not of judgment and brimstone—these traits all helped. Singing and playing a harmonium, Ira Sankey, Moody's musical assistant, drew the crowds into the spirit of the moment with catchy, rollicking revival hymns and tunes which the crowds easily learned and never forgot. Antiphonal group singing and a large choir added to the excitement. All the major popular revivalists after Moody felt it necessary to have a musical leader to assist them.

Moody's religious beliefs were simple and never thought through very systematically. He expressed his views in graphic, rough-hewn sermons studded with homely anecdotes. He possessed a practical, not a formal, theology. An explicit Arminianism, combined with a constant stress upon God's love and a minimal doctrine of the church, made his message easy to accept and practice. He was a biblical literalist, believed in the necessity of a personal conversion experience, and harbored premillennialist beliefs about the second coming of Christ, all of which made him a religious conservative in a time of great cultural flux. These attitudes also added to his public appeal, providing reassurance to people living in a new and sometimes frightening industrial, urban world.

From 1875 to 1885, Moody conducted revivals averaging several weeks in length in all the major cities and many lesser ones of the United States. It is impossible to pass judgment in any final sense about their success or failure. Moody's supporters cited the thousands of people who pressed into the "inquiry rooms" located at the edges of the revival auditoriums and either renewed their faith or for the first time "gave their hearts to Christ." Statistical analysis of these results, however, suggested that many were "repeaters" or lapsed evangelicals. There is not much evidence to suggest that Moody effectively reached the poorest elements in the new urban centers. He consistently attracted middle-class people or those who aspired to middle-class status, even though he fretted often about the "lapsed masses" of the cities who seemed to him nearly impervious to all formal religious influences.

In the 1880s Moody began to alter his work significantly. He still conducted revivals on a regular schedule, but increasingly he organized decentralized revivals in local churches in different parts of a metropolis rather than at a large downtown auditorium. He also began less frenetic, more leisurely campaigns, often lasting several months instead of an intense few weeks. Popular revivalists have always viewed their work as twofold—to convert sinners outside the church and to revitalize backsliders within. Moody seemed to be shifting his emphasis from the recruitment of those largely outside the churches to the "quickening" of people inside. He also seemed to be acknowledging the need to experiment with new techniques of evangelism extending beyond the formal trappings of mass revivalism. These developments were hints that by the mid-1880s Moody's halcyon days as a popular revivalist were coming to an end.

Between the autumn of 1879 and the early months of 1881, the evangelist embarked on two new ventures, establishing in his hometown the Northfield Seminary, a private secondary school for girls, and just across the Connecticut River, the companion Mount Hermon School for boys. They quickly became known as the Northfield Schools. Ever since the days of work with ragged youngsters in Chicago Moody had thought about starting a school. Now he was famous and able to gather around him people eager to help create and run the academies or to provide the large sums of money needed to finance these new ideas. Many back-country young people in and around Northfield and students from overseas responded eagerly to education available at nominal costs and through a self-help work-study program.

Moody never participated in the day-to-day operations of the schools. Instead, college-trained people became the administrators and teachers (the female seminary had especially close ties with Wellesley, because of a friendship between Moody and one of the founders of the women's college). This meant that the Northfield Schools quickly joined the ranks of the private, secondary-level academies scattered all over New England. Yet Moody did place his imprint on his schools. In addition to a Bible-centered curriculum and daily religious activities in which he directly participated, Moody envisioned his schools as a place for creating lay evangelists like himself, "gapmen" or helpers in evangelism, who through their studies and experiences in Northfield would be "well equipped for their work." This was to be a variation on revival work and equally important. The Northfield Schools flourished and are still very much alive today, but soon after they were founded it became clear that they were not training "gapmen." Given the geographical and cultural context in which they were established, this was not surprising. In order to survive they had to be primarily educational institutions and only secondarily nurseries for lay evangelists. Moody accepted that fact, which explains much about the motivations behind his founding of a third school in 1886, the Chicago Bible Institute.

From the outset Moody and his Chicago supporters viewed the Bible Institute as a practical school for city evangelists, in which formal academic training would take a back seat to on-the-job training in preaching and pamphleteering in the streets of the Windy City. Here was an opportunity to work directly with the "unchurched masses" of a great urban center, a long-held concern of Moody's that mass revivalism had never been able to confront fully. The animating purpose of the institute seemed much closer to Moody's original intentions for the Northfield Schools. Long absences from Chicago necessitated by his many other activities and personality conflicts with some of the leaders in the Midwest meant that this third educational venture did not begin to assume concrete shape until about 1890. Yet it, too, has continued to the present as Moody Bible Institute, perhaps the best-known of the evangelist's nonrevival enterprises.

At Northfield Moody initiated another program which departed from revivalism but which was consistent with his desire in the 1880s and after to revitalize the life of the evangelical churches from within. Beginning in 1880 and continuing annually thereafter, he held summer "conferences" on the women's seminary campus, where outstanding evangelical leaders like William Rainey Harper, George Adam Smith, and Henry Drummond spoke both to college students and adult churchgoers. The student gatherings underlined Moody's ability to relate to and deeply influence an entire generation of young churchpeople—eventual ecumenical leaders of American Protestantism such as John R. Mott, Robert Wilder, and Robert E. Speer—who came to Northfield as members of college YMCAs and fell under the evangelist's spell. Out of these college conferences emerged the Student Volunteer Movement, one of the last worldwide evangelical missionary efforts, which sent hundreds of young Americans to remote outposts in the years just prior to World War I.

The adult conferences, while having less long-term impact upon the churches, were also important. Some of the speakers there reflected the earliest hints of theological ideas—premillennialism, concerns for "holiness," emphasis upon biblical inerrancy and a literal interpretation of the Bible—which became taproots of fundamentalism in the first decade of the twentieth century. Indeed, at times in the conferences Moody had to mediate between his conservative brethren and people like Drummond and Harper. These were early signs of the deep splits between religious conservatives and liberals that were to rend American Protestantism in the first quarter of the twentieth century.

Much of Moody's last years was spent quietly in Northfield. Secure economically, he could savor fully his grandchildren, his recognition as a figure of national importance, and a devoted circle of friends and family. However, he continued a strenuous schedule of preaching and revival-making, both in England and in this country. The demands of such endeavors, the fact that he was badly overweight, and worry in the last year of his life over the death of a much-loved grandchild added complications to serious heart problems, which remained largely unattended. Stricken while conducting a revival in Kansas City, he managed to return to Northfield, where he died just before Christmas in 1899.

Moody's chief historical achievement was to adapt popular revivalism, a central aspect of evangelical Protestantism, to a developing industrial urban society. He linked simple preaching to methods of showmanship that attracted mass urban audiences, practices characteristic of American revivalism even today. Moody's life and work also hinted at the transatlantic dimensions of evangelicalism as well as its close connections with education and popular secular cultural trends. His career seemed a nearly perfect model for millions of Americans who throughout the nineteenth century thought of themselves as evangelical Protestants, and his death late in 1899 also seemed to mirror the slow decline of that massive religious and cultural phenomenon.

• The most important collection of Moody's personal papers is located at Yale Divinity School. Other key manuscripts and printed sources are in the archives at the Northfield Schools, at Moody Bible Institute in Chicago, and at the Library of Congress. Numerous collections of Moody's sermons were published during his life. An example is L. T. Remlap, pseud. [Loomis T. Palmer], ed., *The Gospel Awakening . . .* (1883). Moody's youngest son, Paul, has written a revealing essay entitled *My Father: An Intimate Portrait of Dwight L. Moody* (1938). For a scholarly biography, see James F. Findlay, Jr., *Dwight L. Moody, American Evangelist: 1837–1899* (1969). Other relevant historical studies include Virginia Brereton, *Training God's Army: The American Bible School, 1880–1940* (1990); and George Marsden, *Fundamentalism and American Culture: The Shaping of Twentieth Century Evangelicalism, 1870–1925* (1980).

JAMES F. FINDLAY, JR.

MOODY, Harriet Converse (18 Mar. 1857–22 Feb. 1932), entrepreneur and patron of the arts, was born in Parkman, Ohio, the daughter of William Mason Tilden, a livestock broker, and Harriet Converse. William Tilden moved his family to Chicago circa 1867. Educated at home by her mother, Harriet later attended the Howland School, a Quaker institution in Union Springs, New York. She continued her education at Cornell University, where she earned a degree in English literature in 1876. Enrolling at the Women's Medical College of Philadelphia, she returned to Chicago after one year, made her debut, and married Edwin Brainard, a lawyer. The marriage was not a success, and the Brainards were divorced in the 1880s.

The death of William Tilden, whose business had failed, left Harriet with responsibility for her mother, an invalid. In 1889 Harriet became a schoolteacher in Chicago, including among her students Alice Corbin (Henderson), later associate editor of *Poetry* magazine. In 1892 she became a graduate student in the Department of English at the University of Chicago. To support her mother, Harriet began a series of culinary experiments with chicken salad and gingerbread in 1889, leading to her establishment of the Home Delicacies Association, a catering and restaurant enterprise that was a Chicago institution for nearly forty years. She marketed Home Delicacies products at Marshall Field and Company, the Field Museum cafeteria, and the tea room of the Chicago Little Theatre. She maintained a branch at Selfridge's in London. She served clubs and corporations; she stocked Pullman dining cars. Her restaurants, including Le Petit Gourmet on North Michigan Avenue, enjoyed the highest reputation. Home Delicacies offered high-quality homestyle food, preserving the ceremony of dining within the efficient modern household and despite the ascendant kitchenette.

In 1899 Harriet met poet William Vaughn Moody, professor of English at the University of Chicago. Eleven years Harriet's junior, Will Moody shared Harriet's devotion to poetry and to spirituality. Each found an idealization of gender in the other. Their friendship led to marriage in 1909, shortly before Will Moody died of brain cancer. Thereafter Harriet devoted herself to the arts, especially poetry, and to business. Moody became a founding supporter of *Poetry* magazine, contributing Will Moody's "I Am the Woman" to an otherwise novitiate first number. She soon emerged as saloniere and patron of the Chicago literary renaissance. Her talents in business, her generosity, and her commitment to modern art coalesced in an extraordinary array of friendships with writers, musicians, and visual artists. Her skilled networking and articulate critical judgment put her in a strong position to advance the careers of friends. Her large home on the near South Side provided space for guests to live and work; her chauffeur routinely met new arrivals at Union Station. Dinner parties and late-night poetry readings in her drawing room became legendary. Direct, warm, and a brilliant conversationalist, Moody befriended and advised Edwin Arlington Robinson, Edna St. Vincent Millay, Countee Cullen, Richard Eberhart, Amy Lowell, Vachel Lindsay, Hart Crane, Carl Sandburg, Yone Noguchi, Padraic Colum, Edgar Lee Masters, James Stephens, John Masefield, Walter de la Mare, and others. She brought Robinson's "Eros Turanos" to *Poetry*. Her friendships with Robert Frost, from early in his career, and with Rabindranath Tagore, preceding his Nobel Prize and readership in the United States, were notably influential. Not only was her friendship a source of inspiration, but she also helped both poets with decisions that shaped their careers. In 1920 she opened a series of poetry readings at Le Petit Gourmet. Titled Les Petits Jeux Floraux, the readings brought Frost, Lindsay, Sandburg, and Colum yearly; other readers included Maxwell Bodenheim, Countee Cullen, Alfred Kreymborg, Percy MacKaye, Edna St. Vincent Millay, Amy Lowell, Harriet Monroe, Ridgely Torrence, and Margery Swett. Other forms of patronage followed from this work. She arranged readings at a number of universities, including the University of Chicago and Cornell University, where she served from 1912 to 1922 as the only female trustee. Her apartment in Greenwich Village, her farm in West Cummington, Massachusetts, and her summer retreat at Mackinac Island all welcomed visiting artists. Her salon, in effect an art colony, moved with her, offering material means for creative work before public and foundation grants were generally available.

In her later years, Moody's commitment to business took second place to her passion for the arts. In 1929 the Home Delicacies Association failed. Moody supported herself in her last three years by teaching and writing, including *Mrs. William Vaughn Moody's Cook Book* (1931). She died in Chicago.

Moody's name became a byword in the restaurant business in Chicago and beyond; more important to her own sense of fulfillment, she took a position of understated leadership in the Chicago literary renaissance and the *Poetry* magazine circle and thus contributed significantly to the growth of modernism. What sets her apart from other philanthropists is the fact that she was a self-made woman who earned her money largely to give it away.

• Primary sources include the Harriet Brainard Moody Papers and the William Vaughn Moody Papers, University of Chicago. William Vaughn Moody's letters to Harriet Moody are in the Huntington Library, San Marino, Calif. Harriet Moody's letters to Houghton Mifflin Co. are in the Houghton Library, Harvard University. For a discussion of Moody's career, see Susan Albertine, "Cakes and Poetry: The Career of Harriet Moody," in *A Living of Words: American Women in Print Culture*, ed. Susan Albertine (1995). For a biographical memoir, see Olivia Howard Dunbar, *A House in Chicago* (1947). Additional information on Moody can be found in William Vaughn Moody, *Letters to Harriet*, ed. Percy MacKaye (1935); Harriet Monroe, *A Poet's Life: Seventy Years in a Changing World* (1938); Martin Halpern, *William Vaughn Moody* (1964); Maurice F. Brown, *Estranging Dawn: The Life and Works of William Vaughn Moody* (1973); Eleanor Ruggles, *The West-Going Heart: A Life of Vachel Lindsay* (1959); Arnold Grade, ed., *Family Letters of Robert and Elinor Frost* (1972); Lawrance Thompson, *Robert Frost: The Years of Triumph, 1915–1938* (1970); and Dale Kramer, *Chicago Renaissance: The Literary Life of the Midwest, 1900–1930* (1966). An obituary is in the *Chicago Daily Tribune*, 25 Feb. 1932.

SUSAN ALBERTINE

MOODY, James (31 Dec. 1744–6 Apr. 1809), British spy during the American Revolution, was born in Little Egg Harbor, New Jersey, the son of John Moody, a merchant, and a woman known only as Mrs. Holden, a widow. Although James's parents were Anglican the community was predominantly Quaker, and he is assumed to have been educated in the community's Quaker school. As a young adult he made his way to Knowlton Township, Sussex County. There he married Elisabeth Brittain, with whom he had three children. He farmed on five hundred acres given to him by his father, successfully raising sheep and cattle.

For two years after the Revolution's outbreak Moody took no side in the struggle. He was harassed, however, for not accepting the resolutions of the local Committee of Safety or swearing allegiance to the revolutionary government, and on one occasion he was assaulted by men from the committee. On 28 March 1777 a body of rebel militia fired on him as he walked in his fields. He escaped unharmed and within weeks, with seventy-three of his neighbors, made his way behind British lines and joined Cortland Skinner's New Jersey Volunteers, a Loyalist militia regiment commissioned in 1776 by British general William Howe.

Most of Moody's war service entailed deep penetration into enemy territory and more narrow escapes from death or capture than one should count on. Initially his task was to recruit Loyalists behind enemy lines, and in the summer of 1777 he recruited at least five hundred for the king's cause. By 1778 he was also going out with small raiding parties to capture enemy officials and military officers. In June, for example, he took a raiding party of about twenty men into Monmouth County, captured three field officers, two captains, and an assortment of other ranks, destroyed a sizable depot of arms and ammunition, and seized a considerable amount of stores. Despite a fierce skirmish, including a bayonet charge by Moody and his men on forces greatly outnumbering them, they made their way back to British lines.

In October Moody was sent behind enemy lines to gain information on George Washington's army. Again in November he crossed into enemy territory in Pennsylvania to gather information on General John Sullivan's army, from there to Morris County to gather information on Washington's troops, and then on to General Horatio Gates's camp, gaining "the exactest information" on his present and anticipated troop strength. Moody finally made his way back behind British lines, where he was becoming recognized as, in Governor William Franklin's words, "the most distinguished Partizan we then had."

In May 1780 Moody was again behind enemy lines rescuing prisoners from rebel jails and seizing a sizable number of officials and officers. On 17 July, on attempting to return to the British lines, he unsuspectingly stumbled on a Patriot assault on a Loyalist stronghold at Bull's Ferry, New Jersey, and was captured.

Moody was held in several prisons until transferred to West Point, where he was kept in a powder magazine, ankle deep in water and, despite requests from Washington and Benedict Arnold, shackled at the hands and ankles by the officer responsible for him. On 1 September he was transferred to Washington's camp to face court-martial. Because of infection the shackles were removed from his ankles. He was, however, confined in the center of the camp with a guard inside his room, one at the door outside, and four more within yards of the room. On 21 September, having somehow freed himself of his handcuffs, he managed to dash past the inside guard, seize the musket of the outside guard, and escape outdoors before the cry could be raised. He passed himself off as just another Patriot shouldering a musket in search of the villain Moody long enough to find a way past the sentries and make his way back to New York.

Early in 1781, having been promoted to lieutenant, he was asked to go into enemy territory again, to capture Washington's mail. In an eleven-day foray in March, Moody, with a guide and two others, captured the mail and the post rider and returned safely; however, two of the four died not long after from the exposure and hardship of the raid. In May Moody was again sent out for dispatches. This time he was informed on and ambushed. Escaping from one group, he ran into seventy other militia, almost all of whom seemed to have fired at him from a distance of about fifty yards; his clothes were riddled, his hat drilled through, he was grazed, but, remarkably, he escaped back to New York. Almost as remarkable, he was away again the next night, avoided capture once more, managed to seize the mail, and was back in New York by 4 June.

In November Moody and his younger brother John were sent to break into the statehouse in Philadelphia to steal secret congressional papers and plans. They were betrayed. Moody, by hiding in a cornstack for two days, managed to escape. His brother did not and was executed shortly after. Moody's war had ended.

Moody's first wife had died some time after 1778. In 1782 he married Jane Lynson, the widow of a Loyalist. Shortly after, he accepted the offer of a passage to England, where in the fall of that year he wrote *Narrative of His Exertions and Sufferings in the Cause of Government*. Widely read, the narrative awakened much sympathy for the Loyalist cause. In that year the British government awarded him an annual pension of £100. In the following year the Loyalist Claims Commission granted him £1,608, almost all that he had claimed, for property lost and £1,330 for expenses incurred in raising men. On the disbanding of the New Jersey Volunteers he received half pay as lieutenant.

In 1785 Moody left England and in the following year settled in Sissiboo, in southwestern Nova Scotia. He became a prominent member of the community, a leading force in the Church of England, and a builder of ships and mills. He became a member of the Royal Nova Scotia Regiment, a magistrate, a colonel of the militia, and a road commissioner, all symbols of status and good standing with the government in Nova Scotia's small society. He served as a member of Nova Scotia's legislative assembly from 1793 to 1806. His remaining years, however, were difficult ones. He was in very poor health. He had to mortgage his property to cover the debts of his son, John, who then died tragically at sea. Moody died in Sissiboo. His widow, pleading straitened circumstances, had to petition Britain for a continuation of his pension. She was granted £81 annually.

• The most detailed and vivid account of Moody's wartime experience is to be found in his own *Lieut. James Moody's Narrative of His Exertions and Sufferings in the Cause of Government since the Year 1776* (1782; rev. ed., 1783), which has been reprinted, with notes by C. I. Bushnell, as *Narrative of the Exertions and Sufferings of Lieut. James Moody* (1865), and with an introduction by W. S. MacNutt, in *Acadiensis* 1, no. 2 (1971–1972). For more on the Loyalist struggle in New Jersey, see A. E. Jones, *The Loyalists of New Jersey: Their Memorials, Petitions, Claims, Etc., from English Records* (1927), and William S. Stryker, *"The New Jersey Volunteers" in the Revolutionary War* (1887). Paul H. Smith, *Loyalists and Redcoats: A Study in British Revolutionary Policy* (1964), will help explain the British use of and attitude toward Moody, his men, and his regiment. Robert M. Calhoon, *The Loyalists in Revolutionary America, 1760–1781*, is an outstanding study of the Loyalists. Although Moody had a distinguished career and reputation in Nova Scotia, his life there has a sense of epilogue. Details on his life in Nova Scotia can be found in I. W. Wilson, *A Geography and History of the County of Digby, Nova Scotia* (1900); details on the Loyalists in Nova Scotia can be found in Neil MacKinnon, *This Unfriendly Soil: The Loyalist Experience in Nova Scotia* (1986).

NEIL MACKINNON

MOODY, Paul (21 May 1779–8 July 1831), mechanic and manufacturer, was born in Newbury, Massachusetts, the son of Captain Paul Moody, a prosperous revolutionary war veteran, and Mary (maiden name unknown). Captain Moody sent most of his sons to Governor Dummer Academy and two to Dartmouth College, but Paul was eager to earn his living. At age twelve he began his career in textile manufacture by obtaining training from workmen at the Newbury woolen factory of John and Arthur Scholfield. The factory, operated by two English weavers, housed handlooms on which Moody received his training. By age sixteen he had become a practical weaver; he then found employment with Jacob Perkins of Newburyport, who had developed a machine for making nails. The business was a success and moved to Amesbury Massachusetts, in 1798, as did Moody. Under Perkins's tutelage Moody learned to make carding machinery, which was installed in mills in various parts of New England. He married Susan Morrill of Amesbury (recorded variously as in either 1798 or 1800), with whom he had several children, including three who survived him.

Shortly after his marriage Moody entered partnership with Ezra Worthen in order to establish a satinet (a cotton-and-wool fabric) mill in Amesbury. He worked as a mechanic for this firm for about fourteen years. This partnership and his earlier employment prepared him for the important contributions he would make to cotton manufacture after 1812. Knowing how handlooms worked, how to make carding machinery, and how to shape metal, he now learned of the nature of cotton fiber and how it needed to be processed to produce good yarn and fabric.

When Francis Cabot Lowell and other investors formed the Boston Manufacturing Company in Waltham, Massachusetts, they sought someone to help them set up textile machinery and start a mill, and Perkins suggested Moody. In 1814 Moody moved to Waltham with his family and began to work for Lowell, who had recently returned from abroad; he had toured English and European textile mills and returned with extensive knowledge of cotton manufacture. By 1812 Lowell had begun to develop a water-powered loom based on the Miller wiper loom patented in England. The loom used a cam to make the beater move back and forth against the forming fabric. Although Lowell had developed a model loom prior to Moody's arrival in Waltham, it was not operable. Under Moody's supervision the machine shop became a laboratory for improving the loom and developing associated equipment, such as warpers and dressers, which would make the mechanism commercially viable. By 1813 a model and two additional looms had been constructed in the shop, but it took autumn 1814 to make them truly operable. The patent for the loom was issued to Lowell, but subsequent improvements were patented by Moody.

The development of the power loom had an enormous impact on the textile industry. It enabled manufacturers to produce fabrics of simple construction in tremendous quantity and to compete with British manufacturers after the War of 1812. The work Moody performed on the loom, warper, and dresser initiated his many innovations in textile technology; he also suggested significant improvements in dressing, spinning, and doubling. In 1818 Moody's improvement to the Waltham dresser replaced faulty wooden rollers with rollers of soapstone. In 1819 and 1820 he improved the double speeder, according to calculations and suggestions made by Lowell. Between 1819 and 1823 the significance of the patents is evidenced in the exclusivity of the equipment to the industry. Moody also developed a method for spinning filling directly on the bobbin. Moody developed numerous minor inventions between 1814 and 1823 while working with Lowell; his innovations influenced incalculably the growth and development of the textile industry in New England, especially in Massachusetts.

In 1821 Moody, Kirk Boott, Patrick T. Jackson, John Boott, and Warren Dutton formed the Merrimack Manufacturing Company, intending to establish a firm in East Chelmsford, Massachusetts. In 1823 the manufacturers paid Boston Manufacturing Company $75,000 for all their machinery patterns and for Moody's services. This transaction enabled Moody to move to East Chelmsford (now Lowell), Massachusetts, and establish a machine shop there. He was also superintendent of the Merrimack Company and supervised the manufacture of the machines. His new responsibilities left him little time for invention, and other than the introduction of belts for transmission of power to line shafting, he introduced no more innovations to the industry. Moody died in Lowell after a brief illness.

• Several early works described Moody's influence on developing textile technology, including Samuel Bachelder, *Introduction and Early Progress of the Cotton Manufacture of the United States* (1863); Nathan Appleton, *Introduction of the Power Loom, and the Origin of Lowell* (1858); James Montgomery, *A Practical Detail of Cotton Manufacture of the United States of America* (1840); and J. D. Van Slyck, *Representatives of New England Manufactures* (1879). More detailed descriptions of the technology and his contributions are in David Jeremy, *Transatlantic Industrial Revolution: The Diffusion of Textile Technologies between Britain and America, 1790–1830s* (1981); and George Sweet Gibb, *The Saco-Lowell Shops Textile Machinery Building in New England 1813–1949* (1950).

GAIL FOWLER MOHANTY

MOODY, William Henry (23 Dec. 1853–2 July 1917), cabinet officer, member of Congress, and justice of the Supreme Court, was born in Newbury, Massachusetts, the son of Henry Lord Moody and Melissa Emerson, farmers. Moody graduated from Phillips Academy, Andover, Massachusetts, in 1872 and received an A.B. from Harvard in 1876. He studied at the Harvard Law School for four months and then left to read law in the office of Richard Henry Dana (1815–1882). After eighteen months of study, Moody was admitted to the Massachusetts bar in April 1878.

Moody's law practice in Haverhill, Massachusetts, soon took him into politics. He became a member of the city school board and served as city solicitor from 1888 to 1890. He was appointed U.S. district attorney for the state's Eastern District in 1890 and prosecuted the murder case of Lizzie Borden for allegedly butchering her parents in 1892. Although Borden was acquitted, Moody came out of the case better known and respected. Running as a Republican, he won a special election in November 1895 to fill the unexpired term of William Cogswell (1838–1895), who had died. By this time he had become friendly with Theodore Roosevelt (1858–1919), who called him a "very good young fellow."

In the House of Representatives, Moody gained attention for his skill in debate and his mastery of legislative detail. By his second term he was chosen for a seat on the powerful Appropriations Committee. His closeness to Roosevelt made him a likely choice for a cabinet position after Roosevelt became the president in September 1901. In May 1902 Roosevelt named Moody secretary of the navy to succeed John D. Long.

During the next two years, Moody worked hard for Roosevelt's organizational reforms of the navy, a buildup of the size of the fleet, and improved naval readiness. He recommended unsuccessfully that a general naval staff be created. Roosevelt said that the secretary "has run the Navy Department as it must be run." The friendship between Moody and Roosevelt grew stronger during this period.

When Attorney General Philander C. Knox left the Department of Justice in June 1904, Roosevelt named Moody as his replacement. For the next two years, Moody was one of the president's closest advisers on a variety of domestic issues. He played a large role in the legislative struggle to enact the Hepburn Law regulating railroads in 1906.

Moody's work in the Justice Department dealt primarily with the trust issue that was high on Roosevelt's agenda. The attorney general personally conducted the prosecution of the Beef Trust in 1904–1905 and argued the case to victory before the Supreme Court in *Swift and Company v. United States* (1905). Moody agreed with Roosevelt's distinction between "good" trusts that, in the president's mind, served the public interest, such as United States Steel and International Harvester, and "bad" trusts, such as Standard Oil, that failed to fulfill a socially useful purpose. Moody accepted Roosevelt's strategy of private arrangements instead of antitrust prosecutions for U.S. Steel and International Harvester. For Standard Oil, however, the Justice Department pursued an aggressive enforcement of antitrust law.

By 1906 a weary Moody wanted to retire from public life. For some time Roosevelt had been trying to fill a vacancy on the Supreme Court with William Howard Taft. After Taft definitively declined in August 1906, Roosevelt considered a southern Democrat for the opening and then turned to the more ideologically compatible Moody as a man who was a "follower of [Alexander] Hamilton [1755–1804] and [John] Marshall and not a follower of [Thomas] Jefferson and [John C.] Calhoun." Moody was appointed on 12 December 1906, and the Senate confirmed his nomination five days later.

Moody's service on the Supreme Court was anticlimactic. By April 1909 he had begun to suffer from rheumatism that first crippled and then incapacitated him. Before illness overtook him, he gave promise of being the kind of progressive jurist that Roosevelt had hoped he would be. In the First Employers' Liability Case (1908), Moody dissented from the Court's view that the Federal Employers' Liability Act was unconstitutional. The power to regulate interstate commerce, Moody contended, gave the federal government the power to oversee relations between workers and their employers. Other cases indicated that more than his colleagues on the Court Moody's liberal nationalism would have led him to uphold the federal government's power of regulation. On the other hand, he sustained the right of New Jersey courts to comment when a criminal defendant refused to testify in his own behalf in *Twining v. State of New Jersey* (1908).

As Moody's illness worsened after 1908, his participation in the work of the Supreme Court declined. To facilitate his retirement, Congress enacted a law in 1910 granting him retirement benefits despite his few years of service. Moody remained active as long as his strength permitted. During 1910 he advised Roosevelt about constitutional issues and sent him speech material that Roosevelt used when he articulated the doctrine of the powerful regulatory state to pursue social justice that became known as the New Nationalism. Roosevelt regarded Moody's illness and his resignation from the Court in 1910 as "a real calamity from the public standpoint."

Moody lived for seven more years in increasing pain, unable to move his arms or legs or to read and write. He had never married, and his sister nursed him until his death. Late in his life he told a friend that he had forsaken the "pure individualism" he had learned years before in college and now believed that those who wanted to lessen the effects of industrialism "were not mere meddling intruders upon private business." By the time Moody died in Haverhill, Massachusetts, he was a forgotten figure.

Moody's personal tragedy was a great loss for the cause of moderate progressive reform during the first decade of the twentieth century. His appointment to the Supreme Court represented Roosevelt's attempt to leave a judicial legacy for the regulatory economic policies of the Square Deal. Moody's resignation allowed the new president, Taft, another appointment to take the Court in a conservative direction. Roosevelt said of Moody's departure, "there is not a public servant, at this particular time, that the public could so ill afford to lose." The record of public service that Moody provided in Congress, the cabinet, and on the Supreme Court offered striking evidence of the accuracy of Roosevelt's verdict.

• Moody's personal papers are at the Manuscript Division, Library of Congress, and at the Haverhill (Mass.) Public Library. The papers of Felix Frankfurter, Theodore Roosevelt, and Elihu Root at the Library of Congress contain additional information on Moody. For an example of his writing, see William Henry Moody, "Constitutional Powers of the Senate: A Reply," *North American Review* 174 (Mar. 1902): 386–94, and his *Annual Reports* as secretary of the navy and attorney general. Contemporary assessments are Louis A. Coolidge, "The New Secretary of the Navy," *Independent* 54 (Mar. 1902): 744–46, and Isaac Marcosson, "Attorney General Moody and His Work," *World's Work* 13 (Nov. 1906): 8190–94. Paul T. Heffron, "Theodore Roosevelt and the Appointment of Mr. Justice Moody," *Vanderbilt Law Review* 18 (Mar. 1965): 545–68 and "Secretary Moody and Naval Administrative Reform, 1902–1904," *American Neptune* 29 (Jan. 1969): 30–53, treat aspects of Moody's life. There is no published biography of Moody, but James F. Watts, Jr., "William Moody," in *The Justice of the United States Supreme Court 1789–1969*, vol. 3, *1801–1822*, ed. Leon Friedman and Fred L. Israel (1969), and Judith R. McDonough, "William Henry Moody" (Ph.D. diss., Auburn Univ., 1983), provide informed treatments of his career. An obituary is in the *New York Times*, 2 July 1917.

LEWIS L. GOULD

MOODY, William Vaughn (8 July 1869–17 Oct. 1910), poet, playwright, and educator, was born in Spencer, Indiana, the son of Francis Burdette Moody and Henriette Emily Stoy. Prior to Will's birth, Burdette Moody was captain and part-owner of two Mississippi riverboats, one of which was confiscated by the Confederacy at the outbreak of the Civil War. Never recovering from this financial setback, "Captain Moody" dutifully abandoned the freedom and adventure of the river to work the rest of his life as a secretary in the Stoy family's ironworks at New Albany, Indiana, where Will spent his childhood. Henriette, an accomplished artist but an invalid for much of her life, nourished Will's interest in the arts and encouraged his devotion to Methodism. From this environment, Will developed a respect for the Protestant ethic, which later warred with his humanistic values and devotion to freedom.

Following the traumatizing deaths of his mother and father in 1884 and 1886, respectively, and his graduation as valedictorian of a class of twenty, Moody spent one tedious year teaching in a rural Indiana public school to earn money for college, then entered Riverview Academy, Poughkeepsie, New York, for preparatory training in the classics, earning the highest academic average in the school's history. In September 1889 he entered Harvard, where he completed his course work in three years. During that same period he enjoyed a rich literary life, contributing poems and essays to the college literary magazines. While still a freshman, he was elected to serve on the editorial board of the *Harvard Monthly* and became part of a circle of young intellectuals that included Robert Herrick, George Santayana, Norman Hapgood and Hutchins Hapgood, and Robert Morss Lovett. Yet to most of his colleagues Moody seemed defensive and enigmatic, combining, as one classmate noted, "intellectual candor and personal reserve in a way that many found bewildering." But Robert Morss Lovett, who perhaps knew Moody best, described him as especially companionable to intellectuals "who like himself had seen the vision and not been disobedient to it." During his senior year Moody enjoyed what was destined to be the first of many stimulating trips to Europe, this time as the tutor to Ingersoll Bowditch; he returned in the spring of 1893 to graduate second in his class and be elected class poet.

After two more years at Harvard, during which he earned an M.A. in English and served as an instructor in the English department, Moody accepted an appointment as instructor of English at the University of Chicago, a position to which he brought his customary energy and dedication. In addition to his heavy teaching load, Moody continued to develop as a poet and editor, producing scholarly editions of Bunyan, Coleridge, Milton, Scott, and Pope, among others. After the stimulation of Harvard, however, the Chicago environment seemed bleak and culturally shallow. Also, teaching proved uncongenial. Students found him distant, labeling him "The Man in the Iron Mask," and the time spent preparing lectures and grading papers seemed more and more a betrayal of his aesthetic ideals. "I cannot do it," he ultimately told his departmental chairman. "At every lecture I slay a poet." By 1897 he had fallen into the pattern of teaching but half of the year, using the other half for travel and writing, and during 1900 he did not teach at all. Finally, in 1902, with the success of *A History of English Literature*, coauthored with Lovett, Moody achieved economic independence from teaching. Though he remained a member of the University of Chicago faculty until 1908, the last eight years of his life were devoted to literary projects and extensive travel within the United States and abroad.

Moody's first published volume of poetry was *The Masque of Judgment* (1900), a closet drama consisting of a prelude and five acts written in blank verse interspersed with songs. Conveyed primarily through a dialogue between the archangels Raphael, mankind's champion, and Uriel, initially an apologist for the wrathful Calvinistic God, the action dramatizes man's rebellion against the Creator, who, impatient with sin and willfulness, demands that His subjects surrender their free will. When most refuse, God destroys them and Himself, having failed to realize that only through human struggle is temporal and spiritual perfection achieved. Moody described the *Masque* as "a vindication of individual will and passion as a means of salvation."

For *Poems* (1901), Moody drew upon a decade of work, choosing twenty-three selections that represent a variety of poetic voices and techniques and range chronologically from the medieval allegories of his Harvard years to statements on the American scene at the turn of the century. Arranged thematically, most, like "The Daguerreotype" and "Good Friday Night," are quite introspective, while some, like "Gloucester Moors" and "Ode in Time of Hesitation," express outrage at social or political evils such as capitalistic exploitation and the annexation of the Philippines. Ironically, the poems of social protest, least typical of Moody, have been most frequently anthologized and seem most likely to keep his reputation as a poet alive. After the publication of *Poems*, Moody turned his attention largely to drama.

The Fire-Bringer (1904), a three-act verse drama based on the Promethean myth, was conceived as the first of a trilogy, *The Masque of Judgment* to be the second. Written in blank verse interspersed with songs, the play celebrates the rebellion of Prometheus, who accepts punishment at the hands of Zeus to save humankind, thereby providing a humanistic model of dignity and self-assertion that humans must follow to reach ultimate fulfillment. Based on Greek models, *The Fire-Bringer* was written for stage performance but never produced.

The prose style and contemporary setting of *The Great Divide*, produced in 1906, were departures for Moody; however, the play's emphasis on human fulfillment was not. As the title suggests, the action focuses on the failed marriage of a puritanical New Englander, Ruth Jordan, whose commitment to repentance and self-denial have led her to abandon her husband, Stephen Ghent, a generous but uninhibited and morally immature westerner who earned Ruth's hand by saving her from a rape in which he initially intended to participate. In the end, however, love and empathy triumph, allowing the couple to rise above their cultural conflicts and achieve a more fulfilling union. Featuring the actors Margaret Anglin and Henry Miller (1860–1926), *The Great Divide* proved to be one of the great critical and popular successes of its time, running for two years on the New York stage and repeating its success in London. Twice, it has been adapted for motion pictures. Moreover, because of its character complexity, authenticity of dialogue, and underlying sexual themes, the play contributed significantly to the movement toward realism in American drama.

Moody's last completed play, *The Faith Healer* (1910), was a failure. Written in prose and employing a contemporary rural setting, the play follows the fall and rise on Easter morning of the Christlike Ulrich Michaelis, who fears that his mystical healing power has been destroyed by his passion for Rhoda Williams. Ultimately, however, he triumphs over his doubts and the derision of scientific skeptics when he realizes that his power and passion are both divine gifts, vitalizing each other. *The Faith Healer* opened to poor reviews and had only a brief run in New York, even though in some ways it demonstrated Moody's growth as a dramatist. Critics generally agree that the play's realistic medium is incompatible with its spiritual message.

In 1908, with his health deteriorating, Moody was elected to the National Academy of Arts and Letters. The next year he married Harriet Brainerd, a businesswoman eleven years his senior, thereby ending a nine-year courtship carried on largely through correspondence. On their honeymoon in England, Moody experienced the onset of blindness caused by a brain tumor. He died in Colorado Springs in 1910, leaving unfinished the third play of his projected verse trilogy. In *The Death of Eve*, Moody had planned to dramatize the triumph of love and the reconciliation of God and humanity. Only one act was completed; yet, that fragment has been called Moody's "finest achievement" (Halpern, p. 168).

Since the early years of the twentieth century, when Moody was viewed as potentially a major voice in American literature, his reputation has dimmed considerably. The loftiness of his diction, his eclecticism, his fondness for myth, his ambitions for verse drama, and his faith in the perfectibility of humanity all seem alien to modern tastes and seem artificial, pretentious, and perhaps irrelevant. A minor poet and playwright, Moody's writings are chiefly available in anthologies and literary histories.

• Unpublished Moody papers are available at the Houghton Library at Harvard University, the Princeton University Library, and the University of Chicago Library. Other significant primary sources include John M. Manly, ed., *The Poems and Plays of William Vaughn Moody* (1912); Daniel Gregory Mason, ed., *Some Letters of William Vaughn Moody* (1913); Robert Morss Lovett, ed., *Selected Poems of William Vaughn Moody* (1931); and Percy MacKaye, ed., *Letters to Harriet* (1935). Major studies of Moody's life and works are David D. Henry, *William Vaughn Moody: A Study* (1934); Martin Halpern, *William Vaughn Moody* (1964); and Maurice F. Brown, *Estranging Dawn: The Life and Works of William Vaughn Moody* (1973).

RICHARD W. DOWELL

MOON, Lottie (12 Dec. 1840–24 Dec. 1912), missionary, was born Charlotte Digges Moon at "Viewmont," in Albemarle County, Virginia, the daughter of Edward Harris Moon and Anna Maria Barclay, plantation owners. Lottie was one of the best-educated women of the antebellum South. A graduate of Virginia Female Seminary at Botetourt Springs (later Hollins Institute), she took the master of arts degree in languages at Albemarle Female Institute, a pioneering school for women's education. As the Civil War came to a close, Moon worked on her parents' plantation and took occasional appointments in private schoolteaching.

Moon was baptized by the illustrious John A. Broadus at the Charlottesville, Virginia, Baptist church in 1858, beginning her pilgrimage as a Christian worker. Between 1866 and 1873 she taught school in Danville, Kentucky (1866–1873), and Cartersville, Georgia (1873). On 7 July 1873 she was appointed a missionary by the Southern Baptist Foreign Mission Board in Richmond, Virginia. She was to join her sister Edmonia as a missionary to China. The Baptists of Georgia were asked to support Lottie as those in Virginia supported Edmonia. Following Lottie's arrival in China in late 1873, the sisters became involved in the operation of a school for boys and evangelistic work. Edmonia's health steadily declined, and she fell prey to serious respiratory problems. In 1876 Edmonia and Lottie returned to the United States, Edmonia's missionary career at an end. In 1877, however, Lottie returned to China for a stay of more than thirty years.

Moon originally went to China to teach and assist the male missionary force of the Southern Baptist Foreign Mission Board. After seven years, however, she tired of managing a boarding school at Tengchow and moved to the interior of Shantung Province in 1885, establishing her base at Pingtu. From that central walled city, she conducted evangelistic work and started several schools in neighboring villages. Through political unrest, inadequate support from her sponsoring board, and ultimately starvation, Moon remained among the Chinese people. She became a strong advocate of the need for Westerners to wear Chinese clothing. While she urged increased American financial support for the missionary endeavor, she favored a self-support policy for the Chinese churches, and she lived a lifestyle of self-denial to provide a model for the new Christians.

Moon took a special interest in Chinese women, and she saw herself as an evangelist to women. She derived her appreciation of Chinese culture from Samuel W.

Williams's *The Middle Kingdom* (1883) and decided that she would affirm the culture rather than try to Westernize it. She was shocked by the Chinese practice of footbinding and determined to free women from degrading customs. Her strategies were personal evangelism and establishment of schools where girls could learn the art of motherhood and spousal relations on a more equitable plane. Her desire to improve the lot of women also extended to the missionary force. Originally, in the service of Southern Baptists, women were expected to assist men; Moon, however, urged the Southern Baptist Foreign Mission Board to raise their appreciation of women's work and even to grant women equal status with men in decisions on the mission field. Her classic article, "Missions," in the periodical *Religious Herald* (28 Aug. 1873) was the inspiration for eventual transformation of board policy.

Within the Baptist community in the United States, Moon is best remembered for her advocacy of the role of women in missions. Early in her overseas career she wrote that the advance of women in missions was the emerging issue of the era; in this regard Southern Baptists were following a trend set among other religious groups. Her reports from China and her sense of urgency for greater financial support were major catalysts in organizing the Women's Missionary Union of the Southern Baptist Convention in 1888. In 1887 she wrote, "What we want is not power, but simply combination in giving in order to elicit the largest possible giving." She held that contributions to missions flow naturally from one's Christian experience. An annual offering and day of prayer for overseas missions were named in her honor.

As time moved on, Moon gained the respect of most social classes in Tengchow City and Shantung Province. During the Chinese war with Japan in 1895, government officials prevailed upon missionary personnel to remain and give the impression of confidence and security. During the bombardment of her city, the general population in flight, Moon remained in her bombed home as a symbol of strength and resistance to the Japanese. She visited 118 villages in spite of the war.

In 1903–1904 Moon returned on furlough to the United States. She lectured widely across the Southeast and visited many churches. Her themes were respect for the Chinese people, sympathy for their progress, and requests for more American missionaries in China. She also managed to make important statements about the incongruity of sending missionaries to Africa while turning aside the needs of blacks in the United States.

Back in China for her last term, Moon faced her stiffest challenge in 1910–1911 with the downfall of the Manchu Dynasty and an outbreak of the plague. In addition, famine evolved in central China, and the effects were severe in Shantung Province. Moon was quarantined for a time, assisted with relief among the villages, and deprived herself of food to distribute to others. Her strength depleted, in December 1912, with the assistance of her nurse, Cynthia Miller, she departed reluctantly from China, and on board the ship *Manchuria* in the harbor of Kobe, Japan, she died.

One of the most intriguing episodes in Moon's life was her relationship with Crawford H. Toy. During Moon's studies at Albemarle Institute, Toy taught her English. He later went on to teach Hebrew and the Old Testament at Southern Baptist Theological Seminary in Louisville and was dismissed for heterodox views. Eventually he took an appointment at Harvard College. Toy and Moon had planned to marry in 1881, but Moon declined after studying the relevance of Toy's position on the origins of the Bible. The broken engagement led her to have a singular devotion to overseas missions, and to a personal rejection of what she called the "new theology," which she held to be an obstacle to the missionary spirit. She never married.

• Moon's correspondence is included in the archives of the Southern Baptist Foreign Mission Board in Richmond, Va., and additional material is in the archives of the Women's Missionary Union in Birmingham, Ala. Her own writings are few, typically periodical articles such as "Some Truths about China," *Seminary Magazine* 6 (1872): 128–31. Biographies include Una R. Lawrence, *Lottie Moon* (1927); Helen R. Monsell, *Her Own Way: The Story of Lottie Moon* (1958); and Catherine B. Allen, *The New Lottie Moon Story* (1980). A survey of her missionary work is in William R. Estep, *Whole Gospel, Whole World: The Foreign Mission Board of the Southern Baptist Convention, 1845–1995* (1994).

WILLIAM H. BRACKNEY

MOONEY, James (10 Feb. 1861–22 Dec. 1921), anthropologist, was born in Richmond, Indiana, the son of James Mooney and Ellen Devlin, Irish immigrants. His father died soon after his birth. His mother, who made her living as a housekeeper, supplemented her son's public school education with the legends of her native County Meath, stories about the former grandeur of Irish culture, and memories of alien British rule. She also raised him to be an ardent Catholic. After graduating from high school in 1878, Mooney taught public school for one year and then joined the staff of the Richmond *Palladium*. Charles Stewart Parnell, who toured the United States in late 1879 on behalf of the newly formed National Land League of Ireland, stirred Mooney's passion and idealism. Mooney helped organize a local Richmond chapter of the Land League and served as its first secretary. When the English Parliament passed land reform measures shortly thereafter, much of the original enthusiasm for the league dissipated. Mooney late in 1884 tried to gain employment at the Smithsonian Institution's Bureau of Ethnology (later renamed the Bureau of American Ethnology), which had been founded in 1879 to organize anthropological knowledge in the United States and thereby provide the national government with solutions to the vexing "Indian problem." A former mayor of Richmond introduced Mooney by letter to Major John Wesley Powell, the director, as "the young and devoted anthropological Irishman." Powell had no position to offer. Mooney visited Washington,

D.C., in April 1885 ostensibly on his way to explore the upper Amazon River. When Powell viewed the work Mooney had begun as a hobby ten years before, principally a tribal "synonymy" (a dictionary of tribal names and their synonyms; this eventually grew into the multiauthored *Handbook of American Indians North of Mexico* [1907]) and a very large and detailed map locating current and former homelands of North American Indians, he hired Mooney on the spot. Mooney became a resident of Washington, D.C., where he made his home and eventually married Ione Lee Gaut in 1897; they had six children.

Mooney remained deskbound at the Smithsonian his first two years in Washington. Under the tutelage of Dr. Washington Matthews, curator of the Army Medical Museum, contributor to bureau publications, and an Irish expatriate, Mooney learned that to be a successful ethnologist one must first gain the complete confidence of the informant. To achieve this confidence, one must respect the informant's culture in all its particulars. When stationed among the Sioux and later among the Navajos, Matthews had learned their languages. Under Matthews's influence, Mooney was meticulous in his research and would learn Cherokee, Kiowa, and some Comanche. He began his field studies during the summer of 1887 among the Eastern Cherokees of the Great Smoky Mountains. Years of research that followed among the Cherokees of eastern Tennessee and western North Carolina who had escaped forced removal in the 1840s led to the publication of the monographs "Sacred Formulas of the Cherokees" (*Seventh Annual Report of the Bureau of Ethnology* [1891]), "Myths of the Cherokee" (*Nineteenth Annual Report of the Bureau of American Ethnology* [1900]), and the posthumous *The Swimmer Manuscript: Cherokee Sacred Formulas and Medicinal Prescriptions* (1932), named for one of the shamans and traditional healers who resisted forced assimilation and preserved Cherokee traditions. As Mooney's biographer George Ellison has suggested, no greater testimonial can be offered to Mooney than the reliance placed on his work by anthropologists, general readers, and especially the various North American Indians he so diligently chronicled. In the 1970s Richard Mack Bettis, President of the Tulsa (Oklahoma) Cherokee Community stated that he and his contemporaries grew up holding the writings of James Mooney on the Cherokees in a reverence that is usually reserved for scripture.

Mooney is, however, best remembered for his research and writing on the Ghost Dance Religion. When he visited the Indian Territory in late 1890 to complete research among the western division of the Cherokees, he witnessed the ghost dance in full performance at the Cheyenne and Arapaho reservation. He spent the next three years conducting research throughout the West and writing on one of the greatest social and religious movements to affect American Indians in the nineteenth century. Mooney's "The Ghost Dance Religion and the Sioux Outbreak of 1890" (*Fourteenth Annual Report of the Bureau of Ethnology*, part 2 [1896]), is generally considered his greatest work and has earned him an enduring reputation among anthropologists and historians. It was the first accurate history of the religion, and it has served generations of ethnohistorians as a major source of evidence about the religion and the Sioux rebellion. In the book Mooney came very close to articulating a theory of revitalization expounded by anthropologists during the second half of the twentieth century. In lyrical prose he compared the religion of the Paiute prophet Wovoka to other religions, including Christianity.

While in the Indian Territory in 1890–1891, Mooney also encountered the burgeoning Peyote Religion at the Kiowa and Comanche reservation, detected what he believed to be a heraldic system among plains Indians borne out by designs that appeared on tipis and warrior shields, and found pictographic calendars of the Kiowas. A Kiowa storyteller would use the pictographs on his calendar as a sort of mnemonic device to recall the memories of that particular year or "winter." The Kiowa calendars (and those found among the Sioux about the same time) exposed the falsity of the assertion that American Indians were people without a "written" history.

Following completion of his manuscript on the Ghost Dance, he finished his "Calendar History of the Kiowa Indians" (*Seventeenth Annual Report of the Bureau of American Ethnology*, part 2 [1898]). Along with his other research interests, he would continually return to his heraldry studies and the Peyote Religion during the next thirty years, though he never finished books on either subject. Indeed, his sympathetic treatment of the peyote ritual led to his being barred from conducting research on Indian reservations. In 1918 he assisted in the chartering of the Native American Church of Oklahoma, an act that defied federal policy aimed to outlaw the use of peyote. For that reason, the Secretary of the Interior issued the ban of his research. He tried unsuccessfully for the remaining three years of his life to get the ban lifted. He died at his home in Washington, D.C., from the cumulative effects of heart disease that had first appeared in the early 1890s. A member of the first generation of professional anthropologists, he left behind a wealth of ethnographical and historical data.

• There are no James Mooney papers. The majority of his correspondence and all of his unfinished manuscripts and research notes may be found in the National Anthropological Archives, National Museum of Natural History, Smithsonian Institution, Washington, D.C. Mooney's other major writings include "The Cheyenne Indians," *Memoirs of the American Anthropological Association, 1905–1906* (1908), and "The Aboriginal Population of America North of Mexico," *Smithsonian Institution Miscellaneous Collections*, no. 52 (1928). A splendid, short biographical introduction by George Ellison is in James Mooney, *History, Myths, and Sacred Formulas of the Cherokees* (1992). Two biographies of Mooney exist, one by William Munn Colby, "Routes to Rainey Mountain: A Biography of James Mooney, Ethnologist" (Ph.D. diss., Univ. of Wisconsin, 1977), and L. G. Moses, *The Indian Man: A*

Biography of James Mooney (1984). See also Curtis M. Hinsley, Jr., *Savages and Scientists: The Smithsonian Institution and the Development of American Anthropology, 1846–1910* (1981). An obituary is in *American Anthropologist* 24 (1922): 209–14.

L. G. Moses

MOONEY, Thomas Joseph (8 Dec. 1882–6 Mar. 1942), labor leader, was born in Chicago, Illinois, the son of Bryan Mooney (also called Bernard), a coal miner, and Mary Hefferon (or Heffernan). Mooney lived in Washington, Indiana, until he was ten, when his father died. The family then moved to Holyoke, Massachusetts, where his mother found work in a paper mill as a ragsorter. Mooney left school at fourteen for a job in a local factory and in 1898 entered the iron molding trade. He joined the molders' union, a membership he maintained the rest of his life. With opportunities for employment scarce, he began traveling around the country, doing whatever work he could find. In 1907 his journeys took him to Europe, and there he discovered socialism. Returning home, he began drifting again, this time traveling as far west as Stockton, California. There he joined the Socialist party, worked for the presidential campaign of Eugene V. Debs, and spent a winter in Chicago learning more about the party.

In 1909 Mooney set off again, this time seeking to win a round-the-world trip in a subscription-selling contest sponsored by a socialist magazine. He lost, but so narrowly that the magazine paid his way to attend the International Socialist Congress in Copenhagen in 1910. He then returned to California, this time settling in San Francisco. He belonged briefly to the Industrial Workers of the World, but, finding them too sectarian, he aligned himself with the radical minority of the local Socialist party and served as circulation manager for their short-lived newspaper, *Revolt*. He ran on the Socialist party ticket for superior court judge in 1910 and for sheriff in 1911. He also helped organize molders for the tiny left-wing Syndicalist League of North America. He was married in 1911 to Rena Ellen Brink Hermann; they had no children.

In 1913 Mooney and Warren Knox Billings, another young radical, became involved in a bitter electrical workers' strike against the Pacific Gas and Electric Company. Billings was caught with a suitcase full of dynamite, and although Mooney does not appear to have been involved, he heard that he too was about to be arrested. He went underground for several months, then tried to slip away by boat, but was caught and charged with illegal possession of explosives. Three trials followed, the first two ending in hung juries and the third (1914) in his acquittal. Once released, Mooney resumed his labor activism.

By 1916, with World War I in Europe nearly two years old, many Americans were calling for a military build-up. Others, including many labor leaders and radicals, opposed the idea, arguing that it would only hasten the country's entry into what they saw as a corrupt and imperialist war. On 22 July 1916, during the period when Preparedness Day parades were being held throughout the country, a bomb exploded in the midst of San Francisco's parade, killing ten people and wounding forty more. Although there was almost no physical evidence, the press immediately blamed political radicals, while District Attorney Charles M. Fickert concluded that the bomb had been brought to the scene in a suitcase. With encouragement from the private detective at Pacific Gas and Electric who had tracked down Mooney and Billings in 1913, Fickert quickly arrested both men, along with Mooney's wife and several other people.

Billings, who was tried first, was found guilty of second-degree murder and sentenced to life imprisonment. Mooney's trial for first-degree murder followed in January 1917. A rancher named Frank Oxman, who had not appeared in the Billings trial, testified that he had seen both men carrying a suitcase near the bomb scene, and although his statement contradicted other prosecution testimony, Mooney was convicted and sentenced to the gallows. Subsequent investigations discredited Oxman's testimony, but under pressure from local business interests and the Hearst press, Fickert refused to reopen the case. In the meantime, Mooney's wife was tried (without Oxman's testimony) and acquitted.

Until Mooney's conviction, most of his support came from fellow radicals, in addition to a few public-minded lawyers, led by Bourke Cockran. Once the trial was over, however, Mooney's circle of supporters expanded to include a wide array of mainstream labor leaders, civil libertarians, reformers, public officials, and members of the general public. The case attracted worldwide attention, and when mobs in Petrograd stormed the American embassy to protest Mooney's conviction, President Woodrow Wilson urged the governor of California to consider giving Mooney a new trial. Some months later, at the suggestion of Colonel Edward House (Wilson's closest adviser), the case was reviewed by the Wickersham National Commission on Law Observance and Enforcement, which was studying labor strikes. On the basis of questions raised by the commission, Mooney's sentence was commuted to life imprisonment in November 1918.

Mooney was saved from execution, but he was still in San Quentin Prison, with no new trial on the horizon. For the next twenty years his supporters struggled to maintain public interest in the case and to win his freedom. They encountered innumerable political and legal obstacles, however, and Mooney's irascibility and distrust made their task more difficult. Nevertheless, they persevered; Frank Walsh, Mooney's attorney from 1923 to 1939, is said to have spent $50,000 of his own money in pursuing various appeals. In 1934 Upton Sinclair, running for governor, promised to set Mooney free if elected; this ray of hope disappeared when Sinclair was defeated. A U.S. Supreme Court decision on one of Mooney's appeals (*Mooney v. Holohan*, 1935) set important new precedents in federal habeas corpus proceedings, but Mooney remained a prisoner.

Mooney failed in a personal appeal to the California state legislature in 1938 and shortly thereafter was rejected for the last time by the U.S. Supreme Court. Finally, in January 1939, Governor Culbert L. Olson granted Mooney a pardon. (Billings was released from prison when his sentence was commuted ten months later, and he was officially pardoned in 1961.) Mooney had a brief tour as a labor hero and then sank into obscurity, burdened with debts, estranged from his wife, and suffering from bleeding ulcers. He died in San Francisco.

Mooney did not become a dissident hero by choice; there is no evidence that he had anything to do with the bombing that sent him to prison. Nor was he a hero by nature; his complaints and resentment strained the loyalty of his supporters almost to the breaking point. Nevertheless, his experience forced him into a hero's role, providing the beleaguered labor movement with a martyr and leading many ordinary citizens to conclude that the American system could be very unjust.

• Mooney's papers are in the Bancroft Library at the University of California, Berkeley, while documents relating to his trial are to be found in the papers of Fremont Older, also at Berkeley; the papers of Bourke Cockran, Frank P. Walsh, and the American Civil Liberties Union at the New York Public Library; the papers of the Governor's Office in the California State Archives, Sacramento; the Thomas McDade Collection and Warren K. Billings Papers, University of Wyoming, Laramie; the Warren K. Billings Papers, Library of Congress; the Joseph Labadie Collection, University of Michigan, Ann Arbor; and the American Civil Liberties Union Mooney Collection, Columbia University. Other archival collections containing Mooney documents are listed in the *National Union Catalog of Manuscripts*. See also Richard H. Frost, *The Mooney Case* (1968); Henry T. Hunt, *The Case of Thomas J. Mooney and Warren K. Billings* (1929); Ernest J. Hopkins, *What Happened in the Mooney Case* (1932); Wickersham Commission on Law Observance and Enforcement, *The Mooney-Billings Report* (1932); Curt Gentry, *Frame-Up: The Incredible Case of Tom Mooney and Warren Billings* (1967); and James McGurrin, *Bourke Cockran* (1948). An obituary is in the *New York Times*, 7 Mar. 1942.

SANDRA OPDYCKE

MOORE, Aaron McDuffie (6 Sept. 1863–29 Apr. 1923), physician, was born in Rosindale, Columbus County (now Bladen County), North Carolina, the son of Israel Moore, a free African-American farmer, and Eliza (maiden name unknown). Moore's family was of African-American, Native-American, and Caucasian descent and had owned land and farmed in the Columbus County area since the early nineteenth century. He worked on the family farm and attended the local public elementary schools available to African Americans between the harvesting and planting seasons. After completing the eighth grade he attended the Whitin Normal School in Lumberton, North Carolina, and then the normal school in Fayetteville, North Carolina. His schooling was interspersed with periods when he worked on his father's farm and taught in the county school.

In 1885 Moore enrolled in Shaw University, an African-American institution located in Raleigh, North Carolina. He entered the university's Leonard Medical School, which had opened in 1882, and completed the four-year curriculum in three years. In 1888 he took his examination for a North Carolina medical license along with thirty whites and nine other blacks. He passed his state examination, second in rank, and became the first African-American physician to practice in Durham, North Carolina. In 1889 Moore married Cottie S. Dancy, daughter of John C. Dancy, one of North Carolina's leading early African-American political figures. They had two children.

In 1888 Moore ran for county coroner but found whites so antagonistic to his campaign that he withdrew from the race and never again stood for elected office. Henceforth he directed his energies to his medical practice, various business and public enterprises for African-American self-improvement, and his Baptist church.

In October 1898 Moore, John Merrick, a Durham barber and businessman, and five other black community leaders met in Moore's medical office for the purpose of establishing an insurance company. African-American insurance companies were first organized in the American South in the mid-nineteenth century; white companies actively competed for African-American business during the mid- to late nineteenth century. In 1881, after a study by the Prudential Insurance Company that argued that there was an excessive loss rate on policies for African Americans, white insurance companies reduced the size of policies they were willing to write for blacks and significantly increased the premiums. This provided the opportunity for African-American companies to compete for business. Moore, Merrick, and their associates formed the North Carolina Mutual Life Insurance Company. Originally housed in Moore's medical office, the company benefited from his financial support and guidance. Moore served as its secretary-treasurer and medical director and, from 1919 to 1923, company president. Ultimately the company grew to become the largest African-American financial institution in the United States.

Durham's Lincoln Hospital, also founded by Moore, was granted a charter in February 1901. The facility was erected with a gift of $85,550 from Washington Duke, a noted businessman and philanthropist whose name Duke University carries. It had at first been proposed to add an African-American wing to the existing city hospital, but Moore opposed the idea, because he believed that adding a separate wing on a white hospital would not provide facilities for the practice of black physicians or for the training of black nurses. Duke had in mind erecting a monument on the campus of Trinity College (now Duke University) to the memory of African-American slaves for their loyalty during the Civil War. Moore, in cooperation with Dr. S. L. Warren and Merrick, convinced Duke that a hospital for the care of the descendants of the slaves would be more appropriate. The hospital opened as a

125-bed acute-care facility, with Moore as its superintendent. It served Durham's African-American community until the 1960s, when it merged with the white community hospital, Watts Hospital, to form Durham County General Hospital.

In 1895 Moore helped launch the Bull City Drug Company, a pharmacy staffed by a black pharmacist and designed to serve Durham's African-American community. In 1907 he helped found the Mechanics and Farmers Bank and served that institution as a member of its board of directors and as vice president. In 1913 he also helped establish the Durham Colored Library, which had begun with Moore's donations in the basement of the White Rock Baptist Church. Many people would not utilize a library located in the church, so Moore secured a building and enlisted city and county funds to support the facility and served as president of the library. Later in life Moore became deeply involved in the rural education movement for the black schoolchildren of North Carolina. In 1914 he personally paid the salary of North Carolina's first rural school inspector as an initial step in demonstrating the need for such a program. The inspector visited rural schools and recommended steps for improvement. Moore successfully petitioned for state funds to sustain the program and obtained a matching grant from the Rosenwald Foundation.

Moore was chairman of the Board of Trustees of Shaw University for ten years, a founder of the Durham Young Men's Christian Association, a trustee of the Colored Orphan Asylum, and chairman of the board of deacons, superintendent of the Sunday school, and member of the board of trustees of Durham's White Rock Baptist Church. He was president of the Baptist State Sunday School Convention and worked for the Lott Cary Foreign Missionary Convention and used funds he raised in the United States to travel to Haiti (at his own expense), where he founded the Haitian White Rock Baptist Church. During World War I he accepted an appointment as special agent and supervisor of Negro economics in North Carolina. He was influential in securing jobs for African Americans and assisting African-American farmers.

Moore died in Durham. His life was devoted to improving the status of African Americans through health care, self-help business enterprises, and the church.

• The definitive scholarly history of the North Carolina Mutual Life Insurance Company, and Moore's association with it, is Walter B. Weare, *Black Business in the New South: A Social History of the North Carolina Mutual Life Insurance Company* (1973). The founding of the Lincoln Hospital and its place in African-American health care are described in Charles D. Watts and Frank W. Scott, "Lincoln Hospital of Durham, N.C.: A Short History," *Journal of the National Medical Association* 57 (1965): 177–83; Mitchell F. Rice and Woodrow Jones, Jr., *Public Policy and the Black Hospital: From Slavery to Segregation to Integration* (1994); and *Charter of the Trustees of Lincoln Hospital, as Amended, and By-laws, Rules and Regulations of the Trustees of Lincoln Hospital*, 2 Feb. 1948, in possession of the Duke University Medical Center Library. Biographies of Moore appear in Vivian O. Sammons, *Blacks in Science and Medicine* (1990), and William S. Powell, *Dictionary of North Carolina Biography* (1994). An obituary is in the *Journal of the National Medical Association* 16 (1924): 72–74.

EDWARD C. HALPERIN

MOORE, Addison Webster (30 July 1866–25 Aug. 1930), philosopher, was born at Plainfield, Indiana, the son of John Sheldon Moore and Adaline Hockett, farmers. After completing his studies at Plainfield Academy, Moore turned down an offer to remain there as a teacher. He entered DePauw University, from which he received an A.B. degree in 1890 and an A.M. degree in 1893. In 1891 he married Ella E. Adams, whom he met at the university; they had one child.

In 1893 Moore began work toward a Ph.D. in philosophy at Cornell University, which was at that time a center of neo-Hegelian idealism. Similar to the absolute idealism then being taught by Josiah Royce at Harvard, this approach to philosophy emphasized conflict and dialectic. Its method involved the resolution of opposites through struggle and the preservation of their pertinent aspects within a higher synthesis. All this activity, the idealists argued, took place within a stable organic whole.

Even though idealism offered brilliant analyses of past cultures and institutions, Moore became convinced that it provided little in the way of plans of action for the future. He was interested in exploring a more experimental and future-oriented philosophical method. So when he learned that John Dewey had accepted a position at the University of Chicago, he moved there in order to be a part of the school of instrumental pragmatism that was growing up around Dewey. Dewey's work was already well known for its concern with practical action and experimental results. An added consideration in the move to Chicago was his wife's graduate work in English. The couple considered the University of Chicago more hospitable to women.

In 1898 the University of Chicago awarded Moore a Ph.D. degree and hired him as an instructor. In 1901 he took a leave of one year to study in Berlin. His doctoral dissertation, directed by Dewey and James R. Angell, was published in 1902 as *The Functional versus the Representational Theories of Knowledge in Locke's Essay*. A revised version was published the following year (in a larger work) as "Existence, Meaning, and Reality in Locke's Essay and in Present Epistemology."

In these essays Moore argued that reality is not separate from meaning and existence, as Locke had argued, but is constituted by it. Because Locke had identified reality with meanings or ideas, he was forced to find some way of connecting meanings to extramental existences. His solution was to appeal to a correspondence between meanings and existences supported by God or nature. Moore thought that

Royce and other absolute idealists faced similar problems. Since they held that movement and development are confined to meanings, they were unable to explain how such movement could reflect reality, which they characterized as static and completed. Moore's proposal was to treat reality as dynamic. Meaning and existence are aspects of reality, not reflections of some reality apart from them. They are intelligible only in the context of the reconstruction of lived, habitual responses. Meaning and existence are thus separated only in the context of a problem to be solved, and then only until the solution is reached. In March 1903 William James wrote to Dewey that "I have just read, with almost absurd pleasure, A. W. Moore's *Existence, Meaning and Reality*."

Moore was promoted to assistant professor in 1902, to associate professor in 1904, and professor in 1909. He was elected president of the Western Philosophical Association in 1911 and president of the American Philosophical Association in 1917. During 1918 he was a lecturer at Harvard University.

Moore played an important role in the development of what William James termed the "Chicago School" of instrumentalist pragmatism. The school was instrumentalist in that it treated concepts, institutions, and even logical objects as tools by means of which human beings adjust to evolving conditions. It was pragmatic in that it emphasized the practical bearings that, it insisted, philosophical debate must evince in order to be meaningful.

In *Pragmatism and Its Critics*, published in 1910, Moore sought to defend pragmatism from its critics as well as to develop its central themes of instrumentalism, experimentalism, and practical relevance. This, his single book-length monograph, was well received as the most authoritative volume, apart from Dewey's own, to come out of the Chicago School. Several of its chapters, including "Truth Value," "Pragmatism and Its Critics," "Professor Perry on Pragmatism," "Pragmatism and Solipsism," "The Social Character of Habit and Attention," "The Ethical Aspect," and "The Pragmatic 'Universal,'" had previously appeared in professional journals.

Moore's presidential address at the 1917 meeting of the American Philosophical Association, published as "The Opportunity of Philosophy," took dead aim at the position advanced by A. O. Lovejoy, his immediate predecessor in that office. Moore argued that Lovejoy's positivism, his attempt to reduce the diversity of philosophical inquiry in order to render philosophy one of the hard sciences, was misguided. Rather than "attempting to substitute scientific concepts for values, or conversely," he argued, philosophy ought to "proclaim science as the method of its values." By this he meant that both the subject matter and the methods of science should be utilized as tools for the formation of values. He argued that his view would avoid two extremes: first, Lovejoy's view that the natural sciences offer a paradigm for all other types of knowing; and second, the view that science ought to be the servant of supernatural or "spiritual" values.

Following the death of Moore's wife in 1924, his health began to deteriorate. On the advice of his physician, he retired as professor emeritus in 1929. Despite his weakened condition, he completed a 6,000-mile motor tour of Europe. He died of pneumonia following a stroke in London, on his way from the Continent to attend an international philosophical conference at Oxford.

On 8 November 1930 Moore's life and work were commemorated in a memorial service held at the University of Chicago. Moore's colleague George Herbert Mead wrote of him that he "became in the philosophic world after Mr. Dewey the most important and most authoritative member of the so-called Chicago school." Like his mentor and friend Dewey, Moore took it as a principal task to deliver philosophy from both arcane speculation, at one extreme, and subservience to the physical sciences, at the other. His was a vigorous philosophy that called for the ongoing intelligent reconstruction of lived experience.

• Some of Moore's papers are in Special Collections at Dartmouth College Library. Other important essays by Moore include "Some Logical Aspects of Purpose," in *Studies in Logical Theory*, 2d ser., vol. 11 (1903), pp. 341–82; "Bergson and Pragmatism," *Philosophical Review* 21 (July 1912): 397–414; and "Reformation of Logic," in *Creative Intelligence: Essays in the Pragmatic Attitude* (1917), pp. 70–117. Sources of information about Moore's life and work include Elizabeth Flower and Murray G. Murphey, *A History of Philosophy in America* (1977); Darnell Rucker, *The Chicago Pragmatists* (1969); "Addison Webster Moore: Memorial Service," *University Record* (Univ. of Chicago), Jan. 1931, pp. 45–50; and Benjamin Wolstein, "Addison Webster Moore: Defender of Instrumentalism," *Journal of the History of Ideas* 10 (Oct. 1949): 539–66. Obituaries are in the *New York Times* and the *Chicago Daily Tribune*, both 26 Aug. 1930.

LARRY HICKMAN

MOORE, Andrew (1752–24 May 1821), U.S. congressman and senator, was born at "Cannicello" near Staunton in Augusta (now Rockbridge) County, Virginia, the son of David Moore and Mary Evans, farmers. Moore was educated at Augusta Academy (now Washington and Lee University) and at the College of William and Mary, where he read law under George Wythe. In 1774 he gained admission to the bar and began practicing law in Augusta County. In the same year he fought in Lord Dunmore's War, participating in the bloody battle of Point Pleasant, where the Virginia militia defeated the Shawnee.

Like most of his Scotch Irish Shenandoah Valley neighbors, Moore was an ardent patriot. When the American Revolution began, he helped raise a company of riflemen from Augusta County, was commissioned lieutenant, and marched off to fight the British. His company was attached to the Ninth Virginia Regiment of the Continental Line. When General George Washington ordered Colonel Daniel Morgan to organize a select corps of five hundred expert riflemen to join General Horatio Gates's army in New York, Moore's company became part of Morgan's Rangers.

Promoted to captain, Moore led the Augusta Rifles at Saratoga in the fall 1777 battles of Freeman's Farm and Bemis Heights. Morgan's Rangers played a major role in defeating General John Burgoyne's army. Saratoga was the high point of Moore's military service. He fought in subsequent campaigns until 1779, when a surplus of officers prompted him to resign his commission. A courageous soldier and able officer, he later rose to the rank of major general in the Virginia militia.

Moore, once out of the army, found plenty of opportunities to serve on the political front. Virginia confronted major challenges in making political, economic, and social adjustments to independence. In 1780 Moore was elected to the House of Delegates, beginning a political career in the state and nation that spanned three decades and involved him in twenty-nine elections, only one of which he lost. In the Virginia Assembly he allied himself with James Madison, whose efforts to disestablish the Episcopal church and extend the boundaries of religious freedom Moore strongly supported. He served ably in the assembly during the periods 1780–1783 and 1785–1788.

Moore was a delegate to the state convention of 1788 that met in Richmond to consider the new federal Constitution. Since 1785 he had supported efforts to strengthen the national government, and he stood for election in 1788 as a proponent of the new Constitution. Augusta freeholders petitioned him to oppose ratification, but he allied himself firmly with Madison in the ratification struggle.

Although the Augusta voters were unhappy with Moore's support of the Constitution, they did not lose faith in him; they elected him to represent them in the new nation's first four congresses, from 1789 through 1797. In Congress Moore continued his alliance with Madison, whom he served loyally as political lieutenant. He resisted efforts to make radical changes in the Constitution. In general, he opposed Alexander Hamilton's financial policies, especially the national bank. He recognized the necessity of funding the national debt but opposed the plan outlined by Hamilton because he thought it benefited speculators. He also opposed Hamilton's excise tax, which he thought taxed western citizens disproportionately.

Moore did not run for reelection to Congress in 1796. The previous year he had married Sarah Reid, daughter of Andrew Reid of Augusta County, and personal business required his attention. Public service had eroded his financial position; he had to devote more time to his legal practice and rebuild his financial base in order to provide security for the family he had begun, which before many years would number four children. When another political crisis developed, however, he returned to the political arena.

In 1798 the Federalist-dominated Fifth Congress passed the Alien and Sedition Acts. Like Republican party leaders Jefferson and Madison, Moore saw in these measures a serious threat to freedom of speech, and he returned to the Virginia House of Delegates to help secure passage of the Virginia Resolutions drafted by Madison to oppose the objectionable laws. The following year he joined with Madison to uphold the Resolutions against Federalist attacks and to gain passage of the Report of 1800, which became the fountainhead of conservative Republican political philosophy. In this same 1799–1800 legislative session, Moore supported changes in the state's electoral laws that gave the dominant Republican party the advantage in the coming presidential election. In January 1802 he was appointed federal marshal of the Western District of Virginia, a post he held only until March, when the district was abolished with the repeal of the Judiciary Act of 1801.

The Republican victory in 1800, together with some improvement in his financial situation, induced Moore to return to Congress. He was elected to the Eighth Congress, which convened 4 March 1804, but he served only until August, when he was appointed to a vacancy in the U.S. Senate. For the next five years he supported the Jefferson administration and effectively represented Virginia's interests. In 1808, when John Randolph and other conservative Republicans tried to nominate James Monroe over James Madison for president, Moore vigorously promoted his old friend and ally and was pleased when the Republican caucus selected Madison as its nominee.

In 1809 Moore was offered the position of territorial governor of the Louisiana Territory. He declined but accepted an appointment as U.S. marshal for the District of Virginia, a position he held until shortly before his death. Throughout his long political career Moore championed franchise extension. He believed that all tax-paying, arms-bearing white males above the age of twenty-one should be able to vote. He earnestly promoted the economic and social development of western Virginia, focusing especially on enhancing educational opportunities for the region's youth. He was an active trustee of the institution that became Washington and Lee University, which he served faithfully from 1782 until his death at his home in Augusta.

• There is no large collection of Moore's papers, but several archives hold a few items. The Andrew Moore Papers at the Library of Congress include one letter from 1807, and the Andrew Moore Papers at the University of Virginia contain a few miscellaneous items. More useful are the Zachariah Johnston Papers, 1772–1800, at the Virginia State Library in Richmond, which contain some of Moore's correspondence relating to his support of Jefferson's and Madison's efforts to establish religious freedom in Virginia and his involvement in the ratification contest of 1788–1789. One letter from Moore to Madison is in the James Madison Papers at the Library of Congress. There is a short biographical sketch of Moore by Hugh B. Grigsby in *Washington and Lee Papers*, no. 2 (1890): 56–62, an even briefer sketch in *Biographical Directory of American Congresses* (1928), and a useful article by Charles W. Turner, "Andrew Moore—First U.S. Senator from West of the Blue Ridge Mountains," *Filson Club Quarterly* 28, no. 4 (Oct. 1954): 354–70. Scattered information can be found in J. A. Waddell, *Annals of Augusta County, Virginia* (1902).

CHARLES D. LOWERY

MOORE, Anne Carroll (12 July 1871–20 Jan. 1961), librarian, was born in Limerick, Maine, the daughter of Luther Sanborn Moore, a lawyer and state senator, and Sarah Hidden Barker. She was christened "Annie" but later changed it to Anne to avoid confusion with Annie E. Moore, who also wrote about children and books. As the only girl, and the youngest of eight surviving children, she was exposed to "boy" games as well as girlish pursuits and enjoyed a happy childhood. Her father often took her through rural New England on legal business trips, and she developed a taste for law. She was educated at the Limerick Academy, went on to Bradford Academy for Women in Massachusetts, from which she graduated in 1891, and began to read for the law, but she was forced to give it up when her father suddenly died and no other lawyer would take on a girl as an assistant.

In 1895 Moore went to study librarianship at Pratt Institute in Brooklyn, New York. She did not start out in children's work but gladly accepted Mary Wright Plummer's invitation to design services for the new Children's Library of Pratt Institute and "do with it whatever you have it in you to do" (quoted in Sayers, p. 41). There was a great deal that she had in her to do, and in 1906 she went to work for the New York Public Library (at the request of Arthur Bostwick, head of circulation), to establish library service for children in the Central Children's Room of the main library, then under construction at Fifth Avenue and Forty-second Street, as well as in the fourteen libraries that had joined the New York Public Library and the sixty-five branches that were to be set up with money from Andrew Carnegie.

Moore, who saw boredom as a danger in childhood, believed that all children deserved to be introduced to the best aspects of their culture. She encouraged exhibits and celebrations to spark interest in all kinds of subjects and to promote a love of reading unrelated to schoolwork. She once wrote, in a letter to someone worried about protecting children from fascism and communism, "You can only give them what you've found to be the highspots of life. . . . After every war, people want to wipe the decks clean and tell children what they ought to think. Little will come of it" (quoted in Sayers, p. 236). She believed that giving children a sense of the world as an exciting, joyful place would be more effective than any amount of moral instruction in making them value life and other human beings. In an effort to give children the "highspots of life," in the early decades of the twentieth century, when books were costly and demand was high, Moore set up reading rooms as well as circulating collections. Children would line up around the block, waiting to borrow a book. At these reading rooms, they had access to popular books and safe, quiet places to read in a crowded and noisy city. These collections stood libraries in good stead during the dark days of war and depression, for even when budgets severely limited the acquisition of books, the reading rooms always had one copy of the best books for children.

Long before the late twentieth-century concern for multiculturalism, Moore purchased books for New York's immigrant children in their native languages as well as English translations of favorite tales from their countries of origin. The few surviving books of this kind in the New York City public libraries testify to the rich variety of European cultures that have added vitality and diversity to American life.

One of Moore's most lasting contributions to the field was her advocacy of oral storytelling. She invited storytellers who were used to high society's drawing rooms and ballrooms into the New York Public Library and celebrated such occasions with flowers and candles. Among the famous authors who were drawn by Moore to the Central Children's Room were Walter de la Mare, Ludwig Bemelmans, Stephen Vincent Benét, and Carl Sandburg. To this day, the sharing of oral literature continues in children's libraries around the United States.

Moore was not a storyteller herself, but she did talk to groups of children, sometimes with the assistance of her little carved wooden doll, Nicholas, named in honor of the city's Dutch founders. She was rarely seen in a group of children without Nicholas, and she wrote two books about him, *Nicholas: A Manhattan Christmas Story* (1924) and *Nicholas and the Golden Goose* (1932). Some have ridiculed her attachment to this toy, but it served her well with shy children and often formed a bridge to adults as well. Many famous authors and illustrators sent cards and gifts to Nicholas.

With her reviews of children's literature, Moore's concern for books of literary value, rather than those of moral didacticism or poor quality, reached beyond the New York Public Library system. Her column "The Three Owls" ran in the *New York Herald Tribune* from 1924 until 1930, when it was dropped for financial reasons related to the depression. In 1936 she began writing "The Three Owls Notebook" for the *Horn Book* and continued writing it until her death. Several collections of her columns for the *Herald Tribune* were published in book form. She loved reviewing and did an extraordinary job of exciting interest in children's literature.

Moore's life centered on children's literature, but her experience was not limited to books. She became involved in a cause célèbre of anti-Semitism when Leo Frank, who had used Pratt library as a child in Brooklyn, was accused of murdering a girl in Atlanta in 1913. To demonstrate her trust, she visited him while he was on trial. She initiated petitions and visited him in prison while he waited to see if his death sentence would be commuted by the governor of Georgia. She, along with much of the world, was horrified when he was lynched while serving his life sentence.

She also loved to travel and went to Europe several times, including trips to help France after World War I. On a trip to England, she accepted an invitation to visit Beatrix Potter at Hill Top Farm, and they became quite friendly.

Moore retired in 1941 but continued to teach and write until her death twenty years later in New York

City. Her enormous impact on children's library service and on children's literature led to her being honored with many awards, including the Diploma of Honor from Pratt Institute (1932); the first Constance Lindsay Skinner memorial award (1940), presented annually to a woman considered to have made "an outstanding contribution to the world of books"; and the Regina Medal of the Catholic Library Association (1960). She was also the recipient of two honorary doctorates.

• Moore documents can be found at Pratt Institute and at the New York Public Library. The American Jewish Archives in Cincinnati, Ohio, has her correspondence with Leo Frank. There are several compilations of her reviews and literary criticism: *The Three Owls*, bks. 1, 2, and 3 (1925; repr. 1928 and 1931), and in her *Roads to Childhood* (1920), *New Roads to Childhood* (1923), *Cross-roads to Childhood* (1926), and *My Roads to Childhood* (1939). She edited, with Bertha Mahoney Miller, *Writing and Criticism: A Book for Margery Bianco* (1951) and also wrote an appreciation for *The Art of Beatrix Potter* (1955, repr. 1972). Frances Clarke Sayers, Moore's successor at the New York Public Library, wrote *Anne Carroll Moore: A Biography* (1972). There are two master's theses about Moore: Nancy Meade Akers, "Anne Carroll Moore: A Study of Her Work with Children's Libraries and Literature" (Pratt Institute Library School, 1951); and A. M. Poor, "Anne Carroll Moore: The Velvet Glove of Librarianship" (Southern Connecticut State College, 1966). Other writings about Moore or her work include Barbara Holbrook, "Anne Carroll Moore, of the Golden Age," *Wilson Library Bulletin*, Dec. 1938, pp. 246, 249; Mabel William, "Anne Carroll Moore," *Bulletin of Bibliography*, May–Aug 1946; "Autobiographical Sketch," in *The Junior Book of Authors*, ed. Stanley J. Kunitz and Howard Haycraft (1951), pp. 265–66; Aylesa Forsee, "Librarian from Limerick," in *Women Who Reached for Tomorrow* (1960), pp. 36–55; Eleanor Estes et al., "Tribute to Anne Carroll Moore," *Top of the News*, Dec. 1961, pp. 31–43; Joan Blodgett Peterson Olson, "An Interpretive History of the 'Horn Book Magazine,' 1924–1973," (Ph.D. diss., Stanford Univ. 1976); Grace Hogarth, "A Publisher's Perspective," *Horn Book Magazine*, May-June 1987 and Nov.-Dec. 1987, pp. 372–77; and Margaret K. McElderry, "Remarkable Women: Anne Carroll Moore & Company," *School Library Journal*, Mar. 1992, pp. 156–62. The New York Public Library published a festschrift in her honor, *Reading without Boundaries: Essays Presented to Anne Carroll Moore*, ed. Frances Lander Spain (1956), which includes a bibliography of her writing through 1955. An obituary is in the *New York Times*, 21 Jan. 1961.

AMY SPAULDING

MOORE, Carl Richard (5 Dec. 1892–16 Oct. 1955), endocrinologist, was born in Brighton, Missouri, the son of Jonathan Newton Moore and Sarah Frances Harris, farmers. At the age of nine he moved with his family to nearby Springfield, where he grew up. He matriculated at Drury College in Springfield and paid his tuition by working as a janitor, window washer, and paperboy. Although he had originally planned to become a physician, he soon developed such an interest in conducting laboratory experiments that he decided to become a biologist instead. After receiving his B.S. degree in 1913, he remained at Drury as a laboratory instructor while working toward his M.S. degree, which he received the next year. He then enrolled at the University of Chicago, where he studied and taught zoology and spent his summers conducting research at the Marine Biological Laboratory in Woods Hole, Massachusetts. He received his Ph.D. degree in zoology in 1916.

Moore remained at Chicago as an associate in zoology and was promoted to instructor two years later. At the suggestion of Frank R. Lillie, his dissertation director and the department chairman, he embarked on a project to produce experimentally a freemartin, a normally sterile female calf born as a twin of a male calf. Lillie believed that freemartinism occurs because the female's sex hormones are inhibited by her twin's male hormones, and he convinced Moore that such a study would reveal much about the supposed antagonism between male and female hormones. Although Moore spent the next thirty-eight years working on this project, he never produced a freemartin. However, his efforts in this regard eventually resulted in much more important contributions to the physiology of mammalian reproduction.

Working with rats and guinea pigs, by 1919 Moore was routinely grafting testicles to young females with ovaries and ovaries to young males with testicles. In both cases the rejection rate of the transplanted gonads was virtually nil, thereby proving conclusively that antagonism does not exist between female and male sex glands despite leaving the question of antagonism between sex hormones unanswered. In 1920, the same year that he married Edith Naomi Abernethy, with whom he had three children, and two years before his promotion to assistant professor, he became involved in a controversy concerning testicle transplants in humans. The Viennese scientist E. Steinach began claiming he could rejuvenate elderly men by transplanting testicles from either sheep, goats, or chimpanzees, and the Russian-French surgeon S. Voronoff made the same claim for vasectomies. Hundreds of so-called Steinach operations were performed in Europe and the United States as a result. In an effort to debunk such claims, Moore studied various conditions of testicular degeneration in order to determine their relationship to the production of male hormones. In the process of proving beyond a shadow of a doubt that Steinach operations did not increase the secretion of male hormone and were therefore useless, he also discovered why testicles, unlike ovaries, are contained outside the human trunk in the scrotum. His experiments involving cryptorchidism, the failure of the testes to descend into the scrotal sac, led him in 1924 to the realization that spermatogenesis cannot take place in the relative warmth of the abdomen; only when located in the slightly cooler scrotum can the testes produce sperm.

In 1927, two years after his promotion to associate professor and a year before his promotion to full professor, Moore collaborated with his colleagues at the University of Chicago T. F. Gallagher and F. C. Koch in a series of experiments designed to determine how male hormones affect the development of accessory reproductive glands. By administering lipid extracts of bull testes to castrated mammals and fowl, he demonstrated that male hormone prevents the effects of castration on the development of tissue, cells, and secretions in such glands as the prostate, vesicles, and vas deferens. These experiments also led to the discovery in 1929 of the male hormones androsterone, which primarily influences the growth and development of the male reproductive system, and testosterone, which induces and maintains secondary male sex characteristics. He also attempted to answer the old question of sex hormone antagonism by administering male and female hormones individually and together to intact and gonadectomized rats. The findings were such that the antagonism theory, although seemingly valid in some cases such as the inhibition of testicle growth by the administration of female hormone, did not properly explain the interaction of the hormones. In 1932 he and Dorothy Price postulated the Moore-Price negative feedback concept, also known as the Moore-Price Law and the push-pull theory, which suggested that the gonads and the anterior pituitary gland work together in such a way that an excess secretion of a sex hormone serves to inhibit rather than enhance the effect produced by normal quantities of the hormone. This theory was later adapted and used by Gregory Goodwin Pincus in the 1950s to develop the birth control pill, which prevents ovulation by administering large doses of female hormone.

In 1934 Moore became chairman of the Department of Zoology, a position he held until his death in Chicago. He served as vice president of the American Society of Zoologists in 1926, managing editor of the *Biological Bulletin* from 1926 to 1929, vice president of the American Association for the Advancement of Science's Section F in 1943, and president of the Association for the Study of Internal Secretions in 1944. He received the National Academy of Arts and Sciences' first Francis Amory Award in 1941, the American Urological Association's Award in 1950, and the Endocrine Society's Medal in 1955. He was elected to the National Academy of Sciences in 1944.

Moore was a pioneer in the study of animal reproductive organs and the internal secretions related to sexual differentiation. His studies concerning the role played by male and female hormones in mammalian growth and development contributed to a more nuanced understanding of the ways in which the sex hormones work. His investigation into the workings of the testes and the purpose of the scrotum contributed to a better understanding of the physiology of mammalian reproduction.

• Moore's papers have not been located. A biography, including a bibliography, is Dorothy Price, National Academy of Sciences, *Biographical Memoirs* 45 (1974): 385–412. Obituaries are in the *New York Times*, 17 Oct. 1955; *Journal of the American Medical Association*, 26 Nov. 1955; and *Science*, 23 Mar. 1956.

CHARLES W. CAREY, JR.

MOORE, Carl Vernon (21 Aug. 1908–13 Aug. 1972), research physician and educator, was born in St. Louis, Missouri, the son of Carl V. Moore, a policeman, and Mary Kamp, the owner of a small confectionery. Although his eventual enrollment in college was probably never doubted, Moore augmented his parents' incomes as a youth by working at a number of jobs, including a pharmacy assistant, an elevator operator, and a steel mill laborer. At age fifteen he graduated from high school and began his college education at Elmhurst College (Ill.) with the intention of joining the ministry. He became interested in medicine while at Elmhurst, however, and after three years he transferred to Washington University in his hometown. After completing the requirements for his B.A. in 1928, he immediately enrolled in medical school at Washington University, which he completed in 1932. He took his house staff training at Barnes Hospital in St. Louis, and in 1934 he accepted a National Research Council fellowship in medicine at Ohio State University (OSU). During his time at OSU, Moore began studying hematology and formed a strong friendship with his mentor there, Charles Austin Doan. Also initiated at OSU was a longlasting collaboration with Virginia Minnich, then a graduate student, who was studying nutrition. Another important personal connection made at OSU was meeting and marrying Dorothy Adams; they had one daughter. Moore stayed at OSU for four years, attaining the rank of assistant professor before returning to Washington University, also as assistant professor, in 1938.

Moore's research interests were iron metabolism, anemia, and immunohematology. His role as a pioneer in iron metabolism and the fledgling specialty of hematology was well grounded from his preparation at Washington University. Minnich joined Moore at Washington University and was coauthor of many of his almost 150 scientific publications. In 1950 Moore was selected as one of five hematologists to serve on an advisory committee to the Red Cross for the development of policies for new blood banks. Moore, as an authority on iron metabolism, served on the Food and Nutrition Board of the National Academy of Sciences during reviews of the benefits of enriching bread and flour with iron. He was elected to membership of both the National Academy of Sciences and its Institute of Medicine (1970). In 1971 he received the Abraham Flexner Award from the Association of American Medical Colleges, in recognition of his outstanding contributions to medical education, including his dedication to the administration and promotion of Washington University School of Medicine and to building the foundation for its place as one of the nation's top medical schools. Moore was also on the editing staff of numerous journals and served as president of both the American and the International Society of Hematology.

At Washington University Moore flourished as an educator and administrator as well as a research physician. He was described by his closest associates as a clear and simple speaker, taking the utmost care in preparing and explaining materials, both in the classroom and at the patient's bedside. Patient cases were woven into his lectures and discussions, and his knowledge of the medical literature was extensive. His manner seems to have belied his status, and his modesty prompted him to conduct discussions with every member of the medical school's faculty, staff, and student body as equals, a trait perhaps dating from his interest in the ministry. As early as 1942 Moore entered into the administration of the medical school, when W. Barry Wood was appointed chair of the department of medicine. The two men developed a method for joint administration of the department, wherein one actively participated as chairman while the other pursued research interests. This allowed both to follow their inquisitive minds and use their skills as leaders to promote the development of the school. The idea of a joint chair was emulated by numerous schools, and while it came to a temporary end in 1955 when Wood returned to Johns Hopkins, the advantages of joint administration returned in 1964 when Sol Sherry joined Moore at the helm. Moore served as dean from 1953 to 1955, during difficult negotiations with Barnes Hospital. He naturally succeeded Wood as chair of the department of medicine in 1955, also receiving the title of Busch Professor of Medicine. He held the position of vice chancellor for medical affairs from 1964 until 1965. In 1964 he was elected president of the medical school. He served in these capacities until his sudden death from a heart attack while on vacation with his family in Manistee, Michigan.

Moore's strongest contributions were initially in the world of research, but as his career developed it became apparent that the growth of his medical school depended on his leadership. Through invited lectures he advocated interinstitution cooperation for the distribution of facilities and technology to wider populations, the auditing of medical care to ensure high-quality diagnosis and treatment, continual education for physicians and scientists to stay abreast of increasingly rapid advances, and promotion of preventive medicine as an important part of the duties of hospitals to their communities. Moore's overall support and dedication to the field of hematology and simultaneously to his institution prompted respect and admiration from colleagues.

• The collected papers of Carl V. Moore are in the archives of the Becker Medical Library at the Washington University School of Medicine. *Who's Who in the Midwest* is a good source of Moore's personal information. His view on the enrichment of bread and flour with iron is in *Nutrition*, Mar. 1972. Obituaries appear in *Blood* 40 (1972): 771–75, *Lancet* 2 (1972): 439, and the *New York Times*, 15 Aug. 1972. Further insight is provided by obituaries in *Progress in Hematology* 8 (1973): v–viii; *Medical Journal of Australia* 1 (1973): 314; and *Transactions of the Association of American Physicians* 86 (1973): 28–30.

JOANNA B. DOWNER

MOORE, Charles (20 Oct. 1855–25 Sept. 1942), city planner, journalist, and historian, was born in Ypsilanti, Michigan, the son of Charles Moore, a merchant, and Adeline MacAllaster. His parents died when he was fourteen years of age, and his brother-in-law became his guardian. Moore's parents left an inheritance that permitted him to attend Harvard College (now University), where he studied humanities and eventually became the editor of the student newspaper, *Harvard Crimson*. During his student years he also wrote for the *Detroit Post* and the *Detroit Tribune*. He graduated in 1878, and shortly thereafter on 27 June, he married Alice Williams Merriam from Middleton, Massachusetts. They had two children.

Moore began his career by leasing the rights to publish his hometown newspaper, the *Ypsilanti Commercial*; two years later he purchased a Detroit newspaper called *Every Saturday*. In 1883 he invested heavily in the *Detroit Times* but lost his investment the next year to a fire. His inheritance gone, he worked for the next five years as a reporter for the *Detroit Journal* and the *Detroit Sunday News*. It was during an assignment to report on the 1888 elections that Moore met James McMillan, a senatorial hopeful.

The next year the newly elected senator named Moore his political secretary, a position in which he used his writing and newspaper savvy behind the scenes to achieve good results. Moore's most notable accomplishment was passage of a bill in 1901 authorizing a commission to study park improvements in the District of Columbia. He asked Daniel Burnham, president of the American Institute of Architects, to chair the commission. Moore had respected Burnham's work on the Chicago Exposition of 1893 that had showcased the City Beautiful movement—so much so that in 1921 he wrote a biography, *Daniel H. Burnham, Architect, Planner of Cities*. (He also eventually wrote about another architect on the commission, Charles F. McKim, in 1929.) The team working on the 1901 plan developed a model for the public buildings, parks, and mall calling for a return to Pierre L'Enfant's original designs from 1791. This required moving the railroad tracks that ran through the middle of the mall. Moore remained in Washington after Senator McMillan's death to work for passage of the bill that funded the track's relocation. In 1899 he received his M.A., and in 1900 his Ph.D., in history from Columbian University (renamed George Washington University in 1904). He also wrote the book *The Northwest under Three Flags, 1635–1796* (1900).

In 1903 Moore moved to Sault Sainte Marie, Michigan. He worked for a year as private secretary to Frances H. Clergue in the steel, railroad, and power industries. He next worked for the Union Trust Company of Detroit. In 1906 he became chairman of the Submarine Signal Company in Boston and then returned to Detroit two years later as vice president of the Security Trust Company.

Moore changed his focus when his wife died in 1914. He left business, wrote the *History of Michigan* (1915), and accepted the chairmanship of the Fine Arts Commission, a position he held for twenty-two years (1915–1937). He had earlier become an original member of the commission in 1910, when President Taft appointed him to the post. Now five years later he led that organization on its mission of beautifying Washington. Some of the nation's greatest monuments and buildings were conceived and built during his tenure.

Although Moore was not an artist himself, he had gained a great appreciation for art during his time at Harvard studying under Charles Eliot Norton. Moore, like his teacher, believed architecture to be as much an art as sculpture and painting, and he was a staunch supporter of the classical revival style. He defended the architecture of the Lincoln Memorial when it came under fire as inappropriate for a self-educated man coming from a log cabin. Charles believed time had shown that classical buildings endured because of their beauty. His chairmanship through six administrations accomplished most of the original goals for Washington in spite of the depression years. Seven major buildings were built, comprising what may be the largest collection of Beaux-Arts buildings in the world. The Arlington Memorial Bridge was completed, and the mall was made free of railroad tracks. Moore brought credit to others for these accomplishments, rarely taking any for himself.

Moore's affiliations with organizations were important, as their members contributed support and provided design resources necessary to the development plans. Some of these organizations included the National Sculpture Society, Planning and Civic Association, American Society of Landscape Architects, New York Architectural League, American Institute of Arts and Letters, the Cosmos Club in Washington, and the Century Club in New York.

Moore was acting chief of the division of manuscripts in the Library of Congress from 1918 to 1927. He served as treasurer of the American Historical Association and was instrumental in selecting sites of American war cemeteries in Europe in 1923.

On 23 May 1935 the Fine Arts Commission celebrated its twenty-fifth anniversary by honoring Charles Moore. He received a gold medal designed by one of its members and a portrait painted by Eugene Francis Savage. In 1937 he received the Friedsam fellowship gold medal award from the New York Architectural League and the Carnegie Award for Services in the Arts in America. Moore had led committees that were cohesive and most often unanimous in their recommendations. He had written several books about the District of Columbia and its builders. Now in his eighties he was seeing new sharp criticism for the now-completed designs in Washington. The country had moved toward modernism and the classical forms of architecture were not as appreciated, especially in light of their cost. He retired in 1937 from the commission, having worked for more than twenty years to achieve permanence and beauty for the nation's capital. He left the area to live with his son, MacAllaster, in Gig Harbor, Washington, where he later died.

Moore's friends at the Library of Congress Manuscript Division remembered his career in an essay as "one of varied experience in business, in the political world, and in cultural upbuilding."

• Business papers, memoirs, and correspondence may be found at the Manuscript Division, Library of Congress. Minutes and other materials from the Fine Arts Commission are located at the National Archives, in Washington, D.C. (Record Group 66). Charles Moore, *Daniel H. Burnham* (2 vols., 1921), is a biography but contains information about Washington's development. For other information relating to the development of Washington, see Sally Kress Tompkins, *A Quest for Grandeur: Charles Moore and the Federal Triangle* (1993), and John William Reps, *Monumental Washington: The Planning and Development of the Capital Center* (1967). See also William Harlan Hale, "The Grandeur that Is Washington," *Harpers Monthly Magazine*, Apr. 1934, pp. 560–69; and *Development of the United States Capital* (1930), a collection of addresses by various speakers on the development of the national capital at a series of meetings in 1929. An obituary is in the *Washington Star*, 26 Sept. 1942.

C. Kelly Lohr

MOORE, Charles Herbert (10 Apr. 1840–15 Feb. 1930), painter, scholar, and educator, was born in New York City, the son of Charles Moore, a lace merchant, and Jane Maria Berendtson (anglicized as Benson). He attended New York public schools and began taking drawing lessons from the landscape painter Benjamin Coe by age thirteen. While still a teenager Moore began exhibiting his paintings at the National Academy of Design, supporting himself by selling landscapes to New York art dealers and teaching drawing and painting from Coe's studios at New York University. During the early 1860s Moore's sketching tours of the Hudson River valley increased in frequency and duration. His efforts during these trips are represented by four landscapes given to Vassar College by Matthew Vassar in 1864 (*Upper Palisades* [1860], *Morning over New York*, *Down the Hudson to West Point*, and *Catskills in Spring* [all 1861]). Moore was a founding member of the American Pre-Raphaelite Brotherhood, organized as the "Society for the Advancement of Truth in Art" in 1863. He was a contributor to the group's short-lived periodical, the *New Path*, though only two articles carry his name.

After marrying Mary Jane Tomlinson in 1865, Moore and his bride moved to Catskill, New York. It was probably while painting in the Berkshires that summer that he met Charles Eliot Norton, with whom he began a lifelong friendship. In 1871, at Norton's recommendation, Moore accepted the position of instructor of freehand drawing in Harvard's Lawrence Scientific School. His move to Cambridge ended his painting career. Three years later Norton chose Moore to join him in establishing the college's new art department, making the study of the fine arts part of Harvard University's liberal arts education.

To prepare for his new teaching assignment, Moore was granted a one-year paid leave of absence during which he traveled to Europe in 1876. With a letter of introduction from Norton, Moore, his wife, and their ten-year-old daughter Elizabeth called on John Ruskin and were warmly received. The Moores and Ruskin later rendezvoused in Venice, Italy, where they spent four months discussing aesthetics, sketching architecture, and copying paintings of the old masters. Overwhelmed by the riches of Europe and his interaction with Ruskin, Moore extended his one-year leave to two years. In 1878 he returned to Harvard to begin teaching "Principles of Design in Painting Sculpture and Architecture." Reflecting Ruskin's methods, Moore's combination of lecture and practical exercise in his Fine Arts 1 course complemented Norton's purely historical approach in Fine Arts 2.

In January 1880 Moore's wife died. Two years later, in December 1881, he married Elizabeth Fisk Hewins. The first of his many books, *Facsimiles or Examples in Delineation Selected from the Masters for the Use of the Student in Drawing*, was published in 1882. A year later a second volume, *Examples for Elementary Practice in Delineation, Designed for the Use of Schools and Isolated Beginners*, was completed.

During a second trip to Europe in 1885 Moore focused his attention on the architecture of France. This new interest in architecture resulted in his most important book, *The Development and Character of Gothic Architecture* (1890; rev. ed., 1899). A turning point in his career, this book reveals a shift in Moore's allegiances from the principles of Ruskin to those of Eugène Emmanuel Viollet-le-Duc. This publication elevated Moore's reputation from a skilled painter and respected teacher to an internationally renowned scholar of architectural history. He was soon awarded honorary membership in the American Institute of Architects as well as in the Royal Institute of British Architects. Though he never attended college, he received an honorary A.M. degree from Harvard in 1890 and was promoted to assistant professor the following year.

In 1896 Moore achieved the rank of full professor and was appointed the first director of Harvard's Fogg Museum of Art. He was instrumental in building that museum's early educational collections. In 1905 he published *The Character of Renaissance Architecture* (1905) as a companion to his medieval study.

Moore retired from Harvard in 1909 and moved to England, making his home in Hartley Wintney in Hampshire. In retirement he published a final architectural treatise, *The Mediaeval Church Architecture of England* (1912), and contributed thirteen articles to the *Architectural Record* and the *Journal of the Royal Institute of British Architects*. He died in Hartley Wintney.

As a painter, Moore demonstrated exceptional promise before terminating his career. Had he continued to paint, according to Frank Jewett Mather, Jr., "he might have made himself the best American landscape painter of his generation" (p. 15). As an educator and museum director, he was a pioneer in integrating the fine arts into the liberal arts curriculum. As a scholar, he forced a redefinition of Gothic architecture.

• The Charles Herbert Moore Papers are in Houghton Library, Harvard University. For an account of Moore's career weighted toward his painting, see Frank Jewett Mather, Jr., *Charles Herbert Moore: Landscape Painter* (1957), which remains the most thorough study of Moore's life. Discussions of Moore within the context of the Pre-Raphaelite movement in the United States can be found in David Howard Dickason, *The Daring Young Men: The Story of the American Pre-Rapaelites* (1953; rev. ed., 1970), and Linda S. Ferber and William H. Gerdts, *The New Path: Ruskin and the American Pre-Raphaelites* (1985). Michael W. Brooks discusses Moore's contributions to architectural history in "New England Gothic: Charles Eliot Norton, Charles H. Moore, and Henry Adams," in *Studies in the History of Art*, vol. 35 (1990), pp. 113–25.

RANDY J. PLOOG

MOORE, Clara Sophia Jessup Bloomfield (16 Feb. 1824–5 Jan. 1899), novelist and etiquette writer, was born in Philadelphia, Pennsylvania, the daughter of Augustus Edward Jessup, a mineralogist, and Lydia Eager Mosley. Moore attended Westfield Academy in Westfield, Massachusetts, and Mrs. Merrick's School in New Haven, Connecticut. In 1842 she married Bloomfield Haines Moore, a Philadelphia Quaker, with whom she had three children. Her husband joined her father in forming the successful Jessup & Moore paper-manufacturing firm; by the time of his death in 1878, her husband had amassed a fortune of several million dollars.

Clara Moore was active in Philadelphia society and civic groups. During the Civil War she was corresponding secretary of the Women's Pennsylvania Branch of the United States Sanitary Commission. She helped create the Union Temporary Home for Children and actively supported the Cooper Shop Soldiers' Home of Philadelphia.

Moore's writing career began in the 1840s, soon after her marriage, with the publication of her stories and poems in magazines and local newspapers. She donated the money she earned from her writings to various charitable causes. An early story, "The Estranged Hearts," reportedly received the first prize in a competition with 400 entries, and later stories such as "Compensation" and "Emma Dudley's Secret" and the collection *Tight Times; or, The Diamond Cross and Other Tales* (1855) were also commercially successful. Three novelettes, all published anonymously, appeared before the Civil War: *The Hasty Marriage, The House of Huntly and Raymond*, and *Mabel's Mission*.

After the war Moore continued her writing. She sometimes wrote under various pseudonyms, including Clara Moreton, Mrs. Bloomfield-Moore, and Mrs. H. O. Ward. Her best-known novel was *On Dangerous Ground, or Agatha's Friendship: A Romance of American Society* (1876). Other fiction and poetry includes *The Warden's Tale* (1875), *Three Eras in a Life* (1875), and *Gondaline's Lessons and Other Poems* (1881). Her work was considered sentimental and romantic reading suitable for ladies. She also published a number of children's books, some of which she collected in her *Stories for Children* (1875). One of her children's books, *Master Jacky's Holiday*, was published in more than twenty editions.

Moore's most popular writing, however, was that in which she dispensed advice about etiquette. In March of 1873 she published anonymously "Some Unsettled Points of Etiquette" in *Lippincott's Magazine*. The article attracted considerable attention and criticism, because she argued the need for uniformity in manners, citing cases of the wide variation in customs throughout the country. Later that year she published a revised edition of Eliza Farrar's 1836 manual *The Young Lady's Friend*, a book that Clara's father had given her when she was a girl.

In 1878 Moore published her most famous work, *Sensible Etiquette of the Best Society* (using the pen name Mrs. H. O. Ward). This compilation of rules for social manners is filled with anecdotes and examples demonstrating either appropriate or unseemly behavior. The book covers numerous social situations and implies that there is one correct standard for each, whether or not any reason is given. For example, "Ladies in escorting each other never offer or take the arm." The tone is heavily moralistic throughout. The book places special emphasis on the duty of mothers to train their children and, almost equally, their husbands, who, like men in general, are in need of the "beneficial corrective influences of refined and pure-minded women."

Sensible Etiquette went through twenty revised editions, becoming one of the most popular etiquette books of the time. Moore maintained that good manners signaled one's spiritual worthiness; etiquette made a truly Christian civilization possible by creating "fitness for the enjoyment of a spiritual existence."

Although Moore argued that women did not need the vote, because they had moral influence over men, she did write in favor of education and college training for women, particularly in her last major work, *Social Ethics and Society Duties: Thorough Education of Girls for Wives and Mothers and for Professions* (1892). To her, "education" meant training in respectable behavior, now applicable to work outside the home as well as to women's primary roles as wives and mothers.

After her husband died in 1878, Moore spent many years traveling and living in Europe. In her houses in London and St. Moritz, she entertained artists, musicians, and authors. Of particular importance to her was her friendship with Robert Browning, whom she met in London in 1879. For many years, particularly from 1881 to 1895, she provided financial support to John Ernest Worrall Keely, who in 1874 had announced that he was creating a motor to be powered by the "harmonic vibrations" of atoms. After Keely's death in 1898, it was discovered that his model machines were powered secretly by compressed air; apparently he had run an elaborate hoax for decades, and Clara Moore, who never lost faith in him, was his generous source of funds. Moore's last years brought financial worries, partly as a result of this generosity to Keely, whose personal magnetism obviously held attraction for her; and her grief after Keely's death contributed to her own demise, less than two months later, in London.

• For articles in reference books, see Lina Mainiero, ed., *American Women Writers* (1981), where she is listed under the name Bloomfield-Moore; J. S. Hart, *Female Prose Writers of America* (1852), which includes Moore's short story "The Young Minister's Choice"; *The National Cyclopedia of American Biography* (1907); E. T. James et al., eds., *Notable American Women, 1607–1950* (1971); and Frances E. Willard and Mary A. Livermore, eds., *A Woman of the Century* (1893). An obituary is in the *New York Times*, 6 Jan. 1899.

LOIS A. MARCHINO

MOORE, Clarence Lemuel Elisha (12 May 1876–5 Dec. 1931), mathematician, was born in Bainbridge, Ohio, the son of George Taylor Moore, a grain dealer, and Lydia Ann Bradshaw. He taught school for some years before enrolling in The Ohio State University and earning a bachelor's degree in 1901. He did graduate work in mathematics at Cornell University, receiving an A.M. in 1902 and a Ph.D. in 1904. At this time he spent a year on a study trip in Europe, where he worked with a number of the influential geometers of the period, such as the Italian Corrado Segre. Moore was hired by the Massachusetts Institute of Technology (MIT) in 1904. He was promoted from instructor to faculty status in 1909 and had risen from assistant to associate to full professor by 1920. Moore married Belle Pease Fuller in 1913. They had one daughter.

Moore's chief area of interest in mathematics was projective and differential geometry. Indeed, his earliest work dealt with systems of spheres and circles in algebraic geometry. Although his methods as a young man were largely descriptive, his studies helped to lay the foundation for the analytical research of algebraic geometry and led Moore personally from the consideration of systems in Euclidean (or three-dimensional) space to researches of systems in higher dimensions, differential geometry (the full-scale application of differential calculus to analytic geometry), and manifolds, or surfaces, first identified by George Friedrich Bernhard Riemann in the mid-nineteenth century. Moore also built up the calculus of vectors for hyperspace and, together with H. B. Phillips, a fellow professor at MIT, applied vector analysis to geometry. Later Moore applied the methods of Matteo Ricci to the geometry of higher dimensions, which circumvented some of the shortcomings of the approach, which used calculus. His secretary typed one of the few copies of Ricci's lithographed book, *Lezioni sulla teoria delle superficie* (Lessons on the theory of surfaces [1898]), available in the United States. Finally, Moore combined the study of general properties of manifolds with an investigation of special manifolds in additional work in differential geometry. He found several useful specific results.

In addition to his own research, Moore played a role in the MIT mathematics department's transition from servant of an engineering school to prestigious center of research and scholarship. Mathematical activity increased at MIT over the course of Moore's career, in part because of his vision that the department had possibilities for original research on the level of Harvard and Princeton, two of the earliest and most renowned American mathematical research communities. He believed that research in mathematics was marked by constant production and communication of results, which arose from the study of problems that held both interest and promise for the individual mathematician. Further, he felt research work was essential for every mathematician, and especially for those who trained graduate students. One other way in which Moore supported research was through his role in founding in 1921 and then editing for ten years the *Journal of Mathematics and Physics* at MIT, now *Studies in Applied Mathematics*.

Even though these contributions to mathematical research were significant, Moore's most lasting influence may have been through his encouragement of younger mathematicians. His contemporaries noted that his personality was ideally suited to being a mentor, describing him as friendly, direct, insightful, and sympathetic. Junior colleagues felt free to discuss any concern in academic life or mathematics with him. Two well-known recipients of his counsel were Dirk J. Struik, the differential geometer and historian of mathematics, who remarked in his remembrances of MIT that Moore was one of the few to understand Struik's tensor analysis in its early stages, and Norbert Wiener, the mathematical logician. In his first autobiography, *Ex-Prodigy: My Childhood and Youth* (1953), Wiener wrote of Moore, "Though his field of work was different from mine, he encouraged me with a fatherly interest in my possibilities, which was just what a diffident and awkward young man needed to bring him out" (pp. 277–78).

Moore supervised the second student to receive a Ph.D. in mathematics at MIT, as well as a number of other advanced students, but his caring also extended to undergraduates. For eleven years, he was in charge of Course IX, MIT's course in general science, which was unique in the large number of choices of classes for the student and included an option in mathematics; he advised many of the undergraduates who elected the course.

Moore was elected a fellow of the American Academy of Arts and Sciences in 1914. He was a charter member of the Mathematical Association of America and a member of the American Mathematical Society and the Circolo Matematico di Palermo. An instructorship was founded in his name after his death, which occurred in Cambridge, Massachusetts, at a relatively young age after a surgical operation. Moore had also struggled throughout his career with serious eyesight problems.

• Scattered collections of papers are at the Institute Archives and Special Collections, Massachusetts Institute of Technology. Most of Moore's early papers were published in the *Proceedings of the American Academy of Arts and Sciences*, while his later ones are found in the *Journal of Mathematics and Physics*. Some of his most influential works include his dissertation, "Classification of Surfaces of Singularities of the Quadratic Spherical Complex," in *American Journal of Mathematics* 27 (1905): 248–79; "An Algebra of Plane Projective Geometry," with H. B. Phillips, in *Proceedings of the American Academy of Arts and Sciences* 47 (1912): 735–90 and "A Theory of Linear Distance and Angle," also with Phillips, in *Proceedings of the American Academy of Arts and Sciences* 48 (1912): 43–80, which center on the measurement of linear distance in projective geometry; and "Minimal Varieties of Two and Three Dimensions Whose Element of Arc Is a Perfect Sphere," in *Journal of Mathematics and Physics* 4 (1925): 167–78. A complete list of his publications is in the memorial piece by Dirk J. Struik, "C. L. E. Moore," *Journal of Mathematics and Physics* 11 (1932): 1–11. Another substantial obituary is Philip Franklin, "Clarence Lemuel Elisha Moore (1876–1931)," *Proceedings of the American Academy of Arts and Sciences* 67 (1932–1933): 606–8. Some reminiscences of Moore are also included in Dirk J. Struik, "The MIT Department of Mathematics During Its First Seventy-Five Years: Some Recollections," in *A Century of Mathematics in America, Part III*, ed. Peter Duren (1989).

AMY ACKERBERG

MOORE, Clement Clarke (15 July 1779–10 July 1863), scholar and poet, was born in New York City, the son of Benjamin Moore, a clergyman, and Charity Clarke. Moore graduated from Columbia in 1798 as class valedictorian.

Although Moore had prepared for the ministry, he was never ordained, preferring the life of the scholar, somewhat in the style of the traditional polemical divine, of anti-Jeffersonian bent. In 1804 he published *Observations upon Certain Passages in Mr. Jefferson's Notes on Virginia, which Appear to Have a Tendency to Subvert Religion and Establish a False Philosophy*, and in 1807 *A Letter to Samuel Osgood, Esq. Occasioned by His Letter upon the Subject of Episcopacy, Addressed to a Young Gentleman of This City, by Philalethes*. Then, in 1809, he published the *Hebrew-English Lexicon*, which became a standard resource. He was also published frequently in periodicals of his time such as the *Portfolio* and the *New York Evening Post*. In November 1813 Moore married Catharine Elizabeth Taylor; they had six children, four of whom survived to adulthood, before her death in 1830.

Moore's strong ties to the Episcopal church led him in 1818 to contribute the land in Chatham Square for the General Theological Seminary being planned. Then, in 1821, he became professor of Greek and Hebrew literature at that institution, a position he held until his retirement in 1850. He published an edition of his father's sermons in 1824 and a condensation of Jacques Lavardin's work *History of George Castriot, Surnamed Scanderbeg, King of Albania* in 1850.

Moore's principal claim to fame, however, came with his 1844 publication of a book titled simply *Poems*. In that book appeared the poem "A Visit from St. Nicholas," familiarly known as "The Night before Christmas." The poem had been appearing without any authorial attribution in various publications since 1823, when it was printed in the *Troy (N.Y.) Sentinel*. His claim to authorship, though ambiguous at first, became more definite as years passed and went as far as the production of a holograph version, written and signed "Clement C. Moore" and dated 13 March 1862.

Conflicting claims to authorship of the poem have come forth over the years since it first came to light, principally from the family of one Henry Livingston, Jr., also known as Major Livingston. The most telling of those arguments, perhaps, has been that Livingston was adept at writing in the difficult anapestic rhythms of the poem in question, while for a time it appeared that no other poems accredited to Moore were anapestic, and Moore's poems have little of the grace and wit of the poem so familiar to countless people around the world.

However, Samuel White Patterson, Moore's principal biographer, steadfastly supported Moore's authorship and even reconstructed the Christmas Eve gathering of 1822 at which he believed Moore first read the poem to his young family. In support of his veracity, Patterson wrote: "The accounts of the memorable Christmas Eve of 1822 in Chelsea House are many. Now and then they seem a bit confused, but tradition based on a good deal of fact makes us reasonably sure of the picture just given. The grain of truth, at least, runs through it" (p. 10).

The most solid "grain of truth," however, for dissuading those who are swayed by the evidence of Major Livingston's well-documented virtuosity in anapestic lyrics may well be Patterson's quotation of a poem by Moore that begins and continues for several pages in the following meter:

> On a warm summer day, in the midst of July,
> A lazy young pig lay stretched out in the sty,
> Like some of his betters, most solemnly thinking
> That the best things on earth are good eating
> and drinking.

With that inconsequential, porcine poem the claims of the Livingston adherents are met on their own literary grounds.

Moore died in Newport, Rhode Island.

• Primary sources on Moore are in the records of the New York Genealogical and Biographical Society; Trinity Church, New York City; and Trinity Church, Newport, R.I. Livingston sources are in the William L. Thomas Papers, New-York Historical Society; Adriance Public Library, Poughkeepsie, N.Y.; the Livingston Family Papers, Clermont State Historic Site, Clermont, N.Y.; the New York State Archives, Albany; and the Museum of the City of New York. Samuel White Patterson, *The Poet of Christmas Eve* (1956), is the main defense of Moore's authorship. Patterson devotes an appendix to the controversy (pp. 167–71), repeating the claims while holding his ground in favor of the Moore authorship. He also includes an exhaustive bibliography. The principal challenges to Clement Moore's authorship of "A Visit from St. Nicholas" are, first, William S. Thomas, "Henry Livingston," in the *Year Book of the Dutchess County Historical Society* 5 (1919), pp. 32–46. Thomas was a relative of the Livingston family. His claim was repeated and amplified by Helen Wilkinson Reynolds in vol. 27 of the same journal (pp. 85–104). Henry Noble McCracken, former president of Vassar College, expanded the claim even further in *Blithe Dutchess* (1958), pp. 370–90.

ALFRED H. MARKS

MOORE, Donald Wynkoop (1905?–7 Apr. 1986), magazine editor and writer best known for his work on comic strips and teleplays. His birthplace and his parents' names and occupations are unknown. He graduated second in his class with a bachelor's degree in English from Dartmouth College in 1925. For several years after graduation he worked as a journalist, first in his parents' hometown of Miami, Florida, at the *Miami News* and the *Miami Beach Beacon*, then in the Bahamas. There he founded the Nassau News Bureau (later the Bahama News Bureau) and acted as correspondent for both the Associated Press and United Press International. His *New York Times* obituary quoted him about his work for the wire services: "I was careful not to tell the one I worked for the other. I scooped myself frequently."

In 1928, after what Moore laughingly termed "yrs of starvation and plenty as an alleged newspaperman, publicity man, AP correspondent, youmorist, whatnot," he obtained an associate-editing position at *Argosy All-Story Weekly*, an adventure and mystery magazine that gave him experience with fantasy fiction. He also worked for a time as an editor for *Cosmopolitan*. In 1934, about the time of his first marriage (to Isabel Walsh, whom he divorced in 1946), King Features hired him at $25 a week to write for a new comic titled "Flash Gordon." Drawn by Alex Raymond, the strip was inaugurated in response to a rival syndicate's "Buck Rogers" comic and quickly developed its own large following.

The eponymous hero of "Flash Gordon" was a muscular, polo-playing Yale graduate destined to save the universe for democracy. Flash and his loyal beloved, Dale Arden, were forced by a mad scientist named Zarkov to journey with him to the planet Mongo, domain of the totalitarian "Ming the Merciless" and his daughter Princess Aura. The blond Flash's struggle against the tyranny of the "yellow peril" Ming—and the lust of brunette Aura—lasted for years. Arthur Asa Berger has described the strip as chronicling "the heroic exploits of a bold adventurer, who brings freedom and democracy to alien worlds, fights injustice and tyranny, and destroys all kinds of hideous monsters and brutal despots along the way." Ming and his cohorts were eventually overthrown or reformed, and Flash went on to similar, if less memorable, enemies. The romance, democratic fervor, and xenophobia of the strip attracted audiences before and during World War II who also flocked to its successful adaptation into film serials starring Buster Crabbe.

Moore also scripted another Alex Raymond creation, "Jungle Jim," although that comic was never so popular as "Flash Gordon." "Jungle Jim," which attempted to cash in on the success of "Tarzan," started out as a jungle epic but evolved into a story of international intrigue. Jungle Jim Bradley journeyed about the Orient with an Indian servant named Kolu and a Dietrich-esque female assistant named Lil.

Moore stayed with King Features for twenty years, taking time along the way to work as a captain (later a major) in the Signal Corps, the Adjutant General's Office, and the War Department Bureau of Public Relations between 1942 and 1944. After the war he worked briefly as a story editor for Warner Bros. and RKO Pictures and for CBS-TV. He continued his television work, combining it with his experience in science-fiction writing, with two early space-adventure series in that medium, *Rod Brown of the Rocket Rangers* and *Captain Video*. The latter proved to be one of the runaway successes of early television, despite its abysmally low budget and inconsistent plots.

In 1956 Moore coauthored his only book, *The Naked Warriors*, with F. D. Fane. In 1958 he moved from New York to California to supervise the production of the TV anthology *Studio One* for McCann-Erickson Advertising Agency and met his second wife, Eris Crowe, whom he married in that year. His career thereafter proved inconsistent. He served for a time as story editor for *Death Valley Days* and for Screen Gems and MGM-TV. He also scripted episodes for a variety of television programs, including *Sea Hunt* and *Rawhide*. "TV being famous for alternate chicken and feathers," he reminisced in the 1960s, "I've also done publicity writing. Was advertising manager of a health food magazine, then a group of business magazines." After a near-fatal asthma attack in 1964, Moore returned to magazine advertising, working for a group of business and trade journals on the West Coast. It is not clear whether Eris Moore died or he divorced her, but eventually he married a woman named Anne (maiden name unknown). In 1969 he retired to Venice, Florida, where he could indulge in his hobbies of golf and snorkeling. He died there.

• The Dartmouth College Archives include a very few papers relating to Moore. Information about "Flash Gordon" and "Jungle Jim" can be found in Russell Nye, *The Unembarrassed Muse* (1970); Martin Sheridan, *Comics and Their Creators* (1971); Arthur Asa Berger, *The Comic-Stripped American* (1973); and Maurice Horn, *World Encyclopedia of Comics* (1976). Moore's TV space programs are discussed in Alex MacNeil, *Total Television* (1984); Tim Brooks and Earle Marsh, *The Complete Directory to Prime Time Network TV Shows* (1985); and Linda Rosenkrantz, "Captain Video First TV Space Explorer," *Antiques and Collecting*, Jan. 1991, p. 22. An obituary is in the *New York Times*, 10 Apr. 1986.

TINKY "DAKOTA" WEISBLAT

MOORE, Douglas (10 Aug. 1893–25 July 1969), composer and teacher, was born Douglas Stuart Moore in Cutchogue, New York, the son of Stuart Hull Moore and Myra Drake, both editors. His father, who represented the ninth generation of Moores to inhabit Long Island, worked for *Ladies' World*, one of America's earliest women's magazines. His mother, an amateur pianist, counted both Miles Standish and John Alden among her ancestors. Given this musical and literary environment as well as his strong roots in the American soil, it is not surprising that Douglas Moore's reputation as a composer was won in the medium of opera and in the "Americanist" musical idiom.

While preparing at the Hotchkiss School for Yale University, he met Archibald MacLeish, the first of several American poets with whom he collaborated. Moore had taken piano lessons as a boy but received no training in music theory; nevertheless, he set some of MacLeish's poems to music in 1910 as his first compositions. The following year he enrolled in a liberal arts program at Yale, where at first his only musical activity was writing popular songs. One of these, "Naomi, My Restaurant Queen," became his first published work. In his junior year, Moore enrolled in a harmony class; he also wrote music for a campus production of *Quentin Durward*. Having thereby captured the attention of Horatio Parker, Moore began to study with this famous professor of composition who had been the teacher of Charles Ives. Now increasingly drawn toward a musical career, Moore completed his bachelor of arts degree in 1915. He remained at Yale two more years and earned a bachelor of music as well.

During one of his summer vacations from college, Moore continued to write songs while living at the MacDowell Colony, a New Hampshire artists' retreat to which his family had made a financial contribution. During a period of service in the U.S. Navy in World War I he did further songwriting, this time in collaboration with John Jacob Niles on an amusing volume called *Songs My Mother Never Taught Me*. Discharged from the military in 1919, Moore resisted pressure to enter the family publishing business. Instead, he used a modest inheritance from his father, who had died the previous year, to support two years of music studies in Paris with Vincent d'Indy and Nadia Boulanger. These were interrupted in the fall of 1920 by Moore's brief return to the United States to marry Emily Bailey, with whom he subsequently had two daughters.

While in Paris, the composer met Stephen Vincent Benét, who became his second major literary influence. Through the ensuing years, Moore set many of Benét's poems for both solo voice and chorus. Their most important collaboration would take place in 1939, when Benét's short story "The Devil and Daniel Webster" became the first of Moore's operas to gain widespread recognition. Moore met Vachel Lindsay, a third important poetic force in his life, through a chance encounter in the library of the Cleveland Art Museum, where Moore was employed as the director of musical activities from 1921 to 1925. During these years he also studied composition with Ernest Bloch, acted at the Cleveland Playhouse, and played the organ at Adelbert College of Western Reserve University.

Lindsay opened the composer's perceptions to the flavor of American life and the possibilities of its musical expression. This new direction inspired an orchestral suite, *The Pageant of P. T. Barnum* (1924), which was performed by the Cleveland Orchestra and which established Moore's reputation. This work also won him a Pulitzer Traveling Fellowship to Europe in 1925, after which he joined the music faculty of Columbia University and settled down to a long distinguished academic career (1926–1962). From 1940 to 1962 he was head of the music department, and from 1943 to 1962 he also held the McDowell Professorship of Music. For many years, his course in twentieth-century music had a particularly strong following among the Columbia undergraduates, and he distilled the essence of all his lectures on music literature into two volumes called *Listening to Music* (1932) and *From Madrigal to Modern Music* (1942).

Moore's designation as an Americanist comes from the pen of Gilbert Chase, the first and still one of the most important chroniclers of America's musical history. It relates first of all to Moore's choices of subject matter in all genres. Among these were the orchestral works *Moby Dick* and *Overture on an American Tune*; a setting of Benét's "Ballad of William Sycamore" for voice and chamber orchestra; and a number of operas, especially *The Ballad of Baby Doe*, which was first produced in 1955 and has since become a staple in the American repertoire.

The other principal component of Moore's Americanism is his musical language. Aaron Copland found it to be "highly evocative of the homely virtues of rural America" in its "simplicity and unadorned charm," while the conductor Thomas Scherman praised "Moore's very personal melodic drive [and] the inherent dramatic variety and contrast in his music." The composer himself described his artistic intentions in similar terms. "The particular ideal which I have been striving to attain," he explained, "is to write music which . . . will reflect the exciting quality of life, traditions, and country which I feel all about me."

Moore was elected to the National Institute of Arts and Letters in 1941 and five years later became a member of the board of directors of the American Academy in Rome. He served as president of the American Academy of Arts and Letters from 1959 to 1962 and was also a director of ASCAP.

Moore composed his final American opera, *Carrie Nation*, in 1966, three years before his death in Greenport, Long Island. His reputation persists as a major definer and interpreter of the American musical idiom.

• Columbia University holds the major collection of Moore's papers, including manuscripts and correspondence. A listing of his works may be found in the *New Grove's Dictionary of Music and Musicians* (1980). For the most complete treatment of his life and work, see David Ewen, *American Composers* (1982). See also Otto Luening, *Modern Music* (May 1943): 20–248; and Ruth C. Friedberg, *American Art Song and American Poetry*, vol. 1 (1981), for specific discussions of Moore's style in various genres of composition; and Madeleine Goss, *Modern Music Makers* (1952), for a detailed view of his life and career to that date. Three theses on Moore's compositions were produced in the decade following his death: Jay Harold Weizel, *A Melodic Analysis of Selected Vocal Solos in the Operas of Douglas Moore* (Ph.D. diss., New York Univ., 1971); Donald Joseph Reagan, *Douglas Moore and his Orchestral Works* (Ph.D. diss., Catholic Univ. of America, 1972); and Randie Lee Blooding, *Douglas Moore's "The Ballad of Baby Doe": An Investigation of Its Historical Accuracy and the Feasibility of a Historical Production in the Tabor Opera House* (D.M.A. thesis, Ohio State Univ., 1979). An obituary is in the *New York Times*, 28 July 1969.

RUTH C. FRIEDBERG

MOORE, Edward Chandler (30 Aug. 1827–2 Aug. 1891), designer and silversmith, was born in New York City, the son of John Chandler Moore, a silversmith, and Margaret (maiden name unknown). He apprenticed with his father, who produced silver for John P. Marquand and for Ball, Tompkins, and Black, and then he became his father's partner in 1848, when he turned twenty-one years of age. By 1851 he took over his father's shop and began an association with Tiffany and Company that would last four decades.

In 1868, when Tiffany's became incorporated, Moore sold his shop to Tiffany's and became an officer of the company and the director of its silver department. He played a pivotal role in expanding the department and establishing Tiffany and Company's international reputation as the maker of some of the most significant nineteenth-century American silver. At Tiffany's Prince Street factory he had established in the 1860s a sort of craft school for silversmiths, which was modeled after the French system he had seen on trips abroad in 1855 and again in 1867. Combining the skills of business management with design capabilities, Moore was able to manage the industrialization of Tiffany's production while maintaining high artistic standards.

Moore was deeply committed to producing silver in the Japanese style, and objects with oriental decoration and using oriental techniques were perhaps his greatest contribution to the look of Tiffany silver. But he was also interested in Islamic (which he called Saracenic) art and the art of many other cultures. His collection of about 2,500 ancient, medieval, oriental, Islamic metals, textiles, lacquers, armor, and other objects was bequeathed to the Metropolitan Museum of Art on his death, along with his working reference library of some 556 books; both had been essential sources for his silver designs. His surviving sketchbooks also demonstrate his intense study of many different kinds of objects from a variety of traditions. The silver Moore created was noted for its utility and beautiful form and also for its experimental nature. He developed the use of mixed-metal designs, etching, enameling, oxidation, and other innovative manufacturing techniques. While heavily influenced by historic and exotic sources, Moore's silver achieved an air of individuality through its combination of design elements and fine craftsmanship.

Moore's silver frequently won medals and honors at the important international fairs and expositions of the last half of the nineteenth century, beginning in 1867 at the Paris Exposition Universelle and including the 1876 Centennial Exposition at Philadelphia. The "hammered silver" (with visible hammer marks left on the surface, rather than being planished out) designed by Moore and exhibited by Tiffany's at the Paris Exposition of 1878 received the Grand Prix and helped establish the United States as the international leader in silversmithing, winning honors in competition with the finest wares from England and France. His Saracenic work was similarly honored at the 1889 Paris fair, when Moore was also named a chevalier of the Legion of Honor by the French government.

Moore died at his home in Hastings-on-Hudson, New York. He had been married and was the father of four sons. He was a member of the Chamber of Commerce and of the Union League, Century, Manhattan, and Aldine Clubs, and of the Architectural League. At his death, the *Illustrated American* (29 Aug. 1891) remembered him as "easily the foremost silversmith in the United States. It is largely due to his skill and industry that American silverware has reached a degree of perfection that makes it celebrated all over the world. He practically developed a new industry here: but modest and retiring, almost morbidly averse to publicity of any kind, he passed through life without assuming in the eyes of the general public the credit he so well deserved." One of his grandsons, John C. Moore, was president of Tiffany's from 1907 to 1938 and chairman to 1947.

Although Moore was widely known in his own lifetime, his name quickly became eclipsed by the more famous names of Charles L. Tiffany and Louis Comfort Tiffany. Beginning in the 1970s, however, scholars such as Charles Carpenter and Mary Grace Carpenter resurrected Moore's reputation, recognizing his essential contribution to the history of American Victorian silver.

• Moore's professional life is documented in the Tiffany Archives, Parsippany, N.J.; Moore's own working library of reference works is at the Metropolitan Musuem of Art, along with his collection of ancient, medieval, oriental, and Islamic decorative arts. Charles H. Carpenter, Jr., and Mary Grace Carpenter, *Tiffany Silver* (1978), remains the best survey of Tiffany's during the Moore era. See also Bruce Kamerling, "Edward C. Moore: The Genius behind Tiffany Silver," *Silver* 10 (Sept.–Oct. 1977): 16–20, 10 (Nov.–Dec. 1977): 8–12; and Doreen Bolger Burke et al., *In Pursuit of Beauty: Americans and the Aesthetic Movement* (1986), which includes many bibliographical citations on pp. 472–73. For a recent survey placing Moore's work in context, see Charles L. Venable, *Silver in America, 1840–1940: A Century of Splendor* (1994).

GERALD W. R. WARD

MOORE, Edwin Ward (June 1810?–5 Oct. 1865), U.S. and Texas naval officer, was born in Alexandria, Virginia. After receiving a secondary education at the Alexandria Academy, he enlisted in the U.S. Navy as a midshipman in 1825 and was promoted to lieutenant in 1835. In these years he served first in the West Indies on the brig *Hornet* (1825–1827) and aboard the sloop *Fairfield* (1828–1829), then in the Mediterranean on the ship of the line *Delaware* (1829–1830). In 1831–1832 he was again aboard the *Fairfield* in the West Indies. After promotion to lieutenant, he served aboard the sloop *Boston* (1836–1839).

Moore resigned his U.S. Navy commission in 1839 to join the navy of the independent Republic of Texas. During its war of independence with Mexico, Texas had developed a navy using letters of marque and reprisal to commission privateers. However, in 1839 Texas organized a formal fleet, purchasing a steamer, two brigs, three schooners, and a sloop of war, the *Austin*, which was to serve as flagship of the fleet. Moore was appointed commodore of the fleet and sailed aboard the *Austin*. He recruited sailors from the U.S. Navy and was briefly arrested in the United States for violating the Neutrality Act of 1818. The Texas government posted Moore's bond.

In 1840 Moore took five of the ships of his small navy sailing along the coast of Mexico. Acting under orders of the president of Texas, Mirabeau Lamar, he established relations with the rebellious province of Yucatán. Over the next three years, Moore successfully cooperated with Yucatán against the Mexican government. However, in 1842, when Sam Houston became president of Texas, Moore found himself in disfavor with Texas authorities because Houston never understood the navy's role in the Texas Revolution and believed that Moore's actions undermined his diplomatic authority and strategy. Nevertheless, Moore continued to sail under the Texas flag, with financial and logistics support from the Yucatán authorities. After several sailors on one of his vessels staged an unsuccessful mutiny in February 1842, he ordered their execution, which took place in April 1843. For this act, President Houston declared Moore guilty of murder.

In the battle of Campeche Harbor on 30 April 1843, Moore, in command of the *Austin* and the brig *Wharton*, engaged a larger Mexican force, which included two newly constructed, British-built steamers, *Guadeloupe* and *Montezuma*. The steamers evaded Moore's guns, but on 16 May 1843 Moore again attacked, driving the Mexican ships from the area. Reputedly this was the only recorded battle in which sailing vessels defeated steamers and the first battle in which both sides fired exploding shells.

President Houston ordered Moore to return to Galveston to protect his ships, but Moore evaded the orders for several weeks, operating with finances from Yucatán. Houston then declared Moore a pirate and outlaw. Faced with the possibility of capture and execution by the British or Mexican governments, Moore finally sailed his fleet back to Galveston, where he was received as a hero at mass meetings and public celebrations. When Houston issued a dishonorable discharge to Moore, his fellow officers resigned in protest. The sheriff of Galveston refused to arrest Moore when he presented himself for that purpose. Moore published a pamphlet presenting his case, including documents regarding the history of the Texas navy. At his trial he was cleared of all charges except four minor counts of "disobedience of orders."

Despite the pleading of Moore and coastal residents, the Texas government ordered the fleet of ships sold. The auction failed, however, as local residents intimidated potential bidders into silence. Despite the disbanding of Moore's navy, the Texas Congress indemnified him with the grant of a large tract of land and a cash award.

When Texas was annexed to the United States, Moore's fleet was incorporated into the U.S. Navy, although only the *Austin* was seaworthy. Moore and his officers sought U.S. financial benefits. However, Houston, as U.S. senator from Texas, was able to block awards to Moore, who was also denied an opportunity to rejoin the U.S. Navy. Eventually a compromise was passed in 1855 by which Moore and his fellow officers were awarded leave pay to cover the period from annexation to the passage of the bill. For Moore the pay amounted to some $17,000. After the settlement, Moore resided in New York City, working on mechanical experiments and inventions, until his death there. He never married.

Moore, as a trained U.S. naval officer who left to operate independently under the flag of Texas, had a remarkable career. His willingness to evade orders and on occasion to directly disobey them made him into a colorful hero of Texas independence. However, his longstanding disputes with President Houston over naval policy coupled with his support by the Texas Congress and the residents of Galveston made him one of the more controversial figures in the tumultuous short history of the Texas Republic.

• Small collections of papers pertaining to Moore and the Texas navy are at the University of Texas at Arlington and the University of Texas at Austin. Moore's publications include *A Brief Synopsis of the Doings of the Texas Navy under the Command of Com. E. W. Moore* (1847) and a survey of the Texas coast, *The Coast of Texas* (1848). See also Elizabeth Silverthorne, "Sam Houston vs. Edwin Moore and the Texas Navy," *Oceans*, May 1982. An obituary is in the *New York Herald*, 10 Oct. 1865.

RODNEY P. CARLISLE

MOORE, Eliakim Hastings (26 Jan. 1862–30 Dec. 1932), mathematician, was born in Marietta, Ohio, the son of David Hastings Moore, a Methodist minister, and Julia Sophia Carpenter. Moore studied both mathematics and astronomy as an undergraduate at Yale from 1879 to 1883. He remained there until 1885, when he earned his Ph.D. under the direction of Hubert Anson Newton for his thesis, "Extensions of Certain Theorems of Clifford and Cayley in *the Geometry of n* Dimensions" (*Transactions of the Connecticut Academy of Arts and Sciences* 7 [1885]: 9–26). With Newton's encouragement, Moore next proceeded to Germany for a year of postgraduate study.

His Wanderjahr began at Göttingen University, where he prepared himself linguistically for the courses he subsequently attended at the University of Berlin. There, two of the nineteenth century's premier mathematical figures, Karl Weierstrass and Leopold Kronecker, attracted numerous auditors from both Germany and abroad. While direct influences of this German study tour on Moore's subsequent mathematical career are difficult to isolate, it is undeniable that Moore returned to the United States with a sense of the importance and desirability of the active and sustained pursuit of original research, a fundamental characteristic of the German research ethic of the latter half of the nineteenth century. In 1892 he would transplant this ideal into the congenial environment of the newly founded University of Chicago, after serving for one year as a teacher at the academy associated with Northwestern University, two years as a tutor at Yale (1887–1889), and three years as an assistant, then associate, professor of mathematics back at Northwestern (1889–1892). Also in 1892, Moore married Martha Morris Young. The couple had two children, one of whom survived to adulthood.

The president-designate of the University of Chicago, William Rainey Harper, had come to know Moore as early as 1890, when he had tried to recruit the young mathematician as a teacher at Chautauqua, the institution in upstate New York that had been spearheading a movement in popular education since the 1870s. Moore had declined the invitation, explaining that his own development as a researcher was more important at the time than relatively low-level teaching. In 1891 Harper approached him with another offer that would presumably lend itself to his research objectives, a position at the University of Chicago. When the university opened for business in October of 1892, Moore was in place as the acting head of its Department of Mathematics. He became head in 1896 and served in this capacity until 1931.

Moore proved unusually effective as an administrator. Together with Harper, he brought together a singularly distinguished faculty in mathematics, which consisted of himself and the two German mathematicians, Oskar Bolza and Heinrich Maschke. In 1893 Moore and his colleagues, along with Henry Seely White of Northwestern University, organized the mathematical congress associated with the World's Columbian Exposition in Chicago, the country's first international mathematics meeting. In 1894 they approached the New York Mathematical Society (founded in 1888) in an effort to secure the publication of the congress's proceedings. They not only won the society's financial support but also spurred it to change its name to the American Mathematical Society (AMS) and adopt an increasingly national orientation. In 1896 Moore forced the further westward expansion of the society's power base by spearheading the organization of what would become, in 1897, the Chicago Section of the AMS. This section, and the others that soon followed in the West and Southwest, held regular meetings at which mathematicians were invited to share their latest findings. This provided a key communications outlet for those who were geographically far removed from New York City, the site of the society's monthly meetings. Moore's national activism also manifested itself in 1899 in the formation of a new research-level journal, the *Transactions of the American Mathematical Society*. As this journal's editor in chief from its inception until 1907, he instituted and maintained high editorial standards that almost immediately established a favorable reputation for the new publication at home and abroad.

Moore's initiatives on behalf of mathematics in the United States were widely recognized and appreciated by his peers. In 1898 he won election to the vice presidency of the AMS, and he served as its president from January 1901 through December 1902. Moore used his presidential address, "On the Foundations of Mathematics" (*Science* 17 [1903]: 401–16), as a forum for the promotion of improved mathematics education at all levels. In fact, he argued for a hands-on approach to mathematical pedagogy reminiscent of the ideas of his former colleague at Chicago, John Dewey.

The fifteen years from 1892 to 1907 witnessed not only Moore's active participation in mathematics at the national level but also his blossoming as a major figure in mathematical research and in the training of advanced students. From 1893 until the end of the century, Moore's work focused primarily on questions in group theory. In particular, he proved the existence of a new class of finite simple groups as well as an important classification theorem in the theory of finite fields in his contribution to the Chicago congress, "A Doubly-Infinite System of Simple Groups" (*Mathematical Papers Read at the International Mathematical Congress*, pp. 208–42). By 1900 Moore's interests had shifted to problems in the foundations of geometry raised by the then-recent and pivotal work of Göttingen University's David Hilbert. In the paper "On the Projective Axioms of Geometry" (*Transactions of the American Mathematical Society* 3 [1902]: 142–58), Moore showed that there were redundancies in the axiom system Hilbert had proposed. Finally, by 1906, Moore had changed mathematical direction for the third and final time when he launched an ambitious research program in the foundations of analysis. Called "general analysis," Moore's theory aimed to subsume various areas of analysis under one overarching, abstract, and general theory. He presented a first version of his ideas in "Introduction to a Form of General Analysis" (*New Haven Colloquium* [1910]) and a second in the posthumously published book *General Analysis: Part 1* (1935), coauthored by Raymond Walter Barnard. Moore is perhaps best remembered for the notions of the so-called Moore-Smith limit and Moore-Smith convergence, both of which arise within the context of his general analysis.

During each of his three distinct research phases, Moore succeeded in directing the doctoral research of a student who would become a leading American—and, indeed, international—figure in the field. In 1896 Leonard Eugene Dickson completed his thesis research on linear groups; in 1903 and 1905, Oswald Veblen and Robert L. Moore, respectively, earned their doctorates for work on the foundations of geometry; and in 1907, George David Birkhoff produced a dissertation in analysis, although not in the sort of general analysis that engaged his adviser at the time. As this list evidences, Moore's style of teaching—characterized by a quick-paced presentation of new research ideas and what could be a stinging impatience with those who failed to follow—certainly proved effective, at least for the most talented. Moore was a man of high intellectual and academic standards; he expected much from himself, his students, and his colleagues.

Moore partially retired from active teaching in 1931. Among his many honors and awards were an honorary doctorate from Göttingen University (1899), membership in the National Academy of Sciences (from 1901), and the presidency of the American Association for the Advancement of Science (1921). He died in Chicago.

Moore established the first self-sustaining graduate program in mathematics in the United States at the University of Chicago. As early as the 1890s his department, unlike any in the country, taught a curriculum at both the undergraduate and graduate levels comparable to that at the best of the precedent-setting German universities of the day. It succeeded, largely through Moore's initiative and energy, in training much of the first generation of American-educated mathematical researchers and in animating the professional community so crucial to the subject's further development on these shores.

• The papers of E. H. Moore are housed at the Joseph Regenstein Library of the University of Chicago in nineteen boxes and include correspondence dating from 1889 to 1931, student notes from his courses, reprints of his published papers, and Moore's own working papers. Additional correspondence between Moore and William Rainey Harper dealing with the organization and running of the Department of Mathematics may also be found in the University Presidents' Papers 1889–1925 and in the William Rainey Harper Papers, also at the University of Chicago. Among Moore's other influential works are *Mathematical Papers Read at the International Mathematical Congress Held in Connection with the World's Columbian Exposition Chicago 1893*, ed. E. H. Moore et al. (1896); "Definition of Limit in General Integral Analysis," *Proceedings of the National Academy of Sciences* 1 (1915): 628–32; and (with H. L. Smith), "A General Theory of Limits," *American Journal of Mathematics* 44 (1922): 102–21. On Moore's life and work, see, for example, Gilbert A. Bliss, "Eliakim Hastings Moore," *Bulletin of the American Mathematical Society* 39 (1933): 831–38; Leonard Eugene Dickson, "Eliakim Hastings Moore," *Science* 77 (1933): 79–80; Gilbert A. Bliss, "The Scientific Work of Eliakim Hastings Moore," *Bulletin of the American Mathematical Society* 40 (1934): 501–14; and Raymond C. Archibald, *A Semicentennial History of the American Mathematical Society* (1938), pp. 144–50. The latter two works contain a complete list of Moore's works. Moore's pivotal role in the early American mathematical community receives extensive treatment in Karen Hunger Parshall and David E. Rowe, *The Emergence of the American Mathematical Research Community 1876–1900: J. J. Sylvester, Felix Klein, and E. H. Moore* (1994).

KAREN HUNGER PARSHALL

MOORE, Ely (4 July 1798–27 Jan. 1860), labor leader and congressman, was born near Belvidere, New Jersey, the son of Moses Moore and Mary Coryell, farmers. His early years are obscure. He attended public schools, learned the printer's trade, and moved to New York City in the early 1820s. He later claimed to have studied medicine there. Around that time he married Emma Coutant, whose father, a Democrat, was elected county registrar, and in 1830 appointed Moore assistant county registrar for New York County (Manhattan). Moore displayed his oratorical skills in Coutant's struggle against the charter of the New York & Harlem Railroad, which threatened the livelihood of local carters. Moore and his wife had six children; following her death, he married Clara Baker, with whom he had no children.

Several issues riled New York craft workers. In the 1810s and 1820s an expanding economy had given them economic security and the feeling of being the social equals of the small merchant class. But they were increasingly paid in paper money from chartered banks, whose value fluctuated; the cost of credit seemed manipulated by speculators, and prison labor cut into their sales. There also was a feeling of growing social inequality. In response, New York City craftsmen and mechanics created labor unions and in 1833 formed the General Trades' Union (GTU). Moore, who had not worked as printer in a decade, saw his opportunity. He joined a local typographical union in 1833, became its delegate to the GTU charter meeting, and after a rousing speech was elected its president. In 1834 he became president of the National Trades' Union, a league of six East Coast city unions including the GTU, and the publisher of its organ, *National Trades' Union*. He was now a prominent labor leader.

In 1834 New York State governor William Marcy, a Democrat, appointed a committee to study prison labor. Moore was on it and was the Tammany Hall candidate for Congress. He won handily on his reputation as defender of labor. But the report, issued in the spring of 1835, advocated only small changes, and Moore's voters took his endorsement of it as "a barefaced piece of treachery," as the *New York Evening Post* commented. Moore was not reelected president of either the GTU or the National Trades' Union, and he ceased to have any official relationship with organized labor. In the fall of 1836 he was reelected to Congress, finessing his way through the main issue, whether to charter more state banks, which Democratic leaders wanted and working-class voters opposed. He became political editor for the *New York Evening Post* in 1838. In Congress Moore served on the Committee on Naval Affairs, trying without success to raise the pay of enlisted men and pass a bill to limit the work day on all public works to ten hours. He also defended the right of workers to organize against charges that unions were a conspiracy against trade. But on the whole he was a quiet congressional freshman.

Moore's equivocation over labor issues, which contrasted with his fiery rhetoric, reflected partly his recognition that the American political elite opposed any reform. But he was moved not only by self-interest. Like many workers then, Moore believed in American exceptionalism. As a land of freedom and plenty "born free" through the Revolution, the United States was by nature a harmonious society. The present tensions were quirks caused by oligarchic conspiracies to acquire monopolies, by the "heartless cupidity of the privileged few," as he told Congress on 5 May 1836. Reform was not needed, only the restoration of unfettered individual competition as it existed in Thomas Jefferson's day. The only reform he advocated was better public education.

A long economic depression began in May 1837. President Martin Van Buren wanted to restore credit through an independent treasury system based on state banks. This was attacked by workers who wanted specie, and Whigs who argued that this gave patronage to local oligarchies and did not square with the Jacksonians' opposition to a national bank. Moore stood by Van Buren and, in November 1838, went down to defeat. Thankful, Van Buren appointed him surveyor of the port of New York. But he was dismissed after the Republicans won the presidency in 1840. His attempts at a political comeback were thwarted by labor leaders John Windt, Mike Walsh, and John Commerford, who considered him an opportunist. Tammany Hall refused in 1844 to nominate him for mayor. That same year he ran for Congress but lost. President James K. Polk, a Democrat, made him U.S. marshall for southern New York in 1845, but he was dismissed in 1849 after the Republican Zachary Taylor became president. Moore then bought the *Warren Journal* in his native Belvidere, but his financial situation deteriorated.

In 1853 Moore was appointed agent for several First Nations in Kansas, and from 1855 to 1860 he served as registrar of the United States land office in Lecompton, Kansas. He died on his nearby farm.

Moore was the first labor spokesman in Congress. Taking his speeches at face value, older labor historians took his career as proof that labor played a major role in the Jacksonian coalition. Historians at the end of the twentieth century are less certain of that and see Moore more as an opportunist who used the nascent labor movement as a stepping stone for his career.

• Documents about Moore are in the Kansas State Historical Society in Topeka, especially in the papers of his son Ely Moore, Jr. Moore's speeches are found in New York City newspapers and the *Congressional Globe*. He is usually mentioned in labor histories of the Jacksonian era. Detailed treatments are Walter E. Hugins, "Ely Moore: The Case History of a Jacksonian Labor Leader," *Political Science Quarterly* 65 (1950): 105–25, and in his *Jacksonian Democracy and the Working Class* (1960); Edward Pessen, *Most Uncommon Jacksonians* (1967); and Sean Wilentz, *Chants Democratic* (1984).

THOMAS REIMER

MOORE, Eva Perry (24 July 1852–28 Apr. 1931), women's club leader, was born in Rockford, Illinois, the daughter of Seely Perry, occupation unknown, and Elizabeth Benedict. She attended Vassar College, graduating in 1873, and traveled in Europe for three years. In 1879 she married Philip North Moore, a mining engineer, to whom she was married for fifty-one years, until his death in 1930. They had two children. Her husband's work caused the family to move around the country for ten years, until they settled in St. Louis in 1889. There, Moore distinguished herself in local women's organizational efforts and climbed to statewide and national leadership roles.

She was a charter member of the Wednesday Club, a women's literary society, in 1890 and its president from 1892 to 1894. As president of the Missouri Federation of Women's Clubs (1901–1905), she organized local arrangements for the St. Louis Biennial Conference of the General Federation of Women's Clubs in 1904. She had a lifelong interest in music and served as president of the St. Louis Music Club (1892–1903), vice president of the budding National Federation of Music Clubs (1901–1903), and vice president of the St. Louis Symphony Society until 1918. In the arena of education, she served as a trustee of Vassar College (1900–1908) and president of the Association of Collegiate Alumnae (1903–1907), which later became the American Association of University Women. She also devoted considerable volunteer effort to social service causes, holding office in the St. Louis Provident Association, the Visiting Nurse Association, the Missouri Tuberculosis Society, and the National Society for Organizing and Advising Charities.

Moore rose to national prominence in the General Federation of Women's Clubs, holding several offices: corresponding secretary (1894–1898), treasurer (1898–1900), vice president (1904–1908), and finally president (1908–1912). As president, she traveled 75,000 miles, meeting with many American and Panama Canal Zone clubwomen in the organization of two million members. Among the civic goals she addressed during her administration were vocational education in public schools, workmen's compensation, safety for factory and mine workers, peace, prevention of white slave traffic, conservation, establishment of a department of education and a department of health, creation of a federal bureau of national parks and of a children's bureau, cleaner journalism, a pure-food law, agricultural extension programs, good roads, roadside planting, an employers' liability bill, women as police and immigration officers, hygiene in public schools, uniform marriage laws, and birth registration.

She quickly moved to the presidency of the largest organization of American women, the National Council of Women, an alliance of thirty-six national organizations, including the General Federation. She served from 1914 to 1925, hosting the international meetings of forty national networks in Washington, D.C. She was vice president of the International Council of Women from 1920 to 1930, traveling around the world to attend many of its meetings.

During World War I, she went to Washington, D.C., as secretary of the Women's Committee of the Council of National Defense (1917–1919). In 1919 she traveled with President Woodrow Wilson, campaigning on behalf of the League of Nations. She was a member of the Executive Committee of the League of Nations Non-Partisan Association (1923–1931) and the International Commission of the Pan-American Scientific Congress in Peru (1924) and Costa Rica (1930).

She died in St. Louis three days after returning from the Vienna conference of the International Council of Women, where she was awarded an honorary vice-presidency for life. Widely respected for her modest demeanor, zeal for service, upstanding character, and leadership abilities, Moore held more high offices in major women's voluntary organizations than any twentieth-century woman. She devoted herself to a public life of organizing women for social reform.

• Biography files can be found at General Federation of Women's Clubs headquarters in Washington, D.C., and at the Missouri Historical Society in St. Louis. The latter owns useful women's club scrapbooks as well. See also "Federation Matriarch Active Today," *General Federation News*, Dec. 1929, pp. 15–24. Obituaries are in *Clubwoman*, July 1931, pp. 9, 26, and *Missouri Clubwoman*, June 1931, p. 5.

KAREN J. BLAIR

MOORE, Frederick Randolph (16 June 1857–1 Mar. 1943), journalist and politician, was born in Prince William County, Virginia, the son of Eugene Moore and Evelina Diggs. Information concerning the parents' occupations is unavailable. Having left Virginia in early childhood, Fred Moore grew up in Washington, D.C., where he attended public schools and sold newspapers to help support himself and his family. At eighteen, he began work as a messenger for the U.S. Treasury Department and became personal messenger a few years later for the Secretary of the Treasury. He worked under six successive secretaries and traveled to Europe in 1887 with Secretary Daniel Manning. Also in 1887 Moore resigned from the Treasury Department and moved to New York City, where he became a clerk at the Western National Bank, which later merged with the National Bank of Commerce, a position he held for eighteen years.

Moore began his journalistic career in New York City as general manager and then editor and publisher in 1904 of the *Colored American Magazine*. Originating in Boston in 1900, the magazine changed, under Moore's editorship, from a mainly literary magazine into one that primarily stressed black economic advancement. Moore's purchase of the magazine and its removal to New York were aided by the secret financial support of influential black educator Booker T. Washington. Washington wanted a publication that promoted his philosophy of black economic development, and he supported editors who accepted his conservative position on black political and civil rights. Washington also intended to silence opponents like W. E. B. Du Bois and William Monroe Trotter, who condemned him repeatedly for emphasizing vocational training rather than challenging lynching, disfranchisement, and "Jim Crow" legislation. Moore shared Washington's belief in cultivating economic development in the black community as a means for gaining political equality. Black unity was key to Moore's political and economic philosophy. He believed African Americans should own their own homes and businesses in their communities. Black success in this endeavor, Moore thought, would mean political and economic equality.

Consequently, as editor of the *Colored American Magazine*, Moore explained that the new focus of the periodical was to illustrate "the successes of our people as a whole and as individuals." In this way, the editor hoped that the magazine would reach "the masses of the people" not merely "those who are highly educated and cultured." The *Colored American Magazine* became a didactic tool that encouraged African Americans to become entrepreneurs and, equally important, to patronize black businesses. The majority of black Americans needed, Moore argued, "information of the doings of the members of the race rather [than] the writing of dreamers or theorists." Yet, Moore did not ignore political issues. He consistently published articles and wrote editorials that condemned disfranchisement and lynching. At the same time, Washington's public policy of accommodationism and gradualism regarding southern black political and legal rights was promoted through articles by Washington and pro-Washington writers. Also, Tuskegee Institute, Washington's agricultural and vocational training school in Alabama, received extensive coverage. Most important, there were no longer attacks on Washington in the *Colored American Magazine* as there had been before Moore became editor.

In 1907 Moore again advanced through Washington's clandestine maneuvering and financial support by becoming editor and publisher of the New York *Age*. Published under various names and editors, the weekly newspaper had become the most prominent black paper in the country under the editorship of T. Thomas Fortune. Fortune supported Washington's goals, but not his accommodationist strategy or his loyalty to the Republican party. Under Moore's editorship the *Age* became a much more partisan paper. However, even though he was a devoted Republican, Moore did not endorse Washington or Republican party policies completely; in fact, he challenged them on the editorial pages of the *Age*, condemning Republican quiescence on lynching and disfranchisement and criticizing white southern political inequities and brutality.

Moore redirected the *Age* toward his own interest in black business development and highlighted such activities. Numerous articles featured the successes of black businessmen and women stressing not only their achievements but also a work ethic of industry, frugality, and sobriety. Moreover, Moore almost entirely ignored black radicals like Du Bois, Trotter, and Marcus Garvey. And, as he had done with the *Colored American Magazine*, which died under new editorship in 1909, Moore increased the circulation (to about 27,000 in 1937) and the volume of the New York *Age* and added special features.

After Washington's death in 1915, Moore was more outspoken in his support for southern black migration and political protest, two activities Washington had decried. After a trip to the South, Moore in 1917 urged southern blacks to agitate for fair treatment: "Now is the time for the Negroes of the South to speak out for their rights—not offensively but frankly." He began publishing speeches by selected liberals like Adam Clayton Powell, Sr., who called in 1917 for blacks to take advantage of the nation's need for manpower and wage a "bloodless war" for constitutional rights. By 1924 the *Age* focused extensively on Harlem, where Moore had moved, and revealed his concern for social issues, including medical services for Harlem residents. In the 1920s and 1930s, the pages of the *Age* supported boycotts of white Harlem merchants who refused to employ blacks in their stores and advocated city government investment in the rehabilitation of substandard housing for the poor. Moore's last contributions to the *Age* were during the early years of U.S. involvement in the Second World War when he supported A. Philip Randolph's March on Washington Movement, which demanded fair employment practices in the defense industry. Still, Moore's firm belief in black economic development and black patronage of black business remained a prominent theme in the newspaper.

Moore's career in journalism coexisted with the development of his own business interests. Consistent with his philosophy of racial solidarity and black economic development, in 1893 he helped establish the Afro-American Investment and Building Company which bought New Jersey and New York property and sold it to blacks at reasonable interest rates. By late 1904 Moore was owner of the Moore Publishing and Printing Company, which published both the *Colored American Magazine* and the New York *Age*. Moore noted with pride that the company was black owned and "that all of the mechanical work of construction connected with publishing the magazine has been done by members of the race exclusively." Also in 1904, he was organizer and in the following year general secretary of the National Negro Business League, an organization Washington created to promote black business. Moore was secretary and treasurer in 1904 of an investment company, the Afro-American Realty Company, which purchased Harlem property to sell or rent to New York City blacks in need of decent housing. Although the company failed in 1908, Afro-American Realty played a significant role in creating a predominantly black Harlem community.

Additionally, Moore was a politician and community activist. Always a faithful Republican, he began his political career as district captain in his Brooklyn community. In 1904 he was appointed deputy collector of internal revenue but resigned within a few months to become organizer of the National Negro Business League. Moore also acted as a delegate or alternate delegate to several Republican National Conventions and served on the National Negro Republican Committee from 1908 to 1920. Although he quit after three months and did not actually leave the United States, Moore was appointed Minister of Liberia by President William Howard Taft in 1912. After moving to Harlem, Moore was elected to the New York City Board of Aldermen for the nineteenth district in 1927, replacing a white incumbent. He was reelected to this position in 1929.

Moore's community activism is illustrated by the fact that until his death at 85 he was president of the Parent Teacher's Association of the local public school in his neighborhood. More important, Moore helped found the National Urban League in 1911. The Urban League grew out of several interracial northern urban service organizations established to help the great wave of black migrants from the South. Moore had served on the board of several of these groups and was founder and chairman of the New York Association for the Protection of Colored Women in 1905, an organization created to protect southern black women migrants from labor exploitation in the North. He was also active in the National League for the Protection of Colored Women founded the following year.

Moore married Washington, D.C., native, Ida Lawrence, in 1879. The Moores had eighteen children, six of whom lived to adulthood. Actively involved with the *Age* until 1942, Moore died in New York City.

As editor and publisher of one of the nation's major black newspapers, Moore both reported on and influenced black public opinion during a critical period of African-American life. His career reveals the complexity and diversity of black thought, particularly conservative philosophy, and shows that at specific times and under certain circumstances black conservatism in his era was often liberal and militant.

• Useful information about Moore can be found in the Booker T. Washington Papers at the Library of Congress, in the Emmett J. Scott Papers at the Soper Library at Morgan State University in Baltimore, Md., and in the Robert R. Moton Papers at Tuskegee Institute. His editorials are available in numerous issues of the *Colored American Magazine* and in the New York *Age*.

Informative sources about Moore's involvement with the periodicals include August Meier, "Booker T. Washington and the Negro Press: With Special Reference to the *Colored American Magazine*," *Journal of Negro History* 38 (Jan. 1953): 67–90; Emma L. Thornbrough, "More Light on Booker T. Washington and the New York *Age*," *Journal of Negro History* 43 (Jan. 1958): 34–49; Frederick Detweiler, *The Negro Press in the United States* (1922; repr. 1968); and Roland Wolseley, *The Black Press, U.S.A.* (1971).

Other information about Moore is available in Louis R. Harlan, *Booker T. Washington: The Wizard of Tuskegee, 1901–1915* (1983); Edwin R. Lewinson, *Black Politics in New York City* (1974); Guichard Parris and Lester Brooks, *Blacks in the City: A History of the National Urban League* (1971); Emma L. Thornbrough, *T. Thomas Fortune, Militant Journalist* (1972); Richard Bardolph, *The Negro Vanguard* (1959); Gilbert Osofsky, *Harlem: The Making of a Ghetto* (1963); and Seth M. Scheiner, *Negro Mecca: A History of the Negro in New York City, 1865–1920* (1965).

RITA ROBERTS

MOORE, Gabriel (1785?–6 Aug. 1844), U.S. representative and senator, Alabama governor, was born in Stokes County, North Carolina, the son of Matthew Moore, a farmer and iron worker, and Letitia Dalton. He received his education and studied law in North Carolina. By 1810 he migrated to Huntsville, Madison County, Mississippi Territory, to open a law practice and entered public service soon thereafter, first holding the position of assessor and collector of taxes for Madison County, then the most populous county in the area that ultimately became Alabama. He represented Madison County in the House of Representatives of the Mississippi Territorial Legislature from 1811 to 1817, serving as its speaker from 1815 to 1817. After Alabama became a separate territory, Moore represented Madison County in the House of Representatives of the Alabama Territorial Legislature, serving as speaker for the first session in January and February 1818. However, he did not serve as speaker for the second session in November 1818. During that session, the legislature granted his wife, whom he had married earlier that year, a divorce from him and granted her petition to resume using her maiden name of Mary Parham Caller. Soon afterward, Moore wounded his former wife's brother in a pistol duel.

As Alabama became a new state Moore assumed important leadership roles. He served as a member of the convention that drafted the state constitution in 1819. Upon statehood Moore won election as the first state senator from Madison County in 1819 and 1820, serving as speaker the latter year. In 1821 he won an election to finish the unexpired term of William Kelsey as U.S. representative from Alabama, serving as Alabama's representative at large. For his next three terms, beginning in 1823, Moore represented the northern district, one of three districts in the new state. During his four terms as a congressman, he worked to liberalize provisions for land purchase, an effort that helped make him an affluent attorney, popular with ordinary voters. As a contemporary observed: "Moore was a skilful [*sic*] electioneer, and courted the lower stratum of society" (Saunders, *Early Settlers*, p. 284).

In 1829 Moore won the governorship of Alabama without opposition. As governor, even though he disliked federal tariffs, he complied with them and opposed nullification. He embraced the idea of instruction, suggesting that Alabama's congressional delegation receive instructions to vote against the recharter of the Bank of the United States. He also supported two important intrastate construction projects: the Tennessee River canal designed to bypass Muscle Shoals to make the river navigable across northern Alabama and the state's first railroad from Tuscumbia to Decatur. He also advocated the establishment of a state penitentiary and the revision of the penal code. During his term more lands opened to settlement when the Choctaw Indians surrendered their lands in Alabama to the U.S. government by the Treaty of Dancing Rabbit Creek. On 3 March 1831, during his last year in office, Moore resigned as governor when the state legislature elected him U.S. senator.

As senator Moore encountered serious political opposition that limited his later chances for successful election to public office from Alabama, a state that then heavily favored Jacksonian Democrats. When he assumed his senate seat in December 1831, he professed his support for Jackson and praised especially the president's Indian policy, foreign policy, and fiscal restraint, but had asserted that he would only support administration measures if he approved them and oppose others if he disapproved them. In 1832, allying with John C. Calhoun's anti-Jacksonians, Moore spoke against confirmation of Jackson's nominee for American minister to Great Britain, Martin Van Buren, and voted against his confirmation. Moore soon realized the full negative political impact of his vote against Jackson. The Alabama legislature requested him to resign his seat, but he refused. He served the remainder of his full term until 1837, sometimes in open opposition to the president. For example, he opposed the Force Bill to authorize the president to use force against South Carolina when it nullified the tariff, yet he supported Jackson's opposition to the recharter of the Bank of the United States. In 1837, because he had been an inconsistent Jacksonian, Moore lost an election for a seat in the U.S. House of Representatives, his first defeat at the polls. He never held elective office again.

Following his involuntary retirement from public service, Moore experienced financial setbacks that coincided with the Panic of 1837. Between 1841 and 1843 the circuit court of Madison County issued judgments against him in favor of his creditors. He then relocated west of Alabama in 1843, renting a plantation in Panola County, Mississippi. In 1844 he moved to the Republic of Texas, where he died; he was buried near Caddo Lake in Harrison County. Through provisions in his will and subsequent litigation, he emancipated some of the slaves that he had moved from Alabama to Texas.

Moore's death in relative obscurity outside the state contrasted sharply with the prominence he had enjoyed as a gifted politician who had for over twenty years held elective office. He had helped to shape the constitution and the initial government structure of Alabama and found his greatest success in championing the concerns of the common people, such as increasing the possibility of their acquisition of public lands. Professing the Jacksonian rhetoric of the common people and lambasting aristocrats, he found much favor with Alabama voters. When he later began to support Jackson only selectively, his electoral following eroded.

• No major comprehensive collection exists of Moore's personal or public papers. His gubernatorial papers are located in the Alabama Department of Archives and History. His divorce appears in *Acts Passed at the Second Session of the First General Assembly of the Alabama Territory* (1818). His migration from Alabama to Texas is documented in affidavits filed in a series of lawsuits over claims against his estate, as determined by his will that was probated in Harrison County, Texas. See records of the county probate court and state supreme court in Texas. Evidence of his early public career appears in Edwin Clarence Carter, ed., *Territorial Papers of the United States*, vol. 6 (1938). Some contemporary comments appear in Thomas Hart Benton, *Thirty Years' View*, vol. 1 (1854), and James E. Saunders, *Early Settlers of Alabama* (1899). James M. Martin provides an informative account, "The Senatorial Career of Gabriel Moore," *Alabama Historical Quarterly* 26 (Summer 1964): 249–81.

HARRIET E. AMOS DOSS

MOORE, George Foot (15 Oct. 1851–16 May 1931), professor of religion, was born in West Chester, Pennsylvania, the son of William Eves Moore, a Presbyterian minister, and Harriet Francina. Moore's early education was shaped by considerable tutoring from his father, enabling him to enter Yale as a junior (1870–1872, A.B.). While teaching after graduation, he studied theology independently, so that he was able to enter the senior class of Union Theological Seminary (1876–1877). He was ordained a Presbyterian minister in 1878. That same year he married Mary Soper Hanford, with whom he had one son, and he began a pastorate in Zanesville, Ohio (1878–1883), while continuing his private study. The prodigious academic abilities of this largely self-taught man shaped his professional career for the next forty-five years. He was invited first to serve as professor of Hebrew and Old Testament literature at Andover Theological Seminary (1883–1902) and then as professor of the history of religion at Harvard University (1902–1928).

Moore's international stature as a Hebrew and Old Testament scholar bridged the scholarship of Europe and the United States at the turn of the century. In 1885 he studied for one year in Germany, and he later accepted the German emperor's invitation to return as a lecturer for a year at the University of Berlin (1909–1910). He helped introduce the radical innovations of German biblical scholarship into the United States, endorsing Julius Wellhausen's *Prolegomena* (1883), established a documentary prehistory for the initial books of the Old Testament. Moore served as assistant editor of the *Andover Review* (1884–1893) and editor of the *Journal of the American Oriental Society* (1896–1900), and he was a founding editor of the *Harvard Theological Review* (1908–1914, 1921–1931). He also served as president of a number of academic societies, including the American Academy of Arts and Sciences (1921–1924), the Massachusetts Historical Society (1925), and the American Oriental Society (1911–1913).

The quality of this prolific writer's scholarly work is attested by the continued republication of a number of his contributions nearly a century after their initial appearance. One of his most significant and abiding works, *A Critical and Exegetical Commentary on Judges* (1895), remains a classic in the field of biblical studies, unsurpassed in breadth or depth by any other commentary on the topic. His studies of the history of religion in general and Judaism in particular also represented major contributions at the time. His two-volume *History of Religions* (1913–1919) and *Judaism in the First Centuries of the Christian Era* (1927–1930) epitomize his synthetic analysis and expertise in a number of disciplines. The latter work was unusual in its insistence upon a thorough acquaintance with Jewish sources and religious traditions.

Moore's powerful frame and impressive stature gave him a commanding presence, but he was not easily moved to enthusiasm. His students found him devoted to his advanced pupils though not always patient with those less gifted. His peers admired him for his encyclopedic knowledge and his ability to acquire and retain information. He died in Cambridge, Massachusetts.

• Sources of further information regarding Moore include *Harvard Graduates' Magazine*, June 1931, pp. 539–41; *Harvard Theological Review* 24 (1931): 153–54; and *Journal of the American Oriental Society* 52 (1932): 273–74. Also see *Yale Obituary Record* (n.d.) and the *Alumni Catalogue of the Union Theological Seminary* (1926).

SAMUEL A. MEIER

MOORE, Grace (5 Dec. 1898–26 Jan. 1947), opera singer and motion-picture personality, was born Mary Willie Grace Moore in Slabtown (now Nough), Tennessee, the daughter of Richard L. Moore, a retail merchant, and Tessie Jane Stokley. Educated in the elementary schools of Jellico, Tennessee, where her family resided, Moore later enrolled in the Ward-Belmont School in Nashville, but her penchant for defying curfews and other school rules soon ended her association with the academy.

A short time later, with her father's reluctant support, Moore enrolled in the Wilson-Greene School of Music in Chevy Chase, Maryland, with more lasting results. There she heard and met Alma Gluck and Mary Garden, who were concertizing in nearby Washington, D.C. Garden soon became her idol, and Moore kept up a weekly correspondence with her for a long time afterward. By then, the young woman had matured from a self-described "skinny, long-legged ugly girl, good at sports, much disliked by the other girls," into a lithe beauty with a promising lyric-soprano voice.

In 1919, while still at the Wilson-Greene School, Moore earned a spot as an assisting artist with Giovanni Martinelli when the renowned tenor gave a Washington-area concert. Unfortunately, Moore's choice of music was too taxing for her immature voice, and the critics were unimpressed. But the experience was enough to spur the young woman to move to New York City to advance her career.

After a six-month stint as a café singer Moore damaged her voice, though fortunately not irreparably. Desperate for help, she sought out P. Mario Marafioti, a throat specialist and voice teacher who had been one of Caruso's personal physicians. Marafioti accepted Moore as a pupil, remedied the damage she had done, and gradually refined the flaws in her vocal production. Beyond improving her technique, he taught her to concentrate not merely on the musical score but especially on the emotional content of the words she was singing.

Moore's first significant engagement came not in opera but as an ingenue in a musical, *Suite Sixteen*, where her dancing served her more than her voice. This initial success propelled her into a singing role in a Broadway musical, *Hitchy Koo*, a 1922 production by Raymond Hitchcock with songs by Jerome Kern. Her success with Kern's music led Irving Berlin to engage Moore for his *Music Box Revue* (1923), an annual production then in its third year. Although paired with well-established Broadway personalities on the Berlin playbill (including tenor John Steel, who had introduced Berlin's "A Pretty Girl Is Like a Melody" to great acclaim in the Ziegfeld *Follies* of 1919), it was Moore to whom the critics meted out the most praise. Afterward, Berlin engaged Moore for another edition of the *Music Box Revue* (1924) and gave her some of his most memorable ballads to introduce.

For all her newfound success with popular music, however, Moore viewed Broadway as a stepping stone to an opera career—a path that Rosa Ponselle had established for American-born singers in 1918, when she went directly from vaudeville to a Metropolitan Opera debut opposite Caruso. Moore wanted to take that same path, and with encouragement from financier Otto H. Kahn, who wielded great influence with the Metropolitan Opera management, she was given two auditions. However, she was not successful on either occasion. After a brief but intensive period of study with Richard Barthélemy in France, Moore again asked Kahn to intervene and in late 1927 he obtained for her a third audition. This time she prevailed; she made her Metropolitan debut as Mimì in Puccini's *La Bohème* on 7 February 1928. Puccini's frail heroine also served her later that season, when she made her debut at the Paris Opéra-Comique.

Her first-season reviews at the Metropolitan Opera were mixed ("When she had rid herself of nervousness," W. J. Henderson wrote of her debut in the *New York Sun* [8 Feb. 1928], "she sang her upper tones with more freedom and something more like focus"), but she went on to become one of the Metropolitan's most popular sopranos. Her best roles, in the opinion of most critics, included Fiora in Montemezzi's *L'Amore dei tre re*, and the title roles in Charpentier's *Louise* (which, as with the Montemezzi work, she prepared under the composer's direction), Massenet's *Manon*, and Puccini's *Tosca*—parts that require a substantial lyric-soprano voice and, ideally, a comely appearance. But though no one questioned Moore's physical assets in these and other roles, her voice and acting were not uniformly regarded by the critics. "Her faults were so abundant," Virgil Thompson said of her in 1942, "that it has often been occasion for wonder that so much energy and hard work should be deployed on so seemingly hopeless an errand. And somehow, by sheer good will, hard work, and intellectual modesty, [she] manages to produce the best performance now available in that tradition" (*New York Herald Tribune*).

In Hollywood, Moore's physical and vocal beauty proved to be a potent draw in early sound films, of which she made nine during the 1930s: *A Lady's Morals* (1930), based on the life of Jenny Lind, which Moore filmed in two versions for English and French audiences, respectively; *New Moon* (1930), based on the Sigmund Romberg musical and costarring Metropolitan Opera baritone Lawrence Tibbett; *One Night of Love* (1934), which Moore considered her best film; and four others that she and most of the critics dismissed as the same plot under four different titles (*Love Me Forever* [1935], *The King Steps Out* [1936], *When You're in Love* [1937], and *I'll Take Romance* [1937]). In 1931 Moore married Spanish actor Valentin Parera, with whom she maintained a villa in France and a historic farmhouse in Connecticut. They did not have any children.

In France in 1938, under the direction of Abel Gance, Moore performed the title role in a film version of Charpentier's *Louise*, which is generally considered her most significant cinematic work. Between films, she made her London debut at Covent Garden in 1935. In 1937 she returned briefly to the Opéra-Comique, then came back to the Metropolitan Opera and remained there until 1946. Meantime, she developed a large following as a concert artist both in Europe and the United States, once drawing an estimated 22,000 at New York City's Lewisohn Stadium.

During World War II, she toured Latin and South America under the sponsorship of the U.S. State Department. She also bolstered Allied troops in Europe and frequently entertained at military canteens and service organizations. After the war, she resumed her concert career. Following a concert in Denmark, she was killed instantly when the airplane in which she was traveling crashed at the Copenhagen airport.

• Moore's autobiography, *You're Only Human Once*, was published in 1944. She is also the subject of a biography by Rowena Rutherford Farrar, *Grace Moore and Her Many Worlds* (1982). Although flawed in several ways because of inadequate research, Farrar's biography does correct a number of important details about Moore's life and career (including her birth year, usually cited as 1902 during the singer's lifetime). Critics' reviews of Moore's New York concert appearances are referenced in Richard Aldrich, *Concert Life in New York 1902–1923* (1941), and in Olin Downes, *Olin Downes on Music* (1957). Moore's Broadway success in Irving Berlin's *Music Box Revue* is discussed in Laurence Bergreen, *As Thousands Cheer: The Life of Irving Berlin* (1990). Her association with RCA Victor is recounted in the personal reminiscences of former recording director Charles O'Connell, *The Other Side of the Record* (1947). An excellent summary of her life and career, as well as a critical review of a representative sampling of her recordings, may be found in Edward H. Pearson, "Grace Moore, 'Love Me Forever,'" *Opera Quarterly* (Autumn 1996). The singer is also profiled at varying lengths in Charles Wagner, *Seeing Stars* (1940), in David Ewen, *Men and Women Who Make Music* (1945), in Gladys Davidson, *Opera Biographies* (1955), and in Robert Tuggle, *The Golden Age of Opera* (1983). Obituaries are in the *New York Times*, 26 and 27 Jan. 1947.

JAMES A. DRAKE

MOORE, Harry Tyson (18 Nov. 1905–25 Dec. 1951), educator and civil rights activist, was born in Houston, Florida, the son of S. Johnny Moore, a farmer and store owner, and Rosalea Alberta Tyson, an insurance agent. An African American, Moore grew up in rural, northern Florida when racial segregation was in full force. After attending public schools in Daytona Beach and Jacksonville, in 1925 Moore graduated from Florida Memorial College in Live Oak with an A.A. degree. (Not until 1951 did he receive a B.S. degree from Bethune Cookman College.) In 1926 Moore began his teaching career at Cocoa Junior High School in Cocoa, Florida. As a public school teacher, he knew firsthand that a separate school system shortchanged black students and faculty in providing unequal facilities and financial resources. In 1926 Moore married Harriette Vyda Simms; they had two children.

Moore's concern about discrimination prompted him to join the National Association for the Advancement of Colored People (NAACP) in 1934, and that same year he founded and became president of its Brevard County, Florida, branch. Under Moore's NAACP leadership in 1938, a local school teacher filed litigation challenging the lower salaries black teachers received in comparison with those of whites under state funding schedules. Though the plaintiff lost, the case prepared the way for improvements in the equalization of teacher salaries a decade later. During the 1940s, Moore and the NAACP expanded their activities along several fronts. In the wake of the U.S. Supreme Court's 1944 decision overturning the all-white Democratic primary in Texas (*Smith v. Allwright*), Moore campaigned to expand political participation for blacks in Florida. Because the NAACP was a nonpartisan organization, in 1944 he formed the Florida Progressive Voters League (chartered under Florida law in 1946) to sign up African Americans for the Democratic party primaries from which they had been previously excluded. Besides conducting suffrage drives, the league screened candidates for office and issued endorsements aimed at the black electorate. Under the banner of "A Voteless Citizen is a Voiceless Citizen," the group helped increase black voter registration from 49,000 in 1947 to over 116,000 in 1950.

During this period Moore's efforts were stimulated by American involvement in World War II. The war against fascism abroad provided powerful ammunition for black southerners to combat racism at home. Pressured by another Florida native, A. Philip Randolph, who was a labor and civil rights leader, the federal government established a Fair Employment Practice Committee in 1941 to investigate racial discrimination in federal employment and defense-related jobs. Once the war ended, black veterans who had fought for democratic ideals abroad returned home eager to pursue first-class citizenship rights long denied them. Moore did not get called up for military service at the outbreak of the war, but he continued to wage the fight to defeat racism in this country. On weekends and summer vacations he gathered his family into his car and drove for miles around Florida on NAACP business. As a result of these recruiting forays and inspired by the war, black Floridians expanded the ranks of the NAACP, increasing the number of branches from nine in 1941 to seventy-seven in 1947. To keep pace with this growth Moore served as president of the Florida State Conference of branches from 1941 to 1946 and executive secretary from 1946 to 1951.

In the middle to late 1940s the rising militancy against Jim Crow laws and black disfranchisement produced a white backlash throughout Florida and the South. In 1947 Moore and his wife were fired from their jobs at Mims Elementary School where he was principal and teacher of fifth and sixth grades and she taught third and fourth grades. By 1950 the Ku Klux Klan was on the rise in central Florida near the area where the Moores lived. Faced with white resistance and financial problems, the state NAACP declined in membership, and the number of branches dropped to fifty-nine in 1950. Consequently, in November 1951, Moore took the unpaid position of State Coordinator of Branches. His resolve remained firm, however, and he told his family, "I know eventually they'll try to kill me, but I have to do what I'm doing" (Dukess and Hart, p. 17).

Moore fought his final battle over the sensational Groveland rape case. In mid-July 1949, a seventeen-year-old white woman accused four black men of raping her and assaulting her husband near Groveland, Florida, in rural Lake County, west of Orlando. One of the suspects was shot and killed by a sheriff's posse, and of the remaining three, who were subsequently convicted of the crime, two were sentenced to death. NAACP attorneys appealed the verdict, and the U.S. Supreme Court ordered a new hearing for the two death-row prisoners on the grounds that their original trial had been prejudiced by unfavorable publicity and a mob atmosphere. In November 1951 while transporting the defendants to a pre-trial hearing, Lake County Sheriff Willis McCall shot the two prisoners, whom he claimed were attempting to escape, and he killed one.

Moore vigorously protested the action of the sheriff and called for his dismissal from office by Governor Fuller Warren. The shooting gained wide publicity, and the NAACP emphasized that the case damaged Florida's reputation and hurt the United States in the international arena. At the height of the Cold War, the Soviet Union turned this incident into propaganda, with the Soviet delegate to the United Nations accusing the United States of hypocrisy by discussing human rights while a police officer shot down unarmed blacks. On Christmas day 1951, after celebrating the holiday and their twenty-fifth wedding anniversary, the Moores returned to their home in Mims, Florida, halfway between Jacksonville and Palm Beach. After they went to sleep a powerful dynamite blast exploded under their bedroom instantly killing Harry Moore. His mother and one of his daughters, who were also in the house, survived the blast, but a little over a week later Harriette Moore died of her wounds. Though the killers were never apprehended, the evidence points strongly to members of the Ku Klux Klan as the culprits.

Harry T. Moore was the first civil rights leader assassinated during the modern phase of the black freedom struggle. Though largely unknown outside of Florida, he can be counted with other black southerners who organized at the state and local levels to obtain racial equality in the years before the Supreme Court's decision in *Brown v. Board of Education* (1954) outlawed public school segregation, and the nation heeded black demands for first-class citizenship. The successes won by the civil rights movement after 1954 had their origins in the campaigns conducted by unsung activists such as Harry Moore.

• Biographical information was obtained in correspondence to the author from Moore's daughter Juanita Evangeline Moore, 21 June 1993, and in subsequent telephone conversations with her, 25 Aug. 1993 and 19 June 1994. Moore's NAACP correspondence is in the NAACP papers at the Library of Congress. The most detailed account of Moore's career with the NAACP can be found in Gloster Current, "Martyr for a Cause," *Crisis* 59 (Feb. 1952): 72–81, 133–34. Steven F. Lawson, *Black Ballots: Voting Rights in the South, 1944–1969* (1976), covers Moore's voter registration efforts, and Steven F. Lawson et al., "Groveland: Florida's Little Scottsboro," *Florida Historical Quarterly* 65 (July 1986): 1–26, examines the rape case that contributed to Moore's murder. Two journalistic accounts that also provide valuable material, particularly concerning Moore's death, are Karen Dukess and Richard Hart, "The Invisible Man," *Tropic* [*Miami Herald*], 16 Feb. 1992, and James C. Clark, "The Assassination of Harry T. Moore," *Orlando Sentinel*, 11 Oct. 1991.

STEVEN F. LAWSON

MOORE, Sir Henry (7 Feb. 1713–11 Sept. 1769), British colonial governor, was born in Vere, Jamaica, the son of Samuel Moore, a planter, and Elizabeth Lowe, the daughter of Samuel Lowe of Goadby, Leicestershire, England. His roots were deep in the Caribbean, for his grandfather, John Moore, had settled in Barbados, then had moved to Jamaica. He was educated in England at Eton and at Leyden University in the Netherlands. After returning to Jamaica, he married Catharina Maria Long, with whom he had one child, named John Henry Moore. He also enrolled in the militia and became active in politics. First elected to the legislative assembly, he was appointed to the council in 1752 and became its secretary a year later. In 1755 he became lieutenant governor of the colony under a dormant commission and took up residency in Spanish Town. When the governor, Admiral Sir Charles Knowles, was recalled in 1756, Moore assumed the office of governor, a position he held without interruption for the next three years. During that time he proved himself to be a judicious and tactful administrator, settling quarrels between local legislators and moving forcefully in 1759 to assert his authority against the council by removing recalcitrant members. He established a reputation as an "accurate" administrator, unlike his predecessor, and pursued a program for the erection of handsome public buildings in Spanish Town, which he made the capital of Jamaica.

In 1759 Moore was replaced as governor by Sir George Haldane, but when he died after only a few weeks in office Moore was restored to power. On Easter Monday 1760 he was confronted with a dangerous slave insurrection, which quickly developed into a guerilla war that lasted for more than a year. Proclaiming martial law, he took command of the British regiments stationed in Jamaica, carrying out speedy and resourceful operations against the insurgents that placed him in great physical danger. On two occasions, he was ambushed with his troops and almost killed, and at another time he saved himself when riding alone only by shooting his pistol at an assailant. In February 1762 he gave up his administration and sailed for England. Two years later he was rewarded for his Jamaican services with a baronetcy, and in July 1765 he was appointed governor of New York.

Arriving at his new post four months later, just as the Stamp Act crisis was reaching its peak, Moore found the lieutenant governor, Cadwallader Colden, ensconced in Fort George and practically under siege by the Sons of Liberty, organized to oppose and to thwart collection of the tax. At first, he insisted to the council that the Stamp Act must be enforced, but when he received no support from that body, he adopted a more popular policy. He suspended enforcement of the law, at the same time dismantling the fort, which the citizens saw as threatening, in hopes that economic pressure eventually would force the colonists into line. Disgusted by what he perceived as Moore's pusillanimity, Colden wrote, "He has yielded every thing in order to quiet the Minds of the people, & notwithstanding of this Riots & Mobs have continued frequent & as much insulting on Government as ever." Despite Moore's generally conciliatory attitude, he put teeth into his program by refusing to allow seaborne commerce or the normal functioning of the courts while the law was not in force. But his scheme did not work, and the Stamp Act crisis was not resolved until Parliament rescinded the law in 1766. As Colden acidly noted, "Our present Governor acts oddly, & does not please those whose favour he courts" (*Colden Letter Books*, vol. 2, pp. 106, 118).

The truth of Colden's words was brought home forcefully to Moore when the assembly refused to cooperate with him and General Thomas Gage in accepting the provisions of the Quartering Act, which required colonists to provide housing and supplies to British troops in America. Enraged at the legislators' intransigence, Moore threatened to prorogue the assembly and call new elections but finally decided not to because, as he noted, the same people would be returned in any case and he would derive "not a single advantage . . . from it." A year later, Parliament acted for him and suspended the assembly until it should accept the Quartering Act, but Parliament relented after a time and allowed the assembly to meet. In 1766 Moore and the New Yorkers were on the same side of a political altercation when they pleaded with the Board of Trade to permit the colony to override the Currency Act of 1764 and issue new money; his support of the colony's bid to the board helped it to succeed. He also settled a boundary dispute between New York and Quebec, and he tried without success to do the same for the boundary between New York and Massachusetts. Encouraging good relations between whites and Indians, he worked diligently on matters of Indian policy and twice visited the Five Nations tribes in the northwest of his province. When he died in office in New York after a sixteen-day illness, he left a reputation as a man who was amiable, courteous, and not a little indolent, whose administration on the whole had been advantageous to New Yorkers. Consequently, he was remembered favorably by all parties in the colony, with the exception of the Presbyterians, who were disgruntled at his unsuccessful efforts in 1766 to establish a playhouse, which they found morally offensive.

• Primary sources on Moore's life are Edmund B. O'Callaghan, ed., *Documentary History of the State of New-York* (4 vols., 1849–1851) and *Documents Relative to the Colonial History of the State of New York*, vols. 7–8 (1856–1857); *Colden Letter Books*, New-York Historical Society, *Collections, 1876–77* (2 vols., 1877–1878); *Letters and Papers of Cadwallader Colden, 1711–75*, New-York Historical Society, *Collections, 1917–23, 1934–35* (9 vols., 1918–1924, 1935–1936); and *The Montresor Journals*, ed. Gideon D. Scull, New-York Historical Society, *Collections, 1881* (1882). Moore's family background is covered in George E. Cokayne, *The Complete Baronetage* . . . , vol. 5 (1906). His Jamaican career is analyzed in William J. Gardner, *A History of Jamaica* . . . (1971). For a succinct discussion of his political problems in New York, see Merrill Jensen, *The Founding of a Nation: A History of the American Revolution, 1763–1776* (1968).

PAUL DAVID NELSON

MOORE, James (c. 1650–1706), politician, soldier, and explorer, emigrated from Barbados to Carolina in 1675. Sometime in the 1670s he married Margaret Berringer, stepdaughter of Carolina governor Sir John Yeamans; they had ten children. He acquired land grants in the Goose Creek region of Carolina and settled his family there. In 1684 he imported thirty-seven indentured servants to Carolina, for whom he obtained headright grants, thereby adding to his landholding. In addition to his plantations, Boochawee Hall and Wassamassaw, Moore was an Indian trader and a trader in Indian slaves. In 1690 he explored the Appalachian Mountains in northwestern Carolina in search of gold and silver.

Moore led the "Goose Creek men," a political faction in Carolina united by their Anglican faith, geographic proximity, and opposition to the ruling Dissenter party in the province. Despite his opposition to the religious toleration and moderate Indian policies of the Lords Proprietors of Carolina, the proprietors named him to the Grand Council, the colony's "upper house" and privy council. He served on the council in 1677 and 1682–1683 but was removed from his post because of his activities in the Indian slave trade.

In 1692 Moore represented Berkeley County in the First Commons House of Assembly. As a House member he adopted a conciliatory attitude toward the proprietors and the Quaker governor, John Archdale. Moore's policy succeeded. He reclaimed the good graces of the proprietors, and they reappointed him to the Council. In 1698 he was named secretary of the province, and the following year he became receiver general and chief justice of the province. Having gained power on the Council, Moore sought the governorship. On 11 September 1700, following the death of Governor Joseph Blake, Moore protested that the Council's nominees for the office, Deputy Governor Joseph Morton and Edmund Bellinger—dissenters and pro-proprietary men—were ineligible because they held royal commissions as admiralty judges. Moore convinced a majority of the Council to appoint him interim governor. He served as governor of South Carolina until 1703, when the proprietors' appointee, Sir Nathaniel Johnson, took office.

As governor, Moore actively engaged in imperialist policies toward French and Spanish settlements in the Southeast. Prior to the announcement of the beginning of Queen Anne's War, Moore projected an assault on Spanish Saint Augustine. The Commons House approved his plan, partly because notice of the war declaration arrived in Charles Town during its deliberations. But dissenters in the Commons House strongly opposed his aggressive action. They objected to the cost of the plan and feared retaliation by the Spanish. During the fall of 1702 Moore led a combined land and amphibious assault upon Saint Augustine. His army, composed of Englishmen and Indian allies, captured the city and surrounding villages but, lacking mortars, could not take the fort. They besieged the castillo but had to withdraw when Spanish reinforcements arrived from Havana. Abandoning the siege, Moore and his army burned the city and were back to Charles Town in January 1703.

At the next session of the general assembly Moore again faced opposition to the campaign. The expedition had cost considerably more than expected and had failed in its main purpose. Moore's Dissenter opponents attacked and ridiculed Moore, claiming that at times the governor had been too intoxicated to lead his troops. They tried to block legislation to pay the costs of the campaign. This vote became a test of which party, Moore's Anglicans or the Dissenters, would control Carolina's government. When the Dissenters failed to kill the appropriation for the campaign, they determined to bring the provincial government to a halt. On 23 February 1703 Moore's opponents walked out of the assembly and boycotted its proceedings.

During the interim between the end of that assembly and the election of the next, Moore turned over the governorship of Carolina to Johnson. By splitting the Commons House into two antagonistic factions, Moore had paved the way for Johnson's High Church party to pass the Exclusion Act and the Establishment Act of 1704. These two acts aimed to ensure the Anglican party's political hegemony in South Carolina. The first required that all Commons House members prove they were communicants in the Church of England, and the second made Anglicanism the official, state-supported religion of the province. Resuming his place on the Council, Moore remained a powerful leader in Carolina. He was church commissioner under the Church Act of 1704 and held the posts of attorney general (1703–1706) and receiver general (1702–1706).

In January 1704 Moore led a military campaign against Spanish missions among the Apalachee Indians southwest of Carolina. These raids reduced Spanish influence in the Southeast and captured a considerable number of Indians for the slave markets of Charles Town. Moore claimed vindication as a military leader as a result of this campaign, which decimated the Apalachees and strengthened English control over the region. The Spanish retreated into Florida and the Gulf coast. Two years after this expedition Moore died of yellow fever in Charles Town.

Imperialistic and self-aggrandizing, Moore successfully merged his public and private will to power. He was a frontier entrepreneur who used public office to enrich himself and to create a political dynasty in South Carolina. As governor, he helped to establish the Anglican ascendancy in South Carolina, and as an imperialist he promoted British ascendancy in the Old Southwest.

• Moore's account of the 1690 expedition to the Appalachian Mountains is printed in *Calendar of State Papers, America and West Indies, 1699*, no. 202i, and his report on the 1704 Apalachee raid is in Bartholomew R. Carroll, ed., *Historical Collections of South Carolina*, vol. 2 (1836). His genealogy is in Mabel Webber, "The First Governor Moore and His Children," *South Carolina Historical Magazine* 37 (Jan. 1936): 1–23. Biographical sketches of Moore are in the *Biographical Directory of the South Carolina House of Representatives*, vol. 2, ed. Walter B. Edgar and N. Louise Bailey (1977), and John Raimo, *Biographical Directory of American Colonial and Revolutionary Governors, 1607–1789* (1980). The best secondary accounts of Moore's life and career are found in Verner W. Crane, *The Southern Frontier, 1670–1732* (1928), and M. Eugene Sirmans, *Colonial South Carolina, A Political History, 1663–1763* (1966).

ALEXANDER MOORE

MOORE, James (1737–15 Apr. 1777), revolutionary war general, was born in New Hanover County, North Carolina, the son of Maurice Moore, a planter, and his second wife, Mary Porter. Nothing is known of Moore's childhood or education. He married Ann Ivie (year unknown), with whom he had four children. The Moores lived on the Cape Fear River at "Rocky Point Plantation," which he inherited from his father.

For two decades Moore's service to his province and state encompassed both the civil and the military arenas. His public life began during the French and Indian War with his appointment as a militia captain and in 1758 as commandant of Fort Johnston on Cape Fear. After the war he was elected from New Hanover County to the lower house of the General Assembly, serving from 1764 to 1771 and again in 1773. Moore was a leader of the opposition to the Stamp Act, yet during the backcountry Regulator disorders Governor William Tryon appointed him colonel in command of artillery for the 1768 expedition and the 1771 campaign that led to victory over the Regulators in the battle of Alamance.

In the forefront of the growing revolutionary movement, Moore was a member of the Wilmington Sons of

Liberty and also active on the New Hanover Committee of Safety. A delegate to the Third Provincial Congress in 1775, Moore was appointed colonel of the province's First Continental Regiment on 1 September 1775. Janet Schaw, a contemporary who opposed the rebellion, wrote of Moore that he was the Crown's most dangerous adversary in the province. She held him in both "dread and esteem" because his high principles, virtue, and "unblemished character" contributed to his extraordinary popularity.

In early 1776 the royal governor, Josiah Martin, persuaded the Scottish Highlander settlers of the lower Cape Fear valley to rise in support of the Crown and attempt to link up with a promised contingent of British regulars at the mouth of the river. In overall command of the Whig militia, Moore was responsible for the concentration of forces at Moore's Creek Bridge that interdicted the Scottish march and crushed it in battle on 27 February 1776. According to Hugh F. Rankin, Moore skillfully maneuvered several thousand raw militia with "all the finesse of a master chess player," thwarting the Loyalist moves and forcing them to battle under unfavorable circumstances. The result of his masterful campaign was Moore's appointment by the Continental Congress on 1 March 1776 as a brigadier general in command of North Carolina. His first assignment involved fortifying Wilmington and harassing the British fleet blockading the Cape Fear.

After General Charles Lee (1731–1782) was recalled to the North in September, Moore succeeded him as commander of the Southern Department. Dividing his time between Wilmington and Charles Town (later Charleston), South Carolina, Moore labored tirelessly to recruit and train troops for the defense of the southern colonies. While preparing his forces for a march north to reinforce General George Washington, Moore died suddenly in Wilmington from "a fit of Gout in his Stomach." Considered North Carolina's "ablest military leader" of the period, Moore through his untimely death in his second year of service denied his country the talents of a potentially great commander who had demonstrated his strategic grasp and his tactical brilliance in a minor campaign and department.

• Moore's official papers are in William L. Saunders, ed., *The Colonial Records of North Carolina*, vols. 6–10 (1888–1890) and Walter M. Clark, ed., *The State Records of North Carolina*, vols. 11–13, 15, 18, 19, 22 (1895–1907). See also Hugh F. Rankin, *The North Carolina Continentals* (1971) and "The Moore's Creek Bridge Campaign, 1776," *North Carolina Historical Review* 30 (Jan. 1953): 23–60. For a contemporary characterization of Moore, see Janet Schaw, *Journal of a Lady of Quality*, ed. Evangeline W. Andrews (1921), pp. 167, 205, 318–19.

LINDLEY S. BUTLER

MOORE, James (1764–22 June 1814), Episcopal priest, was born in Rockbridge County, Virginia. Nothing is known about his parents. He studied at Washington College (now Washington and Lee University) in Lexington, Virginia, and in 1790 he married Margaret Todd; the number of their children is unknown. In 1791 or 1792 he moved to the Bluegrass Valley in Kentucky to join a large colony of Presbyterians and to become a Presbyterian minister. The family settled in Lexington, Kentucky, and almost immediately Moore applied to the Transylvania Presbytery to become a candidate for the ordained ministry. He was accepted on 27 April 1792.

For the next year Moore prepared himself for examinations before the Presbytery; but the Virginia Synod forbade the Presbytery to proceed with the examination until Moore's congregation in Lexington had sent documents stating that he was baptized, confirmed, and a member in good standing of the congregation. These documents, known as testimonials, also testified to the education the candidate had received. As a result of this action, the Presbytery suspended Moore as a candidate for the ministry until "these obstacles be removed," but it noted that its action did not result from "any fault we find with the natural abilities, literary acquisitions, or moral or religious character of the candidate" (Swinford and Lee, p. 12). Several months later he was reinstated as a candidate, and he spent much of the next two years preparing for his examinations and preaching several times before the Presbytery. Unfortunately, some members of the Presbytery were absent when Moore preached his final round of sermons and requested that he preach the two sermons again. He refused, and the Presbytery dropped him from its list of candidates.

At about the time that Moore had begun the process for ordination, he had accepted a position of leadership at the Transylvania Seminary, located near Danville, Kentucky. This was the first public educational institution in the area. On 8 April 1793 the trustees of the seminary voted to locate the school permanently in Lexington, and Moore continued to be in charge until February 1794, when he was succeeded by Harry Toulmin.

By this time Moore had decided to enter the Episcopal church and to seek ordination to the priesthood. A small group in Lexington known as the Episcopal Society endorsed him for ordination. Since Kentucky had no Episcopal bishop, Moore returned to Virginia, where Bishop James Madison ordained him as a deacon on 27 December 1794. Madison also later ordained him as a priest on an unrecorded date.

Some of the Presbyterians who sought control of Transylvania Seminary believed that Toulmin was a Unitarian, or a "Socinian." Socinianism was derived from the teachings of Lelio Francesco Maria and Fausto Paolo Sozzini of Siena, Italy, in the sixteenth century. It taught that God was not triune and that Jesus Christ was not the eternal Son of God but the son of the one eternal God. The Socinians established a rival school near Pisgah and named it the Kentucky Academy. Since they knew Moore was an educator and an Episcopalian, they asked him in April 1796 to be the second principal of the academy. He accepted the position. In September he was also called back to be the president of Transylvania Seminary. A little over two years later, on 22 December 1798, the general assembly granted a charter that merged the Kentucky Academy and Transylvania Seminary, effective 1 January 1799, into a single institution known as Transylvania University. Moore served as its president and professor of logic, metaphysics, moral philosophy, and belles-lettres until 1804, when he resigned.

Moore resigned in order to give more time to his ministry. The Episcopal church was weak in Kentucky: not until 28 May 1775 had an Episcopal worship service been held in the area. On that day Colonel Richard Henderson recorded that "divine service, for the first time in Kentucky, was performed by the Rev. John Lyth, of the Church of England" (Smith and Didlake, p. 2). In his *History of Kentucky* (1824), Humphrey Marshall claimed that in 1792 "the country had many Episcopalians but no church and no parson: It might have been hazarded as a public conjecture that no Episcopalian Church could ever be erected in Kentucky" (Johnston, p. 1).

Moore was to prove him wrong. He was the first practicing and permanently located Episcopal priest in the state. After being ordained, he took over the leadership of the Episcopal Society in Lexington, and that group became the nucleus of the first organized Episcopal church in Kentucky. Under his leadership, the Episcopal Society was organized on 3 July 1809 as Christ Church.

During 1812 Moore was ill, and Christ Church appears to have gone without a minister. He partially recovered in 1813 and consented to renew his ministry and officiate every Sunday when his health permitted. This arrangement did not work, and later in 1813 he retired. Moore died in Lexington. Christ Church, which in 1897 became Christ Church Cathedral, is today the Cathedral of the Diocese of Lexington, and Moore is honored as the father of the Episcopal church in Kentucky.

• The most reliable information on Moore is in Frances Keller Swinford and Rebecca Smith Lee, *The Great Elm Tree: Heritage of the Episcopal Diocese of Lexington* (1969). Also helpful is Elizabeth King Smith and Mary LeGrand Didlake, *Christ Church, 1796–1946: A Brief History of Its One Hundred and Fifty Years in the Service of Christ* (1946); Lloyd E. Johnston, *The First Hundred Years of the Episcopal Church in Kentucky* (1896); and John D. Wright, Jr., *Transylvania: Tutor to the West* (1975). There is also a fictionalized account in James Lane Allen, *Flute and Violin and Other Kentucky Tales and Romances* (1891).

DONALD S. ARMENTROUT

MOORE, James, Jr. (1675?–1724), provisional governor and militia commander of South Carolina, was born in that colony sometime between 1675 and 1680, the son of James Moore, Sr., also a governor of South Carolina as well as a prominent planter and Indian trader, and Lady Margaret Yeamans. Although he represented Berkeley and Craven Counties in the Commons House of Assembly between 1706 and 1708, little is known about Moore before the Tuscarora War in 1713. On 20 March his force of some forty whites and 800 Cherokee, Creek, and Catawba allies destroyed the Tuscarora castle at Nooherooka. In so doing they took 392 prisoners and 192 scalps, with total casualties amounting to, in Moore's estimation, nearly 1,000 in contrast to 57 killed (35 Indians, 22 whites) and 82 (58 Indians, 24 whites) wounded among the attackers. This blow crushed the Tuscaroras and obliged them to remove to New York where the nation was incorporated into the Iroquois confederacy.

Two years later the Yamassee War broke out with devastating effect on South Carolina's southern frontier. In August 1715 the frantic assembly created a 1,200-man army including 600 white Carolinians, 100 Virginians, and a number of Indians and free persons of color and placed Moore in command with the rank of lieutenant general. This force, augmented by troops from North Carolina, stabilized the situation until an autumn offensive cleared the South Carolina frontier. Moore also served as an agent in the crucial negotiations with the powerful Cherokees that persuaded that nation to intervene against the Indians threatening South Carolina. This deal secured South Carolina's trade with the Cherokee, which at that time constituted a pillar of the colony's economy. The success of this diplomacy doomed the league of Yamassees, Creeks, Catawbas, and other peoples that had formed against the Carolinians.

Yet the devastation wrought by these enemies before they subsided advanced the perception, held by Moore and other Carolinians after 1700, that the lords proprietor of the colony were distracted by other matters. These people feared that South Carolina's close escape in the Yamassee War represented a symptom of this apparent lack of concern; the next time, the colony might not be so fortunate. Moreover, security threats lurked everywhere: the survivors of the war bent on revenge, the Spaniards at St. Augustine, and the pirates who continued to plague the South Carolina coastline.

The lack of vigor demonstrated by the lords in dealing with these problems, along with their desire to keep the lands captured in the Yamassee War for themselves and their attempts to change the nature of South Carolina's governmental institutions, convinced these Carolinians that the interests of governors and governed had diverged to the breaking point. Unless, these leaders reasoned, the Crown assumed direct control, the colony would continue to suffer politically and economically under the haphazard rule of disinterested proprietors.

On the eve of a parliamentary election in November 1719, a rumor spread that the Spanish were planning to invade South Carolina. This alarm prompted the formation of an association, which asked proprietary governor Robert Johnson to assume the government in the king's name on 26 November. The association also appointed a committee to present grievances, but before the governor could respond the disaffected group went home. When the Commons House of Assembly convened on 10 December, however, it transformed itself into a "convention" that would hold the government in the colony until the Board of Trade considered their petition for royalization of the colony. Moore almost certainly played a central role in these events, since the convention named him governor on 21 December after Johnson refused to break his loyalty oath to the proprietors.

As provisional governor Moore's primary concern was to maintain order until the Board of Trade answered the petition of the Commons House. However, his government did pass an excise law and other revenue measures and set salaries for Moore, the chief justice, and the colony's agent in London. It also passed legislation governing the province's courts, made rice legal tender for the payment of debts, and issued £25,000 worth of new bills of credit that were to be retired by a tax on rice.

Moore's position was made uneasy by the continuing presence of Johnson, who retained the colony's records and who hoped to become royal governor after the Crown granted the colony's petition on 11 August 1720. Other factors included the machinations of place-seekers like William Rhett and Nicholas Trott, as well as his government's lack of legitimacy. But Johnson made only one overt attempt to overthrow Moore. In the spring of 1721 Moore ordered the colony's Anglican ministers not to perform marriages unless he had signed the license. Johnson countered by ordering the clergy to ignore Moore, which the clergy did, albeit reluctantly. At the same time Johnson received the support of the commanders of two men-of-war that had arrived in Charles Town. Supported by this force and by forty militiamen who answered his summons, Johnson sought to bring the convention to heel by force. However, when the Charlestonians under Moore refused to surrender their arsenal or their forts, Johnson subsided without violence.

Moore surrendered his governorship to the Crown's appointee, Sir Francis Nicholson, who arrived in Charles Town in May 1721, and returned to the more familiar area of Indian affairs. The royal takeover of South Carolina produced reforms in the colony's policy toward the Indians. In 1724 a procedure was established whereby the assembly appointed, in conjunction with the council, a single commissioner for handling Indian matters, replacing a three-person body. Moore, who was Speaker of the Commons House as well as an authority on Indians, became the first of these commissioners with the sole authority to oversee the activities of South Carolina's traders in "Indian country." However, Moore died before he could make any effort to regulate these important agents of commercial, diplomatic, and cultural interaction.

Moore married Elizabeth Bereford, but the year of the marriage is not known. The couple had six children.

• There are no Moore papers. Consequently, the early history, education, and private life of this shadowy figure of proprietary South Carolina remain largely unknown, and no secondary literature exists. Yet, Moore's public activities entered the historical record to the degree that several studies of early Carolina accord some treatment to his career. See Verner Winslow Crane, *The Southern Frontier, 1670–1732* (1929); Edward McCrady, *The History of South Carolina under the Proprietary Government, 1670–1719* (1897); M. Eugene Sirmans, *Colonial South Carolina: A Political History, 1663–1763* (1966); and Mabel L. Webber, "The First Governor Moore and His Children," *South Carolina Historical Magazine* 37 (1936): 1–23.

L. H. ROPER

MOORE, John (24 June 1834–30 July 1901), Roman Catholic bishop, was born in Castletown-Devlin, County Westmeath, Ireland, the son of William Moore and Marcella O'Farrell, farmers. As a boy Moore experienced the devastation of famine due to the potato blight in Ireland, so in 1848 he emigrated to Charleston, South Carolina, where a community of Irish worked as longshoremen and laborers and where the Irish-born bishop, John England, had established a seminary. In October 1848 Moore entered St. John the Baptist Seminary in Charleston and quickly demonstrated intellectual promise. Sent to the College of Courbree in Courbree, France, in July 1851, he then attended the Urban College of Propaganda in Rome in 1855. Receiving a doctorate in theology in 1859, he was ordained a priest in Rome on 9 April 1860. Returning to his diocese after his ordination, from 1860 to 1865 he served as assistant pastor at St. Finbar Cathedral, Charleston. During the Civil War he traveled throughout the state to attend to wounded and dying soldiers on both sides of the conflict. Appointed pastor of St. Patrick's Parish, Charleston, in 1865, he was also director of the Catholic Boys' Asylum and later named vicar general of the diocese in 1872. On 16 February 1877 he was appointed the second bishop of St. Augustine and was ordained a bishop 13 May at St. John the Baptist Pro-Cathedral, Charleston, by Bishop Patrick Lynch. He was installed in St. Augustine on 20 May 1877.

Moore's foremost concern was the recruitment of sufficient priests to serve his scattered flock. To this end, in 1887 he handed over to Benedictine priests the pastoral care of three counties on Florida's west coast. In 1889 he commissioned the New Orleans Jesuits to pastorally care for southern Florida, more than one-third of his diocese. Moore also went to Ireland to recruit seminarians for Florida. By the 1890s he had a half-dozen Irishmen ordained to serve the diocese of St. Augustine, a trend that would increase in subsequent years.

Besides personnel shortages, Moore was beset with financial difficulties. His cathedral was destroyed by fire in 1887; for the next fourteen years he struggled to raise funds to rebuild it. An able financier, he traveled to northern U.S. parishes to beg money for his missionary diocese. In Florida, millionaire railroad magnate Henry Flagler, a Presbyterian, befriended Moore after the cathedral fire in 1887. From then on Moore could count on Flagler as a benefactor for special projects.

With no ecclesiastical bureaucracy, Moore managed his diocese not from behind a desk but "on the road" by letter or personal visitation. He visited every parish at least once a year. In 1877 he instituted an annual report for every parish and Catholic institution in the diocese.

Despite pressing challenges, Moore's ecclesiastical interests and involvements extended beyond his missionary diocese. He attended the Third Plenary Council of Baltimore, a meeting of all American bishops in 1884. Archbishop James Gibbons of Baltimore asked Moore to be a member of a committee to bring the decrees of the Third Plenary Council—which included recommending the establishment of parochial schools in every parish, the encouragement of black Catholic schools, the publication of a uniform catechism, the restructuring of seminary education, and the establishment of a "superior grade of seminary" (which in 1889 led to the opening of the Catholic University of America)—to the Vatican for approval. In March 1885 Moore traveled to Rome with fellow committee members Bishops Richard Gilmour of Cleveland and Joseph Dwenger of Fort Wayne and Monsignor Denis O'Connell. In early July Moore met personally with Pope Leo XIII, who subsequently approved virtually all of the council's pronouncements.

Moore also involved himself in controversy that risked his personal reputation and probably short-circuited his further advancement. In 1886 he wrote Gibbons opposing the proposed establishment of an apostolic delegation to the United States. Along with many other American Catholic bishops, Moore feared that such an action would provide ammunition for nativists who railed against Catholic immigration and who claimed that Catholicism represented foreign interventionism by the pope. But Moore's most risky involvement was his personal campaign to get the New York activist priest Edward McGlynn reconciled to his archbishop and to the church. McGlynn, a Catholic social gospel advocate, associated himself with the socioeconomic theories of Henry George and backed George in his 1886 mayoral campaign, against the expressed wishes of his archbishop, Michael Corrigan. As a result, Corrigan suspended McGlynn from the priesthood and delated him to Rome for possible excommunication. From 1887 until 1893 Moore, a classmate of McGlynn's in Rome and his loyal friend, conducted an unremitting epistolary and personal campaign of diplomacy to aid McGlynn's readmittance into the church. Against all odds and the advice of many of his fellow bishops, Moore sent letters and petitions to members of the American hierarchy and to Roman officials. He traveled to New York several times to convince the stubborn and vacillating McGlynn to cooperate with his efforts. In May 1893 Moore went to New York again to escort McGlynn to a ship sailing for Rome so that McGlynn's reconciliation might be effected. Thanks largely to Moore's herculean efforts, McGlynn was reconciled in June 1893.

Although well read and well educated, Moore's simplicity of manner and missionary lifestyle made him easily approachable to both clergy and laity. During his 24-year episcopacy, he rebuilt his cathedral and increased his parishes from eight to fifteen, his missions from twelve to twenty-five, and his clergy from ten to thirty. In August 1899 he suffered his first stroke while fundraising in Wilkes-Barre, Pennsylvania; by June 1900 he had his third stroke in Allegheny, Pennsylvania. He died in St. Augustine, Florida.

• Moore's correspondence can be found in the Archives of the Diocese of St. Augustine, the Archives of the Archdiocese of Baltimore, the Archives of the Diocese of Charleston, and Archivo Segreto Vaticano, Vatican City State. His time in Charleston is mentioned in Richard C. Madden, *Catholics in South Carolina: A Record* (1985). His episcopacy is discussed in two books by Michael J. McNally, *Catholicism in South Florida, 1868–1968* (1984) and *Catholic Parish Life of Florida's West Coast, 1860–1968* (1996). Moore's relationship to the McGlynn affair is considered in Gerald P. Fogarty, *The Vatican and the American Hierarchy from 1870 to 1965* (1985).

MICHAEL J. MCNALLY

MOORE, John Bassett (3 Dec. 1860–12 Nov. 1947), lawyer, judge, and government official, was born in Smyrna, Delaware, the son of John Adams Moore, a physician and state legislator, and Martha Anne Ferguson. Because of health problems, he was educated by his parents and then attended a private school. At the age of seventeen he entered the University of Virginia where he studied the liberal arts and the law. Forced to leave college because of ill health, he nevertheless continued his legal studies and was admitted to the bar in 1883. At the urging of influential Delaware political leaders, he became a clerk in the U.S. Department of State in 1885 and third assistant secretary from 1886 to 1891. In 1890 he married Helen Frances Toland; they had three children.

In 1891 Moore left the State Department to become the Hamilton Fish Professor of Diplomacy and Law at Columbia University, where he wrote books on international law and arbitration during the next two decades. Among his notable publications were the six-volume *History and Digest of International Arbitration* (1898) and the eight-volume *Digest of International Law* (1906). In 1898 Secretary of State William R. Day asked Moore to be assistant secretary of state when the war with Spain seemed imminent. Moore played an important role in shaping the armistice that ended hostilities in August 1898 and in the decisions that led to the acquisition of the Philippine Islands. He traveled to Paris as secretary and counsel to the peace commission that negotiated the treaty of peace with Spain. Even though he was a Democrat, Moore accepted the expansionist policies of the William McKinley administration as the legitimate result of the war with Spain. He resigned his position in 1899 but continued to advise McKinley and his secretary of state, John Hay, about their policies in the Far East through 1900.

Moore's diplomatic service continued into the presidency of Theodore Roosevelt (1858–1919). He helped to shape the Hay-Pauncefote Treaties of 1900 and 1901, which gave the United States authorization to build a canal in Central America. During the crisis with Columbia in 1903 he advised Roosevelt that the United States had a legal right to seize Panama, which was based on an 1846 treaty with New Grenada (the earlier name for Colombia) that gave Washington a "right of war" across Central America. He also counseled the president about the treaty with Panama when it was sent to the Senate. During the decade that followed, Moore held a number of appointed positions, which included service at the Dominican Arbitration in 1904, membership on the delegation to the Fourth International Conference of American States, and membership on the Permanent Court of Arbitration at the Hague, to which President William Howard Taft named him in 1912.

The election of Woodrow Wilson in 1912 gave Moore the opportunity to return to government service with his own political party. Round-faced and bearded, Moore was described as "a little fat jovial man" by this time (West, p. 56). He was named as counselor to the State Department in 1913 and spent a year in the post. However, service in the Wilson administration was not a happy experience for Moore. He did not work well with the secretary of state, William Jennings Bryan, and was "full of his own importances," according to Mrs. Bryan (West, p. 62). Moore found Wilson a man of "supercilious ignorance" (West, p. 49) who was "singularly uninformed" when it came to the history of diplomacy or international law (Megargee, p. 169). As time passed, Moore's advice had less and less influence with Bryan and Wilson, and he learned of one key appointment when he read about it in the newspaper. He disagreed strongly when the president implied that the state laws of California might supersede a treaty with Japan in 1913, and Moore also differed about the president's policy toward Mexico, where he favored recognition of the government of Victoriano Huerta. Moore believed that the "missionary diplomacy" of Wilson and Bryan often ignored issues of international law that loomed large in Moore's "realistic" approach to foreign affairs. Moore resigned in March 1914.

When the First World War began, Moore was privately critical of Wilson's policies, which he believed would lead the nation into war. He favored equal application of the principles of neutrality to both German and Great Britain. Though initially a member of the League to Enforce Peace, after the war Moore became a critic of the Treaty of Versailles and the League of Nations, which he thought had been "founded in a welter of nationalisms, not in a mood of unifying sentiment" (Megargee, p. 301). In 1921 he was named the first American to serve as a judge on the Permanent Court of International Justice at the Hague and held the position until 1928. He urged the court to insulate itself from political and national influences and advocated that the United States become an adherent of the court on the condition that it would not be bound by any advisory opinions that the court might render. Moore advised the Senate to incorporate such language when it approved adherence in January 1926. During his tenure as judge he presided over an international conference in 1923 that wrote rules for the use of airplanes and radio during wars.

Moore retired from his teaching position at Columbia in 1924 and stepped down from the court four years later. He spent most of his later years working on his *International Adjudications* (1936). Moore supported neutrality legislation during the 1930s and attacked what he saw as Franklin D. Roosevelt's increasingly dictatorial policies. After concluding in January 1940 that "all the President's acts and utterances look toward involving us" in the war (Megargee, p. 366), he endorsed Wendell Willkie in the 1940 presidential election. A series of strokes affected Moore's health before his death at his home in New York City.

Moore was the most prominent American authority on international law during the first half of the twentieth century. His writings on international law remain important contributions to the literature of that field. He was a significant participant in the foreign policy decisions of the McKinley and Roosevelt administrations. When his service with Woodrow Wilson proved unrewarding, Moore became an effective critic of the growth of presidential power in foreign affairs.

• A large collection of Moore's papers is in the Library of Congress. The papers of Thomas F. Bayard, William McKinley, Theodore Roosevelt, William Howard Taft, and Woodrow Wilson, all at the Library of Congress, document Moore's public career. Edwin Borchard et al., eds., *The Collected Papers of John Bassett Moore in Seven Volumes* (1944), provides a guide to Moore's thought. In addition to the works already mentioned in the text, Moore wrote *American Diplomacy: Its Spirit and Achievements* (1905) and edited *A Digest of International Law* (8 vols., 1906). Two unsigned articles, "New Counselor of the State Department," *Outlook*, 29 Mar. 1913, pp. 693–94, and "The Loss of Mr. Moore," *Literary Digest*, 4 Mar. 1914, pp. 539–40, offer contemporary views of Moore. The only biography is Richard Megargee, "The Diplomacy of John Bassett Moore: Realism in American Foreign Policy" (Ph.D. diss., Northwestern Univ., 1963). Rachel West, *The Department of State on the Eve of the First World War* (1978), has an interesting sketch of Moore. An obituary is in the *New York Times*, 13 Nov. 1947.

LEWIS L. GOULD

MOORE, John Trotwood (26 Aug. 1858–10 May 1929), author and journalist, was born in Marion, Alabama, the son of John Moore, a state circuit judge, and Emily Adelia Billingslea. After receiving his early education in Marion, he enrolled at Howard College, a local Baptist institution, in 1874. Upon graduation in 1878, Moore served as associate editor of the *Marion Commonwealth*; he then spent the next six years teaching school in Monterey and Pineapple, Alabama. During this period he studied law and passed the bar examination, though he never practiced. Moore probably used the pen name "Trotwood," drawn from a character in Charles Dickens's *David Copperfield*, for the first time in a letter published in the *Commonwealth* on 16 January 1879. He became so associated with its use that he eventually adopted Trotwood as his middle name.

On 17 February 1885 Moore married Florence Allen. The couple soon left Pineapple and moved to Maury County, Tennessee. Here, on a farm near Columbia in the bluegrass region of middle Tennessee, and later in Nashville, Moore lived for the remainder of his life. Becoming increasingly interested in horses and horse lore, he began raising blooded stock on the farm. Like his neighbors, Moore became concerned with the development of a harness racing horse that would pace rather than trot. He began to champion the virtues of the pacer, first in the Columbia *Herald*, then in his own pacing department in the Chicago *Horse Review*. He remained a regular contributor to the latter publication until 1904.

In his writing for the *Horse Review*, Moore was able to combine his passion for the pacing horse with his love of literature by injecting stories and verse into his column. By doing so, he gradually made the move from journalist to fiction writer. In his efforts to portray accurately his region, he practiced his belief that a writer must first observe, then write. Close observation of people's manners and habits should be coupled with good listening. Like many southern writers of his generation, Moore was attuned to the South's oral tradition, to storytelling and the power and beauty of the spoken word. Known as an excellent talker himself, he developed an awareness of speech rhythms and patterns, especially those of blacks. As a writer Moore was influenced by several literary approaches to portraying the southern experience, including the historical romance, the work of the southern humorists, and the local color tradition with its emphasis on intimate acquaintance with a specific locality. Unfortunately, he had difficulty weaving these strands into a consistently unified artistic voice. Nevertheless, Moore's writings provide an important link between the earlier historical romances of writers like William Gilmore Simms and later, more realistic treatments, as in the work of William Faulkner.

An infant son born to the Moores early in 1896 died shortly thereafter. Moore was struck another blow when Florence died on 23 December 1896. In 1897 Moore published *Songs and Stories from Tennessee*, local color sketches and poems collected from his writings for the *Horse Review*, including his best-known racing story, "Ole Mistis," and tales of Uncle Wash, his famous black character. On 13 June 1900 Moore married Mary Brown Daniel; they had three children, one of whom, Austin Merrill Moore, became a psychiatrist and well-known poet. With the publication of his first novel, *A Summer Hymnal* (1901), Moore entered his most prolific period as a writer, publishing seven books between 1901 and the end of 1911. Moore's most significant work is *The Bishop of Cottontown* (1905), which deals with the important changes that industrial forces were bringing to southern life while realistically depicting the travails of child labor. Other novels of this period include *Uncle Wash: His Stories* (1910) and *The Gift of Grass* (1911), the "autobiography" of a racing horse.

One of the reasons that Moore had resigned from the *Horse Review* in 1904 was that he wished to establish his own magazine. In 1905 a group of businessmen in Columbia, Tennessee, helped him organize the Trotwood Publishing Company to publish *Trotwood's Monthly*. Designed to bring quality literature to a rural audience, its pages were filled with stories, poetry, historical sketches, and literary criticism. The magazine was virtually a one-man operation, with Moore as its most prolific contributor. The merger of *Trotwood's Monthly* with *Bob Taylor's Magazine* in early 1907 to create the *Taylor-Trotwood Magazine* did little to change Moore's management and direction of the journal. Suffering from financial problems, no dependable roster of contributors, and an overworked editor, the magazine ceased publication at the end of 1910.

In subsequent years, Moore's interests turned increasingly to Tennessee history. He became state librarian for Tennessee in 1919, working diligently to collect records and original documents and to preserve historic sites. With A. P. Foster, he edited the four-volume *Tennessee: The Volunteer State* (1923). Moore's *Hearts of Hickory: A Story of Andrew Jackson and the War of 1812*, his best-known historical novel, was published in 1926. During his last years, Moore wrote occasional articles on historical subjects for the *Saturday Evening Post*. He was at work on an unfinished novel when he died at his home in Nashville.

Although they needed to be better focused and developed, Moore's gifts as a writer were those of a storyteller who based his work on the South's history and geography as well as its people. His stories and tales helped to keep alive the southern tradition of frontier humor and realism during a time of literary transition.

• The standard work on the life and writings of Moore is Claud B. Green, *John Trotwood Moore: Tennessee Man of Letters* (1957). See also W. M. Bunting, "John Trotwood Moore," in *Library of Southern Literature*, ed. Edwin T. Alderman et al., vol. 8 (1907) pp. 3693–94; Thomas M. Owen, *History of Alabama and Dictionary of Alabama Biography*, vol. 4 (1921), p. 1230. Obituaries appear in the *Nashville Banner*, 10 May 1929; *Nashville Tennessean*, 11, 12, 19 May 1929; and *Horse Review*, 77, 15 May 1929, pp. 448–49.

L. MOODY SIMMS, JR.

MOORE, John Weeks (11 Apr. 1807–23 Mar. 1889), music historian and newspaper editor, was born in Andover, New Hampshire, the son of Jacob Bailey Moore, a physician and amateur musician, and Mary Eaton. After attending high school in Concord, New Hampshire, and Plymouth Academy, Moore became an apprentice at the *New Hampshire Patriot*. In 1828 he moved to Brunswick, Maine, where he edited and published the *Androscoggin Free Press*, the state's first weekly newspaper. He sold the paper in 1831 and returned to Concord to establish the *Concord Advertiser*. There he married Emily Jane Eastman of Concord in 1832; they had three children. From 1838, when they moved to Vermont, until 1851 (except for the years 1842–1846), Moore edited and published the *Bellows Fall Gazette*, a staunchly Whig newspaper. A fine amateur musician who played the piano, violin, and flute, Moore began publishing editions of music in 1840. In Vermont he issued three collections of instrumental and vocal music: *Sacred Minstrel* (1842), *American Collection of Instrumental Music* (1856), and *Star Collection of Instrumental Music* (1858). From 1840 to 1848 he also edited the *World of Music*, at its time the longest running music periodical in the United States.

His most extraordinary and influential work was published while in Vermont: the *Complete Encyclopedia of Music, Elementary, Technical, Historical, Biographical, Vocal, and Instrumental* (1854), at that time the most ambitious work of its kind in the English language. Moore claimed to have compiled the information for this volume seventeen years before publishing it. Most of the *Encyclopedia* is devoted to antiquarian European art music and it is based on summaries of the work of several important European music historians. But, unusual for the period, Moore also included material on the art music of his own time, for which he believed that his fellow music historians had shown "neglect and almost supercilious disregard." For this he solicited biographical data directly from the musicians themselves. Altogether, there are entries on about 4,000 musicians, definitions of more than 5,000 terms, and two hundred short essays on musical topics, collected in a single volume of more than 1,000 dense pages.

In 1863 Moore moved to Manchester, New Hampshire, where he edited the city's *Daily News*. From 1867 to 1870 he also edited and published *Moore's Musical Record*. In 1875 he supplemented a reprinting of his *Encyclopedia* with an extensive appendix, and the next year he issued *A Dictionary of Musical Information*, in essence an abridged version of the *Encyclopedia*. The *Dictionary* is noteworthy for its "List of Modern Musical Works Published in the United States from 1640 to 1875," which includes several thousand compositions. This suggests that Moore had somewhat rethought his position on American music history since 1854, when he had written, "It is impossible that American music can do more than reproduce the music of other ages and nations. We are too open to the world, too receptive of all influences from abroad, too much a nation made up of others to possess a music of our own." His publishing career was capped in 1886 with publication of a work whose subject was his own trade: *Moore's Historical, Biographical and Miscellaneous Gatherings . . . Relative to Printers, Printing, Publishing, and Editing . . . from 1420 to 1886*. Moore died in Manchester.

Moore's work supports the claim that he was the first important American scholar of music history. He collected and edited a wide range of information on the music of Europe and the United States, organized it conveniently, and published it at a price "sufficiently small to place it in the hands of all persons in any way interested in musical affairs." Composer and singing teacher Moses Ela Cheney recognized Moore's importance, writing in May 1878 that "no other man in America has ever brought into form, tangible to the reader and student, so much valuable information upon music and musicians." His *Encyclopedia* justly deserves to be called a monument of English-language music history. Moore's special focus on the art music of Western Europe and his encyclopedic approach helped shape the historiography of music in this country for well over a century.

• Information on Moore's life is scattered. Simeon Pease Cheney noted that Moore "never cultivated the faculty of boasting his merits before the world" and partly corrected the situation in a short biographical piece for his *The American Singing Book* (1879), p. 201. F. O. Jones, another contemporary, included Moore in his *A Handbook of American Music and Musicians* (1886), pp. 102–3. Bits of Moore's life can be pieced together from Ezra S. Stearns, ed., *Genealogical and Family History of the State of New Hampshire*, vol. 2 (1908), pp. 492–93, and Lyman Simpson Hayes, *History of the Town of Rockingham, Vermont* (1907). A bibliography of many of Moore's publications, prepared by himself, is published in *Bibliography of Manchester, N.H.* (1885), pp. 35–36. Obituaries are found in the *New York Times*, 25 Mar. 1889, the Concord, N.H., *Daily People and Patriot*, 28 Mar. 1889, and the *Proceedings of the New Hampshire Press Association* (1890). The most important recent assessment of Moore's contribution is provided by Robert Stevenson, "American Musical Scholarship: Parker to Thayer," *19th Century Music* 1, no. 3 (1978): 201.

DALE COCKRELL

MOORE, Joseph Earle (9 July 1892–6 Dec. 1957), physician and medical researcher, was born in Philadelphia, Pennsylvania, the only child of Joseph Howard Moore, an executive at a corset-manufacturing company, and Adelaide Marie Lovett. The parents separated when Moore was eight years old, and his mother departed for Kansas City, Missouri, with her son. Earle (as he was known) attended public schools in Kansas City until he enrolled at the University of Kansas in 1909. When he left Kansas in the spring of 1914, he had earned a B.A. and had finished two years of training in medicine. That fall he entered Johns Hopkins Medical School, from which he graduated with an M.D. in 1916. He then accepted a position as a resident house officer in medicine at Johns Hopkins Hospital.

Shortly after the official entry of the United States into the Great War in 1917, Moore joined the multitudes of young American men who stepped forward for military service, entering the army as a medical officer, with the initial rank of first lieutenant. Just before he sailed for France, in May 1917, Moore married Grace Douglas Barclay, who had graduated from the Johns Hopkins School of Nursing; they had no children. Moore arrived in France ahead of the bulk of American troops known as the American Expeditionary Force, initially serving with a British field ambulance. When the AEF began to take shape in France later in 1917, Moore joined ranks with his American comrades, eventually rising to the rank of captain.

Moore's superiors assigned him to work with many other physicians in the control of venereal diseases among the American troops—an effort which AEF commander-in-chief, General John J. Pershing, identified as holding extreme military and moral significance.

The effort to achieve greater medical understanding of—and clinical control over—sexually transmitted diseases continued as the focus of Moore's career after this world war and through the next global military conflict. He returned to Johns Hopkins in 1918 to serve as co-director (with Alan M. Chesney) of the Syphilis Clinic at Johns Hopkins Hospital, which became, under Moore's energetic leadership, one of the world's leading centers for the treatment and study of venereal diseases. In 1929 Moore became the sole director of the clinic and continued to hold this position until his death. He published his first book in 1933, *The Modern Treatment of Syphilis*, which quickly became recognized as an authoritative text for clinicians. During the interwar years, Moore also assumed the editorship of the *American Journal of Syphilis, Gonorrhea, and the Venereal Diseases* in 1935.

When the United States entered World War II, the protection of American troops against venereal disease once again became a military and medical problem of the highest order. Moore served as a consultant on VD to both the U.S. Public Health Service and the U.S. Army during this national emergency. Even more significantly, he chaired the venereal disease subcommittee of the National Research Council, to which the federal government delegated great responsibility in determining the allocation of unprecedented levels of funding for research on sexually transmitted diseases. In this administrative capacity, Moore played an important role in one of the noteworthy triumphs of wartime medical research: the establishment of penicillin as an effective treatment for syphilis. For his work during the war, Moore was awarded the Medal of Merit of the United States in 1946.

Moore compiled the knowledge that had been gained during and immediately after the war on the use of antibiotics for the treatment of syphilis in the second major book of his career, *Penicillin in Syphilis* (1946). With the advent of penicillin, Moore and his colleagues achieved such success in the fight against syphilis that they found themselves forced to turn elsewhere in their research. Rather than focus tightly on another medical problem, Moore broadened the scope of his interests to encompass all chronic diseases. In practical terms, he convinced the administrators at Johns Hopkins to convert the syphilis clinic that Moore had directed for decades into a facility for the study of a range of chronic diseases. Similarly, Moore changed the name and scope of the journal he had long edited; in 1954 the *American Journal of Syphilis* became the *Journal of Chronic Diseases*.

Throughout his long and distinguished career as a medical researcher and academic, Moore maintained an active private practice, with many devoted patients. He was also widely liked and admired by his colleagues. On his sixtieth birthday in 1952, former U.S. surgeon general Thomas Parran hosted a dinner in Moore's honor, which was attended by more than 100 colleagues and former students. Moore maintained relationships with medical friends from around the world and had a reputation as a generous host, as was colorfully recounted by a British colleague: "It has happened to me, as to others, to find on our arrival in Baltimore, Earle waiting at the station in his Cadillac to tell us that the hotel reservations had been canceled and that we must be his house guests." This same colleague provided a powerful summation of Moore's professional reputation: "the best-known venereologist of his generation" (*Lancet* 273 [21 Dec. 1957]: 1292).

After the death of his wife in 1954, Moore married later that year Irene Mason Gieske. He died in Baltimore at the Johns Hopkins Hospital—the institution that had been his professional home for more than four decades.

• An excellent general history of venereal disease in the United States that gives some attention to Moore is Allan M. Brandt, *No Magic Bullet* (1985; repr. 1987). Moore himself produced a participant's history of VD research during World War II in the chapter he wrote for *Advances in Military Medicine*, ed. E. C. Andrus (1948). Some of Moore's research activity at Johns Hopkins is treated in A. McGehee Harvey, *Adventures in Medical Research: A Century of Discovery at Johns Hopkins* (1976), pp. 248–54. Obituaries are in *Journal of the American Medical Association* 166 (8 Feb. 1958): 660; *Lancet* 273 (21 Dec. 1957): 1292; *British Medical Journal* (28 Dec. 1957): 1548; the *New York Times*, 8 Dec. 1957; and the *Baltimore Sun*, 7 Dec. 1957.

JON M. HARKNESS

MOORE, Joseph Haines (7 Sept. 1878–15 Mar. 1949), astronomer and administrator, was born in Wilmington, Ohio, the son of John Haines Moore and Mary Ann Haines, distant cousins. Moore's father pursued a variety of professions, as weaver, cabinet maker, miller, merchant, and farmer. Moore did his undergraduate studies at Wilmington College, where he became interested in astronomy and earned his A.B. in 1897. He then began his graduate work at Johns Hopkins University, but his preparation was inadequate, and he had first to take two years of advanced undergraduate courses. Thus he spent six years at Hopkins, studying and working especially on spectroscopy under Henry A. Rowland, Joseph S. Ames, and Robert W. Wood. Moore was a very well trained spectroscopist when he received his Ph.D. in physics in 1903, and he was immediately hired as an assistant in spectroscopy at Lick Observatory, the University of California research institution on Mount Hamilton, California. Moore married Fredrica Chase, A Vassar graduate who was an assistant at Lick Observatory, in 1907; they had two children.

At Lick Observatory, W. Wallace Campbell had begun his program of measuring spectroscopically the radial velocities of stars, fundamental data that had only recently become obtainable. Spectroscopic analysis was to be the major research program of the observatory for all the many years of Campbell's directorship and long after it. Moore worked closely with Campbell until he sent Moore to Chile to take charge of the Lick Observatory southern station in Santiago from 1909 until 1913. Campbell had started this outpost in 1903 to obtain the same radial-velocity data for stars too far south in the sky to be observed from Mount Hamilton. When Moore returned to California in 1913 he became effectively Campbell's right-hand man for running the radial velocity program, as the busy director became more and more involved in national and international scientific leadership. After 1923, when Campbell moved to Berkeley as president of the university but retained the Lick directorship, Moore was in nearly complete charge of the radial velocity work, except for the overall control that Campbell continued to exert.

The main product of this research was measured radial velocities of stars, and Campbell and Moore published a large volume containing these results in 1928. A byproduct of this work was the discovery of many spectroscopic binaries, double stars in orbits about one another but so distant that they appear in the sky as a single point of light; their natures are revealed by their periodic variations in radial velocity. Moore became an expert in spectroscopic binaries, and over the years he compiled several successive catalogs of these objects, as more and more of them became known. Campbell and Moore also measured the radial velocities of many planetary and other gaseous nebulae by the same spectroscopic method. While he was at the Lick southern station in Chile, Moore had obtained the radial velocities of several bright nebulae in the Large Magellanic Cloud, which were important in understanding its nature. In 1928 he, with Donald H. Menzel, then a young Lick staff member, succeeded in measuring spectroscopically the rotational velocity (and hence the period of rotation) of the planet Neptune, a result that held up well into the Space Age and has been only slightly improved since. In 1930 Moore and Menzel confirmed, by the same spectroscopic method, the rotational velocity and period of Uranus, which had been measured previously at Lowell Observatory.

Moore also accompanied Campbell on several Lick Observatory expeditions to remote locations to observe total solar eclipses and himself headed the expeditions to Camptonville, California, in 1930 and Fryeburg, Maine, in 1932. At these eclipses Moore obtained excellent spectrograms for measuring the emission lines of the sun's chromosphere and corona. The wavelengths he obtained from them were among those used by many spectroscopists and astronomers over the years in their attempts, ultimately successful in 1939 and 1941, to identify the coronal emission lines.

In 1942, when William H. Wright retired as director of Lick Observatory, Moore, who by then had been named assistant director, was appointed to succeed him. He was sixty-three years old, and his appointment was an interim, wartime measure. He kept Lick Observatory in operation during World War II and advised and encouraged President Robert G. Sproul to authorize a large telescope for Lick Observatory, to be constructed as part of the postwar University of California capital-building program. By then, however, the elderly Moore and Wright had been worn down by the Great Depression, and their expectations for a telescope were relatively modest. Meanwhile, other, younger astronomers demanded as large a telescope as possible; they prevailed, and Moore worked with them to help start this project.

Very soon after World War II ended, Sproul named C. Donald Shane (who had been Sproul's second choice for the job in 1942, but who had not accepted because of the war) as the new Lick director. Moore, who had suffered from heart trouble at Mount Hamilton, gladly moved to Berkeley in November 1945 to finish out his career in the astronomy department on campus. There he retired in 1948 and died the following year of a heart attack.

Raised as a Quaker, Moore had a quiet, retiring personality. Yet in his many years at Lick Observatory he built up a tremendous repertoire of stories about astronomers, scientists, and the world at large, which he delighted in telling to younger faculty members, assistants, and graduate students through the long, quiet nights at the telescope. His whole career had been built around collecting large quantities of unusually accurate data in programs others had begun.

• The main collection of Moore's letters is in the Mary Lea Shane Archives of the Lick Observatory, in the University of California, Santa Cruz Library. Among the most important of Moore's papers are, with W. W. Campbell, "Radial Velocities of Stars Brighter than Visual Magnitude 5.51 as Determined at Mount Hamilton and Santiago," *Publications of the Lick Observatory* 16 (1928): 1–399; "A General Catalogue of the Radial Velocities of Stars, Nebulae and Clusters," *Publications of the Lick Observatory*" 18 (1932): 1–229; and, with F. J. Neubauer, "Fifth Catalogue of the Orbital Elements of Spectroscopic Binary Stars," *Lick Observatory Bulletin* 20 (1948): 1–31, which gives references to the earlier catalogs. See also J. H. Moore, "Fifty Years of Research at the Lick Observatory," *Publications of the Astronomical Society of the Pacific* 50 (1938): 189–203. Two published memorial biographies are Robert G. Aitken, "Joseph Haines Moore: 1878–1949: A Tribute," *Publications of the Astronomical Society of the Pacific* 61 (1949): 125–28, and William H. Wright, "Joseph Haines Moore," National Academy of Sciences, *Biographical Memoirs* 29 (1956): 235–51; the latter contains a complete bibliography of Moore's published scientific papers. For more on Moore's work at the Lick Observatory see Donald E. Osterbrock et al., *Eye on the Sky: Lick Observatory's First Century* (1988).

DONALD E. OSTERBROCK

MOORE, Julia A. (1 Dec. 1847–5 June 1920), poet, was born in Plainfield, Michigan, the daughter of Alanson Davis and Melinda (maiden name unknown), farmers. Much of the available information about Moore's evidently uneventful life comes from her own poems. For example, we know that her childhood was difficult only because she writes that, with three younger siblings "And dear mother being sickly, / Their care it fell on me" ("Sweet Singer of Michigan"). Her formal education was presumably minimal. She married Fred Moore, a farmer and storekeeper, in 1865; of the Moores' ten children, six lived to maturity. She lived her entire life in or near small towns north of Grand Rapids, Michigan, and died at her home near Manton, Michigan.

Moore's first book of poems, *The Sentimental Song Book* (1876), was published in Grand Rapids. In 1877 a book of her poems was published in Cleveland; it was also titled *The Sentimental Song Book* but added, on the title page: "The Sweet Singer of Michigan Salutes the Public." Moore has ever since been known, affectionately and ironically, as "the Sweet Singer of Michigan": appropriately also, since she composed her lyrics to fit existing tunes and in her public performances sang at least some of her poems. Half a dozen editions of her poems were published from 1876 to 1878.

From the beginning Moore was celebrated for the technical incompetence and maudlin tone of her verse. She did not at first recognize irony in the enthusiastic responses to her work. When in May 1877 some citizens of Grand Rapids rented an opera house for a reading by Moore, the *Grand Rapids Daily Eagle* reported that she was received with the "uncontrollable . . . adulation of the multitude"; "the renditions of this talented authoress and elocutionist are wholly beyond the pale of legitimate criticism" (quoted in Greenley, p. 16). This tone of sarcastic praise exemplifies the responses to her published poems also: she was widely and caustically reviewed across the country, and reviews from newspapers in Illinois, New York, Connecticut, Pennsylvania, Ohio, Massachusetts, and Michigan were reprinted in *The Sweet Singer of Michigan* (1878). During 1877 and 1878 she recited her poems in various towns in the Grand Rapids area.

The drama of Moore's poetic career was her gradual recognition that she was being ridiculed. In her final performance in Grand Rapids, in December 1878, she finally realized the extent to which her audience was ridiculing her, whereupon "her husband forbade her writing any more [poetry] for publication, an injunction which she evidently obeyed" (Greenley, p. 19). She turned to prose instead and in 1880 published, in eight installments in the *Cedar Springs (Mich.) Clipper*, a short novel titled *Sunshine and Shadow*, which shows all the stylistic flaws of her poetry except that special inability to follow a pattern of meter or rhyme by which her poems continually surprise the reader. The publication of this novel in book form (in 1915, one year after her husband died) indicates that she maintained literary aspirations throughout her life, although, as she commented in her only venture into criticism, "Literary is a work very difficult to do. It needs to be thoroughly studied to make it as it should be" ("Address to the Public"). Moore's biographer A. H. Greenley documents a number of Moore's poems written after 1878 and published in newspapers, as well as two book collections in 1900 and 1912. Whether Fred Moore approved is not known.

Moore's subjects include patriotism, politics, famous disasters, temperance, cricket, and Michigan towns, but her abiding theme is death. "William Upson," Mark Twain's favorite, is exemplary. She was not familiar with the young Civil War soldier who died; it matters only that he died pathetically and left sobbing mourners behind: "And oh, how his parents weep, / But now they must in sorrow mourn, / Billy has gone to his heaven home." In Moore's poems the individual case is incidental except as it calls up the appropriate emotions. As subjects, children work best for maximum heart wrenching, and Moore worked children, one might say, to death. In each poem the author slides from pathos to bathos in presenting her "infant" subjects, from "Little Andrew," whose "little soul was free from sin— / He was looking in the water, / When, alas, this child fell in," to "Little Libbie":

> While eating dinner, this dear little child
> Was choked on a piece of beef.
> Doctors came, tried their skill awhile,
> But none could give relief.

From here it is one small step to Emmeline Grangerford, in Mark Twain's *Adventures of Huckleberry Finn* (1885), whose immortal "Ode to Stephen Dowling Botts" differs from Moore's best work only in being funny *by intention of the author* (Twain, not Emmeline). Young Botts's "soul did from this cold world fly / By falling down a well."

Moore's poems reduced to absurdity the sentimentality scorned by writers like Mark Twain. But her technical disability combined with her invincible naïveté and sincerity has continued to endear her poems to readers. Twain wrote in *Following the Equator* that he found in her work a "deep charm," the "subtle touch . . . that makes an intentionally humorous episode pathetic and an intentionally pathetic one funny." For Stephen Leacock, who coined the term "supercomic" to signify humorous poems that are not intended to be humorous, she was "probably the greatest super-comic poet who has lived since Milton" (*Humor and Humanity*, p. 183). Similarly William Harmon invented a term for such work as hers: "A Prismatic—and Mrs. Moore is such a writer *par excellence* and *sui generis*—is a writer so transcendently, surpassingly, superlatively bad that he or she belongs in a special genre in which normal rules and habits of judgment are magically suspended" (p. xx). For Walter Blair "her songs endure the test of true literature by charming the reader." This charm is in the combination of her high poetic seriousness, her inability to command rhyme, rhythm, imagery, tone, or coherence, and her ignorance of this inability. Her tongue, all critics agree, was never in cheek; anyone who thought otherwise (but no one ever has) would miss the special appeal of her poetry. She is more than the "poet laureate" of the "dreadful decade" (the 1870s; the description is Blair's); she transcends her age and will be read with delight as long as readers value poetry.

• The fullest collections of Moore texts are at the Library of Michigan, in Lansing, and the Grand Rapids (Mich.) Public Library. No manuscripts are known to exist. The posthumously collected edition of her poems, *The Sweet Singer of Michigan, Poems by Mrs. Julia A. Moore*, ed. Walter Blair (1928), includes her "Address to the Public" and an introduction by Blair. A. H. Greenley, *The Sweet Singer of Michigan Bibliographically Considered* (1945), is the definitive source for both bibliography and biography, though even he relies on Moore's poems for some biographical information. The most notable commentaries on Moore by her contemporaries are in Bill Nye, *Bill Nye and Boomerang* (1890), and Mark Twain, *Following the Equator* (1897). Moore has been anthologized in D. B. Wyndham Lewis and Charles Lee, eds., *The Stuffed Owl* (1930); James Camp et al., eds., *Pegasus Descending* (1971); and William Harmon, ed., *The Oxford Book of Light American Verse* (1979). Stephen Leacock discusses Moore in *Humor: Its Theory and Technique* (1935) and *Humor and Humanity* (1938), and Kit Lane in *Michigan's Victorian Poets* (1993). For Moore's influence on Mark Twain see Blair, *Mark Twain and Huck Finn* (1960), and L. W. Michelson, "Four Emmeline Grangerfords," *Mark Twain Journal* 11 (Fall 1961): 10–12.

DAVID BARBER

MOORE, Lillian (20 Sept. 1911–28 July 1967), dancer, teacher, and dance historian, was born in Chase City, Virginia, the daughter of William Cabler Moore and Margaret Watkins Goode. She began studying dance at the age of twelve at the Peabody Conservatory in Baltimore, Maryland, where she remained as a student until 1928. She then moved to New York and continued her studies with prominent teachers at the Metropolitan Opera Ballet School and the School of American Ballet.

Moore's career as a performer was varied and extensive. She danced in the corps de ballet of the Metropolitan Opera from 1928 to 1934 and performed as a soloist from 1939 to 1942. From 1935 to 1938 she danced with George Balanchine's American Ballet, also performing in concerts and operas. From 1940 to 1946 Moore was leading dancer, choreographer, and ballet mistress for the Cincinnati Summer Opera. During World War II she toured with the Stars of the Metropolitan Opera and with U.S. Army Special Services in Europe. In the 1950s Moore danced at Jacob's Pillow and made several solo tours of the United States. She stopped performing in 1954 to devote her time to teaching, research, and writing.

From 1950 to 1958 Moore taught ballet and dance history at New York's High School of Performing Arts. She then taught ballet at Robert Joffrey's American Ballet Center for the next nine years, during which time she developed special classes designed for the intensive study of various forms of pirouettes. She also assisted Joffrey during the early years of his own ballet company, stimulating his interest in dance history and staging dances from August Bournonville's nineteenth-century ballets.

Although her most immediate concerns were performing and teaching, Moore is best remembered as a writer. From 1950 to 1965 she served as an associate dance critic for the *New York Herald-Tribune* and wrote dance reviews regularly for the London *Dancing Times*. She contributed articles on various facets of contemporary ballet to a number of magazines and to the *Encyclopedia Britannica* and the Italian *Enciclopedia dello Spettacolo*.

Moore's most important writing was done as America's pioneer dance historian. She had no opportunity for formal, academic training, since no courses in the subject were available at that time. Moore spent countless hours—often snatched between classes and rehearsals—at the New York Public Library, perusing dim, old newspapers and worn letters to confirm facts and bring to literary life the careers of ballet stars of the past.

Moore's first published article, dealing with Fanny Elssler's American career in the 1840s, was published by *Theatre Guild Magazine* in 1929. Her first book, *Artists of the Dance*, a collection of ballet biographies, was published in 1938. A number of her monographs written for the journal *Dance Index* were vanguard research studies of nineteenth-century dancers in America. It was an unusual theme, for at the time ballet was generally considered an art form associated almost exclusively with Europe. With her essays "John Durang, the First American Dancer" (1942), "Mary Ann Lee, the First American Giselle" (1943), and "George Washington Smith" (1945), Moore was the first to call attention to these fine, American classical dancers. For *Dance Perspectives*, Moore wrote "The Duport Mystery," which explores the careers of two Louis Duports (or was it only one?), who danced in France and the United States in the late eighteenth century. Moore's continuing concern with dance in her native land was reflected in the posthumous anthology *Echoes of American Ballet* (1976).

Moore was awarded a Rockefeller Grant in 1955 to finance her preparation of a definitive history of theatrical dance in the United States. But she found she could not limit her activities to this project. A longstanding interest in Russian ballet prompted her editing of the translated memoirs of Marius Petipa, published as *Russian Ballet Master* (1958). She served as an adjudicator for the National Association for Regional Ballet from 1959 to 1966 and as a member of the President's Advisory Commission on the Arts from 1960 to 1967. Moore's *Images of the Dance: Historical Treasures of the Dance Collection 1581–1861*, which describes a number of distinguished prints, was compiled to honor the move of the New York Public Library's performing arts divisions to Lincoln Center in 1965. An interest in Danish ballet led to her book *Bournonville and Ballet Technique* (1961), coauthored with Erik Bruhn, which stimulated American interest in both the ballets and the teaching methods of the nineteenth-century master. Moore never completed the proposed history of American dance.

Moore was married to David Craine Maclay, a librarian with the New York Public Library, in 1935; they had no children. Their small apartment overflowed with her collection of books, prints, scrapbooks, correspondence, statuettes, and a vast variety of memorabilia. She died in New York City.

Lillian Moore was the pioneer of American dance historians. Her formal teaching was limited, since there were no college courses in dance history during her lifetime. But through informal, personal contacts, she inspired many young people to follow the paths she had laid out in dance research and writing.

• The David Maclay Collection in the Dance Collection of the New York Public Library includes early diaries, newspaper clippings, scrapbooks, photographs, programs, research notes, and correspondence. See also Ivor Guest, "The Legacy of Lillian Moore," as a preface to *Echoes of American Ballet* (1976). An extensive obituary is in *Dance Magazine*, Sept. 1967.

SELMA JEANNE COHEN

MOORE, Marianne (15 Nov. 1887–5 Feb. 1972), poet, critic, and translator, was born Marianne Craig Moore in Kirkland, Missouri, the daughter of John Milton Moore, a construction engineer and inventor, and Mary Warner. Moore had an older brother, John Warner Moore. She never met her father; before her birth his invention of a smokeless furnace failed, and he had a nervous and mental breakdown and was hospitalized in Massachusetts. Moore's mother became a housekeeper for John Riddle Warner, her father, an affectionate, well-read Presbyterian pastor in Kirkwood, until his death in 1894. Moore's mother, always overly protective, moved with her children briefly to Pittsburgh, Pennsylvania, and then to Carlisle, Pennsylvania, where Moore attended the Metzger Institute (now part of Dickinson College) through high school. In 1905 she entered Bryn Mawr College, in Bryn Mawr, Pennsylvania; published nine poems, including "A Jelly-Fish," in its literary magazines *Tipyn O'Bob* and the *Lantern*; and majored in history, law, and politics, graduating with a B.A. in 1909. Much—perhaps too much—has been made of Moore's later casual assertion that laboratory studies in biology and histology caused her to consider studying medicine; at any rate, one result of such work was her love of intricately shaped animals and also a lifelong respect for precision in description. She also expressed a desire to become a painter. After taking secretarial courses at Carlisle Commercial College (1910–1911), she taught bookkeeping, stenography, and typing and commercial English and law at the U.S. Industrial Indian School at Carlisle with admirable success until 1915. One of her students was Jim Thorpe, the famous Native American athlete.

In the summer of 1911 Moore and her mother traveled in England, Scotland, and France, and while abroad they visited art museums in Glasgow, Oxford, London, and Paris. In 1915 Moore began to publish poems professionally. Seven poems (including "To the Soul of 'Progress,'" displaying her early habit of rhyming single-syllable lines, sometimes spaced apart) appeared in the *Egoist*, a London bimonthly edited by Hilda Doolittle (H.D.) and featuring modern imagist poets, whose delicacy and compression she admired. Four (including "That Harp You Play So Well" about David the psalmist, and two about Robert Browning and George Bernard Shaw) appeared in *Poetry: A Magazine of Verse* (Chicago), which featured innovative writers quickly admired and influential. And five (including two on William Blake and George Moore) were published in *Others*, a magazine Alfred Kreymborg coedited. During these years Moore was reading much avant-garde poetry and criticism and was beginning to publish subjective reviews and critical essays.

In 1916 Moore moved with her mother from Carlisle to Chatham, New Jersey, to help keep house for her brother, by then a Yale University graduate and a Presbyterian minister. When in 1918 he joined the U.S. Navy as a chaplain, Moore and her mother moved to Manhattan. By this time she was friendly with Kreymborg, photographer Alfred Stieglitz, and poets Wallace Stevens and William Carlos Williams and was also esteemed by H.D., T. S. Eliot, and Ezra Pound. H.D., with the help of her patron Bryher (Winifred Ellerman), who was then H.D.'s lover, selected twenty-four of Moore's poems, many of which had appeared in the *Egoist*, and published them in a small book titled *Poems* (1921) without her knowledge. From 1921 until 1925 Moore worked part-time in the Hudson Park branch of the New York City library. Her London book was expanded to include fifty-three poems and was published in the United States as *Observations* (1924). In 1924 she won an award of $2,000 for achievement in poetry given by the *Dial*, the distinguished monthly pro-modernist magazine edited and partly financed by wealthy Scofield Thayer, whom Moore had met in 1918 and who was regularly publishing her verse. Especially significant in winning the award were three poems. "A Graveyard" (later called "A Grave") is a Melvillean picture of the ocean, seemingly inviting but in reality rapacious and devouring. It was Moore's first poem to be translated into a foreign language and appeared in *Anthologie de la nouvelle poésie* (1928). Her "New York" criticizes the city for general viciousness (synecdochized as a fur-trade center) but also praises it as a center for experience-seekers. And "An Octopus," one of Moore's most splendid long poems, is a scientifically accurate, highly colored word picture, with annotated quotations, of Mount Rainier, in Washington State, which she had climbed in 1920 with a group including her brother.

In 1925 Moore took over from Thayer as editor of the *Dial*, remaining there until 1929, at which time the journal was discontinued. After this, never marrying, Moore supported herself by freelance writing and with occasional help from former *Dial* backers. In 1929 she and her mother moved to Brooklyn, where Moore remained after her mother's death in 1947 and until her own final move back to Manhattan in 1966. Moore's years at the *Dial* were part of a hiatus in her publishing life. But in 1933 she was awarded the Helen Haire Levinson Prize from *Poetry*, which gained her national attention and spurred her to renewed creativity. Her next volume, *Selected Poems* (1935), which included several of the fifteen poems she had recently published between 1932 and 1935 in periodicals and anthologies (including "Camillia Sabina" in *Active Anthology*, ed. Ezra Pound [1932]), confirmed her position as a leading modernist poet. T. S. Eliot provided a laudatory introduction for the collection, writing in part: "My conviction . . . for the last fourteen years . . . [is] that Miss Moore's poems form part of the small body of durable poetry written in our time; of that small body of writings, among what passes for poetry, in which an original sensibility and alert intelligence and deep feeling have been engaged in maintaining the life of the English language." Despite Eliot's well-founded praise, the book sold poorly, and in 1940 nearly 500 copies were remaindered at thirty cents apiece.

Some critics feel that from about this time in her career Moore made little progress; she herself described her artistic development as jerky. In addition, such evolution as there was seems hard to track because of her habit of revising old poems for republication, composing new poems—for example, "To Victor Hugo of My Crow Pluto" (1961) and "To a Giraffe" (1963)—on subjects similar to those of old efforts, and creating later poems with fresh or at least newly modulated insights—for example, "Rescue with Yul Brynner" (*New Yorker*, 20 May 1961), praising the actor's relief work for refugee children, and "Baseball and Writing" (*New Yorker*, 6 Dec. 1961), celebrating her beloved Yankees but mainly comparing two painful arts. It is also true that the first version of "Poetry," undoubtedly her best-known work, first appeared in *Others* in 1919. Considerably revised, it contains her arresting dictum that poetry should offer true-to-life toads in gardens of the imagination. Furthermore, "No Swan So Fine" and "The Jerboa," both often anthologized, were first published in 1932. "No Swan So Fine" suggests that a beautiful china swan, symbol of art, has serenely outlasted Louis XV of France, its cocky whilom owner. "The Jerboa" celebrates the enviable naturalness of the jerboa, an African jumping rat, interfering with which will curse you.

Moore continued to place poem after poem in reputable periodicals such as the *Kenyon Review*, the *Nation*, the *New Republic*, and the *Partisan Review* and then collect them, and others, in book form—for example, in *The Pangolin and Other Verse* (1936), *What Are Years?* (1941), and *Nevertheless* (1944). The title pieces of these books are excellent. "The Pangolin" stunningly equates the pangolin, a scaly African and Asian ant-eating mammal, with Leonardo da Vinci, both being alike artists and engineers, and goes on to compare the pangolin's graceful, functional form to that of the spruce cone, the artichoke, and Westminster Abbey ironwork. Moore's annotations make it clear that while her sources may include direct observation they are mainly esoteric reading. "What Are Years?"—a stellar lyric—ends by paradoxically equating a bird's joyful song with both mortality and eternity. In "Nevertheless" Moore implicitly praises her own life and creativity when she images the red of the cherry as the miraculous result of a bit of thread-thin sap. In 1945 she was awarded a Guggenheim fellowship for creative writing and a year later a $1,000 joint grant from the American Academy of Arts and Letters and the National Institute of Arts and Letters. With leisure thus provided, she followed her friend W. H. Auden's suggestion and began meticulously translating the *Fables choisies, mises en vers* of Jean de La Fontaine, whose realistic moral messages and ingenious craftsmanship she had long admired. The project took too much of Moore's creative energy for almost a decade and cost her considerable self-confidence when the first publishing firm to which she submitted the work rejected it. While laboring over this work, she occasionally conferred with Pound, then confined to Saint Elizabeths Hospital in Washington, D.C. During this time she also wrote Pound and sent him a little spending money.

The 1950s brought Moore several more awards and growing public recognition, which thereafter never abated. Her *Collected Poems* (1951) won the Pulitzer Prize and the National Book Award in 1952 and the Bollingen Prize in 1953; it sold almost 5,000 copies by 1952. When she formally accepted the National Book Award, she made the often-quoted remark that her work is called poetry for lack of any other category to put it in and added that she was "a happy hack." Her *Fables of La Fontaine*, after going through four painstaking drafts, finally appeared in 1954. Although many reviewers praised her translations, some found fault in them, and the prevailing opinion is that they do not represent her best poetic accomplishment. The French government, however, was sufficiently impressed by her *Fables* to award her the Croix de Chevalier des Arts et Lettres. Her critical essays on writers and artists such as Louise Bogan, Jean Cocteau, E. E. Cummings, Pound, and Anna Pavlova, among many others, are collected in *Predilections* (1955). Moore saw Pavlova in November 1921 and wrote H.D. and Bryher (10 Nov. 1921) a long description as minutely detailed as a five-minute color film. In "Anna Pavlova" (*Dance Index*, Mar. 1944) Moore reveals her awareness of the interrelationship of various art forms when she defines Pavlova's performance as "flawless" because "she affectionately informed her technique with poetry." Moore gathered more poems in *Like a Bulwark* (1956), *O to Be a Dragon* (1959), and *Tell Me, Tell Me* (1966) and more prose pieces in *Idiosyncrasy and Technique* (1959) and *Poetry and Criticism* (1965).

While Moore was steadily writing during these years, she also emerged as somewhat of a celebrity. Her tricorn hat and black cape became her personal insignia at public events. She liked the shape of such hats, she said, because they concealed the defects of her head, which, she added, resembled that of a hop toad. She was featured in *Life* magazine, the *New York Times*, and the *New Yorker* and acted as an unofficial hostess for the mayor of New York. She was even asked by Ford Motor Company officials to suggest names for a new series of cars. She gamely offered at least nineteen, the worst being "Magigravue," "Pastelogram," and "Turcotingo," and the best perhaps including "Chaparral," "Mongoose Civique," and "Silver Sword." Declining all of her suggestions, Ford chose the name "Edsel." A climax of a sort came for Moore when, though in poor health, she tossed out the baseball to open the 1968 season at Yankee Stadium. She once said she would give much to have invented the admirably intricate stitch pattern of baseballs. Publishing only six poems after the summer of 1968, Moore suffered a series of strokes, was a semi-invalid for nearly two years, and died in her New York City home.

Moore has proved to be an engaging puzzle, not only to critics of her time but to later ones as well. It is seen that her themes broadened to a degree as she matured. In early works she emphasized a need for discipline and heroic behavior. Later she stressed the need for spiritual grace and love. To survive, she hinted, one must be alert, disciplined, and careful. Gradually she moved from scrutinizing one object to comparing several objects. She delighted in whimsically describing characteristics of animals and athletes, seeing both organisms as subjects and exemplars of art. Never dogmatic in propounding her morality, she often distanced herself and remained furtive by attributing declarative dicta to others and by commenting on quotations and even photographs expressing the point of view of others. For these reasons, critics have not yet reached a consensus—is she modern or anachronistic, imagistic or objectivistic? Regardless, Moore tremendously relished her quietly intense, largely bookish, often convivial life, made memorable to a host of friends by her rapid-fire talk. She was superb at her chosen craft. Her expression is notable for deftness and sharpness of detail, linguistic experimentation, and integration of fresh observation and obscure reading. She teases the reader into looking at reality with keener vision, as though, like her, seemingly for the very first time; challenges the reader to accept the relationship of big and little, animate and inanimate, ideal and object; and invites the reader to note, and practice, the power of words. To those who complained that her poetry often seemed obscure, she once replied that something that was work to write ought to be work to read. Her life displayed and her writings expressed the virtues of courage, loyalty, patience, modesty, spontaneity, and steadfastness.

• Most of Moore's manuscripts, letters, notebooks, and diaries are in the Rosenbach Foundation in Philadelphia, Pa. Other repositories are the Humanities Research Center of the University of Texas, the Beinecke Rare Book and Manuscript Library at Yale University, and the Newberry Library in Chicago, Ill. Collections of her writings are *A Marianne Moore Reader* (1961), *The Complete Poems of Marianne Moore* (1967; rev. ed., 1981), and *The Complete Prose of Marianne Moore*, ed. Patricia C. Willis (1986); although neither of the last two books is "complete," both are generously representative. Craig Stevens Abbott, *Marianne Moore: A Descriptive Bibliography* (1977), and his *Marianne Moore: A Reference Guide* (1987), list, respectively, primary and secondary material. Margaret Holley, *The Poetry of Marianne Moore: A Study in Voice and Value* (1987), includes a chronology of Moore's published poems, pp. 195–202. *The Selected Letters of Marianne Moore*, ed. Bonnie Costello et al. (1997), reveals much personal information. Charles Molesworth, *Marianne Moore: A Literary Life* (1990), is an illuminating biography. The following discuss Moore's professional friendships: Celeste Goodridge, *Hints and Disguises: Marianne Moore and Her Contemporaries* (1989); Joan Feit Diehl, *Elizabeth Bishop and Marianne Moore: The Psychodynamics of Creativity* (1993); and Robin G. Schulze, *The Web of Friendship: Marianne Moore and Wallace Stevens* (1995). The following analyze Moore's subjects, themes, and techniques: Donald Hall, *Marianne Moore: The Cage and the Animal* (1970); Pamela White Hadas, *Marianne Moore: Poet of Affection* (1977); Taffy Martin, *Marianne Moore: Subversive Modernist* (1986); John M. Slatin, *The Savage's Romance: The Poetry of Marianne Moore* (1986); Darlene Williams Erickson, *Illusion Is More Precise Than Precision: The Poetry of Marianne Moore* (1992); and Linda Leavell, *Marianne Moore and the Visual Arts: Prismatic Color* (1995). Bernard F. Engel, *Marianne Moore*, rev. ed. (1989), valuable throughout, is especially admirable in treating Moore's *Fables of La Fontaine*; Elizabeth Phillips, *Marianne Moore* (1982), also fine throughout, explicates "An Octopus" especially well. Numerous critical essays on Moore are collected in Charles Tomlinson, ed., *Marianne Moore: A Collection of Critical Essays* (1969); Harold Bloom, ed., *Marianne Moore* (1987); and Joseph Parisi, ed., *Marianne Moore: The Art of a Modernist* (1990). An obituary, beginning on the front page and with two photographs, is in the *New York Times*, 6 Feb. 1972.

ELAINE OSWALD
ROBERT L. GALE

MOORE, Mary Carr (6 Aug. 1873–9 Jan. 1957), composer, was born Mary Louise Carr in Memphis, Tennessee, the daughter of Colonel Byron Oscar Carr, a federal inspector of steam vessels, and Sarah Amelia Pratt, a writer and Unitarian minister. She spent her early years in Louisville, Kentucky, where her parents entertained such diverse figures as Henry Clay Barnabee, Robert G. Ingersoll, Colonel Henry Watterson, and Ulysses S. Grant. There she had her first piano lessons from Emma Dewhurst, a student of William Mason (1829–1908).

In 1881 her father resigned his appointment, and the family moved to St. Helena, California, where her mother's large family was already well established. Educated mainly at home by her parents and private tutors, she also went to a one-room school adjacent to the family's vineyard for one term and later attended private girls' schools in nearby Napa and Santa Rosa. She first studied voice with Walter Bartlett and harmony and counterpoint with her uncle John Haraden Pratt, a Leipzig-trained organist and teacher in San Francisco.

Financial setbacks ended her family's bucolic life in the Napa Valley and made her planned European study impossible. In 1889 the family moved to San Francisco, where Moore supported her own further study (with Henry Bickford Pasmore for voice and Pratt for composition) through teaching and a position as a church soloist. At nineteen, having already written numerous songs and short piano pieces, Moore composed her first stage work, *The Oracle,* an operetta for which she wrote both text and music and in which she sang the principal role in an 1894 production at Golden Gate Hall. Two years later fainting spells and migraine headaches ended her apprenticeship as an opera singer, and she rejoined her parents in rural Lemoore, California. There she resumed her teaching career, married physician John Claude Moore, and gave birth to the first of three children before moving to Seattle in 1901.

All this seems slim preparation for *Narcissa; or, The Cost of Empire,* a four-act grand opera set to a libretto written by her novelist mother on the 1847 massacre of missionaries Narcissa Prentiss Whitman and Marcus Whitman in the Oregon Territory (near present-day Walla Walla, Wash.). Moore was inspired to embark on this major project in 1909 by the turn-of-the-century American music movement, which sought to elevate the status of serious music composed by Americans and advocated an identifiably "American" style of art music. She herself conducted the premiere in Seattle (1912), which was favorably reviewed in *Musical America*; it was later performed in San Francisco (1925) and Los Angeles (1945). Although unrecognized as such, *Narcissa* has a legitimate claim as the most important American opera of the early twentieth century. Its lyrical arias, dramatic ensembles and choruses, and flexible English recitative reflect and synthesize the influences of church, European opera, popular theater, and domestic music-making on the music of white Americans up to that time. Among other novelties the opera casts Narcissa Prentiss Whitman as the leading character, sensitively portraying her not as the focus of an amorous triangle, but as a missionary with her own powerful commitment to church and country as well as to her husband. The opera clearly presents Native Americans' ambivalence toward the European-American settlers and their perception of the disastrous conditions created by the settlers' presence. It also depicts the imperial style of the Hudson's Bay Company and the heedless patriotism of the overland settlers bearing the Stars and Stripes.

Following a divorce Moore lived in or near San Francisco from 1915 to 1926. Her principal works from this period include a sonata for violin and piano, incidental music for a reading of Robert Browning's *Saul* (later a quintet for piano and strings), the quartet cycle *Beyond These Hills,* and the operetta *The Flaming Arrow*.

In 1926 Moore moved to Los Angeles. There she was freed from restrictive family obligations and ended her nine-year marriage to Arthur De Celles dit Duclos, but was forced to support herself by teaching long hours at the Olga Steeb Piano School and California Christian College (later Chapman College). Nonetheless, this period in Moore's life marked the most productive portion of her career. She composed an Italian opera on Mary Queen of Scots (*David Rizzio,* produced 1932); an opera on early Los Angeles (*Los Rubios,* produced 1931); an operetta on an Oriental subject (*Flutes of Jade Happiness,* produced 1934); and a French opera set in the fifteenth century (*Legende Provençale,* unproduced). In addition she wrote more chamber music, a piano concerto, and a steady stream of songs and other short works.

Throughout her career, Moore was a tireless champion of American music, organizing performances of music by local composers wherever she lived. In Los Angeles she organized a manuscript club for her own students as well as other young composers. While serving on the advisory board for the local Federal Music Project from 1935 to 1942, she encouraged performances of music by Americans through the California Society of Composers, which hosted festivals of new music in 1937 and 1938, and then through the Society of Native American Composers. As a teacher Moore excelled at nurturing talent, fostering every student's productive growth. She died in Los Angeles.

Over her sixty-year career as a composer, Moore's compositional style evolved substantially. Especially in her iconoclastic pursuit of opera, she achieved a distinctive, pioneering voice. Sex discrimination played a restrictive role in her career, however, limiting her access to suitable performance venues and perceptive critical interchange. One influential Los Angeles musician described Moore as "a society lady" who "wasn't a member of the profession" (interview, Philip Kahgan, 1983). A more insightful view came from the first musicologist at the University of Southern California: "Yes, I can see her in my mind's eye, just the way she looked—very, very attractive, very petite, very tiny, full of motion, of course, very, very vital. How in the world the woman ever had the stamina and the courage to do all those operas . . . you don't have that amount of creative energy unless you have the possibility of creating something substantial" (interview, Pauline Alderman, 1980).

• Piano vocal scores for two operas, *Narcissa; or, The Cost of Empire* (1912) and *David Rizzio* (1937; repr. 1981), and about forty songs and piano pieces were published in Moore's lifetime. Moore's manuscripts, most of the published music, a typed memoir of her early years, scrapbooks, and microfilms of other scrapbooks and datebooks are located in Special Collections, Music Library, University of California, Los Angeles. A recording of Moore's songs was issued by Cambria Records (1985). The most complete account of Moore's life and works is Catherine Parsons Smith and Cynthia S. Richardson, *Mary Carr Moore, American Composer* (1987), which includes a catalog of Moore's music and a bibliography. See also Barbara Jean Rogers, "The Works for Piano Solo and Piano with Other Instruments of Mary Carr Moore (1873–1957)" (D.M.A. diss., Univ. of Cincinnati, 1992).

CATHERINE PARSONS SMITH

MOORE, Maurice (1735–1777), colonial jurist, was born in New Hanover County, North Carolina, the son of Maurice Moore, a planter, and his second wife, Mary Porter. He was educated in New England and by profession was an attorney. A member of one of the state's most distinguished families in the revolutionary era, Moore was the brother of James Moore (1737–1777), the brother-in-law of John Ashe, and the father-in-law of Francis Nash, all of whom were revolutionary generals. Moore married Ann Grange, and they had three children. Both of Moore's sons served in the Revolution; Maurice was killed in 1776, and Alfred Moore later became an associate justice of the U.S. Supreme Court. The Moores resided in Brunswick, a port town founded by his father on the Cape Fear River.

Moore entered public life in 1757 when he was elected from the borough of Brunswick to the lower house of the North Carolina General Assembly, where he served in most of the sessions until 1774. As early as 1757 Governor Arthur Dobbs, citing Moore's "good disposition to support his Majesty's Interest," had recommended him for the Governor's Council, and finally in 1760–1761 Moore was appointed to fill a temporary vacancy. In 1763 the governor named Moore an associate judge of the provincial superior court. Except for a two-year suspension in 1766–1768 for his opposition to the Stamp Act, Moore remained on the court until its demise in 1772. Moore's suspension from the court by Governor William Tryon was a result of his 1765 pamphlet criticizing the Stamp Act, *The Justice and Policy of Taxing the American Colonies in Great Britain, Considered*. Moore's key argument against parliamentary taxation was based on a rejection of the concept of virtual representation, the principle that members of Parliament in Britain also represented the colonies. During the Regulator troubles, a back-country protest against eastern domination and government corruption, the governor appointed Moore colonel of a troop of light dragoons in the 1768 expedition to Hillsboro (now Hillsborough). After the battle of Alamance in 1771, Moore served on a special court that condemned twelve Regulators to death for treason, but following the trial he began publicly to counsel leniency. In 1772 he was appointed a judge to the special court of oyer and terminer, serving until 1774.

Although not involved in the early stages of the revolutionary unrest, Moore was elected a delegate to the Third Provincial Congress in August 1775, in which he served on the key committees to convince former Regulators and conscientious objectors that they should support the Revolution, to draw up a test oath, to state the causes of the "present Controversy," and to prepare a plan of government. As the revolutionary movement gathered momentum, Moore's ambivalence led him away from separation from Great Britain. His public statements at the time evinced the desire to return to the relationship with Britain that existed prior to the Stamp Act. In January 1776 he expressed in a letter to Governor Josiah Martin the opinion that North Carolina might yet be reconciled to the Crown. Martin, not trusting the enigmatic Moore, characterized him as capricious and "a most whimsical visionary in politicks . . . strongly tinctured with republicanism." After the Whig victory at Moores Creek Bridge in February, there was no turning aside from independence, and Moore effectively retired from public service. Although elected to the Fifth Provincial Congress, which convened in November 1776, Moore was now so estranged from the revolutionary movement that he did not attend. He died at his home in Brunswick.

• Moore's official papers are found in William L. Saunders, ed., *The Colonial Records of North Carolina*, vols. 6–10 (1890). Moore's pamphlet has been republished in W. K. Boyd, ed., *Some Eighteenth Century Tracts concerning North Carolina* (1927), and in William S. Price, Jr., *Not a Conquered People: Two Carolinians View Parliamentary Taxation* (1975). Also useful for background are Edmund S. and Helen M. Morgan, *The Stamp Act Crisis: Prologue to Revolution* (1953), and Lawrence Lee, "Days of Defiance: Resistance to the Stamp Act in the Lower Cape Fear," *North Carolina Historical Review* 43 (Apr. 1966): 196–202.

LINDLEY S. BUTLER

MOORE, Merrill (11 Sept. 1903–20 Sept. 1957), poet and psychiatrist, was born Austin Merrill Moore in Columbia, Tennessee, the son of John Trotwood Moore, a poet, novelist, and historian, and Mary Brown Daniel, a writer. From 1919 to 1929 his father served as director of libraries, archives, and history for the state of Tennessee, a position later filled by his mother. John Trotwood Moore was a leader in literary circles around the South, and his son credited him with developing his interest in literature.

Moore had a strong linguistic background. He was tutored in French at nine and later went on to teach it at Fisk University in Nashville. Grade school instruction in Latin and Spanish enabled him to read some classics in their original tongue. In college he specialized in German, learned a considerable amount of Greek, and mastered some elements of Sanskrit. He also learned the basic vocabulary and root forms of Hebrew and Yiddish. He regularly read books in French, German, and Spanish. During World War II, while stationed in New Zealand and China, he learned the basics of the Maori tongue, Pidgin English, and Mandarin.

Moore began writing poetry in high school. While attending Montgomery Bell Academy, his aptitude for sonnet writing was discovered and nurtured by his English instructor, Isaac Ball. Later, at Vanderbilt University, from which he received a B.A. in 1924, he began writing two or three sonnets a day, a habit that resulted in the composition of more than 100,000 sonnets during his lifetime. At Vanderbilt he joined a group of young writers who called themselves the "Fugitives." This group began as a reaction to the imagism and free verse advocated by writers such as Amy Lowell and Ezra Pound, a style that seemed too narrow and technical. Loosely organized by Sidney Hirsch, a playwright living in Nashville, and his brother-in-law, businessman James M. Frank, the group in 1922 began publishing a bimonthly literary magazine titled the *Fugitive*. Contributors to the magazine included writers such as Allen Tate, Donald Davidson, Robert Penn Warren, and John Crowe Ransom.

The *Fugitive* was an immediate success. It attracted attention in the United States and England for its regional conservatism and the quality of its verse. When Moore's first entry appeared in the second issue of the magazine, he was the youngest member of the group. By the time it ceased publication in 1925, Moore had published forty-six sonnets and sixteen short poems in the magazine. In 1927 he published an anthology of poems, *Fugitives: An Anthology of Verse*. With this publication, the group ceased to be a reality; personal endeavors scattered its members across the United States and Europe. After the Fugitives split up, Moore adopted the sonnet-writing techniques of John Crowe Ransom, whose sonnets made unconventional use of conventional forms.

Moore's writing did not interrupt his training in medicine and psychiatry. In 1928 he earned his M.D. from Vanderbilt Medical School and interned at St. Thomas Hospital for one year. In 1929 he moved to Boston. His first year was spent as house officer in neurology at Boston City Hospital, and in 1930 he became the resident physician in neurology. From 1931 to 1932 he served as assistant physician at Boston Psychopathic Hospital, and from 1933 to 1934 he was graduate assistant in the Psychiatric Clinic of Massachusetts General Hospital. He received psychoanalytical training from 1931 to 1933. He also taught neurology, neuropathology, and psychiatry in several schools, including Harvard Medical School. From 1936 to 1938 he directed an alcoholism survey and syphilis project for Boston City Hospital, served in the U.S. Public Health Service, and was a staff psychiatrist at Chelsea Marine Hospital. All this, plus his writing, was done in his first ten years after graduation.

In that first decade, Moore published three books of sonnets—*The Noise that Time Makes* (1929), *Six Sides to a Man* (1935), and *M: A Thousand Autobiographical Sonnets* (1938). Louis Untermeyer, anthologist and a valued friend to poets, helped Moore select and revise the sonnets for the volume *M*. Moore also befriended Robert Frost and William Carlos Williams. Williams acquainted Moore with New Directions Press, a company that published many of Moore's sonnets and opened up new literary connections for him. In 1930 Moore married Ann Leslie Nichol, a Nashville woman educated at Smith College. They had four children. In 1935 he set up a private practice in Boston, and over the years he contributed more than 150 articles to medical journals and became recognized as a psychiatric authority on alcoholism and suicide.

Moore volunteered his psychiatric services to the U.S. Army during World War II, serving in New Zealand and the South Pacific. Between 1938 and 1940 he assisted Jewish physicians fleeing Nazi Germany. In 1946, after being promoted to the rank of lieutenant colonel, he was sent to China to direct medical services around Nanking. When the war ended, he resumed his private practice and teaching duties in Boston.

Moore was also a sportsman, photographer, and conchologist. He had begun taking pictures during his Nashville years and had well over 50,000 photographs documenting his travels and important world events. He had a full record of the Bougainville campaign and more than 200 pictures of General George C. Marshall in China during World War II. Moore began collecting shells at the age of five and amassed thousands of them, which he photographed and classified. He also studied geology, geography, astronomy, chemistry, and zoology. He died in Quincy, Massachusetts.

Moore said that his psychiatry and poetry supplemented each other. He believed that science helped his poetry from becoming vague and abstract and that his poetry helped him understand people. Blending science and his imagination, he analyzed fear, love, and death. His poems are marked by sympathy, humor, common sense, and a deep understanding of human nature.

• Moore's papers are in the Library of Congress. Other materials can be found in the Joint University Libraries, Nashville. Other works by Merrill Moore include *Ego* (1938), *Some Poems for New Zealand* (1944), *Clinical Sonnets* (1949), *Case Record from a Sonnetorium* (1951), *More Clinical Sonnets* (1953), *Fugitive Sonnets* (1953), *Merrill Moore and the American Sonnet* (1954), *Verse-Diary of a Psychiatrist* (1954), and another edition of *Fugitive Sonnets* (1954). Henry W. Wells, *Poet and Psychiatrist: Merrill Moore* (1955), contains a bibliography of Moore's medical and psychological writings as well as an appraisal of 200 sonnets.

ELIZABETH A. ARCHULETA
SUSAN E. GUNTER

MOORE, Milcah Martha (1740–1827), editor and compiler of eighteenth-century women's poetry, was born Milcah Martha Hill on the Atlantic island of Madeira, the daughter of Quaker parents Richard Hill, a doctor and merchant, and Deborah Moore. Leaving six of their nine children in the care of their eldest daughter and her husband in Philadelphia, Pennsylvania, Richard and Deborah Hill settled at Funchal, the port town where Milcah Martha was born. Deborah Hill died in 1751, and in 1752 Milcah Martha returned to Philadelphia to be raised by her sister and brother-in-law, Hannah and Samuel Preston Moore. Richard Hill died in 1757. Despite these losses, throughout her life Milcah Martha enjoyed the company of an extensive kinship network in the Delaware Valley, including several sisters and their spouses and many of the most prominent eighteenth-century Quaker families.

In 1767 Milcah Martha Hill married her cousin Dr. Charles Moore, causing a breach with the Society of Friends. While many elite Quaker families married close kin (in fact, Milcah Martha's sister Hannah had married Charles Moore's brother in 1739), by the 1760s a reform movement advocating closer adherence to teachings such as that prohibiting consanguinity had made such marriages untenable. The Moores were disowned. This break was painful, and the object of much discussion among their close-knit extended family. By all accounts each continued to practice tenets of the Quaker faith, and when Charles Moore died in 1801, Milcah Martha immediately rejoined the Society of Friends. The Moores had no children of their own, but they both became involved in children's education. Trained as a physician in Scotland, Charles

Moore apprenticed the sons of family and friends in medicine. In the mid-1780s Milcah Martha Moore opened a school for girls at their home in rural Montgomery township, then part of Philadelphia County. It is not known how long she operated the school, but surviving records show she had at least thirty-eight students. Her interest in education remained keen.

Long a keeper of diaries and commonplace books of prose, poetry, and extracts of Quaker writings, in the 1780s Moore collected material for a book published as *Miscellanies, Moral and Instructive in Prose and Verse*. This volume contained primarily extracts of poetry by British men such as Alexander Pope and Edward Young. Multiple editions of the *Miscellanies* were published in Burlington, Philadelphia, London, and Dublin as early as 1787 and as late as 1829. The book's purpose, Moore noted in the introduction, was didactic. It was published to address the "want of proper Books for the Use of Schools," with this volume of extracts collected "by a Female hand, who had no intention at the Time, but her own Information & Amusement & who from Motives wholly disinterested, has lately by the request of her Friends, consented to their Publication." The book was also intended for the "improvement of young persons of both sexes." The *Miscellanies* was praised by Benjamin Franklin, who wrote a review of the book for early Philadelphia editions. Similarly, Elizabeth Graeme Fergusson wrote a poem for the *Colonial Magazine* in June 1788 called "Lines on Reading Martha Moore's Selections."

While Moore's *Miscellanies* achieved some success, her greatest contribution to American history may be her collection and preservation of eighteenth-century women's writing. Known to have written only one poem herself, about the death of her husband, Moore was an important preserver of other women's writings. During the American Revolution Moore compiled a commonplace book (c. 1770–1778) that featured the poetry of her cousin and close friend Hannah Griffitts and the largest extant collection of writings by Quaker poet, family friend, and renowned intellectual Susannah Wright. The book included some of Wright's meditative verses, as well as a collection of Griffitts's political satires, including her well-known poem "The Female Patriots" (sometimes incorrectly attributed to Moore). Also included in the commonplace book was an excerpt from Fergusson's journal of her trip to England in 1764–1765. Praised by contemporaries as a peerless depiction of English manners and social life, this journal is now known only through the extract preserved by Moore.

Moore died in Burlington, New Jersey, where she had lived with her sister Margaret Morris, author of a famous revolutionary war diary. Moore sustained her interest in education, particularly for girls, for in her will she left a bequest of $800 to educate poor girls from Montgomery and neighboring townships, the site of her former home and her school.

• The largest accumulation of Moore's letters and commonplace books is in the Edward Wanton Smith Collection at Haverford College. Family letters were published in John Jay Smith, *Letters of Dr. Richard Hill and His Children* (1854). A smattering of Moore's letters can also be found at the Historical Society of Pennsylvania. A number of research libraries, including the Library Company of Philadelphia and the American Antiquarian Society, have copies of Moore's *Miscellanies*. Moore's commonplace book, which included the poetry of Griffitts and Wright and the excerpt of Fergusson's journal, has been published as *Milcah Martha Moore's Book: A Commonplace Book from Revolutionary America*, ed. Catherine L. Blecki and Karin A. Wulf (1997). Introductory essays in this volume contain the fullest treatment to date of Moore's life and work.

KARIN A. WULF

MOORE, Raymond Cecil (20 Feb. 1892–23 Apr. 1974), geologist, was born in Roslyn, Washington, the son of Bernard Moore, a Baptist minister, and Winnifred Denney. Moore graduated from Denison University in 1913 with a degree in geology and received a Ph.D. in geology from the University of Chicago in 1916. That year he moved to the University of Kansas, where he was assistant professor in the geology department and director and state geologist at the Kansas Geological Survey. In 1917 Moore married Georgine Watters, with whom he had one child. Moore and his first wife were divorced, and in 1936 he married Lillian Boggs. The number of their children, if any, is unknown.

Moore's appetite for work and accomplishment was legendary, as was the force of his personality. He was fluent in nine languages and sketched artistic portraits of his peers. In 1923 he accompanied a U.S. Geological Survey crew through the Grand Canyon and became the first geologist since John Wesley Powell to traverse this stretch of the Colorado River. He was involved with the creation of many of geology's journals and professional societies in the 1920s and 1930s, and almost single-handedly brought the Kansas Geological Survey to the forefront of state geological surveys in the United States. By the end of his career, he was author or coauthor of nearly 600 scientific papers and books. One of his former students remembered him as a man who "possessed a large ego or, perhaps more appropriately, was comfortable in his knowledge of his own worth."

Moore's achievements can be grouped into four primary areas: administration, studies in invertebrate paleontology, research into cycles of sedimentation, and participation in scientific societies. Moore was the Kansas survey's director from 1916 until 1954, a period during which he also served three times as chair of the university's geology department. After 1954 he was the survey's "principal geologist" and in 1958 was named the university's first Solon E. Summerfield Distinguished Professor. During his time as director of the Kansas survey, the organization produced the first detailed stratigraphic columns of the state's rocks and the first large-format geologic map of the state. He began cooperative water research with the U.S. Geological Survey and opened a branch office of the survey in Wichita. He once wrote that the survey should be "first of all, a scientific research bureau," and he was largely responsible for molding an organization in which research was given high priority. Before Moore's tenure in Kansas, the survey was largely involved with reconnaissance geology and statistical reports on mineral production. Under Moore, the organization achieved substantial scientific prestige, based largely on his work and that of colleagues he brought to Kansas, such as Kenneth K. Landes, Norman Newell, and John C. Frye.

Moore's personal field of research was invertebrate paleontology. He had an almost childlike desire to collect and describe every type of invertebrate fossil in the midcontinent, but he concentrated on corals and crinoids, naming many new species. His long article, "Environment of Pennsylvanian Life in North America" (American Association of Petroleum Geologists, *Bulletin* 13 [1929]: 459–87), was one of a number of papers that established his scientific presence. In 1948 he began the *Treatise on Invertebrate Paleontology* (vol. 1, 1953), the standard reference in the field, which continues to be revised and published with the proceeds from Moore's will. In 1952 he was coauthor of *Invertebrate Fossils*, a classic text.

Moore's name is also closely associated with the concept of cycles of sedimentation. Cyclic sedimentation was recognized in the Midwest before Moore's arrival in Kansas, but he developed models of the cycles in which rocks were deposited. These models, called cyclothems, described alternating layers of limestones and shales, mostly the result of sea-level fluctuation at the time the rocks were deposited. Moore was not greatly interested in the mechanisms that caused worldwide sea-level change, or eustasy. He was far more interested in the rocks themselves, the conditions under which they were deposited, and the fossils they held. The cyclothem model, and several of Moore's ideas, continue to dominate discussion of midcontinent geology to this day.

Moore was influential throughout the science of geology. He wrote the texts *Historical Geology* (1933) and *Introduction to Historical Geology* (1949). He was president of the Paleontological Society in 1947, the Geological Society of America in 1957–1958, and the American Geological Institute in 1960. He edited the *Bulletin of the American Association of Petroleum Geologists*, the *Journal of Paleontology*, and several other major geological journals.

Moore has retained a reputation for energy and self-discipline. He is said to have been able to lose himself in editing a manuscript while at a university basketball game. But he is also remembered for self-promotion and a sometimes abrasive personality. For example, Moore supposedly named a rock formation the Aarde Shale because he wanted to be responsible for the first name in the U.S. Geological Survey's alphabetical lexicon of names for rock units. Moore was proud that he had become so well known that he was mentioned as "Ol' Professor Ray Moore" in the nationally syndicated comic strip "Pogo" in 1954. He died in Lawrence, Kansas.

The scientific institutions and publications that Moore created had a sustained impact on the geologic study of the midcontinent, on thought about cyclic sedimentation, and the field of invertebrate paleontology. He was, in short, the premier invertebrate paleontologist of the first half of the twentieth century, and his presence reverberates still.

• Moore's papers are collected at the University of Kansas Archives, Spencer Research Library, University of Kansas. In addition to Moore's publications listed above, his other major works include, with W. P. Haynes, "Oil and Gas Resources of Kansas," Kansas Geological Survey, *Bulletin* 3 (1917); and "Paleoecological Aspects of Kansas Pennsylvanian Permian Cyclothems," in *Symposium on Cyclic Sedimentation*, Kansas Geological Survey, *Bulletin* 1, no. 169 (1964): 287–380. The only substantial discussion of Moore's life is Christopher G. Maples and Rex Buchanan, "Raymond Cecil Moore (1892–1974): Memorial and Bibliography" (in celebration of the one-hundredth anniversary of the Kansas Geological Survey), *Journal of Paleontology*, memoir 25 (Nov. 1989), which includes a chronological bibliography of Moore's published works. See also Curt Teichert and Ellis L. Yochelson, eds., *Essays in Paleontology and Stratigraphy: R. C. Moore Commemorative Volume* (1967), and Buchanan and Maples, "R. C. Moore and Concepts of Sea-Level Change in the Mid-Continent," in *Eustasy: The Historical Ups and Downs of a Major Geological Concept*, ed. Robert H. Dott, Jr. (1992), pp. 73–81.

REX C. BUCHANAN

MOORE, Richard Bishop (6 May 1871–20 Jan. 1931), chemist, was born in Cincinnati, Ohio, the son of William Thomas Moore, a minister of the Disciples of Christ, and Mary (maiden name unknown). In 1878 Moore's parents moved to England, where Richard received the greater part of his education. He studied at University College, London, under William Ramsay, the discoverer of several inert gases, from 1886 to 1890. He became a chemistry instructor in a high school and then at Birkbeck Institute, London, until 1893. After two years of study in the British Museum, Moore returned to the United States and earned a bachelor's degree in a year from the University of Chicago (1896). He remained at Chicago as an assistant for another year and from 1897 to 1905 was a chemistry instructor at the University of Missouri, where he conducted his first experiments on radioactivity. In 1902 he married Callie Pemberton of Auxvasse, Missouri.

The science of radioactivity was new and exciting in the century's first decade. Early progress had been made in the study of the physical properties of the radiations; now it was the chemists' turn to investigate the radioelements themselves. American leaders in this field, Bertram B. Boltwood and Herbert N. McCoy, sought to establish reproducible standards and determine the relative activities of the components of the decay series. In this work they had the valued support of scientists of the second rank, such as Moore. With his colleague at Missouri, Herman Schlundt, Moore in 1905 measured the radioactivity of several deep wells near their school. Later he surveyed the thermal waters of Yellowstone National Park for their radioactive properties. Ground water, air, soil, and even the mist at Niagara Falls were found to be active in this period, so this work fit in well with proof of the widespread occurrence of radioactivity. Moore and Schlundt also devised techniques for separating uranium X from its parent uranium and made the exciting claim that the former emits an alpha particle. This theory was important in helping to account for the twelve mass units between uranium and radium. Their conclusion was wrong (the alpha came from an unsuspected radioelement, uranium II), but their work was a valuable step in ferreting out the components of this decay series.

Moore next served as chemistry professor at Butler College, in Indianapolis, Indiana, until 1911, after which he spent a dozen years in the U.S. Bureau of Soils and the Bureau of Mines. As chief of the Bureau of Mines' laboratory in Denver, Moore in 1912 made the first detailed survey of the carnotite deposits in Colorado and Utah. He revealed that this uranium mineral was the largest source of radium in the world. Concentrated ore was shipped abroad for purification, and the tiny amount of radium extracted was sold in the United States for medical use at prices over $100,000 a gram. Charging that such prices were excessive, Moore led successful efforts to devise efficient separations techniques and build a domestic radium industry. Promoted to chief chemist of the bureau in 1919, Moore was put in charge of work with helium. Since the alpha particle is actually a helium nucleus, and much helium originates from radioactive decay, Moore's interest probably derived from his student days with Ramsay and a leave he spent in Ramsay's laboratory from 1907 to 1908, during which he worked on inert gases. He was an early advocate of helium's use in balloons and airships, and he encouraged the U.S. government to protect this resource.

From 1923 to 1926 Moore was employed by the Dorr Company, an engineering firm in New York. His last appointment was as professor of chemistry and dean of the school of science at Purdue University. In 1924 he married Georgie Elizabeth Dowell of Dallas Texas. They adopted five-year-old Carol in 1930. He died in New York City.

• An obituary is in *Industrial and Engineering Chemistry, News Edition*, 10 Feb. 1931, p. 40. Information may also be found in Lawrence Badash, *Radioactivity in America: Growth and Decay of a Science* (1979).

LAWRENCE BADASH

MOORE, Richard Channing (21 Aug. 1762–12 Nov. 1841), Episcopal bishop, was born in New York City, the son of Thomas Moore, a merchant, and Elizabeth Channing. He was baptized and raised in the Episcopal church at Trinity Parish in New York City. In 1784 Moore married Christian Jones; they had three children. After studying and practicing medicine for a short time, he became interested in the ministry; he became a communicant of the Episcopal church and decided to seek ordination.

Moore began a course of theological study under Bishop Samuel Provoost of New York and was ordained a deacon on 15 July 1787 as Provoost's first ordinand. Provoost ordained Moore as a priest on 19 September 1787, and Moore began his ministry as rector of Grace Church in Rye, New York. In 1789 he left Rye to become the rector of St. Andrew's Church on Staten Island. While at St. Andrew's, Moore gained a reputation as an excellent preacher. Although he wrote most of his sermons, he was also able to preach extemporaneously with great effect. He was accused of "enthusiastic and methodistical preaching," and some compared him to the revivalist George Whitefield. This illustrates his early commitment to evangelical practices and doctrines. After the death of his wife in 1796, Moore married Sarah Mersereau in 1797; they had six children.

In 1808 Moore served as a deputy to the General Convention of the Episcopal Church, where he was the chair of the committee of the House of Deputies on hymnody. At the time the *Book of Common Prayer* had only twenty-seven hymns. Under his leadership the committee endorsed the addition of thirty more.

In the spring of 1809 Moore left St. Andrew's to return to New York City as the rector of St. Stephen's Church. The new parish had but twenty communicants and thirty families. When he left in 1814 it had more than 400 communicants, and the building was crowded to capacity at Sunday worship services.

Conditions were far different in Virginia. The Committee on the State of the Church of the House of Bishops reported at the General Convention of 1811 "that the Church in Virginia is, from various causes, so depressed, that there is danger of her total ruin, unless great exertions, favored by the blessing of Providence, are employed to raise her" (*Journal of General Convention, 1811*, pp. 380–81). On 4 May 1814 Moore was elected the second bishop of Virginia. He was consecrated on 18 May 1814. For the next twenty-seven years he provided the "great exertions" necessary to revive the church.

Moore took up residence in Richmond and assumed the rectorship of Monumental Church. It became the center of his activities and another parish reinvigorated by his efforts. In 1819 he toured the Diocese of Virginia and also crossed over into North Carolina, which had no Episcopal bishop. Moore bore the weight of episcopal duties in North Carolina in addition to those in Virginia until 1823, when the Diocese of North Carolina elected its first bishop.

Moore's plan to revive the church in Virginia called for strict adherence to the doctrines and services in the *Book of Common Prayer*. In an address to the Virginia Convention in 1826, he spoke of the liturgy as "combining with the soundest sense the purest and most sublimated devotion." Believing that the Anglican liturgy had "commanded the respect and admiration of some of the greatest and most enlightened men who have lived since the reformation," he charged his clergy "to attend to the rubrics, without the least deviation" (Henshaw, p. 184).

One of Moore's more effective means of reviving the church in Virginia was to turn the diocesan conventions into religious meetings. The convention had been mainly a business session, but Moore subordinated the business to religious services that featured preaching, Bible study, and prayer meetings. The conventions usually lasted a week, and people came from throughout the state to attend them. They functioned as revival meetings.

Moore's interest in missions led him to participate in interdenominational agencies. He served for years as the president of the Virginia Bible Society. He was willing to work with others in missionary enterprise but only so long as the character of the Episcopal church was not compromised. At the same time he opposed union church buildings—that is, buildings constructed and used by two or more denominations. He thought that when opposite doctrines were proclaimed from the same pulpit, "the minds of the young" were confused.

Moore believed that the historic episcopate (the office of bishop) was divinely instituted and necessary for the perfection of the church. The episcopate ensured that the Episcopal church had an apostolic ministry. At the same time he was reluctant to dismiss ministries in other churches as invalid. While he stressed the apostolicity of the Episcopal ministry, he did not "unchurch" other clergy.

While Moore was a leading evangelical in the Episcopal church, he was not a Low Churchman. He was in the evangelical tradition of Bishop Alexander Viets Griswold of the Eastern Diocese but differed with Bishop John Henry Hobart of the High Church tradition more in practice and emphasis than in doctrine. Moore was an evangelical sympathetic to the High Church view of the church as a divine institution. He stressed preaching but did not deny the grace of the sacraments.

Although Moore died before the Oxford movement deeply influenced the Episcopal church in the United States, he expressed some opposition to it. He was one of the earliest leaders of the American church to warn against what he saw as its dangerous tendencies, especially its criticism of the Atonement as the center of Christian theology.

The leading impulse of Moore's life was his overwhelming desire to win people to the discipleship of Jesus Christ. This he did by preaching the hopeless condition of humanity, the atoning death of Christ, and the doctrine of justification by grace through faith. He saw preaching as the primary means of winning persons to Christ, and the defining feature of his own ministry was his effective preaching. Moore revived the Episcopal church in Virginia. He rebuilt church buildings, reorganized parishes, established new churches, and increased the number of communicants. After a ministry of fifty-four years, Moore died in Lynchburg, Virginia.

• Moore's papers are in the archives of the Bishop Payne Library at the Protestant Episcopal Theological Seminary in Alexandria, Va. The two major studies are John Prentiss Kewley Henshaw, *Memoir of the Life of the Rt. Rev. Richard Channing Moore, D.D., Bishop of the Protestant Episcopal Church in the Diocese of Virginia* (1843), and John Nicholas Norton, *The Life of the Right Reverend Richard Channing Moore, D.D., Bishop of Virginia* (1857). The most insightful study is Lawrence L. Brown, "Richard Channing Moore and the Revival of the Southern Church," *Historical Magazine of the Protestant Episcopal Church* 35 (1966): 3–64. See also Susan H. Godson, "Bishop Richard Channing Moore and the Renewal of the Antebellum Episcopal Church of Virginia," *Virginia Cavalcade* 32 (Spring 1983): 184–91. An obituary is in the *Richmond Enquirer*, 16 Nov. 1841.

DONALD S. ARMENTROUT

MOORE, Robert Lee (14 Nov. 1882–4 Oct. 1974), mathematician, was born in Dallas, Texas, the son of Charles Jonathan Moore, owner of a hardware and feed store, and Louisa Ann Moore (*née* Moore). While in high school in Dallas, Moore taught himself a substantial amount of calculus from the required textbook at the University of Texas at Austin before entering that institution at the age of sixteen. In 1901 he obtained both a B.S. and an M.A. With the encouragement of mathematics professor George Bruce Halsted, Moore proved that one of the axioms in David Hilbert's *Foundations of Geometry* was not independent of the other axioms. The work, though published under Halsted's name, gave Moore full credit and brought Moore to the attention of Eliakim Hastings Moore (unrelated to Robert), the leading mathematician at the University of Chicago. After spending a year as a teaching fellow at the University of Texas and a further year teaching at a high school in Marshall, Texas, a fellowship became available for R. L. Moore for graduate study at the University of Chicago.

In the active center of mathematics at Chicago, Moore worked especially with E. H. Moore and Oswald Veblen in geometry. He obtained his doctorate in 1905 with a dissertation entitled "Sets of Metrical Hypotheses for Geometry." He then taught at the University of Tennessee for one year, followed by appointments at Princeton University (1906–1908), Northwestern University (1908–1911), and the University of Pennsylvania (1911–1920). In 1910 he married Margaret MacLelland Key of Brenham, Texas; they had no children. He welcomed his return in 1920 to the University of Texas as an associate professor of mathematics. Three years later he was promoted to professor.

From 1907 to 1932 Moore published fifty papers that helped to open up a new field of mathematics, analysis situs, which later became known as point-set topology. He supervised three doctoral students at Pennsylvania and eight at Texas during this period. From 1914 to 1927 he was associate editor of the *Transactions of the American Mathematical Society*. He was elected to the National Academy of Sciences in 1931 and appointed the fifth visiting lecturer of the American Mathematical Society—the first American so honored—for 1931–1932. He was elected president of the AMS for 1937–1938. During the next thirty-seven years at the University of Texas, Moore published seventeen additional papers and supervised thirty-nine doctoral students.

By 1950 the success of Moore's distinctive method of teaching became well known in the mathematical community as the "Moore method." Moore had each student create their own proofs and theorems within the framework of definitions and conjectures laid out by Moore. This work was to be done without reference to any textbooks or other publications and without consulting with other students. Results were presented to the class at the blackboard while Moore participated more as a fellow researcher than as a final authority. A former student, Lucille S. Whyburn, said of a Moore course: "A student seeking a large body of information or expecting to be a passive member of a student group had best avoid the course." In a film about his teaching, *Challenge in the Classroom*, made in 1965 by the Mathematical Association of America, Moore gave as one of his guiding principles: "That teacher teaches best who teaches least." Moore regularly taught undergraduate courses in the belief that it was important to reach potential students early in order for them to benefit from his method. For Moore, who even during the summer months did not take time from teaching to do research, teaching mathematics and creating mathematics were inseparable. Many of his students carried on as researchers in various branches of topology and as teachers using some variant of his methods. These included John R. Kline, R. L. Wilder, G. T. Whyburn, F. Burton Jones, R. D. Anderson, R. H. Bing, and Mary E. Estill Rudin.

Moore's invited colloquium lectures for the AMS in 1929 were published in an extended form as volume thirteen in the AMS Colloquium Publications series in 1932. This work, *Foundations of Point Set Theory*, represented the culmination of his researches to date and provide the foundation for future developments made largely by his students and their own protégés. Many of the principal results produced by this growing school were cited by Moore in his second and last edition of *Foundations* (1962). The geometrical space explored by this school is built on the primitive terms "point" and "region," whose properties are determined by axioms that are introduced one by one. The initial space is thus a very general one that has, for example, no means of measuring distance in it but that nevertheless has an interesting structure to be explored. The additional axioms in *Foundations* allow a Euclidean space to be determined. One of the mathematical tasks is to clarify precisely the most general space in which individual properties hold. This approach has revealed many properties hitherto thought to be exclusively Euclidean that in fact hold in more general spaces. Moore's student R. L. Wilder described *Foundations* as "a very general compendium of point set results which has served, among other functions, as a reference point for many subsequent investigations."

Although Moore was allowed to continue teaching well beyond the usual mandatory retirement age of seventy-five, some university administrators at Texas apparently felt that Moore's very success led to his having an unduly high influence within the mathematics department, which might, for example, have discouraged other outstanding mathematicians from joining the faculty. Moore was retired, over the protests of a number of his students, in 1969. The university honored him by naming its new physics, mathematics, and astronomy building after him in 1973. Moore died in Austin.

• Moore's papers, library, and memorabilia from his home are in the Archives of American Mathematics at the University of Texas at Austin. The most detailed assessment of Moore's work is R. L. Wilder, "The Mathematical Work of R. L. Moore: Its Background, Nature and Influence," *Archive for History of Exact Sciences* 26 (1982): 73–97, which also includes a bibliography of his publications. D. Reginald Traylor et al., *Creative Teaching: Heritage of R. L. Moore* (1972), documents the Moore method and lists successive generations of Moore's students to 1972, along with their publications. See also Lucille S. Whyburn, "Student Oriented Teaching—The Moore Method," *American Mathematical Monthly* 77 (1970): 351–59, based on interviews with a number of Moore's students as well as personal experience; and F. Burton Jones, "The Moore Method," *American Mathematical Monthly* 84 (1977): 273–78.

ALBERT C. LEWIS

MOORE, Stanford (4 Sept. 1913–23 Aug. 1982), biochemist, was born in Chicago, Illinois, the son of John Howard Moore, a law student, and Ruth Fowler. At age six he moved with his family to Gainesville, Florida, after his father accepted a teaching position at the University of Florida Law School. Subsequent career moves by his father took the family to Macon, Georgia, and in 1924 to Nashville, Tennessee, where Stanford completed his secondary education. In 1931 he matriculated at Vanderbilt University and for two years studied chemistry and aeronautical engineering before opting to major in chemistry. After receiving his B.A. in 1935, he attended the University of Wisconsin on a fellowship from that school's Alumni Research Foundation and received his Ph.D. in organic chemistry in 1939.

Moore's dissertation, which identified seven monosaccharides such as glucose as derivatives of the double-ring chemical compound known as benzimidazole, brought him to the attention of the German chemist Max Bergmann. In 1939 Bergmann was studying the structural chemistry of proteins at the Rockefeller Institute of Medical Research (now Rockefeller University) in New York City. He convinced Moore to turn down a four-year fellowship at Harvard Medical School and come to the institute as his research assistant. On his first assignment, Moore and William H. Stein, another research assistant, set out to precipitate selectively the amino acids present in solutions of the proteins albumin and fibroin and estimate their proportions by weighing the precipitants. By 1942, when their work was postponed by the entry of the United States into World War II, they had successfully used aromatic sulfonic acids as reagents to separate trace amounts of serine, alanine, phenylalanine, and leucine.

After serving for two years as a technical aide with the Office of Scientific Research and Development's National Defense Research Committee, Moore in 1944 joined the army's Chemical Warfare Service. The latter position involved investigating the physiological effects of chemical warfare agents, particularly the reaction of mustard gas with methionine, the principal sulfur-containing amino acid in humans, and developing countermeasures against the potential use of chemical warfare by the Japanese.

In 1945 Moore returned to the institute and resumed his collaboration with Stein. In an effort to separate larger quantities of amino acids from protein solutions, they turned to partition chromatography—an innovative filtering technique developed during the war by the English researchers Archer Martin and Richard Synge—and adapted it to their own purposes. In simple terms, Moore and Stein packed potato starch into a very narrow tube or column, poured a solution of protein and reagent into one end, and measured and identified what dripped out the other end—which in each case was a different amino acid fraction, depending on the solution's reagent. By 1948 they had successfully fractionated reproducible quantities of phenylalanine and leucine, as well as isoleucine, methionine, tyrosine, and valine.

Although the starch-column method provided greater yields than other filtering techniques, it took up to two weeks to complete a single run of a protein solution and required that the amino acid fractions be measured manually, a tedious and imprecise task. In 1949, the same year that Moore was promoted to associate member at the institute, he and Stein developed an automatic fraction collector that used a photoelectric cell to count the number of drops of each fraction as it dripped from the tube. Because it saved time and improved accuracy, the collector was quickly adopted by a number of biochemical researchers for use in a variety of applications. In 1951, the year before Moore was promoted to professor, he and Stein began using the techniques of ion-exchange chromatography, whereby the positively or negatively charged filtering medium exchanges ions with the part of the solution that is to be filtered out. By replacing potato starch with sulfonated polystyrene resins, they greatly reduced the amount of time needed to run a protein solution while also making it possible to analyze very small amounts of biological fluids such as urine, plasma, and protein-free tissue extracts.

In 1953 Moore and Stein set out to identify the amino acid composition of ribonuclease, the enzyme that catalyzes the hydrolysis of ribonucleic acid and therefore plays an important role in cellular protein synthesis. By applying the same methods of ion-exchange chromatography that they had employed earlier and by developing a more sophisticated version of the fraction collector, they confirmed in 1963 the sequence of amino acids in ribonuclease and described the relationship between its structure and its activity. This achievement, the first complete amino-acid sequence description of an enzyme, gained for them a share of the 1972 Nobel Prize for chemistry.

Moore served as president of the American Society of Biological Chemists from 1966 to 1967 and the Federation of the American Societies for Experimental Biology from 1970 to 1971. He also served as chairman of the panel on proteins for the National Research Council's committee on growth from 1947 to 1949; as secretary of the commission on proteins of the International Union of Pure and Applied Chemistry from 1953 to 1957; and as chairman of the organizing committee for the Sixth International Congress of Biochemistry from 1961 to 1964 and of the National Academy of Sciences' Section of Biochemistry from 1969 to 1972. He was also a member of the editorial board of the *Journal of Biological Chemistry* from 1950 to 1960. He received the American Chemical Society's Award in Chromatography and Electrophoresis in 1964, its Theodore William Richards Medal in 1972, and the Linderstrøm-Lang Medal of Copenhagen in 1972. In 1960 he was elected to membership in the National Academy of Sciences and the American Academy of Arts and Sciences. Except for the 1950–1951 academic year, which he spent at the Universities of Brussels, Belgium, and Cambridge, England, Moore spent his entire career at Rockefeller. A confirmed bachelor, he suffered from a degenerative nerve and muscle disease for several years before taking his own life in New York City.

Moore made two important contributions to the development of biochemistry. His work with chromatography placed powerful new techniques and equipment in the hands of researchers. His work with amino acids contributed to a better understanding of the molecular structure and activity of proteins and enzymes.

• A biography of Moore, including a bibliography, is Emil L. Smith and C. H. W. Hirs, National Academy of Sciences, *Biographical Memoirs* 56 (1987): 355–85. Obituaries are in the *New York Times*, 24 Aug. 1982, and *Newsweek*, 6 Sept. 1982.

CHARLES W. CAREY, JR.

MOORE, Thomas Overton (10 Apr. 1804–25 June 1876), governor of Louisiana, was born in Sampson County, North Carolina, the son of John Moore, a planter, and Jean Overton. Nothing is known of his educational background; however, it can be assumed it was average to above average for the time. As a young man, he moved from North Carolina to the parish of Rapides, near Alexandria, Louisiana, in 1829 to manage his uncle's plantation. Under the tutelage of his maternal uncle, General Walter H. Overton, a hero of the battle of New Orleans and a local political leader of some renown, Moore learned not only the fine points of running a plantation but also was introduced to the intricacies of Louisiana politics. After managing his uncle's plantation for almost a year, he purchased a plantation of his own. His marriage in 1830 to Bethiah Jane Leonard substantially increased his holdings and his political standing in the parish. (This marriage produced four sons and one daughter. Only the daughter lived to adulthood.) His wife was the owner of the "Emmafield" plantation, which, combined with his own plantation "Mooreland," made Moore one of the largest landowners in the parish. By 1860 the census records show he owned 226 slaves to work his plantations.

As a leading citizen of the parish, Moore embarked on his political career in 1842, serving as a member of the parish police jury. He won election to the state legislature in 1848 and then the state senate in 1851. He left public service after the legislative session in 1852 to manage his properties but was reelected in 1856 to the state senate. While Moore was serving in the state senate, his leadership skills and positions on public affairs attracted the notice of the leadership of the John Slidell wing of the Democratic party, and in 1859 the party nominated him as its standard bearer for the governor's chair. In what was reported in the local newspapers as a very close and spirited (a La. euphemism for mudslinging, no holds barred) election against Thomas J. Wells, also of Rapides Parish, who ran as an independent, he managed to win a narrow victory.

Inaugurated in January 1860, Moore was six months into his term when the national Democratic convention deadlocked over the selection of a candidate for president. Later that year, when the party split, Moore, a resourceful and practical politician who knew where the majority of the Louisiana politicians and white citizens stood, supported the Breckenridge-Lane ticket. During the actual presidential campaign, however, Moore did not take a prominent position, preferring to let others take the lead. He directed the campaign from backstage and used the powers of the governor to the advantage of the Breckenridge-Lane ticket, which carried Louisiana.

As a large plantation owner, slave owner, and dedicated states' rights supporter, Moore was convinced that the election of the Lincoln-Hamlin ticket was a clear signal that the Union had been dissolved by the northern and western states. Personally convinced that the Republicans intended to run roughshod over the doctrine of states' rights, he also could not see how slavery could continue to exist under an Abraham Lincoln presidency. Moore called a special session of the general assembly to meet on 10 December 1860. In his address to the assembly he argued, "I do not think it comports with the honor and self-respect of Louisiana, as a slave-holding state, to live under the government of the Black Republican President." He also requested that the legislature refer the matter to the people and call a convention to determine the course of action the state should take. He further requested that a Board of Military Affairs be created and $500,000 be expended to secure weapons and military accouterments. Moore, however, did not wait until the convention before seizing federal property within the state. Acting as commander in chief of the Louisiana militia, he ordered state troops to seize the forts on the lower Mississippi and the Federal arsenal at Baton Rouge on 11 January 1861. An astute politician, he fully recognized that his action would gain approval from the majority of citizens, and he also realized this would push the convention toward the goal of secession that he desired.

Indeed, when the convention was called by the legislature, the majority of the delegates supported immediate withdrawal from the Union. On 26 January 1861 Louisiana seceded. Moore next guided the state into the southern Confederacy, into which Louisiana was admitted on 21 March 1861.

Moore was determined that Louisiana would have a leading role in this new confederation. When the call for volunteers came from Jefferson Davis, Louisiana overfilled its quota for the ranks of units in what would become the Army of Northern Virginia. Women's units were organized to help the men at the front by taking care of families of the less fortunate.

The high point of Moore's governorship was 1861, for from January 1862 through the remainder of his stewardship of Louisiana he encountered one calamity after another. To face the immediate threat of Union troops invading Tennessee, the Confederate government stripped Louisiana of troops. Moore's worries that the state was defenseless were well justified when on 24 April 1862 the Union fleet under Flag Officer David G. Farragut ran past the forts and steamed up the river to New Orleans. On 1 May 1862 Federal troops under Major General Benjamin Butler occupied New Orleans. Soon thereafter Union troops occupied Baton Rouge, the state capital. Moore was forced to move the Confederate state government to Opelousas and later Shreveport. Until the end of his term he directed the efforts of the Confederate state government to include construction of meat-packing plants and weapons procurement. His government continually battled both the Union forces and, in many cases, the Confederate bureaucracy and enterprising military officers, who appropriated Louisiana-bound weapons and equipment. He recommended that troops be sent to Louisiana to keep the Mississippi crossing open and that the Red River be fortified to protect the army's food sources. Only after the state was literally bled dry did the Confederacy assign General Richard Taylor to the state, although he did not bring additional men or equipment. Moore became more and more discouraged as his recommendations and suggestions were ignored, but he never publicly criticized the Confederate government, as did some other southern governors.

The 1845 Louisiana Constitution prohibited a governor from succeeding himself, so Moore could not run in the 1863 election. Henry W. Allen won the governorship, and Moore retired to his plantation upon completion of his term in January 1864. Even then his suffering did not end, for during Nathaniel P. Banks's Red River campaign of 1864, Moore's property was seized, and the sugar mill and plantations were destroyed. He moved with a large number of slaves to Houston County, Texas, to keep from being captured by Union forces. Fearing for his life at the end of the war because the Louisiana Radical Republican government had issued a warrant for his arrest, he fled to Mexico and then to Havana. Only after receiving a presidential pardon from Andrew Johnson in 1867 did he return to his ruined plantations to resume his life. In 1868 he was elected to the chairmanship of the Rapides Parish Democratic party. His political involvement ended in 1874, when he was stricken with severe rheumatism, from which he never recovered. He died on the Emmafield plantation.

• Moore's papers were published by J. P. Whittington, ed., "The Papers of Thomas O. Moore," *Louisiana Historical Quarterly* 13 (1930): 10–31. His career is discussed in Van D. Odom, "The Political Career of Thomas Overton Moore, Secession Governor of Louisiana," *Louisiana Historical Quarterly* 26 (1943): 975–1054; Mary Lilla McClure, "The Elections of 1860 in Louisiana," *Louisiana Historical Quarterly* 9 (1926): 601–702; J. K. Greer, "Louisiana Politics, 1845–1861," *Louisiana Historical Quarterly* 12 (1929): 381–402, 555–610, and 13 (1930): 67–116, 257–303, 444–83, 617–54; and Edwin C. Bearss, "The Seizure of the Forts and Public Property in Louisiana," *Louisiana History* 2 (1961): 401–9.

ROY R. STEPHENSON

MOORE, Thomas Patrick (1796?–21 July 1853), congressman and diplomat, was born in Charlotte County, Virginia, but spent his childhood and most of his adult life near Harrodsburg, Kentucky. The names and occupations of his parents are unknown. As a youth he received only common schooling. After brief military service in the War of 1812, Moore attended Transylvania University in Lexington and later read law under John Green. When the panic of 1819 stymied Kentucky's economic boom, Mercer County sent Moore to the state house of representatives, where he served from 1819 through 1820 and sat on the committees on grievances and courts of justice. He became associated with the "Relief" faction that in the early 1820s pushed through a host of radical measures intended to relieve the financial crisis, including stay laws against immediate foreclosures, abolition of imprisonment for debt, and creation of the Bank of the Commonwealth with broad power to issue unbacked paper currency. Most of the Relief leaders—men like William T. Barry, Amos Kendall, Joseph Desha, and Moore himself—organized the early Jackson movement in Kentucky.

First elected to the U.S. House of Representatives in 1822, Moore served until 1829, defending the interests of the small slaveholding farmers who grew hemp, tobacco, and flax in the Harrodsburg area. More importantly for his political future, he ingratiated himself with the growing Jacksonian clique in Washington. He usually avoided speaking from the floor but, by 1828, participated actively as one of the two westerners on the nine-member House Committee on Manufactures. As a member of Congress he regularly supported protective tariffs, beginning with Henry Clay's bill in 1824, but complained that his section was consistently denied tariff consideration equal to that given to nascent manufacturers in the Northeast. As he saw it, western farmers were being asked to purchase eastern manufactures without a reciprocal guarantee of market in the East for the fibers and foodstuffs they themselves produced. Along with fellow Kentuckian Charles A. Wickliffe, Moore spearheaded a vain effort in 1827 to broaden tariff protection of industry to include producers of hemp and spirits distilled from grain. With western goods still facing ruinous competition from abroad in 1828, Moore, in one of his few House speeches, declared "any system which transfers wealth from one section to another" to be "unjust and tyrannical." Moore's party loyalty and his committee position make it likely that he had some involvement in the scheme behind the 1828 "Tariff of Abominations." In a plan to embarrass President John Quincy Adams without losing support in the protariff states, Jacksonians framed a bill with exorbitant rates, expecting it to fail because of presumed tariff hostility in New England. With surprising support from New Englanders, the bill passed, including the protection for Kentucky hemp and flax that Moore personally wanted. Sectional interest also motivated his regular support of legislation in the 1820s to extend and repair the Cumberland Road.

More important historically than his positions on public issues was Moore's role in the crusade to make Andrew Jackson president and put Jackson's followers in positions of power by the end of the decade. He was one of a new breed of rough-and-tumble politicians and writers who plotted to keep the hero of New Orleans in the political limelight and make his appeal national. Moore's championing of Jackson in Kentucky came early. It began no later than 1824, when he stood in the pro-Jackson minority of the Kentucky House delegation that voted 8–4 for Adams and helped secure the New Englander's presidential victory in an election that had been thrown into the U.S. House of Representatives. Believing Clay had corruptly furthered Adams's cause, Jackson functionaries started planning their leader's revenge. Key in their 1828 strategy was swinging Kentucky, Clay's own backyard, into the Jackson column. Moore led the charge, along with Amos Kendall and George M. Bibb, mounting a blizzard of pro-Jackson propaganda and organizing an endless series of dinners and meetings to unify lingering elements of both Kentucky factions—pro- and anti-Relief—behind the rising Tennessean.

True to his image as spoilsman, Jackson divided the booty of office among those most loyal to him. Moore's share was generous, a prestigious appointment in March 1829 as minister to Gran Colombia, replacing William Henry Harrison. The elevating of one so inexperienced in foreign affairs drew scorn from former president Adams and the previous secretary of state, Clay. Moore's reputation for shady behavior was catching up with him too, not only among partisan enemies but also within the Jackson camp. John Pope, another Kentuckian, warned the new president against his appointment: "Moore is an efficient man of sense and management and although he has not much moral weight and has not done for you one tenth part of what is pretended, yet he has fought the battle with zeal and boldness. He regards neither truth nor principle to carry his point."

Moore's performance as a diplomat lent credibility to doubts about his character. Instructed to support Simón Bolívar and encourage the spread of republicanism, the new minister stood helplessly while the Liberator died of tuberculosis in 1830 and the dream of Latin American union disappeared in a cesspool of Colombian anarchy, corruption, and greed. Moore's mission as promoter of revolutionary ideals was quickly reduced to protesting the 1831 restoration of heavy import duties on American flour. Discouraged by political events, he wasted no time finding a way to turn his position for personal profit. That came in return for arranging private commercial advantages for the well-connected Washington merchant Elisha Riggs. Though not technically illegal by the vague standards of the day, his dealings were not consonant with the traditional role of an American foreign minister.

Having achieved little but the filling of his own pockets (and those of Riggs), Moore came home in June 1833 and ran for Congress against Robert P. Letcher. He claimed victory, but charges of fraud and miscounted votes inspired Congress to call a second election, which Moore lost. This bad news afforded Moore the unexpected luxury of retiring to private life and financial comfort in Harrodsburg, until the Mexican War revived his martial enthusiasm in March 1847. He used political influence to land a lieutenant colonelship in the Third Regiment of U.S. Infantry, switched to the Third Regiment of U.S. Dragoons, and served in Mexico until the war's end in 1848.

Moore's final public role came as Mercer County delegate to the Kentucky Constitutional Convention of 1849–1850. He died in Harrodsburg, probably of a stroke. He is reputed to have married three times and to have been survived by three children. The names of these family members are not known.

• With Moore's papers generally scattered, the best primary source on his career in Congress is Joseph Gales and William W. Seaton, comps., *Register of Debates in Congress* (29 vols., 1825–1837). His activities as minister to Colombia can be traced in the Riggs Family Papers and the papers of Martin Van Buren, both in the Library of Congress. Valuable bits and pieces on Moore's role in Kentucky politics can be unearthed in *The Papers of Henry Clay*, ed. James F. Hopkins et al. (10 vols., 1959–1992). Especially helpful secondary sources include Robert V. Remini, *The Election of Andrew Jackson* (1963), and John M. Belohlavek, *"Let the Eagle Soar": The Foreign Policy of Andrew Jackson* (1985). An obituary is in the *Louisville Daily Democrat*, 26 July 1853.

JOHN R. VAN ATTA

MOORE, Undine (25 Aug. 1904–6 Feb. 1989), composer and teacher, was born Undine Smith in Jarrat, Virginia, the daughter of James William Smith, a brakeman for the railroad, and Hattie Turnbull. When Undine was four, her family moved to Petersburg, Virginia, but returned to Jarrat every summer to visit family. Moore felt that her early years spent in Jarrat "among the rich musical culture endemic to 'Southside' Virginia" were the inspiration for quite a few of her later compositions. Instilling in their children the importance of education, the Smiths were very supportive of Moore's early interest in music. They were able, despite their limited financial resources, to provide their daughter with a Steinway piano. While in Petersburg, Moore began to study with Lillian Allen Darden and was able at the age of eight to provide accompaniment for a local high school graduation.

Moore continued her musical study at Fisk University in Nashville, Tennessee, particularly under the influence of choral director John W. Work, Jr., and keyboard instructor Alice Grass. Graduating at the top of her class, she received a B.A. and B.Mus. (piano and theory) in 1926 from Fisk University. Many people thought Moore would begin a career as a concert pianist, but she decided to pursue the profession of teaching. She received the M.A. professional diploma from Columbia University Teachers College. She also attended the Juilliard School as Fisk's first scholarship recipient, later studying theory and composition at the Manhattan School of Music and the Eastman School of Music in Rochester, New York.

For several years Moore taught in the school system of North Carolina before joining the faculty of Virginia State College (now University) in Petersburg in 1927. In a 1980 interview with *Black Creative Artists*, Moore, as well as others, expressed their dismay "that each generation appeared to know less and less about Black achievement." Utilizing a grant from the National Endowment for the Humanities, she cofounded with faculty colleague Altona Trent Johns the Black Music Center at Virginia State University establishing a repository of African-American music materials and a venue for the presentation of concerts and workshops. The idea behind the Black Music Center was to focus not only on classical music but on what Moore and Johns felt was the "true Creative genius of the black people in the ditches and the sawmills." Because the project did not receive the support she felt it merited, she resigned from the university in 1972. Among her students during her long tenure in Petersburg were jazz pianist Billy Taylor, opera singer Camilla Williams, conductor Leon Thompson, gospel singer Robert Fryson, music educators Michael V. W. Gordon and James Mumford, and composer Phil Medley. While at Virginia State University she met James Arthur Moore; they married and had one daughter.

Moore's best-known works are marked by an affinity with the tradition of the spirituals, although her early works illustrate a more venturesome vocabulary (e.g., *Before I'd Be a Slave*, for piano). She was most comfortable in the medium of keyboard and choral music, venturing into chamber music with *The Afro-American Suite*, written for D. Antoinette Handy's Trio Pro Viva ensemble (flute, violoncello, and piano), and one large-scale work, *Scenes From the Life of a Martyr*, an oratorio in tribute to Dr. Martin Luther King, Jr., that was prepared with the assistance of Donald Raescher. This oratorio was nominated for a Pulitzer Prize. Her deep appreciation of African-American folklore coupled with her devotion to classical European literature in her teaching and lectures are reflected in her music with texts by Sappho, William Blake, John Milton, and Michelangelo, as well as Langston Hughes. Moore was quite active in her retirement. She held residencies at Richmond's Virginia Union University and on three Minnesota campuses (Carleton College, St. Benedict College, and St. John's University). Respected as a matriarch among African-American composers, she secured frequent performances of her choral works, particularly on college campuses, where her dignified bearing and warm personality were greeted with enthusiasm.

• Moore's archival materials are primarily with her daughter, Nary Moore Easter, a cultural historian and dance specialist. Moore articulated her aesthetic concerns at a 1971 conference whose proceedings were published in Dominique-René de Lerma, ed., *Reflections on Afro-American Music* (1973). Extensive attention to her music is provided in Carl G. Harris, "A Study of Characteristic Stylistic Trends Found in the Choral Works of a Selected Group of Afro-American Composers and Arrangers" (Ph.D. diss., 1971). A register of Moore's recorded works and their publications appears in Dominique-René de Lerma, *The Black Composer: A Discography* (1996).

DOMINIQUE-RENÉ DE LERMA

MOORE, Veranus Alva (13 Apr. 1859–11 Feb. 1931), veterinary pathologist and bacteriologist, was born in Houndsfield, Jefferson County, New York, the son of Alva Moore, who farmed and worked on the Lehigh Valley railroad, and Antoinette Eastman. When Moore was thirteen years old his father died of malaria and left the family in financial straits. Moore interrupted his education to work on a farm and contribute to the family's support. A farm mishap at age fourteen in which he stepped on a nail led to a serious bone infection that required periodic hospitalization for the next ten years. Moore used crutches until he was twenty-five years old.

Between stays at Bellevue Hospital in New York City, Moore taught in the Oswego County, New York, district schools. He received his common school teaching certificate in 1880, graduated from Mexico Academy in Oswego in 1883, and entered Cornell University, where he majored in the biological sciences. Despite his disability, he worked his way through college and received his B.S. degree in 1887.

After graduation he joined two other Cornell graduates, Daniel E. Salmon and Theobald Smith, as a research assistant at the Bureau of Animal Industry (BAI) of the U.S. Department of Agriculture in Washington, D.C. The BAI, formed in 1884, had the first laboratory in the United States devoted to the study of infectious diseases of livestock. Under the guidance of Salmon and Smith, the country's leading animal disease experts, Moore became one of the foremost veterinary pathologists and bacteriologists in the country. He succeeded Smith in 1895 as chief of the Division of Animal Pathology.

While at the BAI Moore attended evening classes at Columbian (now George Washington) Medical School, completing his M.D. in 1890. After graduation he supplemented his income by working at Columbian as a demonstrator in anatomy, and as professor of normal histology from 1894 to 1896. He never practiced medicine. Moore had married Mary Louise Slawson in 1892; they had three children.

A year after the New York State Veterinary College opened at Cornell University in 1895, Moore joined the faculty as professor of comparative pathology, bacteriology, and meat inspection. He held that position from 1896 to 1908, when he was appointed to succeed James Law as dean of the veterinary college. During Moore's twenty-one years as dean, the veterinary college flourished, becoming one of the premier schools of its kind. Moore's work in disease investigation, education, and institution-building made him a leading influence in veterinary medicine. When he began his career there were few scientifically trained veterinarians anywhere in the United States. During his deanship alone, the New York State Veterinary College graduated 550 veterinarians—a substantial portion of the scientifically trained veterinarians in the country.

Moore insisted that the top faculty stay in the classroom to serve as inspirations to the students. He taught classes at the veterinary college throughout his career, adding bacteriology courses for the Ithaca division of Cornell Medical School from 1898 to 1910. He also worked to update veterinarians trained before the era of scientific medicine through veterinary conferences he established in 1909. Two of his best-known books were for the classroom, *Laboratory Directions for Beginners in Bacteriology* (1898; rev. eds., 1900, 1901, 1905, 1914) and *Principles of Microbiology: A Treatise on Bacteria, Fungi, and Protozoa Pathogenic for Domesticated Animals* (1912; rev. ed., 1916).

Moore was in great demand as a consultant to state and federal governments and to the livestock industry. His pathology and bacteriology department at the New York State Veterinary College served as the investigative laboratory for the New York state veterinarian. Moore conducted field investigations of disease outbreaks and was especially well known for his work on bovine tuberculosis. His 1913 book *Bovine Tuberculosis and Its Control* provided methods for dairymen to rid their herds of tuberculosis and cope with the costly impact of public health laws designed to protect the milk supply. Between 1905 and 1911 Moore investigated the effect of toxic smelter smoke on livestock for the Anaconda Copper Company during a lengthy trial brought by Montana ranchers.

Following the scandal over the meat packing industry raised by journalist Upton Sinclair in *The Jungle*, President Theodore Roosevelt appointed Moore to the commission to review the new meat inspection laws of 1907. He also served Roosevelt as a member of the International Conference on Tuberculosis. The Hoover administration appointed him to the Conference on Child Life. During World War I Moore organized the Veterinary Medical Corps of the U.S. Army. In 1930 he was the second American to be elected a fellow of the Royal College of Veterinary Surgeons of England. He served as president of the Society of American Bacteriologists in 1910 and was active in numerous national veterinary organizations.

A man of great personal integrity, Moore was a widely admired civic leader in Ithaca. He served for twelve years on both the board of education and the board of health, and was a trustee of Ithaca Memorial Hospital from 1918 until his death. He was instrumental in the construction of a contagious disease wing at the hospital and helped establish the Tompkins County Public Health Laboratory. Following his retirement in 1929 from Cornell, the hospital implored him to help solve its financial and organizational problems. He took over its management and served as superintendent until his death in Ithaca.

• Moore's papers are deposited in the Department of Manuscripts and University Archives, John M. Olin Library, Cornell University, Ithaca, N.Y. The collection (1870–1931) includes correspondence, laboratory reports, class lecture notes, personal account books, pamphlets, and papers relating to animal disease. Ellis Pierson Leonard's two volumes, *A Cornell Heritage: Veterinary Medicine 1868–1908* (1979) and *In the James Law Tradition, 1908–1948* (1982), provide biographical information and the history of the New York State Veterinary College. Moore provides his own account in "Veterinary Education and Service at Cornell University 1896–1929," *Cornell Veterinarian* 19, no. 2 (1929): 199–243. In addition to numerous pamphlets and reports on livestock disease Moore wrote *The Pathology and Differential Diagnosis of Infectious Diseases of Animals* (1902; rev. eds., 1906, 1908, 1916). Useful biographical accounts written by his Cornell professor and colleague Simon Henry Gage are in the *Journal of Bacteriology* 22 (1931): 1–5, and *Science* 73 (22 May 1931): 550–51.

PATRICIA PECK GOSSEL

MOORE, Victor Frederick (24 Feb. 1876–23 July 1962), actor, was born in Hammonton, New Jersey, the son of Orville E. Moore, a restaurateur, and Sarah Annette Davis. Educated locally and in Boston, Moore appeared onstage at age ten carrying a banner for the Brothers Minstrels and by age seventeen had made his acting debut in *Babes in the Wood*. Leaving Boston in 1895, Moore, always stocky and never handsome, played bits in New York comedies such as *Rosemary* (1896), with John Drew, Ethel Barrymore, and Maude Adams, and *Spiritisme* (1897), starring Maurice Barrymore.

By 1900 Moore had invented a "neat, refined and novel" vaudeville act for himself and in 1902 experienced his first real success after buying a sketch called "Change Your Act, or Back to the Woods." In this act, a vaudeville duo survives the heckling of stagehands and the threat of firing from a smart-aleck stage manager by improvising new songs and dances. Moore married his second costar in the act, Emma Helwig Littlefield in 1902. They had three children before her death in 1934.

Over the next twenty-three years Moore regularly returned to "Change Your Act, or Back to the Woods." After seeing the act, producer Sam H. Harris had his partner, George M. Cohan, write Moore into *Forty-five Minutes from Broadway* (1906). As a former racetrack tout renouncing love because it would have involved marrying for money, Moore, who also introduced Cohan's famous title song, showed an appealing decency and sentimentality.

Although *Forty-five Minutes from Broadway* ran for nearly two years on Broadway and on the road, its sequel, *The Talk of New York*, ran for only a half-year, and Moore returned briefly to vaudeville before costarring in the musical comedy *The Happiest Night of His Life* (1911) and the comedy *Shorty McCabe* (1912). More variety work preceded Moore's earliest films, including two directed by Cecil B. DeMille in 1915 about Chimmie Fadden, a bumbling, good-hearted lad from the Bowery. In others he played a milkman-heir to an English title saved from snobbery by the love of a good woman and a self-sacrificing clown.

After returning to vaudeville in 1916–1917, Moore toured in *Patsy on the Wing* (1918) and as a philandering husband in *See You Later* (1919), a musical by Guy Bolton, P. G. Wodehouse, and composer Jean Schwartz. He then played the vaudeville circuit until 1925 when, balding and much heavier, he returned to the screen to play The Pessimist in the prison film *The Man Who Found Himself*; he also played an eye-catchingly ineffective crook in Owen Davis's comedy *Easy Come, Easy Go*.

Moore's career as a beloved clown truly began at age forty-nine, when he played Shorty McGee, a bumbling rumrunner, in the Bolton-Wodehouse-Gershwin musical comedy *Oh, Kay!* (1926). Supporting English star Gertrude Lawrence, Moore displayed sure but seemingly bare command of a wobbly walk and a wobbly voice. Moore's ability to project to an audience a belief that he was not at all funny stemmed from what Cole Porter's biographer George Eells called his "usual gloomy self." Moore apparently "believed producers and authors kept hiring claques to rock the theatres with laughter." Alfred Simon, a Gershwin biographer, recalled Moore as "a timid . . . lovable man who would arrive at the theater even on the sunniest days with an umbrella in hand."

After a brief turn in the revue *Allez-Oop!* (1927), Moore rejoined the Gershwins and their producers Alex Aarons and Vinton Freedley as a timid jewel thief in *Funny Face* (1927); for these producers he also proved an ideal foil to Bert Lahr's outrageous prize fighter in *Hold Everything!* (1928). Capitalizing on his previous role as a lovable buffoon, Moore played another bootlegger for the Richard Rodgers and Lorenz Hart musical comedy *Heads Up!* The operetta *Prince Charming* (1930) closed quickly.

Moore's two 1930 films, one an adaptation of *Heads Up!*, were inconsequential, and he spent the remainder of his career shuffling between stage and film. After a brief outing in the farce *She Lived Next to the Firehouse*, Moore rejoined the Gershwins, Aarons, and Freedley for the George S. Kaufman–Morrie Ryskind political satire *Of Thee I Sing* (1931), the first musical comedy to win a Pulitzer Prize. As Alexander Throttlebottom, the vice president ashamed to let his mother know what he did for a living, Moore midwifed a word into the American idiom: throttlebottom, an ornamental elected official. Musical historian Ethan Mordden analyzed the Moore character: "The naif entangled in a web of deceits and larks who never quite disentangles himself . . . the sort of character the musical could never have enough of." Moore and the fast-talking William Gaxton, as President Wintergreen, played together irresistibly. Mordden said, "Gaxton would handle the songs, the love plot and the schemes. . . . Perhaps Moore's gift was his ability to *listen* to the scripts. . . . no bystander or interferer but someone at the center of the action." For the next fifteen years Moore and Gaxton were musical comedy's most illustrious pair.

Of Thee I Sing's sequel, *Let 'Em Eat Cake* (1933), may have failed partly because the audiences who loved Moore were offended by the sight of Throttlebottom's head about to be cut off (he had helped his potential executioners repair the guillotine). In *Anything Goes*, the 1934 Cole Porter musical comedy, Moore was Public Enemy Number 13, masquerading as a clergyman.

Moore's film roles were rarely memorable; he was a radio sponsor in *Gift of Gab* (1934) and the owner of a romance magazine in *Romance in the Rain* (1934). There was a bit more substance to his aging hypochondriac in *Gold Diggers of 1937* and to Pop Cardetti, a cupid and pickpocket in the Fred Astaire–Ginger Rogers *Swing Time* (1936), who danced ineptly with Helen Broderick.

After eight films in 1937 and 1938, the most interesting of which was *Make Way for Tomorrow* (1937), a bleak comedy about a septuagenarian cut adrift by warring relatives, Moore returned to musical comedy in Porter's *Leave It to Me!* (1938). As the U.S. ambassador to the Soviet Union, Moore's character yearns to return to pitching horseshoes in Kansas, but even kicking a Nazi envoy in the stomach only enhances his reputation—until he comes up with a workable plan for world peace. Critic John Mason Brown wrote, "He is the happiest combination of a justice on the bench and a baby in distress."

In *Louisiana Purchase* (1940) Moore opposed Gaxton as a senator investigating corrupt practices who is finally defeated by his own idealism because he cannot cross a key picket line to hold his hearings. Except for a brief revival of his vaudeville act in *Keep 'Em Laughing* (1942), Moore spent the next three years in film, most notably in *Ziegfeld Follies* (1946), in which he wails, "Pay the two dollars" to his blowhard partner Edward Arnold as disasters and penalties pile up. In 1942 Moore married Shirley Paige; they had no children.

Moore teamed up with Gaxton twice more: in 1945 as Joseph Porter to Gaxton's Dick Live-Eye in a short-lived modernization of Gilbert and Sullivan's *Hollywood Pinafore* and in 1946 as a ferryman hoping to beat a newspaperwoman in her race against Phileas Fogg's round-the-world record in *Nelly Bly*. His later films included *It Happened on Fifth Avenue* (1947), *We're Not Married* (1952), and *The Seven Year Itch* (1955).

Moore returned to the stage in the revival of Paul Osborn's drama *On Borrowed Time* (1953), winning the New York Drama Critics Award for best actor. Discarding his usual mannerisms, Moore played an elderly man who keeps Death waiting in order to help his grandson. His last role was as the Starkeeper in the 1957 revival of Richard Rodgers and Oscar Hammerstein II's *Carousel*. Moore died in East Islip, New York. Playwrights Howard Lindsay and Russell Crouse said in his eulogy, "He was someone that all the members of the audience wanted to take home with them."

• Although Moore had reportedly begun his memoirs, no manuscript has surfaced. The files of the Billy Rose Theatre Collection at the New York Public Library for the Performing Arts, Lincoln Center, are useful. Histories of the musical theater and the biographies of his contemporaries provide substantial insights into Moore's genius. Among the best of these are Ethan Mordden, *Broadway Babies* (1983); Stanley Green, *The Great Clowns of Broadway* (1984); George Eells, *The Life That Late He Led: Cole Porter* (1967); and Edward Jablonski, *Gershwin* (1987). Enjoyable and gleefully unreliable is P. G. Wodehouse and Guy Bolton, *Bring on the Girls* (1953). An obituary is in *Variety*, 25 July 1962.

JAMES ROSS MOORE

MOORE, William (6 May 1699–30 May 1783), justice and politician, was born in Philadelphia, Pennsylvania, the son of John Moore, a lawyer and collector of customs for Pennsylvania, and Rebecca Axtell. Little reliable information about his early life has survived. He may have followed his elder brothers to England to be educated, and he possibly graduated from Oxford University in 1719. However, his name does not appear in the university's list of graduates. About 1722 he married Williamina Wemyss, reputed to have been the sister of James, the fourth earl of Wemyss, in Scotland. However, Sir James Fraser's *Memorials of the Family of Wemyss of Wemyss* makes no mention of a Williamina Wemyss. What is certain is that, after Moore's marriage, his father gave him 240 acres of land in the prosperous rural area of Chester County in southeastern Pennsylvania. On the land he built a sawmill, a tavern, and his home, "Moore Hall," where he lived for much of the rest of his life. Moore had twelve children, five of whom survived him.

John Moore was one of the founders of Christ Church, Philadelphia, and William Moore succeeded his father as a leading figure among the Pennsylvania Anglicans. He was elected to the provincial assembly from Chester County in 1733 and was reelected each autumn until the resurgence of Quaker popularity in

1740. In 1741 Governor George Thomas appointed Moore justice of the peace and a judge of the Chester County Court. From 1750 until 1776 he was usually the presiding judge. He doubtless made many enemies, for, according to J. Smith Futhey and Gilbert Cope's *History of Chester County* (1881), he "was haughty in temper, and none too gentle in the exercise of power."

Moore was naturally aggressive and frequently at odds with the Quaker-dominated assembly. In 1747 he was elected colonel of militia in Chester County. There is no evidence that he took part in any military action, but the French and Indian War brought him into open conflict with the assembly. The defeat of British general Edward Braddock at the battle of the Monongahela on 9 July 1755 and the consequent American Indian incursions threw many Pennsylvanians into a panic. Moore wrote to the assembly, informing them that 2,000 men of Chester County would march on Philadelphia to compel them to pass a militia law. The letter caused a series of reprisals. For the next two years Moore was accused of tyranny, injustice, and extortion. The assembly ordered him to account for himself and on 28 September 1757 asked Governor Denny to remove him from office. In an address on 19 October 1757, Moore stoutly defended himself, attributing the accusations to the "Fools of the Late Assembly." Moore published his address in the *Pennsylvania Gazette* on 1 December 1757 and, through the offices of William Smith, in the *Philadelphische Zeitung* on 31 December 1757.

Moore's involvement with Smith contributed to his arrest and imprisonment. Smith was the first provost of the College of Philadelphia (now the University of Pennsylvania) and an influential figure in Anglican circles. Even more belligerent than Moore, Smith in 1755 and 1756 had published two pamphlets attacking the assembly for its pacifism. These latest attacks were too much for the assembly, which, on 6 January 1758, had both Moore and Smith arrested for libel. The two men remained in jail for three months. Chief Justice William Allen refused writs of habeas corpus on the grounds that the assembly would simply rearrest them the next day, but after the assembly adjourned, he released them on 8 April 1758. On 26 August 1758 Governor Denny dismissed the charges against Moore. Far from idle in jail, Smith courted Moore's daughter Rebecca, and they married at Moore Hall in June. Later in 1758 Smith went to England to take the case to the Privy Council, which censured the assembly for breach of royal prerogative and individual liberty.

During the Revolution, Moore remained faithful to the British Crown. Two incidents show that age had not dimmed his spirit. The first occurred in June 1775, when he was visited by a patriot committee that forced a written statement of loyalty from him. His response is recorded in Samuel W. Pennypacker's *Annals of Phoenixville*: "I have of late encouraged and will continue to encourage learning the military art, apprehending the time is not far distant when there may be occasion for it. I hope Gentlemen, this will be satisfactory to you" (p. 89). The irony of his words apparently escaped them, for they accepted his statement. The second incident occurred when a detachment from the American army, detailed to deprive local Tories of arms, visited Moore Hall and found a sword with a handle inlaid with gold and silver. Grabbing the sword, Moore snapped the blade from the handle and contemptuously threw the blade at the soldiers, saying, "There, take that if you are anxious to fight, but you have no business to steal my plate" (*Annals of Phoenixville*, p. 111).

Moore died at Moore Hall and is buried under the porch of St. David's Church, in Radnor, Pennsylvania. The inscription on his gravestone praises his work as a judge, magistrate, and community leader. To this it might be added that he provided an example of independence in the face of coercion in two wars, sustained by his pride in the connection with the Wemyss family.

• Moore's papers are in the Historical Society of Pennsylvania. Biographical sketches are in Samuel Pennypacker, *Annals of Phoenixville and Its Vicinity* (1872); Pennypacker, *Historical and Biographical Sketches* (1883); and J. Smith Futhey and Gilbert Cope, *History of Chester County* (1881). Horace Wemyss Smith, *Life and Correspondence of William Smith* (1880), details the Smith-Moore trial and has an inaccurate genealogy, which is corrected by Sir William Fraser's *Memorials of the Family of Wemyss of Wemyss* (1888). Documents of the Smith-Moore trial are in *Minutes of the Provincial Council of Pennsylvania*, vols. 7–8 (1851–1852), and Leonard W. Labaree, ed., *The Papers of Benjamin Franklin*, vol. 8 (1965). Reliable brief summaries of the trial and its aftermath are in Albert F. Gegenheimer, *William Smith, Educator and Churchman* (1943), and William S. Hanna, *Benjamin Franklin and Pennsylvania Politics* (1964). William R. Riddell, "Libel on the Assembly," *Pennsylvania Magazine of History and Biography* 52 (1928): 176–92, 249–79, 342–60, is exhaustive. An account of the trial's significance for jurisprudence is in Joseph Henry Smith, *Appeals to the Privy Council from the American Plantations* (1950).

ROBERT LAWSON-PEEBLES

MOORE, Zephaniah Swift (20 Nov. 1770–30 June 1823), clergyman and college president, was born in Palmer, Massachusetts, the son of Judah Moore and Mary Swift, farmers. Moore moved with his family to Wilmington, Vermont, in 1778 and spent the next ten years working on his father's farm. Having demonstrated a natural inquisitiveness and desire for learning, he attended Bennington (Vt.) Academy and then entered Dartmouth College in 1789. Graduating from Dartmouth in 1793 with an A.B. in classical studies, he spent the next academic year as principal of the Londonderry (N.H.) Academy. Moore felt called to the ministry and devoted the next two years to theological study with the Reverend Charles Backus in Somers, Connecticut.

Licensed to preach by the Association of Tolland County (Conn.) on 3 February 1796, Moore then preached at various churches before accepting a call to the First Congregational Church at Leicester, Massachusetts. Ordained there on 10 January 1798, he remained in the pastorate for the next fourteen years. Moore served as trustee of the Leicester Academy throughout his ministry and from July 1806 until October 1807 also served the institution as principal preceptor. He married Phebe Drury of Ward (now Auburn), Massachusetts, in 1799; they had no children.

In October 1811 Moore accepted an offer from his alma mater to become professor of learned languages. At Dartmouth he taught Greek, Latin, and Hebrew and attracted the attention of the trustees of Williams College. He became the second president of the Williamstown, Massachusetts, institution in May 1815, succeeding Ebenezer Fitch.

After an initial period of prosperity following its opening in October 1793, Williams College had fallen on hard times. Enrollment stood at fifty-eight students, the faculty consisted of two professors and two tutors, the physical plant contained only two buildings, and there was an annual budget deficit. The condition of the college was such that the Reverend Leonard Woods of Andover had been named as president of the college at the same trustees meeting that had nominated Moore. After Woods declined the position, Moore, the contingent choice, received the offer and accepted. Also at that meeting an issue surfaced that was to overshadow Moore's entire administration. One of the trustees, the Reverend Theophilus Packard, successfully introduced a motion to consider relocating the college to central Massachusetts. It was widely believed that Williams's isolated location in northwestern Massachusetts was at least partly to blame for the college's decline in fortune, and the subject was carefully investigated by a committee appointed by the trustees. A report by the committee to the trustees in September 1815 rejecting the relocation seemed to end the matter.

The Moore administration spent the next three years quietly attempting to build up the college. Prospects appeared brighter until the commencement of 1818, when Packard introduced another proposal to the trustees. He recommended relocation and the merger of Williams with the proposed Amherst College in central Massachusetts. Although Moore declared his support for the proposal, the trustees flatly rejected it. In a subsequent meeting in November 1818, Moore himself proposed relocating the college. He claimed that he was led to believe at the time of his inauguration that the college's future plans were based on removal; Moore threatened to resign his office if the proposal was rejected.

The trustees agreed to put the matter before the state legislature (which had granted Williams its charter in 1793). In May 1819 another trustee committee recommended that the college be relocated to the town of Northampton, Massachusetts. By this time the debate over the issue was widespread in all three communities. In November 1819 the trustees of Williams formally petitioned the legislature for permission to move the college and also proposed a merger of the two schools to the Amherst trustees, provided that Amherst itself located in Northampton. The Amherst trustees, although agreeable to the merger in principle, rejected the latest proposal, insisting that the Amherst institution had to remain in Amherst.

The issue was finally resolved by the state legislature in February 1820. The request for removal was denied on the grounds that it would violate the intent of the original charter and also would constitute a betrayal of the financial donors to Williams.

Frustrated and exhausted, Moore subsequently accepted the presidency of Amherst College in May 1821 and traveled to Amherst on horseback (along with Packard and fifteen Williams students). He also assumed the professorship of theology and moral philosophy at the new school. Moore insisted that the college hold the same admission requirements as Yale, which did no harm to enrollment. A second building was begun during his tenure, as was a $30,000 subscription fund to pay college expenses. The library opened in the fall of 1821, and two literary societies were formed. The heavy burdens of his office wore mightily on Moore, however, and he died in Amherst after a short illness.

Zephaniah Swift Moore belongs solidly in the tradition of nineteenth-century clergymen-turned-educators. Although his administration at Williams was preoccupied with the removal issue, and death cheated him of a long tenure at Amherst, the evolution of the two institutions into strong, respected colleges (a development that belied the fears of those who believed that neither would survive) is attributable at least in part to him.

• The papers of Moore are scattered among the archives of Williams College, Amherst College, and Dartmouth College. The best source of information concerning his career at Williams is Calvin Durfee, *The History of Williams College* (1860). The best secondary source on his brief tenure at Amherst is Claude M. Fuess, *Amherst: The Story of a New England College* (1935). An obituary is in the *Boston Daily Advertiser*, 4 July 1823.

EDWARD L. LACH, JR.

MOOREHEAD, Agnes (6 Dec. 1900–30 Apr. 1974), actor, was born Agnes Robertson Moorehead in Clinton, Massachusetts, the daughter of John Henderson Moorehead, a Presbyterian minister, and Mary Mildred McCauley, who had been a singer before her marriage. In 1904 Moorehead's family moved to Hamilton, Ohio, and, in 1916, to St. Louis, Missouri. In 1920 Moorehead entered Muskingum College in New Concord, Ohio, from which she received a B.A. in English in 1923. She pursued graduate study for a year at Muskingum but did not receive a degree. Deciding on a career in acting, she began to study in 1927 at the American Academy for Dramatic Arts (AADA) in New York City and graduated in 1929 with honors. At AADA Moorehead met her first husband, actor John Griffith Lee. They were married in 1930 and later adopted a son.

The coming of the depression made stage work difficult to find, so Moorehead turned to radio. During the 1930s Moorehead appeared in up to eight radio shows a day. She was particularly noted for her ability to play haughty straight women in comedies. On the radio version of "The March of Time" (1931–1945) she regularly impersonated political figures including Madame Chiang Kai Shek and Eleanor Roosevelt. The first lady herself stipulated that only Moorehead could play her.

In the mid-1930s Moorehead met Orson Welles, with whom she began to work extensively. On the popular radio thriller "The Shadow" (1937–1939), Moorehead played Margot Lane, secretary to Lamont Cranston (Welles), the show's millionaire title character. In 1937 Welles asked Moorehead to join his theatrical troupe, the Mercury Theatre. When Welles received his 1939 movie contract from RKO, which allowed the "boy genius" to bring his troupe with him, Moorehead went to Hollywood.

Following nearly a year of bickering between RKO and Welles, his first film, *Citizen Kane* (1941), appeared. In *Kane*, Moorehead gave a brief but powerful performance as title character Charles Foster Kane's mother, a stoic, Colorado pioneer. In Moorehead's—and Welles's—second film, *The Magnificent Ambersons* (1942), Moorehead had a much larger role as neurotic spinster Fanny Minifer, for which she garnered the 1942 New York Film Critics Award for best actress and the first of her four Oscar nominations for best supporting actress.

After Welles's and his company's contract with RKO expired in 1942, Moorehead was able to get a stock contract with MGM. Moorehead soon became one of the most highly paid character performers in film. Often playing unpleasant, emotionally unstable characters, she could become the dominant personality in a movie, even in small roles, such as that of the vengefully murderous Madge Raft in *Dark Passage* (1947). Moorehead also received two more best supporting actress Oscar nominations in quite different roles: as a sympathetic socialite in *Mrs. Parkington* (1944) and as a stern country woman in *Johnny Belinda* (1948). Among Moorehead's most notable films during her MGM years were *The Big Street* (1942), *Journey into Fear* (1942), *Jane Eyre* (1944), *Since You Went Away* (1944), *Tomorrow the World* (1944), *Our Vines Have Tender Grapes* (1945), *The Lost Moment* (1947), and *Showboat* (1951), which was her last film made under her MGM contract.

Moorehead was a featured performer on CBS's popular radio show "Mayor of the Town" (1942–1949). In 1943 she premiered her most famous radio role in *Sorry, Wrong Number*, a one-woman thriller about an invalid who accidentally hears a phone conversation plotting her murder. This radio play by Lucille Fletcher became one of the best-known broadcast dramas of all time; Moorehead would frequently reprise her role on the air.

After Moorehead's MGM contract expired in 1950, she began to freelance. She appeared most frequently in the sorts of roles with which she had become associated: gritty pioneers and other quirky, independent women, often spinsters or widows. *Caged* (1950) and *The True Story of Jesse James* (1957) were among her most important films of this period. In 1951 and 1952 she appeared on stage in *Don Juan in Hell*—a dramatic reading of the final act of George Bernard Shaw's *Man and Superman*—which was a critical and popular success on tour in the United States and Britain and later on Broadway. In 1954 she premiered her one-woman show *An Evening with Agnes Moorehead* (later titled *The Fabulous Redhead*), which she would perform more than 500 times over the next two decades. In the 1950s Moorehead also began coaching drama in Los Angeles. Moorehead and Lee were divorced in 1952 amid Moorehead's accusations of abuse. In 1953 she married the much younger Robert Gist, but they were separated within a year. Gist and Moorehead divorced in 1958.

In the 1950s Moorehead ventured into television through guest appearances on various shows. One of her best known and most effective television performances was as a stoic, extraterrestrial pioneer woman in "The Invaders," a 1961 episode of Rod Serling's "The Twilight Zone." In 1964 Moorehead began her most famous television role as Samantha's (Elizabeth Montgomery) mother and fellow witch Endora on ABC's popular situation comedy "Bewitched" (1964–1972). Although a comic role, Moorehead's haughty and manipulative Endora was not entirely unlike her earlier screen persona. She would win her only Emmy (for best actress in a single performance) for a guest appearance as a feminist in the Old West on a February 1967 episode of "Wild, Wild West." During the last decade and a half of her life, Moorehead continued to make a number of films, including *Hush . . . Hush Sweet Charlotte* (1964), for which she received her fourth, and final, Oscar nomination for best supporting actress; *Twenty Plus Two* (1961); *How the West Was Won* (1963); and *Charlotte's Web* (1973). Moorehead died in Rochester, Minnesota.

Moorehead enjoyed a varied career in radio, television, stage, and film. Her most significant efforts were the character roles she perfected in more than sixty Hollywood films. Moorehead's film characters tended to be tough or neurotic. Often, they were rather unattractive personalities. Moorehead herself was quite different from the women she portrayed. By all accounts a kind and private person, Moorehead was also a devout Christian, who characterized herself as a "fundamentalist" and usually had a Bible with her on set. She was fiercely dedicated to her craft. John Payne, who appeared with Moorehead in *The Blazing Forest* (1952), noted that "when you face Agnes in front of a camera, you know you've got to catch a fast ball or get hit right in the face." Moorehead herself came from an old school of acting. She told an interviewer late in life,

> I don't believe in playing a whole game in front of an audience. . . . My attitude is: "All right, I'll start the tears, but you do the crying." That's because I myself have to keep composed and know what I'm doing up on that stage. I can't constrict my voice, nor can I have my

nose run, nor the tears go out and my mascara get messed up. But I can give an effect through which you become so involved that *you* cry, and you think that I'm doing it. . . . The exciting thing is to be able to characterize and get people to believe what you are characterizing.

Nevertheless, as her career progressed, her performances tended to become more "over the top"; Moorehead's critics often accused her of overacting and scene stealing. But the same roles that earned her the most criticism often also earned her the most praise. Moorehead posthumously became a gay icon, owing to her frequently campy performances and to persistent rumors that she and Debbie Reynolds had had a long-running affair. Although Reynolds and Moorehead were close, there is little if any evidence to suggest that they were sexually involved or even that Moorehead was gay.

• The Agnes Moorehead Papers are housed at the State Historical Society of Wisconsin in Madison. The single best biographical source on Moorehead, Lynn Kear, *Agnes Moorehead: A Bio-Bibliography* (1992), provides a good biographical sketch and complete annotated lists of radio, stage, film, and television appearances, as well as an annotated bibliography and discography. James Robert Parish, *Good Dames* (1974), features a first-rate, extensive biographical sketch of Moorehead. Mike Steen, *Hollywood Speaks* (1974), includes a long and informative interview with her.

BENJAMIN L. ALPERS

MOORLAND, Jesse Edward (10 Sept. 1863–30 Apr. 1940), book collector and religious leader, was born in Coldwater, Ohio, the son of William Edward Mooreland (*sic*), a farmer, and his wife Nancy Jane Moore, members of a black family that had been free for several generations. Raised by his maternal grandparents because of his parents' early deaths, Moorland, an only child, attended Northwestern Normal University in Ada, Ohio, and the theological department of Howard University. In 1886 he married Lucy Corbin Woodson; they had no children. Moorland was ordained to the ministry in the Congregational church in 1891, and became the organizing pastor of a church in South Boston, Virginia, as well as secretary of the Young Men's Christian Association (YMCA) in Washington, D.C. From 1893 to 1896 he was minister of Howard Chapel, Nashville, Tennessee, and then went to Mt. Zion Congregational Church in Cleveland, Ohio.

A social gospel preacher who believed in working to uplift poor urban blacks and protect them from vice by providing a more wholesome environment, Moorland joined William A. Hunton in 1898 as a secretary for negro work with the Colored Men's Department of the YMCA, the association having decided to form separate racial branches. Moorland's intent was to establish centers where athletics, Bible study, job training, and other positive activities would serve as alternatives to the social and economic disintegration and ethical demoralization of the growing black ghettos in major cities.

Given the absence of adequate facilities, Moorland began an ambitious fundraising campaign for construction of the Twelfth Street YMCA in Washington in which he combined solicitation of African Americans on the basis of betterment and race pride and white philanthropists on the basis of betterment and paternalism. The formula was successful and Moorland went to Chicago to raise money for a YMCA building there. He convinced Julius Rosenwald to give $25,000 to any black YMCA in any city that raised $75,000 independently. Over the years Moorland realized over $2 million for construction, much of it from African Americans committed to social improvement and self-help.

Moorland served as a senior YMCA secretary from 1898 to 1923 and relocated to New York along with his office in 1920. After his retirement in 1926, he took on the presidency of the National Health Circle for Colored People. At this stage of his life, however, he also became an influential member of the Howard University Board of Trustees, which he had joined in 1907, and he now devoted much of his time and energy to the university. Moorland was considered something of a statesman on the board, able to rise above the frequent frays and negotiate practical compromises. In fact, he usually sided with Howard's conservative white presidents, even the thoroughly unpopular J. Stanley Durkee, and represented them and their interests to the black faculty and alumni. During the stormy administration of Mordecai W. Johnson, Howard's first black president, Moorland was chairman of the board's executive committee, where his gifts for conciliation and compromise were put not only to great use, but to the test.

Jesse Moorland is now best remembered not for his service to church, YMCA, or university, but for his extensive library devoted to black history and culture, especially the history of slavery. He inherited a book collection from his uncle, Dr. William C. Moore, and added to it over the years—books, pamphlets, engravings, documents, manuscripts, clippings, portraits—until he had amassed over 3,000 items. Kelly Miller and Alain Locke of the Howard faculty had long hoped to establish an African-American research collection—a "Negro Americana Museum and Library," as they said—in order to make Howard a center of black scholarship and even eventually establish a chair in the field. Influenced by Miller and by Howard's president Stephen M. Newman, "who unconsciously inspired me with the desire for historic research," Moorland in 1914 gave the university his library. It was then considered the largest and most comprehensive private collection of materials by and about people of African descent, and it was valued at between $2,000 and $3,000. The university established the Moorland Foundation, a Library of Negro Life, which was housed in a separate location in the new Carnegie library building.

Moorland was a Republican, a Mason, a member of Alpha Phi Alpha, and a trustee of the Frederick Douglass Home Association. He was also a member of the prestigious but ineffectual American Negro Academy and its executive committee. In 1919 he opposed the academy's invitation to A. Philip Randolph to speak on "The New Radicalism and the Negro," but his was a lone voice of disapproval and he reduced his participation in the academy as a result. Moorland was secretary-treasurer of the Association for the Study of Negro Life and History, but he had a falling out with its founder, the contentious Carter G. Woodson, who found him too accommodating to the white establishment. Moorland died in New York City.

Fair-complected enough to pass easily for white, Moorland consciously and intentionally devoted his life to what was then called racial uplift. His positive relationships with white philanthropists, however, influenced him to be something of a cautious mediator and broker between the races. His nonideological practicality kept him from taking unpopular positions, and his penchant for cooperation kept him from controversial views. Moorland's lasting contribution was the gift of his library to Howard. W. E. B. Du Bois commented at the time, "I think you have a fine beginning in Negro Americana. I trust that the University will take immediate and thoughtful steps to make Howard University Library a great center in this line." The Moorland collection made Howard the first university research library committed to collecting materials on African Americans.

• The Jesse Moorland Papers are in the Manuscript Division, Moorland-Spingarn Research Center, Howard University. Two important essays by Moorland are *The Demand and the Supply of Increased Efficiency in the Negro Ministry* (1909) and "The Young Men's Christian Association Among Negroes," *Journal of Negro History* 9 (1924): 127–138. There is as yet no biography. An account of the gift of his library is "The J. E. Moorland Foundation of the University Library," *Howard University Record* 10 (1916): 5–15. An obituary is in the *Journal of Negro History* 25, no. 3 (July 1940): 401–3.

RICHARD NEWMAN

MOOSMÜLLER, Oswald William (26 Feb. 1832–10 Jan. 1901), Roman Catholic priest and Benedictine monk, was born into a wealthy family in the village of Aidling, Bavaria. His father was a forester and a gamekeeper, but his parents' names are not known. Baptized William, he began his formal education in the parish school of Aidling and subsequently enrolled at the monastic school of St. Michael's Abbey, Metten. While studying at Metten, he learned of the missionary work undertaken among German immigrants in North America by Father Boniface Wimmer, a former member of the Metten community. Moosmüller entered the novitiate of the Benedictine community in Metten at the age of nineteen. One year later, in 1852, he was sent to St. Vincent Priory, the new Benedictine foundation of Wimmer in Westmoreland County, Pennsylvania. He entered the novitiate at St. Vincent in January 1854, taking the name Oswald in religion. He made solemn vows in January 1855 and was ordained to the priesthood on 18 May 1856 by Bishop Michael O'Connor of Pittsburgh.

For the next ten years, Moosmüller was given an amazing variety of assignments. He did parish work in Carrolltown, Pennsylvania, Covington, Kentucky, and Brooklyn and Roundout, New York, almost all with German-speaking immigrants. From 1861 to 1862 he was sent to Canada as a superior of a group of monks that took over the administration of a college in Sandwich, Ontario. In late 1862 Moosmüller was sent by Wimmer to Brazil to investigate the possibility of sending other American monks to that country. Moosmüller stayed a year in Brazil, narrowly escaping death—from encounters with a jaguar and a python—and returned to Pennsylvania in 1863. In that same year he was appointed superior of St. Mary's Priory in Newark, New Jersey, a post he kept for three years, during which he put that community on a solid financial footing.

It was evident that Wimmer had great confidence in the ability and talent of his young monk. This was affirmed in 1866 when, after Wimmer secured permission to establish a House of Studies for American Benedictines in Rome, Moosmüller was appointed its first superior, as well as Roman agent for the American Cassinese Congregation of monks. However, when troops of King Victor Emmanuel occupied Rome in the summer of 1870, the House of Studies had to close and Moosmüller returned home to St. Vincent. There he was appointed prior and procurator of the community and took up teaching duties once again at the college. He was also commissioned by Wimmer to write the first history of St. Vincent, published in German in 1873 as *St. Vincenz in Pennsylvanien*. Moosmüller took well to the intellectual work and had other writing projects planned when, in 1874, he was sent by Wimmer to St. Benedict Abbey, in Atchison, Kansas. There, during the ensuing three years, Moosmüller turned the fortunes of a declining community around.

In 1877 Wimmer sent his troubleshooter to another floundering foundation in the diocese of Savannah. There Moosmüller established an industrial school for African Americans on Skidaway Island and a school and monastery in Savannah. Moosmüller's commitment to Savannah was such that, when his St. Vincent's community elected him first abbot of a new foundation in North Carolina in 1885, he sent a brief telegram back to Wimmer: "Thank you for the honor, but I cannot accept." Two years later, in August of 1887, Moosmüller was sent to Alabama, one of Wimmer's last appointments. The patriarch of St. Vincent's and Moosmüller's mentor died in December of 1887.

In February 1888 Father Andrew Hintenach was elected to succeed Wimmer as abbot. As affirmation of his confidence in Moosmüller, he named him as second-in-command, or prior, at St. Vincent. Along with his administrative role and teaching duties in the school, Moosmüller renewed his historical studies. He published a biography of Wimmer, *Bonifaz Wimmer, Erzabt von St. Vincent in Pennsylvanien* (1891). His work was received so favorably that he was offered a chair of history at the new Catholic University of America; he declined the seat.

It was shortly after his return to St. Vincent that Moosmüller began to display reservations about the lack of true monastic observance there. He believed that the rapid missionary expansion at St. Vincent—an expansion that he had been very much a part of—had compromised the contemplative spirit of community life. Partly in reaction to this, Moosmüller envisioned a monastic community that would incorporate his design of Benedictine religious observance and literary work. In 1892 he received permission to start a new monastic community in the small Southern Illinois town of Wetaug, in the diocese of Belleville. The model of this Benedictine community was the medieval monastery of Cluny, thus the name "New Cluny" was given it. As Moosmüller wrote at the time: "The reason why I volunteered for this mission was because I prefer to live in a poor and quiet place where I could devote my time to literary work, especially to the publication of the *Legende*, and where I could train others so as to enable them to continue the same work after my death." The *Legende* was the principal literary and historical activity of New Cluny. It was a German translation of the Latin lives of the saints, adapted to the reading level of the average reader.

The monastic experiment seemed doomed from the beginning. The monastery was located in wetlands that were a breeding ground for malaria-carrying mosquitoes. It was surrounded by a Protestant population that was innately suspicious of Catholics in general and monks in particular. Moreover, Moosmüller's refusal to accept requests for his monks to staff parishes in the local area alienated even his fellow Catholics. The *Legende* had to be discontinued because of rising costs in 1898. Neither the agricultural nor educational ambitions, which some had considered utopian from the beginning, came anywhere close to being accomplished. Father Oswald Moosmüller died at New Cluny in surroundings appropriate to his monastic ideal: on a straw mattress surrounded by books from his library. The remaining monks of New Cluny abandoned Wetaug and accepted a mission to German Catholics in Saskatchewan, Canada, in 1903. Moosmüller's body, buried in Wetaug, was removed to St. Peter's Abbey, Saskatchewan, in 1928.

Moosmüller was an extraordinarily gifted man, whose missionary zeal, model of monastic piety, business acumen, and scholarly achievement found few equals among the religious of his day. In the end, one can say that Moosmüller was too much the visionary and too little the practical person to translate his monastic ideal of contemplation and study into action. As an agent of the American missionary monasticism of Boniface Wimmer he was a success. As a superior who wanted to restore the contemplative and intellectual dimension of medieval monasticism, he appeared as an idealist, unable to adapt to American frontier conditions. As one of many transplanted Europeans who devoted his entire life to the task of bringing the monastic "charism" to the United States, he was at once a model of religious observance and a tireless promoter of the institution of monastic life.

• Most of the letters of Moosmüller to Boniface Wimmer and other monastic correspondents from 1866 to 1901 are in the archives of St. Vincent Archabbey, Latrobe, Pa. Further Moosmüller correspondence is in the Reuss Collection of the American Catholic Historical Society of Pennsylvania. There are a number of shorter historical studies of Moosmüller. These include Felix Fellner, O.S.B., "Father Oswald Moosmüller, The Pioneer Benedictine Historian of the United States," *Records of the American Catholic Historical Society of Philadelphia* 34 (1923): 1–16; Peter Beckman, O.S.B., "Oswald Moosmüller in Kansas," *American Benedictine Review* 7 (1957): 263–81; and Jerome Oetgen, "Oswald Moosmüller, Monk and Missionary," *American Benedictine Review* 27 (1976): 1–35.

JOEL RIPPINGER

MORAIS, Sabato (13 Apr. 1823–11 Nov. 1897), rabbi and founding president of the Jewish Theological Seminary of America, was born in Livorno, Italy, the son of Samuel Morais and Buonina Wolf. He studied privately with rabbis and tutors, mastering classical Hebrew studies as well as Italian, French, and Spanish. In 1845 three of his teachers awarded him rabbinic ordination. In 1846 he became the Hebrew master of the orphanage of London's Spanish and Portuguese Synagogue. Five years later he emigrated to Philadelphia to become minister and spiritual leader (*hazzan*) of Mikveh Israel synagogue, one of the oldest congregations in America. In this post Morais helped keep the synagogue a bastion of traditional Judaism against the tide of nineteenth-century Reform Judaism. At the same time he showed himself open to innovation by crafting programs such as adult education classes and a supplementary school, which were becoming hallmarks of the American synagogue. In 1855 he married Clara Esther Weil; they had seven children.

Morais's tenure at Mikveh Israel, which lasted until his death, was the longest of any nineteenth-century American rabbi and was not without its difficulties. He worked to unite the often divisive elements within the congregation, whose different European traditions (Sephardic or Spanish versus Ashkenazic or German backgrounds) created tensions. When his public stance in favor of abolition alienated one of his influential congregants, Henry M. Phillips, a congressman and friend of President James Buchanan, the congregation muzzled Morais's preaching for a year. Over time his views on the larger national and Jewish communal issues of his day became widely known. His protests against Christian language in government proclamations marked him as a bold champion of a very broad interpretation of the separation of church and state. He staunchly supported immigrants and open immigration. During a disastrous cloakmakers strike in 1890, he preached social justice for the workers, which dismayed some of the wealthy congregants who employed them.

Involved in almost every aspect of American Jewish life, Morais was a principal member of the "Philadelphia Group" of scholars and intellectuals who shaped not only the Philadelphia Jewish community, but also many of the institutions of American Jewish life, among them the Jewish Theological Seminary of America. Although he had earlier supported Reform Rabbi Isaac Mayer Wise's efforts to unify American Jewry, he was essentially a traditionalist. He believed that Jewish law was binding upon all Jews but could conceive of changes in Jewish custom and law, provided that they were made by rabbis faithful to the tradition. Consequently, he was dismayed by the radical actions and statements contravening Jewish law made by Reform rabbis. When a leading member of Mikveh Israel attempted to introduce the reforms of an organ and choir into the congregation in 1869, Morais forcefully opposed the innovations. He viewed these innovations and others, such as eliminating the separate seating of men and women in worship mandated by Jewish law, as imitative of gentile ways. The theory of higher biblical criticism, which argued that the Torah was authored by man, not God, was anathema to him. In 1886 he and a number of like-minded rabbis and Jewish communal leaders founded the Jewish Theological Seminary Association in order to create in New York City a new school—an alternative to Reform's Hebrew Union College in Cincinnati—to train rabbis faithful to Jewish tradition to be the leaders of American Jewry.

As president of the faculty of the Jewish Theological Seminary of America, Morais taught Bible and biblical exegesis and led the seminary to its first building on Lexington Avenue. Originally, he envisioned the school as "the Orthodox Seminary" but ultimately adopted the model of the Jewish Theological Seminary of Breslau, which trained men who were educated in both Jewish and secular studies, for a modern rabbinate. This distinct approach would mark the Jewish Theological Seminary as the fountainhead of Conservative, not Orthodox, Judaism in twentieth-century America. During his long career Morais translated a number of Italian Hebrew works into English, which were posthumously collected in *Italian-Hebrew Literature* (1926). He died in Philadelphia, just as he was completing a translation of the book of Jeremiah, which had been commissioned for the Jewish Publication Society's new translation of the Bible (1917).

• The principal sources on Morais are unpublished materials. The only full-scale biography is an unpublished dissertation, "Champion of Orthodox Judaism: A Biography of the Reverend Sabato Morais, LL.D.," by Max Samuel Nussenbaum (D.H.L. diss., Yeshiva Univ., 1964). Among the printed works that discuss aspects of his life and career are biographical sketches by his son, Henry Samuel Morais, in *The Jews of Philadelphia* (1894), and "Sabato Morais, a Memoir," in *Proceedings of the Sixth Biennial Convention of the Jewish Theological Seminary Association* (1898). Other works include Julius H. Greenstone, "Reminiscences of Old Seminary Days," *United Synagogue Recorder* 6, no. 4 (1926); Moshe Davis, *The Emergence of Conservative Judaism* (1963); Herbert Parzen, *Architects of Conservative Judaism* (1964); Maxwell Whiteman, "The Philadelphia Group," in *Jewish Life in Philadelphia, 1830–1940*, ed. Murray Friedman, (1983); and Robert E. Fierstein, *A Different Spirit: The Jewish Theological Seminary of America, 1886–1902* (1990).

PAMELA S. NADELL

MORAN, Benjamin (1 Aug. 1820–20 June 1886), diplomat and writer, was born in Chester County, Pennsylvania, the son of William Moran, a textile mill manager. His mother's name is unknown. Moran completed public school and then left home for Philadelphia, where he found employment in a printer's shop. Apparently he received some additional education at the Franklin Institute, developed an interest in writing, and as a young man published some poems and sketches. Intent on making his mark as a writer, Moran left the printer's trade and in 1851 sailed for England. His literary career was brief and undistinguished. An account of his travels, *The Footpath and Highway; or, Wanderings of an American in Great Britain in 1851 and '52*, was published in 1853. Among Moran's other literary accomplishments, the most noteworthy was his contribution to a history of American literature entitled *Trübner's Bibliographical Guide to American Literature* (1859).

During his wanderings in Britain in 1852, Moran married Catherine Goulder, an English mill girl almost ten years his senior; they had no children. She died in 1857 after a lengthy, debilitating illness. Moran never remarried. His clerical and routine administrative duties at the American legation in London, where he unofficially began his diplomatic career as a private secretary to Minister James Buchanan in 1854, became the focus of his life. In 1857 the State Department formally appointed Moran as assistant secretary of legation under Minister George M. Dallas, and in 1864, under Charles Francis Adams (1807–1886), he was promoted to secretary of legation. On numerous occasions he served as chargé d'affaires in Adams's absence and during the change of ministers. In late 1874 Moran was promoted to minister resident in Portugal and remained in that position until 1876, when the post was abolished. Moran concluded his diplomatic career as chargé d'affaires in Lisbon, retiring from the diplomatic service in 1882. He died at Bocking Hall, in Essex, England.

During his long service at the American legation in London, Moran became the indispensable bureaucrat for newly appointed ministers because of his command of the legation's day-to-day administrative routine and his vast knowledge of its archives. Hardworking and dedicated, he also acquired the reputation for being irascible, petulant, and easily slighted. After returning home in 1868 at the conclusion of his mission to England, Adams described Moran as a "drudging clerk . . . invaluable to the Legation" but personally unpleasant, because he was "afflicted with a temper so irritable and a spirit at once so fawning to superiors and insolent to those under him, that it is very difficult . . . to act with him." Adams conceded that Moran invariably had been "submissive and pliant" to him, although he suspected his secretary disliked him "at bottom." As he painfully recorded in the journal he regularly kept throughout his years in the London legation, Moran did resent being cast and treated as a social inferior by the successive ministers and their families, whom he served.

In addition to containing accounts of social slights and extensive personal commentary on the host of Americans who passed through the legation in the years 1857–1874, Moran's voluminous journal details the inside workings of Anglo-American relations during the Civil War era and remains an indispensable firsthand account of the period. Although a Buchanan Democrat and virtual expatriate, he unswervingly supported Abraham Lincoln and the Union. Ever suspicious of British actions and motives, and well exceeding his official capacity at the legation, Moran on several occasions acted to prevent British intervention in the American conflict. In one instance, in July 1862, during a House of Commons debate on Mr. William Schaw Lindsay's motion to recognize the Confederacy, Moran circulated a private telegram among British leaders that proved the armies of George B. McClellan (1826–1885) had not surrendered and that the Confederacy had not triumphed; this timely action contributed to Lindsay's decision to withdraw his motion. As the *Times* of London acknowledged in December 1874, Moran was an exemplary representative of the United States who played a critical role in averting an open break between the two nations during the Civil War.

Moran also must be credited for recording the first private acceptance of the Monroe Doctrine by a British foreign secretary. In his journal for 10 April 1858, the American wrote of a meeting between Minister Dallas and Lord Malmesbury, in which the foreign secretary "stated, in the course of the conversation that the Monroe Doctrine was right. We must, said he, agree to it; and it is folly for us to oppose what every body sees must be,—and what is natural and just—your occupancy ultimately of the whole Continent." This remarkable unofficial and unexpected concession, after years of public resistance by successive British governments to the implications of James Monroe's declaration, amazed Moran and led him to conclude that "Malmesbury's adoption of the Monroe Doctrine—called a *dictum* by Clarendon—seemed to indicate a full determination to be peaceful" and revealed that the British leader "intended to adopt a Foreign policy honorable and flattering to the Nation." However, Moran's optimism about England's acceptance of Monroe's principles was somewhat premature; it would be almost a half-century before a British leader would say publicly what Malmesbury had said privately.

Throughout his service in London to six ministers, including three post–Civil War diplomats—Reverdy Johnson, John L. Motley, and General Robert C. Schenck—Moran sustained the continuity of American diplomacy. He was popular and well known among members of the British ruling class and in London's literary circles not only as a diplomat but also as a businessman who had acquired considerable wealth as a promoter of railroads, telegraphs, and transatlantic cables, entrepreneurial activities that were illegal but tacitly overlooked by his superiors at a time when American diplomats were poorly paid and not yet recognized as a professional foreign service. Perhaps the definitive assessment of Moran's diplomatic achievement was offered in the 1874 tribute by the London *Times*, when it editorialized that the "United States never had an abler nor a more honest representative, and if the exigencies of party politics could be thrust aside, no American citizen could be chosen better qualified to sustain the dignity and watch over the interests of his nation at the capital of the British Empire." That contemporary British judgment appeared inflated from an American perspective, but in the end it may illustrate Moran's most significant accomplishment—his contribution to Anglo-American understanding.

• Moran's forty-one volume *Journal* spans the years 1857–1875 and is located in the Manuscripts Division, Library of Congress. Worthington C. Ford, who purchased the *Journal* in 1915 for the library, published extracts in the *Proceedings of the Massachusetts Historical Society* 48 (1915): 431–92. Fourteen volumes of the diary, with introductory material and explanatory notes, were published in Sarah Agnes Wallace and Frances Elma Gillespie, eds., *The Journal of Benjamin Moran, 1857–1865* (2 vols., 1948). For Adams's comments on Moran, see Martin Duberman, *Charles Francis Adams, 1807–1886* (1960). For laudatory accounts of his service in Britain, see *Times* (London), 22 Dec. 1874, and 22 and 23 June 1886. American obituaries are in the *New York Times*, 26 June 1886; Philadelphia *Evening Telegraph*, 22 June 1886; and *Appletons' Annual Cyclopedia 1886* (1887).

EDWARD P. CRAPOL

MORAN, Daniel Edward (12 Apr. 1864–3 July 1937), civil engineer, was born in Orange, New Jersey, the son of Daniel Edward Moran, a banker, and Annie Augusta Blake. Moran was not Irish, as is usually supposed, but of mixed English and Belgian ancestry. Growing up in Brooklyn, he attended local schools and Brooklyn Polytechnic Institute before entering in 1880 Columbia University's School of Engineering, then still its School of Mines. After graduating with a degree in civil engineering in 1884, Moran worked at minor jobs, starting as an apprentice in an ironworks. He surveyed railroads in the West, made maps in New York, and worked as a draftsman for engineer William Barclay Parsons.

A turning point in the young man's career came in 1889 when he met Charles Sooysmith, a pioneer in the designing and building of difficult foundations for bridges and other structures, particularly those needing pneumatic, or compressed air, work. Sooysmith hired Moran as his assistant and sent him to Iron Mountain, Michigan, to supervise the sinking of a mine shaft through quicksand, which he stabilized by a freezing process devised by Sooysmith. Moran next worked on the foundations of Boston harbor's Deer Island Lighthouse, the piers for the Harlem River's Mc-

Comb's Dam drawbridge in New York, and a railroad bridge over the Missouri River at Sioux City, Iowa. He also did the foundation work on New York City's American Security Building, only the second building in history to be supported by pneumatic foundations.

A natural innovator and inventor, the young engineer designed the Moran Air Lock. This was a pneumatic chamber that made possible the hoisting of buckets of excavated material to the open air from underwater working surfaces of a caisson, as opposed to a cofferdam. (A cofferdam is a boxlike structure placed in shallow water and pumped dry. A caisson is a similar structure, but in deep water with compressed air and an air lock keeping the work area free of water.) In 1896 Moran married Sarah V. Kelly in Glasgow, Scotland; the couple had five children. More interested in the potential of skyscrapers than was Sooysmith, Moran left the employ of his mentor in order to become a consultant and special partner in the firm of John Monk & Son. Four years later he organized his own Foundation Company with Franklin Remington and Edwin S. Jarrett, and soon made it into the foremost builder of deep and difficult foundations in America. When the partnership broke up in 1910 because of disagreements among the three men, Moran ran a business on his own. In 1917 he organized a civil engineering firm, Moran, Maurice and Proctor, later Moran, Proctor and Freeman, in Philadelphia, which he continued running in New York City till his death.

During the height of Moran's career, most major construction projects with foundation difficulties sought his expertise—his personal inspection and approval. Among these were the Woolworth, Equitable, Bank of the Manhattan Company, Farmers' Trust, and Port of New York Authority buildings in New York City. Especially demanding were the caisson-cofferdam foundations of New York's Federal Reserve Bank and the New York Telephone Company Building. His company also supervised work on foundations in Pennsylvania, Ohio, and Canada. But Moran came to be remembered more for his bridges than his skyscrapers, starting with the foundations of the Delaware River Bridge, or Camden Bridge, connecting Philadelphia with Camden, New Jersey (1926). He worked on the foundations of the Mid-Hudson Bridge at Poughkeepsie, Detroit's International Bridge, and New York's Triborough Bridge. He hit his stride with his contributions in 1931 to the Bayonne Bridge, spanning the Kill van Kull between Staten Island and New Jersey, and in 1932 to the George Washington Bridge across the Hudson.

The high point in Moran's career came near its end, in 1935, when his genius made possible the longest bridge in the world of its time (8.4 miles long including all of its approaches, and more than 4.5 miles over open water), the San Francisco–Oakland Bay Bridge. Not even the Golden Gate Bridge's engineer, Joseph Strauss, would have dared to try to bridge the two miles of much-navigated deepwater (to 100 feet) between San Francisco's waterfront Embarcadero and Yerba Buena Island, or Goat Island, in mid-bay. Chief Engineer Charles H. Purcell called in Moran as his consultant-assistant to solve a problem deemed impossible by government engineers in 1924. Moran's solution was to built a skyscraper-sized concrete pier up from bedrock in the middle of the "stream." It would serve as a common center-anchorage gripping the cables of *two* suspension bridges in tandem, the only such pair in the world. One would run from San Francisco's Rincon Point and the other from Yerba Buena Island, to meet on Moran's Pier W-4 (West #4).

East of the island, bridging was easy; only a double cantilever span over deep water and a long trestle-like bridge over the shallows and mudflats to Oakland were necessary. But to erect his lofty W-4, Moran first had to build the world's largest (92 by 197 feet) caisson on a Moore Drydock Company shipway in Oakland, launch it like a vessel, tow it and anchor it, and, finally, sink it precisely in place. The huge steel excavating "box" looked like a gigantic egg crate, an open-topped honeycomb of fifty-five vertical dredging cells, cylinders fifteen feet in diameter capable of being capped with steel domes to use air pressure. Liquid cement was poured from floating mixers into the spaces between the tubes, and as the boxy work platform sank lower and lower, its sides were raised and the cylinders extended upwards and capped with new cones, welded on. In the cylinders, clamshell buckets lifted mud to the surface at the rate of 6,800 pounds per scoop. When rock bottom was reached, sharp-pointed steel "gads" were dropped down the cylinders to break up the rock and create a level footing for the sharp-edged bottom of the caisson (Moran would not use explosives). Once that work was done, Moran's caisson became the heart of a great steel-reinforced concrete block that was Pier W-4, a concrete isle ready to grip the 40,000-ton tension of the suspension cables. Moran's center anchorage rose 226.7 feet above the low tide mark to give ships plenty of clearance. It was taller than the highest San Francisco skyscraper and bigger than the largest pyramid in Egypt, and it gobbled up more concrete than New York's Empire State Building.

Moran's career after his work on the Bay Bridge and the foundations for New York's Yankee Stadium, finished in 1923, was cut short by heart trouble. A Democrat and member of the American Societies of Civil, Mechanical, and Consulting Engineers, Moran was also a member of the University and Downtown Clubs and an honorary member of the New York Zoological Society. He died at his Mendham, New Jersey, home.

Moran, fondly called Uncle Dan, may have enjoyed the fact that his peers acknowledged him as the "Dean of Foundation Engineers." San Francisco paid him a wonderful compliment by calling Pier W-4 "Moran's Island." But, alas, the name did not stick. President Herbert Hoover described the Bay Bridge as "the greatest bridge yet erected by the human race," and the American Society of Civil Engineers named it in 1955 one of the Seven Wonders of Engineering. The society gave most credit to Purcell but did single out the unique pier, W-4, as a great advance in engineering design. The society noted the extreme difficulty of sinking a caisson of unprecedented size in a great depth of water, 100 feet, in a 7.5-knot current, so that work could be carried out, by virtue of compressed air chambers at a greater depth by chief diver Bill Reed and his men than ever before. Perhaps Mother Nature paid Moran the highest compliment in 1986, when the Loma Prieta Earthquake buckled the Bay Bridge east of Yerba Buena Island, at the cantilever section. Thanks to Moran's Island anchorage, the twin suspension spans rode out the seismic storm undamaged—for safety's sake, plans have been made to anchor the piers more firmly to the bedrock, which was found to be fractured in places, and to tether them down with steel cables—while the rest of the bridge required a major refitting.

• Small assessments of his career appear in *Who's Who in Engineering* (1936) and the *Transactions* of the American Societies of Mechanical and Civil Engineering in 1938. Moran is also treated in Henry Petroski, *Engineers of Dreams* (1995); H. Shirley Smith, *The World's Great Bridges* (1953); and Joseph Gies, *Bridges and Men* (1963). For overall description of the construction of the San Francisco–Oakland Bay Bridge, see Peter Stackpole, *The Bridge Builders* (1983); Harold Gilliam, *San Francisco Bay* (1957); and, especially, Richard H. Dillon, *High Steel* (1979).

RICHARD H. DILLON

MORAN, Edward (19 Aug. 1829–9 June 1901), painter, was born in Bolton, Lancashire, England, the son of Thomas Moran and Mary Higson, home handloom weavers. Edward was the elder brother of the painters Thomas, Peter, and John Moran. Moran joined his parents working at the handloom at an early age. The Moran parents, like other home textile workers of the time, supplemented their income with work from their children. In April 1844 the family immigrated to the United States, landing in Philadelphia, and soon settled in Baltimore, Maryland, where the elder Moran was employed in a textile factory. In 1845 Thomas Moran, Sr., moved the family to Kensington, Pennsylvania, near Philadelphia. After briefly trying other occupations, including carpentry and house painting, Edward Moran returned to the textile industry, not as a weaver but tending a power loom. After he had worked at the factory for seven years, Moran's supervisor (who, according to family legend, found Moran drawing instead of tending the loom) arranged an introduction to the prominent marine painter James Hamilton.

Apprenticeship was the standard career path for an aspiring artist. Hamilton, probably in need of an assistant for a major commission, took Moran on, and the two worked together for the next two years. When Hamilton left for London in 1854, Moran gravitated to the circle of the German-born landscape painter G. D. Paul Weber, who, though only six years older than Moran, was already an established artist.

Now living and working in a small studio in Philadelphia, Moran exhibited his first painting, *View of the Susquehanna* (unlocated), at the Pennsylvania Academy of Fine Arts in 1854. After working briefly as a lithographer with little success, in 1855 he exhibited four paintings at the Pennsylvania Academy and completed *The Storm* (1855, Washington and Lee University). It was in the same year that his younger brother Thomas came to live with him. By that time Edward was exhibiting a number of paintings at the Pennsylvania Academy each year, had received attention in the art magazines, and was patronized by a number of prominent Philadelphians. In 1857 he exhibited at the National Academy of Design in New York and the recently formed Washington Art Association. In 1858 he exhibited even farther from Philadelphia, at the Boston Athenaeum.

With his career taking hold, Moran married Elizabeth McManes in 1859, and his younger brother Peter came to live with the couple. The couple had two children, Edward Percy and John Leon, who became minor painters. Soon after Elizabeth's death, Moran married, in 1869, Annette Parmentier, with whom he had a son, Thomas Sidney, also a painter.

Moran and his brother Thomas traveled to England in early 1861. Edward toured the English coast, making numerous sketches before returning to Philadelphia in October. The following year he exhibited seventeen works at the Pennsylvania Academy. He took part in two charity exhibitions in the 1860s: the first, in 1864, to raise funds for Union soldiers fighting in the Civil War, and the second, in 1865, for the Artists' Fund Society.

Moran, who had been exhibiting with the Pennsylvania Academy since 1854, fell into violent disagreement with its board of directors in 1868 when he felt his works were given an unfavorable position in the annual exhibition. He expressed his anger by cutting one of his paintings from its frame and covering others with an opaque (but removable) wash. John Sartain, acting on behalf of the board, censured Moran until he formally apologized for his behavior. Drawing widespread press coverage, the incident increased attendance at the academy, leading the directors of the academy to propose extending the exhibition. Moran, however, withdrew his paintings on the appointed closing day and displayed them at a commercial gallery, which earned him even more publicity. Going further, he refused to apologize and resigned from the academy.

Though he continued to exhibit in Philadelphia, his exhibition opportunities there were constrained by his break with the Pennsylvania Academy, and Moran decided to move to New York. An exhibition and sale in 1871 of seventy-five paintings achieved the two goals of raising funds for French victims of the Franco-Prussian War and cutting down on the number of paintings to be stored or transported during his move. After settling in New York in 1872, Moran was elected an associate of the National Academy of Design.

In the presence of works by Martin Johnson Heade, John Frederick Kensett, and Sanford Robinson Gifford at the National Academy of Design, Moran began to experiment with luminism. The use of filtered light, hazy brushwork, and the portrayal of mood over subject became a characteristic trait of Moran's throughout the 1870s. One example of Moran's experiments with luminism is *Foggy Afternoon, New York Bay* (1872, Heckscher Museum of Art, Huntington, Long Island, N.Y.).

Moran met the sculptor Frédéric A. Bartholdi in early 1876, on the occasion of the dedication of the Frenchman's statue of the marquis de Lafayette in Union Square. It was then that Moran was introduced to Bartholdi's idea for a monumental statue, *Liberty Enlightening the World*, to be erected in New York harbor. Inspired by Bartholdi's plan, Moran executed the monumental painting *The Commerce of Nations Paying Homage to Liberty* (private collection), which was displayed in October 1876 in New York City at a reception in Bartholdi's honor. The painting was subsequently displayed at various fundraising functions for the American Committee on the Statue of Liberty.

Inspired to travel again to Europe, Moran auctioned sixty-five of his paintings and a large collection he owned of works by other artists. Realizing $12,000 from the sale, he left for France in 1877. His travels exposed him to the work of the French Barbizon School and other plein-air painters. Moran returned to New York sometime before the spring of 1879, when he exhibited his "European" paintings at the National Academy of Design and the Brooklyn Art Association.

The 1880s saw Moran hailed as the leading American marine painter and praised in the *Art Journal* (Sept. 1880) for his "simple and easy naturalism." Discussing his technique in a series of articles for *Art Amateur*, Moran discussed not only the technical details of marine painting but also his working habits and the opinion that marine painting is a "particular branch of landscape painting" subject to all the same difficulties. *Casco Bay, Coast of Maine* (c. 1889, Heckscher Museum) is an unusual work from Moran's marine painting in its lack of anecdotal detail.

In the 1890s Moran turned to historical marine scenes, a genre he had not generally worked in before. Thirteen canvases were completed between 1891 and 1898 depicting the maritime history of America. The series, which includes *Landing of Leif Eriksson in the New World in 1001*, *Return of the Conquerors*, and *Burning of the Frigate Philadelphia*, is now in the collection of the U.S. Naval Academy Museum in Annapolis.

At the time of his death in New York City, Moran was eulogized as "having no superior in America" as a painter of the sea. Moran's achievement was soon neglected, however, and his fame eclipsed by that of his brother Thomas.

• Moran's works are included in the collections of the U.S. Naval Academy; the Museum of the City of New York; the Philadelphia Athenaeum; and others. The Moran Family Papers are part of the Long Island Collection, East Hampton Free Library, N.Y. Moran's primary statement on his art is contained in two articles on marine painting for *Art Amateur* 19 (Oct. 1888): 101–3, and 19 (Nov. 1888): 127–28. Moran was profiled in "American Painter—Edward Moran," *Art Journal* (Sept. 1880): 258–59. Theodore Sutro, *Thirteen Chapters of American History Represented by the Edward Moran Series of Thirteen Historical Marine Paintings* (1905), includes a romantic sketch of the artist's life in unabashedly idolatrous terms; his account of Moran's early life is often at odds with the historical record. The catalog accompanying the exhibition at the Delaware Art Museum, *Edward Moran (1829–1901), American Marine and Landscape Painter* (1979), includes a useful biography by Paul D. Schweizer. A small exhibition brochure from the Heckscher Museum of Art, *The Moran Family* (1965), includes a useful family tree showing the relationships of the numerous artists in the Moran family. An obituary is in the *New York Times*, 10 June 1901.

MARTIN R. KALFATOVIC

MORAN, Eugene Francis (24 Mar. 1872–13 Apr. 1961), marine industry executive, was born in Brooklyn, New York, the son of Michael Moran, an Irish immigrant who had risen from poverty to found the Moran Towing and Transportation Company, Inc., and Margaret Haggerty. In 1888, when Eugene was sixteen, he began working in the family business as second deckhand on the tugboat *M. Moran*. His father determined, however, that Eugene was not physically suited to work on a tugboat. "You're not big and strong enough to handle six-inch and eight-inch fast lines and hawsers," his father told him. "I'm looking ahead to the day when you join me in the office, helping me run things" (*Tugboat*, p. 48).

Moran's father convinced him to learn the marine insurance business and take an increasingly active role in company management. Moran began work at the Lancashire Fire Insurance Company; after work he would run errands and generally familiarize himself with his father's company.

On reaching his mid-twenties, Moran assumed increasing personal and professional responsibilities. In 1897 he married Julia Claire Browne of Brooklyn; they had six children. The following year he took over the management of Moran Towing and Transportation after the previous manager left to form his own business. He continued to rely heavily on the advice of his father, and he also took over his father's role of organizing port celebrations involving Moran ships.

After becoming manager of the firm, Moran oversaw the rapid expansion of his company, which grew in proportion to the growth of the regional shipping trade. He participated in efforts to reduce congestion in the New York harbor, deepen the Coney Island Channel, and relocate coastal dumping grounds hazardous to transatlantic liners. Moran also promoted the use of diesel engines in tugs, converting some steam-driven tugs to diesel power in 1923, and he purchased his fleet's first diesel in 1936.

By the late 1890s, the Moran company operated tugs in New York and other harbors, and the firm grew into one of the largest tugboat companies in the world. Moran tugs towed huge ocean liners, barges, lighters, and scows. One of the firm's early big contracts, from 1900 to 1902, was for hauling the rock and dirt excavated from what became the tunnels of New York City's first subway. Under Moran's management, the company's annual revenues increased rapidly from $98,000 in 1898 to $786,000 in 1910. During the Spanish-American War, Moran tugs both docked and undocked army transports and did other general towing functions for military operations in New York harbor and at Fort Pond Bay at Montauk Point on Long Island, from which troops and supplies transferred back and forth to the Cuban front.

In 1906 Michael Moran died and Eugene became president of the Moran company; he became chairman of the board in 1930. He also was active in maritime, commercial, and educational civic institutions. He joined the Maritime Exchange, the National Board of Steam Navigation, and the Association for the Protection of Commerce. He also joined school boards and participated in the activities of the Friendly Sons of St. Patrick. Moran's main interest and fascination remained, however, with the tugboat.

Moran came into contact with Franklin D. Roosevelt in 1917 at the New York Yacht Club. Roosevelt, then assistant secretary of the navy, presided over a meeting of marine executives to organize a minesweeping effort to be based on Staten Island. In March 1917 Moran was commissioned a lieutenant in the naval reserve. For a brief while Moran was engaged in monitoring a dwelling that, it turned out, housed spies radioing information to German ships in the Atlantic. Next Moran joined the Special Board for Patrol Vessels. His specific duties there were to purchase and outfit fifty patrol boats to be used in England and France. In April 1918 Moran was relieved of active naval duty and began working with the Shipping Control Committee as consulting expert on harbor floating equipment.

In 1935, under his leadership as chairman of the Rivers and Harbors Committee of the Maritime Association of the Port of New York, the depth of port was increased. In response to the difficulty the large French ocean liner *Normandie* had in entering its slip at Pier 88 on its maiden voyage in June 1935, a French maritime executive wrote Moran and noted that with great advances in ship size and capacity, ship designers now had to consider the capabilities of ports in designing their ships, whereas earlier ports were designed to accommodate ships. Consequently, Moran recommended a deepening of the New York harbor so that it could more easily accommodate the large ships. Moran's efforts at deepening the port were successful, and by 1939 between Pier 80 and Pier 92 on the North River, an estuary of the Hudson, there was enough docking room for ten liners of 355,000 total tons.

From 1942 to 1959 Moran served as a commissioner of the Port of New York Authority. On 3 May 1953 he was appointed a member of the New York City Transit Authority, but he served on this body for only five months, in part because he had also been elected in 1954 to the position of vice chairman of the Port Authority. In 1959 the Port Authority honored Moran with its Distinguished Service Medal in recognition of his lifelong service to the "people, ships and cargoes of New York" (*New York Times*, 14 Apr. 1961). Moran loved the sea, and he led his life in the tradition of his father and his father's friends who lived for and on the sea; he enjoyed deep-sea fishing as well. A Roman Catholic and an active Knight of Malta, Moran died in Palm Beach, Florida, the day before he planned to return to his home in New York.

• The primary source on Moran is his autobiography, Eugene F. Moran with Louis Reid, *Tugboat: The Moran Story* (1956). Moran also wrote *Famous Harbors of the World* (1953), a children's book. An obituary is in the *New York Times*, 14 Apr. 1961.

CHRISTOPHER CASTANEDA

MORAN, Mary Nimmo (16 May 1842–25 Sept. 1899), painter and etcher, was born in Strathaven, Lanarkshire, Scotland, the daughter of Archibald Nimmo, who was probably a weaver, and Mary Scot. Her mother died when Nimmo was very young, and in 1847 her father brought her and her older brother to the United States. They settled in Crescentville, Pennsylvania, near Philadelphia, where she attended grammar school. In 1862 Nimmo married her neighbor, the landscape painter and etcher Thomas Moran, and settled in Philadelphia. He taught her to draw and paint. The couple had three children.

Moran maintained her painting and etching career around her family responsibilities. Her husband frequently traveled to the western United States to fulfill illustration commissions, so she took responsibility for the child care and the household and business management. She also assisted her husband in his work; her responsibilities included making the finished drawings from sketches he made in the field for many of his illustration commissions. Three etchings she made to reproduce his paintings were published in his 1886 exhibition catalog by Ortgies & Company, New York. She occasionally taught drawing and etching in her studio, including a class for children in the late 1870s.

In 1879 Moran produced her first etchings in Easton, Pennsylvania, near Philadelphia, where she lived for the summer. After a ten-year residence in Newark, New Jersey, the Morans moved in 1881 to New York; her etchings from this period reflect Manhattan's transition from a rural to an urban landscape. Influenced by peaceful summers spent in East Hampton, Long Island, in 1884 the family built a home there. Moran traveled with her husband to the West in 1872 and to Florida in 1877 and 1887. On a trip to England, Scotland, and Wales in 1882, they met John Ruskin, who bought many of their etchings. They went again to Europe in 1886. Moran's subjects included scenes abroad as well as in Florida, but she is best known for her landscapes of East Hampton. She died in East Hampton of typhoid fever.

Moran was the first woman elected a fellow of the Royal Society of Painter-Etchers, London. She was one of only two women who were members of the prestigious New York Etching Club. Twice her etchings were published as frontispieces to New York Etching Club exhibition catalogs. The curator, Sylvester Koehler, published her etching *Solitude* in the *American Art Review* (1881). He selected four of her etchings for publication in deluxe etching portfolios (*Original Etchings by American Artists* [1883], *Twenty Original American Etchings* [1885], *Gems of American Etchers* [1885], and *American Etchings* [1886]) and published *Twilight* as the frontispiece for the catalog of the second venue of the Women Etchers of America exhibition at the Union League Club, New York (1888). She also produced drawings to illustrate the *Illustrated Library of Favorite Song* (1873) and *The Aldine Almanac* (1874).

Moran exhibited her paintings at the National Academy of Design and the Pennsylvania Academy of the Fine Arts. More frequently exhibiting her etchings, she showed regularly with the New York Etching Club, including eleven in their first show in 1882. The next year she exhibited seventeen with the Philadelphia Society of Etchers. Koehler selected fifty-four of her etchings for the first museum exhibition of women artists' work, the "Women Etchers of America," in 1887 at the Museum of Fine Arts, Boston. She also exhibited in several world fairs, including in the Fine Arts Building and the Woman's Building at the 1893 World's Columbian Exposition. Christian Klackner produced an exhibition and catalog of Mary and Thomas Moran's etchings in 1889. The first comprehensive listing of Mary Moran's work in etching, it catalogs fifty-eight prints.

Moran was the most prominent of the many women who participated in the etching revival of the 1880s. Critics praised her etchings for having the richest painterlike qualities of any by an American artist. Her dramatic, atmospheric use of light and shade she acquired from the influence of John Ruskin and J. A. M. Whistler. Her plates combine etching with more painterly techniques of mezzotint, scotch stone, sandpaper, and roulette. In two of her most popular prints, *Twilight—East Hampton* (1880) and *'Tween the Gloaming and the Mirk When the Kye Come Hame* (1883), a title that reflects her Scottish heritage, she combines the use of the roulette, a wheel used in engraving that when rolled over the plate breaks the etching ground with patterns of tiny dots to create texture; sandpaper and scotch stone, both of which rough up the plate to create tonal effects; and retroussage, a method of carefully wiping the ink on the plate with a rag to create the effects of paint. One writer called her *Twilight—East Hampton*, which strongly exhibits these expressive qualities of light "in the greatest profusion," the "high-watermark of etching in America." Etchings like *Solitude* (1880) and *Haunt of the Muskrat—East Hampton*, one of her series of linear etchings from 1884, were highly regarded for their poetic, intimate portrayal of the quiet aspects of nature.

Because her work was considered bolder than that of her husband, her etchings were often compared to a supposedly masculine aesthetic. The critic Mariana van Rensselear wrote in 1883 that *Solitude* was a "preeminently manly" piece of work. She said Moran's work would "never reveal her sex—according, that is, to the popular idea of feminine characteristics" and was "above all things, direct, emphatic, bold—exceeding in these qualities, perhaps that of any of her male co-workers." Several years after her death another writer declared that her plates "had about them no suggestion of a woman's hand."

Moran was one of hundreds of women who made etching a significant part of their professional artistic production in the late nineteenth and early twentieth centuries. While she represents a traditional approach to training for women, having access because she was a member of an artist's family, her work is progressive in terms of boldness and experimentation. As the producer of perhaps the most significant and memorable prints during the 1880s etching revival, she inspired the vitality of the next etching revival, in the early twentieth century.

• Archival materials are in the Thomas Moran Biographical Collection, East Hampton Free Library, East Hampton, N.Y., and the Thomas Moran Studio Collection, Thomas Gilcrease Institute of American History and Art, Tulsa, Okla. The Thomas Gilcrease Institute, the East Hampton Free Library, and the New York Public Library have the largest collections of her etchings. The most thorough biographies and descriptions of her etchings are Marilyn G. Francis, "Mary Nimmo Moran: Painter-Etcher," *Woman's Art Journal* 4 (Fall 1983/Winter 1984): 114–19, and Thomas Gilcrease Institute of American History and Art, *Prints of Nature: Poetic Etchings of Mary Nimmo Moran* (1984). See also Thurman Wilkins, *Thomas Moran, Artist of the Mountains* (1966), and Amy O. Bassford, ed., *Home-thoughts, from Afar: Letters of Thomas Moran to Mary Nimmo Moran* (1967). Nineteenth-century accounts of her career include A. DeMontaigu, "A Pen Picture of Mrs. M. Nimmo Moran," *Art Stationer* 1 (July 1888): 4–6, and Morris T. Everett, "The Etchings of Mrs. Mary Nimmo Moran," *Brush and Pencil* 8 (Apr. 1901): 1–16. For descriptions of her career in the context of the etching revival, see Phyllis Peet, "The Emergence of American Women Printmakers in the Late Nineteenth Century" (Ph.D. diss., Univ. of California, Los Angeles, 1987) and *American Women of the Etching Revival* (1988). An obituary is in the *East Hampton Star*, 29 Sept. 1899.

PHYLLIS PEET

MORAN, Thomas (12 Jan. 1837–25 Aug. 1926), artist, was born in Bolton, Lancashire, England, the son of Thomas Moran, a weaver, and Mary Higson. In 1844 Moran left England with his mother and siblings to join his father, who had recently immigrated to Philadelphia. After an elementary education, he was indentured in 1853 to a wood engraving firm, a position he left in 1856. Moran then worked closely with his elder brother Edward, also a painter, and with him became an informal student of Philadelphia marine artist James Hamilton. Hamilton may have introduced them to the work of J. M. W. Turner and to a belief in close study of nature as the foundation for painting. Moran exhibited landscapes at the Pennsylvania Academy of the Fine Arts for the first time in 1856, was elected an academician in 1861, and continued to exhibit there through 1905. In the summer of 1860 he began an enduring practice of travel with a journey to the Pictured

Rocks on Lake Superior. During 1861–1862 Moran and his brother Edward lived in London, where the former devoted himself to a study of Turner's work.

Moran returned to Philadelphia in the summer of 1862 and soon after began to teach at the Philadelphia School of Design for Women in order to supplement his income from the sale of pictures. In 1863 he married Mary Nimmo, who later described herself as a lifelong student of her husband; they had three children. Moran and his wife formed an artistic partnership. They frequently traveled together, worked closely as printmakers, and created an artistic domestic environment that inspired one of their children to become an artist.

In June 1866 Moran traveled with his family to Europe and settled in Paris for nine months to paint and to study art. Although he sought out J. B. C. Corot and enjoyed an afternoon of discussion with the aged artist, Moran tried to distance himself from European models in order to paint American subjects in what he deemed an American style. The Morans concluded their European trip with a stay in Italy and traveled over the Alps back to Paris, where Moran's burgeoning reputation was acknowledged by the exhibition of two of his paintings, *Children of the Mountain* (1866, Anschutz Collection, Denver) and *Autumn on the Conemaugh, in Pennsylvania* (location unknown), in the American section of the Fine Arts Department at the Exposition Universelle. He also showed *Une forêt en Amérique* (location unknown) in the concurrently running Salon of 1867.

After returning home from Europe, Moran turned for inspiration to American romantic literature, such as Henry Wadsworth Longfellow's *The Song of Hiawatha* (1855). He set literary subjects in landscapes that reveal a close observation of nature and yet remain otherworldly, as in *The Spirit of the Indian* (1869, Philbrook Art Center, Tulsa, Okla.).

While in Philadelphia, Moran began what became a long association with *Scribner's Monthly*, one of whose editors, Richard Watson Gilder, had been a boyhood friend. Moran's illustrations appeared in *Scribner's* beginning with the first issue in November 1870, but his greatest opportunity was a commission to illustrate N. P. Langford's series of articles on the newly explored Yellowstone area of the Wyoming Territory, which appeared in the magazine in May and June 1871. Moran's career took a dramatic turn with this assignment, and he asked to join Ferdinand V. Hayden's governmental expedition to the Yellowstone. From the last week in July through about 10 August 1871 Moran and the expedition's photographer, William Henry Jackson, collaborated in selecting scenes to paint and photograph as they explored what soon after became major sites of Yellowstone National Park.

To finance the trip Moran had borrowed money from *Scribner's* publisher Roswell Smith (he used his painting *Children of the Mountain* as collateral) and from financier Jay Cooke, one of the directors of the Northern Pacific Railroad, to whom he promised watercolors of the region. Through his ties to the publishing industry, Moran established connections with eastern investors in the business of art and exploration. Editors were anxious to sell magazines, railroad investors were eager to encourage travel along their routes, and explorers needed increased governmental funding to continue their work. Each wanted imagery to enhance the texts they published, which, in part, were intended to convince legislators and the public of the value of expansionist policies. It was a mutually beneficial arrangement since publishing, rail, and exploration businesses sought to authenticate their texts with pictures, and Moran saw a chance to further his career by being the first artist in Yellowstone, a region that had become legendary almost overnight. Although other painters had traveled in the West, Albert Bierstadt's western travels were the only ones that had been widely reported in the press and that had attracted the patronage of railroad barons. Moran may have hoped to identify himself with Yellowstone as Bierstadt had linked his success to Yosemite.

Moran returned to the East at the end of the summer and by late autumn 1871 had moved his family to Newark, New Jersey, to be closer to New York City's publishing industry, from which he anticipated increased work. Established in a new studio, Moran used his own field sketches and Jackson's photographs as resources for illustrations for several periodicals (among them *Scribner's*, *Aldine*, and *Harper's Monthly*) and for watercolors for exhibition and sale. With his highly finished watercolors, which he often sold as pieces in a series, Moran gained a range of new patrons, including Mrs. George Franklin Edmunds, the wife of the senator from Vermont who advocated passage of the Yellowstone bill, and William Blackmore, a British investor in western land schemes and one of the principal financiers of the Denver and Rio Grande Railway.

Moran also painted a large (7′×12′) canvas titled *The Grand Cañon of the Yellowstone* (1872, U.S. Department of the Interior, on extended loan to the National Museum of American Art). The work, which was the first landscape the government hung in the Capitol, was purchased in June 1872, just three months after Congress voted to establish the Yellowstone area as the country's first national park.

A large number of commissions in 1872 prevented Moran from accepting either Hayden's invitation to spend a second summer in the Yellowstone or the offer of John Wesley Powell, another leader of the so-called "Great Surveys," to accompany his Colorado River expedition. But in August 1872 Moran and his wife made a hurried trip west, primarily to see the Great Salt Lake and to sketch scenes along the rail route. They also made a side trip to Yosemite Valley, by then a lively tourist area made popular in part by Bierstadt's paintings.

By 1873 Moran was in demand as an exploration artist. His work had been widely published, and *The Grand Cañon of the Yellowstone* had been favorably reviewed in newspapers and journals. Major Powell asked Moran to join his expedition's photographer,

John K. Hillers, on his governmental survey of the Rocky Mountain region along the Rio Virgin and the Colorado River in the summer of 1873. This arrangement served each of them: Moran had reported an "intense desire to see the Grand Cañon [of the Colorado]" (Moran to Hayden, 28 June 1873, National Archives), and Powell needed illustrations to accompany the narratives of his explorations.

Moran discovered an ideally dramatic theme for a new painting in a ferocious thunderstorm that he and J. E. Colburn, a writer for the *New York Times*, witnessed when they accompanied Powell to the plateau bearing the major's name. *The Chasm of the Colorado* (1873–1874, U.S. Department of the Interior, on extended loan to the National Museum of American Art) is a forbidding scene that repels rather than entices a viewer's entry. Moran departed from the precedent he had set in *The Grand Cañon of the Yellowstone*, where he lured viewers through a shadowed foreground with engaging details to join two figures at an overlook in contemplation of the sunlit canyon. In contrast, by propelling viewers of *Chasm* directly into the picture's turbulent drama, Moran emphasized the river's simultaneously destructive and regenerative forces and echoed Powell's belief in the necessity of acknowledging the antithesis of a river raging through otherwise arid land. By July 1874, when Congress purchased the *Chasm* to hang next to the *Yellowstone* in the Senate lobby, Moran had successfully challenged Bierstadt's domination of western landscape painting, and in doing so he propounded his ideas about the past and future of the West to a national audience.

In August 1874 Moran joined another of Hayden's expeditions, this time for the sole purpose of seeing the Mountain of the Holy Cross in Colorado. Moran apparently yearned to be the first painter to reach this remote site (in an area that Hayden's men had surveyed and photographed only the previous year), and Hayden must have anticipated another monumental Moran canvas to provide documentation and support for his ambitious surveys. From the few sketches Moran drew under arduous climbing conditions, his vivid memory of the site, and Jackson's photograph of the year before, he created a composite view in *Mountain of the Holy Cross* (1875, Gene Autry Western Heritage Museum, Los Angeles), which won a gold medal at the 1876 Philadelphia Centennial Exposition. Moran's journey to the mountain resembled a pilgrimage to a holy site, and the painting, in which clouds part to reveal the mountain's deep, snow-filled gorges in the shape of a cross, reinforced popular views of this inaccessible place as one that embodied the Christian sanctity of American land, a subject that had preoccupied many painters before him. Moran sent *Mountain of the Holy Cross* on tour in England, where in 1880 it was purchased by William A. Bell, a founder of the Denver and Rio Grande Railway. Bell displayed it prominently in his house in Manitou, Colorado, and made it available for the public to see.

Eighteen seventy-six marked a high point in Moran's career, with publication of his watercolors in Louis Prang's portfolio of fifteen chromolithographs, *The Yellowstone Park, and the Mountain Regions of Portions of Idaho, Nevada, Colorado, and Utah.* This deluxe edition marked the first time Moran's published work appeared in color. Prang engaged Hayden to authenticate the scientific accuracy of the published images and to write the accompanying commentary. The portfolio was heralded as a superb technical achievement and contributed dramatically to Moran's reputation.

As he continued to travel and sketch in the American West, Moran responded to opportunities for other illustration commissions and sought out new subjects. His extensive and varied travels in the United States and abroad mirrored the practices of other American artists in the decades following the Civil War. Frederic E. Church, whom Moran greatly admired, Martin Johnson Heade, and Bierstadt, Moran's rival in the realm of western landscape, all traveled as ceaselessly. In 1877 and again in 1887 and 1891 Moran and his wife visited Fort George Island at the mouth of the St. Johns River in Florida. In 1881 Moran and his family traveled to Niagara Falls. They spent most of 1882 in the British Isles and for three months stayed in London, where they met critic John Ruskin, from which followed a brief correspondence. In 1883 Moran took a sketching trip to Mexico, the first of several visits. Journeys to Venice, Italy, in 1886 and 1890 provided him visual experiences that inspired some of his most dramatically colorful and ethereal views, somewhat reminiscent of Turner's.

Moran moved his family to New York City in 1881 and participated even more fully in the art world there. His memberships in artistic social organizations included the Century Association, the Lotos Club, and the Salmagundi Club. He also belonged to the American Society of Painters in Water Colors and was a founding member in 1877 of the New York Etching Club and of the Society of American Artists. Moran was elected an associate member of the National Academy of Design in 1881, a full academician in 1884, and exhibited there from 1866 through 1900. In 1881 he was elected a Fellow of the Royal Society of Painter-Etchers and Engravers in London, and in 1889 he served on the jury for the American entries to the Paris Exposition Universelle. In addition to an award presented at the Centennial Exposition, Moran's work won medals at the 1891 Pan-American Exposition in St. Louis, the 1893 Chicago World's Columbian Exposition, the 1901 Pan-American Exposition in Buffalo, and the 1902 American Art Society in Philadelphia.

On a visit to East Hampton, New York, in 1878 Moran took up etching, and over the next decade he enjoyed critical and financial success with his prints, culminating in 1889 at the Klackner Gallery in New York in a joint exhibition with his wife, who was gaining recognition as one of the country's finest etchers. Mary Nimmo Moran was accepted as the first woman member of both the New York Etching Club and the Royal Society of Painter-Etchers and Engravers. Her work won a gold medal at the World's Columbian Exposition in 1893. After 1878 the Morans spent part of each summer in East Hampton, and in 1884 they designed and had built a house and studio on property they had purchased two years before.

By providing images for railroad pamphlets in return for funding for his first western trip and gratis travel, Moran entwined his career with the post–Civil War growth of the rail industry. Beginning in 1853 leaders of each of the four governmentally funded Pacific Railroad Surveys hired artists to accompany their parties and to provide images for publications of prospective routes (twelve such illustrated volumes appeared between 1856 and 1861). But it was not until after completion of the transcontinental rail route in 1869 that the rail companies fully exploited visual advertising in posters, pamphlets, and guidebooks dedicated to promoting the scenic wonders of the West. Moran was closely connected to the Denver and Rio Grande Railway, an association that had begun in 1872 with the sale of watercolors to Blackmore and continued in 1881 with a special train trip organized to provide Moran, Jackson, and writer Ernest Ingersoll with comfortable access to sites in Colorado and northern New Mexico. They, in turn, were expected to extol the area's scenic wonders in illustrations for forthcoming publications. Many of Moran's views of Colorado were reproduced in the Denver and Rio Grande's promotional literature during the 1880s and 1890s, none more often than his *Mountain of the Holy Cross*.

Other rail companies also sponsored trips for Moran, including the Union Pacific Railroad (through Donner Pass, Lake Tahoe, the mountains of northeastern Nevada, and the Wasatch Mountains of Utah) in 1879, the Baltimore and Ohio Railroad in 1881, and the Atchison, Topeka, and Santa Fe Railroad in 1892. After 1901 the Santa Fe promoted its exclusive spur to the Grand Canyon by sponsoring Moran's trips there and by purchasing his paintings, from which they made souvenir reproductive prints as well as illustrations for their guidebooks. In the early years of the twentieth century Moran's name was linked with the Grand Canyon in the same way it had been with Yellowstone in the 1870s.

Moran did not limit his travel to areas accessible by rail. He made several arduous journeys to remote areas in the West, among them the Tetons in 1879 and Devil's Tower in 1892. Moran published an account of this last trip, made with Jackson, in the *Century Illustrated Monthly Magazine* (1894).

Following his wife's death in 1899 Moran traveled almost every summer. He returned to favorite spots, especially the Grand Canyon of the Colorado, Venice, and England. In 1916 he began to spend winters in Santa Barbara, California, and he moved there permanently in 1922.

During the last decades of his life, in which he produced a large body of work, Moran continued his practice of painting the subjects that had established his reputation, particularly Yellowstone, the Grand Canyon, and Green River, Wyoming. He simultaneously broadened his range with a monumental painting of icebergs, *Spectres from the North* (1890, Thomas Gilcrease Institute of American History and Art, Tulsa, Okla.). Moran's paintings did not acknowledge development in the West, either the increasing public use of the parks or the growth of towns that the railroad had opened. Rather, as revealed by his devotion for more than four decades to the subject of the cliffs of Green River, he presented a pristine wilderness inhabited, if at all, by explorers and American Indians who are obviously awed by the vision of untouched wilderness, as Moran intended his public to be.

Moran wrote little concerning his aesthetic principles, but the few statements he made help to reconcile the apparent contradiction between replication and invention in his landscapes. He stated, "I place no value upon literal transcripts from Nature. My general scope is not realistic; all my tendencies are towards idealisation. . . . Topography in Art is valueless" (G. W. Sheldon, "American Painters: Thomas Moran and Joseph Rusling Meeker," *Art Journal*, n.s., 5 [Feb. 1879], p. 43), but also, "I have to have knowledge. I must know the geology. I must know the rocks and the trees and the atmosphere and the mountain torrents and the birds that fly in the blue ether above me" (Thomas Moran, "Knowledge a Prime Requisite in Art," *Brush and Pencil* 12 [Apr. 1903], p. 14). Moran harmonized these two statements in his own work, in which the foundation of firsthand experience in nature is subsumed in the final, imaginative painting constructed wholly in the studio. So even as he called for scientists to verify the geographical accuracy of his painted rocks, Moran allowed himself quite literally to move mountains in his compositions. This is most notable in *Mountain of the Holy Cross*, whose foreground waterfall is in actuality on the opposite side of the mountain yet whose "truth," Moran believed, went beyond literal transcription to an expression of a natural Christianity.

Moran's resignation in 1879 from the Society of American Artists signaled his aesthetic separation from the younger artists who comprised most of the society's membership. Beginning in the late 1870s, moody, atmospheric, French-inspired painting held sway among the avant-garde and dominated critical writing on art. Moran was hostile toward the newer movements in European and American art, deriding Barbizon painting and impressionism. Nonetheless, his landscapes of nonwestern subjects, such as those of East Hampton and the few he devoted to urban industry, evince a lyrical harmony critics recognized as different from the obvious drama of his western scenes, which were coming under increased criticism. But since Moran's career had been built and was sustained on images of celebrated western sites, he continued to be categorized as a traditional western artist. He seemed only to confirm this association by becoming a founding member in 1901 of the Society of the Men Who Paint the West and by being named an honorary member of Painters of the West in 1924. His loss of support among prominent critics did nothing to quell popular interest in his printed and painted work.

Moran, unlike the critics, did not divide his work into categories. Throughout his career he viewed his paintings as embodiments of essential characteristics of the places he interpreted: the fantastic geologic formations of Yellowstone, the almost incomprehensible gorge of the Grand Canyon of the Colorado, the aquatic dream of Venice, and the lyrical atmosphere of East Hampton.

Through government patronage and widespread reproduction of his work, Moran's reputation extended beyond the small group of people who could afford to purchase his paintings. His monumental pictures of naturally dramatic sites and his easel paintings that evoke a land of perpetually pristine beauty shaped popular perception of the West in the late nineteenth and early twentieth century. Increasing scholarly attention is being given to the popularization of his western images in order to understand the role the works played in endorsing expansionist values. Yet other examples of Moran's oeuvre, such as his field sketches, poetic landscapes of eastern Long Island and Venice, and etchings, should also stand with his oils of the West in any assessment of his seventy-year career, sustained in productivity until the last months of his life. He died in Santa Barbara.

• Moran's papers are at the Thomas Gilcrease Institute of American History and Art in Tulsa, Okla., and at the East Hampton Free Library in East Hampton, N.Y. Some letters have been published in Amy O. Bassford, ed., *Home-Thoughts from Afar: Letters of Thomas Moran to Mary Nimmo Moran* (1967), with an introduction and notes by Fritiof Fryxell. The most important source for biographical information is Thurman Wilkins, *Thomas Moran: Artist of the Mountains* (1966). On his western work see William H. Truettner, "'Scenes of Majesty and Enduring Interest': Thomas Moran Goes West," *Art Bulletin* 58, no. 2 (June 1976): 241–59; Carol Clark, *Thomas Moran: Watercolors of the American West* (1980); and Joni Kinsey, *Thomas Moran and the Surveying of the American West* (1992). On his watercolors and drawings see Thomas S. Fern, *The Drawings and Watercolors of Thomas Moran (1837–1926)* (1976); and on his prints see Anne Morand and Nancy Friese, *The Prints of Thomas Moran in the Thomas Gilcrease Institute of American History and Art, Tulsa, Oklahoma* (1986). An obituary is in the Washington, D.C., *Evening Star*, 27 Aug. 1926.

CAROL CLARK

MORAWETZ, Victor (3 Apr. 1859–18 May 1938), lawyer, was born in Baltimore, Maryland, the son of Leopold Francis Morawetz, a physician, and Elise Meyer. Morawetz spent his early years in Baltimore and, with his younger brother, was sent to Europe when he was fourteen. For three years his education was largely unsupervised, although he spent at least some time at the Sorbonne. Morawetz also spent several months in Spain as an aide-de-camp to one of the leaders of the Carlist revolution. He returned to the United States in 1876 and in September matriculated at the Harvard Law School. He completed its two-year course and graduated with an LL.B. in 1878.

For two years Morawetz practiced law in Chicago but was not a success. He wrote his sister, "I should be as much surprised to see a client's footprint in the dust before my office door as Robinson Crusoe was when he saw the footprints in the sand of his man Friday." Morawetz became convinced that a modern textbook on corporations law was needed and persuaded his father to support him for a year and a half while he wrote it. In 1882, at the age of twenty-three, Morawetz published *A Treatise on the Law of Private Corporations Other Than Charitable*. With this work he began the first of his three careers, that of legal scholar. Morawetz produced a two-volume second edition, roughly twice the length of the first edition, in 1886. Although he never revised the treatise after 1886, Morawetz was an active scholar throughout his life, publishing numerous law review articles on corporate and financial matters and two other books, *Banking and Currency Problems in the United States* (1909) and *Elements of the Law of Contracts* (1927). He lectured on corporation law at Columbia Law School from 1888 to 1890 while maintaining a full-time law practice.

Private Corporations quickly became the standard work on corporations. Even though the first edition was only four years old, James Barr Ames of the Harvard Law School wrote in 1887 that it was "generally conceded to be the best treatise" on corporations. In 1911 the legal historian Charles Warren included *Private Corporations* as one of thirty-seven important treatises published between 1870 and 1900. As late as 1932 Berle and Means called Morawetz the standard commentator on matters of classical corporate law. The genius of *Private Corporations* was in its structure and the timing of its publication. Prior corporations treatises had focused primarily on municipal and charitable corporations; private business corporations were quite rare before the Civil War. From 1870 on the modern business corporation took on the prominence and power it has today. Morawetz was the first to treat thoroughly the legal problems of these entities. Morawetz recognized that corporations were really aggregations of the shareholders that owned them, even though the law considered them to be separate entities. He thought much of corporate law could only be understood by appreciating the aggregate nature of corporations rather than insisting that corporations always be regarded as entities. Morawetz's recognition of this dual nature of the corporation helped make his treatise immensely useful both to practitioners and academics because it gave them a workable framework for analyzing corporate law issues.

With the success of *Private Corporations*, Morawetz moved in 1882 to New York, where he quickly began his second major career as an important corporate lawyer at the New York bar. His book brought him referrals from other lawyers, and one such referral was Andrew Carnegie. Morawetz remained Carnegie's personal attorney until he retired from the bar. His intellect and the Carnegie connection helped him establish a professional relationship with one of the premier law firms of the city, the predecessor of Cravath,

Swaine & Moore. That relationship became more intense, and in 1887, at the age of twenty-eight, he joined the firm as a partner. In 1890 his name was added to the firm's.

Morawetz spent nine years with the firm, primarily involving himself with complex railroad reorganizations. The railroads had issued bonds to finance the expansion of their track, but many defaulted in the depression of the early 1890s. The solution was to change the railroads' capital structure to ensure that creditors, bondholders, and stockholders all shared the cost of default and to provide a structure that promised the railroads a realistic chance of financial success. These reorganizations were complex both because of the difficulty in accommodating the different economic interests among the factions and because many different jurisdictions regulated railroads and their bonds.

The most important railroad reorganization Morawetz handled was for the Atchison, Topeka & Santa Fe Railroad. After three years' work on the reorganization, he left private legal practice in 1896, at the age of thirty-seven, and became general counsel for the railroad. Thus he began his final career, that of railroad executive. He quickly became chairman of the board, a post he held for thirteen years, until 1909. Louis D. Brandeis, whom Morawetz knew at Harvard, called him the "controlling intellect" of the Santa Fe's great economic success. On occasion Morawetz undertook other interesting corporate matters; most notably he drafted many of the documents establishing United States Steel Corporation in 1901.

In 1909 Morawetz retired to an estate near Charleston, South Carolina, where he died. During his nearly thirty years of retirement, he remained engaged in intellectual matters, writing two books and several articles. He was particularly interested in the teaching of economics as a separate discipline at the college level. He was also among the influential lawyers who founded the American Law Institute in 1922. He married Violet Westcott in 1911; she died in 1918. Morawetz married Marjorie Nott in 1924. He had no children in either marriage.

Although for twenty-seven years Morawetz was an important lawyer and corporate leader whose prominence carried through his retirement for almost thirty years more, his enduring achievement was finished when he was twenty-three and had spent barely four years in the law. *The Law of Private Corporations* provided the first satisfactory framework for understanding the legal nature of business corporations. That framework influenced the practitioners and judges of Morawetz's day and was the starting point for two generations of legal scholars interested in corporations. It remains the primary source for discovering late nineteenth-century conceptions of corporate law and remains an intellectually rich resource for fundamental corporate questions.

• The best single source on Morawetz's life and legal career is Robert T. Swaine, *The Cravath Firm and Its Predecessors, 1819–1947*, vol. 1 (1946). Another helpful source is George Rublee, "Memorial of Victor Morawetz," *Year Book, Association of the Bar of the City of New York* (1938). Obituaries are in the *New York Times* and the *Charleston (S.C.) News and Courier*, 19 May 1938.

ERIC A. CHIAPPINELLI

MORDECAI, Alfred (3 Jan. 1804–23 Oct. 1887), army officer and military technician, was born in Warrenton, North Carolina, the son of Jacob Mordecai and Rebecca Myers. His father was founder and principal of an academy that Mordecai attended. He received appointment to the U.S. Military Academy in 1819 and graduated first in his class. Appointed second lieutenant on 1 July 1823, Mordecai remained at West Point as assistant professor of philosophy and engineering until 1825. He subsequently assumed the duties of assistant engineer during the construction of Fortress Monroe and Fort Calhoun in Virginia. In 1828 Mordecai transferred to Washington, D.C., as assistant to the chief of engineers and functioned in this capacity until 30 May 1832, when he was promoted to captain. Having distinguished himself in all his assignments, Mordecai also became one of ten officers selected to serve in the newly organized Ordnance Department.

Mordecai served in the Ordnance Department for the next twenty-nine years and established himself as one of the most scientifically minded officers of the army. His efforts proved instrumental in advancing and refining U.S. military technology, particularly the artillery. Mordecai commanded the important government arsenals at Washington, D.C., in 1833 and from 1855 to 1857; Frankford, Pennsylvania, in 1836; and Watervliet, New York, from 1857 to 1861. At these arsenals he conducted extensive research on weapons, ammunition, and ballistics and also authored a number of scientific treatises, including *The Ordnance Manual* (1841), *Report of Experiments on Gunpowder* (1845), and *Second Report of Experiments on Gunpowder* (1849). In 1839 Mordecai was appointed to the Ordnance Board, which was created to standardize army weaponry and which helped promulgate the first uniform system of artillery. These principles were enunciated in his influential tract *Artillery for the United States Land Service* (1849). By 1842 Mordecai was functioning as assistant inspector of arsenals and subsequently served as assistant to the chief of ordnance. The following year he was on the Board of Visitors to the U.S. Military Academy. During the Mexican War he commanded the Washington arsenal, distinguishing himself in the shipping of valuable ordnance supplies, and received brevet promotion to major on 30 May 1848. On 31 December 1854 he became a full major at the Ordnance Department, and by 1860 he also served on a board appointed to revise the curriculum at West Point.

In addition to his technical duties, Mordecai was dispatched on a number of important missions abroad. In 1840 Secretary of War Joel R. Poinsett sent him to Europe, where he studied, evaluated, and reported on the manufacture of weapons. In 1855 Secretary of War

Jefferson Davis sent Mordecai to report on the Crimean war in concert with Major Robert Delafield and Captain George B. McClellan (1826–1885). His insightful observations were subsequently published by order of Congress as the *Military Commission to Europe in 1855 and 1856* (1860). Among Mordecai's recommendations was adoption of the bronze "Napoleon" cannon, which became a standard ordnance piece in both Union and Confederate armies. Mordecai also visited Mexico in 1855 at the behest of President Franklin Pierce to investigate fraudulent war claims.

The commencement of the Civil War in 1861 forced Mordecai to undertake a monumental decision. Unwilling to abandon his country and reluctant to take up arms against the South, he resigned his commission on 5 May 1861. Mordecai remained in Philadelphia throughout the war, teaching mathematics. In 1865 he secured appointment as assistant engineer on the Mexico and Pacific Railroad but departed in 1867 following the overthrow of the Emperor Maximilian. Mordecai returned to Philadelphia and found employment as secretary and treasurer of the Pennsylvania Railroad Company. He held this position until his death at Philadelphia.

Mordecai's career exemplifies the growth of professionalism and technology in the U.S. Army. With intelligence and foresight, he oversaw the development, testing, and evaluation of increasingly complex weapons. Metallurgy, production, and uniformity were all advanced during his tenure at the Ordnance Department. Mordecai's precise methodology, coupled with effective writing, greatly contributed to the growing body of professional literature on that subject. The qualitative improvement in American artillery, amply demonstrated during the Civil War, was a direct outcome of Mordecai's quiet and persistent efforts. Mordecai married (date unknown) Sarah Hays and had six children. One son, Alfred Mordecai, Jr., attended West Point, fought for the Union, and like his father, enjoyed a lengthy and distinguished military career.

• Mordecai's official correspondence is in RG 156, Office of the Chief of Ordnance, National Archives. Large collections of personal papers are at the Manuscript Division, Library of Congress; Syracuse University Library, Syracuse, N.Y.; and the American Jewish Historical Society, Waltham, Mass. The only detailed study remains Stanley L. Falk, "Soldier-Technologist: Major Alfred Mordecai and the Beginnings of Science in the United States Army" (Ph.D. diss., Georgetown Univ., 1959). See also James A. Padgett, ed., "The Life of Alfred Mordecai as Related by Himself," *North Carolina Historical Review* 22 (1945): 58–108. For an overview of his impact on military ordnance consult Falk, "Artillery for the Land Service," *Military Affairs* 28 (1964): 94–122; and William E. Birkhimer, *Historical Sketch of the Artillery, U.S. Army* (1899).

JOHN C. FREDRIKSEN

MORE, Nicholas (1638?–1687), colonial Pennsylvania politician and officeholder, was born in England. His parents have not been identified. He was educated as a physician, and throughout his life he was identified as a "doctor of physic." Although he remained an Anglican, his marriage in 1670 to Mary Hedge, the daughter of a prosperous Quaker merchant of London, gave him entry into the group of wealthy Quakers interested in American colonization. In October 1681 he purchased 10,000 acres of land in Pennsylvania from William Penn. He also subscribed £300 sterling to the Free Society of Traders, a joint-stock company organized by Penn to promote the economic development of Pennsylvania, and was elected president of the company. In April 1682 he witnessed the proposed constitution, or frame of government, that Penn issued for the new colony, and in May of that year he witnessed the Laws Agreed Upon in England, a fundamental legal code to accompany the frame of government, which included a ratification of the corporate charter that Penn had granted to the Free Society of Traders.

More arrived in Pennsylvania with his family in October 1682. He evidently expected to play a prominent role in the government of the colony, as the Free Society's corporate charter included a guarantee of three seats for its officers on the provincial council, with one seat presumably assured to More as the company's president. Accordingly, More quickly became involved in the public life of Pennsylvania. As a representative of Philadelphia County, More dominated the first legislative assembly held by Penn in December 1682; although it is now recognized that More was not the Speaker of that assembly, he clearly managed its daily proceedings. Nevertheless, despite the presence of More and other officers of the Free Society as representatives, the assembly failed to ratify both Penn's proposed frame of government and the Laws Agreed Upon in England. Deprived of a seat on the provincial council by the assembly's failure to ratify the Free Society's charter, More also failed to gain a place in either the provincial council or the assembly when elections were held in February 1683. His exclusion led More to denounce as treasonable the alterations that Penn and the 1683 assembly made in the frame of government to provide for a provincial council and assembly with fewer members than had been delineated in Penn's original constitution. More was forced to apologize to Penn and the provincial council for his "unreasonable and imprudent" criticism.

As if to appease More for his exclusion from the legislature, Penn appointed him secretary of the province in May 1683. Since January of that year More had also been president justice of the Philadelphia County courts, styling himself "President of the Free Society and Court of Justices." In 1684 More was again elected to the Pennsylvania legislature from Philadelphia County, becoming that year Speaker of the assembly. Before Penn returned to England that August, he commissioned More the first chief justice of the provincial supreme court. More's high-handed conduct as chief justice, however, alienated so many influential individuals that they combined against him to expel him from the 1685 assembly, in which he was again representing Philadelphia County, and to impeach him from his office of chief justice as an "aspiring and corrupt minister of state." The assembly preferred a ten-article bill of complaint against More to the provincial council and demanded that he be removed from office. The charges, which included badgering witnesses and jurors, refusing to hear cases, and overturning verdicts of other courts, were revealing of More's imperious nature. More was also accused of denying the authority of the provincial council. Nevertheless the council ultimately refused to convict him, perhaps realizing that the impeachment amounted to little more than a personal vendetta against More. The council, however, removed him from the bench in June 1685.

Meanwhile the Free Society of Traders had failed to fulfill the expectations of its investors as a result of overextension of credit and the inattention of its officers, including More, who preferred to concentrate on their private pursuits. More resigned the company presidency early in 1684, and later that year he obtained a bond from the society for payment of the arrears of his salary. As the fortunes of the company continued to decline, in March 1685 More offered to arrange for the reversal by the provincial court of a £500 judgment against the company. In exchange the company was to buy out his stock at par, although it was by then worth only half its face value. More's impeachment and dismissal from the provincial court prevented the implementation of this disreputable but mutually advantageous agreement, but when the financially strapped Free Society refused to pay the bonds, More brought suit against the company. More's political antagonist Thomas Lloyd, the powerful Quaker president of the provincial council, attempted to intimidate the court into finding for the Free Society by observing the proceedings from a large armchair placed in the center of the courtroom, and More and Lloyd jousted verbally during the trial; nevertheless the jury returned a verdict for More. With Lloyd's assistance, the company then appealed the verdict to the provincial court, claiming that More had obtained the bonds by fraudulent means. The verdict on the bond for More's stock was overturned, and More received only the market value of his stock. The result of the appeal on the bond for his salary is not known.

In spite of More's expulsion from both the provincial court and the assembly and his questionable proceedings with the Free Society of Traders, he evidently retained the confidence of William Penn. More was included in a five-member board commissioned by Penn in February 1687 to serve collectively as deputy governor of Pennsylvania. Penn hoped to resolve factionalism in the colony by granting More and Thomas Lloyd, and their supporters, each a share in the government. More's autocratic temperament and the mutual antipathy between him and Lloyd, whose arrogance equalled More's, undoubtedly would have made the scheme unworkable. In any case, until after More's death, the commission was suppressed by the Quaker political leaders in Pennsylvania, a fact of which Penn was not apprised.

More was one of the most controversial figures in the earliest years of Pennsylvania. Arrogant and abrasive of temperament, he quarreled with his fellow officers of the Free Society of Traders and with the Quaker political leaders in the colony (frequently the same individuals), contributing to the factionalism that divided the leadership of Pennsylvania after Penn's return to England. More's Anglicanism set him apart from most of the early leaders of Pennsylvania, who were Quakers, and probably contributed to the antagonism between him and Thomas Lloyd. More expressed a distaste for Quakers in government and ridiculed the provincial councillors as "fooles and Loggerheads." More's irascible disposition was exacerbated by frequent ill health. He died in Pennsylvania, prior to 15 March 1687 (exact date and location unknown), considerably in debt both in the colony and in England. After his death his 10,000-acre "Manor of Moreland" was divided among his five children. More's estate, "Greenspring," in the Northern Liberties of Philadelphia, and portions of Moreland were eventually sold to satisfy More's debts.

• Manuscript sources for the career of Nicholas More are located in the Penn, Gratz, Etting, and Chew collections, as well as in other collections, at the Historical Society of Pennsylvania. Published manuscript material is found in Richard S. Dunn and Mary Maples Dunn, gen. eds., *The Papers of William Penn*, vols. 2 and 3 (1982, 1986). More's political career can be followed in the minutes of the assemblies in which he served in Gertrude MacKinney, ed., *Pennsylvania Archives*, 8th ser., vol. 1 (1931), and in Samuel Hazard, ed., *Minutes of the Provincial Council*, Colonial Records, vol. 1 (1852). His career is also discussed in Gary B. Nash, "The Free Society of Traders and the Early Politics of Pennsylvania," *Pennsylvania Magazine of History and Biography* 89:147–73, and in Nash, *Quakers and Politics: Pennsylvania, 1681–1726* (1968). The most complete biography of More is in Craig W. Horle et al., *Lawmaking and Legislators in Pennsylvania: A Biographical Dictionary*, vol. 1: *1682–1709* (1991), pp. 548–53.

JEFFREY L. SCHEIB

MORE, Paul Elmer (12 Dec. 1864–9 Mar. 1937), essayist and philosopher, was born in St. Louis, Missouri, the son of Enoch Anson More, a brigadier general during the Civil War and a businessman, and Katharine Hay Elmer. Perhaps rebelling against his father's rigid Presbyterianism, More studied German Romanticism and Oriental and classical languages and literatures, first at Washington University, where he earned his undergraduate degree in 1887 and an M.A. in 1892, and then at Harvard University, where he received a second M.A. in 1893. He tried university teaching at Bryn Mawr between 1895 and 1897, but the experience was not a happy one for either him or his students. More "retired" from academia at the ripe age of thirty-three, and, in a gesture reminiscent of Henry David Thoreau, spent two years thinking and gardening on a farm in Shelburne, New Hampshire. The significance of these brief years for More is indicated by his publication of two series of *Shelburne Essays* (14 vols., 1904–1936). "Plato and a garden, what more should human nature desire?" (Hoeveler, p. 12) he wrote during his Shelburne years, and the classicist and religious subtexts held even more meaning for More with each passing year.

His *Helena*, a volume of poems, was published in 1890, followed by *The Great Refusal* (1894), an early volume of letters, and a translation of *A Century of Indian Epigrams* (1898). Following his marriage in 1900 to Henrietta Beck, with whom he had two children, he entered upon a career of journalism, working as the literary editor for the *Independent* (1901–1903), the New York *Evening Post* (1903–1909), and the *Nation* (1906–1909). He took the position of editor of the *Nation* in 1909, only to retire again from full-time employment in 1914 in order to write a series of books published under the general title of *The Greek Tradition* (1921–1931). He accepted a lecturing position in ancient philosophy (later in classics) at Princeton University in 1918 but demanded and received reduced institutional responsibilities. He lived in Princeton, New Jersey, until his death.

Along with *Irving Babbitt*, More was one of the founders of the New Humanist movement in American letters, a broadly Arnoldian critical practice that emphasized ethics over modern science and artistic expression, "man" over nature, the universal over the merely cultural. Highly prolific, he wrote more than eight hundred items and thirty books on literature, religion, philosophy, and law.

Always controversial and often under attack from both the right and the left in American letters, More's best-remembered aphorism suggested that "the rights of property are more important than the right to life." Like a Whig of the early republic, More believed that property signified long-accumulated moral and intellectual worth, and he further suggested that intelligence and moral rectitude should be the criteria for cultural and political authority as well as economic advantage. More often wrote of a "faculty of inhibition," or "inner check," by which superior individuals might "exercise the ethical will" and rise above nature and its base impulses toward neo-Platonic truths and ideals. In later years, particularly in *Christ the Word* (1927) and *The Catholic Faith* (1931), More returned with much earnestness to Christianity and began to treat the story of Christ as a literal enactment of such a process. But seldom if ever did More spell out the practical, social implications of his admittedly elitist tendencies. In a *New York Times* review of *On Being Human* (1936), More's last volume of *Shelburne Essays*, Peter Monro Jack suggested that a better title for More's book and his entire life work might be "On Being Undecided." Jack declared humanism "so unclear that, to this point, the revival of humanism in America has resulted in little more than a protestation and a quarrel over terms" (24 Jan. 1937).

Bordering on the reclusive and never comfortable with the modern world and its intricacies, More, said New Humanist colleague Stuart Sherman, "has never, like Rosetti, gone to market before breakfast to paint a calf in a farmer's cart." More prefigured his own monklike attitudes and lifestyle in *The Great Refusal*, writing, "Henceforth my way must lead through the solitudes of abstraction and meditation; no human care shall touch me more." Nevertheless, Sherman rightly referred to him as the "bishop of our criticism," and More, in his *Nation* years, served a function comparable to that of William Dean Howells two generations before, shaping tastes and the literary canon by the parceling out of reviews. Many of the most important critical debates of the 1920s and 1930s swirled around his writing, particularly the title essay and others in *The Demon of the Absolute* (1928). More is also a significant figure in the tradition of literary scholarship that is infused with a knowledge of intellectual history as well as a sense of the necessity of a cultural tradition. He died at Princeton.

• More's papers and manuscripts are at Princeton University and Harvard University. Arthur Hazard Dakin, *A Paul Elmer More Miscellany* (1950), includes a massive bibliography. Handy collections are More's *Selected Shelburne Essays* (1935); Byron C. Lambert, ed., *The Essential Paul Elmer More* (1972); and Daniel Aaron, ed., *Paul Elmer More's Shelburne Essays on American Literature* (1963). The only modern biography is Dakin, *Paul Elmer More* (1960), although Robert Shafer, *Paul Elmer More and American Criticism* (1935), written during More's lifetime and with his cooperation, is quite useful. More's chief autobiographical works are "Marginalia, Part I," *American Review* 8 (Nov. 1936): 1–30, and *Pages from an Oxford Diary* (1937). Francis X. Duggan, *Paul Elmer More* (1966), and Stephen L. Tanner, *Paul Elmer More: Literary Criticism as the History of Ideas* (1987), are recent studies of More's writing. The best study of the New Humanist movement is J. David Hoeveler, Jr., *The New Humanism: A Critique of Modern America, 1900–1940* (1976). An obituary is in the *New York Times*, 10 Mar. 1937.

SCOTT MICHAELSEN

MOREHEAD, James Turner (24 May 1797–28 Dec. 1854), lawyer and politician, was born near Shepherdsville, Bullitt County, Kentucky, the son of Armistead Morehead, a banker, and Lucy Latham. Morehead's family, recently arrived from Virginia, soon relocated to Russellville in Logan County, where his father served as the first county clerk. After beginning his education there, Morehead studied at Transylvania University from 1813 to 1815. He studied law under Judge H. P. Broadnax and John J. Crittenden, a Russellville resident. Morehead commenced his legal career at Bowling Green, where his parents then resided, in early 1818.

Morehead's interest in politics first surfaced in letters to local newspapers commenting on public issues during the years 1816 to 1818 under the pseudonyms "Public Good" and "Aemilius." Elected a representative to the state legislature in 1828, 1829, and 1830, Morehead was an active proponent of state-supported internal improvements and served as chair of a legislative committee seeking a state subsidy for the Maysville-Lexington Turnpike. Internal improvements would remain a major interest throughout his public career. Morehead was also an active proponent of public school reform as well as a founding member of the board for the Kentucky Education Society (1829) and the Kentucky Common School Society (1834). In 1831, while attending the National Republican convention in Baltimore, Morehead was nominated the party's candidate for lieutenant governor of Kentucky and was elected in August 1832. Upon the death of Governor John Breathitt, a Democrat, in February 1834, Morehead became governor and served until September 1836. One of the major achievements during his tenure as governor was rapid progress in internal improvements. Under his leadership, the Kentucky legislature resumed its program of river surveys and navigational improvements. Governor Morehead served as ex-officio president of the newly organized Kentucky Board of Internal Improvements in February 1835. His successor as governor, after a change in the law in 1838, commissioned him as president, a position he held until 1841. As of March 1837, Morehead worked as a state sales agent for internal improvement bonds. Many of these programs were stalled, however, by the panic of 1837. Morehead's tenure as governor was noted also for judicial reform, public education, and his opposition to abolition.

After his work as governor, Morehead practiced law at Frankfort, the state capital. He was again elected to the state assembly in August 1837. In late 1839 the legislature sent him and John Speed Smith as special emissaries to Ohio to urge that state to enact legislation that would assure the return of fugitive slaves. Morehead also worked outside the legislature for the protection of slavery in Kentucky. He was an active supporter of the Kentucky branch of the American Colonization Society (established with the purpose of settling free blacks in Liberia), including a turn as its president.

Shortly after the success of the mission to Ohio, Morehead was elected to the U.S. Senate, serving 20 February 1841 to 3 March 1847. As senator, Morehead staunchly supported the programs of Henry Clay, particularly the bill to reestablish the Bank of the United States and Edward Everett's nomination as minister to London. Morehead opposed the annexation of Texas and only reluctantly supported the Mexican War.

Morehead enjoyed a reputation for being a magnetic public speaker, and his Senate speeches drew large audiences to the galleries. His most famous address, however, occurred outside the realm of legislative politics. On 25 May 1840, at a public ceremony honoring the original pioneers at Boonesborough, the former governor and amateur historian of early Kentucky delivered "An Address in Commemoration of the First Settlement [settlers?] of Kentucky," subsequently published in newspapers and in a separate edition. Morehead was one of the first to collect materials on early Kentucky settlement, and his library was generally regarded as one of the finer historical collections in the state. Morehead's other published work reflects his accomplishments as a lawyer, *Practice in Civil Actions and Proceedings at Law* (1846).

Morehead had married Susan A. Roberts of Logan County in 1823. She died in 1838, and Morehead married Lavinia Epsy in 1840. After his term as senator, Morehead made his home in Covington, where he died and was buried. His remains were reinterred in the State Cemetery at Frankfort a short time later.

• The papers of James Turner Morehead are housed at the Kentucky State Historical Society. For a published version of his most famous speech see James Turner Morehead, *An Address in Commemoration of the First Settlement of Kentucky* (1840). Biographical sources include G. Glenn Clift, *The Governors of Kentucky, 1792–1942* (1942); Lewis and Richard H. Collins, *History of Kentucky*, vol. 1 (1874); Lowell H. Harrison, ed., *Kentucky's Governors, 1792–1985* (1985); J. M. Morehead, *The Morehead Family of North Carolina and Virginia* (1921); and "Governor James T. Morehead," *Register of the Kentucky Historical Society* 2 (1904): 17–18. For information on his political activities see W. R. Jillson, "Early Political Papers of Gov. James Turner Morehead," *Register of the Kentucky Historical Society* 22 (1924): 272–300 and 23 (1925): 36–61; *Journals of the House of Representatives of Kentucky, 1828–38*; and *Journals of the Senate of Kentucky, 1834–36*. An obituary is in the *Louisville Courier*, 30 Dec. 1854.

ELLEN T. ESLINGER

MOREHEAD, John Motley (3 Nov. 1870–7 Jan. 1965), electrochemist, diplomat, and philanthropist, was born in Spray (now Eden), North Carolina, the son of James Turner Morehead, a prominent textile manufacturer, and Mary Elizabeth Connally. After preparatory and military school training, he entered the University of North Carolina and graduated with election to Phi Beta Kappa in 1891.

Following graduation, Morehead became chemist for Willson Aluminum Company in Spray, a company financed by his father. The company intended to make aluminum, then considered a semiprecious metal, in an electric arc furnace, based on an ore reduction process patented by Thomas L. Willson. Although the process was a failure, in an experiment on 2 May 1892 Willson accidentally discovered a cheap way to make calcium carbide, which reacts with water to yield combustible acetylene gas. However, there were no known commercial uses for either of these products, and the company ultimately went bankrupt.

Morehead then took a job with a New York bank and then moved on to Westinghouse Electric Corporation. Meanwhile, Willson induced a Chicago gas company to enrich its water gas with acetylene to give a much brighter light. Other gas companies followed suit, and by late 1894 the carbide business was booming. Morehead then rejoined the industry. During 1895 and 1896 he oversaw the building of carbide plants in England, Sweden, Germany, and Niagara Falls, New York. In 1896 he joined Peoples Light, Heat and Power Company in Chicago, and when this firm merged with others to form Union Carbide Corporation in 1898, he became chief engineer for the new firm. As new uses for acetylene were found in farm lighting, miners' lamps, oxyacetylene welding, and, later, chemical synthesis, the company grew accordingly. By the 1950s it was one of the largest chemical companies in the United States, and Morehead was one of its principal stockholders.

Between 1900 and 1926 Morehead was granted ten patents covering carbide manufacturing, arc furnaces, metal smelting, and apparatus for the analysis of industrial gases. He published *Analysis of Industrial Gases* (1905), helped revise the *Gas Chemist's Handbook* (1916), and authored several articles on gas analysis. As an outgrowth of his research into chemical reactions at extremely high temperatures and pressures, Union Carbide became America's first producer of polyethylene plastics.

Morehead was a member of the American Electrochemical Society, a fellow of the American Institute of Electrical Engineers, vice president of the American Gas Association, and first vice president of the American Welding Society. He was twice president of the International Acetylene Association and in 1922 established its James Turner Morehead Award.

In 1918 President Woodrow Wilson appointed Morehead to the War Industries Board to address acute shortages of toluene, a key ingredient in explosives. Morehead averted the crisis by severely restricting nonmilitary use of toluene. While in this post, he held the rank of major in the U.S. Army, General Staff; he was promoted to lieutenant colonel in the reserves at the end of the war.

In 1919 Morehead moved from Chicago to Rye, New York, where he was elected a village trustee in 1925 and served as mayor from 1926 to 1930. From 1929 onward he was chairman of the board of Leaksville Woolen Mills, a business started in Spray by his grandfather. From 1930 to 1933 he was U.S. envoy-extraordinary and minister plenipotentiary to Sweden; he was the first foreigner to receive the gold medal of the Royal Swedish Academy of Sciences. He returned to Union Carbide Company in early 1933.

In midlife Morehead began the educational and charitable philanthropy for which he became noted. In 1927 he raised $1.25 million for the United Hospital in Rye, and in 1931 he was codonor of the Morehead-Patterson Bell Tower and Chimes at the University of North Carolina. In 1945 he established the Morehead Foundation at the university, and in 1949 he presented it with the Morehead building, planetarium, and art gallery. The Morehead Scholarships, which he established in 1955 for "tall academic timber," by 1996 had benefited more than 2,000 students. He was also a benefactor of Morehead High School and Morehead Hospital in Eden, North Carolina, in the late 1950s. In 1961 he capped his generosity to the university with a gift of 50,000 shares of Union Carbide stock. In 1964, when the city of Rye was about to borrow $300,000 to build a new city hall in a style he did not like, he gave $500,000 for one built in the Federal style.

Morehead's interest in genealogy led him to publish *The Morehead Family of North Carolina and Virginia.* (1921). He was a member of the Society of the Cincinnati, the Society of Colonial Wars, the American Legion, and the Order of the Fleece. He had an abiding interest in timepieces and in 1936 secured a 200-year-old, tall, case clock for the Rye town hall. He carried his handmade Swiss pocket watch tied to a shoe string "to remind him of his humble beginnings."

Long after fashion dictated change, Morehead continued to dress the part of a successful 1920s businessman, with a trademark high "Hoover" shirt collar. Late in life he justified this eccentricity by saying, "I'm old enough and rich enough to dress as I please." He had a dry wit and once told students at the University of North Carolina that, while money might not bring happiness, it helped quiet the nerves. In a 1954 interview, he said that he would never consider himself wealthy until he could write a check without entering the amount on the stub.

Morehead was married twice: in 1915 to Genevieve Margaret Birchoff of Chicago; and after her death in 1945, to Leila Duckworth Houghton in 1948. He had no children. Morehead never retired; he commuted daily between Rye and New York City. He died at home in Rye.

Morehead's technical skills advanced the chemical industry; his management skills served local and national governments; and his philanthropy continues to provide substantial college scholarships for the education of some of the best and brightest students.

• Some of the anecdotal material in this article comes from correspondence and oral communications between Morehead and the author in 1954. The principal biographical sketch of Morehead is by Herbert T. Pratt in *American Chemists and Chemical Engineers*, ed. Wyndham D. Miles (1976), pp. 346–48. Trustees of the John Motley Morehead Foundation (Chapel Hill), *John M. Morehead: A Biographical Sketch* (1954), gives a useful chronology of his life. Several accounts of the discovery of the commercial carbide process give undue credit to Morehead and his father at the expense of Willson; a more balanced account is Pratt, "Willson Aluminum Company, Spray, North Carolina (1892–1896)," *Journal of Rockingham County History and Genealogy* 17 (June 1992): 1–26. Morehead's work to solve the 1918 toluene shortage is summarized in Williams Haynes, *American Chemical Industry: A History*, vol. 2 (1945), pp. 134–35, 354. His accomplishments as mayor of Rye are covered by Marcia Dolphin, *Fifty Years of Rye (1904–1954)* (1955), pp. 60–73, 94, 123. An obituary is in the *New York Times*, 8 Jan. 1965.

HERBERT T. PRATT

MOREHOUSE, Chauncey (11 Mar. 1902–31 Oct. 1980), percussionist, was born in Niagara Falls, New York. His parents' names are unknown. The family lived in Chambersburg, Pennsylvania, from 1906. Morehouse became a drummer in his high school orchestra, in Bill Sonderman's band, and with his father, a ragtime pianist who played for silent movies. From 1919 to 1920 (or 1921) Morehouse's own Versatile Five worked summers in Ocean City, New Jersey. After graduating from high school, Morehouse toured to Pittsburgh with the Harrison-Hollins orchestra. He may next have joined Ted Weems's band; the chronology is unclear. In 1922 he joined Paul Specht's Society Serenaders in Columbus, Ohio, and went with the band to London the following year. Specht worked at the Addison Hotel in Detroit before playing an engagement into 1924 in the pseudo-African Congo Room at the New Alamac hotel in New York. During these years Morehouse recorded with both Specht's orchestra and with Frank Guarante's Georgians, a small group drawn from the ranks of the Society Serenaders and modeled after the Original Dixieland Jass Band.

After brief periods with Howard Lanin's Benjamin Franklin Hotel Orchestra, including recordings in 1925, and with Weems, Morehouse joined Jean Goldkette's orchestra at the Graystone Ballroom in Detroit in 1925. He remained with Goldkette's band for performances in New York's Roseland Ballroom, where, on the testimony of Fletcher Henderson's own musicians, it outplayed Henderson's big band. The orchestra made a number of recordings during this period, but evidently the producer's musical tastes were such that Goldkette's men were not permitted to record their best jazz and dance arrangements. Nonetheless, Morehouse was able to take part in acclaimed small-group performances involving Goldkette's sidemen Frankie Trumbauer and Bix Beiderbecke. Trumbauer's "Riverboat Shuffle" (May 1927) is characteristic. It reveals a conception of drumming that was devoted to the articulation of melody by means of irregular accents coordinated with arranged passages, and one that focused on crisp cymbal work. On occasion Morehouse used wood blocks in addition to cymbals, as on Beiderbecke's "At the Jazz Band Ball," and he played vibraphone (one of the first jazzmen to use it), as on "I'm More Than Satisfied," recorded by Beiderbecke and Trumbauer under the pseudonym the Chicago Loopers. These two titles were recorded in October 1927, a month after Goldkette's orchestra broke up and while its intended successor, Adrian Rollini's all-star jazz band, was failing.

Morehouse worked in Don Voorhees's pit orchestra for the Broadway show *Rain or Shine* for about a year from February 1928. Continuing as a freelance in jazz and popular studio bands, he recorded with Red Nichols from 1927 until 1929 (including "Original Dixieland One-step," 1928), the Dorsey Brothers Orchestra (1928–1929), baby-voiced "boop-boop-a-doop" singer Helen Kane ("I Wanna Be Loved by You," 1928), Joe Venuti (1928–1929, 1933), Hoagy Carmichael's band including Beiderbecke (1930), Connee Boswell (intermittently, 1930s), and Claude Thornhill's band with Maxine Sullivan (1937). During the 1930s Morehouse adopted the prevailing approach to drumming and thus shifted his style from irregular accentuation to steady timekeeping patterns. He also invented and attempted to perfect a circularly mounted set of fourteen "n'doma drums" used for playing melodies. These he demonstrated on his own recordings from 1938, "Kuli-a" and "Mazi-pani," but tuning proved difficult and the experiment was inconsequential.

In the meantime, Morehouse had reoriented his career toward radio broadcasting. From around 1935 he played for seven years in Peter Van Steeden's Ipana Troubadours on comedian Fred Allen's CBS comedy show, and in that same year he was an original member of the Lucky Strike Orchestra on "Your Hit Parade" on NBC. He performed under Leigh Stevens on the "Saturday Night Swing Club" on CBS from 1936 until 1938 and in Larry Clinton's orchestra on NBC in 1937. Beginning in 1939, his wood blocks sounded hoof beats for "On the Trail" as diminutive Johnny (Roventini) put out a "call for Philip Morris" in a famous commercial for the Philip Morris Playhouse on CBS. Beginning in 1940 Morehouse rejoined Voorhees in the orchestra for the Bell Telephone Hour on NBC.

From around 1939 into the 1940s, Morehouse recorded as a vibraphonist with a vocal quartet, the Merry Macs. In the 1950s he worked with Paul LaValle and the Cities Services Band. He played on television in bands for quiz shows, including "The $64,000 Question." By the late 1960s he was retired, but he still played bass drum for summer concerts in Central Park and performed at jazz concerts and festivals. A widower, he had been married to Evelyn (maiden name unknown); they had two children. In the early 1970s he married Virginia Horvath Bamford, a widow and an acquaintance from his years with Goldkette. In 1975 he was reunited with surviving members of the Goldkette orchestra for a concert at Carnegie Hall, and at about that time he participated in the New York Jazz Repertory Company's re-creation of Beiderbecke's music. Morehouse had lived for some time in Vincentown, New Jersey. He died in Medford, New Jersey.

Morehouse's significance to earlier jazz and dance band drumming stemmed from his playing with Goldkette's pioneering jazz big band and in small groups with Beiderbecke.

• Morehouse had suffered a stroke and substantial memory loss by the time of an interview conducted by Edgar Hutto, Jr., in 1976 and held on tape and in transcript at the Institute of Jazz Studies in Newark, N.J. More useful information can be found in published surveys of his career by Jerry Kline, "Chauncey Morehouse," *Mississippi Rag*, May 1980, pp. 1–4 (including numerous photos), and Warren Vaché, Sr., "The Forgotten Ones: Chauncey Morehouse," *Jazz Journal International* 25 (Aug. 1982): 19–20. An obituary is in the *Philadelphia Inquirer*, 4 Nov. 1980.

BARRY KERNFELD

MORENO, Luisa (30 Aug. 1906–3 Nov. 1992), labor organizer, was born Blanca Rosa Rodriguez Lopez in Guatemala City, Guatemala, the daughter of wealthy parents, whose names and occupations are unknown. She traveled to the United States and attended grammar school at the Convent of the Holy Names in Oakland, California. Returning to Guatemala City, she organized female students who were concerned about the lack of educational opportunities for women at the country's universities. Moreno later worked as a correspondent for a Guatemalan newspaper in Mexico City. She and her artist husband left Mexico in 1928 for New York City. (The date of her marriage and her husband's name are unknown.)

Unable to support an infant daughter, her only child, as a writer, Moreno got a job as a seamstress in a factory located near Spanish Harlem. The low wages and sweatshop conditions led her to join a group of leftist Latino workers deeply involved in labor activism. She helped organize Puerto Rican female garment workers and participated in a 1933 strike of the Needles Trades Workers Industrial Union, which later combined with the International Ladies' Garment Workers' Union (ILGWU). Because the ILGWU did little to organize Spanish-speaking women, Moreno in 1935 joined the American Federation of Labor (AFL) and worked among Cuban cigar makers in Florida. She disagreed with her superiors over contract matters and was reassigned to Pennsylvania. AFL leaders concentrated on organizing skilled workers and did not support Moreno in her effort to recruit unskilled laborers. She broke with the union and joined John L. Lewis and other disgruntled AFL officials, who established the Congress of Industrial Organizations (CIO) in 1938. The CIO gave women responsibility in union recruitment and assigned Moreno to work among people toiling in cigar factories in New York City and Philadelphia.

The plight of rural labor was of equal concern to Moreno. Greatly influenced by economist Paul S. Taylor's studies of the exploitation of Mexican workers in the United States, she moved to San Antonio, Texas, in the mid-1930s and participated in a large pecan shellers strike. She joined the newly formed United Cannery, Agricultural, Packing, and Allied Workers of America (UCAPAWA), a militant CIO union representing mostly racial minorities and women. Armed with leadership skills and experience, she organized Mexican field hands in Florida, Louisiana, Texas, and Colorado. Bert Corona, a longtime labor organizer in California, recalled that Moreno possessed "a very powerful gift for persuasion" and recruited union members with "the weight of her logic, her ease of words, and her speaking abilities" (Garcia, *Memories of Chicano History*, pp. 117–18).

The growth of unionism among Latino workers persuaded Moreno of the need for a broad civil rights organization that would unite Mexican and other Spanish-speaking people in the United States. She traveled throughout the country, spoke to numerous Latin-American groups, and assembled committees for a National Congress of Spanish Speaking People (*El Congreso de Pueblos de Habla Española*). Meeting in Los Angeles in 1939, El Congreso attracted labor union officials, educators, religious leaders, and community organizers. Moreno and other activists assigned the delegates to panels to discuss such matters as health needs, work, education, and racial discrimination. The three-day convention concluded with resolutions calling for, among other things, decent health care and housing, more governmental aid for unemployed laborers, safeguarding of civil rights, and a Spanish-language newspaper to help in the organization of Latino unionists.

El Congreso received considerable support from CIO unions and helped move Moreno to the front ranks of the labor movement in California. She became vice president of the state CIO executive board. In 1940 the officials of the UCAPAWA put her in charge of Local 75, which represented Mexican women employed by the California Sanitary Canning Company, one of the biggest food processing plants in the Los Angeles area. She encouraged cannery workers to voice openly their grievances and enforced contract provisions and governmental regulations concerning labor rights. The following year she was elected international vice president of UCAPAWA.

America's entry into World War II provided a greater opportunity for Moreno to display her organizing skills. Canning and packing companies received large contracts from the federal government and hired many minority workers. Moreno, along with other union professionals, recruited Latino women in canneries and packing houses throughout California. Tobacco workers also joined UCAPAWA, leading the union to change its name to the Food, Tobacco, Agricultural, and Allied Workers of America (FTA) in 1944.

The late 1940s were a different and difficult time for Moreno. The U.S. Congress overrode President Harry Truman's veto of the Taft-Hartley Act in 1947. One provision of the act required the National Labor Relations Board to withhold certification of a union as a legal bargaining representative until its officers signed affidavits disavowing membership in the Communist party. Moreno and other FTA leaders refused to comply with the affidavits, drawing much hostility from anticommunist organizations. The California Un-American Activities Committee interrogated Moreno in 1947. The following year the Immigration and Naturalization Service started deportation proceedings against her. Among the evidence used against Moreno was a signed statement by a Bexar County (Tex.) sheriff, who alleged that she was a Communist party leader. She was deported to Guatemala in 1949.

In Guatemala Moreno gave speeches in support of the democratic government of Jacobo Arbenz Guzmán until it was overthrown in 1954. Moreno visited Cuba shortly after the revolution of 1959 and helped draft the curriculum for that country's new system of education. She went to Mexico and spoke out strongly in support of the Sandinista revolution in Nicaragua in the late 1970s and early 1980s. She died in Guatemala.

Moreno made important contributions to the labor movement in twentieth-century America. One of the first women to hold a leadership position in the hierarchy of an international labor union, she brought a great number of minority people into the trade unions, enabling them to exercise some control over their working conditions. Nurturing a class consciousness among Mexican women, she established a permanent position for them in the field of labor relations in California and other southwestern states.

• Moreno's early life, union work, and political activity are carefully described in Albert Camarillo, *Chicanos in Califor-*

nia: A History of Mexican Americans in California (1981); Vicki L. Ruiz, *Cannery Women, Cannery Lives: Mexican Women, Unionization, and the California Food Processing Industry, 1930–1950* (1987); and Mario T. Garcia, *Memories of Chicano History: The Life and Narrative of Bert Corona* (1994). Rodolfo Acuna, *Occupied America: A History of Chicanos* (1988); and Garcia, *Mexican Americans: Leadership, Ideology, and Identity, 1930–1960* (1989), also provide valuable information on her role in American labor organization and Latino activism in the 1930s and 1940s.

MARTIN J. SCHIESL

MORFORD, Henry (10 Mar. 1823–4 Aug. 1881), author and journalist, was born in the village of New Monmouth, Monmouth County, New Jersey, the son of William Morford, a merchant, and Elizabeth Willett. The Morford family had emigrated from England to New Jersey, where they engaged in farming as well as mercantile, coal, and lumber businesses. The Morfords were devout Baptists, and they were politically active as Whigs and, later, Republicans.

Educated in the village school of New Monmouth, Henry Morford worked in his father's mercantile business, one of only two stores in the New Monmouth community. He also served as postmaster for New Monmouth. Described as having a Greek face and long, curly brown hair, Morford wrote verses as a hobby and at a young age had poems published in the *New Yorker* and the *Saturday Evening Post*. Morford's best poetry was inspired by the desire to imitate the incomparable Lord Byron's *Don Juan* in the form of a sequel published in 645 stanzas under the title *The Rest of Don Juan* (1846). Morford apparently was attracted to *Don Juan* and Byron in part because of a morbid fascination with the poet's theme of fatalism and the youthful death of Byron. His other published collections of poetry, *Rhymes of Twenty Years* (1859) and *Rhymes of an Editor* (1873), both of which included a biographical sketch of the author, showed a mastery of the poetic form yet lacked any distinctive originality.

In 1852 Morford launched a weekly newspaper, the *New Jersey Standard*, from his father's store. The site was soon moved to Keyport and in 1860 to Red Bank. One of thirty-nine New Jersey newspapers begun in the decade of the 1850s, the *New Jersey Standard* later became a daily after Morford gave it up. In addition to editorial duties at the *Standard*, Morford often contributed poetry and reminiscences of his mercantile career. By 1855 he had sold the paper. He soon moved to New York City, where he was employed as an editorial writer for newspapers, including the obscure New York *Atlas*. During the Civil War and shortly after, Morford served as clerk for both the Court of Common Pleas (1861–68) and the Board of Aldermen in New York City. Although this period included the infamous "Boss" Tweed scandals, the Republican Morford was not implicated in the Democratic Tweed ring activities.

Morford had the opportunity to meet and talk regularly with other lesser-light authors at Pfaff's, a popular New York City gathering spot. Morford, enthralled by the war, wrote several novels with the conflict as a setting, including *Shoulder-Straps* (1863), *The Days of Shoddy* (1863), and *The Coward* (1864). While reflecting the wartime environment, the stories revealed unsophisticated character development and were filled with contrived details and rhetorical flourishes. Later novels such as *Utterly Wrecked* (1866) and *Only a Commoner* (1871) reflect mediocre talent at best. Morford also dabbled with drama, writing several plays, including *The Merchant's Honor* and *The Bells of Shandon*. The latter was set in Ireland and produced with John Brougham on the stage of Wallack's Theater in New York City in 1867. A collection of essays, *Sprees and Splashes*, published in 1863, reflected Morford's proclivity for anecdotal, albeit hackneyed, humor. An 1868 essay by Morford in *Lippincott's Magazine*, entitled "Woman and American Chivalry," revealed Morford's conservative social views. He questioned the wisdom of the feminist movement for sexual equality and reminded women of important protection accorded them as a result of their traditional social roles.

In part for reasons of health, Morford traveled to Europe in 1865, visiting England, Scotland, and France. He recounted his travels in *Over-Sea* (1867), which showed that his skills in composing descriptive travelogues surpassed other literary efforts at poetry and fiction. Indeed, upon returning to America, Morford concentrated on writing additional guidebooks. He published *Morford's Short-Trip Guide to Europe* in 1868 and a counterpart, *Morford's Short-Trip Guide to America*, in 1872 for Europeans visiting the United States. Morford returned to Europe in 1878 and recounted the trip in *Paris and Half-Europe in '78* (1879). All of Morford's guidebooks went through numerous editions and showed the talent as well as sustained interest of the author in the genre. In 1876 Morford even established a bookstore in New York City that specialized in travel literature.

Upon his return to the United States from his second European journey, Morford moved to Brooklyn. There he founded and edited a journal, the *Brooklyn New Monthly Magazine*, during 1880–1881. This venture followed an unsuccessful periodical known as *Morford's Magazine* which had had an even briefer life in the 1870s. In 1881 Morford became ill while visiting friends in Manhattan. He planned a trip to Maine for his health but died before leaving.

Despite being a prolific writer, Henry Morford's travel descriptions were the only books that both commanded extensive attention and reflected a degree of literary ability. His verses were not widely known or respected by contemporary critics, and he did not remain long enough with any newspaper or periodical to establish a journalistic reputation. Thus, his experience as a journalist seemed best suited to descriptive rather than aesthetic or provocative literature.

• Fourteen Morford letters can be found in the archives of the Historical Society of Pennsylvania in Philadelphia. The New Jersey Historical Society possesses copies of the *New Jersey*

Standard for the period of Morford's ownership. Morford and his family are mentioned briefly in T. H. Leonard, *From Indian Trail to Electric Rail* (1923), and Franklin Ellis, *History of Monmouth County, New Jersey* (1885). H. S. Ashbee analyzed Morford's poetry in "The Rest of *Don Juan*," *Bibliographer* 7 (1883): 25–28.

DANIEL WEBSTER HOLLIS, III

MORGAN, Abel (1673–16 Dec. 1722), Baptist minister, translator, and biblical scholar, was born in Alltgoch, Llanwenog, Cardiganshire, Wales, the son of Morgan ap Rhydderch ap Dafydd, a Baptist pastor; his mother's name is unknown. Although the details of Morgan's formal education are obscure, his accomplishments indicate that care was taken, for he followed in the traditions of an uncle, a great-uncle, and a great-grandfather, all of whom were noted as poets, writers, or translators.

By 1692 Morgan began his career as a preacher in Llanwenarth. He was called to be ordained as the first pastor of the congregation in Blaengwent, Monmouthshire, in 1696. Active in the Welsh Baptist Association, he served on several committees that dealt with questions of doctrine and discipline. He was once asked to preach the opening sermon for the gathering, a sign that his talents were recognized within the larger Baptist community.

In August 1709 Morgan was invited to become the pastor of the Pennepek Baptist church in Pennsylvania, the most influential church among the founding members of the Philadelphia Baptist Association. Welsh Quakers had purchased 40,000 acres of land from William Penn in 1681. Forming themselves into seven companies, they were responsible for recruiting settlers from among their country people. In 1683 the first Welsh Baptist colonists founded Pennepek Church in Lower Dublin Township. Morgan's brother, Enoch, had been among those who emigrated in 1701 to the "Welsh Tract," where the first Baptist meeting had been briefly served by Elias Keach. Morgan indicated his willingness to accept this call late in 1710. Custom dictated that his congregation approve his plans to emigrate, which they did with some regret at a special meeting in 1711; whether this conference occurred in April or August is disputed. After false starts and delays, Morgan's ship arrived in Philadelphia on 14 February 1712. His first wife, Priscilla Powell, and a son died during the voyage; a daughter survived. Morgan's second marriage was to Martha Burrows; they had no children. Following her death, he married a widow, Judith Griffiths Golding, with whom he had four children. The dates of his marriages are unknown.

Morgan's ministry concentrated on the organization of Particular Baptist churches in both the Welsh- and English-speaking settlements of Pennsylvania, Delaware, and New Jersey. Particular Baptists, in contrast to General Baptists who believed that Christ died for all who would accept him on faith, were strict Calvinists who believed that Christ died only to save those predestined to heaven, or the elect. Morgan advocated the formation of separate churches organized around one minister who preached and administered the sacraments, assisted by elders in secondary roles. Concerned about proper church order, he worked to regularize statements of faith and selection of church officers. He frequently preached in meetings lacking a settled minister, including the Philadelphia meeting, which did not have a resident pastor during this period. He was a respected member of the Philadelphia Baptist Association.

At the request of his Pennepek congregation, Morgan translated the 1689 London "Century Confession" of faith into Welsh. Adopted by one hundred congregations in England and Wales, it formed the basic statement of faith for British Baptists and eventually for Particular Baptists in the American colonies. Morgan added articles twenty-three and thirty-one from an alternative version of the confession published by Elias and Benjamin Keach in 1697. These provided for church covenants, the singing of psalms during worship, and the laying on of hands at baptism, all important practices within the Welsh tradition. Adopted and signed at a meeting of the Baptist congregation in Pennepek in February 1716, Morgan's translation marks the first time a version of the "Confession" entered into formal use in America, although it had earlier been used to settle doctrinal disputes. While the translation does not appear to have been published, other Welsh-speaking congregations subsequently accepted the document as the foundation for their doctrines and practices. The Morgan/Keach additions to the "Century Confession" were adopted by the Philadelphia Baptist Association when it adopted a confession of faith in 1742.

Concerned about the survival of the Welsh language in the colonies as well as the spiritual welfare of Baptists in his homeland, Morgan compiled the first Welsh concordance to the Bible. Virtually complete at the time of his death, this folio volume of 234 pages was revised, corrected, and seen through the press by his brother Enoch and a fellow minister. *Cyd-Gordiad Egwyddorawl o'r Scrythurau: Neu Daflen Lythyrennol o'r Prif Eiriau Yn y Bibl Sanctaidd. Yn Arain dan y Cyfryw eiriau i fuan ganfod pob rhyw ddymunol ran o'r Scrythurau. A Gyfan-soddwyd Drwy Lafurus Boen Abel Morgan, Gwenidog yr Efengyl er Ill's y Cymru* (*A Concordance of the Sacred Scriptures; or, A Complete Alphabetical Index to the Principal Words in the Holy Bible, By Which Any Portion of the Scriptures Desired, Can Be Immediately Found. Compiled Carefully and with Much Labor. By Abel Morgan, Minister of the Gospel, among the Welsh*), published by Samuel Keimer and David Henry in 1730, was the second Welsh-language book printed in the American colonies. It circulated widely in Wales as well. It is this contribution, as well as his role in the formation of the doctrinal basis of the Philadelphia Baptist Association, for which Morgan is most notable.

• For additional information on Morgan, see H. D. Davies, *Transatlantic Brethren—Rev. Samuel Jones (1735–1814) and*

His Friends: Baptists in Wales, Pennsylvania and Beyond (1995); Morgan Edwards, *Materials Towards a History of the Baptists in Pennsylvania . . .* (1770); Horatio Gates Jones, "The Rev. Abel Morgan, Pastor of the United Baptist Churches of Pennepek and Philadelphia," *Pennsylvania Magazine of History and Biography* 6 (1882): 300–10; and Francis W. Sacks, *The Philadelphia Baptist Tradition of Church Authority, 1707–1814: An Ecumenical Analysis and Theological Interpretation* (1989).

SALLY SCHWARTZ

MORGAN, Agnes Fay (4 May 1884–20 July 1968), nutrition scientist and home economics administrator, was born Jane Agnes Fay in Peoria, Illinois, the daughter of Irish immigrants Patrick John Fay, a laborer and builder, and his second wife, Mary Josephine Dooley. Morgan graduated as an outstanding student from Peoria High School and with financial aid from a local citizen briefly attended Vassar College and then the University of Chicago, from which she received the B.S. (1904) and M.S. (1905) in chemistry.

Morgan taught chemistry for one year each at Hardin-Simmons College, Missouri, and the University of Montana. At Montana she met and in 1908 married a university student, Arthur Ivason Morgan, who was a veteran of the Spanish-American War and a high school teacher, football player, and coach; the couple had one child. In 1910 Morgan went with her husband to Seattle where, at the University of Washington, she taught for two years and founded a chemistry honor society for women that later merged with Iota Sigma Pi. Then, with the support of her husband, she resumed her studies with Julius O. Stieglitz, chair of the chemistry department at the University of Chicago, receiving her Ph.D. in physical and organic chemistry in 1914.

In 1915 Morgan accepted a teaching and research position at the University of California, Berkeley, with Myer E. Jaffa in the College of Agriculture's Division of Nutrition. To prepare for that position, in the fall of 1914 she had studied with the well-known nutritionists at Columbia University, Henry C. Sherman and Mary Swartz Rose. In the fall of 1916 a new department of home economics was created in the College of Arts and Sciences at Berkeley, and Morgan was made head of its Division of Household Science. The division became a separate department in 1918, and she was named associate professor and chair. Several students accompanied Morgan from Agriculture to Arts and Sciences, and in 1917 they were the first of more than fifty who received their advanced degrees under her direction. Morgan was promoted to professor in 1923. The department was transferred back to the College of Agriculture and renamed home economics in 1938, with Morgan continuing to serve as its head until her retirement in 1954. During some of the later years of her administration she also had responsibility for the home economics program at the Davis campus of the university and for coordinating her programs with the home economics programs at the Los Angeles and Santa Barbara campuses.

Morgan successfully combined departmental administration with an outstanding research career. Her research program was a pragmatic blend of fundamental research and the seeking of solutions to practical problems of interest to Californians. She measured the vitamin content of processed foods and showed that sulfur dioxide, used in preserving some foods, lowered their vitamin B-1 value and protected vitamin C. She demonstrated the benefit of adding certain nutritious foods to the diets of schoolchildren and showed that heat lowered the nutritional value of protein, in part by making the essential amino acid, lysine, less available for use by the body. During World War II she developed improved methods for food dehydration for the military. Her major contribution is her work on relationships between vitamins and hormones, including the effects of large doses of vitamin D on the secretion of parathyroid hormone and the effect of a deficiency of the B-vitamin pantothenic acid in damaging the adrenal glands. In 1940 she reported that rats deficient in pantothenic acid exhibited a graying of their normally dark hair due to adrenal damage; later this observation was extended to dogs, foxes, and other animals.

From 1936 to 1950 Morgan served on the Experiment Station Committee on Organization and Policy, a national committee providing overall direction to the work of the state agricultural experiment stations. From 1946 to 1950 she also served on the U.S. Department of Agriculture's Committee of Nine, the group responsible for approving the regional and national program of research undertaken by the experiment stations. Both of these assignments were unusual for a woman at that time.

Morgan received many awards for her work, including the Garvan Medal of the American Chemical Society (1949) and the Borden Award of the American Institute of Nutrition (1954). In 1950–1951 she was named the faculty research lecturer at Berkeley, the first woman to receive the highest honor given by that faculty. In 1962 she was the first recipient of the research award of the Society of Medical Friends of Wine for her work on vitamins in wine and the effects of alcohol and wine on cholesterol metabolism in animals. In 1959 she was made a fellow of the American Institute of Nutrition, the first woman so honored. In 1961 the home economics building on the Berkeley campus was renamed Agnes Fay Morgan Hall. In 1964 the *San Francisco Examiner* named her one of the ten outstanding Bay Area women of 1963 and awarded her the Phoebe Apperson Hearst Gold Medal.

After her retirement, Morgan continued her scholarly work, adding more than forty papers to the more than two hundred she had published earlier. Her most significant postretirement project was in analyzing and summarizing more than 175 publications from a coordinated national research program on the nutritional status of various age groups that was carried out by agricultural experiment stations across the country. *Nu-*

tritional Status U.S.A., written by Morgan and published by the California Agricultural Experiment Station in 1959, marked the first attempt at a nationwide assessment of nutritional status in the United States. Morgan also published a history of the women's chemistry honorary, Iota Sigma Pi, in 1963.

Morgan has been described as a "skilled administrator [who] became known and feared as a powerful personality" (Nerad, p. 160) and as having "research imagination and the ability to choose problems . . . [that secured] outside support in the days of limited university resources" (Okey, p. 1104). Morgan was revered as a mentor by her many students who have themselves achieved positions of leadership in dietetics, nutrition education, and nutrition science. She was recognized as a good teacher, writer, and speaker. Morgan took pride in the scientifically based home economics program that she developed at the University of California. The decision by campus administrators in 1956 to retain the nutrition program at Berkeley, when the rest of home economics was moved to the Davis campus, confirmed her belief in its quality. Morgan was widely honored as a leading scientist and remained professionally active until her death in Berkeley, California.

• Morgan's papers are in the Bancroft Library of the University of California, Berkeley. A complete bibliography of Morgan's publications is available from the Department of Nutritional Sciences, University of California, Berkeley. Morgan's longtime colleague Ruth Okey assesses her life in "Agnes Fay Morgan (1884–1968), a Biographical Sketch," *Journal of Nutrition* 104 (1974): 1102–7. The history of the home economics program at Berkeley is discussed by Maresi Nerad in "Gender Stratification in Higher Education: The Department of Home Economics at the University of California, Berkeley 1916–1962," *Women's Studies International Forum* 10 (1987): 157–64. An obituary is in the *San Francisco Examiner*, 22 July 1968.

PATRICIA B. SWAN

MORGAN, Anna (24 Feb. 1851–27 Aug. 1936), speech and drama teacher, was born in Fleming, New York, the daughter of Allen Denison Morgan, a gentleman farmer, and Mary Jane Thornton. After the death of her father in 1876, Anna moved with her family to Chicago, where she studied elocution at the Hershey School of Music. She soon earned a local reputation as a dramatic reader with a naturalistic approach that contrasted with the current fashion of more stilted and stylized speech. Her repertoire included selections from plays by Shakespeare, Schiller, and Maurice Maeterlinck, and poetry by authors that ranged from Robert Browning to Paul Laurence Dunbar. Morgan's fame as a reader spread throughout the Midwest and then to New York and Boston when she toured for the Redpath Lyceum Bureau, one of many booking agencies for lectures and readings, from 1880 to 1883.

In 1884 Morgan joined the faculty of the Chicago Opera House Conservatory, which was later renamed the Chicago Conservatory. It was here that her interest in dramatic pedagogy flowered, and while she continued to give recitals and private elocution lessons, education became her major interest. She developed a curriculum that included theater and literary history, as well as acting and playwriting, and she was highly respected for the performances by her students that she staged at the conservatory. Her classes presented American premieres of Henrik Ibsen's *The Master Builder* (1895), George Bernard Shaw's *Candida* (1898), and W. B. Yeats's *The Hour Glass* (1905).

Morgan left the Chicago Conservatory in 1898 to found her own school, the Anna Morgan Studios. Her focus remained on education, and she concentrated on the development of her students' literary and interpretive skills rather than on the training of professional actors. Located in the Chicago Fine Arts Building, Morgan's studio was a center of activity and discussion during the early twentieth century, a period of dynamic cultural growth and artistic creativity in Chicago. She helped to found the Little Room, a salon for lively discussions by artists and members of local society, which included editor Harriet Monroe and writer Hamlin Garland. As an influential and respected member of Chicago's artistic community, Morgan helped to make the study of speech a serious intellectual enterprise. She believed in presenting works in context and in teaching her students more than the techniques of acting. For this reason, she stressed historical study as well as technical expertise. For a brief period, Morgan studied the Delsarte Method of using gesture and body position to convey particular emotions, although this was not wholly consistent with the rest of her methodology or pedagogy. One of her three books, *An Hour with Delsarte* (1889), describes her experience using this method. Morgan retired from active teaching in 1925, and she died in Chicago a decade later.

• Morgan wrote an autobiography, *My Chicago* (1918), and her scrapbooks and letters are housed in the Chicago Historical Society. The most comprehensive work on Morgan is Joyce Sozen, "Anna Morgan: Reader, Teacher, and Director" (Ph.D. diss., Univ. of Illinois, 1961). See also Henry B. Fuller, "The Upward Movement in Chicago," *Atlantic Monthly*, Oct. 1897, pp. 534–47; Herman Clark, "The Little Room, A Famous Artist Group in the Chicago of Yesterday," *Townsfolk*, May 1944; and Bernard Duffey, *The Chicago Renaissance in American Letters* (1954).

BARBARA L. TISCHLER

MORGAN, Anne Tracy (25 July 1873–29 Jan. 1952), philanthropist, was born in Highland Falls, New York, the daughter of John Pierpont Morgan, a financier, and Frances Louisa Tracy. She was educated by tutors and at Russell Sage School, spending her summers abroad with her family and a large retinue of servants. Isolated in the opulence of her family life, she developed strong athletic interests, including horseback riding, golf, tennis, fishing, and yachting, giving her a physical stamina that served her well in later years.

A decisive influence on Morgan was her association with Elizabeth Marbury, a theatrical and author's agent; Elsie De Wolfe, a fashionable designer; and Florence Harriman, a New York socialite, in the founding of the Colony Club (1903). This was intended to provide social and recreational facilities to prominent women similar to those of exclusive men's clubs and was the first of its kind in New York. Marbury and De Wolfe shared a house in the city and later a villa at Versailles, France, and through them Morgan greatly enlarged her intellectual horizon and circle of acquaintances.

Turning next to the needs of working women, Morgan became active in the National Civic Foundation, founding through its women's branch in 1909 a clubroom and restaurant in the Brooklyn Navy Yard where workers could purchase nutritious meals at cost. She served as a volunteer factory inspector in New York and New Jersey for the purpose of improving the working conditions of women. In the bitter strike of the women's shirtwaist makers in 1909–1910 she was prominent among those supporting the union. She worked also for the Vacation Committee (later Vacation Savings Fund of New York), which provided a way for working women to save money for vacations in modest increments, and later she was active in the American Woman's Association (AWA). An outgrowth of this work was her essay "The American Girl: Her Education, Her Responsibilities, Her Recreation, Her Future," which was published in *Woman's Home Companion* in 1914–1915 and in book form in 1915.

In 1912 Morgan added a wing to the "Villa Trianon," Marbury and De Wolfe's residence at Versailles, and some years later bought out Marbury's share when the latter decided to concentrate her work in New York. The villa became a favored haunt of the French political and intellectual elite, wealthy Americans, and European nobility. De Wolfe's memoirs *After All* (1935) describe with amusement the numerous noble suitors of "depleted fortune" who sought in vain the hand of the magnificent American heiress, who never married.

Morgan was in France at the outbreak of the First World War. Her love of the country and firsthand experience of the destruction, chaos, and brutality of the war caused her to concentrate her resources and effort on assisting the victims, military and civilian. Returning home in September 1914, Morgan was immediately active in the drive to collect clothing, food, and relief packages for the French. Her main interest was to create an American women's organization along the lines of the women's auxiliary support groups of the British armed forces. To this end, she returned to France in 1916, despite the risks from submarines, and visited the Somme and Verdun, commissioning a report on the structure and operation of the British organizations. This led in the following year to the creation of the National League for Women's Service as well as the American Fund for French Wounded. Because of her wealth, experience, knowledge of France, and executive abilities, she was a natural leader of this effort, and the special role of the Morgan Bank in financing both the Allied war effort and the French government after the war of 1870 gave her immediate access to the French political and military leadership of the time.

The carnage and destruction in northern France, through combat and systematic atrocities of the invaders, was on a scale hitherto unknown, and Morgan was among those who sought to inform the American public of its extent ("Rekindling Home Fires in France," *Delineator*, Feb. 1918; "What Must Be Done in France," *Forum*, May 1918). The Comité Américain pour les Regions Devastées (CARD) was formed in 1917, with Morgan as chief executive officer and headquarters at Blérancourt in the Aisne region.

The committee, under the direction of Morgan and Anne Murray Dike, imported and distributed food, agricultural implements, seed, and livestock; formed agricultural cooperatives; and assisted in the task of reconstruction. Their work was destroyed by a renewed German offensive and the Allied counteroffensive (Mar.–Oct. 1918). The committee's task was divided: the military wing ran ambulances and canteens in teams of two American women with a vehicle. They fed as many as 7,000 soldiers a day and 45,000 a week, sleeping exhausted in their trucks at night, then moving on with the advancing front. The refugee teams concentrated on the thousands of displaced people who fled the fighting or had to abandon their destroyed villages.

With the armistice in 1918, the women returned to the Aisne to find the devastation worse than before, with close to 90 percent of the housing, public buildings, schools, and industry destroyed and 80 percent of the prewar population killed, maimed, or homeless. Over the next four years the women established a network of clinics, schools, community centers, and a home visitation program, and they provided clothing, medicine, agricultural tools, and social services to over one hundred devastated towns and villages in the Aisne and neighboring areas. Besides directing this operation, Morgan herself served in all aspects of the work and in addition spearheaded a fund drive that raised more than $5 million. Her report gives a detailed presentation of the work of this organization (*Summarized Statement of Work of the American Committee for Devastated France, Inc., from April 1, 1918 to March 31, 1924* [1924]). Before she left France in 1924, Morgan founded a French national museum of Franco-American cooperation at her old headquarters at Blérancourt; the French government awarded her the Croix de Guerre and made her a commander of the Legion of Honor, the first American woman so honored.

Back in New York, Morgan assumed the chair of a committee of the AWA raising money to build a 27-story building in Manhattan, and she held meetings for 200 to 300 clubwomen four nights a week in her own home. In 1928 she was elected president of the AWA, serving in that capacity for fifteen years and continuing thereafter as honorary president and member of the board of governors.

By 1938 Morgan was convinced that war in Europe was inevitable, so she presented to the French army a plan for civilian relief under a newly formed Comité Américain de Secours Civil (CASC). The following year she returned to Blérancourt, and she and her team went to work once again on ambulance duty and evacuation of refugees from the Aisne and Ardennes regions, quitting Blérancourt only a half-hour before its occupation by the Germans. When France capitulated, Morgan was one of the few Americans to remain. She returned to Paris and demanded permission of the German ambassador to return to Blérancourt to resume her work. The German authorities soon found her committee too effective and independent for their liking, so Morgan was forced to return to New York, where she continued fundraising and preparation of relief shipments despite frequent bureaucratic interference.

In 1946 Anne Morgan returned again to France to survey the work of the CASC. She was dismayed at the damage done by Allied bombing in the north of France, the effects of which had been downplayed in the American press. Fundraising was difficult, as the American public was tired of the war, and Morgan's health had begun to give way.

Morgan's imperious, impatient manner; tall, handsome figure; stately presence; deep, resonant voice; and intense, unswerving sense of purpose made a lasting impression on all who dealt with her. Memory of her was still vivid in northern France forty years after her death.

The American relief effort in France, to which Anne Morgan devoted her time, energy, organizational skills, and wealth, was the first of its kind in scale and complexity. She was the most visible and influential of numerous American women who left comfortable circumstances to face the danger and drudgery of a war-ravaged countryside. As a leading independent woman in American society, she championed numerous projects and organizations to improve the working conditions and social and economic position of women in her own country.

The CASC continued its work until 1951, with Morgan as president in name only. She retired to her estate in Mount Kisco, New York, where she died.

• The main repositories of Anne Morgan's papers are the Morgan Library, New York, and the Musée de la Coopération franco-américaine, Blérancourt, France; additional material is in the files of the Association Anne Morgan, Soissons, France. Her publications include "Sidelights on the Woman Question" and "Copy Cats," *Saturday Evening Post*, 26 Mar. 1927 and 6 Oct. 1928, respectively. Biographical sketches include Margaret K. Leech, "Profiles: Lady into Dynamo," *New Yorker*, 22 Oct. 1927, pp. 21–23, and Mary F. Watkins, "Anne Morgan: An Intimate Portrait," *Woman Citizen*, n.s. 12 (Aug. 1927): 8–9, 31–32. The fullest study of her relief work in France is Evelyne Diebolt and Jean-Pierre Laurant, *Anne Morgan, une Américaine en Soissonnais (1917–1952), de l'Aisne devastée à l'action sociale* (1990); her work in the Second World War has been described by Lilla Pennant, *Anne Morgan, Eva Dahlgren, Rose Dolan, and the Aid They Brought to French Refugees 1939–1949* (1990). Recollections of her as a child are in Elizabeth Drexel Lehr, *"King Lehr" and the Gilded Age* (1935), pp. 17–18. Her early work in New York and her life in France just before the First World War are best known from Elizabeth Marbury, *My Crystal Ball* (1923), with portrait opposite p. 252; other photos are in "A Life of Rebuilding the Wreckage of War," *Life*, 11 Feb. 1952. Her relations with her family are discussed by Ron Chernow, *The House of Morgan* (1990), pp. 140–44. An obituary is in the *New York Times*, 30 Jan. 1952.

BENJAMIN R. FOSTER

MORGAN, Ann Haven (6 May 1882–5 June 1966), zoologist and ecologist, was born in Waterford, Connecticut, the daughter of Stanley Griswold Morgan and Julia Douglass. Ann Morgan, who was christened Anna, grew up in Waterford, where she explored the area's forests and streams, developing an early interest in biology. She attended the Williams Memorial Institute at New London.

In 1902 Morgan began studies at Wellesley College but transferred two years later to Cornell University, a campus with fewer restrictions for female students. Morgan completed an undergraduate zoology degree in 1906 and was hired as an assistant and instructor at Mount Holyoke College. By 1909 she had returned to Cornell, where she studied at the Limnological Laboratory with James G. Needham, who had admired Morgan before she was his student, submitting her name in 1908 for membership to the Entomological Society, to which she was accepted.

Morgan was inspired by Needham, whom she claimed "helped her to see things in the water," as she studied the aquatic biology of insects. An assistant and instructor, Morgan was nicknamed "Mayfly" Morgan by her freshmen lab students because of her dissertation "A Contribution to the Biology of May-flies." She changed her legal name to Ann on this work, which earned her a Ph.D. from Cornell in 1912 and was published in the *Annals of the Entomological Society of America* in 1913.

Morgan agreed to teach at Mount Holyoke and quickly advanced through the ranks to chair of the Department of Zoology in 1916 and full professor by 1918. She focused on reforming the science curriculum at Mount Holyoke and throughout the United States, urging her colleagues at other institutions to integrate an ecological perspective into courses. Defining herself as a "general zoologist," not a specialist, Morgan taught courses on water and winter biology (the study of how wildlife survives, copes, and adapts during severe weather and how it readjusts in the spring), emphasizing conservation to her students. She took her classes on field trips to conduct primary observations and research, as stressed by her mentor, Mount Holyoke biologist Cornelia Clapp. Through her teaching, Morgan intrigued many talented women in the field of zoology.

Beginning in 1918 Morgan taught and researched echinoderms at the Marine Biological Laboratory at Woods Hole, Massachusetts, and returned for several summers during the early 1920s. She pursued investigations on William Beebe's preserve at the Tropical Laboratory at Kartabo, British Guiana, in 1926. Morgan was also a visiting fellow at Harvard and Yale Universities and was judged one of a group of "master grantswomen" at Mount Holyoke, securing research funds from the National Academy of Sciences, National Research Council, and Rockefeller Foundation. Morgan was starred in three editions of *American Men of Science*, designating her as one of a select group of scientists, most of whom were male.

Morgan published three books, all deemed zoological classics. The first, *Field Book of Ponds and Streams: An Introduction to the Life of Fresh Water* (1930), was a popular guide lauded as an "angler's favorite" by amateur naturalists. Explaining how to study and collect stream and pond specimens, Morgan's text emphasized the role of aquatic insects in the ecosystem. "This book began in ponds where frogs sat on the lily-pads and by swift brooks from which mayflies flew forth at twilight," she wrote. "I hope that it may be a guide into the vividness and variety of their ways" (p. vii). She illustrated her text with her own drawings and photographs, describing algae, liverworts, mosses, leeches, crustaceans, snails, mussels, salamanders, turtles, and snakes. She credited her colleagues for her zoological insights, especially Clapp's enthusiasm and Needham, who "first showed me how to look for things in the water."

Morgan's *Field Book of Animals in Winter* (1939), written for both amateurs and professionals, analyzed the "ways in which animals meet the crises and depressions of winter." Morgan presented survival strategies, such as hibernation and migration. Considering it "invigorating" to explore how insects, mammals, birds, amphibians, fish, and reptiles secured shelter and food and endured hardships, Morgan admired their "persistence which must hearten any human being to contemplate." She assisted the *Encyclopedia Britannica* in making an educational movie about her book and published related articles in *Anatomical Record*.

Morgan retired in 1947, enabling her to research and write other than at the holidays and "odd hours" that had been her creative time while teaching. She became increasingly interested in conservation and the environment. A mentor to Elizabeth Adams, a Mount Holyoke zoologist, Morgan invited Adams to travel throughout the western United States with her to assess projects for the National Commission on Policies in Conservation Education. At home, Morgan planned conservation projects for the Connecticut River valley and taught summer workshops to teachers, sharing her knowledge and enthusiasm for conservation and ecology. She urged educators to incorporate conservation topics in the science curricula, writing about her efforts in the *Mount Holyoke Alumnae Quarterly*. When not teaching, she was happiest wading in "some particularly oozy mudhole" to snare specimens.

In Morgan's third book, *Kinships of Animals and Man: A Textbook of Animal Biology* (1955), she observed that "humanity is facing two very old problems, living with itself and living with its natural surroundings. . . . Conservation is one way of working out these problems, an appreciation and intelligent care of living things and their environment. It is applied Ecology" (p. 792). She outlined animal behavior, revealing how animals cooperate and compete and urging humans to preserve the environment and coexist with wildlife. "Now that the wilderness is almost gone, we are beginning to be lonesome for it," she warned. "We shall keep a refuge in our minds if we conserve the remnants" (p. 792). Used as a basic zoology textbook, Morgan's treatise enabled the public to access and understand conservation topics.

A "true pioneer in the taxonomy and biology of mayflies" (Alexander, p. 1), Morgan was also lauded as a science educator both in the classroom and as an author. Her promotion of local and global conservation and her lucid analysis of environmental threats to natural habitats alerted both professional and amateur naturalists to protect ecological concerns, mobilizing the conservation movement. Suffering from stomach cancer, Morgan, who never married, died in South Hadley, Massachusetts.

• Morgan's manuscripts and papers are available at Mount Holyoke College's Williston Library and the Cornell University Archives. A biographical account is Charles P. Alexander, "Ann Haven Morgan, 1882–1966," *Eatonia* 8 (15 Feb. 1967): 1–3. Morgan's career is discussed in Marcia M. Bonta, *Women in the Field: America's Pioneering Women Naturalists* (1991), and Margaret W. Rossiter, *Women Scientists in America: Struggles and Strategies to 1940* (1982). An obituary is in the *New York Times*, 6 June 1966.

ELIZABETH D. SCHAFER

MORGAN, Arthur Ernest (20 June 1878–15 Nov. 1975), college president and first chairman of the Tennessee Valley Authority (TVA), was born in Cincinnati, Ohio, the son of John Morgan, a surveyor and schoolteacher, and Anna Wiley, also a schoolteacher. Shortly after Arthur's birth, the family moved to St. Cloud, Minnesota, where he grew up. If his father influenced Arthur to become an engineer, his mother influenced him to become hard working, disciplined, and self-righteous; to seek perfection in all his pursuits; and to hold others to his elevated personal standards. Morgan's lifelong inability to tolerate behavioral and moral differences in associates and subordinates alike originated in childhood.

Morgan's formal education ended at high school in St. Cloud. In both 1897 and 1898 he enrolled at the University of Colorado but, citing an unspecified illness, quickly dropped out. Here as throughout his life, his general good health, bolstered by regular vigorous exercise, gave way to temporary complaints of sickness whenever major personal or professional problems arose. Not surprisingly, Morgan was sometimes called a hypochondriac.

In 1904 Morgan married Urania Jones, an osteopath. A son was born a year later, but shortly thereafter Urania died of typhoid fever. In 1911 Morgan married Lucy Griscom, a Wellesley College graduate and chemistry and home economics instructor. They later had two children. Lucy influenced Morgan, a Baptist, to become a Quaker. Morgan's subsequent commitment to reaching a Quaker-like consensus and avoiding conflict proved difficult to reconcile with his prior but persistent harsh judgments of others' alleged failings.

Morgan became an engineer because it was then still possible to avoid school-based professional training and to acquire expertise on the job—a key part of his later curricular endeavors as an educator. He shrewdly specialized in the emerging field of flood control and soon became America's foremost hydraulic engineer. Taught basic skills by his father, whose small surveying business he took over in 1905, Morgan began treating rivers as components of larger environmental systems, a perspective that later shaped his vision of TVA.

In 1907 Morgan moved to Washington, D.C., to work for the Agriculture Department's Office of Drainage Investigations. Although he spent most of his time away on on-site drainage planning, he was stimulated by the growing conservation movement centered in the capital. It reinforced his holistic and moralistic conception of his calling. If, like other progressive conservationists, Morgan considered himself a kind of scientific manager of the natural environment, he simultaneously believed that the alteration of the landscape brought about by his often large-scale engineering projects benefited society.

Notwithstanding his visionary bent, Morgan left his government post in 1910 in order to earn more income. Capitalizing on his government service and contacts, he established an engineering firm in Memphis, Tennessee. Morgan Engineering Company's growing financial success complemented its president's prized certification by the American Society of Civil Engineers as an associate member. Despite the absence of any degrees, Morgan was made a full member in 1913 and in 1927 was elected a vice president.

In 1913 Morgan and his family moved to Dayton, Ohio, where Morgan had been appointed chief engineer of what, within two years, became the Miami (Valley) Conservancy District, the largest flood control project to that time. Its regional autonomy presaged that later granted TVA. Likewise, the social engineering that Morgan embraced at TVA had its origins here, including comfortable housing for workers, educational and recreational opportunities for both them and their families, and limited self-governance at each of the five district dam sites.

In 1921 Morgan left the district to accept the presidency of Antioch College in nearby Yellow Springs, Ohio. Founded by educational reformer Horace Mann in 1853, the college faced bankruptcy when Morgan, already a trustee, took over. In addition to financial improvements that kept Antioch alive, Morgan extended cooperative education, or combined academic and practical work programs, to the liberal arts; it had hitherto been restricted to engineering schools. Morgan was not hesitant to boast of his accomplishments in the national press and to have others praise him in print as well.

On 18 May 1933 newly installed president Franklin Roosevelt signed the legislation creating TVA and announced Morgan's appointment as chairman of TVA's three-member board of directors. Morgan did not know Roosevelt and had in fact voted for fellow engineer Herbert Hoover (1874–1964) for president the year before; exactly who recommended Morgan to Roosevelt remains unclear. Their initial meeting nevertheless convinced Morgan not only that Roosevelt shared his vision of comprehensive, multipurpose regional planning but also that TVA would be free from politics altogether. Both were dubious assumptions.

From the outset, Morgan repeatedly clashed over virtually everything with his more pragmatic fellow directors, Harcourt Morgan (no relation), a low-key specialist in agricultural resource management, and David Lilienthal, an ambitious public utilities lawyer and regulator. Gradually the latter two prevailed, not only in Knoxville but also in Washington, D.C. Arthur Morgan was eventually dismissed by Roosevelt in 1938 after failing to document repeated public charges that the other directors were guilty of malfeasance and lack of integrity. A subsequent congressional investigation found no basis for those charges and further damaged Morgan's public image and, ironically, his reputation for integrity. Morgan's lifelong inability to accept legitimate dissenting views and his naive belief that apolitical engineering values and practices could readily be applied to so political an agency as TVA proved his undoing. Morgan had misread Roosevelt and the extent of Roosevelt's support for him. Paradoxically, Morgan was, with greater justification, accused by Lilienthal and others of being much too willing to compromise with the private utilities generally hostile to TVA in order to reach a consensus at all costs. Far from simply being pragmatic in a conventional sense, however, Morgan was trying to follow the Quaker discipline of avoiding conflict.

By 1938 TVA had made cheap power production its hallmark, and Morgan's broader vision of social and moral engineering had been largely cast aside. Significantly, Lilienthal's very popular book *TVA: Democracy on the March* (1944) omitted not only Morgan's achievements but his very name. Lilienthal emphasized TVA's efficient public administration, its responsiveness to local concerns, and its "grass-roots democracy." All were at best exaggerations of the truth. Yet Morgan's engineering accomplishments—above all, the original dams and their professional staffs—were crucial to TVA's technical and economic successes.

After his dismissal, Morgan returned to Yellow Springs, where he lived the rest of his life. He devoted much of his time to Community Service, Inc., an organization he founded in 1940. He advocated small communities as the cornerstone of economic and moral uplift, a notion he had tried out at TVA with limited success. On their behalf he wrote and traveled extensively until late in life.

In 1944 Morgan published three books on Edward Bellamy, whose influential *Looking Backward* (1888) he had first read in 1893, and a fourth book on utopias two years later. No other modern professional engineer has embraced utopianism to this degree, but Morgan saw social and material engineering as complementary, together leading to perfection.

Morgan's charter membership and active participation in the American Eugenics Society was a related pursuit. He was even asked to lead the organization while chairman of TVA but declined. Like so many others of that persuasion, Morgan deemed white Anglo-Saxons as the truest and best Americans, as those who alone could perfect the nation. Not surprisingly, Morgan proved no better than other TVA administrators in providing adequate employment, training, and housing opportunities for qualified African and Native Americans. He died in Xenia, Ohio.

As TVA has lost its early luster and become widely identified as yet another bloated government bureaucracy—and as an expensive and environmentally destructive power producer—Morgan's original comprehensive vision has been seen in an increasingly sympathetic light. So, too, has his aversion to politics. Whether, however, Morgan's TVA legacy will ever rival Lilienthal's remains uncertain.

• Morgan's papers and publications are in Antioch College's Olive Kettering Library. Other significant materials are in TVA's technical library and in TVA's central files, both in Knoxville. Morgan's most important book is probably his last one, *The Making of the TVA* (1974). His other significant books are *My World* (1928); *The Long Road* (1936); *The Small Community, Foundation of Democratic Life* (1942); *Edward Bellamy* (1944); *Nowhere Was Somewhere: How History Makes Utopias and How Utopias Make History* (1946); *The Miami Conservancy District* (1951); and *Dams and Other Disasters: A Century of the Army Corps of Engineers in Civil Works* (1971). The most complete modern assessment is Roy Talbert, Jr., *FDR's Utopian: Arthur Morgan of the TVA* (1987). See also Erwin C. Hargrove and Paul K. Conkin, eds., *TVA: Fifty Years of Grass-Roots Bureaucracy* (1983). Older, more personal, but still useful assessments are Lucy Griscom Morgan, *Finding His Way: The Story of Arthur E. Morgan* (1928); Clarence J. Leuba, *A Road to Creativity, Arthur Morgan: Engineer, Educator, Administrator* (1971); and Walter Kahoe, *Arthur Morgan: A Biography and Memoir* (1977). An obituary is in the *New York Times*, 17 Nov. 1975.

HOWARD P. SEGAL

MORGAN, Clement Garnett (1859–1 June 1929), attorney and civil rights leader, was born in Stafford County, Virginia, the son of slaves. After being emancipated during the Civil War, the family moved to Washington, D.C., where Morgan attended the well-regarded Preparatory High School for Colored Youth. He left school and worked briefly as a barber in Washington before moving to St. Louis, Missouri, where he worked as a teacher for four years.

In 1885 Morgan moved to Boston to attend the Boston Latin School. After graduating in 1886, he enrolled in Harvard College, where he and W. E. B. Du Bois were then the only African-American students. While at Harvard, Morgan supported himself by working as a barber and by giving readings and speeches at summer resorts. Sizable scholarships for academic excellence took care of most of his tuition costs. In 1889 he won the Boylston Prize for oratory (Du Bois finished second). In his senior year Morgan was named class orator. After graduating from college in 1890, Morgan entered Harvard Law School, receiving his LL.B. in 1893. That year he passed the bar and established a law office in Cambridge.

In addition to his law practice, Morgan developed a career in local electoral politics. Running as a Republican in 1895, he became the first African American elected from predominately white Ward Two to the Common Council of Cambridge. In 1898, after serving the two-year term on the common council, he successfully ran for a two-year term as alderman. He then ran unsuccessfully for the state legislature in 1899, 1900, and 1908. In 1897 Morgan married Gertrude Wright.

In the late 1890s Morgan became a part of the so-called "Negro Radicals," a group of prominent African-American intellectuals, attorneys, and activists that included Butler R. Wilson, Archibald H. Grimké, George Forbes, and most notably, William Monroe Trotter. This group, which advocated agitation for full civil rights, led the opposition to Booker T. Washington's politics of accommodation for African Americans. Morgan served as an attorney for Trotter when the latter was charged with inciting what came to be known as the "Boston Riot" of 1903, when several of the Radicals disrupted a speech being given by Washington.

In 1904 Morgan helped form the Committee of Twelve for the Advancement of the Interests of the Negro Race, a short-lived coalition of Radicals and Washington's followers that attempted to reconcile the two factions. In 1905, after the Committee of Twelve fell apart, Morgan joined the Niagara movement, an organization founded by Du Bois that split sharply from Washington in its strident denunciations of Jim Crow laws and militant advocacy for African-American rights. Morgan was named as the head of the Massachusetts branch of the new organization.

Morgan soon became involved in factional disputes that ultimately led to the demise of the Niagara movement. He feuded with Trotter over support for Massachusetts governor Curtis Guild's reelection. In exchange for supporting Guild, Morgan had been nominated for the state legislature by the Republicans. Trotter opposed the governor on the grounds that Guild had approved of giving state funds to Jamestown, Virginia, for the town's segregated tricentennial exposition. In 1907 Morgan excluded Trotter from the planning of a Niagara fundraising event in Boston. The Niagara Executive Committee sided with Trotter and voted to remove Morgan from his position as president of the Massachusetts branch. Du Bois then interceded and convinced the executive committee to retain

Morgan. A subsequent split developed between Du Bois and Trotter over another Boston event in which Morgan was involved, leading to the virtual disintegration of the Niagara movement by 1909.

In 1910 Morgan and Du Bois joined the newly formed National Association for the Advancement of Colored People (NAACP). From 1912 to 1914 Morgan served on the executive committee of the Boston branch of the NAACP. In the last years of his life he continued his law practice in Cambridge and remained active in local civil rights work. He was a leading organizer of the campaigns to stop the showing of the film "The Birth of a Nation" in Boston in 1915 and 1921. Morgan died in Cambridge.

• Information on Morgan is in several works on Du Bois and Trotter, including David Levering Lewis, *W. E. B. Du Bois: Biography of a Race, 1868–1919* (1993); Elliott M. Rudwick, *W. E. B. Du Bois: Propagandist of the Negro Protest* (1969); and Stephen R. Fox, *The Guardian of Boston: William Monroe Trotter* (1970). Obituaries are in the *Boston Globe*, 3 June 1929, and the *New York Age*, 8 June 1929.

THADDEUS RUSSELL

MORGAN, Dale Lowell (18 Dec. 1914–30 Mar. 1971), historian, editor, and bibliographer, was born in Salt Lake City, Utah, the son of James Lowell Morgan, an office machine salesman, and Emily May Holmes, a schoolteacher. Morgan's father died when he was six years old, and the burden of caring for the family of four children fell on his mother, who taught in the Salt Lake City public schools. Morgan was a gifted student, but his contracting spinal meningitis at age fourteen seriously changed his life; he was left totally deaf.

Morgan eventually graduated from the University of Utah in 1937 with a degree in art but was unable to find work. His skills in writing, however, led to his involvement in the Utah Historical Records Survey under the Works Progress Administration (WPA). In 1940 he was appointed state supervisor. While working for the WPA, he helped prepare the *Inventories of County Archives of Utah* (1939–1941) and, in 1941, *Utah: A Guide to the State*. These early projects show the attention to detail as well as the descriptive ability that would characterize his later work in western American history.

From 1942 to 1954 Morgan was engaged in a number of research and writing projects, and for three of these years (during World War II) he worked as an information specialist, Department of Information, in the Office of Price Administration in Washington, D.C. During this time he was able to do historical research in the Library of Congress. Using monies from a Guggenheim Fellowship, from 1947 to 1949 he traveled and researched extensively on a projected three-volume history of the Church of Jesus Christ of Latter-day Saints (Mormon). While he never composed more than a few chapters, this intensive period of research formed the basis for his important bibliographical work on the Latter-day Saints. From 1949 to 1954 he worked for the Utah State Historical Society and in 1954 moved to the Bancroft Library at the University of California, Berkeley, first to research the Navajo Tribe Land Claim case, then to edit the Guide Program of Manuscripts. He remained at the Bancroft until his retirement in 1970 and died of cancer shortly thereafter in Accokeek, Maryland. He never married.

From 1940 to his death Morgan authored or edited over forty books on Mormonism, the California Gold Rush, the history of the fur trade, and the Overland Trail. In addition to his meticulous editions of important sources for western Americana, his introductions and extensive annotations added greatly to the scholarly value of the individual works.

While his own history of the Mormon church was never completed, the initial chapters were gathered together with selective correspondence and published in 1986. In addition to his work with the WPA, he prepared *A History of Ogden* (1940) and *Provo, Pioneer Mormon City* (1942). His collection of documents relating to the proposed Mormon State of Deseret in 1849 remains an essential text for students of Utah history (see *Utah Historical Quarterly* 8 [Apr., July, Oct. 1940]). His *The Great Salt Lake* was published in 1947 and his bibliography of Mormonism was significantly expanded and eventually published by Chad J. Flake, *A Mormon Bibliography, 1830–1930: Books, Pamphlets, Periodicals, and Broadsides Relating to the First Century of Mormonism* (1978). Morgan also served as a mentor of a number of students of Mormon history, including Fawn M. Brodie and Juanita Brooks.

Morgan's work on the California Gold Rush consisted of editing a number of important texts, such as William S. McCollum's *California as I Saw It . . .* (1960), and in assisting Carl Wheat on the important five-volume *Mapping the Transmississippi West, 1540–1861* (1957–1963).

Some of Morgan's very best work was on the history of the fur trade. His biography *Jedediah Smith and the Opening of the West* (1953) and his editing of *The West of William H. Ashley: The International Struggle of the Fur Trade of the Missouri, the Rocky Mountains, and the Columbia, with Explorations Beyond the Continental Divide, Recorded in the Diaries and Letters of William H. Ashley and His Contemporaries, 1822–1838* (1964) are standard works on the topic.

Morgan also manifested his careful historical sense in studying the western trails. His careful study *The Humboldt: Highroad of the West* (1943) was followed by a number of edited texts, the most important of which were *The Overland Diary of James A. Pritchard from Kentucky to California in 1849* (1959) and *Overland in 1846: Diaries and Letters of the California-Oregon Trail* (2 vols., 1963). His professional relationship with individual rare book and manuscript dealers for whom he occasionally worked, like Ernst Ederstadt and Fred Rosenstock, gave him additional insight into the literature of the American West. He started a series of book reviews of western history and fiction for the *Saturday Review of Literature* in 1945. His bibliographies remain valuable guides to their topics.

During his lifetime Morgan received a number of awards for his research and writing: Fellow Award, Utah State Historical Society, 1970; Henry R. Wagner Memorial Award, California Historical Society, 1961; Award of Merit, American Association for State and Local History, 1965, 1969; Silver Buffalo Award, New York Westerners, 1966; and John Simon Guggenheim Fellowships, 1945, 1970.

• Morgan was a prolific writer and researcher. His voluminous personal papers (66 linear feet) are housed in the Bancroft Library, University of California, Berkeley. The collection was microfilmed in 1992. An extensive register to the collection is available. A copy of the microfilm has been deposited in the J. Willard Marriott Library, Special Collections, University of Utah, Salt Lake City. The papers of Madeline McQuown and Fawn M. Brodie, both friends of Morgan, as well as those of a cousin, T. Gerald Bleak, are housed in the Marriott Library and all contain Morgan material. An extensive collection relating to the Utah WPA Writer's Project is in the Utah State Historical Society, Salt Lake City.

The most comprehensive guide to Morgan's writings is Richard L. Saunders, *Eloquence from a Silent World: A Descriptive Bibliography of the Published Writings of Dale L. Morgan* (1990). Copies of Morgan's extensive bibliography of transcriptions of materials on Mormonism in early American newspapers are in Harold B. Lee Library, Brigham Young University, Provo, Utah; the Henry E. Huntington Library, San Marino, Calif.; Utah State Historical Society Library; and the Beinecke Library, Yale University.

A useful collection of correspondence and the first printing of Morgan's unfinished history of early Mormonism is *Dale Morgan on Early Mormonism, Correspondence and a New History*, ed. John Phillip Walker (1986). Short biographical tributes by a former colleague at the Utah State Historical Society are Everett L. Cooley, "In Memoriam, Dale L. Morgan, 1914–1971," *Utah Historical Quarterly* 39 (Winter 1971): 85–88, and Cooley, "A Dedication to the Memory of Dale L. Morgan, 1914–1971," *Arizona and the West* 19 (Summer 1977): 102–6. See also Richard Saunders, "'The Strange Mixture of Emotion and Intellect': A Social History of Dale L. Morgan, 1933–43," *Dialogue, a Journal of Mormon Thought* 28 (Winter 1995): 39–58.

DAVID J. WHITTAKER

MORGAN, Daniel (c. 1735–6 July 1802), revolutionary war general, was born in either Bucks County, Pennsylvania, or Hunterdon County, New Jersey, the son of James Morgan, a farm laborer and ironmaster, and Eleanor (maiden name unknown). His parents were immigrants from Wales. Morgan, estranged from his father, at age eighteen went to Frederick County in Virginia's Shenandoah Valley. He worked as a farm laborer and as a wagon driver. Soon he was able to afford his own wagon and team and became a teamster. In this capacity he served in the Braddock expedition of 1755. He knocked down a British officer and was sentenced to 500 stripes; Morgan later boasted that he had received only 499. After the war, the burly six-foot Morgan eventually settled on a 255-acre farm that he purchased, eleven miles east of Winchester. Morgan held local public office as a surveyor, deputy sheriff, road supervisor, and militia captain. By 1774 he owned ten slaves. During Lord Dunmore's War (1774) Morgan headed a volunteer company on an expedition to the Ohio Indian country but did not see action.

Morgan lived ten years in a common-law relationship with Abigail Curry, the daughter of poor parents in Berkeley County. A son was born out of wedlock. After the couple was married in 1773 they had two daughters.

Answering Congress's first call for troops for a Continental army, Morgan raised a company of riflemen and, in the rank of captain, led them to George Washington's headquarters at Cambridge, Massachusetts, in the summer of 1775. He volunteered for Benedict Arnold's expedition to Canada, in which he commanded three rifle companies. Captured in the ill-fated assault on the Lower Town of Quebec on 31 December 1775, Morgan remained in the city as a prisoner of war until paroled on 11 August 1776. Returning to his home in Frederick County, Virginia, he was exchanged in January 1777 and thus free to fight again.

Congress, on 12 November 1776, had appointed Morgan colonel. Morgan fought in the skirmishing in New Jersey in early 1777; in August of that year he joined Horatio Gates's Northern army, in charge of a corps of riflemen whom Washington had selected from the main army. Morgan's rifle unit was the only one in the American armies. His troops were especially effective with their long (Kentucky) rifles, which had a range of 200 yards, twice that of a musket. As snipers and "wood-fighters," Morgan's men were capable of harassing enemy marches and supply lines at a distance. Morgan emerged as a hero of both battles of Saratoga: Freeman's Farm, 19 September, and Bemis Heights, 7 October 1777. Morgan's riflemen exacted a heavy toll in the forest at the British army's right in both battles. General John Burgoyne wrote that Morgan's men "hovered upon the flanks in small detachments and were very expert in securing themselves and in shifting their ground."

Morgan next joined Washington's army at Whitemarsh, Pennsylvania, where in December 1777 his men repelled an advancing British column under General Charles Grey. Morgan stayed with the army at its encampment at Valley Forge. In the confusion of the battle of Monmouth, 28 June 1778, his men came up after the main action. Morgan then went on an indefinite furlough. Resenting Anthony Wayne's appointment as commander of the newly created light infantry corps instead of himself, Morgan took an honorable furlough from the army on 18 July 1779.

Disheartend by Gates's defeat at Camden, South Carolina, in August 1780, Morgan on his own joined the Southern army. On 13 October 1780 Congress made him a brigadier general. General Nathanael Greene, Gates's successor, gave Morgan charge of light infantry and in mid-December 1780 sent Morgan to collect militia and to take position between the Broad and Pacolet rivers. Lieutenant Colonel Banastre Tarleton and his legion, detached from General

Charles Cornwallis's army, accepted the challenge. At the battle of Cowpens, 17 January 1781, Morgan demonstrated his tactical genius in disposing his troops in three broadly separated lines down a gentle sloping terrain—largely militia holding the first two lines, with the Continentals in the third position. Mounted infantry and dragoons were kept at the rear. When Tarleton rushed into an attack, the militia held briefly, as planned, and regrouped with other units further back; the American cavalry swept down the flanks, and Tarleton was caught in a double envelopment. Congress voted a medal honoring Morgan for the victory at Cowpens on 9 March 1781, which, however, he did not receive until 1790. After Cowpens, Morgan provided the rear guard for Greene's escape across the Dan River, while being pursued by Cornwallis. Suffering from sciatica and rheumatism, Morgan went home on a leave of absence.

In 1781 Morgan aided Lafayette's army against Cornwallis in Virginia by raising recruits and sending on supplies. After a brief time in the field, he had to return home because of his physical ailments.

During the Whiskey Insurrection of 1794, Morgan (appointed a major general of Virginia militia in 1793) led light infantry troops as the federalized militia army marched into western Pennsylvania. The army met no resistance. General Henry Lee, the commander, left Morgan and 1,500 troops in charge of the "Whiskey country." Morgan showed leniency to the rebels by allowing leaders not included in a general pardon to go home on parole. The troops were disbanded in May 1795.

Morgan, as a Federalist, served in the House of Representatives from 4 March 1797 to 3 March 1799. His main legislative contribution was to support the war initiative against France and the Sedition Act. Because of ill health he did not seek another term. After the war Morgan had become a large landholder, in Virginia and west of the Alleghenies. In 1797 he purchased a house in Winchester. Incapacitated for six months from crippling arthritis and infirmities of old age, he died there.

Of humble origins and a product of the frontier, Morgan was an officer with whom the common soldier could identify. Untried as a commander of a whole army or in grand strategy, he was, nevertheless, with resourcefulness and cunning, a superb tactician.

• Chief sources for Morgan papers are the Theodorus B. Myers Collection at the New York Public Library; the Horatio Gates Papers at the New-York Historical Society; and Richard K. Showman, ed., *The Papers of General Nathanael Greene*, vol. 7 (1994). The book-length biographies are James Graham, *The Life of General Daniel Morgan . . . with Portions of His Correspondence* (1859); Don Higginbotham, *Daniel Morgan: Revolutionary Rifleman* (1961); and North Callahan, *Daniel Morgan: Ranger of the Revolution* (1961).

HARRY M. WARD

MORGAN, Edwin Denison (8 Feb. 1811–14 Feb. 1883), merchant and politician, was born in Washington, Massachusetts, the son of Jasper Morgan and Catherine Avery, farmers. When Edwin was nine years old the family moved to Connecticut, where he received a sparse formal education that ended when he was fifteen. At seventeen he became a clerk in an uncle's general store. Quickly displaying an acumen for business and politics, he became a partner in the store at twenty and a member of the Hartford Common Council the next year. He married his cousin Eliza Waterman in 1833; of their five children only the first born, Edwin, survived infancy.

Lured by the larger commercial opportunities of New York City, Morgan in 1837 began there a lucrative mercantile career, coming to specialize in importing and distributing sugar and coffee. Decisive, tireless as he was taciturn, he soon established a reputation for shrewdness, integrity, competence, and a penchant for politics. In 1849 he won election as a Whig to the city's Board of Assistant Aldermen, which named him as president. His skill in dealing with the city's affairs and the cholera epidemic that ravaged the metropolis led to his election later that year to the state senate.

Morgan rose rapidly in state and national politics. During four years in the senate, where he was president *pro tempore* and chairman of its financial committee, he formed close associations with antislavery Whig leaders Thurlow Weed, William H. Seward, and Hamilton Fish. In 1855 when the Whigs fused with the newly created Republican party, Morgan swiftly embraced the party and became state chairman. He helped organize the coalition of state factions opposed to the extension of slavery and became the first national chairman of the Republican party, a post he held in all for twelve years. Throughout the turbulent year 1856, Morgan strove energetically to guide the process of party realignment and to raise campaign funds. Though he failed to procure enough money for the presidential contest in Pennsylvania, he took consolation in his belief that he had helped found a powerful antislavery party.

While in the senate he introduced and saw through a measure establishing Central Park in New York City. From 1855 to 1858 he served as a commissioner on the New York State Board of Emigration, a courageous act for an aspiring politician in view of the strong anti-foreign sentiment in the nation. He also became president of the Hudson River Railroad, which was later merged into the New York Central system. Despite his sympathy for immigrants, his railroad connection, and his silence on temperance, he won election as governor in 1858 in a four-cornered contest, cutting into Democratic strength in New York City.

During his first term as governor Morgan improved the state's tangled finances, secured a voter registry law, and vetoed legislation sought by special interests, including a group of notoriously corrupt New York City railroad bills favored by Weed. In 1860, still national party chairman, he swallowed his disappointment when Seward failed to gain the presidential nomination. Believing Abraham Lincoln's victory essential to the party's survival, he bent his efforts to raising money, especially for the critical states of Pennsylvania and Indiana. He was gratified by Lincoln's victory over what he considered southern domination of the nation as well as by his own reelection in 1860 by the largest majority ever won by a New York governor.

Throughout the secession crisis Morgan's was a voice of moderation, recommending New York's participation in the Virginia-sponsored peace convention and repeal of its personal liberty law, though he believed the latter move would chiefly unite the North as a defender of the Constitution. The surrender of Fort Sumter, however, prompted quick action on his part in enrolling and equipping troops, appropriating money, and dispatching forces to Washington. Morgan was one of a handful of New Yorkers whom Lincoln enlisted to aid the secretaries of the army and navy in forwarding troops and supplies. In 1861 and 1862 he tirelessly sent forward over 250,000 men. He offered a premium to those who enlisted thirty-two recruits, paid a bounty to volunteers, and endorsed the Militia Act of 1862 though he advised against using it to draft men on the eve of the fall elections.

Worn by his labors and aware of the Democrats' growing popularity in the state, Morgan chose not to seek a third term as governor. Backed by Weed, however, he won election as United States senator. In 1863 he counseled the War Department on the New York City draft riots, seeing the violence as resulting in part from exemptions for cash payments; he also advised the president on military arrests, saying resolutions condemning the government and favoring the peace party "had best be permitted to go on." The following year he so firmly opposed a New York appointment put forward by Secretary of the Treasury Salmon P. Chase that the secretary resigned from the cabinet. Calling to order the Union party convention during the 1864 presidential election, Morgan, after consulting with Lincoln, urged adoption of an emancipation plank. He relinquished the party chairmanship and served on the Union executive committee, distributing campaign speakers and documents. Early in 1865 he refused Lincoln's offer to appoint him secretary of the treasury.

Working diligently but speaking little, Morgan discharged his senatorial duties, succeeding in abolishing military exemption by payment of money. Though loyal to Lincoln he voted for the Wade-Davis bill by which Congress sought to take control of Reconstruction. With war's end he at first supported President Andrew Johnson. Committed to racial equality, however, he supported the 1866 civil rights bill, and failing to persuade the president to agree on black citizenship he voted to override the veto. He sided both with the Radical Republicans in passing the Military Reconstruction Acts that placed the South under military rule and with New York's attempt to enfranchise blacks in 1867. In the impeachment proceedings he voted to convict Johnson.

Defeated for reelection to the Senate in 1869, Morgan returned to an active life in New York as merchant, president of the Erie Railroad, politician, and philanthropist. He again served his party as national chairman from 1872 to 1876, refused the Russian ministry in 1874, ran unsuccessfully as party candidate for governor in 1876, and for a second time declined the post of secretary of the treasury in 1881.

A patron of the arts whose collection was sold after his death for $79,000, and a philanthropist who gave Morgan Hall to Williams College and $400,000 to Union Theological Seminary as well as other benefactions, he generously devoted his last years to private and public affairs without suffering the stains on his reputation that afflicted many of his contemporaries. He died in his Fifth Avenue mansion and was laid to rest in Hartford in a tomb designed by Stanford White and embellished by Augustus Saint-Gaudens.

• A large collection of Morgan papers is in the New York State Library in Albany. Some materials may be found in the New York Public Library and the New-York Historical Society, both in New York City, and in the Thurlow Weed Papers in the University of Rochester Library. The only biography is James A. Rawley, *Edwin D. Morgan: 1811–1883: Merchant in Politics* (1955).

JAMES A. RAWLEY

MORGAN, George Thomas (28 June 1925–7 July 1975), country singer and songwriter, was born in Waverly, Tennessee, the son of Zachariah "Jack" Valentine Morgan, a farmer and laborer, and Ethel Turner. Two weeks before George was born, his father had an accident when his boot laces got caught in a railroad switch and his leg was severed by a train. George was raised in Barberton, Ohio, where Jack Morgan supported the family by hauling coal and later working for a rubber company.

George Morgan's parents were avid listeners to the Grand Ole Opry. In an interview with Dixie Deen, Morgan said, "I grew up listening to country music and my love for it was instilled because to my folks it was something from 'down home.'" Morgan learned to play guitar as a young boy and even wrote songs. He dropped out of school in the eleventh grade and as a young man held a variety of jobs, including working as a truck driver, salesman, and in a restaurant. He enlisted in the army in 1944 but after three months received an honorable discharge on medical grounds.

In 1947 Morgan formed his own band and performed on radio stations in Ohio, writing his signature song, "Candy Kisses," during this time. Morgan and his band got a job as the opening act on local radio station WWST in Wooster, Ohio. The band tired of the early morning shift, but Morgan continued on, gaining an audience, eventually working into a better time slot, and performing on WAKR in Akron, Ohio, as well.

When Hawkshaw Hawkins left WWVA's Jamboree in Wheeling, West Virginia, Morgan auditioned for the spot and was hired. Although a popular performer, he was beginning to become discouraged when the station manager persuaded him to make a demo of "Candy Kisses." The demo was sent to RCA in Nashville, where an executive happened to play it for representatives from station WSM, who were on the lookout for talent because Eddy Arnold had resigned from the Opry. Morgan's style was similar to Arnold's smooth, crooner delivery, and on the strength of the demo Morgan was invited to audition for the Grand Ole Opry. Columbia Records signed Morgan to a recording contract in September 1948 but could not record him until January 1949 after the Petrillo ban had ended (the Petrillo ban prevented all union musicians from playing for recording sessions; it came about when American Federation of Musicians president James C. Petrillo called two strikes during the 1940s over musicians' wages). Other Opry perfomers earned their living through personal appearances, but since Morgan did not yet have a record, WSM employed him as a disc jockey to tide him over.

Morgan loved to tell the story of his first Opry appearance. In his excitement he could not find the Ryman Auditorium, then the home of the Opry. According to Morgan, he "was walking along a dark street, getting more frantic by the minute, when I saw these two fellows, talking near a street light. Walking up to them I timidly asked, 'Could you tell me where the Ryman Auditorium is?' I looked closer and identified that one of the men was Eddy Arnold."

In 1949 "Candy Kisses" was released and went to number one. It was a phenomenal hit for Morgan, who named his band the Candy Kids. Besides his version, the song had three other top-ten releases by Cowboy Copas, Eddie Kirk, and Red Foley and would be covered by many other artists, including Bill Haley (for a small Philadelphia label under the name "Bill Haley and the Four Aces of Western Swing"), Dean Martin, and Tony Bennett. That same year Morgan had more top-ten hits with "Please Don't Let Me Love You," "Room Full of Roses," "Rainbow in My Heart," and "Cry-Baby Heart." For a time it looked as if he might surpass Arnold as the king of country pop.

But it would be another three years until Morgan had another top-ten hit, with "Almost" in 1952. His record sales for Columbia were steady but not spectacular. While he landed many songs in the lower charts, there were few big hits. Morgan's other hits during the decade were "(I Just Had a Date) A Lover's Quarrel" in 1953 and "I'm in Love Again" in 1959. In 1956 he hosted a television show that was carried over 120 stations nationwide.

During the 1960s Morgan had one big hit, "You're the Only Good Thing," which charted in 1960. On 6 December 1964 he was dropped from the Opry roster along with other stars, including Kitty Wells, Faron Young, Ray Price, Don Gibson, and Ferlin Husky, for not having met the rule of appearing at the Opry at least twenty-six weekends during the previous twelve months. Morgan was later reinstated and continued to be a popular performer at the Opry. Throughout the 1960s and 1970s Morgan was a guest on television variety shows and continued making personal appearances.

In 1966 Morgan left Columbia and recorded first for Starday and later for other labels. During the 1970s he had two top-twenty hits, "Lilacs and Fire" in 1970 on the Stop label and "Red Rose from the Blue Side of Town" in 1973 for Decca/FourStar. For a brief period Morgan was president of the Association of Country Entertainers.

In May 1975 Morgan suffered a heart attack while installing an antenna on the roof of his home. He recovered and resumed his appearances at the Opry, celebrating his fifty-first birthday with the Opry debut of his daughter Lorrie Morgan. Ironically, Morgan dedicated "From This Moment On" to a friend recovering from heart surgery, only to learn a few days later that he himself needed open-heart surgery. Morgan suffered complications from the operation and died several days later in Madison, Tennessee.

Morgan was married to Anastasia "Anna" Paridon, with whom he had four daughters and one son. In 1979 his voice again graced the airwaves when a duet, "I'm Completely Satisfied with You," with daughter Lorrie charted. Lorrie Morgan went on to become a major country artist in her own right. Morgan was known as a devoted father, no doubt affected by his own father's example. Recalling his father's struggles to support the family, Morgan told Deen in a 1973 interview, "These are not pleasant things, but it is pleasant in my mind to know how much dad loved us to go through all this."

While Morgan's style of singing waned in popularity, he always maintained his star appeal as a performer at the Grand Ole Opry. He was popular with fans and fellow performers alike. Some of the songs that Morgan recorded later charted as pop songs sung by other artists, and he was one of the few country singers to record with pop vocalists. Morgan was the first country performer to record with a full symphony orchestra. In an article in the *John Edwards Memorial Foundation Quarterly* (Winter 1979) Norm Cohen wrote, "The country music of the years immediately after the second World War has fallen between the cracks of the reissue business. Too late to catch the interests of old-timey enthusiasts, too old for contemporary country fans, too country for bluegrassers, it has been neglected by almost everyone." Within the crooning genre, Morgan remained true to country music. He did not have a rural sound, but he championed the traditional sounds of country music throughout his career.

• Although Morgan was a popular performer, little has been published about his life or career. The entry in the *Encyclopedia of Folk, Country and Western Music* (1969) is very descriptive, although it borrows considerably from Dixie Deen's article in *Music City News*, Mar. 1967, pp. 14, 27. Chet Hagan, *Grand Ole Opry* (1989), has a good overview of Morgan's early life and career. *The Guinness Encyclopedia of Popular Music* (1992) lists his albums. An obituary is in the *New York Times*, 8 July 1975.

MARILEE BIRCHFIELD

MORGAN, Sir Henry (1635–25 Aug. 1688), buccaneer, planter, and lieutenant governor, was born in Llanrhymny, Wales, the son of Robert Morgan. His mother's name is not known. Little is known of Morgan's years in Wales. In a letter that he wrote to the Lords of Trade in 1680, Morgan said of his education that he "left the schools to [*sic*] young" and that he had been "more used to the pike than the book." Morgan went to the West Indies as a member of General Robert Venables's army, sent in 1654 by Cromwell to expand England's holdings in the West Indies by capturing Hispaniola. When Venables failed at Hispaniola, he invaded and captured Jamaica in 1655.

In the early 1660s, not yet able to or inclined to acquire land and begin a plantation, Morgan was an active member of the large contingent of buccaneers operating in the Caribbean, based primarily on the northern coast of Hispaniola, on the island of Tortuga, and in Port Royal, Jamaica. From late 1661 to early 1663, Morgan commanded one of several ships in a buccaneer expedition that successfully attacked Santiago, Cuba, and the city of Campeche, on the Yucatán Peninsula. In 1663, flush with these successes and his share of the booty, Morgan joined with several other buccaneers to organize and lead an eighteen-month privateering expedition to the Spanish-American mainland, first to the province of Tabasco on the Yucatán Peninsula, then to Trujillo, a city in what is now Honduras, and finally, in 1665, to the city of Granada, on the shores of Lake Nicaragua. Returning to Port Royal in late 1665, he discovered he was a hero. Morgan discovered, too, that Governor Thomas Modyford was withdrawing his commission (because of a shift in diplomatic policy).

In 1664, while Morgan was absent from Jamaica, his uncle Edward Morgan had been appointed lieutenant governor and relocated to Jamaica, where he accepted a military post and a royal grant of land to begin a plantation. Morgan's uncle died during a campaign against the Dutch island of St. Eustatius, and when Morgan returned to Jamaica in 1665, he met for the first time his six cousins, who would become his extended family. In early 1666 Morgan married his cousin Mary Elizabeth (Edward's eldest daughter), purchased his first sugar plantation, and settled into the life of gentleman-planter for the next two years. The couple had no children.

By late 1667 England's relations with Spain were worsening, and Jamaicans felt threatened by a possible invasion of Spanish forces said to be assembling in the region. With new royal permission to issue commissions to privateers—and as the only way to assemble a substantial defense force—Governor Modyford again authorized expeditions against the Spanish possessions in the Caribbean. Morgan was Modyford's natural choice to lead these renewed efforts. In 1667 and 1668 Morgan led his forces on a raid of Puerto del Principe, the third-largest city in Cuba. From Cuba, the expedition sailed to Portobelo, now in Panama, one of the two or three largest cities on the coast of the Spanish Main, successfully attacking the city and capturing substantial treasures. The buccaneers returned to Port Royal but did not remain for long, launching another expedition, this time attacking Maracaibo and Gibraltar in the Gulf of Venezuela, once again capturing substantial prizes. But when he returned again to Port Royal in mid-1669, Morgan lost his commission once more: the attack on Maracaibo violated the spirit of the governor's commission, and Modyford was under intense pressure from England to control the buccaneers' ventures against the Spanish. At the time, England was in the middle of sensitive peace negotiations with Spain.

Morgan turned his attention to being a planter, acquiring a second plantation of more than 800 acres. But by mid-1670, because the peace negotiations in Europe had not stopped Spanish aggression in the Caribbean, Modyford called on Morgan again, returning his commission. In early 1671 Morgan launched his last and most daring expedition as a buccaneer, traversing what is now the isthmus of Panama, from the Caribbean to the Pacific, and capturing the city of Panama. Morgan returned to Port Royal in April 1671 to find his reputation at its height, not only in the Caribbean, but in England and Europe, too. Unfortunately, while Modyford and Morgan were initiating this last expedition, England and Spain had signed a peace treaty, in July 1670. Unknown to him or Modyford, Morgan's Panama expedition had been conducted illegally, without the blessing of the Crown, which had withdrawn Modyford's authority. To pacify Spain's outrage, Modyford was arrested and returned to England in 1671. Not long after, in early 1672, Morgan was also arrested and transported to England.

As a result of shifting court politics and because of Morgan's popularity with the English public, both Morgan and Modyford were eventually exonerated. Early in 1674 Morgan was named lieutenant governor of Jamaica. In addition to his office, Morgan also received a knighthood, and in early 1676 he returned to Jamaica and to his wife. Over the next eight years, Morgan served in several official capacities, including terms as acting governor in 1678 and in 1680, as head of the admiralty court, and as general of the militia. Soon after his return to Jamaica, in 1676, Morgan added a third sugar plantation of nearly 4,000 acres, and in 1680 he acquired another 1,200 acres, on the northern coast of the island, increasing his total holdings to more than 7,000 acres and making him one of the larger landowners on the island. Morgan was an effective and respected administrator. Charles Leslie, in *A New History of Jamaica* (1740), reports that Morgan "was looked upon as one that was the ablest . . . to rule a Colony" (p. 114).

In 1683, after several years of local political infighting, Morgan lost all his government positions. In 1684 the English translation of Alexandre Olivier Esquemeling's 1678 *The Buccaneers of America* appeared, after having been circulating in Dutch and Spanish for five years. Esquemeling had served under Morgan on several of his expeditions. Morgan objected to the ways that he was represented in Esquemeling's accounts. In particular, Esquemeling wrote that Morgan had been an indentured servant in Barbados before coming to Jamaica. And in several of Esquemeling's descriptions of the buccaneers' dealings with their Spanish captives, he claims that Morgan condoned and participated in acts of torture and rape. Morgan sued the English publishers of the translations, prompting both to issue apologies and corrections and to pay damages of £200. However, the retractions and clarifications were not printed in most subsequent editions of Esquemeling's accounts, and generations of readers learned about Morgan from Esquemeling.

A local legend and a hero and friend to many, after more than thirty years in the West Indies and Jamaica, Morgan spent his last years in ill health. He died in Port Royal. During his life and after his death, Morgan was revered by many Jamaicans and Britons, not only because of his buccaneering exploits, but also because of his role in securing Jamaica as the centerpiece of the British empire in America. Leslie considered Morgan to be a model colonial citizen: "He shewed the World, that he equally understood the Arts of Peace and of War; that he was qualified to govern as well as to fight, and that in all Stations of Life he was a great Man" (p. 115).

• The most scholarly of the numerous accounts of Morgan's life is Dudley Pope, *The Buccaneer King: The Biography of Sir Henry Morgan, 1635–1688* (1978). Pope includes a thorough bibliography of primary and secondary sources. Two earlier biographies complement Pope's later work: Philip Lindsay, *The Great Buccaneer* (1951) , and W. Adolphe Roberts, *Sir Henry Morgan: Buccaneer and Governor* (1933). The *Calendar of State Papers, Colonial Series: America and West Indies* includes the extensive correspondence of Governor Modyford, who regularly reported Morgan's exploits to the Lords of Trade. The English translation of Esquemeling's *The Buccaneers of America* is available in several reprinted editions. Esquemeling's book provides accounts of Morgan's buccaneering expeditions. And though Esquemeling's precision with dates is suspect, the details of his accounts have been confirmed, for the most part, as accurate, matching Spanish accounts in most particulars.

GLENN BLALOCK

MORGAN, Jacob Casimera (14 Sept. 1879–10 May 1950), Navajo political leader, was born at Nahodeshgizh, New Mexico, near the Navajo reservation. He was born into a traditional Navajo family, which herded sheep in the area near Crownpoint. His father's given name was Casimera; his mother's name is not known. Morgan enrolled in school at the age of seven. Most Navajo children of the era did not attend school, but Morgan's decision was prompted by his father's joining the U.S. Army in 1886 to serve as a scout in a final campaign against the Apaches. Young Jacob visited his father at Fort Wingate and saw another Navajo boy dressed in a school uniform. Admiring the look of the outfit, Morgan chose to attend the other boy's school at Fort Defiance, Arizona. Soon after his arrival, he volunteered through the act of raising his hand, but not knowing what he was agreeing to, to transfer to another government boarding school in Grand Junction, Colorado. In the spare new surroundings of the Colorado institution, Morgan learned to play the cornet, was converted to Christianity, and gained increasing fluency in English.

Morgan attended the Grand Junction school for nine years and then was admitted to Hampton Normal and Agricultural Institute in Virginia, one of the few schools to offer additional training at this time to Indian students. Hampton had been established to educate African Americans, but it had opened its doors as well to Indians in 1878, at the urging of Captain Richard Henry Platt, who would in the following year establish the influential Carlisle Indian Industrial School in Pennsylvania. About 20 percent of Hampton's students were Indian during Morgan's stay, but he proved to be one of the few to complete the requirements for graduation. Morgan studied carpentry and played in the school band. After graduating in 1900, he returned briefly to Navajo country. He worked for a time as a carpenter in Tohatchi, New Mexico, and as night watchman at the Phoenix Indian school. Dissatisfied with such employment, he returned to Hampton in 1901 for more training in carpentry as well as preparation in bookkeeping and general business. Morgan again played in the band as a soloist and wrote for the newspaper. Illness at school prompted his return home in 1903.

Once more, Morgan appeared unable to gain satisfactory employment. He did not hold any position for long before 1910, when he started to work for Christian missionary organizations. His prior training allowed him to help as a teacher or carpenter, and his good command of both English and Navajo made him an obvious choice as a translator. During one of his assignments, at the Christian Reformed church mission in Rehoboth, just outside of Gallup, New Mexico, he met and married (Aug. 1910) a Navajo employee, Zahrina Tso.

In 1914 Morgan took a job with the Bureau of Indian Affairs. He returned to the area where he had spent his first years, teaching industrial arts and conducting the band at the Crownpoint boarding school. Morgan enjoyed witnessing the kind of transformation formal education had brought to his life; his small school bands were great favorites in the eastern portion of the Navajo reservation and at the New Mexico state fair in Albuquerque. By the end of the decade he had also become a leader of the Navajo Progressive League, made up of young, educated Navajos who pushed for economic and educational opportunities for members of the tribe.

In the early 1920s Morgan moved to Shiprock, where he again taught at a Bureau of Indian Affairs school. It was in the Shiprock area that Morgan became politically active. His fluency in Navajo and English, his talents as a speaker, and his concern for the Navajo future soon made him an important figure in tribal politics. Morgan was chosen to represent Shiprock in the newly established tribal council. This body had been formed in large part because the federal government needed an official Navajo entity to approve leases of oil reserves near Shiprock. Chee Dodge chaired the first council, with Morgan one of the twelve delegates and one of the two translators. A regionalist rather than a Navajo nationalist, Morgan did not approve of money gained from resources in his area going to the Navajo nation as a whole. He clashed repeatedly with Dodge, a wealthy livestock owner from the southern portion of the reservation, whose affiliation with the Catholic church inspired Morgan's bitter antagonism. Few Navajos belonged to any Christian denomination and the Native American church, which used peyote, had yet to arrive in Navajo country; most of the people attended traditional Navajo ceremonies. Morgan's continuing battles with Dodge, of course, also involved the ambitions of both men. They continued to vie for political supremacy for many years.

In 1925 Morgan went to work as an assistant to Reverend L. P. Brink at the Christian Reformed mission just east of the reservation in the border town of Farmington, New Mexico. He continued to serve on the tribal council, which by 1928 included only one other delegate who had been a member of the initial body. The early councils disproportionately included returned students, such as Morgan, and their influence aroused the ire of more traditional and less well educated members of the Navajo population. By 1933, for example, a clear majority of the council had attended school, in an era when few of the people had done so. Morgan was one of the delegates perceived to be able to comprehend the difficult issues before the council and follow discussions with and presentations by Bureau of Indian Affairs employees who could not speak Navajo.

In 1933 the New Deal of Franklin Delano Roosevelt was accompanied by the so-called Indian New Deal under Commissioner of Indian Affairs John Collier. Collier's support of traditional Indian religions and his general rejection of the assimilationism that had dominated Bureau of Indian Affairs policies for the previous half century quickly brought him and Morgan into conflict. The commissioner's advocacy of livestock reduction earned him the wrath of most Navajos, who did not want their herds of sheep, goats, and cattle diminished in number. Collier's unpopularity played into Morgan's hands. When a new form of tribal government was proposed under the terms of the Indian Reorganization Act of 1934, Morgan campaigned vigorously against it. The Navajos split in their referendum on the proposal, with Chee Dodge's district voting in favor of it while Morgan's region rejected it overwhelmingly. Thanks to the vote from the Shiprock area, the IRA did not pass on the Navajo reservation, and the tribe did not come under its terms. Morgan's opposition also doomed efforts in 1937 to draft a tribal constitution.

Morgan finally gained the chairmanship of the Navajo Tribal Council in 1938, but his four-year term at the helm of tribal government demonstrated that he was more effective as a critic than as an administrator. Despite strident Navajo protests, the federal government carried out a harsh program of livestock reduction, and Morgan was powerless to do much about it. The outbreak of the Second World War accelerated Collier's declining influence, just as the New Deal itself had largely run out of steam by the end of the 1930s. With Navajo attention increasingly focused on the world situation, the attempted reforms of Collier could not be carried out as quickly or as fully. Morgan's grudging acceptance of livestock reduction as a fait accompli may have reflected recognition of federal power, but it did not enhance his own. Chee Dodge easily defeated him for the chairmanship in 1942.

Morgan spent the remaining years of his life in relative obscurity. One of his sons was killed in the Pacific campaign. He worked for some time at the Methodist Mission in Farmington, where he died and was buried in the mission cemetery. To the end he advocated what he perceived as a more progressive approach to the demands of life in the twentieth century, which included adopting Christianity, the English language, and a kind of Protestant work ethic. He is still remembered among his people for his opposition to Collier and the program of livestock reduction, as well as for his advocacy of regionalism within an increasingly nationalistic Navajo world.

• This portrait of Morgan relies primarily on Donald L. Parman, "J. C. Morgan, Navajo Apostle of Assimilation," *Prologue* 4, 2 (Summer 1972): 83–98. Additional information about Morgan may be found in Robert W. Young, *A Political History of the Navajo Tribe* (1978), and Parman, *The Navajos and the New Deal* (1976).

PETER IVERSON

MORGAN, John (16 Oct. 1735–15 Oct. 1789), physician, was born in Philadelphia, Pennsylvania, the son of Evan Morgan, a shopkeeper and merchant, and Joanna Biles. While his father was a Baptist and his mother a Quaker, Morgan eventually joined the Anglican communion. After attending the academy of the Reverend Samuel Finley at West Nottingham, Pennsylvania, he was apprenticed in 1750 to Dr. John Redman of Philadelphia. He served from 1755 to 1756 as apothecary of the Pennsylvania Hospital and attended the College of Philadelphia (now the University of Pennsylvania), from which he received an A.B. in its first class in 1757. Meanwhile Morgan had received a commission in the Pennsylvania provincial forces and served four years as a military surgeon on the western frontier. In 1760 he traveled to London, where he enrolled as a pupil at St. Thomas's Hospital. Attending the lectures of the anatomist Dr. William Hunter, he learned how to prepare anatomical specimens by injecting wax into the vessels and then corroding away the solid matter. He matriculated at Edinburgh University in 1761. With the benefit of the introductions he carried from Benjamin Franklin (1706–1790) and others, as well as his intelligence and personal charm, Morgan was soon a welcome guest in the homes of Sir Alexander Dick, president of the Royal College of

Physicians, George Drummond, lord provost of Edinburgh, and Professor William Cullen; and he received the freedom of the cities of Edinburgh and Stirling. He submitted a dissertation on the formation of pus and received an M.D. in 1763, graduating, in the words of a friend, "with an Eclat almost unknown before." He was elected a Fellow of the Royal College of Physicians of Edinburgh in 1765. Morgan was also elected a Fellow of the Royal Society in 1765, the most impressive distinction an American man of science could receive in the late eighteenth century.

Morgan spent the winter of 1763–1764 in Paris, where he observed medical practice at the Hôtel de la Charité. There he presented his dissertation on pus and demonstrated to the Académie royale de Chirurgie the method of preparing anatomical specimens that he had learned from Hunter. In the spring of 1764, accompanied by Samuel Powel of Philadelphia, he set out on the Grand Tour to southern France and Italy. It was the most famous excursion of the kind that any American had made up to that time. From Florence, Morgan and Powel traveled to Rome in the party of the Duke of York. In Rome they had a private audience with Pope Clement, were admitted as members of the Accademia degli Arcadi, and had their portraits painted by Angelica Kauffmann. In Turin they were presented to the king of Savoy; in Padua Morgan visited the great pathologist Morgagni, who gave him a copy of his work on *The Seats and Causes of Diseases;* and in Switzerland they spent an afternoon with Voltaire at Ferney. On his return to England Morgan was elected a licentiate of the Royal College of Physicians of London. In 1765 he married Mary Hopkinson; they had no children.

For several years American students at Edinburgh had discussed how to raise standards of medical education and practice in the colonies. Taking the first step toward this end, in 1762 Edinburgh graduate William Shippen, Jr., delivered a course of private lectures on anatomy and obstetrics in Philadelphia. On Morgan's return home in 1765, he proposed to the trustees of the College of Philadelphia that they establish a medical school and name him professor of medicine. He was elected to the chair on 3 May, and on 30–31 May he publicly presented his plan for a medical school. He followed this with a statement of the requirements of "regular" practice—the separation of medicine from surgery and of both from the sale of drugs. In 1766 he formed a medical society, which he expected would receive authority to license physicians who met these requirements. Unfortunately, Morgan had not consulted Shippen or any of the older physicians in town. On Morgan's recommendation, Shippen was elected professor of anatomy in the college, but he deeply resented Morgan's having put himself at the head of the affair. The rift never healed and continued to vex the medical profession in Philadelphia for almost half a century.

Morgan was active in 1766–1767 in organizing the American Society for Promoting Useful Knowledge (which merged into the American Philosophical Society in 1769). He was also a physician to the Pennsylvania Hospital, a vestryman and warden of Christ Church, and a member of the Philadelphia Society for Promoting the Culture of Silk. The paintings and other works of art that he collected in Europe were studied by aspiring artists like Henry Benbridge and Henry Pelham, and his paleontological specimens, which had been collected by his brother George in the Ohio country, were eventually studied by European scientists to identify the mastodon as a distinct species.

In 1775 Morgan was appointed by the Continental Congress as director-general of the Hospital of the army then assembled at Boston. His problems were daunting. Medicines, instruments, bandages, bedding, and other supplies were lacking and had to be found and assembled. Smallpox erupted and threatened to decimate the troops. An entire medical service had to be established and organized. These problems were complicated by the fact that neither Congress nor the commander in chief had experience in organizing medical care for an army or even understood the vital importance of the health of troops. Furthermore, the common soldiers preferred to be treated in their own regimental hospitals by familiar surgeons—a preference in which the company officers supported them. Every failure and want of success was blamed on the director-general. Opposition to Morgan centered around his old rival Shippen, who was supported by his influential relatives and allies in Congress. As a result, just as the army was moving into New Jersey, Morgan's authority was restricted to the area east of the Hudson River, and Shippen was put in charge of medical affairs in the field of action. In 1777 Morgan was dismissed from his post and was soon replaced by Shippen. Morgan spent the next two years seeking vindication, which Congress granted him in June 1779. He then formally charged Shippen with fraud and speculation in hospital supplies. Shippen was court-martialed and resigned in 1781.

Drained by the long controversy and suffering from ill health, Morgan increasingly withdrew from practice after 1785. He had not taught in the medical school since 1775. As one of the original Fellows of the College of Physicians of Philadelphia in 1787, he inaugurated its library with a gift of books and took a lead in obtaining a charter for the society from the state. He published several papers in the *Transactions of the American Philosophical Society* in 1786, but they added nothing to his reputation, and one of them was dismissed, quite properly, by a London reviewer as "too ridiculous for comment." He died in Philadelphia.

Morgan has sometimes been denominated "the father of medical education in America." The phrase is too inclusive. Benjamin Rush offered a sounder judgment at his colleague's death: "The historian, who shall hereafter relate the progress of medical science in America, will be deficient in candor and justice, if he does not connect the name of Dr. Morgan with that auspicious era in which medicine was first taught and studied as a science in this country."

• No single large collection of Morgan manuscripts survives. The principal holdings are in the College of Physicians of Philadelphia, University of Pennsylvania, Historical Society of Pennsylvania, American Philosophical Society, New York Academy of Medicine, and National Archives (for the Continental Congress Papers). Photocopies or transcripts of most of these documents, as well as of those in other institutions and private ownership, are in the College of Physicians. His *Journal . . . from the City of Rome to the City of London, 1764,* was transcribed by Julia Morgan Harding and privately printed in a small edition (1907). Broadsides, handbills, newspaper and magazine articles, as well as Morgan's pamphlets, are listed in Francisco Guerra, *American Medical Bibliography, 1639–1783* (1962). Whitfield J. Bell, Jr., *John Morgan: Continental Doctor* (1965), is the only complete biography. The earliest contemporary account and estimate is Dr. Benjamin Rush, "An Account of the late Dr. John Morgan," *American Museum,* 6 (1789): 353–55. Mary C. Gillett, *The Army Medical Department, 1775–1818* (1981), provides background and a broader view of Morgan's service as director-general of the Hospital of the Continental army.

WHITFIELD J. BELL, JR.

MORGAN, John Hunt (1 June 1825–4 Sept. 1864), soldier and Confederate general, was born in Huntsville, Alabama, the son of Calvin Cogswell Morgan, a wholesale merchant and planter, and Henrietta Hunt, the daughter of an entrepreneur. When Morgan was six years old, his family relocated to Fayette County, Kentucky, near Lexington. He attended Transylvania University but was suspended for dueling and never completed his studies. During the Mexican War he served in a volunteer cavalry regiment that distinguished itself at Buena Vista in 1847. Desiring a career in the military but denied the opportunity, Morgan became a businessman, investing in hemp manufacturing and the woolen industry, as well as the slave trade. He also was active for several years in the Kentucky militia, forming a sixty-man company known as the "Lexington Rifles." In 1848 Morgan had married Rebecca Bruce. After giving birth to a stillborn child, she lingered as an invalid for eight years prior to her death in July 1861. Seventeen months later, Morgan married twenty-one-year-old Martha Ready of Murfreesboro, Tennessee.

Born in the South and with business connections firmly linked to the southern economy, Morgan cast his lot with the Confederacy. On 27 October 1861 he was sworn into the Confederate army and was soon elected as captain of a squad of cavalry scouts. Six feet tall, athletic, and handsome, Morgan was a romantic figure. On 4 April 1862 he was promoted to colonel of the Second Kentucky Cavalry, a rank he held at the battle of Shiloh, his first and only full-scale military engagement. For much of the war, Morgan preferred and excelled at irregular (guerilla) warfare. He relied on taking the offensive, plunging behind enemy lines, gathering intelligence, disrupting communications, capturing supplies, and using deception, the cover of darkness, and sometimes disguises; high risk activities, to say the least, but he avoided decisive battles at all costs. Morgan can be compared to Francis Marion, the so-called Swamp Fox of American Revolution fame, who attained a hero's status as a successful guerilla fighter. Indeed, Morgan was given the sobriquet the "Marion of the War," a comparison he particularly relished.

Morgan is best known for launching a series of raids behind enemy lines. Three of these raids occurred during the second half of 1862. Morgan's men, mostly Kentuckians and Tennesseans and numbering scarcely more than 3,000 at any one time, rode hundreds of miles through the central Bluegrass, destroying and disrupting transportation and communication lines and capturing prisoners and supplies, while at the same time suffering relatively few casualties. The raids were politically embarrassing to the North and caused the Union commanders to commit thousands of troops in an effort to apprehend Morgan's men. The raids also gained notoriety for plundering and other outrages against northern citizens, ostensibly in retaliation for similar treatment of southern citizens by Federal troops. Southerners admired Morgan's daring and panache. Once, after capturing some mules during a raid, Morgan and his men had the audacity to telegraph a complaint about the quality of the livestock to none other than Abraham Lincoln. On 11 December 1862, following his second raid into Kentucky, Morgan was promoted to brigadier general. Several months later, after the completion of yet another successful raid, he received a commendation of gratitude from the Confederate Congress.

In the spring of 1863 Morgan decided, against orders, to take the war further north, this time into Indiana, Ohio, and West Virginia. Leaving Tennessee on 20 June 1863 and crossing the Ohio River at Brandenburg, Indiana, on 8 July, the raid ended on 26 July at New Lisbon, Ohio, about ninety miles from Lake Erie. It was the longest cavalry operation of the war, covering some 700 miles in less than one month and sometimes averaging fifty to sixty miles per day. Morgan was captured, and his command was broken and dispersed; he spent the next four months in the Ohio State Penitentiary at Columbus, until 26 November 1863 when he and six of his officers managed a spectacular escape.

Placed in command of the Department of Southwest Virginia, Morgan embarked in July 1864 on yet another Kentucky raid. But this one did not fare as well as had those earlier in the war. Morgan was still without many of his former officers, though they would soon be exchanged and join him on one last campaign, and Federal forces were better prepared and equipped to turn back Morgan, who was thus forced to flee rather than risk being captured again. Nevertheless, Morgan's exploits were not over. In September 1864 Morgan embarked on his final foray, this time into East Tennessee, a region that was strongly supportive of the Union. After launching a surprise attack on Federal forces near Knoxville, Morgan encamped on the evening of 3 September at Greeneville, Tennessee. Learning from a number of different informants that Morgan was the leader of this band of raiders, early the next morning the Federals moved into Greeneville, where they surprised Morgan and his staff. Morgan attempted to escape through the garden near the house where he had been sleeping but was shot in the back and killed by a Federal private who, ironically, formerly served under him as a Confederate. Morgan's remains were temporarily buried at Abingdon, Virginia, and later at Richmond, before finally being reinterred at Lexington in 1868.

Morgan gained renown for his endurance, daring, and dash. To the enemy he was a common thief, murderer, and outlaw, and while imprisoned in Ohio he and his fellow officers were treated as such. Yet the northern press also admired his courage, exaggerated his significance, and helped to make him a folk hero. Morgan's name became a household word throughout the nation, and he remains a legendary figure and a symbol of the Confederate cause, ranking with J. E. B. Stuart and John S. Mosby.

• Manuscript material regarding Morgan is scattered and incomplete. Aside from official documents found in various Confederate record groups in the National Archives, the best single body of personal correspondence and family documents is located at the Southern Historical Collection, University of North Carolina, Chapel Hill. There are also various papers in the University of Kentucky and the University of Tennessee archives. A number of Morgan's men wrote postwar accounts of their experiences with Morgan; see particularly Basil Duke, *History of Morgan's Cavalry* (1867), by Morgan's brother-in-law and second-in-command. Also useful are Thomas F. Berry, *Four Years with Morgan and Forrest* (1914), George D. Mosgrove, *Kentucky Cavaliers in Dixie: Reminiscences of a Confederate Cavalryman* (1895), and Sydney K. Smith, ed., *Life, Army Record, and Public Services of D. Howard Smith* (1890). See also R. B. Rosenburg, ed., *"For the Sake of My Country": The Diary of Col. W. W. Ward, 9th Tennessee Cavalry, Morgan's Brigade, C.S.A.* (1993). Morgan has been the subject of a number of popular biographies, including Howard Swiggett, *The Rebel Raider: A Life of John Hunt Morgan* (1937), and Cecil F. Holland, *Morgan and His Raiders: A Biography of the Confederate General* (1942). The most scholarly and reliable biography is James A. Ramage, *Rebel Raider: The Life of John Hunt Morgan* (1986).

R. B. ROSENBURG

MORGAN, John Pierpont (17 Apr. 1837–31 Mar. 1913), investment banker, was born in Hartford, Connecticut, the son of Junius Morgan, a merchant banker, and Juliet Pierpont, daughter of a Unitarian minister. J. P. Morgan was educated at the Hopkins Grammar School in Hartford, the Hartford Public High School, and finally Boston's English High School, from which he graduated in 1854. He then attended the Institution Sillig at Vevey in Switzerland and spent two years at Germany's Göttingen University.

In 1854 Junius Morgan moved to London to become a partner in George Peabody's merchant bank. Peabody controlled one of London's most prominent American-owned financial institutions. In 1857 Junius arranged for Alexander Duncan of New York's Duncan, Sherman & Company to give his son J. P. a job. New York City was locked in a battle with Philadelphia for American financial supremacy. The United States was vastly different from Great Britain; compared to England, the American government had little control over finance. Although the U.S. Congress had nominally tied the dollar to a specie standard (based on gold and silver), the United States lacked a central bank. In 1857 the individual states set the banking laws. There was no centralized control over the issue of bank notes or other forms of credit, nor guarantee that banknotes could be converted on demand into specie. American banks were subject to panics that saw banks either fail or suspend specie payments.

Unlike England, which had a capital surplus, America needed to import funds. From the 1850s to the 1890s the building of a railroad industry especially created an enormous demand for capital. The 1870s through to the 1890s saw a railroad boom as transcontinental lines expanded from the Midwest to the Pacific Coast. Railroads—both established, such as the New York Central, and new ventures, such as the Northern Pacific—provided an almost insatiable demand for foreign capital, and Morgan rose to power by organizing the funds. From the 1880s onward, great new industrial ventures grew in such fields as steel, agricultural machinery, and electrical machinery. Morgan also became a source of funding for these enterprises.

For the English investor, American securities carried at least two types of risk. First, there were the questions associated with any business: Could it pay dividends on its shares and interest on its bonds? The second major risk involved currency exchange. The specie standard, which after 1873 became a gold standard, fixed the value of the dollar in terms of the yellow metal. One gold-backed English pound sterling was worth about $4.83. Morgan worked to keep the United States on the gold standard because it minimized the risk of foreign investor losses through adverse currency exchange rates. Morgan's stands helped to maintain the inflow of European funds that were so necessary to American expansion. However, Morgan's actions brought him into conflict with farmers and many other railroad users.

For J. P. Morgan the year 1857 provided a brutal training ground. Soon after his arrival, financial panic struck. For a while it seemed that both Peabody in London and its New York agent, Duncan, Sherman, might fail. Only the support of the Bank of England kept Peabody afloat, and the English house in turn saved Duncan, Sherman. The lesson of this was clear to J. P.: avoid rash speculation.

Morgan started his own firm in 1861. Like his later firms, J. P. Morgan & Company was a private wholesale bank. Akin to the English merchant bank or issue house, the private wholesale bank formed syndicates that jointly underwrote new issues of bonds or stock. Underwriting contracts committed the bank to sell securities at a minimum price, say 97 percent of par or face value of the security. Morgan normally acted as a lead banker, taking as much as 50 percent of an issue and placing the rest with other houses. He then tendered these shares to retail stockbrokers, commercial banks, and rich individuals who were clients of the house. Investment bankers made money if they could sell securities above the contract price. All underwriting was risky since unforeseen events such as wars, financial panics, and natural disasters could destroy confidence in the stock market, making an issue unsalable. Investment bankers needed good relations with commercial banks and other cash-rich organizations such as insurance companies, from whom they could borrow during the underwriting process. Above all, they needed a reputation for honesty, integrity, and fair dealing and would gradually benefit from a record of successful floats and for being associated with issues that appreciated in value over time. Morgan acquired an unparalleled reputation for successful floats and for protecting the interests of those who purchased the securities that his firm underwrote.

By purchasing an exemption from the draft, Morgan was able to avoid service in the Civil War. When George Peabody retired in 1864, Morgan's father took control of the London house, which became known as J. S. Morgan & Company. From that point father and son worked to channel British investment into the United States. They came into their own with the 1870s railroad boom.

J. P. discovered that there were two quite different types of railroads and that these required two kinds of financiers. Three of the original transectional American railroads—the Baltimore & Ohio (B&O), the Pennsylvania, and the New York Central, were characteristic of the first type. Each was soundly financed and served territories that generated substantial freight and passenger traffic. The fourth transectional railroad, the Erie, was of the second type. It was not well financed and ran through a region almost devoid of passengers or freight. The Erie could survive only by taking a large amount of the interregional traffic moving between the Midwest and the Atlantic seaboard from prosperous lines such as the B&O, the Central, or the Pennsylvania. To attract traffic, the Erie engaged in ruinous rate wars that threatened the financial stability of the prosperous lines.

Investment bankers dealing in blue chip railroad securities, such as the B&O and the Pennsylvania, made money through underwriting. In contrast, the Erie attracted speculators such as Jay Gould and James Fisk. Gould was the mirror opposite of J. P. Morgan. While Morgan handled gilt-edged securities, which he hoped would appreciate over the long term, Gould made his money through stock market manipulation. It was in the interest of lines such as the B&O, the Pennsylvania, and the Central to limit competition to keep rates and fares high. While collusive agreements to fix rates and fares might be reached between railroad leaders, such pacts were unenforceable under U.S. law. Gould pretended to join alliances but then lowered rates surreptitiously, thus stealing traffic from the more prosperous lines. In 1869 J. P. saw three outstanding personalities dominating American railroads: Thomas Scott of the Pennsylvania, Cornelius "Commodore" Vanderbilt of the New York Central, and Jay Gould. Of these, Gould was "the disturbing influence . . . a ruthless destroyer of values. . . . Other men built railroads, J. Gould wrecked them, reorganised them, unloaded their securities onto the public and began over again" (Satterlee, p. 133). Morgan first clashed with Gould and Fisk in 1869 over the control of the 142-mile-long Albany & Susquehanna. During the resulting war Gould and Fisk used nearly every trick, including physical force and legal manipulation, but failed to win the day.

In 1871, at the urging of his father, Morgan merged with Philadelphia's long-established investment bank Drexel & Company. J. P. Morgan became head of Drexel's New York office, which was renamed Drexel, Morgan & Company, and a partner in both the Philadelphia bank and the Paris firm, Drexel, Harjes & Company. The Drexels reinforced Morgan's association with blue-chip railroads because the firm had been a banker for both the B&O and the Pennsylvania. In 1875 Junius Morgan became the B&O's English merchant banker. Soon thereafter came a stunning coup. In 1877 Vanderbilt, who controlled the New York Central, died and left most of his shares to his son William. In 1879 William decided to sell most of his shares and employed Drexel, Morgan to sell hundreds of thousands of them at $120 each. Selling William Vanderbilt's inheritance took a number of years and resulted in a permanent alliance between Drexel, Morgan, and the New York Central, and J. P. Morgan became one of the railroad's directors.

Despite Gould's departure from the Erie in 1870, the relationship between the eastern trunk lines remained troubled. In the early 1880s a consortium built a line along the Hudson River's west shore paralleling the New York Central. The Pennsylvania gave the West Shore line tacit encouragement. At the same time, the Pennsylvania and the Central engaged in rate wars severe enough to imperil the Central's dividend. On 10 July 1885 Morgan arranged a meeting of the Central and the Pennsylvania's leaders on his yacht, the *Corsair*, that resulted in a compact. The Central got control of the West Shore and the South Pennsylvania went to the Pennsylvania. Both systems agreed to cease rate wars. Morgan threatened to make it difficult for a road in default of the agreement to gain further financing. The *Corsair* compact caused a rise in the share value of eastern railroads and greatly increased Morgan's prestige.

Throughout the 1880s and 1890s Morgan led many railroad reorganizations. He refinanced the Baltimore & Ohio, the Chesapeake & Ohio, and the Reading twice, in 1885 and in 1890. In the 1890s Morgan built the Southern Railroad (currently the Norfolk Southern) out of the bankrupt Richmond Terminal. Morgan's men ended up on the boards of directors of the refinanced rail systems, and he often selected the president of the corporations. He stressed cooperation between lines and his hand-picked directors voted against rate wars.

Morgan also financed important new railroad ventures, especially in the Northwest. In the early 1880s Morgan arranged the funds to complete the Northern Pacific Railroad, whose failure in 1873 had destroyed the rival house of Jay Cooke & Company. Morgan also became banker for James J. Hill, the entrepreneur building the Great Northern Railroad. It was typical of Morgan to serve as banker to two rival railroads. This tactic enabled him to influence management of each firm and to avoid cutthroat competition.

In 1887 J. P. Morgan tussled with Edward H. Harriman, who outwitted him in a fight over the Dubuque and Sioux City Railroad. An angry Morgan saw Harriman's tactics as "a recurrence of the J. Gould methods of resorting to lawyers and technicalities" (Satterlee, p. 244). He never forgave Harriman and this led to one of the most infamous incidents in the history of the New York Stock Exchange. Harriman, using Jacob Schiff of New York's Kuhn, Loeb & Company, gained control by 1901 of a large network that included the Union Pacific and Southern Pacific railroads. Harriman's lines, which ran from Nebraska to California, Arizona, and Oregon, did not go east of Omaha, Nebraska, and he coveted the well-run Chicago, Burlington & Quincy (CB&Q) as a Chicago connection. Harriman's plans threatened Hill and Morgan. Hill's roads, in common with Harriman's, did not reach Chicago but terminated in St. Paul, Minnesota. If Harriman gained control of the CB&Q he would be in a position to wage a rate war for traffic between the Midwest and the Pacific Northwest. Control of the CB&Q lay in the hands of the Northern Pacific Railroad, which owned a large number of its shares. In a daring plan, Harriman, backed by Schiff and the New York financier William Rockefeller, nearly snatched control of the Northern Pacific. Many New York brokers did not understand that Hill and his rivals were secretly buying all Northern Pacific shares on offer. These outside brokers therefore sold Northern Pacific short (that is, they sold shares they did not own hoping to pick them up later at a lower price and deliver them).

Northern Pacific common went from $110 per share on 9 May 1901 to $1,000 a share the next day. Much of Wall Street found itself technically insolvent, unable to deliver the Northern Pacific shares they sold to either the Morgan or the Harriman camps. The panic associated with the Northern Pacific "corner" caused both Morgan and Schiff to rethink their positions. Although it was Morgan who actually won control of more then 52 percent of the crucial Northern Pacific common shares, to stop the panic Morgan and Schiff bailed out most of Wall Street and London shorts. More revealing was Morgan's strategy to ensure that the hard-won war stayed won. In past rail reorganizations, Morgan had maintained control through selecting company presidents and by placing his men on the boards of directors. These devices seemed inadequate to lock up control of the railroads involved. To retain control, Hill and Morgan used New Jersey's relatively new holding-company legislation and on 12 November 1901 organized the Northern Securities Company to hold the shares of the four railroads.

Morgan miscalculated the force of the political changes shaping America. During the 1870s, 1880s, and 1890s southern and midwestern farmers opposed Morgan and the gold standard that they saw forcing down the prices of their commodities. Many of the Minnesota wheat farmers, who started antirailroad Granger parties in the 1870s, later in the 1890s became William Jennings Bryan populists. The farmers saw Morgan setting high freight rates for the benefit of English, German, and Wall Street capitalists. Morgan understood his difference with midwestern farmers. He supported gold Democrats such as Grover Cleveland and conservative probusiness Republicans such as William McKinley. What Morgan did not appreciate was the complexity of America's reaction to big business.

In 1890 Congress passed the Sherman Antitrust Act, which forbade combinations in restraint of trade. Much of its appeal was to businessmen in the small- and medium-sized cities across the United States who voted Republican but feared the financial power of men like the Morgans, Vanderbilts, and Rockefellers. McKinley, a "Wall Street Republican," did not take antitrust seriously; not a single suit was brought under the law during his administration. Theodore Roosevelt was different. He was a Republican but sensitive to Main Street as well as to Wall Street. Roosevelt feared that if big business excesses were not curbed, real radicalism such as Bryanism or even outright socialism might result.

Morgan established the Northern Securities Company nearly two months after Roosevelt became president. He was unconcerned that Wall Street, under his leadership, had created a railroad monopoly in states such as Minnesota. The state of Minnesota, which had voted Republican in 1896 and 1900, brought suit against the Northern Securities Company under the antitrust act. Roosevelt supported the Minnesota mainstreeters and ordered his attorney general to enter the case. In March 1904 the U.S. Supreme Court ruled the Northern Securities Company in violation of the Sherman Antitrust Act and forced its dissolution. This was the first trust "busted" under the act. The editor of the *Wall Street Journal*, Serano S. Pratt, commented that the court's ruling made business reform a "new national issue," and he saw the desire for change extending beyond the railroads to the nation's financial sector, which meant Morgan.

From the 1904 Northern Securities decision and its aftermath, J. P. Morgan reaped much of what he had sown in the previous three decades. Ever since the Civil War he and his father had fought for the right to serve as bankers to the U.S. government. During the war, Philadelphia's Jay Cooke & Company had a near monopoly of government business. After the war the United States, which had been forced off the gold standard, took steps to return to gold. This meant refinancing the Civil War debt. In 1870 Congress launched a massive refinance of long-term Civil War debt. Cooke had the inside track, but the firm's failure in the panic of 1873 left four major American investment banks: two Yankee firms, Drexel, Morgan & Company and Morton, Bliss & Company, and two firms of German-Jewish origin, J. & W. Seligman & Company and August Belmont & Company.

The key to raising overseas money, much to Morgan's annoyance, was the London branch of the House of Rothschild, which favored its New York agent, August Belmont. In the first postpanic loan, Rothschild took a 55 percent interest, and the rest was split equally between Junius Morgan and the Seligman brothers. The younger Morgan wrote his father, "We are entire nonentities. We are never consulted or informed & have no more idea of what is being done than if we had no interest or liability in the matter" (Carosso, p. 184). But try as he might, J. P. Morgan could not freeze out Belmont, and in the remaining refinancing of America's long-term debt, Rothschild took the largest share (41.25 percent) as opposed to a combined total of 33.75 percent of the next two largest subscribers, Drexel, Morgan and J. & W. Seligman, who took equal amounts.

During the gold crisis of 1894–1895, repeal of the Sherman Silver Purchase Act and a major depression, characterized by massive railroad and industrial insolvencies, caused a run on gold. While President Grover Cleveland supported gold, he was handicapped because many in his political party were silverites. In January 1895 it seemed possible that the government would be forced off gold. Morgan sprang into action. On 4 February he arrived in Washington, D.C., determined to meet Cleveland. "I have come down to see the President," he said, "and I am going to stay here until I see him" (Carosso, p. 325). Their meeting was the genesis of a private contract that provided for the purchase of more than $62 million in gold for the U.S. Treasury and saw J. P. Morgan guarantee the Treasury against gold withdrawals from February through the end of September 1895. The contract gave the loan to four merchant banks, N. M. Rothschild & Sons and J. S. Morgan in London, and J. P. Morgan and August Belmont in the United States.

Morgan was the leader. He came under bitter attack from Joseph Pulitzer's *New York World*, which called the agreement a "Wall Street conspiracy" (Carosso, p. 335), a conclusion enhanced by the financial success of the agreement. Actually, the Morgan firm earned more than $295,000 on the deal, less than the sum estimated by Morgan's enemies. Morgan himself concluded that the Treasury rescue was "the proudest accomplishment of his life" (Carosso, p. 337).

The J. P. Morgan firm was always considered a Yankee bank. The fierce rivalry with Jewish firms, especially August Belmont in the 1870s and Jacob Schiff during the fight over the Northern Pacific, often caused Morgan to be considered unfriendly toward Jews. The record is much more confusing. As the 1895 gold crisis demonstrates, J. P. worked effectively with young Belmont. Furthermore, Jacob Schiff, who had set up a New York branch of Kuhn, Loeb Company in 1875, openly praised Morgan's 1895 Treasury rescue. Morgan often included Jewish firms in his syndicates and participated in theirs. Despite Morgan's Yankee heritage he was at home in the United Kingdom and, since the alliance with Drexel, he had a Paris office, which in 1895 became Morgan, Harjes & Company. Nor did Morgan limit his firm to New Englanders. In 1876, at J. P.'s insistence, Italian-born Egisto Fabbri, who as a New York merchant had a long association with both Junius and J. P., became a Morgan partner. Philadelphia's Anthony Drexel was not happy to have a "foreigner" in the firm, but J. P. felt otherwise. He wrote to Junius that Fabbri had been in America "long enough to become naturalised in every respect."

Morgan played a major role supplying capital to industry. Such ventures came later than railroads because transportation systems required initial massive capital infusions. In contrast, industrial firms were usually initiated by either a single entrepreneur or a family and started small and expanded by plowing back profits. In the beginning manufacturing had little need for investment bankers. They became important to entrepreneurs when the businesses got big and the owners considered selling or merging their properties. There were, however, some industries that needed investment banks from the outset because of the large amounts of capital required to develop and market such products as incandescent lights and electric motors. J. P. Morgan admired Thomas Edison and underwrote the development of the incandescent light.

In 1881 Edison installed incandescent lights in Morgan's New York residence; it was the first house in the world to have them. The installation required a steam engine in Morgan's backyard to run the dynamo, the noise of which annoyed his neighbors. Edison's first central generating station, which came online in September 1882, supplied 106 incandescent lights in the J. P. Morgan office building. Morgan's relationship with electricity was no passing fancy. He invested in many of the Edison companies that were formed to generate and distribute electric power in American cities. In 1892 he financed the creation of a giant electrical manufacturing combination, General Electric.

Modern technology and science captivated Morgan. He took pride in owning the latest gadgets. This characteristic was in stark contrast to his deeply conservative social, religious, and artistic views. Morgan became a major collector of ancient Egyptian relics and medieval and renaissance paintings. He detested the impressionist artists such as Cézanne or Matisse and disliked contemporary music and novels.

Morgan's most significant industrial financing occurred in the steel industry. By 1890 the United States was the world's preeminent steel producer; its annual tonnage surpassed the United Kingdom, France, and Germany combined. During the 1890s American steel mills were highly competitive, and prices were volatile. In the early 1890s Morgan served as banker to Illinois Steel, whose counsel, Chicago lawyer Elbert H. "Judge" Gary, impressed the New York financier. Gary wanted to compete with Carnegie, America's most efficient producer, who at the time owned 20 percent of the nation's steel capacity. In 1898 Morgan backed the creation under Gary's leadership of Federal Steel, which was a vertically integrated steel firm combining Minnesota iron ore mines, lake steamships, Illinois coal, and various steel mills. Unfortunately, Carnegie could undercut Federal Steel and take away its markets at will.

In 1901 Morgan began a series of mergers that produced the United States Steel Corporation. His primary motive was to protect two Morgan companies, Federal Steel and National Tube. The U.S. Steel Company was the world's largest industrial corporation, with a capital of nearly $1.4 billion. The new firm, headed by Gary, included the Carnegie Steel Company, Federal Steel, National Tube, and a number of formerly independent firms. Many critics objected to Morgan's strategy, which was to stabilize the steel industry by ending competition. Morgan and Carnegie did not admire each other. Carnegie had been miffed in 1885 when Morgan brought peace between the Pennsylvania and the New York Central. Carnegie had hoped to use the dispute between the two railroads to drive down freight rates. Morgan disliked Carnegie's fierce independence and competitive spirit. He feared that if Carnegie remained in control of his mills, he would use his power to drive down steel prices.

Critics of Morgan's consolidation complained that he paid inflated prices to the owners of the firms merged into U.S. Steel. The federal Bureau of Corporations asserted that as much as 47 percent of U.S. Steel securities were "water." Others objected to Morgan's underwriting profits, which exceeded $11 million. Many disliked U.S. Steel's market power. The corporation controlled approximately 60 percent of America's steel capacity.

Morgan and Gary successfully overcame the problems of antitrust and President Roosevelt's hostility. They moved quickly to build good relations with America's remaining steel producers. During the 1890s, for example, steel rail wholesale prices varied from an average high of $31.78 per ton in 1890 to lows of $18.75 and $17.63 per ton in 1897 and 1898, respectively. Morgan made it clear that U.S. Steel would not take away markets from existing mills, nor would he tolerate having its market stolen. U.S. Steel fixed steel rail prices at $28 per ton in 1902. That price remained constant until 1915. Morgan placed a "price umbrella" over competing firms. He set prices low enough to deter new entrants and high enough to protect those already in the market. Some benefits went to labor because the steel mills tended to work continuously without the unemployment associated with the boom and bust period of the 1890s. In 1911, when the Taft administration filed an antitrust suit against U.S. Steel, its competitors rose to support Morgan's creation.

U.S. Steel was the largest of a number of Morgan industrial consolidations. In 1902 he underwrote International Harvester, a merger of two large farm machinery manufacturers, the McCormick Harvesting Machine Company and the Deering Harvester Company. (This merger helped U.S. Steel preserve its market because it ensured that the big agricultural machine makers did not vertically integrate backward into steel production.) Not all of Morgan's combinations succeeded. Among the worst failures was the International Mercantile Marine Company (IMM) formed in 1900 to merge a number of American and British shipping corporations that served the North Atlantic route. By 1905 IMM had run up big operating losses, and Morgan's bank had suffered substantial underwriting deficits.

Some of Morgan's worst mistakes resulted from his relationship with the New York, New Haven & Hartford Railroad (New Haven). In 1903 Morgan backed the New Haven's new president Charles S. Mellen, who wanted to create a New England transportation monopoly by uniting all of the region's major railroads, including the New Haven, the Boston & Maine, and the Maine Central with the region's street and interurban electric railways and coastal shipping firms. Even in the best of circumstances such a grandiose plan was dubious, especially since Morgan accomplished the buyouts by increasing the New Haven's capitalization more than four times, from $93 million in 1903 to $417 million in 1913.

In common with nearly all financial experts of his day, Morgan refused to take the automobile seriously. He regarded the motorcar as a plaything for the rich and placed his bets on the railway and streetcar, which in New England, however, proved highly vulnerable to competition. Yankee railroads carried mostly passengers and high-value factory outputs: traffic easily diverted to automobiles, buses, and trucks. By contrast, railroads in the nation's mid-Atlantic, southern, and western regions moved large quantities of heavy freight such as coal, wheat, and iron ore over long distances, a transportation challenge that motor carriers could not meet. Because heavy freight was a much smaller part of the traffic in New England, Morgan forced increased debt on the New Haven, thereby ensuring that the railroad would fail.

The panic of 1907 witnessed Morgan's greatest triumph and, at the same time, brought together many of the forces arrayed against him. America's banking system was as disorganized and volatile at the beginning of the twentieth century as it had been in 1857. There were three main types of retail financial institutions, state-chartered banks, federally chartered "national" banks, and trust companies (organizations that had state charters and many of the characteristics of banks). In New York State, both state and federal banks were subject to government regulation that specified reserve requirements. The nearest thing to a central bank was the state's Clearing House—an institution created by the state's banks to oversee the transfer of funds between them. The Clearing House could act to mitigate a run on a member bank, but it lacked the resources to serve as a true bank of last resort. The trust companies were technically not banks. Most were not members of the Clearing House and depended on the true banks to serve as agents for them in the transfer of funds to other institutions. The trust companies did not have to maintain substantial reserves. Nevertheless, to the general public they seemed indistinguishable from banks since they took deposits, lent money, and allowed their customers to access their deposits by writing checks.

Morgan disliked the trust companies because they were often controlled by speculators. The Knickerbocker Trust had close ties to F. Augustus Heinze, a notorious stock market gambler who on 16 October 1907 failed in an attempt to corner the shares of United Copper. The full force of the panic of 1907 struck while Morgan was in Richmond, Virginia, attending a general convention of the Episcopal church. When Morgan arrived back in New York City on 20 October, the Knickerbocker Trust was experiencing a run that was threatening to spread to other trust companies associated with Wall Street speculators. Morgan, as the most powerful and respected American banker, was enlisted by the nation's financial sector to lead the fight against the panic. In this he was joined by James Stillman of New York's National City Bank, a retail institution closely associated with the Rockefeller family. Although others participated in the struggle against the panic, J. P. Morgan's influence towered over all. He decided which financial institution should live and which should perish. With the country on the brink of financial ruin and the government lacking a central bank, no observer challenged Morgan's judgment. Morgan sent his men to investigate the Knickerbocker Trust. They found it wanting, and he let it fail. Years later Morgan's judgment was subject to strong criticism because it was discovered that the Knickerbocker's assets were nearly enough to pay creditors one hundred cents on the dollar. Many asserted that Morgan had used his awesome power during the crisis to settle private grudges against certain Wall Street speculators, an action that damaged many "innocent" bystanders.

The Knickerbocker Trust failure heightened the panic that then spread in full force to the Trust Company of America and the Lincoln Trust. Morgan's investigating team determined that the Trust Company of America was solvent, a conclusion that led Morgan to make his famous statement "This, then, is the place to stop this trouble" (Allen, p. 129). Morgan systematically led a successful rescue effort that combined investment and commercial banks as well as the federal government. Even Morgan's strategy, which saved the Trust Company of America, was later criticized. In the congressional investigations that followed the panic, it was asserted that Morgan used his power to force the New Haven Railroad to invest in what became worthless securities of a competitive interurban electric railway, the New York, Westchester & Boston, which ran parallel to the New Haven's tracks. Morgan's motive, it was alleged, was to bail out Oakleigh Thorne, who was the dominant financial power in the Trust Company of America.

As soon as Morgan had stopped the trust company runs, he was faced with the collapse of the Wall Street brokerage house Moore & Schley. Morgan feared that if this house failed the panic would reignite. His rescue of Moore & Schley brought him more controversy since he arranged to purchase a controlling interest in the Tennessee Coal, Iron & Railroad Company, whose shares Moore & Schley held. Morgan's action raised opposition because Tennessee Coal controlled rich iron and coal deposits near Birmingham, Alabama. Morgan proposed to rescue Moore & Schley only if he could purchase the shares for U.S. Steel. The problem was that the ownership of the Tennessee Coal Company would push U.S. Steel's dominance of America's steel industry well above 60 percent and place the corporation in a position to dominate the increasingly important southern steel market. Morgan would only act after he sent his men, Elbert Gary and Henry Clay Frick, to Washington to get President Roosevelt's agreement not to undo the deal through antitrust prosecution. On 4 November 1904 Roosevelt agreed to Morgan's terms. Morgan's enemies asserted that he had duped the president.

Morgan received widespread acclaim for his role in stopping the panic. Nevertheless, the panic made it clear that the nation needed banking reform. Morgan took little part in the deliberations that preceded the formation of the Federal Reserve System in 1913. He preferred a more centralized reserve bank, closer to the model favored by Senator Nelson Aldrich than the one actually adopted by Congress.

For Morgan, the aftermath of the panic turned sour as his critics urged a massive investigation of his power and the uses of it. In 1912 Congress, through the actions of the House Banking and Currency Committee, established a subcommittee to conduct an inquiry into the financier's activities. The chairman was Arsène Pujo of Louisiana, but the actual investigation was led by New York lawyer Samuel Untermyer, who virtually put J. P. Morgan on trial. One of the major attacks against Morgan was his use of "interlocking directorates" in major American firms where Morgan, his representatives, or banks allied with him, such as New York's National City Bank, sat on literally hundreds of boards of directors of America's big industrial and commercial companies. Morgan argued eloquently that there was no "money trust" and, predictably, convinced few of his critics. But he did not produce the strongest evidence—that he had not profited from his actions during the panic of 1907. In 1907 his firm lost \$21.5 million as opposed to profits of approximately \$23 million for the four years preceding the panic.

Morgan's private life was as controversial as his public career. His first marriage, in 1861, to Amelia "Mimi" Sturges, the daughter of Jonathan Sturges, was tragic. He married Mimi knowing that she had tuberculosis; she died less than five months later. In 1865 he was married again, this time to Frances Louisa Tracy, the daughter of a leading New York lawyer. This marriage was long-lasting and produced four children: John Pierpont, Jr., Louisa Pierpont, Juliet

Pierpont, and Anne Tracy. Throughout his life Morgan was a strong supporter of the Protestant Episcopal church. He also was a founder in 1873 of the New York Society for the Suppression of Vice, an organization dedicated to outlawing "indecent" pictures and "filthy" literature. These pursuits contrasted sharply with his unorthodox married life. He often traveled alone to Europe. At other times the two took different ships. The actress Maxine Elliott was alleged to be his mistress, and rumors circulated that Morgan had financed the building of a New York theater for her. Whatever the truth, Morgan's private life brought strong criticism from many contemporaries, including Andrew Carnegie.

Morgan died in Rome on the way home from a trip to Egypt. His estate (exclusive of artwork) was valued at $68.3 million. This was a modest sum compared to the wealth of John D. Rockefeller and Andrew Carnegie, who said on learning the value of Morgan's estate, "and to think, he was not a rich man" (Carosso, p. 644). Morgan was, however, the single most powerful financial leader in the United States from the 1890s until his death. Although he never held public office, he exercised more influence on the American economy than any government leader of his day, even Theodore Roosevelt at the apex of his presidential power.

• Morgan manuscripts are housed at the Pierpont Morgan Library in New York City and at the Guild Hall Library in London. Published material on J. P. Morgan is voluminous. Much of the early writing about him was hindered by the refusal of either the Morgan family or the Morgan banks to make any material available to outsiders. Not until the 1980s were professional historians allowed to use the Morgan manuscripts. Nevertheless, there were ample public records. From the 1870s onward, J. P. Morgan underwrote a very large number of securities issues. This activity, one of Morgan's most important, can be traced through advertisements and articles in the *Commercial & Financial Chronicle* (N.Y.) and later in the *Wall Street Journal*. Of the major congressional investigations involving Morgan, the most important is the Pujo Money Trust Investigation of 1913, U.S. House of Representatives, subcommittee of the Committee on Banking and Currency, 62d Cong., 3d sess., Investigation of Financial and Monetary Conditions in the United States Hearings (2 vols.). Morgan's connection with the New Haven Railroad can be traced in S. Doc. 543, 63d Cong., 2d sess., which includes the Interstate Commerce Commission report on the financial transactions of the New York, New Haven and Hartford Railroad.

Many biographies of Morgan have been published. Most of the early ones, such as J. K. Winkler, *Morgan the Magnificent* (1930), are unscholarly, unreliable, and sensational. Two of the best popular works dealing with Morgan were written by Frederick Lewis Allen, *The Lords of Creation* (1935) and *The Great Pierpont Morgan* (1949). An important but uncritical glimpse into J. P. Morgan's private life is in Herbert L. Satterlee, *J. Pierpont Morgan* (1939). The most scholarly and definitive work, which is based on a meticulous use of the Morgan papers both in the United States and England, is Vincent P. Carosso, *The Morgans: Private International Bankers 1854–1913* (1987); it contains a superb bibliographic guide to the Morgan source material. Ron Chernow's *The House of Morgan: An American Banking Dynasty* (1990) is readable and authoritative; however, it lacks the scholarly depth of Carosso and rakes over the scandalous parts of Morgan's career. An obituary is in the *New York Times*, 1 Apr. 1913.

STEPHEN SALSBURY

MORGAN, John Pierpont, Jr. (7 Sept. 1867–13 Mar. 1943), investment banker, was born in Irvington, New York, the son of John Pierpont (J. P.) Morgan, an investment banker, and Frances Louisa Tracy. Jack, so called by his family and associates to distinguish him from his illustrious father, graduated from Harvard in 1889. In 1890 he married Jane Norton Grew, daughter of Henry Sturgis Grew, a member of a powerful New England merchant and manufacturing family. They had four children.

In 1890 Morgan went to work for Jacob C. Rogers, the Boston agent for his grandfather's London merchant bank, Junius S. Morgan & Company. In 1891 he and his wife moved to New York City, where he joined his father's firm. The younger Morgan quickly became a partner, albeit a minor one; in 1885 his interest was only 2 percent. The death in April 1890 of Junius Morgan, who dominated Junius S. Morgan & Company, left that firm without an obvious leader, and as there was no ready candidate available, the London leadership remained an open question for a number of years. In 1898 J. P. Morgan finally sent his son to London to become a resident partner.

Jack Morgan's residence in England converted him into an Anglophile. The Morgans became close to the royal circle, including Lady Sibyl Smith and Lady Antrim, a lady-in-waiting to Queen Victoria. Morgan cheered the British victories in the Boer War. In his love of England he differed from his father who, while comfortable there, was almost equally at home in continental Europe.

Morgan returned to New York in January 1906. Even though he was the heir apparent to the House of Morgan, he never had an easy relationship with his hard-driving father. He lacked his father's brilliance and aggressiveness. At times he had regarded his London stay as an exile. He was so out of touch with New York that he learned about some of his father's most famous exploits, such as the 1901 formation of United States Steel, from newspapers. Nevertheless, he was neither rebellious nor bitter. He admired his father and willingly stood by him during the Pujo committee's 1912 congressional money trust investigation.

After J. P. Morgan's death in March 1913, Jack Morgan took control of the House of Morgan. Where his father had demanded subservience from his partners and seldom held regular meetings to plan strategy, now in contrast he had daily meetings, and the decisions were reached by consensus. The Morgan partners, especially Henry P. Davison, Thomas Lamont, and George Whitney, held him in warm affection. Whitney commented that Jack "was never given credit, because he was shy, but he kept that bunch of primadonnas working, the partners, and he was the unquestioned boss and there was never any argument about it. . . . He wasn't a buccaneer like his father, but he was a hell of a guy" (Chernow, p. 167).

Morgan took over the firm at a time of vast change. His father stood at the apex of America's financial system. The attack on Morgan by the Pujo committee and the creation of the Federal Reserve System in 1913 ensured that never again would a private person have the power or responsibility to act as the United States' banker of last resort as J. P. Morgan had done in 1907. After 1913 the House of Morgan retreated to the more traditional functions of an investment bank—the underwriting of funds for new issues of bonds and shares. Other changes were equally important, although they were barely recognizable in 1913. Throughout his entire career the elder Morgan had worked to channel European, especially British, funds into a capital-short American economy. During the time of his son's ascendancy, New York was replacing London as the world's financial capital. The United States had become a creditor nation and was lending more abroad than it borrowed. For the Morgans the emphasis shifted from domestic to international loans, especially to sovereign entities.

World War I thrust Jack Morgan into international lending in a major way. Although President Woodrow Wilson tried to keep the United States neutral, Morgan disliked Germany and vehemently supported the United Kingdom and its ally France. As the war dragged on, Britain and France required an ever greater amount of goods, especially food and armaments such as gun powder, shells, and rifles. On 15 January 1915 Morgan became the British purchasing agent; a few months later he accepted a similar commission from France. Before the conflict's end, and largely before America's entry into the war in 1917, the Morgans purchased $3 billion of war supplies for Britain and France. This was half of all goods sold by the United States to the Allies. Commissions on these transactions brought Morgan $30 million in fees. In organizing this flow of goods, the House of Morgan came to dominate much of America's industrial economy, and Jack Morgan's reputation rose to new heights as the bank prospered as never before.

Morgan's stint in London from 1898 through 1905 had made England his second home, and it seemed natural to him that his firm should not only finance Britain's war effort but act as a British intelligence agency as well. His pro-British stand caused him to be the target of an assassination attempt in July 1915 when a crazed pro-German gunman, Erich Muenter, invaded the Morgans' Long Island family home and fired two bullets into Jack's groin. Fortunately, they missed his vital organs, and he recovered quickly.

The war revealed an ugly side of Morgan's character. Wall Street had a number of powerful Jewish financial firms such as Goldman, Sachs, whose partners openly praised German culture; Kuhn Loeb, whose principals spoke German at home; and the Seligman brothers. The Morgans had always regarded these firms as rivals. J. P. Morgan, however, came to respect these Jewish bankers, and in the crunch always managed to paper over ill feelings. Not so with his son. On 15 November 1915 Morgan wrote his London partner Edward Grenfell "that most of the Jews in this country are thoroughly pro-German and a very large number of them are anti–J. P. Morgan & Company" (Chernow, p. 199). As time went on, he lunged into cruder anti-Semitism. In May 1920 he wrote to President A. Lawrence Lowell of Harvard University opposing the selection of a Jew to the university's board of overseers. "The Jew is always a Jew first and an American second," Morgan wrote. He had similar views about Roman Catholics. These statements distorted his perspective in the 1920s and 1930s and indelibly stained his reputation.

Peace brought Morgan both opportunities and dangers. He feared the rise of Communist power in Central Europe and Russia and actively opposed socialism in America. In 1920 he hired William "Wild Bill" Donovan (who became the head of the Office of Strategic Services during World War II) to investigate the Communist International. The same year an English radical, Thomas Simkin, attended the Morgan church in New York and fatally shot Morgan's physician in the mistaken belief that he was attacking Morgan. On 16 September 1920 a horse-drawn wagon with 500 pounds of nuts, bolts, and other small pieces of metal exploded in front of Morgan's building at 23 Wall Street, killing thirty-eight people, including two Morgan employees, and slightly injuring Junius Morgan II. The damage to the stonework of the Morgan office building is still visible.

Morgan had mixed feelings about the world order emerging after 1918. He disliked President Wilson, whom he associated with the money trust investigation in 1912. However, he favored Wilson's League of Nations. For this reason he felt uncomfortable about the isolationist bent of many Republicans. Nevertheless, his bank became an intimate supporter of the Republican administrations of Warren G. Harding and Calvin Coolidge, which politically dominated the 1920s. His internationalist views coincided strongly with the House of Morgan's position as the world's premier investment bank. From 1917 through 1926 the Morgan house floated $1.7 billion worth of securities for foreign countries. In contrast, Morgan's domestic underwriting (largely to private corporations) during the 1920s totaled $4 billion. He watched with alarm the economic chaos in Germany that culminated in the disastrous inflation of 1922, which severely damaged that country's middle class. He recognized that something must be done to ensure an orderly redevelopment of Central Europe, and hence he softened his stand toward the former enemy. In 1924 he represented the Coolidge administration at a conference that spawned the Dawes Plan to restructure Germany's debts. This scheme effectively placed Germany in receivership to ensure that Germany would be able to manage its international debt, especially its restructured war reparations obligations. As a part of the Dawes Plan, Morgan underwrote a massive German loan.

In the United States the House of Morgan continued to function as a conservative and prudent lender and avoided most of the worst financial excesses that led to the stock market boom that produced the Wall Street crash of 1929. Nevertheless, Morgan's judgment was not infallible. The house underwrote Cleveland's Van Sweringen Brothers as they put together their series of unsound holding companies, which they used to control a vast railroad empire that included the Erie, the Chesapeake & Ohio, the Nickel Plate, and the Missouri Pacific. Even in 1930, when the brothers were in serious financial strife, Morgan underwrote a secret loan of $40 million in a vain attempt to shore up their financial structure. In 1935 the Van Sweringens defaulted on this loan, and Morgan took charge of liquidating their holdings.

In 1929, prior to the stock market crash, Morgan engaged in the Paris conference, chaired by Owen D. Young, to help Germany again reschedule its reparation debts. Morgan supported the resulting Young Plan and sponsored yet another German loan that amounted to nearly $100 million. The stock market crash on 24 October, "Black Thursday," occurred while he was in Europe. As the nation's premier private bank, the House of Morgan took the lead in a consortium that included Seward Prosser of Bankers Trust, Charles Mitchell of the National City Bank, Albert Wiggin of the Chase National Bank, and William Potter of Guarantee Trust. Together these men pledged $240 million to support the stock market and stop the panic. They were unable to stem the tide, and the market fell dramatically on 29 October, "Tragic Tuesday." The House of Morgan survived the crash but suffered losses exceeding half of its capital. The greatest loss, however, was to the firm's reputation. As in the aftermath of the panic of 1907, Wall Street was the subject of a major congressional investigation, this time conducted by Ferdinand Pecora, a lawyer for the Senate Banking Committee.

Morgan had an unreal worldview. His perspective had been severely distorted by the 1912 Pujo attack against his father and the various physical attacks against him during and immediately after the First World War. He reacted by looking inward. He resented the brash new America in which immigrants from eastern and southern Europe were playing an increasingly important part. Morgan's reaction was to create a secret world beyond the view of the general public. He privately held Pecora, a New York Democrat who had been born in Sicily, Italy, in contempt. He maintained that his bank was private and that he was not even required to produce balance sheets for the Senate committee's inspection. Morgan hired as his lawyer John W. Davis, the Democratic presidential candidate against Coolidge in 1924. Acting on Davis's advice, he faced the Pecora committee with a different strategy than his father had adopted before the Pujo committee in 1912. Whereas J. P. Morgan was arrogant and bombastic, his son was courteous to the point of meekness. While Pecora could find little to expose in the Morgan business, which was honestly and conservatively managed, the public picture that emerged did not flatter Morgan, who admitted that he had paid no income tax during the years 1930–1932. While his actions were legal, the public was surprised at the disclosure, especially since Morgan's testimony on the subject of taxes was confused and hesitant.

The New Deal banking reforms of 1933 included the passage of the Glass-Steagall Act, which forced the separation of commercial from investment banking. Since the House of Morgan engaged in both activities (it took deposits from many of America's largest corporations, including DuPont, the New York Central Railroad, U.S. Steel, Montgomery Ward, General Electric, and American Telephone & Telegraph) it had to reorganize. On 5 September 1935 the House of Morgan was split. Morgan and most of his partners stayed with the J. P. Morgan firm, which became a public chartered commercial bank, and a new firm, Morgan Stanley, took over investment banking. Both of these operations prospered, but their collective influence waned throughout the 1930s and early 1940s.

Jack Morgan died in Florida. Like his father he left a comparatively modest estate of $16 million, which was reduced by taxes and expenses to $4.6 million. Although obituaries praised his role in holding the House of Morgan together and noted the bank's power and prestige, the consensus was that he had added little to the economic or political life of the nation. After his death, leadership in the Morgan banks passed to non-Morgans.

• For additional information see the article on J. P. Morgan, Jr., in John N. Ingham, *Biographical Dictionary of American Business Leaders* (1983), and John Douglas Forbes, *J. P. Morgan Jr., 1867–1943* (1981). Also useful is Vincent P. Carosso, *The Morgans: Private International Bankers 1854–1913* (1987); Ron Chernow, *The House of Morgan: An International Banking Dynasty* (1990); and Frederick Lewis Allen, *The Lords of Creation* (1935). An obituary is in the *New York Times*, 13 Mar. 1943.

STEPHEN SALSBURY

MORGAN, John Tyler (20 June 1824–11 June 1907), U.S. senator, was born in Athens, Tennessee, the son of George Morgan, a frontier merchant, and Frances Irby. The Morgans moved to Benton (now Calhoun) County in east-central Alabama in 1833. After attending public school in Tennessee for three years, John Tyler continued his education under the tutelage of his mother, the well-read daughter of an Episcopal clergyman. In 1840 Morgan moved to neighboring Talladega County to read law with his brother-in-law, William P. Chilton. He passed the bar in 1845 and became a prominent and successful attorney, first in Talladega and after 1855 in Selma. Although Morgan cultivated no land, he did own six slaves who probably functioned as household servants. While living in Talladega, Morgan married Cornelia Willis, with whom he had five children.

With his move to Selma, Morgan also emerged as a key supporter of William Lowndes Yancey and Alabama's secession movement. While Morgan's early political affiliations are obscure, he ended a brief flirtation with the American party in 1855 by making a lifelong commitment to the Democrats. Articulating the southern fear of dependence, acute concern for honor, and determination to preserve the South's political and economic equality within the Union and slavery's equal access to the new territories, Morgan declared his region's "vital liberties" endangered. He warned of the "utter overthrow" of Alabama's "entire social system" and of "personal and political subordination" to African Americans and their northern allies (Fry [1992], p. 12). Morgan served as a delegate to the Democratic State Convention in January 1860 and campaigned actively as a presidential elector for John C. Breckinridge. With Abraham Lincoln's election, Morgan represented Dallas County in the secession convention, where he was instrumental in marshaling the secessionist majority and chaired the committee that wrote Alabama's new constitution.

When war ensued, Morgan was elected a major in the "Cahaba Rifles" and accompanied the Fifth Alabama Infantry to northern Virginia, where he was promoted to lieutenant colonel in November 1861. During spring 1862 he resigned his commission, returned to Alabama, and raised a cavalry unit, the Fifty-first Alabama Partisan Rangers, over which he was appointed colonel. Morgan and the Fifty-first fought as a part of the Confederate Army of Tennessee, and he was commended for bravery at Chickamauga Creek and later during fighting near Knoxville. Promoted to brigadier general in November 1863, he was abruptly arrested and relieved of his command in June 1864. It was rumored that he had been charged with drunkenness, but the documentary evidence is inconclusive. By August he was restored to the command of two cavalry regiments and fought against William T. Sherman in Georgia until March 1865, when he was assigned to recruit black soldiers in Mississippi. Attempts by Morgan and other Confederates to enlist their slaves revealed the depleted condition of southern armies and the final dissolution of the war aimed at preserving black bondage.

In the immediate postwar period, Morgan returned to Selma and concentrated on rebuilding his law practice and his family's finances. Beginning in 1868, he regained public prominence as a leading opponent of Republican Reconstruction and a champion of the "Bourbon" strategy of local autonomy, governmental economy, and rigid white supremacy. Morgan campaigned throughout the state in five crucial elections from 1874 through 1876, in which the Democrats regained political dominance. In the latter year, the state legislature rewarded him with the position of U.S. senator, an office to which he was subsequently reelected five times.

The experiences of secession, war, and Reconstruction left Morgan acutely apprehensive of sectional dependence. Upon assuming his duties in Washington, he complained of a "Solid North" attempting to make Dixie into the "Ireland of the American Union" (Fry [1992], p. 47). This fear provides the key to understanding Morgan's senatorial career, which focused on an unrelenting search for southern autonomy and a professed determination "to wring justice for Alabama from any hands, however unwillingly" (Fry [1992], p. 46).

When addressing Gilded Age domestic issues, Morgan endorsed a number of mechanisms for increased southern economic independence from the Northeast: free coinage of silver to augment the currency supply, state banks to make credit more readily available, lower tariffs to decrease the cost of manufactured goods, and an income tax to raise the relative tax burden of the more prosperous North. These issues also reflected his principal concern for the interests of the agricultural South, especially black-belt planters over industrial interests, North or South. While the senator attended to the interests of the emerging Birmingham iron and coal district, his priorities always relegated industry secondary to agriculture. Rejecting the politics of class and the fundamental reform embodied in the subtreasury plan, Morgan opted for the politics of sectionalism and race, which was always his basic domestic consideration. He had previously opposed the Republican-sponsored Blair Education Bill, Lodge Election Bill, Interstate Commerce Act, and Sherman Antitrust Act out of the fear that a more active federal government would interfere with southern racial practices. When the Populists challenged Democratic one-party dominance, he emphasized race, arguing that only the solidarity of white southerners precluded northern interference. Following the Populist defeat, Morgan ran successfully for reelection in 1899–1900. By making the need for black disfranchisement a key issue in his campaign, Morgan helped pave the way for Alabama's 1901 constitutional convention that deprived African Americans of the vote.

Although Morgan followed domestic issues closely, he considered economic and territorial expansion the most promising avenues for achieving southern economic prosperity and political independence. First appointed to the Senate Foreign Relations Committee in 1878, he served continuously and actively until his death. By increasing the South's export sales of cotton, coal, iron, and timber, Morgan hoped to generate indigenous sources of capital and to free Dixie from the control of northern and British merchants and investors. By adding new territories, he hoped to incorporate states sympathetic to the Democratic South and thereby augment the region's voting power in the Senate. By constructing an isthmian canal, he hoped to convert the Gulf of Mexico into an American Mediterranean, Mobile into a flourishing international port, and Mount Vernon, Alabama, into a shipbuilding center. While pursuing these goals, Morgan tirelessly supported expanded trade with Latin America, Asia, and the Congo, endorsed the construction of a modern U.S. Navy and merchant marine, welcomed the annexation of Hawaii, Puerto Rico, and the Philippines, and championed a canal through Nicaragua.

By the time of his death in Washington, D.C., such stands had rendered Morgan the Gilded Age South's most aggressive economic and territorial expansionist and the nation's most relentless proponent of an isthmian canal. On the domestic front, where he was Alabama's most important late-nineteenth-century public figure, Morgan had been in the vanguard of state politics from secession through the defeat of the Populists and was an ardent defender of the South on the national scene. As such, he bequeathed a legacy of rigid states' rights, elite domination of politics, proplanter economics, and oppression of African Americans.

• Morgan's personal papers are in the Library of Congress and the Alabama State Department of Archives and History in Montgomery. The *Congressional Record* and pertinent Senate documents and reports are fundamental to tracing his senatorial career. The basic published source is Joseph A. Fry, *John Tyler Morgan and the Search for Southern Autonomy* (1992). For Morgan's foreign policy positions, see August C. Radke, "Senator Morgan and the Nicaraguan Canal," *Alabama Review* 12 (1959): 5–34; Joseph O. Baylen, "Senator John Tyler Morgan, E. D. Morel, and the Congo Reform Association," *Alabama Review* 15 (1962): 117–31; and O. Lawrence Burnette, Jr., "John Tyler Morgan and Expansionist Sentiment in the New South," *Alabama Review* 18 (1965): 163–82. See also Fry, "An Unlikely 'Friend' to Native Americans: John Tyler Morgan and Gilded Age Indian Policy," *Hayes Historical Journal* 11 (1993): 5–18. Obituaries and tributes are in the *Washington Post* and the *New York Times*, both 12 and 13 June 1907.

JOSEPH A. FRY

MORGAN, J. P. *See* Morgan, John Pierpont.

MORGAN, J. P., Jr. *See* Morgan, John Pierpont, Jr.

MORGAN, Julia (20 Jan. 1872–2 Feb. 1957), architect, was born in San Francisco, California, the daughter of Charles Bill Morgan, a mining engineer, and Eliza Woodland Parmelee. At an early age Julia heard about Paris and the École des Beaux-Arts from Pierre LeBrun, her cousin's husband, an architect of distinction in New York. Her education at the University of California at Berkeley, however, was in engineering, as there was no architectural school in the West. She graduated with a degree in civil engineering in 1894. Influenced by her professor of descriptive geometry, architect Bernard Maybeck, she worked in his office until 1896, when she convinced her parents that the program in the Section d'Architecture at the École des Beaux-Arts would best prepare her for the career she had chosen.

Although there had never been a woman in this part of the École, Morgan set out for Paris with a college friend who went on to study economics in Germany, while Morgan prepared in an atelier for the formidable entrance examinations, written and oral, that would ultimately lead to a certificate from the architectural section. This course was a prerequisite for government architects in France, although a quota of foreigners was admitted. There was no rule against a woman student, but such a candidate had never applied. The first woman in the world to be accepted, Morgan competed successfully for prizes and medals, mastering the difficult programs in French for the certificate that was hers in February 1902. Travel in Europe was also a significant part of her studies, and she did not return to the United States during her six years in France.

On Morgan's visit in New York while en route to her family home in California, she was invited to practice in her cousin Pierre LeBrun's firm in New York, but she was determined to lead her professional life in her native area of the San Francisco Bay. Morgan found a position with John Galen Howard at Berkeley, where he was in charge of a major campus expansion, including plans for an architectural school. Howard, who had completed his own education at the École, respected Morgan's training and gave her real responsibility on the Hearst mining building as his assistant and the job of project architect for the Greek theater. During this period (1902–1904) Morgan began a practice of her own and passed the state examination as California's first woman licensed to practice architecture. Her most conspicuous design of this period was the Mills College reinforced concrete bell tower, the first campus bell tower in the West. It was the precursor of several Mills campus buildings by Morgan (the library, the gymnasium, the student center, the alumnae building, and the infirmary) that established the character of the Oakland women's college as a veritable museum of architectural design in California.

In 1904 Morgan left her position at Berkeley just as the architecture school was shaping up, with a faculty position almost certainly to be hers. She took with her as junior partner Ira Wilson Hoover and set up an office in San Francisco, Morgan and Hoover. That office was completely destroyed by the earthquake of April 1906. Morgan rallied to take over the rebuilding of the Fairmont Hotel by 1907, and next came work on the Merchants Exchange Building, where she established her own office, hers only until she closed it in 1951 with about 800 buildings to her credit. Hoover left San Francisco late in 1910 for the East Coast.

Morgan's devotion to architecture gave her almost no time for a life outside of her family and her work. She never married, and her favorite recreation was trips alone by freighter to Mexico, South America, and Europe. Her clients often became her friends, but all evidence indicates that architecture was the vocation and the love of her life. When Morgan felt unable to continue her practice in 1951, she disposed of what records her clients did not claim by requesting that the building manager, Otto Haake, see to their incineration in the furnace of the Merchants Exchange Building. Her faithful secretary took some of the material to her own home, and Morgan saved her École drawings, Paris memorabilia, the Hearst correspondence, and her library (including the library of Pierre LeBrun, willed to her at his death) in her San Francisco house where she died. Her nephew, Morgan North, disposed of her estate.

Morgan wrote no books or articles, refused to seek or permit interviews, and is reported to have said, "My buildings speak for me." Much of her practice consisted of work for women's nonprofit organizations with new needs for new kinds of buildings, and there was no publicity beyond word of mouth, although she also designed churches, banks, newspaper offices, and a public market. Domestic architecture was balanced with institutional for steady work in her office, while Morgan's personal attention to each job regarding both design and progress on the site made her as popular with construction workers as with clients.

Morgan's most conspicuous clients were Phoebe Apperson Hearst and her only son, William Randolph Hearst. Phoebe Hearst's interest dated from Morgan's years in Paris and in Berkeley; she commissioned the young architect to complete her elaborate estate, the "Hacienda," designed originally by August Schweinfurth before his untimely death. While working on this project (1902–1910), Morgan was introduced to the National Board of the Young Women's Christian Association and was commissioned to design and build their conference center, Asilomar, at Monterey Bay. This work (1912–1932) led to that organization's program of building centers for young women who came to cities to work in offices and factories but could not find appropriate housing. Morgan responded with group residences and recreation centers. For the YWCA in World War I, Morgan designed "hostess houses" at army posts in the West, where family visits with soldiers took place and recreational activities were sponsored. These were Crafts-style, wooden, one-story buildings with large fireplaces, open-trussed ceilings, small areas for some privacy, and large central spaces for dances and showing films. Two of these in California continue in service, one adapted as a restaurant in Palo Alto and another as part of a YWCA in San Pedro. In larger cities the more formal YWCAs still in active use include those in Honolulu, Oakland, San Francisco, Pasadena, and Salt Lake City. Their symmetry as they face the street is softened by inner courtyards, colored tiles, daylighted pools, and loggias or balconies, evidence of Morgan's concern for amenities in what served "working girls."

At the death of his mother in 1919, William Randolph Hearst finally came into his fortune, although it was carefully restricted by corporate lawyers. He went to Morgan's office for a plan to build on a central coast hilltop, the site of family picnics and part of his father's thousands of acres. This plan, dedicated to his mother, gradually emerged as a lifetime project for both client and architect, a setting for his collections, and ultimately a state monument visited by a million people each year. Morgan, as sole architect, dedicated her weekends to San Simeon for more than twenty years, often leaving an office staff member at the site while she worked on her many other diversified commissions. Hearst deferred to her, contractors and engineers answered to her, and she designed and supervised the labor camp and developed a poultry farm and zoo (the largest private collection in America). In a letter of September 1921 to Arthur Byne, a purveyor of Spanish artifacts and an old friend from her Paris days, Morgan wrote, "We are building for him a sort of village on a mountain top overlooking the sea and ranges of mountains, and housing his collections as well as his family. Having different buildings allows the use of varied treatments, as does the fact that garden work is on steep hillsides, requiring endless steps and terracing." On 7 May 1924 she wrote, "The place on the hill grows and from a distance begins to assume the look of a hill town. There is no effort to make the buildings themselves other than modern." Her many letters, along with the buildings she designed, remain the greatest source for understanding her work.

The San Francisco Bay area continued to prize Morgan's designs for their use of light and her meticulous attention to detail, but the architectural press ignored her until about 1976, when *Women in American Architecture*, edited by Susana Torre, appeared along with an exhibition at the Brooklyn Museum to stimulate interest in many little-known members of the profession. That same year marked the Museum of Modern Art's exhibition of nineteenth-century drawings from the École des Beaux-Arts, noted by *New York Times* critic Ada Louise Huxtable as "one of its most important contributions to tastemaking and art scholarship since 'The International Style' formally introduced modern architecture to this country in 1932." The Oakland Museum showed Morgan's drawings in the same year. Julia Morgan has become an architect to be reckoned with in architecture schools, not only as the most distinguished and prolific woman architect but as an important member of the profession in American architectural history.

• Documentary sources include the Bancroft Library, University of California, Berkeley, especially the Regional Oral History Office, which contains transcripts, tapes, and a two-volume publication edited by Suzanne B. Reiss, *The Julia Morgan Architectural Project* (1976). The Bancroft Library also has a collection of cataloged documents. Berkeley's College of Environmental Design has a documents collection in the architectural library, with correspondence, drawings, specifications from Morgan's Paris years, her diary from a 1947 trip to South America, and material from the Forney-Stone, Steilberg, and Hussey collections. The M. H. deYoung Memorial Museum in San Francisco has archival material on the monastery imported from Spain by Hearst and a card table–sized model of Morgan's proposed Museum of Medieval Art. By far the most inclusive collection is from Morgan North, the architect's nephew; it is in the Special Collections at the Robert E. Kennedy Library, California Polytechnic State University, San Luis Obispo, organized in *A Descriptive Guide to the Julia Morgan Collection* (1985). The only full-length biography is Sara Holmes Boutelle, *Julia Morgan, Architect* (1988). An obituary is in the *San Francisco Chronicle*, 3 Feb. 1957.

SARA HOLMES BOUTELLE

MORGAN, Junius Spencer, Sr. (14 Apr. 1813–8 Apr. 1890), merchant banker, was born in West Springfield, Massachusetts, the son of Joseph Morgan, a farmer and investor, and Sarah Spencer. In 1815 Junius's father purchased a stagecoach inn and tavern in Westfield, Connecticut; in 1817 his father moved to Hartford, where he started the Exchange Coffee House.

Joseph also became a successful real estate investor, bought into a local bank, and became a founder of the Aetna Insurance Company.

Junius attended primary schools in Middletown and East Windsor, Connecticut. In 1829 his father apprenticed him to Alfred Welles, a Boston general merchant. Against his father's wishes, in 1833 Junius joined Welles in a partnership that quickly ran into financial difficulties. Joseph Morgan bailed out the firm, and the partnership ended in 1834. Almost immediately, thanks to his father's financial support, Junius became a partner in Morris Ketchum's private New York City bank. In 1836, Junius Morgan left New York to join Howe Mather & Company, a Hartford wholesale dry goods business that sold its wares to the South. Young Morgan helped steer the firm through the panic of 1837 when he traveled from Virginia to Florida systematically collecting the firm's debts. He quickly learned the complex nature of the commercial world and found it possible to receive payment not in specie (gold or silver) but in bills drawn on English merchants who had purchased southern cotton. In 1836 Morgan married Juliet Pierpont, daughter of John Pierpont, the passionate abolitionist pastor of Boston's Hollis Street Unitarian Church. The Morgans had five children.

In 1850 Morgan moved to Boston, where he entered a partnership with James M. Beebe, who ran one of the United States's largest wholesale dry goods and importing firms. Morgan had a 35 percent interest in the resulting firm, J. M. Beebe, Morgan & Company. In 1853 Morgan traveled to London, then the world's financial capital. He called on George Peabody, a rising merchant banker who had helped finance America's cotton trade and lent money to U.S. import houses. Peabody also sold American railroad securities to British investors. Prior to the Civil War most American railroads imported British iron rails, and the exporters often accepted American railroad securities in payment.

When Morgan visited Peabody, the bachelor merchant was fifty-eight years old, in failing health, and was looking for a partner. Morgan was highly respected not only in Boston but in New York City, where he was on good terms with Peabody's agent, Duncan, Sherman & Company. He was also well known in the South, where he had made good contacts as a Hartford merchant. In September 1854 Morgan agreed to a ten-year partnership and moved to London. Peabody kept 65 percent of the business, Morgan gained 28 percent, and a third man, Charles C. Gooch, took 7 percent. Morgan entered the London financial world when England and Russia were engaged in the Crimean War, which increased the demand for American cotton and grain.

Despite Peabody's business in railroad securities, at the time of Morgan's entry the firm was primarily a granter of commercial credits. During the Crimean War, Peabody & Company unwisely overextended loans to a number of American import houses. The war ended in 1856 and was followed by the panic of 1857, which began in the American commercial banking system and then spread to wholesale merchants. The collapse of these American firms spread the panic to England. Soon Peabody's New York agent and largest debtor, Duncan, Sherman, where Junius had placed his son J. P. Morgan, was near financial collapse. Peabody's good reputation in London saved his bank. Thirteen English guarantors, including London's prestigious Joint Stock Bank, approached the Bank of England, which on the strength of their guarantees bolstered by the collateral of American securities held by Peabody, agreed to a credit line of £800,000. Morgan did much of the work in arranging the rescue and used part of the funds to save Duncan, Sherman. Peabody needed only £300,000 of its credit line. By Christmas 1857 Peabody was profitable. Nevertheless, the panic was sobering. At the height of the danger Morgan wrote his son in New York, "Let what you now witness make an impression not to be eradicated. In making haste to be rich how many fall, '*slow & sure*' should be the motto of every young man" (Carosso, p. 64).

In February 1859 Peabody turned over active management of his firm to Morgan. After the panic, Morgan cautiously restricted major American loans to businesses operating in large northern and midwestern cities. This strategy enabled the firm to ride out the collapse of the southern cotton trading houses, which resulted from the American Civil War.

After the war, between 1865 and 1890, much of Morgan's success came from financing America's railroad boom. He profited from his experience with the Ohio & Mississippi (O&M), a railway that linked Cincinnati with St. Louis. Peabody had started to underwrite the O&M's bonds in 1853, but during construction the railroad threatened to default on its debt. Especially during the middle and late 1860s, Morgan witnessed outside experts force financial, operational, and construction plans on the O&M that ensured the company could pay its bondholders. Morgan learned early the value of a merchant bank acting to protect the interest of its clients.

While Morgan always remained a fiscal conservative, he took some risks in the support of new technology. He backed Cyrus Field's pioneering of the Atlantic Telegraph Company that in 1858 succeeded in establishing cable communication across the Atlantic. Unfortunately, the cable broke after four weeks, and it took eight years to replace. However, Morgan never lost faith and rejoiced when Field established permanent cable service in 1866. In the United States, Morgan's son J. P. proved an equal enthusiast for science-based inventions. The Morgans used technology to increase their firms' visibility and image.

Peabody retired on 30 September 1864. Morgan took over on 1 October and, at the insistence of Peabody, changed the firm's name to Junius S. Morgan & Company. More than 80 percent of the bank's capital of approximately £350,000 represented Morgan's funds. His approach to the business differed from Peabody's in one major respect. While Peabody used agents and correspondents to carry out the American end of his business, Morgan used his son to build a true transatlantic financial institution. He arranged for Charles H. Dabney, the most conservative member of the Duncan, Sherman firm, to join his son. The resulting Dabney, Morgan & Company began in November 1864. Morgan furnished $200,000 of its $350,000 capital. In 1871 he orchestrated the merger of one of Philadelphia's leading investment banks with his son's business, and the new partnership, Drexel, Morgan, quickly assumed financial leadership in New York.

Morgan recognized that a successful London merchant bank that underwrote American ventures needed two strengths. It had to have a U.S. representative to evaluate and seize opportunities, and it had to build its reputation on its ability to protect the bondholders' and shareholders' investments. Morgan used his son's investment bank for these purposes. He tried to restrict underwriting to rail systems with strong managements such as the Pennsylvania, the Baltimore & Ohio, the Lehigh Valley, and the New York Central. He publicly floated the securities of all of these systems and raised many millions of pounds for them between 1869 and 1879. Prior to 1879 Morgan underwrote in England for the Pennsylvania alone securities valued at more than $20 million. His ability to channel English funds to his son's clients elevated J. P. Morgan & Company into America's leading investment bank by the time of Junius Morgan's death. He also participated in a substantial number of loans to European and South American nations.

Junius Morgan, who remained an American citizen, died in England near Eze as a result of an accident while riding in a horsedrawn carriage. He left an estate (excluding artwork) of approximately $12.4 million, of which nearly $10 million represented Morgan's own capital in his firm. J. P. Morgan was his sole heir, thus assuring the rising New York banker a solid English financial base.

• The following books provide useful information on Morgan: Vincent P. Carosso, *The Morgans: Private International Bankers 1854–1913* (1987); Fritz Redlich, *Moulding of American Banking* (2 vols., 1947–1951); Dorothy Adler, *British Investment in American Railroads 1834–1898* (1970); and the entry on Morgan in John Ingham's *Biographical Dictionary of American Business Leaders* (1983).

STEPHEN SALSBURY

MORGAN, Lee (10 July 1938–19 Feb. 1972), jazz trumpeter and composer, was born in Philadelphia, Pennsylvania. Little is known about his parents except that his father was a pianist for a local church choir. Morgan's older sister, Ernestine, was influential in his musical education. When he was in his early teens she took him to hear alto saxophone legend Charlie Parker and bop pianist Bud Powell at the Earle Theatre. She also gave Morgan his first trumpet at age fourteen. Aided by his parents' support, Morgan amassed a substantial record collection, and many of his colleagues congregated at his home to listen to his library.

Philadelphia in the late 1940s and 1950s was a vital and active center for modern jazz. Morgan studied trumpet privately as well as at his high school, Mastbaum Tech, which was known for its depth of young jazz talent. Considered a prodigy, Morgan astonished local contemporaries. At age fifteen Morgan began to perform professionally with his own group that included at various times pianist Bobby Timmons, drummers Albert "Tootie" Heath and Lex Humphries, and bassists Spanky DeBrest and Henry Grimes. In addition, Morgan participated in many jazz workshops at the Music City instrument shop. It was through these sessions that he had the opportunity to play with such jazz legends as trumpeters Miles Davis, Kenny Dorham, Roy Eldridge, and Dizzy Gillespie; saxophonists Sonny Rollins and Sonny Stitt; drummers Art Blakey, Kenny Clarke, and Max Roach; and pianist Bud Powell.

Morgan viewed trumpeters Fats Navarro and Clifford Brown as most directly influential upon his personal style. His favorite trumpeters, in the order of his personal preference, were Navarro, Brown, Gillespie, Davis, and Dorham.

The year 1956 proved to be significant for Morgan. He performed with both Navarro and Brown in Philadelphia. Morgan first recorded as a leader for the jazz labels Blue Note (*Lee Morgan Indeed*) and Savoy (*Introducing Lee Morgan*), both in 1956. Gillespie, another significant figure in Morgan's musical development, hired him for the trumpet section of his big band in the summer of 1956. Morgan toured and recorded with the band until its dissolution in January 1958. Several albums from 1957 that feature Morgan with Dizzy include *Birk's Works*, *Big Band Sound of Dizzy Gillespie*, and *Dizzy Gillespie at Newport*. Pianist Wynton Kelly, a colleague of Morgan's in the Gillespie band of 1957, and Hank Mobley, who performed with Gillespie in 1953, were also among the musicians with whom Morgan first recorded. Noted critic Nat Hentoff, in the liner notes to the 1960 album *LeeWay*, discussed the first time he heard Morgan soloing with Gillespie in 1957 on the standard "Night in Tunisia": "a trumpet soared out of the band into a break that was so vividly brilliant and electrifying that all conversation in the room stopped . . . ."

Morgan performed prolifically during 1957. His solo endeavors with Blue Note included *City Lights*; *Lee Morgan, Volume 3*; *Candy*; and *The Cooker*. Featured artists on these albums include alto saxophonist Gigi Gryce; tenor saxophonist Benny Golson; baritone saxophonist Pepper Adams; pianists Kelly, Sonny Clark, and Timmons; bassists Victor Sproles, Doug Watkins, and Paul Chambers; and drummers Billy Higgins, Art Taylor, and Philly Joe Jones. As a sideman, Morgan, along with trombonist Curtis Fuller, pianist Kenny Drew, Paul Chambers on bass, and Philly Joe Jones on drums, was featured on tenor saxophonist John Coltrane's legendary 1957 album *Blue Train*. Another remarkable appearance in 1957 was on tenor saxophonist Johnny Griffin's appropriately named *A Blowing Session*, which featured Griffin with

Coltrane and tenor saxophonist Mobley, along with the rhythm section of Kelly, Chambers, and Blakey, in a very casual setting much in keeping with club-style jam sessions. Fellow Philadelphian jazz organist Jimmy Smith included Morgan on similarly oriented sessions for two albums in 1957 and 1958. *The Sermon* in 1957 included trombonist Fuller, alto saxophonist Lou Donaldson, tenor saxophonist Tina Brooks, guitarists Eddie McFadden and Kenny Burrell, and drummers Donald Bailey and Blakey. *House Party* in 1958 used mostly the same personnel, with the substitution of George Coleman on alto sax and the sole use of Blakey on drums.

Griffin's and Smith's recordings highlighted some of Morgan's style traits from his early years, best described as effervescent, flashy, and even arrogant. Bending and smearing of tones via a half-valve technique, precarious leaps in rhythmically unstable areas, and unexpected bold swooping passages musically depicted the raw feelings of maliciousness that were associated with the style later dubbed "hard bop."

This style reached a zenith during the late 1950s with Morgan's incorporation into the Jazz Messengers. Blakey invited Morgan in 1958 to join the recently formed cooperative venture that would serve as one of the most important crucibles for young jazz musicians over nearly four decades. Throughout Morgan's tenure with the group, he performed with tenor saxophonists Golson, Mobley, and Wayne Shorter; pianist Timmons; bassist Jymie Merritt; and Blakey. At the forefront of jazz during the late 1950s and early 1960s, the Messengers were major sponsors of the hard bop and funky jazz movements. Morgan performed on club dates and recorded often, most significantly on the albums *Moanin'* (1958) and *A Night in Tunisia* (1960), the title track of which was a Gillespie standard. Morgan's association with the Jazz Messengers was perhaps one of the greatest achievements of his career. Noted scholar Gunther Schuller said of Morgan's playing within Blakey's group: "this is brass playing of very rare excellence."

Morgan's efforts as a leader during the period 1958–1961 included the 1958 album *Peckin' Time* and three albums in 1960, *Here's Lee Morgan*, *LeeWay*, and *Indestructable-Lee*. Notable sideman appearances included a series of recordings for Blue Note with Brooks (1958–1961); *Wrinkles*, a 1959 album led by Kelly that also included tenor saxophonist Shorter, bassist Chambers, and drummers Jones and Jimmy Cobb; and the 1960 Thad Jones album *Minor Strain*.

The years 1958–1961 marked a transition for Morgan in which he tended toward greater critical selectivity of melodic and rhythmic material. This maturity, in large part, was due to the influence of Blakey's Jazz Messengers. *Moanin'* reflected the beginning of this change, and with *A Night in Tunisia*, Morgan had nearly attained his mature style, displaying a commanding sense of rhythmic, tonal, and formal mastery.

Morgan left the Jazz Messengers in 1961 and returned to his hometown for a year to bring an increasingly overwhelming drug addiction under control. While in Philadelphia he performed with tenor saxophonist Jimmy Heath but reduced his recording activity. Morgan appeared on Blakey's *The Freedom Rider* in 1961 and recorded *Take Twelve* in 1962, which featured tenor saxophonist Clifford Jordan, pianist Barry Harris, bassist Bob Cranshaw, and drummer Louis Haynes. In 1963 Morgan returned to New York City, and later that year he appeared as sideman on Mobley's *No Room For Squares* with pianist Andrew Hill, bassist John Ore, and drummer Jones. The album, which included modal, gospelish blues, and ballad styles, marked Morgan's resurgence to popularity. Morgan's style achieved full maturity during this period, with a considerable emphasis upon melodic and rhythmic discrimination, and a darkening of his tone to reflect a cynical, sardonic character present in his later recordings.

Morgan returned to the forefront of jazz and popular music with a vengeance in 1964 with two landmark recordings: as a leader on his signature album *The Sidewinder*, which comprised original compositions by Morgan, and as a sideman on trombonist and composer Graham Moncur III's *Evolution. The Sidewinder*, which featured tenor saxophonist Joe Henderson, Harris, Cranshaw, and drummer Billy Higgins, became one of Blue Note's all-time bestsellers. It showed up on juke boxes, was adopted as a television theme, made *Billboard*'s Top 200 LP list in 1964, and was even featured in a Chrysler television advertisement. This level of popularity was almost nonexistent in the jazz community at the time, since virtually no jazz albums produced the economic interest found in other segments of popular music. The title track's rhythmic vitality, danceable beat, and energetic playing by Henderson and Morgan made for a recording that has become a time-honored standard. The popularity of this album caused Blue Note to delay the release of two sessions recorded at the same time, *Search for a New Land* and *Tom Cat*; the latter was released in 1980.

Within weeks of recording *The Sidewinder*, Morgan participated in a memorable session for Moncur's *Evolution*. According to Morgan's brother, James, in the fall 1989 newsletter *Blue Notes*, Morgan considered the album *Evolution* a critical point in his style development. Moncur placed Morgan and Cranshaw alongside the team of alto saxophonist Jackie McLean, vibraphonist Bobby Hutcherson, and the extraordinary seventeen-year-old drummer Tony Williams. McLean and Morgan proved to be an ideal pairing for blend of sound. This album foreshadowed the gradual elimination of the stylistic "barriers" placed by hard bop's creators around its basic tenets, frenetic melodic activity and the malicious contempt of jazz within the context of bebop.

Additional albums led by Morgan in 1964 included the notable *Search for the New Land*, with Shorter, guitarist Grant Green, pianist Herbie Hancock, bassist Reggie Workman, and drummer Higgins; and *Delightfulee Morgan*, with Joe Henderson, pianist McCoy Tyner, Cranshaw, and Higgins. Morgan performed on Shorter's *Night Dreamer* alongside Tyner, Workman, and drummer Elvin Jones.

Morgan continued to record for Blue Note as a leader throughout the mid- to late 1960s. Of his many recordings since 1964, of special note were *The Gigolo* and *The Rumproller*, both recorded in 1965, as well as *Cornbread* and *The Rajah*, both recorded in 1966. *The Rumproller*, although a fine album in its own right, failed to achieve the success of its conceptual predecessor *The Sidewinder*. Other albums of this period included *Tom Cat*, *Infinity*, and *The Cat* (all 1965); *Charisma* (1966); *The Procrastinator* (1967); and *Caramba* (1968). Morgan returned to the Jazz Messengers in 1965 and remained with the group for another year. During this time he recorded *Indestructible*, which featured trombonist Fuller and on which pianist Timmons was replaced by Cedar Walton. As a sideman, Morgan appeared with Mobley in 1965 on *Dippin'*; with McLean on *Consequence* (1965) and *Jacknife* (1966); with Joe Henderson on *Mode for Joe* (1966); and with keyboardist Lonnie Smith on *Think* (1968).

The early 1970s saw Morgan active in a crusade for musicians' rights. A leader of the short-lived Jazz and People's Movement, he helped to combat perceived media ignorance and indifference toward jazz artists. As part of the group's efforts to gain regular access to television for jazz groups, it picketed and disrupted the talk shows of Johnny Carson, Merv Griffin, Dick Cavett, and David Frost.

Notable recordings by Morgan during the early 1970s included the 1970 performance *Live at the Lighthouse*, with reedman Bennie Maupin, pianist Harold Mabern, bassist Merritt, and drummer Mickey Roker; the 1971 release *Capra Beach*; and Morgan's last completed project for Blue Note, a 1972 two-record set completed six weeks before his death, simply titled *Lee Morgan*. Sidemen on this album included saxophonist Billy Harper, Mabern, Merritt, Workman, and drummer Freddie Waitts. On 19 February 1972, a quarrel erupted between Morgan and his longtime companion Helen More while Morgan performed with his quintet at the New York City nightclub Slugs. The argument escalated, and Morgan was shot through the heart at close range. He died instantly, and More was charged with the homicide.

Morgan displayed explicit virtuosic command of chord changes with bold conviction. A master of formal manipulation, his intelligent phrasing often featured irregularities that supported his advanced harmonic and melodic delineation. Morgan's playing style came across as sassy and brash early in his career—half-valving, bending, and smearing were favorite techniques and epitomized the "badness" of hard bop style. Calm assuredness directed his mature solo recordings with purpose. His extensive range and bold, clear sound, combined with great precision and accuracy in his solos, made an enormous impact upon subsequent jazz trumpeters. Morgan was widely perceived as the direct successor to Clifford Brown because of their remarkably similar trumpet styles. Many of Morgan's stylistic characteristics found their way into his numerous, blues-based compositions, which became more modal in orientation in the latter half of the 1960s and early 1970s.

• David Rosenthal, *Hard Bop: Jazz and Black Music 1955–1965* (1992), opens with a lengthy biographical and stylistic discourse of Morgan and promotes him as the epitome of hard bop style. A wonderful contextual discography, Tom Piazza, *The Guide to Classic Recorded Jazz* (1995), offers an insightful account of Morgan's performances as leader and sideman. Len Lyons and Don Perlo include a biographical sketch of Morgan in *Jazz Portraits: The Lives and Music of the Jazz Masters* (1989), as does Gérald Arnaud and Jacques Chesnel in *Masters of Jazz* (1991). What is considered to be Morgan's last interview, with Mike Bourne in *Down Beat* 39, no. 8 (1972): 11, provides insight regarding his crusade for jazz musicians' rights, as well as his musical philosophy late in life. See also John Litweiler, *The Freedom Principle* (1984). Obituaries are in *Down Beat* 39, no. 6 (1972): 11, and *Rolling Stone*, 30 Mar. 1972, p. 18.

DAVID E. SPIES

MORGAN, Lewis Henry (21 Nov. 1818–17 Dec. 1881), anthropologist, was born near Aurora, New York, the son of Jedediah Morgan and his second wife, Harriet Steele, farmers. Early in his life Morgan's parents let their farmlands and moved to Aurora, New York, on the eastern shore of Lake Cayuga. Morgan was educated at Cayuga Academy there and proceeded to Union College in Schenectady for his junior and senior years, graduating in 1840. He read law and was admitted to the bar two years later. Because of the economic depression following the panic of 1837, he delayed starting a practice and remained at home in Aurora until the fall of 1844. He then moved to Rochester, where he became successful in his profession, residing there until his death.

It is, however, for his accomplishments in anthropology, not as a lawyer, that he is remembered, beginning with his writings on the Iroquois. Morgan liked to represent the circumstances of his start in anthropology as a happy accident. In 1842, in Aurora and at leisure due to the depression, he joined a literary club called the Gordian Knot. "We soon concluded to cut this knot," he later wrote, and they turned the club into a secret society with an Indian theme, taking the name Cayuga after the Iroquois nation that formerly lived there. Membership grew to some 400, encompassing neighboring towns, and a constitution was devised based on the Iroquois league, a confederacy of five nations (Mohawk, Oneida, Onondaga, Cayuga, and Seneca; a sixth, the Tuscarora, was added later) and the eight "tribes" or clans into which the nations were divided (Wolf, Bear, and so on). The group took the name of the Grand Order of the Iroquois (GOI), and the various "council fires" in different villages were named after a particular Iroquois nation and clan. It was a secret society made up of young bachelors that lasted five or six years until its members took up their careers. The "accident" that brought Morgan to anthropology was largely of his own making—he was probably the instigator of the transformation of the Gordian Knot into the Cayugas, for example. The organization served him as a pretext for developing a serious interest in the study of Iroquois life under the cover of fun.

Morgan was the constitutionalist for the GOI. As such, his interest took the form of acquiring information about the structure of the Iroquois league in order to use it as a model for his organization. During a trip to Albany to gather information on treaties with the Iroquois, Morgan made the acquaintance of Ely S. Parker (Hasanoanda), a young Seneca who was then serving as interpreter for a delegation of his leaders who were meeting with the governor. Later Morgan and some of his fellow members of the GOI visited the Tonawanda and other reservations, where they became acquainted with the life of the Iroquois and the traditions about the structure of the Iroquois league with Ely Parker's help. Morgan was surprised to learn that the Iroquois clans were matrilineal and that the fifty chiefships that made up the leadership of the league were owned by matrilineal clan segments, such that chiefships passed not from father to son but from uncle (mother's brother) to nephew (sister's son). This contradicted what he had found in published histories. Similarly the matrilineal principle governed the Iroquois longhouse, which grouped together the women of a clan and their husbands and children into a large household. He came to see that the political structure of the Iroquois league rested upon the kinship structure.

These and other matters Morgan committed to writing, first as addresses to the Grand Order, then as a paper delivered before the New-York Historical Society (in 1846), then published in the *American Whig Review* in the form of fourteen "Letters on the Iroquois, by Skenandoah," his moniker in the GOI, addressed to statesman and pioneering ethnologist Albert Gallatin. At about the same time Morgan began collecting and studying Iroquois material culture in response to a general appeal from the regents of the University of the State of New York for Indian artifacts to form a state collection. Morgan's collections are published in the 2d (1849), 3d (1850), and 5th (1852) *Annual Reports of the Regents of the University on the Condition of the Cabinet of Natural History* and are the basis of "The Fabrics of the Iroquois" (*Stryker's American Register*, July 1850, pp. 319–43). By this time, however, the GOI had waned and died.

Morgan came to think that he must abandon his ethnological research if he were to build up his law practice, and so he cast these writings into his first book, *League of the Ho-de'no-sau-nee, or Iroquois* (1851) in an attempt to bring this work to a conclusion. He dedicated the book, "the materials of which are the fruit of our joint researches," to Ely Parker, who went on to have a notable career as adjutant to Ulysses S. Grant during the Civil War and as commissioner of Indian Affairs during Grant's presidency. That same year Morgan married Mary Elizabeth Steele of Albany (his mother's brother's daughter), presenting her with a specially bound copy of his book as a wedding present. It was to have been his swan song as an anthropologist, as he turned to the serious business of making money and raising a family. (The couple had three children, but two daughters died in childhood.)

He continued, however, to be drawn to scholarly associations. Before the Rochester Athenaeum and Mechanics' Association he gave a lecture (later published), *Diffusion against Centralization* (1852), arguing that the diffusion of wealth in American capitalism will prevent the formation of a hereditary monied class inimical to democracy. Then, in 1854, Morgan and several associates formed another literary society, the Club of Rochester (often called the Pundit Club), with Morgan as secretary. Papers he gave in the opening years are on geology, slavery, and animal psychology but not anthropology. Then in 1857 he attended the annual meeting of the American Association for the Advancement of Science (AAAS), held in Albany that year, and it served to reawaken his dormant ethnological interests. At the AAAS meeting of the following year he gave a paper on "Laws of Descent of the Iroquois," and most of his scholarly work for the next ten years or so were devoted to the study of kinship.

Morgan's guiding hypothesis during this period was that the underlying pattern of kinship among the Iroquois was the same in all the American nations. There were essentially four elements to that pattern: one, clans, which he considered to be gigantic families; two, matrilineal descent; three, "classificatory" kinship (words for kin that were distinguished in English were "classified" or merged in the Iroquois languages such that, for example, a father's brother was a "father" and a mother's sister was a "mother"); and four, the longhouse as a form of collective living. Morgan's anthropology largely devoted itself to the problems of the relations among these features of Iroquois kinship and the question of their generality. If the underlying pattern or a part thereof could be shown to be universal in the Americas and found in Asia as well, it would demonstrate what philological comparisons of American Indian languages had been unable to: that the Indians were all one people and that they had come to America from Asia.

In the 1850s Morgan was associated with Rochester businessmen investing in railroads and iron mines in the Upper Peninsula of Michigan, work that took him to Marquette on Lake Superior each summer for several years. During his visit of 1858 he used the occasion to look for the Iroquois pattern of kinship among the Ojibwa (Chippewa). He found that their clans, unlike those of the Iroquois, were patrilineal but that, like the Iroquois, their terminology of kinship was classificatory. He believed that this common semantic patterning showed the Iroquois and Ojibwa to be related historically even though the vocabulary and grammar of their languages retained no trace of such a relationship. During the following four summers (1859–1862) Morgan made field trips to the West, going to Kansas and Nebraska Territories, up the Missouri River to the Rockies, and to Lake Winnipeg in

Canada. During these trips he collected information on Native-American classifications of kin for some 200 genealogical positions among eighty nations. He also undertook a vast correspondence with missionaries and consuls around the world (later assisted by the Smithsonian Institution), collecting information on kinship terminologies by means of a printed questionnaire and circular letter that gave a trenchant overview of the project ("Circular in Reference to the Degrees of Relationship among Different Nations," *Smithsonian Miscellaneous Collections* 2, no. 10 [1862]). At the end of the first of his summer field trips he obtained, from a missionary returned to his village in New York on sick leave, information on kinship systems from South India (Tamil and Telugu), which, Morgan believed, were sufficiently similar to the Iroquois "classificatory" pattern to be regarded as identical and therefore as proof of Asiatic origin.

The results of these labors were published in *Systems of Consanguinity and Affinity of the Human Family* (1871), a large quarto volume of more than 600 pages with massive tables of kinship terms. The final version of the text was complete in 1868, but publishing it made such demands on the finances of the Smithsonian Institution (strained by the fire of 1865) that Morgan was obliged to wait three years for it to appear, all the while his irritation and fears mounting at the thought of being forestalled. In the final version of Morgan's argument, the "classificatory" kinship system in America and Asia was interpreted as an evolutionary stage leading to the "descriptive" kinship system of Europe and the Near East via a series of different forms of marriage progressing from primitive promiscuity to monogamy. Morgan rushed this theory into print in "A Conjectural Solution of the Origin of the Classificatory System of Relationship" (*Proceedings of the American Academy of Arts and Sciences* 7 [1868], pp. 436–77). In the same year he published *The American Beaver and His Works*, another outcome of his trips to Michigan's Upper Peninsula and the longest of a small group of publications dealing with animal psychology.

By the mid-1860s Morgan had amassed a small fortune as a lawyer, which allowed him to retire from his practice and devote himself full time to his anthropological research. Morgan took the grand tour of Europe with his wife and son in 1870–1871. It was during this year, when his kinship book came out, that he met the leading lights of British anthropology: Sir John Lubbock (Lord Avebury), president of the newly formed Royal Anthropological Institute, John Ferguson McLennan, and E. B. Tylor as well as H. S. Maine, the historian of comparative Indo-European family law, Charles Darwin, and others. Sometime after their return to the United States, Morgan began work on the third of his three major anthropological works and the one for which he is best known, *Ancient Society*, published in 1877.

Ancient Society is Morgan's grand synthesis, upon the scale of universal history. Like the contemporary writings of his British counterparts, it is a work of high Victorian social evolutionism, tracing "the lines of human progress from savagery through barbarism to civilization," and like them its strongly progressive or developmentalist thesis was a response to the dramatic lengthening of human history with the discovery, at Brixham Cave in 1859 (among other sites), of human remains in association with long-extinct animals. In *Ancient Society* Morgan deploys the stages-of-development idea to the problems first posed for him by Iroquois matrilineal clans, classificatory kinship, and communal living. The book has four parts: the "growth of intelligence through inventions and discoveries"; the "growth of the idea of government," in which Morgan brings the Iroquois clan to bear on the understanding of Aztec, Greek, and Roman clan-based government; the "growth of the idea of the family," in which he elaborates the stages of the evolution of marriage adumbrated in the *Systems of Consanguinity*; and the "growth of the idea of property."

In the closing years of his life Morgan devoted much of his attention to the sociology of domestic architecture—late-bearing fruit of his early interest in the Iroquois longhouse—putting in writing ideas that had to be excluded from the *Systems of Consanguinity* because of its great bulk. The theme of these writings is that the material form of Native-American houses expresses the principles of family organization, which, as in the longhouse, is clan-based and collective: "communism in living," as he called it. This principle explained, among other things, the form of the Pueblos of the Southwest. Morgan argued that the features of living Indian societies provide the key to the real structure of Aztec polity, which the Spanish accounts misinterpreted by confusing it with European feudalism. Thus Montezuma's "palace" is really the joint tenement of a clan, and Aztec "kingship" is actually a clan-owned chiefship. The most memorable work in this vein is the polemic article "Montezuma's Dinner" (*North American Review*, Apr. 1876, pp. 265–308), an attack on Hubert Howe Bancroft's *Native Races of the Pacific States* (5 vols.,1874–1876) and, more generally, on the historians of the Aztecs in favor of an anthropological approach. Morgan's last book, *Houses and House-life of the American Aborigines* (1881), appeared just before his death in Rochester.

Morgan played an important role in the formation of anthropology as a community of specialists with a coherent subject matter and techniques for investigating it. In the 1860s and 1870s, with the revolutionary lengthening of human history as a result of the sudden discovery of a prehistoric period, anthropology took on definition as a body of specialists to provide authoritative answers to newly posed questions about the human past. Anthropology formed itself in the learned societies, outside the universities, as the modern research university was only beginning to be imagined. Morgan presided over the creation of an anthropology section of the AAAS in 1875, and his election as president of the AAAS in 1879, as well as his election to the National Academy of Sciences in 1875, served to mark the emergence of anthropology as a self-conscious and publically recognized entity and to acknowledge Morgan as its leading practitioner in the United States.

The institutional formation of anthropology presupposed its intellectual definition, and in this matter Morgan's role is very clear. The anthropology of his time—aside from the study of race—had two parts to it, the study of primitive religion and the study of kinship and social organization. Morgan, together with European scholars such as J. J. Bachofen, J. F. McLennan, H. S. Maine, and Fustel de Coulanges, invented kinship as a field of study, and there is no doubt that his was the most original and formative contribution. Thus Morgan was the principal architect of one of the two legs upon which anthropology initially stood.

Of Morgan's three great books, *League of the Iroquois* and *Ancient Society* were widely read and have remained in print more or less continuously. The *League* has continued to be viewed as the best single book on Iroquois life. *Ancient Society* has had a more complex fate. Very influential in its time, its evolutionism went out of favor with the succeeding generation of anthropologists, who (in the United States under Franz Boas) wanted to redirect anthropology away from conjectures about the prehistoric past and toward the more immediate issues of diffusion and function. Social evolutionism has never recovered the strength it enjoyed during the Victorian period (although it has never entirely disappeared), and, accordingly, *Ancient Society* looks very much the prisoner of its time. On the other hand, the book was closely studied by Karl Marx at the close of his life, and after Marx's death, his friend and collaborator Friedrich Engels used his notes to write the book that Engels said Marx had intended, *Der Ursprung der Familie, des Privateigenthums und des Staats, im Anschluss an L.H. Morgan's Forschungen* (The origin of the family, private property, and the state, after the researches of Lewis Henry Morgan, 1884). The attraction for Marx was that Morgan had shown that bourgeois forms of property and marriage had been preceded by the "communism in living," of which the Iroquois longhouse had been an expression. The fact that Morgan was a Presbyterian, a Republican, and an opponent of socialism made him an unimpeachable witness. His book has been much read in Marxist countries, resulting in a fame that certainly would have surprised him.

The third of Morgan's major books, the *Systems of Consanguinity*, is too technical and demanding ever to have gained the popularity of the other two, but it has remained a living text within anthropology among specialists on kinship. The major types of kinship systems that Morgan identified and the methods of description and analysis he devised remained in use by anthropologists in the twentieth century. The profound originality of this work continues to be as evident as it was when it first appeared, and it has had an important influence on such noted anthropologists as W. H. R. Rivers, A. R. Radcliffe-Brown, and Claude Lévi-Strauss.

• Morgan's papers, which include six volumes of manuscript field notes, are at the University of Rochester Library. Leslie A. White has published several manuscript materials, including an important autobiographical statement, "How Morgan Came to Write *Systems of Consanguinity and Affinity*," *Papers of the Michigan Academy of Science, Arts, and Letters* 42 (1957): 257–68, and *Lewis Henry Morgan: The Indian Journals 1859–62* (1959), which gives extensive extracts from the field notes. Thomas R. Trautmann and Karl Sanford Kabelac, "The Library of Lewis Henry Morgan," in *Transactions of the American Philological Society* (1994), includes a catalog of Morgan's books and a register of the Morgan papers. Trautmann, *Lewis Henry Morgan and the Invention of Kinship* (1987), is an intellectual biography. The earlier biography by Carl Resek, *Lewis Henry Morgan, American Scholar* (1960), remains useful for information on other aspects of Morgan's life not dealt with in Trautmann. Elisabeth Tooker has published valuable studies of aspects of Morgan's life, especially "The structure of the Iroquois League: Lewis H. Morgan's Research and Observations," *Ethnohistory* 30, no. 3 (1983): 141–54, and "Lewis H. Morgan and His Contemporaries," *American Anthropologist* 94, no. 2 (1992): 357–75. The most important assessments of his work include two pieces by contemporaries of Morgan, John Wesley Powell, "Sketch of Lewis H. Morgan, President of the American Association for the Advancement of Science," *Popular Science Monthly* 18 (Nov. 1880): 114–21, and Rev. J. H. McIlvaine, *The Life and Work of Lewis H. Morgan, LL.D., an Address at His Funeral* (1882; repr. in *Rochester Historical Society Publications* 2 [1923]: 48–60). Among more recent titles, Meyer Fortes, *Kinship and the Social Order: The Legacy of Lewis Henry Morgan* (1969), is indispensable.

THOMAS R. TRAUTMANN

MORGAN, Mary Jane (c. 1830–3 July 1885), art collector, was born in New York City, the daughter of Francis Sexton, an importer; her mother, whose name is unknown, was the daughter of William Ross, a wealthy carriage manufacturer. Morgan's forebears were siblings to two signers of the Declaration of Independence, George Ross and William Ellery. She was educated at several area schools, finishing at Dr. Schroeder's school at Flushing, Long Island, where she began teaching French and mathematics at age seventeen. While teaching at Schroeder's school in Greenwich Village, either in 1851 or 1852, she married shipowner Charles Morgan, the father of one of her pupils. Morgan quickly became her husband's confidential assistant and bookeeper, helping him build, expand, and manage what became Morgan's Louisiana and Texas Railroad and Steamship Co., called "the largest, most prosperous, and best managed enterprise of the kind in the South" (*New York Times*, 9 Nov. 1881). Both were reclusive. When her husband died in 1878, he left it to Morgan to distribute his estate, a situation that led to bitter recriminations and lawsuits.

It is unclear if Morgan began buying art before Charles died, but thereafter she became the most enthusiastic purchaser of paintings in the United States. She bought all but one of her 240 pictures from five New York dealers, ofter paying record prices to get what she wanted. She purchased more Barbizon paintings than any other collector in New York, eventually owning eight Corots, eleven Millets, seven Rousseaus, and numerous other examples. Like most millionaires of that era, she bought few American works. Her nine American pictures included two works by the obscure artist Albert Pinkham Ryder. Morgan maintained a costly greenhouse of orchids and owned impressive collections of prints, oriental ceramics, silver, and miscellaneous objects d'art. She had just hosted her first art receptions when she suffered a final attack of Bright's disease, or kidney failure. She died in Saratoga, New York, while undergoing its mineral spring treatments.

Scandal ensued following Morgan's death because she had given to a married clergyman, the Reverend Nathaniel W. Conkling, a house and more than $600,000. Morgan's administrator and her attorney both told reporters that she made these gifts and bought her art during bouts of an illness that impaired her judgment. The latter declared "when her mental faculties were clouded she was quickly elevated to the position of the leading patroness of art in America" (*New York Sun*, 28 Nov. 1885). No other accounts refer to such a malady, and such statements seem efforts to demean a strong, independent woman.

The auction of Morgan's pictures in 1886 created a national sensation. Over three nights her 240 pictures fetched $885,300, the largest sum realized by an art auction during the nineteenth century. News of the high prices paid for her Barbizon paintings spread interest in these works from the wealthy collectors, who already admired their pastoral ideal, to middle-class art lovers, who previously found them unappealing because they lacked narrative detail and verisimilitude. The sale of a recent picture, Jules Breton's *The Communicants* (1884), for $45,500 stunned readers and corroborated critics' recent assertions that art was a good investment. This seemed confirmed a few days later when Morgan's tiny Peachblow vase, her most publicized possession, was reported sold for $18,000 to William T. Walters, founder of Baltimore's Walters' Art Gallery. (Much uncertainty still surrounds this transaction.) The splendor of her sale lent chic to art auctions, and American collectors began on this occasion to pay premium prices for works from celebrated collections. The total proceeds of the sale of Morgan's several collections reached $1,205,090.

Morgan's importance rests on the paintings she collected and the results of their sale. The paintings amply represented leading styles of the day; their diversity reflected the eclectic tastes of an age that judged the importance of a collection by its comprehensiveness. Although not particularly bold or pioneering in her tastes, she was more discerning and more personally involved in collecting than Alexander T. Stewart or William H. Vanderbilt, the only contemporary New York collectors of comparable importance. These men's collections have received much attention. Morgan's total obscurity remains the strongest documentation of historians' shameful neglect of women collectors, especially those who did not patronize avant-garde artists. Nevertheless, Morgan was a key figure in the evolving social history that allows women and popular artists to replay the important roles they originally filled during the nineteenth century.

• Miscellaneous letters from dealers and other documents concerning Morgan's collection and sale are in the records of the American Art Association, Archives of American Art, Smithsonian Institution. The only modern publication treating her at any length is Wesley Towner, *The Elegant Auctioneers* (1970), a chatty, unscholarly history of Parke Bernet. Morgan is mentioned in passing in other histories of Sotheby Parke Bernet, including James P. Baughman, *Charles Morgan and the Development of Southern Transportation* (1968), and Katherine S. Howe et al., *Herter Brothers: Furniture and Interiors for a Gilded Age* (1994).

Scholars are utterly dependent upon contemporary newspapers and journals for information on Morgan. The best obituary is in the *New York Times*, 6 July 1885. The key discussion of the Conkling scandal and Morgan's sanity is the *New York Sun*, 28 Nov. 1885; see also the *New York Daily Tribune*, 27 Nov. 1885, and the *New York Times*, 29 Nov. 1885. The best general discussions of the art collection are Charles de Kay, "An American Gallery," *American Magazine of Art* (1886): 245–49, and Mrs. Schuyler van Rensselaer, "Fine Arts. The Morgan Collection," *Independent*, 4 Mar. 1886, p. 11, and 11 Mar. 1886, pp. 7–8.

Morgan's sale was the first in New York to have a deluxe, limited-edition, illustrated catalog in addition to a regular one: *Catalogue of the Art Collection Formed by the Late Mrs. Mary Jane Morgan* (1886); the standard catalogs issued for the sale contain the only full listing of her miscellaneous objects, books, and other items. Extensive reports on the auctions of the paintings appeared in the New York newspapers between 4 and 6 Mar. 1886. The most systematic and useful accounts are in the *Art Amateur* 14 (Apr. 1886): 98–100 and 117. The sale of her other collections is chronicled in the *New York Times* and elsewhere between 9 and 16 March 1886.

SAUL E. ZALESCH

MORGAN, Mary Kimball (8 Dec. 1861–13 Oct. 1948), Christian Science educator and college president, was born in Janesville, Wisconsin, the daughter of Freeman Aaron Kimball, a Union officer in the Civil War and later a merchant, and Helen Maria Chapin. Mary was educated in the St. Louis, Missouri, public school system and later tutored at home. Poor health prevented her from attending college. In 1885 she married William Edgar Morgan; they had two children.

Morgan's continued health problems caused her in 1888 to be receptive to the ideas of Christian Science, a newly emerging American religious movement founded by Mary Baker Eddy. According to Eddy, the purpose of Christian Science was to "organize a church designed to commemorate the word and works of our Master, which should reinstate primitive Christianity and its lost element of healing" (*Manual of the Mother Church* [1901], p. 17). In Christian Science, healing and the worship of God are directly related. The sufferer receives not just physical healing but spiritual healing as well. After studying the religion, Morgan's health improved; as a result, she and her husband became lifelong workers for the cause of Christian Science. In 1896 Morgan became a recognized Christian

Science practitioner and authorized teacher involved in the full-time healing ministry of the church.

Although not a trained educator, Morgan began an experimental school, first by teaching her sons and one other boy at home. She understood her most important work to be the development of the moral character of young people. This ideal generated interest among other parents, and on 17 October 1898 Morgan officially opened a small school above a store in St. Louis, Missouri, for the children of Christian Science families. The school was named the Principia, a derivation of the Latin word *principium*, meaning "principle." Morgan's theory of education was unique because it was based on the metaphysical concept of "Principle," which in Christian Science is a synonym for God.

The school expanded, graduating its first high school class in 1906. It added a junior college curriculum in 1910 and was established as a four-year liberal arts college in 1932. In 1935 the four-year college moved to Elsah, Illinois.

The desired end of Morgan's educational theory was moral discipline based not on psychology but on the "divine mind." Her experimental school was the means to that end. In her book *Education at the Principia* (1966) Morgan explained that the Principia was founded to surround children with "an environment of scientific thought until such time as they should be sufficiently mature to take their stand on Principle through a certain amount of working knowledge of its operation" (p. 11).

Morgan designed the school to create an atmosphere that fostered truthful thinking based on the unchanging, supreme Principle. The concept of truthful thinking is significant because it relates to the central doctrine of the "unreality" of disease, sin, and death. According to Christian Science, because God is totally good and creates only that which is good, it follows that evil and suffering are illusions caused by incorrect perceptions. As Eddy asserted: "We weep because others weep, we yawn because they yawn, and we have small-pox because others have it; but mortal mind, not matter, contains and carries the infection" (*Science and Health with Key to the Scriptures* [1934], pp. 126, 497). Thus, it is essential for Christian Scientists to cast off mortal mind and to think with the reality that is divine mind or Principle.

In establishing the Principia, Morgan established a community based on Christian Science. Faculty and staff were Christian Scientists and students were the children of Christian Scientists. The composition of the community was intended to produce a unity of ideals and purpose. According to Morgan, "More can be taught by example than by precept" (*Education at the Principia*, p. 12). The strict adherence to the "one mind" places each human being in relation to his or her fellow human beings in all matters of life. The result is a collective spirit that affects the acts of individuals. When this happens, a moral community has been established.

A 1930 speech to college men by Morgan illustrates this point:

> A real Principia product is a well-balanced individual whose whole nature is expanding under the guidance of Principle. . . . Since you have become a member of our family at Principia, you have automatically assumed a new responsibility . . . [and] incurred the responsibility of honestly helping Principia give truthful evidence of its purpose in being. (*Education at the Principia*, p. 195)

Morgan was actively involved with the college and academy until shortly before her death. She chaired the board of trustees from 1912 to 1942. Her sons, Frederick E. Morgan and William E. Morgan, Jr., succeeded her as administrators. Morgan died at her home on the college campus in Elsah, having lived long enough to participate in the fiftieth anniversary celebration of the institution she founded. Her legacy continues in the lives of the students influenced by her maxim "there is no success in life outside of obedience to Principle."

• The best repository of sources on Morgan is the archives of Principia College in Elsah, Ill. Information about Morgan and the school can be found in Edwin S. Leonard, Jr., *As the Sowing: The First Fifty Years of the Principia* (1948). An obituary is in the *New York Times*, 14 Oct. 1948.

MARSHA MIHOK

MORGAN, Morris Hicky (8 Feb. 1859–16 Mar. 1910), classical scholar, was born in Providence, Rhode Island, the son of Morris Barker Morgan, a merchant, and Isabelle Manton. He entered Harvard with the intention of pursuing a career in law or business, but he fell under the influence of the Latinist George Martin Lane, who impressed on him not only the beauty and humanity of ancient literature but also the deep satisfaction of passing that knowledge on to students. He maintained these values throughout his career, which began after his graduation in 1881, when he returned to his prep school, St. Mark's, in Southboro, Massachusetts, as tutor in Latin and Greek for three years. Morgan married Eleanora Semmes Gibson in Baltimore in 1896; their marriage was without issue. Though his teachers Lane and William Watson Goodwin had been trained in Germany, Morgan remained at Harvard, where he received an A.M. and Ph.D. in 1887 and was rewarded with employment as instructor in Greek (1887–1888), tutor in Greek (1888–1891), assistant professor of Latin and Greek (1891–1896), assistant professor of Latin (1896–1899), and professor of classical philology (1899–1910), succeeding Frederic De Forest Allen. He became, in the words of his colleague H. W. Smyth, "A treble-headed power, . . . at once an inspiring teacher, a productive scholar, an effective administrator," though much of his promising career as a scholar was lost in his devotion to the service of his university. He was chairman of the classics department (1898–1906), university marshall (1908–1910), and member of the library council for fifteen years and spent many hours tending the details of

President Abbott Lawrence Lowell's inauguration and supervising admission applications. He was named a fellow of the American Academy of Arts and Sciences in 1902.

In the tradition of Lane he was a humane and humorous teacher, known more for his clear and well-organized lectures than for charm or depth of learning. Typical was his claim that his Lowell Lectures of 1907–1908, "The Private Life of the Romans," contained no original scholarship. He taught a full range of Greek and Latin authors, including Homer, Aeschylus, Demosthenes, Virgil, and Cicero, with a specialty in ancient literary criticism and the history of classical scholarship. Consequently, his book-length publications are basically school editions and translations that could be useful in the classroom. He edited with his colleague and former teacher John Williams White *An Illustrated Dictionary to Xenophon's Anabasis* (1892); revised *The First Four Books of Xenophon's Anabasis* (1894), edited by White and Goodwin; edited Lane's *Latin Grammar for Schools and Colleges* (1898, 1903) and decocted from it *A School Latin Grammar* (1899); and edited *Eight Orations of Lysias* (1895), Tacitus's *Agricola Germania*, and *Dialogus* (1904). With Edward Parmelee Morris of Yale he edited a series of nine Latin texts known as the Morris-Morgan series. He translated Xenophon's *The Art of Horsemanship* (1893) and Terence's *Phormio* (1894). His most congenial author for wit and morality may have been Persius, on whom he wrote grammatical notes (*Harvard Studies in Classical Philology* 7 [1896]: 191–203) and *A Bibliography of Persius* (1893; 2d ed., 1909), a bibliography of over 1,000 items, many of which were included in his personal library of over 660 books on this author, bequeathed to Harvard.

Morgan's training in philology might have led him to produce an edition of Persius, but there was another side to his study of antiquity evident as early as his dissertation and manifest in his final work, an interest born of his teaching impulse to show how the Greeks and Romans solved certain problems of daily life and how their technology bears on our own. To answer these problems he sought out not only ancient sources but also the expertise of modern engineers, architects, and public administrators. His dissertation, *De ignis eliciendi modis apud antiquos commentatio* ("A Study of Ways of Lighting Fires among the Ancients"; 1887; printed in *Harvard Studies in Classical Philology* 1 [1890]: 13–64), dealt with ways in which the ancients lit their fires; his interest in how the Romans got their water ("Remarks on the Water Supply of Ancient Rome," *Transactions of the American Philological Association* 33 [1902]: 30–37) led to a study of Vitruvius, the great Roman writer on architecture ("Notes on Vitruvius," *Harvard Studies in Classical Philology* 17 [1906]: 1–14; "Critical and Explanatory Notes on Vitruvius," *Harvard Studies in Classical Philology* 21 [1910]: 1–22), that became the chief object of his later career. Morgan spent over a decade preparing an edition of Vitruvius's ten books on architecture, aiming his notes more at architects and archaeologists than at philologists, but his death from pneumonia while recuperating from another illness in Newport, Rhode Island, deprived us of what would have been a great American edition to set alongside K. F. Smith's *Tibullus* (1913) or A. S. Pease's *Aeneid IV* (1935). The depth of learning and attention to clarity and detail in his posthumously published translation, edited by Albert Andrew Howard (1914), limns the potential of what was lost. In the words of M. N. Wetmore, the volume "represents the highest development of classical scholarship to-day" (*Classical Weekly* 9 [1915–1916]: 117). Morgan's early death followed by only a couple of years the deaths of two other colleagues of approximately the same age, Minton Warren and John Henry Wright. The loss of these three men had a devastating effect on the Harvard classics department, for with the death of Morgan, as Basil L. Gildersleeve said, "Harvard has lost not only one of her chief forces in the classical field but she has lost perhaps the most typical representative of the Harvard spirit in philology." Gildersleeve found "the literary finish, the sense of reserved force, this toying with a subject the speaker has well in hand, this gentle irony of one who feels his mastery" (*American Journal of Philology* 31 [1910]: 243) in two essays, "The Student of the Classics" and "The Teacher of the Classics," both in *Essays and Studies* (1910), published two days before his death.

A professional manner, excruciating attention to detail, and inexhaustible energy are the common threads that characterize Morgan's contributions as teacher, scholar, and administrator. His style of teaching and engagement in the life of the university, elegantly expressed in the early essays of *Essays and Studies*, is that of an easy, gracious, and humane age of education, in which intellectual rigor and attention to the needs of students were of greater value than the publication of original ideas or sweeping theories.

• Morgan's papers, including A. S. Pease's student notebook of Morgan's class in the history of classical studies, are in the Harvard University Archives. There is no full account of his life, but among the more important obituaries are those by B. L. Gildersleeve, *American Journal of Philology* 31 (1910): 243–44; C. H. Moore, *Classical Journal* 5 (1909–1910): 338–39; H. W. Prescott, *Classical Philology* 5 (1910): 357; and *Memorial Minute of the Class of 1881* (1910). A bibliography with inaccuracies and omissions is in *Harvard College Class of 1881 Twenty-Fifth Anniversary* (1906), pp. 225–26.

WARD W. BRIGGS

MORGAN, Sam (18 Dec. 1887–25 Feb. 1936), cornetist and bandleader, was born in Bertrandville, Louisiana, the son of a railroad worker. Samuel Barclay Charters gives Morgan's year of birth as 1895, but on his tombstone in Holt Cemetery exact dates appear, together with the inscription "age 48 years." His parents, whose names are unknown, sang in a Baptist church, and his brothers Isaiah, also a cornetist, and Andrew, a clarinetist and saxophonist, played with Sam; the youngest brother, Albert, a string bassist, also played with Isaiah's group but had a separate, distinguished career in jazz.

After playing in brass bands in Plaquemines Parish, Sam Morgan moved in 1915 to New Orleans, where he led the Magnolia dance band and the Magnolia brass band while working as a track laborer for the Grand Island Railroad. He suffered a stroke in 1924. By the fall of 1926 he was sufficiently recovered to join Isaiah's Young Morgan Band, founded in 1922. Sam Morgan took over its leadership, as he was better known and had access to better jobs. The group, now known as Sam Morgan's Jazz Band, primarily played at dances in New Orleans. It comprised two cornetists (Sam and Isaiah), a trombonist (Jim Robinson), two reed players (including Andrew from 1925), a banjo player, a string bassist, and a drummer. Occasionally a pianist was added, notably for two recording sessions in 1927. That same year, the band began broadcasting regularly from Meridian, Mississippi, on a radio show sponsored by Regal Beer. It toured occasionally at first, usually in the deep South, but also made a trip to Chicago in 1929. Their regional touring became more frequent in the early 1930s as the depression worsened. In 1932, while performing in Bay St. Louis, Mississippi, Sam suffered a second stroke. Isaiah reassumed the group's leadership until it disbanded in 1933. Sam played in a Works Progress Administration band in 1934, but ill health forced his retirement the following year. He died of pneumonia in New Orleans. It is not known if he ever married or had children.

Morgan's significance was threefold. In deference to the church, Sam Morgan's Jazz Band did not play hymns at dances, but at the request of its producers it recorded versions of "Sing On," "Down by the Riverside," and "Over in the Gloryland." These recordings of 1927 anticipated by more than a decade a key component of the repertory of the New Orleans jazz revival, and more broadly, they hinted at the intertwining secular and sacred roots of jazz. His band's prominent use of saxophones, rather than clarinets, offered testimony against the stereotypical view of the role of the clarinet in the New Orleans jazz style; moreover, the instrument is played in a manner more central to the jazz tradition than that of contemporary recordings by Oscar Celestin's Original Tuxedo Orchestra that used the same instrumentation that same year. Most important, Morgan's renditions of "Steppin' on the Gas" and "Bogalousa Strut" (also from these sessions of 1927) are believed to be among the best and most authentic documents of early jazz, exhibiting a devotion to collective improvisation and a wonderful rhythmic drive.

• Interviews with Morgan's brothers are in the archives of Tulane University; transcripts appear on microform as *New York Times Oral History Program: New Orleans Jazz Oral History Collection*, no. 46 (1979), chaps. 123–25. Samuel Barclay Charters IV, *Jazz: New Orleans, 1885–1963* (1963), summarizes the careers of Morgan and his brothers. Morgan's early years are discussed in Karl Koenig, "Four Country Brass Bands," *Second Line* 36 (Fall 1984): 13–23. Detailed but confusing memories of Morgan in the 1920s appear in Koenig, "Nathan 'Big Jim' Robinson: Jazz Trombonist," *Second Line* 35 (Winter 1983): 24–35. Enthusiastic descriptions and assessments of the band's recordings are in Gunther Schuller, *Early Jazz: Its Roots and Musical Development* (1968), pp. 75–77, and William J. Schafer, "Hot Dancing in New Orleans: The Black Bands," *Mississippi Rag* 7 (July 1980): 6–7.

BARRY KERNFELD

MORGAN, Thomas Hunt (25 Sept. 1866–4 Dec. 1945), biologist, was born in Lexington, Kentucky, the son of Charlton Hunt Morgan, former U.S. consul to Messina, Italy, and Ellen Key Howard, granddaughter of Francis Scott Key. Morgan became interested in natural history at an early age while roaming the countryside around Lexington and the Cumberland Mountains of Maryland where his family visited in the summers. A graduate (B.S., 1886) of the State College of Kentucky (now the University of Kentucky), Morgan pursued graduate studies at Johns Hopkins University under William Keith Brooks, the last student of Louis Agassiz. He received his Ph.D. in 1891, conducting original work in morphology, a prominent field in the late nineteenth century that combined comparative embryology and anatomy, cytology, and evolutionary theory to trace the phylogenetic history of organisms. Morgan's dissertation was on the evolutionary relationships of the Pycnogonids (sea spiders) to other arthropods. By detailed microscopic analysis of the earliest embryonic stages (cleavage), Morgan determined that the Pycnogonids were more closely related to the Arachnids (true spiders) than to the Crustaceans (crabs, lobsters) that they resembled.

As a result of his own early work, Morgan became dissatisfied with morphology, finding it too descriptive and speculative. A summer (1891) and later a full academic year (1894–1895) at the Stazione Zoologica in Naples convinced him of the importance of an experimental, as opposed to a primarily descriptive, approach to biology, a theme that he pursued for the remainder of his career. In collaboration with Hans Driesch, one of the founders of the new field of *Entwicklungsmechanik* (developmental mechanics), Morgan began experimental work on the early causes of differentiation in embryos. He pursued this new line of work in the 1890s and early 1900s at Bryn Mawr College, where he taught from 1891 to 1904, and continued with it after moving to Columbia University in 1904. His many publications on embryonic development in sea urchin eggs and on regeneration in the earthworm, together with his comprehensive book *The Development of the Frog's Egg* (1897), introduced a whole generation of students to the exciting problems of embryonic development and differentiation that were emerging in the work of European and American biologists. Morgan also championed the use of marine organisms in experimental work through his association with the Marine Biological Laboratory in Woods Hole, Massachusetts (founded in 1888 based on the model of the Naples Stazione), where he worked virtually every summer from 1890 until 1943. Many of his publications bear the Marine Biological Laboratory name as well as his university affiliation.

Morgan was always skeptical of what appeared to him to be speculative theories in science. Not only did he reject morphology as largely guesswork about animal evolutionary relationships, but early in his career he also rejected Darwin's theory of natural selection as a major explanation for the process of evolution. From 1900 until 1910 he also rejected Mendelian explanations for heredity and, in the same period, the chromosome theory put forward by his close friend and colleague at Columbia, Edmund Beecher Wilson. To Morgan, both theories were preformationist, postulating preformed particles in the germ cells as an explanation for the appearance of adult hereditary traits. It was only after he began his own breeding studies with the fruit fly, *Drosophila melanogaster*, in 1910 that Morgan became a strong advocate of both theories.

Beginning in 1910 Morgan, along with his laboratory group of undergraduates Alfred H. Sturtevant, Hermann J. Muller, Calvin B. Bridges, Alexander Weinstein, and others (all but Muller later to take their graduate degrees under Morgan), carried out numerous breeding experiments demonstrating the correctness of the Mendelian theory and, most important, the bold assertion that Mendel's "genes" could be viewed as discrete segments of the long rod-shaped chromosomes in the cell units. At Morgan's suggestion in 1911, Sturtevant developed a method of mapping the order of genes on chromosomes by using data on the frequency of crossing-over or breaking of linkage between genes on the same chromosome. Morgan hypothesized that the farther apart two genes were on the same chromosome, the more frequently the linkage would be broken during the process of crossing-over in meiosis (chromosome reduction in germ cell production). Using frequency of recombination of traits obtained from breeding experiments, Sturtevant produced the first genetic map in 1911, published in 1913. The group quickly adopted this method for mapping gene positions within the four chromosome pairs of *Drosophila*. The mapping technique was used by many other workers, including Rollins A. Emerson's active maize group at Cornell and, later, William E. Castle's mammalian genetics group at Harvard.

The value of the mapping technique for genetics was multifold. First, it provided a means of demonstrating the precise location of a gene, with respect to other genes, on the linear chromosome structure. (It was found, for example, that a change in position along the chromosome altered the gene's expression.) Second, mapping brought together the previously separate theories of Mendelian genetics (concerned with data from breeding experiments) and cytology (the study of chromosome structure and activity, as in working out the details of meiosis), substantiating each theory by showing its concordance with the other. Third, the mapping technique provided a precise, experimental, and quantitative technique that Morgan thought could make biology a rigorous science like chemistry and physics. Finally, the mapping procedure showed that Mendelian genes were not abstract or idealized entities but real material entities, thus reinforcing Morgan's materialistic view of science.

Through the work of the Morgan group many new genetic principles were brought to light, for example, the ideas of modifier genes (where one gene affects the expression of others), position effect (where change of a gene's position alters its expression), sex determination, sex-linkage, and phenocopy (change in a gene's expression by changing environmental conditions during development). The Morgan lab (the so-called Fly Room) at Columbia University became the world center for the "new genetics," attracting numerous graduate and postdoctoral students from the United States and abroad, including Curt Stern from Germany, Otto Louis Mohr from Norway, and Theodosius Dobzhansky from the Soviet Union.

In 1927, at the invitation of trustee George Ellery Hale, Morgan agreed to establish the Division of Biology at the California Institute of Technology. There he championed the pursuit of rigorous experimental and quantitative work not only in genetics but also in neurobiology, plant physiology, and biochemistry. Among those in the next generation of geneticists to be brought together as part of the Caltech group were not only Dobzhansky (who went with Morgan from Columbia) but also George Beadle, Boris Ephrussi, Edward L. Tatum, Linus Pauling, Frits Went, and Sidney W. Fox. More than almost anyone of his generation, Morgan was responsible for showing that biology need not be rooted in unprovable speculations about evolutionary history, but could be rigorous, quantitative, and experimental.

Morgan was known to his friends, colleagues, and students as a down-to-earth, humorous, and informal person who encouraged collaborative efforts and the free exchange of ideas. His *Drosophila* group was one of the first models of the sort of collaborative scientific groups that later became routine. Some students, such as H. J. Muller, felt that Morgan and the group sometimes failed to give full credit to individuals for their ideas, but the majority of group members felt that they gained more from the collaborative effort than they gave up. All agreed that the work could not have proceeded as rapidly or produced as many innovative ideas or techniques without the close collaboration that Morgan encouraged.

In 1904 Morgan had married Lilian Vaughan Sampson, a graduate student at Bryn Mawr and an accomplished biologist in her own right. They had four children, one of whom, Isabel Morgan Mountain, contributed significantly to the development of the polio vaccine.

Morgan was the recipient of many honors during his long academic career. He was awarded the Nobel Prize in physiology or medicine in 1933, in addition to the Darwin Medal (1924) and the Copley Medal (1939) of the Royal Society (London). He was a member of the National Academy of Sciences (president, 1927–1931), the American Philosophical Society, the Genetics Society of America, the American Morphological Society (president, 1900), and the American Society of

Naturalists (president, 1909). He served as president of the Sixth International Congress of Genetics, held in 1932 in Ithaca, New York, and was a trustee of the Marine Biological Laboratory in Woods Hole from 1897 to 1945. He died of complications from a bleeding ulcer in Pasadena, California.

Morgan was a major architect of the Mendelian-chromosome theory of heredity, that is, the view that genes are discrete units arranged in a precise linear order along the chromosomes. The work that he and his research associates carried out at Columbia University and at Caltech provided the basis for understanding a number of problems in heredity, from agricultural breeding to human genetic disease.

• No single collection of Morgan's papers exists, though a relatively large collection from his later (post-1928) years is housed in the archives at the California Institute of Technology, and another, somewhat smaller collection is held at the American Philosophical Society (APS) among the Otto L. Mohr Papers; in addition, the APS has microfilm of Morgan's letters to Hans Driesch. Morgan's letters to other scientists can be found in their collections, many of which are in the superb history of genetics archive maintained at the APS (see, e.g., Morgan's letters to William Bateson, A. F. Blakeslee, Charles B. Davenport, H. S. Jennings, Raymond Pearl, and Milislav Demerec). Additional Morgan letters can also be found in the extensive archives of E. G. Conklin (Princeton) and Ross G. Harrison (Yale).

Morgan wrote twenty-two books, the most important of which, in addition to the *Development of the Frog's Egg*, include *Regeneration* (1901), *Evolution and Adaptation* (1903), *Experimental Zoology* (1907), *The Mechanism of Mendelian Heredity* (1915, with A. H. Sturtevant, C. B. Bridges, and H. J. Muller), *A Critique of the Theory of Evolution* (1916; rev. ed., 1925), *The Physical Basis of Heredity* (1919), *Experimental Embryology* (1927), and *Embryology and Genetics* (1934). Among his most important papers (he wrote more than 370) are two collaborative efforts with Hans Driesch in *Roux' Archiv für Entwicklungsmechanik der Organismen* 2 (1895): 205–15, 216–24; an enthusiastic impression of the Naples station in *Science* 3 (1896): 16–18; his first paper on the white-eyed mutant in *Drosophila* in *Science* 32 (1910): 120–22; and a summary of his ongoing work in genetics in the *Carnegie Institution of Washington Annual Reports* from 1916 on. His Nobel acceptance speech, tracing the relationship between genetics and medicine and physiology, is in *Scientific Monthly* 41 (1935): 5–18.

There are two substantial accounts of Morgan's work. Garland E. Allen, *Thomas Hunt Morgan: The Man and His Science* (1978), is the more complete, while Ian Shine and Sylvia Wrobel, *Thomas Hunt Morgan: Pioneer of Genetics* (1976), provides an accessible introduction. A. H. Sturtevant's obituary of Morgan in *Biographical Memoirs* (National Academy of Sciences) 33 (1959): 283–325, is a mostly factual account but contains a complete bibliography. A major essay on Morgan's early embryological work is in Jane Maienschein, *Transforming Traditions in American Biology, 1880–1915* (1991), pp. 231–60, while aspects of his studies in genetics and development, and their reception, are covered in E. A. Carlson, "The Drosophila Group," *Genetics* 79 (Suppl. 1975): 15–27; Nils Roll-Hansen, "Drosophila Genetics: A Reductionist Research Program," *Journal of the History of Biology* 11 (1979): 159–210; Scott Gilbert, "The Embryological Origins of the Gene Theory," *Journal of the History of Biology* 10 (1978): 307–51; Garland E. Allen, "T. H. Morgan and the Split between Embryology and Genetics, 1910–1935," in *A History of Embryology*, ed. T. J. Horder et al. (1986), pp. 113–46, and "T. H. Morgan: Materialism and Experimentalism in the Development of Modern Genetics," *Trends in Genetics* 1 (1985): 151–54, 186–90; and Jonathan Harwood, "The Reception of Morgan's Chromosome Theory in Germany: Interwar Debate over Cytoplasmic Inheritance," *Medizinhistorisches Journal* 19 (1984): 3–32. From a philosophical point of view, Morgan's commitment to empiricism has been carefully analyzed by Marga Vicedo, "T. H. Morgan, Neither an Epistemological Empiricist nor a 'Methodological' Empiricist," *Philosophy of Biology* 5 (1990): 293–311.

GARLAND E. ALLEN

MORGAN, William (7 Aug. 1774–12 Sept. 1826?), leader of the Antimasonic movement, was born in Culpeper County, Virginia. Information about his parentage has not survived. He served as a stonemason apprentice to Joseph Day in Madison County, Virginia, then removed to the west (probably Kentucky), finally settling in Richmond, Virginia. For a time he worked on the construction of the Orange County (Va.) Courthouse. It is believed by some that Morgan fought in the War of 1812, thus adopting the title, if it was not his rank, of captain. In 1819 he married Lucinda Pendleton of Virginia and moved to western New York State by 1823. They had two, possibly three, children and resided in Batavia, where it is assumed he pursued his trade, sometimes having to move far afield of his home to find work. Extant correspondence from 1824 reveals that Morgan was literate, even eloquent, and a responsible spouse and caring parent.

In May 1825 Morgan was admitted to the Leroy Lodge of the Freemasons and became a Royal Arch Mason. Later in 1825 or in early 1826, the Masons of Batavia, including Morgan, petitioned the Grand Lodge of New York State to establish a chapter in their town, and a list of proposed members was drawn up. A leader in the petition drive named Ganson, who operated a saloon in Batavia where Morgan maintained a circle of friends, felt, along with other leading Masons, that owing to Morgan's lower-class friends and his reputation for drunkenness he should not be included. Thus a second petition was drawn up without his name and submitted to the state lodge. When the charter was approved and returned to Batavia, Morgan determined that his name had been excluded and so he turned on the fraternity. The Masons believed that he entered into a plan with David C. Miller of Batavia to republish an eighteenth-century English Antimasonic tract, *Jachin and Boaz*, to create a sensation and make money. The result was *Illustrations of Masonry*, for which Morgan registered copyright in August 1826. It was said that he had come to believe that the bane of civil institutions was Masonry and that he owed it to his country to expose its dangers.

During the summer of 1826 Morgan was involved in several legal charges, ultimately imprisoned for nonpayment of debts. On 11 September he was arrested on an allegation of petty theft and taken to Canandaigua to answer the charge. Six men entered the Canandaigua jail and abducted Morgan; the jailer's wife stated that he had demeaned her care of inmates and told coarse jokes.

According to the most plausible account of what then happened, Morgan's abductors took him to Fort Niagara, a state post near Lewiston, New York, and had him incarcerated in the blockhouse or powder magazine there. From that point on he was never reliably seen again. Edward Giddings, the ferry keeper at Fort Niagara, testified in 1831 before a Niagara County Special Court of Inquiry that he was approached by a stranger on 12 September 1826 to transport a "perjured scoundrel to the Masons of Canada to do with him as they thought proper." Giddings believed that he was the last to see Morgan in the United States alive.

In October 1827 a human body washed up on the Lake Ontario shore near Oak Orchard, New York. A coroner's report with minute details of the body reached the attention of Morgan's friends, and they hastened to inspect the body and called for a public inquest. Based solely on the written descriptions, Mrs. Lucinda Morgan and friends declared that the body was that of her husband. When the coffin was opened, she changed her opinion, and the essential mystery of Morgan's disappearance was reborn. The body was later identified as that of Timothy Munro, a Canadian. But on the strength of Mrs. Morgan's first opinion, the enterprising Rochester newspaper editor Thurlow Weed publicized the find and declared a conspiracy. After the remains were properly identified, to avoid embarrassment, Weed called the body "good enough Morgan" because of its publicity value, and he began a public campaign against the Masons. Subsequently, in 1828 Weed began publication of a partisan newspaper, the *Antimasonic Enquirer*.

Morgan's disappearance was the catalyst for the Antimasonic movement. In 1826 and the following year, a campaign against the Masons broke out and several investigations were launched. New York State governor DeWitt Clinton, himself a Mason, offered a reward for the discovery of the body or the identity of Morgan's murderers. Candidates of the newly founded Antimasonic party were elected to office throughout western New York and eventually in the national election of 1832. Morgan became a symbol of egalitarian rights against secret societies of the privileged. His book, *Illustrations of Masonry*, was published by Colonel David C. Miller of Batavia, the publisher of the *Batavia Republican Advocate* and a Morgan enthusiast. Following Morgan's disappearance, Miller published in 1827 a paper called the *Morgan Investigator* and more editions of Morgan's book. Owing to the mystery surrounding its author, several editions were printed and translations made for a wide distribution.

Morgan's character has been variously interpreted. Masonic interests depict him as the town drunk in Batavia in 1826. Pro-Masonic reports exist of his being deranged and a public nuisance. Sympathetic accounts speak to his family devotion and his being excluded from the Freemasonic fraternity because he was not a member of the social elite. Later religious writers considered him a victim of a criminal and immoral conspiracy.

After a respectable time, Lucinda Morgan married George W. Harris in 1831; she then was married again in 1838, as a plural wife to Joseph Smith, the founder of the Church of Jesus Christ of the Latter Day Saints. Some historians and critical analysts of the *Book of Mormon* argue that William Morgan figured posthumously in the creation of that work, suggesting that the name "Mormon" is a portmanteau word derived in part from "Mor" and in part from "Mon" roe County, New York, where the events of the Morgan affair took place.

Morgan became the symbolic martyr for the antisecret society cause of many religious groups. An impressive monument to his memory was erected in 1882 in the Batavia Cemetery by the National Christian Association. The 38-foot monument was erected in the plot of David C. Miller at an expense of $2,500 and involves a life-size figure of Morgan. The association was organized to combat Masonry and enjoyed a wide patronage among evangelical holiness leaders, notably Benjamin T. Roberts and Charles Blanchard of Wheaton College in Illinois. A hymn in Morgan's honor was written by Jonathan Blanchard and can be found in some nineteenth-century collections.

• Useful materials, including some manuscripts, are in the Genesee County History Department in the Holland Purchase Land Company Museum in Batavia, N.Y., and in the New York State Archives in Albany. *Illustrations of Masonry, by One of the Fraternity Who Has Devoted Thirty Years to the Subject* (1827) contains an introduction by Colonel David C. Miller. Ezra C. Cook Publications, Inc., of Chicago, Ill., has issued an undated reprint.

It is useful to compare Morgan's book with *Jachin and Boaz: An Authentic Key to the Door of Freemasonry, both Ancient and Modern, by a Gentleman Belonging to the Jerusalem Lodge* (1762). Biographical investigations of Morgan include the sympathetic Samuel D. Greene, *The Broken Seal; or, Personal Reminiscences of the Morgan Abduction and Murder* (1870); the critical Thomas A. Knight, *The Strange Disappearance of William Morgan* (1932); and Stanley Upton Mock, *The Morgan Episode in American Free Masonry* (1930). The most thorough pro-Masonic account is Rob Morris, *William Morgan; or, Political Antimasonry, Its Rise, Growth and Decadence* (1883). Other useful insights are found in David Bernard, *Light on Freemasonry* (1858); Pope Catlin Huntington, *The True History of William Morgan* (1886); and William H. Brackney, *Religious Antimasonry: The Genesis of a Political Party* (1976), which treats the religious implications of the Morgan incident. An interesting theory on Morgan's fate and its further interconnections with the Mormon movement is found in Fawn Brodie, *No Man Knows My History: The Life of Joseph Smith, the Mormon Prophet* (1945).

A woodcut likeness of Morgan of unconfirmed origins was circulated in Boston, Mass., at the time of Morgan's disappearance and was the basis of the sculpture on the Batavia Cemetery monument. Masons held that the portrait was a modification of DeWitt Clinton's portrait.

WILLIAM H. BRACKNEY

MORGENSTERN, Oskar (24 Jan. 1902–26 July 1977), economist, was born in Goerlitz, Silesia, Germany, the son of Wilhelm Morgenstern, proprietor of a modest business, and Margarete Teichler, said to have been an illegitimate daughter of Frederick III of Prussia. When he was quite young, his family moved to Vienna, where Oskar grew up, attending high school and the University of Vienna, at which he obtained his doctorate in 1925. He received a Laura Spelman Rockefeller Memorial postdoctoral fellowship, which enabled him to travel and study from 1925 to 1928 at Harvard and Columbia Universities in the United States and at the Universities of London, Rome, and Paris.

His first major work was *Wirtschaftsprognose* (Economic prediction), his 1928 thesis for appointment to the faculty of the University of Vienna. This work considered the problems and paradoxes of prediction, especially when those whose behavior was being predicted could themselves react to the predictions. This work started Morgenstern on a line of inquiry that was to lead to his greatest contribution, the collaboration with John von Neumann on applying the theory of games to the social sciences.

Morgenstern was made a professor of economics in 1935, but in a pattern that persisted for the rest of his career he seems to have found more satisfaction in off-campus activities than in formal teaching. From 1931 until his dismissal from his Vienna posts following the German absorption of Austria in 1938, he was director of the Austrian Institute for Business Cycle Research, a journal editor, an adviser to the Austrian national bank, and a member of a League of Nations statistical team. While head of the institute, he was able to provide employment for the brilliant mathematical statistician Abraham Wald, who was denied a regular post at the university because of anti-Semitism. Wald instructed him in modern mathematical and statistical analysis, in addition to contributing to the research of the institute. Morgenstern was associated with the "Vienna Circle," the distinguished intellectual group with which were also associated Rudolf Carnap, Karl Popper, Kurt Gödel, and mathematician Karl Menger.

During this Vienna period Morgenstern edited several volumes related to work done at the institute and wrote a book on the limits of political economy. Most importantly, however, he wrote a paper in 1935 on perfect foresight and economic equilibrium, which continued the theme of his 1928 work and again took up his favorite prediction problem, the pursuit of Sherlock Holmes by Professor Moriarty, in which each tries to base a strategy on what he thinks the other thinks he will think the other thinks he will think, and so on. After hearing the verbal presentation of the paper in Karl Menger's colloquium, the mathematician Edward Čech drew Morgenstern's attention to the similarity of some of the questions raised to those examined in von Neumann's 1928 classic paper on game theory. Čech outlined the von Neumann work and urged Morgenstern to read it, but he did not do so at the time. He had the misfortune to be away from Vienna in 1937 when von Neumann, whom he was very anxious to meet and who was by then at the Institute for Advanced Study in Princeton, spoke at a subsequent meeting of the colloquium.

In 1938 Morgenstern received a Carnegie Visiting Professorship to the United States. The incorporation of Austria into Germany took place while he was abroad, and Morgenstern (who was not Jewish) was dismissed from his university post as politically unacceptable. He accepted an offer from Princeton University as lecturer in economics for three years, choosing it over other possibilities because of the prospect of working with von Neumann, whom he met soon after his arrival there.

Von Neumann attended a talk on business cycles that Morgenstern gave to the Nassau Club early in 1939; this led to discussion on games, experiments, and predictions. Morgenstern now set out to study von Neumann's 1928 paper, which led to many conversations with the author on its content and significance. Morgenstern decided to write a paper explaining the nature of game theory and its significance for economists. Von Neumann offered to read the partly finished manuscript and suggested that it needed expansion if it were to be comprehensible to someone new to the subject. After reading the expanded paper in the fall of 1940, he apparently was still not satisfied and suggested that he and Morgenstern collaborate on a new version.

The collaborative version kept growing in size until it was clearly too large to be published as a standard scientific paper, even spread over two parts. It was decided to approach Princeton University Press with a proposal for a monograph of about 100 pages, and the press accepted the idea. The authors worked intensively through 1941 with seemingly endless discussions, but the close contact ended in 1942 when von Neumann moved to the Office of Naval Research in Washington, D.C. However, the two were able to meet at Christmas of 1942 to write the last few pages. The 100-page pamphlet had become a manuscript of 1,200 typed pages, and the press said it could not now publish it without a subsidy, which Morgenstern was able to obtain but whose source was not revealed. The book finally went to press in 1943 and was published in September 1944 as *Theory of Games and Economic Behavior* (a title chosen after considering several alternatives), with von Neumann listed as first author.

The book generated an initial wave of interest with its promise of a new way to approach the analysis of economic behavior, replacing older concepts of the competitive process with new ideas expressed in terms of games of strategy. It was reviewed enthusiastically in leading economic journals and received front-page treatment in the *New York Times* book review section, so that the first edition sold out quickly and was followed by second and third editions in 1947 and 1953 (and many later editions). This initial enthusiasm soon faded, however, since the theory as set out in the book turned out not to be easily or directly applicable to economic analysis at that stage. It took two decades or more for the next generation of game-theory pioneers to develop solution concepts and approaches that truly linked game theory to economics. By the 1980s, however, game theory had become a dominant theme in economic analysis, and the promises of the original authors were well on the way to being fulfilled.

Morgenstern's exact contribution to the collaboration has always been a matter of some dispute. It seems certain that he was the entrepreneur and was responsible for reviving von Neumann's interest in game theory, on which the latter had written nothing since his 1928 paper; and he is certainly responsible for the orientation of the work toward economics and the problems of rational behavior and prediction—his Moriarty-Holmes problem reappears, now as a formal game. Morgenstern was responsible for an important contribution of the book, which came to be widely used in the analysis of decision making under uncertainty even in nongame contexts, the introduction of what became known as "Von Neumann–Morgenstern utility." This is a criterion for making decisions when outcomes are uncertain but have associated probabilities, based on a series of plausible axioms about rational behavior under these circumstances, but preserving a role for individual preference. The formal mathematical analysis of game theory itself obviously is entirely von Neumann's. Even Martin Shubik's friendly memoir notes Morgenstern's difficulty in reproducing the formal proofs in his seminar on game theory. It has been said that Morgenstern was a problem *setter*, von Neumann a problem *solver*. This appears to sum up the relationship between the two and account for the success of their collaboration.

Morgenstern, who had been given a regular faculty appointment at Princeton as associate professor of economics in 1941, was promoted to professor in 1944. In 1948 he married Dorothy Louise Young, at a somewhat late age for a first marriage; they had two children. Despite his professorship, he remained somewhat of an outsider with respect to both the economics department at Princeton and the American economics profession generally, at least until the last years of his life. In spite of the success of the game-theory book, there was skepticism as to his own contribution. The young mathematical economists who appeared in the 1950s were more attracted by linear programming and other new developments than by game theory. He was not a popular classroom teacher and was regarded as too much in the European "Herr Professor" tradition for those used to American informality. Game theory flourished at Princeton, but in the mathematics department rather than the economics department.

As in Vienna, Morgenstern was much involved with activities outside the university. He carried out research for the Office of Naval Research for many years, was an editor of the *Naval Research Logistics Quarterly*, and a consultant for the Atomic Energy Commission and the National Aeronautics and Space Administration (NASA). He was on the editorial board of the postwar revival of the *Zeitschrift für Nationalökonomie*, the journal he had edited in his Vienna days. In 1971 he founded and was the first editor of the *International Journal of Game Theory*. He was a cofounder in 1959 (later chairman) of "Mathematica," a research and consulting firm in Princeton, which remained an important center of his activity for the rest of his life. He had considerable influence on the young mathematicians and economists working on his various research projects, more important than the influence he wielded through formal teaching activities.

Although Morgenstern's membership among the most distinguished economists is based primarily on his contribution to the theory of games, he worked on other themes. One of these was the extension of another contribution by von Neumann, the model of an expanding economy, which had been published in 1937. (It was the presentation of this work that Morgenstern had missed in Vienna.) In a collaborative paper with J. G. Kemeny and G. L. Thompson, published in 1956, the model was generalized and linked closer to game theory. Morgenstern never finished entirely with any theme he introduced (as he had shown in pursuing the problem of prediction), and he continued working on the expanding-economy model until near the end of his life, publishing *Mathematical Theory of Expanding and Contracting Economies* in 1976 (with G. L. Thompson). Other themes of his included skepticism as to the accuracy of economic data and the statistical analysis of stock prices and similar economic series. He also wrote on problems of defense and politics.

Morgenstern retired from Princeton in 1970 and accepted a distinguished research professorship at New York University, which he held until his death at his home in Princeton, New Jersey. Unlike von Neumann, who had died twenty years earlier, Morgenstern lived to see the beginning of the incorporation of game theory into economics. In 1976 he was made a Distinguished Fellow of the American Economics Association and awarded the Golden Cross of the Republic of Austria.

• *Selected Economic Writings of Oskar Morgenstern*, ed. Andrew Schotter (1976), contains Morgenstern's most important shorter papers, translated into English where necessary. His "Collaborating with von Neumann" (a recollection) appears in the *Journal of Economic Literature* 14 (1976): 805–16. Martin Shubik, Morgenstern's former student and one of the major figures in the application of game theory to economics, wrote several evaluations of Morgenstern's contribution, the most extensive being in the *International Encyclopedia of the Social Sciences, Biographical Supplement* (1979). A more personal memoir by Shubik, "Oskar Morgenstern: Mentor and Friend," appears in the *International Journal of Game Theory* 7 (1978): 131–36. An obituary is in the *New York Times*, 27 July 1977 (with a correction note on 29 July).

KELVIN LANCASTER

MORGENTHAU, Hans Joachim (17 Feb. 1904–19 July 1980), legal scholar, was born in Coburg (the capital of the duchy of Saxe-Coburg-Gotha), Germany, the son of Ludwig Morgenthau, a physician, and Frieda Bachmann. As a schoolboy in Coburg, Morgenthau, who was Jewish, was the victim of a virulent form of anti-Semitism. When he received an award for best academic record, many in the audience held their noses. The effect of this experience left a fear of rejection that remained with Morgenthau for the rest of his life.

Although Morgenthau wanted to study art and philosophy, his father persuaded him that he was not qualified to study at the University of Berlin and that these interests would not make profitable occupations. Morgenthau thereby left the study of philosophy at the University of Frankfurt and in 1924 went to the University of Munich to study law.

Another factor that influenced Morgenthau's education was Germany's severe inflation beginning in 1918. In the fall of 1923, when the mark was stabilized, one 1914 gold mark was worth one billion paper marks. This development had a shattering effect on those who lived on fixed incomes, including Morgenthau's father and grandfather, who had money in war bonds. Much as the Nazis spoke of Jews as traitors responsible for "the stab in the back" defeat of Germany, they held them responsible for the devastating effects of inflation. Partly for these reasons, in 1931 Morgenthau emigrated to Geneva, Switzerland, and later to Spain and the United States.

Morgenthau received a doctoral law degree in 1929 from the University of Frankfurt, with a thesis titled "The Nature and Limits of Judicial Function in International Law." From 1929 to 1931 he worked for a famous labor and criminal lawyer writing briefs for him for the German supreme court. He then became an assistant to a Professor Baumgarten, a legal philosophy scholar at the University of Geneva, who was the only German disciple of William James and of pragmatism. Baumgarten sponsored Morgenthau for a tenure position but faced insurmountable difficulties because of Nazism and anti-Semitism. Consequently, Morgenthau left in 1931 for Geneva, where he taught international law, international organization, and international relations at the Graduate Institute for International Studies. His approach was at odds with the dominant view that held that the League of Nations and the Kellogg-Briand Pact of 1929 outlawing war would bring peace. One professor was quoted as saying that anyone who didn't believe that the Pact of Paris made war impossible simply lacked political imagination. Yet these were the declining days of the League of Nations, and the Nazis were rearming in a massive way. With German factories humming to produce more and more war materials, the drafting or revising of legal texts seemed of little value. Morgenthau's colleagues were taken aback by his views, and some saw him as a disturbing influence.

In 1935 Morgenthau married Irma Thorman; they had two children. In that same year he left Geneva for Madrid, where he gained his first paid appointment at the Institute for International and Economic Studies. Its director, Antonio de Luna, became Morgenthau's friend and sponsor, as did other staff members. Faced with the threat of the Spanish Civil War, Morgenthau on 28 July 1937 left for the United States only to find that the one professor he knew there who had promised to help him had died the previous spring. After many unsuccessful attempts to obtain a teaching position, he was hired finally by Brooklyn College for nine hours of teaching in the evening session. At the time, Brooklyn College was considered friendly to radical thought and Morgenthau's realism led him to oppose its utopian and revolutionary views. Both the low pay and hostility to his anticommunist position made Brooklyn unattractive to him, and in 1939 he went to the University of Kansas City, where, until the fall of 1943, he taught courses on subjects ranging from American government to torts and wills. Despite tremendous pressure from an administration that exploited the faculty, Morgenthau there completed a substantial part of *Scientific Man vs. Power Politics*, in which he attacked the prevailing philosophy of social sciences and political science, and passed the Missouri bar examination. He also published several law journal articles.

In 1943 Morgenthau accepted a six-month appointment at the University of Chicago to replace Quincy Wright, who was serving as an advisor to Justice Robert Jackson at the Nuremberg Trials. His appointment was extended for six months, and in 1946 he was named to a tenured professorship. In 1946 Morgenthau published *Scientific Man vs. Power Politics*. In it he argued that there was a tragic dimension to policies and that rational solutions were less fruitful than political ones in which leaders sought to live with reality. In 1948 he published his most successful book, *Politics among Nations: The Struggle for Power and Peace*. It became the leading text in international relations, and Morgenthau was heralded as the major theorist of political realism. He served as a consultant to the Policy Planning Staff in the Department of State from 1949 to 1951, and early in 1951 he was sent to Austria to assess the changeover from military to civilian rule. In 1950 he published *Principles and Problems of International Politics* with Kenneth W. Thompson and in 1951, *In Defense of the National Interest*. From 1962 to 1965 he was a consultant to the Defense Department. Although his major interest remained philosophy, he concentrated on foreign policy because he concluded that human survival depended on a sound U.S. foreign policy.

From 1961 to 1975 Morgenthau opposed the Vietnam War and U.S. involvement. He had earlier been considered a hard-liner in foreign and defense policy, but he opposed U.S. policy in Vietnam on the basis of a principle set forth in 1948 in *Politics*: never put yourself in a position from which you cannot retreat without loss of face and from which you cannot advance without undue risk. In 1958 he published *Dilemmas of Politics* and in 1962, a three-volume collection of his writings, *Politics in the Twentieth Century*, whose volumes included *The Decline of Democratic Politics*, *The Impasse of American Foreign Policy*, and *The Restoration of American Politics*. In 1972 he published *Science: Servant or Master*. His most important work on the goals of the United States was *The Purpose of American Politics* (1960). He died in Manhattan.

• Morgenthau's personal papers are located at the Library of Congress. For more on Morgenthau's life and work, see Kenneth W. Thompson and R. J. Meyers, eds., *Truth and Tragedy: A Tribute to Hans J. Morgenthau* (1977). Thompson provides another tribute to his colleague in *Power and Policy in Transition*, ed. Vojtech Mastny (1984). An obituary is in the *New York Times*, 20 July 1980.

KENNETH W. THOMPSON

MORGENTHAU, Henry (26 Apr. 1856–25 Nov. 1946), lawyer, real estate agent, and diplomat, was born in Mannheim, Germany, the son of Lazarus Morgenthau, a cigar manufacturer, and Babette Guggenheim. After his business failed, Lazarus Morgenthau immigrated to the United States in 1866 and became an insurance salesman. Henry Morgenthau attended public high school, graduating in 1870, the same year he entered the City College of New York. He remained there only one year before financial pressures compelled him to work. Employed as an errand boy at a law firm, Morgenthau slowly learned the business, becoming expert in title searches and mortgage foreclosure sales. In 1875 he quit his job to enter Columbia Law School, supporting himself by teaching at night. He graduated in 1877 and was admitted to the bar.

Along with two friends, Morgenthau founded the law firm of Lachman, Morgenthau and Goldsmith in 1879. He focused on real estate transactions, at which he became extremely successful. In 1883 he married Josephine Sykes; they had four children, one of whom, Henry Morgenthau, Jr., became secretary of the Treasury under President Franklin D. Roosevelt. Morgenthau, Sr., left the law firm to found the Central Realty Bond and Trust Company in 1899 and the Henry Morgenthau Company in 1905, both of which dealt in real estate. In 1913 Morgenthau closed both of his businesses and devoted himself to public service.

Morgenthau was an active philanthropist and social lobbyist. A Reform Jew, he in 1907 helped found and acted as first president of the Free Synagogue. Radically opposed to the Orthodox emphasis on religion, the Free Synagogue was more concerned with broad-based community service. He worked on the Committee on Congestion of the Population (1908), which advocated tenement reform, and the Committee of Safety (1911), which was formed in reaction to the Triangle Shirtwaist Company fire and lobbied for improved industrial safety laws. In 1911 he founded the Bronx House, a settlement and music school, and was a lifelong patron of the Metropolitan Opera. A supporter of Woodrow Wilson, Morgenthau donated over $30,000 to Wilson's presidential campaign in 1911–1912 and served as chairman of the Democratic National Committee's finance committee in 1912.

President Wilson appointed Morgenthau ambassador to Turkey in 1913. Morgenthau was untrained in diplomacy, and the position was initially difficult for him. His most laudable action in office was in foreseeing the looming isolation of Jewish settlers in Palestine with the onset of the First World War, and he obtained $50,000 from the American Jewish Committee to prevent their starvation. After Great Britain, France, Russia, and the other Allied countries broke off diplomatic relations with Turkey when the latter entered the war in October 1914, Morgenthau was left as the only western ambassador in the country, and he was overwhelmed by demands for evacuation and help. He handled the situation with such tact that he was decorated by the British and French governments for service to their nationals and was also offered a cabinet post by Turkey. Morgenthau resigned his ambassadorship in 1916, sickened by the Turkish slaughter of Armenians. He returned to the United States to increase public awareness and to raise funds for Armenian relief. He also served on President Wilson's reelection campaign. In June 1917 he was sent on a secret mission to negotiate a separate peace between Turkey and the Allies. This mission was prematurely aborted under pressure from Britain and Zionists, who feared the compromising of their own interests.

Morgenthau was involved in many subsequent international diplomacy and relief efforts. In February 1919 he was part of a speaking tour to promote U.S. membership in the League of Nations; in March of that year he was a delegate in Cannes at the conference for the creation of the International Red Cross; he advised on Turkish questions at the Paris Peace Conference in 1919; he served on the Harbord Commission (1919), which recommended American policy on Armenia; and he was vice chairman (1919–1921) of the Armenian Relief Committee, later the Near East Relief, Inc. President Wilson used him frequently as an emissary abroad. Morgenthau traveled to Poland in the summer of 1919 at Wilson's behest to investigate the persecution of Jews. The president appointed him ambassador to Mexico in 1920, but because of turmoil in the country his appointment was not confirmed by Congress. He chaired the League of Nations Refugee Resettlement Commission in Athens, which was faced with the problem of 1.25 million Greeks who had been summarily expelled from Turkey. Their successful resettlement was one of Morgenthau's greatest achievements, and he recounted the story in his memoir, *I Was Sent to Athens* (1929).

Morgenthau's political involvement continued into his old age. He was a strong supporter of Franklin Roosevelt and his New Deal and served as technical delegate to the World Monetary and Economic Conference in London in 1933. Morgenthau died at his home in New York City.

• Morgenthau's papers are in the Library of Congress. His autobiography, *All in a Lifetime* (1922), and his account of his diplomatic service in Turkey, *Ambassador Morgenthau's Story* (1918), are excellent sources of information on his life. Information on Morgenthau's family, including his son Henry Morgenthau, Jr., is in Henry Morgenthau III, *Mostly Morgenthaus* (1991). Information on Morgenthau's involvement in the Wilson administration and international diplomacy and relief is in William F. McCombs, *Making Woodrow Wilson President* (1921); Josephus Daniels, *The Wilson Era* (2 vols., 1944–1946); and James L. Barton, *The Story of Near East Relief* (1930). An obituary is in the *New York Times*, 26 Nov. 1946.

ELIZABETH ZOE VICARY

MORGENTHAU, Henry, Jr. (11 May 1891–6 Feb. 1967), secretary of the treasury, was born in New York City, the son of Henry Morgenthau, a businessman and entrepreneur, and Josephine Sykes. His father, of German-Jewish ancestry, amassed a considerable fortune through investment in real estate properties in the Bronx and Harlem. Both of his parents were activists in the Democratic party and in social welfare causes, including the Henry Street Settlement, the Bronx House, and efforts to improve fire safety conditions in depressed areas of New York City. The senior Morgenthau served as head of finance for the Democratic National Committee in 1912 and again in 1916 and was ambassador to Turkey during World War I. Morgenthau felt a particularly heavy burden of paternal expectations because he was the only son and bore his father's name. His youth was beset by personal anxieties that the financial ease assured by his father's wealth could not dispel.

Morgenthau entered Phillips Exeter in 1904 but did poorly. He remained only two years, completing his college preparation at the Sachs Collegiate Institute in New York City with the help of private tutoring. Admitted in 1909 to Cornell to study architecture, he left in the middle of his second year. For a time he worked at odd jobs, including timekeeper for a construction company, machinist with a typewriter company, and bank teller. He also did volunteer work with Lillian D. Wald at the Henry Street Settlement, and that experience implanted an empathy for the poor that never left him.

Morgenthau found his métier in 1911, when he went to Texas in an effort to regain his health after a bout with typhoid fever. While there he became interested in farming and decided to pursue a career in agriculture. In later explaining his decision, he recalled that his father "was crazy to have me in business with him. . . . In a desperate move to get out from under him I moved to the country" (Blum, *From the Morgenthau Diaries*, vol. 1, p. 5). Morgenthau returned to Cornell for a time, then ended his formal education and traveled extensively, observing farming practices throughout the United States. In 1913, when he was twenty-two, his father helped him purchase 1,000 acres in Dutchess County, New York, and shortly thereafter an additional 700. He applied himself to making the largely depleted farmlands profitable, enjoying success in apple and dairy farming. During World War I he assisted Herbert Hoover's U.S. Food Administration in a program to provide badly needed tractors to French farmers. Toward the end of the conflict he accepted a gentleman's commission as a naval lieutenant.

Within two years of moving to Dutchess County, Morgenthau became acquainted with Franklin D. Roosevelt. Roosevelt tried to persuade Morgenthau to run for county sheriff. He declined, but over the years the two developed a close friendship. Roosevelt, some ten years older than Morgenthau, came to exercise an influence on the younger man nearly as powerful as that of Morgenthau's own father. It was as if Morgenthau, troubled by a lingering sense that he had not fulfilled his father's expectations, chose to see in Roosevelt an alternative father—an older man who cheerfully and unreservedly accepted him as he was.

In 1916 Morgenthau married Elinor Fatman, a charming and brilliant Vassar graduate whom he had known since childhood. They had three children. Elinor Morgenthau and Eleanor Roosevelt also formed an enduring and mutually supportive friendship, working together in Dutchess County relief and educational projects.

The ties between the two families were strengthened after Roosevelt's polio attack in 1921. During the convalescence Roosevelt and Morgenthau spent much time together playing board games and discussing common interests. Among these was a concern for the plight of farmers, which led Morgenthau in 1922 to purchase the moribund *American Agriculturalist*. He proceeded to revivify the journal, making it an eloquent voice for reclamation, conservation, and scientific farming. The two men also pursued a common interest in building up the Democratic party in the heavily Republican rural areas of New York State to counter New York City control of the party.

It is thus no surprise that Roosevelt found a place for Morgenthau in Albany when Roosevelt was elected governor in 1928. Roosevelt first named his friend chairman of the Agricultural Advisory Committee, with special responsibilities for strengthening the Democratic party in the economically depressed New York hinterlands. After his reelection in 1930, Roosevelt appointed Morgenthau commissioner of conservation. Elinor Morgenthau confided to Roosevelt that Henry was enthusiastic about working with and under him. She said, "It gives Henry a chance to grow, so that your friendship can continue to be cemented by a community of interest as well as by the deep affection with which he holds you" (Blum, *From the Morgenthau Diaries*, vol. 1, p. 21). Morgenthau worked ably in this position, implementing, with Harry L. Hopkins, later one of Roosevelt's closest advisers, a state reforestation project that created employment for thousands of men and planted nearly ninety million trees.

When Roosevelt was elected president, Morgenthau hoped to be appointed secretary of agriculture. Though disappointed, he nonetheless served enthusiastically as head of the Federal Farm Board until he became acting secretary of the treasury, replacing the ailing William Woodin on 13 November 1933. When in January 1934 it became clear that Woodin could not continue, Morgenthau became secretary. Morgenthau remained at the post for the next eleven years, longer than any of his predecessors except Andrew Mellon.

Morgenthau's time in Washington was plagued with controversy arising from doubts in some quarters as to his capacity for high public office and from his outspoken positions on major policy issues. He and Roosevelt took lunch together each Monday, and his closeness to the president made him the envy of many administration officials. While still with the Farm Credit Administration, he encouraged the president to implement the inflationist theories of Cornell agricultural economists George F. Warren and Frank A. Pearson by devaluing the dollar. Between 25 October 1933 and 31 January 1934 the president raised the price of gold from $20.67 to $35 an ounce. Seen by some as near-blasphemous monetary tinkering, the action had little positive effect on the economy, but it did free the president to pursue an expansionist economic policy in other areas.

Thoroughly schooled in Progressive era commitments to balanced budgets and efficiency in government, Morgenthau saw it as his special responsibility to accomplish these goals for Roosevelt's administration. With signs of recovery evident in early 1937, Morgenthau concluded that the time was right to deliver on the president's long-delayed promise to balance the federal budget. That fall, however, the economy took a serious downturn. Deeply concerned about the fate of the New Deal, Morgenthau entered into a major policy debate within the administration over how to deal with the Recession of 1937–1938. As the downturn deepened, he insisted that balancing the budget was necessary now not as a consequence but as an agent of recovery, while Marriner S. Eccles, chairman of the Federal Reserve Board, urged a resumption of deficit spending. When Eccles and like-minded New Dealers finally persuaded Roosevelt to renew spending in April 1938, Morgenthau threatened to resign. Though he backed away from the threat after a talk with Roosevelt, he continued to see the decision as a major turning point in the evolution of national economic policy, recalling years later, "A balanced budget had never been tried and might have worked" (Blum, *Morgenthau and Roosevelt*, p. xiii).

When war broke out again in Europe, Morgenthau involved the Treasury in a series of key issues. He opposed the relocation of West Coast Japanese Americans in 1941. His sensitivity to atrocities against Jews in Nazi Germany made him an early advocate of American aid to the Allies. He helped to establish the War Refugee Board as an agency to assist Jews and other refugees from Europe. He worked at stabilizing the dollar against near fiscal anarchy as Europe moved toward war. When Germany attacked Poland in 1939 he established a procurement service in the Treasury that facilitated purchase of munitions by France and Britain. He was outspoken in his opposition to the sale of scrap metal and other strategic supplies to Japan. In 1941 he proposed a plan, rejected by Secretary of State Cordell Hull, to appease Japan with a $2 billion loan at 2 percent interest. Morgenthau participated in private efforts to help Brigadier General Claire L. Chennault, of China's Flying Tigers, to begin purchase of fighter planes and in efforts to provide aid to China over the Burma Road.

The difficult task of financing the war became his major preoccupation from 1942 through 1945. As part of this effort he encouraged the purchase of war bonds by civilian Americans, the bonds not only helping to fund the war, but also diverting funds from the spending stream that might have accelerated inflation. His aim, through his time as Treasury head, however, was to provide the basis for a sound, predictable currency. His work at the Bretton Woods conference in 1944 was directed to that end and included the establishment of the International Monetary Fund and the World Bank. His "Morgenthau Plan" for dealing with postwar Germany, announced in September 1944, proposed the complete demilitarization of Germany, including dismantling of industrial plants and granting of East Prussia, the Saarland, and Silesia to neighboring states and internationalization of the Ruhr basin. The remainder of Germany was to be divided into two agricultural states. The highly controversial plan was initialed at the Quebec Conference that year but was dropped thereafter by policy makers who felt a strong postwar Germany was necessary for stability in Europe.

After Roosevelt's death on 12 April 1945, Morgenthau remained in office, hoping to continue until the end of the war in the Pacific. He worked uncomfortably with President Harry S. Truman, who was cool toward the Morgenthau Plan. In July 1945, when Truman rejected his wish to attend the Potsdam Conference, Morgenthau tendered his resignation and returned to his farm in Dutchess County. Elinor died in 1949, and in 1951 he married Margaret Puthon Hirsch. He devoted much of the rest of his life to philanthropies. He was chairman of the United Jewish Appeal between 1947 and 1950 and chairman of the Board of Governors of the American Financial and Development Corporation for Israel from 1951 to 1954, helping promote bond issues to assist in the economic development of Israel.

Morgenthau was often inarticulate and awkward in press conferences and other public appearances, causing many to underrate his competence. Treasury Department minutes show him to be a sound administrator, an articulate defender of policies he advocated, and above all a man sensitive to human needs and suffering. His personal insecurities and occasional poor judgment nonetheless limited his effectiveness as a public official and lowered his reputation among the Washington Press Corps and some New Deal colleagues. While it was widely observed that he had little aptitude for finance, he is credited with keeping the dollar sound during an unparalleled economic crisis and successfully financing America's involvement in the war. He was impeccably honest and open as secretary of the treasury and devoutly loyal to Roosevelt. In his resignation letter to President Truman he mentioned an understanding between Roosevelt and him that "when he was through we would go back to Dutchess County together" (Blum, *Morgenthau and Roosevelt*, p. 644). Deprived of the friend and mentor whose confidence, as Elinor Morgenthau understood, drew out his best qualities, Morgenthau was content to spend the rest of his days as a gentleman farmer and philanthropist. He died in Poughkeepsie, New York.

• Morgenthau's secretary, Henrietta Klotz, saved nearly every item that passed over his desk during his long Washington career. This collection, known as the Morgenthau diaries, totals over eight hundred volumes and provides an indispensable day-to-day account of Roosevelt's administration from Morgenthau's perspective. The collection is at the Roosevelt Presidential Library in Hyde Park, N.Y. John Morton Blum has published three volumes drawn from the collection, appropriately titled *From the Morgenthau Diaries* (1959–1967). See also Blum, *Roosevelt and Morgenthau* (1970). Elmus Wicker examines the 1933 revaluing of gold in "Roosevelt's 1933 Monetary Experiment," *Journal of American History* 57 (1970): 864–79. Dean L. May examines Morgenthau's role in the Recession of 1937 in *From New Deal to New Economics: The American Liberal Response to the Recession of 1937* (1981). The Morgenthau Plan is thoughtfully discussed in J. K. Sowden, *The German Question 1945–1973* (1975). Still useful are Arthur Schlesinger's three volumes on *The Age of Roosevelt* (1957–1960).

DEAN L. MAY

MORINI, Austin M. (4 Mar. 1826–29 July 1909), Catholic priest, philologist, and historian, was born John Morini in Florence, Italy, the son of Paul Morini, a goldsmith and designer, and Anna Bartolini, an embroiderer. He received his early education at the school of the Piarist Fathers in Florence; then in 1844, at the age of eighteen, he entered the novitiate of the Servite Friars (Servants of Mary) at SS. Annunziata church in Florence. At that time his name was changed to Austin. He completed his philosophical and theological training at SS. Annunziata and was ordained to the priesthood on 1 May 1850. He received the degree of master of theology in 1856.

From 1853 to 1862 Morini taught Latin, Greek, and the Italian language at SS. Annunziata. During this same period, "for the love of the language" and to attract greater attention to texts in humanistic and renaissance Italian, he began to work on a new edition of the *Epistole di s. Girolamo*, translated by Giovan Francesco Zeffi in the Florentine language of the end of the fifteenth century. In preparing this edition, the last section of which was printed in 1861, Morini entered into correspondence and developed friendships with the intellectuals in Florence (Luigi Razzolini, Gino and Carlo Capponi, Fausto Lasinio, Cesare Guasti, and Pietro Fanfani), in other parts of Italy (Niccolò Tommaseo, Giovanni Battista De Rossi, Celestino Cavedoni, Alfonso Capecelatro, and Giuseppe Bardelli), and in other countries (Victor de Buck, Ivan Martinof, and Ivan Gagarin). These epistolary exchanges included discussions of contemporary political and cultural events, so his correspondence is, in a sense, a political and cultural chronicle of the early years of unified Italy. The Bollandist Victor de Buck wrote this evaluation of Morini's work: "I read your last work with all the interest that I have for you. But stop being an editor—you write better than all those whose writings you publish. If I knew French or Flemish as well as you know Italian, I would exercise much influence in my country by the pen." During this period Morini also began his study of Servite history, collecting documentation that would serve him in later years.

As an intellectual Morini was "liberal," open to the truth from whomever it might come, even from those, such as Gino Capponi, whose political views he did not share. He defended his friends when their scholarly research put them at odds with authorities. Some of his own historical conclusions went contrary to the received traditions of his order: he showed that the medieval philosopher Henry of Ghent was not a member of the Servite Order and that the story of sixty-four Servite martyrs in Prague in the fifteenth century was a fabrication.

As a priest, Morini saw the danger of the small Order of Servants of Mary being completely extinguished by the growing demands for the suppression of religious orders in Italy. Because of this concern he and Philip Bosio established a foundation in England in 1864, and six years later Morini led a group of four friars to the United States to found the Servite Order in Menasha, Wisconsin. While in Wisconsin he helped support the parish and the growing Servite community by giving retreats and lectures.

In 1874, at the invitation of Bishop Thomas Foley, Morini founded the parish of Our Lady of Sorrows, then on the western outskirts of Chicago. This became the motherhouse of the Servite Order in the United States. Almost immediately he established contacts with Catholic intellectual circles in Chicago, and that fall he gave a lecture on Savonarola to the Union Catholic Library Association at the request of its president, William J. Onahan. In reporting on the lecture, the *Chicago Tribune* (30 Nov. 1874) described Morini as "of the intellectual Latin type of mankind, whose pronunciation of English smacks very pleasingly of his soft and thrilling mother-tongue."

In addition to his office of vicar general of the Servite Order in the United States, Morini was also the pastor of the growing parish of Our Lady of Sorrows from 1874 to 1885 and novice master for young men who wished to enter the Servite Order. He did not, however, give up his intellectual endeavors, for he was able to maintain a limited correspondence with his Florentine friends. While in Chicago he prepared for publication an account of the foundation of the Servite Order that he believed dated from the fourteenth century, although later studies have shown that it actually dated from the late 1600s. It was printed in Italy in 1882 during his first visit to Italy in fifteen years.

That year John Paul Moser, an Austrian Servite who had worked with Morini in Wisconsin and Chicago for three years, wrote this private estimation of him to a friend: "He is a quiet man, not making much noise or show, but ready for every sacrifice; not jealous but happy if good is done by anyone, and anyhow wonderfully blessed by God. [He is] the best man for introducing common life and leading his house quietly to good discipline."

While in Chicago, Morini translated a lengthy life of St. Philip Benizi from French to Italian; it was published in Rome in 1885. Upon his return to Rome in 1888 he published a critical work on the thirteenth-century founders of the Servite Order. In Rome he was named to such important offices as secretary to the prior general, a member of the general council of the order, and postulator of causes of canonization. At the same time Morini continued his research and writing, publishing, in addition to numerous articles, a monograph on the origin of the cult to Our Lady of Sorrows in 1893. In 1897 he founded, together with Peregrine Soulier, the *Monumenta O.S.M.*, a twenty-volume series of documents relating to the history of the Servite Order. Many of the contributions in this collection are his.

Toward the end of his life, between 1904 and 1907, Morini wrote his recollections of the founding of the Servite Order in England and in the United States. For this work he used the many letters and other documents he had collected. Although the order numbered only two priories and sixteen members when Morini left the United States in 1888, the foundation grew to two separate provinces and 355 professed members at its peak in 1964. Soulier captured Morini's spirit when he wrote in the obituary that appeared in the *Monumenta O.S.M.* that Morini was "never idle, but always occupied either in reading or writing" (vol. 11 [1910], p. 10). Morini died in Rome, leaving his confreres and friends a legacy of true intellectual dedication and the wisdom and foresight to reach out beyond the known to new geographical areas, coupled with a pastoral concern for those away from major cultural centers.

• Morini's correspondence and other papers are found in the Servite General Archives in Rome; letters by Morini to the Bollandists are found in their archives in Brussels, and those to his Florentine friend Alessandro Carraresi are found in the Biblioteca Nazionale of Florence. The best general biography of Morini, with a listing of his published works, is Justin M. Ryska, "Austin Morini, Servite Scholar and Founder (1826–1909)," in *Contributi di storiografia servitana* (1964). His philological and literary activity has been discussed in two articles by Filippo M. Berlasso, "Correspondenza di Bartolomeo Sorio con fra Agostino Morini (1861–1864)," *Studi Storici O.S.M.* 40 (1990): 203–73, and "La ripresa degli studi agiografici servitani nella corrispondenza Caselli-Morini-Simoni (1855–1865)," *Studi Storici O.S.M.* 43 (1993): 171–98. For Morini's contribution to founding the Servite Order in England, the best work available is Gerard M. Corr, *The Servites in London* (1952). Morini's account of the foundational years in the United States is published as *The Foundation of the Order of Servants of Mary in the United States of America (1870–1883)*, with English translation and notes by Conrad M. Borntrager and the Italian text edited by Odir J. Dias (1993).

CONRAD M. BORNTRAGER

MORISON, George Shattuck (19 Dec. 1842–1 July 1903), civil engineer, was born in New Bedford, Massachusetts, the son of the Reverend John Hopkins Morison and Emily Rogers. His father was the minister in a small church. Four years later the father was asked by citizens of Milton, Massachusetts, to take charge of their Unitarian parish, an appointment that lasted over fifty years.

After some schooling in Milton, Morison, like his father, attended Phillips Exeter Academy and then Harvard College, where he received an A.B. in 1863 and an LL.B. in 1866. At the college, where he was ninth in a class of 121 and a member of Phi Beta Kappa, he was said by a classmate to be "not otherwise prominent." The same may be said of the law school, where he won the Bowdoin Prize and acquired a respectable but not illustrious place in the class.

During this period Morison was somewhat unsatisfied with himself. For a year after college he became a government superintendent of plantations in St. Helena Island, South Carolina. His purpose was to find the possibility of order in a continuing Civil War. Unsatisfied in this situation, he came back to Harvard Law School and from there entered the great firm of Evarts, Southmayd, and Choate in New York City. His experiences up to that time only convinced him of the things he did not want to do. Looking back on these years he said they were a "blunder and a waste."

What shook Morison loose from this position was his belief that the development of the western lands offered "a unique opportunity to an original and ambitious mind." Accordingly, he determined to enter a field for which he had no preparation and a profession that scarcely existed in the United States; he decided to become a civil engineer. To start, he wrote out a program that began with how he would spend his evenings (studying) and ended with the state of engineering. First, he said, he would spend a season in the field seeing how locomotives and trains worked. Then he would go abroad for a year to study French and German and "the acquirement of scientific knowledge." Morison's interest in engineering stemmed from a desire to rise above "mere money making."

Evarts, Southmayd, and Choate gave Morison almost a year to figure out what he wanted to do and then gave in with grace as he decided "to measure and calculate the cubical contents of stone for the masonry pier of a bridge." He went to Kansas City, Missouri, to a project that was to bring the Kansas City and Cameroon Railway into the city over the Missouri River. The manager of this enterprise was Octave Chanute, a perfect match for Morison. He had "the Gallic power of clear expression" and "a truly scientific spirit." He was working on his first big bridge and was something of a wit.

When Chanute left the project to be the chief engineer of the Erie Railroad, he asked Morison to come with him as his deputy. But Morison took three more years finding out about rivers, railroads, and bridges, before rejoining the older engineer. Not long after, the Erie Railroad confronted a fire on the main line at Portage, New York, where the longest wooden viaduct in the world was burning to the ground. Morison was put in charge of the restoration with instructions to replace wood with iron. Four days after the destruction of the viaduct he had in hand the plans for the future.

Eighty-six days later the structure was open to traffic: a new bridge made of iron with the measurement of 818 feet and 2 inches between abutments. The bridge was highly praised.

For the next twenty-five years Morison's main task was bridge building. On the whole self-taught on jobs that were always different, he built up a remarkable record. He concentrated on the territory between the Mississippi and the Rockies, but in fact he would build any kind of bridge anywhere: nine bridges over the willful Missouri, five over the Mississippi, four in the Far West, and a good many in between. He always worked with the newest materials and procedures. His handling of foundations was skillful. Morison undertook numerous demanding bridge construction projects, developing a singular reputation in the United States and internationally.

Morison in fact led several other lives. For years he reported to Baring Brothers in London on the state of locomotives, trains, and railroads in this country. He traveled a great deal in the United States and abroad; he bought back most of the familial land in Peterborough, New Hampshire, that over the years had been let go. And he served for many years as chairman of the board of trustees of Phillips Exeter Academy.

In his later years he was on several presidential committees; the most important was the Isthmian Canal Commission to choose the site in Central America that ultimately became the Panama Canal. To fulfill this task Morison took two trips to Europe, spent four months in Central America, and attended fifty-five sessions in Washington. The arguments for a proper site were heated and prolonged. At one time, he was the only person in favor of Panama; he is now recognized as the influence that settled the canal in its present site.

A proud, determined, austere man who reached the very top of his profession, Morison had no time for small talk or idle chatter; he was rude to waiters; he didn't trust people who were good with horses; and when he said he would meet someone at 10:15 A.M. he meant not a minute before or after. Although he had a sister and a brother for most of his career he had no home but parlor cars, Pullman cars, and clubs scattered around the country. During the 1890s he built an astonishing brick house in Peterborough, which he said was to celebrate Thanksgiving with his family and to watch the sun go down over Mount Monadnock. In all, he spent forty-nine nights in the house before he died in New York City.

After Morison's death his brother, Robert, put together some of his speeches in a small book, titled The New Epoch as Developed by the Manufacture of Power (1903). Morison saw farther ahead than his fellows; his writing offers insights in science, technology, culture, and the nature of life as these subjects exist and interact together.

• Morison's personal and professional files are available in Peterborough, N.H. Additional information is in L. A. Morison, *The History of the Morison or Morrison Family* (1880); and E. Gerber et al., *Transactions of the American Society of Civil Engineers* 54 (June 1905): 513–23. A memoir by George Abbot Morison, *George Shattuck Morison* (1932), was published by the Peterborough Historical Society. See also David McCullough, *The Path Between the Seas* (1977). An obituary is in the *New York Tribune*, 3 July 1903.

ELTING E. MORISON

MORISON, Samuel Eliot (9 July 1887–15 May 1976), historian and educator, was born in Boston, Massachusetts, the son of John Holmes Morison, a lawyer, and Emily Marshall Eliot. He was raised in the fashionable Beacon Hill home of his grandfather, the historian Samuel Eliot, and he enjoyed many of the privileges associated with a patrician background, including preparation for Harvard, where he enrolled in 1904. At Harvard (1904–1908), Morison took a wide range of courses that anticipated the eclecticism of his later career. Enrolled primarily in European history classes taught by Charles Homer Haskins, Roger Merriman, and George Santayana, Morison was exposed to the study of the past at a time when the discipline of history was in transition. In the late nineteenth century, most history was taught primarily from institutional and political points of view, emphasizing the role of monarchs and political leaders and employing methodologies specific to judicial rulings and parliamentary debate. By the early twentieth century, however, new and challenging sociocultural approaches were being introduced that made use of folk customs, literature, and songs. Morison was influenced profoundly by these trends. After his graduation in 1908, he studied briefly at the École des Sciences Politiques in Paris. He then returned to Harvard to earn a Ph.D. (1913) in American history, under the "great triumvirate" of Edward Channing, Albert Bushnell Hart, and Frederick Jackson Turner. From Channing, Morison learned the significance of scholarly research and attention to detail; from Hart, he gained an appreciation for developmental philosophy and cultural criticism; and from Turner, he discovered the methods of social-scientific analysis and the importance of challenging established doctrine. Morison's dissertation on his great-grandfather, the lawyer and statesman Harrison Gray Otis, was later published as a two-volume biography (*The Life and Letters of Harrison Gray Otis* [1913]). After a brief stint teaching at the University of California at Berkeley in 1914, Morison returned to Harvard, first as a teaching instructor and later as an assistant professor of history. He remained at the university until his retirement in 1955.

Morison's career as a historian was marked by many transitions and a slow but steady rise to national prominence. Prior to World War I, he engaged in numerous enterprises to prove the "usefulness" of history—he taught night classes in history and government for electricians and plumbers at trade schools, he edited historical documents for use by schoolchildren, and he helped found the New England History Teachers' Association. These activities linked him to the "usable past" tradition of "New Historians" like James Harvey Robinson, Charles Beard, and Carl Becker, who hoped the techniques of the professional historian could be applied to the concerns of contemporary society.

Morison was politically active as well, supporting the Democratic policies of Woodrow Wilson and entering the army during World War I on the strength of the president's call for the active involvement of scholars in the restoration of peace in Europe. Morison came out of the war profoundly disillusioned with American idealism, a disenchantment he shared with many intellectuals. When he returned to Harvard in the fall of 1919, he found himself less receptive to the excesses of his students and the general materialism of American university life. America had degenerated into an "orgy of extravagance, profiteering, and soaring cost of living," he noted later in an autobiographical memoir, as well as "intolerance, hypocrisy, cruelty to foreigners, [and] shortsighted persecution of Reds."

Morison's disillusionment with postwar America profoundly altered his career. It hastened a withdrawal from the usable past tradition with which he had been linked before the war by eliminating the utilitarian impetus for his early scholarly work. If prior to World War I Morison had required history to be the handmaiden of reform, then after the war it was obligated only to serve the casual, indefinite needs of a general reading audience. Arguing that the arcane and unnecessarily technical language of professional scholarship prohibited most Americans from appreciating the important historical research professors were accomplishing, Morison began work on a maritime history of Massachusetts directed at general readers. It was an attempt to "dish up a bit of unwritten history in a form and style that the dear reading public—especially 'he-men' would come to read," he wrote to historian and former senator Albert Beveridge. "If they take the bait, I shall go ahead along the same line," he added, "if not, I shall return to the small clientele which appreciated my first book." The experiment was a success. *The Maritime History of Massachusetts, 1783–1860* (1921) was praised by the *Boston Globe* as a "fresh, sparkling" contribution to nautical literature, with the "odor of the sea" about it.

In addition, such scholarship widened doors of academic opportunity for Morison, who, like so many during the postwar period, seemed anxious to escape reactionary America for the freer intellectual climate of Europe. Granted a leave of absence from Harvard, Morison became the first Harmsworth professor of American history at Oxford University, where he was associated with "the most humane and intelligent group of people" he had ever known. He later described his stay (1922–1925) as his days of "wine and roses."

Although tempted by an offer to remain in the Harmsworth chair for a decade, Morison returned to the United States in 1925, in part because his wife, Elizabeth "Bessie" Shaw Greene, whom he had married in 1910, worried that their four children would grow up unaware of their country of birth. He also returned in part because members of the Harvard history department were growing restless about the length of his absence and partly because he had become disillusioned by the "debunking" activities of the disaffected Americans he met in Europe. Oxford had given him time "to read and think and appreciate the solid worth and essential character of America."

He returned home with a renewed faith in his country's future. This new conviction was reflected in the tone of his *Oxford History of the United States* (2 vols., 1927; later retitled *Growth of the American Republic* [1930], with Henry Steele Commager), a textbook that sought to reconcile differences among recent surveys of American history, especially disparities of region like those separating Morison's mentors Edward Channing of New England and Frederick Jackson Turner of the West, whose antithetical theories are intermingled with some success throughout the work.

Morison's hope for a more unified national vision was also reflected in his new attitude toward his alma mater. His postwar pessimism about higher education in general and Harvard in particular gave way in the late 1920s to unbridled optimism; so much so, in fact, that he became the tercentenary historian of Harvard in the early 1930s. Attracted while in Europe to the "history of ideas as expressed through academic institutions" and the need to acknowledge the staying power of tradition against transitory educational reform, Morison's five-volume history of his college represented a declaration of allegiance to the stabilizing forces of profession and university. In his tercentenary history of Harvard (1929–1936) as well as in his *Builders of the Bay Colony* (1930) and *The Puritan Pronaos* (1936), Morison identified with the Puritans as righteous upholders of tradition and professionalism in the face of spurious and misdirected challenges to authority. He attacked journalistic historians like James Truslow Adams and Van Wyck Brooks for their tendencies to obscure facts and twist meanings and accused them of working deceitfully on the "ragged edge of truth." As a means of lending what he perceived to be a much-needed professional authority to the journalistic study of the New England past, Morison founded the *New England Quarterly* in 1928 with Harvard colleague Kenneth Murdock and former student Perry Miller—the "three Ms" of Puritan revisionism as Morison, Murdock, and Miller were later known.

Because Morison's intellectual allegiances had shifted from those of a progressive, reform-minded pragmatism to a more conservative defense of tradition, he found himself naturally at odds with historian Charles Beard, whose career had taken a parallel but opposite course. An academic who had resigned from Columbia University during World War I to become a leading spokesperson for the debunking of American institutions in the 1920s (especially democratic capitalism), Beard had written a highly popular and rival textbook to Morison's titled *The Rise of American Civilization* (1927). In this and other works, Beard stressed economic interests, particularly class conflicts. Morison disclaimed Beard's brand of "dialectical materialism," arguing that it had contributed to the "mass murder of historical characters" through books containing "no great men or leading characters, only automata whose speeches, ideas, or aspirations are mentioned merely to give the historian an opportunity to sneer or smear." The disagreement between Morison and Beard came to public attention in 1938, when each challenged the nomination of the other for the directorship of the new library at Hyde Park, New York, being built to commemorate the presidency of Franklin Roosevelt.

Morison rejected the Hyde Park position in part because by 1938 he was hard at work on a new biography of Christopher Columbus, a work that he had hoped would reestablish the Italian mariner as a truly memorable American hero and provide an object lesson about how to pursue historical research in a professional and even "scientific" manner without slipping into pedantry. In what would later become known as his "participatory" style of history (modeled after the techniques of Francis Parkman and Thucydides), Morison retraced the voyages of Columbus in a chartered ketch, the *Capitania*. Crisscrossing the Atlantic and the Caribbean in search of corroborating evidence for speculations regarding nautical position and landfalls in Columbus's journals and sea logs, Morison demonstrated the power of histories written with professional attention to detail about maritime venues essentially unchanged in five centuries of European experience in the Americas.

The result of this work was *Admiral of the Ocean Sea* (1942), which earned Morison the Pulitzer Prize. In the writing of his Columbus volumes, Morison consciously alternated between the detached voice of the twentieth-century professional historian, who disdained the "unprofitable speculations" of armchair students of Columbus, and a less objective, more empathetic presence that introduced imaginative solutions to questions not subject to scientific verification. Some readers complained that Morison's technical, scientific, and objective vision struggled unsuccessfully at times against an artistic, poetic, and subjective one; others noted that Morison's "controlled imagination" was but a perverse variety of the reckless subjectivity he had accused journalistic historians of employing. But whether justified or not, the dual personality of Columbus (both practical mariner and impractical dreamer) recapitulated in revealing ways Morison's own struggle as a historian to meet the needs of both professional and nonprofessional readers. Issued in a two-volume edition for scholars and in a Book-of-the-Month Club edition for general readers, *Admiral of the Ocean Sea* was the most popular piece of writing Morison ever completed.

While in Europe in the late 1930s researching the Columbus biography, Morison had become sensitive to the fragile European political scene. Eyewitness to the Spanish civil war as well as German submarine activity off the coast of Portugal, Morison began writing his Harvard classmate, President Franklin Delano Roosevelt, as early as the summer of 1939, urging a greater U.S. role in the war in Europe. Arguing that "this country is right now in greater danger of losing her freedom of action and national integrity than at any time before 1861 or since 1864," Morison advised the president that "it will be cheaper in the end to help the Allies now than fight Germany alone, with perhaps Japan on our backs."

When war did come, Morison sought to play a significant role in it. Too old to be considered for active duty, he received a commission from FDR to serve as the "official" historian of naval operations during the war. This appointment determined the direction of Morison's work for the next twenty years. Given permission to participate firsthand in the historical events he was to record and interpret, Morison gained berths on patrol boats, destroyers, and heavy cruisers; participated in planning sessions for invasions of northern Africa; and conducted postoperational interviews with commanders in the Pacific theater. He was in Guadalcanal when it came under Japanese air attack, participated in the storming of Makin Island, and "narrowly escaped death" at the hands of a Japanese kamikaze pilot during the invasion of Okinawa. Throughout these operations, Morison was viewed with suspicion by some in the military, who characterized him as a "long-haired" eccentric unfamiliar with the "Navy way," and with utter contempt by others, who resented his assessments of their military actions. Morison's fifteen-volume history of naval operations during the war embroiled him in continual controversy of this sort, but general readers accepted its critical stances and applauded its pervasive spirit of nationalism.

Nowhere was this spirit more evident than in the public reaction to a historiographic controversy that emerged in the wake of the publication of volume three of Morison's naval series, *Rising Sun in the Pacific*. In 1948 Morison's old nemesis Beard had published *President Roosevelt and the Coming of the War* in which he suggested in a now well-established line of argument that FDR knew of the impending attack on Pearl Harbor but chose to ignore it because he desired an excuse to push America into war with Japan. In *Rising Sun in the Pacific*, Morison took direct aim at Beard's interpretation, arguing that it was but a confirmation of Beard's debunking tendencies, his general suspicions of government leaders, his midwestern isolationism, and his dialectical materialism.

In several inflammatory articles, including one facetiously titled "History through a Beard," Morison argued that Beard was "endeavoring to inculcate in the rising generation the same self-pity about being tricked into war that bedevilled the generation of the 1920s and 30s." Noting that in his book Beard was "simply indulging in hate against the late Mr. Roosevelt and all he stood for," Morison pointed to the "disquieting resemblance" of Beard's platform "to the economic autarchy practiced by Hitler." He proclaimed *President Roosevelt and the Coming of the War* "the most dishonest work calling itself a history I ever remember reading, excepting some of the Nazi stuff." Supporters of Beard dismissed Morison as a hired gun, a "court historian" paid to cover up the dangerously aggressive and hawkish actions of the Roosevelt administration. Others, like Howard K. Beale, viewed the entire disagreement as a function of Morison's Harvard and New England elitisms.

Despite these outbursts of anger against the historical tendencies of writers like Beard, Morison cultivated a reputation for being "balanced" and evenhanded in his scholarship. In his 1950 presidential address before the American Historical Association, Morison gave voice to a new mode of historical writing, characterized by him with reference to the French word *mesure* (balance) but dubbed "consensus history" by its critics. If Beard and other historians had emphasized the role of conflict in American culture (section versus section, class versus class, ideology versus ideology), then seekers of *mesure*, Morison noted, pursued unified and holistic interpretations of the past, emphasizing the continuity and stability of American history.

Morison's brand of consensus history had deep roots in the nationalism of the postwar period, of course, and its critics complained that it was so "strikingly conservative" in outlook that it threatened to obscure all history of dissent and conflict in American culture. Beale linked Morison to the anticommunist crusade of the 1950s, characterizing Morison's philosophy of history as a McCarthyesque device to stifle freedom of academic expression. But Morison demonstrated frequently that for him *mesure* implied at least rhetorical commitment to both unity and diversity of opinion. In *Freedom in Contemporary Society* (1956), he acknowledged that he feared the "menace of [the] bloated and irresponsible administrative arm" of government more than he feared communism itself, and he urged President Dwight D. Eisenhower not to use government to endanger political freedoms in the name of controlling communism.

While immersed in the controversies of contemporary events, Morison continued in his pursuit of more conventional historical topics as well. In 1957 he received his second Pulitzer Prize for *John Paul Jones: A Sailor's Biography*, and in 1962 he found unexpected success with a small autobiographical volume written during a short period of convalescence titled *One Boy's Boston*. His crowning glory, however, was *The Oxford History of the American People* (1965), an American history textbook written so that students might "love their country's past instead of considering it a bore." Referring to his volume as a variety of that "social history" he had first learned at Harvard sixty years before, Morison focused on how Americans had lived and amused themselves, what sports they had followed, and what arts they had pursued. Indulging his own preferences in a manner in which he had not since the publication of *The Maritime History of Massachusetts*, he was hailed by *Newsweek* as a "matchless anecdotalist," whose opinions were those of "a civilized man talking in a personal, idiosyncratic, crotchety, opinionated, even dogmatic voice."

The histories that Morison produced in his last years retained some of this "breezy" style of presentation while continuing to be grounded solidly in archival and observational research. In the mid-1960s Morison traveled extensively throughout Mexico and Japan to complete a biography of Matthew Calbraith Perry titled *Old Bruin* (1967). Research for two highly readable volumes on the age of discovery in the Americas, *Northern Voyages* (1971) and *Southern Voyages* (1974), took him around the world in pursuit of aerial photographs of ocean currents, landfalls, and colonial outposts.

Morison "retired" unofficially from writing history in 1976. His decision was based not only on the effects of advancing age (he was eighty-eight), but also on a series of personal calamities that had touched his life. In the summer of 1945 Morison's wife of thirty-five years had died of heart failure; in 1949 he had married again, this time to a distant cousin twenty years his junior, Priscilla Shackerford. This singer and Baltimore socialite radically altered Morison's disposition by bringing him, in his own words, passion, variety, and a "light-hearted gaiety that he had never known"; but in 1974 she, too, died, and that loss proved nearly unbearable for Morison.

Never an easy person to get to know, Morison's somewhat crusty and intimidating personality made companionship difficult in the last years of his life. Nor could he rely on his other love, sailing, which was now physically too demanding for him. The final blow to Morison came in May 1976, when he suffered a debilitating stroke and died in Boston.

Morison died as he had lived, the tradition-bound "dean of American historians." Many of his colleagues, even those who had become increasingly distant in recent years, found it hard to believe he was gone. "The end comes as a bit of a shock," wrote one, "as with the cutting down of a tree that has been a neighborhood landmark." Another observed that Morison had "filled the shoes of Francis Parkman for so many years," and that he had "covered so much territory in them" that readers naturally expected him to walk in them forever. Perhaps the most fitting tribute to Morison came from Arthur Schlesinger, Jr., whose father had taught with Morison at Harvard. "One feels that his death breaks a last link to the classic past," Schlesinger wrote. "He was in the apostolic succession, the last heir of the great New England tradition—Bancroft, Parkman, Prescott, Motley, Henry Adams—and there is no one to come after."

So how will Morison be remembered? First and foremost perhaps for the great breadth and diversity of his scholarship. His life and works constitute a virtual chronicle of the American historical profession in the twentieth century, touching nearly all the major personalities and topics of interest over seven decades of development. Additionally, in an age when scholars were increasingly specialized, Morison was eclectic in his interests. Comfortable in discussing fifteenth-century navigation, seventeenth-century ecclesiastical law, or the anticommunist purges of the twentieth century, Morison was one of the last of the truly well-rounded and diverse leaders of the profession. Morison will also be remembered for his narrative style. Whether describing the capriciousness of Columbus, the frailty of the elder John Paul Jones, or the uncertainty of life at sea during war, Morison wrote with a flair that has seldom been approached. Finally, Morison will undoubtedly be remembered for his attempt to carve out a middle ground between the demands of professional scholarship on the one hand and the need to reach a popular audience on the other.

• The most valuable source of information about Morison's career as a historian is the Samuel Eliot Morison Collection, Harvard University Archives, Pusey Library. A smaller holding of Morison papers at Harvard's Houghton Library is mainly associated with the historian's earliest published works, and a substantial collection related to the *History of the United States Naval Operations in World War II* is at the Naval Operations Archives in Washington, D.C. In addition to the published works cited in the text, Morison also wrote *A Prologue to American History: An Inaugural Lecture* (1922), later reprinted in *By Land and by Sea: The Essays and Addresses of Samuel Eliot Morison* (1953); *The Tercentenary History of Harvard* (4 vols., 1930–1936); *Three Centuries of Harvard, 1636–1936* (1936); *Second Voyage of Christopher Columbus* (1939); *Portuguese Voyages to America in the Fifteenth Century* (1940); *History as a Literary Art* (1946); *History of the United States Naval Operations in World War II* (15 vols., 1947–1962); "Faith of a Historian," *American Historical Review* 56 (1951): 261–75; and *Vistas of History* (1964). See also Emily Morison Beck, ed., *Sailor Historian: The Best of Samuel Eliot Morison* (1977).

Gregory M. Pfitzer, *Samuel Eliot Morison's Historical World: In Quest of a New Parkman* (1991), is the only complete book-length study of Morison's life. Other useful biographical sources include Walter Muir Whitehill, "Portrait of the Admiral as a Renaissance Man," *Boston Magazine*, Sept. 1965, pp. 19–24, 52–58; Wilcomb Washburn, "Samuel Eliot Morison, Historian," *William and Mary Quarterly*, 3d ser., 36 (July 1979): 325–52; and P. A. M. Taylor, "Samuel Eliot Morison: Historian," *Journal of American Studies* 2 (1977): 13–26.

GREGORY M. PFITZER

MORLACCHI, Giuseppina (8 Oct. 1836–23 July 1886), ballet dancer, was born in Milan, Italy, the daughter of Antonio Morlacchi and Maria Raimondi (occupations unknown). At the age of six Morlacchi's parents entered her in the ballet school attached to Milan's La Scala Opera House, where she studied with Carlo Blasis, Augusto Hus, and Salvina Calversi. She made her debut in the spring of 1856 at the Teatro Carlo Felice in Genoa in Jules Perrot's ballet *Faust*. Soon thereafter she received an invitation from Benjamin Lumley, director of Her Majesty's Theatre in London, to join the ballet attached to his theater as a second-ranking dancer. For the next eight years she danced in spectacles, pantomimes, and incidental ballets in London. In 1866 Morlacchi toured Europe, performing in Rome, Turin, Naples, and Lisbon. While in Lisbon she met Don Juan de Pol, a theater manager who hired her to come to the United States as the leading dancer in *The Devil's Auction; or, The Golden Branch*, which opened at Banvard's Opera House in New York City on 23 October 1867.

American audiences greatly admired Morlacchi. Slender, graceful, and composed, she did not play the coquette on stage as did many of her Italian colleagues. In *A Book about the Theatre* (1916), Brander Matthews, American dance and theater critic, wrote that "she has skill and style, and poetry; she is a fine pantomimist; she loves her art, and she feels fully that it is an art; she has the tact and the taste to conceal all trace of effort, knowing the hiding of artifice is the supreme proof of art."

In November 1868, with the aid of her business manager, Major Thomas Burke, Morlacchi formed her own dance company, hiring six dancers and several supernumeraries. For repertory she revived ballets she had performed at La Scala, including *Esmeralda* and *La Bayadère*, and choreographed new dances. The company, which performed primarily in Boston with occasional engagements in New York, was well received by critics and was a financial success for Morlacchi. It performed at James Fisk's Grand Opera House in New York City in Shakespeare's *The Tempest* (Apr. 1869), followed by Offenbach's *La Périchole*.

Through these early years in the United States Morlacchi gained a reputation with theater managers as the champion of dancers, those in her company as well as those working elsewhere. Injustices such as the unfair scale of fines (to guard against various backstage infractions) levied by theater managers against performers or the standings of companies of dancers in small towns outside New York, often with no money to pay for tickets home, became occasions for Morlacchi to intervene. She gave benefits in support of the dancers and even took managers to court to correct wrongdoings.

In December 1869, Morlacchi bought a forty-acre farm in Billerica, a community outside Boston, to which she moved her father and her sister. The farm became a frequent refuge from an expanding touring schedule and a rehearsal space where members of her company gathered. In the 1870 season Morlacchi performed *Bluebeard* at Boston's Adelphi Theatre, followed by a transcontinental railway trip to California for an engagement at John McCullough's California Theatre, and then one at Piper's Opera House in Virginia City, Nevada. Morlacchi performed *Masaniello; or, The Mute of Portici* and *The French Spy* as well as *Mytrillo; or, The Orphan of the Pyrenees*. She mimed and danced the leading roles in these productions in the following season as well.

From December 1871 to December 1872 Morlacchi's company toured Philadelphia, Cincinnati, Charleston, and St. Louis. In December 1872 she was asked to join "Buffalo Bill" (William Cody) and "Texas Jack" (John Omohundro) in a new sensational drama, *The Scouts of the Prairie*, in Chicago at Nixon's Opera House. The play was a dramatized version of Ned Buntline's dime novel, *Buffalo Bill's Last Victory; or, Dove Eye the Lodge Queen*. Perhaps the first stage western, this play featured Morlacchi in her first speaking role as the Native American "Dove Eye." In addition to dancing an "Invocation to the Great Spirit" in a buckskin dress and pointe shoes, she spoke her lines clearly, although one critic commented, "her strongly accented English sounds strangely enough coming from the lips of an Indian maiden." Despite general agreement that the play had no literary merit whatever, it succeeded. So impressed were audiences with onstage real-life heroes, bad guys, Indians and renegades, battles, war whoops, shootings, scalpings, stabbings, and maidens in distress that the theater was sold out. The play continued to fill theaters for most of its subsequent tour to St. Louis, Cincinnati, Rochester, Boston, Philadelphia, Richmond, and New York City.

On 31 August 1873 Morlacchi and "Texas Jack" were married in Rochester, and Tom Burke announced Morlacchi's intention to retire from the ballet stage to assist her husband in his theatrical ventures. Although Morlacchi did travel with her husband and Buffalo Bill for most of the 1874–1875 season, she gathered her company together for engagements in the summer. While Omohundro guided foreign visitors on hunting tours of the West, Morlacchi performed in *The Black Crook* and *La Bayadère*. The couple bought a home in Lowell, Massachusetts, a fast-growing mill town close to Billerica. They remained childless.

In 1877 Omohundro broke away from Buffalo Bill and formed his own touring company organized around a star performer. He toured with his wife in three entirely new plays: *Texas Jack on the Plains*, *The Great Divide; or, The Scouts of the Prairie*, and *Texas Jack in the Black Hills*. For the next three years they performed together and separately during the theatrical season. In the spring of 1880 Morlacchi and her husband arrived in Leadville, Colorado, for what were to be their final engagements. Morlacchi was performing in *The Black Crook* at the Grand Central Theatre and Omohundro in *Humpty Dumpty* when he came down with a cold that developed into pneumonia. Although Morlacchi resigned her position to give full attention to her husband, Omohundro died at the age of thirty-three on 28 June 1880. Morlacchi was inconsolable, disbanding her company and retiring from the stage. She returned to Lowell to live with her sister. Although she never returned to professional theater, she did participate in amateur theatricals in Lowell, occasionally choreographing and teaching the local mill girls to dance. She did not establish a school, but she did contribute her talent to the community without compensation. Morlacchi died of cancer at her Billerica farmhouse; she left the bulk of her estate to the Actor's Fund.

Morlacchi is remembered as a major figure in post-Romantic European ballet, whose simple, unaffected performances gave tribute to the excellent training of Carlo Blasis and to the superiority of the Italian school. In the United States she gained a reputation as a versatile actress and dancer, a pioneer performer who took her own company of ballet dancers by overland stages and railroad to mining towns in the West and performed principal roles in ballets within operas, with special success in mime roles. In addition, she acted and danced in early Wild West shows, exposing audiences that had never seen ballet to the best of European dance.

• For discussion of Morlacchi's contribution to American dance see Lillian Moore, "Ballerina and Plainsman: Giuseppina Morlacchi and Texas Jack," in *Echoes of American Ballet*, ed. Ivor Guest (1976), and Barbara Barker, *Ballet or Ballyhoo: The American Careers of Maria Bonfanti, Rita Sangalli and Giuseppina Morlacchi* (1984), which provides useful information on her life. For information on *The Scouts of the Prairie* see Don Russell, *The Lives and Legends of Buffalo Bill* (1960). Materials on Morlacchi's early performances in Italy can be found in the Dance Collection, New York Public Library for the Performing Arts, Lincoln Center, and in the archives of the Museo Teatro alla Scala, Milan, where programs for her apprentice performances between 1852 and 1855 are available. Records of Morlacchi's performances in New York City are in George C. D. Odell, *Annals of the New York Stage* (15 vols., 1927–1949), especially vols. 8, 9, 11. An obituary is in the *New York Dramatic Mirror*, 30 July 1886.

BARBARA BARKER

MORLEY, Christopher Darlington (5 May 1890–28 Mar. 1957), man of letters and editor, was born in Haverford, Pennsylvania, the son of Frank Morley, a mathematics professor at Haverford College, and Lilian Janet Bird, a musician and poet. She taught him to read, and he soon became a voracious reader. The family moved in 1900 to Baltimore, Maryland, where Morley's father taught at Johns Hopkins University and Morley attended school and frequented the Enoch Pratt Library. He enrolled at Haverford College in 1906, published in the school's *Haverfordian*, was on its editorial board, edited his class yearbook, helped write, produce, and act in plays, and was a member of the cricket and soccer teams. After graduating in 1910 as valedictorian of his class, he became a Rhodes scholar at New College, Oxford University, where from 1910 to 1913 he studied modern history. While there he published *The Eighth Sin* (1912), a slim book of poems. Returning to the United States, Morley began a versatile career as poet, novelist, essayist, critic, and editor, supporter of theatrical ventures, book-club judge, and friend of neglected old writers and emerging new ones.

In 1913 Morley obtained an editorial position with Doubleday, Page and Co., publishers, on Long Island, New York. In 1914 he married Helen Booth Fairchild; they had four children. They moved to Philadelphia, where Morley helped edit the *Ladies' Home Journal* (1917–1918); he published his first novel, *Parnassus on Wheels* (1917), another book of poetry (1917), two books of essays (1917, 1920), and *The Haunted Bookshop* (1919); and he wrote for the *Philadelphia Evening Public Ledger* (1918–1920). In 1920 the Morleys moved permanently to Roslyn Heights, Long Island, where he began a column for the *New York Evening Post*, continued until 1923 and followed by a column in the *Saturday Review of Literature* from 1924 to 1938. Meanwhile, his next novel, *Where the Blue Begins* (1922), was one of his most charming. In 1924 he cofounded the *Saturday Review of Literature* and for the next seventeen years edited and wrote for it. In 1925 came *Thunder on the Left*, his most fantastic novel. In 1926, when the Book-of-the-Month Club was founded with Henry Seidel Canby as chairman of the board, Morley was named one of the original members of the book-selecting committee, along with Heywood Broun, Dorothy F. Canfield Fisher, and William Allen White, all of whom were his close friends. For the next twenty-eight years Morley not only read fifteen or so books a month to prepare for his choices but also wrote brief reviews of scores of selections for the club's newsletter. His laudatory introduction to a 1926 edition of Walt Whitman's two *Leaves of Grass* prefaces did much to promote his favorite American poet. An indication of his fecundity is the fact that Doubleday, Page in 1927 issued the "Haverford Collected Edition" of his works in twelve volumes. From 1928 to 1930 he coproduced revival melodramas at two theaters in Hoboken, New Jersey. The experiment ended when an associate embezzled $30,000; Morley repaid the theater loans personally.

During the 1930s Morley was intensely busy. In 1931 he published two of his best novels, *John Mistletoe* and *Human Being*, followed a year later by a weak little one, *Swiss Family Manhattan*. He lectured widely; his series at the University of Pennsylvania was published as *Ex Libris Carissimis* (1932), and another at the University of Hawaii as *Shakespeare and Hawaii* (1933). He cofounded the Baker Street Irregulars in 1934 for Sherlock Holmes fans like himself. He coedited Bartlett's *Familiar Quotations* (11th ed., 1937). In the 1930s Morley collected many of his essays in five books, published his tenth book of clever, tender verse, and provided prefatory material for editions of works by three authors he especially revered—H. H. Munro (1930), William Shakespeare (1936), and Laurence Sterne (1938).

Morley's sensational novel, *Kitty Foyle*, rounded out the decade dramatically when it appeared in 1939. It made the bestseller lists that year and the next and was the basis of a 1942 movie starring Ginger Rogers. *Kitty Foyle* is the stream-of-consciousness narrative, once shocking (and even banned in places) but now mild enough, of a modern working girl. She vigorously loves a Philadelphia scion but aborts his baby to permit his marrying another whom his stuffy family approves; she survives the depression and becomes a successful, witty career woman of the sort Morley long observed and much admired.

In the 1940s Morley edited material by Whitman (1940), Sir Francis Bacon (1944), and his close friend, the humorist Don Marquis (1946). He also laboriously reedited Bartlett (12th ed., 1948), replacing some former favorites with items from recent poets (including himself). His last novel was *The Man Who Made Friends with Himself* (1949). In 1951 he suffered a severe stroke, followed by two others that limited his productivity. Three days after he died in Roslyn Heights, a message sending his "unchanged love" and "gratitude" to his professional and personal friends appeared in the *New York Times* and the *New York Herald Tribune* (both 1 Apr. 1957). Although Morley hated it when reviewers labeled his writing "whimsical" and once called the word an "emetic epithet," this tender farewell to his chums is precisely that.

Although Morley wanted most of all—at least early in his career—to be a poet, his novels attracted his widest audience and perhaps best reveal his versatility. *Parnassus on Wheels* tells of a traveling bookseller; he meets a farmer's sister who wants to write and buys his van, and off they go together. *The Haunted Bookshop* continues the story of their married life in Brooklyn; it has a subplot involving a German bomb threat and is marred by bookish digressions. *Where the Blue Begins* is an allegorical, satirical dog story; Gissing, a philosophical dog named after George Gissing (another of Morley's favorite authors), leaves Canine Estates in search of life's meaning, becomes a floorwalker for Beagle and Co., and tries being a clergyman and then a sailor, pondering all the while. *Thunder on the Left* is a fantasy in which children at a boy's tenth birthday party become adults whose lives the boy, while remaining a child, spies on and participates in; many reviewers, including Babette Deutsch and Lloyd Morris, praised it greatly.

The autobiographical *John Mistletoe* narrates the hero's years at Haverford, Oxford, Paris, and back home; noteworthy is its style, which expertly skirts close to the precious and the didactic while remaining simply polished. *Human Being* presents in flashbacks the efforts of an old businessman to lay out revealing events in the life of a seemingly drab employee, now dead; the reader never sees the subject directly, but a few key experiences define him as quietly, heartbreakingly human. *Swiss Family Manhattan* describes a family crash-landing atop the Empire State Building and descending to observe ugly Americans at street level. A reviewer of this strained work noted, unkindly but perhaps correctly, that Morley "writes too much and too easily to reach the heights of his possibilities" (*Saturday Review of Literature*, 9 Jan. 1932).

The Man Who Made Friends with Himself, which Morley wrote carefully, was the work that he considered most challenging, and it was his favorite. It features a literary agent who vigorously loves not only his psychiatrist's body but also her mind, values and seeks individuality, and meets his Doppelganger. Reviewers lauded the novel's sparkle, which includes erudite diction, literary allusions, James Joyce–like puns, and aphorisms, some of which are a little bitter—for example, "Letters, like prayers, should have no expectancy. . . . They . . . [are] the divinely casual dysentery of the day."

Morley, whose works became neglected after his death, was a keenly intelligent, prolific, versatile writer. He was the close and loyal friend of unnumbered fellow literary and "ordinary" people, and he was what he called a "mediator," ever at pains to explain to the public that literature is a treasure that can enrich all lives. In 1966 "The Knothole," a cabin he built behind his Roslyn Heights home to write and entertain in, was moved and made part of Christopher Morley Park in Nassau County, New York, a memorial to his desire to reach the general public with literature.

• Most of Morley's papers are in the Berg Collection of the New York Public Library and in libraries at Haverford College and the University of Texas at Austin. Guy R. Lyle and H. Tatnall Brown, Jr., *A Bibliography of Christopher Morley* (1952), is exceptionally thorough. John T. Winterich, "Certain Essential Preliminary Footnotage," humorously glosses time-obscured references and allusions in a reprint of *Parnassus on Wheels* (1955), pp. 7–15. *Bright Cages: The Selected Poems of Christopher Morley and Translations from the Chinese*, ed. Jon Bracker (1965), is a representative collection, but the "translations" included are merely imitations. Morley's prefaces and introductions were gathered into *Prefaces without Books* (1970). Helen McK. Oakley, *Three Hours for Lunch: The Life and Times of Christopher Morley* (1976), is a detailed biography. John Tebbel, *Between Covers: The Rise and Transformation of American Book Publishing* (1987), discusses Morley's relationship with the publisher Frank Nelson Doubleday. Charles Lee, *The Hidden Public: The Story of the Book-of-the-Month Club* (1958), explains Morley's work for the club. Richard D. Altick, "Average Citizen in Grub Street: Christopher Morley after Twenty-Five Years," *South Atlantic Quarterly* 41 (Jan. 1942): 18–31, is an insightful essay. Mark I. Wallach and Jon Bracker, *Christopher Morley* (1976), provides broad biographical and critical coverage. An obituary is in the *New York Times*, 29 Mar. 1957.

ROBERT L. GALE

MORLEY, Edward Williams (29 Jan. 1838–24 Feb. 1923), chemist, was born in Newark, New Jersey, the son of Sardis Brewster Morley, a Congregational minister, and Anna Treat, a former teacher. First educated at home, in West Hartford, Connecticut, and Attleboro, Massachusetts, as his father moved to pulpits of successively higher-status churches, Morley showed an early interest in chemistry and studied popular author Jane Marcet's *Conversations on Chemistry* (2 vols., 1809) and Yale chemist Benjamin Silliman's textbooks. In 1857 he entered, as a sophomore, Williams College, his father's alma mater, where the teachings of the college's president, moral philosopher Mark Hopkins, and of astronomer Albert Hopkins proved most influential. After earning a B.A. in 1860, Morley remained at Williams for about a year to work with Albert Hopkins, under whose direction he mounted a transit instrument and measured the college's latitude.

Following his father's lead, Morley then began preparing for the ministry and entered Andover Theological Seminary in 1861. After three years, he was licensed as a minister of the gospel in the Congregational church, and in the fall of 1864 he joined other well-educated northerners in avoiding military duty by becoming a relief agent for the U.S. Sanitary Commission at Fort Monroe, Virginia. There he served the needs of convalescent Union soldiers in the last months of the Civil War. He then taught several subjects, including chemistry, through 1868 at the South Berkshire Institute, New Marlboro, Massachusetts, and in that year accepted the pastorate of a Congregational church in Twinsburg, Ohio. Soon after moving west, however, he accepted the offer of Western Reserve College in nearby Hudson, Ohio, of a professorship of chemistry, botany, mineralogy, and geology in order to avoid the chore of preaching. He entered his new position on 1 January 1869, a week after he married Isabel Ashley Birdsall of West Winsted, Connecticut. The couple had no children.

At Western Reserve College, Morley established a program of chemistry teaching that soon displaced his other duties and involved more laboratory instruction than similar contemporary programs. He supported it with personal subscriptions to at least thirty European chemical journals, and his reading of them soon completed his education in chemistry. In 1873 he also began to teach at the Cleveland Medical School as professor of chemistry and toxicology (a position he held through 1888), and soon thereafter he began a fairly lucrative consulting practice in analytic chemistry. At Western Reserve he also began a research program in chemistry that continuously demonstrated his interest in precision measurement, particularly of, what he called, the constants of nature. His first scientific paper, on the latitude of Williams College (*Proceedings of the American Academy of Arts and Sciences* 6 [1866]: 384–90), had already illustrated this interest, and his penultimate paper, presented in 1912, bore the title "Fundamental Chemical Constants."

Morley's research program focused successively on three major problems. In the early 1870s Yale meteorologist Elias Loomis theorized that winter cold snaps derived not from blasts of arctic air but instead were caused by cold air falling from high altitudes. Morley reasoned that, since oxygen itself is heavier than the air of which it is a relatively small component, air from higher altitudes would be less rich in oxygen than that from lower altitudes, so that, if Loomis were correct, colder air would contain less oxygen than warmer air. Throughout the 1870s Morley analyzed hundreds of samples of air collected at different temperatures by weather stations throughout the United States and, in doing so, gradually evolved continually more precise techniques of gas analysis. His conclusions, published in 1880, supported Loomis's theory, but chemists read with greater interest Morley's series of twelve papers, published between 1879 and 1881, that described how he modified standard laboratory equipment to allow him to analyze air samples rapidly, accurately, and precisely.

In 1882 Western Reserve College moved to Cleveland as Western Reserve University, and in his new setting Morley gradually implemented a fifteen-year research program that was designed to determine the precise relative atomic weights of oxygen and hydrogen. Like most chemists before him, he focused his attention on the reaction through which these gases form water, and the procedures he developed eliminated all identifiable sources of experimental error and all impurities in the gases he used. At each experimental stage he measured all relevant quantities, and his data thus allowed him to perform two independent calculations of oxygen's relative atomic weight: one that was based on direct weighing of the gases and their product, and another on volume and density measurements. In 1895 Morley determined the relative atomic weight of oxygen (within one part in ten thousand) to be 15.879. His colleagues honored his achievement by electing him to the National Academy of Sciences in 1897, and to the presidencies of the American Association for the Advancement of Science in 1895 and the American Chemical Society in 1899. They also awarded him three gold medals, and in a 1903 survey they ranked him as the second most eminent American chemist, after Ira Remsen of Johns Hopkins. In "A Completed Chapter in the History of the Atomic Theory," his 1896 address as retiring president of the American Association, Morley argued that his experiments had finally laid to rest Prout's hypothesis of 1815, which suggested that all atoms comprise conglomerations of hydrogen atoms.

In the mid-1880s Morley collaborated with Albert A. Michelson, a physicist at the nearby Case School of Applied Science, whose interest in the phenomena of light had led him to try to measure the "ether drift" postulated by all contemporary wave theories of light. Despite his extensive grant support, Michelson lacked the experimental skills that characterized Morley's work, and he looked to his colleague for assistance. Morley apparently thought Michelson's experiments might yield insights into the constants of nature, and he refined Michelson's procedures and apparatus; for example, he mounted Michelson's interferometer, which split beams of light in two, on a stone platform that floated in mercury, and thus eliminated sources of optical distortion. Their experiments failed to detect any ether drift, and some argue that its null result helped lead Albert Einstein in 1905 to his theory of special relativity. Neither Michelson nor Morley accepted their own results, and after Michelson left Cleveland in 1888 Morley continued experiments designed to detect ether drift with Dayton C. Miller, Michelson's successor at Case.

In 1906 Morley retired to West Hartford, Connecticut, where he spent the rest of his life. There, in a chemical laboratory in his home, he analyzed many geological samples collected in what is now Indonesia by his neighbor Joseph P. Iddings. Morley died in West Hartford.

In arguing that all atoms comprise protons, neutrons, and electrons, late twentieth-century chemists accept an updated form of Prout's hypothesis and thus understand that the uneven atomic weight that Morley measured derives from mixtures of different isotopes of oxygen. Because late nineteenth-century chemists lacked this perspective, they honored Morley for attacking, and apparently solving, one of science's longest-lived problems. Morley enjoyed their esteem, but, according to some colleagues, his excessive modesty prevented him from achieving even more by attracting greater support for his work. Like many of his contemporaries, however, Morley rarely saw himself as a professional scientist in the same way that Michelson, for example, did. His career thus represents, for better or for worse, that of the last generation of "gentlemen scientists."

• A collection of Morley's letters is in the Manuscript Division of the Library of Congress, Washington, D.C., and in photocopy form at the Case Western Reserve University Archives, Cleveland, which also hold his laboratory notebooks. His collection of chemical journals may be consulted at the Case Western Reserve University Library. Morley's principal work, *On the Densities of Oxygen and Hydrogen*, appeared in 1895. A full biography by Howard R. Williams, *Edward Williams Morley: His Influence on Science in America* (1957), contains a full list of Morley's publications, as does an obituary by Frank W. Clarke in National Academy of Sciences, *Biographical Memoirs* 21, no. 10 (1926): 1–8. An obituary by Olin Freeman Tower in *Science* 57 (1923): 431–34, also is useful. Stephen S. Visher, *Scientists Starred, 1903–1943, in "American Men of Science"* (1947), reports the American chemical community's 1903 ranking of its members.

MICHAEL M. SOKAL

MORLEY, Frank (9 Sept. 1860–17 Oct. 1937), mathematician, was born in Woodbridge, Suffolk, England, the son of Quaker parents, Joseph Roberts Morley, the proprietor of a china store, and Elizabeth Muskett. Morley's early passion and skill in chess led him to meet the Astronomer Royal, Sir George Biddell Airy, who shared the same enthusiasm. This friendship, combined with Morley's strong scholastic record at the Seckford Grammar School, enabled him to win an Open Scholarship to King's College, Cambridge. Morley entered Cambridge in 1879, where illness delayed completion of his undergraduate studies until 1884. At Cambridge he did not adjust well to the strenuous demands required for achieving a high place in the Mathematical Tripos. Although recognized as being in no way commensurate with his abilities, Morley's poor showing precluded him from receiving a fellowship. Unable to remain in Cambridge, he accepted a school mastership at Bath College (1884–1887), where he regained his health and mathematical confidence.

In 1887 Morley came to the United States as an instructor at Haverford College in Pennsylvania. From 1888 to 1900 he served as professor of mathematics there. In 1889 he married Lilian Janet Bird of Hayward's Heath, Sussex, England; they had three sons, all of whom achieved prominence. Morley's Haverford years were likely the most congenial and mathematically creative of his life as they involved his close association and friendship with the Cambridge-trained mathematicians Charlotte A. Scott and James Harkness, both of nearby Bryn Mawr College. With Harkness, he wrote *A Treatise on the Theory of Functions* (1893), which was later improved and reissued as *Introduction to the Theory of Analytic Functions* (1898). Well received on both sides of the Atlantic, these were among the first advanced level textbooks on pure mathematics to be produced in the United States.

They still offer a valuable perspective on the state of function theory as it existed at the end of the century. Almost half of Morley's mathematical publications appeared in his Haverford period, and during this time he became well known through his editorial service for the *Bulletin of the American Mathematical Society* and the *American Journal of Mathematics*.

In 1900 Morley's life underwent a radical change when he was called to the Johns Hopkins University as professor and head of the mathematics department. The latter position included editorship of the *American Journal of Mathematics*, and he discharged these duties for the next thirty years. The Hopkins program in mathematics had been initiated by the great British mathematician James J. Sylvester, who had been one of the university's first professors (1876–1883). Between 1878 and 1900, the Hopkins mathematical program had flourished and produced over a third of the American doctorates awarded in mathematics. In 1900, however, the program was in disarray, and the appointment of Morley was intended to remedy this situation. Morley, who largely fulfilled these expectations, proved himself a wise choice. He served as professor and department head until his retirement in 1928 and continued to supervise doctoral students until 1931, producing a total of forty-eight Hopkins doctorates. In 1903, when *American Men of Science* rated the leaders in American science, Morley was rated seventh on a list of eighty mathematicians. In 1919–1920 he was president of the American Mathematical Society.

Morley was an inspiring teacher who was particularly concerned with finding problems that were appropriate to his doctoral students' abilities. His son Frank V. Morley recalled that such duties, and the seemingly endless stream of students, prompted the family to bestow the nickname "Doctors" on the elder Morley. Many of his most promising ideas were passed on to his students, and Morley published *in toto* only some seventy-five research papers.

Morley's mathematical interests were unusual and largely concerned with isolated geometric problems and configurations. As he would have readily admitted, pleasant questions with elegant and unexpected answers held a lasting fascination for him. His often ingenious results include the remarkable Morley's theorem (c. 1899), Morley chains (1900), and the clever use of complex numbers and inversions in geometric problems. This last topic was a favorite of Morley, and a twenty-year collaboration with his son F. V. Morley, led to the book *Inversive Geometry* (1933). Perhaps his most characteristic work, it has remained the only definitive study of the subject. Today much of Morley's research seems of less than compelling significance, and one is tempted to regard his interests as those of a talented amateur—an artist who took delight in small and beautiful things—rather than those of a professional mathematician. Yet, whatever significance one chooses to attach to them, Morley must be given credit for both finding and solving such questions. Morley died peacefully at his home in Baltimore. Although a U.S. resident for almost fifty years, he died a British citizen.

Morley's contribution to American mathematical life rests primarily on his three books; his impressive number of doctoral students, who were much in demand by American universities; and his yeoman service to the mathematics program at Johns Hopkins. At a critical juncture he was largely responsible for saving this program, which, in less capable hands, might well have ceased to exist. He was fondly remembered by his colleagues and friends as a kind and courtly gentleman who was gifted with a lively imagination.

• Morley's retiring address as president of the American Mathematical Society, "Pleasant Questions and Wonderful Effects," *Bulletin of the American Mathematical Society* 27 (Apr. 1921): 309–12, provides an interesting glimpse of his style and taste. F. V. Morley, *My One Contribution to Chess* (1946), contains a number of personal reminiscences. A biographical sketch of Morley by R. C. Archibald in *A Semicentennial History of the American Mathematical Society, 1888–1938* 1 (1938): 194–201, includes a roster of his doctoral students and a complete list of his publications. Obituary notices containing detailed comments on his research can be found in the *Bulletin of the American Mathematical Society* 44 (Mar. 1938): 167–70, and the *Journal of the London Mathematical Society* 14 (Jan. 1939): 73–78. An obituary is in the *New York Times*, 18 Oct. 1937.

JOSEPH D. ZUND

MORLEY, Sylvanus Griswold (7 June 1883–2 Sept. 1948), Maya archaeologist and epigrapher, was born in Chester, Pennsylvania, the son of Colonel Benjamin Franklin Morley, a professor of chemistry, and Sarah Eleanor Constance de Lannoy. When Morley was ten years old, the family moved to Buena Vista, Colorado, where he began to express serious interest in archaeology. He nevertheless attended the Pennsylvania Military College and received a degree in civil engineering in 1904, a year after his father's death; he then immediately enrolled at Harvard University to study archaeology. Under the tutelage of Frederic Putnam and Alfred Tozzer, Morley abandoned his plan to study Egyptology and instead turned to the lesser known ancient Maya. At Harvard he earned a B.A. in 1907, followed by an M.A. and a fellowship in American research in 1908. During these years he made several trips to Yucatan and also worked in the Southwest. He never pursued a Ph.D. but received an honorary doctorate from the Pennsylvania Military College in 1921.

As a fellow at the School of American Archaeology in Santa Fe, New Mexico, an affiliate of the Archaeological Institute of America (later the School of American Research), from 1909 to 1914, Morley launched his career in Maya archaeology. He spent the years from 1910 to 1912 at Quiriguá, Guatemala, which led to the eventual publication of *Guidebook to the Ruins of Quiriguá* (1935). The restoration work at Quiriguá, much of it overseen by Morley, was the first to be undertaken at any Maya site.

In 1914 the Carnegie Institution of Washington accepted Morley's proposal to excavate Chichén Itzá,

Yucatan. A year later the institute appointed him research associate in American archaeology. These achievements marked a turning point in his career and brought the powerful Carnegie Institution into the Maya field, a development that shaped the course of pre–World War II Maya archaeology. Many new excavations were undertaken, and a battery of distinguished Mayanists got their start on these projects, usually at Morley's personal invitation. Morley headed the Carnegie program until 1929, when Alfred Vincent Kidder was named the director of the Division of Historical Research; Kidder's appointment effectively took administrative control of the Maya program out of Morley's hands.

Political turmoil in Mexico delayed the Chichén Itzá project until 1924. In the interim, Morley proceeded with a second grand scheme, "a plan for a comprehensive study of the Maya inscriptions." In the mold of earlier explorers like Alfred Maudslay and Teobert Maler, Morley embarked on daring expeditions into the remote jungles of Mexico and Guatemala to record new sites and monuments. His greatest single achievement in exploration came in 1916 with the discovery of Uaxactún; the site yielded some of the most important archaeological findings in pre–World War II Maya research. Morley has one of the most impressive records of any explorer of the Maya region, and he returned there annually from 1909 until the year of his death. Although he was not a robust individual and disdained the hardships of a tropical environment, he was so intent on finding new hieroglyphic inscriptions or, as he colorfully put it, to "bring home the epigraphic bacon," that he returned year after year.

Morley was at heart an epigrapher. His early work on Maya hieroglyphic writing culminated in *An Introduction to the Study of Maya Hieroglyphs* (1915), the most influential general book on the subject until mid-century. He later published *The Inscriptions at Copan* (1920), which in its ambitious scope as the first exhaustive study of the inscriptions of a single Maya site set the stage for his magnum opus, the five-volume *Inscriptions of Petén* (1937–1938). This work won him the Duc de Loubat Prize from Columbia University and the Guatemalan Order of the Quetzal.

Morley was mainly interested in the chronological portion of texts and paid little heed to "unknown hieroglyphs," that is, the historical portion of texts unrecognized as such in Morley's day. His epigraphic research led to the decipherment of a variant of the *tun* (360-day period) glyph, the end of *tun* glyph, and the five-*tun* and ten-*tun* anniversary glyphs. He established the general lunar significance of the Supplementary Series (a set of glyphs following the major calendrical glyphs that lead off many Maya descriptions) in "The Supplementary Series in the Maya Inscriptions" (*Holmes Anniversary Volume* [1916]), a study that was also a stepping-stone in the decipherment of Glyph A, which specifies the length of a lunar month. Morley is less well known, however, for breakthrough epigraphic discoveries than for amassing an enormous database of primarily calendrical inscriptions through his relentless field explorations. He was also the first to decipher hundreds of dates on stone monuments.

Known as "Vay" to his friends, Morley was a generous, outgoing man whose boundless enthusiasm for the Maya made him one of their greatest popularizers. According to Maya archaeologist Alberto Ruz, Morley considered Maya culture "the most brilliant on the planet." Morley's lectures and articles, especially those appearing in the 1920s and 1930s in *National Geographic* with dramatic scenes in brilliant color, stimulated public interest as never before. He made his vast knowledge accessible to a wide audience in *The Ancient Maya* (1946), his final, great synthesis of the pre-Hispanic Maya, which set a standard for future works of this genre.

Morley's marriage in 1908 to Alice Gallinger Williams, with whom he had his only child, ended in divorce in 1915. He married Frances Ann Rhoads in 1927. His American home base was Santa Fe, where he played an important role in architectural preservation. He was appointed director of the School of American Research in 1947 and, at the time of his death in Santa Fe, had planned to assume that post on retirement from the Carnegie Institution.

• Morley's personal papers related to his Carnegie years are at the Peabody Museum of Archaeology and Ethnology, Harvard University. Robert L. Brunhouse, *Sylvanus G. Morley and the World of the Ancient Maya* (1971), is the most complete biography. The flavor of Morley's ebullient personality emerges most fully in a collection of anecdotes in Arthur J. O. Anderson, ed., *Morleyana* (1950), and a hilarious personal reminiscence by Ed Shook, "Recollections of a Carnegie Archaeologist," *Ancient Mesoamerica* 1, no. 2 (1990): 247–52. A critical view of Morley's role in the history of Maya hieroglyphic decipherment is in Michael D. Coe, *Breaking the Maya Code* (1992). Noteworthy obituaries are by Ralph L. Roys and Margaret W. Harrison in *American Antiquity* 3 (1949): 215–19, and J. Eric S. Thompson in *American Anthropologist* 51 (1949): 293–97.

ANDREA STONE

MORPHY, Paul Charles (22 June 1837–10 July 1884), chess champion, was born in New Orleans, Louisiana, the son of Alonzo Morphy, a Louisiana Supreme Court justice, and Louise Therese Felicite Thelcide LeCarpentier, composer of operettas. Morphy grew up in a wealthy, prominent family in antebellum New Orleans, receiving private tutoring and a deeply religious training in the Roman Catholic faith. He fit the commonly accepted definition of a child prodigy. By age eight, he had gained mastery in chess over his father and uncle, both recognized club players in the city. He also gained notoriety at that age by defeating General Winfield Scott in a two-game match. In 1850, just after his thirteenth birthday, he astounded the chess world by besting Janos J. Lowenthal, a Hungarian master, in a three-game match. After completing academy training in New Orleans, Morphy attended Spring Hill College, a Jesuit institution in Mobile, Alabama, and then finished the two-year legal curriculum at the University of Louisiana. In 1858 he passed the Louisiana bar exam with ease because he had memorized the entire Louisiana Civil Code in both English and French.

Since Morphy had to wait a year before taking the bar exam, he accepted an invitation from the nation's most prestigious chess clubs to participate in the first National Chess Congress in New York in 1857 to determine the first American chess champion. The "experts" from Boston, New York, and Philadelphia paid little attention to the slightly built, softspoken 21-year-old from New Orleans. To their astonishment, however, Morphy easily captured first place with fourteen wins, one loss, and three draws. In the final match for the championship, Morphy crushed his rival, Louis Paulsen of Dubuque, Iowa, with five wins and one loss. In the second of his wins against Paulsen, Morphy made a spectacular sacrifice of his queen in a game that has remained a favorite of chess fans ever since.

Prompted by his sensational victory at the National Chess Congress, Morphy's American supporters urged him to match his skills with the leading European players. He was especially eager to play Howard Staunton of Birmingham, England, an eminent Shakespearean scholar who was widely acknowledged as one of the world's top players. Staunton accepted a challenge from Morphy for a match, with a stake of $5,000. However, when Morphy arrived in England in June 1858, Staunton repeatedly found excuses to avoid playing. For two months, Morphy played and defeated England's other leading players.

In September 1858 he journeyed to Paris, where he challenged the best players on the Continent. While in Paris, the young American could be found most nights at the renowned Café de la Régence demonstrating his amazing ability. On 27 September he played eight strong opponents simultaneously, with his back to the board. The ten-hour exhibition resulted in six wins and only two draws for Morphy. He became a celebrity in the French capital, feted and toasted at innumerable banquets and parties, and besieged by eligible young ladies of Parisian society. Morphy often accepted invitations by members of the nobility to accompany them to the opera, and on 2 November 1858 he played what is perhaps his most famous game. While attending a performance of *The Barber of Seville* as the guest of the duke of Brunswick and Count Isouard de Vauvenargue, Morphy defeated his noble opponents with successive sacrifices of his knight, bishop, rook, and queen. The caliber of his opponents was quite low, but Morphy's game proved so aesthetically pleasing that it remains a favorite of chess fans.

In October 1858 Morphy challenged Adolf Anderssen, a German mathematics professor generally considered the world's strongest player, to a match for the world championship. In early December 1858 the match took place. Morphy scored a decisive seven wins, two losses, and two draws victory, leaving him unquestionably the best chess player in the world. Although no official world championship of chess existed at the time, Morphy's preeminence was universally acknowledged. In May 1859 Morphy returned to the United States, where he was feted at huge testimonial banquets in New York and Boston. Such luminaries as Oliver Wendell Homes, Jared Sparks, Henry Wadsworth Longfellow, Louis Agassiz, and Edward Everett lauded his spectacular triumph. In early 1860 Morphy issued a challenge: he would play anyone in the world, giving the odds himself. After no one accepted his offer, Morphy retired from active chess competition. With the exception of a few off-hand games with friends, he refused to play competitive chess. He opened a law practice in New Orleans, but potential clients regarded chess players as athletes and would not respect his legal ability. He spent the Civil War years in Havana, Cuba, and Paris and, other than a brief visit to Paris in 1867, spent the remainder of his life in New Orleans. In the 1870s and 1880s, Morphy displayed symptoms of mental illness. He aimlessly wandered the streets, borrowing money and vehemently denouncing anyone who mentioned chess. Morphy never married. He was found dead in his bathtub in his home in New Orleans. His personal physician listed the cause of death as "apoplexy and heat prostration."

Morphy has been called the "pride and sorrow of chess" because of his fantastic ability and because of his abrupt retirement from active competition at the height of his powers. Several psychoanalytical studies of Morphy have been written, attributing his refusal to play chess again to such "disorders" as homosexuality, an overreliance on his mother, and a paranoic fear of losing mastery over his game. Such hypotheses, of course, cannot be verified. While there is insufficient evidence to accurately explain Morphy's behavior from 1860 until his death, it can be stated with accuracy that by retiring at such an early age Morphy deprived chess devotees of many years of the highest quality examples of this complex, fascinating game.

Like his twentieth-century American counterpart Bobby Fischer, who also retired at the height of his powers, Morphy remains one of the most enigmatic figures in the history of chess. He so towered over his competition that his true abilities were never really tested. Like all chess players, Morphy made mistakes he could have avoided and lost games he could have won. Some of his games exhibit a distinct unease with such closed systems as the French defense. Of far more significance, Morphy emphasized rapid development of the pieces and demonstrated his ability to discern the significance of the control over certain dark and light squares. His defense to the Ruy Lopez, the most popular, widely used of all chess openings, has not been improved on, while his maneuvering of the pieces to obtain a favorable position for the endgame remains a trademark of contemporary chess masters. The brilliance of his games and the widespread adulation he received for them enormously enhanced the popularity of chess at home and abroad and made Morphy one of the most revered names in the game's history.

• No collection of Morphy's writings is known to exist, although individual letters and manuscripts of his games can be found in the Paul Morphy Collection at the Cleveland, Ohio, Public Library. Of the numerous books about Morphy, published in over a dozen languages, the most reliable is David Lawson, *Paul Morphy: The Pride and Sorrow of Chess* (1976). For a scholarly study, see Michael L. Kurtz, "Paul Morphy: Louisiana's Chess Champion," *Louisiana History* 34 (1993): 175–99. Another work worth perusing is Philip W. Sergeant, *Morphy's Games of Chess* (1957), especially valuable for the moves of most of his games.

Morphy is the central character in a novel by New Orleans author Frances Parkinson Keyes, *The Chess Players* (1960). His games have undergone continuous analysis since they were played, with *Chess Life* containing the most valuable studies, including Arthur Bisguier, "Morphy vs. Fischer: The Inevitable Comparison," Sept. 1987, pp. 32–37. A personal reminiscence of Morphy by Charles A. Maurian is "Paul Morphy," New Orleans *Picayune*, 17 Jan. 1909. An obituary is in the New Orleans *Times-Democrat*, 11 July 1884.

MICHAEL L. KURTZ

MORRELL, Benjamin (5 July 1795–1839), sealing captain and explorer, was born in Rye, New York, the son of Benjamin Morrell, a shipbuilder. His mother's name is unknown. When he was less than a year old, the family moved to Stonington, Connecticut, on the shore of Long Island Sound, where his father began his shipbuilding career. Benjamin was a sickly child until he was ten years old, at which time, as his health improved, his interests focused on the sea. In March 1812 he ran away to sea, sailing from New York on the ship *Enterprise*, captained by Alexander Cartwright, with a cargo of contraband flour. The cargo was sold at Cadiz, despite its being under bombardment by the French. Morrell calls the experience of being in a city under siege "grand and sublime," and says that from that time he "became romantically fond of hazardous and desperate enterprises." During the return voyage, on the Banks of Newfoundland, the ship was captured by the British sloop *Hazard*, and the entire crew was confined in a prison ship at St. John's for about eight months.

Returning home and hearing of the American naval victories against the British in 1812–1813, he rejected his father's advice to improve his minimal education but instead, seeking glory, signed on to the American privateer *Joel Barlow*. The ship eventually took on a cargo for France as well as passengers, including Mordecai M. Noah, consul to Tunis. After an unremarkable cruise, the *Joel Barlow* was captured by the British frigate *Briton*, and Morrell spent almost two years at Dartmoor prison. Subsequently, he made a number of deep-sea voyages as a sailor on commercial vessels, mostly to the Pacific, until Captain Josiah Macy took an interest in him and saw to it that he learned what he needed to know to qualify for officer rank.

In 1819 Morrell was married, though his *Narrative of Four Voyages, to the South Sea, North and South Pacific Ocean, Chinese Sea, Ethiopic and Southern Atlantic Ocean, Indian and Antarctic Ocean. From the Year 1822 to 1831* (1832), on which his reputation rests, does not mention his wife's name. By 1822 he had his first command, the schooner *Wasp*. That sealing voyage (1822–1824) was followed by three more, also in schooners: one in the *Tartar* (1824–1826), and two in the *Antarctic* (1828–1829, 1829–1831)—the last two focused largely on exploration. In June 1824 he returned from the *Wasp* voyage to learn that his wife and their two children had died in his absence. Before leaving again on 19 July, he married his fifteen-year-old cousin Abby Jane Wood, who later accompanied him on the second *Antarctic* voyage and also "wrote" her own narrative of it (1833—actually ghostwritten by Samuel L. Knapp, author of *Lectures on American Literature*).

Morrell's later travels produced no notable results. Though his commercial voyage to the Pacific in the schooner *Margaret Oakley* (begun in 1834) seems to have been promising, the vessel was blown onto the beach at Madagascar and wrecked. By report, the indefatigable Morrell sometime later fitted out a trading vessel in the West Indies and sailed for the Pacific by way of Mozambique—where he died of fever.

Though a sealer, and a trader always on the lookout for profitable ventures, such as in *bêche-de-mer*, Morrell sought renown in exploration. His accounts of contact with the islands of the South Pacific do remain important, whatever one may think of his ethnocentric interpretations of those peoples and his killing numbers of them in apparent self-defense. His assertions of discovery and primacy, if true, would make him significant in Antarctic exploration. He claims to have been the first American captain to cross the Antarctic Circle, reaching 70°14′S, where he found the Weddell Sea free of ice—justifying his belief that if only he had not had to turn back for water and fuel he might have been able to sail virtually to the South Pole. Morrell also claims to have seen "New South Greenland," discovered earlier by Captain Robert Johnson, near 67°S, 48°W.

Morrell's Antarctic claims have been challenged, and in some cases proved wrong. Sir Ernest Shackleton, for example, disproved the existence of New South Greenland in 1915. Morrell's too-frequent errors in position are probably due in part to carelessness, but also to his having to rely solely on a magnetic compass and his inability (because of weather) to take frequent sun sights. He had no chronometer. Morrell has been accused of being "the Baron Munchausen of the Pacific," and, somewhat less pejoratively, his descriptions have been called more imaginative than true. Since he described nonexistent ruins in Patagonia and equally imaginary albatross-penguin rookeries, the judgment of an overactive imagination seems reasonable. His style—melodramatic, clichéd, sentimental, and self-justifying—raises doubts. But such qualities may be largely due to the poet Samuel Woodworth, who made Morrell's notes and materials into a book under an arrangement with Morrell's publishers, J. and J. Harper. Since it is distorted by inaccuracy, altered by imagination, and presented in deficient prose, Morrell's *Narrative* will no doubt remain a work of dubious value.

• Morrell's manuscripts may no longer exist. The only other firsthand account of his exploring and commercial activities is Thomas Jefferson Jacobs, *Scenes, Incidents, and Adventures in the Pacific Ocean . . . during the Cruise of the Clipper Margaret Oakley under Capt. Benjamin Morrell* (1844). Significant twentieth-century commentary on Morrell and his claims includes Rupert T. Gould, *Enigmas* (1929); E. W. Hunter Christie, *The Antarctic Problem* (1951); Philip I. Mitterling, *America in the Antarctic to 1840* (1959); and Burton R. Pollin, "The Narrative of Benjamin Morrell: Out of 'The Bucket' and into Poe's *Pym*," *Studies in American Fiction* (1976). The true authorship of Morrell's *Four Voyages* is revealed in Eugene Exman, *The Brothers Harper* (1965).

HASKELL SPRINGER

MORRIL, David Lawrence (10 June 1772–28 Jan. 1849), physician, clergyman, and politician, was born in Epping, New Hampshire, the son of Samuel Morril, a clergyman, and Anna Lawrence. David grew up in a comfortable, stable home. His father and paternal grandfather were Harvard-educated Congregational ministers; his maternal grandfather, David Lawrence, was a wealthy farmer in Epping. But when his father died in 1785, young David was sent to live first with his paternal grandfather, who wanted him to become a physician, and then with his maternal grandfather, who wanted him to run his farm. Not until his mother married Dr. Timothy Johnson of Epping was it decided that David should go into medicine. He spent the winter of 1790–1791 at Phillips Exeter Academy, studied for a few months with his stepfather, and then moved to Natick, Massachusetts, to practice medicine with his uncle Dr. Isaac Morril. By 1793 David Morril had set up his own practice in Epsom, New Hampshire, and within a year was married to Jane Wallace and building a house. The couple had no children. Morril later recalled that he was "quite happy" and that "a kind Providence smiled" upon him.

Morril's contentment ended at midday on 27 July 1799 when he underwent a profound religious experience. A bright light seemed to shine about him, and the earth seemed to open up, exposing the "awful terrors" of hell. "Overwhelmed by guilt" and convinced that he had little hope of "escape" from "Hell and destruction," he gave up his medical practice, left home, and traveled about seeking guidance from Baptists and New Light and Old Light Congregationalists. He was soon drawn to the doctrines of the Congregationalist Samuel Hopkins, who preached a God of love and called on his followers to abandon self-interest and to live a life of benevolence. Hopkins was one of the first Congregational ministers to oppose slavery. After studying for a year and a half with the Reverend Jesse Remington of Candia, New Hampshire, Morril went on a preaching tour and in March 1802 was ordained as pastor of the Presbyterian-Congregational Church of Goffstown, New Hampshire. When his wife finally joined him that October, Morril seemed once again set on his life's work.

Within a few years, however, the Presbyterians had left his church, and he was finding that many of the Congregationalists had "hard hearts" when he preached against "frolicing" and "total depravity" and warned them of "everlasting perdition." The strains of his pastorate became so great that by 1808 he was complaining of neck pains and headaches and a year later asked the congregation for dismissal. In 1811 his request was granted.

Morril had already resumed his medical practice and had entered politics. In 1808 he was elected moderator of the Goffstown town meeting and representative to the state house of representatives, positions that he held, with one minor exception, until 1817. It was a propitious time to be entering politics, for a new generation of politicians, including Isaac Hill and Levi Woodbury, was beginning to replace the old leadership. Morril showed his Republican colors in 1808 by voting against a New Hampshire house resolution attacking Thomas Jefferson's trade embargo. He gained more attention in 1811 during a floor fight in which the Republican majority accused the Federalists of treason for opposing James Madison's trade restrictions. When former Federalist governor John Taylor Gilman angrily demanded proof, Morril responded by quoting from Federalist speeches and sermons. Elected Speaker in 1816, he played a major role in securing passage of the judiciary and Dartmouth College bills during the session.

In 1817 Morril was one of two Republicans elected by the legislature to replace the two Federalists in the U.S. Senate. He immediately established himself as an opponent of slavery by backing efforts to strengthen the law against the African slave trade and by opposing efforts to require the states to enforce the fugitive slave law. On 17 January 1820 he made a strong antislavery speech supporting Rufus King's amendment to keep slavery out of Missouri and later in the session voted against the first Missouri Compromise. In 1821 he voted in favor of the second Missouri Compromise, admitting Missouri, even though the resolution did not deal directly with a clause in the Missouri constitution excluding free blacks from the state. Also while in the Senate he made unsuccessful efforts to have military officers dismissed for dueling.

When his term expired in 1823, he joined the factional struggle that was going on within the New Hampshire Republican party. Allied with Isaac Hill, he defeated incumbent governor Levi Woodbury in 1824 in a close election that had to be settled in the legislature. The following year he was reelected with no opposition, but when he and Hill split in 1826, Morril barely managed to win a third and final term. While governor he secured passage of several reform bills in the legislature, including one regulating the schools in the town of Portsmouth.

Throughout the rest of his career Morril sought other ways to promote reform and religion. Still devoted to the ideas of Samuel Hopkins, he published "Observations on Genesis 3: 4, 13" and "Thoughts on Revelation 20: 10" in the Providence (R.I.) *Hopkinsian Magazine* (1828). Moving to Concord, New Hampshire, in 1831, he served as editor of the *New-Hampshire Observer*, "a plain, evangelical periodical" devoted to biblical doctrine, religious revivals, Sabbath schools, Sabbatarianism, temperance, and other reform movements. Although more than ever opposed to slavery, he did not believe that emancipation could be achieved until the number of blacks in the United States had been reduced by colonization in Africa. He served as president of the New Hampshire Missionary Society, the New Hampshire Colonization Society, the New Hampshire branch of the American Education Society, and the American Tract and Book Society; he was vice president of the American Sunday School Union and the Home Missionary Society.

After the death of Jane Morril in 1823, Morril a year later married Lydia Poore; the couple had three children who survived infancy. He died in Concord. Despite the many turns of a long career, he had lived faithfully according to his religious beliefs. Physician, clergyman, and reformer as well as politician, he was one of the most versatile political figures in the early republic.

• The New Hampshire Historical Society has a small collection of Morril papers. The most valuable item in the collection is his diary for the years 1799–1810, which starts with a brief sketch of his early life and contains a detailed account of his religious conversion and his pastorate in Goffstown, N.H. The society also has his governor's messages and some of his religious writing in published form. Another useful source is the Concord *New-Hampshire Observer*, which Morril published and edited between 1831 and 1833.

An excellent short account of Morril's life is William H. Brown, "David Lawrence Morril," *Historical New Hampshire* 19 (Summer 1964): 3–27. For Morril's life in Goffstown see George P. Hadley, *History of the Town of Goffstown* (2 vols., 1924), which contains a picture of Morril, reproduced from the original in the State House at Concord. Mabel Frances Plante provides a detailed study of Morril's political career in "David Lawrence Morril" (M.A. thesis, Univ. of New Hampshire, 1955). Additional material may be found in Nathaniel Bouton, *The History of Concord* (1856); James O. Lyford, ed., *History of Concord, New Hampshire* (2 vols., 1903); and Everett S. Stackpole, *History of New Hampshire* (4 vols., 1916). For genealogies see Annie Morrill Smith, *Morrill Kindred in America* (2 vols., 1914); and Katharine L. Morrill, "Morrill Genealogies" (1903), an unpublished paper available at the New Hampshire Historical Society. The review of Morril's life in the *New-England Historical and Genealogical Register*, vol. 3 (1849), p. 199, is based on an excellent obituary in the Concord *Independent Democrat & Freeman*, 1 Feb. 1849.

DONALD B. COLE

MORRILL, Edmund Needham (12 Feb. 1834–14 Mar. 1909), banker, congressman, and governor of Kansas, was born in Westbrook, Maine, the son of Rufus Morrill, a tanner and currier, and Mary Webb. He was educated in the common schools and at Westbrook Academy, where he graduated in 1855. For one year he was the academy's superintendent, but he moved with a colony of settlers in 1857 to Brown County, Kansas Territory, and established a sawmill a few miles west of present-day Hiawatha. The mill failed after a fire in 1860, but Morrill repaid all of his creditors.

Like other Kansans, he was caught up in the slavery controversy and, as an opponent of slavery, served in the territorial legislature in 1857. In December he was elected by "a bolters' convention" of Free State men who disagreed with the movement's majority, which did not want to participate in government, to be a representative under the Lecompton constitution, the proslavery document eventually defeated in Congress. In October 1861 he enlisted as a private in the Seventh Kansas Volunteer Cavalry, the infamous "Jennison's Jayhawkers," and rose to the rank of sergeant before Vice President Hannibal Hamlin, also of Maine, secured an appointment for him as commissary of subsistence with the rank of captain. From August 1862 until he mustered out in October 1865, most of Morrill's service was spent in Tennessee, where he controlled army stores. He was brevetted major for meritorious service.

Morrill married Elizabeth A. Brettun in 1862; she died in 1868. He then wed Caroline J. Nash on Christmas Day in 1869; they had three children. His life following the Civil War was spent in business and politics, and although he was not a particularly adroit political leader, he was popular with voters. A Republican, he settled in Hiawatha and was elected clerk of the district court (1866–1870), county clerk (1866–1873), state senator (1872–1874, 1876–1880), and a member of the U.S. House of Representatives (1883–1891). In the state senate he was chairman of the Ways and Means Committee and president pro tem.

In Congress Morrill was an at-large delegate, 1883–1885, and after the state was reapportioned, he represented the First Congressional District. He served continuously on the Committee on Invalid Pensions, which he chaired when Republicans regained control of the House during his last term. Among various pensions he recommended was a precedent-setting law for Union army prisoners of war. According to opponents, it was the first time pensions were granted by general category. More importantly, the Morrill Dependent Pension and Disability Act of 27 June 1890, sometimes called the Omnibus Pension Act, granted pensions to veterans of the Union army who had served for at least ninety days and were then or thereafter physically or mentally disabled and thus unable to earn a living. It also provided pensions for minor children, dependent parents, and widows who had married veterans before 1890.

Congressman Morrill was a moderate conservative who exemplified the late nineteenth-century western Republican's tendency to support activist government that favored his constituency. Legislation he championed included building a bridge over the Missouri River at Leavenworth, navigation and flood control improvements to the Mississippi River, construction of a national penitentiary in his congressional district, sale of Potawatomi and Kickapoo reservation lands, and legislation to aid state and local control of the sale of liquor. Some of his most important votes included support for the Texas Seed Bill, an eight-hour day at the Government Printing Office, almost any law that supported the national banking program (especially expansion of its currency), and the continuation of a two cents per pound tax on oleomargine. He opposed downward revision of the tariff in 1887 and 1888, and not wishing to face the wrath of reformers or railroads, he joined 136 other congressmen in abstaining on the vote that reclaimed as part of the public domain railroad land grants that had been unused. The bill passed in 1889.

Refusing to stand for reelection in 1890, Morrill allowed his name to be advanced for the gubernatorial position in 1892, although he failed to secure the nomination. Two years later he was nominated and elected to serve as Kansas's thirteenth governor. With the help of Cyrus Leland, Jr., Kansas's political leader par excellence, he defeated the incumbent, Lorenzo D. Lewelling, the state's first People's party governor. Morrill's campaign profited from a variety of revelations of Populist mismanagement and corruption, from his advocacy of tariff protectionism and the unlimited coinage of silver mined in the United States on a parity with gold, and from the candidacy of the Democrat David Overmyer, who took previous Fusionist votes from Lewelling. Although the tariff and free silver were extraneous to the office he sought, they were important, because many Kansans blamed Grover Cleveland's advocacy of tariff reductions and the gold standard for the depression of 1893.

Despite Morrill's activist views while in Congress, as governor he did little. Faced with an agricultural economy suffering from debt, a shortage of capital, and drought and destitution in the western part of the state, he announced that government could not improve things because the "laws of trade which . . . control business . . . cannot be repealed by any statute." Moreover, he felt legislation that might "disturb" or "restrict trade" should be avoided (Clanton, p. 171). Legislation he advocated included lower taxes, a law banning lotteries, a longer legislative session, and an increase in the state judiciary. He also supported the calling of a constitutional convention to set limits on state expenditures and local debts and to grant the governor a line-item veto on appropriation bills.

Prohibition proved to be a major problem for him. A teetotaler and early advocate of temperance, he failed to use the considerable powers given Kansas governors by the Metropolitan Police Law to enforce Prohibition in the state's larger cities. He justified his inaction on the grounds that a law could not be enforced where local sentiment opposed it. A leading member of the Kansas State Temperance Union said of him, "A more weak, truckling, subservient, cowardly administration never was elected" (Bader, p. 125). In addition to losing Prohibition support in 1896 when he stood for reelection, Morrill also lost the undivided support of Leland, who had been appointed a cochairman of President William McKinley's western campaign in Chicago. Leland was not only unable to help, he was likewise unwilling, because of Morrill's weak showing as governor.

After losing reelection to his Populist-Democrat opponent, Morrill returned to his business affairs, which were substantial. He continued as president of the Morrill and Janes Bank in Hiawatha, an institution he founded in 1871. He was also president of the First National Bank in Leavenworth and a director of the Interstate National Bank of Kansas City, Kansas. He owned an Atchison loan company and had extensive landholdings in Kansas, including an 880-acre apple orchard. Toward the end of his life, he was one of the richest men in the state.

Among Morrill's civic involvements were membership on the Board of Managers of the U.S. Soldiers' Home, membership on the Committee on the Centennial Celebration of the Washington Inaugural, and the founding of the Morrill Free Public Library and the Hiawatha Academy. The city of Morrill in northwestern Brown County is named for him. He died in San Antonio, Texas, where he had gone to escape the harsh Kansas winter.

• Both the private and public papers of Morrill are located at the Kansas State Historical Society in Topeka. Information regarding his career in Congress is found in the *Congressional Record* (1883–1890). Useful small biographies include James C. Malin's *Dictionary of American Biography* entry; Robert Sobel and John Raimo, eds., *Biographical Directory of the Governors of the United States, 1789–1978*, vol. 2 (1978); Frank W. Blackmar, *Kansas: A Cyclopedia of State History*, vol. 2 (1912); and William E. Connelley, *A Standard History of Kansas and Kansans*, vol. 2 (1918). Special studies of value include Leverett W. Spring, *Kansas: The Prelude to the War for the Union* (1885); Robert Bader, *Prohibition in Kansas: A History* (1986); O. Gene Clanton, *Kansas Populism: Ideas and Men* (1969); and Walter T. K. Nugent, "How the Populists Lost in 1894," *Kansas Historical Quarterly* 31 (Autumn 1965): 245–55. An obituary is in the *Topeka Daily Capital*, 15 Mar. 1909.

ROBERT S. LA FORTE

MORRILL, Justin Smith (14 Apr. 1810–28 Dec. 1898), businessman, politician, and legislator, was born in Strafford, Vermont, the son of Nathaniel Morrill, a blacksmith, and Mary Hunt. Morrill left school at fifteen after studying at the common school in Strafford and at Thetford and Randolph Academies. He wrote later, with obvious regret, "I desired to obtain a college education, but my father said he was unable to send all his boys to college and felt that he ought to give all an equal chance" (Parker, p. 23).

Morrill worked as a clerk in Strafford general stores for four and a half years and as a bookkeeper in a dry goods store in Portland, Maine, for four years. In 1834 he returned to Strafford as the partner of Judge Jedediah H. Harris in a retail business, where he had clerked from 1827 to 1830. Harris was the leading merchant in Strafford, a successful farmer, and a local political leader. He had great influence over the young Morrill, and they remained close friends until Harris died in 1855. Their partnership flourished and, for a time, operated four stores in Vermont towns. In 1840 Nathan Smith Young joined the partnership, and by 1848

Morrill had so prospered that he could retire to a small farm nearby.

Apparently Morrill also finally felt secure enough to wed. In 1851 he married Ruth Barrell Swan, and they settled in the house that he had newly built on his farm. They had two children, one of whom died in infancy. In later years, Morrill's sister-in-law, Louise Swan, was also a member of their household. Morrill was a Unitarian and an abstemious nonsmoker.

During Morrill's years in business, he gained the status of a leading citizen of the community and was, thereby, drawn into public affairs. He chaired the county Whigs, attended party conventions, and served on the Whigs' state committee, among other duties. With his retirement from business, his political involvement increased, including service as a delegate to the 1852 Whig National Convention. For many years he refused repeated offers of nomination to elective office, except that he served one year each as town auditor and as justice of the peace.

In 1854, however, he accepted the virtually unanimous Whig nomination for Congress from the Second Vermont District and beat a Democrat and a Free Soiler in the general election with a 59-vote majority. Thus began one of the longest and most distinguished careers in the history of the U.S. Congress. During his forty-four years of service there, he delivered more than one hundred set speeches and intervened in the proceedings 2,477 times.

In 1855 the Whig party collapsed, and Morrill became one of the leading founders of the Republican party in Vermont. His legislative record conformed well to mainstream Republican positions. He was an abolitionist, a moderate protectionist on tariff questions, an indefatigable advocate of "sound" money, and the leader in the fight against Mormon polygamy. He promoted those policies as a temperamental moderate, a fine legislative stylist, and a persuasive though not eloquent speaker.

During his twelve years in the House, he served on Committees on the Territories, Agriculture, and Ways and Means, rising to the chairmanship of the last in 1865. He became perhaps the most influential member of Congress on tariffs and public finance. According to a contemporary journalist, during his last three years in the House, "the tariff and the revenue laws of the country have been shaped much more by his hand than by any other member of either branch of Congress." His influence may have been enhanced by his commonsensical, practical approach; his quiet, courteous manner; and his imposing physical appearance. He was six feet tall and angular; with deep, penetrating blue eyes; a prominent nose; thick, wavy, dark-brown hair; and side whiskers.

Morrill's principal legislative achievements in the House were the Morrill Tariff of 1860, the Internal Revenue Act of 1862, and the Morrill Land Grant Act of 1862. The former two laws were the foundation of public finance during the Civil War. The revenue bill introduced the income tax to American practice. The tariff that bore Morrill's name was solidly protectionist and was so popular with Congress that it survived repeated efforts to lower it, including by Morrill himself, until long after the Civil War.

Morrill is best known today for the 1862 Land Grant Act. It provided that each state receive 30,000 acres of federal land for each member of Congress representing it. The proceeds from the sale of the land were to be used to establish "colleges of agricultural and mechanical arts." He had been inspired by agricultural schools in Europe, but he added training for "mechanics," partly out of respect for his father's trade. He was also influenced by the ideas for practical college education of Alden Partridge, founder of Vermont's Norwich University, and Jonathan Baldwin Turner of Illinois College. No doubt, his motivation came largely from his own frustration at being denied a college education. The fruit of the Land Grant Act was the establishment of some three score institutions of higher learning that have educated hundreds of thousands of Americans at modest cost. He ensured that they would not be denied what his father had been unable to afford for him.

Support for practical higher education was a hallmark of Morrill's political career. He had expressed such a commitment at least as early as 1848 and had introduced a bill to involve Congress in that effort within three months of being seated in the House of Representatives. After the passage of the 1862 act, he worked ceaselessly to ensure greater federal assistance for the land grant schools, finally succeeding in 1890 with the passage of legislation providing annual cash grants. Also, he was an incorporator and longtime trustee of the University of Vermont.

Throughout Morrill's 32-year career as a senator, which began in 1866, he served on the Buildings and Grounds and Finance Committees. He chaired the former committee from 1869 to 1877 and the latter in the years 1877–1879, 1881–1893, and 1895–1898. His name was not attached to any major pieces of legislation during his Senate service (except the second Land Grant Act), but he was probably the most influential senator on public finance policy and took a special interest in the physical landscape of the nation's capital. He conducted a career-long campaign to sustain and enhance the beauty of the public areas in Washington. One of his first major accomplishments in Washington was the creation of the Hall of Statuary in the Capitol in 1864. Through his long-term membership on the Senate Committee on Public Buildings and Grounds, he provided the legislative leadership for the completion of the Capitol and the Washington Monument, the construction of the Library of Congress, and the landscaping by Frederick Law Olmsted of the Capitol grounds. His last official action as a senator was to secure the enactment of the bill authorizing the acquisition of the land on which the Supreme Court Building stands.

Morrill was a staunch Republican party loyalist. He served in the House during the impeachment of President Andrew Johnson and in the Senate during his trial. He was a member of the Joint Committee on Reconstruction but not a leader in that struggle. He voted with his party both to impeach and to convict Johnson to preserve party unity, despite his reservations on the substance of the issue. Similarly, he disapproved of the "Liberal Republican" revolt of Charles Sumner and Horace Greeley in 1872. He opposed legislating an eight-hour workday and woman suffrage but supported civil service reform.

In foreign affairs, however, Morrill never shared his party's passion for expansion. He was one of only two senators to oppose the purchase of Alaska and the only Republican to vote against the accession of Hawaii. He was against the proposed annexation of Santo Domingo in 1870 and the Spanish-American War at the very end of his life. He deviated from that principle in his lifelong belief in the inevitability of union with Canada.

Morrill's personal life was serene and tranquil, although his wife was often ill and predeceased him by seven months. He traveled to Europe twice, first, in the summer of 1867, with James G. Blaine and later, in the summer of 1880, with his wife, son, and sister-in-law. The handsome home he built on Thomas Circle was a Washington social center, especially for his annual birthday parties, and housed his small art collection.

Morrill had modest literary ambitions. As a youth he had published a few articles in local newspapers. He included literary phrases in the diary that he kept for many years. In 1882 he published privately Self-Consciousness of Noted Persons, a small book of brief anecdotes about famous persons that illustrated their awareness of their own abilities and renown. He expanded it to 171 anecdotes in an 1887 edition and was preparing a third edition at his death. In his last years he also wrote nearly a score of magazine articles on public affairs.

Morrill remained active in the Senate almost to the end. He delivered his final speech on 13 December 1898 and fell ill a week later. He died in his Washington home. His record of continuous service in Congress was not broken until December 1956, by Carl Hayden. He had lived an exemplary life, in public and private. He was one of the great legislators of American history and a gentleman who was respected and admired by all who worked with him.

• Most of Morrill's papers are available on fifty-two reels of microfilm at the Library of Congress. Morrill's life is the subject of William Belmont Parker, *The Life and Public Services of Justin Smith Morrill* (1924), and Randal Leigh Hoyer, "The Gentleman from Vermont: The Career of Justin S. Morrill in the United States House of Representatives" (Ph.D. diss., Michigan State Univ., 1974), which provides a guide to literature on the context of Morrill's life. Biographical articles on Morrill include James Barrett, "Early Life of Justin S. Morrill," *Vermonter* 2 (1896): 61–68; and T. D. Seymour Bassett, "Nature's Nobleman: Justin Morrill, a Victorian Politician," *Vermont History* 30 (1962): 3–13. His most important legislative achievement is the subject of William Edwin Sawyer, "The Evolution of the Morrill Act of 1862" (Ph.D. diss., Boston Univ., 1948). An obituary is in the *New York Times*, 28 Dec. 1898.

WILLIAM G. ANDREWS

MORRILL, Lot Myrick (3 May 1813–10 Jan. 1883), governor, U.S. senator, and secretary of the treasury, was born in Belgrade, Maine, the son of Peaslee Morrill, a farmer, storekeeper, and sawmill operator, and Nancy Macomber. He attended district schools and in 1833 briefly enrolled in Waterville (later Colby) College, then served for a year (1833–1834) as principal of a private academy in western New York. He studied law in Readfield, Maine, and began practicing his profession there soon after being admitted to the bar in 1839. In 1841 he moved to Augusta, where, adhering to the political views of his father, he became active in the state Democratic party and as a legislative lobbyist. In 1845 he married Charlotte Holland Vance, with whom he had four daughters.

From 1849 until 1856 Morrill chaired the state Democratic committee and was a member of the Maine House of Representatives in 1854, the same year his brother Anson Peaslee Morrill was elected governor as an antislavery candidate. In 1855 he began to break with his party by opposing any further congressional concessions to the southern slave oligarchy. Notwithstanding his resignation as party chairman in 1856, he was that same year chosen as president of the state senate by the Democratic majority to elevate him to a largely ceremonial position so that he would not be as effective in behalf of republicanism as if he remained on the floor. Before the year was over he openly declared his adherence to the newly formed antislavery Republican party.

As a Republican and a longtime temperance advocate, Morrill was three times elected governor of Maine (1858–1860), during which time he successfully resisted repeal of his state's prohibition law and consistently aligned himself with its most radical antislavery politicians. In 1861 he was chosen by the state legislature to replace U.S. senator Hannibal Hamlin, who was soon to become vice president. At the Washington Peace Conference of February 1861, although threatened with physical violence by a hulking proslavery delegate, the slightly built Morrill, described by an onlooker as retiring and effeminate, quietly but boldly delivered such a strong repudiation of secession sentiment that he became a celebrity in New England. His stature in his own region was further enhanced when, in his initial speech in the Senate the following month, Morrill condemned the so-called Crittenden compromise, backed by congressional conservatives, as "a proposition . . . which is to incorporate into the Constitution a recognition of the slavery of the African race."

During the Civil War Morrill insisted upon the confiscation of "rebel" property and the emancipation and enfranchisement of southern slaves, and he was easily reelected to a full Senate term in 1863. Predominantly owing to his instigation, laws were adopted emancipating the slaves in the District of Columbia, providing for their education, and granting males of this class the right to vote. In 1868 he delivered a lengthy Senate speech, justifying military Reconstruction of the South, that was one of the most eloquent defenses of Radical Republican doctrines and legislation ever uttered. That same year he voted to remove the impeached president, Andrew Johnson, so that Benjamin Wade, the president of the Senate whose Radical views resembled Morrill's, could become the nation's chief executive.

Early in 1869 Morrill was opposed for reelection to the Senate by former vice president Hamlin, whom Morrill had replaced eight years earlier. A fierce struggle took place in the Republican caucus of the Maine legislature, ending in a 75 to 74 majority for Hamlin. However, upon the death in September 1869 of Maine's other senator, William Fessenden, the governor appointed Morrill to fill the vacancy. He easily won reelection in 1871 and continued to serve as chairman of the Appropriations Committee. He worked indefatigably on a voluminous report, issued 2 June 1876, that traced in minute detail all of the expenditures and revenue measures of the U.S. government from its inception until the time of the document's completion.

Morrill resigned his seat on 7 July 1876 to enter the cabinet of President Ulysses S. Grant as secretary of the treasury, which office he filled with distinction for almost eight months. In March 1877 President Rutherford B. Hayes offered Morrill the ministry to Great Britain, but poor health, dating from an attack of nervous prostration in 1870, induced him instead to accept appointment as collector of customs at Portland, Maine. That position enabled him to live, albeit in an enfeebled state, at or near home until his death in Augusta.

Lacking the relentless intensity of Fessenden, the rustic gentility of Hamlin, or the shrewd opportunism of James G. Blaine, his three most famous Maine contemporaries, Morrill nevertheless obtained, by virtue of his unflappable principled eloquence and his lifelong dedication to selfless public service, the admiration of political associates and the respect of opponents. Perhaps his greatest contribution to the restoration of the American Union was his early insistence upon the necessity of combating secession and armed rebellion by using the presidential war powers to seize property and liberate slaves in the South, presaging the policies of confiscation and emancipation that followed.

• George F. Talbot, "Lot M. Morrill: A Sketch of His Life and Public Services," Maine Historical Society, *Collections and Proceedings*, 2d ser., 5 (1894): 225–75, is the fullest biographical treatment available. See also Augustus F. Moulton, *Memorials of Maine: A Life Record of Men and Women of the Past . . .* (1916); Francis Fessenden, *Life and Public Services of William Pitt Fessenden* (2 vols., 1907); Charles E. Hamlin, *The Life and Times of Hannibal Hamlin* (1899); and James G. Blaine, *Twenty Years of Congress: From Lincoln to Garfield* (2 vols., 1886). Obituaries are in the *New York Times*, 11 Jan. 1883, the *Portland Advertiser*, 10 Jan. 1883, and the *Daily Eastern Argus*, 11 Jan. 1883.

NORMAN B. FERRIS

MORRIS, Caspar (2 May 1805–17 Mar. 1884), physician, was born in Philadelphia, Pennsylvania, the son of Israel W. Morris, a merchant, and Mary Hollingsworth. He was educated in Philadelphia, at the Pine Street Meeting House, a private school, and at the William Penn Charter School. Morris pursued his childhood dream of studying medicine by entering the University of Pennsylvania and by becoming an apprentice to Joseph Parrish, a local physician. During his training, he was employed in a drugstore. He received his M.D. in 1826.

Morris had a fear of surgery and was at first insecure about his diagnostic abilities. His fears proved unfounded when he correctly diagnosed in detail a specific case of fractures of the base of the skull and parietal and frontal bones. When the skull was examined after the patient's death, Morris's diagnostic abilities were confirmed. Compassionate as well as knowledgeable, he took home and nursed to health a fellow student who had contracted smallpox. His kindness would extend to the care of poorer residents of Philadelphia throughout his medical career.

In 1827 Morris went to sea as a ship's surgeon on the *Pacific*. To break the monotony of the long days on the ship, he studied Greek. On his return to Philadelphia in 1828, Morris was appointed physician to the Philadelphia Dispensary. The following year he married his cousin Anne Cheston; they eventually had six children.

Morris was an active member of the community in Philadelphia. A founder in 1825 of the Pennsylvania Historical Society, he contributed to its journal a paper titled "Early History of Medicine in the Province" shortly thereafter. More important, he dedicated himself to the care of the poor, despite his high social position. He founded the House of Refuge for the poor and served as a physician there from 1830 to 1834. Morris also helped to establish the Pennsylvania Institute for the Instruction of the Blind, becoming its first physician and managing the facility from 1838 until his death. An active member of the Episcopal church, Morris was nevertheless an admirer of the Quakers and throughout his life dressed as they did. He also became a regular lecturer on the practice of medicine at the Philadelphia Medical Institute and was active in it from 1838 until 1844.

To bring attention to the need for more hospital facilities in Philadelphia, Morris published a pamphlet addressed to the bishop of his diocese of the Episcopal church, and this began a movement to found the Episcopal Hospital of Philadelphia. He then managed this institution for some years. He was also a member of the National Academy of Sciences and the American Philosophical Society. In 1871 he traveled to Egypt, the Holy Lands, and Europe in the company of his wife and brother. On his return, having observed several medical institutions during his trip, he contributed his suggestions for the building plans of the Johns Hopkins Hospital in Baltimore in 1875.

In addition, Morris published several essays on scarlet fever, including *Lectures on Scarlet Fever* (1851) and *An Essay on Pathology and Therapeutics of Scarlet Fever* (1858). He enjoyed verse and wrote a volume titled *Heart Voices and Home Songs*, which he privately published. He also wrote a brief life of William Wilberforce, the English evangelical, abolitionist, and philanthropist. Morris never fully recovered from an attack of anthrax in 1868, and he died in Philadelphia.

• A few of Morris's manuscripts and lecture notes are at the College of Physicians of Philadelphia. For further information on Morris, see J. Cheston Morris, "A Biographical Sketch of Caspar Morris, M.D.," *Transactions and Studies of the College of Physicians of Philadelphia*, 3d ser., 10 (1888): xxxiii–liii; *Medical and Surgical Reporter* 50 (1884): 416; and John Welsh Crosky, *History of Blockley* (1929).

DAVID Y. COOPER

MORRIS, Charles (26 July 1784–27 Jan. 1856), naval officer, was born in Woodstock, Connecticut, the son of Charles Morris and Miriam Nichols, farmers. He had little formal education after the age of ten, apparently staying home to help out on the family farm. His father was a purser in the American navy during the Quasi-War with France, however, and he helped his son win a temporary appointment as a midshipman on 1 July 1799, when young Charles was not quite fifteen.

Morris had a successful voyage with the *Congress*, although he did fall from the main mast during a storm in January 1800, breaking his arm and receiving a concussion. Given a permanent appointment when the Quasi-War ended, he took advantage of his leave time to study at Woodstock Academy for nine months. In August 1803 Morris sailed with Commodore Edward Preble in the *Constitution* against the pasha of Tripoli. Stephen Decatur chose him to participate in the raid that resulted in the burning of the captured American frigate *Philadelphia*, and Morris was the first American to reach the deck of that ship. Promoted to lieutenant in 1807, Morris served aboard the *Hornet* and the *President*, and he was the executive officer of the *Constitution* under Captain Isaac Hull when the War of 1812 began. When the *Constitution* was in danger of being caught by a superior British force on a calm sea, Morris suggested the technique of kedging—dropping an anchor one-half mile ahead and then pulling forward—that allowed the Americans to gain a vital advantage. He also distinguished himself the following month in the epic battle against the British frigate *Guerrière*, receiving a wound as he climbed the rail in order to lead the boarding party onto the enemy's deck. Congress awarded him a silver plate for that action and promoted him to captain.

In his own ship, Morris was less lucky. He commanded the 26-gun corvette *John Adams* in 1814 and captured ten enemy ships, but he was forced to sail up the Penobscot River and was trapped there by a superior British sea and land force. Morris attempted to make a stand on the land, but he was greatly outnumbered; when the American militia fled, he set his ship on fire and escaped with his men. A court of inquiry cleared him of any dereliction of duty. In February 1815 Morris married Harriet Bowen of Rhode Island. The couple had four sons and six daughters.

Morris had a long and distinguished career in the peacetime navy. He served on the *Congress* from 1815 to 1817 and then commanded the Portsmouth Naval Station until 1823, when he was appointed to the Board of Naval Commissioners as one of three senior officers meant to assist the secretary of the navy. He served on the board until 1827 and then again from 1832 to 1841, becoming actively involved in all aspects of naval development and building a reputation as an expert on naval affairs. In 1825 and 1826 he went to sea again, carrying the marquis de Lafayette back to France after Lafayette's tour of the United States. Between 1827 and 1832 Morris was in charge of the Boston Navy Yard. He commanded squadrons off Brazil and in the Mediterranean from 1841 to 1844. Morris was chief of the Bureau of Construction from 1844 to 1851 and chief of the Bureau of Ordnance and Hydrography until his death in Washington, D.C. He served fifty-seven years in the navy, twenty-one of those at sea, and was on leave less than three years in all.

Morris wrote an autobiography for the benefit of his family, who allowed the U.S. Navy to publish it posthumously. It contains impressive descriptions of the author's battles and of his naval activities generally. There is also thoughtful analysis, as with Morris's argument that American victories in the ship-to-ship fighting of the War of 1812 were owing, in general, to the intense patriotism of the American seamen and, more particularly, to highly skilled gunnery, the result of sustained practice. The autobiography is also an uplifting tale of a young man who raised himself through hard work as well as bravery. Morris's technical acumen, for example, resulted from systematic self-study while at sea. The reader is also impressed with a young naval officer who uses his first trip to Paris to familiarize himself with the artwork available in that city.

Morris was one of a small number of men in the early Republic who made the American navy a force to be reckoned with. Less well known than other American heroes of this period, Morris is still significant, particularly because he served the navy in peacetime as well. His autobiography deserves to be more widely known.

• The best source is Charles Morris. *The Autobiography of Commodore Charles Morris* (1880). See also Edgar Stanton McClay, *History of the United States Navy from 1775 to 1901* (1906–1910); Theodore Roosevelt, *The Naval War of 1812* (1882); and Donald R. Hickey, *The War of 1812: A Forgotten Conflict* (1989).

S. CHARLES BOLTON

MORRIS, Clara (17 Mar. 1848–20 Nov. 1925), actress, was born in Toronto, Canada, the daughter of Charles La Montagne and Sarah Jane Proctor (who later assumed the last name of Morris). The separation of Morris's parents when she was a small child left her mother in poverty to support herself and Clara as a seamstress or housekeeper. Much to her mother's horror, Morris was invited to join the Corps de Ballet in John Ellsler's Cleveland Academy of Music when she was thirteen years old. Morris's progress toward stardom was typical. While a member of the ballet corps she was given a small secondary speaking role, then assigned boys' parts, and later given an opportunity to understudy more important roles until finally, after proving her ability, she was given a regular acting position in one of the "lines" of business. From her start in the ballet corps, however, she made enough money to become the wage earner in the family. Much later, writing of the actress's life, she would commend acting as a realistic choice in the limiting world of Victorian-era America, which usually demanded servitude of women. Don't ask, she wrote in *Stage Confidences* (1902), whether acting is a perfect profession; rather ask, "What advantage has it over other occupations for women?"

Morris's first starring role was in 1870 when she debuted in Augustin Daly's Fifth Avenue Theater in New York City, playing the role of Anne Sylvester in *Man and Wife*, an opportunity that arose from the refusal of Daly's leading lady to accept the role. Shortly afterward she moved from Daly's to A. M. Palmer's Union Square Theatre, where she starred for most of her thirty years in the theater. In 1874 Morris married Frederick C. Harriott of New York City. They had no children.

Morris was one of the most popular performers of her time, and during her years as a star she amassed a fortune. For over thirty years she was well known as the unchallenged queen of the emotional school of acting. By contrast, Sarah Bernhardt was perceived to be a colder, more cerebral player. Drama critics were divided about Morris's talents. Most, like Willard Holcomb, drama critic for the *Washington Post*, conceded that she was immensely popular and unsurpassed in certain melodramatic roles but saw her as never more than a mediocre talent whose "natural talent unrestrained" was never refined by a "technique developed to absolute art." On the other hand, John Ranken Towse wrote in *Sixty Years of the Theater* that Morris was "one of the very few American actresses to whom the gift of genius may be properly ascribed." Her famous roles, performed over the course of years with different companies, included Cora in *L'Article 47*, Lucy Carter in *Saratoga*, Madame D'Artigues in *Jezebel*, Fanny in *Divorce*, Marguerite Gautier in *Camille*, Jane Eyre, Esther in *The New Lady Macbeth*, and Mercy Merrick in *The New Magdalen*.

By 1890 Morris was too ill with arthritis and other ailments to continue acting on a regular basis and instead turned to lectures, making occasional stage appearances, and writing. Her eyesight failed in 1909 and only partially returned by 1914. In severe financial straits, Morris wrote eight books in eight years. *Little Jim Crow* (1899), a children's book, *A Silent Singer* (1902), and *Life on the Stage* (1901) are all collections of personality sketches. *Life on the Stage* may well be Morris's most valuable literary contribution. An account of her early childhood and rise to stardom and concomitantly an excellent picture of theatrical life, the book also defends the stage and its actresses, both of which were constantly under attack at the time. Morris stressed the advantages of independence and dignity that the stage bestowed on actresses. "The working girl," she wrote, "is expected to be subservient, she is too often regarded as a menial, she is ordered. An actress, even of small characters, is considered a necessary part of the whole. She assists, she attends, she obliges. Truly a difference" (p. 133). Still, Morris admitted that few actresses were accepted into polite society and that all were subject to clerical denunciation.

Morris's novels reflect the same melodrama that characterized her acting, and several contain autobiographical elements. *Left in Charge* (1904) is set in the Ohio frontier of her youth. *A Pasteboard Crown* (1902) moralizes about an actress's hopeless love for a married man. *The Trouble Woman* (1904) is another sketch of frontier life. Her bestselling novel was the intense melodrama *The New East Lynne* (1908).

The literary strengths and weaknesses of Morris's work—stock melodramatic characters and stories and rapidly moving plots—derived from the domestic tragedies in which she appeared as an actress. Despite the superficiality and trite situations in much of her fiction, Morris's books reveal the problems of women of her time: constant "neurasthenia," the sexual double standard, the plight of the single woman, and the burden of urban and rural poverty. While none were bestsellers or of great literary merit, Morris's novels are invaluable as historical sources.

In her last years, her considerable fortune exhausted, Morris battled poverty and arthritis. Several benefits staged for her by her fellow actors failed to save her house from creditors, and she died in poverty in New Canaan, Connecticut.

• Clara Morris's own works, particularly *Life on the Stage: My Personal Experiences and Recollections* (1901), are the best sources of information about her life. Although no biography has been written about her, information on her acting style and personal life can be found in some theatrical memoirs, including Alfred Ayers, *Actors and Acting* (1894); Willard Holcomb, *Famous American Actors of To-day* (1896); Lewis C. Strang, *Players and Plays of the Last Quarter Century* (1903); John Ranken Towse, *Sixty Years of the Theater* (1916); Garff B. Wilson, *A History of American Acting* (1966); and William Winter's two-volume *Wallet of Time* (1913). A front-page obituary is in the *New York Times*, 21 Nov. 1925.

CLAUDIA DURST JOHNSON

MORRIS, Earl Halstead (24 Oct. 1889–24 June 1956), archaeologist, was born in Chama, New Mexico Territory, the son of Scott Neering Morris, a teamster and construction engineer, and Juliette Amanda Halstead, a schoolteacher. Morris's father's work, building railroads and freighting supplies to the mines, provided uncertain support for the family, and although his mother's schoolteaching was a source of income, Morris had to help the family at a very early age. Firewood chopped and delivered was worth twenty-five cents a cord and constituted a day's work. Helping his father find American Indian antiquities in the Farmington, New Mexico, area was Morris's introduction to prehistory.

In 1904, while trying to get one of his drivers out of a brawl, Morris's father was shot and killed. After a trying adjustment, Morris graduated as valedictorian from high school in Farmington, New Mexico, in 1908. A local benefactor who recognized his promise helped send Morris to the University of Colorado in Boulder. He majored in psychology, played in the band, and worked on the school paper. He also became acquainted with Junius Henderson, the university museum founder and director, who commissioned Morris to spend some of his student summers finding ancient pottery and other artifacts to enrich the collections. Beginning in 1912 he excavated in the La Plata River valley of Colorado and New Mexico.

In 1914 Morris earned an A.B. from the university and joined the honorary Phi Beta Kappa and Sigma Xi societies. In 1916 he earned the M.A. in anthropology at Colorado for describing the La Plata sites. His thesis was published by the Bureau of American Ethnology in 1919. During this interval Morris spent time with archaeologists, including Jesse L. Nussbaum and Edgar Lee Hewett, in New Mexico, and he was able to accompany Hewett to Quirigua, Guatemala, in 1912. In 1914 Morris returned there with Neil M. Judd. In 1917 he spent a year studying anthropology under Franz Boas at Columbia University. While in New York City, Morris became acquainted with Clark Wissler of the American Museum of Natural History's anthropology department. In 1916, on Wissler's recommendation, the museum put Morris in charge of the excavations at its so-called Aztec Ruin at Aztec, New Mexico, which he continued to direct until 1924. This huge, multistoried Indian pueblo site produced many remains. It was located in such a dry environment that wood, leather, basketry, and even the human burials were preserved in excellent condition. The stone walls and log roofs were so well constructed that many rooms had not collapsed in the site's roughly 800 years of existence. The enormous great kiva (a semisubterranean religious structure) that Morris restored at the site became a major attraction for the visitors to what is now Aztec National Monument and remains the only great ceremonial structure of its kind that has been reroofed. The artifacts from his excavation are in the American Museum of Natural History.

The age of the Aztec pueblo was not known when Morris was excavating. However, the well-preserved roof timbers attracted the attention of astronomer Andrew E. Douglass, who was trying to find old trees whose sequential patterns of thick and thin annual growth rings would enable him to discover past climatic variation. This new science, labeled dendrochronology, became the most precise archaeological dating method in the world. Using this method, Douglass estimated that the Aztec Ruin had been built about 100 years after Pueblo Bonito and other big ruins in nearby Chaco Canyon. With excitement Morris informed Douglass that temporal changes in ceramic decoration found at the site supported the tree-ring dating. Thereafter Morris became an avid collector of dendrochronological remains. Eventually he excavated specimens near Durango, Colorado, that dated from the centuries immediately before and after the time of Christ. For many decades these were the earliest dated archaeological specimens in the Southwest.

In 1923 Morris married Ann McCheane Axtell; they had two daughters. The following year he was employed by the archaeological research department of the Carnegie Institution of Washington, for which he worked until the time of his death. Between 1924 and 1929 he was in charge of excavating and restoring the Temple of the Warriors at the Maya ruins of Chichen Itzá in Yucatán, Mexico. This impressive structure, with its magnificent bas-relief sculpture and painted panels, became even more interesting when a second decorated temple mound was found buried underneath it. Besides contributing to the annual reports of the Carnegie Institution of Washington, Morris published a popular book, *The Temple of the Warriors* (1931). Additionally, he coauthored a generously illustrated two-volume scientific monograph under the same title in 1931 with Jean Charlot and his wife, Ann Axtell Morris. The restored temple and the associated buildings have been visited by millions of visitors and have served as examples of the benefits of restoration for many other splendid Mesoamerican ruins.

During the rainy summers when fieldwork was impossible in Yucatán, and after his work at Chichen Itzá was completed, Morris returned to the Southwest to excavate at Canyon de Chelly, Arizona; a number of sites near Shiprock, New Mexico; and at Basketmaker period caves and villages near Durango, Colorado. A number of articles resulted from this work, and the collections of the artifacts were deposited at the University of Colorado, the University of Arizona, the American Museum of Natural History, the Aztec National Monument, and at Mesa Verde National Park.

Drawing on his expertise in rebuilding and restoration, Morris worked at Balcony House and Cliff Palace in Mesa Verde National Park and at Mummy Cave in Canyon del Muerto at de Chelly National Monument, strengthening these ancient structures to withstand the impact of modern visitors. Uniquely qualified for this task, Morris made use of the frontier engineering skills developed during his youth in the railroad and mining camps.

In his later years, and as the onset of World War II caused the cessation of fieldwork, Morris spent his time in laboratory analysis of his finds. His book *Anasazi Basketry* (1941), coauthored with Robert F. Burgh, was one result of his research efforts. He was working on a detailed monograph on beautifully woven and elaborately decorated Anasazi yucca fiber sandals at the time of his death. This book was later prepared for publication by his daughter Elizabeth Morris and colleagues. After his wife's death in 1945 Morris married Lucile Bowman, a former schoolteacher, the following year. They had no children.

It has been stated that Morris did not like to write, but his long list of publications indicates otherwise. Beginning with "The Cliff Dwellers of the San Juan," an article printed in the 1911 issue of *Colorado Magazine*, and ending with his meticulously detailed monograph coauthored by Burgh, *Basketmaker II Sites Near Durango, Colorado* (1954), he was a prolific producer. He wrote seven books and more than thirty articles in addition to book reviews and annual reports. Any sensitive reader of his popular articles in *Natural History* and *National Geographic* or of his many scientific articles and monographs will recognize a dedicated scholar and perceptive observer of human beings even through the dust of ages and the fog of time.

Invited by Alfred Vincent Kidder, the "dean of southwestern archaeology," to the First Pecos archaeological conference at the Pecos Ruin in New Mexico in 1927, Morris was in regular attendance into the 1950s. This regional conference, where current field research is presented and discussed, has contributed significantly to archaeological theory. A courteous, respected, and well-liked scholar, Morris was there at the beginning of the conference and his contributions continue to be important.

In 1931 Morris received the Norlin Medal presented annually by the University of Colorado to one of its distinguished alumni. In 1953 he received the Alfred Vincent Kidder medal for outstanding achievement in both Mesoamerican and southwestern history from the American Anthropological Society. An endowed scholarship in his name is awarded from time to time to an outstanding archaeology student from the University of Colorado.

Morris died at his home in Boulder, Colorado. His ashes were scattered at the Aztec Ruin, to which he had given so much.

Morris was largely self-trained and loved his archaeological work. Besides using his frontier survival skills to provide access for himself and others to remote ruins of the southwestern United States, Morris brought the painstaking perception of an artist and the reasoning of the scientist to his archaeological endeavors. To collections of artifacts from dozens of ruins may be added his contributions to dendrochronology, to ceramic and architectural taxonomy, and to his meticulous analysis of rare specimens of basketry and yucca fiber sandals. His restoration of ancient structures in Yucatán and the Southwest has helped bring their builders to life for a multitude of viewers.

• Morris's papers, including correspondence, notebooks, and photographs, are in the museum at the University of Colorado, Boulder. Among his most important publications not mentioned in the text are the American Museum of Natural History anthropology series and *Archaeological Studies in the La Plata District* (1939). Robert Lister and Florence Lister have written *Earl Morris and Southwestern Archaeology* (1968), *The Earl H. Morris Memorial Pottery Collection* (1969), *The Aztec Ruins on the Animas: Excavated, Preserved, and Interpreted* (1987), and *Aztec Ruins National Monument: Administrative History of an Archeological Preserve* (1990). The University of Colorado Museum published *Among Ancient Ruins: The Legacy of Earl H. Morris* (1985), a volume of photographs accompanied by quotes from Morris and introduced by Joe Ben Wheat, the museum's curator of anthropology and a longtime friend. This museum also published *The Morris Code* (1983), a traveling exhibit of many enlarged photographs. Ann Morris's two popular books, *Digging in the Southwest* (1933) and *Digging in Yucatán* (1931), delightfully describe the adventures of an archaeological couple. Roy L. Carlson published two monographs on Morris's work, *Basketmaker III Sites Near Durango Colorado* (1963) and *Eighteenth Century Navajo Fortresses of the Governador District* (1965). See also Hannah Huse, "Identification of the Individual in Archaeology: A Case-Study from the Prehistoric Hopi Site of Kawaika-a" (Ph.D. diss., Univ. of Colorado, 1976), and, by his daughter Elizabeth Ann Morris, *Basketmaker Caves in the Prayer Rock District of Northeastern Arizona*, Anthropology Papers of the University of Arizona (1980). Obituaries are by Robert F. Burgh, in *American Anthropologist* 59, no. 3 (1957); by Alfred Vincent Kidder, in *American Antiquity* 22, no. 4 (Apr. 1957): 390–97; and by Hugo G. Rodeck, in *Southwestern Lore* 22, no. 3 (1956). *American Antiquity* and *Southwestern Lore* include bibliographies of his works.

ELIZABETH ANN MORRIS

MORRIS, Edward Dafydd (31 Oct. 1825–21 Nov. 1915), minister and professor, was born in Utica, New York, the son of Dafydd Edward Morris, a shoemaker and grocer, and Anne Lewis. Both parents being of Welsh descent (his father migrated to the United States as a youth), Morris grew up in Utica speaking both Welsh and English. Enrolling at Yale as a sophomore in 1846, he paid his own expenses, campaigned for the Free Soil party, wrote scholarly articles, and compiled an impressive academic record. Following his graduation in 1849, he completed a degree in 1852 at Auburn Theological Seminary, where he was strongly influenced by leading New School Presbyterian theologian Laurens P. Hickok. After being ordained by the Cayuga presbytery, he served as a minister of the Second Presbyterian Church of Auburn, New York. In 1852 Morris married Francis Elizabeth Parmelee of Fair Haven, Connecticut. They had four children. From 1855 to 1867 he pastored the Second Presbyterian Church of Columbus, Ohio. His first wife died in 1866, and the following year Morris wed Mary Bryan Treat of Tallmadge, Ohio, with whom he had two children. His inspiring and innovative leadership of his Columbus congregation, coupled with his scholarly abilities, prompted Lane Theological Seminary in Cincinnati to appoint him in 1867 as a professor of church history. He served in this capacity until 1874, when he moved to the chair of systematic theology. During his twenty-three years in this position Morris played a crucial role in the life of the seminary.

Between 1837 and 1869 the Presbyterian Church, USA (PCUSA), separated into Old School and New School branches. The division arose because New Schoolers opposed slavery, supported interdenominational voluntary societies, endorsed the theology and practices of antebellum revivalism, and tolerated theological diversity much more than did Old Schoolers. A New School pastor from 1852 to 1869, Morris enthusiastically promoted the reunion that occurred the latter year. While he strongly endorsed the Westminster Standards (the Westminster Confession of Faith and the Shorter and Larger Catechisms) as the doctrinal basis of the reunited denomination, he argued for latitude in interpreting them. Morris never personally accepted the progressive orthodoxy or evangelical liberalism popular during the late nineteenth century that stressed human goodness rather than original sin; God's immanence and love rather than his transcendence, judgment, and wrath; religious experience rather than doctrine; and Christ's moral example rather than his atonement for sin. For a while, however, he insisted that other PCUSA ministers had the right to espouse these views. Despite his election as moderator of the denomination's General Assembly in 1875, his tolerance of progressive orthodoxy made it necessary for Morris to defend his own theological views against attacks by former Old School proponents during the late 1870s and 1880s. By the 1890s he had adopted a stricter view of the extent to which PCUSA ministers should be permitted to disagree with the denominational standards and did not offer any active assistance to Charles Briggs of Union Theological Seminary or Henry Preserved Smith of Lane Seminary when they were tried by the General Assembly because of their theological beliefs. As a member of a committee appointed to revise the Westminster Confession of Faith, Morris fought to preserve the creed's Calvinism and sought simply to soften its language in order to make Presbyterian preaching and witness "more practical, . . . irenic and friendly to other evangelicals," goals achieved by the revision the denomination adopted in 1903 (*Theology of the Westminster Symbols*, 808–9).

After 1875 Lane suffered from low enrollment, inadequate finances, and theological controversy. Morris, who not only taught at Lane for thirty-one years, but also served as a trustee for many years and as an interim treasurer and superintendent, helped to preserve the seminary during these difficult years. In 1893 all of Lane's faculty except Morris resigned in protest over the General Assembly's interference in their institution's affairs, especially its rebuking of Lane's trustees for retaining Henry Preserved Smith after the presbytery of Cincinnati suspended him. At age sixty-eight Morris managed to provide instruction for the twenty-three students who attended Lane during the critical 1893–1894 academic year and to keep the seminary alive until it could be reorganized. After retiring in 1897, Morris resided in Columbus, taught occasional courses at Lane, preached widely, and continued to write.

While providing important service to his denomination and seminary, Morris also contributed to American Protestantism between 1880 and 1910 through his many publications. His numerous periodical articles dealt with a wide array of theological, ethical, and cultural issues. Two of his books were especially important because they clarified and defended Reformed views of the church and theology and helped shape the thinking of many of his contemporaries: *Ecclesiology: A Treatise on the Church and the Kingdom of God on Earth* (1885) and *Theology of the Westminster Symbols: A Commentary Historical, Doctrinal, Practical, on the Confession of Faith and Catechisms and the Related Formularies of the Presbyterian Churches* (1900). In *Ecclesiology* Morris argued that individual salvation was "the substantial basis of all social or generic changes" and that "Christianity must aim at nothing less than the regeneration of humanity in every aspect and every relation" (p. 5). The chief instrument God used to save souls and Christianize society, he averred, was the church. To play its divinely commissioned role, the church must avoid two historical patterns: the tendency to ascribe too much power to the church and to make it as important as Christ in the process of redemption, and the opposite tendency to undervalue the authority of the church and to depreciate its supernatural calling, sacraments, and mission. By explicating "the divine idea of the Church as given in Scripture," Morris sought to help resolve contemporary debates about church polity, administration, and discipline; the nature and practice of worship and the sacraments; and proper observance of the Sabbath (p. 12). In his 858-page *Theology of the Westminster Symbols* Morris defended the historic standards of the PCUSA against their many detractors by explaining their historical context, comparing them with other Christian creeds, elucidating their "grand underlying unities," and showing their relevance to his own era. By analyzing the teaching of various confessional documents drafted by the Westminster Assembly in the 1640s on doctrines such as the authenticity and authority of the Bible, the attributes and activities of God, the fall and free will of humanity, the incarnation and mediatorship of Christ, the plan and process of salvation, the nature of the Christian life, the relationship of church and state, and eschatology, Morris hoped to produce a positive, irenic, scripturally based systematic theology that could advance the vigor and success of American Protestantism. Its inherent vitality and "impregnable foundation and warrant in Holy Writ," he argued, had enabled Calvinism to thrive despite extensive opposition for three centuries and to provide the "muscular system in the great body of evangelical Christendom" at the turn of the twentieth century (pp. 809, 832).

When Morris died in Columbus, *The Continent* praised his "guidance and gover[n]ance" of his denomination, his "inspiring teaching," and his "serene and elevated" Christian life (p. 1615). A committed Calvinist, a gifted teacher, and a careful scholar, Morris labored diligently and effectively to preserve the peace and unity of the PCUSA.

• The best source on Morris's career at Lane Theological Seminary is his *Thirty Years at Lane, and Other Papers* (1896). See also Morris, "Lane Memoranda, 1879–1886," in the Lane papers, McCormick Seminary Library. Many of the letters

Morris wrote to Charles Briggs are preserved in the Dr. Charles A. Briggs Transcript at Union Theological Seminary Library in New York City. Morris wrote a number of pamphlets on different issues pertaining to the Presbyterian Church, USA. These include *The Doctrinal Platform of Our Church* (1882), *A Calm Review of the Inaugural Address of Prof. Charles A. Briggs* (1891), *A Friendly Talk on Revision; Being a Discussion of the Report presented to the Last General Assembly* (1891), and *A Defense of Lane Seminary* (1893). He also published *Outlines of Theology* (1880), *Is There Life after Death? A Treatise on the Gospel in the Intermediate State* (1887), and *A Book of Remembrance: The Presbyterian Church, New School, 1837–1869* (1905). To understand the context of Morris's labors, see Lefferts Loetscher, *The Broadening Church: A Study of Theological Issues in the Presbyterian Church since 1869* (1954), and Gary Scott Smith, *The Seeds of Secularization: Calvinism, Culture, and Pluralism in America, 1870–1915* (1985). Obituaries are in *The Continent* (New York), 2 Dec. 1915, and *Herald and Presbyter* (Cincinnati), 24 Nov. and 1 Dec. 1915.

GARY SCOTT SMITH

MORRIS, Edward Joy (16 July 1815–31 Dec. 1881), legislator, author, and diplomat, was born in Philadelphia, Pennsylvania, of unknown ancestry. He attended the University of Pennsylvania and graduated from Harvard College in 1836. He studied law and was admitted to the Philadelphia bar in 1842, while serving in the Pennsylvania assembly, 1841–1843. Morris served one term as a Whig in Congress, 1843–1845. When his bid for reelection failed, he resumed his law practice. In 1847 he married Elizabeth Gatliff Ella of Philadelphia, with whom he had two daughters.

As a young man, Morris traveled extensively in Europe and the Near East, developing impressive credentials as a linguist, until he was fluent in French, German, and Italian and able to converse in Greek, Turkish, and Arabic. In 1842 he published *Notes of a Tour through Turkey, Greece, Egypt, Arabia Petraea, to the Holy Land*, which, along with frequent travel sketches and literary commentaries published in newspapers and magazines, won him distinction before he reached his fifties.

On 10 January 1850 President Zachary Taylor appointed Morris as chargé d'affaires to the Kingdom of the Two Sicilies. At Naples until 26 August 1853, Morris had the opportunity to travel and study, out of which leisure time emerged three volumes he translated from German, Alfred de Bessé's *The Turkish Empire* (1854), Theodor Mügge's *Life and Love in Norway* (1854), and Ferdinand Gregorovius's *Corsica, Picturesque, Historical and Social* (1855), all well received by critics.

As a member of the Pennsylvania House of Representatives in 1856, Morris became a protégé of U.S. senator Simon Cameron and a leader in the state's new Republican party. Elected as a high tariff and antislavery Republican to the U.S. Congress, he served from 4 March 1857 until 8 June 1861, when he accepted President Abraham Lincoln's appointment (secured by Cameron) as U.S. minister resident in Turkey. In this position, with the active support of American Christian missionaries living in the region, he negotiated a commercial treaty (Feb. 1862) that helped to triple American exports to Turkey during his residence there. He also persuaded the Ottoman government to publish an order (Mar. 1862) prohibiting Confederate privateers from preying on U.S. merchant vessels in local waters.

On 25 October 1870, after his first wife died, Morris resigned his post in Constantinople in order to make it available for Wayne MacVeagh, Senator Cameron's son-in-law. Returning to Philadelphia, Morris flirted with the Liberal Republican movement, even accepting the nomination of that anti-Grant faction for Congress, but in November 1872 he voted reluctantly to reelect President Ulysses S. Grant. In October 1876 he married Susan Leighton and lived quietly in Philadelphia until his death there.

• References to Morris's life and work may be found in Erwin S. Bradley, *The Triumph of Militant Republicanism* (1964), Harry N. Howard, *Turkey, the Straits and U.S. Policy* (1974), and Catharine Newbold, "The Anti-Slavery Background of the Principal State Department Appointees in the Lincoln Administration" (Ph.D. diss., Univ. of Michigan, 1962). A brief but inaccurate obituary is in the *New York Times*, 1 Jan. 1882.

NORMAN B. FERRIS

MORRIS, Elizabeth (1753?–17 Apr. 1826), actress, was born probably in England, although no information is available concerning her birth and parentage. Known as the second Mrs. Owen Morris, she married the comedian after his first wife drowned in 1767 but before Elizabeth appeared with the Old American Company at Philadelphia in November 1769. It is not known if Elizabeth and Owen Morris had children.

By 1773 Elizabeth Morris had matured on the stages of the Old American Company in theaters in Annapolis, Philadelphia, New York, and Charleston, South Carolina, in roles such as Catherine in the afterpiece *Catherine and Petruchio*, Mrs. Hardcastle in Oliver Goldsmith's *She Stoops to Conquer*, and Queen Elizabeth in *The Earl of Essex*. Her portrayal of the Abbess in the American drama *Conquest of Canada, or The Siege of Quebec*, drew British army and navy detachments volunteering to appear in the battle and parade scenes.

In September 1774 Morris and the company arrived to open New York's John Street Theatre but were thwarted by the prerevolutionary Congress's resolution banning plays. During the American Revolution the company resettled in the loyal West Indies, allowing Morris, "a beautiful, stately, and pretentious woman," to develop her repertoire.

After struggling against postwar resistance to theater in New York in 1785–1786, Old American Company managers Lewis Hallam and John Henry returned in 1789–1790 to Philadelphia, where in competition with Mrs. Henry the youthful Morris was often cast to advantage against her aged husband. Thomas Wignall, champion of Morris's career, was prevented from entering management by Hallam and Henry because the latter championed the career of his prima-donna wife. In October 1791 Wignall and musician Alexander Reinagle formed Philadelphia's Chestnut Street Theatre company, and Morris and her husband joined them.

In August 1792 the Chestnut Street company defied local ordinances and attempted Boston's first theater season. Authorities grew intolerant and ended the season on 5 December during *The School for Scandal* by arresting Elizabeth and Owen Morris as they performed. Elizabeth remained based in the newly constructed Chestnut Street Theatre from its February 1794 opening until 1811, succeeding in roles such as Lady Townley in *The Provok'd Husband.* After Owen died in 1809, Elizabeth erected a monument to him at Philadelphia's St. Peter's churchyard. For many of these Chestnut Street seasons, she also performed on the circuit of Baltimore, Washington, and Annapolis, a lucrative arrangement that provided her near year-round employment.

Well past renown in the summer of 1811, Morris appeared with Philadelphia's unsuccessful Apollo Theatre company. Cast lists advertise "old Mrs. Morris," reflecting her outmoded "personal and professional style." Early in 1812 she had two short engagements at Philadelphia's Olympic Theatre. In 1812–1813 she joined the dissatisfied, unemployed, and destitute Theatrical Commonwealth. Formed to combat managerial exploitation, during 1813 and 1814 the troupe contended for audiences by alternating short engagements between Philadelphia and New York. In 1815 Morris evidently traveled with the remainder of the commonwealth to New York's Anthony Street Theatre, appearing in roles such as Kathleen in *The Poor Soldier*, a favorite of George Washington's, which in her prime in Philadelphia she had undoubtedly performed for him.

The last documented engagement for "old Mrs. Morris" was from April to June 1818 in Philadelphia with managers James H. Caldwell and James Entwisle. Morris possibly continued on the stage until 1825. According to the burial records of St. Peter's Church and *Poulson's American Daily Advertiser*, 19 April 1826, the "formerly . . . eminent actress" died in Philadelphia on 17 April 1826.

Enchanting to her audiences, Morris also fascinated off the stage. Her sharp-featured portrait depicts her eccentric attire of 1776, particularly a tall turban low on her brow and a white cravat covering her chin. Charles Durang noted that her "fantastic etiquette," considered "very oûtre," included "formal and quaint cut" short-waisted dresses with long trains and high-heeled shoes. W. B. Wood also remarked on her "peculiarities of dress," including heels "of such dangerous altitudes as required the utmost caution in her locomotion."

Wood further recorded Morris's "very mysterious manner," which some thought arose from her "reserved and retiring nature." A "tall, imposing, well-formed person," Wood noted, she attracted unwanted attention walking between her Maiden Lane lodging and New York's John Street Theatre. Consequently, with permission from one of Wood's relatives, Owen Morris installed a garden gate so she could bypass Broadway by a private path, avoiding "the vulgar eye of day."

Elizabeth Morris's spirited acting made her "the dashing high comedy lady" with the Old American Company and secured her founding membership of the Chestnut Street Theatre. She performed with grandiloquence and proper carriage of the classical style of her era. By 1796, however, her dominion on the American stage was being challenged by new arrivals, such as "that divinity of an actress" Anne Brunton Merry, whom Durang contrasted with Morris, referring to the latter as "professionally *passé*." While Morris was being remembered as "the toast of NY before 1792," newer performers were cultivating the romantic style of acting, avoiding the appearance of bombast by employing more emotion and grace. This stylistic transition evidently prompted Philadelphia's "Theatrical Censor" of 1806–1807 to criticize Morris as Lady Sneerwell in *The School for Scandal* for injurious zeal and passion. Wood later came to believe that Morris had been "greatly overvalued" for her attractiveness, considering her faulty enunciation, meager "mental qualifications," and poor "retentive memory." Regardless of how Morris's stage worth modified as her appearance and acting styles changed during her long career, Durang noted that she made "few concessions to the modern styles." Once "the favorite of the fashionable world," admired for her performances in stylish comedies and grand dramas, Elizabeth Morris was among the first celebrated women on the American stage.

• Major sources of primary material on Morris include Charles Durang, "The Philadelphia Stage, from the Year 1749 to the Year 1855. Partly Compiled from the Papers of His Father, the Late John Durang, with Notes by the Editors (Of the Philadelphia *Sunday Dispatch*), May 7, 1854 to July 8, 1860"; William Dunlap, *A History of the American Theatre* (1832); and W. B. Wood, *Personal Recollections of the Stage* (1855). Respected secondary sources, whose authors are considered to have had access to primary materials now largely unavailable, include Arthur Hornblow, *A History of the Theatre in America from Its Beginnings to the Present Time* (1919); J. N. Ireland, *Records of the New York Stage* (1866); G. C. D. Odell, *Annals of the New York Stage* (1927); Thomas Clark Pollock, *The Philadelphia Theatre in the Eighteenth Century* (1933); George O. Seilhamer, *History of the American Theatre* (1888); Eola Willis, *The Charleston Stage in the XVIII Century* (1924); and Richardson Wright, *Revels in Jamaica, 1682–1838* (1937). More recent scholarship that parenthetically expands on Morris's career and the theater scene includes Gresdna Ann Doty, *The Career of Mrs. Anne Brunton Merry in the American Theatre* (1971), and M. Julia Curtis, "The Early Charleston Stage: 1703–1798" (Ph.D. diss., Indiana Univ., 1968). Nan L. Stephenson, "The Charleston Theatre Management of Charles Gilfert, 1817 to 1822" (Ph.D. diss., Univ. of Nebraska, 1988), contains a full discussion of the activities of the Theatrical Commonwealth.

NAN L. STEPHENSON

MORRIS, Esther Hobart (8 Aug. 1814–2 Apr. 1902), suffragist and justice of the peace, was born in Spencer, Tioga County, New York, the daughter of Daniel McQuigg and Charlotte Hobart. Her mother died when Morris was a young girl, and she lost her father before she had reached maturity. Orphaned at an early age, she was fully aware of the need for women to be able to support themselves and to live independently. Forced to earn her own living, Morris started a millinery shop through which she enjoyed relative success and prosperity. In 1841 she married Artemus Slack, a civil engineer with the Erie and Illinois Central railroads; they had a child the following year. Her husband died in 1845, and Morris moved with her son to Illinois to claim land owned by her late husband. At that time, however, Illinois did not recognize the right of women to own or inherit property, and the difficulties Morris encountered in the settlement of the estate showed her that women needed legal rights equal to those of men. In Peru, Illinois, in 1845 she met and married John Morris, a prosperous merchant from Poland. The couple lived in Illinois for more than twenty years and had twins, born in 1851, and a third child who died in infancy.

In 1868 the lure of gold fever drew John Morris to South Pass City, Wyoming, where he took up mining and saloonkeeping. Esther joined him in 1869 and soon became a leading citizen of the frontier town. She nursed the sick of the community and was respected for her "strong character, positive will and dominating spirit." She was outspoken in her support of woman suffrage, and the miners liked her direct way of speaking. Standing six feet tall and weighing 180 pounds, she was bound to attract attention.

Wyoming Territory elected its first legislature in September 1869. According to legend, Esther Morris invited both candidates from South Pass City, Herman G. Nickerson and William Bright, and a large number of women to a tea party in her cabin. She then extracted a pledge from the two candidates to support an act conferring the right to vote on the women of the territory. William Bright won the election and proceeded to introduce the first bill granting full equality to women at the polls. After much ridicule and opposition, the bill finally passed on 10 December 1869. Thus, Wyoming became the first state to grant women full political rights.

Although Nickerson was responsible for circulating the story that Morris was the instigator of woman suffrage, the true extent of her influence on Bright is not known. Clearly, her outspoken support of women's rights was known to him, and many claim that she was very helpful as midwife to Mrs. Bright. Others argue that Bright introduced the bill for a variety of reasons, many of which were unrelated to Morris. First, Edward M. Lee, who was secretary of the territory and a supporter of the national woman suffrage movement, may have influenced Bright and actually drafted the bill for him. Also, Bright, originally from the South, was devoted to his wife and felt that women deserved the right to vote as much as blacks did. Other legislators voted for the bill to gain publicity for the state in order to encourage settlers and attract more women, who were then greatly outnumbered by men in the territory. Finally, many of the legislators who were Democrats hoped to embarrass the Republican governor, John Campbell. They expected him to veto the bill, thus insulting the women of the territory.

Under the suffrage statute women gained not only the right to vote but also the right to hold office in the territory. The Sweetwater County Commission appointed Morris to be the justice of the peace on 17 February 1870 as a replacement for Rufus Barr who had resigned his position to protest the suffrage statute. As the first woman in American history to hold a judicial office, she performed in an exemplary manner. She tried seventy cases with none appealed or reversed by a higher court. Her partial term ended on 1 November 1870, when she was not nominated for another term by the people of Sweetwater County.

Morris left South Pass City in 1871 to live with her son Edward, who was a newspaper publisher in Laramie. Alcoholism may have precipitated her separation from her husband. She once swore out a warrant for his arrest for assault and battery but dropped the charges. On 25 July 1874 she left Wyoming for a time to take up residence in New York. She had long since returned to Wyoming when she participated in the statehood celebration of 1890 in Laramie, where she lived with Edward and where she later died.

Morris's final years were marked with continued political activity on behalf of women. She attended national suffrage conventions and was nominated for a seat in the Wyoming legislature in 1873, but she withdrew her name. In 1894, at the age of eighty, she served as a delegate to the Republican National Convention.

Esther Hobart Morris exemplifies the rugged, independent spirit of America's pioneer women. Having overcome the trials of a young orphan and then a widow, she could identify with the principles of the woman suffrage movement and forcefully promote the cause. She is honored in Wyoming as the "Mother of Woman Suffrage" because of her outspoken support for women. She deeply believed in equal legal rights for women, although she supported the idea of separate spheres for men and women. Her statue has been placed in front of the Wyoming state capitol and in the Statuary Hall in Washington, D.C., commemorating her role as proponent of women's equal rights.

• Morris's papers are in the Hebard Collection of the University of Wyoming Coe Library, Laramie. Cora M. Beach, *Women of Wyoming* (1927), is the principal source of biographical information. The controversy concerning Morris's role in the passage of Wyoming's suffrage amendment is discussed in two master's theses, Miriam Gantz Chapman, "The Story of Woman Suffrage in Wyoming, 1869–1890" (Univ. of Wyoming, 1952), and Virginia J. Scharff, "South Pass since 1812: Woman Suffrage and the Expansion of the Western Adventure" (Univ. of Wyoming, 1981); see also Bacil B. Warren, "How Wyoming Gave Women the Right to Vote," *Denver Post*, 14 Dec. 1969; Minnie Woodring, "Famed

South Pass City Woman in Hall of Fame," *Cody Enterprise* 14 Apr. 1960; and T. A. Larson, *History of Wyoming*, rev. ed. (1978).

JANET CLARK

MORRIS, George Pope (10 Oct. 1802–6 July 1864), poet and journalist, was born in Philadelphia, Pennsylvania. Information concerning his parents, siblings, and the first ten years of his life is lacking. Apparently from a modest family background and having no formal education, his literary skills were primarily self-taught. The precise year he arrived in New York City is unclear, but he began his lifelong literary career there around age ten as an apprentice in the printing shop of writer Samuel Woodworth. By age fifteen he was publishing poems in such newspapers as the *New York Gazette* and the *American*. Morris was an extremely popular antebellum poet and songwriter and, through his editorship of several magazines, a significant member of the "Knickerbocker" school of New York literati from the 1820s to the 1850s.

Morris's literary career began to flourish in 1823, when, seconded by Woodworth, he founded the *New-York Mirror and Ladies' Literary Gazette*, which appeared weekly from 1823 to 1842. When Woodworth left the magazine in 1825, Morris assumed principal editorship and subsequently worked with several associate editors, notably Theodore S. Fay and Nathaniel Parker Willis. Along with its rival, the monthly *Knickerbocker Magazine*, Morris's *Mirror* was one of the period's key literary periodicals. It promoted the genteel, middlebrow, moderately conservative literary values of the Knickerbocker school and published most of its best-known authors, among them William Cullen Bryant, James Kirke Paulding, N. P. Willis, Fitz-Greene Halleck, Gulian Verplanck, Willis Gaylord Clark, and William Leggett. After financial problems closed the *Mirror* in 1842, Morris founded and coedited with N. P. Willis two short-lived successors, the weekly *New Mirror* (1843–1844) and a daily newspaper, the *Evening Mirror* (1844–1845), both of which met with similar difficulties. His next venture, however—the weekly *National Press*, founded in 1845 and in 1846 renamed the *Home Journal* (also with assistant editor N. P. Willis)—had great success and returned him to prosperous editorship for the remainder of his life. Like the earlier *Mirror*, the *Home Journal* was influential in promoting younger New York writers, and it made Morris a leader of the journalistic establishment.

While Morris's editorial work stands as his most significant accomplishment in historical terms, he was best known to contemporaries as a critically and financially successful poet and songwriter. His lyrics, in the words of Kendall B. Taft, were "brief, simply phrased, and unaffectedly sentimental." Described by N. P. Willis as the "song-writer of America" and by Edgar Allan Poe as "our best writer of songs," Morris produced the most widely known and appreciated lyrics of the antebellum years. The most famous is "Woodman, Spare That Tree!" (1837); other well-known titles, such as "My Mother's Bible," "We Were Boys Together," or "I Have Never Been False to Thee," convey the spirit of these popular works, which were set to music by prominent composers, including Henry Russell, Charles E. Horn, and Stephen C. Foster. Morris's facility and sure touch in song composition were legendary. N. P. Willis claimed that Morris and Henry Wadsworth Longfellow were the only writers of the period who could earn the sum of $50 for a lyric sight unseen.

Morris published four volumes of verse. Each met with great success and went into several editions: *The Deserted Bride and Other Poems* (1838, 1843, 1853); *The Whip-poor-will* (1843, 1846); *The Songs and Ballads of George P. Morris* (1844, 1846, 1852); and *Poems by George P. Morris* (1853, 1854, 1855, 1858, 1860). He also wrote *Brier Cliff* (1826; published 1935), a drama set during the revolutionary war; *The Maid of Saxony* (1842), an opera libretto; and *The Little Frenchman and His Water-Lots* (1839, 1844), a volume of humorous prose sketches. Alone or with coeditors, he also edited several anthologies of contemporary verse and songs.

In the early 1820s Morris married Mary Worthington Hopkins, the daughter of New York printer and publisher George F. Hopkins, and with her had three children. From the 1830s on, he was a respected and well-liked society figure. Active in philanthropic organizations and in the New York State militia (his honorary rank of brigadier general earned him the nickname "General" Morris), he enjoyed his later years at "Undercliff-on-the-Hudson," a country estate near Cold Springs in Westchester County, New York.

• Collections of Morris's papers and manuscripts are in the Library of Congress, Harvard College Library, the Historical Society of Pennsylvania, the New York Public Library, and the New York State Library. The drama *Brier Cliff* was published in the *Magazine of History*, extra number 194 (1935): 27–57. No biography exists, but outlines of Morris's career and additional information can be found in Kendall B. Taft, *Minor Knickerbockers* (1947), and Jean Folkerts, "George Pope Morris," *Dictionary of Literary Biography* 73: 221–24. See also Nathaniel Parker Willis, *Hurry-Graphs* (1851); James Grant Wilson, *Bryant and His Friends* (1886); and Richard Henry Stoddard, *Recollections* (1893). An obituary is in the *New York Times*, 8 July 1864.

PHILIP BARNARD

MORRIS, George Sylvester (15 Nov. 1840–23 Mar. 1889), philosopher, was born in Norwich, Vermont, the son of Sylvester Morris, a tanner, and Susanna Weston. Morris was raised in a strict Congregationalist home. Morris's father was outspoken in his support for abolition and temperance, and the family home in Norwich was a station on the Underground Railroad. After completing his college preparation at the Kimball Union Academy in Meriden, New Hampshire, Morris entered nearby Dartmouth College in the fall of 1857 and graduated first in his class in July 1861. During the 1861–1862 school year, Morris was the principal of Royalton Academy in Royalton township,

Vermont. He resigned his position in 1862, intending to accept a full scholarship to attend Auburn Theological Seminary. However, after President Abraham Lincoln's call for volunteers for the Union army at the beginning of August, Morris enlisted in the Sixteenth Regiment of the Second Vermont Brigade. Morris, who as regimental postmaster did not serve on the "firing line," was present at several major battles, including Gettysburg. He was remembered by his comrades for leading readings of Shakespeare after hours in the orderly's tent. He was mustered out as a corporal in August 1863, again intending to enroll at a seminary. With no scholarship money available, however, he took a position as a tutor at Dartmouth, where he remained for a year while he completed his master of arts degree in July 1864.

In September 1864 Morris entered Union Theological Seminary in New York, where he studied with Henry B. Smith, an influential scholar who helped to introduce the study of German philosophy to American universities. On the advice of Smith, Morris left the seminary in December 1865 to study philosophy in Germany from April 1866 until August 1868. While in Germany, he studied with Friedrich Adolf Trendelenburg, whose revitalization of Aristotle and criticisms of Immanuel Kant significantly influenced Morris's philosophical development. Following his return to the United States, Morris served as a tutor for the family of New York banker Jesse Seligmann, while he began his important translation of Friedrich Überweg's *History of Philosophy* (1871 and 1873) for a series edited by H. B. Smith and Philip Schaff. In 1870 Morris became professor of modern languages and literatures at the University of Michigan. During 1874 and 1876 Morris published several significant philosophical papers on the role of final causes in knowledge, mind, and art that helped to establish his reputation as a philosopher. In June 1876 Morris married Victoria Celle at Ann Arbor, Michigan. They had a son and a daughter.

In 1877 Morris was invited to become a lecturer at the Johns Hopkins University, where he presented several lecture series during January 1878 and 1879. He joined the faculty at Hopkins in February 1880 and shortly thereafter published *British Thought and Thinkers*, a series of lectures given at Hopkins. In these lectures he criticized British empirical philosophy for treating human intelligence as fundamentally passive, merely receiving the experienced world, rather than as having an active role in constructing it. Since Morris's appointment at Hopkins was part-time, Michigan arranged for him to rejoin the faculty part-time as professor of ethics, history of philosophy, and logic. Morris became the editor for a series of philosophical textbooks on German philosophy in 1881 and wrote the first volume, *A Critical Exposition of Kant's Critique of Pure Reason* (1881). Morris returned to Union Seminary in 1883 to give the prestigious Ely Lectures, which were published later that year as the volume *Philosophy and Christianity*. In 1885, after his position was not renewed at Hopkins, Morris returned to Michigan as the head of the Department of Philosophy. During the summer of 1885 Morris returned to Europe and met with a number of the most significant philosophers of the day, including F. H. Bradley, Edward Caird, and T. H. Green, and the German psychologist Wilhelm Wundt. After his visit to Europe, Morris published a second volume in his German philosophy series, *Hegel's Philosophy of the State and of History* (1887). During a stay at the family vacation home at North Lake, Michigan, Morris caught a "severe chill" and died.

In his philosophical work, Morris attempted to understand the connections between individuals and society and humanity and the natural world. Against religious and philosophical idealism of the sort represented by German idealism, Morris argued for the importance of experience and the role of environment in understanding the world. Against mechanistic science and empirical philosophy of the sort represented by British empiricism, he argued for the constructive role of individuals and society in making the reality we experience. In order to join these disparate views, Morris proposed an organic conception of "intelligence" that held that knowledge is the result of an interaction between knowers and the world. The purpose of philosophy, as a mode of knowledge, was to understand the universe as a whole and so to provide guidance for the progress and use of special studies in science and religion. Morris's work found its greatest influence in the philosophy of John Dewey. Morris was Dewey's teacher and mentor at Hopkins and gave Dewey a position in the philosophy department at Michigan after Morris's graduation. Like Morris, Dewey's philosophy involves the rejection of the philosophical separation of individuals from the world, an organic conception of knowledge, and an activist conception of philosophy. Although Morris is often viewed as offering an ill-formed combination of Aristotle's empiricism and German idealism, his work is better understood as a part of the American philosophical tradition with its emphasis on the role and responsibility of individuals within society and the reality or "givenness" of the natural world.

• Morris's papers are at the University of Michigan. Other significant published works include "Friedrich Adolf Trendelenburg," *New Englander* 33 (1874): 287–336, reprinted as Appendix A in Marc Edmund Jones's biography, *George Sylvester Morris* (1948), pp. 335–84; "The Final Cause as Principle of Cognition and Principle in Nature," *Journal of the Transactions of the Victoria Institute, or Philosophical Society of Great Britain* 9 (1874): 176–204; "The Theory of Unconscious Intelligence as Opposed to Theism," *Journal of the Transactions of the Victoria Institute, or Philosophical Society of Great Britain* 11 (1876): 247–91; "The Philosophy of Art," *Journal of Speculative Philosophy* 10 (1876): 1–16; "Philosophy and Its Specific Problems," *Princeton Review* 9 (1882): 208–32; "University Education," *University of Michigan Philosophical Papers* (1886); and the unused introduction to Morris's 1887 Hegel volume published as Appendix B in Jones's *George Sylvester Morris*, pp. 385–412. Another biography of Morris is R. M. Wenley, *The Life and Work of G. S. Morris* (1917). Also see John Dewey, "The Late Professor Morris,"

The Early Works, 1882–1898, vol. 3 (1969). For Morris's influence on Dewey, see Dewey, "From Absolutism to Experimentalism," *The Later Works, 1925–1953*, vol. 5 (1984), and Neil Coughlan, *Young John Dewey: An Essay in American Intellectual History* (1975). Herbert W. Schneider, *A History of American Philosophy* (1946), provides a useful summary of Morris's work and its relation to the American philosophical tradition.

SCOTT L. PRATT

MORRIS, Glenn Edward (18 June 1912–1 Feb. 1974), Olympic decathlon champion, was born in Simla, Colorado, near Fort Collins, the son of farming parents (names unknown). Morris was acknowledged the best high school track and field athlete and the best football player in the state, and he continued both activities at nearby Colorado State University, where he earned All-America honors in the two sports in his senior year (1934). At one track meet he won eleven events. At the national level, he won junior and senior Amateur Athletic Union (AAU) competitions in the 400-meter hurdles. From 1934 to 1936 he devoted himself to the arduous task of Olympic Games preparation in the ten-event decathlon, the most difficult event on the Olympic program. Morris qualified as a member of the U.S. Olympic Team and headed for Berlin in the summer of 1936. At twenty-four years of age he stood six feet tall and weighed 200 pounds. He was sufficiently handsome to attract Hollywood motion picture scouts even before his victorious world record results in the Olympic decathlon were printed in the world's sporting pages.

The Berlin Games were the biggest and most competitive of the Olympics up to that time, all amid the specter of Adolf Hitler and the Nazi party. Morris had the best two days of his career, breaking the Olympic and world records in the decathlon. He scored 7,900 points; a fellow American, Robert Clark, was second (7,601 points), and their compatriot, Jack Parker scored 7,275 for third place. The three Americans led the scoring after the first day. On the second day the rivals were to toil for ten hours in a cold rain. The stadium lights were turned on for the last event, the "metric mile" or 1,500-meter run. Morris ran a magnificent time of 4 minutes, 33.2 seconds to guarantee victory. The handsome American became a world celebrity, second only to the four gold-medal winner and African American Jesse Owens. Morris's 7,900 points remained on the record book for fourteen years. The Associated Press called Owens the greatest athlete of the Games, but the American AAU, angered at accusations of athletic professionalism leveled at Owens, voted Morris to receive its highest honor, the Sullivan Award trophy. He retired as a decathlon athlete; according to Bill Mallon, he was "one of the few track and field athletes never defeated in his major event."

In December 1936 Morris married his college friend Charlotte Edwards, a professional nutritionist who had supervised his training diet. In 1937 Morris signed a quarter-million-dollar contract with Twentieth Century Fox Studios, and the next year he starred in *Tarzan's Revenge*, sharing the screen with multiple Olympic swim champion Eleanor Holm. Morris appeared in *Hold That Coed* (1938), with John Davis and John Barrymore. An early biographical sports film titled *Decathlon Champion: The Story of Glenn Morris* (1936) gave him a kind of immortality.

Morris played professional football in 1940 as a wide receiver and defensive end with the Detroit Lions. Following the attack on Pearl Harbor, Morris joined the U.S. Navy and served as a chief specialist in the Pacific, where he was seriously wounded. After World War II, never fully recovered from the trauma of war, Morris worked in the construction industry in Menlo Park, California, until his death in the adjoining city of Palo Alto.

• Morris's early years are described in I. G. Klinghorn, "Glenn Morris, Olympic Star," *Rotarian*, Jan. 1937, p. 56. Also see Bill Mallon's essay in David L. Porter, ed., *Biographical Dictionary of American Sport: Outdoor Sports* (1988). Again, Mallon and Ian Buchanan are helpful in *Quest for Gold* (1984), p. 327. Morris's achievments in Berlin and prior to these 1936 Olympic games are detailed in Frank Zarnowski, *The Decathlon* (1989), pp. 70–72; Duff Hart-Davis, *Hitler's Games: The 1936 Olympics* (1986), p. 226; William J. Baker, *Jesse Owens: An American Life* (1986), pp. 144–45; F. A. M. Webster, *Olympic Cavalcade* (1948), p. 213; and Alexander M. Weyand, *The Olympic Pageant* (1952), p. 268. On Morris's movie career, see David Fury, *Kings of the Jungle: An Illustrated Reference to "Tarzan" on Screen and Television* (1994), pp. 135–36. There are scores of articles on Morris in the *New York Times* dealing with his athletic and film-making adventures. Obituaries are in the *New York Times* and the *Los Angeles Times*, both 2 Feb. 1974.

JOHN A. LUCAS

MORRIS, Gouverneur (30 Jan. 1752–6 Nov. 1816), framer of the Constitution and diplomat, was born at the family manor, "Morrisania," in what is now The Bronx, New York, the son of Lewis Morris, Jr., a judge of the court of vice-admiralty in New York, and his second wife, Sarah Gouverneur, daughter of a Speaker of the New York Assembly. His grandfather, Lewis Morris (1671–1746), was a governor of New Jersey. Gouverneur attended the Academy of Philadelphia (1761–1764) and King's College, New York (1764–1768), with a year off (1766–1767) to recover from a scalded right arm and side. Tall, handsome, rich voiced, and self-assured, he admitted that he spoke "too often and too long," but even a critic acknowledged that he was "an ingenious orator, who possesses an exuberant fertility of invention, and is capable of decorating the product of imagination with all the ornaments of language" ("Lucius," *Freeman's Journal*, 30 May 1781).

As the youngest of three sons, he received a limited inheritance of £2,000 and opted for a legal career. After a three-year apprenticeship in the New York office of William Smith, Jr., he received a license to practice and an M.A. from King's College. With the outbreak of the Revolution, he at first advocated compromise lest the colonies fall under "the domination of a riotous mob" (Sparks, vol. 1, p. 25). Possibly his brilliance, which he took "no pains to conceal" ("Narrative of the Prince de Broglie," *Magazine of American History* 1 [1877]: 234), made of him an elitist. But after the battle of Lexington, as the inheritor of a family tradition of colonial self-government, he sided with the patriots. On 8 May 1775 he was elected from Westchester County to the newly formed New York Provincial Congress. There he proposed the issuance of a Continental paper currency, which the Continental Congress adopted. He advocated in an eloquent oration the elimination of separate colonial identities and a congress chosen from national districts. In the framing of a constitution for New York State, he secured a £20 freehold voting qualification but unsuccessfully argued for a strong governor with veto and appointive powers. He defeated attempts to deny religious freedom to Catholics and advocated abolition of slavery "so that in future ages every human being who breathes the air of this State shall enjoy the privileges of a freeman" (*Journals of the Provincial Congress*, vol. 1 (1842), p. 887).

On 3 October 1777 the provincial congress elected Morris a delegate to the Continental Congress. He promoted army reforms requested by George Washington, notably officers' half pay for life, which, however, the Congress reduced to seven years. Upon the arrival of conciliatory British negotiators, he drafted the Congress's rejection of any terms short of independence and issued a white paper that concluded with a call to create "an Assylum to mankind. America shall receive to her bosom and comfort and cheer the oppressed, the miserable and the poor of every nation and of every clime" (Committee of Congress, *Observations on the American Revolution* [1779], p. 132). With the signing of the Franco-American treaty of alliance, he headed a committee that drew up instructions for Benjamin Franklin (1706–1790), minister plenipotentiary, proposing a Franco-American invasion of Canada. Washington, however, objecting that this would beggar his southern campaigns and might tempt France to repossess Canada, persuaded the Congress to abandon the scheme. In the dispute between two of America's commissioners to France, in which Silas Deane declared that the supplies furnished by the financier Caron de Beaumarchais were a private loan and not an obligation of the French government, as Arthur Lee maintained, Morris sided successfully with Deane. He also successfully opposed the New England congressmen's demand that Newfoundland fisheries rights be an ultimatum in the peace negotiations. As a precocious nationalist, Morris introduced sweeping proposals for reforms later adopted by the Constitutional Convention: state cession of western land claims to the national government; elimination of state currencies in favor of a single national issue; removal of interstate commercial restrictions in favor of a national tariff; and the creation of a "chief of states" responsible to the Congress. In the New York Assembly, his localist opponents charged him with inattention to its land claims to the New Hampshire Grants (the future state of Vermont) and on 1 October 1779 removed him from Congress.

On 6 July 1781 Robert Morris (1734–1806), superintendent of finance, appointed Gouverneur (no relation) as his assistant; he served three and one-half years. Gouverneur Morris drafted a proposal for the Bank of North America, chartered by Congress on 31 December 1781 and financed with a $254,000 French loan, and himself purchased a $400 share. He also drafted the "Report on Public Credit," which has been described as "the most important single state paper on public credit ever written prior to Hamilton's First Report on Public Credit" (Clarence L. Ver Steeg, *Robert Morris, Revolutionary Financier* [1954], p. 124). It called for national assumption of state war debts at face value, a 5 percent ad valorem duty on imports, a $1 poll tax on freemen and male slaves, and a ⅛$ excise tax on alcoholic beverages. The Morrises enlisted the support of the army officers, desperate for pay, whom Gouverneur urged to "associate themselves together in one common Interest" with all public creditors. He bluntly asked Henry Knox, commander of the northern army, and Nathanael Greene, commander of the southern army, to support use of force, but both refused. When Washington, at Newburgh, appealed to his officers for patience, the "conspiracy" collapsed.

On 14 May 1780 Morris was thrown from a phaeton and his left ankle broken. The leg was removed below the knee. Thereafter his oaken leg became his trademark but did not interfere with his reputation as a gallant. He remained in Philadelphia and as an attorney successfully represented the Bank of North America in defeating attempts to repeal its charter and incorporate a competing bank. As a businessman, with loans from Robert Morris, he joined the partnership of William Constable and Company, purchased a St. Lawrence River township of 60,641 acres, and invested in a share in John Fitch's steamboat company. After the death of his mother, he purchased on 4 April 1787 the nearly 1,400-acre Morrisania estate from the family heirs for £2,500 in cash and £7,500 on credit.

The Pennsylvania General Assembly elected him a delegate to the federal Constitutional Convention on 30 December 1786, against his wishes and by a bare majority of thirty-three out of sixty-three. James Madison (1751–1836) reported that Morris insisted on "the political depravity of men, and the necessity of checking one vice and interest by opposing them to another vice & interest," but was willing to change his mind, "making the best of measures in which he had been overruled" (Sparks, vol. 1, p. 286). He considered property the foundation of society and defended a market economy against abridgment or regulation. He argued unsuccessfully for a legislature with an upper house appointed by the executive for life, a lower house elected by freehold suffrage, greater representation for the maritime than the western states, and rejection of representation based on three-fifths of a state's slave population. He smoothed acceptance of the "great compromise" by the large states, however, with the provision that direct taxation be proportioned to representation. His major contribution was to the formation of the executive. He preferred an independent executive popularly elected for life and unimpeachable but settled for a reeligible term of two years, impeachment for treachery and bribery, and a veto over Congress subject to a three-fourths override. Then, as the spokesman for a committee of eleven, one from each attending state, he proposed the electoral college system for a four-year reeligible term, with the president's treaty-making power limited by two-thirds of the Senate, and nomination of Supreme Court justices and ambassadors confirmed by a Senate majority. Concerning civil rights, Morris opposed bills of attainder, religious tests for public office, and suspension of the writ of habeas corpus except during threat of war. Appointed to the committee on style, he condensed the original twenty-three articles into the final seven. In the preamble, he substituted "People of the United States" for "People of the [enumerated states]," thus interposing a potential bar to state separatism, and he added the invocation to "form a more perfect Union, establish Justice, insure domestic Tranquility, provide for the common defence, promote the general Welfare, and secure the Blessings of Liberty to ourselves and our Posterity."

On 18 December 1788 he departed for France, sent by his business associates to promote their tobacco contract with the French Farmers General, sale of lands in the St. Lawrence and Genesee river valleys, and purchase from France of the American debt of $34 million at fifty cents on the dollar. On 21 January 1790 he received an appointment from President Washington as an informal emissary in London to inquire whether Britain would comply with the 1783 peace treaty by evacuating the northwest forts and paying for the slaves taken by the departing British armies, and whether a treaty of commerce could be negotiated. Morris believed that Britain would agree only under duress, and he secretly schemed, through correspondence with friends and French and Spanish officials, to exacerbate the then-developing Nootka Sound Controversy into a general European war of Spain and Spain's allies against Britain. Spain, however, acceded to Britain's demands, and war was averted.

On 12 January 1792 Washington named Morris minister plenipotentiary to France. Morris's diary while there is a major record of the times. He was an open partisan of the monarchy, fearing the destruction of the old order before the people were prepared for a new one. Predicting that a revolution would only pave the way for the rise of a demagogic dictator, he preferred a limited monarchy. He antagonized the Jacobins by arranging the aborted flight of Louis XVI, providing refuge for royalists in his residence, and refusing to treat with the new government for payment of an advance on the American debt. He refused to extradite Thomas Paine, who as a naturalized French citizen had been elected to the National Assembly but was then jailed for his Girondist convictions. In 1794 the French requested Morris's recall in retaliation for the American rejection of Edmond Charles Genet. Afterward, although a private citizen, Morris journeyed to England and pressed upon Prime Minister William Pitt an unsuccessful invasion plan to restore the French monarchy. In 1798, enriched with land speculations but having failed to purchase the French debt, he returned to America.

In 1800 the Federalist-controlled New York legislature elected him to a three-year unexpired term as U.S. senator. He proved to be a partisan Federalist, heatedly opposing repeal of the Judiciary Act of 1801, and, as a continuing opponent of Napoleonic France, supporting James Ross's unsuccessful resolutions for an attack on New Orleans. In retirement, for once disagreeing with his Federalist friends, he approved the purchase of Louisiana as a shield against a French invasion. He opposed the embargo and charged that the War of 1812 was a plot of the slaveholding states to conquer Canada. He endorsed the Hartford Convention but criticized it as too timid and advocated the secession of New York and New England from the Union. Yet two months before his death he conjured the Federalists to "forget Party and think of our Country." Concluding his career in New York, he teamed with DeWitt Clinton to propose the construction of the Erie Canal.

He married Anne Cary Randolph on 25 December 1809, unmoved by charges never legally proved that she had committed adultery with her brother-in-law, Richard Randolph. Morris died at Morrisania of a chronic obstructive uropathy. His oft-quoted strictures against popular government have obscured his achievements in the Constitutional Convention as a principal architect of the presidency and the stylist of the Constitution. He saw no contradiction in championing private property and defending civil rights.

• Morris's youthful manuscripts and lifelong correspondence are at Columbia University; his diaries and letterbooks, beginning in 1789, are in the Library of Congress. Published writings are in Jared Sparks's prudishly pruned *Life of Gouverneur Morris, with Selections from His Correspondence and Miscellaneous Papers* (3 vols., 1832); the selectively edited *Diary and Letters of Gouverneur Morris*, ed. Anne Cary Morris (2 vols., 1888); the faithfully and sprightly edited *Diary of the French Revolution by Gouverneur Morris*, ed. Beatrix C. Davenport (2 vols., 1939); and the Parke-Bernet Galleries 7 Apr. 1970 manuscript sale 3019 catalog of excerpts, *Americana . . ., Including Selections from the Papers of Gouverneur Morris* (1970).

Max M. Mintz, *Gouverneur Morris and the American Revolution* (1970), is comprehensive, with an extensive bibliography. Earlier biographies are Theodore Roosevelt, *Gouverneur Morris* (1888); Daniel Walther, *Gouverneur Morris, Témoin de Deux Revolutions* (1932; English trans. 1934); Howard Swiggett, *The Extraordinary Mr. Morris* (1952); and Mary-Jo Kline, "Gouverneur Morris and the New Nation, 1775–1788" (Ph.D. diss., Columbia Univ., 1970). On the Morris family genealogy, see Eugene R. Sheridan, *Lewis Morris, 1671–1746* (1981). On Morris as assistant superintendent of finance, see E. James Ferguson and John Catanzariti, eds., *The Papers of Robert Morris, 1781–1784* (1973–). On Morris as an "aristocratic capitalist," see Jennifer Nedelsky, *Private Property and the Limits of American Constitutionalism: The Madisonian Framework and Its Legacy* (1990). On Morris as the convention "floor leader" of the advocates of an independent presidency, see Charles C. Thach, Jr., *The Creation of the Presidency, 1775–1789* (1922).

MAX M. MINTZ

MORRIS, John Gottlieb (14 Nov. 1803–10 Oct. 1895), Lutheran pastor, entomologist, and Baltimore cultural leader, was born in York, Pennsylvania, the son of John Samuel Gottlieb Morris, a physician, and Barbara Myers. Raised in a pious middle-class household, Gottlieb, following his father's death in 1808, lived much of his life in unusually close relationship to his mother and his brother, Charles. After studying at the College of New Jersey (later Princeton University) and graduating from Dickinson College in 1823, he studied theology at Princeton Seminary and at the infant Gettysburg Seminary. He married Eliza Hay in 1827; they had three children.

Licensed (1826) and ordained (1827) by the Maryland and Virginia Synod of the Lutheran church, Morris became pastor of First English Lutheran Church, Baltimore, Maryland, in 1826, serving there with distinction until 1860, when he became the librarian for the new Peabody Institute. In 1867 he resigned as librarian to become the pastor of Third English Lutheran Church in Baltimore, serving until 1873.

From his earliest days Morris was vigorous, faithful, progressive, and successful. First English Lutheran Church grew and flourished under his leadership. He also was active in the larger issues that shaped nineteenth-century American Lutheranism. An influential preacher and teacher, he was elected seven times as president of his church's Maryland Synod and twice chosen head of the General Synod, the first national Lutheran church body.

Until the mid-1840s Morris advocated "American Lutheranism," identified with a broader Protestant evangelicalism. He was also the founder and first editor of its journal, *The Lutheran Observer*, and a promoter of the Sunday School movement, the establishment of Bible societies, and various reform efforts. But after 1845 his own studies in Lutheranism, together with the theological trends brought from Germany, led him to move to a more conservative theological position and a greater emphasis upon the Lutheran Confessions. He became a major figure in the more conservative wing of the General Synod, which split in the 1860s, and later led efforts to draw together the separated bodies, primarily through organizing Free Diets in the 1870s.

Through six decades Morris labored energetically to build an English-speaking Lutheranism that would take its place in American life and share in building cultural, scientific, and political institutions. His writings and speeches presented to an American public the heroic figure of Martin Luther as the father of modern liberty and Lutheranism as the mother denomination of modern Protestant, American civilization. For five decades Morris served on the boards of the seminary and the college at Gettysburg and was a frequent lecturer. In 1843 he helped found the Lutheran Historical Society, served for many years as its president, and secured American Lutheran publications for its collection.

Morris also distinguished himself as an entomologist and promoter of scientific interests in America. He enthusiastically searched for butterflies and moths and created systematized collections for them. As a teacher at Gettysburg (then Pennsylvania) College he created and purchased specimen collections in the 1840s and led movements to form the Linnaean Society and erect a campus building for the study of natural history. In the next decade he developed for the Maryland Historical Society a broad and useful collection of natural history specimens and exhibits. A founding member of the American Association for the Advancement of Science in 1848, he later served as chairman of its entomology subsection. Interested in reconciling the Genesis account with scientific theory, he lectured in natural theology for both church and civic gatherings.

In the field of science Morris's most enduring and significant publications were *Catalogue of the Described Lepidoptera of North American* (1860) and *Synopsis* (1862), both published by the Smithsonian Institution. His biographer, Michael Kurtz, rightly named him "a pioneer in the arena of American natural science."

One of the most remarkable aspects of Morris's career was his indefatigable efforts on behalf of the cultural life of Baltimore, of Maryland, and of German Americans. In the 1830s Morris participated in the early phase of the Lyceum movement. Through hundreds of lectures on scientific, literary, and historical topics, through popular readings in famous literature, and as a teacher of elocution and president of the Baltimore Lyceum, he became prominent in the city's cultural and civic life. Many of his lectures and writings brought history—especially biography—to a wide audience. He also interpreted German literature for American audiences, partly to encourage his German-American colleagues to take pride in their heritage while also taking part in American public life.

Morris's most significant impact on cultural affairs was through the Maryland Historical Society. There his energy, organizational skills, and interests combined for the shaping of a major and public research library for the city of Baltimore. Beginning in 1855 until the end of his life he served as director. Morris also served as a board member of the Peabody Institute and was its first librarian (1860–1867).

Perhaps the best example of Morris's interest in civic and church life was his establishment of Lutherville, Maryland. Using his own summer home, and then with the help of a private corporation that he formed with money from friends and early Lutherville residents, he built a female seminary and sold lots for residences. Lutherville—now a Baltimore suburb—was a pleasant rural village with summer homes for the well-to-do of the city. Morris believed firmly in the importance of education for women and wanted a good school for his own daughters. The seminary opened in

1854 and for three decades he was virtually its owner and primary director. Despite his efforts direct support for the school from Lutheran synods never materialized, yet it served both church people and the broader community. Morris died in Lutherville.

• The bulk of Morris's papers is in the Archives of the Lutheran Theological Seminary at Gettysburg, which complement documentation on Morris contained in the institutional records of the seminary and the college at Gettysburg, the Maryland Historical Society, and the Peabody Institute. His own reminiscences are contained in *Fifty Years in the Lutheran Ministry* (1878) and *Life Reminiscences of an Old Lutheran Minister* (1896). A definitive and well-annotated biography is Michael J. Kurtz, *John G. Morris: An American Patriot and Scholar Informed by Faith* (1996).

FREDERICK K. WENTZ

MORRIS, John McLean (1 Sept. 1914–8 Apr. 1993), reproductive biologist and physician, was born in Kuling, China, the son of DuBois Morris, a Presbyterian missionary and pastor of Presbyterian Church in Manhattan, and Alice Buell. The suffering and cruelty Morris witnessed in China as a child had a lasting influence on his life. He later spoke of seeing people stepping over the bodies of the dead and dying in the streets. His interest in women's health and reproductive issues stemmed from the widespread infanticide of baby girls he saw in China.

Morris earned his A.B. from Princeton in 1936 and his M.D. from Harvard Medical School in 1940. He joined the navy when the United States became involved in World War II and served four years in the Pacific as a lieutenant commander in the Navy Medical Corps. Morris married Marjorie Stout Austin in 1951; they had five children.

Just after World War II Morris identified and described a rare sexual disorder, testicular feminization. The condition, also known as Morris' Syndrome, causes genetic males to develop as females because they have faulty receptors for testosterone, the hormone responsible for the development of male traits. After the war, and possibly as a result of his experience in the Navy Medical Corps, Morris also became an advocate of radiation treatment for cancer, especially tumors of the ovary. Radiation treatment for cancer was a new idea in the United States and was not commonly taught in medical schools or practiced as it was in Europe. In 1951, therefore, Morris went to Sweden on a year-long fellowship to study radiation therapy.

When he returned from Sweden in 1952, Morris joined the faculty of Yale University. There he began a radiation center and was the attending gynecologist at the Yale University School of Medicine and the Yale-New Haven Medical Center. He was also a consulting gynecologist at Meriden Hospital; the Veterans Administration Hospital in West Haven, Connecticut; Middlesex Memorial; New Britain General Hospital; and Uncason-Thames Hospital. He twice acted as chairman of obstetrics and gynecology at Yale. He became full professor of gynecology there in 1961.

As a surgeon, Morris developed new techniques in pelvic surgery for treatment of ovarian cancer. His interest in birth control led him to design new versions of the intrauterine contraceptive device (IUD). He was a medical adviser to Planned Parenthood and the World Health Organization and a lifelong advocate of population control. Morris also maintained ties with China by acting as chairman of the Yale-China Medical Committee.

In the early 1960s Morris began researching the safety and effectiveness of the morning-after pill. Funded by the Population Council of New York and collaborating with Gertrude van Wagenen of the Yale medical school, he showed that the estrogen compounds in the pill prevented a fertilized egg from implanting in the uterus for up to six days after conception. Morris and van Wagenen presented their work in April 1966 to a meeting of the American Fertility Society. The popular press and the scientific community both lauded the development as the first safe and effective means, other than abortion, of post-intercourse birth control. Europe quickly adopted the new form of birth control, but the United States was slower to make full use of it, limiting its use mostly to college students. Morris remained active after his retirement in 1987 as a proponent of population control and a consultant, until his death of prostate cancer in Woodbridge, Connecticut.

Morris made lasting contributions to research on many gynecological topics, including field surgery and radiation therapy, cancer, dosimetry, radiation sensitivity, ovarian tumors, endocrinology, intersexuality, urinary diversion procedures, and drugs that affect the development of fertilized eggs. With Robert E. Scully, Morris wrote *Endocrine Pathology of the Ovary* (1958).

Morris served effectively on the National Board of Medical Examiners, the American Board of Surgery, and the American Board of Obstetrics and Gynecology. He held membership in the American Gynecological Society, the American Fertility Society, the Society of Pelvic Surgeons, the New England–St. Paul Surgical Society, the New Haven Obstetrics Society, the New Haven County Medical Society, Sigma Xi, and Alpha Omega Alpha.

• Accounts of Morris's discovery of the morning-after pill are in *Time*, 6 May 1966, p. 60; and *US News and World Report*, 4 Oct. 1965, pp. 56–58. Obituaries are in the *New York Times* and the *New Haven Register*, 11 Apr. 1993; the *Los Angeles Times*, 12 Apr. 1993; and *Yale Medicine* 27, no. 1 (1992–1993): 54.

BETH MARTIN

MORRIS, Lewis (15 Oct. 1671–21 May 1746), chief justice of New York and royal governor of New Jersey, was born in New York City, the son of Richard Morris, who had recently migrated from Barbados to pursue a career as a merchant, and Sarah Pole. A member of a Welsh gentry family, Richard Morris had fought for Parliament during the English Civil War and then became a sugar planter on Barbados. Orphaned by the deaths of his parents less than a year after his birth, Lewis Morris was raised by his father's brother Lewis, a strict Cromwellian Quaker and also a sugar planter, who moved from Barbados to New York to care for his nephew. Morris was educated by at least two tutors, one of whom was George Keith, the noted Quaker apologist. But the high-spirited Morris rebelled against his stern uncle's efforts to raise him according to the precepts of the Inner Light and ran away to the West Indies in about 1689, returning home shortly before his uncle's death in February 1691.

The magnificent inheritance Morris received from his uncle made him a member of the landed elites of New Jersey and New York, whose values he espoused and whose interests he defended for the rest of his life. At an estimated value of £16,818, the main elements of this inheritance were the 6,200-acre manor of "Tinton" in New Jersey, complete with a profitable iron works; the 1,900-acre estate of "Morrisania" in New York (for which Morris obtained manorial status in 1697, making him the only colonial manor lord in two different provinces); and a seasoned workforce of at least sixty-six black slaves, which made him the largest slaveholder in the history of the Middle Colonies. In November 1691 Morris wed Isabella Graham, the daughter of James Graham, the Speaker of the New York Assembly, beginning an enduringly affectionate marital relationship that produced fifteen children, eleven of whom reached adulthood. Sometime later Morris entered the Anglican church and remained at least a formal member until his death, having by middle age privately rejected Christian orthodoxy and embraced deism.

Morris devoted much of his life to a relentless effort to exemplify the norms of English gentility. He acquired a knowledge of Greek, Latin, Hebrew, and Arabic and accumulated a library of 3,000 volumes. He read widely in classical and modern history and literature and wrote poetry, mostly political satires. He loved music, becoming a fiddler of dubious merit, and was keenly interested in natural science, amassing an impressive collection of fauna.

Morris's great wealth, high social status, acquired gentility, and driving ambition were the mainsprings for one of the most remarkable political careers in colonial history. An unabashed elitist, Morris believed that political power follows the balance of property. He never doubted that the landed elite should play the leading political role in the two colonies where he resided. Despite their frequent affluence, he viewed merchants as too concerned with private profit and too at variance with the interests of the agrarian majority to pursue the common good of society. Moreover, it was axiomatic to him that artisans, craftsmen, laborers, and ordinary farmers ought to follow the lead of those he deemed their wiser social betters. Only members of the landed elite possessed the proper blend of wealth, prestige, talent, honor, and wisdom to provide the effective political leadership and concern for the public interest he regarded as essential for a well-ordered polity.

Morris's long and eventful political career began in October 1692 when he was appointed by Governor Andrew Hamilton to the East Jersey Council and the East Jersey Court of Common Right and Chancery. Attaching himself to the proprietary interest, Morris labored at first in obscurity. Then in April 1698 newly arrived Governor Jeremiah Basse, whose authority Morris had refrained from recognizing because of Basse's lack of the royal approval required for colonial governors by a 1696 act of Parliament, dismissed Morris from his conciliar and judicial offices, propelling him to the forefront of East Jersey politics. Once out of office, Morris undermined Basse's administration by mobilizing popular opposition to him and the proprietary regime through a series of "Red-Hot" letters to various towns calling for the royalization of East Jersey and criticizing Basse's alleged venality. Morris's actions accelerated the final crisis of proprietary government in East Jersey, forcing the proprietors to replace Basse with Hamilton and to begin negotiations with the imperial administration for the surrender of their governing rights.

In order to expedite these frustratingly slow negotiations, Morris embarked on a resoundingly successful mission to London in 1701–1702. He served as the chief intermediary between the East Jersey and West Jersey proprietors and the board of trade and was one of the main architects of the settlement. The proprietors surrendered their rights of government to the Crown in return for the establishment of a unified royal colony of New Jersey, the confirmation of proprietary rights to the soil, and the creation of an electoral system designed to secure the dominance of the landed elite through high property qualifications for assemblymen and voters. For this the imperial administration made Morris the senior member of the New Jersey Council and acting chief executive of the colony until the arrival of its first royal governor, Edward Hyde, Lord Cornbury, in 1703. While in London Morris became the first American member of the Society for the Propagation of the Gospel in Foreign Parts, an influential Anglican missionary organization. He also paved the way for his appointment in 1703 as American business agent of the West Jersey Society, a group of English land speculators with interests in various northern colonies, a position he held until 1736.

Lord Cornbury's assault on key elements of the settlement Morris had helped to fashion in London led Morris to assume the role of defender of popular liberties and proprietary privilege on his return to New Jersey. Cornbury turned against the proprietary party, suspended Morris from the New Jersey Council, destroyed the restrictive electoral system Morris favored, and threatened the landed prerogatives of the East Jersey proprietors with whom Morris was allied. Morris then won election to the New Jersey Assembly in 1707 and induced it to petition Queen Anne to remove the noble lord from office on the ground that he was a threat to constitutional liberties and proprietary rights. The imperial administration removed Cornbury in 1708 and also restored Morris to the New

Jersey Council. Morris gradually consolidated his victory over the next five years by securing a restoration of proprietary control over the New Jersey Council as well as over land distribution and the collection of quitrents in the colony.

Morris retained his seat on the New Jersey Council and continued to play a leading role in the colony's political affairs, but beginning in 1710 he shifted the focus of his attention to New York. He formed a political alliance with Governor Robert Hunter, on whose behalf he undertook to manage the New York Assembly, to which he was elected in 1710. Morris gradually built up a court party, based on the landed interest, that won firm control of the New York Assembly by 1715. Under Morris's leadership the New York Assembly provided Hunter with a five-year Support Act financed by duties on trade rather than taxes on land, thus ending a grave political and constitutional crisis that had pitted the governor against the assembly and had stalemated New York politics for many years. At the same time Morris prevailed on Hunter to agree informally to expend public funds as the assembly specified by recommendatory resolutions in its journals, thereby satisfying the assembly's long-standing wish for greater control over the public purse while preserving the Crown's fiscal prerogatives nominally intact. Hunter rewarded Morris for helping to maintain the rudiments of balanced government in New York by appointing him chief justice of the New York Supreme Court in 1715. Morris continued to manage the New York Assembly for Hunter and his successor, William Burnet, until 1725, when the rival merchant interest led by Adolph Philipse won control of that body and made it impossible for Morris to transact the governor's business.

Morris emerged as a staunch defender of the royal prerogative in New York in response to the Philipsite repudiation of his constitutional compromise on control of provincial finances. When the New York Assembly under Philipse's leadership asserted a unilateral right to determine the salaries of royal officials in 1726, Morris perceived a grave threat to balanced government in New York. He criticized the assembly for usurping the Crown's right to reward its servants and persuaded Burnet to resist its effort to reduce his salary as chief justice. In 1729 Governor John Montgomerie finally acquiesced in the New York Assembly's determination to reduce Morris's salary as chief justice, and the imperial administration ignored a strong protest against Montgomerie's action by Morris's son, Lewis Morris, Jr., a provincial councillor. Morris then sought unsuccessfully to compensate for his declining political fortunes in New York by seeking an appointment as royal governor of New Jersey.

During the final phase of his career in New York, Morris assumed the role of a country party leader in opposition to the arbitrary rule of Governor William Cosby. Morris was dismissed as chief justice of the New York Supreme Court by Cosby in April 1733 for opposing Cosby's attempt to settle a legal dispute with New York councillor Rip Van Dam by circumventing the jury system. Morris responded by forming the most radical country party in New York before the American Revolution. Denouncing Cosby as a despotic governor who threatened the constitutional liberties of New Yorkers, Morris won election to the New York Assembly and helped to launch the *New-York Weekly Journal*. The first avowedly opposition newspaper in New York, the *Weekly Journal* called for an independent judiciary, a legislatively independent council, and a stronger assembly, all the while arraigning Cosby and his closest supporters for being on the wrong side in the age-old contest between power and liberty. But the Morrisites could not break Cosby's control over the New York Assembly. When in November 1734 the governor struck back by having the printer of the *Weekly Journal*, John Peter Zenger, arrested on a charge of seditious libel, Morris decided that his only recourse was to outflank the governor by undertaking a second mission to London. During his 1735–1736 stay in London Morris failed to achieve any of his primary objectives—Cosby's removal as governor, his own restoration as chief justice, or the enactment of the Morrisite reform program. He did, however, win the patronage of two highly influential Royal Navy admirals, Sir John Norris and Sir Charles Wager, who prevailed on the Walpole ministry to appoint him royal governor of New Jersey in 1738.

Morris's vertiginous political career came to a stormy climax when he reverted to the role of defender of the royal prerogative against legislative encroachments during his gubernatorial administration in New Jersey. Concerned to reverse what he took to be a dangerous decline of royal authority, stemming from the governor's excessive dependence on the assembly for financial support, Morris informed the New Jersey Assembly in 1738 that henceforth as governor he would be the ultimate arbiter of the public good in the colony and that the provision of revenue for the government would no longer be contingent on prior gubernatorial approval of popular legislation. However, to quell fears of arbitrary executive power, he strengthened the independence of the judiciary by commissioning the chief justice of the New Jersey Supreme Court to serve during good behavior and enhanced the independence of the New Jersey Council by absenting himself from its legislative sessions. The two actions nicely mixed principle and nepotism, since the judge in question, Robert Hunter Morris, the governor's youngest son, also served on the council. But Morris's efforts to reinvigorate royal authority in New Jersey ran afoul of the province's long-standing drive for greater autonomy within the British empire. Morris soon found himself involved in a succession of increasingly bitter disputes with the assembly over his refusal to approve popular laws that ran counter to imperial policies, his vigorous support for imperial military expeditions against Spain in the West Indies and the French in Canada, and his staunch defense of colonial subordination to Parliament. At length, in 1744, the New Jersey Assembly refused to provide any further revenue for his administration unless he first approved a number of popular acts, one of the few times in colonial history an assembly took such a drastic step. Rather than compromise, Morris appealed to the imperial administration for the passage of an act of Parliament to make him and other royal governors in America financially independent of their legislatures—a plea imperial officials ignored because of their preoccupation with the war against Spain and France. Thus Morris and the New Jersey Assembly remained deadlocked until his death. Morris died near Trenton, New Jersey, but not before he had sown one of the seeds of the American Revolution with his call for radical parliamentary intervention to shore up royal authority in America.

• The most important collections of Morris's papers are the Morris Family Papers in Rutgers University Library, the Lewis Morris Papers in the New Jersey Historical Society, and the Rutherfurd Collection in the New-York Historical Society. Key selections of these papers are printed in Stanley N. Katz, ed., "A New York Mission to England: The London Letters of Lewis Morris to James Alexander, 1735 to 1736," *William and Mary Quarterly*, 3d ser., 28 (1971): 439–84, and William A. Whitehead, ed., *The Papers of Lewis Morris* (1852). The most comprehensive edition of Morris's papers is Eugene R. Sheridan, *The Papers of Lewis Morris, 1698–1746* (3 vols., 1991–1993). See also Eugene R. Sheridan, ed., *Lewis Morris, 1671–1746: A Study in Early American Politics* (1981), and John R. Strassburger, "The Origins and Establishment of the Morris Family in the Society and Politics of New York and New Jersey, 1630–1746" (Ph.D. diss., Princeton Univ., 1976).

EUGENE R. SHERIDAN

MORRIS, Lewis (8 Apr. 1726–22 Jan. 1798), the third and last lord of Morrisania Manor and member of the Continental Congress, was born on the family estate in Westchester County, New York, the son of Lewis Morris and Tryntje Staats. His grandfather and namesake was the redoubtable first lord of Morrisania Manor, chief justice of the New York Supreme Court, and royal governor of New Jersey.

Morris's education was the subject of considerable concern on the part of both his father and grandfather. Early on, as the presumptive third lord of the manor, he was introduced to the management of Morrisania, with its many slaves, tenant farmers, and artisans. His early schooling prepared him for college, yet in 1746 he left Yale without a degree. Returning to Morrisania, he played an increasingly larger role in running the estate with his father, who also was a judge in the vice admiralty court and was influential in provincial politics. Morris concentrated on developing the resources of Morrisania and making the manor operate more effectively; he did not add to the estate's nearly two thousand acres. In 1749 he married Mary Walton, the daughter of Jacob Walton, a wealthy New York City merchant. They would have ten children.

Upon his father's death in 1762, Morris became the third lord of Morrisania Manor. Perhaps encouraged by his brother Richard, who also owned lands in Westchester County and who succeeded to the vice admiralty judgeship once occupied by his father, Morris became much more involved in politics. Winning election to the provincial assembly in 1769, he joined the Livingston faction in the assembly in opposition to the faction identified with the De Lancey family, whose members were wealthy New York City merchants and neighboring landlords in Westchester County. The De Lancey party challenged the legitimacy of Morris's election from the borough of Westchester, wherein Morris owned land although he lived outside the town itself, and he was expelled from the assembly. His expulsion further embittered the political rivalry between the Morrises and the De Lanceys, which dated back to the 1720s. A staunch Anglican, as were the De Lanceys, Morris nevertheless supported the unsuccessful efforts of the Livingston faction to give all Protestant churches equal standing before provincial law, much to the chagrin of various Anglican clerics. Moreover, as England and its American colonies argued over parliamentary taxation, he became increasingly outspoken in his criticism of British imperial policy.

The De Lanceys accused Morris of acting out of malice and jealousy, and he obviously resented the powerful connections that the De Lanceys had in England. But in fact, Morris feared parliamentary pretensions, even though he was a conservative Whig who also worried about the "democratic spirit" that the controversy with Britain was unleashing. He also understood that his family's wealth and status might well be lost in any military confrontation with the mother country. Except for Morris and Pierre Van Cortlandt, the large landlords and most of the other inhabitants of Westchester County showed little enthusiasm for colonial resistance to imperial policy. Nevertheless, after the provincial assembly refused either to endorse the Continental Association or to appoint delegates to the Second Continental Congress, Morris supported a countywide meeting at White Plains, where delegates from Westchester County were to be chosen and sent to the provincial congress called for April in New York City. At White Plains, despite the powerful opposition of landed families like the Pells and Philipses as well as the De Lanceys, Morris was chosen chair of the Westchester delegation to the state gathering. He was also among the delegates sent by the New York provincial congress to the Second Continental Congress in May 1775.

While serving in this first provisional government of the United States for two years, Morris performed a number of administrative duties. Because a British invasion of New York was imminent, he was initially assigned to a committee that explored the best ways to defend the vulnerable province. His other committee assignments included arranging military supplies and treating with the western Indians. In June 1776, as the British invasion of New York began, Morris took a leave of absence from the Continental Congress and accepted an appointment as brigadier general of the Westchester County militia. He took part in the New York campaign as British general William Howe pursued General George Washington across Long Island

and Manhattan and through Westchester County. As a result, Morris was not in Philadelphia when the Declaration of Independence was adopted, but he did attend the New York provincial congress that shortly thereafter approved of breaking free of Great Britain; he later returned to Philadelphia and added his signature to the Declaration in his capacity as a member of the Continental Congress.

Leaving the New York delegation in 1777, Morris was replaced in the Continental Congress by his half-brother Gouverneur Morris. Although he remained a general in the state militia, he performed mainly civil duties for New York state for the rest of the American Revolution. In 1777 and 1778 he was a judge for northern Westchester County, the only part of the county under American control. Between 1777 and 1790 he also served periodically in the New York Senate. Occupied by British troops during much of the war, his beloved Morrisania was plundered by both sides. Much of its woods were cut down by the British, and several of its buildings were burned. The manor house itself was wrecked. In 1783 Morris retired from the state militia with the rank of major general. Thereafter he gave most of his attention to restoring the family estate, but he still maintained a considerable political presence in the New York Senate.

Although allied with popular governor George Clinton, Morris remained a conservative Whig—very much concerned, as were the Livingston, Van Cortlandt, and other landed families, that the property and political influence of the patriotic landlords should be protected. Well into the 1790s the masterful Clinton, whose political base was primarily the yeomanry of Orange and Ulster counties, succeeded in keeping most conservative Whigs such as Morris and his brother Richard within his coalition party. In 1784 Morris was appointed to the board of regents for the University of the State of New York, on which he remained until his death. In 1786 he served on the Council of Appointments, an influential body that selected many important county officials. However, Morris differed sharply with Clinton over the ratification of the federal Constitution. In 1788, the year after his half-brother Gouverneur had helped shape the Constitution, Morris was at the Poughkeepsie Convention as an ally of Alexander Hamilton in support of the proposed document.

As a patriotic leader, Morris had risked his life and his property in defense of American freedom. But he was always a conservative Whig dedicated to the protection of the property and privileges of the patrician class to which he belonged. His last foray into politics was as an elector for John Adams and Thomas Pinckney in 1796. His final years were spent refurbishing his estate, his pride and joy, and living the life of a country gentleman in Westchester County. He died in Morrisania Manor.

• Morris's papers are widely scattered in the collections of contemporary figures, including Alexander Hamilton, John Jay, George Clinton, and Gouverneur Morris. Broad details of his life and career are given in Franklin Bowditch Dexter, ed., *Biographical Sketches of the Graduates of Yale College* (6 vols., 1885–1912). Insight into the Morris family and his early life can be found in Eugene R. Sheridan, ed., *The Papers of Lewis Morris* (3 vols., 1991–1993), esp. vol. 3. Also of interest with regard to his service during the American Revolution are "Letters to General Lewis Morris, 1775–1782," *New York Historical Society Collections* 7 (1875): 433–512. The political environment that Morris entered in 1769 is described by Leopold S. Launitz-Schurer, Jr., *Loyal Whigs and Revolutionaries: The Making of the Revolution in New York, 1765–1776* (1980). His association with the Clinton coalition is discussed in Alfred F. Young, *The Democratic Republicans of New York: The Origins, 1763–1797* (1967). His role at the Poughkeepsie Convention is mentioned by Linda Grant DePauw, *The Eleventh Pillar: New York State and the Federal Constitution* (1966), and in the essays in Stephen L. Schechter, ed., *The Reluctant Pillar: New York and the Adoption of the Federal Constitution* (1987).

RONALD W. HOWARD

MORRIS, Nelson (21 Jan. 1838–28 Aug. 1907), cattle trader, breeder, and meatpacker, was born in Hechingen, Germany, a province of Hohensollern; his parents' names are unknown. His father had raised cattle in the Black Forest but, implicated in a plot to unite the area with Switzerland, fled to America. Morris thus arrived with his family in 1851 in Philadelphia, Pennsylvania, utterly poor, without formal education, and speaking no English. He had already worked in Germany selling rags, skins, and copper for his father; in America he took whatever odd jobs he could find and peddled for two years. In 1853 he headed north, working as a charcoal hauler in Lakerville, Connecticut; he then traveled west, working on boats on the Erie Canal and the Great Lakes. When he arrived in Chicago, he took a job cleaning animal pens at John B. Sherman's Bull's Head Yard (Sherman later founded and promoted the Union Stock Yards). In winter he would work all night, watching hogs to ensure against their crowding together and suffocating. By the time Sherman moved his operations to his Lake Shore Yards, Morris was the feedmaster.

While still working for Sherman, Morris began in 1856 to purchase crippled and smothered hogs, which he sold to renderers. Morris often made his purchases at the end of the market week, taking whatever had not been sold when farmers were ready to accept almost any price. He soon expanded his venture by buying cattle as well, principally from farmers in Blue Island, which he sold to Sherman. In 1859 Morris was ready to become a full-time livestock broker (he was not Chicago's first; that distinction belongs to Solomon P. Hopkins). Sherman encouraged him to do so, lending him money to get started and offering advice. In 1863 Morris married Sarah Vogel; they had five children.

Morris's firm began in 1859 as a partnership with Isaac Waixel, a recent German immigrant knowledgeable about livestock. They soon established themselves as a leading firm by securing a major contract to provide meat for the Union army. By the end of the Civil War they were the sole meat provider for the

Army of the West. Building on this experience, Morris would sustain goods links to governments, handling major contracts for the American, French, British, and German governments. This foundation propelled Morris into leadership in the live cattle trade from Chicago to Atlanta and made him a pioneer in transatlantic shipments, which he initiated in 1868 with shipments to Glasgow and London. By 1885 he had perfected techniques for handling livestock on ships, such as the design of stalls and specialized vessels, and among seagoing cattle mortality had dropped to below 1 percent. Morris also did some of the earliest experiments with shipping frozen beef to eastern markets, shipping frozen sides during the winter in standard boxcars (this succeeded only when the weather cooperated). Morris was a pioneer in transporting dressed beef to the seaboard.

With Hopkins and Samuel Allerton, Morris became the first, in 1865, to move his firm to the Union Stock Yards, creating the first consolidated stockyard with extensive, direct railroad connections. (Although John B. Sherman founded the Union Stock Yards, he was not himself a packer or a major trader.) The move was an immediate, unparalleled success, quickly putting all of the old, dispersed yards out of business. Morris's own facility there eventually covered thirty acres. By 1873, when his revenues exceeded $11 million, Morris also began to handle pork, and by 1877 he was sufficiently established to expand his pork packinghouse. He then added packing plants in three other cities: East St. Louis, Illinois; St. Joseph, Missouri; and Kansas City, Kansas. In 1883 Morris joined Nathaniel Fairbank in a firm that produced and shipped dressed beef, canned meats, and butterine; in 1884 he began building his own refrigerated railroad cars and establishing branch sales houses. By 1888 he had nine branches spread throughout eastern cities and was the third largest meatpacker in the country. Thus, Morris followed a pattern of rarely pushing innovation himself but quickly exploiting techniques that others—principally Gustavus Swift—had demonstrated were successful.

In 1889 the practices of the "Big Four" meatpackers (Armour, Hammond, Morris, and Swift), which included price fixing and division of sales territories, came under scrutiny in a Senate investigation chaired by Senator George G. Vest; its report in 1890 was highly critical of the meatpackers, accusing them of collusion to control the meat market. Even if true, these alleged practices gave Morris little benefit in the 1890s: though slaughtering 5,000 to 8,000 cattle a day and as many pigs and sheep, and though generating nearly $1 billion in sales, the company's profits were barely .5 percent. In 1893 Morris turned most management responsibilities over to his son Edward. Over the next thirty years, the company decreased in significance, and in 1923 Armour bought its physical assets.

Morris, like Swift, was an expert butcher in his own right, as well as a skilled cattle buyer. After he married, Morris built a large frame home at Indiana and Twenty-fifth Streets, just a "buggy ride away" from the yards. He arrived at his office when the yards opened at 6 A.M., coming in with the regular employees. Although Morris often struck people as cold and cruel, those close to him judged him as "warm-hearted."

In addition to his importance as a meatpacker, Morris did significant work in breeding, which he carried out on a 300,000-acre ranch in Texas, another 30,000-acre spread in Indiana, and a third ranch of 30,000 acres in Nebraska. He was perhaps the first to import Polled-Angus and Galloway cattle. These large operations also made him at one point the largest cattle finisher in North America, handling 75,000 head annually.

In addition to serving as the president of both Nelson Morris & Company and Fairbanks Canning Company, Morris served as a director of the First National Bank, the First Trust and Savings Bank, the National Live Stock Bank, the People's Trust and Savings Bank, the New England Stockyards Company, the Brighton Stockyards Company, the St. Joseph Stockyards Company, the Western Meat Company, the South Omaha Land Company, the San Francisco Land Improvement Company, and the Union Rendering Company. He was also a major owner of Chicago real estate. He established the Nelson Morris Institute of Pathological Research and was a major contributor to Chicago's Michael Reese Hospital. He died in his beloved Chicago home.

Morris was one of the principal actors in the development of the modern meatpacking industry, especially in developing export markets in Europe. Although he was rarely himself an innovator, he was an aggressive competitor who quickly exploited opportunities, thus pushing others to do the same.

• The only extant original sources are Morris's correspondence, included in the Jeremiah McLain Rusk Papers at the State Historical Society of Wisconsin. The autobiography of Ira Nelson Morris, *Heritage from My Father: An Autobiography* (1947), provides limited information on Morris's career. There is substantial literature on the development of the meat-packing industry, the central role that it played in the development of refrigeration technology, and its sometimes bitter relationship with railroads. See Oscar Edward Anderson, Jr., *Refrigeration in America* (1953); Rudolf A. Clemen, *The American Livestock and Meat Industry* (1923); Wilfred V. Casgrain, *Memorandum on the Life of George H. Hammond, 1838–1886* (1945); and Mary Yeager Kujovich, "The Refrigerator Car and the Growth of the American Dressed Beef Industry," *Business History Review* 44, no. 4 (Winter 1970): 460–82. See also Jimmy M. Skaggs, *Prime Cut: Livestock Raising and Meatpacking in the United States, 1607–1983* (1986); Mary Yeager, *Competition and Regulation: The Development of Oligopoly in the Meat Packing Industry* (1981); and Louise Carroll Wade, *Chicago's Pride: The Stockyards, Packingtown, and Environs in the Nineteenth Century* (1987).

FRED CARSTENSEN

MORRIS, Richard (15 Aug. 1730–11 Apr. 1810), lawyer and judge, was born in Westchester County, New York, the son of Lewis Morris, second lord of the manor of Morrisania, and Tryntje Staats. He was the brother of Lewis Morris, the third and last lord of Morrisania Manor and signer of the Declaration of Independence, and the half-brother of Gouverneur Morris, who wrote the final draft of the Constitution of 1787.

Morris's early education was supervised by his grandfather, Lewis Morris, the first lord of Morrisania Manor, who had been chief justice of New York and who became governor of New Jersey in 1738. Both his father and grandfather groomed him for the bar. He learned Latin, graduated in 1748 from Yale, and soon began pursuing a legal apprenticeship. In 1750, while he was still studying law, the general assembly appointed him clerk of the Courts of Oyer and Terminer and General Gaol Delivery for provincial New York. Two years later he was commissioned an attorney at law and opened his office in New York City. His father, judge of the vice admiralty court, made Richard his deputy.

Morris married Sarah Ludlow in 1759 and established his country home at Mount Fordham, not far from Morrisania; the couple would have three children. However, the focal point of his work was New York City. In 1761 he was appointed clerk of the New York Supreme Court. Following his father's death in 1762, Morris succeeded to the judgeship of the vice admiralty court for New York, New Jersey, and Connecticut. Few young lawyers enjoyed such an extensive practice. Indeed, Morris possessed both the legal skills and the family influence so crucial to success at the bench and the bar in colonial America. The coming of the American Revolution threatened his successful career, however.

Unlike his brothers Lewis and Gouverneur, Richard did not participate in the American protest to parliamentary taxation. However, despite pleas from William Tryon, the royal governor of New York, that he continue in the vice admiralty court, Morris resigned his judgeship in the fall of 1775. His reluctance to espouse publicly the patriotic cause, combined with his well-known aristocratic temperament, led the provincial committee charged with deterring conspiracies to question his "equivocal neutrality." Yet when New York's provincial congress set up its own court of admiralty in 1776, Morris was asked to become its judge. Citing family exigencies following the destruction of his Westchester County estate, which was apparently ravaged by both American and British troops, Morris declined the position.

Morris returned to public life in 1778 after the New York State Assembly appointed him to replace a senator from the southern district, as the area around New York City occupied by the British was called. He served in the senate until 1780. In 1779 he was appointed chief justice of the supreme court of New York, the position for which he is best known; in so doing he succeeded his friend John Jay. Like Jay and his brothers Lewis and Gouverneur, Morris was a conservative Whig who wanted to protect the interests of the propertied classes from the more reform-minded politicians who followed Governor George Clinton, the champion of New York's yeoman farmers. Sympathetic to the plight of former Loyalists, Morris urged that they be allowed to return to New York unmolested. In 1785 the chief justice appealed personally to Governor Clinton to pardon a Loyalist soldier convicted by a Westchester jury and sentenced to be executed because he had been a member of a Tory regiment that hanged a patriot in 1781.

Like most conservative Whigs, Morris was a strong supporter of the proposed federal Constitution of 1787. Elected as a delegate from New York City to the Poughkeepsie ratifying convention, he played a major role, along with his brother Lewis, former loyalist Samuel Jones, and Alexander Hamilton, in convincing the initially anti-Federalist majority into ratifying the Constitution with recommendations. The divisions that appeared at the Poughkeepsie Convention threatened the Clintonian coalition and foreshadowed the development of the Federalist party in New York state politics. In 1789 the Federalists seriously considered running Morris for governor against the popular Clinton, finally deciding instead upon Robert Yates, an anti-Federalist judge. Morris was also a leading contender for one of New York's U.S. Senate seats, but that too proved elusive.

Having gotten his fill of politics as well as the bench and the bar, Morris retired from public life in 1790. Following the American Revolution, his estate having been seriously damaged by the war, he built another house at Scarsdale in Westchester County and purchased farm lands around the town of Greenburgh. He lived the remainder of his life as a country gentleman. He died at Scarsdale.

• Relatively few of Morris's papers have survived. Letters to and from him may be found in the collected papers of Alexander Hamilton, John Jay, George Clinton, and Gouverneur Morris. Information on his early life is in Eugene R. Sheridan, ed., *The Papers of Lewis Morris* (3 vols., 1991–1993), esp. vol. 3. His life is reviewed in Franklin Bowditch Dexter, ed., *Biographical Sketches of the Graduates of Yale College* (6 vols., 1885–1912). His roles in confederation politics and in the ratification of the U.S. Constitution are discussed in Alfred F. Young, *The Democratic Republicans of New York: The Origins, 1763–1797* (1967); Linda Grant DePauw, *The Eleventh Pillar: New York State and the Federal Constitution* (1966); and Stephen Schechter, ed., *The Reluctant Pillar: New York and the Adoption of the Federal Constitution* (1987).

RONALD W. HOWARD

MORRIS, Richard Brandon (24 July 1904–3 Mar. 1989), historian, was born in New York City, the son of Jacob Morris, a supervisor in the garment industry, and Tillie Rosenberg. As a high school student at Townsend Harris Hall, Morris developed a strong interest in history. Encouraged by his teachers, the fifteen-year-old Morris in 1920 published an article in the *American Hebrew and Jewish Messenger*, "Alexander Hamilton as a Hebraist," which noted the Old Testament foundations of early American law—foreshadowing his scholarly career.

Morris's "love affair with history," as he termed it in a *William and Mary Quarterly* interview (vol. 41 [July 1984]: 455), gathered intensity at the City College of New York, from which he graduated cum laude as a history major in 1924. His interest in legal history had been whetted by Morris Raphael Cohen's course in the philosophy of law, and Morris promptly embarked on graduate study at Columbia University under the tutelage of colonial historian Evarts B. Greene. His master's paper, "Massachusetts and the Common Law," was published in the *American Historical Review* in 1926. Convinced that to write legal history he needed courses in the law, Morris persuaded Columbia Law School traditionalists—who saw law and history as separate disciplines—to admit him to three years of law classes, taken simultaneously with his full graduate history program. Morris was awarded an M.A. in 1925 and a Ph.D. in 1930. A law school paper, "Primogeniture and Entailed Estates," which appeared in the *Columbia Law Review* in 1927, became the second chapter of his dissertation, *Studies in the History of American Law*, published in 1930.

Studies set forth in four chapters a revisionist view of the legal foundations of the United States. Rather than emphasizing the transplantation of legal principles and institutions from England to the colonies, as was then fashionable, Morris took his stand squarely in seventeenth-century America. Surveying three spheres of legal practice common to the colonies—the distribution and alienation of land, women's position in the law, and legal liability in an agrarian society—he argued that in cases where the common law was excessively technical or offered little guidance, the colonists had shaped legal practices to fit their social and environmental circumstances. Such colonial innovations, though curbed after 1690 by imperial reforms and the rise of a provincial propertied class, demonstrated the "refreshing originality" (p. 258) of what Morris termed "American law."

It was a bold interpretation that drew praise from scholars appreciative of Morris's effort at synthesis. But some law professors, suspicious of legal reasoning that rested so lightly on the weighty tomes of English jurisprudence, clearly resented Morris's foray into their terrain. Undeterred, Morris pursued his interest in legal history in journal articles and in edited works such as *Proceedings of the Maryland Court of Appeals, 1695–1729* (1933), with Carroll T. Bond, and *Select Cases of the Mayor's Court of New York City, 1674–1784* (1935).

While teaching undergraduate classes at City College in the 1930s, Morris, married in 1932 to Berenice Robinson and soon the father of two sons, supplemented his meager salary by serving as secretary to the American Historical Association's Committee on Legal History. Charged with locating and publishing court records from the period before 1790, the committee dispatched Morris on a search of local repositories from Maine to Florida. This spell in the archives convinced him that the role of law in society should become the prime focus of his scholarship.

Perhaps partially in response to his critics' charge that *Studies in the History of American Law* lacked a sufficient empirical base, and by his own account stimulated by the New Deal's involvement with labor issues, Morris in 1946 produced his formidable *Government and Labor in Early America*. Based on about 20,000 cases—primarily unpublished inferior court records, supplemented by statutes, town ordinances, and vestry records—*Government and Labor* explored in scrupulous detail the working conditions, regulation, and concerted actions of free and bound workers in colonial America. The role of labor was no more than a gleam in history's eye in 1946, and Morris's study offered a pioneering examination of many aspects of the subject. In 1960 he and others attracted to the topic founded a journal, *Labor History*, with Morris serving as chair of its editorial board for sixteen years.

With the publication of *Government and Labor* Morris vaulted to the top of his field, as was shown by the honors soon bestowed on him: the first of three Guggenheim fellowships (1947, 1961, and 1982); a visiting professorship at Princeton University's graduate school; a stint at the Institute for Advanced Study; and in 1949 a tenured professorship at Columbia University. Although Morris would later take up visiting professorships at the University of Hawaii, the Free University of Berlin, and the Hebrew University of Jerusalem, Columbia—where he was named Gouverneur Morris Professor of History ("no relation," he delighted to point out)—became his permanent academic home.

At Columbia Morris's teaching responsibilities focused on the period of the American Revolution and the Confederation and Constitution; soon his research interests shifted accordingly. Beginning in the 1950s he published a brief history of the American Revolution and a volume on Alexander Hamilton as a founder of the nation. With Henry Steele Commager he edited the popular sourcebook *The Spirit of 'Seventy-six: The Story of the American Revolution as Told by Participants* (1958). Morris's interest in the leaders of the Revolution came to center on a man he considered the era's most neglected figure, New Yorker John Jay; Columbia had purchased his papers from the Jay family, and Morris was chosen to edit them.

The first fruit of this project was Morris's magisterial study of Jay and other diplomats who forged the treaty ending the revolutionary war, *The Peacemakers: The Great Powers and American Independence* (1965). Here was Atlantic-world history of the highest order; Morris had burrowed through the archives of ten countries. While he was attentive to the basic documents of diplomatic give-and-take, his prime objective in *The Peacemakers* was to scrutinize the personal relations and discern the inner drives of the leading negotiators. As Morris noted, "Nations are notoriously prone to apotheosize their war heroes and forget their peacemakers" (p. 438). The book won almost universal praise, including a Bancroft Prize (1966). A Pulitzer Prize was also within Morris's grasp, but the

Pulitzer board overrode its nominating jury's recommendation of *The Peacemakers* to bestow a posthumous award on Perry Miller's *Life of the Mind in America*—a blow that temporarily reduced the usually buoyant Morris to a state of subdued disappointment.

Morris was soon back at work, however, producing two volumes in 1967. His Anson G. Phelps Lectures at New York University appeared as *The American Revolution Reconsidered*; the Gaspar G. Bacon Lectures at Boston University were published as *John Jay, the Nation, and the Court*. From his sixth-floor office at the top of Fayerweather Hall, Morris now became a close observer of the radical tide rising at Columbia and other universities around issues of civil rights and the Vietnam War. As a student of revolutionary turmoil, he could see elements of both nihilism and moral conviction in the new radicalism. Yet Morris's personal defense of the American liberal ideal against "egregious distortion" (p. xi) by its critics was vigorously asserted in *The Emerging Nations and the American Revolution* (1970), in which he proclaimed the American Revolution a still-relevant model for twentieth-century independence movements—a position that prompted some criticism.

Morris's long-held belief that historians had an obligation to address the broader public had already borne fruit in works such as *Fair Trial: Fourteen Who Stood Accused from Anne Hutchinson to Alger Hiss* (1952), six books of American history for children, *The Making of a Nation: 1775–1789*, with the editors of *Life* (1963), and *Seven Who Shaped Our Destiny: The Founding Fathers as Revolutionaries* (1973). Morris formally retired from Columbia in 1973. While continuing to teach part time and to edit the papers of John Jay, Morris now put his undiminished energy at the service of the coming bicentennial of the American Revolution. He served on national and international commissions, advised on television series and "Bicentennial Minutes," and lectured on the meaning of the Revolution in exotic places such as Iran and Afghanistan.

A signal recognition of his eminence was Morris's election in the bicentennial year 1976 as president of the American Historical Association. During his presidency he organized (with James McGregor Burns, his counterpart at the American Political Science Association) a ten-year educational program, Project '87, designed to stimulate public interest in the origins of the U.S. Constitution for its bicentennial in 1987. Although Morris often jested that he did not expect to be around for that anniversary, he survived two years beyond it. His last writings focused on the framers of the Constitution; his respect for their achievements was evident in *Witnesses at the Creation: Hamilton, Madison, Jay, and the Constitution* (1985).

Morris's final years were filled with honors, including the Society of American Historians' Bruce Catton Prize for Lifetime Achievement in the Writing of History (1988). Perhaps most satisfying, he was widely recognized not only as a prolific and versatile scholar but also for having made seminal contributions to increasingly important sectors of American history such as legal, labor, women's, and public history. He died in New York City.

• Morris's papers are in the Special Collections Library, Columbia University. In addition to the interview cited, Morris expresses personal opinions in "The View from the Top of Fayerweather," in *Freedom and Reform: Essays in Honor of Henry Steele Commager*, ed. Harold M. Hyman and Leonard W. Levy (1967), and other essays listed by Mary Jo Kline in *Perspectives on Early American History: Essays in Honor of Richard B. Morris*, ed. Alden T. Vaughan and George Athan Billias (1973). Major works not mentioned in the text include *The Forging of the Union, 1781–1789* (1987); the *Encyclopedia of American History*, which appeared in six editions between 1953 and 1982 and a seventh edition in 1996 under the supervision of Jeffrey Morris; and two edited volumes of Jay papers, *John Jay: The Making of a Revolutionary* (1975) and *John Jay: The Winning of the Peace* (1980). An excellent assessment of Morris's contributions to American legal history is Stephen Botein, "Scientific Mind and Legal Matters: The Long Shadow of Richard B. Morris's *Studies in the History of American Law*," *Reviews in American History* (June 1985). An obituary is in the *New York Times*, 6 Mar. 1989.

PATRICIA U. BONOMI

MORRIS, Robert (20 Jan. 1735–8 May 1806), preeminent merchant and revolutionary financier, was born in Liverpool, England, the son of Robert Morris, Sr., an ironmonger and later a tobacco agent in Maryland, and Elizabeth Murphet. Shortly after Morris joined his father in Maryland in 1747, his father placed him in the care of Robert Greenway of Philadelphia, who obtained an apprenticeship for Robert in the established Philadelphia mercantile house of Charles Willing. Morris quickly displayed exceptional talent and resourcefulness in commerce, sometimes serving as supercargo on the firm's vessels. He also became a lifetime friend of Charles Willing's son Thomas. They established the firm of Willing and Morris on 1 May 1757, developing a network of mercantile connections in Great Britain, Portugal, Spain, and the West Indies. By 1773 the firm owned no less than ten vessels and chartered others for specific voyages; by 1775–1776 Morris had become, in effect, the managing partner. Meanwhile, in 1769 Morris had married Mary White of Maryland, with whom he had seven children.

When differences arose between Britain and its North American colonies after 1763, Morris opposed the revenue measures adopted by Parliament. In 1765 he signed the nonimportation agreement protesting the Stamp Act and with six others persuaded the Philadelphia collector to give up his appointment. In June 1775 Morris was appointed to the Pennsylvania Council of Safety, with special assignments to procure arms and ammunition and to serve as its banker. In October he was elected to the provincial assembly and made vice president of a renewed council of safety.

On 3 November the Pennsylvania legislature elected Morris as a delegate to the Second Continental Congress, where he served on the influential Secret Committee of Trade, Congress's war department; the critical Committee of Secret Correspondence, Congress's department of foreign affairs; and the Marine Committee, Congress's naval department. His dominance of these committees quickly established him as a leading member of Congress. Until December 1776 Morris wrote most of the essential diplomatic correspondence of Congress, but his assignment to the Secret Committee of Trade overshadowed other responsibilities.

As chairman of the Secret Committee of Trade after 14 March 1776, Morris took charge of much, if not most, of its vital activity, which included contracting with merchants and business firms to obtain needed war matériel and purchasing commodities for export as remittances. He often used Willing and Morris's network of commercial agents to implement the committee's task. The firm's warehouses became so crowded with Continental supplies that Continental guards were assigned to protect them. The complexity of the enterprise overtaxed the available accounting and communication techniques, with the result that the records of the committee became hopelessly tangled. Inevitable complications arose from the war. Often years elapsed between the time a contract was made, goods were purchased abroad, and the ships, if not captured, arrived, often carrying private as well as public consignments. Because of his central role, Morris was drawn into controversy regarding the disposition of government money and goods, which critics later used to cast a shadow on his reputation.

The decision for independence did not come easily to Morris. He and John Dickinson, another delegate from Pennsylvania, abstained from the crucial ballot of 2 July so that the state could vote for independence. However, Morris signed the finished draft of the Declaration of Independence and, thereafter, backed independence with enthusiasm. His energy, experience, and talent were best displayed when Congress, having withdrawn to Baltimore to escape advancing British forces, vested him with the authority to act on its behalf in Philadelphia in 1776–1777. Among other decisions, he issued orders to the Continental vessels in the Philadelphia harbor, prepared for the evacuation of stores, and sent supplies and money to General George Washington. Congress praised Morris's actions: "Your whole Conduct since our Flight is highly approv'd," wrote John Hancock. In 1778 Morris completed his term as a congressional delegate.

As a merchant, Morris regarded the release from British trade restrictions and the domestic demand for goods as a golden business opportunity. "Profits are now so great it is well worth risquing largely," Morris wrote William Bingham, his agent in Martinique. Willing and Morris developed an interconnection of partners and agents throughout America, the West Indies, and Europe. Beginning in 1777 Morris also engaged in privateering. When Willing refused to leave Philadelphia after the British captured the city, Morris terminated the firm in July 1778 and developed a new and enlarged mercantile and business network that included no less than nine major partnerships throughout the country as well as agents abroad.

By 1781 Morris, now often referred to by contemporaries as the "Great Man," was regarded as the foremost merchant in America and probably its wealthiest citizen. It was this reputation that prompted the Continental Congress to take the unprecedented step on 20 February 1781 of appointing Morris by a unanimous vote to a new position in the Confederation government, superintendent of finance. In this capacity, Morris made his most important contribution to the nation.

After clarification of his authority, including the power to dismiss all persons involved in the expenditure of public monies, Morris confronted a disastrous situation. The credit of the Confederation government had collapsed. Paper money issues, which had paid for approximately 70 percent of the Continental expenditures by 1781, were now worthless. No one wished to purchase Loan Office certificates, the bonds of the Confederation. The issuance of certificates of indebtedness by procurers of supplies met increasing resistance. Requisitions from the states produced almost no income. For all practical purposes, the Confederation government was insolvent.

Morris believed that the public credit of the Confederation could be revived only by utilizing private credit. He took steps to achieve two goals: in the short term to provide the military with supplies to win the war; and, more important, in the long term to introduce a comprehensive national financial program to strengthen the Confederation politically. On 17 May, three days after accepting office, Morris submitted a bold plan to establish the first national bank, the Bank of North America. Congress responded by adopting an ordinance of incorporation on 31 December 1781. In a letter to John Jay, Morris explained his political objective: the bank was to "unite the several States more closely together in one general Money Connexion, and indissolubly to attach many powerful Individuals to the Cause of our Country, by the strong Principle of Self Love, and the immediate Sense of private Interest" (*Papers*, vol. 1, p. 287). During his term, Morris borrowed funds from the bank for Continental purposes well in excess of its capitalization, and the bank notes served as currency. The financier also employed his personal credit to bolster that of the Confederation by issuing "Morris's Notes" which—together with the bank notes—became the accepted national currency during his term of office. "My personal Credit, which thank Heaven I have preserved throughout all the tempests of the War, has been substituted for that which the Country Had lost," Morris wrote Benjamin Harrison, governor of Virginia, in January 1782. "I am now striving to transfer that Credit to the Public" (*Papers*, vol. 4, p. 46).

Meanwhile, Morris responded to Washington's urgent plea for help in the Yorktown campaign by using his business connections to supply flour, foodstuffs, and boats to transport the army to Virginia. When necessary, he pledged his personal credit. Beginning 1 January 1782 Morris also introduced a novel system of contracting with businessmen to furnish supplies for the Continental army, which reduced costs by as much as one-half and, according to Washington, enabled the troops to be better fed, housed, and clothed. Congress also augmented Morris's responsibilities by appointing him agent of the marine, thus giving him full control over naval affairs.

The financier, however, gave primacy to his long-term goal: funding the "public debts" by means of a permanent national revenue. The promises made to the creditors, he asserted, had been made by a government of the union of states, not the states individually. Distribution of the public debts to the states, he argued, implied disunion. By placing funding of the public debt in this context and giving it his highest priority, Morris assumed a leading role in the nationalist movement that led eventually to the replacement of the Articles of Confederation by the Constitution.

In August 1781 Morris sent Congress a proposal to settle the chaotic accounts incurred in the struggle for independence so that the public debts of the Confederation could be specifically defined. Congress approved the proposal by resolutions in January and February 1782, authorizing him to appoint commissioners in each state to settle all accounts, including those of the quartermaster, commissary, hospital, clothier, and marine departments. Morris also appointed receivers of continental taxes in each state to reinforce ties to the central government.

Morris next dispatched a comprehensive message to Congress on 29 July 1782, the most important single American state paper on public credit written prior to 1790. It extolled the advantages of funding for all citizens, husbandmen as well as enterprisers, asserting it would result in a flourishing national economy. Moreover, he argued, a public debt with a permanent Continental revenue to pay the interest and to provide a sinking fund to reduce it would serve a higher goal, strengthening the ties of "Union which seems not to have been sufficiently attended to, or provided for, in forming the national Compact." Funding would also "give Stability to the Government, by combining together the Interests of the moneyed Men for its Support" (*Papers*, vol. 6, p. 59). Congress failed to act, in part because word arrived that Rhode Island had voted against a Continental impost on imports, thus ending the drive for an independent Continental revenue.

Morris became concerned that news of a peace settlement would encourage states to neglect funding the public debt. When representatives from the army appeared before Congress to obtain back pay, he urged them to make "common cause" with other public creditors. Convinced that the only way the army pay demands could be met was to use his private credit, Morris stunned Congress by submitting his resignation, without warning, on 24 January 1783, to become effective 31 May. His dramatic gesture was less effective than he anticipated because Congress kept the letter confidential. When it was made public at Morris's request, anonymous newspaper articles viciously attacked Morris's actions and accused him of scheming to persuade the army to act in his behalf.

Morris has been charged by some historians with fomenting mutiny. Although he never directly corresponded with the military officers involved in what is called the Newburgh Conspiracy, Morris was certainly aware of letters by Gouverneur Morris, his assistant, and Alexander Hamilton written to their friends in the army, urging them to cooperate with other public creditors; and in his discussions with Congress over army pay, Morris declined to act without the assurance of funds to draw on. Morris sought additional allies to support Continental funding, but there is no document to suggest he advocated any militant action. Eventually, he provided partial pay using Morris's Notes.

Between midsummer of 1783 and November 1784, when he formally vacated his position, Morris concentrated on fulfilling his last obligations as superintendent of finance. The final accounts of his administration show a small but favorable balance of $20,000, a substantial achievement considering the disastrous situation that prevailed at the time he was appointed.

Near the end of 1783 Morris reentered private business, establishing the firm of Willing, Morris and (John) Swanwick. Its single most innovative enterprise involved participation in outfitting the *Empress of China*, the first ship to sail from the United States for the Orient, departing from New York harbor in February 1784. It returned after a profitable voyage, opening the United States–China trade that was eventually exploited by others.

Morris was much sought after by European merchants, bankers, and businessmen as well as by American entrepreneurs. Among his most ardent pursuers were the Farmers General of France, who held a monopoly of the French tobacco trade. Morris signed a secret contract with the farmers in 1785 to deliver 20,000 hogsheads of tobacco annually for three years. The contract itself was valued at £900,000 sterling, reputedly the largest "private contract" during the *ancien régime* and approximately four times the revenue obtained from the states during Morris's term as financier. Whether Morris profited from the contract has never been satisfactorily resolved because of the incomplete and tangled accounts, but the evidence indicates that he became badly overextended and that the debts he incurred led him to borrow far beyond his means to repay. As a result, he was forced to halt all shipping to France early in 1789. Nonetheless, Morris's taste for innovative and monumental enterprises did not abate. He mistakenly believed that no venture was beyond his capacity to execute.

Morris did not abandon politics. In 1785 he was again elected to the Pennsylvania assembly. He was appointed a delegate to the Annapolis Convention in 1786, and the following year he represented the state at the constitutional convention. He did not participate in the debates, relying instead on friends—Hamilton, James Madison, Gouverneur Morris, and James Wilson—to argue the case for a stronger union. During the convention, Washington made his home with the

Morrises, a practice that had begun during the war whenever Washington came to Philadelphia.

Upon ratification of the Constitution, the Pennsylvania legislature on 30 September 1788 elected Morris as senator to the newly established federal government. He served with characteristic energy on forty-one committees, more than any other senator, and provided committee reports on fifteen. His primary focus was on trade and commerce, followed by ways and means, as well as the settlement of accounts. He left public service at the end of his Senate term.

In the late 1780s and into the 1790s Morris engaged in far-flung land speculation. His entry into major landholding began in western New York when in August 1790 he bought one million acres from the state of Massachusetts, part of a tract known as the Phelps-Gorham purchase, for approximately $116,000. He sold the vast holding to a London group in March 1791 for approximately $330,000.

This handsome return seemed to spur Morris into a mania of land speculation. He became involved with John Nicholson, who, having gained uncertain title to some four million acres of land, now needed capital. In 1794 Morris and Nicholson established the Asylum Company, a vehicle for selling about one million acres of Pennsylvania land to prospective French settlers. Although their expectations were not fulfilled, the company continued to 1819. In 1795 Nicholson and Morris were joined by John Greenleaf, a businessman who had returned from Europe after dealing in U.S. securities in Holland, to form the North American Land Company, an elaborately organized corporation often regarded as the largest land trust ever established in America. The company pooled some six million acres of land located in New York, Pennsylvania, Virginia, North and South Carolina, Georgia, Kentucky, and what became Washington, D.C. Differences between the principals and dishonesty in the use of joint funds by Greenleaf resulted in Morris and Nicholson buying out Greenleaf in 1796. The extensive holdings became involved in legal tangles when neither partner was able to raise sufficient cash to meet their obligations, and both men became bankrupt. The problems of the company were still in litigation as late as 1869. Morris was also forced to surrender his individual holdings, involving millions of acres, to claims of creditors. In February 1798 Morris was imprisoned for debt. After passage of a federal bankruptcy law, he was released in August 1801. He died in Philadelphia.

Morris's letters reveal a commanding, optimistic, even visionary individual with an extraordinary grasp of detail. He exuded generosity and good will, even when imprisoned, which set him apart from the petty vindictiveness of some of his critics. In the line of succession that includes Alexander Hamilton and Albert Gallatin, Morris should be considered the first of three great treasury secretaries who laid the financial foundation of the United States.

• At the time of his death, Robert Morris retained most, if not all, of his letterbooks and other manuscript materials; subsequently, they became scattered, and some were lost or destroyed, introducing serious gaps in the record. Almost every major archival repository along the Atlantic seaboard has some material, with key clusters at the Library of Congress, the National Archives, the Historical Society of Pennsylvania, the Pennsylvania Archives, and the New York Public Library. The Henry E. Huntington Library, San Marino, Calif., also holds an important collection. For the only reliable printed materials, consult the *Papers of Robert Morris, 1781–1784* (8 vols., 1973–1995), edited successively by E. James Ferguson, John Catanzariti, and Elizabeth M. Nuxoll and Mary A. Gallagher, with detailed notes leading to a wide range of essential manuscript sources and secondary works. The modern scholarly study, Clarence L. Ver Steeg, *Robert Morris, Revolutionary Financier; with an Analysis of His Earlier Career* (1954), has, as yet, no substitute. Ferguson, *The Power of the Purse: A History of American Public Finance, 1776–1790* (1961), supplies needed context. Nuxoll, *Congress and the Munitions Merchants* (1985), is essential for the Secret Committee of Trade. Barbara Ann Chernow, *Robert Morris, Land Speculator, 1790–1801* (1978), is useful, but needs to be supplemented by older studies such as Paul D. Evans, *The Holland Land Company* (1924), and Shaw Livermore, *Early American Land Companies* (1939). For Morris and the Farmers General, Jacob Price, *France and the Chesapeake: A History of the French Tobacco Monopoly, 1674–1791, and of Its Relationship to the British and American Tobacco Trades* (2 vols., 1973), has no parallel. Ellis P. Oberholtzer, *Robert Morris: Patriot and Financier* (1903), is uncritical but contains information on Morris's personal and home life.

CLARENCE L. VER STEEG

MORRIS, Robert (31 Aug. 1818–31 July 1888), Masonic lecturer and poet, according to most biographers, including his son, was born near Boston, Massachusetts, the son of Robert Morris and Charlotte (maiden name unknown), teachers. However, the reliable twentieth-century Masonic historian Henry Wilson Coil in his *Masonic Encyclopedia* asserts that he was born Robert William Peckham in New York City and at age seven, after the death of his father, went to live in Massachusetts and western New York State with John Morris, from whom he acquired his surname. If the latter account is true, it may help explain why the ritual themes of Freemasonry, which are centered around the martyred death of a widow's son, provided such fertile ground for his creative work.

While still a teenager, Morris taught school, and after moving to Mississippi around 1840, he continued to teach. He married Charlotte Mendenhall of Athens, Alabama, in 1841; they had seven children. After conducting classes near the town of Oxford, he soon became principal of the area's Mount Sylvan Academy, the position he held when he joined the Masonic fraternity in 1846. Masonry quickly absorbed nearly all of his energies, and details remain sketchy on how he earned his livelihood in later years. Chiefly, it seems, he put together a living as a Masonic lecturer, writer, and journal editor in an era when fraternal activists functioned partly as circuit riders supported by the contributions of lodge members and the statewide grand lodges and partly as entrepreneurs. Due to his large family, the precariousness of his financial situation remained a constant problem throughout his life. "I find myself at this late day," he noted despairingly in September 1861, "after eleven years of consecutive and most arduous labor as a Masonic teacher, out of employment, and uncertain where to turn to make a support" (quoted in Denslow, p. 84). A fellow Mason described him as an unsuccessful businessman who spent freely and would give his last penny to someone who asked for assistance.

As a Freemason, however, Morris excelled in his career, becoming the most widely known member of the American fraternity during the middle decades of the nineteenth century, years when the organization was still recovering from the blows inflicted by the powerful Antimasonic movement of the 1820s and 1830s. He entered the brotherhood through Oxford Lodge, number 33, but after moving with his family to Kentucky in 1853, his major work was carried out from his home base in the town of La Grange, near Louisville, where they lived for most of the next thirty-five years. There he amassed a library of some 1,200 volumes and authored over fourteen books on Masonic topics, covering virtually every field of interest to the fraternity, from Masonic origins, law, biography, and institutional history to poetry, memoirs, and essays on the quality of Masonic life. He also edited and published two leading Masonic journals, the *American Freemason* (1853–1858) and the *Voice of Masonry* (1859–1867), produced numerous ritual guidebooks, and published the thirty-volume Universal Masonic Library, a compilation of fifty-six classic works by Freemasons that found its way into hundreds of American lodge libraries. In addition to his literary endeavors, he traveled unceasingly, visiting, by his own count, over 2,000 lodges in the United States and Canada and lecturing frequently before Masonic audiences. He also helped originate the Order of the Eastern Star, the auxiliary body for female relatives of Masons, and composed its ritual.

There was no aspect of mid-nineteenth-century Masonry that did not engage Morris's interest and usually his comment, but he contributed most significantly to the brotherhood as a poet and ritualist. His two most widely read books, both during his lifetime and after, were his two collections of poetry, *Masonic Odes and Poems* (1864) and *The Poetry of Freemasonry* (1888). Both contain his most renowned composition, "The Level and the Square," reprinted in countless lodge manuals and journals throughout the world (sometimes under different names and in slightly altered versions), which sounded its elegiac notes in its famous opening and closing lines, "We Meet Upon the Level and We Part Upon the Square." George Oliver, Morris's contemporary and the leading British Mason of his day, said of the poem and its author, "He has breathed out his depths of feeling, fervency and pathos with brilliancy and vigor of language, and expressed his faith in the immortal life beyond the grave" (*Poetry of Freemasonry* [1895], p. xvii). Indeed, overcoming the fear of death through joyous faith in the Masonic message formed the most prominent theme in all his poetry. When he was honored on 17 December 1884 as the "Poet Laureate of Freemasonry" at a ceremony attended by several thousand Masons in New York City, his son called the moment "the crowning point of a wondrous life."

Morris's extensive activities as a Masonic ritualist proved more controversial. Although he participated in all of the ceremonies of the fraternity, his primary love remained the liturgy of Craft Masonry, the rituals of the first three degrees. He was elected to the highest statewide office in Craft Masonry, grand master of Kentucky's grand lodge, in 1858–1859. It was not as an administrator that he undertook his most zealous work, however, but as an itinerant "lecturer," the Masonic term for a ritual instructor. In this capacity, he journeyed by horseback as well as by train to hundreds of lodges, particularly in the Midwest. "In the lodge or out of it," recalled an early assistant, "he was ever seeking or communicating Masonic light." His son wrote that even in the midst of the Civil War, Morris "talked of nothing but Freemasonry" (*Poetry of Freemasonry* [1895], p. xviii).

At the heart of his endeavors lay his commitment to bring precision and uniformity to the language of the rituals. As early as 1848 he had begun to collect the different versions of the rituals then in practice within the lodges of the various states. Scrupulously investigating their genealogies, checking their references against biblical and ancient sources, and consulting with senior Masons known for their ritualistic proficiency and knowledge, Morris became an expert in the field and began promoting what he deemed to be the true descendant of the brotherhood's ancient rites. His efforts culminated in the formation of an elite group within the national fraternity known as the Conservators of Symbolical Masonry, whose task was to bring reformation and uniformity to the ritual within five years of its date of inception, 24 June 1860. Morris named himself the Chief Conservator, and some 3,000 Masons responded to his call by joining the organization. But the group failed to achieve its goal, causing bitter accusations among the fraternity's leaders. The failure of Morris's campaign reflected a number of factors: namely, that Masonic ritual in the United States, with the principal exception of Pennsylvania's practice, was already fairly uniform; that most statewide grand lodge officials opposed the movement as an attempt to undercut their own authority; that the group violated the tradition of Masonic secrecy by printing an encoded version of the ritual to aid in its propagation; and, not least of all, that the Conservators' efforts coincided with the years of the Civil War, a case of poor practical judgment reflecting the insularity to which the esoteric world of religious ritualists is often prone.

Following the demise of his attempts to reform the Masonic ritual, Morris devoted himself to demonstrating the origins of Freemasonry within the world of biblical antiquity. An inveterate organizer, he again took to traveling in support of a new body, the Masonic Holy Land League, which funded his own trip to

Palestine in 1868 and led to his most ambitious book, *Freemasonry in the Holy Land* (1872). The league, which reached a membership of 8,000 by 1879, sponsored trips by other Masons to Palestine and evolved into the Oriental Order of the Palm and Shell, an allied organization within the Masonic family, complete with its own degree ceremony, developed by Morris, based on the story of Nehemiah's rebuilding of Jerusalem's city walls.

Morris died at La Grange and was given a Masonic funeral that drew a very large attendance. He may be remembered as a leading figure of mid-nineteenth-century American Freemasonry: a man of strong religious conviction, meticulous mental energy, and tireless organizing ability who acted to revitalize the fraternity following its years of disrepute in the 1820s and 1830s.

• In addition to the titles mentioned above, Morris's leading works include *Lights and Shadows of Freemasonry* (1852), *Life in the Triangle; or, Freemasonry at the Present Time* (1854), *Code of Masonic Law* (1856), *History of Freemasonry in Kentucky* (1859), *Tales of Masonic Life* (1860), *The Masonic Martyr: The Life of Eli Bruce* (1861), *Dictionary of Freemasonry* (1867), and *William Morgan; or, Political Anti-Masonry* (1883). He coauthored with Albert G. Mackey *Lights and Shadows of the Mystic Tie* (1878). Morris's own library, following a fire that partially destroyed it, was sold to the Grand Lodge of New York, where it became the nucleus of the Masonic library in that state. There is no scholarly biography of Morris, but valuable summaries and discussions of his life and work can be found in various Masonic sources. Most useful are Henry Wilson Coil, *Conversations on Freemasonry* (1976) and *Coil's Masonic Encyclopedia* (1961), and Ray V. Denslow, *The Masonic Conservators* (1931). The principal source of information used by all later commentators is the "Biography of Rob Morris, LL.D., Masonic Poet Laureate," published without a designated author but based on "official data furnished by his son, Robert Morris, Jr., of Franklin, Kentucky," which serves as an introduction to the 1895 edition of Morris's *The Poetry of Freemasonry*. Two older accounts of his life are Thomas R. Austin, *The Well Spent Life: The Masonic Career of Robert Morris* (1878), and Lucien V. Rule, *Pioneering in Masonry: The Life and Times of Rob Morris* (1922). An obituary is in the Louisville (Ky.) *Courier-Journal*, 1 Aug. 1888.

TONY FELS

MORRIS, Robert (8 June 1823–12 Dec. 1882), lawyer, was born in Salem, Massachusetts, the son of York Morris, a waiter, and Nancy Morris, free blacks. He came of age at a time of strident anti-black prejudice. Although Massachusetts had abolished slavery and had indeed even proclaimed that blacks and whites were equal before the law, vigorous social and economic discrimination ensured that few blacks could aspire to any but the most menial of occupations.

Morris was educated in the common schools of Salem. At the age of fifteen he left his parents' household to become the servant of Ellis Gray Loring, a Boston attorney and abolitionist. Loring quickly became impressed with young Morris and allowed him to read his law books in his spare time. Soon Morris became Loring's law clerk, formally studying law through apprenticeship, the principal route to the legal profession in nineteenth-century America.

Admitted to the Suffolk County, Massachusetts, bar in February 1847, Morris quickly began an active practice. His first case, in which he successfully represented a black man in a labor dispute, was the first occasion in which a black lawyer represented a client in an American court. That action ensured Morris's fame and brought him to the attention of abolitionists and civil rights activists in antebellum Boston, as well as to the city's black community.

Morris's first effort at civil rights litigation would prove to have a long-reaching effect on the jurisprudence of race in the United States. At the request of black activist Benjamin Roberts, Morris brought suit against the Boston School Committee for requiring that Roberts's daughter attend the segregated "colored school" instead of the common school closer to her home, which was reserved for white students. Morris lost the case at the 1848 trial and later joined Charles Sumner in appealing it to the Massachusetts Supreme Judicial Court. Although the claim brought by Morris and Sumner that segregation was inherently stigmatizing and thus violated the free and equal provision of the Massachusetts Constitution was rejected in an opinion written in 1849 by Chief Justice Lemuel Shaw, the argument would nonetheless have an important life in American jurisprudence. The equation of legal segregation with stigmatization would later be considered and rejected by the U.S. Supreme Court in *Plessy v. Ferguson*. That claim would finally be adopted by the Court in the school desegregation case *Brown v. Board of Education* decided in 1954, more than a century after the argument was first made by Morris and Sumner.

Like many in Boston's antebellum black community, Morris actively opposed the federal Fugitive Slave Act of 1851. Involved in many of the famous fugitive slave cases of the era, including the cases of Anthony Burns and Thomas Sims, Morris was best known in this regard for aiding one fugitive slave, Frederick Wilkens—also known as "Shadrack." Morris represented Wilkens in court and later aided his escape from the courtroom. For this Morris and other antislavery activists, including Charles Sumner and Richard Henry Dana, were tried and acquitted on criminal charges.

In addition to his prominence as a civil rights activist, Morris had a strong reputation as a trial attorney. His clientele was evenly divided between blacks and whites, the latter group mainly consisting of poor Irish immigrants. He was able to build up a fairly lucrative legal practice. Due to his prominence, he was appointed as a magistrate in Massachusetts in 1852, one of the earliest judicial appointments of a black man, albeit a minor appointment, in the United States. In 1866 Morris unsuccessfully ran for mayor of Chelsea, Massachusetts.

Morris had married Catherine Mason in 1844, and the couple had one child, Robert Morris, Jr. Morris sent his son to France and England to be educated, partly to shield him from the social prejudices of the day. His son was admitted to the Massachusetts bar in 1874. Morris died in Boston.

Morris, the second American of African descent to be admitted to the practice of law in the United States, had a professional career that spanned some thirty-five years. During that time he was a pioneer civil rights litigator, prominently involved in fugitive slave cases, efforts to desegregate Boston's public schools, and cases involving discrimination in public accommodations. Morris was also a highly successful trial attorney in a variety of criminal and civil cases.

• James Oliver and Lois E. Horton provide a valuable discussion of Morris's life and work, placing both within the larger context of the antislavery and equal rights struggles of Boston's antebellum black community in *Black Bostonians: Family Life and Community Struggle in the Antebellum North* (1979). J. Clay Smith provides important insights into Morris's career as an attorney in *Emancipation: The Making of the Black Lawyer, 1844–1944* (1993). A good discussion of *Roberts v. City of Boston* (1848) and its enduring significance in American jurisprudence is Roderick T. Baltimore and Robert F. Williams, "The State Constitutional Roots of the 'Separate but Equal' Doctrine: *Roberts v. City of Boston*," *Rutgers Law Journal* 17 (1986): 537–52. A useful early biography is Pauline E. Hopkins, "Robert Morris," *Colored American Magazine*, Sept. 1901. An obituary is in the *Boston Evening Transcript*, 13 Dec. 1882.

ROBERT J. COTTROL

MORRIS, Robert Hunter (c. 1713–27 Jan. 1764), landed aristocrat, political leader, and judge in New Jersey and Pennsylvania, was born at "Morrisania," the New York manor of his parents, Lewis Morris, a prominent landholder and politician, and Isabella Graham. Educated at home by his parents and tutors, Morris was heavily influenced by his father, whose argumentativeness, interest in natural science, flair for poetical political satires, and deism he shared. Indeed, though far more convivial than his austere father, Morris was even more outspoken in his repudiation of Christian orthodoxy, earning a reputation for himself as "a profest enemy to all revealed Religion." Morris never married, but he did father four children out of wedlock, one of whom, Robert Morris, became New Jersey's first chief justice after independence. Morris managed "Tinton," the family's New Jersey estate, until his father died in 1746, and thereafter he inherited it outright.

Morris's disputatious political career as a staunch defender of royal authority and proprietary privilege began under the auspices of his father. He accompanied Lewis Morris as a secretary during the latter's 1735–1736 mission to London to seek redress against the arbitrary rule of Governor William Cosby, and the elder Morris's appointment as royal governor of New Jersey in 1738 was accompanied by the naming of his son to the New Jersey Council. Moreover, in 1739 Governor Morris commissioned him to serve as chief justice of the New Jersey Supreme Court during good behavior, a coveted tenure since most colonial American judges served at pleasure, and one that he used to professionalize the court's procedures. Morris strongly supported his father's efforts to reinvigorate royal authority in New Jersey, making himself unpopular with the provincial assembly. He further increased his unpopularity by becoming a member of the East Jersey Board of Proprietors in 1742 and taking the lead in trying to have Governor Morris as chancellor enforce highly contentious proprietary land claims against certain settlers in eastern New Jersey, a strategy that provoked a decade of serious land riots in the colony beginning in 1745. Dissatisfied with the failure of his father's successor, Governor Jonathan Belcher, to quell the rioters, Morris embarked in 1749 on a mission to London, where he sought unsuccessfully to persuade the imperial administration to station British regulars in New Jersey to end the riots, to strengthen royal authority by inducing the New Jersey Assembly to provide a perpetual revenue for Crown governors, and to appoint him either governor of New Jersey or lieutenant governor of New York.

Morris returned to America in 1754 as deputy proprietary governor of Pennsylvania, having won the patronage of the Penn family during his stay in London. Taking office when the conflict between the English and the French for control of the Ohio Valley was exploding into the Great War for Empire, Morris spent most of his administration locked in a series of bitter disputes with the Quaker-dominated Pennsylvania Assembly over his efforts to promote the defense of the colony while protecting proprietary privilege. He insisted that the assembly provide men and money for provincial defense without taxing proprietary lands, and even though the resulting controversy was finally settled late in 1755, when the assembly appropriated £60,000 for defense and the proprietors promised to contribute £5,000 for the same purpose, Morris resigned in 1756 because the assembly's refusal to provide him with a salary made the deputy governorship insufficiently profitable for his taste.

Coming back to New Jersey, Morris devoted himself full time to his duties as chief justice, an office he had continued to hold while serving as deputy governor of Pennsylvania, although he could then only attend sporadically. Following a second mission to London in 1757–1759, during which he tried in vain to resolve the disputed New Jersey–New York boundary and obtain a monopoly over salt production in British North America, Morris arrived back in New Jersey to find the office of chief justice being held by Nathaniel Jones, an English barrister appointed by the imperial administration to serve at pleasure. By arguing that his good behavior commission entitled him to priority over Jones, Morris prevailed on the New Jersey Supreme Court in 1760 to accept his claim to the chief justiceship. Morris held this office until he died of heart failure after a festive evening of dancing with the wife of a local minister. Shortly after Morris's death, William Smith, Jr., a close friend and the first historian of colonial New York, mourned him as a "Natural genius . . . penetrating and solid," with a "Knowledge of Men and Books extensive," and a "very agreeable Companion."

• The two main collections of Morris's papers are the Robert Hunter Morris Papers in the New Jersey Historical Society and the Morris Family Papers in Rutgers University Library. His London diary is in Beverly McAnear, ed., "An American in London, 1735–1736," *Pennsylvania Magazine of History and Biography* 64 (1940): 164–217, 356–406. See also Donald L. Kemmerer, *Path to Freedom: The Struggle for Self-Government in Colonial New Jersey, 1703–1776* (1940); James H. Hutson, *Pennsylvania Politics 1746–1770: The Movement for Royal Government and Its Consequences* (1972); and Edmond Dale Daniel, "Robert Hunter Morris and the Rockey Hill Copper Mine," *New Jersey History* 92 (1974): 13–32.

EUGENE R. SHERIDAN

MORRIS, Roger (28 Jan. 1727–13 Sept. 1794), British soldier and Loyalist, was born in Yorkshire, England, the son of Roger Morris and Mary Jackson, daughter of Sir Peter Jackson. On 13 September 1745 Morris was commissioned a captain in the Forty-eighth Regiment of Foot. In that regiment he accompanied General Edward Braddock to America in 1755. Morris along with George Washington and Captain Robert Orme were the three aides-de-camp on the ill-fated Braddock expedition to the Monongahela River. At the battle near Fort Duquesne, 9 July 1755, Morris was wounded early during the fighting. Morris also served as an aide-de-camp to generals William Shirley and Daniel Webb during the campaigns in New York, 1755–1757.

In 1758 Morris married Mary Philipse, one of the wealthiest women in the colonies. She had inherited on the death of a sister and her father, Frederick Philipse, second lord of Philipsborough Manor, 51,000 acres, comprising parts of the manor (in Westchester County) and the Highland Patent (Putnam County). These estates brought a handsome income from many tenants. Five days before the wedding Roger and Mary signed a prenuptial agreement that they would jointly hold a life lease of the estate, which then would be inherited by any children of the marriage. This factor was most important because it clouded the legality of confiscation of the estate during the Revolution. The Morrises had four children; one son, Henry Gage Morris, became a rear admiral in the British navy.

Mary Philipse was regarded as a great beauty. Tradition has it that George Washington had considered marrying her. Washington stayed at the home of Beverley Robinson (a friend of Washington's who had married Sussanah Philipse, sister of Mary, and had settled on the Philipse estate) twice during his journey to and from Boston in early 1756. Here he met Mary. Douglas Southall Freeman, biographer of Washington, noted "that a match between them had been considered a possibility" (vol. 2 [1949], p. 160n). Roger Morris, whom one contemporary, Joseph Chew, referred to as "a Ladys man, always something to say," was the successful suitor. Mary, or "Polly" as she was called, was said to have had a domineering personality.

On 16 February 1758 Morris received a major's commission, which he had purchased. In May he was ordered to duty at Halifax, Nova Scotia. He commanded the Seventeenth Regiment in General Jeffery Amherst's successful siege of Louisbourg (surrendered 27 July 1758). From fall 1758 to spring 1759 he commanded at Fort Frederic, at the mouth of the River St. John in the Bay of Fundy, occasionally leading sorties against hostile Indians.

Morris served with General James Wolfe at the victory over the French at Quebec in September 1759. When the French returned to attack Quebec in April 1760, Morris, with the Thirty-fifth Regiment, fought in the battle of Sillery (several miles from Quebec near the Plains of Abraham). Brigadier General James Murray had sought to stop the enemy's advance on Quebec. Morris's unit, kept initially in reserve, came into action during a flanking movement. The British were forced to retreat, but the French did not follow up their victory. On 19 May 1760 Morris was appointed lieutenant colonel in the Forty-seventh Regiment of Foot. In June he supervised the building of a redoubt at St. Foy, five miles from Quebec. Morris commanded detachments of the Thirty-fifth Regiment and Third Battalion of Royal Americans at the successful siege of Montreal (surrendered 8 Sept. 1760).

With his Forty-seventh Regiment about to return to Ireland to be disbanded, Morris, on 15 June 1764, sold his commission to Major John Spital. He and his family then took up residence at a townhouse that he built on the southeast corner of Whitehall and Stone streets, New York City. In December he began ten years service on the royal council for the colony of New York; during the war he held a similar position in the Tory-military government under General James Robertson. The Morrises owned a large tavern on Broadway, which they leased.

In 1765 the Morrises bought from James Carrol a homestead of 115 acres in upper Manhattan Island (Harlem), between 160th and 162d streets and stretching between the Hudson and Harlem rivers. Here they constructed their country estate, sometimes referred to as "Mount Morris," a mansion of nineteen rooms and a garret. It was later known as "Jumel Mansion." During the war it served briefly as a headquarters for George Washington and also for different British generals. Uncommitted to either the American or British side at the start of the war, Morris traveled to England in May 1775; he returned to New York in December 1777. Further opportunity to hold royal office, his Loyalist in-laws, with whom he held joint property, and fear of losing property if the American Revolution succeeded influenced Morris's decision to align himself with the British cause. On 1 January 1779 he was appointed inspector of the claims of refugees, with a rank of provincial colonel; he served in this post in British-occupied New York City until the end of the war.

Morris and his wife were among fifty-eight persons whose estates were confiscated by an act of attainder of the New York state legislature on 22 October 1777.

The total evaluation of the Philipse estate (of which the Morrises had a one-fourth interest) amounted to £235,413 14s. 3d. It was divided into 250 parcels. On 9 July 1784 the Commissioners of Sequestration and Commissioners of Forfeiture sold the Morris mansion property in Harlem for £2,250 to John Berrian and Isaac Ledyard.

In 1783 the Morrises and their four children settled in Yorkshire, England. The Morrises put in a claim to the British government for compensation of £68,384 for their losses in America. The Royal Claims Commission awarded them £12,205 for their life interest in the estate, but since the property was entailed for inheritance by the children, it was considered that the children had reversionary rights to the property. In 1809, after Morris's death in England, John Jacob Astor purchased the reversionary rights from the widowed Mrs. Morris and her children. In 1828 Astor sold these rights to the state of New York for $500,000, which action prevented ejectment against those who had purchased parcels of the estate as confiscated lands.

• The papers of Roger Morris were destroyed by his son Rear Admiral Henry Gage Morris, and copies that Roger Morris made have disappeared. Records pertaining to the Philipse estates are found at the New York State Library at Albany. Materials relating to Morris's claims for compensation from the British government after the war are found in the records of the Commission of Enquiry into the Losses and Services of the American Loyalists (1776–1831), Audit Office Papers, Public Record Office, London; transcripts of this collection are located at the New York Public Library, microfilm. William H. Shelton, *The Jumel Mansion: Being a Full History of the House on Harlem Heights Built by Roger Morris before the Revolution* (1916), contains substantial biographical information. (See p. 21 regarding the loss of Morris's papers.) Also useful as biography are Thomas Glenn, *Some Colonial Mansions and Those Who Lived in Them* (1900); Edward H. Hall, *Philipse Manor Hall at Yonkers, New York* (1912); and William S. Pelletreau, *History of Putnam County, New York, with Biographical Sketches of Its Prominent Men* (1886). Morris's military career may be traced in Arthur G. Doughty, ed., *An Historical Journal of the Campaigns in North America, for the Years, 1757, 1758, 1759 by Captain John Knox* (3 vols., 1769; repr. 1970); William O. Raymond, *The River St. John: Its Physical Features, Legends, and History from 1604 to 1784* (1910); and G. D. Scull, ed., *The Montresor Journals* (1881).

HARRY M. WARD

MORRIS, Thomas (3 Jan. 1776–7 Dec. 1844), the first abolitionist senator, was born in Berks County, Pennsylvania, the son of Isaac Morris, a Baptist minister of Welsh background, and Ruth Henton, the daughter of a Virginia small planter. The family soon moved to near Clarksburg in western Virginia, where Morris was taught to read by his mother, but he received little formal schooling. In 1795 Morris moved to Columbia, a frontier Baptist settlement near Cincinnati, where he worked as a clerk in a small grocery and fell under the influence of his employer and Baptist minister, the controversial Republican politician John Smith.

In November 1797 Morris married Rachel Davis, whose family had come from Lancaster County, Pennsylvania, by way of Mason County, Kentucky. They had eleven children. In 1800 they moved to Williamsburgh, Clermont County, Ohio, where he ran a tavern and was briefly imprisoned for debt. Moving to Bethel and working as a brickmaker, he began to study law in the evenings. Admitted to the bar in 1804, he proved an effective advocate, especially shrewd in cross-examination.

In 1806 Morris was elected state representative for Clermont County and served in the Ohio General Assembly for seven sessions to 1815. Committed to absolute legislative supremacy, in 1808–1809 Morris conducted the impeachment of the Ohio judges who had overturned unconstitutional laws and in 1809 was himself elected to the state supreme court. The assembly, however, soon declared all offices vacant and failed to reappoint Morris. In fury, he changed sides and supported the judicial-review faction, which triumphed in 1812. Though an ardent supporter of war against Britain, he ran unsuccessfully for Congress in 1814 and 1816.

In 1820 Morris reentered the assembly, where he opposed Ohio's canal program on the grounds that it would bankrupt the state and in due course be superseded by railroads. He strongly advocated publicly financed common schools, which apparently led to his defeat for reelection to the state senate in 1823. In the presidential contest of 1824, he initially favored John Quincy Adams but, according to later opponents, shifted to the locally more popular Andrew Jackson and so became a Democrat. He ran for Congress unsuccessfully in 1826, helped Samuel Medary found a local Jacksonian newspaper in 1828, and acted virtually as Jacksonian floor leader in the state senate, where he served for six sessions, 1825–1829 and 1831–1833. Approving of President Jackson's attempts to appease southern dissatisfactions, he cast doubt on the constitutionality of protective tariffs but also authored Ohio's resolutions backing the Union in the nullification crisis. In state legislation, he pressed for social and legal reforms, notably securing the abolition of imprisonment for debt.

In 1832 Morris ran for Congress as an ardent supporter of Jackson's bank veto but was defeated by an independent Jacksonian more critical of the president's policies, Thomas L. Hamer. As a reward for his constancy, the state party elected Morris to the U.S. Senate in January 1833, recognizing his "pure democratic faith, of a strict construction of the Constitution and open war against all peculiar privileges and monopolies" (Zanesville *Muskingum Messenger*, 24 Dec. 1832). In the Panic Session of 1833–1834 he backed Jackson's attack on the Bank of the United States, hoping that its destruction would make "men, instead of depending on borrowing, . . . look to their own industry for support." He criticized congressional extravagance and urged the federal government to "confine its action within the strict letter of the

Constitution, and exercise even then, as little power as possible" (Morris, pp. 353, 348–49).

Morris's commitment to "true Democracy" included a lifelong hatred of slavery, learned from his parents. In January 1836 he presented several petitions requesting the abolition of slavery in the District of Columbia and in April opposed restrictions on the circulation of abolitionist material in the mails. His position was not strictly abolitionist, since he could accept the constitutional right of Arkansas to choose slavery for itself in 1836; rather, he focused on protecting civil liberties, especially the right of petition. In January 1838 he responded to John C. Calhoun's resolutions on slavery by presenting provocative counterresolutions calling on Congress to define precisely the limits of slavery's supposed constitutional privileges. In the course of denying that the Constitution gave any positive protection to slavery, he forcefully condemned "the putrid mass of prejudice, which interest has created, to keep the colored race in bondage" (Morris, p. 58, 85).

When questioned by the state party, Morris said he had "always believed slavery to be wrong, in principle, in practice, in every country and under every condition of things" (Columbus *Ohio Statesman*, 30 Nov. 1838). Accordingly in December 1838 the Ohio Democrats refused to reelect him. As his Senate swan song, on 9 February 1839 Morris made a long and passionate speech attacking the combination of "the slave power of the South and the banking power of the North" that was threatening freedom in America. Openly defending abolitionism, he concluded that "THE NEGRO WILL YET BE SET FREE" (Morris, pp. 85, 119–20, 165, 174).

Inevitably, Morris was read out of the Ohio Democratic party in January 1840 despite his loyal commitment to President Martin Van Buren and antibank principles, and he became the antislavery "lion of the day" and a target for mobs. Salmon P. Chase, who worked with him on the 1842 Van Zandt and other fugitive-slave cases, credited Morris with teaching him "to see the character of the slave power, as an aristocracy, naturally in league with the money power; and the need of an earnest and consistent Democratic organization to counteract its pretensions." In 1843 Morris was nominated as the Liberty party's vice presidential candidate, but soon after the 1844 election he suffered "a fatal attack of apoplexy" on his farm near Bethel (Morris, pp. 166, xi, 404).

Though an undoubted "moral hero," Morris had many faults and more enemies. He was tactless, commonly mistrusted, far from popular in manner, and even friends acknowledged that his lack of "early education and a well-disciplined judgement" prevented him from attaining greater distinction. Though deeply devout in his youth, in later life he was "not a religious man in the church acceptance of that term," but he believed that the Bible, which he frequently quoted at length, expressed the laws of nature. He advocated "strict morality, untiring industry, rigid economy, and a steady perseverance" and opposed lotteries, intemperance, and monopolies (Morris, pp. 402–7). Personally benevolent, he helped young people in need, notably Hamer, his later opponent. Four married daughters all died early, leaving young children, some of whom he adopted and educated. Three of his sons held public office, two as congressmen; a fourth became a Presbyterian minister and biographer of his father, whom he appreciated as a pathbreaking example of an antimonopoly Democrat turned abolitionist.

• No collection of Morris's papers exists. Benjamin F. Morris, *The Life of Thomas Morris* (1856), is essentially a piece of Republican party propaganda but remains the main source of information and selected speeches and correspondence. It was condemned as "very poor" by James B. Swing, "Thomas Morris," *Ohio Archaeological and Historical Society Quarterly* 10 (1902): 352–60, which adds a few details. Scattered information on his political career before 1833 may be found in the papers of his contemporaries and in the local Ohio press, notably the Williamsburgh *Western American*, 1814–1816, and the Georgetown *Castigator*, especially 1832. See also Donald J. Ratcliffe, ed., "The Autobiography of Benjamin Tappan," *Ohio History* 85 (1976): 145–47. The best treatment of his antislavery stand is John A. Neuenschwander, "Senator Thomas Morris: Antagonist of the Old South, 1836–1839," *Cincinnati Historical Society Bulletin* 32 (1974): 122–39. Morris's valedictory was published by the American Antislavery Society as a pamphlet: *Speech of Hon. Thomas Morris of Ohio. In Reply to the Speech of the Hon. Henry Clay. In Senate. Feb. 9, 1839* (1839). The Liberty party's appreciation was expressed in W[illiam] H[enry] Brisbane, *An Eulogium on the Life and Character of the Late Hon. Thomas Morris* (1845).

DONALD J. RATCLIFFE

MORRISON, Harry Winford (23 Feb. 1885–19 July 1971), businessman, was born in Tunbridge Township, Illinois, the son of George William Morrison, a millwright, and Amy Maria Hawkins. Only four when his mother died, young Morrison's grandparents—who owned a nearby gristmill, blacksmith shop, and general store—helped rear him. When not "farmed out" to help neighbors, Morrison attended local public and private schools. He dropped out before completing high school to take a job with a Chicago construction company, Bates and Rogers, for whom he had worked summers as a water boy. With an aversion to farming and believing that success would come with more education, he enrolled in a business college but left after little more than a year to take another job with Bates and Rogers. In 1904 the company sent him to Idaho as a timekeeper. Bates and Rogers had landed a U.S. Reclamation Service contract to build Minidoka Dam on the Snake River in southern Idaho. A hard worker, industrious and opportunistic, the transplanted midwesterner soon joined the Reclamation Service as a construction supervisor. In 1909, while supervising the cement work on a diversion dam project on the Boise River, Morrison met Morris Hans Knudsen, the owner of a small construction company that was digging the diversion canal. With nothing more than "just guts" to contribute, Morrison persuaded Knudsen to take him on as a partner. In 1912, in a one-room office in Boise, Idaho, the two men founded the construction giant known around the world as Morrison-Knudsen Corporation (M-K). Morrison married Ann Daly in 1914 and she became like a partner, helping out in the construction camps and traveling with him to job sites. They had no children.

Morrison was the driving force in the company. Largely through his intelligence, risk-taking, and energy, Morrison, according to business historian Harold Bunderson, "propelled MK from a tiny, undercapitalized, start-up construction business to a world-class heavy construction and engineering company." Morrison took advantage of opportunities resulting from World War I and compounded its growth in the 1920s, which prepared his company to embark on the most colossal construction enterprise of that time, Boulder Dam. In 1931, organizing six of the largest construction companies in the country in a joint venture, he bid on the Bureau of Reclamation's project to build the giant Colorado River dam. The joint venture known as the Six Companies won the bid and over the next five years built what was at 726 feet the highest dam in the world. The companies not only turned a profit, they completed what came to be called Hoover Dam ahead of schedule. After Hoover Dam, then the world's largest construction project, Morrison found no task too big or too complex for his company and surrounded himself with those who thought likewise. "He had great loyalty from his people," said one associate. "Foremen and others would stay with the company forever." He returned that loyalty in kind, setting up a financial program from which employees could draw when there was no work. This was long before government unemployment insurance.

The outbreak of World War II found Morrison's company (by this time Knudsen was inactive; he died in 1943) building huge bases and underground petroleum storage facilities in the Pacific. At the end of the war M-K expanded to become an international builder, often entering into joint ventures with one or more of the original Six Companies that built Hoover Dam. By the 1950s he had built M-K into the largest heavy construction company in the world. He attracted wide media attention in those years. *Time* magazine featured him on the cover of its 3 May 1954 issue and called him a "master builder" and "the man in history who has done the most to change the face of the earth." Extolling the company's international reach, *Business Week* wrote, "The sun never sets on Morrison-Knudsen Company." He and his construction "stiffs" were dubbed the "ambassadors with bulldozers."

In 1957 Morrison's wife died, and in 1959 he married Velma Shannon, who like his first wife was actively involved in his business and served on the M-K board. By 1960, when Morrison retired from the presidency of M-K, he had taken the company from a struggling family partnership to an enormous, diversified construction company whose stock was publicly traded. Besides its massive construction work and dam building (over 150 large dams around the world), M-K mined coal, built ships, rebuilt railroad locomotives, and developed real estate. Through its HK Ferguson subsidiary the company also built large factories. Despite his retirement from the presidency, Morrison continued as chairman of the board until shortly before his death at home in Boise.

Morrison is known not only for the company he helped build and the construction projects it undertook, some of which (especially the massive dams) were and have continued to be controversial, but he pioneered the joint-venture system in the heavy construction industry, enabling companies to pool their resources and expertise to accomplish projects far too large and expensive for any one company to build. A philanthropist and public-spirited citizen, Morrison served on the board of trustees of Boise Community College (later Boise State University). Through the foundation he created and endowed, he built and donated a beautiful park to the city of Boise named after his first wife, Ann. Always wanting to establish a center for the performing arts in the city he came to love, it was not until after his death that the Morrison Center for the Performing Arts was built on the Boise State University campus with monies donated by the Harry W. Morrison Foundation. Over the years the foundation helped to support the arts, education, and health and public-affairs programs. Morrison's generosity also enabled the Boy Scouts of America to build Camp Morrison at McCall, Idaho.

• Morrison's personal papers and company manuscripts are at Morrison-Knudsen's Office of Records Retention, Boise, Idaho. Sources on Morrison are limited, but one should consult Glen Barrett's unpublished manuscript "To Build, To Build . . . : A History of Morrison-Knudsen Company, Inc." (1979), which contains biographical material and places Morrison in the context of the company he helped build. Morrison's wife Ann Daly Morrison published her *Diary of Ann Morrison, Those Were the Days* (1951), which provides information on the couple's construction activities and opinions. Suellen Hoy wrote a brief biography of Morrison that appeared in the *APWA Reporter*, Dec. 1977. See as well the magazine articles about him in *Colliers*, 2 Aug. 1952; *Time*, 29 May 1950 and 3 May 1954; *Fortune*, Aug., Sept., and Oct. 1943, Dec. 1956, and Sept. 1966; and *Business Week*, 20 July 1957. Susan Stacy's anecdote-rich *H. W. Morrison: A Portrait* (1992), and Harold R. Bunderson's *Idaho Entrepreneurs: Profiles in Business* (1992), are enlightening.

ERROL D. JONES

MORRISON, Henry Clinton (7 Oct. 1871–19 Mar. 1945), educator, was born in Oldtown, Maine, the son of John Morrison, a general merchandise store owner, and Mary Louise Ham. Morrison spent his childhood in this lumber and fishing town, where he excelled as a canoeist and axeman. He distinguished himself in college preparatory work such that a local banker assisted in the financing of his tuition to Dartmouth College. Morrison entered Dartmouth's classical course, which concentrated on Greek, Latin, math, English, and foreign languages, and was graduated from the college with a bachelor of arts degree in 1895, one of two students to graduate magna cum laude.

After graduation, Morrison served as a teaching "principal" from 1895 to 1899 at the high school in

Milford, New Hampshire, where he taught classes in Latin, mathematics, history, and the sciences. The school was described as rough, with an overactive group of students who physically intimidated the teachers. Morrison had participated in his share of lumber camp brawls in Oldtown, and within a short period of time Milford became a well-disciplined school under his guidance. Following this success, Morrison was appointed and served as the superintendent of schools for Portsmouth, New Hampshire, from 1899 to 1904. It was during this time in Portsmouth that Morrison married Marion Locke in 1902; the couple had three children.

In 1904, Morrison was appointed the New Hampshire state superintendent of public instruction, although Morrison referred to himself as a "sort of state police officer." Although Morrison is said to have distinguished himself in this demanding position, he resigned somewhat suddenly in 1917 to become the assistant secretary of the Connecticut Board of Education. He served in this position for two years until assuming a professorship of education and the superintendency of the Laboratory Schools at the University of Chicago. Morrison served as superintendent of the Laboratory Schools from 1919 until 1928 and professor of school administration until 1937. It was during his eighteen years at the University of Chicago and his subsequent retirement that Morrison made his greatest contributions to the field of education and, in essence, shaped aspects of classroom instruction in the United States.

Although John Dewey had founded an elementary laboratory school at the University of Chicago only twenty-three years before, Morrison drew little upon progressive thought for the running of the school and, instead, relied much more on a traditional conception of education and the method of empirical observation. Morrison criticized the prevalent view that learning referred only to the acquisition of subject matter and believed that genuine learning was the actual change in the behavior of the learner, what he called an "adaptation." The "unit" was the procedure used for the teaching of an adaptation based on a stimulus-response psychology. This view stems, in part, from Morrison's categorization of learning into a cycle of three phases: stimulus, assimilation, and reaction.

Morrison's landmark publication was *The Practice of Teaching in the Secondary School* (1926), the synthesis of his experiences in New Hampshire and at the Laboratory Schools. Presenting one of the most widely known and used systems of teaching from the late 1920s through the early 1940s, the work has been described by J. Minor Gwynn in 1960 as having the "greatest single effect on the method and technique of teaching" in the United States (p. 178). The book also implicitly attended to one of the fundamental dilemmas of the field of curriculum—the relationship between curriculum and instruction—and marked the beginning of a major conceptual distinction between these two areas.

The Practice of Teaching in the Secondary School was written especially for "executive and staff officers of schools who realize that teaching is by far the most important activity which they have to administer." Morrison configured the secondary school curriculum into units of five types: science, appreciation, practical arts, language arts, and pure-practice. Acknowledging that instruction would vary among the different types of units, Morrison nonetheless identified a five-step pattern for the instruction process of the science unit which became known as the "Morrison Plan" (also called the Morrison Method). The Morrison Plan, eventually applied to all content areas by its devotees, included exploration of the field to be studied, presentation of findings, assimilation, organization of material, and recitation. While similarities can be drawn between the Morrison Plan and the then-antiquated Herbartian steps for learning, Morrison's ideas were not a narrowly conceived teaching technique but a general pattern for the instructional process.

Morrison added another aspect to the instructional methods outlined in *The Practice of Teaching in the Secondary School*, namely the "mastery formula" that was, in his estimation, the only way to ensure that adaptive change takes place. In fact, Morrison proposed that students be expected to attain 100 percent mastery of subject units as a prerequisite for promotion to the next grade. This formula consisted of "pre-test, teach, test the result, adapt procedure, teach and test again to the point of actual learning." Morrison's mastery formula served as a precursor to the educational movements of "individualized instruction" and "mastery learning."

While Morrison's historical significance stems primarily from *The Practice of Teaching in the Secondary School*, he also brought systematic, empirical analysis to the area of school finance in *School Revenue* (1930) and *The Management of School Money* (1932). Morrison standardized many school fiscal practices and proposed a progressive state income tax as the basic means of supporting schools. Morrison's later publications, including *Basic Principles of Education* (1934), *School and Commonwealth* (1937), *The Curriculum of the Common School* (1940), and *American Schools: A Critical Study of Our School System* (1943), focus on the organization and administration of schools. Morrison accepted only state and national sovereignty and argued that the state, not the local municipalities or districts, should be the fiscal and administrative unit for public education. He also recommended that local systems of school organization be consolidated. Morrison did not suggest that local school administration should not exist, however; he maintained that, as the state becomes the basic unit for all decision making, the implementation of policy becomes the responsibility of local government (a position somewhat predictable coming from a former state supervisor).

Morrison has been described as an individual with a commanding presence whose deportment closely resembled that of an Old Testament prophet. His appearance and general demeanor caused him to be "more feared than loved, more respected than admired" (Beck, p. 36). Morrison retired from the University of Chicago in 1937 and remained a resident of Hyde Park, where he died.

• Morrison's unpublished materials, internal memos, and correspondence are housed in special collections, Regenstein Library, University of Chicago. General descriptions of the Morrison Plan appear in Harold Alberty, *Reorganizing the High School Curriculum* (1947), and J. Minor Gwynn, *Curriculum Principles and Social Trends* (1943, rev. 1960). See also Hugo E. Beck, "The Contributions of Henry Clinton Morrison: An Educational Administrator at Work" (Ph.D. diss., Univ. of Chicago, 1962). Eulogies appear in *School and Society*, 9 June 1945, p. 19, and *Nation's School*, June 1945, pp. 380–82. An obituary is in the *New York Times*, 20 Mar. 1945.

CRAIG KRIDEL

MORRISON, Jim (8 Dec. 1943–3 July 1971), singer-composer, was born James Douglas Morrison in Melbourne, Florida, the son of Steven George Morrison, a navy officer, and Clara Clarke. Morrison, one of three children, was considered unusually intelligent by the time he attended high school, first in Alameda, California, then in Alexandria, Virginia, where his English teacher said he read "probably more than any other student in class. But everything was so offbeat I had another teacher who was going to the Library of Congress check to see if the books Jim was reporting on actually existed." He also began writing poems, at least one of which, "Horse Latitudes," survived to be included in one of his early recordings.

Feats of intellectual braggadocio characterized his year at St. Petersburg (Florida) Junior College, when he challenged friends to select one from hundreds of books in his room and read any first paragraph from any chapter, and he would identify the book and author. At Florida State University he enrolled in theater arts classes, where a fellow actor said of his only stage performance, "There was a constant undercurrent of apprehension, a feeling that things were on the brink of lost control." In 1964 he transferred to the film school of the University of California at Los Angeles, experimented with psychedelic drugs, and was an undistinguished student. Repeating his high school behavior, he did not attend ceremonies at which he received a B.A.

For a summer he lived on a rooftop in Venice, California, continuing his experiments with drugs and writing song-poems, later telling *Rolling Stone* magazine (1969), "I was just taking notes at a fantastic rock concert that was going on inside my head." Meeting a former UCLA classmate, Ray Manzarek, on the beach, he sang some of his lyrics. Manzarek, a keyboard player, suggested that they organize a band and "make a million dollars." A guitarist and a drummer, Robbie Krieger and John Densmore, were recruited from a meditation class Manzarek attended. When Morrison told his parents he was joining a band, his father, a navy captain commanding an aircraft carrier, said he was wasting his life.

Morrison named the band the Doors for the title of Aldous Huxley's study of mescaline experiments, "The Doors of Perception," adding, "There are things that are known and things that are unknown and in between are doors." Despite his initial stage shyness, the band found work in a small club on Los Angeles's famed Sunset Strip, moving next to the top venue in the city, the Whisky a Go Go, as backup band in 1966.

The Doors now had forty songs in their repertoire; more than half were Morrison's, and two of those were free-form epic song-poems whose dark themes about transcendence and death set the band's mood and built a cult following. The Doors were fired from the Whisky a Go Go when Morrison included an Oedipal section in one of the songs: "Father, I want to kill you . . . Mother, I want to . . . " followed by a primal scream. By then, the band had signed with Elektra Records, a small label with a reputation for recording folk singers. Their first single, "Break on Through," flopped, but the Doors' second single, "Light My Fire" (1967), written by Krieger, became the number one song of the "summer of love."

Consciously, Morrison forged an image for the 1960s, wearing leather pants and love beads and developing a performance style that featured dives into the audience, along with carefully crafted phrases for the media. "Think of us as erotic politicians," he told *Newsweek*. In his official press biography, he said his parents were dead. Inside the cover of the band's third album (*Waiting for the Sun*, 1968) he proclaimed in a poem to be the "lizard king," boasting "I can do anything." At night, he went "home" to a $10-a-night motel room. Albert Goldman called him a "surf-born Dionysus" in *Life*, and *Village Voice* critic Richard Goldstein called him a "sexual shaman," saying "the Doors begin where the Rolling Stones leave off." All the media followed, from "teenybopper" magazines to *Vogue*.

Although the band's biggest hit, "Light My Fire," was written by Krieger, it was Morrison's darker, more poetic vision that set the mood. When the band performed "The End," with its hypnotic and haunting lament of dread, its lyric ride on a strange blue bus, its image of a seven-mile-long snake, lost in a wilderness of pain (where children were insane), with its message of incest and patricide, it stopped an audience dead.

An arrest for breach of the peace, resisting arrest, and "performing an indecent and immoral exhibition" onstage in New Haven, Connecticut, on 9 December 1968, one day past his twenty-fifth birthday, established the Doors as rebels. Riots occurred at the band's concerts, and following a 2 March 1969 performance in Miami, Florida, Morrison was charged with "lewd and lascivious behavior . . . indecent exposure . . . open profanity . . . [and] drunkenness." The band's manager called it "just another dirty Doors show," but for much of the next year the group was unemployed.

Morrison came to hate his image as a sex idol, gaining weight and growing a beard. He told a friend, Fred Myrow, "If I don't find something else to do within a year, I'll be good for nothing but nostalgia." The Doors produced a documentary about themselves, *Feast of Friends* (1970), and Morrison financed a brief film in which he played a mysterious hitchhiker-murderer, *Hwy* (1971). He self-published three small collections of poetry, *The Lords: Notes on Vision* (1969), *The New Creatures* (1969), and *American Prayer* (1970), and sold the first two to Simon & Schuster. He wrote a screenplay, "St. Nicholas," with beat poet Michael McClure.

A schedule of weekend concerts resumed in 1970, and record sales were good. Morrison's diminished interest in the band and time spent on legal matters contributed to a slowdown in activity, however, forcing the record company to release a live album and an anthology of early hits. The media turned on Morrison, depicting him as a drunken clown. There were new arrests and trials, one in Phoenix, Arizona, for drunkenness aboard a plane, and another in Las Vegas, Nevada. He was convicted on two charges in Miami in 1970. So no one in the Doors organization was surprised in March 1971, after the band completed its seventh album, when Morrison and his longtime girlfriend Pamela Courson went to Paris for an extended vacation.

Courson told police on 4 July 1971 that she found Morrison dead in their apartment bathtub. A heart attack was blamed, yet many fans believed Morrison staged his death as a hoax to win the freedom that anonymity brings. Later statements by Morrison confidants revealed death most likely was caused by an overdose of heroin and alcohol. He was buried at Paris's Pere-Lachaise Cemetiere, near the graves of Moliere, Balzac, Edith Piaf, Chopin, and Oscar Wilde. On his death certificate, he was identified as a poet.

In the years following his death, Doors records sold in greater numbers than when Morrison lived. At least a dozen books about the Doors and Morrison were published—as well as two posthumous books of his poetry—and a major Hollywood film, *The Doors* (1991), was directed by Oliver Stone. In death as in life, Morrison remained a symbol of rebellion and search, drawing an international audience of people who were born after he died. In 1994 his gravesite was ranked the number three tourist destination in Paris, after the Eiffel Tower and the Louvre.

• Morrison's poems are collected in *The Lords and the New Creatures* (1970). His other writings are collected in *Wilderness: The Lost Writings of Jim Morrison*, vol. 1 (1988), and *The American Night: The Lost Writings of Jim Morrison*, vol. 2 (1990), both edited by Frank Lisciandro. For biographical information on Morrison, see Jerry Hopkins, *No One Here Gets Out Alive* (1980) and *The Lizard King: The Essential Jim Morrison* (1992); David Dalton, *Mr. Mojo Risin': Jim Morrison, the Last Holy Fool* (1991); John Densmore, *Riders on the Storm: My Life with Jim Morrison and the Doors* (1990); and James Riordan and Jerry Prochnicky, *Break on Through: The Life and Death of Jim Morrison* (1991).

JERRY HOPKINS

MORRISON, Nathan Jackson (25 Nov. 1828–12 Apr. 1907), educator, was born in Sanbornton (later Franklin), New Hampshire, the son of Nathan Smith Morrison and Susannah Chase. Morrison was educated in a district school during his early years, and studied in his hometown with private tutors. This prepared him for college; he graduated from Dartmouth College in 1853 and started teaching classes at a twelve-week school in Acworth, New Hampshire. In January 1854 he began pursuing an advanced degree at the Oberlin Theological Seminary, where he studied under the prominent evangelical minister and president of Oberlin College, Charles Grandison Finney. While there he taught in the college's preparatory school and tutored individual students. He graduated in 1857 and was ordained in the Congregational church on 11 February 1858. His first pulpit was at the Congregational church in Rochester, Michigan.

On 8 July 1863 Morrison married Miranda Capen Dimond in Brooklyn, New York. They had three children.

In September 1859 Morrison became professor of Greek and Latin at Olivet College in Michigan. The college, founded in 1844, had just received a charter. When its president resigned because of poor health, Morrison served as interim president of the struggling institution, which was adversely affected by the Civil War. Despite trying conditions, Morrison officially became the president of Olivet through unanimous election in June 1864. He also assumed the chair of mental and moral philosophy, a position often reserved for a college's president. As a fundraiser, he was able to secure $50,000 for the college endowment. He held high standards of scholarship for students, and he was careful to select teachers from various colleges, largely alumni of the older New England institutions. Despite his success at Olivet, he resigned in June 1872 and moved on to found a new institution, Drury College, in Springfield, Missouri.

Morrison became interested in starting a new college while passing through Chicago, where he read in *The Advance* about a proposed new college in St. Louis, Missouri. After contacting the Congregationalist minister in St. Louis about his idea, Morrison traveled west with Samuel F. Drury of Michigan, hoping to found an institution dedicated to providing Christian education for that region. Drury, who had helped secure money for Olivet, served again as a fundraiser.

Morrison was elected the first president of Drury College in 1873, and he remained in that position until his resignation in 1888. The college suffered many financial reverses during his tenure, and it did not always have the support or understanding of the community. Morrison was domineering but tenacious and was often able to achieve success in fundraising, but when he left the institution it was $44,000 in debt. He tended to dislike soliciting funds, which he considered a thankless task and one that kept a college president from maintaining the more important roles of scholar and teacher.

Morrison took time to tour Europe in 1884. He served as president of the Missouri State Teachers' Association and completed several publications, including *Memorial Address on Olivet College and Its History* (1866), *The Christian College* (1874), *Essay on Relation of Drury College to the Congregational Churches of Southwestern Missouri* (1877), *Decaying the People's Sense of Duty* (1878), and *Young Men* (1882).

After fifteen years at Drury College, Morrison left administration. He then taught philosophy at Marietta College in Ohio from 1888 to 1895. Despite his advanced age, he became interested in founding another college, the Fairmount Institute in Wichita, Kansas. Fairmount already was in operation, but Morrison became active in raising its status to that of a four-year institution. He became president of the newly elevated college, serving until his death in Wichita.

Morrison remained true to the education that he had received at Dartmouth and Oberlin colleges. He brought to the West an evangelical Christian spirit that viewed education as the means to salvation. Although some thought him difficult and autocratic, he was dedicated to high standards of learning and the scholarly aspects of a college president's job, and there is no doubt that he was successful in his major role in life, the founding of Christian colleges.

• Accounts of various stages of Morrison's career are in Arthur P. Hall, "Historical Address Delivered at the Celebration of the Semi-Centennial of the Founding of Drury College, 1873–1923," published by the college's alumni association (1923); Moses T. Rupnels, *Memorial Sketches and History of the Class of 1853, Dartmouth College* (1895); and Wolcott B. Williams, *A History of Olivet College, 1844–1900* (1901). An obituary is in the *Topeka Daily State Journal*, 12 Apr. 1907.

RITA S. SASLAW

MORRISON, William (14 Mar. 1763–19 Apr. 1837), merchant, was born in Doylestown, Pennsylvania, the son of John Morrison and Rebecca Bryan. Morrison's father, a member of a titled family in County Cork, Ireland, had immigrated to the United States as a young man in the early eighteenth century and established an estate in Pennsylvania. Little is known about the early life of William Morrison; presumably he was tutored at home, but there is no record of a formal education. As a youth he began working in the store of an uncle, Guy Bryan, who was a prominent merchant in Philadelphia. This association led to the formation some years later of Bryan & Morrison, a merchant firm that also included five of Morrison's brothers.

Sometime around 1790, Morrison traveled to Kaskaskia, in the Northwest Territory, as the western representative of Bryan & Morrison. Kaskaskia, located in what is now southwestern Illinois, near the junction of the Kaskaskia and Mississippi rivers, was a major pioneer trading center. Kaskaskia had been founded in 1703 as an Indian settlement and was later controlled successively by France and Great Britain before coming under U.S. authority in 1787; it is considered the oldest town in the American West. There Morrison established a thriving business in consumer goods and fur trading that extended as far west as the Rocky Mountains and from southern Wisconsin to New Orleans. In 1800 he opened a store in Cahokia, another major trading center in Illinois country (which that year became part of Indiana Territory) and not far from St. Louis. This establishment also thrived.

Morrison earned a place in American history in 1804, when he sent an emissary, a Frenchman named Baptiste Lalande, to Santa Fe with a stock of goods to sell. With this venture Morrison became the first U.S. merchant to trade with Spanish-dominated New Mexico, nearly two decades before that territory established formal, full-scale trading relations with the United States.

In addition to his own business, Morrison backed other ventures that prospered, including an expedition of fur trapper Manuel Lisa to the mouth of the Big Horn River in 1807 and the establishment of the St. Louis Fur Company in 1809, the same year that Illinois became a separate territory. In both these efforts he joined forces with fellow pioneer merchant Pierre Menard, a political rival who later presided over the Illinois territorial legislature and still later served as the state's first lieutenant governor.

In the years before Illinois's separation from Indiana Territory, Morrison was active in a political faction that opposed the rule of William Henry Harrison, then governor of the territory. He was also a major figure in a dispute over land claims with the Indiana territorial government; his principal adversary was Michael Jones, the Harrison-appointed register of the land office who accused Morrison and other speculators of fraud. When Rice Jones, the attorney for Morrison's faction, was found murdered in December 1808, Morrison and his associates publicly blamed Michael Jones for the crime. Jones was arrested but later acquitted, after which he sued Morrison for defamation of character and won a $200 judgment against him.

This incident was not a setback for Morrison the merchant, but it undoubtedly curtailed any political ambitions he may have entertained. Although Morrison continued to prosper in his business ventures, he did not play a major role in Illinois's emerging political prominence, first as an independent territory and later, after 1818, as a state. However, belying Morrison's reputation at the time of the Jones incident as hotheaded and unscrupulous, many of his contemporaries, including Illinois governor John Reynolds, later described him as dignified, gracious, and benevolent.

Morrison was married three times and had children—the exact number is not known—with each wife. His first marriage was to Catherine Thaumur around 1794; after her death (date unknown), he married Euphrosine Huberdeau in 1798. In 1801 he built a large stone house in Kaskaskia, where he lived for the remainder of his life. After the death of his second wife (again, the death date is unknown), he married Elisa Bissell in 1813. Morrison died at his Kaskaskia home.

• Biographical information on William Morrison can be found in John Reynolds, *The Pioneer History of Illinois* (1852), and Clarence Walworth Alvord, *The Illinois Country, 1673–1918* (1920; repr. 1987). For an account of the Rice Jones incident, see W. A. B. Jones, "Rice Jones," in the Chicago Historical Society's Collection, vol. 4 (1890). *The WPA Guide to Illinois* (1939; repr. 1983) offers a succinct account of Illinois's prestatehood history, including the settlement of Kaskaskia and Cahokia and the career of Pierre Menard.

ANN T. KEENE

MORRISON, William McCutchan (10 Nov. 1867–14 Mar. 1918), Southern Presbyterian missionary, was born near Lexington, Virginia, the son of James Luther Morrison and Mary Agnes McCutchan, farmers. Morrison's parents hoped he would study for the ministry, as had several generations of his family before him; but Morrison resisted their efforts to convince him, reportedly stating that "for me to preach is for me to be a missionary and I don't want to be a missionary." Consequently, as a young man he entered Washington and Lee University to study law. Shortly before his college graduation in 1886, however, his father died, and this event apparently ended his resistance to his parents' vocational desires for him. Still, he delayed his entry into theological studies for another six years while he taught school in Searcy, Arkansas. He then entered the Presbyterian Theological Seminary in Louisville, Kentucky, at age twenty-six. After graduating, he sailed in November 1896 for the Congo as a missionary of the Presbyterian Church in the United States, commonly referred to as the Southern Presbyterian church.

The initial mission work in the Congo Free State had begun in 1890. Its leadership had been the unlikely but highly effective team of Samuel Norvell Lapsley, the son of an aristocratic southern family from Alabama, and William Henry Sheppard, an African-American graduate of the Stillman Institute from Waynesboro, Virginia, who had been born free only a month after the end of the Civil War. Lapsley's untimely death in 1892 had left the mission struggling, although Sheppard kept it alive by recruiting a number of African-American college graduates from the United States to join the mission effort. The arrival of Morrison at the main station in Luebo in 1897 breathed new life into the project and marked a turning point in the mission's subsequent history.

A strong, determined leader and organizer, Morrison moved quickly to place the mission on a sounder basis. He labored to produce *Grammar and Dictionary of the Buluba-Lulua Language as Spoken in the Upper Kasai and Congo Basin* (1906), which put in writing the oral language of a large indigenous population for the first time. For this accomplishment he was awarded a D.D. degree by his alma mater Washington and Lee. Bible paraphrases and translations of other Christian and Sunday school literature soon followed, and he was working on a New Testament translation at the time of his death. He was a regular contributor to the Southern Presbyterian paper *The Missionary* (renamed the *Missionary Survey* in 1911) and later a frequent writer for leading newspapers and magazines of England and America. In 1901 he initiated the *Kasai Herald* and served as its editor for the next sixteen years. In 1906 he married Bertha Marion Stebbens, whom he had met during a furlough to the United States in the summer of 1905; they had no children, and she died only four years later in Luebo.

It was Morrison's protests against the brutal practices of King Leopold of Belgium against the native Congo population that gained the missionary his greatest renown. The Congo Free State, formed in 1885, fell under the direct personal rule and financial ambition of Leopold and his agents. Sheppard's investigation in 1899 of reported atrocities by one tribe against another at the explicit instigation of the state first led Morrison to publicize abuses against the native people in the Congo. Specifically, he charged that excessively burdensome taxation imposed by the state was ruining traditional African ways of life, that armed natives of various tribes were used to enforce rubber collection for the monopolistic, state-controlled rubber companies, and that slavery, although officially outlawed, continued to exist. Although at least partially motivated by frustration at the Catholic regime's reluctance to give permission for the expansion of Protestant missions, Morrison's charges of human rights violations were authentic and impassioned.

Morrison's charges proved explosive, serving as the catalyst that ignited and fanned the flame of a reform movement already under way. On his first furlough home, Morrison spoke before groups in both England and America, including the Boston Peace Conference of 1904, where he spoke "in the name of an oppressed people who cannot speak for themselves." His efforts aroused many influential members on both sides of the Atlantic to advocate reform measures in the Congo. The Archbishop of Canterbury, Sir Arthur Conan Doyle, and J. Pierpont Morgan were only a few of the varied influential leaders with whom he maintained correspondence and influence. Mark Twain's scathing polemic *King Leopold's Soliloquy* (1905) was based in part on information Twain had received from Morrison and Sheppard.

The resulting international protest movement against the uncontrolled exploitation and mistreatment of the native population led Belgium to directly annex the Congo as a colony in 1908. A massive counteroffensive was mounted by Leopold and his agents to discredit Morrison and his attacks. In February 1909 Morrison and Sheppard were sued for libel by the Compagnie du Kasai, based on an article Sheppard had written and Morrison had published a year earlier, "From the Bakuba Country," in the *Kasai Herald* (8 [Jan. 1908]: 12–14). In his article, Sheppard condemned the "armed sentries of chartered trading companies, who force men and women to spend most of their days and nights in the forests making rubber." In ensuing correspondence with the officials of the company, Morrison condemned the "monopolistic system by which the country is being ruthlessly stripped of its natural products, with the natives getting but little return," while the company reaped enormous dividends. Attorney and socialist leader Emile Vandervelde of Belgium was recruited to defend the missionaries and eventually won them a dramatic acquittal.

Morrison possessed a strong, forceful personality, administrative skill, and a passion for justice. His efforts against Leopold have won him praise as one of the earliest modern crusaders in the international struggle for human rights. He is also remembered among Presbyterians for his missionary successes: on his arrival in Luebo in 1897, the American Presbyterian Congo Mission consisted of one mission station, eight missionaries, and fifty converts. By 1918 the mission comprised six stations, forty missionaries, and 17,000 converts. Morrison died in Luebo of tropical dysentery at the height of his influence, worn down by the demands of two decades of missionary service.

• Morrison's papers, including his extensive correspondence between 1897 and 1918, are in the collection of the Southern Presbyterian mission to the Congo at the Department of History of the Presbyterian Church in the United States of America in Montreat, North Carolina. His diary for 1899 is also included in the collection. Additional primary source material on Morrison's work is in contemporary articles in *The Missionary* and the *Missionary Survey*. See, for example, Morrison, "Africa between the Upper and the Nether Millstones," *The Missionary* 33, no. 2 (Feb. 1900): 64–67, and Morrison et al., "Situation in the Congo Free State—Protestant Missions in Danger," *The Missionary* 38, no. 1 (Jan. 1905): 13–16. An older, uncritical biography that cites extensively from Morrison's pre-1899 diary is T. C. Vinson, *William McCutchan Morrison* (1921). A more recent resource is Robert Benedetto, ed., *Presbyterian Reformers in Central Africa: A Documentary Account of the American Presbyterian Congo Mission and the Human Rights Struggle in the Congo, 1890–1918* (1996), a documentary collection consisting primarily of Morrison's correspondence with world figures on the situation in the Congo and a brief history of the mission. Stanley Shaloff, "The American Presbyterian Congo Mission: A Study in Conflict, 1890–1921" (Ph.D. diss., Northwestern Univ. 1967), also highlights Morrison's role in the conflict between the missionaries and Leopold. An obituary is in the *Missionary Review of the World*, June 1918.

SUSAN WILDS MCARVER

MORRISON, William Ralls (14 Sept. 1824–29 Sept. 1909), congressman and interstate commerce commissioner, was born in Prairie du Long Township in present-day Monroe County, Illinois, the son of John Morrison and Anna Ralls, proprietors of a country store. After Morrison's mother died when Morrison was young, his father married a Miss Ditch (full name unknown), who owned the Waterloo Tavern, moved into Waterloo to become its keeper, and entered politics. Constantly exposed to political discussions in the family tavern, Morrison became a deputy sheriff at twenty-two. The Mexican War had begun, and he soon enlisted as a private in the Second Illinois Regiment and fought at Buena Vista (23 Feb. 1847). After the war he journeyed overland to California in the 1849 gold rush with a party of adventurers from Missouri and "had lots of fun on the way, but reached the Pacific in rather bad plight" (Robbins, p. 2). There Morrison's luck was good, and he returned to Waterloo a year later with $8,000. At twenty-six he realized his educational deficiencies and from 1850 to 1852 attended the Preparatory Department of McKendree College in Lebanon, Illinois. Before completing his studies he married Mary Jane Drury in 1851; they had two children, who died in infancy.

Settling in Waterloo, Morrison entered politics in 1852 and was elected circuit court clerk for Monroe County. Although his in-laws were Whigs and his relatives were anti-Douglas Democrats, Morrison endorsed Stephen A. Douglas's view that popular sovereignty would best determine the fate of slavery in the territories. Morrison was elected as a Democrat to the state house of representatives in 1854, became its Speaker after the election of 1858, and served until 1860. There he earned a reputation for fairness, decisiveness, dispatch, and for being, as Abraham Lincoln later said, "above . . . false pretense" (*Collected Works*, vol. 5 [1953–1955], p. 342). Morrison was also admitted to the Illinois bar on 1 January 1855 and was for a time in partnership with Gustav Philipp Körner, who encouraged the "terse and cautious" Morrison to speak with confidence. Morrison's wife died on 3 March 1856, and in 1857 he married her half-sister, Eleanora Horine, who supported his political ambitions. They had one child, who died in infancy.

Morrison went down to defeat with his idol Douglas in 1860 and, like Douglas, supported Lincoln's call to arms to prevent secession. Commissioned a colonel, Morrison raised and commanded the Forty-ninth Illinois Infantry and was seriously wounded in the hip while assaulting Fort Donelson (13 Feb. 1862). Angered because he was not promoted—for which he blamed the political hostility of Lincoln—Morrison ran for Congress while in the field, was elected as a War Democrat in 1862, and left the army in December 1862. His district was located across the Mississippi River from St. Louis, Missouri, and his constituents were mostly farmers (many of them German-Americans) but also included those engaged in coal mining and manufacturing. In the Thirty-eighth Congress (1863–1865) he backed most war measures but opposed the Thirteenth Amendment (emancipating slaves) and Radical Reconstruction, as embodied in the Wade Davis Bill (1864). Defeated for reelection by seventy-five votes in 1864 and by over 1,000 votes in 1866, Morrison served a term (1870–1871) in the state legislature. In 1872, with Liberal Republican support, he was swept back into Congress, where he remained from 1873 to 1887.

Shy, diffident, and in the Democratic minority, Morrison initially had little influence. Noted for his blunt candor, he was conspicuous as a western opponent of inflation—a "hard money" man—and in his modest, honest way, he was effective in caucuses and conferences. When the Democrats gained control of the House of Representatives in 1875, Morrison backed Michael C. Kerr of Indiana for Speaker; Kerr in turn made Morrison chairman of the Ways and Means Committee. Influenced in general by David A. Wells, the tariff reformer, and specifically by Joseph S. Moore, a New York merchant and former employee of the New York Customhouse, Morrison in 1876 introduced legislation to simplify and lower import tariffs, but in the excitement of the disputed 1876 Hayes-Tilden election, it did not pass. After observing the Louisiana returning board in New Orleans, Morrison believed that Republican fraud combined with Samuel J. Tilden's lack of "pluck" had enabled Rutherford B. Hayes to win. He could also have blamed Democrats in the Illinois legislature for abandoning his candidacy for the Senate to elect David Davis, which enabled that Supreme Court justice to avoid serving on the Electoral Commission and virtually assured Hayes's election. During the crisis Morrison filibustered with those Democrats who wished to force a new election and later served on the Potter committee (1878–1879) in an effort to keep alive the fraud issue.

Although the Democrats retained control of the House, the new Speaker, Samuel J. Randall, supported protective tariffs. In 1877 Randall moved Morrison, who believed tariffs should only be employed to raise needed revenue, from the Ways and Means Committee to the Pacific Railroad Committee, where Morrison opposed subsidizing railroads with land grants. In 1879, however, Randall returned him to the Ways and Means Committee, where Morrison advocated tariff reform without success but with notoriety. He was Illinois's favorite son for the 1880 Democratic presidential nomination and received sixty-two votes on the first ballot. From 1883 to 1887 Morrison served as chairman of the Ways and Means Committee. His Horizontal Bill of 1884 proposed a 20 percent tariff reduction across the board, but when Randall and his "forty thieves" defected to the Republican minority, the tariff was lost, as were "Horizontal Bill" Morrison's aspirations for the presidency. After narrowly missing election to the Senate in 1885, he remained in the House, where he successfully devised rules that reduced the power of the Appropriations Committee, which Randall chaired. In 1886 Morrison introduced another tariff bill with "diagonal reductions" on specific items, but President Grover Cleveland gave it scant support, and Randall joined with Republicans to defeat it. In 1886 an infusion of funds from hostile Chicago Democrats and from protectionist manufacturers combined with the fears of workers that "Horizontal Bill" would reduce jobs along with the tariff to defeat Morrison's bid for reelection.

Although Morrison knew little about railroad regulation, Cleveland appointed him to the newly established Interstate Commerce Commission (ICC). Morrison served on the commission from 1887 to 1897 and during the last six years of his tenure was its chairman. He was warmly sympathetic toward shippers, but his efforts to eliminate discriminatory rates and rebates ended in frustration. During his last year on the ICC, the Supreme Court denied the commission's power to determine railroad rates and destroyed its control over long-short-haul discrimination. While a member of the ICC, Morrison was spoken of as a possible presidential candidate in 1892 and, after Cleveland's victory that year, as a possible head of either the treasury or interior departments, but Cleveland chose John G. Carlisle as his secretary of the treasury, and railroad interests successfully opposed Morrison as secretary of the interior. As a bimetallist opposed to the unlimited coinage of silver, he attracted support in 1896 as a compromise candidate, but his supporters were overwhelmed by the Democratic stampede to "free" silver. In 1896 Morrison voted for but did not campaign for William Jennings Bryan and helped defeat John Peter Altgeld, a fellow Democrat whom he despised, for reelection as governor of Illinois. When President William McKinley failed to reappoint him to the ICC, Morrison retired in Waterloo. There he lived to see the nation accept his views of railroad regulation, and there he died before the nation adopted his tariff reform principles.

• Morrison's papers are in the Illinois State Historical Library, Springfield. David Earl Robbins, Jr., "The Congressional Career of William Ralls Morrison" (Ph.D. diss., Univ. of Illinois, 1963), is indispensable. See also Franklin D. Scott, "The Political Career of William R. Morrison," *Illinois State Historical Society Transactions*, no. 33 (1926): 134–71. Obituaries are in the *Illinois State Register* (Springfield) and the *Chicago Tribune*, both 30 Sept. 1909; the *Waterloo Republican*, 6 Oct. 1909; and the *Journal of the Illinois State Historical Society* 2 (Oct. 1909): 111–13.

ARI HOOGENBOOM

MORRISSEY, John (12 Feb. 1831–1 May 1878), gambler, prizefighter, and U.S. congressman, was born in Templemore, County Tipperary, Ireland, the son of Timothy Morrissey, a factory worker, and Julia or Mary, whose maiden name is unknown. He immigrated with his family to Canada in 1834 and then moved with his family to Troy, New York, where he grew up. As a youth, Morrissey joined several street gangs in Troy and was constantly involved in brawls and gang fights. He worked briefly in a wallpaper factory and in the Burden iron works. He was the leader of a gang called the Downtowns, which engaged in continuing fights with the Uptowns. By 1848, at the age of seventeen, Morrissey began to consider a career in prizefighting after beating a gang of six Uptowns in one afternoon. He got a job as a deck hand on a Hudson River steamer, and about 1849 he married Sarah Smith, the daughter of the ship's captain. They had one child who died in childhood.

In 1849 Morrissey issued a challenge to "Dutch" Charley Duane, a New York City prizefighter. Duane ignored his challenge, and Morrissey traveled to New York to find him at the saloon of Isaiah Rynders, a Tammany Hall politician. Finding that Duane was not there and that no prizefighters were available, Morrissey challenged "any man in the house." He was immediately set upon and beaten up by a group at the saloon, including one man who knocked him down with a spittoon. Rynders was impressed and nursed Morrissey back to health.

After a return to Troy, Morrissey went to work for Rynders as a "shoulder hitter," one who would get out the vote for Tammany. He was just under six feet tall and extraordinarily powerful, with huge hands and arms and a deep chest. He would keep fighting long after others would have given up. Morrissey earned the nickname "Old Smoke" in a fistfight with a hoodlum named Tom McCann over a madame, Kate Ridgely, who operated a popular New York brothel. The two fighters overturned a stove, and glowing coals rolled out on the floor. McCann held Morrissey down on the coals, which burned through his clothes, filling the room with smoke. Eventually Morrissey overcame McCann and kicked and beat him to defeat.

In 1851 Morrissey saved enough money to journey to California, traveling at least part of the distance as a stowaway. In San Francisco he opened a gambling game and amassed a bankroll. He appeared for the first time in a professional boxing ring on Mare Island, California, defeating George Thompson in August 1852 for a purse of $4,000 and a side bet of $1,000. According to some reports, Thompson, intimidated by Morrissey's followers, threw the match. While in California, Morrissey led an abortive expedition to seize gold lands in the Queen Charlotte Islands off British Columbia, outfitting a schooner with weapons, cannon, and a crew of thugs.

Although Morrissey called himself the "Champion of America" following the fight with Thompson, the title was not confirmed until 1853, when he defeated "Yankee" Sullivan in a fight in Boston Corners, New York, in thirty-seven rounds.

Morrissey organized a gang that fought for Tammany and led a group that engaged in fights with a Know Nothing political gang led by Bill Poole. Eventually Morrissey and Poole challenged each other to a fight on the New York docks on 26 July 1854, in which Morrissey was defeated. A vendetta between the two gangs ensued, with several fatalities and serious injuries. On 8 March 1855 Poole was shot and killed, allegedly by one of Morrissey's men. Morrissey was arrested for the murder but was released.

In October 1858 Morrissey fought John C. Heenan, "the Benicia Boy," a fellow resident of Troy, New York, in Long Point, Canada, and won a side bet of $5,000. All of these fights were without gloves, with a round lasting until one or the other fighter fell to the ground. The fight ended only when one fighter could not return to the center of the ring on his feet.

After his defeat of Heenan, Morrissey retired from boxing and gave his attention to saloon ownership, gambling, and politics. He briefly operated two saloons in New York, and with the profits from the saloons and his prizefight winnings, he took over a gambling house on Barclay Street in New York. This "resort" became very popular among politicians and the gambling "sporting" community of New York. He reputedly banked a net profit from this house of $1 million within five years. He continued to work several other gambling houses in New York as well. Although faro-houses and casinos were illegal at the time, they were widely tolerated by the police in return for generous cash payments. In the late 1850s Morrissey emerged as one of the most successful and well-known proprietors of such resorts in New York City.

Morrissey invested in real estate and a gambling casino in Saratoga and held controlling interest in the Saratoga race track after 1863. In 1866 he was elected to the U.S. Congress as a Democrat from New York's Fifth District and, reelected to a second term, served from 4 March, 1867 through 3 March 1871. He took up residence in Saratoga, continuing improvements to the track and gaming house there. In 1875 and 1877 Morrissey was elected a state senator. In politics, he became known as an opponent of William M. "Boss" Tweed. He died in Saratoga Springs, New York. Morrissey's colorful life as a brawler, boxer, political tough, gambling house owner, and politician illustrates the connections between the rough sporting life and the political machines of the 1850s to the 1870s.

• Information on Morrissey is in Elliott J. Gorn, *The Manly Art, Bare-Knuckle Prize Fighting in America* (1986); Rex Lardner, *The Legendary Champions* (1972); Herbert Asbury, "John Morrissey and His Times," in *Sucker's Progress: An Informal History of Gambling in America from the Colonies to Canfield* (1938); and William E. Harding, *John Morrissey: His Life, Battles, and Wrangles* (1881).

RODNEY P. CARLISLE

MORROW, Dwight Whitney (11 Jan. 1873–5 Oct. 1931), investment banker, diplomat, and senator, was born in Huntington, West Virginia, the son of James Elmore Morrow, a mathematics teacher and school principal, and Clara Johnson. Dwight Morrow grew up in a close-knit and intellectually active family, which possessed all the virtues of "right-minded" Presbyterianism, yet was perennially short of money. He was a frail and sickly child who compensated for his diminutive size through precocity of intelligence and tenacity.

Morrow scored at the top of a competitive examination for the U.S. Military Academy and hoped to follow his brother Jay Johnson, the later governor of the Panama Canal Zone, to West Point. A rival candidate, however, exerted influence with the local congressman, and Morrow lost out. A family friend who held a professorship of Greek at Amherst College came to the rescue. Despite straitened finances and defective preparation in the classics, Morrow matriculated there in 1891. Amherst proved a formative influence. Morrow later became a trustee and donor.

At Amherst, Morrow compiled a brilliant academic record in mathematics, history, and philosophy, and as a campus leader honed his skills in negotiation and persuasion. In addition, he developed a dense web of friendships. He befriended one awkward and introverted classmate, Calvin Coolidge, who later became president. During his college years, Morrow met Elizabeth Reeve Cutter, an ambitious and upwardly mobile Smith College bluestocking from Cleveland. A prolonged and rocky courtship led to marriage in 1903. The couple had four children. Their second daughter, Anne, subsequently married the aviator Charles Lindbergh and became a noted diarist in her own right.

After an unhappy interlude as a law clerk in Pittsburgh, Morrow entered Columbia Law School in 1896. Despite an unpretentious manner and sartorial inelegance, he made strategic contacts among the New York social elite. After graduating with distinction in 1899, he joined the law firm later known as Simpson, Thacher & Bartlett, and became the protégé of the senior partner there. Morrow quickly developed a reputation as one of the shrewdest corporate lawyers in the city. In 1905 Simpson, Thacher rewarded him with a partnership. In Englewood, New Jersey, at that time the residence of choice for much of New York's banking and legal elite, Morrow entered politics. He helped draft New Jersey's workmen's compensation law in 1911, and some years afterward chaired the state's Prison Inquiry Commission. After American entrance into World War I, he served as director of the National War Savings Committee for New Jersey.

Through an Englewood neighbor, Thomas W. Lamont, Morrow came to the attention of the investment bank J. P. Morgan & Co. In 1914 J. P. Morgan, Jr., offered him a partnership. Morrow had no particular expertise in banking, and he recognized that a Morgan partnership would likely block his future political ambitions. After much agonizing, however, he accepted and remained a mainstay of the boardroom at 23 Wall Street until 1927. J. P. Morgan figured as the avuncular guiding spirit of the firm, but day-to-day responsibility during the war and postwar periods fell on a small number of partners, chief among them Lamont, Morrow, Henry P. Davison, and later Russell C. Leffingwell. The company played the pivotal role, before American entry into World War I, in helping the Allies to float loans on the American market and in organizing the centralized purchase of foodstuffs, munitions, and supplies necessary to sustain the war effort. After the war, Morgan's took the lead in arranging reconstruction loans for Britain and France and also for the defeated Central Powers. Morrow played a key part in all those efforts. His Morgan partnership gave Morrow national visibility, won him an invitation to join numerous corporate boards, and made him very rich.

Morrow became a central figure on the Allied Maritime Transport Council in 1918. The AMTC played a vital role in the last year of the war in resolving inter-Allied conflicts over the allocation of scarce shipping resources and, by that token, of manpower and supplies. In theory, Morrow served as the U.S. expert on the imports subcommittee of the AMTC executive. In practice, he deployed his marvelous negotiating skills to surmount a variety of logistic obstacles to coordination among the powers. He worked closely with General Charles G. Dawes, chief purchasing agent for the American Expeditionary Force. General John Pershing lauded the "tact and good judgment" with which Morrow had managed to resolve potentially divisive disputes over tonnage. The internationally minded civil servants, businessmen, and bankers who met through the AMTC and its sister organizations remained in contact after the war and did much to foster economic reconstruction. Morrow also maintained an interest in Latin American affairs, and in 1921–1922 helped to reorganize Cuban finances.

Disputes over the payment of German reparations and Allied war debts dominated economic diplomacy in the 1920s. The Morgan firm, as the acknowledged interpreter of American securities markets, became at crucial points the arbiter of the settlements that private investors would underwrite with loans. Because popular sentiment in the United States opposed political involvement in Europe, J. P. Morgan & Co. was thrust by default into making quasi-political judgments. Morrow fretted continually about this problem. "The Morgan firm is an anachronism," he once reflected. "It is accountable to nobody but its own sense of responsibility." Morrow, as opposed to his partners, felt some enthusiasm for the Dawes Committee of 1924 and its revision of the reparations schedule. He hoped to become agent general to supervise German finances under the Dawes Plan. However, the American ambassador to Germany argued that voters in the Middle West would dislike selection of a Morgan partner, and at the last minute President Coolidge backed off from appointing Morrow.

During the 1920s Morrow became restless and nourished the hope that Coolidge would appoint him to high office. He was repeatedly disappointed. In 1925 he was named chairman of a board detailed to study the employment of aircraft in national defense. The assignment was ticklish, since the head of the Army Air Service had demonstrated that aircraft could sink major ships, and public anxiety ran high. Morrow's board made middle-of-the-road recommendations for developing civil and military aviation without offending vested interests. Not until 1927, when he had decided to forgo another term, did Coolidge offer Morrow a major position, as ambassador to Mexico. Elizabeth "Betsey" Morrow minuted her disappointment in her diary. "'No skates or sleds left in my bag!' says Santa Claus, 'but here's a silly little whistle!'" The humorist Will Rogers, echoing more benign public sentiment, described Morrow as the only man who had ever "voluntarily quitted a really first-class business like J. P. Morgan to associate himself with a second-class business such as the government of the United States."

Morrow served as ambassador to Mexico from October 1927 through September 1930. He worked assiduously to improve relations between that country and the United States. In the throes of revolution and radical disorganization since 1914, Mexico had defaulted on American bonds and refused to recognize the subsoil property rights of U.S. oil and mining enterprises. Forsaking diplomatic formality and deploying his fabled charm, Morrow rapidly won the confidence of the rough-hewn and crafty Mexican president, Plutarco Elías Calles. He secured some limited recognition of pre-1917 oil and land holdings by Americans, and also helped mitigate Mexican government persecution of the Catholic church. Those achievements garnered much praise at the time. Yet in retrospect they appear ephemeral. Morrow actually opposed the settlement brokered by his former partner Lamont for rescheduling the defaulted debt. And Mexico's success in expropriating American property interests behind a small figleaf encouraged other Latin American states to do likewise when the depression struck.

Morrow's name was bandied about as a potential secretary of state in 1929, but President Hoover, who had crossed swords with Morrow over the organization of European relief in 1919, did not seriously consider him. Later, however, Hoover grew increasingly respectful of Morrow's advice. He named him a delegate to the London Naval Conference of 1930, where Morrow labored indefatigibly, albeit without success, to get France and Italy to accept limitations on cruisers and smaller ships.

In the fall of 1930, Morrow ran for senator from New Jersey on a platform opposing prohibition, which he abhorred both as a matter of public policy and private conduct. He won handily and, though taking little direct part in Senate deliberations, became a powerful figure in Hoover's entourage. In June 1931 he persuaded the president to proclaim the "Hoover moratorium," a one-year cessation on war debt and reparations payments, which had been elaborated in Morgan offices. In the fall of 1931, he helped the State Department to prepare for the visit of French prime minister Pierre Laval. He was tentatively scheduled to lead the American delegation to the World Disarmament Conference at Geneva.

Morrow died suddenly of a cerebral hemorrhage. He was exceedingly ill served by his official biographer, the British litterateur Harold Nicolson, who slighted Morrow's business career. Nicolson concluded that Morrow had about him "a touch of madness . . . the mind of a supercriminal and the character of a saint." The Morgan partners were dismayed. Morrow's achievements remain essentially unchronicled.

• Morrow's papers, which are quite full, are in the Amherst College Library. Additional correspondence appears in the papers of his partners Thomas W. Lamont (Harvard Business School), Russell C. Leffingwell (Sterling Library, Yale University), and J. P. Morgan, Jr. (Pierpont Morgan Library). The best biography, despite its defects, is Harold Nicolson, *Dwight Morrow* (1935). Nicolson's final assessment is found in his *Diaries and Letters, 1930–1939*, ed. Nigel Nicolson (1968). Hewitt Howland, *Dwight Whitney Morrow: A Sketch in Admiration* (1930), and Mary Margaret McBride, *The Story of Dwight W. Morrow* (1930), do not rise above the level of campaign biography. Family ambience may be gleaned from Joyce Milton, *Loss of Eden: A Biography of Charles and Anne Morrow Lindbergh* (1993).

For Morrow's role in reparations diplomacy, see Stephen A. Schuker, *The End of French Predominance in Europe* (1976), as well as the account of the decision to pass over Morrow as agent general for reparations in K. Paul Jones, "Discord and Collaboration: Choosing an Agent General for Reparations," *Diplomatic History* 1 (1977): 118–39. Morrow's ambassadorship in Mexico is chronicled in Robert Freeman Smith, *The United States and Revolutionary Nationalism in Mexico, 1916–1932* (1972), as well as in Smith's earlier articles cited therein; Richard Meltzer, "The Ambassador *Simpatico*: Dwight Morrow in Mexico 1927–1930," in *Ambassadors in Foreign Policy: The Influence of Individuals in United States Latin American Policy*, ed. C. Neale Ronning and Albert P. Vanucci (1987); L. Ethan Ellis, "Dwight Morrow and the Church-State Controversy in Mexico," *Hispanic American Historical Review* 38 (1958): 482–505; Stanley R. Ross, "Dwight W. Morrow, Ambassador to Mexico," *Americas* 14 (1958): 173–89, and "Dwight Morrow and the Mexican Revolution," *Hispanic American Historical Review* 38 (1958): 506–28. For Morrow's role at the London Naval Conference, see Raymond G. O'Connor, *Perilous Equilibrium: The United States and the London Disarmament Conference of 1930* (1962). On Morrow's 1930 Senate campaign, there is Edmund Wilson's amusing journalistic account, "Dwight Morrow in New Jersey," in *The American Jitters* (1932). Long obituaries are in the *New York Times*, 6–7 Oct. 1931.

STEPHEN A. SCHUKER

MORROW, Honoré Willsie (1880–12 Apr. 1940), novelist, was born in Ottumwa, Iowa, the daughter of William Dunbar McCue and Lilly Bryant Head. She graduated from the University of Wisconsin, earning an A.B. shortly before her marriage in 1901 to Henry Elmer Willsie, a construction engineer. They had no children.

As an aspiring writer, Honoré Willsie spent two years in the West, gathering materials for short stories and articles. During that time she visited friends at a mining camp in Arizona, where she wrote her first novel, *The Heart of the Desert* (1913). After moving to New York, she found a market for her works in magazines such as *Collier's* and *Harper's Weekly*. She wrote on a variety of topics, including Native American issues, divorce, immigration, and the U.S. Reclamation Service.

Beginning to gain a reputation for her freelance articles, Honoré Willsie turned down a position on the *Delineator* (a woman's magazine) when Theodore Dreiser first offered it because she wanted to concentrate on her writing. In 1914, however, she accepted the editorship of that same magazine, a position she held until 1919. During her tenure as editor, she produced five novels, all of which centered on topical issues such as forest conservation, desert reclamation, and the U.S. Reclamation Service. *Benefits Forgot* (1917) was made into the motion picture *Of Human Hearts* in 1938.

In 1922 she and Willsie were divorced; in 1923 she married William Morrow, treasurer of Frederick Stokes Publishing Company. Later, he founded William Morrow Publishers. She and her second husband adopted three children. Her literary efforts continued to focus on aspects of life on the western frontier. This phase of her writing ended in 1924 with *The Devonshers*; she then turned to the type of work for which she is best known, her historical fiction. She based her first such work on the diary of Narcissa Whitman, who, with her husband Marcus, served as a missionary to the Native Americans of the Oregon Territory.

A meticulous researcher who once remarked that because of her bookish parents "facts became like food and drink to me," Morrow spent seven years preparing to write her Abraham Lincoln trilogy, which chronicles Lincoln's years as president. Contemporary reviews were mixed, but, when the three Lincoln works were published together in one volume as *Great Captain*, William Lyon Phelps wrote the preface. Phelps states that Morrow "is at once an eminent research scholar and an eminent literary artist." Her career as a historical novelist continued until her death, but she also wrote biographies of Mary Todd Lincoln, temperance leader John Gough, and Bronson Alcott.

Alcott had been a friend of Morrow's mother's family, and her mother told her daughter vividly recalled stories of Alcott's "misunderstood genius." When Morrow's editor asked her to write an account of Bronson Alcott's life, she traveled to Concord, discovered the fifty-volume diary that documents his educational experiments on his daughter Louisa May, and wrote a vindication of Alcott titled *The Father of Little Women* (1927). In her introduction to that book, Morrow writes of her excitement upon perusing Alcott's works:

> The diaries became living entities to me and out of them grew before my fascinated vision a giant who had been lost, a star that no telescope had been strong enough to bring into our ken.
>
> Bronson Alcott was and is the greatest of all America's schoolmasters. It is as a schoolmaster, as a genius who attempted to remake America's ideas of the functions of education, that I have dealt with him in the pages that follow. (p. 9)

Thus, she fulfilled her mother's wish to have "justice done him."

After the death of her husband in 1931, Morrow moved to England, where she lived with their daughter Ann Penn Morrow in Brixham, Devon. Her last novel, *Demon Daughter* (1939), chronicles the difficulties she had in rearing her "highly-strung" daughter Felicia.

In January 1940 Morrow returned to the United States, planning to retrace the steps of her paternal grandfather, a Methodist circuit preacher in West Virginia before the turn of the twentieth century. Three months later, she died of influenza in New Haven, Connecticut.

During her lifetime, Morrow was known for writing carefully researched, well-documented novels and biographies. Her style is lucid and accessible. Her historical novels captured the attention of the reading public and helped create a market for such works a decade later; but shortly after her death her popularity began to wane. Although the western novels are obviously dated, they provide the contemporary reader with insight into important social issues of the first quarter of the twentieth century in the United States.

• Works by Morrow not already mentioned include *Still Jim* (1915), dealing with her U.S. Reclamation Service experience; *Lydia of the Pines* (1916), with forest conservation; *The Forbidden Trail* (1919), with desert reclamation; *The Enchanted Canyon* (1921), with the Reclamation Service once again; *Judith of the Godless Valley* (1922), with the need for a return to the faith of the pioneers; and *The Exile of the Lariat* (1923), with the need for scientific research to support industry. Morrow also wrote *We Must March: A Novel of the Winning of Oregon* (1925), based on Narcissa Whitman's diary; *On to Oregon!* (1926); *Forever Free* (1927), covering Lincoln's presidency from 1861 to 1863; *With Malice toward None* (1928), concerning Lincoln's presidency from 1863 to his return to Washington after the fall of Richmond; *Mary Todd Lincoln* (1928), a biography; *Splendor of God* (1929), a tale of Adoniram Judson, the first Baptist missionary to Burma; *The Last Full Measure* (1930), the last novel in the Lincoln trilogy; *Tiger! Tiger!* (1930), a biography of John B. Gough; *Black Daniel* (1931), the story of Daniel Webster's love affair with Caroline Leroy; *Beyond the Blue Sierra* (1932); *Argonaut* (1933), the story of a woman in the Alaskan gold rush; *Yonder Sails the Mayflower* (1934), the story of the Pilgrims; and *Let the King Beware* (1936), the story of England immediately before the American Revolution.

Little has been written about Morrow. An obituary is in the *New York Times*, 13 Apr. 1940.

CHERI LOUISE ROSS

MORROW, Jeremiah (6 Oct. 1771–22 Mar. 1852), congressman, U.S. senator, and governor of Ohio, was born near Gettysburg, Pennsylvania, the son of John Morrow and Mary Lockhart, farmers. The family's Presbyterian faith and Scotch-Irish accent revealed a powerful ethnic heritage preserved by western Pennsylvanians. Young Morrow's mastery of mathematics in common schools and his original occupation as a surveyor in Ohio provided basic skills for his most noted service later as the leading congressional expert on public land policy.

Determined to improve himself and to overcome a diminishing supply of open farmland in Pennsylvania, Morrow, at age twenty-four, set out for the Ohio frontier. Settling in the Miami valley, he bought land in Warren County, started his own farm, became proprietor of a large flour mill, and taught school. In 1799 Morrow married his cousin, Mary Parkhill; they raised six children.

With Ohio on the verge of statehood, political opportunities opened rapidly for Morrow and others like him. In the fall of 1800 his neighbors elected him to the territorial legislature, where he became part of the "Chillicothe Junto"—antislavery advocates of Ohio's admission to the Union. Two years later he served as a delegate to the Ohio constitutional convention and, briefly in 1803, as a member of Ohio's first state senate. Morrow entered Congress as a Jeffersonian Republican in late 1803 and served in the House until the Ohio legislature elevated him to the U.S. Senate in 1813. His toughest fight for reelection came in 1806, with a nasty assault from the ambitious, self-promoting James Prichard of Jefferson County. Accused of being a closet Federalist, a tool of designing speculators and of a would-be aristocracy, Morrow and his allies, led by Senator Thomas Worthington, withstood growing demands for "rotation in office." Appealing to the "honest part of the community," Morrow declared, would keep "good old republican principles pretty much in fashion."

During this time, Morrow promoted the commercial development of Ohio's fragile and still largely frontier economy. He saw the Cumberland Road and other projects of internal improvement as "conducive to the interests of the western people." Anticipating territorial gain from Canada and an accompanying boost to regional trade, Morrow supported the declaration of war against Britain in 1812. Grudgingly, in 1816 he backed the Second Bank of the United States, perceived in the Ohio banking community as a necessary evil in light of wartime financial chaos and the need for stability to leaven postwar western growth. The issue that defined his congressional career, however, was reform of federal public land policy, specifically the abolition of the credit system for federal land sales. In both that field and in his specific aim, Morrow inherited Albert Gallatin's mantle of authority.

Beginning in 1800, at the bidding of territorial representative William Henry Harrison, Congress allowed purchasers of the minimum 320 acres four years (and later up to ten years) to pay debts from auction purchases at a minimum $2 per acre. Subsequent modifications in law reduced both the minimum tract sizes and prices per acre, in addition to extending payment deadlines. As chairman of the Public Lands Committee, first in the House and later the Senate, Morrow urged reducing the acreage minimum, slashing the price per acre, and ousting the government from a credit business that had produced a western class of debtors. Partly intended to reduce speculation, the proposals looked to a West dominated by the "independent landholder, secure and quiet in his possession." Elimination of government credit, while making land purchase more difficult for some, was to help stabilize the frontier financially. Despite vociferous opposition from Illinois senator Ninian Edwards, who favored continuing credit, preemption rights for squatters, and more radical price reductions, the Morrow Bill passed the Senate in 1819 but fell short in the House.

With its devastating effects on western commerce and capital, the panic of 1819 made land reform a matter of urgency. "It cannot be correct policy," declared Morrow, "to persist . . . in a system so much affected by circumstances" and in need of "mitigating expedients to preserve its existence." Before the collapse, reckless speculation drove auction prices too high, and the debtor class provided too little federal revenue to finance internal improvement projects that westerners considered vital. Solving both problems seemed necessary to avert political disorder on the remote fringes of the republic. The result was the Land Act of 1820, which sealed the fate of credit sales and reduced the purchase minimum to 80 acres and the minimum price to $1.25 per acre. With plans to run for governor of Ohio in the fall of 1820, "Old Father Morrow" left Washington with the accolades of peers. John J. Crittenden declared him to have "long been our Palinurus" in public land policy. "He has steered us safely through all its difficulties, and with him as our helmsman, we have feared neither Scylla nor Charybdis."

Losing his first bid for the governorship to Ethan Allen Brown, Morrow received the nomination of the Democratic-Republican caucus in 1822 and was elected in a close race against his main rival, Allen Trimble, then reelected in 1824. In a period of economic distress and recovery in Ohio, Morrow, as governor, sought property tax reform, creation of a state-supported common school system, and, most importantly, a canal-building program to link Ohio commercially to the eastern trade network being opened with completion of the Erie Canal in 1825. The key project, started that year, was the Ohio Canal, connecting Lake Erie and the Ohio River. Ironically, the canal boom sunk Ohio in a morass of debt, with the railroad industry supplanting canal transit soon afterward.

Though he retired from the governorship in 1826, Morrow continued service in state politics, first in the state senate from 1827 to 1828, then two terms in the Ohio house, 1829–1830 and 1835–1836. His enthusiasm for domestic manufacturing found expression at the Harrisburg Convention of 1827. A supporter of John Quincy Adams for president in 1828 and Henry Clay in 1832, Morrow followed the national republican trail into the Whig party of the 1830s and 1840s, sharing its passions for protective tariffs and internal improvements. He chaired the Ohio Whig convention that endorsed Harrison for the presidency in 1840 and, for a last hurrah, rode the party crest into Congress that year, staying just one term.

Always a proponent of enterprise, both public and private, Morrow sat on the Ohio Canal Commission in 1820 and 1822 and was the first president of the Little Miami Railroad Company, founded in 1836 and responsible for the first rail line out of Cincinnati. He died at Twenty-Mile Stand, near Lebanon, in Warren County, Ohio.

• The Morrow papers are to be found at the Ohio State Library and the Ohio Historical Society in Columbus. His career in Congress is best traceable in Gales and Seaton, comp., *Annals of the Congress of the United States, 1789–1824* (42 vols., 1834–1856), and *Register of Debates in Congress, 1825–1837* (29 vols., 1825–1837). On his Ohio political background, see Andrew R. L. Cayton, *The Frontier Republic: Ideology and Politics in the Ohio Country, 1780–1825* (1986). For his role as shaper of public land policy, see Daniel Feller, *The Public Lands in Jacksonian Politics* (1984).

JOHN R. VAN ATTA

MORROW, Prince Albert (19 Dec. 1846–17 Mar. 1913), dermatologist, syphilologist, and reformer, was born at Mount Vernon, Kentucky, the son of William Morrow, a planter, and Mary Ann Cox. Morrow attended

Cumberland College and graduated from Princeton College, Kentucky, in 1864. New York University conferred a medical degree on him in 1873. Morrow continued his studies at the École de Médicine, Paris, and in London, Berlin, and Vienna. He began his practice of dermatology and syphilology in New York in 1874. That same year he married Lucy B. Slaughter of New York City. They had six children.

Morrow was a clinical lecturer on dermatology at New York University in 1882. In 1884 he was named clinical professor of venereal diseases and in 1886 of genitourinary diseases. Morrow also served as surgeon for Blackwell's Island, 1884–1904, and as attending physician at New York Hospital and City Hospital. St. Vincent's and City Hospital used him as a consulting dermatologist. In 1890 and 1891 Morrow was elected president of the American Dermatological Association. Highly successful and well regarded, he chaired the section on hygiene and scientific hygiene of the American Medical Association in 1907. Morrow was noted as a medical sociologist and writer. Among the founders of the *Journal of Cutaneous and Venereal Diseases*, he edited the journal from 1896 to 1901. Morrow paid careful attention to changing policies in Europe toward prostitution and venereal diseases. He translated and edited prominent French venerologist Alfred Fournier's *Syphilis and Marriage* from the French in 1880. Among his other medical writings were *Venereal Memoranda* (1885), *Drug Eruptions* (1887), *An Atlas of Skin and Venereal Diseases* (1888–1889), *A System of Genito-Urinary Diseases, Syphilology and Dermatology*, with coauthors (3 vols., 1893–1894), and *Personal Observations of Leprosy* (1889), based on observations after an American tour of leprosy colonies.

In the later years of his career, Morrow emerged as a major social reformer, taking responsibility for founding the American Society of Sanitary and Moral Prophylaxis in 1905. Morrow attended the Brussels conferences on syphilis in 1899 and 1903. At these conferences, Fournier acknowledged the failures of state-regulated prostitution. Physicians searched for a new social policy. Morrow contributed *Social Diseases and Marriage* to the discourse in 1904. He placed the primary responsibility for the contamination of "innocents" on men, opposed a double standard of morality, and pressed for sex education to reduce disease rates. Morrow, in his book, urged punishing those who transmitted venereal diseases. Influenced by Fournier, Morrow placed greater emphasis on moral reform and education as agencies of social hygiene.

A tireless reformer, Morrow worked diligently to enlist the medical professions into the international campaign against syphilis, an initial step in the transformation of social purity into social hygiene. Headquartered in the New York Academy of Medicine, Morrow's society had initial difficulty in alerting physicians to the unpopular cause. In 1903 Morrow reported venereal disease rates in New York City for the Academy of Medicine's Committee of Seven. Although greatly exaggerated, they remained an arsenal for reformers until World War I statistics for draftees, based on the Wassermann tests, corrected them. The Society of Moral and Sanitary Prophylaxis developed branches from coast to coast, giving national prominence to Morrow.

In 1910 the "Page law" provided for the reform of New York City's inferior courts. It established a woman's night court and provided for the fingerprinting and medical examination of suspected prostitutes, with indeterminate sentencing tied to their treatment for venereal diseases. The law was applied to women as a public health measure, but it was not applied to men. Interpreted by social purists and feminists as neoregulationism as advocated by Fournier, they opposed the law, which was eventually declared unconstitutional by the New York Supreme Court. Morrow aligned himself with the objections of the American Purity Alliance and the women's movement to the compulsory examination of suspected prostitutes. When arsphenamine and neo-arsphenamine, Paul Erlich's "magic bullet," were widely accepted as therapeutics, Morrow remained adamant in upholding the single standard of morality on the grounds that these chemical therapeutics did not cure syphilis. He agreed with feminists in advocating premarital testing for venereal diseases in men. His experiences had led him to conclude that male sexual indiscretions had infected wives and infants. These infections contributed, according to Morrow, to most gynecological surgeries on women.

Morrow's sex education activities have been characterized as sexual jeremiads. Through his society, he assembled exhibits in the 1910s that graphically showed the effects of venereal diseases on the human body. A leader among sex educationists, he assumed the presidency of the newly formed American Federation for Sex Hygiene in 1910. The federation subsequently merged with other organizations to form the American Social Hygiene Association, indebted to the leadership, financial and intellectual, of John D. Rockefeller, Jr. Only the New York Society for Moral and Social Hygiene remained outside the Rockefeller-sponsored organization. After Morrow's death in New York City, the New York branch of his society merged with the ASHA.

• A small collection of Morrow's correspondence and his movement's records are in the American Social Hygiene Association Papers, Social Welfare History Archives Center, University of Minnesota. For more on Morrow, see H. A. Kelly and W. L. Burrage, *American Medical Biographies* (1920), and James F. Gardner, Jr., "Microbes and Morality: The Social Hygiene Crusade in New York City, 1892–1917" (Ph.D. diss., Indiana Univ., 1973). Noteworthy obituaries, including summary biographies, are in *Journal of Cutaneous Diseases* 31 (Oct. 1913): 775–78, *Bulletin de la Société française de dermatologie et syphilologic* 24 (Dec. 1913): 546, *Journal of the American Medical Association* (29 Mar. 1913): 1011, *Lancet* (19 Apr. 1913): 1134, *Social Diseases* 4 (July 1913): 103–42, and the *New York Times*, 18 Mar. 1913.

DAVID J. PIVAR

MORROW, Thomas Vaughn (14 Apr. 1804–16 July 1850), physician, was born in Fairview, Kentucky, the son of Thomas Morrow and Elizabeth Vaughn, farmers. He was educated at Transylvania University in Lexington, Kentucky, and received his medical degree from the Reformed Medical College of New York (1829 or 1830). There Morrow first encountered the doctrine of eclecticism, a movement opposed to the excesses of prevailing medical practice such as blood-letting and the indiscriminate use of the heavy metal-containing drug Calomel. The eclectics arose out of a number of disparate "botanic" groups, all of whom supported a doctrine that every region of the earth produces indigenous medicinal plants that are ample for the cure of its local diseases; that is, in its grand scheme Nature provides equally for disease and its remedy. Morrow's mentor, Dr. Wooster Beach, was a leader of the movement and founder of the Reformed Medical College.

By 1829 Beach had initiated the Reformed Medical Society of the United States and desired to extend the field of operation westward. Under the auspices of the society a medical school was established and officially opened in Worthington, Ohio, in December 1830. In 1831 Morrow was selected by the trustees of the society to head the Reformed Medical Department of the Worthington College. In 1836 Morrow and his colleagues established a journal, the *Western Medical Reformer*, to further the aims of the Reformed Movement, which, at the suggestion of Morrow, was renamed the Eclectic Movement. It was Thomas Cooke, a fellow medical reformer, who introduced the term "eclectic" to distinguish the group from other "botanical" groups. Cooke chose the term to indicate a system of medicine that "selected out" single, indigenous plant remedies to effect the cure of specific symptoms or disorders.

During the ten years of its existence under Morrow's leadership, the Worthington enterprise traveled a stormy course. There was internal dissension; criminal charges of grave-robbing were brought against Morrow but were dropped by a grand jury; the financial crash of 1837 and the ensuing depression discouraged supporters; faculty deserted; and enrollment dwindled to twenty students. In the spring of 1839 the medical college building was ransacked by a mob that suspected grave-robbing. The charter of the school was repealed on 20 March 1840, but Morrow continued to practice and carry on some private teaching until he departed with his family from Worthington for Cincinnati in 1842. He had married Isabel Greer of Worthington during his sojourn there (marriage date unknown). Together, they had five children, but only one, Worcester (Wooster) Beach Morrow, a prominent Cincinnati lawyer, survived to adulthood.

Shortly after his arrival in Cincinnati, Morrow opened the Reformed Medical School. For two years classes were held informally; in 1844 the *Western Medical Reformer* was revived; and then in 1845 Morrow filed for a charter from the Ohio legislature for his fledgling medical college. His application received wide city endorsement. In spite of strenuous opposition by the Medical College of Ohio and others, a charter was granted to the Cincinnati Eclectic Medical Institute on 10 March 1845. By 1848 Morrow was successful in establishing the National Eclectic Medical Association and served as its first president (1848–1850).

By placing high value on the quality of teaching at the college, backed by a strong national association of physicians, Morrow was able to attract and retain a well-respected faculty. Since the eclectic/botanic movement was loosely defined, the faculty was broad-based, and "all varieties and shadings of therapeutic practice were represented" (Juettner, p. 366). Recognizing the value of a trained pharmacist, Morrow retained William S. Merrell as the college pharmacist, the first eclectic pharmacist in Cincinnati and one of the first in the nation. Prior to Merrell's research, botanical medicines were prepared as infusions; that is, a large quantity of vegetable matter was soaked or steeped in water or alcohol to extract the active medicinal ingredients. Medicinal doses were large, contained impurities, and frequently led to nausea and other adverse reactions. Merrell's chemical research identified the specific active ingredients in the infusion so that medications became purer, measurable, and more specific. By the last quarter of the century, the school that Morrow founded was the leading eclectic medical institution in the country. Morrow was dean and professor of the theory and practice of medicine and pathology until his untimely death from dysentery at his home in Cincinnati.

In addition to his college duties, Morrow had a large practice. "He gave no calomel and was decidedly for botanic medicines. His favorite alternative, which was perhaps given more than any other, was *macrotys racemosa*. Some of the students called him 'Old Macrotys'" (Felter, p. 13). (Macrotys or Cimicifuga, commonly called Black Snakeroot, was used as a mild sedative and for the relief of pain.) His successor as dean at the college, Ichabod G. Jones, collected Morrow's papers, added his own writings, and published *The American Eclectic Practice of Medicine* in 1853–1854.

Renamed the Eclectic Medical College in 1910, the school remained in operation until 1939 and lost its charter in 1942, the last of its genre in the United States. Although eclectic medicine is no longer practiced, it grew out of a protest against polypharmacy and other excessive measures. By challenging some of the dogma of prevailing practice, the Reformed/Eclectic movement brought an end to a variety of overly rigorous medical practices and introduced a more circumspect approach. Thomas Vaughn Morrow was an early advocate of this approach, and his leadership of the first two eclectic medical schools west of the Alleghenies won him the sobriquet "Father of Eclecticism in the West." "We believe," he said in the *Ohio State Journal* (19 Nov. 1833), "that every individual who takes upon himself the highly responsible duties of the physician should be intimately and thoroughly acquainted with every department of his profession."

As a practitioner, organizer, and teacher of medicine in the mid-nineteenth century, he brought this message to the medical community west of the Alleghenies.

• The most complete archive of the Eclectic College, including material on Morrow, is at the Lloyd Library in Cincinnati. Harvey Wickes Felter, *History of the Eclectic Medical Institute, Cincinnati, Ohio, 1845–1902* (1902); Alexander Wilder, *History of Medicine* (1904); Otto Juettner, *Daniel Drake and His Followers: Historical and Biographical Sketches* (1909); and John S. Haller, Jr., *Medical Protestants: The Eclectics in American Medicine, 1825–1939* (1994), are important sources. Felter also wrote a lengthy account of Morrow's Worthington years, "Worthington College, Ohio, Reformed Medical Department," *"Old Northwest" Genealogical Quarterly of 1903* 4 (Oct.): 157–70. Morrow's scientific writings and his addresses to students and faculty are in various issues of the *Western Medical Reformer*.

STANLEY L. BLOCK

MORSE, Edward Sylvester (18 June 1838–20 Dec. 1925), biologist and expert on Japanese culture, was born in Portland, Maine, the son of Jonathan Kimball Morse and Jane Seymour Beckett. His father was a partner in a firm that dealt in beaver furs and buffalo robes, and his mother was said to be "interested in all branches of science." As a boy Morse collected shells, and at the age of seventeen he joined the Portland Society of Natural History. At the encouragement of other naturalists in the society, Morse began to study the land snails of his state and to correspond with leading American conchologists. After attending preparatory schools he worked as a draftsman in the locomotive shops of the Maine Central Railroad, presumably to save for college. There he demonstrated a fine ability in sketching and creating line drawings, which he used to advantage in his later publications.

From 1859 to 1862 Morse was enrolled as a special student in the Lawrence Scientific School at Harvard University. He then became an assistant to zoologist Louis Agassiz in the university's Museum of Comparative Zoology, but he did not receive a degree. Morse's colleagues at Harvard included Alpheus Hyatt, Alpheus Spring Packard, Jr., Frederic Ward Putnam, Samuel Hubbard Scudder, and Addison Emery Verrill, who all had distinguished careers in science.

Morse married Ellen Elizabeth Owen in 1863; they had two children. He was rejected for service in the Union army during the Civil War (because of his teeth). In 1863 or 1864 he joined the Essex Institute in Salem, Massachusetts, at the urging of Putnam, who was from that city. The institute's museum contained items of natural history and ethnology deposited there through the years from Salem trading ships. Morse became responsible for the collection of shells, while Hyatt, Packard, Verrill, and Putnam worked on other collections. In 1867 George Peabody founded the Peabody Academy of Science (later Peabody Museum) in Salem, which obtained the buildings and anthropological collections of the East India Marine Society and the biological collections of the Essex Institute. The young scientists, except Verrill, transferred to it. The four founded in 1868 the *American Naturalist*, then the only U.S. publication in popular natural history. Morse wrote articles for it and drew many of its illustrations. He was also a lecturer to the general public on subjects in science, especially Darwinian evolution.

Morse became professor of zoology and comparative anatomy at Bowdoin College from 1871 to 1874. In 1873 he was one of the teachers at the remarkably successful summer school for naturalists headed by Agassiz at Penikese Island, Massachusetts. Morse published the textbook *First Book in Zoology* in 1875. Continuing his studies on mollusks, he concluded that they were not closely related to brachiopods, in spite of a superficial resemblance. First from a study of the shells, then from a study of the internal organs and the development of the eggs, he deduced that brachiopods, now placed in a phylum of their own, were more closely related to worms.

Because a number of species of brachiopods had been documented in Japan, Morse traveled there in 1877 and set up a seaside laboratory at Enoshima. He was promptly invited to become professor of zoology at Imperial University in Tokyo, which had determined to improve its scholarly basis. He served in that post from 1877 to 1880, taking a keen interest in the people of Japan and their arts. Some of his students there became excellent zoologists.

On his return to the United States in 1880 Morse became director of the Peabody Museum in Salem until 1916, after which he served as emeritus director. He rearranged the museum's collections, invented a new kind of museum shelf bracket, improved the methods of display, and raised funds to enlarge the building.

Morse's scientific publications began with descriptions of new species of land snails in Maine and continued over many years with descriptions of other mollusks and the classification of brachiopods. As another scientific interest, through long acquaintance with astronomer Percival Lowell, he spent thirty-four nights at Lowell Observatory, observing Mars and recording it in sketches. He published *Mars and Its Mystery* in 1906 and was honored with membership in the astronomical societies of France and Belgium.

In Japan the chance discovery, observed from the train between Enoshima and Tokyo in 1877, of ancient shell heaps from aboriginal people led Morse from research on mollusks to the study of ancient pottery and to collecting Japanese pottery, including items from living potters. "The kinds he wanted are those bearing potters'-marks and specimens from every kiln and for every kind of use, all in the tradition of that old Japan of which he so keenly lamented the passing," wrote F. S. Kershaw of the Boston Museum of Fine Arts. In 1890 Morse placed his collection of pottery in that Boston museum, which purchased the collection two years later and appointed Morse its keeper. In 1901 the museum published his catalog of the collection, which was later translated into Japanese and published by the Japanese government. In 1898 Morse became the first American to receive the Medal of the Order of the Rising Sun from the emperor of Japan, and he also received the Medal of Sacred Treasure from that country.

While teaching in Japan and on a later trip in 1882–1883, Morse also took an interest in Japanese houses, on which he published *Japanese Homes and Their Surroundings* (1888), illustrated with more than 300 of his own line drawings. He extended this interest to China on a trip there in 1882 and published *Glimpses of China and Chinese Homes* (1906).

Morse was considered by colleagues a good lecturer and fine raconteur, although prejudiced by antireligious views. He was a member of a number of scientific societies and was president of the American Association for the Advancement of Science in 1886. He was elected into the National Academy of Sciences in 1876. He died in Salem, Massachusetts.

• Morse's extensive papers are at the Peabody Essex Museum in Salem, Mass., which has a complete bibliography of his publications. A detailed biography is Dorothy Wayman, *Edward Sylvester Morse: A Biography* (1942). Shorter tributes are by F. S. K[ershaw] in *Museum Fine Arts Bulletin* 24 (1926): 11–12; by J. S. Kingsley in *Proceedings of the American Academy of Arts and Sciences* 61 (1925–1926): 549–55; and by L. O. Howard in National Academy of Sciences. *Biographical Memoirs* 17 (1935–1937): 1–29.

ELIZABETH NOBLE SHOR

MORSE, Freeman Harlow (18 Feb. 1807–6 Feb. 1891), congressman and U.S. consul, was born in Bath, Maine, the son of William Morse and Eliza Harlow, farmers. After attending local schools until the age of fourteen, he ended his formal education and became a ship carpenter. Short, stout, and serious, he was physically strong and intellectually curious. He began to read extensively in political history and effectively employed his knowledge as a member of a young men's debating society, in which he espoused the political doctrines of the Whig minority of his state. In 1834 he married Nancy Leavitt, with whom he had two daugthers.

In 1840–1841 and 1843 Morse represented the Bath area in the Maine House and was twice the unsuccessful Whig candidate for the office of Speaker. In 1840 he managed the winning campaign of William Pitt Fessenden to become the first Whig congressman from the Portland district. Morse himself served a term in Congress from 1843 until 1845, after which he was mayor of Bath in 1849, 1850, and 1855. He was a state legislator in 1853 and 1856. In the latter year he became a Republican and as such was returned to Congress, this time serving two terms, 1857 to 1861. Throughout his public career he was an intense moralist, temporarily sacrificing his congressional seat in 1844 by voting against the admission of Texas as a slave state and thereafter consistently speaking out against any territorial extension of slavery.

After representing Maine as a delegate to the Washington Peace Convention of February 1861, Morse was appointed U.S. consul at London, England, by President Abraham Lincoln, owing to the intercession of Senator Fessenden. For the next four years Morse labored with considerable success, at times employing spies and bribing shipyard employees, to assist the U.S. minister, Charles Francis Adams, in obtaining information about Confederate blockade-runners and warship construction in England. Morse's espionage efforts enabled the Navy Department to tighten the Federal blockade of the southern coast and aided Adams in preventing the Confederacy from utilizing the formidable Laird rams. The London consul's hard work also helped to construct a voluminous evidentiary edifice, which enabled Adams in 1872 to obtain substantial monetary reparations at the Geneva arbitration tribunal.

During his years in London, Morse was frequently chosen to preside over dinners and other public events in place of the less gregarious American minister. The social highlight of Morse's consular years occurred on 22 April 1864, when he hosted a breakfast reception for Guiseppe Garibaldi at his London house in Hanover Square.

Continued as consul at London by President Andrew Johnson, Morse was elevated on 16 April 1869 to consul general by President Ulysses Grant. However, opposition to this appointment within the Maine congressional delegation and the death of his patron, Senator Fessenden, led to Morse's replacement in July 1870 by Adam Badeau, a journalist who had attached himself to Grant during wartime and who was living in the White House.

Outraged, Morse decided to make his home in England. Although his wife and daughters soon returned to the United States to live, Morse dwelled in rural retirement until his death at Surbiten in Surrey.

As a member of Congress and as a U.S. consul, Morse held important offices in the midst of some of the most momentous events in American history—the secession winter of 1860–1861 in Washington and the desperate efforts in London to keep Great Britain from intervening on the side of the Confederacy. Yet contemporary newspaper accounts and the diaries and letters of others also involved in those dramatic events hardly allude to him. When they do mention Morse, it is with respect but without much emotion. Hence his role appears to have been that of the conscientious public servant working in the shadows of more magnetic men.

• Morse's dispatches to the State Department have been issued on microfilm as T-168 from RG 59, and letters from Morse are in the papers of Thomas H. Dudley at the Huntington Library in San Marino, Calif., and in the William P. Fessenden Papers at the Library of Congress. Some correspondence is also at the Western Reserve Historical Society in Cleveland, Ohio. Abner Morse, *Memorial of the Morses: Containing the History of Seven Persons of the Nine Who Settled in America in the Seventeenth Century* (1850), mentions Morse in an appendix. *The Journal of Benjamin Moran, 1857–1865*, ed. Sarah A. Wallace and Frances E. Gillespie (2 vols., 1948), has frequent brief references to Morse while he was in London during the Civil War.

NORMAN B. FERRIS

MORSE, Jedidiah (23 Aug. 1761–9 June 1826), geographer and clergyman, was born in Woodstock, Connecticut, the son of Jedidiah Morse and Sarah Child. His father was a local officeholder and a deacon of the Congregational church. Morse attended a local academy and then entered Yale College, from which he graduated in 1783. He continued to study theology in New Haven while teaching at a school for young girls.

For the students at that school Morse wrote *Geography Made Easy* in 1784, which was said by historian George W. White to be the first geography published in the United States. The book sold beyond Morse's "most sanguine Expectations" and was widely praised. A few years later he disparaged this volume as a "juvenile, hasty production" and declared to his father his intent to compile a more complete account of the geography of his country for a mature audience.

In 1785 Morse became pastor of a church in Norwich, Connecticut, and the next year was a tutor at Yale. In the fall of 1786 he arranged to exchange pastoral duties for a few months with an acquaintance, Abiel Holmes, in Midway, Georgia. Morse's purpose was to gather geographical information for his new project. On his way south in October he conferred with and gained the encouragement of such distinguished men as the governor of New Jersey, two faculty members at Princeton University, Benjamin Franklin in Philadelphia, and James Madison, who was then president of the College of William and Mary. In letters to his father Morse described the countryside, the commerce and manufacturing in cities, the climate, and other observations. In South Carolina he noted that the low-lying area must have once been ocean for as much as a hundred miles inland.

Morse returned to New Haven in early spring of 1787 and worked on the manuscript of *American Geography*, which was published in 1789. That same year he married Elizabeth Ann Breese. The couple had eleven children, of whom only three reached maturity; one of these was Samuel Finley Breese Morse, inventor of the telegraph. Also in 1789 Morse became minister of the First Congregational Church of Charlestown, Massachusetts, where he continued until 1819. Not considered an outstanding theologian, he was nevertheless a strong supporter of orthodox views and strongly opposed to Unitarianism.

Morse's sources of information for his geography book were primarily written ones, not his own excursions. In 1787 he began circulating a questionnaire asking for knowledge of their places of residence from "such Gentlemen as are able and likely to furnish answers." His form letter was at times reprinted in weekly newspapers, and Morse received many replies. In addition, he quoted and abstracted from such sources as *Notes on Virginia* (1784) by Thomas Jefferson and from maps by Lewis Evans, Thomas Pownall, Jefferson, and others. He queried "men of Science" for information on natural history and other specialties. He obtained statistics on population from magazines and newspapers. In his published book he did not clearly identify his many sources, and he often quoted works directly. He would not use foreign publications, with the comment that "Europeans have . . . too often suffered fancy to supply the place of facts."

Morse's section on population in *American Geography* well expresses his brisk style and opinions:

> From the best accounts that can at present be obtained, there are, within the limits of the United States, three millions, eighty three thousand, and six hundred souls. This number, which is rapidly increasing both by emigrations from Europe, and by natural population, is composed of people of almost all nations, languages, characters and religions. The greater part, however, are descended from the English; and, for the sake of distinction, are called Anglo-Americans. . . .
>
> A European writer has justly observed that, "if there be an object truly ridiculous in nature, it is an American patriot, signing resolutions of independency with the one hand, and with the other brandishing a whip over his affrighted slaves." . . . The time, however, is anticipated when all distinctions between master and slaves shall be abolished; and when the language, manners, customs, political and religious sentiments of the mixed mass of the people who inhabit the United States, shall have become so assimilated, as that all nominal distinctions shall be lost in the general and honourable name of AMERICANS.

American Geography sold well to the general public and to schools, to about 15,000 copies of the first edition. It was reprinted in London and Dublin in 1792, and English chemist Joseph Priestley called it "an excellent treatise." President George Washington wrote that he felt that the book would bring about "a better understanding between the remote citizens of our States." Secretary of the Treasury Oliver Wolcott pointed out that certain sources used by Morse were not reliable. Botanist Manasseh Cutler noted that "the accounts of both animals and vegetables . . . I conceive to be very erroneous and defective." He then submitted a manuscript on the subject, which Morse included in the edition of 1793. Some southerners were not pleased with the descriptions of their cities, such as Williamsburg appearing "dull, forsaken, and melancholy . . . [with] no industry, and very little appearance of religion." The strongest criticism of the book was the poor quality of its maps.

Morse began to revise his book as soon as it was published. He also expanded it to include the eastern hemisphere in a second volume, against the advice of some of his colleagues. The revision was published in 1793 as *The American Universal Geography*, with volume one (691 pages) on the United States and volume two (548 pages) on the rest of the world. Within two years the new book had sold 6,000 copies of volume one and 4,500 of volume two.

New editions were published in 1796, 1801, and 1805, but the changes were not significant. In 1795 Morse wrote *Elements of Geography* for children of ages eight to fourteen, because, he said, "no science is better adapted to gratify the natural curiosity of youth than Geography." His presentation was in the popular format of a catechism.

In 1797 Morse published his first geographical dictionary, *The American Gazetteer*, two years after the first such work in the United States appeared as Joseph Scott's *Gazetteer of the United States*. Noah Webster, not yet engaged in his dictionary, in 1793 had offered to help Morse with a gazetteer but soon withdrew because of other editing commitments. Morse instead obtained help from the Reverend Samuel Austin. The book was successful but not as profitable as his geography book. He decided to extend the project to the rest of the world, and in 1802 coauthored with the Reverend Elijah Parish of Byfield, Massachusetts, *A New Gazetteer of the Eastern Continent*.

In 1804 some members of Morse's church questioned the time he was devoting to his publications. He told them that he did not intend to produce any new works but expected to continue revising the published ones, to the extent of probably less than an hour a day. He founded and edited a periodical called the *Panoplist* in 1805 to espouse orthodox Congregational religion. He was one of the founders of Andover Theological Seminary in 1808. In 1814 he was a founder of the New England Tract Society to spread religious information, and in 1816 he helped establish the American Bible Society.

Morse began an extensive revision of both volumes of *American Universal Geography* in 1810. He was assisted by his sons, by Serano Dwight (son of Yale president Timothy Dwight), and by "worthy friends," whom he did not name. In the new (sixth) edition he left out overly detailed local information and incorporated material from government reports, the census of 1810, travel accounts, and regional studies. The chapters on each state were revised into "historical geography" and "natural geography." A separate atlas of sixty-three maps was created by Aaron Arrowsmith and Samuel Lewis.

Morse resigned from his ministry in 1819 and moved to New Haven, Connecticut. That same year the final revision of *American Universal Geography* was completed, chiefly by his son Sidney Edwards Morse.

In 1820 Morse accepted an appointment as an agent of the Department of Indian Affairs to determine the condition of various Indian tribes from western New York through the Great Lakes area. After three months of tiring travel, he ended his expedition in Wisconsin and returned to New Haven, where he compiled a narrative of his journey, with appendices of relevant reports on Indian matters.

In 1823, with his son Richard Cary Morse, he published a pocket gazetteer, *The Traveller's Guide*. Morse's final work was a historical compilation titled *The Annals of the American Revolution* (1824). Over the years his first book, *Geography Made Easy*, had gone through twenty editions.

Morse's significance was in producing what, according to historian Ralph H. Brown, "appears to have been the most widely read geographical book ever written in and about America." His style was terse for its day, his sentiments patriotic and moral. Morse died in New Haven, Connecticut.

• Morse's extensive papers are at Harvard and Yale Universities, New York Public Library, and the Massachusetts Historical Society. In addition to the works cited above, Morse's report on the Indian tribes in New York and the Great Lakes area was published in 1822 as *A Report to the Secretary of War of the United States, on Indian Affairs*. A significant biographical source is Ralph H. Brown, "The American Geographies of Jedidiah Morse," *Annals of the Association of American Geographers* 31 (1941): 144–217, with bibliography; it cites (pp. 148–49) much earlier biographical materials on his accomplishments in religion and geography.

ELIZABETH NOBLE SHOR

MORSE, Marston (24 Mar. 1892–22 June 1977), mathematician, was born Harold Calvin Marston Morse in Waterville, Maine, the son of Howard Calvin Morse, a farmer and real estate agent, and Ella Phoebe Marston. Morse graduated from Coburn Classical Institute in 1910 and then entered Colby College in Waterville. He received his A.B. summa cum laude from Colby in 1914, after which he began graduate studies in mathematics at Harvard. There he was awarded an A.M. in 1915, and a Ph.D. in 1917; his dissertation, "Certain Types of Geodesic Motions on a Surface of Negative Curvature," was directed by George D. Birkhoff.

From 1918 to 1919 Morse served as a private in the U.S. Army in France in the Ambulance Corps and was awarded the croix de guerre with Silver Star by the French Army. Subsequently commissioned a second lieutenant, he served from 1919 to 1924 in the Coast Artillery Corps (Reserve). Following his military service, he was the Benjamin Pierce Instructor at Harvard (1919–1920) before becoming an assistant professor at Cornell University (1920–1926), and Brown University (1926–1928). Morse then returned to Harvard, where he successively served as an assistant professor (1926–1928), an associate professor (1928–1929), and finally a professor (1929–1935).

On 20 June 1922 Morse married Céleste Phelps; they had one son and one daughter before their divorce in 1930. In August 1932 Phelps married Morse's Harvard colleague William F. Osgood. This led to a scandal at Harvard that prompted Osgood to retire and became a great shock to Morse.

Following his wartime service and the publication of his dissertation in 1921, Morse almost immediately made a major discovery, the implications of which would ultimately constitute his life's work. Morse first announced the discovery in his paper "Relations between the Critical Points of a Real Function of n Independent Variables" (1925). This paper, together with his subsequent publications on the calculus of variations (1928), led to the creation of a new branch of mathematics commonly known as Morse theory. This theory represented a bold, and quite unexpected, synthesis of analysis and topology (technically known as homology theory). Morse brilliantly summarized this theory in his book *Calculus of Variations in the Large* (1934), and he presented important expositions of it at the International Congresses of Mathematicians in Zürich, Switzerland (1932), and Cambridge, England (1950).

In 1935 Morse became a professor of mathematics at the Institute for Advanced Study, in Princeton, New Jersey, and he held this position until his retirement in 1962 (he remained there as an emeritus professor until his death). He became a consultant for the Office of the Chief of Ordnance and the Coast and Geodetic Survey in 1935, and he held these positions until after World War II began. He chaired the following panels: the War Preparedness Committee of the American Mathematical Society (1940–1942); the division of mathematics of the National Research Council (1950–1952); and the U.S. National Commission on Mathematics (1959–1963). One of the founders of the National Science Foundation, Morse served on its first board from 1950 to 1954. In 1940 he had married Louise Jeffreys; they had two sons and three daughters.

Morse's later mathematical works include the books *Critical Point Theory in Global Analysis and Differential Topology*, with Stewart S. Cairns (1969); *Variational Analysis: Critical Extremals and Sturmian Extensions* (1973); and *Global Variational Analysis: Weierstrass Integrals on Riemannian Manifolds* (1976). While Morse theory undoubtably represents his best-known work, it was only a part of his output of almost 180 papers and eight books and lecture note volumes. The subject range of these publications covers the areas of dynamics and geodesic flows, minimal surfaces, topological methods in the theory of functions of a complex variable, integral representations; pseudoharmonic functions, and differential topology. The remarkable richness and influence of these contributions has continued to be felt in contemporary mathematics.

Morse received many honors during his lifetime, including some twenty honorary doctorates. He was elected a member of the National Academy of Sciences in 1932 and later a foreign member of the Académie de Sciences (Paris), and the Accademia Nazionale dei Linceo (Rome). For the American Mathematical Society he was colloquium lecturer (1931); vice president (1933–1935); president (1941–1942); and Gibbs Lecturer (1952). He shared the 1933 Bôcher Prize with Norbert Wiener, and in 1947 he received a Presidential Certificate of Merit in recognition of his war work. In 1964 he was awarded the National Medal of Science for his mathematical contributions, and his creation of Morse Theory was especially cited. He was also vice president of the International Congress of Mathematicians (1958–1962) and a Chevalier, Legion d'Honneur of France.

Morse was one of the most influential figures in twentieth-century mathematics. While it is not unusual for mathematicians to propose new theories based on an abstraction or refinement of previously known results, very few have created a new theory where none existed before. Morse theory was such a theory, and in creating it Morse followed in the heroic tradition of Henri Poincaré and Morse's mentor George D. Birkhoff. Although Morse Theory has since been recast in more modern and abstract form, its principal results have remained almost single-handedly the work of Morse himself. Ironically, Morse was little interested in abstraction for its own sake; for the last forty years of his life, although he took careful note of current trends in topology, he was little involved in the general abstract development of the modern theory. His abiding interest lay in the great problems of mathematics, such as the three-body problem in celestial mechanics and the open challenge of a topological theory of quantum mechanics. His results—if any—on such topics have remained largely unknown.

Throughout his life Morse retained the stamp of his Maine upbringing in his frugality and industry. He worked long hours and had many collaborators (usually at the postdoctoral level) to whom he transmitted his boundless enthusiasm for mathematics. Many of these collaborators enjoyed distinguished careers in research and teaching. Morse remained mathematically active until his death in his home in Princeton.

• There are two editions of Morse's mathematical papers: *Marston Morse—Selected Papers* (1981); and *Marston Morse—Collected Papers* (6 vols., 1987). His autobiographical sketch in the *McGraw Hill Modern Scientists and Engineers* 2 (1980) contains a noteworthy account of the geometrical and physical aspects of his work. Upon his retirement from the Institute for Advanced Study, a symposium was held, the proceedings of which were published as *Differential and Combinatorial Topology: A Symposium in Honor of Marston Morse* (1965). Although Morse's mathematical writings are generally businesslike and dry, he wrote three expository essays that give revealing glimpses into himself and his feelings for mathematics: "Twentieth Century Mathematics," *American Scholar* 9 (Autumn 1940); "What is Analysis in the Large?" *American Mathematical Monthly* 49 (June-July 1942); and "Mathematics and the Arts," *Yale Review: A National Review* 40 (Summer 1951). The last of these is remarkable not only for its content but for its eloquence. The Mathematical Association of America produced a two-part, 74-minute video cassette, "Pits, Peaks, and Passes," in which Morse gave an engaging description of his theory. The definitive obituary is in the *Bulletin of the American Mathematical Society, New Series* 3 (Nov. 1980). Obituaries are also in the *New York Times*, 26 June 1977, and National Academy of Sciences, *Biographical Memoirs* 65 (1994): 222–40.

JOSEPH D. ZUND

MORSE, Philip McCord (6 Aug. 1903–5 Sept. 1985), physicist, was born in Shreveport, Louisiana, the son of Allen Crafts Morse, an engineer, and Edith McCord, who had been a journalist until marriage. The Morses returned shortly thereafter to the Cleveland, Ohio, home of their families for several generations. Allen Morse worked in telephone system construction, but as the industry consolidated, he earned a tenuous, gradually diminishing income consulting for state utilities commissions in their court battles to control telephone rates. In spite of the family's strained financial circumstances, Edith Morse insisted that all her children be broadly educated, and all went to college.

Morse developed an early interest in science but did not commit to studying physics until his sophomore year (1923–1924) at the Case School of Applied Science (now part of Case Western Reserve University).

For his remaining three years at Case, Morse studied primarily with physicist Dayton C. Miller and with Jason J. Nassau, a mathematician and astronomer. Both instilled in him a dedication to accurate measurement and mathematics. Morse worked with Miller in the latter's extension of the Michelson-Morley ether drift experiments, designed to test the validity of Einstein's theory of relativity. Miller's and Nassau's support of Morse opened doors to graduate study. Both Harvard and Princeton made offers, but Princeton's superior financial deal dictated Morse's choice; he began his studies there in the fall of 1926.

At Princeton, Morse completed a thesis on the behavior of electron flow through low-pressure gas, under the tutelage of plasma physicist Karl T. Compton. His more significant work dealt with quantum theory, which was being developed by Niels Bohr, Albert Einstein, Max Planck, Arnold Sommerfeld, and others. Edward U. Condon and H. P. Robertson, new to Princeton after spending postdoctoral years in Europe, sought to bring quantum theory to the United States. Condon asked Morse to coauthor a textbook with him, resulting in *Quantum Mechanics* (1929), which was the standard text on the subject into the 1960s. Quantum theory's probabilistic epistemology and mathematical sophistication came relatively easy to Morse. The theory also resonated with his undergraduate interests: Miller's principle work had been in acoustics. Morse (with Ernst C. G. Stueckelberg) subsequently extended Erwin Schrödinger's equations to describe molecules and developed the Morse Potential of quantum chemistry, which predicts the energy necessary to pull apart vibrating diatomic molecules.

Morse remained close to Compton, who secured for his student the prestigious Porter Ogden Jacovus Fellowship (1928–1929) and a teaching job at Princeton when Morse graduated in the spring of 1929. Compton also convinced Morse to apply for a Rockefeller Foundation International Fellowship, which allowed him to spend the 1930–1931 year in Munich with Sommerfeld and in Cambridge with Ernest Rutherford, Neville Mott, and Harrie S. W. Massey. The trip resulted in Morse's further collaboration with Stueckelberg on a theory of slow electron collisions, and another with William P. Allis on electron scattering. When Morse returned, Compton (now president of the Massachusetts Institute of Technology) found him a place on the MIT physics faculty.

Compton's mission at MIT was to transform the prestigious engineering school into a major American center for basic research, especially in physics. Toward this end, he appointed John Slater chairman of the physics department. Soon half of the physics faculty consisted of "young Turks" such as Morse, Allis, and Robert J. van de Graaff, all well versed in quantum theory. Morse's job was to build up an outstanding acoustics program from scratch. He soon designed the curriculum and wrote the field's standard textbook, *Vibration and Sound* (1936). Next, Morse built up an academic research team with fellow MIT acoustician Richard Fay and postdoctoral student Richard Bolt. He then initiated contacts with Wallace Sabine's successors at Harvard, F. V. Hunt and Leo L. Beranek. By 1939 the research successes of this thought collective had helped to earn Morse the rank of professor. Ever restless, Morse also made forays into other arenas, especially astrophysics.

Despite this flurry of productivity, Morse gradually came to the disheartening conviction that his upward mobility within the physics profession was limited. He understood his skills to be those of a quick study, able to comprehend the implications of a theoretical or experimental breakthrough. "But I wasn't the one to make the initial breakthrough," he noted later in his autobiography. Fay managed to buoy his spirits, however, and Morse eventually consoled himself by noting that, in the aftermath of the quantum revolution, neophytes needed a competent guide. He also grew increasingly concerned with over-specialization within the physics community, particularly after World War II, and became a staunch defender of the scientific generalist. His first tour of duty as his department's graduate registration officer (1933–1941) began a lifelong commitment to teaching and directing research.

World War II curtailed Morse's teaching and led him to use his expertise in new ways. Between 1940 and 1944 he was a consultant to MIT's Radiation Laboratory, which designed microwave radar units for the National Defense Research Committee. During the same period he chaired the National Research Council's Committee on Sound Control; his influence led to the creation at Harvard of the Electro-Acoustic Laboratory under Beranek and the Psycho-Acoustic Laboratory under S. S. Stevens. Between 1940 and 1942, Morse directed the Navy–MIT Underwater Sound Project, which helped neutralize the threat of German acoustic mines and acoustic torpedos.

Morse's most notable wartime effort, beginning in April 1942, was organizing and directing the U.S. Navy's Antisubmarine Warfare Operations Research Group (ASWORG), later Operations Research Group (ORG). Operations research (OR) had originated in Britain during the late 1930s as scientists helped Royal Air Force officers devise tactics and procedures for new radar technology. It rapidly expanded to the point that both scientists and officers believed warfare was susceptible to quantitative analysis. In the United States, scientific researchers led by engineer Vannevar Bush resisted OR's adoption believing that it diverted attention from the development of military technologies and threatened the delicate boundary between civilian science and the state. By contrast, Morse saw in OR an opportunity to extend scientific analysis beyond the narrow confines of the laboratory. Not the first OR section in America, ORG nevertheless was the first to gain the respect of civilian scientists, partly because of Morse's stature in that community and his influence within the navy. Morse received the U.S. Presidential Medal for Merit for his OR contributions and returned to MIT soon after the war, intending to promote OR in government, industry, and educational institutions.

These plans had to be put on hold. Immediately after his return, Morse was asked by the Associated Universities, Incorporated, to oversee the construction of the Brookhaven National Laboratory on Long Island, New York. The AUI was a consortium of research universities retained by the new Atomic Energy Commission to build and manage nuclear research facilities. Morse started work at Brookhaven in September 1946. Serious design problems soon surfaced, however, and although he blamed the building contractor, Morse lost the confidence of the AUI trustees. He returned to MIT in September 1948.

From then on Morse's contribution to physics was primarily that of teacher and administrator, rather than researcher. He oversaw numerous theses and continued to write influential textbooks, notably *Methods of Theoretical Physics* (with Herman Feshbach, 1953) and *Theoretical Acoustics* (with K. Uno Ingard, 1968). He helped to lay the groundwork for MIT's Acoustics Laboratory during the 1940s and early 1950s. He served a second period as graduate registration officer (1950–1965), was a member of various committees on the MIT library system, and was MIT's faculty chairman (1958–1960). Outside MIT, he sat on the editorial boards of *Technology Review* (1946–1950), *Annals of Physics* (1956–1978), *Journal of Mathematics and Physics* (1959–1968), and *Science* (1960–1964). Morse was president of the Acoustical Society of America (1950–1951), a fellow of the National Academy of Sciences (1955), president of the American Physical Society (1972), and chairman of the American Institute of Physics' Governing Board (1975–1980).

Morse's most significant postwar activities stemmed from his promotion of and work in operations research. His postwar publication record is solidly oriented toward these ends. By 1950 he had assisted the military services in establishing civilian "think tanks" that performed OR—the navy's Operations Evaluation Group (ORG's successor), the air force's RAND Corporation, and the Joint Chiefs of Staff's Weapons Systems Evaluation Group. Morse also encouraged the nonmilitary use of OR. He saw it as a means for the scientifically trained to enrich public discussion over how technology would be used. OR provided Morse with an instrument to demonstrate the importance of the scientific generalist and the dangers of over-specialization. He helped persuade the National Research Council to create the Committee on Operations Research (1949–1955), which encouraged industries, private foundations, and universities to support OR. This committee led to the founding of the Operations Research Society of America (ORSA), of which Morse was the first president (1952–1953). Morse advised an increasing number of government agencies and industrial firms interested in OR. Around 1950 he helped the consulting firm of Arthur D. Little to expand into the field.

At MIT, Morse persuaded the new president, James R. Killian, and the provost, Julius A. Stratton, to support OR, beginning with the establishment of an institute committee that Morse chaired from 1952 until his retirement in 1969. Morse transformed his final ORG report into the first textbook on the subject, *Methods of Operations Research* (with George E. Kimball, 1951), and began overseeing the development of OR courses at MIT. These efforts culminated in the 1956 creation of the Operations Research Center, an interdisciplinary graduate training program for which Morse secured army and navy start-up funds. He also directed the center until he retired.

Morse's interest in operations research and ensuring the effective use of new technologies also prompted him to encourage the use of computers on campus. His chairmanship of various committees on computation led to the 1957 creation of the MIT Computation Center, which he directed for a decade. During his tenure MIT completed its transition to digital technology and rejected analog computing. Morse, through his support of Marvin L. Minsky and John McCarthy, influenced the development of MIT's computer time-sharing. Thus his dual directorships of the OR and computer centers served OR at MIT in material terms; as their mathematical modeling became ever more complex, OR students enjoyed easy access to computing facilities.

Operations research also dominated Morse's professional activities away from MIT. In the post-Sputnik environment of the late 1950s, he persuaded the North Atlantic Treaty Organization to sponsor an advisory panel on OR to spread the activity throughout the alliance. Using his international connections, he urged the formation of another panel of the Organization for Economic Coöperation and Development. He chaired both panels (1960–1965 and 1962–1968, respectively). He also served as secretary general of the International Federation of Operations Research Societies (1961–1964), an organization he helped found.

From the mid-1960s, Morse attempted to expand OR's horizons beyond the military. American involvement in Vietnam disturbed him greatly and created uncomfortable tensions with his new international contacts in Europe and in the developing countries. As a result, the issues of urban planning, transportation, regional development, and third-world modernization came to dominate his agenda, which included numerous trips to Europe, India, Japan, and other nations. Closer to home, his frenetic lecture schedule and other commitments continued long after his retirement.

In his later years, Morse became increasingly disillusioned with the prospects of OR and the scientific generalist, at least in the United States. When a 1971 study by ORSA supported plans for developing anti-ballistic missiles, Morse took it as an affront to himself and other scientists who had publicly spoken against the ABM. Having gradually come to the conclusion that OR had been co-opted by government bureaucrats and self-serving Pentagon officials, Morse nearly resigned from the organization he had helped found. He spent his last years bitterly believing that modern society squandered opportunities for social progress and that its citizens and scientists abdicated individual moral responsibility in favor of a crass technocracy.

Morse had married Annabelle Hopkins of Cleveland in April 1929. They had two children. He died in Concord, Massachusetts.

• Morse's professional papers are in the Massachusetts Institute of Technology Archives. The fullest account of Morse's life is his autobiography, *In at the Beginnings: A Physicist's Life* (1977). For insight into the context of professional physics in which Morse operated, see Daniel J. Kevles, *The Physicists: The History of a Scientific Community in Modern America* (1978); and Stuart W. Leslie, *The Cold War and American Science: The Military-Industrial-Academic Complex at MIT and Stanford* (1992). For an overview of operations research, see M. Fortun and S. S. Schweber, "Scientists and the Legacy of World War II: The Case of Operations Research (OR)," *Social Studies of Science* 23 (1993): 595–642. Schweber also interviewed Morse shortly before his death; the author wishes to thank Schweber for his observations. For Morse's role in the development of the MIT Computation Center, see Larry Owens, "Where Are We Going, Phil Morse? Changing Agendas and the Rhetoric of Obviousness in the Transformation of Computing at MIT, 1939–1957," *IEEE Annals of the History of Computing* 18 (1996): 34–41. A helpful obituary is Herman Feshbach, "Philip McCord Morse," National Academy of Sciences, *Biographical Memoirs* 65 (1994): 243–55.

ERIK P. RAU

MORSE, Samuel Finley Breese (27 Apr. 1791–2 Apr. 1872), artist and telegraph inventor, was born in Charlestown, Massachusetts, the eldest child of Rev. Jedidiah Morse and Elizabeth Ann Breese. Some biographers have emphasized the influence of his father's evangelical Calvinism on Morse, but much of his early life was spent away from home; he was enrolled as a boarder at Phillips Academy in Andover at age eight. He entered Yale in 1805 and graduated in 1810, obtaining some knowledge of electricity (but not of electromagnetism, which had yet to be discovered) from courses with Benjamin Silliman and Jeremiah Day. His interest in art was evidenced only by a few miniatures that he painted to help support himself.

After graduation he persuaded his father to allow him to pursue a career in art and sailed with Washington Allston to study in London in 1811. His terra cotta statue of *Hercules* won a gold medal at the Society of Arts in 1812, and large paintings of *The Dying Hercules* and *The Judgement of Jupiter* won acclaim. But when he exhibited the paintings in Boston upon his return in 1815 he found little public interest, and he turned to portraiture, traveling to different cities to find sitters. He spent three successful winters in Charleston, South Carolina, between 1818 and 1821. In 1823 he established a studio in New York City, where his art matured. His best work of this period is represented by a large painting of the House of Representatives (1822–1823) and two portraits of the Marquis de Lafayette (1825–1826). He founded the National Academy of Design in New York City in 1826 to promote the training and exhibiting of American artists and was its president and guiding spirit until 1842. He was effective as a lecturer in promoting its cause throughout this period.

Morse married Lucretia Walker in 1818, but his work kept him away from his family for long periods of time. While he was in Washington working on the Lafayette portraits in 1825, he learned that his wife had died shortly after birth of their fourth child. His father died the following year and his mother two years after that. Depressed, he left his children with one of his two brothers and sailed for Europe in 1829. He was financed by several commissions for paintings, but his purpose was to gain enough experience to produce a grand painting that would establish his reputation. He saw Lafayette in Paris but spent most of his time in Italy, often in the company of James Fenimore Cooper.

He returned in 1832 with high hopes for *The Gallery of the Louvre*, which he displayed in New York. But it, like *The House of Representatives*, failed to attract public interest. A final disappointment came when he learned that he had not been chosen to paint one of the four panels in the ceiling of the rotunda in the Capitol in Washington, a commission he had long coveted. This rebuff was undoubtedly at least in part a reaction to his strongly expressed political views, which were anti-Catholic and antiabolitionist. (He ran unsuccessfully for mayor of New York in 1836 on the Native-American ticket.)

Frustrated, Morse turned to the field of invention. He had done some experimenting with the paints for some of his portraits. And he and a brother had devised a flexible-piston pump (1817) and a marble-cutting machine (1822); the former was patented but proved impractical, and the essentials of the latter had been anticipated by someone else. On the return trip from Europe a new field presented itself to his imagination. Conversations about electricity with Charles Thomas Jackson (who would later make claims that Morse had stolen the idea of the telegraph from him) led to a consideration by Morse that "if the presence of electricity can be made visible in any part of the circuit, I see no reason why intelligence may not be transmitted instantaneously by electricity."

In 1834 he was appointed professor of sculpture and painting (with no pay) at the nascent University of the City of New York (later New York University). Without funds and without any real technical skills, Morse laboriously began to put his ideas about the telegraph into working form. He made molds and cast thin strips of lead with notches on one side. This "type" was later mounted on a wooden "portrule" (about three feet long), with the notches facing up, and pulled under one end of a wooden lever; pushed by the type, the lever moved up and down, and its other end closed an electrical circuit for long and short periods of time. The analogy with type on a printer's rule is clear and logically may have followed from the circumstance that his brothers were printers.

In 1835, with a new title of professor of literature of the arts and design, Morse moved into the university building overlooking Washington Square. His student fees were not enough even to pay for his rooms. However, by the end of the year he had constructed a crude but workable telegraph instrument. The portrule was the transmitter. A pair of wires, one connected to a battery, led to an electromagnet that pulled against the middle of a lever. One end of the lever was fixed; the other end carried a pencil that marked a wavy line on a strip of paper pulled under it by a wooden clock mechanism. The various parts of this receiver were mounted on an artist's frame (or "canvas stretcher"). The only complex part of the assemblage was the clock unit, which had probably been obtained from one of the many nearby shops that sold such items. Groups of short and long "waves" in the pencil line represented codes for numbers. The numbers in turn represented words. Morse now spent long hours composing a dictionary of numbered words.

This first telegraph was capable of sending messages only a few feet. The basic problem was the small number of turns of wire around the electromagnet. For more than a short distance, therefore, the length of wire in the line was much greater than that on the magnet. Most of the voltage (and electrical energy) was thus lost in transmission through the line; and Morse lacked the benefit of increased magnetism that many turns would give. To understand this, he needed to have some appreciation for the relationship between current, voltage, and resistance that had been enunciated by Georg Simon Ohm in 1827. (This was the year Morse attended a series of lectures on electricity by James Freemon Dana at the New York Athenaeum; they would have refreshed his previous learning but would have contained nothing about Ohm.) Fortunately, Leonard D. Gale, professor of chemistry at the university, was familiar with the work of Joseph Henry, and although Henry himself was unaware of Ohm's law, his work with magnets illustrated its features. Morse showed Gale his apparatus in 1836, and by spring of 1837 the two of them had increased the turns of wire around the magnet. By November, using a more powerful battery, Gale was able to send electrical pulses through as much as ten miles of wire. This was a distance that Morse considered sufficient for a practical instrument, since he had conceived that, in place of a receiver, he might have the magnet activate a switch (or "relay") for a second circuit that could convey pulses for another ten miles, and so on indefinitely.

In September 1837 a student at the university, Alfred Vail, joined the team. Vail had mechanical skills critical for refining the instrument; equally important, his father, Stephen Vail, owned a prosperous iron and brass works in Speedwell, New Jersey. For their efforts, Vail and Gale received one-quarter and one-eighth interests, respectively, in the invention.

Vail constructed a modified instrument that inscribed short and long marks (dots and dashes) in ink on a strip of paper, and the partners made their first public demonstrations. Morse had completed his dictionary in October, and it apparently was used in trials in Morristown, New Jersey, on 6 January and 13 January 1838. But by 24 January, in a demonstration at the university, the marks represented individual letters in a form that would become known as the Morse code. (More precisely, as altered in 1844, this was American Morse; it was further modified for use in Europe to a form known as International Morse.) Further demonstrations were made in Philadelphia and Washington. In 1836 Congress had asked the secretary of the treasury to report on "the propriety of establishing a system of telegraphs for the United States." The secretary issued a circular, with the expectation of receiving proposals for optical (semaphore) systems similar to those that were well known in Europe. Morse was anxious to submit his electrical apparatus for consideration. One of those most impressed was the chairman of the House Committee of Commerce, F. O. J. Smith. In a clear conflict of interest, Smith became a fourth partner in the enterprise, entering a bill requesting $30,000 for a more extended demonstration. (He did absent himself for most of the rest of his term and did not seek reelection.) Later in the spring Morse and Smith left for Europe to apply for patents. In the United States, a patent was issued in 1840.

Morse returned from Europe in 1838 with little to show for his efforts, few prospects in the Congress, and no funds. He had met Louis Daguerre and now set up a studio to take photographic portraits and instruct others (including Mathew Brady). He met and exchanged encouraging letters with Joseph Henry. But there was no reference here or elsewhere to indicate any appreciation for the debt Morse owed to Henry's critical studies of the electromagnet. Henry was justifiably bitter about this in later years. This was a period of substantial poverty; it was finally broken when Congress narrowly passed the $30,000 appropriations bill in 1843.

Rejoined by Gale and Vail, Morse prepared to run a line forty miles from Baltimore to Washington. They were assisted by Ezra Cornell, who devised a plow to lay an underground cable consisting of a lead casing with wires insulated by tar inside. After thirteen miles had been laid they determined that the wires were hopelessly shorted and resorted to conveying bare lines overhead on glass insulators attached to poles. Successful completion was marked on 24 May 1844 with a message from Washington to Baltimore and repeated back: "What hath God wrought." The new instruments were constructed by Vail. The transmitter was a simple "key" with which a finger could make and break contact. At the receiving end two large coils of a relay activated coils of the "register," which caused a metal stylus to press marks on a moving tape.

There has been much dispute over Vail's contributions to the telegraph. Aside from details in construction of the instruments, he himself never claimed more than the use of the stylus and the key. Others have argued that the shift from the use of a dictionary to a letter code also originated with Vail.

Morse wanted his invention to belong to the government, and he offered to sell it for $100,000. There was little interest. An additional grant of $8,000 financed operations for another year. After that, the Morse Electromagnetic Telegraph Company licensed use of the patent in different parts of the country.

Morse played almost no part in the succeeding history of the telegraph. Nevertheless, he received fees totaling hundreds of thousands of dollars. He built a house, "Locust Grove," on the Hudson River near Poughkeepsie in 1847 and the following year married a 26-year-old second cousin, Sarah Griswold, with whom he had four more children. He ran unsuccessfully for Congress as a Democrat in 1854, was (essentially honorary) electrician for the Atlantic cable in 1857–1858, and was a cofounder of Vassar College in 1861. He received numerous honors, most notably a grant of 400,000 francs from a consortium of several European governments in 1858. He made some attempts to paint—mainly landscapes—but found that his talent had left him. He died in New York City.

• The bulk of Morse's papers are in the Manuscript Division of the Library of Congress. Additional items are held in the Smithsonian Archives, Yale University Library, Emory University Library, and the New-York Historical Society, as well as in the papers of Alfred Vail at the Smithsonian Institution, the Library of Congress, and the New Jersey Historical Society Library, and in the F. O. J. Smith Papers at the Maine Historical Society Library. The 1837 telegraph instrument, tape messages from 1838 and 1844, and a copy Morse made of his 1832 notebook are preserved in the Smithsonian's National Museum of American History. A portion of a receiving instrument from 1844 is held at Cornell University. Extensive quotations from Morse's writings appear in Samuel I. Prime, *The Life of Samuel F. B. Morse* (1875), and in Edward Lind Morse, ed., *Samuel F. B. Morse: His Letters and Journals* (2 vols., 1914). A general biography is Carleton Mabee, *The American Leonardo: A Life of Samuel F. B. Morse* (1943). Two more recent studies provide insights into the inventive and artistic sides of Morse's career (and to relationships between them). They are, respectively, Brooke Hindle, *Emulation and Invention* (1981), and Paul J. Staiti, *Samuel F. B. Morse* (1989). An early view of the telegraph invention is contained in William B. Taylor, *An Historical Sketch of Henry's Contribution of the Electro-Magnetic Telegraph; with an Account of the Origins and Development of Prof. Morse's Invention* (1879).

BERNARD S. FINN

MORSE, Wayne Lyman (20 Oct. 1900–22 July 1974), senator from Oregon (1945–1969), was born near Madison, Wisconsin, on the farm of his parents, Wilbur Morse and Jesse White. Morse spent his youth in rural Wisconsin because his father chose to remain on the family farm after completing high school. His mother, however, had received a degree from Downer College in Milwaukee. She insisted that her son travel the eleven miles into Madison rather than attend a nearby one-room school and encouraged his efforts to complete high school. He received a B.A. from the University of Wisconsin in 1923 and an M.A. in 1924. Excelling at oratory and debate, Morse decided to enroll at the University of Minnesota for a graduate degree in speech, but he later changed his course of study and left Minnesota with a law degree in 1928. He completed his education at Columbia University by gaining a doctorate in jurisprudence in 1932. Meanwhile, he had married Mildred Downie in 1924. The marriage produced three children.

In 1929 Morse moved to Oregon, where he served as an assistant professor of law for only two years before becoming dean of the University of Oregon Law School. His first public appointment came in 1938, when Secretary of Labor Frances Perkins named him to the position of Pacific Coast labor arbitrator. Immersing himself in labor law, Morse became an outstanding arbitrator, and in 1942 President Franklin D. Roosevelt appointed him to the newly created War Labor Board.

In 1944 Morse was elected on the Republican ticket to the first of four terms that he would serve in the U.S. Senate. He quickly exhibited the spirited nonconformity and reluctance to compromise that marked his entire Senate career. Fortunately, his stance as a maverick was popular in Oregon; as one close associate noted, Oregonians loved his independence, outspokenness, and courage. He immediately showed his independence by antagonizing the leading members of his own party, particularly the ranking Senate Republican, Robert Taft. A member of the Labor Committee, Morse not only voted against the antilabor Taft-Hartley Act but staged the first of many filibusters in an effort to defeat it. In addition, he was an internationalist whose support for the World Court was so adamant that he antagonized even Senator Arthur Vandenberg, a leader of the internationalist wing of the Republican party. He joined Margaret Chase Smith in repudiating the tactics of Republican Senate colleague Joseph R. McCarthy in his search for Communists.

When Morse was reelected in 1950, the battles between him and his fellow Republicans persisted. An angry Taft refused to appoint him to a seat on the Senate Foreign Relations Committee. Morse, for his part, began to publicly attack both the Republican leaders of the Senate and his party's 1952 presidential candidate, Dwight D. Eisenhower, for their failure to repudiate McCarthy. He decided to leave the Republican party and campaign against Eisenhower. As the Senate assembled in January 1953, Wayne Morse rather dramatically carried a folding chair into the chamber and placed it in the aisle that divided the Republicans from the Democrats. Even though he cast his vote for the Republicans and broke the stalemate over control of the evenly divided Senate, the party leadership eagerly deprived him of his committee positions, especially his place on the Labor Committee.

Bitterly opposed to Eisenhower's policy of promoting private ownership of tidelands oil and private development of dams by electric power companies, Morse campaigned at length for the public construction of the Hells Canyon dam and spoke for more than twenty-two hours in futile opposition to the tidelands oil legislation. The election of 1954 once again resulted in an evenly divided Senate. This time, assured by the Democratic leadership of appointment to the Senate Foreign Relations Committee, Morse voted with the

Democrats. When he defeated his Republican opponent in 1956, he returned to the Senate for a third term as an elected Democrat. He spent the remaining years of the Eisenhower presidency in bitter opposition to the administration's policy on civil rights, its promotion of private ownership of the public domain, and many of its foreign policy decisions, such as those concerning the offshore islands of Formosa.

Following the discouraging response to his decision to run for president in 1960, Morse continued his Senate career and in 1961 became chairman of the Senate's Subcommittee on Education. For the remainder of his years in the Senate his support of federal aid to education constituted his major contribution to domestic policy. He had a long and cooperative relationship with President Lyndon Johnson, dating from the years when Johnson was Senate majority leader, and was a supporter of Johnson's Great Society program. Making use of Morse's talents as a labor arbitrator, Johnson appointed him to two emergency labor relations boards. Unfortunately, in each instance he angered the unions involved, with the result that they worked against his reelection in 1968.

Meanwhile, Morse's attention had gradually turned toward foreign relations. His appointment in 1955 as chairman of the Senate Subcommittee on American Republics stimulated a particular interest in the southern neighbors of the United States. He traveled to most of the countries of South America and supported U.S. aid and technical advice to the region several years before President John F. Kennedy announced the Alliance for Progress.

However, it is his opposition to the Vietnam War that guarantees Morse a place in the history of U.S. foreign policy. Morse made his first speeches against the increasing American role in Vietnam as early as 1961, but it was only after President Johnson expanded American involvement in early 1964 that Morse began the succession of public appearances marking his opposition. When Johnson announced in the summer of 1964 that a U.S. ship had been fired upon in the Gulf of Tonkin, the Senate quickly passed a resolution in support of presidential action in Vietnam. Morse was one of only two senators who voted against the Tonkin Gulf resolution. For the remainder of his career in the Senate, Morse concentrated on promoting opposition to the war. He harassed public officials who would not release information, testified before his fellow legislators, and crossed the country giving speeches. His entire career seemed to have been preparation for his stance on this wrenching turning point in American history.

Public officials contribute to the body politic in a variety of ways. Some become insiders. Others, influenced by a combination of intellectual independence and personality traits, are destined to remain outsiders. Wayne Morse chose to influence the public welfare by remaining the consummate outsider. Throughout his long and controversial career, Morse regarded himself as the conscience of the Senate. Although known for his prodigious intellect, he succeeded in this role because of his impressive personality.

Morse, who had become complacent about his support by Oregon voters, was defeated in 1968 in a very close election. Although his stance on the Vietnam War may have influenced some voters, his controversial decisions on the emergency labor relations boards also contributed to his defeat. Morse was offered positions in law firms and at least one law school, but he could find no substitute for life in the Senate. He ran for the Senate again in 1972 but was defeated. He made a final effort in 1974 and died while campaigning in Portland, Oregon.

• Morse donated his papers to the library of University of Oregon, Eugene. A complete bibliography of works by and about Morse as well as a useful biography can be found in Lee Wilkins, *Wayne Morse: A Bio-Bibliography* (1985). Also see Arthur Smith, *Tiger in the Senate: The Biography of Wayne Morse* (1962). An obituary is in the *New York Times*, 23 July 1974.

ANNA KASTEN NELSON

MORTAR (?–Nov 1774), Upper Creek "Micco" or chief of the town of Okchai (in present-day Alabama), emerged in recorded history at the time of the Seven Years' War (1756–1763). Nothing about his early life can be ascertained; nor is there information on the origin of his English name. He was known by several other names or titles, the spellings of which vary, including Yahatastanage, Otis Mico, and the "Wolf King" of Okchai; because of the last, the French called him "Le Loup."

During the Seven Years' War the Mortar was an advocate of united Indian opposition to British expansion. For two decades he sought intermittently to unite Creeks, Cherokees, Chickasaws, and Shawnees in an anti-British alliance, backed by French or Spanish supplies. During periods when he found peace with the British essential, he denounced both the high prices of British trade goods and the cessions of Creek lands to Great Britain's colonies. Impressed with the Mortar's extensive intertribal efforts, though for the most part they produced only modest results, the historian J. R. Alden has called him "the most talented Upper Creek chieftain of his generation." His leading British opponent, Southern Indian Superintendent John Stuart, called him "a sensible manly Indian" and understood his challenge to Britain to stem from "love to his country."

The Mortar's most important efforts were aimed at uniting Creek and Cherokee militants, but they were disrupted both by persistent Creek opposition and by a failure to find a secure alternative to reliance on British supplies. In 1756 he led emissaries from the militant Cherokee town of Tellico to the French Fort Toulouse at the fork of the Alabama River. This Cherokee delegation, like the Mortar's own supporters, represented only a minority tribal faction, and the French could not provide it with adequate materials. In 1758 the Mortar settled a new town at the mouth of Coosawaitee Creek. A rash of retaliatory border killings by Virginia settlers and Cherokee warriors, escalated rather than diminished by the arrogant diplomacy of South Carolina governor William Henry Lyttelton, led to the Cherokee War at the end of 1759. As tensions mounted, the Mortar called upon the Upper Creek towns for a Creek-Cherokee war against Britain, but he obtained few French supplies and little Creek support.

He attended the 1759 Tukabatchee conference, sponsored by the British to preserve Creek peace. There the first British southern Indian superintendent, Edmund Atkin, who had announced that he intended to place a British trade embargo on any Creek town that was in friendship with the French, was slightly wounded by an opponent of Britain. Although the Mortar has been suspected of complicity in this assault, his involvement is uncertain. Creeks rescued Atkin, and the conference soon resumed. Although no treaty was made at Tukabatchee, the Creeks promised to remain at peace with the colonies.

When a full-scale Cherokee war with Britain broke out in the winter of 1759–1760, the Mortar, despite great efforts, was unable to gain supplies from the poorly supplied French and could offer the Cherokees little aid. In May 1760 he contrived but failed to capture the British garrison of Fort Loudoun. At the same time, his allies among the Upper Creeks slew eleven resident British traders in a clear effort to provoke a Creek war with Britain. The majority of Creeks, however, relied too heavily upon European trade goods to risk war with the British, who were, in these twilight years of New France, the best source of supplies. Upper Creek advocates of neutrality protected other British traders, and Lower Creeks disavowed the killings. By the end of August the Mortar could muster only fourteen Creek followers as proof to the Cherokees of his support. When Chickasaws killed his brother, the Mortar became involved in a brief war against the Chickasaws, a dispute he blamed on British intrigue.

The Mortar rejected as invalid the French and Spanish cessions of Creek lands to Britain that accompanied the formal close of the Seven Years' War. He was widely believed to be behind the killings of fourteen Carolina settlers in the Long Canes region in 1761 and of two British traders among the Upper Creeks in 1763. As Pontiac's War (1763–1765) raged in the North, the British commander of North American forces, General Thomas Gage (1721–1787), fearing a pan-Indian alliance, urged the Mortar's assassination. Many leading Creeks advocated accommodation, and, lacking an adequate following among his own people, the Mortar sent a peaceful message, via another Upper Creek, to Governor James Wright (1716–1785) of Georgia in August 1764. The British prudently responded favorably.

British expansion from Mobile Bay into Alabama drew the Mortar's protests in the fall of 1764, but he nonetheless attended the Conference of Pensacola (1765), which was called to determine the boundaries of the new British possessions at Pensacola and Mobile and to formalize good Creek-British relations. After some initial resistance, the Mortar acceded to the new British settlements. Although he protested the high prices charged by British traders, he accepted a British medal, a symbolic commission from Stuart.

After the British policy of fomenting a war between the Choctaws and the Creeks (1766–1775) became known to the Creeks, the Mortar renounced his medal in the summer of 1766. He also continued to challenge British terms of trade. Meeting with Stuart at Augusta in October 1769, he complained again of British trade abuses. While southern Indians met with the British at Augusta in June 1773, the Mortar was rumored to be visiting an anti-British faction among the Cherokees, to whom northern Shawnees were then proposing an intertribal alliance. Most Cherokees, however, recalling their appalling losses in the recent war with the British, chose not to cooperate with the Shawnees.

A series of border killings and retaliations between Creeks and Georgians in the winter of 1773–1774 provoked a British embargo on trade with the Creeks. The Mortar, seeking a sorely needed alternate trade outlet as the Creeks' war continued with the Choctaws, boldly attempted to reach the Spanish in New Orleans. Descending the Alabama River in November 1774, his party of eighty engaged thirty Choctaws. Mortally wounded, the Mortar, the Creek advocate of intertribal unity, died in an intertribal battle.

The Mortar's hopes of unity ran afoul of Creek dependence upon the British for trade goods, a dependence that led large factions of Creeks, Cherokees, and other southeastern tribes to pursue peaceful relations with the British.

• Discussions of the Mortar's life are in John Richard Alden, *John Stuart and the Southern Colonial Frontier* (1944), and David Corkran, *The Creek Frontier, 1540–1783* (1967) and *The Cherokee Frontier: Conflict and Survival, 1740–1762* (1962). For a contemporary account, see James Adair, *History of the American Indians* (1775).

GREGORY EVANS DOWD

MORTON, Benny (31 Jan. 1907–28 Dec. 1985), jazz trombonist, was born Henry Sterling Morton in New York City. As a child he was taught the trombone by Professor Rohmie Jones and played with the Jenkins Orphanage Band. Morton began playing professionally as a teenager. In 1923 he was hired by Clarence Holiday's orchestra and was soon sitting in with the Fletcher Henderson big band.

In 1926 Morton joined the Henderson band as a full-time trombonist and, at nineteen years old, was the group's youngest member. Despite his youth, Morton gained recognition with a sterling performance on a recording of "Jackass Blues" (1926) by the Henderson band. Morton's flawless technique and light, nimble style quickly earned him a reputation as one of the leading trombonist sidemen in the swing era of the 1920s and 1930s. He was also one of the first members of the Henderson band to employ the elaborate syncopation that became a hallmark of modern jazz. He stayed with the Henderson band until 1928, played with a variety of big bands in 1929, and in 1930 joined Chick Webb's big band. In 1931 Morton left Webb's band to play with Don Redman's orchestra, which was one of the leading African-American big bands of the swing era. Morton stayed with the Redman band until 1937, when he joined the Count Basie Orchestra. He performed with the Basie orchestra for three years and in 1940 was hired by Teddy Wilson to play in a sextet. Morton played with the Wilson sextet until 1943, when he joined Ed Hall's band for a short time. In 1944 Morton formed his own group, which performed until the end of 1945.

From January 1946 through 1959 Morton worked in theater orchestras for Broadway musical productions, including *Guys and Dolls*, *Silk Stockings*, *St. Louis Woman*, and for several Radio City Music Hall productions in 1959. In the 1960s Morton returned to the jazz scene as a freelancer with various New York bands, including ones led by Henry "Red" Allen in 1960, Ted Lewis in 1964, Wild Bill Davison in 1968, Sy Oliver in 1970 and 1971, and with the Saints and Sinners in 1967 and 1970. Morton joined the World's Greatest Jazz Band for a tour in 1973 and 1974 and in 1975 appeared on the PBS television special "The World of John Hammond" with Benny Carter, Teddy Wilson, Jo Jones, George Benson, and Red Norvo. He then continued playing on a freelance basis through the late 1970s and early 1980s. Morton died in New York City.

Though a sideman for nearly all of his career, Morton was nonetheless one of the most accomplished, innovative, and sophisticated trombonists of the swing era and can be considered a pioneer of modern jazz.

• Brief but useful summaries of Morton's career can be found in Barry Kernfeld, ed., *New Grove Dictionary of Jazz* (1988), and John Chilton, *Who's Who of Jazz: Storyville to Swing Street*, 4th ed. (1985). See also Gunther Schuller, *Early Jazz: Its Roots and Musical Development* (1968), and Stanley Dance, *The World of Swing* (1974). A short obituary is in *Down Beat* 53 (Mar. 1986): 13.

THADDEUS RUSSELL

MORTON, Charles (c. 1627–11 Apr. 1698), Puritan clergyman and educator, was born at Pendavy in Cornwall, England, the son of the Reverend Nicholas Morton, the rector of St. Ive, and Frances Kestell. His early years were spent in Southwark, London, where Nicholas Morton had been appointed to the rectory of St. Saviour's shortly before Charles's birth. His mother died when he was quite young, and after the death of his father in 1640, Charles and two younger brothers returned to Cornwall to live with their mother's family. In 1646 he entered Cambridge, his father's alma mater, and joined the Puritan party, which controlled the university throughout the Great Rebellion. When Oxford, which had been a Royalist bastion, surrendered to the Parliamentary forces in 1646, hundreds of scholars and lecturers were ejected to make room for men loyal to the new regime. In 1648 Morton joined the Cambridge Puritans who flocked to Oxford to take advantage of the opportunities at the older institution. He was admitted to Wadham College in 1649, and he took his B.A. the same year. Wadham was then a major center for the study of the "new philosophy," as emerging experimental science was known in the seventeenth century. By the time he took his M.A. in 1652, Morton had acquired a first-rate scientific education.

Morton seems to have begun his ministry in 1653 as vicar of Takeley in Essex. He remained until 1655 when the Presbyterian party in Blisland, Cornwall, discharged the incumbent minister and installed Morton as rector. He left Blisland after the Restoration in 1660, settling for a time in St. Ive, where he preached privately to a few people in the neighborhood. Morton remained in St. Ive until 1666, when losses from the Great Fire forced him to move to London to manage his affairs. The next decade of his life is difficult to reconstruct, but he apparently continued to preach. In 1672 Morton was licensed to preach in his home in Kennington under the Declaration of Indulgence. There, he apparently acted as pastor for a small congregation of Dissenters, as Puritans and others who refused to conform to the restored Anglican church were called.

By this time the Dissenters had begun to set up academies, where their sons, who were barred from the universities by the Test Acts, could obtain a higher-level education. These academies soon became the most progressive schools of higher learning in England. They introduced the study of modern languages, and science was given greater emphasis than in the universities. About 1675 Morton opened an academy at Newington Green, a London suburb, where his fame as a schoolmaster attracted numerous students, including a few of the nobility. Samuel Wesley and Daniel Defoe were among his pupils, and both praised him highly in their writings. Wesley was impressed by the quality of scientific instruction at the academy, and Defoe praised Morton's practice of conducting classes in English, rather than Greek or Latin, and teaching students the proper use of their native tongue. Morton probably would have remained a schoolmaster had the authorities left him in peace, but the academies were harassed and persecuted as hotbeds of heresy and sedition. Morton held out for a time, but heavy pressure finally forced him to close his academy in 1685.

The closing of the academy also closed the English phase of Morton's career. Having maintained close ties with the New England Puritans throughout his life, he now decided to join them. Increase Mather, who had met Morton in England years earlier when Mather was acting president of Harvard, had apparently indicated that Morton would be made president of Harvard if he emigrated. Morton's decision to emigrate seems to have been made with this expectation in mind. By the time Morton arrived in Boston in the summer of 1686, however, his appointment as Harvard president had became politically impossible. The Massachusetts charter had been revoked, and the colony faced an uncertain future. The appointment of a president so clearly out of favor with the English government might have been fatal to the institution, so Morton accepted Mather's invitation to become pastor of the First Church of Charlestown instead. He fit easily into the political and religious life of New England, and he shared the widespread resentment of the arbitrary government imposed by England. In a sermon preached in September 1687, he assured his congregation that the revocation of the charter had been invalid and that the old government would eventually be restored. The governor's council responded by citing him for sedition, but a Boston jury acquitted him of the charge. The trial increased Morton's popularity by identifying him completely with the concerns of New Englanders.

Morton seems to have shared the views of his Massachusetts colleagues on all important questions, including the witchcraft frenzy of 1692. During the Salem trials he played a cautious role and shared Cotton Mather's doubts about the use of spectral evidence. Although Morton never became president of Harvard, he maintained close ties with the institution, occasionally lecturing on scientific subjects and serving as vice president, an office especially created for him in 1697. His *Compendium Physicae*, written during his academy years in England, was copied and recopied in manuscript by Harvard students for use as a science textbook from 1687 until about 1728. Morton's writings reveal him to have been a person of wide erudition. They range from theology and biblical commentary to science, logic, psychology, and practical measures for the improvement of Cornish agriculture.

Though Morton was admired and respected by those who knew him, not much is known of his private life. His wife, Joan (full name and date of marriage unknown), who died in 1693, and a daughter, Mary, accompanied him to Massachusetts in 1686. Another daughter, Alice, was baptized at Blisland in 1654. Apart from that, only the events of his public life are accessible. It was a notable life by any standard. Morton played an important part in a significant phase of English education, and he was an influential minister in New England. He died in Charlestown.

• The only book by Morton published during his lifetime was *The Spirit of Man* (1693), a practical handbook on human behavior that explores human psychology from the standpoint of Calvinist theology. His *Compendium Physicae* did not appear in published form until 1940, in *Publications of the Colonial Society of Massachusetts* 33. The sources for Morton's life are scattered and fragmentary. The most complete biographical accounts are Samuel Eliot Morison, "Charles Morton," *Publications of the Colonial Society of Massachusetts* 33 (1940): vii–xxix; and F. L. Harris, "Charles Morton—Minister, Academy Master and Emigrant," *Journal of the Royal Institution of Cornwall*, n.s., 4 (1963): 326–52. For Morton's life in England, see Edmund Calamy, *The Nonconformist's Memorial: Being an Account of the Ministers, Who Were Ejected or Silenced after the Restoration* (2 vols., 1713), which contains a list of Morton's writings; and Calamy, *A Continuation of the Account of the Ministers, Lecturers, Masters and Fellows of Colleges, and Schoolmasters, Who Were Ejected and Silenced after the Restoration in 1660* (2 vols., 1727), which includes copies of Morton's "Advice to Candidates for the Ministry" and "A Vindication of Private Tutors among the Dissenters," treatises illustrative of his acuity of mind and literary style. For Morton's academy years, see Walter Wilson, *Memoirs of the Life and Times of Daniel De Foe* (3 vols., 1830); Luke Tyerman, *The Life and Times of the Rev. Samuel Wesley, M.A.* (1866); and Herbert McLachlan, *English Education under the Test Acts* (1931). For his life in New England, see Richard Frothingham, *The History of Charlestown, Massachusetts* (1845); William I. Budington, *The History of the First Church, Charlestown* (1845); James F. Hunnewell, *Records of the First Church in Charlestown, Massachusetts, 1632–1789* (1880); Samuel Eliot Morison, *Harvard College in the Seventeenth Century* (1936); William B. Sprague, *Annals of the American Pulpit* (9 vols., 1860–1869); Thomas B. Wyman, *The Genealogies and Estates of Charlestown, in the County of Middlesex and Commonwealth of Massachusetts, 1629–1818* (1879); and "Diary of Samuel Sewall," *Collections of the Massachusetts Historical Society*, 5th ser., 5 (1878): passim. For Morton's place in seventeenth-century science, see F. A. Turk, "Charles Morton; His Place in the Historical Development of British Science in the Seventeenth Century," *Journal of the Royal Institution of Cornwall*, n.s., 4 (1963): 353–63; and Theodore Hornberger, "The *Compendium Physicae*," *Publications of the Colonial Society of Massachusetts* 33 (1940): xxxi–xl.

EDGAR J. MCMANUS

MORTON, Ferdinand Quintin (9 Sept. 1881–8 Nov. 1949), attorney and political leader, was born in Macon, Mississippi, the son of Edward James Morton, a clerk in the U.S. Treasury Department, and Willie Mattie Shelton. Morton's parents were former slaves. His father accepted the position with the Treasury Department in 1890, when the family moved north to Washington, D.C. Morton attended school in Washington, then enrolled at Phillips Exeter Academy in New Hampshire. He graduated in 1902 and entered Harvard. He left Harvard after his junior year, in 1905, seemingly for financial reasons. Despite the fact that he was not a college graduate, he began studying at Boston University Law School that fall. He remained there for only a year and a half, again leaving without a degree, probably because of monetary problems.

Morton next became involved in politics. In 1908 he moved to New York City and began working on the campaign of Democratic presidential candidate William Jennings Bryan, giving speeches on his behalf. Bryan lost the presidency to Republican William Howard Taft, but Morton retained his taste for Democratic party politics. Still possessed with the desire to practice law, he worked as a law clerk for two years, then passed the New York State Bar examination in 1910.

In addition to his work as a lawyer, Morton kept busy in the political arena. Shortly after his experiences with the Bryan campaign, he became a member of the United Colored Democracy, a political group established for the purpose of convincing New York's black population, made up traditionally of Republicans, to switch to the Democratic party. The New York Democratic machine, known as Tammany Hall, was led by Charles F. Murphy, a man who admired Morton's speaking abilities and his intelligence. In 1915 Murphy secured Morton's nomination as leader of the United Colored Democracy in hopes of winning political backing from Harlem.

Balancing politics with his legal career, Morton practiced law for six years. In 1916 he was appointed assistant district attorney for New York County, and in 1921 he was placed in charge of the office's Indictment Bureau. Morton's tenure at that post was short-lived, however, because on 1 January 1922 he was appointed by Mayor John F. Hylan as the first black member of the New York Municipal Civil Service Commission. Morton's position on the commission helped guarantee an increase in the number of blacks employed by the city.

Blacks, however, were facing increased obstacles in other areas. In the 1920s white Democratic leaders tried to bring about the dissolution of the United Colored Democracy and instead incorporate its members into the more traditional Democratic political organizations. Morton refused to allow this to happen, believing that such a measure would do considerable damage to the political power of blacks as a whole, not to mention the harm it would inflict upon his own political clout. Morton eventually left his position with the United Colored Democracy in 1933, when newly elected New York City mayor Fiorello La Guardia threatened to remove him from the Civil Service Commission if he did not. Morton chose to remain on the commission, where his salary exceeded $10,000 per year, placing him among the highest paid blacks employed by the city.

To fill the void left by his departure from politics, Morton in 1935 accepted the job of baseball commissioner of the Negro National League. He served as commissioner for four years, spanning the final two years that the National League was the sole black league and the first two years after the foundation of the rival Negro American League. In his role as commissioner, Morton was rarely called upon to do anything of consequence. His function was limited to appearances at league meetings. When in 1938 he attempted to call a league meeting on his own authority, Gus Greenlee, the powerful owner of the Pittsburgh Crawfords, told the other owners not to bother to attend. The owners complied with Greenlee. Later that year the league abolished the office of commissioner.

On 16 July 1946 Morton was elected president of the Civil Service Commission. He continued as president until 10 January 1948, when the effects of Parkinson's disease forced him to retire. Morton, who never married, died in Washington, D.C., when the hospital bed in which he was receiving treatment caught fire from a lit cigarette.

• Biographical information on Morton is quite limited. Two brief studies in the Schomburg Collection of the New York Public Library provide details of his life, James Gardner, "Brief History of Ferdinand Q. Morton of N.Y," and Samuel Michelson, "History of the Democratic Party in Harlem." He is also included in the *Class Reports* of Harvard College for the class of 1906, even though he never graduated. For information on Morton's experience as commissioner of the Negro National League, see Robert Peterson, *Only the Ball Was White* (1970). Obituaries are in the *New York Times* and the *New York Herald Tribune*, 9 Nov. 1949.

FRANCESCO L. NEPA

MORTON, Henry (11 Dec. 1836–9 May 1902), college administrator and scientist, was born in New York City, the son of Henry J. Morton, an Episcopalian minister, and Helen McFarlan. Morton grew up in Philadelphia, where his father was rector of St. James Episcopal Church. He attended Episcopal Academy in Philadelphia and graduated from the University of Pennsylvania in 1857. While still a student, with two classmates he translated the Greek, demotic, and hieroglyphic inscriptions of the Rosetta Stone, which they published in 1858 in a 172-page report containing 100 illustrations engraved by Morton.

After a postgraduate course in chemistry Morton began the study of law, but he abandoned it in 1859 to teach chemistry and physics at Episcopal Academy. When his popular lectures were opened to the public in 1860, Morton soon became a local celebrity. In 1869 he headed the photographic division of the U.S. Eclipse Expedition to Iowa and showed that a mysterious bright line at the moon's edge, previously attributed to diffraction, was due to chemical action during development of the photographic plate.

Morton married Clara Dodge of New York City in 1862; they had two sons. That same year, he began teaching chemistry both at the new Philadelphia Dental College and at the Franklin Institute. In 1865 he became resident secretary of the institute at an annual salary of $1,500, and from 1867 through 1871 he was editor of its prestigious journal.

To raise money for the institute Morton began in April 1865 a series of science lectures at the 3,500-seat Philadelphia Academy of Music. The first two-hour lecture, on light, packed the house for two successive nights. Similar lectures followed over the next five years; some were repeated in Baltimore, New York, New Haven, and Providence. They were spectacular theatrical productions requiring a cast of actors and a stage crew of as many as fifteen persons. To show the combustion of iron, Morton burned a red-hot steel sword-blade in oxygen while standing atop a fifteen-foot-high altar amid a shower of sparks, against a backdrop of mountains and stormclouds. Many of his demonstrations employed a specially built magic lantern that could project moving images onto a screen forty feet square. This work resulted in at least sixteen publications by Morton on the use of the magic lantern in teaching.

From 1868 to 1870 Morton taught chemistry at the University of Pennsylvania. He coauthored *The Student's Practical Chemistry* (1877) with Albert R. Leeds.

In 1870 Morton became the first president of the new Stevens Institute of Technology in Hoboken, New Jersey, and developed a course of study in mechanical engineering, the first of its kind in the United States. The school was an instant success and became preeminent in its field. An engineering research laboratory, a new idea at the time, was built in 1875, and faculty member Robert Thurston was one of the founders of the American Society of Mechanical Engineers in 1880. A course in marine engineering was added in 1882 and a Department of Analytical Chemistry in 1886. By 1902 the institute had 261 students, 886 alumni, and a faculty of twenty-two.

Although the institute was Morton's primary concern, he did not ignore research. His work on the fluorescence of anthracene and related compounds, as well as a new compound, thallene, which he discovered, resulted in seven publications between 1871 and 1876. Between 1877 and 1883 he published seven papers on the production, toxicity, paraffin content, and calorific value of water gas. In 1879 he showed that the dyes anthrapurpurin and flavopurpurin were distinct compounds, whereas isopurpurin was a mixture of the two. In the same year he studied the elimination of antimony from the human body. In 1880 he published the first thorough investigation of the efficiency of Edison's electric lamp. His development of new materials for filling teeth resulted in widespread changes in dental practice.

From 1878 to 1886 Morton was a member of the U.S. Lighthouse Board and led its research on new fog signals, lighted buoys, fire extinguisher, dynamos, and electric lights. Work as a consultant and as an expert witness made Morton relatively wealthy. He was perhaps America's leading expert on the chemistry of dyes, acting for twenty-five years as consultant to Badische Anilin- & Soda-Fabrik, the world's largest dye manufacturer. In the courtroom he was known for his concise, understandable testimony and composure during cross-examination.

During his 32-year presidency of the institute Morton donated $145,000 or more toward its needs, an amount about equal to the sum of his yearly salaries. His gifts included a machine shop (1881), electrical apparatus and endowment for a department of applied electricity (1883), scholarships (1882), an endowed professorship of engineering practice (1888, 1892), a new boiler house (1901), and general endowment (1901).

Morton was a member of the New York Lyceum of Natural History, the American Dental Society, the National Academy of Sciences (elected 1873), and the Society of American Authors. He also was a founding member of the American Chemical Society in 1876, a vice president (1876–1881) and a director (1880–1884). Frequently he hosted society conferences at the institute; there, around 1879, he introduced fellow members to a "curious instrument that seemed to have possibilities"—the telephone.

A student of biblical criticism, Morton published articles on cosmogony (1897) and on the relationship between science and religion (1888). His interest in archaeology led him to help organize and finance an excavation at Ur of the Chaldees.

Throughout his life, Morton was an avid reader of fiction and a connoisseur of art; he painted and wrote poetry for pleasure. A collection of his poems and illustrations was published privately in 1904. He delighted in lively conversation with friends, saw value in the life of every individual, and believed that true happiness could be found only in helping others. Colleagues characterized him as generous, devout, at home in any social setting, a hard thinker, broad-minded, scholarly, and intellectually superior. He died in a New York City hospital.

• The Samuel C. Williams Library of Stevens Institute of Technology has a collection of Morton's correspondence, materials about him, a copy of the book of his poems and illustrations, and his diaries over twenty-eight years. For biographical sketches, see *Science*, 30 May 1902, pp. 858–61; National Academy of Sciences, *Biographical Memoirs* 8 (1919): 143–51; *American Chemists and Chemical Engineers*, ed. Wyndham D. Miles and Robert F. Gould (1976), pp. 351–52; and Clark A. Elliott, *Biographical Dictionary of American Science* (1979). Details of his life and work and numerous pictures are in Coleman Sellers and Albert R. Leeds, *Biographical Notice of Pres't Henry Morton, Ph.D.* (1902), which describes Morton's Franklin Institute lectures and apparatus and cites references to his publications. F. De R. Furman, *Morton Memorial: A History of Stevens Institute of Technology* (1905), a work started by Morton but completed after his death, includes a 29-page sketch of Morton with many testimonials. An obituary is in the *New York Times*, 10 May 1902.

HERBERT T. PRATT

MORTON, Jelly Roll (20 Oct. 1890–10 July 1941), composer and pianist, was born Ferdinand Joseph Lamothe in New Orleans, Louisiana, the son of F. P. Lamothe, a Creole contractor, and Louise Monette. After his father abandoned the family, his mother married William Mouton, who later changed his name to Morton; they had two daughters. After Jelly Roll's mother died, he and his sisters were raised by their grandmother, who subsequently asked him to move out of the house when she learned he was making money by pimping and performing in houses of ill repute. He performed on piano all his life but also held jobs as a comedian, gambler, nightclub owner, parlor house professor (pianist), pimp, pool shark, and vaudeville comedian.

As a young man Morton came under the tutelage of pianist Tony Jackson, who, according to historical accounts, emphasized notated music, published his own compositions, loved both opera and ragtime, and maintained a heavy schedule of recording dates. Jackson was also significant for Morton as he was the only dark African American Morton is known to have respected. Of Creole descent, Morton preferred Creole musicians over uptown African Americans (witness his preference for Freddie Keppard over Louis Armstrong and King Oliver). Morton grew up within the context of distinct and stratified uptown (dark) and downtown (Creole) traditions.

Though few details are known of Morton's musical training, early experiences included absorbing the musical polyglot of New Orleans: brass bands, quadrilles, blues, jazz, ragtime, and spirituals. Shortly after the turn of the century he was working as a pianist and composing tunes such as "New Orleans Blues" (1902 or 1903); "King Porter Stomp" (1905); "Jelly Roll Blues," "Indian Blues," and "Alabama" (1905); and "Wolverines" (1906), later retitled "Wolverine Blues." By 1904 Morton was traveling extensively throughout Alabama, Florida, Louisiana, and Mississippi. He absorbed other cultural influences during his travels, including African drumming, French opera, Neapolitan music, Haitian rhythm, Cuban melodies, and other Latino and Spanish idioms. The Spanish influence can be heard in "New Orleans Blues" from 1902.

Morton left New Orleans in 1907, traveling throughout the United States and working in Kansas City, Memphis, St. Louis, and by 1911, New York City, where James P. Johnson heard him play "Jelly Roll Blues." Morton's travels continued, and by 1917 he had arrived in Los Angeles, where he renewed his friendship with Reb Spikes (whom he had met in Tulsa in 1912), a publisher and store owner on Central Avenue, famous for African-American entertainment.

Morton enjoyed immense success in Los Angeles, participating in the existing strong New Orleans cultural milieu. By 1921 the New Orleans–to–Los Angeles migration included Bill Johnson's Creole Ragtime Band (1908), Freddie Keppard (1912), Kid Ory (1919), Alton Redd (by the early 1920s), and both Ed "Montudie" Garland and the Angel City Brass Band (1921).

Morton left for Chicago in 1922, another mecca of jazz activity featuring, before 1930, Louis Armstrong, Johnny St. Cyr, Baby and Johnny Dodds, Kid Ory, Bunk Johnson, and Kid Punch Miller. Morton's disdain for uptown African Americans continued in Chicago, distancing him from other musicians and giving way to speculation on the lack of recordings with Armstrong, the Dodds brothers, and King Oliver. Morton did record with the New Orleans Rhythm Kings, and he included in his Red Hot Peppers Johnny St. Cyr on banjo and John Lindsey on bass.

Morton made his first two recordings, "Big Foot Ham" (Paramount 12050) and "Muddy Water Blues," in Chicago in 1923, displaying a mature, nonexperimental, technically secure piano style. He altered the standard New Orleans band orchestration by replacing the trombone with the alto saxophone of Arville Harris alongside Wilson Townes on clarinet and Natty Dominique on cornet.

Morton and the New Orleans Rhythm Kings made five recordings. In "Clarinet Marmalade" Morton's touch can be heard in the swing rhythm, a two-bar lead-in phrase, and a strong driving back beat on the out chorus. On "Mr. Jelly Lord" (*Mr. Jelly Lord*, Paramount 20332), Morton used characteristic double-time rhythm and a triplet pattern. Morton recorded "Mr. Jelly Lord," also known as "Mr. Jelly Roll," several times, including the Gennett version in which Morton uses blue notes and dissonance in a swinging piano solo. Other albums from this period include a series of solo recordings for Gennett in 1923: *Grandpa's Spells/Kansas City Stomp* (Gennett 5218); *The Pearls* (Gennett 5323); *New Orleans Joys*, retitled *New Orleans Blues* (Gennett 5486); and *King Porter Stomp/Wolverine Blues* (Gennett 5289). In 1924 he recorded *Shreveport Stomp* (Gennett 5590) and *Jelly Roll Blues/Big Foot Ham* (Gennett 5552). He recorded *Froggie Moore* as a soloist in 1924 for Paramount (14032).

In addition to making a wealth of solo recordings in the mid-1920s, Morton served as leader on both the Autograph label (*King Porter Stomp* [1924; Autograph 617] and *Wolverine Blues* [1925; Autograph 623]) and the Victor label in 1926 (*Black Bottom Stomp* [Victor 20221], *Dead Man Blues* [Victor 20252], and *Grandpa's Spells* [Victor 20431]) and in 1927 (*Hyena Stomp* [Victor 20772] and *The Pearls* [Victor 20948]). In 1928 Morton married Mabel Bertrand, a New Orleans Creole who was working as a showgirl in Chicago.

Morton moved to New York City in 1928, where he was surrounded by composers and arrangers such as Don Redman, Fletcher Henderson, and Duke Ellington. Morton eschewed their style of unison melodic lines, call-and-response patterns, harmonized ensembles, and solo improvisation, continuing his use of collective improvisation.

In New York Morton recorded both arrangements and original compositions such as "Blue Blood Blues," "Kansas City Stomp," "Low Gravy," and "Tank Town Bump." Although some of his compositions, like "King Porter Stomp" and "Milenberg Joys," enjoyed continued popularity, by the 1930s Morton's compositions and piano style were considered outdated. With the proliferation of African-American styles such as swing, blues, and boogie woogie, New Orleans style and ragtime were less popular.

From the mid-1930s Morton's jazz career was on the decline. He managed a jazz club in Washington, D.C., in 1930 and continued sporadic performances. He recorded two albums for the Circle (USA) label in 1938: *Fickle Fay Creep/Jungle Blues* (Circle [USA] 32-46) and *Hyena Stomp* (Circle [USA] 45-71).

In 1938 Morton met folklorist Alan Lomax. Lomax arranged and conducted an extensive series of interviews with Morton for the Library of Congress (first issued on disc in 1948 and reissued in 1957). In the interviews Morton provides deep insight into the jazz music culture from pre-1900 to the mid-1930s. The interviews are permeated with Morton's personal experiences as well as those of several contemporaries. Morton also performs the styles of some of his contemporaries. Some of Morton's finest (and last) recordings were made in 1940 and include "The Crave," "King Porter Stomp," "Mamie's Blues," and "Whinin' Boy Blues." These recordings rekindled interest in both Morton and New Orleans jazz.

Suffering from asthma and high blood pressure, Morton left New York in 1940 for Los Angeles. He died of a heart attack at Los Angeles General Hospital. Although he remained married to Mabel Bertrand until his death, in his will Morton left everything of value to Anita Johnson Gonzales, a partner and love interest.

Morton's piano style can be described as an amalgamation of ragtime, blues, and other genres. He combined a smooth technique and an appropriate touch with strong melodic concepts and both fewer eighth-note patterns and stronger bass lines than most of his contemporaries. Morton combined a linear melodic concept in his right hand with an elaborate bass line to create a unique style. James Dapogny writes that "Morton's technique involved a variety of first- and third-beat sonorities—single notes, fifths, sixths, sevenths, octaves, tenths and triads—and deviated from a simple statement of the pulse into bass melodic figures, contained within two and a half octaves below and a fifth above middle C" (Dapogny, p. 11). Examples include "Grandpa's Spells" and "Stratford Hunch."

Morton's right-hand style shows his interest in musical contrast (dynamics, timbre). He often punctuated chords and used dissonance, the "Spanish tinge," and cross rhythms against his left hand. These concepts are prevalent in "New Orleans Blues/New Orleans Joys" (1923; 1938), "Chicago Blues/Original Jelly Roll Blues" (1924; 1926; 1938), and "Spanish Swat" (1938). Dapogny also notes that Morton "used the pedals sparingly in his later recordings. The Library of Congress recordings indicate a strong preference for legato playing with the emphasis on quarter-note rhythm" (Dapogny pp. 13–14). The steady quarter-note foot tapping can be heard on the twelve solos that Dapogny transcribed from the recordings, including "Jelly Roll Blues," "Kansas City Stomp," "Freakish," "Jungle Blues," "Bert Williams," and "Spanish Swat."

Morton's expertise as a composer is demonstrated by the adoption of several of his compositions as early staples of the jazz repertoire, including "Chicago Breakdown," "Georgia's Swing," "King Porter Stomp," "Milenberg Joys," "Wild Man Blues," and "Wolverine Blues." These pieces were recorded by musicians such as Armstrong, Benny Goodman, and Henderson. Morton had distinct definitions of ragtime, blues, and jazz. According to Gunther Schuller he considered a blues composition to be structured in eight, twelve, or sixteen bars with a single theme expressed in a set chord progression. He viewed ragtime as a particular kind of syncopation that lends itself to mutithematic development but a limited range of melodies. And he regarded jazz as a looser form able to absorb any type of song or melody, "jazzing" the material with a syncopation much less rigid than that of ragtime.

Morton's early jazz style deviated from the rigid two-four oom-pah rhythmic feel by moving to a flat four-beat concept in his piano improvisations. His pieces included solo breaks, stop-time sections ("Jelly Roll Blues"), melodic bass writing ("New Orleans Blues"), and what appear to be trombone- and clarinet-inspired instrumental lines ("Chicago Breakdown" and "Jelly Roll Blues"). Morton was fond of writing contrapuntal lines and using riffs for contrast in specific harmonic situations. He also experimented with musical form in "Grandpa's Spells," a tri-thematic, pseudo-rondo composition written for seven instruments. The two-bar, four-bar, and sometimes longer phrases are scored in a variety of instrumentations, and the piano interpolations are enhanced by dynamic contrasts. Morton wrote only two known monothematic compositions, "Hyena Stomp" and "Jungle Blues."

From the minor-blues-sounding "Mournful Serenade" (1928) and one-bar modulations found in "Shreveport Stomp" (1928), Morton demonstrated his stature as one of the preeminent jazz composers of his day. The Melrose Brothers Music Company of Chicago published more than a dozen of Morton's compositions over his lifetime, including "Jelly Roll Blues" in 1915, perhaps the first jazz orchestration ever published.

Morton's stature in the history of jazz is secure. Both as a composer and as a performer, he was a significant exponent of a form of music that was still at an early stage of development. His compositions were permeated with innovative orchestral concepts, like the grouping of instruments in "Grandpa's Spells" and the Spanish tinge that he used in "New Orleans Blues," concepts that he adapted to his piano playing. His considerable influence on Ellington and later jazz arrangers/composers indicates that before Ellington started to make his mark, no one was Jelly Roll Morton's equal. One can also gauge Morton's importance by his having defined and synthesized the diverse genres and musical influences of his day into a unique style, an achievement no one else in jazz would duplicate until Ellington's mature compositions began to emerge.

• Perhaps the most scholarly analyses of Morton are those provided by James Dapogny, ed., *Ferdinand "Jelly Roll" Morton: The Collected Piano Music* (1982); Gunther Schuller, *Early Jazz: Its Roots and Musical Development* (1968), pp. 134–75; and Schuller, "Jelly Roll Morton," in *The New Grove Dictionary of Jazz* (1988), pp. 136–39. Whereas Dapogny covers Morton's life and compositional and piano style and includes forty transcriptions, Schuller focuses on a bio-musical portrait. In his autobiography, *Mister Jelly Roll: The Fortunes of Jelly Roll Morton, New Orleans Creole and "Inventor of Jazz"* (1953; 1973), Morton provides insight into Storyville, history, style, and people. Information regarding his tenure in both Washington, D.C., and Chicago can be found in Kenneth Hulsizer, "Jelly Roll Morton in Washington," *Jazz Music*, Feb.–Mar. 1944, and Karl Kramer, "Jelly Roll in Chicago: The Missing Chapter," *Ragtimer*, Apr. 1967. An in-depth assessment of Morton's life and music can be found in Martin Williams, *Jelly Roll Morton* (1963). Insights into the Library of Congress recordings have been presented by Jerry Valenti in "Jelly Roll Morton and the Library of Congress," *Jazz Record*, Mar. 1946, and Martin Williams's liner notes for *Jelly Roll Morton: Library of Congress Recordings* (Riverside Records, no. 9001–9012 [1957]). Additional bio-musical assessments can be found in Frank Tirro, *Jazz: A History* (1993), pp. 155–58, and in James Lincoln Collier, *The Making of Jazz: A Comprehensive History* (1978), pp. 95–108.

EDDIE S. MEADOWS

MORTON, John (1725–1 Apr. 1777), signer of the Declaration of Independence, was born in Tinicum, Ridley Township, Chester County (now Delaware County), Pennsylvania, the son of John Morton and Mary Archer, farmers. Both parents were of Swedish descent. Morton's father died before he was born. When he was about seven years old his mother married John Sketchley, a neighboring farmer of some education and English by birth. Sketchley, an affectionate stepfather, recognized Morton's ability and character. He educated his stepson at home, making up for Morton's minimal formal education, which was possibly as little as three months of schooling. Sketchley also encouraged young Morton to continue his involvement in and support of the Swedish church in Pennsylvania, although Morton later became an active member and a vestryman and warden of St. Paul's Anglican Church in Chester. In late 1748 or early 1749 Morton married Ann Justis, also of Swedish descent; they had four sons and five daughters.

An able and diligent farmer, surveyor, and lawyer (he was probably educated in the law by Sketchley), Morton soon became established economically. He was elected to the Pennsylvania General Assembly from Chester County in a special election on 26 June 1756. His predecessor, William Peters, had resigned as a result of the French and Indian War, which some Quaker assemblymen felt they could not in conscience support. Coming from the southeastern, heavily Quaker part of Chester County, Morton was a strong supporter of the Quaker party in the assembly. However, as an Anglican and not a pacifist, he was able to support war measures. Morton's ability, modesty, and political moderation enabled him to retain the respect and support of his neighbors for the next two decades. Morton's increasing prominence in the assembly led to his selection to serve on the Pennsylvania delegation to the Stamp Act Congress in New York City in October 1765; he presented the delegation's formal report to the Pennsylvania assembly.

While serving in the assembly, Morton began a distinguished judicial career. In 1757 he was appointed justice of the peace, serving until November 1764. The proprietary government probably excluded Morton from the Commission of the Peace that year because he supported Benjamin Franklin's struggle to tax proprietary land holdings in Pennsylvania. From June 1770 until his death Morton served as presiding judge of the Chester County courts. In April 1774 Morton was appointed associate justice of the Supreme Court of Pennsylvania, capping his judicial career.

In October 1766 Morton resigned his seat in the assembly to replace Philip Ford, his wife's recently deceased cousin, as sheriff of Chester County. In 1769 he resigned as sheriff and resumed a seat in the assembly, a position he held until the colonial assembly's final adjournment in September 1776. In March 1775 he was unanimously elected Speaker of the assembly, an indication of his respected position among all factions as the struggle over measures of resistance to Britain deepened.

Morton played a significant role in Pennsylvania's movement toward independence. As Quaker assemblymen grew less willing to support ever-stronger resistance measures in 1775, Morton was part of the crucial Chester County assembly delegation, which provided the slim margin of support for organizing a state militia. Morton tried unsuccessfully to preserve political unity in Pennsylvania as the decision for independence was forced on the assembly in 1776. Although he acknowledged that the colonial assembly was too slow to support independence, Morton opposed the new government organized under the Pennsylvania Constitution of 1776. He believed that the state constitutional convention exceeded its popular support by establishing a radically different form of government for the province and by temporarily serving as a state government. He served as a delegate to the First and Second Continental Congresses and signed the Declaration of Independence, making possible Pennsylvania's three-to-two vote in favor of withdrawal from the British Empire. He chaired the congressional committee that wrote the Articles of Confederation, although he did not live to see them ratified.

By the fall of 1776 Morton's political activities may have been reduced by the illness (probably tuberculosis) that caused his premature death early the next spring in Tinicum, Delaware County, Pennsylvania. His passing deprived Pennsylvania of a seasoned leader who was respected both by Quakers, who could not support the Revolution, and by political conservatives, who accepted independence but strongly opposed the new state constitution.

• The most important unpublished sources concerning Morton are in the Chester County public records at the Chester County Courthouse in West Chester, Pa. Two letters in the Wayne papers at the Historical Society of Pennsylvania illuminate Morton's political attitudes in 1776: Morton to Anthony Wayne, 16 Aug. 1776, and Benjamin Rush to Anthony Wayne, 18 June 1777. The best source on Morton's genealogy and personal life is Ruth L. Springer, *John Morton in Contemporary Records* (1967). Published public documents relating to Morton's career are in *Minutes of the Provincial Council of Pennsylvania*, vols. 9 and 10 (1852), and *Pennsylvania Archives*, 2d ser., 9 (1890).

ROSEMARY WARDEN

MORTON, Julius Sterling (22 Apr. 1832–27 Apr. 1902), Democratic party leader, U.S. secretary of agriculture, and promoter of Arbor Day, was born in Adams, Jefferson County, New York, the son of Julius Morton, who ran a small general store, and Emeline Sterling. In 1834 his family moved to Michigan, where his father prospered as a merchant and banker. Morton attended the University of Michigan but, shortly before graduation in 1854, was expelled, apparently over a dispute with the university president over Morton's defense of a dismissed faculty member. The faculty granted his A.B. in 1858; he also received an

A.B., apparently honorary, from Union College in 1856. In 1854 he married Caroline Joy French. They had four children.

In 1854, soon after their marriage, the Mortons moved to Nebraska Territory, settling in Nebraska City in 1855, and Morton began a lifetime of prominence in Democratic party politics. An impressive orator, he served in the second and fourth territorial legislatures, establishing himself as a leading opponent of wildcat banks. President James Buchanan appointed Morton as territorial secretary in 1858, and he served until 1861, including five months as acting governor.

In 1860 Morton sought election as territorial delegate but lost. Morton supported the Union during the Civil War but was harshly critical of the Republicans, especially over emancipation, and later opposed extending suffrage to African Americans. After 1860 Republicans usually dominated Nebraska politics. Accordingly, when Morton ran for governor in Nebraska's first statehood elections in 1866, he lost and largely withdrew from politics until 1880.

After the Civil War, homesteaders swarmed to Nebraska as railroad companies laid out lines across the new state. Morton was a leading booster for Nebraska's development. He ran a newspaper for a time and filled it with glowing stories about Nebraska's future potential. He wrote for Chicago newspapers, pushed local development, and served as a Washington representative for Chicago companies, especially the Burlington lines. He also helped to establish the Nebraska State Historical Society in 1878.

The Mortons had purchased a farm when they first came to Nebraska, and they developed it over succeeding years, specializing in fruit raising. Active in state agricultural and horticultural societies, Morton promoted efforts to make agriculture more productive and, above all, encouraged Nebraskans to plant trees on their bare plains. At a meeting of the state board of agriculture in 1872, he introduced a resolution designating a day when Nebraskans were encouraged to plant trees. Morton suggested it be named Arbor Day; about the same time, he dubbed the Morton farm "Arbor Lodge." In 1885 the Nebraska legislature specified that Arbor Day henceforth be celebrated on 22 April, Morton's birthday. Arbor Day eventually spread to nearly all the states and to several other countries. Morton was never alone in his efforts to promote tree planting, but he presented the initial resolution for a tree-planting day, always claimed credit for creating Arbor Day, and considered it his greatest achievement.

In the 1880s Morton returned to a more active participation in politics. He served as state Democratic chairman in 1880, sought the governorship in 1882 and 1884, and ran for Congress in 1888. These efforts produced no victories, but he established himself as a strong regional leader within the Democracy. Grover Cleveland's victory in 1884 set off a scramble for patronage among Nebraska Democrats, in which Morton lost control of the state Democratic party to a faction centered in Omaha and led by George L. Miller.

Nebraska politics were transformed in 1890 with the advent of the Populist movement. That year James E. Boyd, an Omaha Democrat, narrowly won the governorship, and William Jennings Bryan won a congressional seat. Morton had initially treated Bryan as a protégé but soon saw him as a threat and then as a menace. To reassert his leadership of the state party and to head off Democratic fusion with the Populists, Morton ran for governor in 1892. He devoted most of his campaign to attacking the Populist gubernatorial candidate and finished a distant third.

Morton's prominence as a conservative western Democrat brought him a place in Cleveland's second cabinet as secretary of agriculture (1893–1897). As secretary, he practiced rigid economy, returning more than 18 percent of the appropriations for his department and reducing the number of employees by 11 percent. He tried, unsuccessfully, to end the program by which the department gave members of Congress free seeds for distribution to their constituents. He also increased the proportion of the department's positions in the classified civil service from just over a quarter to three-quarters.

While in the cabinet, Morton became a favored speaker among conservative Democrats for his attacks on free silver and agrarian radicalism. With Bryan's victory at the Democratic convention in 1896, some looked to Morton to lead the National ("Gold") Democratic ticket; while he supported that effort, he refused to accept nomination. In 1897 he made his last campaign, for university regent, as a Gold Democrat, even though he had already begun to advocate a new Conservative party. In July 1898, with financial assistance from his sons and guarantees of subscriptions by railroad companies, he launched the *Conservative*, a weekly political journal committed to upholding the banner of conservatism, promoting a Conservative party, and attacking what he called "Bryanarchy." He accepted the presidency of the National Sound Money League in 1898 and 1899 and was a vice president of the Anti-Imperialist League in 1899. Disappointed that Bryan took leadership of the anti-imperialist movement, Morton voted for William McKinley in 1900. In 1897 he launched a multivolume history of Nebraska, a project completed after his death. He died at the home of his son, Mark, in Lake Forest, Illinois, where he had gone to seek medical treatment.

Morton's politics were always those of unrestrained individualism. His campaigns tried to persuade voters in favor of minimal government and laissez-faire economics and against such policies as the protective tariff, railroad rate regulation, prohibition, and free silver. In attack he was relentless and sometimes given to extreme statements. What one associate called his "uncompromising and implacable spirit" was his strength but sometimes also led to his defeat. Despite a political career of repeated defeats, his tireless promotion of Arbor Day created his lasting monument.

• The extensive Julius Sterling Morton Collection, Nebraska State Historical Society, is the major source for Morton's career and his political views; it is available on microfilm. James C. Olson, *J. Sterling Morton* (1942; repr. 1972), is a comprehensive and highly readable biography. See also the long biographical sketch in J. Sterling Morton and Albert Watkins, *Illustrated History of Nebraska*, vol. 1 (1905). Other relevant works include C. Fred Phelps, "The Rhetoric of J. Sterling Morton and his Defense of Individualism and Laissez-Faire Government" (Ph.D. diss., Univ. of Missouri, 1966); Margaret V. Ott, *Sterling's Carrie: Caroline Ann Joy French, Mrs. J. Sterling Morton* (1989); Robert W. Cherny, *Populism, Progressivism, and the Transformation of Nebraska Politics, 1885–1912* (1981); Horace Samuel Merrill, *Bourbon Democracy of the Middle West, 1865–1896* (1953); and Addison E. Sheldon, *Nebraska* (3 vols., 1931).

ROBERT W. CHERNY

MORTON, Leah. *See* Stern, Elizabeth Gertrude.

MORTON, Levi Parsons (16 May 1824–16 May 1920), twenty-second vice president of the United States and governor of New York, was born in Shoreham, Vermont, the son of Daniel Oliver Morton, a Congregational minister, and Lucretia Parsons. A member of an old New England family, Morton could count some eighty ancestors living in America before 1650. His family moved to Springfield, Vermont, in 1832 and to Winchendon, Massachusetts, in 1837. Morton attended district schools, but unable to afford college, he instead started work at age fourteen as a clerk in a general store in Enfield, New Hampshire. He later taught in a one-room school in Boscawen, New Hampshire, and then worked as clerk in a general store in Concord, New Hampshire. At age nineteen Morton was placed in charge of the store's Hanover, New Hampshire, branch. When the store's headquarters in Concord failed and its chief creditor approved the continuation of the Hanover store, Morton purchased it. By 1845, when he was twenty-one years old, Morton had become in the words of his biographer "an independent, and singularly successful merchant." He initiated advertising over a wide area, attracting a substantial trade. As his business prospered he took a growing interest in politics, becoming a devoted Whig and leading the local presidential campaign for Zachary Taylor in 1848.

In 1849 Morton was offered a position with one of Boston's leading wholesale firms, J. M. Beebe & Company, at a time when Boston was a major national trading center, importing southern cotton and selling manufactured products. Morton became a junior member of the firm in 1851, along with Junius Spencer Morgan, the father of J. Pierpont Morgan. After making several trips to England for the firm, Morton moved to New York City in 1854 to take charge of a Beebe branch office, known as J. M. Beebe, Morgan & Company. Morton's wealth had grown rapidly, and in 1855 he invested $100,000 with a new partner in a new enterprise, Morton, Grinnell & Co., Wholesale Dry Goods, Commission, a firm primarily active in the cotton wholesale trade. Morton's business grew rapidly but was forced into bankruptcy in May 1861 with the onset of the Civil War. Southern debtors could not pay their debts, and the firm could not buy cotton. Morton's creditors received only 50 percent of what was owed them, but seven years later Morton organized an elaborate dinner to repay the principal and interest due each of his creditors. In 1856 Morton married his longtime sweetheart, Lucy Young Kimball, who died in 1871 following the death of their only child. In 1873 he married Anne Livingston Reade Street; they had five daughters.

Morton obtained financing in 1862 to establish an international banking business at 30 Wall Street, known as L. P. Morton & Co., with partners Walter H. Barns and H. Cruzer Oakley. A short time later he opened a London branch, known as Morton, Rose & Co., in partnership with an Englishman, Sir John Rose. Sir John sold his partnership in 1869 when he became the representative of the British government in the arbitration of the *Alabama* claims, which stemmed from the actions of the British-built commerce-raider during the Civil War. Morton served as the middleman between President Ulysses S. Grant and Sir John in the eventual resolution of the *Alabama* controversy, as well as in collateral issues involving Newfoundland fishing rights and the Canadian boundary in the Puget Sound area. A treaty was ratified by the Senate and the British government and proclaimed on 4 July 1869 by President Grant.

With his banking activities generally regarded as second only to J. P. Morgan, Morton became a candidate for public office. An ardent Republican for many years, Morton was known as a "Stalwart" because of his support of a third term for Grant and "Money Bags" Morton because of his willing financial support for Republican candidates. Although he lost his first race for the Eleventh Congressional District in New York in 1876, two years later he won the seat and moved his family to H and Fifteenth streets in Washington. He served in the special session beginning in March 1879 and the subsequent regular session. Morton was a delegate to the Republican National Convention in 1880 and a leading fund-raiser for the national ticket. After James A. Garfield became the presidential candidate, Morton declined the vice presidential nomination, which went instead to another New Yorker, Chester A. Arthur, an important figure in the "Stalwart" faction headed by Roscoe Conkling. Reelected to Congress that year, Morton accepted and then declined a position as secretary of the navy in president-elect Garfield's cabinet. Garfield then appointed him minister to France. During his four years in Paris he ceremonially drove the first rivet in the Statue of Liberty and later accepted the statue for the United States. In 1881 (while still in Paris), 1885, and 1887, Morton unsuccessfully sought a seat in the U.S. Senate from New York. After the Democratic candidate Grover Cleveland won the presidency in 1884, Morton returned to New York, sold his summer house in Newport, and bought a 1,000-acre estate, which he named "Ellerslie," near Rhinebeck, moving his home from New York City. There he entertained his friends and many grandchildren and developed a model dairy operation.

When Benjamin Harrison (1833–1901) was nominated for president by Republicans in 1888, Morton, who represented a different faction of the party, was made vice presidential candidate on the first ballot. Harrison and Morton won the election over Grover Cleveland and Allen G. Thurman. As presiding officer of the Senate, Morton did not show the partisanship of Speaker of the House Thomas B. Reed. Reed got new strict rules upholding his slim majority in the House, while Morton was accused of placing proposed Republican legislation at risk because of his impartial rulings.

After four years in Washington, Morton moved his family back to Ellerslie, saying "my public career is over." Now seventy years old, he took his family to Europe and returned home in late summer, only to become the compromise Republican candidate for governor of New York in 1894. Morton was elected with substantial Republican majorities throughout the state. He was not the absentee governor that party bosses expected because he had always been easy to deal with before. Instead, Morton worked for civil service reform and for a charter bill that enabled three of New York's largest boroughs to combine, creating the New York City of the twentieth century. Morton was a "favorite son" of New York's Republicans at the presidential nominating convention in 1896, but he declined the vice presidential nomination and later that summer also declined a second term as governor. During the next fifteen years Morton reorganized his businesses, creating the Morton Trust Company, which was eventually absorbed by the Guaranty Trust Company. He used some of his vast wealth to support the new Episcopal Cathedral of St. John the Divine on Morningside Heights. Morton died on his ninety-sixth birthday at Ellerslie.

• The Levi Parsons Morton Papers, which contain private and public letters and business records, are deposited in the New York Public Library. A major biography is Robert McElroy, *Levi Parsons Morton: Banker, Diplomat, and Statesman* (1930). Other Morton materials include a vice presidential campaign biography that Morton published with Lew Wallace, *Life of Gen. Ben Harrison* (1888), newspaper articles and obituaries, and a collection of speeches by U.S. senators in the Fifty-second Congress presented at a testimonial banquet following Morton's service as vice president. Matthew Josephson's *The Politicos* (1938) describes Morton's bank as the second largest in New York and uses the term "Money Bags." William Starr Myers, *The Republican Party, a History* (1928), illustrates Morton's entanglement in shady deals and his involvement in organizing huge industrial-banking enterprises.

HOMER E. SOCOLOFSKY

MORTON, Marcus (19 Feb. 1784–6 Feb. 1864), lawyer, congressman, and governor, was born in Freetown, Massachusetts, the son of Nathaniel Morton, a member of the state's General Court and Executive Council, and Mary Cary. Morton received most of his education at home until he was fourteen, then he was instructed by the Reverend Calvin Chaddock of Rochester. At age seventeen he entered Brown University's sophomore class. The choice of Brown rather than Harvard illustrates the "peculiar role" the Rhode Island university played in the "life of Massachusetts" in the early nineteenth century; the Mortons and other descendants of the Pilgrims who grew up in an orthodox rural environment considered Harvard a "godless place" (Darling, p. 28). Morton's oration at his Brown University commencement pointed to thoughts that would guide his life of public service, especially economy in public affairs. He felt that extravagance led to privilege and inequality. After graduating in 1804, Morton studied law for a year with Judge Seth Padleford in Taunton before entering Tapping Reeve's Law School in Litchfield, Connecticut.

In 1807 Morton was admitted to the bar in Taunton and married Charlotte Hodges, with whom he had twelve children. He opened a law practice in Taunton where he resided for the rest of his life. He began a career of public service that exemplified the "highest type of leadership among the Massachusetts democracy" (Hart, p. 78). Since his college days he had been interested in Jeffersonian reliance on reason, as opposed to adherence with tradition, and was concerned about the rights of man. So he considered the needs of the farmers, working people, and recent immigrants, who were becoming the rural, progressive, liberal element in Massachusetts politics, in contrast to the bankers, manufacturers, and ship owners, who were the aristocracy revolving around Boston. With the numbers of the liberal element growing, democracy and aristocracy became opposing focal points of alliances, and the significance of party labels became blurred.

Morton was appointed clerk of the Massachusetts Senate for the year 1811. Elected as a Jeffersonian Republican to the Fifteenth Congress in 1816 and to the Sixteenth Congress in 1818, he failed to win a third term. Morton later said those years in Congress were "the lamest period of my life . . . some of my doctrines on manufactures and internal improvements would be deemed very heterodox now by myself as well as others" (Darling, p. 44). In other words, Congressman Morton did not oppose protective tariffs and internal improvement programs as Governor Morton would later.

Leaving Washington in 1821, Morton returned to the confused political scene of Massachusetts, in which he played a role for the rest of his life. He was a member of the Massachusetts Executive Council, 1823–1824, and in 1824 he was elected lieutenant governor as a Jeffersonian Republican. Upon the death of Governor William Eustis, Morton became acting governor on 6 February 1825 and served until 26 May of that year. Then Governor Levi Lincoln appointed Morton to the Massachusetts Supreme Court, where he served as a judge for the next fourteen years. He was recognized for his knowledge and his patient, wise application of the law. He was also criticized by some for being a politically active judge.

Indeed, during his time on the bench, Morton's name reappeared on the ballot as candidate for governor. Working to bring liberal and progressive political forces in Massachusetts together into a viable Democratic party, he refused formal nomination but consented to be the candidate of the pro-Jackson wing of the Jeffersonian Republican party in 1828, 1829, 1830, and 1831. Then Morton became the candidate of the Democratic party, but until 1839 liberals could not garner enough votes to elect him. Reflecting political change in the state, however, Morton, as the major opposition to the conservative candidate, gained votes in almost every election and increased the number of towns he carried, generally in the rural areas. He hoped the election of President Andrew Jackson in 1829 would help build the Massachusetts democracy but was disappointed when Jackson compromised with the remaining Federalists and the Whigs in dealing out federal appointments.

Morton won the governorship twice. In 1839 he received 51,034 popular votes to incumbent governor Edward Everett's 50,725. To a legislature controlled by Whigs, he detailed his Democratic ideas that private banks were monopolies tending to inflate currency, corporations should not benefit from special legislation, unqualified aid to railroads was questionable, spending should be curbed rather than increasing taxes, secret ballots should be secured, and the property qualification for voting should be reduced. His program went on to embrace the growing Democratic complexion of his state. It was, however, ignored by the legislature, as the Whigs began immediately to plan for the next election. Whig John Davis took the governorship in 1840, when the popular general William Henry Harrison won a national landslide. In 1842, with three candidates running, Morton received a plurality of the popular vote and was then elected by the state senate for the 1843 term. But the following year he lost his last contest for the office of governor.

Although most of Governor Morton's reform proposals did not meet with legislative approval, he kept ideas alive that would later be translated into programs. He was ahead of his time, and thus a leader, in advocating shorter working hours; distrust of business, abolishing the poll tax for males between sixteen and twenty; repealing the law that closed the voting polls at dark, which had precluded laborers from getting to the polls, and making stockholders individually liable. He streamlined court procedures and achieved some economy in public affairs, the idea he had addressed as a young college graduate.

In 1845 President James K. Polk appointed Morton collector of the Port of Boston. At the "Barnburner" convention in Utica in June 1848, the "radical" Democrats, in rebellion against the more conservative Democrats of the administration, nominated Martin Van Buren for the presidency. When Van Buren's men offered Morton the vice presidential nomination, Morton said he could not accept as an officeholder under Polk. He stated that even for "so righteous a cause" as the slavery issue, he felt "restrained by his subordinates in the Customs House," who would lose their jobs if he left his position (Darling, p. 348). But later that year Morton did resign as collector, for with his lifetime opposition to slavery, he could no longer support the national Democratic party. He eventually joined the Free Soil party, a short-lived party opposed to slavery in principle and to its extension into the territories, and that party was eventually absorbed into the Republican party. As a Free Soiler, he was in 1853 a delegate to the state constitutional convention and served in the 1858 Massachusetts legislature, his last public office.

Morton was on the Harvard Board of Overseers for thirty-two years. Although he was a governor and a congressman, his significance is in the years devoted to building a political coalition to carry out what he felt were needed reforms during the pre–Civil War decades. He supported the Union cause during the Civil War but died in Taunton before it ended.

• Morton's three letterbooks are at the Massachusetts Historical Society, Boston. Arthur B. Darling, *Political Changes in Massachusetts, 1824–1848: A Study of Liberal Movements in Politics* (1925), details Morton's activities, provides a perspective on him as a leader of Jacksonian Democracy, and includes a lengthy bibliography. The best summary of Morton's complicated career is in Robert Sobel and John Raimo, eds., *Biographical Directory of the Governors of the United States, 1789–1978*, vol. 2 (1978). See Joseph E. Kallenbach and Jessamine S. Kallenbach, *American State Governors 1776–1976*, vols. 1 and 2 (1981), for election statistics and a biographical sketch. Albert B. Hart, ed., *Commonwealth History of Massachusetts*, vol. 4 (1930), is an important chronological analysis of the several political parties affecting Morton's checkered career. A death notice is in the *New York Times*, 7 Feb. 1864.

SYLVIA B. LARSON

MORTON, Martha (10 Oct. 1865–18 Feb. 1925), playwright, was born in New York City. (Some sources give 1870 as her year of birth.) Although she claimed several prominent literary forebears, including English playwright John Maddison Morton, Alfred Sutro, and Edward Arthur Morton, and her brother was playwright Michael Morton, the names of her parents are not known. According to Morton, her mother had memorized most of Shakespeare's plays. Morton attended New York City public schools and Normal (now Hunter) College, but ill health interrupted her course of study. Her parents then traveled with her on an extended tour of Europe, where she took special interest in the theaters of England, France, and Germany and read voraciously in those dramatic literatures. Over the years she made several return visits to Germany and by 1904 had also visited Russia.

Morton's childhood penchant for writing led to the publication of some short stories in magazines. After seeing David Belasco's *May Blossom* (1884), she wrote a parody of it that attracted the attention of producer Daniel Frohman. It was performed at the Academy of

Music for a charity benefit. She then attempted to find a producer for her first full-length play, *Hélène*, a drama of a misunderstood woman, set in France. After numerous rejections (one manager commented that a woman playwright "would demoralize the entire company"), Morton produced it herself at the Fifth Avenue Theatre for one performance only (30 Apr. 1888). A revised version was later acted by Clara Morris, but the reviews remained unfavorable. Unable to find a producer for her next play, *The Merchant*, a drama of Wall Street and people living beyond their means, Morton submitted it under a male pseudonym to a playwriting competition sponsored by the *New York World*. The play won first prize and was produced at the Union Square Theatre in May 1891. This initiated her into the practice of supervising rehearsals of her own plays, although her directorial contributions were never acknowledged in programs or reviews.

Augustus Pitou's company produced Morton's third play, *Geoffrey Middleton, Gentleman* (1892), a popular success despite rather mean-spirited reviews. For the lovable, robust comedian William H. Crane, she wrote *Brother John* (1893), *His Wife's Father* (1895), *A Fool of Fortune* (1896), and *The Senator Keeps House* (1911). For Sol Smith Russell, who specialized in comic country "hick" roles, she wrote *A Bachelor's Romance* (1896), which became one of his most enduring vehicles. Effie Shannon played an American heiress who marries an English lord in *Her Lord and Master* (1902), a comedy described as "a sort of international *Taming of the Shrew*." It was still running when *The Diplomat* (1902) opened. In 1904 she won the *Theatre*'s playwriting competition with her comedy *The Triumph of Love*. With *The Movers* (1907), she reprised the theme of financial extravagance as a threat to the family.

In 1891 she described herself as "a disciple of . . . W. D. Howells' school," inclined toward realism but without the dark vision of Émile Zola or Leo Tolstoy. She often told interviewers that her aim was to reflect American life truthfully on the stage. She strove also to depict women taking a role in solving national problems. She commented in 1904 that "woman has come to a time of growth out of the squaw stage of development." Although critics accused her of adhering too closely to the German models that had influenced her, Morton's plays were well supported by the public. Her plays with German sources include *Uncle Dick* (1896), *His Wife's Father* (from *Der Compagnon* by Berlin dramatist L'Arronge), and *On the Eve*, adapted from a play by Leopold Kampf).

Morton wrote approximately thirty-five plays as well as a novel (*Val Sinestre* [1924]); at least fifteen of her plays were produced, and four of them were published. Her efforts in the 1880s and 1890s blazed a trail for the many women who began getting plays produced in the 1900s and 1910s and earned her recognition as "the dean of women playwrights." When she began her career, women were not admitted to membership in the American Dramatists Club. Therefore, in 1907 she founded the Society of Dramatic Authors with a charter membership of thirty women and one man. That same year the two professional associations were amalgamated into the Society of American Dramatists and Composers, with Morton as vice president.

Married to German-born businessman and Zionist activist Hermann Conheim in 1897, Morton lived in a stylish home at 265 West Ninetieth Street. Her luxuriously appointed library held 3,000 volumes. In her later years, she was devoted to philanthropic causes, including support for young writers and the Council of Jewish Women. The Conheims had no children. After her death at her home, her husband established a scholarship fund in her memory at the Hebrew University in Palestine.

• The clippings file on Morton in the Billy Rose Theatre Collection at the New York Public Library for the Performing Arts, Lincoln Center, includes many articles, the most useful of which are "An American Woman Who Writes Plays," *New York Dramatic Mirror*, c. 1895; "Mirror Interview XXI: Martha Morton," *Dramatic Mirror*, 7 Nov. 1891; A. P., "The Theatre's Prize Play Competition," *Theatre Advertiser*, Jan. 1904; Ada Patterson, "A Chat with the Dean of America's Women Playwrights," *Theatre* 10 (1909): 126–30; and Lucy France Pierce, "Women Who Write Real Successes," *Green Book Album* 7 (May 1912): 1058–61. A substantial study of Morton is Rosemary Gipson, "Martha Morton: America's First Professional Woman Playwright," *Theatre Survey* 23 (Nov. 1982): 213–22. A photograph and commentary are included in Felicia Hardison Londré, "Money without Glory: Turn-of-the-Century America's Women Playwrights," in *The American Stage*, ed. Ron Engle and Tice L. Miller (1993), pp. 131–40. An obituary is in the *New York Times*, 20 Feb. 1925.

FELICIA HARDISON LONDRÉ

MORTON, Oliver Perry (4 Aug. 1823–1 Nov. 1877), governor of Indiana and U.S. senator, was born Oliver Hazard Perry Throck Morton in Salisbury, Indiana, the son of James Throck Morton, a shoemaker, and Sarah Miller. After his mother's death in 1826, her family raised Morton on a farm in southwestern Ohio. He returned to eastern Indiana as a teenager and in 1837 briefly attended Wayne County Seminary. Afterward he worked in Centerville as an apothecary's clerk and a hatter's apprentice. Unhappy in these pursuits, Morton enrolled at Miami University in Ohio in 1843. Quitting in 1845 he returned to Centerville and read law. That same year he married Lucinda Burbank; they had five children, two of whom died in early childhood. Morton found work as an attorney in Centerville and served briefly as a circuit judge in 1852. He resumed his legal studies at the law school of Cincinnati College for a few months in 1853 and then formed a new firm in Centerville. He thrived in trial work and prospered in the 1850s, particularly through his services to railroads.

Morton entered politics just as sectional tensions were beginning to disrupt the parties. Initially a Democrat, he proved fairly conservative by northern standards, opposing the Wilmot Proviso and embracing the Compromise of 1850 as a final settlement of the issue of slavery's expansion in the territories. When the Kansas-Nebraska Act of 1854 inspired widespread revulsion in the North against the repeal of the Missouri Compromise, however, Morton, after some equivocation, endorsed the People's party, Indiana's anti-Nebraska fusion slate. He did not immediately sever all ties to the Democracy, but in early 1856 he attended the Pittsburgh convention that began the work of organizing a national Republican party. Later that year Morton received the gubernatorial nomination of what would become Indiana's Republication party but lost his race by somewhat less than 6,000 votes.

In these early years of Morton's political career a distinct pattern established itself. Repeatedly, with respect to the important issues of the moment, he started out at the conservative end of his party's spectrum of opinion, as evidenced by his always being at odds with Indiana Free Soiler and later Radical Republican George Julian. But, either owing to opportunism that certain scholars have found at the core of his character or some more complex and not entirely self-serving responsiveness to the tendency of events and public opinion, Morton generally ended up as a forceful exponent of the positions he had earlier shied away from or repudiated. Thus, through the late 1850s Morton urged Republicans not to become exclusively identified with antislavery politics and even suggested they focus on other issues entirely, such as U.S. expansion in Latin America. Yet when nominated for lieutenant governor in 1860, it was Morton rather than the man at the top of the ticket, Henry S. Lane, who most aggressively agitated the issue of slavery in the territories. With Indiana voters that year electing not only the Lane-Morton ticket but a Republican legislature, Lane was immediately sent to the U.S. Senate and Morton, in January 1861, promoted to governor.

Taking office as the Union was dissolving, Morton, who earlier declared, "If it was worth a bloody struggle to establish this nation, it is worth one to preserve it" (Foulke, vol. 1, p. 93), urged forceful countermeasures. Not one to clamor for war while endeavoring to spare himself and his constituents the hard work of waging it, he proved among the most successful governors in raising men for the Union armies. Assembling 6,000 soldiers within a week of Abraham Lincoln's first call for troops, Morton thereafter mustered more Indianans into service more quickly than even the administration demanded. Even to the point of irritating Federal officials, he saw to it that, once in the field, Indiana soldiers were adequately fed and clothed, well cared for when wounded, and not overlooked in promotions.

Morton's talents as a war governor, however, involved more than zeal. If he evidenced a certain flexibility in terms of his political principles, he displayed a perhaps related talent at improvisation in exercising power. This became apparent in his dealing with immediate military needs, such as establishment of a state-run arsenal that eventually employed 700 workers to manufacture ammunition, as well as in his responses to political circumstances. As the Union effort faltered and the war became less popular, Democrats won control of the legislature in 1862. The lower house then declared for an armistice, denounced Federal policies such as emancipation and the suspension of habeas corpus, and attempted to hobble the Morton war machine. The Republican minority frustrated a plan to parcel out Morton's war powers to a board appointed by the legislature but only at the price of forcing adjournment of the legislature before appropriations had been made. Rather than reassemble the hostile body, Morton ran the state alone for the balance of the legislature's two-year term, funding his purposes by borrowing from the War Department, private banks, businesses, and local Republican officials. On his own authority, he accumulated over $1 million and spent over $900,000. Tarring his Democratic adversaries as enemies of the Union, he repeatedly stressed to Federal officials the threat a disloyal "Copperhead" underground presented to the state and nation. Such alarms led Lincoln reportedly to conclude, "Morton is a good fellow, but at times he is the skeeredest man I know of" (Hesseltine, p. 312). Others have seen more calculation than anxiety in Morton's most prominent sallies against subversion, noting that they came at politically advantageous moments. A wave of much publicized treason arrests in Indiana in late 1864 clearly aided Republicans in reelecting Morton and returning the legislature to party control in the final months of the war.

On the issues born of emancipation, Morton exhibited his familiar tendency to shift with the tide. Initially he had embraced the Emancipation Proclamation only as an expedient of war, but in early 1864 he declared abolition to be the Lord's work. The latter position did not, as far as Morton was concerned, entail support for the enfranchisement of African Americans, however, and at the war's end he attempted to use many white Indianans' hostility to black suffrage as a means to harry the Radical Julian. To Julian's further dismay, Morton endorsed Andrew Johnson's prescription for Reconstruction, involving quick restoration of the southern states with a minimum of congressional intervention. But as Johnson's intransigence led conservative and moderate Republicans to shift against him, Morton shifted too, breaking with the president after his veto of the Civil Rights Act of 1866. In January of the following year, even though he had been crippled by a paralytic stroke late in 1865, Morton was elected to the U.S. Senate. He thereupon resigned the governorship.

In the Senate Morton's penchant for partisan battle and his aggressive waving of the bloody shirt lent him a patina of radicalism. Nevertheless, early on, he was decidedly centrist in his voting, his notions of Congress's powers to superintend the internal affairs of southern states being less expansive than those of certain of his Republican brethren. Yet as Congress felt compelled in 1869 to write more straightforward guarantees of black suffrage into the Constitution, Morton performed what his old enemy Julian termed "a sudden and splendid somersault" (Julian, p. 269). Morton urged upon his colleagues more positive and uniform guarantees of African Americans' right to vote and hold office than the Fifteenth Amendment ultimately provided for but then played an essential role in engineering the amendment's ratification. He overcame northern resistance to the amendment by strong-arming his own state legislature and by having conditions imposed upon the remaining unreconstructed states requiring that they ratify before readmission, thus guaranteeing approval by the requisite number of states even if some northern ones balked.

By the beginning of the 1870s, Morton had emerged as a representative of a new generation of post–Radical Republican leadership, the "Stalwarts," who headed powerful machines in their home states and whose course in Congress seemed dictated more by the imperatives of party building than by firm ideological commitments. But even if driven chiefly by an interest in securing the Republican constituency, Morton proved a more resolute supporter of freedpeople's liberties than some who had been brought to Radicalism by purer motives. He worked hard in support of the Enforcement (or Ku Klux Klan) Act of 1871 and spoke forcefully for the Civil Rights Bill of 1875. Reelected to the Senate in 1872, Morton kept an eye out, too, for the interests of his Indiana constituents. He endorsed federal regulation of interstate railroads in 1874 and opposed a remorseless contraction of the currency, preferring that more paper money be circulated. To promote his presidential ambitions, however, he trimmed a bit on the money question so as not to irreversibly alienate the more financially orthodox sectors of the party. Nevertheless, his efforts to secure the Republican nomination did not survive the first ballot at the 1876 national convection. The nominee, Rutherford B. Hayes, ultimately benefited from Morton's stubbornness in the electoral crisis of the following winter. As a member of the electoral commission, Morton did his best to see that the Republican candidate was given the benefit of every doubt in the counting of the disputed votes. Hayes's inauguration in March 1877 is often taken to mark the formal close of the era of Civil War and Reconstruction, and it is fitting that Morton, "the soldiers' friend" and Senate Stalwart, barely survived its passing. After suffering another stroke, he died in Indianapolis less than eight months after Hayes took office.

• Collections of Morton's personal and official papers are at the Indiana State Library in Indianapolis. William Dudley Foulke, *Life of Oliver P. Morton* (1899), shows its age but is useful in excerpting many of the subject's speeches at length. For a rival's perspective on Morton, see George Julian, *Political Recollections 1840 to 1872* (1884). Works that contain valuable discussions of various aspects of Morton's career include William Gienapp, *The Origins of the Republican Party, 1852–1856* (1987); Kenneth Stampp, *Indiana Politics during the Civil War* (1949); Emma Lou Thornbrough, *Indiana in the Civil War Era, 1850–1880* (1965); William Hesseltine, *Lincoln and the War Governors* (1948); Michael Les Benedict, *A Compromise of Principle: Congressional Republicans and Reconstruction 1863–1869* (1974); William Gillette, *The Right to Vote: Politics and the Passage of the Fifteenth Amendment* (1965); and Eric Foner, *Reconstruction: America's Unfinished Revolution, 1863–1877* (1988).

PATRICK G. WILLIAMS

MORTON, Rogers C. B. (19 Sept. 1914–19 Apr. 1979), politician and cabinet member, was born Rogers Clark Ballard Morton in Louisville, Kentucky, the son of David Cummins Morton, a physician and business executive, and Mary Harris Ballard. Morton came from a wealthy, politically active, Episcopalian family. He was a descendant of the American revolutionary leader George Rogers Clark. Morton's older brother Thruston Morton represented Kentucky in the U.S. Senate from 1957 to 1969.

Morton benefited from his family's wealth and status. Educated at a preparatory school, he earned a B.A. from Yale University in 1937. After briefly studying medicine at Columbia University, Morton returned to Louisville in 1938 to help manage Ballard and Ballard, his family's flour-milling firm. That same year he married Anne Prather Jones; they had two children. During World War II Morton joined the army as a private and attained the rank of captain. He became president of Ballard and Ballard in 1946 and held the post until 1951, when the firm merged with the Pillsbury Company. Morton was a director of Pillsbury's executive committee from 1953 to 1971. Within the Louisville community, he served on the board of Children's Hospital, as a trustee of the University of Louisville, and as finance chair of the local Republican party.

During the 1950s and 1960s Morton pursued business and political interests. In the early 1950s he moved to a farm on Maryland's Eastern Shore. (Morton once quipped that his middle initials stood for "Chesapeake Bay.") He raised livestock and began a cattle-feeding business. Senator Thruston Morton joked: "My kid brother Rog [is] a hog farmer and he weighs anywhere from 235 to 275 pounds. When the price of hogs goes up, he sells them. When the price of hogs goes down, he eats them." A Republican in a Democratic state, Rogers Morton managed Edward T. Miller's unsuccessful campaign for the U.S. House of Representatives in 1960. Two years later Morton himself won a House seat. Marylanders reelected him four times by comfortable margins.

Balancing the wishes of constituents with those of the Grand Old Party, Morton voted as a moderate conservative. After much hesitation, he braved voter disapproval and backed the Civil Rights Act of 1964. Four years later he opposed an open housing law backed by the Republican presidential nominee, Richard M. Nixon. On environmental issues, Morton's record proved mixed. He refused to support federal funding of highway beautification, yet he drafted legislation to establish Assateague Island National Seashore on Maryland's eastern seaboard and advanced a bill to limit oil pollution. During the Ninety-first Congress (1969–1971), he sponsored President Nixon's environmental program.

Always ebullient (colleagues called him a "jolly giant"), Morton rose quickly within Republican circles. During his first three terms in the House, he advised GOP congressional candidates and raised funds for the House Republican Campaign Committee. After the defeat of Republican presidential nominee Barry M. Goldwater in 1964, Morton worked to bind the party's wounds by stumping the country on behalf of Republican candidates. In 1968 he endorsed the GOP frontrunner, Nixon, and served as his floor manager during the party's national convention. After winning the nomination, Nixon asked Morton to be his running mate. Citing lack of experience, Morton withdrew in favor of another Marylander, Governor Spiro T. Agnew. The Nixon-Agnew ticket won a narrow victory.

Morton's star ascended with Nixon's. In 1969 Morton earned a place on the powerful House Committee on Ways and Means, and in April of that year Nixon named him chair of the Republican National Committee. Morton continued to serve in the House.

As party chair, Morton never became a close presidential adviser. Minimally interested in the fortunes of the Republican party, Nixon instead focused on his own reelection in 1972. To that end, he centralized political decision making within the White House. The president used Morton as a spokesman for his administration and accordingly regularly invited him to strategy sessions at the White House. However, Morton's influence on the president proved scant. Morton wanted Nixon to court racial and ethnic minorities and young people to make the GOP the "swinging, action party of the day." The president instead concentrated on wooing white blue-collar workers and southern conservatives.

Nevertheless, Nixon continued to value Morton's loyalty, enthusiasm, and communications skills. Upset over Secretary of the Interior Walter Hickel's criticism of the administration's Vietnam policy, Nixon fired Hickel in 1970 and replaced him with Morton.

Interior secretary Morton exercised minuscule authority over domestic policy. Preferring to develop initiatives within the White House, Nixon charged domestic adviser John D. Ehrlichman and his deputy, John C. Whitaker, with drafting the administration's environmental initiatives. White House staffers Bradley H. Patterson, Jr., Leonard Garment, and Barbara Greene Kilberg fashioned the president's Native-American agenda. While these matters came within the responsibilities of the interior secretary, Morton's role in them proved small. He urged the return of 40 million acres of federal land to Alaska's natives. Over the protests of environmentalists, he approved construction of the Alaskan oil pipeline. When Native Americans seized the Indian Affairs Building in Washington, D.C., in late 1972, Morton spoke on behalf of the administration. He assumed a similar role six months later, during a standoff between federal officials and the Oglala Sioux at Wounded Knee, South Dakota.

Following Nixon's resignation on 9 August 1974, President Gerald R. Ford appointed Morton to his transition team and named him commerce secretary in 1975. Ford made Morton counselor to the president and chair of his election campaign in 1976. Ailing with cancer, Morton proved less than dynamic. After Ford lost several primaries to Republican challenger Ronald Reagan, a reporter inquired if Morton was considering a change in strategy. He responded, "I'm not going to rearrange the furniture on the deck of the *Titanic*." Ford won the Republican presidential nomination, but Morton resigned as campaign chair shortly before Ford's loss to Democrat Jimmy Carter. Morton died in Easton, Maryland.

Morton's public years spanned an era when the White House extended its grip over political and policy decisions. Nixon and Ford recognized Morton's talents, and their appointments advanced his career. Unfortunately, Morton served as a party and cabinet official when both institutions exercised less and less policy influence. Thus, his achievements in those positions proved minimal.

• Morton's papers are at the Department of Special Collections, Margaret I. King Library, University of Kentucky, Lexington. Archival material on Nixon's political, environmental, and Native-American decisions is in the Nixon Presidential Materials, National Archives, Washington, D.C. For Morton's relations with Nixon, see Richard Nixon, *RN: The Memoirs of Richard Nixon* (1978), and H. R. Haldeman, *The Haldeman Diaries: Inside the Nixon White House* (1994). Nixon's domestic policies are covered in Joan Hoff, *Nixon Reconsidered* (1994). For Morton's service under Ford, consult John Robert Greene, *The Presidency of Gerald R. Ford* (1995). An overview of the evolving American presidency is Fred I. Greenstein, ed., *Leadership in the Modern Presidency* (1988). An obituary is in the *New York Times*, 20 Apr. 1979.

DEAN J. KOTLOWSKI

MORTON, Samuel George (26 Jan. 1799–15 May 1851), physician and physical anthropologist, was born in Philadelphia, Pennsylvania, the son of George Morton, a merchant, and Jane Cummings. His father died soon after his birth, and his mother moved her family to West Farms, in Westchester County, New York, where Morton attended Quaker schools. On her remarriage in 1812 (to Thomas Rogers, an amateur mineralogist), the family returned to Philadelphia, where Morton continued to attend Quaker schools until 1815, when he was apprenticed to a merchant. His teachers—notably John Gummere of Burlington, New Jersey—and stepfather encouraged his continuing interest in things scientific, and in 1817 (at his mother's death) Morton began studying medicine privately with Philadelphia physician Joseph Parrish. He also attended medical lectures at the University of Pennsylvania, which awarded him an M.D. degree in 1820. With support from his father's wealthy brother—John Morton of Clonmel, Ireland—Morton then studied medicine at the University of Edinburgh, from which he earned a second M.D. in 1823.

On his return to Philadelphia later that year, Morton found that other young physicians had better contacts with the city's medical establishment, and he sought other means to build his practice. He wrote on treatments for fever and for pulmonary consumption, served as physician to the Almshouse, joined with others to continue Parrish's teaching through the Philadelphia Association for Medical Instruction, served (from 1839 through 1843) as professor of anatomy in the Medical Department of Pennsylvania College (later Gettysburg College), prepared (in 1836) an American edition of John Mackintosh's well-respected *Principles of Pathology and Practice of Physic*, and, most notably, wrote *An Illustrated System of Human Anatomy* (1849). His professional stature (and income) grew gradually through this activity. Early in his career, in 1827, he married Rebecca Grellet Pearsall, with whom he had eight children.

While Morton's medical practice grew slowly, he had the time (and the continuing support of his Irish uncle) to pursue his scientific interests. These typically centered around the Academy of Natural Sciences of Philadelphia, which he served as recording secretary (1825–1829), corresponding secretary (1831), vice president (1840), and president (1849). His earliest scientific papers, on the mineralogy of Bucks County (north of Philadelphia), illustrate the continuing influence of his stepfather and of Edinburgh geologist Robert Jameson, whose lectures he had attended. His interests gradually shifted toward paleontology, and later practitioners of the science (including Jules Marcou of Harvard) portrayed his 1834 description of the fossils collected by Meriwether Lewis and William Clark, in his *Synopsis of the Organic Remains of the Cretaceous Group of the U.S.*, as the starting point of much of their own work.

Morton's most influential scientific work from 1830 focused on human craniology, a pursuit that spun off from his anatomical and paleontological concerns and derived in part from an interest in the then-influential science of phrenology. He pursued his studies with a collection of contemporary and older skulls that eventually included over 1,000 specimens. His network of correspondents (including military officers, diplomats, physicians, and missionaries) gathered and identified crania for him in all parts of the world, and Morton developed ingenious techniques to measure their capacities. His analyses, first published in detail in the well-illustrated *Crania Americana* (1839), supported the then-common division of humans into five races—Caucasian, Mongolian, Malay, American, and Ethiopian—and concluded from his measurements "that the American race differs essentially from all others, not excepting the Mongolian, . . . that the American nations, excepting the polar tribes, are of one race and one species, . . . [and] that the cranial remains discovered in the mounds from Peru to Wisconsin, belong to the same race." Morton also argued that his studies showed that "the physical characteristics that distinguish the different Races, are independent of external causes," a conclusion he reinforced and extended in *Crania Aegyptiaca* (1844), based on a study of 137 skulls collected by George R. Gliddon, U.S. consul in Cairo. In this volume, he argued that the ancient Egyptians were Caucasian, that "Negroes were numerous in Egypt, [that] their social position, in ancient times, was the same as it is now; that of servants or slaves," and that the physical differences between the races he found in the skulls he measured existed "from the beginning."

Most scientific readers, including reviewers for Yale's *American Journal of Science* and Harvard naturalist Louis Agassiz, praised the empirical basis of Morton's work; for example, Harvard anatomist Jeffries Wyman emphasized its "freedom [from] air-woven hypotheses" (*North American Review* 51 [1840]: 173–86). So too did southern American supporters of slavery, and physician Josiah C. Nott of Mobile, Alabama, cited it regularly in claiming that the human races had different origins and did not belong to the same species. (Nott and Gliddon even dedicated their "polygenetic" *Types of Mankind* [1854] "to the memory of Morton" and prefaced it with Henry S. Patterson's "notice" of Morton's "life and scientific labors.") Some contemporary critics of Morton's work, including Philadelphia physician Samuel Florry, wrote against his implied criticisms of biblical chronology and "monogenism." Others, such as Lutheran minister (and well-respected amateur zoologist) John Bachman of Charleston, South Carolina, claimed that the fertility of human beings with parents of different races proved the unity of the human species. Morton's last major scientific work, on the hybridization of animals, argued at length against these claims.

Morton rarely enjoyed good health, and an 1848 bout with pleurisy seriously damaged both his lungs and heart. He died in Philadelphia before he could begin the *Elements of Ethnology* that (friends reported) he had planned to write. These friends spoke of his modesty and courtesy and "gentleness of manner," and he avoided addressing the political and social implications of his craniology. But those who followed him—especially the pompous Gliddon and aggressive Nott—never hesitated to do so, and his work thus took on added significance. Late twentieth-century observers thus remeasured the crania Morton collected and recalculated his averages. But their (usually implicit) challenges to his integrity clash sharply with the views of earlier historians—who spoke of an "American School" of physical anthropology that Morton established—and especially those of his contemporaries. Even as one religious paper regretted the "infidel tendency" of some of his work, the *New York Tribune* (20 May 1851) mourned the death of "one of the brightest ornaments of our age and country."

• Useful collections of Morton's papers include those at the American Philosophical Society Library (most useful for his early years) and the Library Company of Philadelphia. The papers of American archaeologist Ephraim G. Squier at the Library of Congress also include much Morton correspondence. Three informative memorial notices—by Charles D. Meigs (1851), George B. Wood (1853), and Henry S. Patterson (1854, in Nott and Gliddon's *Types of Mankind*)—appeared soon after Morton's death. William Stanton, *The Leopard's Spots: Scientific Attitudes toward Race in America,*

1815–59 (1960), traces Morton's craniological work in detail within the context described by its subtitle. Frank Spencer, "Samuel George Morton's Doctoral Thesis on Bodily Pain: The Probable Source of Morton's Polygenism," *Transactions and Studies of the College of Physicians of Philadelphia* (1983), effectively reviews Morton's interests during his years in Edinburgh. Both Stephen Jay Gould (in *The Mismeasure of Man* [1981]) and John S. Michael (in his Macalester College honors paper, 1986) recalculated Morton's averages and came to opposite conclusions about the accuracy of Morton's analyses. (Michael also remeasured the crania in Morton's collection.)

MICHAEL M. SOKAL

MORTON, Sarah Wentworth Apthorp (Aug. 1759–14 May 1846), poet, was born in Boston, Massachusetts, the daughter of James Apthorp and Sarah Wentworth, both members of New England's most distinguished and wealthiest mercantile families. Her birth date is unrecorded, but her baptismal certificate at King's Chapel is dated 29 August 1759. From her birth until about 1767, she lived in the Apthorp mansion on King (later State) Street, a home to which she would return after her marriage. In the late 1760s her family moved to Braintree, Massachusetts, where the Adamses, Quincys, and Hancocks had also established homes. The patriot ferment of Braintree most likely encouraged her ardent support of the American Revolution, even though many of the Wentworths and Apthorps were Loyalists. Her poetry indicates that she was widely read in literature and history, but our only information about her education is contained in a poem dedicated to John Trumbull titled "To Pollio" (1793), in which she praises Trumbull for his direction of her early reading.

In 1781 Sarah married Perez Morton, a well-connected lawyer and brilliant speaker famous for his 1776 funeral oration for General Joseph Warren. An important political figure in Massachusetts throughout his life, Perez Morton served as a representative in the lower state house and later as attorney general. In 1784 the couple acquired and made the Apthorp mansion their home; the home had been confiscated as Loyalist property. They had six children, five of whom survived infancy.

Morton first came to public notice because of two scandals, one minor, the other tragic. The first concerned the couple's participation in the short-lived Sans Souci Club in the winter of 1784–1785, an assembly for card playing and dancing. The club was attacked for promoting luxury and frivolity in a series of articles in the *Massachusetts Centinel* and in a dramatic satire titled *Sans Souci, alias, Free and Easy* (1785), in which Morton is caricatured as Madam Importance (Pendleton and Ellis, pp. 29–30). Soon after its founding, the club was disbanded. More damagingly, the Mortons became a subject of public gossip in the summer of 1788 when Morton's younger sister, Frances Apthorp, committed suicide after giving birth to an illegitimate daughter fathered by Perez Morton. A coroner's inquest determined that Perez Morton played a role in Frances's death and implicated him. To quiet the scandal, John Adams and James Bowdoin, family friends chosen by the Apthorps to handle the affair, published a letter in the *Massachusetts Centinel* on 8 October 1788 exonerating Perez Morton and blaming Frances Apthorp's suicide on insanity. *The Herald of Freedom*, however, dismissed the letter as a whitewash (9 and 13 October 1788). The family was further ridiculed when a duel between Morton's brother Charles and her husband was prevented by a sheriff, an event that inspired numerous satires including *Occurences of the Times* (1789) and a newspaper dialogue in the *Boston Gazette* on 9 February 1789 that depicts both duelists as cowards. The affair between Perez Morton and Frances Apthorp again threatened to bring unwanted public scrutiny when William Hill Brown published *The Power of Sympathy* (1789), which thinly disguises the scandal as the Ophelia-Martin subplot. Although this episode occupies only three chapters of Brown's novel, it was given prominence by the frontispiece, which depicts Ophelia's suicide by poison. Because of the plot's connection to her family, the anonymously published *The Power of Sympathy* was erroneously attributed to Sarah Morton by Francis Samuel Drake in *The Town of Roxbury* (1878), a mistake repeated in a number of late nineteenth- and early twentieth-century literary studies.

However traumatic and disappointing the years of 1788–1789 must have been to Morton, they also mark her emergence as a public poet. Although Morton began writing poetry while an adolescent and may have published anonymously in her youth, the first published poem known to be by her is "Invocation to Hope," which appeared in the July 1789 issue of the *Massachusetts Magazine*. Using the pseudonym "Constantia" and later "Philenia," Morton became a frequent contributor to the *Massachusetts Magazine* and the *Boston Columbian Centinel* in the early and mid-1790s. Her work in these publications reveals characteristic themes and formal considerations. "Ode to the President" (1789), "Beacon Hill" (1790), and "Philadelphia, an Elegy" (1793) reflect her interest in patriot themes, while "Tears for Humanity" (1791), on the other hand, illustrates Morton's penchant for moral contemplation, especially in reaction to disappointment or loss. Morton's early poems are often imitative of British neoclassical and early Romantic models. Her verse correspondence with "Alfred" in the *Boston Columbian Centinel*, for example, is modeled on the *London World's* effusive verse correspondence between "Della Crusca" and "Anna Matilda." Yet Morton was also interested in innovative verse forms. Although she frequently wrote in neoclassical couplets, Morton was one of the earliest American writers of sonnets. That Morton's short verse found favor with both readers and contemporary arbiters of literary taste is demonstrated not only by the verse appreciations of "Euphelia" and other magazine poets, but also by the frequent reprinting of her poems in the *New York Magazine*, the *Gazette of the United States* in Philadelphia, the *Federal Orrery* in Boston, and Joseph Dennie's *Farmer's Weekly Museum* in Walpole, New

Hampshire (Pendleton and Ellis, p. 50). Moreover, nine poems by Morton appeared in the earliest anthology of American poetry, Elihu Hubbard Smith's *American Poems, Selected and Original* (1793). She was the only woman poet so honored.

In 1790 Morton published her first long poem, *Quabi; or, The Virtues of Nature*, a verse romance in heroic couplets based on a story titled, "Azakia, A Canadian Story," which appeared in the September 1789 *American Museum*. Morton's poem, which was critically well received in both America and England, advances an interracial love story within the conventions of the noble savage theme. The poem inspired the composer and organist Hans Gram to set "The Death Song of an Indian Chief" from *Quabi* to music in 1791, thus creating one of the earliest American orchestral scores. (Gram had already set Morton's "Ode to the President" to music in 1789.) *Quabi* also provided the foundation for an English play, James Bacon's *American Indian* (1795). Two other long poems by Morton followed: *Beacon Hill, a Local Poem, Historic and Descriptive* (1797), the first part of a projected five-part verse epic, and *The Virtues of Society: A Tale Founded on Fact* (1799). An ambitious attempt to mythologize the American Revolution, *Beacon Hill* invokes the muse of history, narrates pivotal events of the conflict beginning with the Battle of Bunker Hill, eulogizes revolutionary heroes from every colony, and concludes with a "prophetic Apostrophe to the Progress of freedom throughout the World." Despite the freshness of her subject, Morton's unimaginative use of epic conventions and stilted language resulted in an undistinguished poem. Because of its lukewarm reception, Morton declined publishing the four remaining parts of her epic, although *The Virtues of Society* (1799), is undoubtedly a reworking of the epic's projected third part ("Apology for the Poem," *Beacon Hill*). Dedicated to Abigail Adams and based on the adventures of Lady Acland, *The Virtues of Society* presents an episode of the revolutionary war from the perspective of the brave British wife of a Canadian soldier.

In 1797 the Mortons moved to Dorchester (later Roxbury), Massachusetts, first living in a house designed by Morton and in 1808 moving into a house designed by her husband. During their years in Dorchester, she maintained an active literary and social life, taking fashionable trips to Philadelphia and Washington. During a stay in Philadelphia, Morton sat for Gilbert Stuart who painted three artistically notable portraits of her, the last left unfinished. In gratitude, she wrote one of her finest lyrics; "To Mr. Stuart" (1803). Her homes in Dorchester became a refuge for writers and scholars, including Joseph Dennie, Robert Treat Paine, Jr., and Isiah Thomas. Although apparently discouraged by the reception of her long poems, Morton continued to write for herself and friends and published occasional verse in Dennie's *Port Folio* (Philadelphia) and the *Monthly Anthology and Boston Review*. In addition to poems praising friends and hosts, Morton memorialized public events, such as President George Washington's visit to Boston and various patriot heroes, including John Adams, John Jay, Daniel Webster, and Commodore Perry. She also continued to write contemplative poetry, her most notable production being "Reanimation, A Hymn for the Humane Society" (1804), a meditation on death and eternal life. Her personal devotion to the Episcopal Church not withstanding, Morton wrote several poems demonstrating religious toleration, including the broadside *Dedicatory Hymn. Composed for, and to Be Sung at the Opening of the West Boston Meeting House* (1806), which also includes "Stanzas in Honor of Bishop Cheverus, First Primate of the Roman Catholic Church in New England."

My Mind and Its Thoughts (1823), Morton's last published work and the only one to appear under her real name, reflects Morton's growing sense of grief following the deaths of her only son in 1809 and her youngest daughter in 1816. Explaining her purpose in an "Apology" to this collection of fugitive poems, essays, and sententia—some of it highly autobiographical—Morton expresses the hope that persons in distress may find consolation in reading her "poor fragments" just as she eased her own mind through "a series of disappointments . . . cruelly agravated by the premature death of her very dear children" by writing them. Recalling Anne Bradstreet's "Meditations" and "Contemplations," Morton's final work in tone and form belongs simultaneously to the traditions of Christian contemplative writing, New England exemplary biography, and Romantic consolation in thought about nature (Bortoff, pp. 13–14). Nothing Morton wrote after 1823 has been preserved. After her husband's death in 1837, Morton moved back to her childhood home in Braintree (then part of Quincy), where she spent her last years.

Although Morton long outlived her fashionableness as a poet, she was one of the few women of her day to adopt the role of public poet, chronicling and celebrating the aspirations and achievements of the young republic. Aside from religion, the central intellectual experience of her life and work was the American Revolution and its meaning, as she understood it, both for her times and for subsequent generations. Her passion for this cause led her not only to write extravagant paeans to military and political heroes, but also to reach some uncomfortable conclusions about the injustice of slavery and the abuse of Indians. While the conventions of her age, birth, and gender precluded her taking a politically active role in social reform, Morton was an early proponent of radical themes explored by later and more radical New England writers such as Lydia Maria Child and Catherine Sedgwick.

• The Huntington Library in California houses a large collection of manuscripts by Morton. For biographical accounts, see Emily Pendleton and Milton Ellis, *Philenia: The Life and Works of Sarah Wentworth Morton, 1759–1846* (1931); and William K. Bottorff's introduction to the 1975 reprint of *My Mind and Its Thoughts*, which provides a concise acount of her life and a sensitive appreciation of her miscellany. A largely unsympathetic overview of Morton's poetry can be found in Emily Stipes Watts, *The Poetry of American Women from 1632 to 1945* (1977). An obituary is in the *Boston Transcript*, 15 May 1846.

JEANNE M. MALLOY

MORTON, Thomas (c. 1580–1647), colonist and writer, was born probably in the West Country of England. His identification on the title page of his *New English Canaan* (1637)—as "of Cliffords Inne gent"—shows that he had studied law. In his book he refers to himself as the son of a soldier and identifies himself as "having bin bred in so genious a way" that he "had the common use" of hunting hawks. Almost nothing is known otherwise of his parentage or his rearing. Morton was a traveler, for, in addition to his three trips to New England in the 1620s and 1640s, he reports that he had been so near the equator that "I had the sun for my zenith." On 6 November 1621 he was married to Alice Miller, a widow. Other evidence shows that he was, according to the social standards of his day, a gentleman and a person of means.

In the spring of 1624, Morton traveled to the New World aboard the *Unity*, under a Captain Wollaston. The group landed at what is now Quincy, Massachusetts, and began a colony at a then-deserted place that the Native Americans called Passonagessit. The colonists first named it Mount Wollaston for the ship captain. It was located about thirty miles from the Plymouth colony and not far from a group headed by Captain Robert Gorges at Wessagusset. Morton reported that he was able to explore the area and was vastly impressed by both the land and its original inhabitants: "a Country whose indowments are by learned men allowed to stand in a parallel with the Israelites Canaan"; the Indians "may be accompted to live richly, wanting nothing that is needfull; and to be commended for leading a contented life."

Morton managed to become the leader of the colony, which he renamed Ma-re Mount, perhaps signifying a hill by the sea. (Others called it Merrymount.) Morton established there a system of trading by which the Indians were given spirits and firearms in exchange for highly valued furs. To confirm the merriment suggested by the colony's name, the colonists set up a maypole and performed "Revels and merriment after the old English custom." The Indians of the area also took part. Morton later recorded the events, including the text of a poem prepared for the occasion. A less sympathetic account appears in William Bradford's (1590–1657) *Of Plymouth Plantation*, in which Bradford explains that the Plymouth colonists were so distressed by Morton's supplying the Indians with firearms that in 1627 they rallied other colonists and collectively reprimanded the Merrymounters. When their protest was ignored, Morton was forcibly taken to Plymouth the following year and then shipped back to England to be prosecuted for his offensive behavior.

The allegations against him were unsubstantial, and in 1629 Morton returned to Plymouth and then to Ma-re Mount. When John Endecott, leader of the advance party of the Massachusetts Bay Company, tried to get Morton to agree that the trade in beaver skins was to be a company monopoly, Morton refused. But once the substantial body of Massachusetts Bay colonists under Governor John Winthrop (1588–1649) arrived in 1630, Morton was again arrested for failing to recognize the authority of the Bay colony, whose charter gave it jurisdiction over the territory where Morton and his associates lived. Morton's house was burned, his property confiscated, and he himself banished from Massachusetts.

Back in England again, Morton worked as an attorney for Sir Ferdinando Gorges to challenge the authority of the Bay Company. Though for a time they appeared to be successful, ultimately they failed. Morton then tried an alternative: the writing and publication of his *New English Canaan*, which satirizes both the Plymouth and the Bay colonists. He hoped that his detailed reports on the Puritans' radical departure from the established practices of the Church of England would result in the revocation of the colony's charter. Agents of the Bay Company apparently were able to make it difficult for Morgan to have his book published. The first printing was seized before publication, and only two copies survive. The book was ultimately printed in 1637 in Amsterdam, where agents of the Massachusetts Bay Company could not interfere.

In 1643 Morton made another trip to New England, his last. He was permitted to stay in Plymouth during the winter and then to travel to both Maine and Rhode Island. In September 1644 Morton was arrested again by the Massachusetts Bay Puritans for challenging the authority of the Bay Company and also, as John Winthrop's journal records, for setting forth "a book against us," though neither Winthrop nor any of the other officials had seen it. They sent to England for evidence against him, and meanwhile Morton was kept in jail. In 1645 he described himself in an appeal: "the petitioner coming into these parts, which he loveth, on godly gentleman's imployments," he had been arrested, then judged on false evidence. He was soon released and, though ill, was able to make his way to Maine. He died there in 1647.

In his book Morton uses the term *New Canaan* both to celebrate New England and to mock what he considers to be the religiosity of the Pilgrims and Puritans. *New English Canaan* has three parts, called "Books." In the first, on the Native Americans, Morton writes that when he arrived in New England he found "two sortes of people, the one Christians, the other Infidels; these [latter] I found most full of humanity, and more friendly than the other." He describes the "great mortality" that had so reduced the native population a short time before the arrival of the Pilgrims of Plymouth. Morton's graphic and admiring account of the Indians' houses, clothing, religion, child-bearing practices, and especially their personal characteristics is both informative and entertaining.

The second book provides "a description of the Country with her natural indowements." Morton's is a lavishly admiring account, but it too is full of interesting observations, such as this one: "Lobsters are there infinite in store in all parts of the land, and very excellent. The most use that I made of them, in 5. yeares after I came there, was but to baite my Hooke for to catch Basse; I had bin so cloyed with them the first day I went ashore." These first two books are promotional, rather like some of the writings of Captain John Smith (1580–1631), though Morton's writing is more self-conscious, full of references to Latin mythology and literature. Morton saw himself as a poet, and his prose reflects the identity he assumed.

Nothing in *New English Canaan* thus far prepares a reader for the third book, a history of the Europeans in New England. Now Morton is both satirical and argumentative—also often so obscure that one needs to read the work in the heavily annotated edition of Charles Francis Adams (1835–1915). Showing a strong sense of humor, Morton proffers an extended mock-epic account of New England history. He regularly refers to himself as "mine host," Miles Standish as "Captaine Shrimp," John Endecott as "Captaine Littleworth," and John Winthrop as "Master Tupperwell." Readers of early New England histories have found Morton's *New English Canaan* a healthy antidote to the dour sobriety of such writers as Bradford and Winthrop. Among the attractions of Morton's book are his skills as a satirist and as writer of poetic prose and Ben Jonson-like verse. Morton expresses vigorous opposition to religious intolerance and celebrates individualism and pleasure.

More attractive than his book has been the image that he created of gaiety in the wilderness of New England. "And upon Mayday they brought the Maypole to the place appointed, with drummes, gunnes, pistols and other fitting instruments for that purpose." Englishmen and Native Americans danced together, with a "barrell of excellent beare" at hand. One imagines that meanwhile, not far away to both north and south, Puritans were dedicating themselves to virtue and high seriousness.

• Charles Francis Adams wrote about Morton at length both in his edition of Morton's *New English Canaan* (1883) and in his *Three Episodes of Massachusetts History* (1892). His accounts are corrected in Charles Edward Banks, "Thomas Morton of Merry Mount," *Massachusetts Historical Society Proceedings* 58 (1925): 147–93, and 59 (1926): 92–95; Banks also includes Morton's will and other documents. Donald F. Connors then corrected Banks's account in "Thomas Morton of Merry Mount: His First Arrival in New England," *American Literature* 11 (1939): 160–66. Connors provides an account of *New English Canaan* as literature in his *Thomas Morton* (1969), which includes a useful bibliography. Information about the publication difficulties faced by Morton's book can be found in Paul R. Sternberg, "The Publication of Thomas Morton's *New English Canaan* Reconsidered," *Papers of the Bibliographical Society of America* 80 (1986): 369–74.

EVERETT EMERSON

MORTON, Thruston Ballard (19 Aug. 1907–14 Aug. 1982), Republican political leader, congressman, and U.S. senator, was born in Louisville, Kentucky, the son of David Cummins Morton, a physician, and Mary Harris Ballard. He was raised in an old-line Kentucky family of substantial wealth. Morton attended Woodberry Forest School in Orange, Virginia, and received a bachelor of arts degree from Yale in 1929. In 1931 he married Belle Clay Lyons; they had two sons.

Morton worked in the family's grain and milling business, Ballard and Ballard, and eventually became president in 1946. The prosperous firm was acquired by Pillsbury Mills, Inc., in 1951. Morton enlisted in the navy prior to Pearl Harbor, serving for fifty-one months on minesweepers and destroyers in the Pacific. In 1946 he won election to Kentucky's Third Congressional District seat. A political moderate, Morton often said he was "just two degrees to the left of center." He supported the Harry S. Truman administration's Greek and Turkish aid program, the Marshall Plan, Point Four, and American participation in the North Atlantic Treaty Organization. He also became a vigorous critic of Senator Joseph McCarthy and a defender of established federal social and economic policies and the Tennessee Valley Authority. He attracted considerable attention as a border state Republican when he advocated civil rights legislation at a time when racial segregation remained an integral part of American life. After serving three terms in the House of Representatives, he announced that he would not seek reelection in 1952. He gained favorable notice that fall for his management of the successful campaign of John Sherman Cooper for the U.S. Senate.

Morton joined the Dwight D. Eisenhower administration in 1953 as assistant secretary of state for congressional relations. In this capacity he worked successfully with other administration officials to prevent by a narrow margin Senate passage of the proposed "Bricker amendment" to the Constitution, a complex and controversial proposal that would have required senatorial ratification of executive agreements. His leadership in this effort was roundly denounced by conservative groups, especially the John Birch Society.

In 1956 Morton won election to the U.S. Senate in a narrow, 6,981-vote victory over incumbent Earle Clements. Morton benefited from a serious rift between his opponent and Governor A. B. "Happy" Chandler as well as the coattails of Eisenhower. In the Senate, Morton's middle-of-the-road stance on most issues made him almost a perfect embodiment of Eisenhower's "Modern Republicanism" credo. He was appointed Republican national chairman in 1959, a position he held for two years. He easily won reelection in 1962 and for a time was prominently mentioned as a possible 1964 presidential candidate before he withdrew his name from consideration. Although unhappy with the nomination of staunch conservative Barry Goldwater, Morton loyally supported his party's ticket while serving as chairman of the Republican senatorial campaign. Although he favored civil rights and Great Society programs designed to address poverty in Appalachia, he opposed most of Lyndon Johnson's other domestic programs, apparently motivated largely by partisan considerations. He voted for the Civil Rights Acts of 1964, 1965, and 1968.

Morton initially supported American military involvement in Vietnam but became disenchanted with that policy in 1967, calling for a cessation of bombing in North Vietnam and the withdrawal of American troops. At one point he caustically said that the "military-industrial complex" had "brainwashed" Johnson into believing victory was still possible. In 1968 he served as an adviser to Nelson Rockefeller's campaign for the Republican nomination. In February of that year he shocked political observers when he announced that he would not seek a third term. "To use an old Kentucky expression," he told the press, "I am just plain track sore." Friends privately confirmed that he was suffering from exhaustion and depression, the latter apparently the result of the anguish he felt over the war in Vietnam and its impact on American society.

Upon returning to Louisville, Morton continued his longtime involvement in banking, investment management, and community affairs. Throughout his adult life he was especially active in thoroughbred horse circles, serving as chair of the board of directors of Churchill Downs and president of the American Horse Council. After several years of general declining health, Morton died in Louisville.

• Morton's private papers, containing 296,000 items, are in Special Collections at the University of Kentucky Library in Lexington. An excellent oral history that focuses on the politics of the 1950s is in the John Foster Dulles Collection in the Princeton University Library. A good source of information on Morton is Sara Judith Smiley, "The Political Career of Thruston B. Morton: The Senate Years, 1956–1968" (Ph.D. diss., Univ. of Kentucky, 1975). An obituary is in the *New York Times*, 15 Aug. 1982.

RICHARD O. DAVIES

MORTON, William Thomas Green (9 Aug. 1819–15 July 1868), dentist and introducer of ether anesthesia, was born at Charlton, Massachusetts, the son of James Morton and Rebecca Needham, farmers. In 1840, after early experiences as a clerk and salesman in Boston, Morton studied dentistry at the College of Dental Surgery in Baltimore. In 1842 he set up in practice in Farmington, Connecticut. In the winter of 1842–1843 he practiced jointly with Horace Wells in Boston. In March 1844 Morton matriculated at Harvard Medical School and attended two courses of lectures but never graduated, and he continued to practice as a dentist. In 1844 Morton married Elizabeth Whitman; they had one child, a son.

Morton is best remembered for administering ether to a patient undergoing successful surgery at the Massachusetts General Hospital on 16 October 1846, an event that is clouded in controversy. His attempts to secure for himself all the glory and any profits accruing from the technique resulted in a dispute so virulent that it obscures even some of the basic chronology of the events in the summer and fall of 1846. Morton was by no means the first to administer a general anesthetic agent or to conceive of its surgical uses. By the nineteenth century, surgery, which had long been held to be one of the lesser healing arts, had become a technically complex and, for the most successful practitioners, a socially prestigious occupation. To facilitate their increasingly protracted operations, mainly on bones and joints and on the teeth and jaws, a small number of surgeons and dentists had experimented with anesthetic techniques. Gas chemistry had been created in the late eighteenth century and in 1800 the English chemist Humphry Davy had suggested that the recently discovered gas nitrous oxide might be used with advantage during surgical operations. In the 1820s, in England, Henry Hill Hickman had experimented with gases on animals with the explicit intention of developing surgical anesthesia. In the 1840s mesmeric techniques had successfully been used by a number of surgeons to perform pain-free operations. In 1842 Crawford W. Long, practicing in Jefferson, Georgia, had performed several operations on patients under ether. By the time Morton had come to experiment with anesthesia, the possibility of making surgery pain-free was by no means unrealized.

In December 1844 Horace Wells, Morton's erstwhile partner, had a tooth extracted successfully under nitrous oxide, and thereafter he used the gas on a number of patients. In 1845 he approached Morton, who introduced him to two of the surgeons at Massachusetts General. Wells's demonstration of nitrous oxide anesthesia at the hospital was a failure, possibly because the patient inhaled an insufficient quantity of the gas, and the surgeons were unimpressed. By now Morton also was thinking about the possibility of anesthesia, especially for his own dental work, a great deal of which involved extensive reconstruction. Thus, as his legal adviser Richard H. Dana was later to write, Morton had a "direct pecuniary motive" (Duncum, p. 99) to alleviate pain. Any number of sources could have suggested to Morton that ether was a potentially useful anesthetic. In 1844, before Wells's demonstration, Morton was a student and boarder of Charles T. Jackson, a professor of chemistry at Harvard, and at his suggestion Morton had used ether drops as a local dental anesthetic. Jackson also demonstrated the narcotic power of ether in his chemistry classes, although Morton later claimed to have learned of this power from a standard text on materia medica. Knowledge of ether's properties was widespread, for it was also inhaled for fun at "ether frolics." According to his own account and those of his later supporters, Morton was experimenting secretly with ether vapor through the summer and fall of 1846, first on animals and himself and then on his assistants. By the end of June he was so preoccupied with his ether experiments that he engaged a partner, Grenville G. Hayden, to supervise his dental business. In 1848 Hayden recounted that when the partnership was formed Morton confided that he had an idea of something that "would be one of the greatest things ever known." He further disclosed that this "thing" was a way to extract teeth without pain

(Duncum, p. 100). Hayden reported that it was clear to him that Morton thought that the agent that would effect this possibility was ether. In March 1847 two of Morton's student apprentices recounted the events of the previous summer. One of them, William P. Leavitt, recalled being sent to buy ether in July 1846 and also being instructed to ask the chemist whether ether would affect india-rubber (Wells had used a rubber bag to administer nitrous oxide). The other apprentice, Thomas R. Spear, recalled that in August 1846 he had inhaled ether at Morton's request. It seems clear that at this point Morton was convinced about the value of ether but unhappy with the technical details of its administration. At the end of September a critical episode in the history of etherization occurred; Morton consulted with Jackson about gaseous anesthesia. By his own account, Morton withheld from Jackson at this interview the fact that he, Morton, was experimenting with ether. At the end of October 1846, however, Jackson was claiming that it was at this meeting that he had informed Morton about the anesthetic power of ether. All the evidence, except for Jackson's own, points against this being the case, but it does seem clear that Morton had gleaned some valuable information from Jackson, either about anesthetic administration or about ether preparations.

On 30 September a willing patient, Eben H. Frost, was anesthetized with ether by Morton and had a tooth extracted. Morton immediately tried to patent etherization. Frost had been anesthetized by ether dropped on a handkerchief. Subsequent attempts to anesthetize patients in this way were failures, and Morton constructed an inhaler. Morton now sought to bring his technique to public notice and he contacted the senior surgeon at Massachusetts General, John Collins Warren. Warren expressed interest in Morton's work, even though Morton kept his agent a secret. Morton was promised an opportunity to demonstrate. On 15 October Morton worked frenetically on his inhaler. The next day Warren removed a tumor from the neck of a young man anesthetized by Morton using an ether-soaked sponge contained in a glass vessel. Afterward Warren is said to have made the famous remark, "Gentlemen this is no humbug." A second operation, to remove a tumor from a woman's arm, was completed successfully the following day. The surgeons at the hospital endorsed the value of the technique, and Morton frantically attempted to exploit his success. On 19 October he wrote to Wells that he had successfully carried out more than 160 dental extractions under his "preparation" (Duncum, p. 111).

Rumors of the Boston experiment abounded, and Morton received so many letters inquiring about his technique that he was obliged to employ a secretary. He published pamphlets recording successful cases and had a great number of inhalers made. His agent, sulfuric ether, was still his secret, and he was still without a patent. Jackson now claimed joint priority for the discovery of the technique. Jackson, a Harvard professor, was a man of influence in Boston with friends at the patent office. Morton was persuaded that with Jackson's name on the patent greater personal benefit might accrue, and with some reluctance he applied for a joint patent on 27 October. The patentees claimed they had "invented or discovered" that sulfuric ether could abolish the pain of surgical operations (Duncum, Appendix A). The inhaler also was patented. Jackson immediately agreed to assign all his rights in the patent to Morton, for which concession Jackson was to receive 10 percent of the profits from American sales of the patent. A second joint patent to cover sales abroad was also issued. The surgeons of Massachusetts General Hospital, meanwhile, denounced Morton's secrecy and marketing strategy and banned the use of Morton's agent in the hospital. He, in need of their support, agreed that they were not to be bound by the patent. On 7 November an amputation was performed under ether at the hospital. On 15 November Jackson began to claim that Morton had merely acted on Jackson's instructions from the beginning. On 18 November the surgeon Henry Jacob Bigelow announced the success of the technique in the *Boston Medical and Surgical Journal*. At a meeting at the hospital between Morton and Bigelow and Dr. Oliver Wendell Holmes on 21 November, Morton's secret agent was designated Letheon.

By now Jackson was attempting to ensure for himself the profits from any European sales. Wells also entered the fray, claiming in print that he was the originator of the principle of gaseous inhalation for pain-free surgery. The next twenty years of Morton's life were spent in bitter litigious controversy. Instead of making a fortune he soon fell into debt, having neglected his dental business. Around 1850 he took up farming but continued his as yet unsuccessful attempt to enforce his patent, the government itself having infringed it; both the army and the navy had used etherization without permission or payment. Applications by Morton to Congress for financial reward failed to produce a result. In 1852 Crawford Long's supporters persuaded him to claim priority for the use of ether. On 19 April 1854, a bill passed the Senate "to recompense the discoverer of practical anaesthesia." But on the grounds of "multiplicity of claimants"—Morton, Jackson, Long, Wells—it was rejected by the House of Representatives (Duncum, p. 128). Shortly after this, Morton received personal assurances from President Pierce that the patent would be protected. In 1858, on the basis of this assurance, Morton, heavily in debt, initiated a test case against the government, specifically against the superintendent of the United States Marine Hospital at Chelsea, near Boston. The government, however, failed to come to his aid, and in 1862 the case was dismissed on the grounds that the patent was not valid. Morton lived in poverty on his farm from 1862 until 1868, when a pamphlet from Jackson prompted him to file a suit in New York. His death, brought on by a stroke in New York City, relieved him of further litigation.

Morton lived in a world in which the paying patient was the key to medical and dental success. Competition was fierce, and the most successful practitioner was the one who could offer some unique service to his clientele. Morton also lived in a world that regarded and rewarded discovery as the fruit of individual dedication and genius. In spite of his knowledge of the endeavors of others, Morton saw himself as the sole discoverer of inhalational anesthesia. It was acting on this perception that destroyed Morton. Discovery is not a momentary intervention by a unique individual, however, but a process. It is clear that Morton had an important place as midwife to anesthesia. It was not a role that no one else could have played. Much wider determinants were at work. Morton's work was spawned by very general changes in the practice of surgery, and by very local influences on the practice of dentistry. He doggedly dedicated himself to realizing a principle that was not enunciated solely by him or anyone else, and he promoted an agent that had not been discovered by him or whose actions were known only to him. No one person "discovered" anesthesia. Morton did, however, make an early persuasive public demonstration of the power of ether to restrict pain during surgical operations.

• A volume of Morton's letters and papers relating to ether is in the Massachusetts Historical Society, Boston. Morton's published works, and early works about him, are nearly all polemical interventions into the priority dispute. From 26 Nov. 1846 he published, usually weekly, *Circular: Morton's Letheon*, containing the results of his researches (see the back page of the *Boston Medical and Surgical Journal*, 9 Dec. 1846). Morton began to include in these sheets correspondence and news clippings, and they were then reissued in pamphlet form (first ed., 1846) with the same title and the significant subtitle *Cautioning Those Who Attempt to Infringe upon His Legal Rights*. In 1847 he published *Remarks on the Proper Mode of Administering Sulphuric Ether by Inhalation*. In the same year from Paris a pamphlet appeared documenting Morton's claims, *Mémoire sur la Découverte du Nouvel Emploi de l'Éther Sulfurique Suivi des Pièces Justificatives*. In 1850 he issued a brochure in response to James Young Simpson's claims for chloroform, *On the Physiological Effects of Sulphuric Ether and Its Superiority to Chloroform*. In the same year also appeared *Remarks on the Comparative Value of Ether and Chloroform, with Hints upon Natural and Artificial Teeth*. *The Index-Catalogue of the Library of the Surgeon General's Office* also lists a dental publication from 1848, the second edition of *On the Loss of the Teeth and the Modern Way of Restoring Them*. Early accounts of Morton's career are all polemical, including B. P. Poore, *Historical Materials for the Biography of W. T. G. Morton* (1856); N. P. Rice, *Trials of a Public Benefactor, as Illustrated by the Discovery of Etherization* (1859); and H. J. Bigelow, "A History of the Discovery of Modern Anaesthesia," in *A Century of American Medicine* (1876). Pamphlets relating to the priority dispute can be found in the annotated catalog by John F. Fulton and Madeline E. Stanton, *The Centennial of Surgical Anesthesia* (1946). The best modern secondary source dealing with the early history of anesthesia is, without question, Barbara M. Duncum, *The Development of Inhalation Anaesthesia* (1947).

CHRISTOPHER LAWRENCE

MOSBY, John Singleton (6 Dec. 1833–30 May 1916), Confederate partisan officer, was born in Powhatan County, Virginia, the son of Alfred D. Mosby and Virginia McLaurine, farmers. When John was five or six years old, his father moved the family to Albemarle County, where he prospered. John attended local schools before enrolling at the University of Virginia in 1850. In March 1853 Mosby shot and wounded a man. He was found guilty of "unlawful shooting" and spent nearly seven months in jail. Upon his release in December, he read law at the office of his prosecutor, William J. Robertson, and then opened a practice in Howardsville. In 1858 he moved to Bristoe with his bride, Pauline Clarke, daughter of a former congressman and diplomat from Kentucky. They had eight children.

When Virginia seceded in April 1861, Mosby volunteered as a private in Company D, First Virginia Cavalry. The regiment fought at First Manassas, and during the next year Mosby rose to the rank of lieutenant, serving briefly as the regiment's adjutant. In April 1862, when an officer whom Mosby disliked assumed command of the regiment, he resigned his commission. An excellent scout, Mosby unofficially joined the staff of J. E. B. Stuart, commander of the Confederate army cavalry. Throughout the summer and fall, Mosby performed valuable scouting and reconnaissance duties for Stuart.

On 31 December 1862 Mosby received permission from Stuart to conduct guerrilla operations behind Union lines in northern Virginia. Mosby began with a nucleus of nine men—soon increased to fifteen—that eventually evolved into the 43d Battalion of Virginia Cavalry. For the next twenty-eight months, operating from a base in the Virginia counties of Fauquier and Loudoun that became known as "Mosby's Confederacy," Mosby and his rangers rode forth in raids against enemy supply lines, railroad and wagon trains, outposts, and detachments. The command provided Robert E. Lee with valuable intelligence information, seized hundreds of thousands of dollars worth of federal material, and captured thousands of enemy troops. Mosby never surrendered, disbanding the battalion on 21 April 1865, twelve days after Lee surrendered at Appomattox.

Mosby began a legal practice in Warrenton after the war. He eventually became friends with President Ulysses S. Grant, joined the Republican party, and served in various government posts. He served as a consul in Hong Kong, a lawyer in the General Land Office, and an assistant attorney in the Department of Justice. Many southerners condemned him for his actions, but his reputation as a Confederate officer silenced much overt criticism. He wrote *Stuart's Cavalry in the Gettysburg Campaign* (1908) and *The Memoirs of Colonel John S. Mosby*, published in 1917 after his death. Mosby died in Washington, D.C.

John Mosby was one of the finest guerrilla officers in American military history. Small and thin, he possessed a keen intellect and a fearless nature. He created the 43d Battalion, planned its operations, and disciplined its members. A restless man, he fought the war as if it were a personal conflict. Warfare suited him, and he emerged from it as a matchless partisan commander. Unlike some partisans, however, he did not engage in ruthless efforts against civilians. A pragmatist, Mosby accepted the defeat of the Confederacy and chose to heal wounds. He saw no conflict in accepting a Republican post.

• Collections of Mosby letters and manuscripts are located at the University of Virginia; Duke University; the Virginia Historical Society; and the General Stuart–Colonel Mosby Museum, American Historical Foundation, Richmond. Several memoirs by members of his command have been published, the best being John Scott, *Partisan Life with Col. John S. Mosby* (1867), and James J. Williamson, *Mosby's Rangers* (1896; 2d ed. 1909). A popularly written but undocumented biography of Mosby is Virgil Carrington Jones, *Ranger Mosby* (1944). Kevin H. Siepel, *Rebel: The Life and Times of John Singleton Mosby* (1983), provides an excellent account of Mosby's postwar years. The most recent work on Mosby and the battalion is Jeffry D. Wert, *Mosby's Rangers* (1990), a scholarly study of the command's wartime operations.

JEFFRY D. WERT

MOSCHZISKER, Robert von. *See* Von Moschzisker, Robert.

MOSCONE, George Richard (24 Nov. 1929–27 Nov. 1978), mayor of San Francisco, was born in San Francisco, California, the son of George J. Moscone, a guard at San Quentin Prison, and Lena "Lee" Monge. Moscone graduated from St. Brigid Elementary School and St. Ignatius High School. From a family of modest means, he won an athletic scholarship to the College of the Pacific (later University of the Pacific), where he received a B.A. in 1952, and an academic scholarship to the Hastings College of the Law, where he received a J.D. and an LL.B. in 1956. In 1954 he married Eugenia "Gina" Bondanza; they had four children.

Following service in the U.S. Navy, Moscone practiced law in San Francisco from 1957 to 1963, when he was elected to the board of supervisors, the governing body for the county and city of San Francisco. A skilled politician and coalition builder, he ascended steadily in the city's Democratic party power structure. In 1966 he was elected to the California Senate, where he served for nine years, rising to the position of majority leader. In the state senate he distinguished himself as an advocate of nutrition programs for children and an early proponent of government intervention on issues of marital and family violence as chairman of the senate's Subcommittee on Nutrition and Human Needs.

In 1975 Moscone was elected mayor of San Francisco. His brief administration was marked by outreach to the city's increasingly vocal gay community and advocacy for the city's poor and disadvantaged. Just a few days before his assassination his administration was rocked by the mass suicide in Jonestown, Guyana, of members of the People's Temple, recently relocated to the South American jungle from San Francisco. The Reverend Jim Jones, the charismatic leader of the People's Temple and instigator of his congregation's final self-destructive act, was a former Moscone appointee as head of the San Francisco Housing Authority. Moscone, along with many other San Francisco political leaders, deferred to Jones as a populist spokesman for a sizable segment of the city's poor. But Jones, an ostensibly humanitarian religious visionary, proved to be a deranged cult leader. California congressman Leo Ryan, a Moscone ally, was murdered in Jonestown.

On 27 November 1978 former San Francisco supervisor Dan White murdered Moscone in the mayor's office at San Francisco City Hall. Moments later White also murdered Supervisor Harvey Milk, the city's first openly gay elected official and a national leader of the emerging gay rights movement. White, a handsome, 32-year-old, clean-cut former city police officer and firefighter, was a law-and-order conservative often at odds with the progressive mayor. Unable to support his family on a supervisor's salary of $9,600, White resigned his position just over two weeks before he murdered Moscone and Milk. White almost immediately regretted giving up his seat on the board of supervisors and unsuccessfully lobbied Mayor Moscone to reappoint him to the post. Moscone was scheduled to announce the appointment of Don Horanzy, a political ally, to White's vacant seat on the day White killed him.

White won his seat on the board of supervisors from a blue-collar district in an overtly antigay campaign. On the board, White often clashed with his colleague Milk, although the two maintained an outwardly congenial relationship. Milk was originally a close political ally of Moscone, and White may have suspected Milk of influencing the mayor against his bid for reappointment. Ironically, the relationship between Moscone and Milk was quite strained at the time of the murders. Moscone gave Milk's political career a major boost in 1975 when he appointed Milk to the city's board of permit appeals, making Milk the first openly gay city commissioner in the United States. But the mayor soon disavowed his controversial appointee when Milk decided to run for the state assembly against Art Agnos, Moscone's choice for the assembly seat, less than five weeks after taking office on the board of permit appeals. When Milk was elected to the board of supervisors in 1977, he and Moscone were frequent allies because of the convergence of their political views, but their relationship remained formal and cautious.

• Useful oral histories of Moscone's life and career were compiled under the auspices of the Regional Oral History Office of the Bancroft Library of the University of California, Berkeley, and are available at that library and at the California State Archives in Sacramento. A brief biographical entry on Moscone is in Gladys Hansen, ed., *San Francisco Almanac* (1995). Events surrounding his assassination are explored in detail in Mike Weiss, *Double Play: The San Francisco City Hall Killings* (1984), and in a play by Emily Mann, *Execution of Justice* (1986). A retrospective on the Moscone assassination is Paul Krassner, "The Milk-Moscone Case Revisited," *Nation*, 14 Jan. 1984, pp. 9–12. Extended obituaries, including assassination details and analysis of his career, are in *Time*, 11 Dec. 1978, pp. 24–26; *Newsweek*, 11 Dec. 1978, pp. 26–28; *U.S. News and World Report*, 11 Dec. 1978, pp. 22–24; and *Rolling Stone*, 25 Jan. 1979, pp. 45–46.

FREDERICK J. SIMONELLI

MOSCONI, Willie (27 June 1913–16 Sept. 1993), pocket billiards champion, was born William Joseph Mosconi in Philadelphia, Pennsylvania, the son of Joseph William Mosconi, a boxing trainer and pool hall owner, and Helen (maiden name unknown). Mosconi was born to the game of pocket billiards, being raised over a gymnasium where a pool table was available to the boxers his father trained. His father, who hoped that Willie would eventually join his uncles in their vaudeville act, resisted Willie's learning the game because it had a bad reputation. But when the boy sneaked out of his room to play pool with a broom handle for a cue and potatoes for pool balls, his father conceded. He began to display his inborn talent on the table owned by one of his uncles, a vaudevillian and dance instructor. His uncle's show business background motivated him to use Willie's talent in public, and as a six-year-old prodigy Willie soon defeated most local players, although he had to stand on a crate to make most of his shots. He made a good income for his family in these exhibitions and even played against billiards champion Ralph Greenleaf, but he "retired" at age 10 to pursue more normal childhood interests.

After attending public school in Philadelphia and, for a short time, Banks College, Mosconi ended his formal education in order to take care of his ailing parents. He became the family breadwinner at the beginning of the Great Depression by working at an upholstery shop for a family friend. Following an argument with his boss in late 1931, he quit his job and entered a pool tournament, easily winning the $75 first prize. He began to play in every tournament in Philadelphia, making as much money as he had upholstering. Deciding that he had enough talent to play full-time, he entered his first World Championship in 1933. He won the regional title in New York, then qualified for the nationals in Minneapolis. He then advanced to the World Championship in Chicago, where he lost his first game by one ball and the tournament by one game. Mosconi's fourth-place performance attracted the attention of the management of Brunswick-Balke-Collender, the leading manufacturer of billiard tables. The company paid him $600 a month to travel the country with twenty other professionals giving exhibitions. In his first tour Mosconi was paired with Greenleaf, his opponent during childhood; by the end of the tour Mosconi was regularly defeating Greenleaf. Playing against Greenleaf proved valuable for Mosconi. He acquired the maturity necessary to hone his raw talent and learned how to handle the pressures of constant travel and performance.

Throughout the 1930s Mosconi could defeat the top players in the world, but he did not win any championship tournaments. In 1939 he retired from competition and moved to California. The following year he married Ann Harrison; they had two children. Finding no work in California, Mosconi played in a series of exhibitions against Greenleaf. In 1941 he won his first championship, a marathon 224 games in several cities over six months. In this tournament Mosconi proved to be a master, as he consecutively ran the winning 125 balls five times, on one occasion doing so in 30 minutes. This accomplishment was the pocket billiard equivalent of Joe DiMaggio's 56-game hitting streak and Ted Williams's .400 batting average. Mosconi defended his championship in 1942 and won the title again in 1944 and 1945.

Following the outbreak of World War II, Mosconi moved to his wife's home state of Michigan and took a job in a defense plant. A factory accident badly cut a finger on his left hand, but he managed to avoid any ligament damage, which could have ended his pool career. He changed to a less dangerous job, but it was so dull that he made himself available for the draft. Inducted into the U.S. Army in early 1945, he had no overseas duty. He had given exhibitions for soldiers prior to his induction and continued to do so while in the service. Mosconi left the army on a hardship discharge shortly after the war ended; his wife had abandoned him and his two children, and she had disappeared.

Mosconi moved with his children to New Jersey, living with his brother's family and sister's family in their father's house. He went back on the road, giving demonstrations and representing Brunswick. After the war there was a huge upsurge in the popularity of billiards, but only Irving Crane was talented enough to challenge Mosconi's hold on the title. With the exception of one tournament loss in 1949, Mosconi dominated the game for fifteen years. In 1953 he married Flora Marchini; they had one child. In 1954, in the midst of a slump in interest in the game, the Billiard Congress of America (BCA) ceased its sponsorship of world championship tournaments. When Crane attempted that same year to hold his own tournament and bill it as the world championship, Mosconi stood by the BCA and brought suit in federal court against Crane. The two professional rivals became personal rivals as well, especially when Crane defeated Mosconi in a sanctioned tournament in 1954; an overwhelming victory by Mosconi in a challenge match returned the title to him the following year. His final tournament victory was in 1956, after which several years passed without the BCA sponsoring any championships. The following year Mosconi suffered a stroke, and he retired permanently from competition.

The popularity of pocket billiards returned with a vengeance after the 1962 release of the motion picture *The Hustler*, for which Mosconi was technical adviser. In this capacity Mosconi gave private lessons to the film's star, Paul Newman, who had never held a pool cue. Within four months Newman proved a talented student and became a skilled player. *The Hustler* proved such a popular film that Brunswick rehired Mosconi to go back on the exhibition circuit. Now in his sixties Mosconi was retired, but he came back for one tournament in 1966; his second-place finish convinced him that he did not have the necessary drive to play at the level he expected from himself.

In the late 1970s Mosconi returned to the public eye as an expert commentator for ABC television in a number of matches featuring self-promoting pool hustler Minnesota Fats. Fats's claim that he had consistently beaten all the great players irked Mosconi, who challenged him in public to play anytime, anywhere, for any amount of money. His $100,000 challenge failed to draw a response from Fats. The two eventually did meet in 1978 through the auspices of ABC, and Mosconi won handily. Although he had little respect for Fats, Mosconi accepted the offer to go on national tour with him in a series of televised matches.

Mosconi received a small speaking part in the movie *The Baltimore Bullet* (1979) and was brought back as adviser for *The Color of Money* (1988), the sequel to *The Hustler*. His representation of sporting goods companies and his occasional television appearances brought him the best income of his life. He spent a few years as a professional host for Harrah's casino in New Jersey, but it was not to his liking. He retired completely but for a few exhibitions per year. He died in Haddon Heights, New Jersey.

Mosconi loved and respected the game of pool, but he always viewed it as a job in which he excelled and could make a decent living. He could walk away from the game periodically and not miss it, but when playing he had an intensity that was almost frightening to his opponents. No pool player in the twentieth century could match his number of championships or records in shooting.

• The most complete account of Mosconi's life is his autobiography, *Willie's Game*, written with Stanley Cohen (1993). Mosconi wrote two books on pool-shooting techniques, *Willie Mosconi on Pocket Billiards* (1954) and *Winning Pocket Billiards* (1957).

PAUL K. DAVIS

MOSES (1829?–25 Mar. 1899), chief of the Columbia Sinkiuses, a band of Interior Salish speakers of the mid–Columbia River in present-day Washington State, was the son of Sulktalthscosum (Piece Split from the Sun, or Half-Sun), a powerful Columbia River Plateau chief, and Karneetsa (Between the Robes), his favorite wife, a half-Spokane. Moses bore the childhood name Loolowkin. In native fashion he bore other names during his lifetime, the most important of which was that of his chieftain father. The name Moses, by which he was known to white settlers, was given to him by the Reverend Henry H. Spalding when for a short time he attended Spalding's American Board mission school at Lapwai (Idaho).

Moses was said to have been born in the general area of the confluence of the Columbia and Wenatchee rivers. The natives were cited by Merriwether Lewis and William Clark as having been at the Long Narrows of the lower Columbia when these explorers were there in 1805. Apparently the first white person to visit Moses's people in their Columbia River homeland was David Thompson of the North West Company on his "Journey of a Summer Moon" down the Columbia in 1811. Thereafter, Moses's people had contact with Astorian fur traders, other "Nor'Westers," and after 1818, men of the Hudson's Bay Company who introduced to them such things as cattle and potatoes.

Horses, which Moses's ancestors had acquired around 1750, enabled the Sinkiuses to travel to the Great Plains to hunt buffalo. Like other peoples of the Columbia Plateau they became expert horsemen. On one of his people's journeys "to buffalo," Moses, despite his youth, was said to have dispatched a full-grown Blackfeet warrior with a knife. Around 1850 his father was killed in a continuing revenge cycle pitting warriors of the plateau against those of the plains.

Like other young men of his tribe Moses was involved in conflict with encroaching white settlers. Following the Indian wars (1855–1858) he confessed that during these conflicts his hands had been "dipped in blood." These wars had followed treaties effected by U.S. officials and coast and plateau Indians. Headmen of the latter had signed these pacts in the Walla Walla valley in 1855, but disgruntled at having alienated their vast lands, they sought to turn the tide of post-treaty white invasion and restore their lands to their aboriginal purity. It was during this time of troubles that Yakima Chief Kamiakin assumed leadership of warring tribal elements, including that of Moses, and brought them together in opposition to federal troops and territorial volunteers. Following the death of his older brother, Quiltenenock, at the hands of Canada-bound miners in 1858, Moses assumed leadership of the nontreaty peoples of the mid-Columbia. By that time he had abandoned his belligerent stance against white people and their government, very possibly remembering the words of his former tutor, Henry Spalding, that the approaching settlers were as numerous as sands of the sea or leaves of the trees.

Moses's peaceful posture, however, was threatened during two conflicts; one involved his friend, the Nez Percé Chief Joseph in 1877, and the other involved the Bannock-Paiute-Umatillas the following year. White cattlemen and others seeking to oust Indians from Columbia Plateau grasslands had accused Moses of killing a white couple actually slain by Umatillas fleeing northward after their defeat by American forces. After a brief incarceration in a Yakima reservation jail, Moses, the shrewd negotiator, sought a favorable settlement of the conflict with white settlers in conferences with General Oliver O. Howard of the U.S. Army. For his agreement to not go on the warpath Moses received promises of land and many gratuities from the government for himself and his followers. During a visit to Washington, D.C., in 1879 he received from government officials the Columbia Reservation (also known as the Moses Reservation) stretching north from Lake Chelan to the Canadian border. After its northern portions were withdrawn by an agreement on 7 July 1883, the entire reservation was restored to the public domain. Moses had never moved his followers onto the reservation but did collect rents from white cattlemen who ran their herds on it.

During his second journey to the national capital in 1883 Moses wrangled from the government a promise to settle himself and his people on the Colville Reservation just east of the Columbia Reservation. In Washington he also managed to secure benefits for his people and a $1,000 annuity for himself. Indians of the Colville, such as Okanagons, Sanpoils, and Nespelems, were unhappy with Moses, whom they considered an intruder in their midst. They also did not take kindly to the 1885 arrival of Chief Joseph and his band under Moses's auspices, who were returning to the West from confinement in Indian Territory (Oklahoma) following their retreat from government forces in 1877.

On the Colville, Moses and his people awkwardly tried to accede to the government's wish to make farmers of them; these proud former mounted tribesmen undertook the tasks with little enthusiasm. In fact some of their government-provided equipment was never used and eventually came into the hands of white farmers in the Big Bend country of the Columbia to the south. A poor role model for these would-be agrarians, Moses sought pleasurable escape at various white Fourth of July celebrations attired in the best Indian finery, his shirts adorned with celestial body trappings. Perhaps he so accoutred himself because of his friendship with Francis Streamer, who in the latter nineteenth century traveled throughout Indian country, writing Moses's letters to the government enumerating his various complaints. Streamer not only served as Moses's amanuensis but believed himself to be an intermediary between solar powers and the Indians. At various celebrations Moses, now too obese to race horses, was at the forefront wagering on his favorite riders and mounts. Such gatherings stimulated his consumption of liquor, which he rationalized as proper since it was produced, introduced, and consumed by white men.

Moses succumbed to a respiratory disorder. Long after his death his numerous progeny continued to lionize him. The non-Indian community also remembered him for his friendship to white settlers, and in 1989 at the time of the Washington State Centennial he was named to the Hall of Honor. In Washington State his name has been given to a city, its surrounding lake, and a coulee.

• Biographical writings on Moses include Robert H. Ruby and John A. Brown, *Half-Sun on the Columbia: A Biography of Chief Moses* (1965), and "In Search of Chief Moses's Lost Possessions—Stolen from His Grave," *Columbia, the Magazine of Northwest History* 1, no. 3 (Summer 1992): 21–28. Further information on Moses and his times can be found in Jessie A. Bloodworth, "Human Resources Survey of the Colville Confederated Tribes," *Field Report of the Bureau of Indian Affairs*, Portland Area Office, Colville Agency, Nespelem, Washington (1959); Ann Briley, *Lonely Pedestrian: Francis Marion Streamer* (1986); M. Gidley, *Kopet: A Documentary Narrative of Chief Joseph's Last Years* (1981); M. Gidley, *With One Sky above Us: Life on an Indian Reservation at the Turn of the Century* (1979); and Ruth Scofield, *Behind the Buckskin Curtain* (1977).

ROBERT H. RUBY

MOSES, Franklin J., Jr. (1838–11 Dec. 1906), politician, was born Franklin Israel Moses (he substituted the initial "J." for his middle name) in Sumter District, South Carolina, the son of Franklin J. Moses, a lawyer and judge, and Jane McLelland. In 1853 Moses enrolled in South Carolina College, but he did not complete a degree. He married Emma Buford Richardson, also of Sumter, on 20 December 1859. They had at least one child, a daughter. A year after his marriage he entered politics when, as an avid secessionist, he became the personal secretary of Governor Francis W. Pickens, serving through the expiration of Pickens's term in 1862. Conflicting accounts relate that Moses raised the Palmetto and Confederate flags over Fort Sumter in April 1861. During the war he was conscripted into the Confederate army, rose to the rank of colonel, and served as an enrolling officer.

In 1866 Moses resumed his career in politics, acting as secretary at the convention to endorse President Johnson's Reconstruction policy. He promoted Johnson's conservative program as editor of the *Sumter News* in 1866 and 1867. In addition, he was admitted to the state bar on 28 November 1866.

At this point Moses abandoned the policies of his white southern colleagues and became a Radical Republican, earning the epithet "scalawag." His alliance with the Radicals paid off when he was elected a delegate to the state constitutional convention of 1868. Gaining support of the Union Leagues, secret societies organized to garner African-American support for Radicals, he laid the groundwork for his rise in Reconstruction politics when he opposed a poll tax to fund public education on the grounds that it could disenfranchise African-American voters. At the convention, nominations were made for state legislators, resulting in a Republican slate of candidates that mirrored the membership of the convention. When the election was held, only those voting in favor of the new constitution could choose legislators. The result was a Republican-controlled general assembly and a position for Moses in the state house of representatives. Although African Americans constituted a numerical majority in the Reconstruction legislature, the limits of their political power were apparent when Moses defeated Robert Brown Elliott, an African-American representative, for the speakership on the first ballot.

While speaker, Moses was appointed adjutant and inspector-general of the state militia by Governor Robert K. Scott. In both positions, Moses used political power for personal aggrandizement. He contracted with gun manufacturers for the refurbishing of 10,000 state muskets and earned a "royalty" of $10,000 drawn from public funds. As speaker, he took bribes to orchestrate house proceedings, including blocking an impeachment resolution against Governor Scott in return for the governor's canceling a personal debt owed him by Moses. These abuses of power went largely unpunished; at the Republican state convention of 1872, Moses was named candidate for governor with the support of African-American delegates, especially chairman Robert B. Elliott. His nomination resulted in a Republican party split, as bolters followed the lead of former governor James L. Orr and denounced the abuses of the Scott administration. Because the opposition did not field a candidate, Republican factionalism resulted in a party contest, and, with the support of African-American voters, Moses defeated the Reform Radical candidate Reuben Tomlinson.

Like his tenure in the legislature, Moses's gubernatorial administration was marked by corruption. He bought a $40,000 mansion in Columbia and used public funds to finance his growing personal debt. He sold pardons, releasing hundreds of convicts. He diverted state money to his personal creditors by issuing warrants on a contingent fund the governor controlled; this practice resulted in a scandal when a warrant was issued for Moses's arrest for misuse of the contingent fund. He resisted arrest by calling out the state militia for his protection; a trial found that charges could not be brought against Moses unless he was impeached by the legislature, which he controlled.

Throughout the country, Moses's administration came to symbolize corruption in the Reconstructed South. Thomas Nast satirized South Carolina's political corruption in the pages of *Harper's Weekly*, and James S. Pike, a Republican and journalist for the *New York Tribune*, imparted condemning, if racist, descriptions of the administration in *The Prostrate State*. As the "Robber Governor" (Thompson), Moses contributed to the failure of Reconstruction in South Carolina by personifying the failures of the political system for both Democratic and Republican opposition. Held in disrepute by citizens of both his native state and the nation, he was thoroughly discredited and had no chance of reelection when his term concluded in 1874.

Moses's life then began a prolonged downward spiral. Extravagance in his personal life contributed to debts of almost $100,000, which caused him to file for bankruptcy in 1875. In the same year he was elected circuit judge by the legislature, but his successor, Governor Daniel Chamberlain, refused to grant his commission. When the Democrats gained control of the state in 1877 and conducted an investigation of the Radical Republican administrations, Moses alienated his remaining supporters when he testified against his former colleagues. His wife divorced him in 1878 after he stole household property and deserted her to live with a prostitute. Members of his family changed their surname to Hanby in disgrace.

Leaving South Carolina, Moses moved among cities in the North, attempting to support himself and a drug habit by minor jobs in journalism and, more often, by fraud and petty larceny. The former governor was incarcerated in New York, Cambridge, Boston, Chicago, and Detroit. He eventually settled in Winthrop, Massachusetts, where he returned to his earlier vocation as a writer and edited the *Winthrop Sun* (1892–1905). He also served sporadically as town moderator. When his editorship ended, he was hired briefly by the owner of the *Boston Daily Tribune* to write a history of Reconstruction. Moses then entered into a conspiracy with associates to profit by financially ruining his employer. At the time of his death, he was unemployed and living in poverty in a Winthrop boardinghouse. His death certificate testified to his fall: the former governor was identified as a white male writer who was born in Charleston of unknown parentage and died of accidental poisoning by either opium or gas. Moses's notorious political career and the disreputable years that followed symbolize the decline in public morality in the years after the Civil War.

• The most complete treatment of the life of Moses is R. H. Woody, "Franklin J. Moses, Jr., Scalawag Governor of South Carolina, 1872–1874," *North Carolina Historical Review* 10 (1933): 111–32. Francis Butler Simkins and Robert Hilliard Woody, *South Carolina during Reconstruction* (1932), is the classic work on the era. For Moses's role as secretary to Pickens, see John B. Edmunds, Jr., *Francis W. Pickens and the Politics of Destruction* (1986), and C. Vann Woodward, *Mary Chesnut's Civil War* (1981). Henry T. Thompson describes Moses's failures as speaker and governor in his critical if biased consideration of Radical Republicans, *Ousting the Carpetbagger from South Carolina* (1927). Additional sources include Richard Zuczek, *State of Rebellion: Reconstruction in South Carolina* (1996); Richard Nelson Current, *Those Terrible Carpetbaggers* (1988); Thomas Holt, *Black over White: Negro Political Leadership in South Carolina during Reconstruction* (1977); and Peggy Lamson, *The Glorious Failure: Black Congressman Robert Brown Elliott and the Reconstruction of South Carolina* (1973). Primary sources include Moses's 1877 testimony against his former colleagues in *Report of the Joint Investigating Committee on Public Frauds, 1868–1877* (1878). See James S. Pike, *The Prostrate State: South Carolina under Negro Government* (1874), for a northern journalist's account of the era. Moses's infamous later career is mentioned in Edward P. Mitchell, *Memoirs of an Editor* (1924). Obituaries are in the *Columbia State* and the *Charleston News and Courier*, 12 Dec. 1906.

CHRISTINE DOYLE

MOSES, Grandma (7 Sept. 1860–13 Dec. 1961), painter, was born Anna Mary Robertson on a farm in Washington County, New York, the daughter of Russell King Robertson, a flax grower, and Margaret Shannahan. Like her nine brothers and sisters and other farm children during that era, she attended school sporadically. As a child, she loved to draw pictures and color them with grape and berry juice. Her father, who encouraged his children's artistic talents by providing them with blank sheets of newsprint, admired her work; her mother, however, told her to spend her time in more practical pursuits.

In her early teens Anna Mary Robertson was hired out to a neighboring farm. In 1887 she married Thomas Moses, the hired man on the same farm. Traveling north after a wedding trip to North Carolina, they decided to settle in the Shenandoah Valley, near Staunton, Virginia, and rented a farm with $600 in savings.

After eighteen years there, during which Moses gave birth to ten children (only five survived to adulthood), the couple returned to New York State and in 1905 bought a farm in Eagle Bridge, not far from her childhood home. Following the death of her husband in 1927, Moses remained at the farm, which she ran with the help of several of her children.

In her late seventies Moses retired from farmwork and, at the suggestion of a daughter, began to make embroidered pictures to pass the time. Advanced arthritis in her hands soon made it impossible for Moses to hold a needle, however, and one of her sisters, recalling how Moses had loved to draw and color as a child, suggested that she make pictures with oil paint. Thus, at the age of seventy-eight, the woman known to family and friends as Grandma Moses became a painter.

Grandma Moses painted her first work on thresher cloth using old paint she had found in the barn. At her sister's urging she purchased a box of artist's paints and brushes from a mail-order house and then began to copy illustrated postcards and Currier and Ives prints using masonite as a surface. She soon turned to subjects from her own experience, painting primitive rural scenes that combined landscapes with figures engaged in such everyday activities as apple picking and collecting maple sugar. She gave most of her paintings away but sold some locally for modest amounts.

Louis Caldor, an engineer and art collector from New York City, was traveling upstate in 1939 when he came upon a for-sale display in a drugstore window in Hoosick Falls, New York. Four of Moses's paintings were in the display, and he bought them all. The next day he drove to the Moses farm, where he bought fifteen more. In October of that year he loaned three of the paintings to the Museum of Modern Art in New York for inclusion in an exhibition called Contemporary Unknown Painters.

The paintings of Grandma Moses had immediate and wide appeal, perhaps due to their nostalgic evocation of an earlier time and an America that was far removed from the depression and the threat of war. In October 1940 the Galérie St. Étienne in New York staged a one-woman show of thirty-five of Moses's masonite paintings, all mounted in old mirror frames from the family attic. A month later, Gimbel's, a New York department store, held a Thanksgiving exhibit of her pictures, along with her preserves and jams. The eighty-year-old Moses, on her first visit to New York in twenty-two years, opened the exhibit and addressed visitors. She ignored her pictures, however, and instead charmed those in attendance with a discourse on canning and preserving.

From the start Grandma Moses's paintings were appreciated by critics as well as the general public. Favorable reviews followed her first show in 1940, after which she was often cited as America's leading folk painter. Through the years art critics commented most often on her eye for color; they also praised improvements in the spatial arrangement of her scenes.

The career of Grandma Moses was carefully managed by Otto Kallir, director of the Galérie St. Étienne, who bought her entire output of more than fifteen hundred canvases. Between 1940 and 1961 he staged hundreds of individual and group exhibitions throughout the United States and during the early 1950s, fifteen different exhibits in major European cities. Kallir also helped establish Grandma Moses Properties, which copyrighted her pictures and made her name a trademark; reproduction rights were sold to several companies, including Hallmark, the greeting card company, and several of her paintings were widely reproduced on Christmas cards. During her lifetime she earned an estimated $500,000 through the sale of her artwork.

Kallir described Moses's work as a harmonious unit that balanced figures and landscape to express a single event. He classified her paintings according to the four seasons: white, or winter, pictures depicted snow scenes; light green pictures captured spring; deep green was the predominant color of her summer scenes; and autumn pictures were done in shades of brown. Kallir, a perceptive critic, was careful to differentiate among Grandma Moses's paintings and exhibit only those he deemed the best. Among her most-famous works are *Sugaring Off* (1939), *Black Horses* (1941), *Catching the Thanksgiving Turkey* (1943), *From My Window* (1946), and *The Old Checkered House* (1945).

Grandma Moses was very matter-of-fact about her artistic activity, which she viewed as just another form of work. She painted, she said, to occupy her time; too old to raise chickens, she painted pictures instead. Painting from memory, in her bedroom, which she used as a studio; she worked on the flat surface of a wooden mixing board covered with newspaper and resting on a pine table. Each masonite "canvas" was first treated with linseed oil, then given three coats of flat white paint. She painted the sky first, then the ground, and finally the figures. She usually painted three or four pictures at once in order, she claimed, to save paint and time. Her paints were stored in old coffee cans, and she softened her worn brushes in discarded cold cream jars.

Grandma Moses continued to paint until August 1961, when she was hospitalized at a health center in Hoosick Falls after a fall at her home. Her death at the center four months later was announced on the front pages of newspapers in both the United States and Europe.

Grandma Moses, considered a unique figure in modern art, is America's most-renowned primitive painter. Her paintings hang in leading museums around the country, including the Museum of Modern Art and the Metropolitan Museum of Art in New York, the Phillips Gallery in Washington, D.C., and the Minneapolis Institute of Arts.

• For additional biographical information see Otto Kallir, ed., *Grandma Moses: My Life's History* (1952); Otto Kallir, *Grandma Moses* (1973); and Jane Kallir, *Grandma Moses: The Artist Behind the Myth* (1982). See also the exhibition catalog *Four American Primitives: Edward Hicks, John Kane, Anna*

Mary Robertson Moses, Horace Pippin (1972, ACA Galleries, New York). A chapter devoted to Moses is in John Vlach, *Plain Painters: Making Sense of American Folk Art* (1988). An obituary is in the *New York Times*, 14 Dec. 1961.

ANN T. KEENE

MOSES, Robert (18 Dec. 1888–29 July 1981), city planner, highway builder, and entrepreneurial public servant, was born in New Haven, Connecticut, the son of Emanuel Moses, the owner of a department store, and Bella (maiden name unknown), the daughter of a wealthy German-Jewish New York family and founder of the Madison Settlement House. The family moved to New York City, where Robert was raised among the well-to-do. He graduated Phi Beta Kappa from Yale in 1909 and from Oxford in 1911, where he was awarded the M.A. in political science.

Returning to New York City in 1912, Moses matriculated at Columbia and earned the Ph.D. in political science in 1914, publishing his dissertation *The Civil Service of Great Britain* in the same year. He immediately began attempting to implement his ideas about civil service reform, such as liberal paternalism and meritocracy, in his first job at the Bureau of Municipal Research. In 1915 he married a secretary at the bureau, Mary Louise Sims; they had two children. Following the death of his first wife, in 1966 he married Mary A. Grady, who remained his wife until his death.

The reform mayor John Puroy Mitchel of New York appointed a new Civil Service Commission in 1915 that in turn chose Moses as a technical expert. His *Detailed Report on the Rating of the Efficiency of Civil Service Employees* insisted on a meritocracy in the heyday of boss rule, and it and Mitchel were soundly defeated in the election of 1917. Fortunately for Moses, the Tammany Hall politician Alfred E. Smith was elected governor in 1918. Smith, through an introduction by Democratic strategist Belle Moskowitz, became a lifelong friend and supporter of Moses.

Moses's first job with Smith was as staff director of the Reconstruction Commission, an organization formed to rewrite the New York State Constitution to streamline its structure. Bitterly opposed by Tammany and the Republican regulars, only bits and pieces were passed into law. Elected again in 1922, Smith appointed Moses president of the Long Island State Park Commission. Moses wrote the legislation to establish the commission, creating the first of many virtually autonomous commissions and authorities through which he manipulated the politics of development in both New York City and the state for more than a generation. He served as chairman of the commission for thirty-nine years.

Using powers that insulated, in the name of reform, the president of the Long Island State Park Commission from politics, Moses built the Northern State and Southern State parkways, grabbing the property of some of the wealthiest people in the country under the power of eminent domain. The Jones Beach Park project (completed in 1929), combined with the highways leading to it, had a powerful and unprecedented impact in stimulating automobile use and in shaping the ways in which large public projects were subsequently built.

By the onset of the Great Depression, Robert Moses was known as an expert on civil service, government organization, public works planning, and highway construction. He was lionized in the newspapers of the day and considered to be a dedicated manager and reformer above the petty dishonesty of common politicians. He was not, except for a disastrous gubernatorial loss to Democrat Herbert Lehman in 1934, an office-seeking politician. Rather he was, as the title of Robert Caro's famous biography argued, *The Power Broker*. He ruled by serving on authorities (Triborough Bridge, 1934–1968), as an appointed city commissioner (New York City Parks Department 1934–1960), and in numerous roles that appeared to be technical and innocuous and not positions of obvious power and political influence. Frequently he served in temporary advisory roles, as in the case of the United Nations Building (1946), Lincoln Center (1960–1967), and the New York World's Fair Corporation (1960–1967). But his hold on construction of bridges, parks, and highways in and around New York exceeded that of any of his contemporaries.

He was particularly astute at invoking the constitutional prohibition of impairment of contract when elected leaders attempted to overrule his decisions. He did this by "rolling over" bonds issued by the various authorities he directed, thereby creating a fiduciary relationship that no legislature could readily undermine. Thus the proceeds from one bridge could be used to fund the construction of another. Typically, the extent of this power was not understood by the New York legislature until it was too late. Moses usually wrote the legislation himself, as he had done in the creation of the Long Island Park Commission. Although he had a close association with many politicians like Smith and Fiorello La Guardia, the reform mayor of New York, he was often at odds with men of power, including Franklin D. Roosevelt, whom he had once excluded from a parks council appointment.

Interestingly, FDR could do little to Moses during the depression because he was, as in the case of the Triborough Bridge (finished in 1940), so technically skilled in design, budgeting, and management that his proposals were virtually always the first approved on their merits. When the paralysis of the depression hit the construction industry most seriously, Moses's Triborough Bridge project employed more architects, engineers, skilled tradesmen, and laborers than any contemporary project, thus winning millions from FDR's Public Works Authority (PWA), an Interior Department agency created to prime the pump of recovery. As parks commissioner, Moses put thousands to work in rebuilding city facilities, including zoos, parks, playgrounds, and monuments. He was enormously popular, being seen by most people as a can-do, around the clock manager who had only the public interest at heart.

The immediate post–World War II construction boom and the resumption of normal civilian life brought even more power Moses's way. In 1946 he became New York City construction coordinator, a post he would hold until 1965. He was also chairman of the mayor's Slum Clearance Committee from 1948 until 1960. These roles, combined with others, permitted Moses to dominate all aspects of city planning, highways, urban renewal, public housing, and construction during this period.

Moses's power and ego isolated him from the consequences of many of his decisions. His public works dispossessed hundreds of thousands of low-income people without properly relocating them during the 1950s. His housing projects, and in particular the expressways that conveyed millions to and from the suburbs, divided neighborhoods and created schisms in areas that had enjoyed reasonable racial and ethnic integration. His high-handed attitude toward public protest and his lifelong love affair with the automobile slowly began to earn him the hostility of the newspapers that had fervently supported him for so many years. His friends in the banking community, in the construction unions, and in politics continued to support him, but others like John Lindsay, reform mayor of New York, opposed his autocratic domination of the affairs of the city.

More significant was the opposition of Governor Nelson Rockefeller, who slowly but surely maneuvered the aging Moses out of many positions of power, beginning with the New York Council of Parks, from which Moses habitually threatened to resign when politicians failed to see things his way. When he mistakenly threatened Rockefeller in 1963, the governor accepted his resignation, thus ending Moses's thirty-year term. He also resigned from the New York State Power Authority and the Long Island State Park Commission at the same time. Rockefeller planned to merge Triborough into a new Metropolitan Commuter Transportation Authority (MTA) with William Ronan, head of the New York Development Authority, in charge. The governor promised Moses a seat on the new board of what was to be an enormous superagency that would dominate all forms of transportation. Moses accepted and gave up his last centers of power only to be passed over for the MTA board.

The publication of Caro's *The Power Broker* in 1974 left Moses stigmatized and isolated, although he continued to give occasional speeches and wrote until his death in New York City. Moses's reputation has remained in some dispute. The balance of opinion between community-based decision making and expert managerial direction tends to define one's view of Moses. His accomplishments in building engineering gems like the Triborough Bridge and parks like Jones Beach contrast with his contributions to the automobilization of big cities and his arrogant disregard for the people who lived in them.

A product of an essentially elitist reform movement, Robert Moses became an usher of modernity, a public servant with little accountability, save his conscience. His contributions to contemporary life will doubtless outlast memories of him. For better or worse the people of New York will live with the physical results of his enormous energy, intellect, and political power for generations to come.

• The papers of Robert Moses are in the many agencies in which he served. Moses wrote an autobiography, *Public Works, a Dangerous Trade* (1970); also valuable is Robert A. Caro, *The Power Broker* (1974). An analysis of Moses appears in Eugene Lewis, *Public Entrepreneurship* (1980).

EUGENE LEWIS

MOSESSOHN, David Nehemiah (1 Jan. 1883–16 Dec. 1930), dress industry arbitrator and editor, was born in Ekaterinoslav, Russia, the son of Nehemiah Mosessohn, a rabbi and publisher, and Theresa Nissenson. Mosessohn came from a long line of rabbis, and his grandfather had once been chief rabbi of Odessa. In 1888 the entire family emigrated to the United States, and David grew up in Portland, Oregon, where he graduated from high school in 1900. He attended the University of Oregon and received his law degree from that university in 1902. That same year his father also received his law degree, and they were the youngest and the oldest graduates in 1902. Between 1902 and 1918 Mosessohn engaged in a general law practice while a senior member of Mosessohn and Mosessohn. Between 1908 and 1910 he served as deputy district attorney of Multnomah County. Together with his brother Moses Dayann Mosessohn, Mosessohn also served as publisher of the weekly *Jewish Tribune*, which his father had founded in 1903. In 1905 he married Manya Lerner; they had one child.

Mosessohn's career changed dramatically when, with his father and brother, he moved to New York City in 1918. Soon after his arrival in New York, he became acquainted with J. J. Goldman, a leader in the garment industry. Goldman invited him to study the dress industry's problems, and Mosessohn came up with the idea for an organization of dress manufacturers that came to be known as the Associated Dress Industries of America. Mosessohn became executive director of this organization in 1918, and in 1923 he became its executive chairman. Mosessohn had no previous experience in the dress business, but his background in law and Jewish ethics suited many of the manufacturers who sought to raise the standards in what was essentially a Jewish industry.

As the leader of the Associated Dress Industries, Mosessohn sought to bring order to a chaotic industry characterized by cutthroat competition. He worked with bankers to stabilize lines of credit to both manufacturers and retailers; he aided manufacturers in developing means to avoid overproduction and to spread out production through the entire year; he sought to put the dress industry on a "higher plane" by exposing fraudulent manufacturers; he established an arbitration board that could settle disputes among manufacturers, retailers, and creditors without resort to the courts; above all, he sought to tame the frenzy of speculation that had made the dress industry so unstable. Mosessohn believed that business, rather than being just a "money making opportunity," was a "part of life," and many of his ideas paralleled those of Herbert Hoover, who as secretary of commerce tried to spread the cooperative idea to industry. After becoming president, Hoover in December 1929 named Mosessohn a member of the National Business Survey Conference.

By the late 1920s the Associated Dress Industries included over 600 manufacturers, but Mosessohn proved only partly successful in implementing his ideas. Dress manufacturers continued to have the highest turnover rate of any sector in the ready-to-wear industry, and in 1928 only 28 percent of all manufacturers had been in the business for over four years. As editor of *Dresses*, the journal of the Associated Dress Industries, Mosessohn spoke in optimistic tones, but the ease of entry, disputes among partners, sudden changes in fashion, and the runaway shop (companies that moved to outlying areas mainly to escape labor unions) all continued to make dress manufacturing a highly unstable business.

After his move to New York, Mosessohn also remained active as a publisher and editor. In 1918 the *Jewish Tribune* absorbed the *Hebrew Standard* and expanded its format. Mosessohn became editor of this journal when his father died in December 1926. Under David Mosessohn's editorship, the *Jewish Tribune* continued in the direction established by his father. Although it paid attention to religious affairs, most of its articles dealt with secular matters. A strong supporter of Zionism, it regularly reported on events in Palestine and on developments within the Zionist movement. A relentless foe of anti-Semitism, it gave extensive coverage to events affecting Jews in Eastern Europe. Emulating the style of American popular magazines, it contained features on Jews prominent in film, theater, music, art, politics, and sports. Anxious to see Jews Americanized, the *Jewish Tribune* also warned about the perils of assimilation. In unsigned editorials, Mosessohn in his thoughtful and common-sense style urged Jews to settle their disputes amicably and to avoid divisions that could damage their interests.

Mosessohn also played a prominent role in New York Jewish affairs. In 1924 the *Jewish Tribune* began to sponsor forums, where Mosessohn often spoke, that aired a wide variety of issues of concern to Jews. A founder and vice president of the Jewish Education Association, he was also active in the United Synagogue of America. Although concerned primarily with Jewish interests, Mosessohn also sought to build bridges with the Gentile world. A serious-minded man who valued reason, moderation, and toleration, Mosessohn hoped to see Jews and other immigrants accepted into the American mainstream. Quite characteristically, on hearing about Henry Ford's recantation of his anti-Semitic diatribes in the *Dearborn Independent*, Mosessohn suggested that in the "spirit of American fair play" Ford sponsor "a world wide campaign of education against national chauvinism, religious bigotry and racial antagonism."

Mosessohn died of arteriosclerosis at his home in New York City. His death, at age forty-seven, cut short a highly unusual career in which he had become prominent in the world of business and in the world of Jewish publishing. Despite his strenuous efforts, Mosessohn only had limited success in his effort to bring stability to the dress industry. He had more success in his publishing endeavors, and in the 1920s the *Jewish Tribune* fulfilled its claim of being "the foremost English language publication of general Jewish interest in America." A Conservative Jew, Mosessohn always remained firmly anchored in the Jewish world. Nevertheless, he recognized the opportunities available to Jews in the freer atmosphere of the United States. Regardless of his activities, Mosessohn consistently spoke for the need for reason to prevail over emotion, and his emphasis on law and ethical behavior represents a stage in the secularization of the Jewish rabbinic and talmudic tradition.

• There are no Mosessohn papers. Mosessohn's ideas can best be followed in the two journals he edited, *Dresses* and the *Jewish Tribune*. The *New York Times* also gave frequent coverage to the activities of the Associated Dress Industries. Background on the family can be found in the *Jewish Tribune*, 24 Feb. 1928 and 19 Dec. 1930, the latter containing a noteworthy obituary. See also John Walker Harrington, "The Benevolent Despot of the Dress Industry," *Popular Finance*, Sept. 1923, pp. 49–53.

DAVID J. GOLDBERG

MOSHER, Clelia Duel (16 Dec. 1863–22 Dec. 1940), physician, professor, and medical researcher, was born in Albany, New York, the daughter of Cornelius Duel Mosher, a doctor, and Sarah Burritt. After graduating from the Albany Female Academy in 1881, Mosher returned home for eight years to conserve her delicate health. With her father's help, she opened a florist business, earning enough money for four years' tuition at Wellesley College. During her sophomore year illness forced Mosher to withdraw from school. By the summer of 1891 renewed strength and a growing interest in science prompted her to study entomology at Cornell, followed by courses at the University of Wisconsin during 1891 and 1892. She received a bachelor's degree in zoology (1893) and an M.A. in physiology (1894) at Stanford University.

Mosher's oscillation between convalescence and education was symbolic of a widespread belief in late nineteenth-century America that female bodies were too fragile to withstand rigorous schoolwork or other demanding activities. Such concerns escalated into public discussions of the "Woman Question," an intense national debate about women's natural qualities and roles. The prevailing view, biological determinism, maintained that the intellectual and physical attributes of men and women were markedly and innately different. The issue of sex differences—their extent, origins, and implications—framed Mosher's career as a teacher and researcher.

Mosher's master's thesis, for instance, tested physiologists' contention that men breathed diaphragmatically, whereas women breathed with their upper chests, or costally, because of the demands of pregnancy. Observation led Mosher to conclude that sex differences in respiration were due not to biology, but to habit, specifically women's inactivity and restrictive clothing. As an instructor in hygiene at Stanford in 1894–1896, Mosher also began investigating menstruation. By tracking the cycles of several hundred of her students, Mosher hoped to discover the normal pattern of "functional periodicity" and the factors that disrupted it.

In 1896 Mosher enrolled in the newly founded medical school at Johns Hopkins, one of thirteen women in a class of forty-one. She received her M.D. in 1900. After one year as an extern in the Johns Hopkins Hospital dispensary and as a gynecological assistant in Howard Kelly's sanatorium, Mosher returned to Palo Alto and endured nine lean years as a private practitioner with little time or funds for her research. In 1910 she became an assistant professor of personal hygiene, medical adviser for women, and director of the Roble Gymnasium at Stanford University. These positions enabled Mosher to continue her study of female physiology.

In a 1911 article Mosher defied conventional wisdom by arguing that normal menstruation was not a disabling or pathological condition. Dysmenorrhea, or painful menstruation, she wrote, resulted from poor posture, chronic constipation, weak muscles, unsuitable clothing, "morbid apprehensions," and other correctable habits. Believing that women could be comfortable throughout their cycles, Mosher developed a series of deep-breathing exercises to relieve dysmenorrhea; these became known at Stanford and elsewhere as the "moshers." By 1915 her interest in posture led to the co-invention (with a Stanford engineer) of the schematograph, a device that reproduced an individual's silhouette on graph paper. Considered a simple and scientific means of analyzing posture, the schematograph became familiar equipment in physical education departments around the country. Mosher's ideas also received general attention with the publication of her popular book *Woman's Physical Freedom* (3d ed., 1923). Originating in 1915 as an address for the Young Women's Christian Association, the book, first published in 1916 as *Health and the Woman Movement*, offered practical advice about female health and summarized Mosher's views on menstruation, "based on the study of more than 2000 women during 12,000 menstrual periods" (p. 19). In collaboration with Ernest G. Martin, a Stanford physiologist, Mosher next studied sex differences in muscular strength using college students as subjects. In a 1918 report Mosher and Martin concluded that observed disparities in men's and women's strength were not innate but arose from different patterns of muscle use or disuse in daily life.

During World War I Mosher served in France with the Children's Bureau and the Bureau of Refugees and Relief, two agencies of the Red Cross. On returning to the United States in 1919 she studied trends in the average height and weight of female students at Stanford since the 1890s. Mosher applauded women's increased size, attributing it to improved diet, dress, and exercise.

Mosher also conducted but never published a remarkable survey of female sexuality. Beginning in 1892 and continuing for nearly thirty years, she collected detailed questionnaires from female patients and acquaintances about their sexual attitudes and experiences. Rediscovered in the 1970s, the surviving responses refute the late-Victorian claim that women were passionless, with no sexual urges other than for reproduction.

In 1929 Mosher retired from Stanford as a full professor. Only two other female faculty members achieved that rank during Stanford's first four decades. She died in Palo Alto.

As the United States debated the Woman Question, Mosher subjected the claims of biological determinism to scientific scrutiny. Invariably she concluded that women's apparent physical limitations were acquired and correctable, not innate and permanent. "As step by step scientific knowledge of [woman's] physiology advances," Mosher wrote, "her traditional incapacity and the physical weakness supposed to be inherent in her sex have been shown to be due not to sex but to other and removable causes" (*Woman's Physical Freedom*, p. 1). In her research and teaching Mosher invited each woman to reject "the old ideal of physical weakness and dependence" and to seize "the opportunity of tasting the richness of physical perfection and the fullness of life which comes in its train, making of herself a better citizen, a better wife, a better mother" (*Woman's Physical Freedom*, p. 87). Along with other female academics in the biological and social sciences during the early 1900s, Mosher combined research and feminism. By emphasizing the role of social, rather than biological, factors in human behavior, they affirmed women's right and capacity for unhindered development.

In a shirtwaist dress, with starched collar and four-in-hand tie, walking confidently and working earnestly, Mosher was herself the model of strong, independent womanhood. That public self, however, concealed Mosher's private life as a sensitive, lonely woman. Without close friends, Mosher tended her beloved garden and wrote prose, diary entries, and letters to an imaginary confidante, reflecting poignantly on her seemingly contrary longings for intellectual stimulation and emotional intimacy. As a counterpoint to her public accomplishments, Mosher's private world testifies to the personal conflicts that many professional women in America faced during the early twentieth century.

• The two major collections of Mosher's personal and professional papers are at Stanford University: the Department of Special Collections in Green Library and the Archives of the Hoover Institution for the Study of War and Peace. Among her noteworthy publications are "Functional Periodicity in

Women and Some of the Modifying Factors," *California State Journal of Medicine* 9 (1911): 4–8; "A Physiologic Treatment of Congestive Dysmenorrhea and Kindred Disorders Associated with the Menstrual Function," *Journal of the American Medical Association* 62 (1914): 1297–1301; "The Physical Training of Women in Relation to Functional Periodicity," *Woman's Medical Journal* 25 (1915): 71–74; "The Muscular Strength of College Women," *Journal of the American Medical Association* 70 (1918): 140–42; and "Some of the Causal Factors in the Increased Height of College Women," *Journal of the American Medical Association* 81 (1923): 535–38. Mosher's sex survey is described in Carl N. Degler, "What Ought to Be and What Was: Women's Sexuality in the Nineteenth Century," *American Historical Review* 79 (1974): 1467–90, and reprinted in *The Mosher Survey: Sexual Attitudes of Forty-five Victorian Women*, ed. James MaHood and Kristine Wenburg (1980). The most complete biography, with a full listing of Mosher's works, is Elizabeth Brownlee Griego, "A Part and Yet Apart: Clelia Duel Mosher and Professional Women at the Turn-of-the-Century" (Ph.D. diss., Univ. of California, Berkeley, 1983). Shorter but informative pieces are Griego, "The Making of a 'Misfit': Clelia Duel Mosher, 1863–1940," in *Lone Voyagers: Academic Women in Coeducational Universities, 1870–1937*, ed. Geraldine Jonçich Clifford (1989), pp. 147–82, and Kathryn Allamong Jacob, "Clelia Duel Mosher," *Johns Hopkins Magazine* 30 (1979): 8–16. A friend's recollections are in Mary Roberts Coolidge, "Clelia Duel Mosher: The Scientific Feminist," *Research Quarterly of the American Association for Health, Physical Education, and Recreation*, supp. to vol. 12 (1941): 633–45. Obituaries are in the *Palo Alto Times*, 23 Dec. 1940, and the *New York Times*, 24 Dec. 1940.

MARTHA H. VERBRUGGE

MOSHER, Eliza Maria (2 Oct. 1846–16 Oct. 1928), physician and health educator, was born in Cayuga County, New York, the daughter of Augustus Mosher, a farmer, and Maria Sutton. Her parents were educated Quakers who were interested in antebellum reform. An early penchant for nursing, resulting from rather harrowing experiences with family sickness and death, convinced Mosher, while still a teenager, to become a doctor. Her enthusiasm, coupled with the fact that three women schoolmates entered medicine, softened her mother's initial opposition. Mosher began reading medicine with her family physician and in 1868 became one of five intern-apprentices at the female-run New England Hospital for Women and Children in Boston. A year later she returned to Boston for a six-month term as assistant to Dr. Lucy E. Sewall.

In 1871 she entered the University of Michigan medical school, newly opened to women, where she received the M.D. degree in 1875. Opening a private practice in 1875 in Poughkeepsie, New York, with Dr. Elizabeth Gerow, one of her childhood friends, she gradually acquired a special interest in the physiological development of adolescent girls. She delivered physiology lectures for ladies at the local YMCA and in the 1880s lectured on anatomy and hygiene to women students at the Chautauqua summer school of physical education. She taught Sunday school classes and did temperance and social purity work, campaigning against prostitution and male sexual promiscuity and exhibiting the deep religious commitment that remained characteristic of many women doctors of her generation.

In 1877 she was persuaded by Massachusetts governor John D. Long to come to the new Reformatory Prison for Women at Sherborn as resident physician. While there, she legally adopted one of the prisoners, treating her like a daughter and providing her with education and nurse's training. The two women kept in close touch throughout Mosher's life.

Released from her duties at Sherborn in 1883 because of a knee injury that gave her several years of pain, until she herself devised an operation to cure it, Mosher settled into joint partnership in Brooklyn, New York, with Dr. Lucy Hall, another Michigan graduate. For several years thereafter the two alternated semester stints as resident physician at Vassar College. In keeping with her interest in adolescent development, Mosher also devoted herself to pediatrics, posture, and physical education, designing several different types of posture chairs and subway seats. In 1896, after a year's delay in negotiations because of the reluctance of the medical school to appoint a woman to its faculty, she became the University of Michigan's first dean of women and professor of hygiene, although the unrelenting medical school insisted the appointment be made through the literary department. With the encouragement of President James B. Angell, she established a rigid system of preventive medicine, health records, and physical education for Michigan's coeds.

Returning to Brooklyn in 1902, Mosher continued her teaching, lecturing, social purity work, civic reform, and professional medical activities. She founded the American Posture League, served as senior editor of the *Medical Women's Journal* from 1905 until her death, and participated in the establishment of the Medical Women's National Association (today the American Medical Women's Association) in 1915. She ardently supported the suffrage movement and, during World War I, helped found the American Women's Hospitals Service, an organization that sent women physicians abroad for war and postwar relief work.

All her life, Mosher felt keenly the burdens and special responsibilities of being a woman physician, warning her colleagues in the American Medical Women's Association, shortly before her death, to beware of "narrowing and concentrating their vision upon the purely physical to the exclusion of the psychic and human." She believed that women doctors played a significant role in disease prevention. Although she was beloved by many individuals and enjoyed warm friendships, she never married, claiming that no man ever captured her heart. She died in New York.

• Mosher's *Health and Happiness: A Message to Girls* (1912) provides insight into her work in preventive medicine and health education. Her papers, which consist of a rich correspondence, clippings, memoirs, and other memorabilia, can be found in the Michigan Historical Collections at the University of Michigan. Also on deposit there is a detailed unpublished biography by Florence Woolsey Hazzard, who also published two articles about Mosher in the *Michigan*

Alumnus Quarterly Review, 11 May and 27 July 1946. See also Burke A. Hinsdale, *History of the University of Michigan* (1906); Dorothy Gies McGuigan, *A Dangerous Experiment: 100 Years of Women at the University of Michigan* (1970); the article on Mosher in the *Woman Citizen*, 5 Apr. 1925; and the *New York Times*, 17, 18, 20 Oct. 1928. See also numerous articles on her life in *Medical Woman's Journal* 29 (Oct. 1922), 32 (May 1925), 33 (Nov. 1926), 35 (Nov. 1928), 42 (Apr. 1935), 55 (Feb. 1948), 57 (May 1950); and in *Bulletin of the Medical Women's National Association* 23 (Jan. 1929) and *Literary Digest* 85 (Apr. 1925). For Mosher's achievements in historical context, see Regina Morantz-Sanchez, *Sympathy and Science: Women Physicians in American Medicine* (1985).

REGINA MORANTZ-SANCHEZ

MOSKOWITZ, Belle Lindner Israels (5 Oct. 1877–2 Jan. 1933), social reformer, was born in Harlem, New York, the daughter of Isidor Lindner, a watchmaker, and Esther Freyer. Her parents had emigrated together from East Prussia in 1869. Belle attended city schools and Horace Mann High School for Girls and then, for one year, Teachers College at Columbia University. In 1900 the Educational Alliance, a Jewish settlement on New York's Lower East Side, hired her as a resident social worker, eventually appointing her director of entertainments and exhibits.

In 1903 she resigned her job to marry Charles Henry Israels, an architect. She remained active in volunteer social service, doing part-time editorial work for the social reform journal *The Survey* to pay for domestic help. She pursued projects for the United Hebrew Charities, the New York State Conference of Charities and Corrections, and the Council of Jewish Women–New York Section, rising in each of these organizations to hold offices or serve on boards of directors. Her work concentrated on providing urban working-class girls with decent recreational and vacation resources. In 1908 she launched a successful drive to license, regulate, and create substitutes for New York's commercial dance halls, a cause that social workers elsewhere eventually took up in their own regions.

Charles Israels died of heart disease in 1911. To support their three children, Belle Israels wrote a pamphlet on child care (*The Child*) for the Metropolitan Life Insurance Company and then worked as commercial recreation secretary for the Playground and Recreation Association. In January 1913 she took a job with the Dress and Waist Manufacturers' Association, a group that had set up, with labor, joint grievance and arbitration procedures in order to prevent strikes. She worked for this group almost four years, settling thousands of grievances and rising to head its Labor Department. By the fall of 1916, however, her employers had become dissatisfied with her prolabor sympathies. After electing a new board, they fired her.

In 1914 Belle Israels married Henry Moskowitz, a settlement worker, industrial mediator, and then president of the Municipal Civil Service Commission of New York. They had no children. Having lost her job with the dress manufacturers, Belle opened a firm in the new field of industrial consulting. In 1918, after long affiliation with independent Republican, Progressive party, and city "fusion" causes, the Moskowitzes threw their support behind Democrat Alfred E. Smith for governor. Moskowitz's organizing the women's vote for Smith (New York women could vote after 1917) brought her to his attention.

Smith's victory, which came as World War I ended, prompted Belle Moskowitz to urge him to appoint a Reconstruction Commission to plan the course of the state's future. Accepting her idea, he appointed her the commission's executive secretary. The commission's reports, issued between April 1919 and March 1920, covered labor and industry, the rising cost of living, public health, education, and government reorganization and retrenchment. They reflected the fundamental progressive-era idea that government should spur business interests to cooperate voluntarily in reform, but when voluntarism failed the state needed to interfere. Smith's later reforms, including his Reconstruction Labor Board, State Highways Transport Committee, State Housing Board, and expanded powers for the Department of Farms and Markets, reflected his adoption of many Reconstruction Commission ideas.

During his first two-year term, Smith relied increasingly on Moskowitz, turning to her for advice on issues of strategy and filling government posts. When he lost the 1920 election and became head of the group planning a bistate authority for the Port of New York–New Jersey, he asked Moskowitz to devise the group's public relations program. After winning reelection in 1922 (thanks in strong measure to Moskowitz's publicity work), he offered her a job in state government. She declined, opting instead to create her own post, that of publicity director for the State Democratic Committee. In this post she acted as Smith's public relations counselor, writing his speeches, preparing and monitoring legislation, and finding appointees for vacant posts. The job made her a central figure in the governor's unofficial "kitchen cabinet."

Moskowitz oriented her work for Smith around three interrelated goals: to win support for his policies, to reelect him, and after 1924 to make him president of the United States. She developed public relations programs to increase backing for his legislation, sending out weekly news releases, distributing copies of Smith's speeches, and planting favorable editorial comment in newspapers. Working through citizens' committees, in 1924 she produced all the publicity and correspondence related to his presidential ambitions. When in 1926 his fourth gubernatorial victory swelled his popularity outside New York State, Moskowitz coordinated the response and maintained a card file on Smith boosters across the country. In 1928 this network of supporters helped Smith win the primaries and, ultimately, the presidential nomination.

During the 1928 race, Belle Moskowitz, the only woman on the executive committee of the Democratic National Committee, directed the national campaign's publicity program. Despite her best efforts, Smith lost to Herbert Hoover. In the aftermath Moskowitz stayed on as Smith's press agent, trying to help him retain his leadership of the state and national Democratic organizations. The effort was in vain. Franklin Delano Roosevelt, New York's new governor, refused to hire Moskowitz and gave little attention or deference to Smith. In 1932 Roosevelt defeated Smith for the Democratic nomination and won the presidency. In December Moskowitz fell down the steps of her Upper West Side brownstone, suffered an embolism while recovering from broken bones, and died.

The era of Smith's ascendancy in the national Democratic party was one when women, unless related by blood or marriage to political figures, never achieved proximity to power. Moskowitz succeeded by offering Smith a total and selfless loyalty, a strategy interpreted at the time as reflective of her "modesty." In fact, the strategy was essential to secure her influence over Smith without threatening his status. It had serious personal consequences for Moskowitz, however. When his career fell into decline, so did hers, and she remained a generally forgotten figure until the modern movement to restore women to history revived an awareness of her many accomplishments.

• Moskowitz's papers, mostly of a private nature and saved only from the last few years of her life, are at Connecticut College in New London. A complete biography is Elisabeth Israels Perry, *Belle Moskowitz: Feminine Politics and the Exercise of Power in the Age of Alfred E. Smith* (1987). For related material, see Mary R. Beard, *Woman's Work in Municipalities* (1915); David Burner, *The Politics of Provincialism: The Democratic Party in Transition, 1918–1932* (1967; repr. 1975); Robert Caro, *The Power Broker: Robert Moses and the Fall of New York* (1974); Paula Eldot, *Governor Alfred E. Smith, the Politician as Reformer* (1983); and Matthew Josephson and Hannah Josephson, *Al Smith, Hero of the Cities: A Political Portrait Drawing on the Papers of Frances Perkins* (1969). An obituary is in the *New York Times*, 3 Jan. 1933.

ELISABETH ISRAELS PERRY